V&R

International Handbook of Cooperative Organizations

edited by Eberhard Dülfer
in cooperation with Juhani Laurinkari

and with the participation
of V. Beuthien, E.-B. Blümle, H. Bonus,
R. Bratschitsch, W.W. Engelhardt, P. Erlinghagen, B. Großfeld,
W. Großkopf, W. Grüger (DGRV), O. Hahn, A. Hanel, V. Laakkonen,
L. Marcus (ICA), H.-H. Münkner, J. v. Muralt (ILO),
J. Perkowski (WOCCU), H. Seuster, B. Thiemann (DG BANK),
G. Turner, O.W. van Verschuer (IRU), W. Weber, J. Zerche
and further renowned scholars and
experts from throughout the world

Vandenhoeck & Ruprecht in Göttingen

MEMBERS OF THE EDITORIAL STAFF:

Brockmeier, Thomas / Broicher, Ingo / Evitts, Stacey / Fährmann, Elke
Grafen, Barbara / Herrmann, Elke / Kluge, Dr. Arndt / Lellep, Irene
Meyer, Christine / Schreiter, Dr. Carsten / Stremme, Jörg
Tegtmeyer, Kerstin

Die Deutsche Bibliothek – CIP-Einheitsaufnahme

International handbook of cooperative organizations /
ed. by Eberhard Dülfer in cooperation with Juhani Laurinkari
and with the participation of V. Beuthien ...
and further renowned scholars and experts from throughout the world. –
Göttingen : Vandenhoeck und Ruprecht, 1994
ISBN 3-525-13225-5
NE: Dülfer, Eberhard [Hrsg.]; Beuthien, Volker

© Vandenhoeck & Ruprecht, Göttingen 1994
All rights reserved. No part of this publication may be reproduced,
stored in a retrieval systems, or transmitted in any form or by any means,
electronic, mechanical, photocopying or otherwise,
without the prior permission of Vandenhoeck & Ruprecht
Printed in Germany by Hubert & Co., Göttingen

Editor's Preface

COOPERATION – what does it mean? Human beings are born as individuals, but right from the beginning they enter into communication and interaction, i.e. into social relationships: first with their mother and other family members, later on with friends, colleagues, partners, clients and foreign people. The more self-reliant individuals become the more their interactions either are pure exchanges of information and goods, or conscious, goal-directed common action in the sense of '*cooperation*': cooperation in games and sports, cooperation in vocational areas, cooperation in business.

In societal and economic contexts human interactions are dominated by certain *systems of order*: ranging from the pure hierarchical system of command, like in the historical Inka State or the former Soviet Union, to the pure market system of exchange directed by Adam Smith's "invisible hand". Between these extremes, diverse forms of conscious common action occur which can be subsumed under the term "*cooperation*" in the broadest sense.

There is renewed interest in various ideas and forms of cooperation in the face of the collapse of *real socialism* in the Soviet Union and its former satellites as well as the unsatisfactory effectiveness of the *pure market economy* to bring about the socio-economic transformation of a centralized system into a decentralized one. This can include cooperation between individuals of different age or social situation, cooperation between entrepreneurs or boards of enterprises, cooperation between employees or workers within a business undertaking, cooperation between enterprises and authorities on different administrative levels, cooperation everywhere in society.

There are quite *heterogeneous institutional patterns* of cooperation, one of them being the classical *co-operative society* and its contemporary versions. In this book we thus distinguish between *co-operation* in the form of co-operative societies or related institutions and *cooperation* (spelled without hyphen) beyond the classical co-operative societies, unions, and federations.

Co-operative societies are an important element of all national economies in the *Western world*. Over a period of 150 years, they developed as credit co-operatives, handicraft and commercial co-operatives, consumer co-operatives, and housing societies. There is a renaissance of co-operatives in the post-socialist countries after a period of their communist denaturation. The most instructive example of this phenomenon is the restructuring of co-operative banks and enterprises in the new (Eastern) federal states of re-united Germany. Finally, co-operatives are very much appreciated in the *Third World*, partially referring to well-known classical European patterns. Partially, historical local forms are being revitalized, or new patterns are being developed, intentionally distinct from colonial heritage.

Other traditional forms of *cooperation* exist in manufacturing industries, e. g. as *syndicates* or *cartels*, both of which are problematic in the view of antitrust legislation and policy. Here new patterns have also been developed, such as national and international *joint ventures, strategic alliances* and *informational networks*.

During the first three decades after World War II, cooperative organizations were mostly interesting on the national level. At present, however, large systems of *international economic interaction and cooperation* are developing, e.g. the European Union (former European Community), the European Free Trade Association (EFTA), the North American Free Trade Association (NAFTA), and the American-Pacific Economic Cooperation (APEC). Others will be developed in the course of West/East European adaptation.

Thus, cooperation is of immediate interest, though quite *different meanings and concepts* of cooperation can be found in the various parts of the world, e.g. among the members of the European Union or among international organizations, e.g. of the United Nations family. It seems to be an important task of social science to promote knowledge and discussion about the possibilities of cooperation worldwide.

Cooperation in the widest sense and co-operation by co-operatives, however, is the subject of a number of *scientific disciplines*: sociology and social psychology, jurisprudence, economics, management science, industrial relations, technology, social engineering, ergonomics, etc. They use different paradigmatic approaches and analytical methods and are interested in different forms and aspects of cooperation.

This book intends to present the different *national and cultural concepts of cooperation* from the perspective of various scholarly disciplines and to stimulate *international discussion* on content, concepts, and methods of cooperative action in all kinds of cooperative organizations. It picks up the thread of the „Internationales Handwörterbuch des Genossenschaftswesens", a German-language volume edited in 1927 by Professor Totomianz in Paris. The subject, however, has been extended in accordance with present-day situations and needs, but publishing house and editor agreed not to exceed the size of one volume. The result is a collection of 197 contributions, each of up to 12 columns, presented in alphabetical order.

Thus, this book has the character of an encyclopaedia (in German literature: 'Handwörterbuch'), although the title reads "handbook". This follows the well-known example of the "Handbook of German Business Management" and bears distinction from the concept of a 'handbook' in the Anglo-American use. 500 *key words* were suggested by the members of the Institutes of Co-operative Science in Germany and abroad which belong to the Association of University Institutes for Co-operative Science (AGI). 200 were selected by the editor and his colleages. The other ones were initially considered "dead headwords" which referred to other terms. In the course of the preparatory process, however, many additional headwords generated interest. Therefore we decided to join them in the *Subject Index* on the end of the book.

The 153 contributors are from Europe, North and Latin America, Asia, and Africa: scientists and practitioners, economists, sociologists, lawyers, as well as presidents, managers, and board members of co-operatives, other enterprises, and federations. Names and institutions are included in the *List of Contributors* found before the indexes. The authors present their different scientific or pragmatic approaches to co-operative action and cooperative organizations. In the acquisition and coordination of this large circle of authors from all parts of the world I received considerable assistance from my dear colleague, *Prof. Dr. Dr. Juhani Laurinkari,* University of Kuopio (Finland) who initially brought to AGI's attention the interest held by Scandinavian co-operators for such a publication.

A market study confirmed a potential demand worldwide. Thus, the AGI decided to start work on this project in 1988. Many contributions were written during these first years. Therefore, some facts and relations reported do not represent the most current state of affairs, e.g. in the context of East/West-harmonization. In these cases, however, the authors or the editor added short comments or revised the text. I am greatly endebted to the authors for their qualified and willing cooperation.

93 authors wrote their contributions in English. We thoroughly appreciated the effort involved because it very much facilitated the preparation and financing of this book. These contributions are presented, of course, in their original (English or American) version. The appropriate English translations of the remaining 104 contributions proved to be a very particular challenge. Mary E. and Bertel Fassnacht, Albert Jennings, and David Smith (in chronological order) – three of them native speakers – undertook this difficult task and mastered it in an excellent manner. The translations have been scrutinized (with respect to technical terms) by the editorial team and the authors. The translator's initials can be found in parentheses behind the author's name. In some cases, further translators are indicated at the end of the article. The problem of homogeneous terminology was very hard. In some cases, we invented unique technical terms, like "promotion mandate" (Förderauftrag) or "joint-production co-operative" (Produktivgenossenschaft) in spite of various other common English terms for the same object.

As to the financing of this project, I owe sincere gratitude to the *Wissenschaftsfonds der DG-BANK* (Germany), which provided the main financial support. Nevertheless, the project could not have been finished without the personnel and financial resources put to the disposal of the editor by the Institut für Genossenschaftswesen an der Philipps-Universität Marburg (Germany) and the devoted work of numerous staff members, above all Barbara Grafen and Thomas Brockmeier. They all are to be thanked by the inclusion of their names in the list of the staff members below.

Last but not least I have to thank the publishing house of Vandenhoeck & Ruprecht, Göttingen, for its commitment in this unusual project, and for its smooth and productive cooperation which remained a permanent feature throughout this extensive project.

June 1994   Eberhard Dülfer

Contents

Editor's Preface V
 Eberhard Dülfer

Recommendations for Use XIV

Accounting in Co-operatives 1–8
 Herrmann Siegfried Rinn
Agricultural Credit and Co-operatives 8–11
 Ottfried C. Kirsch
Agricultural Trade and Co-operatives 11–15
 Egon Wöhlken
Ambelakia Syntrophia 15–16
 Stavros Mariadis
Anti-Trust Laws and Co-operatives 17–23
 Bernhard Großfeld/ Guido Lenfers
Assessment of Success and the Distribution of Benefits and Surplus in Co-operatives 23–28
 Jens Jokisch
Association of Co-operatives Science Institutes 29–31
 Eberhard Dülfer
Assortment Policies of Co-operatives 31–36
 Jerker Nilsson
Auditing, Co-operative 36–42
 Konrad Mose
Authorities, Co-operative 42–46
 Peter S. Akpoghor
Autochthonous Co-operatives 46–51
 Paul Trappe

Bank Rating in the USA 52–53
 Werner Boos
Bauhütte Movement 53–57
 Klaus Novy
British–Indian Pattern of Cooperation 57–63
 Hans-H.Münkner
Buchez, Philippe Joseph Benjamin (1796–1865) 63–64
 Emmanuel Kamdem
Building and Loan Associations, Co-operative 64–68
 Horst Kleiner
Business Policies, Co-operative 68–74
 Helmut Lipfert
By-laws of the Co-operative Society 74–79
 Hartmut Becker

Central Co-operative Institutions 80–85
 Gunther Aschhoff/ Eckhart Henningsen

China, Actual Co-operative Development in 85–92
 Korinna Hana
Classical and Neo-classical Contributions to Co-operative Theory 92–100
 Rolf Eschenburg
Classification and Typologies of Co-operatives 100–106
 Werner W. Engelhardt
Co-determination in Germany 106–110
 Wolfgang H.Staehle
Combine, Co-operative 110–115
 Jürgen Zerche
Commercial Purchasing and Service Co-operatives 115–120
 Georg C. Neumann
Commonwealth, Co-operative 120–123
 Lajos Varadi
Commonweal Economy and Co-operatives 123–127
 Jürgen Zerche/Ingrid Schmale
Communal Settlements 127–131
 Yaacov Oved
Competition and Co-operatives 131–135
 Walter Hamm
Conceptions, Co-operative 135–142
 Werner W. Engelhardt
Configuration of Co-operative Society, The: Macrosociological Aspects of Co-operatives 142–146
 Robert Hettlage
Consulting for Co-operatives 146–150
 Carl E. Krug
Consumer Co-operatives 150–157
 Johann Brazda/Robert Schediwy
Controlling in Co-operatives 157–163
 Hans-Jürgen Wurl
Co-operative Banks 163–169
 Oswald Hahn
Co-operative under Public Law 169–170
 Bernhard Großfeld/Cornelius Renken
Cooperativismo Sanitario (Health care co-operativism) 170–179
 Salvador Mussons
Corporate Culture of Co-operatives 179–186
 Eberhard Dülfer
Credit Unions, World Council of 186–189
 Christopher Baker
Cybernetics and Cooperation 189–193
 Bernd Schiemenz

Data Processing in Co-operative Organizations 194–198
Walter Bausch

Desjardins, Alphonse (1854–1920)/ Filene, Edward A. (1860–1937) 198–199
Roland Pohling

Development of Co-operatives in Africa, South of Sahara 199–205
Samuel C. Chukwu

Development of Co-operatives in Eastern Europe 205–211
Tadeusz Kowalak

Development of Co-operatives in Israel .. 211–216
Yehuda Don

Development of Co-operatives in Latin America 216–222
Dieter W. Benecke

Development of Co-operatives in North America 222–226
J.G. Craig

Development of Co-operatives in Northern Africa 226–234
Jamil Chaabouni

Development of Co-operatives in South Asia 234–242
Arvind Vyas

Development of Co-operatives in South-East Asia 242–247
Ali Mahmood Khan/Y. Bhatti

Development of Co-operatives in Turkey 248–254
Ismail Duymaz

Development Policy, Co-operatives in ... 254–259
Jochen Röpke

Discriminatory Analysis Procedures for Corporate Assessment 259–265
Jörg Baetge/Markus Feidicker

Diversification Strategies of Co-operatives 265–271
Axel Bänsch

Dual or Double Nature of Co-operatives . 271–273
Alfred Hanel

Early Warning Systems for (Credit) Co-operatives 274–281
Eberhard Dülfer /Jost W. Kramer

Economic Order and Co-operatives 281–287
Walter Hamm

Economie Sociale 287–292
Claude Vienney

Education and Training in Africa, Co-operative 292–299
Anthony N. Nchari

Education and Training in Asia, Co-operative 299–309
Ganesh P.Gupta/ Dharm Vir

Education and Training in Europe, Co-operative 309–313
Johann Brazda/Tode Todev

Education and Training in Germany, Co-operative 313–321
Walter Swoboda

Education and Training in Latin America, Co-operative 321–329
Benjamin Ramirez

Education and Training in North America, Co-operative 329–334
Lou Hammond Ketilson/Brett Fairbairn

Environmental Protection and Co-operatives 334–339
Eberhard Seidel

Equity Capital, Co-operative 339–343
Horst Seuster

Ethics and Co-operatives 343–346
Juhani Laurinkari/Vesa Laakkonen

European Community (Union) and Co-operatives 346–349
André Van Hulle

European Cooperation of Co-operative Central Banks 352–355
Friedbert Malt

Evaluation of Co-operative Organizations 355–363
Eberhard Dülfer

Federation Statistics of Co-operative Organizations 363–367
Peter von der Lippe

Federations, Co-operative 367–372
Peter Schwarz

Financial Accounting Law for Co-operatives 372–376
Erich Weinerth

Financing of Co-operatives 376–382
Horst Seuster

Forms of Cooperation in the Agricultural Sector assuming non-Co-operative legal forms 382–385
Eberhard Schinke

Franchising in Co-operative Business ... 385–387
Georg C.Neumann

GACOPEA/AMSAC 388–392
Gabriele Ullrich

GDR, Co-operatives in the Former 392–397
Gerhard Rönnebeck/Thomas Pfeiffer

Gierke, Otto von 397–398
Friedel Linneborn

Goods, Individual, Private, Collective ... 398–403
Ulrich Fehl

Group Theory, Co-operatives in the 403–407
Paul Trappe

Group, Common Innitiative 407–409
Emmanuel Kamdem

Group, The Co-operative 409–412
Friedrich Fürstenberg

Guilds 412–417
   Alfred Kieser

Haas, Wilhelm (1839–1913) 418
   Horst Seuster
Health Care System, Co-operatives and
   Other Institutions in the 419–424
   Jürgen Zerche
History of Co-operative Ideas 424–429
   Werner W. Engelhardt
History of Co-operatives before 1800 429–436
   Julius Otto Müller
History of Co-operatives in Europe in
   the 19th Century 436–440
   Julius Otto Müller
Honorary Office, Co-operative 440–445
   Günther Ringle
Housing Reform and the Housing Reform Movement 445–449
   Helmut Jenkis
Housing Co-operatives 449–453
   Jürgen Zerche
Huber, Victor Aimé (1800–1869) 553–457
   Helmut Jenkis
Human Resource Management in the
   German and Austrian Co-operative
   Banking Industry 457–460
   Dudo von Eckardstein

Incentives of Co-operatives 461–464
   Günther Ringle
Industrial Relations, An Integrative Concept 464–469
   Hans W. Hetzler
Informal Co-operatives 469–472
   Julius Otto Müller
Institutional Economics: Co-operatives .. 472–477
   Holger Bonus
Insurance, Co-operative 477–484
   Hans-Dieter Wehlmann
Intercompany Cooperation 484–489
   Rudolf Bratschitsch
International Co-operative Alliance 489–491
   Bruce Thodarsson
International Co-operative Organizations 491–499
   S.K. Saxena
International Raiffeisen Union, The 499–503
   Willi Croll
Internationalization of Co-operative
   Trading Enterprises 503–510
   Annette Gobbers

Joint Stock Company, Co-operative 511–517
   Martin Luther
Joint-Production Co-operatives 517–521
   Eberhard Dülfer
Joint Ventures 522–527
   Klaus Macharzina

Kaufmann, Heinrich (1864–1928) 528–529
   Heinz Stoffregen
Kolkhozes 530–532
   Jerzy Kleer

Labour-Management 533–538
   Ernst Fehr
Landwirtschaftsanpassungsgesetz–
   LAG 538–540
   Horst Seuster
Law Concerning Company Groups and
   Co-operatives 540–543
   Peter Erlinghagen
Law, International Co-operative 543–550
   Hans-H. Münkner
Law, National Co-operative (example:
   Germany) 551–553
   Volker Beuthien
Legal Form, Co-operative 553–559
   Volker Beuthien
Legal Transformation of a Co-operative . 559–563
   Peter Erlinghagen
Liability of Co-operative Boards 563–568
   Peter Erlinghagen
Linking Banks and Self-Help Groups ... 569–573
   Hans Dieter Seibel

Machinery Associations and Machinery
   Rings in Agriculture 574–579
   Johannes Kuhn
Management in Co-operatives 579–584
   Helmut Wagner
Management Teams 584–586
   Hartmut Kreikebaum
Managerial Economics of Co-operatives 587–592
   Eberhard Dülfer
Marketing Co-operatives 592–596
   Eduard Mändle
Marketing Strategies of Co-operatives 596–602
   Jerker Nilsson
Marshall, Alfred (1842–1924) 602–603
   Thomas Brockmeier
MATCOM 603–607
   Gabriele Ullrich
Mergers and Consolidations in the
   Co-operative System 607–613
   Ulrich Fehl/Carsten Schreiter
Mill, John Stuart (1806–1873) 613–615
   Thomas Brockmeier
Mondragon 615–620
   Robert Hettlage
Motivation for Cooperation 620–622
   Juhani Laurinkari
Multi-Use Credit Co-operatives 623–626
   Emmerich Bakonyi

Nachschußpflicht (member obligation to make further contributions) 627–632
Peter Erlinghagen
New Co-operatives 632–638
Marlene Kück
Non Profit Organizations 638–640
Wolfgang Pelzl

Officialization of Co-operatives 641–647
Alfred Hanel
Oligarchy in Co-operatives 647–651
Rainer Vierheller
Operational Size of Co-operatives 651–654
Ernst-Bernd Blümle
Oppenheimer, Franz (1864–1943) ·....... 654–656
Oswald Hahn
Organizational Structure of Co-operative Societies......................... 656–661
Hans-H. Münkner
Organizational Structures, Co-operative: Mesosociological Aspects of Co-operatives 661–665
Robert Hettlage
Owen, Robert (1771–1858) 665–667
Sydney Pollard
Own Production, Consumer Co-operative 668–670
Johann Brazda/Robert Schediwy

Partnership Enterprises 671–678
Richard Weiskopf/Stephan Laske
Periodicals, Co-operative 679–682
Herbert Wendt
Pfeiffer, Eduard (1835–1921) 682–684
Heinz Stoffregen
Plunkett, Sir Horace (1854–1932) 684–685
Elise Bayley
Plunkett-Foundation, The 686–687
Edgar Parnell
Policies for the Promotion of Co-operatives in Developing Countries 687–692
Alfred Hanel
Pre-co-operative Forms of Cooperation 693–700
Hans-H.Münkner
Pricing Policy among Co-operatives 700–705
Ulrich Fehl/Jürgen Zörcher.
Principle of Cost Coverage 705–708
Jens Jokisch
Principles of the Co-operative System 708–716
Juhani Laurinkari
Privatization and Collectivization by Co-operatives .... 716 –721
Ulrich Fehl/Carsten Schreiter
Producer Associations 722–726
Egon Wöhlken
Production Co-operatives 726–731
Theodor Bergmann

Produktionsförderungsgenossenschaften (Co-operatives for the Promotion of Production) 731–736
Johannes G.F.Wörz/Ottfried C. Kirsch
Promotion Balance Sheet, Promotion Report, Promotion System 736–739
Wilhelm Weber/ Johann Brazda
Promotion Mandate 740–745
Werner Großkopf
Public Benefit Orientation and Co-operatives 745–750
Helmut Jenkis
Public Services in Latin America, Co-operatives for 750–754
Hermann Schneider/Dante Cracogna

Raiffeisen, Friedrich Wilhelm (1818–1888) 755–756
Horst Seuster
Ratio-based Credit Rating Procedures Used by Co-operative Banks 756–762
Gert Schemmann
Register, the Co-operative 762–765
Christian Schwarz
Reimbursements, Co-operative 766–769
Eberhard Dülfer/Carlos Bienefeld
Relationship Patterns, Co-operative: Microsociological Aspects of Co-operatives 770–773
Robert Hettlage
Religious Co-operatives, Cloisters 773–775
Friedrich Fürstenberg
Rochdale Equitable Pioneers Society, The 776–778
Roy Garratt
Rural Co-operatives 778–784
Hans H. Gessner
Rural Peoples Communes in China 784–786
Jerzy Kleer

Schulze-Delitzsch, Hermann (1808–1883) 787–789
Eberhard Dülfer
Security Mechanisms within the Federal Association of German Co-operative Banks (BVR) 789–794
Wolfgang Grüger
Selection of Members 794–796
Juhani Laurinkari
Self-help Organizations and Third-World Development 796–802
Herbert Kötter
Social Policy and Co-operative System 802–806
Vesa Laakkonen/Juhani Laurinkari
Socialist Co-operative Theory under Real Socialism 807–810
Jerzy Kleer

Socialist Critics of Co-operatives 810–815
Karl-Hans Hartwig
Societal Form, Co-operative as a 815–820
Robert Hettlage
Solidarity 820–823
Mario Patera
State and Co-operatives in a Market
  Economy 823–828
Walter Hamm
State and Co-operatives in Socialism 828–833
Tadeusz Kowalak
Strategic Alliances 833–841
Dietger Hahn/Lutz Kaufmann
Strategies Employed when Establishing
  Co-operatives 841–846
Julius Otto Müller
Strategic Planning in Co-operatives 846–850
Hartmut Kreikebaum
Structural Changes among German Co-
  operative Banks 850–853
Bernd Kubista
Structural Types of the Co-operative 853–858
Eberhard Dülfer
Subsidiarity among Co-operatives 858–861
Reiner Vierheller
Supply Co-operatives 861–864
Werner Großkopf

Taxation of Co-operatives 865–871
Rüdiger Philipowski
Theory and Science of Cooperation 871–879
Werner Wilhelm Engelhardt

Theory of Co-operative Cooperation 879–885
Rolf Eschenburg
"Third Way", Co-operatives as a 885–887
Paul Trappe
Trade Unions and the Co-operative System 887–895
Achim von Loesch
Transport Co-operatives 895–897
Ulrich Schumacher

United Nations System and Co-operatives 898–906
Jürgen von Muralt

Walras, Léon (1834–1919)/ Pareto, Vilfredo (1848–1923) 907–909
Thomas Brockmeier
Women and Co-operatives in Developing Countries 909–916
Sabine Becker(ILO)
Worker Co-determination in Co-operatives 916–919
Klaus Bartölke

List of Contributors 921–923

Index of Persons 925–939

Subject Index 940–961

Recommendations for Use

1. The **Headword Articles** (Stichwortartikel) of the IHCO are presented in alphabetical order. They all are organized in the same pattern:

- Other *Headwords* related to the subject addressed are listed at the beginning of each article.
- These are followed by a *List of the main headings/sections* of the article.
- In the text all proper names are printed in italics. Technical terms with specific national or cultural origin are presented in the original language (e.g. Landwirtschaftsanpassungsgesetz; champs communs).
- Each article has a *Bibliography* in alphabetical order.

2. **References** (Verweise) accord with the following rules:

- There are *cross-references* to other articles in the International Handbook.
- *References* within the text give author (and year of publication) of the work cited. When a source is quoted *verbatim*, page numbers are also given. Full details can then be found in the *Bibliography* at the end of the article concerned.

3. A number of **Indexes** have been added to facilitate the use of the International Handbook:

- The List of *Contents* at the beginning of the volume lists the Headwords of the Handbook and their authors.
- The List of *Contributors* (names and related institution).
- The *Subject Index* in addition to the headwords (titles of articles, appearing in bold print) includes further keywords, technical terms and institutional names and refers to the page they are to be found.
- *Abbreviations of institutional names* are included in the Subject Index, and refer to the page where the full name is to be found.
- The *Index of Persons* includes all proper names mentioned in the text as well as in the bibliographies.

Accounting in Co-operatives

HERMANN SIEGFRIED RINN [J]

(see also: *Financial Accounting Law*; *Auditing*; *Controlling*; *Taxation*; *Evaluation*; *Promotion Balance-sheet*)

I. Legal-organizational Framework; II. Objectives, Interests and Expectations; III. Success Orientation; IV. Critical Judgment.

I. Legal-organizational Framework

The rendering of accounts and/or reporting are tasks inherent in the broad range of responsibilities determining the possibility to duplicate operations objectively or subjectively, the overall success of which can be measured in individual cases, in periods or according to company categories.

The annual financial statement is the central element of accounting which German co-operatives are obligated to draw up according to *HGB* (*Handelsgesetzbuch*, German Commercial Code), *GenG* (*Genossenschaftsgesetz*, German Co-operative Law), other special laws (e.g. *KWG* [*Kreditwesengesetz*, German Banking Law], *WGG* (Rent Subsidy Law)) and ordinances as well as to their own by-laws, rules of procedure and other internal regulations (→ *Financial Accounting Law*). "Accounting" should be understood as comprehensive documentation and demonstration of the foundations and developments of a commercial undertaking. Co-operatives thereby do not fundamentally differ from companies assuming other corporate forms.

Leffson sees the hierarchy of norms involved in accounting resulting from the identification of the legal nature of the principles of orderly bookkeeping and/or the balancing of accounts. The following figure of information fields was developed out of the various attempts to present the term "accounting" in an all-encompassing manner (c.f. *Schierenbeck*, p.466; *Jacob*, p.404; *Leffson*, p.62):

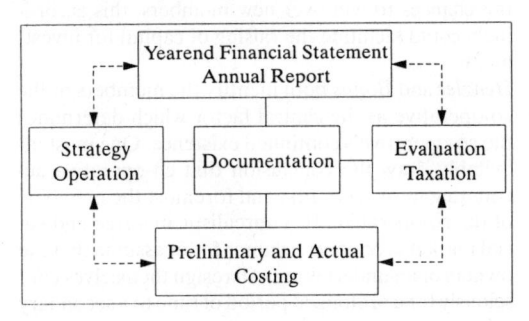

Figure 1.

In general one can continue with *Leffson's* train of thought which derives the obligation for reporting from goals associated with the transmission of information – namely for the sake of creditor and proprietary protection. Reporting embraces retrospectives and prognoses and substantiates itself in documentation. Corporate strategies and operations can dispense with documentation just as little as can evaluating and taxation. Preliminary and actual costing are invariably quite closely tied together with documentation, which represents the central binding factor of the entire information system.

Lawmakers very clearly demand corporations to provide appropriate representation of their actual financial status with respect to the content of their annual financial statements (*HGB*, § 264, Subsec.2). The Law provides for additional details to be presented in an appendix when special circumstances prevent the company from providing such appropriate representation in their annual financial statements. The general norm previously mentioned is to be applied to co-operatives according to *HGB*, § 336, Subsec.2 as long as the provisions found in *HGB*, 337 ff. do not specify otherwise. According to *HGB*, § 242 the annual financial report consists of a balance sheet as well as a profit and loss account; it also includes an appendix according to *HGB*, § 264, Subsec.2 in combination with *HGB*, §§ 284288 which is of considerable importance for the rendering of accounts in a registered co-operative.

A representation of the various types of balance sheets with their grounds, content and functions is provided by *Schierenbeck*, p. 482. Figure 2 includes approaches of both functional and group-oriented accounting which lawmakers can only partly take into consideration on account of their greater interest in general public matters and of the extent accounting provisions are used to form the parameters for all enterprises. This diagram has been supplemented with the category " → *Promotion Balance Sheet*" so that the connection to the central task of co-operative accounting procedures is not overlooked.

Registered co-operatives are defined as commercial traders in *GenG*, § 17, Subsec.2 and are obligated to render accounts according to *HGB*, §§ 238 ff. (→ *Legal Form, Co-operative*).

II. Objectives, Interests and Expectations

Co-operatives pursue economic goals – the promotion of their members' enterprises and households – via their joint business unit. Lawmakers commit co-operatives to these economic functions and only in exceptional situations allow them to pursue public benefit purposes in a limited scope.

Type of Balance Sheet	Reason	Content	Functions
Commercial balance sheet	Annual financial report prescribed for in HGB, 242	Comparison of assets and capital on the balance sheet date according to commercial balance sheet and assessment provisions.	Accountability (with respect to creditors, employees, the general public), documentation of earnings and the financial situaion; numerical basis for corporate political decisions.
Tax balance sheet	Year-end tax report prescribed for in EStG, § 5	Similar to commercial balance sheet; only supplemental orientation around special provisions for the balance sheet and assessment (authoritative principle of the commercial balance sheet.	Ascertain taxable profits from a period through a (pure) net worth comparison, corrected for contributions and withdrawals according to EStG, § 4–7.
Consolidated balance sheet	Year-end financial corporate group according to HGB, § 290	Comparison of assets and capital companies belonging to the corporate group; exclusion of double accounting.	Information about the earnings report of a of all affiliated and financial situation of the corporate group.
Period balance sheet	Supplements the year-end financial report	Ascertainment of inventory changes between 2 consecutive reporting dates; indication of only the balance (change in balance) or separate reports of inventory changes after additions and disposals (flow statement).	Presentation of financial transactions (application of funds, source of funds, liquidity).
Social balance sheet	Supplements the year-end financial report	Not a balance as such, but rather solely a systematic and consequential presentation of social services (societal advantage from corporate activities) and social costs (societal detriment, e.g. environmental damage by company).	Accountability of societal consequences caused by the company's economic processes; social information for management and staff.
Promotion balance sheet	Supplements the year-end financial report	The success of the jointly run business enterprise seen as provided utility and the attained increase in promotion potential.	Accounting and reporting as an element of self-administration intended according to GenG, § 1.

Figure 2.

According to *Bonus* the co-operative is a hybrid organizational form, that is a characteristic, independent organizational form of entrepreneurial activity fused together out of market and heirarchical elements. This concise formula of the unique co-operative character differs from those developed by *Dülfer* (1977) and *Henzler* (1970). *Bonus* names central and peripheral production factors which in the long term can only be ideally combined when those individuals shouldering the undertaking recognize the real factor contribution in the accounts of the promotional undertaking, and when they can freely decide about their own participation.

Henzler (1970) addresses the problems co-operatives confront in a growing economy. He comes to the conclusion that improving the situation of members as investors in the co-operative will increase the chances to win over new members; this accordingly could facilitate the raising of capital for investments.

Henzler and *Bonus* both identify the members of the co-operative as the central factor which determines the co-operative's continued existence. One must inevitably draw the conclusion that co-operative accounting must serve first and foremost the members of the co-operative. It is unrealistic in a free and social market economy to clamor for or assume that the owners of an undertaking will resign themselves consciously for a prolonged period of time to a secondary role.

Model analogous to Leffson/Baetge 1976, p.23.

```
                        Regulation of Interests
                       /                        \
        Regulation of Promotion              Regulation of Information
       /         |          \                           |
Maintenance  Reimbursement  Regulation of      Documentation and Reporting
of Promotion               Profit Distribution        /          \
Capability                                        Internal    External
```

Central Tenet: The year-end financial report of the registered co-operative is a compromise determined by lawmakers which compensates diverging interests held by co-operators

---

Model analogous to Leffson/Moxter 1976, p.91/100.

```
                    Principles of Adequacy
                   /                      \
          Bookkeeping                    Reporting
                                        /         \
     Functions                General Principles   Core Principles
     – Itemization            – Truthfulness       Orientation around
     – Journal                – Totality           – Addressees
     – Accounts               – Clarity            – Decision making
                                                   – Hazards
     Verifiability
     – Documentation
     – Storing Past Information
```

Central Tenet: Differing core and general principles which ensure adequate accounting must correspond to the various accounting and reporting functions.

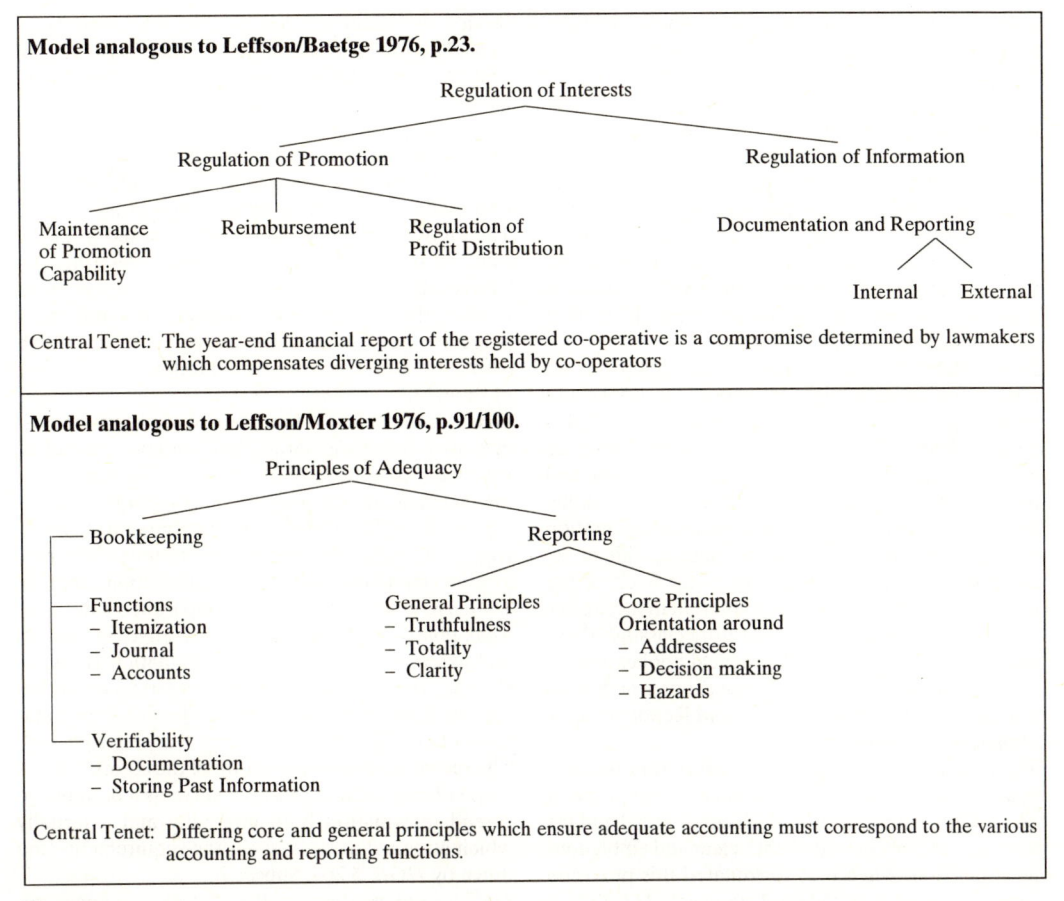

Figure 3.

Members' interest in the rendering of accounts is directly relative to:

- the degree of integration and dependency of the member enterprises on the co-operative business operation as well as their competitive situation with respect to the co-operative;
- the direction and extent of the co-operative's entrepreneurial activities;
- members' risk contribution;
- members' motive for investment participation.

One must agree with *Bonus* that it is of equal importance for the co-operative as a type of business enterprise to prove its economic efficiency and to safeguard the trust of its members. Co-operative accounting must in particular address this task, whereby members could develop a behavior and/or disposition which either stabilizes or endangers the basis. Priority must insofar be given to the level of member information both in a retrospective and prognostic sense. Only in this context can *Großfeld* and *Reemann* be understood who expressly warn against the co-operative's public image being determined by brochures and association speeches.

Lawmakers underline the primacy of member's rights and claims to information stated in *GenG*, § 147. *GenG*, § 60 also states that members should receive important information firsthand with regard to the position and development of special and critical co-operative situations. *Baetge* and *Moxter* closely associate the demands placed on accounting with the "natural" state of information in and about companies. Figure 3 renders the corresponding model conceptions to the co-operative circumstances.

Members' right to information as well as management's obligation to render accounts are as a matter of course restricted by higher level protection rights. Co-operative by-laws thus reserve the right to deny access to information.

The extensive accounting procedures without a doubt also fulfill in part creditor and minority investor protection with respect to members on account of their frequent function as creditors and the openly public nature of general and representatives' assemblies.

Employees of co-operatives also attain knowledge through numerous channels, in particular through information provided by members which they can use to protect their own interests, such as in the situation of a potential merger for the accomodation of conflicting interests.

Dicussion is not necessary concerning the rights of the general public to have access to an adequate rendering of accounts – and in particular when co-operatives enjoy local, regional, professional, branch-specific or market-regulating importance (c.f. residential building, dairy and supply co-operatives). Co-operatives must accordingly have an interest in convincing the general public through "offensive" accounting that they are promotional facilities for all market partners who are willing to cooperate.

Due to their claim to tax monies, tax authorities retain an independent right to inspect the books and renderings of co-operative accounts (c.f. *AO* ([*Abgabenordnung*, German Fiscal Code], §§ 140 ff. as well as the tax laws for transportation, net worth and earnings) (→ *Taxation*). The authoritative principle, the reversed authoritative principle and the retention option are of importance on the material side of accounting when the co-operative avails itself of the corporate-political advantages inherent in these principles and options. *Schlüter* therefore classifies these matters within the scope of practical application involving the *HGB* and *GenG* provisions which were altered through the Accounting and Reporting Law (*Bilanzrichtliniengesetz*).

The board fundamentally must ensure that the necessary co-operative account books are kept properly and orderly with respect to both commercial and tax laws. Lawmakers provided both clear and ambiguous legal positions when they formulated this provision found in *GenG*, § 33, Subsec.1, to which *AO*, § 140 is related. *Schaffland* trains his attention to the fact that co-operatives are subject to the obligation to render accounts according to *HGB*, § 238, Subsec.1, Sent.1 and to the obligation to draw a balance sheet according to *HGB*, § 242; in both cases this must correspond to the *GoB* (*Grundsätze ordnungsmäßiger Buchführung*, Principles of Proper Bookkeeping Documentation). The quantity and nature of the necessary account books are contingent on the individual situation and on the *GoB*.

III. Success Orientation

Co-operatives would be endangering their existence as companies and business undertakings if they merely fulfilled the legally prescribed minimum of accounting functions, that is if they solely followed the codified and generally accepted *GoB* procedures. Accounting procedures in co-operatives should make use of and develop means and tools that serve the level of entitlement enjoyed by those people interested in the rendering of accounts and/or their addressees. The DGRV (German Co-operative and Raiffeisen Union) has published guidelines for the annual financial reports of credit, commodity and service co-operatives since 1974 (now in its third edition). This publication contains a collection of all provisions and standardized forms serving proper bookkeeping, reporting, and balance sheet needs.

Every co-operative is free to take advantage of all explained alternatives and potential lee-way for the sake of its own interests and is accordingly obligated to provide mandatory or optional reporting.

The DGRV guideline handbooks proceed from the rules of transformation in the sense described by *Baetge* which resemble the rules of orderliness practised by the auditing federations and which thereby possess a general or consultative character. *Bergmann* and *Ohlmeyer/Bergmann* follow a similar line of thought.

Whereas the external reporting of the registered co-operative follows generally binding laws (excluding the listed exceptions in *HGB*, § 336, Subsec.2), the management of the respective co-operative is reserved the right to inform its members through retrospective and prognostic interpretations of the promotion mandate and about promotion success. *Dülfer/Kramer* illustrate to an unparalled extent the weak points affecting credit co-operatives in internal and external accounting; this explanation is just as clear as their discussion on the understandable human inclination to undertake subjective interpretations of risk situations (→ *Early Warning Systems*). The recognized sensitive nature of the co-operative's scope of information must not serve as a pretense to spread information both internally and externally which attempts to circumvent the requirements laid down by *HGB*, § 264, Subsec.2.

Dülfer/Kramer discuss the "market-linkage co-operative" and allocate the co-operative identity principle strategic importance (→ *Structural Types*); this is because business conducted with non-members as a capacity factor to an extensive degree is irreplaceable and therefore is unavoidable as a disruptive factor. Whereas on the one hand the combination of competition management and cooperation management is referred to, other authors address → *corporate culture* or the co-operative's attachment to its members.

The objective and comprehensive rendering of accounts both internally and externally in the sense of reporting presents the opportunity to attend most closely to member relationships; this is the conclusion of all empirical research results and theoretical observations. At the same time, however, in crisis periods the rendering of accounts harbors the danger of crippling the market-linkage co-operative or instigating its self-destruction. Within this wide range of potential consequences the established and optional elements of information should be carefully weighed out – information which serves the members and at the same time protects the existential interests of the co-operative.

Among the clearly dominating principles of self-administration and self-responsibility the demand for critical analysis and careful planning must be met just as conscientiously and thoroughly as the intention to contribute to motivation with respect to management and the development of new markets. Co-operatives should pursue information management on the basis of dependable and rational techniques, systems and procedures in the sense of availing themselves of all data at their disposal (→ *Data Processing*). Elements of accounting can be coupled with strategic and operative approaches of corporate policy when information is regularly collected and utilized in a directed manner. Formulated somewhat differently, the provision of information in the planning and controlling systems (→ *Controlling*) assumes the same level of importance as in the field of marketing. *Schulte* undertakes to juxtapose the components of a credit co-operative's marketing controlling system with those of a finance controlling system on account of their common information basis. FINCON, MACON and GBICON procedures are identified as elements of an incomplete BVR-controlling concept in the sense of an allround information system.

Ebert explains the terms "strategic" and "operative" controlling in his articles addressing new management instruments. The following Figure 4 designed especially for this provides a great number of approaches to corporate management. According to the position of the DGRV works committee (1986) the precondition for an objective rendering of accounts external to the co-operative is a functioning internal controlling and information system. The supervisory boards (→ *Organizational Structure of Societies*) must know their element and functional methods and use them to oversee the company with the necessary and expected scrutiny (*Metz*). Operational reporting is suitable for this, that is, a system directed along maintaining the corporate policy decided upon by the board. According to the DGRV works committee (1990), external auditing must ascertain the extent the accounting system is constructed and used as a management instrument (→ *Auditing*).

Konrad and *Vikas* presented the following management functions (→ *Management in Co-operatives*) in a case study found in the collection edited by *Jacob*.

The connection between corporate goals, control information and accounting's control function is clearly presented in Figure 5 Financing objectives as well as profitability and asset structure goals require voted approval in a co-operative and an uptodate control mechanism with respect to their realization (→ *Financing*). The verifiable dimension of attained promotion goals not only determines the extent the members are attached to their co-operative but also the degree of truth in internal and external accounting, which in general should fulfill the following requirements:

1. Produce the most dependable data pool possible;
2. Operate according to strategic planning;
3. Impart real information.

Jacob provides assistance oriented around daily practise by differentiating between project accounting and periodic accounting as well as between internal and external accounting. Attention should be cast to *Jacob's* note concerning the problems in calculating performance in the combine group; more attention should be cast to member and/or customer relationships with their contribution margins. The obligation to promote the members (→ *Promotion Mandate*) should be pretense enough to concentrate accounting procedures in the co-operative bodies on this aspect. A project-related presentation of the employment of means as well as intended and achieved results can facilitate members in their identification process with the co-operative.

IV. Critical Judgment

A detailed enterprise accounting system which is oriented around the strategic and operational goals of the co-operative without a doubt sets the best preconditions for the responsible bodies to be suitably informed in order to make the best possible professional decisions affecting the undertaking as a whole. The transparency of the decision-making basis greatly facilitates ongoing control of the development and evaluation of the periodic, group or project-related results undertaken by the management and its bodies entrusted with surveillance functions.

Extensive unanimity among the elected member representatives – above all those on the board and supervisory board – with respect to the principles of evaluating the goals and success of the company is of considerable importance for the credibility of the co-operative's rendering of accounts. *Richter* concedes that the diversity of members' goals alone complicates every calculation of the results. For him "operational" is not identical with "quantifiable". It is a reasonable demand that goal realization must be verifiable.

The supervisory board must address these questions and its position to them in its mandatory annual progress report – above all in its position to the board's yearend report. According to *Dülfer*, the expert opinion of this surveillance body bridges a gap in the control system and as such fulfills the initial precondition for members to vote and discharge the board.

Direct member participation in the results remains the most important element of cooperation in co-operative organizations. *Manewald* interprets the introduction of commodity reimbursements in credit co-operatives as an opportunity to reorient activity around promotion as it was formerly practised. According to *Berge* concerns about the co-operative's

Controlling

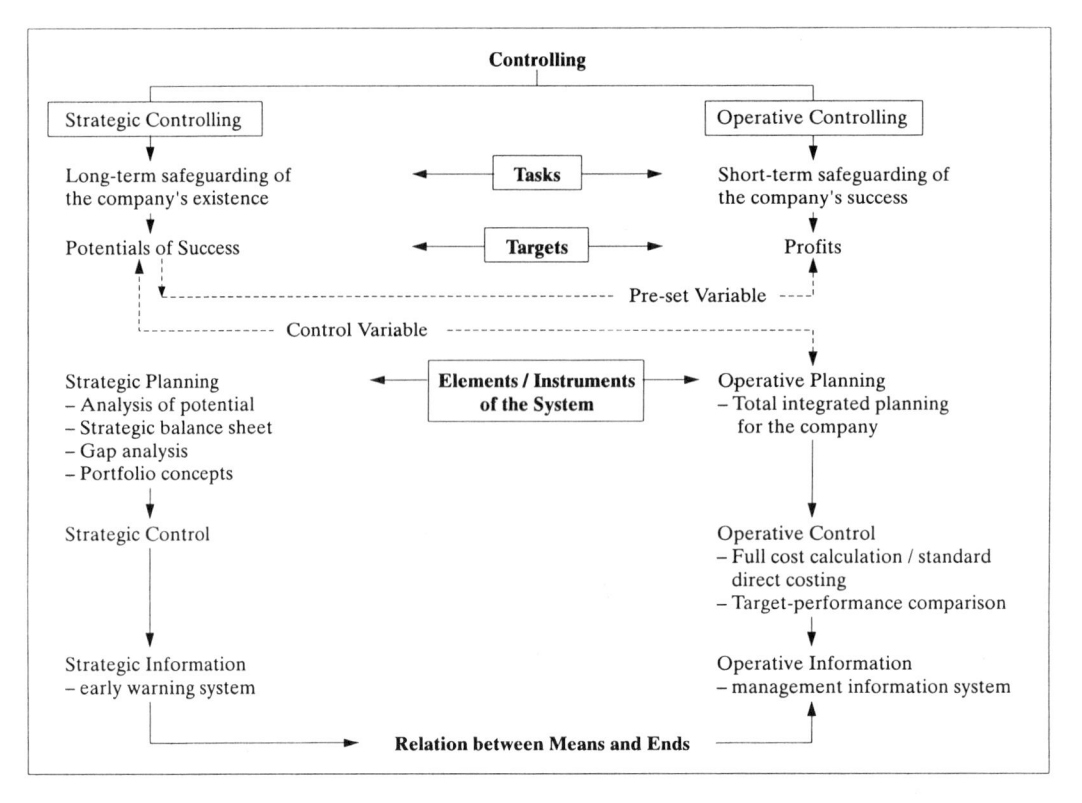

Strategic Controlling
Long-term safeguarding of the company's existence
↓
Potentials of Success

Operative Controlling
Short-term safeguarding of the company's success
↓
Profits

Tasks ← → Tasks
Targets ← → Targets
Pre-set Variable
Control Variable

Elements / Instruments of the System

Strategic Planning
– Analysis of potential
– Strategic balance sheet
– Gap analysis
– Portfolio concepts
↓
Strategic Control
↓
Strategic Information
– early warning system

Operative Planning
– Total integrated planning for the company
↓
Operative Control
– Full cost calculation / standard direct costing
– Target-performance comparison
↓
Operative Information
– management information system

Relation between Means and Ends

Figure 4: Breakdown of Controlling.

Management Functions

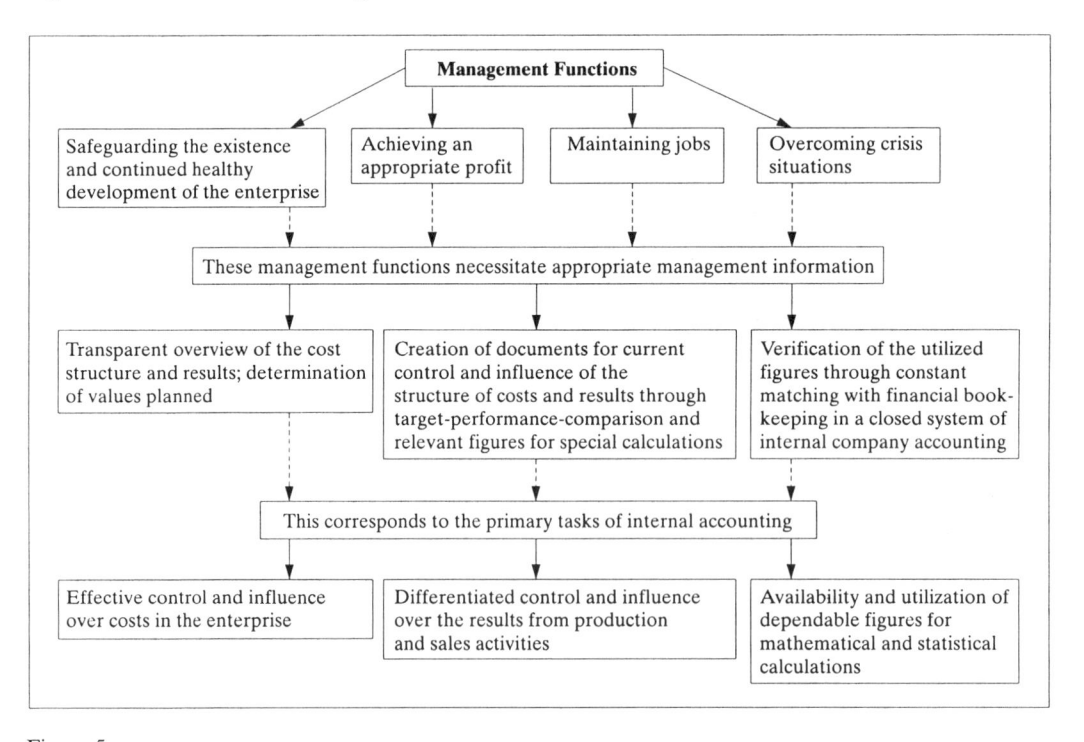

- Safeguarding the existence and continued healthy development of the enterprise
- Achieving an appropriate profit
- Maintaining jobs
- Overcoming crisis situations

These management functions necessitate appropriate management information

| Transparent overview of the cost structure and results; determination of values planned | Creation of documents for current control and influence of the structure of costs and results through target-performance-comparison and relevant figures for special calculations | Verification of the utilized figures through constant matching with financial bookkeeping in a closed system of internal company accounting |

This corresponds to the primary tasks of internal accounting

| Effective control and influence over costs in the enterprise | Differentiated control and influence over the results from production and sales activities | Availability and utilization of dependable figures for mathematical and statistical calculations |

Figure 5.

ability to provide promotion also arise when two-thirds or so of the achieved surplus in a fiscal year is directed to the formation of reserves and thus relinquished to the tax authorities.

Jacob emphasizes the importance internal performance and earnings reports have for trade and production sectors, above all with respect to entrepreneurial decision-making. *Schotenroehr* in turn addresses the situation that additional classification problems arise for co-operative and corporate combine systems. Complete coverage and calculation of outputs and costs as well as an accurate classification of their source and cause are preconditions for a correct distribution of earnings, which can only be executed in the scope of established norms. Alongside this formal balance-sheet law the co-operative must also address the following question through its accounting practises: the extent assessment lee-way and optional approaches as well as certain liberty with respect to the annual financial report and the status report influence the actual amount of the annual surplus which is to be indicated in one sum and divisible (for distribution).

Schlüter summarizes the experience the co-operative sector has gathered with preparing balance sheets according to amended laws in such a manner that the preconditions for uniform co-operative accounting practises are encouraged and furthered. *Schüter* includes the following considerations in the "problem" category (pp.18–22): the provision for valuation continuity (*HGB*, § 252, Subsec.2); rights for optional depreciations and valuations (*HGB*, §§ 253, Subsec.4; 254) in connection with restricted disclosure (*HGB*, § 284, Subsec.1). According to *Schlüter's* position, depreciations according to *HGB*, § 253, Subsec.4 are not justifiable when based on unrealistic fears, purely subjective moments and extreme assessments.

The provision of discretionary freedom is considered by *Großfeld/Reemann* as insufficient as such because they maintain that quiet reserves which more than cover the liabilities are inadmissible. They see the co-operative as a "special association", the economic constitution of which *Weber* addressed in his 1984 dissertation.

Großfeld/Reemann maintain that the free formation of reserves and the promotion obligation are incompatible. Dangers rest in the

- functionaries' interests,
- self/serving goals of the co-operative,
- impediments to free withdrawal,

and ultimately in the co-operative losing its credibility as an institution which promotes its members. The accounting system in a registered co-operative should not only fulfill the three requirements listed previously but it should also develop into an instrument to control the operation of the market co-operative, itself based on voluntary participation with those persons interested in developing the highest possible level of identification with it. It can thereby convey the actual image of a → *corporate culture* worth striving for and worthwhile of participation to all those people either interested in or directly addressed by the co-operative. This goal can be achieved through

- the board exercising selfcontrol functions;
- effective surveillance of the supervisory board;
- members exercising discriminating partnership, and extensive external audits.

Bibliography

Baetge, Jörg/Moxter, Adolf/Schneider, Dieter: Bilanzfragen, Festschrift für Ulrich Leffson, Düsseldorf 1976.
Berge, Helmut/Philipowski, Rüdiger: Zinsrückvergütung in Kreditgenossenschaften, Marburg 1986.
Bergmann, Joseph: Das neue Bilanzrecht für Genossenschaften. In: ZfgG, vol. 36 (1986), pp. 85–98.
Bonus, Holger: Die Genossenschaft als modernes Unternehmenskonzept, Münster 1987.
Die Fachgutachten und Stellungnahmen des IdWP, Düsseldorf 1991.
DGRV (ed.): Jahresabschluß der Kreditgenossenschaft, 3rd edition, Wiesbaden 1990.
DGRV (ed.): Jahresabschluß der Waren- und Dienstleistungsgenossenschaft, 2nd edition, Wiesbaden 1990.
DGRV (ed.): Die Prüfung des internen Kontrollsystems, Schriftenreihe Heft 4, 5th edition, Wiesbaden 1986.
Dülfer, Eberhard: Der Förderauftrag als Gegenstand von Geschäftsberichten und Pflichtprüfungen, Marburg 1981.
Dülfer, Eberhard/Kramer, Jost: Schwachstellenanalyse und Frühwarnsysteme bei Genossenschaftsbanken, Marburg 1990.
Ebert/Koinecke/Peemöller: Controlling in der Praxis, Landsberg am Lech 1985.
Ebert, Günter: Controlling, Managementfunktion und Führungskonzeption, Nürtingen 1990.
Frankenberger, Wilhelm: Der Aufsichtsrat der Genossenschaft, 3rd edition, München 1985.
Großfeld, Bernhard/Reemann: Die neue Genossenschaftsbilanz; in: Bilanz- und Konzernrecht, Festschrift für Reinhard Goerdeler, Düsseldorf 1987.
Havermann, Hans: Der Aussagewert des Jahresabschlusses. In: Die Wirtschaftsprüfung, Heft 21, Düsseldorf 1988.
Henzler, Reinhold: Betriebswirtschaftliche Probleme des Genossenschaftswesens, Wiesbaden 1962.
Henzler, Reinhold: Der genossenschaftliche Grundauftrag, Frankfurt 1970.
Jacob, Herbert: Moderne Kostenrechnung, Wiesbaden 1978.
Lang/Weidmüller (Metz, Egon/Schaffland, Hans-Jürgen): Genossenschaftsgesetz, 32rd edition, Berlin 1988.
Leffson, Ulrich: Die Grundsätze ordnungsmäßiger Buchführung, 7th edition, Düsseldorf 1987.
Manewald, Petra: Zinsrückvergütungen bei Bankgenossenschaften der Primärstufe, Berlin 1988.
Ohlmeyer, Dietrich/Bergmann, Joseph: Das neue genossenschaftliche Bilanzrecht, Wiesbaden 1986.
Richter, Oswald: Möglichkeiten der Operationalisierung des genossenschaftlichen Förderauftrages, Düsseldorf 1981.
Schierenbeck, Henner: Grundzüge der Betriebswirtschaftslehre, 10th edition, München/Wien 1989.
Schlüter, Manfred: Bilanzierung nach neuem Recht – Erfahrungen im Genossenschaftssektor, Münster 1990.
Schotenroehr, Harald: Die Konsolidierte Deckungsbeitrags-

rechnung in kooperativen und konzernmäßigen Verbundsystemen, Göttingen 1975.
Schulte, Heinz-Werner: Controlling in Kreditgenossenschaften, Berlin 1988.
Weber, Heinz-Otto: Die eingetragene Genossenschaft als wirtschaftlicher Sonderverein, Göttingen 1984.

Agricultural Credit and Co-operatives

OTTFRIED C. KIRSCH

(see also: → *Development Policy*; *Co-operative Banks*; *Policies for Promotion*; *Rural Co-operatives*)

I. Problems Facing Small-scale Farmers in Traditional Agricultural Societies; II. The Effect of Government Intervention; III. Credit Schemes and Types of Co-operatives; IV. The Revival of Solidarity Groups; V. Saving Funds and Credit Programmes; VI. Trends within Rural Co-operatives.

I. Problems Facing Small-scale Farmers in Traditional Agricultural Societies

In traditional agricultural societies various factors combine to exclude small-scale farmers from the formal credit sector, thus making them totally dependent upon usurers. Firstly, since these farmers are often mere tenants rather than landowners, they lack the collateral required by the formal credit sector. Secondly, even if they do happen to own their land, they are often unable to afford the cost of registering it in order to use it as collateral. Thirdly, the transaction costs for small-scale formal agricultural credit are so high that the extension of such credit holds little attraction for the financial institutions. Finally, formal agricultural credit tends to be strictly production-oriented, whereas the small-scale farmers frequently need consumption credit in order to be able to pay for weddings or funerals, or to tide them over after a natural catastrophe. For the sake of accuracy it should, however, be pointed out that since consumption credit often represents the only chance of survival for these farmers, it is essential for maintaining the productivity of human capital, and therefore it is highly questionable whether such loans can properly be regarded as consumption credit at all (*Schultz*).

Since the small-scale farmers have little chance of obtaining loans from the formal credit sector, they are forced to turn to private money-lenders. These money-lenders, who are often village traders, offer all kinds of informal credit. In such a face-to-face system, transaction costs are extremely low. However, since these money-lenders enjoy a virtual monopoly in the field of consumption credit, they are able to charge usurious rates of interest. Therefore they also insist that those to whom they grant consumption loans come only to them for production loans or to market their products. As a result, these usurers also enjoy a monopoly in the field of marketing and are thus able to offer the farmers low and unfair prices for their products.

The only chance the farmers have of breaking out of this vicious circle of exploitation is working together to create their own alternative sources of credit, such as *credit and savings co-operatives* (→ *Co-operative Banks*). The advantage of this sort of co-operative is that the farmers' lack of collateral becomes irrelevant because they are able to secure loans by means of joint liability. Such co-operatives need not to put the private money-lenders completely out of business; it is sufficient if they introduce an element of competition and thus force the usurers to offer fairer terms. However, in order to compete successfully with the usurers, such co-operatives must be able not only to offer all kinds of credit, including consumption credit, but also to provide the farmers with funds to repay existing debts to private money-lenders (→ *Development Policy*). Unfortunately, most credit co-operatives simply do not have sufficient financial reserves to meet these requirements.

II. The Effect of Government Intervention

It will be clear from the above that the small-scale farmers in traditional agricultural societies need help if they are to succeed in breaking out of the vicious circle of poverty and exploitation (*Kirsch* et al.). In developing countries this help often comes from government agencies (→ *Co-operative Development in Third World Countries*). Unfortunately, however, these government agencies tend to be more interested in pursuing their own goals than in promoting the idea of self-help. For example, the government departments responsible for planning and implementing agricultural credit programmes often pursue so-called "production campaigns" in which cash crops are promoted instead of individual farms. In addition, by using rural co-operatives to distribute credit in remote areas, they force these co-operatives to become instruments for encouraging production rather than participatory organizations promoting the idea of self-help. A further drawback with promotion through government institutions is that an institutional and legal framework tends to be imposed from above instead of the idea of self-help developing from below. Finally, the ready availability of government money sometimes causes the farmers to develop something of a gift mentality.

The amount of government influence exerted on self-help structures as a result of government-sponsored credit programmes varies according to the terms of the loans involved. Long-term loans for settlement and land development are much more of a bind on farmers than short-term credit, such as crop advances and seasonal production loans. Thus, government-sponsored settlement co-operatives and land development co-operatives leave little room for their members' participation, and although they are supposed to be organized according to the "educational model", they often turn into co-operatives of the "administrative model" (*Dülfer*). The same applies to co-operatives set up within government-financed inter-farm mechanization schemes.

All of this contrasts starkly with the manner in which the European co-operative movements were founded. There the external promoters were committed individuals, such as → *F.W. Raiffeisen*, who introduced the target groups to the idea of self-help. These individuals remained independent of government institutions, a fact which greatly facilitated the development of autonomous, dynamic co-operative movements.

III. Credit Schemes and Types of Co-operatives

Agricultural credit schemes provide either short-term production loans (e.g. for input supply), short-term crop advances (to facilitate joint marketing and processing), medium-term loans (e.g. for livestock development, implements and machinery) or long-term loans (e.g. for buildings, land development and settlement). In most agricultural co-operatives short-term loans are the most common form of credit. Medium-term loans are difficult to monitor and thus, even today, are very uncommon. Long-term loans are generally only available for government-sponsored settlement co-operatives (→ *Linking Banks*).

In Europe, agricultural co-operatives, which originally were based on a thrift and loan society model developed by *Raiffeisen*, soon developed into multi-purpose co-operatives aimed at the supply needs of the farmers (→ *Rural Co-operatives*). However, when introducing the Raiffeisen model in developing countries, the external promoters, in particular government agencies, tended to concentrate on single-purpose credit and savings co-operatives and to entrust marketing activities to special marketing co-operatives. This was especially the case in India and certain other anglophone countries during the colonial period (→ *Co-operative Development in South Asia*).

Since then, many of these single-purpose credit co-operatives have taken on procurement and marketing functions, thereby developing into multi-purpose co-operatives (→ *Multi-Use Credit Co-op*eratives). Conversely, some → *marketing co-operatives* have taken on credit functions. In other cases, a link-up system between credit and marketing co-operatives serves the same purpose. In West-Cameroon, for example, a link-up system is being developed between agricultural marketing co-operatives and community-based → *credit unions* (i.e. local savings and credit co-operatives). Whereas the agricultural marketing co-operatives are under the supervision of the ministry of agriculture, the credit unions represent an autonomous co-operative movement which tries to avoid government influence as much as possible. The credit unions have lent some of their own assets, which consist purely of members' savings, via their central fund to the agricultural marketing co-operatives. This enables the latter to give crop advances to their members, many of whom are also members of the credit unions. As a result of an agreement between the agricultural marketing co-operatives and the credit unions, the marketing board may only distribute the marketing revenues among the marketing co-operatives once the credits unions have been repaid (*Kirsch/Göricke*).

Many agricultural extension services coordinate "supervised credit" programmes. In order to prevent the misallocation of funds, the agricultural development bank gives "credit in kind" (e.g. seed, fertilizers, pesticides) according to a strict production plan. In some of these programmes, in order to ensure repayment, the credit agreement includes an obligation on the part of the farmer to market his produce via a particular institution. As in the above-mentioned link-up system, the farmer is only paid for his produce once the agricultural development bank has been repaid. *Ruthenberg* propagated this approach under the fitting name of "production under close supervision". In such programmes the farmer is often relegated to the role of a mere contractual producer. When supervised credit programmes are implemented through multi-purpose co-operatives, the latter become → *co-operatives for the promotion of agricultural production*. Such co-operatives tend to develop into complex organizations requiring full-time, professional → *management*. However, since the co-operative personnel in most developing countries is provided, or at least trained, by the government, the above-mentioned trend of co-operatives developing into government-controlled institutions (co-operatives of the administrative model) rather than genuine self-help organizations is further strengthened. Instead of creating a dynamic → *organizational culture* aimed at promoting the members' interests, the management adopts the hierarchical organizational culture found in government institutions (→ *Officialization*). In such an environment, agricultural credit becomes seen not as a self-help activity, but rather as a kind of self-service method of distributing government funds. The members fail to identify themselves with their co-operative and therefore have no scruples about evading loan repayments by marketing their produce on the black market. The co-operative is soon paralysed by these overdue and bad loans and is therefore excluded from further government funding. As a result, it eventually becomes dormant and continues to exist on paper only. This phenomenon to some extent explains the large number of "inactive co-operatives" which appear in official registers.

IV. The Revival of Solidarity Groups

In order to improve the low level of repayment in externally funded credit programmes, joint guarantee groups are sometimes set up within co-operatives (→*Policies for Promotion*). The extension of new credit to group members is then made dependent upon the level of repayment rates within the group as a whole. It is thus hoped that pressure from within the group will encourage those members who would otherwise default to repay their loans. Members who continue to default despite such pressure are usually excluded from the group by the other members (*Schäfer-Kehnert*).

In South-East Asia some commercial banks have developed a similar system of group loans in which the banks contract directly with the farmers rather than via a co-operative structure. In such groups, which are kept fairly small, an elected group leader is responsible for negotiating such loans. He is also responsible for production planning, marketing and joint purchase of input. He thus fulfils the same functions as the management of formal co-operatives in the other schemes.

Other programmes have been developed in which groups are formed with the sole aim of establishing better contact between individual group members and the formal credit institutions. It is hoped that this will improve the members' chances of receiving credit from the banks (*Kropp* et al.). Such programmes, however, require relatively large and efficient individual member farms. Joint guarantee funds, partly supplemented by external funds, have proved useful in this respect (→ *Linking Banks and Self-help Groups*).

V. Saving Funds and Credit Programmes

A precondition for the successful integration of agricultural credit programmes with co-operative activities is a possibility to stimulate savings within the co-operatives in order to build up equity capital. With this in mind, some programmes have been developed which make a member's participation in the credit programme dependent upon his having saved regularly over a specific period. Other programmes require part of the money lent to a member to be immediately deposited in a savings account or used to purchase share capital.

VI. Trends within Rural Co-operatives

Originally, agricultural co-operatives, in particular savings and credit co-operatives, were organized on the basis of unlimited liability. This was aimed at strengthening the financial position of the co-operatives. Nowadays, however, with the co-operatives drifting away from genuine, autonomous self-help organizations, unlimited liability has lost its importance and limited liability has become quite common. Channelling agricultural (often government-subsidized) loans through co-operative structures, particularly through savings and credit co-operatives, tends to minimize the members' own efforts at capital formation (→ *Equity Capital*). There are, however, a few exceptions. Some genuine savings and credit co-operatives (i.e credit unions) refuse to accept so-called "easy government money" because they feel it prevents the development of self-reliance and participation. Thus, for instance in Korea and Thailand, government funds are not accepted by the local → *credit unions*. External funds are only accepted by the national credit union federations to finance their so-called "central funds", which serve as interregional financial institutions. In general, credit unions are enjoying a revival in the form of an autonomous co-operative movement restricted to thrift and loan activities.

The trend which can be observed in the industrial countries is a shift away from the multi-purpose co-operatives towards considerably larger and more specialized co-operatives. As a result, double membership in co-operatives with different functions is quite common and allows an effective link-up between credit, supply and marketing. In the course of this development, multi-purpose Raiffeisen co-operatives, which in the past carried out marketing and supply functions as well as credit and savings functions, have been separating off their banking business and merging it with other credit co-operatives to create genuine → *co-operative banks*. In such co-operative banks, long-term loans are secured by real property, whereas working capital is provided in the form of personal loans. In this respect, therefore, co-operative banks scarcely differ from commercial banks.

Bibliography

Adams, Dale W. et al. (eds.): Undermining rural development with cheap credit. Westview Special Studies in Social Political and Economic Development, Boulder and London 1984.

Armbruster, Paul G.: Finanzielle Infrastruktur und organische Entwicklung durch Genossenschaften in ländlichen Räumen der Dritten Welt, Göttingen 1990.

Dülfer, Eberhard: Operational efficiency of agricultural co-operatives in developing countries. FAO Agricultural Development Paper No. 96, Rome 1974.

FAO: Agricultural credit through co-operative and other institutions. FAO Agricultural Studies No. 68, Rome 1965.

Kirsch, Ottfried C./ Göricke, Fred V.: Scope and impact of the credit union movement in selected African countries, Mainz 1977.

Kirsch, Ottfried C. / Armbruster, Paul G. / Kochendörfer-

Lucius, Gudrun: Self-help institutions in developing countries: cooperation involving autonomous primary groups. Studies in Applied Economics and Rural Institutions, Vol.13, Saarbrücken - Fort Lauderdale 1984.
Kropp, Erhard et al.: Linking self-help groups and banks in developing countries. APRACA and GTZ, Eschborn 1989.
Ruthenberg, Hans: Types of organization in agricultural production development, in: Quarterly Journal of International Agriculture, Vol.12 (1973) No. 3/4.
Schaefer-Kehnert, Walter: Success with group lending in Malawi. In: Quarterly Journal of International Agriculture, Vol.19 (1980) No.4.
Schultz, Theodore W.: Investment in human capital. In: American Economic Review, Vol.51 (1961) No.1.
Stockhausen, Joachim von: Staatliche Agrarkreditpolitik und ländliche Finanzmärkte in Ländern der Dritten Welt, Berlin 1984.

Agricultural Trade and Co-operatives

EGON WÖHLKEN [J]

(see also: → *Rural Co-operatives*; *Agricultural Credit*; *Competition; Producer Associations*)

I. Functions; II. Institutions; III. Competition; IV. Development; V. Market Shares; VI. Outlook.

I. Functions

1. Line of Products

Those institutions are identified under the rubric of agricultural trade and co-operatives (the latter in the sense of rural trade co-operatives) which fulfill the identical function: trade with agricultural products. The term agricultural commodities trade is frequently used as a general categorical term for both of these institutions. On the purchasing side of agricultural enterprises, agricultural commodities in the product line include typical working materials such as seed, fertilizer, pesticides, fuel, lubricants, mixed feed and supplemental fodder. On the sales side the agricultural commodities trade collects the products for sale, predominantly grain, oil-bearing seeds and legumes; this is because a great deal of other agricultural products is delivered to product-specific institutions within the trade for further preparation or sale. Examples of this are the grape harvests passed on to the wine growers' co-operatives, milk brought to dairies, and livestock in the cattle trade - either at livestock processing co-operatives or direct at the butchers or slaughterhouses.

2. The Characterization of the Market for Agricultural Goods

The products that agricultural enterprises sell are in the most part nutritional raw materials and are to a considerable degree homogenous in contrast to the food products manufactured from them. The differences according to each product category in the agricultural working materials range from minimum to substantial. Fertilizers and, to a partial degree, additional fodder are comparably homogenous bulk goods; there is a considerable amount of heterogeneity among seeds and pesticides.

A further characteristic of the agricultural market is the insufficient transparency of the market a great number of farmers have who run relatively small enterprises. The agricultural trade and the co-operatives who are market partners of the farmers are disproportionately better informed (*Heidrich*, p.9).

The exceptional feature of the agricultural commodities market is that agricultural enterprises as well as the business of agricultural trade operate in a limited region. In particular, this results from high transportation costs for low priced goods farmers are selling.

3. Range of Activity

Seen from the view of the farmers, the agricultural commodities trade serves the function of a middleman for a limited assortment of agricultural products: to the producers of input goods on the purchasing side and to the processing companies on the sales side.

The following functions fall under the range of activities of agricultural trade and co-operatives along the lines mentioned above: *Trade* in the sense of transactions; *workmanship* in the form of typical trade preparation of the goods collected from the farmers (e.g. cleaning, sorting); *maintaining stock* in order to make the assortment ready and available and, above all, to serve as stockpilers holding tiding-over reserves between harvest and selling for processing, *financing* purchases of working materials, and *consulting* not only with respect to purchasing and selling goods but also concerning production.

II. Institutions

1. Organizational and Legal Forms

Both institutions, agricultural trade and co-operatives equally avail themselves to the functions of agricultural commodities trade. They can, however, be differentiated with respect to their legal and economic status.

The essential difference lies in the economic-political goal orientation of attaining profit in agricultural trade undertaken by individuals as opposed to the promotion commitment that co-operatives undertake (...promoting the earnings or the economic situation of their members through a collective enterprise...). To a certain extent the establishment of this promotion relationship determines the organizational structure of the co-operative; in the ideal situation all members are simultaneously business partners, and all business partners are members (*Dülfer*, col. 1859). The legal form of rural commodities co-operatives on the primary level is therefore almost exclusively that of a registered co-operative according to the Co-operative Law of 1889. The individually administered rural trade works predominately as a private enterprise with one or more persons as owner (entrepreneurs).

Within the group of rural commodities co-operatives, the purchasing and marketing co-operatives which are only involved in commodities business can be differentiated from the credit co-operatives involved in the trade of goods which, aside from banking, additionally run commodities business and therefore fulfill the same function as the purchasing and marketing co-operatives.

2. Regional Distribution

Agricultural trade and co-operatives prove to have typical differences with respect to regional distribution. Agricultural trade enterprises are more heavily represented in regions which have more favorable size structures of the farms, such as in northern Germany (*Prüße*). The rural commodities co-operatives are present all over the total Germany but have a particular dominance in the southwest of Germany predominated by smaller farms (*Prüße*). This is because co-operatives, following their promotion commitment, assume the provision of working materials and the collection of products for sale also in those regions where the smaller farms produce higher collection and distribution costs.

The internal structure of the rural commodities co-operatives as purchasing and marketing co-operatives or as credit co-operatives involved in commodities trade is also different along the lines of regional distribution. According to their sheer number and turnover, the purchasing and marketing co-operatives have their domain in Lower Saxony and North Rhine-Westphalia, whereas credit co-operatives involved in commodities trade dominate in the southern German states, but also in Schleswig-Holstein (*Prüße*).

3. Tiered Organization

The organizational structure of agricultural trade and co-operatives is three-tiered in its arrangement (→ *Federations*). The vertical cooperation between primary co-operatives on the local and lowest level with the main co-operatives on the middle level as a regional center and the Deutsche Raiffeisen Warenzentrale GmbH as the central institution on the national level also made the organization arrangement of vertical cooperation with institutions on the regional and national level necessary for agricultural trade.

From the organizational point of view it is also quite noteworthy that the majority of the regional associations of the sellers of agricultural products have chosen the registered co-operative (→ *Legal Form, Co-operative*) as their legal form (*Jessen*). On the national level, this resulted in the organizational consolidation into the *"Vereinigte Landwarenkaufleute, Bundesvereinigung e.V."*, while the economic consolidation took the name *"Agrarhandelsunion der Vereinigten Landwarenkaufleute GmbH"*.

III. Competition

Agricultural trade and co-operatives generally are in → *competition* with each other because they can both offer farmers identical or similar services. The competition can therefore be characterized by the rivalry which exists between the majority of market participants on each side of the market, the subjective awareness the market participants have of the competition, as well as through the uncertainty of success of the activities on the relevant market (*Mändle*, 1980).

The farmer decides which market partner he will take for the appropriate purchasing or sales transactions; because agrarian production is geographically stationary this decision determines the relevant market with respect to the accessibility of the market partner. As a general rule, the radius of activity is usually larger for the purchase of working materials than for the sale of agricultural products. Through the course of time this radius of activity for agricultural operations has expanded due to improved infrastructure and transport facilities. As in former times, however, the time shortage during the harvest period for the taking over of products still plays an important factor in how the farmer selects a buyer. The buyer can increase his own attractiveness by providing decentralized collection facilities. Similarly, the construction of a system of branch centers also increases the potential of competition (*Kühl*).

One can determine from the presented discussion that statements concerning competition between agricultural trade and co-operatives are only feasible when observing a small area (*Kühl/Hanf*). The relevant market must be defined objectively, spatially and temporally (*Hamm*).

The market form for agricultural commodities as a situation of competition in which suppliers and buyers find each other is an oligopoly with respect to its market structure (*Krelle*). This is so because only a few buyers are present to purchase the farmer's products; possibly more suppliers are accessible for the purchase of equipment and supplies under acceptible conditions. Survey results are also available which lead to the conclusion that agricultural trade and co-operatives have oligopolistic market behavior (*Busch*).

One question still remains open: Do forces influence the competitive position of the two organizational forms of agricultural commodities trade based on the previously mentioned differences in the goal orientation of agricultural trade and co-operatives (profit attainment vs. promotional commitment) or with respect to characteristics intrinsic to each enterprise form?

Agricultural trade is identified by autonomy and independence whereas a special, functionally based relationship exists between a co-operative and its business partners in which the latter as members are represented in the decision making process of the co-operative. This can easily lead to limitations in the corporate policy.

Survey information from central headquarters of agricultural trade and co-operatives indicate that the subjective estimation of the intensity of competition was exclusively rated as "very high" or "high", and that the competitive intensity has increased in the course of time (*Prüße*). By differentiating the statements according to products, the competitive intensity was judged higher for purchases than for sales; within sales, competition for grain was more intense than for potatoes. Both purchases and sales inclined to have stronger and higher levels of competitive intensity within agricultural trade than within co-operatives (*Prüße*). Therefore a certain difference in respect to the organizational form of the agricultural commodities trade can be determined.

According to their own estimations, rural trade co-operatives have seen their competitive position become stronger in the course of time with respect to agricultural trade (Prüße). Because of the shrinking agricultural sector and reductions in purchases and sales, the competition among the rural trade co-operatives for market shares will certainly become stronger (*Kalefeld*).

IV. Development

Agricultural commodities trade is statistically assigned to wholesale trade. It is very clear from tax statistics that the number of obligatory tax payers in the economic sector "wholesale trade of grain, seed, feed and fertilizer" (without definite categorical classifications) fell from 2,200 in 1980 to 1,800 in 1986. The taxable turnover climbed in the same time period from DM 25.3 billion to DM 28.1 billion; this means that taxable turnover per taxpayer increased from DM 11.7 million in 1980 to DM 15.4 million in 1986 (BML, table 328). When the inflation rate of the entire economy is taken into consideration, this is only a very marginal increase in actual turnover per taxpayer.

For the presentation of this development one can consult the results of the Trade and Restaurant Census 1979 and 1985 which detail the development of the economic sector "Wholesale trade of grain, seed, feed and fertilizer" as follows (BML, table 331):

	1979	1985
enterprises	3,063	2,637
work sites	4,223	3,449
number employed (thousands)	25.8	21.2
turnover previous year (DM billions)	33.3	29.9
„ per enterprise (DM mln)	10.9	11.4
„ per employee (DM mln)	1.29	1.41

By taking the inflation rate of the entire economy from 1979–1985 into consideration, the turnover per enterprise and the turnover per employee have fallen in real terms which signalizes the necessity of further rationalization progress.

A strong reduction in the number of enterprises active in agricultural trade is also visible during earlier periods of time. Their number fell from 3,500 in 1970 to 2,100 in 1982, but their turnover climbed during these same years from DM 5 billion to DM 20.5 billion; the average turnover per enterprise thus increased from DM 1.4 million in 1970 to DM 9.8 million in 1982 (*Schürmann*, p.30). This was almost a four-fold increase in the actual turnover per enterprise when the inflation rate of the entire economy is considered.

The development of the number and turnover of the rural trade co-operatives is well documented statistically and is also available for the previous years. In order to make a comparison with the information from agricultural trade possible, the following data were selected for three different years (DRV, p.14).

	1970	1982	1989
Marketing & purchasing co-ops			
enterprises (number)	1,740	957	697
turnover (DM billions)	3.17	7.90	6.99
„ per enterprise (DM mln)	1.83	8.26	10.03
Credit co-ops involved in trade of goods			
enterprises (number)	4,920	2,236	1,613
turnover (DM billions)	3,442	8,063	5,888
„ per enterprise (DM mln)	0.70	3.61	3.65
Primary co-operatives			
enterprises (number)	14	12	11
turnover (DM billions)	3.96	17.55	15.80
„ per enterprise (DM mln)	0.63	1.46	1.44

Under consideration of the inflation rate, observable actual growth in turnover per enterprise from 1970 to 1982 switched over to a period of stagnation in the marketing and purchasing co-operatives and shrinkage for the other two groups from 1982 to 1989.

V. Market Shares

With exception of the quantitative statistics for grain production which is presented below, there are only estimates available from individual authors of the market breakdown of agricultural trade and co-operatives for the other sales products, for equipment and supplies, and their respective shares in the sales and purchasing markets in the institutional branches.

In 1977–78 the turnover from co-operatives had the following shares of total purchases in West German agriculture (*Kopplin*, p.62): fertilizer 73%; pesticides 64%; seed 64%; agricultural machinery 29%. The co-operative share of proceeds on farmers sales was quoted by the same author for all products at 46%; for vegetable products (which include vegetables, fruit and wine) the figure was 36% (*Kopplin*, p.62). According to the official statistics for the same year (1977–78), the share of grain realized by co-operatives was 53% of all grain sales in agriculture (BML, 1980, table 203).

The eleven main and central co-operatives had a 30% share of the national market in 1975 for the production of mixed feeds (*Schwier*, p.73). The co-operative share on turnover in the entire agricultural commodities trade in 1980 was estimated at approximately 42% in sales transactions and 63% in purchase transactions (*Prüße*, p.90). The turnover of agricultural trade in 1980 consisted of approx. 30% from receipts on sales products and 70% from consignments of agricultural working materials such as equipment and supplies (*Prüße*, p.90).

The development of the market shares of agricultural trade and co-operatives can only be traced for the sales item "grain" with the help of official statistics for a longer period of time up to the present. The three harvesting institutions have the following percentage shares in grain sales (BML, 1989, table 195):

	1970/71	1980/81	1988/89
trade	34	35	37
co-operatives	50	52	53
processing companies	16	13	10

The direct grain sales from processing firms proportionately slipped during this period of time. Agricultural trade and co-operatives have been able to win shares to the detriment of the processing firms.

VI. Outlook

Because the multitude of factors which can affect and determine agricultural commodities trade are so difficult to estimate, statements concerning the developmental tendencies of this trade are not possible in a quantitative form. Nevertheless, several probable tendencies can be aluded to.

The existent rationalization pressure up to now which has left rash structural changes in agricultural trade and co-operatives in its wake will become more accentuated in the future because of two influential events: 1) the unification of the two German states and 2) the completion of the European Common Market. Adjustments in the pre- and post-harvest areas of agricultural commodities trade must have taken place anyway during the transformation of the operational size structure in agricultural production. Nonetheless - inspite of the probability that the operational sizes in agricultural production will be reduced in the territory comprising the five new German states - the operational structure of agricultural enterprises in these German states will presumably assume such a form that repercussions can be expected in the structure of operational size in the older German states; this in itself will further necessitate appropriate adjustments.

The completion of the European Common Market (→ *European Community*) also intensifies competition - so much that an enlarged enterprise form is necessary at least on the level of the main or central co-operatives. This may be demonstrated by the planned fusion of the central business institutions in Münster, Oldenburg and Osnabrück. Financing larger investments will also have consequences on the legal forms of organizations, particularly as the co-operative increasingly is transformed into a public limited company.

Cooperation must not only intensify horizontally; the vertical bonds and associations will likewise be affected as the traditional three-tiered system becomes more and more a two-tiered system (Mändle, 1990). In addition to the influence which derives from the organizational size structure of the pre-and post-harvest agricultural commodities trade, the reduction of agrarian protection in the EEC as a result of the EEC agrarian reform beginning 1993/94, which is the consequence of the negotiations in the Uruguay Round of the General Agreement on Tariffs and Trade (GATT) will not only influence the range of agricultural production but also the structure of production. Furthermore, future agricultural production will also be affected by intensified ecological measures. This will lead to a reduction of the intensity level of agricultural production and have a stifling effect on the agricultural commodites trade, both on the amount of ordered purchases and on the amount of products for sale.

The competition between enterprises on the same market level will therefore also become more accute as purchase and sales amounts stagnate or fall. At the same time, super-regional competitors in the pre-harvest market will be seeking direct contact to farmers, eliminating present sectors of the agricultural commodities trade (*Meyer*).

Against the background of stagnating or actually sinking conditions in the agricultural market, an early recognition of the situation and a directed, enterprising action are required for the continuance and survival of agricultural trade and co-operatives.

Bibliography

Bundesministerium für Ernährung, Landwirtschaft und Forsten (BML): Statistisches Jahrbuch über Ernährung, Landwirtschaft und Forsten der Bundesrepublik Deutschland 1989 sowie frühere Ausgaben.
Busch, E.: Entwicklung des Landwarenhandels in Schleswig-Holstein, Hamburg und Berlin 1974.
Deutscher Raiffeisenverband (DRV): Jahrbuch 1989.
Dülfer, Eberhard: Zielsystem der Genossenschaft, in: Mändle, E./Winter, H.W. (eds.): Handwörterbuch des Genossenschaftswesens, Wiesbaden 1980, cols. 1857–1872.
Hamm, Walter: Marktstellung und Marktentwicklung landwirtschaftlicher Genossenschaften, in: Agrarwirtschaft, no. 32, vol. 4 (April 1983), pp. 121–124.
Heidrich, Rüdiger: Strukturplanung für ländliche Warengenossenschaften. Fallbeispiel Kreis Minden-Lübbecke, Gießen 1989.
Jessen, L.: Der private Landwarenhandel in der BRD, Hamburg, Berlin 1976.
Kalefeld, Klaus-H.: Wettbewerbsstrategien im Agribusiness als Problem genossenschaftlicher Verbandpolitik, Münster 1983.
Kopplin, Dieter: Marktstellung und Marktentwicklung landwirtschaftlicher Genossenschaften in der Bundesrepublik Deutschland, Dissertation rer. oec., Kiel 1982.
Krelle, Wilhelm: Preistheorie, Tübingen, Zürich 1961.
Kühl, Rainer: Wettbewerbstheoretische Analyse des Landwarenmarktes in der Bundesrepublik Deutschland, Kiel 1986.
Kühl, Rainer/Hanf, C.-H.: Der Landwarenhandel in der Bundesrepublik Deutschland – Struktur – Entwicklung – Analyse, Kiel 1985.
Mändle, Eduard: Wettbewerb und Genossenschaften, in: Mändle, E./Winter, H.W. (eds.): Handwörterbuch des Genossenschaftswesens, Wiesbaden 1980, cols. 1697–1717.
Mändle, Eduard: Entwicklungstendenzen ländlicher Warenhandelsgenossenschaften, in: Ernährungsdienst vol. 45, no. 102 (4.9.1990), pp. 11–12.
Meyer, A.: Der Landwarenhandel in der Bundesrepublik Deutschland, Münster 1983.
Schürmann, Karl: Landwirte und deren Handelspartner – Ein empirischer Beitrag zur Marktstellung, Bonn 1984.
Schwier, D.: Struktur und Wettbewerb auf dem Markt für Mischfutter in der Bundesrepublik Deutschland, Frankfurt am Main 1987.

Ambelakia Syntrofia

STAVROS MARIADIS

(see also: *History of Ideas*; *Autochthonous Co-operative*; *Pre-co-operative Forms*)

I. History; II. Analysis.

Although today a small mountain village indistinguishable from the many others of its kind, Ambelakia on the Greek island of Thessaly possesses a unique socio-economic history which places it among the forerunners of contemporary co-operative structure. The *syntrofia*, or Common Companionship, emerged as a form of limited partnership (→ *Partnership Enterprises*) which assumed characteristics typically associated with co-operative business structures. Although the *syntrofia* never referred to itself as a co-operative body, numerous historians later bestowed the title to it; if it is to be seen as a co-operative organization, it would predate the Rochdale co-operatives of Britain. Particular elements of the original articles of association dated 1780 and 1795 indicate, however, that this company was too substantially based on non-co-operative principles to consider it a co-operative enterprise (→ *History before 1800*).

I. History

During the period of Turkish occupation of Greece around the beginning of the 18th century, a handicraft industry started to develop in the community of Ambelakia. Like other similarly sized Greek towns (4000–6000 inhabitants), Ambelakia was "free", meaning that it had its own self-administration. Workers were organized in guilds called *sinafia* and primarily produced red thread which was particularly popular abroad. Greek tradesmen travelling abroad looked for new markets and started investing in these guilds slightly before the Industrial Revolution took place in England.

Because of increased competition at the beginning of the 18th century, tradesmen were forced to make partnerships or *syntrofia* with each other to concentrate capital. The first one was founded in April, 1771; others were founded afterwards to avoid competition between the dyehouses which numbered 24 by the end of the 18th century.

In 1778, the first Common Companionship (C.C.) was founded by 80 large merchants. The smaller companionships which were united in this organization sought the security a larger organization could offer them under the arbitrary actions of the Turkish conquerer. The first copy of the statutes (→ *Bylaws*) of this organization are, however, available for 1780 which imply in their formulation that they were a reworking of previous articles of association.

The "brotherhood" (→ *History of Ideas*) formed through these statutes was a type of limited partnership with shareholders coming from different classes and trades: landowners, upon whose land the cotton was grown; capitalists (merchants and salesmen) who marketed the thread; and craftsmen (technicians) who actually produced the products. Since the price was too high for an individual purchase, the craftsmen, however, also purchased stock in the *syntrofia* as a group.

Because of a remarkable network of markets in Central Europe was developed, the level of economic and social prosperity of Ambelakia was incredibly high for its date and place. According to the results of *Iannis Michailidis*' research, enormous amounts of profit were raised, up to 100%. To maximize capital investment in the Common Companionship, dividends were set at 10%. Furthermore, money was set aside for taxes (to the Turks), the Church, for education, social welfare programs, public works, rent, administrative and travel expenses.

This Common Companionship did not remain a harmonic unity for long. A competing companionship was founded in 1783 and the C.C. ceased to exist in 1790. The French historian *Beaujour* noted that greed played an important role among the large stockholders as well as the fact that everyone wanted to give orders rather than follow those of others.

The second Common Companionship was founded on January 1, 1795. Now, the articles of association and the text, respectively, were not only constructed much better, but more closely stressed the role of the partnership as well as the foreign offices in Europe, implying that problems were more probable there than in the local production centers in Ambelakia. Discord broke out among the stockholders again, however, and the C.C. was dissolved for good in 1811.

II. Analysis

The word "co-operative" is never mentioned in the texts of the Ambelakia Syntrofia, but rather it is referred to as an "association", "common companionship" or even "company". Against the background of the accepted definition of a co-operative as cooperation between captial and labor to solve social problems, I have come to the conclusion that the C.C. of Ambelakia cannot be characterized in any way as a co-operative with today's concept for five reasons.

1) The articles call for the designation of "special supervisors" equivalent to managing directors of today's companies. Large merchants were specifically named to fill these positions, thus making the organization resemble a partnership.
2) As initial share ownership level deviated between 5,000 and 20,000 piasters, an inequality existed among members. This is similar to the "popular base company of today".
3) The corporate logo was laid down in the articles as that of "Schwarz Brothers & Co.", two of the most prominent merchants and stockholders in the C.C. This does not represent the unification of capital and labor but rather is a poignant example of how certain individuals acted as majority shareholders, self-appointed administrators not elected by the general assembly.
4) The partners in the C.C. did not have equal levels of liability; the larger stockholders covered for the less wealthy ones.
5) The internal lending rate was a full rate of 12%. Internationally, it has become accepted that shares should only be lent at an interest not exceeding half of the bank rate.

Although a limited partnership, the C.C. was not purely capitalistic because of certain characteristic co-operative features. It promoted social solidarity by financing medical clinics, schools, libraries and scholarships for study abroad. Furthermore, its membership was open to all people of Ambelakia, an important co-operative principle (→ *Principles*). Also, profits were proportionally distributed. Based on the level of participation capital capitalists did earn more than laborers did. But what is important is that workers were included both in the company and in the distribution of profits, unlike in most companies today. Lastly and perhaps most interestingly, the membership composition represented different classes and trades, forming a collective spirit. Through this mixed membership a vertical economic process developed, from the production of raw materials through processing up to the eventual marketing.

This model had many characteristics in common with the "Villages of Cooperation" of → *Owen*, the "Phalanstéres" of *Fourier*, and the co-operative models of → *Raiffeisen* and → *Schulze-Delitsch* upon which the contemporary co-operatives are based. This implies that it was studied by the pioneers of the co-operative movement as long as it was well known in Europe through its sub-branches and through the literature of British, French, and German traveller-writers of that time.

If, because of the reasons mentioned above, the Common Companionship can not be considered the first contemporary co-operative of the world, enough evidence exists to justify it as a parallel co-pioneer form. The cooperation which existed between the various productive sectors of capital, land, and labor remain a useful model for today's world.

Bibliography

Abelidis, Parmenion: To agrotiko syneteristiko kinima stin Ellada, Athens 1975.
Anagnostiadis, Christos: I ikonomiki diarthrosi ke i nomiki morfi tou syneterismou ton Ambelakion, Thessaloniki 1973.
Boulanger, Felix: Ambelakia ou Les Associations et les Municipalités Helliniques, Paris 1875.
Filaretos, Giorgos: Synergatiki Syneterismi, Athens 1927.
Georgiou, Ilias: Neotera stichia peri tis istorias ke tis Syntrofias ton Ambelakion, Athens 1950.
Kordatos, Giannis: Ta Ambelakia ke o mythos ja to synterismo tous, Athens 1973.
Mariadis, Stavros: Die Entwicklung der Agrarfrage in Griechenland seit Entstehung des neugriechichen Staates (1821) bis zum zweiten Weltkrieg, Dissertation, Bonn 1966.
Michailidis, Giannis: Ta Ambelakia tis Thessalia, periodiko "ISTORIA", T. 31, Feb. 1971, Athens.
Moutsopoulos, Nikolaos: Ta thessalika Ambelakia, efimerida to "Vima", Athens 17.4.1966.
Pepelasis, Adamandios: Diakosia chronia apo ta Ambelakia, efimerida "Vima", Athens 4.5.1980.
Tsambasis, P.: Ta Ambelakia Thessalias, ekdosi A.T.E., Athens 1963.
Xytsas, Vasilios/ Kosmanos, Dimitrios: Ta istorika Ambelakia, Thessaloniki 1974.

Anti-Trust Laws and Co-operatives

BERNHARD GROSSFELD / GUIDO LENFERS [J]

(see also: *Law, National*; *Law, International*; *Forms of Cooperation*; *Economic Order*; *Competition*)

I. Introduction; II. Legal Foundations; III. Consequences for Co-operatives; IV. Exemption According to *GWB*, § 5b; V. Exemption According to *GWB*, § 5c; VI. Legal Exceptions; VII. Closing Word.

I. Introduction

Historical overviews often associate cartels and forms of cooperation closely with one another. The typical form of cooperation, the co-operative, has always played an important role in the discussion concerning anti-trust law. This itself is understandable if one considers the general background and development of anti-trust legislation. At the beginning of the 19th century freedom of trade (Gewerbefreiheit) was introduced into extensive parts of the German Reich. Trade privileges and prohibition of association that had existed up to this time hereby disappeared (→ *History in 19th C.*). Initially no particular type of competition protection seemed necessary, but following World War I cartels formed to a great degree in Germany and Austria. Cartelization later increased in England, France and Italy; international cartels likewise were formed more rapidly.

The first strict and effective anti-trust laws were initially developed after World War II. The German anti-trust law was drafted under certain assumptions and understandings, namely that the free market economy can only be successful when the system of competition functions; a further goal was the provision of the best possible consumer protection. Competition is understood to be a system which brings about an approximate balance of power between business partners and prevents social and political supremacy.

II. Legal Foundations

1. Origin

The German Law against Restraints of Competition (*Gesetz gegen Wettbewerbsbeschränkungen, GWB*) dating July 27, 1957, came into being following an intensive debate over its fundamental concept. One view argued that monopoly agreements which lack state approval should be declared void from the start (rule of per se illegality); others maintained that the state should only intervene when cartel agreements are abused (principle of abuse). The more stringent principle of prohibition prevailed fundamentally as can be seen in § 1 of the *GWB*, the central provision against restraints of competition. In accordance with this provision, among other things, all contracts which bind companies together for a common purpose are declared void if and when they likewise could lead to an infringement of market relationships by restricting competition. If a contract is declared invalid according to *GWB*, § 1, the Anti-trust Authority can enforce an interdiction (so-called objective procedure, *GWB*, § 37a, Subsec.1). Moreover, the Anti-trust Authority can impose penalty charges on companies and their managers who entered into such contracts if they make light of or ignore the invalidity of the particular contract or resolution (*GWB*, § 38, Subsec.1, Num.1; Subsec.4).

Alongside the prohibition of cartel contracts (agreements) and decisions found in § 1 of the *GWB*, concerted practices have also been prohibited since 1973 (*GWB*, § 25, Subsec.1). In other words, any non-contractual concerted action is enjoined if and when such an action in the form of a contract or cartel decision would have fallen under *GWB*, § 1. In practical application of anti-trust legislation, however, § 25, Subsec.1 of the *GWB* is only used guardedly; the terms "cartel agreement" and "cartel decision" found in *GWB*, § 1 are instead interpreted more widely. Both authorities and courts include typical cases of "concerted practice" (*GWB*, § 25, Subsec.1) under *GWB*, § 1, which today is the central standard for restraints of competition through forms of corporate cooperation.

2. Change in Interpretation of GWB, § 1

Ever since the *GWB* was enacted in 1957 it has remained contested how the elements of rule in § 1 should be interpreted. Two such elements of rule found in *GWB*, § 1 are particularly important for anti-trust rulings affecting co-operatives:

– common purpose
– restraint of → *competition*.

Aside from the interpretation of each of these elements, the relationship between the two is also contested.

a) Theory of Subject Matter of Contract (Gegenstandstheorie)

According to the "Theory of Subject Matter of Contract" the cartel element of rule found in *GWB*, § 1 must be interpreted narrowly. Such a contract in the sense of the rule is either a deed of partnership or similar partnership agreement. The restraint of competition must be an subject matter of the contract; it can, for example, result from the common purpose. A cartel contract (cartel agreement) is accordingly at hand when the members of the cartel are contractually obligated to a particular conduct which restrains competition; there must be a legally tangible tie bonding the parties together in the cartel. The Theory of Subject Matter of the Contract was conceived above all with the co-operative in mind and initially was prevalent. The practical application of anti-trust legislation upon the creation of the *GWB* is based on this theory.

b) Theory of Eventual Consequence (Folgetheorie)

Increasing opposition mounted in the course of time against the Theory of Subject Matter, and the "Theory of Eventual Consequence" won over supporters in literature. The Theory of Eventual Consequence differs substantially from the Theory of Subject Matter in that it states a cartel element of rule without redressing the purpose or content of the contract. According to the Theory of Eventual Consequence a contract is found to be in violation of the anti-trust legislation if and when it can effect competitive restraints on the structure of the relevant market, on the behavior of those involved and/or on other market participants. The decisive factor therefore is the external effect of the contract; the cartel element of rule in *GWB*, § 1 is thus viewed quite broadly.

c) Court Rulings

Court rulings with regard to *GWB*, § 1 have not decisively endorsed either the Theory of Subject Matter of Contract or the Theory of Eventual Consequence; they rather have come to choose an intermediary solution (the so-called *"Theory of Purpose"*). This can be seen in two judgements, each grounded in facts in which the interpretation of the elements of rule as defined in *GWB*, § 1 played a decisive role. In order to throw light onto the course of these legal decisions, the judgements themselves must first be presented in short.

aa) ZVN Decision

The following facts of the case (greatly abbreviated) lay at the root of the ZVN decision handed down by the German Federal Supreme Court. The Norddeutsche Zementwerke (North German cement factories) entered into a marketing cooperation and for this purpose founded the Zementverkaufsstelle Niedersachsen GmbH (ZVN, cement outlet Lower Saxony). This cement outlet signed marketing and supply agreements with the cement factories. The ZVN in turn sold the contract goods at agreed upon purchasing prices on its own name and account and granted each supplier most-favored treatment. A mandatory delivery obligation was expressly not included for goods to be supplied to ZVN; each cement factory could operate on its own on the market.

The German Federal Supreme Court (Bundesgerichtshof, BGH in WRP, 1975, p.665) considered this marketing cooperation a violation against *GWB*, § 1, as had the Court of Appeals at Berlin (Berliner Kammergericht) in the preceding instance. It was not decisive that restraints of competition themselves are direct elements of the contract; it was irrelevant that no contractual obligation existed to sell the products via the sales cooperation. Such an obligation could however be replaced

"through the common expectation of reasonable business behavior from each party involved in the contract seen from the view of commonly held goal conceptions" (BGH, ibid., p.668).

This decision thus lies somewhere between the Theory of Subject Matter and the Theory of Eventual Consequence: On the one hand the competitive restraint is done away with as an element of the contractual obligation, but on the other hand it does not suffice that the cooperation agreement

"leads de facto to a market situation in which competition is exposed to certain restraints" (BGH, ibid., p.667).

This position was named the "Theory of Purpose" (Zwecktheorie).

bb) Selex + Tania Decision

This case dealt primarily with the interpretation of the element of rule "restraint of competition" found in *GWB*, § 1. The decisions of the Federal Cartel Office and the Court of Appeals (Kammergericht) indicate the limits of business cooperations involved in purchasing activities. Facts of this case (greatly abbreviated): The Selex+Tania-Gruppe came into being through the merger of two previously independent companies, the Selex Handelsgesellschaft mbH & Co KG and the Tania–Vereinte Handelsgesellschaften mbH & Co KG. Ten large companies also belonged to this conglomerate (including Kaufhof, Ratio, Wertkauf). A complicated system of arrangements existed between S+T and its members concerning vertical and horizontal agreements. Selex+Tania AG, acting as a holding company, intended to assume tasks for its members in the following fields: purchasing of goods, supervision of payments, negotiating minimum conditions, central envoicing and del credere transactions.

The Federal Cartel Office prohibited this corporate cooperation. The Court of Appeals also shared this injunction: The strong concentration of purchasing activities accordingly limits competition on the demand side of the market. It is not necessary for those cooperating individuals with a particular demand to obligate themselves to place purchases either legally or in a de facto manner. S+T had negotiated prices for its members, and at these prices it was a dictate of reason for members to buy from the suppliers (→ *Pricing Policy*). The members of the cooperation were therefore obligated not to undermine the settlements made by the central organization by making offers of their own to the suppliers. Such a situation of unified demand causes suppliers to endure a shortage of alternatives, something they usually have in a typical situation when competition exists among buyers. The decision and position in this case set the precedent for the formation of purchasing cooperations.

III. Consequences for Co-operatives

The element of rule found in anti-trust laws affects companies and corporate associations regardless of their legal form. If this were not the case, companies could elude anti-trust laws by simply changing their legal form. Co-operatives therefore in principle must also be measured against § 1 of the *GWB*. This is not the case in Austria: Industrial and provident co-operative purchasing societies are excluded from the anti-trust legislation as long as they do not exceed the bounds of Co-operative Law through a cartel contract (Austrian Anti-Trust Law, § 5, Subsec.1, Num.6).

1. Co-operative Characteristics and the Element of a Cartel Rule

As the preceding discussion presented the various interpretations of *GWB*, § 1, we now turn our attention to the extent co-operatives fulfill the standard elements of rule. *GWB*, § 1 encompasses at first only companies and corporate associations. Both registered and non-registered co-operatives (→ *Register, Co-operative*) whose members are themselves companies fall under this categorization. → *Consumer co-operatives* (Co-operative Law, [*GenG*], § 1, Subsec.1, Num.5) and home building societies (→ *Building and Loan Societies*) (*GenG*, § 1, Subsec.1, Num.7) accordingly are not subject to the cartel prohibition as their members constitute private households.
The essence of *GWB*, § 1 encompasses at least all "contracts" that are partnership agreements, thus including all co-operative → *by-laws*. In the case of co-operatives, the "common purpose" presupposed in § 1 of the *GWB* is the purpose of promotion (cf. *GenG*, Art.1: Co-operatives strive to promote the commercial situation or economic benefit of their members through a common business enterprise) (→ *Promotion Mandate*).
Ultimately, however, it is difficult to determine the extent co-operatives' fixed purpose of promotion fulfills the final element of rule found in GWB, § 1:

> "to influence the production of goods or market relationships concerning the flow of goods or commercial services through restraints of competition."

This question is primarily raised in connection with how purchasing co-operatives (→ *Commercial Co-operatives*) should be treated, and this co-operative group therefore needs to be considered in particular.

A differentiation must thereby be drawn between co-operatives with a mandatory purchasing obligation and co-operatives which, although lacking a contractual mandatory purchasing clause, result in "de facto purchasing concentrations".

2. Exclusive Dealing

Purchasing co-operatives with mandatory purchasing obligations for their members are generally seen to be unlawful cartels in the sense of *GWB*, § 1. This is true for co-operatives which have included a mandatory purchasing clause in their → *by-laws*. This is likewise true for co-operatives that coerce their members to purchase from them by charging indemnity or associational fines on those members who do not meet their demand for goods through the co-operative (indirect coercion). These prohibitions may not be eluded through agreements not included in the by-laws: A direct or indirect purchasing obligation therefore must not be included in the individual skeleton delivery contracts settled with each co-operative member (so-called "Sternverträge"). Such contracts, together with the by-laws, are measured as one composite unit against *GWB*, § 1. If a violation against the cartel prohibition is determined, the skeleton delivery contract according to law of obligation, if not more, is declared void. The Cartel Office can invalidate such contracts according to *GWB*, § 37a, Subsec.1.

3. Co-operatives without Mandatory Purchase Obligations

It is contested to what degree purchasing co-operatives without either direct or indirect purchase obligations on their members fall under *GWB*, § 1. How these co-operatives are ultimately judged is decisively determined by how the element of rule "restraint of competition" in *GWB*, § 1 is interpreted. Purchasing co-operatives exercise demand-side pressure on suppliers; the purpose of concentrating demand is the promotion of the membership body. It remains questionable, however, whether companies which coordinate their purchases via a co-operative thereby bring about an unlawful contractual restraint on competition.
The Theory of Subject Matter and the Theory of Purpose do not pass sentence on the formation of co-operatives as such. The Theory of Eventual Consequence regularly permits co-operatives to restrain competition: Based on their purpose of promotion and therefore on their legally determined structure, co-operatives are always seen as cartel societies (per se cartel). A two-fold restraint on competition is present with regard to *GWB*, § 1: The co-operative concentrates the demand of its members and in doing so prevents business transactions between the in-

dividual co-operative members and suppliers. Secondly, the concentrated strength on the demand side puts disproportionate pressure on the supplier when terms and conditions are being negotiated.

4. Legislation and Daily Practise

Purchasing co-operatives (→ *Supply Co-operatives*) free of any mandatory provision or delivery clauses cannot ideally be differentiated from prohibited cartels. The goals of the anti-trust law and the Co-operative Law (→ *Law, National*) rather need to be taken into consideration and weighed out against each other.

"The prohibition of cartels does not mean the prohibition of cooperation" (Report of the German Federal Cartel Office for 1978/88, DB 1989, pp. 1276, 1278).

The legislative goal of anti-trust and co-operative laws is the promotion of mid-sized company forms of cooperation. In its 1963 publication on co-operatives (*Die Kooperationsfibel*) the Federal Ministry of Economics therefore stated the following:

"Purchasing societies are permissible with regard to anti-trust legislation. The companies involved, however, must not place any restraints on their own independent purchasing activities through contractual arrangements. They must have the freedom to satisfy their demand needs through other suppliers aside from the purchasing co-operative."

This position was stated in a more differentiated manner in the second edition of the *Kooperationsfibel* issued in 1976; here the ZVN decision was taken into consideration. Later amendments to the Anti-Trust Law (GWB) indicate, however, that it remains the intention of lawmakers to promote forms of mid-sized business cooperation (cf., e.g. BT-Drs. 7/765, p.4). The particular valuations in Co-operative Law must also be considered; the extent these specific co-operative qualities suffice to make an exception to the general prohibition of cartels remains contested. (cf. *Großfeld/Strümpell; Baumann*, 1981).

In practical application the Federal Cartel Office and lawmakers share the identical intention:

"...the Federal Cartel Office considers cooperation between independent trading companies in purchasing activities as something positive for competition as long as it serves to improve the competitiveness of small and mid-sized companies in the face of large corporations" (Report of the Federal Cartel Office 1987/88, DB 1989, pp.1276, 1278).

This indicates that the aim of the law and practical application of it by the Federal Cartel Office is to provide mid-sized companies with effective protection and promotional support. This can only be achieved when purchasing co-operatives without mandatory purchasing clauses are as a rule exempted from *GWB*, § 1. The sole question remaining to be answered is where the line should be drawn for intentional protection of mid-sized companies (→ *Operational Size*). It has in part been proposed to apply *GWB*, § 38, Subsec.2, Num.2 in an analogous manner (see *Baumann*, 1981, pp.23–28 for a thorough explanation). This rule of law details the exact preconditions under which promotion of mid-sized companies is permissible (see *GWB*, § 38, Subsec.1. Nums.11, 12).

5. Competitive Restraint

Purchasing co-operatives without mandatory purchasing obligations as a rule do not aim to induce any type of "restraint of competition" in the essence of *GWB*, § 1. *Beuthien* grounds this position as follows (DB-Beilage, 5/77): Co-operative members do not intend to restrict sales competition with respect to other purchasers when they become co-operative members and enter into business transactions with their co-operative. They do not strive to make uniform purchases from the co-operative but rather to make individually favorable purchases. Because no purchase obligation exists, other suppliers who compete on the market with the co-operative have the chance to sell their goods to the co-operative members. The co-operative concentrates demand and thereby puts pressure on the producer, thus fracturing competition into more pieces and directions. If co-operatives did not exist the member enterprises would namely place purchases with "some other large wholesaler" and not buy directly from the producer. The purchasing co-operative becomes an additional player on the demand side of the market. The co-operative can furthermore only attract and maintain members by providing a market input; it must constantly hold its own against other large-scale wholesalers through effective (promotional) inputs. The strength accrued on the demand side as a result of competitive performance is in conformance with competitive practise. A restraint on competition at least is not at hand when the purchasing co-operative assumes independent market functions with respect to its members, bears its own market risk and convincingly fulfills its → *promotion mandate*.

IV. Exemption According to GWB, § 5b

Inasfar as a co-operative falls under *GWB*, § 1 it can receive exemption based on *GWB*, § 5b (the so-called cooperation cartel or cartel of mid-sized companies). *GWB*, § 5b states that *GWB*, § 1 is void when the cartel agreements

"have as their object the rationalization of business procedures through a type of intercompany cooperation other than that named in § 5a".

Furthermore it is necessary that the cartel

"does not considerably hamper competition on the market, and that the contract or resolution serves to promote the productivity of small and mid-sized companies."

If the preconditions for § 5b are at hand, the co-operative can contact the Cartel Office and register those contracts and resolutions which fell under *GWB*, § 1 (*GWB*, § 9). As long as the Cartel Office does not oppose the contract, it and/or the resolutions become effective (*GWB*, § 5a, Subsec.3). The cooperation cartel then is subject to control of abusive practices through the Federal Cartel Office (*GWB*, § 12).

V. Exemption According to GWB, § 5c

In the course of amending the anti-trust law lawmakers recently provided a special exemption provision for purchasing co-operatives, *GWB*, § 5c, effective since January 1, 1990:

"GWB, § 1 does not apply to those contracts or resolutions which have as their purpose the common purchase of goods or the common provision of commercial services without substantiating a mandatory purchase obligation when competition on the market is not seriously impaired and when the contract or resolution serves to improve the competitiveness of small or mid-sized companies" (German Civil Code (BGBL) 1989 I, p.2486).

It has been the object of debate whether this provision is necessary; among co-operatives its necessity was contentious. It was feared that *GWB*, § 5c could become a new "Supervisionary standard" for purchasing co-operatives and seriously constrict their field of activities. The co-operatives demanded much more attention to the fact that purchasing co-operatives without mandatory purchasing obligations usually do not fall under *GWB*, § 1 anyway; a special exemption for them therefore is not necessary. Inasfar as a special exemption provision such as *GWB*, § 5c exists, it was argued that the antitrust laws practice would have an easier time declaring purchasing co-operatives illegal cartels according to *GWB*, § 1. Lawmakers wanted to create legal security through *GWB*, § 1 (cf. the in-depth explanation in BT Drs. 11/4610, pp.14–17). They maintained that the admissibility of purchasing co-operatives with respect to anti-trust legislation had also not been sufficiently clarified in legal decisions (see above). Faced with this situation lawmakers felt it their task to settle such questions. Nevertheless, it was emphasized that the new provision § 5c should not alter interpretation of *GWB*, Art.1. *GWB*, § 5c presupposes that the elements of rule found in *GWB*, § 1 have been fulfilled. The registration of the purchasing co-operative (*GWB*, § 9) and control of abusive practices (*GWB*, § 12) comply with the existent regulations for cooperation cartel as determined in *GWB*, § 5b.

GWB, § 5c extends the exemption possibilities which already exist through *GWB*, § 5b. Lawmakers justified the need for this elaboration as follows: *GWB*, § 5b does not suffice to legalize purchasing cooperations. The element of rule "rationalization of business procedure through intercompany cooperation" found in *GWB*, § 5b – which is related to the element "promotion of productivity" - is not fullfilled by all purchasing cooperations in a satisfactory manner from the point of view of competition policy (→ *Economic Order*). The mere aim of achieving more favorable conditions based on stronger negotiating ability resulting from the consolidation of purchasing volumes does not suffice for the necessary improvements in a company's internal relationship between expenses and revenue (productivity) which are prescribed in *GWB*, § 5b. The new § 5c makes exemptions possible in such cases. Inasfar as purchasing co-operatives in individual cases fall under *GWB*, § 1, they can attain exemption according to *GWB*, § 5c.

VI. Legal Exceptions

§§ 99–105 of the *GWB* forsee exceptions for the applicability of anti-trust law (in part only for particular standards) for some contracts in certain economic sectors. Exceptions for sectors are in part *ipso jure*, but in part the contracts must also be registered with the Cartel Authority or at a specialized authorization office. The exceptional economic sectors also include certain sectors of the co-operative economy.

1. Credit Co-operatives

a) General Information

GWB, § 102, subsec.1 prescribes a special element of rule which can be applied alongside the general exemption elements found in *GWB*, §§ 2–8 for the sectors of credit business (→ *Co-operative Banks*) and insurance trade (→ *Insurance, Germany*). *GWB*, Art.102 was fundamentally changed in the course of recent amendments (January 1, 1990). The rule of per se illegality was introduced in the place of the principle of abusive practices. Lawmakers thereby adapted German laws on competition to those of the European Community which do not include any general or comprehensive exceptions of the rule of per se illegality for entire economic sectors (→ *European Community*). *GWB*, § 102, Subsec.1 concerns long-term cooperations and vertical contracts as well as recommendations that are not limited to isolated situations (*GWB*, § 102, Subsec.2). Such contracts, resolutions and recommendations which according to *GWB*, §§ 1; 15; 38, Subsec.1, Num.1 are prohibited can become legalized through their registration with the Cartel Authority in the scope of the prescribed protest procedures. In the co-operative sector it is above all the credit co-operatives which are affected by *GWB*, § 102.

b) Formal Preconditions

GWB, § 102, Subsec.1, Sent.1, Num.1 contains the formal preconditions for exemption: Only those banking and insurance businesses are accordingly qualified for exemption which are subject to the surveillance or approval of the appropriate supervisory authority. The Federal Supervisory Office for the Banking (BAK) executes this supervisory function for credit institutes. §§ 1 ff. of the Credit System Law (*KWG, Gesetz über das Kreditwesen*) define the term "credit institute"; *KWG*, § 1, Subsec.1 in particular lists types of banking operations. Exemption from prohibition of competition can only be granted for bank-specific transactions; the special state of affairs is not effective for restraints on competition arising through ancillary or sideline business. The exemption is applied most often in determining the extent of a bank's performance, conditions and fees as well as for reciprocal delimitation agreements according to both geographic and material criteria.

c) Material Preconditions

GWB, § 102, Subsec.1, Sent.1, Num.2 lists the material preconditions for exemption. A business cooperation can accordingly be exempted when the cooperation is both suitable and necessary to bring about the productivity increase striven after. No other alternative can therefore exist that restricts competition to a lesser degree. Increases in productivity are at hand when all companies involved in the cooperation can improve their technical, administrational or organizational efficiency. Exemptions from the cartel prohibition can include internal company rationalization programs as well as cooperations involving banks and insurance companies which either maintain or increase the productivity level among the cooperation partners as a whole.

A further precondition for exemption is that the cooperation better satisfies the demand needs on the other side of the market. This in particular is the case when the cooperation creates a new service or improves its palette of services. A vertical contract must likewise improve the satisfaction of demand needs. Furthermore, the level of success expected from the cooperation must remain in appropriate relation to the competitive restraints associated with it. Lawmakers wanted to provide a margin of discretion in *GWB*, § 102, Subsec.1, Sent.1, Num.2 concerning the measurement of this element of rule but called for particular care in this undertaking when vertical price and/or condition ties are involved (cf. BT Drs.11/4610, p.29).

d) Registration

GWB, § 102, Subsec.1, Sent.2 calls for contracts, resolutions and recommendations to be registered with the Cartel Authority according to Sent.1. This registration must be substantiated according to *GWB*, § 102, Subsec.1, Sent.3, including an explanation of where the competitive restraint lies, why it is necessary and the extent demand needs can be satisfied through it. The Cartel Authority should accordingly be able to have an overview of the dimensions and effects of the registered competitive restraint.

e) Transitional Regulation

GWB, § 102, Subsec.6 contains transitional regulations for those contracts, resolutions and recommendations which restrain competition and became effective according to former law. These remain in effect without any renewed registration as long as the Cartel Authority does not declare the contracts or resolutions invalid or the recommendations inadmissible within three years. Those competitive restraints which were in effect according to former law must hereby be measured against the criteria established in the new § 102, Subsec.1, Sent.1 of the *GWB*.

2. Agricultural and Forestry Co-operatives

a) General Information

GWB, § 100 contains an extensive sectoral exemption for agriculture (→ *Rural Co-operatives*) but does not completely remove this economic sector from the reaches of anti-trust legislation; *GWB*, § 1 is alone declared inapplicable under certain preconditions. *GWB*, § 100, Subsec.1 permits extensive agricultural cartels regardless of their market power as long as they do not completely eliminate competition (*GWB*, § 100, Subsec.1, Sent.3). A legalization procedure with respect to anti-trust laws is not necessary. *GWB*, § 1 does not have validity over the following:

> "Contracts and resolutions from production enterprises, associations of production enterprises and groups of production associations inasmuch as they effect the production or the marketing of agricultural products or the use of common facilities for the storage, cultivation or processing of agricultural products without fixing prices."

The exemption from the prohibition of cartels is grounded on the structural difficulties and the branch-specific competitive disadvantages faced by agricultural producers. The exemption essentially serves to facilitate all self-help measures which tend to restrain competition in the agricultural sector. The control of abusive practices established according to *GWB*, § 104 hardly corrects this. *GWB*, § 100, Subsec.8 extends the created leeway even further through various laws on market regulation and structure as well as through European-wide market order regulations.

b) Specific Details

The following outlines several individual elements of rule as found in *GWB*, § 100, Subsec.1:
- "Production enterprises" according to § 100, Subsec.6 and in connection with Subsec.5, Num.1 are companies (natural or juristic persons) which undertake primary agricultural production (including the growing of vegetables and fruit, gardening and wine-growing), bee-keeping, and fisheries (→ *Classification*). Privileges are restricted to the producing branches; a farmstead is not however necessary. It is likewise irrelevant whether these enterprises produce these primary products in an industrial manner. Enterprises which cultivate or process primary agricultural products are not production enterprises. The cultivation or processing of agricultural products only then falls under the benefit of privileges when such activities are executed by the producer himself (e.g. dairy or winegrowers co-operative).
- The "association of production enterprises" most frequently appears in the form of a co-operative. The legal form is not however of importance (→ *Forms of Cooperation*). If the co-operative expands its assortment with purchased goods above and beyond its members' products, as an association of producers it only receives privileges for those products grown by its members.
- The term "groups of producer associations" encompasses above all central co-operatives (→ *Central Institutions*) and marketing centers. Commercial companies on the identical business level as the affiliated producer associations may not be members, for example a private diary cannot be a member of a co-operative central dairy without the later losing its exemption status with respect to cartel prohibition.
- "Contracts and resolutions" in *GWB*, § 100, Subsec.1 are defined exactly as they are in *GWB*, § 1 (see above).
- "Production" encompasses every type of primary growing procedure and the creation of new products through cultivation and processing. Agreements and resolutions must directly relate to production.
- "Marketing" describes the route agricultural products take from the grower to the consumer. The most important marketing regulation is the obligation to deliver all grown products via a particular organization or to a particular processing center. This supply obligation as such fulfills the element of rule in *GWB*, § 1 as the producer no longer can enter the market on his own as a seller. *GWB*, § 100, Subsec.1 in this case makes an exemption from cartel prohibition.
- Finally, so-called compulsory utilization is permissible: Members can be obligated to use common facilities for warehousing, cultivating and/or processing agricultural products.

IV. Closing Word

The subject of anti-trust laws and co-operatives is not particularly suitable as the object of comparative law as both components of this subject are organized too varyingly in different countries. On the one hand, the term "co-operative" is used internationally for the most varied of organizational forms, and on the other hand, anti-trust laws in individual countries vary quite dramatically. This presented overview can therefore only illustrate the situation in Germany.

Bibliography

Baumann, Horst: Einkaufsgesellschaften und -genossenschaften im Kartellrecht, in: Schriften zur Kooperationsforschung, B. Vorträge, vol. 13, Tübingen 1981.
Baumann, Horst: Der Mittelstandsgedanke und § 1 GWB, in: Zeitschrift für das gesamte Genossenschaftswesen, Göttingen vol.35 (1985), pp. 229–249.
Beuthien, Volker: Einkaufsgenossenschaften und Kartellverbot, in: Der Betrieb, Düsseldorf 1977, Beilage No. 5/77.
Beuthien, Volker: Kartelle und Genossenschaften. Handwörterbuch des Genossenschaftswesens, Wiesbaden 1980, cols. 1009–1035.
Beuthien, Volker: Genossenschaften und Kartellrecht. Das Kartellamt als Orakel- Durch unbegrenzte Auslegung zum offenen Kartellrecht?, in: Vorträge und Aufsätze des Forschungsinstitutes für Genossenschaftswesen der Universität Wien, no.12, Wien 1987.
Großfeld, Bernhard/ Strümpell, Harald: Genossenschaften, Kartellgesetz und Mittelstandsempfehlungen, in: Schriften zur Kooperationsforschung, B. Vorträge, vol.6, Tübingen 1976.
Steindorff, Ernst: Sind Handelsgenossenschaften Kartelle?, Heidelberg 1978.

Assessment of Success and the Distribution of Benefits and Surplus in Co-operatives

JENS JOKISCH [F]

(*see also: Theory of Co-operatives*; *Evaluation*; *Business Policies*; *Financing*; *Reimbursements*)

I. The Problem; II. On the Existence of Specific Benefits that are Typical of Co-operatives; III. On the Relationship between Performance and Price Policy of Co-operatives; IV. On the Distribution of Benefits and Surplus in Co-operatives.

I. The Problem

The measurement and assessment of the success and benefits of co-operative enterprise are central topics in the theoretical explanatory systems on co-operatives and are a relevant practical problem of co-operative management and membership as well. What is controversial is the exact nature of success and benefits as aimed for by co-operatives and the extent to which co-operatives strive to achieve these aims. Furthermore, there is no unanimous opinion on the different groups which have a role in setting goals in a co-operative.

The questions to be investigated here are whether there is a specific meaning of enterprise success and enterprise benefits typical for co-operatives and whether there exists a distribution of benefits and surplus which is typical for co-operatives. Thus, questions on generating and utilizing profits in the co-operative enterprise are to be the subject of the following analysis. The analysis does not deal with the measurement of benefits of co-operative activities as they are reflected in the businesses or households of the members – which are the objects of promotional efforts of the co-operative (→ *Evaluation*) – but rather it deals with questions of co-operative theory and business policies on assessing and distributing the benefits obtained by the co-operative business enterprise promoting the member businesses or households. The special problems of benefits in co-operative productive societies are not to be dealt with here. What will be discussed, however, is the feasibility of distinguishing, as suggested in scientific literature, between the two aspects of co-operative success: success in the market and success in the promotion of members' interests.

II. On the Existence of Specific Benefits that are Typical of Co-operatives

The concept of co-operatives as it came up around the middle of the 19th century was based – in accordance with the bourgeois-liberal concepts of society that had developed at the time – on the assumption that economic activity in co-operatives is determined by the co-operative members alone, independent of any influence from outsiders and free of the influences of power and domination by political or other rulers (→ *History in 19th C.*). This one-sided perspective oriented solely to the interests of the members has been gradually modified as new knowledge of organization theory has been taken up into the theory of business administration. Some hold the view that a realistic explanation of developments in the co-operative system is possible only through an analysis taking into account the multiple structure of processes for formulating goals. This means that the influence of all interest groups on the formation of goals and on the co-operative's concrete business policies must be analyzed – the influence of the members as market partners and as investors, of outside capital investors, of management, of employees, of contractors for supportive business with the co-operative, of non-members, etc..

However, in older scientific literature on business administration dealing with the typology of enterprises, co-operatives were looked upon solely as instruments for the promotion of their members, over against profit-making enterprises, whose object is to pursue the interest of capital investors, and over against enterprises for public benefit, whose purpose is to promote the interest of a general public not specifically defined. The principle that co-operatives must promote the interests of their members was looked upon as a criterion differentiating them from profit-making enterprises and enterprises for public benefit, but also as a criterion for decision-making in questions of business policies of the co-operative enterprise (→ *Managerial Economics*).

From statements to be found in organization theory on the formation of goals, one can come to conclusions about specific co-operative goal systems and therefore about criteria for evaluating the success or benefits achieved by co-operatives. Success criteria which are typical just for co-operatives, however, can exist only if the essence of the individual goals is clearly different from those of other types of enterprises. If, on the other hand, the process of goal formulation is similar in the different types of enterprises, because comparable interest groups with a similar distribution of power between the interest groups participate in the negotiation process in the political system of the co-operative, then it is probable that the result of the goal-formulation process, and thus of the criteria for success as well, are not particularly influenced by whether the enterprise in question is a co-operative or a profit-making business.

Whoever accepts the views of organization theory on goal formulation can no longer accept uncritically the assumptions of traditional business administration about the content of goals and the instrumental function of co-operatives in promoting their members' interests and of profit-making businesses in promoting the owners of capital. Therefore the attempt to construct a co-operative goal system determined by the members' interests and, with that, to raise the question of success criteria which are typical for co-operatives, is doomed to failure from the viewpoint of organization theory, because the members' interests are only one out of many input variables of the political system, whereas the success criteria developed from the goal system have come about through a compromise made by all participating interest groups and are part of the output of the political system. Since the members are not the dominant goal-formulating interest group in co-operatives, member promotion (→ *Promotion Mandate*) must not be made the sole or primary criterion by which to judge the co-operative's success and benefits.

In co-operative theory it has been maintained that one can differentiate between two kinds of success or benefits of co-operatives: success in the market, and success in member promotion (→ *Business Policies*).

In this distinction, market success refers to traditional business administrative yardsticks for success, such as profit, sales, share in the market, etc. Success in member promotion, on the other hand, reflects the degree of fulfillment of functions of the co-operative for the affiliated member businesses or households.

The hypothesis has been put forward that, if the members formulate goals for management in too unspecific a manner, then management can disguise a lack of success in member promotion and make it appear to have been a success after all by switching the emphasis from the promotional benefit which was not realized (but which is also impossible to measure) to a market success. The more managers tend to refrain from demonstrating member promotion and to limit themselves to demonstrating market success, the more this will support the tendency, according to the view referred to here, to undermining and breaking up the co-operative as an enterprise for promoting members' interests. From this it has been deduced that the interests of members must be defined more exactly and spelled out as a verifiable goal formulation for management. If the function of co-operative to promote their members were thus put into operational terms, then they could be used as criteria for an assessment of the success of co-operatives in promoting their members' interests.

But argumentation of this sort merely reproduces a thought pattern of traditional co-operative theory by making the realization of more or less concretely formulated interests of co-operative members the criterion for the identification of a co-operative. Types of enterprises that are structured as co-operatives but are temporarily or possibly even permanently not pursuing or not attaining the interests of their members are thus not included among the research subjects of traditional co-operative theory.

It is doubtful, however, whether the success of a co-operative can be measured with instruments based on enterprise type, because the division into co-operative success in the market and success in member promotion, which division underlies the argumentation, is not clean-cut. Success in the promotion of members' interests is unthinkable without success in the market, but success in the market is very well possible without success in promoting members' interests. Knowing the regulations of co-operative law pertaining to decision-making, and knowing the potentialities of co-operative members in influencing business policies, one can assume, however, that in well-functioning co-operatives the influence of the members is strong enough to transform market success into success in promoting the interests of the members.

For co-operative theorists, it is interesting to consider the case in which a co-operative enterprise is not in a position to bring about a continuous, measurable promotion (or additional promotion) of its members' interests. The reasons for this development might lie in socio-economic change, in political or economic discrimination against co-operatives, and/or in individual management mistakes, and should by all means be made subjects of research in co-operative theory and business administration. In this context the question comes up as to whether these businesses, which are no longer co-operatives from the viewpoint of enterprise typology, should be dissolved, by the members or some other interested group. In organization sociology, however, it is a verified fact that all social systems oriented toward some goal tend toward self-perpetuation and consequently strive to avoid their dissolution. The business policy of these co-operative enterprises orients itself less around the members and more around interested groups which secure the survival of the co-operative and thereby safeguard its success in the market through their support and demand for services. If the members are no longer the dominant goal-determining interest group, then it follows that not the promotion of members but success in the market must be made the primary criterion for judging the success of the co-operative. Admittedly preference is thus given to a business administrative line of argumentation rather than to a consideration of co-operative theory or co-operative ideologoy.

III. On the Relationship between Performance and Price Policy of Co-operatives

In the following, success is to be understood as the profit or surplus of the co-operative enterprise, in the way in which legal and tax regulations require it to be laid open. In addition, other relevant business administrative goals can be included, such as the cash flow (in its various forms), profitability as related to equity capital and to total capital, or the co-operative's share in the market.

If one assumes that the behaviour of the co-operative in its business policies toward all other interest groups (market partners) is no different from that of other types of enterprise, then the price policy of the co-operative enterprise toward its members and also toward non-members, if the case applies, can be looked upon as the essential determinant of profit-making in co-operatives. If, on the other hand, there is a price policy that is typical just for co-operatives, then this policy would have to be deducible from the specific goals of the co-operative. In keeping with the basic function of the co-operative to promote its members through its services, the co-operative should demand low prices as a purchasing co-operative in its business dealings with its members and pay out high prices as a marketing co-operative. In the long run, however, the co-operative can offer "better" prices than its profit-maximizing competitors only if it runs lower costs and/or if the co-operative is able to calculate its prices with lower profit margins (contributions margins) than its competitors (→ *Pricing Policy*).

Then the next thing to consider is whether the total sum of costs which is to be compensated for through contributions can be kept lower in the case of the co-operative than in the case of comparable businesses. Since the costs or rent, personnel, and goods, etc., are on the same price level anyway, one might even suppose that there is a cost disadvantage at times for the co-operative, because of its weaker position in the purchasing market. Depreciation on production factors are certainly the same, whereas for depreciation on accounts receivable there may be a small cost advantage for the co-operative, because of the closer market proximity to the members. Taxes on cost factors as well as on profits, however, would show no recognizable advantages for the co-operative. Because it is difficult, if not impossible, to put into practice a difference in prices for members and for non-members, it would be just as impossible to obtain higher cost-covering contribution margins in business with non-members than with members. At the most one might obtain additional contributions but not higher ones. Since business with non-members is basically allowed, however, the threshold to becoming a member is made higher for potential members that way – a fact which reduces the co-operative's capital base and increases its costs of financing.

This leads to considerations about the cost of capital, that is, the cost of outside capital and of equity capital to the co-operative. Capital costs are dependent upon the source of capital, i.e. of a particular segment of the capital market, and upon the total risk, as the sum of operating and financial risks of the business. If outside capital is borrowed in the bank-credit market, the co-operatives have to pay the regular market rate of interest. The same is true for financing from the suppliers' credit market, where the deferment of payments has to be paid for by waiving discounts and/or negotiable price reductions.

Generally one enterprise has lower capital costs than another if it is in a more favourable risk situation. Co-operatives have comparatively less equity capital than other businesses (→ *Equity Capital*); and, furthermore, members can give notice on this capital at any time, according to co-operative law, and withdraw it after the interval required for giving notice has elapsed, so there is a risk from the financing viewpoint which in traditional business administration theory has been called the special financing risk of the co-operative (*Henzler*). Therefore one has to expect higher capital costs in co-operative than in other better financed types of enterprise (→ *Financing*).

In this context the issue to consider is whether the co-operative should also have to pay "interest" on its equity capital, in other words, whether in a co-operative lower profits would be expected than in a profit-maximizing enterprise. In traditional co-operative literature the viewpoint has been put forward that a co-operative of the ideal type should make no profits at all, since it would just be "getting rich" on those whose interests it is supposed to represent. More recent literature on co-operative enterprise, however, and co-operative practice indicate the need for co-operatives to accumulate their own reserve capital; they stress the necessity of making profits in order to realize a permanent potential for promoting the interests of members. It is pointed out that the co-operative is not just supposed to cover its expenses, but must also make profits. No statement is made, however, as to how high the intended profits should be.

The next question which must be analyzed is whether the necessary quota of reserve capital accumulated from profits should be set at a lower level in co-operatives than in profit-maximizing businesses. In scientific literature the view is held that co-operatives are in a position to give their members additional promotional help for the reason that they need not earn the same high returns for equity capital which capital investors in profit-maximizing enterprises expect to receive. In the long run, however, the same principle of finance is valid for co-operatives as for profit-maximizing enterprises: when investors cannot expect a return from profits, they do not make their capital available. By giving investors the returns they expect, however, businesses secure for themselves both equity capital and outside capital. Should co-operatives have no need for a comparable incentive for the supply of capital, then one or more of the following preconditions must be fulfilled: firstly, the co-operative's need for capital is not so great as that of a profit-maximizing business; secondly, equity capital is available at lower capital costs, that is, the dividend expectation of the members is lower; thirdly, the cost of equity capital in the co-operative is covered by the rate of earnings set aside for that purpose.

Since the provision of goods and services has to be made with the same volume of capital input, irrespective of the goals formulated for the enterprise, it is not clear why the need for capital in a co-operative should be less than in other enterprises. Therefore the first precondition for lower costs for equity capital seems not to be fulfilled.

The second precondition refers to the attractiveness of capital investment in co-operatives. Limitations on any resale of co-operative shares, the liability of members over and above the amount of their share (or the amount of capital paid in, respectively) that usually applies in a case of bankruptcy, limitations on chances for members with a large sales volume to exert influence upon the business policy of the co-operative, and the low degree of active participation of the members in the affairs of the co-operative as a whole – despite the possibilities provided by the law – these all contribute to the impression that capital participation of the members in the co-operative is not very lucrative. Willingness to go without a high return on capital would seem plausible to the members only if accompanied by a direct financial advantage (for example, in prices), in other words, only if the co-operative offers its members tangible price reductions. An active price policy of the co-operative which would permit only limited profits to accumulate and would pass on service benefits directly to the members would certainly represent a form of co-operative benefit distribution. But on account of competition, a business policy like this is impossible nowadays in many markets, or at least is not expedient, since one might run into ruinous price wars that way. With a highly varied programme of services, it is also hard sometimes to measure the benefits which a co-operative offers its members, a problem which makes it difficult for the members to perceive any direct help being given to them.

On the one hand, it can rightly be asserted that the members of a co-operative display little responsiveness to earnings from capital investments with the co-operative. This elasticity would surely change, however, if the share capital of the individual members were larger. In this sense, the lack of incentives for members to invest capital in the co-operative leads to an undersupply of equity capital and, because this entails the high costs of borrowing outside capital, to an unfavourable financing situation, which has a negative influence on the potential of the co-operative to be successful and benefit its members.

The third precondition for an adequate supply of capital at relatively low cost to the co-operative would be fulfilled if the self-financing rate realized by the co-operative – i.e. the rate of earnings set aside for the purpose – were lower than that of other comparable enterprises. In this context, self-financing does not mean what is most frequently described in textbooks on business administration, namely the statement on the balance sheet (ex post) on retaining profits. After the balance sheet has been set up, the decision to be made on the volume of profits to be distributed to the members or to be retained does not procure the enterprise any additional means of finance and thus fails to fill any needs for capital. Instead, in an act of bookkeeping, that decision merely leads to an exchange of positions on the balance sheet between stated profit (earnings) and the open reserves and/or, more rarely, the share capital of the members.

If the co-operative cannot supply its need for capital through external financing from the market both for equity and outside capital, then this must and can be done only by temporary accumulation of financial resources through self-financing from marketing turnover. Underlying this self-financing process is a price policy which includes in the calculation not only the actual costs of the period and the rates for depreciation and allowance for contingencies, but also provision for accumulating and retaining additional financial resources. It is not necessarily the case, however, that at the end of the period profits will actually appear on the balance sheet and that a decision will then have to be made as to whether they should be retained or distributed. It is just as possible that these contribution rates for capital formation as well as the rates for depreciation and the contingency allowance can be covered by the market price through marketing efforts for only a mere few months of the business year, at the end of which a loss may have to be indicated.

In business administration there should be no material difference between these contribution rates needed to compensate for finance deficits of the co-operative and the profit rate needed to meet the expectations of investors for returns on the equity capital. It is therefore not at all evident that a co-operative can figure on lower capital costs than other types of enterprise. Thus co-operatives will have considerable difficulty in achieving benefits for their members through a policy of offering them the direct benefit of reduced prices. In the long run this difficulty will lead to efforts to achieve success in the market and then to distribute the results of market success to the members as a promotional benefit.

IV. On the Distribution of Benefits and Surplus in Co-operatives

In co-operative history, various co-operative founders have recommended various forms of distribution of surplus or profits to members. In principle a surplus or profit contained in the balance sheet can be distributed to the members according to criteria yet to be discussed and/or can be retained in the co-operative business through the formation of open reserves. Profit distribution is therefore the allocation of a positive result of co-operative business activity with relevance to financing.

The distribution drawn between retention of profits and distribution of profits is of course not a complete set of alternatives, from the standpoint of financing, since the profit and loss statement to be made by management and to be approved by the general assembly or the assembly of elected delegates, respectively, is based upon acts of evaluation the result of which is ultimately dependent upon the balance of power between management and membership. Through this evaluation, with the formation of hidden reserves, a decision is made in advance as to the extent of the surplus to be retained. On the surplus stated in the annual report, another decision has then to be made as to how much of it is to be retained and how much is to be paid out in dividends on the basis of share capital or on the basis of business patronage. At this point the question comes up of whether one of the alternatives or a combination of alternatives can be given preference from the standpoint of co-operative theory and business policy.

In scientific literature and in the experience of the

international co-operative movement, the principle of the Rochdale Pioneers of 1844 has often been considered as the one and only determining principle for distributing surplus in co-operatives, the principle being to distribute a surplus primarily according to patronage in the co-operative business and beyond that to permit only a limited amount of interest to be paid on capital investment (→ *Reimbursements*). This standpoint was reaffirmed by the Principles of the International Co-operative Alliance (ICA) of 1966. According to this form of surplus distribution, called a dividend for patronage in the co-operative business, the members receive the surplus back which has been achieved through sales, on the basis of their individual sales volume: in purchasing co-operatives this is a refund for overpayment of prices; in marketing co-operatives it is a compensation when the originally paid amounts were too low. This form of surplus distribution is based upon the idea that in this way the surplus is distributed to those who through their patronage of the co-operative have contributed toward achieving that surplus.

On the other hand, *Hermann Schulze-Delitzsch*, who supervised the founding of merchandise and credit co-operatives, recommended the distribution of surplus according to the members' capital investment (amount of share capital) in the co-operative. The German legislatures of 1867 and 1889 took over this method in the Co-operative Law, but with the provision that other forms were permitted to be laid down in the bylaws. *Friedrich Wilhelm Raiffeisen*, in contrast, proposed that in the credit co-operatives established on his initiative and in the agricultural merchandise co-operatives founded afterwards the surplus be retained in an "indivisible foundation fund"; that is, he made it a principle not to distribute the surplus at all.

The different proposals of co-operative founders on the forms of surplus distribution to be applied are not logical results of their views on the co-operative as a type of enterprise, which after all were identical to a great extent; rather, they were ultimately arrived at from specific market conditions which the consumers' co-operatives (*Rochdale*), the industrial purchasing and marketing co-operatives and savings and loan co-operatives (*Raiffeisen*) were facing at the time.

The consumers' co-operatives found themselves in tight competition with private food retailers at the time and could not afford to enter into price wars. They therefore accumulated a surplus in the co-operative and then repaid it to the members as a dividend on the basis of purchases from the co-operative. This rate of dividend, which was considerable at times, was paid without differentiation on all sales, that is, it was also paid on products with a low or even negative contribution to profit. The same was true for additional payments to members in the case of marketing co-operatives. This represented a high incentive for the members to do business with the co-operative. A refund of this sort, however, seemed impracticable in credit co-operatives on account of their heterogeneous bank services in borrowing and lending money. In addition, the possible total credit volume was dependent on the amount of equity capital available. The co-operative banks therefore switched to paying dividends on capital shares of their members, to offer them an incentive for signing up for shares and paying for those shares.

In contrast to this, the rural purchasing and marketing co-operatives had considerable needs for capital which could be met neither from the market for outside capital, which had not been sufficiently developed at the time, nor from the market for equity capital, since the farmer-members with their liquidity problems could participate only with small amounts. As a result, the sales process remained the only essential source of finance, where-upon it was necessary to retain surplusses.

Thus it has ben demonstrated that from the viewpoint of co-operative theory no definite or single form of surplus distribution can be given preference over the others. The historical discussion on price policy and surplus distribution policies in co-operative enterprise are determined by market-oriented considerations.

Bibliography

Bänsch, Axel: Operationalisierung des Unternehmenszieles Mitgliederförderung, Göttingen 1983.
Blümle, Ernst-Bernd: Probleme der Effizienzmessung bei Genossenschaften, Tübingen 1976.
Boettcher, Erik: Die Genossenschaften in der Marktwirtschaft, Tübingen 1980.
Boettcher, Erik: Kooperation und Demokratie in der Wirtschaft, Tübingen 1974.
Dülfer, Eberhard: Betriebswirtschaftslehre der Kooperative, Göttingen 1984.
Etzioni, Amitai: Soziologie der Organisationen, 2nd ed. München 1971.
Henzler, Reinhold: Der genossenschaftliche Grundauftrag: Förderung der Mitglieder, publ. by Deutsche Genossenschaftskasse, Frankfurt/Main 1970.
Henzler, Reinhold: Die Genossenschaft – eine fördernde Betriebswirtschaft, Essen 1957.
Jokisch, Jens: Zur Explikation der Zielbildung in Genossenschaften, Dissertation Hamburg 1974.
Lipfert, Helmut: Mitgliederförderndes Kooperations- und Konkurrenzmanagement im genossenschaftlichen System, 2nd ed., Göttingen 1988.
Mayntz, Renate: Soziologie der Organisation, Reinbek 1963.

Association of Co-operative Science Institutes

EBERHARD DÜLFER [J]

(see also: *Theory of Co-operatives*; *Periodicals, Co-operative*)

I. Members and Executive Bodies; II. The History of its Formation; III. Functions; IV. International Co-operative Science Conferences; V. Journal for Comprehensive Co-operative Studies.

I. Members and Executive Bodies

The "Arbeitsgemeinschaft Genossenschaftswissenschaftlicher Institute" (AGI, Association of Co-operative Science Institutes) is an association of academic research institutes at German-speaking universities engaged with co-operative studies. The legal form of the AGI is a registered non-profit association, and its legal domicile is Frankfurt am Main. It is of public benefit and non-profit standing vis-à-vis German tax legislation and is financed through contributions and an annual grant from the DG-BANK. The ordinary members are the institutes for co-operative studies at the universities of Berlin, Erlangen-Nuremberg, Fribourg (Switzerland), Gießen, Hamburg, Hohenheim, Cologne, Marburg, Münster, and Vienna, including approx. 40 professors of law, economics, social science and agriculture. The extraordinary membership is composed of roughly 20 further university professors who "in the scope of academic research and instruction are concerned with co-operative studies" either in other institutes or in the realm of their own professorial seats. Corresponding members can include:

- "Persons hailing from non-German-speaking regions who are concerned with co-operative studies in the scope of their academic research and instruction;
- university institutes and seminars for co-operative science in non-German-speaking regions;
- other German-speaking research institutes which promote co-operative science."

Among others, the Institute for Co-operative Studies at the University of Helsinki (Finland) numbers among this group.

The AGI is headed by an honorary board comprised of the chairman, deputy chairman, and the particular member responsible for the following academic conference. The election of the board and decisions concerning conferences and other important matters are incumbent on the general assembly which as a rule convenes twice a year. Only the ordinary members are entitled to vote; the extraordinary members assume an advisory function.

II. The History of its Formation

The tradition of scientific research into co-operative problems on the university level stretches back to such university professors as → *Victor Aimé Huber* (Germany), *Charles Gide* (France) and *Hannes Gebhardt* (Finland). Other influential personalities in the formative years of co-operative praxis were active as honorary professors or lecturers on the university level. *Georg Draheim* is exemplary of this in the more recent past.

After the earlier co-operative forms – themselves traceable to the Middle Ages (→ *Guilds*) – had acquired mounting importance in individual national economies through the pioneer work of → *Schulze-Delitzsch*, → *Raiffeisen*, the → *Rochdale Pioneers* and the co-operative socialists in France (→ *Co-operative Socialism*), they increasingly became an object of investigation in the disciplines of economics, economic policy, business administration, soziology, agricultural science and law (→ *Legal Form, Co-operative*). This initially led to the establishment of teaching and research institutes in various European countries, and later extended beyond the European continent. These institutes were in part shouldered and supported by national co-operative organizations, but were also in part integrated in universities. The English co-operative college Stanford Hall (Loughborough) which co-operated with the University of Nottingham attained international acclaim as did the Collège Coopératif in Paris as an arm of the Sorbonne University.

Several German universities offered co-operative seminars in the 1920s, but these were dissolved or abolished both before and during World War II. Re-establishment of these seminars took place in 1947 in Marburg and Münster; the universities in Erlangen and Frankfurt likewise soon undertook such steps as did the University of Vienna in Austria. These "Institutes for Co-operative Studies" at the respective universities carried on independently from one another in the scope of their individual departments. They, nonetheless, entered into co-operation with each other through the establishment of the *Zeitschrift für das gesamte Genossenschaftswesen* (Journal for Comprehensive Co-operation). Although this journal was edited by the Institute in Erlangen, the five institutes met annually in editorial conferences in order to share ideas and discuss the content of the publication (→ *Periodicals, Co-operative*).

A further expression of co-operation came into being based on the impulses of Prof. Dr. *Hans-Jürgen Seraphim* in the form of "International Co-operative Science Conferences"; the first of these took place at the University of Münster in 1954.

Prof. Dr. Georg Draheim provided the stimulus in 1968 to institutionalize this co-operation in the form of the "Arbeitsgemeinschaft Genossenschaftswissenschaftlicher Institute" – AGI which subsequently followed on Sept. 21, 1969, on the eve of the 6th International Co-operative Science Conference in Gießen. The founding members included the co-operative institutes at the universities of Berlin (Freie Universität), Erlangen-Nuremberg, Gießen, Hamburg, Cologne, Marburg, Münster and Vienna as well as the Institute for Co-operative Studies in Developing Countries additionally founded at Marburg in 1963. The present membership body listed at the onset of this article resulted from the subsequent inclusion of the institutes as the universities of Fribourg (Switzerland) and Hohenheim. In 1991, the newly founded institute at the Humboldt Universität in Berlin assumed the seat initially held by the Berlin Institute at the Freie Universität, which had been dissolved in the 1970s. The founding board of the AGI in 1969 included *Prof. Dr. Eberhard Dülfer* (Marburg) as chairman, *Prof. Dr. Walter Hamm* (Marburg) as deputy chairman, and *Prof. Dr. Erik Boettcher* (Münster) as co-ordinator of the following international conference.

III. Functions

The primary objective at the AGI is the preservation and further development of co-operative science as a subject of instruction and examination in the legal science and economics departments and sub-departments at German-speaking universities. The functions of the AGI are defined in detail in Article 2 of the by-laws:
"[The AGI] holds symposiums in which co-operative science problems are discussed and joint research projects are chosen and co-ordinated.
[The AGI] in particular ensures the uninterrupted progression of the International Co-operative Science Conferences.
[The AGI] maintains contact with foreign co-operative science institutes and organizations through the International Co-operative Science Forum.
The association can represent the interests of its members in the scope of a previously determined mandate in matters of common interest."
Biannual symposiums including the meeting of members are held in Frankfurt (usually in the DG-BANK building) in which an academic lecture is regularly held in addition to the discussion of usual matters and current affairs.

IV. International Co-operative Science Conferences

The first six International Co-operative Science Conferences held between 1954 and 1969 were organized by individual institutes, whereby the fellow institutes were also intensely involved. The location, host institute and co-ordinator, general subject matter and number of participants of these are outlined below:
1954: Münster, Institute for Co-operative Studies at the University of Münster; co-ordinator: *Prof. Dr. Seraphim*; "The Function of Co-operatives in the Scope of Modern Economic Policy"; approx. 150 German participants, 50 from abroad.
1957: Erlangen, Research Institute at the University of Erlangen; co-ordinator: *Prof. Dr. Georg Weippert*; "The Cultural, Social and Economic Situation of Contemporary Co-operatives"; 118 German participants, 124 from abroad.
1960: Marburg, Institute for Co-operative Studies at the University of Marburg; co-ordinator: *Prof. Dr. Wilhelm Michael Kirsch*; "International Problems of Co-operation"; 217 German participants, 111 from abroad.
1963: Vienna, Research Institute for Co-operative Studies at the University of Vienna; co-ordinator: *Prof. Dr. Dr.h.c. Wilhelm Weber*; "The Co-operative and the State"; 82 Austrian participants, 292 from abroad.
1966; Hamburg, Seminar for Co-operative Studies at the University of Hamburg; co-ordinator: *Prof. Dr. Reinhold Henzler*; "Planning in the Co-operation"; 169 German participants, 78 from abroad.
1969; Gießen, Institute for Agricultural Co-operative Studies at the University of Gießen; co-ordinator: *Prof. Dr. Paul Meimburg*; "Co-operatives in Economic Growth"; 181 German participants, 70 from abroad.
Upon the founding of the AGI in the course of the Conference at Gießen it was agreed upon that the conferences from then on should be held in the name of the Association. In accordance with the by-laws the colleague elected as the third member of the board should be willing to assume the organization of the academic presentations at the next international conference; the conference location as well as the host institute/seat are thereby likewise determined. Further developments in the progression of the International Conferences occurred as follows:
1972: Münster, Research Institute at the University of Münster, co-ordinator: *Prof. Dr. Erik Boettcher*; "Co-operatives – Democracy and Competition"; 269 German participants, 74 from abroad.
1975: Darmstadt, Chair for Private Law at the Polytechnic University of Darmstadt; co-ordinator: *Prof. Dr. Dietrich Schultz*; "Co-operatives and Concentration"; 152 German participants, 76 from abroad.
1978: Fribourg (Switzerland), Research Institute for Co-operative Studies at the University of Fribourg; co-ordinator: *Prof. Dr. Dr.h.c. Bernd Blümle*; "Is Co-operative Science still actual? Expectations of Co-operative Practice on Co-operative Science"; 145 Swiss participants, 85 from abroad.
1981: Marburg, Institute for Co-operative Studies at the University of Marburg and the Institute for Co-operation in Developing Countries at the University of Marburg; co-ordinator: *Prof. Dr. Eberhard Dülfer*; "Co-operatives in the clash between Member Participation, Organizational Development and Bureau-

cratic Tendencies"; 247 German participants, 169 from abroad.
1985: Münster, Research Institute for Co-operative Studies at the University of Münster; co-ordinator: *Prof. Dr. Erik Boettcher*; "The Co-operative in Competition of Ideas – A European Challenge"; 227 German participants, 85 from abroad.
1990: Stuttgart-Hohenheim, Research Center for Co-operative Studies at the University of Hohenheim; co-ordinator; *Prof. Dr. Werner Grosskopf*; "Origin and Future – Co-operative Science and Co-operative Practice at the Start of the Decade", 235 German participants, 67 from abroad.

V. Journal for Comprehensive Co-operative Studies

The *"Zeitschrift für das gesamte Genossenschaftswesen – Organ für Kooperationsforschung und -praxis"* (Journal for Comprehensive Co-operation – organ for cooperation in research and practice) was founded in 1959 by the Erlangen professors *Georg Weippert* and *Rudolf Pohle* in cooperation with the publisher *Hellmut Reprecht* and has been published ever since by the publishing house Vandenhoeck & Ruprecht in Göttingen. In contrast to the federation magazines of the various co-operative organizations the Journal is conceived as an academic periodical in which current co-operative problems are addressed from an expert scientific point of view. Particular elements of the Journal include editorials entitled "What we think", treatises, regional/state reports, the juristic chronicle which reports about current court decisions affecting co-operatives, and a bibliography for literature on co-operative studies (→ *Periodicals, Co-operative*).

Assortment Policies of Co-operatives

JERKER NILSSON

(see also: *Classification*; *Supply Co-operatives*; *Marketing Co-operatives*; *Marketing Strategies*; *Business Policies*; *Diversification Strategies*)

I. The Concept of Assortment; II. The Concept of Co-operatives; III. Co-operative Assortment Policy; IV. Consumer Co-operatives; V. Supply Co-operatives; VI. Labour and Marketing Co-operatives.

I. The Concept of Assortment

The concept of assortment can be looked at in different ways. In a wide perspective, assortment can be defined as a set of products which an actor possesses for the purpose of using it in a specific type of activity. Here, neither the actor is defined, nor what the products should be used for, nor what the products consist of.
The actor can be a person, a household, a firm, another organization, a public authority - any acting unit. The products can be intended for use as inputs in any type of activity - consumtion, sales, storage, speculation, filing, etc. Products included in the assortment can consist of any goods or services, i.e., all type of material and non-material benefits. It should be noted that an assortment can consist of services, and that every actor selling goods also offers an assortment of services such as payment conditions, guarantees, display and advice (→ *Diversification Strategies*).
This definition is in agreement with *Alderson's* wide definition (1965, p.47): "Assortments are collections which have been assembled by taking account of human expectations concerning future action." It is applicable in the following situations:

1. A manufacturer buys an assortment of raw material to be used in the production of certain products - procurement or purchasing assortment (*Gümbel* 1974, 1976,).
2. When the manufacturer takes up production, an inventory of ready-made products is built up to be stored during a certain period - storage assortment (*Gümbel* 1976).
3. The producer sells part of his storage assortments. The amount of goods sold is a marketing or sales assortment (*Gümbel* 1974; 1976).
4. A reseller acquires goods from different producers to compose an assortment appropriate for buyer purchasing behavior and so also for the reseller's sales - marketing or sales assortment.This is the equivalent of *Alderson's* definition of the seller's assortment (1965, p.47): "Intermediate assortments (trade stocks) have been collected to provide a choice of alternatives for (a) the consumer, (b) others in the trade."
5. When the consumer purchases, he chooses certain goods, pays for them, and then takes them home - procurement or purchasing assortment (*Wind*).
6. In his home (refrigerator, freezer, kitchen cabinet, etc.) the consumer stores a variety of food to be used for cooking and eating - storage assortment. Even this has its equivalent in *Alderson* (1965, p. 47): "Ultimate assortments (Consumer inventories) have been collected by the consumer in the hope and expectation of being prepared to meet future contingencies (probable patterns of behavoir)."

Theoretically, all these situations represent correct interpretations of the concept of assortment, but in discussions of assortment usually alternatives 3 and 4 are referred to, i.e., producing and distributing firms' assortment of products, which are offered for sale to other firms and to consumers. Hence, the American Marketing Association (1960) defines an assortment as "the composition of products offered for sale by a firm or a business unit". This definition is the one relevant for the present analysis. Co-operatives include both producing and distributing firms and they sell to consumers as well as to other firms. An assortment should be appropriate as input to a sales activity and, therefore, to a purchase activity also. However, all of the products making up the assortment are outputs stemming from other activities, primarily from production and storage. The composition of products can never be the same in both situations. There are always variations in the composition of products, which comprise outputs from different production and storage.

This means that an additional *sorting* process is necessary, aiming at putting together the products from storage and production in such a way that the amounts and types become more well-suited to the sales assortment. The sorting process involves a number of steps, including information collection, contacts with suppliers, negotiations, decision-making, transport, storage, finance, sales and market promotion. This sorting is a resourcedemanding process, and therefore, treated in isolation, undesirable.

From a sales point of view, on the other hand, sorting increases the value of the assortment, i.e., a well-implemented sorting results in an assortment giving the seller the opportunitiy to sell more at higher prices and at lower sales costs. The *potency of assortment* is raised (*Alderson* 1957; 1965). The sorting, therefore, is the expression of seller adjustment to buyer demand.

One conclusion of this is that the actors in a distribution chain have different assortments. There are always greater or lesser *discrepancies of assortments*, which means that all actors must carry out a certain sorting activity (*Alderson* 1957; 1965). Because sorting is resource demanding, however, no actor is willing to do more sorting than is absolutely necessary. Hence, in the distribution chain (for example, producer, wholesaler, retailer, consumer), there are some assortments which have greater similarities with the assortment in a previous or subsequent link in the chain and less similarities with another.

All products in an assortment must have certain common characteristics, otherwise they would not belong to the same assortment. There must be certain types and degrees of homogeneity. For example, they should be intended for similar types of use, be directed toward similar buyer categories, be purchased from the same supplier or require the same handling equipment. All these are *partial homogeneities*.

The issue of partial homogeneities is affected by the assortment holder's wish that the activity for which this assortment is an input, is carried out effectively. (*Alderson* 1965). Because of the type and degree of economies of scale and scope, respectively, that is found in each activity, the assortments must be more or less homogeneous in some respects. Therefore, a tobacco retailer has an asssortment which is homogeneous in terms of product character, because, given the buying habits of his clientele, his sales will be more effective.

II. The Concept of Co-operatives

1. Classification of Co-operative Business

The assortment policies differ significantly between different types of co-operatives. A farmer co-operative slaughterhouse and a consumer co-operative grocery store have different assortment policies as the products in their assortment come from different activities and are intended as inputs in different activities. Hence, co-operatives must be classified in a way allowing for a greater homogeneity in each category in terms of assortment policy.

A categorization based on two criteria is proposed, viz., the role of the firm for members (disposal or acquisition of products) and the type of member (private individual or enterpreneur). When these two categories are combined four types of co-operatives emerge:

→ *Consumer co-operatives:* Acquisition of products for private persons, e.g., grocery stores or insurance.
Supply co-operatives: Acquisition of products for enterpreneurs, e.g., retailer associations or farm inputs supply.
Labour co-operative: Disposal of services (labour) for private individuals, e.g., worker-owned workshops.
→ *Marketing co-operatives:* Disposal of goods and services for enterpreneurs, e.g., a farmer-owned slaughterhouse.

The concept of assortment concerns the relationship between seller and buyer. The co-operative categories represent the seller side. On the buyer side, two types are identified, namely consumers and purchasing organizations. (for discussion of different market types, see → *Marketing Strategies*).

Given the four types of co-operatives and the two types of markets, there are eight classes of assortments covered:

Marketing organization	Consumers	Buying org.
Consumer co-operative	A;A*	B
Supply co-operative	C	D;D*
Labour co-operative	E	F
Marketing co-operative	G	H

There are such similarities among these classes that they can be dicussed together:

- Consumer co-operatives' assortment offered to members (A): Section IV.
- Supply co-operatives' assortment offered to members (D): Section V.
- Labour and marketing co-operatives' assortment

offered to consumers and purchasing organizations (E-H): Section VI.
- Consumer and supply co-operatives' assortment offered to non-members (A* and D*): → *Marketing Strategies*.

2. Partial Vertical Integration

Co-operative activity can be viewed as *partial vertical integration* (Staatz). Integration is a concept based on co-ordination. There are two ways to co-ordinate activities such as sales and purchase, viz., market mechanism (co-ordination by feedback) and hierarchical control (co-ordination by plan).

Market co-ordination implies interaction between a large number of buyers and sellers, all fully capable of safeguarding their own interests (homo oeconomicus). The products and needs are homogeneous; information channels function perfectly; etc. Hence, no actor can force another to adapt to him, so co-ordination takes place by everyone adjusting him- or herself to others, based on information about how others react to one's own behavior. There are no ties between actors; everyone is completely independent. The degree of integration is zero.

Hierarchical co-ordination means that coordination takes place within an organizational hierarchy. Decision-makers on higher echelons of the hierarchy decide under which conditions coordination has to take place. This is a situation of full integration.

Partial integration is a synthesis: co-ordination takes place through a combination of market information and organizational planning. Co-operative activity is always partial integration between the members and the co-operative firm, i.e., co-ordination takes place as a result of both member decision to trade (giving feedback information from the market) as well as member decision in the governing bodies (giving hierarchical coordination).

The fact of cooperation being a partial integration is a result of the insufficiency of the market mechanism, i.e., the existence of *market failures*. If markets function imperfectly from either the sellers' or the buyers' perspective, then sellers (buyers) can escape the market solution by integrating forward (backward), i.e., establishing a co-operative. Because of the large number of preconditions for markets to function properly, there are many types of market failure. Among others, some examples are (→ *Marketing Strategies*):

- No counterpart exists (buyer or seller).
- The counterpart has a monopsony or a monopoly.
- Actors cannot assess counterparts or the products bought or sold, so there is a risk for deceptive behavior.
- Actors are economically or socially tied to the counterpart.
- High transaction costs (→ *Institutional Economics*).

III. Co-operative Assortment Policy

1. Vertical Integration

The assortment policy of a firm is related to its degree of integration with its trading partners. If a firm is fully integrated with another, it has no degree of freedom at all. Its assortment consists of products decided upon by the headquarters. If the degree of integration is zero, i.e., the firm interacts with others through market relations, the firm decides its own assortment (high degree of freedom). The bases for the decisions are the expectations of need and supply concerning the other market partner, and the task of the firm is to adjust its assortment to demand as much as possible.

As co-operative activity represents a form of partial integration, co-ordination between the co-operative enterprise and its members takes place with the help of a combination of the market mechanism and hierarchical control. Therefore, the conditions for a close relationship between assortment policy at different levels of the processing/distribution chain exist. The assortment of → *marketing* and → *consumer co-operatives* can be planned in conjunction with member desires as to products, and the assortment of supply and labour co-operatives can be linked with member production.

Vertical integration is also apparent in terms of how large parts of the processing chain are included in the activities of the firm. The question is to what extent the co-operative firms should pursue strategies which involve further vertical integration (→ *Franchising*):

- Should a farmer-owned slaughterhouse sell butchered carcasses to independent processing plants, or should it produce consumer products at wholesale, or should these products be sold through own retail outlets?
- Should a consumer co-operative chain buy goods from independent suppliers, or should it have its own factories where an assortment of the demanded goods is produced?

There are no simple answers to these questions. In each specific case, the solutions are determined by the respective market relationships. If there are functioning markets, there is no reason to integrate. If, however, market imperfections exist, continued integration is a sound possibility. Hence, the same principles apply here as those which influence people to join together into co-operative organizations (see Section II.2).

2. Homogeneities

Because the definition of assortment requires that it be an input well-suited to a certain type of activity, the degree of homogeneity in terms of buyers' needs and demands is important. A firm trying to serve a heterogeneous clientele has a handicap in the form of higher costs resulting from the lack of economies of scale as well as from lower revenues due to poor market adjustment. Efficiency losses occur in all activities, but they are especially discernible in assortment policy given its central role in marketing.

For the capitalistic firm, the solution to the problem of heterogeneity is a simple one, since it can choose categories of buyers which are homogeneous enough to be served efficiently. To a large extent, this is also true for the labour and marketing co-operatives. Consumer and supply co-operatives cannot, however, choose buyers in the same way. They are tied to their clients who, at the same time, are their members. This entails certain problems.

There are different solutions for these problems. First, the society can try to change the composition of membership so that it becomes more homogeneous. Second, the firm can influence current members to be more homogeneous. This can be done through communication, differentiated prices, service levels, etc. Third, the firm can differentiate its activities by establishing different member categories, chosen so as to ensure a high degree of homogeneity within each category.

IV. Consumer Co-operatives

Both → *consumer* and → *supply co-operatives* have assortment policies which are aimed at their members. Hence, member needs determine the products to be included in the assortment. The situation can appear to be similar in a capitalistic firm, as its assortment is determined by the demands of the buyers. However, there is, a difference due to the nature of co-operative activity as a partial integration, i.e., the task of the co-operative is to compensate for market imperfections.

→ *Consumer co-operatives* can be conditioned by many types of market imperfections and, therefore, it is not possible to deal with all of these here. Instead, the presentation is limited to market failures which occur because consumers have insufficient resources in the form of knowledge, analytical ability, overview, etc. as well as unclear goal perceptions, i.e., their demand, motives, and criteria are not in harmony with their needs (*Nilsson* 1983). First, the concepts of need and demand must be examined. Every actor has a great number of goals, connected with each other in a complex net of interrelationships. For the sake of simplicity this can be represented by a hierarchy having an overall goal at its top. At lower levels, there are goals which are operationalized from the overall goal. At the base of the hierarchy, there are the detailed goals guiding concrete action, such as decision criteria. In this goal hierarchy, needs are found at the top, and demands at the bottom (→ *Competition*).

In the operationalization process, disturbances can result in a less than perfect harmony between the two levels. One is where the actor has limited resources of different types - knowledge, overview, etc. Another is where other actors, such as capitalistic firms, exercise influence. These conditions lead to a specification of goals at lower levels, possibly creating conflicts with overall goals. The actor can thus unintentionally work against his own interests.

The capitalistic firm is indifferent to whether the consumer satisfies his needs. What is significant is consumer purchasing behavior which is guided by demands, as it is this activity which affects the sales of the firm.

The co-operative firm finds itself in a different situation. In its contacts with members playing the role of consumers, it receives the same signals as the capitalistic firm does. Other types of signals, however, come from the members in their role as owners. The democratic system allows the members to influence the firm's assortment policy. These signals represent thoroughly thought-over and well-informed opinions, originating from the overall goals.

These circumstances have consequences for the assortment policy of consumer co-operatives:

- fewer fancy products;
- greater emphasis on health, safety and reliability;
- low prices are important;
- the goods give more factual and less emotional information;
- the assortment is shallower - fewer goods which are de facto similar but appear to be different;
- lower frequency of rotation in product assortment;
- thorough product analyses precede assortment decisions;
- products are analyzed from the consumer's perspective when assortment decisions are made;
- independence relative to outside suppliers is important;
- there is a tendency to use distributor brands.

V. Supply Co-operatives

→ *Supply co-operatives* are also the result of the existence of market failures (Cf. *Sauer*). A farmer co-operative selling inputs such as seed, fertilizer, feed, and machinery is chosen as an example. This firm has been established as an alternative to a capitalistic regional monopoly which would not function to the satisfaction of farmers.

The capitalistic monopoly could maintain a high price level as well as an assortment of goods not being well-suited to client needs, require long delivery time for specialized inputs, etc. The firm could exploit clients in situations where needs arise suddenly, e.g. when a spare part to a combine harvester is needed in the busiest period of the harvest. By establishing a supply co-operative, farmers can eliminate the risk of being exploited.

The assortment of the co-operative firm is decided upon the basis of both market information (sales data) and organizational planning (needs as expressed by members and democratically elected bodies) (→ *Organizational Structure of Societies*). This two-sided stream of information facilitates better co-ordination:

- The members can agree to standardize their demand in a way allowing the firm to limit its assortment and keep costs and prices down.
- The firm can decide not to extract the total costs from the individual customer, and to defray these costs from a general account, when supplying unusual goods, at non-business hours and in acute need situations. This means that the prices of other products will include a certain insurance premium.
- Certain types of services are provided at little or no cost.
- The close ties between firm and members allows the firm to invest more in long-term product development. The risk that demand will fail is less.
- The firm can implement a streamlined system for ordering, deliveries, billing, and payment.
- The flow of information between firm and clients can be made more effective. Advertising and other communication can be replaced by integrated, even computerized, systems.

VI. Labour and Marketing Co-operatives

The assortment marketing and labour co-operatives offer their buyers consists of products that the firm produces on the basis of inputs from their members - raw materials such as animals and grain, or labour and skills. These two types of co-operatives exist to market member resources in more or less processed form.

This fact can appear to be a limit to the ability of the firm to design an assortment policy. The assortments are designed from the perspective of the supplier/employee, not of the buyer. Thus, there probably is a minor discrepancy in the relationship with the members, while there is a large discrepancy with buyers (*Cobia & Anderson*). The firm can have difficulties in making its assortment homogeneous enough to be suitable for demand. This necessitates an analysis of how serious this limitation is:

- The firm should not regard all products as one large assortment but rather as several minor ones. There are probably many market segments, each with its own characteristics, and so, one should distinguish between different assortments for each category.
- The assortment of the labour and marketing co-operatives is highly dependent on the way the firm is organized. The greater the gap between suppliers/employees and buyers and the more important it is to adapt to demand, the more urgent it is for the firm to have an effective marketing department, being able to close the gap between suppliers and buyers.
- The marketing or labour co-operative can build up an attractive assortment by adding certain products from outside suppliers, primarily products supplementing those produced within the co-operative, that is products having the same buyers, products buyers will purchase at the same time, or products being distributed and stored together. Hence, own products are given sales support, i.e., the potency of the assortment increases. Also, costs are kept low as a result of economies of scale and scope, respectively.
- The co-operative firm may buy products from outside suppliers which are substitutes for the products from member input. This is a radical step in that it implies competition with members, but under certain circumstances it can be worth considering. The outside products can generate a profit greater than the sum of the profits of the members and the co-operative.
- New products can be developed within the co-operative firm, based on those products which members deliver.
- The firm can integrate forward in the processing chain, and thus develop new products based on its previous ones.
- Product development can be done with members, that is in an earlier phase in the processing chain. The co-operative can function as a catalyst for member-oriented product development - improving quality, new varieties, techniques, etc.
- The firm can promote other member interests than before. An example may be a farmer co-operative whose members have the possibility of renting out vacation cottages to tourists. The firm can then expand its assortment of dairy or meat products to also include vacation rentals.

Bibliography

Alderson, Wroe: Marketing Behavior and Executive Action, Homewood, IL 1957.
Alderson, Wroe: Dynamic Marketing Behavior, Homewood, IL 1965.
American Marketing Association: Marketing Definitions: A Glossary of Marketing Terms, Chicago, IL 1960.
Cobia, David W. & Bruce Anderson: Product and Pricing Strategies, Cooperatives in Agriculture, Engelwood Cliffs, NJ 1989, pp.174–194.
Gümbel, Rudolf: Sortimentspolitik, Handwörterbuch der Absatzwirtschaft, Stuttgart 1974, cols.1884–1907.
Gümbel, Rudolf: Sortiment und Sortimentspolitik, Handwörterbuch der Betriebswirtschaft, vol.I/3, Stuttgart 1976, cols.3563–3573.
Nilsson, Jerker: Det konsumentkooperativa företaget (The Consumer Co-operative), Stockholm 1983.
Nilsson, Jerker/Viggo Høst: Reseller Assortment Decision Criteria, Greenwich, CT 1987.
Sauer, Klaus: Das Einkaufsentscheidungsverhalten im ge-

nossenschaftlichen Lebensmitteleinzelhandel. Eine empirische Untersuchung, Göttingen 1982.
Staatz, John M.: A Theoretical Perspective on the Behavior of Farmer's Cooperatives, Michigan 1984.
Wind Jerry: Toward a Change in the Focus of Marketing Analysis: From a Single Brand to an Assortment, Journal of Marketing 41 (1977), pp.12 & 143.

Auditing, Co-operative

KONRAD MOSE [J]

(see also: *Federations*; *Law, National*; *Financial Accounting Law*; *Controlling*; *History in 19th C.*)

I. Historical Development; II. Co-operative Auditing Federation: The Organization of the Co-operative Auditing; III. Mandatory Co-operative Audit (GenG, § 53); IV. Audit Upon Formation; V. Additional Audits and Auditing Federations; VI. International Comparison of Co-operative Auditing.

The German co-operative auditing is considered one of the most developed in the world, and it therefore is the focus of attention of this exposition. The original designations "comptrollership" (Revision), "comptroller" and "comptrollership association" were renamed into "audit", "auditor" and "auditing federation" (Prüfungsverband) in the Genossenschaftsgesetz (*GenG*, German Co-operative Law) dating from October 30, 1934.

I. Historical Development

Soon after their establishment in the middle of the 19th century the first co-operatives expressed the desire to have competent auditors provide them with consultation and conduct audits (→ *History in 19th C.*). Business administration was almost exclusively in the hands of honorary managers and board members. One could not speak of professionalism per se; the supervisory board (→ *Organizational Structure of Societies*) had no experience in auditing procedures. The administration, in particular the bookkeeping, therefore often exhibited numerous incompetencies and shortcomings which later lead to business failures. → *Schulze-Delitzsch*, who was confronted with the demand to introduce an external audit in 1864, initially refused this requisition. He saw this as intervention into the self-administration of the co-operative and maintained that the supervisory board was better qualified to undertake the necessary auditing procedures on account of its insight into the local conditions than an external auditor. → *Haas* similarly refused outside audits for many years. → *Raiffeisen* in contrast advocated a detailed and dependable audit of the books and an assessment of management undertaken by selected individuals as well as comprehensive consultation and assistance for the administrative bodies as early as 1866 (*Raiffeisen*; *Hildebrand* 1913). In 1873 he engaged itinerant teachers as auditors and consultants and consistantly expanded the system of voluntary audits. Obligatory audits were introduced in all affiliated co-operatives in his federation in 1883. *Haas* followed his example in 1883/84. *Schulze-Delitzsch* altered his defiant position as a result of increasing demands from co-operatives as well as from the effect of a slew of grave bankruptcies and liquidations. In order to prevent legal mandatory revisions through state authorities which were called for in 1881 (proposed by Rep. *Ackermann* in the Deutscher Reichstag), he advocated routine voluntary audits through the co-operative federations and developed auditing principles in the course of the legislative proceedings which he initiated (*Schulze-Delitzsch*).

The *co-operative → federations* (Chapter II) increased their activity in auditing procedures in these years, expanded the scope of the audits and intensified the training of auditors in order to prevent the introduction of a statutory audit by making it superfluous. All of these efforts were nonetheless in vain. The *GenG of May 1, 1889* (Co-operative law) subjected all registered co-operatives to a mandatory audit (§ 51). This was the first legally prescribed, mandatory audit in Germany. State intervention was limited to granting the right to select an auditor, and, if necessary, to rescinding this right. The auditor, not the federation, was responsible for the audit; he was the one entrusted to sign the audit report and issue certification of the audit (§ 61). Membership in the federation was not mandatory, and non-federated co-operatives were allowed which in turn were reviewed by an auditor named by the register court (§ 59). The nature and extent of the audit were not determined by the law but rather by respective specifications in the → *by-laws* of the federation (§ 54). It was, however, added in the statement substantiating the *GenG* that "the periodic audits concern the co-operative management in all branches of administration. (The audit) must in no way only be limited to a mere calculatory review of the balance and business accounts. The auditor's investigation must essentially be based on the financial side of the business management and on the principles to be adhered to as well as on officials in the co-operative organization and the other mechanisms of the co-operative" (*Beuthien/Hüsken/ Ackermann*, p.255). The lawmakers thus to a substantial degree assumed the auditing principles developed by the federations, whereby the exigencies of the term "substantive audit" were strongly contested up until about 1930 (*Mose*, 1984, p.12). The misgivings that mandatory audits would have a negative effect on the development of the co-operatives proved to be unsubstantiated. The audit, with its distinct components of consultation and assistance, became a true review of development and contributed to the further expansion of the co-operative system.

The economic difficulties after World War I lead to various new regulations to intensify the auditing functions. The auditing structure attained a completely new foundation through the *GenG* ratified on *October 30, 1934*. Membership in an auditing federation became mandatory; the auditing regulations were more precisely and thoroughly defined; the auditing federation became responsible for the audit, and the auditor for providing assistance to complete the audit; the institution of a co-operative certified public accountant (Wirtschaftsprüfer) was established; the rights and obligations of the auditing federations with respect to evaluating the audit and redressing shortcomings were considerably extended. Further influence on the auditing structure resulted from the VO affecting publically appointed certified accountants in the co-operative sector from 1935 as well as from the Bilanzrichtliniengesetz (*BiRiliG*, EC code of guidelines for striking a balance) dating December 19, 1985 and the *BiRiliG* from 1990. (cf. chapters II and III for the present conditions in force.)

II. Co-operative Auditing Federations: The Organization of the Co-operative Auditing

1. Development and Present Organization

The formation of the auditing structures within the scope of the legal stipulations is left to the auditing federations. These developed out of the original correspondence offices, which supported and carried out the extensive correspondence of the founders, and into comprehensive consulting and assistance institutions with their own legal person. When the GenG of 1889 became effective, they became *comptrollership* federations. The utilization of the right to appoint auditors was variously (→ *History in 19th C.*). Whereas the "Anwaltschaftsverband" (federation of attorneys) in Neuwied became an auditing federation on November 28, 1889 (*Raiffeisen*), the "Allgemeine Verband" (general federation) (*Schulze-Delitzsch*) at no time acquired auditing rights. These were exclusively practised in the sub-federations, while the sub-federations in the Raiffeisen-Organisation became auditing federations in 1905. This was likewise true for *Haas*' organization.

Alongside these federations the *Verband der Baugenossenschaften* (federation of co-operative → housing societies) was founded in Berlin in 1896 as a sub-organization of the General Federation and attained the right to appoint auditors on March 11, 1897. The co-operative housing societies withdrew from the *Schulze-Delitzsch* organization in 1934 and founded the *Hauptverband deutscher Wohnungsunternehmen (Baugenossenschaften und -gesellschaften) e.V. Berlin* (main federation of German housing enterprises of Berlin) as a central organization with 12 regional auditing associations. The *Zentralverband deutscher Konsumgenossenschaften* (central federation of German consumer co-operatives) was formed in 1903 as a further umbrella organization; the authority to audit was practised by its regional auditing federations. After unsuccesful attempts to unite between the years of 105 and 1913, the two largest rural organizations of *Raiffeisen* and *Haas* merged in 1930 upon the incorporation of various smaller co-operative federations into the *Reichsverband der deutschen landwirtschaftlichen Genossenschaften-Raiffeisen-e.V. Berlin* (Reich association of German agricultural co-operatives-Raiffeisen, Berlin). This organization attained the right to appoint auditors on July 24, 1930, through the resolution of the Reich Council.

A reformation of the auditing structure followed after World War II. In the Federal Republic of Germany there are currently three central organizations (→ *Central Institutions*) with the authority to audit as well as numerous regional and specialized auditing federations:

a) *The Deutscher Genossenschafts- und Raiffeisenverband e.V.* (DGRV, German Co-operative and Raiffeisen Union) in Bonn emerged through the amalgamation of the industrial and rural organizations in 1971. It was granted the authority to conduct audits on February 23, 1972. After several successful mergers the Union could boast 12 regional auditing federations and 6 specialized auditing federations in 1989. As of December 31, 1988, 93 certified public accountants, 1065 federation accountants and 272 assistants were employed.

b) The *Gesamtverband gemeinnütziger Wohnungsunternehmer e.V.* (joint federation of non-profit housing enterprises) in Cologne was allotted the right to audit on September 25, 1951; it had 10 regional auditing associations with 25 certified public accountants, 147 association accountants and 41 assistants as of December 31, 1989.

c) The *Revisionsverband deutscher Konsumgenossenschaften e.V.* (auditing federation of the German consumer co-operatives), the legal successor of the former Zentralverband der deutscher Konsumgenossenschaften after the incorporation of six regional auditing associations which up to then had practised independently, was granted the right to audit on January 1, 1949. As of December 31, 1989 there were two certified public accountants and six federation auditors.

2. Legal Status and Responsibilities of the Auditing Federations

In accordance with § 54 of the *GenG*, each co-operative must belong to a federation which has been entitled to conduct audits. If a co-operative withdraws from an federation, it will be dissolved by the register court if it cannot verify membership in another federation within an imposed period of time (§ 54a). Within this prescribed period the court may appoint another auditing federation to assume the responsibilities layed down in the law (§ 64b). The authority to audit is conferred by the appropriate state authority, as a rule the economic ministry in whose jurisdiction the federation has its domicile. The federation is incumbent on the constant supervision of this authority. The right to audit can only then be conferred when the federation can guarantee the fulfillment of all tasks and duties to be assumed. The necessary preconditions for this above all include a sufficiently sized staff of specially trained federation accountants and an adequate administrational apparatus. At least one certified public accountant should belong to the board of the auditing federation or be appointed as special proxy § 30 *BGB* [German Civil Code]; *GenG*, § 63b, Sec.5). A certified public accountant is also managing the auditing service. State authorities can divest a federation of its right to audit when it can no longer guarantee the fulfillment of its given responsibilites or when there is no longer any demand or need for its services.

The law differentiates between *mandatory duties* and *voluntary functions*. According to § 63b, auditing its member co-operatives *must be* an objective of the federation, and the collective safeguarding of its interests *can be* an objective. It may not pursue other objectives. The main function of the auditing federation is the mandatory audit. *Beuthien's* position that the mandatory audit need not be the main objective of the federation remains contested (*Meyer/Meulenbergh/Beuthien*, comment 4 to *GenG*, § 63b). Despite extensive consultational and support functions (such as in law, taxes, business administration, marketing, data processing) which the federation members can make use of as they will, the auditing federation tend to place more and more emphasis on the mandatory audit as their main responsibility. Other audits or reviews are supplemental.

The → *federation* should have the legal form of a registered association. Their members can only be registered co-operatives and other enterprises irrespective of their legal form which either are completely or extensively in the hands of a registered co-operative or which serve the co-operative sector. Those enterprises which are not registered co-operatives and which are subject to other statutory auditing procedures remain subject to the other auditing procedures and not to those of the *GenG* despite their affiliation to the association (§ 63b). The by-laws of the auditing federation can nonetheless also prescribe additional audits for these companies (cf. Chap. V).

III. Mandatory Co-operative Audit (GenG, § 53)

1. Legal Framework

§ 53 of the *GenG* states that "the *facilities*, the *financial position* and the *management* of the co-operative are to be audited every other business year in order to assess the business conditions and the properness of the management. An annual audit is to be conducted on those co-operatives whose balance sheet total does exceed DM 2 million. Within the scope of this audit the annual financial statement (→ *Financial Accounting Law*) is to be inspected in light of the status report and accountancy. The auditing procedures determined in the Handelsgesetzbuch (*HGB*, German Commercial Code) § 316, Sec.3; § 317, Sec.1, Sents.2–3 group statement are to be applied appropriately." As of January 1, 1991, *HGB* § 340k (formerly § 27 of the Kreditwesengesetz [*KWG*, German Banking Code]) is additionally applicable in the audit of the annual financial statement of credit co-operatives. The co-operative is audited by the federation to which it belongs. The federation engages employed auditors who have sufficient training and experience in co-operative auditing procedures. The auditing federations thus continually host high quality training and further education courses for this purpose. Members of the board of directors and supervisory board of the co-operative to be audited as well as employees and members may not conduct the audit. If the federation has a pertinent reason it can appoint another auditor (not one of its employed auditors); this may only be another auditing federation, a certified public accountant or a chartered accounting office. One such plausible and important reason is when no orderly audit (legal, legitimate in content, and in due time) can be otherwise guaranteed (*Meyer/Meulenbergh/Beuthien*, p.421). A federation's *authority to audit* of an federation is *rescinded* when a member of its board or its special proxy (*BGB*, § 30) is a member of the board of directors or supervisory board, a liquidator or employee of the co-operative to be audited. In such a situation the central apex organization to which the federation belongs must appoint another auditing federation, another certified accountant or another chartered accounting office upon the behest of the board of the co-operative in order to avoid any conflicts of interest (*GenG*, § 56).

2. The Execution of the Audit

a) The objects and method of the audit

The audit is conducted following the auditing principles and instructions issued by the auditing federations as well as in accordance with professional guidelines set by the Chamber of certified accountants. It is both a financial assessment of the management and a temporally fixed audit encompassing all branches of the enterprise. In order to meet the legally prescribed auditing deadlines it frequently takes the form of a cyclical audit with annually rotating concentrations; it is likewise often broken down into a preliminary and general audit and carried out in selected samples. The investigation and ascertainment of the present cirumstances, the determination of standards, the assessment and the disclosure of the report are the components of the audit.

The audit can follow either announced or unannounced. The federation must notify the chairman of the supervisory council in time about the beginning of the audit. The supervisory board must become involved in the audit upon the insistance of the federation or the auditor. The auditor must immediately notify the chairman upon making important findings which require immediate measures from the supervisory board.

The audit of the financial position is concentrated above all on the situation of assets, finances and revenue as well as on efficiency and profitability. It is based on bookkeeping; the audit itself includes the totality of assets and liabilities at their full value, hidden reserves, acute and latent risks, uncertain payables and expenses, imminent losses from pending business, the formation of sufficient reserves/depreciation reserves (→ *Financial Accounting Law*). Conclusions and evaluations concerning the structure and suitable application of equity result from this, along with observations and assessments of the financial situation and structure as well as liquidity position (→ *Equity Capital*). When considering and evaluating the revenue situation the auditor must direct his formal observations to a certain degree to how the board has pursued the co-operative promotion principles (→ *Promotion Mandate*).

The *management assessment* must ascertain both formal and substantive regularity within management. It must be investigated whether the necessary personnel and material measures have been undertaken in accordance with the law, the → *by-laws* and the business policy (→ *Business Policies*), and whether these measures can be viewed as appropriate in the framework of the co-operative principles and business structure. The assessment is concerned with the management as an institution and organization, with the management mechanism and its activity. The management functions include organization, planning, information, auditing, internal comptrollership, bookkeeping, personnel policy, and technical operating ability. The organization as a component of this functional mechanism includes both the internal and external organization of the co-operative. The audit also encompasses management policy, planning and supervision. In particular the fulfillment of the promotional policy and the observation of the principles regarding equal treatment of all members are to be studied. The assessment and/or judgement of the promotional factor frequently proves to be problematic (*Dülfer*) (→ *Assessment of Success*). This is likewise true for the evaluation (→ *Evaluation*) of the expediency of the corporate policy and the commercial measures which the auditor must assess (*Hildebrand*, 1936; DGRV, 1979; *Mose*, 1984). The expediency falls under criticism if inappropriate actions determined in the course of the audit simultaneously indicate an infraction against the prescribed orderly behavior or an infringement of the order of promotional (DGRV 1982, p.9). The audit also serves to assess the *personal dependability and specialized qualifications of the management*, which are to be measured on the level of their resonsibility according to *GenG*, § 34. The composition and activity of the supervisory board are likewise assessed.

The auditor presents an oral report in the *final auditing meeting* with both the board of directors and the supervisory board about the presumable results of the audit. The final outcome of the audit is reflected in the written *audit report* of the auditing federation. The board of directors and the supervisory board must deliberate the results of the audit immediately following the submission of the audit report (Art.58). The supervisory board must report about the essential findings and/or objections raised by the audit in the general assembly.

b) The aftermath of the audit

Lawmakers have granted the auditing federations extensive influential power over the audited co-operative with respect to the mandatory audit in order to ensure that any existing shortcomings are redressed by the board. The federation and/or the auditor have the following rights: to participate in the consultational meeting with the administration concerning the audit report (§ 58, Sec.4); to assume a consulting role in the general assembly in which the audit report is presented (§ 59, Sec.3); to call an extraordinary general assembly when the resolution concerning the audit report has been unduly delayed or when the general assembly has been insufficiently informed about the most important findings and/or objections of the audit report (§ 60); to demand a written reply from the board in accordance with the by-laws of the auditing federation and to engage the consulting department of the federation to redress any shortcomings; the authority to inform affiliated co-operatives and central co-operative offices of the co-operative sector about the content of the audit report, as well as the right to submit a copy of the report to the central auditing federation; to conduct an extraordinary audit, as a rule for clarification of certain circumstances/items in connection with the mandatory audit (§ 57, Sec.1).

IV. Audit Upon Formation

1. Legal Stipulations and the Objective of the Audit

The initial audit upon the establishment of a co-operative through the auditing federation and the register court was added to the GenG through the law ratified on October 9, 1973. Before this time, a mandatory audit existed through an unwritten law (*Meyer/Meulenbergh/Beuthien*, comment 1 to § 11a). The co-operative undertakes this audit in the initial stage of its formation in order to acquire legally prescribed entry into the co-operative register. According to §11, Sec.2, Item 4 the *certificate of admissability from the auditing federation* as well as its *expert opinion* are necessary; these determine whether the personal and/or financial conditions of the co-operative, in particular the extent of its assets, present an endangerment of the interests of the co-operators or of the creditors of the co-operative. A submitted assessment of the profitability along with an audit of the proceedings leading to the formation and registration are required for the expert opinion. The audit of the establishment and registration by the auditing federation are not expressly prescribed by lawmakers, but it is nonetheless a component of an orderly audit upon formation. The audit prescribed for the register court in § 11a is basically identical with that of the auditing federation; they are therefore not separately delineated. If the co-operative has not been formed and registered in due order, the court must refuse its entry; this is likewise so when the interests of the cooperators or creditors are endangered by insufficient capital. The audit and expert opinion of the auditing federation should serve as a basis for the audit conducted by the register court and facilitate its assessment. The court is not, however, bound to the federation's report, but it will not enroll the co-operative when it considers the federation's position convincing with regard to a denial of enrollment (*Meyer/Meulenbergh/Beuthien*, comment 5 to § 11a). The court can also procure further expert opinions. For credit co-operatives § 32 of the *GenG* (authorization) and *KWG* § 43.1 (registration proceedings) are also applicable upon formation. (→ *Strategies when Establishing Co-operatives*)

2. The Financial Audit and Personnel Assessment

An endangerment of the interests of members and/or creditors can be based on meta-economic factors, but above all can be found in economic spheres. It can be caused by the members themselves in the form of insufficient ability or engagement, capital contributions (paid-up shares) and even possible additional contributions (→ *Financing*) which they need to provide in order to maintain the necessary continual input-output relationship with the co-operative. An endangerment might also lie in the insufficient qualifications of the manager; the audit thus must judge his personal and professional suitability. The postulates in *KWG* § 33 with regard to the qualifications of the manager and the structure of the financial means of the co-operative (→ *Equity Capital*) for credit co-operatives (→ *Co-operative Banks*) are to be taken into consideration analogously.

The audit of the financial situation should illustrate the shape of assets, finances and revenue in the formative stage and assess the presumable development. Thus the existing/planned supply of capital (extent of the participatory interest and paid-up shares, participatory capital, formation of reserves), liquidity position, foreseen extent of business, earning power, and the structure and development of risks must be studied. For this the organizational structure, detailed corporate plans, investment and financial plans, etc. must be taken into consideration. The audit is essentially one of the future which is based on prognoses, and thus considerable factors of uncertainty are involved. The auditing federation cannot be charged with a false estimate of future development or of the general economic situation of a particular economic branch based on its scrutinous assessment of factors at the time of audit (*Lang-Weidmüller*, comment 17 to § 11). According to prevalent opinion, the auditing federation and the register court need not evaluate the economic expediency of the co-operative enterprise (*Meyer/Meulenbergh/Beuthien*, comment 7 to § 11 and comment 5 to § 11a). This should not, however, be practised in an unrestricted manner: If the audit undertaken upon formation should namely indicate that efficiency and profitability will not be at hand, that the promotion principle cannot be fulfilled, and that the interests of the members and creditors are threatened, enrollment into the register must be denied.

3. International Regulations

As a rule authorization from a responsible public authority or enrollment into a public register are necessary in order to secure legal capacity. This entails formal and/or financial audits. There are no uniform regulations in → *international co-operative law*, and a comprehensive presentation will not be undertaken at this point. Chapter VI details corresponding regulations.

V. Additional Audits and Auditing Federations

Alongside the mandatory audit (Chap. III), the audit upon formation (Chap. IV) and extraordinary audits (*GenG*, § 57, Sec.1), the auditing federation conducts among other things the following examinations:

- *Annual audit and group audit in accordance with HGB § 340k* for incorporated *credit co-operatives* (normally within the scope of the audit prescribed

in *GenG* § 53), inasfar as over half of the members of the board of the auditing federation are certified public accountants. This is likewise applicable for incorporated credit institutions with the legal form of an incorporated society;
- *Audit of custodianship accounts* according to § 30 and *incidental audits* according to *KWG* § 44, Sec.1 for credit co-operatives upon instruction from Federal Banking Supervisory Office (Bundesaufsichtsamt für das Kreditwesen);
- *Annual audits* for members of the federation who have the legal form of an AG (corporation) or a GmbH (private limited company) in which the majority of shares and the majority of voting rights are in the hands of co-operatives, non-profit housing enterprises or co-operative auditing federations, and when over half of the members of the board of the auditing federation are certified accountants (*Introductory Law to HGB,* § 25, Sec. 3 [also note Secs.1,2]).

The necessary requirements for an auditing federation to make an *expert opinion* include the following examinations, whereby the term "audit" is not used by lawmakers:
- *Audit of a merger* according to *GenG* § 93a ff.;
- *Audit of a resumption* according to § 79a upon the continuation of business activities following its dissolution;
- *Audit of conveyance* in liquidation (§ 88a) and bankruptcy procedures (§ 108a);
- *Audit of enforced settlement* (§ 115e);
- *Audit for compensation* (§ 111 of Code of Compensation Regualtions);
- *Audit upon restructuring* from a registered co-operative into an AG (*AktG,* § 385m [Corporation Law]).

VI. International Comparison of Co-operative Auditing

Audits are an essential element to ensure the correctness of a business enterprise. This realization has apparently become accepted worldwide in co-operative business structures although no uniform regulations exist in matters concerning the various higher supervisory authorities, the objective of the audit, the auditing organizations and institutions, the nature, extent and methods of the audit. The following examples should illustrate this point, whereby an extensive comparison is not possible in the scope of this article.
Austria: To a very large degree in concurrence with the German auditing regulations. *Great Britain*: Annual audits of the account books and the yearly statement are conducted by chartered accountants, and the audit report is presented to the registrars. The regulations for the majority of the *Commonwealth* countries as well as for *Asian* countries are the same or similar; only the subject matter of the audit and the legal capacity of the registrars vary in part. *France*: No uniform legal structure exists. Periodical audits are conducted on co-operatives which are publically supported, and occasional audits are conducted on all co-operatives by *commissaires aux comptes*. Federations also conduct voluntary audits, above all in the agricultural sector. The subject matter of the audits differ in the various co-operative groups. *Belgium*: There is no co-operative law and no mandatory audit. Voluntary audits are undertaken by auditing federations and resemble in part a management assessment review. The central Raiffeisen bank is the auditing authority for its organization. Similar regulations exist in *the Netherlands* for the Rabo banks. Here, a co-operative federational structure exists, but without obligatory membership and mandatory audits. *Switzerland*: No mandatory audits are conducted. The general assembly appoints an auditor to review the management and the balance. Individual certified accountants or authorities are allowed alongside the auditing federations. *Denmark* and *Norway*: There is no legally stipulated audit, but the dominant form is through auditing federations. The extent of the audit varies from pure bookkeeping to management reviews. *Sweden* and *Finland*: Regular financial audits are conducted by qualified independent auditors chosen by the general assembly. Audits are likewise conducted through auditing federations, but membership is not mandatory. *Greece*: Co-operative laws date from 1979 and 1982. The co-operative sector is controlled by the state. Agricultural co-operatives are subject to the supervision of the agricultural minister and/or the agricultural bank. The biannual audit includes analyses of the financial situation, the organization and management. *USA*: Audits of varying degree are conducted by auditors external to the co-operative. *Latin America*: The solutions here are particularly heterogeneous; audits varying in their extent are conducted by the state, by auditing federations, or by publically appointed auditors.

Bibliography

Beuthien/Hüsken/Ackermann: Materialien zum Genossenschaftsgesetz, vol. II, Göttingen 1989.
Deutscher Genossenschafts- und Raiffeisenverband: Grundsätze ordnungsmäßiger Prüfung der Geschäftsführung bei Genossenschaften, Schriftenreihe no. 10, Wiesbaden 1979.
Deutscher Genossenschafts- und Raiffeisenverband: Der Beruf des Verbandsprüfers, Schriftenreihe no. 19, Wiesbaden 1982.
Dülfer, Eberhard: Der Förderungsauftrag als Gegenstand von Geschäftsberichten und Pflichtprüfungen, no. 3 of Marburger Schriften zum Genossenschaftswesen, Marburg/ Lahn 1981.
Ebert, Kurt Hanns: Genossenschaftsrecht auf internationaler Ebene, vol. 1, Marburg/ Lahn 1966.
Hildebrand, Karl: Die Einführung der obligatorischen Ver-

bandsrevision, in: Landwirtschaftliches Genossenschaftsblatt, Neuwied, no. 11 (1913), pp. 377–380.
Hildebrand, Karl: Wegweiser für genossenschaftliche Prüfungen, vol. XVI, Wegweiser für Wirtschaftsprüfer, Berlin and Leipzig 1936.
Meyer/Meulenbergh/Beuthien: Genossenschaftsgesetz, 12th ed., München 1983.
Mose, Konrad: Prüfung der Ordnungsmäßigkeit der Geschäftsführung bei Genossenschaften, no. of Marburger Schriften zum Genossenschaftswesen, Marburg/Lahn 1984.
Mose, Konrad: Die genossenschaftliche Verbandsprüfung – Aspekte und Perspektiven, in: ZfgG, vol. 36 (1986), pp. 241–255.
Lang/Weidmüller. Genossenschaftsgesetz, 32th ed., Berlin/New York 1988.
Münkner, Hans-H.: Die Organisation der eingetragenen Genossenschaft in den zum englischen Rechtskreis gehörenden Ländern Schwarzafrikas, dargestellt am Beispiel Ghanas, Marburg/Lahn 1971.
Münkner, Hans-H.: Genossenschaftsprüfung bei staatlich geförderten Genossenschaften in Südostasien, in: Perspektiven der Genossenschaftsrevision, Wien 1986, pp. 282–296.
Raiffeisen, Friedrich Wilhelm: Die Geschäfts- und Rechnungsrevisionen eingetragener Genossenschaften und die Gesetzgebung, in: Landwirtschaftliches Genossenschaftsblatt, Neuwied, no. 1 (1879), pp. 61–62, no.9, pp. 66–68.
Schmidt, Ferdinand: Prüfung von Genossenschaften, Herne/Berlin, 2nd ed. 1969 (1st ed. 1968).
Schulze-Delitzsch, Hermann: Material zur Revision des Genossenschaftsgesetzes, Leipzig, 1883, pp. 84–95.
Selchert, Friedrich-Wilhelm: Die genossenschaftliche Gründungsprüfung als Spezifikum eingetragener Genossenschaften, in: ZfgG, vol. 30 (1980), pp. 93–99.

Authorities, Co-operative

PETER S. AKPOGHOR

(see also: *State and Co-operatives, Market Economy*; *Development in different Parts of Third World*; *Law, International*; *Policies for Promotion*; *Development Policy*)

I. Introduction; II: Organization, Role and Functions of Co-operative Authorities; III. Co-operative Authorities in Selected Countries; IV. Arguments For and Against Involvement of Co-operative Authorities in Co-operative Development; V. What to Do.

I. Introduction

All over the world, Co-operatives are recognized as offsprings of and instruments against socio-economic stress. In Europe, they began as a result of the severe effects of the industrial revolution and sectoral problems of farmers and independent craftsmen. Consequently, the Movement was born before laws were made to regulate its operations. The only exception is India where the British colonial power introduced the so-called Classical British Indian Pattern of Co-operative laws based on the experience in Europe (*Münkner* 1971) (→ *British-Indian Pattern*).

In countries where the Co-operative movement sprang up from the initiative of the people, the law governing it has been accordingly liberal (→ *Schulze-Delitzsch*). On the contrary in Africa, Asia and the Caribbean where the state has been its promoter from inception, the resulting laws have been sometimes less liberal. This has brought the Co-operative Movement very close to the government, a situation which, according to *Draheim* (1955, p.210) is typical of the Movement.

The direct result of this close relationship is the establishment of so-called Co-operative Authorities in many developing countries. For the purpose of this essay, Co-operative Authorities are Co-operative departments and all such agencies established by the government to promote and regulate the Co-operative Movement. The rationale behind their establishment is (i) to protect their members and their business partners (ii) to guide the predominantly illiterate membership and (iii) to harness their involvement in the pursuit of government policy objectives (→ *Policies for Promotion*). In Nigeria, Strickland recommended that the Registrar should "take the initiative and exercise *control* over the Movement in a degree quite *unsuitable* to the conditions of an advanced and educated population" (1934, p.1.).

In some countries, the Co-operative Authorities may be spread in several government agencies such as in Indonesia, or merely a part of an agency that looks after other issues as in the United Kingdom or in Germany where issues pertaining to Co-operatives come under the Federal Ministry of the Economy. In a few countries such as Belgium and Denmark there are no Co-operative laws and therefore no Co-operative Authorities in the context of this paper.

In order to facilitate a better understanding of this exercise, it is divided into five sections. Section II describes the organization, role and functions of Co-operative Authorities. In Section III four case studies of Co-operative Authorities in Africa and Asia are presented, while in Section IV arguments for and against government involvement in Co-operatives are succinctly articulated. The paper is concluded with suggestions on what should be the continuing role of Co-operative Authorities in the developing countries so as to set the Movement on the path of sustainable growth.

II. Organization, Role and Functions of Co-operative Authorities

Most Co-operative departments in Africa and Asia are headed by the Director of Co-operatives, Registrar, Chief Registrar or Commissioner. He is supported by an appropriate staff complement. Each department is divided into various divisions to handle specific functions such as promotion and development, arbitration, inspection and supervision, etc. Ancillary functions are subsumed under the divisions.

The role of the Co-operative Authorities is to promote and generally control the Co-operative Movement. In the advanced countries, the role of the ministry or department charged with Co-operative matters is, in the main, limited to administration of the Co-operative law, where one exists, ensuring that all societies are registered and work according to the law. In Africa and Asia, the Co-operative Authorities are endowed with powers which could mean life or death to their Movement (→ *Law, International*).

The statutory duties of Co-operative Authorities are many and include registration, audition and amalgamation, etc. (→ *Bylaws*). The Authorities also perform *non-statutory* functions such as education and training, policy formulation, seeking of foreign technical assistance as well as state financial assistance to the Movement. Some of these non-statutory functions are self-imposed because their performance is necessary for the orderly development of the Co-operatives. It is noteworthy that the traditional distinction between statutory and non-statutory functions has lost its importance as the latter functions have metamorphosed into statutory functions through subsequent legislation (*Münkner*, 1971). In Nigeria, for example, policy formulation and education and training, etc. have been made provisions of the Co-operative Development Decree 1974 which established the Federal Co-operative Department.

An important function of the Co-operative Authorities is the presence or representation of the Director at general meetings of societies. In Nigeria as in many English-speaking African states, the Director or his representative must be present at all the general meetings of societies under his jurisdiction. Although he is there in an advisory capacity, his presence is intimidating and a source of worry to discerning Co-operators. In countries where governments are particularly sensitive to criticism of any kind, the presence of the Director is a sure cause of concern.

Although government involvement in Co-operative development was supposed to be transitional, this original aim has never been defined or time-framed. This is one of the dilemmas of the Movement today. Whatever critics say of the system, however, never bothers the Co-operative Authorities. They are getting more involved by the day and seem to forget that the Registrar of companies does not have to attend the general meetings of companies registered by him. The Authorities' stand, however, demands a sympathetic view as government's aim is to promote the people through Co-operatives.

In some countries, Co-operative policy formulation still remains a non-statutory function. Such policies may be formulated alone by functionaries of the Co-operative Authorities or with concurrence of government agencies with similar interests or with the Co-operative leadership. Where there is no such consultation between the Co-operative Authorities and the Movement, the result is normally unbridled criticism from the Movement. There is even more acrimony if such policy leads to a new legislation (→ *Law, International*).

Policies made must be implemented. This is where the Co-operative Authorities fail sometimes. Because of frequent changes of governments and policies in developing countries, Co-operative policies suffer from unsustained implementation. Sometimes abrupt changes are introduced mid-stream resulting in fragmented development and inconsistency on several fronts.

III. Co-operative Authorities in Selected Countries

The Co-operative Movement evolved spontaneously in the advanced countries. Government's role was to pass a suitable law for its growth. In Britain the Co-operative Authority, if it may be so called, is in the office of the Registrar of Friendly Societies. His duties start and end with the registration and cancellation of the certificate of registered societies. In the Federal Republic of Germany, the Wirtschaftsministerium (Economic Ministry) administers the Co-operative law. In the USA, there are federal and state laws "designed to legalize Co-operative action, to provide means of incorporating associations ... and to promote Co-operatives... to compete on a more satisfactory basis with others in the economy" (*Roy* 1976, p. 97). In all these countries there is no agency with identical structure as the Co-operative Authorities in developing countries. This is because Co-operatives in the market economies are allowed considerable leeway in their operations (*Dülfer*). Close intervention and interference are absent but the countries all pursue policies which are conducive to Co-operative growth (*Heckman* 1969).

The picture is different in the developing countries. In the last segment of this section of the paper, therefore, four case studies are briefly presented to illustrate the operations of Co-operative Authorities in Africa and Asia (→ *Development, Africa*; → *Development, South Asia*; → *Development, South-East Asia*).

1. Nigeria

Nigeria ia a federation of 30 states with a Federal Capital Territory, Abuja. It has two Co-operative departments at national level and thirty States Co-operative departments. The Federal Co-operative Department is in the Federal Ministry of Labour and Productivity. It was established by decree No.5 of 1974. The Federal Department of Agricultural Co-operatives was created in 1979 under the Federal Ministry of Agriculture. It has been under the Directorate of Food, Roads and Rural Infrastructure since 1991.

The Federal Co-operative Department performs the usual statutory functions of registration and supervision of national apex organizations as well as education and training and policy formulation, etc. Its counterpart in Agriculture was established as a policy measure to promote agricultural Co-operatives. *It has no statutory powers.*

In order to coordinate Co-operative activities in Nigeria, two conferences, namely the conference of Minister and Commissioners (State Ministers) responsible for Co-operative matters and the conference of Directors of Co-operative, have been instituted. They meet at least once yearly to review Co-operative activities, set goals and formulate policies. The conference of Directors serves as source of input to the conference of Minister and commissioners. The Minister of Labour is in addition advised by the 15-man National Advisory Council for Co-operative Development whose members are drawn from the relevant sub-sectors of the economy, including the Universities.

2. Republic of Cameroun

Barring recent political changes, there are two main Co-operative Authorities in the Cameroun. They are the Co-operative Department established in 1954 for West Cameroun and the Commission Centrale de Surveillance des Societé Indigène de Prévoyance established in 1937 for French-Speaking Cameroun. In the West, the Registrar exercised the conventional statutory functions and non-statutory and advisory services (*Gabelmann* 1971).

The main function of the Commission Centrale des SIP was to oversee the operations of the SOPs. In 1959 the Director de la Coopération et de la Mutualité was established to, among others, *control* and advise existing Co-operatives and promote the formation of new ones. It was headed by a Director. It had two sections, namely the Service de Controle and the Service d'Etudien, d'Assistance et de Developpement. The Control Service (Agency) had overwhelming powers, including *control of internal management of Co-operatives*. In 1967 the Service de la Information et de la Propaganda was created to carry out research into Co-operatives and prepare syllabi for Co-operative training, among others.

In 1969 the first Central Co-operative Authority was established under UNDP and ILO technical assistance. Known as the Federal Centre for the Development of Co-operative Enterprises (CEFDEC), it was established to carry out studies on proposed and existing Co-operatives, render advisory services and train Co-operative management and administrative personnel.

Recently the Cameroun government embarked upon a fundamental change in its Co-operative law designed to liberalize its grip in the Movement. The results of these changes remain to be seen.

3. Republic of Indonesia

Indonesia (*Baldus*, n.d., pp. 97-115) comprises 13,000 islands. It is a former Dutch colony. The country's government interest in the Co-operative Movement began on the attainment of independence. Today, Indonesia has nine agencies responsible for Co-operative Development. The prominent ones are:

a) *The Department of Trade and Co-operatives* – responsible for the establishment, guidance, organization and supervision of Co-operatives, legal assistance and education and training.
b) *Ministry of Agriculture* carries out five statutory functions including guidance, motivation of farmers, assisting to obtain production inputs and the marketing of farm products.
c) *The Ministry of Industry* provides assistance in the fields of education and training, surveys and research, technical and managerial advice, etc.

The other six agencies are the Ministries of Home Affairs, Trade, Public Water and Electrical Water and Finance, the Bank of Indonesia and the Provincial Governors. The danger of duplication of efforts cannot be ruled out in these elaborate arrangements but *Baldus* (p. 111) states that "Although the promotional approach is top-down until now it is the expressed intention of the government to develop a self-reliant Co-operative Movement based on the initiative of the people themselves".

4. The Republic of (South) Korea

The Republic of Korea covers an area of 100,000 sq.km. Its government involvement in the Co-operative Movement began after the country's liberation from Japan in 1945. In the subsequent constitution, the government expressed a desire to "encourage the development of Co-operatives founded on the self-help of farmers..." (*Baldus*, pp. 118-119). In 1961 it passed a Co-operative Law to, among others, improve "... the economic and social status of farmers through independent Co-operative organisations of farmers" (*Baldus*, p. 119).

The Ministry of Agriculture and Fisheries is the government agency for Co-operative development in Korea. The apex National Agricultural Co-operative Federation (NACF) is under the Ministry. The *Saemaul Undong*, New Village Movement, was established in 1971 to reduce the gap between incomes and living standards in rural areas. It is located in the Ministry of Home Affairs. Both the NACF and the Saemaul Undong receive enormous government patronage and bear the attendant control and interference.

IV. Arguments For and Against Involvement of Co-operative Authorities in Co-operative Development

The involvement of Co-operative Authorities in Co-operative development has evoked considerable controversy. The following are some arguments for and against the system.

1. Arguments for Government Involvement

These include:
a) There is need to develop the national economy in all its ramifications and use the Co-operatives to strengthen *the disadvantaged* in the nation.
b) Co-operatives have inherent weaknesses and need government promotion for growth.
c) Co-operative members and the public should be protected from the shortcomings of Co-operatives.
d) The government and Co-operatives are partners in progress and share the same ideals towards the weak.
e) Government can use any instrument, including Co-operatives, for pursuing its socio-economic objectives.

2. Arguments Against Government Involvement

The academics and other commentators are very critical of government involvement in Co-operative development. Their arguments include:
a) Nothing has been done to fix a *time-frame* for government involvement which was designed originally to be temporary.
b) Operations of Co-operative Authorities stunt the growth of the Movement. In East Africa, *McAusian* (1970, pp. 81-120) lists an array of functions of the Co-operative departments which include approval of by-laws, the signing of Co-operative cheques by Co-operative officials and dissolution of a society or removal of its management committee if found wanting by an official enquiry.
c) Frequent changes in governments and government policies adversely affect the Movement.
d) Co-operative leaders tend to enjoy government patronage and rest on their oars but are quick to accuse government of interference and thereby court animosity. In summary, it should be said that although government involvement is desirable, it should be ingeniously handled and reviewed as set out below (→ *Officialization*).

V. What To Do

I think governments in developing countries have a right to use whatever instruments, including the Co-operatives, available to them to pursue the national socio-economic goals. Thus, the government, in my view, will continue to be closely linked with the Movement for many years to come. But changes are inevitable in tune with the wind of liberalization currently sweeping through the world. The following are some suggestions in this connection (cf. *Akpoghor*, 1991).

1. There should be a comprehensive policy review and reorientation based on the wide-ranging study of government involvement in Co-operative promotion. The emerging policy should form the basis of a new liberal Co-operative law.
2. The Co-operative Movements in all developing countries with strong Co-operative Authorities should be studied to identify (a) viable societies requiring no government assistance for survival (b) societies capable of being helped to stand on their own with minimum government assistance and (c) those that cannot be nurtured to maturity. In carrying out this study, attention should be paid to the various sectors of the economy (→ *Development Policy*). In Nigeria, thrift and credit societies especially those in Ministries and in industry fall under category (a) while consumer societies and societies in the informal sector fall under category (b). The time-frame for assistance in (b) must be pre-determined.
3. Co-operative Authorities should take a definite stand on unviable societies and dissolve them, just as unviable companies go into voluntary liquidation.
4. Co-operative Authorities should cease auditing the annual accounts of Co-operatives. Instead, a Co-operative Auditors Association should be established in appropriate developing countries to undertake the annual audit with the approval of the Director of Co-operatives. Competent retired Co-operative officials could form the nucleus of such a body.
5. There should be institutional strenghtening of tertiary Co-operative organizations. At present too many depend too much on government for assistance. The leadership of the Movement in appropriate Third World countries should be sensitized to address themselves to their responsibilities in their Movement.

In conclusion, it should be stressed that in spite of their severe criticism, the world should learn to continue to live with the phenomenon of the involvement of Co-operative Authorities in Co-operatives while efforts are being made towards an effective liberalization of the system. A state of laissez faire may be the ultimate goal. In many developing countries this may yet be long to achieve. At best, developing countries will continue to promote Co-operatives while they gradually free themselves from controlling and interfering in their internal management.

Bibliography

Akpoghor, Peter S.: Liberalisation of Government Involvement in Co-operative Development in Nigeria, (Unpublished Individual Development Project submitted to the Administrative Staff College of Nigeria, Badagry 1991).
Baldus, R.D.: "Government Promotion and the Development of Self-Help Organizations – Case Studies: Indonesia, Korea, Malasia, Philippines and Thailand." in Baldus, R.D./Hanel, Alfred/Münkner, H.-H. (eds.): Government Promotion of Co-operatives and other Self-Help Organizations for Rural Development, Berlin (no date). The information on Indonesia and Korea is based on this work.
Draheim, Georg: Die Genossenschaft als Unternehmungstyp, 2nd revised edition, Göttingen 1955.
Gabelmann, Ekkehart: Die Genossenschaft in Kameroun, Marburg 1971.
Heckman, John H.: "The Role of Government in Co-operative Development", in Mcgrath, Mary Jean (ed.): Guidelines for Co-operatives in Developing Economies, Madison 1969.
Mc Ausian, J.P.W.B.: "Co-operatives and the Law in East Africa," in Widstrand, Carl Gosta (ed.): Co-operatives and Rural Development in East Africa, Uppsala 1970.
Münkner, Hans-H.: New Trends in Co-operative Law of English – Speaking Countries of Africa, Marburg 1971.
Roy, Ewell Paul: Co-operatives: Development, Principles and Management, Danville 1976.
Strickland, C.F.: Report on the Introduction of Co-operatives into Nigeria, Government Printer, Lagos 1934.

Autochthonous Co-operatives

PAUL TRAPPE

(see also: *Classification*; *History before 1800*; *Development, Africa*; *Development, South Asia*; *Development, South-East Asia*; *Pre-co-operative Forms*; *Informal Co-operatives*; *Societal Form, Co-operative*)

I. Definition and Sources; II. Africa; III. Latin America; IV. Asia; V. Cooperation as an ubiquitous phenomenon.

I. Definition and Sources

The term "*autochthonous co-operatives*" refers to co-operative organizations whose existence can be traced to "pre-European" eras, or which have been modelled on neither western nor eastern European types of co-operative society.
Anthropological jurisprudence towards the end of the nineteenth century, and continued contemporary research whose aim is to produce "monographs" about ethnic units in the most varied parts of the world, have gradually heightened interest in research into co-operative societies and similar associations in non-European cultures. Twentieth century development policy has added new concerns to this field of research, which has furnished evidence of a wealth of co-operative societies, which existed *prior to* any influence by the co-operative movements of the industrialized states. In their own culture-specific moulds these have been able to remain in operation down to the present. We have "pre-co-operatives", "co-operatives proper", "simple forms of cooperation", even *Alfred Vierkandts's* "cooperative forms of society" and *G.D.H. Cole's* "primitive co-operative enterprise", and many more.

As long ago as 1931, *Alfred Vierkandt's* pioneering work was an important milestone: "The co-operative form of society is here opposed to the hierarchical... In the co-operative society this (unequal division of power among various subgroups, P.T.) does not exist: Power is essentially equally divided among the various individuals and subgroups (family, kin, etc.); rank and class exist, if at all, only in embryonic form. Instead of the state there is a much looser political organization..." The literature on autochthonous co-operatives flourished especially in the 1960s and 70s, based largely on reactions to early travelogues, and through politicians involved in the development of newly independent states. Thus, attempts were made, especially in agrarian societies, to harness autochthonous co-operatives, or even proto-forms of co-operative societies to the development process (→ *Development Policy*). These usually took the form of work groups, but longer-lived, economically oriented groups were by no means rare.

Autochthonous co-operatives are not, however, limited to non-European cultures, but also exist in industrialized nations, especially in so-called development regions (less developed, almost exclusively agricultural regions of the Mediterranean countries). Autochthonous forms have also been preserved here and there in the industrial centres, although these are generally based on agricultural or other primary sector activities. The essential socio-economic function of autochthonous co-operatives was, and is, in the "informal sector" (→ *New Co-op*eratives). For the theory and practice of co-operative societies, the "discovery" of autochthonous co-operatives resulted in considerable broadening of horizons and relativization of the claim that cooperative forms of this type were manifestations of European economic and social history (→ *History in 19th C.*).

II. Africa

In *Africa*, which, compared to other regions of the world, came under direct European economic and social influence relatively late (essentially only after the Berlin conference of 1884–85), the density of autochthonous co-operatives is particularly striking, since here the most varied traditional forms of cooperation have managed to survive (→ *Development, Africa*).

Relevant concepts for similar or even culture-specific forms of cooperation among individuals, families or groups can probably be attested for all African languages. Just a few examples may serve as an illustration: the terms are "gaya" and "gandu" in Hausa, "humbe" in Tiv, "tafar" for the Kanuri, "shirka" among the Shua-Arabs, and "nafir" and "faza" in Kordofan and Darfur.

M. Bardeleben, writing on forms of organization in the Nuba Mountains, states that: "The members of the association (baramka) choose a leader and deputy leader who are responsible for the organization of labour, particularly for sowing, picking and cleaning of the short-staple cotton planted in this area. If a member of the group is prevented from joining in the work on the appointed day, he is obliged to make a small contribution to the group's petty cash from which tea and sugar are purchased. If he fails to contribute, he is excluded from the baramka." This is especially the case where the social structures are organized in a *segmentary* way (in *Emile Durkheim's* sense), or where such segmentary systems have managed to survive in spite of processes of (*Überlagerung*) subjugation to many other forms of organization. Of these segments, those that do not consist only of related individuals are especially interesting for the study of co-operative movements. Furthermore, they evidence "proto-democratic" political structures (cf. *George Peter Murdock's* survey).

In particular research carried out in recent decades has shown that in the whole of sub-Saharan Africa we find recurrent forms of economic cooperation (→ *Pre-co-operative Forms*) combined with solidarity-based socio-political structures which could well be described as "co-operative societies". They occur especially in non-centrally-organized systems "without rulers", in the sense of *John Middleton* and *David Tait's* "Tribes without Rulers". Self-help and autonomy are taken for granted.

Such forms of cooperation can take the form of agricultural activities and bush clearing; the gathering of building materials and construction of huts, houses, and storehouses; savings societies based on "substitute currencies"; and artisans' associations and specialized subgroups of workers to coordinate fishing, fish processing, transport over relatively great distances and through several middlemen to the consumer (e.g. fishing and fish processing at Malamfatori and Vulgo on Lake Chad), and the sale of dried fish in cities of northern *and* southern Nigeria.

Fishermen's associations displaying great similarities in their constitution and norms, are widely found around the great lakes of sub-Saharan Africa. Rather less frequent are the typical forms of farmers' associations concerned with artificial irrigation, since such developments, especially in pre-European times, took place only in a few parts of Africa. Where they existed they took advantage of very limited opportunities for cultivation (e.g. the distribution via ingenious canal systems of glacier melt waters from Mt. Kilimanjaro to intensively cultivated market gardens and cattle farms).

Some of the systems of cooperation did not restrict their activities to single ethnic groups but operated uniformly, especially in West Africa, over large areas, borne by members of highly differentiated populations. They were mostly spread by populations (like the Dioula of the Ivory Coast and Ghana, and the Hausa of Northern Nigeria) who had supraregional trade interests. The special credit banks which in West Africa are usually called "esusu" or "tontines" must be included among these *all-embracing systems* which covered wide areas. W.R. Bascom defines it thus: "The esusu is a fund to which a group of individuals make fixed contributions of money at fixed intervals; the total amount contributed by the entire group is assigned to each of the members in rotation." As *Hans Dieter Seibel* and *Michael Koll* have demonstrated, these still occur in several West African countries as unregistered co-operatives.

Of greatest significance, and yet apparently most commonplace, are the groupings engaged in agriculture. These are specialized work groups, usually tied up with African *age group systems* and the typical *division of labour* among the sexes in the region. Work groups are not only widespread in Africa; they could almost be regarded as a sociological universal, just as the family has proved to be an universal institution (cf. *P. Wilhelm Schmidt*). In this respect it is remarkable that such work groups are gathered as required for a specific purpose and that co-operative activity stops as soon as their goal (bush clearing, house building, boat buildung, extraction and working of meteoritic iron, etc.) has been achieved. However, they reappear as groups once their particular task again becomes necessary.

Of special significance are the *norms* evolved in particular among fishermen's work groups. *Hans Cory* and other government anthropologists have uncovered in their recording of such norm systems (among previously non-literate peoples) true co-operative statutes or even co-operative laws which had probably been passed on down the ages by means of oral tradition and practice before the advent of writing. Among fishermen, too, especially in areas with Islamic populations, specific normative systems can be traced back to Islamic law or Islam-influenced common law. These are similar in Senegal and Gambia as well as along the East African coast. However, such forms of cooperation were often led by single individuals who succeeded in replacing traditional co-operative groups of equals with smaller fishing enterprises emplying waged workers.

The same goes for the associations of artisans usually found in traditional urban environments or large semi-urban villages in West Africa which have been described in various places as "guilds" (→ *Guilds*). In the 60s *Michael Koll* carried out pioneering research on these in Yoruba cities. While in the urban environment diverse handcrafts were organized into "guilds" (metal workers, weavers, tailors, tanners, transport, and other activities), in the rural environment it was in the first instance smiths and their suppliers of raw materials, and in the Sahel (indigo) dyers and weavers who did so.

Interest in these forms of cooperation was more academic than social or focused on development policy, which sometimes prepared the ground for the practical realization, *consolidation and/or furtherance* of existing forms of cooperation. The most comprehensive efforts in this direction had already in colonial times been consciously led along this path in anglophone Africa. In any case, on independence, the majority of these countries, especially in East Africa, had at their disposal coherent systems of modern co-operative societies which viewed themselves as continuations of autochthonous co-operative forms.

For the most part they had developed via intermediate forms (farmers' associations) into modern co-operative societies following the introduction of colonial or state co-operative society laws, which remarkably enough led to the marketing co-operative society becoming most widespread. These were in the main concerned with marketing cash crops, in particular products aimed at world markets, such as cotton, coffee, cocoa, cashew nuts, etc. In isolated instances not only the raw product was co-operatively marketed but also various phases of manufacture were organized on co-operative lines. For decades the Kilimanjaro Native Co-operative Union (KNCU) in Moshi, Northern Tanzania (coffee), or the Kenya Co-operative Creameries, were taken as paradigmatic examples.

In the years following independence there was a return to traditional roots which has taken hold in the conception of *African socialism* in particular and has made its most far-reaching, if unsuccessful mark in Tanzania's *ujamaa policy*. This initiative, in spite of many setbacks, is still regarded as one suited to local conditions, even though the setbacks can be attributed to internal misdevelopments (management, taxation, etc.) and external factors (terms of trade, rising oil prices, population explosion, desertification, etc.).

The concept was already outlined in the year of independence (1961) by *Julius K. Nyerere*, and underwent further elaboration in theory and practice through the decades. The traditional principles of co-existence in (kinship-based) self-sufficient units was to serve as the guiding light for nation buildung. *J. Nyerere* has written that: "In traditional African life the people were equal, they co-operated together, and they participated in all the decisions which affected their lives. But the equality was an equality of poverty: the co-operation was on small things; and their government was only the government of their own family unit, and of their clan, or at most of their tribe. Our task, therefore, is to modernize the traditional structure so as to make it meet our new aspirations for a higher standard of living."

It was acknowledged that society, in the process of becoming "more complex", also required new social concepts which were, however, to be developed in accordance with the principle of ujamaa: "In the larger national society where the possibilities of high productivity are exploited, it will be difficult to organize the fair sharing of both work and reward. It will also require institutions and a degree of understanding which were not necessary when everyone knew everyone else in the family community, and it will take time and experience before we get things working smoothly. But the purpose remains the same as in the traditional society. That is, the welfare of every individual in the context of the needs of the society of which he is a member." Precisely this projection onto larger social units than the village community was unsuccessful, not so much due to conceptual weakness as excessive haste in social reconstruction, the population explosion, a decrease in tillage area, and financial structures.

Initiatives on the lines of the Tanzanian model were applied elsewhere in Africa, for example in Madagascar, which is atypical of Africa. The two can be compared as follows:

Fokonolona/Madagascar	*Ujamaa*/Tanzania
Villages as traditional settlement type of various kinship groups.	Scattered homesteads as traditional kinship-based settlement type.
Private property (held by head of family; but also by individual members of family).	Land held by tribe, right of occupancy with head of family, no private propert.
Leasing system (métayage).	No leasing.
Wages work (permanent or seasonal).	Limited wages work.
Functionaries (President, secretary and council members) elected by village community.	Leadership externally appointed (TANU youth organization function-aries).
Large degree of ethnic homogeneity in village community.	Ethnic heterogeneity village community (to combat tribalism).
Party ideology (AREMA) affects only development, not village affairs, as these could function traditionally without an explicit ideology.	Strong party ideology (TANU) with detailed development plans (mostly based on the ideas of J. Nyerere).
Individual cultivation with "groupements paysans", "coopératives de culture".	Individual cultivation with "self-help-groups" on traditional models, co-operative marketing of cash crops.

Misdevelopment is exemplified by the extraordinary haste in implementing the comprehensive villagization and detribalization policies that grew out of the theory. The latter policy led for example to widespread and inadequately prepared desmantling of mature co-operatives, without however permitting viable new procedures for even short-term reintegration to become effective.

The express aim of linking up with autochthonous forms of cooperation, and corresponding attitudes can be attested, though with various nuances, in countries from the Atlantic to the Indian Ocean, from the Sahel to southern Africa: especially worthy to mention, apart from the ujamaa principle, are the concepts of "Zambian Humanism", the "Common Man's Charta" in Uganda, the "Communaucratie" in Guinea, and diverse formulations with only minor differences in Senegal, Mali, Nigeria and other countries. It is remarkable that anglophone countries in particular tried to carry out this programme, and were also most successful. It is also remarkable that at times *a single* clearly outlined programme, usually with *a single* goal, has been formulated and followed as the co-operative intention when autochthonous co-operative societies have been exploited: in most cases it is marketing. Collectivist co-opertive forms have not been realized on this basis, although experiments in this direction have been unsuccessfully carried out. Moreover, the concept of ujamaa itself consistently applied a notion of collectivism which had neither African nor European roots: namely that of the large collectives of the People's Republic of China.

III. Latin America

In *Latin America* there are autochthonous forms of co-operative societies in the areas of the earlier high cultures, like the Inca, and in relatively isolated Indian cultures that have not been subjected to European forms, such as for example the *Mapuche* of Chile. The forms of community and cooperation in the former Inca empire, presumed to be "agrarian communism", has come in for special attention from Peruvian scholars, foremost among them Luis Valcárcel, whose pioneering research in the 60s stimulated the national development policy for the Highland Indians ("Plan Nacional de Desarrollo Popular") under President *Belaunde Terry*.

Valcárcel bases the notion of the Indios' "agrarian communism" on the assumption ("ideology") of the indigenous (Quechua-speaking) population that: "All goods are gifts from the earth. Devotion to 'mama pacha' (the earth as the mother of all things under the sun) amounts to sun worship, and as the sun belongs to no single individual, so the earth cannot be the possession of one man. The linking of these two concepts in the ideology of the indigenous population resulted in agrarianism, i.e. common ownership of land and community worship of the sun." As *J.C. Mariátegui* has said: "The 'ayllu', the village community, was the fundamental unit of the Inca empire, but they did not create the fundamental unit. The order they established certainly reflected the already existing natural situation..."

Even the title of one of *Valcárcel's* major works ("Del Ayllu al Imperio") stresses this form of village co-operative, which even under subjugation to the Inca empire's hierarchical organization not only formed the basis of the administrative system but was also the basic agrarian economic unit of self-help and local government. The ayllu community was founded on kinship, common ownership of land and water, individual use; furthermore, the sale of land to insiders and outsiders alike was forbidden. It was believed that the ayllu could be discerned in the "communidades" of the Spanish and post-Spanish eras, although in these times in particular it was subjected to a renewed period of subjugation and consequent withdrawal of autonomy.

In spite of the "Leyes de Indias" of 1542, enacted for the protection of the indigenous peoples, their way of life, social structure, and last but not least their environment, were virtually wiped out. As *Mariátegui* has written: "In general the colonial agrarian system led to a large proportion of the native rural village communities being replaced by large estates in the hands of individuals which were cultivated by the indios in a state of feudal dependence." Nonetheless the opinion persisted, as in many other cases of "discoveries" of autochthonous co-operative societies, that the alienated remnants could be revitalized to form the basis of a compensatory development process.

This widely held opinion was most notably expounded in the 20s and 30s by the "indigenismo" movement (also known as "pro-indigena"), which numbered among its most prominent representatives *L. Valcárcel, J.C. Mariátegui* and *Hildebrando Castro Pozo* ("Nuestra Communidad Indigena"). *Mariátegui* cites *Castro Pozo* as follows: "The ayllu or village communities have retained their natural peculiarity, their character of quasi-familial institutions..." Consequently it became almost commonplace to admit in practice that links with historical forms are not sufficient in themselves, but that the social and economic environment, and especially the natural environment must also be taken into consideration. Spanish feudalism and/or special forms of estate ownership had, however, meant that precisely the environmental conditions had in fact not developed in a manner advantageous to the villages survival as autonomous, self-sufficient units. Reactivation of the "communidades" on dispersed estates failed several times in Peru (e.g. the "Vicos" project, conceived by a team from Cornell University, USA).

In other Latin American countries, too, even comprehensive, well-funded national programmes like the "Ejido" plan following the first Mexican revolution failed, in spite of some very promising developments. *J.C. Mariátegui's* parallels with the "Mir" under Russian semi-feudalism are important in this respect.

IV. Asia

In *Asia*, with its high cultures developed over millenia, there are still traces of multifarious forms of self-help groups which have evolved since time immemorial. Basically, it can however be claimed, in accordance with the ideas of *Karl August Wittfogel* and others, that subjugation to centralized authority and forms of rule hampered self-help activities on any large scale. This was already mentioned (for India) by *Karl Marx* in his reports on the "oriental mode of production". In *Marx's* view, the "stereotypically recurring" social forms were "too primitive" to give rise to "voluntary associations", co-operative societies included. Both regard the state of the social structure (Asiatic and semi-Asiatic despotism) as the crucial cause of the non-functioning of "voluntary associations" (*K. Marx*).

More recent research, especially into various populations on the Indian subcontinent, have demonstrated however that even under an extremle rigid caste system self-help groups and autonomous units existed on a broad basis. The great Indian social reformers of the twentieth century, like *Mahatma Gandhi* and *Vinoba Bahve*, have attempted to exploit precisely these structures and build democratic systems of administration upon them. From these highly regarded initiatives grew numerous political programmes and social ideologies which placed self-sufficiency and autonomy in the centre.

S.K. Dey's work has highlighted the concept of Panchayat Raj in the context of the co-operative movement, and *Detlef Kantowsky* has written on the principle of Sarvodaya in India and Sri Lanka. As *S.K. Dey* puts it: "The co-operative form of organization has the merit of combining individual initiative with the advantages of large-scale enterprise and is the most effective tool for economic decentralization..." Obviously, the tendency to form co-operative societies was considerably promoted under British colonial administration (presumably through their anchoring in law alone). From there cooperative society laws and there resulting co-operative projects gave considerable impetus in other British dependencies (such as the influence in anglophone Africa of the introduction of a co-operative society law that had already been tested in Assam and Sri Lanka, then still Ceylon).

China experienced a special development in which centrally organized systems of rule certainly promoted the development of a strong peasant class (*Wolfram Eberhard*). In the nineteenth century the peasants revolted on a number of occasions in attempts to achieve autonomy and increase productivity through numerous agrarian innovation (e.g. the combination of rice cultivation with fish and cattle farming in manageable mutual aid groups), and they achieved at least some of their aims.

The range of organizational forms in urban environments is of special interest for current policies aimed at developing co-operative societies. In many Asian countries, in India and South East Asia especially, but also in Nepal and in the great cities of India, programmes have been adopted with the aim of stimulating the "informal sector", because the most elementary forms of traditional associations and group relations could form the nucleus of credit and savings societies. As *Hans Dieter Seibel* has pointed out with regard to Java, initial experiments in the 60s and 70s gave rise to social movements, especially in Indonesia.

V. Cooperation as an ubiquitous phenomenon

In *Europe's Development Regions* again and again traditional forms of cooperation have been set aside when comprehensive agrarian reform projects have been proposed and put into action (as in Spain and Italy). Usually in such circumstances "fraternities" (hermandades) and artisans' associations were encountered, whereas the agricultural population had no organizations of their own, not even in any real sense among small farmers and agricultural workers. Agrarian reforms were frequently carried out in late feudal systems in which subsequent newcomers were obliged to participate in modern co-operative activities (compulsory co-operatives). The modern co-operative societies, then, came into being in areas which had been "co-operative deserts", where they made substantial, though as a rule unsuccessful, efforts to achieve autonomy for their members. Lack of *co-operative discipline* has frequently been regarded as the cause of failure.

There are in Europe some historically very old organizational forms peculiar to particular regions and nations which can be regarded as autochthonous co-operatives. Examples might be political co-operatives like the "Eidgenossenschaft", (i.e. the Swiss Confederation), Alpine drovers' associations, irrigation societies, mill and bakery societies, societies organized for the extraction of slate, turf, clay, and other raw materials, and burial societies.

The greatest density of co-operatives seems to occur in politically and economically decentralized systems where inheritance and land distribution have given rise to structures based on "small-holdings". There the advantages or necessity of "unifying association" among landowners and/or entrepreneurs was obvious. Proof of this is not yet available in the literature (counterevidence may be submitted: i.e. no cooperation of any kind in areas with identical infrastructures, as for example in several wine-producing areas on the Rhine and Moselle).

To what extent the early "Eidgenossenschaft" was based on peasant cultures working co-operatively, or whether only the more prosperous and more powerful were "co-operatively" organized, is an issue on which Swiss historians disagree (e.g. *Roger Sablonier, Peter Pfrunder, Werner Meyer, Ulrich Im Hof*).

However, world-wide and independent of one another, specialized associations whose members share common interests can also be found across cultural boundaries. The most frequent impulse taken into consideration seems to be relations of neighbourhood. "Co-operative" creameries (coordinating milk production and processing which would not be profitable for members on their own) can be regarded as supra-regional autochthonous co-operative societies. Likewise the diverse forms and economic intentions of "artels" in pre-revolutionary Russia were supra-regional: "The Russian people call any association of several persons for a common task an "artel", regardless of both the character of the activity and its organization" (*A. Ulitin* in *V. Totomianz'* "Handwörterbuch", with further literature and numerous cases). The limits of the social group in the sociological sense cannot be unambiguously drawn in this case. Nevertheless, artels – the word is derived from "orta" (community) and "ortak" (communal) in a Turkic language – include work groups (of hunters, smallfarmers, and artisans) as well as housing and production co-operatives (like *A. Ulitins's* example of the "peculiar artel organization" of the "Saporog cossack samp"). The extremely numerous types of artel, varying not only in structure and purpose but also intent (of which there may be several), and comparisons with identical or similarly structured associations in other cultures (above all in black Africa and South America) have not been discussed to date in the literature on the theory of co-operative societies.

A differentiated analysis of autochthonous co-operative societies in intercultural comparison would pave the way for a (considerable) relativisation of a eurocentric theory of co-operative societies.

Translation: Kevin McCafferty

Bibliography

Bardeleben, Manfred: The Cooperative System in the Sudan, München, vol. 82 (1973).
Bartu, Friedemann: Die Agrargesellschaften – Sociedad Agricola de Interés Social (Sais) – als Träger der wirtschaftlichen und sozialen Entwicklung in den Anden Perus, Diessenhofen 1979.
Bascom, W.R.: The Esusu: A Credit Institution of the Yoruba, London, vol. 82, no. 1, (1952), pp. 63–69.
Faust, Helmut: Geschichte der Genossenschaftsbewegung, Ursprung und Weg der Genossenschaften im deutschen Sprachraum, Frankfurt am Main 1965.
Dey, S.K., Sahakari Samaj: The Cooperative Commonwealth, London 1967.
Holmberg, Allan R.: "Participant Intervention in the Field", Human Organization, Oklahoma City 1955.
Im Hof, Ulrich: Mythos Schweiz, Identität-Nation-Geschichte 1291–1991, Zürich 1991.
Iwu, Eugene: Die Bedeutung ursprünglicher sozio-ökonomischer Organisationsformen in Afrika für die Industrialisierung, Marburg 1973.
Koll, Michael: Crafts and Cooperation in Western Nigeria, A Sociological contribution to Indigenous Economics, Freiburg i.B. 1969.
Mariátegui, José Carlos: Siete ensayos de Interpretacion de la Realidad Peruana, Lima 1928.
Mead, Margaret: Cooperation and Competition among Primitive Peoples, Enlarged Edition, Boston 1961.
Middleton, John and David Tait: Tribes without Rulers, Studies in African Segmentary Systems, London 1958.
Münkner, Hans-H.: Wege zu einer afrikanischen Genossenschaft, Marburg 1980.
Murdock, George Peter: Africa, Its Peoples and their Culture History, New York 1959.
Nyerere, Julius K.: After the Arusha Declaration, Dar es Salaam 1967.
Nyerere, Julius K.: Ujamaa – The Basis of African Socialism, Dar es Salaam 1962.
von Oertzen, Eleonore: Revolution und peruanische Wirklichkeit. José Carlos Mariátegui, ausgewählte politische Schriften, hgg. und eingel. v. E.v. Oertzen, Frankfurt am Main 1986.
Pakistan Academy for Rural Development: An Evaluation of the Rural Public works Programme East Pakistan, Fourth Annual Report, 1962–1963, Comilla 1963.
Seibel, Hans Dieter: Finance with the Poor, by the Poor, for the Poor, Financial Technologies for the Informal Sector, Basel, vol. 3, no. 2 (1989).
Seibel, Hans Dieter and Andreas Massing: Traditional Organizations and Economic Development, Studies of Indigenous Co-operatives in Liberia, New York 1974.
Seibel, Hans Dieter and Michael Koll: Einheimische Genossenschaften in Afrika, Formen wirtschaftlicher Zusammenarbeit bei westafrikanischen Stämmen, Freiburg i.Br. 1968.
Trappe, Paul: Soziale Breitenwirkung einer Entwicklungsintervention, "Lac Alaotra – Grenier de Madagascar", Basel, vol. 19 1987.
Trappe, Paul: Entwicklungssoziologie, Social Strategies, Basel, vol. 12 (1984).
Trappe, Paul: Die Entwicklungsfunktion des Genossenschaftswesens am Beispiel ostafrikanischer Stämme, Neuwied-Berlin 1966.
Valcárcel, Luis: Ruta Cultural del Peru, Lima 1945.
Valcárcel, Luis: Del Ayllu al Imperio, La Evolucion politico-social en el antiguo Peru, y otros estudios, Lima 1925.
Vierkandt, Alfred: Die genossenschaftliche Gesellschaftsform der Naturvölker. Handwörterbuch der Soziologie, (Stuttgart 1931), Unveränderter Nachdruck 1959.
Wittfogel, Karl August: Die orientalische Despotie, Eine vergleichende Untersuchung totaler Macht, 1962.

Bank Rating in the USA

WERNER BOOS

(see also: *Co-operative Banks*; *Insolvency Prognosis*; *Ratio-based Credit Rating*; *Data Processing*)

Bank rating provides a classification of the overall solidity of banks and their short- and long-term issues in a ranking system for investor protection purposes, particularly focusing on deposit securities and liability regulations in case of insolvency. A rating can be defined as a standardized indicator of an investor's risk and the issuer's credit quality concerning his ability to repay his debt obligations punctually.

Ratings are accomplished by private, profit-oriented agencies; the most popular and leading ones are Standard & Poors Corporation (S & P) and Moody's Investors Service (Moody's), both of which started their activities at the beginning of the century. Today more than 3000 companies all over the world have a Moody's rating.

Ratings often start with the issuer's application for one; the ranking agency deserves open and continuous direct contact to the issuer's management and its financial functions and affairs. Aside from qualitative elements like the core business position, management quality, strategies, risks/weaknesses, and opportunities/strengths of the company, the agencies analyze a large number of key financial figures. Moody's, for example, chose 91 indicators to determine the strength, stability, and predictablility of the financial and profit levels of an issuer.

The rating agencies see their ratings rather as opinions, than as recommendations; the investor is not relieved from undertaking credit rating evaluations on his own. Ratings do, however, provide the international capital market with a consistent framework for comparing the quality of rated debt securities, regardless of the currency of the obligation, the accounting rules used, the legal form or the country of the issuer. They increase the investor's ability to analyze the credibility of companies operating nationally and internationally, and enable him to manage his portfolio according to profit and credibility criteria (→ *Early Warning Systems*).

In principle, participation in the rating evaluation is voluntary, but in the USA a good rating is a *must* for banks to place their issues on the market. Ratings are made available to the international financial community, and they are regularly reviewed and adjusted, especially before new issues. A review may lead to an up- or downgrading. The results of a downgrading can be serious: The rating not only has an impact on the success of the issue but also on the cost of debt. The better the rating, the better the conditions for the debtor. Companies with a low rating have to pay a risk-uplift on the interest rate.

Different symbols are used for rating short-term and long-term debts. Moody's rates short-term debts (maturity less than one year) from category Prime–1 down to Not Prime and long-term bonds from Aaa down to C (see accompanying table), while S & P rates with A–1 to D, from AAA to D, respectively. Long-term securities issued by a single issuer can carry different ratings due to different indenture provisions.

The growing complexity of the markets not only caused an enormous growth of the two market leaders but also lead to new company establishments in the USA, like Duff & Phelps or Fitch Investors Service. These firms do not only rate American companies but rather have expanded their activities more and more to Europe and Japan.

Table: Long term debt ratings used by Moody's Investors Service

Aaa	(bonds judged to be of highest quality and to carry the smallest risk for investors – "gilt-edged bonds"): Interest payments are protected by a wide or exceptionally stable margin, and the principal is secure. While the various protective elements are likely to change, these changes usually do not impair the fundamentally strong position of such issues.
Aa	(bonds judged to be of high quality by all standards): Together with the Aaa group they comprise what is generally known as high-grade bonds. They are rated lower for (one of) the following area: The margin of protection is judged to be not as high as in Aaa securities, or the fluctuation of protective elements may be of a greater amplitude. There may be other elements present which make the long-term risk appear somewhat higher than with Aaa securities.
A	(upper-medium grade obligations with many favorable investment attributes): Factors giving security to principal and interest are considered adequate, but elements may be present which suggest a susceptibility to impairment sometime in the future.
Baa	(medium-grade obligations): Interest payments and principal security appear adequate for the present, but certain protective elements may be lacking or may be characteristically unreliable over any great length of time. Such bonds lack outstanding investment characteristics and have speculative elements.

Ba (bonds judged to have speculative elements; their future cannot be considered well-assured): Often the protection of interest and principal payments may be very moderate and therefore is not well safeguarded during both good and bad periods in the future. Bonds in this class are characterized by an uncertainty of position.

B (bonds that generally lack characteristics of the desirable investment): Assurance of interest and principal payments or of maintenance of other terms of contract over any long period of time may be small.

Caa (bonds of poor standing): Such issues may be in default, or there may be elements of danger present with respect to principal or interest.

Ca (speculative obligations to a high degree): Such issues are often in default or have other marked shortcomings.

C (the lowest rated class of bonds): These bonds can be regarded as having extremely poor prospects of ever attaining any real investment standing.

Ratings Aa to B are additionally classified from 1 to 3 to indicate the ranking within the category.

Bibliography

Eckhardt, Jens: Die Wertpapierbörse hört auf ihr strenges Urteil, Handelsblatt, 31.5.91, P.D.
Moody's Global Ratings, vol. IV, no.5, May 1991.
Moody's Credit Options / Financial Institutions, USA, March 1991.
Moody's Corporate Credit Report, USA, Sept. 1987.
Moody's Credit Ratings (Capital Market), USA, 1990.
Standard & Poor's Debt Rating Criteria, USA, March 1991.

Bauhütte Movement

KLAUS NOVY [F]

(see also: *Housing Societies*; *Housing Reform*; *Joint-production Co-operatives*; *Guilds*; *Co-operative Socialism*)

I. Beginning and Ideological Background; II. Transformation from a Productive Society to *Bauhütte*; III. Formation of Associations and Unions; IV. Development up to 1933; V. Decline and End.

I. Beginning and Ideological Background

The *Bauhütte* Movement, which had its zenith during the German Weimar Republic, is a concrete adaptation of guild socialism to a particular branch of the economy. In its conception, this was a middle way between state socialism and syndicalism. Guild socialism originated in Great Britain prior to the First World War, when the struggle of the workers' movement through political action and trade unions seemed to have exhausted itself in a number of considerable defeats. Guild socialism wanted to give the trade unions a new perspective as initiators and supporters of a branch/oriented socialistic structure of the economy. A flood of programmatic writings appeared by *G.D.H. Cole*, *A.J. Penty*, *St. Taylor*, and others. As "economic federalism", guild socialism differed on the one hand from state-centered socialism and on the other hand from the industrial separatism of syndicalism. It proclaims a self-administration of the individual branches. Guilds themselves, going back to medieval craft guilds (→ *Guilds*), are a union of all those who work with their heads and their hands in one branch of the economy. Built up from the local to the national level, all the craft guilds together from the guild parliament. This parliament of organized producers was then to have a counterweight in the political parliament comprising the interests of the consumer and the overall public. The guilds were intended to evolve out of occupational associations and trade unions. *O. Bauer, R. Hilferding*, and *K. Kautsky* made a mark by their introduction of guild socialism into the German debates on socialization after 1918.

In effect, guild socialism played a certain role in trade-union policy after 1918, particularly in the construction field (guilds of construction) (→ *Trade Unions*). In Great Britain, Italy, Palestine, Holland, France, Spain, Czechoslovakia, Austria, Switzerland, and Germany there arose very heterogeneous construction guild movements, which in 1922 organized themselves into the short-lived "International Construction Guild Association", with Berlin as its seat, with the president of the construction workers' union *F. Paeplow* as its president, and with *M. Wagner* as its secretary. British construction guilds failed after just a few years, due to a course of action which overtaxed the guilds' resources: their practice of providing social and economic security for their employees independently of the volume of orders coming in. When the guilds appealed to the trade unions for financial support, the unions refused, with the legitimate explanation that one could not use tradeunion means to enable guild employees to obtain special privileges for themselves. The Housing, Dwelling, and Construction Guild in Vienna, Austria, whose secretary was *O. Neurath*, and which had emerged primarily out of the cooperation of Viennese housing co-operatives (cf. *Novy/Förster*) with the building society for public benefit *Grundstein*, also blossomed for only a short time (1921–1924) and then fell victim to the communal socialism of "Red Vienna" (→ *Housing Societies*). Today one can find institutional remnants of this programme only in the Swiss Association of Social Building Enterprises, which was founded in 1932 by the trade unions, and which today comprises about forty building productive societies.

II. Transformation from a Productive Society to *Bauhütte*

In Germany the construction guild movement developed independently, achieving a significance which was qualitatively noteworthy, but which has been historically completely neglected. The German *Bauhütte* movement sprang from two sources: the efforts of unemployed construction workers and building engineers to help themselves through the formation of productive societies (→ *Joint-production Co-operatives*); and the establishment of the *Bauhütte Berlin*, Social Building Society, Limited, as a model, in conformity with the plan of *M. Wagner* and with the help of capital contributed by certain provincial organizations. Both of these efforts were made separately in the autumn of 1919. The two sources were brought together by the socialistic construction workers' trade union, which as of the sixth of May, 1919, began to stand up programmatically for socialization through self-help, if necessary from the grass roots. Within the next two years about 200 building productive societies were set up by socialist trade unions and about 20 by Christian trade unions. How was it possible in the construction field, the second largest industry in Germany, for co-operatives to make a break-through? The answer lies in the fact that the construction business required relatively little capital investment, drew largely upon craftsmen and the middle-class, and in addition had run into a crisis because of World War I and the squeeze of sky-rocketing building costs and sinking wages. Thus the new workers' joint-production Co-operatives had a rather easy time getting into the market. Their rapid rise to success was also made possible through their price policy. They broke away from the price agreement, which existed even at that time, of the private construction business; their prices were between 10 and 30 per cent lower than those of the cartel.

But as the private building sector began to organize itself into associations to ward off the competition and to fight back with low prices, then the structural weaknesses of the productive society came fully to light, as → *F. Oppenheimer* had already foreseen they would with his "transformation law". There were four of these structural weaknesses:

1) lack of financial means;
2) lack of organizational experience and leadership qualification;
3) the danger of each society's thinking just of itself and not of the movement as a whole, known as business egotism; and
4) the absence of organized marketing channels and therefore vulnerability to fluctuations in the market and to competition.

These structural weaknesses of the joint-production society made a thorough-going discussion on basics necessary, which was carried out in the main by the Berlin city councillor for construction *M. Wagner* and the chief editor, *A. Ellinger*, of *Grundstein*, the weekly publication of the German Union of Construction Workers. During the course of this debate, Wagner developed his concept of a new form of enterprise, which he called *Bauhütte*. He wrote the following statement about it in 1924: "The main reason for founding *Bauhütte* for me was the fact that the social polarity between labour and business capital had to be bridged over, that the building business needed to be set up on a new efficient basis, and that the existing relationship of mutual mistrust could not possibly be beneficial to the joint work of producer and consumer, that is, of the entrepreneur constructing the building and of the person conferring the building contract." The *Bauhütte* idea represents a forgotten milestone in the otherwise meagre history of projects for economic reform. In the *Bauhütte* idea it was possible to find solutions for the four above-mentioned problems of the isolated co-operative society, however only at the price of the loss of its legal status as a co-operative, since *Bauhütte* became a company with limited liability, in which the decision-making bodies were structured to give half of the votes to the employees (that is, until 1925; after that the employees were entitled to only 25 per cent) and half to the assembly of the shareholders. The shareholders came from a group of people who sympathized politically with the *Bauhütte* movement: local trade unions, building and consumer co-operatives, and above all municipal governments. The capital which these befriending organizations contributed was not intended to produce a high return but was set at a moderate interest rate of three to five per cent. By means of this mixed structure, whereby the co-operative members lost their double status as both shareholders and employees, it was possible to solve two of the four above-mentioned difficulties: capital from socially-minded sources began to flow in; and the tendency toward business egotism on the part of the employees was given a check by the co-determination of shareholders who represented interests beyond those of the individual societies.

III. Formation of Associations and Unions

For *Wagner* there was more at stake than just the reform of isolated individual enterprises. What was important to him was a strategy of economic reform whereby guild socialism could be fought through branch by branch by means of a new trade-union policy. In the fall of 1919 it was decided in the construction workers' trade union to summon a conference for the purpose of sharing experience and knowledge. The letter of invitation stated, "We must face the fact that under the present circumstances a socialization of the building industry from above, that is, a socialization with the help of legislation, is not to be expected for the time being... Construction workers have come to realize that they themselves are the ones who must pave the way for socialization and actually begin to put it into effect... We have the intention of calling into being an Association of Social Building Enterprises, in order to give young socialized businesses their own strong backbone and a strong association, which at the same time should serve as a counterweight to the associations of entrepreneurs." The Association of Social Building Enterprises (in German *VSB*), of which *M. Wagner* became the first executive director, developed rapidly into an organ of strategic action. Parts of the trade-union dues were used as "contributions to socialization", in other words in effect as a private socialization tax, toward building up *Bauhütte* enterprises. To develop and transmit a theoretical groundwork, the association magazine *Soziale Bauwirtschaft* (Social Building Economy) was brought into being, which took up questions of socialization and production policy. Through the exchange of knowledge and experience and the debates on theory, it was soon possible to set up a model statute for *Bauhütte* which was meant to be an answer to the discipline problems of productive societies (→ *Bylaws*). Difficulties of the joint-production co-operatives in staying solvent due to inflation, as well as the efforts of the association to enlighten people about its work, helped the unification process to move forward rapidly: building joint-production societies were transformed into *Bauhütte* companies; regional and business-wide associations were set up; divisions for building materials were added on; courses and training programmes at the *Bauhütte* school were set up to teach efficiency skills and spread the knowledge of modern organizational techniques. Thus the second above-mentioned problem of inadequate organizational experience was tackled. The fourth problem – the absence of organized marketing channels – was broached in 1924 with the strategic move of establishing the DEWOG Association, the German Joint-Stock Company for Providing Housing for Civil Servants, Employees, and Labourers, described below. The *Bauhütte* movement needed marketing organizations, that is to say, organizations of groups of people desiring to erect buildings, who would patronize them and systematically organize the market supply for them, for example with regard to housing construction. The trade unions had thus broadened their programme and now considered themselves the instrument of a socialization policy from the grass roots upward.

In 1923 the Association of Social Building Enterprises (VSB) took up contact with the top organizations of the socialistic trade unions for the purpose of founding a society, organized by trade unions and co-operatives, for providing housing for workers. VSB also tried to interest the church-oriented trade unions in the new society, but in vain; the church-oriented trade unions put their efforts, programmatically and actually, into setting up a Christian-oriented economy. Just as with the *Bauhütte* companies and their Association of Social Building Enterprises, so here, too, it was *M. Wagner* from whom the conception and realization of the new association originated. In a speech in 1924 on "New Possibilities for Building Small Dwellings", *Wagner* developed the idea of the need for a three-level vertical association on the basis of mutual cooperation among building societies, communities, and trade unions, as still exists to this day in the Swedish Building Co-operative Association. Then on the 14th of March, 1924, the DEWOG was founded, the German Joint-Stock company for Providing Housing for Civil Servants, Employees, and Labourers, mentioned above, by socialistic trade union associations. *R. Linneke, Wagner's* successor in VSB and DEWOG, described DEWOG's roles in the association journal *Wohnungswirtschaft* (Housing Economy) in 1927 in the following way: "The intention was to bring the *Bauhütte* movement into a closer, organic relationship with organized consumers, because it is simply impossible in the long run for productive enterprises for public benefit to find their orders exclusively on the free market, to be exposed there to all the shortcomings and contingencies adherent to this type of competition for orders, and never to be able to get free of the irregular, fitful, and therefore inefficient type of business which that kind of competition for orders involves. On the contrary, the *Bauhütte* movement needed to be co-ordinated with consumers, to be given a substructure which – if not previously, then at least from then on – linked it organically to the consumer market. This was and is to a great extent the purpose of the DEWOG movement." The Christian Building Productive Societies – called "Building Unions, Registered Co-operatives" – founded an organization of their own similar to VSB, the Imperial Association of German Building Productive Societies, though much smaller than VSB; and in 1927 with the foundation of German Home Construction they set up a functional equivalent to DEWOG as a housing marketing organization. In contrast to the socialistic *Bauhütte*, however, the Christian group held fast programmatically to the legal form of co-operative.

IV. Development up to 1933

Within one decade the socialistic Bauhütte companies had erected, in addition to high-rise and industrial buildings, nearly 100,00 flats, of which a growing proportion was designated each year for the DEWOG association's own building societies and societies for providing housing. At the time of its greatest success in 1929, the DEWOG association comprised 128 social construction businesses, 29,367 employees (peak for the year), and 17,615 erected flats, of which 73 percent had been built to fill orders from within the organization, for people within its own association for public benefit. As a complement to housing-co-operatives, these DEWOG societies formed a pillar in the german movement for housing reform; and it is thanks to them that Bauhaus architecture, the new Way of Building, was able to make a break-through. *Bauhütte* companies were instruments of social modernization within a backward industry. Paradoxically enough, in the twenties they took over the role of dynamic innovators which *Schumpeter* had ascribed in theory to entrepreneurs.

V. Decline and End

On the 2nd of May, 1933, all trade union undertakings were seized and put under the national-socialist "German Work Front" (DAF). Many people feared that *Bauhütte* companies would now be dissolved; but despite pressure in this direction put on by middle-class craft associations, they were not dissolved, because the DAF leadership soon recognized the economic potentiality of these companies. Only accessory building businesses had to be sacrificed to the pressure of the middle-classes. Nonetheless, with the national socialists' elimination of all political oppositions and the conversion of *Bauhütte* into an instrument of nations-socialist economic and social policy, the idea behind *Bauhütte* became list. The elected *Bauhütte* managers were arrested or forced out of their jobs. *M. Wagner* emigrated to the United States. *A. Ellinger*, the second intellectual leader of the *Bauhütte* movement, committed suicide in 1933. Nazis moved into the businesses on all levels and made even the *Bauhütte* companies impossible as places where people could collectively work under cover until conditions improved. In 1936 the Bauhütte companies were centralized into *Deutsche-Bau-AG* (German Joint-Stock Construction Company). The trade-union housing enterprises with the DEWOG association were also absorbed into the DAF, and after 1938 their name was changed to *Neue Heimat* (New Home).

The story of the *Bauhütte* companies after 1945 constitutes one of the least known chapters in the history of trade-union enterprise for public benefit. In the development as a whole, one can clearly discern three phases: 1945–1957 resumption, but without any programme or active movement; 1957–1963 reorganization and new impetus of the *Bauhütte* companies; 1964–1980 end of *Bauhütte*: regression from a parent organization to a meaningless subsidiary company within the private business economy. After 1945 individual *Bauhütte* companies were founded again at the former old locations with the support of local trade unions, consumer co-operatives, or municipal governments. All these new establishments were initiated essentially by individual "old-timers" of the earlier *Bauhütte* movement. The economic capacity of the *Bauhütte* companies to produce was unsatisfactory. Everything was lacking, compared with the time prior to 1933: among neither the employees nor the management nor the trade unions was there a sense of enthusiasm for new things, comparable to the years after 1919. The *Bauhütte* companies lacked sufficient capital, were poorly managed, and had no socio-political purpose due to lack of interest on the part of the other workers' organizations. They had lost their lead in technical development during the years of the Third Reich. Although *Bauhütte's* democratic business statute, which had passed the test of probation long before 1933, could have had significance as a model for efforts at socialization being put forth at the state level, still the German trade unions failed to make propaganda use of their historical and currently relevant experience with the *Bauhütte* model. At a trade-union convention in Bielefled in 1951, it became apparent that most of the delegates were unfamiliar with the trade-union project *Bauhütte*. In the mid-fifties, there were only about 1,600 workers and employees involved in the association businesses.

In 1957, as a result of trade-union decision, there was a reorganization, concentration, and tightening up of the remaining *Bauhütte* companies. Trade-union president *G. Leber* spoke out for expanding *Bauhütte* policy. Key words in his reasoning were that *Bauhütte* represented a "regulator of social order" with which to combat the immorality and price abuses of the private building industry; promotion of economic, social, and technical advancement in the building industry; full employment the whole year long; encouragement of the younger generation; new forms of employed co-determination and profit-participation; distribution of seats on the supervisory board into three equal parts, one for representatives of the employees, one for representatives of the ownership, and one for representatives of organizations giving contracts and of the public at large.

The VSB was restructured into the *Deutsche Bauhütte GmbH* (German Bauhütte, Ltd.), with its head-office in Frankfurt. Key phrases of the new concept were as follows: making work methods in the trades more efficient, preparing work carefully, setting up production plans, making running cost-calculations at the time, not afterwards, prefabricating building elements, and using new technologies such as tunnel sheathing. By means of periodic business news-sheets, training programmes, and management conferences, the improvements were to be made more widely known. Efforts, however, toward a closer cooperation between *Deutsche Bauhütte* and *Neue Heimat*, analogous to the association between VSB and DEWOG prior to 1933, in order to cut costs through a larger proportion of mass production and longer-range joint planning, were unsuccessful, failing to bring about an agreement even on the basic level of principle. By 1963, however, the reorganization had progressed so well that not only the sources of deficit had been eliminated, but also the basis had been laid for *Deutsche Bauhütte* to get a head start in competition. The internal consequence was that for the first time in the German building industry, the employees of a company received a share of the profits and further benefits over and above their agreed wagescale.

The final development has remained non-transparent to this day. In this situation, the association's decision to take over a private-enterprise construction company in a state of overdue bankruptcy, in order to achieve a diversification into fields of civil-engineering and high-rise construction, led inevitably to an insurmountable accumulation of negative factors. In 1966, after the third attempt on the part of trade-union enterprises to put *Deutsche Bauhütte* on a sound financial footing again, the relationship betweeen *Deutsche Bauhütte GmbH* and private construction companies had reversed itself. The "mother" had turned into the "daughter" company. The reorganization, which was carried through at great loss by the trade-union *Bank für Gemeinwirtschaft* (Bank for Public Benefit), culminated in the relinquishment by the Industrial Construction Trade Union (*IG BAU*) of its shares in *Deutsche Bauhütte*. This meant that the pillar of the *Bauhütte* idea all through its history, the trade unions, now withdrew from the circle of its shareholders. With the transformation of *Deutsche Bauhütte GmbH* into a normal private construction enterprise, the history of the *Bauhütte* movement as a trade-union effort towards reform was finally closed.

Bibliography

Ellinger, August: Die Sozialisierung des Baugewerbes, Hamburg 1920.
Ellinger, August: Die Bauhüttenbewegung, Berlin 1927.
Ellinger, August: Sozialisierungsströmungen im Baugewerbe, Dresden 1919.
Ellinger, August: Zehn Jahre Bauhüttenbewegung, Berlin 1930.
Garbei, August: Die Bauhütten. Vergangenheit und Zukunft, Hamburg 1928.
Loesch, Achim von: Die gemeinwirtschaftlichen Unternehmen der Gewerkschaften, Köln 1979.
Mersmann, Arno/Novy, Klaus: Gewerkschaften, Gemeinwirtschaft, Köln 1991.
Novy, Klaus/Förster, Wolfgang: Einfach bauen. Die Wiener Siedlerbewegung, Wien 1985.
Novy, Klaus/Prinz, Michael: Illustrierte Geschichte der Gemeinwirtschaft, Bonn 1985.
Novy, Klaus: Self-Help and Co-operative in Germany, Bonn 1989.
Wagner, Martin: Die Sozialisierung der Baubetriebe, Berlin 1919.
Wagner, Martin: Neue Wege zum Kleinwohnungsbau, Berlin 1924.
Werbik, Gerhard: Bauhütten. Gemeinwirtschaft auf eigenen Wegen, Frankfurt 1960.

British–Indian Pattern of Cooperation

HANS-H. MÜNKNER

(see also: *Law, International*; *Principles*; *Development, South Asia*; *Development, Africa*)

I. The Origin of the Classical British–Indian Pattern of Cooperation; II. The Concept of State-sponsored Cooperation; III. Changes that Occurred Between 1912 and 1946; IV. Spreading of the British–Indian Pattern of Cooperation; V. The Development of the British–Indian Pattern of Cooperation after Independence; VI. Assessment of the Strengths and Weaknesses of the Model; VII. Summary.

I. The Origin of the Classical British–Indian Pattern of Cooperation

1. Problems to be Solved

At the end of the 19th century, the British Colonial Government of India had to face serious economic problems and social unrest caused by the indebtedness of the Indian farmers and by permanent famine. Attempts to find solutions to these problems by setting up agricultural credit schemes and by taking legal measures against usurers failed.

Attracted by the successes of co-operatives in Europe in solving similar problems (→ *History of Ideas*), the British Colonial Government of India decided to study the possibility of introducing co-operative credit societies of the Raiffeisen type (→ *Raiffeisen*). This decision was based on a careful study of co-operative development and co-operative law in several Western European countries including Germany, carried out by *F.A. Nicholson*, who concluded his report with the suggestion to "find an Indian Raiffeisen".

2. A Model Specially Designed for Developing Countries

The officials of the British Colonial Government of India were aware of the fact that the transfer of a model of organization like co-operatives from one continent to another would need special efforts to be successful. Therefore, a set of measures was planned including:

- the promulgation of an experimental legislation to be later amended and improved in the light of experience gained,
- the creation of a special Government machinery for propagating the new model of organization and implementing the co-operative legislation,
- the training of co-operative promoters who, although they were government officials, had the task to teach co-operative principles and practices, to advise and guide inexperienced cooperators, to supervise co-operative activities and to protect members and the public against malpractices.

Instead of introducing the legislation governing co-operatives in the United Kingdom (e.g. the Industrial and Provident Societies Act of 1852), the British Colonial Government of India developed a new model of a co-operative Law, combining elements of the continental European co-operative legislation in force at the turn of the century (mainly the German Co-operative Societies Act of 1889) with elements of the Industrial and Provident Societies Act and using British techniques of drafting laws. The resulting model of state-sponsored co-operative development has become known as the *"British–Indian Pattern of Cooperation"*.

It is important to note that this model was developed and implemented by the colonial authorities without consultation of the population called upon to put it into practice. Furthermore, the model was devised to solve the problems of the colonial government (economic crisis and social unrest in the colony) by helping the poorer strata of the population to solve their problems by way of organized self-help (→ *Development Policy*). This colonial origin of the British–Indian Pattern of Cooperation, being a model introduced from the top and from outside has been influencing the image of co-operative societies in the developing countries before and even after independence.

II. The Concept of State-sponsored Cooperation

The original concept underlying the British–Indian Pattern of Cooperation was summarized in a speech by *Sir Denzil Ibbetson* introducing the Co-operative Credit Societies Bill in the Indian Legislative Council in 1903. *Ibbetson's* speech is proof of a deep understanding of the mechanics of organized self-help and of government's role in promoting it, as is shown by the following quotations:

"... if an institution of this sort, which depends upon the people themselves combining for their mutual advantage, is to succeed, it must be as far as possible an indigenous and natural growth. An exotic type may be forced by artifical stimulus to flourish for a while but we can never expect it to take vigorous roots, or to continue to flourish when the stimulus is withdrawn" (p. 102).

"The Registrar (i.e. the head of the governmental co-operative development agency), to whom somewhat extensive powers have been given to secure that our legislation is not taken advantage of by bogus societies ... should be a full time officer, specially selected for this work. For the first few years at least he will constantly be going around and watching their (the societies') progress, criticising and assisting them, but as a friendly advisor rather than as an inspecting officer. As experience is accumulated and the societies gain strength and are able to stand alone, and as their numbers multiply, the 'drynurse' element will disappear from his duties, which will become more purely official" (p. 107) (→ *Authorities, Co-operative*).

"Societies must learn to swim before being thrown into deep water, to take care of their own money before they are entrusted with much of ours. To allow them to regard themselves as mere agencies for the distribution and recovery of government advances would wholly defeat the object of their creation" (p. 108).

From *Ibbetson's* statement and from *Calvert's* commentary to the Indian co-operative legislation it can be concluded that the salient features of the British–Indian Pattern of Cooperation were the following:

- To create autonomous, self-reliant co-operatives of the Raiffeisen or Rochdale Pioneer type in the long run but to substitute the lacking technical knowledge and initiative of the population for a transition period by the know-how of officials of a specialized government agency (*Calvert*, pp. 35, 105 et seq.).
- To provide a team of well trained government officers who during an initial stage have to:
- teach the methods of co-operative organization to persons interested in practicing organized self-help along co-operative lines,
- help to establish co-operative societies after solid preparation of the prospective members,
- to give advice and technical assistance to registered societies upon request.
- To build up a government machinery for the promotion and supervision of co-operatives headed by a Registrar of Co-operative Societies, whose duties and powers are far beyond those of the British Registrar of Friendly Societies, who is mainly in charge of registering co-operative societies in England.

In the Classical British–Indian Pattern of Cooperation the Registrar of Co-operative Societies is perceived as a central figure.

"The success and failures of a co-operative movement ... must depend very largely on the choice of person as Registrar. Registrars will normally be drawn from persons who have already had experience in cooperation and co-operative departments and whose other qualifications fit them for their work" (Colonial Office Memorandum, Enclosure).

"The Registrar of Co-operative Societies should not only be a man of outstanding ability but should be temperamentally suited for the work of running a popular movement of this kind" (*Calvert*, p. 108, Co-operative Planning Committee, 1946, p. 155).

According to the original concept the Registrar and his staff have to encourage and supervise the formation of new societies, to advise and audit registered societies and to liquidate non-viable, inactive or defaulting societies. In order to enable him to exercise these functions effectively, the Registrar and his staff were given the following powers under the Indian

Co-operative Societies Act of 1912 (statutory powers):
- to decide at his discretion whether to register a new society or to refuse registration (Sec. 9);
- to decide upon registration of by-laws or amendments of by-laws, a power, which could be (mis-) used to impose model by-laws, drafted by him (Sec. 9, 11);
- to carry out audits and to conduct enquiries into the affairs of co-operative societies upon request or at his own motion (Sec. 17, 35);
- to settle disputes within and between co-operative societies as an arbitrator (Sec. 43(1)) and
- to decide at his discretion to dissolve co-operative societies (Sec. 39, 42).

It was the intention of the law-makers and the agreed policy underlying the law, that:
-the Registrar should exercise his wide discretionary powers only during an initial phase until co-operative societies were strong enough to do without government assistance;
- during this initial phase of state-sponsored co-operative development the Registrar should be more of an educator helping co-operatives to become self-reliant than an administrator supervising registered societies;
- the Registrar should avoid creating the impression that co-operatives were public institutions run by the government rather than private business organizations run by their own members;
- the Registrar should act mainly as an advisor. He was not expressly given authority to force members of co-operatives to accept his advice or to punish them if they refused to accept it.

Only in emergency cases, the Registrar was assumed to have powers to interfere directly with the day-to-day management of registered co-operative societies. However, these emergency powers of direct intervention were not expressly provided for under the Act, but rather were derived from the Registrar's overall responsibility to protect the interests of the members and of the public (non-statutory powers).
Following the tradition of British law making, none of these assumptions on which the concept underlying the British–Indian Pattern of Cooperation was based, were written into the law.
Given the fact that the Indian Co-operative Societies Acts of 1904 and 1912 were experimental legislation and that for the sake of a maximum of flexibility, detailed provisions were avoided, many matters were left open for future decision or to be provided for in regulations made under the Act, also the basic questions of how far and for how long government assistance to co-operatives should go, were left without an answer.
As will be shown in the following, this vagueness of the legal text with regard to the underlying policy and the lack of precision regarding the relationship between co-operatives and the state turned out to be the main reasons for ultimate failure of the entire concept.

III. Changes that Occurred Between 1912 and 1946

When putting the British–Indian Pattern of Cooperation into practice, it proved to be difficult to implement some of the main assumptions on which the concept was based.
The Registrar's office or Co-operative Department being part of the public administration, it turned out to be impossible to prevent bureaucratic procedures from penetrating co-operative development programmes. Where plans to form certain numbers of new co-operatives in a given period of time were drawn up, it proved to be difficult to wait until the future members of co-operatives had learned about the advantages of forming a co-operative society and had decided to do so. However, where the government officers went ahead to form co-operatives for the members, these co-operatives were seen as being the responsibility of government (→ *Officialization*). Once co-operatives were formed which the members were not able to run and to control themselves, the government officers of the Co-operative Departments could no longer limit their role to that of educator and friendly advisor. In order to avoid inexperienced or unscrupulous board members or managers making wrong decisions or causing damage to the society, preventive measures were introduced by the Registrar and his staff rather than to wait until the damage done was discovered during the annual audit. These preventive measures which were originally not contained in the law but practised as "non-statutory functions" included:
- inspection of the books of registered societies,
- submission of potentially dangerous decisions of the board of directors and of the general meeting to the approval of the Registrar,
- direct interference in the day-to-day management of registered societies,
- dismissal of unfit officers of the society,
- removal of the entire board of directors of a co-operative society and appointment of a temporary care-taker committee and
- convening of special general meetings.

With a growing number of co-operative societies to be advised and supervised, these "non-statutory" emergency powers, meant to be used in exceptional cases only, gradually became routine powers and found their way into the regulations made under the Co-operative Societies Act, thereby turning them into statutory powers. The assumption that the Registrar should be a highly qualified professional specially selected and trained for this difficult task, ceased to be valid, when the post of Registrar of Co-operative Societies became more and more a normal civil service position, filled with officials of the required level, but without experience in this field, who held the position only for a relatively short period and used it as a stepping stone in their civil service career.

The idea to provide a team of well trained and highly motivated promotors working in the Co-operative Department to explain the co-operative law and to preach the co-operative gospel, select the places in which co-operatives are best likely to succeed and convince the people that they should try to take action themselves (*Ibbetson*, p. 107) was defeated, if the service conditions of the Co-operative Department were not attractive enough to recruit and retain in service the right caliber of co-operative development officers. Accordingly, where Co-operative Departments were not construed as closed, technical departments and given a special scheme of service, the quality and motivation of field staff took a downward turn and instead of educating, promoting and helping cooperators to run their own co-operatives for their own benefit and at their own risk, inspection, supervision and control of co-operatives became more and more predominant, entangling co-operatives in a cobweb of administrative and bureaucratic procedures.

In 1946, when the British Colonial Office published a Model Co-operative Societies Ordinance and Model Co-operative Societies Regulations for use in the overseas dependencies, the Model Ordinance contained basically the same provisions as the Co-operative Societies Act of India, 1912, proposing to the Governments of all British dependencies who had not already adopted it, to adopt the Classical British–Indian Pattern of Cooperation. After more than 30 years of practical experience, the legislation still maintained its enabling and experimental character, leaving many important matters open to be decided in regulations made under the law. However, the changes that had occured over the many years of practical application, were reflected strongly in the Model Regulations, where the process described earlier of turning non-statutory emergency powers into statutory routine functions became clearly visible. Although in the Enclosures to the Circular Despatches of 1946, containing the proposed model legislation, it was stated that the original concept underlying this model of state-sponsored co-operative development was still valid, the legislation for state-sponsored co-operatives had become a legislation for state-controlled co-operatives. This made the legislation to some extent ambiguous.

IV. Spreading of the British–Indian Pattern of Cooperation

The Classical British–Indian Pattern of Cooperation as introduced by the Co-operative Societies Acts of India, 1904, 1902 was applied not only in India but also in other British dependencies, e.g. Ceylon (Sri Lanka), Cyprus, Palestine, to mention only a few.

In 1931, a law very similar to the Indian Co-operative Credit Societies Act of 1904 was introduced in Gold Coast (Ghana), in 1932 a co-operative law based on the Co-operative Societies Ordinance of Ceylon was promulgated in Tangayika (Tanzania) and in 1935, Nigeria adopted a co-operative law following the British–Indian Pattern of Cooperation (→ *Development, Africa*).

The spread of this model was advocated by *Stickland*, an officer of the British Colonial Civil Service, who had served as Registrar of Co-operative Societies in India and wrote a book, "Cooperation for Africa", published in 1933, in which he propagated the British–Indian Model for use in Africa.

In Africa, co-operatives were mainly used by the Colonial Governments for two purposes:

– to improve the quality and to control the marketing of cash crops and
– (less important) to organize thrift and credit co-operatives among salary earners.

Especially after the Second World War, co-operatives were increasingly seen as instruments to teach democratic procedures and to prepare the citizens of British dependencies for independence. After the Second World War, the Model Co-operative Legislation of the British Colonial office of 1946 already mentioned earlier, was recommended to all governments of British dependencies and taken over without many changes by most of these governments from the South Pacific Island States through South East Asia (Singapore, Malaysia), Africa (e.g. Sierra Leone, Gambia, Uganda, Kenya, Zambia, Northern Rhodesia (Zimbabwe), Lesotho (Botswana), to the Carribean (e.g. Jamaica, Barbados)).

The original concept was maintained, which among other things can be proved by the fact that the most widely used textbook and commentary to the Model Co-operative Societies Ordinance and Regulations, the Manual of Co-operative Law and Practices by Surridge and Digby quotes extensively the standard textbook on the Indian Co-operative Societies Act of 1912 by Calvert.

In practice it was proved that where all unwritten assumptions on which the concept is based were met, the model could be applied successfully. During the years 1950–1960, the Co-operative Departments in many former British dependencies managed to develop co-operatives to a high level of efficiency and helped to establish co-operative federations and unions which took over part of the functions of the Co-operative Departments (e.g. education, consulting and audit). This was achieved through massive training inputs, highly qualified staff, effective government services and a clear government policy to make co-operatives self-reliant.

V. The Development of the British–Indian Pattern of Cooperation after Independence

After independence, most of the former British dependencies retained the co-operative legislation based on the British–Indian Pattern. However, the political environment for co-operatives changed. In Ghana, for instance, the post of Registrar was filled with a political appointee, co-operative apex organizations established during the last years of colonial government were dissolved and political party structures were registered as co-operative societies. The size of Co-operative Departments kept growing and these Departments developed into highly stratified bureaucracies with Chief Registrars, Joint Registrars etc. Some countries even created Ministries in charge of co-operative development.

In Kenya, Tanzania and Zambia the powers of the Registrar were vested in a Director of Co-operatives or Commissioner for Co-operative Development, who either replaced the Registrar or became the superior of the Registrar. In other countries like Uganda, most of the powers of the Registrar were vested in the Minister in charge of co-operative development.

Only a few English-speaking countries drastically changed their Co-operative Development System and left the British Indian Pattern of Cooperation, like Tanzania, which dissolved all co-operatives of the "traditional" type and replaced them with village collectives (ujamaa) in 1975. However, this experiment ended in complete failure and since 1982 attempts are being made to come back to the previous pattern (→*Autochthonous Co-operatives*).

Many countries introduced socialist ideas into their co-operative development policy but retain the British–Indian Pattern of Cooperation as the legal basis. This move helped to strengthen a general trend to increase government's powers over co-operatives and to use co-operatives as instruments for the implementation of government's programmes.

New statutory functions of the government agency in charge of co-operative development include the following powers of direct intervention in the affairs of registered co-operative societies:

- Compulsory amendment of by-laws,
- recision of decisions of general meetings and board of directors,
- freezing of bank accounts,
- secondment of government officers to act as managers,
- suspension of the activities of the society,
- compulsory amalgamation or division of societies,
- orders to remedy defects disclosed during audit, inspection or inquiry.

New statutory powers intended to prevent registered co-operative societies from taking potentially dangerous decisions are:

- Power of government officers to attend meetings,
- the legal requirement of the Registrar's approval for business plans and budgets, decisions on financial matters like taking of loans, investment of funds, distribution of surplus, use of reserves, voluntary amalgamation or division.

Finally, new corrective statutory powers of the Registrar include police functions like surcharge and attachment of property, prosecution of persons who cause damage to registered co-operative societies. According to the original concept underlying the Classical British–Indian Pattern of Cooperation, most of these new statutory powers should not have been enacted at all, and where they had been introduced, procedural safeguards should be taken, that these powers could only be used in case of emergency and for good reason. The idea to limit government's supervision of co-operatives to an initial phase until co-operatives could organize their own development and audit machinery, proved in practice to be unrealistic. There is a clear trend to perpetuate these government powers and to increase them even further.

VI. Assessment of the Strengths and Weaknesses of the Model

1. Strengths

The British–Indian Pattern of Cooperation pioneered in the field of development law. It was the first systematic attempt to solve socio-economic problems in developing countries by devising not only a law introducing new rules of organization and norms of behaviour but also a government machinery for the dissemination of information on the new law and for its implementation.

Where this development oriented concept was systematically applied and the unwritten requirements for its implementation were met i.e.:

- a clear government policy treating co-operatives as private business organizations serving primarily the interest of their members,
- strict limitation of government assistance to the initial phase of co-operative development and preparing the cooperators for their work but leaving them alone to run their societies,
- turning the co-operative department into a special, well-equipped technical unit with qualified and motivated staff headed by an experienced Registrar of high caliber, who has the resources and the political backing to encourage the development of a self-reliant, member-oriented co-operative movement,

the results were positive.

However, in most of the countries following the British–Indian Pattern of Cooperation, a modified model of state-controlled co-operatives is applied and the unwritten success criteria are absent.

2. Weaknesses

Building the British–Indian Pattern of Cooperation on unwritten assumptions has been one major reason for the gradual transformation of state-sponsorship of co-operative development into state-control. But there are also other reasons why co-operative legislation and its practical application have drifted far away from what was originally intended.

During colonial government as well as under the national governments of the independent states, co-operatives were mainly seen and treated as development tools for the implementation of programmes planned from above. Co-operative development was accelerated artificially by providing them with external funds, fiscal priveleges and monopoly positions. This in turn was used as an argument to increase government's control over co-operatives to avoid misuse of public funds.

Once co-operatives had been registered which were incapable of working on their own, the Registrar and his staff could not restrict their functions to that of an educator and advisor, but had to interfere and supervise. Co-operative Departments often turned into huge bureaucratic structures without the human and financial resources required to promote, supervise, audit and control a growing number of co-operative societies (→ *Officialization*). Despite a steady increase of statutory powers, the services rendered by Co-operative Departments became less efficient. There is a clear trend to turn field work (informing, training and advising cooperators how to solve their practical problems) into office work.

VII. Summary

90 years after the inception of the British–Indian Pattern of Cooperation, there is doubt whether the involvement of the state in promoting co-operatives is a workable concept under present day conditions. The unwritten assumptions on which the British–Indian Pattern of Cooperation was based and which were essential for its success, have proved to be difficult to implement.

- Despite the intention to limit government's help to co-operatives to an initial phase only, government assistance to co-operatives has become a permanent feature,
- instead of phasing out government's involvement in co-operative development there has been a clear trend to increase and strengthen government's influence continuously,
- instead of teaching members of co-operatives how to run their own co-operative societies to satisfy their own needs, governments continue to see co-operatives as their development tools administered under government control to achieve objectives set by external planners.
- The idea of building a cadre of well-trained, highly motivated promoters within the civil service structure for carrying out mainly educational and advisory functions, appears to have become unrealistic under current government structures.
- What started as a programme of temporary state-sponsorship has turned into a programme of permanent state control.

In view of these conceptual problems and of the fact that many governments of developing countries are under budget constraints and cannot afford to finance and equip a heavily staffed government machinery for co-operative development, which in practice has proved to be largely ineffective, the time has come to consider a new approach to co-operative development.

After decades of → *education and training* and much progress made in the field of mass media, the citizens of developing countries have become more aware of ways and means to defend their legitimate interests and to form their own organizations. They should not be continuously guided but treated as self-responsible adults.

The government can now limit its role to that originally perceived under the British–Indian Pattern of Cooperation as the ultimate stage:

To provide a legal framework for the formation of autonomous co-operatives and a registration service with the main task of registering co-operatives upon application, if the applicants meet the legal requirements, to keep a file for each co-operative, which has to submit its annual reports and audited balance sheets and to monitor that all registered co-operatives comply with the provisions of the co-operative law.

This would allow governments to reduce their expenditure for subsidies and privileges granted to co-operative societies and for the supervision of co-operatives. At the same time it would require cooperators to build up their own organizations with their own means corresponding to their own needs.

In this way co-operatives would become what they should be: one of several forms of organization which the citizens can choose to solve their problems by working together.

Bibliography

Baldus, R.D./Hanel, A./Münkner, H.-H. (eds.): Government Promotion of Cooperatives and other Self-help Organizations for Rural Development, DSE, vol. 1 and 2, DOK 1063 A/a S 79–88–80.

British Colonial Office: Circular Despatches dated 20th March and 23rd April, 1946 from the Secretary of State for the Colonies to the Colonial Governments, HMSO, col.No.199.

Calvert, H.: The Law and Principles of Cooperation, 5th ed., Calcutta 1959.

Ghai, Yash: Co-operative Legislation in East Africa. In: Widstrand, Carl Gösta (ed.): Africa Co-operatives and Efficiency, pp. 39–61, Uppsala 1972.
Ibbetson, Sir Denzil: Approach to Legislation on Co-operative Credit 1904. In: National Co-operative Union of India, An Anthology of Co-operative Thought, vol. 1, pp. 99–109, New Delhi 1975.
Maini, Krishan M.: Co-operatives and Law with Emphasis on Kenya, Nairobi, Dar-es-Salaam, Kampala 1972.
McAuslan, J.P.W.B.: Co-operatives and the Law in East Africa. In: Widstrand, Carl Gösta (ed.): Co-operatives and Rural Development in East Africa, pp. 81–120, Uppsala/New York 1970,.
Münkner, Hans-H.: Die Organisation der eingetragenen Genossenschaft in den zum englischen Rechtskreis gehörenden Ländern Schwarzafrikas, dargestellt am Beispiel Ghanas, Marburg 1971.
Münkner, Hans-H.: New Trends in Co-operative Law of English-speaking Countries of Africa, Institute for Cooperation in Developing Countries, Papers and Reports, No. 4, Marburg 1971.
Münkner Hans-H.: Co-operative Law as an Instrument for State-sponsorship of Co-operative Societies, ILO Co-operative information, 1/73, pp. 27–42.
Münkner, Hans-H.: Co-operative Law and Co-operative Development in Ghana. In: The Plunkett Foundation, Year Book of Agricultural Cooperation (1976), pp. 126–144.
Münkner, Hans-H. (ed.): Comparative Study of Co-operative Law in Africa, Marburg 1989.
Nicholson, F.A.: Report regarding the possibility of introducing land and agricultural banks into the Madras Presidency, vol. I, Madras 1895, vol. II, Madras 1897.
Odede, O. and Verhagen, K.: External Supervision as an Integral Part of Promoting Co-operative Development. In: Konopnicki, M. and Vandewalle, G. (eds.): Cooperation as an Instrument for Rural Development, ICA, pp. 98–108, London 1978.
Strickland, C.F.: Cooperation for Africa, London 1933.
Surridge, B.J. and Digby, M.: A Manual of Co-operative Law and Practice, 3. ed., Cambridge 1967.

Buchez, Philippe Joseph Benjamin (1796–1865)

EMMANUEL KAMDEM

(see also: *History in 19th C.*; *History of Ideas*; *Joint-production Co-operative*)

Buchez was a medical doctor, philosopher, and French politician. He is one of wellknown precursors of co-operatives in France. Born in Matagne-la-Petite, (Belgium, Ardennes) in 1796, he died in Rodez (France) in 1865. *Buchez* was a disciple of *Saint-Simon* and is considered as the father of Christian socialism and Christian democracy. In 1821, during his medical studies, he joined the Charbonnerie, a political secret society created in France under the Restoration. *Buchez* participated in many political complots and was taken to court because of the Belfort Conspiracy.
As Deputy Mayor of Paris in February 1848, *Buchez* was in charge of National Security. He also had to establish national workshops on Handicrafts. Elected as member of the Constituent Assembly in 1848, *Buchez* became its first Chairman (5th may – 6th June 1848). Against *Louis Napoléon Bonaparte*, *Buchez* gave support to *Cavaignac*. *Buchez's* defeat in the legislative election of May 1849 marked the end of his short political career. He wrote the "Traité de Politique et Science sociale" which was published after his death in 1866.
Buchez is the founder of the "Association ouvrière de Production" (Workers Production Association). He first collaborated with the *Saint-Simonism* movement from 1825 to 1830, but abandoned it in 1830 because of its pantheist philosophy. Together with some other dissidents, he then tried to defend the "veritable" doctrine of *Saint-Simon*. He tried to synthesize the tenets of Christianity and socialism as well as the aims of the French Revolution.
In 1832, he founded the "Européen" (European) review. The first articles emphasized a "European federation" that *Buchez* believed to be feasible once the "equality and the freedom proclaimes by the Christian law are established in fact and legally as the basis of society". In 1834, he published "L'Histoire Parlementaire de la Révolution" (Parliamentary History of the French Revolution). He developed the "Théorie de l'Association Ouvrière" (Theory of Workers Association) and founded in 1834 the "Association Artisanale d'Ouvriers Bijoutiers" (Jewellery Workers' Craft Association) which ,from 1840 to 1850, published the Newspaper "L'Atelier" ("The Workshop"). "L'Atelier" accepted the principles of class struggle and energetically fought the capitalistic system and the payment by salary. In its concern to protect the worker's dignity, it also rejected all forms of charitable assistance.
In opposition to the Utopian *Fourier*, *Buchez* developed certain principles which greatly influenced the French workers as well as other precursors of the Co-operative Movement, such als *Louis Blanc* in France, *John Stuart Mill* (→ *Classic/Neo-classic Contributions*), and the Christian Socialists in Britain. *Buchez* was a social idealist with a specific vision for the future. He envisioned the Workers' Co-operatives (→ *Joint-production Co-operative*), which he recommended and created, as institutions which would benefit the future generations through their programmes and activities.
According to *Buchez*, the working class should pursue self-help activities independently, that is without government intervention or philantropical assistance. The associated workers were to bring together the tools they owned and the little capital they had saved. In time, the capital of the association would increase through the accumulation of realized surplus. For *Buchez*, the production association was to be founded freely among the members of a same profession. The members would elect among them-

selves two trusted individuals to run the enterprise. Members of the association earned their wages according to their capabilities and according to the standards existing in their respective professions. Each day, they were to put aside an amount equal to the part due to the entrepreneur. At the end of the year, 80% of this amount (as a net surplus of the co-operative) was to be distributed among the members proportionally to their respective wage-share, i.e. according to the work they had accomplished. The remaining 20% was to be set aside to provide for the accumulation of capital. This capital was to be inalienable and constitute an indivisible and indissoluble fund. In case of liquidation of the society, it was not meant to be distributed among the members but rather be used towards the funding of some other association, preferably in the same area of production. *Buchez* thought that the accumulation of all such inalienable funds would transform the whole of society into an association of a State Labour Bank. Thus, the indivisible fund would have worked towards the reform of society along a co-operative path, due mainly to the transfer of the means of production to the workers. Despite the fact that each worker is mortal (as is any member of human society), and although the associations can be subject to dissolution some time, *Buchez* stressed the point that human society as such, however, is eternal. Because of its link between the past, the present and the future, the permanent human society should have a permanent fund at its disposal. So the fund should continue to exist even after dissolution of the co-operative. This idea was also shared by *Louis Blanc*, → *Raiffeisen*, and the → *consumer co-operatives*. Two workers co-operatives (→ *Joint-production Co-operatives*) were created by *Buchez* along his principles: a Carpenters Co-operative (created in 1832 and quickly liquidated), and an Jewellers' Association (created in 1834, lasting until 1873). Those co-operatives reserved 1/7 of their surplus to the inalienable fund, the rest being distributed as follows: half was allocated to a reserve fund and the other half to the members or the co-operative.

Buchez's contribution to the co-operative movement was significant and rests on his Guiding → *Principles* of:

a) Self-help;
b) Non-intervention of the State in co-operative business;
c) Reserve Fund;
d) Self-management;
e) Non-distribution of the reserve fund in case of liquidation.

One of the two workers' co-operatives created by *Buchez* lasted more than forty years (1834–1873) and can be considered successful. The concept of workers' co-operatives is still very actual at the end of the 20th century. Indeed, some authors think that workers' co-operatives can contribute to the solution of present economic and unemployment problems.

Bibliography
Bertrand, Louis: Histoire de la coopération en Belgique, Tome 1, Bruxelles 1902.
Cuvillier, Armand: Buchez, le fondateur en France de l'Association ouvrière de production, in: Revue des Etudes coopératives, 1ère année, No.1.
Lambert, Paul: La doctrine coopérative, Troisième édition augmentée, Bruxelles 1964.
Mladenatz, Gromoslav: Histoire des doctrines coopératives, Paris 1933.
Müller, Julius Otto: Voraussetzungen und Verfahrensweisen bei der Errichtung von Genossenschaften in Europas vor 1900, Göttingen 1976.

Building and Loan Associations, Co-operative

HORST KLEINER [J]

(see also: *Co-operative Banks*; *Combine, Co-operative*; *Housing Societies*)

I. International Comparison of Building and Loan Associations; II. Parallels between Co-operatives and Building and Loan Associations; III. The Development of Schwäbisch Hall, a co-operatively owned Building and Loan Association; IV. How modern Building-saving functions; V. Documentation of the Contractual Building-saving Business; VI. The Importance of Building-saving for the Contractual Building-saver; VII. The Importance of Building-saving for Both the State and Society.

I. International Comparison of Building and Loan Associations

Building and Loan Associations are "Credit institutions, the main function of which consists of the accumulation of savings capital in order to grant loans to promote home building, particularly that of private family housing" (*Lehmann*, 1977). One can essentially differentiate between three international varieties of the same form:

The British "Building Societies" and the US-American "Saving and Loan Associations" (→ *Development, North America*) are today predominantly open institutions on the capital market. They procure the means to grant building loans from investment-seeking savers and, to an increasing degree, from the capital market. The borrower need not have been a former saver. The equilibrium between the investment-seeking savings capital and the demand for loans results from variable interest rates.

Characteristic for contemporary French building-saving is the system of "épargne-logement" which banks offer as a special form of savings and financing in two varieties ("plan d'épargne logement" PEL and "comptes d'épargne-logement" CEL). The building-saver must provide a certain level of savings before he can receive a loan. The French building and loan system thus has similarities with the system of collective building-saving. It is very strongly determined by support from the state.

According to § 1 of the Law on Building and Loan Associations (Gesetz über Bausparkassen), German Building and Loan Associations "...are credit institutions, the business of which is directed towards accepting deposits from building-savers (contractual building-saving deposits) and granting the building-savers monetary loans (contractual building-saving loans) from the accumulated amounts for measures in the field of housing (contractual building-saving business)". The latter may only be executed by Building and Loan Associations.

The efficiency and capacity of a Building and Loan Association is determined by the contributions of its members. The German system of collective building-saving, which is also practiced similarly in Austria, thus is based on the principle of self-help (→ *Principles*). Through his savings contributions the building-saver makes credit possible for other building-savers to whom their accumulated savings balance together with their contractual building-saving loan is payed out at the end of the savings period. The building-saver himself simultaneously acquires a legal claim to a contractual building-saving loan by way of his savings contributions.

II. Parallels between Co-operatives and Building and Loan Associations

The German and Austrian Building and Loan Associations can therefore be considered co-operative in a fairly broad sense of the term. They function according to the collective system which exhibits a close relationship to the basic co-operative idea. *Friedrich Wilhelm* → *Raiffeisen* established agricultural co-operative banks (→ *Co-op. Banks*) because the farmers of his day and age were not considered creditworthy for the commercial banks. The English laborers, who were the first to develop the idea of building-saving, were also dependent on self-help towards the end of the 18th century (→ *History before 1800*). Each individual can build considerably faster if willing savers unite as if each person individually saves for his own property and construction costs. The savings of the individual are completed by the savings of others. The collective system of building-saving came into being in Germany after World War I in a similar situation of housing shortage and lack of capital after a forerunner institution failed to gain acceptance at the end of the 19th century (→ *History in 19th C.*).

Further parallels between Building and Loan Associations and co-operatives can be drawn based on *Draheim's* work.

Building and Loan Associations and co-operatives are enterprises which must stand their ground on the market; in other words, economic principles are valid for both of them. All the same they are committed to particular social conduct because their clientele is dependent on them. Efficiency and competitiveness do not contradict the social obligation but rather condition it.

The notions of self-help and service are in the foreground for Building and Loan Associations and co-operatives. Both of them are obligated to the interests of all present and future members / building-savers and not in a partial manner to the interests of an individual.

Building and Loan Associations and co-operatives comprise members who are connected to each other through common interests. In as much as the members of a co-operative can attain their collective goal only with each other, in principle there is also no opposition between the individual building-savers of a Building and Loan Association. Each must first save to receive a loan afterwards, set at a fixed interest rate. A conflict of interests which is inevitably produced on the capital market between building-savers and borrowers because of fluctuating interest rates is out of the question in the collective system of building-saving.

The parallel between Building and Loan Associations and co-operatives is also apparent in terminology. One speaks of the co-operative movement the same as one speaks of the building-saving movement (→ *Conceptions, Co-operative*).

III. The Development of Schwäbisch Hall, a co-operatively owned Building and Loan Association

Because of the many parallels between co-operatives and the notion of building-saving it does not astonish that the latter has been able to flourish especially well in Germany in close contact with the co-operative banks. The development of the Schwäbisch Hall Building Society to the leading German Building and Loan Association exhibits this connection well. This enterprise, which can be considered a co-operative Building and Loan Association in a narrow sense, was founded by craftsmen in Cologne in 1931 and named "Deutsche Bausparer AG, Bau-, Spar- und Entschuldungskasse". The enterprise rapidly gained importance, moved in 1934 to Berlin and developed close relations to the co-operative banking sector. During this time, trailblazing corporate decisions were made. The Building and Loan Association concentrated its activities on second mortgages. The connections to the *Volksbanken* (urban credit unions) (→*Co-operative Banks*) offered further opportunities of taking a first mortgage at an institution with which friendly relations were shared. What the Building and Loan Association was then introducing would be required for all such institutions five years later through a reform. In 1936 a change of name also accentuated this policy, "Gesellschaft für zweitstelligen Grundkredit, Deutsche Bausparer AG".

This early contact to the co-operative banking sector led to a lasting cooperation in the following years. In 1941 the German *Volksbanken* participated in the capital of the enterprise. This step led to the renaming of the enterprise into "Bausparkasse der Deutschen Volksbanken AG". After evacuating from the destroyed city of Berlin and relocating in Schwäbisch Hall, the connection to the co-operative organization was strengthened even further. In 1956 the *Raiffeisenbanken* (rural credit unions) (→ *Co-operative Banks*) also joined. The "Bausparkasse Schwäbisch Hall AG" was formed from the "Bausparkasse der Deutschen Volksbanken AG". The new partners invested more than just their financial strength in the enterprise. The overall presence of the Building and Loan Association on the market was expanded to a considerable degree through this cooperation. Today the Combine of Co-operative Banks and the Schwäbisch Hall Building Society are represented in almost every township in Germany with a most intertwined network of branch offices – over 19,000 in all.

The co-operative banking partners and Schwäbisch Hall together have further developed the product of building-saving into a highly flexible instrument of both service and consulting for provisional savings and building finance. Today the building-saving contract is a standard item in the range of financial services offered by *Volksbanken* and *Raiffeisenbanken*. This close partnership and cooperation, which has lasted for decades, has secured a top market position for the Building and Loan Association. This is reflected by 6.6 million building-saving contracts amounting to a total contractual sum of over DM 233 billion. With its close to 4.5 million customers, Schwäbisch Hall has the largest number of customers of all Building and Loan Associations in Germany; every fourth building-saver in the Federal Republic is a Schwäbisch Hall customer. The contractual building-saving deposits, which play a prominent role in the market position of a Building and Loan Association, attained a record level of DM 32 billion in the 1992 business year.

Co-operative building-saving has become a successful, interlocking system of service in the past 30 years which has been in great demand. Building and Loan Associations and banks have invested specialist competence, educational programs and technological capacities in this product. Banks and Building and Loan Associations work hand in hand from customer consulting services to the conclusion of contracts, from residential construction to complementary financial services. This results in a highly individual level of consultative competence and comprehensive services for the customer.

IV. How modern Building-saving functions

Collective building-saving is today a modern savings and financing system, the functions of which can be presented as follows from the perspective of the building-saver:

The building-saver concludes a building-saving contract for an amount of contract chosen by him. First, he regularly saves and deposits equity into his building-saving account.

Upon termination of the contract and the savings procedure the building-saver attains a right to a building-saving loan, which as a rule is as much as the money saved on his account.

The interest rate for this loan lies between 4.5% and 6% and is completely independent from the developments on the capital market. This interest rate corresponds with an appropriate interest on savings of between 2.5% and 4%. The difference between interest on savings and on credits is 2%.

Upon disbursement of the loan the amortization begins according to the levels agreed upon, which usually lasts between 6 and 11 years.

Example: A building-saver who has signed a contract for 100,000 marks has his share of equity of 50,000 marks as well as a loan share of 50,000 marks at his disposal.

The procedure from the viewpoint of the Building and Loan Association is as follows:

The Building and Loan Association receives deposits from building-savers and grants loans for measures in the field of housing from the accumulated amounts.

The system of financing within the Building and Loan Association is thus self-contained. It is fed out of the savings plus credit interests, and amortization amounts.

The amounts flow into one fund out of which the total contractual sums – the savings deposits plus the loan – are paid out in a particular succession. The term "allotment" has been generally adopted for this procedure.

The allotment method is based on the principle of "time multiplied by money"; the point in time at which the building-saver can lay claim on his loan depends on the savings period and the size of the savings amounts.

After allotment, the loan is to be amortized by the building-saver within a set time period, as we have already mentioned.

As in the savings process the building-saver has flexibility as well in amortization. The building-saving tariffs vary according to the different interest rate combinations as well as rates of savings and amortization. The building-saver can tailor his own saving contract and adjust it to his own individual demand and needs even after signing the contract.

Building-saving today thus poses a complex financial and mathematical process from the point of view of the Building and Loan Association; because of reasons of competition this will constantly continue to develop. Inspite of numerous changes the basic idea behind it all has remained unchanged: "Building-saving is an aid to self-help".

V. Documentation of the Contractual Building-saving Business

The realm of business activities of a Building and Loan Association is calculated through numerous turnover and balance levels which are oriented towards the various stages and phases in the course of a building-saving contract. New business, the contract portfolio and allotments also are included, whereby one must differentiate between the number of contracts and the total contractual sum. Other important sales indicators are the receipts in the allotment fund and its main components of savings receipts and amortization payments. Building-saving deposits and the portfolio of contractual building-saving loans are branch-specific indicators of the balance sheet. The entire loan portfolio additionally includes the allotment of pre- and interim credits. The balance sheet total represents the entire activities including all non-collective sideline business. The question thus arises according to which criteria the market position of Building and Loan Associations should be established. This is at the same time the general question of building-saving: Which of the varying business indicators express best the building-saving business as a whole?

The suitable criteria for the market position as a whole are the amounts of monetary receipts flowing into the allotment fund (the accumulation of savings receipts, interest on deposits and net amortization) and the receipts for building-saving deposits as itemized on the balance sheet (Glandorf). Both business indicators take into consideration the former business development and influence future development. The building-saving deposits do, of course, put more emphasis on the development of previous years. The choice between receipts in the allotment fund and the building-saving deposits depends on the extent the development in the past should be considered.

New business and the contract portfolio are important indicators for the development of the building-saving business; they are, however, less suitable for a comparison of the market position among all Building and Loan Associations. New business and the contract portfolio affect the actual savings and amortization receipts differently, depending on set rates for savings and amortization contribution and the line of conduct of these two practises. Savings and amortization receipts themselves, as well as the building-saving deposits indicated on the balance sheet, can represent the market share and market position of a Building and Loan Association considerably better. The balance sheet total is not considered because it also includes non-collective business. Pre- and interim financing can also be undertaken by partner banks and thus do not belong to the relevant market.

VI. The Importance of Building-saving for the Contractual Building-saver

The activities in the building-saving business experienced an unprecedented upswing in Germany after World War II. Building-saving contributed decisively to the reconstruction of the destroyed cities and towns. The contract portfolio at German Building and Loan Associations continued to expand between 1950 and 1989 from 400,000 contracts to almost 26 million contracts. The volume has reached approximately DM 900 billion today; forty years ago it was just at DM 4 billion. Since the end of the War the Building and Loan Associations in Germany have been involved in the financing of 10 million homes. Nearly 80% of all living space in owner-occupied houses and condominium apartments in Germany is financed in whole or part by Building and Loan Associations.

The importance of building-saving business remains undiminished even after German reconstruction and economic consolidation. Savings preceeding the loan are essential for most citizens when purchasing housing property. Building-saving as a goal-oriented savings plan is particularly suitable for owner-occupied housing because building-savers reach their savings goal faster than other savers. Continually more young families are able to take the step to owning their own homes through building-saving; in comparison to earlier years, the average age for purchasing home property has duly sunk. Aside from this, building-saving has also contributed to the fact that more and more families with children and with average incomes can purchase their own homes.

The accumulation of equity capital (→ *Equity Capital*) by building-saving is completed by the security that the low interest rate on the building-saving loan offers over the entire duration. The monthly interest and amortization rate is a constant basis of calculation for financing home building. This is particularly important also for low income earners or for families with many children who can only with difficulty cope with the heavier burdens resulting from the variable rates on the capital market.

A particular feature of building saving is the ability to raise a second mortgage on a property, and that up to 80% of the mortgage value. This is possible without public guarantees.

Because of its great socio-political importance, building-saving is officially promoted by the state in Germany. All single persons who have a taxable income not exceeding DM 27,000 as well as all married couples with taxable income up to DM 54,000 can lay claim under the current legal situation to the so-called building-saving bonus as well as to the employee savings bonus. The building-saving bonus of 10% is granted to personal savings up to DM 800 for singles and DM 1600 for married couples annually. The employee savings bonus is for contributions which the employer transfers to a building-saving contract within the scope of the Law on Asset Accumulation (*Vermögensbildungsgesetz*). The employee savings bonus amounts to 10% on deposits up to DM 936 yearly.

Building-saving contracts are applicable in many situations. Building-saving means can be employed in numerous methods providing both premium and tax privileges. The building-saver can use his allotted building-saving means in order to:

- purchase a property upon which to build a house;
- have a house built, or buy one;
- rebuild or modernize a house, or to make other such improvements;
- enlarge a house;
- purchase a condominium or similar property with a right for long-term occupancy;
- build or buy a garage adjacent to a house;
- build or buy a vacation house which, based on the construction design, is suitable for permanent living and which will not be used for commercial purposes;
- invest in the financing of a building in order to have an apartment reserved for him;
- pay out co-heirs in order to purchase property from the estate;
- purchase particular real estate certificates;
- modernize an apartment as a tenant;
- finance the costs of the inhabitable part of a mixed-use building;
- repay building debts which have arisen in connection with one of the measures mentioned above.

Today there are 17 million building-savers in the Federal Republic of Germany. Building-saving contracts are in the possession of single persons and families from all social groups; there is thus no "typical building-saver". The rough characteristics of the social structure of the German population at large also are appropriate for the group of building-savers (*Kleiner*, 1986). Two out of every three building-saving customers are employed persons; wage workers compose one-fifth, salaried staff one-third and public servants one-tenth of all German building-savers. This shows that building-saving is an esteemed and frequently used method of asset accumulation for employed persons, especially for wage workers.

VII. The Importance of Building-saving for Both the State and Society

Building and Loan Associations are the main sources of financing in residential construction in Germany. Payments of building loans from these associations in 1989 once again reached more than DM 40 billion; this represents around 40% of payments from capital accumulation funds for the entire branch of housing construction. The importance of building-saving for housing construction is, however, only insufficiently reflected by the share of building-saving investment in construction financing. This purely quantitative consideration does not express the contribution which building-saving makes to the materialization of financing. Even more important than the quantitative share is the qualitative share of building-saving for financing home construction. The building-saving contract is the basis for financing for almost all builder-owners and initially makes construction possible.

The German system of building-saving is one of the few dependable mainstays for the construction of owner-occupied housing. This is because the volume of building loan payments is to a large extent independent from business cycle situations and from the interest levels on the capital market. The level of payments concerning building loans of Building and Loan Associations is much more determined by the level of deposits of all building-savers, in the form of savings and amortization amounts. Building-saving thus secures jobs and positions, particularly in middle-sized construction and development companies, affecting the entire national economy.

Bibliography

Draheim, Georg: Zur Ökonomisierung der Genossenschaften. Gesammelte Beiträge zur Genossenschaftstheorie und Genossenschaftspolitik, Göttingen 1967.

Glandorf, Karl-Heinz: Marktanteilsermittlung bei Bausparkassen. Die Vergleichbarkeit bei den einzelnen Geschäftsgrößen und die Kriterienauswahl für die Marktstellung insgesamt, Dissertation, Stuttgart-Hohenheim 1989.

Kleiner, Horst: Bausparkasse Schwäbisch Hall und Kreditgenossenschaften. Aktive Verbundkooperation. Aspekte künftiger Zusammenarbeit unter veränderten Marktbedingungen, in: Bankinformation, vol. 13 (1986), no.4, pp. 10–18.

Kleiner, Horst: Wer sind die Bausparer?, in: Hahn, Gernot v./Otto, Klaus-Friedrich (eds.): Ein Zuhause für Menschen. Festschrift für Walter Englert, Frankfurt/M. 1986, pp. 121–129.

Laux, Hans: Die Bausparfinanzierung. Die finanziellen Aspekte des Bausparvertrages als Spar- und Kreditinstrument, 5th ed., Heidelberg 1983.

Laux, Hans: Fortgeschrittene Bauspartechnik, Heidelberg 1985.

Lehmann, Werner: Beiträge zur Entwicklung des privaten Bausparwesens, Berlin 1940.

Lehmann, Werner: Die Bausparkassen (Frankfurt/M. 1963), Frankfurt/M. 1977.

Lehmann, Werner/Schäfer, Otto/Cirpka, Ekkehard: Bausparkassengesetz und Bausparkassenverordnung unter Berücksichtigung des Gesetzes über das Kreditwesen. Kommentar, 3rd ed., Bonn 1987.

Business Policies, Co-operative

HELMUT LIPFERT [F]

(see also: *Promotion Mandate*; *Management in Co-operatives*; *Economic Order*; *Managerial Economics*; *Diversification Strategies*; *Strategy Planning*; *Dual Nature*)

I. Set of Objectives; II. Co-operative Policies in Primary Co-operatives; III. Competition Policies in Primary Co-operatives; IV. Business Policies in the System in which Co-operatives are Linked Together; V. Policies for Distributing Benefits to Achieve Long-Range Promotion of Members' Interests.

In the various branches of the economy in which co-operatives are active, they must face competition from participants in the market who are not co-operatives (→ *Competition*). Co-operatives are expected to offer the whole breadth and variety of services, in their respective branches, which business policies and market success require. This article, however, will concentrate on specific business policies typical for co-operatives due to their "inborn" nature, as far as possible treating them irrespective of individual branches.

The article will deal with the science of business policy in an interdisciplinary way, including psychology and sociology. The author also considers it necessary to go into various norms of co-operative business policy, at the risk of being criticized for appearing norm-oriented.

I. Set of Objectives

Enterprises of all legal types can attain lasting success in market economies only if they devote themselves intensively to benefitting their customers (i.e. other enterprises, public authorities, private people). Courted by business, these customers – who are links in economic service chains (*Porter*) – must be persuaded that their own portion of the total economic value, arising as a whole from the respective chains, will be maximized solely by this very service offered to them by the enterprise.

1. Promotion of Members through the Chain of Co-operative Services

With the help of *Porter's* theory on economic service chains (analysis and consequences for business policy), we can detect clearly the basic difference between non-co-operative and co-operative business policies, namely the different set of objectives aimed for. Suppliers who are not co-operatives try to increase benefits to their customers with the goal of optimizing the scope and durability of the profits solely of their own enterprise.

The unique commission given to co-operatives, however, at the base or primary level as well as to their central co-operatives and associations, which is to promote the interests of their members (→ *Promotion Mandate*), imposes on the co-operative a double set of objectives: the dominating goal is to maximize the business success or private benefit for the last link in the service chain, that is, for the business or private members of co-operatives at the base level of the chain, which includes private members, primary-level co-operatives, and secondary-level co-operatives. This maximization is possible in the long run only if in promoting the last link of the chain, the capacity of all the other links of the service chain up to the last one is kept fully intact. In addition to the fulfillment of its commission to serve its members then, there is a second objective of co-operative business policy, which is to secure in the long run the success-potential of the co-operative's regional or national association.

2. Success in Business Competition and the Optimal Form of Cooperation

On the one hand, business policies of co-operatives at the primary and centralized levels, formulated with the help of the associations, must prove that they can hold up against competition in their respective branch situations, in order to be able to promote the last link in the chain by offering services that are competitive. On the other hand, those who uphold these business policies must be able to count on the members' actually taking advantage of the services offered by the primary co-operatives as well as on the primary co-operatives' taking advantage of the services provided by the central organizations (→ *Central Institutions*). This guarantee that their service relations potential (*Bänsch*) will indeed be used is absolutely essential, because in contrast to non-co-operative suppliers, the primary co-operatives and the central organizations are not free in their search for purchasers of their services, but quite to the contrary they are very much limited in their search by their orientation to their members and their region.

Business policies in co-operative systems always have the double task, both tasks completely interdependent on each other, of achieving success both in competition outside the system as well as in close cooperation with members within the system. This is a difficult task, not the smallest reason for it being that it calls simultaneously for "soft" cooperation with other human beings "on the inside" and "hard" specialized competition in the markets. Only for the sake of keeping a clear overall view will these two interlocking areas of co-operative business policies – cooperation policies and competition policies – be dealt with here separately.

II. Co-operative Policies in Primary Co-operatives

1. Positive Interactional Synergy as a Factor for Increasing Performance

"The term co-operative is used everywhere where a number of people join together for a common project, because the joint effort makes possible an amount of strength which is greater than the sum of the individual amounts of energy." In accordance with these words of *Müller's*, which have become "classic" today, the synergy potential (the whole equals more than the sum of the parts) takes on crucial significance as a factor of increasing co-operative performance. The concept of synergism (*Ansoff* has stated that two and two make five) requires an attitude of cooperation in the co-operative triangle made up of members, management, and employees. Antagonistic mutual mistrust, on the other hand, is counter-productive (two and two makes three). What is crucial here is that, in accordance with *Deutsch's* "elementary law of social relationships", and given a basis of cooperation which is functioning well, the relationships of positive synergetic cooperation tend to intesify.

Synergy is not to be confused with harmony or lack of differences. Rather, it is the optimal integration of optimal union of what was heretofore differentiated or distinctly different. The previous state of differentiation is especially important, because the farther away a new thought or combination of feelings is from the normal everyday patterns of thoughts and feelings, the greater is its synergetic potential.

2. Obligation of Management to Orient Itself to Members

Henzler (1957) and *Draheim* (1967 and 1972) have not thrown into question what is understood here as positive interactional synergy in co-operatives; quite to the contrary, in their books they have set forth their concepts of how the synergy potential can be more intensively utilized.

Eschenburg (1971), who characterizes the two above authors as representatives of a "harmony theory", is himself the founder of the "conflict theory" (→ *Theory of co-operative Cooperation*). He assumes that between members and managers there exists a relationship of potential conflict. "In reality there is, of course, no complete harmony of interests between members and managers of co-operatives. To the contrary, fairly serious conflicts can be expected to crop up over and over again." (*Eschenburg*, 1972)

As explained above in I.2., those responsible for co-operative business policies are just as dependent on successful internal cooperation as they are on successful external competition in the market; and these two forms of success are simply inconceivable without a clear orientation to the members. Even if in extreme cases managers thought only of their own personal ambition (high income, etc.), they would nonetheless be forced to make the most intensive efforts possible to meet the promotional interests and human aims of the members (→ *Management in Co-operatives*). If they did not, then in the long run they would not be able to safeguard the fulfillment of their own self-centered interests.

This fact is not refuted in any way by the very few though alarming criminal or pathological cases in which reprehensible motives have predominated and/or the boundless self-overrating of managers' own abilities in the process of managing co-operatives has prevailed.

3. Cooperate Identity

a) Identity Problems of Co-operatives

It is symptomatic not just of marginal orientational weaknesses and identity problems in the co-operative system when co-operatives turn away from certain fundamental characteristics hitherto typical of co-operatives to orient themselves to profit-maximizing, capitalistic patterns (→ *Dual Nature*). This can happen while keeping the abbreviation e.G. (registered co-operative), or transforming the co-operative into an *AG* (joint stock company) while still keeping – either in fact or in name only – the character of an organization oriented to promoting its members' interests. *Neumann* has stated: "As a matter of fact, the environmental conditions under which co-operatives today have got to survive have undergone such huge changes over against the conditions existing at the time when co-operatives were founded that a new orientation of their understanding of themselves has become absolutely necessary and has already actually occurred in many places, of course without one's being fully aware of the fact everywhere."

Evidently it is necessary, through a conscious fostering and emphasizing of co-operative identity, to enable the co-operative members and employees as well as the general public to identify the co-operative's unique character. It can help capture this character and keep it identifiable to introduce and use the term "cooperate identity". (*Lipfert*, 1984) (→ *Corporate Culture*).

b) Orientation to Common Values and Meanings

In all legal forms of enterprise, leadership oriented to identity consists of measures to build up confidence in the organization, measures which are intended, through emphasis on the enterprise's own personality, to promote a feeling of belonging within the enterprise and its standing with the public outside the enterprise.

For members, customers, management, and employees of primary co-operatives and central organizations, co-operative identity consists of the connection between matter-of-fact business service relationships and relationshps of human communication. "Co-operative identity is manifested in the way the co-operative organization conceives of itself, in its consciousness of being oriented around mutual values and meanings (the purpose of the enterprise being the promotion of the interests of its members) and in the image which members and employees as well as business partners and the public have of this co-operative organizations." (*Lipfert*, 1988)

Leadership oriented to cooperate identity in the co-operative system has the task of fostering credibility and trust by bringing into unison self-image, behaviour, and communication, in order to make clear the value of cooperation relationships. This way a threshold can also be erected against tendencies to level off differences between co-operatives and other legal forms of enterprises, tendencies which are evident in legislation and administration (as in the new German credit law, in tax legislation (→ *Taxation*), and in the government office for the supervision of cartels (→ *Anti-Trust Laws*)).

c) "The Co-operative Member as Customer is King"

Business management oriented to maintaining the identity of the organization should bind the members to the services offered by the co-operative in an emotional respect, in the sense of creating a feeling of "satisfaction and contentment" (*Henzler*, 1970) and of "group solidarity" (→ *Group, the Co-operative*). A climate of general consensus with regard to co-operative values and meanings can give impetus to an "economy of input and output relations" in the co-operative system as a whole.

Of course it is necessary to have a basis of qualification and authorization through expertise, if employees and full-time as well as volunteer members of boards are to be successful disseminators of cooperate indentity. In addition, all participants have to become sensitized to using, as a matter of course, business practices which are in keeping with the specific character of co-operatives. One should note here that individual identities are by no means always evident, but are sometimes hidden, though present everywhere. Informal coalitions and structures can be decisive for the state of cooperate identity in the organization.

Ideal "transformers" of efforts to get the various heterogenous needs of the members fulfilled, because recognized and accepted by the majority (only thus can every member feel like a "king"), are the voluntary members of boards of directors (→ *Honorary Office*). They are managers and member-customers of directors. They are managers and member-customers all at the same time. The cooperation policies of primary co-operatives simply cannot do without the work and commitment of these board members.

d. Mobilization through Member Participation

Possible institutions for mobilizing awareness of co-operative identity, in addition to the general assemblies of members and the small circles of leadership (such as supervisory boards), can be special organs of participation (*Ringle*), such as advisory committees, counseling circles, groups which pave the way for decisions to be made, advisory bodies for youth affairs, meetings of the up-and-coming generation, etc. (→ *Organizational Structure of Societies*). *Blümle/ Purtschert* favour project teams – teams of experts which are set up *ad hoc* as the need arises, to deal with definite problems that have to be decided on. It is particularly stimulating for a co-operative sense of identity if a consensus of the membership base has to be reached on significant investment decisions affecting the future.

In order to achieve an efficiency potential – a positive cost-benefit relationship – with regard to actual participation, it is necessary to have an optimal degree of participation on the one hand and the management's interest in offering opportunities for participation on the other (*Ringle/Hill*) (→ *Evaluation*). The great positive significance of an intensified membership participation for cooperate identity in co-operatives, for a supportive atmosphere within the organization, and for successful competition outside the organization has, on the one hand, to be brought into harmony with the legal charge aid onto the co-operative boards to manage the organization. On the other hand, it is imperative to persuade partners in participation within the circle of members-customers that the considerable amount of time they unavoidably have to spend informing themselves sufficiently on the factual issues to be dealt with nonetheless bears correspondingly high rewards.

III. Competition Policies in Primary Co-operatives

1. Strategic Positions to be Supported

a) Strengths and Weaknesses

An analysis of strengths and weaknesses of co-operatives has to start out from the fact that co-operatives are "born with certain restrictions" which do not hold true for their competitors in the market: the co-operative's geographical field of business is limited to a certain city or region; it is closely related to its members (including a limited amount of business with non-members); and it is normally active in only one branch of business.

This state of affairs results in both advantages and disadvantages as to policies regarding business competition. The advantage of being a co-operative is the stabilization of service relationships resulting from the membership, which makes a specialized business policiy possible – and necessary – that consciously harmonizes with the intentions of the members.

A considerable disadvantage of primary co-operatives, on the other hand, lies in the fact that they are in a much weaker position than their national or international competitors in the utilization of ways, proven by experience, of reducing costs by operating on a larger scale (every time one doubles the volume of services or goods ever produced, one thereby reduces the real cost of each individual service or product by 20 or 30 per cent).

b) Deviation Analyses

The day-to-day working out of concepts and concrete measures in trade policies related to members' needs requires constant early recognition of opportunities and risks, both in dealings outside the co-operative and in life within the particular special co-operative. It is especially necessary to analyze conditions and expectations in constantly changing external competition with other enterpises in the same branch of business, competition which is above all determined by existing rivalries and possible new competitors.

As to the internal life of the co-operative, it is extremely important to take note of changes in the total number of services requested by the members, as well as of corresponding fluctuations involving individual members. With the help of these deviation analyses, it is possible promptly and reliably to perceive needs for making adaptations in strategy and operations, in the form of strengths to be fostered and weak spots to be eliminated in the competitive situation.

c) Synergetic Differentiation and Diversification Oriented to the Promotion of Member's Interests

Since many of the markets in which co-operatives are active display a low growth rate or a high degree of saturation, in the hard fight for business the co-operatives in their policies of competition are almost always forced to stand out through policies of specialized service differentiation which – based on a prominent cooperate identity – consciously harmonize with the intention of the members. In market niches in which members are involved, the co-operatives should at least maintain their shares in the market and if possible expand them. What they should strive to achieve is market leadership in these niches.

In their policies of competition, co-operatives should make great efforts to distinguish themselves from their competitors through special co-operative features which are oriented to the future and hold promise of business success. The members-customers of the co-operatives should be able to discern clearly the prospects for business success in the range of the co-operatives' services.

Even with a range of services which is customary for the market, the management of co-operatives can build up and expand member-oriented, specific capacity-potentials and thereby strengthen their strategic position for promoting their members' interests through the following means:

- a policy of providing services which is decidedly member-oriented,
- fulfillment of quality standards according to the wishes of the members,
- a high quality of counseling by specially trained sales personnel,
- responsiveness to special problems and needs of the members,
- transmission of the feeling to the members that the co-operatives are always there when needed and always offer their members something unusual (→ *Management in Co-operatives*).

For a specific policy of differentiation for the promotion of the interests of the members, it is advantageous if the range of member-oriented services allows room for a transfer of know-how from service to service, that is, if the range of services displays interdependence. "It is then possible to expect a synergetic effect from the transfer of experience with one product to experience with another, which also makes it possible to reduce the costs of the other products." (*Bänsch*)

2. Risks and Policies for Avoiding Risks

As a possibility for spreading out results to occur around one expected result, risk is an unavoidable component of economic life and thereby of co-operative reality as well. The management of uncertainty is the endeavour to discover and utilize ways and means of limiting the danger of disadvantages (losses) and of increasing the chance of advantages (profit-earning).

a) Diversification Strategies

→ *Diversification strategies* to avoid undue risks are based on research by *Markowitz* on stock markets: *Markowitz* says that a properly assembled portfolio with various types of stocks – that is, a portfolio with low correlation co-efficients – displays a lower risk of loss under a given expectation of returns than a single type of stock does under the same expectation of returns.

Because of "inborn limitations", the possibilities of co-operatives for strategic diversification are greatly reduced. (However, credit co-operatives can endeavour to achieve optimal branch plurality among their middleclass customers.) The general restictedness is relatively easy to accept, because it is possible to diversify away only an "unsystematic" risk. The far more dangerous "systematic" risk of widespread crises – for example, of crashes on the stock market – still remains.

Through joint institutions co-operatives have been

successful today in making provisions to safeguard their stability. These provisions represent arrangements made once diversification has already taken place (*ex post*). Now, however, co-operatives are turning more and more to preventive measures to protect their economic positions. These measures lead to highly desirable policies for avoiding losses in the first place (*ex ante*).

b) Utilization of Active, Flexible Options

Ever more far-reaching and rapid changes in the fields of competition force co-operative managements today to embrace active, flexible policies with regard to risks. While taking the interests of the members fully into account, management should take up new activities which present themselves, in order to gain competitive advantages. Likewise they should drop or curb current activities if considerable losses are to be expected from them or have even already set in.

A formal aid for making decisions on policies for risk control is the step-by-step decision-making system (*Van Horne*) from occurrence to decision, occurence to decision. Cost-oriented legal instruments for overcoming uncertainties, adapted to the situation on hand, are presented by options on the capital and foreign-exchange markets (*Lipfert*, 1992). The participants in these markets who are interested in optimal security pay *ex ante* a sort of insurance premium for the right to decide *ex post*, when they know about the changes occurring during the term of the option, whether to use their options or whether to let them expire. In this way they purchase flexibility.

In situations of uncertainty, primary co-operatives and central co-operatives do well to think over their member-oriented options and the costs of these options: should, for example, a project consisting of several steps, which has been completely accepted by the members, be continued if the situation has changed greatly? Does the extent of the situational changes justify the loss of the option premiums paid up to that point (meaning abandonment of the investment)? How high should one assess the cost of the option premium consisting of the dissatisfaction of the members if the project should be called off? What is the cost of the option of investing in a limited continuation of the project, in the perhaps justified hope that the original situational conditions will return?

It is an important responsibility of the associations and central offices to give advisory assistance to the primary co-operatives in developing and carrying out active, flexible business and risk policies.

IV. Business Policies in the System in which Co-operatives are Linked Together

In competition strategies, the central function of the system in which co-operatives are linked together consists in compensating or even over-compensating for the gap – caused by the "inborn limitations" of primary co-operatives – in their potential for reducing costs by operating on a larger scale (cf. III.1.a). It is possible, of course, to obtain a closely restricted practical compensation for this gap through co-operative business with non-members. But what is crucial is full compensation through the intensification of the link-up of individual co-operatives at various levels. It is the positive interactional synergy of this system which makes possible the opportunity for over-compensation.

Intensification of the association of individual co-operatives requires that all association members be fully determined to cooperate and make conscious efforts to do so, all the way up from the single member of a primary co-operative to the board of directors in the apex co-operative. The principle of subsidiarity, by which the higher levels in the system assume only those functions which the primary co-operatives cannot fulfill equally cheaply, and the *bottoms-up* principle, by which decisons are made from the bottom to the top, may not be interfered with here (→ *Subsidiarity Principle*). Endo-cannibalism within the system is bad, despite all necessary efforts for success in exo-cannibalism outside the system; and a high degree of deflection to outside interests is to be deplored.

According to the inducement-contribution theory (*Barnard*), for the present or potential participant in the link-up organization to decide to remain in the organization or to become a member – that is, the cooperate with the association – he must subjectively consider the total inducements offered by the organization to be higher than the contributions which he is expected to make (or at least not lower than those contributions) (→ *Incentives*).

V. Policies for Distributing Benefits to Achieve Long-Range Promotion of Members' Interests

A distribution of the benefits of the co-operative system made in such a way as to achieve a long-range promotion of the interests of its members must be based on a dynamic analysis of the system's strengths and weaknesses and must be oriented to the future, kept flexible, and geared to anticipating and preventing difficulties, in order for the distribution to be continually adapted to changing patterns of competition and cooperation and for it to contribute to a dynamic fulfillment of the charge to co-operatives to promote the interests of their members. Misconstrued efforts to maintain continuity and spread out benefits indiscriminately are counter-productive.

Co-operative achievement of optimal, long-term success in the future requires mutual, flexible resistance to vulnerability through vulnerability management of the entire co-operative system, with the goal of making the strong ones in the system even less vulnerable and the weak ones less in danger of damage.

A policy of conscious, partial re-distribution of benefits on and between the various levels of the system should not only not interfere with cooperation within the system, but should further it. The well-directed, rather intensive shift of resources toward providing services and training is in accordance with this condition. The cost of acquiring proven, expert, excellent top personnel as management consultants, for example, is a good distribution of benefits, oriented to the future, if this personnel is unreservedly committed to the basic charge to co-operatives to promote the interests of their members.

Bibliography

Ansoff, H.: Corporate Strategy, (New York 1965), Suffolk 1968.
Bänsch, A.: Operationalisierung des Unternehmenszieles Mitgliederförderung, Göttingen 1983.
Barnard, C.I.: The Functions of the Executive, 14. ed., Cambridge/Mass. 1960.
Blümle, E.-B./Purtschert, R.: Förderungsauftrag, Partizipation und intergenossenschaftliche Kommunikation, ZfgG, vol. 33 (1983), pp. 128–134.
Deutsch, M.: A Theory of Cooperation and Competition, Human Relations, vol. II No. 2, London 1949.
Draheim, G.: Zur Ökonomisierung der Genossenschaften, Göttingen 1967.
Draheim, G.: Aktuelle Grundsatzprobleme des Genossenschaftswesens, Marburg 1972.
Eschenburg, R.: Genossenschaftstheorie als Konflikttheorie. In: Boettcher, E. (ed.): Theorie und Praxis der Kooperation, Tübingen 1972.
Eschenburg, R.: Ökonomische Theorie der genossenschaftlichen Zusammenarbeit, Tübingen 1971.
Henzler, R.: Der genossenschaftliche Grundauftrag: Förderung der Mitglieder, Frankfurt/Main 1970.
Henzler, R.: Die Genossenschaft eine fördernde Betriebswirtschaft, Essen 1957.
Lipfert, H.: Devisenhandel und Devisenoptionshandel, 4. ed., Frankfurt/Main 1992.
Lipfert, H.: Genossenschaftliches Konkurrenz- und Kooperationsmanagement als Forschungsobjekt, Hamburg 1984.
Lipfert, H.: Mitgliederförderndes Kooperations- und Konkurrenzmanagment in genossenschaftlichen Systemen, 2. ed., Göttingen 1988.
Markowitz, H.M.: Portfolio Selection. Efficient Diversification of Investments, New York 1959.
Müller, A.: Das deutsche Genossenschaftswesen, Berlin 1922.
Neumann, M.: Das kapitalistische Element in der modernen Genossenschaft, ZfgG, vol. 25 (1975), pp. 32–40.
Porter, M.E.: Competitive Advantage, Creating and Sustaining Superior Performance, New York, London 1985.
Ringle, G.: Mitgliederaktivierung und Partizipation in modernen Primärgenossenschaften – mit einer Stellungnahme von M. Hill, Mitgliederaktivierung notwendig und möglich, Göttingen 1983.
Van Horne, J.C.: Financial Management and Policy, 4. ed., Englewood Cliffs, N.J. 1977.

By-laws of the Co-operative Society

HARTMUT BECKER [J]

(see also: *Legal Form, Co-operative*; *Law, International*; *Responsibility*; *Principles*; *Co-determination*)

I. Introduction; II. The Legal Nature of the By-laws; III. The Extent of Autonomy in Formulating the By-laws; IV. The English Legal System.

I. Introduction

The by-laws constitute the fundamental law of the co-operative, governing the legal relationship between the co-operative and its members (→ *Promotion Mandate*). The co-operative, however, is not completely free in the formulation and enactment of its by-laws. The opposite is true, rather, as the Co-operative Law exactly prescribes the minimum content for each set of by-laws concerning the formation and termination of a co-operative. The regulation of the legal relationship between the co-operative and its members likewise is not subject to complete co-operative autonomy with respect to the by-laws. According to § 18, Sent.2 of the German Co-operative Law (*GenG, Genossenschaftsgesetz*), only those provisions come under legal consideration for the by-laws which are explicitly permissible through the Co-operative Law.

The following exposition illuminates the importance of the by-laws for the internal organization of a co-operative as well as the role the by-laws play in the English legal system (→ *British-Indian Pattern*).

II. The Legal Nature of the By-laws

The by-laws as an essential component of the co-operative's establishment process express the unanimous volition of all those involved in founding a co-operative; they furthermore define which activities the co-operative will execute and which structure it will have. The by-laws, according to their legal nature, are thus a contract which addresses the formation of the co-operative and the creation of objective legal norms for its corporative organization (*BGHZ*, Bk.13, p.11, Bk.21, p.374 [*Entscheidungen des Bundesgerichtshofes in Zivilsachen*, Decisions of the German Federal Court for Civil Issues]; *Lang/Weidmüller*-[Metz], § 5, margin note [m.n.] 2; *Müller*, § 5, m.n.1 [further sources listed]). Therefore, the general statutes of contract law found in the German Civil Code (*BGB, Bürgerliches Gesetzbuch*) are applicable in order that the by-laws become realized in the first place. In any case, the law of general trading conditions does not effect this "corporate-legal contract" (*AGBG*, Art.23 [*Gesetz zur Regelung des Rechts der*

Allgemeinen Geschäftsbedingungen, Law for the Regulation of the Rights of General Trading Conditions]). Nevertheless, the content of the by-laws is not completely free from every control instance. The principle of good faith (*BGB*, § 242), a legal conception particular to the whole of private law, is also applicable to the co-operative's by-laws (*Schubert/Steder*, § 6, m.n.1).

1. Preconditions for Effectuality

In accordance with *GenG*, § 5, the by-laws must be laid down in written form. *BGB*, § 126 serves as the legal prescription for this required form (*Palandt-Heinrichs*, § 126, Note 1). The entire content of the by-laws must accordingly be set down in *one* written document. This document must be signed by each of the charter members individually. The signature can be signed in blank before the text has been completed. The signatory must accept the text above his signature as his declaration and, thus, the validity of the document even when the text does not correspond to his volition and/or personal conception. If necessary, a contestation grounded on mistake or deception can be filed as long as the findings for such action have been constituted.

2. The Legal Consequences of Confirmed Effectuality

A non-registered co-operative comes into being once the original by-laws have been signed by at least seven charter members. The prescriptions in the Co-operative Law are applicable for this "pre-co-operative" with the exception of those clauses which either are replaced through special stipulations regarding formation or which require legal capacity. Co-operative Law already is in effect fundamentally with respect to both the internal and external relationships. Problems arise primarily concerning the extent of procuration – business activities above and beyond those laid down in the object usually require a special power of attorney – and the extent of each member's liability. In this matter, the particular question is raised whether members' liability for the "pre-co-operative's" outstanding debts should be determined along the foreseen liability regulations of the future co-operative or whether members should be personally liable to an unlimited extent for substantiated debts which arise in the time between the formative stage and the entry of the co-operative into the register (*Lang/Weidmüller*, § 13, m.n.4) (*Register, Co-operative*).

The by-laws, at the same time, are the basis for entry into the co-operative register and thus the necessary precondition for attaining legal capacity. The establishment of the co-operative itself can through its by-laws be made contingent on further persons signing the articles, that is up to the moment of entry. Each subsequent membership up to the registration of the by-laws' entry can only result through further signatures to the by-laws. This belated membership can in dubious situations require the approval of all other charter members inasmuch as an elaboration to contract is undertaken. *GenG*, § 15 is effective from the moment the registration is made.

3. The Fundamentals of Interpreting By-laws

In correspondence with the legal nature of the by-laws as a contract of private law, *BGB*, §§ 133 and 137 should be considered for the interpretation of the statutory explications. However, inasmuch as the by-laws determine the corporative organization of the co-operative and thus have immediate consequences beyond the circle of individuals involved in the legal formation, the by-laws must be interpreted according to the applicable principles used in the interpretation of objective legal norms (*BGHZ* Bk.47, p.180; *Müller*, § 5 m.n.25). First of all, the wording of each clause must be considered for the interpretation. Furthermore, objective aspects, such as the object of the co-operative and the conceptualized view of the professional circles found in the co-operative, must also be taken into consideration. The subjective view of the founders and the history of the by-laws' creation are only of relevant importance inasmuch as they can be recognized and objectively established by those involved (Reichs Court Judgement in 1932, No. 1287). Those clauses in the by-laws which solely determine the relationships of the personal rights between the co-operative and the co-operative members should be interpreted following the principles of contractual interpretation.

As long as the by-laws lack certain provisions, they can be provided through the use of a supplemental interpretation (see *Larenz*, p.286 for supplemental contractual interpretation). This is particularly important when certain clauses of the by-laws are invalid according to *BGB*, §§ 134, 138. Through this manner, the content of a clause in the by-laws can be adapted to the alteration of objective circumstances which was applicable to the clause in question.

4. The Invalidity of Clauses in the By-laws

Clauses in the by-laws are invalid insofar as they violate a legal injunction or are contrary to good morals. This is correspondingly true when by-laws contain contradictory provisions from which the priority of one clause over another cannot be determined. Likewise, a clause does not acquire any legal capacity when its content is so indefinite that this defect cannot be cured even with the help of an interpretation (*Müller*, § 5, m.n.28).

If a clause in a set of by-laws is invalid, the effectuality of the remaining sections of the by-laws remains fundamentally intact (*Müko-Reuter,BGB*, § 25, m.n.13). The provision of *BGB*, § 139 is inapplicable. Eventual gaps are to be filled in through the course of a supplemental interpretation.

The invalidity of a clause can invalidate the by-laws as a whole only in one exceptional situation, namely when the remainder of the by-laws does not guarantee a proper regulation of the co-operative's corporative organization. If the co-operative is entered inspite of this flaw, its legal capacity remains unaffected; the consequence is simply either the disincorporation of the co-operative (*FGG*, § 147, [*Gesetz der freiwilligen Gerichtsbarkeit*, Law of Voluntary Jurisdiction]) or the lodgement of a lawsuit for invalidity (*GenG*, § 94).

5. The Voidableness and Invalidity of the Declaration of Intention Made by Charter Members

a) Prior to the assumption of business transactions and prior to entry into the register

As long as the by-laws have not been entered into the register (→ *Register, Co-operative*) and the co-operative has not commenced its business, a founding member can contest his declaration of intention without any type of restriction in accordance with general laws, thus in accordance with every reason for invalidity listed in the German Civil Code which comes into consideration. He can furthermore demand that entry into the register and the commencement of the co-operative's activities are stopped as long as he remains a founding member.

The invalidity of a founding member's declaration of intention at first has no effect on the declarations of the other founding members, or in other words, the by-laws as such remain legally valid. This is only different when the number of remaining charter members falls below seven due to the invalidation of a declaration of intention. As the contestation follows retroactively, the by-laws should be treated as if they had only been signed by six founding members. Under this aspect, each charter member can affect the invalidation of the establishment and thus also demand that the entry and/or assumption of business activity is stopped (*Müller*, § 5, m.n.32, 33).

b) After the assumption of business activity yet prior to entry into the register

If the co-operative commences business activity before being entered, the laws for the de facto company are to be applied for the effectuality of contestation and invalidity appeals (*Baumbach-Hueck, AktG*, § 23, m.n.2 [*Aktiengesetz*, German Stock Companies' Act]). The invalidity or contestation of the declaration of intentions in connection with the by-laws can accordingly only be effected through the termination of the co-operative (see *Hueck, OHG*, p.82ff.[*die Offene Handelsgesellschaft*, general partnership] for information on de-facto-companies). The principles of the de-facto-company are likewise applicable when a member contests his declaration prior to the activation of the co-operative but, nonetheless, remains a co-operative member after business has been assumed (*Müller*, § m.n.34). In this case, he can terminate his membership. The regulations concerning the de-facto-company are, however, not completely applicable without exception. A member can successfully declare his contestation in the following situations even after business transactions have been commenced:

– through the declaration of a minor or a legally incapacitated individual;
– through the lack of a binding declaration (signature forgery);
– when representation occurs without procuration authority;
– through contestation involving a threat against life and limb.

Inasmuch as the declaration of intention is invalid despite the commencement of business activities, each member and even the co-operative itself can appeal the declaration.

c) After the co-operative has been entered

The co-operative attains legal capacity upon entry into the register. From this moment on, complaints with respect to flaws or deficiencies in the formation process, as a rule, can no longer be lodged. This enjoins general interest and trust in the correctness of a public register. Only those reasons listed in *GenG*, § 94 ff. make a declaration of the co-operative's invalidity possible in the course of adjudication. This, however only leads to the liquidation of the co-operative according to the procedures for its dissolution (*GenG*, § 97 ff.) Only those exceptions come into consideration in which a contestation would take effect after the activation of the co-operative. Even in this situation, the invalidity of a declaration of intention does not affect the existence of the co-operative; however, if less than seven valid declarations of intention remain at hand, the co-operative is to be dissolved in accordance with *GenG*, § 80.

6. Modification of the By-laws

The formality contained in *GenG*, § 5 is not applicable to modifications of the by-laws after entry. In other words, the by-laws need not be signed by all members. The particulars are to be found in *GenG*, § 16.

III. The Extent of Autonomy in Formulating the By-laws

The by-laws are the most important fundament for the legal relationship between the co-operative and its members. Because of this, it must be ensured that certain factors are firmly settled in the by-laws of every co-operative.

The necessary content of the by-laws is established in *GenG*, §§ 6,7 and 36, Sec.1, Sent.2. As long as one of the issues listed in these provisions and in need of being settled is not up to norm, the co-operative must not be entered into the register (*Meyer/Meulenbergh/Beuthien*, § 6, m.n.3). This is likewise so when a necessary point to be settled in the by-laws is formulated in either an unclear or ambiguous manner. However, the provisions mentioned only state that certain points must be settled in the by-laws. The wording of the actual content is widely left to the will of the general assembly, the body entrusted with the formulation of the by-laws. With respect to the by-laws, an extensive autonomy for the co-operative seems to exist.

1. The Importance of GenG, § 18

Primarily the compelling stipulations of the relevant law for each business form must be taken into consideration in order to ascertain the extent of a co-operative enterprise's autonomy with regard to its by-laws. These laws define set limits to the freedom of formulation which the co-operative enterprise must not transgress. Frequently, an interpretation must be undertaken to determine which provision is compelling. This matter is settled for co-operatives in the law itself. *GenG*, § 18 reads as follows:

– "The legal relationship between the co-operative and the co-operative member above all is determined by the by-laws. The latter may only deviate from clauses of this Law insofar as this is expressly stated as permissible."

Thus, the priority relationship between the Law and the by-laws is clearly stated. Even if the wording of Sent.1 at first would possibly imply something else, the absolute precendency of the Law over the by-laws is determined in Sent.2. The systematic arrangement of such regulations contains a simplification insofar as one can directly determine from the provisions whether or not the law is flexible and thus grants leeway for the statutory formulations; this, therefore, also contributes to legal surety. The fundamental deviation injunction found in *GenG*, § 18, however, does not state that the by-laws are restricted to those regulations forseen in the Law, be they of a compelling nature or not, or that the by-laws furthermore may not make any arrangements as they lack a certain legal authority. *GenG*, § 18 rather only prohibits deviations "from the clauses of this Law" as far as no legal sanction exists. Thus, the presupposition always is that the Law itself contains a ruling for the issue in question; only then does the question of a deviation arise. Namely, the Law should prevent the autonomy for the formulation of the by-laws from being used in an undesired manner and not completely eliminate this autonomy. The freedom of a co-operative enterprise concerning the settlement of its own matters is fundamental in this regard (*Feuerborn*, p.85). If one proceeds from the clauses of the Co-operative Law while keeping in mind *GenG*, § 18 and traces their effect on restricting autonomy, one then realizes that the Law comprehensively regulates the legal relationships of a co-operative in many details and thus only permits the by-laws to deviate from the legal provisions in relatively few cases (*Ebert*, p.131; cf. *Müller's* list, § 18, m.n.1b). These cases do not solely concern the external relationships, which likewise are relatively strictly standardized for other company forms because of the effects on third parties as well as for the protection of general legal relations (*Teichmann*, p.1): It is rather the structure of the internal order which is prescribed within large parts of the Law. Thus, the co-operative stands in contrast to other company forms, above all the private limited company, in which the members of the company can decide on the regulation of their internal relationships extensively on their own (cf. *HGB*, § 109 for general partnerships or *HGB*, § 161, Sec.2 or § 163 for limited partnerships [*Handelsgesetzbuch*, German Commercial Code]). For these company forms, the adaptation of the corporate contractual conditions to the individual needs of the company members can assume practically any dimension desired. The co-operative, in contrast, is the legal company form with the least amount of autonomy; whether this type of narrow delimitation of the co-operative's freedom of formative arrangements is still justified today, appears questionable. The actual reasoning for this strict form of the law was seen in that the co-operative was earlier considered an organization of "little people" who were to be protected from their own lack of business knowledge and experience through the help of cogent stipulations (*Paulick*, p.61). In the face of the fundamental change that co-operatives have experienced since then, such historic argumentation hardly still seems appropriate today (*Staufer*, p.44). Lawmakers in part took this into account with the 1973 amendment to the Co-operative Law, partially relaxing such limitations. Although *GenG*, § 18 was kept in its unaltered form and still can be traced back to *Schulze-Delitzsch*, the opportunities to develop structural deviations through the by-laws have been expanded, for example concerning voting rights (*GenG*, § 43, Subsec.3, Sent.3) or the procedures for terminating membership (*GenG*, § 65, Sec.2). Notwithstanding, the Co-operative Law today still limits associational autonomy more than such limitations exist for other company forms (*Feuerborn*, p.87).

2. The Co-operative Principles as a Barrier to the Autonomy of the By-laws

The latitude of the co-operative by-laws is furthermore reduced through the generally recognized co-operative principles (→ *Principles*), such as the provision for equal treatment (*Lang/Weidmüller*-[Metz], § 18, m.n.14), co-operative allegiance (ibid., m.n.42) or the principle of self-administration. Thus, in spite of *GenG*, § 24, Subsec.2, Sent.2, it is not permissible through provisions to the by-laws to entrust a third party with the appointment of board members. This would signify inadmissible intervention into the principle of co-operative self-administration. Likewise, the by-laws could not state that only certain members have title to promotional support ("selection" injunction, see *Meyer/Meulenburgh/Beuthien*, § 18, m.n. 1,8).

IV. The English Legal System

In England, no uniform organizational law for co-operatives exists. The Industrial and Provident Societies Act of 1965–1978 was conceived as a co-operative law, but it nevertheless does not create a co-operative company form. It simply states that an industrial and provident society must either be a "bona fide" co-operative or a company which exclusively acts to benefit the general public (Industrial and Provident Societies Act 1965, Sec. 1 (2), a,b). This means that a co-operative can also be registered in the legal form of a company or limited partnership (*Münkner*, p.105). Organizations with co-operative goal orientation can freely choose between the legal forms provided through British company law above and beyond the Industrial and Provident Societies Act. They must simply adhere to the co-operative principles. The Industrial and Provident Societies Act contains neither a definition of the term "co-operative" nor a thorough description of particular co-operative characteristics; furthermore. it does not set standards for the status, rights, and obligations of the corporate entity comparable to those established in German Co-operative Law. Apparently, it was important to British lawmakers on the one hand to provide co-operative company forms with a set legal structure in order to ensure their economic survival (*Poggemann*, p.25), but on the other hand, to grant them extensive authority in their private sphere and/or autonomy concerning the by-laws (*Ebert*, p.136). The Industrial and Provident Societies Act 1965–1978 accordingly lists only the necessary components of the by-laws, inasmuch corresponding to the regulations in German Co-operative Law. Among other things, the attainment of membership, the structure of the company shares, the procedures for amending the by-laws, etc. are settled. The co-operative itself has a greater amount of leeway with respect to the actual content, as no comparable regulation to *GenG*, § 18 exists. The by-laws must only observe the following legal stipulations: The co-operative must evolve from at least seven charter members; the highest amount of company shares a natural person may have in his possession must not exceed 10,000 pounds; the by-laws must arrange for an annual report to be drawn up and audited. As the makeup of the industrial and provident societies does not immediately result out of the Law (is for German co-operatives the case), the by-laws of these co-operatives have a considerably greater importance: the by-laws, in accordance with their legal nature, form a contract between members and their co-operative. The by-laws must furthermore fulfill the requirements of a "bona fide" co-operative (see *Poggemann*, p.26). The registrar examines the effectuality of the by-laws before the co-operative is entered.

The general regulations found in Company Law are valid for co-operatives which become established in the legal form of a company. The question whether the company is run according to co-operative principles dependens on the appropriate statement of object and purpose found in the by-laws. The co-operative organizational structure of smaller companies (under 20 members) which assume the legal form of a partnership is likewise reserved for the by-laws.

In the end, one can maintain that the by-laws acquire a much more extensive importance for English co-operatives than for those under German Co-operative Law. The relationship between state influence and autonomy with regard to the by-laws is arranged in a completely different way. Whereas *GenG*, § 18 as a result of the quite comprehensive regulation in the Law, sets narrow parameters for the autonomy of the by-laws, much more extensive leeway for such autonomy exists in the English legal system due to the more reserved position of British lawmakers.

Bibliography

Baumbach, Adolf/Hueck, Alfred: Kommentar zum Aktiengesetz, 13th ed., München 1968.

Ebert, Kurt Hanns: Genossenschaftsrecht auf internationaler Ebene, vol. 1, Veröffentlichung des Instituts für das Genossenschaftswesen an der Philipps-Universität Marburg, vol. 33, Marburg 1966.

Feuerborn, Sabine: Die statutarische Mitgliederbindung aus genossenschaftsrechtlicher Sicht, Schriften zur Kooperationsforschung des Instituts für Genossenschaftswesen an der Universität Münster, vol.7, 1978.

Hueck, Alfred: Das Recht der offenen Handelsgesellschaft, 4th ed., München 1971.

Lang, Johann/Weidmüller, Ludwig: Genossenschaftsgesetz, 32nd ed., Berlin, New York 1979.

Larenz, Karl: Methodenlehre der Rechtswissenschaft, 4th ed., Berlin, New York 1979.

Meyer, E.H./Meulenbergh, Gottfried/Beuthien Volker: Kommentar zum Genossenschaftsgesetz, 12th ed., München 1983 (with supplement 1986).

Müller, Klaus: Kommentar zum Gesetz betreffend die Erwerbs- und Wirtschaftsgenossenschaften, vol.1, 2nd ed., Bielefeld 1991.

Münchner Kommentar zum Bürgerlichen Gesetzbuch, vol.1, Allgemeiner Teil, 2nd ed., München 1984.

Münkner, Hans Hermann: Selbstverständnis und Rechtsverfassung von Genossenschaftsorganisationen in EG-Partnerstaaten, in: Die Genossenschaft im Wettbewerb der Ideen, Bericht der XI. Internationalen genossenschaftswissenschaftlichen Tagung in Münster, Tübingen 1985.

Palandt, Otto: Bürgerliches Gesetzbuch, 51st ed., München 1992.

Paulick, Heinz: Das Recht der eingetragenen Genossenschaft, Quellen und Studien des Instituts für Genossenschaftswesen an der Universität Münster, Karlsruhe 1956.

Poggemann, Klaus: Genossenschaften in England, Kooperations- und Genossenwissenschaftliche Beiträge des Instituts für Genossenschaftswesen der Westfälischen Wilhelms-Universität Münster, vol.25, 1990.

Schubert, Rolf/Steder, Karl Heinz: Genossenschaftshandbuch, vol.II, Berlin 1973.

Southern, Robert: Das Genossenschaftsrecht Großbritanniens, in: ZfG (vol.IV) 1954/183.

Staufer, Wolfgang: Die Beschränkung der statuarischen Autonomie durch das Genossenschaftsgesetz, Schriften zur Kooperationsforschung, C. Berichte, vol.3, Tübingen 1971.

Teichmann, Arndt: Gestaltungsfreiheit in Gesellschaftsverträgen, München 1970.

Central Co-operative Institutions

GUNTHER ASCHHOFF AND ECKART HENNINGSEN

(see also: *Federations*; *Co-operative Banks*; *International Co-operative Organizations*)

I. Introduction and Definition; II. Central Institutions for Co-operative Banks in Selected Countries; III. A Comparison; IV. International Cooperation of Central Institutions; V. Bibliography.

I. Introduction and Definition

After the successful introduction of (primary) co-operatives in their countries, virtually all the founders of co-operatives concurred in working to found joint entities which would be in the position to take care of certain interests shared by all the co-operatives concerned. In Germany, this holds true for the founder of commercial co-operatives and banks, → *Hermann Schulze-Delitzsch* (1808 to 1883), as well as the founders of the rural trading co-operatives and banks, → *Friedrich Wilhelm Raiffeisen* (1818 to 1888) and → *Wilhelm Haas* (1839 to 1913). It is also true for the initiators of → *consumer co-operatives*, → *Eduard Pfeiffer* (1835 to 1921) and → *Heinrich Kaufmann* (1864 to 1928).

The economic interests of co-operatives as the members of these joint entities may be of two different kinds, as a rule: They may relate to auditing, auxiliary operating services and representing their interests to the outside world, or they may relate to markets. In the first case we speak of federations, in the second of central co-operatives.

The geographical scope in which these joint entities operate may also differ. If it comprises only one region, then we speak of regional → *federations* or regional central co-operatives. If it relates to the whole national economy, then we speak of national federations or national central co-operatives. Since these are the apex institutions of the respective organization, national federations are called central federations, national central co-operatives also central institutions.

Confining ourselves to the banking sector (→ *Co-operative Banks*), in what follows, we want to examine the structure of co-operative central banks in selected countries around the world. We will be using the terms "regional (central) bank" and "(national) central institution".

II. Central Institutions for Co-operative Banks in Selected Countries

Belgium
396 local banks (Raiffeisenbanks, Caisses Rurales)
425,000 members
Central institution: CERA Centrale Raiffeisenkas, Louvain (founded in 1895)

The central institution of the Belgian banking co-operatives is the CERA. Its members include, in particular, the rural merchandise and service co-operatives, as well as the co-operative banks. It is the liquidity manager for the related local banks and acts as their clearing center. CERA provides services in foreign business and in securities trading. Belgian law treats CERA and the co-operative banks as one unit: Although the local banks are legally independent, the regulations regarding minimum capital, the presentation of balance sheets and the balance sheet structure coefficients need not be met by each bank individually but only by the group as a whole. Consequently, the local banks are subject to CERA instructions, supervision and coordination. CERA also performs all the functions of a federation: It performs the annual audit of the local banks, advises them in legal and business matters, and organizes the training of local employees. CERA and the local banks mutually guarantee for incurred obligations.

In neighboring **Luxembourg**, the central institution of the 47 co-operative banks is the Caisse Centrale Raiffeisen, Luxembourg, founded in 1926.

Federal Republic of Germany
3,400 local banks (Volksbanks, Raiffeisenbanks)
11.5 million members
3 regional banks
Central institution: DG BANK Deutsche Genossenschaftsbank, Frankfurt am Main (founded in 1895)

The German Volksbanks (people's banks) and Raiffeisenbanks today belong to one banking system. It also includes three regional banks and the DG BANK as its central institution. More than half of the local co-operative banks operate directly with DG BANK.

The shareholders in the regional banks are for the most part the Volksbanks (people's banks) and Raiffeisenbanks in the respective region. The regional banks serve them as the centers for depositing their surplus liquidity and for refinancing. Furthermore, they are the clearing centers for the settlement of noncash payments (supraregional settlements are performed by DG BANK). Lending transactions with local customers are supported by the regional banks by way of syndicated loans. In the securities business and in commercial transactions abroad, the Volksbanks and Raiffeisenbanks can also rely on the services provided by the regional banks.

The central institution here is DG BANK. It is a corporation under public law, and the task of promoting the entire German co-operative movement is imposed on it by law. A good 90% of its capital is held by the regional banks and other co-operative institutions. The primary task of DG BANK has always been to provide liquidity for – or absorb liquidity from – the co-operative banks. It invests the surplus liquidity of the system in the money and capital markets both in Gemany and abroad. In the other direction it provides refinancing, especially long-term funds which it raises by issuing bonds.

The co-operative organization has issued liquidity rules laying down what minimum percentage of its liabilities a co-operative bank must maintain with its regional banks and, directly or indirectly, with DG BANK.

The lending business of the regional banks and the local co-operative banks is promoted by DG BANK as a syndicate partner. DG BANK is also the "house bank" of the federal centers of the commercial co-operatives. Moreover, it deals directly with borrowers in Germany and abroad which are too big for co-operative banks at the local or regional levels.

The securities business of the co-operative banks is promoted by DG BANK through its activities in domestic and international stock and bond syndicates, and through comprehensive services provided by its investment consultants, plus the contribution made to training securities investment specialists.

To promote the foreign business of the Volksbanks and Raiffeisenbanks, DG BANK makes international financing, investment and hedging facilities available. It also provides services in all sectors of commercial business abroad as well as information, advisory and referral services. Its foreign bases at all major financial and commercial centers are accessible to the Volksbanks and Raiffeisenbanks and their customers.

Finally, DG BANK provides specialized financial services such as mortgage loans, home building loans, leasing, factoring, mutual fund certificates, equity participations and insurance services through subsidiaries or affiliated companies.

Finland

360 local banks
654,000 members
Central institution: OKOBANK, Helsinki (founded in 1902)

OKOBANK is virtually fully owned by the Finnish co-operative banks. Its first and foremost task is to act as liquidity manager for the local banks. It raises liquidity on the national and international money and capital markets, and invests any surplus liquidity there. The fact that co-operative local banks must deposit 12% of their customers' deposits with OKOBANK makes for a particularly close liquidity link between the local level and OKOBANK.

Moreover, OKOBANK is the center for payment transactions of the co-operative banks and the clearing center for settling payments between the co-operative banks themselves. It has an important function in the syndicating business, which it performs together with the co-operative banks. OKOBANK does business directly with large corporations which are not customers of the local co-operative banks. It offers the entire range of services provided by a "universal" type of bank. In Helsinki it operates also as a local bank.

The foreign business of the co-operative banks is handled exclusively by OKOBANK which maintains bases at all major international financial centers. Its position as central institution is emphasized by the fact that it has direct business contact with the Bank of Finland, whereas the local co-operative banks do not.

In neighboring **Sweden**, FB Banken Föreningsbankernas Bank, Stockholm, has been the central institution for the 383 co-operative banks and their regional banks since 1958. In **Denmark**, the central institution for 48 co-operative banks is Danske Andelskassers Bank, Hammershoj, founded in 1969.

France

a) Crédit Agricole
3,056 local banks
5 million members
92 regional banks
Central institution: Caisse Nationale de Crédit Agricole (CNCA), Paris (founded in 1920)

Crédit Agricole is a network of local co-operative banks, regional banks and CNCA. The regional banks, owned by the local banks, assist their banks in their business. At the regional level, the primary task is the implementation of Crédit Agricole's information technology innovations. The regional banks also do direct business with corporate and private customers. However, short-term loans are the only loans that they may grant autonomously; as to medium and long-term loans, they need the consent of CNCA.

In 1988, CNCA was converted from a public law corporation to a joint stock company with the regional co-operative banks holding 90% of the capital. CNCA has a dominant function within Crédit Agricole. It manages all the savings deposits with the group. Of the Crédit Agricole banks, the CNCA is the only one which is authorized to transact foreign business. It also has extensive rights to supervise, audit and check the regional banks.

b) Crédit Mutuel
3,000 local banks
4.4 million members
21 regional banks
Central institution: Caisse Centrale du Crédit Mutuel (CCCM), Paris (founded in 1963)

The Crédit Mutuel local banks have set up regional banks and a central institution. These three levels constitute a close-knit liquidity system: The local banks are obliged to keep 50% of their deposits with the respective regional bank (Banque Fédérative), which, in turn, forwards 2% of its deposits to the CCCM. The regional banks' primary tasks are to manage liquidity, to handle payment transactions and to coordinate the development of technological equipment.

The primary task of the central institution, whose capital is held by the regional banks, is to promote the expansion of Crédit Mutuel in France. Furthermore, it serves as a clearing bank for the regional banks. The CCCM manages the reserve and equity capital of the group. The CCCM does not operate internationally. Foreign business is performed by Crédit Mutuel through the group's regional banks, mainly Banque Fédérative du Crédit Mutuel, Strasbourg.

c) Banques Populaires
31 regional banks
2.9 million members
Central institution: Caisse Centrale des Banques Populaires (CCBP), Paris (founded in 1920)
The central institution of the Banques Populaires, the co-operative banks of the sector of small and medium-sized enterprises, is the CCBP. Its capital is held almost exclusively by the Banques Populaires. Its primary task is the liquidity management for the Banques Populaires which operate as regional banking institutions but are also represented at the local level.

The CCBP is the central clearing bank of the Banques Populaires and provides the information technology network for the group. In foreign business, it coordinates the activities of the Banques Populaires and represents these in the international financial centers, partly through bases of its own.

Italy
a) Rural sector
728 local banks (Raiffeisenbanks, Casse Rurali)
300,000 members
2 regional banks
Central institution: Istituto di Credito delle Casse Rurali ed Artigiane (ICCREA), Rome (founded in 1963)
Unlike the co-operative banks in other Italian regions, the Raiffeisenbanks in Trentino-Alto Adige have established regional banks; their shares are held by the rural co-operatives as well as by the Raiffeisenbanks. Their main function is to manage the liquidity for the local level. They also conduct foreign business for the smaller Raiffeisenbanks.

The central institution is ICCREA. Its capital is held by all the local co-operative banks. It acts first and foremost as a refinancing and depository bank for these banks. ICCREA deals in securities to a limited extent. It advises on and provides technical assistance for the local banks. Moreover, ICCREA provides international correspondent banking relations for the local banks, offers data processing services and manages the central guarantee fund.

b) Commercial sector
114 local banks (Banche Popolari)
1.5 million members
Central institution: Istituto Centrale delle Banche Popolari Italiane, Rome/Milan (founded in 1939)
The central institution of Italy's nonrural co-operative banks is the Istituto Centrale delle Banche Popolari Italiane, Rome/Milan. Its shareholders are the co-operative banks it serves. Its importance as central institution is mainly based on its activities as a giro and cheque-clearing center. For the smaller co-operative banks, it also serves as liquidity manager and by handling their foreign business. The central institution is not engaged in lending to nonbank clients.

Japan
a) Rural sector
5,400 local banks
5.3 million members
82 regional credit federations
Central institution: Norinchukin Bank, Tokyo (founded in 1923)
In Japan, co-operative agricultural lending is performed by agricultural co-operatives and fishing co-operatives with banking departments. At the prefecture level the co-operatives have formed credit federations, whose task is liquidity management. The central institution shared by all agricultural co-operatives, fishing co-operatives and also the forestry co-operatives (which, however, do no banking business of their own) is the Norinchukin Bank. Its capital is held exclusively by these co-operatives.

As the group's liquidity manager, Norinchukin Bank is one of the mainstays of the Japanese money and capital market. The local co-operative banks are obliged to pass on at least two thirds of their surplus liquidity to the credit federations, and these have to deposit half of their own surplus liquidity with Norinchukin Bank. Norinchukin Bank's services concentrate on interregional payments and the collection of payments for the member co-operatives. It is active abroad through bases of its own in important international financial centers.

b) Commercial sector
924 local banks (credit unions, Shinkin Banks)
9.7 million members
Central institutions: National Federation of Credit Co-operatives, Tokyo; National Federation of Credit Associations (The Zenshinren Bank), Tokyo (founded in 1950)
Financial services for small and medium-sized enterprises outside agriculture are provided by two co-operative organizations: The credit co-operatives (credit unions) and the credit associations (Shinkin Banks). The central institution of the credit co-

operatives is the National Federation of Credit Co-operatives. Its primary tasks are liquidity management and forwarding government funds at preferential interest rates for the promotion of small enterprises.

The central institution of the Shinkin Banks, the Zenshinren Bank, also acts as liquidity manager. In addition, it engages in all customary banking activities, grants syndicated loans together with its member institutions, does business abroad, provides electronic banking services and manages a joint guarantee and assistance fund. The capital is held by the Shinkin Banks.

The Netherlands
882 local banks (Rabobanks)
760,000 members
Central institution: Rabobank Nederland, Utrecht (founded in 1898)
Rabobank Nederland is both the central bank and the federation. Its sole shareholders are the local Rabobanks. In its function as a central bank, Rabobank Nederland acts first and foremost as a liquidity manager. The liquidity system is particularly closely-knit: Every Rabobank has undertaken to place 25% of its deposits with the Rabobank Nederland, and excess liquidity must be deposited entirely with the central institution. To fulfill its liquidity management functions, Rabobank Nederland is active in the domestic and international money and capital markets.

It performs central functions for its local banks also in the management of domestic and international payment transactions and securities trading. It also performs all foreign transactions on behalf of the local banks. In its lending business, Rabobank Nederland grants syndicated loans together with local Rabobanks, but it also serves its own direct customers amongst the co-operatives, large corporations and public authorities.

The central bank of the Netherlands has granted Rabobank Nederland the right to audit and supervise the local banks connected with it. The local banks, for their part, have undertaken to adhere to the guidelines and regulations issued by Rabobank Nederland in order to coordinate joint developments and activities. There is a mutual guarantee system linking the local banks and the central institution. As far as the liquidity rules are concerned, the Dutch central bank treats the Rabobank organization as one unit. Consequently, the local Rabobanks are not required to comply with the liquidity regulations separately; it suffices if the Rabobank Nederland does so on behalf of the entire organization.

Austria
a) Rural sector
851 local banks (Raiffeisenbanks)
1.6 million members
9 regional banks

Central institution: Raiffeisen Zentralbank Österreich (RZB), Vienna (founded in 1927)
The Raiffeisenbanks together with their regional banks and the RZB form a three-level system. The regional banks at the "Land" (state) level are partly banks and partly departments of the regional federations. Their capital is held by the local Raiffeisenbanks and other Raiffeisen co-operatives. Their task lies essentially in liquidity management for the Raiffeisenbanks and in providing credit for the rural merchandise co-operatives.

The RZB as the central institution has corresponding tasks. Its capital is held by the regional banks and the central enterprises of the rural merchandise co-operatives. It serves the regional banks primarily as a liquidity manager, operating in the money and capital markets at home and abroad, also through international bases of its own. Under the provision of Austrian banking legislation (Kreditwesengesetz) regulating liquidity reserves, the various Raiffeisenbanks must deposit a certain portion of their liabilities with their central institution, and this strengthens the position of the RZB as the liquidity center. The RZB supports the regional banks in their lending business by way of syndicated loans, but also makes its own loans to the central Raiffeisen merchandise enterprises and other large customers.

b) Commercial sector
103 local banks (Volksbanks)
650,000 members
Central institution: Österreichische Volksbanken AG (ÖVAG), Vienna (founded in 1922)
The ÖVAG is the central institution of the Austrian Volksbanks. According to its charter, its task is to promote the interests of these banks and small and medium-sized businesses. Its fields of activities are liquidity management, the provision of syndicated loans and services (remittances, clearing, foreign business) for the Volksbanks. Under the provisions of Austrian banking legislation (Kreditwesengesetz) regulating liquidity reserves, the various Volksbanks are obliged to deposit a certain portion of their liabilities with the ÖVAG. The ÖVAG holds a stake in various specialized institutions providing insurance, home building loans, leasing and other financial services. As a commercial bank, it also does business of its own with direct customers.

In neighboring **Switzerland**, the central institution of the 1,216 co-operative banks is the Schweizer Verband der Raiffeisenkassen (Swiss Federation of Raiffeisenbanks), St. Gallen, founded in 1902, with its banking department.

Spain
115 local and provincial banks (Cajas Rurales)
865,000 members
Central institution: Banco Cooperativo Español, Madrid (founded in 1990)

With a few exceptions, the co-operative banks in Spain are rurally. They operate in villages or in the form of provincial banks. Their central institution is the Banco Cooperativo Español. Of its capital, 85% is held by the Cajas Rurales and 15% by DG BANK Deutsche Genossenschaftsbank, Frankfurt am Main, one of its founders.

The Banco Cooperativo Español operates as liquidity manager for the co-operative banks in the domestic and international financial markets. It is required to strengthen the range of services offered by the Cajas Rurales and to promote basic and advanced training of their personnel. Furthermore, the Banco Cooperativo Español is authorized to conduct all kinds of business characteristic of a universal bank.

In neighboring **Portugal**, the corresponding activities are performed by the Caixa Central de Crédito Agricola Mutuo, Lisbon, founded in 1984 as the central institution of the country's presently 220 co-operative banks.

USA

15,144 local banks (credit unions)
60.4 million members
42 regional banks (corporate credit unions)
Central institution: U.S. Central Credit Union, Overland Park, Kansas (founded in 1974)

Most local credit unions in the United States belong to one of the regional corporate credit unions which operate at the state level, acting first and foremost as liquidity managers, but also conducting a lending business of their own, mainly with private individuals.

The corporate credit unions hold the capital of the central institution which performs key functions for them, in particular in liquidity management, handling payments, securities trading and data processing. Together with the regional corporate credit unions, the U.S. Central Credit Union constitutes the corporate Credit Union Network. Since most "corporates" deposit their liquidity surpluses almost entirely with the U.S. Central, the liquidity system is very closely-knit.

In neighboring **Canada**, the Caisse Centrale Desjardins, Quebec, founded in 1978, serves as the central institution for the 1,500 Caisses Populaires, while the Canadian Co-operative Credit Society, Toronto, founded in 1953, is the central institution for the 1,300 credit unions and their regional banks.

III. A Comparison

Central institutions for co-operative banks have been in existence since the end of the nineteenth century (→*History in 19th C.*). As was the case at the local level, the foundation of central institutions started in Germany: DG BANK (through its first predecessor, the Preussische Central-Genossenschaftskasse) (→ *Co-operative Banks*) and Belgium's CERA are the central institutions with the oldest tradition – both were founded in 1895. Rabobank Nederland is only three years younger. The Finnish and the Swiss central institutions were founded shortly after the turn of the century (1902).

The worldwide development of co-operative banking accelerated markedly after World War I: Central institutions were founded in France (CNCA, CCBP), Austria (ÖVAG, RZB) and Luxembourg, as well as in Japan (Norinchukin Bank). In 1935, the central institution of co-operative banks was founded in India, four years later the central institution of the Italian Banche Popolari. Of those founded after World War II, the central banks in Canada and in the USA should be given a special mention. The most recent foundations are those of the central institutions in Portugal (1984) and Spain (1990).

Most central institutions are part of banking systems formally comprising two levels. In large countries there are three-level (USA; Canada), or even four-level (India) systems. In countries where there are separate co-operative organizations for rural and nonrural/commercial banks, as in France, Italy, Austria and Japan, the rural (Raiffeisen) sector is usually organized in a three-level, the commercial sector in a two-level structure; in Italy, however, a three-level rural banking sector exists only in part of the country.

The same applies to Germany. Although its rural and nonrural co-operative banks do not belong to separate organizations but to the same system, only part of this system is still organized in a three-level structure. The number of regional central banks has declined (→ *Structural Changes*) substantially in recent years, so that more than half of all German co-operative banks are directly linked with the central institution, DG BANK.

Since in most countries there is only one co-operative banking organization there is also only one central co-operative institution. In France, Italy, Austria and Japan separate organizations exist for rural and for commercial co-operative banks, each with its own central institution. In these countries, unlike Germany, no mergers of the two organizations have yet taken place. The same applies to Canada, where the existence of two different linguistic population groups led to two separate co-operative banking organizations, the Caisses Populaires and the Credit Unions.

Since DG BANK is required by law to promote the entire co-operative system in Germany, its shareholders include merchandise and service co-operatives as well as the co-operative banks, their regional banks and regional co-operative holding companies. No other apex banking institution has a range of tasks at the national level as wide as has the DG BANK. While in other countries there are also central institutions in which nonbank co-operative institutions as well as banks are holding shares, nowhere but in Germany does the ownership of the central co-operative bank represent the entire co-operative system. Most central co-operative institutions concentrate their work on promoting the co-operative banks belonging to their organizations.

In some countries, the central institutions perform both banking and federation activities for their member banks. In these cases, the functions of the co-operative central bank also include supervising and → *auditing*, advising and coordinating, training and developing personnel (→ *Education, Germany* etc.), administration of the deposit guarantee fund, and so on. In most cases, however, the central institutions only do banking business, with liquidity management as the dominant task everywhere. This function is often supported by statutory or internal regulations stipulating that a certain percentage of the local banks' client deposits be placed with the central institution. Other important tasks performed by central institutions are payment transactions and clearing. Areas of growing importance are electronic banking, securities trading, and foreign business.

IV. International Cooperation of Central Institutions

Central institutions have been co-operating internationally for quite some time in various ways. One level of co-operation is represented by the international federations, namely ICA (International Co-operative Alliance), WOCCU (World Council of Credit Unions), CICA (Confédération Internationale du Crédit Agricole), CICP (Confédération Internationale du Crédit Populaire), IRU (Internationale Raiffeisen-Union), and the Association of Co-operative Banks of the EC (→ *European Community*).

Another level consists of business co-operations. For instance, there are agreements relating to the joint development and marketing of bank products (→ *Co-operative Banks*). International co-operation is also reflected by equity capital investments; thus, DG BANK holds shares in the U.S. Central Credit Union, the Canadian Co-operative Credit Society, the Österreichische Volksbanken AG, and the Banco Cooperativo Español, partly indirectly and together with other central institutions. Finally, cooperation is also reflected in numerous international → *Joint Ventures*.

International co-operation has gained particulary great importance in the form of the UNICO Banking Group (→ *European Cooperation of Co-operative Central Banks*).

V. Bibliography

Aschhoff, Gunther: Genossenschaften, Stellung in der Gesamtwirtschaft. Handwörterbuch des Genossenschaftswesens, Wiesbaden 1980, cols. 687–713.
Aschhoff, Gunther/Henningsen, Eckart: The German Co-operative System. Its History, Structure and Strength, Frankfurt am Main 1986.
Die japanischen Volksbanken, in: Die gewerbliche Genossenschaft, no.1/2 (1981), pp.1259–1261.
Engelhardt, Werner Wilhelm: Genossenschaften II: Geschichte. Handwörterbuch der Wirtschaftswissenschaft, Stuttgart, New York, Tübingen, Göttingen, Zürich 1988, III, pp.557–571.
Genossenschaftsbanken in Europa, in: Zeitschrift für das gesamte Kreditwesen, no.10 (1984), pp.441–467.
Guthardt, Helmut: The structure and operational mode of the co-operative bank organizations in West European and North American Countries, in: Co-operatives in the clash between member participation, organizational development and bureaucratic tendencies, London 1985, pp.169–183.
Moody, J. Carroll/File, Gilbert C.: The Credit Union Movement and ed., Madison (Wisconsin) 1983.
The Central Union of Agricultural Co-operatives (ed.), Agricultural co-operative Movement in Japan, Tokyo 1985.
Usui, T.: A Comparison of Agricultural Credit Co-operative Systems and Functions in France, Federal Republic of Germany and Japan, London 1982.

China, Actual Co-operative Development in

CORINNA HANA

(see also: *History of Ideas*; *Development, South Asia*; *Development, South-East Asia*; *Rural Peoples Communes*; *Socialist Co-operative Theory*)

I. History; II. Co-operative Development in the Post Mao Era.

I. History

1. Republic

a) Development

The first (consumers') co-operative in China was established at Beijing University in July 1918. But Chinese intellectuals had come across Western co-operative ideas since the beginning of this century. *Xue Xianzhou* (1871–1927), glorified as the father of Chinese co-operatism, in 1901 had left for the United States. 1905–1911 he stayed in Germany and studied at the University of Berlin. Deeply impressed by the German co-operative development he, after his return to China, propagated co-operatism as the most valid solution for the economic and social problems of China's common people (pingmin). With the foundation of the first co-operative bank (1919) and the constitution of the Pingmin Study Society (May 1920), both in Shanghai, *Xue* initiated China's first co-operative movement. Main platform for the dissemination of the new ideas was the society's weekly

Pingmin Zhoukan. Although the movement began to politicalize in 1924 by forming a coalition with the then strongest political force, the Guomindang (Nationalist Party, GMD), it remained only marginal until its renaissance with the establishment of the Nanjing Government in 1928.

Another early co-operative movement started from Beijing in 1921 and was initiated by the China International Famine Relief Comission. It, too, referred to the Raiffeisen model of rural credit co-operatives but was seen as something imported from outside and never accepted as a true Chinese movement. All the more since it openly supported a government which was heavily attacked by Chinese reformers and revolutionaries. In 1936/7 the supervision over these co-operatives was formally handed over to the GMD government.

b) Legislation

Dai Jitao (1891–1949), a leading GMD theoretician, has been attracted to co-operative ideas since he had studied in Japan 1905–1909. In Nov. 1921 he published his draft of a co-operative law for Guangdong province in the most influential periodical New Youth (Xin Qingnian). The two main sources Dai referred to were the Japanese law for industrial co-operatives of 1900 (which in turn was based on German legislation) and the Russian law issued in March 1917. As in many other cases civil war, here too, stopped any further development before the Nanjing era. Only in 1935 (Sept.1) a national co-operative law together with a model bye-law was issued, after a series of regional and national drafting and provisional legislation.

c) Efficiency

Following the official installation of co-operative policy, a flood of enthusiastic literature poured down on the Chinese people propagating co-operative economy as the true means for the realization of Sun Yixian's third (economic) principle, the principle of levelihood. → *Rural Co-operatives* starting with only about 580 in 1928, mushroomed during the 1930s. But the expected success did not appear. Many of the nearly 47,000 co-operatives in 1937 may well have been nothing more than a bureaucratic file. Imposed on rural socio-economic life and dominated by the rural elite (gentry) the co-operatives had hardly any beneficial effects on the common farmers and did not bring about the necessary change in the traditional ruinous practice of money-lending. Although approximately three-fourths of the co-operatives performed credit functions, their credits in most cases only reached the rich rural elite, a fact which reveils that GMD politics during the Nanjing era did not aim at a fundamental reform of the socio-political relationships in the countryside. One gets the impression that the term *co-operatism* (hezuozhuyi) was a welcome propaganda slogan against *capitalism* (zibenzhuyi) and, most of all, *Communism* (gongchanzhuyi).

2. The People's Republic before 1978

The development of a socialist model of co-operatives in China roots in the early 1920s (→ *Socialist Co-operative Theory*). When the Communists took over political power in 1949 they expanded over the whole country a system they had already experienced in those areas which they had "liberated" and which functioned as their strategic bases (→ *State and Co-operatives, Socialism*). Aiming at the final elimination of private landownership the new rulers – after the land reform law had come into force in June 1950 – began in 1952 to first organize the Chinese farmers into *mutual aid teams* and then gradually to proceed from *lower* to *advanced agricultural producers' co-operatives*. This development finally led to the great leap forward and the establishment of *the people's communes* (remin gongshe) (→ *Rural Peoples Communes*).

II. Co-operative Development in the Post Mao Era

1. Co-operatives in the Context of Economic Reforms since 1978

a) The first stage 1978–1984/5

December 1978 marks the turning point in China's economic policies. Now reforms and the opening up to the outside world were issued as the new political guidelines. The reforms since then can be divided into two major stages. The first one was primarily concerned with the abolition of egalitarianism (the iron rice bowl) and the disintegration of the → *people's communes* through the introduction of new profit oriented economic entities, fostering individual initiative and the principle of competitive advantage. Among them the most important elements are the *rural households* and the *village and township enterprises* (xiangzhen qiye, TVEs). One of the most stimulating and dynamic innovations was the *family contract responsibility system* (chengbao system). It allows the farmers to operate privately and on their own risk after having fulfilled the contracted quota. The formal owner of the collective land property confines himself to activities a single farmer cannot achieve by himself. Although the chengbao system constitutes such a crucial element in the rural reform process there exists only a very general legal basis for it which, moreover, has been provided years after the reforms had begun (1986, general rules of civil law §§ 27–29, 80, 81). One of the milestones was the legal return of private as well as co-operative enterprises in 1982/3. The Chinese Constitution of Dec. 1982 sets in article 8 the decisive course that any kind of co-operatives belong to the socialist economy of collective property, which means that co-operatives are collective economic organizations. In addition, article 10 of the constitution says that in rural areas land now is defined as collective property while in the cities it remains State property.

b) The second stage since 1985

The second stage in its first phase began around 1985 and was designed to pave the way for all kinds of rural economic organizations to enter into commodity economy. Land system building and the system of social services (technology, funds, sales and transportation for rural households) constituted the central topics of economic politics for the rural areas. In order to keep up with these manifold new tasks *rural reform experimental zones* (at present 26) were installed in 1987. Here, with pilot projects and in a concentrated way, five reform programs were and still are to be explored: Land building system, grain purchasing and sales system reform, TVEs development, co-operative economic organization building and rural financial reform. Among them the most outstanding reforms concern the TVEs' *share-holding co-operative system* and the *rural co-operative (credit) foundations*. A third very important but still only partly and not adequately resolved project constitutes the issue of *legal standardization*, also for co-operative organizations.

Meanwhile, since the end of 1991, and vehemently in 1992, reforms have reached the second phase of stage two, a development closely connected with the 14th Party Congress and the clear decision for a market economy. To many reformers' opinion the most necessary target for China should be the transition from an agrarian society into an industrial one. Similar to the revolution of 1949 the point of departure for the economic reforms has to be the countryside. Thus, it is argued, the 1990s must be dominated by reforms in Middle and West China. Share-holding co-operative organizations are seen as most important means to pave the way towards this goal.

2. Co-operative Economy (hezuo jingji)

a) Introduction

Since 1985 a flood of articles on co-operative economy for China appeared in the relevant journals and periodicals. Irrespective to other details in their content they all make obvious that this new development has 1) to distinguish itself very clearly from the former people's communes' centralized system and 2) to do everything to make the term *co-operative* (hezuoshe) psychologically again acceptable. One should keep in mind that in the area of co-operative economy basically everything is still in the experimental phase. As long as this phase has not come to a satisfying result a thorough legislation cannot be expected. So far co-operative organizations of all kinds are classified as a special brand of collective economy. Since collective enterprises enjoy many advantages over private ones there is a strong tendency towards even forcibly subsuming one's enterprise to the co-operative category. Critical scholars point out that quite a few have put on a "red (socialist) cap" where they should rather wear a white one.

b) Legislation (→ Law, International)

Despite the lively and divers co-operative acitivities a national co-operative law is still lacking. The only legislation extant on a national basis are the *provisonal regulations for rural share-holding co-operative enterprises*, issued by the Ministry of Agriculture Feb.12, 1990 (provisional regulation). These regulations go back to those developed in Wenzhou experimental zone in Nov. 1987 which in turn have borrowed from similar regulations for Sichuan province of Dec. 1986. It is a common feature in Chinese legislation that a law or regulations in fact are nothing but the final act that sanctions a long development of experimental practice. This is also true for the *rural share-holding co-operative enterprises* (SCEs), and still, the now existing provisional regulations are only issued on ministry level. In addition to the provisional regulations there exist regional plans for co-operative legislation for communal and specialized co-operatives like in Hebei, Fujian, Guangdong and Sichuan provinces. Drafts are already worked out. It is argued that one should rather, as a first step, concentrate on rules which meet the concrete regional demands than waist any more time waiting for a national law. The rural co-operative (credit) funds sofar are only provided with a governmental circular dealing with problems of more standardization and systematization issued December 1991.

c) Literature and sources

Western literature about actual co-operative development is poor. For the Chinese sources in addition to published material we have drawn on unpublished papers, bye-laws and drafts as well as on interviews. Informations, data and figures, acquirable only like mosaic pieces and poorly co-ordinated want to be treated with caution. To put them together to an overall picture is difficult and debatable. Stages of development differ extremely from one province to another. Some new forms, though important, are not found worthy for statistics (example: specialized co-operatives in Sichuan). Moreover, the mere existence of (provisional) legal prescriptions does not in the least guarantee an adequate translation into practice. Still another problem turns up with regard to terminology which has not yet found a reliable standardization. Thus, when introducing the different kinds of co-operative economic organizations in

China the aim can only be to show fundamental tendencies in recent development and at times, illustrate them with individual cases.

3. New Developments

a) Introduction

The co-operative scene one meets at present in China is rather complex: There still exist those co-operatives which can be classified as "traditional" or "classical" because they have been in operation in the People's Republic of China since the early 1950s: The *supply and marketing co-operatives* (gongxiao hezuoshe), the *industrial co-operatives* (gongye hezuoshe) or the *credit co-operatives* (xinyong hezuoshe). In the course of collectivization after 1956, these co-operatives have lost their independence and merged with the people's communes. Until today they could not get rid of the odour of being a State instrument although attempts have been made to reform them. They all work, in one way or the other, as subdivisions of State run organizations like banks or commercial authorities. A second group – very important because dominant in agriculture – is the group of *communal co-operative economic organizations* (shequxing hezuo jingji zuzhi). They have replaced the former production brigades or teams. Despite some fundamental organizational reforms they, like the first group, are not really free from official interference. A completely new, innovative force constitute all kinds of *share-holding co-operative economic organization* (gufen hezuo jingji zuzhi). These include the *rural share-holding co-operative enterprises* (SCE), the different kinds of non-governmental *rural co-operative credit foundations* (nongcun hezuo jijinhui) and, in recent times, also *communal (agricultural) share-holding co-operative organizations* (shequxing gufen hezuo jingji zuzhi). In addition to these we find *specialized co-operatives* (zhuanye xiehui), *co-operatives for medical service* (yiliao hezuoshe), various forms of *co-operative study societies* (yanjiu hui) etc. In contrast to the first (and to some degree to the second) group they all can be characterized as "run by the local people" (minban) and seen as promising economic forces that have broken through the fatal link-up of political and economic administration dominant throughout the times of the people's communes.

b) Communal co-operative economic organizations

These organizations emerged after the people's communes had been dissolved on the territorial and organizational basis of the former production brigades or teams – today natural of administrative villages. They are agricultural co-operatives ranging from mere agricultural production to multipurpose operation including industry and commerce. On village (cun) or community (xiang) levels these grassroots co-operatives are united into federations (lianheshe). The term *communal co-operative economic organizations* denominates three elements which are closely linked to each other but at the same time operate autonomously. These elements are: The communal co-operatives, the collective enterprises owned by the co-operatives and the individual rural households which – as members of the co-operatives – work independently on their contracted land, only bound by the contract and the co-operative's constitution. The co-operative as the collective landowner gives the land to the rural househoud on a contractual basis. Besides this its internal functions comprise provision of services to its members, development of resources, assets accumulation, etc. To the outside, the co-operative represents its members whenever necessary and seeks economic exchange. Land is contracted in the so-called *two-land-system* (liangtianzhi), which means that the land is divided into *grain ration land* (kouliangtian) and *responsibility land* (zerentian). Other names are *commodity land* (shangpintian) or *economy land* (jingjitian). The latter can, after delivery of the contracted quota, be used for market production. As mentioned above, for this kind of co-operative organizations which constitute the major part of agricultural economic operation some provinces have started to work out a regional legislation. *Co-operative operation* (hezuo jingying) wants, as can be found in any statement or written definition in China, the carrying out of basic co-operative principles like voluntary membership or autonomous democratic management. Yet it is also called for that the special conditions of China need the development of special criteria and principles suitable to meet the Chinese demands. The Sichuan draft of regulations for agricultural co-operatives, for example, more or less follows the standards. It also provides for voluntary membership (ch.I,§5.1). However, this prescription in reality is blocked by factual compulsion. Ch.II,§8 lists the conditions for membership: 16 years of age, recognition of the co-operative's constitution, and household registration within the area of the co-operative. This reveils that the peasant is practically born into a co-operative as a *natural member* (tianran sheyuan). If he wants land to work on he cannot but to be a member of his 'home co-operative'. Withdrawal, on the other hand, only makes sense if household registration changes to another region.

c) Rural share-holding co-operative enterprises (SCE)

These enterprises, incorporated in the sphere of co-operative operation, are defined as a new form of collective economy (→ *Classification*). Among the TVEs, the non-agricultural sector of rural economy, the SCEs are of growing importance and considered as indipensable for China's road towards market economy (until Oct. 1992: commodity economy). They can either result from the transformation of an existing collective TVE or through the association of at least three rural households or individual farmers. After Central Committee and State Council had decreed that TVEs can partly distribute their gains according to shares (Jan. 1983 and again Jan. 1984) and declared that co-operative economy should be promoted, SCEs proliferated all over the country. In order to co-ordinate this development three experimental zones were established in 1987/88 in the provinces of Anhui (Fuyang), Shandong (Zhoucun) and Zhejiang (Wenzhou). Their task was to work on five projects: to clarify the distribution of property (public, collective, enterprise and individual shares), to standardize the management of SCEs, to promote urbanization, to develop non-governmental co-operative credit organizations and to elaborate legislation. Legislation was the domain of Wenzhou (Zhejiang). Already in 1987 the "provisional regulations for some problems with SCEs" have been worked out, followed by "provisional regulations for the standardization in SCEs" in early 1990. Both are still not published. As said earlier, these regulations constituted the model after which the national provisional regulations have been shaped. The latter, issued Feb.12, 1990, lay down the ideal type of an SCE. A model bye-law (→ *Bylaws*) and extensive explanations give further insight. They show that a series of basic co-operative elements are recognized, like voluntary association (here, however, only three founding members are requested, which corresponds to the Chinese prescriptions for public limited companies, May 15.1992), open membership, democratic management and control, equal voting rights, autonomy, and the accumulation of an indivisible reserve fund (→ *Principles*).

Coming to the distribution of the economic results, however, there have arisen some controversies which are still not settled: It is a popular argument in China that for this new kind of economic organization one has picked out the best elements of both, the share-holding and the co-operative systems, and combined them into a co-operation of capital and labor. The dispute concerns the balance between these two parts of co-operation. According to co-operative → *principles* share capital remuneration should be limited in the interest of the enterprise's soundness. §§ 14 and 15 of the national provisional regulations settle the question of profit distribution (→ *Equity Capital*). Share dividends (→ *Assessment of Success*) are divided into two parts. One is named *guxi* (share interest), the other one *fenhong* (dividend), which, according to the commentator, in international usage is the same. *Share interests* (guxi) are to be distributed obligatory within a fixed period according to bank interests. They count as production management costs. *Dividends* (fenhong) are profit-related and fall due after the payment of tax. They shall not transgress 20% of the profit. The "explanations" go into further details. They point out that this practice indicates that the provisional regulations do not clearly distinguish between *shares* (gufen) and *bonds* (zhaiquan). This results from the fact that on the one hand share-regulations for collective enterprises allow *share interests* (guxi) to be payed either before or after tax payment. On the other hand the share-holding co-operative system is only in its initial stage. Thus in the SCEs' case shares are conceptionally differentiated into *common shares* (putonggu) and *preferential shares* (youxiangu). Dividends for the latter are treated like loan interests and thus estimated as costs while dividends for the others are to be payed only in relation to actual profit. 20% of the profit are fixed for social welfare funds and bonusses while 30% go into the common reserve fund. The remaining 30% are only defined by the "explanations". They count as collective property of all shareholders and are as indivisible as the reserve fund. There is no influence on either form of share dividends. The *Wenzhou method* differs considerably and consequently is criticized for distorting the idea of the system. As can be seen from individual bye-laws (the regulations themselves are not published), 25% of the profit are meant for bonusses, social welfare and common reserve funds while another 25% are determined for dividends. The 50% left, designated for extended reproduction, are registered under the individual shareholders' names, thus increasing both kinds of dividends. Some critical commentators calculate that 70%–80% of the profit returns to the share-holders and only little is left for the collective. Standardization is demanded that can provide criteria for the classification of enterprises as co-operative (and thus collective) or private. Cases are cited where a group of three relatives rose the capital to establish an SCE with dozens of hired workers.

d) Communal share-holding co-operative economic organizations

This term gives expression to the fact that the share-holding system is introduced into the communal (agricultural) co-operatives. It is said that while the 1980s have been the decade of the family responsibility system the 1990s will see the high tide of share-holding co-operative organizations. Besides the SCEs among the TVEs only very recently have appeared pilot programs for a fusion of communal co-operative and share-holding systems. So far these experiments are confined to only some localities in the economically highly developed areas around Canton (Tianhe district) and Shenzhen (Bao'an, Henggan, Shajin) in Guangdong province. In 1991, for example, the district government of Tianhe has decided to establish *communal share-holding co-operatives* in all natural and administrative villages. The idea to transform the communal co-operatives into share-holding co-operatives came up when the industrialization in the big cities, spreading across city boundaries, took away arable land. More and more farmers had to leave agriculture and were hired as industrial workers. This caused a difference in income to the disadvantage of the industrial workers. To solve this problem it was decided to convert the collective assets of the communal co-operatives (accumulation of labor) into collective accumulation shares and into shares the farmers can subscribe if their households are registered in the co-operative's area, even if they are no longer engaged in agriculture. However, more than 60% of the shares have to remain collective in order to demonstrate the collective character. Another kind of shares are the so-called *cash shares* (xianjingu) which are meant to stimulate the people to transfer consumption funds into production.

Recent tendencies in this field: 1) In the case of Bao'an (Shenzhen) the collective shares have decreased from 60% to 30% and tend toward zero. 2) It is feared that the preferential treatment of those farmers whose houshold is registered within the co-operative might cause social discontent. Workers from outside, it is argued, contribute a great deal to the economic development of the area and shoud be allowed to also buy shares. Meanwhile in some exceptional cases technicians and longterm workers can buy shares, but no cash shares. Although still only in the stage of the very beginning the development of share-holding in communal co-operative has attracted great attention among the Chinese experts.

e) Non-governmental financial service co-operative organizations (minjian jinrong fuwu hezuo zuzhi)

Background: The provisional regulations for banking adminstration of 1986 allowed private banking institutions in form of co-operatives. Following this pilot programs were established in some experimental zones, as in Fuyang (Anhui) which set up 12 collectivley owned co-operatives for the financial service to the SCEs. In 1988 the State Council has entrusted the newly founded China Agribusiness Development Trust & Investment Company (CATIC) with the reform of the rural investment and financial systems. Supported by the first substantial loans granted by the World Bank, three experimental zones were chosen for the development of true co-operative credit organizations with special attention given to the elaboration of correct bye-laws.

Non-governmental co-operative credit organizations run by the farmers have emerged in quite a number of villages since the mid 1980s. These include *rural Co-operative foundations* or funds (nongcun hezuo jijinhui), *peasants' share-holding funds* (nongmin gufen jijinhui), *deposit co-operatives* (nongcun hezuo chujinhui), *farmers' mutual financial aid societies* (nongmin zijin huzhuhui), to just list some of them. The role of these institutions is to support rural households with small, short-term credits for low investment in agricultural and industrial production. Official credit institutions (like the rural credit co-operatives which are affiliated to the Bank of Agriculture) had restricted their credit policy to village committees while other newly appearing financial institutions prefer loans of relatively low risks and costs.

Pilot programs were implemented in five experimental zones in the provinces Heilongjiang (Shangzhi), Hebei (Yutian), Sichuan (Guanghan), Guangxi (Yulin) and Shandong (Pingdu). Figures given for the end of 1991 say that rural credit co-operative funds have amounted to about 18,000 on township level (33%) and 130,000 on village level (16%). The funds raised reach 9.9 billion yuan (RMB) = 1,7 billion US $. Officially their business field is limited to the communal co-operative economic organizations of the respective communities of villages. Loans should go exclusively to enterprises or farmers' households within the area of these co-operatives. Thus qualification for membership depends not only on share holding but also on household registration (hukou). However, in practice these limitations are very often broken through.

Rural co-operative (credit) funds are only meant as internal fund-raising and -administrating institutions. Thus deposits are not allowed. To avoid this obstacle the method of putting in the so-called 'daiguanjin' (capital the fund administers in place of the capital owner) is introduced. For the 'daiguanjin' one gets interest but no dividends.

f) Rural specialized co-operative associations

These are co-operatives (→ *Rural Co-operatives*) which concentrate on the specialization in production and services. Their aim is to raise the level of production and to widen agricultural production operation. Like the other agricultural co-operatives they operate on the two levels of decentralized individual production and centralized service. Service to the members includes information, technologies as well as capital and material. Exchange of specialized technologies is promoted. The prosperity of specialized co-operatives, however, differs considerably within China. Figures given for the end of 1990 show a general decline from approximately 60% in the East to 30% in the middle and 10% in the West of the total number of 1.154 millions, be it the production-operation type (740,000) or the production-service type (414,000). The drafted co-operative regulations for Sichuan province include the specialized co-operative associations.

g) Specialized research societies (zhuanye yanjiuhui)

These are *non-governmental science and technology co-operative organizations* (minjian kezhi hezuo zuzhi) established for the purpose of resolving technological problems emerging from production. Their main task is to introduce, demonstrate and popularize advanced technolgy for agriculture and to train the farmers.

4. The Gung Ho or Industrial Co-operatives (gungye hezuoshe)

This is a very interesting and, in regard to co-operative practice, promising non-governmental initiative which goes back to the Gung Ho (Indusco) movement 1937–1952. Chinese patriots had started this movement in Shanghai with the support of Rewi Alley from New Zealand, in China highly appreciated, and the well-known American journalist Edgar Snow (*Red Star over China, 1968*) with his wife Helen Foster Snow. It aimed at building up an economic front against the Japanese aggressor. After the first co-operative had been set up in Baoji (Shaanxi) in 1938 the movement spread throughout the country, first supported by the Nanjing Government as well as by the Communists. An International Committee for the Promotion of Chinese Industrial Co-operatives (ICCIC) was established in Hongkong 1939 which managed to win international (financial) help. In 1983 the (Chinese) Association of the Chinese Industrial Co-operatives resumed its activities and in Sept. 1987, with *Rewi Alley* still being the promoter (he died Dec.27, 1987), the ICCIC revived in Beijing. It sponsors four experimental areas in Shandong (Longkou and Penglai), Gansu (Shandan), Hubei (Honghu) and Beijing (Haidian). The target is to develop model industrial co-operatives that may cause other people or enterprises to follow them. Great emphasis is given to education and training as well as to the elaboration and completion of bye-laws following international standards. (Financial) support comes in China from the Central Government and from local authorities but also from sponsors of foreign countries. A newsletter is published irregularly and distributed among the committee members.

5. Managerial Structure

Although there are substantial differences due to genesis, character and targets of the various co-operative economic organizations, provisional and draft legislation, bye-laws and practice correspond in essential parts (→ *Managerial Economics*; → *Organizational Structure of Societies*).
The highest authority or power organ in each case is the *general meeting* (dahui) of the members (communal co-operatives and Gung Ho) or the shareholders (SCE). The general meeting elects the *board of directors* (terminology differs: lishihui, dongshihui, guanli weiyuanhui). This in turn has a *chairman* and vice chairman (communal co-operatives and Gung Ho) or appoints a *factory* or *managing director* (SCEs).
While these are responsible to the board of directors the board for its part is responsible to the general meeting. Chairman or managing director represent the co-operative organization legally in the co-operativs's external relations. Prescriptions differ in regard to supervision. While the Gung Ho type provides for a *supervisory board* (jianshihui) to be elected by the general meeting the SCE type has the *board of directors* to constitute an integrated organ of management and controlling (model bye-law ch.4, § 11.5 and 6). For the communal co-operatives the draft regulations in Sichuan (§34), for example, want an *internal system for auditing*.

6. Conclusion

Common to all kinds of co-operative organization is the equal status of all members or share-holders irrespective to their contribution. Moreover, all types have (more or less detailed) prescriptions for social welfare funds. This is of importance since a national social insurance system is still lacking. Differences can be noticed with regard to the shares. Communal co-operatives, with the exception of the very newly development type around Canton and Shenzhen have no shares at all. The Gung Ho type wants a share contribution in accordance with the economic strength of the applicant as a prerequisite for membership (§10, draft model bye-law.). Shares subscribed to the SCE type, on the other hand, are regarded as financial investment. While Gung Ho shares can be returned in the case of withdrawal, SCE shares cannot or only in exceptional cases under the condition that the registered capital does not decrease. But these shares can be transferred, inherited or made over to others.
Membership in a Gung Ho co-operative requires an age of at least 18 while the communal type only wants 16 years. There is no prescription in the provisional regulations for the SCEs but it is said that child work is forbidden (§ 9).
Promotion of members or *share-holders* is only one and often only a second-rate aim. All kinds in the first line are seen as important factors in rural economic modernization, for China's prosperity and for the development of market (commodity) economy. Communal co-operatives, in addition, emphatically underline the training of their members for being good socialists, patriots and collectivists and to develop a socialist material and intellectual civilization (Sichuan draft, § 6). In reality, however, the members are promoted by various services and organizational support. But it is clear that individual incentives are given mainly in view of achieving the overall goal of China's economic modernization.

Bibliography

Chen Han-seng: Gung Ho! The Story of the Chinese Co-operatives, New York 1947.
Chen Jiyuan and Hu Bin: Lun fazhan nongcun hezuo jijinhui

de shenceng yiyi (The development of rural co-operative funds association in its far-reaching impacts), in: Zhongguo Nongcun Jingji (1992) 9: 14–17.
Chen Yan: Guanyu Wenzhou gufen hezuo jingji de tiaocha yu sikao (Survey and consideration on share-holding co-operative economy in Wenzhou), in: Zhongguo Nongcun Jingji (1991) 9: 24–28.
China International Famine Relief Commission ed.: Herr Raiffeisen among Chinese Farmers, Peiping 1930 (repr. New York/London 1980).
Du Ying and others (State Council, Center for Rural Research, Dept. of Experimental Zones) eds.: Gaige shijian lu (Report on the practice or reform), Beijing 1990.
Durau, Joachim: Arbeitskooperation in der chinesischen Landwirtschaft. Die Veränderung bäuerlicher Produktionsbeziehungen zwischen Agrarrevolution und Kollektivierung (1927–1957), Bochum 1983.
Gu Cunwei and Chen Wei: Guanyu gufen hezuo qiye de jidian sikao (Several considerations on co-operative share-holding enterprises), in: Zhongguo Nongcun Jingji (1991) 9: 29–31.
Gu Yikang: Shehuizhuyi chuji jieduan nongmin gufen hezuo qiye chutan (A tentative exploration on share-holding co-operative enterprises in the primary stage of socialism), in: Zhongguo Nongcun Jingji (1991) 9: 32–34.
Kikuchi Kazutaka: Kônichi sensô jidai no Chûgoku kôgyô gassaku undô (The Chinese Gung Ho movement during the war of resistance against Japan), Rekishi Kenkyû 485 (Oct. 1980): 29–45.
Kikuchi Kazutaka: Chûgoku kokumintô ni okeru gassakusha no kiten to tenkai (The origins of the co-operatives initiated by the GMD and their development), Son Bun (Sun Wen) Kenkyû 9 (Dec. 1988), 1–32.
Kikuchi Kazutaka: Chûgoku kôgyô gassaku undô to kyûkoku kaiha – Chûgoku kôgyô gassaku kyôkai setsuritsu o me gutte (The Chinese Gung Ho movement and the National Salvation Society – on the establishment of the Chinese Industrial Co-operative Association), Rekishi Kenkyû 25 (1988): 97–126.
Münzel, Frank: Accounting and planning in Chinese agricultural co-operatives, Revue of Socialist Law (1978): 27–56.
Münzel, Frank: Landwirtschaftliche Genossenschaften in China. Rechtsprobleme und Reformen. Rabels.Z (1980): 41–65.
Nathan, Andrew James: A History of the China International Famine Relief Commission, Cambridge/Mass. 1965.
Nongmin gufen hezuo qiye (Rural share-holding co-operative enterprises), ed. by the office for village and township enterprises (TVEs), Ministry of Agriculture, Beijing 1990. (Contents: The provisional regulations for rural share-holding co-operative enterprises, the model bye-law and the explanations).
Selden, Mark: Cooperation and conflict. Co-operative and collective formation of China's countryside. The Transition to Socialism in China. New York 1982, 32–87.
Sichuan sheng nongye hezuoshe difang fagui yantaohui lunwenji (collection of papers presented to the symposium on regional legislation for agricultural co-operatives in Sichuan province), ed. by The Sichuan Commission of Rural Work and the Friedrich-Ebert-Stiftung, Chengdu 1992.
Stettner, Nora and Bert Oram: Changes in China. The Role of Co-operatives in the New Socialism, Manchester 1987.
Wang Shiying and Lin Rong: Hezuo fagui (co-operative laws and regulations), Nanjing 1945.
Wu Yuzhang: Zhongguo hezuo yundong xiaoshi (A short history of the co-operative movement in China), Nanjing 1929.

Yang Jianbai ed.: Hezuo jingjixue gailun (Introduction into co-operative economics), Beijing 1989.
Yang Peilun and others: Hezuo jingji lilun yu shijian (Theory and practice of co-operative economy), Beijing 1989.
Zheng Gang and others: Nongcun hezuo jijinhui de fazhan fangxiang yu tixi jianshe (Development orientation and establishment of the system of rural co-operative (credit) funds), Zhongguo Nongcun Jingji (1992) 9: 10–13.
Zhongguo jingji baike quanshu (The encyclopedia of Chinese economy), 2 vols., ed. by Chen Daisun and others, Beijing 1991.
Zhou Jinting and Wu Yihuan: Nongcun hezuozhi de xin fazhan – Guang dong sheng baoanxian henggangzhen gufen hezuozhi fazhanjishi (New development in the rural co-operative system: On-the-spot report of developing share-holding co-operation of Henggang town, Bao'an county, Guangdong province), Zhongguo Nongcun Jingji (1992) 8: 34–37.
Zhou Wanjun, ed.: Hezuo jingji gailun (Introduction into co-operative economy), Beijing 1987.

Classical and Neoclassical Contributions to Co-operative Theory

ROLF ESCHENBURG

(see also: *Biographical articles about Mill, Walras/Pareto, Marshall*; *Socialist Critics*; *Economic Order*; *Competition*)

I. Introduction; II. John Stuart Mill (1806–1873); III. Leon Walras (1834–1910); IV. Vilfredo Pareto (1848–1923); V. Alfred Marshall (1842–1924); VI. Arthur Cecil Pigou (1877–1959).

I. Introduction

Modern co-operatives achieved their breakthrough in 1844 upon the founding of the Rochdale consumer co-operative (→ *Rochdale Pioneers*). As a novel enterprise form they automatically became an object of economic investigation at that early day and age following their formation and further development. From the beginning economists analyzed co-operatives under a two-fold approach as they did other business undertakings or organizations. On the one hand the question was addressed whether or not and/or under which circumstances co-operatives were advantageous to the economy as a whole, thus socio-economically desirable and eventually also deserving of support. On the other hand investigation was directed at the organization of co-operatives: if they function adequately they can truly render their potential contribution to the economy as a whole.

The negative side-effects of the liberal-capitalistic industrialization process form the focus of discourse provided by the individual authors. These side-effects can be broken down into two groups, namely the shortcomings inherent in traditional, hierarchical organizations dominated by capital and the shortcomings inherent in the market-oriented co-ordination of production executed according to a division of labor.

In contrast to the early French socialists *Fourier, Blanc, Buchez* and *Gide* – all of whom hoped to overcome the capitalistic system with joint-production and/or consumer co-operatives – → *Mill, Pareto,* → *Walras,* → *Marshall* and *Pigou* all perceived the co-operative simply as an opportunity to supplement the market economy system in a benevolent manner.

The central positions of the individual authors are provided in the following in a concise form and illustrate that the authors saw numerous opportunities for co-operatives to supplement the system. Many of the arguments presented in their time past have remained quite up-to-date and have not lost any of their convincing power. This in particular is evident when the discourses formulated by the individual authors with regard to co-operatives are more closely examined.

II. John Stuart Mill (1806–1873)

1. Freedom, Competition and Evolution

Mill views co-operatives – above all → *joint-production co-operatives* – fundamentally in a positive light based on his understanding of the economy. Co-operative cooperation is understood as a self-help measure and as such is not out of line in his fundamental conception of political order, itself grounded in utilitarianism, individualism and the concept of evolution.

The supreme norm is that of utilitarianism with its maxim the greatest happiness of the greatest number, whereby *Mill* by no means simply concentrated on material happiness. Personal autonomy and human self-realization rather are to a greater degree values in themselves. The norm of individualism states that the utilitarian norm can be pursued through institutional control while the individual freedom of all persons is preserved. The co-ordination of individual actions necessary to achieve "the greatest happiness of the greatest number" should be guaranteed through competition and voluntary cooperation (in particular co-operative) in the scope of an appropriate social and economic order and on the basis of a corresponding → *education and training* system. On account of their success, co-operatives promote in particular those positive moral and economic characteristics inherent in man which are necessary for economic success, and by doing so they fulfill an important socio-economic function.

2. Co-operatives and an Efficient Production System

According to *Mill*, in order to approach the goal of "the greatest happiness of the greatest number" a production system must be found which is both economically efficient and at the same time socially advanced. Economic efficiency can be achieved through the division and consolidation of labor, through the unification of factor prices, as well as through overcoming indivisibilities, i.e. through specialization, → *competition* and large-scale operational production. *Mill*, nonetheless, considers the traditional capitalistic system of production "disintegrational" and inefficient; it namely requires restrictions to be placed on individual freedom and thus guarantees only limited opportunities for personality development (self-actualization). As a whole it thus only offers slight performance incentives.

Mill sees the chance to realize the advantages of large-scale operational production without incurring the disadvantages previously discussed in the transition to a method of production along the lines of a joint-production co-operative. The expectation of being in the position to prevent motivational losses from arising is grounded in profit sharing and in particular in the shared identity between capital owners and employees. If workers are placed in the appropriate relation to their "work", they will gain the incentive to work as much as possible as compensation for their pay rather than work as little as possible (→ *Incentives*). This allows the conflict between labor and capital to be settled and evokes a new feeling of security and independence.

According to *Mill* and expressed in today's language, → *joint-production co-operatives* can provide the allocative efficiency of large-scale production methods as well as the motivational efficiency (X-efficiency) of small-scale, craft-like production methods. Since the days of *Mill* co-operative science (→ *Theory of Co-operatives*) has thus known that co-operatives can combine the advantages of large-scale operations with the advantages of small-scale operations. This is not only true for joint-production co-operatives but rather also for service co-operatives. *Mill* namely also recognized the opportunity of making capital-intensive inventions in farming technology available to small-scale farming enterprises through the multi-enterprise employment of machinery.

Mill did not, however, just note the opportunities that co-operatives (above all joint-production co-operatives) provided in his day and age, but he also believed that these opportunities could and would be utilized. He personally had the vision that the joint-production co-operative would prevail in grand style with its socially progressive and economically superior production system. He, nevertheless, was not lured into granting the establishment and development of joint-production co-operatives priority over the principle of free competition and/or the norm of individualism. He maintained that co-operatives should hold their own in competition with other organizational forms and thus prove their socio-economic superiority. He fundamentally foresaw no success in a revolutionary restructuring of the economic order, not even in a revolution benefiting co-operatives. Competition for him is certainly not the optimal means of incentive, but he nonetheless felt it to be essential as it cannot be foreseen in advance when it would become superfluous for continued progress.

According to *Mill*'s conceptions, socio-economic progress proceeds slowly in an evolutionary process of trial and error. State intervention to the benefit of co-operatives could accelerate this process (→ *State and Co-operatives, Market Economy*). It is, however, the task of the state to prescribe the skeleton conditions for people's actions, be they individual or collective in nature (e.g. assuming the form of a voluntary cooperation). How else could interventions for co-operatives be justified without likewise justifying each and every intervention in the private sector which promises progress? State intervention – even to the benefit of co-operatives – does not fit into *Mill*'s basic understanding of political order. Even without a glimmer of a doubt concerning the professional quality, integrity and fastidiousness of civil servants he saw no reason for state encroachment into the private sector.

He feared detrimental consequences on the development of workers' economic and, in particular, entrepreneurial skills among workers especially from state aid in the form of capital: this would reduce their chances to act in a self-responsible and entrepreneurial manner and improve their social and economic situation. *Mill*, furthermore, feared that state intervention would homogenize the variety of co-operative efforts. Aside from this, he maintained that extensive state financing of co-operatives was not feasible due to a lack of capital as well as out of distributional-political reasons.

The superiority of the production system in joint-production co-operatives can only result from a higher level of motivational efficiency. Avoiding the demarcation into labor and capital itself does not ensure sufficient motivational efficiency. Rather, performance incentives are necessary in the form of profit sharing and above all in an arrangement fairer to rendered performance. *Mill* placed particular importance on the latter as one can gather from his reference that up to then all experiments had failed which had dispensed with compensation systems fair to rendered performance. This statement can still be upheld today.

Mill saw with equal clearness the true imperfections of competition in reality. The main causes of these are non-economic behavior factors like tradition (apathy, carelessness, notions of justice), a lack of mobility spurred by an insufficient will to react, inadequate reaction skills (due to dependencies such as charging goods on credit) as well as insufficient information. During his era the imperfections in competition caused considerable misallocations, above all in retail trade; this led to the squandering of resources traceable to overstaffing and overcapitalization, exaggerated distribution costs and inflated prices for inferior quality products (→ *Pricing Policy*).

Mill maintains that it is here that competition can be intensified to a considerable degree through consumer co-operatives, thereby achieving a superior allocation of factors. The introduction and maintenance of the principle of cash payments in the → *consumer co-operatives* paved the way for abolishing the custom of charging goods on credit with its related costs. Consumer co-operatives fulfill the special function of exposing the costs of such credit business in their full dimension (approx. 20% surcharges), thus motivating its full abolishment.

3. Co-operatives and the Social Question

In order to explain the impossibility or difficulty in improving the social situation of workers the classical economists developed two wage theories: the theory of the minimum existential wage and the theory of the wage fund. According to the former the natural wage level lies at the existence threshold inasmuch as further populational development is dependent on the level of wages. The theory of the wage fund is derived from the assumption that a portion of available capital forms the so-called wage fund which cannot be varied through redistribution. An increasing population must therefore bring about falling average wages. Socio-political measures and unions are inappropriate due to the failure of redistribution measures. In order to raise wages the wage fund must grow faster than the population. The distribution side of the problem, however, remains to be resolved as the wage fund increases disproportionally slowly due in particular to the accumulation of fixed capital; property distribution therefore is shifted to the detriment of workers. It is accordingly all the more important to overcome the antagonism between capital-owning employers and wage-dependent employees. *Mill* is of the opinion that this cannot happen through trade unions but rather must occur through joint-production co-operatives.

Joint-production co-operatives provide the opportunity to kill two birds with one stone. On the one hand the social question can be solved (→ *Social Policy*) in that the antagonism between capital and labor is resolved. On the other hand, workers can take advantage of the higher motivational efficiency of production organized in joint-production co-operatives. For this, however, *Mill* maintains that it is necessary to increase the workers' willingness and their ability to save because of his renunciation of capital assistance from the state.

In order to increase workers' ability to save, wages must be considerably higher than the minimum existential wage in a long-term perspective. This is only possible when population growth can be reduced and maintained at a low level through appropriate temperate behavior. *Mill* holds that this in turn necessitates a corresponding education as well as an upbringing stressing farsightedness and self-discipline – characteristics that workers nonetheless require for successful cooperation in joint-production co-operatives. Insofar the joint-production co-operative must inevitably represent *Mill*'s ideal means to an end.

III. Leon Walras (1834–1910)

1. Primary Goal: The Reduction of Human Suffering

The central problem of science and politics is human suffering (rooted in natural, individual and social causes). According to *Walras*, the social causes of human suffering form the point of departure for economic theory and policy with regard to the best possible solution to production and distribution problems in the economy. The goal of distribution is equally as important to him as the goal of maximum production, and thus the two are in well-balanced relationship. Competitive order created and protected by the state is the appropriate means to achieve maximum production. With regard to the distribution goal, *Walras* proposes nationalizing land and thus land rents. For him the decisive factor for an unfair income distribution lies in (the unfair distribution of) land property in private hands.

2. Co-operatives as Self-Help Organizations

Walras, in contrast to *Mill*, does not adjudge co-operatives any type of social reform qualities. He strictly differentiates between areas of state responsibility (*action collective*) and sectors of involvement for private economic subjects (*action individuelle*). Among the former number the creation of an appropriate framework for competition which enables the optimal development and utilization of productive forces on an individual basis, as well as social reform which resolves the social question.

For *Walras* allocating co-operatives social reform functions would mean entrusting them with state tasks. Nevertheless, he recognizes that co-operatives solve special problems and therefore can fulfill an important social function. In his concept, however, they solely play a supplementary role to the system at large. Co-operatives are an element of the private economic sector and must therefore be integrated in it (→ *Economic Order*). *Walras* accordingly does not see any reason for co-operatives to receive any kind of state support.

Nonetheless, *Walras* thoroughly recognizes the special characteristics of co-operatives. In his concept societal property is broken down into the three main categories of land, capital and human capital (mental-physical capabilities). Property owners attain income through economic employment in the form of ground rents, interest and wages. An essential characteristic of social progress is identified in that all individuals have a greater and greater share in all forms of wealth, but in particular that workers have continually improved access to property in the form of capital. *Walras* sees the decisive co-operative characteristic in the fact that co-operatives provide economically weaker individuals the opportunity to build capital collectively, to invest it and put it to good use.

For *Walras* the consumer, joint-production or credit co-operatives are commercial, industrial or credit-granting undertakings created out of their own resources. In principle all co-operatives have positive production and distributive effects and contribute to the integration of economically weaker individuals into the capitalistic, competitive economy. They offer such economically weaker persons the opportunity and incentive to use their capabilities in a profitable manner – capabilities which would otherwise go unutilized. He, nevertheless, envisions the engagement of co-operatives to be limited to those situations in which they can hold their own in competition with other market participants and organizational forms.

3. Principles of Co-operative Organization

In *Walras*' thinking the role of the state with regard to co-operatives solely extends to the determination of commercial-legal regulations. The state thereby only must establish the content of the provisions regulating the protection of third parties and the public at large in external relations. The regulation of internal relations is solely the concern of the members which have joined together in self-reliance and who thus act within the realm of the autonomy granted by their → *by-laws*. In principle co-operatives are nothing more than one form of commercial undertaking among numerous others, and as such are not entitled to any privileges.

One must also accept the fact that under certain socio-economic circumstances co-operatives have no prospect to achieve success. An example is the consumer co-operative in a large urban area. On the one hand, the large geographic distances and the high level of fluctuation endanger the cohesion among members; on the other hand, competition constantly improves consumers' access to foodstuffs. He envisioned successful prospects for joint-production co-operatives primarily in the sector of mid-sized enterprises (→ *Operational Size*). In contrast he sees practically unlimited success for credit co-operatives. These seem to him the most important type of co-operative due to their function of paving the way for other co-operative forms. He was influenced in his opinion here by → *Schulze-Delitzsch*, whose contributions he was both familiar with and held in esteem.

With regard to the question of expedient guidelines for organizational structure, *Walras* explicitly discusses financing, decision-making procedures and the distribution of the surplus. As a *financial model Walras* suggests that members gradually raise their capital share through variable personal payments, whereby the amount of the payments can be set somewhat higher than a cost-specific minimum contribution based on each member's individual ability to pay. In *decision-making matters* a sound compromise must be reached in the conflict between democracy and economy. Here, *Walras* envisions dispensing with direct self-management and delegating decision-making authority to administrative and supervisory bodies. The "one man, one vote" principle should be applicable in the general meeting regardless of capital participation (→ *Principles*). The *distribution of the surplus* (→ *Assessment of Success*) should take place periodically and be structured according to capital participation levels.

IV. Vilfredo Pareto (1848–1923)

1. Principle of Hedonism and Co-operative Ideology

Pareto took issue with *Gide's* concepts of solidarity both in general and in connection with co-operatives and refuted his concept that increasing solidarity is a result of and a presupposition for socio-economic development (→ *Conceptions, Co-operative*). According to his opinion, development is possible through human action based on self-interest. He constructed an action theory with a far-reaching field of application in which human action is divided into logical and illogical categories.

The purpose and primary goal of human action is sensuous or intellectual pleasure according to the so-called principle of hedonism. Economic theory applies hedonistic fundamentals inasmuch as it assumes that economic subjects primarily have their own unsatiated needs in mind and as rational actors maximize a utility index function in which their own unsatiated needs are used as arguments (maximization of individual utility).

Pareto sees no reason to assume that the members of a co-operative undertake an action motive which deviates from the hedonistic principle. Their individual endeavors to attain individual economic utility is considered the basis for the formation and maintenance of co-operatives. Members in every type of co-operative are always only interested in their individual economic advantage. Non-economic goals propounded by numerous co-operatives proponents, promoters and founders need to be differentiated from this.

The establishment and promotion of co-operatives out of non-economic motives – e.g. the realization of a better, non-capitalistic economic order – are to be allocated to "illogical" behavior according to *Pareto* and thus lie beyond economic analysis. A co-operative ideology and ideological motives are however of importance in an economic sense because the ideological mobilization of skills and resources can increase a co-operative's economic success. An animated co-operative ideology fulfills the economic function of facilitating successful co-operative collaboration.

2. The Competitiveness of Co-operatives

Pareto sees practically no chances for co-operatives to survive in markets which are sufficiently structured with → *competition*, or in other words, in markets where dynamic competition functions. On the other hand, successful prospects can be found on markets in which competition is restricted and can be intensified by co-operatives. He is of the opinion that consumer co-operatives and joint-production co-operatives have quite differing opportunities. Competition in the trading sector is to a great degree imperfect, thus providing consumer co-operatives with substantial functions and prospects. In contrast to this, he sees practically no prospects for joint-production co-operatives in industry under the competitive conditions of his day and age.

Unlike *Mill, Pareto* considered the joint-production co-operative to be inferior to the private, non-co-operative business undertaking due to organizational reasons. He, furthermore, indicated losses to national welfare brought upon by joint-production co-operatives. The employment guarantee attached to membership in a joint-production co-operative can on the one hand result in a suboptimal allocation of factors and, on the other hand, occasion reduced adaptability to the business cycle. *Pareto* also cannot support the property-political argument for joint-production co-operatives: the formation of capital in the hands of the worker need not result in capital investment in his own company; furthermore, workers' savings capital must be invested in a particularly safe manner, i.e. elsewhere.

Gide's conception of co-operativism assumes that co-operatives – above all consumer and joint-production co-operatives – can be enlarged to any desired extent. This presupposes the "open door principle" by which each person seeking membership has the right to join if he meets objective entry conditions. The "open door principle", frequently and confusingly misnamed the "open membership principle", is not compatible with *Pareto's* notions of cost development associated with an increase in enterprise size. Proceeding from the "law of increasing costs" resulting from ever stronger bottleneck factors, it is argued that an optimal enterprise size and a corresponding optimal membership group size can be determined for consumer and joint-production co-operatives. The optimal enterprise size is determined by the minimum level of long-term unit costs. It would contradict the interests of older members to accept further members once this minimum has been reached, and entry into the co-operative should thus not be made accessible to further members.

3. Effects of Co-operatives on the Economy as a Whole

Pareto, like *Walras*, considered the economic advantages for members to be the decisive reason behind the establishment and continued existence of co-operatives. He likewise understood co-operatives to be economic self-help organizations and therefore investigated the bases for co-operative advantages benefiting all parties involved and evaluated the co-operative role in the economy as a whole. Co-operative literature today differentiates in this connection between the cost advantages and the competitive advantages of co-operative endeavors. One can find a plethora of allusions to both categories in the older literature.

Pareto especially sees the opportunity consumer co-operatives have to realize cost advantages. They can reduce exaggerated transaction costs brought upon by usurious prices and adulterated products and take advantage of their operational size (economies of scale). All co-operatives can realize cost advantages through the collective outsourcing of functions and through specialization (due to specialization advantages). Possible cost disadvantages traceable to the democratic structure and the management of the co-operative through "hired servants" can, however, emerge alongside these potential cost advantages. On account of their limited suitability to undertake greater risk in dynamic competition, co-operatives furthermore tend to assume the role of the imitator rather than that of the pioneer. Regardless of this, all cost advantages resulting from productivity advancements in co-operative endeavors are desirable not only for the individual enterprise but rather for the entire economy.

The emergence of power structures in markets causes losses to welfare through the misallocation of resources and the redistribution of income. According to *Pareto* individual or collective monopolies usually are successful only because their continued existence is either directly or indirectly a result of legislation. *Pareto* therefore ascribes only minimal prospects to the political enforcement of a liberal economic order. He furthermore is very reserved in his assessment of the chances state competition policy has to succeed. In contrast he ascribes consumer co-operatives in particular – as defensive associations of consumers – the chance of intensifying competition to their advantage. He furthermore recognizes a positive effect on competition through the preventive waive of market power abuse alone in the fact that consumer co-operatives come into being and heighten competition.

Alongside from investigating the effects of competition *Pareto* also more closely analyzed optimal co-operative pricing policy.

V. Alfred Marshall (1842–1924)

1. The Co-operative and Socio-Economic Development

Moral consciousness, an occupation with contemporary social problems and optimism in the face of development induced *Marshall* to orient himself and his scientific work around reality and to strive for both applicability and influence in economic practice. This is likewise true for his treatment of co-operatives which to him seemed particularly worthy of attention on account of their economic and social orientation. Two distinct realms can be identified in *Marshall's* system of thinking. The first encompasses his occupation with the problem of human behavior as the basis for his theory of social-economic evolution. The second realm addresses his occupation with the application of the partial-analytical mechanism for allocation calculation. *Marshall's* occupation with co-operatives can be identified in conjunction with both of these realms.

The analysis of long-term socio-economic development can be identified as one of *Marshall's* supreme objectives. With this higher objective in view, itself referring to development theory, the static analysis of equilibrium is of instrumental importance. For him the decisive impulse for socio-economic development is the enlargement and differentiation of human needs.

The creative needs are of crucial importance for socio-economic development. Their satisfaction results in energetic initiative and entrepreneurial daring on the basis of reason, frugality, industriousness and sincerity. *Marshall* sees the positive development function of co-operative self-help organizations in the fact that co-operatives provide the opportunity to transgress from the first stage – dominated by physiological needs – into the second stage which is characterized by creative needs (→ *Development Policy*); in this context he foresees great prospects for joint-production co-operatives.

For *Marshall* the development function of co-operatives has two aspects. On the one hand, co-operatives make socio-economic development possible by embracing social, non-economic aspects. On the other hand co-operatives make it possible for the "working classes" to continually develop their higher human capabilities and needs without undertaking revolutionary steps; in other words, co-operatives open the way for evolutionary socio-economic development.

2. Destructive and Constructive Cooperation

According to *Marshall* economic development goes hand in hand with increasing emancipation from conventional behavioral traits tied to tradition and thus with increasing economic freedom. Individual economic subjects can make decisions both consciously and freely with greater frequency; they can and even must determine their lives with a mounting degree of self-responsibility. Competitive behavior and cooperation are thereby behavior alternatives between which they can in principle freely decide. Competition for *Marshall* signifies individual behavior which is oriented in an oppositional manner and which is directly determined by aspirations to achieve individual utility. In contrast, cooperation is behavior oriented more collectively and based on deliberate arrangements; cooperational behavior is thus characterized by indirect, carefully considered aspirations of individual utility. In the ideal situation, exclusive altruistic behavior would even exist. *Marshall* considered it a mistake of the early socialist advocates, however, to assume such an ideal as a basis (→ *Socialist Critics*).

Marshall's non-idealistic perspective allows him to recognize that cooperation beyond the voluntary restrictions to an individual's latitude (for action) in principle always restricts competition. On the one hand, the actual form of cooperation and its respective effects on competition must be investigated; on the other hand it must also always be checked whether the advantages brought upon by cooperation outweigh the disadvantages which go hand in hand with competitive restrictions. Cooperation – like concentration – presents both advantages and disadvantages for the economy at the same time. Cooperation is destructive, if the disadvantages are prevailing. The greater the freedom of association is for economic subjects, the more pressing it is to have effective controls against abuse in order to avoid destructive cooperation. Cooperation as a rule is destructive when it aims to disadvantage third parties through power-specific distribution advantages among cooperators. *Marshall* above all sees the danger of economically destructive cooperation in the fields of sales and marketing, particularly in price agreements. Destructive cooperation is advantageous for cooperators individually by collectively sheltering them from performance competition. *Marshall*, however, sees this entailing a high degree of group discipline, and the consequence is that individual initiatives are stifled and entrepreneurial skills remain unutilized. The greatest danger of destructive cooperation, however, is rooted in that the dynamics of the competitive process are interrupted, thus creating a tendency for structural crisis.

According to *Marshall* cooperations are constructive when either internal or external economies of scale can be harnessed from them. *Internal economies of scale* are size advantages which undertakings can draw from on account of larger enterprise sizes, better organization and more experienced management. Their realization is dependent on the decisions of the respective enterprise. *External economies of scale* are agglomeration advantages which come into being through positive external effects. These are thus the long-term, advantageous consequences of positive, external effects which assume the character of public goods, for example a pool of qualified workers in certain regions which has emerged over the generations from years of experience in producing specific quality products. Discoveries, innovations and experience which can also be utilized by third parties are the fundaments of these external economies of scale.

3. Cooperation and Economies of Scale

Constructive cooperation is thus always associated with external and/or internal economies of scale (→ *Operational Size*). *Marshall* names in particular economies of materials, economies of machinery, economies of highly organized buying and selling and economies of skill. In each case these entail size-specific specialization advantages.

Economies of material: In contrast to large-scale operation production, small-scale operation production cannot take advantage of all potential applications of working materials, for example utilizing waste products by adding on respective production facilities. Cooperation thus offers small-scale enterprises the opportunity to realize specialization advantages through greater diversification. *Marshall* transposes and applies these considerations to the labor element as "working materials". For him workers' potential skills and qualifications can be utilized better through cooperation in joint-production and/or promotional co-operatives. The improved utilization and development of latent capabilities furthermore paves the way for external savings.

Economies of machinery: The employment of special machines – with which good quality work can be accomplished at low cost when the quantities are sufficiently high – is often not worthwhile in small-scale enterprises. Cooperation provides the opportunity to take advantage of such specialization, for example above and beyond mutual specialization in smaller enterprises (→ *Machinery Associations/Rings*). Cooperation in promotional co-operatives through the collective outsourcing of functions in particular permits small economic units to have certain outputs produced for them at favorable costs in a collective enterprise using modern technology.

Economies of highly organized buying and selling: Larger enterprises can function with more favorable costs than small-scale enterprises not only in the production of outputs but also in the commercialization of such outputs and in the acquisition of inputs (→ *Commercial Co-operatives*; → *Supply Co-operatives*).

Promotional cooperation assistance offers small undertakings the opportunity to realize specialization advantages through the collective execution of purchasing and marketing functions. On the other hand, *Marshall* also identifies the formation of market power involved in this and therefore the danger that the cooperation could turn destructive. *Marshall* alludes in numerous situations to consumer co-operatives as well as to agricultural supply and marketing co-operatives; using the example of an American marketing co-operative for citrus fruits he detailed how market research and the development of new markets can function in a co-operative framework (→ *Marketing*). In contrast to this he leaves the credit co-operatives largely unmentioned.

Economies of skill: Small-scale undertakings in comparison have fewer chances to avail themselves of specialists versed in management and business execution. The managers of small-scale undertakings are rather necessarily "burned out" by their everyday job activities and are prevented from fully developing their creative skills. Cooperation particularly in a common promotional undertaking provides the chance to unburden managers through the outsourcing of service functions, which in turn realizes specialization advantages. A model example of this for *Marshall* is cooperation in a promotional or complementary or more generally – in a service co-operative. All in all *Marshall* is, however, especially interested in → *intercompany cooperation* in the fields of research and development. Such cooperation has a minimum of destructive elements, strengthens the dynamics of competition, preserves independent business undertakings and promotes the utilization and diffusion of technological progress.

VI. Arthur Cecil Pigou (1877–1959)

1. Co-operatives and Social Welfare

Pigou's investigations are derived from considerations of welfare theory, whereby he casts particular interest to economic welfare emerging from real goods and services as well as to income distribution. The analysis of his economic theory thus addresses two primary problems: the optimal allocation of factors and the optimal distribution of income. Co-operatives for him in the first place are of importance for the optimal allocation of factors; this is because information limits and re-allocation costs exist on the one hand as well as external effects on the other hand which are rooted both in the production system and in market relationships. Misallocations of resources result from this which, if the occasion arises, can be corrected by co-operatives.

2. Co-operatives and Impediments to Adaptation

Pigou distinguishes between two primary reasons for the misallocation of factors: impediments to adaptation and external effects. The following three implications lead to a less than ideal allocation of factors – above all that of capital – when co-ordination is left to the market alone: *insufficient information, insufficient risk compensation and fluctuations in demand*. Promising investment activity and thus an optimal application of capital require a high level of information about profitable investment plans, a targeted evaluation of this information (e.g. using carefully thought out investment calculations) and constant surveillance of investment activities in order to reduce risk. Financial institutions can provide assistance in numerous ways in this connection.

Pigou sees the social and personal proximity of members to each other as a particular advantage of co-operative financial institutions (credit co-operatives). This enables dependable information about investment risks and chances to be passed to members and secures a better control over the application of credits. Positive welfare effects accordingly result. Financial institutions are active as negotiators in capital transactions between savers and investors. They thus provide savers a certain *risk compensation* as the collective risk of all investments is equally distributed among all savers. *Pigou* ascribes shared liability in the credit co-operative (as a guarantee basis) particular potential as a far-reaching component of risk compensation.

Short- and mid-term *fluctuations in demand* as a rule overstrain companies' abilities to adjust their capacities to demand. Advantages in exhausting capacities in the common co-operative enterprise can be realized through the collective orientation on the average level of fluctuating demand. According to *Pigou's* opinion these advantages are not compensated by the fact that other non-co-operative undertakings can satisfy fluctuating demand.

3. Co-operatives and External Effects

Individual company decisions concerning the organizational structure of voting procedures and production processes possibly overlook external effects of corporate organizations. According to *Pigou* the social marginal returns of a company organization exceed its private marginal returns when it offers entrepreneurially-minded individuals room for personal development and chances for job promotion; the entrepreneurial potential of the economy as a whole is thereby strengthened in the long term and better utilized. *Pigou* maintains that promotional and joint-production co-operatives in particular have such effects on account of their co-operative-democratic organization. Such investments above all in joint-production co-operatives can achieve increases in welfare which are tied to education and training for workers; these in turn contribute to the formation of all-round, usable human capital. Inasmuch as such positive external effects can be expected, *Pigou* sees reason for the state to initiate the establishment of co-operatives.

Promotional co-operatives encompass both sides of a market. They thus in principle are suitable to internalize all (particularly the negative) external effects determined by market form. This must, however, by no means be achieved with negative consequences for non-members (third parties). *Pigou* sees Hilfsgenossenschaften having three effects. *Firstly,* they can avoid economically unproductive advertising costs which in general are a concomitant phenomenon of monopolistic competition. Advertising is only economically advantageous inasmuch as it serves as consumer information. *Secondly,* they can avoid the economically unproductive costs inherent in the struggle for income in a bilateral monopoly; they could in particular counteract all eventual dishonesty in the form of false information, inaccurate weights and adulterated goods. *Thirdly and lastly,* they can avoid economic losses resulting from the decelerated vertical diffusion of improvements. The conflict of interests between buyer and seller exacerbates vertical diffusion above all in a monopolistic market form. According to *Pigou* this conflict is abolished in a promotional co-operative.

4. Applicational Limits of Co-operatives

Having an advantageous position in principle does by no means imply that the advantages will always appear. It is not enough to anticipate increases in welfare from an idealistic point of view in the transition to co-operative cooperation (e.g. through the founding of a co-operative) when insufficient market co-ordination is prevalent (e.g. resulting from monopoly power). The situation can namely arise that re-allocation costs, the costs of co-operative co-ordination and frictional losses can nonetheless lead to welfare losses through inadequate co-operative co-ordination. The engagement of co-operatives is accordingly only of value when the co-operative coordination of the economic activity of the affected economic subjects within a co-operative as a whole yields such great advantages in comparison to market co-ordination that the re-allocation costs can be more than compensated for in a forseeable timeframe.

Bibliography

Eschenburg, R.: Konzeption der Genossenschaften in Entwicklungsländern. In: Boettcher, E. (ed.): Die Genossenschaft im Wettbewerb der Ideen – eine europäische Herausforderung, pp. 191–192, Tübingen 1985.
Hoppe, M.: Die klassische und neoklassische Theorie der Genossenschaften, Berlin 1976.
Marshall, A.: The Future of the Working Classes, 1873. In: Pigou, A.C.(ed.): Memorials of Alfred Marshall, London 1925.
Marshall, A.: Principles of Economics, vol.1, vol.2: remarks, 1920, Editor: Guillebaud, C.W., London 1961.
Marshall, A.: Industry and Trade, London 1923.
Maslow, A.H.: Motivation and Personality, New York 1954.
Mill, J.St.: Grundsätze der politischen Ökonomie mit einigen ihrer Anwendungen auf die Sozialphilosophie, 1871, 7th edition, vol. 1+2, translated by Gehrig, H., Jena 1924.
Mill, J.St.: Closing speech on the Co-operative system, printed under the title: Further Reply to the Debate on Population. In: Archiv für Sozialwissenschaften und Sozialpolitik, vol.62, Tübingen 1929.
Pareto, V.: Cours d'économie politique, vol.1+2, Lausanne, 1896.
Pareto, V.: Les systèmes socialistes, 2nd ed., vol.1+2, Paris 1926.
Pareto, V.:Lettre d'Italie: Les sociétés coopératives. In: Busino, G.(ed.): Oeuvres complètes de V. Pareto, vol.4, Libre-Echangisme, Protectionisme et Socialisme, Geneva 1965.
Pigou, A.C.: Some aspects of Welfare Economics. In: Newman, P.C./Gayer, A.D./Spencer, M.H.(ed.): Source Readings in Economic Thought, New York 1954.
Pigou, A.C.: Volkswirtschaftlicher und privatwirtschaftlicher Reinertrag und die Lehre von der Maximalbefriedigung. In: Mayer, H.(ed.): Die Wirtschaftstheorie der Gegenwart, vol.3, Einkommensbildung, Vienna 1928.
Pigou, A.C.: The Economics of Welfare, 1932, 4th edition, newprint London 1952.
Walras, L.: Les associations populaires de consommation, de production et de crédit, Paris 1865, new print Rome 1969.
Walras, L.: Etudes d'économie sociale, Lausanne-Paris 1896.
Walras, L.: Etudes d'économie politique appliquée, Lausanne-Paris 1898.

Classification and Typologies of Co-operatives

WERNER W. ENGELHARDT [F]

(see also: *Conceptions, Co-operative; Theory of Co-operative; Commercial Co-operatives; Consumer Co-operatives; Housing Societies; Production Co-operatives; Rural Co-operatives; Supply Co-operatives; Joint-production Co-operatives*)

I. Historical and Conceptual Approach; II. Differences between Class and Type; III. Typology of Basic Ideas; IV. Typology of Present-Day Forms of Cooperation; V. Types of Co-operatives in the Light of Different Scientific Disciplines and Their Main Features; VI. Types of Co-operatives and Other Forms of Cooperation as Viewed from the Discipline of Business Administration.

I. Historical and Conceptual Approach

Ever since the human race began to settle down, and perhaps even before then, it has developed, in many parts of the world, business units of a rudimentary character that were based upon associations of persons, upon some form of community. Ever since the Middle Ages, as circumstances have changed, these business units and associations of persons, tied to each other in 'dual nature' (*Draheim*), have become designated in the German language as *"Genossenschaft"* (*von Gierke, Schulze-Delitzsch*), more recently in German as *"Kooperativ"* as well (*Dülfer*). These terms correspond to the English *"co-operative society"* and the French "co-operative" or *"association"*. In modern times, and especially since the beginning of industrialization in the 18th and 19th centuries, co-operatives have evolved with a great variety of purposes and forms. It has therefore been difficult to reach a definition for them that is valid universally, although this has been attempted for a long time. As an initial approach to our object of empirical and cognitive concern here, we can understand co-operatives as voluntarily or involuntarily formed associations of persons, associations, or groups which simultaneously embody features of business enterprises established by these associations, including their subsidiaries. Both components – that of business and that of an association of persons – are entities *sui generis* (*Draheim*) tied to each other, having specific efforts of their own. In very extensive modern forms, co-operatives contain not only dual but triple centers of gravity when, in the case of "Integrated co-operatives" (*Dülfer*) (→ *Structural Types*), even business enterprises owned by individual members are fully integrated into the co-operative tie-up. Elaborating specific features and relations of co-operative dual and triple natures and their subsystems according to their purposes and forms, both in order to differentiate and to re-group, is the main task of morphological research on classes and types of these enterprises.

II. Differences between Class and Type

By forming classes on the one hand and types on the other, we can differentiate or group co-operatives, as well as other enterprises or organizations, in morphologically very different ways (*Castan, Dülfer, Engelhardt, Hahn, Schwarz, Tietz* et al.). Conceptual constructions that lead to *"classes"* lay down, in the sense of classical Aristotelian logic, one or more characteristic features of define as class concepts larger or smaller quantities of sub-classes. These concepts can be of interest in themselves but will more frequently be formed as contradictory or contrary pairs. Frequently one arrives at the construction of complete pyramids of concepts by the method *genus proximum et differentia specifica*. In this case one determines for each class concept the respective higher class and names the specific feature that characterizes the particular concept.

As far as *"types"* are concerned, the term is frequently used for class concepts. More specifically, however, it is used to mean relational or ranking concepts (*von Kempski*) in the sense of more recent non-classical logic denoting position in a series. "Ideal types" (*M. Weber*) are an early and widely-applied form approximating relational terms of this kind. Furthermore, under relational terms one can differentiate among type conepts in the narrow sense, *Gestalt* concepts, and concepts dealing with complex effects (*Oppenheim, Hempel* et al.).

In co-operative science, ideal types and the various so-called "proper" relational concepts, just like class and type concepts, take on great significance. In spite of these considerations, a differentiation in detail between co-operative classes and co-operative types must be foregone in this paper. It is also not possible to go into the question – considered important today with regard to the formation of empirical theory – of idealizing co-operatives through evolving ideal types to describe them (*Albert, von Hayek*). The same applies to problems of evolving normative and explanatory types as part of research on guiding images and other utopias, which research would also be important if one went into utopias more deeply (*Engelhardt*). Instead, examples are to be given here for types of co-operatives according to purpose and form, always built upon one guiding characteristic, usually including numerous sub-features in detail. These examples demonstrate the variety of phenomena of a co-operative nature in the industrial age.

III. Typology of Basic Ideas (Sinngehalte)

The basic ideas of co-operatives go back mainly to subjective, "utopian" ideas, to institutionally determined conception (*Weisser*), and to the actual behaviour of a co-operatives's owners, its leadership, and its employees. To ascertain "types of basic objectives", which are at the heart of this typology, it may also be important to consider other non-personal criteria and to give heed to behavioural effects. If one premises seven ideal-type objectives in industrial society – "profit-seeking" or "individual self-help", "private outside help", "purely subjective self-help", "community", "mutual self-help", "public assistance", and "public welfare" (*Engelhardt* 1985) – then one can distinguish among the following types of co-operatives:

1) *Co-operatives for commonweal* (→ *Commonweal Economy*) *or public benefit* (→ *Public Benefit Orientation*) are autonomously established "from below" and by direct and partly voluntary initiative. Also called "free co-operatives for public benefit" ("Frei-gemeinwirtschaftliche Genossenschaften"), these co-operatives are institutionally and practically devoted not merely to their respective members or specific groups beyond them, but to the general public (the "common welfare"). They may arise not only "naturally", as they usually did up to the high Middle Ages (→ *History before 1800*), on the basis of common descent, of the neighbourhood, and of the bond of

estate. They can also become established by deliberate policy decisions which directly or indirectly lead to co-operatives for public benefit. This has frequently been the case in Western Europe during the past two centuries. In the Federal Republic of Germany co-operatives of this kind were established in this way in the housing field up until 1990 (*Engelhardt/Thiemeyer, Lambert, Jenkis, Münkner, Novy, Watkins, Weisser* et al.).

2) *Foundation-type co-operatives* are based upon a more or less altruistic motivation of their leaders and other members, that is, they are subjectively, institutionally, and in practice bound to the "public weal" (*Weisser*). Their founders presuppose that one can set objectives to benefit others, as was explicitly the case, especially in the beginning phase of modern-age co-operatives, in German welfare associations and associations for public benefit (→ *Victor Aimé Huber*, → *Schulze-Delitzsch*, → *Raiffeisen*). Later on, this motivation continued to be of some importance for the activity of co-operatives, and in a less noticeable way it is a contributing factor even among co-operative types with a different basic orientation. Because of their similarity to co-operatives for public benefit, these foundation-type co-operatives can also be considered as co-operatives for indirect public benefit.

3) *Co-operatives of the group-economy type* take advantage of the legal and actual possibilities for formulating their by-laws and executing their business. That happens, when over and above the respective economic or non-economic interests of the members, aims are set up which serve the middle class, the working class, or other groups in society, which step may be quite legitimate. The co-operative as an institution intended for permanent existence is not necessarily under any obligation solely toward the present generation or the one which it helped to organize. In fact, it frequently effects solidarity among generations, that is, it attempts to even out inequalities of an intertemporal character. In so doing, it builds upon latent or already established organizations, to which the potential members already have a more or less close relationship (*Dülfer, Schnorr von Carolsfeld* et al.).

4) *Co-operatives for the purpose of promoting members' interest* are, if one interprets narrowly § 1, subsec. 1, of the German Co-operative Law in the Federal Republic (→ *Law, National*), under exclusive obligation toward their members. However, the wording of the law states merely that the promotion of the members' businesses or economic welfare is to be the "purpose"; it does not specify that this has to be achieved. Furthermore, one has to consider that the responsibility to serve the members' interests is not laid down by the legislators directly. The legislators simply set down the existence of a promotional relationship as a prerequisite for recognition as a co-operative. Thus, not only the letter of the law but also the autonomy of membership groups to formulate their by-laws play a role in the establishment of co-operatives for the purpose of promoting members' interests. It is probably this type which is still the most prevalent type today (*Beuthien, Boettcher, Dülfer, Paulick* et al.).

5) *Co-operatives for providing a maximized income* for their members are co-operatives that have been transformed, at least with respect to their intended purpose. During the last century, they first developed among workers' co-operative societies whose original purposes had not been to maximize income; but today, profit maximizing co-operative societies can also be found among other co-operatives. They have become similar to other private and profit-maximizing competitors or opponents up to a degree where they cannot be distinguished from them any more. They serve exclusively or at least predominantly the individual interests of members as leaders or part-owners and disregard the wider range of service functions in kind or financial support. Such changes naturally do not exclude promotion of their members in the same way other profit-maximizing businesses "promote" their customers, in some cases to a very large extent, as a consequence of profit-orientation (*Engelhardt, Potter-Webb, Thiemeyer, Weisser, Witte* et al.).

6) *Co-operatives intended to serve a centrally administered economy* carry out functions for a compulsory economic system within a society (*Ritschl*). They have existed as transformed co-operatives ever since the earliest states of absolutistic rule in ancient history. During recent decades, they have been a wide-spread phenomenon under totalitarian regimes of Communist countries. Since the demise of these regimes, they have been rapidly dissolving, with a few exceptions such as in Cuba. As exceptions one can also imagine them in free-market economies in areas like agriculture or transport. As they function one hundred per cent as "instruments" (*Thiemeyer*), one can rule them out as free enterprises for public benefit because compulsion is their constituting element, and they are based not upon "being born into them" nor upon voluntary establishment nor upon democratic decisions (*Ritschl, Thiemeyer, Weisser* et al.).

IV. Typology of Present-Day Forms of Cooperation

If one disregards the two types of transformed co-operatives, then for the remaining types of co-operatives several differentiations in form take on great relevance. Under this aspect one can differentiate among the following:

1) *Co-operatives in the legal sense*, e.g. registered co-operatives according to the above-mentioned German Co-operative Law of 1889 or according to any co-operative law of any country. Here, one can also include the types of legal co-operatives of earlier historic periods, largely based upon common law fixed by custom, and in the present age those of the Anglo-Amercian legal tradition. With regard to the first group, *von Gierke* has differentiated among "free" co-operatives under the old German law, "dependent corporations under private law", and "free" co-operatives under the new law.

2) *Co-operatives in the economic sense* in the most varied forms possible of private or public law or in marginal cases without any legal form. In the Federal Republic of Germany there are co-operatives at present in the legal form not only of registered co-operative (eG) but also, among others, of association under civil law, of registered association (eV), of open trading company (OHG), of limited company (KG), or of corporation or public law. If formulations of the by-laws make the necessary provisions, then co-operatives are also conceivable and actually found in the other legal forms of limited company (GmbH, GmbH & Co KG), with or without limitation by shares, or of joint-stock company (AG). One has to consider that not every co-operative in the legal sense is to be counted automatically as a co-operative in the economic sense, even if requirements of "legal limitation as to type of enterprise" (*Paulick*) are fulfilled (*Beuthien, Blomeyer, Ebert, Münkner, Paulick, Schnorr von Carolsfeld, Westermann* et al.).

3) *Other co-operative types of cooperation*
These mainly include pure associations of persons with no joint business, or, at the most, associations with only rudimentary business activity. Here, one can include mere savings clubs, school co-operatives, and – recently some up in the Federal Republic of Germany – "self-help groups", of which there are thousands, especially in the health sector, in social services and employment projects (*Eschenburg, Kück, Novy, Nutzinger* et al.).

4) *Non-co-operative types of cooperation*
These are found e.g. as teams of as "cooperation in ownership" (*Eschenburg*). Most of all, they exist as forms of cooperation among profit-oriented businesses known as "cartels" or "syndicates" (→ *Anti-Trust Laws*) (*Boettcher, Eschenburg, Hamm* et al.). Between all forms of cooperation and types of co-operative purpose-orientation there are transitional forms and gradual differences which cannot be dealt with here.

V. Types of Co-operatives in the Light of Different Scientific Disciplines and their Main Features

Types of co-operatives have been considered and formulated systematically in various scientific disciplines thus far, for example in legal science, history, sociology, social policy, economics, and particularly often in business adminstration. Since co-operatives are of interest nowadays first and foremost as enterprises and as associations of enterprises, this category of types will be dealt with in a later section.

1) With regard to characteristics singled out by *legal science*, and in addition to the categorization developed by *von Gierke* (already mentioned) according to the main legal turning points in co-operative development in Germany, one can also take up typologies in the manner of the predominating corporation theory. Thus, in addition to the co-operative according to old German law, not only constituted by the members but closely tied to them by relationship of "social law", one could even include corporations in the tradition of Romanic law in the sense of *universitas*, in which the rights of the corporation were kept absolutely separate from those of the individual members (*Thieme*).

2) Under *historical aspects* of the changing *basic co-operative Gestalt*, following *von Gierke*, one has differentiated among co-operatives tied to families or clans and other tied to castes the states, to individual enterprises, social classes or a social order (*Seraphim, Schachtschabel*). Another historical differentiation can be made according to the historical era in which co-operatives were formed, whereby one distinguishes among co-operatives of prehistoric times, of ancient history, of the Middle Ages up to the beginning of the modern period, and among "modern" co-operatives of the industrial age (Back et al.).

3) Seen from the *sociological characteristic* (→ *Societal Form, Co-op.*) of the type of personal ties prevailing in co-operatives, one can differentiate between co-operatives structured as *Gemeinschaft* and others structured as *Gesellschaft* (*Tönnies, Weippert*). Further differentiations in this scientific discipline take into account the power distribution within the co-operative or the occupations of members or their roles within the organization. In the first case, a distinction has been made between a more co-operative form of society with power evenly distributed and a more ruler-dominated form *(Vierkandt, von der Gablentz* et al.). With regard to occupations represented, there are at present co-operatives and similar forms of cooperation for agriculturalist, farmers, forest-owners, hunters, wine-growers, water-suppliers, fishermen, ship-owners, miners, transport businessmen, taxi-drivers, lorry-drivers, bakers, butchers, shoemakers, hairdressers, re-

tailers, architects, specialists in construction statics, doctors, pharmacists, etc., but also for unemployed persons, refugees, women, school children, and others.

4) Under aspects of → *social policy*, one can differentiate according to the living situations of members, that is, between co-operatives of less well-to do and those of economically saturated members (*Albrecht, Weisser*). According to the extent to which co-operatives have a role in safeguarding the economic existence of their members, there are also various types, such as "augmentary" and "full" co-operatives.

5) As far as the various possibilities for differentiation and grouping *in economics* go, those criteria are especially important which touch the relationship of the co-operative to the state. There are self-help co-operatives (*Schulze-Delitzsch*), self-help creating co-operatives (*Dülfer, Weisser*), co-operatives that build upon state assistance (*Lassalle*), and collective state enterprises (*Draheim*). But distinctions are also important according to the position of the co-operatives within the co-operative system, as well as according to the branch of the economy to which the co-operatives belong. In the first case, there are primary and central co-operatives, the latter divided into secondary and tertiary co-operatives. Under the aspect of the branch of the economy to which the co-operatives belong, there are agricultural, forestry, and fishery co-operatives, as well as others in energy distribution, handicraft, industry, retail and wholesale business, transport, and other services, including those that serve consumers directlcy.

VI. Types of Co-operatives and Other Forms of Cooperation as Viewed from the Discipline of Business Administration

1) With regard to their business features, one can differentiate, depending on the *degree of improvisation or organization* which the co-operatives in the economic sense or other forms of cooperation display, between activity-oriented (*process-oriented*) and formalized (*institutionalized*) forms of cooperation.

a) Under the aspect of the categories of *enterprises or households* which are the shareholders of these co-operatives, one has differentiated for a long time now – supported, for example, by the German co-operative Law – between business co-operatives (in the German Law *Erwerbsgenossenschaften* of the urban business or agricultural or rural type) and household co-operatives (in the German Law *Wirtschaftsgenossenschaften*, that is, consumers', housing, health care, insurance, and school co-operatives).

b) Under the aspect of the *main purpose of co-operative activity*, one can differentiate between merchandising co-operatives (of consumers, craftsmen, retailers and wholesalers, farmers, etc.) and credit or credit guarantee co-operatives (of the urban business or rural type, some of them organized especially for consumers), which can also exist in mixed forms. It is the merchandising and credit co-operatives which are definitely the dominating type in the industrial age. But aside from all these, from time immemorial there have been labour co-operatives for marketing their members' work capacity, which societies either just group wage-earners into "work co-operatives" (in the USSR these often exist in the form of "attached" co-operatives at the present time) or which were intended as full-production co-operatives in overcoming the dependency of wage-labourers on the employer (in agriculture these are sometimes called "joint production co-operatives"). Co-operatives that solely provide services tend to have been founded more recently, e.g. in the transportation and the tax-consulting business.

c) Under the aspect of the *number of business functions* the co-operative assumes, one can differentiate among single-purpose, multi-purpose, and universal co-operatives, of which the last-mentioned are hard to bring into being and are therefore rare.

d) Under the aspect of the *kind of business functions* taken over by the co-operative, one has usually differentiated thus far between purchasing and marketing co-operatives (e.g. *Henzler*). It might be useful, however, to consider other central functions of modern business administration as differentiation criteria as well, in so far as co-operatives or other forms of co-operation make these functions a basis of their activity. In this respect there are production co-operatives, financing co-operatives – including credit guarantee associations, guarantee co-operatives, and investment groups – and administration co-operatives, e.g. book-keeping associations. Many further typologies based on one or several business dimensions are possible, but cannot be presented here (cf. *Engelhardt* 1984).

2. Of greater importance for present-day business administration and for disciplinary as well as interdisciplinary research are types of *multidimensional differentiation and re-grouping*.

a) Some of these have become known as *development types, structural types,* or structural development types. In respect to the intensity of business relations between the co-operatives and their members' businesses, one originally differentiated among co-operative shops, co-operative enterprises, and joint co-operative enterprises (*Henzler*) and among traditional co-operatives,

market co-operatives, and integrated co-operatives (*Dülfer*) (→ *Structural Types*).
b) In a much more broadened approach (→ *Managerial Economics*) involving system theory and decision theory, *Dülfer* has recently not only renamed these types, referring to co-operative terminology mentioned earlier. By means of statements on highly differing co-operative subsystems to be found not only in western industrial nations but also in developing countries, *Dülfer* has also offered a more complete description of these types of co-operatives. Similar to the concept mentioned earlier of co-operatives having a triple nature, *Dülfer* considers as three subsystems of a co-operative the members' businesses or households, the co-operative group, and the co-operative business enterprise. A further and different relationship results if we answer the question about what keeps each of these subsystems together. Under this aspect, he differentiates among communication systems having to do with the functioning of the business (BKS), with legal aspects of the organization (OKS), and with interpersonal relationships within the organization (IKS). From these three basic subsystems a fourth communication system has been derived, the "management-membership information system", which essentially reflects the technical consequence of daily communication. Of greater importance for typology is *Dülfer's* new characterization of structure types in place of the earlier development types: "In the case of an "executively operating" it is the members' own businesses and households which control and give impetus to the business activity of the operational unit ("Organbetrieb") through their actual demands for promotional services.". "In the case of a "market-linkage co-operative", the members' businesses and the operational unit operate more or less independently of each other, held together only loosely by the basic responsibility ("Grundauftrag") of the co-operative to promote members. In the case of the "integrated co-operative" it is the operational unit which largely controls and gives impetus to the economic activities of the members' businesses, on the basis of their voluntary acceptance (with feedback effects) of decisions and recommendations made by the co-operative enterprise through its superior level of information" (*Dülfer* 1984).
c) In partial reference to *Blümle*, and by means of a feature matrix which is also system-oriented, *Schwarz* (→ *Federations*) has attempted a morphology and typology of all forms of cooperation and association among business enterprises. The author takes into consideration a total of 34 individual characteristics and many more feature gradations from the first through the third degree. His approach differentiates among the total of included phenomena first according to the cooperation strategy employed and arrives at cooperation for co-ordination, cooperation for representation, and cooperation for economizing. Through consideration of the specific function as a further charcteristic, *Schwarz* comes up with a total of nine types: functional groups, promotional co-operatives, service associations, special interest associations, bargaining associations, associations for trade regulation, cartels, co-operation for specialization, and vertical co-operation. Of interest here, under the aspect of co-operatives in the legal or economic sense, and of other forms of co-operation, are beside the promotional co-operatives, the functional groups, forms of co-operation for specialization, and forms of vertical co-operation. By functional groups the author means groups of enterprises that work together to make their activities more effective, either by setting up a joint enterprise or by co-operating with a leading firm in order to take care of purchasing, provision of goods and services, and marketing for the purpose of increasing efficiency and improving their competitive position. Co-operation for specialization includes not only specialization along product lines in marketing but also division of labour in internal business functions such as research and development. Vertical co-operation, as between producers and traders or wholesalers and retailers, is principally an agreement on trade relations but can also be extended to other activities. In a delivery system or an agreement on exclusive sales representation, the group would be small, whereas in asymmetrical co-operation between wholesalers and retailers there could be large groups (*Schwarz* 1979).

Bibliography

Albert, Hans (ed.): Theorie und Realität (Tübingen 1964) Tübingen 1972.
Blau, Peter M./Scott, Richard: Formal Organizations. A Comparative Approach, London 1963.
Blümle, Ernst-Bernd/Schwarz, Peter (eds.): Wirtschaftsverbände und ihre Funktion, Darmstadt 1985.
Castan, Edgar: Typologie der Betriebe, Stuttgart 1963.
Draheim, Georg: Die Genossenschaft als Unternehmungstyp (Göttingen 1951) Göttingen 1955.
Dülfer, Eberhard: Betriebswirtschaftslehre der Kooperative, Göttingen 1984.
Dülfer, Eberhard: Zur Frage des Unternehmenscharakters der Genossenschaft, ZgGenW, Göttingen, 6 (1956), pp. 265–274.
Engelhardt, Werner W./Thiemeyer, Theo (eds.): Genossenschaft – quo vadis? Supplement 11 of ZögU, Baden-Baden 1988.
Engelhardt, Werner Wilhelm: Allgemeine Ideengeschichte des Genossenschaftswesens, Darmstadt 1985.
Engelhardt, Werner Wilhelm: Grundprobleme der Einzelwirtschaftstypologie, Cologne Dissertation 1957.
Engelhardt, Werner Wilhelm: Unternehmungstypen, Gablers Wirtschaftslexikon, Wiesbaden 1988, col. 2178–2184.

Engelhardt, Werner Wilhelm: Zur Relevanz morphologischtypologischer Theorieaspekte für die Genossenschaftslehre, Genossenschaften und genossenschaftswissenschaftliche Forschung, Regensburg 1989, pp.35–48.
Engelhardt, Werner Wilhelm: Zur Unterscheidung von Arten und Typen der Genossenschaften und diesen verwandter Kooperativen, ZgGenw, Göttingen, 34(1984), pp. 6–20.
Hahn, Oswald: Struktur der Bankwirtschaft, vol. 1, Banktypologie und Universalbanken, Nürnberg 1981.
Hamm, Walter: Sind Genossenschaften Kartelle? ZögU, Baden-Baden, 4(1981), pp. 1–18.
Henzler, Reinhold: Die Genossenschaft eine fördernde Betriebswirtschaft, Essen 1957.
Kück, Marlene: Betriebswirtschaft der Kooperative, Stuttgart 1989.
Lambert, Paul: La Doctrine coopérative (Brussels/Paris 1959) Brussels 1964.
Münkner, Hans.H.: Ausprägungen genossenschaftlicher Struktur in Westeuropa, Tübingen 1985.
Paulick, Heinz: Die eingetragene Genossenschaft als Beispiel gesetzlicher Typenbeschränkung, Tübingen 1954.
Potter-Webb, Beatrice: The Co-operative Movement in Great Britain (London 1891) London 1930.
Schwarz, Peter: Morphologie von Kooperationen und Verbänden, Tübingen 1979.
Thiemeyer, Theo: Wirtschaftslehre öffentlicher Betriebe, Reinbeck 1975.
Tietz, Bruno: Bildung und Verwendung von Typen in der Betriebswirtschaftslehre, Köln/Opladen 1960.
von Gierke, Otto: Rechtsgeschichte der deutschen Genossenschaft (Berlin 1868) Darmstadt 1954.
Weisser, Gerhard: Form und Wesen der Einzelwirtschaften, vol.1 (Stuttgart 1947) Göttingen 1955.

Co-determination in Germany

WOLFGANG H. STAEHLE

(see also: *Industrial Relations*; *Workers Co-determination*; *Managerial Economics*)

I. Historical Roots of Contemporary Co-determination in Germany; II. Range of Application; III. Structure and Responsibilities of Co-determination Bodies; IV. The Process of Co-determination; V. The Reality of Co-determination. Co-determination refers to the legally codified participation of employees (or their representatives) in decision-making of management at various levels of a company. Participation offered by management to employees (e.g., management by objectives, quality circles) that is not covered or prescribed by law is not subsumed in the concept of co-determination.

I. Historical Roots of Contemporary Co-determination in Germany

Whereas in the nineteenth century the entrepreneur as employer acted like an absolute monarch (corporate governance based unilaterally on the interests of capital), the industrial relations system today takes both capital and labor into account. In other words, the interests of the employees (labor) are organized in a system of representation alongside the traditional chain of command organized by capital. Demands for co-determination through works councils, so-called factory committees, were first raised in the Constituent National Assembly in Frankfurt in 1848. It was not until the constitution of 1919 that works councils were mandated by law. Companies with at least twenty employees were obliged by the Works Council Act of 1920 (Betriebsratsgesetz) to set up works councils. This practice ended when Hitler took over in Germany in 1933. After World War II, the Allied Control Council Act No. 22 of 1946 (Kontrollratsgesetz) again legalized the establishment of works councils. Shortly thereafter, the first attempts to legalize co-determination at the board level were stated in the British-occupied zone. The idea of the British Military Government was to weaken the former Germany military-industrial complex (the iron and steel industry) through massive worker and union co-determination. In 1951 an act establishing the co-determination of workers in the supervisory and management boards of companies in the coal, iron, and steel industry (Montanmitbestimmungsgesetz) was passed. In other parts of the industry, co-determination at the board level is regulated by the Co-determination Act of 1976. At the plant level, the Works Constitution Act of 1952 (Betriebsverfassungsgesetz) took up the tradition of the 1920 Works Council Act for all companies with at least five employees. (This law was considerably amended in 1972 and 1989.) For this and the following sections, the English terminology for the German co-determination laws largely follows the translation by the International Labor Office (publishing by the German Federal Minister of labor and Social Affairs) (→ *United Nations System*).

II. Range of Application

Under German law not all employees enjoy co-determination rights. The individual regulations are highly fragmented and differentiated. Several factors determine whether individual employee interests are represented by legally prescribed collective bodies inside companies (co-determination through company-level works councils and at the supervisory-board level) and/or by trade unions across the boundaries of plants and companies (the so-called dual system of industrial relations). Being completely voluntary, the latter arrangement will not be treated in this article (see Industrial Relations in Germany).
For an employee to be entitled to exercise co-determination rights (either actively as a representative or passively as a voting member of an organization), it is important for that employee's company to be subject to one of the co-determination laws.

Size of the plant, legal form, and type of industry
In a plant that normally has *five* or more permanent employees, works councils shall be elected, regardless of the legal form and type of industry. If the establishment belongs to the private sector, the Works Constitution Act is applicable; if it belongs to the public sector, the Staff Representation Act (Personalvertretungsgesetz) is used. According to *Chmielewicz* (1990, p.419), some 60% of all German employees have co-determination rights under these laws.

In a joint-stock company with more than *five hundred* employees, regardless of the type of industry, co-determination at the plant level (works councils) is complemented by representation of labor on the supervisory board (one third of the members; the other two thirds of the members represent capital interests). Co-determination rights of employees in this size group are also regulated in the Works Constitution Act of 1952.

Persons working in a joint-stock company with more than *one thousand* employees in the coal, iron, and steel industry enjoy the strongest co-determination rights in Germany (see section I). Since only thirty companies comprise this sector of industry (approximately 4% of all employees), it is no doubt a group of extreme symbolic importance, but in terms of numbers it is negligible. One half of the supervisory board members represent labor (parity co-determination), including external trade-union representatives. Deadlock situations, which are always possible because of the even number on each bench (capital and labor), are resolved through the neutral member. This eleventh member cannot be elected against the majority vote of either labor or the shareholders and thus has the confidence of both benches. In addition there must be a labor director on the management board in charge of social and personnel affairs. This person cannot be elected without a majority of the votes cast by the representatives of labor on the supervisory board. The far-reaching co-determination rights in this sector are regulated by the Montan-Mitbestimmungsgesetz of 1951.

In a joint-stock company with more than *two thousand* employees, regardless of the type of industry, co-determination at the plant level is complemented representatives of labor on the supervisory board (who hold half of the seats). Unlike the solution in coal, iron, and steel industry, however, deadlock situations are resolved through a second vote cast by a chairman. Since the chairman represents the shareholders, we speak of imperfect parity in the supervisory board. Another difference is that the labor director may be elected against the will of the labor bench. This means in reality that the labor director is almost a representative of capital. Co-determination rights in this size group are regulated by the Co-determination Act of 1976. Some five hundred companies, representing approximately 20% of all employees, belong to this group.

In addition to the size of the plant/company, its legal form, and the type of industry, co-determination rights differ according to employee status.

Employee status
German law distinguishes between three groups of employees:

- Executives (leitende Angestellte)
- White-collar workers, or salaried employees (Angestellte)
- Blue-collar workers, or wage earners (Arbeiter)

Executives are differentiated from salaried employees by their managerial status and their right to hire and dismiss personnel. Executives thus have the position of an employer. Consequently, they are excluded from all representation at the plant level (works council). Since 1989 executives may vote for an executive council (Sprecherausschuß) if ten or more managers enjoy executive status. But the co-determination rights of executive councils, namely, the right to be informed by the management board, are only very weak compared to those of the works council. At the company level, the Co-determination Act provides for at least one representative of the executives on the labor bench of the supervisory board, a right that is clearly at odds with this member's status as an employer.

White-collar and blue-collar workers constitute two bodies that separately elect their representatives to the works council and the labor bench of the supervisory board. Thus, the composition of these bodies corresponds to the total number of employees belonging to each group in the plan/company.

III. Structure and Responsibilities of Co-determination Bodies

1. Works Council

Works council elections are held every four years. Immediately after its constitution, the works council elects two of its members as chairperson and vice chairperson. If the works council consists of nine or more members, it sets up a works committee for dealing with day-to-day business and may establish additional committees if necessary. The works council meets during working hours, and any expenses incurred by its activities are covered by the employer. Works council members are released from their other duties without loss of pay. In plants with more than three hundred employees, at least one member of the works council is released from all other duties. The works council may call a works meeting (composed of all wage and salary earners of the plant) during working hours once in every calendar quarter and reports on its activities and plans. Section 80 (1) of the Works Constitution Act of 1972 lists the following general *responsibilities* of the works council:

1. To see that effect is given to acts, ordinances, safety regulations, collective agreements, and works agreements for the benefit of the personnel
2. To make recommendations to the employer for action benefiting the establishment and the personnel
3. To receive suggestions from the personnel and the youth delegation and, if they are found to be justified, to inform the relevant personnel about the status of corresponding negotiations with the employers
4. To promote the rehabilitation of disabled persons and other persons in particular need of assistance
5. To prepare and organize the election of a youth delegation and to collaborate closely with it in promoting the interests of the young employees; it may invite the youth delegation to make suggestions and to state its views on various matters
6. To promote the employment of elderly workers in the establishment
7. To promote the integration of foreign workers in the establishment and to further understanding between them and their German colleagues

The *rights* of the works council are divided into three areas:

- Social matters (e.g., daily working hours, vacations, wage structure, suggestion schemes)
- Personnel matters (e.g., personnel planning, vocational training, hiring, transfer or dismissal of employees)
- Economic matters (e.g., investment, production, marketing, organization structure)

The extent of these rights differs considerably, decreasing from social to economic matters. The strongest are co-determination rights (Mitbestimmungsrechte), including the rights to oppose, refuse consent on, and veto management decisions. Participatory rights (Mitwirkungsrechte) are weaker and include the mere right to be informed or to be consulted. Section 87 (1) of the Works Constitution Act of 1972 lists the social matters where the works council has a right of co-determination insofar as they are not prescribed by legislation or collective agreement:

1. Matters relating to the work regulations of the establishment (Betriebsordnung) and the conduct of the employees in the establishment
2. The commencement and termination of the daily working hours, including breaks and the distribution of working hours among the days of the week
3. Any temporary reduction or extension of the hours normally worked in the establishment
4. The time, place, and manner of remuneration
5. The establishment of general principles for leave arrangements and the preparation of the leave schedule as well as the fixing of the period during which leave is to be taken by individual employees if no agreement is reached between the employer and the employees concerned
6. The introduction and use of technical devices designed to monitor the behaviour or performance of the employees
7. Arrangements for preventing accidents at work, preventing occupational diseases, and protecting health on the basis of legislation or safety regulations
8. The form, structure, and administration of social services limited to the establishment, company, or combine
9. The assignment of and notice to vacate accommodation that is rented to employees by virtue of their employment relationship as well as the general fixing of the conditions for the use of such accommodation
10. Questions related to remuneration arrangements in the establishment, in particular the determination of principles of remuneration, the introduction and application of new renumeration methods or the modification of existing methods
11. The setting of job and bonus rates and comparable performance-related remuneration, including cash coefficients (i.e., prices per time unit)
12. Principles for suggestion schemes in the establishment

2. Supervisory Board

Co-determination at the company level exists only in joint-stock companies with more than five hundred employees (who hold 33% of the seats); joint-stock companies with more than one thousand employees in the coal, iron and steel industry (50% of the seats); and joint-stock companies with more than two thousand employees in any industry (50% of the seats). Since representatives of labor on supervisory boards enjoy the same rights as all other board members, the rights and responsibilities of board members as laid down in the Public Limited Company Act (Aktiengesetz) apply. Important rights of the supervisory board are to elect and dismiss the members of the management board, approve the annual accounts prepared by the managing board, and approve all major investments and transactions of the company. Its responsibility is to monitor and oversee the management board in the interests of the owners and the employees. But it is prevented by law from interfering with day-to-day management action.

IV. The Process of Co-determination

The basic philosophy of postwar co-determination in Germany is consensus, not conflict, between labor and management. According to Section 2 (1) of the Works Constitution Act, the employer and the works

council shall work together in a spirit of mutual trust (Prinzip der vertrauensvollen Zusammenarbeit).
If, nevertheless, consensus is not reached on matters requiring co-determination (especially Section 87 of the Works Constitution Act), the conflict is referred to the conciliation commitee (Einigungsstelle), half the members of which are appointed by the works council and half by the management. The conciliation committee is headed by a neutral (external) chairperson.
Agreements reached by this committee by majority vote are binding for both parties. If there is no such agreement, the committee can appeal to the labor court for a final decision. Labor-court decisions are an important source of change in the German industrial relations system in general and in co-determination in particular.
In the case of participatory rights, the works council has only to be informed and sometimes consulted (e.g., lay-offs, economic decisions). In the end, management is free to proceed as planned. This means, for example, that rationalization measures cannot be prevented but that the works council may ask for compensation of the workers affected. Bargaining starts between managements and the works council on a works agreement, which can turn out to be a social compensation plan that reconciles the interests of both parties in cases of major organizational change. If no agreement is reached, the matter is referred to the conciliation committee. On account of the principle of cooperation in good faith, however, this course of action is not the regular procedure. Most disputes are settled without involving the conciliation committee.

V. The Reality of Co-determination

Although by law works councils are to be elected in all plants with five or more permanent employees (see section II), most small companies ranging in size from five to fifty employees and a large number of medium-size companies have no works council. Only the larger companies (those with over five hundred employees) fully comply with the co-determination laws. As far as co-determination at the company level is concerned, this kind of employee participation is widely accepted by German entrepreneurs.
This was not always the case. In the late 1970s, when the Co-determination Act was passed, many companies tried to evade co-determination on supervisory boards, sometimes by splitting the company into two smaller establishments if it had over two thousand employees, or by changing its legal form from a joint-stock company to a partnership and thereby creating companies not subject to the Co-determination Act of 1976. Today, the attitude has become more liberal; owners are no longer reluctant to accept co-determination. On the contrary, most entrepreneurs and chief executives have found co-determination to be very helpful in implementing difficult management decisions that require the full support of all the employees. Early information and intensive consultation with employee representatives is deemed to be the key to successful management of change and a key to Germany's success as a leading competitor in the world.
Another important part of reality in German co-determination is that the representation of employee interests is not strictly separated between trade unions and works councils (dual system) as stipulated by law. About 75% of all works council members are also union members, and works councils are heavily supported and influenced by trade union officials. In all larger companies, the unions can also rely on elected or appointed union representatives known as shop stewards (Vertrauenleute) as major sources of information and as communications links between unionized workers, works-council members and the union administration.
Another strong personal overlap exists between co-determination at the plant and company levels, since in most cases works council members are also members of the supervisory board. Usually, the works council chairperson is simultaneously the deputy chairperson of the supervisory board. In reality, the chairpersons of the management board, the supervisory board, and the works council constitute the inner circle of the company's top leadership. In this group all critical questions are discussed informally before information is given to the legally prescribed bodies.
Whereas entrepreneurs in the early postwar period tended to regard co-determination only as costly and time consuming because it increased bureaucracy and delayed important decisions, it is accepted today as an important way to keep social peace by mitigation and channeling conflicts or – through early information and consultation – by anticipating possible confrontation and eliminating the sources of conflict in advance.
From the viewpoint of the trade unions, co-determination does not go far enough. At the company level there is only imperfect parity on the supervisory board (see section II); at the plant level, works councils enjoy only the weakest participation rights where important economic matters are concerned. In any case, no significant changes in German co-determination laws are foreseeable, except for the necessary adaptation to new EC standards (see the First Directive on the structure of public limited companies and the powers and obligations of their organs).

Bibliography

Federal Ministry of Labor and Social Affairs (BMA) (ed.): Co-determination in the Federal Republic of Germany, Bonn 1980.
Federal Ministry of Justice (BMJ) (ed.): Bericht über die

Verhandlungen der Unternehmensrechtskommission [Report on the negotiations of the Commission on Corporate Law], Cologne 1980.
Säcker, Franz J./Zander, Ernst (eds.): Mitbestimmung und Effizienz [Co-determination and Efficiency], Stuttgart 1981.
Wächter, Hartmut: Mitbestimmung (Co-determination), Munich 1983.
Endruweit, Günter/Gaugler, Eduard/Staehle, Wolfgang H./Wilpert, Bernhard (eds.): Handbuch der Arbeitsbeziehungen, Berlin, New York 1985.
Gladstone, Alan/Lansbury, Russel/Sticher, Jack/Treu, Tiziano/Weiss, Manfred (eds.): Current Isspective, Berlin, New York 1989.
Chmielewicz, Klaus: Co-determination. Handbook of German Business Management, Berlin 1990, col. 412–428.

Combine, Co-operative

JÜRGEN ZERCHE [F]

(see also: *Federations*; *Central Institutions*; *Classification*; *Anti-Trust Laws*; *Principles*)

I. The Problem; II. The Phenomenon of Cooperation in Theory and Practice; III. Combines in Various Co-operative Sectors in Germany; IV. Co-operative Combines in Western Europe; V. Outlook for the Future.

I. The Problem

1. Differentiation of Terms

For the term 'co-operative combine' there is neither a legal definition, nor can such a definition be derived from concrete norms (*Westermann*). Thus, the attempts to define it in scientific literature are correspondingly varied. Etymologically the term 'combine' (Verbund) expresses the effect of bringing formerly separate entities together into one whole (*Grochla*). In politics and the Church, one speaks of "confederation".
When members with their businesses join together into a primary co-operative, this alone leads to the creation of a co-operative business combine or a primary combine. When co-operatives join together at a higher level, then one speaks of a secondary combine (*Dülfer*).
Frequently the entire co-operative organization or system is included under the term combine (*Leffson*). In this article here, however, a more particular differentiation is meant: a combine as the specific form of voluntary economic cooperation among co-operatives at a higher level, both horizontally and vertically (*Schultz/Zerche*), with the purpose of promoting primary units.

2. Historical Roots in the Example of Germany

There is no exact date for the establishment of the co-operative combine system. But the idea of combining has been immanent in the co-operative movement from the beginning and is contained in the promotion mandate laid down by co-operative pioneers as the purpose of the co-operative (*Reiners*). In the beginning, problems of finance were the reason for horizontal cooperation of primary co-operatives. A pooling of financial resources was to take care of the problem within the organization and to make possible more efficient activity to promote members (→ *History in 19th C.*).
In 1860 a central correspondence office took over the task of co-ordinating these efforts among industrial co-operatives, and only five years later the first central bank owned by co-operatives was founded under the name of "Deutsche Genossenschaftskasse von Soergel, Parrisius & Co". The first central bank among agricultural co-operatives was founded in 1872 (→ *Central Institutions*).
As straight on as this development appears to have been in retrospect, in reality it was quite devious. In the so-called systemic dispute ("Systemstreit") between → *Schulze-Delitzsch* and → *Raiffeisen* in the 1870's, all the problems over supervision, power, and liability in a multi-level organization were touched on, which still characterize the discussion on combine policy today (*Noelle, Pfüller, Zerche*).

II. The Phenomenon of Cooperation in Theory and Practice

1. Cooperation as a Universal Principle

Co-operative behaviour can be observed in all areas of life. Scientific disciplines as far apart as biology, psychology, political science, sociology, or even mathematics in the form of game theory find cooperation to be a subject of research (→ *Theory of co-operative Cooperation*).
In economics as well, the phenomenon of human cooperation is of central importance. Its potential to form structures and to organize is a basis of every economy. Dimensions of cooperation range from unconscious cooperation of economic entities in an economy of division of labour (invisible hand) to deliberate agreements to attain a common goal through joint action (*Eschenburg*). Under certain market conditions, co-operative behaviour can be the only rational way to behave. A solution for the classical "prisoners' dilemma" occurs when one deals with regularly or frequently repeated situations of cooperation with a great number of partners who can be chosen freely (*Tullock*). We also find forms of cooperation among businesses and others in all economies, independent of the type of economic sys-

tem or of the relative importance of industries. In this context it is to distinguish co-operative combine systems from cartels and company groups.

2. Organizational Principles of Co-operative Combine Business

The basic principles of economic cooperation in the co-operative combine are → *solidarity* on the horizontal level and subsidiarity in the vertical direction. The horizontal combine consists of primary co-operatives of equal rank, operating in limited geographic areas, each co-operative legally and, as a rule, economically independent, and assuming liability for each other e.g. by standing guaranty for each other in a common guarantee institution. The vertical combine, on the other hand, comprises enterprises of various levels of business activity; in addition to the primary co-operatives as members of the economic units at higher levels, this includes secondary and tertiary level units and their subsidiaries and separate enterprises in which they own parts of equity capital (→ *Federations*). They all serve the purpose of equalizing risks as well as of adjusting quantities and qualities to their needs, in order to achieve a more effective fulfillment of functions and a strengthening of market power. The higher levels of organization take over transferable function whenever these can help promote the members of primary co-operatives, and whenever the primary level is not in a position to provide these functions at the same quality. The initiative for such business activity remains with the primary level for each of these functions.

According to paragraph 1 of the German Co-operative Law, co-operatives have the right to participate financially in other enterprises only in cases where this activity as a rule helps them to fulfill their basic mandate, as laid down in the same paragraph of the Law (→ *Legal Form, Co-operative*). An exception to this rule can be seen only in a provision in §1, subsec. 2 No.2 of the Co-operative Law which permits common welfare-oriented activities as a side purpose.

The activity of the combine can therefore not be directed to making profits for the top organization or apex banks (*Westermann*). Rather, the focus and yardstick of success of all combine activity remains the individual self-administered co-operative (*Bungenstock*); one also speaks of the *Förderungsauftrag* (→ *promotion mandate*) of the co-operative combine (*Henzler*).

a) Discipline within the Combine versus Co-operative Autonomy

In certain cases, superordinate group interests can begin to compete for priority with the promotion mandate of the individual entity and can work against it, at least in the short run. This leads to the question of what is to be understood as discipline in a combine and how it is to be achieved without infringing on co-operative autonomy.

If one defines co-operative autonomy as the opportunity for members to decide independently on the principles for realizing their promotion interests, then measures taken by a third party, even if their intention coincides with what is provided in §1, subsec.1 of the German Co-operative Law, can come into conflict with co-operative autonomy (*Metz*).

A demarcation of this type, however, puts too much emphasis on internal solidarity at the expense of outward solidarity. Economic cooperation within the combine can strengthen the position of co-operatives in the competition among groups only if it is extensively used. Its basis is therefore reliability and reciprocity and presupposes a willingness to compromise among all combine participants (*Horlacher*).

The top organization of the combine possesses the right neither to make leadership decisions binding on the whole combine nor to influence the business management of its affiliated co-operatives in a legal way by appointing their policy-makers or managers. Thus there can be a tendency to develop disciplinary means of imposing guidelines in the co-operative combine. For example, it would be conceivable to issue warnings or impose sanctions in the use of combine facilities, e.g. in the form of exclusion from promotion measures and credit facilities (*Westermann*). This does not apply, however, to those services which are open for participation in a free-rider position. At the same time one should not overlook the problem that the top organization of the combine could gradually become more and more independent or that the balance of power could be shifted at the expense of the primary level (→ *Business Policies*).

b) Combine and Company Group

The differences between a combine and a company group are significant (→ *Laws Concerning Company Groups*). While the top of a company group unites and controls legally independent enterprises under a unified leadership, the top level of a co-operative combine is expected to provide services for its constituent owners, the primary co-operatives. The combine is thus like a group pyramid turned upside down; in the relation between company group and combine, reflects the opposition of decentralization and centralization as organizational principles. Solution in establishing combines thus tend to combat trends toward concentration more than do solutions in establishing company groups.

Sometimes, however, relationships are also to be found in a co-operative combine which resemble a genuine company group. Thus central co-operative banks (→ *Central Institutions*) often have subsidiaries which the banks as mother companies set to work to promote members' interests. In organizational theory a form of this type is designated as a hybrid.

The degree, the intensity, and the capacity of the powers-that-be in a company group to enforce their will is sometimes more and sometimes less pronounced, depending on the arrangement oriented at integration or a contractual or a more de-facto relationship.

In this connection the fact is disturbing that in the co-operative combine today there often exist structures similar to those of company group-in-effect. This is especially true for personal and organizational links, e.g. crossties in appointments and accumulation of offices in the hands of individuals responsible for decisions at the top of the combine. A decreasing representation of simple members in favour of more full-time managers on the boards of directors and boards of supervisors of the combines also raises the question of how much supervision is actually possible for the real owners of the combine, the members of primary societies (*Großfeld/Jäger/Lenfers*).

c) Combine and Cartel

The larger the optimum or minimum sizes of businesses become, and the stronger the units of competitors grow to be, the more vital becomes economic cooperation on the combine level in the co-operative sector (*Henzler*). In such cases, the combine helps to build up an alternative, countervailing power and thus does not eliminate competition, but makes it truly possible.

Nonetheless, co-operatives and their combine cooperation are not per se free of the suspicion of being cartels. In principle, the German law on competition (→ *Anti-Trust Laws*) is neutral as far as the legal forms of enterprises are concerned and grants no special status to co-operatives. Therefore the effect of co-operative combine activity upon competition has to be examined in each case (*Beuthien, Köhler*).

It is possible, in principle for coalition both on the demand side (purchasing co-operatives) and on the supply side (marketing co-operatives) to produce effects which harm competition (→ *Commercial Co-operatives*; → *Marketing*).

III. Combines in Various Co-operative Sectors in Germany

The various areas of the co-operative movement (→ *Classification*) take advantage in differing ways of the possibility to transfer individual functions to different levels of the combine. But generally a two-level arrangement prevails; often additional specialized combine enterprises are organized as subsidiaries of central co-operatives (*Bungenstock*).

1. Credit Co-operatives

The basis of the co-operative banking group (→ *Co-operative Banks*) comprises more than three thousand credit co-operatives, all active at the local or regional level. In addition to people's banks and Raiffeisen banks, these also include some banks set up as co-operatives for occupational groups. They present themselves nowadays mainly as universal banks.

The regional central banks as a secondary level of the co-operative banking combine (→ *Central Institutions*) mainly provide an exchange of liquidity and serve as a refinancing unit and depository bank for the primary level. At the same time they carry on a credit business; and, in cooperation with the apex bank of the German co-operative banking group, which is the "DG BANK Deutsche Genossenschaftsbank", they act as the contact point for trade with foreign countries.

According to the DG BANK Law, the DG BANK as the tertiary level has the mandate of promoting all branches of co-operative activity above the regional level and in all industries. Otherwise it is active in the same areas as the central banks. The credit co-operative sector as a whole has a share of 16.9 percent (1988) of the business volume of all banks in Germany (Deutsche Bundesbank). This set-up is augmented by special banking institutions in the combine (1988: 4) offering specialized financing services nationwide. In this manner the co-operative combine was able to offer an all-finance package long before this concept became generally known (*von Harder*).

In recent years the co-operative banking combine has been marked by moves toward concentration (*Zerche*) and by controversial debates on restructuring the combine organization. In a medium-term plan the banking business of the regional central banks and of the DG BANK would be brought together and the ownership of the DG BANK and other important combine enterprises of the co-operative finance sector are to be re-organized (*BVR*) (→ *Structural Changes*). Thus far several central banks have already merged with the DG BANK. There is debate about whether a streamlining of the combine like this will really lead to strengthened rights of participation and supervision for local co-operative banks, or whether the consequence will not be an increase of power for the top institution and a reversal of the line of authority to influence policy (*Geilen*).

2. Rural Commodity and Service Co-operatives

The combine of rural commodity merchandising co-operatives and service co-operatives (→ *Rural Co-operatives*), also called the Raiffeisen organization, consists of three levels. The nearly six thousand local commodity, marketing, and service co-operatives (1988: 5705), mainly credit societies with merchandising, supply and marketing co-operatives, co-operatives for processing dairy and milk products, cattle marketing co-operatives, fruit and vegetable co-operatives, and wine-growers' co-operatives, comprise the first level. Here again the local societies are the owners of the central co-operatives that are active at the regional level (1988: 55). On the third level there are several central co-operatives that are active nationwide (*DG BANK*).

For individual products the economic importance of these co-operatives varies greatly. As an average figure one can estimate that co-operatives do over 50 percent of the business in these products.

3. Industrial Commodity and Service Co-operatives

The primary level in this branch of the co-operative sector includes co-operatives of food and beverage retailers, the non-food trade, of butchers and bakers, of non-food craftsmen, of various professions and other branches of economic activity (→ *Commercial Co-operatives*). The weight of these co-operatives in the economy varies greatly. Joint-Production co-operatives, which have no great importance in the West German economy, also belong to this group (1988: 737).

With the exception of bakers' and confectioners' co-operatives, which have central co-operatives at the level, there are no central co-operatives at the regional level. At the national level, however, central co-operatives are active over the whole country (1988: 15). Thus one can say that in this area combines generally have two levels (*DG BANK*).

4. Consumer Co-operatives

Most of the still existing → *consumer co-operatives* do business under the internationally used sign "co-op". The same is true for many consumer co-operatives that have been converted into → *joint stock companies* and for other enterprises closely associated with consumer co-operatives.

The co-op group has a two-level structure. The base is composed of consumer societies with partly local and partly regional areas of activity. Their share in the market in the turn-over of food retailing amounted in 1988 to 10 percent, in the total retail trade to three percent (*DG BANK*).

Since 1974 the central enterprise has been the co-op joint stock company (Co-op AG) in Frankfurt. It presents itself as the top organization of the company group in the consumer co-operative group. In a steady process of streamlining and centralizing originally independent consumer co-operatives, it has created a hierarchically structured big enterprise with its own retail branches, which no longer exhibits the characteristics of a self-governed association of persons with the purpose of promoting the interests of its members (*Schultz/Zerche*).

Criminal actions by the board of directors have led to heavy debt-overload of the enterprise and in 1989 made an overall reconstruction necessary. The upshot of the development was an offer by a group of competitive retailers in 1990 to take over ownership of co-op, which has since been accepted and has led to the break-up of the co-op group.

5. Transport Co-operatives

Transport co-operatives include co-operatives of road transport, taxi-owners, river and canal transport, and other (1988: 74) (→ *Transport Co-operatives*). Road transport and taxi co-operatives each have their own central co-operative, but all other branches comprise one level only. Of special importance are the road transport co-operatives for long-distance transportation of goods, with a share in the market of 94.3 percent (*DG BANK*).

6. Housing Co-operatives

In the sector of German housing co-operatives, a consistent one-level structure has been arrived at (→ *Housing Societies*). Since 1970 the primary co-operatives (1988: 1176) have no longer had a regional or national secondary co-operative (*DG BANK*).

IV. Co-operative Combines in Western Europe

The most important characteristic of the co-operative combine organization in Western Europe is its diversity. There is not even a generally recognized definition for the term co-operative: what is considered an important element of co-operative structure in one country is in other countries a criterion for exlusion from the co-operative movement (*Boettcher*). All the more remarkable are the variations displayed by the forms of co-operative combines existing in Western Europe. This applies to their structures as well as to the way they fulfill their functions. Historical circumstances have determined the time of origin and the emphasis on branches of the economy and on certain regions. Consequently, the degree to which co-operatives have permeated society today, i.e. the number of co-operative members and the share of the market achieved by co-operative enterprises, varies from country to country. The problem of the number of levels in a vertical combine has also been variously solved; there are one-level, two-level, or three-level types of structures. Furthermore, in certain cases, e.g. in Finland, the rule has been broken that lower levels of the combine emerge before higher levels do.

As far as the functions of combines are concerned, one can observe that in several countries, e.g. in Belgium, Greece, and Italy, a close interlocking of co-operative → *federations* and combine organizations exists (*Zerche/Guthard*).

In the following, features peculiar to different countries will be demonstrated on the example of the co-operative banking combine.

The relationship between primary and secondary co-operatives has taken shape in widely different ways. Duties and rights in a combine for liquidity exchange vary as do the degrees of dependence on each other. The great majority of the local co-operative banks accept deposits on their own account and utilize these funds independently. In Sweden and France, however, the banks pass the funds on directly to the central banks, and in the Netherlands, Finland, and Austria a certain percentage of the funds must be passed on in this way. In Germany there are also so-called liquidity calculation forms which help to determine what recommended percentage of deposits should be passed on to the central banks. Belgium, France, Luxemburg, Austria, and Switzerland have regulations which go even beyond this; in these countries the cental banks take over all liquidity surpluses. In close connection with these rules there are regulations which determine the extent of centralism in further business policy decisions. Thus the authority to determine conditions and loan regulations sometimes lies not with the local co-operatives, as in Germany, but with the top enterprise of the combine. The principle of exclusiveness is also regulated differently from country to country (*Guthardt*).

In principle one can say that as the responsibility of the local level diminishes, the need for co-ordination also decreases, but that at the same time the basic co-operative idea of self-responsibility (→ *Principles*) becomes distorted.

V. Outlook for the Future

With a view to the European Community's open market, the multitude of ways shown here in which different nations in Europe have organized co-operative combines is in need of being brought into harmony. If in the sense of group competition, co-operatives are to work together over and above national boundaries, then not only better knowledge of one another is necessary, but also the willingness to compromise. The same holds true for present day developments in Eastern Europe.

Bibliography

Beuthien, Volker: Genossenschaften und Kartellrecht. Das Kartellamt als Orakel – Durch unbegrenzte Auslegung zum offenen Kartellrecht?, Wien 1987.

Boettcher, Erik (Hrsg.): Die Genossenschaft im Wettbewerb der Ideen – eine europäische Herausforderung -, Bericht der XI. Internationalen Genossenschaftswissenschaftlichen Tagung 1985 in Münster, Tübingen 1985.

Boettcher, Erik: Einführung: Autonomie und Verbunddisziplin in der Genossenschaftsorganisation. Autonomie und Verbunddisziplin in der Genossenschaftsorganisation, Tübingen 1982, p. 5f.

Bungenstock, Wilfried: Verbundbildung und Verbundformen im deutschen Genossenschaftswesen. Genossenschaften und Gnossenschaftswissenschaft. Systematische, strukturelle und ordnungspolitische Aspekte des Genossenschaftswesens. Freundesgabe für Professor Dr. Erik Boettcher, Westfälische-Wilhelms-Universität Münster zum 65. Geburtstag, Wiesbaden 1984, pp. 173–184.

BVR Bundesverband der Deutschen Volksbanken und Raiffeisenbanken: Verbundstruktur für die Zukunft. Gemeinsam die Märkte von morgen gewinnen. Untersuchung der Verbundstruktur im Auftrag des Verbandsrates des BVR, Bonn 1989.

Deutsche Bundesbank: Monatsberichte der Deutschen Bundesbank, 41. Jg., No. 4 (April 1989).

DG BANK Deutsche Genossenschaftsbank: Die Genossenschaften in der Bundsrepublik Deutschland 1989. Statistik, Frankfurt 1989.

Dülfer, Eberhard: Organisation und Management im kooperativen Betriebsverbund. VI. Internationale Genossenschaftswissenschaftliche Tagung Gießen 1969, Thema: Genossenschaften im wirtschaftlichen Wachstum, ZfgG, Sonderheft Bd. XX, Göttingen 1970, pp. 76–103.

Eschenburg, Rolf: Ökonomische Theorie der genossenschaftlichen Zusammenarbeit, Tübingen 1971.

Geilen, Bernd: Zur Problematik der zwei- oder Dreistufigkeit des genossenschaftlichen Bankenverbundes, ZögU, Vol. 13 (1990), H.1, pp. 22–39.

Grochla, Erwin: Betriebsverband und Verbandbetrieb. Wesen, Formen und Organisation der Verbände aus betriebswirtschaftlicher Sicht, Berlin 1959.

Grossfeld, B./Jäger, W./Lenfers, G.: Tradition und Zukunft im Genossenschaftsrecht. Die Genossenschaft im Spiegel des Rechts, Ansprachen auf dem Akademischen Festakt "100 Jahre Genossenschaftsgestz" am 12. Juni 1989 im Schloß und im Rathaus zu Münster, Münster 1989, pp. 73–101.

Guthardt, Helmut: Struktur und Wirkungsweise des genossenschaftlichen Bankenverbundes in den Ländern Westeuropas und Nordamerikas. Die Genossenschaften zwischen Mitgliederpartizipation, Verbundbildung und Bürokratietendenzen, Arbeitsergebnisse der X. Internationalen Genossenschaftswissenschaftlichen Tagung 1981 in Marburg, Sonderband der ZfgG, Göttingen 1983, pp. 124–136.

Henzler, Reinhold: Die Genossenschaftsunternehmung und der Genossenschaftsverbund. Methoden und Probleme der Wirtschaftspolitik. Gedächtnisschrift für Hans-Jürgen Seraphim, Berlin 1964, pp. 283–297.

Horlacher, Hellmut: Verbund, genossenschaftlicher. Handwörterbuch des Genossenschaftswesens, Wiesbaden 1980, cols. 1557–1574.

Köhler, Helmut: Genossenschaften im Spiegel von Kartellrecht und Antitrust-Recht, ZfgG (1983), Vol. 33, pp. 105–127.

Leffson, Ulrich: Genossenschaftliche Verbundbildung als Mittel zur Effizienzsteigerung der Mitgliederbetriebe. Genossenschaften und Genossenschaftsforschung. Festschrift zum 65. Geburtstag von Georg Draheim, Göttingen 1968, pp. 154–169.

Metz, Egon: Genossenschaftsautonomie und externe Verbandprüfung. Autonomie und Verbunddisziplin in der Genossenschaftsorganisation, Tübingen 1982, pp. 7–21.

Noelle, Birgit: Genossenschaftsverbund und Mitgliederförderung, Frankfurt am Main 1989.

Pfüller, Reiner: Der Genossenschaftsverbund, Göttingen 1964.

Reiners, Josef: Bankwirtschaftliche Verbundsysteme und ihre Stabilität, Wiesbaden 1977.

Schultz, R./Zerche, J.: Genossenschaftslehre, 2., vollständig neu bearbeitete Auflage, Berlin-New York 1983.

Tullock, Gordon: Adam Smith and the Prisoners' Dilemma, The Quaterly Journal of Economics, Vol. 100, Supplement 1985.

v. *Harder, Peter C.*: Chancen für Banken und Versicherungen im genossenschaftlichen Verbund, Vortrags- und Diskussionsveranstaltung in Marburg am 14. Okt. 1988. Marburger Beiträge zum Genossenschaftswesen 15, Institut für Genossenschaftswesen an der Philipps-Universität Marburg 1989.

Westermann, Harry: Zum Rechtsbegriff des Verbundes bei Genossenschaften. Genossenschaften und Genossenschaftsforschung. Festschrift zum 65. Geburtstag von Georg Draheim, Göttingen 1968, pp. 196–210.

Zerche, Jürgen: Aufbau des Genossenschaftssektors in den Ländern der Europäischen Gemeinschaft. Internationales Lehrbuch für Genossenschaftswesen, München 1990.

Zerche, Jürgen: Konzentration und Kreditgenossenschaften. Finanz-, Bank- und Kooperationsmanagement. Beiträge zur Betriebswirtschaftslehre nationaler und internationaler Unternehmungen. Festschrift zum 65. Geburtstag von H. Lipfert, Frankfurt am Main 1989, pp. 261–279.

Commercial Purchasing and Service Co-operatives

GEORG C. NEUMANN [J]

(see also: *Classification*; *Supply Co-operatives*; *Schulze-Delitzsch*; *Structural Types*; *Assortment Policies*; *Pricing Policy*; *Internationalization*)

I. Functions and Scope of Activity; II. Historical Development; III. Co-operative Models in the Private Enterprise System and in Socialism; IV. Productivity and Cost Advantages in Co-operative Organizations; V. Structural Models and Legal Forms; VI. Services Provided by Commercial Co-operatives; VII. The Effects of Competition; VIII. Co-operatives and their Legal Fundaments; IX. Federations of Commercial Co-operatives.

I. Functions and Scope of Activity

Commercial purchasing co-operatives, referred to more aptly as merchandise and service co-operatives (→ *Classification*), are voluntary associations of tradesmen (wholesalers, retailers, craftsmen) and practitioners of professional trades who wish to foster and promote their companies and practices through the inputs of a collectively borne co-operative enterprise (→ *Promotion Mandate*). The typical co-operative identity between customer and member develops accordingly (→ *Dual Nature*).

As a rule, co-operative activity concentrates on wholesale merchandise trade and the assumption of service and marketing functions for the membership body. Wholesale trade activities include business on one's own account (inventory sales, advance payments), transactions for third persons (delcredere functions, centralized account settlement) and agency business. Business in some branches is predominantly undertaken for one's own account in the form of inventory sales or advance payments, whereas co-operative wholesale trade in other branches mainly operates as a central collection office or agency. Aside from assuming marketing functions related to merchandising activities, co-operatives also provide members with service functions in the form of general management tools. Continuing education programs for member enterprises and their employees are likewise becoming more important (→ *Education, Germany*). Though variable according to branch and sector, the importance that service and marketing functions have in general for co-operatives above and beyond classic wholesale trading functions is, nevertheless, increasing everywhere.

Commercial merchandise and service co-operatives constitute the most varied type of co-operative form with respect to the branch or sector their members belong to. Co-operatives exist in the grocery and retail luxury food industry not only for classic retail food trade but also for retailers of health food, dairy products, and tobacco products. Co-operatives exist in the non-grocery retail sector for drugists and pharmacists as well as for retail trading of household items, hardware, office supplies, paper goods, shoes, textiles, toys, furniture, and household appliances. There are co-operatives for vocational trades such as for bakers, butchers, roofers, glassmakers, tailors, hairstylists, carpenters, painters, plumbers, locksmiths, shoemakers, chimney constructors, and plaster of Paris workers. In addition, wholesalers from various branches and industrial enterprises have joined together in co-operatives. Co-operatives exist within the transportation industry for navigators of inland waters, taxi drivers, and commercial forwarders. Among professional circles, co-operatives have been formed by lawyers, tax consultants, engineers, doctors, management consultants, and court bailiffs (→ *Classification*).

II. Historical Development

The two major catalysts for the development of commercial co-operatives were industrialization occurring in the early 19th century (→ *History in 19th C.*) and the expansion of transportation networks which exposed locally operating tradesmen to increased competitive pressure. The first established co-operative recorded in history was founded in 1832 by → *Philip Buchez* for carpenters. In 1834, a further co-operative was founded for goldsmiths. The national workshops established in France in 1848 can also be seen as a forerunner of (worker) co-operatives for craftsmen. The first successful co-operative wholesale company, however, was founded in 1849 by → *Hermann Schulze-Delitzsch* in the town of Delitzsch, located in Saxony. This was a carpenters association for raw materials which served to achieve lower purchase prices for its members through efficient acquisition practises with larger quantities. The co-operative furthermore served to ensure its members improved sales opportunities and to open up new business channels. *Schulze-Delitzsch* founded another association of this nature for shoemakers in 1850. After the concept of these co-operatives was anchored to the principles of self-help, self-responsibility, and self-management, co-operatives gradually started spreading throughout all German-speaking regions in 1850. By 1859, the designation "co-operative" had been introduced to replace to term "association".

Retail trade co-operatives came into existence relatively late as a reaction to the encroachments made by new enterprise forms and large, centrally managed companies. The first co-operative in the grocery and luxury food industry was established in Frankfurt/Oder by provision merchants in 1888. Numerous other company establishments rapidly followed in this branch, soon making interregional federations possible. Co-operatives for non-food retailing sectors were initially founded after the turn of the century and, in particular, after World War I.

Commercial co-operatives spread throughout practically all countries where self-employed retail traders and craftsmen were active following the initial establishments in the 19th century. In socialist countries, the commercial co-operatives to the most part were completely integrated into the state trade organizations (insafar as they were not abolished as a relic of private enterprise activity), thus preventing independent, entrepreneurial activity (→ *State and Co-operatives, Socialism*).

III. Co-operative Models in the Private Enterprise System and in Socialism

The co-operative concepts found at the root of the commercial co-operatives can be allocated to one of two co-operative models according to the promotional mission and property rights of the members: either to the co-operative model of the private enterprise system or to the socialist co-operative model of the social economy.

The co-operative model of the private enterprise system is characterized by the principles of self-help, self-responsibility, and self-management (→ *State and Co-operatives, Market Economy*). The corporate objective of co-operatives oriented along the lines of private enterprise is exclusively directed to the economic promotion of the membership body (→ *Promotion Mandate*). The co-operative is exclusively borne and supported in its activities by the economic strength and participation of its members. The members of such co-operatives claim the exclusive right to utilize the facilities of the co-operative, to appropriate the surplus resulting from this utilization, and to exercise all their rights with respect to the co-operative.

The obligations the co-operative members have to the state and society in this concept, do not exceed those obligations effective for other private enterprise companies. Co-operative members, just like those persons involved in other legal forms, are free to pursue their individual goals through the co-operative. The particularity of the co-operative rests solely in its special manner of distributing the achieved surplus: members' companies, due to their intensive customer relationship and economic ties, are taken more substantially into consideration to the detriment of the co-operative "company" than stockholders of a free enterprise corporation are, who in turn only can expect proceeds in return for their investments.

In contrast, socialistic and social economic co-operative models are rooted in the conviction that co-operatives are not to serve the economic promotion of their members but rather to pursue general political or social-political goals (→ *State and Co-operatives, Socialism*). As a rule, socialistic and social economic co-operative models foresee weakening and reducing members' rights to property in order to ensure the political orientation in the organization – as long as they have not been conceived for central administration purposes. Members have no claim to the exclusive utilization of co-operative facilities (e.g. through the forced enrollment of new members); the surplus resulting from utilization must be used for certain prescribed, political goals, and members are prevented from exercising all their rights with regard to the co-operative enterprise. If a co-operative enterprise is sold or liquidated, the revenue resulting therefrom must be passed on to the state or to social institutions.

Despite numerous experiments since the beginning of the 19th century, in market economies, co-operatives based on the socialistic/social economy model have not been blessed with any success worth mentioning (→ *Socialist Critics*). The co-operatives were not attractive to "net payers" as their payment contributions were not reciprocated with equalivalent co-operative outputs. Long-term subsidization of other members produces a one-sided economic and social dependency and leads to distribution conflicts within the co-operative. Co-operatives oriented along socialist or social economic lines, therefore, cannot be organized under competitive conditions (→ *Competition*).

IV. Productivity and Cost Advantages in Co-operative Organizations

Co-operative enterprises and their members as a corporate entity are characterized by relatively high organizational costs in comparison with subsidiary companies as a result of their decentralized structure. The competitiveness of the co-operative group (→ *Competition*) is safeguarded in that the cost disadvantages of a decentralized structure are offset by productivity advantages which are unattainable in centrally managed companies (→ *Principle of Cost Coverage*). Co-operative companies make the advantages of centrally managed companies accessible to their autonomous members, but they also ensure their members the advantages arising from independent, self-responsible involvement in the market. These advantages primarily exist in the form of informational and motivational effects based on self-reliance. With regard to local markets, an independent operator has substantially more information than a centrally managed company. As the independent entrepreneur not only bears the capital risk of his company but also can reap all surpluses resulting from his business activity, it is likely that he will be more motivated than a branch manager to take advantage of local market opportunities that might arise.

Because the market success of co-operative organizations is so decisively based on the advantages of independent activity on local markets – advantages which could not be realized in a centrally managed organization -, commercial co-operatives confront their own limits when standardized distribution concepts are introduced. The dominant position of branch companies in the discount sector can be explained in that the informational and motivational advantages of the independent retailers do not have an effect when standardized assortments are distributed without taking local circumstances into consideration.

V. Structural Models and Legal Forms

Commercial merchandise and service co-operatives can be differentiated according to the following characteristics: the number of organizational tiers; the nature of the marketing concepts realized by members, particularly among retail co-operatives; the extent and intensity of the organizational relations between the co-operative company and member enterprises; the legal form of the co-operative company (→ *Law, International*).

The fundamental model of the co-operative organization is a local, regional or interregional co-operative which is supported by members in its geographic district and which has no organizational relations to other companies with regard to purchasing or marketing. A two-tiered organization results when several such co-operatives collectively found a regional or interregional central co-operative. The primary co-operative on the lowest level maintains the identical relationship to the secondary or central co-operative as the members of the primary co-operative do to their organization. In a three-tiered co-operative organization, several regional central co-operatives sustain an interregional central co-operative (→ *Central Institutions*).

In multi-level commercial co-operative organizations, not all organizational levels assume the identical tasks. As advantages in centralization are more likely at hand concerning the provision of services, the commercial central co-operatives largely concentrate on third party business, agency activities, and other services. The advantages of decentralized organizational structures among single-level co-operative organizations active interregionally can also often be realized with the help of regional distribution warehouses.

Retail co-operatives can furthermore be differentiated according to the type of marketing structure available to their members. The breadth of such organizational possibilities ranges from discount-similar sales structures to traditional specialty shops, and modern large-scale enterprise forms. If several clearly different marketing structures are at hand within a co-operative, the organization of inputs and outputs involved in the relationship between the co-operative and its member enterprises must be differentiated in order to do justice to the demands of the various marketing structures and to avoid conflicts (→ *Marketing*).

Commercial cooperation can also be designated to one of three types of co-operative structure according to the differentiation introduced by *Dülfer*, namely: traditional, market-linkage, and integrated co-operatives (→ *Structural Types*).

The traditional co-operative restricts itself to offering its members advantageous supply channels. It acts purely as a wholesaler and is not actively involved in its members' sales markets. The traditional co-operative does not have close command over the organizational relationship with its members, who can easily switch over to another co-operative group or retail supplier.

The market-linkage co-operative not only assumes classic merchandising functions for its members but also offers them selective marketing and additional services. The activities of the co-operative company become oriented much more vertically, or in other words, they are tuned to the members' sales markets. Therefore, the organizational relationship between the co-operative company and its members is clearly consolidated and expanded.

The integrated co-operative in turn is characterized in that all opportunities for cooperation are exhausted as thoroughly as possible, whereby the distribution of tasks and the entrepreneurial autonomy of members are maintained. Furthermore, a comprehensive co-ordination of all market activities of the co-operative enterprise and the member enterprises is necessary – to such a degree that this confederation can be referred to as organized co-operative planning. The co-operative enterprise and the member enterprises enter the market as one intact entity. Corresponding to the close cooperation with its member enterprises, the co-operative not only provides those services associated with supplying wholesale merchandise but rather also a complete palette of marketing functions and other services.

When assigning actual commercial co-operatives to these three structural categories, one must bear in mind that this development is by no means inevitable in all branches, although co-operatives, as a rule, have developed from traditional to integrated co-operatives. A considerably more differentiated pattern of structural types has developed for many co-operatives involved in the trade of consumer goods; this pattern more closely relates to the connections between the extent of offered services and the intensity of organizational relationships with members (Ifo–Institute).

Commercial co-operatives can furthermore be differentiated according to the legal form chosen for the cooperation (→ *Forms of Cooperation*). The business concept of the co-operative as a federation of enterprises wishing to further themselves through the inputs of a collectively supported co-operative company can be realized in most countries through a variety of legal forms. Aside from the legal form especially designed for co-operatives, other legal forms which regularly come to question are those of a stock corporation and a → *joint-stock company* (with limited liability). The differences between the co-operative legal form and those of the stock corporation and limited company are predominantly rooted in the fact that the object of the co-operative legal form must be based on the promotion of the membership body achieved through certain inputs; the corporate object of companies, on the other hand, is open to each and every kind of capital employment, and promotion of members and/or shareholders through certain inputs or services only then occurs when this has been specified in company → *by-laws* or contracts.

VI. Services Provided by Commercial Co-operatives

Within the scope of classic merchandise trading, commercial co-operatives can engage in three forms of activity. When trading on their own account, co-operatives act as a principal; they purchase goods in their own name, on their own account, and at their own risk in order to resell them to their members. Such sales can result through a co-operative warehouse (inventory sales), or else the delivery can proceed directly from the supplier to the member (advance payment) (→ *Business Policies*).

When trading for third parties, the co-operative wholesaler operates in the name of a third party and either on its own account or that of a third party in the scope of delcredere transactions and/or central collection. The co-operative company negotiates with suppliers and signs contracts with them settling prices as well as delivery conditions and payment terms (→ *Pricing Policy*). The members then place their orders individually with the suppliers, and sales contracts are drawn between the individual members and the suppliers. The co-operative wholesaler assumes payment of its members' invoices from the suppliers – even when the individual member has not yet paid the invoice amount to the co-operative company (delcredere).

In agency transactions, the co-operative compiles a list of suppliers with whom it has arranged skeleton contracts involving prices, discounts, delivery conditions, and payment terms. It presents this list to its members who then immediately enter into contracts with the listed suppliers, i.e. without any further involvement from the co-operative. In commission dealings, the co-operative company assumes the role of a purchasing agent, or in other words, it buys goods in its own name on its members' accounts.

Members achieve economic advantages through these various forms of third-party transactions since their respective purchasing costs drop considerably. Third-party transactions executed by co-operatives particularly reduce members' costs with regard to information about suppliers, prices, and the quality of goods. These costs, however, are not only reduced for the members but rather also for the suppliers, in particular with respect to business risks.

Alongside providing classic merchandising functions, commercial co-operatives also offer their members their own unique brands and other marketing services. Goods are carried which are marked with the brand name or company logo of the co-operative wholesaler. Having brands of their own, helps members achieve a clearer market profile. Common marketing inputs include providing advertising budgets, hosting produce exchanges, conceiving special advertising campaigns, and making consumer information available. As a rule, additional services are offered which are not directly related to the distribution of goods. These include securing consultational advice for legal, tax and insurance matters, executing settlement proceedings, management consulting, accounting assistance, and financial help. Within the field of marketing, co-operatives support their members by providing information on assortment and goods, assisting in the selection and examination of business sites, settling leasing arrangements, designing store interiors, running apprenticeships and other continuing education programs, designing and distributing advertising materials, hosting produce exchanges, and offering sales promotion measures, special sales products as well as special sales campaigns.

As a result of mounting competitive pressure, marketing and additional service functions have become increasingly more important for the entire palette of co-operative inputs. As a rule, co-operatives lacking such "full-service" functions are not in the position to sufficiently assist their members in maintaining their market position.

VII. The Effects of Competition

The rapid market success of co-operatives even in the 19th century resulted in the insistency of limiting their field of activity, for example in business transactions with non-members (→ *Marketing*). Regulations regarding this matter at first only affected credit and consumer co-operatives, leaving the sector of commercial co-operatives untouched. In contrast to this, even today discussion continues concerning whether or not commercial co-operatives in particular effect competitive restraints and whether they should be considered a cartel (→ *Anti-Trust Laws*). The positive effects co-operatives have on market structure for small and mid-sized companies are recognized in competition policy. The majority of small and mid-sized companies (→ *Operational Size*), particularly those involved in retail trade, would no longer remain competitive in the face of large-scale company forms (multi-outlet companies) without their co-operative organizations providing inputs and services. Co-operatives thus contribute to the maintenance of a diverse supply structure.

Even today, the question concerning the cartel-like characteristic of co-operative groups remains unanswered (→ *Anti-Trust Laws*). It nevertheless seems certain that the business success of commercial merchandise and service co-operatives is not based on the typical monopoly-like effects of income redistribution but rather on real resource savings among members and suppliers. Commercial co-operatives thus ensure an efficient combination of production factors involved in the distribution of goods. Qualifying co-operatives as a cartel likewise seems inappropriate insofar as their business activity does not differ from that of other wholesale and service companies (e.g. factoring banks); their only special characteristic is the customer-member identity.

VIII. Co-operatives and Their Legal Fundaments

The relevant legal framework for the activity of commercial co-operatives can be found in organizational law (Co-operative Law, Companies Act, Law for Private Limited Companies) as well as in Competition Law, Tax Law, and Constitutional Law (→ *Law, International*; → *Anti-Trust Laws*).

The co-operative organizational system can be subdivided as follows:

1) Supported organizations which are composed of their collective membership bodies;
2) Companies which aim to make available certain outputs; aside from the legal form of a co-operative, they can assume that of a stock corporation or private limited company.

Co-operative tax privileges fundamentally contradict orientation around self-help as they can be considered subsidies which effect a loss of autonomy. Current observations indicate that special tax treatment for co-operatives is a tendency of the past. Co-operatives as juristic persons are subject to the various tax obligations just as all other companies or owners are, following tax assessment by virtue of their legal form and/or on account of their asset structure. Exceptions to this are either sector-specific (agriculture) (→ *Rural Co-operatives*) or based on social reasons (non-profit standing/public economic interest). Commercial co-operatives, as a rule, are not affected by such exceptions. Nonetheless, the co-operative legal form does present a particular disadvantage regarding accessibility to capital markets. The typical co-operative business interests (customer = member) present a barrier to the interests of pure capital employment maintained by outside investors. Accordingly, a tax break for equity accumulation could compensate for this (→ *Taxation*).

The special social quality still being attributed to co-operatives (to a considerable degree out of ignorance) has lead to a particular emphasis to be placed on the co-operative system in many constitutions following World War II. Dictates placed on the state to undertake the protection or expansion of co-operative self-help are usually seen in connection with the demand to promote independent small or mid-sized enterprises involved in agricultural, trade, professional craft, and commercial/industrial sectors. The influence these constitutional demands have on actual policy, however, cannot be seen. Competitive market structures are the result of market processes and cannot be standardized through constitutions.

IX. Federations of Commercial Co-operatives

The first early forms of co-operative → *federations* were founded in the commercial sectors in 1852 under the influence of → *Schulze-Delitzsch* (→ *History of Ideas*). In many other countries, the rapid expansion of commercial co-operatives at the end of the 19th century and beginning of the 20th century also brought about the establishment of correspondingly structured co-operative federations. The first international association of co-operative federations, the → *International Co-operative Alliance*, established in London in 1895, developed essentially under the influence of → *consumer co-operatives* and does not have any relation worth mentioning to commercial co-operatives and their federations. In its place, the national federations of commercial co-operatives have joined together under special umbrella organizations in light of specific international organizations. The European umbrella organization *UGAL* (Union des Groupements d'Achat Cooperatifs de Detaillants de L'Europe) emerged out of a federation of purchasing co-operatives composed of independent European grocery retailers active in wholesale trade; in the meantime, this organization represents all merchandise and service co-operatives. Aside from the Italian Federation *ANCD,* the *UFCC* in France, and the ZENTGENO (Central Association of the Co-operative Wholesale and Service Agencies) in Germany (→ *European Community*), a further 18 co-operative groups and/or federations in the *EC* and *EFTA* belong to *UGAL*.

Bibliography

Boettcher, Erik/Großfeld, B./Wagner, H. (eds.): Die Genossenschaftsidee im Widerstreit der Meinungen, Münster 1984.
Boettcher, Erik: Die Genossenschaft im Wettbewerb der Ideen, Tübingen 1985.
Boettcher,Erik/Westermann, Harry (eds.): Genossenschaften – Demokratie und Wettbewerb, Tübingen 1972.
Deter, W.: Deutsche Konsumgenossenschaften, Karlsruhe 1968.
Deutscher Genossenschaftsverband e.V. (ed.): Schulze-Delitzsch – Festschrift zur 150. Wiederkehr seines Geburtstages, Wiesbaden 1958.
Draheim, Georg: Zur Ökonomisierung der Genossenschaften, Göttingen 1968.
Engelhardt, Werner Wilhelm/Thiemeyer, Theo (eds.): Marketing als Unternehmensführungskonzeption von Handelsgenossenschaften, Schriften zum Genossenschaftswesen, Vol. 21, Berlin 1987.
Faust, H.: Geschichte der Genossenschaftsbewegung, 3rd edition, Frankfurt/M. 1977.
Gesellschaft zur Kooperationsförderung im Handel (ed.): Die innere Erneuerung der Verbundgruppen des Handels, Köln 1987.
Laurinkari, Juhani (ed.): Die Prinzipien des Genossenschaftswesens in der Gegenwart, Nürnberg 1986.
Loesch, Achim von: Die gemeinwirtschaftliche Unternehmung, Köln 1977.
Mändle, Eduard/Swoboda, Walter (eds.): Genossenschaftslexikon, Wiesbaden 1992.
Mändle, Eduard: Genossenschaften – Wesen, Unternehmensziele, Entscheidungsstruktur, Ordnungspolitische Einstufung, Geschichte, Schriftenreihe der FH Nürtingen, Nr. 9, 1989.
Ohlmeyer, D. (ed.): Selbsthilfe zum Beispiel – Eine Chronik der Genossenschaften, Hannover 1984.
Olesch, G./Tiedtke, H (eds.): Die wirtschaftliche Bedeutung der Einkaufsverbände des Einzelhandels, Frankfurt/M. 1981.
Olesch, G.: Die Einkaufsverbände des Einzelhandels, Frankfurt/M. 1980.
Olesch, G.: Die Kooperationen des Handels, Köln 1991.
Paulick, H.: Das Recht der eingetragenen Genossenschaft, Karlsruhe 1956.
Seraphim, H.-J. (ed.): Die Genossenschaften des gewerblichen Mittelstandes in der Wettbewerbswirtschaft, Institut für Genossenschaftswesen, Heft 5, Münster 1954.
Weisser, Gerhard/Engelhardt, Werner Wilhelm (eds.): Genossenschaften und Genossenschaftsforschung, Göttingen 1968.
ZENTGENO (ed.): Zukunftsaspekte genossenschaftlicher Kooperationen im Einzelhandel und Handwerk, Bonn 1988.

Commonwealth, Co-operative

LAJOS VÁRADI

(see also: *History of Ideas*; *Conceptions, Co-operatives*; *Socialist Co-operative Theory*; *Economic Order*)

I. The "Perfect Society" and the Co-operative Idea; II. A Historical Look Back; III. A Dichotomic Development; IV. The Co-operative Principles; V. Co-operative Evolution.

I. The "Perfect Society" and the Co-operative Idea

Mankind's eternal dream is to bring about a "perfect society", where economic welfare and social justice prevail (→ *History of Ideas*). Several attempts have so far been made to reach this goal (one could quote the Essenes, early Christianity, the French Revolution, communist ideas and various religious sects, etc.). None succeeded entirely: they were either swept away because of their tyrannical methods to assure "Paradise on Earth" to their subjects (regardless whether these subjects wanted it or not), or by becoming a part of the "normal" societal establishment. An example of the former category is the communist system, which has just collapsed before our eyes, and, for the latter, the established religions. To a certain extent, ideas or trends wishing to accomplish the task of redeeming humanity, should bear the characteristic of a quasi "religious obsession", otherwise they be unable to mobilize the masses for the common goal. Their adepts are ready to sacrifice themselves for the "just cause", but very frequently others, for having opposed or thought to have opposed their endeavours. Once again, one can recall the burning auto-da-fés of the Inquisition, the gas chambers of the Nazi regime, or the gulags of the defunct Soviet system with their millions of victims.

These examples are, of course, extremes and cannot be lumped together with "Co-operative Commonwealth", the subject of the present study. They only serve to show how naive and dangerous is any ideology, which strives to monopolize by excluding and forbidding anything which does not fit strictly into its view of world.

A mild version of the "redemption of the world" was an attempt to reorganize the economic and social order on co-operative lines (→ *History of Ideas*), i.e. converting the whole society – and later the whole world – into a Co-operative Republic, or Commonwealth.

The very first co-operatives came into being as early as the 1830s, but officially the first co-operative was born in Rochdale, near Manchester, in England in 1844 (→ *History in 19th C.*). A group of 28 weavers, the Equitable Pioneers Society as they called themselves, started business based on principles which still serve today as a compass to the World's Co-operative

Movement. The main principles laid down by the → *Rochdale Pioneers* are the following:
1) The division of the surplus amongst the members in proportion to their purchases.
2) The right of all members to a share in control, irrespective of capital holding.
3) The sale of goods at ordinary market prices.
4) The vesting of the assets of the society in the collectivity of the members.

These four points with the principle of unrestricted and democratic membership (open and voluntary membership, one member one vote) enshrine the very characteristics of the co-operative movement worldwide (→ *Conceptions, Co-operative*).

II. A Historical Look Back

Before reaching this stage of co-operative development, we have to make a little historical look back on the forefathers of the modern co-operative movement.
First of all, we have to mention → *Robert Owen*, who was born in 1771 in Newtown, United Kingdom, and died in 1858 (the same place). His main book "New View of society" outlining his ideas was published in 1813. He acquired a spinning mill in Scotland (New Lanark Mills), where he organized the work on the line of his ideas, to experiment how they functioned in practice. *Owen* thought that he was morally obliged to provide a good living to his employees and a good education to their children. His conviction was that, through education, one can change society. He submitted a "Plan" that the Government should set up "Villages of co-operation" (based on the New Lanark model). They should be self-supportive, i.e. they should raise the produce needed for their own consumption.
Owen sought fresh experience and left for the United States of America, where he founded the "Co-operative Community of New Harmony". This proved to be a complete failure. After having returned to Great Britain, where trade unionism was just emerging, 1832 he established the "National Equitable Labour Exchange", where co-operative products could be exchanged on the basis of the New Lanark principle. The "Rochdale Pioneers" were also inspired by *Owen's* principles when they started their → *consumer co-operatives*.
In France, we have to mention the names of *Charles Fourier, Saint-Simon* and → *J.P. Buchez*. In Germany, *W. Weitling* and mainly, → *F.W. Raiffeisen*, whose principles spread to many countries in the field of credit and agricultural co-operatives (→ *Rural Co-operatives*). A further co-operative ideologist well-known in German speaking countries was → *Schulze-Delitzsch*. It may be said that the very origins of the → *consumer co-operative* movement may be traced back to England, to the Rochdale Pioneers, the producer (or worker) co-operatives (→ *Joint-production Co-op*eratives) to France (*Buchez*), and credit and agricultural co-operatives to Germany (*Raiffeisen*).
One should say that with the establishment of the Rochdale Consumer Co-op Society, a chapter was opened in history, but at the same time another was closed. Why? *Robert Owen* and his followers worked for the creation of the future co-operatives to a certain extent with a religious zeal and considered Co-operation as a New Religion, which finally would lead mankind to suppression of exploitation and to a general social and economic justice. It is no mere coincedence that many of the early co-operative pioneers were priests, who, seeing the dire living conditions of large sectors of the population, started to think of possible solutions to alleviate poverty.
A further impulse to the co-operative idea was given by Marxism and the growing Trade Union movements. From about the middle of the XIXth century, the co-operative movement turned to this direction (with the exception of the German Raiffeisen agricultural and credit co-operatives). *Friedrich Engels* and *Karl Marx* (→ *Socialist Critics*) studied the conditions of workers in England, where the first co-operatives started to function. And it was in nearly the same year (1847) that *Marx* formulated his Communist Manifesto.

III. A Dichotomic Development

One can conclude that the birth of the co-operative movement was a reaction to the enormous extremes in standards of living (at misery level for large masses), to the unbearable working conditions, to the absence of social security, etc., as was the creation of political parties (Socialist and Labour Party) in different European countries. From the very beginning, close relationships were maintained between them. But, from this very moment on, we can already witness a certain scission in the co-op movement. One part allied itself with left-wing political parties and trade unions (with atheistic trends), while the other part called itself Christian Socialist or Christian Democrat. This difference lead later on to the creation of separate co-operative Federations at the beginning of the XXth century (Lega versus Confederazione in Italy; SOK and OTK in Finland, etc.). The division was even more evident on a sectorial basis.: the rural co-operatives (agriculture, savings and credit) were in the majority so-called "conservative" ones, as against the consumer and other urban related co-operatives, which generally supported the Social Democratic Party of their countries.
Some national organizations had succeeded in overcoming differences between "socialist" and "neutral" co-operatives, like in France where, at the National Congress held in 1912 in Tours, delegates agreed on the merger of the two movements. The French co-operative movement of that time was characterized

by names like *Jean Jaurs*, *Charles Gide* and *Ren Poisson*. The latter devoted most of his time to the creation of a Co-operative Republic. This Republic should have been created as a solution to social problems, since (consumers') co-operatives would bring about a new economic society in which not only would the means and instruments of exchange be the collective property of the consumers, but the production of wealth would also be directed by the consumers in association as owners of the means of production and exchange.

IV. The Co-operative Principles

The co-op society should be ruled according to four principles (→ *Principles*):

a) Division in proportion to purchases;
b) Equality of members;
c) Sale at market prices;
d) Collectively owned capital.

a) Division in proportion to purchases

In a capitalist society, the profits gained from an economic activity will be distributed according to the capital invested (→ *Assessment of Success*). The co-operative way distribute profits according to the efforts made by each co-operator to assist the business. However, co-operation is not a simple negation of the existing economic system. Rather it wishes to improve it (→ *Economic Order*). The more loyal a co-operator is to his society, the more he profits from it after his purchases. No account is taken of his subscription to the share çapital. What counts is his purchase from the co-operative society. This practice was so common that those members who had purchased nothing from the society over a certain period, were excluded. In neglecting the share capital held by members, some societies even refused to pay a nominal interest rate after the capital or tried to keep it down as low as possible. Consequently, members were not really interested in investing in the society's capital, which very soon caused funding problems (societies had to seek these funds from bankers and other lenders at substantially higher rates) (→ *Equity Capital*).

Even the word "profit" was not used any more. Instead, expressions like "discount" or "co-operative surplus" were utilized. This distinction sought to make clear that the purpose of the society was not the pursuit of profit-making, or the renumeration of the vested capital, but rather that consumer had rights arising from his purchasing and was entitled to recover his investment. A capitalist producer produces something to sell, a co-operative society produces to distribute the products to its members. Some co-operative societies replaced payment in the form of money with payment in goods of special services (e.g. insurance).

b) Equality of members

A co-operative society is essentially democratic or self-governing, based on the equality of its members and on equal rights to share in control. This principle is often summed up as "one man one vote". In a private company, the owner decides alone; in a joint-stock company, the most important shareholders decide in proportion to the capital held. In a co-operative society, it is all the same whether a member has one share or several shares, in voting it is the member alone who is counted and not the amount of the shares held by him (→ *Group, the Co-op*erative).

This principle might shock some people at first sight, but it is already applied as a democratic formula of universal suffrage to determine the conduct of public affairs. So, co-operative society is a model for economic democracy (→ *Societal Form, Co-op*erative).

c) Sale at market prices

The co-operative society works in an economic system of free competition, so it has to take into account the existing rules of the economic game (→ *Competition*). Sales therefore are made at current commercial prices or slightly less, at fair prices. The question may arise, why not sell at cost prices? (→ *Pricing Policy*). This would leave the co-op society without working capital, i.e. there would not be money to make advantageous wholesale buying. The society's destiny would depend on day-to-day business and would stagnate, etc. Therefore, there is a need to work within the usually accepted commercial market prices, incorporating margins used normally by competitors. Beyond that, the co-op society does not sell only to its members, but also to external consumers (→ *Business Policies*), and it would not be fair that they should share the same advantages as members.

d) Collectively owned capital

The surplus assets of a co-op society belong to the society as a whole and none of their members have any individual right to them (the indivisibility of the fund). In all countries legal regulations require all economic entities, including co-operatives, to build up reserve funds from the profits as insurance against bad times. Besides that, there might also be an obligation to set up a development fund. This fund will also be part of the indivisible assets of the co-operative society. In a capitalist society these funds must be divided sooner or later among the shareholders and the share value will increase or fall, depending on the success or failure of the enterprise. The co-operative system is different. The share value does not change, since it is not quoted on the exchange. That a member pays in, he can withdraw it – but only the amount he paid in, having no claim to any of the reserve. If a co-operative society is disbanded and there is a surplus at hand, it will be handed over to another co-operative society (or to a fund held jointly by co-operatives), or to a benevolent institution. This principle is one of the most characteristic features of cooperation.

V. Co-operative Evolution

After the governing principles, let us look at the opportunities for extension of a co-operative society. These might be summed up as follows:
- extension of membership (it is a permanent goal to recruit more and more members);
- extension of business operations (the co-operative tries to look for more and more needs of the members);
- extension by coordination of efforts (co-operative societies they to multiply the services to be offered to members by coordinated actions, like wholesaling);
- extension of activities to production and finance of goods (like bakeries, co-op banks, agricultural production, etc. The guiding idea was that the co-operative consumption will be supported totally by co-operative production (→ *Own Production*). For example, the Co-operative Wholesale Society in U.K. is one of the largest agricultural producer in the country).

The economy is constantly developing from small-scale to large-scale industry. The co-operative society is a part of the economic environment and has to follow the trend (→ *Operational Size*). The hypothesis of creating a Co-operative Republic was to involve practically all the households in retail consumer co-operative societies, which, in their turn, would supply all the material needs of mankind, from foodstuff to clothing, from housing to insurance services, etc.
The outcome of that solution would bring an end to the increasing divergence between methods of the production of wealth and the manner of its distribution. There would be no room for "parasites" and practically everybody would become a productive worker. Collective property was to be instituted not as the absolute right of the worker, but for the benefit and under the control of the great masses of consumers. The consumers would enjoy the profits of the retail and wholesale trade, and of manufacture, as well as interest on capital and the rent of land. Consumption would govern production, the Co-operative Republic would put things in order.
The pioneers of the Co-operative Commonwealth had also questioned whether this hypothesis was valid, whether co-ops could ensure themselves the development outlines by them. The co-operative movement was not alone in the world, was a part of an existing economic (capitalist) system, which it tried to reform or "eat away". But could not his capitalist society also envolve, transform itself and leave co-operation with its mission unfulfilled?

To-day (1992), when we look back to this idea, we already know the answer. The idea of a better so, since any ideolgy which seeks to organize human society in line with one accepted and authorized theory should be doomed to failure. Those men an women who fought for the creation of such a Co-operative Commonwealth certainly were absolutely honest and convinced about their "just cuase". They wanted to eliminate exploitation and profit-seeking, the very essence of capitalist society, and share the wealth on an equal footing by distributing it according to the spirit of co-operation.
Co-operatives (all types) grew stronger in the meantime and became established in practically all countries of all continents. Certainly, they have to struggle each day to mange to continue working in the growing world of competition, and consequently they have to adapt themselves to new challenges. They also have to seek for profit and not simply to distribute wealth. When doing so (forced by the rules of the economic game), however, they should not forget → *solidarity*, honesty, caring and equity which should always characterize a co-operative society, and distinguish it from other types of enterprises.

Commonweal Economy and Co-operatives

JÜRGEN ZERCHE/INGRID SCHMALE [J]

(see also: *Economic Order; Non Profit Organizations; Principles; Theory of Co-operatives; Economie Sociale; Legal Form, Co-operative*)

I. Introduction; II. The Co-operative as an Economic and Legal Form; III. The Commonweal Sector and Undertakings with a Commonweal Character; IV. Co-operatives and Commonweal Entities from the Point of View of the Theory of Economic Order; V. Underlying Methodological Concept and Morphological Considerations.

I. Introduction

The manifestations of co-operative structures found in the Western European region indicate multi-various and strongly varying relationships to the commonweal sector and/or to undertakings which aim to satisfy needs through commonweal orientation. Similarities between co-operative and commonweal undertakings result from the classification of both economic forms to the sector of → *non-profit organizations*.
For quite some time there has been a controversial discussion in Germany concerning how the relationship between co-operatives and the commonweal economy should be identified. This discussion is led

by co-operative practitioners and theoreticians and reflects various positions in the theory of economic order. Various economic approaches and methodological starting points with regard to the investigation of corporate structures must be referred to from both a macro-economic and, above all, micro-economic perspective.

After identifying the co-operative as both an economic form and a legal form and providing analytical observations of the commonweal economic sector and/or undertakings structured along such commonweal lines, points of contact and problems between these two empirical objects in their relationship will be presented. International manifestations of this matter will likewise be addressed.

II. The Co-operative as an Economic and Legal Form

Co-operatives are an economic and legal form. The co-operative economic form must fulfill certain basic co-operative values in order to be considered as such. *Laurinkari* and *Brazda* reduce the co-operative form of cooperation to one principle and ascribe to cooperation the necessity of collective action for emancipation from material, social and political dependencies (*Laurinkari/Brazda*, 1990). The expressions of the existential co-operative principles defined by co-operative scientists – namely solidarity, democracy, identity, self-administration, management by members (Selbst-Organschaft) and self-help – must be seen in connection with their respective historic situations, that is with respect to the legal and political circumstances, the level of a country's economic development, and the personal self-consciousness of those involved.

At its conference in Vienna in 1966, the International Co-operative Alliance determined principles which fundamentally characterize the co-operative as an economic form through:

- open membership on a voluntary basis,
- democratic self-administration, whereby all members enjoy identical voting rights,
- limitations on interest payments on capital,
- reimbursement of surpluses in proportion to the level of transacted business,
- co-operative further education to develop a sense of solidarity,
- cooperation on various geographical and regional levels.

The reference to a needed extension or concretization of these principles through the *identity principle* (*Münkner*, 1992) which designates the identity between the member as the upholder of the co-operative and the customer (purchasing co-operative) supplier (marketing co-operative) or employee (workers' co-operative) directly addresses the heart of the matter to be discussed – the relationship between co-operatives and the commonweal economy.

At least four characteristics are constitutive for the *legal form* of the registered co-operative in Germany. §1 of the German Co-operative Law (GenG) defines co-operatives as "*companies* with a non-finite number of members which endeavor to *promote* their *members*' enterprises or households through a *common business enterprise.*"

Alongside the characterization of the co-operative as a people-oriented affiliation with voluntary and variable membership which maintains a business enterprise of its own for its goal of membership promotion, other characteristics of the co-operative are also raised: the *limitation* of activities to those providing *economic promotion*, the *variability of capital* associated with the variable number of members, *democratic management* and *control*, the *subordinate function of capital* to promotion, and *limited business contact with non-members* (*Münkner*, 1985).

This legal foundation proves to be a narrow parameter for co-operative action inasmuch as the goal of membership promotion assumes the form of direct operational relationships between member households ("Wirtschaft") and/or member enterprises ("Erwerb") and the common, co-operative business enterprise (identity principle). Goal orientation which is directed primarily at the commonweal or at common welfare, in other words the promotion of third parties, is at least problematic in this legal characterization.

The identity principle as a delimiting criterion does, however, lose its stringency when potential future members are embraced in the promotion efforts. Business with non-members is problematic: it should never be the primary purpose of co-operative activity but rather should only be seen as supplementary in nature or as business intended to win over new members. Co-operatives must accordingly be classified to the sector of non-profit organizations, just as those undertakings with a commonweal economic character. In contrast to profit-seeking companies the foremost tasks of this sector are in the needs-economy; profit attainment most clearly has the character of a means or instrument and is not an end in itself.

III. The Commonweal Sector and Undertakings with a Commonweal Character

Whereas *Münkner* defines a company oriented around the commonweal as one whose upholders "render benefits to promote third parties" (*Münkner*, 1985, p.15), *Thiemeyer* continues in *Weisser's* tradition and sees the activities of companies oriented around the commonweal directed at "public interests", "the interests of the general public" or "in interest of a higher totality". This objective is chosen either freely or on account of a public contract (*Thiemeyer*, 1990, p.324). "The totality of these 'enterprises with a commonweal character' in the scope of an otherwise fundamentally private economic system is called the "commonweal economy (*Thiemeyer*, 1990)."

Terms closely related to "commonweal economy" are "public benefit orientation" and "orientation around common welfare". The concentration of activities exclusively and directly around purposes serving the general public is a characteristic of the definition of "public benefit orientation" and is thereby at least an indication of how closely it is related to the term "commonweal economy". The term "public benefit orientation" is therefore applied by several authors synonymously with the terms "commonweal economy" and "orientation around commom welfare" in the sense of "doing business in favor of others" (e.g.*Engelhardt*).

State recognition of public benefit orientation in Germany with respect to taxation means that such an organization is extensively *tax-exempt* for income accrued through its activities. This is commensurate with the subsidiarity principle – when private (non-state) institutions which execute public functions are exempted from a tax obligation. In the German Fiscal Code (AO) public function sectors are listed such as the promotion of science and research, education and upbringing, art and culture, religion, youth assistance and welfare provision, sports, etc. The criteria against which public benefit orientation is measured for recognition are focused on the serving function of capital and resemble co-operative characteristics. The term "public benefit orientation" in the sense of tax purposes (non-profit) deviates from the general use of the word.

Up until January 1, 1990, there was a separate public benefit housing law in Germany for public benefit housing companies (→ *Housing Societies*); this law provided tax exemption when codified procedures were maintained by public benefit housing companies, such as obligatory construction, price maintenance and proprietary protection. *Engelhardt* characterizes this law as "an essential element of a mixed tertiary economic, societal and social structure, an element which the social market economy was in the position to mold and shape" (*Engelhardt*, 1992, p.239). Approximately 95% of all housing co-operatives can be classified to this public benefit housing economy. Co-operatives and other companies which work and produce for the general public are quite closely involved with one another in this sector.

Engelhardt formulates five categories which are of considerable significance for the classification of a company to the commonweal economy:

1) subjective basis of action (subjective motivation/goal orientation);
2) institutional action bases;
3) other objective action bases;
4) actual behavior of all persons involved;
5) intended and non-intended consequences of behavior (*Engelhardt*, 1993).

The reference to the public interest makes it obvious that alongside the respective explanation of what the "public interest" is in each case, the self-perception of the commonweal economy always is involved in the discussion. Particular commonweal functions recognized as such can become obsolete in the course of economic development (c.f. *Thiemeyer*, 1978). The differentiation in literature (and traceable to *A.Wagner*) between "compulsory commonweal entities" and "free commonweal entities" refers to actual organizations: compulsory commonweal entities are state undertakings which fulfill public tasks or functions; self-help enterprises numbering among the free commonweal enterprises include co-operatives (a contested issue in Germany!) and charitable economic enterprises which dedicate themselves to the welfare of third parties (e.g. religious institutions, union companies). Discussion furthermore continues concerning how publicly affiliated and/or regulated undertakings belong to the commonweal economy (e.g. transport, energy, credit and insurance businesses, doctors' practices, pharmacies, etc.) (c.f. *Thiemeyer*, 1990).

IV. Co-operatives and Commonweal Entities from the Point of View of the Theory of Economic Order

The theoretical discussion of the position of the commonweal economy within the economic order revolves around the question whether the free commonweal economy can be considered a third sector alongside the "state" and the "market" (c.f. *Gretschmann*). *Wagner* and *Schäffle*, the "classic financial theoreticians" who worked out idealistic approaches for the determination of "common welfare", considered free commonweal entities to be organizations characterized by the solidarity principle – in contrast to the "charitable" system which is lead by altruistic motives. Their primary occupation with the allocation of state functions might have contributed to the situation that scientific and political disputes (particularly following World War II) often equated commonweal economies with planned economies and centrally administered economies. (*Wagner's* law stated that state involvement increases on account of problems related to functions and consequences of market allocation and distribution.) The commonweal sector was first rediscovered by many people in Germany as a possible third, autonomous sector at the end of the 1970s in the course of the discussion around the state financial crisis.

In other countries of the European Community such as in France (*secteur d'économie sociale*), Italy, Luxembourg, Portugal and Great Britain (the consumer co-operatives) there has been unanimity for many years about the notion of socially responsible economic activity in a third sector between market and state economies (→ *Economie Sociale*). Moreover, this third sector has even been ascribed the power to alter society (c.f. Zerche, 1990).

An understanding of co-operatives is present in these countries which is focused on reciprocal assistance and which casts interpersonal solidarity between the strong and the weak in a particularly favorable light. Co-operatives with commonweal objectives are considered particularly worthy of promotion, or in other words, desirable (c.f. Münkner, 1985). The four fundamental criteria for classification in the "social economy" in France are compatible with co-operative characteristics: voluntary membership, democratic administration, freedom of action (independence from state reglementation) and the preclusion of endeavors for personal profit. Co-operatives (*secteur coopératif*), mutual insurance associations (*secteur mutualiste*) and associations pursuing public benefit (*secteur associatif*) belong to the social economy. Co-operatives are (financially) supported by the state in Italy as institutions pursuing self-help; the possibility of state reglementation is therefore extant.

V. Underlying Methodological Concept and Morphological Considerations

As an underlying scientific-theoretical concept the neo-classic axiom of identifying the individual maximization of utility and income as human behavior is thus closely related to theoretical classificational observations, but it also is fundamental for macro- and micro-economic considerations (c.f. Zerche, 1992) (→ *Classic/Neo-classic Contributions*). The consequence of this axiom is that cooperation can only be analyzed with others under the aspect of the individual maximization of utility. Behavior along the line of solidarity in the sense of a renunciation of potential individual utility in order to aid others and/or to realize social reform concepts cannot be analyzed. Analytical observations of "doing business benefiting third parties" are accordingly only possible to a most limited extent.

The following criteria are listed in the specialized literature for the commonweal economic orientation of co-operatives: a needs-economy; distribution of the surplus accordingly to the level of utilization and not to capital share; elimination of the market between the co-operative and its members; voting principle oriented around people and not capital; collaborative concept of co-operatives (particularly in the pan-co-operativeness in France borrowing from *Charles Gide* and the Nimes School)(→ *Conceptions, Co-operative*); the joining of those groups whose promotion is in the "general public interest"; the mobilization of important business capabilities among those involved through self-responsibility and self-management; the option of building up anonymous "social capital" through co-operatives; the "double nature" (*Draheim*) of co-operatives on the one hand as associations of individuals in the sense of a community (*Tönnies*), and on the other hand as business enterprises (→ *Dual Nature*).

Mändle (1992) in contrast sees principle characteristic differences between co-operatives and commonweal entities and identifies the lack of the co-operative "double nature" in the commonweal economy, the missing character of an auxiliary or supplemental economy and thus a self-help organization for members, and the missing identity principle. Commonweal business enterprises operate in the legal form of corporations whose shares are in the hands of organizations concerned with propagating ideal concepts (churches, unions) ("Tendenzbetriebe"). Neither a direct nor an indirect member democracy is therefore existent; in contrast the corporate goals of commonweal enterprises are determined externally.

The argument that co-operatives are group-oriented but that commonweal entities wish "to serve all people of a particular state" (*Mändle*, 1992) is based on the notion that the "interests of the general public" only corresponds with the provision of purely public goods. If, on the other hand, it is recognized that group-specific public goods can be offered "in the interest of the general public", *Mändle's* arguments are thus reduced to a quite narrow interpretation of co-operatives' legal functions in Germany and/or to the dedicative type of promotion co-operative in which the identity principle is fully realized.

The least common denominator within the German discussion remains "that both types of undertakings are not ends in themselves but rather means to certain ends; they strive for the identical secondary corporate objectives (production, purchasing, financing goals, etc.), they are active within the market economy and ultimately also exert positive effects on competition" (*Mändle*, 1992, p.240)(→ *Competition*). It remains to be seen whether other European conceptions of co-operatives, the commonweal economy, and the social economy can approach this denominator or whether a renaissance of economic activity for others (either in or with co-operatives) can evolve in Germany in the course of European assimilation.

Bibliography

Engelhardt, Werner Wilhelm: Gemeinwirtschaft und Genossenschaft. In: Mändle, Eduard/Swoboda, Walter (ed.): Genossenschaftslexikon, pp. 238–239, Wiesbaden 1992.

Engelhardt, Werner Wilhelm: Gemeinwirtschaftliche Unternehmen. In: Wittmann, Waldemar et al (ed.): Handwörterbuch der Betriebswirtschaft, col. 1388–1396, Stuttgart 1993[5].

Gretschmann, Klaus: Steuerungsprobleme der Staatswirtschaft, Schriften zum Genossenschaftswesen und zur Öffentlichen Wirtschaft, vol.4, Berlin 1981.

Laurinkari, Juhani/Brazda, Johann: Genossenschaftliche Grundwerte. In: Laurinkari, Juhani (ed.): Genossenschaftswesen, Hand- und Lehrbuch, pp. 70–77, Munich/Vienna 1990.
Mändle, Eduard: Gemeinwirtschaft und Genossenschaften, Abgrenzung. In: Ders., Swoboda, Walter (ed.): Genossenschaftslexikon, pp. 239–240, Wiesbaden 1992.
Münkner, Hans-H.: Ausprägungen genossenschaftlicher Struktur in Westeuropa, Schriften zur Kooperationsforschung, speeches, vol.19, Tübingen 1985.
Münkner, Hans-H.: Prinzipien, genossenschaftliche. In: Mändle, Eduard/Swoboda, Walter (ed.): Genossenschaftslexikon, pp. 509–511, Wiesbaden 1992.
Thiemeyer, Theo: Symbiose zweier Bereiche. In: ÖWG 1, pp.9–12, 1978.
Thiemeyer, Theo: Zur Abgrenzung von Genossenschaften und Gemeinwirtschaft. In: Laurinkari, Juhani (ed.): Genossenschaftswesen, Hand- und Lehrbuch, pp. 324–336, Munich/Vienna 1990.
Zerche, Jürgen: Aufbau des Genossenschaftssektors in den Ländern der Europäischen Gemeinschaft. In: Laurinkari, Juhani (ed.): Genossenschaftswesen, Hand- und Lehrbuch, pp. 385–402, Munich/Vienna 1990.
Zerche, Jürgen: Neoklassische Theorie und Genossenschaften. In: Mändle, Eduard/Swoboda, Walter (ed.): Genossenschaftslexikon, pp. 469–471, Wiesbaden 1992.

Communal Settlements

YAACOV OVED

(see also: *Development, Israel*; *History of Ideas*; *Conceptions, Co-operative*)

I. Definition of Communal Settlements; II. Religious Communes; III. Socialist Communes; IV. Hutterites and the Bruderhof; V. Modern Communes; VI. Australia and New Zealand; VII. Japan; VIII. Europe.

I. Definition of Communal Settlements

A communal settlement is an autonomous community, whose members have voluntarily agreed to live communaly according to the principle of 'from each according to his ability and to each according to his need'. There are various kinds of communal organizations, whose common denominator is collective ownership, the abolition of private property, collective work and consumption, as well as an autonomous community life. Such settlements are usually based on a common social ideology or religion.

II. Religious Communes (→ *Religious Co-operatives*)

Various forms of communal settlements developed throughout modern history. To begin with, they were inspired by the Jewish-Christian tradition and later by utopian socialism, anarchism and a large number of modern environmental, and spiritual theories. The first religious communities were the *Essenes*, who lived in the first century B.C. and the *Apostles*, in Jerusalem whose tradition was adopted by Christianity as a model way of life. When Christianity was made a state religion, these radical traditions were adopted by marginal groups, primarily in monastic orders and eventually in various heretic sects that emerged since the 11th century.

Under the prevalent social and economic conditions in Europe, followers of communal traditions were prevented from forming autonomous communal communities in their homelands. When the New World, with its wide open spaces and religious tolerance was opened up for settlement, various sects emigrated. Ever since the 18th century, hundreds of communal settlements were established in northern America, but most did not survive more than a few years.

First were the *German Millenarian* sects which established communal settlements in Pennsylvania. The most outstanding was *Ephrata* (1732–1813), whose members led a life of abstinence and seclusion; they established a communal farm that provided their modest needs. A turning point in communal history were the *Shaker* settlements, established by English Quakers who arrived in America on the eve of the War of Independence. By the end of the 19th century, they had established 18 communal settlements, in which about 5000 men and women lived in abstinence. Their communal farms and workshops prospered and most of their settlements survived for over a hundred years and some even two hundred.

Early in the 19th century (→ *History in 19th C.*) German Separatist sects emigrated to America and established *Harmony* in 1805, (which survived for about a hundred years) followed by *New Harmony* and *Economy*. Although these communities achieved an impressive economic prosperity, they eventually disappeared for lack of natural increase. The Inspirationalist German sect established *Amana* (1842) seven settlements in the State of Iowa, maintaining federative relations and prosperous industrial enterprises. They survived form 1843 until 1932, when they gave up their communal way of life.

The spiritual upheaval in the American society during the 1830s/40s, led to the establishment of *Oneida*. It was an American commune, whose members came from among New England circles. Oneida was founded by the Perfectionist sect under the spiritual leadership of *John Humphrey Noyes*. They introduced the 'complex marriage' according to which all members were married to one another. In the 1860s, the commune tried to adopt a form of birth control called stirpiculture. *Oneida* was a prosperous, stable, well organized and culturally active commune; its members introduced a system of mutual critisism as a means of socialization and supervision. It survived until the 1880, when it ceased to exist due to pressure by the church which resented to its 'immoral' family relations.

III. Socialist Communes

During the second decade of the 19th century, America experienced its first crisis as an emerging industrial society, leading to social unrest. The socialist reformer, → *Robert Owen*, visited the United States from 1825 to 1829. During that period he founded *New Harmony*, in which he tried to realize his theories of a model future society. The commune merely survived for three years, but it was to serve as a turning point and during the 1820s many other communal settlements were established.

The 1837s depression led to a reform movement when Fourierist utopian ideas were brought to the United States by the American *Albert Brisbane*. *Fourierism* presented a comprehensive plan of reconstruction based on cooperation and harmony and it reached its apex between 1843–1846, when scorces of communal settlements were established in various Eastern states. When the depression passed, Fourierism abated and as a result the communal settlement movement came to a standstill for thirty years. Even so, several communes were founded by European immigrants, the most outstanding by followers of *Cabet* and the French *Icaria* movement. In 1848 they established their communes in the Midwest surviving for over fifty years.

During the 1880s, communal activities were renewed mainly by a socialist organization the Brotherhood of Coopertive Commonwealth, the BCC, which proposed communal settlements in the Western states as a solution to unemployment. Their settlements centered around *Puget Sound*, Washingtion State and members were a heterogenous group without any prior training. This impaired their development and led to their desintegration after 4–5 years.

During the first half of the 20th century, the most stable among the socialist communes was *Llano del Rio* (1914–1938), which was established in California and later moved to Luisiana. Its founders were socialists who had become disillusioned with the political struggle. It attracted many workers, but many merely passed through.

IV. Hutterites and the Bruderhof

In 1874, survivors of the Hutterian communes, that had existed in Europe since 1530, arrived in the United States. They had started as an Anabaptist, pacifist group, that found refuge on Bohemian and Moravian estates where they laid the foundations for their communal communities. Their first spiritual leader was *Jacob Huter*, who gave the movement its name. The sect flourished during the 16th century, when its 60.000 members made their living on farms and in the service of their aristocratic masters. During the Thirty Years War, they were severely persecuted by rival religious armies and the few survivors led to Transylvania, Hungary and Rumania. Finally, they reached Russia, where they remained until the end of the 19th century. However, during the final years of that century the official policy was changed and when their sons were forcefully enlisted into the army, the Hutterites decided to emigrate to America. On their arrival in the United States, the Hutterites established prosperous agricultural settlements in South Dakota. During the First War their young people refused to enlist and as a result many were imprisoned, two even tortured to death. This tragic event prompted them to move to Canada in 1920, but eventually they agreed to return to the Midwest and nowadays a network of settlements is spread out on both sides of the border. Since the arrival of about 300 Hutterites in 1874, their numbers have steadily increased to 40.000 members who live in 390 communes today. The settlements are mainly based on agriculture, using modern machinery. They have no industry, but due to their diligence and agricultural know how they manage to produce a surplus and acquire additioal lands for new settlements. Although the Hutterites maintain economic relations with their neighbors, they seclude themselves against any alien influence. Their children study at local schools and do not receive higher education; they do not try to make souls and their only relations in modern history have been with the Bruderhof sect which arrived in the United States 1954.

The *Bruderhof* Movement was established in Germany in 1920. Its founder and spiritual leader was *Eberhard Arnod*, a young theologian whose study of Christian origins led him to pacifism and Anabaptism. After the World War he was active in the Student Christian Movement and from among its members formed a communal community in Sannerz (1920). They adopted a communal way of life, making a living from agriculture and educational institutions. After *Hitler* came to power, tensions ensued and they decided to flee Germany. At first they went to Lichtenstein, but realizing that they were not safe enough there, they moved on to England, where they settled in the Cotswolds on the eve of World War II. Although the authorities were quite tolerant, their neighbors were hostile and suspicious and eventually they decided to seek refuge on the American continent. The only country willing to accept them was Paraguay, where they settled in 1941. However, conditions were very hard and the Bruderhof experienced its worst crisis. Finally, they decided to move to the United States and together with a pacifist community they established a communal settlement *Woodcrest* in New York State. Making a living mainly from toy manufacture "Community Playthings", the Bruderhof sought to establish relations with the Hutterites and in 1974 and both movements merged.

Since 1954 the Bruderhof has established six communes in the USA, one in England and one in Germany. They maintain a religious, economic and financial interrelationship; collectively they manufacture toys and equipment for the handicapped. Their union with the hutterites has led them to adopt the latter' customs and clothing, but there are distinctive differences between the settlements: Bruderhof children study at regional high schools and some even go to universities; their settlements are larger and at present they have some 2000 members. Combined, they form the second largest communal movement after the Israeli kibbutz movement (→ *Development, Israel*).

V. Modern Communes

During the 1960s, a communal tide swept the Western world as a result of the student's revolt and the appearance of the flower children. Its center was in the United States and within a short while thousand of communes were established. In December 17th 1970, the New York Times reported that about 2000 communes existed in 34 states, some of them rural communities and others urban communes. Most members joined the communal movement in reaction to an alienated and materialistic world. They aspired to return to nature and live a simple life of freedom. They formed small communities based on harmony and on a new kind of inter relationship. Seeking ways of creativity, they made a living from handicrafts and organic agriculture, developed solar enery and grew their own food. However, tensions ensued and many communes disintegrated; only a small number managed to survive. Following are a few examples:

The Farm was established by a group of San Francisco hippies inspired by *Steven Gaskin*, one of the outstanding figures in the local student revolt. In 1971 he set out on a lecture tour throughout the country, accompanied by his followers in a convoy of buses. They ended up in Nashville, Tennessy and acquired a tract of land to establish what was to become the largest commune in the United States. They called their commune *The Farm* and members had to agree to a frugal and collective way life. Each member got a limited budget and his needs were provided by a general store. This system worked until the early eighties, but now there is a trend to adopt co-operative methods and limit collectivity. In 1983 members were permitted to have private property, keep bank accounts and accept payment for work, while paying for services received. Land and accommodation are commonly owned and have to be payed for. They maintain their autonomy and manufacture their own food. The most important of their many enterprises, is 'Plenty' which offers aid to the third world; established in 1973. The commune has an elementary and a high school, where they attempt to instil their children with their own values.

The Federation of Egalitarian Communities, is a group of communal settlements spread across North America. Originally inspired by behavioral psychologist *B.F. Skinner's* utopian novel Walden Two, they range in size from small homestead-oriented groups to village-like communities. All have been in existence for several years; the first, *Twin Oaks*, was founded in 1967. They all have a common base:

1) they hold their land, labor and other resources in common;
2) they assume responsibility for the needs of their members, receiving the products of their labor and distributing these and all other goods equally according to need;
3) they practice non violence;
4) they use a participatory form of government in which members have a direct vote;
5) they do not deny membership nor promote inequality among members through discrimination on grounds of race, creed, age or sex;
6) they assume responsibility for maintaining ecologically sound production and consumption.

Padanaram (God's Valley), was founded in 1966 at the height of the hippie movement and has religious priniciples. *Daniel Wright*, an undenominational minister, his wife and twelve pioneers founded it in a forest in Martin county, Indiana. Originally, the economic basis was agrarian but because of poor soil the farming venture gave way to saw-milling in 1968, providing the basis for a growing population and improved living conditions. By 1977, the sawmill had expanded to a point that it was moved to Bloomington, Indiana becoming the business complex Imperial Lumber Co., the largest sawmill in the State. The community has an open door policy; its members are employed in the sawmill, construction, child care, kitchen, school, etc. They have their own apartments and live in family units. Meals are taken togehter in the dining hall. Half the population is under 18. In the local school work and intellectual pursuits complement one another, students share village work responsibilities. Graduates can go to college under village sponsorship. They claim that their aim is 'an international communal utopia'.

VI. Australia and New Zealand

Australia has a history of communal settlements extending back to the start of European settlement. During the 1890s there was a rash of communal settlement that lasted some time, leaving behind a tradition which resufaced during the 1930s and again in the early 1970s as part of the radical student revolt against the Vietnam war. Many commune members are environmentalists and involved in ecological issues. They aspire to achieve 'inner peace, integral living and personal growth'. There are religious as well as secular communes and several assert that they have no ideology. Most of the communes leave a broad scope of choice and inividual autonomy to their members. Their sets of rules are only limited to specific areas in which they aspire to a consensus.

Most of the communal settlements are in *New South Wales,* each with an average of 200 members. Mostly they have no independent work branches and are employed in the neighborhood, or live off the dole, which they justify by claiming that they have returned to nature without harming the environment. Recent studies have pointed to a trend of progressive decline in the ideological zeal of communalism but even so, the movement increases in size.

There are several communal settlements in *New Zealand* and the most famous is *Riverside*, which was established in 1941 by a pacifist religious group that tried to adopt a collective way of life as an alternative to the existing order. During the war many of them spent long periods in detention camps. After the war the commune expanded and in 1972 they abolished their principle of accepting Christians only, but maintained their philosophy of nonviolence, frugal living and pacifism. Each member receives a weekly budget regardless of his/her contribution. Most work in the community and some outside. Riverside has about 100 members.

VII. Japan

Japan has a long and diversified tradition of communal experiments. The oldest is *Itoen*, which was founded in 1905 by *Tenko Nishida*, a wealthy merchant who gathered a group of followers to live collectively. In 1919 the group expanded, turned into a movement and moved to the outskirts of Kyoto where they started a printing press. They have a primary and a highschool, open to all neighborhood children. When *Tenko San* died in 1968, the leadership passed on to his son *Takeshi Nishida* and later to his grandson, but they also have an administrative council. They advocate mutual aid and frugal living. The commune has several industries, agriculture and a construction firm. They also care for Lepers who find no place on other nursing homes. Itoen numbers about 270 members and their families.

The most extensive communal movement is Yamagishi Kai that was founded in 1953 by *Miyoso Yamagishi*, an expert chicken farmer who had studied philosophy. He taught his followers Kensan, a philosophy of nonviolence and no private property. The movement gradually expanded and new communes were established, all expert chicken farmers. When the founder died in 1961, their movement declined; nowadays there are about 30 communes (with an average of 25 members each). *Toyasato* with about 400 members, is the largest and the center of Tensan. All communes have a communal store and every member helps himself; they have a communal dining hall and public halls for reading and relaxing. Children live with their parents up to the age of six and then are moved to children houses. The community is administered through a mixture of democracy and hierarchy. Having no fixed work hours, they work seven days and rest whenever they feel like it. In the words of their founder, "all those who are ready to work for nothing, wearing rags... come to us."

VIII. Europe

Even though Europe was the cradle of communal sects and utopian socialism, communes did not materialize there until after the student revolt of the 1970s. Most of the communes were urban ones and just a few established stable settlements.

The conspicuous European communal movement is *Longo Mai* which was founded in 1973 on the foothills of the Alps in Southern *France*. At first it had 25 members who pooled their resources to buy an abandoned stretch of land. To avoid dependence on the outside market, they developed mixed agriculture, small industries and crafts. It expanded during several years and them abruptly declined. The cooperative's membership is stable and all important decisions are made at general meetings. Although several additional cooperatives have been established, the movement has lost its momentum. *Community of the Ark* was founded by *Lanza del Vasto*, in the Haut Languedoe (France). There are three communities with about 150 companions, who vow to commit themselves to the service of others, in the manner of Gandhian non-violence. They do manual work, live frugally, and are commited to the cause of peace. Their independence of all religious or potential affiliation, enables the Ark to welcome everyone as member. They own 120 acres of arrable land and being vegetarian, produce their own food. All resouces are held in common and everyone contributes what they can and receive according to their needs. All important decisions are made by consensus.

Danish Production communes came into being during the 1960s, when the demand for social change in *Denmark* became overwhelming. One of their imperatives was to create a new way of life according to their vision of an intergrated community within a capitalist society. In order to withstand the pressure of the outside world, they organized as a legal entity devoted to production and services. The most famous, the *Svanholm Collective* was established in 1978 and is based on ecological farming. In addition they have a packing factory, a publishing house for books on the environment, an apple orchard, a candle factory, etc. The community consists of about 75 adults. Most work at home and some have outside jobs. They maintain a collective economy and all income is pooled. They live in 'house groups' in various buildings. All eat supper in a communal dining hall. Small children are taken care of in the kindergarten and the older ones have a 'youth club'. The communal meeting serves as a decision making authority.

Germany, from which the religious sects set out to form communes in the New World, did not provide fertile ground for communal settlements until after the World War II. During the Weimar Republic and the youth movement era, communes such as the Bruderhof were established, but the movement was abolished in the Nazi era. During the 1960s there was a renaissance and communal movements such as the *Integrierte Gemeinde* emerged. However, there has been no significant settlement movement since, and only recently several nuclei of communal groups have emerged (→ *New Co-op*eratives) which may eventually become independent settlements such as the Michaelshof (Bruderhof).

In *The United Kingdom* communitarianism has existed over the past two centuries. The 19th century communes were generally more closely embedded in a process of political change than their successors. Utopians socialists (like → *Robert Owen*) and agrarian socialists (like *Feargus O'Connor*) attracted working class supporters, and a variety of communities were formed to further the socialist cause. Later in the century, the writings of *Morris, Kropotkin* and *Tolstoy* inspired a new generation of anarchists to seek their own brand of change through community. Nor was religious communitarianism absent, for in the ferment of change, messianic leaders attracted their own following.

In the early 20th century, community formation continued less concerned with political change and more with the immediate spiritual and practical advantages of living in community. To this is added a surge of activity in the form of pacifist communes in the 1960s when communes offered opportunities to work towards an alternative society and to pioneer many elements of modern life such as environmental issues, patterns of work and social responsibilities. Several communes (like Findhorn) have proved to be remarkably enduring and adaptable to changing needs. As the end of the century nears, uncertainties surrounding the mainstream society and the challenge of environmental and other issues will create conditions for a new phase of communitarianism; the need to ask questions and to offer novel answers remains as urgent as ever.

Bibliography

Bestor, Arthur: Backwood Utopias, Univ. of Pennsylvania Press 1978.
Clark, Margaret Munro: Communes in Rural Australia, Hale & Oremonger 1986.
Cock, Peter: Alternative Australia, Quarter Books 1979.
Fogarty, Robert R.S.: Dictionary of American Communal and Utopian History, Greenwood Pr., USA 1980.
Hardy, Dennis: Alternative Communes in 19th Century England, London 1979.
Hinds, Williams: American Communities (reprint 1908 ed.), Porcupine Press 1974.
Hostetler, John: Hutterite Society, John Hopkins U.P. 1974.
Holloway, Marc: Heavens on Earth, Dover Press 1966.
Kantor, Rosabeth: Commitment and Community, Harvard Univ. Press 1972.
McLaughlin, Corinne/Davidson, Gordon: Builders of the Dawn, Stillpoint Publ., New Hampshire 1985.
Nordhoff, Charles: The Communisitic Societies of the United States (Harper 1875), Schocken 1965.
Noyes, John H.: History of American Socialism (Lippincott 1870), Dover 1966.
Oved, Yaacov: Two Hundred Years of American Communes, Transaction Books, U.S.A. 1988.
Popenoe, Cris & Oliver: Seeds of Tomorrow, Harper & Row, U.S.A. 1984.
Zablocki, Benjamin: Alienation and Charisma, A Study of Contempory American Communes, The Free Press, U.S.A. 1980.

Competition and Co-operatives

WALTER HAMM [J]

(see also: *Economic Order; Classic/Neo-classic Contributions; Pricing Policy; Business Policies; Anti-Trust Laws*)

I. The Functions of Competition in a Free Market Structure; II. The Tasks of Competition Policy; III. Co-operatives as an Element of Competitive Structure.

I. The Functions of Competition in a Free Market Structure

Competition is commonly understood as an incessant process of advances and pursuits on markets: individual suppliers or those in demand of goods and services strive to surpass competitors by making particularly enticing contractual offers to their business partners. Competitors endeavor to defend themselves against imminent turnover or profit losses by either neutralizing competitive advances through the emulation of successful policy measures or by attempting to respond through their own advances. An expedient legal framework for the course of the competitive process (see Part II) can ensure that the participants of the competitive process, each seeking his own advantage, either intentionally or unwillingly accomplish important functions affecting the entire economy (→ *Anti-Trust Laws*). Freedom of discretion for all actors regarding their utilization of instruments (action parameters) to outstrip competitors is the necessary precondition for the realization of competitive processes; this, in particular, concerns pricing (→ *Pricing Policy*), product quality, research and development, terms and conditions, advertising, and customer service.

What is the nature of the most important functions of competition affecting the entire economy? Above all, the following tasks must be mentioned:

– *Safeguarding Autonomy*;
The actors themselves decide on their goals and the appropriate policy measures to pursue them within state-established bounds. They are not subject to any sort of arbitrary constraint and can determine their behavior autonomously. Competition is thus a constitutive element of a liberal structure.

– *Co-ordinating Economic Plans*;
Individual goals can only then be achieved with a prospect of success when the current behavior/policy of other actors as well as forseeable actions and reactions are taken into consideration. In this manner, an interactive relationship evolves between all important economic subjects being reciprocally affected. A particularly effective and permanent solution to the coordination problem ("spontaneous co-ordination") is secured through the engagement of individual interests. The more complex a national economy and its structure is, the more dependent it is on the effectiveness of spontaneous efforts (*v. Hayek*).

– *Creating Effective Incentives;*
Rewards and penalties must ensure that all participants decisively strive to mobilize their strengths. This occurs in such that positive and negative incentives (→ *Incentives*) are directly fixed to the prevalent individual economic goals. Competitive success is reflected through income and capital advantages, failure through losses or even bankruptcy. Experience shows that this system of incentives is particularly effective. The extent of the reward or penalty results from the non-authoritarian harmonization process of the market (in contrast to the distribution of bonuses through the authorities in a system of central state economic planning and control). Because profits resulting from a certain advantage can be reaped by trailing participants (rapid propagation of preeminent knowledge), the incentive to continue undertaking new advances remains preserved.

– *Supporting Evolution;*
Competition is furthermore a process of discovery. It is worthwhile for actors to discover new knowledge and test it on markets (competition as a "process of discovery"). This explains the lively innovative activities and the marked dynamism of free market processes. There is substantial evidence that the discovery of new facts and data is likewise a function of the number of companies operating independently of one another.

– *The Economical Utilization of Scarce Resources;*
Competition is advantageous for the economy as a whole as companies are induced to utilize means of production in an economical manner. The reduction of unit costs (→ *Principle of Cost Coverage*) facilitates an improvement in company returns. With the amount of available resources more goods can be supplied to the economy as a whole than otherwise possible without the effects of increased efficiency arising from competition.

– *Controlling Economic Power;*
Competition provides contractual partners with the opportunity to make selections. In order to prevent economic power from being misused to the detriment of a contractual party, those affected can protect themselves by switching over to other competitors. If this is not possible, potential competition becomes activated (newcomers). These controls, stemming from the self-interests of actors, seem to be considerably more effective than state bureaucratic controls, inasfar as market accessibility is free.

– *Peacefully Solving Conflicts of Interest;*
Suppliers and purchasers have opposing interests. Buyers wish to acquire products with a specific quality at a low price. Suppliers, on the other hand, strive to achieve the highest possible price. Competition regularly proves to be a procedure to solve such conflicts of interest peaceably. Buyers as well as sellers recognize that market competition determines limits as a non-authoritarian procedure of interest settlement. On the other hand, state (authoritarian) price regulation as a rule does not satisfy one side of the market which thus considers itself unjustly treated and accordingly complains in public of its disadvantaged treatment. Competition, therefore, also has a peacemaking effect.

II. The Tasks of Competition Policy

Competition fulfills the functions enumerated above only under certain conditions; state authorities must ensure that these preconditions are fulfilled (→ *State and Co-operatives, Market Economy*). Because competition is understandibly considered by many companies as irksome (performance pressure), and inasfar as less competition among suppliers frequently leads to considerable financial advantages, a wide spectrum of corporate measures exists to restrain trade. These, likewise, have influential effects on politicians to limit competition. Only a strong state can withstand such pressures. Experience shows that all too often politicians in many countries have yielded to this lobby pressure.

Which preconditions must be provided for in order for competition to produce the desired effects on the entire economy?

– *Open Markets*;
Competition is only then in the position to control economic power effectively and ensure high output stimulating dynamics when entry into a market is free. Potential competition (from companies ready to enter the market) must not be restricted. Both private and state restraints to market entry can stand in the way of this principle. Free entry is in fact complicated or denied by private industry when companies new to the market must reckon with embargos,

delivery refusals or underbidding practices by those companies (or cartels) with a strong market position. Guaranteed shelving contracts within retail trade can produce similar effects. An abuse of market strength can be assumed when either new competitors are not drawn to the market or when market share among existing competitors does not mount despite rising prices and above average profits at a company dominating the market.

State authorities frequently create barriers to entry. Above all, two reasons come to the fore: Either public companies should be protected from competition arising from private competitors (e.g. electric supply, telecommunication, quasi-public corporations on the local level, rail and air traffic), or market entry is limited through pressure from private interests, thus leading to an artificial scarcity of supply and to mounting profits (e.g. the trucking industry). In all of these situations, competition policy has the responsibility to ensure open markets. If, on the other hand, market entry is a factor of professional qualification to serve the public welfare (e.g. doctors), such impediments to free entry are to be accepted.

– *Free Determination of Action Parameters;*
The anticipated effects of competition can furthermore only then materialize when companies are free according to their own discretion to determine the parameters of their actions within the laws of the legal framework. Competition restraints exist which stem from private industry as well as from the state. Cartels obviate autonomous corporate decision making among cartel members, for example in pricing issues. Other forms of binding collective decisions concerning the determination of action parameters likewise represent trade restraints. Competition policy is entrusted to forestall such limitations.

In numerous cases, companies are prevented from determining their action parameters by state regulation. Price intervention, above all in the form of set prices or price floors and ceilings, which restricts the freedom of corporate decision-making on many markets and produces cartel-like effects needs to be mentioned. Grave, undesired economic developments, such as the supply surplus on agricultural markets, can be traced to national or international pricing intervention which has prevented the anticipated positive effects on the economy as a whole from being realized. Working towards deregulation in special sectors of restricted competition policy is thus an important task for politicians involved in such policy making.

– *The Prohibition of Unfair Competition;*
Rewards and penalties resulting from competitive processes must solely be dependent on economic performance if competition is to fulfill its functions. State regulatory guidelines must therefore prevent companies from attempting to achieve revenue advantages through misleading or defamatory advertising, false claims or by bribing the employees of competing companies. The strict connection between financial advantages and economic performance must be safeguarded; otherwise, competition would degenerate to a lawless battle conducted with foul means – likewise to the detriment of consumers.

– *Preventing the Abuse of Market Power;*
Economic power must not be abused in order to limit competition, to achieve an exploitative pricing policy or to exercise arbitrary power over others. Monopolies commissions can effectively combat the abuse of power by tracking down and forestalling practices that restrict competition. The forces of competition are particularly successful when it comes to leveling down above average profits. Additional competition brings along alternative companies which can be turned to when market dominating companies try to exercise arbitrary pressure.

The laws of competition in many countries subject leading market companies to state supervision with regard to competition (→ *Anti-Trust Laws*). Aside from a limited number of obvious cases of power abuse (e.g. boycott, delivery refusals, cartel-like pricing agreements, tying agreements), numerous other practices exist which can only with great difficulty be definitively proven to present a misuse of economic power. Causal therapy, or the elimination of barriers to entry (also for foreign suppliers) facilitates the tasks of antitrust authorities. Curing the symptoms (e.g. investigating "exaggerated" prices and demanding their reduction) is a drawn-out process which entails extensive problems in establishing proof. The non-bureaucratic method of introducing competitive forces achieves the objective both faster and surer. Inasfar as market entry is hindered by state regulation, the elimination of this intervention must be pressed for.

III. Co-operatives as an Element of Competitive Structure

1. The Effects of Co-operatives on Inducing Competition

Co-operatives normally promote their members by opening more favorable supply channels, offering better terms and conditions through collective purchases, by making new sales channels accessible, through consultation, and through the co-operative production of goods/services at prices lower than individual members would otherwise be able to produce (→ *Promotion Mandate*). Members can thus hold their own in competition with greater success.

The co-operative regularly serves as an additional option for small and mid-sized companies or for households. The entry of yet another competitor heightens competition between available business partners. Joint co-operative action makes it possible for more small and mid-sized companies to hold their own in competition, something they otherwise would not be able to do without such a concentration of strengths. This means a greater number of independent decision making centers, more opportunities for innovative competitive action, as well as a wider selection of business partners for the co-operative members' customers.

Competition is therefore stimulated and intensified on all levels and in all of its facets. In the case of a wholesale co-operative (→ *Commercial Co-operative*), a further supplier with an extensive product/service assortment enters the market alongside the private wholesaler. Those companies already active on the market are forced to improve their performance, which in turn has an influential effect on the purchasing co-operatives. More mid-sized companies are able to survive the competition due to collective cooperation; positive effects from competition likewise arise at this stage. All parties involved are forced to increase their endeavors, which in the end benefits consumers.

Co-operatives are permanently subjected to a test of their performance. Members can withdraw from their co-operative when they receive offers for more favorable conditions and better outputs from competitors. Membership in a co-operative by no means implies a survival guarantee for mid-sized companies: It is only possible to endure competition with a good corporate performance. The incentives and pressures to perform are not any lower for co-operative members. Because co-operatives enable an effective utilization of scarce means of production in members' enterprises, competitors likewise become forced to improve their efforts. In conclusion, it can be determined that co-operative activity on all levels produces positive effects which incite competition.

2. Possible Consequences of Co-operative Activity which Restrain Competition

Co-operatives, just like companies which have assumed other legal forms, are subject to state statutory guidelines for competition. Individual co-operatives, on account of their strong market position, could also be tempted to promote their members by limiting competition, by reducing their purchasing costs through the abuse of their economic power, or by achieving disproportionally high profits from the sales of their goods. Co-operatives dominating a market must, therefore, also be subject to the identical antitrust authorities that other companies are. Positive effects inciting competition do frequently result from co-operatives (as described in Part III.1); these, nevertheless, do not make supervision through an antitrust authority superfluous.

Which practices are seen to restrict competition and are thus regularly prohibited by lawmakers? Above all, the following states of affairs should be considered:

– *Corporate Mergers:*
Monopolies commissions are legally entrusted to prevent market dominating companies from emerging through external growth (corporate mergers, lease of a running concern, and similar agreements). Because market dominating companies can likewise emerge through mergers, it is essential that mergers within the co-operative sector are both legally registered and audited (→ *Mergers and Consolidations*). Most of the numerous mergers among smaller credit and retail co-operatives are cases almost irrelevant with respect to antitrust laws. To the most part, these merging co-operatives are active on different geographic markets; they only have negligible market shares and are in stiff competition with companies of different legal forms. On the other hand, occasional merger attempts arise which could restrict competition and which, therefore, need to be forestalled. Above all, the mounting strength on supply markets are watched.

– *Conditions limiting the Autonomy of Suppliers:*
The (contractual) pressure a market dominating company exerts to the detriment of its suppliers is a restraint of competition insofar as no other buyer would be granted such low prices or favorable conditions (forced discrimination to the disadvantage of competitors). Such a supplier would no longer be free to institute his own marketing instruments according to his own discretion. The strength of a contractual partner is thus abused to restrict the discretionary freedom of others. Monopolies commissions must prevent such types of coercion.

– *Conditions limiting the Autonomy of Members:*
The question remains contested concerning the extent co-operatives may force their members to work together with the co-operative enterprise and fully accept the collectively determined marketing strategies. In principle members should be free to decide to what extent and how closely they wish to be tied to their co-operative. Members make use of the services of a purchasing co-operative to a great degree and without any pressure when the services are good. "Co-operative loyalty" among members (a large share of total purchases from the co-operative) can, therefore, not be concluded without further investigation of mandatory purchases (→ *Supply Co-operatives*).

Furthermore, members should be ensured discretionary freedom regarding the employment of their marketing instruments: only through this manner competition between the co-operative and its market competitors as well as competition between the co-operative members can be maintained. Members involved in collective advertising must, however, adjust their assortment and pricing policy to the publicized services/outputs (→ *Anti-Trust Laws*).

– *Territorial and Position Protection:*
Basically, entry into a co-operative is open to all those who are interested in co-operative support and

who are willing to participate actively. It would be objectionable if a purchasing co-operative denied entry to a new member on the grounds that another member already offers his services to the local market (protection of position). Beyond any doubt, such behavior would constitute a restraint of competition if the purchasing co-operative had a dominant market postion.

Contractual obligations between co-operatives (e.g. credit co-operatives (→ *Co-operative Banks*)) which prevent contracts from being signed with business partners located in the territory of another credit co-operative function like a territorial cartel. It should be welcomed rather than objected to when credit co-operatives, as a consequence of their promotional policy concentrate their activity (in particular their lending transactions) on their members. Furthermore, the creditworthiness of business partners in one's own regional territory can be evaluated better than that of unknown customers living elsewhere. From the viewpoint of the cartel stipulations, this close cooperation between a co-operative and its members should by no means be frowned upon. This is not a practice intended to restrict competition, but rather a legally defined and pursued business policy. At any rate, several banks in other legal forms are usually existing as competitors.

3. Closing Valuation

Understandibly, only very few large co-operatives (→ *Operational Size*) are at the center of attention of monopolies commissions and in the public light; only occasionally do practices become noticed which restrain trade and competition. On the other hand, there is practically no notice taken of the tens of thousands of small and mid-sized co-operatives and their regular stimulation of competition. This fact must be emphasized in order to place the proper importance in competition policy. In the highly developed industrial nations, co-operatives are surely no longer the "children of need" as they were at the time of the formation of the first modern co-operatives around the middle of the 19th century. Nevertheless, they are an important keystone for small and mid-sized companies to preserve their independence. This ultimately means that co-operatives contribute to the preservation of more numerous autonomous corporate decision centers and, thus, to the stimulation of competition.

Bibliography

Aberle, Gert: Wettbewerbstheorie und Wettbewerbspolitik, Stuttgart 1980.
Dülfer, Eberhard: Betriebswirtschaftslehre der Kooperative, Göttingen 1984.
Eucken, Walter: Grundsätze der Wirtschaftspolitik, 5th edition, Bern/Tübingen 1975.
Hamm, Walter: Staatsaufsicht über wettbewerbspolitische Ausnahmebereiche als Ursache ökonomischer Fehlentwicklungen, Ordo, vol. 29, Stuttgart 1978, pp. 156–172.
Hamm, Walter: Die genossenschaftliche Idee – bewährt und zukunftsweisend. 125 Jahre Genossenschaftsverband Hessen/Rheinland-Pfalz, Frankfurt 1987, pp. 61–75.
Homrighausen, Fritz H.: Wettbewerbswirkungen genossenschaftlicher Einkaufszusammenschlüsse, Göttingen 1980.
Herdzina, Klaus: Wettbewerbspolitik, 2nd edition, Stuttgart 1987.
Schultz, Reinhard/ Zerche, Jürgen: Genossenschaftslehre, Berlin 1983.
Woll, Artur: Wirtschaftspolitik, München 1984.

Conceptions, Co-operative

WERNER WILHELM ENGELHARDT [F]

(see also: *History of Co-operative Ideas*; *Theory and Science of Co-operatives*; *History in 19th C.*; *Principles*; *Managerial Economics*; *Combine, Co-operative*; *Promotion Mandate*)

I. Terminological Categories and Present-Day Relevance; II. Ideologies, Policy of Economic Order, Systemic Disputes; III. Institutional Meaning, Legal Spheres, Principles; IV. The Promotion Mandate, Co-operative Consciousness, Co-operative Identity.

1. Terminological Categories and Present-Day Relevance

Co-operative ideas or utopias (cf. the article on the History of Co-operative Ideas) are the result of instinctive impulses (*Watkins, Claessens*), but even more the result of personal and subjective thinking of an intellectual, psychological, and linguistic kind (*Buber, Engelhardt*). These ideas (utopias) lead to conceptions of co-operatives, if they are exposed to logical and normative requirements and empirical facts (→ *History of Ideas*). The ideas, or utopias, as well as the conceptions can be characterized and approximately defined as "co-operative guiding principle" (→ *Principles*) or "co-operative philosophy" or "co-operative culture" (→ *Corporate Culture*), as has recently often been done (e.g. by *Dülfer, Hahn, Großkopf*, and others).

As a matter of distinction, there are co-operative conceptions of practitioners as well as those of scientists. The former kind have also been called "co-operative programmes" and "co-operative strategies", ever since the work of the → *Rochdale Pioneers* and the founding of international co-operative organizations (cf. *Hasselmann, Boettcher, Bonus*, and *Zerche*). The latter kind can be further sub-divided, especially with regard to scientific theories (→ *Theory and Science of Co-operatives*). Between the two kinds of conceptions, practical and scientific, come co-operative ideologies, which, as general prescriptions for taking a stand (*Albert, V. Kraft*), create a co-operative consciousness in a more or less dogmatic way and are intended to contribute to a co-operative identity. Co-operative ideologies often take up ideal-type dedications as well as utopias (cf. the article on classification and Typologies and Co-operatives; further cf. *Weippert, Fürstenberg,* and *Hettlage*), and they also often form bridges to political concepts of economic order. More recent scientific conceptions of co-operatives in the industrial age often pursue the purpose of concretising co-operative basic or → *promotion mandates* (*Henzler, Bänsch*) into systems of goals (*Dülfer, Münkner*). If the terms used are not made workable, then these mandates – which also exist in public enterprises, as, for example, in savings banks – constitute somewhat empty phrases, even though guiding principles have gone into their making (*Grünfeld, Draheim, Engelhardt*). However, in the various legal spheres of industrial and developing countries in which co-operatives exist (cf. *Ebert, Dülfer, Hanel, Kuhn, Münkner,* and *Trappe*), the intended institutional purpose of the co-operatives were early laid down through commentary and application of the respective laws (→ *British–Indian Pattern;* → *Law, International*). From the legal and constitutional norms and objectives of these organizations, but also partly from the subjective intentions and actual actions of the pioneers and later members, co-operative principles have been derived.

At the present time, co-operative organizations in many countries are striving to find a new purpose or role for their co-operatives (cf. *Engelhardt* and *Thiemeyer,* eds.: *Genossenschaft quo vadis?*, 1988). What they have in mind is either an active continuation of the earlier, dominant orientation of co-operatives to the common welfare (→ *Commonweal Economy*), or else a mere recognition of the interests of their organized or potential membership groups, whether those interests be rightly understood or actually expressed. In the second case of mere recognition of members' interests, and faced with the ever more urgent demands of the market, these organizations supposedly suggest only that their co-operatives react to the situation as best they can. Over against an "economism" which has partly become a purpose in itself in the rest of the economy (*Weisser, Rich*), and which corresponds to the trend toward "enterprise as such" (*Rathenau, Witte*) in the area of individual enterprise, at least parts of the international co-operative movement nonetheless still hold fast to their traditonal socio-economic political-economic orientation.

Co-operatives in an economic or legal sense and other forms of cooperation (→ *Forms of Cooperation*) can actually make considerable contributions to ways of "thinking in order", which have been built up through scientific efforts as well as through practical experience, and which admittedly (*Eucken, Lampert*) still have gaps (→ *Economic Order*). Given a new evolution of forms of cooperation in the present day (cf. *Axelrod, Wiesenthal,* and others), the economic and non-economic outputs or services could even remain permanently in demand, depending on how successfully these forms of cooperation resist the trend to adapt themselves to present-day tendencies and pressures.

II. Ideologies, Policy of Economic order, Systemic Disputes

Basic co-operative ideologies include co-operativistic as well as non-co-operativistic ones. Sometimes the former kind are also called co-operatistic, solidaristic, or labouristic conception (→ *Pfeiffer, Pesch, Nell-Breuning,* and others). The latter can be sub-divided into individualistic, or private-enterprise-oriented, and collectivistic, or central-administration-oriented, ideologies, whereby, however, the "économie collective" or "économie sociale" in French-speaking countries is to be interpreted partly as central-administration-oriented and partly as co-operativistic and oriented to commonweal enterprise (*Milhaud, Lambert, Lasserre, Lavergne,* and others). The non-co-operativistic ideologies lead to derived ideological conceptions, which came to have great importance in the co-operative movements of the 19th and 20th centuries (→ *History in 19th C.*).

Individually, the co-operativistic ideologies can be sub-divided, according to *Hettlage*, into pan-co-operativistic and insular co-operativistic ones. Both types stem from the older essentialisms and ideolgies of corporativism, which were of particular importance in the time of historical co-operatives of the Middle Ages, shaped by German social law, and which are now being revived in the form of neo-corporativism (→ *von Gierke, Huber, Thieme, Böhret*). But co-operativistic ideologies are also connected with partly very old utopias and partly new ones having to do with natural law or the natural order of government and society, of the economy, and of social services and welfare. Frequently in the past a thing has been and in the present still is declared by certain authors to be an ideology and therefore a thing to be spurned, which with other authors is considered simply a policy dealing with economic systems and is highly regarded. Ever since the important systemic disputes in the previous century and the more recent controversies between the supporters of varying interpretations of co-operatives – those oriented to private enterprise, and those oriented to commonweal economy – there have been many examples proving the truth of this statement.

1. Pan-co-operativistic Ideologies of Dominance

According to the opinion put forth by the author of this article – of course, it is not the only opinion possible – utopias today as well as in the past can be distinguished from ideologies, although in the area of integrated utopias there is an overlapping. Integrated or great utopias are understood here to be uncompromising subjective views, that is, subjectivisms with definitely irrational aspects (*Popper, Albert*). In contrast to selective utopias, these integrated or great utopias have the trait in common with ideologies, among other traits, that they claim absolute validity. Supporters of these utopias fail to distinguish sufficiently between normative validity, empirical truth, and logical correctness in their assertions.

The ideologies of co-operativism have many founding fathers, among them → *Eduard Pfeiffer, Charles Gide, Peter Kropotkin,* and *James Peter Warbasse.* In analysing these ideologies, it is a good idea to start out with the distinction already mentioned between pan-co-operativistic ideologies, with the envisioned dominance of co-operatives (*Bourgeois*), and pluralistic insular ideologies, in which there is merely an equality of rank or even an inferiority of rank with regard to the co-operatives' position (e.g. *Weippert*). In the variants of both types of ideologies, however, ontological or "value-philosophical" essentialisms play a role, which means that the problem of attempting to give reasons in principle for reforms in society, in the economy, and in the social system (cf. *Gehrig* and *von Krockow*), as well as the chances for mastering that problem through essence-oriented pragmatism and institutionalism (*Dewey, Katterle*), are usually too little recognised.

One of the most outspoken early adherents of pan-co-operativism was probably *Pfeiffer*, who, like *Gide* later, at first placed his hopes particularly on the spread of consumer co-operatives. *Pfeiffer's* main statement – which seemingly avoided all doctrinairism, but contained it anyway – was the following: "We want to be careful not to fall into the same mistakes which communists and socialists make; we don't want to set up a finished system which has been worked out to the last detail. This cannot be established a priori; but one can surely determine the principle and the direction of reform; and if it is then to be viable, the reform must lock arms with life, and in developing it will thus adjust itself to varying conditions everywhere, in one place in one way, in another place in another way."

Pfeiffer then makes the transition to the co-operative movement: "This process is exactly what we observe in cooperation; and therefore one can with assuredness predict success and ultimate victory for the new system (which we wish to call cooperativism, in contrast to socialism and communism), because it is not a matter here of overthrowing everything at one blow, of creating entirely new conditions, but of gradually altering existing circumstances for the betterment of the least fortunate social classes. Furthermore, no reform is to be imposed here from above, but rather the least fortunate class itself, drawing on its own strength, is to bring about the reform. In this way alone will better conditions, once reached, be able to withstand every upheaval."

2. Insular Co-operativistic Pluralistic Ideologies

Whereas supporters of the monistic trend toward a → *co-operative commonwealth* assumed that in its fully and partially integrative variants (i.e. of → joint-production societies and societies intended to assist their members), the co-operative movement was to be striven for as the dominant structure in society and would – at least eventually – succeed as such, supporters of pluralism felt and still feel differently. They gave and still give no chance ever for predominance to co-operatives in a legal or economic sense, nor do they do so to more or less co-operative-type of (according to *Hettlage*) congruent forms or to forms which in their character of self-help, self-administration, and participation have an affinity to co-operatives (→ *Relationship Patterns*).

For protagonists of this line, the co-operative movement, according to *Hettlage*, is "always tied to a definite economic order, within which it fulfills certain supplementary functions." Advocacy of a "third way" (e.g. *Back, Fauquet*), however, or of "third" or "middle economic orders" (*Watkins, Weippert,* and others) is by no means thereby excluded. Pluralists simply approach it differently from monists. For example, *Weippert* has referred to agreements as a basis of a third economic system, and *von Loesch* has referred to insular functions of co-operatives or of free enterprises for public benfit. Apart from the fact that it is hardly possible to speak of "the" one monistic or pluralistic line or even school of thought, but only of the various supporters of both trends belonging to different schools of world-views, political opinions, and scientific attitudes, still the differentiation of terms between monistic and pluralistic approaches is to be approved of.

Weippert's concept of "agreements as a third principle of economic order" is a pat example of pluralistic co-operativism, which is the reason why his approach is to be gone into here in some detail. To commence with his earlier essentialistic statements on co-operative sociology, *Weippert* says that the co-operative "exists and is viable only insofar as it is firmly rooted in the social community." For him (as for *Faust*, as well), the meta-economic dimension of the phenomenon of modern co-operatives is "always immanent everyhere." It belongs to the "essence of the co-operative", no matter whether the co-operative is ascribed to the *Tönniesian* ideal type, structured according to communal groups, or to the ideal type structured according to society as a whole (→ *Societal Form, Co-operative*).

In a theoretical study of economic systems, *Weippert* then proves that apart from the classical forms of coordination known as market and plan, mutual consultations and consensus – including the "agreement" among co-operative members to accept a "co-operative contract" – represent a third, logically independent principle of coordination. Unlike *Eucken*, *Weippert* attributes great importance to this principle for an analysis of real types of market economies. One by one *Weippert* differentiates between voluntary arrangements between persons and groups, agreements, and coordinations of actions, on the one hand, and forced or automatically-resulting arrangements on the other hand. Agreements have to do with markets in money and goods and, in the case of co-operatives, serve mainly to defend the social position of members. The reason "why co-operative agreements represent a → *third way* is that the co-operative principle accords not only with the fact of sociality but also with that of personality, in other words, with the needs of the individual to be himself as well as with the requirements of the group to live together" (*Fürstenberg*, in addition to *Weippert*) (→ *Group, the Co-operative*).

3. Derived Ideologies

Of course, there are many more ideologies in the field of co-operatives than have been set forth thus far in this analysis of the central ideologies of dominating and pluralistic co-operativism. Basically, all democratic and technocratic, all authoritarian and totalitarian ideologies which one normally comes across in social, economic, and political life can also be noted in the field of co-operatives in the various countries. In many cases, however, they have undergone refinements, i.e. have assumed additional attributes, or else they fall back on borrowed intentions. For this last reason, ever since *Grünfeld*, they have come to be called derived ideologies. They focus on special features of agricultural production processes, for example, or on craftsmen's way of life, or on general or special needs of consumers.

Referring to *Weippert*, writers have spoken of "special ideologies", all of which are supposedly undergoing decline. In contrast to these ideologies, *Weippert* has put forward the ideology of a "unified society", an ideology which is difficult to grasp but presumably impossible to overlook. It must be borne in mind and reiterated "as long as the self-image of a social unit fails to coincide with the actual circumstances of that unit and contains within it traits of mere self-justification." Modern individualism and of course radical collectivism are also to be considered ideologies. *Weippert* has distinguished between a-capitalistic and anti-capitalistic occupational classes, in particular among strata of farmers, craftsmen, and proletariat, each with their early special ideologies. In the area of cooperation *Weippert* has differentiated according to ideologies of the *Raiffeisen* movement (→ *Rural Co-operatives*), of *Schulze-Delitzsch* co-operatives (→ *Commercial Co-operatives*), of → *housing co-operatives*, and of → *consumer co-operatives*.

Seraphim, taking up similar distinctions from *Sombart*, has used the expression "economic conviction". However, he does not yet use the term in speaking of the beginning of the co-operative movement in the industrial age. "For the initial phase of the development of co-operative ideas, it is the predominance of conceptions of social reform, aiming for the reshaping of the whole social order, which was characteristic." In the same context, *von Loesch* speaks of an "economy for a commonweal economy as a co-operative overall system," which he contrasts with an "commonweal economy as a co-operative economy (self-help)." Between the two world wars, *Grünfeld* wrote along similar lines, whereas *Liefmann* (and later *Reinhardt*) tended toward individualistic interpretations of self-help. To cite *Weippert* once more, everywhere where the idea of self-government began to be genuinely accepted, including even free socialism and commonweal economy, *Weippert* spoke of "the co-operative principle", toward which, in his opinion, one should be especially open-minded and receptive.

4. Recent Discussions on Policies of Economic Order

In view of such varying characterizing terms, it is not surprising that particularly in the past decade the discussion has flared up again as to which world-view co-operatives should be classed under: whether under criteria of individualistic private enterprise, under criteria of a collectivistic-administered economy, or under criteria of commonweal oriented free enterprise. It cannot be denied that all these interpretations of co-operatives have also led to ideologies in which particularized intellectual approaches have been passed out as general approaches (*Fürstenberg*) and have been uncompromisingly put forward. From the ideas or utopias of *Schulze-Delitzsch*, of the *Rochdale Pioneers*, and of many other initiators, there have developed – to leave out ideologies of an administered economy for the moment – general instructions on action to be taken for the middle-class, for workers, and for consumers. Not just collectivistic conceptions of planning, but also these general instructions have up to the present day been often enough upheld as a doctrine of policy of economic order, although by no means by all their supporters. According to *Thiemeyer*, the perspective on policy of economic order contained in the concept of the commonweal oriented free enterprise emphasizes numerous traits which co-operatives and public enterprise have in common. This occurs on the basis of a critical-realistic orientation to the common good in the sense of *Kant*, which can be distinguished not only from rationalistic but also from idealistic orientations to the common good. According to the unorthodox supporters of a commonweal economy, both types of enterprise – co-operatives and public enterprise – are to become active only when and insofar as others, in the predominating political opinion of the time, fail to fulfill the task just as well (the theory of bridging the gap, which coincides to a large extent with the principle of subsidiarity). As far as co-operatives are concerned in particular, a "many-faceted social life" (*Weisser*), in the sense of a "post-modern precept for pluralism in ways of viewing things, organizing things, and living" (*Novy*), has many advantages over the "bisectoral world-view" (*Gretschmann*) of free market economists or of economists of a planned economic system. "What is to be striven for is a pluralistic market economy made up of many different forms of enterprise and organizations, all bound up in a number of coordination mechanisms, whereby, after the well-known experience with state-run alternatives, the market itself should be the dominant coordination mechanism" (*Novy*).

Boettcher, on the other hand, has attempted to define anew the position of co-operatives with regard to policies on the economic order and the social system, considering co-operatives as private enterprises to be grouped together with other profit-oriented enterprises. *Boettcher* has taken pains here to connect up, by means of a definition of the nature of co-operatives, with the idea of cooperation put forth by *Schulze-Delitzsch* and with the Co-operative Law of 1889, which *Schulze-Delitzsch* was so instrumental in bringing about, but not with other possible authors (as, for example, → *Walras*, *Liefmann*, and *Reinhardt*). *Boettcher* writes: "According to paragraph one of the Co-operative Law, only those organizations may obtain the legally protected form of a registered co-operative whose ownership group pursues the goal of promoting itself by means of a jointly-owned enterprise. If we accept this definition, we can do two things: we can class co-operative together with private enterprise, and on the other hand we can separate them from the commonweal economy as well as from the public sector. Only co-operatives which belong to private enterprise can fulfill the ... function given them to improve the competitive market system." (→ *Competition*)

5. Historical Systemic Disputes in Germany

The study of a debate on basics between *Schulze-Delitzsch* and *Raiffeisen* shows that the former, in contrast to the latter, gave priority to the individual striving for gain, even in the field of co-operatives. To that extent it seems justified to group *Schulze-Delitzsch* with the private economy and *Raiffeisen* with the commonweal economy (*Finis*). A more thorough reconstruction of *Schulze-Delitzsch's* ideals and concepts, however, together with their realisation, reveals that initially, at any rate, this co-operative pioneer definitely sympathised with commonweal-oriented interpretations of his actions, so that it is possible here to speak of public benefit orientation as a "by-product" (*Herrmann*).

Only a part of the industrial co-operative movement of the previous century and of the first decades after that adhered to *Schulze-Delitzsch's* preference for individual and common self-help and disapproval of outside state assistance. In this connection it is worth mentioning the work of *Korthaus*, in particular, who founded the Central Federation of German Industrial Co-operatives, which competed with the first co-operative federation – the General Federation – established by *Schulze-Delitzsch*. *Korthaus* turned, as *Faust* has explained, against the "extreme economic liberalism and the rejection of state help" practiced by the General Federation. Logically enough, this was one of the main reasons why *Korthaus* was included among the advisers to the Prussian minister of finance, *von Miquel*, when in 1895 the latter founded the Prussian Central Co-operative Bank (→ *Central Institutions*).

Within the agricultural co-operative movement, the main disputes took place between *Raiffeisen* and *Haas*. But even *Haas* disagreed with *Schulze-Delitzsch* over the question of governmental aid and approval for central co-operatives. → *Haas*, who was the second significant pioneer in the rural co-operative movement, and despite his basic position favouring national-liberal policies, nonetheless tended to assume a pragmatic standpoint with regard to economic questions. Most of all, he opposed *Raiffeisen's* supposedly or actually doctrinaire attitude of basing his co-operative on extraeconomic, religious principles. *Haas'* own opinion of absolute neutrality in religious and political respects nevertheless included, rather than excluded, the education of farmers to act together for a common purpose.

III. Institutional Meaning, Legal Spheres, Principles

As was mentioned at the beginning of this article, utopian concepts held by dedicated people on the basis of their convictions can, if those concepts are put to the test of logic and norms and experience, result not only in ideologies and concepts of political systems, but also – when success begins to set in – in institutionalized expressions of purpose in law and business administration (→ *Law, National*). These expressions, if they come to be, occur gradually, whereby the first-mentioned, in addition to laws in the legal sense, take the form of → *by-laws* and manifestations of legal policy (*Weisser, Thiemeyer*). Strictly speaking, of course, institutional meaning does not emerge as a group of features until organizational regulations of a legally normative or practical kind, despite initial resistance to them, come to be generally recognized, as demonstrated in public opinion, for example.

From the kind of institutional or institutionalized meaning (or purpose) which can be classified according to various legal systems, one is able to derive individual legal and procedural principles. In many cases the needs of business adminstration procedures are also taken into consideration thereby. In this context *Henzler* has spoken out in favour of a strict separation of absolute principles inherent in the nature of co-operatives, which must meet essential needs of their members, and variable procedural principles. *Dülfer*, on the other hand, has especially advocated a further development of the approach on procedural principles, because he distinguishes among co-operatives according to the type of their structural development. His basic assumption is that the co-operative operational unit or business establishment has a decidedly instrumental character. However, he does not characterise the enterprises as mere neutral instruments in the sense of a specific business-administration ideology of a technocratic, technological sort, but rather he definitely commends them with regard to policies on business, membership, and development (→ *Structural Types*).

Moreover, instead of referring to institutional purpose, *Dülfer* speaks of the "Organisationsrechtliche Kommunikationssystem" (legal-organizational communication system). To this system belong all legally-recognized normative ties or obligations which result from laws, decrees, court decisions, association and bilateral contracts, and so on, and which lead to a close dove tailing of service relationships for the purpose of reconciling differing interests (→ *Managerial Economics*). Since co-operative organizations can be set up not only in the legal form of a co-operative, but also in almost any other desired organizational form under private and public law (cf. *Westermann, Großfeld, Beuthien, Blomeyer*, and others), these legal forms and their typology or intended limitations of types (*Paulick*) should also be dealt with, to be exact, in order to determine institutional meaning (→ *Legal Form, Co-operative*; → *Co-operatives under Public Law*. In addition to these forms there have also emerged legal spheres in co-operative law which differ from each other from country to country, as has already been mentioned. Besides the German sphere with its own characteristic co-operative features, there is an Anglo-American, a French, and perhaps also a slavic, communist legal sphere (cf. *Ebert, Dülfer, Hanel, Münkner, Trappe*, and others) (→ *Law, International*).

In a comparative evaluation of German, English, and French co-operative literature, *Münkner* has come up, among other things, with the following characteristics and → *principles* of co-operatives as legally relevant, tracing them back to general ideas from which they stem:

(1) mutual aid;
(2) promotion of members' interests;
(3) sense of identity;
(4) democratic decision-making processes;
(5) economic efficiency;
(6) voluntary association;
(7) autonomy in determining one's own by-laws;
(8) fair distribution of earnings;
(9) open membership;
(10) indivisible financial reserves;
(11) promotion of education.

These characteristics and principles, which have also been called the "dynamic elements of the co-operative idea", overlap in part with the original *Rochdale* Principles, which, however, were also derived from actual practice. The principles, still valid today, of the International Co-operative Alliance (cf. *Watkins* and *Hasselmann*), which have come back under discussion ever since the congress of the organization in Stockholm in 1988, also definitely make reference to actual behaviour and practice. Principles play a greater role, by the way, in countries like Great Britain and Switzerland, where even today there is no special law regulating the organization of co-operatives, than in countries with special co-operative legislation.

With particular reference to the situation in Germany, *Münkner* has with urgency reopened the discussion on the question of fundamental legal organizational principles in co-operatives. Although in the opinion of some co-operative organizations, there is no special need for action in this respect, in *Münkner's* view, and also in the opinion of most of the lecturers at the 12th International Conference on Co-operative Science in Stuttgart in 1990, new ways have to be found to guarantee better than heretofore the commitment of co-operative leaders and business management to the purpose of co-operatives to promote the interests of their members. Above all, "what is missing is a catalogue of norms against which to evaluate the promotion of members' interests under the aspect of the proper business management of a co-operative." Through alterations in the law, model by-laws handed down by the federations, and the strict application of these by-laws, central organizational principles – that is to say, the exercise of members' rights and self-government in the form of honorary leadership and control – have been greatly curbed or even undermined. As far as the federation level is concerned, the principle of subsidiarity is rightly considered as the only suitable basis for producing the strategic norms needed for a future-oriented structural concept of a co-operative superstructure. Particularly for credit co-operatives, the orientation to this concept has meanwhile come to be regarded as indispensable (*Schierenbeck*).

IV. The Promotion Mandate, Co-operative Consciousness, Co-operative Identity

Nowadays, of course, the general reference to co-operative principles no longer suffices, according to *Großkopf*. What is still lacking, in his view, is an up-to-date, future-oriented definition of the promotion mandate. The clearly recognizable "deficits in the self-image" of present-day boards especially in co-operative banks – but the same holds true for wholesale and retail co-operatives as well (cf. for example *Hanel, Schmid*, and *Straaten*) – endangers not only the sense of identity of co-operative enterprises in the long run but also their image-profile over against their non-co-operative competitors. In a situation of this sort, co-operative business management is "simply under obligation" to make strategic use of its promotion mandate as a distinctive co-operative feature, and to take advantage of the opportunities still inherent today in making this supreme goal concrete in a specifically co-operative way (also *Blümle, Richter, Patera, Röhm, Seuster*, and *Bakonyi*). But co-operative business managers often have to act "on their own responsibility" thereby, i.e. give the members a "promotional plus" (*Henzler*) on the basis of merit, as it were, in the sense of an increased promotion of their interests in comparison to the promotion which their profit-seeking competitors give.

What counts, then, is to meet the challenges of the market with means that are specific to co-operatives. In addition to the business-administration efficiency and performance of co-operative enterprises and to their working together in a co-operative enterprise combine (Verbund), only an achieved or restored sense of co-operative identity can provide a unique, unmistakable image-profile (→ *Combine, Co-operative*). To strengthen this sense of identity, it would be necessary to renew the promotion mandate and to build up membership awareness once more. The original principle of identity, which made sure that every advantage of cooperation became at the same time an advantage for the members, has indeed become watered down by extensive business done with non-members. But the distribution of surplus income and particularly reimbursements continue to provide points where specific co-operative characteristics can take effect, not only for wholesale and retail co-operatives, but also for credit co-operatives (cf. *Berge, Manewald*, and *Schmid*). Through suitable operationalisation of the promotion mandate and through its strict, supervised implementation, decisive contributions could be made even today to strengthen co-operative consciousness and thereby ensure a sense of co-operative identity.

What is essential, in *Großkopf's* view, is to set up a new typology – of "pure customers", "nominal members", and "co-operative members", on the one hand, and of "basic advantages" for all customers and "exclusive advantages" for co-operative members only on the other hand – and according to this new typology to reassess, for example, the promotion portfolios at co-operative banks and furthermore, by means of indicators, to put them into concrete terms. *Großkopf* writes: " The introduction of exclusive advantages leads ultimately to a differentiated promotional strategy in the sense of a membership marketing, which furthers the sense of co-operative identity and guarantees the loyalty of the members to their co-operative, as well as the other way around, the loyalty of the co-operative to its members (previously *Richter, Schmid*, and others as well).

However, not only loyalty, but also the reactivation of group structures, the participation of members, with all its possibilities, and the solidarity among members could probably be decisively furthered in this way. The dangers of a transformation of promotional co-operatives in the direction of "member enterprises" with traits similar to those of joint-production co-operatives or influenced by social policies (*Betsch, Hahn*), into foundation-like "enterprise as such" (*Rathenau, Draheim, Witte*), or even just into ordinary profit-oriented enterprises, with the goal-system of maximising earnings or of efficiency as an end in itself – these dangers will probably not be excluded this way, that is true; but perhaps they will be thereby perceptibly reduced.

Bibliography

Arbeitskreis für Kooperation und Partizipion e.V. (ed.): Das Zentrum für Kooperation und Patizipation, Baden-Baden 1987.

Arbeitskreis für Kooperation und Partizipion e.V. (ed.): Kooperatives Management, Baden-Baden 1990.

Axelrod, Robert: The Evolution of Cooperation, New York 1984.

Boettcher, Erik (ed.): Die Genossenschaft im Wettbewerb der Ideen, Tübingen 1985.

Boettcher, Erik (ed.): Führungsprobleme in Genossenschaften, Tübingen 1977.

Büscher, Horst: Solidarische Selbsthilfe als innovatives kooperatives Handeln. In: Arch.f.ö.u.fr.U., vol. 12, Göttingen 1980, pp. 33–60.

Derfuß, Joachim: Erfolgsermittlung bei gewerblichen und ländlichen Genossenschaften, Wiesbaden 1974.

Dülfer, Eberhard: Betriebswirtschaftslehre der Kooperative, Göttingen 1984.

Dülfer, Eberhard: Die „Unternehmenskultur" der Genossenschaft – Ein traditionsreiches Thema in neuer Aktualität. In: Laurinkari, Juhani (ed.): The International Cooperative Movement – Changes in Economic and Social Policy, Geneva 1988, pp. 157–188.

Engelhardt, Werner Wilhelm: Allgemeine Ideengeschichte des Genossenschaftswesens, Darmstadt 1985.

Engelhardt, Werner Wilhelm: Über die Bedeutung der Kategorie „Genossenschaftlicher Grundauftrag" für die Genossenschaftslehre und Praxis. In: Gemeinnütziges Wohnungswesen, vol. 13, Hamburg 1960, pp. 227–232.

Engelhardt, Werner Wilhelm: Utopien im Verhältnis zu Ideologien und politischen Konzeptionen, In: Die Mitarbeit, vol. 22, Göttingen 1973, pp. 108–125.

Fürstenberg, Friedrich: Die Genossenschaft als sozialer Integrationsfaktor. In: Jahrbuch für Sozialwissenschaft, vol. 15, Göttingen 1964, pp. 243–255.

Gide, Charles: La Coopération, (Paris 1900), 4th ed., Paris 1922.

Gretschmann, Klaus: Steuerungsprobleme der Staatswirtschaft, Berlin 1981.

Großfeld, Bernhard: Genossenschaft und Eigentum, Tübingen 1975.
Großkopf, Werner: Strukturfragen der deutschen Genossenschaften, Part I, Frankfurt/Main 1990.
Häcker, Axel: Genossenschaftliche Zukunftsperspektiven in marktwirtschaftlich geprägten Industriegesellschaften, Berlin 1990.
Hahn, Oswald: Die Unternehmensphilosophie einer Genossenschaftsbank, Tübingen 1980.
Henzler, Reinhold: Der Genossenschaftliche Grundauftrag: Förderung der Mitglieder, Frankfurt/Main 1970.
Hettlage, Robert: Genossenschaftstheorie und Partizipationsdiskussion, 2nd ed., Göttingen 1987.
Kuhn, Wolfgang: Gedanken zur Konzeption einer genossenschaftsadäquaten Geschäftspolitik der Kreditgenossenschaften. In: ZgGenW, vol. 36, Göttingen 1986, pp. 5–13.
Laurinkari, Juhani (ed.): Genossenschaftswesen, München/Wien 1990.
Loesch von, Achim: Die gemeinwirtschaftliche Unternehmung, Köln 1977.
Manewald, Petra: Zinsrückvergütungen bei Bankgenossenschaften der Primärstufe, Berlin 1988.
Meyer, Bernd: Ein Zielsystem der Genossenschaft für die 80er Jahre, In: Zerche, Jürgen (ed.): Aspekte genossenschaftlicher Forschung und Praxis, Düsseldorf 1981, pp. 127–134.
Münkner, Hans-H.: Co-operative Principles and Co-operative Law, Marburg 1974.
Münkner, Hans-H.: Strukturfragen der deutschen Genossenschaften, part II, Frankfurt/Main 1990.
Novy, Klaus: Genossenschafts-Bewegung, Berlin 1983.
Pfeiffer, Eduard: Über Genossenschaftswesen, Leipzig 1863.
Rheinberg, Wilhelm: Grundsätzliche und aktuelle Fragen der Beratung im Bereich der Kreditgenossenschaften, Berlin 1987.
Richter, Dieter: Möglichkeiten der Operationalisierung des genossenschaftlichen Förderungsauftrages, Düsseldorf 1981.
Schmid, Günter: Marketing als Unternehmensführungkonzeption von Handelsgenossenschaften, Berlin 1988.
Schulte, Heinz-Werner: Controlling in Kreditgenossenschaften im Wettbewerb der Bankengruppen, Berlin 1991.
Thiemeyer, Theo: Gemeinwirtschaftlichkeit als Ordnungsprinzip, Berlin 1970.
Verein zur Förderung des Genossenschaftsgedankens e.V. (ed.): Perspektiven der Genossenschaften, part I, Darmstadt 1990.
Vierheller, Rainer: Demokratie und Management, Göttingen 1983.
Warbasse, James Peter: The Co-operative Way, Chicago 1946.
Watkins, William Pascoe: Co-operative Principles Today and Tomorrow, Manchester 1986.
Weippert, Georg: Jenseits von Individualismus und Kollektivismus, Düsseldorf 1964.
Zerche, Jürgen: Management Philosophy and Business Strategies of Credit Co-operatives. In: Treacy, Mary and Varady, Lajos (eds.): Co-operatives Today, Geneva 1986, pp. 529–541.

Configuration of Co-operative Society, The : Macrosociological Aspects of Co-operatives

ROBERT HETTLAGE [J]

(see also: *Societal Form, Co-operative*; *Relationship Patterns*; *Organizational Structures, Co-operative*; *Group Theory*; *Economic Order*)

I. Co-operative Principles and Co-operative Social Structure; II. Changes in Society Brought About by Co-operatives.

In contrast to microsociology with its concentration on interpersonal action within small groups and to the sociological analysis of the mesostructural level, devoted to the problems of the social organization, macrosociological observation involves large social aggregates and far-reaching social processes. The object of macrosociological study entails societies, mostly as a whole, and their interaction. As a result, the individual members themselves are no longer concerned but rather only the structural regularities, functional dependencies and/or tensions between partial sectors and structural elements. Beyond the analysis of value classifications and the conditions of social structure (e.g. institutionalized systems of inequality), it is undertaken to identify similarities and differences in superstructure, conditions for stability, as well as the overall nature and tendency of change and transition within the states of societal structure. Co-operatives are an important object of sociological investigation within the study of society as a whole. The economic, social and political-legal standing of the "association" in societal structure are put to discussion. This fundamentally can be researched from two viewpoints: on the one hand, the importance of co-operative → *principles* in society, and on the other hand, the conceptions – varying in magnitude – of society being infused by co-operative organizational structures (→ *Organizational Structure of Societies*). Both statements overlap each other as societal transformation on levels other than those purely economic in nature is also frequently striven for with the help of co-operative principles, above and beyond the propagation of the co-operative as an organization.

I. Co-operative Principles and Co-operative Social Structure

Social structure is meant when a relatively stable network of social relationships and expectations is discussed in which both a cause and effect relationship and a relationship of reciprocal dependency are recognizable. One may speak of familiar, organizational, pan-societal or other social structures according to the units one chooses to observe. If one brings into question the particular quality of these relationship patterns, among other things the distribution of power between individuals and groups (→ *Group, the Co-operative*), as well as their life chances must be examined. In this regard co-operative social structures (fundamentally egalitarian, autonomous and self-administered) are traditionally differentiated from hierarchical social structures (*Gierke* 1954, *Vierkandt* 1959, *Oppenheimer* 1959, *Weber* 1964, *Geiger* 1972). The latter form is at hand when the power of disposition over people and affairs to a great degree is unfairly distributed between individuals and groups, thus resulting in pronounced pre-eminence and subordination. Not everything that was previously considered a co-operative, for example the semi-feudal "farmstead co-operative", was in fact one. The co-operative is only then at hand when its principles (equal standing within the association, elimination of class differences, management through "primus inter pares", camaraderie, social morals, → *solidarity* in action) (*Engelhardt*, 1985; *Bernsdorf*) are given and/or fulfilled in accordance with the intention. The social validity of hierarchical principles, according to wide-spread opinion, is a late phenomenon of human history. Recently it has been sharply contested whether a hierarchy is better suited for complex social relations. The need to reconsider the co-operative principles and to pave the way for experiments involving elements of co-operative structure seems evident in modern societies, even though the concept of the co-operative is frequently not used (any longer). Verification of its importance in society as a whole so far has been provided from various positions:

1. The Theoretical-Sociological Starting Point: Types of Socialization and Decentralization

It is little known that *F. Tönnies* set his famous classification of the stages of societal development, "community and society" (Gemeinschaft, Gesellschaft), against a necessary third state in the form of "commonweal socialism" (→ *Group Theory*). He therewith meant the co-operative, which, due to its dual communal-social nature, could thus form the essential synthesis of values and future point of departure for an ethically based world culture capable of evolution.(c.f., *Balla* 1990).
R.F. Behrendt (1963) goes on from K. *Mannheim's* postulate of "fundamental democratization". Modern, highly complex and efficient societies which break down the division of labor harbor two dangers: the decision-makers becoming an → *oligarchy* and the collective becoming emotionally robbed of its meaning. The decentralized engagement of as many as possible in the societal responsibility of order becomes a modern exigency of the system. A renunciation of centralization and hierarchical structure on the national and international level in favor of federative principles is to be qualified as "co-operative".

2. The Historical-Sociological Starting Point: Legal Culture and Lifestyles

A. Gasser (1976) determined in his historical studies that the European national constitutions can be distinguished into two fundamentally different schools of thought. The "traditionally free" nations (England, Scandinavia, the Netherlands, Switzerland) are structured according to the autonomy of communities and citizens' freedom, which stem from medieval times; therefore in today's day and age they still exhibit a strong tendency towards a "co-operative" decentralization of administration. France, Germany and Italy meanwhile broke away from this early way of thinking involving local self-administration; these countries therefore are more likely to be exposed to the dangers of absolutism, centralism and "top-down" intervention (→ *History before 1800*; → *History in 19th C.*).

G. Eisermann remarks that co-operative thought has today also begun to assert itself in other sectors of society. On the one hand, he identifies the search for a revitalization of "community", social obligation, "affliction" and participation (e.g., civil initiatives/movements). On the other hand he sees a trend to a new "co-operative" distribution of power within and between groups. This includes an egalitarian style of child raising and education, womens' emancipation, alternative economy, co-determination coupled with plans for asset accumulation, as well as the elimination of class boundaries. All attempts to increase the participation level of those affected are accordingly qualified as "co-operative". It remains an unanswered research question how far these principles can determine a populational group's method of thinking, its disposition to act and the actual formation of entire social sectors, or to what extent they influence social learning processes.

II. Changes in Society Brought About by Co-operatives

The initial points of departure for a macrosociological co-operative theory can be found when the opportunities of engaging the co-operative as an *organization* are examined.

1. Co-operative Society and the Conception of its Objectives

The notion that the co-operative organizational form could fundamentally serve to alter the lifestyle and economic practice of entire societies was closely tied to the modern co-operative system from its beginning. The early socialists who introduced these ideas were therefore branded by *Marx* (1962) as "utopian" – not because he considered their goal false but rather because he maintained that the co-operative was useless as a *means* (→ *Socialist Critics*). These utopian ideas, nevertheless, stubbornly lived on and periodically achieved higher levels of interest and endorsement in times of social crisis and extensive upheaval (*Hettlage* 1989) (→ *History of Ideas*). The modern *alternative co-operatives* make this particularly evident. Criticism aimed at both the government and the market intertwines and becomes criticism aimed at civilization, whereby co-operatives should be allotted a decisive role as the upholders of a new culture. These transformational theories mostly commence with the economic system (convergence theory, theory of the "third track" (→ *"Third Way"*) between capitalism and socialism) in order to proceed and encompass the entirety of political and social life ("co-operativization"). The transition in many cases is fluid.

a) The system of co-operative exclusivity

Monists strive to establish co-operatives in the middle or long term as *the* dominating economic entity as they attribute co-operatives a higher level of efficiency – on account of their double nature – than other company forms. One can either lay stake on joint-production co-operatives (the "social workshops", "modern employee self-management" of *Proudhon*, → *Buchez, L. Blanc*), allot central tasks to agriculture (*R. Oppenheimer's* settlement co-operatives) (→ *Communal Settlements*), prefer the → *consumer co-operatives* (→ *R. Owen, Ch. Gide, E. Poisson*), or see the driving force arise from "administrational co-operatives" which combine consumers, producers and administration (*B. Lavergne's* "administrative enterprises" (1927)). The extent of the intention to create a new social order can be exemplified through the completely integrative settlement experiments (USA, Paraguay, Israel), by *J. Nyerere's* "ujamaa" development concept in Tanzania (→ *Autochthonous Co-operatives*), in the political goals of a co-operative state structure (regional, national and international versions of → *"cooperative commonwealth"*, *J.P. Warbasse* 1946) or in the dismantlement of state structures (*Kropotkin, Landauer*).

b) The system of supplemental co-operative order

The *pluralists* do not set quite such lofty objectives. They consider "pan-cooperative activity" neither feasible nor practical. The main function of co-operatives is not to replace market or planned economic systems but rather to supplement and relativize them, for they represent an "agreement", a "logically independent principle of order" (*G. Weippert* 1963). There is room for neither voluntary associations, agreements nor group settlements within the conception of system dualism oriented on the ideal types.

Their real social importance as "organizations dedicated to public welfare" is, however, considerable. They unite society and individual personality and through this cultural synthesis are able to improve a mixed economy system – even to alter structure – by transforming the given order from the inside out (→ *Economic Order*). Once again it becomes evident that a wider social range of co-operativization, namely that of the propagation of the co-operative idea as a long-range objective, likewise is not precluded in this more restricted version.

2. Chances for Realizing Co-operativization

Such notions will fall verdict to being "utopian" and "not of this world" as long as the conditions for their realization are not also provided. Nevertheless, they remain relevant for many as they are cognitive and volitional models which mold activity. They anticipate reality, which both constitutes their fascination and stimulating power as well as their weakness.

All early socialistic experiments ended in failure. We are a long way away from a co-operative monism; co-operatives, even under pluralistic conditions, must struggle hard to survive economically (→ *State and Co-operatives, Market Economy*), not to mention the functional problems within the co-operatives themselves ("activity" and "capacity" factors).

Further external macrosociological barriers (and chances) should be presented at this point: the effects of the social *environment* (the economic structure, the legal foundations, the political and cultural system), or in other words, genial or hostile macrostructures with regard to co-operatives. The "exosystem" determines the conditions for opportunity in these far-reaching systems of thought and the actual design and form of co-operative organizations ("possibility factors").

These macrosociological influences are mentioned time and time again in the case studies of the factors affecting the establishment of co-operatives in the developing or industrializing countries, but they have not been systematically researched (*Trappe* 1966, *Finis* 1980, *Brentano* 1980). (→ *Self-help Organizations*) Three aspects need to be alluded to:

a) The role of the legal and economic environment

In co-operative theory, one question was lively debated for years, namely which *economic* and *legal* structural preconditions must be at hand for co-operative enterprises even to form and hold their ground. It was discussed under the heading "compulsory co-operative" whether those co-operatives planned by higher authorities should be considered co-operatives as such. It became apparent that external initiative is not the determining criterion for co-operatives: The lee-way granted for autonomous subsystems proved more important. Conditions ensuring continuance at a later point in time are more decisive than the initial formative phase in determining whether and to what degree economic-political → "*officialization*" and the demands of self-management are compatible with one another (in developing and state capitalistic countries). Thus the problem is also addressed concerning which economic structure is compatible with and supportive of co-operatives, or whether the co-operative is not in need of the identical environment/political structure that capitalist companies are (contractual freedom, competitive performance, property rights, autonomous corporate entity).

b) The role of the political environment

Political order is also a background condition which needs to be studied. This is quite obvious, almost exemplary, in the traditional co-operative systems of many developing countries. Inasfar as their structures are relatively egalitarian ("absence of hierarchy") they can be modernized by being combined with modern co-operative organizations (*Trappe* 1966). It cannot, however, be ruled out that hierarchical forms thereby adapt themselves to modern exigencies and formalize themselves throughout the co-operative administration functions, thus "modernizing" and stabilizing themselves therein (*Bergmann* 1967) (→ *Production Co-operatives*). At least parallel structures are feasible which in conflict situations continue to favor the traditionally legitimized procedural methods. If the traditional political power systems remain efficient, co-operatives are then frequently "instrumentalized" in the hierarchy and infiltrated. This can be proven using the example of clientele (and mafia) relationship patterns which were able to take root in co-operatives without resistance and which furnish the usual "big men" and "brokers" with additional opportunities to exercise domination and control (*Giordano/Hettlage* 1979).

c) The role of the cultural environment

The numerous examples of internal emptiness and the depletion of purpose and meaning within co-operatives exemplify that the *cultural system* plays a central role in the success of co-operatives (values, inner morals, circle of acquaintances and contacts, communication methods and habits, world perspectives, ethnic nationality, co-operative ethic, trust, individualism, familism). Practices in child up-bringing and societal forms are determined through these factors; these are important for the development of a particular co-operative inclination as well as for the decisiveness and durability of collective engagement. If individualism, pessimism, a hierarchical understanding of the world, mistrust and defensive behavior were internalized, these then would have the destructive effect of a self-fulfilling prophecy on the process of co-operative integration. The same is true for narrow and/or wider circles of confidences and acquaintances concerning the esteem or disregard of certain virtues supportive of collective action, such as self-control, fairness, dependability, openness, sense of order, etc. (→ *Corporate Culture*).

Micro-, meso- and macrosociological observation of the co-operative system herewith comes full circle. Even in defining environments favorable for co-operatives the questions remain debated concerning the necessary conditions for realizing action in an organizational context which treats cooperation fairly (→ *Relationship Patterns, Co-operative: Microsociological Aspects of Co-operatives*; → *Organizational Structures, Co-operative: Mesosociological Aspects of Co-operatives*). Without an answer to these questions there remains too little reliable information to be gained about the standing co-operatives have in the world: in industrial and developing countries, in the East or the West, in classic or alternative organizational forms. Above all, there is little reliable information whether co-operatives also truly function "co-operatively" according to the typical intentions of their actions and the organizational principles that are derived from them.

Bibliography

Balla, B.: Das Drei-Stadien-Denken, ein Grundmuster von Sozialtheorien, und seine Elemente bei Ferdinand Tönnies. In: Schlüter, C./Clausen, L. (eds.): Renaissance der Gemeinschaft? Stabile Theorie und neue Theoreme, pp. 93–129, Berlin 1990.

Behrendt, R.F.: Dynamische Gesellschaft, Bern/Stuttgart 1963.

Bergmann, T.: Funktionen und Wirkungsgrenzen von Produktivgenossenschaften in Entwicklungsländern, Frankfurt 1967.

Bernsdorf, W.: Genossenschaftliche Gesellschaftsform. In: Bernsdorf, W. (ed.): Wörterbuch der Soziologie, vol.2, Frankfurt 1972.

Bretano, D. von: Die Bedeutung der Solidarität in Genossenschaften und bei genossenschaftlichen Gründungsvorgängen, Archiv für öffentliche und freigemeinnützige Unternehmen, pp. 11–31, 12 (1980).

Eisermann, G.: Wandlungstendenzen der modernen Gesellschaft. In: Eisermann, G. (ed.): Wirtschaft und Kultursystem, pp.100–130, Erlenbach-Zürich/Stuttgart 1955.

Engelhardt, W.W.: Allgemeine Ideengeschichte des Genossenschaftswesens, Darmstadt 1985.

Engelhardt, W.W.: Die Funktion von Utopien in der Entwicklung von Wirtschaftsordnungen. In: Wagner, H.-J. (ed.): Anpassung durch Wandel. Evolution und Transformation von Wirtschaftssystemen, pp. 139–171, Berlin 1991.

Finis, B.: Wirtschaftliche und außerwirtschaftliche Beweggründe mittelständischer Genossenschaftspioniere des landwirtschaftlichen Bereichs, Berlin 1980.

Gasser, A.: Staatlicher Großraum und autonome Kleinräume, Basel 1976.

Geiger, Th.: Führung. In: Kunczik, M. (ed.): Führung, Theorien und Ergebnisse, pp. 52–61, Düsseldorf/Wien 1972.

Gierke, O. von: Das deutsche Genossenschaftsrecht, vol.1: Rechtsgeschichte der deutschen Genossenschaft, Darmstadt 1954 (original 1868).

Giordano, Ch./Hettlage, R.: Persistenz im Wandel. Das Mobilisierungspotential sizilianischer Genossenschaften, Tübingen 1979.

Hettlage, R.: Cooperatives beckon in times of crisis: On the origins and sociopolitical significance of the sociological theory of cooperatives. In: Wallimann, I./Dobkowski, M. (ed.): Research in Inequality and Social Conflict. A Research Annual 1, pp. 95–130, 1989.

Lavergne, B.: Les régies co-operatives, Paris 1927.

Mannheim, K.: Freedom, Power and Democratic Planning, London 1950.

Marx, K.: Kritik des Gothaer Programms. In: Marx-Engels-Werke, vol.19, pp. 11–32, Berlin 1962.

Oppenheimer, L.: Machtverhältnis. In: Vierkandt, A. (ed.): Handwörterbuch der Soziologie, pp. 338–348, 2nd edition, Stuttgart 1959.

Tönnies, F.: Vorrede zur 3.Auflage von "Gemeinschaft und Gesellschaft". In: Tönnies, F.: Soziologische Studien und Kritiken, Jena 1925.

Trappe, P.: Die Entwicklungsfunktion des Genossenschaftswesens am Beispiel ostafrikanischer Stämme, Neuwied 1966.

Vierkandt, A.: Die genossenschaftliche Lebensform der Naturvölker. In: Vierkandt, A. (ed.): Handwörterbuch der Soziologie, pp. 191–201, 2nd edition, Stuttgart 1959.

Warbasse, J.P.: The Cooperative Way. A Method of World Reconstruction, Chicago/New York 1946.

Weber, M.: Wirtschaft und Gesellschaft. Grundriß der verstehenden Soziologie, 5. ed., Tübingen 1964.

Weippert, G.: Vereinbarung als drittes Ordnungsprinzip. Jahrbuch für Sozialwissenschaften, pp. 169–178, 14 (1963).

Consulting for Co-operatives

CARL E. KRUG

(see also: *Federations; Auditing; Development Policy*)

I. External Consulting for the Improvement of Co-operative Performance; II. Types of Consulting; III. Structural Features of Consulting; IV. Specific Features of Consulting for Co-operatives, V. Short Definition: Consulting for Co-operatives; VI. Organization Development as an Instrument of Consulting for Co-operatives.

I. External Consulting for the Improvement of Co-operative Performance

Co-operatives like other enterprises are faced by various problems and challenges, which result e.g. from structural changes in the economy, internationalization of markets, the pressure for innovations or from internal growth.

In order to overcome these more and more complex issues and for the improvement of their performance, co-operatives increasingly demand consulting services from external sources. This is especially beneficial if the problems cannot be sufficiently identified internally, because of time constraints of staff members, in case special knowledge and experiences are needed, when strict neutrality and impartiality are mandatory, or if internal differences of opinion prevent a solution from being realised.

Apart from these considerations the decision whether to request external consulting services is a usual make or buy decision and it is mainly based on cost-benefit considerations.

II. Types of Consulting

The large variety of possible types of consulting is reflected in the various terms for consulting, which can be found in scientific publications and in practice. These terms are often used unprecisely and inconsistently. This diversity of terms is aggravated by the fact that in most countries neither the offer of consulting services nor the respective occupational titles are legally protected.

In the following the most important types of consulting are listed:

- economic consulting (this term is now rarely used)
- business consulting in a broad sense: generic term for the general consulting of enterprises and for consulting in specific fields of management
- business consulting in a narrow sense: consulting for specific aspects of management i.e. taxes, financing, personnel, data processing, marketing etc.
- management consulting: integrated consulting, taking into consideration problems in their entirety, applicable not only for enterprises, but also for public institutions or non-profit organizations
- organizational consulting: special type of management consulting utilizing modern methods of planned organizational change.

Independently from these types of consulting distinctions can be made according to the economic sector, location and size group of the enterprise, as well as stage in the cycle of enterprise growth. A distinction is normally not made according to the legal form of the enterprise. Therefore the concept of a special consulting for co-operatives has so far not been discussed extensively in scientific publications or in practice. A definition for the consulting for co-operatives is presented in V.

III. Structural Features of Consulting

The object matter of consulting is generally distinguished according to institutional, functional and instrumental features (*Stutz* 1988, S. 117ff).

1. Institutional Features

The institutional aspects deal with the recipients of consulting services (client system), the entity providing such services (consultant system) as well as with the area of interaction between the parties involved (consulting system). The client system comprises the directorate, management, staff members and all other participants of the consulted enterprise/organization, who are relevant for the consulting operation. Participants of the consultant system are those staff members of a consulting firm, who provide the consulting services. In order to be classified as a consulting firm the following criteria should be fulfilled: externality with regard to the client, i.e. legal, organizational and financial independence from the client, consulting at least as main activity, on a permanent basis and being offered at least at cost recovery.

The consulting system represents a social system, which exists only during the individual consulting operation, in which participants of the client system and the consultant system produce the consultancy effort. In an organizational view a consulting operation can be interpreted as a project task, i.e. as a complex, singular, risky task with time limit as well as determination concerning contents and budget.

2. Functional Features

The functional aspects relate to the material contents of the consulting operation as well as to the interaction-relationship between participants of the client system and consultant system.

The possible contents of consulting operations can be summarised as follows: assistance in the solution of entrepreneurial problems through identification of problems, proposals for solutions, and help in implementing them. The objective is the recovery or improvement of the performance of an enterprise/organization through more effective use of production factors (incl. management, planning, organization).

In general a distinction is being made between consulting, which follows an integrated approach (management or organizational consulting) on one hand and business consulting in specific fields of management on the other hand (business administration, taxation, personnel, technical issues, legal advice etc.).

Modern scientific publications classify the consulting operation as an interaction-relationship between participants of the client system and consultant system. According to such views this operation can be categorized relating to: contents, specifications on the side of client and consultant, environment of the consulting operation, supporting methods for the interaction and the roles of client and consultant during the consulting process.

The consulting operation demands on both sides sensibility and the willingness, to deal with possible conflicts. As a working basis complete and correct information from the consulted organization is mandatory. If needed this information should also reveal possible deficiencies and inappropriate developments. All persons affected by the consulting operation and by its possible consequences should be integrated in the process.

3. Instrumental Features

Instrumental features comprise mainly: the organizational structure within the consulting organization, the employed management tools and consulting methods.

Complex consulting tasks are normally accomplished by teams of consultants, who collaborate in a specific subsystem (project system) within the consulting organization. The main aspects to be regulated are: hierarchic relationship, reporting system, right of access to information, authority to instruct, delegation of competencies, definition of steps in the consulting process and of their order, fixing of time limits and prestructuring of expected results.

IV. Specific Features of Consulting for Co-operatives

It has to be stated here that a theory of consulting with special regard for co-operatives has not been developed yet. Based on the general features presented above the object matter of consulting for co-operatives may be described as follows.

1. Client System

Concerning its client aspects consulting for co-operatives is determined institutionally as refering to consulting of organizations, which possess legally or economically the main characteristics of co-operatives. This comprises primary co-operatives and central co-operative enterprises. The case of co-operative federations as objects of consulting is not treated here.

The main structural feature of co-operatives is their → *dual nature* (Doppelnatur) as business enterprise and as grouping of individual members, which distinguishes them fundamentally from enterprises with different legal form. Therefore the recipients of consulting inputs in co-operatives may represent all components of the co-operative complex: the co-operative bodies Board of Directors and Supervisory Committee, management and staff members of the co-operative enterprise as well as the members in their function as owners of the co-operative enterprise.

A different case, which is not treated here is members' consulting, i.e. the assistance provided by primary co-operatives or co-operative federations to individual members in their function as owners of enterprises or households.

2. Consultant System

In the first years of development of co-operatives (in the following demonstrated with Germany as an example) the leadership of co-operatives used to discuss existing problems with their collegues from neighboring co-operatives with the aim to develop solutions through exchange of experience and mutual learning. The promotion of this indirect form of consulting was from their beginning one of the most important functions of the co-operative federations. When compulsory audits were introduced in 1889 the task of consulting was partly taken over by auditors, who were at that time not staff members of the co-operative federations, and it was performed beside their main function as auditors. With the amendment of the co-operative law in 1934 the task of auditing was exclusively handed over to the co-operative federations. Since then they are also the main performers of consulting services for co-operatives.

Consulting and auditing as important external interventions in co-operatives are partly interrelated. The identification through an audit of possible weaknesses in organizational set up, in management or in member-related performance can lead to the request of subsequent consulting. However, due to its very formal character auditing is hardly compatible with an open interaction and cannot replace consulting services.

In general various institutions may perform the task of consultants for co-operatives.

- In the co-operative movement a department or a subsidiary of the co-operative federation or an independent consulting firm closely collaborating with the federation,
- a consulting company acting independently from the co-operative federation, especially those who have specialised on the consulting of co-operatives.
- a governmental or non-governmental co-operative promotion institution (ministry, department, registrars office, self-help promotion institution or a project in the context of technical cooperation).

It has often been proposed that a consulting organization within the co-operative movement is in the best position to fulfill the special demands on consulting for co-operatives.

Based on their specific experience gained e.g. through auditing, their consultants possess better insights into the problems of co-operatives. As responsibility towards a member co-operative continues to exist even after the completion of the particular contract, consulting within the movement aims more at contributing to long-term development rather than at short-term elimination of problems. Those clients who are at the same time members of the respective federation, can partly influence the conditions of consulting.

The establishment of consulting capacities at secondary level also reaps the benefits of economies of scale, with central consulting departments replacing or complementing the respective activities at primary level.

If co-operative federations intend to become service centers for their member co-operatives consulting belongs to the basic services to be offered (beside auditing and training).

This is also the self interest of such federations, who want to secure their own existence through strengthening of the performance of their member co-operatives.

Consulting services can also be offered by consulting firms, which have developed special instruments for co-operatives as clients. The competencies in the consulting of co-operatives can be gained through consulting activities and through direct experience of the consulting enterprise with co-operative organizational structures.

Consulting firms have several possibilities to utilize such structures. The coordination of a group of legally independent small consulting firms with different areas of specialization in a supply co-operative may help to obtain contracts jointly and at lower cost. This allows a more stable flow of orders. The main features of consulting firms are the high degree of self determination provided for the consultants, hierarchic structures similar to a partnership and a co-operative style of leadership. The organizational type of a productive co-operative provides the advantage of personal identity between accomplishment of tasks and participation in leadership and financing. In practice the legal form of the co-operative is rarely chosen by consulting firms.

Consulting firms outside of the co-operative movement which have been specialised on co-operatives mostly concentrate on consulting of co-operatives and self-help organizations, institutions and projects of self-help promotion in the framework of technical cooperation.

In many developing countries co-operatives are promoted because of their positive effects for development. For this purpose consulting services can be offered by governmental institutions (ministries, development agencies), non-governmental organizations for self-help promotion or development projects. In a strict sense this assistance through advice can only be classified as consulting if the criteria of externality and professionalism (services at least partly at cost recovery) are fulfilled and if it does not interfere with the independence of the co-operatives.

3. Contents of the Consulting Operation

With regard to its contents several forms of consulting for co-operatives can be distinguished.

Business consulting is related to specific areas of management (e.g. taxes, finance, personnel, data processing). It aims at the improvement of the operational performance of the co-operative e.g. through elimination of bottlenecks as well as assistance in the fulfilment of legal requirements. This type of consulting has to take into consideration conditions which are explicitly relevant for co-operatives (e.g. co-operative law, by-laws, accounting principles). If seen from the composition of participants of the consulting system and from the methods of interaction there are in principle no differences to the consulting of enterprises in other legal forms. However, a specialisation on the problems of co-operatives on the side of the consultant can lead to advantages of efficiency.

With the functions of management getting more complex, increasing pressure from competition and further internationalization of co-operative enterprises there is need for assistance in additional areas of management (e.g. organization, controlling, marketing) which demand new types of business consulting as well as consulting for sector-specific problems.

As primary co-operatives become larger entities they possess the capacity to solve these operational problems internally. At the same time such co-operatives tend to be confronted with unsurmountable problems in the field of strategic development. This leads to the demand of external assistance in the form of management consulting. This type of consulting is based on the perspective of the co-operative in its entirety and takes the interdependence of its subsystems into consideration. It aims at the improvement of the overall performance of the co-operative especially with regard to rentability, competitiveness and ability for change. Consulting for better strategic management employs the following instruments: analysis and assessment of all aspects of the co-operative concerning its interaction with members and the environment; establishment of appropriate strategies for the improvement of the co-operative's strengths, for the elimination of weaknesses and for the optimal reaction to existing external opportunities and threats.

4. Process of Interaction

This sequence of various types of consulting illustrated above (IV.3) is characterized by an increasing need for the consideration of co-operative specific aspects with regard to the organizational set up and the regulations of the consulting system, the composition of its participants and the choice of methods of interaction.

Most of all management consulting or strategic consulting has to respond to the dual function of co-operatives as enterprises and group of members, to the overall objective of member promotion and to the normative value of intensive members' participation. These circumstances are reflected in the composition of participants of the consulting system on the side of the co-operative, which should also include the members. All interaction processes have to be implemented with inclusion of the members and with a high degree of transparency.

In order to secure successful consulting operations the following preconditions should be fulfilled by the co-operative and the consulting institution.

Preconditions on the side of the co-operative: open information policy, readiness for self criticism and external assessment, discussion on strengths and weaknesses of the co-operative, consequent implementation of strategic concepts, involvement of staff members and members in the process of change. Preconditions on the side of the consulting institution: customer-oriented provision of services, highly trained and experienced personnel especially with regard to the problems of co-operatives, provision of services at least at cost recovery, strict neutrality. In the case of co-operative auditing associations organizational separation of auditing and consulting should be secured.

A consultant for co-operatives must be able to respond to specific demands from the various subsystems of the co-operative. The management expects in him a partner for dialogue, who can assess the actual position of the co-operative, an analyst in the search for better performance and a moderator for discussions between management, board of directors, supervisory committee and members. The board of directors on the other hand expects an expert in the search for alternative strategies and activities and in the elaboration of a strategic concept for the co-operative. Furthermore it seeks an analyst of the conditions existing in the co-operative's environment and of their future development.

All this demands consultants with excellent communicative skills, up-to-date expert knowledge, a high degree of responsibility and a thorough understanding of the internal structure and decision making system in co-operatives.

The co-operative principle of subsidiarity demands from the consulting institution to strengthen the self reliance of the client co-operative. The consulting intervention should enable the management and leadership of the co-operative to solve similar problems in future without external assistance (*Weinkauf* 1992).

V. Short Definition: Consulting for Co-operatives

Consulting for co-operatives describes an interactive process between a consulting institution and the participants of a co-operative client system, in which the strengthening of the co-operative's performance is being sought, ranging from solving operational management problems and strategic development to the optimization of member promotion. These services are offered by external consultants as market related services and are implemented in consideration of the structural characteristics of co-operative organizations.

VI. Organization Development as an Instrument of Consulting for Co-operatives

In the course of consulting operations a change of the organizational set up of a co-operative may become necessary. The advantages expected from this in novation in the formal system can be set off by inefficiencies in the informal system (interpersonal communication system of the co-operative, *Dülfer* 1984) due to unknown behavior patterns of the persons concerned (→ *Managerial Economics*).

The consulting concept of organization development seeks to improve the acceptance of changes in the formal structure of an organization by influencing the behavior of the organization's participants. It aims at improving the organization's effectiveness and at the same time at a better realization of the individual expectations of the organization's participants (*Zipp* 1985).

Organizational development as a method for external consulting is based on the approach, to enable the participants of the organization to identify their problems by themselves, to try out interpersonal relationships and to create conditions within the organization, which are compatible with the individual needs of the participants and with the requirements of the organization. In short this concept attempts to make planned organizational change feasible.

Consulting interventions in co-operatives must take the specific organizational set up and the existing interpersonal relationships into consideration. Therefore organization development seems to be a very appropriate instrument for the consulting of co-operatives. It aims at influencing the behavior of all organizational participants of the co-operative complex (i.e. leadership, management, staff and members). It seems most appropriate in the case of changes in the formal organization structure of the co-operative and for the improvement of the willingness and the ability of the co-operative's members to participate actively (*Zipp* 1985). The legal bodies, management, staff and members of the co-operative must be involved in the process of organization development. Effective instruments for this purpose are: open information policy for the benefit of members, assessment of members needs and expectations, training of members in order to enable them to actively participate in the governing bodies of the co-operative or in subsystems (work teams) within the co-operative. In order to be effective, changes in the behavior of the organization's participants should be supported by changes in the formal structure.

Processes of organizational development demand the functions of various moderators. It is the task of the Change Agent to identify possible problem areas in the co-operative enterprise, to make clear the need for a process of change and to formulate objectives and instruments for the planned change. A further contributor is the Change Catalyst, whos task is to eliminate differences of opinion between change agent and the members of the client system.

Organization development inputs are most effective if they are implemented by an external consultant for the following reasons: limited capacity of the co-operative, insufficient expert knowledge and the need for strict neutrality. Possible external moderators of processes of planned organizational change are: consulting departments in co-operative federations, consulting enterprises within the co-operative movement or private consulting firms, who possess special experience in processes of planned organizational change.

Bibliography

Ansoff, H.I.: Implanting Strategic Management, Englewood Cliffs 1984.
Attems, R.: Organisationsentwicklung und Genossenschaften, in: Vorträge und Aufsätze des Forschungsinstitutes für Genossenschaftswesen an der Universität Wien, Wien 1982.
Dülfer, Eberhard: Betriebswirtschaftslehre der Kooperative, Göttingen 1984.
Jones, G.N.: Planned Organizational Change – A Study in Change Dynamics, London 1968.
Krug, Carl E.: Consultingunternehmen, genossenschaftliche, in: Mändle, Eduard/ Swoboda, Walter (Eds.), Genossenschaftslexikon, Wiesbaden 1992, pp. 106–107.
Röpke, Jochen: Strategic Management for Self-help Organizations, Marburg 1992.
Steyrer, Johannes: "Unternehmensberatung" – Stand der deutschsprachigen Theorienbildung und empirischen Forschung, in: Hofmann, Michael (Ed.), Theorie und Praxis der Unternehmensberatung, Heidelberg 1991, pp. 1–44.
Stutz, Hans-Rudolf: Management-Consulting, Organisationsstrukturen am Beispiel einer interaktiven Dienstleistung, Bern / Stuttgart 1988.
Weinkauf, Walter: Unternehmensberatung für Genossenschaften, in: Mändle, Eduard/Swoboda, Walter (Eds.): Genossenschaftslexikon, Wiesbaden 1992, pp. 654–655.
Zipp, Wolfgang: Genossenschaften als Betriebsverbände, Möglichkeiten zur Integration der Mitglieder in die genossenschaftliche Organisationsstruktur, Bergisch Gladbach / Köln 1985.

Consumer Co-operatives

JOHANN BRAZDA / ROBERT SCHEDIWY

(see also: *Classification*; *Kaufmann*; *Pfeiffer*; *Own Production*)

I. Historical Origins; II. Country Survey; III. The Present Situation and its Problems.

I. Historical Origins

The consumer co-operative has been a *vital factor* in the modernization process of industrial societies. In recent years, however, its *difficulties to adapt* to a rapidly changing retailing environment have been obvious.

On the European continent most consumer co-operatives before 1885 (→ *History in 19th C.*) were sponsored by "enlightened benefactors" such as aristocrats and industrialists. Laissez-faire liberalism saw co-operatives as mild *antidote* to the social problems of the age. Austria's law on co-operatives dating from 1873 e.g. was meant to *"mitigate the social question"* (i.e. the mass poverty brought about by the industrial revolution) *"without questioning the property of the possessing classes"* whilst *"extracting the poorer classes from the erroneous teachings of communism"*. The ideology of consumer co-operatives (→ *History of Ideas*) was spread in Europe by Holyoake's book on the → *Rochdale pioneers* in the 1860's. It was mostly taken up by lower middle classes and an economic elite of industrial workers. The marxist radicals at first opposed the consumer co-operative concept (→ *Socialist Critics*). Nevertheless the birth of thousands of consumer co-operatives around 1900 all over Europe was a true grass-roots labour movement. Leading examples were the politicized Belgian co-operatives, with their organizational and financial links between co-operative, party and unions. Christian and rural co-operators, however, were opposed to the co-operative as an "instrument of classstruggle" and pointed out its economic risks.

Party politics also played a role in the sense that labour leaders tried to control the creative chaos of the "founding wave". Many of the then predominant one-shop co-operatives were in great difficulties and represented a risk for the political workers' movement. Therefore experts and far-sighted politicians pressed for mergers, for creating wholesale companies and for industrialized → *own production*. Thus the "technocratic trend" in consumer cooperation was started already before 1914. The principle of formal political neutrality had some of its first breakthroughs too at that time.

All over Europe the effect of World War I on consumer co-operatives was one of *consolidation and success*. They acquired a reputation as fair distributors of scarce goods. Also the *wholesale companies* were strengthened. These companies (founded mostly around 1900) became privileged importers and "quasi-official" institutions. By the end of the war some wholesale companies – e.g. KF in Sweden – had established a very strong influence on their "mother co-operatives".

The desire for scarce goods increased also the membership on the retail level.

The consumer co-operatives started the period between the wars with a solid financial basis and a positive reputation. The *economic efficiency* of co-operation became a vital concern for the members as well as for management. Around 1920 *brilliant leader figures* were about to emerge, who were to mould the culture of co-operative enterprises well into the 1950's or even 1960's.

These pioneers believed in co-operation as a vision – but they also believed strongly in solid accounting → *Principles* and in a clear chain of authority. *Albin Johansson*, the "monarchical" ruler of KF from the 1920's to the 1950's can be regarded as the epitome of the highly motivated, idealistic, innovative co-operative autocrat. (Similar figures would be *Goedhart* in the Netherlands, *Tanner* in Finland, *Everling* in Germany or *Sagmeister* and *Korp* in Austria.) A similar figure was *Gottlieb Duttweiler* (→ *Conceptions, Co-operative*). His Migros in Switzerland copied many co-operative strategies, broke cartels in a defiant way and thus became a dangerous competitor to existing consumer co-ops. (It was later turned into a co-operative group not recognized by the → *ICA*.)

Where the wholesale societies and their leading technocrats had not become so dominant, the consumer co-operative successes were less impressive. Strong *elected officials* (e.g. in parts of Great Britain and France) tended towards a commercial conservatism that made for slower growth rates. *Interco-operative co-operation* on an international scale was then advocated strongly e.g. by *Albin Johansson* with the creation of Nordisk Andelsförbund and with the Scandinavian Luma-project. However the transnational companies' hierarchical organization proved to be more effective than the federative principle of co-operation.

Co-operative democracy became somewhat subdued during that period. Member participation tended to be more passive than around 1900. Few co-operatives were founded after 1920 (except for Italy and Japan). In *Max Weber's* terms we can regard the consumer co-operative movement of the interwar-period as one that was already transforming from a charismatic movement to a bureaucratic organization. Already then there were complaints that the consumer co-operatives had given up the "true co-operative spirit", often voiced by radical minorities, e.g. communists.

In spite of the great depression of the 1930's many consumer co-operatives in different parts of Europe did surprisingly well – thanks to their honest, efficient managers. From a long-term point of view the period of the "great autocrats", however, produced some economic problems too. In many cases they left their jobs a little too late as happens often with great leader figures. When they were not able to destine a "heir" in time, collective leadership and its built-in slowness of decision-taking made its appearance. As regards the wholesale organizations the leaders of the emerging big regional co-operatives made it quite clear in time that they were not willing to tolerate domination by their "common subsidiary". The central organizations thus had to realize that their local and regional merger concepts (→ *Mergers and Consolidations*) were challenging their own power base (an example is *E. Poisson's* regionalization plan for France).

In addition to these pluri-central tendencies there were also dualities and rivalries on the central level between *ideological organizations* (that also performed some economic activities such as auditing, printing etc.) and the *wholesaling organizations*. Usually the wholesalers finally took over most tasks of the "ideologues". But this usually happened only in the 1960's and 1970's. For the interwar years we can note that those movements with a unitary central organization (KF or the "neutral" SOK in Finland) usually fared better than those with a dual one.

Another bipolarity materialized where early mergers had formed *extremely powerful retailing co-ops in capital cities* such as Stockholm, Copenhagen, Helsinki or Vienna. These were the earliest "regional kingdoms" in the world of consumer cooperatives, often admired and somewhat feared by smaller rural coops. The latter tended to flock around their wholesaling organization where they controlled the majority of votes.

In the 1920's and 1930's when most of retailing still consisted of small independent business consumer co-operatives still enjoyed some economies of scale. In Northern Europe these were their most successful years. Italian fascism and German nazism, however, undermined independence and growth. In Northern Spain, where consumer co-operatives played an important role in the economic war effort on the Republican side they were practically annihilated after 1939. In Germany and Austria they had to be re-founded after 1945 because they had been turned into instruments of the Nazi party organization. In Germany the consumer co-operatives were not even given back the right to offer savings accounts to their members after the war – a right they had lost in 1935. Still, up to the 1960's, consumer coops in many European countries found themselves in a *relatively favoured position*. Private businesses were still largely unorganized, even though grocers' cooperatives and chain store movements responded to the co-operative challenge since the 1930's. The co-ops had a national image, store fronts largely followed a unified pattern. – However, this unity was more apparent than real because it camouflaged the pluricentrism mentioned above.

The more pragmatic and "technocratic" movements served as *innovators in European retailing*, largely by adapting models from the U.S. Self service was imported at the end of the 1940's and beginning of the 1950's with consumer co-ops often taking the lead. Large-scale sales outlets (supermarkets and hypermarkets) were also often pioneered by cooperatives in the 1960's. However, closing small neighbourhood shops in favour of a big new store was not well accepted by elderly, less mobile cooperators. Thus the management – dominated Swedish cooperatives were more (technically) "progressive" than many traditional British or French working-class cooperatives, and the Italian consumer co-ops became innovators only after they had shaken off traditional mentalities at the end of the 1970's. Even more reluctance was shown by co-operatives to adopt the "discount store revolution" that became apparent in the 1970's and is still going on.

The minimization of personnel in discount operations went against the usually strongly entrenched trade union interests in consumer co-operatives (→ *Trade Unions*), the limited assortment went contrary to the tradition of the co-op as "universal provider". The tendencies of the 1970's and 1980's of retailing markets to split up into high quality outlets and extremely cheap operations left the co-ops in an uncomfortable middle ground. Where they went into discounting they usually did so as belated "followers" (as in Austria) or buyers of formerly private chains (as in Finland), not as pioneers. Costly experiments with sophisticated department stores went against the lower middle-class image of co-ops and were less successful than anticipated. Nevertheless, up to the 1960's, the consumer co-operative world seemed to be in order. Some movements even had become very rich: their enormous mass of real estate helped to cushion the first operational losses, which were mostly regarded as temporary and not as signs of a great crisis to come.

II. Country Survey

Consumer co-operatives in Great Britain, however, were more advanced in their life cycle. There the "*Gaitskell-Report*" came to alarming results already in 1958. It named the following causes for the *stagnation of British consumer co-ops*: Their shops were badly situated, old fashioned and did not cater to the changes in tastes that increases in consumer incomes had brought about. Prices and qualities were often not up to competitive standards. The commission observed poor standards of management due to interference by lay bodies and claimed that internal recruitment patterns should be changed by admitting people with a higher education. Closer contacts to the private sector in order to stay in touch with new trends were also recommended. The structure of the movement, independent local co-ops, did not allow for economies of scale. A national organization for the sale of consumer durables was recommended. But this "technocratic" report was not taken seriously by a movement that still felt self-confident and where distrust against academic "experts" was strong. Neither took the other movements this warning seriously, because the British and the French co-operatives were seen as the most "old-fashioned" ones. The consumer co-operative decline in Great Britain has continued up to the end of the 1980's. There have been some positive developments in recent years but it is not yet clear whether the downward trend really has been broken. Up to now the private competitors seem to have kept the upper hand.

However, the British decline was only the precursor of more dramatic events in other co-operative movements. The *Netherlands* were characterized by an extremely keen competition in retailing already in the 1960's. At that time a Dutch commission of experts came to the conclusion that the 18 big retail societies and their wholesale subsidiary Coop Nederland had to form a single company within short delay. In 1970 11 regional co-operatives merged in order to form Coop u.a.

But this was in fact the beginning of the end, because only the weakest of the regional co-ops had flocked around the wholesale company and the latter was not strong enough to cure them. In the crisis of 1973 Coop Nederland and Coop u.a. had to be sold to private competitors, a feat that was possible because they had still rather interesting production facilities. Otherwise a more dramatic solution might not have been avoided. Some of the strongest remaining co-operatives chose to change their character and to become private enterprises or to sell out too.

Parallel but less spectacular events happened in *Quebec* and in *Belgium*, once a model of consumer co-operation, where the co-ops are now a relevant factor only in the pharmacy sector.

In *West Germany* a major catastrophe could be avoided around 1975 mainly by the Bank für Gemeinwirtschaft stepping in to reorganize the weakest parts of the consumer co-operative movement. Attempts at autonomous structural reform in 1967 and 1972 had failed. The sector had not been ready for a common effort, because each co-op that could afford it wanted to guard its full independence. In spite of a dramatic revolution in German retailing (with a massive increase in sales area and a concomitant threat for the weakest participants to be pushed out of the market) the consumer co-ops were not able to develop fundamentally new strategies. Only when their biggest creditor stepped in – temporarily helped by some international co-operative solidarity from the Scandinavian countries – a structural reform was possible. Most societies gave up their juridical quality of co-operatives and were organized in a hierarchical holding. However the strongest co-operatives who felt that they could survive on their own (ASKO, Coop Dortmund) did not participate in that solution because their management was not willing to subordinate its sphere of decision to the new central coop-AG.

Thus the rescue operation of the mid-seventies involved only the weakest co-ops and it brought about a disintegration of the consumer co-operative sector. The formation of the coop AG group was finished in 1985. But a somewhat excessive expansion course led the trade union and Scandinavian co-operative capital to be withdrawn from the rather intransparent enterprise. A large number of shares was placed on the stock market – just before the crash of October 1987. Already at that time there were rumours that the group was in financial difficulties. A full-fledged crisis broke out in 1989, when it had to be admitted that the losses had annihilated own capital. The creditor banks consequently had to give up 75 per cent of their claims in order to rescue co-op AG from bankruptcy. Lack of control by the owners and creditors had encouraged a quasi-autonomous management to engage in risky experiments. Since 1990 co op AG was sold in part to German and foreign competitors.

The *"big merger" solution* has been discussed everywhere from the 1960's onward, but has been put into practice only in Austria and in the "progressive" E-movement of Finland. Usually it has been favoured by the central institutions, especially the wholesale companies. It has usually been fiercely resisted by the stronger primary co-operatives who did not want to give up their independence in order to be reorganized by a company "owned by them".

Austria, was the actual pioneer of the "one country – one co-operative" solution in 1978. More than 95 per cent of consumer co-operative sales volume thus could be integrated into one giant co-operative (only some small societies in alpine regions stayed out). This was made possible by the political support of Austria's powerful trade union federation (ÖGB). Also, some big co-operatives were in very bad shape and in fact too big for the traditional rescue operation by regional merger. 16 different companies had to be merged into one entity, a formidable task that created some initial chaos and a constant danger of bureaucratisation. The central bodies, the wholesaling society (GÖC), its financial institutions and the co-operative union (Konsumverband) were not strong enough to impose their dominant role, which was covertly played by the big consumer co-op of Vienna, (after World War I the biggest consumer co-op in the world). Unfortunately the economic results of the first 15 years of this giant co-operative are not too encouraging. The strong involvement of ÖGB and its president *Benya* may have delayed cutting personnel cost to competitors' levels. Furthermore, the sheer size of the company and its image as the "red giant" in retailing may have created an unrealistic feeling of confidence. A high rhythm of investment was kept up in spite of rising operational losses. Finally – by the end of 1992 – Konsum Austria was forced to engage in a "mega-deal" with the Swiss MIGROS group (alongside with a private competitor). MIGROS is a co-operative in form but still bears a strong resemblance to its private origins under *Gottlieb Duttweiler*. The rather complicated arrangement is to create a group that would dominate 33 per cent of the Austrian food market. It would actually represent the first attempt at effective transnationalization by a (more or less) co-operative group.

The Austrian solution of 1978 has served as a model for the "progressive" wing of the *Finnish consumer co-operation* (the "neutral" wing has been considering a big merger too, but is characterized by a strong spirit of local autonomy). In Finland, consumer cooperation has played a dominant part in retailing (but also in the hotel and restaurant business) for decades. The last twenty years have been economically disappointing, however, for both main co-operative groups, who lost billions of Finnmarks. When the situation of the "progressive" E-movement became critical, its wholesale organization went for a unification on the Austrian model (also with political support by party and unions). However, ELANTO in Helsinki was not allowed to play the dominant part that Vienna had played and thus stayed out of the EKA merger. EKA has adopted an offensive strategy, and has split its shops into several "chains". These measures are regarded as commercially sound, but the merger was a last-minute operation. EKA is linked to an insurance group and a big building enterprise and it is hoped that these two "strong brothers" will help the retailing branch to recover. SOK has taken a less centralizing approach. In view of a closer interco-operative co-operation a Central Union of Finnish Consumer Co-operatives has been founded at the beginning of 1992.

In *Sweden* as well the economic results of the last 20 years were unsatisfactory. There the much admired co-operative foothold in the non-food-market turned into a problem. Engel's law proclaims that rising incomes will lead to a decreasing share of income to be spent on food, thus it seemed wise to invest in department stores. However, this sector turned during the 1970's from an asset to a liability. Many co-operatives had been proud to dominate the central areas of their towns with their "flagship" department stores. They often had pioneered hypermarkets too. But while the latter usually turned out successes, the department stores often became money losers and hard to get rid of. The structure of the movement for a long time followed the traditional pluricentral model but with increasing tensions between money-making and money-losing co-operatives. An internal reform of KF (KF'85) aimed at splitting the giant complex up into many profit centers. However KF was unable to reform weak retailing co-operatives, since its "hospital society" SHF which could take over the management of sick co-ops was dissolved in the "fat" 1960's following the wishes of autonomy-minded primary co-operatives.

Still, KF had to bear the ultimate responsibility for the solvency of the movement. Due to a dramatic downturn in many primary co-operatives' economic results around 1990 a new nationwide retailing organization had to be created in 1992 (with a proposed number of 6 to 8 regional co-operatives mainly left to organize neighbourhood shops). *Roland Svensson* from Konsum Stockholm has been put at the helm of KF which is reported to have experienced a record loss in 1992. The strongest regional co-operatives (such as Värmland) chose to stay outside the big merger, however – a structural aspect that could be noted already at the formation of Coop AG in Germany. The KF-group has recently lost its dominant position in Swedish retailing to the private ICA-group – a chain system organized by wholesalers on the basis of semi-independent private retailers. ICA has started its co-operation in the 1930's as a weapon against the then triumphant consumer co-ops and is thus in a way a heir to their organizational impulse. Today Swedish Consumer Co-operatives are experimenting with a franchising model too.

In Denmark, one of the pioneer countries of consumer co-operation (especially own production) an over-expansive capital city co-operative had to be taken over by FDB, the country's wholesaling organization. But FDB is having serious troubles with a chain bought in 1982. As in Sweden new acquisitions in order to increase an already substantial market share have shown to be problematic. In 1991 several small but prosperous consumer-coops have left FDB.

The *French crisis of 1985–86* with the collapse of FNCC and SGCC (the ideological and commercial central organizations) was characterized by the desintegration of a traditionally weak central authority. The lack of big city co-operatives (Paris, Marseille, Lyon etc. have been co-operative wastelands for a long time) may be due to the fact that the strong communist wing of the French worker's movement would regard co-operatives mostly as a tool in class warfare. Thus (predominantly moderate leftist) French consumer co-operatives were only important in the industrial North. In some relatively rural areas the Christian, politically neutral co-operative ideology took roots. Where pragmatic technocrats held the reigns these co-operatives were able to develop with the rhythm of French-retailing.

In the north of France coops tended to form islands of commercial traditionalism that were flooded by the hypermarket revolution of the 1960's and 70's. For many years the wholesaler SGCC was forced to subsidize these structurally backward co-operatives who originally had a large share of their market but lost most of it as their old faithful members gave way to a younger, less ideologically committed generation. Some other co-ops tried to jump the hypermarket train belatedly and ruined their finances by overinvestment. This situation led to a rebellion of the soundest regional co-operatives in 1985 who probably had no other choice but to sacrifice their wholesale company and the weaker co-operatives in order to retrieve the credits extended to it. The process was accentuated by a financial panic and has not yet come to a clear end, but it seems that only the co-operatives of Saintes and Strasbourg will have a fair chance to survive on their own. Those areas where the traditional cooperative spirit had been strongest, however, seem to have little chance to recover.

In *Switzerland* the once private MIGROS co-operative movement and the traditional Coops are dominating retailing since the 1940. Whether it may be termed a true cooperative organization or not – MIGROS had a pioneering role in Switzerland as regards the creation of more dynamic retailing markets. MIGROS' active price policy, its mobilisation of consumers already started in the 1920's and continued after the childless founder, *Gottlieb Duttweiler*, had "handed his enterprise over to the consumers" in 1941. This competition was a healthy challenge to the traditional co-ops. As a consequence, the two cooperative giants are today dominating Swiss retailing with a market share of 22 per cent (MIGROS) and 15.7 per cent (coop). Maybe the economic success of consumer co-operatives in Switzerland is actually due to this creative rivalry.

The traditional Swiss coops had been faced with a supplier's boycott before World War I and had been forced by this factor to concentrate and to start their own production plants already at that time. In the 1960's the efficient and strongly centralized MIGROS organization with its only 13 regional coops forced the traditional coops to engage in another big step towards restructuration. This is a process that is continuing well into the 1980's due to strong resistance by independent primary cooperatives facing up to the arguments and financial pressure of the central organizations. At present there are still about 28 local and regional coops. Their amalgamation into bigger units is now pursued in a "soft" way. MIGROS serves as a model also where shop structure and marketing strategies are concerned. MIGROS introduced the first self-service shops in central Europe (1948), it pioneered supermarkets and hypermarkets as well as special shops. MIGROS is also increasingly active in the non-food area and started to expand its area of operation at the beginning of 1993 in the direction of Austria as well as France (probably motivated by the Swiss referendum decision against the adhesion to the European Economic Area). The MIGROS cultural program (financed by the statutory one per cent of turnover destined for culture) has contributed enormously to the positive image of the organization. The new consumer tendencies towards a more active interest in protecting the environment (→ *Environment Protection*) and health food were also taken account of at an early stage.

In all of these areas the traditional Swiss Coop organization is the follower and not the leader. A more restricted financial sphere of action and the higher autonomy of elected officials and members may play a limiting role in this context. Democratic revolts against technocratic centralised leadership have occasionally happened at MIGROS too. The so-called MIGROS-Spring movement of 1980 has continued a tradition of unsuccessful revolts that started already at the time when *Duttweiler* was still at the helm of his new "cooperative". This may be a sign of the fact that even a pro-forma democracy can show signs of real life, especially in a society with strong democratic traditions like Switzerland. At the same time the dominant position of a successful management vis a vis such a democratic revolt is also reaffirmed by this example.

In *Spain, Portugal* und *Greece* there are only a few consumer co-operatives. Greek co-operative development has been fomented in recent years with the help of Swedish KF.

In general we can resume that the lot of consumer co-operatives in Europe (→ *European Community*) has been not to easy in recent years. At present only the *Norwegian movement* seems on a path of strong expansion – but it is still very fragmented and may benefit more from its strength in the savings area than from a true comparative advantage in retailing. Concentration processes have been started but find their obstacles in the geographic nature of the thinly populated country. In Northern *Italy* co-operatives seem to be faring rather well too, but Italian retailing with its many small independent shops is one of the most backward in Europe. Differences of opinion between the commercial (technocratic) "basis" of the movement and its political-bureaucratic "superstructure" (LEGA) have arisen in recent years: an indication of an ongoing process of managerialization and de-ideologization.

In *Japan* retailing is also a legally protected realm of small private enterprises. In this environment the co-operatives have been so successful in recent years that they have even prompted unfriendly law projects inspired by their private competitors (as in Europe around 1910 and 1933). A peculiar aspect of this success story are the "Han", collective buying groups where the socially discriminated Japanese housewifes find an accepted field of action. More important for possible imitators may be the aspect that young environmentalists from university co-ops – later active in the "normal" co-op sector -succeeded in Japan to give the co-ops a very "green", flavour appealing to the new middle classes. Europe's consumer co-operatives on the contrary have generally not succeeded in becoming the champions of environment-minded-retailing (despite some early advantages in this field). Japan thus may be regarded as a model.

III. The Present Situation and its Problems

In conclusion we may state that the *present crisis* of consumer co-operatives is due to a variety of reasons.

1) The increasing → *competition* in retailing has lead to a downward pressure on margins which has made seem some "*social aspects*" of co-operatives costly luxuries. Privileged relations with trade unions, a reluctance to close money-losing shops or a wish to avoid discounting or other ways of minimizing personnel cost are bound to lead to losses.
2) The downward pressure on margins has made it difficult to earn the *traditional dividend* (→ *Fi-*

nancing) which is often still regarded as the trademark of consumer co-operation. Since withholding part of the dividend has been a traditional tool of self-financing and since members confronted with a "dividend pause" may choose to call back their shares the build-up of own capital is severely hampered. Recent "bonus cards" attempts to revitalize the dividend with increasing percentages according to the cumulative volume of the member's purchases are promising but do not avoid the risk of "paying bonusses out of losses" (→ *Reimbursements*).

3) The wealth accumulated by consumer co-operatives up to the 1950's and 1960's made it all too easy to *"overlook" the first serious losses*, to regard them as temporary, or to blame outside factors (unfriendly governments, the business cycle, shifts in consumption patterns etc.).

This led to a *"culture of not facing problems"*, and an art of explaining them away, that has proved very detrimental. Problems that are not faced early on tend to become too big to handle, and a fall from imagined strength to depressed resignation may ensue. If losses are not fought early, financial charges also tend to become a burden.

4) The consumer co-operatives that had and have the biggest problems seem to have been those *most closely linked to traditional labour movement culture* (→ *Corporate Culture*).

5) *Tensions between parallel organizations on a central level* (typically an "ideological" one and a commercial one) have in general led to a victory of the "businessmen" over the "ideologues". But more problematic are the problems of a pluricentrism created by large regional mergers, where the central organizations tend to become the battlefield of feuding "regional barons".

6) The central bodies had the duty to guarantee the solvency of all co-operatives without having the concomitant right to guarantee good management. *Strong regional co-ops tend to resent, however, the fact that they have to pay for subsidies to weak co-ops* via higher wholesale prices, low interest on loans to central bodies etc. This presents a centrifugal danger, if strong regional co-ops decide to buy cheaper outside the sector.

The "coop AG" model functioning as a holding company with strong central authority solves some of these problems but at the price of the traditional co-operative model. The supermerger is another possibility but it has yet to prove its commercial viability. Today most successful models in retailing tend to minimize bureaucracy and opt for at least a limited degree of local flexibility.

7) The role of the *members* and of their *elected representatives* has become very modest. Members tend to become pure customers and to judge co-ops mostly by their performance compared to other shops. The old ideological commitment is dying out. Everywhere shows and little presents have to be used to attract 5–10 per cent of members to grassroots meetings. Members' representatives often seem to be self-recruiting elites rather out of touch with the mass of member-customers. Managers of co-operative enterprises usually regard them as "the problem and not the solution".

From the "technocratic" point of view many co-operative movements should be reorganized according to the *holding company model*. But then economic arguments alone are not all that counts. There is an enormous potential of creative idealism in our "post-industrial" society, and even the old co-operative spirit can come alive occasionally as is shown by *"alternative" health-food co-ops and workers' co-ops*. Today's educated young consumers may also be potentially interested in having a say in the firm that they buy their goods from. Some "traditional" co-operatives like the one in Dortmund are still faring quite well.

In a recent study we were able to formulate the following hypotheses about the *"best performers"* in the consumer co-operatives field:

1) Consumer co-operative organization with a *dominant and enlightened monocratic leadership tend to be "good performers"*.

2) Consumer co-operatives which have *emancipated themselves relatively early and to a large extent from party politics and labour union politics* seem to weather the storms of high pressure competition better than those who have not.

3) Consumer co-operatives *located in traditionally oriented agrarian or small urban environments* where the full pressure of the modernisation processes in retailing is less obvious than in the industrial metropoles seem to be better performers. (Thus a better economic situation of a consumer co-operative would not necessarily be due to better management. This redardation phenomenon seems to be valid also on a national level (e.g. Italy or Japan).

4) Consumer co-operative enterprises that are *receptive for new trends in consumer behaviour* are better performers than those where a certain traditionalism impedes quick adaptations.

The general picture of today's consumer co-operatives is, admittedly, rather bleak. The minimum the member (customer) is expecting from his co-operative today is obviously that *price, quality and service are comparable to that of the competitors*. Only on this basis an additional (social and human) plus of "co-operative togetherness" can be achieved. *"New consumer co-operatives"* of a biological, alternative character (→ *New Co-operatives*) tend to be member-oriented, anti-hierarchical; often members contribute their work effort just like at the beginning of today's established consumer co-ops around 1900.

This shows that the cooperative spirit may be reborn. On the other hand the new biological co-ops show some of the negative aspects of the founders' wave too.

As industrial societies have become quite well-to-do membership motives may focus today in the personal sphere: friendship, family relationships and the specific problems arising from that personal sphere could be addressed in membership circles. Our value systems have changed: interpersonal relations, shopping not only as an economic act but also as a social activity, active interest in environmental issues – in these post-materialistic areas cooperatives could play an important role, provided their truly economic function is at an efficient level. Members' study groups in areas like health food and other non-economic activities could create that feeling of togetherness. But the decisive basis for all of this lies in an efficient and competitive sales and production network.

Bibliography

Brazda, J. and R. Schediwy (Eds.): Consumer Co-operatives in a Changing World, Geneva 1989.
Brazda, J. and R. Schediwy: In Search of Consumer Co-operative Excellence, Lessons of the Past and Present in Order to Master the Future, in: What are the viable co-operative models and contributions for the future? Proceedings of the Tokyo Forum, 1992.
Ilmonen, K.: The End of the Cooperative Movement, Helsinki 1992.
Innovation within Cooperatives as We Approach the 21st Century, Report of the Yokohama International Symposium on the Theory of Cooperatives, Yokohama 1993.
Kylebäck, H.: Konsumentkooperation i strukturomwandling, Kungälv 1983, 1989 (2 volumes).
Nilsson, J.: Det konsumentkooperativa företaget, Stockholm 1983.
Saxena, S.K. and Craig, J.G.: Consumer Co-operatives in a Changing World A Research Review, Annals of Public and Cooperative Economics 4/1990, pp. 489–517.
Schediwy, R.: Federative Structures of Co-operative Organizations – Indispensable or Outdated? Paper for the conference: Well-Being in Europe by Strengthening the Third Sector (May 27th to 29th in Barcelona).
Svensson, C.: Strategi i federativa organisationer – teori och fallstudier, Lund 1992.

Controlling in Co-operatives

HANS-JÜRGEN WURL [J]

(see also: *Management in Co-operatives*; *Accounting*; *Financial Accounting Law*; *Auditing*; *Data Processing*; *Cybernetics*)

I. Introduction; II. Goals and Tasks of Controlling in Co-operatives; III. Relevant Controlling Instruments; IV. Organizational Integration of Controlling in Co-operatives; V. Problems and Perspectives.

I. Introduction

The concept of controlling was developed in the USA, and its roots can be traced back to the end of the 19th century. The actual development and propagation of controlling as a separate operational function, however, first began in the 1930s during the years of the depression as a reaction to the existential problems which numerous business undertakings were confronting at that time.

This development initially went practically unnoticed in Europe. The controlling concept first caught on in the European countries in the 1970s, in particular in the German speaking regions, and quite rapidly achieved almost revolutionary importance.

This phenomenon can be ascribed to a variety of causes.

- The globalization of competition even for small and mid-sized companies necessitated the internationalization of corporate activities. As a consequence management must adapt itself more and more to unfamiliar influences inherent in foreign cultures.
- A result of this internationalization process has been the tendency to create larger and larger operational economic units through expansion, mergers, participational share holding and corporate acquisitions; recently this development has occurred through → *strategic alliances* and cooperation arrangements. The increased complexity resulting from this extends the need of coordination. Shortcomings in the coordination of operational activities inevitably jeopardize the synergy effects which are striven for.
- Furthermore, as *Ansoff* convincingly proves, today's corporate environment not only is gaining dynamics, but it is rather also increasingly determined by structural changes and discontinuities. Empericism is tending to lose importance as the basis for operational decision-making, and the available time for necessary operational adaptation processes continues to wane.

What the term "controlling" ultimately encompasses remains heatedly discussed; the spectrum of differing opinions is relatively broad. In the USA, controlling is frequently seen as an original management function alongside "planning", "organizing", "staffing"

CONTROLLERSHIP

PLANNING FOR CONTROL
To establish, coordinate and administer, as an integral part of management, an adequate plan for the control of operations. Such a plan would provide, to the extent required in the business, profit planning, programs for capital investing and for financing, sales forecasts, expense budgets and cost standards, together with the necessary procedures to effectuate the plan.

REPORTING AND INTERPRETING
To compare performance with operating plans and standards, and to report and interpret the results of operations to all levels of management and to the owners of the business. This function includes the formulation of accounting policy, the coordination of systems and procedures, the preparation of operating data and of special reports as required.

EVALUATING AND CONSULTING
To consult with all segments of management responsible for policy or action concerning any phase of the operation of the business as it relates to the attainment of objectives and the effectiveness of policies, organization structure and procedures.

TAX ADMINISTRATION
To establish and administer tax policies and procedures.

GOVERNMENT REPORTING
To supervise or coordinate the preparation of reports to government agencies.

PROTECTION OF ASSETS
To assure protection for the assets of the business through internal control, internal auditing and assuring proper insurance coverage.

ECONOMIC APPRAISAL
To continuously appraise economic and social forces and government influences, and to interpret their effect upon the business.

Figure 1: Scope of Functions for Controlling according to the "Financial Executive Institute" (1962).

and "directing" (*Koontz/O'Donnell*). On the other hand, in the German speaking regions controlling is mostly interpreted as a *support concept* for management (→ *Management in Co-operatives*). Proponents of this interpretation maintain that on the one hand individual personal space must be afforded for necessary innovative adaptational processes through the delegation of rational, comprehensible management tasks considering the altered demands placed on management; on the other hand, the procurement of information is allotted greater importance particularly in light of potential problems arising through shifts occurring to the environmental constellations in and around the operation and their anticipated effects on the operational system of objectives. Thus, the following remarks will proceed from the latter approach dominating in the German speaking countries.

In this sense, controlling can be differentiated into strategic and operative components. Whereas strategic controlling addresses the long-term safeguarding of competitiveness, operative controlling is to a greater degree oriented around short-term profit goals.

II. Goals and Tasks of Controlling in Co-operatives

Controlling goals are ultimately derived out of the corporate philosophy being pursued. The service function imputed in controlling entails that the controlling activities must be so oriented as to improve management's efficiency. In view of the changing demands placed on management the controlling goals are concretized in the endeavor to promote the *adaptability* of management on the one hand, and to safeguard the *coordination* of operational processes on the other.

Both controlling goals are in principle applicable to co-operatives. The → "*promotion mandate*" as a constitutive element of the affiliated co-operative system does, however, under certain circumstances stipulate that the goal concept be broadened to an extent. Controlling in co-operatives could therefore not only serve the management of the co-operative enterprise but also include providing members with controlling services; a considerable promotional effect is associated with such a service palette (→ *Business Policies*). This is particularly the case when members are not in the position to undertake controlling functions on their own in their enterprises or have such functions executed by members although they nevertheless are dependent on such services in order not to endanger their competitiveness. The goal concept need not be broadened either in co-operatives whose members constitute private households or in the so-called → "*joint-production co-operatives*".

Empirical investigations reveal that the tasks allocated to controlling differ considerably in their content. One of the oldest listings of controlling tasks is the recommendation of the "Financial Executives Institute" (FEI) dated 1962 (see Figure 1).

In the meantime, the views of what controlling should encompass have in part changed to a considerable degree. The attempt to delineate the extent of these controlling tasks according to their content, based on representative surveys of such undertakings in which such controlling concepts have been realized, not only proves difficult in its methodology but likewise must fundamentally be considered question-

Structural Determinants

internal / external

- Co-operative Structural Typology
- Size of the Co-operative
- Corporate Philosophy
- Management Style
- Objekt of the Promotion Mandate

→ Co-operative Controlling Concepts ←

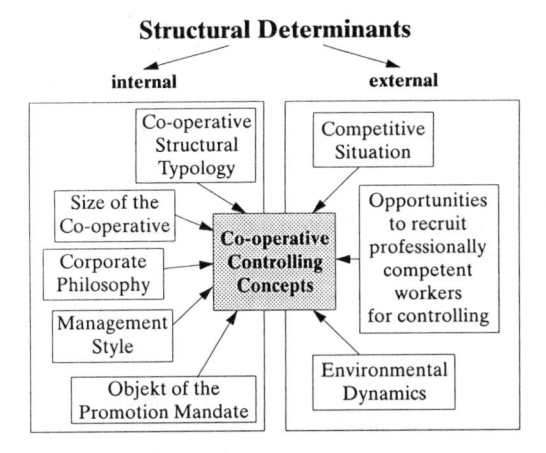

- Competitive Situation
- Opportunities to recruit professionally competent workers for controlling
- Environmental Dynamics

Figure 2: Structural Determinants of Co-operative Controlling Concepts.

able. It seems more consistent in a logical sense to derive controlling tasks out of controlling goals.

An essential precondition for management's adaptability in the light of altered environmental circumstances is the comprehensive and dependable provision of relevant information. Above all it is important to detect problems which could jeopardize the results being pursued and competitiveness in general at the earliest stage possible. It is, however, also important that appropriate reaction alternatives are ascertained as quickly as possible and analyzed with regard to the foreseeable efficiency of their effect, as reaction speed is a decisive factor for → *competition*. As a result controlling is allocated the tasks of conceiving, implementing and maintaining information systems which satisfy these demands; controlling must nonetheless also ensure that internal company communication is free of all interference (e.g. reporting systems) (→*Accounting*). Furthermore, the development of an appropriate *member information system* along the lines of those proposed by *Vierheller* or *Dülfer* is part of this complex of tasks for co-operative organizations (→ *Managerial Economics*).

In principal, there are several possibilities to guarantee the coordination of operational processes. Planning systems with integrated control mechanisms prove a particularly efficient instrument for coordination. Controlling accordingly is entrusted with the tasks of developing suitable planning concepts and implementing them as well as synchronizing the various planning processes – strategic and operative – with regard to their substance and implementation (→ *Strategy Planning*). Controlling's responsibility and competency should in all cases also extend over the necessary controllership activities as such are fit to identify indications as acute problems. It cannot be unequivocally determined from the controlling goals whether steering functions should be assigned to them as has been exacted.

It is evident that planning and control mechanisms must be co-ordinated with the systems of information procurement in a manner fitting to the goals at hand. *Küpper*, nevertheless, correctly indicates that the problems of coordination in principle do not only concern this one component but rather *all* components of the management system. Organization and planning must be synchronized with each other, for example, and planning in turn can only then be efficient when it is adapted to the envisioned goals of the corporate policy as comprehensively as possible. Coordinational tasks involved in controlling should therefore fundamentally encompass all of the latest designated management functions.

It cannot be determined in general how the controlling concept for each individual co-operative should be structured in form and substance; this must rather be decided according to the situation. *Figure 2* illustrates which contextual factors should be taken into consideration.

The co-operative corporate philosophy indicates, for example, whether or to what extent controlling services should be provided by the co-operative enterprise for the members. The size of the co-operative is insofar of importance in that it reflects the degree of operational compexity, therefore at least tending to mirror the extent of coordinational problems (→ *Operational Size*). The need for controlling services is likewise influenced by the management style being practised. Under a participative management style controlling is assigned other tasks, and under certain circumstances, more competencies than is the case under a more patriarchal co-operative administration. Decisive factors for the contextual dimensions of the controlling concept also include co-operative structural typology (as detailed by *Dülfer*) and, above all, the palette of real outputs concretized in the promotion mandate (→ *Structural Types*). For example, the controlling tasks in a credit co-operative must inevitably be defined differently than those in a co-operative house-building society.

These "internal" contextual factors stand opposed to those ("external") structural determinants which affect the co-operative from the outside and as a rule are not influenced by the members. Strong competitive pressure as well as a heightened environmental dynamic reinforce willingness for extensive controlling. On the other hand, difficulties in recruiting competent employees entrusted with controlling duties have a restrictive effect.

The departmental function "internal auditing" (→ *Accounting*) is confronted with a conceptional problem as to its proper allocation. On the one hand, the internal audit like "controllership" fulfills surveillance functions and could insomuch be subordinate to controlling. However, inasfar as the controlling processes constitute an object of the internal audit, it is recommendable *not* to integrate the latter into the controlling system in order to guarantee autonomy between the parties responsible for the internal audit and the controlling (*Heigl*).

Equally contested is the question whether controlling should also be responsible for external bookkeeping and taxation problems of the enterprise. Whereas both partial functions are seen as traditional components of controlling in the USA, this position in general is not shared in the German speaking regions where the dominating notion of controlling – as a management support system – above all is oriented around future company involvement and action.

III. Relevant Controlling Instruments

All methods held suitable either to enable or facilitate the fulfillment of controlling tasks number among the instruments for controlling. Aside from certain exceptions the direct application of these instruments is *not* subordinate to controlling. Competency is predominantly limited to the initiative function and the supervision of implementation.

Controlling processes are as a rule circular processes. They are initiated once shortcomings either in management's procurement of information or in the coordination of operational activities are identified and in principle proceed along the following scheme of phases:

1) The quest for appropriate instruments to overcome the sighted shortcoming;
2) Assessment of the ascertained alternatives and the selection decision;
3) Implementation;
4) Overcoming (internal operational) acceptance barriers;
5) Critical supervision of involvement under efficiency aspects.

If it should be determined in the final phase that the procedures or models utilized no longer suffice to address the demands at hand – e.g. due to altered environmental circumstances – a new controlling process must be introduced which is oriented around the proper problem. If interference is determined, this process is limited to the initiation of appropriate correctional measures or procedural modifications.

One must note in this connection that the executors of the controlling function under certain circumstances – in particular in phases 2 through 5 – must themselves make use of selected controlling instruments, for example in the benefit analysis involved in the assessment of alternatives.

The most important controlling instruments are systematically arranged in *Figure 3* according to functional criteria and possible implementation in co-operatives. The ranks of appropriateness are presented in ordinal symbols and are not theoretically grounded. They should solely serve to provide orientation.

The selection of the ultimate instruments for implementation is once again contingent on situational conditions. Important determinants for the selection decision include the importance of the sighted problems, financial and personnel restrictions, professional qualification of co-workers as well as the nature and structure of the co-operative service palette.

IV. Organizational Integration of Controlling in Co-operatives

Fundamentally, the controlling concept can be anchored in the co-operative organization in one of two ways: either through the institutional solution or through waiving institutionalization.

Above all, in smaller co-operatives the question of establishing an independent controller position would never be raised, not least due to financial reasons. In such cases the board members or other management staff are entrusted with controlling tasks. The coordination of controlling activities can be guaranteed through arrangements made in regularly held commission meetings. The problematic features of this solution include the following two situations: on the one hand necessary controllership know-how is rather often lacking, and on the other hand the additional work load inevitably impairs the fulfillment of function-specific responsibilities. Consequently, the danger arises that the controlling concept ultimately fails to be realized *and* the sought after improvements to the undertaking's competitiveness fail to materialize. A solution to this dilemma could be the temporary requisition of external consulting services hailing from either state or private institutions, and under certain circumstances even international organizations.

The institutionalization of controlling mechanisms is more apt for larger co-operatives. Three possible organizational forms of such an attachment can be differentiated: staff jobs, line positions, or cross-section areas (see *Figure 4*).

Conveying controlling responsibilities to a staff post is problematic inasmuch as the controller not only needs to provide consultational services but also must enforce structural measures, for example the introduction of innovative planning methods, under disadvantageous conditions – sometimes even against internal company resistance. The establishment of a pure line position for controlling tasks would once again contradict the accentuated support function that controlling offers management. It thus seems more expedient to present controlling as a cross-section area according to the structuring concepts of matrix organization and then attach certain functional decision-making and directing competencies to this position.

If decentralized controller positions in individual functional sectors or branches are to be established above and beyond the central controlling mechanism in larger co-operatives, it is necessary to regulate the

Controlling Instrument			Potential Implementation			
			Primary co-op		Secondary co-op	
			in central unit	for services	in central units	for services
Planing	Strategic	Procedures for long-term prognoses (e.g. scenario techniques)	*	*	***	***
		Analysis of strengths and weaknesses	**	*	***	***
		Portfolio methods (e.g. analyses of market share, market growth)	**	*	***	**
		Analyses of the competition	**	–	***	**
		Systems of experts	–	–	*	***
		Methods to further creativity, (e.g. Brainstorming)	*	–	**	–
	Operative	Procedures for short-term prognoses, (e.g. exponential smoothing)	***	**	***	***
		OR-Procedures (e.g. PERT, techniques for network plans)	*	–	*	**
		Concepts for cost calculation (e.g. activity based costing)	***	**	***	***
		Investment analysis (e.g. method of capital value)	**	***	**	*
		Rationalization procedures (e.g. zero base budgeting)	**	*	**	–
Control	Strategic	Strategic Early Warning Systems	*	–	***	***
		Ex post facto analyses	**	–	***	***
	Operative	Operative Early Warning Systems	**	***	***	**
		Comparisons of Targets and Actual Standing	**	**	***	***
		Ratio Analysis	***	***	***	**
Reporting		Analysis of Information Needs	***	*	***	**
		Communication Structure	**	**	***	**
		Standardization of Reporting	**	***	***	**
		Safeguarding Measures against Interference and Manipulation	***	*	***	**
Additional tasks		Examples: Analysis of Organizational Efficiency Procedures for Corporate Assessment Techniques for Motivation and Conflict Resolution	*	*	**	**

*** : particularly suitable * : less suitable
** : suitable – : hardly suitable

Figure 3: Classification of Important Controlling Instruments according to Functional Criteria and Potential Implementation Sectors in Co-operatives.

relations between the various hierarchical controlling levels. A frequently practiced solution to this organizational problem is the so-called "dotted line principle" in the following version: The decentralized controller is subordinate in a disciplinary sense (*which* tasks should be attended to *when*?) to the function and/or branch managers to whom they are assigned, whereas the authority of functional instruction (*how* should these tasks be attended to?) is anchored in the centralized controlling field.

It cannot be determined without further ado which organizational model can operate optimally for controlling in co-operatives; the mechanisms for action associated in the possible organizational forms have yet to be sufficiently investigated in view of the co-operative goal system. Relevant determinants for this decision include the size of the co-operative, its particular type (according to *Dülfer*) (→ *Structural Types*) as well as the existing organizational structure. One must thereby note that hybrid forms and temporary transition arrangements also come into consideration for the organizational attachment of controlling mechanisms aside from the basic variants described above.

Although the integration of institutionalized controlling in the second management level (as illustrated in organizational diagram, *Figure 4*) corresponds with the usual recommendations found in the literature on the subject, this solution is itself not problem-free. The integration of the controller in the board may seem worth deliberation – above all in smaller co-operatives; such an arrangement would, however, not provide the controller with the necessary distance for a grounded, critical analysis of the board's work. A lower hierarchical attachment is also conceivable.

V. Problems and Perspectives

Whereas the idea of controlling has already won thorough recognition in industry, this is not yet universally the case in the co-operative sector. One of the reasons for this could be the dominance of smaller operational units. It is also conceivable that the advantages of controlling are either not generally known in the co-operative decision-making bodies or else not correctly appraised. Acceptance problems rooted emotionally must ultimately also not be excluded. In spite of it all, co-operatives must make themselves more accepting to the notion of controlling in the future in order not to lose ground competitively. This process could be accelerated through more intensive educative endeavors undertaken by umbrella organizations and/or institutions (co-operative authorities, auditing federations and centralized computing centers, international organizations). It is, however, in itself insufficient to support the diffusion process for the controlling idea solely through information. It is of at least equal importance that knowledge of controlling is imparted through targeted training programs in the various branches of co-operative activity. The success of controlling in the end rests on the professional competency of the workers entrusted with controlling responsibilities.

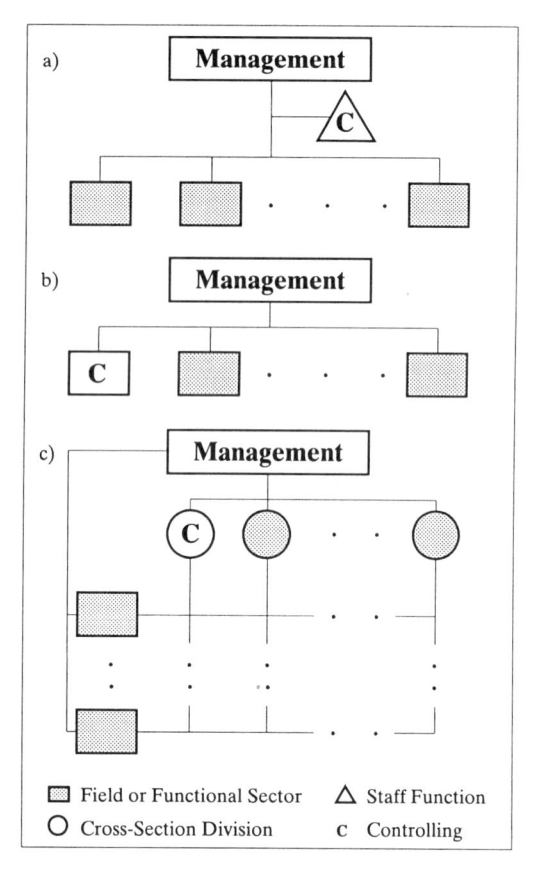

Figure 4: Basic Forms of Organizational Attachment.

▨ Field or Functional Sector   △ Staff Function
○ Cross-Section Division   c Controlling

Bibliography

Ackoff, R.L./Finnel, E.V./Gharajedaghi, J.: Zukunftssicherung durch Contolling, Stuttgart 1989.

Albach, H./Weber, J.(ed.): Controlling, Zeitschrift für Betriebswirtschaft (additional volume), Wiesbaden 1991.

Ansoff, H.J.: Strategic Management, London/Basingstoke 1979.

Boettcher, E. (ed.): Die Genossenschaft im Wettbewerb der Ideen, Tübingen 1985.

Coenenberg, A.G./Baum, H.-G.: Strategisches Controlling, Stuttgart 1987.

Dülfer, Eberhard: Betriebswirtschaftslehre der Kooperative, Göttingen 1984.

Financial Executives Institute (ed.): Controllership and Treasureship Functions Defined by FEI,. In: The Controller, 30th vol., p. 289, 1962.

Hahn, D.: Planungs- und Kontrollrechnung – PuK, 3rd edition, Wiesbaden 1985.

Hahn, D./Taylor, B. (ed.): Strategische Unternehmensplanung – Strategische Unternehmensführung, 5th edition, Heidelberg 1990.

Heigl, A.: Controlling – Interne Revision, 2nd edition, Stuttgart/New York 1989.
Hinterhuber, H.H.: Strategische Unternehmensführung, 4th edition, Berlin/New York 1989.
Hinterhuber, H.H./Hammer, R.: Organisation und Implementierung des Strategischen Controlling in Unternehmen. In: Controlling, vol. 4, pp. 190–197, München/Frankfurt 1991.
Horváth, P.: Controlling, 4th edition, Munich 1992.
Jackson, J.H.: The Comptroller: His Functions and Organization, 2nd printing, Cambridge, Mass. 1949.
Koontz, H./O'Donell, C.: Principles of Management: An analysis of managerial functions, New York 1955 (8th edition 1984, with co-author H. Weihrich).
Kreikebaum, H.: Strategische Unternehmensplanung, 4th edition, Stuttgart/Berlin/Köln 1991.
Küpper, H.-U.: Konzeption des Controlling aus betriebswirtschaftlicher Sicht. In: Scheer, A.-W. (ed.): Rechnungswesen und EDV, pp. 82–116, Heidelberg 1987.
Küpper, H.-U./Weber, J./Zünd, A.: Zum Verständnis und Selbstverständnis des Controlling – Thesen zur Konsensbildung. In: Zeitschrift für Betriebswirtschaft, pp. 281–293, Wiesbaden 1990.
Laurinkari, J. (ed.): Genossenschaftswesen, München/Wien 1990.
Mayer, E./Weber, J. (ed.): Handbuch Controlling, Stuttgart 1990.
Probst, G.J.B./Schmitz-Dräger, R. (ed.): Controlling und Unternehmensführung, Bern 1985.
Serfling, K.: Controlling, 2nd edition, Stuttgart 1992.
Spremann, K./Zur, E. (ed.): Controlling, Wiesbaden 1992.
Vierheller, R.: Unternehmensführung und Mitgliederinformation in der Genossenschaft, Marburger Schriften zum Genossenschaftswesen, vol. 42., Göttingen 1974.
Wagner, G.R./Janzen, H.: Ökologisches Controlling. In: Controlling, Vol. 3, pp. 120–129, München/Frankfurt 1991.
Weber, J.: Einführung in das Controlling, 3rd edition, Stuttgart 1991.
Welge, M.K.: Unternehmensführung, vol. 3: Controlling, Stuttgart 1988.

Co-operative Banks

OSWALD HAHN [J]

(see also: *Classification; Agricultural Credit; Central Institutions; Credit Unions; Early Warning Systems; Linking Banks*)

I. The Nature of Co-operative Banks; II. Palette of Services and Membership Body; III. Organizational Forms; IV. Structural Types and the Promotion Mandate; V. The Importance among the All-purpose Banks.

I. The Nature of Co-operative Banks

Differentiation is made with respect to co-operative banks (as for numerous other business forms) between the narrow juridical term (the legal form) and the much broader economic concept (goal formation and targeted recipients). The focus of the following treatise is directed at the dimensions of the economic concept of co-operative banks which, by all means, are limited in part by the formation of → *federations*. Three characteristics distinguish co-operative banks in international comparisons: Firstly, it is the most recent of co-operative forms. It came into being around 1850, thus following considerably after → *production co-operatives* (15th century) and → *consumer co-operatives* (1750), and directly after housing and merchandising co-operatives. Secondly, co-operative banks are the youngest form of banking institution and were preceded by private banks and public credit institutions (17th century). They are considered a separate banking group in all countries but nevertheless are subject to common banking laws and/or special legislation to varying degrees. Thirdly, co-operative banks dominate world-wide with regard to their sheer number but have the smallest operational size among institutes within national banking systems. A study of co-operative banks from an international standpoint requires face-to-face comparisons, which in turn necessitate appropriate criteria (Parts II through V).

II. Palette of Services and Membership Body

By using the criterion of "services provided" in connection with the particular customer body actually being served, one can differentiate between three types of co-operative banks: consumer oriented co-operative banks, investment oriented co-operative banks, and co-operative banks oriented around small and mid-sized businesses.

1. Consumer-Oriented Co-operative Banks

Co-operative banks centered around consumers constitute the oldest form of co-operative structure. Nonetheless, they were only able to develop into financial banks for particular target groups in a handful of regions, thereby assuming one of the three following constellations:
a) Financially underdeveloped institutes concentrating on cost deferment for customers (*financing credit purchases*). The most significant example of this form are the British consumers' co-operatives.
b) The *credit unions* found in North America. These have a completely different character which has nothing to do with the merchandising activities of the → *consumer co-operatives*. The founders of this movement, *Alphonse* → *Desjardins* (1854–1920) and *Edward. A. Filene* (1860–1937), did however draw from → *Friedrich Wilhelm Raiffeisen's* concept. Aside from their co-operative orientation, no relationship exists between the credit unions and the agricultural credit co-operatives. Within the reaches of their deposit function, the → *credit unions* are limited to accepting savings deposits, and within their lending business they only grant consumer credits. In the meantime, they have spread throughout the world to those locations where small business co-operative

banks are not accessible to consumers. In principle, the *Co-operative Savings Societies* found in the English speaking African countries are active on the identical level (→ *Development, Africa*); these organizations (as in India) (→ *Development, South Asia*) serve as substitute for savings banks which are missing on the local level.

c) The prototypical *savings bank* oriented along co-operative lines. These are found in Switzerland where the co-operative principle meanwhile has become subordinate to the interests of group integration as represented by "regional banks and savings banks".

2. Investment-Oriented Co-operatives

No homogenous form or group exists within this category; differentiations are possible according to three distinct forms:

a) Issuing and Guaranty Associations

i) The oldest form of investment-oriented co-operatives is surely the (German) "*Landschaft*", a predecessor of the modern mortgage bank. This form came into being through Dutch initiative in the form of the oldest Prussian "Landschaft" of *Frederich the Great* (1769). These early institutions can be considered debtor guaranty and issuing associations which can only be categorized under the "co-operative" heading based on economic criteria. The two following types of co-operatives are based on this concept.

ii) The *central issuing and/or underwriting authorities* of various banking groups: These developed in Austria and Switzerland as special centralized institutes of the regional mortgage banks. Central banks for conglomerate groups are more common (central clearing banks, central co-operative banks) which undertake such business in the scope of their all-round functions.

iii) The *Swiss "Bürgschaftsgenossenschaft"* (*surety co-operative, 1921*) was the first modern promotional institution which served to transform collateral for personal credit into securities in kind. This institution was embraced only by a few countries; state support for such undertakings dominates world-wide (in Germany: credit guaranty associations).

b) The Anglo-Saxon → Building and Loan Societies

The lack of a system of mortgage banks prompted the savings and loan idea to arise, which itself developed out of co-operative thought. In England, this took the form and name of *Building Societies* (1775) and in the United States *Savings and Loan Associations* or *Building and Loan Associations* (Philadelphia, 1831). In the course of time, however, these institutions transformed into commercial undertakings. On the European continent, the idea of building and loans arose much later due to the success of mortgage banks. The only gap in the market they could fill was that for second mortgages; the co-operative idea could not develop in that business realm.

c) Institutes for Self-Financing

The emergence of equity investment companies (H.J.Persé) as well as the commercial savings banks for targeted investments (*Otto Mayer*) were not able to be realized as the third model of investment-oriented co-operatives. These are not self-help institutions aiming to cover short-term credit needs with the available excess liquidity of other members (as the classic credit co-operatives were). The notion of self-help in this case requires long-term consumer temperance and sacrifice. Such a deferred waiting period is possible for savings and loans, but it is not achievable within the sector of manufacturing investment credit and seems to lack permanent growth there. One could, however, imagine that two different types of mid-sized business subjects would coalesce for a common action: On the one hand a company seeking equity but unable to issue debentures, and on the other hand self-employed individuals seeking a promising investment. However, the typical co-operative element is not present here: the member constantly embodying both creditor and debtor. This problem was resolved in the identical manner as was the situation involving the provision of security, namely through state assistance.

3. Small Business Co-operatives

This final type has achieved the broadest international expansion as well as the greatest national importance. Small and mid-sized companies join together to form credit co-operatives with the goal of making savings available to the group as a community; the practise of lending this savings out to members is based on their personal creditworthiness.

a) Traditional and Modern Co-operative Banks

In general, only the modern "Small Business Co-operative Movement" is categorized under such credit co-operatives, including commercial and farming credit co-operatives, co-operative banks in both cities and villages, or *Schulze-Delitzsch* Co-operatives (1855) as well as *Raiffeisen* Co-operatives (1864). In many underdeveloped countries, these institutions are in opposition to "traditional co-operatives" which many governments consider competitors to the "modern" co-operative concepts adopted from Europe in which the state is financially involved. This frequently leads to opposition against the modern conception (*Hämke-Kievelitz*). The following is restricted to observations of modern co-operative banks.

b) All-purpose Co-operative Banks

i) Alongside the notion of credit unions, only those concepts developed by → *Raiffeisen* and → *Schulze-Delitzsch* have developed practically world-wide into all-purpose banks. These are represented in urban *"Volksbanken"* and rural *"Raiffeisenbanken"* or savings and loan banks.

ii) Each group is found world-wide to a varying degree. Only the Raiffeisen Movement has really achieved an "international" position. Those co-operatives in the tradition of *Hermann Schulze-Delitzsch*, on the other hand, can be found above all in Europe (particularly in EC member countries, Austria and Switzerland) and in Japan. The commercial credit co-operatives in Malaysia and Indonesia can be traced back to Dutch influences, those in Argentina and Chile to German models. The much greater frequency of "Raiffeisen" co-operatives in contrast to "Schulze-Delitzsch" co-operatives is based on the fact that the provision of banking services for small companies has gradually been guaranteed in urban areas, whereas the rural regions of many countries are still today neglected by both private and state banks.

iii) Mergers between both banking groups commenced in 1971 in the Federal Republic of Germany and were completed throughout the country in 1989. In contrast, the other countries which have kept both groups have maintained the former structure, which in part is contingent on varying orientation (France, Italy, Austria).

c) Group Formation within the Raiffeisen Organization

i) In the United States the "farm credit system" is referred to in general instead of a group of rural credit co-operatives. The "Farm Credit Administration", which includes state, private and co-operative institutions, dominates the credit system there. The following breakdown describes the individual groups belonging to this organization.

The *Land Bank System* is composed on the one hand by joint stock banks in the form of private stock-mortgage banks and, on the other hand, by local "National Farm Loan Associations" which are assisted on the regional level by 12 state-run "Federal Land Banks".

The *Federal Intermediate Credit System* encompasses 12 central "Federal Intermediate Credit Banks" which refinance all types of local banks involved with agricultural credits.

The *Production Credit System* works with "Production Credit Associations" as local co-operatives and 12 state-run "Production Credit Corporations" as refinancing centers.

The *Bank for Co-operative System* is composed of the "Federal Bank for Co-operatives" and 12 "District Banks for Co-operatives" which provide refinancing for merchandising co-operatives.

ii) The *French* rural co-operative banking sector is split into two parts. Firstly, the three-tiered system of the *Crédit Agricole Mutuel* belongs to the *secteur bancaire* semi-public (private savings banks on both the local and regional level which receive state subsidies, and an apex state institute, the "Caisse Nationale de Crédit Agricole"). The other division is the *Crédit Agricole Mutuel Libre* which likewise has a three-tiered structure but in contrast does not receive any support from the state and, therefore, is fairly autonomous.

iii) Originally, *the Netherlands* likewise had two agricultural credit systems, each two-tiered in stucture and grounded firmly on a pure co-operative basis: the Raiffeisenbanken with the "Coöperative Centrale Raiffeisen Bank" in Utrecht and the Boerenleenbanken with the "Coöperative Centrale Boerenleenbank" in Eindhoven. These two groups merged in 1971 and formed the Rabobankgruppe (Rabobanken with the Central Rabobank).

iv) A particularity of Asian and Latin American countries bordering coastal waters is the additional existence of *fishery co-operatives* (→ *Classification*). Such co-operatives actually arose first in Great Britain but never really undertook credit business there. These co-operatives have a particularly important position in Japan and Korea. Furthermore, the independent section of Japanese *Forestry Co-operatives* also deserves mention. However, agricultural, fishery, and forestry co-operatives in Japan are united on the national level through a central bank.

III. Organizational Forms

Throughout the world, the co-operative banking system is structured in a multi-tiered manner. Aside from development in geographically small countries, a three-leveled system evolved from an early stage on in most instances, in India even a four-leveled system. This multi-tiered structure assumes a variety of organizational forms: a co-operative solution, that of consolidated companies, and that of a trust.

1. The "Co-operative" Form

The "co-operative" form is the "normal" manifestation: the banking system is broken down into several legally independent levels. "Primary co-operatives" (co-operative banks) are differentiated from "central co-operatives" (here the co-operative central banks). Seen in the course of development, the primary co-operatives as "local banks" existed at the beginning. In this system, the regional central banks established their own interregional central bank vested with usual subsidiary functions (reserve and refinancing bank, issuing bank; an institute to execute "more advanced" business, above all foreign transactions, brokerage activities, and clearings). An interregional central bank (→ *Central Institutions*) is characteristic for most countries (for example, in Germany the Deutsche Genossenschaftsbank – DG BANK; the Caisse Centrale des Banques Populaires – CCBP, and the Crédit Agricole Mutuel, Paris; the Instituto di Credito delle Casse Rurali et Artigiane – ICCREA, Rome; Rabobank Nederland, the Netherlands; Raiffeisenzentralbank Österreich and the Österreichische Volksbanken AG, Austria; Okobank, Helsinki).

The two-tiered system was realized in Germany in part between 1985 and 1989; it had been discussed since 1974 and has received mixed appraisals. Three-tiered systems can still be found in Europe only in France, Austria (Raiffeisen), and in Sweden; they otherwise can still be found on the American continent.

2. The "Trust" Form

In the course of historical development, the "corporation" form should be contrasted with the "co-operative" form, but in the actual chronology the "trust" form evolved, a "central" co-operative with legally independent branches. This form emerges through two methods:

a) through its *establishment* (as exemplified by the Schweizer Volksbank, 1869, and the Co-operative Bank Ltd, Manchester). Such institutes are founded centrally which then in turn open branch offices.

b) through → *mergers* (as exemplified by the Nederlandsche Middenstandsbank). The development of such mergers is forecasted in various ways to serve as a model for the two-tiered German system.

3. The "Shareholding" Form

The shareholding model of co-operative banking can usually be traced back to a lack of capital on the lowest organizational level.

a) *Finland* was the first country to go in this direction. A central co-operative bank based on the Raiffeisen idea was founded in 1902 by *private individuals* (Osuuspankkien Keskuspankii Oy, OKO). The first local savings and loan banks came into being six months later once trust had been established in this top-level institute.

b) The Finnish system was "rediscovered" in the USA and still serves as a characteristic model for *developing countries* (→ *Policies for Promotion*). There, central and/or regional co-operative banks or "agricultural banks" are founded by the state in the initial phases of a newly directed and institutionalized co-operative movement (which does not take into regard the traditional system of customary rights). These co-operatives in turn assist in the foundation of local credit co-operatives by purchasing participation in them. At the basis of such a conception, itself determined by the farming populations's lack of capital, lies the goal of "divestiture" at a later date: This would happen initially by the central bank selling its share of the local co-operatives to the co-operative members; secondary development is pursued when the local credit co-operatives assume state-owned equity in the central banks.

c) Vertical concentration can ultimately also be the result of *crises* on the local co-operative level. It could be that the central bank simply does not increase its level of investment participation, or that thorough reorganization is necessary.

IV. Structural Types and the Promotion Mandate

The three structural types propounded by *Eberhard Dülfer* (→ *Structural Types*) are likewise realized among co-operative banks, though to varying degrees on both the primary level and within the vertical combine.

1. Structural Types on the Primary Level

a) The "Traditional Co-operative"

Every newly founded co-operative bank which is characterized by the membership managing the bank's business activities can be assigned to this category. Initially all activities are executed on an honorary basis. These co-operative banks aim to redress a situation of scarcity, which itself can come to light in several forms, such as a lack of banking offices in the vicinity of potential customers/members. Assuming they are present, private banks only provide credit against underlying securities in kind, or else at exceptionally high interest rates. By joining together, members can pool their savings in a concentrated manner; the honorary board of directors personally knows each borrower (origin of the credit worthiness investigation), and affordable interest rates can be charged on account of the administration working at cost-price (primarily honorary activity). Today, such a situation can still be found in many underdeveloped countries, in sparsely populated regions of the North Atlantic (North America, Scandinavia, Switzerland) or in neglected regions (Alsace, Southern Tyrol).

b) Market-linkage Co-operatives (→ *Structural Types*)

The activities of the co-operative banks enable their members to become capable bank customers and are, therefore, a factor for economic development. As the extent of development increases, co-operative banks enter into competition with commercial banks; this is the reason why the classical promotion mandate (credits granted on the local level, low interest rates and no underlying collateral) is cast aside. The co-operative bank thereby confronts two alternatives: It can either seek out new opportunities in other situations of scarcity (gaps in the market) and abandon its previous activities, or it can reformulate its promotion mandate. In the latter case, demand exists primarily for the co-operative bank to assume overall economic functions (providing countervailing power on the market, supporting mid-sized banking structures) and/or promote its members not as borrowers but rather as investors (business stocks as a revenue instrument) or as fellow owners (not only participating in the election of the administrative body but also actively shaping business policy through branch office management).

c) The Integrated Co-operative

In contrast to the merchandising co-operatives which assume considerable parts of their members' main commercial function, the co-operative banks solely assume components of the financial function. An integrated co-operative would expand its promotion mandate to include all financial functions of its members, which would correspond to bank-conducted cash management. In such a situation, the integrated co-operative (→ *Structural Types*) would be realized: The member lacks the necessary heightened information level in the field of finance which is why the co-operative enterprise would manage all of his financial activities in the integrated co-operative system. This model has not, however, been realized on the co-operative level but rather is provided by all banks in a commercial manner. Thus, the situation involving the integrated co-operative does not exist on the level of the relation between the co-operative bank and its member.

2. The Structural Types of the Vertical Co-operative Combine

a) The discussion above is analogously applicable to the *traditional co-operative central banks*: Their formation through the primary banks is undertaken for the identical reason that the co-operative banks resulted through their members. Today, however, there are only a few vertical combine systems on this "traditional" level (Switzerland, South Tyrol, Alsace); the other co-operative banks have continued their development into market or integrated co-operatives.

b) The *market economy situation* is typical of co-operative banks in most of the industrial countries where primary banks free themselves from their central banks as their operational size increases; they accordingly choose to employ the services of other institutes. In the industrial countries, three constellations of this situation can be found in practise:

i) The central bank continues to fulfill the classical promotion mandate for smaller institutes; it is considered executively operating unit by each co-operative bank.
ii) Larger institutes solely see the central bank as a source of assistance in times of need; they otherwise are drawn to the central bank only when it offers better conditions than those available on the market.
iii) The final group of member banks remains loyal to the concept of executively operating units. Every central bank, therefore, finds itself in a conflict situation when mergers on the local level are recommended. In such a case, the integrated co-operative provides a solution.

c) The *integrated co-operative constellation* can evolve in two ways:

i) In the under-developed countries, modern co-operative banks are formed "top down", which is nothing other than the "shareholding solution" presented above: A state central bank is founded which participates in the establishment of local co-operative banks. A centralized decision making is at hand from the beginning which, at best, could gradually lead to de jure co-decision participation on the basis level.
ii) In the highly developed countries, such integrated co-operatives evolve as a form of reorganization rather than through initial establishment. As competition heightens and/or as the competition exhibits greater banking concentration, the situation develops which *Dülfer* described, namely that the primary banks suffer an information deficit compared to the competitors. The central bank assumes the function of a central franchise organization, initially as an alternative to a merger, but later as an adaptational maneuvre for the organizational structure with regard to the competition. Such integration provides the local co-operative banks with the necessary information they previously lacked. The integrated co-operative to a great extent manages the business activities of the member banks. This type of an integrated vertical combine for co-operative banks is achievable in the Federal Republic of Germany once the merger goal of 500 to 1000 local banks has been reached (→ *Structural Changes*); it would serve as an alternative to and/or preliminary basis for a total merger.

V. The Importance among the All-purpose Banks

The criteria under consideration are product/service assortment, market share, operational size, and local distribution.

1. The Product/Service Assortment of Co-operative Banks

Based on this criterion, three model constellations can be constructed.

a) The highest level of development can be found in Europe (excluding the majority of the former COMECOM countries), Japan, and several threshold countries (China) – countries with a co-operative banking system which is firmly integrated in the banking system as a whole. It would be too much in the scope of this article, however, to individually highlight the numerous finer differences between these countries.

b) The second constellation can be found in the Anglo-Saxon countries – exhibiting a co-operative banking system in which the credit co-operatives, to a certain extent, are limited in their field of activity. Great Britain heads the list of most restrictive, whereas Australia has the most advanced credit co-operatives in the Commonwealth.

c) The third constellation is to be found in developing countries in which co-operatives pursue classical parallel business activity: On the one hand they accept daily deposit savings and, on the other hand, they grant short and mid-term amortizing loans. There are, however, considerable discrepancies in the level of development starting with Latin America and proceeding to the Indian subcontinent, the remainder of Asia and lastly Africa.

2. Market Shares

The greatly differing methods of statistical tabulation make it quite difficult to provide a comprehensive comparison of market shares (and the length of this article likewise prevents such presentation). Therefore, attention will be limited to typical countries and groups of particular states (see *Table I*). Three country categories can be differentiated:

a) Countries in which the credit co-operatives' share of the balance volume from all commercial banks combined is below five percent. Most of the member countries of the Commonwealth, Switzerland, Sweden, Spain, Israel, America, and Africa number among this group.

b) Economic regions in which co-operative banks have a market share between 10 and 15%. Belgium, Korea, and Norway are examples here.

c) Countries in which the co-operative share lies between 20 and 30%. These include Italy, Germany, Finland, France, Austria, and the Netherlands, all of which are countries in which the co-operative banks have developed the character of successful market co-operatives. By far the leading country with regard to co-operative banking activity Japan is.

Table I: The Importance (Market Share) of Co-operative Banks among All-Round Banks in Selected Countries (expressed as percentage of total balances)

	Commercial Banks	Savings Banks	Co-operative Banks
Australia	20	75	5
Belgium	86	5	9
Germany	32	47	21
Finland	44	31	25
France	56	18	26
India	84	12	4
Italy	55	26	19
Japan	62		38
Korea	56	33	11
New Zealand	67	32	1
the Netherlands	63	12	25
Norway	58	16	26
Austria	42	30	28
the Philippines	92	2	6
Sweden	74	21	5
Switzerland	85	11	4
Spain	63	35	2
Thailand	88	9	3
USA	89	7	4

3. Local Presence

a) The classic co-operative bank characteristically assumes a monopoly position on the local level. The lack of a bank in the proximity was itself the situation of scarcity which prompted the formation of co-operative banks. In the meantime, a definite change can be noted. As competition has increased, the commercial banks have set up branch offices in locations which were previously the territory of classic co-operative banks; market co-operatives in turn strive to establish branch offices in the vicinity of their competitors.

b) For the most part, co-operative banks today maintain the largest network of branches within the entire banking structure. This is the case for both those countries in which the co-operative market share of banking business is greater than 10% as well as for the developing countries. Considering the share of total bank branch offices, credit co-operatives in the industrial countries have developed an ever smaller share (e.g. Germany: a decrease from 54% to 43% between 1957 and 1990), whereas credit co-operatives in the developing countries indicate increasing proportions.

c) Certain discrepancies exist among those industrialized countries in which the co-operative banks have a small market share (below 5%). Commercial banks and savings banks dominate here. The low percentage share of co-operatives within the total network of branches is primarily based on the fact that the banks in this group retained their classic promotion mandate and have not sought further competition.

One observation can however be established for all countries bordering the Atlantic, above all those in the Alpan regions, in Scandinavia, and in North America: The high economic standard, particularly in their rural areas, is not least a result of the high density of bank branches in the co-operative sector. There is general disappointment that the wave of co-operative formations in developing countries has not reaped success. In such countries, the rural infrastructure in many regions seems to correspond more closely to that of 17th or even 16th century continental Europe rather than that of the 19th century.

4. Operational Size

Co-operative banks are characteristic by their small operational sizes (→ *Operational Size*). Furthermore, the traditional co-operative bank ("village bank", *Hahn*) has no branches. Based on international observations, three situations can be ascertained :

a) Those countries with a *newly developed co-operative system* indicate permanent growth in the number of independent co-operative banks. This was likewise the situation in Germany and Austria up through the middle of the 1930s, and in Switzerland up to 1975. Current examples of this development are Bolivia, Columbia, Equador, individual Arab states, and all African countries.

b) The number of institutes remains constant in the *"consolidation phase"*. It could be that no new banks are founded (e.g. Switzerland, USA) or that new bank formations are offset by a reduction in numbers due to mergers (such as on the India subcontinent and in numerous Latin American countries).

c) The *"merger phase"* is considered characteristic for industrial countries where co-operatives enjoy a large market share. The concentration process (→ *Mergers and Consolidations*) began during the 1960s in Scandinavia, made its way to Germany during the 1970s (→ *Structural Changes*), continued to Austria the following decade, and in the meantime has spread to all remaining countries on the continent. Two opposing challenges have resulted from this: On the one hand, rationalization is strived for through mergers, resulting in a reduction of costs (synergy effect) and improvements in efficiency. On the other hand, estrangement between the bank and members increases because of this, and a new promotion mandate (oriented around the member as investor and co-owner) is therefore conceived which strives to reduce this new development. The problem remains to find the optimal operational size. This cannot be set in general terms but rather is determined by local conditions and, above all, by the "dispositive factor" (management).

By any rate, the competitor's "size multiplier" lies above the average operational size of the co-operative banks throughout the world. *Table II* serves to illustrate this situation, using central Europe as an example; in all cases, the multipliers are higher in the other countries than they are in Germany.

Table II: Size Multiplier among the Competitors of Co-operative Banks (multiple of the average operational size of the co-operative bank)

Country	Year	Regional Banks	Savings Banks	Bankers
Germany	1950	243	41	53
	1965	123	41	17
	1990	18	10	5
Austria	1989	33	9	3
Switz.	1989	269	17	10

With respect to customer proximity, the co-operative banks are in a much better position than their competitors.

Bibliography

Note: There are no complete international comparisons. Monographs tend to concentrate on their author's native country. The archives of co-operative studies institutes (e.g. Zeitschrift für das gesamte Genossenschaftswesen, annual bibliography) (→ *Periodicals, Co-operative*) provide information for descriptions of individual countries; organizations provide statistical overviews (e.g. Association of Cooperative Banks of the EC, Brussels (→ *European Community*); → *International Co-operative Alliance*, London; → *World Council of Credit Unions*, Madison/Wisconsin, USA; → *International Raiffeisen Union*, Neuwied, Germany; Confédération Internationale du Crédit Populaire, Paris).

Benecke, Dieter/Eschenburg, Rolf: Las Cooperativas en América Latina, Sao Leopoldo 1987.
Benecke, Dieter/Eschenburg, Rolf: Genossenschaften in Lateinamerika, in: ZfgG, vol. 38 (1988), pp. 105–118.
Croteau, John T.: The Economics of the Credit Union, Detroit 1963.
Draheim, Georg: Die Genossenschaft als Unternehmungstyp, 2nd edition, Göttingen 1955.
Dülfer, Eberhard: Betriebswirtschaftslehre der Kooperative, Göttingen 1984.
Hämke, Kerstin/Kievelitz, Uwe: Traditionelle kreditgenossenschaftliche Systeme in Ländern der Dritten Welt und ihr entwicklungspolitisches Potential, in: ZfgG, vol. 37 (1987), pp. 310–321.
Hahn, Oswald: Die Unternehmensphilosophie einer Genossenschaftsbank, Tübingen 1980.
Hahn, Oswald: Struktur der Bankwirtschaft, 2nd edition, Berlin 1989.
Hahn, Oswald: Die klassische Raiffeisenbank: Die Dorfbank als Nostalgie oder Notwendigkeit?, Nürnberg 1986.

Co-operatives under Public Law

BERNHARD GROSSFELD; CORNELIUS RENKEN [F]

(see also: *Classification*; *Legal Form, Co-operative*; *Law, International*; *History in 19th C.*)

I. Introduction; II. Terminology; III. Diversity of Functions.

I. Introduction

There are many organizations which are called co-operatives under public law (→ *Classification*). For a number of these the designation as co-operatives results from the language of the statute, e.g. for hunting co-operatives. For others their classification as co-operatives under public law is clear, even though the statute does not say so, e.g. for water and land associations, associations for the consolidation of landholdings, chambers of commerce, and craftsguilds. There is no uniform concept of the co-operative under public law. It can be similar to a co-operative under private law (→ *Legal Form, Co-operative*), but it can also be so different that there is hardly any similarity at all. Whether an association is a co-operative under public law can often be established only in the individual case. Therefore it is preferable to call them corporations under public law with co-operative elements (cf. II. 2. d) below).

II. Terminology

1. Public Law and Co-operative

The essence of the co-operative idea is the joining together of persons into an association for the purpose of mutual aid. → *Otto von Gierke* distinguished between co-operatives in a narrow sense and those in a wider sense. Among the former he saw all corporations of German common law based upon free associations and with legal personality. As co-operatives in a wider sense he considered all associations with additional characteristics determining their structure, thus including the state and local communities. Parallel to the changing concept of the corporation in the 19th century (→ *History in 19th C.*), state and local communities ceased to be part of the traditional co-operative. But some corporations under public law continued to be called co-operatives. Today the co-operative under public law is generally considered as a special corporation under public law. The corporation under public law brings a group together that has to implement special public functions through its corporate form (*Quadflieg*). This historical background explains why certain types of public corporations are called co-operatives under public law.

2. Corporation under Public Law

a) Corporation

Under German law so-called "legal persons" can have rights and duties. Legal persons can be associations, established to last indefinitely and to be independent of any changes in membership, and other organizations for a specific function on a long-term basis. Co-operatives are associations of persons which form a legal entity, and are not impaired by any changes in individual membership (*Wolff/Bachof/Stober*, §84 II 1 a). Associations of this kind are typical corporations.

b) Public Law

Whether a corporation is considered to be under private law or under public law is determined by the manner in which it is established. The corporation under private law comes into being through a private act which determines the existence, legal form, and the character as a legal person (*Flume*, I/2). The corporation under public law, on the other hand, comes into being through governmental action. The governmental act establishing such a corporation is a statute of parliament or an administrative act based on a statute. Thus, a hunting co-operative comes into existence directly by virtue of a statute, the Federal Hunting Law (§ 9 BJagdG), whereas a craftsguild comes into existence only when its → *by-laws* are approved by the competent public authority.

c) Further Characteristics

An essential characteristic of the corporation under public law is its governmental function, in particular the power to use compulsory measures. That does not mean, however, that all its activities are actually governmental acts. It is enough that these measures are at the corporation's disposal (*Forsthoff*) (→ *State and Co-operatives, Market Economy*).
Another characteristic of the corporation under public law and therefore of the co-operative under public law is governmental supervision. Of course, co-operatives under private law are also subject to some governmental supervision. But only where there is an all-inclusive legal supervision, extending beyond the limits of general governmental supervision over associations, we find a public corporation and a co-operative under public law (cf. *Fortshoff, Wolff/Bachof/Stober*, § 84 IV 2 e).

d) Definition

A public corporation is therefore "an association under public law, organized on the basis of membership and capable of possessing legal rights, which has governmental functions and public authority under government supervision" (*Forsthoff*, p. 491). For historical reasons, corporations with co-operative structure are called co-operatives under public law. The term is somewhat unclear, however, and should therefore be used with caution (*Mändle* is apparently of a different opinion). Since public law is the core, it would be better to speak of corporations under public law with co-operative characteristics.

3. Other Characteristics

There are two features which are usually pointed out as co-operative characteristics for corporations under public law:
- position of members
- implementation of special function.

a) Position of Members

Every public corporation exists on the basis of membership. Membership in a corporation can have various aspects. Corporations with a co-operative structure are oriented around occupational, economic or social aspects. Whether membership is voluntary or obligatory makes no difference (→ *Group, the Co-operative*).

An important question, however, is whether membership is structured in a co-operative sense. This is the case when all members have the right to exert immediate influence on the affairs of the organizations, either by electing the board of directors or by voting in an assembly (*Quadflieg; Klein*). The decisive criterion is whether the members make the fundamental decisions directly or at least indirectly through the election of executive or supervisory boards (*Forsthoff; Quadflieg*) (→ *Organizational Structure of Societies*).

b) Special Functions

The modern private co-operatives which started around the middle of the 19th century promoted self-help and self-administration for less affluent population groups (small farmers, craftsmen). They wanted and want to assist their members through a joint business enterprise.

The public corporation with co-operative features follows this pattern. It is created when there are certain public functions which can be implemented by common action and which cannot be left to the chance of private action. The legal form of a corporation under public law may be chosen for public functions only. A function is considered public if the public has an interest in its fulfillment (*Peters*). Because of the difficulty in defining the term more exactly, the Federal Constitutional Court has left the decision as to whether a particular function is a public function or not to the discretion of the legislature (Decisions of the Federal Constitutional Court, BVerfGE 10, 89 (102); 38, 281 (297)). If a specific public function needs implementation, the legislature may create the legal basis for a corporation under public law with co-operative attributes.

The particular purpose of a public corporation must be laid down in the statute. This statute, together with the by-laws of the corporation, is the constitution of the association; it creates and limits the association's functions. The advantage of the association under public law is that membership may be compulsory and that aims of the association can be enforced. In contrast to private associations, the constitution of public corporations can, if the statute grants such power, even bind non-members. The disadvantage, however, is that acts of the corporation are only valid if they are within the limits of the purpose. Other measures are *ultra vires* and automatically invalid (Decision of the German Federal Supreme Court in Civil Cases, BGHZ 20, 119 (122 ss.); also *Wolff/Bachof/Stober*, § 97 I 4).

An essential characteristic of the public corporation with a co-operative structure is the fact that it has specific public functions. It serves the public function and the private interests of its members at the same time. There is at least partially an identity of private and public interests; the pursuit of the one will benefit the other (*Köttgen*; *Quadflieg*). However, there are nowadays attempts to destroy this identity of interest: water and land associations are used as instruments for nature preservation; public interest and membership interests may then conflict with each other (cf. the report *Bericht der Forschungsgesellschaft für Genossenschaftswesen an der Universität Münster* 1989).

III. Diversity of Functions

Legislation has conferred a variety of functions on co-operatively structured corporations under public law. Some of these functions will be presented here briefly (cf. the listing in *Wolff/Bachof/Stober*, § 98 III).

1. Occupational Co-operative

An occupational risk co-operative provides industrial accident insurance for employees under the social security programme law. It pays compensation whenever an employee suffers an accident at or on the way to his work place. In addition, the co-operative tries to reduce work accidents through preventive measures (cf. Insurance Regulations of the German Empire RVO, § 537). Every enterprise in the area covered by the occupational risk co-operative must be a member (RVO, § 658).

2. Water and Land Associations

The legal basis of water and land associations is still the First Water Association Regulation of the German Empire of September 3, 1937, which was based on the Water Association Law of 1937. The association must improve the agricultural production, regulate water resources, secure the water supply, and provide for sewage disposal. To this may be added the protection of certain land against flooding (dike associations) and the safety of waterways. Every landowner who has to maintain natural water resources must join the water and land association. The association handles this responsibility partially or entirely on behalf of its members.

3. Hunting Co-operative

According to the Federal Hunting Statute (BJagdG, §§ 7, 8, and 9), in conjunction with the hunting statutes of the federal states, all landowners whose grounds are too small for hunting rights and obligations must join a hunting co-operative (cf. BJagdG, § 7); the co-operative takes over these rights and obligation (BJagdG, § 10).

4. Fishery Co-operative

Fishery co-operatives come into existence through state statutes. In Northrhine-Westphalia, for example, all fishing rights within a community, are united to a single fishing district. All holders of fishing rights within the district form a fishing co-operative, that jointly manages and utilizes the available fishing waters.

5. Forestry Co-operative

The formation of a forestry co-operative may be compulsory as a matter of state law (cf. § 4 ss. of Forestry Statute of Northrhine-Westphalia). A forestry co-operative has to manage the forests of its members according to a common plan in the interest of the forest owners and of the forest area in general. Everybody who owns or has a right to utilize forest in a certain area must be a member of a forestry co-operative.

6. Association for the Consolidation of Landholders

The formation of associations of participants to help execute land consolidation schemes can be compulsory, according to the Land Consolidation Statute (FlurbG, §§ 1 and 16). According to § 1, these associations are to promote agricultural and forestry production and to contribute to proper land utilization and land development in general. The method used is a planned redistribution of landholdings. Every owner of agricultural or forest land in a certain area must, according to §§ 10.1 and 16 of the statute, become a participant in or member of the respective association.

7. Chambers of Industry and Commerce

§ 1.1 of the Statute of Industry and Commerce (IHKG) lays down that these chambers have to support affiliated enterprises. All individuals and associations who carry on a commercial activity in the area of the chamber must be members (IHKG, § 2.1; cf. the comprehensive investigation by *Irriger*).

8. Chambers of Handicrafts and Craftsguilds

Craftsguilds, according to the Handicraft Regulation Act (HandwO, §§ 54.1.1 and 54.4) are to serve the interests of their members. Members are always self-employed craftsmen of one craft or at least similar crafts that are technically and economically closely related (HandwO, § 52.1). Membership is voluntary – an exception among corporations of public law (cf. HandwO, § 58.1). Every craftsman, however, who meets the requirements for membership has a right to be accepted as a member (HandwO, § 58.3).
In Chambers of Handicraft, however, membership is compulsory; all craftsmen and owners of similar businesses in a particular district are automatically affiliated (cf. HandwO, § 90.2). These chambers serve the interest of the craft and mediate between individual craftsmen and their organizations (HandwO, §§ 90 and 91.1; here again cf. *Irriger*).

Bibliography

Flume, Werner: Allgemeiner Teil des Bürgerlichen Rechts, vol. 1, part 2, Die juristische Person, Berlin 1983.
Forsthoff, Ernst: Lehrbuch des Verwaltungsrechts, vol. 1, Allgemeiner Teil, 10th ed., München 1973.
Gierke, Otto von: Deutsches Genossenschaftsrecht, vol. 1, Berlin 1968, Reprint Graz 1954.
Irriger, Ulrich: Genossenschaftliche Elemente bei öffentlich-rechtlichen Körperschaften – dargestellt am Beispiel der Industrie- und Handelskammern und der Handwerksorganisationen, Thesis Münster 1992.
Klein, Friedrich/Berlin H.: Die Fischereigenossenschaften in der Bundesrepublik Deutschland und ihre steuerliche Behandlung, in: ZfgG 13 (1963), p.197.
Klein, Friedrich/Leidel, H.: Die Jagdgenossenschaften in der Bundesrepublik Deutschland und ihre steuerliche Behandlung, in: ZfgG 12 (1962), p.1.
Klein, Friedrich/Leidel, H.: Wassergenossenschaften und Wasserverbandsrecht, in: ZfgG 10 (1960), p.1.
Klein, Friedrich/Scheder, T.: Die Waldgenossenschaften in der Bundesrepublik Deutschland und ihre steuerliche Behandlung, in: ZfgG 17 (1967), p.241.
Klein, Friedrich: Die Genossenschaften des öffentlichen Rechts, in: ZfgG 7 (1957), p. 145.
Köttgen, A.: Die rechtsfähige Verwaltungseinheit, in: VerwArch 1939, p.1.
Mändle, Eduard: Zur Frage des genossenschaftlichen Charakters öffentlich-rechtlicher Genossenschaften, Archiv für öffentliche und freigemeinnützige Unternehmen, vol. 12 (1989), p. 219.
Peters, Hans: Öffentliche und staatliche Aufgaben, in: Festschrift für Hans Carl Nipperdey zum 70. Geburtstag, vol.2, Berlin 1965, p.877.
Quadflieg, Friedrich: Die Teilnehmergemeinschaft nach dem Flurbereinigungsgesetz v. 14.7.1953 als Genossenschaft des öffentlichen Rechts, Stuttgart 1967.
Schulin, Bertram: Sozialrecht, 3rd ed., Düsseldorf 1989.
Wolff/Bachof/Stober: Verwaltungsrecht II, 5th ed., München 1987.

Cooperativismo Sanitario (Health care co-operativism)

SALVADOR MUSSONS

(see also: *Health Care System*; *Social Policy*; *Classification*)

I. Public Health Care Systems: Social Security; II. Health Care Co-operativism; III. Conclusions.

I. Public Health Care Systems: Social Security

1. Overview

The main role of health care systems is nowadays held by the State, who sets the rules, and directly or indirectly controls the funding of health expenditures. The State decides, and doctors follow the established views (→ *Health Care System*). State-controlled Medicine, as a notion, is feasible during periods of economical growth; when said growth slowdowns or disapperars, it is necessary to reduce costs, and this results in limitation or elimination of the most expensive items, and the appearance of waiting lists, both for certain analysis and for hospital availability of beds. The public sector is as dehumanized as a very big company, and for sure, amongst the many problems it must face, the economical one is not only the most serious one, but as well very difficult to handle, since health care expenditures, anticyclical as all social costs are increasingly higher.

Welfare State is currently undergoing a crisis. The notion according to which a public system can protect people from birth to death, has been dropped long ago, not for ideological but for economical reasons, since the cost of bureaucracy is higher than the costs of services provided (*Morgas*). The health care division of Social Security, belonging to the public sector, which results in bureaucracy, operative inefficiency and stagnation, has tried to cover endless requirements with limited resources, a problem which has arisen in most developed countries.

The performance of the public health care system gives place to both hope and despair, since whatever decisions are made today, will shape the future situation. Health policies must deal with life, suffering and death, as well as with those methods created by western societies to face these issues.

2. Social Security and the European Economic Community (European Union)

Social Security may be considered as the major European concern, considered as such by the community itself, which has officially stated this global problem (→ *European Community*). Though admitting that each country, owing to its peculiar socio-economical situation, has distinctive features, the different systems aim at similar goals; but means, services and/or methods employed are different.

All of the systems provide for illness, motherhood, unemployment, accidents, labour resulting diseases, family coverage, disablement, old age and death; nevertheless, management systems differ; funding also differs, budget percentages allotted to social security are also different. The truth is that Social Security expenditures have grown out of proportion in Europe, and both unemployment and pensions disbursements are frightening; medical expenditures are enormous and it is increasingly difficult to find public resources to cover all these needs. The States' possibilities of facing this increasing expenditures growth is becoming slowly reduced to good intentions. Therefore, it is necessary to reconsider the ideology that promotes growth for the sake of growth itself.

The positive effects of this huge expenditure effort aimed at maintaining Social Security achievements cannot be discussed; nevertheless, we believe that regarding health, Health Care Co-operativism, *cooperativismo sanitario* (→ *Classification*), might help, either as a complement or a replacement, since it implies change, and it can provide motivation and effectiveness.

The current crisis in *Spain*, and the attempts to revamp Social Security, is no exception amongst European countries. Though admitting the socio-economical differences mentioned above, the common background results in a likewise overall crisis of Social Security itself.

3. Brief Analysis of Social Security Crisis

Our analysis is based on three major issues:

First, Social Security systems were in no case created "ex ovo", but on the basis of preexisting social insurance systems which conditioned the new social Security regulations. Some countries managed to work out better solutions to such a complex change, but all in all, resulting systems have a poor rationale, since logical conclusions have not been easy to achieve, and problems have always arisen from political or private convenience. All of them resulted in systems which had to be gradually modified, hoping for a better final outcome, which in many cases has not been totally achieved, weighing on the overall situation of Social Security.

Second, the group of factors which result in this crisis and shape its further evolution, are common to all European countries. The said crisis is indoubtedly the outcome of the economic crisis of the seventies. Social security arose and developed during a period of full employment and high economic growth. Its generally accepted major goals were full coverage of all of the population, provision for those who had to drop their work either due to disease, disablement or age, income levels similar to those of fully employed people.

The ongoing economic growth could smoothly cover

the increasing expenditures of social coverage. The economic crisis at first slowed down and then limited economic growth; it reduced the availability of resources to face social coverage costs; persisting mass unemployment, which not only increases the needs for coverage, but also reduces income provided by sharply reduced employed population, and companies' difficulties to take charge of greater contributions, has forced a debate to decide whether the originally developed and globally accepted Social Security model, is still adequate in face of current needs. The *third* issue refers to demographic evolution. Birthrate fall has been very sharp in Europe. On the other hand, the increase of life expectancy jointly lead to the increasing ageing of working population, which in turn increases dependent rates; according to 1985 data, the latter amounted to 12% in Spain, to 13.8% in Belgium, to 14.8% in Germany, 21.2% in Netherlands, 15.1% in United Kingdom and 12.9% in Italy and France. Population ageing is one of the most important social and economic phenomena of the end of this century and the beginning of the next. The said phenomenon, which affects all European countries, clearly shows that governments by themselves will not be able to cope with the problem.

According to a survey on quantitative aspects of old age, developed by the Ministry of Welfare in Spain, in 2010 population over 60 years of age will amount to some 8.35 million people, over a fifth part of overall population (Health care forecast). Relating the increase in the number of pensioned people with a higher life expectancy and a simultaneous improvement of their life standards is not an easy problem, neither for present nor future governments of EEC member countries.

Birthrate fall in all European countries is obviously another very important problem. Indeed, children being born nowadays in western Europe will reach their retirement in a peculiar social environment, since overall population will have decreased, and the number of aged people will double those under 20 years of age. Experts state that young parents must be guaranteed the necessary resources to be able to upbring several children; that is, in view of unheard of fall suffered by birthrate, family aid is an urgent and compulsory issue.

4. Ways of Possible Restructuring Social Security

In spite of some local differences, this crisis is affecting all European countries, though none has globally restructured the Social Security System. It is still generally considered that urgency services must be maintained, while trying to develop an ideal formula adapted to present times, or understanding that it is necessary to develop a new Social Security model which reduces coverage to a minimum, leaving complementary coverage to the private sector. This problem reaches beyond the decisions made by individual countries, becoming a global European Economic Community debate, bearing in mind that though the issue is urgent, it must be dealt with very carefully.

Even though a EEC regulation will not offer a global solution, it can clarify issues regarding replacement, reprivatisation or correction of present systems, a solution some sectors consider necessary for the sake of peace, in order to achieve a uniform community Social Security system. Possible corrections could imply privatisation measures regarding health care, as well as complementary pensions, and possibly a certain restriction of the level of social expenditures. In brief, quoting the President of France, "... obviously Social Security implies an expenditure, but its existence, maintenance and development must be paid for". The truth is that a health care model must be defined to be able to act accordingly. It has been adequately stated that "... we should not accept an increasing influence of the State on the medical field, on the basis of social considerations". (*Ernst Jünger*).

II. Health Care Co-operativism – Cooperativismo Sanitario

We truly believe that the chance of overcoming the current health care sector Social Security crisis basically lies in being socially innovative and politically daring, since economic restrictions are hindering the promotion of social issues, affecting social welfare frameworks. This undeniable fact probably implies a challenge to change towards a new social stage whereby certain groups take on the responsibility of participating for their own and consequently the overall community's benefit.

Regarding these notions, Dr. *José Espriu* has wisely conceived, promoted and developed a new concept of social or collective medicine, structured on the basis of wider-ranging cooperation, aimed at the undeniable fact that an ill person must always have the right of not only receiving adequate attention, from a technical and scientific point of view, but the same humanitarian care rendered to a private patient, in full obeyance of professional ethics, and because of its undoubted therapeutic value.

1. Principles of Health Care Co-operativism

The principles which, legally structured, shape health care co-operativism may be briefly stated as follows:

a) Unquestioned admission of every doctor applying for admittance, free from all possible discrimination.
b) Service and not profit oriented economic policy.
c) Admittance within a solidary, democratic and responsible framework, implying full participation of all those self-willingly entering this self-managed system. That is, true democracy within a co-operative structure, which in turn protects democracy itself.

d) Allocation of possible profits to improve services, or increase medical fees, or benefit existing welfare institutions.

Dr. *Espriu's* basic goals, which are truly far-reaching, clearly perceived the existence of users as a similarly powerful group to that represented by doctors, and which could by no means be disregarded. Indeed, his goals were clear and strict: preserving both doctors' professional image and patients as human beings, both included in peculiar self-managed system, since health care co-operativism, free from commercial interests, is solely concerned with providing sound, satisfactory and responsible health care. This is true both for those who provide and those who receive the services, allowing patients to recover the elementary right to choose a doctor at all levels, and to have a private room while being at hospital, and the equivalent right of being paid for each professional service rendered.

This basic principle regarding free choice, applying both to doctors and patients, implies the elimination of all intermediation between these two main members, doctors and patients, thus safeguarding their dignity, as the focal point of a new kind of health care organisation. Indeed, public health cannot be affected by profit seeking investments, since such and exacting and qualified matter as aiding the ill and caring for the healthy, can be submitted to no profit expectation whatsoever. This field of social economy must adapt itself to common benefit goals.

2. Co-operative Health Care Co-management

Over thirty years ago, *Espriu*, following his notions, set up a health care co-operative system, which started in Barcelona, and later extended throughout Spain, though at first with no legal acknowledgement. Nowadays it includes medical producers' co-operatives (→ *Classification*); user co-operatives which manage their own health care facilities, and family health care co-operatives which accept both doctors and patients as members; the whole of these modalities is what according to *Espriu* we call health care co-operativism.

These different co-operatives, while keeping their independent management, merge at a higher level into a second degree co-operative, which unifies the group shaping a co-management health care system, which owing to its drive and solidarity is a full example of a truly free notion of human beings (→ *Solidarity*). Health care co-management is fully embodied at this second degree level, since shared management enables the merging of separate co-operative interests into common interests. It aims at achieving a unity, based on the specific features of each of the different co-operatives, which keep their independent management, but abide with the criteria and goals of this higher level group in charge of providing unity to the diverse components (→ *Managerial Economics*).

Health care co-management has been and will continue to be the core of health care co-operativism, as a responsible and fully participative attitude (→ *Workers Co-determination*), in defense of freedom and democracy within a highly important field such as health: a very gratifying co-managed health system. Health care co-operativism could be thus defined as an innovative organisation, which excludes business profit as a goal, and provides for common needs within individual freedom. It thus becomes a health care co-managed system where all members are involved in the cooperation: doctors and users, with equal rights and duties; democratic particpation which comes true specially through a co-operative framework, having freedom interwoven into the co-operative pattern.

The co-operative health care system synthesizes features of both individual and social health care; it is at the same time centered on the community and on the individual person. Its basis is the individual human being, its attitude is social; it thus perfectly suits the co-operative framework.

3. Health Care Co-operativism: Facts

The following co-operatives are the embodiment of this health care system:

1. *"Autogestio Sanitaria"*, a medical producers' co-operative is located in the city and province of Barcelona, includes 4,207 doctors, providing health care to over 200,000 people, members of the users' co-operative. In full agreement with Dr. *Espriu*, we believe that a Social or collective medicine requires not just improving the best features of public health care, but taking advantage of *health care co-operativism*, since in spite of excluding business profits as a goal, it has the possibility of offering individual coverage, and renders the same importance both to doctors and to users of health care services.

2. *"SCIAS-Barcelona, Sociedad Cooperativa de Instalaciones Asistenciales Sanitarias'"*, is a users co-operative, which having received no external funding whatsoever has created its own hospital, the "Hospital de Barcelona", with 367 individual rooms and the most advanced technology equipment. This users co-operative is aimed at eliminating the inefficiency and slacks of the state system, as well as the business profit goal of other private health care systems. Thanks to its members it has reduced the costs of hospital attention, benefitting its users. Dr. *Espriu* decided to create this hospital in view of the lack of available quality hospital rooms. Through the SCIAS co-operative, members are not only the owners of the hospital, but they have as well a right to participate at the second degree level in the improvement of

their own health care, both within and outside their hospital.

a) Co-operative committees

Considering the special case of Barcelona, where co-operativism has greatly developed, and always following *Espriu's* concern over participation, these co-operative committees were created to group members according to their residence. These committees are in turn grouped by the General assembly and the Ruling Council. They consult with and advise the said council, informing their local members, who can inversely offer as many suggestions as they wish. They strengthen at the same time co-operativism, fostering co-operative and health care training amongst members through adequate courses; therefore, information reaches all members of the co-operative.

b) Co-operative hospital

As it is centered in the individual human being, SCIA's Hospital de Barcelona has a limited number of members, to preserve the quality of medical services, because of members' regional residence location, and because decentralization is an obliged requirement, since macro-structures and macro-economics are quite unsuitable for co-operativism as they lead to bureaucracy, massification and dehumanisation, all of which must be avoided by all means. As for the premises themselves, the Hospital de Barcelona is located on the city's most important avenue, it covers 43,996 square meters and it has twenty floors, three of which are underground.

Its operative scheme is basically structured along assistance areas, diagnoses and therapies areas and catering and maintenance areas.

The distribution of individual rooms is as follows:
17th. Floor Hemodialysis (8beds)

16th	„	Psychiatric Unit	16
15th	„	Surgery	16
14th	„	„	30
13th	„	„	30
12th	„	„	30
11th	„	„	30
10th	„	„	30
9th	„	„	30
8th	„	Paedriatic Unit	16
8th	„	Prematures (20 beds)	
7th	„	General Practice	22
6th	„	„	30
5th	„	„	30
4th	„	Obstetric Unit 27 Nursery (40 beds)	
3rd	„	Obstetric and Gynecologic Unit	30
2nd	„	Intensive care (10 beds) Coronaries Unit (6 beds)	

Total number of individual rooms	367
Total number of beds	451

3. *"SINERA"*, families health care co-operative, being presently developed, accepts both doctors and users as members. In most EEC countries, social Security health care is mainly based on the public hospitals network, and the traditional role of the family doctor has been replaced by a dehumanized technolgy which is very often inadaquately employed. This co-operative aims at achieving a complete direct health care preventive and communitarian assistance, promoting as well a health care and co-operative training for its members. The development of first aids care undoubtedly reduces the need for later treatment demanding more expensive hospital assistance and more sophisticated technological resources.

4. *"Lavina"*, is another medical producers' co-operative, offering countrywide coverage, which has over 22,000 doctor members throughout Spain, servicing approximately one million people.

5. Other SCIAS's co-operative societies

Other health care users' co-operatives have been created in Spain following Barcelona's SCIAS example. They are presently "co-operativizing" the following already existing facilities:

SCIAS

Sevilla	–	Santa Isabel clinic	118 beds
MURCIA	–	Ntra.Sra. de Belén clinic	80 „
Albacete	–	Ntra.Sra. del Rosario clinic	31 „
Granada	–	Ntra.Inmaculad Concepcion – clinic	131 „
Huelva	–	Los Naranjos clinic	17 „
Badajoz	–	Ntra.Sra. de Guadalupe clinic	63 „
Málaga	–	El Angel clinic	120 „
Alicante	–	S. Carlos clinic	32 „

SCIAS Madrid has already acquired the piece of land to build a 250 bed clinic. More SCIAS projects are either already under way or being planed in other Spanish provinces.

6. Second degree co-operativism

The development of this co-operative health care system has implied effort and sacrifice, all the more noteworthy since insurance co-operativism (→ *Insurance, Germany*) has not been legally acknowledged in Spain until recently, so great amounts of strong will and imagination were required to achieve the same co-operative goal via indirect insurance procedures (→ *Insurance, North America*).

Integrating different co-operatives, this system sets up at first a levelled solidarity (→ *Solidarity*) amongst them, and a further inclusion in the higher second degree level. Therefore, integration goes beyond the first co-operative level to expand at the widest level of the health care co-operative movement. This principle of integration (→ *Structural Types*) is the tool which can turn health care co-operativism into the great democratic solution for health care, since it takes on the responsibility of caring for collective needs within individual freedom.

Health care co-operatives follow the line of what is already known in Europe as the "new cooperation", which implies employing the co-operative method in unusual or unheard of socio-economical fields (→ *New Co-operatives*). Solutions offered by health care co-operativism to the real need for health care regarding common diseases and everyday accidents, through co-operative self and co-managed means, has been truly positive, showing real social usefulness and financial efficiency.

As in all other fields, health care co-operativism is a self-willing and democratic popular organisation, which structures a new Social or Collective Medicine notion. This view carries out a double function, as health care provider, and at an economical level, withing a self-managed framework, which implies obvious financial advantages, since doctors set their own fees. This, on the one hand levels the system, on the other hand it is also levelled by users themselves, since through this co-operative system they cannot only create their own health care facilities, but also control the actual use of medical services, enabling the due correction of inadequate or deviated consumption.

7. Montepio de Previsión Social

Espriu founded the first health care co-operativism "Montepio", setting up a retirement system at 70 years of age, which allows a continued professional practice. He afterwards created the "Grupo Especial de Vida", to benefit a member's family upon his/her death. Furthermore, he set up a life insurance which benefits impaired children of the deceased member. LAVINIA, the countrywide medical producers' co-operative has created the second "Montepio de Previsión Social" which offers services similar to those above mentioned.

8. Computer services

Maintaining service excellence is a daily challenge, because of constantly increasing needs, complexities and costs. One of the key factors to achieve this goal lies in information availability, quality and updating. Computer networks fulfill the needs of all important organisations (→ *Data Processing*), whereby this division has also been created, to service not only the management areas, but within the co-operative hospital itself, where software has been duly adapted to make them quicker, wider and more profitable.

9. Gabinete de Estudios y Promoción del coperativismo Sanitario (Health Care Co-operativism Research and Promotion Department)

The "AUTOGESTIO SANITARIA", SCIAS Barcelona and "LAVINIA" co-operative, following Dr. *Espriu's* suggestion, fostered the set up of this "Gabinete", which includes different experts devoted to researching this very specific subject of health care co-operativism along its many by-ways. Furthermore, it also carries out a task of co-operative training and education are basic to co-operativism itself (→ *Education, Europe etc.*). At the beginning, the "Gabinete" had to work out adequate legislation, since owing to its novelty, health care co-operativism had no legal coverage: insurance co-operativism itself has only recently been properly regulated.

This legal promotion has been partly achieved thanks to Dr. *Espriu's* drive and reputation (→ *Law, National*; → *Law, International*). Regarding other fields, it has also promoted the formation of users co-operatives, and has organized seminars, workshops and courses at the Universidad Politécnica de Madrid, and the Universidad Complutense de Somosaguas. It has as well participated in national health care and co-operativism meetings, paying due attention to international relations. Another important task carried out by the "Gabinete" has undoubtedly been that of editing its own publications, which are distributed free of charge references.

It is worth mentioning that in view of the social and health care importance of health care co-operativism, Banco de Santander summons an annual contest, the "Premio José Espriu", which awards a Pesetas two million prize. Coordinated by "LAVINIA" co-operative, this prize is awarded to the author or authors who best contribute to health care co-operativism, including all possible research fields (legal, economic, sociologic, medical, health care, management, etc.) which may positively add to this activity.

10. Fundación Espriu

In spite of Dr. *Espriu's* unwillingness, because of his lack of self-compliance, the groups of doctors and users which partake of health care co-operativism have created a foundation which bears his name, to render due respects and hommage to the founder of such a peculiar health care system, and to look after his achievements.

Besides carrying out co-operative and cultural activities, this foundation obviously is concerned with continued research and promotion of health care co-operativism, whereby the Gabinete de Estudios y Promoción del Cooperativismo Sanitario, while maintaining its original goals, has been absorbed by the foundation which has a farther reaching services range.

Amongst the foundation's activities, including those now pertaining to the "Gabinete", it is specially worth mentioning that it plans setting up its own training school. Indeed, in view of the many different co-operatives included by our system, the school will, on one hand take care of the health care and co-operative training of our users' co-operatives' members, aimed at an active participation in health care co-operativism. On the other hand, it will dedicate its greatest efforts to the members of medical producers' co-operatives, to promote its solidarian ideology as it is displayed in everyday co-operative health care practice, management training and medical training updating.

As any other kind of cooperation, health care co-operativism must be understood as a life experience, and the foundation must aim at promoting this system on the basis of its essential features, contributing to a true interaction between the social environment and co-operative everyday facts.

11. International Projection

Our peculiar health care co-operative system has drawn great attention from international renowned representatives of the health care field, wanting detailed information on our structural framework, and wishing to visit our co-operative Hospital de Barcelona. Thanks to suggestions received from the said visitors, we have introduced our movement at different international cooperation meetings, where it has been most positively received. So much so, that it is being presently studied in different American countries, including Canada, in spite of their deeply rooted public health care system, and several Central and South American countries, in which public Social Security is highly inefficient.

In *Brazil*, for instance, the Confederacion de Cooperativas Médicas (medical co-operatives' confederation), is starting to set up the essential user participation, by means of the building of its own hospital in the city of Sao Paulo. Our movement has had great acceptance in *Colombia*, and the cities of Medellín and Bogota are launching co-operative health care systems, according to the original Spanish model, based on users-doctors co-management. Furthermore, the Ministry of Energy and Mining in Peru is considering the possibility of servicing the mining sector with this system, which might be afterwards extended to the global Social Security system. Many other medical co-operatives in South America are likewise proceeding to modify their structures and management according to our model.

We believe that the innovative character of our health care co-operativism must be duly acknowledged, because of its fast and steady acceptance throughout Spain, and its wide international recognition, because of the quality of its services, the equalitarian participation of services' users and providers, for leveling care demand and available resources, achieving a high resource effectiveness. Also for promoting an adequate agreement regarding health care provided through public funds. For speeding up the decision-making process, for its responsible and independent management, and for the number of members it has collected, in a totally popular, democratic and self-willing manner.

We should point out that the system renders better results within the co-operative than within the public sector. We, therefore, believe in the need for a close collaboration between both sectors, which would as well put an end to present forceful double user payments: social security payments and private payments.

III. Conclusions

In view of increasing health care costs, deep demographic changes, social changes, and technical-medical advances. Public health care systems should be revised and modified, taking advantage of all public and private resources, to proceed afterwards to their due incorporation to the National Health System. Owing to public sector inefficiencies, society as a whole must try to satisfy its health care needs by way of private entities, which results in the above mentioned double payments.

It must be understood that the state cannot possibly take care of everything, even when it is responsible for the financial and legal organisation of social services. The German system is particularly interesting since it is a mixed system, public-private, which offers a truly effective equilibrium.

Bibliography

Publications by the Gabinete de Estudios y Promoción del Cooperativismo Sanitario:

1st Meeting on Health Care and co-operativism, 1982, Zaragoza, Collected papers and communications.

2nd. Meeting on Health Care and co-operativism, 1982, Madrid, Collected papers and communications.

3rd, Meeting on Health Care and co-operativism, Sevilla, 1984, Collected papers and communications.

4th. Meeting on Health Care and co-operativism. 1st. Meeting on Users health care co-operativism, Barcelona, collected papers and communications.

5th. Meeting on Health care and co-operativism. 2nd. Meeting on Users health care co-operativism, Madrid, 1986, collected papers and communications.

6th. Meeting on health care and Co-operativism. Second degree co-operativism, Santander, 1987, collected papers.

7th. Meeting on Health care and Co-operativism. Health care co-operativism and a National Health Care System, Madrid, 1988, collected papers and communications.

8th. Meeting on health care and co-operativism. Member participation, Barcelona, 1990, collected papers and communications.

Alexander, Philippe and Delors, Jacques: En sortir ou pas, Paris 1985, Ed. by Grasset.

Alonso Soto, Francisco: El Cooperativismo sanitario en la nueva Ley General de Cooperativas, Revista Sanidad y Economia Social, No 4, Madrid, C.I.R.I.E.C.

Alonso Soto, Francisco: La alternativa del cooperativismo sanitario, 1985 Espriu Prize.

Azurmendi, José: El Hombre cooperativo, published by Editorial Caja Laboral Popular, Mondragón 1984.

Ballesteros, Enrique: Economía Social y empresas cooperativas, Madrid 1990, Ed. Alianza Editorial.

Belenes Juarez, R. et al: Estudi comparat dels Sistemes de Seguretat Social, Serveis Nacionals de Salut i Exercici Mèdic al la C.E.E. i a Espanya, published by GAPS, Gabinet d'Assesoria i Promoció de la Salut del Col.legi de Metges de Barcelona, 1981.

Castaño Colomer, Josep: Cooperativismo sanitario integral, 1988 Espriu Prize.
Economic security and insecurity, memorandum presented by the European Institute of Social Security at the 3rd. Conference of European Social Security Ministries, 9–11 December, published by Revista de Seguridad, 1985. Social, No 28. Also published by the Ministry of Labour, 25 Sept. 1989, Cuenca, Universidad Internacional Menendez Pelayo and AECOOP.
Espriu José, et al: Cooperativismo y asistencia sanitaria. 1st. Symposium on free medical insurance health care, Madrid 1979.
Espriu José: Hacia und nueva fórmula de Medicina Social (Cooperativismo sanitario). Lecture at the Barcelona Royal Academy of Medicine, 19 February, 1980, published by ELAIA.
Espriu, José: Cooperativismo sanitario, 1986.
Espriu, José: Cooperativismo y Asistencia Médica, communiation at the Symposium on Health Care Proposals, 8–9 May 1981, Vitoria.
Gutierrez del Alamo, Joaquin: Estudio juridico del cooperativismo sanitario, 1987 Espriu Prize.
Hernandez, Santos: Macrocooperativas y Cooperativismo Sanitario, 1990.
Junger, Ernst: Interview published by "La Vanguardia", 7 November, Barcelona 1989.
Machancoses, Francisco: Las relaciones sanitarias en el cooperativismo de la sanidad, 1987 Espriu Prize nominee.
Minc, Alain: La máquina igualitaria. Crisis en la sociedad del bienestar, Barcelona, 1989, Ed. Planeta.
Moragas, R.: Interview published by "AVUI", Barcelona, 3rd. June, 1990.
Münkner, Hans H.: Principios cooperativos y derecho cooperativo, Marburg 1987, Spanish version.
Mussons, Salvador: La perspectiva del cooperativismo sanitario, presented at the 5th. Meeting on Improvement of Health care Services, 7–8 May, Ed. by EADA (Business School), 1990.
Mussons, Salvador: Sistema público de Seguridad Social y Cogestion Sanitraia Cooperativa, published by Gabinete de Estudios y Promoción del Cooperativismo Sanitario, 1988.
OCDE Report, El Estado Protector en Crisis, published by the Ministry of Labour and social Security, Madrid 1981, 1985.
Previsión Sanitaria magazine, Madrid 8 May 1990.
Rius Mosoll, Ramón: Conversaciones con el Doctor Espriu, 1989 Espriu Prize (in press).
Rius, Ramón: Cooperativisme sanitari, nous camins, noves iniciatives. Lecture published by Revista Cooperació Catalana, No 90, 1988.
Rosembuj, Tulio: Jornadas sobre principios cooperativos, Unión de Cooperativas de Consumidores y Usuarios de España, Madrid 1988.
Rovira, Juan and Vidal, Isabel: Posibilidades de desarrollo del cooperativismo en el sector sanitario español, 1986 Espriu Prize.
Salinas Ramos, Francisco: Temas cooperativos, Nov. 1982, Ed. by Caritas Española 1a.
Schulte, Bernd: La Financiación de la Seguridad social en la Comunidad Europea, Revista de Seguridad social No 38, published by the Ministry of Labour and Social Security, Munich 1988.
Technical meeting on Health Care and Social Security within Autonomous Governments, 1–3 March, published by Departament de Sanitat i Seguretat Social, Generalitat de Catalunya, 1984.
Velarde Fuertes, Juan: El tercer viraje de la Seguridad Social en España (Aportaciones para una reforma desde la perspectiva del gasto), Madrid 1990, Ed. by Instituto de Estudios Económicos.
Velaverde Fuertes, Juan: Glosas sobre la Financiación de los Servicios de Salud, Social Economy, published by Karpos, 1982.
Various publications from Institut per a la Promoció y la Formació Cooperativa del Department de Treball de la Generalitat de Catalunya.

Corporate Culture of Co-operatives

EBERHARD DÜLFER [J]

(see also: *Business Policies*; *Managerial Economics*; *Management in Co-operatives*; *History of Ideas*; *Conceptions, Co-operative*; *Principles*)

I. The Concept of Corporate Culture; II. Corporate Culture in Co-operatives?; III. Co-operative Corporate Culture in the Present Day.

I. The Concept of Corporate Culture

1. The Catalyst for the Discussion about Corporate Culture

The term "corporate culture" is unknown in classic and neo-classic economic theory which attempts to trace entrepreneurial behavior back solely to the rationalistic calculation of costs and revenue typical of homo oeconomicus (→ *Classic/Neo-classic Contributions*). At the same time it is assumed that this model enjoys general, pan-cultural validity; cultural influences are not taken into consideration in such a factoral, theoretical approach. Economic efficiency accordingly results exclusively from the optimal combination of production factors. Even in classic management studies the determining elements are technical, organizational and management-related know-how. *Katz's* approach identifying three types of "management skills" is characteristic of this direction of investigation.

Seen in international comparison at the beginning of the 1980s, American companies appeared by far to be at the head of this pack, a fact empirically confirmed using the comparative management concept conceived by *Farmer/Richman* (1965). This conviction, deeply set as it had been for many years, nonetheless began faltering as American companies found themselves pressured by recent Japanese competition particularly in high technology fields. In 1985, the American business magazine *Business Week* wrote, "America's leading position in each and every electronic market has been eroded; the trends reflect nothing less than a crisis for American hi-tech." 1984 had witnessed the first US deficit in its import-export relations with Japan, and this even in the classic American domain of automobile production. The question thus arose whether a better business methodology existed than that of the Americans.

2. Classic American Contributions to Corporate Culture

In the face of the apparent contradiction to the thesis presented by *Farmer/Richman* the question raised above was taken up by American economists. Inasmuch as the performance results of Japanese production methods were clearly superior to American ones despite their technical-operative similarity, it was realized that something else must play a role – some influential factor rooted in the different culture. The initial publications on the subject of corporate culture, the monographs written by *W.G. Ouchi* (1981) and *Pascale/Athos* (1981), therefore concentrated on these factors. These authors apparently observed varying attitudes and behaviors in operational processes and undertook to describe them in a cultural context, even if their efforts come across as superficial at first.

The term "culture" in this early phase of discussion was still focused on the national environment of the company and oriented around the cultural circle of this environment, exactly how it is understood in normal language use. This could be characterized as the macrolevel method of observing cultural influences on labor and management behavior. In subsequent studies the specific effects of this general culture on the living, working and management conditions were then investigated for individual companies, and these effects were compiled according to particular traits. The term "corporate culture" or "organizational culture" thus emerged as a micro-level manifestation of the respective national culture in individual situations. This manifestation was then however specified to the individual social entity – to the individual company. This is particularly true for the third American classic on this theme, *Deal/Kennedy's* book entitled *Corporate Culture* (1983).

This same approach could already be found, however, in the work of *Pascale/Athos* and their presentation of the *7–S model* of management instruments. These two scientists had developed this model in a project group at McKinsey Consulting, which is the reason behind its propagation as the McKinsey Model in the publications of *Peters/Waterman*. In this model the traditional "hard" management instruments (strategy, structure, management systems) are set in opposition to the so-called "weak" instruments (superior goals, skills, management style, skeleton staff). Their thesis was that Japanese success is traceable to the preference placed on weaker instruments. The emphasis of the observations made by *Deal/Kennedy* on the other hand is on the orientation of co-workers. They formulate the term "hero" to whom they allot central importance for processual efficiency. They expressly do not emphasize charismatic effects but focus rather on particularly involved work behavior.

For the first time the *pratice-oriented* approach comes to light in connection with these two authors, something quite evident in the German translation of the book's title, "Unternehmenserfolg *durch* Unternehmenskultur". The instruments of such a management method are symbols, rituals, company myths, and in particular the communication network within the company itself. *Peters/Waterman's* publication *In Search of Excellence* (1982) was the book which by far enjoyed the greatest success among the American classics on this subject (more than four million copies). This apparently was due above all to the orientation the authors chose for their work: they freed discussion for the first time from direct intercultural comparisons between Japan and America and concentrated solely on comparing "excellent" American companies with less excellent ones. Instead of assuming a strongly defensive/critical angle of observation like other authors, they represent an offensive/optimistic view of management opportunities in the US.

3. Edgar Schein's Contribution

Inasmuch as the basic values analyzed by Peters/Waterman were described even by the authors as "common sense" to the largest part and lacked scientific verification despite their brilliant journalistic style, the question remained unanswered for some time as to what exactly the term "corporate culture" should mean and/or encompass. This question was first addressed in an academic manner in the monographs published by MIT-professor *Edgar Schein*, "Organizational Culture and Leadership" (1985). In this work a systematic methodology was developed for the first time which afforded the term precision and critical review. This systematic approach was based on a three-tiered structure in which the visible "artifacts and creations" of the company derive from only partially perceivable "values", which in turn are derived from wholly invisible/intangible "basic assumptions" which exist only in one's unconscious.

Schein stressed emphatically that organizational culture is not identical with business climate, company philosophy or social relationships. However, all of these phenomena are components of the organizational culture. Schein's derivation of the term "culture" is also particularly plausible. He describes how he encountered the influence of foreign cultures on company structures through his foreign involvement in Europe and Mexico. He determined that the majority of these large-scale international enterprises were able to articulate their own corporate culture which had developed within their companies as well as defend and preserve it on the international level.

They successfully prevailed over foreign cultural influences on the local level. Schein therefore deduces the micro-level terminological use of "corporate culture" from the original macro-level intercultural comparison.

There are of course other derivations, such as the one proposed by *Peters/Waterman*. These authors rely more on sociological theory found in American literature when laying the groundwork for their term "corporate culture". In such literature the "way of life" of certain minority groups or partial social suborders (→ *Informal Co-operatives*) is investigated; as a "subculture" it is set in contrast to the all-embracing national society. Here observed cultural traits serve to characterize a partial number or subgroup of society.

In this context it also becomes clear that the term "culture" is used differently in American English than it is, for example, in German, which more often than not reserves it for macro-cultural use. The most precise formulation of corporate culture interestingly enough can be found in a book published in London back in 1951, *Jaques'* manuscript "The Changing Culture of a Factory": "The culture of the factory is its customary and traditional way of thinking and of doing things, which is shared to a greater or lesser degree by all its members, and which new members must learn and at least partially accept in order to be accepted into service in the firm." (p.251)

4. Methodological Problems

Regardless of efforts to define more precisely the term "corporate" or "organizational culture", complicated methodological questions remained unaddressed. For example, it is difficult to explain how values, value conceptions or ethical norms can be compiled in an empirical manner. Such factors only exist in people's heads and influence individual behavior in ways which cannot be precisely delineated and/or reconstructed. Nonetheless it is necessary from the scientific approach to compile such observations when and if corporate culture is to be investigated as the object of true scientific research. In the meantime it should be well uncontested that this is a relevant phenomenon of human society. The difficulty lies, however, in interpreting observable traits and behaviors and reducing them to determining values and basic assumptions. Attempts are made in the methodological research on this problem to build on such stimuli as the method called "verstehen" introduced by *Max Weber* and to attain substantiated results with the help of particular interview methods ("narrative interview") and theoretical fundaments ("interpretative paradigm").

A further problem arises in the pratice-oriented questions as to the extent corporate culture can be influenced and altered through measures undertaken by management staff. In management literature an overly optimistic position is often assumed which borders on naivety. This in part could be traceable to the concepts put forward by consulting firms. Management personnel exhibiting a large degree of personal magnetism – characterized in the sense of *Max Weber* as charismatic management – can without a doubt influence the value conceptions and behavioral norms of midlevel management staff and co-workers within the company, and in certain situations even vary or modify such conceptions and norms. The composition of the working staff and their interpersonal relationships ultimately determine the degree this is possible and when this could occasion a counter reaction. The formation of subcultures within the company can also subsequently ensue. Whether or not the respective personnel/co-workers hail from a people or nation which in the past had negative experience with state-political efforts to exercise ideological indoctrination could play a role in this connection.

II. Corporate Culture in Co-operatives?

The discussion held world-wide both in science and in practical application concerning the existence and aspects of corporate culture has of course been followed by co-operatives. The question arises in this context whether the concepts and descriptions presented so far are relevant for co-operatives to an equal degree or whether it is possible that a specific corporate and/or organizational culture exists for them.

1. Different Reference Points

Indeed an important difference can be discerned in this matter from the first glance: The American considerations about organizational culture are in reference to the management staff and co-workers present in the respective enterprises. This was a thoroughly remarkable and radical change for American business practise in the 1980s as it reflected an altered view of the company as such. The company in general was understood previously as an institution to attain interest on invested capital and in which one could easily "hire and fire" employees and workers as they were needed. Now, however, the company is conceived as an association of individuals structured with a division of labor and in which human resources represent an essential component of its success. The early scientific concepts put forth by *Cyert* and *Simon/March* which in Europe had been part of classical management schooling for some time were embraced by the Americans at a later point in time. According to this approach corporate culture is the entirety of common value references held by the "organizational participants" (*Simon*).

Among co-operatives throughout the world, however, the *membership group* is the point of departure for the creation of the organization (→ *Group, the Co-operative*) – in contrast to the previous approach. The members found and shoulder the *common business enterprise*, bearing in mind the needs their own households or enterprises have for outputs/services. The well-known promotional relationship and the → *promotion mandate* directed at the co-operative enterprise by the member enterprises result from this, which in some countries (e.g.Germany) is directly addressed in its Co-operative Law (→ *Law, National*;→ *Legal Form, Co-operative*).

In contrast to this and inasmuch as the co-operative enterprises were often small and only had a marginal number of employees (→ *Operational Size*), the internal organizational structures in the enterprise, or in other words the relationships between management staff and co-workers, at least in the past only played a small role in co-operatives (→ *Managerial Economics*). In the more recent past these aspects have appeared more pronounced considering enterprise expansion in the industrial countries and in connection with the development of co-determination in enterprises and the enforcement of internal company by-laws.

The question of corporate culture for present-day co-operatives is dualistic in nature: On the one hand it refers to the question of value conceptions and basic assumptions held by the members (→ *History of Ideas*), and on the other hand to the value conceptions and norms noticeable in the relationship between management personnel and staff members in the co-operative enterprise. Here it is apparent that a certain predetermination in both fields as well as a connection between both fields is at hand through the promotion mandate.

2. Value References in Co-operatives in Earlier Times

If we look at the first aspect more closely we can see that considerations about value references in the co-operative membership group do not represent anything new, not even for their basis of orientation in commercial behavior. This concerns groups of individuals who have joined together because of a commonly held goal. The phenomenon of group culture in the sense of a subculture is therefore almost automatically present and stretches all the way back to early phases of the history of mankind (→ *History before 1800*). Such a retrospective in management studies is by all means not generally the rule. Critical accusations are raised in this connection in that management considerations only evolve from contemporary conditions; in order to explain environmental influences, however, it also is necessary to study earlier times. This is true for co-operative organizations to an exceptional degree.

Our observation must be limited to the four largest sectors of → *rural co-operatives*, of → *commercial co-operatives*, of → *consumer co-operatives* and → *housing societies* and at best should include → *joint-production co-operatives*. We are aware that the respective organizational concepts and the actual organizational complexes which emerged from them can be assigned quite clearly to certain value-oriented conceptions of the 19th century. Historical works on co-operative development (e.g. *H. Faust, J.O. Müller and W.W. Engelhardt*) must be referred to here for specifics (→ *History in 19th C.*).

The apparent value and/or ideological orientation of the co-operatives in the second half of the 19th century was clearly determined by two main influential factors. On the one hand, the amalgamation of individuals in the co-operative resulted from the respective plight faced by groups of individuals sharply cut off in their social condition: mainly farmers, craftsmen, small-scale commercial operators as well as wage-earners in industry. *Engelhardt* notes that co-operative science strongly proceeds from this living situation in the sense of a "concept of plight" (1989) (→ *Theory of Co-operatives*).

The other large influential factor was composed of certain intellectual currents which had formed in the years of upheaval from the Middle Ages (→ *Guilds*) to the modern times as a result of the philosophy of the enlightenment and subsequent political and economic liberalization, which in turn was influenced by a flood of inventions and technological advancements.

These two influential factors would not have directly led to the establishment of co-operatives had not a third component had a type of catalyzing effect: The great *founder personalities* and pioneers of the co-operative system, for example the → *Rochdale Pioneers* in the sector of consumer co-operatives in Great Britain as well as → *Friedrich Wilhelm Raiffeisen* and → *Hermann Schulze-Delitzsch* in Germany respectively for the agricultural sector and the sector of artisans, small-scale commercial operators and later merchants. The organizational and action-oriented concepts hit upon by these practitioners were refined and systematized in part by intellectuals and scientists such as *the Fabiers* in Great Britain (→ *Sir Horace Plunkett*) and → *Victor Aimé Huber* in Germany. These great founder personalities knew the traits and reasons for the specific plight faced by the respective groups based on their own experience and degree of information. They then developed operative concepts for assistance based on the intellectual foundations of their respective out-looks on life to which they were inclined. Historical coincidence therefore also played a role.

Expressed in a simplified manner we can determine that the Rochdale pioneers owed their success and propagation to the support provided by the Christian Socialists. → *F.W.Raiffeisen* made strong reference to the Christian concept of neighborly love, whereas →

Schulze-Delitzsch as a progressive, liberal politician based the corpus of his thoughts solely on the enlightenment and the tenets of political economic liberalism which subsequently developed. The consumer co-operatives in Germany also originally were rooted in this direction. They quickly recognized, however, that they were falling into conflict with the other co-operative groups and locked on to *Lasalle's* worker movement, which in turn was based on the theses and interpretational approach to "scientific socialism" (→ *Socialist Critics*). Socialist conceptions both utopian in nature and in advance of scientific analysis likewise brought about co-operatives, above all joint-production co-operatives in France. The housing co-operatives were related and closely tied to the consumer co-operatives for a long period of time; following 1945 in Germany, however, they developed separately as the housing co-operatives became subject to the Law of Public Benefit (→ *Housing Societies*). Value orientations were thus at hand to a considerable degree in all early co-operative organizations. This was typified at an earlier time as the "ideological substance" of the co-operative concepts (→ *Conceptions, Co-operative*). In such cases where, for example, workers were needed in great numbers at an early point in time for consumer co-operatives' own production, the majority of such workers hailed from the identical population groups as the members of the consumer co-operative, and were even members themselves. The internal corporate culture of the enterprise was thus also determined in this case by the subculture of the membership group. This is similar still today among the co-operative banks.

3. Differences according to Structural Types

When studying the more recent development of co-operative enterprises in the industrialized countries one must take into consideration the variations among them described in their structural typology (*Dülfer*, 1956; 1969) (→ *Structural Types*). In the early years of the 20th century the "traditional co-operative" was still dominant. In this form (*Typ*) the ethical, moral and manneristic norms of the respective membership group determined the parameters in which decisions concerning material matters were made which also affected commercial relationships. The respective organizational-cultural nature of the membership group also is reflected through the economic actions it pursues in its business operations. This changed later quite considerably through the development of the "market-linkage co-operative". A relaxation of the relationships thus resulted between the group of member enterprises on the one hand and the co-operative company on the other hand which was involved more intensely in the mounting competition. Quasi-market relationships developed between these two parties. This constellation led to the situation in which commercial operational methods were determined less through the value conceptions of the members than through those of the managers. These operational methods in turn oriented themselves predominantly around the situation on the market and competitors' behavior. A combination of these two was then achieved in the "integrated co-operative", whereby extensive acceptance among the members can be determined with regard to the business practises pursued by the managers due to competitive restraints and challenges on the market.

These three structural types can be found today worldwide. Their development could be traced the clearest in Germany, one of the countries in which a classic development of co-operatives occurred. Here the consequences of World War II led to a new orientation of the co-operative organizations, which after the war reemerged to the greatest part in their former structure. These were primarily concerned with the material reconstruction of the various economic and social sectors. The occurrence of the War not only brought about a drastic reduction in the living standard of wide sections of the population but also contributed to their loss of feeling for life, for immediate goals and for personal endeavors. The co-operative organizations were therefore fully concentrated in their new group structures and compositions to solve the pressing problems of reconstruction and the material provision of their members. In the face of the general lack of resources it was important to find the most rational method to solve the problems of provision, thereby using resources as appropriately as possible. The all-round compulsion to improvise and to find unconventional methods to solve pressing existential problems created a pronounced type of pragmatism. Theoretical, conceptual explanation was consciously dispensed with, a matter which found considerable approval among the membership as the population had developed a deep-set aversion against any form of ideology in their economic and social life through the misuse of value terminology in the exaggerated political propaganda of earlier years. The market-linkage co-operative and the integrated co-operative subsequently evolved against this backdrop.

4. The Revitalization of Principles in the New Context

All of this occurred in the scope of the new state and economic order based on democratic parliamentarism, the principle of the rule of law and the concept of order in the social market economy. It is noteworthy that all umbrella co-operative organizations which in the past could be assigned to varying political directions and social structures professed this new concept of order after a relatively short phase of development. They thus shared strong similarities in their basic assumptions, in their new vision of the world, in their forced improvisation, in their pragmatic attitude, in their scepticism of other proclaimed doctrines of social salvation, and in their extensive willingness to provide and receive reciprocal assistance on the basis of common goals.

In the further course of time a special corporate and organizational-political conception then developed in the various organizations. Interestingly enough, reference was drawn primarily to the former founding figures, although outstanding management personalities were also active in this phase.

A phenomenon running parallel to this was the careful revitalization of the so-called *principle catalogues* (→ *Principles*). Seen from an international perspective, the recommendation of the → *International Co-operative Alliance* should be noted which at that time suggested reducing the Rochdale principles down to four fundamental theses. From the perspective of managerial science it can likewise be ascertained that the respective principle catalogues were decisive for the formulation of certain communication standards. Insofar they can be interpreted without a doubt as "values" as applied by *Schein*, for they were consciously used as educational and training instruments within organizations, and their content was internalized as norms for action.

III. Co-operative Corporate Culture in the Present Day

When one studies these evocations of classic notions it becomes obvious that the concept of organizational culture does not represent something novel for modern co-operatives. Terms such as self-help, self-administration and self-responsibility – in the sense of certain values meant be observed – descend from the Rochdale Pioneers and *Schulze-Delitzsch*. Nonetheless, one needs to raise the question whether a new conception of the meaning of value references in corporate policy and corporate management has indeed come to light. *Lipfert* (1987) indicated this development and coined the term "co-operative identity".

1. The Dominance of the Promotion Mandate

Each and every concept of co-operative management both in the present and future is primarily determined through the promotional needs of the member enterprises. Accordingly a *structural* organizational concept of the promotional relationship between the co-operative enterprise and the member enterprises remains at hand; this is especially the case in the manifestation of the integrated co-operative. The relevant problem thereby rests in whether more comprehensive value conceptions and value terms can be jointly formulated and internalized in the sense of an "identity consciousness" within such a construction above and beyond the material promotional needs of members and their enterprises. Something more substantial than simply an organizational structure would thereby come into being – namely a specific organizational culture through which the particular institution can distinguish itself in society, and above all in competition with other institutions and corporate groups.

2. Can Corporate Culture be Shaped?

We herewith do not merely address the question of observing an actual, given organizational structure and the organizational culture which results from it but rather how it can be potentially influenced or molded. In this regard it must be noted once again that a certain allergy against ideological manipulation exists in general in modern society, not just in countries with a certain totalitarian political past. The fact must not be overlooked that membership bodies in existent co-operatives are likewise partial subgroups of the national society. As a consequence individual persons are also confronted with the plethora of notions and intellectual currents which are currently being identified by sociologists and social psychologists.

The "generation problem" also plays a role in this context. Top-level management positions in co-operative organizations are also held in the majority of cases by people of earlier generations, whereas the change in values is noticeable above all in the younger and middle generations and thus in the primary level of co-operative organizations.

The question as to what exactly this change in values consists of or encompasses cannot be answered incidentally in the context of this treatise. For sure, however, this does not exclusively concern the appreciation or non-appreciation of material provision as is said from time to time. Even in the phase of reconstruction the actual incentive for action did not rest in meeting material needs: The quest for new solutions, improvisational skills, and the renouncement of former codes of behavior to the benefit of non-conventional modes of behavior played a substantial role instead. Personality traits were accordingly respected which individuals needed to experience success and enjoy the "esteem by others" as described by *Maslow*. This scenario disappears to an extensive degree in a production and consumption situation characterized by routine processes in which problem solving rarely has components of individualism.

The reduction of working hours is a further factor on top of this. The effects of structural unemployment and the obvious shift of interests to leisure activities are the aftermath of this development. Furthermore, interests require certain goals. Goals in turn are based on preferences and value conceptions. It is therefore not surprising in this altered situation that the younger generations are on the quest for new value conceptions which give direction to their individual endeavors. Perhaps the recent and in part still amateurish efforts to establish co-operatives in so-called alternative sectors should be seen and understood in such light. These are not merely a statement of negation but rather an attempt at further development and improvement.

When the question is raised as to what can be done concretely to shape and mold specific organizational or corporate cultures in co-operative organizations, one must surely proceed from the argument that two diverging development tendencies can be observed in today's economy and society.

3. Current Development Tendencies

The first current tendency is the increasing professionalization of operational decisions; this is achieved with the help of shrewd calculation and the employment of electronic data processing systems in order to achieve a high degree of rationality in the allocation of resources for a given goal (→ *Managerial Economics*). The other divergent tendency which perhaps is precipitated by this former development is modern man's endeavors to come to the fore as a fully entitled citizen and organization participant. Man strives to be involved in decisionmaking in all affairs which affect his/her life, including the organization in which he/she is a member or co-worker. Desires and requirements of participation emerge in all branches and levels, including within the co-operative and the → *co-operative combine*. The conditional diversity of goals and the necessary compensation of interests is reflective of the contrast drawn by Max Weber between "purpose rationality" and "value rationality". In our day and age these must constantly be tied to one another although they could produce varying consequences. In the context of co-operative praxis of all branches seen at once, this means that both tendencies are in effect in the realm of member relationships as well as in the realm of co-worker management within the enterprise; furthermore, these tendencies require appropriate answers which further their development. In the scope of the structural typologies this usually signifies a development in the direction of stronger integration. The following examples illustrate this situation.

4. Branch-specific Examples

In all industrialized countries an alteration in the corporate policy of → *co-operative banks* has resulted from the depletion of the bank market. Competitive relationships escalated because additional target groups could no longer be found and addressed. In this situation the institutionalization of the member relations represents a competitive advantage for the co-operative banks, one they should accommodate in the future through a company policy oriented around their members instead of around their customers, as they had practised in the past. This requires the reformulation of corporate principles and values within the co-operative enterprise and entire combine. Economic measures such as the introduction of interest reimbursement payments could be quite effective in this connection but are nonetheless only a partial component in the scope of development of a specific organizational culture.

In the sector of the consumer co-operatives structural development has already led in part to a complete alteration of the organizational structure and corporate culture. It is interesting in this light, however, that local consumer co-operatives continue to exist in the industrialized countries. Reports from the United States tell of how members in small consumer co-operatives are obligated to provide honorary services, whereby they accordingly receive mentionable price discounts. Business conducted with members thereby is clearly distinctive from business with non-members, which likewise is undertaken intensively.

In the sector of housing co-operatives it is reported that local membership groups (→ *Group, the Co-operative*) are formed in which the operational problems of housing maintenance and floor plans are discussed on the local level. Participational contributions to company management from the viewpoint of members' interests thus also play a role here. This is a specific type of internal cooperation.

Efforts can be identified in all types of co-operatives in the direction of both diverging tendencies described above to activate value rationality and competence among members for management through additional measures either in general or through specific projects. This can occur for example through the introduction of an advisory board (Ringle, 1986) (→ *Organizational Structure of Societies*). Among the member combine companies with large numbers of co-workers, the attempt has been made to accentuate co-operative principles in the management and labor relationships as well. Indications of specific corporate cultures are evident here, such as through special rituals (the award ceremony for inner company competition among the R + V → *insurance co-operatives*) or through symbols of identity (e.g. logo of the co-operative banks). In this context one must not forget admonishments against superficial efforts; in contrast to corporate identity, corporate culture is not susceptible to manipulative efforts in any manner and extends greatly beyond mere external appearance.

5. Summary

As a whole it can be determined that the concept of organizational and corporate culture which became propagated through American publications by no means represents a completely novel innovation in Germany. This is likewise the case for those countries rooted in the tradition of co-operative organizations.

This is rather a long-overdue reminiscence of the earlier developments in the home countries of the *Rochdale Pioneers*, or *Raiffeisen* and *Schulze-Delitzsch*. Nonetheless this is not a matter of simply reviving former policies which were effective at an earlier day and age but rather of bringing them together with current development tendencies and the actual demands which have resulted from these developments.

For co-operatives it is quite clear that their long-maintained tendency of avoiding as much as possible value or ideological orientation and merely pursuing a pure, matter-of-fact business policy needs to be rethought. It would surely be a curiosity if private companies, which from the neoclassic view are ascribed profit maximization as their only formulated goal, would outdo co-operatives in their recognition of organizational and corporate culture – especially if they undertook such measures while drawing reference to principles which are associated with the classic value conceptions of the early co-operative pioneers. The concept of organizational culture is thus especially of current importance to co-operatives as it presses them into a discussion to which they have a great amount to contribute on account of their substantial experience in the past. Despite this past it is not simply a matter of reiterating the opinions of co-operative forefathers but rather of seeking accords which do justice to the social, socio-psychological and ethical-moral needs of modern society both today and in the future.

Bibliography

Deal, Terrence E./Kennedy, Allen A.: Corporate Cultures – The Rites and Rituals of Corporate Life, Reading, Mass. 1982
Draheim, Georg: Die Genossenschaft als Unternehmenstyp, Göttingen 1952.
Dülfer, Eberhard: Betriebswirtschaftslehre der Kooperative – Kommunikation und Entscheidungsbildung in Genossenschaften und vergleichbaren Organisationen, Göttingen 1984.
Dülfer, Eberhard: Die Unternehmenskultur der Genossenschaft – ein traditionsreiches Thema in neuer Aktualität, in: Marburger Beiträge zum Genossenschaftswesen, Vol.12, Marburg 1987, pp.17–47.
Dülfer, Eberhard (ed.): Organisationskultur – Phänomen, Philosophie, Technologie, 2.ed., Stuttgart 1991.
Ebers, Mark: Organisationskultur – ein neues Forschungsprogramm?, Wiesbaden 1985.
Farmer, Richard N./Richman, Barry M.: International Business: An Operational Theory, Homewood, Ill. 1966.
Heinen, Edmund: Unternehmenskultur als Gegenstand der Betriebswirtschaftslehre, in: Heinen, Edmund et al. (ed.), Unternehmenskultur, Perspektiven für Wissenschaft und Praxis, München, Wien 1987.
Lipfert, Helmut: Mitgliederförderndes Kooperations- und Konkurrenzmanagement in genossenschaftlichen Systemen, Göttingen 1986.3
Matenaar, Dieter: Organisationskultur und organisatorische Gestaltung, Berlin 1983.
Müller, Julius Otto: Voraussetzungen und Verfahrensweisen bei der Errichtung von Genossenschaften in Europa vor 1900, Marburger Schriften zum Genossenschaftswesen, Serie B, Vol.11, Göttingen 1976.
Münkner, Hans H.: Co-operative Principles and Co-operative Law, Marburg 1974.
Ouchi, William G.: Theory Z. How American Business Can Meet the Japanese Challenge, Reading, Mass. 1981.
Pascale, R.T./ Athos, A.G.: The Art of Japanese Management, Applications for American Executives, New York 1981.
Peters, Thomas J./Waterman, Robert, H.: Auf der Suche nach Spitzenleistungen, Landsberg am Lech 1986.
Ringle, Günther.: Mitgliederaktivierung und Partizipation in modernen Primärgenossenschaften, Vol.2, Hamburger Schriften zum Genossenschaftswesen, Göttingen 1983.
Schein, Edgar H.: Organizational Culture and Leadership, San Francisco, Washington, London 1985.

Credit Unions, World Council of

CHRISTOPHER BAKER

(see also: *Classification*; *Co-operative Banks*; *Desjardins/Filene*; *Development, North America*; *Business Policies*)

I. Introduction; II. What is a Credit Union?; III. International Credit Union Operating Principles; IV. History; V. Strategy; VI. Services; VII. Conclusion.

I. Introduction

The World Council of Credit Unions (WOCCU) is the worldwide representative organization of credit unions and similar co-operative financial institutions (→ *Co-operative Banks*). Its mission is to assist members to organize, expand, improve, and integrate credit unions as well as related institutions as effective instruments for the economic and social development of people throughout the world (→ *Development Policy*). The World Council serves as a forum for the exchange of ideas and information, provides services for its members, promotes membership, development and growth, represents members' interest, and extends co-operative financial services to areas where people want and need these services.

As of June 1993, the international credit union system encompasses credit unions and related co-operative financial institutions in 87 countries, including 77 countries in the developing regions of Africa, Asia and the Pacific, Latin America and the Caribbean. The direct members of the World Council include seven regional or national credit union confederations and four free-standing leagues (→ *International Co-operative Organizations*).

Confederations

ACCOSCA	African Confederation of Co-operative Savings and Credit Associations
ACCU	Asian Confederation of Credit Unions
CCCU	Caribbean Confederation of Credit Unions
COLAC	Latin American Confederation of Credit Unions
CUCC	Credit Union Central of Canada
CUNA	Credit Union National Association (USA)
CUSCAL	Credit Union Services Corporation (Australia) Limited

Free-Standing Leagues

ABCUL	Association of British Credit Unions, Ltd.
FCUL	Fiji Credit Union League
ILCU	Irish League of Credit Unions
NZACU	New Zealand Association of Credit Unions

Associate and observer members of the World Council include the following ten organizations:

Associate Members
Austrian Raiffeisen Association
Confédération du Crédit Mutuel (France)
CUMIS Group Ltd. (Canada)
CUNA Mutual Insurance Group (USA)
Groupe Desjardins (Quebec, Canada)
Eccu Assurance Company Limited (Ireland)
Finafrica Foundation (Italy)
International Raiffeisen Union
Association Mutualiste des Fonctionnaires des organisations Intergouvernementales ayant leurs sièges ou des bureaux permanents en Europe (AMFIE)
International Co-operative Banking Association of the ICA

The World Council, in turn, is a member of the following international bodies: International Liaison Committee on Co-operative Thrift and Credit (CLICEC), Committee for the Promotion and Advancement of Co-operatives (COPAC), Federation of International Institutions in Geneva (FIIG), and International Co-operative Alliance (ICA).

The World Council has also established relations with: Economic and Social Council of the United Nations (consultative status), Food and Agricultural Office of the United Nations (special consultative status), International Fund for Agricultural Development, (observer status), and International Labor Office (special NGO status). The World Council maintains its home office and principal staff complement in Madison, Wisconsin, USA, with two additional offices in Washington, DC, USA, and Geneva, Switzerland.

II. What is a Credit Union?

A credit union is a co-operative financial organization owned and operated by its members on a not-for-profit basis according to democratic principles (→ *Conceptions, Co-operative*). Its purpose is to encourage savings and to pool members' funds to make loans to each other at reasonable rates of interest. Members are united by a common bond such as employment, church or community group (→ *Group, the Co-operative*). All members are equal owners of the credit union and have equal privileges and opportunities.

Credit unions are governed by the International Credit Union Operating Principles (→ *Principles*), approved by the World Council's Membership Council on August 24, 1984, and summarized below. The operating principles, as put forth by the World Council, are founded in the philosophy of cooperation, equality, and social responsibilty. At the heart of the principles is the concept of human development expressed by people helping people to achieve a better life for themselves and their community.

III. International Credit Union Operating Principles

Democratic Structure
Membership in a credit union is voluntary and open to all within the accepted common bond, regardless of race, nationality, sex, religion, and politics. All members are owners of the credit union and have equal voting rights (one member, one vote) and responsibilities. Credit unions are autonomous within the framework of law and regulation, and its elected officers are voluntary and uncompensated.

Service to Members
Service to members (→ *Promotion Mandate*) are designed to improve the economic and social well-being of all members. Credit unions encourage thrift through savings and offer a fair rate of interest on savings and deposits. Any surplus arising out of the operation of a credit union belongs to the members, is distributed among them or directed to improve services to them.

Social Goals
Credit unions promote thrift and the wise use of credit among their members. Moreover, they help teach democratic and mutual self-help principles. Credit unions actively cooperate with other credit unions and co-operative organizations in order to best serve the interests of their members and their communities. Their vision of social justice and human development extends to credit union members and to the community at large.

IV. History

Although the World Council of Credit Unions was not conceived until 1970, the historical origins of credit unions can be traced back to the early credit co-operative societies of mid–19th century Germany. Two men, → *Hermann Schulze-Delitzsch* and → *Friedrich Wilhelm Raiffeisen* were responsible for establishing the first credit co-operatives as a means of providing financial services to the poor.

In 1864, *F.W. Raiffeisen*, the mayor of Heddesdorf, Germany, formed the first true credit union, and set forth the co-operative guiding → *principles*, which still govern most of the credit unions in the world today: (1) credit unions were democratically run institutions (one member, one vote), (2) loans were made for prudent and productive pruposes and were based on the character of the borrower rather than collateral alone, (3) only people who were members should borrow there.

The concept of co-operative credit societies quickly spread to other European nations and to North America. *Alphonse Desjardins*, a French-Canadian journalist, was the first to bring the concept to North Amercia. In 1900, he established the first credit union (caisse populaire) in Levís, Quebec, and eight years later helped organize the first credit union in the United States in Maryland, New Hampshire, today known as St. Mary' Bank.

Edward A. Filene and *Roy Bergengren* were instrumental in spreading and developing the credit union movement in the United States (→ *Development, North America*). In 1935, the Credit Union National Association (CUNA) was established as the trade association for credit unions in the United States. As requests for assistance from overseas parties continued to grow, CUNA established the World Extension Department in the 1950s to address these needs. This effort, complemented by those undertaken by sister co-operative movements in Canada and Europe, led to the organization of credit union movements in nearly all parts of the world.

In order to represent global leadership within CUNA's organizational structure, CUNA changed its name to CUNA International in 1965. In 1970, CUNA International voted to create a separate entity, the World Council of Credit Unions, to address the needs of all credit union movements. Shortly after, regional and national credit union confederations in Asia, Latin America, Africa, and the Caribbean joined other movements in Canada, Ireland, New Zealand, Fiji, Australia, Great Britain, and the United States to form the World Council of Credit Unions (→ *Policies for Promotion*).

V. Strategy

From the outset, institutional development has been the operational strategy of the international credit union system. This approach is based on a model comprised of local credit unions providing members with essential financial services, supported by national and regional organizations providing needed technical and savings, credit and related services. In order for the system to operate on a sustainable basis, development efforts focus on building the requisite capabilities at each level.

The World Council assists at each level to develop the managerial, technical, and financial resources necessary to provide essential and sustainable service to local credit unions. This building-block approach has been largely responsible for the evolution of an international system that now encompasses nearly 42,000 credit unions with total assets of US $ 434 billion, serving 89 million individuals in 87 countries.

VI. Services

As the international organization of credit union associations, the World Council possesses unique skills in the development of credit union systems. It provides informational, developmental, representational and resource mobilization services, and draws upon the skills and experience of its members as well as those of its own staff to provide extensive technical services.

Representation and Co-ordination

The World Council co-ordinates periodic meetings to address the evolving roles and needs of the worldwide savings and credit unions movement, and it represents movements before national and international organizations to increase visibility and support for the international credit union movement.

Technical and Development Services

The World Council provides technical and developmental services for its developing country members, including the design and implementation of long-term programs in institutional development, short-term technical assistance and training projects, and assistance in mobilizing human and financial resources.

Long-term development projects are usually 3–5 years in duration and generally employ one or more resident advisors. For country-specific projects, technical assistance is focused on institutional and financial strenghthening at all levels of the system to promote the safety and soundness of credit unions.

The World Council conducts numerous consultancies (→ *Consulting*) to improve the technical capabilities of its member organizations. Examples of consultancies include: legislative reform, management-information system development, stabilization programs, strategic and business planning, financial policy development, and savings mobilizations.

Training Services

The World Council offers various specialized training services for executives, managers, and leaders such as study tours including short visits, lectures, and technical exchanges; short-term training courses in the operation of financial markets, credit union regulation and examination, finance and marketing; internship programs; design and implementation of institutional development and train-the-trainers programs; on-the-job training and advisory services for credit union staff and regulators (→ *Education, North America*).

Publications
The World Council publishes a variety of informational/promotional materials on the activities of the World Council and the international credit union movement (→ *Periodicals, Co-operative*):
WOCCU Annual Report – summary of world Council's and member organization's activities.
WOCCU Statistical Report – annual compilation of country-by-country, regional and international credit union statistics.
World Reporter – journal covering topics of interest to both credit unions and development organizations.
Technical Reporter – a technical series providing information on credit union operations and management.
Perspectives – a monthly newsletter summarizing activities of the World Council and the international credit union movement.
Beyond Barriers – a semi-annual newsletter promoting the development of women, men and credit unions.
CEE Update – provides information on World Council's activities in Eastern and Central Europe.
In addition, the World Council has also produced various technical publications on the topics of financial management, savings mobilization, membership promotion, central finance programs, and small business lending.

Information Services
The World Council maintains an Information Center to serve the information needs of the international credit union system and other organizations involved in international development activities. The Information Center has a variety of information resources on credit union and international development, allowing it to respond to a multitude of information requests and to assist in the preparation of feasibility, design, evaluation and research studies.
The World Council also maintains a statistical database of member credit union movements and financial markets in member countries (→ *Federation Statistics*). In addition to processing financial data in local currencies and US dollars, in both nominal and real terms, this country-by-country, regional, and international bases.

Resource mobilization
The World Council mobilizes human and financial resources of public and private agencies supportive of credit union development activities to assist credit union organizations in the developing world. The World Council collaborates with member organizations to develop funding proposals, and it represents these organizations with identified funding agencies.

VII. Conclusion

Credit unions are unique financial institutions. They provide savings and credit services to population groups not generally served by the formal sector, and they are uniquely suited to meet the financial needs of middle and lower-income individuals in developing countries. Besides promoting thrift and the wise use of credit, credit unions help teach democratic and mutual self-help principles (→ *Self-help Organizations*).
To support these institutions, a vast international system has been established which links each credit union into a worldwide network of national and regional service organizations, headed by the World Council of Credit Unions. Through this network or people helping people, credit unions have proven to be effective tools of economic and social development.

Cybernetics and Cooperation

BERND SCHIEMENZ

(see also: *Theory of Co-operatives*; *Managerial Economics*; *Theory of co-operative Cooperation*)

I. Fundamentals of Cybernetics; II. The Use of Cybernetics for Co-operative Organizations.

I. Fundamentals of Cybernetics

1. The Development of the Scientific Discipline Cybernetics

Cybernetics has several sources. The joint cognition was that on a specific level of abstraction the problems of communication and control are of general nature and appear as well in living organisms as in machines and in combinations of both. Several researchers of different disciplines had this idea nearly at the same time. It, however, found its clearest expression in the group around the mathematician *Norbert Wiener* who in 1947 gave the discipline its name and distributed the findings in his book "Cybernetics – or control and communication in the animal and the machine" (*Wiener*).
Soon it became clearly understood that questions of many other disciplines like psychology, medicine, pedagogy, sociology, political sciences, law, economics and management could be reduced to the same

problems. Parallel to this expansion, cybernetics experienced a deepening of its fundamental theories, theorems and techniques. We partly find a crossfertilization with other approaches like general systems theory, systems analysis and systems engineering, systems dynamics, synergetics and catastrophe theory, which together form an influential systems movement.

Typical of cybernetics as of other members of this systems movement is a process-view of the world. The different real and informational processes are interconnected and can be controlled partly. The merits of cybernetics may be found especially in the elaboration of the conditions and techniques of controlling complex systems.

2. Control

Cybernetics helped much to clarify the possibilities, preconditions and consequences of different types of control.

Open-loop control (see fig. 1) is the process in a relatively isolated system in which the controlling system influences the controlled system by one or several input-signals without measuring the output-signals of the controlled system, that are the controlled variables.

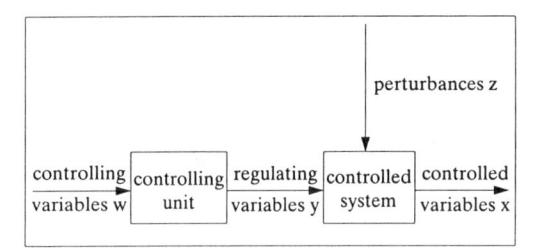

Fig. 1: Open-loop control.

Precondition that the controlled variables x of the controlled system reach their desired level w is the exact knowledge of the behaviour of the controlled system by the controlling system. If there are also external perturbances z, having influence on x, the controlling system has to know them, too, as well as the reaction of the controlled system on them.

If, e. g. a production co-operative wants to sell exactly its production w, using pricing-policy only, it needs the knowledge of the price-demand-function of the corresponding market. Then it can calculate that price y that makes the demand x equal to its desired level w. If there are more influences on this demand, not under control of the co-operative, like actions of the competitors, these actions as well as their influence on the demand have to be known as well.

Seldom has the controlling system all this necessary knowledge. Then a difference between output x and its desired level w would remain. The second type of control, feedback control (see figure 2), tries to avoid this remaining difference. The result x is fed back to the controlling system, the regulator, which compares it to w and changes its control signals in order to reduce this difference.

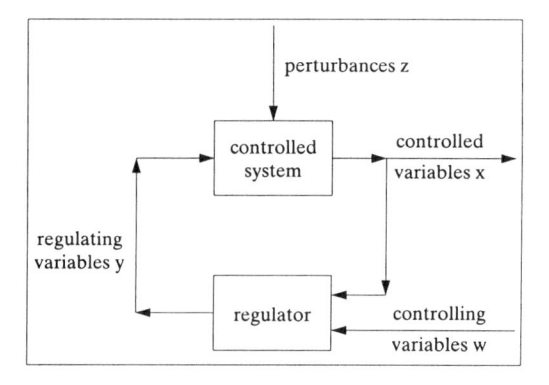

Fig. 2: Feedback control.

This type of control is very powerful and in principle works with little knowledge about the behaviour of the controlled system and external perturbances. Naturally, the better this knowledge is, the better the control becomes. Here, feedback control offers an additional advantage. Correlating controlled variables and regulating variables leads to a better model of the controlled system which even follows its changing behaviour. Feedback therefore makes highly adaptive control processes possible that use all possible actual information.

There is, however, also a disadvantage of feedback control. Especially when there are delays in the system and the system is not designed very carefully, oscillations may occur, even with increasing amplitude. Examples for this are the zigzagging when driving a car or a ship and the well known pig-cycle in economics.

An important and frequently mentioned and discussed result of cybernetics is the "Law of Requisite Variety" (*Ashby*). It deals with the necessary number of own alternative actions one needs to compensate the actions of a competitor or the different possible states of the environment so that a desired result is obtained.

	states of the environment					
	s1	s2	s3	s4	s5	s6
a c t i o n s	a1	b	d	e	c	f	g
	a2	h	b	i	j	c	k
	a3	l	m	b	n	o	c

Fig. 3: Decision matrix for the law of requisite variety.

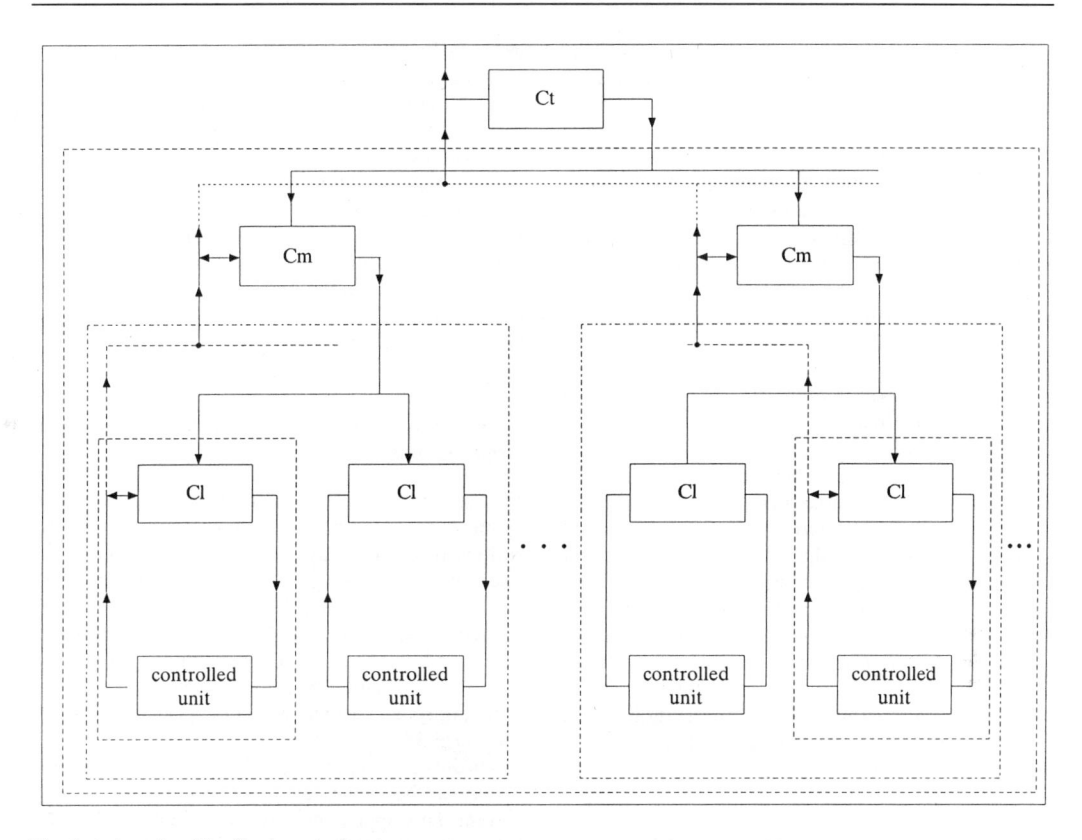

Fig. 4: A three-level feedback control system.

In fig. 3 the controller has n = 3 (discrete) alternative actions (a1...a3) at his disposal, the environment may have m = 6 different states (s1...s6). The outcome of one action varies from state to state (b...g; h...k; l...c). The variety of the outcome then cannot be kept lower than the quotient m/n = 6/3 = 2. Variety here means the number of distinguishable elements of a set. In the case of fig. 3 the controller has to accept the two different outcomes b and c. If he wants to reduce this variety, he has to increase the variety of the actions. Only variety of the controller's actions can compensate the variety of the environment so that a specific outcome results.

In the situation described, the law is absolutely exact. It, however, must not be misinterpreted. In practice, first the outcomes might not change from state to state, second variety of the actions might be expensive and third some actions might be more efficient than others to keep the output within acceptable boundaries. The Law of Requisite Variety, therefore, can only give a first general guideline.

3. Hierarchy

Feed-forward as well as feed-back control establish a kind of hierarchy. The controlled system shall follow the signals of the controlling unit or regulator in order to obtain the aims and objectives given to or developed by the latter. This hierarchy can be extended to a multi-level hierarchy. Fig. 4 shows as an example the case of a three level feedback control system.

In fig. 4 the top-level controller Ct controls several medium-level controllers Cm which control the lower-level controllers Cl. The Cl's finally control a controlled unit each.

Especially when the controllers are human beings with their own aims and objectives, multi-level feed-forward (open loop) control will hardly work. Feed-forward 'control' would leave them uncontrolled. A broadly understood feed-back control of this multi-level-multi-goal-system (*Mesarovic* et al.), on the other hand, may be very effective and efficient. That means, it may obtain the right objectives in the best way. For this, feed-back information must not only contain the results of the respective controlled unit. It must also include information about the capacity of the behaviour, the state of the environment and especially the respective aims and objectives. The controller thus gains more the property of an integrator or moderator than that of a dominator.

The type of hierarchy, we were talking of until now,

may be called inter-systems hierarchy, because it is a hierarchy between systems where one controls the other. Besides this type, cybernetics and systems theory elaborated another type, the intra-systems hierarchy (*Scholz*). This type corresponds to the specific systems view according to which any part of the real world may be seen as a system, existing of systems of lower order which are related to another. The system is part of a system of higher order, which itself is part of an even higher system etc. This recursive relation holds true to the large and to the small nearly indefinitely. The dotted rectangles in fig. 4 are to indicate this aspect of hierarchy.

Hierarchy in this sense of intra-systems hierarchy is the central construction principle, any architect of a concrete or abstract system must use, if he wants to overcome complexity. Nobel laureate *H. A. Simon* proves this by his famous fable of the two watchmakers *Hora* and *Tempus* and many examples: A complex system is only then stable, if it is composed of relatively stable subsystems. This principle therefore has been included also in the viable systems approach of *Beer* (1984) and the living systems approach of *Miller*. Connected to this principle are aspects like internalization of externalities as well as → *solidarity* and subsidiarity of the catholic social doctrine, which, however, can not be elaborated here (see *Schiemenz* 1982).

4. Theory and Technique of Information Systems

The intentions and aspirations of cybernetics go beyond the discussed aspects of control and hierarchy. From the very beginning (see *Wiener*), cyberneticians tried to quantify what might be quantifiable, thus drawing the consequences from a thesis of *Kant*, that in any natural philosophy there is only as much real science to be found as there is mathematics in it (see *Steinbuch*, p. 323).

And cybernetics dealt with the modelling and automation of the nervous system and the brain. Cyberneticians therefore work, with a deep theoretical insight, also in such fields as expert systems and approximate reasoning, robotics and manufacturing, artificial intelligence, parallel distributed processing in man and machine, etc. (see e.g. *Trappl*).

II. The Use of Cybernetics for Co-operative Organizations

1. Cybernetics and General Management

The cybernetic approach, methods and results are used in different disciplines like control, mechanical and electrical engineering, informatics, biology, pedagogy, psychology, political sciences, sociology, economics, and especially business administration and management. These disciplines are, in various ways, influencing each other and the management practice (*Schiemenz* 1984). A proof for this can be taken from the proceedings of the congresses of the various international organizations for cybernetics and systems. In Germany the Gesellschaft für Wirtschafts- und Sozialkybernetik e. V. promotes and spreads these ideas (e.g. *Schiemenz/Wagner, Fischer, Fahrion*). Furtheron, there are different books on cybernetics or systems theory and management (e. g. *Beer* 1959, *Schiemenz* 1972 and 1982, *Baetge, Ulrich/Probst*) giving evidence of the influence of cybernetics on management.

2. The Importance of Cybernetics for Co-operative Organizations

Because of this importance for general management, cybernetics is of importance for co-operative organizations too, especially for the management in co-operative organizations (→ *Managerial Economics*). It is *Dülfer*, who most consequently uses this approach – respectively general systems theory – as a new paradigm, "because they enable the integration of different disciplinary aspects in a closed explanatory approach which was not possible so far" (*Dülfer/p. 33*).

According to this paradigm, the co-operative organization can be viewed as a socio-technical economic system. This opens one's eyes for the part-whole relation in co-operative organizations as well as of the latter in their environment and shows the necessity of the development of appropriate organizational structures.

These structures must make an intensive use of feedback. Feedback loops prove to be a very important tool to control co-operative organizations. They first allow the coordinating and integrating institutions to recognize, how far the objectives have been obtained and to take the appropriate counter-measures. Feedback allows also to learn about the reactions of the members and customers as well as their needs, objectives, capabilities etc. Only feedback makes real cooperation possible.

Using this approach, *Dülfer* develops "Strukturtypen der Genossenschaften" (→ *structural types* of co-operatives) that systematize and explain their historical form and give indications for their further development.

The concepts of hierarchy and especially self-organization (e.g. *Probst*) for co-operative organizations are not yet completely exploited. Here further research may be helpful.

The same applies to the recent developments of information and communication theory and technique which may prove to be a strategic weapon especially for co-operative organizations (*Schiemenz* 1987; see also → "*Data Processing* in Co-operative Organizations").

Bibliography

Ashby, W. Ross: An Introduction to Cybernetics, 5. impr., London 1963.
Baetge, Jörg: Betriebswirtschaftliche Systemtheorie, Opladen 1974.
Beer, Stafford: Cybernetics and Management, London 1959.
Beer, Stafford: The viable system model, Journal of the Operations Research Society, vol. 35 (1984), pp. 7–25.
Bertalanffy, Ludwig v.: General System Theory, New York 1968.
Bleicher, Knut (ed.): Organisation als System, Wiesbaden 1972.
Dülfer, Eberhard: Betriebswirtschaftslehre der Kooperative. Kommunikation und Entscheidungsbildung in Genossenschaften und vergleichbaren Organisationen, Göttingen 1984.
Fahrion, Roland (ed.): Kybernetische Aspekte moderner Kommunikationstechnik. Wissenschaftliche Jahrestagung der Gesellschaft für Wirtschafts- und Sozialkybernetik am 9. und 10. Oktober 1987 in Heidelberg, Wirtschaftskybernetik und Systemanalyse, vol. 14, Berlin 1988.
Fischer, Thomas (ed.): Betriebswirtschaftliche Systemforschung und ökonomische Kybernetik. Wissenschaftliche Jahrestagung der Gesellschaft für Wirtschafts- und Sozialkybernetik am 17. und 18. Oktober 1986 in Stuttgart, Wirtschaftskybernetik und Systemanalyse, vol. 13, Berlin 1987.
Mesarovic, M. D. et al.: Theory of Hierarchical Multilevel Systems, New York 1970.
Miller, J. G.: Living Systems, New York 1978.
Probst, Gilbert J.B.: Selbst-Organisation – Ordnungsprozesse in sozialen Organisationen aus ganzheitlicher Sicht, Berlin/Hamburg 1987.
Schiemenz, Bernd: Regelungstheorie und Entscheidungsprozesse. Ein Beitrag zur Betriebskybernetik, Wiesbaden 1972.
Schiemenz, Bernd: Betriebskybernetik – Aspekte des betrieblichen Managements, Stuttgart 1982.
Schiemenz, Bernd: Fortschritte des kybernetik- und systemtheoriegestützten Managements, in: Schiemenz; Bernd/ Wagner, Adolf (eds.), Angewandte Wirtschafts- und Sozialkybernetik, Berlin 1984, pp. 231–248.
Schiemenz, Bernd: Mehr Informationstechnik für Genossenschaften!, ZfGG, vol. 37 (1987), pp. 1–22.
Schiemenz, Bernd/ Wagner, Adolf (eds.): Angewandte Wirtschafts- und Sozialkybernetik, Berlin 1984.
Scholz, Christian: Betriebskybernetische Hierarchiemethodik, Bern 1981.
Simon, Herbert A.: The Architecture of Complexity, Proceedings of the American Philosophical Society, Vol. 106 (1962), pp. 467–482.
Steinbuch, Karl: Automat und Mensch – Kybernetische Tatsachen und Hypothesen, 3. edition, Berlin/Heidelberg/New York 1965.
Trappl, Robert (ed.): Cybernetics and Systems '88, Part 1 and 2, Dordrecht – Boston – London 1988.
Ulrich, Hans/ Probst, Gilbert: Anleitung zum ganzheitlichen Denken und Handeln, Bern/Stuttgart 1988.
Wiener, Norbert: Cybernetics – or control and communication in the animal and the machine, 2. ed., New York/London 1961.

Data Processing in Co-operative Organizations

WALTER BAUSCH

(see also: *Federations*; *Federation Statistics*; *Controlling*; *Auditing*)

I. Basic Features; II. History of Computing Centres; III. Co-operative Data Processing Today; IV. Co-operative Data Processing Tomorrow; V. Outlook.

I. Basic Features

Data processing in the co-operative sector cannot be understood without knowing specific features of co-operatives on the one hand and data processing, in particular electronic data processing (EDP), on the other. Thus, the purpose of this first chapter is to selectively highlight some of them. It is for obvious reasons we are drawing our examples predominantly from the co-operative banking sector (→ *Co-operative Banks*) in Germany.

1. Co-operatives

In any economy, co-operatives are generally quite large in numbers. In return, the single institutions are usually relatively small in size (→ *Operational Size*) compared to the average firm in their respective industry.

As a consequence, it is impossible for many of the co-operatives to employ specialists for each line of business in their industry. From their customers' point of view, they are often not proficient enough in carrying out advanced tasks. This seems to be particularly true in the German banking sector, where the private banks are market leaders e.g. in the securities business (see *Hagedorn/Pelzl*).

The co-operative banks try to overcome this disadvantage by forming → *central institutions* working regionally or even nationwide. Besides the central co-operative banks and chartered accountants, there are also organizations like BIK (supporting in questions of business administration) (→ *Managerial Economics*) and GIS (an information provider). Last but not least there are regional data processing centers supplying services to their co-operative customers.

Since the co-operative banks are legally independent companies, they have a high degree of freedom on their business policies (→ *Business Policies*). When it comes to coordinate strategies, there often arises a natural conflict between the individual objectives and the objectives of the co-operative sector as a whole. This is an issue we are going to return to when talking about the co-operative data processing centers.

2. Electronic Data Processing

Years ago, banks had to employ a great number of people for more or less routine work. Interest calculation was a very time consuming issue. Hence, the application of new labour replacing technologies in the beginning primarily was important for enhancing economic efficiency. Taking into account the increased diversity of the banking business today, it is of at least equal importance to use electronic data processing as an information source and a toolbox for bank employees.

Typically, it takes specialists from different disciplines to create an appropriate system to support banking activities. Although it is not within the scope of this article to give a complete list of functions needed we should, nevertheless, name a few to give some flavour: data base designers, network experts, job controllers, operators, system engineers.

Another relevant feature of computer application is the existence of economies of scale. By "economies of scale" we mean in this case that production costs for a unit of output are decreasing with total output. Some causes of this effect may convince you that the assertion is indeed true (→ *Principle of Cost Coverage*):

1. Taken total cost for developing a new system as given, the cost share of each user decreases with the total number of users.
2. Given a certain equipment, an increasing number of operations performed does not require an equiproportional increase in the number of operators.
3. If there are no differences in other technical features, the unit cost (per byte) of storage space usually decrease with size.

II. History of Computing Centres

Experts noted early that, in many cases, a central computer center was the only possible way to keep the local touch of co-operative banks and to allow, at the same time, access to sophisticated information technology. (See, e.g., *Bausch/Abele* who refer to the origin of today's FIDUCIA founded in 1960.) The markets require the use of such a technology to grant for high quality service and low cost. Independence of the single co-operative banks means that it is at their own discretion to work with a common computer service centre. Hence, the growth of such an institution is directly related to the benefits the banks expect from their participation. Consequently, the remark of *Gitzinger* that from the beginning more banks have joined than have left a central computing centre is a most important observation concerning the service standards of these centres.

The local banks used to insist on keeping a reasonable influence on their central institutions. Thus, they founded several regional computing centres. As in this situation further economies of scale still exist, some centres have merged in the meantime. *Fig.* 1 shows the current centres and the regions they are servicing.

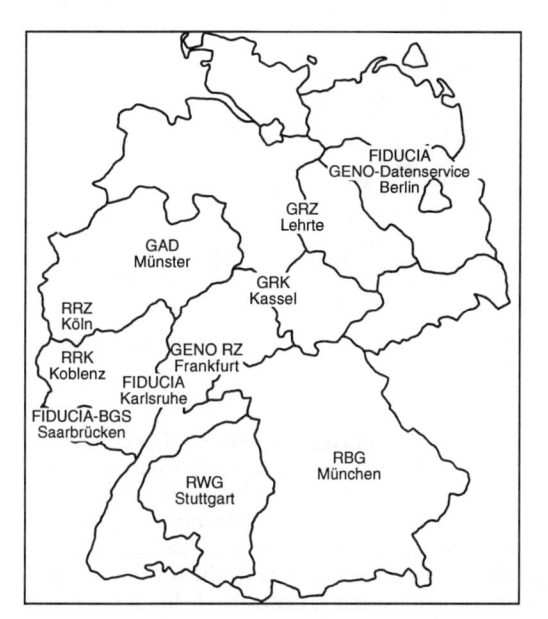

Fig. 1: Co-operative Data Processing Centers.

(It is still an open question, how many of these centres, and of course which ones, will be able to survive.)

Despite all the advantages of common data processing mentioned, there are still some co-operative banks working with own computers. They seem to apply standard banking software. An example is reported by *Benseler/Kengerter*.

Describing the beginning of co-operative data processing would be incomplete without pointing to another technical and organizational aspect. When joint electronic data processing came up, great numbers of punchcards had to be transported each day. This was the origin of courier services which are still important today for delivering printed output. These transaction costs certainly reduce the advantages of joint processing. They decrease with the introduction of online systems and decentralized printing.

III. Co-operative Data Processing Today

When analyzing the state of electronic data processing in co-operative organizations today, the economic and political conditions as well as the state of technology have to be referred to.

1. Competition

The computer centres shown in the last picture are directly affected by the structure of the co-operative sector in the respective region. *Figure* 2 showes the diversity of structures with respect to the balance sheet totals of banks serviced.

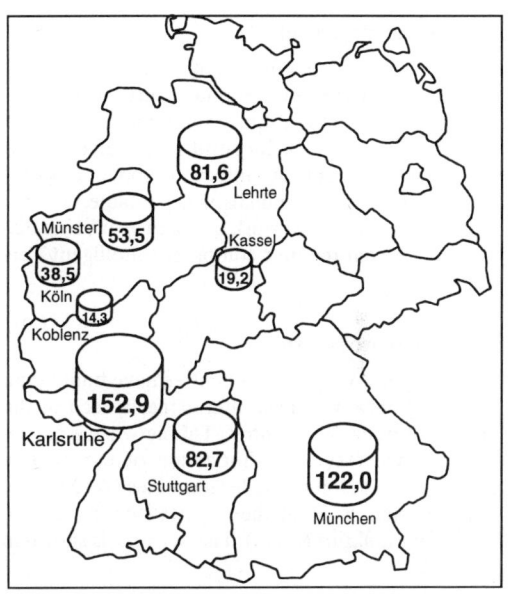

Fig. 2: Balance Sheet Totals of Credit Co-operatives serviced by Co-operative Data Processing Centers (Mrd. DM 1992).

In their own regions, the centres, using different software, are basically monopolists (→ *Competition*). Yet, the informal contacts between the banks of different areas are putting some indirect pressure on them. This is done by comparing the economic performance of the computing centres as well as the quality of their systems. At present (June 1990), the alliance GAD/GRZ compete with FIDUCIA/RBG: the former are developing a new system to cope with future demands, whereas the latter believe that an evolutionary change is more beneficial for their banks.

2. Commonality

Economies of scale not only exist in the processing of data but also, among others, in system design, training, and hardware selection. For this reason the co-operative computing centres founded a working group named AGR (Arbeitsgemeinschaft genossenschaftlicher Rechenzentralen) in 1986. A very important strategical product currently being prepared under the auspices of the AGR is software for bank controlling (→ *Controlling*). Three of the computing centres are involved in developing parts of the system. Eventually, there will be a common data base for controlling purposes without creating a need to redesign the other systems applied by the single computing centres. This data base can be used for many different evaluations which could also be procured jointly.

3. Real-time Processing

An increasing number of co-operative banks has on-line connections to their computer centre. The operation mostly occurs real-time, i.e., input data is processed immediately and the results are available right away (Dialogsystem). An important tool in this process are intelligent terminals which enable the user to do some parts of his work in the case of being disconnected from the host computer (intelligent Terminals).

4. Co-operative Network

The co-operative computer centres have built up an advanced network which interconnects each of the co-operative banking centres. This network is particularly suited for the authorization of eurocheque cards used at automatic teller machines (ATM). The authorization is altogether centralized in a data centre in Frankfurt (Main). The network is shown in *figure 3*.

5. Customers

So far, we have pointed out the role of co-operative computer centres for co-operative banks. Our presentation would not be complete without mentioning other customers of the computer centres. In the case of FIDUCIA as a fairly representative example, the local co-operative banks are the most important customers, followed by the regional central bank of the co-operative sector. Other co-operative customers (e.g., dairys) and central co-operative institutions have also been working with a computing centre. A group that will probably deserve more attention in the future are the non-co-operative customers. The trends in electronic banking indicate that it is necessary for the banks to supply their customers with computer know how and assistance. In this relation, the computer centres of the co-operative sector have the task to assure a high service standard to provide their banks with a comparative advantage above competitors.

6. Full Service

The finance industry seems to experience an increasing demand for integrated financial services world-

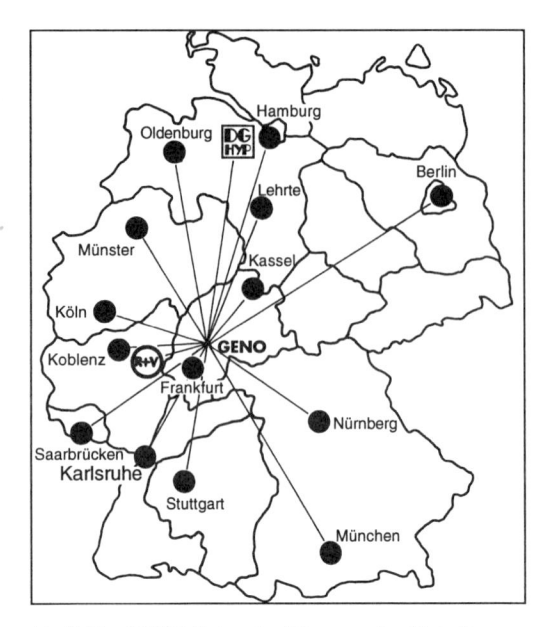

Fig. 3: The GENO-Network of Co-operative Data Processing Centers.

wide. It is not sufficient any more to offer only a small selection of products: the customers request a thorough presentation of alternatives. For a computer centre, this implies that a wide variety of products must be supported: interest must be calculated, reports required by clients or by the law must be generated automatically, electronic help on the use of products and programs must be supplied, and so on. Above their original work the computer centres have expanded to cover a wide range of activities for their own customers, i.e. the banks. Examples of the current lines of business include: hardware leasing, production of software for sale, consulting.

IV. Co-operative Data Processing Tomorrow

It is difficult to make forecasts how data processing in the co-operative sector will look like in a few years. From our perspective, there are at least three main issues that must be taken into consideration: political and economic changes in Europe (→ *European Community*), trends in the banking industry, and technological as well as organizational developments in the information industry.

1. Changes in Europe

Until very recently, the consequences of further liberalization in the common European market were on the top of every company's agenda. For the German banking industry, e.g., the Cecchini report forecasts a 10 per cent drop in revenue (*Priewasser*, p. 1128). More competition across borders and more diversity

in product offerings were generally expected. In the last months, however, the German reunification has been the leading topic. The final outcome of this process is still to be determined, and even the status quo is not fully known. As far as co-operative banks in East Germany are concerned, the situation is as follows:
The co-operative sector is split into subsectors which have their emphasis on industry, respectively agriculture. Some electronic data processing is available. But since this has to be more or less replaced, there is an exceptional opportunity to install a common system for all co-operative banks in the former German Democratic Republic. It is the fervent competition among the western computer centres which might make such a solution impossible. Because of the difficulties concerning prediction of future developments in East Germany, we will refrain from a thorough analysis here. Also, there is a high probability that the situation in the East will sooner or later approach the status quo of the West. In this case, a detailed examination of the GDR was obviously obsolete.

2. Banking in the Future

Trends in future banking have been widely discussed. The reader may consult e.g., *Priewasser* and the other papers on that issue, or *Schimmelmann*. Here we shall only give some keywords: increasing competition, decreasing margins, more innovative products, mobile sales force, increasing importance of consultancy. Quite generally, it can be stated that market power will continue to shift from the banks to their customers. For the co-operative banking sector it will, in addition, matter very much how the two merging processes will go on: the first one which yields bigger institutions on the local level, and the second one which integrates the regional central banks into the head institute, the DG-Bank (→ *Central Institutions*). From an organizational point of view, it seems to be one of the key issues whether or not we will see branch offices without any employees, i.e., purely automatic teller centres.

3. Effects on the Information Industry

The effects on the information industry are manifold. Above all, there is and will be a continuous pressure for rapid development of software needed to process the new products. At the same time, the requirements are becoming more and more complex. The computer centres themselves can expect some relief in this situation from the applicaton of CASE (computer aided software engineering) tools. Other major technological changes include the advance of relational databases. They are much better suited for applications by the end user than any other data base technology before. Combined with decreases in the price and increases in the performance of personal computers, this enhances decentralized solutions (see below) including local area networks (LAN).
Another growing branch of software technology is the broad area of artificial intelligence in general and expert systems, respectively knowledge based systems in particular. These tools provide help in difficult situations, making them especially worthwhile for the co-operative sector, since the small individual firms often precisely lack such expert knowledge due to their size. For the computer centres, location factors will increase in importance. Among them are not just the level of wages, but also the supply of qualified manpower. Emphasis will particularly be on contact with universities having a strong background in computer science.

4. Centralized and Decentralized Processing

In the co-operative sector, the discussion about advantages of centralized versus decentralized processing is always alive. The aspects are basically all known and will not be repeated here. Still, we shall like to highlight two issues:
The changes in the finance industry (→ *Financing*) mentioned imply that many programmes must be written. Apart from many other tasks, auditors checking the banks are required to examine the data processing in general. It is a remarkable, but often forgotten financial advantage of computer centres that this needs not to be done at every single bank, since there is a thorough test of the centre which can be referred to by all auditors (→ *Auditing*).
What has changed dramatically over the past years is the attitude of bank employees. In the beginning of the computer age, many were quite sceptical with respect to the new tools and their organizational implications. Now, there are more and more young people entering the banking business who like personal computers and often have one at home (→ *Human Resource Management*). This new type of employee is used to the generally high comfort they provide. Consequently, the users, in many cases, are not satisfied with, the graphical capabilities and the response times of host systems run by computer centres.

V. Outlook

Anyway, computer centres will continue to play a major role in the co-operative sector in the years to come. They will, however, be forced to support some division of labour: on the one hand, the processing of large amounts of data will still take place in these centres, but, on the other hand, the centres will enable users to amend this work by giving them access to appropriate data bases for the banks' own information systems.

Bibliography

Bausch, Walter/P. Abele: Datenverarbeitung bei einer flächendeckenden Buchungsgemeinschaft, IBM Nachrichten, Vol. 242 und 243 (1978), pp. 301–308, 394–400.
Benseler, Hans und Günter Kengerter: Siemens-KORDOBA bei der Volksbank Schorndorf, Bank und Markt, Vol. 7 (1988), pp. 347–360.
Gitzinger, Siegfried: Entscheidungskriterien für das EDV-Konzept einer Genossenschaftsbank. Aspekte bankwirtschaftlicher Forschung und Praxis, Frankfurt 1985, pp. 347–360.
Hagedorn, Ellen/Wolfgang Pelzl: Das Effektengeschäft der Genossenschaftsbanken, Zeitschrift für das gesamte Kreditwesen, Vol. 12 (1989). pp. 567–569.
Priewasser, Erich: Die Banken in Europa, Zeitschrift für das gesamte Kreditwesen, Vol. 24 (1988), pp. 1126–1128.
Schimmelmann, Wulf von: Technologie ist kein Wundermittel, Bankkaufmann, Vol.4 (1988), pp. 15–20.
Schneider, Walter: Gedanken zur Zweigstellenpolitik und Zweigstellenstruktur einer Genossenschaftsbank, Bank und Markt, Vol. 10 (1989), pp. 5–14.

Desjardins, Alphonse (1854–1920) / Filene, Edward A. (1860–1937)

ROLAND POHLING

(see also: *Credit Unions*; *Schulze-Delitzsch*; *Raiffeisen*; *IRU*)

I. Alphonse Desjardins; II. Edward Albert Filene.

Alphonse Desjardins and *Edward A. Filene* are internationally considered the founders of the *"credit union movement"* (→ *Credit Unions*).

I. Alphonse Desjardins

Alphonse Desjardins was born on Nov. 5, 1854 at Lévis, Québec/Canada. After visiting the Collège de Lévis he entered journalism on a local newspaper and later worked on the *Canadien*. He edited at his own risk the Debates of the Quebec Legislature from 1879 to 1890 and later after a one year's returning to journalism served as an official reporter of the House of Commons in Ottawa from 1892 to 1917.
Inspired by House debates on excessive interest rates imposed on low-income people *Desjardins* conceived the idea of co-operative savings-and-loan societies on a parish basis, which could satisfy the credit needs especially of the labouring classes. He had already studied the co-operative credit systems in Europe and examined the publications of → *Hermann Schulze-Delitzsch,* → *Friedrich Wilhelm Raiffeisen* (Germany), *Luigi Luzzatti* (Italy) and *Henry W. Wolff* (England) when *Wolff* (by that time chairman of the Executive Bureau of the International Co-operative Alliance, London) encouraged him to establish such a society. The first savings and credit co-operative on the North American continent (*"Caisse Populaire"*) was founded on Dec. 6,1900 in Lévis, where it began operation on Jan. 23, 1901, although there was no legislation under which it could have been incorporated. The first deposit received was ten cents and the total received on the first day was $ 26.40. Despite this humble start and rather slow development in the first years, the co-operative all of a sudden became the point of departure for what later was called *"Le mouvement des caisses populaires Desjardins"*.
According to the conception of *Desjardins* the savings-and-loan society should not only procure financial means but procure at the same time education for its members in order to motivate and enable them to accurately deal with money and also to bring them to a better perception of themselves as responsible partners in the co-operative and in the parochial community. The joint orientation towards economic and social educative goals characterized these co-operatives from the beginning and effected fruitful relations with the clergy, to whom the movement owed enduring support.
In the following years *Desjardins* took up the cause of co-operative organizations. In 1907, the first Canadian legislation with respect to the *caisses populaires* was enacted by the Legislature of Quebec under the title *Quebec Co-operative Syndicates Act* (→ *Law, International*). In 1909, *Desjardins* also became instrumental in the founding of the first savings-and-loan societies in the USA, where a group of French-Canadians organized such a co-operative in St. Mary's Parish in Manchester/New Hampshire; others were founded in French sectors of two towns in Massachusetts. Since US authorities, however, did not accept the translation *people's bank* in the USA this type of co-operative was henceforth named *credit union* (→ *Co-operative Banks*). By that time *Desjardins* also worked closely together with *Edward A. Filene* and *Pierre Jay* (Banking Commissioner of Mass.) in preparing the Credit Union Act in that State, which was enacted in the same year.
Desjardins became widely renowned already during his lifetime. He was selected to membership by the American Economic Association, the American Academy of Political and Social Science, and the Permanent American Commission of Agricultural Finance, Production, Distribution and Rural Life. In recognition of his work and for his further support in establishing and promoting *caisses populaires* he was conferred the Order of St. Gregory by *Pope Pius X* in 1913. When he died in his native town on Oct. 31, 1920 he had initiated and assisted the foundation of 206 caisses: 173 in Québec, 24 in the province of Ontario and 9 in the USA.

II. Edward Albert Filene

Edward Albert Filene, LLD, was born on Sept. 3, 1860 in Salem, Massachusetts /USA. After visiting high school he together with his younger brother *Lincoln* took over the management of their father's department store in Boston, which soon succeeded extraordinarily. *Edward Filene* proved himself as pioneer in applying scientific methods of management and efficient organization in retail distribution. Beyond his own business affairs he concerned himself with common interests of trade and was active as a planner and co-organizer of the local, state, national and international chambers of commerce.

After taking exit from his mere business career, *Filene* turned to projects for human betterment while maintaining that *"his social and economic views represented the enlightened self-interest of a businessman rather than altruism"*. During a visit to India, he learned the method of operating a co-operative credit institution shaped after the co-operative model of → *F. W. Raiffeisen*, an experience which led him to the conviction that the American of modest income could solve his problems of credit by associating himself and his co-workers to organize their savings and loan business on a co-operative basis. He engaged himself in the *credit union movement* by mobilizing liberal businessmen for its support and by considerable contributions out of his private means. Organizational instruments for his social activities were the *Co-operative League* and later the *Twentieth Century Fund*, which he had set up especially for this purpose.

When the Credit Union Act of Massachusetts had become effective in 1909, *Filene* set up a national committee on people's banks to encourage and direct the establishing of credit unions throughout the US, which, however, met with little success and in 1921 was organized anew as *Credit Union National Extension Bureau (CUNEB)* for the head of which he introduced *Roy F. Bergengren*. On *Filene's* and *Bergengren's* initiative credit union laws were prepared and effected in 32 federal states from 1929 and the first *Federal Credit Union Act* was passed in 1934 as well. In the same year *Filene* induced the foundation of the *Credit Union National Association (CUNA)* to take over the tasks of CUNEB and to function as apex organization of the credit unions in the US. He became the first president.

Filene's activities in favour of the social and public weal were hardly restricted to the credit unions. Among other activities he was founder and first president of the *Consumer Distribution Corporation*, the central organ for a national league of co-operative department stores (1935), vice president of the American Association for Labor Legislation, chairman of the Massachusetts State Recovery Board (1933–34), vice chairman of the executive committee and chairman of the finance committee of the League to Enforce Peace, and organizer and financial sponsor of European Peace awards in Great Britain, France, Germany and Italy. *Filene* is author of The Way Out (1924), More Profits from Merchandising (1925), The Model Stock Plan (1930) and of Successful Living in this Machine Age (1931). In honour of his services *Filene* was nominated Officer of Legion of Honor (France); Cavaliere of Order of The Crown (Italy), Commander of Order of the White Lion (Czechoslovakia) as well as of the Great Gold Cross of Merit (Austria). He died in Paris on Sept. 26th, 1937.

Development of Co-operatives in Africa, South of Sahara

SAMUEL C. CHUKWU

(see also: *Development, Northern Africa*; *Development, South Asia*; *Development, South-East Asia*; *Development, Latin America*; *Classification*; *Education, Africa*; *Pre-co-operative Forms*; *Autochthonous Co-operatives*)

I. French-born Approaches to Co-operatives; II. British-born Approaches to Co-operatives; III. Co-operative Development After Independence; IV. Areas of Co-operative Activity; V. Secondary Co-operative Institutions.

Co-operative development in Africa greatly reflects colonial activities especially the English and French and, after independence, activities by African governments and co-operatives themselves. Before these, however, many, varied *indigenous forms of co-operation* existed (*Seibel* 1968) (→ *Autochthonous Co-operatives*). Most common were the rotating savings and credit associations. Despite variations, they all revolve around savings and/or loans (→ *Pre-co-operative Forms*). Basically, members contribute at fixed regular times to a joint purse given to one member after the other until all have been served and a new cycle may begin. Although popular, several shortcomings exist e.g. corrupt leadership, inequity, default by early receivers, fraud, inadequate accounting and inadequate loanable funds, common to these and the modern co-operative is especially the spirit of mutual effort towards meeting commonly felt needs. They could thus have been launching pads for the modern co-operatives; but this was rare since e.g. many colonial administrators sought to replace them with those co-operatives. Different approaches were adopted especially by the French and British.

I. French-born Approaches to Co-operatives

While the French tried assimilating Africans, on the co-operative (institutional) level, they tried replacement. Between 1910 and independence in the sixties, they tried some variations (→ *Development, Northern Africa*).

The *Societes Indigenes de Prevoyance* (SIP), created by government order, were introduced as from 1910. Each one covered an administrative district with a chairman nominated by the colonial governor after consultation with an elected district supervising board. Because of poor response, voluntary membership gave way to compulsion in 1915. Member subscriptions were collected alongside regular taxes and were perceived as one and the same thing by natives. The head of the colonial district administration was the ex-officio chairman. The policies of the SIP were public oriented and its powers also wide. It could e.g. seize land for public use and had to maintain buffer food stocks against emergencies; procure, stock and supply agricultural inputs; buy, process and sell agricultural produce and, arrange for extension services and loans.

As co-operative oriented structures, they neither met the basic criteria nor the member oriented aims. Though conceived as voluntary and democratic, in reality, they were fully dominated by the colonial officials. Natives scarcely took active part. The administrative council, though elected, was such that members could not challenge or contradict an official who was both chairman of the SIP and district officer concurrently. The SIP was seen as a branch of the public service or parastatal, which left the native no room for initiative or independence. Also, in some instances they were very large, covering up to 200 villages each, with membership of up to 100,000.

Criticisms and demands for genuine co-operatives grew. For a brief period, therefore, rapid, indiscriminate establishment of producer cooperatives took place which, for lack of co-operative education, management skills etc. mostly failed. Thus arose a new variation of the SIP, the *Societe Mutuelle de Production Rurale* (SMPR) or Mutual Association for Rural Promotion in 1953. Its tasks were the same as those of the SIP, but it aimed at gradually reducing the powers of the government administration, increasing democracy and development of proper co-operatives. It had a meeting of elected delegates from constituent villages of the district, an administrative council (elected from the delegates and ex-officio members, technical advisers, territorial counsellors etc.) and a president elected from the non-ex-officio members. Membership was obligatory and open to groups. The SMPR was divided into specialised departments (production, marketing, services etc.) under special committees of the administrative council. Despite this apparently increased democracy, because of compulsory membership, actual administration and finance being the same as in the SIP and, emphasis on cash crops as against natives' emphasis on subsistence crops, it failed to attract natives.

To regenerate the SMPR, they were turned in 1956 into the *Societe Mutelle de Development Rurale* (SMDR) or Mutual Associations for Rural Development which acted as intermediaries for loans, inputs etc. to peasants. They were meant to become regional bodies for development on co-operative lines but were otherwise administered like their forerunners with obligatory membership. They were, likewise, generally unsuccessful. They limped on into the independence era (the sixties) in the different countries.

II. British-born Approaches to Co-operatives

Regarding the British, indirect rule rather than assimilation was propagated using existing indigenous institutions. There was, however, no such use of indigenous associations which, rather, were to be replaced by the imported co-operatives. The basic concept was the → *classical British-Indian Co-operative pattern* developed from mainly German (→ *Raiffeisen*; → *Schulze-Delitzsch*) and British (→ *Rochdale Pioneers*) home experiences enriched with those of India, Burma and Ceylon/Sri Lanka and then transferred to the Gold Coast/Ghana (1931), Tanganyika/Tanzania (1932) and Nigeria (1935) etc.

Its aim: state sponsorship of co-operatives which should ultimately develop into autonomous, self-reliant, viable units on the Rochdale/Raiffeisen lines, after a period of guidance, supervision and advice by the office and staff of the government Registrar of cooperatives in each country. The registrar and his staff were thus to make up for the lacking technical know-how. Interested natives were to be first taught modern co-operative organisation prior to establishing societies and, helped to establish and register them (→ *Policies for Promotion*). The registrar was to audit, advise and assist in their administration and to liquidate eventually unviable ones. Emphasis was on → *education* rather than administration, under normal circumstances avoiding interference which could give the impression that the co-operative belonged to, or was run by the government.

However, this was not achieved; rather, *state control* (→ *officialization*) slowly replaced sponsorship. This resulted from very rapid numerical increases of the societies and quantitative inadequacy of the advisory staff. It has run into the post-independence era. Rather than slowly nursing societies into viable units before registration, as from 1946, the process was often short-circuited. The registry staff concentrated increasingly on supervision, registering more and more economically inviable societies with unenlightened members and committees. An attempt to counteract the resultant inadequate self-management and control was sought in giving increased powers to the registrar to interfere in the day-to-day management and control of societies and, sometimes, to even act on their behalf.

A striking feature in the colonial period especially in those areas with European settlers was the racially segregated co-operatives in Kenya, Zambia, Zimbabwe and the "co-operative" settlements (colonatos) of Angola and Mozambique. Furthermore, like in the SIP, compulsory membership existed for a while in the native coffee co-operatives of Kenya in the 1940's and, in those around the Kilimanjaro coffee areas (Tanzania) in the late 1920's. In addition, contrary to popular belief, the co-operatives were sometimes spontaneous by natives e.g. in the Kilimanjaro area (early thirties); Ghana (1928); Sierra Leone (forties); Uganda (1913). Also contrary to popular belief, colonial governments were not always positively disposed to such co-operative establishment e.g. in Uganda and, also Ghana (1925). The rather high rate of failure of such attempts, therefore, sometimes resulted from this unsupportive attitude (e.g. in Sierra Leone).

Thus, in many countries, the first significant increases followed the unavoidable enactments of the co-operative laws and appointment of registrars e.g. Kenya (from 1945); Zambia (1948); Ghana (1931); Nigeria (1935); Tanzania (1951), Uganda (1946) etc. This resulted generally from the registrar's promotional and enlightenment work. However, enthusiasm was not always generally and spontaneously high since sometimes, the high standards set and increasing government control raised native suspicions e.g. Nigeria (1935/36); Uganda (1948); Kenya (1940's) and, most especially, Zimbabwe, where the co-operatives were under the then Ministry of Internal Affairs, a key agent of pre-independence racial oppression.

III. Co-operative Development after Independence

The second, and till date, the greater impetus to co-operative development came with political independence in the late fifties and the sixties, the new government encouraging co-operatives for different reasons (→ *Development Policy*).

The early part of that era saw the co-operative sectors of francophone Africa having relatively few orthodox urban co-operatives and dominated by the different variations of the basic pre-cooperative SIP, while anglophone Africa was domiated by gradually officialised Rochdale/Raiffeisen oriented types. Independence, however, did not bring these directions together. In the francophone countries two broad directions have emerged, exemplified by Senegal/Ivory Coast on one side and Niger/Mali/Burkina Faso on the other (*Münkner* 1984).

The Rochdale model co-operatives in Senegal (as from 1942), due to poor management and bad loan activities etc. had failed by 1952. A period of socialism (1960) also affecting the co-operatives and spearheaded by some state bodies (e.g. Regional Centres for Development Aid-CRAD etc.) ended in 1962, followed in 1963 by new attempts at state induced autonomous co-operatives overseen by another parastatal (National Board for Co-operative and Dev. Aid – ONCAD) with Co-operatives covering 4 to 8 villages each. It failed in 1980 leaving behind various rural, mostly (1,987) marketing societies. The trend was then to turn each village of those large co-operatives into a section, represented at the co-operative itself by elected delegates.

Unofficial/*Probationary societies* and *village groups* initiated by state and other agencies also exist in large numbers. The aim is to achieve an autonomous orthodox movement of all these with secondary etc. bodies not yet realised but whose functions are now handled by parastatals and a cooperative development. The Ivory Coast shares this aim as well as comparable experiences. In 1966, all her existing cooperatives technically became probationary pre-co-operatives (*groupement à vocation coopérative – GVC*) and, like any subsequently new ones, had a maximum of 3 years to prove their viability and be registered as proper cooperatives or, liquidate (→ *Pre-co-operative Forms*).

In e.g. Niger/Mali/Burkina Faso on the other hand, beside small numbers of orthodox urban co-operatives, following failures of state interventionist attempts, the emphasis is now fully on pre-cooperatives and *all-purpose village groups* e.g. 10,360 in Niger (1983); 8,310 in Mali (1967) and 3,594 in Burkina Faso (1981). Guided by different state and private (aid) agencies these are expected to eventually mature into viable, *adjusted African "co-operatives"*. Structurally they are informal, spontaneous, nonconformist and heterogenous, following normal local village customs. Membership may be group (the village) rather than individually based (e.g. Mali; Niger) and share-holding is not always a pre-condition (e.g. Niger).

These governments, as well as those of the anglophone countries generally see the co-operatives as one instrument for, among other things, improving earnings and living standards. In some cases (e.g. Zambia) especially the humanistic element was seen to tally with that of traditional African society while in e.g. Tanzania; Senegal (1060–62) they were considered to be ideologically close to local versions of African socialism and, in other cases, (e.g. Uganda, S. Leone, Tanzania) they were a means of bringing natives into the mainstream of hitherto totally or sectorally foreign dominated national economies (e.g. Asians in East Africa and Lebanese etc. in the West) (→ *Groupe d'initiative*).

This encouragement gave rise to great numerical increases (e.g. of over 400% in Zambia between 1966 and 1969; approximately 100% in Kenya, 1963–66; 77% in Tanzania, 1961–65; and 142% in Nigeria, 1960–70) as well as in their fields of activity, starting from the originally mostly marketing co-operatives to group farming/settlement societies; supply, credit and multi-purpose agricultural ones, fisheries, poultry and cattle rearing; insurance, credit and banking and also, especially in the urban areas, consumer supplies, crafts and small-scale industrial production and supply activities. They have, however, been most important in agriculture (marketing), thrift and credit and to a lesser extent, consumer supplies, on which this paper subsequently concentrates. They have not gained prominence in the other areas of their existence.

IV. Areas of Co-operative Activity

1. Marketing

In *Marketing*, the co-operatives mostly concentrate on cash/export crops (→ *Marketing*). They are part and parcel to the Marketing Board system. Their secondaries etc. are licensed buying agents among others, or enjoy monopoly rights for specific crops. They generally exist as primaries integrated into secondaries and apexes.

Their activities cover e.g. assembly, transport and/or processing and storage till the produce is taken over by the marketing board. They thus help check e.g. collusion between middlemen; buying rings; manipulation of farm gate prices and monopoly of transport, all of which leave producers defenceless and exploited. In very few cases, indigenous governments have, therefore, granted them monopoly rights e.g. Tanzania (coffee); Uganda (Cotton); Senegal (groundnuts) while e.g. Zambia (early eighties) even replaces the MB with them. Malawi is exceptional in keeping them off marketing her major cash crop, tobacco.

Over time, the fortunes of these co-operatives have varied. They guaranteed good quality, which led to premiums and popularity and, sometimes, the requirement that they also serve non-members e.g. coffee in S. Leone; groundnuts and maize in Zambia. In e.g. Ghana, their share of cocoa handled rose from approx. 2% to 11% in 1939–48, 30% in 1960/61, 25% in 1967/68 while in S. Leone (1959/60) they controlled 50%. Regarding Uganda's cotton and coffee, before monopoly rights for cotton in 1969, they had increased their share from 1% in 1950 to 20% in 1960 and 60% in 1965. The generally much higher percentages recorded in East and Central Africa reflect in part, the generally more preferential treatment enjoyed there.

In many cases, marketing has been combined with other activities e.g. supply of often government subsidized inputs (→ *Supply Co-operatives*). Since application of these are still not widespread, their scale of operation has remained modest and, *purely agricultural supply societies* hardly exist (→ *Rural Co-operatives*).

2. Credit and Banking

Credit activities have been relatively more important, taken up partly because private buyers lure members with them, thereby increasing indebtedness and disloyalty to their cooperatives and also, partly because of the advantage of increased loan recovery through linking marketing with credit (→ *Co-operative Banks*). Unlike in Asia, therefore, credit has followed marketing in most cases, rather than vice versa.

A much smaller number of orthodox (*Raiffeisen* type) *savings and/or credit cooperatives* of any consequence have existed mainly in Mauritius, Sierra Leone and Nigeria (East). Not only did colonial co-operative sponsors often discourage credit, believing that indebtedness was not high, input supplies to be possibly credit financed have been low and the usual necessary collateral, land, has not been easily available, because of widespread group ownership. In Sierra Leone, the big push came with 25 co-operatives in 1953 growing to 163 in 1959, 364 registered plus 200 unregistered ones in 1963 and 629 in 1968. In Nigeria, they started in 1938 in the south-east, many evolving from indigenous rotating savings and credit associations. They soon (1945) were too many for the government promoters to cope with thus encouraging growth of regional and provincial unions. In Mauritius, they grew from 20 in 1913 to 36 in 1923. They fell to 28 in 1932, leading (1939) to their activity being linked with sugar cane marketing, reduced levels of default and evolution to 66 virtually multipurpose societies in 1944 and 175 in 1983 (*Jeetun* 1988).

While savings also came from non-members, the major credit activity covers mainly short-term loans to members. Whereas the loans cover production and consumption aims in Mauritius, in Nigeria, they have been dominantly for small-scale trading. While in Sierra Leone (1967/68) and elsewhere, their contributions to agricultural activities have been on the decline along with the marketing societies, in Nigeria, they generally have not been a prominent agricultural loan source. *Purely savings co-operatives* have not been common even in these 3 cases. In e.g. Mauritius, they numbered 11 in 1966/67, falling to 7 in 1980/81. They have also been concentrated in urban areas and (e.g. in Nigeria), since many members see little advantage in saving only, the societies tend to be transformed into urban savings and credit societies which increased from 182 to 219 in 1942, and 405 as early as 1951. As the post office savings system and the commercial banks spread into the rural areas and increase mobile banking services or become more accommodative, the attraction of these societies tends to wane. A relatively new entrant in the field are the North American style → *credit unions* (*Kirsch* 1977).

Mostly introduced after independence (e.g. Ghana,

1955; Ehtiopia, 1964; West Cameroon, 1964; Kenya, 1973 etc.) between 1970 and 1974 e.g. membership and savings increased respectively in Zambia approx. 65% and 165%; Ethiopia, 163% and 622%; Kenya, 211% and 85%; W. Cameroon, 195% and 769% and Ghana, 203% and 264%. By 1975, they were most common in S. Leone (425 societies), Ghana (417), Nigeria (251), Tanzania (230), W. Cameroon (177), Kenya (155) Uganda (80), Zambia (63) etc. They are mostly urban oriented (exception: Cameroon where 66% are rural). Organizationally, they often exist in 3 tiers: primary, national apex and regional chapters which are informal non-legal entities but rather, branches of the apex. Their establishment is usually that of bottom – apex – middle instead of the classical bottom-middle-apex, or, as in most developing countries, top, and then middle or bottom, interchangeably.

As confirmed by the above statistics, the little success of the orthodox savings and credit co-operatives cannot be simply explained away by a lack of savings potential; rather, the success of the C.U. goes back to being mostly initiated by missionaries within their parish stations, and thus being free of the environmental and human frailties common to other cooperatives; intensive pre-co-operative education, orientation and enlightenment; restriction to financial activities; insistence on a solid common bond and, much less interference from, or dependence on government agencies which limit themselves to the minimum statutory duties, leaving promotion, supervision, advice and sometimes, even audit, to the CU movement itself. Unlike the other co-operatives, the CU's are united in a continent-wide association, the Africa Cooperative Saving and Credit Association (ACOSCA) (*Münkner* 1978), in Nairobi, which was established in 1986 and is open to all CU national associations or national promotion committees or primary CU's. Its aims include, promotion, co-ordination, consultancy, advisory and representation, fund raising, technical assistance, training etc. activities for CU development in Africa.

CU's have tended to avoid much functional contacts with other co-operatives, Cameroon (where they have linked up with agricultural cooperatives) being an exception. Unlike the other cooperatives which scarcely contain women members, female representation is high in the CU's in Nigeria, Sierra Leone, Lesotho and Botswana.

Their major problems among others include: their distinct single-purpose nature being contrary to the increased tendency towards multi-purpose co-operatives; their basically urban orientation being contrary to the present emphasis on rural development; their basic voluntary unpaid management not leading to the required management calibre and yet they often do not have enough funds to employ professionals.

3. Farming on Co-operative Lines

Regarding the other co-operatives, the following are some key problems: inadequate capital; unenlightenment, poor management, supervision and control; high loan defaults; corruption and fraud; inability to pay cash for members' produce; untimely delivery of loans and supplies; margins from the marketing boards being too low; stiff and often unfair competition from private sources etc.

A variety of *farming on co-operative lines* have also existed e.g. in Zaire, Zambia, the Ivory, Coast, Benin, Burkina Faso, Togo, Nigeria, Uganda (*Dülfer* 1974). They aim at e.g. employment and increased income generation; introduction of improved technology; increased food supply; checking the rural-urban drift and achieving demonstration effects etc. The settlement schemes (→ *Communal Settlements*) in Nigeria and the special SONADER model of Benin are of special interest. However, the farming cooperatives generally, have not been successful. Key problems include internal disagreements; lack of feelings for common property; ineffective division and organisation of labour; high overheads; poor management and, a civil service mentality etc. The most prominent case is the *Ujamaa* of Tanzania (*Baldus* 1976) (→ *Autochthonous Co-operatives*).

They were preceeded by unsuccessful (colonial) government and private attempts and were based on President Nyerere's ideas articulated as from 1962 and reflected in the Arusha Declaration (1967). The settlements were to be eventually based on common ownership of land, installations, food etc., with settlers working and living together etc. characteristic of the African extended family. The government was to provide basic infrastructural, advisory and credit facilities but the settlement was to be democratically self-governing in a form of African socialism (→ *Conceptions, Co-operative*).

Villagisation implied clustering nomads and, often, isolated homesteads of between 250 and 600 each, thus making feasible, the supply of basic social, extension and other productive services. As from 1968, they could register as co-operative societies; based on persuasion, they increased (1967–71) from 48 to 4,464 societies with a population of 1.5 million, far short of the target 14 million and thus prompting a call in 1973 for attaining the target by 1976. This new tempo increased the villages from 5,628 (1973) to 8,000 with 13 million villagers (1977) under a transition which was not always smooth or based a persuasion. Under a 1975 law, each of them was automatically deemed a multi-purpose co-operative while all other orthodox rural co-operatives were abolished (Abolition also took place in Ghana on an even greater scale (Nov. 1960), followed likewise by re-instatement in 1966).

A full Ujamaa socialist village was to evolve in 3 stages starting with registration and then, increasing communal activities until no individual identification of farms etc. would exist in the last stage. Ujamaa was, however, generally unsuccessful for reasons including: self-government was not actualised as bureaucrats virtually took over; poor planning; compulsion; non-fulfilment of government promises; farmer resistance; inadequate sites, management, attitude to common property, commitment and competence by relevant parastatal staff; and, preference by settlers for private individual farms etc. Non-performance led to the re-instatement of the hitherto abolished rural co-operatives in 1982.

4. Consumer Co-operatives

→ *Consumer co-operatives* have also been tried, started usually in periods of great shortage. Their aims include equitable distribution of essential goods; checking hoarding, black markets, conditional sales, profiteering, inflation; and, (e.g. Uganda), encouraging native participation in commerce. They have not been prominent, highest numbers (1965–70) being Mali (151), Senegal (97), Mauritius (56), Ghana (53) Tanzania (50) etc. They sometimes exist in 3 tiers: importation, wholesale, retail (Ghana; Nigeria) or also only as retail units (Kenya).

They have tended to increase at the economically most difficult periods, encouraged sometimes by positive but rarely practicalised government statements guaranteeing supply of minimum quotas of local and imported items to the societies (e.g. Ghana, Nigeria) or, by grant of monopoly or preferential treatment regarding importation and/or internal distribution (Tanzania, 1962; Mali, pre- 1968). Generally urban oriented, other rural societies may have consumer supplies only as sidelines (e.g. Zambia, Sierra Leone, Senegal;) while the consumer ones may also turn multi-purpose (e.g. Burkina Faso).

Generally, they have not been successful for reasons including (*Hanel* 1967) incompetent, dishonest management and staff; inadequate capital; stiff, unfair and unequal competition with large corporations (Botswana, Lesotho, Cameroon) or multi-nationals (Nigeria) and also with a host of small traders who have virtually no overheads; internal ideological/political rivalries (Chad); inadequate supplies; adoption of a foreign fixed price system; refusal of credit sales as practised by competitor traders and, a high level of subsistence production by the majority rural folk.

V. Secondary Co-operative Institutions

Cooperation banking was first reported from Kpeve, Togo (1938) (*de Graft-Johnson* 1958). By 1962, they existed in Nigeria (4 units beginning 1953) and, Ghana (1946), Mauritius (1948), Uganda (1964), Kenya (1965), Sierra Leone (1971), Botswana (1974) which have them as national apexes (→ *Central Institutions*). Their aims include saving/capital mobilisation; financing co-operatives in order to reduce costs (interests to other lenders; preferential rates to them in Nigeria, Ghana, Botswana); co-ordinating co-operatives' finances; creating a greater security base for other lenders; channelling funds under national/international schemes to co-operatives (e.g. Kenya); co-operative education and training (Botswana).

In Nigeria and Kenya, they exist under both the cooperative and the company laws and, though originally meant to serve only members, they often go fully commercial, lending to non-members (Nigeria, Ghana, Botswana) and even state governments (Nigeria) such that these become the dominant borrowers (Nigeria-East). Major problems include variously; inadequate capital leading to periods of dormancy (e.g. Uganda), use of other banks as agents (Kenya), sponsorship by other banks (S. Leone) or government (Ghana, Nigeria) leading, in turn, to interferences or even take-overs (Nigeria, Kenya); doubtful credit-worthiness, management and viability of member co-operatives and projects; high overheads, inadequate liquidity etc. In this situation, their work has often been supplemented by other state financial bodies (mostly state agricultural banks e.g. Nigeria, Ghana, Uganda, Senegal, Ivory Coast, Niger).

Other secondaries and apexes have also existed (vertical integration), many of them tending to be multipurpose, reflecting the nature of most of their primary affiliates. While they are still to develop in the francophone areas (parastatals take their place there) some of them have done well in anglophone areas (*Hyden* 1973; *Münkner* 1985).

Relatively recently beset (like the francophone parastatals) by corruption, inefficiency, inadequate committeemen, sectionalism and poor quality services, poor capital base etc., state sponsorship and concentration of powers in government hands have greatly increased. To the classical government function (of e.g. promotion; administration of the law), much of internal administration in secondaries and primaries has been increasingly added, while (e.g. in Kenya), extra-ordinary powers of the government now also cover: compelling membership of primaries in secondaries; ordering amalgamations; approving divisions; instituting inquiries and consequently removing elected management committees and appointing interim ones including managers; approving resolutions of general meetings, society budgets and high level appointments e.g. by secondaries. Misuse of such wide powers cannot be ruled out.

VI. Summary

As against the post-independence explosion of co-operatives and the above functions and powers, the staff strength of the *relevant government departments* have not kept pace by any means; pay and conditions of service have not been commensurate and, drifting of the able staff to other establishments is common. With increasingly dwindling resources and huge internal and foreign debts, the governments cannot keep up the present option which is also unfair to the other tax paying non-co-operative sectors. *De-officialization* is thus preferable, if adopted gradually and accompanied by effective education with specific target dates for individually differentiated societies and movements. The better experiences of the Credit Union support this option.

Bibliography

Apthorpe, R. (ed.): Rural co-operatives and Planned Change in Africa – Case Materials, Geneva 1970.
Baldus, R.: Zur operationalen Effizienz der Ujamaa Kooperative Tanzania, Marburg 1976.
Brycesson, D.: Second Thoughts on Marketing Co-operatives in Tanzania, Oxford, not dated.
Commonwealth Institute: Ujamaa in Tanzania, London 1978.
COPAC (Rome): Co-operatives Information Notes (especially Nos.) 2. Kenya; 11. Nigeria; 12. Ghana; 14. Zimbabwe; 15. Botswana; 18. Lesotho; 28. Mali; 29. Niger; 30. Senegal; 9. Revisd and 9. Burkina Faso/UperVolta.
COPAC: Commodity Marketing through Co-operatives. Some Experiences from Africa and Asia, Rome 1984.
de Graft-Johnson, J.C.: African Experiment, London 1958, especially p. 139 and p. 47ff.
Dülfer, E.: Agricultural Co-operatives and Related institutions in Ghana-Country, Dossier, Marburg 1969.
Dülfer, E.: Operational Efficiency of Agricultural Co-operatives in Developing Countries, Rome 1974, pp. 75ff.
Dülfer, E.: Der genossenschaftliche Kredit in afrikanischen Ländern, in: Zeitschrift für das gesamte Kreditwesen, 21. Jahrgang, Heft 12, pp. 559ff.
Fischer, P.H.: Genossenschaften in West Afrika. Bericht erstattet im Auftrag des Bundesministeriums für Wirtschaftliche Zusammenarbeit – Dahomey, Elfenbeinküste, Niger, Obervolta (Manuskript), Marburg 1970.
Friedrich Ebert Stiftung: Die Genossenschaften in Afrika (translation), Bonn 1965.
Hanel, A.: Genossenschaften in Nigeria, Marburg 1967, pp. 22ff.
Hyden, G.: Efficiency Versus Distribution in East African Countries, Nairobi 1973, pp. 75ff.
Jeetun, B.: Appropriate Management Systems for Small Agricultural Co-operatives (AMSAC), Marburg 1988, pp. 39ff.
Kirsch, O.C./Göricke, F.N.: Scope and impact of the Credit Union Movement in Selected African Countries, Mainz 1977.
Kuhn, J.: Agrarverfassung und landwirtschaftliche Siedlungsprojekte in Nigeria, Marburg 1967
Münkner, H.-H. (ed.): Credit Union Development in Africa, Mainz 1978.
Münkner, H.-H.: Comparative Study of Co-operating Law in Africa, Marburg 1989.
Münkner, H.-H.: Die Organisation der eingetragenen Genossenschaft in den zum englischen Rechtskreis gehörenden Ländern Schwarzafrikas, dargestellt am Beispiel Ghanas, Marburg 1971.
Münkner, H.-H.: Legal Problems in the Building of Vertical Organizations in Co-operatives, with special reference to the situation in Developing Countries, in: Dülfer, E./Hamm, W. (eds.): Co-operatives in the Clash between Member participation, Organisational Development and Bureaucratic Tendencies, London 1985, p. 217ff.
Münkner, H.-H.: New Trends in Co-operative Law of English-speaking Countries of Africa, Marburg 1971 and 1973.
Münkner, H.-H.: Possibilities and Problems of Transformation of Local Village Groups into Pre-Co-operatives, in: Law in Alternative Stratgies of Rural Development, Third World Legal Studies, 1982, p. 174ff.
Münkner, H.-H.: The Role of Government Development Bureaucracies in Promoting self-help Organizations, examples from French-speaking Africa, in: Münkner, H.-H. (ed.): Adjusted Patterns of Co-operatives in Developing Countries, Bonn 1984, pp. 3 ff.
Ojo, A.T./Adewunmi, W.: Co-operative Banking in Nigeria, Lagos 1980.
Pössinger, H.: Landwirtschaftliche Entwicklung in Angola und Mozambique, München 1968.
Roider, W.: Form Settlements for Socio-economic Development – the Nigeria Case, Munich 1971.
Seibel, D./Koll, M.: Einheimische Genossenschaften in Afrika.
Widstrand, C.G. (ed.): African Co-operatives and Efficiency, Uppsala 1972.
Widstrand, C.G. (ed.): Co-operatives and Rural Development in East Africa, New York, 1970.
Yearbook of Agricultural Co-operation – series of articles in Editions: 1954; 1960; 1961; 1962; 1963; 1965 and especially 1971 and 1977.

Development of Co-operatives in Eastern Europe

Tadeusz Kowalak

(see also: *State and Co-operatives, Socialism*; *Co-operative Socialism*; *Socialist Critics*; *Classification*; *Law, International*)

I. History Until 1945; II. Socialist Co-operatives; III. Co-operatives in the Economies of the Eastern European Countries; IV. Trends of Change.

I. History Until 1945

The first co-operatives in Eastern Europe emerged in the middle of the 19th century (→ *History in 19th C.*). These were consumer co-operatives based on Rochdale principles (→ *Rochdale Pioneers*) which were followed by other types of co-operatives generally based on the concepts of →*Raiffeisen* and → *Schulze-Delitzsch*. The legal basis of those co-operatives on present day Polish territory (under Prussian rule until 1918) and those in the former German Democratic Republic (GDR) was the German Co-operative Law of 1889. The co-operatives on the present territory of Czechoslovakia and Yugoslavia, as well as in the Austrian partition of Poland, were based on the Austrian Co-operative Law of 1873.

Hungarian co-operatives were controlled by the Hungarian Trade Act of 1875. Latest of all, at the end of the 19th century, the first co-operatives in Russia emerged. Co-operatives had already achieved an important economic position in the eastern part of Europe before the outbreak of the First World War, especially in the sectors of credit (→ *Co-operative Banks*), agricultural supply and marketing (→ *Supply Co-operatives*), milk processing (→ *Rural Co-operatives*) and retail trade (→ *Commercial Co-operatives*). Housing co-operatives (→ *Housing Societies*), fruit and vegetable processing co-operatives, cattle and pig marketing co-operatives (→ *Marketing*), as well as some insurance and workers' productive co-operatives (→ *Joint-production Co-operatives*) came into being, too.

Before the outbreak of the First World War, co-operatives in regions inhabited by nations deprived of political independence played not only an important economic, but also a specific socio-political role, giving economic support to national, cultural and political movements.

Between the two World Wars, co-operatives in Eastern Europe grew both in number and kind. A great majority of them were affiliated with upper level economic and auditing organizations. Co-operatives were mostly connected with the agricultural sector, predominantly being of the savings and credit type. In Poland, for instance, among the total of 13,741 co-operatives in 1938, there were 6,567 co-operative banks, 5,344 consumer and 1,475 dairy co-operatives. At the same time in Hungary there were 1322 co-operative banks, 970 dairy, 80 housing, and 50 workers' productive co-operatives; 5,699 co-operatives existed in Romania in 1945, including 3,475 for savings and credit, and 1,557 supply and marketing co-operatives. In the USSR, after a short period of development of a great variety of co-operative organizations (NEP), the centrally planned economic system eliminated co-operative banks, dairy and processing co-operatives, the majority of housing co-operatives, as well as workers' joint-production co-operatives between 1956 and 1960. In 1940 there were 32,400 consumer co-operatives organized in the one centrally co-operative union, *Centrosojuz*, some 13,000 less than in 1927.

II. Socialist Co-operatives

1. Main Principles and Tendencies

The Second World War disturbed the development of co-operatives in Eastern Europe. Co-operative organizations underwent a complete change of character and purpose in all countries dominated by the Soviet Union. Under Communist rule, co-operatives have been reshaped into an instrument used for the construction of the socialist system. The theoretical concept of the socialist co-operative is based on the principle that the co-operative represents a transitional form of economic activity. Their ownership is socialist, subsumed, however, to the highest form of socialist ownership — that of the state (→ *State and Co-operatives, Socialism*).

The philosophic foundation of co-operatives which existed up to this point in time was replaced. The principle of democracy was substituted with that of democratic centralism, i.e. the subordination of primary organizations to those of a higher level; the principle of the promotion of members' enterprises and households was changed into the principle of serving the needs of the entire society; the principle of self-sufficiency disappeared under the monetary policy of the state; the material liability of members did not play any role in the co-operative's existence; the value of members' shares became negligible. Members, in spite of legal regulations, were deprived of their right to freely elect the management of the co-operative. The centrally planned economic system reduced the right of members to decide about the economic activities of their co-operative to a bare minimum. Co-operatives became mass organizations in which the masses had not only nothing to say, but people often did not even realize that they were co-operative members. Co-operatives served the economic and social policy of the totalitarian state and became one of the instruments of state control over the lives of those in the society. The system of obligatory membership of primary co-operatives in central, territorial and branch co-operative unions became a tool for imposing tasks on co-operatives and state control over their activities.

Although described in a very simplified way, this development of philosophic and organizational foundations was extended to all Eastern European countries. There were, however, essential differences among those countries as far as their traditions, their level of civilization and their economic and social structures were concerned. There were also some differences in the approach central decision-makers in particular countries took toward co-operatives. The conviction about the transitional character of co-operative forms of economic activity in socialism was therefore not sufficient to introduce a uniform co-operative system in the region. On the contrary: the development of co-operative organizations was not uniform at all. Their legal regulations, as well as their forms of organization and of economic development, were different; there were important differences in the dynamics of growth in particular branches of co-operative organizations, in their tasks, and in the realm of their activities. In some countries, certain kinds of co-operatives did not exist, whereas at the same time they played an important role in other countries.

The acknowledgement of co-operatives as a part of the centrally managed socialist economy resulted in their important quantitative development. The increase of the number of co-operatives and their monopolistic position, especially in supplying the population with elementary commodities, resulted in an important increase in the number of co-operative members. In Hungary, half of the population were co-operative members in the 1980s; in the USSR, 55.9%; in Poland, 39%; in the GDR, 23.5%. In Bulgaria 20% of the population belonged to consumer and workers co-operatives.

2. Co-operative Functions

The socialist co-operative doctrine (→ *Socialist Critics*) originated from Lenin's so-called co-operative plan (of 1923), which prejudged their instrumental character. Their main task was "to build socialism". This meant that in practise they were to accomplish functions which served the specifically understood interests of society as a whole. Co-operatives performed:
a) structural functions, such as transforming private property into social property, e.g. the collectivization of agriculture; socialization of privately owned handicraft and small-scale industrial enterprises; creation of social property (integration of the dispersed financial means of the population, accumulation of reserve funds, construction of economic and social infrastructure); development of democratic forms of management in enterprises;
b) economic functions, such as supplying farms and handicraft industries with means of production; supplying the population with consumer goods; producing all kinds of commodities; marketing of agricultural and industrial products; rendering manifold services; construction of houses, farm buildings and production sites; the collection of savings and granting of credits to individual farmers and craftsmen;
c) social functions, such as running professional schools; professional training of co-operative employees and members; rehabilitation of disabled persons; supervising kindergartens and infant nurseries; providing medical and dental services to co-operative members and their families; coordinating cultural and educational activities; providing vocational and social guidance; promoting sport organizations and events, and administrating aid to the aged. Social functions were especially developed in rural areas where following the principles of self-help was more effective and less expensive than direct state intervention.
Up until approximately 1948, some co-operative organizations identified themselves with particular political orientations, e.g.consumer co-operatives in Poland and in Czechoslovakia were under the influence of the Social Democrats, agricultural co-operatives were oriented along the lines of the Christian Democrats. The introduction of a one party dictatorship brought an end to any independent political functions of the co-operative movements. In spite of the important economic potential of co-operatives and their great, formal social functional range, they have not played any role in politics since 1948.

3. Types of Co-operatives and their Number; The Co-operative Movement

The most developed co-operative sector in the region exists in Poland. In rural areas there are supply and marketing co-operatives, horticultural co-operatives, co-operative banks, dairy co-operatives, agricultural production co-operatives and co-operatives of agricultural circles. An important co-operative sector exists in urban areas, too, consisting of consumer, housing, workers' productive, supply and marketing co-operatives for craftsmen, as well as students' and school co-operatives. The USSR has the greatest number of co-operatives (about 250,000), followed by Poland (15,000), the former GDR (4,500), Hungary (2,600) and Czechoslovakia (3,500). A dramatic growth in the number of co-operatives took place in the USSR after 1988 as the result of new economic policy and of the new Co-operative Law, passed in May, 1988. An important increase in the number of co-operatives was noticed in Poland and Hungary in the 1970s and 1980s. There were no major changes in the other countries in the region in this respect.
After the Second World War new kinds of co-operatives emerged. All socialist countries started the collectivization process of private farms in 1949. Following the lines developed in the USSR, agricultural production co-operatives were established on a great scale. Aside from Poland, where farmers dissolved the great majority of co-operatives of this type in 1956, private farms practically ceased to exist in all other countries in question. In order to render technical services to individual farms in Poland, a specific form of co-operative called co-operative of an agricultural circle was introduced which was not known in the other countries of the region. In Poland, too, housing co-operatives were entrusted with the solution of the national housing problem. This resulted in the creation of several different types of housing co-operatives and in important growth of their number.
An important number of workers' productive co-operatives came into being in Poland, Hungary and Czechoslovakia. They employed 7% of the total professionally active population in Poland. Workers' productive (or work) co-operatives belong mainly to small and middle-scale industries. Their share in the total production of some branches and commodities, however, was important, e.g. in Hungary they provided the home market with 39% of furniture, 60% of clothing and 80% of children's goods; in Poland 42% of clothing and 24% of leather commodities were manufactured by workers co-operatives; in Czechoslovakia workers co-operatives produced 20% of furniture, 20% of clothing and 9% of all shoes. They

played yet a more important role in rendering different services to the population. In Hungary a legal framework for the so-called "small" workers co-operatives, mostly rendering services and producing only one commodity, was created in 1982. Their internal organization was simplified and some deregulation was implemented. Within the framework of workers co-operatives a form of disabled persons' co-operative emerged. This played a complementary role in the social welfare system and is an instrument of professional and social rehabilitation for the disabled.

In all countries of real socialism, the state decided arbitrarily about the vicissitudes of co-operatives. In Czechoslovakia in 1949, activities of consumer co-operatives were strictly limited to rural areas; in Bulgaria in the 1970s all agricultural production co-operatives were merged with state farms to form "agricultural complexes"; in the USSR during the 1960s and '70s some, agricultural production co-operatives were arbitrarily transformed into state farms, and between 1956 and 1960 all workers co-operatives were transferred to the state industries. In Poland in the 1970s, workers co-operatives were transferred to the state industry, but, in contrast, all grocer's shops were transferred from state organizations to consumer co-operatives in 1975; at the same time all co-operative shops with industrial commodities became state enterprises.

In the majority of the Eastern European countries, primary co-operatives were obligatorily affiliated with control co-operative unions. In some countries, regional and specialized co-operative unions, in addition to consulting and promoting the development of their affiliated co-operatives, also exerted economic influence in the spheres of supply, marketing, investment and financial assistance. They served as transmitters of the tasks of the central economic plan to the co-operative organizations and, accordingly, as an instrument of state control over co-operative activities. Auditing was the responsibility of the central unions. Due to structural economic changes in Poland, Hungary and the USSR, the power exerted by national unions on primary co-operatives and regional co-operative unions started to relax, especially at the end of the 1980s.

With the exception of the USSR, the former GDR and Bulgaria, Supreme Co-operative Councils existed in all other countries of this region, and umbrella organizations served all national co-operative unions. They differed from each other as far as their functions were concerned. Some, like in Poland, had a representative character, with no power of decision; others, like in Czechoslovakia, played an important role in the organization, legislation and co-ordination of the economic activities of particular co-operative branches. In Bulgaria, all co-operative organizations were affiliated directly with the Central Co-operative Union, which was furnished with powers similar to those of state authority. The affiliation of primary co-operatives with national unions was obligatory until 1987 in Poland, till 1988 in the USSR and till 1990 in all other Eastern European countries.

III. Co-operatives in the Economies of the Eastern European Countries

The share of co-operative activity in creating gross national product (GNP) illustrates the role they play in the economies of Eastern Europe. Co-operatives produced 23% of GNP in Hungary, 11.2% in Poland, 10% in Czechoslovakia (1986), 9.4% (estimated) in the USSR (1975), and 4.3% in Bulgaria (1984), There is no data available for Romania and the former GDR (→ *GDR*). In Poland, Hungary and Czechoslovakia, the share of co-operative activity in the respective national economies grew slowly between 1975 and 1988. It dropped in Bulgaria by 50% because of the transfer of agricultural production co-operatives to the state sector.

In the former GDR, 87.1% of arable land was cultivated by agricultural production co-operatives (1987); in Hungary 60%; in the USSR 30.3%; in Poland 3.6%. The co-operative share in the production of food is approximately the same. Co-operatives produced 2.2% of the total volume of industrial production in the USSR; in Czechoslovakia, 4.1%; in Hungary, 6.5%; in Poland, 12% (1986). The co-operative sector's share in retail trade turnover was 70% in Poland, 36.1% in Hungary, 34.4% in the former GDR, 30.1% in Bulgaria, 27.2% in the USSR, and 25.3% in Czechoslovakia (1986). Housing co-operatives constructed 72% of all new housing units in Poland; 44.2% in Czechoslovakia; 25% in the former GDR; 6% in the USSR, and 2.7% in Hungary (1986). 1600 co-operative banks in Poland collected 18.5% of total savings in 1987; in Hungary, 260 savings and credit co-operatives accumulated 15% of total savings of the population in 1984. In Czechoslovakia this form of co-operative ceased to exist early in the 1950s. In the USSR the Co-operative Law of 1988 recognized this form of co-operative organization, limiting its activities to financial services for other types of co-operatives. In Bulgaria a discussion recently started about the possible introduction of savings and credit co-operatives within the framework of consumer co-operatives.

Some co-operative organizations enjoyed a monopolistic position on the home markets. Dairy co-operatives in Poland purchased and processed close to 100% of all milk. For the majority of Poles the only way to get a flat was through housing co-operatives; supply and marketing co-operatives in rural areas were the only organizations in Poland where the rural population could shop; likewise, farmers could buy means of production there as well as sell their agricultural products. Consumer co-operatives in rural areas of the USSR, Czechoslovakia and Bulgaria were the only retail trade organizations from which the population could buy food and other necessary commodities.

The first demonopolization steps within co-operative structures took place in Poland, where individual farmers were authorized in the 1950s to sell their products directly to consumers. During the 1980s, the strict delimitation of the areas of particular consumer co-operative activity was dropped, and more freedom was granted in starting private trade enterprises. In the USSR this process started in 1986 when the Central Committee of the Communist Party and the Council of Ministers issued a joint decision allowing co-operatives operating in the same branch, especially industrial and agricultural production co-operatives, to compete on the market. Starting in the mid 1980s, regulations were softened in this respect in Czechoslovakia, Hungary and Bulgaria, allowing consumer co-operatives to open stores in some towns.

IV. Trends of Change

The first breaches in the tight corset of socialist co-operative doctrine and practice took place in Poland as one of the consequences of the national rebellion of October, 1956. The Law on Co-operatives and Their Unions of 1962 proclaimed the principle of voluntary and open membership as well as democratic management. The purpose of a co-operative was still legally defined as activity within the framework of national economic plans, and thus a realization of the interest of society as a whole, but the fulfillment of members' needs was also mentioned, albeit as a secondary purpose. In Hungary in 1968 the theoretical concept of co-operatives' instrumental role and their subordinated position in relation to the state economy was questioned, and the idea of equal rights for both state and co-operative forms of socialist ownership was openly discussed. Consequently, the Hungarian Co-operative Law of 1971 went a step further in comparison with the Polish Law of 1962, placing priority on the promotion of the material well-being of co-operative members rather than on the fulfillment of the needs of society as a whole. Political upheavals in 1980 and 1981 lead to further liberalizations of Co-operative Law in Poland in 1982.

There was a strong concentration tendency in all co-operative organizations of the Eastern European countries until the 1980s. This was a result of more general policy implemented in all sectors of the socialist economies. Mergers and/or absorptions of small co-operatives by larger ones became the rule. In 1975 an average consumer co-operative in Poland had 58,400 members (the biggest one had over 250,000); a rural supply and marketing co-operative had over 3,200 members, a work co-operative about 445 members. Excessive concentration proved to be detrimental to both the economic and social effectiveness of co-operatives. A process of decentralization and promotion of small co-operatives was characteristic of the situation in the Soviet Union, Hungary and Poland at the end of the 1980s. Transformations of co-operatives into state enterprises and vice-versa ceased to occur.

The first signs of a basically new approach to the question of land ownership in agricultural production co-operatives appeared. At the beginning of 1990 the Hungarian Parliament decided that members of agricultural productive co-operatives or their heirs are free to decide whether they allow the co-operative to use their land in return for rent, or if they wish to sell it to the co-operative; furthermore, they can ask for other land equivalent to their own to be allocated with which they can carry out private farming. As 39% of all land utilized by such co-operatives belongs legally to members or to their heirs, this decision must be considered rather revolutionary. Up until 1990 there were no signs of any move in the Soviet Union in the direction of denationalization of land. Nevertheless, land tenancy by individual persons was made possible in 1990.

Starting in the 1970s numerous forms of direct participation of co-operative members in the decision-making processes were introduced in all countries of the region as a part of the more general attempt to animate economic development. The by-laws of consumer co-operatives in the former GDR lists six different co-operative organs within one co-operative, each taking part in the decision-making process; statutes of large Polish and Hungarian co-operatives introduced "groups of members" furnished with the right to decide about certain minor matters. Legal regulations had, however, a limited influence on the existing reality. Neither the principle of central planning nor the practice of designating co-operatives' managing organs by Communist Parties or state authorities were abandoned. Radical changes in Poland and then in the other countries in this region in 1989 and 1990 opened the way for authentic member participation.

The process of the de facto re-orientation in co-operative doctrine and practice began in Eastern Europe in the second half of the 1980s as the result of reformatory changes in politics and economy gradually introduced in reaction to an obvious stagnation of economic growth. For the first time in history, the Parliament of the Soviet Union passed a comprehensive Law on Co-operatives in May, 1988. The law defined the nature and regulated the activities of all kinds of co-operatives, including kolkhozes. In Poland, compulsory affiliation of co-operatives to co-operative unions was rescinded (1983, 1987); in Hungary, liberal principles for small scale workers co-operatives were introduced (1987). In the rest of the Eastern European countries, discussion about necessary changes had not yet been concluded by the beginning of 1990. The changes in co-operative laws in Poland, Hungary and, to some degree, the USSR are based on the following principles: the recognition of the promotion of co-operative members' enterprises and households as the main purpose of a co-operative; the cancellation of development barriers restricting co-operative organizations; the introduction of the principles of independence, self-government and self-financing; and voluntary affiliation of co-operatives with co-operative unions.

As a result of the above mentioned changes in laws and in the attitude to co-operatives in general, a rapid increase in the number of small scale industrial and service co-operatives in the Soviet Union can be noted. At the beginning of 1990 in the USSR, 193,400 industrial co-operatives of the type provided for by the new Co-operative Law of 1988 existed. They employed 8,850,000 members and employees, and the volume of their production in 1989 was five times higher than in 1988. They produced consumer goods and services of all kinds. An important increase in the number of work and housing co-operatives can be noted in Poland and Hungary. In Poland between 1975 and 1987, more than a threefold increase in the number of housing co-operatives was noted (from 876 to 3,085). Their membership grew in the same time period from 2.1 to 3.3 million. The number of workers co-operatives increased in Poland during this same time from 1,600 to 2,500. New co-operative unions have recently been established.

In the USSR a new Union of Productive Co-operatives within the national organization of consumer co-operatives was created in 1988. A similar union emerged in Bulgaria in 1989. Co-operative associations were created in all districts of the former GDR as instruments of "lobby" organizations in the process of co-operation between co-operatives and state authorities, banks, industry and other partners.

The economic activities of co-operatives in Eastern Europe showed a growth tendency in the 1980s, especially in the sectors of agricultural production processing and in industrial commodities production for both domestic and foreign markets. A great number of situations hamper the development of co-operatives: the remnants of socialist methods of management, the lack of experience in acting within a democratic system, the conservatism of older managers, lack of know-how concerning new market economy conditions, lack of membership participation, inadequate co-operative equity and strong dependence on credits from state banks. The reintroduction of co-operatives and the co-operative movement as a whole to the features of an authentic, democratic, and socio-economic method of organization will likewise afford numerous improvements in the information system, the introduction of far-reaching changes in co-operative legislation, and extensive educational and economic efforts. The difficult economic situation of this region of Europe should, theoretically, ensure a strong position of co-operatives in the new market economy system. Their role in respective national economies will, however, most probably diminish as a result of the emergence of a new, competitive private sector. The Soviet Union will be the probable exception to this possible development during the first few years because the process of privatization will need much more time. The first signs of a quantitative drop in the number of workers' productive co-operatives can be noted in Hungary, where the recent legal regulations allow the transformation of co-operatives into joint stock companies. Pressure for the "privatization" of co-operatives is imminent in Poland, too.

It is generally recognized that the introduction of far-reaching changes in co-operative legislation (→ *Law, International*) are urgently needed to help the co-operative movements in Eastern Europe adjust themselves to the new political and economic systems emerging after the collapse of the socialist concept of managing the economic and social life in these respective countries. The promotion of members' enterprises and households as the principle purpose of a co-operative should be unequivocally recognized by law. Co-operative property should have the same rights as other forms of ownership, enjoying no privileges and suffering no discrimination. Co-operatives should become authentic, democratic structures based on the principles of self-help and self-responsibility, independent and self-sufficient. The structures of the co-operative movements should be changed with an eye on decentralization within the limits imposed by existing market conditions. The links between members and co-operatives should be strengthened. Flexibility and liberty in establishing new forms of alternative co-operatives could open the way to continuous co-operative development.

The Hungarians have already introduced an important modification to the Law on Co-operatives. The amendment, passed in 1990, revoked the principle of the indivisibility of collective co-operative property by introducing the provision that up to half of the joint property may be changed into personal property belonging to members through the general assembly's appropriate decision. Recent regulations in Hungary are aimed at strengthening the independence and autonomy of co-operatives. In Poland, the 1991 amendment to the Co-operative Law of 1982 allows the transfer of half of the co-operative reserve funds to a members' share fund, complying with the new political and economic situation. Czechoslovakia enacted a new Co-operative Law in 1990 which introduces democratic solutions concerning formations, management, mergers, the division and liquidation of co-operatives, and the establishment of co-operative unions – generally correcting former alterations.

The way, however, is long. The decree of the Council of the National Salvation of Romania dated February 8th, 1990, says that the purpose of a co-operative is "to develop an activity in common" (Art.1), but "through its whole activity (the co-operative) brings its contribution to the prosperity of the economic and social life of Romania" (Art. 2). A year and a half after the Soviet Law on Co-operatives was introduced (1988) a Soviet paper presented in March, 1990, at the International Co-operative Alliance meeting in Geneva reported that the collective form of co-operative management had not yet been introduced, that co-operatives were still ruled by state and higher level co-operative organizations, and that the population had an aversion to co-operatives because they set the prices too high.

Lack of stability and the nervousness of the decision-makers can be illustrated by the decision of the Supreme Soviet entrusting the control of co-operatives to the UGB at the end of 1990. Years will have to pass until stabilization can be achieved in the region as a whole, including the situation of respective co-operative movements. It is expected that co-operative organizations will lose a part of their economic importance but will emerge as private enterprises owned and controlled by members.

Biliography

Ehm, Michaela: Die polnischen Genossenschaften zwischen Privat- und Zentralplanwirtschaft, Münster 1983.
Herzog, Hans-Joachim: Genossenschaftliche Organisationsformen in der DDR, Tübingen 1982.
Janic, Janina: Rozwoj spoldzielczosci w krajach RWPG. The Development of Co-operative Movement in the Countries of Mutual Economic Aid, Manuscript in Polish, at the Co-operative Research Institute, Warsaw 1989.
National Co-operative Council (ed.), Hungary: Hungarian Co-operative Movement. A short Survey of the History and the Activities, Budapest 1986.
Watkins, William Pascoe: Die Internationale Genossenschaftsbewegung, Frankfurt/Main 1969.
Texts of co-operative law of: Bulgaria (1983), Czechoslovakia (1988), German Democratic Republic (1982), Hungary (1971–1988), Poland (1982, 1983, 1987, 1990), Rumania (1984, 1990), USSR (1988).

Development of Co-operatives in Israel

YEHUDA DON

(see also: *Classification*; *Conceptions, Co-operative*; *Communal Settlements*)

I. Early Co-operative Foundations in the Former Jewish Palestine; II. Co-operatives under the British Mandatory Regime; III. The Kibbutz Movement and other Settlements; IV. Co-operatives in the State of Israel.

I. Early Co-operative Foundations in the Former Jewish Palestine

The history of the co-operative movement in modern Jewish Palestine, and as of 1948 in the State of Israel, is an accurate reflection of the socio-economic history of modern Jewish Palestine and then the State of Israel.

Attempts to conduct economic activities through co-operative organizations go back to the early stages of modern colonizatory efforts of Zionist immigrants in Palestine. Furthermore, the sectorial cleavage between the Socialist and the non-Socialist economic sectors, which was so typical of the economic scenery of Palestine and has continued to characterize economic life in independent Israel, made its appearance in the initial phases of the co-operatives development as of the beginning of the 20th century.

Early forerunners of co-operatives in modern Jewish Palestine can be traced back to the late 19th century. *H. Viteles* reported about groups of settlers who had founded co-operative-like associations for housing as well as for the provision of community services such as bakeries, ritual baths etc.

The first documented and registered co-operative was a general purpose agricultural association, established by nine citrus growers in 1900, entitled "PARDES". Its foundation was assisted by the colonizatory-philantropic administration of *Baron Edmond de Rothschild* being active during the pre Wold War I era in the promotion of numerous rural enterprises. So was formed in 1905, and reorganized in 1908, an association for cattle insurance and in 1906 the famous "CARMEL winegrowers co-operative" which now encompasses the largest group of wine growers and wine producers in Israel. Up to World War I, quite a number of co-operatively functioning groups were founded, for the provision of agricultural services and credit. Co-operative formuli were also found expendient for the financially sound supply of credit to individual farmers in the new Jewish colonies. In 1914, 45 such groups existed with 1800 members. These co-operative enterprises, mainly agricultural service and credit societies, functioned on behalf of and for the non Socialist sector.

Initial experimentations with co-operatives by the forefathers of the Socialist sector, the young idealistic, yet penniless immigrants of the pre World War I years, were of different character. Their objective was to alleviate their living conditions as hired workers through mutual aid. Consequently, the first co-operative efforts focused on the provision of consumers' services. A further step in co-operative self-help were attempts to set up contractors' associations to ease the hardship of unemployment. Yet, since the formal credit worthiness of such workers' co-operatives was very low, no commercial credit was obtainable for the initial sustenance. As a result, their average lifespan was exceedingly short. Of the numerous attempts one should single out the rather large contractors' co-operative for farming and construction "AHVA" which was founded in 1915 by 100 workers, and functioned for two years. In 1916, to alleviate the grave economic hardship of the workers, they established a countrywide network of consumers' co-operatives, named *MASHBIR*. In due course, it has developed into one of the largest consumers' outlets of the Socialist sector.

The most significant co-operative achievement of the pre World War I era was the Collective Colony, better known as the Kibbutz. The first kibbutz, Degania, founded in 1909 by a group of seven workers, opened a new epoch in the history of Jewish resettlement in Palestine. Its birth was the result of a search by immigrant workers for new modes of existence in their recently adopted homeland. The status of the hired Jewish laborers in Jewish colonies, in a situation of incessant competition for employment with the more experienced Arab laborers, generated deep dissatisfaction among the immigrants as its dull substance seemed remote from the high ideas of nation building through physical labour. The vision of workers' colonies as an alternative to the prevailing reality did not suggest any one specific formula of interaction among members of such colonies. Various models were propagated, each of them containing a high degree of mutual help (→ *Joint-production Co-operative*). The best known among those models was F. Oppenheimer's detailedly elaborated blueprint of a co-operative colony. It was envisioned to take off as a co-operative – non collective – agricultural colony which in due course would develop into an agro-industrial complex in which private initiative, reinforced by a network of co-operatively supplied services, would safeguard efficiency and prosperity. The model was implemented in 1911 in the Co-operative Colony Merhavia which turned out to be the only experiment along the lines of the Oppenheimerian colonizatory blueprint, although it was designed to become the prototype of workers' colonies in Palestine. Merhavia was dissolved in 1918.

Degania, on the other hand, was not organized along any pre-conceived blueprint, and its only maxim was to "enable us how to run our lives and to create economic equality and equality between the sexes" (*J. Bussel*, a prominent founder). Its final ideological maxim of collective production and consumption, based upon the principle of "from each according to his ability and to each according to his needs", was the outcome of a long process of trial and error lasting a decade.

The Degania type of colony proved successful both socially and economically, and it was followed before World War I by two kibbutzim, and during the war by four more. After World War I, the Kibbutz model proliferated rapidly.

II. Co-operatives under the British Mandatory Regime

Following the arrival of the British Mandatory regime in 1920 (officially in 1923), co-operative organizations consolidated and entered a stage of rapid expansion.

1) Consumers' cooperation, unlike in Great Britain and other European countries, had started in the rural areas among agricultural workers, who fought inefficient and exploitative retailing practices. The *HAMASHBIR*, founded in 1916 and reorganized in 1930, split its operation into three divisions. One developed into a wholesale society of consumers' goods and agricultural inputs for the kibbutz movement. The second specialized in rural consumers' and agricultural supply services for the non-collective sections of the socialist sector, the small-holders' Moshav movement. The third devision, later renamed *HAMASBIR HAMERKAZI*, (Central Supplier), became the basis for the urban Consumers' Co-operative network which used the central purchasing and producing bodies of *HAMASHBIR* as the wholesale suppliers of the retail primary stores. Following the establishment of a proper consumers' network, an Audit Union for consumers' co-operatives was founded in 1932. The development of urban consumers' cooperation up to 1947 was anything but spectacular; only a small fraction of the non-rural consumers found the utilization of co-operatives useful.

2) Non rural production cooperation, which had its roots in the pre World War I years, has been sponsored, assisted and controlled by the socialist sector. In 1920, 76 production co-operatives employed about 800 workers. Thus, the typical co-operative plant was in fact a small workshop with about 10 employees. Production co-operatives employed a mere 2.3 per cent of the total urban Jewish labor force. In the interwar years, expansion was modest with a rate of growth below that of the Jewish urban labor force. In 1947, about 5,000 workers found employment in 123 co-operative plants reducing the ratio of urban labor in production co-operatives to 2.1 per cent. The "Central Union of the Production and Service Co-operatives", established in 1927 under the wings of the Histadrut, provided an apex body of control and intercession, and formalized the political link of the production co-operatives to the Histadrut.

3) Credit Cooperation, which was unenvely but clearly divided between the socialist and non-socialist sectors grew very rapidly during the British Mandate. From 700 members with a total sum of £ 4,760 deposits, credit co-operatives grew to a membership of 108,500 with more than £ 11.2 million deposits. Such a rapid growth rate indicated a real need of the middle and lower middle classes for decent saving and banking services as well as small scale credit. Such services were, apparently, not offered by the commercial banking network. The impressive penetration of co-operative credit into the Jewish population is clearly indicated by the crude percentage of Credit Society membership in total Jewish population. Co-operative Credit in 1947 comprised 14.2 p.c. of all banking credit.

The sectorial division of co-operative credit created two competing credit networks. The one representing the non-socialist sector controlled about two thirds of all societies and memberships, while the other network, is linked to the Histadrut.

4) *Agricultural marketing* obviously reflected the profound growth and diversification of agricultural production. The sectorial division of co-operative marketing reflected that of agricultural production. Due to the dominance acquired during the 1920s in the production of locally consumed produce by the Kibbutz and Moshav movements (see next section), the marketing vehicle of these movements, *TNUVA*, became the dominant co-operative organization for internally marketed agricultural produce. *TNUVA*, formed in the late 1920s, through a series of amalgamations is a co-operative central society, the membership of which is comprised of agricultural settlements. Its share in the home market since the 1930s has been about 75 p.c. In the course of the 1930s, *TNUVA* branched out into exports (*TNUVA EXPORT*). It has also entered the industrial processing of farm produce and is now a very important factor in the food processing industry.

5) *Co-operative agriculture* made during the era of the British Mandate the most conspicuous progress. It became by far the most important co-operative sector in Jewish Palestine.

III. The Kibbutz Movement and other Settlements

The 1920s were the formative period for the Kibbutz movement, which expanded rapidly following World War I. The highly intensive pioneering spirit of the post war immigrants, mainly from Eastern Europe, led to experimentations with various forms of co-operative living, mostly based upon a high degree of collectivism and economic equalitarianism. Among the major models, the most radical undertaking was the countrywide commune known as *GDUD HAAVODA* (Labour Battalion), formed in 1920, which attempted to organize a network of workers' communes, encompassing all Jewish workers in the country, to pool their incomes and redistribute them in equality. The members of the Battallion were to establish agricultural and urban communes, "Companies", and operate them along the lines of its regulations. *GDUD HAAVODA* at the height of its influence in 1923, had 780 members in nine "Companies", located both in urban centers and in the countryside. In 1923 and 1924, following a series of splits, the Battalion disintegrated. Some of its left wing members returned to the Soviet Union.

A second Kibbutz Pattern closely connected with the Battalion in its early days, was the *EIN HAROD* model. It emerged from the awareness of the the intrinsic limitations of the original Kibbutz model, developed in *DEGANIA,* to serve as an effective vehicle for the absorbtion of the immigrating pioneer-workers, and for the promotion of nation building in Palestine. The *EIN HAROD* kibbutz model advocated the concept of the "Large and Expanding Kibbutz", in which all economic activities, including agriculture, industry, and employment as hired hands, were equally legitimate. The communal form of distribution, consumption, and education was carefully preserved, however, the policy of absorption was more liberal and optimum membership less constrained than in the *DEGANIA* model.

The *DEGANIA* model chrystallized in the course of the decade long experience of the first kibbutz. It emphasized the importance of close and intimate interpersonal relationships among the members, which together with the limitation of employment to only agriculture on the land of the commune, aimed to create a way of life of close community experience in a rural, rudimentary environment. The size of membership was, consequently, heavily constrained, and when the number of applicants to join *DEGANIA* surpassed the projected size of the kibbutz, its members preferred to relinquish a part of their land and sponsor the establishment of a twin but separate collective, *DEGANIA B.*

A third kibbutz model was the "organic collective". It was conceived by immigrating youth groups most of whom originated from middle class families in Poland and Galicia and were members of the elitistic Boy-Scoutish *HASHOMER HATZAIR* youth movement. The essence of this movement was the search for a new way of life, based on intensive group togetherness and ideological concord of pioneers who live by their own toil within their closely knitted collective community. This mode of kibbutz neither accepted the principle of open admission for all those who adhere to the basic premises of collectivism, nor endorsed the concept of the small family like introvert community of the *DEGANIA* model.

The Kibbutz as the most popular pattern of agricultural settlement proliferated rapidly in the 1920s. In May 1925, there were 22 kibbitzim with a population of 1,611. Two years later, in 1927, the overall population in 27 kibbitzin was estimated at 2,261, comprising 1.5 p.c. of the total Jewish population in Palestine. The growth of the Kibbutz movement necessitated the establishment of apex organizations. An attempt in 1925 to form one all embracing federation for the whole movement failed because of unbridgeable ideological and conceptual differences among the adherents of the three major kibbutz models. In 1927, the "organic collective" movement formed its countrywide organization, named *HAKIBBUTZ HAARTZI.* In the same year, the "Large and Expanding Kibbutz" colonies model amalgamated into the *KIBBUTH MEHUHAD* federation, and in 1933 the *DEGANIA* type kibbutzin federated under the *HEVER HAKVUTZOT* organization.

The Kibbutz movement continued to grow during the 1930s, both in terms of population and the number of settlements. In fact, kibbutz polulation increased almost three times as fast as the Jewish population in Palestine, which itself increased between 1927 and 1939 at an annual rate of 9.7 p.c.

Table I: Development of the Kibbutz Movement 1927–1939 (Number of Settlements)

	K	M	A	Others	Total
1927	10	9	5	3	27
1939	29	35	37	6	107
Increase in No.	19	26	32	3	80
Increase in p.c.	190	289	640	100	296

K = HEVER HAKVUTZOT; M = KIBBUTZ MEUHAD; A = HAKIBBUTZ HAARTZI

Source: Z. TZUR: The Hakibbutz Hameuchad in the Settlement of Eretz, Israel, Tel Aviv, 1979, vol I, P. 325, (Habrew).

Collective settlements were not the only way of co-operative colonization in Palestine. The establishment of small holders' villages, entitled *MOSHAV OVDIM*, in which the family was to be the basic producing unit and in which individual effort and ingenuity were to be directly rewarded, was advocated even before World War I.

In a way, the moshav was a reaction to the dominance of the kibbutz as the leading settlement model, and a number of the founding fathers of the first moshav *NAHALAL,* in 1921, were renegades from *DEGANIA*. The moshav was designed to combine the motivating power upon productivity of individual incentives with the benefits of cooperation in overcoming handicaps of small size. The basic maxims of the moshav were:

1) private operation of the farm on national land on long lease;
2) performance of all work with the labor force of the family;
3) mutual aid;
4) co-operative marketing.

For important segments of the immigrating pioneers the moshav became a popular alternative to the kibbutz, so that on the eve of World War II 60 moshavim, with over 10,000 members and their families, functioned in Palestine.

A third model of co-operative settlements, entitled *MOSHAV SHITUFI*, attempts to combine moshav type family based consumption patterns with the economic advantages of large scale kibbutz type production. Despite such a challenging synthesis, the moshav shitufi did not gain popularity, and up to World War II only three such settlements took roots.

When the State of Israel was established, the country had a complex and highly developed co-operative network.

In consumption, transportation, credit, and agricultural production the extent of co-operativization was momentous. About one fourth of all Jewish households were associated with a co-operative store, and one out of two had a registered member in a credit co-operative. Public transportation on busses was monopolized by co-operatives, and 75 percent of all inhabitants in rural communities lived in either a kibbutz or a moshav.

IV. Co-operatives in the State of Israel

The formation of a sovereign Jewish State in 1948 has had an overwhelming impact on the development of the co-operative movement. Distinction should be made between the short and the long runs. On the short, during the first decade of independent statehood, the major events were both the massive immigration and the consolidation of the State's bureaucratic machinery. Immigration created instant demands for goods, services, and employment. The infant state of State bureaucracy led to the recourse to existing pre-statehood institutional frameworks, such as the co-operatives, which were considered perfect and loyal surrogates for State organizations for the implementation of State sponsored policy objectives. The utilization of co-operative institutions, particularly of the socialist sector, was indeed flawless in

Table II: Co-operative Societies & Estimated Membership by Branch, in 1956

Branch	No. of Societies		Membership	
	No.	Growth from 1948 p.c.	No.	Growth from 1948 p.c.
Consumers' (society)	312	173	135,000	125
Consumers'(stores)	1230	785		
Producers'	270	80	5,282	– 0,3
Transport	27	–51	7,001	?
Agricultural (excl.settlements)	345	– 3	?	?
Housing	4 84	59	44,000	340 units
Credit & Pension Funds	530	53	378,322	202 (credit only)
Kibbutz	232	102	38,300	47
Moshav	253	336	93,000*	325*
Moshav Shitufi	20	233	1,603	129

Source: Ministry of Labour, Dept. of cooperation: Co-operative Societies in Israel 1956. Jerusalem, 1957

* – no information on working population; the number 93,000 represents total population; the growth rate of 325 per cent refers to total population which, in 1948, was 21,900.

view of the ideological concord between that co-operative sector and the dominant socialist parties in the Government. Thus, though losing much of its independence by becoming a policy instrument, the co-operative movement entered a period of rapid expansion. From 1949 to 1956, 2,037 new societies were registered, as compared to 2,755 societies in the preceding 26 years of existence of the Co-operative Registrar's office.

Table II reveals the problems co-operatives were assigned to solve and the results of their endeavor. The shortage in consumers' retail outlets, particularly in food, led to the massive expansion of co-operative stores, especially in new villages, towns, and urban neighbourhoods. The 785 new stores indicated an expansion rate of 176 per cent, yet membership grew only by 125 per cent, pointing to the increasingly effective competition of the small private shopkeepers with the co-operatives. Indeed, complaints about business losses in consumers' co-operatives were widely reported in the 1950s.

In view of the strict rent control which discouraged residential construction for renting, the housing of new immigrants was solved by public housing projects. One convenient legal device to organize neighbours' collaboration in large apart houses was the housing co-operative. Housing co-operatives, thus, thrived by conveniently filling a legal gap for the housing authorities.

Credit co-operatives prospered, primarily as a result of the rather sharp increase in consumption (in constant prices, 85 p.c. from 1950 to 1956) and the high rate of inflation (192 p.c.). Expectations for further inflation made borrowing lucrative, and it was difficult for the monetary authorities to effectively exercise credit control over the numerous small credit co-operatives. Thus, although there was only a modest increase in the number of credit societies, membership tripled.

The most conspicuous change in the co-operative movement took place in agricultural production. In the course of eight years, 225 new moshavim were founded, and the number of moshav settlers quadrupled. Between 1948 and 1956, over 110,000 new inhabitants settled in co-operative agricultural settlements. Of them, 65 p.c. joined moshavim – old and particularly new ones – and only 33 per cent joined kibbutzim. The principal cause of such radical change in the agricultural settlement patterns was the age and sociological composition of the immigrating masses to Israel after the implementation of its open gate policy towards Jewish immigrants. In contrast to former waves of immigration which included strong elements of young, single, pioneering individuals, the mass migration of 1949 – 52 was comprised mainly of large families. Most immigrants had had no previous ideological preparedness to espouse the kibbutz way of life. On the other hand, thousands of immigrating families were conducted, directly on their arrivals, to skeletons of new rural settlements, designed to be structured as moshavim. Consequently, although these new settlement skeletons did not subscribe to, or even were aware of the existence of the classical moshav principles, as of the early 1950s the moshav movement became the largest federation of agricultural settlements.

The kibbutz lost much of its quantitative primacy, declining to 21 p.c. by the end of 1952 in the rural population. Besides its diminishing popularity among the new immigrants, the kibbutz went through a painful schism in the largest inter-kibbutz federation, the *KIBBUTZ MEUHAD,* which split in 1952 on the issue of allegiance to the Soviet Union's version of Socialism. The rupture led to a hitherto traumatic organizational realignment of the kibbutz movement, whereby the splinter part of the *KIBBUTZ MEUHAD* joined the politically moderate *HEVER KVUTZOT* to form the non-leftist federation *IHUD HAKIBBUTZIM VEHAKVUTZOT.* The schism was a tragic event, which terminated life-long comradeships and in some cases even ruptured families over abstract ideological issues. After the split was accomplished, for about thirty years the kibbutz movement functioned within three equally sized, politically differentiated federations. In the early eighties, when the original raison d'etre of the schism was of no relevance anymore and political differences faded, the federations *IHUD HAKIBBITZIM VEHAKVUTZOT* and *KIBBUTZ MEUHAD* amalgamated to found the "United Kibbutz Movement" (*TAKAM*), which now encompasses about 60 per cent of all 268 kibbutzim. Rapid improvements in agricultural productivity and the heavy decline in the growth rate of demand for food, due to reduced levels of immigration, threatened the rural sector with the hazards of overproduction. The kibbutzim averted such danger by shifting increasing shares of their labor force and capital from agriculture to manufacture. Thus, as of the 1960s, more and more kibbutzim, originally conceived as agricultural colonies, turned into agro-industrial collectives. The moshav kept its place as the largest rural settlement model, though its declining share in rural population.

Among the major difficulties were the perils of overproduction in agriculture. The moshav, unlike the kibbutz, could not adjust to manufacture due to structural factors. On the other hand, agro-technological progress enhanced the disadvantages of small scale agriculture, reducing the competitiveness of many family farms and driving large numbers of moshav farmers to part time farming. These changes were complemented by the coming of age of the second generation of the demographically fecund immigrant settlers of the 1950s. The combined effects of all these developments strengthened feelings about the inevitability of structural changes in certain segments of the moshav movement.

Consumers' co-operatives have also been exposed to

the consequences of modernization. The Israeli consumer has developed tastes and standards of expectations which are remote from the austere subsistance concepts of the founding fathers about co-operative consumerism in Palestine. Changes were observable in two spheres. The number of independent co-operatives drastically declined. Parallelly, the emergence of competing supermarket chainstores imposed upon the enduring co-operatives radical restructuring through the amalgamation of hitherto independent societies, the numbers of which developed as follows:

1956	1967	1976	1982
312	46	30	27

Notwithstanding such drastic decline, consumers' cooperation, with its chain of well over 200 large and modern supermarkets, has maintained an important position in the consumers' food market. Obviously, very little has survived of the Rochdale model. Yet, consumers' cooperation still plays a significant and constructive role in Israel's retail trade.

Credit co-operatives which generated remarkable power before 1948 and continued to exert influence on the market of small and medium credit in the first decade of statehood, fell victim to its own significance. As of the beginning of active monetary policy by the Bank of Israel, in the late 1950s, the existence of numerous small co-operative banking institutions were considered an impediment of effective monetary control by the Central Bank. Consequently, a policy of narrowing the scope of activities for the credit co-operatives was pursued and, as a result, more and more such societies went out of business. The process was intensified by a trend of mergers in the banking industry in general, which led to the concentration of almost all banking business in the hands of five large banks of Israel. Thus, more and more credit co-operatives were taken over by the large commercial banks, so that today credit cooperation in its real sense has become insignificant.

Producers' cooperation has displayed remarkable endurance, in spite of many emerging disadvantages. The Israeli industry, in accordance with global trends, has developed towards production patterns with increasing capital intensity and growing human skill requirements, which have had adverse effects on co-operative production plants. Nevertheless, production of certain goods and services in labor-owned and -managed enterprises continues to employ over 20,000 workers in Israel. Admittedly, well over two thirds of those workers belong to one co-operatively structured public transportation company named EGGED, which is the monopolistic bussing company in public transportation. Furthermore, about one half of all employees in the producers' co-operative sector are hired workers, which is a reprehensible phenomenon in the Israeli co-operative code. Notwithstanding, producers' cooperation remains an ongoing experiment, which serves as a model for post industrial business organizations.

The co-operatives of the late 1980s are amid a process of rethinking and regeneration. It may well be that the movement which will emerge will be a rejuvenated organization, capable to contribute to the improvement of the socio-economic reality in Israel in the next century.

Development of Co-operatives in Latin America

DIETER W. BENECKE [J]

(see also: *Education, Latin America*; *State and Co-operatives, Market Economy*; *Economic Order*; *Policies for Promotion*; *Development Policy*)

I. Names and Terminology; II. Rudiments and Preconditions; III. Quantitative Development; IV. Qualitative Development; V. Future Perspectives.

I. Names and Terminology

Cooperativas, the common term in Latin America for co-operatives, basically only means people working together, but it was originally an adjective used to describe associations (*asociaciones, sociedades*). The co-operative term derived from French and English terminology on the one hand is indicative that the cooperation undertaken in a community or association is not pursued so seriously; the stability of the cooperation is stressed less than the achievement of immediate results. On the other hand, the term alludes to the origins of co-operative thought. The ideas of the French socialists (→ *Co-operative Socialism*), in particular those of *Charles Gide*, as well as the lofty principles of the → *Rochdale Pioneers* stand sponsor to the initial co-operative movement. → *Raiffeisen's*, → *Schulze-Delitzsch's* or → *Haas'* co-operative ideas based on self-help, self-responsibility and self-management – (→ *Principles*) and above all *Draheim's* and *Henzler's* later corporate and commercial considerations – in contrast only had isolated influence on the formative efforts of the co-operative founders and organizers.

It thus proves to be quite difficult to evaluate co-operative development through the eyes of contemporary West European functionalists who proceed from *Draheim's* notion of the co-operative exhibiting a "double character" as an enterprise and as an association of individuals (Draheim) (→ *Dual Nature*). The associative character among the majority of co-operatives in Latin America has precedence over the more long-term character of a cooperation based on self-responsibility which consciously addresses both its goals and problems. The enterprise character as a rule is as weakly manifested as the associative character of partnerships found today in Europe (→ *Partnership Enterprises*).

II. Rudiments and Preconditions

The notion of cooperation is deeply anchored in pre-Columbian society. The *ayllus* and other co-operative organizations in the Inca Empire were considered highly developed forms of joint production among neighbors, providing for times of need as well as meeting the needs of the Inca aristocracy (→ *Autochthonous Co-operatives*). The motive of progress by all means was not existent in these organizations, an understandable situation in such an age in which wide sectors of the population were exclusively concerned with securing their existence and not achieving surpluses. This was presumably also the situation in the other advanced pre-Columbian civilizations dominated by ruling priests. If the motive of economic progress had been stressed over that of subsistence in these → *self-help organizations*, the central and hierarchical domination of these agrarian societies would hardly have been preserved for so long.

Even the *ejido*s which were established after the Mexican Revolution (starting in 1917) and often compared to agricultural worker's co-operatives reflected the former relationship to subsistence-oriented cooperation under a central state hierarchy (→ *Policies for Promotion*). In addition, the all-dominating Party of the Institutionalized Revolution (PRI) demanded control functions itself. The results of this cooperation – ultimately determined by external forces although formally self-responsible – remain slim, as can be expected (→ *Officialization*). One can say the same for the co-operative efforts undertaken in the settlement territories of the South American Indios in the 1960s. Several non-government organizations such as *DESEC* in Cochabamba (Bolivia) or the Federation of Coffee Farmers' Co-operatives in Guatemala (*FEDECOCAGUA*) made use of more suitable national and mentality-specific methods, incorporating sociological and psychological factors more expediently. In several cases they were even so successful in combining commercial thinking with traditional forms of cooperation that advisors and consultants were able to disengage themselves from their former client associations.

Alongside co-operative associations which continued in the tradition of early forms of cooperation, isolated co-operatives were established even before the 1960s. These were usually set up by European emigrants and had the typical character of auxiliary co-operatives, such as in Brazil, Argentina, Uruguay and Chile. Services such as purchasing, marketing and processing were predominantly directed around the farming sector and contributed to overcome market distance or problems in communication and information. Community life-oriented workers' co-operatives established by emigrant religious groups such as the Mennonites in Paraguay were likewise successful for their members.

Discussions of → *development policy* commenced in the 1950s, and in their course the spectrum expanded, even in the co-operative sector. The idea was initially pursued in Latin America to achieve development primarily through capital accumulation in the industrial sector. This dominant "development strategy" did by all means bring strong economic growth up through the beginning of the 1960s, but it likewise introduced the characteristics of dualism typically associated with such growth as defined by *Myrdal* (*Myrdal*). Poles emerged in development which syphoned off dynamic elements. The diffusion effects (trickle down effects) which *Hirschman* described were without a doubt at hand, but they were not effective to the extent expected (*Hirschman*).

Seen theoretically, this dualistic development is the ideal starting point for the creation of commercially oriented co-operatives. They can consolidate the impulses in the underdeveloped regions and population groups; due to the accumulated capacity of numerous small potential members they can absorb innovations from other sectors and implement them in these disadvantaged sectors; as "spontaneously imitating entrepreneurs" (*Heuß*) they can propagate the development process analyzed by *Schumpeter* und ultimately incite this process themselves to the benefit of their members (Benecke, 1972). In order for this theoretically feasible process to produce actual positive effects, dynamic and well-controlled co-operative entrepreneurs, or stated more modestly, business managers, are needed. Furthermore, relatively well informed members are needed who are motivated for a long-term cooperation along commercial lines. Suitable "leader personalities" are to be found in all Latin American countries in which the Caudillo principle enjoys a long tradition; control exercised by members and supervisory board (*juntas de vigilancia*) has, however, been mostly ineffective (→ *Organizational Structure of Societies*).

The general atmosphere for co-operative promotion has had an even worse effect. Instead of grappling with the concrete problems and chances of dualism, in most situations discussion has concentrated on social-utopian principles. Co-operatives were imputed the capacity of educating individuals to act primarily out of solidarity; because of the importance of this socialization function, the state was sought as a promoter, financial supporter and controller. Other societal institutions such as churches and unions participated in this type of well-meaning, albeit paternalistic promotion. As it is well known, this does not necessarily have negative effects when such promotion is concentrated on and limited to the initial outrigging, education and training or imparting of information to (potential) members. If this attention is extended too long, however, the organization only learns at a late point in time to function independently.

The excellent preconditions for the establishment of effective co-operatives in Latin America were indeed recognized in the 1960s, but these were mostly only used ideologically. A numerical explosion in the number of co-operative establishments occurred, but aside from exceptional cases the practical effects – understood as improvements in the level of their members' production and wealth – remained slight in most countries.

III. Quantitative Development

Systematic research and statistical documentation of co-operative development in Latin America commenced initially at the end of the 1960s. An exact calculation of the previous years is not possible due to poorly kept registers. The first co-operative institute founded in Chile at the Catholic University in cooperation with the University of Münster (Germany) (→ *AGI*) traced numerous co-operatives in the state co-operative registers which in actuality no longer existed and found numerous co-operatives in a field study which were not registered (*Benecke*, 1969). This situation was similar in other Latin American countries.

The quantitative dimension found in Chile should be similar to that of the majority of countries in Latin America. 246 co-operatives were founded between 1925 and 1955, but in contrast almost 1,300 were founded between 1960 and 1968 under the influence of governments which pursued social reform policies (*Benecke*, 1970). Substantial, steady development can be ascertained in Argentina (predominantly commercial co-operatives); up to the end of the 1960s, there was practically no co-operative development in Venezuela, Panama and Ecuador (see country reports in *Benecke*, 1976). After the early 1970s Argentina, Uruguay and Chile led in numerical development (see *Appendix I*). Secondary co-operatives were also developed to the furthest extent in these countries. Between 1972 and 1984, one can identify healthy numerical growth among primary co-operatives and their members in Colombia, Venezuela and Ecuador, a certain concentrational tendency in Argentina and Uruguay (mounting membership with a constant number of primary co-operatives), and a clear decrease in Chile (*Appendix II*).

It is particulary apparent in Chile – a reverse situation of what was occurring in Colombia during its steady democratic development – how important the nature and form of governments are for numerical development. Right-wing dictators maintain a skeptical position with respect to co-operatives, that is when they let them remain in existence at all. A rigid application of the Chicago model of a free market economy and a drastic process of economic reform determined development in Chile between 1974 and 1980 (→ *State and Co-operatives, Market Economy*). There was no longer any room for the social-utopic approaches cultivated between 1964 and 1970; in the market one was forced to seek his own niche and chance. Free competition which permits uncontrolled concentration, such as in the trading and agricultural sectors, made it difficult for co-operatives to achieve surpluses and guarantee that modernization would be carried out. Members above all belonged to the low-income classes and therefore supported the policy of "the best price now" rather than "waive profit now and invest for the best price tomorrow". The result of this was the failure of two of Latin America's star co-operatives, the consumer co-operative chain *UNICOOP* and the purchasing co-operative for building materials, *SODIMAC*; both of these served as economic and social models for organizations abroad.

Total development throughout the 1970s and the beginning of 1980s is captured in a extensive research study (*Benecke/Eschenburg*) based on an analysis conducted by the author in 1970 (*Benecke*, 1976) for all Latin American countries with the exception of Panama, the Guyanas and the Carribean states. Based on these results one may conclude that orientation around a concrete membership promotion mandate has gradually prevailed in Latin America. The increase in the rate of penetration is considerably higher than the population growth rate, in other words, the share of the population organized in co-operatives compared to the population as a whole.

IV. Qualitative Development

In the formal structural sense co-operative development in Latin America can in essence be considered finished or completed. Various sectoral co-operatives are found in almost all countries; almost all sectors in turn have secondary co-operatives and tertiary organizations for → *financing*, → *insurance* and vocational education – also in part for auditing functions and co-operative representation with respect to society and the state (→ *Education, Latin America*). The performance potential of these organizations is by all means quite varied both for the individual sectors and for the individual co-operatives in these sectors. As a whole one must consider the movement quite heterogeneous. Due to well-organized secondary co-operatives a certain homogenization in the performance level has been achieved for affiliated co-operatives in exceptional cases, such as among the credit co-operatives in Colombia and Bolivia, the co-operative home-building societies in Chile and the coffee farmers' co-operatives in Guatemala and Costa Rica.

Country	Year	Population (1000)	Primary Co-operatives				Secondary Co-operatives			Apex and spezialized Co-operatives				
			Member	Member (1000)	Penetration (%)	Size (5:4)	Member	Member Co-oper.	Integration (%)	Apex Federation	Education	Finance	Audit	Insurance
1	2	3	4	5	6	7	8	9	10	11	12	13	14	15
Argentine	1972	24.000	4.400	4.745	54,4	1.078	33	3.301	75,0	CIA	ESEC	Genoss. Banken	Banco Nación	AACMS FACS
Bolivia	1973	5.200	1.459	124	11,9	85	6	518	35,5	–	COOP AS	–	–	–
Chile	1972	10.343	3.452	834	22,2	242	23	1.131	26,7	CONFE COOP	ICE COOP	IFI COOP	AUDI COOP	UCO SEG
Costa Rica	1972	1.426	270	77	10,5	218	6	119	44,0	UNA COOP		INFOCOOP	–	–
Ecuador	1972	6.595	910	128	5,4	141	8	–	–	–	ICE	Genoss. Bank	–	–
Columbia	1972	21.362	1.480	1.113	14,3	752	11	452	30,6	AS COOP	INDE SCO	FINANCIACOOP	–	–
Mexico	1973	53.645	2.886	344	1,7	119	66	–	–	CNC	IMEC	–	–	–
Panama	1972	1.515	282	40	7,3	142	7	93	35,0	–	–	–	–	–
Peru	1973	14.630	2.010	926	17,5	461	27	417 392 416	20,7 19,5 20,7	Confederación	–	BANCOOP	–	COSE INCA SEG. COOP
Uruguay	1972	3.068	918	261	23,4	284	3	55	6,0	–	IDEAL COOP CCU	–	–	–
Venezuela	1973	11.563	292	74	1,9	253	6	–	–	CNC	Mérida, Gumilla	ICC	–	–

Appendix I: The Co-operative System of Latin America (General Survey, 1972).

Country	Year	Population (1000)	Primary Co-operatives				Secondary Co-operatives			Apex and spezialized Co-operatives				
			Member	Member (1000)	Penetration (%)	Size (5:4)	Member	Member Co-oper.	Integration (%)	Apex Federation	Education	Finance	Audit	Insurance
1	2	3	4	5	6	7	8	9	10	11	12	13	14	15
Argentine	1982	28.539	4.198	9.468	100	2.255	45	–	–	CIA COOPERA CONIN AGRO	ALCECOOP	–	–	–
Bolivia	1983	6.082	2.218	216	11	97	8	484	22	–	–	–	–	–
Brasil	1983	129.660	3.309	9	1.138	65	–	–	–	see report CONFE	–	–	–	–
Chile	1984	11.879	2.261	–	–	–	8	–	–	COOP COPAGRO	ICECOOP	–	AUDI COOP	–
Colombia	1983	27.880	2.410	1.314	14	545	43	–	–	Confederación de Cooperativas de Colombia	(10)	FINANCIA COOP	–	–
Costa Rica	1984	2.460	464	268	33	578	19	–	58	UNACOOP	–	INFOCOOP	–	–
Ecuador	1982	8.000	4.378	760	29	174	7	1.409	32	–	CEC ICE	Banco Cooperativo	–	–
El Salvador	1984	4.828	1.110	59	4	53	6	335	32	COACES	–	–	–	–
Guatemala	1985	7.916	882	209	8	237	10	301	34	CONFE COOP	CENDEC	–	–	–
Honduras	1984	4.192	892	131	9	146	7	354	40	CHC	IFC	–	–	–
Mexico	1984	76.950	6.221	551	2	89	117	–	67	CONA COOP	UCPEET	BANPESCA FOSOC	–	–
Nicaragua	1984	3.137	2.738	168	16	61	1	32	1	–	–	–	–	–
Paraguay	1984	3.105	178	50	5	287	4	91	51	–	–	–	–	–
Perú	1981	18.000	2.032	2.060	34	1.014	43	843 336 350	42 17 17	Confederación	–	BANCOOP	–	COSE INCA Seg. Coop.
Uruguay	1984	2.994	794	582	58	733	8	403	51	–	CIDCOOP CCM y CAD	–	–	–
Venezuela	1985	16.278	550	145	3	264	16	467	85	CECONA VE	–	SIF	–	–

Appendix II: The Co-operative System of Latin America (General Survey, 1984).

The causes for this lack of homogenization are multifarious. The ideological/paternalistic impulses for founding co-operatives mentioned above hindered the more enduring determination for self-help. Economic difficulties, a mentality stressing wind-fall profits, the lack of manager personalities, their insufficient exercise of control or even in part their quite pronounced need to flaunt themselves were factors which hindered stronger sectoral cooperation and the exchange of practical knowledge.

A further hurdle to progress is the "inclination for premature complacency" among members caused by internal difficulties. The cooperation was accepted or desired in order to improve the current situation. If this is achieved only to a modest degree compared to other potential opportunities, members express their contentment; if one perhaps fears the endangerment of that which one has achieved, one tends to let further cooperation endeavors fall to the wayside. If, for example, one joins a credit co-operative in which one can receive a credit amounting to 300% of one's savings according to the terms of business, there is a strong inclination to save only up to that amount needed to have a justifiable claim to the credit striven for. Cooperation oriented around more long-term efficiency can only be stimulated in such situations by expanding the co-operative's palette of bank-oriented services (→ *Co-operative Banks*).

As a result, qualitative outputs and/or services with a greater degree of influence – such as structuring of competition, increasing the employment rate, reducing inflation, providing credit and information and influencing democratic development – remain either slight or nonexistent. Because a generalization of the co-operative movement's qualitative effects does not seem appropriate in the light of the heterogeneity of the movement, and inasmuch as a detailed and differentiated analysis is not possible in the limited dimension of this treatise, we wish to refer readers once again to the volumes "*Las Cooperativas en America Latina*" in which they can find a more detailed description of the individual sectors and organizations. The attempts to establish co-operative integration on the continental level are also addressed, such as The Organization of American Co-operatives (*OCA*), The Latin American Confederation of Industrial Workers' Co-operatives (*COLACOT*), The Association of Financial Institutes (*SIDEFCOOP*), Vocational Training Institutes (*ALCECOOP*) and Research Institutes (*CIUDEC*).

If one views the qualitative development of Latin American co-operatives in a rather skeptical light – as is the case in this presentation – one must bear three restrictive considerations in mind:

1. Co-operatives' success up through the present is not viewed skeptically in general, but skepticism rather results when their achievements are compared with the given theoretical potential of co-operative effort as well with the actual necessary performance level of these organizations for development policy.
2. Above all it is the ideologically motivated state promoters of co-operatives who deserve low marks – promoters such as the *SINAMOS* farming advisors in Peru at the beginning of the 1970s, who were more rooted in their own structured utopia than the reality of their country, or the state farming authorities in Chile who played a notorious and ultimately frustrating role for the rural population rather than motivating cooperation.
3. The role of numerous – but by all means not all – co-operative management personalities should also be seen critically, persons who tend to eye their position as a "political role" rather than serving as leaders of a social movement, acquiring proper training as co-operative managers or at least offering their business managers proper training. These management personalities in addition neglected auditing and controlling authorities.

This critique of co-operative performance in Latin America appears to contradict their numerical development. If observed in the light of the restrictions listed here – in particular in comparison to the high expectations placed on co-operative functions in the general development process – this criticism is more than justified and should be understood as a source of concrete improvement suggestions for the future. It must also be stressed that the situation of co-operative members and even non-involved third parties (*Olson*) in most cases would be considerably worse without the co-operatives and their work. The provision situation would be precarious for many consumers, and the products expensive; numerous persons would not have invested their modicum of savings nor have been in the position to receive a loan; electrification and water provision projects would not have been executed; the processing and marketing of agricultural products as well as the purchasing of means of production would not have been undertaken; numerous small houses and dwellings would not have been built; truck and bus drivers would not have been able to protect their independent status.

It remains a speculative question whether it is better or worse for the development process of a country to provide a certain "something" which does not achieve the needed level of efficiency, or not to provide it at all and wait for potentially more efficient means or procedures. Cooperation without a doubt was always the better road to take for those in question – the co-operative members – rather than for them to wait for others to provide a solution to their problems.

V. Future Perspectives

Had this article been written 10 years ago when dictatorial or less firmly democratic governments determined policy in the majority of the countries in Latin America, one would have considered the chances quite minimal that a qualitative improvement in Latin American co-operatives would have followed their quantitative development. Today one can be somewhat more optimistic. Since priority has been given to democratic development in all Latin American countries and the collapse of the socialist experiments in the former Eastern Block robbed the advocates of this ideology of their societal illusion – at least for the present time – more favorable general conditions exist for the co-operatives' further qualitative development.

By all means the difficulties and threats must not be misjudged which have become more grave in Latin America since the beginning of the 1970s. Attention should be cast above all to the more extensive poverty affecting wider sectors of the population, the lack of education among the poorer population groups, the problems of urbanization and continuing rates of extreme population growth.

If co-operatives are to undergo noticeable qualitative improvements they require several additional further measures. Priority should be placed on more intensive economic consultation of existent co-operatives. Further attention should be cast on providing co-operative members with more comprehensive information about operative procedures. More effective activity would be needed from the auditing → *federations*, who in turn should judge their success on the progress made by the co-operatives they audit and consult (→ *Auditing*).

A wide range of involvement also avails itself for international cooperation. Europeans would, nevertheless, have to accept the fact that consultation, training and auditing functions strictly oriented around operational and economic factors are insufficient. Co-operatives in Latin America also fulfill a social function which they will probably be forced to continue excercising in the future due to the lack of other alternatives. A compromise must thus be found between economic efficiency and social functions which is suitable to the mentality in Latin America in order for co-operatives as a model to win over or retain the emotional involvement of their members.

Bibliography

Baudin, L.: El Imperio Socialista de los Incas, 5. edition, Santiago/Chile 1962.
Benecke, Dieter W.: Kooperation und Wachstum in Entwicklungsländern, Tübingen 1972.
Benecke, Dieter W.: Einige Aspekte des Genossenschaftswesens in Chile. In: Zeitschrift für das gesamte Genossenschaftswesen, vol. 19, pp. 54–68, 1969.
Benecke, Dieter W. (ed.): Las Cooperativas y el Estado, Santiago/Chile 1970.
Benecke, Dieter W.(ed.): Das Genossenschaftswesen in Lateinamerika, Münster 1976.
Benecke, Dieter W./Eschenburg, R.: Las Cooperativas en America Latina, Sao Leopoldo 1987, vol. 1, I–XXI, published German version: Genossenschaften in Lateinamerika, Results of a study, Münster 1987.
Benecke, Dieter W.: Cooperativas – Escuela de la Democracia en America Latina, pp. 369–389, Münster 1988.
Benecke, Dieter W.: Demokratie und Verschuldung in Südamerika. In: Wagner, W.(ed.): Die Internationale Politik 1983–1984, pp. 368–382, München 1986.
Draheim, G.: Die Genossenschaft als Unternehmenstyp, Göttingen 1952.
Eschenburg, R.(ed.): Formas Cooperativas en America Latina, Münster 1988
Heuß, E.: Allgemeine Markttheorie, Tübingen/Zürich 1965.
Hirschman, A. O.: Die Strategie der wirtschaftlichen Entwicklung, Stuttgart 1967.
Myrdal, G.: Ökonomische Theorie und unterentwickelte Regionen, Stuttgart 1959.
Olson, M. jr.: Die Logik des kollektiven Handelns, Tübingen 1968.
Ritter: Dorfgemeinschaften in Peru, Göttingen 1966.
Schumpeter, J.: Theorie der wirtschaftlichen Entwicklung, 6. edition, Berlin 1964.

Development of Co-operatives in North America

J.G. CRAIG

(see also: *Development, Latin America; Development, Northern Africa; Development, South Asia; Development, South-East Asia; Credit Unions*)

I. Historical Overview; II. Credit Unions; III. Agricultural Co-operatives; IV. Consumer Co-operatives; V. Other Co-operatives; VI. Critical Issues Facing Co-operatives.

I. Historical Overview

The co-operative idea came to North America with immigrants from Europe in the 19th century (→ *History in 19th C.*), but it was in the early part of the 20th century that the movement became strong. The socio-economic circumstances were different from those in Europe and co-operatives evolved differently. Agricultural co-operatives (→ *Rural Co-operatives*) were developed first and still are the strongest sector. They developed amongst new immigrants in the new frontier, where farming by Europeans was being started. The communities were relatively classless (compared to Europe) with poor economic infrastructures to service the farmers (*Mac Pherson*). In the larger urban centres, → *credit unions*, housing co-operatives (→ *Housing Societies*), and service co-operatives like daycare and health co-operatives (→ *Health Care System*) have developed but → *consumer co-operatives* are few and relatively small scale organizations.

Two national apex organizations (→ *Central Institutions*) in Canada represent the movement internationally, the Canadian Co-operatives Association (CCA – Anglophone) and Le Conseil Canadien de la Cooperation (CCC – Francophone). In the United States, the National co-operative Business Association (NCBA), the National Council of Farmer Co-operatives (NCFC), and the Credit Union National Association are the main national → *federations*.

Rationalization of local units has been rapid in the 1970s and 80s as local co-operatives and regional federations have merged to form stronger economic units (*French et al.*). In the 1980s, mergers at the regional level particularly in the United States have produced some very large well integrated co-operatives. Fifteen have annual sales close to or over a billion dollars. The five largest co-operatives appear on the 1988 list of the largest 100 diversified service companies by Fortune Magazine.

1. Canada

Canada has one tenth the population of the United States, a larger land mass, and two founding language groups. As a result, the movement has evolved differently from the United States. There are two apex organizations, both members of ICA. They are not formerly connected but for most of this century the working relationship has been close.

The strongest part of the movement is agricultural marketing (see table 1) (→ *Marketing*). → *Consumer co-operatives* have had a turbulent development and are declining in market share with some notable exceptions. The → *credit unions*, → *housing co-operatives*, and co-operatives in the Arctic amongst the *Inuit* have grown significantly in the 1970s and 80s. The Arctic co-operatives have become the largest employer (next to government) of indigenous people in the North West Territories and Nouveau Quebec (Iglauer).

Quebec is a distinct society within Canada, with 6 million francophones surrounded by 20 million English speaking Canadians and 260 million Americans. The Caisse Populaires (→ *Co-operative Banks*) were started in 1901 by → *Alphonse Desjardin* and, with about 45% of personal savings deposits, are the largest financial institution in Quebec. Quebecs' strong agricultural movement is focused around milk co-operatives and has a major share of the market. The younger movements in housing and worker co-operatives are energetic and dynamic and growing rapidly (*Roy*, 1988, pp.22–23). In Atlantic Canada, the focal point for the movement came in the 1920s with the adult education approach promoted by the extension workers from St. Francis Xavier University in Antigonish Nova Scotia. All types of co-operatives developed from this approach and leadership from Antigonish (→ *Conceptions, Co-operative*) played a key role in the development of co-operatives in Atlantic Canada.

Ontario, the largest and most wealthy province, has the weakest movement. Agricultural co-operatives started around the turn of the century, have a long tradition but have faced strong competition and difficult financial problems in the 1980s. The Ontario credit unions market penetration has also declined during the 1980s and was burdened with deficits. In the urban areas the credit unions continue to develop along with housing co-operatives and daycare co-operatives.

The bread basket of Canada has been the strongest movement in English speaking Canada. Co-operatives have handled 70% of the cereal grains marketed since the late 1920s and agricultural → *supply co-operatives* remain strong. Consumer co-operatives in the largest cities have been in decline with the notable exception of Calgary.

2. United States of America

Agricultural co-operatives (→ *Rural Co-operatives*) were organized in the later part of the 19th century (→ *History in 19th C.*). In the early part of the 20th century, ideological differences occurred. Some co-operatives (bargaining co-operatives) developed to market farm products to privately owned processors with the purpose to bargain for better prices (→ *Pricing Policy*). Others developed on a pooling basis with the object of marketing (→ *Marketing Strategies*), processing and packaging the product for consumers. This difference is still evident. The bargaining co-

Table 1: Co-operative Share of Agricultural Marketing Activity*

Year	USA 1982	1986	1989	1991	Canada 1982	1986	1989	1991
All farm products	30%	26%	26%	28%	44%			
Dairy	77%	78%	80%	81%	51%	57%	56%	59%
Grain	36%	27%	36%	38%	76%	73%	75%	74%
Cotton	36%	35%	43%	36%				
Vegetables	20%	4%	18%	18%	9%	10%	11%	12%
Fruit		18%			17%	22%	17%	15%
Honey & maple					25%	20%	26%	23%
Livestock	11%	8%	7%					
– Hogs					13%	13%	12%	18%
– Beef					17%	15%	19%	23%
– Poultry	7%	8%			35%	34%	35%	39%
Eggs					3%	3%	4%	5%

* Market share statistics come from several published sources and are estimates only. For Canada *Co-opration Canada*, Ottawa: Co-operative Secretariat, Gouvernment of Canada. For the United States, *Farmers Cooperatives*, Washington: US Department of Agriculture/Agric. Cooperative Services.

operatives are virtually invisible to consumers but a number of large marketing co-operatives have developed national brands and are very highly visible.
Rural Electric Associations (REAs) (→ *Classification*) were first organized in 1935 to provide electricity to rural households. They purchased electricity from government and privately owned plants (many now have their own generating facilities) and were responsible for rural electrification (*Knapp*). REAs currently retail to over 25 million rural households. → *Supply co-operatives* developed alongside → *marketing co-operatives* to provide animal feed, fertilizer, and petroleum to farmers. Banks for co-operatives (→ *Co-operative Banks*) have played an important role in providing debt capital for rural co-operatives and are part of Farm Credit System (→ *Agricultural Credit*), a government program to provide credit to farmers (*Abrahamsen*).
Unlike Europe, the consumer food co-operative movement never received strong support from organized labour and its members have not become major retailers. Other consumer owned co-operatives are important in urban America. Without a government medical plan, medical co-operatives started as medical insurers, but have evolved to owning hospitals, medical clinics, and laboratories. → *Housing co-operatives* are important providers of urban social housing for low and moderate income earners and insurance co-operatives are major underwriters.

II. Credit Unions

→ *Alphonse Desjardin*, a reporter in the house of commons in Ottawa, became distressed at the inaction of the Members of Parliament in dealing with usury. After studying the co-operatives started in Rochdale UK, in Germany by → *Raiffeisen* and → *Schulze-Delitzsch*, and in Italy by *Luzzatti*, he organized the first caisse populaire in 1901 in Levi Quebec. The caisses were organized on a parish basis to provide credit to the poor on the basis of character (*Moody and Fite*). Their success influenced the development of credit unions in the industrialized centers in the United States, which organized on the common bond of work place. The common bonds are still present, now credit unions with industrial bonds, community bonds, religious and ethnic bonds work together in state and provincial federations.
La Confederation des Caisses Populaires d'economie Desjardins du Quebec is a three-tiered organization with an affiliate membership of 4.6 million and combined assets of $33.4 billion in 1989. The Canadian Co-operative Credit Society is the apex organization for the Credit Union Centrals in the nine anglophone provinces with an affiliate membership of 4.1 million and combined assets of $24 billion in 1989.
In the United States, the Credit Union National Association (CUNA) is the apex organization for the state leagues with an affiliate membership of 54.5 million and combined assets of $184.7 billion in 1989. Working relationships with the movements in the two countries have been close and in 1970, the → *World Council of Credit Unions* (→ *International Co-operative Organizations*) was created to assist credit union development in the less industrialized countries. Although the largest members are in Canada and the United States, the combined world wide membership in 79 countries is 77.6 million people and combined assets of $255 billion in 1989.

III. Agricultural Co-operatives

Agricultural co-operatives (→ *Rural Co-operatives*) are important in the marketing of agricultural products beyond the farm gate (→ *Marketing*). North America is one of the largest food producing areas in the world and farmers market 26% of their produce in the United States and 44% in Canada (see table 1). In the United States, the dairy sector is dominated by co-operatives having a market share of nearly 80% and in Canada the dominant sector is grain marketing. Co-operatives also supply about 1/3 of the farm supplies (see table 2). In fresh vegetables, 73 associations in the USA served about 8,000 members, mostly in the West and South In 1986,they account for only 4% of the market share but a sales volume of $218 million. Bargaining co-operatives are important in the fruits and vegetables sector.

Table 2: Co-operative Share of Agricultural Supply Activity*

Year	USA				Canada			
	1982	1986	1989	1991	1982	1986	1989	1991
All farm supplies	28%	26%	24%	28%	33%	33%	31%	30%
Feed stuff	18%	18%	18%	20%	30%	28%	26%	27%
Fertilizer	42%	46%	42%	45%	32%	32%	36%	36%
Chemicals	30%	31%	24%	28%				
Seed	17%	17%	15%	14%	25%	25%	20%	19%
Machinery					17%	15%	12%	7
Farm fuel	36%	3%	39%	43%	42%	47%	52%	52%

* Market share statistics come from several published sources and are estimates only. For Canada *Co-opration Canada*, Ottawa: Co-operative Secretariat, Gouvernement of Canada. For the United States, *Farmers Cooperatives*, Washington: US Department of Agriculture/Agric. Cooperative Services.

US agricultural co-operatives have had the National Bank for Co-operatives organized on a regional basis to provide a source of credit. The national system ran into difficulties in the recession of the early 1980s. Most regional banks were merged into one national bank called CoBank in 1988. It has assets of $12 billion (1989), its loan portfolio included 39% to marketing co-operatives, 255 to rural utility co-operatives, 7% to farm supply co-operatives, and

23% to finance products exported to international customers (USDA).

Animal feed is a major expense in livestock production. In 1987, almost 3,000 USA co-operatives provided to their members feed valued at nearly $3 billion. The number of co-opertaive feed mills grew by 18% to 1,913. Expansion of mill capacities and feed production increased proportionally. The trend is toward mills with larger capacities to gain greater economies of scale (→ *Operational Size*). However, market share in both countries has declined by 2% during the 1980s, and the market share of all farm supplies has remained constant at about 1/4 in the United States and 1/3 in Canada.

IV. Consumer Co-operatives

Although → *consumer co-operatives* have a very small market share in North America, over 3.4 million consumers are members. In rural and many isolated areas they are important suppliers of food and household supplies. In some regions, notably Atlantic Canada, they are located in most cities and currently have 20% of the food market share. The Calgary Consumers Co-operative is the largest consumer co-operative in North America with 14 stores, membership of over 250,000, and annual sales exceeding $440 million for about 35% of the food market share in its trading area.

The large consumer co-operatives with food stores in the 1950s and 60s like Berkeley, Palo Alto, and Washington D.C. have gone out of business or discontinued food operations. The exception is the Hyde Park Co-operative which markets food in the Chicago area. The over 7,000 consumer co-operatives are mainly small organizations serving a particular niche in the market place (*Cotterill*).

V. Other Co-operatives

The new movements are growing and vibrant, this includes the *indogenous co-operatives* in the arctic which are multi-purpose, they market carvings and handicrafts, operate retail stores, coffee shops, tourist facilities etc. Housing co-operatives are growing in both countries. In Canada, they are continuous organizations (members own part of the co-operative, not their housing unit), being a major supplier of social housing (Laidlaw). Usually, members are from low and moderate income levels, a fact reducing the social stigma and social problems usually associated with income segregates social housing in North America. Besides continuous co-operatives, the United States also have equity housing co-operatives which are numerous in many large cities. Housing co-operatives are linked nationally by the Housing Federation of Canada and the National Association of Housing Co-operatives in the USA.

There are thousands of small service co-operatives in North America that are unaffiliated, but meet local needs. These include co-operative farms, machinery co-operatives, transportation, funeral co-operatives, recreational facilities, farmers markets, and many others.

VI. Critical Issues Facing Co-operatives

1. Decline of Agriculture and Rural Communities

Agriculture is in crisis in North America and co-operatives, as major organizations in agriculture, are under great pressure to become more efficient and more active in speaking for agricultural interests.

2. Capital Crisis

Agribusiness organizations are becoming more vertically integrated into more countries. Co-operatives are responding to this transnational challenge by moving more into food processing (→ *Own Production*) and provided more value added to the products. The capital needs to expand are problematic as cash short farmers need capital to invest in their own operations (→ *Financing*). Credit unions are faced with similar challenges with a need to build reserves and member equity (→ *Equity Capital*). In times of high inflation, the traditional methods used by co-operatives to raise capital are not effective. New innovative devices that are consistent with the essence of cooperation are needed and some innovative experiments are underway.

3. International Cooperation

With globalization, the private sector competitors are growing. Co-operatives have developed multinational commercial organizations but they are insignificant to compete with the growing competitors. Co-operatives have great potential to cooperate at the international level, but the potential is not being realized (*Craig*).

4. Co-operative Education

North American educational systems have dichotomized the economy into private and government sectors. The co-operative sector has been ignored. The land grant universities in the United States have taught courses to agricultural students about co-operatives, but for most of the twentieth century co-operatives have not been a part of public education. This is slowly changing. Now, there is more university based research and school curriculum materials. Co-operatives are often seen as one of North Americas best kept secret (→ *Education, North America*).

Bibliography

Abrahamsen, Martin A.: Agricultural Co-operatives in the United States, Oxford 1980.
Cobia, David W. (ed.): Co-operatives in Agriculture, Englewood Cliffs NJ 1988.
Cotterill, Ronald (ed.): Consumer Food Co-operatives, Danville Ill 1982.
Co-operative Secretariat: Cooperation in Canada, 1988, Ottawa 1990.
Craig, John G.: Multinational Co-operatives: An Alternative to World Development, Saskatoon Sask 1976.
French, Charles E./ John C. Moore/ C.A. Kraenzle and K.F. Harding: Survival Strategies for Agricultural Co-operatives, Ames Iowa 1980.
Knapp, Joseph G.: The Advance of American Co-operative Enterprise: 1920-1945, Danville Ill 1973.
Laidlaw, A.: Housing you can afford, Toronto 1977.
Mac Pherson, Ian: Each for all: A history of the co-operative movement in English Canada, 1900-1945, Toronto 1979.
McBride, Glynn: Agricultural Co-operatives: Their Why and Their How, Westport 1986.
McLanahan, Jack & Connie (Eds.): Co-operative/Credit Union dictionary and Reference: United States, Canada, World, Richmond Kentucky 1990.
Moody, J. Carroll/ Gilbert C. Fite: The Credit Union Movement: Origins and Development, 1850-1970, Lincoln 1971.
Roy, Alain: "Forestry Co-ops Predominate, National Survey Shows, Worker Co-op Magazine, 1988, vol. 8, no.2, pp. 22-23.
Roy, Ewell Paul: Co-operatives: Development, Principles and Management, Danville, Ill. 1976.
Sekerak, Emil and Art Danforth: Consumer Cooperation: The Heritage and the Dream, Santa Clara 1980.
USDA (United States Dept. of Agriuclture): Farmers Co-operatives, Washington D.C., Jan. 1990, p.18, Feb. 1989.

Development of Co-operatives in Northern-Africa

JAMIL CHAABOUNI [J]

(see also: *Development Policy*; *Development, Africa*; *Strategies when Establishing Co-operatives*; *Pre-co-operative Forms*; *Autochthonous Co-operatives*; *Law, International*; *Education, Africa*)

I. Statement of Problems and Definition of Terms; II. Pre-Co-operative Organization Forms Prior to Colonization; III. Co-operatives During the Colonial Era; IV. Outset of Co-operative Development in the Three Countries after Independence; V. Closing Comments.

I. Statement of Problems and Definition of Terms

The development of co-operatives in Africa north of the Sahara (the countries of Tunisia, Algeria and Morocco will be considered in this treatise) began following the colonization of these countries by France. *Pre-co-operative Forms* in the agricultural sector already existed in the three countries to varying extents. After gaining independence the development authorities – above all in Tunisia and Algeria – became engaged in co-operative development. The co-operative movement of Morocco, however, first received substantial attention in the 1970s and '80s. The question to be raised and addressed are:

– which strategies were used for the establishment and development of co-operatives in the three countries (→ *Strategies when Establishing Co-operatives*), whether the co-operative movement has been of use to the pre-co-operative forms of reciprocal assistance (→ *Pre-co-operative Forms*) in order to thereby acquire a larger legitimacy among the population, encouraging their active involvement and participation;
– the degree of autonomy that the co-operative management was granted, as well as the results which were reached.

Co-operative organizations (co-operatives) are understood in this context according to *Dülfer*'s definition (1979):"contractual or institutionalized combinations of business operations (or households) which strive to achieve economic advantages for the members of their organizations (who pursue their own goals) through direct cooperation or through the establishment and maintenance of collective business enterprises."

II. Pre-Co-operative Organization Forms Prior to Colonization

The traditional form of cooperation in Maghreb are anchored in religious law and traditional practice. Although they vary between tribes and locations, they generally assume the following forms in the agricultural sector:

1. The Use of Collective Land

Land is collective property of the tribe (*tribu*); each member has utilization rights. Collective property can neither be mortgaged, sold nor divided.

2. "Maâouna"

The *Maâouna* – reciprocal assistance or *Taâoun* (*Taâounia* means "co-operative" in the Near East) – is a pre-co-operative form propagated in North Tunisia in the Tell Region. Farmers work the privately held fields together during sowing and harvesting seasons.

3. "Touiza"

Propagated in Morocco, the *Touiza* is a collective labor service for the common good which is provided without payment. Examples include the construction of grain silos (*Citadelle d'Agadir*), underground irrigation systems and their maintenance or field work on the private property of social groups who themselves cannot undertake such work, e.g. widows and orphans. Participation in the Touiza can take the form of either work or monetary payments.

4. "L'Ouiza"

This is a form of association for the collective purchase of products or services (foodstuffs, livestock feed). Other forms of such group organizations include the *Mouzarat*, in which workers and landowners plant wheat and divide the harvest, and the *Mussakat*, which is like the *Mouzarat* but for irrigated land.

The traditional forms of cooperation represent situation specific solutions made by social actors. They have, nonetheless, not led to the development of a "co-operative spirit" in the three countries under consideration.

III. Co-operatives During the Colonial Era

After conquering the Maghreb countries the French administrative authorities found themselves confronted with the task of controlling farming and introducing a market economy. The French position was based on the assumption that the system of agricultural credit and the provision of welfare to the autochthons resulting from this would bring the *Fellachen* (peasant farmers) under French control. This position was undertaken in the three countries – although at different points in time – through the ratification of necessary legislation.

The first attempts (in Algeria in 1869) led to the establishment of agricultural credit and welfare associations (Sociétés de Crédit et de Secours Mutuels, *SCSM*), which were disbanded in the French-Algeria War. These associations inspired the establishment of the newer Sociétés de Prévoyance et de Crédit Agricole, *SPCA* (1882), which were later renamed the famous *SIP* (Sociétés Indigènes de Prévoyance, Secours et Prêts Mutuels) (through Law and Enactment in Algeria in 1893; Ordinance in Tunisia dating 1907; *Dahir* [Law] in Morroco dating 1907). Seen juristically, the *SIP* are co-operative associations which should distribute credits to small farm holders from public monies; the lack of comprehensive reform in the farming sector altered these credits into mere monetary support and/or lost subsidy money.

The *SIP* (in Morocco for example) were responsible for the following tasks:

- Selection and purchasing of seed, cleaning grain for the *Fellachen*;
- Fertilizers; facilities for model enterprises;
- Purchasing and maintaining technical facilities;
- Founding farming co-operatives.

Even when the *SIP* according to law were administered by an elected council, the president of which being the *Kaid* (mayor) – as was the case in Tunisia – the indigenous population, nevertheless, developed the impression that the welfare associations were French instruments for the expropriation of land and the extraction of capital.

The *SIP*, which basically were entrusted with the political task of appeasing the rural population's opposition to the French, were practically robbed of their co-operative character before they were actually even established.

A spontaneous co-operative movement acting independently of the colonial authority came into being as late as 1905 among the European farmers in northern Tunisia. They founded the Caisse Locale de Crédit Agricole Mutuel which functioned according to the co-operative principles although no legal foundation was in existence. These banks of sort quickly spread, but the level of indigenous members remained low. The movement developed upon the foundation of agricultural service co-operatives for French farmers: La Coopérative Central des Agriculteurs de Tunisie, *CCAT*, (supply, warehousing, marketing), La Coopérative de Motoculture, *MOTOCOP*, (supply co-operative providing fuel), La Caisse Mutuelle d'Assurances Agricoles, *CMAA*, L'Union des Coopératives Viticoles de Tunisie, *UCVT*, (bookkeeping, supply, marketing).

The first workers co-operatives were founded by union leader *Mohamed Ali* in Tunisia in 1920. This move later greatly influenced the development program of the Tunisian federation of unions which was embraced in the 1960s by the government.

Starting in 1927, the *SIP* in Morocco dispensed with financial contributions from the *Fellachen*, a move later followed by Algeria and Tunisia. The *SIP* evolved into banking and administrative bodies for welfare provision in the agricultural sector. A new policy phase began in 1936 through the incorporation of subsidy policies and the introduction of machine technology; the establishment of production and service co-operatives resulted from this. The main concern during World War II was to secure France's autarky with respect to the provision of grain.

The *SIP* amalgamated into the Office Interprofessionel du Blé (*ONIB*) in Algeria, Office du Blé en Tunisie (*OBT*), and Office Chérifien Interprofessionel du Blé (*CIB*) in Morocco, whereby the *CIB* represented the first effort to group the *Fellachen* together in pre-co-operative like associations for collective purchase and sales activities (→ *Autochthonous Co-operatives*). The administrative bodies of the "Offices" were tied together with the ministerial trade departments; obligatory grain deliveries to the offices were imposed on the *Fellachen*. This interference on the side of the authorities smothers any autonomous co-operative development.

Following World War II, the welfare organizations

once again took on a new appearance in the form of Sociétés Agricoles de Prévoyance, *SAP*. The *SAP* in Algeria, the *SOCAP* in Morocco (Sociétés de Crédit Agricole et de Prévoyance), and the *STP* in Tunisia (Sociétés Tunisiennes de Prévoyance) were committed to the modernization of the traditional rural economy. Although the *SAP* were not as centralized as the *SIP* they, nonetheless, were initially run in a similar manner. A law was passed for the first time in Algeria in 1952 that foresaw elected members assuming seats on the board of directors alongside those appointed members. Following Morocco's example, the *SAP* in Algeria grouped together in local associations called Secteurs d'Amélioration Rurale, *SAR*. The *SAP* spread professional know-how among the *Fellachen* through monitors and adapted their credit policy to the needs of the farmers. As their directors were frequently commercial clerks, concentration became placed on financing and the principles of profitability: They promoted creditworthy farmers and thereby neglected the multitude of *Fellachen* (*Plum*, 1967).

In Tunisia, every *Kaidat* (mayor's office) had a *STP*; the administrative organization was further extended after 1962 (Union Régionale de Développement). The *STP* acquired a central bank (Caisse Central des *STP*) which following independence developed into the *BNA* (Banque Nationale Agricole). Although the ordinance dating from 1945 expressly foresaw the development of co-operatives, the local initiatives were preserved. Despite this, several co-operatives came into being in the farming, crafts, and fishing sectors.

In Morocco, the *SMP* (Secteurs de Modernisation du Paysanat), the *CMA* (Co-opératives Marocaines Agricoles), and the *SCMA* (Sociétés Co-opératives Marocaines Agricoles) developed seperately from each other alongside the *SOCAP*. A confusing bureaucratic organization thereby resulted whose administrative structure was composed of three bodies:

- the Section Council of the community administration with loyal Muslim *notables*;
- the board of directors, composed of the *Kaids*, a French comptroller, one or more *Khadis* (judges), as well as representatives of the financial directors and the responsible technical department;
- the Treasury.

The *SOCAP's* influence on the traditional *Fellachen* farming sector was minimal because of its confusing bureaucratic organization and its vague policy. Its administration fell apart even before Morocco gained independence. The *SMP*, which can be considered pre-co-operative institutions, fell victim to distrust on the side of the *Fellachen* and the French farmers. The *CMA*, whose members included numerous support banks which were far from being true co-operatives, evolved into pure instruments of government control. The *CAM* and the *SCAM* outlived the French protectorate status by marketing products hailing from the traditional farming sector. Not receiving stimulus from the state, they lost their importance year for year and only had a modest number of members. They were not mentioned in either the First or Second Development Plans (1965–67).

The procedural manner with which the colonial power established the *SIP* and *SAP* as dummy co-operatives left behind deep impressions in their wake which have also influenced the policy pursued by the independent nations. The legacy is a procedural manner of establishing co-operatives and/or making changes to their structure which can be characterized as a "top-down" strategy. Traits of this procedural manner include:

- the authorities pursuing a state controlled strategy for the formation, administration and supervision of co-operatives;
- an overemphasis placed on the role of the state concerning technical and administrative assistance and credit policies which prevent self-initiative and the further development of those involved;
- the expropriation of farmed land.

These characteristics were predominantly applicable to Tunisia and Algeria on their initial development plans, whereas the co-operative movement in Morocco at first had no set priorities due to land distribution, also taking place there, and its preferred liberal economic policy supported from the beginning. Nevertheless, the co-operative movement gained importance in Morocco in the middle of the 1970s as an instrument of development policy (→ *Development Policy*).

IV. Outset of Co-operative Development in the Three Countries after Independence

1. The Tunisian Experience

a) The first approaches, 1956–62

The first official approach for the co-operative movement was made by the ruling Néo-Destour Party, after its Congress in 1959 recognized that the parcelling of thousands of hectares of land was uneconomical (following the expropriation of settler's property and the disbandment of religious foundations [*Habus*]). An attempt was undertaken on the regional level; in each of the 13 *gouvernorate* (provinces) a youth collective was to organize a farm, manage it and keep it in their possession.

With the exception of only two cases, the youths, however, could not afford any investment shares, were not allowed as members of the co-operatives which they had organized and built.

A new attempt to provide promotion through the credit system of the co-operative movement was undertaken in 1961 with the founding of the Banque d'Etat pour les Coopératives. This bank was to undertake the responsibilities of the *CCAM* (Caisse Centrale de Crédit Artisanal et Maritime). Its involvement in all sorts of co-operative problems beyond its realm of jurisdiction led to its dissolvement in 1962.

A further impulse for the credit system was given by the *UGTT* (Union Générale des Travailleurs Tunisiens) in 1962 by the establishment of the Banque du Peuple; 51% of the capital was owned by the union, 49% by the union co-operatives. It should be mentioned in this context that it was the *UGTT* in 1920, after the failure of *Mohamed Ali*, which gave workers the initiative to join together in co-operatives (Congress of 1956). In the course of the following years two co-operative types evolved: those co-operatives which were centrally managed by the union, and those associations which were spontaneously formed by workers and small-scale entrepreneurs.

These first endeavors led both to rapid growth in the number of co-operatives (from 70 to 250) and to an increase in related problems (in mentality, organization and management). This state of affairs forced the government in the summer of 1962 to undertake direct intervention (→ *Policies for Promotion*).

b) State controlled development policy, 1962–69

aa) The paradigms of co-operative development

The co-operative policy, administered in a strict manner by the Ministry of Planning, was documented in three-year plans and in ten-year perspectives. The co-operative system was allotted a particularly strong position as an efficient instrument for social and economic development. Co-operatives were not only seen as a route to technical modernization and the propagation of economic advancement, rational production and distribution but also as an "impetus for structural reform – for the promotion of people based on a collective rather than an individualistic basis" (*Hirschfeld*, 1963). It was intended to realize a specific kind of socialism (*socialism destourien*) for the country.

The government decided to proceed step by step in order to achieve this goal: the registered co-operatives were first to be recognized before new ones were founded; a firm groundwork resting on economic and social science, pedagogy, and administration was to be established. New laws, a new banking system, and an appropriately trained management were to provide the needed support for the development of the co-operative system.

bb) The legal scope and the co-operative bodies

Co-operatives were established in 1962, based on the laws which had been adopted. The first new legal groundwork came into being through the Law of 1963 (for agricultural co-operatives), the Law of 1964 (the authorization of co-operatives), the Ordinance of 1965 (the activities of the authorization commission), and above all through the Law of 1967 (general status of co-operatives, an amendment of the Law of 1955). A Conseil Supérieur de la Coopération was later founded by law which was entrusted with the determination of guide lines. According to the Law of 1967, co-operatives are joint-stock and partnerships which carry out activities in sectors prescibed in the national plans and which fulfill the specific principles of the co-operative system.

The co-operative bodies include: the general assembly of members (each member has one vote) which elects the board of directors (conseil d'administration), which in turn appoints its president (→ *Law, International*). The general assembly appoints an auditing commission composed of at least three members. The co-operatives are required to join the appropiate regional co-operative union *URC* (Union Régionale des Coopératives) established in each *gouvernorat* for assistance and consultational purposes as well as for representation with regard to third parties.

According to the initial → *by-laws* the *URC* had the identical administrative bodies as each member co-operative with great autonomy and responsibility reserved for the president. A director, however, had to be added to the model by-laws by the Ministry of Planning who represented the *URC* both to the state and third parties and who acted independently in his administration. The *URC* ultimately proved to be an institution through which the Ministry of Planning could exercise control over the co-operatives.

Central unions (Union Centrale, *UC*) have been planned and/or established for individual economic sectors alongside the multi-purpose co-operatives, *URC*.

cc) Co-operatives in the Agricltural Sector

Agricultural co-operatives were formed on the basis of "production units" (UCPA, Unité Co-opérative de Production Agricole). A state demesne usually formed the heart of a co-operative, and the neighboring small farm holders were petitioned to join the co-operative "voluntarily". The arable acreage was then distributed among the farmers and land workers in parcels but, nevertheless, farmed using collective machinery.

The Law recognized four types of production units and one type of service co-operative:

- production co-operatives in the north of the country (cultivation of wheat fields),
- the multi-crop and processing co-operatives in the middle and south of Tunisia,
- the production co-operatives on publicly irrigated lands,
- livestock co-operatives.

Service co-operatives pursued the following goals:
- purchasing all products in the interest of the co-operative members,
- collective canning, processing and marketing of all agricultural products,
- purchasing farming machinery and tools.

All rural co-operatives have a standard set of by-laws according to their particular nature.

The state, convinced that the rural population was not prepared for modernization and legal formalities, reserved the right to interfere in the co-operative management and take control of it (Art. 41 and 42). With this in mind, the UCPA for example had a technical assistant appointed by the Ministry of Agriculture and a director alongside its usual prescribed legal bodies. The decisions of the board of directors with regard to the organizational structure, the budget, the number of employees and their wages were subject to the approval of the Ministry of Planning and/or Agriculture (→ *Officialization*).

The nation-wide apex organization *UNC*, Union Nationale des Coopératives, was founded in 1969, thus replacing the "Direction de la Coopération" in the Ministry of Planning. A few months later, the government decided to put a stop to the co-operative program.

dd) Trade co-operatives

The founding of trade co-operatives was intended to reorganize the domestic market by abolishing middlemen, to organize distribution and ultimately stabilize prices. Shareholders of such co-operatives included traders, commercial agents, and consumers. They were organized on two levels: on the community level as regional co-operatives (*délégation*) and as trading units (sales outlets). A central union for trading co-operatives *UCCC* (Union Centrale des Coopératives de Consommation) was also planned which in turn was to be a member of the *UNC*. The complete Reform Law was finally ratified in 1969.

ee) Industrial co-operatives

These encompass the worker production and artisan co-operatives (→ *Joint-production Co-operatives*). The first artisan co-operatives were quite old and more likely to be found in the traditional economic sectors. The new artisan co-operatives were expected to attain a rational organization of production, serving as a transition to batch production.

ff) Co-operative training

Training was executed on two levels:
- Propagation of co-operative thought among members,
- Training of co-operative managers and administrators.

After several attempts the decision was taken that "co-operative subject-matter" should be conveyed and taught on the basis of the everyday activities of the co-operative members. This indirect teaching method required highly qualified teachers, while these were supplemented by party officials. The professional and technical co-operative training, on the other hand, did not pose as many problems, although there was a lack of teaching personnel here, too. Great emphasis was placed on co-operative instruction in the agricultural vocational schools as well as in middle and secondary schools. In order to curb the deficit of specialized workers, the *ENC* (Ecole Nationale de Coopération) was founded in 1964 which offered year-and-a-half, one-year and two-year training programs (→ *Education, Africa*).

c) The suspension of the experiment and the current situation of the co-operative movement

The government decided in 1969 to halt the co-operative movement. At the end of 1969 and beginning of 1970, co-operative members received circular letters, leaving it up to their judgement whether or not to withdraw from their co-operatives. The disbandment of the co-operatives occured faster than their establishment had. The withdrawal movement took place too quickly in the sectors of trade, artisanry, and farming. The official retrospectives, inspite of it all, document hardly any indices of a failed national economy; the social atmosphere, nonetheless, was quite tense in 1969. The co-operative movement gave traders and wealthy property owners the impetus to invest in private industry and thus divest collectivization efforts of their capital.

In retrospect, three important factors can be identified which impeded co-operative development in Tunisia:

- *Bureaucratic intervention*

  The co-operatives were not founded voluntarily but, rather *per décret*. The principle of democracy was replaced with a "state controlled democracy", including a triumvirate consisting of an appointed co-operative director, a technical assistant and sometimes even the elected president. The local administrative authorities meddled in the management of the co-operative, which was an arm of quasi-state organizations (→ *Officialization*). The management was determined by bureaucrats; endless administrative channels developed out of this which hampered flexibility and reinforced dependency on the administrative authorities. Decisions of central importance were made outside the co-operative. The co-operative members were either badly informed or not informed at all about the actual economic situation of their enterprise.

- *The behavior of the co-operative members*

  This situation and compulsory membership led to passivity among members. They considered them-

selves wage workers, but when they were appointed to the board of directors they felt themselves to be government officials. The co-operative was considered a state institution by many members – and even as a welfare organization.
- *Technical reasons*
The decision was made to pursue mechanization in the agricultural sector. This led to limitations in the number of jobs and to intensive utilization of borrowed capital. The co-operatives were often in debt, and technical consulting and commercial assistance was insufficient.

The co-operative has also continually lost importance through privatization measures since 1970. Tunisia is no longer taken into consideration by international statistics recording co-operative activity. The number of co-operatives in the agricultural sector has also diminished. In the face of the inflicted social damage it will still take quite some time until the population has overcome its aversion to co-operatives.

2. The Algerian Experience

a) The socialist sector after independence

When Algeria gained its independence in 1962, the nationalization of settlers' lands received priority attention; in the course of time it fell under the possession of the *ONRA* (Office Nationale de la Réforme Agraire). The structural reforms were not initiated from the administrative authorities but rather from the field workers who spontaneously seized the estates now absent of their former owners (*biens vacants*). This de facto "socialization" could not be rescinded at a later time and was even legalized through the Ordinance of 1963. The standard structure of the *self-administrated demesnes (enterprise autogérée)* foresaw the following bodies:
- the plenary assembly, as a highest decision-making body elects a worker commitee and/or a board of directors as executives;
- the president, responsible for contacts with the general public;
- a director installed in office for state control.

Above and beyond the socialized sector, farmers were called upon to join together in associations and co-operatives.
Sporadic movements to form co-operatives were registered from the *FLN* (Front de Libération Nationale), the *ANP* (Armée Nationale Populaire), and the union *UGTA* (Union Générale des Travailleurs Algériens). Following the *coup d'état* in 1965 up to 250 co-operatives were established by war veterans (anciens combattants), the *CAPAM* (Coopératives Agricoles de Production des Anciens Moudjehidines) in the self-administrated demesnes under pressure exerted by the *FLN*.

It should be noted here that the majority of agricultural reforms were executed by local-level administrative authorities. It became a matter of course that the spontaneously formed worker adminstrative committees were placed under the control of the subprefects. Lawmakers entrusted the community council with important functions.
The founding of "co-ordinating committees" on the regional level in 1962 was intended to co-ordinate the intervention of the local-level administrative authorities and the political organizations. They were grouped together on the national level in the *MCA*, Mouvement Coopératif Algérien, but nevertheless never played an important role in the Algerian co-operative movement. The "Institut de Promotion Coopérative" was established in 1966, practically neutralizing the *MCA*. The economic difficulties the self-administrated demesnes were facing occasioned their reorganization in 1968. These difficulties included the marketing of products, a usurious bureaucracy controlling credit, production and marketing which crippled the production process through its intervention, as well as an inappropriate payment method for workers.
The restructuring process of 1968 was subject to the general goal of decentralization. The national office for farming reform *ONRA* was replaced by the Ministry of Agriculture *MARA* (Ministère de l'Agriculture et de la Réforme Agraire) as highest level planning authority. The credit system was transferred into the hands of the *BNA* (the Algerian national bank). A slue of national offices for supply and marketing were established. The autonomy of the self-administrated enterprises was to be strengthened through new legislation. The office of the installed director was dismantled step by step; by 1969, he was only allowed an advisory role but nonetheless retained his right to veto rulings. In 1971, however, he was once again entrusted with an influential function upon the founding of the higher-level multi-use service co-operatives *CAPCS* (Coopérative Agricole Polyvalente Communale de Services); because of this, the propagated principle of self-administration must be considered questionable.
In 1971, the amalgamation of the self-administered demesnes into regional and national associations was decided upon in order to promote reciprocal support. State co-operatives were furthermore set up on the basis of the *"Wilaya"* for bookkeeping and accounting, activities which up to then had been conducted in part quite chaotically. Against the backdrop of the unsatisfactory development of the self-administrated demesnes and mounting pressure from the population, agrarian reform which had already been planned was put into effect in 1971.

b) Agrarian reform in 1972

The agrarian reform (considered an agrarian revolution in Algeria) endeavored to restructure the private sector and publically held lands in the possession of the state, communities and religious foundations (*Habous*) in a revolutionary manner. Through the redistribution of landed property they aimed to mobilize land reserves and improve the economic, social and cultural conditions of small land owners, tenant farmers and field workers.

The land gained in this manner was to be farmed in co-operatives. Entry into the co-operatives was to be voluntary, but it became imposed in the haste of the local authorities. Marketing and technical structures were established to meet the needs of the newly established co-operative sector. Four types of co-operatives became recognized:

- service co-operatives,
- co-operatives for collective labor and reciprocal help,
- joint-production co-operatives,
- livestock raising co-operatives.

In the initial stage of the agrarian reform the public lands and those in the hands of the *Habous* were distributed under the supervision of a local people's assembly supplemented with representatives of the ruling party and associations. In the second stage (1973–75) expropriation was undertaken of those properties formerly in the possession of large-scale landowners and of those individuals no longer in the country. The large-scale land owners were allowed to retain a determined share of their former land and operational facilities/equipment based on the size of their operation and labor capacity. Thus, the benficiaries of the agrarian reform lacked the necessary stock and equipment through this manner.

The third stage of the agrarian reform (1975–77) concentrated on the steppe regions. As in the second stage, livestock raising co-operatives were established on the basis of expropriation. Grazing land that became the property of the state was divided into three categories of utilization: one for the state-organized livestock raising co-operatives *CEPRA* (Coopérative d'Elevage Pastorale de la Révolution Agraire), one for the private livestock ranchers, and a third one for the regeneration of the surface vegetation on the pasture land.

The co-operatives founded during the agrarian revolution have great similarities in their adminstrative bodies. The highest decision-making body was the plenary assembly of co-operative members which, as was the case with the self-administered demesnes, determined the policies of management. It elected a board of directors which in turn appointed a chairman. The accountant was recommended by the Ministry of Agriculture upon endorsement by the Ministry of Finance. The director installed by the state only played a role in the local multi-use service co-operatives (*CAPS*) and in the marketing co-operatives for fruit and vegetables (Coopérative de Commercialisation des Fruits et Légumes de Wilay, *COFEL*).

The structure of the co-operative system was organized as follows:
- The pre-co-operative groups formed the lowest rank (GMPV; Groupement Précoopératif de Mise en Valeur);
- The second level consisted of the agricultural production co-operatives *CAPRA* (Coopérative Agricole de Production de la Révolution Agraire) and the livestock raising co-operatives *CEPRA*;
- The motor of the agrarian revolution for the *GMPV*, the *CAPRA*, *CEPRA*, the co-operatives of war veterans and the self-adminstrated demesnes were the *CAPCS*, the local multi-use service co-operatives.
- Special co-operatives were established on the *Wilayate* level which in part replaced former national offices.

The agrarian reform in general was executed without the active and organized participation of its beneficiaries (*Badrani*, 1987). As was the case with the self-administrated demesnes, the state and local authorities interfered with management, thus decreasing the attractiveness of the co-operatives. Co-operative members demonstrated similar behavior found in the self-administrated sectors and preferred work beyond the bounds of the co-operatives. The limited economic success of the co-operatives led to the situation that members actually became dependent on state family assistance due to their lack of income. The low level of productivity in part can be explained in that the co-operatives never had control over the means of production supplied to them or of the sales of their products. It must also be added in conclusion that the state up to the beginning of the 1980s had conceded the agricultural sector only a minor role in the development process.

c) Restructuring after 1980

The following measures were undertaken in order both to increase agricultural production and to minimize and/or do away with the burden of subsidies on the state budget:
- free access to markets for self-administrated demesnes and co-operatives;
- physical restructuring of the production co-operatives;
- dismantlement of the local multi-use sevices co-operatives *CAPCS* (1983–84).

The dualism between the self-administrated demesnes and the co-operatives was established in that the *CAPRA* members could decide either to join a self-administrated demesne or divide their land into parcels. The *DAS* (Domaines Agricoles Socialistes) came into being in the place of the *CAPRA* and the self-administrated demesnes. The *CAPS* were replaced with specialized supply co-operatives. As these measures did not bring around the desired

goals (*Bessaoud*, 1989) a new set of measures was embraced in 1987:
- The members of a *DAS* could join together into groups based on their own discretion;
- Groups formed in such a manner shared land, buildings, stocks and equipment among each other;
- Each group acquired non-expiring utilization rights;
- The utilization rights became transferable;
- Land, however, remained in the possession of the state.

These measures were to be tried out in 1987, and generalized in the following years.

3. The Moroccan Experience

No such co-operative movement comparable to that in Algeria or Tunisia developed in Morocco. The monarchy shied away from the establishment of co-operatives for the small farm holders out of political reasons (fear of a revolutionary movement). The *Dahir* of 1957 established the *ONMR* (Office National de la Modernisation Rurale) which in turn absorbed almost all institutions of agricultural modernization and welfare. The *ONMR* and the *ONI* (Office National de l'Irrigation) founded in 1961, discontinued their activities in 1964 and officially joined the newly formed *OMVA* (Office de Mise en Valeur Agricole), which itself was soon disbanded in order to make room for seven regional authorities.

When the *Fellachen* attempted to go beyond the suggestions of the *ONI* by wanting to establish production co-operatives, they found themselves impeded by the antisocial credit system and the conservative legal system of the monarchy (*Plum*, 1967).

The "agrarian revolution" resulting from the *Dahir* of 1972 led to the founding of 64 co-operatives in the agricultural sector. The co-operative movement received new momentum in the middle of the 1970s (opening of *ODCO*, Office de Développement de la Coopération; ratification of *Charte Coopérative*). According to official statistics 3,853 registered co-operatives were counted in 1989 in 32 sectors (of these 2,900 were in the agricultural sector) (*Ghazali*, 1990). The number of consumer co-operatives and co-operative home-building associations increased between 1978 and 1985. The first worker co-operatives were founded in 1984 in the scope of Moroccan guest workers returning home. Artisan co-operatives account for approx. 11% of the total number of co-operatives in Morocco.

The co-operative movement was obviously promoted by the Moroccan development policy in those economic sectors which received priority attention. The co-operative herewith served as a means to control the economic actors through adminstrative and technical supervision. This is evident in the manner co-operatives function. According to law the plenary assembly is the highest adminstrative body of the co-operative; it elects the *conseil d'administration* which in turn manages the co-operative with the chairman as its head. In practical application (and particularly among the agricultural co-operatives) the co-operative is constantly controlled on the inside by the representatives of the administrative authorities; the co-operative is actually managed by the appointed director and the technical and administrative supervisors (e.g. bookkeeper) who are paid directly through the administrative authorities. The decisions of the plenary assembly are prepared in such a manner that they are ultimately made to the liking of the *OMRVA* and the *MARA* (Ministère de l'Agriculture et de la Réforme Agraire).

The co-operative movement in Marocco has apparently not learned very much from its neighboring countries. The government's withdrawal from the co-operative movement, announced in 1990, probably does not mean any greater autonomy for the co-operatives. The question remains unanswered whether the existence of many co-operatives will be threatened or not without subsidies.

V. Closing Comments

The analysis of the development of co-operatives in the three Maghreb countries indicates that the co-operatives remained an instrument of the state to steer either individual economic branches, the entire economy and/or the process of structural reform both during and after the colonial era. Even when spontaneous co-operative or pre-co-operative forms emerged, they were either obstructed or else the initiatives were wrested from the promoters (sponsors). The state interfered to a great degree in the business activity of the co-operatives through legislation, administrative bodies, the granting of credits, control measures, consultation and supervision. By doing this the state failed:

a) to observe the reaction of the social groups in a serious manner, avail themselves of it and integrate it;

b) to remember that the principles of democracy and participation cannot simply be assigned to co-operatives through law in practical application.

The "top-down strategy" because of this remained practically blind. The bodies of state control overlooked the fact that social actors are in the position to develop strategies that not only substantially separate state measures from their original goals but which also make use of the state measures in order to attain personal advantages. These actor strategies should have been recognized, and those promising success should have been integrated into the concept of co-operative formation.

The various reforms and ultimately the withdrawal of the state in all three of the Maghreb countries is evidence that the planned economic goals could not be attained through the formation of co-operatives.

Bibliography

Abdallah, C.: Aspects et problèmes de l'intensification des systémes de production du secteur agricole coopératif. L'exemple des UCP de Medjejez-El-Beb, in: Revue Tunisienne de Géographie, no. 6, 1980, S. 9–40.

Adair, P.: Mythes et réalités de la réforme agraire en Algérie, in: Etudes Rurales Paris, no. 85, 1982, S. 49–65.

Ait-Amara, H.: Enquête sur la participation dans l'autogestion agricole algérienne, in: Archives internationales de Sociologie de la coopération, no. 29, 1971, S. 119–153.

Bedrani, S.: Algérie: Une nouvelle politique envers la paysannerie?, in: Revue de l'Occident Musulman et de la Méditerranée, no. 45, 1987, S. 55–66.

Ben Lalah, A.: Les terres collectives en Tunisie, in: série : Etudes de Droit et d'Economie, CERP, Tunis 1973, vol. II.

Bessaoud, O.: La réforme agricole: Unouvelle tentative d'issue à la crise de l'agriculuture algérienne, in: Mondes en Développement, vol. 17, no. 67, 1989, S. 117–127.

Bouami, A./Raki, M.: Politique agricole et limites du développement de l'agriculute marocaine, in: Revue du Droit et d'Economie du Développement, no. 8, 1984, S. 131–151.

Boulet, D.: Les coopératives, no. 167, 1972, S. 95–98.

Chaulet, C.: Les ruraux algériens et l'Etat, in: revue de l'Occident Musuman et de la Méditerranée, no. 45, 1987, S. 67–79.

Dülfer, E.: Leitfaden für die Evaluierung kooperativer Organisationen in Entwicklungsländern, Göttingen 1979.

Dülfer, E.: Kooperative Organisationen in Entwicklungländern, in: HWO, Stuttgart 1980, Sp. 1117-1130.

El Ghazouani, A.: Vers un Transit marocain: d'économie coopérative en économie sociale, in: Archives internationels de Sciences Sociales, de la Coopération et du Développement, no. 181, 1987, s. 115–119.

Elleuch, T.: L'expérience des coopératives agricoles en Tunisie, in: Revue des Etudes Coopératives, no. 167, 1972, S. 85–93.

Ghazali, A.: Droit, Etat et coopération au Maroc, in: Revue Juridique et Economique du Maroc, no. 24, 1990, S. 151–175.

Gheroune, N.: Femmes coopératives et coopératives de femmes, in: Archives Internationales de sciences Sociales, de la Coopértion et du Développement, no. 79, 1987, S. 102–111.

Granges, C.: La coopération dans le secteur artisanal au Maroc, in: Revue des Etudes Coopératives, no. 202, 1980, S. 75–99.

Guen, M.: La coopération et l'Etat en Tunisie, Tunis 1964.

Hirschfeld, A.: La coopération en Tunisie. Bilan et perspectives in: Revue des etudes Coopératives, no. 133, 1963, S. 281–299.

Hirschfeld, A.: L'evolution récente du mouvement coopératif tunisien, in: Revue des Etudes Coopératives, no. 149, 1967, S. 326–337.

Hirschfeld, A.: Quelques données sur le mouvement coopératif au Maoc, in: Revue des Etudes Coopératives, no. 181, 1975, S. 19–37.

Le Coz, J.: Dynamique de la révolution agraire algérienne; la phase de la „bataille de la gestion", in: Méditerranée Aix-en-Provence, vol. 35, no. 1–2, 1979, S. 93–97.

Marthelot, P.: Problèmes de participatin dans la Socieété rurale au Maghreb, in: Archives internationales de Sociologie de la Coopération, no. 24, 1968, S.60–72.

Marzouki, I./Chekir, H.: Les méthodes traditionnelles d'entraide en Tunisie, in: Les Cahiers du CERP, 1990.

Moncef, D.: Le socialisme tunisien à travers l'action gouvernenmentale, thèse de doctorat, 1983.

Müller, A.: Le projet coopératif tunisien et son avortement, in: Archives Internationales de Schinces Sociales, de la Coopération et du Développement, no. 28, 1970, s. 57–79.

Payot, A.: Traditions et coopération au Maroc, in: Revue des Etudes Coopératives, no. 140, 1965, S. 141–161.

Plum, W.: Sozialer Wandel im Maghreb, Schriftenreihe des Forschungsinstituts der Friedrich-Ebert-Stiftung, Hannover 1967.

Reboul, C.: Le lent apprentissage de l'autogestion: les coopératives de production agricole d'Aabadia, Agéreie, in: Méditerranée Aix-en-Provence, vol. 35, no. 1–2, 1979, S. 65–72.

Trautmann, W.: Entwicklung und Probleme der Agrarreform in Algerien, in: Erkdkunde, vol. 33, no. 3, S. 215–226.

Villiers, G. de: La révolution agraire et le pouvoir communal en Algérie, in: Cahiers du CEDAF, no. 2-3-4, 1986, S. 139–155.

Development of Co-operatives in South Asia

ARVIND VYAS

(see also: *History in 19th C.*; *Self-help Organizations*; *Policies for Promotion*; *Articles on Co-operative Development in Other Continents*)

I. Aim and Objectives of the Paper; II. Historical Background; III. Areas of Activities of Co-operatives – Countrywise; IV. Development of Co-operatives in South Asia: Problem Areas; V. Summary and Conclusions.

I. Aim and Objectives of the Paper

The object of this paper is to examine different aspects of the development of the co-operative movement of co-operatives in South Asia – with special reference to India, Pakistan, Bangladesh and Sri Lanka. By the term co-operative is meant "to work together" derived from Latin "*cooperare*". Of all forms of working together, working done by any association of all persons, on the basis of joint self-help (→ *Self-help Organizations*), and in accordance with the co-operative principles, for the elimination of middlemen, profit making and having as their object their social and economic betterment, is termed co-operative in its *sui generis* (unique) sense. Such an association is called a co-operative which has the following characteristics: voluntary and open membership, democratic control, limited interest on capital, and equitable distribution of profit (→ *Principles*).

II. Historical Background

The problem of developing co-operatives in these economies of South Asia arose in order to break the stranglehold of the moneylanders who charged usurious interest rates on the weaker and poorer sections of the agrarian population. This basically, triggered off a series of legislative acts which are considered together in this section of the contribution, since till 1947 and 1948 all the countries constituted part of the British empire (→ *British–Indian Pattern*).

In the sub-continent, the first co-operative legislation named "Co-operative Credit Societies Act" was passed in 1904 was enacted for the organisation and regulation of agricultural credit. In 1912, another act was enacted to broad base the scope of co-operative law. The third stage in the evolution of co-operative law began with the constitutional reforms in 1919 when co-operatives became provisional subjects which empowered them to enact their own laws. Subsequently the Government of Bombay passed the Co-operative Societies Act of 1925 to replace the act of 1912. Thus, at the time of independence (1947) there were two laws operative in the areas comprised to Pakistan. The province of Sindh operated under the act of 1925 by reason of its having been part of the Bombay Presidency before 1936, while in the rest of Pakistan, the act of 1912 continued to operate (cf. International Co-operative Alliance). In Sri Lanka, the co-operative movement got a thrust by the passing of an ordinance to give legal recognition to co-operative societies but the first societies were organised in 1912 and three of them were registered in February-March 1913 soon after the appointment of Registrar of Co-operative Societies, in February 1913 (*Ibid*, p.455).

The period 1911–1942 marked the era where the credit co-operatives were expanded and their operation widened. The growth of co-operatives was rather slow; further there were numerous operational problems with the result that the establishment of co-operatives had to be carried out with great caution. The state officials played a vital role in educating and motivating people and at the same time developed the rudimentary systems of auditing (→ *Auditing*) and supervision (cf. International Co-operative Alliance).

III. Areas of Activities of Co-operatives – Country-wise:

India: After independence, the National Development Council (NDC) emphasized the need for simplification of the co-operative law by removing restrictive provisions from it. Another important landmark in the development of the co-operative law was the implementation of the recommendations of the Comitte on Cooperation (1965) which made important recommendations for the incorporation of co-operative principles, viz, devolution of the powers of the registrar of co-operative societies, incorporation of provisions for removing vested interests, promotion of co-operative leadership and the development of genuine co-operative societies.

In the very recent past, the Government of India appointed an expert committee on co-operative law for democratising and professionalising the management of co-operatives which became important in their multidirectional expansion (→ *Policies for Promotion*).

Before presenting a broad overview of the areas in which the co-operative movement is active, special mention may be made regarding the provision of rural credit. In 1954, the Reserve Bank of India (RBI) carried out a rural credit survey in the country and it also assessed for the first time the rural credit need in the country, which was placed at *Rs* 750 million per year. It interalia recommended the following: (i) ensuring state partnership in co-operatives; (ii) establishing a national level bank to extend its activities more and more in rural areas with preference to co-operative institutions and the creation of various funds like the *National Agricultural Credit* (long term operations) and the *National Agricultural Credit* (stabilisation) Fund. Both these funds have been transferred to the National Bank for Agriculture and Rural Development (NABARD). The setting up of NABARD in 1982 was a major landmark in the history of the rural credit movement in India. During this period, a large number of national federations have been set up such as: National Co-operative Union of India (NCUI); National Agricultural Co-operative Marketing Federation of India (NAFED), etc. – further details are given below;

(i) National Federation of Industrial Co-operatives (NFIC)
(ii) National Co-operative Land Development Banks Federation (NCSLDBF)
(iii) National Federation of Co-operative Sugar Factories (NFCSF)
(iv) National Federation of State Co-operative Banks (NFSCB)
(v) All India Federation of Co-operative Spinning Mills (AIFCOSPIN)
(vi) National Co-operative Housing Federation (NCHF)
(vii) National Co-operative Dairy Federation of India (NCDFI)
(viii) National Federation of Labour Co-operatives (NFLC)
(ix) National Federation of Fishermen's Co-operatives (FISHCOPFED)
(x) National Federation of Urban Co-operative Banks and Credit Society (NFCUB)
(xi) National Co-operative Tobacco Growers Federations (TOBACCOFED)

The co-operative movement has become an important sector of the economy since independence. In terms of its institutionalisation, membership and operations, it does not have a parallel in the world. The co-operative movement is characterised by its expansion and diversification in various fields – in the

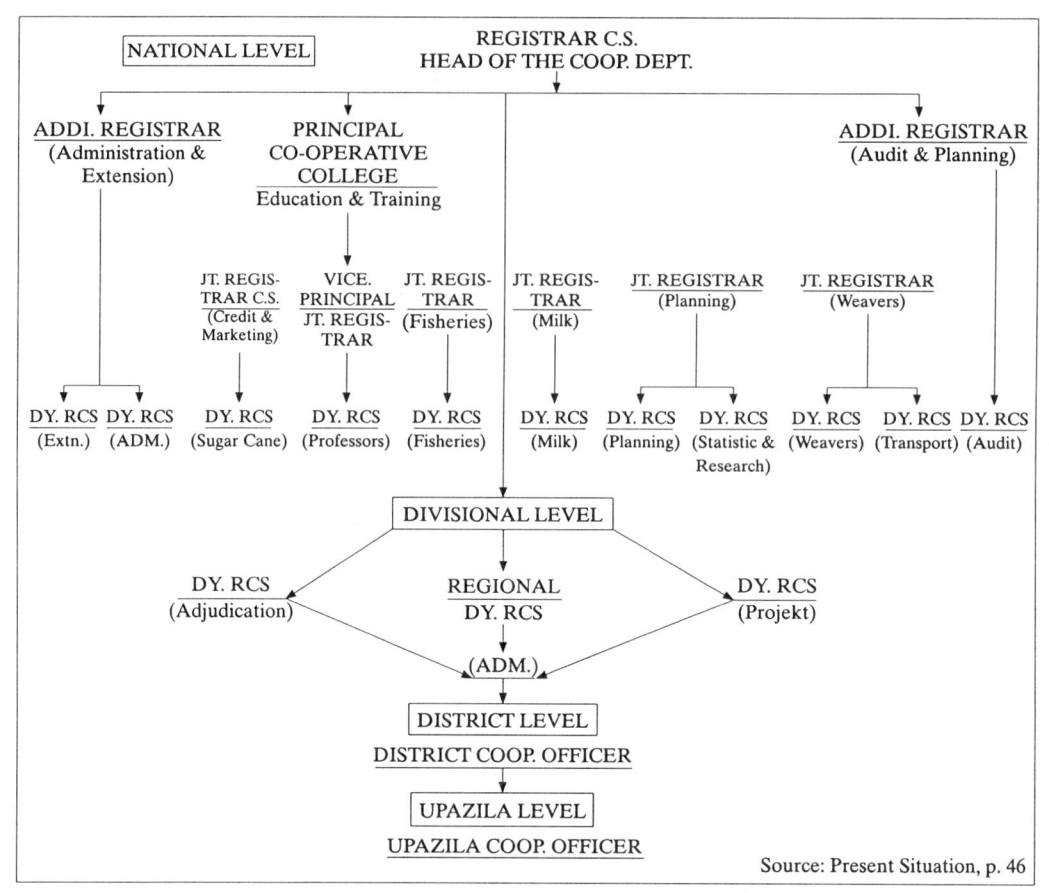

```
┌─────────────────────────────────────────────────────────────────────────────────────┐
│  ┌───────────────────┐           REGISTRAR C.S.                                      │
│  │  NATIONAL LEVEL   │       HEAD OF THE COOP. DEPT.                                 │
│  └───────────────────┘                                                               │
│        ↓                    ↓                              ↓                         │
│  ADDI. REGISTRAR       PRINCIPAL                     ADDI. REGISTRAR                 │
│  (Administration &   CO-OPERATIVE                    (Audit & Planning)              │
│     Extension)          COLLEGE                                                      │
│                      Education & Training                                            │
│                                                                                      │
│             JT. REGIS-   VICE.    JT. REGIS-  JT. REGIS-  JT. REGISTRAR  JT. REGISTRAR│
│             TRAR C.S.   PRINCIPAL   TRAR        TRAR       (Planning)    (Weavers)   │
│             (Credit &  JT. REGIS- (Fisheries)  (Milk)                                │
│             Marketing)   TRAR                                                        │
│                                                                                      │
│  DY. RCS DY. RCS  DY. RCS    DY. RCS    DY. RCS  DY. RCS DY. RCS DY. RCS  DY. RCS DY. RCS DY. RCS│
│  (Extn.) (ADM.) (Sugar Cane)(Professors)(Fisheries)(Milk)(Planning)(Statistic &(Weavers)(Transport)(Audit)│
│                                                                   Research)          │
│                         ┌─────────────────────┐                                      │
│                         │  DIVISIONAL LEVEL   │                                      │
│                         └─────────────────────┘                                      │
│         DY. RCS              REGIONAL              DY. RCS                           │
│      (Adjudication)          DY. RCS              (Projekt)                          │
│                                                                                      │
│                               (ADM.)                                                 │
│                         ┌─────────────────────┐                                      │
│                         │   DISTRICT LEVEL    │                                      │
│                         └─────────────────────┘                                      │
│                         DISTRICT COOP. OFFICER                                       │
│                         ┌─────────────────────┐                                      │
│                         │   UPAZILA LEVEL     │                                      │
│                         └─────────────────────┘                                      │
│                         UPAZILA COOP. OFFICER                                        │
│                                               Source: Present Situation, p. 46       │
└─────────────────────────────────────────────────────────────────────────────────────┘
```

Fig. 1: Organogram of the Co-operative Departments in Bangladesh.

agricultural sector in the disbursement of credit, manufacture and distribution of fertilizer and other inputs, marketing of agro-processing, etc.

To sum up: the co-operative movement in India is significant in the following fields: marketing and storage, oilseeds, sugar co-operatives, spinning, handlooms, fruits and vegetables, dairy co-operatives, India's total milk production (not of course, per capita) ranks 3rd in the world – next to USSR & USA (→ *Classification*). The dairy co-operative in Anand, Gujarat, is one of the few cases of a producer's co-operative, fisheries and finally the housing co-operative societies – at the moment there are approx. 26,000 housing societies which have completed 0.65 mln. houses and 0.31 mln. houses are under construction.

Sri Lanka: Co-operatives were initiated in Sri Lanka with credit societies of unlimited liability. The present extent of diversification is shown in the following statistics relating to the end of 1986: Amalgamated multi-purpose co-operative societies (MCPS) with a membership of 20,84798. Their retail trade had a turnover of 10,954 million (1,095.4 crores). Credit/ – 4406 with a membership of 483,345, tea, rubber and coconut producers' societies with a membership of 11,327, milk producer societies/ – 154 with a membership of 29,758, fisherman's societies/ – 68 with a membership of 21,464, labour societies/ – 57 with a membership of 3353, school co-operatives/ – 775 with a membership of 263,195, hospital societies/ – 7 with a membership of 11,486, small industry societies/ – 190 wih a membership of 24,576, textile weavers' societies/ – 31 with a membership of 61,075 Young Farmers' Societies/ – 19 with a membership of 2503. Other types – 267 with a membership of 139,283, grand total 6330 societies with a membership of 3,141,163.

Bangladesh: Before discussing the role of co-operatives it might be useful to look at the organisational structure which is given in Fig. 1.

Persons engaged in agricultural sector have variegated credit needs, such as, for *short term, medium term and long term utilisation*, sometimes even for bare subsistence. They are occupied in various

Category of Primary societies	Indication about area of operation of individual societies	Total number of societies	Total membership (Individuals)	Remarks
A. Departmental Co-operatives				
Union Co-op. multipurpose society (UCMPS)	One Union	4,110	1,310,245	Union based multipurspose agri-co-op. to provide overall support in agricultural operations to farmers.
Krishi Sambaya Samity (KSS) Agricultural Co-op.	Village or part of a village	25,613	1,126,843	Village based multipurpose agri-co-ops. to provide overall support in agricultural operations to farmers.
Bitrahin Symbaya Samity (BSS) assetless farmers Co-op.)	-do-	443	25,901	Organised for landless or nearly landless farmers to provide support to them in their agricultural and other operations.
Sugar Cane Growers' Co-op. Society.	-do-	681	124,448	Organised around sugar mills to meet the needs of sugar cane growers.
Milk Producers Co-op. Soc.	-do-	210	28,476	Organised in Milk Producing belts to meet the needs of milk producers.
Salt Producers Co-op. Society	-do-	254	21,405	Organised in the salt producing coastal belt to meet the needs of salt producing farmers.
Colonisation Co-op. Soc.	One Village or groups of villages	18	5,626	Organised for rehabilitation of groups of displaced farmer usually in usettled govt.-owned lands.
Land Mortgage Bank (LMB)	One District	53	60,592	Originally organised to stop alienation of land & for agric. development work.
Oil Producers Co-ops.	Village or part of a village	74	3,195	Organised in oil seed growing areas to meet the needs of oil producers.
Tobacco Growers Co-ops.	Village or part of a village	26	7,135	Organised in tobacco growing areas to meet needs of tobacco growers.
'Pan' (Betal Leaves) Growers Co-op.	-do-	36	2,432	Organised in 'pan' growing areas to provide support to the growers.
Vegetable Growers Co-ops.	-do-	15	439	Organised in vegetable growing belt to belt to provide support to the growers.
Fish Cultures Co-ops.	-do-	391	15,215	Subsidiary occupation co-ops. for farmers.
Poultry Farmers Co-ops.	-do-	4	280	Subsidiary occupation co-ops. for farmers.
Bazar (market)	-do-	61	27,007	Subsidiary occupation co-ops. organised to manage rural market places.
Rickshaw Pullar Co-ops.	-do-	343	22,452	Subsidiary occupation co-ops. also for persons displaced from agric.-sector.
B. B.R.D.B. Co-operatives				
Krishak Sambaya Samity (KSS) (Agri-co-ops.)	-do-	56,529	1,968,082	Village based multipurpose agric.-co-op. to provide overall support to farmers in agricultural operation.
Mahila Sambaya Samity (MSS) (women co-ops.)	-do-	9,284	273,041	Village based women's co-ops. for women's development.
Bittahin Samabaya Samity (BSS) (assetless farmers co-ops.)	-do-	1,452	327,211	Organised for landless or nearly landless farmers to provide support to their agricultural & other operation.
Other Rural Co-ops.	-do-	822	22,535	Subsidiary occupation co-ops for displaced farmers.
Total		110,420	5,366,489	

economic activities, as farming of various crops, after following off-season or lean season subsidiary occupations. Such activities also call for occasional, seasonal and also long term financial accommodation. There are also farmers who might have turned landless or assetless, over the years, but whose main livelihood centre around agriculture and allied occupations. As such, various categories of separate primary societies grew up and came to be organised in the agricultural sector in an effort to cover common grounds, in as many related fields as possible.

To provide an idea as to the total range of activities covered, a statement showing categories, numbers of various primary societies organised together with rural membership in cash category (also with an indication about respective areas of each individual society) is furnished on page 237.

Besides 910 primary women's co-operatives operate under the departmental sector. These operate mainly in the urban and semi-urban areas and only a small section of the membership is involved in the agricultural activities.

The size of primary societies often prove to be too small, average membership per society have to be 49 to permit viable business operations, and *audit* and other reports show that quite a large portion of them run at a loss. Societies with small membership are often dominated by rural power groups, who in order to maintain their hold in the society discourage and prevent enlargement of membership. It would also be seen that more than one society with the same objectives operate in the same area, limiting each others' business operations. Overlapping and duplication of efforts result in under utilisation of facilities and in increasing overhead expenses. Economic benefits of amalgamation of co-operatives offering similar services in the same and contiguous area are yet to capture the imagination of the members of the coops and more particularly of the Government authorities. Rural power groups are yet big stumbling blocks in enlarging the size of primary societies and in merging the smaller societies into larger and viable ones.

Pakistan: Here the co-operative movement is the most weakly developed – a point to which we shall return, the areas of activities are confined to two provinces – Punjab and Sindh which are as follows:

(i) Development and marketing of sugar-cane in Faisalabad – Tobu Tek Singh District,
(ii) Co-operative Supply and Marketing Federations,
(iii) Co-operative Training Centre, Rawalpindi,
(iv) Sheep shearing in tribal areas.

In Sindh, there is a co-operative farm service sector, a district co-operative house in Sukkur, Research and Development Co-operative Societies, a co-operative workshop in Hyderabad, a Fisherman's co-operative Society in district Dadu, and a co-operative farm service centre at Garhi.

The State Bank of Pakistan is the principal source of finance for the co-operative movement. It provides funds primarily for agricultural credit to the provincial co-operative banks which, in turn, finance their member societies. As the provincial co-operative banks have very small funds of their own, they depend almost entirely on the State Bank for their needs of credit and a crisis develops if the arrival of funds is delayed. The provincial co-operative bank of Punjab is in a slightly better position than other banks.

The State Bank has been traditionally interested in the development of agricultural co-operatives. It used to deal directly with the provincial co-operative banks but now it channels funds to them through the Federal Bank of Co-operatives. The Federal Bank functions as an agent of the State Bank in all matters relating to co-operative finance and exercises extensive supervisory powers over the provincial co-operative banks.

IV. Development of Co-operatives in South Asia: Problem Areas

India: As mentioned earlier, we first discuss some general problems relating to the functioning of co-operatives, and then examine some more basic issues. As early as 1958, it was pointed out that there was excessive official interference in co-operatives as a result of the existing legislation (→ *Officialization*). It was felt necessary to decentralise the functions of co-operatives, in particular, to reduce the powers of the registrar of co-operatives. In 1965, it was felt that there was a mushrooming growth on non-genuine co-operatives. A committee appointed that the benefits of the co-operatives should go to the actual users and the needy ones.

In 1977, the Government of India brought out a 12 point policy resolution on co-operation which is given below (→ *Policies for Promotion*).

(i) Co-operatives are to be built up as one of the major instruments of decentralised labour intensive and rural oriented economic development.

The above is the official government view-point. Serious scholars in India – Pattanaik, (1972, 1976), Rundra, (1972) Bhaduri (1984), et. al. emphasize that such a view is biased in that the co-operative has made virtually no impact on the dominant capitalist mode of production in Indian agriculture, Bhaduri attempts to demonstrate that in parts of backward Eastern India "semi-feudal relations" of production still prevail and that the grip of moneylenders, and traders is still very strong on the vast masses of the rural population. In short, co-operatives have had virtually no impact on the relations of production which are, of course, different in different parts of the country.

A similar point has been made by an eminent Soviet Indologist, *Granovski* (1988), when he says: "In the individual countries of the region (i.e. South Asia) two qualitatively different modifications of the capitalist mode of production emerge, that have nevertheless many similarities. In Pakistan and emphatically in Sri Lanka, the integrating role of the modern capitalist sector stimulates gradual overcoming of the dualism of a colonial type, and a slow painful growth of a more or less homogeneous system of capitalist relations, prone however, to social turmoil. In turn, in India and Bangladesh the intensity of these integrational trends is polarising the overall socio-economic structure of capitalist production". (p. 329).

The above issues can, of course, be debated at length, however, for reasons of space we cannot go into these questions further. However, the above problems must always be borne in mind when evaluating the co-operative movement.

(ii) Close association of co-operatives with the process of planning and social change;
(iii) Co-operatives to be developed as "shield for the weak";
(iv) Promotion of co-operative development on a national basis and removal of regional imbalances in the co-operative growth.
(v) Development of cooperation as an autonomous and self-reliant movement free from undue outside interference and excessive control as also from politics;
(vi) Removal of corruption and mal-practices from the co-operative movement;
(vii) Development of co-operative based enlightened participation of broad-based membership, free from donation of vested interests;
(viii) Development of a strong and viable integrated co-operative system for total and comprehensive rural development;
(ix) Development of a net work of agro-processing and industrial units;
(x) Development of consumer co-operative movement to strengthen the public distribution systems;
(xi) Formulation of streamlined organisation systems. Simple and rationalised procedures for cooperatives;
(xii) Development of professional managements for co-operatives.

Government Objectives of Co-operative Development:

Cooperation has been accepted as an instrument of economic planning by the state. The National Development Plan, which lays down strategy for development, recognises co-operatives as the most effective vehicle for socio-economic transformation particularly in regard to removal of poverty and creation of employment opportunities. The 20-point-programme, 1986 given to the nation by the Prime Minister for renewing national commitment to eradicate poverty, raise productivity, reduce income inequalities and to improve quality of life of the people emphasises revitalisation of co-operatives and local institutions for poverty alleviation programmes.

The objectives of development are outlined by the plan documents. A study of plan documents shows that till the third five-year-plan which ended in 1966, the long term objectives of cooperation development set out by the government was to establish self-reliant and decentralised economic system through co-operatives. The following observations contained in various plan documents will be relevant to mention:

(a) The first five-year-plan stated "as it is the purpose of the plan to change the economy of the country from an individualistic to social and co-operative basis, its success should be judged among other things, by the extent to which it is implemented through co-operative organisations;"
(b) The second five-year-plan maintained, "building up co-operative sector as a part of scheme of planned development was one of the central aims of National Policy."
(c) The third five-year-plan observed, "a rapidly growing co-operative sector with special emphasis on the needs of the peasants. The workers and the consumers becomes a vital factor for expansion of employment opportunity and for rapid economic development."

After 1969, with the adoption of multi-agency approach to development, long-term objective of co-operative development was redefined, particularly, for ensuring increased agricultural production, promotion of rural development, public distribution system and generation of employment opportunities. The fourth plan outlined the approach to co-operative development thus, "it will be a part of the policy during the fourth five-year-plan to ensure that the opportunity before co-operatives should be as large and as varied as they can utilise".

A similar approach was adopted by successive five year plans.

Problems and Tasks of Agricultural Co-operatives:

Bangladesh:
Primary societies are those based on which the whole structure of agricultural co-operatives are built but these suffer from various weaknesses and deficiencies which stem from their small size and low membership. The national average membership is 49. For BRDB primaries it is 33 and for the department pri-

Sl. No. Particulars	1950–51	60–61	70–71	80–81	85–86	86–87
I. All-Coops-Overall view:						
i. No. of societies (1000s)	180.00	332.00	320.00	299.00	315.00	
ii. Membership (million)	13.70	35.20	64.40	106.20	141.05	
iii. Working capital (billion)	2.76	13.12	68.09	208.80	377.69	
II. Primary AGRL Credit Societies:						
i. No. of societies (000)	105.00	212.00	160.00	95.00	92.00	
ii. Membership (million)	4.40	17.00	42.90	57.50	69.18	
iii. % of rural population covered (estimated)	7.00	24.90	36.10	55.90	67.25	
III. Agricultural Credit (Rs. in billion):						
i. Short & Medium term loan advanced	0.22	2.02	5.78	17.63	26.67	
ii. Long-term loans advanced	0.01	0.12	1.68	3.63	5.39	
IV. Marketing of AGRL Produce:						
i. Agricultural Produce marketed by Coops (in billion)	0.47	1.69	6.48	19.50	30.32	41.93
V. COOP Sugar Factories:						
i. No. of Factories in production	2.00	30.00	73.00	149.00	186.00	194.00
ii. Sugar produced (00 tonnes)	5.00	450.00	1262.00	2903.00	4113.00	4754.00
iii. Percentage to National production	0.50	14.90	33.80	56.40	58.60	56.00
VI. Cooperative Stores:						
i. No. of godowns	na	5000.00	17930.00	29947.00	49620.00	52526.00
ii. Storage capacity owned (million tonnes)	na	0.80	3.00	5.10	8.56	9.40
VII. Percentage Share of COOPS to Total National Figures:						
i. Total institutional credit						
ii. Of fertilisers distributed					54.00	50.00
iii. Of national production of sugar as on 31.3					20.00	35.00
iv. Produced by coops for parastatal institutions					58.60	56.00
a) wheat					24.92	23.80
b) cotton					39.80	19.00
c) jute					37.00	37.00

Fig. 2: Cooperative Movement in India (Trends).

maries it is 86, the department primaries (except their KSS) usually having larger areas of operation. Another alarming feature of the situation is that membership in many societies of both the streams have remained static for years, which may be due to unwillingness of an inert or a vested-interest group to share the benefits of the society with others. The minimum number of 10 members prescribed in the law to register a co-operative also contributes to keep the membership low. Because of its small size the primary society is

- unable to do sizable business to earn profit,
- can hardly diversify its business,
- cannot employ paid professional staff to look after its business and,
- is unable to meet its obligatory charges out of its revenue income and therefore suffers persistent loss.

The way out appears to be in increasing the membership in the existing societies and/or enlarging the area of operation of the societies and/or through merger or amalgamation of activities with appropriate societies of the neighbouring area. The existing rules regarding merger and amalgamation of societies may be simplified to make the amalgamation process easier and less time-consuming for the societies to follow. The prescribed minimum of members needed for registration of a society may also be raised from 10 (ten) by the society in disbursing credit. What is required to be accomplished by the co-operative sector is not merely providing loans and recovering but introducing a 'sound' credit culture which could be spread and sustained.

Sri Lanka:
The role of the agricultural co-operatives should be viewed in the background of this small holder agricultural system of the country. Both the strength and the weaknesses of the co-operatives depend on the degree and extent to which they have succeeded in penetrating this system and providing the supplies and services to the small in an organized manner. The wide range of services that are necessary to support the small farmer-dominated agricultural system can-

not, of course, be provided by co-operatives alone nor can it be done by thinly spreading its support over the entire system. It is therefore necessary to identify the most effective and the convenient points of entry to this system. It appears that this point of entry consists of two critical areas in the rural agricultural sector, namely credit and marketing.

Credit has been the most important requirement in the lives of the rural agricultural community (→ *Agricultural Credit*). In fact this was identified as the basic necessity of the agrarian society long ago and the earliest co-operatives were established solely for the purpose of providing credit. However, problems of rural credit have not yet been satisfactorily resolved although a multiplicity of agencies are currently engaged in this task.

There are two types of credit, namely, institutional credit and non-institutional credit. The first category is provided by the state such as government departments, commercial banks, and co-operatives. The second category is the informal system of obtaining credit from the private trader and the rural money lender. There has been a gradual increase of rural indebtedness notwithstanding all efforts taken by the state to redress it (→ *Linking Banks*).

The role of the private money lender also increased significantly in spite of the exorbitant interest rates levied by him. The drift towards non-institutional credit demonstrated the weaknesses of the state sponsored credit systems. These were the results of inherent difficulties, redtapism, built-in-delays in disbursement of credit. Officials who manned those state sector credit institutions often were insensitive to the plight of the people to the extent that their attitudes have turned the people away from the credit institutions to be received warmly by the private money lender.

Providing rural credit therefore seems to be the most important service that can be extended by the co-operatives. What has to be emphasized here is that although specialized co-operatives have been set up their involvement seems to be inadequate.

The spread and the coverage of these institutions are insufficient to the task and therefore the opportunities available through co-operatives to reduce rural indebtedness are limited. The credit therefore is the door to the complex small farmer agricultural system from where the co-operatives should widen their tentacles to encompass all aspects of rural life.

The weakness displayed by the co-operatives in providing rural credit are not problems of the co-operative system but largely the results of policy announcements, and rules promulgated by the banking sector. The people's bank is the principal donor agency of rural credit which is channelled through the co-operative rural banks. All conditions, such as security for loans, treatment of defaulters, risk minimization, lending procedures, interest rates and disqualifications of defaulters, to obtain loans are determined by the registrar of co-operative societies and the people's bank and the co-operative rural bank has become an unfortunate implementer of some of unsympathetic regulations. Loans other that cultivation loans exceeding Rs. 5,000 required security in immovable property. No risk permitted to be taken by the society even through the board of directors would like to do so. Re-scheduling of previous loans are done often but no flexibility rests with the society to devise their own system of recoveries by developing social pressures. Loans default under co-operative law is a dispute which has to be resolved through arbitration and enforced by the courts of law. Cumbersome procedures such as numerous form filling and repeated visit to credit institutions discourage the rural people. Therefore it is unfortunate that the MPCSs are not fully geared to providing the most important input of rural development, namely the credit.

Pakistan:

The government not longer gives direct subsidies to co-operatives, except a small amount to the National Co-operative Union. The provincial governments make contributions to the share capital of the provincial co-operative banks only and also stand guarantee for repayment of the amounts borrowed by them from the Federal Bank. There are no cases of joint government-co-operative enterprise of foreign collaboration for co-operative projects but such joint projects are permitted by policy.

Preferential treatment to co-operatives in the matter of permits or licences or in the allotment of land is no longer available. Similarly, no special incentives are given to co-operatives, and local government funds are deposited only in the nationalised banks. The Federal Bank for Co-operatives gives modest grants and subsidies now and then for educational and extention programmes.

Co-operatives are exempted from payment of stamp duty and fees for registration of documents. Surplus resulting from business done with genuine members is also exempt from corporate tax. No other fiscal concessions are given.

Co-operatives are treated on a par with the private sector and receive no preferential treatment. In fact, the private sector has a distinct advantage where permits, licences and industrial loans are concerned as the applicants from that sector are usually persons with political or social influence. Prominent co-operative leaders would rather seek government favours for themselves that for co-operatives. The public sector being the government's own enterprise is, of course, entitled to special consideration and co-operatives cannot claim any comparison with them. In short, co-operatives rank No. 3 when compared with the private and the public sector.

V. Summary and Conclusions

1. We have examined the following problems: the historical development of the co-operative movement (→ *History in 19th C.*), the areas in which co-operatives have been operating (→ *Classification*), the organisation framework within which they function (→ *Organizational Structure of Societies*), and finally some of the major problem areas of the co-operatives in the four countries of South Asia (→ *Self-help Organizations*).

2. The co-operative movement is the weakest in Pakistan and relatively much more developed in India followed by Sri Lanka and Bangladesh. Even in India, however, the movement has not made any significant impact on production relations, and has failed to make a dent on poverty. Even in official circles, it is admitted that 40% of the population lives under conditions of extreme poverty. It should, however, be mentioned that given India's vast population, considerable benefits have percolated to the upper and lower middle classes and may have trickled down via provision of rural credit, marketing and in the field of co-operative housing. The trickle-down hypothesis is itself debatable and in case would have to examined separately and not only in terms of the development of co-operatives.

3. Finally, is the co-operative form of ownership "superior" or more "efficient" that individual or corporate forms of ownership? The question assumes a novel topicality in the context of the changes (both actual and envisaged) taking place in the so-called "socialist" economies of USSR, Eastern Europe and China. This indeed, would be a fascinating area for future research. Some discussion on the problem may be found in Vyas, A. and Vernikov, A.V. (1990) in Chs. 2 and 4.

Bibliography

Bhaduri, A.: The Economic Structure of Backward Agriculture, Mcmillan, Delhi 1984.
Chattopadhyay, P./Rudra, A.: Farm Size and Productivity revisted. Economic and Political Weekly, vol. 11, no. 39 (1975/76), pp. 104–111.
Granovskii, A. E.: Ekonomicheskii Rost v Stranakh Uzhnoi Azii (Economic Growth in Countries of South Asia in Russian, with an English Summary), Moscow 1988, pp. 329–331.
Loan Waiver fatal for co-op. Credit Business Times, The Times of India, New Delhi, November 13, 1990.
Pattnaik, U.: Economics of Farm Size and Farm Scale. Economic and Political Weekly, vol. 7, no. 31 (1972), pp. 1613.1621.
Pattnaik, U.: Class differentiation within the peasantry. Economic and Political Weekly, vol. 11, no. 39 (1976), pp. 82–103.
Present Situation Regarding the Co-operative Movement in India, Sri Lanka, Philippines and Bangladesh: International Co-operative Alliance, New Delhi, 1990.
Role of Government in the Co-operative Movement, International Co-operative Alliance, New Delhi 1989.
Rundra, A.: Farm Size and Yield per acre. Economic and Political Weekly, Bombay, Spl. no. July (1968).
Vyas, A./Vernikow, A. V.: The Economics of Perestroika, Ajanta International, New Delhi 1990.

Development of Co-operatives in South-East Asia

Mahmood Ali Khan/ Y.Bhatti

(see also: *Development, South Asia*; *Development, Africa South of Sahara*; *Development, Northern Africa*; *Development Policy*; *Policies for Promotion*; *Self-help Organizations*)

I. Development of Co-operative Movements; II. Role of the Government; III. People's Participation; IV. Selected Innovative Experiences; V. Issues in Co-operative Development

I. Development of Co-operative Movements

1. Early Initiatives

Co-operatives as legal and institutional organizations in South and South-East Asia (S&SEA) are an outcome of specific interventions of the colonial powers during the early twentieth century. Since Western Europe had successfully solved the problem of peasant indebtedness through a co-operative system, the colonial authorities preferred to apply the same approach to the problem of peasant indebtedness in their respective colonies to save the farmers from extreme poverty and misery (→ *British–Indian Pattern*).

For many decades, credit co-operatives dominated the co-operative movements. The scope of co-operatives was later expanded to allow the development of diversified activities (primarly marketing) and an appropriate vertical structure through amendments in co-operative laws. These laws, in general, empower Registrars (governments) to regulate and restrict the working of co-operatives. However, the laws in Thailand, Philippines, Indonesia and Singapore are such that the intervention posssibilities for the government are limited (→ *Law, International*).

In socialist countries like Burma, Laos and Vietnam, co-operative laws are, a priori, democratic, but in practice, co-operatives are controlled by the political party in power and are widely used as an instrument for regulation of prices, food distribution, farm input supplies and cooperativizing farms and cottage industries (→ *State and Co-operatives, Socialism*). The family crafts are turned into co-operative organizations.

2. Post–Independence Expansion

After the independence of the countries in Asia, co-operative development has undergone a great deal of expansion, diversification and experimentation. Some countries like Sri Lanka have even funeral associations to cover the expenses of burial rites.

Any structural changes, reforms of legislative amendments have been invariably brought by the top bureaucracy. Sometimes, these changes are introduced to achieve broad national objectives such as accelerating distribution of farm inputs, managing land reforms, promoting settlement, migration of refugees, retired army personnel, tribals and others.

The measures may be described either as expanding or consolidating. Expansion was sought in terms of numbers, forms and types of activities to reach out to a large number of people and bring them into the mainstream of development. The consolidating approach consisted of restructuring and providing financial support and training to improve the co-operative management (commonly measured in terms of recovery of loans), the marketing of farm inputs and farm produce, and enhance the knowledge of co-operative functioning among members. Such measures succeeded most in Indian Punjab, where they occurred while the agricultural transformation (green revolution) was taking place, but had limited success in Sri-Lanka as no parallel development in agricultural production was in vogue.

Urban co-operatives have not been subjected to many reforms. These are mostly thrift, credit, industrial production, and consumer supply oriented. Many are quite active where the support of the employer is available as railways consumer co-operatives in Pakistan, employees' consumer co-operatives in various urban industrial units in Thailand and among five star hotels of Indonesia. → *Consumer co-operatives* have also been organized by the staff of various jails.

3. Recent Trends

Co-operatives are no longer ideologically and conceptually the same as conceived by the early initiators. The rich organize co-operatives to take advantage of fiscal concessions allowed by the governments to co-operatives, whereas the poor form co-operatives to improve their socio economic conditions. In all the cases, co-operatives are registered under the same law. Co-operatives are, therefore, used by all those, who may be in favour or against co-operatives. Indian Government has, in particular, promoted various industrial co-operatives by participating in capital and management. Examples may be cited of Indian Farmers Fertilizers Ltd., Krishak Bharte co-operative Ltd., Petrofils co-operative Ltd. (synthetic yarn production) and the sugar co-operative associations. Government has participated in the co-operative insurance system in the Philippines and special co-operatives for the small farmers and the landless have also been organized as in Nepal and Bangladesh.

Since the recovery of bad loans through Registrar of co-operatives is much easier than having a recourse to a court of law, co-operatives are also used by the banks for advancing loans. For example, fishermen were advanced loans by a bank through co-operatives to buy fishing boats and engines in Sri Lanka. Technical assistance projects and NGOs organize informal groups on co-operative lines to reach out to the people for ensuring popular participation. In brief, co-operatives are used in all possible ways, many times in quite disregard to the spirit of co-operative principles. For example, Indonesia made a policy anouncement in 1988–89 that foreign and domestic investors could undertake production in partnership with co-operatives.

II. Role of the Government

1. Policy Framework

Co-operatives are essentially a component of the private sector and are basically economic enterprises. Working capital should, therefore, come from individuals. Governments are required primarily to provide an appropiate policy. ILO recommendation 127 of 1968 has laid down specific guidelines, as (a) enumeration of various types of activities for the low income groups, (b) ability of governments' aid and encouragement of economic, financial, technical, legislative or of other character, (c) integration of co-operative development into the national development plans, (d) training of the management cadres and member education, and (e) ensuring autonomy and independence of co-operatives (→ *United Nations System*).

Most of the above stated elements are not acted upon. Co-operative development does not even form any part of the national development plans in market economy countries of S&SEA. India and socialist countries are exceptions. National Corporation for Co-operative Development in India undertakes some planning for co-operative development. The national plans of socialist countries provide for certain targets to be achieved by the co-operative sector. Many countries allow certain fiscal and monetary concessions to the co-operatives, as income tax exemptions, registration fees, subsidized interest rate and provide financing facilities through the banking structure. These concessions are mostly misused and have not been appropriate to a large number of co-operatives which are small in size, have very limited turnover and do not qualify to pay any taxes.

Another element of the policy is the governments' technical assistance. The early initiators called the governments' field staff as friends, philosophers and guide of the movement. Today, they act as managers and controllers of the co-operatives. Co-operative legislation provided the basis not only for promoting and organizing co-operatives (→ *Policies for Promotion*) but also for the excessive governments' intervention in the co-operative affairs (→ *Officialization*).

All these elements of policy support have been available in different periods and in varying proportions. For example, co-operatives were allowed a monopoly of fertilizer distribution in Pakistan for a number of years and purchase of paddy in Japan. Sometimes co-operatives are preferred for a specific activity over individuals, as in the case of housing co-operatives in Pakistan and Malaysia, and land settlement programmes in Thailand (→ *Communal Settlements*).

The objectives of the policies are defeated if proper beneficiaries are not identified and the defined procedures in executing the programmes are not followed. A number of co-operatives have been ultimately dissolved due to these reasons.

2. Financial Support

Governments play a dominant role in providing financial support; provided through government controlled apex institutions. In India and Indonesia, governments stood guarantors to loans advanced to co-operatives. India has developed a very innovative and effective mechanism of financing industrial co-operatives through National Finance Corporation for Co-operative Development (→ *Financing*). Thailand follows a package approach consisting of credit, training and management; rendered partly by the bank and partly by the government staff. In Pakistan, the needs of small and marginal farmers are met through primary co-operatives. Interest free seasonal loans are granted which are recovered when the crop is harvested.

Despite governments' financial support, co-operative are able to satisfy only around 105 of borrowers' needs. The non-institutional credit sources still play a big role in meeting the credit needs. The membership has not exceeded 20–255 of the national households.

3. Training and Member-Education

The member-education (→ *Education, Asia*) is done either by the co-operative unions or by the departments or by both. Governments have established permanent staff and colleges for this purpose. Singapore is, however, a unique example where neither any permanent staff nor college exists. The co-operative union organizes short term courses, as and when needed, by hiring the part time staff and space. In Thailand, the national bank financing the co-operatives is also providing the in-service training.

The need is, to train the low paid staff. Since most of the co-operatives are economically weak, they hire relatively less qualified staff and train them, except in the case of Singapore, where the co-operatives are economically viable and can, therefore, afford to hire the professional staff from the open market.

III. People's Participation

1. General Awareness

Although co-operatives have been operating in S&SEA since the beginning of the present century, the common people are still not aware of their concept. People, particularly in the rural areas, still consider them as government institutions as they are run by the officials of the co-operative department. The lack of awareness may, in general, be attributed to three major factors. Firstly, co-operatives are sometimes born overnight under government policies and programmes and, in this way, no proper education is imparted to the people as to why a co-operative should be organized. Secondly, the high rate of illiteracy is often cited as a cause. Finally, a large number of co-operatives in various countries are not operating and out of the operating ones, only about 305 of the members are actually involved in activities. Therefore, it may be said that members' awareness is limited due to the inactivity of co-operatives (→ *Self-help Organizations*).

2. Participation and Decision Making

The key to the participatory process and democratic control is decentralization. The basic unit is the primary co-operative which is supposed to be autonomous. This, however, does not ensure members' effective participation. People participate in it to benefit by sharing the development activities.

People's participation is hindered by numerous factors. For example, bureaucrats are biased and doubt whether people will be able to manage their affairs themselves, particularly if government funds are involved. In India, the Multi-State Co-operative Societies Act (section 41(1)) provides for nomination of governmental officals on boards of directors.

Another limiting factor is the conflict between the rich and the poor. Since the elites exploit the limited resources for their personal use, the benefits are not extended to a large number of medium, small and marginal farmers. The low literacy level in many countries also plays a role in low people's participation. The training material in many countries is still available in english, which can be utilized only by few members. Moreover, contents of the training consist of members' rights, obligations, co-operative principles, periodic meetings and general meetings, which do not meet members' current needs.

3. Co-operative Leadership

Co-operative development demands an effective leadership. The example of late President Park of South Korea, who led Samuel Wondung to success through his personal interest and commitment, is outstanding. The same is true for Pandit Nehru and Dr. Hatta, the late prime ministers of India and Indonesia, respectively. Indonesia has committed itself to the co-operatives in its constitution of 1945 and adopted co-operatives as a means of socio economic development. In India and Pakistan, quite a number of parliamentarians hold positions among co-operatives. But they do not have any lobby. The national leadership rests with the office bearers of national unions. In some countries, these leaders are elected today, who mostly come from the rural elites or retired government officials for their political primary benefits (United Nations, p.11).

The co-operative local leadership is influenced by the socio economic structure. The benefits are mainly exploited by the management committee (Khan and UNRISD). Co-operatives tend to reproduce the existing social structure among the rural and urban communities along with the control of elites, the role of the government bureaucracies, the indifferent attitude of the common people, and common man's attitude to co-exist with the prevalent leadership and power structure without much effort to exercise countervailing power. Such state of affairs suit the bureaucracy and local leadership who in connivance with each other perpetuate the status quo.

IV. Selected Innovative Experiences

As the traditional approach to co-operative development failed, in general, various planners who were civil servants in the governments have been looking for some alternatives and innovative programmes which may provide a solution to various development problems. A number of experiments were, therefore, launched. A few are reported hereunder.

1. India

a) National Co-operative Development Corporation (NCDC)

NCDC was established in 1963, through an act of parliament, with the functions to plan, promote and finance processing, storage and marketing of agricultural produce, food stuff, and notified commodities like fertilizers, insecticides, agricultural machinery, lac, soaps, textile, etc., through co-operative organizations. NCDC is a semi-autonomous body. It is allowed grants and loans by the federal government to meet its expenses. Its performance has been creditable. Its assistance to various co-operative programmes has exceeded 10 billion rupees. During 1986–87, its assistance level was about 110 million rupees. Over the past decades, it has promoted more than 200 co-operative sugar factories, 100 co-operative spinning mills, 3 co-operative oil seed processing and marketing units, and three fertilizer plants owned and operated by Indian Farmers Fertilizer Co-operative (IFFCO). It has also created about 10 million tons capacity for co-operative storage.

NCDC places special emphasis on assisting weaker sections of the society. The disbursements to co-operatives of the scheduled castes, tribals and women increased from 8 to 15 million rupees between 1978–79 and 1984–85. The involvement of people also increased from 7 to 10 million. To improve the equity capital, NCDC increased its share capital contribution from RS. 20,000.00 to RS. 200,000.00 for each large sized multipurpose co-operative. At the end of 1987, NCDC had also advanced loans for the construction of 1634 godowns/workshops, for the purchase of 187 transport vehicles, for the setting up of 132 processing units, for establishing 633 rural consumer projects, and for the assistance to 64 other co-operatives in tribal areas. NCDC promoted 45 Coir projects for women through co-operatives by March, 1987. It has also achieved an enormous progress in co-operative marketing, and production of fertilizers. NCDC has largely contributed in diversifying the co-operative activities and ensuring economic viability.

b) The Kaira District Co-operative Milk Producers Union Ltd. (AMUL)

AMUL was organized with five Village milk Producers' Co-operatives on December 14, 1946. Pasteurization of milk was started in 1948. At that time, only 250 liters milk was collected from only two co-operatives. Today, there are 895 co-operatives with 357,000 milk producers participating with 750,000 liters per day. The technical services provided to the farmers are veterinary care and artificial insemination. Men and women are taught not only about co-operatives but also about animal husbandry and milk quality control.

The key to AMUL's success is the organizational structure, scientific management, technical assistance and extension services to the dairy farmers, governments's commitment to the programme, member education, discipline, and technical and financial assistance from abroad. AMUL is a two tier Union, where the village co-operatives collect milk and transport it to the district Union. The Union processes and sells it. AMUL has ensured members fair prices, i.e. 20 to 405 higher than what they would have received without the co-operative system. The Board of Directors consists of 17 members (12 elected and 5 nominated).

2. Indonesia

Relatively speaking, Indonesia has always had greater political commitment to the co-operative development than any other developing country of Asia. In terms of action programme, however, India perhaps is the leading country. Indonesia attempted some new approaches, which are as under:

a) BUUD Organization

BUUD is an area level organization to provide integrated services for development. It federates five to ten rural co-operatives in a sub-district. There are today 27,000 BUUDs, nearly as many as sub-districts. A BUUD consists of an advisory board, made up of elected members from the village co-operatives, an elected manager and the members.

Indonesia's rural economy is basically rice growing. BUUDs were encouraged to be involved in all phases of rice production, i.e. from production to consumption. They were particularly expected to stabilize the price of rice by providing farm inputs, undertaking rice processing and purchasing rice when its price falls below the established floor price and thereby eliminate the role of middlemen. BUUDs were, therefore, allowed subsidized credit to buy small scale rice hullers and rice polishing equipment.

Due to the dominating role of the civil administration, BUUDs could not gain the confidence of rural people. Increase in the number of BUUDs diluted government's support. Moreover, government's rice procurement policy at low prices severely affected BUUD as the latter failed to safeguard members' interest. In brief, BUUD could not gain the confidence and support of people and, hence, could not become participative area level development insitutions.

b) Workers Co-operative Alliance (INKOPAR)

INKOPAR has been organized at the national level to provide facilities to the urban co-operatives and a political profile to the movement. It has a three tier system. The intermediate level is called PUSKOP-KARS, which also act in many cases as a wholesale supply organization and provides education and training services to the members.

There are about 1666 urban co-operatives of various kinds, mostly consumer and services co-operatives. A great number of them belong to industrial and commercial enterprises. Many are quite successful primarily due to employers' support regarding management, capital formation and premises for business; prompt and full recovery of credit sales due to workers' regular income; and coincidence of co-operative and trade union leadership (→ *Trade Unions*).

A workers' co-operative, established in 1982 with 550 members at Hotel Kartikaplaza (WCKP), in Jakarta may be mentioned as a typical example. The activities of WCKP consisted of mobilization of savings, extending of loans (cash & kind) and providing basic consumer goods at competitive prices. It accumulated a compulsory deposit of 14 million, admission fee of 2.5 million over a period of five years, and a turnover during 1985 was reported to be 200 million Rupiah with a net profit of 35 million. Depositors received 22% return on savings and the dividend on purchases was declared to an extent of 44%.

3. Pakistan

Farmers Organization (Idara-i-Kisan–IK)

IK has been promoted through a Livestock Production Project; being run in about 52 villages of Kasur & Okara districts of Punjab under a technical assistance programme of the Federal Republic of Germany. The small livestock farmers have organized themselves into co-operative like groups in each village called Village Milk Collection Centers (VMCC) guided by a local representative called Nomainda. VMCC collects milk, ensures the quality of milk supply and makes payment for milk collected. It is served by three workers called village milk collector, extension worker and veterinary assistant. All these workers have either been elected or selected by villagers themselves, duly trained by the project, and are paid according to the services rendered by them. Each center is self supporting as all the costs of milk collection, transportation, etc., are borne by the milk suppliers.

At present, there are about 72 groups and more than 50 Nomaindas. These Nomaindas make up the electoral college for the IK who elects 8 members to the board of management. IK is running a milk plant and 3 chilling units.

IK has been quite successful in raising the farm gate milk price and reducing farmers' dependence on middle-men for milk sale, supply of credit and other inputs. It has still problems related to its democratization, optimum utilization of the milk plant, self reliance of IK in terms of provision of services to the livestock farmers, and developing cooperation and collaboration with the government agencies, particularly the livestock and dairy development department.

4. Philippines

Samahaang Nayon Pre-Co-operative (SN)

SNs are closely related to the land reform measures undertaken during the 70's. According to Presidential decree No. 37, all tenanted rice and corn land over and above 7 ha is to be distributed among tenant farmers, who will pay in accordance with a 15 year amortization plan. In order to enable tenant farmers to pay for the land, SN programme was put into operation. SNs, which are Barrio Associations, are "pre-co-operatives" to train the farmers as future co-operators. At the same time, it should collect enough resources of its own in order to benefit from the land reform programme and obtain transfer deeds.

SNs were introduced with an eye on the future. Lessons were learned from the failure of FACOMA. (Farmers Co-operative Marketing Associations).

The maximum number of members of a FACOMA was supposed to be 200. But it exceeded to 5000 in some cases, causing organizational, managerial and sociopolitical problems. Therefore, the SN membership could not exceed 200. Its main activity is limited to continued education, capital building (savings promotion) and discipline among the members. SNs are not supposed to engage themselves in any business undertaking. Each member must first receive necessary education and training before becoming a member. A minimum of 25 members can form a SN; with only one SN in a Barrio.

Members are obliged to follow the prescribed saving programme, i.e. Pesos 10 as membership fee, Pesos 5 as annual fee, 50 kg of palay (rice) per ha. per harvest, 5% deduction on any insitutional loan to be credited to a special barrio saving fund, and a minimum contribution of Pesos 5 per month by non-borrowers. Barrio saving funds thus collected, were to be used to buy shares of co-operative rural banks.

A SN needs to graduate in terms of having obtained training, implementation of savings programme and discipline. Thus, a SN may be promoted to a Kilusang Bayan (KB), a full-fledged co-operative centralizing all barrio based economic activities of the association. SN provides the lowest tier of secondary level cooperatis. One is called Area Marketing Co-operatives (AMC), which undertake supply of farm inputs, processing, storage and sale of agricultural commodities. The second is Co-operative Rural Banks (CRB) for banking services.

V. Issues in Co-operative Development

1. New Directions

Co-operative development is today proceeding in all directions. But they may not fulfill all the requirements laid down in the law. For example, the membership may not be open to all. The original membership may only be restricted to the close friends and relatives in some cases or it may change hands with the sale/purchase deed as in the cases of housing co-operatives. A co-operative is sometimes organized by a group of businessmen to enjoy the privileges of a co-operative, like tax exemptions, or the Registrar is obliged to register a co-operative through political pressure exercised by some influential people for their own motives. This may cause failure of co-operatives giving ultimately a bad name to the movement.

Small farmers are provided seasonal loans, mainly for fertilizers, by co-operatives. However, the condition for refinancing is the 100 % recovery. Since this is almost impossible, the co-operatives with outstanding loans become dormant and new co-operatives are formed to take advantage of the new loaning facility (as in Pakistan). This enables the bureaucrats to show their performance regarding the development of co-operative movement. Thus, co-operatives are organized to (a) meet the objectives of a government's policy, (b) take advantage of exemption from taxes and (c) benefit from the government's policy for special preference to co-operatives as land allotment for houses.

2. Self-reliance

A co-operative movement can reflect the true aspirations of its constituent only if the co-operatives are self reliant, free and autonomous (→ *Self-help Organizations*).

The governments' involvement in the affairs of co-operatives is very high. Some state control may be accepted, since governments have provided financial support. But the long term objective should be to make the co-operatives independent and autonomous (Weerman) (→ *Officialization*).

Many a governments run co-operatives as a means to an end. The bureaucracy takes care whether co-operatives comply with the directives given, without taking any notice of their willingness. Co-operatives could perhaps refuse any bad business if they were free and autonomous in a functional sense.

Self reliance is positively correlated with the size (volume of business) and the laissez-faire attitude of the bureaucrats. As long as governments promoted small sized co-operatives, self reliance would remain a distant goal. Conversely, large size capital intensive co-operative enterprises are likely to be self reliant and could resist bureaucratic interventions.

3. Non-Governmental Organizations

NGOs have been quite successful in reaching out to the poor in some countries in respect of socioeconomic activities, as Grameen Bank and Prosika in Bangladesh, Bina Swadya in Indonesia, Agha Khan Rural support Programme in Pakistan, grass root Rural Integrated Development (GRID) in Thailand, and Philippines Business for Social Progress (PBSP) and PROCESS in the Philippines. The number of NGOs has mushroomed in many Asian countries. There exist even various national associations of NGOs.

NGOs are small and generally operate among a range of 5 to 500 villages. However, when they grow big like PROSIKA in Bangladesh, they face problems of leadership, organizational and managerial character.

Bibliography

Khan, Mahmood Ali: Co-operatives Dilemma, Lyallpur 1972.
United Nations: Popular Participation in Decision Making for Development, New York 1975.
UNRISD: Rural Co-operatives as Agents of Change, Geneva 1975.
Weerman, P.E.: A Model Co-operative Societies Law, ICA, x, New Delhi 1978.

Development of Co-operatives in Turkey

Ismail Duymaz [J]

(see also: *Development, Eastern Europe*; *Israel*; *Law, International*; *Principles*)

I. Introduction; II. Preconditions for Development and Functional Involvement of Co-operative Cooperation in Turkey; III. Historic Development and Aspects of Jurisdiction; IV. Actual Weak Spots and Shortcomings of Co-operative Development in Turkey; V. Current Results and Prospects for the Future.

I. Introduction

Turkey can count some 7.5 million co-operative members dispersed in 54,684 primary and 336 secondary co-operatives among its total population of 58 million inhabitants. These co-operatives are active in all economic sectors and address numerous enterprise and household functions (see *Table I*). It would be impossible in the scope of this article to provide a complete overview of co-operative development in Turkey. For this reason only the essential characteristics, tendencies and perspectives of this development will be illuminated. Following a brief and general account of Turkey's socio-economic situation, discussion will primarily concentrate on the legal-organizational and economic development tendencies of co-operatives as well as on their shortcomings.

Co-operatives have been established in Turkey since 1930, in part through government initiative and in part through members' own initiative. High expectations have been placed on them as they were intended above all to contribute to the improvement of the material, personal and institutional market infrastructures. They were intended to instigate suitable market opportunities for credit availability, purchasing, consulting and marketing as well as to provide both chances and incentives to modernize traditional, stagnating enterprises; they ultimately were to facilitate or accelerate the integration of those individuals involved in the market process. Anticipated and actual achievements, however, today prove to be rather distinct. Claims placed on them have only been fulfilled in exceptional cases by co-operatives which have approached fulfilling their own expectations.

II. Preconditions for Development and Functional Involvement of Co-operative Cooperation in Turkey

The socio-economic conditions today in Turkey also provide a fertile basis for co-operative activity in greatly varied functional sectors in both rural and urban areas which have witnessed tremendous changes since the 1960s. Despite these structural changes, Turkey still remains a semi-developed country in which almost half of the population lives from farming. Per capita income amounted to $ 2,622 in 1992. Considerable economic growth, nonetheless, cannot hide general disappointment in the fact that intrasectoral, intersectoral, and regional development discrepancies have not been substantially reduced. The dualistic break-down of the economic and social structure is reinforced through continuing growth and the social changes achieved through such growth. The country's afflictions have increasingly switched from those rooted in underdevelopment to those rooted in the uneven, incoherent and unorganized development in and among sectors and regions; there are not any clearly identifiable symptoms of a soon integration process.

Agriculture has always assumed a substantial share of total employment (48%) although it plays an ever-decreasing role in real net output (16% in 1992; ITO, 1992). On the one hand, modern, capital intensive farming enterprises have arisen which orientate their production more intensely around the market. On the other hand, increasing stagnation has befallen the small-scale structures in rural areas forced to face a progressing marginalization process; such structures are the source of internal population migration. Many factors offset rapid developmental progress: the fragmentation of enterprise structures, insufficient capital, inadequate knowledge of production techniques, a lack of production alternatives, and low institutional efficiency in production and in the marketing organizations. Small-scale producers working alone are rarely in the position to undertake marketing on their own and to transform their potential surpluses into market outputs. Their products must pass through only a few marketing channels, but these are both long and multi-leveled.

Turkish agriculture is not "poor" in natural resources in the usual sense of the word. Nonetheless, a widespread and fateful "poverty" in the form of organizational deficits is prevalent in almost all functional divisions within the farming enterprises. The degree of organization among growers indeed is high in number, but the level of efficiency is considerably low. Functional private business organizations are needed which are actually in the position to work in an autonomous manner on the market level and in the interest of their members, to effect member participation and address member interests in full, and ultimately to embody a permanent institutional culture. There are an estimated 4 million farming enterprises, 96% of which cultivate their own land. 62% of all farms are smaller than 5 hectares. Subsistence production varies according to product and region and is estimated at approx. 20% of marketed production. Urban areas likewise grow and their problems with them. The material and social infrastructure in large metropolitan areas are no longer capable of shouldering annual population growth rates between

4 and 6%. Above all municipal housing and public utilities are directly affected by this rapid process. Urban areas, for example, require 460,000 new housing units annually. The construction boom in and around urban conglomerations knows neither boundaries, norms, nor standards. There are also numerous reasons to organize consumer co-operatives. Objective deficiencies as well as inadequacies related to the application of market power exist among the municipal utilities. Producers with little market power experience drastic price decreases and are at the mercy of the one-sided, dominant practices of those actors in agribusiness. With only few local exceptions to report, producers as well as urban consumers have failed to join together into market-relevant and functioning organizations acting as "countervailing power". Instead of dedicating themselves to the founding of autonomous, private interest organizations as instruments of market regulation and the revitalization of competition, they have tended to rely on (quasi-)state or communal initiatives and expected them to rectify grievances and abuses. In general, the producer markets are also gradually changing into buyer's markets; this tendency is, however, overshadowed by oligopolistic market structures in agribusiness as well.

Urban trade and industry are extensively conducted in small-scale enterprise structures. About 98.5% of all enterprises in processing industries are small-scale operations which often face predatory competition and high risks without a social safety net. As a result of the competitive dominance of the large-scale enterprises they more frequently fall victim to stagnation.

The depressing urban employment situation and its social consequences is thereby much graver than the annual inflation rate of 70% which in particular greatly handicaps the situation of wage-earners. The informal sector (underground economy) thus blooms with both advantages and disadvantages. Marginal city residents live below the absolute poverty level. The social net encompasses only about half of the population.

Turkey, therefore, has a particularly favorable climate for the creation and diffusion of co-operatives, that is a climate which is fostering the development and spread of co-operatives. The socio-economic situation of wide population groups, both in cities and on the land with limited material means or rudimentary/inadequate market accessibility, forms a suitable foundation and presents an objective problem to be redressed. Eventual co-operative development is spawned by the consequences on small-scale enterprise structures, powerlessness in the face of organized purchasers and/or suppliers, and the extreme discrepancies in the distribution of income. Given structural situations thus make an organized undertaking of affected actors necessary in numerous functional fields. Barriers to market entry, risks and the dependencies of individual economic units with regard to industrial or agricultural purchasing, financing and marketing are all relatively high for sole (individual) economic units and could be substantially reduced through co-operative action.

In contrast to this situation, however, the insight of those in question concerning the necessity and advantageous nature of co-operatives in their respective fields of engagement – in other words a particular co-operative consciousness – has developed only fragmentarily. In many cases an ambivalent position is at hand. Neither Turkish farmers or artisans nor urban traders and consumers have a particularly developed sense or inclination to cooperate based on behavior rooted in economic → *solidarity*. An individualistic behavior of self-interest is generally typical of them, even when they concede that individual effort has certain disadvantages when they critically observe the shortcomings and weaknesses of their own situations. They only show a propensity for co-operative efforts when they see an organizational-technical necessity or a material advantage which can be gained in the short-term; at the same time, their individual sphere of production must remain sovereign. The strong inclination to individualism, above all in the sphere of production, which has been attributed to Turkish farmers or artisans for centuries itself has many dimensions and complex back-ground causes of both an economic and social nature. The individual cultivation of land has always been the rule in Turkey. Collective economic methods, for example co-operative farming, have found neither interest, popularity nor application. Land remains untouched in agricultural co-operatives; collective property and responsibility (→ *Joint-production Co-operatives*) is generally unpopular. Furthermore, the slogan "small is nice as long as it belongs to me – even when it doesn't help much" is embraced today by small-scale artisans and merchants. This social-psychological fact in part hinders the willingness among those in question to cooperate. The Turkish farmer, artisan or consumer therefore does not judge (his) co-operative(s) under the aspects of social solidarity or a particular ideology but rather simply according to the material prosperity he can expect in the short term. Clear distinction is thus drawn between levels of social and economic solidarity. The relatively strongly developed propensity for social solidarity in multi-generational families and neighborhoods, therefore, does not automatically and unconditionally lead to a blind inclination for solidarity and/or cooperation in business matters. The value of cooperation for them is contingent on the effect of technical-economic advantages and not, however, on the potentially attainable social effects. Rather than ideology it is the economic character of the co-operative which surfaces in the foreground of all considerations and/or calculations revolving around co-operative membership. This phenomenon, however, has not yet been registered carefully and sufficiently by both the state and the academic community. Among other things, the counter propaganda in the 1970s and '80s caused many people to decrease their willingness to cooperate and to distance themselves from co-operatives. Each and every step in the direction of reform was branded as "socialistic" and therefore "harmful". Traditional dependencies in the context of quasi-feudal rural structures, above all in the southeast of the country, caused lethargy and had a retarding effect on co-operative development. In contrast to this, the religious-cultural elements and norms in essence neither prevented nor delayed the creation and further development of co-operatives.

Members' capacity to cooperate is quite varied according to the co-operative branches; in general, however, it is weak when it comes to providing adequately to meet the economic demands of the co-operative enterprise. This general handicap for the operational ability and competitiveness of the co-operative enterprise affects self-financing (even when the paid-up share are relatively inexpensive, e.g. DM 80.00) as well as claims to the economic output/service placed on the enterprise by its members as customers and/or suppliers. Considerable problems exist in raising outside financing. Co-operatives must often fight with their relatively "bad" reputation. There is no co-operative bank. Alone the housing co-operatives are favorably financed through a special fund.

III. Historic Development and Aspects of Jurisdiction

1. Co-operatives: Their Phases and Levels of Development

The Turkish system of co-operatives today can look back over a 130–year tradition. Three phases of development can thereby be distinguished (→ *History in 19th C.*).

The first phase began in 1863 through the establishment of "country banks", a type of credit co-operative conceived by *Mithat Pascha* to protect against usurers and was the first co-operative initiative in the Ottoman Empire. The respective articles and by-laws were applied to the entire country in 1867. The "country banks" can thus be considered the first co-operative form in the Near and Middle East. Their subsequent transformation into state-controlled "benefit banks" in 1882, and their assumption of a pseudo-co-operative character paved the way for their dissolvement in 1888, through the establishment of the Turkish Agricultural Bank, known today as TCZB. This institution is a state bank for the entire agricultural credit sector. Prior to World War I, purchasing co-operatives for artisans and consumers were founded in Instanbul which, however, only proved to be short-lived experiments.

The founding of a marketing co-operative by fig growers in Aydin deserves particular attention. This initially assumed the form of a producers' association in order to evade the exploitation of Levantine merchants in Izmir. This true self-help organization was augmented and furthered by the foundation of a credit institute (Milli Aydin Bankasi). A powerful regional association, TARIS, later evolved from this rather modest first initiative.

The second and, in the literal sense, actual co-operative developmental phase first began upon the founding of the Turkish Republic in 1923. The state assiduously involved itself in the agricultural sector during this phase; it established both governmental authorities and co-operatives for the purchasing and provision of important farm products in order to facilitate the development of a functionable market infrastructure. Hoped-for expansion and reinforcement, however, were first afforded once amendments to two special laws were passed in 1935: No.2834 for agricultural marketing co-operatives (AMCs) and No.2836 for agricultural credit co-operatives (ACCs). The approach to co-operative development strategies, pursued in the 1930s, can be clearly identified today as a "top-down" method. The existent structural state of markets and production sectors as well as farmers' traditional mentality with respect to economic matters were cited as justification for these state-initiated and executed strategies; today, these reasons hardly seem to validate, justify or make plausible the legitimization of state interference into co-operative affairs. Nonetheless, these laws later proved to have grave consequences and seem to have stunted the notions of self-help rather than promoted them because they placed AMCs and ACCs perpetually under further state supervision. The subsequent amendments, passed to these laws in 1985, only served to strengthen this tendency.

The third phase commenced once the General Co-operative Law No.1163 became effective in 1969 (→ *Law, International*). The new Co-operative Law opened up new orientation and spheres of activity, provided a suitable foundation for a "bottom-up" strategy (→ *Development Policy*), and even paved the way for the democratization of development and its de-officialization (→ *Policies for Promotion*). Inasmuch as the special laws for AMCs and ACCs, mentioned above, were maintained and remained in effect for their respective spheres of influence, a legal and operational fission and/or polarization became programmed for once and for all in co-operative development. Alongside the "top-down" method, co-operative development "bottom-up" was also intended as an operative strategy; in the course of time, however, attempts failed at harmonizing these strategies and introducing development which favored the concepts and notions inherent in the Co-operative Law.

The levels of regional co-operative development

today indicate a differentiated landscape. The socio-economic conditions in individual regions are quite varied and accordingly affect the level of co-operative development. Farming co-operatives are predominantly scattered around the west and south of the country where farmers today indicate a higher level of market orientation and enjoy their proximity to industrialized areas. In such regions, innovative behavioral patterns as well as the willingness and ability to involve oneself in cooperation are developed to a greater extent than in regions in which large land owners, semi-feudal production relationships or tiny farm units are predominant. Southeast Anatolia as well as certain districts in the east of the country are typical examples of such conditions, as can be easily proven using statistical data (TOKB, 1985). Among the rural co-operatives the village development co-operatives and their regional centers (KÖY-KOOP) stand in esteem as democratic, autonomous projects which are perpetually involved in conflicts with the state. In urban areas, the residential and artisans' settlement co-operatives above all dominate. Furthermore, → *consumer co-operatives* organized by union-affiliated workers and their central organizations such as *Yol-Koop, Es-Ko* and *Körfeztükobirlik* receive particular notice (→ *Central Institutions*).

2. Aspects of Disparate Jurisdiction

At present, co-operatives fall under the jurisdiction and influence of three laws.
a) Co-operative Law No.1163 passed in 1963 encompasses all urban and rural co-operatives (except AMCs and ACCs). According to Turkish legal understanding in the sense of the Co-operative Law, the co-operative is a juristic person in private law which comes into being with at least seven founding members, when its by-laws have been approved by the responsible ministry, and when it has been enrolled in the local trade register. Economic goal orientation is not presumed. The purpose of the co-operative is thus the safeguarding and protection of certain economic/professional interests which members have. The Co-operative Law upholds the → *principles* recognized internationally: members have the same rights and obligations; limited liability is the rule; Co-operative Law extensively regulates how executive bodies are formed, how they function, the rules of profit distribution and the formation of reserves, and states their competencies. Co-operatives must siphon off 1% of their year-end profit to a fund managed by the responsible state ministry for the sake of attending to and propagating co-operatives as well as for the promotion of co-operative education.
Co-operatives do not receive any special incentive or treatment in tax matters (→ *Taxation*). One tax code statute does grant limited privileges as long as business is conducted only with members, when no surplus is distributed and when the capital shares are not interest bearing. All co-operatives are prohibited from becoming active politically.
b) Special laws are effective for AMCs (No.3186) and ACCs (No.3223). The framework for a legal definition as well as for the formation of executive bodies and their functions, as specified in the Co-operative Law, are only assumed by the AMCs and ACCs in a formal sense. This is, however, de facto impossible: The state employs the AMCs and ACCs in agriculture exclusively as its own instrument for support buying practices (AMC) and for financing (ACC); it treats them as an object of state expansion policy and thereby determines all aspects of their business activities. This rather peculiar piece of legal interpretation de facto completely precludes members' interests, their right to voice opinions as well as their participation. The state no longer exists alongside the co-operatives but rather in the co-operatives themselves. Although the co-operative administrations are formed de jure, such elected bodies are in fact merely a facade, inasmuch as they have no right to voice their opinions, as they de facto cannot secure any influence over business practices, and as they themselves therefore do not assume any real functions. Even the directors appointed by the responsible ministry can neither act autonomously nor work to serve the membership. They are the heads of elected boards which singularly must take note of the instructions given by the ministry (→ *Officialization*).

3. Co-operatives: Between Tutelage and Autonomy

Two fundamental types of co-operatives have arisen on the basis of such disparate legal interpretation.
a) AMCs and ACCs are under state tutelage. Guidelines for their co-operative structure do not exist either de jure or de facto. These are regulated, quasi-co-operatives and show indications of abnormity and degeneration, as the following aspects should illuminate.
The AMCs are product-specific co-operatives which strive to promote their members' enterprises through the provision of inputs and collateral loans, as well as through marketing, warehousing, transportation, consulting and processing functions for the agricultural products they purchase. At least 10 founding members, each assuming a capital share of approx. DM 80.00, are needed to found an AMC with limited liability. Professional contact with the agricultural sector is furthermore a precondition for membership (as is also the case for the ACCs).
The AMCs have, without a doubt, provided considerable service and performance in the various functions listed above. Their input contributed substantially to the increase in the degree of commercialization and vertical intensification of agriculture as well as promoted the infrastructure for a market

economy. They, furthermore, have constructed tremendous agro-industrial facilities which today have enormous tractive power and thus paradoxically serve as an object in the privatization discussion.

Support purchasing undertaking by the AMCs is done in the name and under the responsiblity of the state. The financial source of such purchasing activity hails from credits made available by the TCZB. Absolutely no difference is drawn between members and non-members when purchases are undertaken; membership, thus, frequently becomes burdensome. Up to now the state has always failed to operate in an attentive manner, to work at a profit and to distribute surplus earnings. Losses are transferred to the national budget as "operational losses". The AMCs therefore are seen today as a bottomless pit for the squandering of public funds and mismanagement practices. The AMCs are considered by the state to be their own purchase outlet and are not at all accepted by their members as they enjoy no real participation. This produces substantial deviation in the rate members as customers and/or suppliers lay claim to and utilize the services of the operation. They immediately switch camps when they find larger alternative advantages elsewhere. Co-operative loyalty and membership frequency thereby quickly reach their potential limits.

The situation of the ACCs does not vary from that of the AMCs; their numerical development and the existence of 16 regional centers must not disguise their own functional shortcomings. The ACCs are not organizations promoting the formation of savings and capital but rather are intermediaries and distributors of monetary and collateral means from sources located in the TCZB. They are practically rural branches of the TCZB and are "administered" in their substructure and superstructure by appointed state officials.

b) In contrast to these two organizational forms the co-operatives which arose in the scope of the Co-operative Law are based on the three co-operative concepts of self-help, self-responsiblity, and democratic self-administration (→ *Conceptions, Co-operative*). They are rather tolerated by the state than promoted and are financially dependent on themselves and their slight capital and business bases. Stated in an overly exaggerated manner, they still save the dignity of co-operative endeavors in the Turkish context and are a source of hope for the future.

IV. Actual Weak Spots and Shortcomings of Co-operative Development in Turkey

The Turkish co-operative system today, in general, attempts to maintain its existence – without an academic research and training institute, without a credit institute of its own, and without an auditing association of its own. Day-to-day practice thereby rests on shaky ground and lacks fundamental foundation; on the other hand, it is heavily in the shadow of state influence. The deficits in the development can be summarized as follows.

1) Co-operatives operate in two fundamentally different spheres and lack any visible chance of an intersection in the sense of the Co-operative Law. One portion of the co-operatives rests firmly in the hand of the state with no prospect of disengaging itself from its custody. The other portion in contrast attempts to develop a democratic, autonomous movement, to hold its ground on its own and to serve as a counterweight to the state co-operative form. The schism in development will remain unavoidable in organizational and orientational terms as long as there is not uniform legislation and legal interpretation on the grounds of the Co-operative Law.

2) The system of co-operative federations has developed quite varyingly in individual branches. The integration process comes to pass very sluggishly. The Co-operative Law provides for a fourtiered federation structure. At least seven primary co-operatives in the same branch are needed to establish a secondary co-operative. Such central co-operatives in the same sector can join together on the third tier in a central federation. Central co-operatives in one branch may not found a second central federation. Central federations above all are assigned training and auditing functions which today can hardly be availed of. Cooperation between at least seven secondary and/or tertiary co-operatives in different branches was the precondition for the establishment of the fourth organizational structure in spring of 1992, the National Co-operative Organization of Turkey (TMKB). This umbrella organization is solely shouldered by democratic, autonomous co-operatives and presently finds itself in a phase of quest, searching for a concretization of special functions and a suitable internal organizational structure. The AMCs and ACCs distance themselves from this development on account of their reserved position.

National tertiary co-operatives up to now have only been formed in a handful of co-operative sectors. Of these, the housing co-operatives and the village development co-operatives lead the pack (see *Table I*).

3) Up through today, the system of co-operative auditing and consulting has been completely neglected. Individual branches have expanded their secondary and/or tertiary co-operatives to include internal auditing and consulting functions. The audit in principle is attended to by the state, which can in turn contract the audit out to the central organizations. Nonetheless, the audit in most cases is a simple look into the books and as such does not satisfy the formal and material expecta-

Table I: Fields of Co-operative Activity and Numerical Representation of Development (1992)

Type of Co-operative	# of Primary co-ops	# of Members	Regional Secondary Co-ops #	Mem.	Central Federation #	Memb. (sec. co-ops)
1. Agricultural Marketing Co-ops*	421	685,319	17	397	–	–
2. Agricultural Credit Co-ops*	2,474	1,480,394	16	2,474	1	16
3. Tobacco Marketing Co-operatives*	22	9,500	–	–	–	–
4. Village Development Co-operatives	3,602	523,744	74	1,366	–	–
5. Sugar Beet Co-ops	28	1,421,482	1	28	–	–
6. Co-ops for Water Products	252	17,119	8	82	–	–
7. Irrigation Co-ops	1,282	124,388	4	33	–	–
8. Guaranty Co-ops for Artisans and Traders	820	800,000	26	820	1	26
9. Housing Co-operatives	37,145	1,557,889	145	3,359	1	25
10. Settlement Co-ops for Light Industry	916	149,505	6	143	–	–
11. Artisan Co-ops	372	14,332	5	60	–	–
12. Transport Co-ops	2,062	82,831	10	91	–	–
13. Purchasing and Distribution Co-ops	221	7,753	–	–	–	–
14. Tourism Co-ops	232	15,113	4	34	–	–
15. Consumer Co-ops	3,512	496,690	17	175	–	–
16. Joint Production and Marketing Co-ops	285	26,028	2	17	–	–
17. Workshop Construction Co-ops for Artisans	856	88,825	1	10	–	–
18. Processing Co-ops	64	9,791	–	–	2	35
19. Other Co-ops	18	1,847	–	–	–	–
Total	54,684	7,512,550	336	9,089	5	77

Source: Association for the Turkish Co-operative System, Ankara

* Law No. 3186 is effective for LMCs; Law No. 3323 for LLCCs; Law No. 1196 for tobacco marketing co-operatives. All other co-operative sectors fall under the jurisdiction of Law No. 1163.

tions and criteria of a real audit as intended by the promotion mandate.

4) Co-operative research and training is likewise in a crisis, a situation for which academicians themselves are also to blame. Not only the co-operatives but also researchers have in part fallen victim to an → *"officialization"*. Intellectual fatigue in scientific undertakings has paralyzed reciprocal enrichment between research and practical application; even the position of co-operative science has yet to be fundamentally decided. Understanding about co-operatives is unclear in many situations, and notions about what co-operatives in essence are range from "special business undertakings" to "social institutions".

The demanding responsibility of conducting research and training is not sufficiently attended to by either the co-operatives or the state. No nation-wide, consistent training program for co-operative practitioners is in existence. Modest internal training programs for an operation's own staff are offered in only a few sectors. Only very few university faculties offer lectures about co-operative science (→ *Theory of Co-operatives*); these, nonetheless, lack praxis-oriented research opportunities. There is also not a national institute for research and training. The newly founded umbrella organization TMKB could pave the way for such facilities.

V. Current Results and Prospects for the Future

Turkish co-operatives today oscillate between optimism and crisis. The crisis exists both in the sense of market failure as well in the sense of legitimization for state activities (state failure). So far co-operatives have not been able to instigate efficient production and distribution effects on a wide basis. Co-operative-specific effects remain limited to certain sectors and regions. The state is thereby answerable for the calamities in the Turkish co-operative system as it has always been skeptical about democratic, autonomous actors organized "from below" and thus consciously never ceded the principle of subsidiarity any substantiation. The state over-extended itself in its involvement and set unreasonable expectations without admitting its own short-comings. At the same time, it stood in its own way when it attempted to fulfill its expectations with the help of bureaucracy. Bureaucracy, however, was the wrench thrown into the gearwork of potential reform. The state has demonstrated an inability to learn and has repeatedly corrected old mistakes with new ones. It was interested in the numerical development rather than productivity and efficiency and thus often failed to support positive aspects and developments. Negative development, however, could not be redressed. The conflicting relationship between the state and co-operatives limited potential effects of their cooperation; mistrust cultivated on both sides paralyzed forces which encouraged sensible and reciprocal supplementation.

Intensive state involvement in co-operative affairs clearly accelerated their numerical development, but this almost sufficating attention at the same time led to considerable losses in co-operative values.

These conflicts will only increase in the future as long as the state continues to consider its citizens obedient subjects and continues to have problems accepting creative impulses which come from full-standing citizens. Today, Turkish citizens shows a growing sensitivity for the legitimization, quality and costs of political decisions, even when the road from an authoritarian state – or a regulated democracy – to a political democracy is long and hard and strewn with hurdles from the past. Self-consciousness with respect to the formulation and insistence of one's interests is increasing. Today, both co-operatives and members demand more participation, equal treatment, more autonomy and greater lee-way with respect to state actors. They also are increasingly developing the opinion that economic solidarity, self-initiative and/or self-responsibility, and autonomy can no longer tolerate state tutelage, and that state assistance no longer represent a charitable act but rather must only be seen as an emergency response.

Bibliography

DIE: Statistical Yearbook of Turkey 1990, Ankara 1992.
DPT: Kücük Sanayi, Vi. BYKP, ÖIK Raporu, Ankara 1988.
Findikoglu, Z.F.: Kooperasyon Sosyolojisi, Istanbul 1967.
Hazar, N.: Kooperatifcilik Tarihi, Ankara 1970.
ITO: Ekonomik Rapor, Istanbul 1992.
Musto, S.A.: Die türkische Landwirtschaft, DIE-Manuskript, Berlin 1988.
Mülayim, Z.G.: The Fundamental Problems of Turkish Co-operatives and Proposals for their Solution, FES., Istanbul 1990.
Mülayim, Z.G.: Kooperatifcilik,Ankara 1992.
TOBB: Köy Envanter Etüdleri-Türkiye 1981,Ankara 1985.
TOBB: 1991 Yili Ekonomik Raporu, Ankara 1992.

Development Policy, Co-operatives in

JOCHEN RÖPKE

(see also: *Policies for Promotion*; *State and Co-operatives, Market Economy*; *Self-help Organizations*; *Officialization*)

I. Historical Background; II. Conceptional Framework; III. Co-operative Entrepreneurship and Its Stimulation.

I. Historical Background

While co-operatives have produced impressive results during the industrial and agricultural transformation of the now industrialized, high income economies, they were not an explicit part of governmental development strategy, and this has remained so up to now.

Co-operatives in the West evolved in a process of competitive "natural selection", according to their respective comparative advantages, unhampered but also unhelped by governmental action (→ *Competition*).

But already during colonial times, a more activist approach towards co-operative development can be detected in the colonial dependencies. The British, French, and Dutch colonial administrations were quite active in promoting specific types of co-operatives in their respective empires (*Münkner*). Their motives were as ambivalent as those of contemporary governments in developing countries: Mobilizing local resources through co-operative self-help, but also promoting national (colonial) development by channeling inputs and credit and siphoning local produce for national and international marketing (→ *Policies for Promotion*). In some countries, the causes of co-operative failure definitely could not be blamed on laissez-faire and lack of administrative creativity, a case in point being British Burma, where the main pioneer co-operative movements from Europe have been given a try, starting with → *Schultze-Delitzsch*, followed by → *Raiffeisen*, and only to be superseded by *Luzzati*, all co-operative types characterized by a lack of commercial success. But compared to government involvement in co-operative scheming and projecting since independence, and measured against objective needs for external promotional help, it seems fair to conclude that colonial administrators tended more to an underpromotion of co-operative projects.

This neglect of co-operatives during colonialism seems to have been one motive for a more activist, even overpromoting approach since then (mirroring similar shifts in other areas of economic policy: import substitution instead of free trade, industrialization instead of agricultural transformation, etc.). The impressive results of member-controlled co-operatives in Europe and North America and the ideological and political attractiveness of the co-operative model as a "third" – progressive – "way"(→ *"Third Way"*) between capitalism and socialism created a strong inclination of post-independence governments to use co-operatives as an integral instrument for national development policy. Unfortunately, the favorable experience with co-operatives in the industrialized countries could not be repeated in the Third World.

A systematic and comprehensive analysis of the causes of the generally poor performance of co-operatives in developing countries is not provided here, but an overview of the more pervasive difficulties and possible solutions will be given.

II. Conceptional Framework

People are attracted to co-operatives because they expect a better satisfaction of their needs; governments make use of co-operatives in order to better achieve their own goals or to indirectly promote the welfare of beneficiary groups – by assisting co-operatives.

For a government to make a rational and controlled use of co-operatives in strategies and programs of development, a conceptional framework linking its co-operative activities to the ultimate policy targets will be necessary (see *figure*).

First: What are the "causes" of the problems addressed or the difficulties to be overcome (low income, insufficient employment, fluctuating prices, poverty, lack of access to market, etc.)?

Second: Can co-operatives influence the "causes" of the respective problems? If co-operatives cannot influence the magnitudes of the variables ("causes") – responsible for the problems (e.g. poverty) – they cannot be used as institutions (agencies) for promoting the members/target groups. With what kind of co-operative or with what type of co-operative activity (credit supply, provisions of inputs, etc.) can co-operatives – potentially – affect the causes of the problems? Fortunately, we know a lot about these cause-effect relationship (linkage 1).

Third: Our knowledge – theoretical, empirical, practical – will be much more limited, if we move to the crucial third linkage. Under what conditions do co-operatives have a *comparative* advantage in providing those services/activities, on which the solution of the problems depends? To answer this question, we would have to look into the "causes" of the comparative performance of co-operatives. If we do not have adequate knowledge about the factors on which comparative co-operative advantages and, respectively, successful performance depends, any outside intervention, promotion and guidance on behalf of co-operatives will be severely limited, and consequently: the *direct* use of co-operatives in development policy would be severely handicapped.

```
(1)         Policy targets
                ↑
         Performance of co-operatives concerning incomes,
         employment, poverty reduction etc.
                ↑
(2)           CAUSES
                ↑
            Co-operatives
(3)             ↑
             Conditions
(4)             ↑
         Co-operative promoting agencies  } (5b)
(5a)            ↑
         Government policy and strategy
```

Figure: *Causal structure of co-operative policy*

On the other hand, in an *indirect* promotion ("grassroots") approach, or in a strategy of fostering a spontaneous evolution of co-operatives, the double cause-effect-relationships (linkages 1 and 3) will mainly take care of themselves.

In such an indirect and evolutionary policy regime, co-operative development would primarily consist of a discovery process, driven by co-operative entrepreneurs: the relevant knowledge about the cause-effect-relationships would be discovered in the process of co-operative action itself, and it would be limited mostly to those participating in the grassroots-process of co-operative learning and development, thereby not being available for a centralized approach of steering co-operatives according to explicit policy targets.

Fourth: If we know the "causes" of the comparative performance of co-operatives, we can try to link these potential performance conditions with external assistance/promotion and policy measures, aiming at the creation of (or helping in creating) those conditions on which comparative co-operative performance depends. This last linkage can include the strategic steering of co-operative projects by cooperative (self-help) promotion agencies.

Fifth: The last part of the framework consists of causally linking government policy/strategy with either the co-operative promoting agencies (5a: providing financial and other assistance) or to the direct influence of the conditions on which the comparative performance of co-operative depends (5b: e.g. legal framework; subsidies).

Since the strategic paradigm employed by the government influences directly (5b) or indirectly (5a) the space open for co-operative action in realizing developmental objectives, in our framework, government occupies the "highest"level.

In a certain sense, it summarizes and reflects the policies practiced in many developing countries, where the governments act as "top managers" in a linear, rational, analytic "co-operative system", with the results (measured as attainment of the goals) being expected to be proportional to the initial forces (initiating conditions) influenced or created by governmental action.

Unfortunately, since there is no clear way of attributing to co-operatives a specific mission or role in development policy, the situation is much more complicated. The causal framework provided contains black and grey boxes, making the causal framework non-linear and non-deterministic. Therefore, the results of policy action are non-proportional to the magnitude and direction of the initiating forces and hence uncontrollable.

First: We lack a theoretical basis and framework for creating linear (deterministic) causal relationships between co-operatives and the attainment of goals. In other words: causal relationships are non-linear if not even indetermined.

In addition: the specific contribution of co-operatives to development depends on how they are able to move into the "play of action" opened up by their comparative advantage which often is not given or à priori available.

Finally, the specific contribution of co-operatives depends on the kind and effectiveness of government policy/strategy itself, especially concerning the creation of property rights and incentives for co-operative entrepreneurs, who are the agents of initiating new co-operative activity. Consequently, the possibilities for cooperative action are not given in any objective sense but, rather, strategy-dependent.

Co-operatives can successfully compete with other types of economic organizations (owner-managed firms, partnerships, corporations) when they do have a comparative competitive advantage. But as theoretical and empirical analysis indicates, co-operative institutions seem to possess such net advantages only under very specific conditions, which – unfortunately for policy-makers – are difficult to discover and to implement.

Given the experience with regard to co-operative development and given our theoretical knowledge concerning the comparative advantage of co-operative institutions, we can conjecture that the potential contributions of co-operatives to economic development have probably been "oversold". Even in developed countries with a strong co-operative sector, the co-operative contribution to Gross Domestic Product is well below 10 per cent. Why is it, that not more economic transactions are governed by co-operatives? Or to paraphrase a famous question of *Ronald Coase*: Why is not all production carried out by co-operatives?

In development policy, the causes of comparative co-operative underperformance are rarely acknowledged. The superiority of co-operative institutions is deduced – if not directly from ideological and essentialistic premises – by comparing an ideally functioning co-operative with an imperfectly working real market economy.

In order to survive in a competitive economy, a co-operative must supply goods/services at conditions comparable to or better than those of other forms of organization and still cover costs (→ *Competition*). If co-operatives are seen as objects and instruments of development policy, the question has to be answered, why and how cooperative organizations can survive side by side with competing forms of organizations. Sadly, this answer is not available, if we exclude reasons irrelevant from a comparative advantage view as co-operative survival because of privileges of the state, such as favourable tax treatment.

In his famous article on "The nature of the firm" *Coase* argued that the equilibrium size of an economic organization is indeterminate when the cost of transacting (as opposed to transformation) is zero.

Consequently, transaction costs (including costs of obtaining information, monitoring behavior, recompensing middlemen, and enforcing contract) must be an important variable in explaining the variation in economic organization (*Williamson*). Others have applied transaction-cost-economics to co-operatives (*Baldus et al; Bonus*) and found conventional arguments (economies of scale; monopolized market structure; etc.) unconvincing (→ *Institutional Economics*). If we allow for uncertainty, asymmetrical information, and mutual dependency, additional comparative advantages of co-operative structures can theoretically be created, leading to more complex arguments, which by no means are exhausting all possibilities for explaining the comparative advantage of co-operative organizations.

Whatever may be the merits of the new insights concerning the relative advantage of each type of organization, they corroborate the conjecture that cooperative structures are able to function effectively and efficiently only under very specific internal and external conditions, about whose precise "local" existence we do not know very much.

III. Co-operative Entrepreneurship and Its Stimulation

We can offer only one solution to this policy challenge: enter cooperative agents, so-called entrepreneurs as "gap fillers", knowledge creators and opportunity implementors. Their primary function consists of discovering and implementing co-operative opportunities: the entrepreneur has to discover, whether in a specific location a co-operative does have a comparative advantage, based on some of the factors scientists have detected so far – as transaction costs – or on unnoticed causes.

Therefore, co-operative entrepreneurial action together with the resulting development and diffusion of co-operatives has to be considered as a process of discovering opportunities and learning to implement these effectively and efficiently.

The necessity to focus on co-operative entrepreneurship will require a restructuring of the cognitive field of policy makers, and a shift in the paradigm, strategy, and content of development policy concerning co-operatives and the contributions co-operatives can make to attain developmental objectives. New evolutionary pathways must be encouraged in order to make fuller use of co-operative structures in development policy.

In a static competitive economy with full information and no transaction costs, there is no need for localized initiative or for a co-operative entrepreneur. Consequently, entrepreneurial action could be erased from the political economy of co-operatives. The management literature on co-operatives – by dedicating itself mainly to the routine management of cooperative affairs – has similarly banished *intra-preneurial* action from its reasoning and policy prescriptions.

From this entrepreneurless paradigm was derived the belief that "blue print" or "top-down" invigoration of decision makers was not only feasible, but could produce better results even quicker than a patient "bottom-up" building of the co-operative framework, the phases of which can be sketched as follows: In co-operative development, it is useful to distinguish between three stages of a "learning process", each of which emphasizing a different learning task (*Korten*). In the first stage, the goal is "effectiveness" ("doing the right things") in assisting (promoting) the members. The main challenge will be to discover a comparative advantage (opportunity recognition), and then establish the organization for implementing the opportunity. At the heart of this process is the cooperative entrepreneur. Since initially, the level of knowledge is low and ignorance high, a lot of mistakes will be made until an effective co-operative program has been discovered. To provide the co-operative entrepreneur with information and feedback a high level of member participation will be required. If the stage of learning to be effective is managed "top-down", we can derive the theoretical conclusion vindicated by rich experience from the Third World, that co-operatives of this type have immense difficulties in competition and in promoting their members effectively: the process of co-operative search, discovery, and learning will be handicapped by technocratic management and bureaucratic regulation.

Bureaucratic entrepreneurs are oriented towards the political and administrative centre – to comply with development targets, to satisfy their superiors, to lobby for and be alert for personal gains that come with the implementation of development programmes.

Learning to be effective, requires freedom to experiment, to make mistakes. Co-operative entrepreneurs must be able to act without regulative constraints and bureaucratic control. The → *officialization* of cooperatives does not fit with the requirements of localized co-operative initiative under conditions of dispersed knowledge.

If effectiveness has sufficiently been established and the proper channel for promoting the members has been set up, the focus of co-operative entrepreneurship shifts on to *achieving efficiency* ("doing things right"). By now, uncertainty and complexity will have sufficiently been reduced; it becomes feasible to find out how the resources available can be used more efficiently.

Finally, in the third stage of *learning to expand*, the focus of co-operative development can shift to giving more members the effective and efficiently produced co-operative opportunity, to set up co-operative "branches" in similar situations.

A Schumpeterian approach to co-operative development (→ *Classic/Neo-classic Contributions*) does not imply a laissez-faire attitude to co-operatives, but a strategic shift to the promotion of cooperative entrepreneurship, especially during the initial phase of learning to become effective. The theoretical logic is similar to but not identical with the well-known argument concerning "infant industry protection".

From the co-operatives' perspective, the reasons for insufficient co-operative entrepreneurship resulting in an underperformance of the cooperative sector (not only in developing countries) can be external and internal ones. Laws, regulations, socio-cultural constraints, and ill-designed and -implemented intervention may discriminate against and demotivate co-operative entrepreneurs.

Focusing on the internal factors, co-operative organizations are characterized by a far-reaching difficulty – a kind of entrepreneurial *incentive failure* (→ *Incentives*), which cannot be addressed properly by conventional policy prescriptions. Because of their peculiar construction and property rights structure (identity of owners of the enterprise and users of the services), co-operatives face serious handicaps to attract and reward entrepreneurs.

A co-operative entrepreneur creates wealth (net benefits, welfare) mainly not for himself but for others, a fact setting him apart from conventional entrepreneurship: benefits which accrue to the co-operative entrepreneur himself (a), benefits which are appropriated by the present members (b), advantages for new (potential) members (c) and advantages which are external to the co-operative (d: non-members, the general public).

As seen from the co-operative entrepreneur, the advantages b, c and d are *external* beneficial consequences of his own action, reducing the net benefits available to him.

In addition, the co-operative's residual income, the

sum that remains when those resource-owners with fixed pay-off contracts have been paid, is appropriated by the member-owners. Thus we expect a co-operative entrepreneur to produce a "public good" (→ *Goods*).

If the net benefits produced by the entrepreneurs are indeed fully internalized by the co-operative (if benefit d = 0), the traditional infant co-operative argument for protection/promotion becomes invalid.

Nevertheless, *within* the co-operative, external net benefits of entrepreneurial action will exist. Because of the co-operative property rights structure (identity of owners and users), the members have an interest to maximize these external benefits on behalf of themselves, thereby reducing the probability that any co-operative entrepreneur would be willing to provide those co-operative public goods, in which the members so freely participate.

Historically, various patterns of co-operative entrepreneurship have evolved to overcome incentive failure. Co-operatives have been externally promoted (by bureaucratic and catalytic entrepreneurship), or they have emerged spontaneously out of the actions of their own members or managers. The latter types (member- and manager-entrepreneurs) can derive adequate entrepreneurial rewards by trying to capture part of the benefits which otherwise might be available to the members. In this way, a reduction of incentive failure may be possible but negative consequences of such *self-initiating* co-operatives – widely documented in literature (*Unrisd; Sira and Craig; Attwood and Baviskar*) have to be considered:

- a more unequal distribution of benefits,
- a lower level of member participation, even disintegration of the co-operative,
- rent seeking, corruption and looting of the co-operative.

Under conditions of highly uncertain benefits and costs, i.e. in the crucial experimental and pilot phase of learning to become effective, a substantial financial contribution of the potential beneficiaries (the members) cannot be expected.

To overcome internal entrepreneurial difficulties, external assistance/promotion is economically justified (infant co-operative promotion), either in the form of bureaucratic or catalytic entrepreneurship.

Bureaucratic entrepreneurs, sponsored by the government or quasi-officialized institutions, may indeed overcome the problems of underpromotion and underinvestment in co-operative ventures. Unfortunately, this can only be done at the expense of creating new difficulties: restriction of local entrepreneurial freedom to take initiatives, localized experimentation, flexibility, and member participation, instrumentalization of co-operatives for state (official) goals, leading to a low level of effectiveness and efficiency, tending to be overcome by additional doses of financial assistance, provision of monopoly rights, privileges, leading to an overpromotion and a collapse of self-help promotion. That is, new interventions are needed to cope with second, third etc. generation problems caused by the original, blue-printed program.

To overcome the difficulties of incentive failure and bureaucratic promotion, catalytic entrepreneurs try to promote co-operatives outside conventional bureaucratic channels. In addition, the local co-operatives initiated by catalysts remain autonomous, self-organizing structures.

The catalytic approach to co-operative development implies that co-operatives, to a limited extent, can be used only for the fulfillment of governmental goals. Government policy concerning co-operatives shifts from direct intervention and promotion of state goals within a framework of control-oriented planning and management procedures to indirect assistance and promotion of member goals: creating better conditions for the supply and motivation of catalytic entrepreneurs, creating and securing the autonomy of co-operatives, and fostering responsiveness to the inevitable and sometimes irreducible uncertainty and complexity inherent to co-operative development.

The government could, of course, try to implement its priorities by manipulating the catalytic promotion agencies: the rebirth of the blueprint approach at a higher level.

But since no optimal way has been discovered so far, to assist and promote cooperatives and co-operative entrepreneurship, such a strategy would in the end be self-defeating. Any wise government may well restrict itself to sponsoring the competition of approaches to cooperative development, thereby equipping co-operative policy with the *evolutionary* dynamics lacking so far.

What actually works, cannot be invented, designed and synoptically engineered at the armchair, but rather has to be discovered by trial and error, by doing, by entrepreneurial initiative. Because so many factors are involved, nothing but *competing approaches* have any chance to discover effective solutions. No "master theory" being available, we have to rely on the "micro-theories" of competing agencies and co-operative (catalytic) entrepreneurs.

The evolution of a more effective co-operative strategy, and consequently, the effective use of co-operatives in development policy is possible only when suitable strategic variation and selective pressure exists to choose among the most promising (effective and efficient) variants. The vigour of competition between catalytic agencies, and implicitly, their promotion strategies will be essential to co-operative success and, in the long run, will determine the contribution of co-operatives to economic development.

Co-operatives may very well possess a greater potential than is reflected in their meagre actual contributions to the creation of national income and wealth. Since to policy makers (linkage 4) neither the conditions for co-operative success (linkage 3) nor a best way to promote/assist co-operative ventures via promoting agencies is available, the conventional method to realize the co-operative potential via an activist, blueprint, synoptic approach, runs a high risk of failure.

This knowledge can only be created by and, therefore is, the *result* of a competitive-evolutionary process of discovery and institution building and unavailable for top-down invigoration by decision-makers.

A policy of top-down intervention needs to simulate co-operative entrepreneurship sucessfully, to create participatory feedback mechanisms at all levels of the intervention hierarchy, and it requires a high level of intervention competencies (beginning with the acceptance of appropriate ethical-cultural norms up to professional expertise), conditions usually absent in developing countries.

Given these requirements, widespread failure of co-operative based development initiatives and disillusionment with "modern" co-operatives in general will be the predicted outcome. Thus, to realize the potential of co-operatives in development policy, requires a strategic shift in co-operative policy:

- government policy targeting via co-operatives has to give way to member promotion;
- indiscriminate assistance has to be replaced by selective intervention within a policy environment of decentralized co-operative competition and co-operative promotion strategies;
- instead of wholesale, indiscriminate promotion of the co-operative sector, co-operative entrepreneurship has to be nurtured, special emphasis given to catalytic ventures.

Bibliography

Attwood, Donald.W./Baviskar, R.S.(eds.): Who Shares? Co-operatives and Rural Development, Delhi 1988.
Baldus, Rolf D./ Röpke, Jochen/ Semmelroth, Dieter: Einkommens-, Verteilungs- und Beschäftigungswirkungen von Selbsthilfeorganisationen in Entwicklungsländern, Köln 1981.
Bonus, Holger: The Cooperative Association as a Business Enterprise, Journal of Institutional and Theoretical Economics, vol. 142 (1986), pp. 310–339.
Korten, David C.: Community Organization and Rural Development: A Learning Process Approach, Public Administration Review, vol. 40 (1980), pp. 480–511.
Münkner, Hans-H.: Die Rolle der staatlichen Entwicklungsbürokratie bei der Förderung von Selbsthilfeorganisationen, Rabel Zeitschrift, Tübingen, 1980, pp. 17–40.
Röpke, Jochen: Cooperative Entrepreneurship. Entrepreneurial Dynamics and their Promotion in Self-help Organizations, Marburg 1992.
Rondinelli, Dennis A.: Development Projects as Policy Experiments. An Adaptive Approach to Development Administration, London and New York 1983.
Sira, F.N./ Craig, J.G.: Dilemmas in Cooperative Development in Third World Countries, Annals of Public and Co-operative Economics, vol. 60 (1989), pp. 229–249.

UNRISD (ed.): Rural Institutions and Planned Change, vol. I – VIII, Geneva 1969–75.
Uphoff, Norman: Local Institutional Development: An Analytical Sourcebook with Cases, West Hartford, Conn. 1986.
Williamson, Oliver E.: The Economic Institutions of Capitalism, New York 1985.

Discriminatory Analysis Procedures for Corporate Assessment

JÖRG BAETGE/MARKUS FEIDICKER [J]

(see also: *Early Warning Systems*; *Accounting*; *Financial Accounting Law*; *Auditing*)

I. Objective of Analysis: Indication of Financial Standing on the Balance Sheet; II. Analyses of Financial Statements using Multivariate Discriminatory Analysis; III. Application of Multivariate Discriminatory Analysis in Theory and Practice; IV. The Opportunities and Limitations of the Application of the Discriminatory Analysis Procedure to Appraise Companies.

I. Objective of Analysis: Indication of Financial Standing on the Balance Sheet

The number of corporate failures dropped slightly around the end of the 1980s, but they, nevertheless, still cause billions of marks worth of damage. Because of this fact it remains necessary for all market participants *to identify corporate crises as early as possible*. The primary objective is the appraisal of short and long-term solvency for those companies under scrutiny. The careful analysis of a company's financial standing is above all necessary from the vantage point of creditors in order for them to calculate the risk tied to their credit involvement. The warning of an impending corporate crisis must occur at such an early stage that the endangerment of creditors' capital employment can be prevented through appropriate measures (→ *Early Warning Systems*). Alongside the *economic situation as a whole*, *relationships within particular branches*, *specific market conditions* as well as the *products*, the *management* and the *breakdown of functions* within the company under appraisal, the financial statement constitutes an essential source of information in the process of data acquisition. Inasmuch as we only choose to address the corporate analysis, the following treatise is limited to the analysis of the financial statement and thus the *financial standing as indicated on a company's balance sheet*.

The *early identification of corporate crises* is one of the most responsible and yet difficult functions for balance sheet analysts as they find themselves facing a dilemma. If the financial standing of a company is either prematurely or (eventually) unjustifiably classified as "critical", the danger arises on the one hand of a self-fulfilling prophecy. On the other hand, creditors can hardly avoid losses when the analyst gives either no warning signal or one too late despite the presence of a grave crisis.

Balance sheet analysts can only solve this problem when early warning of a crisis is not solely based on subjective assumptions but rather can be grounded on objective, i.e. intersubjectively verifiable facts. An objective indicator is sought which can provide timely warning signals; it must indicate the *short-term solvency* of a company and render an appraisal of the *enduring situation of results (Heno)*. The *enduring attainment of results* is the future precondition for the company to render interest and redemption payments as stipulated. At the same time an indicator gained from the financial statement should objectify, facilitate and rationalize the credit investigation process.

II. Analyses of Financial Statements using Multivariate Discriminatory Analysis

1. Shortcomings of Traditional Financial Statement Analysis

The declarative potential of financial statement analyses with respect to corporate appraisals is restricted through a number of factors. The financial statement can *only provide quantitative information* about *previous accounting periods* (→ *Financing*). The information in financial statements is only conditionally useful for a liquidity analysis in the first place because it is *chronologically restricted to earnings and expenses* provided in the financial statement, i.e. these must be recalculated as revenue and expenditures (→ *Accounting*). Secondly, the financial statement is often only *available for analysis months after the balance sheet date*. Furthermore, varying approaches as well as evaluation and reporting rights of choice open to discretion create *leeway in balance sheet policy* which complicates insight into to the actual net worth position and the financial and revenue situations of the company. Every analyst must be aware of these short-comings. Nevertheless, financial statements clearly illustrate persistent negative development in the scope of a company's stability, that is its net worth and financial and revenue situations in the course of time. A downward trend in the course of time associated with negative corporate developments is always evident as the reserves accumulated in the good years are consumed; an intentional positive presentation of the economic situation is no longer possible through the appropriation of hidden reserves.

In the previous attempts to identify negative corporate developments at an early point in time on the basis of a single company's financial statements, in other words using traditional financial statement analysis, the analyst was not able to provide reliable answers to the following questions:

1) Which of the numerous feasible ratios actually indicate negative corporate development in an empirically dependable manner?
2) How many of these dependable ratios need to be taken into account in order to draw an appraisal?
3) How should contradicting assessments about one company based on multiple ratio analysis be handled?
4) How can dependable, indicative ratios be consolidated into one non-contradicting indicator of the economic situation?
5) At which value should such an indicator sound the alarm for a potential endangerment of the company?

It is impossible to answer these five questions using traditional financial statement analysis as such a method lacks the capacity to resolve contradictions. These questions can only be answered objectively using statistical methods and through the analysis of financial statements from numerous healthy as well as ailing companies.

2. The Procedure of Statistical Financial Statement Analysis

The objective of financial statement analysis is the clearest possible differentiation of companies into two groups, namely *healthy* and *ailing* companies. For such an undertaking one requires a statistically representative number of financial statements from healthy and ailing companies. From this mass of data the most significant distinguishing characteristics (ratios) between these two groups are formed, consolidated and weighted in such a manner that the companies to be classified can clearly be assigned to one group or the other. Other companies in the future can be analyzed and assigned to these two groups using the cutoff criteria gained through this method.

One can differentiate between *univariate* and *multivariate discriminatory analysis* according to whether the statistical analysis of the financial statements is pursued with one or with several ratios simultaneously. The linear form of the discriminatory function proves in the case of multivariate analysis to be more accurate than the quadratic discriminatory function when companies are to be classified which were not included in the sample used to calculate the function. Because of this reason, *linear multivariate discriminatory analysis* was used in the majority of investigative studies, and we will restrict our presentation to this subject. This function form in addition avails itself to a particularly graphic interpretation of results, a factor which increases its acceptance in practical application. Such a linear discriminatory function can in general be expressed as follows:

$$D = -a_0 + a_1 * X_1 + a_2 * X_2 + ... + a_z * X_z$$

In this function the most discriminating ratios X_1 through X_z are multiplied with their respective weights a_1 through a_z. The sum of these weighted ratios and the absolute term a_0 amount to the discriminatory value D with which a company can be classified. The graphic determination of this function can be illustrated using two ratios in the following graph: In *Diagram 1* the values of twelve healthy (H) and twelve ailing (A) companies are plotted for the ratios profitability (X_1) and indebtedness (X_2). If each ratio is observed in isolation, in other words using univariate analysis, the optimal cutoff value would be approx. 5% for the profitability ratio and approx. 60% for the indebtedness ratio; using these values the number of incorrectly classifed cases is thereby kept to a minimum. With univariate analysis of the *profitability* criterion which is higher for healthy companies (H) than for ailing companies (A) according to our hypothesis, four ailing and four healthy companies would be incorrectly classified using the proposed 5% cutoff margin. The second univariate separation of the 24 companies under investigation with the ratio *percentage of indebtedness* results in X_2. For this calculation the hypothesis is pursued that healthy companies (H) have a lower *indebtedness* than ailing companies (A). In this case, using the proposed 60% cutoff margin three companies are incorrectly classified in each of the two categories.

Neither of the two ratios alone provides for a sufficiently precise separation between the two groups of companies because the area of overlap between the ratio distributions is quite large. Aside from this, one acquires *contradictory statements* for all companies above and to the right of the dotted demarcation lines as well as below and to the left of them: according to one ratio these are healthy companies, but according to the other they are classified as ailing. This is illustrated by the actually ailing company U which is classified as healthy with a 50% rate of indebtedness and simultaneously as ailing with a 2% rate of profitability.

A bivariate discriminatory analysis of the 24 companies is undertaken in *Figure 1* alongside the two univariate analyses. The result of the analysis shows the bivariate discriminatory function D, which is composed of the ratios "indebtedness" and "profitability", and indicates the respective bivariate demarcation line. With the help of the *bivariate discriminatory analysis* both ratios are weighted and consolidated in such a manner that the determined crisis warning value D with its respective demarcation line can much more satisfactorily differentiate than the two

Explanation:
- • = Ailing Company (A)
- □ = Healthy Company (H)

Bivariate Discriminatory Function:
$D = -a_0 + a_1 \cdot X_1 - a_2 \cdot X_2$

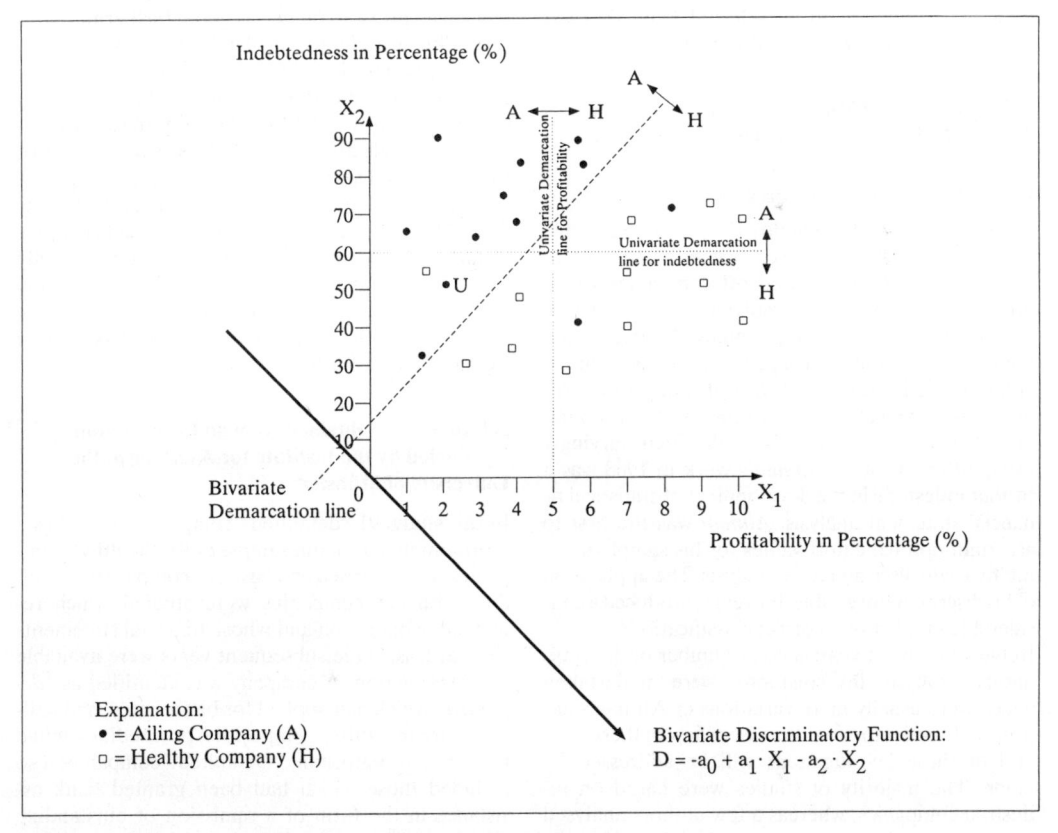

Figure 1: Determination and Presentation of the Discriminatory Function

calculated univariate demarcation lines; above all it can differentiate without producing contradictory statements. Company U which is truly ailing lies to the left of the diagonal demarcation line. The number of incorrect classifications also is considerably reduced in comparison with the univariate analysis. Only one healthy and two ailing companies are incorrectly classified.

Through bivariate discriminatory analysis the two ratios "profitability" and "indebtedness" are weighted in such a manner that the total classification error is considerably reduced. This means for example that a company with a low profitability is not considered in danger when its level of indebtedness is correspondingly low, or in other words when it has sufficient equity capital to cover future losses which it eventually may incur. On the other hand, a company with high profitability is not classified as "healthy" when its indebtedness is too high. Such a company is not soundly financed and would quickly fall into the red on account of interest payments if the economic cycle slowed or when the branch-specific situation deteriorated (leverage risk).

Discriminatory analysis does not always only weight and aggregate two ratios as in the bivariate case illustrated above. The *multivariate procedure* rather provides for those ratios which together can provide thorough distinction to be selected from the vast number of possible ratios, and weighted.

III. Application of Multivariate Discriminatory Analysis in Theory and Practice

1. Development up to the Present

Beaver was the first to employ the procedure of discriminatory analysis for the early identification of insolvency in 1966. He paired off companies which proved to be solvent and insolvent in the course of time, compared their average values and ascertained the univariate ratios which provided the best differentiation for his sample. *Beaver* also faced the problem when applying various ratios on actual companies that a company could be classified varyingly using different ratios. *Altman*'s work in 1968 was a further milestone in the development of statistical financial statement analysis. *Altman* was the first to ascertain optimal cutoff values for his sample using multivariate discriminatory analysis. The application of his discriminatory value, however, produced a considerable number of incorrect classifications.

In the subsequent years a great number of discriminatory analysis investigations were undertaken which were usually mere variations of Altman's approach. In order to provide an overview of these, several of these investigations will be addressed by name. The majority of studies were based on industrial companies, whereas a few authors analysed various branches, e.g. banks (*Sinkey, Martin,* *Dhanani*), third party property risk insurers (*Barniv*), brokerage firms (*Altman/Loris*) or small-scale companies (*Edminster*). Discriminatory analysis procedures for the early identification of corporate crises were also employed outside of the United States, e.g. in Germany (*v.Stein, Thomas, Gebhardt, Lüneborg, Niehaus*), in Austria (*Bleier*), Switzerland (*Weibel*), England (*Taffler*), the Netherlands (*Bilderbeeck*), or in France (*Altman*, among others).

Several investigations endeavored not only to identify corporate risks at an early stage but also analysed the influence of inflation (*Alwabil*) or the consequences of assessment procedures on the prognostic capacity of ratios (*Elam, Aly*). Other models strove to predict industrial bond ratings (*Pinches/Mingo, Chen/Shimerda*), the performance level of credit investigators compared to multivariate discriminatory analysis results (*File*) or the declarative content of quarterly balance sheets (*Baldwin*). Alongside the various parametric discriminatory analyses, other non-parametric procedures were also tested in part (*Weinrich, Bilderbeeck, Gebhardt, Lüneborg, Niehaus*). Attempts were also undertaken using logit and probit analyses to improve results (*Martin, Ohlson, Zavgren, Gentry/Newbold/Whitford*). Linear multivariate discriminatory analysis has nonetheless produced classification results up through the present day which prove to be just as good; furthermore this procedure is easier to calculate (*Zavgren*).

The results of the individual studies are not presented in this treatise (c.f. *Rösler*) because they are hardly comparable with each other. The differences with respect to the selection of ratios, the size of the sample, the source and structure of the data and the procedure for estimating errors are often considerable. The following discussion therefore presents the procedural method and results of an empirical study which was conducted in the scope of a cooperation undertaken between the Institute for Auditing in Münster and the Bayerische Vereinsbank AG in Munich (*Baetge/Huß/Niehaus*).

2. Experience Obtained from an Investigation Conducted by the Institute for Auditing at the University of Münster

In this study, 91 "defaulted" companies as well as a representative random sample of 91 "healthy" companies were assessed as a basis for comparison; in addition further companies were studied which remained in operation and whose financial statements from at least three subsequent years were available for investigation. A company was identified as "*defaulted*" which had applied for bankruptcy, had petitioned for instituting composition proceedings or had filed for a moratorium. "Defaulted" companies also included those which had been granted bank assistance in the form of a remission of outstanding claims or similar waivers or for which the bank had undertaken itemized allowances for bad debts (*Niehaus*). The most recent of the financial statements drawn by the defaulted (ailing) companies and included in the analysis dated between 7 and 18 months prior to the date of the default.

The *working hypothesis* of either A > H or A < H was formulated for each of the 42 ratios analysed in the study. The hypothesis A < H with respect to the profitability ratio, for example, signifies that the average values of the ratios from the defaulted companies (A) in average are smaller than the average of the ratio values from the healthy companies (H). Not all of these ratios are, however, equally suitable for the credit investigation of companies. The objective of this project was to ascertain which ratios indicate the most dissimilar characteristics for healthy and ailing companies and to consolidate them into a crisis indicator. Because we wanted to calculate and employ only one discriminatory function for the point in time three years prior to insolvency which likewise should reliably distinguish between ailing and healthy companies both one and two years prior to the default, the working hypothesis needed to prove itself for each discriminating ratio every year prior to the default. If the working hypothesis of a ratio's average value in one particular year could be falsified it had to be excluded from the group of empirically usable ratios. If this were not the case it would generate a positive response in the discriminatory function for group differentiation in one year and a negative response another year, thus increasing the number of incorrect classifications.

We tested the working hypotheses in a *comparison of ratios' average values* from healthy and defaulted companies in a three-year period. Several of these ratios had to be excluded from the discriminatory analysis as the comparison of their average values proved the unsuitability of these particular ratios.

The relationships between the ratios were studied using correlation and factor analyses. As a result seven ranked factors could be ascertained, the ratios of which are highly interrelated among each other but which indicate only a slight correlation to the ratios from other factors. These seven factors are: *profitability, financial strength, liquidity, capital structure, equity-to-fixed assets ratio, short-term debt*, and *record of meeting payments*.

In a step-by-step discriminatory analysis all ratios from those factors were systematically excluded which were already represented through other ratios in the function. Through this manner the following ratios were ascertained which differentiate between "healthy" and "endangered" companies and which prove to be particularly declarative in nature:

$$X_1 = \frac{\text{equity capital}}{(\text{balance sheet total}) - (\text{liquid funds}) - (\text{real property})}$$

$$X_2 = \frac{\text{cash flow I}}{\text{balance sheet total}}$$

$$X_3 = \frac{\text{cash flow II}}{\text{short-term borrowed capital}}$$

The quantities "equity capital", "cash flow I" and "cash flow II" are defined as follows:

equity capital =
subscribed capital + reserves + result brought forward + shareholders loans + 50% of special items related to reserves – unpaid subscriptions

cash flow I =
operating result (pre-tax) + ordinary depreciations + allocations to retirement reserves

cash flow II=
cash flow I – operating tax – changes in inventory – other goods and services for own account + financial extraordinary result

The aggregate ratio – the discriminatory value D – is formed from these ratios as illustrated:

$$D = -a_0 + a_1 * X_1 + a_2 * X_2 + a_3 * X_3$$

The coefficients a_1, a_2 and a_3 weight the ratios and result from the multivariate discriminatory analysis. The origin of the discriminatory axes is established as the origin of the coordinate system through the absolute term a_0. The *discriminatory results* attained with this function are provided in *Figure 2* for companies included in the total study, in other words companies not taken into consideration in the sample. These results attest to the high suitability of this procedure to identify corporate crises at an early point in time.

A gray zone was introduced for those companies which could not unequivocally be classified as healthy or ailing using the discriminatory value. Between 82.4% and 89.8% of all companies which actually defaulted were properly identified as ailing in the time frame prior to the default (between one and three years before the default occurred). The relatively high number of incorrect classifications of the actually healthy companies (26.9% to 28.5%) proved not to be a problem as these errors were able to be quickly spotted and clarified in the course of the subsequent audit conducted by the credit specialists at the bank (*Baetge*).

IV. The Opportunities and Limitations of the Application of the Discriminatory Analysis Procedure to Appraise Companies

Although multivariate discriminatory analysis has been successfully applied in Germany for example by the Deutsche Bundesbank (*Thomas*) and the Bayerische Vereinsbank, this procedure faces in part considerable scepticism in day-to-day practical application. Criticism above all is directed at the procedure's lack of a theoretical foundation for the early identification of corporate crises: such identification is not based on a theory of insolvency or of its causes

	Years	Classification as		
		"white" ("healthy")	"grey"	"black" ("ailing")
Classification of defaulted (ailing) companies approx. 500 financial statements p.a.	3 years prior to default	7.3%	10.3%	82.4%
	2 years prior to default	6.6%	9.7%	83.7%
	1 years prior to default	5.3%	4.9%	89.8%
Classification of non-defaulted (healthy) companies approx. 14,500 financial statements p.a.	1981	50.7%	22.4%	26.8%
	1982	51.0%	27.7%	27.3%
	1983	51.9%	21.2%	26.9%
	1984	50.1%	22.5%	27.4%
	1985	48.3%	23.1%	28.5%

Figure 2: Classification Results from Parent Population Data *(Baetge).*

but rather is undertaken in the form of a *black box analysis.* The discriminatory function, nonetheless, contains three ratios; a tested working hypothesis lies at the root of each one of these, and each has been successfully used both in managerial theory and in practical application.

The procedure furthermore exhibits certain advantages which cannot be achieved through traditional methods. The crisis indicator ascertained using multivariate discriminatory analysis enables one to rank a company as healthy, as "gray" or as endangered. Contradicting statements like the ones raised in the course of traditional financial statement analysis are precluded in this procedure. The balance sheet analyst can manage in multivariate discriminatory analysis without needing to weight subjectively partial findings which are based on individual ratios and under certain circumstances prove to be quite divergent. The allround assessment is intersubjectively verifiable through the evaluation of a wide empirical basis and thus is objective.

Discriminatory analysis is therefore most suitable as a *rationalization instrument* for institutions which must evaluate scores of financial statements every day. Those companies which can clearly be identified as healthy require hardly any further analysis. Those companies identified as ailing on the other hand necessitate *supplemental audits* as the incomplete data on the financial reports as a rule do not provide for more extensive investigation into the causes of a corporate crisis. The assessment of a company based on discriminatory analysis therefore must not be seen as a comprehensive and exclusive instrument of analysis but rather as the *first step in corporate analysis.* In order for a bank to work with a concrete discriminatory function for its corporate clients, it usually needs to *calculate its own function on the basis of a representative sample of its own corporate clients.* Results from other studies can namely only then be transposed when their underlying bases as a whole have similar structures.

Discriminatory analysis must not be misunderstood as an instrument to forecast corporate insolvency. It must solely be used as an objective basis to provide early warning of negative corporate developments in order that promising countermeasures can be undertaken to prevent corporate insolvency (*Baetge*).

Bibliography

Altman, Edward I.: Financial Ratios, Discriminant Analysis and the Prediction of Corporate Bankruptcy. In: The Journal of Finance, vol.23, pp. 589–609, New York 1968.

Altman, Edward I.: Corporate Financial Distress, New York etc. 1983.

Altman, Edward I. et al: Financial and Satistical Analysis for Commercial Loan Evaluation, A French Experience. In: Journal of Financial and Quantitative Analysis, vol.9, pp. 195-211, Seattle 1974.

Altman, Edward I./Loris, Bettina: A Financial Early Warning System for Over-The-Counter Broker-Dealers. In: The Journal of Finance, vol.32, pp. 875–900, New York 1977.

Alwabil, Wabil Ali: The Effect of Inflation on the Predictive Ability of Financial Ratios, diss., Columbia 1983.

Aly, Ibrahim M. Mohamed: Prediction of Business Failure as a Criteria for Evaluating the Usefulness of Alternative Accounting Measures, diss., Denton 1986.

Baetge, Jörg: Möglichkeiten der Früherkennung negativer Unternehmensentwicklungen mit Hilfe statistischer Jahresabschlußanalysen. In: Zeitschrift für betriebswirtschaftliche Forschung, vol.41, pp. 792-810, Düsseldorf/Frankfurt am Main 1989.

Baetge, Jörg/Huß, Michael/Niehaus, Hans-Jürgen: Die statistische Auswertung von Jahresabschlüssen zur Informationsgewinnung bei der Abschlußprüfung. In: Die Wirtschaftsprüfung, vol.39, pp. 605-613, 1986.

Baetge, Jörg/Huß, Michael/Niehaus, Hans-Jürgen: The Use of Statistical Analysis to identify the Financial Strength of Corporations in Germany, Studies in Banking and Finance, vol.7, pp. 183-196, North-Holland 1988.

Baldwin, Jane Nora: Bankruptcy Prediction Using Quarterly Financial Statements Data, diss., Arkansas 1986.

Bar-Niv, Ran: Insolvency Prediction for Property-Liability Insurers, New Statistical Measures and the Effects of Alternative Accounting Practices, diss., Ohio 1983.

Beaver, William, H.: Financial Ratios as Predictors of Failure, Empirical Research in Accounting, Selected Studies, Supplement to Journal of Accounting Research, vol.4, pp. 71-111, Chicago 1966.

Bilderbeeck, Jan: An Empirical Study of the Predictive Ability of Financial Ratios in The Netherlands. In: Zeitschrift

für Betriebswirtschaft, vol.49, pp. 388–407, Wiesbaden 1979.
Bleier, Ernst: Unternehmensanalyse aus dem Jahresabschluß, Wien 1989.
Chen K. H./Shimerda, T. A.: An Empirical Analysis of Useful Financial Ratios. In: Financial Management, pp. 51–60, Albany, Spring 1981.
Dhanani, Karim A.: An Empirical Study of Financially Distressed Commmercial Banks: A Discriminant Model for Predicting Future Bank Failures, diss., Louisiana 1986.
Edmister, Robert: An Empirical Test of Financial Ratio Analysis for Small Business Failure Prediction. In: Journal of Financial and Quantitative Analysis, vol.7, pp. 1477–1493, Seattle 1972.
Elam, Rick: The Effect of Lease Data on Predictive Ability of Financial Ratios. In: The Accounting Review, vol. 55, pp. 25–43, Sarasota 1975.
File, Richard Garrison: Auditor Prediction of Client Firm Failure, diss., Austin 1981.
Gebhardt, Günther: Insolvenzprognosen aus aktienrechtlichen Jahresabschlüssen, Wiesbaden 1980.
Gentry, James A./Newbold, Paul/Whitford, David, T.: Classifying Bankrupt Firms with Funds Flow Components. In: Journal of Accounting Research, vol.23, pp. 146–160, Chicago 1985.
Heno, Rudolf: Kreditwürdigkeitsprüfung mit Hilfe von Verfahren der Mustererkennung, Bern/Stuttgart 1983.
Keysberg, Gerhard: Die Anwendung der Diskriminanzanalyse zur statistischen Kreditwürdigkeit im Konsumkreditgeschäft, Diss., Münster 1988.
Lüneborg, Konrad: Konstruktion und Tests statistischer Verfahren im Rahmen der Kreditwürdigkeitsüberprüfung anhand der Jahresabschlüsse kleiner und mittlerer Unternehmen, Diss., Bochum 1981.
Martin, Daniel: Early Warnings of Bank Failures. In: Journal of Banking and Finance, vol.1, pp. 249–276, Amsterdam 1977.
Niehaus, Hans-Jürgen: Früherkennung von Unternehmenskrisen, Düsseldorf 1987.
Ohlson, James A.: Financial Ratios and the Probabilistic Prediction of Bankruptcy. In: Journal of Accounting Research, vol.18, pp. 109–131, Chicago 1980.
Pinches, G. E./Mingo, Kent A.: A Multivariate Analysis of Industrial Bond Ratings. In: The Journal of Finance, vol.28, pp. 1–18, New York 1973.
Rösler, Joachim: Entwicklung der statistischen Insolvenzprognose, Krisendiagnose durch Bilanzanalyse, Köln 1988.
Sinkey, Joseph, F. Jr.: A Multivariate Statistical Analysis of the Characteristics of Problem Banks. In: The Journal of Finance, vol.30, pp. 21–36, New York 1975.
Stein, Johann Heinrich von: Zur Weiterentwicklung der Kreditbeurteilung. In: Betriebswirtschaftliche Blätter, vol.33, pp. 218–222, Bonn 1984.
Taffler, Richard I.: Empirical Models for the Monitoring of UK Corporations. In: Journal of Banking and Finance, vol.8. pp. 199–227, Amsterdam 1984.
Thomas, Karl: Erkenntnisse aus dem Jahresabschluß für die Bonität von Wirtschaftsunternehmen, Der Jahresabschluß im Widerstreit von Interessen, Düsseldorf 1983.
Weibel, Peter F.: Die Aussagefähigkeit von Kriterien zur Bonitätsbeurteilung im Kreditgeschäft der Banken, Bern/Stuttgart 1973.
Weinrich, Günter: Kreditwürdigkeitsprognosen, Wiesbaden 1978.
Zavgren, Christine V.: The Prediction of Corporate Failure, The State of the Art. In: Journal of Accounting Literature, vol.2, pp. 1–38, Gainsville 1983.

Diversification Strategies of Co-operatives

AXEL BÄNSCH [F]

(see also: *Marketing*; *Business Policies*; *Goods*; *Marketing Strategies*; *Pricing Policy*; *Strategy Planning*; *Management in Co-operatives*)

I. Introduction; II. Diversification Activity of Marketing Co-operatives; III. Diversification Activity of Purchasing Co-operatives; IV. Summary.

I. Introduction

Co-operatives which wish to diversify and broaden their field of activity by venturing into product and marketing areas which have previously not been part of their service programmes (→ *Marketing*). It is customary to distinguish among horizontal, vertical and lateral diversification.

In the case of horizontal diversification, there occurs an extension of the programme which is related to the existing product-market set-up, either with respect to production (for example, using the same basic materials or the same production process) or with respect to sales (for example, working with the same purchaser group or the same marketing organization).

In the case of vertical diversification there occurs an expansion of the service programme into or out of preceding or succeeding service levels, whereby the difference between vertical diversification and vertical integration lies in the fact that entering into the new service level leads to an activity in new product-market areas.

In the case of lateral diversification, new activities are taken up that vary so much from the traditional programme that no horizontal or vertical relationships to the prevailing product-market set-up any longer exist. The main reasons why co-operatives, as well as other organizations, desire to diversify are presumably to develop further opportunities for growth, to realize synergic effects and/or to disperse risks. These are suitable secondary goals supporting the co-operatives' primary goal of promoting their members' interests (→ *Promotion Mandate*).

II. Diversification Activity of Marketing Co-operatives

The following figure of the possible directions in which the services of marketing co-operatives can flow gives an overall picture of the imaginable approaches to diversification which marketing co-operatives can take up.

If the basis is a marketing co-operative (→ *Marketing*) serving only members, then this co-operative has been selling certain products supplied by its members

on its traditional market, with or without processing (service-flow O). A co-operative of this type possesses the following possibilities for horizontal or lateral diversification: development of new marketing fields through
1) taking up processing the same products as obtained heretofore, or taking up new forms of processing them (horizontal diversification),
2) making full use of the existing needs of members (horizontal diversification),
3) making full use of the potential needs of members (horizontal diversification),
4) taking up business with non-members (horizontal or lateral diversification).
   Vertical diversification is basically possible through
5) acquiring or establishing supplier firms subsidiary to the co-operative (backward diversification),
6) acquiring or establishing marketing firms subsidiary to the co-operative (forward diversification).

1. Diversification through taking up processing or new forms of processing

In this case, the marketing co-operative changes over to processing, or to a new form of processing, the → *goods* and services which have been offered to it by its members thus far, which – by the definition of diversification – gives the co-operative access to a new market. Hereby the co-operative becomes active in a new product-market area in its supportive business, i.e. in corresponding activities which facilitate the purpose of the co-operative, without having to make any changes in its basic-purpose business, i.e. in the activitiy for which the co-operative was originally formed. This type of diversification is in keeping with the primary goal of the co-operative, if the promotion of members' interests can be better secured or enhanced. This seems possible by securing or increasing the proceeds which the co-operative achieves on the supportive business level.

Should there be a stagnation in the traditional market or even a retrogressive market development, then the co-operative acts entirely in the (long-range) interests of its members when it arranges, through appropriate (new) forms of processing, for access to new markets which promise more growth and thereby greater returns. As a practical example, one could mention a potato-marketing co-operative which has hitherto been limited to dealing strictly in potatoes. By processing potatoes into potato-chips or into convenience-food packages of potato-pancake or po-

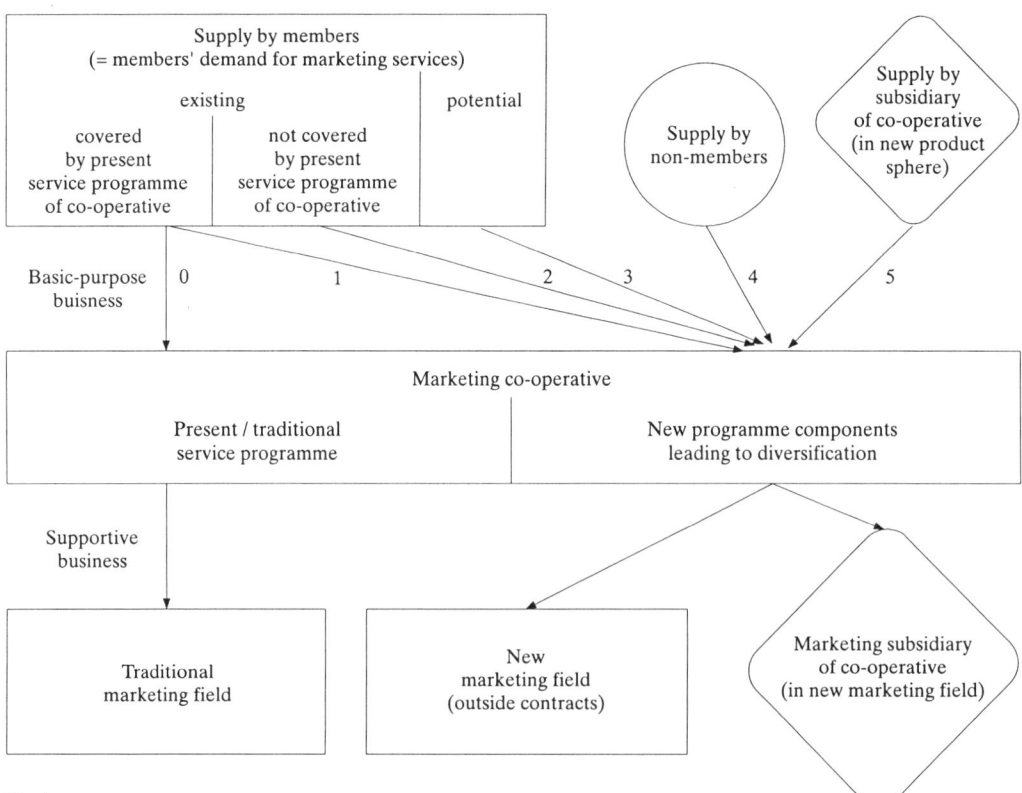

Fig. 1

tato-dumpling mixes, then a diversification could be reached which would open up opportunities for growth, because the processed products mentioned possess a considerably greater elasticity with regard to income changes than the raw product does.

2. Diversification through making full use of the existing needs of members

A further diversification strategy, which is generally directly in keeping with the requirement of the co-operative to promote its members' interests, is open to those marketing co-operatives which have not thus far been able to respond to all aspects of the service needs of their members because of their prevailing service programmes.

It is precisely the exploitation of this opportunity which is nothing new for co-operatives, since every change from a single-purpose to a multiple-purpose co-operative can lead to diversification. In an extreme case, an individual co-operative could try to satisfy all of its members' needs for marketing services, could thereby become active in a variety of marketing fields, and could achieve a high degree of risk dispersement.

However, in practice to try to satisfy all the needs of members is advisable only in extreme cases. The explanation for this lies in the scattering of services and the cost burden which usually results from this attempt, as well as in the diversification risk which stems from the fact that the co-operative scarcely possesses the necessary know-how in all the product-market fields coming into consideration or – for economic reasons – is unable to build up that know-how.

3. Diversification through making full use of the potential needs of members

If in shaping these programmes co-operatives are called upon to react dynamically to changes in the market, it must be born in mind that services which it is possible for co-operatives to render to their members depend to a decisive extent on the services rendered by the members themselves.

If, for example, a co-operative has already exhausted all the possibilities present in the existing needs of members through corresponding new forms of processing, then, if it remains limited to its circle of members, it can undertake (further) diversification only by inducing its members to broaden or restructure their own supply. If the co-operative has received findings of marketing research which indicate chances for growth in certain areas that neither it nor the members have hitherto ventured into, then it is the responsibility of the co-operative to arouse its members' interest in these areas. The co-operative is called upon here to take up new fields of activity in new product-market areas, in order to open up new promotion opportunities for itself and new sources of income for its members. An agricultural marketing co-operative for farm products, for example (→ *Rural Co-operatives*), can persuade its members to make vacation quarters availabe and can market these for its members under the slogan "vacation on a farm". Since with the co-operative concept of the promotion of members' interests it is absolutely in keeping for the co-operative not to wait to take steps until the members themselves first assume the initiative, this diversification strategy is fundamentally in harmony with co-operative goals.

4. Diversification through business with non-members

If a marketing co-operative should find out about the existence of needs in a marketing field which are not yet fulfilled or which could be created, but if the present membership is not, or is not sufficiently, interested in satisfying these needs, then the co-operative should consider working with non-members. There are no complications in the consistence of this approach with the responsibility of the co-operative to further the interests of its members, if by this approach the co-operative attains an immediate increase in memberhsip leading to stabilization or augmentation of its capacity to promote its members' interests, through dispersement of risks and/or utilization of opportunities for growth.

Non-members who are interested in this new service area under consideration by the co-operative may initally hesitate to become members of the co-operative, because they first want to test the possible advantages they derive from this step, without any of the responsibilities inherent in membership (capital investment (→ *Equity Capital*) as well as a possible membership fee and assumption of liability (→ *Nachschußpflicht*). If this is the case, then business dealings of this type with non-members, carried on prior to membership, can also be justified by the responsibility of the co-operative to promote membership interests, because these dealing can eventually lead to gains in membership.

A diversification strategy begun with non-members is only then incompatible with a marketing co-operative's responsibility to its members, if it becomes apparent that this programme strategy can be realized only by dealings with non-members on a permanent basis. Business dealing with non-members on a permanent basis create a foreign element in a joint enterprise oriented to members and are therefore incompatible with a co-operative.

5. Diversification through the establishment of acquisition of supplier firms subsidiary to the co-operative

If a marketing co-operative sets up or buys a supply company subsidiary to the co-operative on the level of the members' own enterprises, then this step is equivalent to backward diversification only if the co-operative thereby obtains access to new product-market areas (→ *Commercial Co-operatives*).

If this backward diversification means that the subsidiary in question channels goods or services to the co-operative which may be new merely for the co-operative market programme, but which are not new as far as the business activity of the members is concerned, then the approach would seem to be a mistake, because an approach of this type leads the co-operative away from its responsibility to serve its members. The co-operative begins to lead a life of its own that way which brings it into competition with its own members. Not only does it thereby cause disagreements with its members, but is also alienates itself from its duty to promote the interests of its members. Instead of this backward-oriented vertical diversification, the co-operative should choose the horizontal diversification approach number 2 mentioned above, that takes up existing needs of members which have not yet been fulfilled by the co-operative marketing programme.

However, a backward diversification can indeed be in conformity with the responsibility of the co-operative, if the reason for adding on a subsidiary supplier firm is to provide members and/or potential members with a model company for learning or for advisory purposes or to prevent the company's falling into the hands of a competitor group. In the latter case, the co-operative must turn around without delay and permit its members or potential members to purchase this company. Thus, if the co-operative acts in keeping with its responsibility toward its members, the backward diversification lasts but a short time and soon merges into a horizontal diversification.

In the former case, in which the reason would be to acquire a model company, the motivation becomes especially important if the programme of the subidiary supplier firm transcends the needs of present and/or potential members. Then the company in question can assume the function of demonstrating new methods, can thereby arouse new needs in the co-operative's members' minds, and can thus introduce and help shore up the approach number 3 mentioned above. For example, if an agricultural marketing co-operative should perceive unsatisfied demands for agricultural products which meet certain dietetic requirements (for instance, for intensively cultivated, unsprayed, naturally fertilized vegetables or fruit) or for fine fish such as carp or trout, then by means of its own experimental company, the co-operative can provide its members and/or potential members with demonstration lessons and can give them incentives and help in initiating their own projects.

6. Diversification through the acquistion of marketing companies subsidiary to the co-operative

Parallel to what has been said thus far about backward diversification, forward diversification depends in an integrated marketing company upon a programme which leads the co-operative into a new product-market area. Otherwise it is just a case of pure forward integration, not forward diversification. The approach of establishing or acquiring marketing firms subsidiary to the co-operative presents an alternative, consistent in principle with the co-operative's purpose, to opening up new product-marketing areas with outside contracting parties.

If the initiative for setting up or acquiring a subsidiary firm in the marketing field holds (long-range) promise of reducing costs, increasing returns, and/or stabilizing business, then this approach is to be preferred. But is is undeniable that this alternative also contains considerable risks and can thereby burden the co-operative group with an unacceptable amount of insecurity. It is theoretically possible, for example, for agricultural marketing co-operatives to decide to diversify in the field of dietetics and set up or acquire health-food stores for marketing purposes (→ *Health Care System*). But among other practical obstacles there will probably be a lack of know-how, insufficient funds, difficulties in assembling an assortment of goods which meets customers' needs, and defensive reactions from groups of long-established healthfood stores.

III. Diversification Activity of Purchasing Co-operatives

The diagramme of possible directions in which the services of purchasing co-operatives can flow shows that, in contrast to marketing co-operatives, there are additional diversification approaches open to purchasing co-operatives which have no effect on the programme of supportive business, but that, on the other hand, all diversification approaches lead to changes in the programme of basic-purpose business. The difference stems from the fact that the diversification is directed toward marketing.

Proceeding from the traditional flow of services O (no sales to non-members), one can distinguish among the following approaches to diversification. New sales possibilities can be opened up horizontally or laterally through

1) making full use of the existing needs of members (horizontal diversification),
2) making full use of the potential needs of members (horizontal diversification),
3) taking up business with non-members (horizontal or lateral diversification).

The vertical approach for opening up new sales possibilities implies

Fig. 2

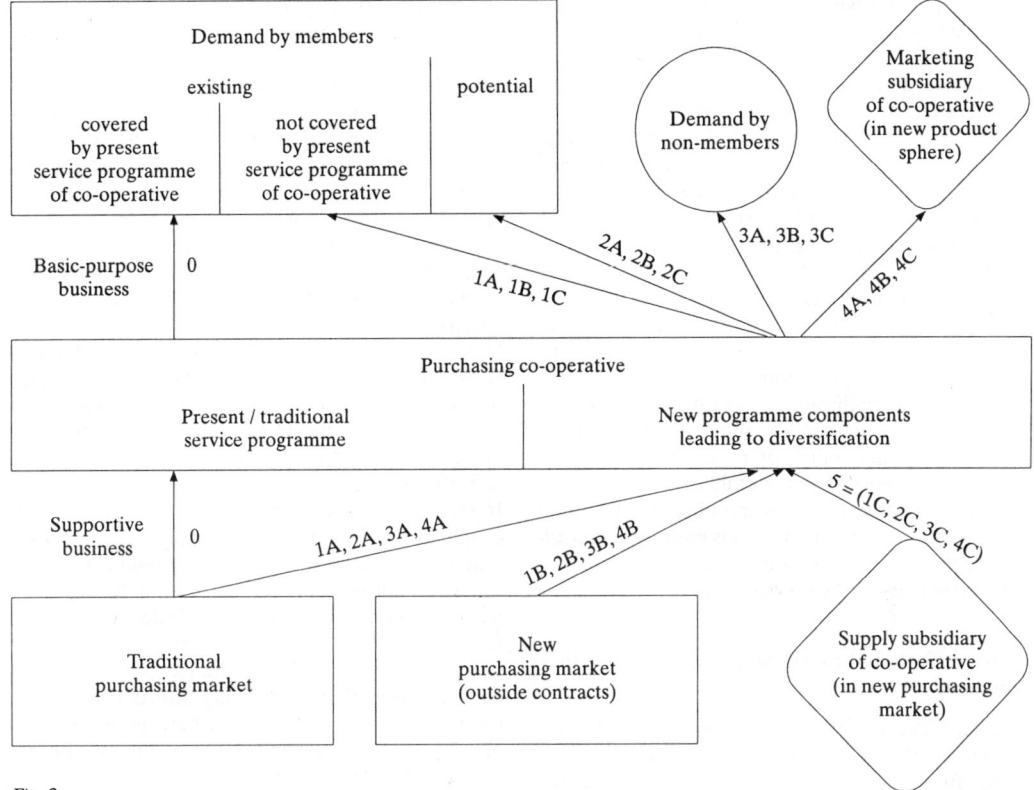

Fig. 2

4) acquiring or establishing marketing or processing firms subsidiary to the co-operative (forward diversification).

The new product lines necessary for setting up these forms of diversification can be created through

A) taking up processing, or new forms of processing, whereby supportive business would continue to be conducted on traditional purchasing markets,
B) turning to new purchasing markets,
C) acquiring or establishing supplier firms subsidiary to the co-operative in the sense of a backward-directed vertical diversification (see number 5 in the diagramme and in the text below).

1. Diversification through making full use of the existing needs of members

If the co-operative should decide to diversify in order to satisfy existing needs of members which have either not been met by the co-operative or else not been covered at all thus far, then the co-operative acts basically in accordance with its purpose, because this way it fulfills a large portion of the exisitng total needs of its members, either through taking up processing or new forms of processing (case A above) or through turning to new purchasing markets (case B above). If, for example, → *consumer co-operatives* should take up processing agricultural raw products and should thereby set up completely new services (such as the processing of cucumbers into cosmetic cucumber lotion or of fruit into fruit brandy) or if they should turn to new purchaing markets (such as tourism or insurance, thereby providing their members with favourable offers for holiday travel or for insurance policy services), then for the co-operative this may mean not only safeguarding sales (distributing risks) or increasing turn-over and thereby stabilizing or increasing the potential of the co-operative to promote its members' interests. It also means that the co-operative can satisfy the needs of its members directly to a higher degree.

2. Diversification through making full use of the potential needs of members

In the case of purchasing co-operatives (→ *Supply Co-operatives*), both diversification through taking up processing or new forms of processing (case A above), as well as diversification through turning to new purchasing markets (case B above), can lead to offers for which there is as yet no need among the members, but for which a need could be created, for example through types of advertising which stimulate new needs.

In the case of agricultural and industrial purchasing co-operatives, this approach to diversification is to be judged just as in the case of the approach with marketing co-operatives. In other words, should any promising new service areas become apparent to a purchasing co-operative working for agricultural, trade, or industrial enterprises, then the co-operative must draw this fact to the members' attention and must offer them the necessary service input factors. Creating needs in this fashion which improve the income chances of its members is directly in harmony with the purpose of the co-operative. If, for example, an agricultural purchasing co-operative should create on the part of its members an interest in bee-farming or in raising mushrooms or in acquiring or establishing a professional riding stable, and if it should offer its members the corresponding service input factors, then the co-operative acts entirely in accordance with its purpose, so long as there are good business prospects for the service areas involved.

3. Diversification through taking up business with non-members

In accordance with the above definition of diversification, it is also possible to devote new service areas to the fulfillment of existing and/or newly created needs of non-members, not just of members. In this regard the reader is referred to the corresponding text above on marketing co-operatives. If, either at once or after a trial period, it is possible to gain new members through these new service offers, then this increase in a co-operative's membership can help stabilize or augment the co-operative's potential to serve its members (→ *Business Policies*). Long-range service relationships with non-members, on the other hand, are not compatible with the co-operatives's purpose.

If consumer co-operatives, for example, declare in their by-laws that running restaurants and hotels is to be part of their programme, then there is a great likelihood that these branch businesses can be maintained only through a considerably large proportion of service relationships with non-members. Here, in other words, is an approach to diversification which contains a great danger that the co-operative may deviate away from its responsibility to serve its members' interests.

4. Diversification through acquiring or establishing marketing or processing firms subsidiary to the co-operative

A forward-directed diversification comes into being when through the newly acquired or newly established co-operative marketing firm, it becomes possible for a purchasing co-operative to market services which were not previously included in its programme.

As with the comments made above on backward-directed vertical diversification of marketing co-operatives, one can say with regard to the forward-directed approach of purchasing co-operatives that this approach is fundamentally incompatible with the co-operative purpose, for this approach separated the co-operative from its members' interests by setting up a self-contained element and creates at least a potential competitor with its own present and prospective members.

However, an approach of this kind can indeed be consistent with the co-operative's goal of long-range promotion of members' interest, if it helps to interest members and prospective members in new product-market areas promising good returns or to secure enterprises in these areas for its members.

If, for example, retailing members of a co-operative, caught in the rut of tradition, display little individual initiative to depart, when they set up their assortment of merchandise, from their orientation to their own particular line of goods and have little inclination to follow the trend toward orientation around consumer needs and consumer hunger for excitement and adventure, then a subsidiary firm, demonstrating the possibilities for success in new assortments of merchandise, can effectively help support the advisory work of the co-operative.

A purchasing co-operative of traders, craftsmen, and other businessmen can thus provide its members with protection for the future by pointing out in a practical way the possibilities of creating new combinations of goods. An example here would be new combinations of food and non-food areas with a greater involvement of services (repair services, restaurant services, travel services, leisure-time and fitness exercise services).

Through activities of this sort, the co-operative can achieve a headstart on the market for its members without exposing the individual member singly to the risks of experimenting with new types of merchandise collections. Trial collections and model enterprises which have overcome the experimental stage can then be turned over by the co-operative to its members or prospective members, so that the purchasing co-operative is in each case only temporarily active on the level on which the members themselves are in business.

5. Diversification through acquiring or establishing supplier firms subsidiary to the co-operative

Acquiring or establishing a supplier firm subsidiary to the co-operative constitutes a backward-directed form of diversification, if it leads the co-operative into new product-market areas. It thereby constitutes an alternative to opening up new purchasing markets for new lines of products by means of outside contracts.

As with the comments made above on forward diversification in marketing co-operatives, it is true to say that the initiative of the co-operative to acquire or set up a subsidiary on the purchasing market seems justified if in the long run, in comparison with working with outside business partners, it holds promise of reducing costs, increasing returns, and/or stabilizing business.

A food-purchasing co-operative, for example, which decides to diversify and expand its programme to include special-diet foods, can acquire or set up farms, agrobusinesses and horticultural firms which are specialised for this purpose.

IV. Summary

Considering the approaches to diversification as a whole, one can say that fundamentally co-operatives can make use of all types of diversification (horizontal, vertical, and lateral diversification). Compared with profit-making businesses, however, their use is more limited, on account of the relationship which the co-operative must maintain with its members (consideration of the potential or actual intentions of the members).

Diversification is compatible with the co-operative purpose of promoting members' interests if it brings about positive effects in synergy, growth, and/or dispersement of risks.

Synergy advantages come about through making full use of the existing service potential of a co-operative in such a way that, on the one hand, given services spread out their influence into new services and that, on the other hand, innovative effects arise and reflect back on given services through new knowledge gained from product-market areas which were heretofore, at least to the enterprises involved, unfamiliar territory. Diversification will produce a relatively high degree of synergy if it helps create a service programme permitting the largest possible number of functions (research and development, production, marketing, administration, and so on) to exert their influence and be influenced.

Whereas in the case of horizontal diversification, there is likely to be a possibility of connecting with existing potentials in basically all branches of activity in an enterprise, from vertical to lateral forms of diversification there is a tendency for these possibilities to decrease.

The degree of risk dispersement attainable is determined by the type and strength of the correlation between the products marketed prior to diversification and the products marketed once diversification has taken place. In the extreme case of a completely positive correlation, here will be no reduction of risks; but in the case of a strongly negative correlation between the two markets, a high degree of risk dispersal will result. Since in the case of horizontal diversification, positive correlations with markets prior to diversification can be generally expected, but in the case of vertical diversification (this tends to be even greater in lateral diversification) negative correlations are more likely, those who make the decisions are confronted with the dilemma that a project which may be highly attractive as far as synergy is concerned is often ineffective with regard to risk dispersal, and vice versa.

Bibliography

Aaker, David A.: Strategic Market Management, New York 1984.
Bänsch, Axel: Diversifizierung – eine genossenschaftsadäquate Programmstrategie?, In: Zeitschrift für das gesamte Genossenschaftswesen, vol. 26 (1976), pp. 209–226.
Bühner, Rolf: Strategie und Organisation, Analyse und Planung der Unternehmensdiversifikation, Wiesbaden 1985.
Salter, Malcolm/Weinhold, Wolf A.: Diversification through Acquisition, New York 1979.

Dual or Double Nature of Co-operatives

ALFRED HANEL

(see also: *Conceptions, Co-operative*; *Theory of co-operative Cooperation*; *Theory of Co-operatives*)

I. The Concept; II. Interpretations; III. Practical Consequences of Different Approaches towards the Dual Nature.

I. The Concept

The terminology and original concept of the 'double' or 'dual' nature of the co-operative ("Doppelnatur der Genossenschaft") was introduced by *Georg Draheim* (1951). Thus, in the second edition of his publication 'Die Genossenschaft als Unternehmungstyp' (1955, p. 16) he emphasized that every co-operative is of a double/dual nature. It is principally on the one hand (a) an association, a group in the sociological and sociopsychological sense, whose members are the individuals owning and maintaining the co-operative, which, on the other hand is also (b) a jointly undertaken enterprise of the members' individual economies (households, individual farms and businesses). The owners of the co-operative enterprise are the individual members of the co-operative group.

II. Interpretations

The socio-economic background of this concept was, according to *Dülfer* (1986), the phase of reconstruction and rapid development of the West German and other West European market economies, in which co-operatives developed successfully as business institutions in competition with private enterprises and other conventional businesses. Consequently, the traditional approach regarding the co-operatives as cohesive groups of individuals characterized by manifold interactions, pursuing various social and socio-political goals, and using a joint economic establishment as a subordinated tool for attaining specific group purposes, was changed through the experience that successful co-operative businesses had to be managed as efficient business enterprises in order to succeed in a market competition and to be able to offer the goods and services expected by the individual members' economies. This tendency was sometimes characterized as an 'economization' of co-operatives. During this period the *type of an executively operating co-operative* was often developed into or replaced by the *type of market-linkage co-operative* (*Dülfer*) (→ Structural Types).

At that time the dual or double aspects of the nature of co-operatives had also been pointed out in the non-German co-operative literature, e.g. by *Richard Philipps* (1951), who - as *Henzler* (1957, p. 13, footnote 19 quoting *Robotka* (1955, p. 162) mentioned – in his economic analysis of the nature of the co-operative association, make a clear distinction between the co-operative association consisting of multilateral agreements between the individual members and the co-operative activity as their jointly owned and maintained economic unit or enterprise.

However, it was *Georg Draheim* who emphasized the dual nature and used this approach as the basis of his famous analysis of the co-operative as a (specific type of a) business enterprise (Die Genossenschaft als Unternehmungstyp). Consequently, his terminology and concept of the double/dual nature of the co-operative influenced considerably – but by no means only – the scientific literature on co-operatives published in the German language.

Many authors are referring to *Draheim's* double/dual nature of the co-operative, when they intend to emphasize the double or especially the dual – in the sense of dualistic or conflicting – aspects of the co-operative group and the co-operative enterprise. However, when using the term 'dual nature of the co-operative' they do not always clarify whether they are using only *Draheim's* terminology or are also applying his theoretical concept. Quite often *Draheim's* approach seems to be integrated and interpreted differently in various theoretical, practical and ideological conceptions of co-operatives.

Thus, there are controversial opinions on the dual nature of co-operative (c.f. for example, *Ter Woorst*, 1966; *Frieteema*, 1968; *Dülfer* 1984) which is related to the centre of co-operative theory and practice. Theoretically, co-operatives are mostly characterized as groups of individuals who jointly own and maintain a business institution or enterprise for the promotion of their individual households, farms or businesses. Therefore, the dual nature is referring to these subsystems of the co-operative organization and closely connected with theoretical approaches analyzing the structure and explaining the behaviour of co-operative organizations. Such theories may influence considerably the action-oriented concepts of co-operatives, in particular the corporate identity and policies of co-operative organizations and the ideologies of co-operative movements. Considering this, some principal aspects of different theoretical interpretations of the dual nature of co-operatives may be mentioned briefly:

(1) The 'dual' or 'double' nature of co-operatives?
Therefore, the terms double or dual nature may indicate a first distinction. It may be generally accepted that co-operatives have insofar a double nature as they consist of groups of individuals and economic institutions, which - as subsystems of the co-operative organizations (*Dülfer*, 1984) – may be governed by different internal relationships, which have to be integrated consistently in accordance with the co-operative organizations' interests and goals. It is questioned that – as *Draheim* and especially some followers maintain – all co-operatives are always characterized by a dual (in the sense of dualistic) nature which means that the interests, goals, behaviour or relationships within and of the co-operative groups are in contradiction to those of the co-operative enterprise; both positions seem to refer to different historical structures of co-operatives.

(2) One or more basic internal structures of co-operative organizations?
As mentioned, *Draheim's* analysis was obviously influenced by early post-war experiences in Western Europe, when many co-operative businesses developed from relatively small and simple economic institutions (often managed by members on honorary basis) into larger efficiently operating economic enterprises. In this transition phase the contradictions between the formerly often close relationships in small cohesive co-operative groups, on the one hand, and the increasing economic rationality within successfully developing co-operative enterprises, on the other hand, caused contradictions and resulted in the conceptional interpretation of the dual (or dualistic) nature of co-operatives. Expressed in *Dülfer's* terminology, the type of the 'traditional' co-operative or 'executively operating' co-operative was often transforming into the type of the 'market-linkage co-operative'. Following this latter approach, it can be concluded that co-operatives may be interpreted to be of a double nature which in specific cases can turn out to be a dual (or dualistic) one. However, this view

is in sharp contrast to the essentialistic interpretations.

(3) Essentialistic or nominalistic interpretations of the double or dual nature? The dual nature of co-operatives has also been interpreted in an essentialistic sense, thus considering definitions to be true characterizations and theoretical interpretations of the phenomena concerned. *Draheim* – influenced by the phenomenalism of *Husserl* – was inclined to share this view. Modern theories of co-operatives apply mostly a nominalistic approach, which means that definitions are considered as conventions and used as tools for theoretical analyses and explanations and can be criticized by using criteria such as usefulness, appropriateness and practicability (for the essentialist and nominalistic methods of definition cf. *Popper*, 1957, vol, II).

Since the dual nature is related to the interests, goals and values of the co-operative group and enterprise, normative and positive interpretations can also be distinguished.

(4) Normative or positive interpretations of the double nature?

Apart from essentialistic positions, the dual nature is sometimes interpreted in a normative sense. It is proclaimed that the co-operative (is and) shall be governed by (whatsoever defined) social relationships (eventually also of a charitable nature), solidaric behaviour and democratic principles, whereas the co-operative enterprise (is and) shall be organized hierarchically and managed through applying economic principles and rationality. 'Nostalgic' positions regret and deplore the increasing economization of co-operatives. In contrast to normative views positive approaches analyse eventually existing conflicts between the social norms of the group and the need for economic efficiency, or between democracy and the required competitiveness of co-operatives in market economies. Thus, according to *Bonus* (1986, p. 311) '*Draheim* claimed, for instance, that workers' co-operatives usually fail because of abnormal strains pertaining to the 'human association' factor".

(5) Disciplinary or interdisciplinary interpretations of the dual nature?

Furthermore, disciplinary analyses apply sometimes the concept of the dual nature by regarding the co-operative group (→ *Group, the Co-operative*) and the co-operative enterprise as isolated systems which are (to be) analysed separately in different scientific disciplines (→ *Group Theory*); then the co-operative group is considered as the object of sociology (→ *Relationship Patterns*), psychology and political science, whereas economic research is (to be) oriented towards the co-operative enterprise (→ *Classic/Neoclassic Contributions*).

Contrary to such positions the systems' approach applied to co-operative organizations emphasizes the interdependent relationships and the need for interdisciplinary theoretical and conceptional approaches towards the co-operative group and the co-operative enterprise (cf. *Dülfer*, 1984, 1986). In this regard economic analyses of the co-operative enterprise based on the concept of transaction costs and new institutional economics (→ *Institutional Economics*) emphasized specific advantages of institutionalized cooperation through making use of positive relationships between the co-operative group and the co-operative business institution (cf. *Bonus*, 1986).

III. Practical Consequences of Different Approaches towards the Dual Nature

Although the dual nature is in the centre of co-operative-oriented theories and ideologies, considerable consequences for the co-operatives' activities may be the outcome of different theoretical approaches. If we agree that the 'best guideline for practical actions are good theories', then appropriate analyses of the double or dual nature may be considerably relevant for the formulation of successful policies and the activities of co-operative organizations and co-operative movements.

Bibliography

Bonus, H.: The Co-operative Association as a business enterprise: A Study in the Economics of Transactions, in: Journal of Institutional and Theoretical Economics 142 (1986), pp. 310–339, Zeitschrift für die gesamte Staatswissenschaft.

Draheim, G.: Die Genossenschaft als Unternehmungstyp, Göttingen 1952, 2nd edition, 1955.

Dülfer, E.: A System Approach to Co-operatives, in: Treacy, M., Varady, L. (eds.), Co-operatives Today, International Co-operative Alliance, Geneva 1986, pp. 131–148.

Dülfer, E.: Betriebswirtschaftslehre der Kooperative, Göttingen 1984.

Frietema, H.J.: Draheims Lehre von der Doppelnatur der Genossenschaft, in: Weisse, G., unter Mitarbeit von W.W. Engelhardt (eds.), Genossenschaften und Genossenschaftsforschung, Göttingen 1968, (2nd ed. 1971), pp. 14–20.

Henzler, R.: Die Genossenschaft, eine fördernde Betriebswirtschaft, Essen 1957.

Patera, M.: Doppelnatur der Genossenschaft, in: Mändle, E., Swoboda, W. (eds.), Genossenschaftslexikon, Wiesbaden 1992, pp. 140–141.

Philipps, E.: Economic Nature of the Co-operative Association, Diss. (unpublished), Iowa State College Library, 1951.

Popper, K.R.: The Open Society and its Enemies, Vol. II, The High Tide of Prophecy, Hegel, Marx and the Aftermath, Third Editon (revised), London 1957.

Robotka, F.: Eine Theorie des Genossenschaftswesens, in: Zeitschrift für das gesamte Genossenschaftswesen (ZfgG), Vol. 5, Göttingen 1955, pp. 155–175 (revised edition of a paper presented at the Annual Meeting of the American Farm Economic Association, 27–12.1946 in Philadelphia; printed in: Journal of Farm Economies, vo. XXIX; published as No. J-1423 of the project No. 725 of the Iowa Agricultural Experiment, Ames/Iowa.

Ter Woorst, G.J.: Coöperatie als vorm van economische organisatie, Diss., Tilburg, Arnheim 1966.

Early Warning Systems for (Credit) Co-operatives

EBERHARD DÜLFER / JOST W. KRAMER [J]

(see also: *Classification; Co-operative Banks; Credit Unions*)

I. Origin and Purpose of Early Warning Systems; II. The Need for Early Warning in Co-operative Banks; III. Relevant Early Warning Systems for Bank Management; IV. Early Warning Assistance for Supervisory Boards and Federation Auditors.

I. Origin and Purpose of Early Warning Systems

Most people are familiar with the term "early warning system" from meteorology or in a similar formulation used in medicine. All such activities are rooted in the notion that certain symptoms can be determined which indicate the development of a process endangering the recipient of the information (a brewing storm or the outbreak of an illness). The value of the early warning thus rests in the temporal interval between the observation of the initial symptom and the onset of the threatening imperilment. The following treatise should address the question whether such early warning is also relevant to co-operatives or to co-operatives of a particular nature.

1. The Genesis of Early Warning Systems in Management Related Fields

An early warning is always in reference to occurrences or processes which unexpectedly appear and thus are never anticipated in the course of continous normal happenings. This is the reason why the term "early warning system" has only recently been taken up in economic practice and managerial science. Theory and practical application of operational planning had concentrated on improving the methods of extrapolation and trend calculation for planning figures following World War II in order to perfect company prognoses. A good deal of success was attained during this period of time – marked by continued growth for individual companies, markets and business relationships as a whole – under a relatively constant framework of conditions. Inasmuch as considerable augmentations and perfections were simultaneously taking place to mathematical decision-making procedures (operations research), it is no wonder that a general inclination to the application of quantitative methods could be observed. This is even all the more so as the rapid development of electronic data processing occurring at the same time facilitated the application of such procedures – or even opened the way for their practical execution.

Against this backdrop one can determine that a truly shocking change took place in the middle of the 1970s in corporate-political thinking: Above all precipitated by the experience of the first oil crisis (1973) but also in connection with the ensuing political and economic developments on the world stage, the influence of environment conditions became acutely and radically obvious. Military interventions in some continents, the Islamic Revolution in Iran sparking unexpected advances of fundamentalist ideologies also in other Islamic countries; the relocation of financial centers as a consequence of the oil crisis; and the debt crisis of the Third World resulting from this which rattled the international monetary system – these unforeseen events with their far-reaching economic effects were responsible for the discussion about "turbulence" in the environment developments. A global discussion ensued about obvious "discontinuities" and even encompassed notions of catastrophy theory and chaos management.

In managerial planning the limited applicability of operational planning methods was quickly recognized, and greater attention was cast to qualitative changes. The "strategic planning" was developed which attempts to indentify the relevant environmental influences from the vantage point of each individual company in order to compare and contrast individual strengths and weaknesses. The American *Igor Ansoff* made a particular name for himself in this development (underway since the early 1970s). Ansoff indicated the existence of *"weak signals"* which, when carefully identified can instigate timely prevention against unexpected risks. He further developed this planning notion into a concept for practical action in the form of "strategic management" (1976). The term "early warning" thereby became firmly implanted in theory as well as in business practice.

2. The Development of Early Warning Systems in Specialized Literature

A retrospective of the literature (*Hahn/Taylor* 1986) indicates a three-staged development of early warning systems starting in 1973. The initial stage introduced periodic comparisons of targets and actual standings following the shocking experience of 1973. Computer aided calculations could forecast when planned levels were exceeded or not met. The superiority of this "expectation calculation" was solely restricted to the feed back effect. The rudiments of the controlling concept are to be found here. In the second stage of the development of early warning (starting in 1977) it was recognized that certain "indicators" enable the advance identification of deviating tendencies. Ratios from production and sales divisions and relevant economic data were used as to construct "*indicator systems*" in order to recognize internal and external sources of risk.

An explicit formulation of strategy first resulted in the third stage (starting in 1979) in which the concept of "weak signals" prevailed for good. The concept of a "strategic radar" emerged and pushed analyses and considerations of the environment to the center of attention. The actual strategic formulation of the application of "*early warning systems*" became clearly recognizable in this stage. Further development of controlling mechanisms also took place parallel to this in which the original, strongly operative orientation likewise made way for a more "*strategic controlling*" (→ *Controlling*).

The early impulses in American literature were also quickly taken up in German studies (e.g. *Kirsch/Trux, Hahn, Bleicher*). Deliberations were, however, almost exclusively directed to manufacturing enterprises. The notion quickly arose that the concentration on early warning aspects represented a much too one-sided approach to risks. Positive situations or "chances" should in contrast also be considered, and thus it would be more all-encompassing to speak of an "*early identification system*". However, practical experience shows that risk identification is a more pressing issue. Further, consensus can be reached among the responsible decision makers much faster with regard to risk identification than to the assessment of chances. The practical effect of early warning systems therefore rests above all in the identification of risk.

3. Early Warning Systems for Individual Types of Business Operations

The first suggestions for early warning systems, conceived for industrial enterprises, are at best of interest to producers' co-operatives, although their perspectives are usually determined by the member enterprises supplying them. Several suggestions for trading companies – in modified form – could be of interest to purchasing associations and → *supply co-operatives*.

Risk analysis for such co-operatives is not, however, of such grave importance as it is for credit co-operatives (as banking institutions). The prospect of chances in this sector is less likely than, say, that of the product policy for an industrial enterprise. On the other hand, the timely identification of risks in the banking system is not only of particular importance from the corporate-political vantage point but also from the view of the economy seen as a whole. We therefore wish to develop considerations about the relevance of "early warning systems" for co-operatives using the *example of* → *co-operative banks*.

II. The Need for Early Warning in Co-operative Banks

Inasmuch as we choose to discuss the relevance of early warning systems not only for banks in general but rather specifically for co-operative banks, such discussion must take the uniqueness of this group of banks into consideration.

1. Operational Concept of Co-operative Banks and their Risks

Detailed explanation of the → *Schulze-Delitzsch* Volksbanken and the → *Raiffeisen* savings and loan institutions cannot be provided with regard to their particular characteristics. Their special goal orientation is to be understood in the context of the contemporary conditions at their time, which is embodied in the well-known catalogues of principles composed by their founders. The following traits accordingly are well to the fore:

- Each primary co-operative is not only legally independent but likewise autonomous in its management, taking the mandate of member promotion as its basis. They therefore require a management like that of any other commercial bank which is in the position to act in a manner of accountable self-responsibility. In this regard bank management in several countries is subject to special governmental-public control (in Germany e.g. the Federal Banking Supervisory Office according to the *KWG* (German Banking Code).
- The co-operative bank of the 1990s in the industrialized countries to the most part is a true universal bank. Although the concentration of business activity might differ among individual banks according to region and customer group, in principle all types of banking operations are provided.
- The advantage of this construction and concept is rooted in the customer's proximity to the decision-making process; if necessary the member (bank customer) can directly contact the board and quickly receive a final answer and/or ruling.
- Compared to other banks the disadvantage of a relatively small operational size is thoroughly compensated through the well-structured and quickly functioning co-operative combine involving specific combine institutions such as mortgage banks, building and loan associations and insurance companies.

The efficiency of the individual primary co-operatives is determined under these preconditions according to the qualifications of its management staff and the intensity of communication with the other combine member companies. Additional risks come into play here (in contrast to other banks) which eventual early warning systems must likewise cover. With regard to the concretion of these specific risks, documented experience stretching back over the past 20 years can be drawn upon in the case of Germany. Several years ago the media reported of several instances of impending insolvency among co-operative banks, as was the case for other banking groups. There was actually a noticeable increase in the number of impending insolvencies among credit institutions in general in the second half of the 1980s against the backdrop of the rapid escalation of insolvencies in the economy as a whole; co-operative banks numbered among these. These (in West Germany) must, however, be seen in the context of the enormous quantitive and qualitative developments of the co-operative banking combine which had previously taken place. The registered cases nonetheless gave occasion to investigate the causes of the impending insolvencies and to track down the potentially weak points in co-operative banks. *Dülfer/Kramer* undertook this task (1991).

2. The Organizational Differentiation of Early Warning Systems for Co-operative Banks

Early warning systems are information systems to aid decision-makers. Inasmuch as the functions of management, execution and monitoring are undertaken by different groups of persons (bodies) in the co-operative bank, relevant early warning systems must also be differentiated for these various groups of task holders.

According to the (German) → *co-operative law*, management responsibilities rest exclusively on the board (§ 27, *GenG* [German Co-operative Law]) (→ *Responsibility*). Within the internal breakdown of bank functions, decision-making must nevertheless be delegated among subordinate, competent employees all the way down to the simple decisions and tasks related to transactions carried out at the bank counter. In correspondence with the different demands of these various ranges of responsibility one can broadly distinguish between those tasks reserved for company policy and administration – to be exclusively executed by the board itself – and those daily banking tasks in the individual business departments, executed by the bank employees. This differentiation is taken as a basis when a distinction is made between early warning systems in the *scope of corporate policy* and those in the *scope of banking operations in business departments*. Both of these fall under the board's scope of responsibilities. In both cases it is accordingly a question of early warning in a *management control system* (*Dülfer*, 1986).

The monitoring of the board's management activities is the responsibility of the supervisory board according to (German) co-operative law: It is therefore an element of a *control and/or surveillance system for administrative bodies*. It will be discussed separately whether a suitable early warning system exists on this level. The co-operative bank as a corporate form lastly is subject to the legally prescribed final audit by the federation. A *monitoring system via the mandatory audit* is thus in existence (in Germany) in which early warning aspects can likewise be identified. The identification of such aspects is, however, no longer a matter for the individual co-operative banks but rather the concern of the responsible auditing federation.

Unexpected risks can crop up in all three control/monitoring systems; timely risk identification would be striven for through early warning systems. Early warning systems thus are a legitimate requirement for co-operative banks. The much more difficult question to answer, however, is that of the particular nature of such systems.

III. Relevant Early Warning Systems for Bank Management

With regard to the marked need for timely risk identification in co-operative banks it is at first necessary to refer back to the available premises, even they essentially refer to industrial and commercial enterprises. The majority of such systems cannot simply be transposed onto the banking sector. Necessary adaptation and further-reaching development of them which takes into consideration the particular circumstances of the (co-operative) banking trade has been addressed in only a handful of publications.

In presenting a suitable option for the adaptation and/or extension of such a system it seems advisable to start off with the above mentioned three-staged development of early warning systems. Through this it becomes evident that the dichotomy of (predominantly quantitative) operative procedures and (predominantly qualitative) strategic procedures not only mirrors historical progression, but that further developments in both areas have occurred, as the following discourse illustrates.

1. Operatively Geared Procedures

This first procedural form always involves ratios which to varying degrees borrow from quotients used in accounting.

a) Logical-deductive ratio systems

Logical-deductive ratio systems were drawn on in the initial phase of development. The individual ratios are derived with an ultimate business goal in mind. The most well-known examples of this type of procedure were developed very early on by the American firm DuPont de Nemours & Co. and by the central Federation of Electronics Industries. Because the latter system boasts of a high degree of abstraction, it could prove sensible to use it once it has been adapted accordingly to bank-specific features. Further development in this direction was undertaken by *Hölscher* (1987) whose ratio system picked up on the specific types of risk encountered by banks. For this 20 ratios were used. The advantage of such a system is found in its consideration of limitational or threshold values prescribed in the "principles" of the *KWG* as well in the presentation of the ratio structure. In general it would be advisable to also include organizational ratios, in the case of co-operative banks the promotion mandate and the risk of losing members. As a whole one can state that the methods of logical-deductive ratio analysis are well-known to business administrators and easy to apply as a comparison of target and actual standings. Problems do not arise out of the application as such, but rather that deviations ascertained through the applied procedure become apparent at a relatively late point in time. Consequentially, a true early warning effect as a rule cannot be attained. Usually it is only possible to reduce damage and not to prevent it.

Because of such reasons the original ratio systems were frequently developed into indicator systems. Although the indicators are so chosen to describe threats which through normal accounting calculations would be identified at a later point in time, such indicator systems ("adapted indicator systems", *Kuhn* 1980) are based on a comparison of target and actual standings. Further developments from logical-deductive systems have led to those which include qualitative factors ("extended indicator systems") or which steer in the direction of empirical-inductive procedures ("empirical-inductive indicator systems").

b) Operative empirical-inductive ratio systems

The ratios of the empirical-inductive systems have been determined through investigation and selected based on heuristic considerations. *Simon* (1986) provides an overview of potentially relevant indicators. Application is essentially undertaken using the procedure of *discriminant analysis* (→ *Insolvency Prognosis*). The classes into which the objects are to be placed are determined in advance, e.g. groups of solvent and insolvent enterprises.

The disadvantage of discriminant analysis is that a 100% differentiation cannot be achieved. The danger always exists of an incorrect classification resulting in a twofold manner: An undertaking which should actually be appraised negatively can be positively assessed according to the classification rules (Type I mistake), or an undertaking which should be appraised positively can be classified negatively (Type II mistake). Grave consequences can result in both cases.

The primary problem of this procedure rests in the calculation of the discriminant function which should provide maximum differentiation with regard to the identification goal. A (scalar) value (Z) is determined which is compared to a "critical value" in order to decide upon the particular group into which it is to be classified. This procedure does not serve to ascertain the ratios or combination of ratios itself but rather can only indicate "*accuracy*" or "*precision*" on the grounds of the prescribed combination of ratios. The main difficulty involved in the application of discriminant analysis consequently is to determine the appropriate ratios. Research undertaken by *Baetge* (1989) and *Niehaus* (1987) in non-banking sectors concludes with convincing results (→ *Insolvency Prognosis*).

The notion of applying this method to classify co-operative banks has gained ground in that all-round appraisals of individual banks are executed by the Federal Regulatory Commission in the USA (→ *Bank Rating*) in connection with the provision of bank insurance (*Erdland*, 1977). The regulatory authorities and the insurance industry work together to classify banks into several groups, whereby only the top group is reserved for problem-free cases. A "list of problem banks" is kept, and a "National Bank Surveillance System" is striven for based on the application of discriminant analysis.

American literature covering such bank applications is addressed in the work by *Meyer/Pifer* (1970), who conclude that a sufficiently accurate classification enables a prediction of insolvency up to two years prior to its occurrence. *Sinkey* (1975) presents extensive investigation for American banks.

c) Special considerations for early warning in the sector of co-operatives and savings banks

Up to now four different procedures have attained particular significance in the sector of co-operative banks and savings banks.

Schemmann's procedure of → "*ratio based credit rating*" (1989) arose within the co-operative sector. The aim of this procedure in the scope of appraising customer credit rating (of non-bank customers) is namely the determination of a credit rating using selected ratios from the annual statement which corresponds to ratings executed usually by experts. Such a rating should be possible based on a single annual report. The values at the root of this procedure likewise are based in the past; a true prognosis can therefore not be achieved, but rather only a statement of the robustness of an undertaking supported through the analyses of a proposed balance.

Another ratio-based procedure was developed explicitly for banks by the Austrian Organization of Savings Banks (*Raab*, 1988). A system for the timely identification of insolvency was conceived following the amendments made to the *KWG* in 1986. The ratios defined by the federation are calculated by every member institute in the "Sparkassen-Haftungsgesellschaft" (Savings Bank Liability Association) and interpreted by the federation. If a warning indication arises appropriate counter measures are taken by a controlling and reorganization committee. Complete implementation of the system occurred in 1988, but extensive experience has not yet been published.

Research work undertaken by *von Stein* (1982/83) likewise hails from the savings bank sector. This comprehensive treatise was intended as a tool to identify credit risks in advance and thus directs attention to non-banking sectors. The STATBIL balance interpretation system developed by *von Stein* is nonetheless applicable to co-operative banks – that is as long as balance sheet values and ratios of a sufficient number of companies clearly identifiable as "good" or "bad" are available. The companies being investigated are subsequently evaluated using the "nearest neighbor" procedure according to which an undertaking's standing is judged more positively when its balance values are close to those of companies in the "good" category. Its standing is accordingly worse the farther its values are removed from those in the "good" category, that is the closer they are to those of the "bad" companies.

In closing the efforts of the co-operative data processing centers with regard to the further development of controlling programs (→ *Controlling*) should be mentioned. The concept of such programs is not restricted to early warning; they rather attempt to implement the early identification of risks in the various company departments and/or divisions within an all-encompassing controlling system. An example of this is the "Finance Controlling Program" developed by *FIDUCIA*. This program is applied to the "condition balance", "interest revenue balance" and "profit and loss account". The progress here lies in the conscious coupling of this concept with strategic bank planning and marketing (*Schulte*, 1988).

2. Strategically Geared Procedures

Compared to the previously discussed operatively geared procedures, the strategic procedures for early warning provide numerous interesting impulses but few concrete indications for bank-specific application. The qualitative procedures must confront the difficult dilemma of selecting characteristics because the observed situations and problems are "poorly structured". Assistance in this regard can be provided by the Delphi Method of determining expert opinion and the Scenario Method for "playing through" alternative concepts. As a whole extensive attention is cast to the environment.

The methods of strategic early identification in the scope of strategic planning (→ *Strategy Planning*) fundamentally distinguish between the extroverted environment analysis and the introverted analysis of strengths and weakness within a company. The most well-known early identification systems of this kind were developed by *Ansoff* (1976), *Mann* (1979) and *Glueck* (1980), but none of these is directed along banking lines. Continued development of strategic early identification resulted in the scope of the portfolio concept.

Von Stein's procedure mentioned above in connection with his research project on the savings bank sector (1982/83) presents an interesting approach in this connection and also serves as further development of the portfolio concept. Focus is trained on an empirically determined table of characteristics and/or combinations of the same for companies threatened with insolvency. Such a concept could in principle be realized for co-operative banks, whereby further intensive research work is first necessary into the personality characteristics of the bank manager responsible for the impending insolvency.

The question concerning the need for early warning also arises for the individual business divisions within the banking trade, even if to varying extents. The relevance of ratio-based credit rating and the *STATBIL* system for the credit policy division with regard to corporate clients has already been aluded to. In this context one could also add specialized expert systems for the analysis of the financial situation and condition of individual clients.

IV. Early Warning Assistance for Supervisory Boards and Federation Auditors

1. Aspects of Early Warning in Control Systems for Administrative Bodies

The *GenG* (§ 38) allocates the supervisory board with the task of "monitoring the board and its execution of management in all fields of administration" (→ *Responsibility*). Based on this request one would then expect that the supervisory board would also identify the situation of a co-operative bank's impending insolvency even when the board either did not see or did not want to see such development. This was however not the case, and the conclusion could be drawn that the monitoring function prescribed by legislation is only conditionally effective. If the supervisory board of an affected bank identifies impeding insolvency at all, it is usually already too late for prophylactic measures.

The necessity of early warning systems for supervisory boards is obvious, but the practical possibilities are quite limited. If it had been the case in the formative years of co-operative banks that the members of the supervisory board and the board of directors as a rule had comparable levels of professional knowledge, this relation in today's universal co-operative bank has clearly changed. Based on the *KWG* (§33) a relatively high level of banking qualification is usually ensured for board members; the members of the supervisory board in mid-sized and large co-operative banks in contrast are typically qualified professionals in their own field of activity but tend to lack the specific knowledge of the banking trade that the bankers on the board have accumulated through their years of experience. Even if the level of professional qualification is the same, supervisory board members cannot fathom decisions made by the board without further ado when they do not have access to the same information.

This illustrates the limits of any type of supervisory board activity in the modern business world, limits which likewise require an altered self-perception. It cannot inevitably be a matter of the qualitative control over the individual business decisions made by the board but rather much more a matter of whether the activities of the Board of Directors can be compatible with the interests and expectations of the represented groups.

Early warning systems which in particular provide the supervisory board with needed information do not exist and are not feasible due to cost factors. In order to reduce its information deficit the consciously responsible supervisory board must rely on particularly detailed reports from the board; it must be extensively briefed (on a monthly basis) about the business developments and important involvements based on regular reviews and hold numerous meetings throughout the year.

2. Early Warning and Personnel Policy

The analysis of weak points carried out by *Dülfer/Kramer* (1991) came to the remarkable conclusion that the causes of impending insolvency in co-operative banks only rarely are exogenous in nature. Faulty personal behavior from board members was responsible for disastrous situations in the majority of cases. This in turn was less a matter of insufficient professional qualifications than it was of inherent personality deficits which led to either active/ fraudulent action or exculpatory/veiled behavior.

A second aspect of the activities of the supervisory board arises at this point: the selection and appointment of board members. According to Co-operative Law this duty is incumbent on the general assembly or assembly of representatives, but in practical application is conveyed to the supervisory board. In the face of experience gained from cases of insolvency among banks, an "early warning system for personnel policy" would be desirable. The application of proper selection and test procedures, however, poses problems of its own; the recommended procedures in the literature are rarely applied – never for top management positions. More important consideration is given to long-term personal knowledge of a candidate, trust-worthy references or actual, proven leadership achievements.

A personnel-oriented early warning system therefore could only then come into being when coupled with a long-term personnel development strategy (→ *Human Resource Management*). This proves problematic for individual co-operative banks based on two reasons: Firstly, such a system would entail immense costs, overtaxing even mid-sized banks. Secondly, candidates for board positions in a bank as a rule do not hail from the institution itself and therefore cannot be observed and assessed over a longer period of time. A potential solution should logically thus be applied to the federation and/or combine level. Adaptation of *von Stein's* procedure described above would be conceivable, tied together with a detailed personal study (quickly executed and evaluated) of the board members of credit co-operatives threatened with insolvency. Through this manner a "negative list" of characteristic combinations could be compiled which would preclude appointment to the board of those candidates exhibiting corresponding characteristics. One could take this thought a step or two further: personality assessments could be carried out in qualification seminars for certain job levels based on candidates' approval; these could then be made accessible at a later point in time at the wish of the candidates during the application procedures for board positions. In this connection the procedure of the "Biographical Questionnaire" (*Schuler/Stehle*, 1986) or assessment center methodology (*Seibert/Elser*) would come under consideration.

3. Early Warning in Mandatory Auditing and Surveillance Systems

The necessity also exists in the field of mandatory auditing and surveillance systems for effective early identification of corporate dangers. Granted the individual primary bank is an autonomous enterprise, through its business policy solely responsible for its members and not bound to accept instructions from anybody; at the same time, however, it is subject to strict professional control through the mandatory audit executed by the federation (→ *Auditing*). The legally prescribed audit extends significantly beyond the "formal" audit of a joint-stock company. This, too, is likewise undertaken to check that all legal regulations are being adhered to; it continues, however, with a "material" examination of the co-operative bank which also entails an assessment of the quality of the business management. This tends, however, in practical application to occur in a truly general manner in that it is soley ascertained whether fundamental business goals are being pursued in accordance with the by-laws. To date the operative criteria as well as the appropriate measuring procedures do not exist for a true and detailed evaluation of the quality of the business management.

Notwithstanding, certain assessments are calculated in the scope of the annual audit (e.g. bank liquidity, equity structure, profitability, credit standing of borrowers in large credit involvements). These evaluations take place yearly, thus enabling early warning effects to arise in the scope of normal auditing procedures. As a result, many cases of impending insolvency are identified in the scope of the audit. Nonetheless, certain limits to the efficiency of the audit have become obvious (*Dülfer/Kramer*, 1991) which to a great degree are rooted in the orientation of the audit to a particular point in time. Frequently no direct evaluation is stated with regard to the situation report, but rather only that it has been properly drawn. Individual risks, either at hand or potential, are rarely named. Seen as a whole, the audit predominantly is based on the facts at the moment of the audit itself and on data referring to the past. Aspects of early warning are hardly an issue, and warnings as a rule are only stated in cases of glaring misguided development.

4. Instruments of Early Warning for Federation Auditors

Early warning instruments are also desirable in the field of auditing in that even the best auditors can only point to those misguided developments which themselves become visible. One of the first points from which to commence here is the interfirm comparison already well developed in the BVR (Federal Association of German Co-operative Banks). This comparison was previously referred to in the audit reports, but mostly with regard to those ratios prescribed by the *KWG* or *GenG*.

In assessing the economic status of the audited bank – particularly in connection with the legally prescribed situation report – an UNIVERSAL bank classification is conceivable as currently undertaken in the USA by the Comptroller of the Currency and The Federal Reserve Bank of New York. The appropriate ratio values would be calculated by the auditor in the institute under investigation and worked on either in the central federation office or on location in the bank itself. In contrast to sample survey data about internal organization stored in a data bank, a machine-calculated credit rating would be possible; this alone cannot and must not serve as a final assessment, but nevertheless it provides helpful orientation in the scope of the final audit as a whole.

Holterhus (1985) suggests drawing up a balance sheet of realization values (Veräußerungswertbilanz) and ascertaining assets at return value (Erfolgswertvermögen) as further tools of assistance; these would be calculated using the commercial balance sheet, realization values which potentially can be achieved, as well as ordinary and extraordinary components of the result. The financial situation accordingly calculated would be an important indicator for future solvency.

Likewise of importance are indications noting weakness in the bank management personnel, as the lack of personal aptitude among management staff was determined to be the main cause of faulty developments in co-operative banks. It would thereby be sensible not only to assess the aptitude of the board members but also to take the supervisory board stronger into consideration with regard to its surveillance responsibilities. Finally the auditor should report whether the board employs early warning instruments to a sufficient degree in the scope of its corporate policy and in the individual business fields. Limits are however set in a two-fold manner preventing the auditor from providing a detailed statement. On the one hand, clear target criteria for co-operative banks have yet to be provided despite continued, extensive discussion. On the other hand, the tasks and competencies of the auditor must not be so greatly enlarged that the bank's autonomy becomes endangered. What is needed is, thus, a relationship for auditing and consulting, not one possibly entailing a transference of decision-making competencies.

Bibliography

Albach, Horst et al. (eds.): Frühwarnsysteme. ZfB-Supplement to journal no. 2 (1979), Wiesbaden 1979.

Ansoff, Harry Igor: From Strategic Planning to Strategic Management, London 1976.

Baetge, Jörg: Möglichkeiten der Früherkennung negativer Unternehmensentwicklungen mit Hilfe statistischer Jahresabschlußanalysen, in: ZfbF, vol. 41, no. 9 (1989), pp. 792–811.

Beaver, William H.: Empirical Research in Accounting: Selected Studies, Supplement to Journal of Accounting Research, no. 4 (1966).

Blei, R.: Früherkennung von Bankenkrisen, Dissertation, Berlin 1984.

Dülfer, Eberhard: Betriebswirtschaftslehre der Kooperative, Göttingen 1984.

Dülfer, Eberhard/ Kramer, Jost W.: Schwachstellenanalyse und Frühwarnsysteme bei Genossenschaftsbanken, Göttingen 1991.

Erdland, Alexander: Die amerikanische Bankenaufsicht heute und morgen, in: Zeitschrift für das gesamte Kreditwesen, no. 2 (1977).

Eschenburg, Rolf (ed.): Schriften des Österreichischen Controller–Instituts, vol. 4, Wien 1986.

Glueck, W. F.: Strategic Management and Business Policy, New York 1980.

Hahn, Dietger/ Klausmann, W.: Frühwarnsysteme und strategische Unternehmensplanung, in: Hahn, Dietger/ Taylor, Bernard (eds.), Strategische Unternehmensplanung und Entwicklungstendenzen, 4th edition, Heidelberg 1986.

Hesseler, H. L.: Presentation of the Du Pont Chart System, in: American Management Association (ed.), Financial Management Series, no. 94, New York 1950.

Hill, George W.: "Why 67 Insured Banks Failed – 1960–1974", FDIC, Washington D. C. 1975.

Hinterhuber, Hans Hartmann: Strategische Unternehmensführung, 2nd edition, Berlin/ New York 1980.

Hölscher, Reinhold: Risikokosten-Management in Kreditinstituten, Frankfurt/M. 1987.

Hofstätter, K.: Die österreichische KWG-Novelle 1986, in: Die Bank, no. 7 (1987).

Holterhus, G.: Früherkennung von Bankkrisen bei der Abschlußprüfung, in: Schierenbeck, Henner (ed.), Schriftenreihe des Instituts für Kreditwesen der Westfälischen Wilhelms-Universität Münster, vol. 30, Frankfurt/M. 1985.

Jeserich, W.: Mitarbeiter auswählen und fördern. Assessment-Center–Verfahren, München / Wien 1981.

Kirsch, Werner/ Trux, Walter: Strategische Frühaufklärung und Portfolio-Analyse, in: Ahlbach, Horst et al. (eds.), Frühwarnsysteme, ZfB-supplement to journal no. 2 (1979), Wiesbaden 1979.

König, Ulrich-Karl: EBIL und Finanzplanung für und mit Geschäftskunden, in: Deutscher Sparkassen- und Giroverband e. V. (ed.): Arbeitskreis 15 des Sparkassen-Prüfertags 1986, Tagungsbericht, Stuttgart 1987.

Mann, Rudolf: Praxis strategisches Controlling, mit Checklists und Arbeitsformularen – Eine Einführung und Anwendung eines Frühwarn- und Steuerungssystems, 2nd edition, München 1981.

Meyer, P. A./ Pifer, H. W.: Prediction of Bank Failures, in: Journal of Finance, vol. 25, 1970.

Niehaus, Hans-Jürgen: Früherkennung von Unternehmenskrisen, in: Baetge, Jörg (ed.), Institut für Revisionswesen der Westfälischen Wilhelms-Universität Münster, 1987.

Raab, Gustav: Kennzahlen zur Beurteilung der Risikosituation von Sparkassen, in: Betriebswirtschaftliche Blätter, vol. 37, no. 5 (1988).

Schemmann, Gert: Kennzahlenorientierte Bonitätseinstufung, in: Bank Information, no. 7 (1989).

Schuler, Heinz/ Stehle, Willi (eds.): Biografischer Fragebogen als Methode der Personalauswahl, Beiträge zur Organisationspsychologie, vol. 2, Stuttgart 1986.

Schulte, Heinz-Werner: Controlling in Kreditgenossenschaften – Funktionale und institutionale Aspekte einer bankgenossenschaftsspezifischen Gesamtlösung, Dissertation, Berlin 1988.

Seiwert, Lothar J./Elser, F.: Assessment-Center = Gruppenbeobachtung: Eine sichere Methode bei der Personalauswahl und Mitarbeiterentwicklung, in: Management-Zeitschrift, vol. 53, no. 2 (1984).

Sinkey, Jr., Joseph F.: A Multivariate Statistical Analysis of the Characteristics of Problem Banks, in: Journal of Finance, vol. 30, 1975.

Zentralverband der Elektrotechnischen Industrie e.V. (ed.): ZVEI-Kennzahlensystem, 3rd edition, Frankfurt/M. 1976.

Economic Order and Co-operatives

WALTER HAMM [J]

(see also: *State and Co-operatives, Market Economy*; *State and Co-operatives, Socialism*; *Co-operative Socialism*; *Economic Order*; *Anti-Trust Laws*)

I. Types of Economic Orders; II. Decision-making Alternatives in the Policy Implementing the Economic Order; III. The Effects of Varying Economic Orders on the Developmental Potential of Co-operatives.

I. Types of Economic Orders

The term "economic order" refers to the totality of rules which are relevant in the course of economic processes in an economy. These rules are determined in the constitution, in laws and in ordinances ("constitution of the economy"), but they likewise can arise from spontaneously evolving or consciously designated behavioral norms which are commonly accepted (e.g. manners and customs). It is apparent from these rules which behavioral modes are admissible or inadmissible and to what extent individuals can enjoy discretionary freedom.

Two fundamental types of economic order are distinguished which indeed cannot be found in pure form: the market economy and the economy centrally planned and steered by the state ("centrally planned economy"). The characteristic distinction between these two forms is the allocation of action and dispositional rights between state bodies and individual economic entities (private households and enterprises). Individual economic entities enjoy rights of action and disposition in the market economy, but they nonetheless must adhere to rules established by the state. Everything which is not prohibited is allowed. Individuals thus have considerable discretionary freedom. In a centrally planned and steered economy rights of action and disposition are in the hands of the state or its appointed administrative bodies. Individuals are bound to directives and are obligated under penalty of law to follow them; they are not left with any discretionary options worth mentioning.

Only mixed forms exist in reality which by all means are more dominantly oriented around one of the two extremes. Economic orders can therefore be discussed which primarily assume the characteristics of a market economy or a centrally planned economy. Of decisive importance here is the nature and method in which the economic activities of the individual economic entities are co-ordinated (see under II.2). Up to 1989, central state planning of the economy dominated in numerous developing countries and in the Eastern Block. On the other hand, market economies, themselves quite varying in nature, are the norm in industrial countries of the Western world.

A country's economic order has decisive influence on co-operatives' existential conditions, their development options and their organizational structure. In those economies predominantly planned in a central manner, state administrative bodies decide the particular circumstances, the objectives and the conditions/stipulations according to which co-operatives can be contracted to fulfill certain functions. The compulsory character of state provisions is reflected in the relationship between co-operatives and their members (→ *State and Co-operatives, Socialism*). In a market economy order on the other hand, it is left to the individual economic entities whether they wish to join together in co-operatives and freely determine their objectives, or whether they wish to continue operating their existing co-operative following either former or altered objectives. The options for development are much more extensive and are solely limited in that the co-operatives must hold their own in competition among each other and with companies which have assumed other legal forms (→ *State and Co-operatives, Market Economy*).

II. Decision-making Alternatives in the Policy Implementing the Economic Order

1. The Essential Elements of Economic Orders

Market and centrally planned economic orders differ fundamentally from each other in various respects. Closer identification of these inherent systemic differences at the same time clearly shows why the character of co-operatives and the conditions of their involvement differ in a fundamental manner according to the politically determined environment. The essential elements of market economic orders are sketched below in a general overview. A descriptive presentation then follows, whereby reference to co-operatives is drawn in both instances.

The first matter of fundamental importance is the co-ordination of activities undertaken by the individual economic entities. It must be insured that the actions of millions of households and enterprises are adjusted in such a manner to each other that people's needs are satisfied in the most efficient manner possible and to the greatest possible extent. Alongside an effective co-ordination of individual economic behavior the motiviation problem must be resolved as a second matter. Effective incentives for productive contributions to the social product must be created. Thirdly, it must be guaranteed that performance and power controls function properly. Fourthly, a dependable information system must be available as the basis for the actions of the individual economic entities. Furthermore, the state must determine the framework for economic activity; otherwise the danger can arise that important political goals are infringed, such as in social policy or environmental protection.

The following areas of policy have proven to be of central importance for the appropriate and expedient solution of these tasks: regulations concerning ownership of the means of production (rights of action and disposition), the organization of competition, monetary policy, foreign trade policy, social security for situations of need (distribution policy) and environmental protection.

2. The Co-ordination of Activities Undertaken by Individual Economic Entities

In an interwoven (national and international) economy with an extensive division of labor, individual economic entities require information concerning which contribution they can most expediently make to the provision of markets. The behavior of the individual economic entities must be adjusted to each other in such a manner that the best possible, trouble-free provision of the market as a whole results. Two procedures exist for the coordination of individual economic entities' activities: central state planning tied with mandatory directives, and autonomous, self-managed, decentralized planning in the individual economic entities ("market economy") which is based on the information system of markets and prices. Commercial success is only then guaranteed when market chances are timely recognized and when demand can be satisfied at conditions (quality and price of output) which at least ensure the coverage of costs which have arisen.

The attempt is undertaken through centralized state planning to direct a national economy's production along set political priorities, whereby an unsurveyable number of reciprocal dependencies between various economic sectors and enterprises must be taken into account. In order to draft the central plan the state planning authorities require an abundance of information about the production potential of each individual enterprise, the most important suppliers, materials usage and the necessary input of human labor and capital. The state planning authorities then decide which goods should be produced, in which amounts, and which production capacities should thereby grow or shrink.

A comparison of the two coordination systems based on practical experience indicates that the centrally planned economy exhibits considerable shortcomings in its steering functions. In society the economic knowledge is scattered throughout the population; it can only be centralized to a minute extent and thus used advantageously by a central planning authority. The enterprises have an interest themselves in feigning a lower output potential than they in actuality have because they can thereby more easily fulfill their expected output level. There is only a slight incentive to produce new knowledge and share it with the planning authorities; this phenomenon can be seen in the lagging level of technical development in countries with a dominant centrally planned economy.

As the numerous shortcomings and bottlenecks in the provision of goods and services illustrate, a centrally planned and steered economy can organize a smooth co-ordination of labor among enterprises at best in a quite imperfect manner. Small and large-scale state enterprises (Kombinate) themselves attempt to redress this situation by including important primary products in their own production, by maintaining oversized stocks in their warehouses, and through (illegal) barter trade beyond the scope of the plan in order to bridge any supply shortages. Productivity losses are tied to the degeneration of the division of labor between enterprises. Large warehouse stocks of both primary and finished products (for barter transactions) lead to an unproductive engagement of scarce capital.

According to all experience accumulated on the matter, the coordination problem in a market economy in contrast is solved in a much better manner: the individual utility of the economic actors is placed in the service of society's goals as a whole. If enterprises wish to increase their income or achieve financial growth, they must detect market chances and provide an effective contribution to the satisfaction of demand. The relative prices of goods on the one hand, and costs which arise in connection with their production on the other hand, are of central importance in this calculation.

Prices freely formed in the course of competition on markets are a highly flexible and sensitively reacting information instrument. Changes in demand, production costs, disposable capacities, technical or organizational progress, the production of new economic knowledge, expected price changes for important substitute goods as well as much further information are reflected in the prices for individual goods and in shifts in relative prices. Hundreds of thousands of enterprises acting in their own interest constantly adjust their production to new market data and cost structures (in order either to avoid disadvantages or to attain advantages) without any centrally issued directives.

It becomes apparent from the characteristics of the two coordination procedures that particularly favorable development potentials are existent in the market economy for co-operatives and their most important membership group, namely independent, small and mid-sized enterprises. The significant innovation potential of the small and mid-sized enterprises as well as their impulses which lead to the invigoration of competition – frequently strengthened by co-operative efforts – contribute decisively to the rapid dynamism in market economies. On the other hand, independent mid-sized enterprises in centrally planned economies – as well as co-operatives – at best live a tenuous existence.

3. Motivation of the Individual Economic Entities

The performance power of a national economy is substantially contingent on whether those involved (both self-employed and employed by others) consider it worthwhile to exert themselves and continually seek methods to improve the results of their performance. Various incentive procedures are used with greatly differing rates of success.

In national economies centrally planned and steered by the state distinctions of all kind, honors and orders are used as a (fairly ineffective) performance stimulus; socialistic competition between similar enterprises is furthermore used in order to increase production. Because of the limited success of such types of performance motivation, financial bonuses ("material prod") are increasingly used (performance bonuses for fulfilling the expected production output in the plan). On the other hand, criminal sanctions (e.g. imprisonment) threaten those who do not achieve the expected output levels according to the plan.

Nevertheless, monetary bonuses and penalties have likewise proven to be unsuccessful. Higher performance levels themselves are usually non-advantageous because of the unattractive supply of consumer goods; urgent wishes cannot be fulfilled through higher wages. A plethora of excuses can explain why the expected plan was not fulfilled (unutilized machine capacities due to missing spare parts or non-delivery). Managers also ensure that the expected production level is set below the actual performance potential of an enterprise ("soft plans"). Potential penalties can thereby be easily avoided, and chances to attain bonuses are improved.

In contrast, the performance incentives immanent in the market economy system have proven to be effective. The willingness to work harder out of individual interests – thereby expanding the supply of goods and increasing the level of wealth and prosperity – is equally prevalent among self-employed individuals and workers alike. Enterprises are forced through competition to continually scout out options which increase their performance and to utilize these chances actively; otherwise they will incur actual losses or damages. Private ownership of the means of production functions well as a stimulus.

The market proves to be a non-deceiving and incorruptible judge with regard to both sanctions (losses, selectivity in competition) as well as to rewards (profits). Understandable personal excuses for poor performance are insignificant in this evaluational procedure, the latter being a product of market processes. Because advances made by innovative and efficient entrepreneurs are often especially rewarded in competition, high dynamism and creative commotion are guaranteed in the market economy. These aspirations for self-serving advantages are, however, only successful inasmuch as the public at large is served in the form of better or less expensive market provision. It can be characterized as a rule of the market economy system that one of the strongest incentives of human action – the individual drive for advantage – is used as an instrument to increase the welfare of the general public.

Experience has shown that even after more than a generation socialism has not succeeded in creating an altruistically thinking individual not oriented around his own self-interest who is willing to give his utmost without any material incentive. The socialistic, centrally planned economy is derived from an illusionary view of man which is estranged from reality; this led to the collapse of socialism in the Eastern Block. The market economy in contrast proceeds from a view of man as he actually is and creates conditions in which the individual can only then attain advantages when he serves the general public through his actions.

The independent utilization of economic knowledge and the activization of the skills and abilities inherent in hundreds of thousands of enterpreneurs in a market economy order has fostered the creation and expansion of co-operatives. Co-operatives must surely confront competition and hold their own in competition. They have proven in numerous markets that they also profit from performance motivation in the market economy and that they can measure up to the competition (→ Competition).

4. Performance and Power Controls

It must be ensured in each and every economic order that the laws set down by the state are not infringed or circumvented to the detriment of the general public. Effective controls are essential.

In a system of central state planning and steering all enterprises must continually be monitored as to whether they strictly adhere to the details of the state plan. An abundant state bureaucracy on numerous levels is exclusively entrusted with this function. All inter-company transactions are monitored in precise detail through complicated ratio systems, through controls in a uniform accounting system and via controls in the movements of goods through the state banking monopoly; all deviations from the plan should be prevented. Nonetheless, there are loopholes, for example in the barter between enterprises (without monetary transactions on accounts).

Control functions are simplified when the number of units to be supervised is reduced (ergo the formation of large-scale state enterprises and the socialization of small and mid-sized enterprises). On the other hand, large monopolies are formed in this manner which frequently elude the watchful eye of the authorities. The power which arises in large-scale state enterprises (Kombinate) can be subjected to bureaucratic control only with great difficulty.

The performance and power controls in the market economy are of an entirely different nature. Above all it must be ensured that the individual freedom of the market participants is not restrained through the abuse of market power; profits must only arise as a consequence of superior performance and not through the utilization of economic power. A consequential competition policy (→ Competition) has proven to be a non-bureaucratic and highly effective instrument of control. Market accessibility must be free on both a national and international level. Private restraints on competition through contracts (cartels), co-ordinated behavior and amalgamations between competing companies (such as mergers) must be prevented; state restraints on competition (for example through barriers to market accessibility, state pricing directives, commercial bans, the monopolization of supply) must be done away with (→ Anti-Trust Laws). Supervision over those companies which dominate the market remains a bureaucratic function for the competition authorities.

Competition organized by the state and protected against corruption (unfair trade practices, deceptive advertising), however, assumes by far the most extensive performance and power controls. The individual interests of customers and competitors are also used as an effective means of surveillance and supervision. Comparatively expensive suppliers with qualitatively inferior products will lose customers; they must be induced to make more favorable offers or else they will be eliminated from competition. Competitors' activities or the concern for new market suppliers (potential competition) insures continued performance pressure. The effectiveness of controls is not contingent on the necessarily limited expertise of a state bureaucracy (as in the centrally planned economy) but rather on market processes and the behavior of highly motivated actors.

5. The Information System

An important precondition for the success of economic activities is the best possible and most dependable information. If this is not the case, the threat arises that resources could be wasted or that goods are produced which cannot be sold at prices which cover their production costs.

In a centrally planned and steered economy the state planning office derives production goals based on previously determined political targets. This is also the case for the supply of consumer goods. On account of the generally poor provision of goods and due to the excess of purchasing power the danger usually does not exist that the supply of products (determined through political decisions) cannot be sold. Private households purchase what is available in the shops. Normally, there are not any alternatives, such as consumer goods purchased abroad. In-depth analyses of marketing options are therefore superfluous for planning authorities. When scarcities abound and when the state lays down priorities, state authorities need not trouble themselves with collecting information about the wishes of the population.

The state conducts itself in a different manner with respect to information concerning its production potential. The state planning office is dependent on receiving realistic data from the large-scale state enterprises and companies concerning their production potential. The enterprises themselves, however, have a fervent interest in playing down their potential production output as much as possible; they can thereby fulfill their expected production level without any difficulty. The information system of a centrally planned economy thus proves to have a grave defect inherent within the system itself.

The most important information medium in the market economy are the prices which come into being on the various markets (→ *Pricing Policy*). Considerable changes both on the demand and supply sides are reflected in price alterations and in the relationship between disparate prices. Suppliers and buyers are thereby prevailed upon to adjust to the altered price structure. If possible, buyers turn to other more favorably priced products. The extensive interdependence among prices also ensures adaptational reactions on the supply side of the market (e.g. intensified efforts to reduce costs, qualitative improvements, adjustments in product assortment, the opening up of new markets).

The chances which co-operatives have in a centrally planned economy are dependent on whether the state planning authority entrusts them with functions or not. Ideological considerations frequently decide whether co-operatives receive a chance. In the market economy on the other hand, entrepreneurial performance – particularly in the procurement of information – decides on success or failure.

6. General State Framework for Economic Activities

The outcome of individual economic activities on the economy and society as a whole is extensively dependent on the promulgation of general regulations by the state which prevent conflicts from arising between the well-being of the public at large and the interests of individual economic entities. Only those individual economic activities are permitted to be lucrative which also serve the general public. Conflicts between individual economic interests and the commonweal regularly develop with respect to external costs, that is when a portion of an enterprise's costs are passed on to the general public (e.g. environmental pollution). Several important framework conditions and their importance will be addressed in the following.

a) Ownership of means of production

Decades of experience throughout the entire world have confirmed the fact that important impulses for expedient economic activity result from private ownership of the means of production. This becomes especially evident in comparison with socialistic countries in which ownership of the means of production through the state or the "people" as a whole clearly dominates. Public ownership of the means of production indeed also exists to a more or less substantial extent in countries with a market economy order. Inasmuch as state and communal enterprises must hold their own in competition with private enterprises, considerable deviations can often not be determined with respect to their behavior and the results of their performance.

Co-operative ownership exhibits quite varied natures in different economic orders. In market economies co-operative ownership serves the promotion of members. The rights of action and disposition are in the hands of the members and the administrative bodies elected by them. In contrast, state bodies are vested with the rights of action and disposition in a centrally planned economy. The co-operatives are then merely enterprises subject to state volition which execute its directives.

Enterprises exhibiting a commonweal economic character (→ *Commonweal Economy*) within a market economy differ from co-operatives in that the addressees of promotion activities are not solely the shareholders (members) of the enterprise but rather all market partners. Such commonweal economic enterprises (including public enterprises and those under trade union ownership) strive to offer their customers more favorable prices and conditions than commercial enterprises (a situation which rarely succeeds due to pursuant competition), or else they channel their attained profits to projects oriented around communal well-being. The action and disposition rights derived from ownership of the means of production as a rule are of decisive importance for corporate goals (→ *Institutional Economics*).

b) The organization of competition

As discussed above, competition in varying economic orders assumes completely different functions. In the centrally planned economy only limited effects can be expected at best which enhance performance. In the market economy on the other hand, competition is entrusted with central functions, above all with the control of power (a function which guarantees freedom), the stimulation of output/performance and with the promotion of innovation.

Inasmuch as contractual partners can regularly fall back on competing contracting parties on the same market, they are in the position to evade the abuse of market power by turning to domestic or foreign alternatives. Even enterprises which assume a dominant market position must reckon with potential competition (new suppliers storming the market) in situations in which market power is being abused. The state is to eliminate barriers to market entry where market accessibility is not free. Inasmuch as effective protection against the abuse of power cannot be achieved in this manner, market dominating enterprises are subject to state regulation of their competition practices. Modes of behavior which precipitate the abuse of market power are inadmissible. Performance pressure arises in competition in that only those enterprises survive which can increase their performance on the market to the same extent as their competitors (the selection by competition). New demands are constantly raised in the progressive competition between innovative enterprises and in the pursuant competition among competitors – all to the advantage of customers.

Profits from a front-runner position which can be achieved by breaking into new economic territory have proven to be a powerful motor for innovation. Inasmuch as these front-runner profits are continually eroded by pursuant competition, incentives for the introduction of novel innovations are preserved. Competition is onerous for entrepreneurs; because of this there are numerous channels to curb competition. One quite important political task is thus to forestall efforts which aim to eliminate competition. Market dominating enterprises which lack any potentially effective competition must therefore be prevented from abusing their economic power by state authorities entrusted with the regulation of competition.

c) Monetary and currency policy

Economies with a substantial division of labor confront considerable problems when they lack a well-functioning monetary policy. Because both the national and international division of labor is one of the most important sources of prosperity, and inasmuch as regression into a primative barter economy looms without stable currencies, great importance is attached to the national monetary policy and the international currency policy.

The domestic money of socialist countries whose economies are centrally planned and steered can only be used within the particular countries themselves. An excess of purchasing power regularly exists when prices are dictated by the state; in other words, there is not a sufficient supply of goods for the money in the hands of private households and state enterprises. The national currency cannot be used to purchase goods abroad because foreigners consider it valueless (there is no opportunity to purchase goods in the country issuing the currency) and because such money usually also cannot be spent abroad. If the domestic currency lacks international acceptance and if the state maintains all monetary contacts with foreign nations, the international trade relations on the money, commodity and service markets will only develop to a modest extent – as can be seen in international statistics.

Countries organized along the lines of a market economy on the other hand facilitate considerably more permissive international trade relations. The convertibility of currencies is regularly guaranteed. Governments which wish to avoid a constant devaluation of their currencies with respect to other currencies are forced under these conditions to pursue a policy of monetary stability in their own countries. If this were not the case, savers and investors would cast a no-confidence vote against their own government. Competition has therefore developed in the western industrial countries for a trustworthy monetary policy.

A stable value of money is not only desirable out of social reasons (protecting small savers from financial losses). Risks caused by fluctuating and high rates of inflation furthermore dampen the willingness to invest and therefore have precarious consequences on the supply of jobs. High rates of inflation likewise trigger the flight of unproductive, real assets (e.g. gold), lead to a misallocation of resources or unleash a flight of capital abroad. The performance-enhancing effects of competition are likewise neutralized by high inflation rates because every supplier – even the least efficient – can market his products when demand is swelled by inflation. Essential preconditions for the most productive possible allocation of scarce resources include a stable value of money (when price formation remains unencumbered) and a liberal currency policy with respect to foreign nations (unrestricted convertibility).

d) Foreign trade policy

Considerable differences exist with respect to foreign trade relations according to the nature of the particular economic order. When economic processes are centrally planned and steered by the state it is imperative that the state dictates the binding nature and range of exports and imports in its central plan or else the goals of the plan remain unachievable. With this objective in mind, state foreign trade monopolies are established which also must equalize differences between domestic prices and those on world markets (usually making imports more expensive and dropping the prices of export goods to the lower world market level). Competition between domestic and foreign producers cannot develop in this manner. Qualitative differences are counterbalanced with price reductions. Trade among countries with centrally planned economies is more fervent than trade with market economy countries but, nevertheless, remains substantially behind the extensive international division of labor among industrialized western countries.

International trade among market economy countries is, however, not free from all administrative fetters (above all duties, quotas, import restrictions for agricultural products). Nevertheless, private initiative in international trade in comparison confronts fewer barriers. Competition which enhances performance, promotes progress and decisively contributes to improvements in all-round market provision is thereby effectively intensified. International mobility offers well-performing enterprises numerous chances, but additional risks surely also arise.

e) Labor law and social policy

Regulations of a social nature number among the especially important framework conditions to be determined by the state with respect to commercial activity. Work conditions in the enterprises must be laid down in a socially acceptable manner, and workers' representatives must be involved in such processes. The rights and obligations of trade unions regarding the negotiation of blanket wage agreements and effective supra-plant labor conditions must be established. Furthermore, the protection of those people lacking employment and income must be guaranteed (health, accident and retirement insurance, social assistance and other social benefits).

These social responsibilities must be regulated irregardless of the economic order of a particular country. One difference does, however, exist: on account of the higher yield of production and the higher standard of living, those national economies organized along the lines of the market economy have more extensive and superior social benefit systems compared to those in economies centrally planned and steered by the state.

f) Environmental protection

Enterprises can save on costs by passing a portion of production-related costs on to the general public, for example in the form of inadequately purified drainage and exhaust. The empirical findings are likewise held to be true that market economy countries can guarantee substantially better environment protection through their general framework than centrally planned economies (→ *Environment Protection*).

III. The Effects of Varying Economic Orders on the Developmental Potential of Co-operatives

In conclusion it can be determined that the conditions for co-operative participation in centrally planned national economies are for the most part unfavourable (→ *State and Co-operatives, Socialism*). Small and mid-sized private enterprises – an especially important membership group for co-operatives – either do not exist or only to a minimal extent. The question whether co-operatives may become involved and in which particular sectors is contingent on external (state) volition and not on the initiative, the performance strength and the competitive energy of the co-operatives and their members.

In a market co-operative on the other hand, co-operatives have free development opportunities within the general framework and conditions set by the state (→ *State and Co-operatives, Market Economy*). Citizens are completely free to join together in co-operatives and collectively pursue promotion objectives. Nevertheless, co-operatives must face competition from other enterprises. Co-operatives are only able to hold their own when they are at least as efficient as their competitors. This competition is also in the interest of their members because the co-operatives are forced to adjust continually to changing market conditions and enhanced performance levels. The liberal order of market economy offers co-operatives extensive chances, by all means also tied with the risk of having to prove themselves in competition.

Bibliography

Röpke, Wilhelm: Die Lehre von der Wirtschaft, (Vienna 1937), Bern 1979[12].
Eucken, Walter: Grundsätze der Wirtschaftspolitik, Bern/Tübingen 1952), Bern/Tübingen 1975[5].
Hayek, F.A.v.: The Constitution of Liberty, (Chicago/London 1960), Chicago 1972[2].
Gutman, Gernot: Grundformen der Wirtschaftsordnung, Kiel 1965.
Hensel, Paul K.: Grundformen der Wirtschaftsordnung, Marktwirtschaft – Zentralverwaltungswirtschaft, München 1972.
Leipold, Helmut: Wirtschafts- und Gesellschaftssysteme im Vergleich, (Stuttgart 1975), Stuttgart 1980[2].
Leipold, Helmut (ed.): Sozialistische Marktwirtschaften, München 1975.
Schüller, Alfred (ed.) et al: Innovationsprobleme in Ost und West, Stuttgart 1983.
Woll, Artur: Wirtschaftspolitik, München 1984.
Peacock, Alan/Willgerodt, Hans (ed.): Germany's Social Market Economy: Origins and Evolution, London 1989.

Economie Sociale

CLAUDE VIENNEY [S]

(see also: *Conceptions, Co-operative; History of Ideas; Commonweal Economy; Social Policy; Public Benefit Orientation*)

I. Contemporary French Manifestations; II. Comparative International Historical Analysis; III. Changes in Social References of Solidarity.

If you rely on the first official text issued by the *Commission of the European Communities* that refers to it explicitly (CEE, 1989) "the notion of social economy (*l'économie sociale*) is nowadays not effective throughout the European Community."
Reviewing all the meanings of the expression in the context of an international handbook requires at least that the following be examined:

1) How it has been reused in France in the seventies and eighties, after a long eclipse, to signify an ensemble of *organizations* which tend to recognize themselves and to be recognized by the State as a sector having specific characters.
2) Why the phenomenon that could have just concerned the institutional economic situation of this one country, has acquired much further reaching historical and geographical responses, to the point of suggesting that the *reasons* for its relative solidarization would not be connected only with the particularities of the French economy and

society, especially in the role the centralized and centralizing State is supposedly playing.
3) Finally, what could be the prospects and stakes involved in the re-emergence of this "sector" of the "mixed" economy during the transition from the 20th to the 21st century, marked by profound transformations in our social references of → *solidarity* in comparison with the 19th.

I. Contemporary French Manifestations

At the end of the year 1981, the expression "économie sociale" enters the actual French law, but it is the final point in a process that began ten years before (→ *History of Ideas*). Since then, the choice of name has caused sufficient conflicts to suggest that the phenomenon is inscribed in a much greater transformation in the relations between the activities, the actors and rules of contemporary economy and society.

a) The first manifestation has a statuatory source: a decree of December 1981 creates the *Délégation à l'économie sociale* (DES) whose area of competence concerns: "the co-operatives, the mutual societies, and the associations whose production activities assimilate them to these organisms." Furthermore, a legislative text consolidates these bases: a law of July 1983, which is "relative to certain activities of économie sociale" regroups texts concerning the different types of co-operatives and creates a new legal category, the unions of social economy, second degree organisms whose members must be co-operatives, mutual associations, and associations. At the same time, a social economy consultative committee brings together representatives of these organizations and those of the public authorities to institutionalize their agreement (Economic and Social Council, 1986) (→ *History in 19th C.*).

Examining it in a more detailed way, one can see that it is a process of reconciliation that was begun ten years before by a number of large national organizations attempting to demonstrate their common characteristics ... and a name which serves to identify *the ensemble* they could tend to form from now on.

- Starting from a first "record of agreement", the National Grouping of Cooperation, the National Federation of French Mutuality, and the Grouping of Mutual Insurance Societies in 1970 create a *National Connection Committee of the Co-operative, Mutual and Associative Activities* [Comité National de Liaisons des Activités Mutualistes, Coopératives et Associatives] (CNLAMCA). Extended to some Federations of "associations gestionnaires", it holds a conference in 1977 to join its members (CNLAMCA, 1977); it draws up a *Charter of social economy* in 1982; it becomes a registered and structured association in 1985.
- Simultaneously, and motivated in a similar way, regional Groupings of cooperation [Groupements regionaux de la cooperation] (GRC) which have been founded at the end of the sixties with a view to "regionalization", transform into GRCM by adding Mutual Societies, subsequently into GRCMA to integrate what is called an "associative component" of social economy.

b) So one is bound to take into consideration that the two aspects of the process of relative solidarization which are included in the term are *interactive*: to be more recognized by the public authorities and various other partners (especially the employers organizations and the employees' trade unions) these institutions tend to unite in the same ensemble; reciprocally, it is to incite them to concerted action that the public authorities legitimize their name, which makes necessary an institutional delimitation.

In any case, the novelty is not the recognition on the occasion of a change in political majority of *each* component organization in the domain. It is the *combination* of a mutual recognition and a recognition by the State of their *common* features rendered necessary by previous changes in their conditions of *insertion* into their economic and social environment.

- Most of the institutions concerned have obtained legal statutes, at least since the end of the 19th century, which identify them and allow them to have access to various forms of public and private aid (*Moreau*, 1982). Now, they do not owe it especially to parliamentary majorities or to socialist governments: they are historically due to extremely different ideological currents (*Gueslin*, 1987), and one can notice that a number of laws under discussion have been treated in Parliament with quasi unanimous votes. Reciprocally, the changes of orientation in governmental politics since 1981 have called into question neither the D.E.S. as such nor the process of legislative development that has been the concern of the principal organizations in this domain for 20 years.

This observation would rather suggest that it is because they were forced to *transform* that these institutions felt the need to unite in order to negotiate these adaptations without losing their respective identities.

c) In the first approximation, the components of the domain of social economy are identified by the following references: the general statute of cooperation (1947) and the laws particular to the different types of co-operative societies; the code of mutuality (1985), the clauses relating to societies with the mutual character of the code of assurances (1989); the law of 1901 concerning the associations. But if one wants to represent even roughly their *common* characteristics, it is on the level of the system of rules one supposes to be contained in all the texts which would have to be examined:

- personal and voluntary character of membership and *reciprocal* identification of the associates and the commonly undertaken activities;
- the right of an *egalitarian* vote in the respective board with a general competence in which the sovereignty of the associates is expressed;
- if there is a division of surpluses, a distribution which is in proportion to the *activitiy* and the limitation of the remuneration of capital;
- *indivisibility* of the net assets in case of liquidation.

If one examines now the principal changes that the legislative and statutory changes reveal in a time when the expression "économie sociale" serves to unite them and allows them to be compared – one will notice that most of the provisions which translate this system of rules into legal norms, have been modified in the texts relating to the co-operatives and mutual associations; at the same time, certain associations (in the wider sense different non-profit organizations without lucrative aims, even for their own members) becoming for their part "enterprises" which tend to acquire relatively analogous rules (*Alix* and *Castro*, 1990).

Owing to the fact that their activities are more and more in direct competition with those of the enterprises operating in the field of profitable market-oriented production, co-operatives and mutual societies conceal their original *personal* characteristics: the circles of steady membership have been enlarged to the point of admitting financing associates who do not participate directly in the activity; the mechanisms of automatic membership multiply as an effect of the admission to the use of these activities; a growing part of the profits can be redistributed proportionally to the parts of capital which are held by the associates to remunerate the non-participating associates; different possibilities of weighting the votes in proportion to the volume of operations and/or of the amount of capital held are reintroduced.

In contrast, the associations which produced their services for other beneficiaries than their members without a direct reference to the costs and prices of the market – thanks to subsidies, contributions or donations – penetrate progressively into the domain of market production. But this obliges them, in relation to the prior historical experience of the co-operatives and mutual associations, to *identify more strictly* these activities and their beneficiaries in order to legitimize the types of aid - public or private – corresponding to their specific social use.

So one can put forward the following hypothesis: if these organizations tended to recognize themselves and to be recognized as a group in the years from 1970 to 1990 while each had previously conquered its own identity in a particular sector, it is because of the conditions of *insertion* of their activities in the economic environment change and demand relatively common responses.

But for that reason the phenomenon extends beyond the framework of its French manifestations, and the expression *social economy* has to be reviewed in terms of a much broader historical and geographical comparison.

II. Comparative International Historical Analysis

Even though the term *"social economy"* only becomes general in the eighties, it refers to the senses which also have been modified since the 19th century, so one refers to the history of social ideas or to the representation of the institutions of industrial capitalism.

a) In the cutting up of the social sciences one can observe such a change on both sides in the fixation of the models referring to the *political economy* called scientific and its Marxist criticism in the last third of the 19th century (*Vienney*, 1986).

Before, the meaning of the expression resides in the articulation of the working rules of economy and of "other" social activities in a fundamental debate, because it concerns their *relations* with those of morals, politics, and religion.

It seems to designate rebellious trends of separation as shown in the two works of *Adam Smith*, "*Theory of moral sentiments*" (1759) and "*Inquiry into the nature and causes of the wealth of nations*" (1776), i.e. of the autonomization – even if it is only relative – of the rules of a profitable market production in competition just as components of economy. It is at least used by those people later called "doctrinaires" to oppose them to the "theorists", even if their sources of inspiration are different (*Desroche*, 1983):

- A conservative Christian tradition, under the influence of the school of *Le Play*, inaugurator and organizer of the "expositions of social economy" from 1855 to the Palace (Palais) of social economy of the universal exposition of 1900.
- A progressive socialist tradition, from *C. Pecqueur* (1840) to *B. Malon* (1883), illustrated by a comment by *Jaures* (1903) on the *Report* of *Gide* concerning this very exposition (→ *Conceptions, Co-operative*).
- *Gide* had presented himself in 1889 as an inventor of a synthesis between these trends. But this was finally, at the turning period suggested above, to substitute contest by complementarity: "We do not see any antagonism between political economy and social economy. They are two disciplines distinguished by their objects" (*Gide*, 1905).

For, *after* the formalization of the models structured by the representation of profitable market production in competition one passes so to speak from the "including" social economy of *Smith* to the social economy "included" by its rules which have become dominant. More precisely, it seems that the studies of social economy attach themselves to the analysis of a certain number of *sub-ensembles* of activities and actors who, whatever may be their reasons, do not principally depend on these central rules which are necessary if the *ensemble* is to work well. → *Walras* (1896) himself foreshadows this new treatment by designating the domain as one of the interventions by the State in the redistribution of social wealth.

When the neo-classical model has become dominant (→ *Classic/Neo-classic Contributions*), the domain will be recognized according to the following principle:
- for the "pure" economy (i.e. scientific) the study of mechanisms of the *production* of social wealth according to its proper rules;
- for the "social" economy that of all the necessary interventions, in reference to the rules which can vary according to the moral norms of the groups concerned to correct the effects considered to be ill-fated to the principal way it functions.

From now on, the expression will serve to designate the domains one can classify, although the two principles generally interfere, it all depends on the nature of *activity* or the personality of the *actors* which make evident the existence of *rules* which are different to the ones of profitable market production in competition.

Here, the *Report* of *Gide* to the Palace (Palais) of the exposition of 1900 is very significant because it restricts and structures the domain by identifying the activities relatively *neglected* by the dominant agents, which are, however, *necessary* for the dominated agents: "social economy does not rely on the free play of natural laws to assure the welfare of mankind, but it believes in the necessity of a wanted, reflected and rational organization which conforms to a certain idea of justice. (...) And still it can be limited among these institutions by those which interest the working classes, because especially for them the conditions of a happy life are missing: with regard to the property-owning classes, the property constitutes a social institution which itself renders all the others nearly superflous" (Ed. 1920, p. 9).

b) But starting from this fact, it is also a modification of the contents of the domain of social economy which manifests this change of perspective. It is no longer the ensemble of the economical domain which is described, but a *sub-ensemble* of institutionalized organizations, whose activities, actors and rulers have particularities which distinguish them at the same time from the others by allowing them to insert. This same *Report* by Gide, which was referred to by the French re-discoverers of the expression in the years 1970 to 1980, also marks an attempt at a synthesis and a change in this point of view.

- It is a *synthesis* to the extent that it presents as a competitor in the organization of the necessary and neglected activities (which are called "purposes" of the institutions of social economy) three modes of assumption of responsibility (which are called their "sources"):
  - the *patronages,* either patrons in the proper sense or charitable or philanthropic institutions which offer voluntary support for others;
  - the *public services*, no matter whether they emanate from the State or from local governments or local communities;
  - the *free associations* of the beneficiaries themselves corresponding to the character of the different types of co-operatives and mutual insurance companies or credit co-operatives.

Violating the doctrinal preferences and the competitions of groups which have analogous activities but opposed references, it suceeds in limiting and structuring the domain of *social economy of 1900* by identifying each institution as the junction of a purpose and a source. This, with a lyrical point, leads to the famous picture of the exhibition as a cathedral: in the central nave "all the forms of free association which tend to the emancipation of the working class using their own possibilities"; in the aisles respectively "all the modes of intervention by the State" and "all the forms of institutions of patronage"; the finalized activities being arranged along the bays, so the visitor can make all the useful comparisons during his tour. Even the remark which is fitting this *universal* palace is not missing: "I will not see any use in conserving the divisions in nationality (...). The lessons would be much clearer, if one saw all the organizations grouped around the original cell which served them as a germ, whatever may be its country of origin." (Ed. cit. ..., pp. 24–25).

- But there is also a *turning point* for two series of linked reasons of which the ones set a high value on the place and role of the *States* in the undertaking of the activities within the domain, the others on the socio-economical and legal diversification of the *associations* manifesting the capacity of auto-organization of their beneficiaries.

In all the countries there emerge at the end of the century *public* social policies in most of the domains where they had been contested before (→ *Social Policy*). Starting from this fact, their institutional frameworks differ according to the function of these national characteristics and in particular the respective weights of the State and of the central administrations on the one hand, and the local communities and decentralized establishments on the other hand. The organizations which have succeeded in *becoming autonomous* with regard to public and private aid by inserting themselves in the production of market services, i.e. the co-operative associations, mutual societies of insurance and credit (→ *Co-operative Banks*) obtain legal statutes which also distinguish them from one another according to their respective sectors as well as those supplying services free of charge by having recourse to donations and subsidies (→ *Law, International*).

Retrospectively, one should not be astonished that the 1900 social economy brightness – at the confluence of doctrinal trends of the 19th century and of the insertion of co-operatives, mutual associations, and associations in the different sectors - was shortlived. Neither that the landscape changed when the expression is used again one century later.

III. Changes in Social References of Solidarity

This historical detour in a wider geographical frame permits one at least to understand that the "exported" construction of the French experience in the 1980s has not immediately been admitted to be operative in all the countries; but on the contrary, the constraints of adaptation, which it manifests, are equally observable in this period when the demands of economic competition disrupt many social references of → *solidarity*.

a) With regard to the French case, it is quite clear that the main point is a change of relations between the State and these organizations, which explains the emergence of this "intermediary" sector (*Gaudin*, 1982), as a reunion of co-operatives, mutual societies and associations gestionnaires of enterprises. The public authorities had played a central role at the same time in their sectorial identifications and their access to privileged circuits of financing, and so it is their relative retreat from these circuits (the "disengagement of treasury") which brings them into the situation of doing "among themselves" what the State did "for them"(*Vienney*, 1987).

It is at least under this pressure that they put forward their common characteristics of enterprises whose rules do not allow them to adress themselves to the financing market in order to collect capital in search of profitable investments, but which are susceptible of mobilizing financial means by supporting each other and by producing evidence to support at the same time their productive *effiency* and their contribution to the defense of the system of voluntary social *solidarity*.

In the other countries, it is especially the inclusion of the *associations* (legal categories which are less strictly connected with the socio-economic structure common to the co-operatives and the mutual insurance and credit companies) which causes problems. It may be that they are not represented as organizations of the *economic* domain, or, when they penetrate it, that they are guilty of "falsifying the competition" starting from the fact that the whole or a part of their costs of production are covered by direct or indirect subsidies of public origin.

In particular, German doctrine is reluctant to admit what is, in reference to its proper juridical categories, considered as an amalgam: on the one hand, the *mutual aid* which refers to the co-operative and mutual characteristics and *the aid for others* which identifies the modalities of charitable or philanthropical associations; on the other hand, *enterprises* in the economic domain and social institutions which do not belong to it (*Münkner*, 1988).

It is a boundary of this type that suggest the delimitation of the domain of social economy by the *Commission* of Brussels in the document that has already been cited by referring to the "Europe Sociale" – this time without any economic reference – all the institutions which do not work according to the rules of market production in → *competition*.

b) But the fact that the organizations of the domain have to face analogous difficulties *in all the countries*, independently of the variety of legal stting in which they had their character inscribed at the beginning of the century, explains also that the phenomenon has echoed in many countries, far from remaining enclosed in its "hexagonal boundaries".

While they had established themselves in those sectors of activity that were mostly *complementary* to the ones of capitalist market enterprises, they are, nowadays, more and more *in direct competition* with them, which cannot but create strong tensions as far as their rules are concerned. In particular, *the cooperatives*, strictly under the constraints of the principles of auto-financing of their activities by their owm members, are looking for the aid of financing partners with whom new arrangements have to be found for sharing profit and power; the mutual associations in the domain of social security have to calculate more strictly the relations between the contributions they demand from their members and the specific cost of each risk which they are committed to cover, which also implies compromises between market logics and redistributive logics on the base of a more or less conscious solidarity; finally the *associations*, when they can no longer rely for their legitimacy on the donations of their benefactors and the benevolent work of their militants, have to identify in a better way the beneficiaries and the professionals involved in their activities, which tend to give them characters which are closer to the "auto-centralized" structure of the co-operatives and the mutual associations (→ *Pricing Policy*).

And this all the more so at a time when the pressure of mandatory contributions as the sources of financing non-market activities, in the context of international competition, incites the *public authorities* if not to disengage totally at least to restrict their aid to the most unfavored social categories. Therefore, the tensions so often mentioned – although the opposition is too simplistic under this form - between the society of assistance for some and the society of opulence for the others, by contracting more the *intermediary* zone in which the organizations in the domain of social economy functioned precisely.

In fact these tensions reveal, in the same measure as they are obliged to arbitrate between their conditions of productive efficiency in competition, and their capacities of solidarization between the producers and beneficiaries of their services, which they combined more often than they opposed them to the "sources" distinguished by *Charles Gide* in his comparative historical and international investigation: *selfhelp* and *help for others* through the internal mechanism that balancing the costs and prices of given services; *market reciprocities and services given to the community* by the allocation of one part of the surplus to the social institutions open to everybody; *voluntary membership and compulsory membership* by way of multiple relations between public bodies and private organisms which are deprived of their respective fields of activities.

Starting from this fact, this could represent threats which are a burden on all the institutions of this intermediary zone between the capitalist market sector and the public administrative sector which could explain the re-emergence of *social economy* as an answer from these institutions which have been identified separately at this point in search of new social references of solidarity.

c) The difficulty of finding an effective definition of the expression – and even the slightly confusing character of the quarrels in the course of which the scientists in this field may have the impression of being prompted to distribute good or bad marks when trying to distinguish whether something belongs to social economy or not – would depend on the following paradox: it is used to circumscribe a "sector" whose components should correspond to *predefined* criteria, while it only acquires its full meaning in problems of institutional *changes*. The recourse to this notion is in fact a way for the organizations of affirming the permanence of their identity while they are changing, the comparative socio-economic analysis showing that they are the results of compromises which are necessarily instable between the forces of *resistance* to the effects of the extension of market production and the capacities of *functional adjustment* to its rules (*Vienney*, 1980 and 1982).

In the contemporary period, it seems that this is the reason why these compromises are threatened, whatever may be the reasons, why they are under the compulsion to form a relative solidarization to obtain a new recognition together. But these adaptative reactions are evidently ambiguous: in certain cases it is a matter of fighting against new social exclusions, in other cases to get rid of rules which are considered to be too constraining to enter into international competition. The difficulties of the definition result from the fact that one is in the presence of a population of institutions *in renewal*, while certain organisms are losing their initial characteristics when others are acquiring them (September 1990).

Bibliography

Addes: Colloques 1983–90 sur les conditions de construction d'une information statistique sur l'économie sociale, Nanterre 1990.
Alix/Castro: L'entreprise associative, Paris 1990.
CEE: Les entreprises de l'économie sociale et la réalisation du marché sans frontières, Communication de la Commission au Conseil, SEC (89) 2187, Bruxelles, 18 XII 1989.
CES: Les entreprises de l'économie sociale, Rapport présenté par Georges Davezac, JO du CES, 12–13 XI 1986.
CNLAMCA: Vingt millions de sociétaires, huit cent mille emplois, Paris 1977.
Desroche, Henri: Pour un traité d'économie sociale, Paris 1983.
Gaudin, Jocelyne: L'économie chachée. Taxinomie, Rome 1982.
Gide, Charles: Economie sociale, Paris 1905.
Gueslin, André: L'invention de l'économie sociale, Paris 1987.
Kaminski, P., Vienney, C., Weber, J.L.: La délimitation et l'organisation du champ statistique de l'économie sociale, Nanterre 1983.
Moreau, Jaques: Essai sur une politique de l'économie sociale, Paris 1982.
Münkner, Hans-H.: Aspects juridiques de l'économie sociale en Europe, RECMA, N° 27, pp. 73–86, 1987.
Vienney, Claude: Le comportement financier des organismes de l'économie sociale, Revue de l'économie sociale, XII, pp. 37–68, 1987.
Vienney, Claude: Les activités, les acteurs et les règles des organismes de l'économie sociale, Université de Paris 1, 1986.
Vienney, Claude: Socio-économie des organisations coopératives, Paris 1980 et 1982.
Walras, Léon: Etudes d'économie sociale, Paris 1896.
Walras, Léon: Les associations populaires de production, de consommation et de crédit, Paris 1865.

Education and Training in Africa, Co-operative

ANTHONY NFORBA NCHARI

(see also: *Development, Africa South of Sahara*; *Development, Northern Africa*; *Education, Asia*; *Education, Latin America*; *Education, Europe*; *Development Policy*; *MATCOM*)

I. The Philosophy and Operations of the Pan African Institute for Development; II. Co-operative Training and Other Promotional Activities Within the Framework of PAID's Activities; III. PAID's Future Role in African Co-operative Development; IV. Summary.

I. The Philosophy and Operations of the Pan African Institute for Development

The International Association of the Pan African Institute for Development (PAID) was established in 1964 out of the realization by a small group of people actively involved in development work, meeting in

Douala, Cameroon, that in African countries there existed a huge rift between the young professional staff returning from France and the rural population who were left to fend for themselves.

Although these young professionals, including those trained in other European and North American universities, were capable of understanding development, they were not adequately equipped to tackle the development problems of the rural areas where the vast majority of Africans live. There was thus the urgent need to train middle-level staff in Africa who would act as agents for rural development between the rural population and elites. It was thought that the best structure would be a college for development staff. The founding fathers by emphasizing development staff training were guided by the principle that man is both a means and an end of development and should therefore become a responsible citizen in his society. Training was seen as the best means for human beings to actively participate in their own development and in that of the local, regional and national communities to which they belong.

The founding fathers thought that the Development Staff College should be established by a Non-Governmental Organization (NGO). Given its private and NGO status, PAID would enjoy a high degree of autonomy which would in turn give it the necessary flexibility of action and in the choice of its partners. With the multiplicity of development systems in Africa, PAID should be able to adopt its actions to the varied conditions.

PAID was thus established as an international association, private and non-governmental. It works closely with African governments, some governments of other countries, regional bodies as well as bilateral and multi-national agencies interested in promoting African development such as UNDP, UNICEF, WHO, FAO, ECA, UNESCO, ILO, EDI/World Bank, COMSEC, EEC, etc. Its vocation is to contribute to the development of Sub-Saharan Africa through the promotion of grassroots development. PAID conducts training, research and provides advisory support services in 44 English and French speaking countries through its four regional institutes, namely Institut Pan-Africain pour le Développement de l'Ouest Sahel (IPD/AOS) (French), based in Burkina Faso, Institut Pan Africain pour le Développement Afrique Central, Cameroun (IPD/AC) (French), and the Pan African Institute for Development – West Africa (PAID/WA) (English), Cameroon and Pan African Institute for Development – East and Southern Africa (PAID-ESA) (English), Zambia.

As a strategic principle, PAID seeks to promote integrated and participative development of both rural and urban populations. It undertakes the training of trainers and action-oriented field studies, as well as project formulation and evaluation for a variety of development partners; it designs training programmes and training tools and publishes the results of its work.

PAID also provides advisory and training support to organizations which are promoting local, regional and national development through the information, mobilization and participation of the populations concerned.

Although PAID's operations are guided by the principle of tri-dimensionality i.e. Training, Research and Support/Consultancy, training has so far been the principal activity.

The long and short courses/units presently organised by the Regional PAIDs (RPAIDs) focus on a limited number of basic areas where general expertise has been developed. These areas include Small-Scale Enterprises Development, Project Planning, Management and Evaluation, Training of Trainers, Community Health and Women's Programmes (Women in Development and Women and Health) and Co-operatives. For both the long and short term courses a total of over 1500 development staff have been trained by the RPAID's and the General Secretariat (PAID-GS) since PAID's establishment in 1964.

Although initially, PAID focused its activities on middle-level development staff, it has since extended its activities to top level and grassroots population.

II. Co-operative Training and Other Promotional Activities Within the Framework of PAID's Activities

1. Role of Co-operatives in African Development

Both the colonial and post-independence African governments realised the vital role that the co-operative form of organization can play in fostering socio-economic development in African countries and consequently promoted their formation and development. Co-operatives were seen as important institutions for transforming the rural areas. They would provide not only the means of integrating the peasants into the monetary economy, but would also contribute to development by capital formation for the benefit of the common man. They would promote their participation in development and would be effective replacements of the foreign middlemen (*Hyden* 1973). Besides, co-operative institutions were seen as appropriate centres for channeling development aid and the right forum for transmitting vital development-oriented information to the rural masses. Tradition also played a vital role in the promotion of co-operatives by post-independence African governments. Mutual assistance and cooperation were seen as an essential ethic in indigenous African life (→ *Autochthonous Co-operatives*). A number of African governments thus launched vigorous campaigns for the promotion of co-operatives, arguing that the principles of mutual assistance stem from Africa's traditional past (*Migot-Adholla* 1970). Thus,

Nyerere and *Senghor* saw in the traditional communal African way of life a basis for African socialism. This was the basis for *Nyerere's* establishment of Ujamaa Villages and Co-operatives in Tanzania (*Nyerere* 1968) (→ *Pre-co-operative Forms*).

Co-operatives have been actively engaged in the marketing of agricultural products, the supply of inputs for agriculture, the provision of savings and credit facilities as well as the performing of a host of other development activities. In spite of the importance attached to co-operatives and the substantial financial, human and material support they have enjoyed from the state and donor agencies during the over 40 years of existence, one can hardly claim an overall success story of African co-operatives, which have hardly lived up to the high expectations of both the promoters and the beneficiaries. An Evaluation Report by the United Nations Research Institute for Social Development (UNRISD) about two decades ago, portrayed a picture of total failure, recommending that co-operatives should be replaced by another form of organization (UNRISD 1972). Although this view has been challenged as being too much on the negative side as the actual picture shows: for instance, Uganda co-operatives made significant contributions to economic growth (*Okereke* 1970), successes have been recorded in a number of Kenya Co-operatives (*Hyden* 1973), the success story of the → *Credit Unions* (CU) in Cameroon (*Deschamps* 1989), (*Nchari* 1991); it irrefutably points to the rather limited success of co-operative ventures. However, the Gaborone Declaration for a Regional Development Decade (1985–1995) by the Ministers responsible for Co-operative Development in East, Central and Southern Africa at the First African Ministerial Co-operative Conference in Gaborone, Botswana in May 1984, portrays the continuous belief by several African governments in co-operatives as important vehicles for promoting development in African countries (ICA, East and Southern Africa 1984).

2. PAID's Guiding Principles Reflected in the Co-operative Principles

From the African perspective, there are quite a number of similarities between PAID's guiding principles and the universally accepted principles guiding the co-operative movement. Both have as raison d'être the development of the human element, particularly the underprivileged and besides, have the field as basis for operations. The cardinal elements of PAID's strategic principle of the Integrated Rural Development (IRD) are basic to the co-operative form of organization. This strategic IRD principle has four principal elements emphasising:

- package programmes for the rural/urban poor in light of the multidimensional needs of an individual;
- participation of the rural population in all aspects of projects and programmes designed for its well being;
- coordination of services provided by various agencies for the same population;
- cooperation in other forms amongst these agencies or institutions.

The Co-operative Principles of Open Membership, Democratic Administration, Education and Patronage Bonus are meant to facilitate active member participation in the decision making process, management, benefits and the monitoring/evaluation of co-operative societies (→ *Principles*). Package programmes are provided through multi-purpose co-operative societies which offer a variety of services to the same community and which in their extreme forms (productive and communal co-operatives) are delegated most functions in the economic and social fields by individual members. Cooperation and co-ordination in the co-operative movement manifest themselves through the co-operative principle of cooperation amongst co-operatives demonstrated through the various forms of vertical and horizontal integration in the co-operative movement. Furthermore, according to systems theory, co-operative societies, being essentially "Open Systems" (*Dülfer* 1984), have to interact with other systems or institutions in their environment.

3. PAID's Co-operative Educational and Training Programmes

a) Problems in Co-operatives and the Necessity for Education and Training

Education is one of the cardinal principles of the co-operative movement and co-operatives can be described as an economic movement employing educational action. Co-operative education should essentially be directed towards solving identified co-operative problems. A Special Committee of Enquiry into the Co-operative Movement of Tanzania by the President of that country in January in 1966 revealed the following problem areas:

- uninformed membership;
- shortage of appropriate manpower;
- lack of democracy at the union level;
- lack of skilled people in the movement with specialist knowledge;
- susceptibility of the movement to political interference (*Westergaard* 1970).

Similar problems have been identified in other countries such as Kenya (*Hyden* 1973, *Ouma* 1990), Cameroon (*Nchari* 1990), and Uganda (*Okereke* 1974). The above shows that educational and trainable needs, necessary to provide the relevant knowlege, skills and attitudes (KSA), are prevalent. *Diallo* (1984) supports this view and sees the lack of adequate training and the inadequate methodological approach as major impediments in the way of the growth of genuine co-operative movements seen as an instrument for authentic self-centred development (→ *Self-help Organizations*).

From the identified problem areas, it is logical that co-operative education and training should be directed towards the membership, including the members of the board of directors, the employees and the general public.

b) Co-operative Training Opportunities in Africa

Many African countries with intensive co-operative activity have specialised national training institutions for the co-operative sector such as Cameroon, Nigeria, Kenya, Zambia, Tanzania, Sudan, Benin, Uganda, Ghana and Botswana. Nigeria alone has 3 federal and 9 State Co-operative Education and Training colleges in the country. Besides, there are 4 polytechnics and 6 universities offering co-operative studies (*Gbenebichie* 1985). Other institutions that offer co-operative education and training are the government co-operative departments or ministries and the national or regional co-operative apex organizations. Besides the national institutions, co-operative training is also received from overseas institutions specialised in co-operative training for developing countries such as Philipps-Universität in Marburg, Germany, that offers Masters Degree courses in Co-operative Economics; the Co-operative University of Paris, France that offers up to post graduate courses in co-operative studies and the Loughborough Co-operative College, Great Britain, offering a variety of co-operative related courses up to the Diploma level (→ *Education, Germany*).

The national co-operative training institutions generally focus their training on the Co-operative Movement and the government departmental staff usually at the certificate and diploma levels. Graduates are capable of serving in various capacities such as supervisors/inspectors in the case of civil servants who have to supervise the existing co-operatives, and undertake feasibility studies for proposed ones and as managers (general) and in specialised areas such as accountants, marketing officers, procurement and supplies officers and personnel officers in the co-operative movement.

The course content for the training for co-operative departmental and movement staff is usually skills-oriented and includes such subject areas as book-keeping and accounts, co-operative principles, co-operative management, co-operative law, general management, development economics and specialised management areas. Membership education/training usually has two dimensions, namely:

(1) The training of Board Members who generally have wide powers including policy formulation, keeping and presentation of audited accounts, to the annual general meeting, appointment of the manager and top level staff as well as overseeing the operations of the entire co-operative enterprise.

(2) Education of the general membership and the public that aims at sensitizing them to inter alia, be aware of the benefits of cooperation, their rights and obligations as members as well as providing them with knowledge on co-operative principles and their role.

c) PAID's Co-operative Educational and Training Programmes

c1) Introduction

As prescribed in its Guiding Principles, PAID's role in promoting African development is essentially one of complementarity. PAID is thus not expected to duplicate services provided for by national training institutions except where these are not adequately provided for or are non-existent.

In its training activities, PAID offers both long term and short term courses.

c2) Long Term Training

Only two out of the four PAID training institutions, namely IPD/AC and PAID/WA, offer regular long term courses with a co-operative component.

IPD/AC serving 13 French speaking African countries in the Central African Region including Angola, Madagascar and Comoros, has the enterprises and co-operative (ECO) units as one of its 4 major units of specialization. The specialization in ECO takes 7 months out of the two year Diploma course for training rural development technicians. The general objective of the ECO unit is to provide the trainees with the relevant knowledge and skills to effectively manage co-operatives and other business enterprises. At the end of the training programme, participants are expected to be able to effectively:

– undertake a feasibility study;
– prepare a project proposal;
– undertake a needs assessment study;
– manage a co-operative society and other business enterprises;
– handle the specialized areas of management notably finance, personnel, production, marketing, procurement and storage.

The ECO specialization unit has 4 modules.
Module 1 concerned with the Formulation and General Management of Business Enterprises and Co-operatives aims at providing trainees with the relevant knowledge and skills in the formation and management of an ECO.

The module covers such aspects as undertaking a Needs Assessment Survey (NAS), undertaking a Feasibility Study (FS) and writing a Project Proposal as well as providing general management knowledge and skills.

Module 2 concerned with Management Techniques for an ECO aims at providing trainees with indepth knowledge and skills in specialized management areas. At the end of the module, the trainees should be able to effectively manage finances, production and personnel as well as market products and build an efficient Management Information System.

Module 3 is concerned with Field Work/Studies by which trainees are attached to a co-operative society or union for a period of two months. The objective of this module is to familiarise the trainees with the actual working of a co-operative enterprise.

Module 4 synthesizes and evaluates the training programme.

Since 1965, a total of 784 participants from 13 countries have acquired co-operative management knowledge and skills from IPD/AC. They are serving as managers in co-operative enterprises or as officials in co-operative departments in their various countries.

In the PAID-WA, co-operative development is one of the major course components in the basic course of the nine-month diploma course in Integrated Rural Development (IRD) held annually with participants drawn from English speaking African countries. The course aims at providing participants with relevant knowledge and some skills on the co-operative form of organization as a basis for promoting IRD and as an instrument for raising the living standards of the population particularly those with very limited means. As learning objectives the participants are expected by the end of the programme to be able to:

- list and explain the Co-operative Principles, their implications and application in the African context; describe and explain at least 5 functional activity areas of African Rural Co-operatives;
- identify situations which call for the establishment of a co-operative society and procedures for establishment;
- organize and manage at least 3 types of co-operative societies;
- integrate some basic needs in a given (existing) rural co-operative society;
- identify the indigenous African co-operative forms and illustrate how these can be used to foster development;
- identify major problems of co-operative management in Africa and how these can be tackled.

The course content reflects these learning objectives. The IRD Diploma course participants also apply knowledge of co-operatives in other phases of the course. During the field studies period, co-operative societies are usually some of the institutions with which the participants come into contact. Their knowledge and skills of co-operatives acquired during the classroom phase facilitates understanding, analysis and preparation of co-operative projects. Some participants write their case studies, an important component of the IRD course, on selected co-operative business enterprises. Others have selected the co-operative development option as their area of specialization.

Since its establishment in 1969, a total of 1159 participants from all English speaking African countries have attended the IRD Diploma Course with Co-operative Development as an integral part of it. In view of the fact that the participants come from various agencies in different countries, the co-operative development course offers each participant the opportunity to practice cooperation in the particular organization served. Some ex-course participants working for the Community Development Department have for instance made use of the knowledge acquired and established savings/credit co-operative societies for the communities they serve as development agents (*Nchari* 1991).

c3) Short Term Training

Each of the four PAID institutions offers short term courses ranging from one week to 3 months in salient aspects of rural development. The short courses are generally tailor-made, i.e. are designed to suit the particular needs of the clients. Clients have usually been organizations, individual African countries or an African region or continent, in cases when problems to be addressed through training cut across.

Co-operative training has been one of those areas of concern for short term training in each of the regional institutions as exemplified by the following examples. IPD/AC organized a series of courses for co-operative credit union staff in Yaounde, Cameroon at the level of managers, cashiers and other employees for a Yaounde based co-operative credit union. It has also organized for managers of the "Caisses Populaires" for other regions of Cameroon as well as short courses in co-operative management for managers of co-operatives in Gabon.

PAID/WA organized an Inter-African Credit Union Training Workshop in collaboration with the African Co-operative Savings and Credit Association (ACOSCA). It has also been organizing a series of courses for managers of women's co-operatives for income generation in Cameroon. It has organized tailor-made training for Senior Store-keepers of the Cocoa/Coffee Marketing Co-operative Societies in Procurement and Store Management, identified as a major area of weakness in the management of these co-operatives.

IPD/AOS has also been quite involved in running short courses in its region of operation. It has organized inter alia a series of courses, each lasting two weeks, on Training Methods and Training tools for all senior co-operative departmental staff in the Ivory Coast on the invitation of the "Office National de

Promotion Rurale (ONPR)" of that country. Though essentially a training of trainers course, focus was also on salient elements of management, communications, work organization and finance.

Most significant amongst the short courses undertaken by PAID-ESA in the co-operative domain was a Co-operative Management Course for top managers of apex co-operative organizations from the East and Southern Africa region. The 25 participants were drawn from 11 countries in the region. Although most of the participating managers already had sound co-operative training, visits to some of the apex organizations had shown some knowledge gaps and revealed the need to continously update their knowledge and skills and to equip them with the necessary analytical tools as basis for making sound investment decisions. Thus equipped they could face the challenges of growth and the rapidly changing environment. Other short term courses organized by PAID-ESA include six weeks training programmes on Strategic Investment Planning and Financial Management for District Co-operative Union Managers from countries of the region (PAID Reports 1976–1991).

Although the training methods used for the various short courses undertaken by the Regional Institutes essentially depended on the content and the level of the participants, generally adult training methods were used with emphasis on discussions and problem solving. Besides, the acquisition of relevant knowledge and skills as per each course design, one basic benefit, particularly from the multinational programmes, has been the exchange of experiences. For instance, PAID-ESA Training for Senior Managers of Apex Co-operative Organizations did not only provide such a forum for the exchange of experiences but also created barter trade links between some of the participating co-operatives and led to the formation of an Association for Co-operative Managers for East and Southern Africa.

4. Other Co-operative Promotional Activities by PAID's Institutions

a) Studies

PAID institutions have also been promoting co-operatives in Africa by undertaking studies either as a basis for taking measures for improvement or for providing information to improve decision making. Thus, IPD/AC undertook a study of the training requirements for savings and credit co-operatives in Zaire. The study revealed an enormous need for training. Consequently, IPD/AC proposed and ran a series of training seminars for various categories of employees. PAID/ESA studied the Ethiopian Peasant Associations and Co-operatives to illustrate people's participation in pural development through co-operatives (*Nchari*, 1984). Studies were also undertaken by IPD/SG on co-operatives in Cameroon to portray co-operatives as decentralised socio-economic institutions (*Nchari* 1990).

b) Support and Consultancy

PAID has also been undertaking support/consultancy services as illustrated by the following examples. IPD/AC has over the years been providing support to the Nylon Craftsmen's Co-operative (COOPAN), Douala, Cameroon, whose aim is to promote development at the grassroots level. This has included assistance in the preparation of financial statements and writing financial reports as well as the provision of logistics support for the storage of equipment. IPD/AOS has been providing management and advisory support to dairy co-operatives in Niger (→ *Consulting*). PAID-WA undertook an evaluation of the North West Co-operative Association, Bamenda, Cameroon as consultant and proposed organizational restructuring and cost reduction measures as well as the introduction of a small-farmers co-operative credit scheme for food growers. PAID's support has also been directed towards national co-operative training institutions such as the National Co-operative College, Bamenda, Cameroon, in the design and implementation of Co-operative Training Programmes for Co-operative Union Managers by PAID-WA; the Somali Institute of Public Administration and Management, Mogadishu, Somalia, in the design of Training Programmes for the Co-operative Component by PAID/ESA; and the Centre Panafricain de Formation Co-operative (CPFC) Cotonou, Benin, in the design and launching of its new training programme for senior level staff by IPD/AOS. At the governmental level, PAID provided one of the consultants in the drafting of the new Cameroon Co-operative Law promulgated in 1992.

c) Organization of Seminars and Symposiums

PAID institutions have also been involved in organizing seminars in the co-operative sector. IPD/AOS assisted in the organization and running of a National Seminar in Burkina Faso organized by the government on the Reforms in the Co-operative Movement. Participants were representatives of the Co-operative Movement, Government Ministries, Non-Governmental Organizations and others interested in Co-operative Development in Burkina Faso. IPD/AOS has participated in other seminars such as the seminar for the Promotion of Insurance Co-operatives for African Populations in Senegal; and the National Seminar on the Appropriate Management of Small Farmers Co-operatives and the Design of Training Programmes in Burkina Faso. PAID-WA participated in the Seminar on Co-operatives in West Africa and the Launching of the International Co-operative Alliance, West Africa located in Abidjan. IPD/AC organized an international symposium in collaboration with the International Co-operative University of Paris (UCI) and the Co-operative Research Centre, Rwanda, on the Training of Peasant Farmers and Functional Literacy. The participants came from 23 African, European and North American countries. The seminar aimed at sharing experiences and knowledge in the field of co-operative training, training of peasant farmers and functional literacy as well as sharing experiences through action-oriented research culminating in a collective piece of work (→ *MATCOM*).

III. PAID'S Future Role in African Co-operative Development

1. Capacity Building of Training Institutions

PAID'S wide areas of activity, in various aspects of development, its continental coverage coupled with very limited resources has made it difficult to do more for the co-operative sector. PAID thus plans in the future to pay greater attention to Capacity Building in Co-operative Training Institutions. Organizing training workshops for staff of these institutions on such areas as Training Needs Analysis, Curriculum Development and Tailor-made Training Programmes, Adult Training Methods as well as on co-operative relevant subject areas, where some deficiencies have been established in terms of know-how, will enable staff members of co-operative training institutions to effectively organize programmes and to meet the particular training needs of their respective countries. Such training of trainers programmes are expected to yield multiplier effects.

2. Promotion of Self-Help Grassroots Associations

Self-help development-oriented rural and urban groupings are increasingly gaining importance in African countries as vehicles for accelerating development (→ *Development Policy*). Although such self-help groups have been organized in almost any area of human endeavour, their organization in the areas of savings/credit and agriculture have been predominant (→ *Self-help Organizations*). Thus, the Oha/Esusu and the thousands of women's associations in Nigeria are playing an important developmental role (*Eze* 1985). Similarly, the Njangis/Tontines to which associations about 50% of Cameroonians belong are proving to be vital tools for mobilizing savings and financing business enterprises in Cameroon (*Nchari* 1990). The failure of agricultural development banks and other rural lenders to reach low-income producers with affordable credit has made lending rural groups and credit co-operatives a popular alternatives (*Huppi* and *Feder* 1990). Some governments and donor agencies have recognized their importance and are actively promoting them.

According to *Münkner* (1985), experience with European-patterned co-operatives in Burkina Faso has not been encouraging. Rather, like in other Francophone countries such as Senegal, the genuine self-help organizations are to be found in the informal sector of village groups. The government of Burkina Faso has expressed its intention to recognise them. The recently promulgated Cameroon Co-operative Law (1992) characterized by the autonomy granted co-operatives, incorporates "→ *Common Initiative Groups*." (Cameroon Government, 1992).

PAID's promotional role has been through training and providing technical assistance in the form of working with the groups as has been the case with the Ford Foundation and the World Bank funded women's groups in Nigeria. The new Cameroon Co-operative Law (1992) earmarks PAID to design simple accounting systems for the common initiative groups. Given its wide experience in working with rural population as well as the growing recognition of these groups, PAID intends to intensify efforts in promoting the self-help grassroots associations and other NGOs using its tri-dimensional approach of Training, Research and Support/Consultancy.

3. Developing Training Materials

The problem of the lack of appropriate co-operative-oriented training materials specific to the African situation requires PAID as an institution familiar with African conditions to develop training materials in relevant subject areas for distribution to co-operative practitioners and training institutions. Preparing case studies that suit the African situation will be an integral part of the training materials development effort.

IV. Summary

The International Association of the Pan African Institute for Development (PAID) has since 1965 been active in undertaking development work in Africa using its tridimensional approach of training African development staff, undertaking research and providing support/consultancy services in various aspects of the socio-economic development in African countries.

The promotion of the co-operative sector in African countries essentially through education and training, but also through research, support/consultancy, has been one of its activity areas to foster African development. Although some successes have been recorded, PAID plans in the near future to achieve greater impact in its co-operative promotional efforts by paying greater attention to capacity building for co-operative training, institutions developing training materials specific to African countries and promoting the strong emerging self-help associations and other NGOs essential for rural development. If PAID goes ahead to implement these intents, the African Co-operative Movement both traditional and imported forms are, ceteris paribus, most likely to experience positive developments in the near future.

Bibliography

Cameroon Government: Law No. 92/006 of 14th August 1992. Decree No. 92/455/PM of 11/23(92. Governing Co-operative Societies, Common Initiative Groups and Their Unions.
Diallo Fousseyni: The Position of Co-operatives in French Speaking Countries of Africa. In: Towards Adjusted Patterns of Co-operatives in Developing Countries, Friedrich Ebert Stiftung, Bonn 1984, pp. 57–73.
Deschamps, Jean-Jacques: "Credit for the Rural Poor: The Experience in Six African Countries: Synthesis Report". Development Alternatives, World Bank, Washington DC 1988.
Dülfer, Eberhard: Betriebswirtschaftslehre der Kooperative – Kommunikation und Entscheidungsbildung in Genossenschaften und vergleichbaren Organisationen, Göttingen 1984.
Eze, E.A. Ewu: The Role of Non-Governmental Organizations in Promoting Rural Development in Nigeria. In: Promotion of Self-Help Organizations. Konrad Adenauer Stiftung, Sankt Augustin 1985, pp. 51–71.
Gbenebichie, S.A.: Role of Co-operatives in Nigeria, Agricultural Development and Government Promotion. In: The Role of Non-Governmental Organizations in Promoting Self-Help Organizations. International Institute of the Konrad Adenauer Stiftung, Sankt Augustin 1985.
Hyden, Goran: Efficiency versus Distribution in East African Co-operatives – A Study of Organizational Conflicts, East African Literature Bureau, Nairobi 1973.
Migot-Adholla, S.E.: Traditional Society and Co-operatives. In: Co-operatives and Rural Development in East Africa. The Scandinavian Institute of African Studies, Uppsala 1970, pp. 17–37.
Münkner, Hans-H.: How to Create an Appropriate Legal Framework for Village Co-operatives – A Case Study Upper–Volta/Burkina Faso. In. Promotion of Self-Help Organizations, Konrad Adenauer Stifutng, Sankt Augustin 1985, pp. 234–247.
Nchari, Anthony Nforba: Co-operatives as Decentralised Socio-Economic Institutions – The Case of Cameroon. In Decentralization Policies and Socio-Economic Development in Sub Saharan Africa, World Bank, Washington 1990, pp. 61–102.
Nchari, Anthony Nforba: Experiences in Training African Development Staff with the Marburg University Educational Background. In: Bildungsinvestitionen in der Dritten Welt. Institut für Kooperation in Entwicklungsländern, Marburg 1991, pp. 67–80.
Nchari, Anthony Nforba: People's Participation in Rural Development Through Co-operatives – The Case of the Ethiopian Peasant Associations. In: People's Participation in Development in Black Africa. PAID and Karthala (Paris) 1984, pp. 247–280.
Nyerere, J.K.: Ujamaa: Essays on Socialism, London 1968.
Okereke, Okoro: The Economic Impact of the Uganda Co-operatives, Nairobi 1974.
Ouma, Sylvester J.: 21 Essays on cooperation and Development in Kenya, Nairobi 1990.
PAID: PAID-Reports 1976–1991, PAID.
UNRISD: Rural Co-operatives and Planned Change in Africa: An Analytical Overview vol. 5, ILO, Geneva 1972.
Vincent, Fernand: The PAID Story (1963–1981), PAID 1982.
Westergaard, Poul W.: Co-operatives in Tanzania as Economic and Democratic Institutions. In Co-operatives and Rural Development in East Africa, Uppsala 1970, pp. 121–152.

Education and Training in Asia, Co-operative

GANESH P. GUPTA/DHARM VIR

(see also: *Education, Europe*; *Education, North America*; *Education, Latin America*; *Education, Africa*; *Education, Germany*; *Development Policy*; *Policies for Promotion*)

I. Co-operative Human Resource Development; II. Scope of the Study; III. Definition of Co-operative Education and Training; IV. Target Group; V. Focus on Member Education; VI. CET Programmes in Southern Asia; VII. CET Programmes in South-East Asia; VIII. CET Programmes in Northern-Eastern Asia; IX. CET Programmes in Central Asia; X. CET Programmes in Western Asia; XI. CET Programmes in Australia and the Pacific; XII. Summary and Conclusion.

I. Co-operative Human Resource Development (CHRD)

According to the ICA policy on human resource development, the concept of HRD in Co-operatives means all the planned information, education, training, mobilisation and manpower development activities undertaken by the co-operatives, so as to create economically efficent organizations, capable of providing services required by the members. A team of well trained and co-operatively educated personnel, both selected for and elected to posts, will go a long way in developing the co-operative organization at any level. This has been successfully done by farmers' co-operatives in major parts of India, with thoughtful help from organizations like National Dairy Development Board (NDDB) and the Indian Farmers' Fertilizer Co-operative Limited (IFFCO). The co-operative movements in Japan and the Republic of Korea also have notably successful examples of HRD and they are being studied by the cooperators elsewhere. However, there is greater need of planning for developing the co-operative sector of national economy of all countries of Asia.

II. Scope of the Study

The Asian and the Pacific Regions are very vast from the geographical and demographic point of view.

From the angle of co-operative development, these regions can be sub-divided into the following sub-regions:
- Southern Asia: Afghanistan, Bangladesh, Bhutan, India, Iran, Maldives, Mynamar (Burma), Nepal, Pakistan and Sri Lanka.
- South-East Asia: Brunei, Indonesia, Kampuchia, Laos, Malaysia, Philippines, Singapore, Thailand and Vietnam.
- Northern-Eastern Asia: China, Hong Kong, Japan, Democratic People's Republic of Korea (DPRK), Republic of Korea (ROK), Taiwan.
- Central Asia: Mangolia, Khajakhstan, Tajakhstan and other CIS countries of Asia.
- Western Asia: Iraq, Israel, Turkey, Jordan and other Arabian countries of the Asian continent.
- Australia and other countries of the Pacific.

Efforts have been made to describe the Co-operative Education and Training (CET) activities in all the sub regions, sufficient information is available about the countries covered by the ICA ROAP. It may be noted that the face of Asia is fast changing due to recent political upheavals and the socio-economic development activities undertaken by the co-operative organizations, government corporations and private enterprises. In addition, multi-national corporations, international development organizations and UN agencies (→ *United Nations System*) and the international financial bodies have been accelerating the process of development and changing the people's life style. Nevertheless, poverty, inequality, erosion of human values, violence and political instability, illiteracy and deteriorating environment are some of the important problems of Asia and the Pacific Region. Co-operatives and the CET programmes were much neglected leading to slow and lopsided development of the co-operative movement in these regions (→ *Development Policy*).

III. Definition of Co-operative Education and Training

The concept of Co-operative education becomes clearer when it is stated as one of the basic Principles of Cooperation and has world-wide acceptance. Co-operative Training is here defined as those training activities that are organized to improve job performance of the co-operative staff and of government employees engaged in support and supervision of co-operatives. (Report of the ILO Regional Symposium, Thailand 1979).

IV. Target Group

In any co-operative organization, the following main groups can be identified for communication, education and training on a regular basis:

i) Members and the active members
ii) Board members and other leaders
iii) Managers and other employees
iv) Special groups such as women, youth, children, rural poor (as prospective members)
v) General public

V. Focus on Member Education

Member Education means all educational and human development activities carried on by co-operatives and their allied organizations aimed at securing contructive member participation, member control and democratic management, effective functioning and growth of their co-operatives. The situation of co-operative member education in the region is confounded by the shortcomings of the policies and programmes of the past. Looking at these shortcomings in retrospect, the considered opinion of the Consultation was that most developing countries in the region have not been able firstly to formulate suitable programmes of co-operative member education and secondly, to implement effectively. Youth education programmes are implemented as a part of the general and women's education programmes.

In some countries cooperation is taught in the schools, colleges and universities. In some educational institutions, students or school co-operatives are successfully organized as in Japan, Malaysia, Singapore and the Philippines. Nevertheless, much more efforts are needed. The movement must realise that due to lack of support and patronage from the younger generation, many organizations stagnate and would deteriorate. The sooner educated youth get active in co-operatives they will bring sustainable development in the community and thus break the vicious cycle of generation gaps in the movement.

VI. CET Programmes in Southern Asia

1. Afghanistan

The first Co-operative Training Institute (CTI) was started by the Ministry of Agriculture and Land Reforms during the first phase of the Project on Agricultural Co-operatives and Credit (PACCA) sponsored by FAO. During the first phase, graduates from the Higher Agricultural Institute and the personnel working with the Ministry of Agriculture, were given training for work in co-operative development. After some time, the Institute was revived and started functioning as a full-fledged centre for the training of personnel working in the Department of Co-operative Development and the agricultural co-operatives in the country. The main task of the Institute is to train the co-operative personnel in co-operative Principles, Legislation, Registration, Marketing, Credit, Supply, Audit, Book-keeping,

Agricultural extension, Agronomy, Sociology and Agricultural Economics. The duration of the course varies from four to ten weeks. Refresher courses of two weeks duration are also organized. It has a well equipped library and an audiovisual cum cinema hall. The CTI undertakes research projects. It is also encouraging participation of women in co-operative activities.

2. Bangladesh

The co-operative movement in Bangladesh which was formally introduced in 1904 for improvement of agro-based rural economy has passed through a long process of trial and error with respect to membership patterns, management, jurisdiction, organizational set-up and CET programmes.
Bangladesh National Co-operative Union (BJSU), The Bangladesh Co-operative College (BCC) and more than 8 zonal co-operative training centres, Bangladesh National Co-operative Federation (BJSF) are the institutions for member education programme. Under the Integrated Rural Development Programme, BJSF and the Thana Training and Development Centres, regular educational meetings for farmers and training meetings for the co-operative leaders, field workers and officers are held in various parts of the country. There are some primary co-operatives undertaking CET programmes. The Co-operative Department and the Department of Rural Development have CET personnel who give assistance.
Some national and international courses, seminars and conferences are held with the assistance of ICA, ILO, ACCU etc. The Co-operative Credit Union of Bangladesh also undertakes CET programmes in collaboration with the Christian Co-operative Association (CCA). Besides, the Centre for Rural Development for Asia and The Pacific (CIRDAP) has also been helping programmes including CET.

3. Bhutan

An acute shortage of qualified and trained manpower, inadequate technical support services are a major constraint to development in all sectors. Agriculture has 370 extension personnel including the supporting staff. Poor infrastructure facilities, remoteness of population centre, poor roads, inadequate coverage of basic communication facilities also put severe constraints on marketing, distribution and extension. The institutional → *agricultural credit* is still in its infancy. Till 1975 some credit for farmers was provided by the marketing co-operative societies. But, in 1975 The Royal Government of Bhutan ordered the closure of the co-operatives, and the Food Corporation of Bhutan was entrusted with the task of recovering the outstanding loans. A big challenge of organizing CET programmes leading to people's co-operatives lies before the international co-operative movement as well as the South Asian Association for Regional Cooperation (SAARC).

4. India

The responsibility for administering and implementing the programme of CET rests with the co-operative institutions at the national and state levels. The centres for training of junior and intermediate workers are looked after by the State Co-operative Unions, while at the central level, the programme of CET has been entrusted to the National Committee for Co-operative training (under the National Co-operative Union of India).
NCUI, the umbrella organization and the official spokesman of the co-operative movement, is responsible for co-ordination, monitoring and supervison of the entire programme of CET. Organizational set-up for CET is a three-tier structure, with NCUI at the national level, 23 State Co-operative Unions, and 325 District Co-operative Unions in the States. A special Committee on Co-operative Education constituted by NCUI advises and guides the programme.
NCUI has built up a large infrastucture for effective implementation of CET programme. This consists of Vaikunth Mehta National Institute of Co-operative Management, Pune, 18 Co-operative Training Colleges and 96 Junior Co-operative Training Centres.

National Centre for Co-operative Education:
The Centre was established in 1957 in response to the need for training and co-operative education instructors working mainly for member education at the primary co-operative level. It organizes short courses for T&D of co-operative leaders working mainly at the district level. The focus of the programme conducted by NCCE is on building up functional efficiency of co-operative education personnel and on leadership development for non-official co-operative leadership for district level co-operatives.

National Council for Co-operative Training:
NCCT, which was established in 1976 and functions under the umbrella of NCUI, is directly responsible for CET programmes for the senior and middle level personnel of co-operative institutions and the government departments. It provides training facilities for foreign scholars on behalf of the Government of India. NCCT has a well integrated 3–tier co-operative training set-up comprised of Vaikunth Mehta National Institute of Co-operative Management at Pune for senior and key personnel; and Junior Co-operative Training Colleges for middle level personnel. NCCT organizes CET programmes in collaboration with ILO, CICTAB (Centre for International Co-operative Training in Agricultural Banking, Pune). National Essays and Debating Competitions

are also organized for University and College students.

Vaikunth Mehta National Institute of Co-operative Management:
VMNICOM infuses a high order of enterprise management in the co-operative sector. It caters to the management development, training, research and consultancy needs. In addition to several long-term and short-term training programmes, it offers Fellowships leading to Ph.D. The Institute closely collaborates with ICA, ILO, FAO, CICTAB and offers training programmes for senior executives of co-operatives in developing countries. Excellent infrastructure of building, training equipment, staff, etc. are available with the Institute.

College of Agricultural Banking:
CAB is run by the Reserve Bank of India and is an apex institution in the field of agricultural banking and training, catering to the training requirements of officers and staff of RBI, and commercial banks involved in agricultural lending.

Over and above the CET activities of above organizations, CET facilities are offered by National Dairy Development Board, National Co-operative Development Corporation, Reserve Bank of India, Petrofils Co-operative Ltd..

All–India Village and Khadi Commission, Housing and Urban Development Corporation, National Federation of Co-operative Sugar Factories, National Federation of Co-operative Spinning Mills, National Federation of State Co-operative Banks, National Federation of Co-operative Rural and Agricultural Development Banks, National Federation of Urban Co-operative and Credit Societies, National Federation of Dairy Co-operatives, National Tobacco Growers' Co-operative Federation, National Co-operative Housing Federation, National Tribal and Co-operatives Federation, National Federation of Labour Co-operatives also provide CET programmes. Few universities offer Graduate and Postgraduate curricula with special in Cooperation, someones optional papers in their Bachelors and Masters Degree programmes.

5. Iran

The Central Organization of Rural Co-operatives, Teheran was founded in 1963 as an autonomous body. It has to secure credit and grants from various sources and arrange farm production inputs for rural co-operatives. CORC also organizes co-operative education and training programmes for elected board members in the Principles of Cooperation, Book-Keeping, Accounting, etc. The Government of Iran provides funds for the promotion of rural co-operatives and also finances CET programmes at all levels including member education at field level. At its Head Quarters, the CORC has a CET Department manned by about 100 persons. At the provincial level, there are special officers and education personnel and filed supervisors who help in organizing educational programmes. One of the most important tasks of the field supervisors is education of the members of rural co-operatives. The educational personnel of the CURC are trained in special courses held mainly by the Co-operative Education Institute of Tehran University.

6. Maldives

In the SAARC region, Maldives is another country which deserves attention from the development agencies for development of CET programmes. In the Island only the Ministry of Agriculture is responsible for CET activities.

7. Mynamar (Burma)

In the beginning of the 20th Century Co-operative ideas were imported from western countries. During 1942–45, Japanese forces occupied the country, the government tried to diversify the Burmese economy and establish co-operatives in the rural areas. In the Ministry of Co-operatives, the Co-operative Department has an Education Division. The Director General of the Co-operative Department is Head of the Central Co-operative School at Yangon (Rangoon). The CCS is well furnished with academic and residential facilities, and is involved both in co-operative education and training pursuits. It also conducts research and development activities. Steps have been taken to promote the CCS as the Central Co-operative College.

In addition, the country has 7 State/Division level Co-operative Schools for CET programmes. The Co-operative School system undertakes CET in cooperation, economics and management field through residential and correspondence courses. These schools have courses for managers, board members as well as for co-operative instructors. Co-operative Training School at Mandlay is being promoted as the Regional Co-operative College.

The Burmese movement is also being served by the Asian Offices of ILO, FAO, WOCCU, etc.

8. Nepal

In 1962, His Majesty's Government of Nepal established a Co-operative Training Centre at Kathmandu under its Department of Co-operative Development with different training tasks. The Centre has been renamed the Centre for Co-operative Development and Training. The CCDT has produced educational material and promotes research in the field of co-operative training and development. With the help of ILO and ICA subjects such as population education and agricultural training were included in the curricula for CET at the local level. CCDT has been conducting mobile member education camps, with the help of district level officers of the Co-operative Department and the staff of agricultural Development Bank, Agricultural Supply Corporation and Agricultural Extension Offices. SAJHA (which means cooperation) has been engaged in promotion of CET activities in Nepal. SAJHA has member co-operatives which deal in consumer and agricultural production goods and services, offices in and outside the national and district level towns.

9. Pakistan

The co-operative movement was initiated by the government in the beginning of the century. Basically, it was a credit providing agency for the peasants. With the creation of Pakistan, the non-muslim traders, bankers and industrialists had to leave the country. To fill the vacuum, the co-operative movement spread itself into new fields of economic activity.

Co-operative Department:
The field staff of the co-operative department in different provinces guide and assist secretaries and committee members in running day-to-day affairs. The Co-operative Educational Instructors and Assistants hold short duration classes for training members, secretaries and office bearers of co-operatives in rural and semi-urban areas in maintaining accounts and management activities.

There are three Co-operative Training Institutes which mainly hold classes for sub-inspectors of the department and the secretaries of development and service societies. There is one residential Co-operative Training College at Lyalpur. There is a Co-operative Union in each province of Pakistan, their main aims being to develop, propagate, publicise, produce literature and safeguard and promote the interests of member co-operative societies. The National Co-operative Union, Lahor, an apex organization of the entire co-operative movement in Pakistan, aims at providing CET to motivate co-operators, to project the concept and principles of cooperation, hold seminars and conferences, advise the government and represent the movement at the national and international level. In addition, Marketing and Supply Federations and some large co-operative societies undertake CET and extension activities in collaboration with apex institutions. Pakistan Academy for Rural Development, National Centre for Rural Development, National and Provincial Governments also provide CET facilities.

10. Sri Lanka

The National Co-operative Council of Sri Lanka is the national apex body of the co-operative movement which is responsible for CET programmes. There are 26 District education Centres which also provide CET. In order to train co-operative employees and junior departmental personnel the NCC has established five Regional Training Institutes. For the training of co-operative employees, NCC and the Department of Co-operative Development share the responsibility. For training of government staff DCD has been running a national level School of Cooperation at Polgolla.

The Sri Lanka Institute of Co-operative Management, Colombo is a statutory body under the Ministry of Foods and Co-operatives. The Institute has been making important contributions towards management training, research and consultancy. One of the authors (Dharm Vir) was working at the CMSC as an ILO Consultant in CET programmes.

VII. CET Programmes in South-East Asia

Most of the countries in the region are covered under ASEAN programme of Social and Economic Development. South-East Asian Forum for Development Alternative (SEAFDA) is a regional network concerned with people's centred development activities in the countries of the Region.

1. Indonesia

The responsibility for CET activities is on the DEKOPIN, the apex co-operative body and the Department of Co-operative Development. Training of board of directors, board of supervisors, managers and other personnel is mainly organized by the co-operative movement and training of officials of the government department is looked after by the Department of Co-operatives. The Department has an extensive infrastructure at the national level as well as at the provincial level and takes major responsibility for CET.

The Indonesian Institute of Co-operative Management:
IKOPIN is a co-operative foundation under the DKI. It is engaged in the education and training of managers and board members of KUD (primary agricultural co-operatives). The Institute also undertakes training of Government Officers. There are long duration courses conducted mainly for the co-operative movement's staff at national level. Completion of the programme makes one eligible for a Graduate degree which is recognised by some of the Universities. Among the young generation, youth university students co-operatives are spreading.

2. Malaysia

For co-operative education of members and committee members of primary co-operative societies, the main responsibilities are with co-operatives and their federal organizations such as the National Co-operative Union (ANGKASA), Co-operative Union of Malaysia (CUM), supported by the Co-operative Development Department and the Co-operative College of Malaysia, Kuala Lumpur. Other government agencies such as FAO, FELCRA, FELGA, RISDA, etc. also undertake member education activities for their specific target groups.

For co-operative employees training, the ANGKASA and the Co-operative College of Malaysia undertake responsibility. The Education and Research Wing of CUM is mainly responsible for education and training within the urban sector of the movement.

Co-operative College of Malaysia is well furnished with academic, audio-visual and residential facilities. The College has been hosting and conducting several regional and international courses in co-operative development. It caters to the training requirements of the co-operatives in neighbouring areas, such as Sarawak and Brunei, and even Singapore. In addition, the sectoral co-operative organizations have their own arrangements for education and training of members and employees.

3. The Philippines

Co-operative Union of Philippines is one of the coordinating agencies in the field of co-operative promotion, education and training. The CET functions are discharged through the Regional Co-operative Union in different regions and member co-operative organizations. There are also several co-operative training centres which are sponsored by the National Association of Co-operative Training Centres Inc. (NATCCO) Manila. The Sugar Co-operative Development Institute of Philippines has its own training arrangements outside Manila. All the above bodies are meeting the CET requirements of the private sector co-operatives and they are assisted by international bodies.

In addition, there is a large official sector of the co-operative movement in the country, under the leadership of Co-operative Development Authority (CDA), under the Ministry of Agriculture. The CET activities in rural areas are conducted by the trained workers with the help of local co-operatives and pre-co-operatives. These farmers' co-operative and pre-co-operatives have their own CET programmes.

The CUP has also been functioning as the lead organization for the Integrated National Co-operative Audit System. The responsibility of training for the government staff for co-operative development is shared by CDA and the Agricultural Credit and Co-operative Institute of the University of Philippines at Los Banos. With the complexity that is increasing in the business activities of co-operatives it is a must that a CET system should be organized from the primary level and upward.

4. Singapore

To look after the CET needs, former Singapore Co-operative Union and the Singapore National Co-operative Federation have had their own Education and Development Committee/Department. There are long established sectoral programmes of CET in Singapore. These are conducted by Singapore Amalgamated Services Co-operative Organization, trade unions sponsored co-operatives such as those for insurance, consumer distribution, taxi service and for medical assistance).

The modern system of co-operative business needs support from modern equipment for educational purposes. To cater to the needs of co-operatives in the field of computer services, a special co-operative was floated in the country. Some training programmes for business and computer personnel have been conducted by this co-operative. Large sized credit and other co-operatives have their own committees and facilities of CET activites.

5. Thailand

CET is the joint responsibility of the Co-operative League of Thailand, Co-operative Promotion Divison and the National Agricultural Co-operative Training Institute. In addition, the CPD is engaged in training of Government officers. CLT has a National Level Co-operative Training Institute in Bangkok having separate divisions for training of co-operative personnel from agricultural and non-agricultural sectors of the co-operative movement. THE CPD has a training division at Bangkok which supervises the Co-operative Study institute and the central as well as the ten regional training centres. Regional Training Centres also operate through Mobile Units. CLT is responsible for training of committee and management staff and employees of non-agricultural co-operatives while the National Agricultural Co-operative Training Institute is responsible for training of personnel in agricultural co-operatives.

The Government of Thailand has long been giving importance to co-operative principles in the well-being of people and, therefore, included the Co-operative subjects in the education curricula starting from the elementary stage up to the university. Some of the universities have special faculties for teaching co-operative courses. School co-operatives are also promoted and supported.

6. Vietnam

Central Council of Supply and Marketing Co-operatives of Vietnam, Hanoi is the new member of the ICA. There is a national level co-operative training centre located in Hanoi. However, the Centre is not well equipped for carrying out CET programmes.

VIII. CET Programmes in Northern-Eastern Asia

1. China (→ *China*)

In the modern chinese economy, the Supply and Marketing Co-operatives (SMCs) with peasants as their members have become most powerful collectives. As a principal component in the socialist economy, they are playing an increasing role in the socialist economy and in the socialist modernisation drive. SMCs boast an extensive network comprising a workforce of over four million people. All-China Federation of Supply and Marketing Co-operatives (ACFSMCs) at the national level is supported by 28 co-operative unions at the provincial level, 2,100 co-operative unions at the country level and 33,000 grassroot SMCs throughout the country. To cater to members' needs better, the SMCs have set up Co-operative Affairs Committees and special associations. Thus, offering farmers comprehensive plans of services including technology transfer and information, and better personnel management. This helped in putting the responsibility system and employees training in SMCs.

Beijing Federation of Supply and Marketing Co-operatives takes active steps to train administrative and managerial personnel. There are 30 schools of different types which are being run in the province. To further improve vocational, technical and managerial abilities of personnel various kinds of training courses are conducted frequently by the promotional department concerned.

Attached to SMCs there are more than 1,400 secondary vocational institutions, out of them two colleges, 79 secondary vocational schools, 179 provincial and prefectural cadre training schools and 1,200 training schools. In the near future, co-operative movement will rationalize the location of its educational institutions and integrate in-service training with pre-job education. In addition to the scientists, co-operative technicians also help in disseminating scientific information and the results of applied researches done in co-operative research institutes run by local and regional co-operatives.

The Chinese SMCs have three kinds of CET programmes, viz. member education, employees' training and education of reserve forces. For members, co-operatives give education in co-operative ideology, management and technical education in agricultural production. For employees' training, it is conducted according to the types of responsibilities of participants. Education of reserve forces, in normal circumstances, are conducted in the two full-time institutions of higher learning or the full-time secondary schools and most of them are assigned to work in co-operative organizations after their graduation.

The ACFSMCs mainly organize the programmes, plan the curricula for courses and study the effects of training frequently held at the local, regional and national level. Duration of the courses depend on training needs, mainly aiming at improving managerial ability of the participants.

Responsiblity of education of pre-co-operative members is on public education organizations and funds are made available by the State. In this way, there is a wide coverage in CET. In addition, the ACFSMCs and the Ministry of Commerce have been running Zhongzhou Grain College, Wuhan Grain Industry College and Anhuei Finance and Trade College as well as Sahn Si Institute of Finance and Economics, for CET and management development.

2. Hong Kong

As there is no separate institution for CET, the Agriculture and Fisheries Department is responsible to its own co-operative staff. CET is undertaken by the departmental staff mainly through audit, supervisory and advisory services.

3. Japan

Co-operative education was started in Japan as early as in 1925 when the first industrial Co-operative School was established by the Central Union of industrial Co-operatives. After World War II, when the entire educational policy in the country was reviewed, the School was succeeded by the Co-operative College. The College, later, became the major educational institution of national co-operative movement in rural Japan. It runs a three year course for rural boys and girls below the age of 22. In addition, short term refresher courses are held for different categories of agricultural co-operative personnel. ZENKYOREN (National Mutual Insurance Federation of Agricultural Co-operative Association) has been running co-operative training programmes and technical education in collaboration with CUAC, which is the promotion body of the agricultural co-operative movement in Japan. The agricultural co-operative movement also offers guidance services for the better management of members' farming at the national, prefectural and regional levels.

The prefectural union held training courses and meetings to train local farm advisers, the guidance staff being trained by CUAC. Women's associations and Youth Club activities are also included in the co-operative programmes. CET programmes of fisheries, forestry and consumer co-operative federations are also conducted by their respective National Co-operative Schools and prefectural level outfits. The main member education, farm guidance and better living activities are held by the primary co-operatives for members and other groups. Farm guidance plays an overall function of agricultural co-operatives and is also defined as a management activity to smoothly carry out the whole process of business activities in a bid to improve members' farm management.

The important feature of the Japanese approach to

CET is that it is well integrated with the life of its members and their household. Women, youth and children are included in this integrated approach. Members education is targeted to individuals, groups and sometimes masses (through A.V. media). The outcome leads to improved image and usefulness of co-operatives and their business gets improved also. These days the co-operative education in Japan is focussed on Co-operative Values and on Environmental issues. Co-operative movement in Japan is getting increasingly conscious for providing technical and financial assistance in the field CET.

Agricultural Co-operative movement has established the Institute for Development of Agricultural Co-operative in Asia (IDACA). Central Union of Agricultural Co-operatives (CUCA) and Japanese International Cooperation Agency (JICA) have been assisting in conducting some development projects for improvement of agricultural co-operatives in Asia and for better involvement of women's participation in co-operatives. CUAC also collaborates with the Afro-Asian Regional Organization for Rural Reconstruction (New Delhi) for exchange visits of farm leaders and conducting international programmes.

I.E.-NO-Hikari Association and Agricultural Co-operative Film Production Federation have also been contributing much towards development of CET programmes in Japan. One such project is on management training for strengthening agricultural co-operatives and the other is strengthening of women's participation in co-operatives in Asia.

4. Democratic Peoples' Republic of Korea

The Central Union of Consumers' Co-operatives and their rural counterparts in the co-operative movement of DPRK are engaged in CET programmes. The adult education and workers education movement in the country coordinate their efforts for promotion of co-operative and consumer education.

5. Republic of Korea

Since the establishment of multi-purpose agricultural co-operatives, particularly in mid–1970, the primary co-operatives have consolidated their organizational base. They have been quite successful in rapidly expanding the volume of their diversified business in banking and credit, supply, marketing and farmer guidance including farm guidance, living guidance, promotion of Saemaul (new farmer) organizations fostering young prospective farmers, and other educational activities. Agricultural co-operatives have been conducting co-operative educational activities in order to enhance the co-operative spirit of member farmers and, to inspire a sense of duty into the minds of the officers and staff members.

The National Agricultural Co-operative Federation (NACF), the apex body of agricultural co-operatives in Korea runs two central level Agricultural Co-operative Training Institutes to foster leading/model farmers. In order to inculcate co-operative spirit in the member farmers, the NACF runs the Agricultural Co-operative Junior College. It also runs a national/central and five provincial Staff Training Institutes to enhance the abilities of co-operatives in business management. Moreover, the new Farmers Technical Colleges attached to the Junior colleges and the Provincial Institutes offer one week courses in modern farm technology on cash crops. NACF also brings out a variety of teaching material including audio-visual aids produced by its own Audio–Visual Centre for use in member information and education. As the rural Korea has a high level of functional literacy, the primary co-operatives issue newsletters which are extensively used for CET. NACF promotes cultural and public relations activities through its monthly magazine New Farmer, monthly Rural Children and the weekly Farmers News-Paper (→ *Periodicals, Co-operative*).

Like NACF there are other member organizations which are engaged in CET and allied activities in their respective fields. In addition, the National Credit Union Federation of Korea, registered in 1973, has its training centre. The Centre trains Credit Union leaders, educators and managers. The CU movement lays great stress on regular co-operative education, training and promotion. NACF has three target groups selected for education and training programmes, namely, the co-operative staff, the member farmers and the potential young farmer members. NACF is one of the few co-operative apex organizations in the world which has established a direct linkage between the business activities and the education/training/guidance activities for the benefit of co-operative members and the staff working for them. Considerable emphasis is, therefore, attached to the education and training of all persons associated with the agricultural co-operative movement.

6. Taiwan

Farmer organizations and the Credit Unions have been engaged in CET programmes and extension services. However, links with outside agencies are limited. The farmers associations are famous for their co-operative development and agricultural extension activities.

IX. CET Programmes in Central Asia

1. Mongolia

The Central Union Mongolian Consumer Co-operative has been active in the field of consumer distribution in urban and rural areas. With the help of ICA ROAP it will be expanding its CET activities.

2. Kazakhstan

After recently joining the ICA, the Union of Consumer Societies is expected to promote CET programmes in the newly established country under the Commonwealth of Independent States (CIS).

X. CET Programmes in Western Asia

1. Israel

In Israel the CET programmes are effective and well organized through the co-operatives, such as Kibutz and Moshavs (→ *Israel*). The Israeli experience in co-operative development is unique and could be shared with advantage by other Asian countries. Former Afro-Asian Institute and the International Institute for Labour Development and Co-operative Studies has proved itself an effective vehicle for communication of Israeli experience of developing countries in Asia and the Pacific Region. ILDEC organizes courses/workshops on Community Empowerment through Co-operatives, Rural Development, mainly for developing countries.

2. Iraq

The Institute of Cooperation and Agricultural Extension has been active in the field of CET. In addition to co-operative organizations and co-operative farming societies, some universities are engaged in CET activities.

3. Jordan

The Jordan Co-operative Organization established in 1977 have the Co-operative Institute, the Jordan Co-operative Federation, the Ministry of Labour and Social Welfare, and the Department of Co-operative Development their members concerned with CET activities. The number of member co-operatives are 115 (agricultural), and 299 (non-agricultural). The Jordanian Co-operative Training Centre is a department of the Jordanian Co-operative Organization. JTC organize pre-service co-operatives as well as seminars/short-term training courses for the members of co-operatives.

4. Turkey

Turkey has a well established co-operative system including the arrangement for CET activities. At Beherin and other Arabian States in Western Asia exist good consumer co-operatives. But, CET programmes are at their initial stages. They need special attention from co-operative development bodies like ICA, ILO, FAO, UNIDO.

XI. CET Programmes in Australia and the Pacific

As in India and Pakistan, the Cooperation and Co-operative development is treated as State level subject by the concerned governments.

1. Australia

The State Federation of Co-operatives in Western Australia has a special department for the organization of CET. Liaison is maintained with State Department of Education for the introduction of cooperation as a subject in high school curriculum. The Federation of Co-operatives in Queensland, New South Wales and Victoria have similar arrangements for CET, covering elected directors and the employees. The Australian Federation of Credit Union Leagues organizes training on a national basis periodically. The Co-operative Federation of Australia, together with the Federal Government of Australia had organized CET programmes for groups of co-operative personnel from abroad. Large sized agricultural co-operatives like West Farmers organized effective member education, agricultural extension and staff training in collaboration with specialized agencies. There is also a national co-operative training and leadership development centre for development of co-operativism among the aborigins in Australia. The ICA Training Development Project located in Australia has been contributing to the development of CET programmes in Australia and nearby countries and islands in the South Pacific.

2. New Zealand

New Zealand is famous for its dairy industry and co-operative dairies in the Hut Valley are most favoured. However, not much information is available on CET programmes.

3. FIJI

The Fiji Co-operative Union Ltd., is the national body of the co-operative movement on the island. The Department of Co-operatives in the Ministry of Co-operatives is responsible for education of committee/board members, general members and pre-co-operative members. Co-operative educators conduct these programmes in the field. Co-ordination of CET is achieved by the co-operative Department with the help of the co-operative movement. For management training the government has been running the Fiji Co-operative Training Centre. There are three mobile-units which are responsible for CET in the field.

There are 3 to 10 weeks long training courses and shorter ones organized by the Co-operative Department for officers and field educators. For member education courses on the islands or at the rural centre, the duration is one or two days.

XII. Summary and Conclusion

In all countries of the Asian region, cooperation has been practiced in its traditional form as a part of peoples' life pattern (→ *Autochthonous Co-operatives*). In the modern sense, the concept of cooperation is often taken as alien and too complex. Most of the people, especially those living in rural areas, are not aware of these complexities. It is, therefore, imperative that they should be acquainted with the concept, principles and practices of cooperation. The governments in the countries have recognized this vital need and have extended financial and administrative support for CET.

The approaches and techniques of CET programmes have changed drastically. Co-operatives are no more perceived a matter of mere faith by most members; they look upon them mainly from the angle of benefit being derived. Keeping this situation in view, the member education activities and employee training programmes have to be re-oriented.

In the co-operative movement of developing countries of Asia, some arrangements for education and training of members and various categories of employees have been made. But, these are not adequate and far below the expected level. These movements have been trying to be self-sufficient and independent from the government and other external controls. In order to achieve this, they should try first to be self-directing as well as self-financing.

As the governments in many Asian countries have gone a long way to lead and assist the co-operative organizations; they are in fact becoming partners in co-operative development (→ *Policies for Promotion*). However, the autonomous character of the movement must be defended vigorously (→ *Officialization*) and possibly enhanced, as is already happening in countries like Korea and Japan. Policies and programmes for co-operative development including CET should primiarily be formed by co-operatives themselves and finally be accepted by them for implementation. The need for monitoring and evaluation of programmes should be realized and put into practice.

The virtue of co-operative movement is that it wants to bring about a fundamental change in the very structure of the society. The chief objective of the CET should be to keep the loyalty of the people in the organization very high so that the faith is not dwindled by any ideology and gets strengthened. The people who are ignorant of co-operative principles cannot act unless told of the same. For this, increasing the knowledge of the people is the need, for which we have to start from down, and not from up. Thus, it becomes essential that the co-operatives be given prime importance to improve the lot of people for a better image of the co-operatives of tomorrow. Above all, all that is needed is a sustained effort to inculcate in people the desire of 'our co-operative'.

Bibliography

ACCU: Asian con News, Bangkok, Jan-Feb 1988.
ACCU: Asian Federation of Credit Unions, Report and Directory, 1986–87, Bankok (Pamphlet), p. 35.
ACF: SMCs on Member Education and Employees Training by Shi Xuming, Bejing, All-China Federation of SCMs, 1993.
AIRD: Aird News, Asian Institute of Rural Development, Vol.6, No. 9, Dec. 1987.
ARRO: Rural Reconstruction, Vol. 20, No. 1, Jan. Afro-Asian Rural Reconstruction Organ. 1987, New Dehli.
Burma: Co-operatives in Mynamar (1993), Yangoon.
CPD: Co-operative Promotion in Thailand, Bangkok, Ministry of Agriculture and Co-operatives.
CUAC: Agricultural Co-operative Movement in Japan, Tokyo, Central Union of Agricult – Rural Co-operatives, 1987, p.50.
CUP: Cup Gazette, Quenon City, Co-operative Union of the Philippines, Vol. 5, No. 7, 1987.
GOP: Government Co-operative Training College (Handbook), Government of Pakistan, Faisalabad, 1986, p. 27.
Gupta, Ganesh P./Chakravorty, Bratati: The Framework of Co-operative Societies as propounded by Noble Laureatte Rabindra Nath Tagore, Proceedings of the 'What are the viable Co-operative Models and Contributions for the Future, International Co-operative Research Forum, Tokyo, Oct. 1992, p. 296–297 (Abstract).
Gupta, Ganesh P.: For the Cause of Co-operative Credit, nay Cooperation too, IRU Courier, International Raiffeisen Union, Bonn, Dec. 1988, p. 4–6.
Gupta, Ganesh P.: Perceptions of the Role of the Co-operatives in Modern Society, Co-operative Perspective, Vaikunth Mehta National Institute of Co-operative Management, Pune, Jan-Mar 1992, p. 28–29.
Gupta, Ganesh P.: Research Priorities in Co-operative Credit, The Cooperator, New Delhi, Oct. 1989, p. 149.
Haederic, LJ: The Co-operative Movement in West Malaysia, Department of Publications, University of Malaysia, 1986.
ICA RO: Consumer Co-operative Movement in Asia and the Pacific, New Delhi, 1993 (Mimeo)
ICA RO: Consumer Cooperation in South-East Asia, New Delhi, 1974, p. 226.
ICA: Co-operative Education Directory, London, 1972 (Mimeo), p. 108.
ICA RO: Co-operative leadership in South-East Asia Bombay, Asia Publishing House, 1963, p.134.
ICA RO: Enhancing Women Participation in Co-operative Activity, New Delhi
ICA RO: Expert Consultation in Co-operative Member Education, New Delhi, 1979, p. 331.
ICA RO: ICA Consumer Co-operative Development Project For South-East Asia, New Delhi, 1987, p. 16 (Mimeographed).
ICA RO: ICA Open Asian Conference on Co-operative Management (Report and Papers), Manila, 1991.
ICA: Review of International Cooperation, Geneva, Vol. 79, No.3, 1986 (Annual Report).
ICA RO: State and Co-operative Development, New Delhi, Allied Publishers, PVT, Ltd. 1971, p. 180.
ICA RO: 29th Regional Council Meeting Minutes, New Delhi, 1987, p.50 (Mimeo).
ICO RO: International Co-operative Seminar, New Delhi, 1993.
ILO: Report on ILO/NOR Regional Project on Co-operative development through Effective Training, Personnel and Organisational Policies, Geneva, ILO, Norway, 1990, p.75.

Imagawa, N.: Educational Activities of Agricultural Co-operatives in Japan, Tokyo, 1993 (Mimeo).
Indonesia: Co-operatives in the Fourth Five Year Plan 1983–88, Jakarta, Ministry of Co-operatives, p. 108.
JCCU: Coojapan Information, Tokyo, Japanese Consumers' Co-operative Union, Nov. 1987.
NCUI: Cooperator Fortnightly, New Delhi, 1992–93.
NCUI: Indian Co-operatives: A Profile, New Delhi, 1990, p.19.
Plunkett: Year Book of Co-operative Enterprises – 1991, Plunkett Foundation Oxford, p. 131–35.
Rana, J.M: Education for Effective Membership Participation, Review of International Cooperation, Geneva, no.1, 1991.
Samiuddin: Co-operative Movement in Arabian Countries Aligarh, 1981.
Stettena, P.L.: Chinese Co-operatives, Plunkett Foundation for Co-operatives, Oxford, 1984, p.67.
Sugakawa, K.: Measures for Promoting Farm Guidance by Agricultural Co-operatives, Tokyo, 1993 (Mimeo).
Vir, Dharm: Adult Psychology and Educational Methods – A Handbook, ICA RO, New Delhi, 1981, p.111.
Vir, Dharm: Co-operative Education and Training in Asia (with information on training facilities abroad), Centre for Promotion of Co-operativism, New Delhi, 1989, p.196.
Vir, Dharm: Co-operative Education and Training in Asia (A study of Policies and Programmes), HRD Consultants, New Delhi, 1990 (Mimeo)
Vir, Dharm: Co-operative Human Resource Development in Asia (CHRD): Indian Experience, HRD Consultants, New Delhi, 1989, p.8.
Vir, Dharm: Provision and Problems of Co-operative Education and Training in Asia, HRD Consultants, New Delhi (unpublished), 1989.
WOCCU: Credit Union World Reporter, Jan. 1988, World Council of Credit Unions, Madison.

Education and Training in Europe, Co-operative

JOHANN BRAZDA / TODE TODEV

(see also: *Education, North America*; *Education, Germany*; *History in 19th C.*; *Human Resource Management*)

I. The History of Co-operative Education; II. Education to Be a Co-operator; III. Education and Training in Europe.

I. The History of Co-operative Education

Co-operatives are centered on the human being. They have been formed as the polar opposite against people's dependency on the power of capital, against ignorance, and against the incapacity to adapt to new conditions in times of rapid economic social and technological change. *There is probably no other modern economic institution whose creation was accompanied by such a strong impetus towards education as co-operatives.* → Robert Owen, → The Rochdale Pioneers, → Friedrich Wilhelm Raiffeisen, and →

Hermann Schulze-Delitzsch did not conceive of their co-operatives just in terms of economic institutions of self-help but also saw them as organizations that were to serve education in the most global sense. Thus, the co-operative principle (→ *Principles*) has been and still is intimately connected with an educational task. The → *development of co-operatives* was one of the numerous new economic strategies developed by people confronted with industrial revolution in the 19th century (→ *History in 19th C.*). This situation was characterized by a sharpening of societal tensions. *Benjamin Disraeli* at that time spoke of "two nations" and a dichotomy of the mass of poor citizens and a rich minority became also part of the influential concepts of Marxism (→ *Socialist Critics*), that was in its formative period at that time. Co-operatives were formed to ease that tension in two ways: people who had fallen into poverty were to be put into a position where they could help themselves in order to be able to benefit from the positive sides of the industrial revolution. Also many co-operative reformers hoped that the new competitive capitalist market order was to be improved or even superseded by a new co-operative order (→ *"Third Way"*).

Since the time of their formation, co-operatives have been engaged in educational activities on three different levels: general education, co-operative education, and professional training.

II. Education to Be a Co-operator

Via this sort of education (or propaganda) various parts of the population were to be enabled to improve their situation via co-operative self-help (→ *Self-help Organizations*). *Co-operative education was regarded as an indispensable foundation for the formation of a co-operative community.* Co-operatives were then not just ment to be a new economic organization but a new form of communal living which was to give man best chances of economic and social development. Economic co-operation was not regarded as a self-evident instinct of man, but future members had to be educated in order to be able to live according to co-operative principles.

1. General Education

General education became part of co-operative education because lack of education, especially illiteracy, was a characteristic of the great majority of the people. In order to promote co-operative and general knowledge, co-operative libraries, reading halls, and educational associations were formed and became a typical aspect of 19th century co-operation. According to → *F. W. Raiffeisen, the members had to be rendered "unbiased and able to judge things on their own" and also able to understand lectures and written material as well as to adapt these sources of information to their practice.*

2. Professional Training

Already during the first waves of co-operative formation co-operatives became aware that the enthusiasm of their prospective members was not enough. A certain basic knowledge in the fields of accounting and in the field of inventory management were indispensable necessity if a newly formed co-operative was to survive. The reports of co-operative unions and → *federations* during the first decades of co-operative development time and again report on the problems of lack of own capital, too large debts, lack of control of financial management, and in general on the lack of experience and general education of co-operative volunteers. Time and again an increasing amount of commercial and organizational expertise on the part of co-operatives' elected officials is demanded in these reports. *Co-operative education in this sense means professional training for the members' representatives and increasingly also the training of co-operative staff.* Out of this branch of co-operative education the first professional training facilities of Europe's co-operative movements developed. Typical in this context was *Albin Johansson's* passion for book-keeping. It was a heartfelt wish of this great Swedish pioneer-entrepeneur of the consumer co-operative field (→ *Consumer Co-operatives*) that every co-operative member should understand the principles of double accounting.

III. Education and Training in Europe

1. Western Europe

As co-operatives became more and more integrated into the core of today's market economy (→ *Economic Order*) and as modern large-scale co-operatives (→ *Operational Size*) and co-operative federative systems became more and more dominant, the scope of co-operative training focussed increasingly on economic tasks in the sense of professional training. Co-operative members did not have to fight for their living any more. They were not situated on the fringe of society anymore and, on the average they were much better trained and educated than their forefathers during the 19th century. *As a consequence of this development, the economic advantages of belonging to a co-operative became more important than the ideological advantages.* The educational impulse to train co-operative staff became more and more dominant. General education was taken care of effectively by other societal institutions.

There were two tendencies that were responsible for this development. Co-operatives became more and more economically oriented organizations and they had to become more like their competitors in their fields of activities under the pressure of a highly integrated world market (→ *Competition*). With this → *internationalization* and a more complex market structure a qualitatively new need for information was also becoming obvious. This new scope for market activities also increased the optimal size of co-operative enterprises (→ *Operational Size*), which meant that a more complex internal organization and management system was necessitated. In today's industrial states successful co-operative movements have attained a highly complex organization on various levels. They are representing substantial group power in today's oligopolistic competition (→ *Competition*) but they are also under constant pressure to rationalize their capital input and their organizational processes. The hierarchization of society, the professional life of co-operative employees have become more and more complex via the generally increasing degree of complexity in today's organizational society.

Thus new pressures of socialization are being put on every individual. Hierarchical and bureaucratical organization has spread rapidly, and via this process a new level of complexity in decision making processes is created that can not be tackled with traditional hierarchical models anymore. Indeed this increasing complexity itself has challenged traditional hierachical patterns. These societal processes have made the traditional educational task of co-operatives appear to be less important. *In the foreground professional training and re-training of co-operative employees and management courses for the top levels of the co-operative professional hierarchy seem to be dominant.* As the general economic environment is changing, there are new tasks for co-operative professional training. During the 1950s sellers' market, it was mostly productivity-oriented (in a rather technical way), in the 1960s the arising buyers' markets necessitated a more client-oriented marketing approach. In the 1970s, a new awareness for societal trends became relevant for co-operative education in terms of professional training. In the 1980s, enterprises were seen increasingly as social systems in which group processes are taking part and thus, the human factor became more important.

Starting from the 1990s, the role of the manager as a person directing social transaction systems is gaining importance. The formation of an adequate organizational culture (→ *Corporate Culture*) today is regarded to be as one of the most important functions of management.

These common trends have to be reckoned with by all Western European co-operatives – even though they may regard themselves (according to national models) as purely economic or rather as social and political organizations. These "ideological" differences are based on different political, economic and social developments in various European countries, but they should not be exaggerated (→ *Conceptions, Co-operative*).

Dominant factors as regards co-operative education in Western Europe are *training institutes of co-operative unions and universities*. In Spain, however, ministries and statal vocational training institutes can be regarded as important centres of co-operative education, too (probably as a result of the corporatist heritage of franquism). According to a survey done by the COGECA the universities of Le Mans and Tours in France, the co-operative college of Loughborough for the UK, the university colleges of Cork and of Dublin in Ireland, the universities in Madrid, Valencia, Cordoba, Santander and Barcelona in Spain, the Agricultural University of Wageningen in the Netherlands, the German universities of Münster, Hamburg, Marburg, Hohenheim, Giessen, Erlangen (→ *AGI*), the technical college of Nürtingen, and the Economic University of Vienna are offering courses programs and/or seminars on co-operative questions, mostly for co-operative staff.

In Belgium, co-operative training activities are taking place sporadically, e.g. organized by the Boerenbond. Most countries are also offering *institutionalized training facilities* according to the various co-operative sectors on a regional and national level. These are basically geared towards the *carreer planning of co-operative personnel*. To some extent, they are also offering courses on *specific co-operative subjects*, such as économie sociale in France, or co-operative consciousness in Italy and Spain and Portugal (In the latter countries co-operative education is regarded as a "school of democracy", too). A similar concept is visible in the traditional French school co-operatives which have influenced the Basque country. This emphasis on co-operative consciousness in the Iberian peninsula – see also programme Seneca in Portugal – may be related to the belated end of dicatorships in these countries.

Training programs may comprise full-year-courses at university level, relatively long seminars for professional training and retraining, and short seminars on topical subjects. They also comprise study tours which have been a traditional instrument of co-operative education for many years.

Co-operative training and educational activities are mostly directed towards co-operative personnel and medium or higher level members representatives. Only in Greece, in some provinces of Spain, in Great Britain and Sweden *members* are eligible for co-operative training, too. Italy and Portugal are also offering courses for young people who want to be active in co-operatives.

In *Sweden*, a country that has an enormously strong tradition in the co-operative field, the level of university involvement in co-operative studies is suprisingly low. Apparently, most work is done by individual researchers that are pursuing the subject on their own. However, there are strong and traditionally influential training facilities for co-operative staff on a vocational and management level, e.g. KF's famous training centre at Var Gard.

In practically all countries the training and educational activities are financed by the co-operatives themselves and by their co-operative federations. To some extent they are also subsidized by the state, with the exception of Denmark, where there are no public subsidies at all for co-operative education.

In addition to international training activities, co-operative education on a *European level* will become important in the near future in the following sectors:

- maintenance of ties between the national organisations mostly via European co-operative unions;
- exchange of experiences, opinions, and information on co-operative education by various co-operative educational and training institutes;
- exchange programs of co-operative teachers and co-operative leaders;
- acceptance of students of co-operative schools for practical training across boundaries;
- exchange of personnel and management across boundaries;
- foundation of co-operative training institutes on a European level (e.g. by C.I.C.P. 1992 in Rome).

2. Eastern Europe

Until the end of the 1980s, the co-operative system of "Real Socialism" in Eastern Europe was part of the *general political and economic system and closely linked to its programmatic task* (→ State and Co-operatives, Socialism). Co-operatives were regarded as useful instruments for increasing the speed of transition from capitalism to socialism. Thus, they were seen as a special model of collective socialist work. This concept was also characteristic for the main goals of basic and higher co-operative education.

The countries of "Real Socialism" (→ *Socialist Co-operative Theory*) developed a rich and highly structured network of educational and training institutions for co-operatives' staff and elected members. Despite their disadvantages of being strongly coloured by propaganda courses, they were at least *relatively well integrated into the statal systems of education*, much more so than in Western Europe (→ *State and Co-operatives, Socialism*). Specific co-operative topics were e.g. integrated into the curricula of higher education. Thus, the problems of co-operative housing and the organizational and financial questions of these co-operatives were part of university courses in Poland and Bulgaria and often statal educational institutions were subsidized by co-operatives. As an example, we can cite the case of the University for International and National Political Economy in Sofia which has an co-operative faculty that was based on financial subsidies by the country's Central Co-operative Union.

Co-operatives recruited their staff from different levels

of the national educational system, from vocational training schools, secondary schools, technical universities, and universities.

There were highly integrated models of cooperation between the co-operatives and the public educational system in the following forms: Students that had to engage in practical activity as part of their university studies could do this in co-operative organizations. Students were engaged in contracts with co-operative organizations which bound them to work for those for several years after the end of their studies. Institutions of higher learning organized special courses and seminars for leading personnel of co-operative organizations.

These statal institutions, however, did not cater to all of the needs of co-operative organizations in terms of professional training. These have created their *own educational systems* basically for the higher and intermediate level of professional training of their employees. They have concentrated these activities in their *central co-operative unions*, financed via the creation of specific funds. This centralization offered the possibility to create a large network of technical colleges, commercial training institutions and so on. Larger countries, such as various parts of the former Soviet Union, have even created their own *co-operative universities* or *technical colleges* with day, evening and correspondence courses (Bulgaria, Poland, Ex-Soviet Union). Specific co-operative courses on co-operative theory, co-operative law, organization and management of co-operatives etc. were and are offered in these institutions alongside more general professional training. Practical field work was done only in co-operatives. Many students of these co-operative schools got a scholarship financing their studies by the co-operative they contracted to work for afterwards. (This was, of course, typical of a situation with at least formal labour shortage, where enterprises had to make sure early on that they would get well-trained staff). There were *specific centres for the training management and higher staff* in all of the former socialist countries of Central and Eastern Europe. The co-operative unions of these countries played a central role in the process of curriculum formation of these educational systems.

Until the period of change after 1989 (→ *Development, Eastern Europe*), permanent education and training was regarded as an obligation and was characterized by dogmatic attitudes that in many cases did not correspond to the real needs of member organizations and participants. After the great change in the direction towards democracy and market economy, there are indications for *new co-operative forms of training and education*. These are focussing on the following aspects:

- the attainment of knowledge about the functioning of co-operatives in market economies;
- more practically oriented training programs;
- a tendency away from the former ideological outlook;
- the propagation of co-operative ideas in their original form;
- new criteria for the selection of participants of courses;
- tendencies to give the participants a say in what they are to be taught;
- the introduction of psychological testing methods for co-operative management;
- introduction of evaluation methods for the quality of educational staff.

a) Bulgaria

The Bulgarian co-operative training system comprises statal schools, co-operative schools, the Economic University and the Economic College and the University for National and International Political Economy, Sofia, training possibilities abroad in Russia, Ukraine, and Western Europe, especially for consumer co-operatives, professional training centres of regional and central co-operative unions. There is a basic training program for new staff members, professional training for new staff members with secondary and higher education, and top level training for leading personnel of co-operatives. During these courses, lecturers are invited from the central co-operative union, and from various ministries and other public institutions, professors from universities and members of research institutions.

b) Hungary

All Hungarian national co-operative unions offer professional training facilities for their staff members in the form of training institutes, but they do not have their own schools. They have created counseling institutions to get in contact with the secondary school graduates. Training institutes are also organizing management training courses that are now dominated by the mangement methods of developed industrial states. During many of these courses, excursions to Western firms are organized.

c) Poland

Up until the dissolution of the central co-operative unions at the beginning of 1990, these were the organizers of co-operative education (their own professional secondary schools offered day, night and correspondence courses). The students got scholarships from co-operative organizations and were thus obliged to work for "their" co-operative for a certain period of time afterwards. There were training centres for top management. Both activities have been taken over by chambers that were set up instead of the central co-operative unions. Since the central co-operative unions did not dispose of their own institutions of higher learning they entered into close co-operation with the universities and many university students did their practical training in co-operative organizations. Students were offered scholarships, and post graduate studies were offered according to the needs of co-operative unions.

d) The Community of Independent States (CIS)

The countries of the former Soviet Union disposed, at the beginning of the 1990s, of ten co-operative educational centres on university level, 128 secondary technical schools, 13 professional schools, and 158 vocational training schools. There were also 15 central institutions for study courses and more than 2,000 enterprises with training facilities. The co-operative colleges and secondary schools now belong to the central co-operative organizations of the states of the former Union since Centrosojus was dissolved.

e) Czechia and Slovakia

In these countries, too, co-operative education and professional training was organized on various levels: the vocational level and professional secondary school level, and the specialized university and management level. Professional training is offered in 40 specialized schools and intermediate professional training institutes. Qualified workers are also trained at co-operatives enterprises themselves. Higher staff members are trained in training centres owned by the co-operative unions on a national and a district level. The co-operative teaching staff is formed at the central co-operative training institute in Prague, which is also offering courses for specialists and management personnel.

Translation: R. Schediwy

Bibliography

40 Years of the Central Cooperative School, in: The Czechoslovak cooperator, Prague 1989.
Kooperazija w stranach sozialisma, Moskau 1985.
Krascheninnikow, A.: Kooperazija w sowremennom mire, Moskau 1987.
Muzik, J.: Erziehung und Bildung im Genossenschaftswesen der sozilaistischen Länder, (unpublished paper), Prague 1990.
Trends und markante Fakten der genossenschaftlichen Politiken und Ausbildungs- und Unterrichtssysteme der einzelnen Mitgliedsländer der Zwölfergemeinschaft, COGECA, Brüssel 1987.
World Council and Assembly on Co-operative Education (ed.): Sixth World Conference on Co-operative Education, Conference Proceedings, Hamilton 1989.

Education and Training in Germany, Co-operative

WALTER SWOBODA [J]

(see also: *Education, Europe*; *Education, North America*; *History of Ideas*; *Conceptions, Co-operative*)

I. Co-operatives and their Understanding of Education; II. The Beginnings of Co-operative Education in Germany; III. Reconstruction of the Co-operative Education System after 1945; IV. The Co-operative Education System since 1970.

I. Co-operatives and their Understanding of Education

The modern co-operatives came into being around the middle of the 19th century in the age of budding capitalism and in a time of radical economic and social change (→ *History in 19th C.*). The objective of the co-operatives, which place themselves in the context of social tension, is to improve the existence of each individual through self-help. Economic advantages should be achieved for each individual through the unlimited consolidation of those economically weaker.

→ *Schulze-Delitzsch* and → *Raiffeisen* also considered the situation of being at the mercy of those economically stronger a result of the insufficient educational level of those economically weaker through the various educational opportunities. Both were under the immediate pressure of usurers and loan sharks who, with numerous tricks, deprived craftsmen, merchants, and farmers of their already minimal income and drove them to destitution and ruin. In this context, *Schulze-Delitzsch* repeatedly demanded that "the propagation of general education (should) for once and for all be energetically undertaken in order to seriously combat the stultification of the population." He was convinced that "education. . .is the essential fundament for economic and all other forms of development. . .The more the education of the population is tended to, the more knowledge it can be conveyed, the more incessantly its moral characteristics are fashioned through education – the greater the share the individual profits from the entire intellectual capacity of humanity, the greater his advancement to freedom will be made possible."
The association for the propagation of national education founded by him in 1871 established public libraries in the following years and hosted lectures and conversation groups in the evenings.
Raiffeisen likewise also saw general educational work as an integral component of co-operative activity. He realized that the catastrophic economic state of affairs among the rural population could not be alle-

viated simply through money. "Much more important is the instruction of how the monetary means to be attained by the society for the improvement of living conditions can also be applied and distributed in the most expedient manner." The credit co-operatives (→ *Co-operative Banks*) should improve both material and moral conditions of their members through the appropriate facilities and institutions.

Well in the foreground were the economic interests of the members in the eyes of → *Wilhelm Haas*; in his opinion, the social situation of the population can only be improved through economic interests. *Raiffeisen's* ethical ideas concerning education (→ *Conceptions, Co-operative*) were pushed into the background; the educational activity of *Haas*' co-operatives concentrated on the economic instruction of their members.

The outlook of the co-operative pioneers centered on people underlines the personal character of the co-operative in contrast to the capitalistic company forms. Every member has a say in the management of the co-operative enterprise and the opportunity to exercise his rightful influence on the agreements and decisions of the organization; he must, therefore, also possess the ability to survey and evaluate the goals and economic situation of the co-operative.

Today, the comprehensive public school system, general compulsary school attendance, and the strong educational tendency of the population no longer make these "basic educational tasks" of the co-operative essential for their members.

II. The Beginnings of Co-operative Education in Germany

Alongside the endeavors of the co-operative founders to improve the general level of education – above all that of the co-operative members –, the undertaking also was pursued from the very start to further train and educate the honorary members of the administration (→ *Honorary Office*) and those employed full-time in the co-operative in their specialized tasks.

Inasmuch as the managing directors (treasurers, bookkeepers) do not belong to the board of the co-operative, as was particularly the case for the Raiffeisen (rural credit) co-operatives, this group of individuals was also included in intensive training activities. Education measures were developed for the members of the co-operative only peripherally.

1. Educational Work among Commercial Co-operatives

a) General association (Schulze-Delitzsch)

The "Allgemeiner Verband der auf Selbsthilfe beruhenden deutschen Erwerbs- und Wirtschaftsgenossenschaften" (General Association of the German Commercial Co-operatives based on Self-help) emerged from the "Ersten Vereinstag deutscher Vorschuß- und Kreditvereine" (First Convention of German Loan and Credit Societies) held in 1859. The first Anwalt (president) of this association was *Hermann Schulze-Delitzsch*. He did not only perceive the extent of the association's work in the representation, counseling, and assistance of the incorporated co-operatives but rather also in the enlightenment and education of vast classes and levels of the population. The resolution of the Twelfth General Co-operative Convention of 1871 should be understood with this in mind: "The societies in the General Association are recommended to utilize a part of their net profit for purposes of educating the population." In 1871, *Schulze-Delitzsch* founded the "Gesellschaft für Verbreitung von Volksbildung" (Society for the Propagation of Popular Education). The association was successful in introducing and expanding instruction concerning the role and importance of the co-operative system in all-round schools, trade schools, and universities.

No independent educational system with organized courses and/or seminars for members of the administrational body, business managers or co-operative members was developed in the Allgemeiner Verband, which continued to exist in this organizational structure until 1920.

Until this point in time, the introduction and instruction of the co-operative business managers was conducted in the scope of the legally prescribed audits carried out by assigned accountants. Apprentices educated in the all-round schools were employed in the various departments as soon as the size of the co-operative permitted this step.

The Allgemeiner Verband considered the *Blätter für Genossenschaftswesen* (*Co-operative Magazine*) its only official educational material. This publication (→ *Periodicals, Co-operative*) came into being in 1864 as an off-shoot of the magazine *Innung der Zukunft* (*Guild of the Future*) which had been founded by *Schulze-Delitzsch* eleven years before. *Schulze-Delitzsch* remained publisher and main author until his death in 1883. In this magazine, which started to be published weekly in 1864, the co-operatives were informed about their general goals and tasks as well as about changes in co-operative, legal, tax and technical conditions. It also reported on current economic questions and thus served as the foundation for the business activity of the co-operatives.

b) General association of industrial co-operatives

Karl Korthaus, born in 1859 in the district of Osnabrück, became secretary of the Chamber of Handicrafts in Osnabrück in 1894 and was intensely involved in improving the economic situation of artisans. As a "wandering mentor" for co-operative affairs, particularly in the Rhine area, in Silesia, and in

Saxony, he inspired the establishment of numerous co-operative organizations – credit societies for artisans and purchasing co-operatives for artisans (→ *Supply Co-operatives*). These co-operatives did not join the Allgemeiner Verband but rather organized themselves in independent regional associations. In 1901, the "Hauptverband deutscher gewerblicher Genossenschaften" (General Association of German Industrial Co-operatives) was founded with *Korthaus*, a lawyer, as its acting business manager. As early as 1902, the Hauptverband started training programs for the business managers of artisan co-operatives. These programs ran several weeks long and were conducted centrally as well as through the regional associations with the generous support from the Chambers of Handicrafts. They were involved in co-operative studies, personal credit within the co-operative framework, legal decisions and stipulations and, above all, with practical co-operative management.

In 1920, the "Allgemeiner Verband der auf Selbsthilfe beruhenden deutschen Erwerbs- und Wirtschaftsgenossenschaften" with its 964 credit co-operatives and 165 merchandise co-operatives joined together with the "Hauptverband deutscher gewerblicher Genossenschaften" with its 459 credit co-operatives and 1,784 merchandise co-operatives to form the "Deutschen Genossenschaftsverbund" (German Co-operative Association). The 62nd Co-operative Convention in 1925 resolved to found a co-operative school and to introduce training courses for members of the executive board and supervisory board.

2. Educational Work among Agricultural Co-operatives

a) General association of German Raiffeisen Co-operatives

F.W. Raiffeisen also assigned both material and idealistic purposes to the co-operative savings and loan societies initiated by him as *Schulze-Delitzsch* similarly had. In his book *"Die Darlehenskassenvereine"* (1881), *Raiffeisen* stated: "It is well known that immaterial well-being cannot be separated from material well-being; constant reciprocal action takes place in this relation." He did not solely see the purpose of these societies in granting members credit, but rather also in the moral, developmental and educational tasks of the co-operative. Each loan society should establish a "Casino" within the co-operative for "instructional purposes". Around the turn of the century, the co-operatives ran numerous libraries, schools for the continuing education of members, elementary schools and courses to meet the demands of the members. In 1903, the Raiffeisen co-operatives ran 1,646 schools for continuing agricultural education in Prussia which served both members and the village inhabitants. In 1904, a law was passed in Prussia for uniform regulation of these schools.

Periodical publications (→ *Periodicals, Co-operative*) were also used as educational material in the Raiffeisen organization. The "Raiffeisen libraries" addressed subjects concerning the co-operative system, whereas the "rural co-operative libraries" carried publications with a scientific/academic character. The *Landwirtschaftliches Genossenschaftsblatt* (*Agricultural Co-operative Paper*), founded by *Raiffeisen* in 1879, was the official organ and contributed to the instruction of the loan societies. The regional associations published their own papers, the *Raiffeisenboten*; the General Association performed the editorial work of the main articles, which appeared alongside those regional in character. The distribution of the regionally and centrally published newspapers reached a level of 300,000 in the 1920s.

The Hessian association located in Kassel held the first one-week bookkeeping course in 1897, which had forty participants. Other associations followed suit with their own educational programs, and in 1925, 47 accounting courses and 135 further courses for board members, members of the supervisory boards, co-operative members, and workers were held.

b) General association of the agricultural co-operatives of the German Reich (Wilhelm Haas)

Wilhelm Haas (1839–1913) made an enduring impression on the three-tiered organizational structure of the agricultural co-operatives. The "Verband der hessischen landwirtschaftlichen Konsumvereine" (Association of Hessian Agricultural Consumer Societies), founded in Darmstadt in 1873, developed into the "Allgemeiner Verband der landwirtschaftlichen Genossenschaften des Deutschen Reiches" in 1890, since 1903 with the new name "Reichsverband der deutschen landwirtschaftlichen Genossenschaften" (Reich Association of the German Agricultural Co-operatives).

In its time, the Allgemeiner Verband put great emphasis on the training and further education of the co-operative business managers (bookkeepers). The first step was the regularly held "accountancy meetings" in which all of the important questions pertaining to the management of the co-operative were discussed. Around the turn of the century, courses were introduced in all provincial associations for co-operative functionaries, for bookkeepers and treasurers, and for members of the executive and supervisory boards. Bookkeeping was the main subject of instruction. In 1898, a dairy school was opened in Saxony which trained dairy managers in six-month courses. Since 1901, accounting and bookkeeping assistance agencies have existed in the associations from which the members of the co-operative boards have learned the fundamentals of bookkeeping. The regional associations undertook a regular circular letter service and provided journals offering comprehensive presentations of specialized problems.

The Reichsverband initially concentrated its educational work on the journal *Deutsche landwirtschaftliche Genossenschaftspresse* (*German Agricultural Co-operative Press*), which can be traced back to *Wilhelm Haas*, as well as on a magazine founded in 1873 by the "Verband der hessischen landwirtschaftlichen Konsumvereine".

In 1904, an agricultural co-operative school was founded by the Reichsverband which commenced its work with a five-week training program for "officials" of this association and the provincial associations. Starting the following year, an annual six-month program was introduced with 750 hours of instruction, along with four-week courses for association managers, auditors, and administrators of co-operative centers. People involved in co-operatives from neighboring nations also frequently took part in the speeches and lectures which assumed in part a university-like character.

c) Reich Association of the German Agricultural Co-operatives – Raiffeisen

Economic crisis, inflation, and the dramatically increasing debt of the German agricultural industry and thus, of its co-operative organizations, lead to the efforts in 1926 to unite the two large agricultural co-operative associations. Ultimately upon the conditions of standardizing the rural co-operative organization, the Reich government, the Rentenbank-Kreditanstalt (a Mortgage Bank) as well as the Central Prussian Co-operative Bank restored the local co-operatives to financial soundness. In 1929 and 1930, regional and central associations were merged together, and on February 13, 1930, the newly unified association was established, the "Reichsverband der deutschen landwirtschaftlichen Genossenschaften – Raiffeisen e.V." (Reich Association of the German Agricultural Co-operatives – Raiffeisen) with 36,339 united agricultural co-operatives (of them 20,592 savings and loan societies, mostly with commodities trade). The educational work was continued based on the principles of *Haas*' Reichsverband.

The establishment of a common organization in the sector of education was interrupted in 1933 through the policy of the National Socialists. The entire agricultural co-operative branch was integrated into the "Reichsnährstand" and subordinated to the state market structures. The agricultural co-operatives thus became a part of the so-called "Erzeugungsschlacht" (productional battle); the credit co-operatives were collection agencies for the necessary financial means for armaments. No developments in co-operative educational work can be determined up to 1945.

III. Reconstruction of the Co-operative Education System after 1945

The political and economic collapse of the German Reich in 1945 also meant the end of the centralized co-operative organizations and its centralized educational facilities. The resumption of educational activity occurred variously in the rural and commercial co-operative structures which gradually started to re-emerge.

1. German Raiffeisen Federation (DRV)

Within the Raiffeisen co-operative organization (banks as well as agricultural co-operatives), instructional activity initially developed exclusively on the regional level. Between 1952 and 1956, co-operative schools were founded in seven regional Raiffeisen associations. The first signs of a comprehensive educational system became visible upon the establishment of a sub-committee for the promotion and training of junior staff within the framework of the "Deutsche Raiffeisenverband" (German Raiffeisen Federation) and its committee of experts for "systems of co-operative organization and association". The "Mayschoss Dialogues", which have taken place since 1954 and which have been continued in Bad-Ems since 1963 as the "Kreditwirtschaftliche Fachtagung" (special congress on co-operative banking), take up current specialized themes and management subjects of the Raiffeisen banks (rural credit banks) and mark the beginning of centralized educational measures.

In 1965, a pedagogical plan for the training of specialists and management in the Raiffeisen banks was presented which supplemented the special training program run through the regional schools with a "Banking Management Seminar" as the ultimate step of the Raiffeisen education system. Until 1970, these twelve-week training programs were held at various places throughout the Federal Republic of Germany. In 1970, the "Bundesgenossenschaftsschule – Raiffeisen e.V." (German co-operative – Raiffeisen School) which was founded the same year was able to move into the training facilities the "Deutsche Genossenschaftskasse" had made available at Schloß Montabaur.

The Co-operative School in Stuttgart-Hohenheim ("Württembergische Genossenschafts-Akademie Hohenheim") founded in 1953 assumed a leading role. In 1960, the first "Hohenheim management seminar" was held for co-operative management staff from various fields and from various geographical areas of the union. From this, specialized seminars emerged, starting in 1964 in the field of agricultural commodities, which are held regularly. So-called "advanced seminars" were introduced as a continuation of the management seminars. The foundation for systematic, nationwide education for the consumer co-operatives was thus achieved.

2. The German Co-operative Federation (Schulze-Delitzsch)

The commercial co-operatives which united in 1959 on the national level as the "Deutscher Genossenschaftsverband (Schulze-Delitzsch) e.V." (The German Co-operative Federation, Schulze-Delitzsch) undertook efforts even in its elemental stage to realize the former plan of a single, central co-operative school. In 1948, at the Second German Co-operative Congress of the Working Committee of Industrial Auditing Associations, a German co-operative school was called for. In 1957, the "Schulze-Delitzsch Institut" was founded which was supported by the Volksbanken, central savings banks, and auditing boards. It started its work with a multi-week training program in Staufen at Breisgau.

The pedagogical work for employees and management staff of the Volksbanken was executed up to 1970 in leased building space in Bad Honnef, Geisenheim, and in Frankfurt/Main. The training program consisted of specialized seminars for the individual banking functions as well as "intermediate" and "advanced" training programs for the management personnel of the Volksbanken. In 1970, the work of the Schulze-Delitzsch Institute could begin to be carried out in the training facilities at Schloß Montabaur, rebuilt by the Deutsche Genossenschaftskasse.

IV. The Co-operative Educational System since 1970

1. The Educational-political Tasks of the DGRV, the German Confederation of Co-operatives

In 1972, a merger occurred between the Deutscher Genossenschaftsverband (Schulze-Delitzsch) and the Deutscher Raiffeisenverband. An all-encompassing umbrella organization named "Deutscher Genossenschafts- und Raiffeisenverband e.V.", DGRV (German Confederation of Co-operatives), was founded for all sectors of commercial and rural co-operatives. In contrast to the three national associations "Bundesverband der Deutschen Volksbanken und Raiffeisenbanken e.V.", BVR (Federation of German Co-operative Banks), "Deutscher Raiffeisenverband e.V.", DRV (German Raiffeisen Federation), and "Zentralverband der genossenschaftlichen Großhandels- und Dienstleistungsunternehmen e.V.", ZENTGENO (Central Federation of the Co-operative Wholesale and Service Agencies) which serve particular partial functions, the DGRV is primarily occupied with social-political tasks. It is furthermore the only auditing association on the national level. Also among its assumed duties are the assertion of educational-political interests and the co-ordination of educational work in the co-operative organization.

The special committee on education in the DGRV lays down the guidelines (both pedagogical and political) of the co-operative organization and provides the basis for the co-ordination of the educational work on regional and national levels. In this committee, all co-operative federations on the national and regional levels as well as the Academy of German Co-operatives are represented both through seating and voting rights. The conference of school principals serves as a sub-committee of this education committee and is composed of the administrators of the regional co-operative education institutions and the Academy of German Co-operatives. The conference of school principals is concerned with conceiving uniform teaching plans on a national level and with technical questions affecting the fields of pedagogy and continuing education based on the fundamentals set by the committee. A further working group also includes those persons appointed by the affiliated enterprises to attend to educational matters and ensures the co-ordination of all educational activities for the primary co-operatives.

2. The Structure of the Educational Institutions

The educational work in the co-operative organization is executed on three levels:
- in the co-operative bank
- in the regional education facilities
- in the Academy of German Co-operatives

Within the educational field of the co-operative organization, "training" characterizes the fundamental profession/vocation education up to the final exam in the training stage. "Continuing education" or "promotion-oriented continuing education" is the systematic accumulation of knowledge in individual professional development directions (career tracks). "Further education" is the continuation of organized education in the sense of expanding knowledge and adapting it to variable contexts, conditions, and new management structures.

The following figure illustrates the contributional share each educational institution has in the levels of professional education.

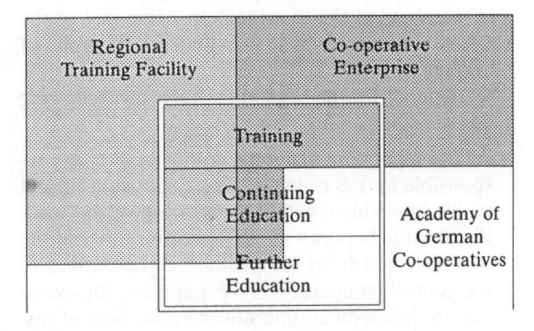

Figure 1.

a) Training at the co-operative company

Vocational education in Germany is organized according to the so-called "dual system": the enterprise doing the training and the vocational school run by the state work as partners and share the work involved in the vocational training. The enterprise thus assumes predominantly the training of the trade to be learned under the supervision of an educator who has passed a qualification exam for the post. The instruction in the vocational school, on the other hand, mostly concentrates on the theoretical knowledge and proficiencies necessary for the trade being studied.

In the majority of cases, the credit co-operatives and the central co-operative banking system train "bank clerks"; in exceptional cases, they also train "office clerks". The agricultural and commercial co-operatives predominantly offer vocational training as "wholesale merchants" ,"import-export merchants" or "retail merchants". Instruction both at the vocational school and on the job is supplemented by classes internal to the co-operative enterprise. Co-operatives frequently join together to form training and study groups in order to delve more extensively into the learning material.

Above and beyond the usual training period, the co-operative company as a place of learning is quite important. Instruction on the job through experienced colleagues, the effect of the management staff as role models and, last but not least, the corporate culture of a co-operative have great influence on both professional and personal development.

b) Regional Education Facilities

The work of vocational education is executed in the German co-operative organizations in affiliation with vocational training in fourteen regional education facilities and, on the national level, through the Academy of German Co-operatives at Schloß Montabaur.

The agency of the regional education facilities is assumed by the regional and the special auditing → *federations*. As of 1990, the regional training facilities are responsible for the approx. 300,000 employees and members of the management personnel of the ca. 8,000 co-operatives in the Federal Republic of Germany.

The regional training facilities have the following fields of responsibility:

– As the superior educational authority, they are responsible for job training in every possible subject or disciple which, within the sharing of the work distribution between the co-operative association, is transferred from the primary co-operatives to the central co-operatives. This applies, for example, to the credit co-operatives in the field of foreign trade and securities. Furthermore, before the final examinations, preparatory classes in the form of tutorials take place.
– They provide the bases of further vocational training by conceiving pedagogical plans for credit, merchandise and service co-operatives.
– They offer continuing education programs to co-operative members.
– They host informational and training events for the honorary members of the co-operative executive and supervisory boards.

The regional education institutions have a teaching staff of their own and employ external lecturers above and beyond this from their own organization, from public schools and universities, as well as private educators. Aside from only a few exceptions, they have training facilities of their own with classrooms and boarding facilities. They are accordingly run as departments of the association supporting them (with only one exception), and are usually able to cover their costs through seminar fees and charges for room and board, which, as a rule, are assumed by the co-operative organizations which are sending the training participants.

c) The Academy of German Co-operatives at Schloß Montabaur

The Academy of German Co-operatives at Schloß Montabaur, the top academy on the national level, came into being on July 1, 1978, upon the fusion of the Schulze-Delitzsch Insitute (for Volksbanken) and the National Co-operative Raiffeisen School. After the two institutions amalgamated in 1978, the seminars and training courses which had up to then been conducted separately were structured in a uniform manner. The agency of the Academy is administered through a registered organization; its members are the national and regional co-operative associations, central business institutions of the various co-operative sectors as well as the "Verein zur Förderung der Akademie Deutscher Genossenschaften" (Society for the Promotion of the Academy of German Co-operatives), whose membership consists of approximately 2,000 primary co-operatives. Ignoring the relatively low membership dues, the Academy finances the training center and the accommodation of the participants from fees and charges which, as was the case with the regional training facilities, are born by the co-operatives which are sending the training participants.

In 1981, the Academy of German Co-operatives was able to purchase Schloß Montabaur with all of its equipment and facilities through the help of contributions from the co-operative organizations within the DG BANK (→ *Central Institutions*). Since then, the Academy has run the school on its own account. The revenue raised from the membership dues of the Verein zur Förderung der Akademie Deutscher Genossenschaften is used to further expand the

Academy or serves to introduce newly planned seminars. In 1990, the Academy had over 230 single rooms at its disposal for the accommodation of participants and guest lecturers as well as class-rooms, space for group work, and recreational and media facilities for the ten to twelve seminars that regularly run parallel to each other at Schloß Montabaur. The Academy educates management and qualified personnel from all German credit, merchandise and service co-operatives in co-ordination with the regional educational institutions.

The Academy of German Co-operatives endeavors to achieve three equally valuable educational goals within the framework of the co-operative education system:

- the orientation of professional work for management and qualified positions based on co-operative company structure;
- the transference, intensification, and expansion of specialized know-how;
- developing personality to assume management functions in the co-operative company.

The Academy has the following responsibilities:

- sustained execution of continuing education courses for qualified junior staff for their promotion;
- transference of specialized knowledge to qualified personnel in the framework of continuing education measures;
- the adaptation of specialized knowledge and management techniques to continually varying circumstances through well-directed continuing training measures for co-operative management personnel;
- measures for both continuing education and further training for management personnel and employees in the central union and member companies in the union.

In its educational work, the Academy relies on its own lecturers, practitioners from all levels of the co-operative organization, as well as on guest lecturers (professors from universities and professional colleges, consulting companies, and independent educators). The work of the Academy is directed at all branches of the co-operative organization: credit, agricultural and commercial co-operatives.

3. Educational Concepts for Credit Co-operatives

The education system of the → *co-operative banks* is structured modularly and consists of seminar units which each individual co-operative bank can make use of according to its organizational structure, its overall size or its business demands related to particular employment positions. The educational structure was based on that of the "generalists" up to 1988. This training goal was predetermined by the structure of the co-operative banks: the small → *operational size* of the individual credit co-operatives did not permit a strong breakdown into job classification. In 1989, however, the co-operative banking organization restructured its educational system according to job-specific training. The operational size had increased through growth, and the larger role of consulting in the banks was able to shoulder the change. An average employment level of 40 workers allows for a job-specific organizational structure based on customers sector, back office and administration, and a horizontal arrangement according to:

- service, consulting and clerical work;
- more individual customer attendence and qualified office work;
- management and supervision.

Job-specific development steps (career tracks) exist within these individual areas.

a) Three seminars for customer consulting, each lasting two to three weeks and completed within approx. two years, precede the final examination to become a banker, as does on the job training lasting one to two years in the co-operative bank for all bank employees, irrespective of their later application or utilization of the training. The completion of these seminars qualifies them to carry out service and consulting functions.

b) The subsequent further training for promotion in each individual direction should develop the employees into qualified consultants and/or office workers. Within the marketing sector, these development tracks include individual customer consulting and assistance, assisting those private customers with large assets at their disposal, consulting commercial customers and assisting people in import-export affairs; within the trade services, the development directions include office clerical work in the areas of credit and foreign trade; in the area of operations, the fields are internal auditor, qualified office clerk for accounting or controlling, or personnel supervisor.

Each development track consists of three seminars lasting three to four weeks. The basis seminar for the initial specialization is followed by a qualification seminar; the development track is completed with a deepening seminar and a final examination. Each of these seminar levels is qualification for a particular job function and can mark the end of training in the area of activity.

c) Educational measures for management and administrative functions commences with a two-day development seminar (assessment center) in which the management potential of those employees foreseen to carry out administrative and supervisional tasks is evaluated. A two-week seminar provides the qualification for the first assumption of management responsibilities and is mainly concerned with leadership behavior and employee responsibility.

A six-week intensive banking seminar at one of the regional training centers provides the qualification for larger management tasks, such as the management of departments and larger branch offices. This includes the elements and functions of the management process and is completed with both an oral and written exam. A successful graduate of this program receives the title "Genossenschaftlicher Bankbetriebswirt" (manager of a co-operative bank).

At the Academy of German Co-operatives there is a "Genossenschaftliches Bank-Führungsseminar" GBF (management seminar for co-operative banks) for the development tracks of authorized clerks, department managers, and junior management staff for the administration of a co-operative bank. The seminar has three sections totalling sixteen weeks and is dispersed throughout a calendar year. The GBF consists of approx. 520 hours of instruction in the fields of co-operative systems, fundamental commercial-political questions, economic policy, general business administration, specific banking management, legal matters, management techniques, accounting and tax law. The participants must take several exams, write a comprehensive research paper and pass an oral exam. Successful graduates may assume the title "Diplomierter Bankbetriebswirt ADG" (bank managers with an Academy degree). The seminar serves as proof of the necessary qualification for the administration of a bank according to § 33 *Kreditwesengesetz* (German Banking Law).

The regional training centers and the Academy of German Co-operatives offer numerous special continuing education seminars alongside those aimed at promotion. At the regional co-operative schools, the comprehensive seminars address individual job areas and product groups, data processing and the application of personal computers, as well as the training and assistance of trainers. The Academy offers such seminars as a six-week trainer seminar with the final title of "Trainer ADG/BDVT", seminars for marketing managers, special seminars for strategy planning and controlling, and organizational development and personnel planning.

4. Educational Concepts for Merchandise and Service Co-operatives

The field of education for both agricultural and industrial merchandise and service co-operatives and the management seminars in the sector of agricultural co-operatives throughout Germany developed in 1960 out of the "Hohenheim Management Seminar", an initiative of the former Württemberg Co-operative School in Stuttgart-Hohenheim. Training programs for commodities trade which were offered nationwide joined this initiative. Upon the founding of the "Bundesgenossenschaftsschule- Raiffeisen" (national Raiffeisen co-operative school) in 1970, it was already foreseen to hold the seminars for commodities trade in Stuttgart-Hohenheim and those for banking at Schloß Montabaur. The expansion of the facilities at the Academy of German Co-operatives at Schloß Montabaur made it possible to relocate the commodities trade seminars to Schloß Montabaur in 1983.

Starting in 1972, the working committee "Lehrgangsplanung der warenwirtschaftlichen Sektion" (planning for training programs in merchandise trading) developed seminar concepts for the National Raiffeisen Co-operative School. This group remained situated at the Württemberg Co-operative Academy in Stuttgart-Hohenheim until 1983 and designed lively seminar activities for agricultural co-operatives. At this point in time, the seminar program consisted of about fifty various seminars in the fields of co-operative company management, co-operative systems, leadership training and personnel administration, labor law, specialized seminars in business administration and branch-specific management seminars.

The further construction and expansion of the training center at Schloß Montabaur in 1983 facilitated the relocation of the commodities trade section so that from then on the field of training there encompassed all sectors of the co-operative organization. In contrast to the sector of credit co-operatives, the agricultural merchandise co-operatives (→ *Rural Co-operatives*) have not been able to realize a nationwide, uniform educational concept. The Academy of German Co-operatives thus developed three areas of cooperation with co-operative associations in the north, middle, and south of the Federal Republic of Germany. The educational concepts in these three zones follow the identical principles but nevertheless take into consideration regional particularities.

The first level of further education leads to the title "Genossenschaftlicher Warenfachkaufmann" (specialized co-operative merchant). The prerequisites to participate in this training program include completed vocational training as a retailer, wholesaler or import-export merchant as well as at least one year's work experience in a trade company. In three block seminars, each lasting fourteen days, the participants intensify their knowledge of business trading, purchasing and storage, marketing, financing and accounting, business organization, company management, labor techniques, and sales training.

Successful graduates can continue in the second level of further education and become a "Handelsfachwirt" (trade specialist) after another phase of work experience. Approx. 500 training hours emphasize economic principles, commercial business training, personnel matters, the leadership of co-workers, and more in-depth analysis of the subjects discussed in the first level. Upon completion of an exam at the Chamber of Commerce, the title "trade specialist" is conveyed.

A four-week management seminar at the Academy of German Co-operatives is the next step, the final goal being a "Genossenschaftlicher Handelsbetriebswirt ADG" (Academy co-operative trade manager), which opens the doors to higher management tasks and responsibilities in merchandise co-operatives. The participants in this third level of further education are occupied with particular questions of company administration. They tackle problems of the development, position, and business policy of co-operative enterprises and train management know-how and behavior in order to successfully lead their workers in the future and to orientate their management around their employees.

5. Educational Concepts of the Commercial Co-operatives

The group of commercial service and merchandise co-operatives which are united in the ZENTGENO (Central Association of Co-operative Wholesale and Service Agencies) in the main includes purchasing (→ *supply*) *co-operatives* from various branches:
- retail trade of foodstuffs and semi-luxury goods
- retail trade of non-food commodities
- trades and crafts involved in food production
- other handicraft branches and their co-operative centers.

The co-operatives in these sectors vary greatly. The large purchasing co-operatives and, above all, the service co-operatives frequently maintain training facilities for the training of the owners of the member enterprises, such as EDEKA, REWE, DATEV, the Nürnberg Federation, as well as the group of purchasing co-operatives in the shoe industry. With the exception of some educational measures, the seminar supplies of the Academy of German Co-operatives were perceived for the own co-worker and executive personnel. The course of further education explained in III c) for agricultural co-operatives (from co-operative specialized merchant to Academy co-operative trade manager) is also much in demand by those involved in the sectors of commercial commodities and service co-operatives.

The co-operative education facilities, particularly the Academy of German Co-operatives, designs internal co-operative seminars for the large merchandise and service co-operatives. At first, the special requirements of the training for the organization are defined, and a concept is developed. The seminars are either centrally held at Schloß Montabaur or in the co-operative companies themselves and thus exclusively are addressed at the workers and management staff of the co-operative itself.

Bibliography

Aschhoff, Gunther: Die Akademie der Volksbanken und Raiffeisenbanken auf Schloß Montabaur, Wiesbaden 1972.
Deutscher Genossenschaftsverband (Schulze-Delitzsch) e.V.: Schulze-Delitzsch 1808/1858, Festschrift zur 150. Wiederkehr seines Geburtstages, Bonn 1958.
Faust, Helmut: Die Geschichte der Genossenschaftsbewegung, Frankfurt/Main 1977.
Raiffeisen, Friedrich Wilhelm: Die Darlehnskassen–Vereine, 1st ed. Neuwied 1866 and 7th ed. Neuwied 1887.
Swoboda, Walter: Der Bildungsauftrag der Akademie Deutscher Genossenschaften, Beitrag zum Bayerischen Raiffeisenblatt No.11, 1984.
Swoboda, Walter: Hoher Stellenwert für Ausbildung und Weiterbildung, Montabaur 1985.

Education and Training in Latin America, Co-operative

BENJAMIN RAMIREZ

(see also: *Education, North America*; *Education, Europe*; *Education, Germany*; *Education, Asia*; *Education, Africa*; *Theory and Science of Co-operatives*)

I. Cooperation and Co-operatives in Latin America; II. The Co-operative Education in Latin America; III. The Praxis of Co-operative Education in Latin America; IV. Future of Co-operative Education.

I. Cooperation and Co-operatives in Latin America

1. Associative Forms of Cooperation in Latin America

Geographically it is not really precise to limit the so-called Latin-American continent. "Latino" is applied to people whose language comes from latin, or in this case includes both countries of Spanish and of Portuguese language, and when locating geographically Latin America we consider Central and Southamerica, including Mexico.

Until 1492, when this continent was discovered by the europeans, a vast part of the territory was densely inhabited. If we define cooperation as a form of working together with other persons whether voluntarily or by force, we can assure, according to historical facts, that cooperation was a form of known action and practiced by primitive people, in some more intensely than others (→ *Autochthonous Co-operatives*). There was not only work in conjunction but also there existed cooperation as a form of joint possession (the case of land) and the cooperation in the use of resources (e.g. with harvested products).

Later on, from Europe we received the cooperation in a more structured form – based on specific → *principles* and establishing afterwards the presently known "co-operatives". The co-operatives were inserted in the form of economical organizations and were recognized by the countries by means of special legislation as "legal bodies" with their own structure and forms of organization (→ *Legal Form, Co-operative*). There are not only co-operatives but also other forms of cooperation that use other denominations, but in its entirety form part of the so-called "associative forms of cooperation".

2. The Creation of Co-operatives in Latin America

After the experiment of Rochdale (→ *Rochdale Pioneers*), the co-operative idea spread worldwide and reached Latin-America with the arrival of the immigrants from Europe. It is only at the beginning of this century, around the third decade, that the co-operatives are introduced as social service organizations backed and promoted by the State. At the same time the first co-operative legislations were approved in these countries: Chile 1925, Colombia 1931, Brasil 1938, etc.

In Latin America, the growth of the co-operative is measured by the number of existing co-operatives. Every country is different and its growth is due to different issues as political and economical, but one of the incentives for its growth are the privileges granted by the State, such as tax exemption or the preference in granting financial credits. There is not a proportion between the number of inhabitants of the country and the number of co-operatives or the number of affiliated in each country.

Usually, the co-operatives in Latin-America are formed at district sections of medium or low income which have more economical problems. In the rural areas, the members are peasants such as small agriculturers or farmers or simply workers of the rural area that are not owners of the land. The urban sectors are formed by labourers, workers of the State or of firms that have a working relation, but there also exist open co-operatives with persons of scarce or medium resources.

3. The Concept of a Co-operative

A co-operative is defined as the association of persons who through an economical-social organization seek to fulfill common objectives (→ *Managerial Economics*).

4. Characteristics of Co-operatives

a) Association of persons

The co-operatives of first stage are grouped or associated by those natural persons that have more or less similar interests (→ *Group, the Co-operative*). The association is a legal entity different from that conformed by the persons, thus has its own structure and patrimony. Here the cooperation appears as a conscious action of the person, this is, when a person forms part of a co-operative, he does it as a result of the selection of various alternatives or at least for one alternative that offers the best outlook. Affiliating with a co-operative is the result of a conscious act of the person. The cooperation in a co-operative is thus a conscious act of the person (→ *Self-help Organizations*).

b) Social-economical Organization

There still exists in Latin-America the concept that the co-operatives must not be seen as an economical type of unit, but which withholds two dimensions: the social and the economical and that in the course of management a balance must be seeked between both aspects.

All companies have a social and economical aspect, but in a co-operative these aspects are understood to be related to the objectives that are pursued. Amongst the most important objectives of the co-operatives are – education and training, both of members as well as administrators. This relates to social objectives. But as an economical unit, the co-operative is in charge of producing assets and services that form part of the economical objective.

This social-economical duality – that the co-operative contains – is a characteristic of its own, that distinguishes it from other types of companies (→ *Dual Nature*). The co-operative as an organization has a structure, and for Latin-America a similar model has more or less been followed with the following components (→ *Organizational Structure of Societies*):

Legislative Instance	→ Assembly	→ Formed by associates
Directive Instance	→ Administrative Board (or Management Board)	→ Formed by associates
Instance of Control	→ Surveillance Board (Fiscal Counsel)	→ Formed by associates
Executive Instance	→ Management	→ Formed by non-associates

The co-operative itself is a different entity (juridical) to that of the members and for its operation has its own financial resources (capital provided by the members) and what can be obtained from other sources (→ *Equity Capital*). As an economical organization it operates as an economical unit within the constellation of the economical system of each country.

c) Own Administration

Another characteristic of the co-operatives is that, at least the directive and control instance is formed by associates elected at the assembly. The executive instances (management) of the big co-operatives are carried out by hired people, whereas with the small ones, for reasons of costs, the administration is assigned to a member (→ *Management in Co-operatives*).

d) The Associates as Object of the Co-operative

Basically the persons create a co-operative to help one another. This means that the main objective of any co-operative (e.g. those of credit) only carry out operations with their associates, although this is not a general rule. Within a competitive market the co-operatives have had to open to operate with non-associates. However, some services, amongst these education and training, are accomplished exclusively with the associates or employees.

5. Types of Co-operatives

Basically, there are two types of co-operatives (→ *Classification*):
- Co-operatives of Production
- Co-operatives of Services or Ancilliaries

The co-operatives of production are destined to produce assets. In this type of co-operative, due to the technical process required, not all members necessarily are involved in the productive system, neither is it supposed that the members are to be the only purchasers of these assets. Many times – in this case – the members fulfill the role of investors.

However, the maximum degree of cooperation is found in organizations of this type when the associates also fulfill the role of workers of their own company. The co-operator is presented as an affiliate and within the productive process as a worker. These two forms of cooperation which are given in one of these cases, within a co-operative of production, seek a sole objective: the member as a member and as a worker (→ *Joint-production Co-operatives*). Likewise, the member is involved with the co-operative also within these two dimensions: member and worker. As a worker it is assumed that most of the income and of the services received depend on the success of the co-operative.

This phenomenon makes the management of a co-operative of production very complicated and thus members require more formation and training in order to succeed.

The co-operatives of services are destined to produce services to the associates. In this type of co-operative, all members are potential users of the services provided by the co-operative (→ *Commercial Co-operatives*; → *Co-operative Banks*).

However, in the event that there are other offers with the same services that are beneficial to the users, they will probably choose the best alternative, although this may not be from their own co-operative. The question is how to maintain the loyalty of the associates within your co-operative? – Through education or by means of economical incentives or, still, better a combination of both.

Another classification of the co-operatives is that they are specialized and multiactive. In Latin-America until a few years ago, nearly all of them tried to cover various economic activities, mainly: savings, credit, consumption. However, to become competitive, they have specialized in a sole economic activity and only in the rural sectors there are multi-active co-operatives.

6. Hierarchization of the Co-operatives

Up to now, we have referred to co-operatives of first stage or first level, that is, those formed directly by natural persons. In each country the co-operatives associate amongst themselves forming organizations of second and third degree (level): federations and confederations (→ *Federations*). Also, there are the centrals, leagues and co-operative banks (→ *Central Institutions*).

At the Latin American level there exists the Organization of Co-operatives of America (OCA), formed by co-operatives of the entire continent, the Latin American Confederation of Co-operatives of Workers and Social Assistance (COLACOT) that comprises only a sector of the co-operatives of workers and the associations of social assistance of various countries. (COLAC: Latinamerican Confederation of Saving and Credit Co-operatives that group all co-operatives of this sector and SIDEFCOOP – Interamerican Society of Co-operative Development and Financing that acts as a financial entity.)

We have mentioned the organizations of second and third degree, as well as other entities called "ancilliary organizations", since one of the activities carried out by these organizations is co-operative education and training.

There also exists the Latinamerican association of third centers of co-operative education "ALCECOOP" with rotational headquaters in different countries. This assocation is dedicated to the encouragement of co-operative education, especially directed to teachers of co-operativism (promoted by the spanish co-operativism).

Also until not so long ago, there existed the association of university centers and institutes of co-operative education – CIUDEC – where departments and centers of co-operative education and investigation were part of certain Latinamerican universities. Its headquarters were rotational and reached its summit with the performance of continental seminars and scientific investigation in the field of cooperation and study of cases regarding types of co-operatives.

II. The Co-operative Education in Latin-America

1. The Concept of Co-operative Education

In the ample sense we define the co-operative education as the learning of elements and methods of cooperation and identification of the objectives to accomplish same.

a) The Education as a Formation Process

The first discussion is whether the cooperation is a human act, that is, a form of behavior or whether it is a knowledge that can be transmitted and learnt. We must start from the human structure, understood that man in its entirety is a puzzle. Many of the behaviors of man are a result of conscious or unconscious individual motivations, that make him act in an individual form. On the other hand, man cannot act on his own to accomplish his ambitions he needs others. The fact of living within a social environment, whether it is only his family, makes man have to share with others aspects of his life.

Of course there are persons with more individualistic character than solidarious. And what the co-operative education does, is search for a balance between his own interests and the interests of others (→ *Solidarity*).

The cooperation is an attitude or form of behavior that requires from the associate willingness to fulfill joint action with others, and share with the rest the product of this common action.

The fact of entering into a co-operative does not imply nor is it a prerequisite condition that the associate leave aside individual interest as such. What it precisely does is achieve these individual interests through cooperation. It is more important not only to seek his own benefits, but these must also be reached by the other associates as set forth by the co-operative, with → *by-laws* and regulations. We neither pretend that the associate with the co-operative education resigns to obtain its individual objectives, he will insist on obtaining better benefits as those of the rest of the associates of the co-operative. Having everybody follow this objective, to reach a reasonable balance, it is necessary to negotiate, as any other negotiation with an offer and a demand. Thus, the co-operative appears as the product of an agreement and its explanation is given by means of co-operative education.

In short, the co-operative education within this context does not pretend to change the attitudes of the associates, neither does it pretend in itself adapting the associate to a special type of behavior. It would be difficult to understand that an associate has one behavior. It would be difficult to understand that an associate has one behavior whilst in the co-operative and a different one when he is out of it.

The co-operative education as formation gives the association a series of information and explanations regarding objectives, principles, values and forms of cooperation, in order to act within one co-operative process in a logical manner.

Now, if the associate as effect of the co-operative education modifies his individualistic behavior to a solidarious attitude, we can ascertain that the co-operative education has reached its utmost objective.

b) The Co-operative Education as Transmission of Knowledge

The co-operative education as developed in Latin-America as yet hasnot a guideline on the contents it must convey or that form part of the apprenticeship.

Under the title of co-operative education, the co-operatives offer their associates a range of courses with different contents – some relate to cooperation and others classified as technical knowledge or general knowledge.

Basically, the knowledge transmitted and related to cooperation correspond to the co-operative doctrine (principle, values, history) and to the structure and operation of the co-operatives. As there is not a science on cooperation, and there are not many investigations of scientific nature that back a theory, these subjects are seldomly dealt with as part of the co-operative education. But certainly and frequently the experiences are dealt with concerning different types of management and administration of co-operatives. However, the co-operative education is not reduced to the simple conveyance of knowledge, it must persuade the person to act in a logical way and conscious within the co-operative. This also implies the element "formation".

2. Levels of the Co-operative Education

In relation to the persons that use the co-operative education and according to which the contents are adapted, we can mention the following levels:

Level I:
Co-operative education to non-members. Here the objective is to try to explain how cooperation operates and the advantages it offers. Its objective is to encourage eventual members or explain the cooperation phenomenon, so that it is understood and comprehended by the public opinion.

Level II:
Co-operative education for members. Deals with more specific subjects regarding the operation of their own co-operatives – and its advantages at short, medium and long term that could be achieved if members remain faithful to their co-operative. Its purpose is to precisely strengthen the persuasion of the associates and encourage active participation in the process so as to achieve the objectives of the co-operative and satisfy the expectations of most associates.

Level III:
Co-operative education for the directors (instances of management and control techniques, as well as administrative items of co-operative enterprises).

Level IV:
Co-operative education for executive level (management) covering specific subjects of enterprise administration in general and of co-operatives. Its purpose is to convey the administrative mechanisms so that the co-operatives become more efficient. In other words, be competitive in the market as well as satisfy the expectations of the associates.

Level V:
Training and Instruction programmes: Covers apprenticeship with emphasis on the practice carried out directly within the co-operative companies. This type of apprenticeship can result from a combination of practical-theoretical apprenticeship (dual educational system). Its purpose is focused to form skills and practical expertness in the areas of co-operative administration or in the handling of specific areas of administration.

Level VI:
Technical, Professional and Post-Degree Formation in the co-operative area. This relates to careers given by institutes or universities that extend professional titles in Sociology, Economy or Business Administration with emphasis in the co-operative area. In this case only a part of the programmes of study correspond to matters that deal with co-operatives. Its purpose is to form groups of directors either as managers, leaders, teachers and investigators or advisors.

Level VII:
Consultancy to co-operatives: The object is to convey experience and knowledge to the directive and/or executive instances to help them in the process of adopting the correct decisions.

3. Components of the Co-operative Education

a) Objectives

As general objectives there are three which are important to outline:
- Make the ideas known regarding cooperation, providing participants with information and knowledge so that cooperativism is known and the range of action of the co-operatives is extended.
- Inform associates of the process of cooperation and its advantages, through courses, seminars, conferences and publication, so that the associates put them adequately in practice and try to reach the expectation they have set forth.
- Train and prepare directors and executives in order to reach efficiency in the administration of co-operative enterprises.

The precise objectives refer to what each co-operative intends to achieve through the educational activities and which are directed to satisfy the needs or lacks to this effect of the associates.

b) Individuals of the Co-operative Education

Basically, the co-operative education is directed to the members in general and specifically to directors and executives. Nevertheless, the co-operative education is also directed to non-members with the object of attracting them as future associates. It is also focused to government organizations and the public in general, in order to make known the co-operative idea and thus ending eventual adverse criticism to the co-operative movement. On the other hand, co-operative education is focussed to prepare future leaders and that eventually could be linked to the co-operatives as executive personnel or as employees of the co-operatives.

c) Contents

We have already mentioned that there is not a guideline that indicates the contents of co-operative education that is offered at the different levels. In this sense, we could divide the contents in those referring to cooperativism and those located out of this context.

Within the contents that refer and correspond to cooperativism we can especially mention:
- the principles and values of cooperativism
- the history of cooperativism
- the co-operative legislation
- the structure and performance of the different types of cooperativism
- the administration and control at the co-operatives
- cooperativism as a development tool
- co-operative economy.

The contents that appear as out of context of cooperativism are so different and depend on the requirements of the co-operatives or the demand of the associates. Only courses or seminars form part of academical studies which are scheduled and form part of the global curriculars that are offered for the careers of studies.

d) Methodology

The open type of co-operative education is offered to the associates, in the form of courses and seminars. The participants are adults and receive these courses only sporadically. We can classify this type of co-operative education as pertaining to the non-formal type, directed to adults. They are mostly theoretical courses which are related to on the job practice. It must be considered that at the courses of members, they being already aware up to certain extent of the cooperation exercise, generally the dialogue method is used, whereby the participants (pupils) provide their knowledge as a result of their experience. Also, different types of educational aids are seldomly used. However, in general the methodology used depends on the teacher or on the indications he receives.

e) Teachers

These are in charge of dictating the courses or directing the seminars. They are also called "instructors", "monitors" or "multipliers". The persons that carry out these courses or seminars are those who from their experience have fulfilled directive posts within the co-operatives, such as independent professionals (lawyers, economists, enterprise administrators or employees linked to organizations of second level).

f) Ways of conveying co-operative education

Co-operative education is conveyed by means of different events such as: courses, seminars, workshops, conferences and panels.

Also communication means are used such as newspapers, magazines, videos, bulletins, radio programmes and more sporadically TV programmes.

Within the formal education system we can mention: professional formation within the dual system and programmes of formation using the presence of the university and the method by distance.

g) Evaluation and Follow-up

The co-operatives occasionally carry out evaluations as to the effects of the co-operative education in the improvement of the operation of the co-operative. Although every event is evaluated, usually the participants are not, though they do evaluate the teachers. However, some co-operatives have a record of educational activities and of the associates that participate and occasionally establishes incentives for those that attend these events.

h) Instances in charge of education

The co-operatives have an educational committee. This committee is in charge of planning and organizing educational events. The large co-operatives like the second degree organizations, have departments and areas with technical equipment and specialized personnel for the educational tasks that are in charge of organizing and fulfilling the educational work.

There are state entities in some countries in charge of planning and conveying co-operative education, as well as the consultancy activities of the co-operatives. There are also non-governmental organizations, specialized in conveying co-operative education, some belong and are financed by the co-operative itself, and others are backed and financed by foreign institutions. In some countries, the Universities have supportive programmes as extension programmes (extra-rural education) and academic formation programmes that are conducive to a title, with a mention in cooperativism.

i) Funds for the Co-operative Education

Most legislations in Latin-America establish that a percentage of the annual profits of the co-operatives must go to co-operative education. This percentage differs according to the country and the type of co-operative, but it ranges between 5 and 25%.

If this was to be considered, the co-operative education will depend on the economic results. The co-operatives with large commerical operations and sufficient profit are able to afford the co-operative education of its members. Meanwhile, the smaller co-operatives or with less marginal profit will not enjoy this advantage. They will have to associate with other co-operatives of second degree to make up for the deficiencies.

The co-operatives of second degree are financed with the share paid by the member and part of these funds are directed to educational co-operative programmes.

III. The Praxis of Co-operative Education in Latin-America

1. Diagnosis of the Co-operative Education in Latin America

According to the statistics of the Economical Commission for Latin America (CEPAL) in 1990 the total inhabitants reached 430 million, of which 42% live in a situation of poverty. It is calculated that for the same year there existed approximately 40,000 co-operatives and 20 million affiliates. A third of the co-operatives are attributed to the agropecuarian sector and 15% to the savings and credit, whereas the production sector only reached 10%.

Most of the co-operative legislations of Latin American countries specify that for the co-operatives to obtain juridical acknowledgement it is necessary that the founder members must have at least taken one co-operative educational course.

Each co-operative has a board or committee of education formed by 2 or 3 members. It also has a percentage of the profits as well as additional funds. The committee must carry out annual planning education activities and see that this is accomplished. At the assemblies it must render reports on the educational activities carried out the preceeding period.

According to this, it is assumed that each co-operative has at least accomplished one course on co-operative education and that each member has participated in an activity of this type.

Nevertheless, with no evaluations available on the co-operative education at the national level and less at the continental level, its efficiency and degree of exact coverage cannot be detected.

The co-operative education in Latin America is mainly focussed on encouraging the participation of members in the decisions of the association on one part and on the other, to improve the administration efficiency level of the enterprises. A sign of the participation of the members is for instance, the presence at the General Assemblies and this, to be honest, is not that significant when observing the Assemblies. It is calculated that only a third of the affiliates participate in the assemblies. When the assemblies are of delegates then the participation is greater, but if this is examined more extensively, for instance, we could have doubts of the involvement of the members in decision making, owing to the vertical system from top to bottom, that they really participate in such decisions.

Regarding the efficiency of the administration (management), it can be said that the executive instances are ever so more efficient as regards to the satisfaction of the members' expectations, but there are no elements that can ascertain that this is due to a direct effect of the educational co-operative. What is certain is that the co-operatives are more than ever seeking in the labour market for their executive instances the best qualified personnel or professionals with university degree.

2. Justification for Co-operative Education

a) Preparation of Members in Decision Takings

As already explained the members of the co-operatives come from a social group where the majority of the persons are of scarce economic resources and of course with quite low education level and very poor knowledge of business administration. If the principle of the co-operative is fulfilled in that they must be administrated by their owners, then the members must consider their preparation in order that they may fulfill this responsibility adequately, especially to the Administrative Committee or Board, which are the instances where the important decisions take place and they are formed by the members. They must learn to process and evaluate the information and take the correct decisions.

b) Preventing Differences between the "Directive" and "Executive" Instances

In general, at an enterprise the executives are best prepared (trained) and have a greater control of internal and external information of the co-operative. This results that if the directive instances (Board of Administration) are not sufficiently prepared, in the practice the executives prepare the decisions and the directors simply approve them. This is not perceived if both instances have the same interests and if there exists a close relationship and cooperation between the two. The problems arise when there are serious discrepancies or extremely different interests, then there are conflicts that can jeopardize the good-standing operation of a co-operative.

On the other hand, considering that the managers are in a subordinate position as regards to the Administration Board, if the members of such Board have no adminstration knowledge of the co-operative to evaluate and understand the information and the advantages and disadvantages of the decisions, they in the end become an embarrassment for the management. Of course, the existence of performance and procedure manuals outline the roles of each instance, but it would be preferable that the members of the directors and administration board also have a degree of formation and information of the executives, so as to avoid the differences in the decision taking or conflicts of the scope of competence.

c) Maintain the Stimulation and Loyalty of the Members

Most of the co-operatives are created with the object of serving the associates and some economically depend on the exclusive operations with the associates especially those concerning supplies. This implies that the co-operatives depend on the loyalty of the members. If there aren't contractual agreements between the co-operatives and its associates, that bind these to fulfill their operations with their co-operatives, they can, as sometimes occurs, trade with the competitors when these offer, although maybe briefly, better conditions. In these cases, the co-operative education in itself is not enough to keep the member faithful. No matter how much one demonstrates the advantages that their co-operative will produce in the medium and short term, this would have no immediate effect, if it is not accompanied by economical incentives. Nevertheless, the co-operative education has an important role with regard to the conscience of the members and commits them to be faithful to their co-operative.

d) Encouraging the Participation of the Associates

Considering that the co-operatives are organizations where democracy is practiced and democracy needs the active participation of its associates, one of the forms of encouraging members to participate is with co-operative education.

e) Encouraging Development

The co-operatives have as main objective to assist the member as a person in his economical, social and cultural development (→ *Self-help Organizations*). The co-operative education helps to improve the levels of knowledge and formation of the associates in order to handle their resources and hopefully learn a new skill. Also the co-operative education stimulates the civic affairs so that the member may be able to act in a better way within its community. Also the co-operative education contributes to encourage the development as they work in sectors economically most unfavoured which in any other way would be difficult for them to solve their economical and social problems.

3. The Execution of Co-operative Education

a) Education to Associates and Directors

It is focussed to form leaders, to create conscious participation and theoretically explain the operation of the co-operative. It is accomplished preferably with courses or seminars of 2 or 3 days, occupying the weekends or the evenings. The number of participants varies between 20 to 50 and attendance is voluntary. The tendency observed is that the members do not show much interest in attending these courses, despite the fact that it has no cost for them, as the co-operatives assume same.

To obtain a greater attendance to the courses, the educational committees have to create various mechanisms of incentives. There are also economical incentives, such as: the co-operatives of credit which provide to those members that attend the courses more points for the credit quota. The large co-operatives and those that have more economical resources can offer more courses and better conditions for the participants. The poorer co-operatives such as those of the rural area cannot carry out educational activities and depend on the second degree organizations or on the government instances in charge of the co-operative promotion.

Within the co-operative education, the co-operatives offer specific courses for the various instances: Board of Administration (Board of Directors), Surveillance Board (Control councils) and for Managers. These activities have more specific contents and a greater participation is achieved.

b) Training Programmes for the Management

The training programmes in the sense of learning by doing as a method to form Co-operative Directors or Managers is not usual in Latinamerican ambit. The only experience is reduced to a type of dual formation, where the courses are formed by a theoretical part in the classroom and the practice carried out at the co-operative. Nevertheless, this practice does not follow set programmes where the student performs the work, but really he is limited to observe how others do the job.

Neither are there specialized educational institutions that carry out these programmes. Only some universities or certain international institutions have tried with specific programmes and sporadically the upper organizations of the same cooperativism.

The human resources for the administration of co-operative enterprises are formed by persons with experience in other firms, including the co-operatives. There is a constant move of executives from one co-operative to another.

At internal level within the same co-operatives, there are no formation or training programmes.

c) University or Post-degree Formation Programmes

In Latin-America it has been discussed whether it is convenient to prepare professionals specifically in cooperativism or if it is preferable to hire professionals of other areas and train them in cooperativism. Certain universities such as the University of La Plata in Argentina, the University of Puerto Rico in Puerto Rico, the Co-operative University of Colombia in Colombia, the University of Chile in Chile and others recently formed have created specific programmes in cooperativism without much success. The reason for this is that the labour market for these professionals is very reduced within the cooperativism. On the other hand, the salaries offered by the co-operatives are not sufficiently attractive to encourage the youth to be interested in this type of studies.

The Universities have decided to introduce in their courses of the careers of economics, business administration (commercial engineering), sociology and law, subjects related to cooperativism through courses, seminars, workshops and surveys. Amongst the main universities with this methodology we can mention "Cordoba" in Argentina, Catholic of Bolivia in La Paz, "Santo Tomas of Cauca", "Risarald and the Co-operative" in Colombia, the Pontiff of Ecuador, of Lima in Peru, that of Uniui, the Federal of Vicosa and Vale dos Sinos in Brasil and the Catholic University of Chile.

This methodology has not had success, since cooperativism is covered with courses for these careers in secondary place or they are optional materials, that furthermore have not much relevance in the context of the studies, and are not related to the praxis.

The alternative that most suits the labour and present situation of Latin-America is that of hiring particular professionals (economics, business administration, engineering, accounting science, law) and train them in cooperativism by means of short courses, seminars or practice.

At post-degree level, there are some experiences. The Universities that have created programmes are the University of Santo Tomas in Colombia, the University of Lima in Peru and the University of Unisinos in Sao Paulo, Brasil. The latter presently valid. These programmes have neither been attractive owing to these reasons of future employment and low salaries.

Sporadically, some universities or certain second degree organizations make agreements with universities to carry out training courses.

However, there is a lack of a closer relationship between the co-operatives and the Universities.

d) Consultancy to the Co-operatives

The co-operatives request consultancy, preferably in the juridical, accounting and taxing areas (→ *Consulting*). Consultancy requirements are not perceived in other areas. It must be considered that consultancy is a form of training and perhaps the most effective since it is carried out on the site and based on definite situations where not only those supervised but also those supervising participate.

4. Offer (Supply) and Demand of the Co-operative Education

In Latin-America, the co-operative education is considered an economical asset and when entering the market, a price is assigned. As offerers (suppliers) there are 2nd and 3rd degree organizations the same organizations; created by the cooperativism, as schools, institutes, training centers, other NGO's with specific programmes, the Universities, establishments and individual persons. As claimants there are co-operatives and organizations of 2nd and 3rd degree, governmental entities, etc.

In this area, supply often exceeds demand. Some organizations of second degree subsidize the cost of the courses, so the user receives this benefit for free. Other organizations have education as a resource of self-financing; some depend exclusively on this. The competition between so many offerers (suppliers) has an influence on keeping the prices low, but also has an incidence on the quality.

The quality does not improve because teachers are not better paid and neither is there investigation nor important innovations that make the co-operative education more attractive or more necessary. On the other hand, the co-operatives themselves prefer providing better services to their members than investing in co-operative education. If the members show an extent of satisfaction with the services that they receive, then the co-operatives do not worry and consider this degree of satisfaction as a form of co-operative education.

Instead of converting the co-operative education into a scope of cooperation, the competition between offerers has made it an area of conflict. This has contributed to a negative image both of the co-operative education and of the institutions that provide same. The offer is concentrated in the urban areas or at places where there are more co-operatives, whereas the rural areas or those further away from the capital cities do not have access, since it is too expensive.

IV. Future of Co-operative Education

The co-operative education forms part of the context of education which is conveyed in the different countries. The education has a direct relation with the social, economical and political structure and forms part of the cultural and spiritual life of the people.

The changes in these structures make it necessary for immediate adjustments in the contents and methods of education and this, at the same time, affects the changing processes of said structures. The co-operative education is not different from any other phenomenon.

Most of the countries have incorporated the model of free market economy. The majority of the public services have been privatized, amongst them education, and the economical sector of production, until recently protected by customs restrictions, have had to modernize and adapt their costs to be able to compete in the market.

The state gradually is less concerned in encouraging the co-operatives and least co-operative education. On the other hand, the co-operatives no longer have the advantage of tax exemption and the favourable credit conditions of the state financial entities.

The co-operatives, like other economical sectors of production of assets and services, have had to change their economic tendency and must alter their mechanisms to act efficiently in the competitive market. The "Co-operative Faithfulness" of the members probably will not resist the influence of competition. In view of these circumstances it is necessary to revise the actual practices of co-operative education with regard to contents and methodology. It is necessary to adapt with time and the new requirements, otherwise many co-operatives will disappear.

The co-operative education and especially the training programmes must be focussed on creating a dynamic and efficient administration. The management (directors and managers) is the central point of these programmes.

It is necesssary to create a new profile for the co-operative education and a new profile for the managers. The co-operative education under these circumstances will more than ever have a decisive role in the future of the co-operative enterprises.

Bibliography

Benecke, Dieter/Eschenburg, Rolf and others: The co-operatives in Latinamerica I, II. Sao Leopoldo, Unisinos 1987.
Castillo, Alfonso/Latapi, Pablo: Education for Adults in Latinamerica, Campiñas S.P. (Brasil) 1985.
CEPAL: Statistics and elemental details on population in Latinamerica and the Carribbean, in: Notes on economy and development, Notes 540 and 541, Santiago-Chile 1993.
International Cooperation Magazine: The co-operatives in Latinamerica, Vol. 23, no. 2, Buenos Aires 1990, pp. 79–85.
Ramirez, Benjamin: Community Promotion and associative forms, Bogotá 1984, 1990.
Ramirez, Benjamin: Theory and Doctrine of Cooperation, Bogotá 1989.
Rojas, Alberto: New Co-operative Legislation, Bogotá 1989.
United Nations/CEPAL: Notes on social development in Latinamerica and the Carribbean, (First Iberoamerican Summit- Guadalajara Mexico 18–19 July 1991), Santiago-Chile 1991.
Uribe, G. Carlos: Basis for cooperativism, Bogota (1965), (1984).

Education and Training in North America, Co-operative

LOU HAMMOND KETILSON/BRETT FAIRBAIRN

(see also: *Education, Latin America*; *Education, Europe*; *Education, Germany*; *Theory and Science of Co-operatives*)

I. Introduction; II. Methodology; III. Co-operative Education and Training in the United States; IV. Co-operative Education and Training in Canada; V. Conclusions.

I. Introduction

The co-operative movements in the United States and Canada share many similarities. Not only did the two evolve from somewhat similar circumstances – mainly in farming regions from the 1880's to the 1940's – but, in addition, the American movement influenced the early development of the Canadian one. In both countries co-operatives and co-operative education remain concentrated in regions – the U.S. Mid-West and South and the Canadian Prairies, Québec, and the Atlantic region. Co-operatives are regionally strong within the wider North American economy.

Yet the two possess differences as well. The movement in the U.S.A. appears less prominent because it is diffused and the organizations are difficult to identify as co-operatives; most do not use the term "co-operative" in their names. Yet 50,000 co-operatives and credit unions are to be found in the United States, located in every state, with a total of 102 million members. In Canada the co-operatives are cohesive and quite easily identified. There are 6,847 co-operatives and credit unions or caisse populaires in Canada, found in every province and territory, and claiming 12 million members. There is a major distinction among the Canadian co-operatives between the French-speaking and English-speaking co-operative movements, each of which has its own institutions for co-operative education and training.

II. Methodology

To gather information for this chapter, contact was made by mail with 115 organizations in the United States and Canada. A follow-up questionnaire was distributed, which drew 33 responses. To complete our data base on 135 North American co-operative education and training organizations, we used the excellent handbook by *Jack* and *Connie McLanahan,* editors, *Cooperative/Credit Union Dictionary and Reference* (Richmond, Kentucky: The Cooperative Alumni Association, 1990). This handbook contains historical and biographical information as well as addresses for the organizations mentioned below. The Cooperative Alumni Association was organized in 1979 to maintain ties among those who have been involved in the co-operative movement.

III. Co-operative Education and Training in the United States

The most striking feature of co-operative education and training in the U.S.A. is its diversity. Our database included 122 agencies that conduct co-operative education or training in the United States (including one in Puerto Rico), ranging from university departments or university-based institutes to independent foundations or associations of co-operatives. This is not a complete list, but it does include the most prominent regional, national, and international agencies based in the United States. The type of education or training also varies greatly, from summer camps for young people, to classes for university students for credit towards their degrees, to certificate courses for managers in co-operatives. Despite this diversity, there are some clear patterns. The bulk of co-operative training and education in the U.S.A. is divided between universities on one hand, which offer primarily credit courses on co-operatives for their students, and, on the other hand, associations or federations of co-operatives, which do training, conferences, or certificate courses for their directors and managers (→ *Theory and Science of Co-operatives*). Both of these activities are usually regional rather than national in scope, typically serving a single state. Official government agencies play only a small role. Of the 122 organizations in the data base, 50 were university departments, 42 of which did courses for their undergraduate students, and 14 of which did training or conferences for other groups. Eight universities reported graduate classes or programs on co-operatives. About equal in number to the universities, 49 of 122 agencies were associations of co-operatives, 34 of which appear to emphasize training programs, while 13 appear to be primarily organizers of conferences for directors, managers, members, and so on. The remainder of the 122 agencies were independent foundations (9), university-based institutes (8), university extension units (5), and one government agency (the Agricultural Cooperative Service of the U.S. Department of Agriculture, about which more is said below).

It is possible that multi-state, university-based co-operative centres will play an increasing role in U.S. co-operative education and training. The 1990 Farm Bill provides for the establishment of such centres under the direction of co-operatives within four to five state areas.

Co-operative education agencies in the United States, like co-operatives themselves, are concentrated in the Mid-West and the South. Of the 122 organizations on which information was compiled, 46 were in the Mid-West region and 37 were in the South. The remainder were distributed as follows: Rocky Mountain states (11); Pacific Coast (10), Mid-Atlantic (7); New England (5); and South-West (4); one was the University of Puerto Rico; and one had no fixed address. The concentration in the Mid-West and the South is apparent for most types of agencies, including universities (18 in the Mid-West and 14 in the South, out of 50), co-operative associations (21 in the Mid-West and 16 in the south, out of 49), university-based institutes (5 of 8 are in the Mid-West), and university extension units (3 of 5 are in the South). The exception is independent foundations, which show no apparent regional concentration and seem to deal on a national level with less developed kinds of co-operatives (housing, employment, and so on).

Agricultural co-operatives (→ *Rural Co-operatives*) are by far the main focus of American co-operative education, to judge by our study results. Of the 122 agencies included in the data base, 68 emphasized education or training related to co-operatives in the agricultural sector, while 41 concentrated on general co-operative training and education. Only 13 concentrated on one or more of the remaining sectors (housing, financial, employment, retail, and service co-operatives). Universities are the backbone of agricultural co-operative education in the United States, making up no fewer than 39 of the 68 agencies that concentrated on the agricultural sector. Most of the agricultural and general co-operative education is regional in scope and organization, whereas agencies that concentrate, for example, on employment or financial co-operatives tend to be fewer, national in scope and concentrated in different regions. From these results one could conclude that co-operative education agencies, and above all the universities, serve the established co-operatives, especially in agriculture, rather than promoting new co-operatives – that is, co-operative education represents a reality of sectoral strength and organization rather than leading or shaping a new reality.

The most common means of delivering co-operative education in the United States are training sessions or courses, classes, and conferences. The primary audiences are directors, managers, and employees of co-operatives, followed by students and distantly by members, the public, and youth. The primary functions of the 122 agencies were as follows: training (58); university classes (40); conferences (13); preparation of resource materials (5); and miscellaneous (6). As for audience, 41 agencies aimed their activities at directors, managers, and/or employees of co-operatives; 36 concentrated on students; only 13 focused on youth, 12 on members, and 11 on the general public.

Among the universities, in particular, the focus was narrow; while 42 of 50 offered classes to undergraduates, only 11 were involved in educational activities for the co-operative sector. Few universities mentioned other audiences: the general public (4), educators (4), youth (4), members of co-operatives (2), or international visitors (2). The universities were narrow in another way. Most of the departments involved were in the fields of agriculture or agricultural economics; 39 of the 50 universities included concentrated on agricultural co-operatives. Not surprisingly, university-based institutes and university extension units, though few, serve wider audiences. Among eight university-based institutes, five mentioned activities aimed at youth, and four aimed at the general public, while two dealt with co-operative directors and managers and two with educators. Of five university extension units, four were involved in youth education. These institutes and units also did proportionately much more for non-agricultural co-operatives (housing, retail, employment, and service) and for general co-operative education.

In short, mainstream university departments appear to teach credit courses on well-established co-operatives for agriculture or economics students, while university-based institutes and extension units have a different role and serve wider audiences among the public and the co-operative sector, including emerging co-operatives.

Against the background of this broad picture of co-operative education and training in the United States, it is useful to consider in more detail a few of the major national- and international-level agencies based in the U.S.A.

The leading national-level agency for co-operative training and education is likely the American Institute of Cooperation (A.I.C.), a private non-profit corporation chartered as a university in the District of Columbia. The A.I.C. conducts conferences and seminars, produces resource materials, and provides special educational services to member co-operatives. The membership of the A.I.C. includes more than 1,000 of the major co-operatives in the U.S.A.. Each year it organizes the National Institute on Co-operative Education, the largest annual co-operative education event in the country, and it publishes the yearbook, *American Cooperation*, as well as the *Journal of Agricultural Cooperation* (→ *Periodicals, Co-operative*).

The University of Wisconsin stands out among American universities as the only landgrant university with a unit where faculty are devoted full time to co-operative education, training, and research. The University Center for Cooperatives in Madison is an autonomous interdisciplinary unit within the College of Agriculture and Life Sciences, where faculty work with regional and national co-operative organizations to develop education and research programs. The Center is also active in international co-operative education. It offers co-operative correspondence courses, short courses, a co-operative management institute, as well as other seminars and programs. The University Center for Cooperatives claims the most extensive library on co-operatives in the U.S.A..

Mention should also be made of the education activities of the larger national-level co-operative → *federations*. The National Cooperative Business Association (N.C.B.A.) is the trade association representing co-operatives of all types and all sectors in the U.S. since 1916, when it was founded as the Cooperative league of the U.S.A.. Based in Washington, D.C., the N.C.B.A. represents U.S. co-operatives to the federal government and to the international co-operative movement, provides training and technical assistance to co-operatives in the U.S.A. and abroad, and promotes co-operative development. The N.C.B.A. publishes the *Cooperative Business Journal*. The Credit Union National Association (C.U.N.A.), headquartered in Madison, Wisconsin, represents more than 90 per cent of credit unions in the United States and makes available a wide range of services, including training of staff in consulting and planning, seminars and conferences, and resource materials. C.U.N.A. was founded in 1934. It publishes weekly, monthly, and quarterly consumer magazines which are distributed to more than one million credit union members.

Other national- or international-level educational agencies include the Association of Cooperative Educators (A.C.E.) and the North American Students of Cooperation (N.A.S.C.O.). A.C.E. holds annual institutes on a rotating basis among eleven geographical regions from Canada to the Caribbean. Its emphasis is liason and professional development for persons engaged in co-operative education, both within co-operatives and in universities or other outside agencies. N.A.S.C.O. links together student housing and other co-operatives from across the continent and provides an annual education and training institute for leaders, members, and employees in the co-operatives.

Within the agricultural sector, an important support role is played by the Agricultural Cooperative Service of the U.S. Department of Agriculture, Washington, D.C.. The service has a mandate to help develop sound and efficient co-operatives. To this end, it conducts research, provides technical assistance, distributes history and statistics, and provides education and information on → *co-operative principles* and practices. It also publishes the monthly *Farmer Cooperatives*.

The National Farmers Educational and Co-operative Union of America, or national Farmers Union for short, is a general farm organization which promotes education concerning co-operatives, especially for youth. Other sector-specific national organizations include: the National Rural Electric Cooperative Assocation of Washington, D.C., which provides conferences, training, and seminars to over 1,000 rural electric co-operatives and similar organizations that provide electricity to more than 25 million people in 46 states; the Cooperative Housing Foundation of Washington, D.C., which conducts workshops and research and prepares manuals to support and develop co-operatives for low-income housing (→ *Housing Societies*); the Institute for community Economics of Greenfield, Maine, which promotes community land trusts as mechanisms for housing and community development; and the Association for the Democratic Workplace of Eugene, Oregon, and National Center for Employee Ownership of Oakland, California, which provide conferences and training to the employment co-operative sector.

Space does not allow mention of many of the other agencies involved in co-operative education and training, though at the risk of arbitrariness it is worthwhile to mention a couple of the regional universities that are active in co-operative education. The University of California at Davis has established a Center for cooperatives, which conducts training, holds conferences, and prepares resource materials that serve co-operative directors, managers, members, and employees as well as youth and educators. The Department of Agricultural Economics (Extension) at Davis is active in co-operative research and education. The University of Wisconsin Agricultural Extension Department at Madison and the Universities of Minnesota, Missouri, and Iowa might also be singled out as significant centres of co-operative education.

IV. Co-operative Education and Training in Canada

As in the United States, diversity is a key feature of co-operative education and training in Canada. Thirteen organizations from across Canada are represented in our data base, ranging from university departments (3) or university-based institutes (3), to independent foundations (2) or co-operative associations (4), to a federal government agency. This list includes regional, national and international agencies. The type of education or training offered varies from university classes for credit toward degrees, to certificate courses for co-operative and credit union managers and employees, to youth camps, to resource materials for school curricula.

Responsibility for the bulk of co-operative education and training is divided between universities, which offer primarily credit courses on co-operatives for their students, and independent foundations and associations of co-operatives, which do training, sponsor conferences, or offer certificate courses for their managers and directors. Large commercial co-operatives do a great deal of inhouse training. Official government agencies play a role of significance only in educational support for co-operative development. Such support is provided in varying degrees by individual provincial government departments.

Co-operative education organizations are dispersed across the width of Canada, but the majority are concentrated in the central provinces of Ontario and Québec. Of the 13 agencies included in the data base, 1 is in the maritime regions, 4 are in Québec, 6 are in Ontario, and 1 each is in the western provinces of Saskatchewan and Alberta. This concentration of agencies does not accurately reflect the concentration of co-operatives, for many more are to be found in the western provinces, particularly Saskatchewan, than in Ontario. The concentration of agencies seems rather to be a reflection of population density, since Ontario is Canada's most populous province.

Not included in the data base are the large commercial co-operatives which provide much of their own education and training inhouse. Some of these co-operatives co-ordinate their programs quite closely with those agencies included in the data base, either through the use of resource materials or having the agency administer specific programs, while others conduct their own programs quite independently. The pattern seems to be dependent on the size and resources of the commercial co-operative.

Of the 13 agencies included in the data base, 4 are "national" in scope, bearing in mind the distinction between the French- and English-speaking movements. The two major national agencies are the Candian Co-operative Association (C.C.A.), which serves all English-speaking co-operatives in Canada, and le Conseil canadien de la coopération (C.C.C.), which serves the French-speaking co-operatives. Although the latter tend to be concentrated in the province of Québec, they also are to be found scattered across Canada. Three of the agencies are international in scope, providing university-based classes and diploma courses for international visitors. Regional co-operative education services are provided by the remainder.

The majority (10) of the co-operative education organizations serve all established sectors (retail, credit, and marketing) relatively equally rather than concentrating on rural or agricultural co-operatives. It is probably fair to say, however, that less work is done on new co-operatives in fields like housing, employment and health care. This is particularly true in the universities. The financial, employment, and housing sectors receive specific focus from three agencies. The relatively broad focus reflects the diversity of co-operative organizational form to be found in Canada.

The most common means of delivering co-operative education in Canada are training sessions of diploma courses, university degree classes, and conferences. The primary audiences are directors, managers and employees of co-operatives, followed by students and distantly by members, the general public and youth. For the 13 agencies included in the data base, primary functions included training (4), university classes (4), conferences (3), development of general resource materials or school curriculum materials (4). (These do not add to 13 as more than one primary function was mentioned by some.) As for audience, 8 agencies aimed their activities at directors, managers, and/or employees of co-operatives; 5 concentrated on students and, to a certain extent, the general public; only 4 concentrated on youth and none on members.

Among the universities, 3 offer classes to undergraduate students; the other 3 focus on courses and training for the co-operative sector, with 2 of these offering a Masters equivalent in co-operative studies. Five of the Canadian universities or university-based institutes provide classes with a focus in the areas of co-operative development and management, while the sixth provides a multidisciplinary offering of courses through 5 colleges.

Since the numbers of co-operative education and training organizations are fewer in Canada than in the U.S.A., it is possible to consider all of them in some detail. The leading national-level agency for co-operative training and education is the Canadian Co-operative Association (C.C.A.), formed in 1987 through the amalgamation of the Co-operative Union of Canada and the Co-operative College of Canada. It is the national association of English-speaking co-operatives and credit unions, with head office in Ottawa. The C.C.A. conducts conferences and seminars, provides resource materials, and provides special educational services to member co-operatives. The inhouse library is extensive, with the C.C.A. providing a lending service across the country. Once every two years, the C.C.A. organizes The Institute of Co-operative Studies, an institute of advanced co-operative studies for managers and directors. Le Conseil candien de la coopération (C.C.C.) provides a function similar to the C.C.A. for the French-speaking co-operatives and caisses populaires. The C.C.C. represents more than 5 million francophone members through its nine provincial conseils and their affiliated co-operatives. It is also located in Ottawa and publishes *Le bulletin Cooppresse*.

Two other co-operative associations deserve mention. The Co-operative Housing Foundation of Canada, located in Ottawa, is a national agency to advance the role of housing co-operatives by lobbying, education, and supporting the development of regional federations and groups. It also provides support to co-operative education in general through the sponsorship of the Laidlaw scholarship, awarded annually to either a masters or doctoral student whose research focuses on co-operatives or credit unions. Fondation Desjardins, a member of the Québec Desjardins Group, the credit union movement in French-speaking Canada, promotes the advancement of education and research.

Two independent agencies form part of the study's data base. The Worker Ownership Development Foundation was formed in Toronto in 1983 as a non-profit charitable organization to provide education and research on worker-owned co-operatives. The foundation sponsors conferences, committees and informal work-shops and provides resource materials to encourage the development of the worker co-operative movement. It publishes *Worker Co-ops* magazine. The Rural Education and Development Association (R.E.D.A.) is located in Edmonton in western Canada and encourages rural education through the development and delivery of training sessions and materials oriented toward co-operative managers and directors. It also provides programs for youth and curriculum materials for schools. It acts as an independent agency, as well as an agent for some C.C.A.-developed programs.

Two universities offer important international programs. The Coady International Institute is a department of St. Francis Xavier University, Antigonish,

Nova Scotia. Training programs for third-world development in the philosophy and methods of social change are conducted both in Antigonish and internationally. A six-month diploma program in social development and two three-week certificate courses are offered. The Institute is self-contained with its own faculty and staff, library, and residential and instructional facilities. The Institut de recherche et d'enseignement pour les co-opératives de l'Université de Sherbrooke (I.R.E.C.U.S.), another international institute, is located in Sherbrooke, Québec. I.R.E.C.U.S. offers a two-year diploma course as well as a Masters degree in co-operative management oriented to students from developing countries. The institute sponsors conferences, develops resource materials, and publishes monographs, occasional papers and *Les Cahiers de la coopération*. York University in Ontario offers a Masters program in co-operative management through the Faculty of Environmental Studies. The program is not specifically oriented to students from developing countries but does attract many from African nations.

Three other universities should also be mentioned. École des Hautes Études Commerciales (H.E.C.) at the University of Montréal offers courses on co-operatives to undergraduate students. This centre claims one of the best collections of materials on co-operatives in its library. It publishes *Coopératives et développement*. Courses focusing on the management of co-operatives are also offered through the Business School at Laurentian University in Sudbury, Ontario. Finally, the newest university-based institute to be mentioned is the Centre for the Study of Co-operatives at the University of Saskatchewan in western Canada, founded in 1984. The Centre's objective is to establish a program of co-operative studies at the undergraduate and graduate levels. The faculty form a multidisciplinary team, teaching classes in five separate faculties. The Centre focuses on teaching, academic research, sponsorship of conferences, the provision of training, and development of resource materials. A library is available for the use of the general public. An occasional paper series is published, in addition to a number of monographs. A final organization deserving brief mention is the Canadian Association for Studies in Co-operation (C.A.S.C.), an academic society. Scholars from Canada, the United States, and abroad come together at the annual meetings to present and discuss academic research on co-operatives, credit unions, and caisses populaires. The organization also strives to bring together practitioners with academics at the annual meetings to share the knowledge base on co-operatives.

V. Conclusions

In both, Canada and the United States, co-operative education and training are regional functions conducted mainly by co-operatives themselves, through political and educational associations, and by universities, mainly through undergraduate classes and in some cases through institutes or centres that also do research and extension education on co-operatives. The role of university-based institutes seems to be increasing. Specialized foundations try to serve less developed or less prominent co-operatives, while the bulk of educational agencies serve established co-operatives. Governments play little role except indirectly through the funding of universities or of extension programs. In both countries, co-operative education is aimed mainly at the leaders of the co-operative sector itself and very little at ordinary members or the general public. Differences include the somewhat greater prominence and centralization of co-operative activities and the relatively broader emphasis in types of co-operatives studied and served in Canada. Despite these differences, both countries show breadth and diversity of co-operative education so that national-level activities are only the tip of the iceberg – an iceberg that may be surprising to outsiders for its depth and size.

Environmental Protection and Co-operatives

EBERHARD SEIDEL [S]

(see also: *Business Policies*; *Management in Co-operatives*; *Managerial Economics*)

I. Preliminary Conceptual Note; II. Behavioural Options for Co-operatives with Regard to Environmental Protection; III. Qualifying Criteria for Co-operative Management of Environmental Protection; IV. Co-operative Affinities with Environmental Protection; V. Conclusion and Prospects for the Future.

I. Preliminary Conceptual Note

If we understand *contingency* as a state of a favoured opportunity but with a lack of necessity, the relation between co-operatives and environmental protection is "contingent" in that sense of the word. In principle, for co-operatives all imaginable *behavioural options* with regard to environmental protection are also feasible (II). Efficient management of environmental protection for co-operatives is based on the same *qualifying criteria* as for any other business enterprise (III.). Nevertheless, there is a considerable *affinity* –

Environmental problem			
Denial	Rejection	Exploitation	Acceptance

Behaviour
⋮
Management

(0) no action

(1) Action

    (1.1) "defensive" merely reactive

    (1.2) "offensive" self-initiated measures

(1.2.1) open rejection "defensive" "conciliatory" "faith-healing"

(1.2.2) covertly (actually) defensive "talking instead of acting"

(1.2.3) mere self-interest "problem free-loaders"

(1.2.4) in the interests of ecology "problem-handling" "environmental protection activity"

(deficits in execution)

"negative" ─── ecology-oriented ─── "positive" management

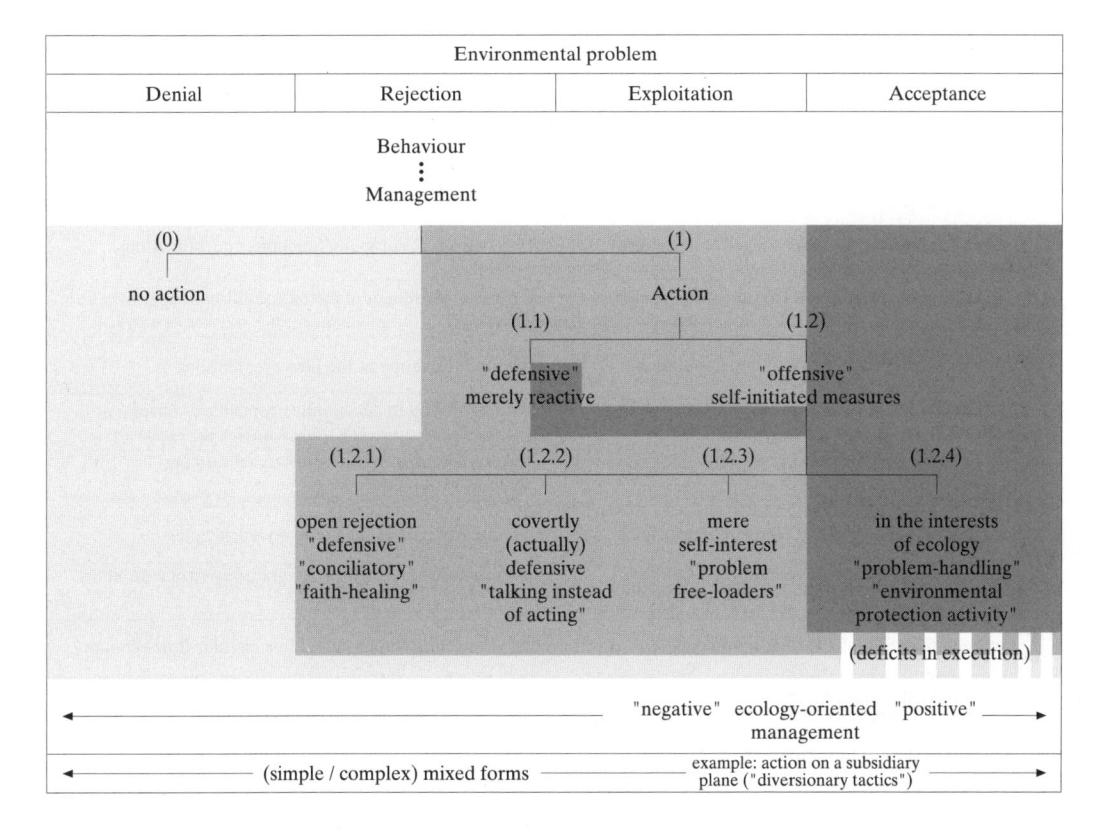

◄── (simple / complex) mixed forms ──── example: action on a subsidiary plane ("diversionary tactics") ──►

Fig. 1: Options for ecology-oriented business management.

actual as well as potential – of co-operative management with the concerns of environmental protection (IV.).

II. Behavioural Options for Co-operatives with Regard to Environmental Protection

With the denial, rejection, exploitation, and acceptance of problems, as well as with the resulting

- passive or active,
- defensive or offensive,
- negative or positive
- behaviour towards environmental protection or management of environmental protection, respectively,

all relevant options of behaviour or action are open to co-operatives; cf. *fig. 1*.
Considered individually, there is a multitude of *mixed* and *transitional forms* of a simple as well as of a complex nature. A typical intermediate form between denying and rejecting problems is, for example, suppressing them; between rejecting and exploiting problems – the mere pretence of solving problems. In practice, various elements of neglect and negative symptoms in the management of environmental protection more or less accompany the actual "positive" management of environmental protection.

III. Qualifying Criteria for Co-operative Management of Environmental Protection

The main qualifying criteria for co-operative management of environmental protection are shown in *fig. 2* – in relation to *fig. 1*. The characteristic features on the right of each figure show the *criteria* for qualified management of environmental protection.
An important prerequisite – not yet a criterion – of such management is to have some *spare leadership capacity* to deal with relevant questions. Many enterprises, particularly small and medium-sized ones, have serious problems in that respect. In connection with this, *unpaid work* is of – positive as well as negative – relevance to co-operatives.
The management of enterprises that are run in an ecologically responsible way, considers all relevant *factors, techniques, systems*, and *products* in relation to environmental protection. As companies providing →*goods* as well as services, their planning is waste oriented. The first criterion for research and development activities is their environmental compatibility. All *life phases of a product* are included in this,

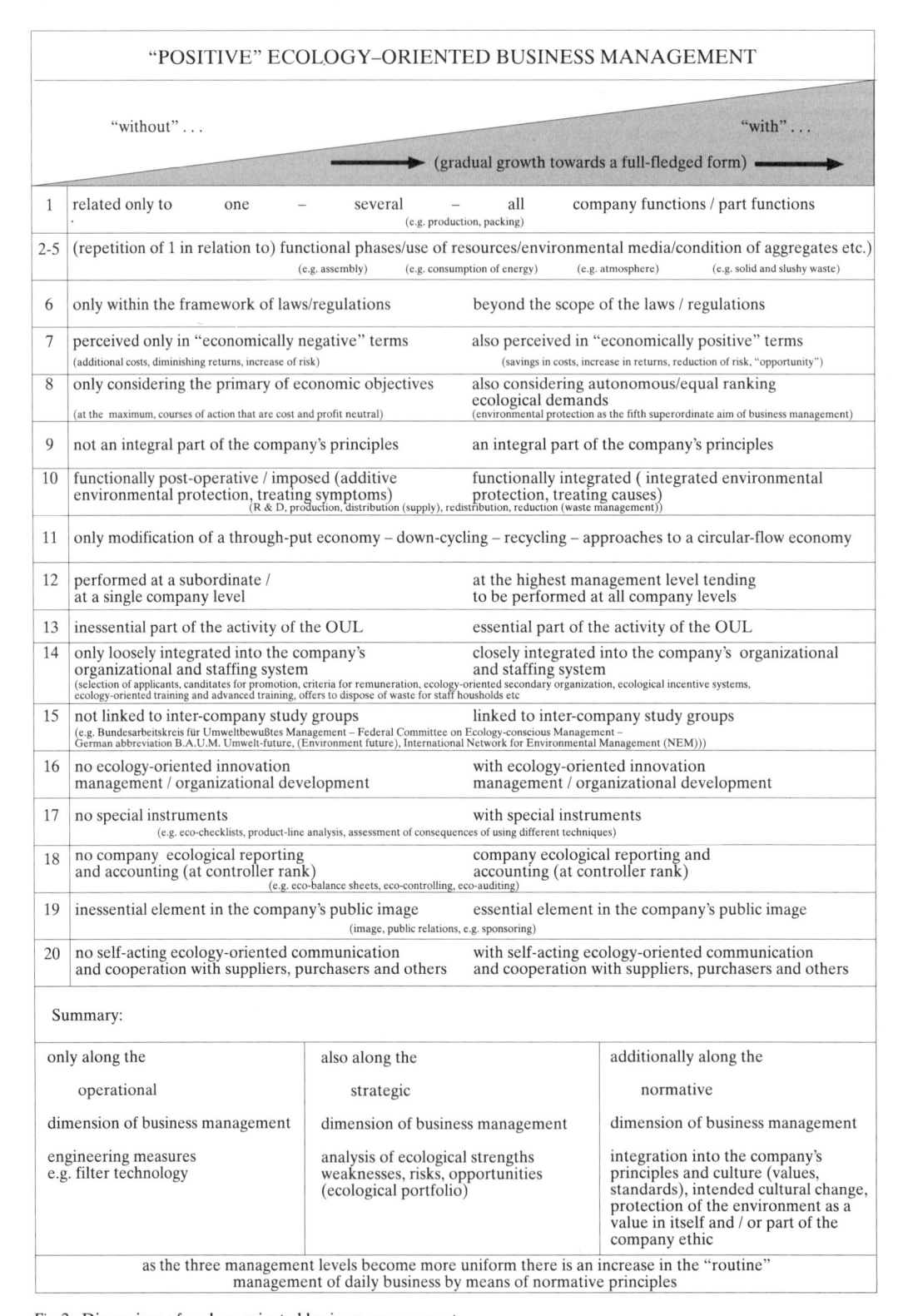

\multicolumn{3}{c}{"POSITIVE" ECOLOGY–ORIENTED BUSINESS MANAGEMENT}		
	"without" … (gradual growth towards a full-fledged form) "with" …	
1	related only to one – several – all company functions / part functions (e.g. production, packing)	
2-5	(repetition of 1 in relation to) functional phases/use of resources/environmental media/condition of aggregates etc.) (e.g. assembly) (e.g. consumption of energy) (e.g. atmosphere) (e.g. solid and slushy waste)	
6	only within the framework of laws/regulations	beyond the scope of the laws / regulations
7	perceived only in "economically negative" terms (additional costs, diminishing returns, increase of risk)	also perceived in "economically positive" terms (savings in costs, increase in returns, reduction of risk, "opportunity")
8	only considering the primary of economic objectives (at the maximum, courses of action that are cost and profit neutral)	also considering autonomous/equal ranking ecological demands (environmental protection as the fifth superordinate aim of business management)
9	not an integral part of the company's principles	an integral part of the company's principles
10	functionally post-operative / imposed (additive environmental protection, treating symptoms) (R & D, production, distribution (supply), redistribution, reduction (waste management))	functionally integrated (integrated environmental protection, treating causes)
11	only modification of a through-put economy – down-cycling – recycling – approaches to a circular-flow economy	
12	performed at a subordinate / at a single company level	at the highest management level tending to be performed at all company levels
13	inessential part of the activity of the OUL	essential part of the activity of the OUL
14	only loosely integrated into the company's organizational and staffing system (selection of applicants, canditates for promotion, criteria for remuneration, ecology-oriented secondary organization, ecological incentive systems, ecology-oriented training and advanced training, offers to dispose of waste for staff housholds etc	closely integrated into the company's organizational and staffing system
15	not linked to inter-company study groups (e.g. Bundesarbeitskreis für Umweltbewußtes Management – Federal Committee on Ecology-conscious Management – German abbreviation B.A.U.M. Umwelt-future, (Environment future), International Network for Environmental Management (NEM)))	linked to inter-company study groups
16	no ecology-oriented innovation management / organizational development	with ecology-oriented innovation management / organizational development
17	no special instruments (e.g. eco-checklists, product-line analysis, assessment of consequences of using different techniques)	with special instruments
18	no company ecological reporting and accounting (at controller rank) (e.g. eco-balance sheets, eco-controlling, eco-auditing)	company ecological reporting and accounting (at controller rank)
19	inessential element in the company's public image (image, public relations, e.g. sponsoring)	essential element in the company's public image
20	no self-acting ecology-oriented communication and cooperation with suppliers, purchasers and others	with self-acting ecology-oriented communication and cooperation with suppliers, purchasers and others

Summary:

only along the operational dimension of business management engineering measures e.g. filter technology	also along the strategic dimension of business management analysis of ecological strengths weaknesses, risks, opportunities (ecological portfolio)	additionally along the normative dimension of business management integration into the company's principles and culture (values, standards), intended cultural change, protection of the environment as a value in itself and / or part of the company ethic
\multicolumn{3}{c}{as the three management levels become more uniform there is an increase in the "routine" management of daily business by means of normative principles}		

Fig. 2: Dimensions of ecology-oriented business management.

down to the disposal of the products after they have been utilized by the ultimate consumer. This means that ecology-conscious enterprises are committed to the idea of *integrated environmental protection, recycling* and *circular-flow economies*. After attending to the problems of avoiding waste and internal waste-recycling, they seek inter-company recycling methods within *cooperation networks* that are as closely meshed as possible.

Ecologically-conscious enterprises attempt not just to observe environmental regulations, but to surpass them whenever possible. Stricter regulations for environmental protection generally find their approval – not least because of the advantage they have in competing with their less environmentally-conscious competitors. The management of enterprises that are run in an ecologically responsible way is open and trusting in its communication with state and society on questions of an *ecology-oriented framework of regulations for business management*. Ecology-oriented management particularly reflects the key problems of *"energy consumption"* and *"intensity of logistics"* in connection with persons and objects. In addition to using the interchange of matter and energy, they also include in their *environmental balance sheet* the space that their business activities require and the landscape that these exploit.

IV. Co-operative Affinities with Environmental Protection

a) Pollution of the natural environment through human business activity depends to no small extent on the size (→ *Operational Size*) of production plants and companies. Large companies not only go hand in hand with ecologically harmful major technologies (so-called "dinosaur technologies"), but also and particularly with business on a spatially large scale, indicating the large-scale, heavy use of transport. From an ecological point of view, these are obvious *"diseconomies of scale"*.

With the exception of self-sufficient co-operatives, generally speaking co-operatives function as *support enterprises* for their associated member economies. As they do this regularly for a large number of associates, they are therefore certainly in favour of an increase in business size (→ *Group, the Co-operative*). Nevertheless, this aspect remains in the background. The main effect is that co-operatives continually promote the relatively small (medium-sized) associated businesses, thus helping them to survive. In addition to that, most co-operatives themselves remain at medium-size level. In this, co-operatives are on the whole relatively close to those *small-scale decentralized solutions* required by all basic proposals for more ecology-oriented business management.

b) A particular facet of the *size problem* is the *cognitive and emotional distance* between the decision-makers and the arenas in which their activities are carried out. Surveys show that serious ecological damage resulting from business activities occur all the more frequently and are accepted more easily, in as much as the centres of decision-making lack spatial (also cultural, historical) proximity to those locations. This finding is, incidentally, *system-neutral*: decisions made by the planning centre in Moscow which affect Siberian landscapes can be used just as well as an example as the decisions made by large multinational companies and their effects on the Third World.

As a rule, people who make decisions for co-operatives are settled in the same natural and economic area where they have their historical, cultural and family roots (→ *Corporate Culture*). This is a substantially more positive basis for *commitment* and *concern*, for a form of sustained business management that prohibits rapid exploitation for its own sake.

c) The affinity of co-operative management with matters of environmental protection becomes especially apparent in the specifically co-operative institutions, namely the "principle of regionalism" and the → *"promotion mandate"*:

– The *principle of regionalism* (→ *Principles*) indicates a limited economic area, which at the same time always represents an immediately perceived, natural and cultural landscape. This stimulates particular interest in, and intimacy with, the region. Thus, the conservation of soil, water and landscape are matters of natural and direct concern.

– It is generally accepted that the proper promotion of causes always means *continuous promotion*. Thus, the *promotion mandate* is especially akin to the idea of *sustainable development*. Today's task of extending and developing this mandate quite naturally is to offer the associated enterprises material aid and services in ecologically-conscious ways and to support their attempts at introducing more environmental protection into their businesses or households. Here, credit co-operatives in particular are faced with the important new task of advising and assisting.

d) The *normative dimension* of co-operative management mentioned in the previous paragraph shows special potential affinities with environmental protection:

– The problem of environmental protection in all its facets – from its emergence to its possible solution – is quite generally *"communicated socially"*. All regulations for sustainable development have certain social implications.

– For this reason, a balance between economic and ecological aspects can – according to many observers – only be achieved by adhering to *economic ethics* – which at the same time means *social and ecological ethics*. In this case, ethics is defined as *communicative or dialogical ethics* (→ *Ethics*).

Co-operatives offer "social communication" with a positive orientation directed towards solving problems, as their very own *principle of organization*. Added to that, *co-operative solidarity* is genuinely akin to communicative ethics. On its own it does a substantial amount of preliminary work in that direction.

e) In general and in summary, it should be stated that environmental protection as a *global task* requires *world-wide human solidarity* in the sense of a global community exposed to hazards, learning processes, changes and self-limitation. Competition has to be partly replaced by direct *co-operation*, something which cannot be conveyed through competition (→ *Competition*). The great teacher and example here is nature: in nature, many non-competing co-operative systems (symbioses) are particularly stable.

These future-oriented, improved combinations of "competition and co-operation" (→ *Business Policies*) are nothing less than the "*essence of the idea of co-operatives*" (→ *History of Ideas*). The significance and scope of this idea in this context cannot be pointed out any better than in *Hardin's* study on "The Tragedy of the Commons" (1968).

In a pre-industrial scenario of archaic pastoral agriculture, *Hardin* – a contemporary of *Adam Smith* – portrays destruction of the environment as a consequence of the urge and need for growth of human business activities. If the land is collective property and the livestock private property, the realization of individual economic interests will lead to the ruin of the pasture.

All approaches towards bridging the gap between individual and global-economic rationality (the *rationality trap*) point to elements of co-operative organization in an institutional dimension.

f) A short remark on organization theory will supplement the points mentioned earlier:

When comparing "ecology" (as a "natural" economy) and "economy" (as an "artificial" ecology), there are, at the same time, fundamentally different, diametrically opposed *principles of organization*: "organic" versus "planned" organization, self-organization versus imposed organization, "evolution" versus "construction". Fitting *secondary*, human artifacts into the *primary*, natural scheme of creation requires improved *adaptation* of the respective principles of organization, which helps towards more unity and stability via a return to greater "self-similarity" of the biosphere (including human business). Not only the – relatively – ecologically sound beginnings of human economies and societies show obvious aspects of co-operative constitution (trustee family), but, as far as is known, this also applies to all later forms of business which were relatively well-fitted and adapted to their natural environment.

Of all forms of business organization so far developed, the co-operative one comes closest to the *patterns of biological organization* in the sense of *organizational bionics*. Without ever having been sufficient for the needs of nature and environmental protection, they nevertheless possess the strongest affinities to their requirements.

V. Conclusion and Prospects for the Future

The affinities pointed out are not so much *actual*, but rather *potential* ones. More disturbing than this fact is, however, that, in the course of their commercialization, co-operatives are tending to allow the basic conditions for these affinities to waste away. In this light, the topic is not only a challenge for co-operatives, but it also gives food for reflection on their own – often neglected – values.

Whether the co-operatives are able to meet the challenge and, if so, whether they will be able to pull through in the end, is – again in the sense of contingency – quite an open question. It is very probable that an unstoppable biospheric macroprocess is unrolling inexorably before our very eyes, which the co-operative principles of organization cannot halt either. Man as a species that has failed in an evolutionary-ecological way is devouring and destroying his biosphere, is in the course of it destroying many animal and plant life forms, and will finally destroy himself.

Although faced with an unpredictable future, one must not give up the struggle for improvement. As the arguments above show, for the cooperative idea and movement this does not mean that co-operatives in their present significance and fields of activity merely accept the challenge. Through the general ecological challenge directed at the economy as a whole, there is a chance for the co-operative movement to initiate a world-wide *breakthrough of its* → *principles*. An efficient environment-oriented economy, especially a waste-disposal and waste-management oriented economy which includes aspects of liability and insurance, could, in the medium term, be given a constitution with a strong co-operative colouring. The pressing problems of environmental protection would then prove to be an important impulse for promoting co-operative principles of organization.

Bibliography

Draheim, Georg: Zur Ökonomisierung der Genossenschaften. Gesammelte Beiträge zur Genossenschaftstheorie und Genossenschaftspolitik, Göttingen 1967.
Hardin, G.: The Tragedy of the Commons, in: Science, 162 (1968), pp. 1243–1248.
Jantsch, E.: Die Selbstorganisation des Universums. Vom Urknall zum menschlichen Geist, Munich et al. 1992.
Meffert, Heribert/Kirchgeorg, M.: Marktorientiertes Umweltmanagement. Grundlagen und Fallstudien, Stuttgart 1992.
Probst, G.J.B.: Selbstorganisation. Ordnungsprozesse in sozialen Systemen aus ganzheitlicher Sicht, Berlin 1987.

Seidel, Eberhard: "Ökologisierung" des Bankgeschäfts. In: BI Bank Information und Genossenschaftsforum, vol. 8, 1992, pp. 16–19.
Seidel, Eberhard/ Menn, H.: Ökologisch orientierte Betriebswirtschaft, Stuttgart et al. 1988.
Steger, U. (ed): Handbuch des Umweltmanagements. Anforderungs- und Leistungsprofile von Unternehmen und Gesellschaft, München 1992.
Ulrich, P.: Transformation der ökonomischen Vernunft. Fortschrittsperspektiven der modernen Industriegesellschaft, Bern et al. 1986.
Umweltbundesamt (German Federal Office of the Environment) (ed.): Umweltorientierte Unternehmensführung, Berlin 1992.
Winter, G.: Das umweltbewußte Unternehmen, 4th edition, München 1990.

Equity Capital, Co-operative

HORST SEUSTER [F]

(see also: *Financing*; *Financial Accounting Law*; *Nachschußpflicht*; *Law, National*; *Law, International*; *European Community*; *Co-operative Banks*; *Linking Banks*)

I. Concepts of Equity Capital; II. Categories of Equity Capital; III. Sources of Equity Capital; IV. The Economic Characteristics of Equity Capital; V. Special Characteristics of Co-operative Equity Capital.

I. Concepts of Equity Capital

1. The Economic Concept of Equity Capital

Equity capital consists of the financial resources brought into an enterprise which belong to the entrepreneur or entrepreneurs (→ *Financing*). Equity capital is thus that part, expressed in monetary terms, which the entrepreneurs or partners own in their enterprise.

Equity capital on the balance sheet is calculated as the difference between total assets and total liabilities (borrowed capital) (→ *Accounting*). In enterprises with the legal form of registered co-operative, joint stock company or limited liability company this equity capital is composed of the nominal capital, capital reserves, and the profits or losses carried forward (→ *Joint Stock Company*). In other legal forms of enterprises one arrives at the amount of equity capital on the balance sheet from the current state of the equity capital accounts.

The effective or actual equity capital includes the equity capital as shown in the balance sheet plus the part of equity capital existing in the form of hidden reserves.

2. Liability Capital

One of the essential functions of equity capital is liability for debts of the enterprise (for details see part IV). With respect to this function, however, there are further possibilities besides the items appearing on the balance sheet, so that equity capital and liability need not be identical. In this regard the hidden reserves come primarily into consideration.

Beyond these, there are financial resources which can, on the basis of legal recognition, have the guarantee function for liabilities even though *de jure* they represent borrowed capital (e.g. profit participation rights; cf. part V, 2). Especially in the case of co-operatives, one should also mention the additional amounts provided for liability sums ("Haftsummenzuschlag"), which do not appear directly on the balance sheet but are declared to have the liability-guaranteeing function (cf. part V, 1).

3. The Equity Capital Concept of Bank Supervision

A form of liability equity capital peculiar to banks (→ *Co-operative Banks*), i.e. equity capital recognized as such by banking supervisors, is of special importance particularly for co-operative banks, because in the banking business the liability function takes priority over all other functions (e.g. operational function) (cf. part IV).

The German Banking Law defines liability capital partly in relation to the legal forms of banks and partly independent of legal forms. For credit co-operatives the following categories are recognized as liability capital (§10, subec. 2, no.3):

- Shares, excluding the capital shares of members who are discontinuing their membership at the end of the year;
- Reserves, excluding the amounts on which members who are leaving can place claims according to §73, subsec. 3 of the German Co-operative Law;
- Additional amounts provided for liability sums;
- Net profit, if it has been credited to share capital or capital reserves;
- Deposits by silent partners, if these deposits meet the requirements laid down in the banking law. Leading scientific authorities on co-operative law have claimed, however, that co-operative law does not permit deposit into credit co-operatives by silent partners (cf. *Licht*, pp. 178–184). The Federal Banking Supervisory Office has also endorsed this opinion;
- Capital with profit participation rights, provided it does not exceed 25 percent of the aggregate of all other liability capital, excluding additional amounts of liability sums, and provided the form requirements laid down in the banking law are fulfilled.

In 1986 the Commission of the European Community presented a proposal for a directive on equity capital in credit institutions, in order to arrive at a uniformity on the concept of equity capital within the EC (→ *European Community*). At the same time the regulation calls for an increase of liability capital from the present rate of three to five percent to eight percent. This directive however differentiates among various categories of equity capital, i.e. nucleus capital on the one hand and augmenting elements of the other.

Nucleus capital includes paid-in share capital (in case of credit co-operations: special co-operative share) and open capital reserves. Augmenting components are revaluation reserves, hidden reserves specific for banks, and other capital items which could be used to cover any losses and are available at any time, e.g. profit participation rights. Augmenting components also include additonal amounts on liability sums in credit co-operatives and debts on which, in case of debtor bankruptcy, claims have a lower priority.

In German banking supervisory laws, the possible acceptance of revaluation reserves, silent reserves specific for banks, and debts with a lower claim priority as augmenting components of equity capital is something quite new. Beyond that, the directive accepts as equity capital components, without limitations, what it calls "means from the fund for general banking risks", without grouping them with either nuclear or augmenting elements. At present, however, the content of this part of the proposal is still rather indefinite. What could be put into this category might be general bad-debt provision as well as valuation adjustments resulting from depreciation privileges specific for banks.

II. Categories of Equity Capital

Equity capital thus consists of the financial resources brought into the enterprise which belong to the entrepreneur or entrepreneurs. In practice there are various opportunities and forms of entrepreneurial activities and thus likewise for financial participation; in addition, the ownership rights to the individual capital reserves differ from each other, a fact which in itself leads to certain differentiations. Irrespective of the legal form of an enterprise, one differentiates among three categories of equity capital, which demonstrate differences in the intensity of ties with the enterprise: a) liability capital; b) items which are similar to equity capital, and c) social capital.

Liability capital (cf. part I.2) is also called equity capital in the narrow sense. But various types of capital fall into this category, depending on the legal form.

Items similar to equity capital are also frequently called extended equity capital. This mainly includes funds from tax privileges and provisions for price increases, substitution requirements, export incentives, housing construction subsidies, and advance payments to compensate those who suffered losses in World War II ("Lastenausgleichsgesetz"). In some branches of industry, special depreciation allowances are also included.

The last category of equity capital, i.e. social capital, mainly includes pension, welfare, and relief funds of enterprises. Its classification as equity capital is, however, under debate, since there are usually legal claims on these funds from others, chiefly from employees. Still, the resources grouped together as social capital are very well in a position to influence for short periods of time the financial situation of an enterprise in a positive way, particularly the liquidity and the relation between equity and borrowed capital, that is, at least as long as the claims by third parties have not yet fallen due.

III. Sources of Equity Capital

From the viewpoint of the enterprise, the most important sources of equity capital can be initially grouped into external and internal sources:

- External sources of equity capital (outside financing)
  a) Paid-up shares;
  b) Financial participations.
- Internal sources of equity capital (internal financing)
  a) Depreciation;
  b) Reserves;
  c) Reserves for special purposes (provisions);
  d) Profits retained (self-financing).

Depending on the influence exerted by capitalowners on the management of the enterprise, the external sources of equity capital (outside financing) are subdivided into deposits and financial participation. From the view-point of the enterprise, however, these are both external resources which may come, for example, from private resources of the entrepreneur or entrepreneurs. In the case of owners who participate in the direction or management of the enterprise, one speaks of deposits, while in the case of owners who do not participate actively in the enterprise, one speaks of financial participation.

In the framework of internal financing, we do consider depreciations (which have been earned in the business) as a means of financing, but technically they do not alter the amount of equity capital of the enterprise (→ *Accounting*). Aside from exceptions, they usually have to be reinvested, to retain the original level of assets.

Reserves are likewise resources that come from the turnover process of the enterprise (self-financing). In the case of co-operatives they consist almost entirely of profits that are retained in contrast to capital allocations. One differentiates here among a) reserves required by law, b) voluntary or open reserves, and c) hidden reserves. When members discontinue their membership in the co-operative, they normally have no claim to any part of the legally required or voluntary reserves. But it is possible nowadays to apportion part of the reserves for members leaving, yet this is a possibility which is only rarely used.

Hidden reserves are formed by undervaluing parts of assets, disregarding increases in value, not activating parts of assets, and/or overvaluing obligations. They are permitted within certain limits as a potential for smoothing out fluctuations in returns. However, they do not appear on the balance sheet, so that outsiders, and this also applies to co-operative members, cannot recognize them and therefore cannot decide upon them. Indeed, hidden reserves are an instrument of the management of an enterprise (a co-operative).

Reserves for special purposes (provisions) are expenditures which have occurred in a previous period but have not yet led to payments. Neither has a fixed due date or amount been stipulated as yet, as a rule. Seen from a dynamic concept of the balance sheet, they serve to determine the success of an enterprise within definite periods, whereas from a static concept of the balance sheet they represent obligations of the enterprise at the date of the balance sheet. From the principle of imparity, there follows fundamentally a general obligation to accumulate reserves for special purposes.

In implementing the Fourth EC Directive, the legislator has prescribed the accumulation of reserves for special purposes for certain definite situations, with a differentiation to be made between reserves for definite expenditure and those for accommodation toward customers: a) uncertain obligations; b) threatening losses from pending business; c) maintenance and rubble clearance yet to be undertaken with impending deadlines; d) guarantees for past deliveries without legal obligation; e) maintenance work yet to be undertaken during the fourth to the twelfth month of the subsequent fiscal year (this category is at the discretion of the enterprise); f) further expenditure insofar as certain legal requirements have been fulfilled.

Compared with the past, the obligation to form reserves has been extended to new areas. In an extensive study of this problem about 30 different instances could be found for which credit co-operatives now form reserve for special purposes.

As far as the volume is concerned, the reserve allowances for pensions play the greatest role. These are formed by an enterprise for future pension payments to its employees. Meanwhile, however, they can very well have a function in financing the enterprise; banks are even permitted to lend out up to 60 percent of pension reserves. Since reserve allowances constitute expenditures for the year in which they are formed, they have the effect at least of shifting taxes due into other periods. One can also characterize them as a special kind of reserves, with the difference from ordinary reserves, however, that they must be used for specific purposes and have a short-term or at the most medium-term character, with the exception of pension reserves. No obligatory, specific manner of valuation for these reserves had been prescribed. The law simply counts on a reasonable valuation according to sound business principles, so the entrepreneur has some flexibility.

There is no doubt that profits are an important, perhaps even the most important source of the means of self-financing in an enterprise, thus of a co-operative, which source naturally depends upon the earning capability of an enterprise. If, however, profits are paid out in cash as capital dividends, as reimbursements or as cost refunds, etc., by a co-operative, then the profits leave the enterprise and are no longer available for self-financing (→ *Reimbursements*). Those parts of profits, however, which are credited to share capital or to legally required or voluntary reserves, will appear in the books of the co-operatives under these positions. This is usually the largest portion of profits from the preceding period. Only a much smaller portion appears as a surplus carried forward into the next period.

Precisely because there are so many possibilities to choose from, the distribution of profits is one of the most important problems in co-operative policy. Whereas the members normally desire a high rate of dividend on their shares, the management mostly prefers to plough surplus back into reserves, which have the advantage of not varying with membership fluctuation and not requiring a certain part of the surplus every time as members do. Thus, year in year out, a compromise has to be found with regard to surplus which is satisfactory to both sides in the co-operative, members as well as management.

In connection with surplus, another possible way of self-financing should be mentioned which has been neglected in most treatises on the subject, namely "temporarily accumulating self-financing" (*Lipfert*). Its origin lies in the fact that surpluses are successively obtained during an accounting period, that is to say, these funds accumulate during the whole of the period, but appear only at the end, on the date of the balance sheet, and are then paid out to the members or are retained by the co-operative for the next period as "self-financing consitutent on the balance sheet" (*Lipfert*). Between the time when the surpluses are made and the time when the enterprise decides how to utilize them, there is a longer or shorter time lag, depending on when in the period the surplus is obtained (cf. *Lipfert, Walther, Seuster/Gerhard*).

IV. The Economic Characteristics of Equity Capital

The economic characteristics of equity capital are in certain respects distinctly different from those of borrowed capital. In contrast to borrowed capital, equity capital 1. has the function of covering liability (securing credit), 2. carries risks, 3. is dependent upon the value of assets, 4. is dependent upon the results of business operations as far as interest in capital is concerned, 5. is usually on hand without time limitation, 6. has a direct influence (in the case of paid-in share capital) or indirect influence (in the case of only financial participation) upon the policies of the enterprise, and 7. the interests earned on it as part of profits are subject to tax on earnings (cf. e.g. *Seuster* 1981). Over and above the criteria mentioned thus far, in the case of bankruptcy equity capital has relevance in two further respects: in the case of inability to pay but at the same time not excessive indebtedness, equity capital guarantees repayment of borrowed capital through the fact that in the liquidation of the enterprise, the claims of the owners will be satisfied only after those of the creditors. In enterprises where the liability of owners is limited to the amount of equity capital, the complete loss of equity capital leads to bankruptcy, in order that with the remaining means the claims of creditors may be compensated. If the owners' liability goes beyond that, then additional liability amounts are also available for that purpose.

V. Special Characteristics of Co-operative Equity Capital

1. Equity Capital on the Balance Sheet and Liability Obligations of Members

Becoming a member of a co-operative means that the individual co-operator is obliged to participate financially in the co-operative. The upper limit for participation of a member is the member's share. This upper limit can be raised, however, by provision in the by-laws, whereby a member is permitted to sign up voluntarily for several shares or is required to take over more than one share, e.g. according to a graduated participation.

Payments by the members can correspond to the amounts of their share capital but are not required to do so. Payments are determined, aside from the members' readiness to pay, by the pay-in regulations of the by-laws. It is only in cases of fully paid-in share capital that share capital and the payments for share capital are the same. The Co-operative Law leaves the → *by-laws* a wide scope for determining the amount of a share of capital and the regulations on payment. The Law requires merely that the by-laws lay down the obligation to make minimum payments. Because of the fact that it is possible for members to withdraw part or all of their share capital, the share capital of a co-operative is at least partially beyond the control of management. It is therefore called the variable part of co-operative equity capital.

The other component of equity capital as it appears on the balance sheet, aside from share capital, is the reserves. Here again the Co-operative Law leaves a wide scope of freedom, as long as the by-laws contain regulations on forming legally required capital reserves. It must just be stipulated how much of the year's surplus is to be put into the legally required reserves, as well as the minimum amount to be paid in. It is up to the assembly of members or the representatives assembly to decide on what additional reserves should be accumulated and how they should be regulated in the by-laws. The Co-operative Law also permits forming additional reserves especially for providing members leaving the co-operative with a definite part of reserve capital, whereas the other reserves cannot be set aside for this purpose. So far, however, co-operatives have hardly made use of this opportunity. Since with the exception of this last instance, reserves are by and large removed from influence by the members, they can be called the fixed or constant part of co-operative equity capital.

Over and above the amount for liability represented by equity capital, it is possible for co-operatives to obligate their members to make further payments in the case of bankruptcy. The following forms of additional liability are possible: 1. unlimited obligation to make further contributions, 2. the limitation of the further contributions to a definite amount (the liability amount), and 3. exclusion of any obligation to make further contribution at all.

With most co-operatives, only limited → "*Nachschußpflicht*" is the actual practice, which can be explained by the only moderate willingness and necessity on the part of members to participate in assuming the burden of unlimited liability. The (additional) amount of liability does not appear on the balance sheet since it does not represent capital. But a statement is required on the total sum of additional liability amounts of all members, as well as on the changes caused by members' joining and members' leaving, in the form of an appendix as a third part of the annual report after the balance sheet and the profit and loss account. The additional liability obligations of the co-operative members over and above equity capital are thus not considered as equity capital or capital, since they do not represent a flow of resources into the enterprise except in the case of bankruptcy. They therefore do not fulfill an important function of equity capital, i.e. the operational function (for acquisition of assets).

Furthermore there are other elements of capital which possess some characteristics of equity capital as well as of borrowed capital. This applies especially to some elements which in their legal form represent capital from creditors (e.g. profit participation rights and obligations with a lower rank of priority in case of the borrower's bankruptcy). Depending upon the success of the enterprise, these can earn interest for the owners of the capital; but in case of financial failure of the enterprise, they take on the function of liability.

2. Profit Participation Rights

Profit participation rights represent property rights which place claims on an enterprise but are not tied to rights of decision-making and participation in decisions on the part of the owner. As there is no fixed legal definition of profit participation rights, there is room for great latitude in shaping these rights. The special relevance of these rights as an instrument of financing lies in the fact that they represent *de jure* borrowed capital but at the same time can fulfill the function of liability for the enterprise, i.e. the co-operative, which issues them. Usually there is a lower rank or priority attached to them in case of bankruptcy, but on the whole they increase the liability volume of the enterprise, i.e. the co-operative.

For example, in the case of credit institutions, and therefore of co-operative banks likewise, since 1984 profit participation rights have been recognized as equity capital with liability. In the regulations to be set up within the EC for co-ordinating the legal supervision of banks, one can also expect that profit participation rights will continue to be recognized as liability capital (cf. *Seuster/Gerhard*).

Seen under taxation auspices, it is relevant that interest distributions on profit participation rights, in contrast to other dividends on share capital or additions to reserves, are recognized as operating expenditure and are therefore deductible from taxable income, so that they lower the amount which is subject to taxation.

Aside from financing by profit participation rights through not paying out dividends on these rights, but by ploughing the dividends back into the enterprise, one also has to examine to what extent profit participation capital can be raised by other means from members, in a form of outside financing. Here there may be even greater possibilities, as far as volume of capital is concerned.

In connection with the question of liability and financing discussed here, profit participation rights with the following features are of interest: 1. title to a share of profits, for which details such as proportion of profits, priority in case of financial failure, fixed minimum share of profit, linking up with the level of share capital dividends, etc., are to be clarified; and 2. title to redemption of the nominal amount after a limited time to maturity.

All in all, financing by way of profit participation rights is a relatively new instrument of business finance, although this possibility has been discussed for quite some time. The point here is not, however, to favour profit participation rights over all other ways of financing, but only to induce the management of every single co-operative to consider seriously this source of financing for its particular case (for details cf. *Schudt, Berge, Seuster/Gerhard*).

Bibliography

Armin, Bernd von: Eigenkapital, Handwörterbuch der Finanzwirtschaft, Stuttgart 1976, cols. 284–289.

Berge, Helmut: Zinsrückvergütungen bei Kreditgenossenschaften als Instrument der Mitgliederförderung und Eigenkapitalbildung, o.O., o.J.

Boos, Karl-Heinz/Mentrup, Horst: EG-Bankrechtsharmonisierung- mögliche Folgen für die Bankenstruktur in der Bundesrepublik, Band I, Vol. 1 (1989), pp. 15–18.

Büschgen, Hans (ed.): Handwörterbuch der Finanzwirtschaft, Stuttgart 1958.

Engels, Wolfram: Eigenkapital, Begriff und Funktion des, Handwörterbuch des Rechnungswesens, 2nd edition, Stuttgart 1981, cols. 419–427.

Fettel, Johannes: Kapital, Handwörterbuch der Betriebswirtschaft, Band 2, Stuttgart 1958, cols. 2959–2963.

Gutenberg, Erich: Grundlagen der Betriebswirtschaftslehre, Band 2, Die Finanzen, Berlin-Heidelberg-New York 1970.

Hahn, Oswald (ed.): Handbuch der Unternehmensfinanzierung, München 1971.

Janberg, Hans (ed.): Finanzierungshandbuch, 2nd ed., Wiesbaden 1970.

Koschka, Helmut: Finanzierung der Genossenschaft, Handwörterbuch des Genossenschaftswesens, Wiesbaden 1980, cols. 459–482.

Kosiol, Erich (ed.): Handwörterbuch des Rechnungswesens, 2nd ed., Stuttgart 1970, 1981.

Lehnhoff, Jochen: Bankeigenkapital für Europa definiert, Band I, vol. 2 (1989), pp. 28–32.

Licht, Wolfgang: Die Beteiligungsfinanzierung der Kreditgenossenschaften, Nürnberg 1980.

Lipfert, Helmut: Optimale Unternehmensfinanzierung, Frankfurt 1969.

Lührig, Klaus: Internationale Eigenmittelnormen für Kreditinstitute – Das COOKE-Konsultationspapier, WPg, 41 (1988), pp. 465–470.

Mändle, Eduard/Winter, Hans-Werner (eds.): Handwörterbuch des Genossenschaftswesens, Wiesbaden 1980.

Rudolph, Bernd: Eigenkapitalanforderungen an die Kreditinstitute im Rahmen der internationalen Bankrechtsharmonisierung, DBW, 49 (1989), pp. 483–496.

Schneider, Dieter: Investition und Finanzierung, 2nd edition, Opladen 1971.

Schudt, Helmut: Der Genußschein als genossenschaftliches Finanzierungsinstrument, Marburger Schriften zum Genossenschaftswesen, Reihe A, Band 43, Göttingen 1974.

Seuster, Horst/Gerhard, Stephan: Verbesserung der Eigenkapitalausstattung bei Kreditgenossenschaften, Manuskript, Gießen 1989.

Streim, Hannes: Eigenkapital, Lexikon des Rechnungswesens, München 1990, pp. 134–136.

Vormbaum, Herbert: Finanzierung der Betriebe, 2nd ed., Wiesbaden 1971.

Walther, Uwe: Finanzierung und Wachstum von Genossenschaftsbetrieben, Schriften zur Kooperationsforschung, C. Bericht, Band 4, Tübingen 1972.

Wittmann, Waldemar: Kapital, betriebswirtschaftliche Betrachtungsweise, Handwörterbuch der Finanzwirtschaft, Stuttgart 1958, cols. 946–951.

KWG: Gesetz über das Kreditwesen vom 10. Juli 1961 (BGBl- I, p. 881).

Ethics and Co-operatives

JUHANI LAURINKARI, VESA LAAKKONEN

(see also: *History of Ideas; Principles; Classic/Neoclassic Contributions; Corporate Culture; Solidarity*)

I. Ethics and Economic Activity; II. Corporate Ethics; III. Ethics in the Historical Development of the Co-operative System; IV. Solidarity as an Ethical Basis for Cooperation; V. Renaissance of Ethics in the Co-operative System.

I. Ethics and Economic Activity

As an expression of decision-making behavior of both economic subjects and the state in the scope of the latter's economic policy, economic activity and ethics are closely entertwined with one another. On the one hand, a precondition for individual behavior is self-responsibility and thus moral justification; on the other hand, the state makes fundamental decisions when determining its economic-political goals and their prioritization – decisions which are of fundamental importance for further societal development. The respective dominant moral conceptions of a society are reflected in the quantity and quality of its economic activities, or in other words, an economy's institutional structure is the result of its dominant conceptions of ethics and morals.

A basic precondition for free moral action is a liberal societal structure which guarantees the individual freedom of decision, that is the choice between given alternatives without any type of restriction (→ *Economic Order*). A structure of this nature can be found extensively in democratic and market economy systems (→ *State and Co-operatives, Market Economy*) but not in totalitarian systems in which only one prescribed behavioral method is allowed (→ *State and Co-operatives, Socialism*); the question of what is moral and what is immoral is never raised in such a system.

II. Corporate Ethics

"Corporate ethics encompasses all justified and/or justifiable material and procedural norms that are put into force in a binding manner by a company attempting to define itself and determine its actions in order to limit the conflict-relevant consequences arising from the principle of profit maximization; this occurs through dialogue with those affected within the scope of concrete corporate activities" (*Steinmann/Löhr*, p. 10). Companies' primary objective is to satisfy the needs of consumers in the best possible and efficient manner; they are there for people and not the other way around. Corporate entities accordingly do not pursue any ends for themselves, and one cannot speak of any type of autonomous corporate ethics in society. Corporate ethics are always a result of economic ethics, which themselves are a result of societal ethics; in other words, the framework for corporate ethics is outlined in a given societal and economic structure, and thus also in economic ethics (cf. *Molitor*).

Corporate ethics thus are only as good or bad as the existing societal and economic ethics. It is therefore futile to discuss corporate ethics in a market economy without also discussing performance components or profit aspirations. One can, however, very well question whether the profit a market economy company attains should merely be the difference between revenue and costs, or for that matter, how costs themselves should even be defined. Must not the costs of environmental destruction also be taken into consideration in accounting practices? Can a company's profit in actuality only be measured as the difference between turnover and expenses, or must one not also include the external effects of individual decision-making behavior in commercial accounting procedures?

III. Ethics in the Historical Development of the Co-operative System

→ *Principles* and ethical questions were of considerable importance in the co-operative system as a social movement whose spiritual roots emerged out of the upheaval of traditional values in the scope of the French Revolution.

The modern co-operative system which developed from this evolved through a process of trial and error with respect to existing, traditional forms of cooperation. The system was a phenomenon which continually knew to adapt itself to the given values and goals of its respective environment in various eras and countries. Its general ethical foundation is anchored in the principles of the co-operative system, which themselves can be traced back to the → *Rochdale pioneers*. The primary objective of the Rochdale Society, aside from achieving numerous improvements of the living situation of the working population of the time, was to create a new society which, from an ethical point of view, should be better than the existing one. In such a society, injustice, disputes and fraud should no longer exist. Economic activity should be undertaken in a fully responsible manner, that is correct measures and weights should be used in a exemplary manner in the sale of goods. No adulterated products should come to the market and correct wages should be paid. The poor, sick and helpless should be aided. The co-operative was conceived of as an institution in which the individual should have the opportunity to expand his knowledge, heighten his abilities and develop his personality to its utmost; it thus was conceived of as the primary basis or germinal seed of a new society.

IV. Solidarity as an Ethical Basis for Cooperation

Draheim characterized the particular corporate form "co-operative" through its two-sided nature as a company and as a mutual community (→ *Dual Nature*). He found the ethical basis for this mutual community to be rooted in the principle of solidarity and attempted to describe co-operative activity as being predominantly collective rather than individual in nature by using this principle. *Raiffeisen* quite appropriately portrayed such activity in the catch phrase "One for all, and all for one".

The solidarity principle emanates from the ideal typified form of "homo cooperativus", or in other words, a "person acting in a collective manner" set in opposition to the ideal typified form of "homo economicus" (cf. *Weuster*, pp. 491–512). This pair of antitheses served as the point of departure for the well-known "controversy between conflict and harmony theory" in co-operative sciences during the 1970s.

According to the harmony hypothesis, all members of a co-operative organization constantly act for the good of each other (cf. *Eschenburg*, p. 52); a harmony of interests is presupposed between the co-operative members and its administration (cf. *Brazda*, p. 31). According to conflict theory (also known as the theory of offsetting interests) (→ *Theory of co-operative Cooperation*), economic subjects act in their own interest in a co-operative; acts of exchange between exchange partners only evolve when each party can achieve an advantage or benefit for his own through the particular action (cf. *Brazda*, p.35). Individual utility in this case is the instigator of co-operative behavior rather than ethical reasons or principles. Vertical and horizontal conflicts or opposing interests exist between the various groups in a co-operative which must be settled and/or compensated (cf. *Eschenburg*, p. 63).

According to *Weuster*, the concept of the ideal typified form "homo cooperativus" is not comprehensive enough to provide a sufficient explanation of behavior in co-operatives (*Weuster*, p. 510). He does, however, state that "homo cooperativus" can be used as an additional criterion to characterize co-operative endeavors as collective rather than individual in nature with regard to the economic behavior of the typified form "homo economicus" (→ *Conceptions, Cooperative*). Economic subjects join together in a co-operative in order to attain benefits out of collective endeavors. Collective activity can therefore be construed as a form of economic activity and must not be elevated to a principle of its own.

It has been undertaken to drive the position that co-operatives – in the past always representing that form of cooperation for the middle class and underprivileged populational groups – therefore are "social enterprises". The principle of open membership among co-operatives is furthermore used to indicate their social character (membership is voluntary and can be discontinued at any time). This principle, however, solidifies the conception of the co-operative as a mass organization which comes into being because of economic or political reasons, but not out of ethical consideration. Co-operatives accordingly are merely instruments through which certain economic or ideological goals can potentially be attained.

A principle of necessity is tied to the social character of co-operatives: Co-operatives stand out in that they are founded by individuals in order to satisfy their most elementary needs (*Laurinkari*). Whereas traditional company forms primarily strive to maximize profits, co-operative tasks are derived from the genuine needs of individuals and their livelihood. Economic behavior in co-operatives is legitimized by only those truly essential needs of their members.

Currently, however, the business or company aspects of the co-operative are continually gaining importance. This development can be accounted for by the intensification of market competitive pressure. Co-operatives find themselves "forced" to adapt their modes of operation to those of stock corporations; consequently, there is no longer any latitude for ethical goals in everyday activity (→ *Structural Types*). Co-operatives – above all large-scale co-operatives backed by considerable amounts of capital – must confront the identical demands that traditional business enterprises do in everyday business practise. This mounting pressure to adapt and adjust, together with the corresponding heightened demands on management, influences and alters the ethical goals which are strived for in the competitive economy.

Current co-operative practices, therefore, often have very little in common with their original intentions. Many of their present goals are no longer in accord with their intrinsic values which they have had to adjust and/or supplant as a result of outside pressure.

V. Renaissance of Ethics in the Co-operative System

The discussion concerning the necessity of corporate ethics in today's day and age has increased in its intensity in the past years and has gained importance in the scope of university curricula for business administration. The discussion presently concentrates on the question of whether corporate managment requires moral principle sat all for its action alongside its goal of profit maximization. Certain academics, such as *Friedman*, reject the idea of companies assuming any type of societal responsibility and espouse the amorality of economic activity.

Seen historically, however, the utilitarians previously argued that the goal of an economy should be the attainment of the greatest level of prosperity for the largest possible number of people, regardless of individual decision-making behavior. This utilitarian principle has once again stepped into the foreground; in the meantime, its norms, based on religious values, no longer found any reception and its legal standards had lost importance on account of their complexity and abstruseness (cf. *Parvinen*).

When formulating a program to determine up-to-date ethical co-operative business principles, the following considerations must without fail be taken into account (*Parvinen*):

- The co-operative management must always be involved in the discussion about moral action. Such views as 'business activities and moral conceptions have nothing in common' or 'morals are not of interest for the daily business of the co-operative' must be revoked.
- Questions concerning corporate ethics must become a set component of co-operative research.
- Ethical values must also be imparted in the co-operative vocational training system alongside economic and technical curricula.
- The co-operative management in large-scale co-operatives must refer to corporate principles based on consensus formation when selecting its objectives.
- In small-scale co-operatives it is sufficient when management bases its actions on the co-operative principles.
- The directives for business activity and fundamental values for co-operatives should be put to paper.

Although ethical action can be coupled with the cession of commercial success, in the long term it is more advantageous for a company to act in a responsible manner rather than only pursue short-term results. Guiding principles of this nature can be found in the corporate principles of *McDonald Douglas*. Moral action is characterized here in four traits:
Guiding moral principles

- are universal, as each individual is subject to the identical regulations in similar situations.
- are prescriptive; they do not describe how things are but rather how things should be, thus presupposing previously determined principles (cf. discussion about basic values in the co-operative system).
- have priority over all other value conceptions and are generally applicable in character.
- are autonomous in that they require no further justification.

Bibliography

Brazda, J.: Genossenschaftswissenschaft als Gestaltungsaufgabe, Vienna 1988.
Draheim, G.: Die Genossenschaft als Unternehmungstyp, 2nd edition, Göttingen 1955.
Eschenburg, R.: Genossenschaftstheorie als Konflikttheorie, in: Boettcher, E., (ed.): Theorie und Praxis der Kooperation, Tübingen 1972.
Laurinkari, J.: Die genossenschaftlichen Grundwerte, in Laurinkari, J., (ed.): Die Prinzipien des Genossenschaftswesens in der Gegenwart. Festschrift für Prof. Dr. Vesa Laakkonen. Publication #24 of the Research Institute for Co-operative Studies at the University of Erlangen-Nürnberg, Nürnberg 1986.
Molitor, B.: Wirtschaftsethik, München 1989.
Parvinen, J.: Suomen hyvinvointi tasapainossa 1995–2000.
Sosiaali- ja terveysiministeriön julkaisuja 1992: 1, Helsinki. (Finnish Prosperity in Equalibrium 1995–2000. Publication of the Finnish Social and Health Ministry 1992:1).
Steinmann, H. & Löhr, A.: Grundfragen und Problemstände einer Unternehmensethik, in: Steinmann & Löhr, (eds.): Unternehmensethik, Stuttgart 1989.
Weuster, A.: Homo economicus und Homo cooperativus in der Genossenschaftsforschung, in: Laurinkari, J., (ed.): Die Prinzipien des Genossenschaftswesens in der Gegenwart. Festschrift für Prof. Dr. Vesa Laakkonen. Publication #24 of the Research Insitute for Co-operative Studies at the University of Erlangen-Nürnberg, Nürnberg 1986.

European Community (Union) and Co-operatives

ANDRÉ VAN HULLE

(see also: *Conceptions, Co-operative*; *Law, International*; *Legal Form, Co-operative*; *Internationalization*)

I. Introduction; II. Representativity and Representation of Co-operative Organizations in the European Community (Part I); III. Legal Statute of a Co-operative Society in the EEC (Part II).

I. Introduction

The European Community (EC) (since 1st Nov. 1993: European Union) is essentially an economic Community. Article 2 of the Treaty of Rome of 25 March, 1957 indeed says that: "The Community shall have as its task, by establishing a common market and progressively approximating the economic policies of member states, to promote throughout the Community a harmonious development of ecomomic activities, ...". The Treaty does not even mention co-operatives as a sector of the economy (→ *Economie Sociale*) neither under the "Policy of the Community" (Part three) nor under the "Economic Policy" (Title II) nor under the "Social Policy" (→ *Social Policy*) (Title III). Under the "Right of establishment" (Title III, chapter 2) co-operatives are mentioned under Article 58, which specifies that "companies or firms" means companies or firms constituted under civil or commercial law, *including co-operative societies ...*".
In the long starting period the European Commission (EC) paid very little attention to the co-operative sector as part of the national economies although this sector represents an important part of the economic life. When in 1962 agricultural co-operatives (→ *Rural Co-operatives*) asked for an exception to the rules on competition under Article 85 of the Treaty, it was conceded under very strong political pressure (Regulation CEE nr 26/62). In the text, however, the

term "co-operative" was expressed by "associations of agricultural producers" and "associations of such associations", under the pretext that the legal notion "co-operative societies" did not have the same meaning in the six Member States (→ *Law, International*). Co-operatives in their capacity of non-governmental bodies are or take no *structural* part in the European Communities. In Part Five of the Treaty the Economic and Social Committee (ESC) is mentioned in chapter 3, Article 193 as a body with advisory status. "The Committee shall consist of representatives of the various categories of *economic and social* activity, in particular, representatives of producers, farmers, carriers, workers, dealers, craftsmen, professional occupations and representatives of the general public". And Article 195 adds to this: "The composition of the Committee shall take account of the need to ensure adequate representation of various categories of *economic and social* activity".

In fact, co-operatives take only part in the various economical sectors where they belong to, as we will indicate further. On the other hand, co-operatives take part in the Advisory Committees, which are set up as advisory bodies by internal decision of the European Commission, whether they are recognized as co-operatives (i.e. agriculture) or participate in recognized organisations in the various economic sectors.

The relationship – representativity and representation – between the EEC and co-operatives should therefore be considered under two main aspects. 1. The gradual upgrading of the representation of co-operatives in the various economic sectors so as to enable them to speak freely and with a certain unity of expression and representation on behalf of the whole of the co-operative movement (Part I). 2. The recognition or admission by the EEC of the legal form of a co-operative society going from efforts to define the legal form of co-operatives in the various Member States to the study of a European statute of a co-operative society (Part II).

II. Representativity and Representation of Co-operative Organizations in the European Community (Part I)

In the most important economic sectors co-operatives have joined forces at European level in interest groups or pressure groups in order to be recognised by the EEC either as direct spokesmen or consultative bodies or as members of a broader representative body of the overall economic sector where they belong to. These interest groups in the broadest sense have been created step by step in the course of time. Up to 1990, the following nine co-operative groups had given notice of their intention to the European Commission and have already joined in a new overall co-ordinating body.

1. European Community of Consumer Co-operatives (EURO-COOP)

(Communauté Européene des coopératives de consommateurs), founded in 1957. Euro Coop's purpose is to represent → *consumer co-operative* organisations and defend consumer interests vis-à-vis the Community institutions, particularly the Commission. It is represented in numerous Advisory Committees in the Commission, in particular the Consumers' Consultation Committee. It groups 16,000 shops and 14 million members.

2. General Committee of Agricultural Cooperation in the EEC (COGECA)

(Comité Général de la Cooperation Agricole de la CEE), founded in 1959. COGECA aims at representing the general and specific interests of agricultural co-operatives (→ *Rural Co-operatives*) in dealing with the EEC authorities and other organizations and bodies. COGECA is represented as such in nearly all Advisory Committees set up in the framework of the Common Agricultural Policy. It groups 48,000 agricultural and fishing co-operatives and 12 million members.

3. European Union of the Social Mutual and Co-operative Pharmacies (UEPSMC)

(Union Européene des Pharmacies Sociales, Mutualistes et Cooperatives), founded in 1961. It groups various national organizations which are involved in distributing and dispensing medicines and represents almost 2,400 pharmacies which serve about 27 million people belonging to its affiliated organisations.

4. Association of Retailer-Owned Wholesalers of Europe (UGAL)

(Union des Groupements d'Achat Coopératifs de Détaillants d'Europe), founded in 1963. UGAL is the European umbrella association for wholesale co-operative buying and service groups set up by independent retailers, primarily in the food sector (→ *Commercial Co-operatives*). It groups 220,000 outlets and about 200,000 members.

5. Association of Co-operative Banks of the EC (CO-OPERATIVE BANKS)

(Groupement des Banques Coopératives de la CEE), founded in 1970. The group's purpose is to further and represent the common interests of its members and their affiliated institution (→ *Co-operative Banks*). Its action is for the most part in the field of harmonization of banking legislation and finance for agriculture and small and medium sized undertakings. It groups 57,000 banking points and about 31 million members.

6. Association of Co-operative Insurers (AACE)

(Association des Assureurs Coopératifs Européens), founded in 1978 (→ *Insurance, Germany*). The Association is a regional section of the International Co-operative Insurance Federation (ICIF) of which it groups the European members. It groups 25 million insured households with 65 million policies, the group employs 140,000 people.

7. European Committee of Workers' Co-operatives (CECOP)

(Comité Européen des Coopératives de Production), founded in 1979. Its goal is first to represent its members (→ *Joint-production Co-operatives*), provide permanent liaison between them and co-ordinate and support their projects. It groups 40,000 co-operative societies with about 900,000 members.

8. European Co-ordinating Committee for Social Tourism (CECOTOS)

(Comité Européen de Coordination du Tourisme Social), founded in 1984. CECOTOS is a European association set up at the instigation of the International Union of Co-operative and Associative Tourism (a member of ICA) and of the International Office for Social Tourism. It groups co-operatives, associations and mutual aid societies of the EEC Member States, which work in the tourism sector, especially in the area of social tourism. Statistics are not yet available.

9. European Committee of Housing Co-operatives (CECODHA)

(Comité Européen des Coopératives d'Habitation), founded in 1986. CECODHA is open to national organizations of housing co-operatives (→ *Housing Societies*) from the EC countries and to those which proceed with the very same objects. Statistics are not available.

Yet, however, the co-operative movements, organized in the European organizations mentioned before, wanted to go further than only to represent the economic interests for which they were founded. They wanted to point out that co-operatives are a particular sort of enterprises of a social-economic nature (→ *Promotion Mandate*) and that they, as a whole, represent an important part of the economy. Therefore, they claimed specific recognition by the EEC. In the eighties, the whole process accelerated.

In the course of 1980, proposals were put forward in the European Parliament to evaluate the role of co-operatives as a particular part of the economy: motions for resolutions were tabled by *Bonaccini* and others (E.P. doc. 1 – 327/80) and by *Filippi* and others (E.P. doc. 1 – 669/80). Both motions were referred by the European Parliament (session of 15 September 1980) to the Committee on Economic and Monetary Affairs (CEMA). From this came out the well known *K.H. Mihr* report (E.P. 74,500 final 1982). This report intended to prove that cooperation in the Community is an economic and social power. European co-operative organizations were strongly recommended to co-ordinate their actions and to create a common platform in their relations with the institutions of the EEC.

On 13 April, 1983 the European Parliament, by a large majority, adopted a resolution which may be considered a milestone in the history of relations between the Community institutions and the co-operative movement (OJC 128/52 of 16 May 1983). The resolution was accompanied by an extensive report by the CEMA on the main issues of the co-operative organization.

Attached to this Report was a list of European co-operative organizations and the texts of the resolutions of the Legal Affairs Committee and the Committees on Social Affairs and Employment and on Agriculture. When preparing its report, the CEMA held a hearing on 26/27 January 1982 with the participation of representatives from the main European co-operative organizations. In the parliamentary debate itself, it became apparent that there was a broad consent among the various political groupings on the general content of the report and on the important role for co-operatives as small and medium-sized undertakings in the European economy (E.P. 1983–84 Session Report of Proceedings, Strassbourg, Wednesday, 13 April, 1983. Supplement to OJ, pp. 112–125). In 1987, another report was made on behalf of the Committee on Regional Policy about the contribution of co-operatives to regional development (Rapporteur Paraskevas Avgerinos – E.P. 101.844 Doc. A2 – 12/87). A third report dates from 1988 on behalf of the Committee on Development and Co-operation (Rapporteur Renzo Trivelli – E.P. 121.497 final Doc. A2 – 0205/88).

As a result of all these issues in 1982 and especially the *Mihr* Report, European co-operative organizations created on 5 November, 1982 in Brussels a co-ordinating body under the name *of Co-ordinating Committee of EEC Co-operative Associations* (CCACC). In doing this, EEC co-operative associations represented in the Co-ordinating Committee wished to foster European collaboration between all co-operative organizations and, going, beyond their interests in specific sectors, together forcefully and unequivocally to defend the theory and practice of co-operative business in their relations with the general public and the authorities. CCACC is not a registered body with statutory structure but is based on a general agreement with ad hoc rules and regulations. It acts on an ad hoc basis to foster exchange of information between member associations; to hold ad hoc working meetings, to draw up joint position papers and to make preparations for concrete action of common interest. This representative body, however, is not substituting the representative function for the individual co-operative groups nor their specific objectives and tasks vis-à-vis the Community institutions.

The European Parliament, the EC Commission and the ESC have given official recognition to this initiative. The *EC Commission* through its speakers in Parliament promised "to look in which the Community Institutions and resources can best be made available to co-operatives". It indicated the importance of the co-operative model for certain Community policies in matters as employment, regional development and development aid. The *Council of Ministers* in its resolution of 7 June, 1984 (OJC 161 of 21 June, 1984) requested the Commission to complete its action by specific studies on subjects such as "legal and fiscal incentives for setting up and developing enterprises including co-operatives and other forms of collective enterprise". The *European Council* in its sessions in 1986 in La Haye and London, requested the Commission to pay attention on further development of co-operatives. In 1986, a new turning point came about in the relations between the EEC and the co-operatives.

In November 1986, the ESC together with CCACC organized a large and well prepared conference under the heading *"The co-operative, mutual and non-profit sector contributions to the building of Europe"*. Three questions were put forward "What contribution can co-operatives, mutual-benefit societies and non-profit bodies make to European integration? What responses can such business organizations offer to the challenges facing the European Community? What do they expect from the various Community policies? (Document, catalogue number ESC 87–003–EN). In preparation of this congress the ESC published (afterwards) an extensive and very detailed handbook (900p.) under the heading "the co-operative, mutual and non-profit sector and its organizations in the European Community".

The conclusions of the ESC conference had important consequences for the disposition and attitude of the Community towards co-operatives. The proposals, however, added another and new dimension to the traditional co-operative sector namely the mutual and non-profit sectors. It was so to say giving birth to a new "deal" that is defined by the French term of → *"Economie Sociale"*, a vague and not always clear outlined or well defined concept. The idea is not accepted with undivided consent. In 1989, further proceedings and negotiations led to some measures taken by the EC Commission. The first and very important one was the setting up of a new service in Directorate General XXIII that has to co-ordinate proposals and studies on the co-operative, mutual and non-profit sector. Second was a communication from the Commisssion to the Council (SEC 89–2187 final) on the "Economie Sociale" sector. This communication proves to be a very important document: – it defines and describes the "Economie Sociale" sector by giving a brief overview of the branches in which its enterprises are active in all Member States; – it identifies the prospects opening up for enterprises in this sector in Europe in 1992, and shows to what extent they are taken into account in Community policies; – it adumbrates the framework for Community action to ensure that enterprises in this sector enjoy access to the frontier-free market on the same footing as other enterprises.

This communication has in Annex a working paper on the subject of business in the Economie Sociale-sector and the frontier-free market. It is a valuable effort to make some notions clear. Co-operative organizations are not happy about putting the three sectors – co-operative, mutual and non-profit – on the same line in an overall concept. Although there is a keen sense of solidarity and they share a number of common features, co-operatives fear that, by lack of a clear differentiation of identity, they will lose their specific principles and character and even the concept of co-operation could be diluted.

We may conclude on representativity and representation of the different co-operative sectors in the EEC that the main and most representative European co-operative organizations have found a platform for mutual information in the CCACC where they can draw up joint positions and take joint actions. One of the most important achievements has been to obtain access to the European Commission through a service especially created for them.

III. Legal Statute of a Co-operative Society in the EEC (Part II)

One of the most fundamental rights assigned to the citizens of the Community is the abolition of internal frontiers, not only for the free movement of goods, services and capital but also free movement of persons. In Article 58 of the Treaty, the right of establishment is granted to companies which have economic aims, co-operatives are mentioned in that article. To safeguard the interests of all those concerned in the various Member States, a whole programme has been set up to harmonize and even coordinate company laws. Co-operative societies cannot escape this development or duck out of its implementation. The successive steps in the way to approachement and eventually unification are the following:

1. *Harmonisation of company law* which sooner or later, in whole or in part, will be enforced in the national legislation (→ *Law, International*). Important parts of company law have already been harmonized by means of Directives. Some national legislations apply them also to co-operative societies.

2. *Co-ordination of company law* is in process of formation.
3. A lot of *preliminary studies on comparative law* has been carried out in connection with agricultural co-operatives. These studies must not be considered as only historical and therefore outdated.
4. *Preliminary drafts of a European statute* of a co-operative society have been prepared and are under discussion (→ *By-laws*).

A more detailed survey of these successive steps:

1. *Harmonisation of company law.* An impressive series of Directives has been adopted until now (1 May, 1990). a) The First Directive of 9 March, 1968 (68/155/EEC) defines a sytem of public disclosure applicable to all companies, the identity of those empowered to represent it, procedures for the winding-up of the company etc. b) Second Directive of 13 December, 1976 (77/91/EEC) deals with the raising, maintenance and alteration of the capital of public limited companies. c) Third Directive of 9 October 1978 (78/855/EEC) introduces a common procedure for company mergers whereby the assets and liabilities of the acquired company are transferred to the acquiring company. d) Fourth Directive of 25 July, 1978 (78/660/EEC) on the annual accounts of limited liability companies. e) Sixth Directive of 17 December, 1982 (82/891/EEC) concerned the scission of a public limited company into several undertakings. f) Seventh Directive of 13 June, 1983 (83/349/EEC) on the consolidated accounts of "groups" of undertakings, parent-companies and subsidiaries. g) Eighth Directive of 10 April, 1984 (84/253/EEC) defines the qualifications to be held by those responsible for the statutory audit of accounts. h) The Directive of 8 December, 1986 (86/635/EEC) on accounts and consolidated accounts of banks and other financial institutions. i) The Directive of 13 February, 1989 (89/117/EEC) on the disclosure of of annual accounts of branches of credit and financial institutions.

Other proposals are still under discusssion (1 May, 1990). a) Fifth Directive on structure and worker participation of public limited companies; b) Tenth Directive on cross-border company mergers; c) Eleventh Directive on disclosure requirements for branches which are created by a company in another member country; d) Twelfth Directive on the creation and operation of limited liability companies by a single person; e) Thirteenth Directive on public bid to purchase stock or exchange against other stock; f) Directive extending the scope of the Directives to include partnership (amendements of the Fourth and Seventh Directives); g) Directive on exemptions for small enterprises in respect of the statements of accounts (amendements Fourth and Seventh Directives); h) Directive for the annuals and consolidated accounts of insurance companies.

Most of the approved (and proposed) Directives only apply to public limited companies and not strictly to co-operative societies. National legislations (e.g. Belgium) want to declare them totally or partly applicable to co-operative societies. In countries where the co-operative legislation has a complete set of rules that do not refer to other parts of company law, co-operative organisations reject harmonization fearing that this would endanger their own national co-operative legislation. Harmonization, however, is essential to establish an equivalent degree of protection throughout the Community which will ensure the protection and safeguard of all interests concerned. In this sense, co-operative legislation may be sooner or later modified and supplemented.

2. *Co-ordination of company law in process of formation.*

a) In 1970, the European Commission made up a first draft (J.O. No C 124 of 10 October, 1970) on the *European Limited Company* based on a specific Community legislation independent of the single national legislations to facilitate cross-border cooperation between companies in the various Member States. This draft was amended in 1975 but the Council of Ministers suspended its discussions in 1982. The European Commission judged it necessary to revive the proposal and submitted a Memorandum in 1988 (COM. (88) 320 final) setting out the main problems and means to resolve them. A new draft was proposed on 25 August, 1989 (COM (89) 268 final – SYN 218 and SYN 219). In its advice on the first draft of the European Limited Company in 1972 and in 1989 (R/ESC 992/89 final) the ESC stated once more that the statute of a European Limited Company should be followed by other legal forms of a private limited liability company and the co-operative society.

b) *European Economic Interest Groupings (EEIG).* By Regulation no 2137/85 of 25 July, 1985 the Council of Ministers created the first entirely common legal instrument facilitating cross-border cooperation. The regulation has been put in force in all Member States since 1 July, 1989. From its registration, the EEIG may operate on the conditions provided for in the contract and with full legal capacity throughout the Community. It may have rights and obligations, place contracts or carry out other legal acts, institute legal proceedings and have its own assets in accordance with the objectives determined by the members. The legal structure of the EEIG comes very near to the idea of what co-operatives intend to do: – it has a legal form inbetween an association and a society (company); – it must be related to the economic activity of its members; – it can only exist in order to enable to develop the own particular activities of its members; – its role is not to manage the activities of each of its members but to co-ordinate some of those activities, for the extension of which it has been made responsible; – the purpose of the grouping is not to make profit for itself. The idea is that the interest and profits of participants lie more in sharing costs and high risks, or in using less costly and more efficient joint services; – all benefits go back to the members; – it may be formed without capital and it is not even required to have any assets.

In the first stage of discussion on the statute of a European co-operative society, it has been objected that the legal form of the EEIG could play the role of a co-operative for cross-border and transnational activities. Co-operative organizations, however, refused to admit such a solution as a final option. The EEIG has indeed some major drawbacks: the unlimited joint liability of its members; its inability to raise public funding (securities); its inability to involve legal persons based outside the EEC; its uncertain tax status. Therefore, co-operative organizations continue to claim an optional, subsidiary legal statute, distinct form that of the European Limited Company (see ESC 451/90, 30 April, 1990).

c) *Preliminary studies on comparative law*. The common Agricultural Policy presupposed an overview of the production and marketing structures and the financial aids to agricultural organizations. Comparative studies were therefore essential. Most of them were not only descriptive, the intention sometimes was comparative law with tendencies of harmonization. These studies have now historical value but remain valuable documents for the history of law and comparative law.

(i) In 1967, an extensive study of comparative law was set up by experts from then six Member States (General Rapporteur *J. Lockhart*) under the title "Agricultural co-operation in the EEC" (Agricultural Series No. 21, Brussels, 1967). The penetrating paper was a rather complete survey of all aspects of agricultural cooperation in the six Member States. As for the comparative method, it went back to an earlier paper "Etude Comparative du Droit de la coopération Agricole en Europe" (Confédération Européene de l'Agriculture, volume 26, Brougg- Suisse 1963).

(ii) In the seventies the European Commission wanted to complete the policy to improve production structures in agriculture by a policy to improve marketing structures and stimulate the formation of producer groups. The purpose was to establish a general Community legislation on a new form of cooperation and with it the aim of keeping national legislations on producer groups (France: groupement de producteurs; Germany: Erzeugergemeinschaften) within reasonable limits. These new forms of cooperation under another name and designation sometimes caused painfull confusion in co-operative organization. Later on, most of these groups joined in the end co-operative structures. A general regulation on producer groups as such never came about. It was integrated in regulations with limited territorial scope of application (Regulation EEC No 1360/78 of 19 June, 1978) and has been adapted to the new Member States in the south.

(iii) In 1974, a new survey of agricultural co-operation in the nine Member States was drawn up by the European Commission under the heading "Les dossiers de la Politique Agricole Commune – la Coopération Agricole" (CEE – D.G. Presse et Information, no 30–31, – December 1974). This paper is limited to a general descriptive survey of economic rather than legal nature.

(iv) In 1976, the European Commission published in its series "Information on Agriculture" a survey of three Member States: United Kingdom, Ireland and Denmark under the heading: "Forms of cooperation between farms for production and marketing in the new Member States" (Information Agriculture no. 20, September 1976).

(v) We have already mentioned (Part I) the comprehensive survey by ESC in 1986 on "The co-operative, mutual and non-profit sector and its organisations in the European Community" this time in the twelve Member States.

d) *Proposals for a European Statute of a Co-operative Society*. In the first period of the Community, co-operative organizations did not feel the need of a European Statute because cross-border trade between co-operatives or undertakings under co-operative statute was only on small scale and because a more flexible right of establishment did no longer impede cross-border cooperation. When, however, legal forms of Community law for cross-border trade came into discussion (see before Part II, 2), co-operatives could no longer lag behind. One of the strongest purposes was that cooperation wanted to keep its range of ideas under its own name and label. This idea was urged on in the context of the achievement of the Single Market.

a) *First draft of European Statute*. As indicated above (Part II, 2), the European Commission worked out a first draft statute for a European Limited Company (societas europea). In a first discussion the European Parliament and the ESC expressed the wish that the European Commission should work out drafts for a European statute for other legal forms than the Limited Company. However, the Commission wanted first to get through with the draft statute of the Limited Company. The main European co-operative organizations – COGECA, EURO-COOP and UGAL (see Part I) – decided to draw up a working paper on an own *European Statute of a co-operative Society*. This paper was handed over to the European Commission in March 1975 together with comments. This working paper has never been studied in detail by the

Commission. As to the content, the draft was inspired by the German Co-operative Law (type association) and as to the modalities by the draft statute of the European Limited Company. The comments were based on following basic arguments: – the Statute of a European Limited Company cannot serve the purpose of co-operatives because they are based on different principles and other distinguishing features as is shown in the national legislations; – there is a need for a specific statute for small and medium-sized undertakings which want to join in European units. This may contribute to economic competition between big and small units; – a European statute should have a general framework of organization or a sort of basic law which can be filled up by the different economical sectors in an own and specific way. The great advantage of this first working paper was not so much the content but the will of the principal co-operative organizations to stick to the idea of a European Co-operative Statute.

b) *Second draft European Statute.* In December 1989, members of the *Co-ordinating Committee of EEC Co-operative Associations* (CCACC) (see Part I) reached an agreement to jointly draw up a working paper on the Statute of a European Co-operative Society. They set up a working party composed of legal experts of all co-operatives groups. A working paper is now under discussion (May 1990). It is a complete worked out statute under Community law, with following specific features:

1. First of all it sets out a specific European legal framework of an EEC co-operative statute that should be independent of the future statute of a European Limited Company and that is open for crossborder activities to members belonging to different Member States.
2. It should supplement but not replace the national legislations. CCACC's member organizations are opposed to the harmonization of national co-operative legislations as such harmonization would anyhow not produce the right integration effect and be extremely difficult to achieve in view of the numerous different rules and structures that exist in Member States. For them, harmonization should be limited to some essential elements of company law which is considered necessary to safeguard the interests of people involved and to avoid unfair competition (see Part II, 1).
3. The statute could consist of fundamental rules independent of national law and could, on the other hand, as to formal aspects (i.e. registration, accounting rules etc.) relate to rules of the country where the co-operative is based or its principal place of business is located.
4. The statute should be uniform, but flexible enough beyond the essential rules of cooperation, to adapt to the economic and financial requirements of the various sorts of co-operatives.
5. The statute must not be compulsory but optional, especially for the co-operatives of those countries that have a rather limited co-operative legislation and in all cases where a co-operative label is the appropriate way.

The working paper is now ready for presentation as a base of discussion to the European Commission and the European Parliament. It may be advisable for the Commission and the Parliament to study and negotiate both European statutes – the Limited Company and the Co-operative – alongside to define their similarities and differences. However, three main peremptory points of discussion should be made in advance:

a) Besides the fact that it is difficult for transnational law to find general and basic rules (i.e. civil law) to refer to in Community law, new basic rules will have to be found to establish new company law (capital-oriented) and society law (person-oriented). In this connection it must be born in mind that basic principles of co-operatives are person-oriented.

b) Tendencies are obvious in national legislations to bring co-operative society law (person-oriented) nearer to company law (capital-oriented) as an instrument for big co-operative societies, in line with what was worked out for second degree co-operatives (co-operatives of co-operatives). Co-operative organizations should take this issue in serious consideration. The simultaneous discussion of both legal forms – Limited Company and Co-operative Society – must bring about a decisive choice in this respect. The review of the co-operative principles may have the advantage not to get out-dated.

c) To conclude, it should be considered very carefully whether Community law would be well served initially with a multiplicity of legal forms (see above "économie générale") especially if they are rather near to one another.

European Cooperation of Co-operative Central Banks

FRIEDBERT MALT

(see also: *Central Institutions*; *Co-operative Banks*; *Data Processing; Development, Eastern Europe; European Community*)

I. From the 1970s to the Early 1990s; II. Towards and Beyond the Completion of the European Single Market and the European Economic Area; III. Outlook.

I. From the 1970s to the Early 1990s

Well into the second half of the twentieth century, the international operations of Europe's co-operative central banks (→ *Central Institutions*) remained confined to comparatively limited activities in commercial business, trade finance and foreign exchange dealing on behalf of large merchandise co-operatives and corporate or institutional clients.

Things began to change, however, during the 1960s. As the economies of western Europe had abandoned post-World War II currency controls, international trade started to increase rapidly, involving a growing number of small and medium-sized businesses of previously local, regional or perhaps national scope; even private households began to demand international products and services such as foreign currency for travel abroad and foreign securities for investment purposes.

In response to requirements of this kind the credit co-operatives (→ *Co-operative Banks*) of old gradually (although at a pace and to a degree varying from one European country to another) had to widen the range of their activities, so that significant numbers of them approached and eventually joined the ranks of full-fledged "universal" banks. An essential prerequisite for this development was a corresponding diversification of the support they received from their central institutions.

At the same time, factors such as the emergence of the Euro(dollar)market (→ *European Community*), rapid growth in cross-border flows of money and capital, and the chain of events that led to the advent of floating exchange rates, motivated an increasing number of large commercial banks all over Europe to establish a presence in key centers of international finance. The major co-operative central banks realized that they had to follow suit for the benefit of their respective systems and in order to sustain their own competitiveness, and it was only natural for them to apply their domestic business philosophy of cooperation to the international level as well.

Initially, their international cooperation was to take the shape of two joint ventures, namely, "London & Continental Bankers Ltd. (LCB)" and "Bank Europäischer Genossenschaftsbanken (B.E.G-Bank of European Co-operative Banks)".

1. LCB

LCB opened for business in the City of London in 1973. It had been established by the central bank of the German co-operative system, the then Deutsche Genossenschaftskasse (which has been known as DG BANK Deutsche Genossenschaftsbank since 1976), in conjunction with S.G. Warburg & Co. Ltd.; but within a few months practically all of Europe's major co-operative central institutions acquired stakes in the new bank's capital. LCB's original objective was to provide the international merchant and investment banking services which its shareholder banks sought from the City for themselves and for the customers of their respective systems. But by the second half of the 1980s, when most of LCB's shareholder banks had opened their own London branches, DG BANK became first the majority and finally the sole shareholder of London & Continental Bankers Ltd., which was renamed DG Investment Bank and ultimately consolidated into the DG BANK London branch.

2. B.E.G-Bank

In a similar way, B.E.G-Bank was founded in Zurich late in 1975 by DG BANK in conjunction with Swiss Volksbank of Berne; they were soon joined by the then Genossenschaftliche Zentralbank AG (since renamed Raiffeisen Zentralbank Österreich – RZB Austria) of Vienna, Caisse Nationale de Crédit Agricole of Paris, and LCB which initially represented numerous other co-operative central banks that subsequently became direct shareholders in B.E.G-Bank themselves. As in the case of London, however, most of B.E.G-Bank's shareholders eventually pursued individual strategies with regard to the Swiss market and sold their shares to DG BANK. Therefore, B.E.G-Bank was renamed DG BANK (Schweiz) in 1987, and since 1991 it has been a wholly-owned subsidiary of its German founder bank.

3. Unico Banking Group

While the joint-venture banks in London and Zurich had served their useful but, as it turned out, temporary purpose as soon as all of their major shareholder banks had firmly established the immediate presence they ultimately needed in these two financial centers, a third joint initiative led to the establishment of a permanent institution: in 1977, six of the then shareholder banks of LCB signed a joint memorandum of understanding and thus formed what was later to become known as the Unico (for United Co-operatives') Banking Group – a basis for non-exclusive, but intensive cooperation with, however, full legal and economic independence for its members.

The Group's overall business strategy is being shaped by a steering committee consisting of the partner banks' chief executives, and implemented by an executive committee of senior officers. Numerous subcommittees and working groups, co-ordinated by a standing secretariat in Amsterdam, deal with technical subjects and prepare proposals for further joint projects.

Step by step, the Unico member banks have been extending their cooperation to a wide range of services and products, from international payments (including the development of a bulk transfer system) and customer accounts to corporate and mortgage loans, from the securities business and mutual funds to capital market activities, corporate finance and leasing.

4. CICP

In parallel with the Unico Banking Group's originally multilateral approach to international cooperation, a number of important bilateral agreements have been concluded by member banks of the CICP – Confédération Internationale du Crédit Populaire, such as Caisse Centrale des Banques Populaires (Paris), Österreichische Volksbanken AG (Vienna) and the central institutions of the German co-operative banking system, namely, DG BANK (Frankfurt am Main), GZB-Bank (Stuttgart), SGZ-Bank (Frankfurt am Main/Karlsruhe) and WGZ-Bank (Düsseldorf). Moreover, CICP member banks from Belgium, Canada, France, Germany, Italy, Spain and the United Kingdom have established the TIPA Network (Transferts Interbancaires de Paiements Automatisés) for the rapid low-cost exchange of bulk payments to be routed through the Interbank File Transfer System of SWIFT (Society for Worldwide Interbank Financial Telecommunication).

II. Towards and Beyond the Completion of the European Single Market and the European Economic Area

The cooperation of the central institutions of the co-operative banking systems of western Europe gained additional momentum as they approached and finally passed January 1, 1993 – the date when the then twelve member countries of the European Community entered the European Single Market and were joined by the seven member countries of the European Free Trade Area in forming the common European Economic Area.

At this historic threshold, the Unico Banking Group comprised eight members: CERA Centrale Raiffeisenkas of Belgium, Caisse Nationale du Crédit Agricole (CNCA) of France, DG BANK Deutsche Genossenschaftsbank of Germany, OKOBANK (Osuuspankkien Keskuspankki OY) of Finland, Rabobank Nederland (Coöperatieve Centrale Raiffeisen-Boerenleenbank) of the Netherlands, Raiffeisen Zentralbank Österreich (RZB Austria), Föreningsbanken AB of Sweden and, as an associated member, ICCREA (Istituto de Credito delle Casse Rurali ed Artigiane) of Italy.

1. General Principles of Cooperation

The advent of the Single Market and the European Economic Area notwithstanding, the co-operative central banks of western Europe entered the new era in the conviction that they should adhere to their tried and tested philosophy of cooperation (as against mutual penetration of one another's domestic retail markets).

The general principle remained, on the one hand, "as much cross-border cooperation as possible", but also, on the other hand, "as many own offices within important markets as necessary" (either in order to enhance co-operative efforts or in response to exceptional competitive situations prevailing on individual member banks' home markets).

In view of the completion of the Single Market and the entry into the European Economic Area, the members of the Unico Banking Group augmented their original memorandum of understanding and other previous multilateral arrangements by concluding numerous bilateral agreements on the specific procedure for and other terms of the mutual referral of corporate customers to partner banks or members of their national systems. As to Germany, several of these agreements were signed by the country's three regional co-operative central banks in addition to DG BANK. With regard to RZB Austria of Vienna, a novel feature of these agreements consisted in the inclusion of services beyond the home market of one of the signatories, namely, the facilities to be made available by the RZB Group in central and eastern Europe.

Examples for cooperation agreements on a partly sub-national level are those between CERA of Belgium and its immediate German "neighbor", the regional WGZ-Bank of Düsseldorf; Banque Fédérative du Crédit Mutuel (Strasbourg) and SGZ-Bank (Frankfurt am Main/Karlsruhe), another of Germany's regional co-operative banks; and between the Network Bancario Italiano (Milan), comprising twelve urban co-operative banks, and SGZ-Bank.

In addition, the home loan savings institutions and insurance groups affiliated with the individual co-operative banking systems – notably those of France, Germany and the Netherlands – have entered into numerous specialized cross-border cooperation agreements.

2. Specific Aspects

In a number of respects, the cooperation practiced by Europe's central co-operative institutions differs from that of comparable commercial banks: in countries with more than one co-operative banking system, separate cooperation agreements have to be concluded by and with either system's central bank if the respective market is to be covered in its entirety; and where, for historic reasons, a co-operative central bank has not (or not yet) been able to achieve a suitable range of operations, some of its sister institutions abroad may prefer to enter into a strategic alliance with a large commercial bank.

Moreover, while the central institutions will make every effort to tailor the contents of their cooperation agreements as closely as possible to the actual or anticipated needs of their regional or local member banks and the customers of those banks, the full fructification of such agreements depends crucially on intensive marketing activities addressing the legally autonomous member banks of the respective systems.

III. Outlook

As the interaction of Europe's economies continues to intensify, the cooperation of their co-operative banking systems will gain further in depth and width: more and more of their millions of corporate and private clients will avail themselves of existing cross-border products and services, and more and more products and services will be included in the "international" range, with an emphasis on the application of electronic banking (→ *Data Processing*).

Furthermore, as the 1990s progress, Europe's co-operative central banks envisage an extension of joint activities mainly in two directions, namely towards eastern Europe and Japan.

1. Eastern Europe

Whereas prior to World War I co-operative banking systems had emerged all over central, eastern and south-eastern Europe, from the Baltic states to Bulgaria, the concept of local banks owned mainly by the individuals they are to serve survived the decades of socialist rule only (and on a reduced scale) in Poland and in Hungary. Under the auspices of the Association of Co-operative Banks of the European Community, the development of these two systems is being supported in the fields of personnel training and technical aid, and the Bank of Hungarian Savings Co-operatives (Budapest) has become a member of the CICP as well (→ *Development, Eastern Europe*). In a field of particular significance for raising the standard of living in Eastern Europe, namely, the development of private housing, co-operative institutions from Austria and Germany literally broke new ground when they participated in establishing a mutual home loan savings bank in Bratislava in 1992; this was the very first institution of its kind in the entire former "socialist bloc".

2. Japan

As to the East Asian member of the global economic "triad", there are three large co-operative banking systems in Japan, their respective central institutions being Norinchukin, Shoko Chukin and Zenshinren Bank. Of these, Norinchukin has been linked with the Unico Banking Group since the 1980s, both as a member of the Unico Consortium that was formed for providing multi-currency facilities to the International Bank for Reconstruction and Development (World Bank), and through a cooperation agreement with DG BANK. Moreover, Norinchukin Bank joined the Unico banks (and the co-operative Caisse Centrale Desjardin of the francophone parts of Canada) in founding the "Unico International Platform" that was established in 1992 for regular discussion of developments in international banking. At the same time, individual Unico banks were also exploring opportunities for closer cooperation with Japan's other two co-operative banking systems.

3. Long-Range View

In setting out a timetable for consecutive steps towards the entry into an age of a single European currency, the Maastricht Treaty of 1992 has put a date of potentially immense significance on the long-range agenda of the co-operative banking systems as well as that of all other financial institutions in and beyond Europe: if and when European countries should eventually indeed reach the stage of irrevocably fixing the mutual parities of their national currencies, the respective co-operative banking systems would be confronted with the question of whether or not it was desirable and feasible to establish a common European apex institution as an additional tier vis-à-vis the supranational European central bank that would have commenced operations by then.

Evaluation of Co-operative Organizations

Eberhard Dülfer

(see also: *Auditing*; *Accounting*; *Assessment of Success*; *Self-help Organizations*; *Policies for Promotion*)

I. Reasons for Evaluating Co-operative Organizations; II. What does "Evaluation" mean? III. The Addressees of Evaluation Results; IV. Why Distinguish Between Project Evaluation and the Evaluation of Institutions? V. The "Tripartite Approach" to Evaluating Co-operatives; VI. The Evaluation Reporting Schemes; VII. Two Examples.

I. Reasons for Evaluating Co-operative Organizations

Co-operative Societies developed in Europe since the Middle Ages as → *self-help organizations*. However, the present organizational and legal forms arose during the 19th century (→ *History in 19th C.*). At the beginning of the development of a Third World, these co-operatives and related institutions have been spread all over the world. It is rather difficult to find a country where this kind of self-help organization (SHO) is not a privileged goal of institution building policy as an instrument of social and economic development (→ *Development Policy*). Their various forms seem to be a very appropriate means of improving the living standard of underprivileged social groups in urban or rural areas, giving them better chances for participation in the economic and political decision-making processes.

However, the practical results of the co-operative organizations established did not correspond to the expectations originally placed in them by both the governmental authorities and the co-operative members.

The main reasons for this imbalance include
- the unadapted implementation of European and US co-operative patterns,
- a lack of know-how in planning and implementing self-help organizations,
- a lack of qualified management personnel,
- the → *officialization* of many co-operative organizations by governmental authorities,
- the limitation of co-operative self-help activities to specific social groups,
- the partial use of co-operative organizational patterns by traditional clienteles for stabilizing traditional social structures.

In view of these facts there is always a need for a better understanding of the special organizational structure of the co-operative (→ *Organizational Structure of Societies*) and a more effective concept of how such organizations should be implemented and managed (→ *Management in Co-operatives*). What are the main goals and objectives of co-operatives as → *self-help organizations* in developing regions? A lot of questions have to be answered concerning their position within the social and economic development process of the countries concerned, the extend the peasant farmers and other involved persons are in a position to assume responsibility in managing co-operative organizations, and the extent to which governmental departments are or can be responsible for promoting and supervising co-operative organizations (→ *Policies for Promotion*).

All these questions should be dealt with and solved by an integrated approach permitting

- an analysis of the actual situation of co-operatives and related institutions,
- an identification of the persons involved and the goal-definers inside and outside the organization,
- a definition of the potentials and capacities of co-operative organizations,
- an identification of their requirements and resources needed for further development.

These aspects are to be included into a procedure of evaluation for co-operative organizations, particularly for its implementation in developing countries. This research task has been given to a group of scientists (of the German universities at Marburg and Göttingen) by the Food and Agriculture Organization of United Nations (FAO) during the seventies and the different separately published results have been summarized (by *E. Dülfer*) in the FAO-publication "Guide to Evaluation of Co-operative Organizations in Developing Countries" (Rome 1981).

However, the actuality of the questions has not diminished in the meantime. The problems of practical implementation of co-operatives are always existing. Nevertheless, evaluation procedures are not very much welcomed by many responsibles. For this reason, the "Tripartite Approach of Evaluation" delivered in the Guide shall be presented here again in order to revitalize the discussion on this subject.

II. What does "Evaluation" Mean ?

An appropriate answer to the question what evaluation does mean presupposes a general statement regarding both the goals and purposes for which co-operatives and related self-help institutions can be used and the operational objectives their activities should be oriented toward. Opinions differ in this respect in theory and practice. Co-operative movements in various countries have long since developed different catalogues of "co-operative principles" (→ *Principles*). According to all these concepts, however, the co-operative institution (co-operative society) seems to possess a specific legitimation and philosophy of action, independent of time and place (→ *Conceptions, Co-operative*). The main purpose of the co-operative enterprise everywhere is to promote the members' economies (enterprises or households). Insofar, the well-known → *"promotion mandate"* really exists. It is, however, a very formal determination, because it does not indicate what the content of the promotional activity should be. It depends on the interests and specific goals of the members of the co-operative concerned what kind of promotion is appropriate in any given case. This is furthermore influenced by the environmental conditions. It needs the "situational approach" for an effective analysis.

The first task in evaluating co-operatives must be to identify the actual goals and objectives of their members. The co-operative enterprise mostly operates on the open market, i.e., in → *competition*. However, there are goals and intentions of the members which can not be achieved under the conditions of competition, e.g. for cost reasons. Thus, co-operative managers very often find themselves in a dilemma situation, torn between the expectations of the members on the one side and the requirements of successful market operation on the other. Because managers want to be professionally successful they are deduced to get a position which conflicts with that of fostering the members' interests (→ *Theory of co-operative Cooperation*).

The analysis of the existing goals and objectives of all decision-making centres (not only the members) within the co-operative is therefore one of the most important tasks of evaluation. It requires the identification of all persons and groups of persons involved in the goal-setting process, which may also include the workers of the co-operative enterprise or their representatives (→ *Relationship Patterns*).

Furthermore, it requires an investigation into the extent to which governmental authorities exert a direct or indirect influence on goal-setting (→ *Policies for Promotion*); and the same question arises again with respect to secondary and tertiary co-operative bodies

(→ *Central Institutions*). As to the managers of the co-operative enterprise, their responsibility is to deploy the natural and financial means at their disposal with reference to the combined system of objectives. The different organizational patterns (→ *Structural Types*) characterizing the co-operative combine as a whole play an important role in this connection. Sometimes, the co-operative enterprise operates more or less independently of the member units (with respect to the quantity and quality offered); in this case we speak of a "market-linkage co-operative". In other cases, the management of the co-operative enterprise provides a "group management" service for the whole combine, including the individual enterprise (or agricultural units) of the members; in this case, we speak of an "integrated co-operative".

When analyzing the different systems of goals and objectives pursued within the co-operative complex, we have to take into consideration:

(a) the personal, individual system of aims and of every single member and the objectives of his individual enterprise (or household),
(b) the system of common aims and objectives of the co-operative member group;
(c) the operational objectives of the co-operative enterprise as deduced from the members' aim system and/or as conceived by the managers;
(d) the personal, individual aims of the managers as factors influencing the co-operatives' course of action;
(e) the aims of employees or workers in the co-operative enterprise as possible influence factors on operational objectives of the enterprise;
(f) further influences on the part of governmental authorities and agencies and/or secondary co-operative bodies.

In face of the scarcity of financial and natural resources, the members and the managers of the co-operative enterprise have a vested interest in making optimal use of those available, i.e., in taking "optimal" decisions. The "economic principle" is valid in the case of co-operatives in the same way as in other enterprises (→ *Business Policies*). The only difference in this respect is that the goals and objectives of co-operative organizations may be more manifold and not exclusively restricted to monetary and financial considerations.

Thus, the achievement of goals cannot always be measured by ratio scales, as is the case for monetary items. Many goals and objectives are of pure qualitative character and can only be measured by ordinal scales and interval scales. Their evaluation requires a very comprehensive set of measuring instruments for supervising the extent and degree of goal achievement in co-operative (and related self-help) organizations (*Dülfer* 1979). A comparison between the planned and actual figures of goal achievement makes a practical feedback possible. This indicates that management and evaluation are closely linked to each other and represent two sides of the same medal (→ *Assessment of Success*).

Because of the multidimensional character of possible goal systems, one of the most difficult problems is how to "amalgamate" the different results in goal achievement. The evaluation method offers specific graphical and mathematical instruments to this end. Finally, any possible deviation between planned and actual goal achievement has to be analyzed with respect to its causes. Recommendations have to be developed to improve the situation and performance of the co-operative concerned.

III. The Addressees of Evaluation Results

The operational system of the goals and objectives of the co-operative enterprise (or the entire → *co-operative combine*) serves as the main criterion for decision-making within this institution. Insofar, the managers of the co-operative enterprise are the first to benefit from evaluation: for them, evaluation serves an important feedback function.

The evaluation also serves the members by assisting them in supervising the managers' activities assuming that the results of the evaluation are made available to the members and/or their representatives.

The governmental authorities responsible for the economic and social development of the country are also interested in the results of evaluation in order to learn what the co-operatives are doing in the context and which positive contributions they are making to the national development. In many cases, they set up special task forces for carrying out evaluation work on behalf of a ministry or department.

In these cases, an important problem arises insofar as the departments often depart from the premise that co-operatives and other SHOs should be effective instruments for the execution of governmental development programmes. This concept may well come into conflict with the self-help character of the co-operative. Whatever the individual goals and objectives of the member groups and the co-operative enterprises may be, their effects can nevertheless be helpful for governmental policies. The evaluation of co-operative activities can thus be an instructive feedback instrument for the promotional activities of governmental departments with respect to co-operatives; and this is relevant at all levels of the administration – at the national, regional, and even at the district one.

IV. Why Distinguish Between Project Evaluation and the Evaluation of Institutions?

During the first development periods, "evaluation" was mentioned mainly with respect to project management and supervision. Yet, it is also of relevance to governmental promotion of co-operative development in whole developing areas. Every promotional activity which requires governmental expenditure must be planned, executed and supervised (evaluated) as a project. The same is valid with regard to the agencies and partner organizations engaged in bilateral or multinational co-operation by way of technical assistance. Building a storehouse for crop farmers, organizing a training seminar for co-operative bookkeepers, or supplying tractors for a co-operative machinery centre – these are typical instances of promotional projects in favour of co-operative institutions.

There are three approaches to project evaluation differentiated with respect to its time of investigation:

a) the ex-ante evaluation;
b) the concurrent evaluation and
c) the ex-post evaluation.

The ex-ante evaluation serves to valuate the expected advantages of a co-operative project in comparison with other ones which could be financed by the available funds. Thus, ex-ante evaluation is a complementary element to feasibility studies and project planning.

Here, the ex-ante evaluation is one method for valuating the expected advantages of a co-operative project in comparison with other possible uses of available funds. Ex-ante evaluation is a complementary element to feasibility studies and project planning. At a later stage, after the project decision has been taken, the concurrent evaluation is required to ensure a permanent feedback to the current project management with respect to the achieved subgoals. Finally, the ex-post evaluation summarizes the positive and negative results of the project in order to enrich the experience of the sponsor organization and to prevent the same mistake in other cases. In practice, however, this kind of ex-post evaluation is mostly not carried out.

Although the classical methods of project evaluation are also relevant to co-operative promotion projects, this whole complex must be strictly separated from the evaluation of institutions, such as co-operative societies and other SHOs (*Dülfer* 1979). In this latter case, it is not a governmental promotion activity in favour of a co-operative institution but the activity of the institution itself which has to be the first object of evaluation.

This calls for a number of differentiations: firstly, a project is defined as a complex of activities which are needed for executing a well-defined event or status as project result (or task). Secondly, the project is calculated with respect to its time consumption (assuming that the total time of the project can be deduced from the time of its single activities). Finally, all operational and detailed objectives of project execution are deduced from the main project purpose (final status) and determined by the project bearer. The project manager and his team are responsible for the execution.

In the case of an institution, the situation is completely different: a co-operative enterprise is founded without any limitation in time. Theoretically, every co-operative aims to exist indefinitely, and the persons or groups of persons involved have a strong interest in ensuring its "survival". Insofar, they have to consider the environmental influences and, if necessary, to change single elements of the system of objectives of the institution (co-operative enterprise) for attaining a better adaptation.

A different method of evaluation is needed in each case in face of these evident differences between project and institution. Nevertheless, some elements may overlap, because the creation of a new institution, like a co-operative enterprise, from the outset until the institution becomes fully self-reliant can be defined as a kind of project; we speak of an "institution-building project". This overlapping, however, must not lead to confusion between the evaluation of the project and the evaluation of the institution concerned. The mandate for all activities pertaining to setting up a new institution is completely different from that for the later activities of the institution itself. There are two distinct objects of evaluation (*Dülfer* 1981 a). The situation becomes more difficult if the co-operative, as explained above, is maintained by different groups of persons who have to bargain for the pursuit of a common system of goals and objectives.

V. The "Tripartite Approach" to Evaluating Co-operatives

Since co-operatives are institutions, the evaluation has to relate to the actual system of objectives in any given case. Let us take the example of an agricultural multipurpose co-operative society. Its system of goals is determined a) by the interests of the members (i.e., → *the co-operative group*), b) by the requirements of market business, and in some instances c) by the personal interests and aims of the managers and eventually d) by those of employees within the co-operative enterprise. The operational system of objectives of the co-operative enterprise thus results from a bargaining process between these persons and groups involved. The extent to which this system of goals is achieved determines the "*operational efficiency*" of the co-operative enterprise. Measuring this efficiency is the content of the evaluation carried out either by the management or an outsider, such as the inspectors of the co-operative department.

On the other hand, the ministry of co-operatives or another governmental authority concerned with the promotion of co-operatives is interested to know to what extent the activities of the co-operative enterprise have contributed to the achievement of national development targets. If they did we can state a *"development efficiency"*. Sometimes, the departments responsible tend to intervene in the management of the co-operative organization; this strategy easily gives rise to a certain bureaucratizing process known as the *"officialization"* of co-operative organization. But even if these authorities or agencies accept the self-help character of co-operatives they often try to influence business policymaking and management within the co-operatives by different incentives or pressures. This is the easier, the more the managers are directly or indirectly dependent on the departments, perhaps because they have been delegated as civil servants of the departments. Thus, the danger exists that the business policy of co-operatives or related SHOs might become adapted to governmental desires without the agreement of the members or even against their will and intentions.

In order to avoid this danger, a third aspect of measuring efficiency must be taken into consideration. It is the degree to which the activities and real effects of the co-operative enterprise serve the real interest and practical wants of the members. This has to be called the *"member-oriented efficiency"* of the Cooperative.

A long-term favourable development of the self-help concept of the co-operative evaluated is only presumable if all three kinds of co-operative efficiency are found to be positive. This makes the tripartite approach indispensable to the evaluation of co-operatives and related institutions..

A further question is, however, how this approach can be implemented in practice being adapted to local and situational conditions. The general concept of the tripartite approach to evaluation is explained in the "Guide to Evaluation of Co-operative Organizations in Developing Countries" mentioned above. This Guide explains in detail the procedure of constructing instruments for measurement and applying the various techniques to specific quantitative and qualitative items. However, an understanding of the methodology presupposes a certain knowledge of management science. Since co-operatives can differ greatly in their stage of development, their main goals, functional orientation and institutional structure, and the evaluation may concern many kinds of co-operatives, as farmers associations, business groups and other socioeconomic institutions, the "Guide" had to adopt a certain level of abstraction to ensure its applicability to a wide range of cases and subjects. In practice, however, evaluation has to be carried out at local level by a large number of field-workers, inspectors and related people who have their own specific obligations and tasks and cannot be expected to be experts in management science.

The tripartite approach has therefore been reduced to standardized schemes for merely reporting on evaluation activity in which the evaluator answers a number of questions. In doing so, he can use his special intimate knowledge of the local situation and relationships without needing an understanding of the theoretical background of the methodology. The tripartite approach has been conretized by the evaluation reporting schemes. The reporting schemes, however, are only able to present a generalized pattern. For application at the local level, they have to be further specified with respect to local or national circumstances or the organization concerned. This specification can easily be done by local managers or district inspectors.

The application of these country-oriented reporting schemes should be explained for use in a very brief and simple manual at the disposal of the evaluator. Some guidance in this connection and can be found in the above-mentioned general Guide to Evaluation.

VI. The Evaluation Reporting Schemes

Whenever an evaluation of a co-operative is made, the results have to be recorded by the evaluator. The evaluator must treat the document as confidential, unless express authority is forthcoming from the commissioning authority for its publication for restricted inspection or for deliberation by the personnel responsible. This aspect should be clearly regulated by the sponsoring organization or authority concerned.

Both, in principle and in numerous points of detail, evaluation resembles the auditing of the annual accounts of public companies (which is regulated under public law in some countries) or the auditing undertaken by the → federations of co-operative societies (→ *Auditing*). But in contrast to a purely formal exercise of supervision with respect to legitimacy, evaluation relates to the measurement of *goal achievement* in the light of the various aspects of efficiency. Nevertheless, the legal auditing principles derived from the practice of certified auditing must likewise be valid for the domain of evaluation. Accordingly, the evaluation report must observe the usual principles of completeness, of true reporting, of impartiality and of uniformity.

In order to facilitate evaluation for the local supervisory and audit personnel, the form of the evaluation is differentiated in accordance with *object* and *purpose*.

Firstly, a distinction is made between the *two main fields* of evaluation: the evaluation of co-operative projects and the evaluation of co-operatives as institutions. As regards co-operative projects, a further distinction is made between co-operative promotion projects and co-operative institution-building projects. Thus, three relevant subjects for evaluation emerge.

Secondly, account must be taken of the various reasons for evaluation explained above:
- ex-ante evaluation;
- the concurrent evaluation and
- the ex-post evaluation.

The combination possibilities of three subjects of evaluation and three aspects of evaluation give a total number of eight instances which have been presented in the FAO-Guide, namely,
- Scheme A: Co-operative Project Feasibility Study (promotion)
- Scheme B: Co-operative Project Feasibility Study (setting-up)
- Scheme C: Project Interim Checking Report (promotion)
- Scheme D: Project Interim Checking Report (setting-up)
- Scheme E: Project Completion Report (promotion)
- Scheme F: Project Completion Report (setting-up)
- Scheme G: Co-operative Periodic Auditing Report (institution)
- Scheme H: Co-operative Liquidation Report. (institution)

VII. Two Examples

Scheme A and Scheme G are given below as examples to demonstrate the structure of such reporting schemes (FAO-Guide 1981).

1. Scheme A:
Co-operative Project Feasibility Study (Promotion)

Classification Scheme for the Ex Ante Evaluation of Co-operative Promotion Projects

1. Evaluation Commission
    1.1 Placing of commission
        (client; commissioning document; form; content; date)
    1.2 Genesis of commission
        (motive and purpose of placing of commission; contexts in which the evaluation is to be seen)
    1.3 Implementation of commission
        (evaluator; collaborators; content, place and time of evaluation transactions; persons supplying information; documents)
    1.4 Result of evaluation in brief
        (description of project; project sponsors; critique as to content and form; most important proposals)
2. Object of Evaluation
    2.1 Previous history of promotion project
        (initiator, causes and reasons; previous attempts; project proposal; project plan)
    2.2 Descrpription of promotion project
        (structure and requirements of target group; institutional and functional description of the co-operative organization to be promoted)
    2.3 General environmental conditions
        (natural environmental situation; social structure; infrastructure; legal system; political structures; Government's conception of development policy)
    2.4 Influences relevant to the project
        (social structure in the project area; state promotion institutions; development programme and measures; relevant legal norms; registration regulations; special project regulations; living conditions of project personnel)
    2.5 Local project resources – location factors
        (raw materials and operating resources; labour force; technology; market situation and possibilities of linkages on procurement or sales side)
    2.6 Planned course of project
        (presentation of individual activities according to content, sequence and use of time according to the project plan, as far as possible in the form of a simple network plan, and with reference to the phase scheme)
    2.7 The project sponsor (partner organization)
        (particulars of the foreign sponsor's partner organization to be implemented; organizational and legal structure; personnel manning, economic situation, political authority and dependencies; form and content of collaboration between foreign sponsor and partner organization, division of responsibilities in the various phases)
3. Project Requirements (arranged according to phases)
    3.1 Requirements of personnel and expertise
        (project appointments plan; counterpart posts; posts for advisors; plan of jobs of the co-operative organization; technical and administrative equipment)
    3.2 Project costs
        (personnel and expertise costs of project implementation)
    3.3 Financing and promotion requirements
        (plan of financing for the project; members' own contributions; promotion needs to be met and assurance of continuing)
4. Forecast of Project Results
    4.1 Forecast of efficiency of promotion measures intended
        (estimate of the effects of project measures with regard to the self-help goals aimed at; forecast of costs and benefits with the application of appropriate ratios; of appropriate, proposals for the revision of goals)
    4.2 Forecast of the overall development effects of promotion measures
        (estimate of the probable contributions of promotion measure to import overall or regionally specific development goals; possible negative effects)
    4.3 Probable reactions of the state authorities responsible
        (possibilities of state promtion and supervision; dangers caused by state intervention)
    4.4 Estimate of time needed for project development according to the phase scheme
        (an attempt should be made to estimate the point in time at which individual phases will be reached)
5. Result of Evaluation (Assessment of Project)
    5.1 Proposal for project decision
        (in weighing the various possibilities of utilization of resources the evaluator should give a summary opinion as to whether the promotion measures should be carried out or whether and on what grounds they seem disadvantageous compared with other projects)

2. Scheme G:
Co-operative Periodic Auditing Report

Classification Scheme for the Concurrent Evaluation of Co-operative Organizations (Institutions)

1. Evaluation Commission
   1.1 Placing of commission
       (client; commissioning document; form; content; date)
   1.2 Genesis of evaluation commission
       (motive and purpose of placing of commissions; contexts in which the evaluation is to be seen)
   1.3 Implementation of commission
       (evaluator; collaborators; content; place and time of evaluation transactions; persons supplying information; documents)
   1.4 Result of evaluation in brief
       (type and structure of co-operative organization; participating partner organization; result of planned/actual comparison; most important deviations; critique as to content and form; most important proposals)
2. Object of Evaluation
   2.1 The co-operative organization evaluated
       (name – form name; address; type of co-operative organization, designation according to local custom in brief form; legal form according to national law; type of operational unit; state of development according to phase scheme)
   2.2 Genesis and development of the co-operative organization
       (impulse and initiator; causes and reason for foundation; previous attempts and preparations; promotion measures of third parties; where appropriate; completion of settin-up project)
   2.3 General enviromental conditions
       (natural environmental situation; social structure; infrastructure; legal system; political structures; Government's conception of development policy)
   2.4 Important influencing factors
       (state promotion institutions and programmes for co-operative organization; relevant legal norms; registration regulations; linkage effects)
   2.5 The co-operative group
       (structure of the self-help group; economic situation of members; motivation and goals of group self-help; contracts with self-help promotion institutions)
   2.6 The co-operative operational unit (e.g., the co-operative enterprise)
       (organizational and legal structure; structure of enterprise management; manner of functioning; resources; linkage effects and market situation; state of accountancy procedures and business planning; structure of assets and financial position, if necessary balance sheet and profit and loss account)
3. Operational Efficiency
   3.1 System of objectives
       (target group of the co-operative organization; statements of individual objectives according to content, degree of achievement striven for and reference to time; explanation of relationships between objectives; possibly graphic representation of system of objectives, priorities)
   3.2 Measurement of achievement of objectives
       (measurement of achievement of objectives in the case of individual material objectives; determination of indicators for measuring formal objectives; statement of measurement scales and indices)
   3.3 Estimation of operational efficiency
       (Objective achievement values of the period and the previous period; if necessary the total objective value; ratios of operational efficiency)
4. Development Efficiency
   4.1 Relevant development objectives
       (explanation of the objectives to be brought into consideration; derived subgoals on the level of the member business or the co-operative organization)
   4.2 Measurement of contributions to development
       (measurement values or coefficients for the different development objectives; measurement of contributions to derived subgoals)
5. Member-oriented Efficiency
   5.1 Procedure of questioning members
       (short explanation of methods of gathering data used)
   5.2 Ascertained expectations of members
       (explanation of attitudes, values and objectives identified)
   5.3 Evaluation of results of collection of data
       (with regard to relevance and statistical significance of results, as well as validity, reliability and objectivity of research method)
6. Deviations in the Development of the SHO from Set-up Planning
   (Deviations in consequence of changed legal norms, changed economic structure; change of objectives system through the members; change of business policy through the management; deviations on the grounds of false estimation in project planning)
7. Results of Evaluation
   (Confirmation of orderliness of business management and accountancy procedures; summary estimation of results of measurement of efficiency; proposals for further development:
   – for the management of the SHO
   – for the participating SHP or sponsor organizations
   – if necessary, for the supervising body)

Bibliography

Baldus, R.-D.: Report to the Government of the Democratic Republic of Afghanistan on Evaluation of Cooperatives in Afghanistan, FAO, Rom 1978 (restr.).

Bauer, P.T./Yamey, B.S.: The economics of underdeveloped countries, (Cambridge Univ. Pr.) Cambridge 1959.

Billerbeck, K.: Kosten-Ertrags-Analyse, (Hessling) Berlin 1968. *Blase, M.G.*: Institution Building: A Source Book, (Agency for Int. Development U.S. Dept. of State) Ann Arbor 1973.

Deutsche Gesellschaft für Technische Zusammenarbeit (GTZ) (Hrsg.), Technische Zusammenarbeit im ländlichen Raum – Projekte zur Förderung von Selbsthilfeorganisationen, Eschborn 1978.

Dichtl, E./Schobert, R.: Mehrdimensionale Skalierung, (Vahlen) München 1979.

Dülfer, E.: An Analytical Method for the Evaluation of (Rural) Cooperatives in Developing Countries, (FAO) Rom 1977.

Dülfer, E.: Kooperative Organisationen in Entwicklungsländern, in: Handwörterbuch der Organisation (HWO), hrsg. von: Grochla, E., 2. Aufl., (Poeschel) Stuttgart.

Dülfer, E. (Hrsg.): Zur Krise der Genossenschaften in der

Entwicklungspolitik, (Vandenhoeck & Ruprecht) Göttingen 1975.
Emory, C.W.: Business Research Methods, (Irwin) Homewood, Ill. 1976.
Etzioni, A.: A Comparative Analysis of Complex Organizations (The Free Press) New York 1975.
FAO (Hrsg): Guidelines for Evaluation of Technical Assistance Activities, Rom 1974.
Fishbein, M.: A Behaviour Theory Approach to the Relations between Beliefs about an Object and the Attitude toward the Object, in: Fishbein, M. (Hrsg.): Readings in Attitude Theory and Measurement, (Wiley) New York 1967.
French, jr. J.R.P./Raven, B.: The Basis of Social Power, in: Cartwright, D./Zander, A. (Hrsg.), Group Dynamics, 3. Aufl., New York/Evanstone/London 1968.
Guttman, L.: A Basis for Skaling Qualitative Data, in: American Sociological Review, Vol. 9 (1944), S. 139 ff.
Halbach, A.J.: Theorie und Praxis der Evaluierung von Projekten in Entwicklungsländern, (Weltforum) München 1972
Hammel, W./Hemmer, H.R.: Zur Methodik der Cost-Benefit-Analyse bei Entwicklungshilfeprojekten, in: Meimberg, R. (Hrsg.: Voraussetzungen einer globalen Entwicklungspolitik und Beiträge zur Kosten- und Nutzenanalyse, (Duncker & Humblot) Berlin 1971.
Hanel, A./Müller, J.O.: Improving the Methodology of Evaluating the Development of Rural Cooperatives in Developing Countries – Case Study Iran, FAO, Rom 1978.
Hanel, A./Müller, J.O.: On the Evaluation of Rural Cooperatives with Reference to Governmental Development Policies - Case Study Iran, (Vandenhoeck & Ruprecht) Göttingen 1976.
ILO (Hrsg.): International Labour Conference: The Role of Co-operatives in the Economic and Social Development of Developing Countries, 49th Session, Report VII (1), Geneva 1965.
Kantowsky, D. (Hrsg.): Evaluierungsforschung und -praxis in der Entwicklungshilfe, (Verlag der Fachvereine) Zürich 1977.
Krech, D./Crutchfield, R.S./Ballachey, E.L.: Individual in Society, (McGraw-Hill) New York 1962.
Kuhn, J./Stoffregen, H.: How to Measure the Effeciency of Agricultural Cooperatives in Developing Countries, FAO, Rom 1975.
Little, I.M.D./Mirrlees, J.A.: Manual of Industrial Project Analysis in Developing Countries, Vol. 2, (OECD) Paris 1969.
Musto, S.A.: Evaluierung sozialer Entwicklungsprojekte, (Hessling) Berlin 1972.
Osgood, C.E./Suci, G.J./Tannenbaum, P.H.: The Measurement of Meaning, Urbana 1957.
Turban, E./Metersky, M.L.: Utility Theory Applied to Multivariable System
US-AID (Hrsg.): Evaluation Handbook, 2. ed., Washington 1974.
Warren, R.D./Mulford, Ch.L./Yetley, M.J.: Analysis of Cooperative Organizational Effectiveness, in: Rural Sociology, Vol. 41 (1976), S. 330 ff.
Weiß, C.: Evaluierungsforschung, (Westdeutscher Verlag) Opladen 1974.
Wettschureck, G.: Indikatoren und Skalen in der Demoskopischen Marktforschung, in: Handbuch der Marktforschung, Bd. 1, hrsg. von: Behrens, K.C., (Gabler) Wiesbaden 1974.
Zangemeister, Ch.: Nutzwertanalyse in der Systemtechnik, 3. Aufl., (Wittemannsche Buchhandlung) München 1973.

Federation Statistics of Co-operative Organizations

PETER VON DER LIPPE [J]

(see also: *Federations*; *Central Institutions*; *Ratio-based Credit Rating*)

I. Field of Attention of Federation Statistics; II. Involvement of the Federations in Government Statistics; III. Statistics Obtained by the Federations themselves; IV. Federation Statistics and Member Enterprises.

I. Field of Attention of Federation Statistics

Recording statistics is one of the tasks → *federations* undertake. In most cases, two functions can be differentiated which the federations fulfill by working with such statistical information.
a) The federations act as intermediaries between the official statistical work executed by the state and the members of the federation, which as companies are also included in the surveys conducted by government statistics offices.
b) The federations organize internal statistics for their entire membership body. Such information can be used above all by members to compare their companies to the branch as a whole. Furthermore, the federation uses internal statistics to make operational comparisons in the scope of its consulting function (similar individual companies are compared to each other on the basis of operational ratios). By exercising this function, the federation acts practically as a staff department of the member companies in the federation (FMC) although it is jointly used by all member companies.

The importance of such statistics for the federation – the amount of composite federation work consumed by such statistical work as well as the importance of this activity in the eyes of the FMCs – is dependent primarily on the nature of the federation and the development level of the country in which it is active. Federations active in branches dominated by small and mid-sized enterprises are usually availed of more strongly in the sense explained above (as external staff departments) than federations in sectors with a higher degree of concentration. On account of their multisided activity and the size of their service palette, large companies not only have a greater demand for a comprehensive and differentiated pool of data but also are in a better position to accumulate such statistical data and utilize it pertinently. A certain branch can also boast of various company forms, and thus of various types of federations. Within the banking industry in numerous countries (a sector repeatedly alluded to in the following discourse), large universal banks, smaller private banks, savings banks and → *co-operative banks* are all active in identical or different market segments. They are affiliated to different federation structures, provided such structures exist at all (large banks are usually not organized in federations). Federations composed of private banks frequently limit their activity to a general information function and provide economic data. The FMCs often do not wish for more comprehensive activities, including those in the field of statistics; one reason for this is their varying fields of business activity. The sector of co-operative and savings banks in contrast is much more homogenous and organized more rigidly. The federation takes more decisive influence on the business policy and accordingly is much more strongly involved in gathering information and making intercompany comparisons.

An extensively developed and independent reporting system for government statistics offices and federations is usually considered a luxury which only highly developed economies can afford. The truth is that there are numerous tasks which federations need to address more imperatively in developing countries than the collection and evaluation of statistical data. Such tasks include providing assistance in the organization of enterprises, in the personnel and training divisions and in marketing as well as representing federation interests with regard to executive and legislative bodies as well as to international organizations.

II. Involvement of the Federations in Government Statistics

The federations exercise their intermediary role mentioned above between the official government statistics and the individual interviewed companies through the following functions:
a) Participation in the *preparation* and
b) in the *execution* of surveys as well as
c) in the *evaluation* of official statistical data in the interest of the federation members.

The federations play a quasi-official role in the production of statistics in the first two functions. The actual, individual tasks allocated to the federations are contingent on the organization of official (state) statistics collection in a particular country. Federations are not, however, only suppliers of particular government statistics (through both informal and institutional participation); they likewise are the most important user of official, published statistical data which, although in principle available to all people, are naturally utilized to varying intensities.

1. The Organization of Official National Statistics

In order to describe the assistance the federations can offer government statistics offices it is helpful to discuss briefly the basic methods of organizing national statistic services. There are also international recommendations which essentially aim to take precautionary measures with regard to organization and procedural methods in order to guarantee

a) the autonomy of the statistics office,
b) the public (and not only state) interests in statistical data, and
c) the protection of those surveyed.

Complex social and economic phenomena cannot be directly grasped through individual observation but rather only indirectly through the medium of statistics, which provides an abstract and numerical sketch of reality (drawn from individual cases). Beyond describing a situation, statistics likewise indicate the need to undertake action, thus serving operational purposes. This is all the more true the more centralized and serious the decisions are (measured against the economic consequences of a bad decision). Therefore the extension of state activities, above all in the field of social services, results in a continually mounting need for data.

According to current-day understanding, statistics is a service provided by the state for all persons and/or institutions and as such constitutes an element of the "informational infrastructure". The state is, however, not only responsible for financing such services but also for guaranteeing the objectivity and methodological correctness of the provided statistical information. On the one hand, this as a rule makes it necessary to obligate those surveyed to provide information, thus entailing state means to guarantee enforceability; on the other hand, the statistics offices must be granted a special status which separates them from the remaining state apparatus. The neutrality of these offices is expedited when they are not answerable to a particular department (e.g. finance ministry), when they are not specialized in one field of activity, when they do not have a political interest of their own concerning the interpretation of the information, and when they must follow strict procedural guidelines and confidentiality regulations.

In the course of the statistical surveys, individual responses are recorded which are then aggregated into typical numerical and anonymous statistical data. The interests of those interviewed to protect the privacy of their responses must be respected; this aspect should be used to gather acceptance for the survey itself. A clean separation must exist between statistics which are only interested in aggregate data and administrative activities which are based on individual data.

The neutrality of government statistics offices is also served in that they themselves do not determine their activities. They thus do not bear any political responsibility whether it is decided to execute a statistical survey or not. In some countries, the basis survey can only be "provided for" by law. The legislative procedures should also ensure that all voiced interests are heard – on the one hand, those interested in survey information and, on the other hand, those who demand that unnecessary survey expenses be avoided.

Despite these precautionary measures the opposition and resistance to statistical surveys continues to increase – not only from individuals but also from organized groups. At the same time, on the national and international level more extensive wishes are articulated for a statistical reporting system. No one seems to be consciously aware of the contradiction between more information and fewer surveys. As a result, more refined skills are needed for survey interviewing; innocuous survey techniques need to be developed which the interviewed companies would regard merely as by-products.

2. Federations and Surveys for Governmental Statistics

The cooperation between the federations and the statistical offices has in the meanwhile become essential to the latter inasmuch as the federations contribute to the atmosphere of acceptance as well as rationalize the way the survey is organized and executed. Branch knowledge accumulated by the federation is also vital for the preparation of the survey. Federations participate in legitimating the survey project, defining the attributes in the survey, adjusting systematics, providing for the preconditions which ensure that the information can be surveyed, etc. When the federations have not been moved to participate in the survey not only is the acceptance among those interviewed often endangered, but the legal foundation for the survey itself may also be threatened. The federations are involved in defining attributes and designing systematics in such a manner as to ensure that the survey reveals meaningful differentiations and useful aggregates. For example, the survey of incoming materials and goods provides a quite important statistic for the estimation of net outputs in the scope of production statistics and national accounts. This statistic registers the inputs of quite different branches. The questions and respective degree of detail concerning the branch-specific inputs can, for example, only be clarified through intensive cooperation between the federations and the official statistics offices. This survey furthermore entails an uncommon amount of effort and expense and, must therefore, contend with a high level of resistance. The federations contribute to the design of this survey in order that it is well-adaptable to the accounting system of the enterprises and encumbrances those surveyed as little as possible. Another example is the definition and delimitation of balance sheet items used in bank statistics. In this day and age of increasing differentiation among monetary and capital market instruments, the federation's relevant experience in the banking sector and in the utilization of bank statistics is particularly in demand.

Both, the continual adaptation to economic developments (e.g. the trend of outsourcing certain service functions, but at the same time the incorporation of further functions in the data processing and development divisions) and the effort to create more international harmonization requires constant revisions to be made to the systematics. This is a challenge for the federation not only with regard to its specialized know-how but also to its interests as a representational body for the branch.

In many surveys conducted by state offices, the federations and their data processing centers are an intermediary stop between those interviewed and the statistics offices and/or Federal Bank (which in the case of German banking statistics is the body conducting the survey and as such is an element of government statistics). The federations serve as a contact person for further inquiries. They can intelligently tie together these surveys with their own federation surveys, help in establishing methodological uniformity and assist in creating or improving technical preconditions for the surveys. Many official state surveys have a considerable planning phase because of the amount of time and energy needed to adjust the data processing instruments on either the enterprise or federation level to the exigencies of the survey.

The federations, acting in their own interest, provide more than their important assistance in the execution of governmental statistics; they are also an important medium for the government bodies concerning the propagation of the data and its interpretation. If it is no longer possible to convince wide sectors of society that statistical data have particular utility, it will be harder and harder for the field statistics to justify its ever more contested existence.

3. Federations and Data from Government Statistics; Methodological Problems

Many federations see it as their task to inform their members about the economic situation using branch-specific statistical information. Numerous federations also undertake investigations which aim to predict branch-specific development. For such predictions internal federation surveys (often involving subjective variables such as "business climate", investment plans, assessments of future developments, etc.) and prognoses from commercial forecasting institutes are processed in addition to the data available through government statistics offices.

All-encompassing explanations of developments in the business cycle as well as prognoses for individual branches (either undertaken as such or derived from a composite economic prognosis) present methodological statistical problems which have yet to be resolved adequately. Further tasks also challenge federation statisticians' knowledge of statistical methods in addition to these methodological problems. Above all, these include methods to construct appropriate descriptive statistics for comparisons; many federations which conduct their own surveys seek methodologies for the planning, execution and evaluation of sample surveys. It must be kept in mind in all cases, however, that federation statisticians must present their statistical considerations and interpretations to non-statisticians. The simple methods of descriptive statistics, therefore, are predominant in the statistical interpretation, because the most important criteria for the utilization of statistics are considered to be e.g. average values and ratios, and above all presentation (graphics), plausability and clearness.

Because federations often intervene in such procedures, the construction and maintenance of a data pool and the development of programs for statistical interpretation and prognoses are rationalized. Both of these functions require continued, intensive effort and engagement which individual companies can often not provide on their own. It is also not sensible to store such data which as such either are not used or only occasionally used in connection with other data only for specific analyses and branch comparisons.

III. Statistics Obtained by the Federations themselves

The statistical activities of many federations only extend to those tasks outlined under II. Nonetheless, many federations continue much further than this by

a) conducting periodic or one-time surveys on their own among their membership (internal statistics) and

b) making intercompany comparisons, that is comparing one individual company with other companies in the same group.

Because the intercompany comparison is an individual case study observation, in the strict sense it is not a statistical operation. Within the federations, the two operational tasks of "statistics" and "intercompany comparisons" are frequently conducted by separate departments. Because the intercompany comparison results from analyses of numerical information and draws upon average values from a comparison group (a defined and appropriate section of the branch) as a means of comparison, it, nonetheless, is methodologically related quite closely to statistics. The construction of relevant ratios and comparison groups is furthermore not only a managerial problem but also a statistical one.

1. Internal Federation Statistics

Continual internal federation surveys are also conducted as supplementation to the government statistics. These either fill the holes with respect to either the investigated facts or the categorization of the data material; e.g. balance sheet data is dominant in German government banking statistics, and certain variables are only recorded as aggregate sums (e.g. securities issued by universal banks and saving banks). Internal federation statistics fill in gaps inasmuch as they record items in the profit and loss account in shorter intervals and with greater actuality and/or investigate balance sheet information with greater detail. German banking statistics is also a good example for the varying emphasis of government statistics on the one hand and private/internal federation statistics on the other. Government statistics is structured around concerns affecting the economy as a whole. Aggregates such as the money supply (within various delimitations), the money level in the central bank or bank liquidity are the main considerations. Aside from data concerning interest levels and interest structure (according to maturity), asset and/or holding levels are predominantly researched. Banking statistics is thus primarily balance sheet statistics. Data from the profit and loss account are only drawn annually and published as a rule six months after the reporting date. In contrast to this, internal federation statistics, for example carried out by the federations of saving banks, is oriented around operational information. It includes, among other things, detailed monthly information about profit and loss accounts. Because of greater personal interest in such data the member companies are much more willing to provide information for federation statistics than for government statistics. One indicator for this is the greater frequency of related questions and inquiries as to when the results will be available. As a general principle, internal federation statistics are voluntary in nature; they do not always claim to be complete or representative in contrast to official (state) statistics. On the other hand, this instrument also provides for information to be collected which is difficult to come upon and accordingly requires a greater level of voluntary willingness to reveal.

Alongside such periodic surveys many federations conduct irregular but nonetheless repeated special surveys which in part assume the form of sample surveys (e.g. with longer intervals, say every five years). These mostly are concerned with questions affecting internal enterprise structure (e.g. training and further education programs) which supplement government statistics and serve to provide a more detailed description of the structure or current problems in a particular branch. An example of the latter is a sample survey investigating how car buyers have availed themselves of new forms of financing through a savings bank federation. Federations can also produce statistical information through special surveys which is of interest to people outside the federations themselves.

2. Intercompany Comparisons

Most of the federations' statistical data, at least for the individual member companies (FMC), serve in one form or another to enable intercompany comparisons to be made – the comparison of an individual company and/or enterprise to the average in the branch as a whole. In the realm of intercompany comparisons, the federation investigates individual FMCs, that is the federation describes and analyzes their performance using numerical bases. Such federation activity is only common in those federations which either provide a great deal of consulting or which can intervene and prescribe the business policy their individual FMCs should follow.

The intercompany comparison is based to a higher degree on the FMC's voluntary cooperation than is the case for the federations' statistical activities in a narrower sense. The federation hereby not only avails itself of information which became evident in the course of the statistical surveys but which was not otherwise published or revealed to (eventual) umbrella organizations because they are submitted to the regulations on data privacy protection; the federation can also utilize additional data especially gathered from both the FMC under investigation as well as from the base comparison group in order to facilitate the intercompany comparison.

IV. Federation Statistics and Member Enterprises

The FMCs are naturally more interested in the results of the federations' statistical activities than in their methodological requirements or in the particulars of the cooperation between the federation and the government statistics offices. Of these considerations the most important is the comparison between an individual company and the "average" in the particular branch characterized through data provided by the official statistics offices and supplemented in part by further detailed results gathered by internal federation statistics. Interest is directed above all to how a particular company performed with regard to certain items on the balance sheet and profit and loss account, to turnover levels for particular products as well as to those important factors which could influence foreseeable trends (e.g. factors which determine demand). In contrast to this, the information which the federation can provide with respect to economic policy – not infrequently related to branch-specific compilations of statistics and prognosis attempts – only plays a subordinate role in the eyes of the FMC. The federation hereby competes with other information sources which in part can more efficiently satisfy special information needs. More specialized and up-to-date information services (such as *Reuter's* monitors) are used by universal and saving banks, above all for money market dealings and investment consulting. The interest and attention which the individual FMCs give to the general economic information and the official statistical data processed by the federations naturally varies. Large FMCs frequently do not need such statistical work conducted for them as they undertake this themselves; small FMCs, on the other hand, often do not feel that they require such statistics because their limited field of business activity is hardly affected by macro-economic factors. One activity of the federation in this sector is nonetheless necessary, even when the FMCs do not avail themselves of the offered services to a degree proportionate to the amount of effort and/or money needed to provide this activity. Such statistics are namely a necessary precondition to fulfill other federation tasks and/or responsibilities, particularly in light of operational consulting and the representation of federation interests with respect to politics and other economic areas. For example, a federation of savings banks is expected to be in the position at any time to lay on the table statistically grounded comparisons between savings banks and universal banks addressing affairs or questions under contention – even if the applied data is of little relevance to the business policy of an individual savings bank.

Bibliography

DG Bank (ed.): Die Genossenschaften in der Bundesrepublik Deutschland (Statistik), verschiedene Jahrgänge.
Schulz, Udo: Die Statistik der gewerblichen Warengenossenschaften in der Bundesrepublik Deutschland, Marburger Schriften zum Genossenschaftswesen, Vol. 34, Marburg 1967.
Von der Lippe, Peter Michael: Wirtschaftsstatistik (4th ed.), Stuttgart 1990.

Federations, Co-operative

PETER SCHWARZ [F]

(see also: *Combine, Co-operative*; *Central Institutions*; *Structural Changes*; *Mergers and Consolidations*; *Federation Statistics*)

I. Origin, Functions, Structures; II. Special Problem Areas of Federation Management; III. Developmental Tendencies; IV. Outlook for the Future.

I. Origin, Functions, Structures

1. Concept and Description of Terms

Federations and co-operatives are considered as "types of cooperations" (*Schwarz* 1984) or "types of co-operative organizations" (*Dülfer* 1984). In this sense federations are organized systems in which independent entities work together and on the basis of common goals withdraw certain individual functions from their autonomous decision-making realm and transfer them to the co-operatives to be fulfilled (→ *Managerial Economics*). Membership in a co-operative of this kind is voluntary, as in Switzerland, or is required by law, as in the Federal Republic of Germany (→ *Legal Form, Co-operative*) and in Austria, where it is obligatory for members to be affiliated with a co-operative auditing federation (→ *Auditing*). "Voluntary" is a relative term, if affiliation is practically the only chance of survival. The members are owners of the co-operative and in democratic decision-making processes determine principal issues in the areas of objectives, potentials, and services. From their own circle they elect an honorary leadership and supervisory body (board of directors, administrative or supervisory council) which exercises the decision-making powers vested in it by the → *by-laws* and supervises the operational unit of cooperation. This unit is responsible for fulfilling the functions and performing the services of the co-operative through employed personnel and managers with their own delegated areas of authority (→ *Management in Co-operatives*). Leadership of the co-operative comes about through a division of labour and through cooperation among members, honorary office-holders, and full-time managers.

Co-operatives are to be distinguished from forms of concentration, in that members of forms of cooperation subject to collective decision-making bodies only those partial functions which they have specifically delegated, remaining independent in all other functions, whereas concentration cancels out all freedom to make decisions on the part of participants and centralizes that freedom in the concentrated enterprise. In the course of their development and growth, however, co-operatives have had the tendency to take over more and more partial functions from their members and thereby to create greater dependencies and closer ties.

Co-operatives are understood here to be primary cooperation whose members are participants in the economy as consumers, businessmen or craftsmen, or agricultural producers. Federations, on the other hand, are understood to be secondary cooperations with co-operative societies as members, or, at a higher level, as federations of federations (tertiary cooperations).

2. Functions and Services

Co-operative federations fulfill the functions conferred on them through production and performance of services. In this they are bound on principle to the *Förderungsauftrag* (→ *promotion mandate*) and to the identity principle: their services are reserved for members only, with the purpose of enhancing the economic activity of members in respect to efficiency

and effectiveness. The federations' service programme can be analysed and subdivided as follows (*Blümle/Purtschert* 1986):
a) Commercial business. Direct promotion of members in their purchasing, production, and sales functions through actual market relations (purchase and sale of goods), with pricing at the most favourable conditions for the members.
b) Services such as information, counselling, education and training, EDP computer centre, etc. depending on the kind and extent of services, there may be fees or prices to pay, or the services may be free (e.g. information or brief consultations). Auditing is also to be counted among services.
c) Representation of interests in the form of lobbying with the government, with apex associations (→ *Central Institutions*), and with organizations, or in the form of collective bargaining (negotiation and agreement) with other organizations, e.g. on the labour market.
d) Co-ordination services in the form of decisions, binding on all members, at the federation level on co-ordination, standardization, and norms, which the members then have to put into effect on their decentralized level in their everyday business.

In the areas of representation of interests and co-ordination, the federation produces so-called collective goods which benefit all participants in the economy, often even those who are not members of organizations (so-called free riders) (→ *Theory of co-operative Cooperation*). These are to be financed out of lump-sum contributions or out of a surplus from commercial business. According to this analysis of services, one distinguishes between single-purpose and multi-purpose federations, depending on whether they are active in one or several functional areas. One can also refer to multi-purpose federations if in the course of time a federation set up for one specific purpose branches out into other areas, for example if auditing federations begin to provide counselling and training services as well, or if lobby federations begin to spread into the performance of services.

3. Structures

For the fulfillment of the above-mentioned functions and services at the secondary level, there are different types of structures (*Bungenstock* 1984):
a) A multi-purpose federation fulfills several or all functions, mostly in the legal form of a registered co-operative. For single services, subsidiary companies (private corporations or public limited companies) can be set up which are entirely owned by the federation. These companies are also found as → *joint ventures* between secondary cooperations on the same level, if necessary with the support of the tertiary national cooperations. This form is common in Switzerland (for example,

agricultural federations, Raiffeisen banks (→ *Co-operative Banks*), and → *consumer co-operatives*).
b) On the secondary level two or even more cooperations are formed, with a tendency to single-purpose federations with a limited range of functions. In Germany and Austria these parallel organizations are inevitable because of the legally required auditing federations, if at the same time commercial business activities are to be conducted at the secondary level. Commercial cooperations at this level are called central co-operatives, central business organizations, head co-operatives, etc.

If the secondary level is on the state or regional level, then there are usually tertiary cooperations at the national level as well, here again as single-purpose or multi-purpose federations, in the latter case as parallel organizations of federations and central business organizations. Beyond them there are, at the most, co-operative apex or top federations comprising several branches of national co-operative organizations. Those federations, central business organizations, and their subsidiaries which are active in one particular branch of the economy are designated all together as a combine. In practice these elements are often interlocked in a complex manner by way of shares in equity capital. There are various legal forms and systems of ownership of the combine enterprises. Figure 1 shows an ideal-type combine model. It is important to point out that these combines are nevertheless built from the bottom up and are characterized by membership structures which ultimately make it possible to tie the whole complex to the interests of the membership basis. In this way, co-operative combines differ, at least in the legal set-up, from groups of profit-oriented companies.

II. Special Problem Areas of Federation Management

1. Nonprofit Character

Co-operatives and federations are designated as organizations which exist to support and promote the purposes of their members. They are structured on the basis of membership and oriented to filling their members' economic needs. These elements of membership and promotions mandate bring about both their character as → *non-profit organizations* and their special management problems, as, for example, the following:
- the organization of democratic decision-making processes and effective membership participation;
- the organization of leadership processes through co-ordinate → *honorary office* with professional management;
- the provision of services which are not subject to

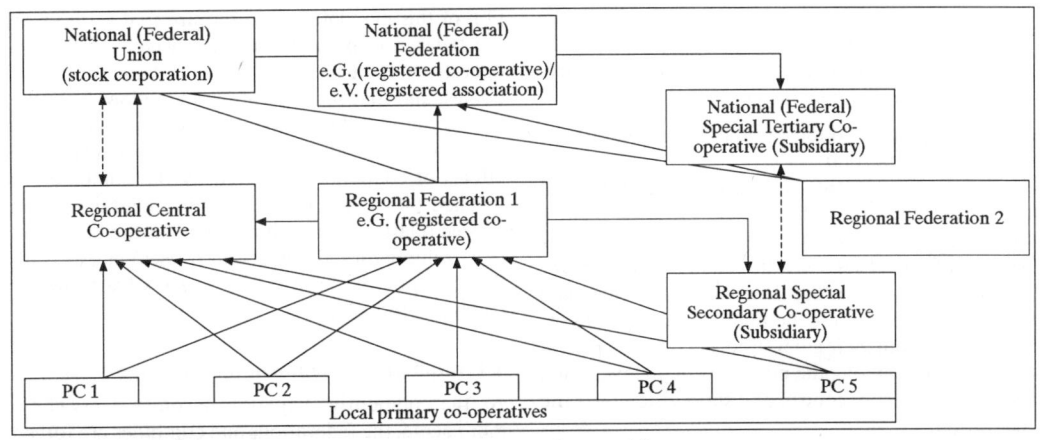

Figure 1: Ideal-type three-tiered structure of a co-operative combine.

the checks of market situations, such as free services and representation of interests;
- the assessment of success and its demonstration in balance sheet and plans of promotion.

Three observations can be made on the basis of this non-profit character:

a) In order to solve these special problems, one needs specific business administration approaches, since these questions do not arise in profit-oriented enterprises.
b) In order to be successful, non-profit organizations must consistently follow the rules of maximum efficiency and effectiveness, just like profit-oriented enterprises, and to this end they must make use of comprehensive leadership instruments, with emphasis on a future-oriented system of setting goals, planning, and supervising.
c) All in all, non-profit management is highly complex, because it has, on the one hand, to manage the operational unit and, on the other, to shape and deal with the democratic structure efficiently.

In what follows, essential problems specific to federations are to be dealt with (*Schwarz* 1984). For questions which apply equally to co-operatives, the reader is referred to the respective articles in this handbook.

2. Formation of Policies and Decision-making

The basic element of decision-making in the federation is the concerted action between the honorary body (board) and the employed business management. In practice the board makes decisions which the managers have prepared. The problem here, known as the staff-line syndrome or as "completed staff work", manifests itself, in the inferior position of the line (decision-making board) against the staff (decision-preparing manager). In federations the dominance of managers is further accentuated by the structural disadvantages of the honorary board compared with managers in terms of expertise, information, and available time. In order to shift this power discrepancy at least partially in favour of the board, the following measures are possible:

- Far-reaching delegation of decision-making powers to managers and limitation of the board to really essential and basic issues and functions, such as objectives, planning, and supervision (no retreating into details).
- Setting up the decison-making process as co-operative interaction, whereby in the first phase, after defining the problems and weighing alternatives, the board lays down individual options for solving the problems and thus makes preliminary decisions, which then serve the managers as binding guidelines for their proposals in the second phase. This interaction in phases demand frequent sessions with the character of workshops for solving problems.
- Election of holders of → *honorary office* at the primary level to the board of the federation. One can expect a deeper expert understanding of federation problems from these people than from members who do not hold office.

In order to ensure more effective participation on the part of the members, steps should be taken to improve the activity of the assembly of delegates:

- Limitation of the number of delegates. Huge assemblies are manipulatable and not capable of reaching decisions;
- Delegation of honorary office-holders from member co-operatives to the representatives' assembly. This will produce a democracy of the elite, which, however, is called for here on grounds of efficiency; but an excessive accumulation of offices by the same persons should be avoided;
- Preparation of the representatives' assembly by decison-making bodies on the primary level in order to obtain effective feed-backs between delegates and the wishes of the members at the base level;

- Retention of fundamental decisons (for example, on federation policies and strategies) by the highest body (assembly) in order to ensure a control over the board and management in basic areas.

Regarding board and representatives' assembly, the following is important:
Exclusion of, or at least limitation of the number of managers representing the primary societies. In principle, these professionals could contribute to a better balance of power vis à vis the federation managers, but, according to conflict theory, this also increases the estrangement of the members of the primary organizations from their federation, encourage a "*do ut des*"-tendency among the managers of all levels, and reduce the effect of control and supervision over the federation.

3. Distribution of Functions among Levels

The extent to which primary co-operatives delegate functions to higher levels rarely remains constant over the course of the years. As already mentioned, there is a definite tendency for the federation to take on more functions of the co-operatives with ever new services. Behind these tendencies there lies a redistribution of functions and ultimately of authority between the levels which co-operatives feel to be a threat to their autonomy. In many instances, however, the division of labour has developed over the course of time and has not been sufficiently clearly defined. To make a grouping of the whole complex of functions of the combine as unemotional as possible, the following analytical categories of functions should serve as the basis:

a) Decentralized autonomous functions which are to be fulfilled by the co-operatives within their own area of jurisdiction (e.g. determining the range of products).
b) Concerted, centrally co-ordinated functions which are to be fulfilled either by all or the majority of the co-operatives in an identical or similar manner or else jointly by co-operatives and the federation, and which require central concepts, guidelines, and instructions (e.g. advertising and public relations).
c) Central functions which are to be fulfilled by the federation alone (e.g. representation of interests).

According to this plan, functions are to be allocated to the various levels solely on the basis of expediency and efficiency. The approach shows clearly that the autonomy of the co-operatives is always only of relative nature, for not even in their decentralized autonomous area can they be considered absolutely independent, because even there they have to abide by superordinate group norms such as guiding ideas, policies, and marketing strategies (see below).
In this allocation of functions, the promotion mandate of the federation plays a role. A strict interpretation of this mandate would require that services by the federation be addressed exclusively to the co-operatives, their members, and their administrative bodies, and that the federation keep aloof from the relationships of the co-operatives to their own members. In practice this is rarely the case, because the effects of cooperation desired by the combine are reached only when the federation maintains direct service relationships with members at the base level (e.g. training for individual enterprises) or exerts influence upon the local markets (e.g. advertising for combine products).

4. Overall Co-ordination of the Combine

As the competitive situation becomes everywhere more acute, the federations and combines are forced to present themselves on the market as the most homogenous group possible in competition with others (→ *Competition*). The name of the federation then becomes a brand name (e.g. → *Raiffeisen* in the banking sector), if the combine succeeds in building up and conveying to the public a co-operative identity (COOPI) (*Purtschert* 1989) embodying the greatest possible uniformity in action, manner, and appearance. Group identity is defined in centralized resolutions at the federation level and is made to take root in the co-operatives by means of a general authorization to issue directives and enforce sanctions. What is more, the co-operative combine is welded together into a group sharing a common fate through joint liability (→ *Financing*) and obligation to make further contributions in cases of failure. No member co-operative may through negligence slip into taking advantage of these joint solidarity services, for this would endanger the existence of the entire combine. This danger can be avoided only if the federation possesses the necessary instruments of crisis management, namely the authority to issue directives and to intervene in the decision-making process of co-operatives in individual cases (e.g. the right of the federation laid down in the by-laws to appeal to the governing body of the co-operative).
Co-operative identity (→ *Dual Nature*) and crisis management give rise to a further restriction on the decentralized autonomous freedom of the co-operatives and a transition to overall co-ordination and combine control by the federation. It is clear that this development toward an integrated co-operative (*Dülfer* 1984) (→ *Structural Types*) cannot take place without internal power struggles; and it will take an outside threat to existence – and not just the determination of the federation manager to expand – to bring about this redistribution of authority.

III. Developmental Tendencies

The economies in fully developed industrial countries are characterized by internationalization or globalization and partly by liberalization of markets, tendencies toward concentration, and continuous technological progress. These factors cause certain courses of development in the co-operative sector which may differ from industry to industry. These effects are more pronounced, the more co-operatives and their members have a small business character, the larger and the more diversified the competing enterprises are, and the shorter the life span of products of the organizations is.

1. Innovation and Diversification

Even though the manifold "economies of scale" continue to justify the transfer of functions to the secondary level, still it is the "economies of skill" which will gain importance in the future (*Engelhardt* 1989). The dynamics of the markets put too much demand upon the co-operatives and their limited capacities. The necessary specialized and professional expertise as well as management and marketing know-how can be accumulated only at superordinate levels. This potential gives to federations and central co-operatives – in comparison to their members – a definite added value which manifests itself in the functions of leadership, drive, and promotion. It is the federations and central co-operatives who early detect trends which are relevant for the group, who formulate strategies, and who push forward the systematic development of the group. They push through product innovations in the marketing offers of the group, go to great advertising and marketing expenditure, and support co-operative employees and members through an intensive training and counselling programme in the fields of merchandising, management, marketing, technology, and computer science. In this way the federations expand their scope of action within the group and diversify their promotion services for their members (→ *Diversification Strategies*).

2. Concentration

Tendencies toward concentration have been apparent in the co-operative sector for years (*Lampert* 1989). Small primary co-operatives with a limited market potential, insufficient financial means, in some cases still parttime administrators, and difficulties in recruiting qualified people for honorary offices, have hardly any chances for survival. In order to achieve optimal or at least viable sizes among co-operative enterprises, federations take up active promotion and support mergers, with the consequence that the number of co-operatives and thus of decision-making centres in the combines becomes drastically reduced (e.g. consumer and → *rural co-operatives*).
Wherever distribution policies call for staying as near to the members or customers as possible, former co-operative units continue to operate as branches of bigger co-operatives. In this connection there is also the increasing tendency among federations and central co-operatives to establish new branch units themselves in order to fill gaps in the distribution network (e.g. consumer shops of agricultural co-operatives), or else to take over units from still-functioning co-operatives on lease and to operate them as branches of the federation (*Hill* 1989).

3. Centralization and "Grouping of Companies"

As the discourse thus far has clearly shown, the expansion of functions at the secondary level and with it the accumulation of power in the central organization to the detriment of primary societies is an apparently widespread and in most cases probably unavoidable and irreversible process. The establishment of branch units originally introduced at the primary level continues as "grouping" at the combine level. Connected with this trend is the tendency legally to convert co-operatives at various levels into joint stock companies, because this legal form can curtail democratic participation in the federation and open up a broader scope of action to offer the managers (*Ringle* 1989). Whether increased centralization actually is always the answer, or whether the benefit of cooperation is not entirely or partially nullified through the loss of small, adaptable, decentralized units with committed honorary officers and business managers, has to be weighed carefully from case to case (→ *Law* Concerning Company Groups).

4. Restructuring in the Co-operative Combine

In connection with centralization, even some combine structures whose origin was occasioned by historical circumstances and which have developed over the decades are being put into question. In order to stop this fragmenting of power and competition between groups, the following measures have been put into practice:

a) Reorganization of federation structures, as has taken place in the Federal Republic of Germany, for example, through the merger of industrial co-operatives (*Schulze-Delitzsch*) with rural co-operatives (*Raiffeisen*) and their integration into a new apex federation (*Schramm* 1985) (→ *Structural Changes*).
b) Reduction in the number of levels, as has been tried in Germany, for example, by the DG-BANK (German Co-operative Bank) by dissolving the co-operative central banks on the regional level (*Lürig* 1989, *Gerlen* 1990).
c) Complete abolishment of the variety of levels through the formation of a nation-wide super-co-operative, e.g. "Konsum Österreich" in Austria (*Rauter* 1983).
d) Establishment of branches to provide services in areas where, for reasons of distribution, federations want to bring their services closer to the co-operatives and their members (such as consult-

ations, training, and marketing support), in order to be able to work with lower costs and build up better personal relations.

IV. Outlook for the Future

In spite of these profound processes of change, often with a considerable weakening of co-operative principles and structures in industrial countries, people working in theory and practice are optimistic and predict that in the future the co-operative sector will continue to have a role to play. More and more co-operative essentials will tend to be sacrificed to increasing centralization, concentration, and integration of combines. But ultimately co-operatives and their federations will keep from losing their characteristic nature only if they maintain their membership-based structure and especially if sufficient well-qualified people remain active in honorary office and commit themselves to the interests of the members (→ *Corporate Culture*). Only through this strong potential of voluntary honorary leadership can the influence of managers be truly counterbalanced in decision-making processes.

Bibliography

Blümle, Ernst-Bernd/Purtschert, Robert: Genossenschaften, Verbände und Genossenschaftsverbände, Unterschiede und Gemeinsamkeiten. Die Prinzipien des Genossenschaftswesens in der Gegenwart, Nürnberg 1986, pp. 15–22.
Bonus, H.: Die Genossenschaft als modernes Unternehmenskonzept, Münster 1987.
Bungenstock, Wilfrid: Verbundbildung und Verbundformen im deutschen Genossenschaftswesen. Genossenschaften und Genossenschaftswissenschaft, Wiesbaden 1984, pp. 173–183.
Dülfer, Eberhard: Betriebswirtschaftslehre der Kooperative, Göttingen 1984.
Engelhardt, Werner W.: Zu theoretischen Analysen genossenschaftsspezifischer Vorteile und positiver Effekte. Finanz-, Bank- und Kooperationsmanagement, Frankfurt a./M. 1989, pp. 139–155.
Gerlen, Bernd: Zur Problematik der Zwei- oder Dreistufigkeit des genossenschaftlichen Bankenverbundes. ZögU Heft 1, Baden-Baden 1990, pp. 22–39.
Grochla, Erwin: Betriebsverbindungen, Berlin 1969.
Hill, Dietrich: Alternativen für das genossenschaftliche Warengeschäft von morgen. Finanz-, Bank- und Kooperationsmanagement, Frankfurt a./M., pp. 157–169.
Lampert, Heinz: Genossenschaften und Konzentration. Genossenschaften und genossenschaftswissenschaftliche Forschung, Regensburg 1989, pp. 49–65.
Lürig, Rolf: Mehr Synergie im kreditgenossenschaftlichen Verbund durch Zweistufigkeit? Finanz-, Bank- und Kooperationsmanagement, Frankfurt a./M. 1989, pp. 191–206.
Purtschert, Robert: Imagewerbung im Verband. Mitteilungen der Forschungsstelle für Verbands- und Genossenschaftsmanagement, Heft 1, Universität Freiburg/ Schweiz 1989, pp. 10–14.
Rauter, Anton E.: Konzentration im Handel, Wien 1983.
Ringle, Günther: Genossenschaften in atypischer Rechtsform? Zur Frage der Umwandlung eingetragener Genossenschaften in Aktiengesellschaften. Finanz, Bank- und Kooperationsmanagement, Frankfurt a./M. 1989, pp. 207–224.
Schramm, Bernhard: Die Neuformierung der genossenschaftlichen Spitzenverbände zum Aufbau einer geschlossenen genossenschaftlichen Bankengruppe. Aspekte bankwirtschaftlicher Forschung und Praxis, Frankfurt a./M. 1985, pp. 427–436.
Schwarz, Peter: Erfolgsorientiertes Verbandmanagement, Sankt Augustin 1984.
Schwarz, Peter: Management in Non-profit-Organizationen. Schriftenreihe "Die Orientierung" der Schweiz. Volksbank Nr. 88, Bern 1986.
Schwarz, Peter: Management in Nonprofit Organisationen, Bern/Stuttgart/Wien 1992.

Financial Accounting Law for Co-operatives

ERICH WEINERTH [J]

(see also: *Financing*; *Law, International*; *By-laws*; *Controlling*; *Equity Capital*; *Nachschußpflicht*; *Promotion Balance-sheet*)

I. Particularities of the Financial Accounting Law for Co-operatives; II. Common Elements of Financial Accounting for Merchants and Companies; III. The Law of Co-operative Financial Accounting; IV. Managing Co-operative Equity; V. Profit and Reimbursement; VI. Co-operative Fundamentals in the Financial Accounting Laws: Are They Taken into Consideration?

The prevailing financial accounting law of the Federal Republic of Germany will be thoroughly discussed in this article.

I. Particularities of the Financial Accounting Law for Co-operatives

The co-operative is an association of individuals striving for the economic promotion of its members through a collective business enterprise. This is how the fundamental task is formulated in co-operative law; the co-operative is to provide its members with economic outputs and/or services. (→ *Promotion Mandate*). These can be described as follows: a) providing a service, output, or benefit; b) transferring the returns of the output or service on to the members; c) creating and maintaining the collective business enterprise. The co-operative initially does not differ from other forms of business activity with its objective of providing a service. The co-operative principle can be so understood as structuring the business in such a manner that members can enjoy the greatest possible utility from it. The service or output should thus be so structured that the members can either have their income increased or their expenses reduced (→ *Assessment of Success*). Co-operatives therefore vary from other business forms which strive to achieve the largest profit possible or highest possible interest on their capital. Output and services are passed directly onto the members by granting them advantages, making co-operative facilities available for use, distributing (a surplus) in the form of commodities → *reimbursement*, and the like. In this context the question arises concerning the treatment of non-members who undertake business relations with a co-operative. Justification for business with non-members includes depleting unused extra capacities, exploiting market opportunities and recruiting new members (→ *Operational Size*).

The co-operative must also ultimately be preoccupied with establishing and safeguarding the collective business enterprise; reserves, a business site, stock, equipment, financial means and personnel are necessary as a rule (→ *Financing*). The means to construct and develop this business enterprise should be made available by the members in the form of business share participation, loans, and the like (→ *Equity Capital*). The financial situation of the co-operative is rounded off by borrowing for long-term investments and capital goods. Reserves should be accumulated to safeguard the financial status; they must ensure that the co-operative remains capable of promotion even when its member enterprises are in a weak position, say through setbacks in the business cycle. Realizing a profit through sufficient write-offs and the accumulation of quiet reserves to an acceptable dimension are thus also justified for co-operatives. According to § 7 of the → *German Co-operative Law* (*GenG*), a necessary item of the articles of association calls for the creation of a reserve fund. It is noteworthy, however, that according to co-operative law and affiliated statutes, no business assets can be paid out to a member before he/she withdraws from the co-operative, no interest or profit shares may be accorded to the paid-up shares, and no co-operative shares may be distributed. The liability of the board of directors according to § 34 of the *GenG* should be referred to.

II. Common Elements of Financial Accounting for Merchants and Companies

According to § 17, subsection 2 of the *GenG*, co-operatives operate like merchants in the sense of the *Commercial Legal Code* (in virtue of their legal form). The regulations of the *Commercial Legal Code* (*HGB*) are thus applicable as far as the *GenG* does not contain any divergent provisions. The obligation to keep account books, to draw up an annual financial statement and provide a situation report is binding on all merchants (*HGB*, Volume III, § 238 ff.). § 33 of the *GenG* details this obligation in that the co-operative board is bound to carry the responsibility that the necessary books are kept and that the annual financial statement and business report are presented to the supervisory board and general meeting. The general provisions of the *HGB* for co-operatives are amended in Volume III of the *HGB*, Part 3 (§§ 336–339). The fundamentals of financial accounting essentially conform to these: The amended provisions concern how the annual financial statement should be drawn up with an appendix and situation report, as well as optional explanations in the profit and loss account and its appendix. Likewise, the reappraisal provision also does not need to be used according to *HGB*, § 280.

III. The Law of Co-operative Financial Accounting

a) Procedures for classification and structure

In accordance with § 243 of the *HGB*, the annual financial statement should be drawn up following the principles of orderly bookkeeping. It must be clear and easy to survey and contain all assets, debts, deferred items, expenses and revenue as far as nothing else has been legally called for (*HGB*, § 246). The clearing of accounts is prohibited in Volume II of the *HGB*, § 242, which states that credit items may not be compensated for by debt items, expenses may not be set off against receipts, nor property titles with encumbrances. Capital assets and current assets, equity capital, debts and deferred items are to be indicated separately and adequately structured (*HGB*, § 247). Only those items are to be identified under the fixed assets which are designated to serve the business enterprise permanently (Vol.II of *HGB*, § 247). Special items with reserve shares are allowed in the liabilities items for tax purposes on income and revenue. Expenses for the establishment and accumulation of equity capital may not be included in the balance sheet (*HGB*, § 348); only those immaterial objects in the capital goods actually purchased may be included in the assets side of the balance.

Reserves should be created in accordance with *HGB*, § 249 for as of yet unknown payables and for potential losses from pending business. Furthermore, an obligatory reserve must exist for postponed maintenance expenses from the current business year which will have to be made within the first three months of the following business year, as well as for postponed waste removal expenses to be made in the following business year, guarantees which are to be fulfilled without legal obligation, and latent taxes. Expense reserves for postponed maintenance and waste removal as well as for fulfilling non-legally binding guarantees must be entered on the liabilities side of the balance sheet. The choice to enter delayed maintenance expenses also exists even if they will not be made within the first three months of the following business year but yet sometime within the following year. This is likewise true for expense reserves according to § 249, subsection 2 of the *HGB* — under the condition that this concerns exactly described expenses which, according to their particularity, must be assigned to the present business year or a previous one, the exact cost of which and whose date of incurrance remain unknown on the fixed-day of the financial statement, although the expenses are either certain or very probable.

The following items are listed under the breakdown of the reserves in the balance: 1) reserves for retirement payments and similar obligations; 2) reserves for taxes; 3) additional reserves. The updated *Commercial Legal Code* obliges all merchants to enter retirement payment obligations on the liabilities side of the balance sheet. This is not a retroactive provision, but rather was instituted for those directly eligible for receiving retirement in the future. The choice of entering pension payments effected before Jan. 1, 1987, and increases in payments which took place before Jan. 1, 1987, on the liabilities register still remains optional. The law affecting reserves, furthermore, contains thorough specifications. Aside from the definition of deferred items in *HGB*, § 250, the information concerning liability status is of particular importance. According to the prescribed structure in *HGB*, § 266, the balance should be drawn in account form. Special provisions concerning the type of blank form are in force for credit co-operatives (→ *Co-op. Banks*). The items listed on the assets and liabilities sides must be separated and identified in the given order; the usual elements of structure are to be followed. Small → *joint stock companies* and co-operatives are allowed to draw up an abridged balance in which only the items identified by letters or Roman numerals are included.

The structure of the balance is such that it is drawn for use as the annual result. As long as no legal provision stands in the way, the balance can also be drawn based on total or partial application of the annual result (*HGB*, § 268, subsection1). If the balance is drawn according to a partial application of the annual report (e.g. allocation to declared reserves), then the items "annual surplus/annual deficit" and "profit c.d./loss c.d." will be replaced with "profit from balance/loss from balance". A carried-down profit or loss item is to be included in the item "profit from balance/loss from balance" and must be noted in the balance or in the appendix.

b) Valuation procedures
The valuation procedures in *HGB*, § 252 apply to all merchants, including co-operatives. Deviations in exceptional, justifiable cases are to be included in the annual financial statement and explained. The valuation procedures were an essential part of the fundamentals of orderly bookkeeping and balance preparation even before they were inducted into law, and include the following: 1) formal continuity in the balance (balance identity); 2) continuation of the enterprise activity (going concern principle); 3) the principle of individual valuation; 4) the principle of fixed-date evaluation; 5) the principle of caution (principles of realization and non-parity); 6) the principle of delimiting time periods; and 7) valuation consistancy.

The fixed and circulating assets must be stated with a value no higher than their purchase or production cost minus depreciation (*HGB*, § 253, subsections 1–3). Upper limits are thus defined for co-operatives which may not be surpassed (see Art.33c, No.1 of *GenG aF*). Commercial undervaluation is permissible in the scope of orderly bookkeeping but is limited by the ban on arbitrariness. The criterion for a lowly quoted value is "reasonable business judgement" according to *HGB*, § 252, subsection 4. Still reserves thus are also permissible as long as they meet reasonable business judgement in the interest of the collective business enterprise of the co-operative. This is an appropriate provision which corresponds to the position of the long-term security of the co-operative business enterprise.

Because the calculation of purchasing or production costs along the lines of the prescribed principle of individual valuation in many cases is not possible or at least entails a large investment of time and/or work (particularly for stock levels), the law allows merchants a simplified valuation procedure in the scope of orderly bookkeeping principles. This concerns the set-value procedure (*HGB*, § 240, subsection 3), group valuation based on a weighed average (*HGB*, § 240, subsection 4), and the methods of tracing use/consumption (*HGB*, § 256).

It has not been layed down in co-operative law how the assets within the capital goods should be written off, although this has always been undertaken based on recognized managerial principles. According to *HGB*, § 253, subsection 2, scheduled depreciations are prescribed for merchants' objects and implements whose utilization is limited temporally. The schedule must distribute the purchase or production costs through the fiscal years in which it can be planned that the objects will be used. It is therefore necessary to estimate the forecasted utilization duration in the year of its procurement and to determine the depreciation method which corresponds to the elements of orderly bookkeeping. The principle of systematic arrangement implies that during the period of depreciation the estimated utilization duration and deprecation method can only be deviated from in exceptional situations. A transition from degressive to linear depreciation calculation is, however, not to be seen as an alteration of method but rather as appropriate to schedule.

In situations of forecasted continual depreciation, non-scheduled write-offs can be made (*HGB*, § 253, subsection 2, Sentence 3). The strict principle of lowest value applies for the valuation of circulating assets (HGB, § 253, subsection 2, Sent.1,2). In situations of depreciation, instead of the purchase or production costs, the lower exchange or market price is to be stated; if such a price is not ascertainable, the attributed value as of the final fixed-date is to be stated. Co-operatives are allowed further depreciation possibilities concerning the fixed and circulating assets according to HGB, § 253, subsection 4. They thus have the chance to create silent reserves (e.g. taxed valuation reserves, aggregate allowances on stock level). This provision is applied based solely on reasonable business judgement. The option that co-operatives also previously enjoyed vis-à-vis retaining a one-time, permissible lower given value even after the reason for this value no longer exists is laid down in § 253, subsection 5 of the HGB. This option to retain has a large importance for co-operatives for both circulating and fixed assets. The given values on the liabilities side are defined in § 253, subsection 1, Sent.2 of the HGB. According to this, liabilities should be stated at their repayment amounts, obligatory retirement payments at their cash values (for those people from whom no service in return can be expected), and reserves only at an amount deemed necessary according to reasonable business judgement. The reappraisal provision binding for joint-stock companies is not applicable to co-operatives.

c) The profit and loss account
According to § 275, subsection 1 of the HGB, the profit and loss account must be presented in graduated form. The profit and loss account is based on gross values; nothing can be balanced. Either the total cost procedure (HGB, § 275, subsection 2) or the sales cost procedure (HGB, § 275, subsection 3) can be used. These procedures vary from one another based on the way the sources of the return are presented. The items listed in the outline of the profit and loss account must be individually separated in the given order (HGB, § 275, subsection 1, Sent.2). Otherwise the structure of the profit and loss account is prescribed in § 265 of the HGB together with the appropriate provisions for the balance. This concerns the consistency of presentation, lists of the previous year's values, the possibility of further classification, and the opportunity of combining all subitems identified with Arabic numerals. Vacant items can be left out as long as no amount was entered under these items the previous year.

IV. Managing Co-operative Equity

Equity (→ *Equity Capital*) consists of the following classification structure in the HGB: 1) subscribed capital; 2) capital reserves; 3) retained earnings; 4) profit and loss carried forward; 5) annual settlement/annual deficit. Instead of subscribed capital, co-operatives must show the paid-up shares of the members in accordance with § 337, subsection 1 of the HGB. This item should be broken down into the paid-up shares of the remaining members, those of former members who have withdrawn, and of cancelled company holdings in accordance with § 67b of the GenG. In contrast to the procedures for joint-stock companies, the paid-up shares of the co-operative members should be listed with their nominal value (the amount paid). The overdue obligatory payments on the company holdings should either be shown separately in the assets or liabilities according to § 337, subsection 1 of the HGB, or noted in the balance under the paid-up shares of the members.

The particular classification procedures are due to the variable calculation of equity based on a company form with open membership. For the state of the co-operative, and also for its presentation to creditors, the indication of possible reductions in the amount of paid-up shares is very important: It is precisely this variability of membership capital which underlines the necessity of creating reserves. The term "capital reserves" has been recently adopted in German Financial Accounting Law. This reserve will most probably not be of much importance to the co-operative; one-time entrance fees, as long as they are still charged by co-operatives, must for example be put into the capital reserves. Co-operatives must indicate reserves from their return, which in effect are the same as their profit reserves. The deviation in the nomenclature of the co-operative in comparison to joint-stock companies expresses the varying goal orientation and objectives; these are reserves which are solely built from business profits.

The reserves from the return are classified into 1) statutory reserves and 2) other return reserves according to HGB, § 337, subsection 2. The creation of the return reserves should especially presented in the balance. It should be indicated which amounts were added by the general meeting from the profit indicated in the balance from the previous year, which ones were entered from the annual surplus of the present business year, and the amounts withdrawn for the current business year. This provision should facilitate an easier comparison of the balance with that of the previous year and easily indicate where any changes can be traced back to. The possibility of creating still reserves through which additional long-term security of the co-operative business enterprise can be attained has already been examined. It is to be noted at this point that arbitrariness is not permissible. This corresponds to the principle that the registered co-operative must not develop any capitalistic business interests of its own with respect to the natural promotion needs of its members in the sense of § 1 of the GenG.

V. Profit and Reimbursement

Co-operative → reimbursement as a specific means of promoting member enterprises is the result of the co-operative's development into a modern company. It has importance both in co-operative law and tax law, and furthermore plays a role in financing. In its legal nature it must be strictly differentiated in the corresponding dividend amounts and the pool of recipients from the profit distribution in connection with the acceptance of the annual financial statement. Profit distribution and surplus distribution (co-operative reimbursement) are two independent institutions and must be treated separately in co-operatives. A member receives the reimbursement due to him not based on the number of business shares subscribed by him or according to the amount of his paid-up shares, but rather entirely based on the level of turnover he himself ran up with the co-operative, from which the surplus accumulated. The reimbursement can be entered as a liability item according to legal tax provisions when the appropriate resolutions have been adopted and when the members have been granted legal claim accordingly in the articles of association.

VI. Co-operative Fundamentals in the Financial Accounting Laws: Are They Taken into Consideration?

Co-operative business studies and literature have been preoccupied with this question again and again. Certainly the efficiency of the promotional measures cannot be seen from the balance the way it is legally defined to be drawn. The problem is the measurability of the promotional success. Accountancy, structured in a business-like manner, is concerned with the economic situation of the enterprise, particularly that of retaining capital as an indicator of the company objective. This, however, is not a compatable instrument with which to measure and indicate co-operative success. The question concerning the presentation of the co-operative's success once again received impetus after the 1974 amendment which specifically called for the managing director to show particular conscientiousness and orderliness. This amendment reformulated the liability provisions for the board of directors and the supervisory board of a registered co-operative. As the law emphasizes the particular function of membership promotion through this formulation, the question must result for the board of how it can develop a co-operative business management, and for the supervisory board of what kind of business management it can expect from the board.

Measurability

The promotional benefit can be measured by the reimbursement. Dividends on capital are not suitable in the typical co-operative calculation procedures based on their character. Alongside payments in kind in the business relationship, there are also the additional services which the co-operative provides its member enterprises in contrast to its competitors. These are essential for co-operative success and are recorded through cost-accounting in the accounts of the co-operative. This is, however, by no means a suitable measure for the utility of the promotion provided for an individual member or group of members. Further measuring instruments must be developed. Inasmuch as commercial accounting is based on monetary values of measurement, it shows above all the limits of its capacity with respect to the measurement and identification of promotional success (→ *Promotion Balance-sheet*).

The annual business report is well suited to present the benefits of promotion. Inasmuch as the employment or application of means to provide the promotional benefit must be thoroughly presented in the explanatory statement, the supplemental report can limit itself to the presentation of the promotion benefits. Verbal commentary should present the contributions of the co-operative in this matter. The law thus did without introducing special procedures which effectuate the presentation of the promotion benefits. Singularly, a special report concerning the benefits the co-operative provided its members can be traced to the wording of the designation of liability for the board of directors and the supervisory board.

Bibliography

Beuthien, Volker: Genossenschaftsrecht woher – wohin?, Göttingen 1989.
Dülfer, Eberhard: Betriebswirtschaftslehre der Kooperative, Göttingen 1984.
Lang-Weidmüller: Genossenschaftsgesetz, 31st ed., Berlin 1984.
Meyer/Meulenberg/Beuthien: Genossenschaftsgesetz, Kommentar, 12th ed., München 1986.
Ohlmeyer/Bermann: Das neue genossenschaftsrechtliche Bilanzrecht, Wiesbaden 1986.
Ohlmeyer: Rückvergütung, genossenschaftliche, in: Handwörterbuch des Genossenschaftswesens, Wiesbaden 1980, cols. 1430–1440.

Financing of Co-operatives

HORST SEUSTER [F]

(see also: *Equity Capital*; *Financial Accounting Law*; *Discriminatory Analysis*; *Controlling*; *Accounting*; *Business Policies*; *Management in Co-operatives*; *Assessment of Success*; *Reimbursements*)

I. Definition of Financing; II. Content and Scope of Financing; III. Principles of Financing; IV. Rules of Financing; V. Possibilities for Financing Co-operatives.

I. Definition of Financing

In the science of business administration, the term "financing" has not been uniformly defined. In the course of time its meaning has been gradually extended. Today the term signifies both the procurement of the means of financing as well as the expenditure of them, including repayment, whereby one must distinguish between a financing concept oriented to a balanced budget and one oriented to decisions (→ *Management in Co-operatives*). Without going any deeper here individually into the many definitions advocated from time to time, the present author determines financing to be understood as the procurement, utilization, and repayment of capital, as well as its planning and supervision (→ *Controlling*). Thus, in addition to the simple procurement of financial means, their use and disposition are also included nowadays among the functions of financing. In contrast to older definitions, therefore, both a broadening of the content of the term financing as well as an explanation of the meaning have taken place.

II. Content and Scope of Financing

1. Vertical Flow of Financing

The overall financing complex includes various individual functions, which, in their teleological sequence, constitute the chain of functions in financing:

1. Planning (rough, overall planning) of finance
2. Clarification (detailed planning) of finance
3. Decision on finance
4. Procurement of means of financing
5. Utilization of means of financing
6. Repayment of means of financing
7. Supervision of means of financing
8. Accounting

(For further information, cf. *Seuster* 1981).

2. Horizontal Structure of Financing

According to *Vormbaum* (p.14), financing in the wider sense comprises the following measures:
Content and Scope of Financing

1. Procurement of capital
   a. From outside (raising of capital)
      1. As equity capital
      2. As borrowed capital
   b. From inside (Capital growth)
      1. Retention of profits
      2. Formation of capital within the enterprise through laying aside reserves
2. Release of capital (Transformation of assets into liquid funds)
   1. Liquidation of parts of property
   2. Depreciations
   3. Other forms of release of capital
3. Capital restructuring
   1. Borrowed capital into equity capital
   2. Equity capital into borrowed capital
   3. Within equity capital
   4. Within borrowed capital
4. Capital drain
   a. Toward the inside (Capital loss)
      1. Of equity capital
      2. Of borrowed capital
   b. Toward the outside (Capital repayment)
      1. From equity capital
      2. From borrowed capital

Because in practice, financing occurs in various types and forms, it is necessary to point out the terms that come up in this connection and their meanings, however with a certain limitation.

According to the frequency or periodicity of occasions requiring financing, a distinction is drawn between one-time financing and recurrent financing.

According to the sources of capital, one can categorize as follows:
a. Financing from own resources
   aa. Financing by shareholders
   ab. Participatory financing
   ac. Self-Financing
b. Outside financing

In contrast to earlier definitions, the concept of financing from own resources has been expanded and is now the categorical form for all sources of capital from the property of the entrepreneur or entrepreneurs. Now at last there is an identity of meaning between financing from own resources and → *equity capital*, as has always been the case between outside financing and borrowed capital.

To be more specific, one speaks of financing by shareholders (aa) when the entrepreneur running the business supplies capital or the means of financing from his own sources, which, however, must come from outside the business, such as from private property. The participatory financing (ab) includes capital from owners or co-owners who are not themselves active in the enterprise (e.g. a partner in a limited company); but this capital also enters the business from the outside.

In contrast to this, self-financing (ac) comes from within the enterprise. Part of the profit as well as the proceeds from depreciation allowances are immediately re-invested. In this last case, however, no additional flow of capital into the business takes place, but merely a restructuring of property. For this reason one also speaks of non-genuine self-financing or simply of shifting or restructuring finances.

In the case of outside financing, capital is also brought into the business from the outside, but in the form of loans. The contributors of capital are creditors, not owners, of the business and have a right to interest payments and repayment of their investment.

Self-financing falls under internal financing (Binnenfinanzierung). On the other hand, financing by share-holders, participatory financing and outside financing fall under external financing. Now and then, however, the procurement of capital on the capital market alone is considered to be external financing. Depending on the direction of the capital flow, there is yet another possible form of differentiation: what the creditor does is then called active financing; and what the debtor does is called passive financing.

Depending on the degree to which a business is equipped with capital, one can speak of normal financing, under-financing, or over-financing. In the case of normal financing, the financial situation of an enterprise is balanced, i.e. all three principles of financing (cf. section III of this article) are taken into account; therefore one can also speak here of optimal financing. But in the case of under-financing a shortage of capital prevails, and in the case of over-financing a surplus.

III. Principles of Financing

1. General Goal

The principles of financing constitute the rules for mastering financing functions in an enterprise in a more or less idealistic way. But the financing functions must be compatible with the higher general economic goal of the enterprise, commonly called the efficiency rule (→ *Principles*). With reference to the finance sector, this main goal can be expressed more concretely as maximization of income (capital income) with regard to the liquidity and stability of the enterprise.

2. Profitability

In the long run the economic goal can be achieved only if the economic process is profitable, i.e. if the return on input is higher than the outlay, given the complete preservation of assets and liabilities and the constant ability to pay. Therefore it is a prime function of the entrepreneur (so well known a principle as to require no further explanation) to determine and realize the optimal input of capital, in view of the given possibilities.

3. Liquidity

An enterprise can exist in a free market economy only if it is able to fulfill its financial commitments to pay at any time. The quantitative expression of this ability to pay is liquidity, specifically liquidity for a given date and liquidity for a given period. Therefore a very important function of the financing policy of the entrepreneur is to create a situation as close as possible to optimal liquidity, which means having as many liquid funds at a given time as necessary, but not more than required. All other situations of liquidity, i.e. surplus or shortage of liquid funds, lead to lower profitability; in the case of insolvency they can even lead to bankruptcy.

4. Stability

The third principle of financing, stability, refers to the volume and structure of the economic assets or the economic capacity of the enterprise and is to be understood in a dynamic sense. An enterprise desiring to maintain its economic position in relation to the economy as a whole or to other enterprises must attain the average growth rate of the economy as a whole. Any devation from this principle signifies a greater than average expansion of the individual enterprise or a loss of economic capacity. This aspect of stability can also be termed prosperity.

Nevertheless, the future of an enterprise is not guaranteed if merely the development of assets and liabilities corresponds to their average development in the overall economy. Not only the absolute or relative capacity (economic potential) of the enterprise must be ensured, but also the structure of the assets. This structure must be so developed as to adapt to changing conditions, to possess what in economic theory is called elasticity or flexibility, especially with regard to re-investments. That this adaptation of the structure of assets should take place without friction is an important prerequisite for ensuring the stability of the enterprise.

Because of the strong interaction of all three principles of financing, it is superfluous to ask which principle takes precedence over another. They must all be put into effect as far as possible, if the enterprise is to function at its economic optimum.

IV. Rules of Financing

1. Optimal Volume of Capital Input

In an enterprise in a market economy, the input of capital i.e equity capital and borrowed capital – is realized according to the so-called principle of expense-backing. That is to say, with regard to profitability a gradual capital input is permissible as long as the capital costs are at least covered by the capital yield. In this case, it is implicit that the factor capital follows the law of diminishing returns. The revenue from invested capital must be at least as high as the expenditure for capital. Therefore, the input of capital may increase up to the point where the marginal capital revenue is equal to the marginal expenditure for capital. But over and above this, the two other principles of financing (liquidity and stability) must also be taken into consideration.

2. Relation between Equity Capital and Borrowed Capital

Another question in financing is what the relation should be between owned capital and borrowed capital. The common answer is that the most expedient capital structure – i.e. the advisable relation between equity capital and borrowed capital – should correspond to the structure of assets. A former maxim states that fixed assets should correspond to long-term capital and current assets should correspond to short-term funds. This is the restrictive implementation of the so-called *golden balance sheets rule*. But an analysis of the balance sheets of actual enterprises very soon reveals that this ideal case cannot be realized in practice (→ *Accounting*). Nowadays the modern maxim is not so restrictive and prescribes that part of the fixed assets can be financed by borrowed capital, but it must be in the form of long-term loans.

3. Utilization of Capital till the Time of Maturity and Capital Life Span

One discusses the utilization of capital till the time of maturity and capital life span only when capital is available solely for a limited time. Apart from some special cases of financing from the enterprise's own resources, a time limit exists only in the case of borrowed capital. The golden rule of financing requires that long-term investments or assets shall be financed by long-term loans and that short-term investments may be backed by short-term funding. The discussion of the problem begins automatically with the interpretation of the term "long-term assets". On the one hand, these are simply what we call fixed assets; but on the other hand they also contain a base stock of current assets. However, the golden rule of financing is correct in requiring that long-term assets shall be backed by long-term capital (equity capital and long-term loans).

There now follow some remarks about the second part of the golden rule of financing, which is that current assets may be financed by short-term loans. With regard to the funding of a single project, this rule holds true. But since the production process of an enterprise is generally not a single operation but normally an on-going, permanent affair, and since with regard to short-term funds there is usually a standing need for such short-term capital in the following period as well as in the present one, the fact of the matter is that in most cases there is a permanent need for short-term funds. However, a permanent need for short-term capital can be filled only if there is a revolving system for obtaining these funds. The second part of the golden rule of financing would then appear to be superfluous.

A permanent demand for short-term funds means that a basic stock of these funds is necessary, in which case it should be considered whether such a permanent demand would not be better financed through long-term credit, which has a lower interest rate than short-term credit. Long-term credit has the further advantages of rendering a liquidity squeeze rarely and, with regard to the stability of the enterprise, of doing away with a part of the uncertainty of financing in the future. Therefore, all three financing principles are served when the basic stock of current assets is financed through long-term credits.

V. Possibilities for Financing Co-operatives

1. General Possibilities

The possibilities for co-operative financing depend to a large extent on the laws of the respective countries (→ *Law, International*). As it is impossible here to go into all the different legal situations in a sufficiently adequate way, the author of this article wishes to limit himself to the situation in the Federal Republic of Germany (→ *Law, National*).

First of all, the following list shows the variety of possibilities for financing co-operatives in Germany:

1. Equity financing (equity capital)
   1.1 Shares in the co-operative (members' equity in the co-operative)
      a. Shares paid in by members
      b. From profits or surplus credited to members
   1.2 Members' liability amount
   1.3 Reserves
      a. Capital reserves required by law
      b. Reserves accumulated voluntarily
   1.4 Short-term possibilities for equity financing
      a. Reserves for contingencies
      b. Hidden reserves
      c. Adjustments of valuation
      d. Temporarily accumulating self-finance funds
2. Profit-participation rights
3. Outside financing (borrowed capital)
   3.1 Long-term loans
      a. Mortgages
      b. Bank credits
      c. Loans from members
      d. Debenture loans
      e. Loans from employees
   3.2 Medium-term and short-term loans
      a. Credit from suppliers (credit on the current account)
      b. Bank credits
      ba. Credit on the current or drawing account
      bb. Discount credit (bills of exchange payable)
      bc. Acceptance credit
      bd. Credit against guarantees
      be. Collateral loans
      bf. Letters of credit
      c. Leasing
      d. Factoring

From this list, the abundance of possibilities for financing will be evident. Since financing from own resources including profit-participation rights will be discussed in a separate article (→ *Equity Capital, Co-operative*), it is possible here to restrict the discussion to the outside financing of co-operatives.

2. Outside Financing

a. Long-term Outside Financing

aa. General Possibilities

Long-term credits are outside funds which are borrowed for a period of more than one year; but in some industries this period is even longer (for example, in agriculture it is ten years or more).

The most common form of long-term credit is a loan;

in this case credit funds are turned over to the borrower for a specified period with the promise of repayment and interest.

Depending on the conditions of repayment, the following forms of loans exist: 1. one-time repayment loan (bullet repayment loan) or cancellation loan, 2. redeemable loan, and 3. annuity loan.

A one-time repayment loan (bullet repayment loan) or cancellation loan is characterized by the fact that at the end of the term the full amount of the loan is repaid in one lump sum. The end of the term can be reached either through cancellation of the loan or through the wording of the credit contract, in which the duration of the loan and thus the deadline for repayment are agreed upon ahead of time. In this form of loan, the full original amount of money is at the borrower's disposal for the entire period of time for which credit has been granted. During that period, only the interest falling due must be paid.

The redeemable loan, on the other hand, is characterized by the fact that instead of a one-time repayment, equal repayment installments are usually agreed upon, dispersed over the entire loan period. Since in this way the amount of credit steadily decreases on which interest must at intervals be paid, the amount of interest itself decreases as repayment of the loan progresses. The borrower's overall annual burden of amortization and interest-payment is thus gradually reduced over the course of the term of the loan.

By contrast, an annuity loan is characterized by a uniform annual burden of debt-repayment and interest payment. Because at the beginning of the loan-term the interest is relatively high, the repayment of the debt itself is at first minimal; but as the loan-term progresses, the proportion of interest to debt-repayment shifts in favour of debt-repayment.

The typical features of, or differences between, the three forms of loans can be summarized as follows: One-time or bullet repayment loan – constant interest payment; redeemable loan – constant rate of loan repayment; annuity loan – constant yearly burden.

With regard to the relative preferability of these loan forms, a decisive role is played not only by the sums to be repaid and the deadlines, but also by the purpose of the loan and its economic effect, as well as by the overall financial and economic state of the enterprise, which by their very nature can be taken into consideration only from case to case.

Financial institutions which deal mainly with medium-term and long-term loans are the following:

1. Mortgage banks;
2. Banks and savings banks;
3. Insurance companies;
4. Building and loan societies.

Mortgage banks lend their money either directly to the consumer or indirectly through banks. Banks (→ *Co-operative Banks*) and savings banks can themselves lend out only a certain percentage of investments in the form of medium-term and long-term loans; over and beyond that they refinance themselves through their central banks or through mortgage banks. Insurance companies invest a portion – the largest portion – of accumulated premiums not needed for insurance reimbursements in medium-term and long-term loans, usually under special conditions. Building and loan societies grant housing or building loans primarily to investors who have accumulated savings with them beforehand; in other words, these are loans for a definite purpose and usually have a lower claim status in case of bankruptcy. A further generally-available possibility for long-term financing is that of debentures, in which case life insurance companies primarily come into consideration as creditors.

Co-operatives cannot obtain long-term outside capital in the form of legally attested securities, because they have no access to the capital market. However, some apex institutions in the co-operative bank sector have issuance rights with which they can obtain credit on the capital market (for example, the German Co-operative Bank and the German Co-operative Mortgage Bank) (→ *Central Institutions*).

bb. *Possibilities for Long-term Financing Specific to Co-operatives*

Besides the usual loans, there are other long-term financing possibilities available particularly to co-operatives, for example loans from co-operative members, which are comparable to loans from partners in partnership businesses. The amounts of these loans do not constitute equity capital of the co-operative; they are outside capital from members. In the framework of government policy to create ownership by having employees participate in savings and share-owning schemes, deposit loans from employees are resorted to most frequently, in addition to employee shares of stock, which predominate in joint-stock companies. Although loans from members and employees can in individual cases quite rightly contribute to the supply of capital of a co-operative, they play only a minor role when compared to the total need for outside capital of all co-operatives together.

b) Short-term and Medium-term Outside Financing

aa. *General Possibilities*

According to generally-applied bank statistics, credits are designated as short-term or medium-term if the periods for which the credits are granted comprise up to three months or one full year, respectively. But here, too, there are differences from one branch of the economy to another, for example, in agriculture.

Particularly in the case of those co-operatives (co-operatives for promoting the interests of their members) which are generally grouped with merchandising enterprises, the trade credit (also called commodity credit or supplier's credit) plays a significant role. It is directly connected with a sales transaction for goods, through the fact that for a certain time the supplier advances on credit the amount which the purchaser owes. Trade credits range from current account credits, in which the trader assumes the keeping of the accounts, to supplier's drafts (among others, bills of exchange), to the granting and utilization of repayment deadlines as well as advanced payments on later deliveries. The trade credit is thus a special form of short-term credit with several distinctive features. The co-operative can become a borrower in relation to the supplier this way, as well as a lender in relation to its members or its customers. Taking everything into consideration, the trade credit has a number of disadvantages, however, in comparison with a bank credit (cf. *Seuster* 1981), so that despite its being widely used, it should be taken up only after careful deliberation.

To span foreseeable times of financial pressure, short-term and medium-term credits are often taken in the form of bank loans, as, for example, seasonal loans. These are granted above all as a current account loan, a discount credit connected with the purchase of commercial bills of exchange, or an acceptance credit, by which is meant the acceptance of a bill of exchange drawn on the bank by a co-operative. The acceptance credit is of special importance in the import and export business.

In addition, certain special forms of short-term and medium-term credits should also be mentioned: the Lombard or collateral loan, the guarantee credit, and the letter of credit. In the case of a guarantee credit, the bank agrees to stand surety for the co-operative up to a certain sum. The Lombard or collateral loan is a credit on the basis of pledging securities or goods. Letter of credit generally means the promise of a bank under certain conditions to make payments for a third party, a form of credit which is particularly frequent in the field of foreign trade. Further possibilities and special features of short-term and medium-term financing (documentary credit, commercial letter of credit, and negotiation) cannot be gone into here.

bb. Substitute Ways of Financing

The possibilities now to be discussed do not constitute financing in the traditional sense, but rather possibilities which enable one to economize on means of financing, such as leasing and factoring.

By leasing is generally meant dealings in renting or leasing property. On the basis of a contract which usually runs for three to five years, the lessor undertakes to put at the disposal of the lessee certain consumer or capital goods in return for a fixed, usually monthly fee, known as the leasing installment rate. In addition to the costs of crediting, this leasing or renting installment rate generally includes still other cost components, for example those for the erection and dismantling, the maintenance, the remaining value, and the risk of the leased property, besides the fee of the lessor. On the whole, the terms of leasing contracts are decidedly flexible, so that only in concrete individual cases is an evaluation possible; but in general leasing contracts can be regarded as favourable only when the leasing installment payments are fully tax-deductible as business expenses and when one can thus save money on taxes. In all cases where tax advantages cannot be brought to bear, the traditional possibilities for financing are usually cheaper, particularly when real securities for long-term credit (that is to say, relatively cheap credit) can be taken advantage of.

According to the type of leasing property, one distinguishes between the following:

1. Leasing of movables (contracts on movable economic goods, i.e. consumer goods and capital goods)
2. Leasing of real estate (contracts on immovable economic goods, i.e. pieces of land and buildings).

According to the position of the lessor, one distinguishes between the following:

1. Direct leasing (contracts which are concluded directly with the producer of the property to be leased)
2. Indirect leasing (contracts whereby an independent leasing company as financing firm is interposed between the producers of the leasing property and the lessee. This company purchases the leasing property for the producer).

According to the nature of the obligations assumed in the leasing contracts, one distinguishes between the following:

1. Operation leasing contracts (normal rent contracts which can be terminated by either party immediately or else after observance of a relatively short period of notice)
2. Finance leasing contracts (contracts which may not be terminated until the end of a rental period agreed upon between the lessor and the lessee).

A special kind of short-term crediting widespread in the United States, known as factoring, is yet to be mentioned. In the factoring system the so-called factor assumes toward others not only a financing function but also a credit-securing function. The claim resulting from the purchasing contract is transferred from the purchaser to the factor, who receives a margin whose extent naturally depends greatly on the type of business to be transacted. But over and above this, the factor often assumes still further functions: billing, collection of amounts owed, customer bookkeeping, counseling of the contract partners, and others. The factoring system thus includes more than the mere granting of credits. All in all, there are definite possibilities for the use of factoring in the co-operative sector, a conviction which day-to-day business dealings also confirm.

Bibliography

Beckmann, Liesel: Finanzierung. Handwörterbuch der Betriebswirtschaft, Stuttgart 1961, Col. 1830–1834.
Büschgen, Hans E. (ed.): Handwörterbuch der Finanzwirtschaft, Stuttgart 1976.
Chmielewicz, Klaus: Finanzierung IV: Finanzierung Planung. HdWW, vol. 3, Stuttgart-Tübingen-Göttingen 1981, pp. 83–97.
Coenenberg, Adolf Gerhard: Die Einzelbilanz nach neuem Handelsrecht, Düsseldorf 1986.
Dichtl, Erwin/Issing, Otmar (eds.): Vahlens Großes Wirtschaftslexikon, München 1982.
Fettel, Johannes: Kapital. Handwörterbuch der Betriebswirtschaft, Stuttgart 1961, col. 2959–2963.
Fischer, Otfried: Finanzierung II: Arten und Formen, HdWW, vol. 3, pp. 31–59, Die Finanzen, Berlin-Heidelberg-New York 1970.
Grochla, Erwin: Finanzierung, Handwörterbuch der Sozialwissenschaften, vol.3, pp. 604–616, Stuttgart-Tübingen-Göttingen 1961.
Hahn, Oswald (ed.): Handbuch der Unternehmensfinanzierung, München 1971.
Heinen, Edmund: Handelsbilanzen, Wiesbaden 1986.
Janberg, Hans (ed.): Finanzierungshandbuch, Wiesbaden 1970.
Kalveram, Wilhelm: Finanzierung der Unternehmung, die Handelshochschule, vol. 1, pp. 1257–1375, Wiesbaden 1929.
Koch, Helmut: Finanzplanung, Handwörterbuch der Betriebswirtschaft, col. 1910–1925, Stuttgart 1956/61.
Kolbeck, Rosemarie: Finanzierung III: Vorgänge, HdWW, vol. 3, pp. 59–83, Stuttgart-Tübingen-Göttingen 1981.
Koschka, Helmut: Finanzierung der Genossenschaft, Handwörterbuch des Genossenschaftswesens, col. 459–482, Wiesbaden 1980.
Kosiol, Erich: Finanzmathematik, Wiesbaden 1966.
Le Coutre, Walter: Vermögen, Handwörterbuch der Betriebswirtschaft, col. 5785–5791, Stuttgart 1956/61.
Lipfert, Helmut: Optimale Unternehmensfinanzierung, Frankfurt 1969.
Mändle, Eduard/Winter, Hans-Werner (eds.): Handwörterbuch des Genossenschaftswesens, Wiesbaden 1980.
Schmalenbach, Eugen: Die Finanzierung der Betriebe, vol. 1, Köln-Opladen 1951.
Schneider, Dieter: Investition und Finanzierung, Köln und Opladen 1970.
Seuster, Horst/Gerhard, Stephan: Verbesserung der Eigenkapital Ausstattung bei Kreditgenossenschaften, Manuskript, Gießen 1989.
Stützel, Wolfgang: Liquidität, Handwörterbuch der Sozialwissenschaften, vol.6, pp. 622–629, Stuttgart-Tübingen-Göttingen 1959.
Swoboda, Peter: Finanzierung I: Theorie, HdWW, vol. 3, pp. 17–18, Stuttgart-Tübingen-Göttingen 1981.
Swoboda, Peter: Finanzierung I: Theorie, HdWW, vol. 3, pp. 18–31, Stuttgart-Tübingen-Göttingen 1981.
Vormbaum, Herbert: Finanzierung der Betriebe, Wiesbaden 1971.
Wöhe, Günter: Bilanzierung und Bilanzpolitik, München 1987.

Forms of Cooperation in the Agricultural Sector Assuming Non-Co-operative Legal Forms

EBERHARD SCHINKE [J]

(see also: *Legal Form, Co-operative*; *Law, National*; *Law, International*; *Machinery Associations/Rings*; *Managerial Economics*)

I. Forms and Definitions; II. Diffusion and Range of Activities; III. Legal Forms.

I. Forms and Definitions

Farmers all throughout the world have united together in legal and organizational forms other than co-operatives (→ *Supply Co-operatives*; → *Marketing*; → *Joint-production Co-operatives*). It is, however, not always universally possible to delimit these other forms clearly from co-operatives. This is true for both those countries which themselves do not have a co-operative law (→ *Law, International*) as well as for those in which a co-operative law exists but where almost identical forms of cooperation can be encountered either as co-operatives or in other legal forms with regard to goal orientation, organization, and range of activity.

Two forms of cooperation can in principle be differentiated from each other (→ *Classification*) according to whether the partner companies found a new collective institution or not. In the former situation, the partners in the cooperation envest the newly founded institution with certain functions which it then executes exclusively for all partners. This situation is likewise at hand when a non-co-operative legal form is chosen whose structure is comparable to that of a co-operative (it likewise assumes certain functions for its members). In the latter situation, the creation of a special institution is dispensed with. Contracts are nevertheless also concluded in which the nature and extent of the cooperation are settled. The delineation between these two forms of cooperation is not always clearly recognizable in practice. On the one hand, arrangements concerning cooperation in other spheres of interest are likewise often made above and beyond the cooperation in a joint institution. On the other hand, both forms are used to achieve the same objective when the function is viewed, and thus both forms resemble each other in the course of their organizational structure. Outside observers, for example, cannot discern without further ado whether the joint utilization of machinery by two neighboring enterprises follows according to the principle of the machinery ring or of the machinery association (→ *Machinery Associations/Rings*). In the former case, only an agreement between the partners needs to exist whereas for the association a jointly run business operation always exists, even when it is comprised of only two members.

If all functions of the partner companies are conveyed to the joint institution rather than only several of them, that is when a full consolidation is executed, one can no longer speak of cooperation in the narrow sense of the word as the cooperating companies as such have ceased to exist. This situation is identical to that upon the establishment of a production co-operative (→ *Joint-production Co-operative*). It should nevertheless be taken into consideration since such a situation frequently marks the completion of a step-by-step, interlocking process of cooperation and, therefore, is generally classified under the category of cooperation.

II. Diffusion and Range of Activities

1. Utilization of Tangible Assets

The multi-enterprise utilization of machinery in farming is by far the largest and most important scope of activity in the agricultural sector both in Germany and its neighboring West European countries. In western Germany, only very few farmers do not work together with professional colleagues in this field in one manner or another. The reasons for this cannot be found solely in enterprise structures and land dimensions which are less than optimal; larger enterprises even vigorously embrace the advantages of financing and capacity utilization which go hand in hand with the employment of machinery on a multi-enterprise level. Multi-enterprise machine employment furthermore facilitates both seasonal adjustments to labor input and improved access to special machines and specialized operating personnel. There are quite a few enterprises which regularly have considerable amounts of their fieldwork taken care of them by personnel and machines hailing from partner enterprises and/or organizations co-ordinating the multi-farm employment of machinery. Western Germany thus serves as a model of this development which can be found in all highly developed countries where an intensive agricultural sector exists.

The machinery association and machinery ring, also known and well-dispersed under the same or similar names beyond Germany, assume a dominating position among the forms of multi-enterprise machinery employment. They are thus discussed under their own heading in this publication (→ *J. Kuhn: Machinery Associations/Rings*). In the agricultural sector, numerous agreements exist alongside these forms concerning the occasional or regular entrustment of machines with or without personnel. These are usually pooled together under the term "community assistance". As mentioned above, these could function through and through as machinery rings, although as a rule they are not named as such. In Poland, a special legal form exists under the name "agricultural circle" (Kolka Rolnicze) in which, among other things, multi-enterprise machinery employment is undertaken to a great extent. This form stretches back historically to the 19th century, was originally co-operative-like in nature, and fell heavily under state control in the communist era; this institution can be found throughout the country and has the legal form of an association.

Cooperations for the collective utilization of capital goods aside from those for motorized vehicles and mobile machines can be found for practically all other capacities, such as for field irrigation and drainage, water supplies for farmsteads, stalls and pastures, the production and provision of electricity, storage, processing, feed production, etc. These are predominantly managed as co-operatives but can assume all other permissible legal forms in a given country such as public and private limited companies, non-trading partnerships, etc. Their diffusion is quite varied both on the local and regional level and is greatly dependent on the extent and quality of offers which third parties make in their particular fields (co-operative and non-co-operative trading and processing companies, communes, state agencies/services). Their diffusion is naturally also based on the given emphasis of production in the agricultural sector. However, no reliable statistics concerning such co-operations are available for any country.

The collective utilization of cowsheds, stables and the like as well as that of the technical facilities affiliated with animal husbandry is substantially less widespread. There are several reasons for this. On the one hand, such matters involve a considerable investment which, in comparison to field machinery, only amortizes itself over a long period of time. On the other hand, the desired effects such as a decreasing trend in costs and labor savings only then become clearly evident when the actual animal husbandry is pursued collectively and not just the collective management of buildings and facilities. This is nothing short of a partial consolidation of the enterprises involved in the particular branch of livestock trade. Not only do the majority of farmers in western Europe view such a joint sectoral operation (in Germany, it is referred to as *Betriebszweig-Gemeinschaft*) sceptically, but such an arrangement entails both a close engagement over a long period of time and an imposed curtailment of their accustomed independence in all management matters. Although these real or supposed disadvantages can be easily calculated and estimated in such production sectors as pig fattening which can be well demarcated from the remainder of the farming operation, this is much more difficult in sectors such as the keeping of dairy cattle which is more tightly interlocked with the entire operation. This is why there are more such joint sectoral operations for pig fattening than for dairy cattle keeping (although still only about 30 in all of western Germany). Joint operations for keeping dairy cattle have even been mostly dissolved in those countries which had developed such cooperations to an extent worth mentioning, such as in Denmark and northern Italy during the 1950s and '60s.

Cooperations in the form of joint sectoral operations are even more rare in farming than in animal husbandry for the reasons provided above. Farming carried out collectively practically resembles a complete consolidation in almost all instances. Associations do exist for the collective use of land, but the type of cooperation in such cases is usually limited to a collective execution of work and thus more or less equivalent to a widely defined machinery association (→ *Produktionsförderungsgenossenschaften*); no collective bookkeeping for earnings and expenses is carried out, and thus it cannot be considered a joint sectoral operation.

Statistics from agricultural associations and register courts indicate a high and increasing number of consolidated agricultural enterprises in many countries. Among these, the most frequent forms of collective enterprise are the *Gesellschaft des Bürgerlichen Rechts* (non-trading parternership) in western Germany, the GAEC or group enterprise in France as well as partnerships and corporations in the USA. Under closer scrutiny, one may doubt whether these are all a matter of cooperation in the usual sense of the word as the vast majority of cases are family companies. For example, over 90% of the French GAECs are run exclusively by closely related family members (father/son, brother/brother). The formation of such joint companies is primarily based on inheritance or tax laws or rooted in the objective to achieve better benefits from state assistance through the new legal form. At the same time, they all clearly qualify as companies and cannot be formally differentiated from the relatively few companies to which the restrictions laid down here do not apply.

The fact that many family companies exist indicates that it is not the complicated legal and organizational matters which deter farmers from becoming involved in cooperations with a high degree of integration, but rather that the attachment to third parties is actually shunned. The fact that a strong, spatial relationship between the agricultural enterprise and the family household exists plays a fairly considerable role in this matter, at least in countries with a peasant farm structure. This problem naturally only plays a negligible role, if any at all, in the family companies mentioned above.

2. Purchasing and Marketing Associations

Associations for purchasing working materials and/or marketing collectively manufactured products are almost always associated with partial consolidations, even when it initially is only restricted to one level of production. The advantages of such purchasing and marketing associations (→ *Supply Co-operatives*) are plain in the face of the predominantly small size of agricultural enterprises; frequently the effects of gradually decreasing costs made possible through the partial consolidation can finally be utilized through the help of collective purchasing and marketing.

Associations for purchasing and marketing, aside from those created through partial consolidations, are also quite numerous. Well known examples for this not only within the → *European Community* but also in other countries are the numerous → *producer associations* which exist. Although these were originally conceived as pure marketing organizations, many of them have developed initiatives in the field of purchasing and additionally exercise influence on the product line of their member enterprises. Thus, it is only natural when members of a producer association frequently work together in another form.

Through this manner, the impetus for further collective activities with the same partners or with other ones emerges from the cooperation undertaken in a limited scope. A nexus of cooperation relationships develops both in co-operative and non-co-operative forms which, for example in the Benelux countries, Denmark, and in the German speaking regions, is quite distinct and affects practically every agricultural enterprise in more than one way.

3. The Employment of Human Labor

Cooperations also exist for the execution of administrative functions such as business planning and accounting. Usually, the agricultural enterprise as such requires substantially less than the manpower of one worker for administrative functions but, on the other hand, must seek and purchase professional know-how to a much greater extent than business active in other branches. Extension rings such as those which have developed in north-western Europe are nothing other than farmer cooperations which collectively employ highly qualified professionals, the likes of which one enterprise would not choose to finance on its own. Upon the assumption and, at least, partial financing of such functions through professional (farmer associations), public (Chamber of Agriculture) or state (Agricultural Ministry) agencies, the co-operative traces are mostly lost or shrouded, but they still exist in some several cases today.

A similar development can be observed concerning the collective utilization of actual agricultural workers through a group of enterprises. The impetus for the development of cooperations for the collective utilization of workers was once again the minimal amount of man-power that each individual agricultural enterprise has at its disposal. When an enterprise is short of man-power of its own (e.g. through illness), it is necessary that a qualified substitute is available for a short period of time. Cooperations between agricultural enterprises which collectively kept workers sprang up initially in Holland; the workers could be used among the enterprises following agreements and according to the enterprises' needs. Today, their employment is no longer restricted to emergency situations but rather also encompasses worker replacements during vacations and the abatement of work in times of peak load. These forms of cooperation, known as *Betriebshilfdienst* (enterprise assistance) in Germany and Austria and meanwhile found in many countries, is only occasionally financed by the participating farmers themselves. The support has predominantly been transferred to professional associations, religious communities (→ *Religious Co-operatives*), co-operatives or machinery rings (→ *Machinery Associations/Rings*). Financing is based to a large extent on the contributions made by social insurance institutions as well as on direct and indirect state subsidies. These vary from country to country and are the highest in Scandinavia.

The multi-enterprise employment of man-power in connection with the co-operative utilization of machinery was discussed above under II.1.

III. Legal Forms

Non-co-operative forms of cooperation within the agricultural sector have various alternatives open to them for the selection of their legal form in accordance with the varying national legal systems. Whereas in Germany, for example, agricultural co-operations can choose any permissible legal form in accordance with commercial and company laws, in France, specific legal forms are prescribed for cooperations between farms (→ *Law, International*). Upon the selection of a legal form, an agricultural cooperation must initially confront the identical problems that companies in other branches do. The consequences with respect to membership rights, management, legal capacity, stability, and taxation must be weighed and appraised. This decision becomes additionally more complicated in agriculture in that measures stemming from state funding policy frequently are tied to certain locations, enterprise sizes, income thresholds, and other such criteria which under certain circumstances cannot be observed. This is the case when the cooperation is considered a company and not simply an addition of many smaller enterprises, as is the case in most countries. Stipulations like that in Germany, which limit the state aid given to a cooperation to three times that to an individual farm, or like that in France which, although only valid for the special form "Groupements Agricoles" (→ *Pre-co-operative Forms*), allow the cooperation to be only ten times larger than the regional average farm size, themselves are the exceptions.

One must also take into consideration that agricultural production greatly benefits from general preferential tax treatment, but the allotment of this is likewise tied to certain conditions. If, for example in Germany, a newly formed cooperation as a whole excedes a certain set threshold value, it loses the tax preference (→ *Taxation*) which each of its members, as a farmer on his own, was most probably entitled to. It furthermore is no longer viewed as an agricultural company and must pay local business tax, something which to a wide extent does not exist in other countries.

Bibliography

Reisch, Erwin/Adelhelm, Reinhard: Kooperative Unternehmensformen in der Landwirtschaft, Frankfurt/ Main, 1980.
OECD: Group Farming, Paris 1972.
Nicht genossenschaftliche Kooperationsformen in der Landwirtschaft, Zeitschrift für das gesamte Genossenschaftswesen, Göttingen, 29 (1979), vol.2, pp. 102–141.
Guide des techniques comptables en g.a.e.c., Paris 1980.
Überbetriebliche Maschinenverwendung in der Landwirtschaft (KTBL-Schrift 244), Münster-Hiltrup 1980.
Überbetriebliche Zusammenarbeit in der Tierhaltung (KTBL-Schrift 245), Münster-Hilturp 1980.
Von Borries, Reyner/Nowak, Gerd und Wesche, Rüdiger: Zusammenarbeit in der Landwirtschaft, Stuttgart 1983.
Schwerpunkt Kooperationen, DLG-Mitteilungen, Frankfurt/Main, 103 (1988), vol. 13, pp. 672–687.

Franchising in Co-operative Business

GEORG C. NEUMANN [J]

(see also: *Supply Co-operatives; Conceptions, Co-operative; Structural Types; Management in Co-operatives; Marketing Strategies*)

I. Definition; II. Legal form; III. Historical Aspects; IV. Forms of Franchising; V. A Tool for Co-operatives?; VI. The European Community and the Laws of Competition.

I. Definition

Franchising concerns a long-term, two-way contract between franchisor and franchisee which, to a great extent, regulates the cooperation between the partners while maintaining their economic independence, whereby no corporate relationship between the partners is necessary. In publications one can even frequently find exclusive sales agreements for brand products with only a few binding obligations and rights regarding purchase and sales under the rubric of franchising (→ *Marketing Strategies*). The definition of the *Commission for the Promotion of Trade and Sales* Related Research in the second edition of its Terminological Catalogue dated 1975 is much more clear-cut and comes to the heart of the matter concerning franchising:

"Franchising is a form of cooperation in which a franchisor, on the basis of a long-term, contractual commitment, grants legally independent franchisees against payment the right to offer certain goods or services with the use of names, trademarks, fittings or other patent rights, as well as the technical or corporate experience of the franchisor, subject to the sales and organization system also developed by him" (Kommission zur Förderung der handels- und absatzwirtschaftlichen Forschung, 1975).

Because franchising presents a contractual arrangement of specific market activities, it is being spoken of as ever more frequently as "contractual marketing".

II. Legal Form

The legal relationships of the franchisees are regulated through individual vertical contracts with the central headquarters (→ *Organizational Structure of Societies*). Contractual or corporate commitments and ties to the other franchisees are not necessary. Practice shows, however, that the pure system of individual contracts can be enhanced through supervisional organizations of the franchisees; examples are the organizations of the partners themselves (e.g. McDonald's Operators Association) or subsequent measures undertaken by the headquarters, such as forming an advisory committee out of the ranks of the franchisees.

By introducing horizontal elements of supervision and consultation the original vertical franchise system structured along individual contracts begins to resemble the classic co-operative associations which have been based on the ideas of → *Schulze-Delitzsch* and → *Raiffeisen* since the middle of the last century.

III. Historical Aspects

The first franchise system developed along the lines of the definition provided above was possibly introduced by the World Radio Corporation in the middle of the 1920s for marketing radio equipment in New England. Retailers were required to pay fees for the marketing support they received. Franchising was first recognized after World War II as a special form of cooperation and subject to closer academic analysis. Whereas existent markets were expanded or even opened up through this form in the U.S., for example in the fast-food industry, the restructuring of existent companies was more prevalent in Western Europe.

In contrast to the U.S, where nonbranch-specific, unspecialized labor contributed to the rapid expansion of the franchise system, cultural and historical opposition stood in the way of a similar expansion in Europe. The → *guild* mentality of the Middle Ages, which was organized in further specific vocational trades along guild lines, continued and thus supported industry-specific self-awareness and the self-employment of workers; this frequently stood in the way of intensive cooperation and clear-cut, binding regulations.

IV. Forms of Franchising

According to *Tietz/Mathieu* one can speak of the following forms of the franchise system based on the origin and the importance of the goal orientation.

1. Product or Assortment Franchising

As with Coca-Cola, this system as a rule only works from the production to the bottler and/or packer as the product assortment is too small for the retail level.

2. Service Franchising

Here are meant those catering services for outfitting and running industrial kitchens and cafeterias as well as specialized systems of filling stations.

3. Sales Franchising

New sales forms are prominent in this classification, for example the Tupperware contracts or the sales structure for Encyclopedia Britannica.

4. Shop-type Franchising

This is the most widely applied form of franchising, particularly in commerce and in restaurant business. The location of the shop or business enterprise is an important criterium for the selection of this enterprise form, whereas certain types of business require a particular locational quality.

The forms of the franchise system are so diverse in practise that one can find attributes of the forms listed above in the most varied of combinations. Two factors, though, are decisive for the success of a franchise system: On the one hand, the neglect of individual wishes and expectations of the partners by the system, and on the other hand, permanent control over the adherence to the rules of the game.

V. A Tool for Co-operatives?

Intensified competition associated with contractional tendencies in the European economies has made the commercial trading and service co-operatives develop from pure purchasing collectives to full-service organizations (→ *Classification*), and ultimately even to marketing associations (→ *Commercial Purchasing and Service Co-operatives, part VI.*).

This development took place in steps for the trading co-operatives, starting with collective purchases (with storage and/or as transfer orders), continuing with collective advertising campaigns, the construction of shops and the introduction of data processing, and resulting in a range of various enterprise types. More and more often it is realized that the effective promotion of members does not end with the procurement of goods or services but rather must be supplemented with intensive sales support in the members' own enterprises. The differentiated structures which have resulted in the co-operatives in the course of numerous decades, for example the assortment or the method of supply among the group of members, must be reorganized along the lines of more homogenous partial groups. The outputs and services of the central organizations are thus more goal directed, making the adjustment to the needs of the market groups more effective.

In order to attain a similar market effectiveness enjoyed by competitors through a centrally controlled branch system, co-operatives must risk retreating from the classic principle of merely giving recommendations and accept the principle of binding cooperation. A technical means to achieve this end is the juncture of services (→ *goods*, advertising, shop construction) together in so-called "packets" which are placed at the disposal of only those members who have opted for such an enterprise form.

For this matter, franchising is a very appropriate organizational tool. By approaching the market with a branch-like structure (having the same company name, the same shop fittings, assortments and pricing policy as well as identical advertising), a high level of familiarity and recognition can be achieved in a relatively short amount of time among consumers. Market penetration (→ *Marketing Strategies*) is faster than in classic purchasing co-operatives. Recently a growing number of co-operatives has proceeded to offer their members franchise-like marketing concepts in order to tauten and make the cooperation more successful between themselves and their members. Examples for the utilization of franchising in co-operatives since the end of the 1960s include the "Quick Schuh" type of enterprise policy introduced by the Nord West Ring e.G. for low-price shoppers, "moda" for fashion-conscious customers and "Forma" for those customers looking for a good fit, or the "Profi-Märkte" for do-it-yourself home repairers developed by the Nürnberger Bund e.G.

Franchising or such similar instruments seem from experience especially suited to revitalize classic co-operatives.

VI. The European Community and the Laws of Competition

Whereas the legal questions in the internal relationship between franchisor and franchisee are based on the principles of contractual freedom as an essential element of the social market economy of the Western World, the effects are judged and based according to the laws of competition, particularly according to the → *anti-trust laws*.

It is laid down in Article 85 of the EC Treaty that all agreements and resolutions are forbidden and invalidated which are so construed as to interfere or impair trade between members states or which strive to effect an obstruction, restriction or distortion of competition in the Common Market. Horizontal as well as vertical contracts are included here in contrast to the German → *Anti-Trust Laws* (GWB) which is essentially restricted to assess and pronounce judgement on horizontal contractual relations. The result of this is that franchised co-operatives are judged more sharply and negatively because of the corporate relations already existent among their partners than pure franchise systems with exclusively vertical contractual relationships. The new § 5c in the German Anti-Trust Laws could provide assistance.

Because the anti-trust laws of the European Community (→ *European Community*) have precedence over the anti-trust laws of the member countries, the Executive Order No. 4087/88, Register L 359, dated December 28, 1988, is of substantial importance for the European franchise system as it has retained an exemption statement for groups in accordance with Article 85 III of the EWGV.

What today (1990) is still lacking and must be attended to is an exemption statement also for co-operatives, particularly when these have just reinforced or wish to reinforce cooperation with their member enterprises with the help of franchising or franchise-like systems. The present legal postion represents a disadvantage for co-operatives in respect to purely vertical franchise systems in both the European and domestic German markets.

Bibliography

Gross, Herbert/Skaupy: Franchising in der Praxis, Düsseldorf and Wien 1976.

Kommission zur Förderung der handels- und absatzwirtschaftlichen Forschung: Katalog E, 2nd ed., 1975.

Love: Mc Donald's Anatomie eines Welterfolgs, München 1987.

Tietz, Bruno: Handbuch: Franchising – Zukunftsstrategien für die Marktbearbeitung, Landsberg 1987.

Tietz, Bruno/Mathieu, E.: Das Franchising als Kooperationsmodell für den mittelständischen Groß- und Einzelhandel. FIW-Series, vol. 85, 1979.

Zentgeno: Zukunftsaspekte genossenschaftlicher Kooperationen in Einzelhandel und Handwerk, Bonn 1988.

GACOPEA – AMSAC

GABRIELE ULLRICH

(see also: *Development Policy*; *Management in Co-operatives*; *Managerial Economics*; *Education, Africa*)

I. Background; II. Context; III. The GACOPEA Concept; IV. The GACOPEA Methodology; V. The GACOPEA Materials; VI. The GACOPEA Network; VII. Review and Outlook of the GACOPEA Programme.

The French abbreviation GACOPEA stands for "Gestion Appropriée de Co-operatives des Petits Exploitants Agricoled" (in English version: Appropriate management Systems for Agricultural Co-operatives-AMSAC). The abbreviation is used for various aspects: for an approach to co-operative management and promotion, for a promotional methodology, for training and information materials, for a promotional programme and for a network of national, regional and international institutions to facilitate its implementation in French-speaking West-African countries. The different aspects of GACOPEA will be elaborated in this article.

I. Background

The first activities of GACOPEA in the West-African French-speaking region started in the early 1980's based on ideas and materials of the English-speaking AMSAC programme, which was initiated by FAO with the Indian Institute of Management, Ahmedabad and other institutions. In the course of the French-speaking GACOPEA activities in which the German Foundation for International Development (DSE), played a major role, the approach underwent substantial developments and changes appropriate to the specific situation of the Region (→ *Development Policy*). In French-speaking African countries (like in other developing countries) co-operatives were introduced by the colonial power as government promoted and controlled organizations to collect agricultural export products (→ *Development, Africa*). The objectives of these organizations were set by co-operative departments or development authorities. The results of increased export production were intended to finance macro-economic targets. After independence co-operatives which in their majority are up-to-date agricultural, remained in most cases in the same situation until their structures started to break down in the 1970's. They were blamed for being a European model parachuted into Africa without necessary adjustment to local conditions, although the similarities to European co-operatives could hardly be recognized anymore. It was in the late 80's that the deficiencies and mistakes were even admitted by the governments and openly declared on different occasions, e.g. at the ILO African Regional Conference in 1988 and at the ICA Regional Conference the same year (→ *United Nations System*). A number of mistakes have been identified; however, the knowledge as to how to implement solutions is still under-developed. They should relate to the following issues:

- promotional activities were mostly geared to formal, registered co-operatives which increasingly lost the confidence of their members and thereby the capability to mobilize local resources. Often informal groups were created which turned out to be competitors of the former.
- the functions were mostly restricted to the collection of agricultural produce and distribution of production inputs, seldom credit and processing. Often the activities were limited to one product (cash crop). As a closely government-linked structure they lost sight of the co-operative purpose to serve the interests of its members who often needed assistance in other fields.
- the population groups involved in economic activities other than cash crop production, particularly women, mostly responsible for food crop production and processing were left out of official co-operative policy and hence major parts of local human resources and material resources were neglected.
- the management of co-operatives (through full-time managers and office bearers) is acting within narrow limitations of fixed prices. State-controlled markets, bound to their supply and marketing system. The scope left to the manager does mostly not allow the development of entrepreneurship in favour of co-operative members. Co-operatives of a smaller size are often not in a position to provide for professional staff.
- the possibility for capital formation of such organisations is extremely limited and keeps them dependent of external financial assistance. Even the little surplus produced is often put into investment of the general community rather than into the co-operative enterprise.
- the → *"officialisation"* of such organisations prevents the development of sound secondary organizations financed and controlled from the primary level. Co-operative departments (→ *Authorities, Co-operative*) take over such functions, however, through administrative procedures which are not appropriate to management of enterprises.

- in general, the above-mentioned aspects of government policy to promote co-operatives are reflected in a lack of system's approach which should take into consideration the interlinkages between the system of the member economy, the system of the co-operative (grouping several of such member economies) and the system of the rural environment. Usually it is neglected that intervention in one of these systems also causes an impact on the others. In the French-speaking African region the members' micro-economies were not seen as holistic entities of household and production; the co-operative system was product- but not function-oriented and lacking self-regulating mechanisms due to continuous outside interventions and control. Hence assistance to co-operatives was consuming too many external resources which became more and more scarce.

II. Context

The French-speaking African countries have certain common characteristics which made the programme GACOPEA applicable to them:
- the masses of the rural population play a key role in the development process. However, their situation has not improved over the last development decades,
- positive developments have been neutralized by high population growth and the living conditions of the small farmers remained poor or even deteriorated which resulted in rural-urban migration,
- large-scale development programmes and government policy failed in breaking the vicious cycle of poverty,
- government policy deviates more and more from social aspects at micro-level to economic aspects at macro-level due to budgetary problems and structural adjustment,
- the countries belong to the environmentally most vulnerable zones of Africa and urgently require measures to protect and reconstitute the natural resources for agricultural production.

Co-operatives as a means of self-organisation of small farmers have the potential to provide assistance to their members and to improve their living conditions. At the same time they can contribute to solving the above-mentioned macro-economic problem areas. However, it is recognized that co-operatives can play this role only if they are seen as voluntary organizations promoting the economic and social interests of their members. Against this background and within this regional context the GACOPEA approach was developed, or more precisely "rediscovered".

III. The GACOPEA Concept

The concept of GACOPEA is based on weaknesses identified in co-operative management in the French-speaking African Region as well as on a systematic approach to assess the co-operative, its environment and the requirements for the assistance from outside to such group organizations. The concept of management is described in nine chapters of the regional GACOPEA Guide with a view to the future shape of co-operative organizations (→ *Management in Co-operatives*). It is more a systematization and recollection of proven co-operative principles and values than the creation of a new concept. Management and external assistance has to be based on this perception: Co-operative management should begin with the understanding of its specific tasks within a system (group of member economies) consisting of self-reliant sub-systems (member economies) (→ *Managerial Economics*).

Co-operative management should then be capable of understanding and analyzing the socio-economic and natural environment (suprasystem) in which the co-operative is acting. Against this background it identifies the possibilities of action of an integrated co-operative which works through forward, backward and horizontal linkages with the market and is not limited to one-product and single-purpose action.

Activities of co-operative management have to focus on the mobilization of human and financial resources, the planning, organization, control and the evaluation for further planning. These activities have to follow common management rules; however, they have to respect the specifics of the co-operative enterprise where the members and office bearers have an active role to play at primary and secondary levels. Such co-operative management is characterized by member participation and a system's approach.

The GACOPEA approach to action refers not only to the tasks of management which is in most cases in West Africa not yet a full-time, professional management and consists rather of voluntary office bearers. Beyond the action described in the regional guide, the GACOPEA approach also makes reference to ways and means of how the co-operative goal of "entrepreneurship for development" has to be reflected in co-operative promotion and assistance to co-operatives as well as in the general environment in which these organizations are acting.

How did the GACOPEA approach perceive the task to contribute to a favourable environment for the development of co-operative management? Two characteristics can be identified: major emphasis is placed on Human Resources Development and action is developed in a step-by-step process. It is crucial in this process to combine local knowledge about possibilities and constraints of economic and social development with external knowledge of possible innovations. The step-by-step action process could be described in phases which can, however, be overlapping, forming a cycle by giving feedback to previous phases. These could roughly be distinguished as follows:

- the orientation phase: the acquisition of knowledge of potentials and needs, the person involved in co-operative action and promotion in the government and non-governmental structures testing through action-research and sensitisation of decision-makers.
- the planning phase: participatory planning for co-operative action and promotion at different levels (members and leader of co-operative groupings, senior officials of servicing structures, political and adminstrative decision-makers). The planning has to be simultaneous and interlinked. Synergetic effects can be mobilized when similar action takes place at local, national and regional level, particularly in training and briefing the persons concerned on the GACOPEA approach.
- the implementation phase: mobilization of local material and human resources currently underused to increase the economic viability of co-operative groupings and hence the income of their members. Only indirect assistance is given in this phase by training of management staff, members of co-operatives and leaders of rural groups, preparation of locally-adapted training materials, consultancy on new production methods and processing techniques.
- the evaluation phase: use of feedback to the orientation and planning phase in a cycle of planning and plan revision (→ *Evaluation*). Monitoring and ongoing evaluation provides the necessary linkages and feedback of the described step-by-step process. The measuring of effects and efficiency of such investment in human resources development is, however, critical, if not impossible. Self-evaluation as participatory reflection and evaluation by the different groups of persons concerned is considered to be a tool for improving orientation, planning and implementing once the approach is appropriated by the different actors.

IV. The GACOPEA Methodology

Efforts to develop an appropriate methodology for GACOPEA activities are being undertaken at all levels of persons involved and for all types of activities. Like the contents, the methods have to correspond at the various levels of implementation. They refer to:

- *the development of the GACOPEA programme* which was inititiated through a dialogue between political and administrative decision-makers (from government and non-government sides) together with some external resource persons. The crystallisation point of this dialogue was the regional management guide for GACOPEA which was step-by-step developed in regional meetings and tested at national and local levels together with the co-operators. Around the discussions of this guide the political, legal, structural and socio-economic environment of co-operative action was assessed. Efforts started at local and national levels to collect the necessary information and to initiate pilot actions. The facilitators of this process were "mixed teams" of national, regional and international experts who accompanied the developments continuously and were trained in participatory methods of communication.
- *the preparation, implementation and evaluation of group events* which were carried out by using participatory methods developed by the German foundation for Development (DSE). These methods were based on techniques of mobile visualization (pin-boards, cards with key ideas elaborated by the participants, mobile to be (re-)structured) developed by the consulting firm Metaplan. Subsequently these techniques were adapted and integrated into a process of participatory group work appropriate to the different levels of participants. The development of these methods formed part of the above-mentioned process and contributed to the mobilization of participants in and after the group event. Essential for the methods was the continuity of the initiated process altenating with regional, national and local events. The process enabled the intended cycle of planning based on previous evaluation, of implementation, of follow-up action planned during the event, etc.
- *the interlinkages of different types and levels of action* which ensures that the methods in different group events are corresponding (not necessarily the same) and action is supplementing and influencing each other mutually, eventually building up a development process rather than projects. Co-operators, trainers, decision-makers and persons-in-charge of external assistance worked with visualization techniques designed for the respective purpose. They all discussed and tested the management guide and related materials. Awareness-creation went hand-in-hand with planning and implementating action.

V. The GACOPEA Materials

The programme's first developed material was the Regional Guide on appropriate management for small farmers' co-operatives (published in French). It was developed step-by-step in several stages of drafts, revisions and editions during various group events. This guide gives only the general framework of that has to be thought of when initiating the development of economically viable co-operatives and some information on methods of planning, organization and evaluation. The regional guide formed the basis for developing national guides and training materials in Burkina Faso, Côte d'Ivoire, Senegal and Togo. The methodological approach to group events was described in a book by introducing and analyzing cases of experiences. Further material was needed to inform decision-makers of recipients and donors on the GACOPEA approach and programme. They were edited in French and German. Country studies produced by the ICA were printed to exchange ideas on practical national work among participants of the programme. Recently, DSE and FAO published a French and English Guide for planning of programmes and projects based on GACOPEA (titles hereunder).

There is still a considerable need for further information and training materials which have to serve these numerous people interested who not had the opportunity to participate in training or other group events. However, it was intended not to duplicate materials already available in other programmes or institutions (e.g. the ILO materials of MATCOM) working in the field of co-operative management and promotion. Concerted efforts are needed to exchange, supplement and develop materials by the various institutions involved.

VI. The GACOPEA Network

Since the first regional conference on GACOPEA in 1982 in Cotonou/Benin a series of regional events have taken place in Feldafing, Germany (DSE-Food and Agriculture Development Centre). Between these regional meetings national and local workshops and training courses were carried out to develop adapted policies, assistance and materials as well as to assess, discuss and revise the action already begun. Out of these activities a network of persons emerged at all levels of decision-making, implementing and facilitating the initiated process. These persons formed a nucleus for the GACOPEA approach who were familiar with the concept, methods and the practical work of GACOPEA. They were frequently able to convince their institutions to participate in and contribute to his network which up to now is not institutionalized. At the last regional conference in Feldafing in 1989 to evaluate the past seven years of the GACOPEA Programme, recommendations were made by high-ranking decision-makers of the region on how such a network could assist movements and governments in their promotional tasks through mutual exchange and systematization of experiences, by establishing a data-base on existing training and research materials and eventually by forming "funds" of human and material resources by external assistance (to ensure appropriate and unbureaucratic help to solve problems related to co-operative management at local and national levels). However, the follow-up of the recommendations turned out to be difficult, particularly as the external support to networks and processes requires pooling of financial resources which administrative procedures of donors do not normally foresee. Nevertheless, what was possible without external help (particularly at the national level) continued to evolve.

Furthermore, at the regional level training courses at the DSE in Feldafing, Germany, and the Co-operative College of Senegal (Ecole Nationale del l'Economie Appliquée-ENEA) contributed at least at the operational level to foster the regional exchange and mutual support of the activities. Participants of such courses reinforce the "GACOPEA-nucleus" in their countries.

VII. Review and Outlook of the GACOPEA Programme

During its existence, the GACOPEA Programme in West African French-speaking countries underwent criticism and setbacks. It tried to draw lessons from them and never claimed to have established a finalized concept and fixed methods. It understood itself rather as an approach to continuously developing solutions in a changing environment and to offering conceptual and methodological benchmarks to facilitate such a process.

One frequent criticism was that the concept offered nothing new and indeed the values identified went back to original co-operative ideas. Though they are also considered to be relevant to the development of European co-operatives the programme did not try to transplant "European models". It rather facilitated the time-consuming process of developing and testing ideas at the level of national promotional structures and of local co-operative action.

Another criticism was that the concept was too complicated and far ahead of the development stage of West-African co-operative grouping. The programme never tried to make believe that the goal of small farmers co-operatively organising themselves, was fast and easily achieved, it revealed that this form of organization and especially the task of managing it, is a complicated one and needs careful preparation. However, as it is one of the few chances for small farmers to self-determine their development, GACOPEA suggested that the complexity of the organization should be taken seriously, not be simplified and all persons concerned should be prepared in-depth and step-by-step for their task even if it is a long way to go. This approach resulted in activities which were often considered "slow" and which always remained "preparatory" especially by donors who are used to rather short-term projects with relatively measurable results. The process of human resources development, where prepartion of persons means already implementation of the process, is difficult to be made understood by conventional administrative structures. Despite or sometimes because of these criticisms the approach of GACOPEA became more and more systematic and explicit. For its facilitators and organizers it is itself an object of a development process, a process of adaptation and appropriation. After more and more understanding of the complex implications of this process in French-speaking African countries, the FAO started "re-transfering" the ideas to other parts of Africa, e.g. Ethiopia where a pilot project is being launched based on the methodological framework of GACOPEA. It is there that feedback can be given to the benefit of the original AMSAC programme.

Bibliography

DSE: Guide pour la préparation de programmes et de projects de promotion des coopératives et groupement ruraux sur la base de concept GACOPEA, Feldafing 1991.
DSE/FAO: Guide pour la gestion approprieé des co-pératives de petits exploitants agricole (GACOPEA) en Africque francophone, 2nd ed., Feldafing 1985.
Lanzendörfer, M.: Angepaßtes Management kooperativer Zusammenschlüsse von Kleinbauern, Ein Überblick (also French version) published by DSE, 1988.
Münkner, Hans-H.: Guide for the Planning of Programmes and projects for the Promotion of Co-operatives and Rural Groups based on the AMSAC Concept (also French version) published by DSE and FAO 1991.
National guides GACOPEA of Burkina Faso, Côte d'Ivoire, Sengegal and Togo.
Ten Country Studies of West Africa published by DSE/ICA 1987.
Ullrich, Gabriele/Jeetun, Beeharrylall: Approches participatives de travail en groupe, DSE, Feldafing 1986.

GDR, Co-operatives in the Former

GERHARD RÖNNEBECK/THOMAS PFEIFFER [J]

(see also: *Socialist Co-operative Theory*; *State and Co-operatives in Socialism*; *Socialist Critics*; *Development, Eastern Europe*)

I. Introduction; II. Co-operatives in the G.D.R.; III. Co-operative Federations; IV. Co-operative Legislation; V. Development Problems for the Co-operatives Prior to the Reform in 1989/90; VI. The Role of the Co-operatives in the Reform Process in the G.D.R..

I. Introduction

This article examines co-operatives in the German Democratic Republic (G.D.R.) prior to the political and economic upheaval which occurred in 1989/90. Following the Second World War a socialistic co-operative model was pursued in the G.D.R. which fundamentally varied from that of market economy co-operatives (→ *State and Co-operative, Socialism*). This model was intended to fulfill certain functions in the development of a socialistic economic and social order. Borrowing from the theories of *Marx* and *Lenin* (→ *Socialist Critics*) in which the antagonism between work and capital is abolished in the co-operative, thus reflecting socialist society "in miniature", the co-operatives in the G.D.R. embodied a *political educative function:* To initiate those societal groups who held to the traditions of autonomy and private property -in particular farmers, craftsmen and small-scale industrialists – into the socialist planned economy and introduce them to collective property. In Marxist-Leninist ideology co-operatives furthermore exercise an economic *transformational function* in the transitional process from private to collective property, or in other words, from capitalism to communism.

Alongside these ideologically based functions, the co-operatives in the G.D.R. fulfilled more pragmatically grounded functions. Whereas incentive systems were instated in the *Volkseigene Betriebe* (VEB; People's Enterprises) which functioned irrespective of economic efficiency, compensation in the co-operatives was oriented around net income; this was intended to stimulate better output and/or higher performance through participation in the distribution of achieved surpluses (*incentive function*). This lead, however, in practical application to unmistakable "free-rider" behavior among co-operative members. Each member wanted to benefit from higher co-operative productivity/efficiency without actually increasing his/her individual productivity level.

Co-operatives in the G.D.R. furthermore were to fulfill a *co-ordinational function* between centralized and decentralized decision-making centers in those economic sectors in which complete central planning and control of the economic processes could not be realized, or if so, only to a limited degree – such as in consumer retail trade or in handicraft trades. The imperfections of the central planning and control system were to be overcome through the assistance of co-operatives.

II. Co-operatives in the G.D.R.

1. Co-operative Banks

a) Bäuerliche Handelsgenossenschaften (BHG, rural trading co-operatives)

The BHG emerged out of the former Raiffeisen co-operatives (→ *Rural Co-operatives*), which they have been turned back into in the meantime. Co-operative farmers, gardeners and wine-growers were organized in them. The settlement of cashless payment transactions, the provision of credits to private customers and/or private companies as well as the supervision of savings accounts – particularly for the rural population – numbered among their business functions. They maintained approx. 2,700 sub-branches with some 1.2 million bank accounts.

Alongside performing deposit and loan functions, the BHG also operated processing enterprises (e.g. dairies, fattening yards) and retail shops (for construction and heating materials, agricultural supplies, etc.) which primarily catered to private individuals and small private companies.

The BHG were subject to the instructions of the *Bank für Landwirtschaft und Nahrungsgüterwirtschaft* (BLN, Bank for Agriculture and Foodstuffs Industry), which in turn was subject to the G.D.R. State Bank; the BLN operated in the name of the State Bank and was responsible for banking matters in the agricultural sector. The G.D.R. State Bank had a mandate and exercised extensive control rights over both co-operative and non-co-operative banking institutions (e.g. savings banks) in that it kept their accounts, determined terms for deposits, made decisions with regard to the provision of refinancing credits, determined banking practices for payment, clearing and credit transactions, and ensured that these were adhered to. The interest rates on both deposits and loans were set by the state.

b) Genossenschaftskassen für Handwerk und Gewerbe (GHG, Co-operative Savings Banks for Handicraft and Commercial Industry)

The GHG developed out of the Volksbanken (urban credit unions) which were dissolved in 1945. In the meantime they too have been reconverted to Volksbanken. Prior to the reforms in 1989/90, 95 GHGs existed as well as two church-affiliated co-operative credit associations. The GHGs were active as commercial banks for private and co-operative handicraft enterprises. The range of their business activity included receiving deposits, keeping business accounts as well as carrying out members' payment transactions. Their business policy was tied to the directives issued by the Ministry of Finance and the State Bank.

2. Co-operatives for Handicraft Industries

Handicrafts, even prior to the reforms, represented that economic sector of the G.D.R. in which private enterprises had a relatively large amount of business latitude, as they had a 60% share in turnover from the entire handicraft industry. Nevertheless, private handicraft enterprises (up to 10 employees) were also bound to state planning directives which encompassed the types of production, assortment policies, delivery ceilings and deadlines, business hours and customer service. Violations of these planning directives could be punished through the revocation of commercial permits.

a) Produktionsgenossenschaften des Handwerks (PGH, Production Co-operatives for Handicrafts Industries)

The first PGHs came into being in 1952 with the political goal of integrating handicraft industries in the general development of socialism (→ *Joint-production Co-operatives*). The PGH model law of 1955, taking into consideration the traditional characteristics of private enterprise inherent in the handicraft sector, foresaw the following PGH types:

PGH-Type 1: Machines, tools, and other means of production remained members' private property; members were directed to make them available to the PGH for a fee.

PGH-Type 2: Members were obliged to sell their means of production to the PGH at book value. Private property with regard to production means was transformed into co-operative/collective property.

This two-tiered system was maintained up to the reform period in 1989/90. There were 2,733 PGHs in 1983 which accounted for approx. 40% of total turnover in the handicraft industry. Membership numbered 156,500 in 1982.

b) Einkaufs- und Liefergenossenschaften des Handwerks (ELG, Purchasing and Supply Co-operatives for Handicraft Industries)

Whereas PGH-members did not pursue any type of self-employed business activity, private handicraft workers and handicraft enterprises were represented in the ELGs (→ *Supply Co-operatives*). The ELGs had a promotional economic character insofar as they offered their members promotional assistance in purchasing and marketing. Notwithstanding, de facto membership was obligatory for private practitioners of handicraft trades as no alternative opportunities existed for them with regard to supply channels – above all for necessary means of production. The ELGs thus were basically state distribution centers for means of production.

3. Mutual Repercussions between State and Co-operative Trade

The private sector had a 8.5% share of the net domestic trade product in 1987. The trading sector, involving 25,600 independent, gainfully employed individuals, ranked behind handicrafts as the second largest economic sector in the G.D.R. with a free economy property structure – above all in retail trade and the restaurant industry. In order to reduce the ever larger deficits present in the provision and distribution of consumer goods, state measures were taken for the promotion of the private economy with respect to trade which, nevertheless, were only limited in their effectiveness. The causes of the mere restricted activation of independent company undertakings were rooted in the existing structural problems of domestic trade within the G.D.R., for example bottlenecks in both production and imports, poor transportation, delivery and storage conditions, etc. Private retail trade was simply granted a supplementary function of sorts to the mammoth company structures of the state trading organizations (HO, *Staatliche Handelsorganisation*) as well as to the consumer co-operatives. The consequence of this was a continual declining share for private retailing and the restaurant trade in the total retail trade turnover within the national economy. Within the last 40 years this share decreased from 53% in 1950 to 8.5% in 1987. Reasons for this decline can be seen in the numerous disadvantages which private retailers had to confront: They were not allowed to set prices on their own, they were supplied with lower quality goods, and they were appropriated insufficient amounts of sales and storage space in unfavorable locations. More intensive entrepreneurial activity, including the willingness to invest more personal energy and assume more risk, could not be encouraged under such conditions.

4. Consumer Co-operatives

The → *consumer co-operatives* formed the third largest mass organization in the G.D.R. with approx. 4.5 million members. Their allotted task, however, was oriented less around providing for the population than it was around carrying out the political educative and integrational functions mentioned above. Nevertheless, alongside the HO shops they were important provision and distribution facilities in the G.D.R. In 1989/90 there were approx. 36,000 sales outlets and restaurants with around 190,000 employees. They had a 33% share in total turnover resulting from retail trade and restaurant business. In addition the consumer co-operatives ran 85 companies and large-scale enterprises (*Kombinate*) for the production of backed goods and meat products (→ *Own Production*). On account of their responsibility of providing for the population and their character as a mass political organization, the consumer co-operatives were much more strongly bound to the central planned economy of the G.D.R. than other co-operative organizations were. Prices for both wholesale and retail trade as well as profit margins were fixed by the state.

5. Co-operative Home-Building Associations

The *Arbeiterwohnungsbaugenossenschaften* (AWG, workers' co-operative home-building associations) were also mass political organizations like the consumer co-operatives (→ *Housing Societies*). Employed members of VEBs, civil servants, university employees, etc. were joined together in the AWGs, which were instruments of state housing policy. Financing for building projects was solely possible through the State Bank, and the AWGs were thus treated exactly the same way state construction companies were. GWGs (*gemeinnützige Wohnungsbaugenossenschaften*), or public-benefit oriented home-building co-operatives (→ *Public Benefit Orientation*), existed alongside the AWGs, but the two differentiated from each other in that membership in the GWG was not constituent on employment in certain enterprises or institutions. On the one hand members of both GWGs and AWGs invested in company shares, on the other hand they were obliged to provide individual labor inputs for the construction of co-operative apartment buildings.

6. Agricultural Production Co-operatives (LPG, *Landwirtschaftliche Produktionsgenossenschaften*)

The LPGs were the dominant agricultural enterprise form in the G.D.R. (→ *Joint-production Co-operative*). They were workers co-operatives which emerged in the process of forced agricultural collectivization and had approx. 900,000 members in 1988. 200 gardening co-operatives (GPG, *Gärtnerische Produktionsgenossenschaften*) with approx. 30,000 members existed alongside the roughly 4,000 LPGs. In average a LPG cultivated between 4,500 and 5000 hectares. The LPG and the GPG are large-scale production enterprises whose members are not independent farmers, but who rather can be designated as agricultural workers. The LPGs provided services for those members who farmed on the side as well as for the remaining small-scale farmers; they provided supplies, made machinery available, processed and sold agricultural products. The specialized large-scale LPG enterprises worked together, usually in the constellation of one plants cultivating enterprise with three to four livestock breeding enterprises. So-called co-operative councils (KOR) were responsible for the co-ordination of the specialized large-scale LPG enterprises; the KORs were entrusted with certain business functions, such as the calculation of arranged prices. Co-operation associations (KOV) were a form of the predominantly vertical co-operation between the producers of agricultural raw materials and the first level of material processing. The KOV furthermore formed the link to those enterprises involved in both the grocery industry and trade which in turn organized the flow of production, warehousing, preparation, processing and marketing of foodstuffs.

7. Councils of Lawyers

The councils of lawyers (*Kollegien der Rechtsanwälte*) were co-operative organizations of lawyers. Through the formation of this organization in 1953 the state attempted to bind independent lawyers to the *socialistic administration of justice*. The attainment of a legal practise license was only possible through membership in this council.

III. Co-operative Federations

The co-operative → *federations* in the G.D.R., rather than acting as large amalgamated organizations serving the interest of the co-operatives incorporated in them, excercised to a much greater extent political functions by conveying the political will of the SED (*Sozialistishe Einheitspartei Deutschlands*, United Socialist Party of Germany) to the population. The federations were tied to the SED and its constitutional directive through their affiliation with the *National Front* (NF). Any actual type of autonomy among organizations or federations was thus out of the question.

1. Coalition of Reciprocal Farming Assistance
(VdgB, *Vereinigung der gegenseitigen Bauernhilfe*)

The objective of the VdgB, which was established in 1946, was to destroy the agricultural Raiffeisen co-operatives which still existed at that time. In the course of land reform and the expropriation of agricultural co-operatives, property was conveyed to the VdgBs. With the help of the machinery loan stations (MAS, *Maschinen-Ausleih-Stationen*) established in 1948 the VdgBs were able to provide *new farmers* with agricultural machines and equipment. Until the end of the 1960s they furthermore settled the purchases of agricultural products through people's collection and purchasing centers. Farming operations were dependent on the state-controlled VdgB for production, financing and marketing. The VdgB could count 596,672 members in 1986, which corresponded to approx. 80% of all co-operative farmers and gardeners. Their services encompassed educational measures, output compensation, maintaining village traditions, village clean-up and improvement measures, etc. At the end of 1950 the VdgB was forcefully amalgamated with all co-operative forms to make the VdgB (BHG).

2. Federation of Consumers' Co-operatives (VdK)

The roughly 4.6 million members of the consumer co-operatives of the G.D.R. were organized in the VdK. Because of its character as a mass political organization, the VdK much more served as a classic instrument for the transmission of the national government's socialist thought than an organization representing the wishes of its members.

3. Federation of the Co-operative Savings Banks for Handicraft and Commercial Industry (GHG)

The federation of the GHG (*Genossenschaftskassen für Handwerk und Gewerbe*) was founded in the 1950s as the successor organization of the former Volksbank federation (→ *Federations*). 95 GHGs amalgamated in the federation, which primarily undertook auditing tasks.

IV. Co-operative Legislation

The co-operatives in the G.D.R. were subject to the applicable business law of the G.D.R.; their internal organizational and legal structure was subject to further legal fundaments such as the LPG Law, labor law and civil law. A co-operative law did not exist. The internal legal relationships were regulated rather by so-called *standard by-laws* which either were provided and binding (e.g. in the case of LPGs and PGHs) or which were to be taken into consideration in the formulation of individual bylaws. The standard bylaws defined the tasks of the co-operative in the framework of state planning, the legal relationship between the co-operative and its members as well as the distribution of property, members' rights and the organizational structure of the co-operative. Co-operatives were founded upon the resolution of the assembly of founding members which decided on the bylaws, tasks, administration and financing of the co-operative. Registration and subsequent state ratification followed from the applicable district council. Co-operative property was considered socialistic property according to the constitution of the G.D.R., as were nationalized property and the property of associational organizations. In contrast to nationalized property which was considered state socialistic property, co-operatives exercised collective property rights over co-operative assets. Those assets provided by members (such as land) formally remained their own property, but achieved returns on such assets were conveyed to the co-operative and thus transformed into collective property.

A particular feature of the co-operative property structure was the formation and accumulation of co-operative *funds*. These were prescribed in the standard bylaws as necessary and served to guarantee an adequate utilization of co-operative property in accordance with the plan. Certain amounts of co-operative property were allocated for particular objectives through these funds, for example for cultural and social programs to the benefit of members and fellow workers (as incentives) or for the financing of incentive bonuses and programs for professional qualification.

V. Development Problems for the Co-operatives in the G.D.R. Prior to the Reform in 1989/90

Co-operatives in a market economy are self-help organizations composed of private enterprises and households, which themselves are autonomous and self-responsible (→ *State and Co-operatives in Market Economy*). Aside from exceptional cases in the handicrafts and retail sectors, the preconditions of free market autonomy concerning property, decision-making and individual action did not exist in the G.D.R. in the past. A necessary fundament for the existence of co-operative self-help organizations was not at hand, namely that of small and mid-sized company structures, which in turn prevented the development of entrepreneurial behavior and personalities. This deficit in turn negatively affected how the co-operative and the enterprises affiliated in it were managed. The co-operative principles of self-help, self-responsibility and self-management were superceded by goals serving the economy as a whole and by procedural principles following socialistic philosophy and policy. The co-operative identity principle, according to which co-operative members on the one hand are customers, suppliers and workers while on the other hand co-owners responsible for decision-making, was replaced by a pure worker-customer relationship. State directives with regard to co-operatives' supply function altered their promotional mission; the entire economy was to benefit from the tasks and services of the co-operatives, which hereby were made an instrument of state socialistic economic policy.

VI. The Role of the Co-operatives in the Reform Process in the G.D.R.

Lenin's co-operative plan formed the basis of the political-economic concept of co-operatives in the G.D.R. Co-operatives accordingly do not serve as self-help organizations for their members but rather should function as an instrument in the class fight to transform private property into collective property and ultimately into societal or state property. This *transformational function* of co-operative activity in socialism is undergoing a fundamental reversal in the current restructuring process of the G.D.R. economy along market economy lines insafar as co-operatives can contribute to the conversion process of a planned economy into a market economy on a level affecting the entire economy. The necessary precondition for the co-operative's reform function to affect the entire economy of the G.D.R. is, however, management reform of its own structures, or in other words, returning to the original promotional character and/or mission inherent in the co-operative organizational form.

These altered co-operatives could assume a reform function affecting the economy as a whole by reducing to a certain degree the social and economic burdens of the population (inflation, unemployment, loss of social security) which arise in the transformation from a planned economy to a market economy; they thereby assume a protectionary function for their members. The original co-operatives established by → *Raiffeisen* and → *Schulze-Delitzsch* assumed a comparable function. One must however recognize that co-operatives could facilitate the growth and development of market economy structures and mechanisms, but they can not bring about a reform process on their own for the entire economy. Co-operative theory confronts a great challenge in this regard: To develop declarative principles for the role of co-operatives in an economic reform process affecting the entire economy and to realize these principles through pragmatic undertakings.

Co-operatives in the former G.D.R. must undergo a reformation of their own organizational structures if they are to contribute to the reform process in any manner at all. For the most part, co-operatives in the G.D.R. were multi-enterprise production co-operatives which must be transformed back into promotional co-operatives. To achieve this, the potential of self-help and corporate self-responsibility among co-operative members must be (re)activated, for example through the dismantlement of the large co-operatives. Alongside these rather technical and legal aspects of co-operative restructuring in the G.D.R. it is particularly important that the population becomes well acquainted with the principles of the market economy and co-operatives (as a component of the market economy) in the framework of a comprehensive campaign process, and that these ideas become firmly anchored in their consciousness. As the first months following the introduction of a market economy in the G.D.R. have shown, the greatest difficulties and strongest resistance result from the decade-long indoctrination through the socialistic leadership of the G.D.R.

Bibliography

Ahrends, K./Luft, H.: Genossenschaften in der DDR, Einheit, no. 10 (1988), pp. 894–899.

Ashauer, Günter: Das Bankwesen in der Deutschen Demokratischen Republik, in: Sparkasse, no. 1 (1990), pp. 8–26.

Bakonyi, Emmerich: Probleme der Leistungsmotivation in landwirtschaftlichen Produktivgenossenschaften, in: Zeitschrift für das gesamte Genossenschaftswesen, vol. 38 (1988), pp. 77–89.

Bengelsdorf, Reinhold: Über die Genossenschaften in Mitteldeutschland, in: Zeitschrift für das gesamte Genossenschaftswesen, vol. 16 (1966), pp. 31–37.

Busche, M.: Über die Entwicklung der Konsumgenossenschaften Mitteldeutschlands (sowjetische Besatzungszone) auf dem flachen Lande, in: Zeitschrift für das gesamte Genossenschaftswesen, vol. 8 (1958), pp. 293–299.

Friedrich-Ebert-Stiftung (ed.): Genossenschaften in der DDR und in der Bundesrepublik, Bonn 1975.

Haendcke-Hoppe, Michael: Neueste Entwicklungen im privaten und genossenschaftlichen Handwerk der DDR sowie in der sonstigen Privatwirtschaft, FS-Analysen, Berlin 1984.

Haffner, Friedrich: Die Genossenschaften in den sozialistischen Planwirtschaften, in: Jäger, W./ Pauli, H. (eds.), Genossenschaften und Genossenschaftswissenschaft, Wiesbaden 1984, pp. 253–268.

Hartwig, Karl-Hans: Konzeptionen der Genossenschaften in den sozialistischen Planwirtschaften Osteuropas, in: Zeitschrift für das gesamte Genossenschaftswesen, vol.34 (1984), pp. 9–13.

Hartwig, Karl-Hans: Konzeptionen der Genossenschaft in Osteuropa, in: Boettcher, E. (ed.), Die Genossenschaft im Wettstreit der Ideen – eine europäische Herausforderung, Bericht der XI. Internationalen genossenschaftswissenschaftlichen Tagung 1985 in Münster, Tübingen 1985, pp. 213–231.

Herzog, Hans-Joachim: Genossenschaftliche Organisationsformen in der DDR, Schriften zur Kooperationsforschung, Berichte, vol. 12, Tübingen 1982.

Homann, W.: Die Arbeiterwohnungsbaugenossenschaften im Rahmen der Wohnungsbaupolitik der DDR, FS-Analysen 5–1981.

Krebs, Christian: Die Entwicklung der ländlichen Genossenschaften in der DDR, Bundesverband der Raiffeisen-Warengenossenschaften, Mitgliederversammlung, Bonn 1975.

Maaß, H.-C.: "Genossenschaftliche Demokratie" in der DDR, Deutschland-Archiv, vol. 2 (1977), pp. 724–731.

Münkner, Hans-H.: Genossenschaftsideale und Genossenschaftspraxis in beiden Teilen Deutschlands, Vortrag im Rahmen der 20. Generalversammlung der Evangelischen Kreditgenossenschaft eG am 11. Juni 1990 in der Evangelischen Akademie Hofgeismar.

von der Neide, Kurt: Raiffeisens Ende in der Sowjetischen Besatzungszone, Bundesministerium für gesamtdeutsche Fragen, Bonn 1952.

Pfeiffer, Thomas: Genossenschaften in der DDR, Studie im Auftrag des Wissenschaftsfonds der DG Bank, Marburg 1990.

Wapenhans, Willi: Über das Wesen der landwirtschaftlichen Produktionsgenossenschaften in Mitteldeutschland, in: Zeitschrift für das gesamte Genossenschaftswesen, vol.11 (1961), pp. 2–22.

Gierke, Otto von (1841–1921)

FRIEDEL LINNEBORN [J]

(see also: *History in 19th C.*; *Law, National*; *Law, International*; *Classification*)

Otto von Gierke was born in Stettin (today Szczecin in northwest Poland) on January 11, 1841, the oldest of five siblings. His father, member of a family residing in this community since 1729, was at the time of his son's birth a vested civil administrator. His mother, Therese, née *Zitelmann*, hailed from an established family of lawyers in Pomerania and was one of *Ernst Zitelmann's* aunts, the internationally renowned advocate of civil law.

Von Gierke commenced his legal studies at the Berliner Universität in 1857. He returned there in 1859 after a four-semester sojourn in Heidelberg. In the following year he attained his doctorate with a dissertatio inauguratis de debitis feudalibus under the supervision of *Karl Gustav Homeyer*, the editor of the "Sachsenspiegel". His professorship was conveyed in 1867 in Berlin following a passage of his work on co-operative law inspired by *Georg Beseler*.

After turning down a chair offered by the University of Zurich, *von Gierke* was named both associate professor in Berlin in 1871 and full professor in Breslau (today Wroclaw). *Von Gierke* began here to expand the horizon of his activities beyond his teaching and pedagogical responsibilities. He advocated social reform in the Society for Social Policy, which he joined in 1872, and at conferences of the Protestant Social Congress which he jointly founded. He was appointed rector of the Breslauer Universität in 1882/83. Just two years later in 1884 he received and accepted a call from Heidelberg as the successor to the civil law professor *Achille Rechaud*. He returned to Berlin three years later, however, where he was bestowed the position of rector in 1902/03.

In the last years of his life *von Gierke* received numerous distinctions and state honors. Harvard University conferred him an honorary doctorate degree in 1909. Two years later he was raised into the heritable nobility. *Otto von Gierke* died in Berlin on October 21, 1921, after a brief illness.

Von Gierke saw himself as an exponent of the historical school of law. Throughout his entire life he firmly held to its fundamental thesis – that law develops out of the spirit of the people. Deviating from the legal thought of his time based on non-popular Roman codes, he emphasized the national and popular elements of the creation of law, as did his mentor *Georg Beseler*. *Von Gierke* called for legal studies based on historic and philosophic observation of German law. His demands were aimed at finding material standards for civil law. He himself saw the material standard in the "idea of rights" which realizes itself "in the concrete legal formations of human co-operatives, which appear and disappear in the flow of history" (*Kleinheyer/Schröder*, p. 97). He was not able himself to describe this contextualization ("Prototypic justice does not reveal herself to us", a quotation found in *Kleinheyer/Schröder*, p. 97); in his opinion the content of this formation was substantially embedded in certain principles of German law.

Co-operative theory formed one area of concentration within his academic/scientific oeuvre. *Von Gierke* took the term "co-operative" to mean each and every "German legal" body based on voluntary association, much beyond the definition contained in § 1 of the Gennossenschaftsgesetz (GenG, German Co-operative Law) (→ *Legal Form, Co-operative*). Through this he recognized a central phenomenon of German legal identity which encompasses all associations, federations or unions structured in the manner of a body, ranging from the family to the state. The individual in the association is an actual rather than simply a fabricated person; he/she forms an organism capable of acting and entering into liabilities, which is at the same time more than only the sum of the individuals joined together in it (tenet of the actuality of the individual in an association). *Von Gierke* established the connection to the social reality of associations; he instructs us how to recognize the differences and correlations between the existence of an association and its legal capacity. Only the legal capacity of an association is a legal matter, not its existence. Both law and the state are confronted with the given individuals who join associations. The juristic personification of this entity is of course a legal matter, but it is in no way subject to the arbitrariness of the state. Juristic persons can come into being not only through state bestowal but rather also on the grounds of a simple legal clause (for example, common law). Inasmuch as *von Gierke* recognized the correlation between the fact of the existence of an association and the legal question of the personality of an association, he shortened the legal-political leeway of the legislative branch with regard to associations and even laid the foundation for subsequent legal development through common law. This is where his importance in legal policy lies.

Gierke was not able to provide a complete, planned dogmatics of the entire co-operative law. The presentation of the rights of associated individuals in the first volume of "Deutsches Privatrecht" (Munich, 1895) as well as the book "Die Genossenschaftstheorie und die Deutsche Rechtsprechung" (Berlin, 1987, Co-operative Theory and German adjudication) can serve in part as a substitute; here he proves that in his day and age, inspite of formal Roman structures, the legal judgements passed down regarding co-operative law to the most part applied German legal principles in their substance. The four-volume work "Das deutsche Genossenschaftsrecht" (The German Co-operative Law) contains the history of the German co-operative (Vol. I, Berlin, 1868) as well as co-operative theory (Vol. II, Berlin, 1873; Vol. III, Berlin, 1881; Vol. IV, Berlin, 1913). In this opus *von Gierke* describes the development of the German co-operative system and its multifarious character. Simultaneously he presents an history of the dogma concerning associations which is unsurpassable in its entirety (→ *History before 1800*).

Today *Gierke's* reputation in the study of civil law is rather slight. On the one hand many of his justified intents were attended to through legislation at the turn of the century. On the other hand *Gierke's* pugnacious, occasionally overly political-ideological style of thinking only pleases a handful of legal scientists. Those who grapple with texts dating prior to the adoption of the *Bürgerliches Gesetzbuch* (BGB, Code of German Civil Law) complain about a lack of necessary seriousness and meticulousness. Many politically active students of private law nowadays are in the habit of not taking notice of such texts; the sociologists of law could ultimately discover stimulating hypotheses, but they nevertheless hardly consider him a forerunner in methodology.

Bibliography

Janssen, Albert: Otto von Gierkes Methode der geschichtlichen Rechtswissenschaft, Göttingen 1974.
Kleinheyer, Gerd/ Schröder, Jan: Deutsche Juristen aus fünf Jahrhunderten, 3rd ed., Heidelberg 1989, pp. 96ff.
Schmidt, Karsten: Einhundert Jahre Verbandstheorie im Privatrecht, Hamburg 1987.
Wolf, Erik: Große Rechtsdenker der Geistesgeschichte, 4th ed., Tübingen 1963, pp. 667 ff.

Goods: Individual, Private, Collective

ULRICH FEHL [J]

(see also: *Economic Order*; *Competition*; *Institutional Economics*; *Theory of Co-operative Cooperation*; *Commonweal Economy*)

I. Individual Goods Versus Public Goods: The Principle of Physical Exclusion; II. Private Goods Versus Collective Goods: The Principle of Legal Exclusion; III. Problems in the Supply and Allocation of Individual and Public Goods; IV. The Importance of Public Goods for the Co-operative System.

I. Individual Goods Versus Public Goods: The Principle of Physical Exclusion

In economic theory the term *goods* is understood as something which is suited either directly or indirectly to satisfy human needs. The concept of a *good* therefore has quite a broad meaning, it by no means solely encompasses physical objects, but rather also services and abstract rights. The set of goods can be devided into partial sets according to varying criteria. For example, if one chooses to distinguish between whether the good serves consumption directly or indirectly one differentiates between *consumer goods* and *capital goods*. One obtains a further distinction into nondurables or durable consumer goods with respect to whether or not the good is used up in one solitary act of utilization.

The classification of goods discussed in this article focusses on the relationship which exists between the good and the individual as soon as several individuals are involved. If a nondurable can be consumed by only one individual or if a durable consumer good can be used by only one individual at the same time for purely physical reasons, one refers to this as an *individual good*. The utilization of the good by one person excludes its utilization by others. Then the *physical* or "*natural*" *principle of exclusion* is in force. Such exclusive use is at hand, for example, when an economic subject consumes a roll or rides a bicycle. An individual good is therefore characterized by the *absolute* → *competition* among economic subjects with respect to the good's utilization or consumption, respectively.

There are, however, goods for which this competition for utilization either does not occur or only to a lesser extent. Such goods are called *public goods*. Collective consumption then is possible in the sense that the individual's utilization of the public good does not preclude its simultaneous use by others; in other words, the principle of natural exclusion does not apply. Public goods, as is the case for individual goods, can be either nondurables or durable consumer goods, whereby services must likewise be taken into consideration. In any case, these are predominantly durable goods, as the following examples illustrate. Light and warmth emitted by the sun can simultaneously be enjoyed by a great number of persons without any utilization competition arising. This is accordingly true with respect to the utilization of knowledge: When a new technological fact is discovered the knowledge resulting from it can be used by various individuals at the same time. The system of legal norms inherent in a market economy also represents a public good: The application of certain legal norms by certain individuals by no means precludes the simultaneous application of these norms by other persons; on the contrary, the legal system tends to be stabilized when simultaneously used by others. Likewise, a theater performance does permit collective consumption without the participants in principle disturbing one another's enjoyment. This is similarly true for the use of a street. A dyke also offers protection to many residents of a coastal area at the same time.

The list of public goods given above is by no means complete, but the examples do clearly illustrate how public goods can appear in differing variants. In the following two criteria which cast some light on these differences will be briefly discussed. First of all, one has to realize that a *capacity problem* as such does not exist for a number of collective goods, whereas such a problem can very well arise for others (so-called "congestion goods" which play a role in the Theory of Clubs). The examples of sunlight, knowledge and legal norms given above belong to the former group. The latter group can be characterized by the example of a street, where, as with all public goods, collective consumption is in principle possible, but "congestion" develops after reaching a certain point; this is when jointness of consumption has come to an end. Ultimately, in the borderline case of a "standstill traffic jam", no one can make use of the public good in its intended purpose. Under certain conditions a capacity problem can also arise with respect to the good "theater performance". Potential audience members can, in fact, be excluded when a certain "attendance threshold" is reached. The question whether or not a capacity problem exists becomes important when rules must be laid down according to which public goods are to be "distributed", thereby making them accessible for use.

Secondly, some public goods can be used without any additional individual goods, whereas in other cases individual goods represent a de facto prerequisite. The example "theater performance" can again be used to illustrate this.

In addition to the actual theater performance each participant must have at his disposal a particular seat in the theater as an individual good, if he is to "consume" the former. On the other hand, the "street" can be used – at least by a pedestrian – without an individual good being necessary as a prerequisite. This second criterion becomes relevant when the production, allocation and financing of public goods have to be arranged.

II. Private Goods Versus Collective Goods: The Principle of Legal Exclusion

The terms "individual" and "public" good used exclusively up to this point refer to the individual's *physical* access to the good in question. These notions must be strictly distinguished from *legal* access in the sense of *rights for disposal and utilization* (property rights). If an individual possesses such rights referring to an individual good this good is called a *private good*. In this case, not only a physical or natural exclusivity is at hand but also a *legal exclusivity* at the same time. The *collective good* is defined analogously to the private good, whereby legal exclusion refers to a *group*. For example, if a theater performance is sold out the participating audience members consume a "collective good"; all other persons meanwhile remain legally excluded from attending.

It has to be stressed that the language used within this subject is anything but uniform. Many authors use the term "collective good" synonymously with the term "public good". Other authors speak of "collective goods" when exactly that is meant which here is referred to as a "public good", whereas they characterize such goods as "public goods" which are produced – or at least offered – by the state. This article makes use of the terminology provided by *Boettcher* (1974). It has to be realized, however, that *Boettcher* himself is not completely clear in his definition of terms: While defining a "collective good" as stated above he gives a further definition in the sense that for such a good the "non-exclusive *physical* opportunity for its utilization" coincides with the "non-exclusive *legal* opportunity for its utilization". Thus, the non-exclusiveness can only refer to the members of the group which consume or use the collective good (durable consumer good or nondurable) but not to individuals outside the group (non-members). That *Boettcher* by using the term "collective good" solely refers to a (non-exclusive) group of individuals can be recognized by the fact that he speaks of a "private good", if non-exclusivity in the *physical* sense is combined with exclusivity in the *legal* sense (for instance, when an individual purchases all tickets to a theater performance). It can be left undecided whether it would not be more adequate then to speak of a "collective good" when legal access to a public good remains open to all individuals. In any case, it is of crucial importance to distinguish between *physical* and *legal* exclusivity.

By making use of the legal exclusion principle it can be determined who may or may not use a particular good. This process is fairly unproblematic with respect to individual goods since such goods can only be consumed or used by one person; it must only be settled who may have disposal over a certain good. In short, legal assignment makes possible a *personal allocation* of the good, thereby allowing – in principle – the production and distribution of such goods through the market. In any case, the execution of the exclusion principle for individual/private goods – that is, safeguarding property rights – certainly entails costs both upon purchase (costs for accumulating information, for paving the way and preparing for the contractual agreement, supervision) as well as for safekeeping such goods (costs for protection/security). These costs are nevertheless trifling in comparison to the expenses for public goods, because in case of the latter, in order to safeguard the legal exclusion, it is necessary to eliminate every possibility that a third party might have to consume such goods. Such possibilities are a direct consequence of the very character of public goods. Such costs can vary extensively depending on the type of public good. In some situations the costs are not only prohibitively high, but the opportunity to apply legal exclusion can practically disappear at all. This can be clearly illustrated by the example of "sun light" as a public good. The public goods "external" and "internal security" can imply costs for exclusion which are prohibitively high, the same being true for the construction of a "coastal dyke". In the latter case all of those coastal residents who are to be excluded from the use of the dyke must be resettled in the higher lying regions in the interior of the country. In other cases potential users of a public good can not be directly barred out due to technical reasons, for example the listeners of a radio broadcast. Here, the principle of legal exclusion can only react in an so-to-say "ex post manner" by tracking down and prosecuting, i.e. punishing those listeners who were not entitled to "consume" the broadcast. It is the threat of punishment that then leads to exclusion from the onset – at least with a certain probability. The costs of exclusion in this case take the form of supervisional control costs. The execution of the legal exclusion principle also turns out to be quite costly for the public good "street", which is why exclusion is reserved for special cases, such as highways. Here, exclusion costs result from construction measures necessary for exercising control measures as well as from personnel expenses. The principle of legal exclusion can always be implemented with relatively few expenses when the public good can be consumed only in connection with a private good, or when arrangements for joint consumption can be made. For example, a movie in a cinema can only be watched in connection with a seat (private good).

III. Problems in the Supply and Allocation of Individual and Public Goods

Although the application of the legal exclusion principle for public goods is not always possible, it is possible in many cases. Often though, when exclusion is not applied this can be attributed to the fact that exclusion costs are too high. On the other hand, the question of whether or not the exclusion principle is applied not only influences the way the public good is used but also is of decisive importance for the question concerning whether and how it should be produced. In order to illustrate this, at first the case of an individual/private good is reflected upon. Anybody who himself does not produce such a good but who wants to use it has to acquire a right to do so by the way of exchange. As a seller the producer will only then waive such a right when the price covers at least the production costs of the good. Thus, the buyer of an individual good is practically "forced" to undertake a share of the production costs of the good.

Things are completely different with respect to public goods, if the exclusion principle either cannot be applied at all or if it is not practiced on account of exorbitant costs. Given that a good of this kind has already been produced, it can, of course, be used by anyone, which follows as a direct consequence from the character of a "public" good. Since no one can be or, in fact, is excluded from using the good – this holds at least in the case of capacity constraints being absent – no one is interested in undertaking a share of the production costs. In other words, every rationally acting economic unit will speculate that others will do the financing at any rate, that is he or she attempts to succeed as a so-called "*free-rider*". If all potential users behaved in such a way, the public good itself would never be produced at all. But since all potential users are fundamentally interested in having the public good at their disposal, they find themselves in a worse situation than they would if they had taken part in financing the production costs – this being a result of their behaviour which, nevertheless, is individually rational. This particular predicament is called "*prisoners' dilemma*" in game theory. One also speaks of "*market failure*" with respect to the public good. The Gordian knot can be cut when *public authorities* become active; they must guarantee the financing of the production by enforcing the mandatory involvement of all potential users in shouldering the costs (i.e. taxes). It is of secondary importance whether the state itself executes the production or simply makes the necessary arrangements for it. In any case, it this can be explained why certain public goods such as external and internal security as well as the material and non-tangible infrastructure of an economy as a rule are provided by the state.

Of course, the implicitly made assumption is quite extreme that each potential user has roughly the same *utility expectation*, which is negligible in comparison to the "total utility" of the public good, so that he can aspire the position of a "free-rider" because of his slight demand. Actually, there are also cases in which the benefit some individuals expect from using a public good outweighs the costs of producing it. Consequently, they decide to produce and/or provide the good in question, regardless whether the other potential users take part in financing the resulting costs or not. The "free-rider" behavior does not disappear in this situation, but it by no means prevents the public good from being produced and offered. For instance, one can imagine a large corporation participating in the political arena as a lobbyist, advocating a legal measure which would then bring about advantages for all firms in the branch – without the other firms having contributed to the costs of the lobbying. It is by no means assumed that the large corporation is behaving in an altruistic manner. On the contrary, one must rather proceed from the assumption that the firm reflects on its own advantage in a thoroughly individualistic manner. On the other hand, one can, however, classify with certain justification the "free-rider-behavior" of the smaller companies as a kind of exploitation with respect to the large firm (*Olson*, 1965).

Finally, one must also bear in mind that "free-rider-behavior" is to be expected primarily when the number of potential users becomes large. Namely in such cases in which the field of participants is relatively small, the production of public goods tends to be performed without either coercion or the presence of a "large" user: Since reciprocal control is possible among a small number of potential users, no one can avoid his participation in financing the costs which occur through the production of the public good. This at least is the case if certain sanctions are available appropriate to "compell" those inclined to "free-riding". Imagine an oligopoly which forms a cartel-like arrangement to raise the price level: If one of the participating firms does not stick to the agreement and cuts the price – either openly or under cover – the others can relatively quickly detect this activity and threaten with a price war; furthermore, they could start such a price war themselves and thus bring about the desired behavior from the "outsider". If, on the other hand, many companies are involved and thus the average market share of each individual firm as a result is smaller, the underbidder can fish in troubled waters much more easily. In other words, he can attempt to substantially increase his sales volume by reducing his prices only slightly, thus refusing to shoulder his part of the "production costs" of the public good "superelevated (above normal) price and/or profit level", costs which have to be borne in the form of a reduction in the quantity offered. It can thus be maintained that group size represents an essential determinant concerning the provision of public goods. If the group of potential users is small, it is a lot easier to reveal the needs pattern, to organize production and to control the financing of a public good than it would be in the case of a larger group. The production and supply of certain public goods are, however, possible even if "large" users are absent and if the group of potential users is large, the precondition being some individual economic units playing the role of entrepreneurs organizing the necessary activities. The potential users of the public good, themselves not excluded from using the good because of its nature, are prevailed upon to participate in its financing by virtue of a private good offered in connection with the public good. An automobile club serves to illustrate this. It provides a public good by representing the interests of the car owners in the political arena. The private goods which serve to keep the membership tied to such a club assume the form of information services (e.g. club magazine) and general services (e.g. towing, insurance, etc.). Most likely, *Olson* (1965) was the first to analyze extensively this strategy to avoid or reduce "free-rider" behavior with regard to the supply of public goods. Nevertheless it remains unclear why the demanders of the private good do not look elsewhere for its provision, at least in situations in which legal exclusion either is not or cannot be practiced; one certainly cannot assume that the producer of a public good can always offer the private good more favorably than a competitor who only provides the market with the private good. This can, however, be the case when synergy effects arise, that is when the combination of both production processes result in cost reductions for the private good. In the absence of such economies of scope, a state of indifference emerges with respect to the supplier of both public and private goods and the supplier who only offers the private good. This indifference can vanish in favor of the supplier of the public good when the demanders are guided by a "social incentive" (*Olson*, 1965), meaning that they are willing to take part in the production of the public good when this at least does not involve any disadvantages (→ *Incentives*).

The preceding considerations clearly show that public goods are in part provided through markets and in part by public authorities; this raises the question concerning the most efficient form of allocation. It is a normative problem that lies at the root of this consideration, and it is instructive to start with a comparison of the circumstances which are typical of individual goods and public goods, respectively. As is well known, in welfare economics when considering individual or private goods the allocation norm *"price equals marginal costs"* is used as a benchmark, provided the market price is assumed to be uniform, that is when price differentiation is excluded. This means that the marginal buyer's willingness to pay must equal the marginal costs. In the case of a public good, in contrast, a *Pareto-efficient allocation* requires the sum of the marginal willingnesses to pay of all buyers to equal the marginal costs for the production of the good (*Samuelson*, 1954).

A yardstick for the evaluation of the respective quantity (supply) of the public good herewith seems to to be at our disposal. Actually, this criterion does not apply directly, just as is the case with respect to the analogous criterion for individual goods. This essentially is due to the fact that welfare theory restricts its view to the analysis of allocation equilibriums, thereby not taking into consideration the processes leading to such equilibriums. Institutional arrangements, information, incentive and decision structures, transaction costs and normative distribution formulas thus remain excluded. But the decision for a particular mode of providing individual and public goods does require a comparative analysis which – at least to a certain extent – takes into consideration all of the factors mentioned. Because there are numerous factors of influence, the respective analysis can only proceed step by step in the direction of concrete results.

Formal analyses (*Blümel*, 1987) indicate that market allocation as a rule is preferable when the costs for exclusion are low. This is true for individual goods as well as for some public goods, as was stated above. If, on the other hand, the costs for exclusion are high, allocation methods which involve public authorities are preferable. The aspect concerning the costs of exclusion must not be overemphasized. A political (voting) procedure or a bureaucratic apparatus are prerequisites for the production and distribution of public goods in those cases in which high costs of exclusion – in order to determine their quality and the mode of their financing – have to be considered. These political or bureaucratic institutions themselves do not operate free of charge, whereby one must also bear in mind that politicians and bureaucrats tend to follow their own objectives, thereby leading to an overproduction of public goods, as greater power or higher income for politicians and bureaucrats is implied. *"State failure"* can thus result as a consequence (*Buchanan*, 1965). On the other hand, pure market allocation of public goods can lead to an insufficient provision of them. It has already been stated that the production of certain public goods can nevertheless be undertaken even when exclusion opportunities do not exist, i.e. in the situation of a single large company becoming active. On the whole it remains a difficult job to evaluate the various allocation methods.

Specific problems arise with respect to the policy-making (voting) procedure which directly correspond to the character of the public good. The maximum willingness to pay of each individual does not need to be revealed for (individual) goods which are provided through the market. If, on the other hand, a Pareto-efficient allocation is to be realized or at least strived for, the respective willingness to pay and thus the preferences for the public good have to be revealed in order to make the sum of all individuals' willingnesses to pay equal the marginal costs of production. In a situation where exclusion opportunities either do not exist or are exorbitantly expensive, no one can be prevented from utilizing the public good – thus producing an incentive to manipulate. In order to keep as low as possible the financial liability being fixed according to the revealed willingness to pay, there is a strong tendency to understate the marginal willingness to pay with the consequence that the revealed preference for the public good will prove lower than it actually is. Therefore, voting procedures are currently being constructed which eliminate this effect: Potential users are prevailed upon to reveal their "true" preferences, or in other words, the endeavor is to guarantee or at least increase the so-called *"incentive compatability" of the policy-making (voting) procedure.*

IV. The Importance of Public Goods for Co-operative Systems

This closing passage should offer a brief overview of the importance public goods have for co-operative theory (→ *Theory of Co-operatives*; → *Theory of Co-operative Cooperation*) and illuminate fundamental positions on this subject.

1) The question of *group stability* investigated by *Olson* (1965) can be applied to the co-operative as well (→ *Group, the Co-operative*). *Eschenburg* (1971) in this context distinguishes between the "saboteur" and the "outsider", the latter being of much more relevance because he is more dangerous. The outsider gains individual advantages out of his behavior, in a way undermining the optimum of the group. This can be explained by the fact that individual profit maximization and group profit maximazation do not coincide. In pursuit of the individual profit the group profits are reduced. The larger the group the more difficult it is to detect such behavior, and seen from the eyes of the individual, the lower are his costs for such behavior.

2) The "countervailing-power-effect" of co-operatives is frequently referred to in co-operative theory. As a consequence, under certain conditions the competition process is intensified leading to a situation similar to that of complete competition. In the case of a purchasing co-operative, for example, both members and other market participants finally achieve the same price at a

now reduced level. This price is *a public good*: While all buyers can benefit from it it was provided for by the co-operative. In such a situation, however, no incentive exists anymore to become a member of the co-operative.

3) Co-operatives themselves can represent a limited public good, referred to as "club goods" in such context: There are goods which are offered privately yet used collectively. Since they can be offered privately, the exclusion of users in principle is possible but not desired, because they are – at least in a limited sense – to be used in common. The utilization of the goods is limited, implying that these goods are not, in principle, free of rivalries. Tractors, for example, can collectively be used only within a time span but not at the same point in time. The same holds true for a tennis court. Collective → *financing* apparently pays off for the members as costs per club member fall faster (in the beginning) than the individual utility. It is important that this cost-reduction – expressed as a percentage – decreases when the number of users increases; in other words, the marginal cost savings per member approach zero while the opportunity costs (lost utility) increase as membership grows. As a rule, the provision of products or services (e.g. by a → *consumer co-operative*) will follow the average preferences of the group. The preferences of the members tend to be similar to one another within small groups. The more homogenous the preferences are, the more specific the design of the product can be, and the less expensive is the policy-making process, or – in other words – the danger that a member has to pay for services which he or she does not desire at all (or in the provided quantity) tends to be slight. On the other hand, an increasing number of members tends to produce heterogeneity among preferences and it reduces individual utility (e.g. a club's exclusiveness will diminish). Thus, opportunity costs arise as the number of members increases, whereby as a rule it has to be assumed that this increase is disproportionally high. Therefore, an optimal membership size (→ *Group, the Co-operative*) for a given club capacity can be determined, based on the development of such costs. The optimal club size can be specified by varying the number of users and the capacity.

Bibliography

Andel Norbert: Zum Konzept der mentorischen Güter, Finanzarchive, N.F. 42 (1984), pp. 640–648.
Backhaus, Jürgen: Ökonomik der partizipativen Unternehmung, Tübingen 1979, Chapter 6.
Blümel, Wolfgang/Pethig, Rüdiger/von dem Hagen, Oskar: The Theory of Public Goods: A Survey of Recent Issues, in: Journal of Institutional and Theoretical Economics, vol. 142 (1986), pp. 241–309.
Boettcher, Erik: Kooperation und Demokratie in der Wirtschaft, Tübingen 1974, esp. chapter 7 and 8.
Brümmerhoff, Dieter: Finanzwissenschaft, 5th ed., 1990, chapter 4, section 5, chapter 10.
Buchanan, James H.: An Economic Theory of Clubs, in: Economica, vol. 32 (1965), pp. 1–14.
Eschenburg, Rolf: Ökonomische Theorie der genossenschaftlichen Zusammenarbeit, Tübingen 1971.
Kirsch, Guy: Die öffentlichen Güter, in: WISU, vol. 2 (1973), pp. 479–484.
Musgrave, R.A./Musgrave, P.B./Kullmer, L.: Die öffentlichen Finanzen in Theorie und Praxis, 5th ed., Tübingen 1990, chapter 3.
Olson, Mancur: The Logic of Collective Action, Cambridge 1965.
Petersen, Hans-Georg: Finanzwissenschaft I, Stuttgart u.a. 1988, chapter C, section I.
Pommerehne, Werner W./Römer, Anselm U.: Ansätze zur Erfassung der Präferenzen für öffentliche Güter, in: WISt, vol. 17 (1988), pp. 222–228.
Samuelson, Paul A.: The Pure Theory of Public Expenditures, in: Review of Economics and Statistics, vol. 36 (1954), pp. 387–389.
Samuelson, Paul A.: Diagrammatic Exposition of a Theory of Public Expenditures, Review of Economic and Statistics, vol. 37 (1955), pp. 350–355.

Group Theory, Co-operatives in the

PAUL TRAPPE

(see also: *Conceptions, Co-operative*; *Group, the Co-operative*; *Societal Form, Co-operative*; *Relationship Patterns*; *Organizational Structures, Co-operative*; *Configuration*)

I. Co-operative as Social Group; II. Primary and Secondary Groups; III. Group Formation in Segmentary Societies; IV: Group Functions.

I. Co-operative as Social Group

In the social sciences and in common usage, it is generally recognized that the term "co-operative" refers to a collectivity of individuals committed to a common (economic) goal. In a complex, pluralist, decentralized society, the co-operative is one of numerous forms of group organization (→ *Group, the Co-operative*). Thus, the co-operative can be seen to exist in terms essentially characterising the "group":

1) Membership is accounted for by "objective distance" (cf. *Geiger*) with regard either to the group's primary or secondary goals.
2) Group-identity of members is determinable and solidarity-based (→ *Solidarity*).
3) Groups are primarily determined by ingroup-relations in clear distinction to outgroup-relations.
4) Furthermore these conditions of existence require longterm (rather than ad hoc) goals.

Draheim refers explicitly to the → *"dual nature"* of the co-operative both as a collectivity of individuals and as a form of corporate existence. Defining the co-operative as a specialized group "insofar as it acts" in the intersection of the sociological group theory and co-operative theory, *Vierkandt* (and others, including *Draheim*) conceives the co-operative in terms fully characteristic of a collectivity that (still) has group size and structure. As the size and the complexity of the "volume" (in *Durkheim's* sense) of the co-operative increases, the possibility of members to determine policies ceases. Thus, self-regulating and the high degree of integration, which determine co-operative membership, suffer when the independence of the co-operative leadership increases. These tendencies of the internal structure of the co-operative to fluctuate have led to its legal status being adjusted to the more complex conditions of group existence (in the shape of transformations into stock corporations or other legal forms) (→ *Forms of Cooperation*; → *Joint Stock Company*). Classifying the co-operative in terms of the two essential types of groups, however, continues to present problems to sociological group theory and co-operative theory.

II. Primary and Secondary Groups

Based upon *Toennies'* fundamental distinction regarding human social relationships between "Gemeinschaft" (community) and "Gesellschaft" (association), *Cooley* classified groups as primary and secondary. The former are small, being defined by personal intimacy, face-to-face interaction and the high integration of the members' human needs. The latter are larger, being typically defined by the commitment to a joint goal (not necessarily economic, although this is generally the case with co-operatives) at the expense of personal interaction between members. They are "objectivized distanced" (cf. *Geiger*) from basic human needs with little intimacy between members. In practice, *Cooley's* ideal distinction is highly relevant and evidence of its applicability has been widely furnished.

In terms of the distinction between primary and secondary groups, straightforward classification of the co-operative group is made difficult by the co-operative being defined by coherent goals: on the one hand, the co-operative, irrespective of size, develops secondary group characteristics to further its goals; on the other hand, responding to basic human needs, co-operatives nonetheless tend towards "Gemeinschaft", i.e. a high degree of social integration of members. Both in theory and practice, co-operatives with secondary group characteristics, which make multiple memberships possible (especially in poly-co-operative village communities), have emerged in western Europe in particular. Thus, on the basis of large membership as a defining characteristic, it is often presumed that the co-operative is discernible as a secondary group. However, identifying the co-operative in terms of secondary group characteristics on principle is problematic, since the specificity of a co-operative is based not on membership size but rather on the mode of social integration, and in particular on the density of ingroup-relations. Hence, internal structures of the secondary group can be equally apparent in small groups. Neither is small group size usually regarded as a legal constraint on the foundation and licensing of co-operatives. In Switzerland, for example, jurisdiction stipulated a membership of seven for the registration of a co-operative. This does not mean that potential 'side-effects' of small or limited membership, i.e. high social integration of members and developed personal relationships, typical of primary groups, are desirable in small co-operatives. *Von Nell-Breuning* has noted that the tendency of Slavic co-operatives towards collectivism is untypical of the western-european co-operative. According to *Schultz*, provisions for the co-operative as "Gemeinschaft" are not made by present western-European co-operative society laws: in the German Co-operative Law, no provision is made for the upgrading of joint-production co-operatives or full co-operatives. According to *Schultz*, it is worth asking whether "the full co-operative exceeds legal boundaries". No more can be inferred from the legal definition of the western-European co-operative than the decisive status of "the specific purposes underlying co-operative, and sub-co-operative, foundation" (cf. *Schultz*; cf. for example, German Co-operative Law, §1; Swiss Federal Co-operative Society Law, Law of Obligations, Art. 828).

Geiger's derogatory reference to the "Kuhstallwärme der Gemeinschaft" implies that the tendency towards "Vergemeinschaftung" (collectivism, cf. *Geiger*) can occur in all social groups, including the co-operative group. Attempts to transfer the social relations of primary groups into secondary groups (e.g. community-based living groups and producer corporations) or, often under ideological pressures, onto even larger collectivities, i.e., "Volksgemeinschaften", have inevitably failed. They have been accompanied by the large-scale disintegration and erosion of social relationships. The pressure towards wide-spread integration ("Kuhstallwärme der Gemeinschaft", cf. *Geiger*), which is often apparently enhanced by that section of the membership striving for strong community-cohesion, is rather a necessary evil, i.e. an illusory replica of a more primitive society, than a truly desirable conditon. Such conceptions of social relationship appear to have been nurtured either by the model of extended families or similar kinship-based groups of else by sectarian influences on group theory, which take the demand for the total commitment to group → *solidarity* for granted. In on-kinship based groups, these forms of social behaviour are practiced although they are untypical. In particular, they are uncommon in legally defined organizations, such as the co-operative, which come into existence primarily on the basis of joint (economic) goals rather than social relationships. "Objectivized distance" (in *Geiger's* sense) thus offers promising conditions for the survival of a co-operative.

Owen's "New Harmony", which managed to exist for three years in the early nineteenth century (beginning in 1825) (→ *Owen*), was an early form of a self-supporting co-operative community. Even in more collectivist-based societies (for example Mir, Kolkhoze, and possibly Kibbuzim) → *joint-production co-operatives* with high levels of membership integration are subject to a continuous pressure of liberalization, which usually occurs when external forces are less threatening or can be met in new ways.

With secondary groups, and hence with co-operatives, membership size and coherent group structure are considered unproblematic as long as joint policies are not undermined or exploited by uncontrollable oligarchic tendencies (in *Michels'* sense) (→ *Oligarchy in Co-operatives*) or by latent fractionalisation, which may then result in the uncharacteristic suppression of the core concepts of self-management, self-responsibility and self-help in group theory. In western-European → *consumer co-operatives*, where membership can exceed hundreds of thousands, the principles of the co-operative group no longer apply, since alternative legal forms, in particular the stock corporation, are in force either de facto or on principle.

In terms of the group pluralism of the complex society, the secondary group co-operative has emerged as the wide-spread type of co-operative world-wide. In non-european cultures, it has been extraordinarily successful given the pursuit of a member-oriented, thus recognizable and commonsensical, goal. In particular, this positive experience was made in colonial times and after independence in anglophone regions (Assam, Sri Lanka, anglophone Africa, etc.) where collectivist co-operative forms never arose. In the years following independence attempted returns to collectivism, such as the Ujamaa–Villagization-Schemes, were stifled in their beginnings by social and economic constraints and subsequently failed.

In terms of the complexity of society at large, group theory brackets the co-operative group under the particular complexity of group pluralism. Thus, the co-operative group is one of many groups (including ideal forms). Their density, number, relation and interdependences are regarded as indicative of the social structure of an entire society. Statistical evidence shows that the density of co-operatives (co-operative memberships per household) is highest in Switzerland. Thus, co-operative pluralism is a factor of general group pluralism, which essentially characterises a society as complex, and defines the form and substance of social change. Social pluralism is based on all groups in which the citizen appears as "homo associativus" (cf. *Meier-Dallach*). In social development, group pluralism functions at an intermediary level between the individual and the state. This position informs the common theoretical and empirical distinction between "socially intermediary powers" and the classical political powers in a society.

III. Group Formation in Segmentary Societies

Vierkandt has shown that there are good reasons for assuming that a "genossenschaftliche Gesellschaftsform" ('social structure built up by co-operative') existed in primitive societies (→ *Societal Form, Co-operative*). This means that they were organized in a segmentary way (i.e. as a system of clans in *Durkheim's* sense), implying a coherent organization and economic policy-making in terms of the three key principles of modern co-operatives: self-help, self-management and self-responsibility. Economic self-sufficiency and comparative political independence define the almost ideal configuration of autonomy of *Durkheim's* "société segmentaire". Writing on the changes afflicting segmentary systems, *Balandier* and *Wallerstein* have noted that these result from the dissolution of the original segments together with the formation of groups whose members neither belong to the original segment nor to the originally dominant kin. It is of interest that groups developing out of the segmentary society often bear traits similar to co-operatives. This similarity can either be explained by the survival of certain forms of economic co-operation from primitive societies or by the association of the original group with on-kinship members being tolerated in economic and/or social terms on the basis of necessarily solidarity-based and common-sensical goals (e.g. associations of artisans, fishermen, cattle-breeders and farmers with joint interests in maintaining infrastructures achieved through co-operation, such as wall-building, house-building, and the building of irrigation systems). This social transition from kinship-based or primary groups (i.e. families, clans, possibly determined by "lineage" in terms of face-to-face interaction and high integration factor of social relationships) to non-kinship based or secondary groups (determined by coherent purposes, "objectivized distance" and restricted social integration) is a remarkable change within the general reorientation of society. Analogous to the "neolithic revolution", this transition could be termed a decisive social revolution of segmentary societies, if the notion of 'revolution' is used to refer to extraordinary long-term development. This revolution means that fundamentally open, co-operative and non-co-operative group forms arise in segmentary systems, which evidence "proto-democratic" associations. In *Marx's* view, parallel developments occur in strict hierarchical social systems, which evidence "stereotypically recurring" social forms of life for the masses ("asiatic despotism" and "oriental means of production"). Social change on the basis of group formations can result in economic differentiation through which "functional chains" (in Elias' sense) arise to help "the civilizing process" get underway (cf. Elias). Although group pluralism is universal, according to Elias' correct assessment, it only exists in preliminary or potential forms. Group pluralism brackets various kinds of group forms, of which the co-operative group is the most recurrent world-wide, and has the best chances of enhancing social and economic change. On principle, the inherent tendency of the co-operative is opposed both to the seeming collectivism of the autarchic kinship-based group and to the Marxist conception of a substitute, "alternative" kinship-based group. Housing co-operatives are regarded as such an "alternative", although they are fundamentally different to long-term and institutionalized kinship-based groups.

IV. Group Functions

Current critical debate is particularly concerned with the functions of specific group formations, such as group pluralism, and how these might be made possible in society at large. Various functions are named in terms of effects: integration effect and performance respectively; stabilization, i.e. the ability of groups to overcome crises without state intervention; "social control", which is the imperative state jurisdiction and general social order; solidification, i.e. "l'union fait la force" (in → *Schulze-Delitzsch's* sense "join those with similar interests to realize your own"); and the communicative function, according to which the reception of everyday and complex political information should be ensured by being processed at group level.

Critical debate has recurrently emphasized the economic function of co-operatives and other groups. Current attempts to mobilize the "informal sector" (in particular in urban areas) in developing countries through "institution building" reflect core developmental policies of the 1960s. These attempts to fight poverty and accomplish large-scale restructuring, even under virtually anomic social conditions, promise success if they are harnessed to pre-colonial (→ *Autochthonous Co-operatives*) or colonial practices ("indirect rule" systems in anglophone regions in particular). Examples from all developmental regions, including Europe, can be cited as evidence. Of particular importance are the social and legal norms anchoring the institutions, which are purpose-directed groups. Thus, institutionalization is a formal pre-condition of socio-economic development (→ *Development Policy*). Its socio-political use, however, does not occur as a matter of course, since it depends on a variety of culture-specific factors, including the degree and dynamics of group density.

Irrespective of the interplay of these factors, however, such development brings new social classes and new power factors to life, though it does not necessarily reduce social inequality or the chasms of social differentiation.

Translation: Mark Kyburz

Bibliography

Albrecht, Gerhard: Die soziale Funktion des Genossenschaftswesens, Abhandlungen und Vorträge, Berlin 1965.
Balandier, Georges: Sociologie des Brazzavilles Noires, Paris 1955.
Cole, George Douglas Howard: Self-Government in Industry, London 1917.
Cole, G.D.H.: Guild Socialism Re-stated, London 1920.
Cooley, George Horton: Social Organization, Human Nature and the Social Order, Glencoe 1956 (1909).
Draheim, Georg: Die Genossenschaft als Unternehmungstyp, 2. ed., Göttingen 1955.
Draheim, G.: Genossenschaften I, Überblick und Entwicklung. In: Handwörterbuch der Sozialwissenschaften, vol. 4, Göttingen 1965, pp. 350–373.
Dülfer, Eberhard: L'efficacité opérationelle des coopératives agricoles dans les pays en développement, Rome 1975.
Durkheim, Emile: De la division du travail social, Paris 1893.
Ehrlich, Stanislaw: Pluralism on and off course, Oxford, New York 1982.
Elias, Norbert: Über den Prozess der Zivilisation, Basel 1939.
Fürstenberg, Friedrich: "Die Genossenschaft als sozialer Integrationsfaktor", in: Jahrbuch für Sozialwissenschaft, vol. 15, Göttingen 1964, pp. 243–255.
Geiger, Theodor: Die Gesellschaft zwischen Pathos und Nüchternheit, Kopenhagen 1960.
Gierke, Otto von: Das deutsche Genossenschaftsrecht, vol. 4, Berlin 1868–1887.
Gierke, Otto von: Das Wesen der menschlichen Verbände (Rektoratsrede), Leipzig 1902.
Henzler, Reinhold: Die Genossenschaft eine fördernde Betriebswirtschaft, Essen 1957.
Lipset, Seymour Martin (ed.): Union Democracy, Glencoe 1956.
Meier-Dallach, Hans-Peter: Die Schweiz zwischen Traditionalität und Modernität, Konflikte und Konfliktregelungsmodelle, Die Schweiz, Stuttgart, Berlin 1988, pp. 100–127.
Middleton, John/Tait, David: Tribes without Rulers, Studies in African Segmentary Systems, London 1958.
Naucke, Wolfgang, Trappe, Paul (eds.): Rechtssoziologie und Rechtspraxis, Neuwied 1970.
Schäfers, Bernhard (ed.): Einführung in die Gruppensoziologie, Geschichte, Theorien, Analysen, Heidelberg 1980.
Schmitt, Günther: Landwirtschaftliche Produktivgenossenschaften in Theorie und Praxis, Zeitschrift für das gesamte Genossenschaftswesen, vol. 41, (1991), pp. 279–297.
Schneider, Bertrand: Die Revolution der Barfüssigen, Ein Bericht an den Club of Rome, Wien, München, et al. 1986.
Schultz, Dietrich: Der Rechtsbegriff der Genossenschaft und die Methode seiner richtigen Bestimmung, Düsseldorf 1958.
Trappe, Paul (ed.): Politische und gesellschaftliche intermediäre Gewalten im sozialen Rechtsstaat (Social Strategies, vol. 22), Basel 1990.
Vierkandt, Alfred: Die genossenschaftliche Gesellschafts-

form der Naturvölker. In: Handwörterbuch der Soziologie, Tübingen 1931.
Wallerstein, Immanuel: The Road to Independence, Ghana and the Ivory Coast, Paris, La Haye 1964.
Weber, Max: Wirtschaft und Gesellschaft, Grundriss der verstehenden Soziologie, Tübingen 1921.
Weippert, Georg: Gruppe. In: Handwörterbuch der Sozialwissenschaften, vol. 4, Göttingen 1965, pp. 718–725.
Westermann, Harry: Der Einzelne und die Gemeinschaft im Spiegel des Genossenschaftswesens, Göttingen 1957, pp. 20–34.

Group, Common Initiative

EMMANUEL KAMDEM

(see also: *Pre-co-operative Forms*; *Autochthonous Co-operatives*; *Law, International*; *Self-help Organizations*; *Development Policy*)

I. Introduction; II. Definition and Functioning of Common Initiative Groups; III. Common Initiative Groups and Traditional Self-help Groups; IV. Common Initiative Groups and Pre-co-operatives; V. Common Initiative Groups and Co-operative Societies; VI. Conclusion.

I. Introduction

Nowadays, because of failure in cooperative promotion in many developing countries (→ *Development Policy*), new forms of organization are developed on the basis of the cooperative principle, but refusing to adopt the name "co-operative". Those forms of cooperation initiated by NGO, farmers, workers, fishermen etc. themselves are neither the traditional form of self-help, nor pre-co-operatives expecting to become co-operatives in the future. They are fully independent forms parallel to classical cooperative organizations.

Those forms are called "farmers' groups", "associations" and many other denominations. In many African countries, co-operative projects or programmes are only accepted by the government or farmers if they are labeled "co-operatives and similar organizations", or "co-operatives and other self-help organizations", or "co-operatives and associative movements", or "co-operatives and groupings" etc... Thus a lot of countries are seeking a legal form for the small-scale farmers and lower-level workers to adopt the "co-operative" as a model, but find the structure too complicated. The grassroots population wants to have a "simple structure" to replace the co-operative, but a complementary one.

It is within this framework that the new law No. 92/006 of August 14, 1992, relating to co-operative societies and common initiative groups in Cameroon, gives a legal form to this new form of organization. However "common initiative groups" should be considered as special types of co-operatives since the law relating to the two forms of organizations is the same, namely the above-mentioned law No. 92/006 of August 14, 1992.

II. Definition and Functioning of Common Initiative Groups

The Cameroonian law No. 92/006 of August 14, 1992 governs both cooperative societies and common initiative groups. However, some provisions are common to both forms and some govern them separately. Sections 49 to 53 of the above-mentioned law govern only the common initiative groups:

Section 49: "Common initiative groups are organizations of an economic and social nature set up voluntarily by individuals having common interests and working together as groups".

Section 50 (1): "Common initiative groups shall be formed by a declaration in writing, drawn during a constituent meeting of at least 5 (five) persons."

Section 50 (2): "A union of common initiative may be formed by 2 (two) such organizations".

Section 51 provides that common initiative groups, as legally constituted co-operative bodies, shall be the only representatives to act for and on behalf of their members which shall have exclusive rights to their services.

For their functioning, common initaitive groups (section 52 of the law) shall freely adopt their articles of association, which shall be in writing, and shall have provisions concerning:

a) the object, main activities, area of jurisdiction, name, head office and duration of the group;
b) the duties of its officials, the duration of their term of office and their mode of appointment;
c) conditions for the admission and withdrawal of members;
d) the organization and functioning of the group, in particular the appointment of officials; the manner in which decisions on loan applications are taken; investment decisions; amendment of articles of association; the dissolution of the group or its change of legal status;
e) the extent of members' activities with the groups;
f) the liability of a member in respect to the debts of the group and the basis on which it is calculated.

Section 50 (3): in addition:

a) Each common initiative group shall appoint a delegate in charge of representing it in all civil matters within the limits of the powers conferred on him by the regulations and discussions of the said group.
b) The officials of each common initiative group shall keep simplified accounts to permit the periodic assessment of the reserves of said groups and justify any changes. The interval between such assessments shall not exceed 2 (two) years.

c) Officials of each common initiative group shall keep an updated register of the members and accounts of individual contributions to the reserves of the said groups.

Section 53 of the above-mentioned law provided that "a common initiative group or a union of such groups may become a co-operative or join a co-operative society or a union of co-operative societies".

Thus the law just gives the guidelines in which the common initiative group should unite and adopt its article for its functioning. This form of organization is new as a legal form, but meets the reality in the field. The background of the Cameroonian policy was to enable the individuals to make a choice and freely elect the form of grassroots organization they wanted for their business. Apart from classical forms of co-operatives the government adopted two other forms of legal organization: the present "common initiative groups" and the "groupement d'intérêt économique" (economist interest group) which we shall not develop here.

The common initiative groups "officialize" the status already existing in the field: at the grassroots level, people have the need to group themselves to undertake together economic activities. However they wish to adopt a simple structure, at least in the beginning, leaving them the option in the future to choose a more complex one as their business grows. The common initiative groups are different from the traditional self-help group, the pre-co-operative and the co-operative; they are a modern form of cooperation without the co-operative status.

III. Common Initiative Groups and Traditional Self-help Groups

The traditional self-help groups are very old informal organizations based on neighbourhood cooperation. Thus they differ from the common initiative groups which are modern, new, recognized organizations. The aims of both organizations might be the same since they are working in the same economic and social areas. The common initiative groups can be considered an answer to whether traditional forms of cooperation can represent a step towards co-operative organization. By adopting such common initiative groups, the traditional form of self-help can obtain a legal status. As common initiative groups are allowed to become co-operative societies, or join a union of co-operative societies, the path followed towards this type of organization seems to be smoother than a direct transformation of common initiative groups into co-operative societies. Another advantage is that the structure of common initiative groups is as simple as the one existing in traditional self-help organizations.

We are thus faced with two co-operative organizations without co-operative status, the one traditonal and the other modern. The main interest of the latter is that it can easily be transformed into a co-operative society.

IV. Common Initiative Groups and Pre-co-operatives

Pre-co-operatives (→ *Informal Co-operatives*) are self-help organizations aiming to become co-operative societies. A pre-co-operative is therefore any kind of organization whose objective is to become a co-operative. Thus it differs from the common initiative group which can remain as such forever. However the common initiative group can become a co-operative if the members so decide; it can also join a union of co-operatives while keeping its legal form. Both organizations are registered in the same register as the co-operatives. While the pre-co-operative constitutes a learning stage before becoming a full-fledged co-operative society, the common initiative group needs no change. The Cameroonian common initiative groups are fully independent at their end stage, in contrast to non-registered pre-co-operatives such as: the "groupements mutualistes villageois (GMV)" in Niger; the "groupement villageois (GV)" in Burkina Faso; registered pre-co-operatives such as the probationary societies in Kenya, Tanzania and Uganda; the "association d'intérêt rural (AIR)" in Sénégal; the "groupement à vocation coopérative (GVC)" in Côte d'Ivoire, and the "Samahang Nayon" in the Philippines.

The use of this nearly independent form of co-operation, governed by the same laws as the co-operative societies, registered in the same place, seems to be more adequate as a stage towards achieving co-operative status than the pre-co-operative forms. It is to hope that the common initiative groups will be tested in other developing countries.

V. Common Initiative Groups and Co-operative Societies

The common initiative group is not an alternative to co-operative societies, in reality it is complementary. The same law governs the two organizations in Cameroon.

The general provisions provide that persons shall be free to set up a co-operative society or a common initiative group, and that no person may be compelled to join or prevented from joining any of them, or a union formed by such bodies.

Section 3 of the law provides that co-operative societies, common initiative groups and unions shall be autonomous private bodies belonging to their members, who shall manage, fund and control them. Their activities shall be carried out without state interventions, subject to the provisions of this law and its implementation decree, or subject to agreement freely entered into, which may also be freely denounced. In opposition to common initiative groups, whose members should only be individuals, co-operative societies can have corporate bodies as members.

Section 8 of the law defines the co-operative society as "a group of individuals of corporated bodies who freely enter into partnership in order to attain common goals by setting up an enterprise which is managed in a democratic manner and to which they are bound by a contract which shall, in particular, lay down the rules governing:

- their activities with this organization;
- the equitable distribution of its capital;
- profit and risk-sharing in the said branch of activity."

Thus, the co-operative society should set up an enterprise, while this is not necessary in the case of a common initiative group. Both organizations can spread their activities to all economic sectors which shall be defined in their articles of association, on the basis of the interests of their members.

Furthermore, the transactions between a co-operative society, or a common initiative group and its members, shall constitute its main activity. That means that each organization should respect the principle of identity between members, co-owners and customers (suppliers or workers).

In general, in the new Cameroonian law, there are common provisions applicable to co-operative societies and common initiative groups, namely section 54 to 86 relating to registration (chapter 1); notification and information (chapter 2); splitting amd merging (chapter 3); dissolution (chapter 4); federation (chapter 5); and miscellaneous, transitional and final provisions.

Section 73 provides that: (1) with a view to representing and defending their common material and moral interests, co-operative societies, common initiative groups and their unions may form federations of co-operative societies and/or common initiative groups; (2) such federations may merge to form confederations; (3) they may seek membership in international organizations having similar objectives...".

VI. Conclusion

The common initiative group (groupe d'initiative commune) is a new form of co-operation without co-operative status, but working under → co-operative principles. It is a legalization of a pre-existing status in the field in many developing countries. It responds to a need felt by co-operators, especially at the grassroots level, where on the one hand farmers often refuse to adapt to co-operatives which they find too complicated, and on the other NGO's and some donors prefer to operate under a simpler form of co-operation.

Common initiative groups can remain as such for ever or be transformed into co-operative ventures. They can also join co-operative ventures, form unions and federations with them, even confederations. It is our belief that the common initiative group should be encouraged as a form, developed and introduced in other countries in order to fill the existing gap in co-operative legislation.

Bibliography

Cameroon, Republic of: Law No. 92/006, August 14, 1992: Relating to co-operative societies and common initiative groups.
Münkner, H.-H.: Le statut juridique de la précoopérative, Friedrich-Ebert-Stiftung, Göttingen 1980.
Schiller, Otto: Die Kooperation in der Landwirtschaft, in: Handbuch der Landwirtschaft und Ernährung in den Entwicklungsländern, Stuttgart 1967.

Group, The Co-operative

FRIEDRICH FÜRSTENBERG [J]

(see also: *Group Theory*; *Organizational Structures, Co-operative*; *Dual Nature*)

I. The Co-operative Group as a Theoretical Paradigm; II. Findings from Cultural Anthropology and Social History; III. Sociological Analysis.

I. The Co-operative Group as a Theoretical Paradigm

Co-operatives are not simply economic organizations but also specific social phenomena. The perception of social relationships between those involved fundamentally determines their goal orientation and self-conception. The paradigm of the co-operative as a group, particularly outlined by *Georg Draheim* (1952, pp.19–48), should be examined in this context. From this angle the co-operative as an association of individuals is at the same time a group founded upon a common feeling of being threatened and oppressed. This co-operative nexus is considered to be rooted anthropologically ("homo cooperativus"). The *perception* of "we" may intensify to an *awareness* or *consciousness* of "we" (*Weippert*), and thereby the co-operative group constitutes a community. In principle, this paradigm can be perceived as a model for co-operative theory, grounded in part empirically, which, in normative application provides the framework for relevant strategies. Evidence drawn from cultural anthropology and social history as well as a systematic sociological analysis should serve to evaluate its empirically based explicative capacity.

II. Findings from Cultural Anthropology and Social History

Indications from ethnologists pointing to the "co-operative character of primitive man" (*Vierkandt*) were influential for the anthropological "group orientation" of co-operative research. In contrast to feudal or hierarchical forms of society, *Vierkandt* saw the co-operative type characterized by an essentially symmetrical distribution of power between the various individuals and groups, resulting in the derivation of particular social manners; the "cardinal values of the co-operative community" above all include self-respect, respect for strangers and self-control. An idealizing model approach of this kind, however, does not hold its ground in the face of serious source analysis. The characteristic of relative freedom from domination and/or a neutralization of power in co-operative organizations, nevertheless, has been hailed as an attribute up to the present. *Draheim*, for example, refers emphatically to the group as the center of co-operative policy making and in this context particularly to the principle of "one-man-one-vote". The "group paradigm" attains support also from socio-historical research on the genesis of modern co-operatives. Especially the concept of "members' living condition" (→ *Conceptions, Co-operatives*) is used as an approach in this connection (*Engelhardt*). The early literature on co-operatives points to the relatively disadvantaged living condition of potential co-operative members which could lead to the expression of common needs suited to foster a co-operative. In contrast to an individualistic interest orientation, being the basis for an "incentive-contribution theory" (→ *Incentives*) claiming purpose-based rationality, such solidaric orientation corresponds to value-based rationality. (see *von Brentano*, p. 140). This is empirically documented in the attitudes of "co-operative pioneers". One might recollect *Robert Owen's* aspirations for social reform, the religious influences on the Rochdale pioneers or *Raiffeisen's* personality, driven by forceful sociopedagogical impulses. The latter, as a pragmatist, also understood that his loan societies were dependent on strong group cohesion for their continued existence and effectiveness. As a consequence of this he undertook to delimit them as small as possible according to the principle of "localization", to organize them in "districts easily surveyable", and, furthermore, especially to promote co-operative education and upbringing.

If we cast our attention to the current establishment of "co-operative enterprises" with "alternative" structures which frequently exhibit co-operative characteristics or similar features, the intentional, value-oriented scope of activity centered around the group also becomes evident.

Characteristics of the ("Idealtyp") "co-operative group" can similarly be identified in co-operatives which are conceived as "cohesive life-long communities" (Vollgenossenschaften) and which maintain themselves as such. This, for example, is true for several co-operative settlements (→ *Communal Settlements*) in the USA predominantly structured along religious lines (Hutterites, Amish). These by any rate are exceptional forms, however, which are atypical for the usual structure of modern co-operatives. As for the rest, *Oppenheimer's* assertion, updated and more clearly stated by *Beyer* and *Nutzinger*, is applicable, especially to companies with co-operative self-management: "They will either die an economic death in pure democratic beauty or else relinquish their basic democratic structure as a result of economic success" (*Beyer/Nutzinger*, p.15).

Ethnological and socio-historical data so only provide limited information concerning the general empirical applicability of the co-operative group paradigm. Nevertheless, there are sufficient references to the importance of social relations within groups for the identification and delineation of preconditions for as well as expressions and effects of co-operative activities. This is justification enough for an attempt to analyze the actual group character of co-operatives systematically and, subsequently, empirically.

III. Sociological Analysis

An appropriate point to commence the discussion is a closer specification of what is implied when using the term "group". The term "group" is used in sociology as a characterization of social relationships (interactions) which exist on a fairly permanent basis between persons and which lead to the formation of common patterns of behaviour and orientation. The *small group* is at the heart of this investigation, one in which the reciprocal relationships are direct and the social roles are relatively non-specific rather than functionally differentiated. Accordingly, emotional relationships could develop intensively. The earlier literature on co-operatives apparently drew reference to this type, particularly when value considerations were theorized permitting the derivation of typical co-operative traits. This orientation around the small group, however, is questionable in the face of the formation of large co-operative organizations with far-reaching functionalization, hierarchical structure and targeted rationalization of action resulting from market orientation. In such cases reality is better addressed by the term "organization", described as a functional social entity which corresponds with a federation or enterprise. Occasionally the terms "large group" or "secondary group" are also used. In contrast to the small group, the decisive characteristics are the determination of a target structure, the appropriate utilization of means which enhance performance, as well as the formal co-ordination of the supporters/participants striving for controlled output efficiency.

Large modern co-operatives exhibit both business and associational structures as they provide economic output as well as representation of member interests. In such organizational forms co-operatives are able to boast a substructure consisting of (possibly) numerous small groups; co-operative centers can thus also serve as the nucleus of co-operative consciousness, just as *Draheim* points out. It is, however, inadmissable to suggest by using the term "group" that a large organization has the same behaviour traits as a small group. *Von Brentano's* advice not to establish uncritically a certain *model* conception (p. 142) should be observed. Otherwise social integration by group awareness is postulated for which there is no real chance or reason.

From a sociological point of view the paradigm of the co-operative group must also be analysed according to its ideological contents. It needs to be contrasted with the verification of the group character of co-operative social phenomena in real life.

It is frequently pointed out that the degree of organizational integration can be negatively influenced by the formation of large co-operatives through the dissolution of the communitarian social structure, and that this in particular weakens the awareness and active expression of solidarity. This, however, must not occur unconditionally. Small co-operative groups facilitate comprehensive solidarity similar to that of cohesive life-long communities. Large co-operative organizations encourage member solidarity to the extent that an integrated goal orientation is possible which, however, is limited to aspects of membership roles and does not cover all social manifestations of the individuals (*Fürstenberg* 1968).

Thus, "the co-operative group" as an actual phenomenon is characterized by varying organizations. Typical social relationships have changed, taking the direction of a more rational goal orientation and more functional role contributions, in accordance with the domination of business co-operatives (Teilgenossenschaften) and their development from primary to secondary co-operatives – even to multi-leveled organizations, some already transnational in their scope. The problems which are posed in this process are not only ideological in character in the sense of a shift in frames of reference, but they also affect the fundamental co-operative task in real life: The promotion of members through co-operative means which are relatively self-determined and participatory. *Claessens* systematically analyzed the problems which arise through the establishment of group associations, amalgamating smaller groups into one large group. He emphasized the tension between the spontaneity characteristic of small groups and the necessity to compensate and balance interests in group associations; this tension can be observed under authoritative as well as co-operative management; in the latter case, however, it is based on a "spontaneity limit" set somewhat higher.

From the sociological point of view the paradigm of "the co-operative group" also refers to the structure of member relationships. This can, however, only be analyzed if the term "group" is not used ideologically but applied in a verifiable manner. The focus of earlier co-operative research thus still remains preserved: The social meaning and real correspondence of the term "co-operative". It is simply presented in a different formulation, not as the postulate of a "collective consciousness" but rather as the potential and experience of participation. Various dimensions need to be considered: *first* the varying number of individuals, *second* the manner the functions and/or roles are allocated, and *third* the method of consensus formation. The decisive determinant is the morphological uniqueness along *co-operative* traits, not simply the size of the group itself. This is expressed in specific aspects of member integration: The activation of a common goal-oriented interest is concentrated on self-help through solidarity; the functional coordination of actions to achieve this goal does not disengage the self-initiative and self-responsibility of the members; ultimately a collective consciousness, a co-operative idea may emerge which extends to the members' live style (*Fürstenberg* 1964).

The relationship between an actual formal "solidaric constitution" (*Hettlage*) of co-operatives and the group characteristics is reciprocally reinforcing (→ *Organizational Structures, Co-operative*). The existence of small groups or intentional associations is an equally insufficient precondition for the continued existence of co-operatives as the presence of a co-operative idea and its codification is to create a corresponding social organization. Only through the integration of these aspects can the formation of a "co-operative group" be achieved.

This sociological understanding of the co-operative system has eminent practical importance, in particular for maintaining co-operative organizations or increasing their size. As one can easily expect, economic goal orientation entails maintaining one's ground in a competitive market. This, however, must additionally encompass the orientation of output and/or performance to members' needs which occurs through the development of specific social relations based on the highest participation level possible. The co-operative as a "co-operative group" or as an intentional association must have strategies at its disposal which in this respect differentiate it from other economic organizations. They substantially concern the internal structure, which, however, should not curb their importance.

The paradigm of the "co-operative group", in spite of frequently being expressed in a form which locks it in time and despite its often insufficiently grounded explicative value, has the important function never to stop addressing the problem of co-operative identity and to continue providing innovative impulses.

Bibliography

Beyer, Heinrich/Nutzinger, Hans G.: Partizipatives Management und Management im Selbstverwaltungsunternehmen, in: Arbeitskreis für Kooperation und Partizipation e.V. (ed.): Kooperatives Management, Baden-Baden 1990, pp. 13–37.
von Brentano, Dorothee: Grundsätzliche Aspekte der Entstehung von Genossenschaften, Berlin 1980.
Claessens, Dieter: Gruppenverbände als Zusammenschluß kleinerer Gruppen zu einer Großgruppe, in: Schaefers, Bernhard (ed.): Einführung in die Gruppensoziologie, Heidelberg 1980, pp. 127–144.
Draheim, Georg: Die Genossenschaft als Unternehmungstyp, Göttingen 1952.
Draheim, Georg: Zur Ökonomisierung der Genossenschaften, Göttingen 1967.
Engelhard, Werner W.: Allgemeine Ideengeschichte des Genossenschaftswesens, Darmstadt 1985.
Fürstenberg, Friedrich: Die Genossenschaft als sozialer Integrationsfaktor. Jahrbuch für Sozialwissenschaft, vol. 15 (1964), pp. 243–255.
Fürstenberg, Friedrich: Ansatzpunkte einer Soziologie des Genossenschaftswesens, in: Weisser, G. (ed.): Genossenschaften und Genossenschaftsforschung, Göttingen 1968, pp. 42–51.
Hettlage, Robert: "Solidarität" und "Kooperationsgeist" in genossenschaftlichen Unternehmen, in: Arbeitskreis für Kooperation und Partizipation e.V. (ed.): Kooperatives Management, Baden-Baden 1990, pp. 123–152.
Vierkandt, Alfred: Die genossenschaftliche Gesellschaftsform der Naturvölker. Handwörterbuch der Soziologie, 2nd edition, Stuttgart (1932) 1959, pp. 191–201.
Weippert, Georg: Gruppe. Handwörterbuch der Sozialwissenschaften, vol.4, Göttingen 1950, pp. 718–725.

Guilds

ALFRED KIESER

(see also: *History before 1800*; *History of Ideas*; *Economic Order*; *Informal Co-operatives*)

I. The Genesis of Guilds; II. The Functions of the Guild; III. Institutional Characteristics; IV. The Decline of the Guild; V. Interpretation of the Specific Institutional Characteristics of the Guild.

I. The Genesis of Guilds

Guilds were medieval corporations of craftsmen or merchants, acknowledged by authorities, which exclusively granted their members the right to practice the respective craft (*Zorn* 1965) (→ *History before 1800*). In Germany, these corporations were first mentioned in documents dating from the early twelfth century (*Wissel* 1971).
For a long time, the genesis of craft guilds was a much debated issue among historians. The "*feudal manor theory*" (*Müller*) proposes that the craft guilds developed out of the feudal manors, which, before the origin of towns, formed the basic social units of mediaval society. These feudal manors were to a high degree economically self-sufficient. With the development of towns, the demand for skilled craftsmen greatly increased and was met by craftsmen moving from the feudal manors into the towns. The feudal manor theory assumes that these craftsmen, once they had settled in the town, had to wait for a considerable length of time before they were eligible to become free citizens. They still belonged to a feudal lord, who, according to their profession, allocated certain streets and quarters of the town to them and put them under the command of master craftsmen who performed a judicial role and collected imposts. According to the feudal manor theory, this structure led to craft guilds as soon as the towns became independent from wordly or ecclesiastical rulers.

The "*office theory*" proposed by *Keutgen* argues that those craftsmen who had moved to the towns advanced so rapidly to the status of a free citizen that their feudal origin did not bear much influence on the subsequent development of guilds. According to this theory, guilds were initiated by offices created by the town magistracies for two reasons: (1) to ascertain that the taxes were paid to the town and church, and (2) to protect the poor from any exploitation and manipulation by the craftsmen and merchants. At this time, markets were fairly new institutions and so the buyers had not yet developed an equitable code of conduct. Soon, the price controls imposed by the offices over the marketplace were extended to measures and weights and, finally, to the production processes, which in turn led to a standardization of procedures. Out of this subordination under a collective control and out of the allocation of marketplaces, stalls, shops, etc. to groups of craftsmen in the same trade, there awoke a joint interest among those concerned that eventually resulted in the development of guilds. Critics of this theory maintain that it by far overestimates the influence of the town magistracies (*Irsigler*).

Below assumes that people of the early Middle Ages had a strong desire for forming associations, and on this assumption he based his "*unification theory*". More recent studies also emphasize the extraordinary co-operative spirit of the Middle Ages (→ *History of Ideas*).

This co-operative spirit can be traced back to the formation period of the North and Middle European societies, during which it was kinship alone that guaranteed protection, honour, and rights. When an individual was uprooted from his kinship by war or trade, the institution of bloodbrotherhood provided an equivalent by creating an artificial kinship relationship with the same rights and duties as the natural one. The bloodbrothers bound themselves to mutual support and blood feud. The *merchant guilds* that are documented since the ninth century obviously fulfilled similar functions to the earlier institution of bloodbrotherhood. The "sworn brothers" (fratres coniurati) of a merchant guild took a solemn oath to support each other in cases of emergencies and feud, to revenge each other, to bury the dead according to the rites, to honour them, and to protect their inheritance. This mutual protection against waylayers, pirates, and the inclemency of the weather and sea was the only one to which the merchants had access during their extended travels. Many features of the merchant guilds were then copied by the craft guilds, e.g., the ritual meal, rituals of admittance, including a solemn oath for mutual support, common public participation in religious cults and obsequies, and an insistence on an independent jurisdiction (*Oexle*). The unification theory assumes that the craft guild was motivated by the co-operative spirit of the early Middle Ages, which had its origin in the kinship system and was inspired by the model of the merchant's guild which, in turn, was built upon the bloodbrotherhood.

Current historical theories on the genesis of guilds refrain from making one specific historical condition responsible for the development of guilds. Rather, they interpret it as the result of a process that was influenced by serveral factors. The co-operative spirit is seen as the driving force and the government structures of the early towns as the frame that directed this spirit into the formation of guilds.

II. The Functions of the Guild

Guilds were essentially religious brotherhoods, which can be concluded from the fact that the oldest documents concerning guilds almost exclusively deal with religious obligations (*Zorn*, 1965). The guilds established and maintained altars in churches that were dedicated to specific saints. The guild members were obliged to participate in the burial of their departed. During the Corpus Christi procession, they marched in special groupings. Guild regulations urged members to follow a strict religious way of life. All rules, even those relating to economic activities, were explicitly based on religious norms.

In addition, the guilds also had political and military functions (*Wissell*, 1971). In Germany, e.g., they played a significant role in the revolts that led to the independence of the towns from the ecclesiastical or secular rulers. For military expeditions, the guilds had to provide men whose equipping was determined by the guild constitution.

Particularly important were the guild's *jurisdictional functions*. The guilds were able to give themselves rules, which, after the authorities had approved them, took on the form of legal norms (→ *Co-operatives under Public Law*). The assembly of all the masters of a guild judged violations and inflicted penalties. The ultimate punishment was expulsion form the guild, of which guilds in other towns were informed so that the outcast member was not accepted anywhere else (*Wissell* 1974). Only criminal offenses were excluded from the guild's jurisdiction. The guild also took on the *responsibility for social security of its members*, above all in the form of reciprocal obligations in assisting sickness and death cases. Some guilds even had money chests to support the unemployed. Social security also applied to widows and orphans. The support was not only material: a journeyman who married the widow of a master became a master more easily than his fellow journeymen.

III. Institutional Characteristics

1. Membership and Demarcation Rules

The major concern of the guild was to preserve and increase the "symbolic value of honour" (*Grießinger*). This is evident by extensive membership and demarcation rules that applied *a craftsman's honourableness* as *the most important criterion*. Whoever was found to be dishonourable, according to the guild's criteria, was not accepted by the guild. Whoever behaved in a dishonourable manner was punished or expelled. However, in the Middle Ages the idea of repute of honourableness was different from that of the present: loss of reputation was tantamount to loss of social status and personal rights (*Wissell* 1974).

Those born illegitimately were dishonourable and could therefore not be accepted into the guild. The reason for this regulation was that it was difficult to prove these persons' descent from free citizens, and only free citizens could become guild members (*Wissell* 1974). Members of certain occupations and their families were also considered as dishonourable and unacceptable, for example, executioners, knackers (persons who collected carcasses), court ushers, tax collectors, watchmen, gravediggers, barbers, shepherds, and jugglers. Such occupations were possibly regarded as disreputable because those who practiced them (or their forefathers) usually were serfs. The masters' wives were subject to the same memberhsip criteria. It is almost self-evident that the chosen wife-to-be had to be a virgin. If something to the contrary was made known or if a child was born "prematurely", those concerned could be expelled from the guild.

From the 1600s onwards, membership and demarcation rules steadily thightened and took on bizarre forms. For example, guild members were strictly forbidden to have any contact with executioners and knackers, to the extent that touching their work tools could bring the guild member into disrepute. Journeymen who worked beside a dishonourable person were themselves claimed to be dishonourable, and they had to pay a penalty in order to regain their honourableness. The killing of dogs or the touching of their carcasses was seen as particularly dishonourable. Many guild members who did this were excluded from their guilds. In general, the dead dog was a symbol of disrepute in the Middle Ages. The journeymen were supposed to live a life of celibacy; they were not even allowed to talk to women of ill-repute. They had to lead a religious life, regularly attend church, and receive the Blessed Sacrament (*Wissell* 1974).

These extensive membership rules did not make it easy for guild members to stay on the path of honourableness, but they gave the guild numerous opportunities to corroborate distinctiveness from other social groups. Thus, all of these rules had the purpose of maintaining professional honour, distinguishing the guild from the outside world, and protecting the solidarity of the guild members.

2. Symbols, Myths, and Rituals

The guild was imbued with rituals, myths, and symbols (→ *Corporate Culture*). Its *core symbol was the chest* in which documents such as seals, privileges, the consitution of the guild, and register of members were kept. It was a cultic shrine like the altar of a church, which it closely resembled. During ceremonial acts such as judicial hearings, entry of apprentices, appointment of journeymen and master craftsmen, it was opened and, while open, hats had to be raised according to the regulations of the constitution and any weapons put down; not a word could be spoken. Violators of these rules were harshly penalized.

Dances and plays were performed during the numerous *guild festivities*, allegorically portraying the beginnings of the guild as well as highlighting important phases of its development. These rituals emphasized the guild's tradition (*Grießinger*). Extensive *initiation rituals* took place for the admission of apprentices and promotions from apprentice to journeyman and journeyman to master. The initiation ceremony for the journeyman was, for example, precisely written down and lasted hours. It was interspersed with rituals of degradation, soiling, and death, each time followed by rituals of purifications, baptism, and resurrections. Journeymen-to-be were given a new name that symbolically bestowed on them a new identity. Rule-abiding and rule-breaking behavior of journeymen was drastically depicted through role playing. All of those rituals were kept confidential within the guild (*Grießinger*).

3. The Economic Philosphy of the Guild and Rules Regarding Economic Activities

Rules regarding the economic function reflected the intention of keeping *production and selling conditions for all members as equal as possible*. No masters should be able to gain an advantage at the expense of his co-masters. Thus, rigid attention was paid so that acquisition of raw materials was under equal conditions, production was carried out with uniform methods, and the selling of goods was at equal prices and under the same conditions. The master was only allowed to employ a restricted number of journeymen, usually two or three, and he was not allowed to choose these men himself. The guild or, later, the brotherhood of journeymen assigned them to the masters. Wages and working hours were also uniformly regulated. The pursuit of customers was strictly forbidden. Sometimes it was also exactly laid down how the master should exhibit his goods. The products were standardized, and the principals of the guild exercised strict quality control.

Weber (1961) considered such regulations as an outflow of the "principle of securing just nourishment", while other authors have maintained that these rules were the result of the town magistracies' policy of attempting to dam up unrestrained profit-striving within the guilds (*Kelter*). *Lütge* proposed a third interpretation: that the monopolistic regulations of the guild were a result of the town magistracies' efforts to establish and guarantee orderly market behavior (→ *Economic Order*). The early craftsmen originated from the closed economies of the feudal manors within which the market and money played little role. In the town, they were now confronted with the demands of markets and a money economy, and the majority was not up to it. In the early Middle Ages, the average craftsman could barely count, and although by the late Middle Ages he mastered addition and subtraction to some extent, division still caused him great difficulties. *Lütge* rightly poses the question whether it can be assumed that a butcher who bought a cow and then sold it by the pound could live up to this task.

Lütge, therefore, considered monopolistic regulations, at least those that were implemented in the first centuries of the guilds' existence, a form of protection for the craftsman against the risks of the market. From the middle 1600s onwards, however, economic interests came further to the forefront and led to a tightening up of these monopolistic regulations (→ *Gierke*). The regulations regarding economic activities were also legitimized by the religious belief system of that time. Striving toward a profit was regarded as being sinful.

Innovations were suppressed. Wordings like "No man should think of or invent something new or use it, but everyman should follow his neighbour in brotherly love" can often be found in guild constitutions (*Braun*). A master gaining an economic advantage from either product or process innovations would have contradicted the guild's spirit. Numerous documents show that innovators were severely punished (*Wissell* 1974). This hostility toward innovations was also legitimized by the world view of the Middle

Ages: only traditional old things and procedures had value (*Gurjewitsch*).

However, the Middle Ages were not without inventions and innovations: e.g., an interlicking series of innovations led to a revolution in agricultural methods. Examples of other revolutionary medieval innovations are the spinning wheel, the casting of iron, the wheelbarrow, the compass, and printing with cast movable type. Although these innovations might seem to refute the hypothesis of the guilds' hostility toward innovation, there are reasons to think they do not. In the first place, most of these innovations did not originate from the guilds' workshops. In the early Middle Ages, the workshops of monasteries were a much richer source of innovations, especially in agriculture and military technology. For innovations originating from craft shops, it can be shown that they came about only under particular conditions that were more conducive to creativity than those of the regular guild: (1) Innovativeness was higher as long as a guild consisted of relatively few members who were not subjected to a lot of pressure from competition within the guild. (2) When products became more complicated and/or new processes (not necessarily highly innovative ones) developed, the guild (not individual members), in agreement with the town magistracies, could decide to branch out a new guild. It usually took some time before procedures for the new guild became standardized, and during this formation period, innovators had more leeway. In the beginning of modern times, rulers intervened and prevented the establishment of tight guild regulations in new crafts in which they took a special interest, such as war technology, astrological instruments, or luxury goods. Very talented and innovative craftsmen were often even placed under the direct protection of the court (*Stürmer*). (3) The innovation barries of guilds were less powerful in towns where the profit-minded patrician merchants could maintain a strong position vis à vis the craftsmen. Nuremberg is an extrem example of such a town; therefore, it is not coincidential that the most famous innovative craftsmen worked there: in 1349, the patricians crushed a guild revolt and from then on successfully suppressed all guild-like activities.

IV. The Decline of the Guild

In Germany, the decline of the guilds began around the end of the fifteenth century. It was characterized by the following vicious circle: The guilds reacted to economic crises by reinforcing their cartels. These maneuvers, however, restricted the adaptability of the guilds and competing institutions such as putting-out systems, manufactories, and factories were increasingly able to expand at the guilds' expense. Pressure on the guild thereby increased, leading to a further reinforcement of cartels, and so on.

The guilds that were very hostile to technological innovations demonstrated an incredible imaginativeness in finding ways to restict admittance. As the number of journeymen rose and it became apparent to the guilds that not all could earn their subsistence, they defined the criterion of honourableness even more restrictively, thereby making it even more difficult to be admitted into the guild as well as raising the chances of expulsion. It became obligatory for journeymen to go on travels lasting up to several years. However, many failed to return, as they were compelled to do military service while they were away (military service made the journeymen dishonourable), and others stayed on as vagrants or married in another town. Those who returned had to complete a probationary period before they could become masters. During this extensive waiting period, the journeymen were forbidden to marry, and they were supposed to behave in a chasteful manner.

Although the journeymens' behavior certainly not always conformed to these strict rules – e.g., there were reports on brothels tolerated by the magistracy and frequented by journeymen (*Schulz*) –, the journeymen could, in principle, be prevented on these grounds from becoming masters, if such a move was considered opportune by the guild. The requirements for masterhood were increased until they were barely attainable. For example, in the early seventeenth century, candidates striving to become masters of a blacksmith workshop had to make up a complete set of horse shoes for a horse that was walked past them only two to three times, allowing them to see it for only a few seconds (*Wissell* 1974).

Costs encountered in becoming a master also rose considerably. The candidate had to entertain the masters with lavish meals when the masters made their frequent visits during the preparation of the masterpiece, but this did not prevent the masters from intensively searching for mistakes. When it became necessary to correct the masterpiece, the candidates had to pay severe fines. The number of prescriptions for the meal that the newly appointed master then had to arrange for his colleagues also increased considerably, leading to higher expenses. It took the new masters years to recover from the debts they had incurred.

These practices prompted changes in attitudes toward the guilds that increasingly deprived the guilds of their legitimation. The absolutist rulers who began to see economic strength as a precondition of political and military strength no longer regarded the guilds as an institution they had to protect but, instead, as an "aggravating ulcer" that ought to be done away with. In the 1600s, they began to pursue a mercantilist economic policy that was not aimed at improving the economic situation of their subjects, but at increasing their own power as well as the income of the court. The guilds' policy of securing just nourishment failed to comply with the concepts of the mercantilists who advised the rulers. Their arguments legitimized the curtailment of the guilds' autonomy by the rulers as well as their right to free talented masters from guilds' chains by offering them the opportunity to work as court masters under the protection of the court (*Stürmer*). The remaining masters of the guild reacted to both this development and to the economic crises triggered by numerous wars by reinforcing cartels and by intensively revitalizing their – in the eyes of contemporaries – strange customs.

Ultimately, the guilds collapsed in the face of the competition from the *putting-out system* as well as the *manufactories and factories* that followed the principle of profit maximization, and were not burdened with any noneconomic functions, therefore being able to produce more efficiently. These alternative organizational forms of production had developed outside the towns or had gained special permission (privilieges) from the rulers. In addition, the rulers sometimes even provided subsidies for these new organizations. At the same time, they increasingly curtailed the rights of the guilds. Freedom of trade, which was established in the German territories during the first half of the nineteenth century, deprived the guilds of practically all their legal and economic influence. The crafts, nonetheless, experienced an upturn during industrialization: the complementary relations between industry and craft were able to develop as the chains of the restrictive economy of the guild were broken.

V. Interpretation of the Specific Institutional Characteristics of the Guild

In this paper, the evolution of work institutions was interpreted within the wider frame of societal evolution. The guild was not a formal organization. It was a social order heavily isolated from all other social orders due to its particular way of life (→ *Informal Co-operatives*); thus, it was *a society within a society* (→ *Configuration*). Generally, social orders were a basic structural element of the medieval society. Each order, including that of craftsmen, had its own norms and laws, its own clothing, its own way of speaking, its own music, and its own way of life, stipulated right down to the last detail, a way of life that was little understood by the members of other orders. But why did these social orders assume such great importance in the Middle Ages? The explanation provided here is based on the assumption that the evolution of society is characterized by a certain direction of progress: those belief systems, institutions, and action systems of individuals that enhance society's ability to adapt have an evolutionary advantage. In this way, the magical belief system was replaced by a religious one, which then gave way to widespread application of worldly – disenchanted – theories (*Weber*, 1978a, 1978b).

During this process, economic philosophies changed as well. For example, striving for profit was considered sinful in the Middle Ages, whereas by the eighteenth century it became increasingly a virtue to do so. This evolution of belief systems triggered evolutionary changes at the level of institutions and was, simultaneously, supported by them. Kinship as the basic structural principle of society was largely replaced by social orders and, finally, by functionally specialized formal organizations. Markets developed and were extended to include more and more goods, production factors, and property rights. These developments brought with them greater autonomy for the individual. They also improved society's ability to solve its problems.

Since the guild was a social order, i.e. a society within the society and not a formal organization, it had to apply a social criterion (such as the craftsman's honourableness) to demarcate itself from other orders. Only by strictly adhering to membership rules based on birth and order-specific behavior could the autonomy of the guild be protected. It was also functional for the guilds to define these membership rules even more closely when their social status was threatened by economic crises or by overcrowding. The stricter the demarcation and membership rules are, the more difficult it is for guild members to stay on the path of honourableness, giving the guild more opportunities to distinguish itself from other social groups and to limit access.

The guilds had to fulfill several functions, since central institutions responsible for the administration of civil justice as well as for social and political duties had hardly developed. This mulitfunctionality led to difficulties in co-ordinating the individuals' activities, as the guilds had to ensure that all functions could be equally fulfilled. Predominantly, the guilds solved this problem by developing a dense network of detailed standards prescribing how members should behave.

If, for example, the guilds had allowed their members greater freedom to concentrate on economic activities, certain members would have striven harder for profit than others, thus forcing members to compete, which would have made it difficult for the guild to fulfill the other functions. In the end, this process would have endangered the continued existence of the guild. Conflicts caused by deviant behavior, such as strikes by journeymen, had an effect similar to that of outside pressures: they inevitably led to an increased number of even stricter rules. At the same time, the guilds had to make sure that their members accepted the extremely restrictive rules, that they saw these rules as morally justified, and that they could identify with them. The moral-religious belief system ensured, by and large, that this was achieved. The intensive use of rituals, symbols, and myths also ensured that these rules escaped critisicsm and that alternative modes of behavior did not occur to the members. Myths and rituals are beyond question. They are handed down from generation to generation and contain profound truths that remain beyond doubt. Symbols, myths, and rituals also created a moral attachment binding members to the guilds, whereas utilitarian attachment prevails in the modern organization.

The multifunctionality of the guilds can also be interpreted as a cause of their restricted ability to innovate. As shown in the first section of this article, a multifunctional social system is affected by several differing selection criteria and, since progress in the direction of one selection criterion usually leads to setbacks with regard to others, an evolution oriented toward one specific selection criterion is prevented. If the guild, for example, had encouraged innovations to increase economic efficiency and profits, this would probably have endangered its social welfare and political functions.

Why were the guilds not able to reform themselves from within? In order to do so, the guild members as collectivities would have had to be capable of reflecting their position within the context of societal development as well as of conceiving of institutional innovations. This was extremely difficult, primarily because the economic system was so closely associated with all other societal functions, another reason being the dense network of restrictive norms that was legitimized by the religious belief system and encapsulated in numerous myths and rituals. Under such circumstances, collective learning was impossible, and threats to the guilds' existence led inevitably to even stricter monopolistic rules and regulations. For the more progressive members of the guild, "exit" (in the form of becoming privileged masters under direct protection of the absolutist courts) proved a much more effective reaction than "voice" or protest and reform from within.

Bibliography

Below, Georg v.: Die Motive der Zunftbildung im deutschen Mittelalter, Historische Zeitschrift, vol. 109 (1912), pp. 23–48.
Braun, Rudolf: Zur Einwirkung soziokultureller Umweltbedingungn auf das Unternehmerverhalten. In: Wolfram Fischer (ed.): Wirtschafts- und sozialgeschichtliche Probleme der frühen Industrialisierung, Berlin 1968, pp. 247–284.
Gierke, Otto von: Rechtsgeschichte der deutschen Genossenschaft, Berlin 1868.
Grießinger, Andreas: Das symbolische Kapital der Ehre. Streikbewegungen und kollektives Bewußtsein deutscher Handwerksgesellen im 18. Jahrhundert, Frankfurt/Main 1981.
Gurjewitsch, Aaron J.: Das Weltbild des mittelalterlichen Menschen, München 1980.
Irsigler, Franz: Zur Problematik der Gilde und Zunftterminologie. In: Berent Schwineköper (ed.), Gilden und Zünfte, Sigmaringen 1985, pp. 53–70.
Kelter, Ernst: Die Wirtschaftsgesinnung des mittelalterlichen Zünftlers. Schmollers Jahrbuch für Gesetzgebung und Verwaltung, 56 (1932), pp. 749–775.
Keutgen, Friedrich: Ämter und Zünfte (Leipzig 1903) Aalen 1965.
Lütge, Friedrich: Die Preispolitik in München im hohen Mittelalter, Jahrbuch für Nationalökonomie und Statistik, 89 (1941), pp. 162–202.
Müller, Walter: Zur Frage des Ursprungs der mittelalterlichen Zünfte, Leipzig 1910.
Oexle, Otto Gerhard: Conjuratio und Gilde im frühen Mittelalter. Ein Beitrag zum Problem der sozialgeschichtlichen Kontinuität zwichen Antike und Mittelalter. In: Berent Schwineköper: Gilden und Zünfte – Kaufmännische und gewerblich Genossenschaften im frühen und hohen Mittelalter, Sigmaringen 1985, pp. 151–214.
Stürmer, Michael: Handwerk und höfische Kultur, München 1982.
Weber, Max: General Economic History, New York 1961.
Weber, Max: Economy and Society. Berkeley, CA 1978b.
Wissell, Rudolf: Des alten Handwerks Recht und Gewohnheit, vol. 1, Berlin 1971.
Wissell, Rudolf: Des alten Handwerks Recht und Gewohnheit, vol. 2, Berlin 1974.
Zorn, Wolfgang: Zünfte. In: von Beckerath, Erich/Brinkmann, Carl (eds.): Handwörterbuch der Sozialwissenschaften, vol. 12, Stuttgart 1965, pp. 484–489.

Haas, Wilhelm (1839–1913)

Horst Seuster [J]

(see also: *History in 19th C.*; *History of Ideas*; *Rural Co-operatives*)

Wilhelm Haas was born in Darmstadt on October 20th, 1839, and died on February 8th, 1913. After completing his high school education he studied law at the State University at Gießen between 1857 and 1861. As a law-clerk he passed through numerous administrational positions in the Grand Duchy of Hesse. He was named to the police board in 1874 and later was entrusted with the office of county councilor for the district of Offenbach.

Haas requested early retirement from the Grand Duke of Hesse in 1900 in order to dedicate himself more fully to his work in rural co-operative structures. Even during his activities as both law-clerk and county assessor he had come into close contact with the rural population; he became acquainted firsthand with their modest standard of living, saw the economic and social problems they faced and recognized the necessity to strengthen people's will to help themselves.

Even in his early years as county assessor *Haas* advocated collective purchasing of agricultural supplies. In 1872, he participated in the establishment of the Agricultural Consumer Co-operative Association in Friedberg and became its director. The following year he made a public notice for the establishment of the Federation of Agricultural Consumer Associations in Hesse, which was founded on June 30th, 1873, in Mayence. *Haas* was elected president and exercised the responsible functions of this office for four decades until his death. Following his initiative, a Federation of Agricultural Loan Associations also came into being alongside the Federation of Agricultural Consumer Associations. A third federation for dairy co-operatives was founded in 1889. A further step in consolidating strengths was the unification of the three federations into the Federation of Agricultural Co-operatives in Hesse. Within the same period of time the Co-operative Center of the Consumer Associations was also established.

The next step, forming a federation of rural co-operatives (→ *Federations*) throughout the German Reich, appeared to be an almost obvious consequence. Soon after being founded the Reich Federation established international relations. The rather lax contacts were drawn more tightly upon the founding of the International Federation of Agricultural Co-operatives. The German Agricultural Co-operative School, which had been recommended by *Haas*, was opened in 1904 (→ *Education, Germany*).

Haas had already become a member of an agricultural association and assumed an active role in the life of the organization prior to devoting himself to co-operative work. He was elected vice president of the Starkenburg Agricultural Association in 1888 and president of the State Commission of the Agricultural Association in Hesse in 1892. When the Chamber of Agriculture evolved from this latter organization in 1906, *Haas* in turn became its chairman.

Haas also was involved in politics. He joined the National Liberal Party and entered the lower chamber of the Hessian State Parliament as a representative in 1881. He was elected president of this chamber in 1897 and exercised the functions of this office in a sovereign manner for 14 years. He was forced to abandon his parliamentary activities in 1912 as a result of his impaired state of health. *Haas* likewise served as representative of the Erbach-Bensheim district in the German Reichstag from 1898 until 1912. Without a doubt *Haas* numbered among → *H. Schulze-Delitzsch* and → *F.W. Raiffeisen* as one of those personalities who decisively shaped and influenced the co-operative system. Whereas *Schulze-Delitzsch* and *Raiffeisen* were active as founders of the co-operative movement, *Haas* is considered the one who gave the co-operative system its organizational form. He likewise was the one who lead co-operatives out of their physical isolation and established the initial international contacts between co-operatives. The organizational form of the co-operatives which he in essence created still fundamentally exists today and thus has proved itself for over a century.

Bibliography

Faust, Helmut: Geschichte der Genossenschaftsbewegung, Frankfurt 1965, pp. 317–335.
Feineisen, Adalbert: Haas, Wilhelm, Gestalter einer großen Idee, Neuwied 1956.
Maxeiner, Rudolf: Haas, Wilhelm, in: Handwörterbuch des Genossenschaftswesens, Wiesbaden 1980, cols. 921–927.

Health Care System, Co-operatives and other Institutions in the

JÜRGEN ZERCHE [J]

(see also: *Social Policy*; *Cooperativismo Sanitario*; *Insurance, Germany*; *History of Ideas*)

I. Definition of Terms; II. The Effect of Co-operatives and Similar Institutions in the German Health Insurance System; III. Summary.

232.7 billion marks were spent on health insurance in the Federal Republic of Germany in 1990. The sector "health" thus had a 10% share in the gross national product. The *gesetzliche Krankenversicherung* (GKV, statutory health insurance), the most important institution, is quantitatively very comprehensive considering the number of members as well as the various services of preventative medicine, treatment, post-treatment care, and rehabilitation covered by the insurance. In 1990, 37.4 million members were organized in the GKV; if one calculates the additional family members also insured, it can be ascertained that almost 90% of the population enjoys protection through the statutory health insurance. Thus, under these quantitative aspects one may speak of a national insurance. The activities of the GKV include treatment through doctors and dentists, pharmaceuticals, bandages and dressings, medication, new teeth, and inhome health care. The costs of the GKV totaled 127.6 billion marks in 1990.

The GKV has its roots in the co-operative self-help institutions of the Middle Ages (→ *History before 1800*), particularly in the benefit funds the organized miners had. In 1883, *Bismarck* made the idea of self-help, which is fundamentally associated with self-administration, a ground stone of the *Sozialversicherung* (SV, social security including the GKV) established during the Reich (→ *History in 19th C.*). Co-operative ideas can, however, also be found beyond the range of the GKV in the German health care system. Of importance here are the co-operatives of pharmacists and doctors as well as the numerous independent self-help groups which have been markedly determined by the co-operative spirit. The institutions of the *gesetzliche Unfallversicherung* (GUV, statutory accident insurance) likewise reveal co-operative elements.

In the following, a definition of terms of co-operatives and similar institutions will be undertaken in which the term "self-help" will also be addressed. Subsequently, a typology of co-operatives will be introduced. Afterwards, the different forms of co-operatives and related organizations and groups in the German health insurance system will be presented and analyzed.

I. Definition of Terms

1. Co-operative

A generally accepted definition of the term "co-operative" does not exist. Nevertheless, two possible definitions of the description of co-operatives stand out and serve as generally accepted starting points. The first is the co-operative term used by the liberal-bourgeois social reformer → *Schulze-Delitzsch*, and the second is the list of characteristics based on the former laid down by the International Co-operative Alliance in 1966.

a) Schulze-Delitzsch's Idea of Co-operatives

In the second half of the 29th century, the German co-operative pioneer, *Schulze-Delitzsch* minted a definition of co-operatives which can be characterized as liberal-bourgeois. Among the characteristics of the co-operative are the promotion mission, the principle of identity, and principle of democracy. At the heart of the co-operative activity lies the promotion of the members. The goal is to overcome a situation of need experienced by members through simultaneously promoting and encouraging their own enterprises (→ *Promotion Mandate*). The output of a co-operative can only be made available to the members. The members of a co-operative are at the same time its customers (*principle of identity*). The decision making process within the co-operative follows a democratic fashion. Each member has the same rights and obligations from membership (*principle of democracy*).

According to *Schulze-Delitzsch*, self-help, self-administration, and self-responsibility belong to the fundament of these three principles and are the basis of co-operative trade (→ *Principles*). These, however, can only be realized when the principles of voluntarism, equality, and equal obligation are fulfilled. *Schulze-Delitzsch* strictly refused any kind of state or outside help.

A difficulty in *Schulze-Delitzsch's* co-operative terms exists in the point that the resulting organizations extend to non-economic or primarily non-economic goals. Thus, the co-operative principles cannot only be applied to economic institutions but also to those transcending strictly economic structures (social institutions).

b) Characteristics of the International Co-operative Alliance (ICA)

The constituent characteristics for co-operatives were developed in Vienna in 1966 at the ICA. According to the ICA, co-operatives are distinguished by:

1) Open membership on a voluntary basis which guarantees free membership and withdrawal; this, however, simultaneously causes the fluctuating level of capital in the co-operatives;

2) Democratic administration, i.e. one vote per member regardless how many shares a member has subscribed; voting is determined by a majority;
3) Limiting the interest rate on capital based on the denial of pure profit attainment. The goal of the enterprise form "co-operative" is not the dividend but rather the promotion mission. Capital is essential but solely has a subordinate function;
4) → *Reimbursement* is based on the level of business transactions in relationship to purchases of goods;
5) Members are brought up and educated in the ideas of collective action;
6) Cooperation among co-operatives takes place on regional, national and international levels.

c) Typology

Co-operatives have been sufficiently characterized through the triad of the promotion mandate and the principles of identity and democracy. They can be typified according to various criteria. In the following, they are differentiated according to the aspects of particular co-operative forms.

aa) Co-operatives and § 1 of German Co-operative Law.

The definition based on § 1 of the *Genossenschaftsgesetz* (GenG, German Co-operative Law) offers a simple, formal starting point in the search for co-operative institutions. It takes up the promotion mandate as the constituent element of nature of a co-operative enterprise. According to this article, co-operatives are "Societies with a non-fixed number of members which strive for the promotion of the employment or the economic situation of their members through a collective business undertaking." (§ 1, GenG)

bb) Co-operatives as public bodies

Adjacent to this form of cooperation laid down in the GenG, there is furthermore the co-operative integration in the legal form of a public body (KöR, *Körperschaft des öffentlichen Rechts*). As a public body under the KöR, the co-operative creates the group of co-operatives in a legal sense (→ *Legal Form, Co-operative*) with the registered, incorporated co-operatives (eG, *eingetragene Genossenschaften*).

cc) Forms of cooperation similar to co-operatives

Alongside the forms of cooperation listed above, there are associations similar to co-operatives (→ *Forms of Cooperation*) whose members strive to realize the ideas of self-help in the legal form of registered clubs (eV, *eingetragener Verein*), as mutual life insurance companies (VvaG, *Versicherungsverein auf Gegenseitigkeit*) or also as loosely connected societies.

2. Self-help

Self-help means that the economic subjects are themselves responsible for seeing that in cases of need to meet individual ends they have securities at their disposal which are appropriate to the particular individual need (→ *Self-help Organizations*). The extent of these securities is dependent solely on the level of previous individual provision. Collective self-help is "when a person in need does not wait for outside measures to remove his troubles, but rather when he undertakes steps himself which can avert them. He can do this alone without the support of others or he can, however, also be accompanied by his fellow sufferers." (*Weisser*) An independent group of subjects, the mustering up of the means from those involved, and self-administration are thus necessary conditions for self-help institutions.

II. The Effect of Co-operatives and Similar Institutions in the German Health Insurance System

The following should investigate those institutions active within the German health insurance system which are organized in a co-operative or similar manner. If one looks for the realization of co-operative ideas in the German health insurance system, the historic roots of the social security system (SV) offer an initial example. In reference to the definition of self-help, the factors of financing the social benefits by those affected themselves with an independent group of supporters exercising self-administration have given cause to have the self-help principle be assumed as a component of the SV.

1. Federal Benefit Fund

Even as early as the Middle Ages (probably already in the 13th century), independent relief funds existed among miners, furnace workers, and hammersmiths to cover risks, illness, accidents, invalidity, and old age. They were taken on by *Bismarck's* social legislation in the 1880s.

The support funds of the mining sector were maintained through dues from the miners as well as from the mine owners. They were organized under the independent management of those affected into self-administrational bodies of "employees" and "employers". In the 18th century, the Prussian State assumed supervision over the funds. The state structured obligatory membership and contribution from all works and plants, thus providing a solid financial basis of the miners' benefit funds. By the end of the 18th century, the funds had assumed obvious characteristics of a public (self-administrated) social security system.

The *Bundesknappschaft* (BKn, Federal Benefit Fund) is a self-administrated public body (KöR) which is financed through dues from employees and employers. The example of the Federal Benefit Fund proves that co-operative characteristics are on hand in the self-administrated bodies of the state health insurance (GKV). For the sake of clarity, "employer" and "insured" should be differentiated. Those insured promote their own economy; the promotional goal of the employers is not necessarily discernable. Those insured join a society against danger in order to obtain risk coverage in the health sector, something that is not available under the same conditions on the market. Those not insured are excluded from the services. The support and financing through the company is historically grounded and is an unknown element in co-operative thought. It can, however, be argued that the employers experience a promotional effect on their economic activity. By insuring their workers, companies strengthen "labor" as a factor production in both the middle- and long-terms.

The duality of the promotional goal is also expressed in the realization of the democratic principle concerning the self-administration of employers and employees in the assembly of representatives, which is composed two-thirds by employee representatives and one-third by employer representatives. The assembly of representatives is newly elected every six years. In turn, it elects the management and the board of the Federal Benefit Fund (→ *Organizational Structure of Societies*).

The identity is closely connected to the promotion mandate. In the Federal Benefit Fund, those insured are, at the same time, "customers" of the insurance and therefore the sole rightful claimants of the services of the insurance. In analogy to that described above, the connection to the employers is indirect; the employers can make use of the services in the form of higher or improved efficiency of those insured.

2. Professional Associations

The professional associations (BGen, *Berufsgenossenschaften*) are the agents of the statutory accident insurance (GUV) in the Federal Republic of Germany. This branch of the SV does not have its origins in the form of voluntarily founded benefit funds but rather in governmental initiation. *Bismarck* wanted to introduce accident insurance for workers as the first step of a structured social security. He failed, however, with the initial idea of a centrally organized insurance institution for the Reich as the agency of this plan as well as organizing the financing from employers and the state. A second attempt also failed until the third proposed concept finally became law in 1884.

The GUV covers the employer for the risk of liability of an employee who is injured on his way to work or at work. Accident insurance is liability insurance for the employer. It is likewise insurance to the advantage of the employee.

The professional associations are public bodies with the right of self-administration. They are under state supervision and are financed by contributions from employers. The promotional goal of the professional associations exists in their offering liability insurance to employers. To this end, an identity exists between the institutions of the co-operative and its rightful claimants. Claims by third parties are not possible. Structuring the principle of democracy is problematic because, in spite of the one-sided financing, parity exists between the social partners in the self-administrative bodies. This contradiction can only be resolved in that the employees are also referred to as "affiliates". One cannot speak of self-help here as the employees have not contributed any means of their own. Therefore, the professional associations can only partially be considered co-operative institutions of the health care system.

3. Co-operatives of Pharmacists and Doctors

In the German health care sector, three pharmacists co-operatives (NOWEDA, Sanacorp) and five doctors' co-operatives are active. They are legally organized as registered, incorporated co-operatives (eG). These enterprises are primarily involved in profit oriented undertakings and are exposed to economic competition; they thus are concerned with equalizing the abundant level of the competition not organized along co-operative lines. The co-operative ideas appear somewhat denatured, but the typical characteristics of the promotion of members, the principle of democracy, and the principle of identity are still present.

In contrast to Germany, where the legal form of an incorporated co-operative (eG) is not the predominant form for pharmacists and doctors, in Belgium, the entire level of retail trade in the sector of pharmaceuticals is organized co-operatively. These co-operatives are united in the umbrella organization "Office des pharmacies co-opératives – OPHACO".

4. Forms of Cooperation Similar to Co-operatives

In the German health insurance system, the objects and forms of the self-help groups being similar to co-operatives are quite various (→ *New Co-operatives*). The number of the active social self-help groups within the German speaking regions is not known; estimates lie between 5,000 and 10,000. Self-help groups have been formed in almost all fields of somatic and mental illness. Frequently, they are organized into registered clubs (eV), but they are also often active in much less strict associations without any statutory footing.

Self-help institutions for diabetics are especially abundant. The most well known self-help group is "Alcoholics Anonymous", an organization founded in 1935 in the USA and active in Germany since the 1950s. Alongside the nationally active self-help organizations such as the German Association of Diabetics, The German League of Rheumatics or the Committee of Self-Help Groups, a wide spectrum of active clubs and non-institutionalized groups exists which are active on a regional level.

If the principles of *Schulze-Delitzsch* are taken as a basis, one can by all means speak of "co-operatives" in this case. *Blümle* uses the term "health co-operatives", the goal of which being the promotion of members, whereby, based on this definition, it can remain open to debate whether this concerns an economic or "entirely" social promotion. The groups provide substitute or complementary services which are either not offered by the GKV or only to an insufficient degree. In most cases, the democratic principle prevails; as a rule, decisions are made after group discussion or in the assembly of all members. The identity of the supplier and consumer of a service is likewise given. Outsiders are excluded from laying claims on the services.

III. Summary

The GKV as well as health care beyond the publically administered level is clearly molded by co-operative elements. The number of these co-operatives and similar organizations and groups is just as large as their heterogeneity. This is largely a product of history and can only be explained historically.

We thus find the "historic" co-operative of the benefit fund which up to today has been an important institution of the GKV. Alongside public bodies, the similar organization of professional associations (which have a completely different background) have become established in the statutory accident insurance (GUK). Adjacent these organizational forms, which can be considered "original" co-operatives, there are numerous "denatured" co-operatives in the German health care system which have chosen the legal form of a registered, incorporated co-operative (eG). These organizations, often founded as purchasing co-operatives, predominantly and exclusively pursue economic interests in contrast to the co-operative institutions of the GKV and GUV.

Lastly, numerous self-help institutions exist in the health care system which are similar to co-operatives and have been formed along the legal lines of registered associations (eV). Alongside the established co-operatives, these other institutions attempt to obviate the lack of care and services existing in the professional sector.

Bibliography

Badura, Bernhard et al.: Sozialpolitische Perspektive, in: Badura, Bernhard/v. Ferber, Christian (eds.): Selbsthilfe und Selbstorganisation im Gesundheitswesen. Die Bedeutung nicht-professioneller Sozialsysteme für Krankheitsbewältigung, Gesundheitsvorsorge und die Kostenentwicklung im Gesundheitswesen, Reihe Soziologie und Sozialpolitik, vol. 1, München, Wien 1981, pp. 5ff.

Behrendt, Jörn-Uwe et al.: Zur Verflechtung von Selbsthilfezusammenschlüssen mit staatlichen und professionellen Sozialsytemen, in: Badura, Bernhard/v. Ferber, Christian (eds.): Selbsthilfe und Selbstorganisation im Gesundheitswesen. Die Bedeutung nicht-professioneller Sozialsysteme für Krankheitsbewältigung, Gesundheitsvorsorge und die Kostenentwicklung im Gesundheitswesen, Reihe Soziologie und Sozialpolitik, vol. 1, München, Wien 1981, pp. 91ff.

Blümle, Ernst-Bernd: Die Genossenschaft als Zusammenschluß von Wirtschaftssubjekten und als Gemeinschaftsbetrieb, in: Laurinkari, Juhani (ed.): Genossenschaftswesen. Hand- und Lehrbuch, München, Wien 1990, pp.78ff.

Faust, Helmut: Geschichte der Genossenschaftsbewegung. Ursprung und Aufbruch der Genossenschaftsbewegung in England, Frankreich und Deutschland sowie ihre weitere Entwicklung im deutschen Sprachraum, 3rd ed., Frankfurt/M. 1977.

Fink, Ulf: Selbsthilfe im Gesundheitswesen, in: v. Ferber, Christian et al. (eds.): Kosten und Effizienz im Gesundheitswesen. Gedenkschrift für Ulrich Geißler, in: Badura, Bernhard (ed.): Reihe Soziologie und Sozialpolitik, vol.4, München 1985, pp. 547ff.

Henning, Hansjoachim: Sozialpolitik III: Geschichte, in: Alber, Willi e.al. (eds.): Handwörterbuch der Wirtschaftswissenschaft, vol.7, Stuttgart 1977, pp. 85ff.

Hunsel, Lothar: Die Bedeutung des Selbsthilfe-Prinzips in der Sozialversicherung, Dissertation, Münster 1979.

Laurinkari, Juhani/Brazda, Johann: Genossenschaftliche Grundwerte, in: Laurinkari, Juhani (ed.): Genossenschaftswesen. Hand- und Lehrbuch, München, Wien 1990, pp.70ff.

Runge, Brigitte/Vilmar, Fritz: Handbuch Selbsthilfe. Gruppenberichte, 900 Adressen, Gesellschaftliche Perspektiven, Frankfurt/Main 1988.

Schultz, Reinhard/Zerche, Jürgen: Genossenschaftslehre, 2nd ed., Berlin, New York 1983.

Thiemeyer, Theo: Gesundheitswesen I: Gesundheitspolitik, in: Albers, Willi (ed.): Handwörterbuch der Wirtschaftswissenschaft, vol.3, Stuttgart 1977, pp. 576ff.

Weisser, Gerhard: Selbsthilfeunternehmen, in: v. Beckerath et al. (eds.): Handwörterbuch der Sozialwissenschaften, vol.9, Stuttgart et al. 1956, pp. 217ff.

Zerche, Jürgen: Krankenversicherung, in: Görres-Gesellschaft (ed.): Staatslexikon, vol.3, 7th ed., Freiburg et al. 1987, cols. 691ff.

Zerche, Jürgen: Das Gesundheitssicherungssystem der Bundesrepublik Deutschland, in: v. Blume, Otto et al. (ed.): Kölner Schriften zur Sozial- und Wirtschaftspolitik, vol.5, Regensburg 1988.

Zerche, Jürgen: Aufbau des Genossenschaftssektors in den Ländern der Europäischen Gemeinschaft, in: Laurinkari, Juhani (ed.): Genossenschaftswesen. Hand- und Lehrbuch, München, Wien 1990, pp. 385ff.

History of Co-operative Ideas

WERNER WILHELM ENGELHARDT [F]

(see also: *History before 1800*; *History in 19th C.*; *Conceptions, Co-operative*; *Classification*; *ICA*; *Articles on Co-operative Pioneers*)

I. The Co-operative Idea as a Formative Principle; II. On the Work of Precursors (Pathfinders) of Co-operatives in the Industrial Age; III. The Great Pioneers (Initiators) of the 19th Century; IV. On Some Leaders of the 20th Century; V. Interrelationships among Various Approaches in Co-operative Research.

I. The Co-operative Idea as a Formative Principle

When the "co-operative idea" is referred to here as a formative principle, it is not *Plato's* holistic understanding of ideas and of utopias which is meant, but rather the concept of *Morus* and his early socialist successors (→ *Theory and Science of Co-operatives*). The words, in that case, mean a "selective utopia" (*Engelhardt*) which can be at least partially made into reality, just as *Morus' Utopia* (1516) can be interpreted approximately as the "practical political programme of a man who could at any moment be appointed a Minister in the English Government". (*H. Oncken*) Although utopias of this sort probably existed in the area of co-operatives even before modern times, it is advisable to talk about a co-operative formative principle chiefly with reference to co-operatives in the Industrial Age (→ *Principles*). The principle is associated with the acts – unconscious at first, perhaps, but then conscious – of individuals who can be characterized either as precursors (who prepare the way) or as pioneers of these co-operatives (who initiate and organize them). (*Draheim, Weuster*)

At the outset of a presentation of personalities like these, it must be observed that most of the local precursors and pioneers are unknown today. But just because they are not mentioned in the annals of history does not mean that they were unimportant. In fact, the opposite is frequently the case. Of those, however, who decidedly did make history – possibly favoured by conditions of their environment – only a selection can be considered in an article concentrating on Central and Western Europe.

Among those personalities selected, there are democratic, liberal-thinking socialists and philanthropic-minded liberals as well as active Christians ("Christians in deed") and constructive conservatives (conservatives in their value systems). (*Grünfeld, Weisser*) It was only ultraconservatives and fascists who often rejected co-operatives completely, naturally with differences among the various countries and with differentiations among the individual types of co-operatives. On the other hand, communist, anarchist and syndicalist movements have usually recognized and accepted their communitarian precursors and innovative thinkers and prophesied for some of their successors from case to case a considerable scope of action in shaping post-capitalistic society.

II. On the Work of Precursors (Pathfinders) of Co-operatives in the Industrial Age

What most precursors of the co-operative movement have in common is their emphasis: most of the co-operatives whose founding they supported or in some cases even undertook themselves were productive co-operatives (→ *Joint-production Co-operatives*) or settlement societies (→ *Communal Settlements*); and this emphasis lay mostly in pedagogical or political and legal directions. Only in the course of the 19th century (→ *History in 19th C.*) did it become more important to pave the way for various types of co-operatives whose function it was to promote individual members' households or businesses (→ *Classification*).

1. Pieter Cornelis Plockhoy (1620–1700)

Just from the long title of a pamphlet by this Dutch Mennonite, dated 1659, one has a very good idea of his programme: "A way propounded to make the poor in these and other nations happy by bringing together a fit, suitable and well-qualified people into one household-government, or little commonwealth, wherein every one may keep his propriety, and be employed in some work or other, as he shall be fit, without being oppressed". (*Faust, J.O. Müller*)

2. John Bellers (1654–1725)

The reform plan of the Quaker John Bellers, *Proposals for Raising a College of Industry*, published in 1696, represents a further milestone in paving the way for productive co-operatives and settlement societies in the realm of mercantilism. Bellers' detailed proposal won for him the reputation of being a "true father" (*Marx*) of co-operatives. It was said he had worked a miracle in the history of political economy. *Hans Müller* detects in his thinking the genesis of the modern co-operative idea. (*H. Müller, Faucherre*)

3. Johann Heinrich Pestalozzi (1746–1827)

Pestalozzi, the great Swiss philanthropist and educator of the people, presented an ideal picture of co-operative activity in his novel on education *Lienhard und Gertrud* (1781), which was influenced by *Rousseau*. Pestalozzi and his follower *Fellenberg* saw in the co-operative "the essential form of active self-education" (*Back*) for people of all ranks of society, but especially for the agricultural poor. According to his early view on the role of the social environment, it is conditions which shape a human being's character; but "human beings are the ones who created those conditions in the first place". (*Faucherre, Faust*)

4. Charles Fourier (1772–1837)

Fourier advocated combined forms of productive, housing and consumers' co-operatives in what he termed "phalansteries" (→ *Consumer Co-operatives*). These can be understood as an attempt to renew the cellular tissue of society (*Buber*). *Fourier's Théorie de l'Unité Universelle* (1822) states that potentially phalasteries could have the effect of "making the collective interest into a compass for individual interests, in a way whereby ambitious people would devote themselves solely to the general interest, which in turn would give individual interests their proper direction". (*Muckle, Faust*)

5. Robert Owen (1771–1858)

Following up the ideas of *Bellers* and *Pestalozzi*, → *Robert Owen* worked to further various forms of settlement societies, but not, however, consumer co-operatives. Using his key work *A New View of Society* (1813–1816) as a basis, he himself founded co-operatives, most of which nonetheless failed. The constitution of the most famous co-operative he founded – in New Harmony, Indiana, USA – provided for "equality of rights for grown-ups, with no distinction as to sex or social standing, and equality of obligations, according to physical and mental capacity; communal ownership of property and co-operative ownership association in the business and pleasures of life". (*Elsässer, Engelhardt, Pollard*)

6. William King (1786–1850)

King – just like *Kingsley, Maurice, Ludlow*, and others later on – was one of those British Christian social reformers who were greatly impressed by the ideas of *Robert Owen*. There were men of this type in other countries as well, as the example of *Saint-Simon* in France proves. In the years 1828 to 1830 in his periodical *The Co-operator, King* developed far-reaching ideas on questions of the formation of co-operative capital, on the co-operative spirit, and on the problem of political and religious neutrality. As a result of this work, over 300 early consumer co-operatives were founded, which, however, were not able to survive. The achievements of the other "Christian socialists" lay mainly in influencing policies of legislation. The British "Industrial and Provident Societies Act" of 1852, for example, was decisively shaped by their proposals. (*Brentano, Faust, Pollard*)

7. Louis Blanc (1813–1882)

The small industrial productive co-operatives which *Blanc* introduced into the discussion, and which were a type of socialized workshops, were meant to be financed by the state and kept, as a general rule, under state supervision. In his book *Organisation du travail* (1840), *Blanc* went on to proclaim the workers' right to work and demanded that this be organized by the respective governments. Yet *Blanc* was no forerunner of a planned economy. Instead he favoured competition among various different forms of types of business enterprises – private ones as well as state-run co-operatives (→ *Co-operative Socialism*). Of course he expected the latter ultimately to prevail. (*Faust, Weisser*)

8. Ferdinand Lassalle (1825–1864)

As a follower of *Saint Simon, Buchez* had approved of productive co-operatives on a self-help basis and had begun to set various ones up, whereby he exerted an influence on men like → *Schulze-Delitzsch*, among others. In a contrary way, Blanc's demand for state aid to help productive co-operatives decisively influenced *Schulze-Delizsch's* German opponent *Lassalle* as well as the catholic bishop *von Ketteler*. In his various writings, among them *Arbeiter-Lesebuch* (Workers' Reader) (1863) and *Herr Bastiat-Schulze von Delitzsch* (1864), *Lassalle* spoke out stronly in favour of joint-production co-operatives but also consistently contested consumer co-operatives (on account of the "Iron Law of Wages") and the general usefulness of craftsmen's credit and purchasing associations. As a true "virtuoso of the Mind" (*Na Aman*), *Lassalle* was in a position to grapple with fundamental aspects of legal philosophy and policies as prerequisites for liberating the working class. (*Bernstein, Faust*)

9. Wilhelm Emmanuel von Ketteler (1811–1877)

Von Ketteler's publication "Die Arbeiterfrage und das Christentum" (Christianity and the Problem of the Worker) (1864) shows that his unorthodox bishop was trying to combine ideas of *Saint Simon's* with those of *Lassalle*. *Von Ketteler* was convinced that co-operatives were in complete harmony with Christianity and that joint-production associations were valuable for improving the conditions of the working class. Long before the social encyclicals "Rerum novarum" and "Quadrogesimo anno" by *Leo XIII* and *Pius XI*, *von Ketteler* developed the concept of the → *subsidiarity* principle (support of local activities only insofar as necessary), which nonetheless definitely included the duty of the state to intervene in questions of social policy. (*Münstermann, Lampert*)

10. Eduard Pfeiffer (1835–1921)

Like *King*, → *Pfeiffer* initially supported the formation of consumer co-operatives, but he characterized the establishment of productive co-operatives as the actual goal of the co-operative movement. He himself became the founder of a large consumer co-operative in Stuttgart and of the first association of German consumer co-operatives. Probably more important was his book *Über Genossenschaftswesen* (On the Co-operative System) (1863), in which he anticipated *Gide's* ideological concepts of co-operativism with emphasis placed on productive co-operatives. This he did in an undogmatic way, however, since, in his words, "We want to take care not to make the same mistakes as the Communists and Socialists and want to avoid setting up a complete system, worked out to the finest detail". (*Hasselmann, Weuster*)

III. The Great Pioneers (Initiators) of the 19th Century

Here it is possible to mention only a few British and German pioneers whose achievements were outstanding.

1. The Rochdale Pioneers (1844 onwards)

These initiators (→ *Rochdale Pioneers*), who were the sole ones to work as a group from the outset, applied two principles which had already been evolved before: the principle of giving patronage dividends which had been instituted in 1812 in the "Lennoxtown Victualling Society" in Scotland, and the principle practices by *King* after 1828 of strict religious and political neutrality. In the pioneer group itself the leadership of the co-founder *Charles Howarth* was probably particularly decisive. Together the group gradually put his guiding ideas into practice, which culminated in the by-laws of the pioneer co-operative of 1844, one of the very earliest examples in which the purpose of individual co-operatives was institutionalized. Lastly, in analyzing the evolution of their ideas and their history, it is important to consider the actual decisions and actions of the boards and individual members of this co-operative as well as of their successors. It is from these decisions and actions, and not primarily from the original concept and first by-laws, that the "Rochdale Principles" were much later derived (→ *Principles*), which then in turn became the basis of the → *International Co-operative Alliance*. (*Cole, Elsässer, Hasselmann, Watkins* among others)

Among the main intentions in the original guiding concept were the goal of mutual self-help and a renewal of older forms of community and of economic activity for the community. However, it was more important at the time to satisfy the pressing material needs of the co-operative's members. This sequence of priorities is clearly revealed in the opening of the first shop on Toad Lane in Rochdale. It also shows, however, that it was ultimately higher goals which the pioneers wished to fulfill, whereby in a → "*co-operative commonwealth*" the interests of all members of society were to become the common concern. The principles which the co-operative group and their successors were guided by are derived primarily from their actual decisions and actions:

1. democratic principles and procedures;
2. open membership;
3. limited interest rates on share capital;
4. refunds according to the amount of individual purchases;
5. accumulation of a reserve fund;
6. payment in cash upon receipt of goods;
7. quality guarantee on goods:
8. further education for members;
9. religious and political neutrality. (*Faust, Holyoake*)

2. Victor Aimé Huber (1800–1883)

Through his travels, this great German pioneer (→ *Huber*) – the earliest one – became acquainted with the efforts of *Robert Owen* and the *Rochdale Pioneers*. He became interested in *Owen's* proposals for housing settlement co-operatives as well as in the Pioneers' plans for eventually erecting houses for members. Proceeding from a standpoint of conservative values, *Huber* tried from 1847 on to find concrete reformative solutions for putting his ideas into practice. He became well-known particularly for his leadership participation in the *Berliner gemeinnützige Baugesellschaft* (Berlin Building Society for Public Benefit) (→ *Housing Societies*). In this way he grew to become an important initiator of new structures of enterprises for public benefit, both of a private and of a public nature, and also an early co-operative theorist of great stature. Integrated into his all-encompassing conservative view of the world, which had crystallized out after early socialistic tendencies, was a "leading concept of the promotion of co-operative self-help" (*Weuster*). In this connection he was thinking above all of help for people to help themselves, to be provided by the more affluent members of society, including aristocratic circles. He favoured private help "from above" (*Jenkis*), that is, "from above and from the outside", rather than "from below and from within" (*J.O. Müller*). State help he decidedly opposed.

In particular, *Huber* analyzed and favoured numerous forms of open and latent cooperation, including company-type or foundation-type associations, among them industrial and other economic associations akin to joint-production co-operatives. With the idea of "inner colonization" in mind, *Huber* strove for a close affiliation of productive societies at their ultimate level of development, that is, in the form of settlement societies, with housing and consumer co-operatives. The "colonies" set up by settlemt societies were to include apartment houses as well as private homes. The residents, originally tenants, were ultimately to become owners. According to *Huber's* publication on the subject *Die Mietgenossenschaft in ihrer vollen Entwicklung* (The Tenancy Co-operative in its Full Development) (1848–49), the tenants' position was to rest on the foundation of revival of a tradition in Germanic law on "corporative overall ownership and was to be dependent on, limited by, and secured by this ownership." Many principles of housing for public benefit can be traced back to *Huber*. They include the following points:

1. the construction of small flats of sufficient size and conducive to health;
2. renunciation of maximum economic utilization of land;
3. limitation on dividends on capital;
4. permanent commitment of assets;
5. freezing of rents;
6. conferral of permanent occupancy rights. (*Jenkis*)

3. Hermann Schulze-Delitzsch (1808–1883)

After a period of trial and error in setting up foundation-type co-operatives with a definite altruistic character, this eminent German pioneer (→ *Schulze-Delitzsch*) also turned to "the practical tact of the English". He repudiated any intention whatsoever of desiring to create and establish a theory similar to that of the early socialists. However, he also had a leading concept, a guiding principle, underlying his actions which, as his efforts became more and more successful, even became the basis of a specific ideology. Guidelines for his actions began to make themselves apparent even in his *Assoziationsbuch für deutsche Handwerker und Arbeiter* (Association Book for German Craftsmen and Workers) (1853). In this book the associations – which were later almost always referred to as co-operatives – were clearly distinguished as "guilds of the future" from the guilds of the Middle Ages. "Not force, but the individual's own self-interest must produce the desire to join" was his motto. For *Schulze-Delitzsch* the co-operative was "a practical means", which nonetheless was regarded not as a technical end in itself but as a decentralized political instrument of the self-employed middle-class working from below. The use of this tool was to begin with elements of society at the time which were capable of being developed, but was to go beyond them. In addition to "material advantages" for the individual and for the middle-class as a whole, the effect to be achieved was to involve a "perhaps less tangible influence on the minds and spirits of the members." This influence was to tend in the direction of "intellectual and moral education", of strengthening the "feeling of belonging to a group", even of awakening a "sense for the public welfare, for working for the common good". *Schulze-Delitzsch* primarily favoured credit unions and people's banks (*Vorschußvereine* and *Volksbanken*) (→ *Co-operative Banks*), associations for obtaining supplies of raw materials (→ *Commercial Co-operatives*) and → *marketing co-operatives* for craftsmen, but also savings associations, genuine consumers' co-operatives, and workers' production co-operatives. He supported joint-production co-operatives as the "highpoint of the system". Despite his advocacy of activities by middle-class groups and approval of "secondary activity toward an economy for public benefit" (*Herrman*), there could be no doubt, in his opinion, about the existing "right to individuality over against devotion to society as a whole." For him, self-help in the field of business meant ultimately "peace", and self-responsibility constituted "the basic order of things". His most important principles, which also served to guide him in the legislative initiatives he took on behalf of the Prussian Co-operative Law (1867) and the Imperial Law on Co-operatives in the Economy (1889) were the following:

1. self-help as an absolute necessity;
2. self-responsibility;
3. equal rights for each individual in the co-operative group;
4. solidarity in the assumption of liability by the group;
5. democratic self-government;
6. strict refusal to accept outside help from the state. (*Dülfer, Hamm*)

4. Friedrich Wilhelm Raiffeisen (1818–1888)

This first great pioneer of agricultural cooperation (→ *Raiffeisen*) was decisively influenced by a protestant pietistic Christian background and world view. In the institutions which he founded as well as in his resulting main work *Die Darlehnskassen–Vereine* (Loan Associations) (1866), he came out, just like the French and British social reformers among the precursors of the co-operative movement, above all for the fulfillment of religious and moral goals. (*J.C. Müller, von Oppen*) The religious uplifting of the members, in the sense of moral demands put upon them by a Christianity calling for good deeds, took priority over the improvement of their livelihood, not only in a chronological but also in a systemic sense. However, Raiffeisen's thinking and actions had their root not in Christian thought alone, which can be traced back all the way to the original Christian community. (*Grünfeld, Siepmann*) He also picked up the early threads of the original forms of co-operatives under older Geman law. This is especially apparent in his understanding of community and in his idea for an indivisible foundation fund as a "new kind of common land but in a money economy framework" (*von Schmoller*). Since the fundamental importance of agriculture for the national economy and for society as a whole was indisputable – during Raiffeisen's lifetime more so than nowadays – he can be characterized as a proponent of economic associations for public benefit. (*Finis*) He spoke up very decidedly for making co-operatives into "seed-beds for genuine Christian community spirit, places where Christians genuinely act together for the public benefit." On the other hand, he evidently saw the dangers of a different set of economic priorities in *Schulze-Delitzsch's* system, dangers which he tried to avoid in his own. Despite his conviction that Christians are known by the later fruit of their deeds, he expected of them active steps for public benefit in the economic sphere at once, and not just as the ultimate effect of their efforts on the general economy. (*Engelhardt*, for a differing view cf. *Seraphim*)

Like *Schulze-Delitzsch*, *Raiffeisen* also began with altruistically motivated attempts to solve social problems. At first he supported charitable associations, then credit associations, and later central co-operatives, wine-growers' associations, dairy co-operatives, and cattle insurance associations. After initial stages, however, in contrast to *Schulze-Delitzsch*, *Raiffeisen* stood up all the rest of his life not just for self-help by those involved. He considered, like *Huber*, the additional use of private outside help to be absolutely necessary; in fact, in contrast to *Huber*, he also held outside help from the government to be absolutely essential. His principles, in particular, were the following:

1. religious and moral as well as material advancement of the members;
2. limitation of the membership groups to small village-size districts;
3. restrictions on share capital and dividends;
4. unlimited mutual liability of the members;
5. voluntary administration of the co-operatives, without pay;
6. accumulation of an indivisible foundation fund.

(*Faust*)

5. Wilhelm Haas (1839–1913)

The life and work of this second great founder personality in the rural agricultural co-operative movement in Germany (→ *Haas*) reaches into the twentieth century. In yet another respect his work represents a cut-off from the old methods and a transition to changed methods and principles. In a long drawn-out dispute about systems, *Haas* turned against *Raiffeisen's* supposed or actual doctrinarism in the moral and religious orientation of his co-operatives. As an important organizer and architect of a special "system of organization" (*Jäger*), *Haas* proceeded from the rather pragmatic standpoint of a national liberal.

In the rural self-help institutions which he supported, he wished to see a more economic grasp of affairs. Although he wanted three problem areas to be distinguished from one another – the morally effective co-operative idea, the likewise socially important effects of co-operatives, and the matter-of-fact, daily business activity "lying between" – he of course devoted himself not just to the last of the three. (*Finis*)

Haas founded numerous "agricultural consumer associations", as the rural merchandising co-operatives which he initiated were at first called. But many credit and dairy co-operatives as well as associations also go back to his initiative. It is also worthy of note that he started central co-operatives with limited liability, a form of co-operative which *Schulze-Delitzsch* as well as *Raiffeisen* had abstained from. Their inclusion in the Co-operative Law of 1889 is further credited to Haas's efforts. What is more, the *Darmstädter Programm* of 1890 contains three organizational principles which were characteristic of his methods and those of later rural agricultural co-operatives:

1. decentralization;
2. specialization, that is, separation of merchandising and credit transactions;
3. neutrality in respect to religion and politics.

IV. On Some Leaders of the 20th Century

The nearer a description of the co-operative movement, based on a history of ideas, comes to the present time, the more creative or innovative the personalities are who come into consideration and the harder it is to choose and present them here under circumstances of limited space. What is more, in addition to leaders in the "basic form oriented to individual enterprise" (*Seraphim*), we must not leave out here entirely those leaders of the "class-oriented" communist basic form, which was important for decades (from the First World War until 1990).

1. Heinrich Kaufmann (1864–1928)

→ *Kaufmann* was the outstanding figure and the "intellectual and organizational leader" (*Hasselmann*) of the German consumer co-operatives, which in 1903 joined together to form the *Zentralverband deutscher Konsumvereine* (Central Union of German Consumers' Co-operatives). Kaufmann was a former teacher and co-worker in educational associations for labouring people. After working with the Hamburg-Harburger Consumers' Co-operative and the co-operative *Großeinkaufsgesellschaft* (Wholesale Society), and together with other capable warriors for the cause (*von Elm, Staudinger* et al.), Kaufmann popularized the idea of an enterprise for public benefit oriented to covering the needs of consumers and developed this idea into a practicable plan. His greatest achievements lay in organizing both centralized purchasing and the production of the co-operatives' own brand goods along business administrative lines, and in setting up a federated association, training for capable auditors, and training programmes generally. (*Hasselmann, Weuster*)

2. Peter Schlack (1875–1957)

In addition to the "Hamburg school" of consumer co-operatives, there was also a "Cologne school", whose spokesman and main formative personality was *Peter Schlack*, the chairman of the so-called "cartel" of the Christian workers' unions, which were sympathetic to the political zentrum party. *Schlack* had founded a consumer co-operative in Köln-Mülheim in 1902, before he took over the chairmanship of the newly-founded *Verband westdeutsche Konsumvereine* (Union of West German Consumer Associations). In his thinking he belonged to those who drew consequences for the Christian workers' movement from the Social encyclical "Rerum novarum" of *Pope Leo XIII*. He was one of the earliest cooperators to work toward instituting a consumer organization and consumer policies oriented toward the idea of serving as a counterbalance to other business. In Sweden *Albin Johansson* had earlier succeeded inputting through something similar, under different political conditions. (*Bock, Weuster*)

3. Wladimir Iljitsch Lenin (1870–1924)

In a treatise written near the end of his life *Über das Genossenschaftswesen* (On the Co-operative Movement) (1923), *Lenin* emphasized the great importance of co-operatives for the new Economic Policy at that time in the Soviet Union (→ *Socialist Critics*). Ultimately in connection with classic marxist works, particularly *Engels*' treatise *Die Mark*, *Lenin* at the same time set the course for the subsequent upswing – at least quantitatively – of the agricultural co-operative movement (→ *kolkhozes*, among others) and also of consumer as well as housing co-operatives in the entire communist power bloc. Of course, these co-operatives, belonging to the basic form oriented to social class, were usually transformed co-operatives from the very outset. They were based on force and fulfilled the function of political instruments one hundred per cent. (*Th. Bergmann, Boettcher*)

4. Otto Klepper (1888–1957)

Klepper was the fourth president of the *Preußische Genossenschaftskasse* (Prussian Co-operative Bank) founded in 1895 by the Prussian Minister of Finance *von Miquel* as an institution under public law. The founding of this enterprise instituted a long period of intensive collaboration between the Prussian state, later the German state, and co-operatives. Contrary to the wishes of *Schulze-Delitzsch*, both agricultural as well as industrial co-operatives had demanded this contact (*Korthaus*, among others). Although *Klepper* headed the organization only from 1928 until 1931, he has gone down in the history of the modern co-operative movement as a great leader. "With skill and not without severity" (*Tillmann*), he pushed ahead the unification as well as the efficiency of the agricultural co-operative movement, which until then had been fragmented (*Raiffeisen* system against the *Haas* system). The "independent but controversial agricultural policy" (*Faust*) pursued by the so-called Prussian Co-operative Bank occurred partly in the period of the oncoming world-wide economic crisis. This agricultural policy proves the usefulness, but also the limits, of a certain role of the central co-operative organizations as political instruments in market economies. (*Faust, Kluthe*)

5. Gottlieb Duttweiler (1903–1972)

In the field of merchandising co-operatives, but also in the areas of non-material services extending beyond merchandising, *Duttweiler* – a Swiss business pioneer and political figure – is one of the outstanding founders and organizers of the 20th century. A remarkable aspect here is that Duttweiler – in reversal of a trend otherwise noticeable among co-operatives – developed step by step from a "wholesaler oriented to his own self-interest into a cooperator oriented to the public good" (*Heister*). In the midst of the Second World War (1940–1941), and out of predominantly non-egotistical motives, he turned over his profit-oriented merchandising enterprise "Migros" to his customers and his employees. In accordance with the regulations regarding co-operatives in the Swiss liability law, he thereby set up a consumer co-operative organization, the second such organization in the country next to the ones patterned after the historic Rochdale co-operatives. According to the type of task to which the organization devotes itself (i.e. according to the people it is intended to benefit), it is a co-operative union for public benefit with a differentiated structure. As the *Thesen aus dem Jahre 1950* (Programmatic Statements for the Year 1950) document, the common weal is to be striven for directly, and is not to be achieved merely as an indirect result. (*Heister*)

V. Interrelationships among Various Approaches in Co-operative Research

As indicated at the beginning of this article, the present account of the history of ideas, limited to co-operatives in modern or industrial times, is the result of a utopia-concept approach. This approach is part of a research programme in co-operative science, including, in addition, both an approach from the perspective of origin and development, all within the actual history of co-operatives, and in addition an approach from aspects and dogmas within the history of teaching (cf. *Engelhardt* and the article on co-operative theory and science). The approach here, based on a utopian concept, has been sketched only halfway. Essential portions of the concepts are missing which have been presented elsewhere (→ *Conceptions, Co-operative*). Genealogically, it should be emphasized that out of utopias or ideas, concepts can result if utopias are brought into confrontation with logic and experience. Applied to the question of whether utopias can be turned into reality or not, one can surmise that in the course of the past few centuries, in comparison to the time when *Morus* was alive, "the scope for the realization of human phantasies based on wishes or fears has been noticeably widened" (*Elias*).

Bibliography

Boettcher, Erik (ed.): Die Genossenschaft im Wettbewerb der Ideen, Tübingen 1985.
Buber, Martin: Pfade in Utopia, Heidelberg 1950.
Cole, G.D.H.: A Century of Cooperation, London 1944; Deutsche Ausgabe Hamburg 1950.
Deutscher Genossenschaftsverband (Schulze-Delitzsch) (ed.): Schulze-Delitzsch. Ein Lebenswerk für Generationen, Wiesbaden 1987.
Elsässer, Markus: Die Rochdaler Pioniere, Berlin 1982.
Elsässer, Markus: Soziale Intentionen und Reformen des Robert Owen in der Frühzeit der Industrialisierung, Berlin 1984.
Engelhardt, Werner Wilhelm: Allgemeine Ideengeschichte des Genossenschaftswesens, Darmstadt 1985.
Engelhardt, Werner Wilhelm: Der Beitrag der Theorie des institutionellen Wandels, von D.C. North zu Theorien der öffentlichen Unternehmen und Genossenschaften, in: Friedrich, Peter (ed.), Beiträge zur Theorie öffentlicher Unternehmen, Beiheft 14 der ZögU, Baden-Baden 1992, pp. 83–98.
Engelhardt, Werner Wilhelm: Die Funktion von Utopien in der Entwicklung von Wirtschaftsordnungen, in: Wagener, Hans Jürgen (ed.): Zur Evolution von Wirtschaftsordnungen, Berlin 1991, pp. 139–171.
Faucherre, Henry: Umrisse einer genossenschaftlichen Ideengeschichte, 2 parts (Basel 1925–1928), 2. ed., Basel 1928.
Faust, Helmut: Geschichte der Genossenschaftsbewegung (Frankfurt 1958), 3. ed., Frankfurt 1977.
Finis, Beate: Wirtschaftliche und außerwirtschaftliche Beweggründe mittelständischer Genossenschaftspioniere des landwirtschaftlichen Bereichs, Berlin 1980.
Grünfeld, Ernst: Das Genossenschaftswesen, volkswirtschaftlich und soziologisch betrachtet, Halberstadt 1928.
Hall, Frederick/Watkins, William Pascoe: Cooperation (Manchester 1937), 2. ed., Manchester 1948.
Hasselmann, Erwin: Die Rochdaler Prinzipien im Wandel der Zeit, Frankfurt/Main 1968.
Hasselmann, Erwin: Geschichte der deutschen Konsumgenossenschaften, Frankfurt 1971.
Heister, Michael: Gottlieb Duttweiler als Handels- und Genossenschaftspionier, Berlin 1991.
Hettlage, Robert: "Solidarität" und "Kooperationsgeist" in genossenschaftlichen Unternehmungen, Kooperatives Management, Baden-Baden 1990, pp. 123–152.
Jenkis, Helmut W.: Ursprung und Entwicklung der gemeinnützigen Wohnungswirtschaft, Hamburg 1973.
Kluthe, Klaus: Genossenschaften und Staat in Deutschland, Belrin 1985.
Lasserre, Georges: L'esprit coopératif et l'efficacité économique, Revue des Etudes Coopératives, Paris, 189 (1977), pp. 53–61.
Laurinkari, Juhani (ed.): Genossenschaftswesen, München, Wien 1990.
Laurinkari, Juhani (ed.): The International Co-operative Movement – Changes in Economic and Social Policy, Geneva 1988.
Manuel, Frank E./Manuel, Fritzie P.: Utopian Thought in the Western World (New York 1977). 2. ed., Cambridge/Mass. 1980.
Müller, Hans: Die Geburt der Genossenschaftsidee aus dem Geiste des Quäkertums, Genossenschafts-Korrespondenz, Halberstadt, 3 (1925), pp. 65–77.
Müller, Julius Otto: Voraussetzungen und Verfahrensweisen bei der Errichtung von Genossenschaften in Europa vor 1900, Göttingen 1976.
Pollard, Sidney: Co-operative Principles in the Modern World, Co-operative College Papers, 13 (1967), pp. 71–80.
Preuss, Walter: Das Genossenschaftswesen in der Welt und in Israel, Berlin 1958.
Seraphim, Hans-Jürgen: Die genossenschaftliche Gesinnung und das moderne Genossenschaftswesen, Karlsruhe 1956.
Tillmann, Hugo: Genossenschaftsgeschichte, Handwörterbuch des Genossenschaftswesens, Wiesbaden 1980, cols. 757–794.
Tönnies, Ferdinand: Gemeinschaft und Gesellschaft (Leipzig 1887), 10. ed., Darmstadt 1963.
Totomianz, Vahan (ed.): Internationales Handwörterbuch des Genossenschaftswesens, 2 vols., Berlin 1928.
von Brentano, Dorothee: Grundsätzliche Aspekte der Entstehung von Genossenschaften, Berlin 1980.
Voßkamp, Wilhelm (ed.): Utopieforschung, 3 vols., (Stuttgart 1982), 2. ed., Baden-Baden 1985.
Watkins, William Pascoe: Die internationale Genossenschaftsbewegung, Frankfurt/Main 1969.
Wegner, Bettina: Subsidiarität und "Neue Subsidiarität" in der Sozialpolitik und Wohnungspolitik, Regensburg 1989.
Weippert, Georg: Zur Soziologie des Genossenschaftswesens, ZgGenW., Göttingen, 7 (1957), pp. 112–114.
Weuster, Arnulf: Theorie der Konsumgenossenschaftsentwicklung, Berlin 1980.

History of Co-operatives before 1800

JULIUS OTTO MÜLLER

(see also: Guilds; History in 19th C.; History of Ideas; Informal Co-operatives; Autochthonous Co-operatives)

I. "Genoz" – Essence and Functions in the European Middle Ages; II. Prehistory and Early History; III. Early Middle Ages; IV. High Middle Ages (12th Century); V. Late Middle Ages (13th to 15th century); VI. Modern Times (16th to 18th century).

I. "Genoz" – Essence and Functions in the European Middle Ages

In Old High German, *noz* means use, benefit; genoz, the co-user, the co-beneficiary. The term *genoze* is used in many ways in sources dating back to the Middle Ages and is abmbigious. A *genosse* (companion) (*paris, comparis, consocius*) is a) a participant in the rights and duties of a community; b) a member of the same standing and, therefore, of equal rank; and c) a partner in a common legal system.

The lord of the manor and the knights acted as partners of their dependents when exploiting and administering *regalia* and when practising livestock keeping jointly. Companions of the same standing in a march, that is, the delimited territory (*marca*), forest, pastures, wild land and waters outside the fields used privately for agriculture, have the same rights. The march is the supreme property of the *lord of the manor* and not the *common or entire possession* of a *march co-operative* which cannot be proved according to the authentic sources. At any rate, the majority of the people share the right of use of the march.

The rights of companions are based principally on the sustainment of *preserving the substance of the object, of increasing it, if possible, and, at the same time, of using it sparingly out of consideration for fellowmen.*

As early as the 6th century already, companions have probably participated to a considerable extent in local and regional security, defence and the maintenance of public rights within the manor and sometimes even against it. As court and later village companions, they participated in ruling the manorial affairs and in applying the law in the relation between the lord of the manor and the peasants. Under specific conditions, they could represent the lord of the manor as member of the court (village court) and proved efficient, later, when 'national co-operatives of lay assessors of the criminal courts were established.' In the case of the economic exploitation of *regalia* (the king's and the state's supreme rights) on the basis of shares administered jointly, the community of companions played a prominent part as a pioneering institution when the state provided fundamental cultural services. The compelling powers of compulsory labour imposed on the serfs by the authorities for working the *regalia*, together with high taxes, were confronted with definite liberties – often overlooked by modern science – which can only be taken on a co-operative basis. They consisted primarily in multiple competent co-operative decisions for a better organization and a collective control of all rights of use within the framework of the prevailing legal order, in the courageous defence of common rights and – within the course of time up to the High Middle Ages – undoubtedly in their exploitation as well, with a view to improving the private and common infrastructures.

II. Prehistory and Early History

Since the dawn of humanity, the confrontation with natural forces and the wildness of fauna and flora as well as with external enemies surely compelled the organized association of kin groups primarily. The struggle for life called for such early human associations for the purpose of taking joint actions in view for protecting and defending hunting grounds, herd management, land occupation and field cultivation. Collective land possessions and the common religious veneration of natural deities in extended family clans are probable at this stage of development. When power structures develop politically imposed co-operative structures, individual forms of property and economy must, under certain circumstances, be adopted. As development increases a free coexistence of collectivism and individualism is also conceivable from time immemorial. The multiple forms of traditional autochthonous cooperation (→ *Autochthonous Co-operatives*), which are known as vital institutions within the context of modern ethnosociology in the so-called developing countries, can present a comparative picture. In scanty traditions from ancient times, ritual structures of cooperation are called the crystallization core of a specific economic cooperation (craftsmen's associations). In Babylon, the *Hammurabi* Codex causes members of the upper class to adopt the common tenancy of large areas with the aim of cultivating them for their joint account and/or of dividing them for independent cultivation. Similarly, co-operative credit institutions are adopted. In ancient Egypt, and probably in China as well, craftsmen's corporation are said to have existed. However, no information is availabe as to their degree of freedom under a strict centralized power.

In all semi-arid zones in Asia, Latin America and North Africa, traditional knowledge of associations for water use has been handed down. These associations were placed under sovereign rather than co-operative management. The same applies to common field cultivation which might not only typify an adopted free agro-co-operative form of primeval economy but also allows the assumption of a communal, however state-co-operative, cultivation at a later date, in the form of the Roman *Centuria* settlements also placed under government authority. In the European cultural region, the Celts and the Romans made serfs and slaves of free peasants – in so far as free communal and individual forms of exploitation prevailed.

III. Early Middle Ages

1. Greek and Roman Late Ancient Times (up to the 6th century)

The roots of co-operative institutions also developed in the Greco-Roman cultural region, i.e., in the religious cult practised jointly, especially in the burial cult, on which forms of mutual help and social life are closely modelled (Greek: thiasis). Communal self-help organizations which had economic and charitable tasks are said to have developed therefrom. The members were townsmen and slaves, foreigners and women, this allowing the conclusion that a relative freedom prevailed. In Greece, such institutions are said to have been legal entities capable of instituting legal proceedings. Industrial colleges – in Greek and Roman territories, venerating resort-deities – that also took political action and opposed the Roman occupying power are probably of the same origin. Many of these institutions are thought to have dissolved as slave labour became widespread. In contrast, ancient Christian communities, organized on a co-operative basis, that surely fulfilled multiple socio-economic functions, have been able to subsist for a long time – in so far as they could escape Roman repression. The Acts of the Apostles (Chapter 1, Verses 44–46) refer clearly to life organization on a fully co-operative basis. More exhaustive sources referring to the free internal organization and absolute self-determination exist besides information supplied by numerous classical authors since the discovery of the scrolls of *Qumran* where the Hebrew confraternity of the *Essenes* had its centre during *Herod's* government. Centres of this fully co-operative working and living community which was based on self-sufficiency and assuming tasks in education and medicine were located in Syria and Egypt (3rd century B.C. until 1000 A.D.). In communication with cosmic and earthly forces, the *Essenes* considered it their task to transmit the consciousness of these forces in order to use them for the individual's activities in continuation of God's creation on earth. Respect of nature, worship of God, discipline in life and work, love of mankind and peace did not only impart to them a lasting spiritual influence and long physical stability. To begin with, their charisma persisted until the late Middle Ages and considerably influenced the spiritual foundations of famous communities such as the *Cathari*, the *Templars*, the *Freemasons* and the *Rosicrucians* as spiritual confraternities. They have not lost their significance for the tasks towards solving the current civilization crises.

The establishment of old co-operative rules that had a great effect on labour in terms of manorial interests for strengthening the economic and political power as well as for safeguarding society has been assumed not only for Roman times. The Roman *Centuria* settlements on generally rectangular areas of approximately 100 arpents or a multiple of this constitute perhaps an example. They were maintained far into the Frankish era and possibly allowed a margin for self-organization. According to *Tacitus*, there was a large number of free small farmers anyway in addition to the characteristic large manors so that basically a relatively free cooperation cannot be excluded altogether. *Cicero* mentions common pasture rights on the harvested fields of others, except on enclosures, in early Roman times (*ager compascuus*).

2. Frankish Era (7th to 11th century)

The aforementioned common field cultivation dating back to Roman times either involving a changing farm pattern and periodical redistribution of fields or strict field community – forms of cultivation that are likely to be connected with cooperation – were surely not the rule in early Frankish times. Similarly, in the regions of Northern Europe subjected to German law, there was neither a co-operative state constitution nor were there political provincial co-operatives. Emerging structures that resembled co-operatives such as *Gemenglage*, three-year field system, compulsory cultivation (*Flurzwang*) can only have emerged at a late date in the train of the population increase.

Taking into account the low population density up to the Carolingian era (9th century), the personal rights of land use (*tera familia*) corresponding to the economic system of the *capitulare de villis* predominated on the socage farm of the lord of the manor. The system of land use was of loan of land for life (vital loan) or for the lifetime of three "bodies" (father, son, grandson). When there was no heir, the land returned to the socage farm to prevent the land from passing on to other hands than those of the members of the farm community. The community of the socage farm- or house companions as an extended family came forward for controlling co-operatively law and justice in all matters pertaining to the farm in association with or in the name of the lord of the manor (farm co-operative). This involves communal and private use in the march. Indeed, the co-operative, under court law, during the Carolingian era was not completely self-administered but had the right to assist in administrative and legal proceedings. Its functions also comprised typical neighbourly tasks such as common fire-brigade, construction and maintenance of wells, burial of the dead, etc.

From the 9th to the 11th century, the population increases threefold; clearing progresses until the 12th century; land becomes scarce; and it becomes necessary to increase wheat yields. In addition to socage farms, large settlements and villages are established. Large peasant families and noble families jointly constitute village settlers' residential, economic, defence, church and legal communities (*village co-operatives*). They enjoy a relatively great autonomy within the village regarding administration and the control of soil cultivation, of rights of use and tax liabilities. Farms that become free as the ruin of the Carolingian *villicationes* progresses are only allocated to the group of court and village companions. Often, clearing and settlement are also co-operative processes for providing individual land use on manorial ground. New forms of common field cultivation are established such as small ploughing co-operatives using 4–8 bullocks. The organization of the three-year field system in *Gewannverfassung* in consideration of other companions, water and pasture rights, the construction of a fence around the fields, etc., either enforced by the supreme authorities or else have been established under co-operative self-responsibility. Finally, this concerns the joint use of the still unlimited march which, later becomes more restricted owing to the commercial use of forest and water by the lord of the manor. It is only in restricted regions of Westphalia and perhaps (those) of the Hesse that the march was common property. March co-operative (*"Markgenossenschaft"*) is a modern term coined in the 19th century and cannot be historically substantiated (→ *Co-operatives under Public Law*). Specific forest and pasture areas, water and harvested fields, as manorial land, belong, to the actual community and are in common use as *algimeinida* (*Allmende*, communal land, land held in common). Within the framework of feudal land tenure, however, the autonomy of peasant communities was still quite extensive. Finally, after 1000, in addition to communities of peasant village, companions, monastic communities should also be presented as co-operative associations with a marked independence.

IV. High Middle Ages (12th century)

1. Rural Development

Following the suppression of the Frankish-Carolingian civil service and the abolition of the socage farm tenure, new feudal lords appear during the transition to feudal tenure. These are small knights who are not so much interested in agricultural as in military development and demand monetary taxes. They could become associate companions. The village co-operative was thus divided into three groups: the knight's family (*familia militaris*), the tenants' (*familia censualis*) and the servants' (*familia servilis*). At the same time, the co-operative connections become closer as a result of compulsory cultivation. Since the village co-operatives and the functions they assumed from the court co-operative were maintained and new co-operative tasks in the *"Gemeng"*-tenure, which they could perform autonomously were added to those, they were also able, within the framework of their participation in agricultural law and petty jurisdiction, to strengthen their position against feudal and manorial power when higher contributions were imposed upon them or damages to the fields caused by hunting had to be adjusted (*"Frühe Bauernbefreiung"*, *"La Solidarité Paysanne"*). Their great co-operative autonomy in almost all local administrative and agricultural tasks constitutes, at a later date, an important condition for the establishment of the modern political rural communities.

One of the most important economic and social functions besides controlling infractions of compulsory cultivation is co-operative livestock farming in individual fields and on common land. In the first case, it becomes possible to improve soil fertility, namely in wheat cultivation, through deliberate heavy grazing and fertilizing of the areas reserved for grain cultivation by co-operative livestock breeding. Thereby, individual pasture rights prevailed according to private shares (contingents) in the common herd. According to livestock species, the size of the herd was jointly determined in consideration of fodder available. Similar rights based on the individual share in the co-operatively kept herd existed in the co-operatives of the Alps since the 12th century. Other special co-operatives emerge: cheese co-operatives in Italy, in the Western Alps, in the Pyrenees and in the Jura, in Switzerland, (*Fruitières*). They also manage the sale of cheese produced in the alpine region, including long-distance transport to urban centres on a co-operative basis. In Russia, since that time, fishermen's and hunters' co-operatives are supposed to have peacefully colonized Southern Russia and Siberia. Finally, this is the period of the first agro-cultural high perfomance of co-operative nature achieved by the Cistercians who, with lay brothers and labourers, cultivate the land in their orders and lay communities, in contrast to the Benedictines. Several monasteries provided, with brotherly charity, for pilgrims' confraternities on their pilgrimages – especially those to Santiago de Compostela – and offered protection, care, advice and provisions for the journey free of charge.

In connection with the economic exploitation of regalia in the rural areas, various industrial structures of cooperation will be introduced: the forest and timber co-operatives, associations for the exploitation of water regalia as operation and transportation means, for running hammer, grinding, and saw mills, for fishery, for regulating water, etc. The exploitation of regalia in mining and metallurgy as well as in salines by a co-operative syndicate by ceding rights of use and shares to the companions and its autonomous operation remain, until the transformation into early capitalistic industrial enterprises, the privilege of relatively free co-operatives.

2. Urban Development

In Central Europe, in the High Middle Ages, the expansion of the urban centres and the development of an urban economy and culture of free citizens constitute the prerequisites for the development of industrial and commercial co-operative societies (corporations). In addition to co-operative institutions for craftsmen and tradesmen, working co-operatives were also established in specific vocational groups. This development is universal from the geographical viewpoint and begins in Italy in the early 10th century; in Northern Spain and in France in the 11th century, and, in England, not until the 13th century. Its origin is generally considered to be independent of the histoy of rural cooperation. A direct relation with the late Roman craftsmen corporations (*collegia*) is less probable than the influence upon a development course extending from Rome to Central and Northern Europe via Byzantium and Ravenna. At the beginning of the 9th century, there is evidence of three corporations for Ravenna: those of the *macellarii* (butchers), *pescatori* (fishermen) and of *negotiatores* (tradesmen). Meanwhile, it is not excluded that suggestions were made by member of manorial associations since, following the dissolution of the *villicationes*, the urban atmosphere liberated precisely the members of such trades. Basically, urban corporations were organized on the free initiative of the people concerned. Their development and economic influence have taken place over several centuries up to the 15th century. From the first, the industrial and commerical corporations of crafts and trade acquire the greatest significance and economic power in urban policy. In authentic sources, the medieval corporations bore various names according to their different purposes: *gilda, corporation, consortium, community, unio, métier, artes, officium, function, craft, guild, master craft, brotherhood, trade union*. The crafts and trade corporations are generally called guilds (→ *Guilds*); those of the merchants brotherhood or *hanse*. As a result of the predominance of the religious institution over the political and economic ones in medieval society, efforts towards attaining salvation were one of the main goals in human life. Therefore, pilgrims' brotherhoods played an important part in medieval society. Just as the wish for common veneration of patron saints of the respective industry and trade among companions of the same standing is common practice. The handing down of numerous corporation and guild charters containing records of statutes and regulations of each of the co-operative proceedings allows much better insights into the internal conditions and regulations of the corporations and guilds in comparison with those of the early rural-agricultural associations. The goals and regulations of the significant craftsmen corporations *(Zünfte)* will be summarized in examples. Apart from the co-operative fulfilment of religious needs, co-operative work is oriented primarily towards

- high efficiency and quality of the labour capacity;
- control of the produced commodities through the joint quality exhibition of the products;
- construction of common stands in the market area in the town in order to prevent, later, in the co-operative shop, individualistic efforts to effect sales.
- Establishment of co-operative institutions for utilizing more sophisticated technological inputs in the processing of raw materials and refining of finished products for individual companions (e.g., bark, fulling, hammer and grinding mills, cloth frames, etc.).
- Efforts towards attaining independence from the urban government which represents the state and its own jurisdiction.
- Independent regulation of industrial production and marketing under prohibition of undesired competition inside and outside the urban centre.
- Imparting the best training to apprentices, journeymen and masters by promoting the co-operative spirit and all the individual interests of the corporations.
- Granting of mutual charitable help and support of poor in the society as well as providing for widows and orphans, especially within the guild.
- Maintaining mundane and religious conviviality and brotherly behaviour together with the veneration of patron saints and the construction of chapels and altars belonging to the guilds.

The constitutive elements of a typical corporation charter – here, once again the example of crafts corporations – can be ascribed to two main characteristics:

a) Equality and solidarity of all the companions of the corporation.

b) The imposition of numerous limitations and prohibitions together with a certain isolation from the outside world (obligation to belong to a corporation ("Zunftzwang")). The principle of equality of all members applied to the benefit of equal privileges with equal rights. Every companion was to have the same opportunities. Therefore, raw materials were obtained jointly. Whoever bought individually had to procure for others and share at cost price. The principle of limitation applied to self-promotion and avoidance of competition as well as to the avoidance of supply problems in a town that was growing too rapidly.

The limitations referred to

- strictly limited admission of masters and apprentices due to admission rules fixed at a high level: socially (neither unfree, illegitimate or of foreign origin), professionally (previous relations with honest occupations, seven years of apprenticeship and travel, expensive "masterpices") and financially (fees, often proof of wealth and high entrance fee for young masters).
- Limitation of the size of enterprises due to a restricted number of journeymen and limited production volume.
- Production and sale of a limited number of pieces.

Prohibition applied to

- unfair competition;
- the organization of the workshop on the basis of

capital economy and the master's development into an entrepreneur with individual use of technical progress;
- the management of several workshops and branches;
- cottage industry for private sale to merchants and publishing firms;
- the employment of women and children;
- night and Sunday work;
- the peddling of products; and
- advertising.

Often, prices were enforced cooperatively – even against prohibition by the authorities. The corporations exercised a highly restrictive influence on the authorization and price formation of commodities which were not produced in the corporations of the same town but imported from external sources (e.g., from peasant production). The power of corporations increased as the masters of the corporations became municipal councillors, especially when industrial privileges (autonomy of the corporation) were conferred by the authorities or when a corporation presented itself as a mighty political institution (predominance in the municipal council). Only those who had been admitted to the corporation could carry on a trade in town (dependent trade).

V. Late Middle Ages (13th to 15th century)

1. Rural Development

In the rural areas, the development of agricultural co-operatives which was marked in the 12th century continued to progress. However, in the Late Middle Ages, it is restricted by the increased *feudal* exploitation and the urban price policy determined by the crafts corporations to the peasants' disadvantage. There is no doubt that the violent repression of numerous peasant rebellions, which began in the 12th century and were organized on the basis of the experience handed down by the village co-operative, on the one hand, and the events of the 14th century (wars, epidemics, reduction of the population to one-third), on the other hand, caused a setback in further co-operative efforts or their ruin. Meanwhile, co-operative livestock farming maintains itself until the 19th century, and food secure for the society by a more intensive wheat production. In addition to the existing rural corporations, *landscape* co-*operatives* ("Landschafts-Zünfte") are established in the metal, textile, timber and stone industry. As far as advantages and disadvantages of their corporative charters are concerned, they are similar to the urban corporations. We also refer to the not very common special agricultural co-operatives such as the "*Hauberggenossenschaften*" for the combined use of tan oaks, pastures, and rye on forest slopes in Siegerland and the "*Gehöferschaften*" for the use of forests and arable land near the Moselle and the Saar – both in Germany-, by order of the manorial authorities.

2. Urban Development

In the urban centres, the corporations increase in nature and number. The merchants' guilds as associations participating in the growing external and foreign trade experience a great boom (→ *Guilds*). They also create common urban quarters, in which stores and offices are run on a co-operative basis. They form solidary associations against the merchants' guilds privileges; the marketing rights for authochthonous goods produced by the guilds for example. Abroad, the offices of the *hanse*, especially in the North, are run jointly at the urban level (in Old Norse, *hanse* means co-operative). Guilds and Hanseatic leagues prevail until the enforcement of the national trade policy in modern times. In the transport industry, co-operative organizations of sailors contribute towards the development of foreign trade. Transport co-operatives partly provided transport faciles on national roads and rivers. Thus, for example, sailors' guilds are established that do their cash accounting jointly, train their members with a view to assuring security, and provide charitable services. Later (since the 16th century), the river shipping co-operatives organize the regular freight traffic. In the mining industry, workers' co-operatives train skilled workers who retain the same rank (no training as masters). Thus, it becomes possible to eliminate irregularities in the train of day labourers' and casual work. They are effective in the service of towns and trade. The co-operative vouches for responsibility and honesty as far as security, weighing, packing, dues and charges are concerned. In this case as well, the earnings often flow into a joint fund for equal distribution. Provision for the disabled and for widows, the grant of death benefits are – as usual in guilds – the forerunners of the national social insurance in the 19th century.

Finally, it should be mentioned that, in the towns, there were a large number of monastic congregations attending society, fraternities of clergymen, corporations of university lecturers, notaries, medical doctors, money changers, and even co-operative organizations for itinerant journeymen, gravediggers, town cleaners, beggars, prostitutes, etc.

The guilds remain economically active until the end of the Middle Ages and then must give way to business forms based on capital economy and organized as enterprises that were asserting themselves. By holding on to privileges, prohibitions against development and the restricted admission to active gainful employment, they brought about the development of an urban proletariat and poverty (mendicity), to which free entrepreneurs refer since the 15th and 16th century in order to introduce the era of industrial manufacture that cause the guilds to become obsolete in the 17th and 18th century at the latest.

Thus, the corporations and guilds made themselves superfluous because of their selfishness and their policy of restrictions, privileges and monopoly. Until the introduction of freedom of trade at the beginning of the 19th century (1810), they subsist formally only while their significance keeps dwindling. This does not detract from their great achievements in craftmanship, education, training, the formation of communities and thus their important contribution to culture in the Middle Ages.

VI. Modern Times (16th to 18th century)

1. Rural Development

In the rural areas, co-operative associations seem to continue to stagnate until new co-operative activities appear in the 17th century: various special co-operatives in the secular field and polyvalent agricultural communities in the religious domain. Among the first, dairy co-operatives see to the distribution of profits according to the producers' shares. Co-operatives for cultivating embankments, heaths and moorland work for the common land clearing and new settlement. Ploughing co-operatives allow an increase in the joint efficiency (*Wales*). Fishermen's and hunters' co-operatives in Russia are probably known since the Middle Ages. There, the self-administered *mir* obtained poll-tax under bondage. Numerous *artells*, work and/or capital fraternities continue to exist with mutual responsibility, in Russia and in the Balkans until the 20th century. Religious, sometimes since Early Middle Ages sectarian communities emerge in Europe where liberal rule allows this: for example, in France, the *communautés*, fully self-administered, self-sufficient institutions founded by Christian and socially-minded landlords; in Germany, the subsistence-oriented communities of "Amana" (1714) and "Ephrata" (1734); in England, the Quakers (1696) and Shakers (1776); in Russia, the Bohemian Brothers (Hutterites) are in exile in the 17th century. In the 19th century, the Doschubors become known. As the oldest religious community, the Bohemian Brothers have existed since 1529 and continue to exist today in the USA, in Canada and in Germany.

On the other hand, individual princely cabinets also prohibited the free association of vassals. Apart from co-operative livestock keeping, many unknown and isolated co-operatives were able to subsist until the 19th century despite their lack of capital by uniting and reducing their standards. Only the separations in the wake of the *Stein's* and *Hardenberg's* reforms, as a result of the land-improvement legislation, cause the communities to split so that the rural forms of cooperation are strongly repressed or abolished. Following the revolutions, liberalism brought about the separation from rule and unfree co-operative since both mean commitment.

2. Urban Development

In the 16th and 17th century, the new system of economy comprising entrepreneurial factories in the cities is introduced. Rural landlords have often assumed entrepreneurial roles and invested capital which they could earn at the cost of agriculture. Many of the former corporative institutions such as shops, mills, quality exhibitions, etc. were handed over to the town and were turned into landlords' capitalistic enterprises. However, the co-operative concept remained alive even in the urban area. It is said that, in the middle of the 17th century already, attempts were made to establish co-operative enterprises. However, they did not prove successful. Other attempts regarding self-help and self-administration independent of entrepreneurial or political power succeed, for example, in Fenwick/Scotland, in 1734, when a consumers' shop which distributed the profits among the parties concerned was established (→ *Consumer Co-operatives*). In England, workers' and consumers' associations emerge, for example in Gowan, in 1777, and Mongewell, in 1794. A workers' joint-productive co-operative was founded by tailors in Birmingham, before 1777; the first grain mill managed by workers on a co-operative basis, in Hull, in 1795. Similar peasants' mills appeared in Rhineland approximately at the same time or later.

The era of independent workers' and consumers' co-operatives had begun. Under the influence of the American Constitution, in 1776, the French Revolution in 1789 and the classical national economy based on economic liberalism (*A. Smith* 1776, *Ricardo* 1817), the secession from feudal control and the latest impact of corporative constraints (freedom of trade in 1810) led into the century of self-responsible co-operatives liberated from external constraints.

Bibliography

Abel, Wilhelm: Geschichte der deutschen Landwirtschaft, Stuttgart 1962.
Bader, Karl Siegfried: Dorfgenossenschaft und Dorfgemeinde, Köln, Graz 1962.
Below, Georg v.: Geschichte der deutschen Landwirtschaft des Mittelalters in ihren Grundzügen, Jena 1937.
Bonnemère, Joseph-Eugène: Histoire de l'association agricole et solution pratique, Paris 1850.
Bordeaux Szekely, Edmond: From enoch to the Dead Sea Scrolls. (Centro Internacional de Salubridad Biogenica), E.I.R.L., Costa Rica 1978, (Frankfurt a.M. 1979).
Clapham, John Harold/Power, Eileen (eds.): The Cambridge Economic History of Europe. From the Decline of the Roman Empire. Vol. 1, The Agrarian life of the Middle Ages, Cambridge 1942.
Dopsch, Alfons: Die freien Marken in Deutschland, Baden, Wien, Leipzig, Brünn 1933.
Dopsch, Alfons: Verfassungs- und Wirtschaftsgeschichte des Mittelalters. Gesammelte Aufsätze, I, Wien 1929, II, Wien 1938.
Duby, George: L'économie rurale et la vie des campagnes dans l'occident médiéval (France, Angleterre, Empire IX–XVe siècles). 2 tomes Paris (1962) 1977.

Franz, Günther: Geschichte des Bauernstandes vom frühen Mittelalter bis zum 19. Jahrhundert, Stuttgart (1963) 1976.
Frauendorfer, Sigmund von: Ideengeschichte der Agrarwirtschaft und Agrarpolitik im deutschen Sprachgebiet. Bd.1, Von den Anfängen bis zum 1. Weltkrieg, Bonn, München, Wien 1957.
Gierke, Otto: Das deutsche Genossenschaftsrecht, Bd.I, Rechtsgeschichte der deutschen Genossenschaft, Berlin 1868.
Kgl. Preuß. Akademie der Wissenschaften (ed.): Deutsches Rechtswörterbuch, Art. Genosse, vol. 4, 1939 – 51, pp. 226–231.
Kulischer, Josef: Allgemeine Wirtschaftsgeschichte des Mittelalters und der Neuzeit, Bd. I, München, Wien (1928), 1965.
Kuske, Bruno: Die kulturhistorische Bedeutung des Genossenschaftsgedankens. Die Genossenschaft, 1. Heft, Halberstadt 1928.
Lütge, Friedrich: Deutsche Sozial- und Wirtschaftsgeschichte, Berlin 1952.
Müller, Hans: (Genossenschaften im) Altertum. In: HWB des Genossenschaftswesens, Berlin 1928, Bd. 1:5–7.
Pirenne, Henry: Sozial- und Wirtschaftsgeschichte Europas im Mittelalter, Bern 1950.
Wernli, Fritz: Zur Frage der Markgenossenschaft, Trübbach S.G. 1961.

History of Co-operatives in Europe in the 19th Century

JULIUS OTTO MÜLLER

(see also: *History before 1800; History of Ideas; Conceptions, Co-operative; Strategies; Classic/Neo-classic Contributions; Marshall; Mill; Walras/Pareto*)

I. Contemporary Conditions; II. Co-operative Concepts and their Promoters, III. Co-operative Realization; IV. Conclusions and Precepts.

I. Contemporary Conditions

The employment of the body of thoughts and concepts that grew out of the Enlightenment in the process of development of the natural sciences, technology and economics had, beginning in England, led in the last third of the 18th century to an increase in the liberal economic and social forms in the leading European nations. On the basis of *Adam Smith's* (1776) and *David Ricardo's* (1817) "classical national economy," the new capitalistic economic system replaced the trade regulations of the Middle Ages and the mercantilistic economic restrictions of the absolutist states. Thus, the privileged craftsmen's corporations and merchants' guilds became obsolete. However, until the second half of the century, the 'free' economic development remained the privilege of the new entrepreneurs belonging to the bourgeoisie connected with high finance. The division and mechanization of labour in the 'factory system' allowed the production of standard commodities. Due to the progress made in transportation facilities, they gained access to the (world) market so that handicrafts, small trade and agricultural work were more and more superseded within the process of growth undergone by a technologically and economically based civilization.

It is true that human rights and democratic principles encouraged the desire for individual freedom in political and economic life (freedom of trade 1810, 1815), but, in contrast to the big industrialists, workers, small tradesmen, craftsmen and peasants could not draw any economic benefits from the newly acquired freedom because of usury, whether in connection with money; commodities or cattle; lack of capital; relative ingorance and exploitative working conditions.

Rational, material and secular ideologies gained ground and, due to the emphasis laid on individual human rights before obligations towards the community and the cultural heritage, led to the loss of cultural, and – in particular – ethical, religious and social values. Values associated with the community and with cooperation in extended families were subsituted for those of the formal society, individualization and egocentrism.

The new bourgeois class-based nation succeeded, until the last third of the century, on warding off all the attempts at politically emancipating the lower classes (socialism) and at unpolitical organization through a politically neutral'association' (common self-help) for fear of subversion. The situation of the workers appeared to be hopeless. Since the end of the 18th century, help in the form of care in social and economic emergency situations had been exclusively provided by the benevolent campaigns of wealthy classes holding humanitarian and Christian views.

II. Co-operative Concepts and their Promoters

As social reforms by the government and improvement in the salaries and the working and living conditions of the lower classes failed to appear and every attempt at politically influencing the dependent workers remained unsuccessful, intellectuals from the economically independent classes who were conscious of their social responsibility stood up for social problems. They all followed the same idea of 'emancipating work' from the economic power of private capital with the objective of improving the economic and social situation of those who, until then, had lived in straitened circumstances by encouraging them to form their own capital with the help of the co-operative association. The intrumental concepts for realizing this idea then followed two basically different conceptual approaches:

a) that of the free co-operative association based on self-help, self-responsibility and independent organization for the autonomous formation of savings from below, while remaining neutral as far as politics and religion are concerned; and

b) that of a politically regimented co-operative association within the conceptual context of theoretical and idealistic socialism.

Both conceptual approaches aimed originally at the participation of the working classes in the ownership of inputs and, in the long run, at the co-operative organization of the overall economy and society and, thus, at the establishment of a new economic and social system. 'In a peaceful struggle,' the power of capital was to be gradually undermined and broken. Concepts orientated towards practice for implementing this plan were concerned at first, around the middle of the century in England (*Cooper* and *Howard* 1844) and in Germany (→ *Schulze-Delitzsch* 1850), with satisfying the immediate individual needs through the formation of savings in small self-help groups of members carefully selected according to economic capacities, sociability and discipline, while safeguarding the personal and economic autonomy of the participating individual economy. They were to stand the test, at first on a small scale level, as preliminary stage for competition with large-scale industry as foreseen for the future for the whole nation. In France, influenced by the strongly restricted personal freedom since the Revolution in 1789, the spiritual advocates of the co-operative movement chose the concepts of collective forms of cooperation. They did not aim at satisfying urgent needs nor at selecting capable members and failed, with notorious exceptions, on account of the too high socio-ethical and socio-theoretical demands for solving the social problems in terms of a socialistic economic system orientated towards the common welfare (→ *Co-operative Socialism*).

The development of creative ideas cannot be severed from the individuals who conceived them and who, as their promoters, transmitted them personally, theoretically or practically to the people concerned. The spiritual concepts for attenuating and dealing definitively with exploitation and social misery are rooted mainly in the ideal of humanity that originated from the philosophy of Enlightenment and from classical literature. At the turn of the 18th century, it was transmitted by famous writers – in Germany, above all by *Goethe*, 'Pädagogische Provinz', in '*Wilhelm Meisters Wanderjahre*' (1821), and pedagogues such as *Pestalozzi* and *Fellenberg* in Switzerland, *King* and the promoters of 'Lincoln's Inn' in England – and had a strong influence on the population's education (education making them autonomous individuals of a humane dispositon). In England, undoubtedly, the Puritan theology, the writings of the Quakers *Plockhoy* (1659) and *Bellers* (1696), whose motives of liberation from the government's religious and political persecution through free, self-sufficient co-operative communities were analogous, had, over a long period, a stimulating effect on the leading minds of social reform (→ *Owen*, *King*, the Christian Socialists).

In the meantime, the forerunners of the Christian and socialistic social reform urged the solution of social problems by organizing economically autonomous co-operative communities or production groups. In France, it was only during the first third of the 19th century that *Saint-Simon* came forward as the precursor of a co-operative socialism of Christian Catholic inspiration within the framework of an economic rather than political public order to be organized on a brotherly basis. → *Buchez*, his follower, demanded a just distribution of the economic resources and products through productive co-operatives and the regulation of production and distribution by a central bank. With exceptions, the organization of free productive co-operatives failed. In England, Christian socialism goes back to *King* who, as a doctor of the poor and pedagogue in Brighton, organized consumers' co-operatives supported by Christian brotherly love, self-help, and moral as well as economic discipline. His journal, 'The Cooperator,' 1828–30, embodied the first comprehensive co-operative theory. His thoughts mark decisively the co-operative movement in Europe which, based on self-help, later became so successful in economic terms. As of 1848, the Christian-Protestant lawyers, theologians and members of parliament from Lincoln's Inn in London (*Ludlow, Maurice, Hughes, Kingsley, Vansittart Neale*) were associated with *King's* work, *Saint-Simon's* and *Buchez*' ideas. They conducted a campaign of enlightenment and reform for civil and parlamentarian participation in the 'proletarian attempts' at social reform and demanded the education of workers and craftsmen as secondary promoters of free consumers' and productive co-operatives. ('Society for promoting working men's associations' 1850, working men's colleges' 1853).

The different ideas of large settlements of productive co-operatives put forward by → *Owen* in England and the USA (since 1817) and *Fourier* in France (*familistères, phalanstères*, around 1830) remained a utopia. In the course of the socialistic takeover of power in 1848, *Blanc* failed when the government established numerous co-operative 'national workshops.'

The concept of free self-help co-operatives gained ground at first in England on the basis of former positive and negative experiences. *Cooper* and *Howard*, two earlier followers of *Owen*, the spiritual leaders of the Equitable Pioneers of Rochdale (1844), organized the world-famous consumers' shop of poor weavers ('penny capitalists') in view of satisfying the most urgent needs through absolute self-help (→ *Rochdale Pioneers*). To the rules of cooperation prescribed by *King*, they only added one which is decisive for the great economic success: the distribution of refunds after having made use of the co-operatives' services, connected with the payment of half dividends to non-members. Thus, after having been strengthened by a small elite group, a sufficiently large group of followers and their fidelity to cooperation became possible: the conditions for a rapid growth from small to large capital without injuring competition. The concept of polyvalent formation and education of the members so that they achieve self-responsibility thereby proved to be indispensable. In Germany, the main spiritual impulses, in additon to the autonomous ideas based on humanitarian or Christian ethics and economic solidarity (→ *Schulze-Delitzsch* since 1850 and → *Raiffeisen* partly as a follower of *Schulze-Delitzsch* since 1864), came mostly from England, but also from France. Thereby, the people understood how to let themselves be inspired by the positive experiences made by the other movements. In that regard, the decisive agents since the middle of the century are → *Huber* and → *Pfeiffer*. Spiritual relationship existed between the individual, not only contemporary holders of ideas and their schools, often beyond national frontiers.

As of the 60s, in France and in Germany, the concept of a cooperative intervention, patriarchally regimented, in view of solving the workers' problems was revived by government and clerical-conservative as well as leftist socialistic promoters. Associated with the interests of the government's and the Church's policy and complemented materially by financial aid as external help without the incitement to form capital under self-responsibility, this idea should be understood as the never-tiring theoretical and practical attempts towards forming independent co-operative groups from below.

III. Co-operative Realization

Differences in the respective histories of countries and concepts and in the cultural characteristics, especially of the political constitution, have, in the individual countries, marked the development of specific forms and types of co-operatives.

Co-operative pioneers and their followers saw to the implementation of the concepts for organizing free co-operatives and adjusting them to specific objectives and requirements, or they created the basis for legal security and economic stabilization. Simultaneously, they imparted technical and human education and placed the movement on an indispensable, ethical basis which took poverty, ignorance and dependence into consideration.

In the individual main countries of Europe (England and Germany), in the 60s of the 18th century already and up to the first third of the 19th century, free associations, of the co-operative type, of workers, craftsmen and farmers (workers' and farmers' mills, bakeries, consumers' shops, loan fund were formed and agricultural corporations ("Gehöferschaften") still existed. They failed, however, due to the lack of legal protection, to fraud, closing down of members' circle, lack of economic advantages and transformation into private capital associations. Caritative and saving associations in the urban and rural areas in England and Germany did not find, sometimes until the 60s of the 19th century, the way to self-help and ceased to exist. In France, on *Buchez*' initiative, quite a large number of free workers' production co-operatives, which, simultaneously, had to serve political purposes (financing new foundations and promoting socialist ideas) are established. After the failure and the prohibition of the nations' socialistic productive co-operatives (*Blanc's* "National Workshops"), in 1849, only a few productive co-operatives based on self-help according to *Buchez* managed to continue to exist – some until the war in 1870 – because they remained faithful to the discipline of strict self-help and the just distribution of profits. However, as a result of the high losses incurred during the war, they failed (e.g. "Gold workers co-operative"). Moreover, the free co-operative development was artificially retained by the conservative government until 1871.

This period of awakening of the free co-operative movement was followed by the period of its economic strengthening and advancement with the foundation of the Rochdale consumers' associations (1844) and of the first craftsmen's co-operative by *Schulze-Delitzsch* (1849). On the political grounds already mentioned, it remained restricted to England and Germany. In contrast to England, it was only after 1860 that a large number were founded. In England, due to the urgent workers' problems there, the co-operative development was concentrated on the type of consumers' co-operatives. Under the influence of the liberalizing laws, forms of vertical integration characteristic of co-operatives came into life already in 1866. The movement grew rapidly and remained stable (1844: 22, 1866: 5,236 members; a turnover of about £300,000 with a dividend of 10–12%). The foreseen institution of self-sufficient settlements in view of undermining capitalism became superfluous with social and co-operative legislation. The Christian Socialists gained great importance by organizing co-operative education, publications, legislation and associations. However, their own attempts to work consumers' and productive co-operatives fail above all as a result of too generous external promotion with initial loans.

In Germany, the consequences of industrial development affected craftsmen and small farmers in a particularly hard way. Therefore, the savings co-operatives for craftsmen (in the beginning for farmers as well) established under *Schulze-Delitzsch* were based on absolute self-help and self-administration and had unlimited liability for capital taken up from the free market. They had the function of people's banks. The craftsmen's co-operatives and people's banks movement was strongly supported by journalistic activities ("Innung der Zukunft" since 1853;

then, "Blätter für Genossenschaftswesen" edited by *Schulze-Delitzsch*) (→ *Periodicals, Co-operative*). In the 'lawyers' societies', *Schulze-Delitzsch* organized advisory, guiding and auditing institutions for primary co-operatives and created the first secondary co-operatives for cash adjustment, the easy purchase of raw materials and sale of commodities (Allgemeiner Verband der auf Selbsthilfe beruhenden Erwerbs- und Wirtschaftsgenossenschaften 1859 – General Association of Industrial and Provident Societies based on self-help, as the precursor of the German Co-operative Association) (→ *Federations*). Thus, the third period, that of economic and social consolidation, was introduced at a later stage than in England. Since 1863, *Raiffeisen's* loan and savings banks turned out to be more appropriate for the long-term credit requirements of small and medium farms. After fifteen years of promoting rural loans through benevolent associations together with the wealthy rural population (savings and insurance associations for medium and upper strata), he became the pioneer of co-operative self-help for the agricultural sector that lagged behind economically and socially. For him, Christian charity was as important as economic development. This is characterized by the accumulation of an indivisible association fund for Christian and welfare purposes. The scope of activities of his co-operatives was limited to members personally known to one another from a vicarage or a civil community. In the beginning, this self-help was supplemented by government aid (borrowing credit from county banks). In this case too, unlimited liability applied at the inital stage; it induced discipline in the strict selection of beneficiaries and in dealing with capital (moral and economic creditability). *Schulze-Delitzsch* and the legislation he provided (Prussia in 1867 and the German Reich in 1889) forced *Raiffeisen*, the father of the poor farmers, to allow the farmers to participate in the autonomous formation of capital (Central Credit Bank, in 1876; lawyers' societies according to *Schulze-Delitzsch's* model, in 1877). At a later stage (1890), *Haas* efficiently reorganized the economy of a complicated secondary organization for advising, guiding and providing capital according to *Schulze-Delitzsch*'s principles. In addition to *Raiffeisen's* activities, there had been, since the 60s, another movement of co-operative purchasing associations for small farmers ("Agricultural Consumers' Co-operatives") later successfully conducted by → *Haas* in terms of *Schulze-Delitzsch's* co-operative policy. Consolidation took place as of 1883 (20 associations and 1319 co-operatives in the General Association of the German Agricultural Co-operatives in 1890; the Reich Association resulting from the union of *Raiffeisen's* and *Haas'* associations, 1903–1905). In 1885, the movement based on *Schulze-Delitzsch's* consisted of 922 loan associations with 466,575 members, 1.5 million Mark of credit accommodation, 1.6 million M shares, 19.4 million M reserve funds, 121.9 million M savings and 6% dividends. In 1885, *Raiffeisen's* movement consisted of 245 assocations (423 in 1888) with 24,466 members. In 1822, the turnover was 141,293 Mark. Thus, the movements in Germany developed into special co-operative institutions orientated towards the credit needs of handicrafts and of the farmers. After initial stagnation or failure, a large number of efficient consumers' and housing construction co-operatives for workers, employees and functionaries were established only during the phase of consolidation, after 1870. It was only much later that transport, machine, bookkeepers' and fisheries associations were added to those. The attempt to found consumers' co-operatives for workers was systematically opposed over quite a long period under the influence of the communist and socialist policy in the wake of *Marx* (→ *Socialist Critics*). They only come to a head after the socialist congress in 1889.

Co-operatives were founded by conservative patrons under conservative governments tolerating, in France, in 1863 (*Napoleon III*), *Cabet's* socialist interests and, at the same time, *Lassalle's* in Germany (*Bismarck*). However, they failed because of lacking self-help and self-responsible force of assertion. Bishop v. *Ketteler's* co-operatives, promoted on the basis of clerical welfare, also failed for similar reasons in Germany in 1863. Further attempts made by patrons to establish co-operatives failed in France, in 1864 under *Napoleon III*, and in 1893, in Germany, under *Wilhelm I* (failure of numerous foundations during the initial phase of the 'Prussian Bank'), since 1895 as a result of tutelage and financial aid from the government. In Ireland, finally, Horace Plunkett had great success in establihsing since 1889 agrarian co-operatives jointly with an effective agrarian structural reform.

The 'International Co-operative Alliance' was founded, in 1895, on the initiative of the English co-operative overall organization (→ *ICA*). The decisive influences of a strategy for the secure formation of capital originated in England and spread over the great majority of other European countries, especially in the consumption sector. In Germany, there arose further organizational impulses to found co-operative associations for handicrafts and agriculture. At the end of the 19th century, they spread as a rule more strongly than the English movement to Switzerland, Italy, Russia and the Scandinavian countries as well as to India and, later on, to Burma (→ *Development, South Asia*; → *Development, South-East Asia*).

IV. Conclusions and Precepts

In the 19th century, as a result of the creation and development of 'free co-operatives', the practical implementation of concepts for the autonomous and conjointly liable organization of new co-operative forms of economy was successful in the dispute between the power of capital and the dependent labour force that was at its mercy. These ideas were presented by theoretical innovators and spiritual leaders belonging to the upper, educated strata within the context of the overall cultural trends of the period, adjusted to the requirements and transmitted, with a charismatic power, to the poor – to be applied by these on their own responsibility in a disciplined manner. Ethical and religious dimensions contributed substantially towards creating, strengthening and perpetuating the free co-operatives. The neutral – in terms of policy and religion – application of Rochdale's 'golden rules' was pioneer work (→ *Ethics*). Therefore, the indispensable conditions of the creation and successful existence of co-operatives in the 19th century (→ *Strategies*) are summarized as follows:

1) According to the economic capacity of social and ethical qualifications, selected members rapidly assume the roles of their promoters as teachers, leaders and administrators of co-operative activities.
2) Promotion and self-help not by order, but rather against the will of the national government in order to maintain the independence from above and outside.
3) Organization of an easily controllable, socio-economically strong primary group from below. Establishment of secondary organizations, in principle at a later stage, on the basis of functioning co-operative primary groups.
4) Economic solidarity on account of unlimited longterm liability for loans as the basis for social solidarity while adjusting the objectives and services of cooperation to the requirement.
5) Flexible adjustment of the objectives of cooperation to the specific contemporary and local-cultural situation.
6) Democratic self-organization and absolute autonomy in all economic activities.
7) Strict self-discipline and loyalty in applying the economic and social regulations (statutes) of cooperation.

These seven elements characterize the open secret of European co-operatives known all over the world on account of their great economic success. This means that the history of co-operatives in the 19th century shows that economic and social success can only be achieved where cooperation originates out of a movement to meet common requirements, widely disclaims foreign support and guidance, and simultaneously courageously enforces the rules of strict self-help, self-responsibility and self-administration.

Bibliography

Brelay, Ernest: Les sociétés coopératives de production, Paris 1887.
Brentano, Lujo: Die christliche-soziale Bewegung in England, Leipzig 1883².
Crüger, Hans: Erwerbs- und Wirtschaftsgenossenschaften in den einzelnen Ländern, Jena 1892.
Engelhardt, Werner Wilhelm: Genossenschaften I Geschichte. Handwörterbuch der Wirtschaftswissenschaft, vol. 3, Tübingen, Göttingen und Zürich 1981, pp. 557–571.
Faucherre, Henry: Umrisse einer genossenschaftlichen Ideengeschichte, Basel 1925.
Faust, Helmut: Geschichte der Genossenschaftsbewegung. Ursprung und Aufbruch der Genossenschaftsbewegung in England, Frankreich und Deutschland sowie ihre weitere Entwicklung im deutschen Sprachraum, Frankfurt a.M. 1977³.
Gide, Charles: Der Kooperativismus, Halberstadt 1929.
Gierke, Otto von: Das deutsche Genossenschaftsrecht, vol. 1–4, (Berlin 1866–1913), Graz, Darmstadt 1954.
Grünfeld, Ernst: Handbuch des Genossenschaftswesens, vol. 1, Das Genossenschaftswesen volkswirtschaftlich und soziologisch betrachtet, Halberstadt 1928.
Holyoake, George Jacob: The History of Cooperation in England: its literature and its advocates. Vol. I–II, (London 1879), (extended) New York 1906.
Huber, V.A.: Reisebriefe aus Belgien, Frankreich und England, vol. 2, Hamburg 1854, 1855.
Hubert–Valleroux, O.: Les associations coopératives en France et à l'étranger, Paris 1884.
Internationales Handwörterbuch des Genossenschaftswesens, (hrsg. v. V. Totomianz), vol. 2, Berlin 1928.
King, W.: The Co-operator (Brighton 1828–30), Manchester 1922.
Müller, J.O.: Voraussetzungen und Verfahrensweisen bei der Errichtung von Genossenschaften in Europa vor 1900, Göttingen 1976.
Pfeiffer, Eduard: Über Genossenschaftswesen. Was ist der Arbeiterstand in der heutigen Gesellschaft und was kann er werden?, Leipzig 1863.
Preuss, Walter: Das Genossenschaftswesen in der Welt und in Israel, Berlin 1958.
Webb, Mrs. Sidney (=Beatrice Potter): Die britische Genossenschaftsbewegung, Leipzig 1893.
Webb, Sidney and Beatrice: The Consumers' Co-operative Movement, London, New York, Bombay 1921.
Zeidler, Hugo: Geschichte des deutschen Genossenschaftswesens der Neuzeit. Staats- und sozialwissenschaftliche Beiträge, vol. I/3, Leipzig 1893.

Honorary Office, Co-operative

GÜNTHER RINGLE [J]

(see also: *Law, National*; *Law, International*; *Management in Co-operatives*; *Relationship Patterns*; *Organizational Structure of Societies*)

I. Characterization of Honorary Office; II. Honorary Office as a Definitive Factor of Co-operatives; III. The Role of Honorary Office in Large Co-operatives; IV. Problem Areas for Honorary Offices; V. Closing Observation.

I. Characterization of Honorary Office

The term "honorary office" numbers among the standard expressions related to co-operative organizations, but at least in German Co-operative Law it is not mentioned (→ *Law, National*). This traditional institution arises rather more strongly in connection with legal provisions which stipulate that positions on the board of directors and the supervisory board are to be filled by members (principle of a self-operating executive unit – "Selbstorganschaft") and which regulate compensation for such activity in an executive body (→ *Organizational Structure of Societies*). The choice between paid, full-time positions and unpaid, honorary part-time positions exists exclusively for the board of directors. The supervisory board and all optional boards or bodies in the co-operative in contrast are prototypically honorary in nature.

An *honorary office* in essence is characterized as unpaid, avocational participation in the bodies of the co-operative exercised by representatives of the membership with the exception of the general assembly. A more precise characterization of this term brings to light the following constituent elements:

- Honorary officers are elected into the respective bodies by the membership assembly (general assembly or assembly of delegates) or by the supervisory board, and as representatives of the membership they participate in consultational, decision-making and control processes in the co-operative;
- Inasmuch as they are not tied to the co-operative business enterprise through an employment contract, those holding honorary office do not receive remuneration for their activity; they only receive compensation for their expenses.

The honorary co-operative office exists to serve an organization in which "individuals themselves have a material interest and from which they expect economic promotion (material advantage) of their own private economies (household or enterprise)" (*Kissling*).

II. Honorary Office as a Definitive Factor of Co-operatives

The history of co-operatives, the structure and constitution particular to such types of organizations and above all the prescribed goal of providing economic promotion mold and form a unique self-conception (→ *History in 19th C.*). Honorary activity for the sake of the cause and not for commercial earnings (*Beuthien*) was decisive in shaping modern co-operatives; in the context of the co-operative principles, this factor today continues to embody the *principle of self-administration* as it did in pioneer times (→ *Principles*). The membership body must accordingly be involved in the decision-making processes in the → *self-help organization* – this can be through a representational body – and must be in the position to articulate common interests and succeed in realizing them.

Lawmakers have bestowed co-operative honorary activity with the status of a *determining element* for this distinct organizational form which should stand in clear and conscious contrast to "*Drittorganschaft*" found in joint-stock companies (*Beuthien*) and distinguish co-operatives from enterprises which have assumed other legal forms. Honorary offices consequently are a *constituent trait* of the unmistakable assemblage of registered co-operatives.

III. The Role of Honorary Office in Large Co-operatives

1. Honorary Office in a System of Salaried, Full-time Management Positions

The importance of the honorary office cannot be given proper attention when isolated from the history of co-operative development:

1) In the formative phase of modern co-operatives, the small social-economic entities (from our present day point of view) were managed exclusively by elected members. *Pure honorary involvement* in the co-operative bodies was suitable to the simplicity and clearness of the business transactions in traditional co-operatives.

2) In the course of growth experienced by co-operatives (enterprise size, number of members) the demands for market knowledge and specific know-how as well as management flexibility increased. The employed business manager answerable to the directives issued by the honorary board handled everyday co-operative affairs. Although the close connection between the honorary board and the remunerated business manager proved a success, employed directors were increasingly inducted into the management bodies (*mixed boards*). Large co-operatives (→ *Operational Size*) in certain sectors ultimately even followed the current trend of *having a board composed exclusively of salaried members* which served as a management body. *Grossfeld* (1979, 1988) categorized this "expulsion of honorary officers" from the board as "the Fall of the recent co-operative system".

The author does indeed see the self-conception of co-operatives jeopardized when professional managers enter the ranks of the board after they have become pro forma "promoting members" and purchased a co-operative share. The *principle of a self-operating executive unit*, according to which the management bodies (board of directors, supervisory board) are to be filled only with persons hailing from the group of co-operative members to be promoted, is violated through this dodgy move.

The example of professionally managed co-operatives (→ *Management in Co-operatives*) with mixed boards shows that honorary offices on the management level must fulfill an important function in internal, co-operative realist politics in the face of discrepancies between the notion of self-administration and its actual expression. In a management system strongly determined by obvious manager dominance, the co-operative management and the membership basis draw distant from one another; alienation in members' relationships to their co-operative accordingly occurs. Conversely, the danger arises that the co-operative management will renunciate its orientation around promotion if and when managers primarily strive to achieve turnover, profitability and corporate growth and neglect members' interests (*Neumann*). Honorary officers are called upon to muster opposition to such development, thereby favoring the fulfillment of the promotion mandate through the co-operative enterprise. In the interest of attaining legitimization of the co-operative corporate policy from the basis, the institution of honorary office must intercede for the sake of achieving higher promotional efficiency from measures which have already been realized (*Jäger*, 1987); "members should be protected from solely rational decisions serving to maintain market position" (*Weinerth*).

2. The Functions of an Honorary Office

The principle of self-administration requires the direct or at least representational participation of the membership in the decision-making and control processes in the co-operative. The involvement of the membership body in the operational activities provides for honorary offices to assume diverse functions:

1) Co-operatives are to promote their members' enterprises over an extended period of time through output/service relationships, or in other words, are primarily to support the attainment of economic goals in an optimal manner. In a democratically structured organization this key goal requires concretization and execution through a promotional policy adequate to the needs at hand and involving member participation. The institution of honorary office should influence the affiliation of the co-operative's corporate policy to the membership basis and serve as a guaranty for the proper fulfillment of the → *promotion mandate* – in short called the *promotion function*. This task is all the more pressing the greater the heterogeneity among members' expectations is, the stronger the relationship "member-management" emerges as an area of potential interest conflict, and the more the co-operative enterprise and all its salaried management is inclined to act independently and serve its own purposes.

2) The *participational function* of an honorary office encompasses all possible honorary activities in which influence can be exercised on management decisions in the co-operative while serving to represent the entire membership body. To begin with, the institution of honorary office in the board can accentuate the membership element in the dispositional processes. If decision making affecting the co-operative's operation is undertaken without collective efforts, the danger arises that current management policy is inadequately directed and oriented around membership's interests.

In accordance with individual co-operative participation requirements, various forms of institutionalized membership participation (advisory boards, project teams) seem suitable – especially for large-scale co-operative entities (→ *Operational Size*). Tasks for those involved can, for example, include assessing management's decisions and plans or directly participating in certain management decisions which greatly influence the development of the co-operative due to their long-term impact (*Ringle*, 1983). The self-determination of common economic interests undertaken by the membership body as well as the co-operative's potential for success are reinforced continually through competent participation in decision-making processes.

3) Honorary offices exercise the function of a connective link serving to intensify communication between the membership basis and the various bodies of the co-operative; this results either as a side product of their consultational, decision-making or control functions or else is consciously undertaken as such. This liaison function on the one hand consists of raising and representing members' needs and wishes in the course of the respective body's activity and of ensuring their realization through appropriate measures. In the other direction the go-between function serves to inform members about important activities in the various bodies (decisions, control measures). The basis is more inclined to identify itself with the work of the co-operative as a whole the more the honorary officers are successful in presenting the promotional relevance of the managment's plans in a plausible manner.

4) Honorary involvement in various co-operative bodies ultimately provides the opportunity to monitor management. The *control function* serves to protect the membership from the one-sided endeavors of the management to achieve market success while neglecting transformation of the same into promotional success. The assumption of this control function in particular lies in the hands of the supervisory board as the actual con-

trolling body legally obligated to monitor the business management. Further opportunities to exercise this control function exist for honorary members by working together with salaried persons in mixed managerial boards. Here management informs them about their decisions and set plans and honorary members verify the correlation of these with members' needs; should a discrepancy arise between target and performance levels they press for stronger promotional orientation in the co-operative's policy.

3. Obligatory Bodies and their Functional Emphasis

Honorary participation itself has specific points of emphasis according to the respective co-operative body; the congruent final goal in all cases is the orientation of the co-operative enterprise's corporate policy around the group interests of the members.

1) Honorary officers on the board are often only peripherally tied to management matters on account of the limited temporal dimension of their participation, for example in determining the guidelines of corporate policy. It is thought that the honorary members of the management body should assume the function of a connective link between the membership basis and the entire co-operative management. Through their personal contacts with both sides they are in the position to remove psychological and communication barriers, to convey expectations from the basis to the business management, and in the reverse direction to present management decisions in a plausible manner. A conceivable identity crisis resulting from internal systematic alienation in the co-operative can be counteracted as a whole through preventative and ameliorating measures.

2) The focus of activity in the co-operative *supervisory board* is the control function, above all in monitoring the business management. In the face of the circumstance that the controlling body in numerous co-operatives has deviated to fulfill additional optional functions such as providing consultational assistance to the board or soliciting new members, such findings deserve exhortation (*Ringle*, 1984). If the supervisory board is so tightly involved in close cooperation with the board – in extreme cases incapable of maintaining a critical distance – and/or if it is too distracted by side activities, its surveillance of the current business in connection with insuring the effectiveness of promotion can suffer. Through a more intense selectional process of supervisory board members strongly oriented around their qualifications, the foundations would be laid for an effective execution of the legally prescribed control function which should serve to counterbalance the self-responsible business management.

3) It is difficult to sketch out a clear point of emphasis and involvement for the *assembly of delegates*. On the one hand, decision-making concerning fundamental matters – the law and the → *by-law*s assign these functions to the general assembly in its capacity as a body of direct democracy – is undertaken by the organizational body emblematic of "indirect" democracy and necessary in larger co-operatives. On the other hand, control is exercised by removing and appointing persons to the other organizational bodies. The delegates should ultimately serve as a communication bridge to the basis in an effort to prevent developments from occurring which destabilize internal democracy; they must maintain healthy contact to the represented "common" members at large.

IV. Problem Areas for Honorary Offices

1. The Problems of Recruitment and Overwork

As in comparable organizations one can observe a growing passivity among members' relationships with their co-operative. Members both personally and professionally suited for such activity frequently do not show any interest in assuming an honorary office. Various individual reasons can lie at the root of this (*Ringle*, 1983):
1) A lack of social ties (→ *Group, the Co-operative*) and weak performance-related connections to the co-operative; 2) high demands placed on individuals from their own enterprises and/or in practiced professions; 3) "free-rider" mentality; 4) the satisfaction of personal needs (the search for esteem and self-realization) beyond the realms of the co-operative.

The passive behavior of enterprising members with regard to exercising an honorary office and the consequent *contraction of the potential recruitment pool* set the background for the more than occasional misuse of honorary offices as a starting gate for "merited functionaries" and for the *overburdening of honorary officers* which is frequently claimed and referred to. In the face of the multi-faceted, complicated nature of their entrusted functions, numerous honorary office holders are in fact hardly in the position to contribute positively to the quality of decisions made in the co-operative and/or to keep effective watch over the business management; such persons are primarily selected on the basis of other criteria rather than according to their professional know-how and discriminatory judgement (*Ringle*, 1984).

The manager profile for modern co-operatives includes a good education, management qualities and the ability to adapt to technical and economic progress. *Wachtel* is skeptical that such requirements could be met by honorary board members. He considers the argument of preserving the element of honorary office in the *board* merely for the sake of membership representation as overly risky both for the honorary board members themselves as well as for the success of the board as a whole (*Wachtel*). This position is rooted in the assumption that honorary offices decelerate activity in market situations which require prompt reaction to changes on the market; honorary offices can delay or even completely prevent enterprising activity which has been identified as being quite successful. An internal allocation of duties within the board has emerged in numerous large-scale co-operatives: honorary officers merely participate in the formulation of corporate policy guidelines and at best are involved with decision-making concerning innovation and strategy. Nonetheless, they are primarily entrusted with the connective liaison function to the membership basis.

The control function of the *supervisory board* has also become more difficult as co-operatives have grown in size. At the same time, however, the control body could gain importance even as the influence on the membership basis in general diminishes. In contrast to this, however, shortcomings within the monitoring function are also present which in numerous situations have precipitated the "flight" from obligatory basic tasks and increased involvement with additional optional tasks.

2. The Problems of Compensation and Liability

In accordance with the essence of co-operatives as self-help institutions, honorary officers receive neither royalties nor other types of remuneration which exceed *compensation for their expenses* (*Meyer/Meulenbergh/Beuthien*). Cost savings was one of the most essential elements of honorary offices even for *Raiffeisen*. The extent the promotion attainable from the co-operative and/or the social prestige associated with holding an honorary office is viewed as adequate "reward" for serving the common organization and is capable of inducing sufficient motivation if determined by subjective value standards. By any means all necessary, entailed costs should be reimbursed in order to preclude any type of financial loss associated with the honorary activity from occurring, or in other words, compensation for losses in earnings or the employment of a stand-in worker to make up for the loss of work in one's own company. Such a material incentive under certain circumstances could compensate for the lack of idealism (*Neumann*).

Appointment to the board of directors loses allure as long as there is no *liability distinction* between salaried and honorary officers on the management level. High levels of liability can make temporaly limited service in the collective organization seem too risky, unreasonable and/or beyond expectation and ultimately endanger the existence of co-operative honorary positions. Who, for example, voluntarily spends his time working without remuneration, even having to answer for decisions made by employed business managers and/or salaried board members – decisions in whose deliberation he was not involved and about which he possibly was not even informed? Whereas advocates of jurisprudence succumb and voice their opinions in individual situations for honorary offices in management bodies to be vested with lower liability levels (*Meyer/Meulenbergh/Beuthien*), co-operative federations tend to use the form of non-differentiated liability anchored in legislation to encourage development in the direction of solely having salaried board members (*Grossfeld*). Conjecture maintains that this has contributed significantly to the progressive professionalization of co-operative boards.

V. Closing Observation

The expediency of honorary offices for small co-operatives can be identified without a doubt; this subject is solely discussed in the context of larger co-operative entities. Whereas justification for honorary offices will also remain uncontested in the future for organizational bodies in which honorary activity is peremptory (supervisory board, optional bodies), the element of honorary offices in the board will most surely remain an object of controversy. Evaluations of this institution so far range from "essential" to "no longer up contemporary" (*Beuthien; Jäger*, 1984; *Wachtel*).

Honorary offices also do not represent "ideological ballast" for larger co-operatives (*Kissling*): the more members lose dispositional influence as management bodies grow in strength, the more important honorary offices become as a factor to stabilize the co-operative's personalistic-democratic character. The involvement of honorary officers can prevent salaried office holders from losing orientation around fulfilling the promotion mandate, such as on account of their preoccupation with market success. The significance of the element of honorary offices is evident not only for preserving self-administration but to the same extent for maintaining the co-operative's credibility to its members and for justifying the co-operative organization form (*Seki/Noelle*).

In the face of the co-operative enterprise's need to hold its own in the market, the responsible execution of honorary offices increasingly requires a greater time investment and high demands on gaining pertinent, function-specific knowledge and skills. Honorary officers are dependent on "informative communication" with management and the membership basis. Targeted training undertaken by the accountable co-operative federation as well as the effects of involvement in organizational bodies are capable of improving honorary officers' ability to function.

Housing Reform and the Housing Reform Movement

HELMUT JENKIS [F]

(see also: *Housing Societies*; *History in 19th C.*; *History before 1800*; *Economic Order*, *Commonweal Economy*)

I. Differentiation of Terms; II. The Housing Reform Movement; III. The Land Reform Movement; IV. De-regulation instead of Housing Reform?

I. Differentiation of Terms

As is the case with many other terms in normative economics, no uniform terms have yet been agreed upon in the field of housing reform. Since what matters are nominal definitions and not real definitions, a differentiation of terms will contribute to a consensus on terminology.

Housing reform is understood primarily to mean the systematic improvement of housing conditions in the cities (housing reform in the narrow sense). The improvement of agrarian colonisation patterns, however, is not usually included in this term. Housing reform can deal with already existing housing as well as with new housing construction. In the first case – reform of already existing housing – the primary purpose is retroactively to correct mistakes made in the past; in the second case – new housing construction policy – the main purpose is to avoid mistakes perceived to have been made in the past.

Housing reform can address housing technology (the shape of the house; technical, sanitary, and hygienic facilities), with the legal system (ownership of land, laws on tenancy), and with the social system (the social structure of owners and tenants, foreigners, socially unintegrated persons and households).

In the course of time, various components of housing reform or of the housing reform movement have increased or decreased in importance. The expression "housing reform movement" appeared for the first time in German scientific literature in the middle of the 19th century (→ *History in 19th C.*), and has come to mean the gathering together of all those scientific, political, and economic groups who considered housing condition unsatisfactory up to that time in economic, legal, hygienic and, last but not least, in overall political respects and who called for an improvement. They strove for this improvement (housing reform) by joining together into an organization which was to exert influence on men responsible for formulating political demands and objectives. Within the housing reform movement, land reform played an important role.

Bibliography

Beuthien, Volker: Genossenschaftliche Ehrenämter – noch zeitgemäß?, in: Genossenschaftliche Ehrenämter – noch zeitgemäß?, Institut für Genossenschaftswesen an der Philipps-Universität Marburg (ed.), Marburg 1983, pp. 19–38.
Großfeld, Bernhard: Das Ehrenamt in der Genossenschaft und im genossenschaftlichen Verbund, in: Zeitschrift für das gesamte Genossenschaftswesen, vol. 38 (1988), pp. 263–274.
Großfeld, Bernhard: Genossenschaft und Ehrenamt. Zeitschrift für das gesamte Genossenschaftswesen, vol. 29, (1979), pp. 217–227.
Jäger, Wilhelm: Genossenschaftliche Selbstverwaltung – Die Bedeutung des Ehrenamtes, Verband westfälischer und lippischer Wohnungsunternehmen e.V. (ed.), Münster 1984.
Jäger, Wilhelm: Zur Problematik der Machtbalance zwischen Ehrenamt und genossenschaftlichem Management, Hardehauser Beiträge, Heft 55, Hardehausen 1987.
Kißling, Reinhold: Genossenschaftliches Ehrenamt, Handwörterbuch des Genossenschaftswesens, E. Mändle/H.-W. Winter (eds.), Wiesbaden 1980, cols. 321–327.
Mändle, Eduard: Zur Tätigkeit ehrenamtlicher Funktionsträger in Genossenschaften, Festschrift für R. Kißling, in: Großkopf, Werner (ed.): Genossenschaften in steter Bewährung, Stuttgart-Hohenheim 1986, pp. 67–89.
Meyer, E.H./Meulenbergh, Gottfried/Beuthien, Volker: Genossenschaftsgesetz (Kommentar), (12th ed.), München 1983.
Neumann, Renate: Rechtliche Möglichkeiten zur Teilnahme an der Willensbildung in der eingetragenen Genossenschaft, Tübingen 1982.
Raiffeisen, Friedrich Wilhelm: Die Darlehnskassen-Vereine, (8th ed.), Neuwied 1966.
Ringle, Günther: Mitgliederpassivität und Partizipation in modernen Primärgenossenschaften, Göttingen 1983.
Ringle, Günther: Überwachung des genossenschaftlichen Managements durch den Aufsichtsrat, Hamburger Beiträge zum Genossenschaftswesen, Institut für Genossenschaftswesen der Universität Hamburg, Heft 2, Hamburg 1984.
Seki, Hideaki/Noelle, Thomas: Das Ehrenamt im Deutschen Genossenschaftsrecht, Zeitschrift für das gesamte Genossenschaftswesen, vol. 34 (1984), pp. 128–141.
Wachtel, Friedrich: Genossenschaftliche Ehrenämter – noch zeitgemäß?, Institut für Genossenschaftswesen an der Philipps-Universität Marburg (ed.), Marburg 1983, pp. 7–12.
Weinerth, Erich: Genossenschaftliche Ehrenämter – noch zeitgemäß? – Überlegungen aus der Sicht eines Prüfungsverbandes, Marburg 1983, pp. 13–18.

II. The Housing Reform Movement

The concept of housing reform and of joining together into an organized movement for that purpose originated in the liberal attitude of mind of the 19th century.

1. From Mercantilism to Liberalism

Not only in the Middle Ages, but also after the Thirty Years' War (1618–1648), the German states were active in housing policy, settlement policy, and population policy (→ *History before 1800*). Examples of the systematic founding of new towns are Potsdam, Mannheim, Kassel, and Darmstadt. At the time of mercantilism and absolutism, the process of locating refugees, such as the Huguenots and the Salzburg Protestants, into new settlements, as well as of furthering handicrafts, industry, and commerce, led to governmental initiatives which were particularly intensive in Brandenburg and Prussia.

After the French Revolution of 1789, mercantilism was gradually replaced by liberalism; and the place of the absolute, centrally co-ordinating state was taken over by the state as a mere night-watchman ("Nachtwächterstaat"), whose function was mainly to serve as a policeman. In this phase of a liberal political, legal, and economic system – which extended until World War I (1914–1918) – industrialization occurred in the second half of the 19th century and brought with it an increase in population and rapid urbanization. These processes took place particularly after 1871: the percentage of agricultural production in relation to the net domestic national product fell from 37.9 percent in 1870/74 to 23.4 percent in 1910/13, while within the same time period the contribution of industry and handcrafts rose from 29.7 percent to 40.9 percent. The population of Germany increased from 40,970,000 in 1871 to 67,790,000 in 1914; the number of cities with a population of more than 100,000 grew from eight in 1871 to 48 in 1910; and the overall number of people residing in cities swelled during that period from 1,970,000 to 13,820,000.

This gradual transformation from an agricultural to an industrial state was especially pronounced during the years from 1871 to 1914, a period in which liberal thought predominated. The fact that government initiative was limited at that time to the mere inspection of housing construction, to make sure that it conformed to building regulations, gave rise to the so-called housing question, which in turn gave rise to housing reform and finally to the "housing reform movement".

2. Housing Reform

As early as the middle of the 19th century, there was criticism of the attendant ills of industrialization, i.e. urbanization and the proletarianization of industrial workers.

→ *Victor Aimé Huber* (1800–1869) and other social reformers made theoretical and practical demands for a housing reform, by propagating the idea of housing enterprises for public benefit and housing co-operatives and by founding these organizations themselves. In 1847 the first housing enterprise for public benefit was set up in Berlin: the Berliner Gemeinnützige Baugesellschaft (Berlin Building Society for Public Benefit), which still exists today as the Alexandra Foundation. After 1889 housing co-operatives gained in importance because the Co-operative Law of May 1st, 1889, introduced limited liability and because invalidity insurance opened up a source of financing with a favourable interest rate. After 1870, regulations were introduced in Prussia which went beyond mere instructions for building and building inspection. These regulations exerted an influence on housing construction, without yet constituting an active governmental housing policy.

In view of the rapid increase in urban population, it became necessary, for example, for communities to acquire the possibility to confiscate property for public purposes. The Law on Expropriation of Pieces of Land, dated June 11, 1874, created the needed leverage to expropriate private property for reasons of the public good, in return for compensation. Of greater significance with regard to the laying-out or alteration of streets and squares in towns and rural communities was another law, the so-called *Fluchtliniengesetz* (Law Regulating the Heigth and Distance of Buildings from the Street, etc.) of July 2, 1875. With the so-called *Lex Adickes* (a law named for *Franz Adickes*, mayor of Frankfurt-on-Main), which was a Law Regulating the Re-apportioning of Property in Frankfurt of July 28, 1902, it became possible to make the re-distribution of pieces of land compulsory. Thanks to the successful application of this law in Frankfurt, the *Lex Adickes* was also introduced in other communities in Prussia after 1918. The Prussian Law on Local Government Taxes of July 14, 1893, introduced the taxation of property according to a fair market value (Gemeiner Wert), a law which served as a model for other German states.

In the scientific realm, it is primarily the Verein für Socialpolitik which devoted itself to the social question in general and to the housing question in particular. Founded in 1872–73, the Verein dealt with the reform of social conditions characterizing the deep cleavage in society at the time. Repeatedly – and for the last time in 1930 – the Verein turned its attention to the housing question in great detail. Critics have commented that an economist is a man who measures workers' dwellings and then says they are too small. *Von Hayek* writes that the "development of opinions in this areas (was) directed almost exclusively by men who were pre-occupied with the elimination of individual evils, and the main question of how the various separate efforts were to be co-ordinated with each other was badly neglected... When one sees the aimless way – evidently without any clear idea of the forces which shape urban development – in which governments handled these difficult problems, then one marvels that the evils have not become even greater than they are" (*von Hayek*, p. 328).

3. The Housing Reform Movement

Industrialization and the concomitant shifts in population led to urbanisation; but meeting the resultant housing needs was left to private initiative and to the real estate market. The building code permitted an intensive exploitation of pieces of property, which led to the dark and poorly ventilated tenement buildings typical for Berlin, with additional buildings or annexes at the backs of the houses. High rents forced industrial workers to live in cramped and unhealthy quarters. To reduce rents, tenants even took on overnight guests. Attention was aroused to these conditions, which were injurious to public health, as early as the middle of the 19th century.

At the end of the 1890's, the groups supporting housing reform joined together in a systematic way. In 1897 the Rheinischer Verein zur Förderung des Arbeiterwohnungswesens (Rhinish Society to Further Housing for the Working Class), was formed under the leadership of *Landrat Brandt*, later known as the Rheinischer Verein für Kleinwohnungswesen (Rhinish Society for Small Dwellings), following which further societies were also founded. The Verein Reichswohnungsgesetz (Society for a National Housing Law) was established on May 25, 1898. According to paragraph 1 of its by-laws, the society pursued the purpose of "instigating and preparing forceful legislation, primarily on the part of the national government, to improve housing conditions." The founder of this society was *Dr. Karl von Mangoldt*. The members of the society came from all political parties, enterprises in the economy, and public administrative bodies.

However, as the goal could not be reached of prompting the national government to an extensive intervention in the realm of housing, a different goal was brought to the fore: the creation of a large organization which was to work toward the spread and implementation of housing reform ideas through its organization and through agitation by means of scientific publications. In the spring of 1904, the society took on the name of Deutscher Verein für Wohnungsreform (German Society for Housing Reform), which it kept until 1940. In petitions and rallies, it expressed its opinion on all questions of housing reform. The outbreak of World War I and the collapse of Germany in 1918 paralyzed its activities. In 1925 the Deutscher Verein für Wohnungsreform resumed its work. In 1938 it received accreditation as a research institute by the National Labour Ministry and in 1940 took on the name Deutsche Gesellschaft für Wohnungswesen (German Society for Housing). In 1941 this society was transformed into the Deutsche Akademie für Wohnungswesen (German Academy for Housing) under the direction of the National Commissioner for Subsidized Housing Construction. The collapse of the Third Reich also put an end to the activity of this institute, and no organization has been set up since to take its place.

In addition to petitions and statements of opinions, the Deutscher Verein für Wohnungsreform organized and held two congresses on housing, one in Frankfurt-on-Main from October 16 to 19, 1904, and the other in Leipzig from June 11 to 14, 1911. In 1916 the society became augmented by the Deutscher Wohnungsausschuß (German Housing Committee). In 1917 the society moved its head office from Frankfurt-on-Main to Berlin. The Deutsche Verein für Wohnungsreform appealed to the public once more in 1925 in a "rally for the continuation of housing reform."

The basic assumption of housing reformers was that it had become a national necessity to achieve a satisfactory solution to housing and settlement conditions. Even if the reformers failed to attain their high goal – a great, unified legislated housing reform by the national government – still they achieved a great deal in individual areas: "Revision of building regulations and development plans in order to favour the spread of small and privately-owned homes with gardens and plots for cultivation; expropriation laws applying to built-up sites; acquisition of cheap land with the help of the government and the community; making public credit available for the construction of small dwellings; reform of mortgage laws, of expropriation laws, of transport, of tenancy laws, and of many other things as well" (*Rose von Mangoldt*, p. 1760).

III. The Land Reform Movement

Whether the issue of land reform (it would be more correct to say land-ownership reform) and the land reform movement constitute a part of the issue of housing reform, or whether these are to be considered independently of each other, is an object of controversy. Here, however, land reform is seen as a part of housing reform.

Land-ownership reform – or, since the imprecise term land reform has become accepted, it will be used here – strives for a reform of the existing land laws, for example of inheritance laws, of housing legislation, and of building regulations. According to *Karl Diehl*, land reformers include socialistic land reformers who work for the elimination of all private ownership, agrarian socialistic land reformers who would also eliminate private ownership but would grant individual persons a right of use, and land reformers in the narrow, actual sense who would keep private ownership but would eliminate only the income which is gained from it without any work – the ground rent – by means of a tax or other measures. Among the proponents of this school of thought in Germany were *Hermann Heinrich Gossen, Theodor Stamm, Michael Flürscheim, Theodor Hertzka*, and *Franz Oppenheimer*; but *Adolf Damaschke* (1865–1935) is considered to be the father of land reform. *Theodor Stamm* founded the Deutsche Landliga (German Land League) in 1880, which supported communal or public ownerhsip of land. This league quickly folded, however, and in 1888 *Stamm* founded the Allwohlbund (Common Welfare Alliance) which also failed. *Michael Flürscheim* (1844–1912) created the Deutscher Bund für Bodenbesitzreform (German League for Land-ownership Reform) in 1888, which strove for a nationalization or communalization of land or of ground rents; later he pursued real political goals. *Damaschke* became chairman of this league in 1898, which called itself the Bund Deutscher Bodenreformer (League of German Land Reformers). In contrast to *Henry George* (1839–1897) who stood for the nationalization of land and ground rents, *Damaschke* held that the mortgage system should be nationalized, the amounts owed on debts paid off, and thereby the ground rents recovered by the state and the communities. By means of a Property Increment Tax on Land, which was instituted in 1911, unearned income was to be siphoned off. Through these land reform measures, land speculation and its influence on housing construction – in particular on costs and rents – was to be lessened.

The land reform movement led to the passage of the Reichs-Heimstättengesetz (National Law on Homesteads) on May 19, 1920, and to article 155 of the Weimar Constitution, whereby the distribution and use of land was to be supervised by the state, in order to prevent its misuse. At the same time the goal was set of securing for every German a healthy dwelling-place and for all German families, especially for families with many children, a homestead where they could live and work. Almost the whole apparatus of active governmental housing policy was developed in the span of time between the two World Wars, whereby basic demands of housing and land reformers were complied with.

IV. De-regulation instead of Housing Reform?

Governmental intervention in the supply of housing, i.e. regulation of rents, took place as early as the beginning of World War I in 1914. After 1918 a system of housing regulation – rent controls, government administration of living space, and tenant protection – was instituted. To a certain extent these included temporary measures called for in 1918 and 1945 by the effects of the wars, but to a certain extent they also included basic corrections in the policy with regard to economic order, corrections of a liberal housing policy in the sense of housing reform and the housing reform movement. After the mid 1920's, government interventions resulting from the war in the form of compulsory regulations were gradually revoked; but during the Third Reich, especially during World War II, and thereafter they were re-introduced and intensified. With the Lücke legislation (Law on the Retraction of Governmental Housing Regulations and on Socially just Tenancy and Housing Rights, enacted on June 23, 1960), the decisive step was taken in the transition to a social market economy in housing.

Active governmental housing policy superimposed itself on the idea of housing reform and eventually made that idea superfluous. Thus the housing reform movement was not brought back to life after 1945. Quite to the contrary, ever since the transition of regulated housing to a social market economy in housing at the beginning of the 1960's, there has been a controversial scientific and political debate over the question of whether and to what extent the state should shape the housing system (→ *Economic Order*). Supporters of the market economy system demand not more, but less state control – thus a de-regulation – in order to stimulate private investment and to put housing at the disposal of free enterprise (→ *State and Co-operatives, Market Economy*). Not making housing socially just, but making it economically efficient, is at the heart of these demands.

Bibliography

Bericht über den Ersten Allgemeinen Deutschen Wohnungskongreß 1904 in Frankfurt a.M., Göttingen 1905.
Bericht über den Zweiten Deutschen Wohnungskongreß 1911 in Leipzig, Göttingen 1912.
Blumenroth, Ulrich: Deutsche Wohnungspolitik seit der Reichsgründung – Darstellung und kritische Würdigung, Münster 1975; abgedruckt in: Deutsche Bau-und Bodenbank Aktiengesellschaft 1923–1973 – 50 Jahre im Dienste der Bau-und Wohungswirtschaft, o.O., o.J. (Frankfurt 1973), pp. 211–411.
Blumenroth, Ulrich: Deutsche Wohnungspolitik seit der Reichsgründung – Darstellung und kritische Würdigung, Beiträge zum Siedlungs- und Wohnungswesen und zur Raumplanung, Vol.25, Münster (Westf.) 1975.
Damaschke, Adolf: Jahrbuch der Bodenreform, Jena 1905–1942.
Die Wohnungsfrage und das Reich. Eine Sammlung von Abhandlungen, Göttingen 1900–1911.
Diehl, Karl: Bodenreform. Handwörterbuch der Staatswissenschaften, vol. II, Jena 1924, pp. 935–954.
Dreißig Jahre Wohnungsreform 1898–1928 – Denkschrift aus Anlaß des dreißigjährigen Bestehens, herausgegeben vom Deutschen Verein für Wohnungsreform e.V., Berlin 1928.
Fuchs, Carl Johannes: Wohnungsfrage und Wohnungswesen. Handwörterbuch der Staatswissenschaften, Jena 1929, (Ergänzungsband), pp. 1098–1160.
Handwörterbuch des Wohungswesens, im Auftrage des Deutschen Vereins für Wohnungsreform e.V., Berlin, hrsg. von Albrecht Gerhard u.a., Jena 1930.

Häring, Dieter: Zur Geschichte und Wirkung staatlicher Intervention im Wohnungssektor – Gesellschaftliche und sozialpolitische Aspekte der Wohnungspolitik in Deutschland, Hamburg 1974.
Hiertsiefer, Heinrich: Die Wohnungswirtschaft in Preußen, Eberswalde 1929.
Jäger, Eugen: Die Wohnungsfrage, 2 Bände, Berlin 1902, 1903.
Jahrbücher der Wohnungsreform, Göttingen 1903–1912.
Jenkis, Helmut: Die gemeinnützige Wohnungswirtschaft zwischen Markt und Sozialbindung – Aufsätze und Abhandlungen, Berlin 1985.
Jenkis, Helmut: Die Mietenpolitik zwischen Ökonomie und Ideologie, ORDO, vol. 32 (1981), pp. 141–184.
Jenkis, Helmut: Die Wohnung: Ein Wirtschaftsgut oder ein Sozialgut? Festschrift für Johannes Bärmann und Hermann Weitnauer, München 1990, pp. 391–433.
Jenkis, Helmut: Kommentar zum Wohnungsgemeinnützigkeitsrecht und zur WGG-Aufhebungsgesetzgebung, Hamburg 1988.
Jenkis, Helmut: Kompendium der Wohnungswirtschaft, München 1991.
Jenkis, Helmut: Ursprung und Entwicklung der gemeinnützigen Wohnungswirtschaft, Bonn, Hamburg 1973.
Lütge, Friedrich: Wohnungswirtschaft (Jena 1939), Stuttgart 1949.
Pergande, Hans-Günther/Pergande, Jürgen: Die Gesetzgebung auf dem Gebiete des Wohnungswesens und des Städtebaues. Deutsche Bau-und Bodenbank Aktiengesellschaft 1923–1973 – 50 Jahre im Dienste der Bau- und Wohnungswirtschaft, o.O., o.J. (Frankfurt 1973), pp. 11–209.
Peters, K.-H.: Die Bodenreform – Ende eines Kompromisses, Hamburg 1971.
Schwan, Bruno: Wohnungsreform (Reform des Wohnungswesens). Handwörterbuch des Wohnungswesens, Jena 1930, pp. 836–838.
Spiethoff, Arthur: Boden und Wohnung, Jena 1930.
Verein Socialpolitik (eds.): Beiträge zur städtischen Wohn- und Siedelwirtschaft, München-Leipzig 1930.
Verein Socialpolitik (eds.): Die Wohnungsnot der ärmeren Klassen in deutschen Großstädten und Vorschläge zu deren Abhilfe, 2 Bände, Leipzig 1886.
Verein Socialpolitik (eds.): Neue Untersuchungen des Vereins für Socialpolitik über die Wohnungsfrage und die Handelspolitik, Leipzig 1898.
Verein Socialpolitik (eds.): Verhandlungen der Eisenacher Versammlung von 1872, Leipzig 1873.
Verein Socialpolitik (eds.): Verhandlungen der Generalversammlung, Berlin 1893, über die ländliche Arbeiterfrage und über die Bodenbesitzverteilung und die Sicherung des kleinen Grundbesitzes, Leipzig 1893.
Verein Socialpolitik (eds.): Verhandlungen der am 24. und 25. September in Frankfurt a.M. abgehaltenen Generalversammlung des Vereins für Socialpolitik über die Wohnungsverhältnisse der ärmeren Klassen in deutschen Großstädten und über innere Kolonisation mit Rücksicht auf die Erhaltung und Vermehrung des mittleren und kleineren ländlichen Grundbesitzes, Leipzig 1887.
Von Hayek, Friedrich August: Die Verfassung der Freiheit, Walter Eucken, Tübingen 1971 (Originalausgabe: The Constitution of Liberty, Chicago and London 1960).
Von Mangoldt, Rose: Wohnungsreform. Handwörterbuch des Städtebaues, Wohnungs-und Siedlungswesens, vol. III, Stuttgart 1959, pp. 1759–1761.

Housing Co-operatives

JÜRGEN ZERCHE [F]

(see also: *Classification*; *Housing Reform*; *Economic Order*; *Commonweal Economy*; *Law, National*; *Law, International*)

I. Introduction; II. Housing Co-operatives as Part of the Housing Economy; III. Position and Economic Significance of Housing Co-operatives in Germany; IV. Housing Co-operatives in Other Countries.

I. Introduction

The housing sector in the Federal Republic of Germany, as in other countries as well, is determined by a multitude of agents and regulating elements. Basically, the market is the dominant influencing factor, considerably restricted by governmental intervention (→ *State and Co-operatives, Market Economy*). Between the extremes of private enterprise agents and public enterprise agents, housing co-operatives and other housing enterprises for public benefit have established a place for themselves ever since the middle of the previous century (→ *History before 1800*). In self-help and solidarity with large groups of the population (cf. *Baumgart*), and oriented to their well-being or that of others, they construct and manage flats, private homes, and in recent times flats for private owners as well (cf. *Riebandt-Korfmacher*).

The concepts which housing co-operatives and building associations have of their role, the tasks they set for themselves, and their development are not the same for all of Europe. The following remarks apply mainly to the situation in the Federal Republic of Gemany. The final chapter will then discuss the situation in other countries.

II. Housing Co-operatives as Part of the Housing Economy

1. Special Features of Supply and Demand on the Housing Market

The need for living space results from the basic human need for a definite place providing security, warmth, protection, etc. This basic need is fundamental to life. Only the concrete creation of housing possibilities can, from the perspective of the science of economics, cause the demand for living space to react flexibly to price. The ability of the demand for housing to react to price will manifest itself mainly when tenants rent new quarters or when living space is purchased. This fact can be explained by the prolonged period of use of the commodity housing and by the high transaction costs (for information, for moving, for the social costs of mobility, etc.). This and the fundamental recognition of the necessity for social protection prevent this area of supply, i.e. housing, from being controlled solely by market prices (cf. *Krischausky/Mackscheidt*). The commodity housing requires intensive capital investment and long-term capital lockup, in which case the individual, private provision of one's own housing appears to be possible only under limited circumstances.

2. Solidarity and Self-help in Solving the Housing Problem, Seen Historically

Solidarity and self-help through setting up housing co-operatives and building societies and through the development of housing enterprises for public benefit were logical answers to the extreme housing need prevalent in the previous century. Above all in the cities there was a flagrant lack of adequate living space. The main victims were families with low incomes and single young people (for exact data cf. *Fuchs*). The totally unsatisfactory living conditions constituted a part of the Social Question of the 19th century.

a) Answers to the Desperate Housing Situation: the Development of Housing Co-operatives

The housing misery of large portions of the population was tackled at first not by the state but by those directly affected helping themselves, by private efforts of individual persons and scientists. (In this context, special mention should be given to → *Victor Aimé Huber*.) In the middle of the 19th century joint stock companies, building societies, building co-operatives, i.e. housing co-operatives and housing construction co-operatives, were formed with the aim of guaranteeing, through solidarity and self-help, the provision of extensive groups of the population with living space (→ *Housing Reform*). They committed their activity to special imperatives with regard to equity capital, attitudes and purposes (cf. *Engelhardt*) which were later incorporated into law as maxims of housing for public benefit. The co-operatives active in the housing sector were mainly consumer or household co-operatives, with the intention of making living space available to their members at reasonable conditions.

At first there was no special legal basis for building co-operatives any more than there was for other co-operatives. Not until the Co-operative Law of 1867, together with the extension of its scope in 1868 and 1873, could co-operatives achieve status as legal entities by being entered in the co-operative register. Especially after the enactment of the Co-operative Law of 1889 (→ *Legal Form, Co-operative*), which, in addition to the re-organization of management, provided for the possibility of limited liability on the part of co-operative members and for the institution of auditing federations, it came about that building co-operatives began to spread. In addition, the invalid and labourer pension scheme, introduced in the same year, made the acquisition of capital easier, since this scheme invested portions of its assets in land and mortgages for the construction of housing for workers (cf. *Schultz/Zerche*).

At first, workers failed to accept the idea of self-help in the form of consumer and household co-operatives as a means of improving their situation. The conflict between labour and capital and thus the problem of the working-class situation was to be solved, they believed, by overcoming ownership maldistribution. Thus, according to *Lassalle*, a more suitable co-operative means would be joint-production co-operatives (cf. *Schultz/Zerche*).

b) Housing Co-operatives and the Bauhütte Movement as Part of the Labour Movement

The co-operative production of housing in the form of activity by → *joint-production co-operatives* never played a big role in Germany. On the one hand, the working class, including the workers party and trade unions, were slow to accept the co-operative movement. On the other hand, the period of the Third Reich was not favourable to joint-production co-operatives, because they were always regarded as a revolutionary means to overthrowing the existing societal order. In addition, further reasons may have played a part which had to do with this particular form of co-operative, with the interests of the members, and with the particular branch of industry (i.e. high capital input). It should be mentioned that "social construction enterprises" (building joint-production co-operatives) in 1924 voluntarily relinquished the legal status of enterprises for public benefit and thus gave up the tax advantages involved, because housing co-operatives for public benefit were already forbidden at the time to act as construction enterprises executing building plans, if they wanted the tax benefits (later generally regulated by law in paragraph 6 of the Law on Housing Enterprise for Public Benefit).

In the 1920's, under the name → *Bauhütte* movement, there was a lively development of joint-production co-operatives in the building field; but this movement was stifled during the Nazi period by the Nazi policy of eradicating everything that failed to conform to the party line. After 1945, housing co-operatives did not pick up the tradition of joint-production co-operatives, particularly because it conflicted with the law on housing for public benefit; but a German Bauhütte, Ltd., was founded anew after 1945.

The Bauhütte movement originated out of the co-operative and Labour Movement, with the goal of producing houses and dwellings with the co-determination of the employees and other groups of the working-class movement. The so-called "soziale Baubetriebe" (social building enterprises) transformed themselves in the years 1921–1924 into Bauhütten with the legal form of limited companies, but with the special feature that the employees with their workshop board and the employee assembly constituted separate bodies apart from management, supervisory board, and shareholders' assembly (*Astor*) (→ *Organizational Structure of Societies*). The shareholders were drawn from institutions of the Labour movement as well as trade unions, building and consumers' co-operatives, workers' banks, and the Social Democratic Party (→ *Consumer Co-operatives*).

III. Position and Economic Significance of Housing Co-operatives in Germany

1. Legal Foundations

In addition to the basic regulations of the housing market and the building sector, the legal foundations which have been of primary relevance for housing co-operatives in Germany are the Co-operative Law and the Law on Housing for Public Benefit (valid until January 1, 1990) (→ *Law, National*).

The charge to co-operatives, laid down in §1 of the Co-operative Law, to promote the interests of their members (→ *Promotion Mandate*), naturally applies to housing co-operatives as well, which set themselves the task of providing their members with living space.

Ninety-five percent of all housing co-operatives enjoyed the status of enterprises of public benefit until January 1, 1990. The remaining few were not recognized as public benefit enterprises because they were too closely linked with the building trade. Recognition as a public benefit enterprise meant exemption from corporation profit tax, property tax, and local industrial tax, as well as certain fees. But there were also restrictions:

- Orientation of all business activity to providing housing for widespread sections of the population,
- Fulfillment of the purpose of benefit to the public through construction of wholesome housing and the obligation to build continuously,
- Independence from the building trade,
- Compulsory membership in a federation and compulsory auditing of the enterprise by the federation, even if it is not a co-operative,
- Formulation of contracts on rent, use, sale, and upkeep in conformity to binding model contracts,
- Restriction of utilization fees and sale prices according to the principle of covering costs and foregoing maximization of profits,
- Coupling of paid-in capital and of profits earned to the purposes of the organizations, through limitation of profit distribution,
- In the case of withdrawal of membership or dissolution of the enterprise, limitation of re-imbursement of the members to the amounts of capital paid in.

Housing enterprises which abided by the basic conditions, especially the limitation of prices to cost coverage, were, from the beginning of building activity for public benefit, exempted from taxes (→ *Taxation*) and favoured by remittance of fees according to the respective national and state regulations, which often varied from case to case.

The essential maxims of housing for public benefit were put on a uniform legal basis by the regulation on enterprises for public benefit of December 1, 1930 (Reichs-Gesetz-Blatt I, p.593), which took over the draft of a law from 1929. A law enacted on February 29, 1940 (Reichs-Gesetz-Blatt I, p. 438), regulated the legal basis of the housing economy for public benefit in every respect, including the objectives of housing policy. In the course of the Tax Reform Law of August 2, 1988, the law on housing for public benefit was repealed, effective from January 1, 1990 (Bundes-Gesetz-Blatt I, p. 1098).

From this, the following regulations result for co-operatives:

- Option possibility according to paragraph 54 of the Law: on application, the tax exemption regulations which were valid until December 31, 1989, could be extended one more year for the tax period 1990, on the condition that the co-operative conducted only business which would have been permitted under the legal regulations for enterprises for public benefit valid until December 31, 1989 (with exceptions permitted under certain circumstances).
- After expiration of the transition period, all housing co-operatives, independently of whether they were formerly recognized as housing enterprises for public benefit or not, on principle acquire the status of a renting co-operative in the sense of paragraph 5, part 1, number 10 of the Körperschaftssteuergesetz (corporation profit tax) as long as they abide by the resulting restrictions on their activity. Business which does not fall into the permitted category is taxable. If the receipts from this business exceed 10 percent of the total income of the co-operative, then the total income becomes taxable.
- By December 31, 1991, or December 31, 1992, respectively, a co-operative could, however, submit a written declaration and relinquish the tax exemption, just that once, according to paragraph 5, part 1, number 10 of the Körperschaftssteuergesetz. After that the co-operative was bound to its relinquishment for at least five years.

Insofar as a housing co-operative does not wish to remain a pure renting or tenants' co-operative, it can provide additional services for members in housing, in care, in financing, and in social and cultural spheres, as, for example, looking after and providing nursing care for the elderly, setting up shared facilities like reading-rooms, hobby rooms and children's day-care centers, and instituting its own savings organizations, etc. (cf. *Pelzl*) (→ *Classification*).

2. Organization into Federations

Housing co-operatives are required to become members of an auditing federation (→ *Auditing*). For the co-operative housing economy there are ten auditing federations, which receive support for their work from additional service institutions in which the auditing federations participate financially, for example, in a technical publishing house for the housing economy. The auditing federations are affiliated (→ *Federations*) with the Gesamtverband der Wohnungswirtschaft e.V. (National Federation of Housing Enterprises), which was formerly the Gesamtverband Gemeinnütziger Wohnungsunternehmen e.V. (National Federation of Housing Enterprises for Public Benefit) until November 30, 1989, which represents common interest primarily toward the public and in the political field.

On the European level the National Federation of Housing Enterprises is a member of and works with the → *International Co-operative Alliance* (ICA): In 1986 the Federation helped to found the European Liaison Committee for Social Housing (CECODHAS). This committee is in turn a member of the "Co-ordinating Committee of European Federations" (→ *International Co-operative Organization*). In developing countries the Deutsche Entwicklungshilfe für soziales Wohnungs- und Siedlungswesen e.V. (German Aid to Developing Countries for Social Housing and Settlements) (DESWOS), founded in 1969 by the Housing Economy for Public Benefit, devotes itself to improving housing in the Third World (→ *Development Policy*).

3. Statistical Data of Housing Co-operatives

Within the overall housing economy for public benefit, housing co-operatives have always dominated numerically. The count, which was 289 co-operatives at the turn of the century, rose to 2,638 in the year 1929 and sank again to 1,176 by the year 1988. This number corresponds to a share of 65.9 percent co-operatives in relation to all housing enterprises for public benefit in the year 1988 (data from the Gesamtverband der Wohnungswirtschaft and the Deutsche Genossenschaftsbank). Their market share of completed housing units in the entire housing economy declined from 7.8 percent in the year 1960 to 5.3 percent in 1970, to 3.2 percent in 1980, and finally to 2.3 percent in the year 1988. The numerically outstanding role of co-operatives within the former housing economy for public benefit stands in contrast to a lower average number of housing units attributed to them. To illustrate: the 1,176 housing co-operatives administered an average of 881 housing units in the year 1988; the 523 housing enterprises registered in the legal form of limited companies, on the other hand, administered 3,153 housing units; and the 59 registered as joint stock companies even administered as many as 11,444. The other 27 housing enterprises for public benefit, which as corporations, foundations, or other associations administered an average of 1,008 housing units, are too few to be of significance.

Structurally and in accordance with the co-operative self-understanding of their position and role, housing co-operatives tend to be small or medium-sized enterprises.

4. Prospects for Housing Co-operatives

With the termination of the legal regulation on housing co-operatives for public benefit, not only the tax privileges went out of effect but also the restrictions, so that now the affected enterprises can define the goals of their enterprises anew. The owners can also change the legal form of the enterprises, if they desire. In view of co-operatives' concept of their role, housing co-operatives will continue in the future to dedicate themselves to the principles of public benefit, as they have in the past. On the other hand, how housing enterprises in other legal forms will develop remains to be seen. A reunified Germany in a unified Europe calls for an active shaping of the housing market, in order to cope with the visible and considerable shifts in demand for housing. In any case, the concepts of solidarity and self-help will continue to be convincing.

IV. Housing Co-operatives in Other Countries

After 1945 the housing economies in the Federal Republic and in the German Democratic Republic went different ways. Up until then, the same tradition and the same legislative foundation had existed (Law on Housing for Public Benefit, enacted in 1940, and the former Co-operative Law). Until recently, in contrast to the Federal Republic, the provision of housing in the GDR, including state control of housing distribution, had the rank of articles of the constitution (cf. *Jenkis*, 1990). At the present time, the area of the former GDR is listed as having about 700 building co-operatives which belong to an auditing federation. The auditing federation was not formerly independent of state intervention, but was attached to the ministry of Finance. Since March 1990, however, there is an independent federation of housing co-operatives. The variety in the way in which co-operatives conceive of themselves and in the legal arrangements in the different countries of the European Community (→ *European Community*), as well as difficulties in the standardization of terms, all hamper a comparison of co-operatives on an international basis (*Münkner*).

Within Europe as a whole, the co-operative movement often tends to be linked more closely with concepts of the common welfare and more strongly with the working-class movement or with other ideological trends than it is in Germany. Housing co-operatives exist in almost all countries of the European Community (for the following remarks, cf. *Amt*). In competition with them there are also building and loan societies, which – partially in the form of co-operatives as e.g. in Denmark – assist in financing living space.

In the United Kingdom and in Ireland, building and loan societies are important institutions on the housing market, whose history can be traced back into the 18th century. Among with them, however, there are also housing and joint-production co-operatives (building guilds). These pursue social-political aims similarly to and sometimes more consequently than the Bauhütten movement in Germany and have put through extensive rights for employees (pay according to need, protection against being given notice, continued payment of wages e.g. in case of sickness, etc.; cf. *Novy*). In the Netherlands there are housing corporations for public benefit which in the year 1983 accounted for 29 percent of all existing housing in the country. However, these are not co-operatives in the legal sense, although they contain forms of democratic representation of members. In France three types of co-operatives are active on the housing market: co-operatives which rent housing with the provision that part of the payment goes toward acquisition of ownership of the dwelling by the tenant member; production co-operatives; and building co-operatives. In Italy housing co-operatives within the co-operative sector are significant purely on account of their quantity (1980: 67, 781 building co-operatives), but most of them are unaffiliated, that is, they do not usually belong to a central co-operative organization. In Spain, Greece, and above all in Portugal in recent times one has been able to observe dynamic developments in housing co-operatives.

In European countries the co-operative movement and particularly the housing co-operative movement has taken a very different course depending on the economic, social, and political conditions in each country. This is demonstrated clearly by the developments in Eastern European societies (cf. e.g. *Piasny*). The legal situations and the various co-operatives' self-appraisal in regard to the tasks they set for themselves differ greatly (→ *Law, International*). This impedes or possibly even hinders the attempts at harmonization within Europe and the creation of a body of co-operative law which transcends national boundaries. On the other hand, this is also a sign of the cultural diversity in Europe; to keep this can also be a worthwhile common goal.

Bibliography

Amt für amtliche Veröffentlichungen der Europäischen Gemeinschaften (ed.): Die Genossenschaften Europas und ihre Verbände, Baden-Baden 1986.
Astor: Arbeiterwohnungsbau. Handwörterbuch des Wohnungswesens, Jena 1930, pp. 10–15.
Baumgarten: Baugenossenschaften. Handwörterbuch des Wohnungswesens, Jena 1930, pp. 49–56.
DG-Bank (ed.): Die Genossenschaften in der Bundesrepublik Deutschland 1989 Statistik.
Engelhardt, Werner Wilhelm: Öffentliche Bindung, Selbstbindung und Deregulierung in der Staatlichen Wohnungspolitik und Gemeinnützigen Wohnungswirtschaft. In: Thiemeyer (ed.), Regulierung und Deregulierung im Bereich der Sozialpolitik, Berlin 1988.
Fuchs, Carl Johannes: Wohnungsfrage und Wohnungswesen. Handwörterbuch der Staatswissenschaft, Jena 1929.
Jenkis, Helmut W.: Kommentar zum Wohnungsgemeinnützigkeitsrecht mit der WGG-Aufhebungsgesetzgebung, Hamburg 1988.
Jenkis, Helmut W.: Wohnungswirtschaft und Wohnungspolitik in der DDR. Ein ordnungspolitischer Effizienzvergleich, Gemeinnützige Wohnungswesen, 3 (1990), pp. 108–126.
Krischausky, Dieter/Mackscheidt, Klaus: Wohnungsgemeinnützigkeit. Zwischen bedarfswirtschaftlicher Tradition und wohnungspolitischer Neuorientierung, Köln-Berlin-Bonn-München 1984.
Münkner, Hans-H.: Selbstverständnis und Rechtsverfassung von Genossenschaftsorganisationen in EG-Partnerstaaten. In: Boettcher, E (ed.): Die Genossenschaft im Wettbewerb der Ideen – eine europäische Herausforderung, Tübingen 1985, pp. 87–116.
Novy, Klaus: Genossenschafts-Bewegung. Zur Geschichte und Zukunft der Wohnreform, Berlin 1983.
Pelzl, Wolfgang: Strategien für Wohnungsgenossenschaften in der Dynamik des Marktes, ZfgG, 1 (1990), pp. 41–53.
Piasny, Janusz: Die Entwicklung der Genossenschaften im Nachkriegspolen. In: Zerche, J./Herder-Dorneich, Ph./Engelhardt. W.W. (eds.): Genossenschaften und genossenschaftswissenschaftliche Forschung. Festschrift des Seminars für Genossenschaftswesen zum 600–jährigen Gründungsjubiläum der Universität zu Köln, Regensburg 1989, pp. 181–191.
Riebandt-Korfmacher, Alice: Wohnungsbaugenossenschaften. Handwörterbuch des Genossenschaftswesens, Wiesbaden 1980.
Schultz, R./Zerche, J.: Genossenschaftslehre, Berlin-New York 1983.

Huber, Victor Aimé (1800–1869)

HELMUT JENKIS [F]

(see also: *History of Ideas*; *Conceptions, Co-operative*; *History in 19th C.*; *Socialist Critics*)

I. Periods of Huber's Life; II. Huber's Intellectual and Spiritual Standpoint; III. Victor Aimé Huber – the Unacknowledged Social Reformer.

Two men, *Hermann* → *Schulze-Delitzsch* (1808–1883) and → *Friedrich Wilhelm Raiffeisen* (1818–

1888), have come to be regarded as the two fathers of the German co-operative movement. Yet it is often overlooked that another man, *Victor Aimé Huber* (1800–1869), was actually the intellectual and spiritual forefather of the movement. The fact that Huber receives less attention than the others may be due in turn to the fact that he was a scholar rather than a practical organizer and entrepreneur.

I. Periods of Huber's Life

Victor Aimé Huber's grandfather, *Michael Huber*, was born in Freising in Bavaria in 1727. In 1742 he emigrated to Paris as a poor farmer lad, later returned to Germany, and became a professor at the University of Leipzig. Of his six children only *Ludwig Ferdinand Huber*, born in Paris in 1764 and later to become the father of *Victor Aimé*, lived to come of age. *Ludwig Ferdinand Huber* made the acquaintance of *Georg Forster* (1754–1794) and his wife *Therese Forster* (1764–1829) and married *Therese* after the death of her husband. *Victor Aimé Huber* was born in Stuttgart on March 10, 1800; his father died only four years later on Christmas Eve, 1804. Thereafter his mother not only managed to support the family through writing but also influenced *Victor Aimé's* thinking deeply.

As his parents preferred the French language, *Victor Aimé* learned French first and German only later. Religion played only a small part in his upbringing. When it came time for him to go to school, *Victor Aimé* was sent to the educational institution run by *Philipp Emanuel von Fellenberg* (1771–1844) at Hofwyl in the Canton of Bern in Switzerland, where the sons of princes and barons from all over the world were educated. Victor Aimé remained at Hofwyl more than ten years. He had come to this school as a gifted, impressionable child; he left it as a youth of strong determination. In Hofwyl *Victor Aimé* met the English manufacturer and social reformer *Robert Owen* (1771–1858) and could never have guessed that he would one day become a supporter of *Owen's* idea of association.

In the summer of 1817, *Victor Aimé* took up the study of medicine in Göttingen, but medicine did not really appeal to him; he preferred to devote his time to literature, history, and languages. Reluctantly he took his preliminary doctor's examination in medicine in Würzburg in 1820. In the spring of 1821 he went to Paris to finish his studies, and in the fall of that year he journeyed to Spain, where he discovered his great love for literature. In 1823 he travelled to Hamburg and on to Scotland and London, where he came into contact with Christian religious groups. It was here that he came to realize that a nation's happiness depends not only on its political constitution but also on the relationship between rich and poor, employers and employees. In 1824–25 he prepared for his final university examination in medicine, but then in Munich he was not admitted to the examination process. Thereupon he joined the staff of the Cotta-owned *Allgemeine Zeitung* (General Newspaper) in Augsburg, traveled to Paris in 1826, was in London for a short time, and served as travel companion for a young man in Italy. In the fall of 1828, his years of wandering came to an end when he took up a post as a teacher in a trade school in Bremen. His first religious contacts and impressions in Scotland had caused him to become a believing, practicing Christian, and he took up membership in the reformed church. On the 15th of June, 1829, his mother died; and not quite a year later, on March 7, 1830, he married *Auguste Klugkist*, daughter of the Senator *Dr. Klugkist* in Bremen.

At the end of 1832 *Victor Aimé Huber* received a call from the University of Rostock for a full professorship in modern history and occidental languages; but because his lectures were not on bread-winning subjects, only a small number of students attended. In the summer of 1836 he received a call from the University of Marburg, where he taught for seven years; and here it was that he published his well-known book *Die englischen Universitäten* (English Universities) in 1839/40 (reprinted in 1990). In 1843 *Victor Aimé* was called to Berlin by *King Friedrich Wilhelm IV* to found a conservative journal; and at the same time he received a professorship for modern philology, literature, and literary history at the University of Berlin. Because of his poor delivery and his anti-liberal attitude, however, his lectures in Berlin found even less resonance than the ones in Rostock and Marburg had done. In 1845 he began publication of the journal *Janus, Jahrbücher deutscher Gesinnung, Bildung and That* (Janus, Yearbooks on German Mentality, Education and Activity). But even these efforts met with no success, and the last issue appeared at the end of March, 1848. Since his political endeavours had failed – the revolution of 1848 had shocked and shaken him – he turned back on politics and turned instead to social reform.

Huber was probably the first German professor to discuss the problem of the modern working class at a German university. At the end of June 1848 he published anonymously the brochure "Die Selbsthilfe der arbeitenden Klasse durch Wirtschaftsvereine und innere Ansiedlung" (Self-help by the Working Class through Economic Associations and Inner Colonization). In 1849 he was asked to become a member of the board of directors of the Berliner gemeinnützige Baugesellschaft (Berlin Building Society for Public Benefit), the first of all housing enterprises for public benefit. From May 1, 1849, until New Year's Day, 1850, at the expense of this society, *Huber* put out the journal *Concordia, Blätter der Berliner gemeinnützigen Baugesellschaft* (Concordia, Journal of the Berlin Building Society for Public Benefit), but even this journal died out. In the cornerstone of the first building erected by the society, a document was cemented in which aptly characterizes *Victor Aimé's* social-policy goal: "Die Verwandlung eigentumsloser Arbeiter in arbeitende Eigentümer" (the transformation of workers who own nothing into working owners).

Fewer and fewer students were attending Huber's lectures; teaching satisfied him less and less and hindered him in his social work. Thus on the 23rd of February, 1851, he requested his release from civil service; his request was granted, and *Victor Aimé* moved from Berlin to Wernigerode in the Harz Mountains. From this retirement spot he made numerous journeys to France, Belgium, and England, attended meetings, and gave talks and wrote articles on social problems and on co-operation. He also took up contact with → *Schulze-Delitzsch*, although there were essential differences between the two men with regard to politics and religion. In 1861 *Victor Aimé* founded yet another journal with the title Concordia, Beiträge zur Lösung der sozialen Frage (Concordia, Contributions to a Solution of the Social Question). It fostered and helped spread his idea of cooperation, but by the end of the year 1861 this journal had also folded up. Among *Huber's* numerous lectures, the one given in Hannover in 1864 should be mentioned: "Über die geeignetesten Maßnahmen zur Abhilfe der Wohnungsnot" (On the Measures most Suited to Relieving the Crucial Need for Housing). In 1855 *Huber* founded a credit association in Wernigerode, and in the same year a school for further training for craftsmen apprentices. In order to unite all branches of this activity under one roof, he created the foundation "St. Theobaldi" in Wernigerode, named after the church nearby. With the exception of slight changes, this building exists to this day under the name of "Kirchliches Tagungs-und Rüstzeitenheim 'Huberhaus'" (Retreat and Conference Center of the Protestant Church 'Huber House'). In the park a bust of Victor Aimé Huber has been erected.

On July 19, 1869, *Victor Aimé Huber* died of a lung infection. He and his wife were buried in the cemetery of St. Theobaldi nearby. The graves have been cared for to this day. Since the reunification of both parts of Germany, there is no longer an impediment of visiting the Huber House and *Huber's* grave in Wernigerode.

II. Huber's Intellectual and Spiritual Standpoint

In the 19th century, liberal constitutionalism and absolute monarchy stood in opposition to each other. *Victor Aimé* came out in support of a christian monarchy, in hopes that the mutual duties of a shared belief of Christians and monarch could reconcile these opposites with each other. The revolution of 1848 came as a shock to *Huber,* because the German Crown proved itself incapable of fulfilling its conservative-reformative tasks. This political standpoint – which was liberal, but not in the sense of a liberal party, and which was also conservative, yet stood in contrast to conservatism was complemented by *Huber's* deep religious belief, which accorded with his ideas of social reform.

During his trip to England in 1844, *Victor Aimé* had seen clearly what the social problem was: the misery of workers in industrial cities. In the uprooting of masses of workers toiling in modern factories, Huber saw the danger that the workers could become poorer and poorer. For him the social question was a moral one; he discerned the greatest danger not so much in the revolution as in moral and social dissolution, in a relapse into heathen barbarianism. Thus he felt that the proletarian masses ought to be organized, in order that they could obtain housing, clothing, and food and be improved morally at the same time. The means to this end, he felt, was the self-help of workers together with the active help of the state, the Church, and the aristocracy, i.e. the aristocracy of mind, birth, and money. As early as 1825, *Huber* had realized that not the preservation of established conditions, but their reform was the truly wise course for the state to take. *Victor Aimé Huber* combined conservative thinking with a monarchical ideal, personal Christian faith with practical Christian love of one's neighbor, Christian life in the community with economic reforms, theoretical demands with practical attempts at solutions to problems.

In the journal *Janus* of which he was editor (number 8, 1846), *Victor Aimé Huber* presented his plans "on inner colonization": that through association there simply had to be some way to provide every family with a small house and garden; that not far from centers of industry, settlements with 150 houses should be erected, each settlement with a main building containing commonly shared facilities. In the text published anonymously at the end of 1848 entitled "Die Selbsthilfe der arbeitenden Klassen durch Wirtschaftvereine und innere Ansiedlung" (Self-help by the Working Classes through Economic Associations and Inner Colonization, mentioned above), *Huber* developed further his plans for associations and settlements. He devoted special attention to the housing problem, because for him housing represented the dwelling-place for body and soul. It was not sufficient, however, just to build good housing; this housing also needed to be within the financial reach of people earning low incomes. *Huber's* criticism of inadequate housing conditions, his demands for a housing reform, and also his active work in the Berlin Building Society for Public Benefit all contributed to make Vicotr Aimé the founding father of the (former) housing for public benefit. On the basis of a resolution of the housing movement for public benefit from December 2, 1960, to honor *Huber*, the Victor Aimé Huber Badge was created – the highest mark of distinction which the organization ever awards. Up to the end of 1989, this badge had been bestowed about forty times.

Victor Aimé Huber got the first inspiration for his idea of cooperation while in England. He distinguished among three forms of assocations:
1. economic association, which includes credit and distribution co-operatives, but above all building and housing co-operatives as well as consumer co-operatives; 2. the industrial association as a joint-production co-operative, about which Huber had his reservations; and 3. latent association, which rests on the responsibility of the aristocracy of birth, wealth, and service to take over the leadership of the working class form above, since the working class itself was not yet in a position to take over that role. The associations have the function of providing not only material help, but also moral and intellectual support; they should be in essence a church institution.

III. Victor Aimé Huber – the Unacknowledged Social Reformer

In his youth *Victor Aimé* was impetuous, revolutionary, and without church attachment; but after this stormy period, he became deeply religious and conservative. He is regarded as a monarchical-conservative social reformer who recognized earlier than most others the perils of industrialization, urbanization, and the proletarianization of the working class. Instead of taking the way out into utopian, communistic settlement plans, as did *Owen* or *Fourier* or *Cabet*, for example, he saw in the association – i.e. the co-operative – and in the debate on the housing question the beginnings of concrete solutions. He stood up for the idea of self-help; but at the same time he realized that the working class was materially and intellectually only partly capable of helping itself. For this reason he called for and pushed latent association, help from above, from the upper class. In his brochure published in 1852 entitled "Bruch mit der Revolution und Ritterschaft" (Break with the Revolution and Lordship) *Huber* made the occasion especially clear and urgent for solving the social problem through association.

V.A. *Huber's* text "Die Selbsthilfe der arbeitenden Klassen durch Wirtschaftsvereine und innere Ansiedlung" appeared in 1848, i.e. a year before *Schulze-Delitzsch* founded his first co-operatives. "Thus we may rightly call *Huber* the first intellectual and spiritual initiator of the German co-operative movement. Through the strong perseverance with which he propagated his co-operative beliefs, he became a pioneer of the co-operative idea in the truest sense of the word. The fact that he placed the factory worker at the focal point of this social and political endeavour shows that he had grasped the signs of the times, a perception which puts him ahead of *Schulze-Delitzsch* and *Raiffeisen* for whom, due to the environment into which they were born, the hardships of craftsmen and farmers were the most important. Yet it was industry and the working class who were decisive in the social developments of the times" (*Faust*, p. 184).

Why, then, has *Victor Aimé Huber* remained almost unknown, and why did his practical attempts at solutions to problems meet with so little success, if with any at all? Even his university lectures were poorly attended, and his journals found few subscribers. Despite the great effort he invested in the preparation of his lectures, his delivery continued weak; and his anti-liberal attitude also contributed to keeping the students away. He reacted to the revolution of 1848 with resignation. After moving to Wernigerode in Sept. 1852, he devoted himself entirely to the "inner mission" movement and to the Association, setting up in Wernigerode a school for further training for craftsmen apprentices and a Christian society for journeymen. As with his lectures, these efforts were not successful.

When *Huber* died in 1869, a man passed away who had self-lessly invested his whole life in service to the people. "The tragic aspect of his life was that in his social endeavors he was far ahead of this time, whereas the political developments he failed to understand in their full depth... The causes of his gradual isolation were surely to be found within himself in many respects; he had not been given the gift of conveying the fullness of his thoughts to his fellow men in an understandable way. Thus his pure wish to do so could often do nothing but trickle away like water in the sand" (*Faust*, p. 191).

In innumerable writings and lectures, *Victor Aimé Huber* sought to win support for his ideas of social reforms, in particular for the idea of association. Other people after him, with more fortunate gifts for organization, have put his ideas into effect.

Bibliography

Birr, J.: Victor Aimé Huber – der Pioneer der deutschen Wohnungsbaugenossenschaften, Gemeinnütziges Wohnungswesen, Heft 2 (1969), pp. 59–64.

Bredendiek, Walter: Christliche Sozialreformer des 19. Jahrhunderts, Leipzig 1953, pp. 69–141.

Elvers, Rudolf: Victor Aimé Huber – Sein Werden und sein Wirken, 2 volums, Bremen 1872, 1874.

Faust, Helmut: Geschichte der Genossenschaftsbewegung, 3rd edition, Frankfurt 1977, pp. 167–192.

Faust, Helmut: Victor Aimé Huber – Ein Bahnbrecher der Genossenschaftsidee, Hamburg 1956.

Jäger, Eugen: V.A. Huber, ein Vorkämpfer der sozialen Reform, in seinem Leben und seine Bestrebungen, Berlin 1880.

Jenkis, Helmut: Victor Aimeé Huber zum 100. Todestag, Gemeinnütziges Wohnungswesen, Heft 7 (1969), pp. 195–204; Heft 8 (1969), pp. 241–247. Erweiterte Fassung in: Ursprung und Entwicklung der gemeinnützigen Wohnungswirtschaft, Schriftenreihe des Instituts für Städtebau, Wohnungswirtschaft und Bausparwesen, Bd. 24, Bonn-Hamburg 1973, pp. 49–59; wiederabgedruckt in: Die gemeinnützige Wohnungswirtschaft zwischen Markt und Sozialbindung, Schriften zum Genossenschaftswesen und zur Öffentliche Wirtschaft, vol. 14/I, Berlin 1985, pp. 17–61.

Lippert: Victor Aimé. Handwörterbuch der Staatswissenschaften, Vol. IV, 2nd edition, Jena 1900, cols. 1230–1232 (mit Schriftenverzeichnis von Huber).
Meitzel, Carl: Huber, Victor Aimé. Handwörterbuch der Staatswissenschaften, 3rd edition, vol. V, Jena 1910, pp. 487–488 (mit Schriftenverzeichnis von Huber)
Paulsen, Ingwer: Victor Aimé Huber als Sozialpolitiker, (Königsberg 1931), 2nd edition, Berlin 1956.
Thier, Erich: Wegbereiter des deutschen Sozialismus, Stuttgart 1940, pp. 25–37.
V.A. Hubers Ausgewählte Schriften über Sozialreform und Genossenschaftswesen, in freier Bearbeitung herausgegeben von *K. Munding*, o.J. (1894), Reprint 1990.

Human Resource Management in the German and Austrian Co-operative Banking Industry

DUDO VON ECKARDSTEIN

(see also: *Co-operative Banks*; *Managerial Economics*; *Workers Co-determination*; *Management in Co-operatives*)

I. Introduction; II. The Development of Co-operative Banking as Background of HR-Strategies; III. Trends in HR-Strategies; IV. HR-Strategies in the Future.

I. Introduction

Banking is a service industry. Services are tightly connected to the activities of the employees. Their performance strongly depends on their motivation and their level of qualification. For the bank to be successful they must be a matter of concern to it. Its human resource strategy is of great importance for its survival in competition. Therefore, the competitive strategy of a bank must to a large extent involve a human resource strategy which motivates the bank's work force to perform in the market place.
The aim of this article is to discuss the main characteristics and recent developments of the HR-strategy, which seems to be typical of German and Austrian c-ooperative banking. Due to the fact that in both countries the structure of co-operative banking is of the same origin and since they resemble each other in many dimensions, both countries can be analyzed together. The differences which, however, do exist will be dealt with later on.

II. The Development of Co-operative Banking as Background of HR-Strategies

HR-strategies cannot be understood without their connections to the environment of a bank and with eventual other factors in context with the prevailing situation.
Between 1975 and 1989, the number of co-operative banks in West Germany sharply declined from about 5,200 to 3,200 mainly due to mergers. In this *concentration process*, the average number of employees per bank rose from 18 to 37 (Exhibit 1), while the total number of employees in the co-operative sector increased from 92,600 to 120,200. This growth of the total number of employees is caused by the general growth of the banking market and the increasing market share of the co-operative banks (→ *Operational Size*).

Exhibit 1: Concentration Process in West German Co-operative Banking

Year	Number of Banks	Employees per Bank	Total of Employees
1975	5.196	18	92.600
1980	4.226	24	101.500
1985	3.660	32	117.700
1989	3.223	37	120.200

(Federal Association of German Co-operative Banks)

At the same time, in addition to the head office numerous co-operative banks opened further branches, so that nowadays most banks dispose of branch networks.
The Austrian concentration process is comparable to the German one, but up to now, there have been two at least partly competing branches of co-operative banking, namely the Raiffeisen Group which operates mainly in rural areas and the Volksbanken Group, mainly situated in small towns and big cities. In Germany, both groups merged a long time ago (→ *Central Institutions*; → *Federations*).
The last two decades were characterized by a high level of *competition* between the banking groups in Germany and Austria. Generally, the saving banks as universal banks are the main competitors in the local markets, especially in rural regions and in small towns. In the cities there is additional competition caused by the local branches of the big commercial banks.
Because of the mostly identical character of bank products offered by the main competitors, the *customer-orientation* of the employees has become one of the most important factors in competition.
It is only by the latter that a bank will get an identity for the customers. Customers expect a professional investment and finance counselling by the bank employees; furthermore, it is no longer unusual that the contact between bank employees and clients takes place in the clients' offices or in the case of private clients in their homes in the evening (→ *Corporate Culture*).
New and more sophisticated bank products demand a *higher professional qualification* of the employees, which means increasing average salaries, a factor which is strengthened by the high demand for well trained employees in the banks' labor market, a de-

mand which is especially intense in the congested urban areas.

In addition, the *decrease in working hours per week* (and nearly six weeks of paid holidays p. a. in Germany, about 5 weeks of paid holidays p. a. in Austria) contributes to increasing labor costs and high labor demand.

III. Trends in HR-Strategies

The objective of the following exposition is to demonstrate the four major fields of influence within the scope of a personnel strategy (*Beer, Spector* et al. 1984). Each will be dealt with independently. However, theoretically and in practice they are to be seen in a unified strategic context (*Hamel* 1989).

1. The Structuring of the Labor Force

Because of the expanding business volume and the concentration process in co-operative banking, the average number of employees per bank doubled in the period from 1975 to 1989 in Germany (Exhibit 1). Big co-operative banks have several hundred employees. Also in Austria, the average size of a co-operative bank has grown considerably. (Furthermore, by law the managing board has to consist of at least two members (→ *Management in Co-op*eratives).) First of all this means that a third and in some cases also a fourth level of hierarchy had to be introduced.

In combination with this quantitative expansion of the labor force, the average level of qualification had to be raised according to the more sophisticated demands of customers and bank products. While in the early seventies many employees working in direct contact with the customers at the bank counter had no specific training in banking, today there are nearly exclusively highly qualified employees with at least two to three years of practical and theoretical vocational training, a fact which pushes average labor costs upwards.

Today recruitment of junior employees mainly refers to a higher educational level: often employees have – in some banks most of them – university entrance qualification, while 15 years ago even junior high school level was unusual.

In comparison to the big commercial and savings banks there is only a very small (1–2 %) percentage of employees with a university degree.

Apparently only few academic applicants are looking for a job in a co-operative bank. On the other hand, the big commercial banks succeed in recruiting the highly talented university graduates. Many co-operative banking officials interpret this difference as a long-term strategic disadvantage. Meanwhile trainee-programs and other measures have been developed in order to get or to stay in contact with those students who have got a vocational training in a co-operative bank before in order to motivate them to come back after having finished their university studies.

Finally, the sex as a distinctive mark of labor structure has to be mentioned: women are represented at the proportion of about 50–60 % at the lower levels of hierarchy; on the higher levels, their proportion strongly decreases and on the boards nearly no women can be found (→ *Women and Co-operatives*). In view of the same entrance qualification of male and female applicants for the vocational training there seems to be a substantial potential in qualification to resolve the recruitment problems of the future.

2. Employee Compensation

Both in Germany and in Austria the basis of pay systems in co-operative banking are labor contracts, negotiated by the union and an employers' association. There are differences concerning the bargaining parties: In Germany, the employees are represented by the industry union which comprises the following sectors: commerce, banking, and insurance (Gewerkschaft Handel, Banken und Versicherungen) (→ *Co-determination*; → *Workers Co-determination*), while the co-operative banks are organized in the employers' association of co-operative banks (→ *Industrial Relations*).

I estimate, that less than 10 % of the employees of co-operative banks are members of this union. Inspite of this low proportion, the agreements are applied to the whole labor force in this industry. (Would the employers refuse to apply the conditions of the agreements to the non-members – which is legally possible – they would compel them to become members, too and thus support the union.)

In Austria, the employees are organized in the union of the employees of all private enterprises, which involves bargaining with the Chamber of Banks (compulsory membership for all co-operative banks), so that the agreed conditions are valid for all employees without regard to their union membership.

Principally, the agreements provide a *time-related pay scheme* with monthly salaries plus 1 or 2 additional monthly payments, so that employees totally receive 13 – 14 salaries p.a. mostly without any relation to their individual performance.

The amount of the salary mainly depends on the job characteristics, i.e. on the qualification required by the job and the responsibility assumed. In addition, the number of years a person is employed by the bank is of importance, especially in Austria, where the agreements contain an elaborated seniority benefit with a seniority-based pay increase every two years, for a period of about 30 years. Hence, the salary on the last seniority step is about 200 % of that of a beginner in the job. In Germany, salary increases due to seniority end after 11 years in the banking sector.

Seniority benefit systems tend to keep labor costs low as long as the work force is growing, because most of the newly hired employees are young and do not earn high salaries. However, with the number of employees being relatively constant at present, the average age of employees is rising and subsequently the average amount of seniority salaries.

In addition, the above mentioned higher average qualification level also induces salary increases. Both tendencies are cumulative and contribute to higher labor costs, which must be compensated by higher productivity rates (Exhibit 2).

Exhibit 2: Changing of Salary Groups and Time of Occupation in Cooperative Banking in (West)Germany (in %). (Federal Association of German Co-operative Banking and calculations by the author)

Years in Banking	Salary Group			Years		
	1–3	4–6	7–9	1980	1985	1989
1–2				7,8	7,4	4,5
3–4				12,0	10,4	8,0
5–5				13,0	10,5	10,1
7–8				10,7	9,2	10,6
9				5,5	6,1	8,1
10				10,8	15,3	11,7
11				40,2	41,1	47,0
1980	13,8	61,7	24,5	100,0		
1985	11,7	62,8	25,5		100,0	
1989	10,7	62,6	26,7			100,0

The individual bank must at least pay the salary fixed in the labor contract. Also, many banks grant voluntary pay rises in addition to the amount fixed in the labour contract in order to prevent employees from changing the employer or to express a special appreciation. Because of the level of the seniority-based salaries for employees who have been in their jobs for many years, banks see almost no latitude to pay further performance-based wage rises in Austria.

There is a discussion about the question whether the income of a bank employee should also be influenced by his/her individual job performance in order to motivate him/her to higher performance. The supporting argument holds that only monetary incentives would enable a bank's sales force to compete with an insurance company or a broker, which motivate their salesforce to a large extent by premiums for sold contracts; the adversary position stresses that apart from the additional costs premiums would induce bank employees to neglect customers' interests. In fact, many co-operative banks pay premiums for sold savings agreements with home savings banks (Bausparvertrag) and for sold insurance contracts, products for which co-operative banks act as agents of allied home loan banks and insurance companies and for which it is relatively easy to measure the employee's (selling) performance. On the other hand, it is methodically difficult to measure the personal performance of the staff members in selling products in the credits and savings business.

Meanwhile some banks have begun to experiment with performance-based pay schemes, but up to now no generally accepted schemes have been developed.

3. Training and Development

Owing to the growing importance of a highly qualified workforce, most co-operative banks make great efforts in training and development (*Kolb* 1990).

The vocational training for beginners as a practical and theoretical comprehensive professional education according to a standardized schedule, which is obligatory for all banks, is a German speciality. As mentioned above, it takes 2 – 3 years corresponding to the level of prior general education. Today nearly all employees in German banks have to complete this training and pass an examination with the Chamber of Commerce before they are definitely hired. Furthermore, most university graduates in business administration and banking who start working with a bank have completed this training before beginning their studies.

In Austria, this kind of vocational training exists as well, but co-operative banks do not consider it a necessary requirement for an employee. They offer a trainee program of some months for their beginners and additionally train them on the job.

The vocational training constitutes the basis of professional work but is insufficient to meet the demands of many jobs, especially the higher ranked ones. In order to prepare the young employees for their future tasks, the bank must offer supplementary training of superior standard which has been developed and organized by the regional co-operative banking associations. Normally, the single bank is too small for organizing seminars on its own. The system of supplementary training consists of a modular system of seminars through which the participants are expected to obtain the qualification for more demanding and specialized jobs. For careers organized according to standardized models (for example counselor for commercial or wealthy private clients, bank accountant, executive of internal services) the seminar modules are aggregated to a training program which lasts for about five years. For those who have successfully completed it, it is quasi coronated by a final management course which is offered by central academies of co-operative banks. Its graduates obtain a certificate which in Germany as well as in Austria is mandatory to become a member of the board of a co-operative bank.

The banks' role in training and development is to plan the employee's career as a sequence of jobs in the bank coordinated with the participation in the modular seminars. Thus the bank has to apply the usual instruments of personnel management such as performance appraisal, appraisal interviews, joint career planning.

On the whole, this training and development system

is of a highly sophisticated standard and seems to be rather efficient. But there are also some critics who point out that this system is too formal and rigid. It does not sufficiently take into consideration the individual demands for development and interests of each trainee as well as leadership behaviour. In addition, some critics say the personal development is neglected, especially in regard to leadership and social skills, while the professional training is strongly emphasized (→ *Early Warning Systems*).

4. Leadership Style and Work Design

As long as the co-operative banking units were small, the leadership style of the head of the units was in a rather "natural state". He/she knew each employee from a daily face to face contact and gave instructions whenever it seemed necessary to him/her. Leadership then was no subject for considerations. This situation changed with the growth of the banks. The daily personal contact between head and most of the employees diminished, sometimes employees working in branches are almost unknown in the central office. At that stage many banks tried to structure the leadership behavior of the supervisors at the newly created second level of hierarchy (→ *Management in Co-op*eratives). The former natural state of leadership was to be replaced by a formal leadership system definining the prerogatives and the expected behaviour of the supervisors in relation to their subordinates. In many banks leadership guidelines and job descriptions were implemented which should serve as a normative basis of leadership. In my view, these first steps towards a rational regulation of leadership, which mostly date back to the seventies, often produced a rather bureaucratic and supervisor oriented leadership style which did not favour cooperation of the employees.

Today, leadership in co-operative banks is characterized by tendencies towards management by (consented) objectives and at the same time by more job autonomy for the employees. The role of supervisors consists more of supporting, coordinating and developing the employees than of giving instructions to them. The high demands of customers and bank products require that the employees mostly work self-controlled (→ *Corporate Culture*).

This tendency is emphasized by the fact that most banks have replaced their former functional organization by new customer-oriented patterns which place the responsibility for the whole business with a customer in the hands of one employee. This enables cross selling to be affected. Hence, the enrichment of their jobs becomes more distinct in comparison to the former functual organization and needs a more self-controlled professional work based on a broad training. In a similar sense the same tendency can be seen with regard to the branch managers who have been made responsible for the branch and its local market.

A trend to more self-controlled work also consists of the implementation of teams (→ *Management Teams*) which are totally responsible for customer groups and which have to organize their work to a large extent by themselves. A further advantage of this organizational pattern is a high degree of flexibility in time regarding the substitution of absenteeism caused by training programs or illness and the reduction of individual working hours per week at constant opening hours of the bank.

An indicator of the reduced hierarchical emphasis in leadership style is the widespread implementation of project groups and in some cases even formal quality circles. They include a large number of employees in the decision-making process, with positive contributions to motivation and personnel development.

IV. HR-Strategies in the Future

Many leading executives of co-operative banks have become aware of the importance of personnel strategies as a significant factor of competition in the banking sector. In order to enhance competitiveness, they systematically derise the adequate HR-Strategies to be adopted. Their effort is focused on two objectives: on the one hand, to cut down labor costs by an economical deployment of labor and on the other hand, to improve performance in particular as regards the quality of customer counselling.

The first objective should be achieved by an efficient organization of the activities resulting from an increased integration of edp (→ *Data Processing*) in the so-called "mass-business". Labor should be substituted by installing automatic teller machines (automatic cash dispensing, printing of account statements and credit transfers by the clients themselves). The improvement of quality in the field of counselling is to be affected by intensified training programs, mbo-systems as well as thorough screening and assignment of employees. At the same time tedious manual tasks in this field should increasingly be computerized. Thus labor capacity could to a larger extent be utilized for counselling services.

Bibliography

Beer, M., Spector, B. et al.: Mananaging Human Assets, Free Press, New York 1984.

Hamel, W.: Innovative Instrumente des Personalwesens für Kreditgenossenschaften, in: Genossenschaften und genossenschaftswissenschaftliche Forschung, ed. by J. Zerche, Ph. Herder-Dorneich, W.W. Engelhardt, Regensburg 1989, pp. 103–112.

Kolb, Christian: Betriebspolitische Maßnahmen zur Sicherung der Wettbewerbsfähigkeit einer Kreditgenossenschaft des kreditgenossenschaftlichen Verbunds, Arbeitspapiere des Forschungsinstituts für Genossenschaftswesen an der Universität Erlangen-Nürnberg, Band 13, 1990.

Incentives of Co-operatives

GÜNTHER RINGLE [J]

(see also: *Promotion Mandate*; *Workers Co-determination*; *Co-determination*; *Human Resource Management*; *Labour-Management*; *Business Policies*)

I. Inducement/Contribution Theory and Co-operatives; II. On the Relevance of Incentives (Inducements); III. Effects of Co-operatives on the Members; IV. Perception of an Individual Value of Incentives; V. Rationally Not Conclusive Behaviour.

I. Inducement/Contribution Theory and Co-operatives

The inducement/contribution theory originated in considerations on coalition theory first proposed by *Barnard* (1938) and developed further by *Cyert*, *March* and *Simon*, among others. Briefly, the core of this basic approach, derived from behavioural theory, is this: a self-determining individual decides to join an organization or, respectively, to maintain an already existing relationship with it, if the total inducements offered him by the organization exceed, or at least equal, the contributions expected of him, that is to say, if he as an individual sees a favourable balance between inducements given and contributions expected.

The principle of this decision process, if specific features are taken into consideration, can be easily applied to co-operatives. Whoever joins a co-operative or keeps up his membership intentionally expects to be able, by partaking in the services and activities of this organization as a member, to utilize the co-operative's potential benefits in order to realize his own individual goals (motives, needs, interests). Benefits (in the widest sense) offered by the co-operative make possible for participants in the organization a better achievement of economic and meta-economic goals through co-operative means.

In reference to *March* and Simon, we include among the benefits just mentioned all the material and immaterial inducements which are given at the moment or are probably to be had in the future from a relationship with the two co-operative sub-systems – membership group and business organization – and which for the recipient possess a subjective satisfaction value or utility. The co-operative, however, does not offer such inducements, relevant for fulfilling individual aims, gratuitously. Recipients of these services are required to make regular compensation in the widest sense (bear disadvantages or burdens). Taken as a whole, these contributions must have a lower (at least not a higher) value in the mind of the individual than the inducements given, so that the complex participatory relationship "member-co-operative" comes into being or, if already established, will be continued.

II. On the Relevance of Incentives (Inducements)

Every organization will make efforts to create inducements or – with a more recent term: incentives which meet people's needs as a means of recruiting new members, of ensuring the satisfaction of individual participants in the organization, or raising obligatory as well as voluntary contributions, and of retaining present membership. Beyond that, what reasons are there for the fundamental importance of incentives for formal organizations such as co-operative systems?

1) First of all, the offering of appropriate incentives serves to protect the organization against dissolution, change of objectives, and/or failure of the cooperation (*Barnard*).
2) The organization, by varying its system of incentives, exerts an influence upon the behaviour of its participants and their decisions on contributions (*Fuchs*).
3) Incentives must be sufficiently attractive to draw in enough contributions to safeguard the survival of the organization (*March and Simon*).
4) The organization must see to it that through a suitable set of incentives it can attract and keep as participants those persons or firms in the economy whose contributions best support the purpose of the organization (*Eschenburg*).

III. Effects of Co-operatives on the Members

1. The System of Potential Incentives

The co-operative is the one who offers incentives. Recipients of those incentives are as a rule individual members or their firms (individual incentives), but they can also be groups from among the members (group incentives). The most important types of incentives characteristic of co-operatives are the following:

a) Incentives which have to do with the economic relationship to the co-operatives:
   – Guaranteed access to markets for affiliated members or their firms.
   – Chances to take advantage of services provided exclusively by the co-operative.
   – Satisfaction of the need for economic security (security for the enterprises of members, pro-

tection of the membership group against disadvantages from sharp competition).
- Chance to obtain services that are comparatively better suited to the needs and wishes of members.
- Financial benefits such as favourable prices and modes of payment, refunds based on patronage, interest on share capital.
- Practical advantages (proximity, parking facilities, opening hours), customer-oriented services, and "humaneness" of the co-operative business (friendly personnel, relaxed atmosphere).
- Ready supply of information and advice from the co-operative relevant for making one's own decisions.

b) Incentives which have to do with a relationship to the co-operative as an organization:
- Concrete incentives to the members or volunteer services (payments or compensation for expenditure, better access to information, experience gained).
- Satisfaction of social needs (contacts with other people, feeling of belonging to the co-operative group, opportunity to participate in co-operative self-government, social contacts, friendships, mutual aid).
- Satisfaction of ego needs (recognition and praise by others, rewards, prestige, chances to exert influence and personal power, self-respect, pride in altruistic dedication).
- Satisfaction of the need for self-fulfillment (welcome changes, utilization of personal freedom in the co-operative, personal growth, achievement, extension of creativity potential).

Interest in participation is primarily determined nowadays by rational and egoistic motives. For members as well as non-members, the attraction of the co-operative stems mainly from the profile of its effectivity as a business partner (*Kleiss*). Participation is expected first of all to be economically expedient (prices and interest rates, dividends or patronage refunds, services, etc.). In this respect cooperation is welcomed as a way of satisfying material needs. But one would over-simplify the facts if one measured the potential of a co-operative to benefit its members solely by the attractiveness of its economic effects. Social and emotional incentives (prestige, esteem, or friendship) or opportunities for co-determination can prove to be equally effective incentives for participation (*Olson, Etzioni, Schwarz*).

For every co-operative the provision of an adequate set of incentives helps maintain the co-operative's existence as well as further its chances of success. However, for potential recipients to react to those incentives, they must become aware of the offered stimuli in the first place, must understand them, and must be guided by → *motives* giving rise to an evaluation of those incentives (*Reber*). The management of the co-operative will have to attend to communication at regular intervals, in order to make known the incentives offered by the co-operative, to explain them, and to bring into effect their potential for influencing behavior and for integrating. After all, the incentives of the co-operative must be effectively used in order for individual benefits to be provided.

2. Interdependence of Incentive Areas

The effectiveness of possible incentives in the economic relationship to the co-operative depend on the extent to which the co-operative facilities are actually utilized (degree of frequency). It will be essential to include them in an internal co-operative communication system – *Dülfers'* management-member information system (MMIS) – which is oriented to the exchange of services and contributions. On the other hand, incentives having to do with a relationship to the co-operative as an organization can be realized through participation in membership meetings, participation in their decision-making, voluntary service in a co-operative body such as the board of directors, supervisory council, advisory board, or project team, or other ways of identifying with the co-operative.

These two incentive areas are by no means isolated from each other. To be sure, incentives regarding the economic relationship to the co-operative serve primarily to influence the behaviour of members as business partners (utilization incentives), whereas incentives regarding the relationship to the co-operative as an organization aim mainly at motivating members (→ *Motives for Cooperation*) to take part in co-operative self-government (active participation incentives). But the acceptance of active participation (→ *Workers Co-determination*) incentives has a positive influence on the acceptance of utilization incentives. By fulfilling ownership functions on all three levels – decision preparation, decison-making, and supervision – the members safeguard the effectiveness of their relationships as customers to the co-operative business. They can at least help determine that the services provided by the co-operative be tailored to the needs of the members and that the other elements of marketing policy (→ *Diversification Strategies*), such as prices (→ *Pricing Policy*), conditions, and service, be oriented to benefiting the member customers.

On the other hand, particularly the inner circle of the membership will take an active interest, through their efforts in the self-government of the co-operative, in keeping up the level of incentives attained by the co-operative in its business relationships with members. From this standpoint, the non-economic stimuli of a co-operative system are part of the prerequisites for its effectiveness.

In every consideration of the various potential incentives of a co-operative, it is obvious that ultimately it is the complete set of incentives which counts for present or potential members, even though its components may be valued differently by different individuals. For example, temporarily inadequate incentives regarding the economic relationship can be compensated for by higher incentives with regard to the relationship to the co-operative as an organization, and vice versa. A decision to join an organization or to continue as a member will be determined by the difference, considered favourable by the individual member, between the value of total incentives given and the value of the total contributions expected (positive incentive/contribution balance).

IV. Perception of an Individual Value of Incentives

1. Urgency of the Needs to be Satisfied

From the point of view of potential or actual participants in an organization, only those services of the co-operative count as inducements which have a subjective value with regard to the fulfillment of real or latent needs. Whether certain material or immaterial services have the effect of incentives depends on how strong individual needs are and to what extent they have in each case been satisfied (the supply situation).

Of course, for a certain portion of those people interested in cooperation, there is an inherent incentive solely in the goods and services forthcoming from an economic relationship with the co-operative, for example in the satisfaction of needs for economic security or in the availability of financial and/or practical advantages. These potential or actual partners do not (yet) expect the co-operative to satisfy any other needs having to do with a relationship to the organization as such. Examples here might be social, ego, or self-fulfillment needs. These needs simply may not be felt to exist, or they may be too rudimentary still, or the co-operative may not be considered a sufficiently satisfactory source of fulfillment.

Improvements in the satisfaction of needs lead to shifts in the urgency with which individual needs are felt. The degree of urgency of specific needs influences the incentive value which a partner attaches subjectively to services rendered by the co-operative. Understandably, the incentive value of services filling dominant needs of a particular individual is higher than the value of services aiming at less urgent motives. When and insofar as there is a predominance of needs which can be satisfied in the sales relationship with the co-operative, then membership is particularly attractive through the fact that member-customers enjoy a clearly recognizable preferential treatment by the co-operative business in comparison to non-member-customers who do not.

These considerations can be summed up, according to *Ackermann*, in the following statement: the higher (or lower) the degree of urgency is which a (potential) participant in an organization feels regarding needs which can be satisfied by material and/or immaterial services of the co-operative, the higher (or the lower) is the incentive value which the participant sees in those co-operative services. A shift in the priority of needs provokes a change in the expectations which individual participants place on the co-operative's incentive system.

2. Suitability of Available Incentives for Satisfying Needs

Given the achieved level at which needs are met, and given the distribution on the scale of urgency with which needs are felt, the incentive value of co-operative services is determined by the extent – perceived by outsiders or members and used as a criterion for their decision whether to join or to remain in a co-operative – to which the co-operative's services might satisfy their needs. A (potential) partner judges the degree of suitability of co-operative services from subjectively perceived "rewards" in the form of basic and supplementary benefits. In addition to the satisfaction of material expectations, a benefit may also be seen in the fulfillment of immaterial needs of an emotional, idealistic, or traditional nature.

The incentive value of a particular service offered by the co-operative is determined by the extent to which it appears capable to the individual of satisfying his needs. Thus one can formulate the statement that the higher (the lower) a potential participant in an organization estimates the degree of adequacy of services for fulfilling his needs, the higher (the lower) he estimates the benefit or incentive value of those services (*Ackermann*). If a service lacks incentives value, then it also lacks suitability for satisfying needs.

V. Rationally Not Conclusive Behaviour

Dülfer warns against a one-sided application of this incentive/contribution concept, which would result from an interpretation of incentives and contributions as monetary quantities in a returns-cost calculation. One must also consider those components which cannot be expressed in monetary terms, and must relate incentives and contributions to the whole motivation structure (also cf. *Schwarz*). According to the incentive/contribution theory, then, the following holds true: the greater the benefits are which an individual expects to gain from joining or continuing working with a co-operative, compared as a whole with the contributions he is expected to make to it, that is, the greater the balance of benefits (of utility) is, the stronger will be his tendency to participate.

In reality, people often behave in a way which is incompatible with a purely rational motivation structure. On the one hand, potential partners outside the organization are approached by members and persuaded to join, or they may decide to participate out of local or family tradition much as they would join a community group like a sport club, the volunteer fire brigade, or the local chapter of a political party. In these cases, a person becomes a member without the rational step of carefully weighing the advantages over against the resulting burdens.

On the other hand, it happens that people maintain their membership in the co-operative and continue to draw services from the co-operative business even though it does not pay economically. As *Louis* has noticed, if members become dissatisfied with the services of the co-operative business, they tend to be very slow about terminating an existing business relationship; and particularly if they have been members for many years, they often do not withdraw their membership even when their own individual balance of incentives and contributions turns out to be negative. *Eschenburg* suggests two explanations for this behaviour (→ *Theory of co-operative Cooperation*) which are not included in rational considerations (the latter might be, for example, a high cost of membership termination): a member may stay in the organization out of loyalty to the co-operative or out of apathy, in which case he foregoes making a purposeful decision entirely.

Neither of these two forms of behaviour – joining a co-operative however paradox the reason may be in the light of the incentive-contribution theory, or not dissolving a membership despite dissatisfaction with the structure of incentives offered by a co-operative or with the intensity of its incentives – refutes the basic reasoning underlying behavioural theory. Actually, it just shows that one has to differentiate between members (or non-members) of a co-operative who decide more or less rationally and others who – under certain internal or external situations with regard to a co-operative – decide in a way which is more irrational and not easy to identify through motivation theory.

Bibliography

Ackermann, Karl-Friedrich: Anreizsysteme. Handwörterbuch der Betriebswirtschaft, 4th ed., Stuttgart 1974, col. 156–163.
Barnard, Chester I.: The Functions of the Executive, Cambridge, MA 1938.
Cyert, Richard M./March, James G.: A Behavioral Theory of the Firm, Englewood Cliffs, NJ 1963.
Dülfer, Eberhard: Betriebswirtschaftslehre der Kooperative (Kommunikation und Entscheidungsbildung in Genossenschaften und vergleichbaren Organisationen). Göttingen 1984.
Eschenburg, Rolf: Zur Anwendung der Anreiz-Beitrags-Theorie in Genossenschaften, Zeitschrift für das gesamte Genossenschaftswesen, vol. 38, (1988), pp. 250–262.
Etzioni: Soziologie der Organisationen, 2nd ed., München 1969.
Fuchs, Michael: Unternehmung und Wirtschaftsverband – das Problem der Beteiligungsentscheidung, Diss. München 1969.
Kleiss, Herbert: Warum Genossenschaftsmitglied? Genossenschaftsforum, No. 2/1979, p.16–17.
Lipfert, Helmut: Mitgliederförderndes Kooperations- und Konkurrenzmanagement in genossenschaftlichen Systemen, 2nd ed., Göttingen 1988.
Louis, Dieter: Zur Stabilität von kooperativen Organisationen, Zeitschrift für das gesamte Genossenschaftswesen, vol. 29 (1979), pp. 295–311.
March, James G./Simon, Herbert A.: Organizations, 3rd ed., New York – London 1961.
Olson, Mancur: The Logic of Collective Action, Public Goods and the Theory of Groups, Cambridge, MA 1960.
Reber, Gerhard: Anreizsysteme, Handwörterbuch der Organisation, 2nd ed., Stuttgart 1980, col. 78–86.
Ringle, Günther: Beitritt zur Genossenschaft als Entscheidungs- und Motivationsproblem, Göttingen 1989.
Schnabel, H.X.: Die Gestaltung der Unternehmensordnung aus interessenpluralistischer Sicht, Gelsenkirchen 1982.
Schwarz, Peter: Erfolgsorientiertes Verbands-Management, Vol.1: Grundlagen der Verbandsbetriebslehre und der Verbandsführung, St. Augustin 1984.
Wartenburg, Günter: Stellung und Aufgaben des genossenschaftlichen Aufsichtsrates, Düsseldorf 1981.
Willeitner, Siegfried: Genossenschaftliche Mitgliedschaft, Handwörterbuch des Genossenschaftswesens, Wiesbaden 1980, col. 1215–1221.

Industrial Relations – An Integrative Concept

HANS WILHELM HETZLER

(see also: *Relationship Patterns*; *Organizational Structures, Co-operative*; *Group Theory*; *Group, the Co-operative*; *Co-determination*)

I. Subject and Definition; II. Conflict and Cooperation; III. Theoretical Development; IV. Criticisms and Modifications.

I. Subject and Definition

The concept of industrial relations originated in Great Britain under the influence of the pioneering work of *Sidney* and *Beatrice Webb*. This endeavour can be interpreted as the equivalent of what in German speaking countries is called the "social question". In a wider sense, it refers to industrial society as a whole. Used in this way, it includes "practically any institutional human relationships which can be distinguished in the industrial context" (*Moore*). Usually, however, it is applied to individual and collective employment relationship, structured as well as unstructured. For some authors the term "industrial relations" comprises both formal and informal aspects, whereas others concentrate on the formal regulations and the bargaining processes which result in collective agreements (*Parker, Brown,*

Child, Smith). Equivalent terms are "labour relations" or "employment relations".

Parallel to the increasing complexity of industrial societies and the conditions of employment, industrial relations became a subject matter of academic interest. In the Anglo-Saxon world this led to the formation of a separate academic discipline. In other countries as in Germany, Austria, and Switzerland the field is treated as an interdisciplinary problem, including economics, labour law, political and social sciences. Because of the great variety of aspects concerning industrial life, it is justified to regard the industrial relations approach as an integrative concept.

The development of industrial relations as a discipline is characterized by an ongoing attempt to primarily substitute descriptive work by more theoretical analysis. Whereas originally emphasis was given to the collective actors involved, in particular to trade unions, subsequent efforts were made to discuss industrial relations within the framework of theoretical models. These attempts took place under the influence of social theory. In the given conflict the dichotomies of differentiation and integration on the one side, and cooperation and conflict on the other are important (*Willke*). These two terminological pairs are related, but they are not the same. Conflict is the result of contradictory expectations between individuals or groups of individuals. The contradictions can be resolved by means of cooperation in the sense of levelling out the disagreements of the opposing parties. Differentiation, in contrast, refers to diverging structures which are relevant for individual or collective action. This view leads to the question of the existence of integrative forces as the basis of a normative orientation.

II. Conflict and Cooperation

It is obvious that social differentiation is a major source of conflict. A well known example is the division of labour. This process is inherent to any society. Its particular importance for industrial societies, however, encouraged social theorists to find an answer to the question why, in spite of the disruptive effects of differentiation society in the sense of an integrated entity is possible. Sociological analysis does not, as classical economics does, concentrate on the usefullness of the division of labour but, rather, on the cohesive elements involved. From a functional point of view, division of labour as long it is not anomic in its character, makes possible solidarity i.e. social integration (*Durkheim*). Whereas the dialectic relationship of differentiation and conflict refers to structural aspects of society, the dichotomy of conflict and cooperation implies the behavioural dimension.

Of the four categories mentioned, conflict deserves primary recognition. It plays not only a role in social thinking since the ancient days of philosophy, it also serves as the key variable to understand industrial relations. There are two ways of explaining the existence of social conflict. One is based on the anthropological assumption of the plural uniqueness of the individual. In the radical version, men appear as wild animals which would destroy each other, unless adequate institutions would enable them to live together in peace (*Hobbes*). A modification of this approach can be found in the social philosophy of utilitarism, where it is argued that, in spite of the persue of private interests or selfish behaviour, social order is the unexpected consequence (*Smith*). For the materialists, conflict is the result of the struggle between capital and labour. As such it is a disruptive element which lasts as long as these two classes do exist.

This point of view is also reflected in industrial relations theory. Marxist authors are reluctant to make use of this approach. In their eyes, the term industrial relations is nothing else but an euphemism for the deeprooted conflict between capital and labour. This means that in the long run, labour relations as they exist today have to be overcome by the joined effort of the working classes. With this perspective in view, in 1975, a British scholar claimed to have developed the first systematic outline for the analysis of industrial relations in the materialist tradition (*Hyman*). The advantage of this procedure can be seen in the fact that it takes into account the dynamic aspects. Insofar, it is of some value for the historical description of the labour relations. Because of its dogmatic assumption, in particular the strict rejection of any integrative effects, it does not provide a theoretical basis for reasonable solutions.

A different and for the treatment of industrial relations more suitable approach with regard to conflict can be found in the sociology of *Simmel*. In his view, not only conformity but also antagonistic behaviour can lead to social integration. He insists that society is the result of both, converging and diverging tendencies. The American sociologist *W.G. Sumner* called this ambivalent kind of social relationship "antagonistic cooperation". He considers it as "the most productive form of combination in high civilization", with the implication that lesser antagonisms are overlooked in order to work together for great interests. Although not coined with regard to industrial relations, this expression fits well into this frame of reference. The division of labour which characterizes industrial society, depends on co-operative behaviour. Both aspects – cooperation and conflict – are two sides of the same coin. On the one hand, there is a contradiction between the parties involved. It is in the interests of the business enterprise to keep costs, including wages and fringe benefits, as low as possible. For the employees, on the other hand, income is the basis of their material existence. Therefore, they try to earn as much as possible. Another source of disagreement are the working conditions. One of the early reasons for industrial conflict was not only the low standard of living of the working classes but also the managerial prerogative of how work has to be done and the expected compliance on the side of the employees. The history of industrial relations, therefore, is marked by the two issues of material improvement of the employees and their demand to participate in the decision making process of the business enterprise to avoid alienation.

Discussing industrial conflict, there is a strong tendency to argue mainly from a moral point of view. The solution is expected to come from changing the nature of men or from the fiction of an egalitarian society. As experience shows, these attempts do not lead very far and often enough they produce inadequate results. This does not mean that moral arguments have to be entirely excluded. In order to handle social conflict, however, they have to be differentiated from the political dimension. Only when these two dimensions are treated separately, conflicts become manageable in an acceptable way. Industrial Relations as an academic discipline provide a conceptional framework for understanding the courses and conditions of labour conflict as well as the institutional possibilities of its settlement.

III. Theoretical Development

In the course of this development, the nature of *industrial conflict* went considerable change which is also reflected in industrial relations theory. Specialists in this field originally concentrated on isolated aspects, in particular on the trade union movement and the chance of industrial democracy. In this context, conflict has been interpreted as a structural problem which could only be resolved violently. This approach has been modified in three ways: first, by reconsidering the functions of industrial conflict; second, by introducing the concept of its institutionalization, and third, by integrating the relevant aspects of industrial relations into a joint theoretical framework. The first major attempt in this direction was taken by *John Dunlop*. His pioneering work "Industrial Relations Systems", published in 1958, is a milestone in the theoretical discussion and empirical research. His endeavour is "to provide tools of analysis to interpret and to gain understanding of the widest possible range of industrial relations facts and practices.".

Systems thinking was established in the natural sciences where it spread out under the influence of the General Systems Theory to overcome the increasing specialization in modern science by "the formulation and derivation of the principles which are valid for 'systems' in general" (*von Bertalanffy*). By definition, systems are integrated wholes. They are separated from the environment by a factual or hypothetical boundary. A particular system consists of a number of elements. The relatively stable interrelations between these parts or patterns in a unified whole are called "structure". The relevance of each part depends on its contribution for the system. Thus, none can be understood isolated from the whole. Therefore, in structural-functional analysis, attention is given first to the structural aspects which in a second step are explained with respect to the functional requirements of the system. With his theory, the American sociologist *Talcott Parsons* makes an attempt to explain the conditions of social order, which is regarded as "one of the very first of the functional imperatives of social systems" (*Parsons* and *Shils*). This means that the system has the tendency to equilibrium and integration. This is the desired state and any deviation is regarded as dysfunctional.

Dunlop adopts this so-called "structural-functional" approach without major alterations. Whereas, the end in the Parsonian model, however, is self-maintenance, *Dunlop* introduces the concept of rule making as the purpose of industrial relations systems. Rules and regulations appear in various forms such as laws, constitutions of collective actors like trade unions or employers associations, collective and individual agreements. *Dunlop* sees it as the central question of his theory "to explain why particular rules are established in particular industrial relations systems and how and why they change in response to changes affecting the system."

The rules themselves he divides into substantive and procedural regulations. The first category refers to the material terms and conditions of employment such as wage rates or working hours. They are the result of negotiations of individual or collective actors, managers or their representatives on the employers side and workers or their representatives on the employees side. In addition to these two parties, the role of the state becomes increasingly important. These three groups of actors constitute the so-called "*tripartite-system*", a major characteristic of modern industrial relations system (→ *United Nations System*).

Whereas the substantive rules refer to the ultimate output of the system, the procedural rules refer to the process of rule making. They are the result of mutual agreements between the actors on how they want to proceed during negotiations in pursuing the interests of their members. With regard to this function, it can be said that these kinds of regulations are the core of what has been called the "institutionalization of industrial conflict" (*Dahrendorf*). What originally appeared as unconditioned struggle between capital and labour has been gradually transformed into a relationship governed by specific rules. Those are partly generated by the actors themselves and partly by state legislation.

This influence is an important variable characterizing various national industrial relations systems. In the Anglo-Saxon countries, for instance in Great Britain, the state traditionally is reluctant to interfere with the relations between capital and labour. In Germany, on the other hand, legalism is one of the main features of the industrial relations system. Differences of this kind can be explained by the specific histories of industrialization and social chance. Thus, Germany is regarded as a "retarded nation", both politically and economically. In comparison to early industrialized countries, especially to Great Britain, attempting to avoid unrest, the German authorities took a far more active role in social policy and social legislation. In the meantime, state intervention became a general tendency all over the world. Nevertheless in this respect there are still significant differences affecting national labour relations in industrialized countries. The systems approach can be applied to different *levels of interaction*. The main ones are the shop floor, the firm, and the level above enterprise. At the same time this means differentiation of the actors involved and the issues being negotiated. It is worth mentioning that the different levels are interrelated. Thus, attention has to be given not only to the interactions going on at the various levels but also between them. In this context, two general tendencies can be observed: first, an increasing emphasis on qualitative in contrast to quantitative issues, and secondly, a shift from collective bargaining at the level above the enterprise to the single firm and even to shop floor bargaining.

Both tendencies are closely interrelated. Increasing demands for technical and organizational flexibility result in negotiations about qualitative issues. They vary from plant to plant and, therefore, cannot become subject of regulations concerning an industry as a whole. Quantitative issues like wage rates or working time, of course, are still important. In some industrial relations systems, however, the center of gravity to the same degree shifts towards the individual plant in which qualitative rule making becomes important. With respect to this development, the question arises whether it indicates "an irreversible trend in European industrial relations" (*Roberts*).

As in structural-functional theory, *Dunlop* distinguishes between the system and its *environmental context*. Like the system, the latter is an abstraction of reality. In the given model, it is restricted to the following three sets of variables which influence the behaviour of the actors and the process of rule making. The first is the technical conditions of the working places. As mentioned above, this part of the environment is of significant influence in the field of industrial relations. It affects not only the forms and functions of organizations but also the interactions between individual and collective actors. For instance, are the operators of a high-tech installation in a better position to exercise pressure than their collegues who work with conventional machinery. As the second segment of the system environment *Dunlop* introduces market and budgetary constraints such as market position, size of the enterprise, homogenity of the market and its expected development in the sense of expansion or contraction. In addition, he takes into consideration the characteristics of labour and other factor markets such as the structure of the labour force, the availability of manpower and the proportion of the labour costs in relation to the overall costs.

The author states that these characteristics are relevant for the distinction of particular industrial relations systems. As the third analytic dimension *Dunlop* uses the environmental influence of power and the states of the actors involved. Among others, the status of the workers, or their organizations depend on their relation with the managerial hierarchy, with public agencies. The status of managerial hierarchies in turn depends on the relations with the workers and their representatives, competing hierarchies, and public agencies. With respect to the status of this group of actors, *Dunlop* distinguishes for idealized types: dictatorial, paternalistic, constitutional, and participative. The third and final segment is the influence exercised by the state administration.

An important issue are the relations among the three corporate actors. In *Dunlop's* model, they are supposed to be independent from each other. In reality, however, there do exist connections, in particular between the state on the one side and the trade unions and employers associations on the other. Whereas, originally, there was a more or less strict separation between the state and the economy, working conditions were the result of market forces. This situation changed with the rise of interest groups and their recognition as legitimate. For example, the trade unions were initially suppressed and forbidden, then they were tolerated, and finally, they became acknowledged. This development paralleled structural and functional changes within the organization. As the trade unions became mass-organizations, they involuntarily changed from an antagonistic opposition to an integrative part of the social-economic-system.

This role implies a variety of contracts and exchanges with the government. The same is true for employers associations. Under these so-called "neocorporatist" conditions, it depends on the dominate political forces, which side can bring its influence to bear with regard to policy making and state legislation.

A problem, deserving further attention is the organization of the interests of labour and capital. They are both *voluntary organizations*. As membership is not compulsory, members enter and stay within the organization as long as they expect that their interests are served adequately. One of the major issues in this context are the results of collective bargaining. They are public goods in such countries as Germany, in which the trade unions and the employers associations are the only bodies entitled to make collective agreements. What they achieve becomes the contractual basis for the whole labour force within an industry, whether members or not. This leads to different consequences for each side. Being mass-organizations, the trade unions have to balance their capacity for compromise between what is offered by the employers and what is expected from the members on the one hand, and their ability to get this compromise accepted by their members on the other hand. The employers associations see themselves confronted with the problem of free riders. This is also true for the trade unions. But organizing a great number of people the latter are less affected by this problem than their counterpart with a comparatively small number of members.

IV. Criticisms and Modifications

Structural-functional theory is an attempt to show the conditions making social order possible. The explanation is based on two assumptions. First, certain "functional requirements" have to be satisfied in order to maintain a given structure. In a macro-theoretical perspective, these functions correspond with certain segments of society such as politics or economy. Second, the integration of the social system requires a minimum of shared values by its members. With respect to these assumptions, *Parsons'* model has been criticised for being static and supporting the social status quo. As *Dunlop* adopts this approach in its essential parts, the objections are more or less the same. In addition, he denies making conflict a central category of his system. In his eyes, "industrial strife" is a surface sympton of more fundamental characteristics of rule administration in a given industrial context.

To a great extend, theoretical development in the field of industrial relations took place by modifying *Dunlop's* model. As a representative of the so-called "Oxford approach", *Flanders* emphasises industrial conflict and its institutionalization by means of industrial bargaining. Others demand the consideration of behavioural variables such as attitudes, beliefs, and motivations. These alterations leave the substance of the original model unchanged. Therefore, the question arises as to which kinds of problems it can be applied.

The concept of institutionalization by itself implies an integrative effect, regardless of the quality of the relationship under discussion. Furthermore, it is questionable whether the premise of common ideologies remains valid in a pluralist society and in industrial relations characterized by divergent interests rather then by ideological consent as their starting point. Finally, it is worth considering whether *Dunlop* was well advised to adopt the macro-theoretical frame of reference from the structural-functional approach with the implication that industrial relations fulfill a functional requirement for society as a whole. Perhaps he in this way intended to underline the disciplinary relevance of his subject.

In evaluating his model, it is important, however, to consider whether it is a contribution to the explanation of macro-theoretical relations or whether it is judged in view of the more modest aim as serving as an instrument for systematic gathering and handling of empirical data. In spite of its theoretical deficiencies, *Dunlop's* model with the differentiation of actors, levels of interactions as well as rules and regulations as their outcome provides an analytical tool which can be readily used for the description of industrial relations systems. In this more restricted sense, his model was fundamental in establishing industrial relations as a recognized academic discipline. It became particulary fruitful in comparing different systems across time, countries, and industries. A great deal of research is carried out by the Institute for Labour Studies, an organization affiliated with the International Industrial Relations Association and the International Labour Office (ILO) in Geneva. The systematic gathering of empirical data on the basis of a framework accepted throughout the world makes it possible to detect general tendencies, which in turn can be used for theoretical purposes.

Dunlop assumes that a distinct system of industrial relations emerges in every country. Moreover, each of these systems is basically consistent with the institutional environment of the society it belongs to. The actual importance of this statement for social politics in Europe can hardly be overestimated. With the completion of the Common Market, questions arise about eliminating economic barriers and how to harmonize various sectors, including labour relations. In other words: most different industrial relations systems have to be integrated on the supra-national level. Finding an adequate solution for this difficult problem is the great challenge to all engaged in the vast field of industrial relations.

Bibliography

Bertalanffy, Ludwig von: General Systems Theory, Harmondworth, 1968.
Dahrendorf, Ralf: Sozialstruktur des Betriebes, Wiesbaden, 1972.
Dunlop, John T.: Industrial Relations System, New York, 1958.
Durkheim, Emile: Über soziale Arbeitsteilung, 2nd. ed., Frankfurt (Main), 1988.
Endruweit, Günter, Gaugler, Eduard, Staehle, Wolfgang H., Wilpert, Bernhard (eds.): Handbuch der Arbeitsbeziehungen, Berlin – New York, 1985.
Flanders, Allan: Management and Unions, The Theory and Reform of Industrial Relations, London, 1970.
Hobbes, Thomas: De Homine, London, 1658.
Hyman, Richard: Industrial Relations, A Marxist Introduction, London, 1975.
Kerr, Clark, Dunlop, John T., Harbison, Frederick H., Myers, Charles A.: Industrialism and Industrialized Man Reconsidered – Some Perspectives on a Study of the Problems of Labour and Management in Economic Growth, Princeton, 1975.

Moore, William E.: Industrial Relations and the Social Order, New York, 1946.
Parker, S.R., Brown, R.K., Child, J., Smith, M.A.: The Sociology of Industry, 2nd. ed., London 1972.
Parsons, Talcott: The social System, London, 1964 (1951).
Parsons, Talcott and Shils, Edward A. (eds.): Toward a General Theory of Action, Cambridge (Mass.), 1951.
Roberts, Benjamin C.: Ist die Verlagerung zur betrieblichen Ebene ein irreversibler Trend in den europäischen industriellen Beziehungen? in: Hetzler, Hans Wilhelm (ed.), Arbeitsstrukturierung durch Verhandlungen, München – Mannheim, 1980.
Simmel, Georg: Soziologie, 4th ed., Berlin, 1958; Smith, Adam, The Theory of Moral Sentiments, 1st. ed., 1759.
Sumner, William G.: Folkways, Boston, New York etc., 1st. ed., 1940 (1906).
Webb, Sidney and Beatrice: Industrial Democracy, London, 1897.
Weiss, Manfred: Labour Law and Industrial Relations in the Federal Republic of Germany, Deventer, Antwerp, London, Frankfurt, Boston, New York, 1987.
Willke, Helmut: Systemtheorie entwickelter Gesellschaften, Dynamik und Riskanz moderner gesellschaftlicher Selbstorganisation, Weinheim und München, 1989.

Informal Co-operatives

JULIUS OTTO MÜLLER [S]

(see also: *Group, the Co-operative*; *Group Theory*; *New Co-operatives*; *Autochthonous Co-operatives*; *Pre-co-operative Forms*; *Relationship Patterns*)

I. "Informal"; II. Informal Co-operatives in History; III. Modern Informal Co-operatives; IV. Sociopolitical Significance; V. Conditions for Functioning and Existence.

I. "Informal"

A co-operative is informal, if the group in question forms an independent co-operative self-help community according to its own conceptions, but at the same time refrains from or escapes being formally recognized for political, social or religious motives. Informal co-operatives are often in opposition to the formal (legal) system of superordinate ruling institutions, generally the state with its political, ideological and social constitution. Therefore, they wish to or need to shut themselves off from the public. If there are legal regulations for co-operative forms of cooperation, such as formal registration in a public register of co-operatives, regular management, supervision, fair distribution of profits, book-keeping and auditing, an informal co-operative will ignore or reject them.

II. Informal Co-operatives in History

Informal co-operatives are as old as social ruling systems. Historically, co-operative organizations are to be considered as informal, if the state did not tolerate them for reasons of assumed or actual threat to its security or for violating binding social norms (→ *History before 1800*).

Therefore, some of these cooperations acted underground. Some popular examples are:

- co-operatively organized traders' "*collegia*" of the late ancient Graeco-Roman era with secret oppositional activities directed against the Roman colonizer;
- village co-operatives of the high and late middle ages, intercommunally and co-operatively organized, that had made the fight against exploitation by the authorities and/or the landowners one of their (secret) aims amongst other aims of their co-operative community (peasant uprisings from the 12th to the 16th centuries);
- spiritual and religious fraternities (→ *Religious Co-operatives*), which could live only according to their spiritual and religious convictions – opposed to state religion – in an informal organization, generally as fully cooperating life companionships, such as the Hebrew Essenes of late antiquity, the Bohemian Brothers (Rebaptizers) since the 16th century, probably the English Quakers in the 17th century, and others (→ *Religious Co-operatives*);
- the free religious "*communautés*" in France (with communal farms and separate families) under the protection of religiously inclined seigneurs.
- socialist joint-production, workers' and consumer co-operatives: in France, where → *joint-production co-operatives* were strictly prohibited after 1848, and where a few secretly survived until the 1870s; in Italy, Brazil, the U.S.A., including the communes of Utopian Socialism (→ *Conceptions, Co-operative*), which failed or were not implemented, connected with names such as *Morus* ("Utopia"), *Campanella* ("Sun State"), *Cabet* ("Icaria"), *Fourier* ("Phalanstère"), → *Owen* ("New Harmony"); in England: socialists and chartists (before Rochdale), with ideas of self-organized cooperation in the political and economic struggle against capitalist economy and the industrial state (in part they were forcibly suppressed). Well known examples in the early 20th century were the artists' and life reformers' commune of "Monte Vérita" (Italy), and those of the "Jugendbewegung" (Germany).

They all had a stimulating influence on the formation of modern informal co-operatives in the late 20th century.

III. Modern Informal Co-operatives

1. Conditions of Formation

In the U.S.A., earlier than in Europe, even at the beginning of the 1960s, there was strong criticism of industrial civilization. The cultural system of late industrial societies suffers from its basic structures, which are determined by the economic institutions: an uncritically optimistic belief in progress, the seemingly unlimited technological possibilities, manipulability in terms of socio-economics and market psychology, dependence on material values, technocratic and bureaucratic excessiveness, the spreading of "imperial" claims to power. To the same extent as progress in industrial development could provide mankind with material advantages and physical relief, man was made superfluous in the production process and his natural everyday needs were neglected. Family structures as the basic structures of society then break down, social relationships tend towards anonymity, the ethical foundations of the basic human order go into a decline. Many people become mentally immature, passive, marginalized and cease to carry responsibility. The gap between rich and poor widens, and so does the poverty rate itself. Also the basic structures of life are more strongly endangered than ever before through the destruction of the biosphere and the ecological equilibrium (→ Environment Protection).

Faced with these manifestations of cultural decline, it is not only larger segments of the younger generations that question or reject the norms and patterns of behavior of industrial civilization. Life styles and work styles, expectations of position, legal norms, food and medicine, behavior towards nature and the earth are equally subject to the question of alternative orientation. Originating in the U.S.A., a movement of sub- and counter-culture develops, within which, after theoretical analysis of its intellectual forerunners – e.g. *Herbert Marcuse, Paul Goodman, Charles Reich, Timothy Leary, Murrey Bookchin* and others, of Eastern religious wisdom (e.g. Zen-Buddhism, Sufi), of *Rudolf Steiner's* Anthroposophy, increasingly practically oriented concepts emerge. Movements towards an alternative and counter-culture gradually spread to all industrial countries.

"Wanting to be different" is related to an ideal image of man in harmony with nature and his mental, physical, spiritual powers and needs. The general aims of these movements tend towards economical use instead of waste, ecological compatibility, the fulfillment of needs instead of profit-making, soft technologies instead of hard ones, a clear and integral concept. Furthermore, the limitation of the analytical concept of nature, opening up of an awareness of more than just economics and technology, self-denial instead of abundance and waste, community instead of isolation, variety instead of specialization and professionalism, openness and exchange in network-like relations, decentralization, co- and self- determination according to competence, non-violence and peace. Such a complex catalogue of aims is, however, expecting too much of the "Alternatives".

"Green Movements" emerge from this direction of thinking and acting, the "counter-culture" becomes an "intermediary culture", in whose projects not only "dropouts", but also sympathizers from the establishment become involved, bringing ideas, knowledge and funding. Co-operative-like informal cooperation and "new" communal co-operatives, often adopted from examples in history, play a considerable part, at least temporarily (→ *New Co-operatives*).

2. Urban Location

In the large and medium-sized towns of America and Central Europe there are organized projects and networks functioning in the form of co-operative-type unions, e.g.:

- → *consumer co-operatives* with affiliated purchase and sale associations to provide their members with healthy food products. Especially in university towns, so-called "*food co-ops*" develop in connection with healthy nourishment;
- the Association of Left-wing Booksellers, which unites into a co-operative informal co-operatively organized bookshop collectives (which are often living communities at the same time) from the times of the '68 students' movement;
- the "Newspaper Co-operative" in Berlin, where several newspapers utilize communal production plants for their papers and publications;
- the "Mehringhof" in Berlin, which unites seven prospering alternative projects on an informal co-operative basis. The people involved jointly purchased a well-preserved building complex, which serves as a communal workshop for 30 different projects. All projects involved are tenant and owner in one. They have equal seats and votes in the "management council". All capital is "neutralized" by means of a special legal construction;
- the "Politische Offensive Verkaufsorganisation (POVO)" (Political Offensive Sales Organization), founded as an initiative of the "Arbeiterselbsthilfe Frankfurt" (a workers' self-help organization), the shepherds' co-operative of "Finkhof" (Allgäu) and a carpenters' and furnishers' co-operative in Vienna are considered examples of border-crossing projects. The aim is to market products from self-managing enterprises all over Europe: watches and clocks by "LIP" in France, jeans by "Salik" in Belgium, wine from rural communes in Occitania and Italy, wickerwork from co-operatives in Portugal, cement by "Erwitte" and glass by "Süssmuth" in Germany;
- numerous "local community networks" on a smaller scale, self-managed in an informally co-operative way, such as town district development projects, organizations of families, shops and individual persons within a town district. They want to revitalize their surroundings on a multi-functional basis, not least in order to reinstate

neighborhood help, cultural identification with the common habitat and a solid network of small and medium-sized enterprises with local money circulation;
- old peoples' communes provide mentally, physically and spiritually stimulating tasks for self-help in the living patterns of senior citizens;
- communal slum redevelopment and community networks are well advanced in the U.S.A.. Informal co-operative organization springs to mind in this case. In so-called "small networks", living communities, families and single persons unite to partly support themselves and to provide handicraft, educational and nursing services together. Forms of communal ownership and communal budgets can be observed. In Switzerland, groups of this sort are mainly located in small towns and rural areas.

3. Rural Location

Beyond the small networks, a multitude of rural communes proliferated in country areas, in the U.S.A. in the 1960s, in Europe in the 1970s. They partly followed old examples, such as the kibbutzim in Israel after 1900, the rural communes of the "German youth movement" in the 1920s, the behaviorist communes on the basis of models of *Skinner's* scientific psychology (e.g. "Walden II", U.S.A.), or Eastern spirituality and American counter-culture projects such as "Hippy" and "Open Land".

"Rural commune" in this case means a type where people with aims in common get together in a family-like, rural living and economic community, in order to achieve a certain socio-economic independence. Gardening, agrarian, domestic and technical activities are usual, providing services and jobs on the side for additional earnings are possible. An important aspect of the community is cultivating of the soil, which is ecological and subsistence-oriented. The products are mostly planned, divided and used jointly, often on the principles of spiritual or secular ideologies. Mutual social, intellectual and economic relationships with the rural, more rarely with the urban surroundings and with other communes are desirable, following the regional network concept, normal weekly markets included. In a (rural) commune all generations can be involved in the communal living pattern. Traditional social patterns of ownership and association, family and sexuality are not necessarily observed. A multitude of models and mixed types of different agrarian and trade communes can be found. The ideal group size will be found, as long as (extended) "family" relations remain possible, and relief from physical work and relative economic profitability can be assured (approx. 50 people with the respective supply of production factors, technical and organizational skills and possibly the necessary exterior contacts for exploitation). Smaller membership numbers – less than ten – predominate and place a burden on everyday work. Widely known communes, such as "Twin Oaks" and "The Farm" (U.S.A.), "Auroville" (India), "Findhorn" (England), "Eden" and "Finkhof" (Germany), "Arche" and "Longo mai" (France) today exist in their second or third generation. But most rural communes disappear again after a short while, because the hard conditions of existence cannot be met.

IV. Sociopolitical Significance

Taking into account the sociopolitical functions informal co-operatives have given themselves, they do not seem to attribute any explicit socially or politically relevant "missionary" significance in the sense of an alternative social economy to the industrial society, especially in the critical formative phases. Geographical isolation, internal human and economic problems, a lack of competence and of the ability to engage in communal life all set constraints to exterior activities of this kind. In the framework of a "dual economy", informal co-operatives can create an informal economic sphere within modern, highly developed industrial societies both in the city and in the country, which does not arise from the need for growth, but from an individual and social fulfillment of basic needs which is at peace with nature and the world. Particularly, functioning informal co-operatives are able to provide people from the industrial sector with additional alternatives for work and survival during economic crises. Examples are projects for provisioning people with healthy food products, nutritional and health therapies for drug addicts and people suffering from psychological problems, useful employment schemes for unemployed juveniles and adults which are satisfying from a human point of view, ecologically directed redevelopment activities in cities, rural areas and forests, etc.

V. Conditions for Functioning and Existence

The realization of the ambitious aims informal co-operatives have – particularly in working and living communities – requires that extensive conditions of existence be fulfilled in a permanent, disciplined way (→ *Strategies*):

- committment to intellectual aims, to a communal idea and/or ideology, which must not be allowed to fall into neglect;
- being prepared to solve socio-economic and sociocultural crises following the decline of industrial society;
- the existence of a clear concept (binding rules, statutes, rights and duties) for arranging work and life, leadership and co-determination, establishing and maintaining the enterprise, participation in the manufacture and consumption of the products;

- selection and rejection of members after a trial period;
- attention to related intellectual attitudes and needs (on a global cultural scale), repudiation of senseless ideas of growth and consumption;
- limitation of the number of members in view of long-term economic and social viability;
- professional skills and competence; having the courage to plan the division of labour jointly;
- respect for individuality, granting freedom for self-actualization (physically, intellectually and spiritually);
- democratic, selfless, limited, temporary leadership without domination (e.g. leadership council), regular re-election;
- alternating mental and physical work;
- legal protection of the economic basis;
- education and self-education of adult members and their children;
- cultivating human contact and economically advantageous external relations.

This canon for the formation and continued existence of informal co-operatives shows the art of cooperating informally. At the same time, it explains the major problems of their existence and why so many people fail when making an attempt at this form of cooperation.

Bibliography

AG Spak: (ed.), Alternative Ökonomie, 3 vols., Berlin 1977–1979.
Borsana, Gabriela et al: Monte Verità. Antropologia locale come contributo alla riscoperta di una topografia sacrale moderna, Milan 1978.
Buber, Martin: Pfade in Utopia. Über Gemeinschaft und deren Verwirklichung, Heidelberg 1950.
Gyzycki, Horst, v., Habicht, Hubert: Oasen der Freiheit, Frankfurt a.M. 1978.
Friedmann, Yona: Machbare Utopien, Frankfurt a.M. 1978.
Horx, Matthias: Das Ende der Alternativen oder die verlorene Unschuld der Radikalität, Munich 1985.
Huber, Joseph, (ed): Anders arbeiten, anders wirtschaften, Frankfurt a.M. 1979.
Huber, Joseph: Jenseits von Markt und Staat. Netzwerke der Selbsthilfe und Eigenarbeit. In: Liberal 1980 H. 17.
Infield, Henrik F.: Utopia und Experiment, Göttingen 1956.
Jarchow, Klaas, Klugmann, Norbert, Heumarkt: Versuche anders zu leben zwischen Stadt und Land, Berlin 1980.
Landauer, Gustav: Beginnen. Aufsätze über Sozialismus, (Neumarkt), Hilversum 1977.
Linse, Ulrich, (ed.): Zurück o Mensch zur Mutter Erde. Landkommunen in Deutschland 1890–1933, Munich 1983.
Morris, David, Hess, Karl: Neighbourhood Power. The New Localism, Washington, D.C. 1975.
Müller, Julius Otto: Alternative Culture and Co-operative Rural Communes. In: Co-operatives in the Clash between Member-Participation, Organizational Development and Bureaucratic Tendencies,pp.66. 147–167, London 1985.
Penth, Boris, Hollstein, Walter: Alternativprojekte. Beispiele gegen die Resignation, Reinbek 1980.
Peters, Jan, (ed.): Die Geschichte alternativer Projekte von 1800 bis 1975, Berlin 1980.
Rossei, Giovanni: Utopie und Experiment. Studien und Berichte, (Zürich 1897), Berlin 1980.
Roszak, Theodore: The Making of a Counter Culture, New York 1968.
Vollmar, Klaus-Bernd: Landkommunen in Nordamerika, Berlin 1975.
Wurm, Shalom: Das Leben in den historischen Kommunen, Cologne 1977.

Institutional Economics: Co-operatives

HOLGER BONUS [J]

(see also: *Conceptions, Co-operative*; *Theory of Co-operatives*; *Theory of co-operative Cooperation*; *Economic Order*; *Societal Form, Co-operative*)

I. Introduction; II. Plastic Production Factors; III. Opportunism.

I. Introduction

In the language of the "new institutional economics", the (classic) co-operative is a hybrid organizational form (*Rubin, Williamson* 1985, *Bonus* 1986) and in this respect is related to → *franchising* (*Rubin*). Whereas the co-operative company operates centrally in the frame-work of a corporate hierarchy, members remain decentralized in terms of their own activities; they are answerable to the market rather than being subject to the co-operative hierarchy (→ *Economic Order*). The co-operative thus presents a situation in which hierarchichal and market elements are fused together.

II. Plastic Production Factors

1. Definition

The term "plastic production factor" (essentially the application of individual experience – a nonquantifiable entity) must be introduced at the outset in order to clarify the above mentioned asymmetry (*Alchian/Woodward*). A broad spectrum of legitimate options is available when putting such factors into practice; those executing them must first assess and then choose among these options without having the selection criteria formalized (*Williamson* 1985). In most cases this concerns job-specific know-how that is gradually accumulated in the course of certain complex activities, which, in colloquial speech, can be called "experience", "instinct", "special feel", or even "sixth sense". First-class results cannot be achieved without the full job-specific application of plastic factors; on the other hand, since such factors are intangible and nonquantifiable, it is impossible to prove whether they have been appropriately applied. After all, there are no standards for their use. An example of this is "doing the job according to regulations": Taken literally, this would mean suspending the application of plastic factors, which in turn would not only lead to failure, but to a situation in which the individual involved could not be held responsible.

2. Peripheral vs. Central Positioning

Such plastic factors can either be applied "peripherally" or "centrally" (*Bonus* 1986). The consequences of an inappropriate peripheral application turn against the individual in command of the factor and do not affect the organization; the quality of the plastic factor input is separable from that of the company output. On the other hand, the consequences of a central factor application turn immediately against the company: the quality of the company's output cannot be separated from that of plastic inputs.

a) Peripheral Positioning: The Farmer

The farmer is an excellent example of peripheral factor application. In his or her daily work the farmer faces and makes decisions that entail risk and that are based on experience or special feel – plastic factors. If a farmer is part of a company hierarchy (e.g. a → *kolkhoze*), the central organization will hold him accountable for mistakes (e.g. failure to take appropriate measures in spite of an approaching storm). However, management can hardly evaluate the local situation and must be prepared to concede that the failure cannot be traced to the negligence of the farmer (→ *State and Co-operatives, Socialism*). In order to protect itself from such a situation, management must issue directives adherence to which can be objectively evaluated. The problem is that such directives rob the farmer of the opportunity to act according to his own judgement, thus precluding the optimal application of plastic factors. The results speak for themselves. One need only look at the state of agricultural production in the former Soviet Union. On the other hand, if a farmer works independently it is in his own interest to optimally utilize accumulated experience and special feel to improve results. If he fails, he alone must bear the consequences. In general, peripheral plastic factors of production should be externalized from the firm, and transactions with them should be conducted across the company boundary.

Skilled craftsmen provide a further example of the need for peripherally applied plastic factors to operate independently. The less standardized local conditions are (in other words, craftsmen must work with greater plasticity), the fewer the advantages of a large company and the greater the importance of autonomy and self-employment. A corporation for craftsmen would not be economical.

b) Central Positioning: The Bank Clerk

The bank clerk provides a counter example. A large degree of experience, prudence and talent are involved in the conversations he holds with customers, in other words, plastic factors. If he worked independently, that is, sold individual transaction settlements on the market for bank commissions ("discrete incentives", see *Bonus* 1986), he would continuously be tempted to abuse his circumspection and talent in order to settle as many transactions and acquire as many commissions as possible. Customers would no longer be served properly, and the bank's reputation would be jeopardized. The bank clerk is therefore positioned centrally and must be a part of the company hierarchy.

c) Discrete versus Cumulative Incentives

Because plastic factors cannot be appropriately supervised from outside, the organizational structure must be such that individuals have an incentive to apply them at their own discretion in the interest of the company. This calls for appropriate institutions: peripherally positioned plastic factors are to be placed outside the firm and subjected to discrete incentives, while the same factors are to be placed within the firm and subjected to "collective incentives"(→ *Incentives*) when they are centrally positioned (*Bonus*, 1986): Thus the bank clerk is not payed according to the current success of his activities, but his salary will reflect the value which the bank expects from him over a longer period of time. In negotiating compensation, the bank is led by his past performance – on his reputation within the company, as it were. This encourages the employee to place particular value and importance on dependability and thoroughness. In order to assess his average behavior and compensate him accordingly, the bank must arrange a longer-term contract with him which, nonetheless, cannot be completely comprehensive.The bank cannot write down all services it is going to expect because it is impossible to foresee what will be required in the future. A relational contract is therefore arranged which is confined to the establishment of an employment relation, whereby the employee is bound to follow instructions from his superior (see *Simon, Williamson,* 1975, 1985). This is how hierarchy emerges.

3. Precarious Relations

a) Franchising

Precarious relations result when a peripheral factor is in some sense also centrally positioned, or when central factors cannot be bound to the company hierarchy. Hybrid organizational forms are called for in such cases. An insurance representative, e.g., is positioned peripherally and should be rewarded by means of discrete incentives (commission). However, his sloppy physical appearance or inadequate dependability can gravely harm the reputation of his employer, i.e., the insurance company. Therefore the agent is remunerated in part by commission while at the same time receiving a fixed salary and being subject to company directives and control. His independent position becomes interspersed with hierarchical elements. Another example is franchising. The franchisor provides the franchisee with know-how and a reputation (→ *Franchising*). The franchisee (e.g. the owner of a wine-tavern) can be adequately employed in a peripheral manner, that is as a sole-proprietor. Insofar as management negligence of the wine-tavern can bring the entire chain into disrepute, the franchise contract must include precise regulations and control devices. Hierarchical instruments are not only in the interest of the franchisor in this case, but also of the other franchisees who are likewise dependent on the reputation of the chain as a whole (*Williamson*, 1985).

b) Co-operatives

Co-operatives are another example of hybrid forms (→ *Theory of Co-operatives*). Their members are peripheral vis-à-vis the co-operative company and must operate independently in order to utilize advantages of smallness; these advantages take the form of a superior overview of the local conditions and a high degree of decentralized flexibility. Simultaneously, the co-operative company utilizes the economies of scale associated with large production runs and bargaining clout in its purchasing and sale agreements. The combination of both the advantages of local smallness and of regional muscle render the co-operative an economically potent and socio-politically attractive configuration (→ *Configuration*).

c) Why Form a Company?

Nonetheless, it remains to be clarified why the independent members decided to set up a company hierarchy instead of contracting on an open-ended basis with selected suppliers or customers. At first glance it would appear that they did so to secure economies of scale in production and to gain shelter from monopoly power. However, closer inspection reveals that this is not true. Neither argument suffices to explain this phenomenon – and thus the hybrid character of the co-operative (*Bonus*).

As *Williamson* (1985) demonstrated, the economic "penalty" for in-house production becomes more burdensome the more pronounced economies of scale from production are; one would accordingly forego "market aggregation economies" if forming a joint company. The existence of pronounced economies of scale is therefore a point against rather than in favor of producing an item in one's co-operative as compared with of buying it on the market from a large supplier who specializes in its production. Another potential argument in favor of establishing a co-operative is that it might be used to weaken the monopolistic power of a supplier or customer. To illustrate this, reference is often made to the usurers found in rural regions of Germany around the time of → *Raiffeisen*. These local money-lenders ended up driving small farmers off their land. However, before arguing this way, one must first establish the reason for the usurers' monopoly power, which was of a local nature, as even co-operatives were helpless against truly large cartels (*Faust*, 1977).

d) The Cost of Information

In the case of the credit co-operatives, the underlying reason for the monopoly power of local money-lenders was the high cost of information. Small-scale farmers, merchants and businessmen were unable to obtain short-term operating credits because at that time it was much too costly for urban banks to get hold of the detailed information it took to evaluate the risk associated with offering loans to individuals, given the small amounts involved. But the same was true for moneylenders, who had to spend much time to collect and to update local information. Due to the limited range of local information, the operating base of moneylenders had to be small and could not sustain more than one of them, which explains the fact that they mutually respected each other's district. The credit co-operatives (→ *Co-operative Banks*) escaped this dilemma by tapping the local information pool and thus taking advantage of the intimate knowledge the members had of each other. Still, the co-operative bank districts had to be small, which implied that the local credit co-operative held a monopoly of its own (*Bonus*, 1986).

e) Co-operative Central Banks

Since the discretionary decision to grant credits, which implies the evaluation of associated risks, represents a highly plastic factor, a precarious relationship emerged between co-operative banks and their customers. The local, viewed as a central and plastic factor of production, should normally be tied into a joint enterprise of the members. At that time, the customers themselves should not be part of such a hierarchy, because they held a peripheral position vis-à-vis the company. This explains how the hybrid form of the co-operative evolved: The bank was made subject to a hierarchy controlled by its own customers, such that the members' transaction-specific dependency from their bank could no longer be turned against them.

Other co-operatives (e.g. dairy co-operatives [*Bonus*, 1986]) (→ *Classification*) can also be seen as hybrid forms which serve the institutional requirements of transaction-specific dependencies.

4. Transaction-specific Quasi-rents

a) Transactions and Specificity

The "new institutional economics" is based on the concept of the transaction, which indicates the transfer of a good or service across a technologically separable interface (*Williamson*, 1985). "Transactional costs" are essentially the costs of getting information and providing institutionalized security for such transactions. Such security is necessary to the extent that the transaction-specific factors are utilized, i.e., factors losing value when applied to something other than their original purpose within a given chain of transactions (dairy equipment, for example, can only be converted to other purposes with great difficulty). Therefore, whoever invests in a chain of transactions is getting dependent on his partner in these transactions according to the degree of "specificity" (that is, the amount of capital tied exclusively to this chain of transactions). Quasi-rents are used to measure transaction-specific dependency (cf. *Klein/Crawford/Alchian; Alchian*): A quasi-rent is that part of the returns from transaction-specific investments that ceases to exist as soon as the transactions are discontinued. In earlier times, if the local credit co-operative would no longer grant credits, then the only alternative was the local usurer. A quasi-rent resulted which consisted of the difference between the financial conditions offered by the co-operative and those offered by the usurer. This difference was large, which constituted a strong (latent) dependency of the members on their co-operative bank.

b) Protective Institutions

High quasi-rents reflect high transaction-specific dependencies and must be safeguarded institutionally because they could be "expropriated" by a transaction partner. This is the way transaction cost economies, basically concerned with transaction-specific-dependencies, developed into an economic theory of institutions. Quasi-rents could have been skimmed off through the local bank, for instance, by attempting to reap profits at its customers' expense through its local monopoly position. Therefore, the customers safeguarded themselves institutionally by means of establishing a co-operative in which the members themselves exercised control.

c) Diminishing Quasi-rents

In the 19th century, co-operatives as an institutional safeguard enabled small economic units to adapt to the evolving markets without becoming dependent on the process. From the point of view of the New Economics, a market difference exists between present-day co-operatives and those of the 19th century. These days, members of a credit co-operative, for example, can receive credits from other banks without any problems; no quasi-rents accrue that must be safeguarded. In the last century, members would sink or swim depending on their relationship with credit co-operatives. Their success was founded on who else was a member to such a degree that the shares were not made transferable. Today, however, members must only risk their payed-up shares and an eventual, extended liability charge. To avoid the risk that some individual members (e.g. the relatively few large landowners) might influence the general assembly to the detriment of the majority of members, each co-operative member was entitled to one vote only, regardless of the number of shares held. This motive likewise is irrelevant today as quasi-rents no longer accrue. Key points of current co-operative law are no longer sustained by economic factors to the extent that they were in the past.

5. Re-interpreting the Promotion Mandate

a) The Need for External Experts

A new interpretation of the wax members should be promoted by modern credit co-operatives is offered by the New Institutional Economics (*Bonus*). Presently, there is little room in the competitive money and financial markets for material promotion in the conventional sense (*Grosskopf*). However, the relationship between the bank and its mid-sized clients is precarious according to the definition provided above. The "small" company of today is part of a closely-knit network of economic relationships, financing agreements, and promotion as well as investment regulations concerning asset values – elements so complex that they can be managed only by specialists (→ *Operational Size*). "Small" companies must be able to function in an independent manner within this complex system of interlocking processes and regulations in order to optimize their competitiveness (→ *Competition*). The "small" company cannot, however, afford a staff of skilled experts like that of large corporations. It must therefore rely on the advice of external specialists, the adequacy of whom it is not in a position to determine.

In today's world, the bank increasingly assumes the position of an external consultant for monetary and financial matters. Viewed as a factor of production, the bank is extremely plastic; it must be vested with comprehensive discretionary judgement while nevertheless playing a central role in advising customers. Plastic and central production factors must be tied to the company hierarchy. It is precisely this configuration that is not possible in a mid-sized company as it could neither use its own experts to capacity nor pay them accordingly. A hybrid organization, like the co-operative, is appropriate in such situations.

b) The Value of Tradition

In modern co-operatives, promotion (→ *Promotion Mandate*) tends to be non-material in nature, taking the form of reliability in the face of precarious ties.

A bank recommends certain options while advising against others. What motives determine its behavior? Only those in the client's interest, or others associated with the size of the commission? Traditions play an important role in the "New Institutional Economics" with regard to precarious ties: What the bank decides to do in unforeseeable or barely controllable situations depends very much on its tradition. A bank with a solidly capitalistic conception of itself will make different decisions in critical situations than a credit co-operative with a firmly rooted co-operative tradition, as the latter will not be primarily interested in profit but rather in its clients' needs. This tradition must by all means be cultivated to make sure that its trust-evoking effect is kept alive. Such a tradition is of invaluable economic significance.

c) Central Banks as Hybrid Forms

The evolution of central co-operative banks (→ *Central Institutions*) can also be interpreted as the result of precarious ties (*Bonus/Schmidt*). As mentioned, the credit co-operatives of the 19th century were geographically confined to small districts whose local informational pools could be used to the banks' advantage. This, however, resulted in a very limited know-how in dealing with larger urban banks on whom they were dependent. For example, when the harvest was sold, the credit co-operative had to invest the surplus revenue profitably, whereas prior to the harvest it had to borrow cash in order to satisfy the demand for local credit. To local credit co-operative, close ties to urban banks would have been quite precarious. Being business partners, the latter would have been operating as plastic factor in a central position; and the local credit co-operative would not have been able to assess the urban banks' standing. The co-operative, then, could not risk depositing their money (entrusted to them by local farmers) with banks unfamiliar to them that they could not in any way supervise. Such banks could invest the money in a risky manner or refuse to place money at the co-operators' disposal even when it was drastically needed. The institutional answer was a hybrid organizational form – a central bank owned by the regional credit co-operatives themselves.

III. Opportunism

1. Bounded Rationality

From this example two important fundamental assumptions of the "New Institutional Economics" can be demonstrated. One of these is bounded rationality. According to this assumption, it is often not possible to fully safeguard oneself by means of contracts against opportunistic abuse of transaction-specific ties to the partner. Either the information prerequisite for such contracts is not at all available, or asymmetrical information is poorly accessible if not intentionally withheld. The second fundamental assumption is opportunism. The opportunist enters coalitions formed in order to institutionally safeguard transaction-specific quasi-rents (*Alchian*) without adhering to the agreed conditions later on. Opportunism transcends the traditional assumption of selfishness, as guile comes into play.

2. Reputation

Taken independently, each of these assumptions is harmless. When, however, opportunism and transaction-specific quasi-rents are jointly present, institutional safeguarding becomes essential (*Williamson*, 1985). Due to limited rationality it is impossible to develop a "watertight" contract; because of transactional dependencies, it is impossible to withdraw from a relationship in a timely manner when something unexpected occurs; and the presence of opportunism renders likely the exploitation of unprotected dependencies (skimming off quasi-rents). In such a situation, a tradition becomes very important as it reduces the likelihood of opportunism. Reputation, the product of continously experienced reliability, relaxes the need for institutional safeguarding. Transaction costs can be dramatically cut this way.

3. The Co-operative Finance Group

a) The Advantage of Being Small

Ties between local credit co-operatives and co-operative central banks are still somewhat precarious these days (*Bonus/Schmidt*). Although the average credit co-operative is much larger presently than it used to be, it is nonetheless much too small to be independently competitive when facing large banks and savings institutions. On the one hand, its strength lies in its smallness, which facilitates fast decisions and flexible local operations. On the other hand, the same smallness amounts to becoming dependent on cooperation with larger banks, which as partners are both plastic and centrally positioned. Failure of a large partner bank to cooperate appropriately turns immediately against the smaller credit co-operative. Furthermore, the larger bank can acquire internal corporate information – for instance while joining a collective meta-credit as it is occasionally granted to a larger customer – which the larger bank might abuse (for example, to entice a customer away from the credit co-operative). Once again, a hybrid form represents the appropriate institutional safeguard of precarious ties. The local credit co-operatives jointly own the regional central bank on which they depend. This hybrid organizational form is the secret of the co-operative banking group's success. It enables credit co-operatives to enter very precarious arrange ments with larger partners (central co-operative bank, Bausparkasse Schwäbish Hall (→ *Building and Loan Societies*), R+V Versicherung (→ *Insurance, Germany*), etc.), because proper safeguarding is provided by means of joint ownership.

b) *The Seduction of Growing Large*

The precarious nature of the co-operative financial group was apparently overlooked during a reorganization effort in Bavaria, Northern Germany and Hessia (*Bonus/Schmidt*). The former central co-operative banks in these regions were transformed into branches of the DG BANK, with the result that the credit co-operatives themselves can no longer exercise any direct influence on them. This jeopardizes the former institutional safeguards and confronts credit co-operatives with the decision to either continue precarious ties without appropriate institutional safeguarding, or withdraw from the co-operative banking group altogether. Both alternatives are "unstable contractually", to use *Williamson's* (1885) expression. Presuming that the credit co-operative opts for the first alternative (no safeguard), then it would no longer be in the position to sidestep directives, uniform conditions and the like, which the DG BANK might introduce in order to standardize business transactions; if the local bank fails to follow suit, then the central organization could gradually tighten its conditions with respect to the reluctant co-operative in order to put it under pressure. If that would happen, however, the hierarchy within the co-operative financial group would be turned upside-down, and after some time the local credit co-operative would be treated as a de facto subsidiary of a corporation. If, on the other hand, the credit co-operative opts to leave the co-operative banking group, then it must cooperate with other larger banks and establish precarious ties with them, again without proper institutional safeguarding. This would sooner or later induce the takeover of such a credit co-operative by the larger partner. Regardless of the way the co-operative decides in such a situation, it will end up becoming a component in a top-down hierarchy – a structure resembling that of a corporation – which would eliminate the specific advantages of the co-operative financial group.

Bibliography

Alchian, Armen A.: Specificity, Specialization, and Coalition. In: Journal of Institutional and Theoretical Economics, 140 (1984), pp. 34–39.
Alchian, Armen A./Woodward, Susan: Reflections on the Theory of the Firm. In: Journal of Institutional and Theoretical Economics, 143 (1987), pp. 100–136.
Bonus, Holger: The Cooperative Association as a Business Enterprise: A Study in the Economics of Transactions. In: Journal of Institutional and Theoretical Economics, 142 (1986), pp. 310–339.
Bonus, Holger: Das Selbstverständnis moderner Genossenschaften, Tübingen 1993.
Bonus, Holger/Schmidt, Georg: The Cooperative Banking Group in the Federal Republic of Germany: Aspects of Institutional Change. In: Journal of Institutional and Theoretical Economics, 146 (1990), pp. 180–207.
Faust, Helmut: Geschichte der Genossenschaftsbewegung, Frankfurt/M. 1977.
Großkopf, Werner: Der Förderauftrag moderner Genossenschaftsbanken und seine Umsetzung in die Praxis, Band 16, Veröffentlichung der DG Bank Deutsche Genossenschaftsbank: Strukturfragen der deutschen Genossenschaften, Teil I., Frankfurt/M. 1990.
Klein, Benjamin/Crawford, Robert, G./Alchian, Armen, A.: Vertical Integration, Appropriable Rents, and the Competitive Contracting Process. In: Journal of Law and Economics, 21 (1978), pp. 297–326.
Rubin, Paul H.: The Theory of the Firm and the Structure of the franchise Contract. In: Journal of Law and Economics, 21 (1978), pp. 223–233.
Simon, Herbert A.: A Formal Theory of the Employment Relation, pp. 183–195. In: Simon, H.A. (ed.): Models of Man: Mathematical Essays on Rational Human Behavior in a Social Setting, New York et al. 1957.
Williamson, Oliver E.: Markets and Hierarchies – Analysis and Antitrust Implications, New York/London 1975.
Williamson, Oliver E.: The Economic Institutions of Capitalism: Firms, Markets, Relational Contracting, New York/London 1985.

Insurance, Co-operative

HANS-DIETER WEHLMANN [J]

(see also: *Classification; Insurance, North America; Financing; Co-operative Banks*)

I. The Principle of Insurance and the Co-operative Idea; II. The Insurance Market in the Federal Republic of Germany; III. The R+V Versicherungsgruppe; IV. The R+V Versicherungsgruppe in its Revised Structure: Facing Europe.

I. The Principle of Insurance and the Co-operative Idea

Living with risks and the problems emerging from them with regard to an adequate safeguarding of one's future are as old as mankind itself. Existence initially became secured through behavioral changes and later through the accumulation of property. In the course of time the natural desire to enjoy security lead to the formation of larger communities in which material losses could be compensated for. Back in the Middle Ages it was possible to protect oneself financially against fire-related catastrophy for a given price: The principle of insurance was thus born (→ *History before 1800*).

In principle, these communities of interest were organized in a co-operative manner. In the course of progressive industrialization one confronted newer and newer risks; the demand for insurance services and benefits grew, but the extent of the individual risks likewise grew. Suitable protection could only be offered by sufficiently large insurance companies.

The natural concern for provisory care lead to the establishment of state and private institutions which offered financial security. In the Federal Republic of Germany, public social insurance undertook basic provisory care for those insured; this is based on a system of adjustable contributions and likewise takes into consideration social aspects. Individual insurance, on the other hand, covers risks according to individual need and one's sense or perception of security. Contributional payments are calculated according to the principle of the insurance industry, that is, each insurance policy – seen statistically – should finance itself (equivalence principle).

The great similarity between the principle of insurance and the co-operative idea (→ *Principles*) is evident when seen against this backdrop. Their common goal is found in the promotion of both the economic development and the existential security of their members and/or customers (→ *Promotion Mandate*). It is merely the manner in which this mission is fulfilled which differentiates co-operatives from the insurance trade.

Co-operative thought rests on the principles of self-help, self-administration and self-responsibility. All institutions affiliated in the co-operative system orientate themselves around co-operative promotion mandate, which should secure the development of the middle classes – wage and salary earners as well as self-employed individuals. The continuing growth of co-operative companies indicates that this idea still possesses great attractivity. Co-operatives are thus an important sustaining element of our prosperity and a guarantee for a pluralistic society.

The insurance business, based on co-operative thought, enables risks that the individual cannot cope with on his own to be borne collectively. An economy evidencing a division of labor above and beyond its national borders in today's world is not imaginable without a differentiated insurance system. This is true analogously for the numerous types of private insurance. Life insurance, for example, is a sustaining pillar of provisory care for old age and surviving dependents. An insurance company must at the same time manage the money entrusted to it by those insured in both a responsible and profitable manner. Redeeming promised insurance benefits, calculating rates in accordance to risks, and generating surplus profit – above all for life insurance – are the common parallels between the insurance business and the co-operative system. The R+V Versicherung in Germany is obligated to the co-operative promotion mandate.

II. The Insurance Market in the Federal Republic of Germany

In order to better understand the importance of R+V Versicherung on the German market and to enable international comparison, several figures of the insurance market should be mentioned. Further explanation of the individual items in Tables I–II is however not necessary.

The safety need in our affluent society, increasing criminality and rising damages by natural forces as well as new laws and technologies favor the development of the insurance industry. Thus, premium receipts rose 9% in 1992 to a current level of 184 billion marks; insurance benefits presently amount to 156,8 billion marks. The over 655,000 employed individuals in this economic sector processed more than 4 million insurance policies, saw to more than 50 million insurance cases and managed financial investments of approx. 840 billion marks. For years both nominal and real growth of payments in the insurance sector have been lying above corresponding GNP growth figures. Premiums in 1992 accounted for a 8.8% share of national income. These figures clearly indicate that security and provisory care are of great importance in Germany.

The Federal Republic of Germany, seen in international comparison, assumes fourth place in the world with per capita revenue from premiums amounting to 2,390 marks. Switzerland has the highest per capita premium expenditure at 4,000 marks, followed by Japan at 3,550 marks and the USA with 3,000 marks. These figures reflect standings as of 1987 as more recent figures are not available for comparison.

The mounting social-political relevance of private provisory care in Germany is represented most poignantly by life insurance. The most important element of private assistance for old age, disability and surviving dependents today, life insurance assumes an influential share in the total volume of provisory care in Germany. Whereas benefits in this branch accounted for only approx. 10% of retirement pensions called for by statutory retirement insurance for wage earners and salaried employees in 1980, this rate had increased to 21.5% in 1992. Within the identical time span, the annual benefits paid to clients increased from 11.3 billion marks to just under 42.5 billion marks in 1992. It can be expected that the services and benefits of life insurance companies will continue to contribute an ever mounting share of total assistance in the years to come.

Provisory care on a personally responsible basis in all branches will most probably continue to increase – also in the other member countries of the European Community. The R+V Versicherung aims to have an appropriate share in this market volume.

III. The R+V Versicherungsgruppe

1. An Historic Overview

The developed structure of the co-operative organization and its close orientation to customers/members as early as the end of the 19th century lead to

Table I: Six Insurance Policies per Resident

	# of Insurance Contracts in millions (annual figures)					
	1980	1985	1988	1989	1990	1991
Life Insurance	65,75	67,48	68,29	69,46	72,38	76,85
Motor Vehicle Insur.	63,00	66,42	71,16	72,73	75,54[5])	87,98[5])
Property Insurance[1])	47,71	52,07	54,84	56,23	57,84	60,53
General Liability	21,90	24,64	26,47	27,40	27,99	30,32
Private Health Ins[2])	20,10	22,56	24,76	26,36	27,40	28,84
Legal Expense Coverage	17,20	20,56	22,73	23,47	24,46	26,58
Private Accident Ins[3])	14,80	17,63	19,71	20,48	21,48	24,88
Other Types[4])p)	110,00	110,00	110,00	110,00	110,00	110,00
Total	360,20	381,36	398,15	406,13	417,04	445,98

These figures include both private and commercial transactions. Source: GDV

1) Insurance for household and personall effects, building, fire, burglary, water damage, plate glass, stormwind; technical insurance; participations included.
2) estimated number of those with set rate policies
3) number of contracts, not identical with the number of individuals vocered.
4) Transport and baggage insurance, additional property coverage (such as livestock insurance), credit insurance, air-risk insurance, nuclear-risk coverage.
5) including area east   p) estimated

Table II: Individual insurance in unified Germany
Estimated Gross Premium Peceipts According to Insurance Branch
(out of policies closed by initial underwriters)

Insurance Branch	1992 [p]		1991		
	Premium Receipts in DM billion (estimated)	Percentage change (estimated and rounded off)	Premium receipts in DM billion	Change in percent	Percentage share of total expenditure
Life Insurance[1])	66.5	+ 9.5	60.774	+13.4	39.2
LAMLE Branches[2])	56.3	+10.2	51.150	+14.9	32.9
Private Health Insurance[3])	22.5	+ 9.6	20.571	+10.2	13.2
Property Coverage	19.7	+ 7.0	18.409	+12.7	11.9
Transport Insurance	2.8	+ 7.0	2.604	+ 9.6	1.7
Credit, Air and Nuclear Risk Insurance[4])	1.8	+ 8.0	1.694	8.5	1.1
GDV Total	169.6	+ 9.3	155.202	+13.3	100.0
– Damage and Accident Coverage	80.0	+ 8.3	73.857	+14.0	47.6
Total Market	184 [p]	+ 9.0	168.906	+14.0	

1) Booked gross premiums by GDV member companies (but not including payments to the reserve fund for the reimbursement of permiums).
2) Liability, Accident, Motor Vehicle, and Legal Expense Coverage (including legal expense coverage for motor vehicles as well as travel service insurance).
3) Including additional benefits, but not those payments out of the reserve fund for the reimbursement of premiums.
4) Nuclear insurance sold both directly and indirectly.
p) Estimated.

co-operative banks including supplemental services – among them insurance – into their palette of offered services (→ *History in 19th C.*). As the formation of a life insurance system even then entailed great requirements, *Friedrich Wilhelm Raiffeisen* initially paved the way for insurance arrangements through the savings and loan associations. When the sale of insurance through banks is mentioned today, one must be aware that → *Raiffeisen* undertook pioneer work in this business sector over 100 years ago.
The continued further development of his vision lead to the establishment of the Raiffeisen Allgemeine Versicherung AG (stock corporation) and the Raiffeisen Lebensversicherungsbank a. G. (mutual society) following the end of World War I in 1922. The Generalverband der deutschen Raiffeisen-Genos-

senschaften founded insurance associations in order to boost credit and consumer co-operatives' efficiency in fulfilling their promotional mission with respect to their members. Bausparkasse Schwäbisch Hall (→ building and loan society) and DG Hypothekenbank (mortgage bank), two companies involved in the combine, were established prior to World War II; the foundations of today's co-operative financial combine were thus laid in the first half of this century. The R+V Versicherungsgruppe needed to start anew in 1946 as customer contacts and financial investments were lost in the confusion following the war. Entrepreneurial initiative was the only asset which survived unscathed, and it was this will to perform which provided the initial company capital upon its fresh start in Niederwall im Rheingau. By the time the companies relocated to Wiesbaden in 1948 the groundwork for a orderly course of business had already been put back to place.

The reestablishment of the R+V Versicherungsgruppe went hand in hand with an expansion of its fields of activity, which included among other things the strengthening of cooperational ties with the commercial co-operatives, the central banks of credit co-operatives (→ Central Institutions) and the Volksbanken (people's banks). Marketing channels through the co-operative banking sector were opened and developed to the advantage of customers and co-operatives alike. The strategy of the combine, "Everything Out Of One Hand" gave decisive impulses to the business development and contributed extensively to the expansion of R+V. The cooperation with marketing partners became clearly apparent in the naming of the co-operative insurance company: "R+V" stands for Raiffeisenbanken and Volksbanken.

Today the following companies belong to the co-operative insurer:
R+V Versicherung Holding AG (holding company)
R+V Allgemeine Versicherung AG (general insurance)
R+V Lebensversicherung AG (life insurance; stock corporation)
R+V Lebensversicherung a.G. (life insurance; mutual society)
R+V Pensionsversicherung a.G. (retirement insurance)
R+V Rechtsschutzversicherung AG (legal expense coverage)
R+V Krankenversicherung AG (medical insurance)
Vereingte Tierversicherung Gesellschaft a.G. (livestock insurance)
Rhein-Main-Rückversicherungs-Gesellschaft AG (reinsurance).

R+V hopes to accompany all active persons on the road to their personal life goals through their advertising campaign "We open horizons". R+V's wide palette of insurance provides freedom and security as well as offers customers new perspectives for realizing the goals they are striving for. More than 11,600 employees, including over 4,300 field agents, in both the headquarters and 16 branch offices ensure that the growing demands of customer service and consultation are being met.

2. Market Position and the Palette of Insurance Services

The individual companies within the R+V Versicherungsgruppe belong to the leading German insurance companies. R+V Versicherung is the largest insurer of banks, the second largest insurer for burglary and theft, the third largest provider of accident insurance, as well as being Germany's fourth largest underwriter of both life insurance and property insurance. This success can primarily be traced to the particular marketing structure and corporate policy oriented around target groups.

The R+V Versicherungsgruppe manages 12,1 million insurance policies which in 1992 brought in gross premium receipts of 6.5 billion marks. Investments of the group amounted to 25.9 billion marks at the end of the 1992 financial year. The following examines the two largest companies more closely, the R+V Allgemeine Versicherung and the R+V Lebensversicherung.

R+V Allgemeine Versicherung AG

R+V assumes a top position among the over 300 composite insurers in the Federal Republic. Gross premium receipts amounted to 3.2 billion marks in 1992 distributed over 8.2 million insurance policies. The development of policy receipts in the past decades (see Graph 1) clearly illustrates the dynamism with which the company has grown. Investments proudly reached 3.6 billion marks by the end of 1992. Despite gross expenditures of 1.6 billion marks for insurance claims in the same year, substantial policy dividends could be granted for automobile and accident insurance. These above-average benefits were made possible through a wide selection of insurance products encompassing all insurance branches.

Overview of Insurance Assortment
Motor Vehicle Insurance
Motor Vehicle Liability Insurance
Automobile Insurance (full and partial comprehensive coverage)
Motor Vehicle Accident Insurance
Travel Service Insurance
Accident Insurance
Individual and Family Accident Insurance
Group Accident Insurance
Travel Accident Insurance
Liability Insurance
Private Liability Insurance
Home and Property Owners Liability Insurance
Business and Professional Liability Insurance
Product Liability Insurance

Property Insurance
Fire Insurance
Burglary and Theft Insurance
Water Damage, Plate Glass and Windstorm Insurance
Related Household Insurance
Related Insurance for Residential Housing
Special Property Insurance
Technical Insurance
Tranport Insurance
Credit Insurance

The goals of the service palette in the sense of the co-operative promotion mandate include the provision of need-specific insurance protection as well as comprehensive consultation, advice and attendance of R+V clients. R+V offers individual solutions for the multifaceted insurance problems inherent to commercial clients. In fulfilling their function as risk managers, the R+V company consultants work together with companies to ascertain insurance needs and to work out sensible coverage concepts.

As the largest bank underwriter in Germany, R+V Allgemeine Versicherung AG has contributed significantly to the development of safeguarding measures for banks through collaborative efforts with Raiffeisenbanken and Volksbanken. In the end such measures and concepts benefit both customers and bank workers.

R+V Lebensversicherung AG
The R+V Lebensversicherung occupied fourth place among German life insurance companies by the end of 1992 with holdings and assets amounting to over 96.7 billion marks. The basis of this capital is formed by 3.4 million insurance policies which produced gross premium receipts of 2.8 billion marks in 1992. R+V Leben boasts of continual, above-average growth analogous to that of R+V Allgemeine (see Graph 2). The company by the end of 1992 has more than 20.4 billion marks in investments at its disposal. These positive results can likewise be traced back to the wide pallete of all types of life and retirement insurance.

Overview of Insurance Assortment
Endowment Insurance
Pure Endowment Insurance
Joint Life Insurance Coverage
Provisional Insurance for Adolescents Equipment
Insurance paid only upon fixed date
Hazardous Insurance
Hazardous Insurance with a Level Sum Insured
Hazardous Insurance with a Falling Sum Insured
Left-over Credit Insurance*
Insurance for Capital Accumulation*
Old-Age Insurance/Annuity coverage
Disability Insurance for Self-Employed Individuals
Old-Age Health Care/Nursing Insurance
Group Insurance
Group Endowment Insurance
Building Hazardous Insurance
Extended Insurance
Extended Accident Insurance
Extended Hazardous Insurance
Extended Workers Disability Insurance

* provided by R+V Versicherung a.G.

The majority of business activity of the R+V Lebensversicherung is to be found of course in the co-operative sector. Those professional groups involved in handicraft trades, commercial trade and agriculture (including gardening and wine-growing) which traditionally have been closely affilitated with co-operative companies likewise form the target group of the R+V Lebensversicherung. As the market position of the company tends to indicate, other target groups composed of both private and commercial customers are furthermore of great importance. Wage and salary earners as well as self-employed individuals of the middle classes in particular have learned to think highly of the R+V's performance on account of its extensive service palette and consultation practices on an individual level. R+V Lebensversicherung considers the demands of all its customer groups as one of its most important tasks and offers a modern, comprehensive palette of services which both meets customers' demands and maintains favorably priced premium payments.

3. Sales Channels

The decisive factors for the sales success of an insurance company include the selection of sales method suitable to the company as well as the respective qualitative and quantitative strengths of its workers active in field service. Essentially the following marketing channels exist within the insurance sector when one breaks it down in general terms:

1) General Agents
2) Part-time Agents
3) Contacts through Professional Organizations
4) Independent Agents, Agency Companies, Insurance Brokers
5) Direct Sales
6) Banks

Because one of R+V's most important objectives is to attain optimal customer and market proximity, the Versicherungsgruppe has armed itself with five marketing channels. These include:

Channel I: "Co-operative Banks"
Channel II: "Rural Consumer, Service and Production Co-operatives"
Channel III: "Commercial Purchasing and Service Co-operatives"
Channel IV: "Independent Agencies on the Market"
Channel V: "Associations"

Within these marketing channels a field service which guarantees individual, needs-related attention through the implementation of specially developed risk solutions is ready for specific customer groups. The integration of insurance products under the roof of the co-operative company enables the banks to offer a complete and attractive assortment of financial services to which the other companies in the combine likewise contribute. This concept corresponds with modern marketing: Orientation around the needs of the customer is the focus of commercial activity. In the face of mounting competition the question should not be raised how the available products should be sold. The focus of concentration must remain the satisfaction of the customers' needs. Each co-operative member and each customer expects an individual solution and not a pat-answer financial solution with regard to all types of problems related to personal investments, money procurement and provisory care.

In the scope of the co-operative financial combine, this cooperation provides the ideal preconditions for joint success. As marketing Channel I is of greatest importance to the company itself, it should be discussed more closely. From the eye of the customer the co-operative banks are all-round suppliers of financial services; specialists within the affiliated companies guarantee all-round financial advice. This division of labor – primarily through this marketing channel – has decisively contributed to R+V Allgemeine and R+V Lebensversicherung establishing themselves among the top German underwriters. The collaboration between the banks and R+V's field service organization is determined through the agency contract, as it is in all sales channels. The bank obliges itself in the scope of this contract to abide by the guidelines of competition set by the Federal Insurance Commission for the insurance sector as well as by R+V's insurance conditions. The contract furthermore includes the agreements regulating sales and collection commissions. The extent of the commission as a rule is based on the degree the field service agent is involved in the actual closing of the insurance contract.

The marketing concept between the bank and R+V provides for standardized products to be independently handled and settled by bank workers over the counter. A specialist from R+V is summoned for those qualified transactions requiring further explanation in order to ensure the best possible customer consultation. In the third level of this interchange the bank simply passes on addresses to the R+V agent. The bank establishes contact between the customer and the agent who then on his own sells insurance to the transferred client.

Because of the varying given preconditions affecting banks – the dimensions of their annual balance sheets, their customer structure and other factors influencing insurance sales – three fundamental models exist for customer attendance, each of which takes into consideration differing preferences and sales capabilities.

In *Model I* of customer attendance – the insurance trade is an arranged field of business – banks acting as basic models are at disposition, but the insurance trade does not represent an independent field of business in them. The R+V field service agents are therefore strongly engaged in normal customer transactions as well as in business divisions involving wealthier private customers, commercial clients, craftsmen and industrial customers. Specialists and experts such as corporate consultants furthermore are present for particular questions which arise in business with corporate clients.

In *Model II* of customer attendance – the insurance trade is a coordinated field of business – bank employees are more intensely involved in both consulting and sales functions in the insurance business conducted with private customers. The R+V employees can thereby more closely attend to wealthier private customers as well as to business with commercial clients, craftsmen and industrial customers. As in Model I it is possible for specialists and experts to clarify special questions corporate customers may raise to a higher professional degree.

Model III of customer attendance – the insurance trade is a fully integrated field of business – presupposes that insurance matters for private customers are pre-dominantly attended to by bank employees. These employees are given back-up support only when particular needs arise by special R+V staff who are exclusively involved in the private customer market. The remaining R+V field service agents can therefore fully concentrate on the target groups of wealthier private customers, commercial clients, craftsmen and industrial customers. A particularity of Model III in the field of personal insurance is that a specialist for financial and retirement consultation is employed for this target group.

The individual classification of the banks to a specific customer attendance model occurs according to set criteria and in collaboration with the particular bank in question. The division of functions which the bank assumes is contingent on the respective classification, and sales commissions for insurance business are also defined accordingly. The more functions the bank assumes in the insurance business, the higher are the commissions it receives.

As a result of Germany's strict principle of separating types of insurance, the R+V Allgemeine and the R+V Lebensversicherung must appear on the market as legally distinct companies, but sales nonetheless are conducted through a joint field service organization. The market can be more extensively exhausted when it is handled in such a coordinated manner, and customer bonds can be more tightly drawn, a factor which in the end safeguards competitiveness. In order to guarantee specialist competency and the quality of consultation advice in the banks, specialists of both insurance fields, R+V Allgemeine and R+V Lebensversicherung, work at the banks. Both field service employees are supervised by a common manager in order that a more efficient, joint market engagement of both companies is ensured. In daily practise this means, for example, that the specialist for R+V Allgemeine primarily is active in the field of property insurance, but if need be, he can nonetheless also sell life insurance as secondary business.

Mounting competitions and the targeted goal of achieving more extensive market penetration in the co-operative financial combine ultimately made further measures necessary (→ *Competition*). In order to intensify market canvassing activities a so-called cross selling arrangement was established, for example with Bausparkasse Schwäbisch Hall, another large-scale company in the financial combine. This agreement enables the field service organizations of R+V and Schwäbisch Hall also to sell products among each other. In acquiescence with the banks such an agreement can also be extended under certain conditions to have bank products sold by R+V and the Bausparkasse (→ *Building and Loan Societies*).

By pushing the idea of cross selling over 5,000 field service agents are actively involved at the banks on the local level without being all-round financial consultants. They maintain their primary function as specialists for their own products, a matter which is of considerable importance for the sensitive banking marketing channels. The high value place on specialist knowledge and the specialist direction of field service work is evident in that further specialist employees of either R+V Allgemeine or R+V Lebensversicherung will be assigned according to the particular needs of the banks. Such specialists include industrial and corporate consultants, health insurance experts, and financial and retirement advisors. A substantial portion of R+V's success up to now can be traced back to this specialization. The cross selling arrangement so seen is a consistent, continued development of the combine's concepts and the mission of co-operative promotion.

IV. The R+V Versicherungsgruppe in its Revised Structure: Facing Europe

1. Preparing for Europe

Underwriters fall under the large service sector, and 7% of the GNP of the European Community is directed alone to financial services. Community contracts therefore forsee liberalization in this branch as one focus of concentration within general harmonization efforts, particularly as national laws have constructed difficult barriers for business extending beyond national boundaries (→ *European Community*).

R+V Versicherung must observe the branch-specific circumstances that result from this development, but at the same time it must also take the demands placed on German → *co-operative banks* and → *consumer co-operatives* into consideration which arise as a result of the common European market (→ *European Community*). The opening of national boundaries entails new chances and risks for all parties involved, including the insurance business.

Overly restrictive regulatory stipulations as well as difficult barriers in part for foreign-run branches have up to now restricted the degree of interrelation within the insurance trade on the largest markets. Insurance business conducted by foreigners in the Community above all assumes the form of participations in insurance companies or branch office openings. As the European Commission and the national regulatory boards are currently extending and/or liberalizing the freedom underwriters have in the provision of services, no final details have been set, and thus no more discussion should be conducted here on this particular matter. Nonetheless it can be sure in any case that competition on all European markets will become more intensified due to greater supply pressure. Reasons for this, among other things, include sharp increases in product variety, thus entailing a broad spectrum of conditions, services and corresponding differences in premium rates.

The continuingly growing amount of cooperation between banks and insurance companies on national and international levels must be alluded to in this connection. The pertinent rule for this all is capital interrelation among financial services. Strong, new group arrangements attempt to achieve a higher level of market penetration through efficient organization forms. As a result competition takes place much more often between these new group arrangements and less between the original branches in this sector, i.e. between the banking and insurance markets. An inclination towards intensification of the processes of corporate consolidation and internationalization within financial services groups on financial services markets results through these current marketing strategies. The co-operative financial combine cannot face this development in a passive manner.

2. New Structures for the Future

Consolidations, regardless of their form, are themselves not a goal of co-operative organizations. The co-operative financial combine must nevertheless keep up with this development to a sufficient degree in order to maintain high levels of both customer service and competitiveness. Small and mid-sized companies as well as consumer co-operatives – in other words the commercial customers of the co-operative banks – will become more integrated in international business relationships as the trade barriers within Europe are further dismantled. The affiliation of R+V Versicherung to the co-operative combine also entails certain obligations, such as accompanying clients along their route to a more unified

Europe by providing necessary services. Organizational changes within company structure were therefore necessary in this regard.

On June 15, 1989, the assembly of member representatives of the R+V Lebensversicherung a.G. and the general assembly of the R+V Lebensversicherung AG ratified the contract for holdings transference and partial company conveyance proposed on May 9, 1989 (company reorganization). R+V Lebensversicherung a.G. accordingly transferred its insurance assets (aside from its asset accumulation and left-over credit insurance) retroactively from January 1, 1989, to the AG (corporation). Policy holders received an indemnity for relinquishing their membership rights to R+V Lebensversicherung a.G. amounting to the extent of the earning value of their assumed assets.

This action fulfilled the preconditions for restructuring R+V Versicherung in preparation for the future. By reorganizing R+V Lebensversicherung into a corporation, the five companies within the R+V conglomerate could be joined together under the common roof of the R+V Versicherung Holding AG. The most important goal of this consolidation was to have the co-operative group take up a stronger financial interest in R+V Versicherung. Furthermore, primary banks are considerably better represented and can participate much more actively in the administrative functions of the R+V companies in accordance with combine conventions. R+V is likewise more tightly drawn to the co-operative financial combine as the underwriter of this organization. The intensified cooperation with all combine partners resulting from this provides the primary co-operatives with the best possible basis for enduring support of their performance ability.

The R+V Versicherungsgruppe is composed of the six corporations of the R+V-Konzern as well as the three mutual underwriters: Vereinigte Tierversicherung Gesellschaft a.G., R+V Pensionsversicherungs a.G., and R+V Lebensversicherung a.G. following its reorganization focusing on asset accumulation and left-over credit. These companies appear on the market together under the banner of R+V Versicherung.

The path for the future has now also been prepared seen from the organizational side through the new conglomerate structure. With regard to further proceedings in the direction of Europe, the company believes a policy of gradual steps forward to be expedient and necessary. Such a policy ensures that the domestic market remains the main direction of orientation and that the employment of workers and capital is apportioned according to their availability. The primary goal of activities abroad is not the acquisition of large market shares. Cooperations which, if the occasion should arise, assume the form of minority participation, fit much better in this initial concept phase than majority participations with considerable corporate responsibility on foreign markets.

R+V Versicherung is also looking for partners beyond the German border whose preferences lie in the co-operative sector. Such partners must however fulfill particular profile requirements with regard to their performance and efficiency levels. Other affiliated companies within the German co-operative combine are naturally also involved in market analyses and in the search for partners as they confront parallel problems and similar negotiation imperatives.

As it has been presented in this treatise, the answers of R+V Versicherung to the challenges of the common European market first and foremost must be seen in light of customer needs in Germany and in affiliation to the co-operative combine. The nature and speed of any proceedings must orientate around available resources: Each individual company in the → *combine* does not have the dimensions of a large, international financial conglomerate. The co-operative financial combine as a whole nevertheless has the strength and ability to play a successful role on the European stage. Decisive requirements for this are closer bondage and thus particular collective action within the entire co-operative organization.

Bibliography

Aschoff, Günther/Henningsen, Eckard: The German co-operative System, Frankfurt 1986.
Baumann, Horst/Falkenstein, Lorenz: Die Volksbanken und Raiffeisenbanken, Frankfurt 1976.
Harder, Peter C. von: Der Europäische Binnenmarkt und die R+V Versicherung, in: Forum, vol. 16, no. 12 (1989), pp. 543 ff.
Harder, Peter C. von: Zusammenarbeit – aber auf verschiedenen Wegen, Börsenzeitung 03.12.1988.
Harder, Peter C. von: Das Versicherungswesen, Informationsschrift der R+V Versicherung, Wiesbaden 1988.
Koch, Peter: Versicherungswirtschaft, 2nd edition, Karlsruhe 1989.
Wirtschafts- und Sozialausschuß der Europäischen Gemeinschaften (ed.): Die Genossenschaften Europas und ihre Verbände, Baden-Baden 1986.

Intercompany Cooperation

RUDOLF BRATSCHISCH [J]

(see also: *Managerial Economics*; *Classification*; *Franchising*; *Joint Ventures*; *Strategic Alliances*; *Combine, Co-op*erative)

I. Definition of Terms; II. Goals; III. Basic Fundaments; IV. Types; V. Realization; VI. Assessment of Objectives and Control Mechanisms.

I. Definition of Terms

Intercompany cooperation refers to activities undertaken by two or more enterprises which result in the formation of an association. This term provides no insight into the content of such relationships, but nevertheless one must keep in mind that no dominating market strengths should thereby evolve which could lead to a distortion in competition. The participating enterprises themselves remain autonomous, whereby the association – the new economic entity – that evolves develops a certain life and dynamic of its own; in the end one can speak of reciprocal influence between the enterprises co-operating together, each of which relinquishes a part of its "autonomy" and places it under the auspices of the association. Many enterprises have certain functions supported through the collective organization (the association). This is not a selective separation (cession) of functions but rather a particular promotion of these functions.

II. Goals

The goals of intercompany cooperation fundamentally involve the enhancement and improvement of economic efficiency, profitability and financial strength. These goals are often achieved through the expansion of market opportunities through which a solidification of competitive ability results. Participants of intercompany cooperation should be supported and furthered to the extent that they can fulfill their functions much more satisfactorily than before. The possibility likewise arises that new functions and/or responsibilities can be assumed through intercompany cooperation.

If each and every enterprise performed all its tasks on its own, resources would frequently be wasted. The decisions concerning which types of functions and their respective intensities should be performed by the individual participating enterprises or by the association can be taken in various manners. These decisions can be traced back to a number of elemental facts; by any means the following objectives should be achieved:

1) Advantages in costs/expenses
2) Quality advantages
3) Financing advantages
4) Time advantages
5) Risk advantages
6) Assumption of new functions
7) Tax advantages
8) Increased ability of the company to concentrate on its main tasks/functions.

These all should ultimately result in an increase in the returns of the individual participants.

The realization of these furtherances will thereby benefit various (partial) divisions of the enterprises, for example, research and development, purchasing, production, etc. These divisions are specified in a recently published volume concerning business administration, and the goals which should accordingly be pursued are likewise elaborated. (See Tables I and II) This ultimately concerns the distribution of functions between the enterprise and the association.

III. Basic Fundaments

The initial basis for the formation of an intercompany cooperation is the willingness to undertake such a step. On the one hand, one must consider that a part of a company's individual autonomy must be sacrificed in such an undertaking; on the other hand, the personal needs of enterprise employees are often satisfied as increases both in prestige and income frequently accompany intercompany cooperations. This essentially concerns irrational matters and not the consideration that the participating enterprises in the end are promoted and supported. The situation will most probably develop, however, that the issue of securing the continued existence of the enterprise in times of increasing internationalization and competitive pressure will make enterprises more inclined to consider more closely these rational aspects regarding promotion and support. It can be seen that the will to co-operate among individual economic sectors (industrial production, craft trades, commercial trade) is quite varied, whereby the necessity arises time and time again to include new forms of intercompany cooperation in strategic considerations. The technical facilities subsequently play a role in determining whether intercompany cooperation will be undertaken or not. This itself is basically a question of exhausting capacities with regard to human input, operating materials and capital. A certain similarity in the structure and size of the co-operating enterprises is thereby a precondition, whereby cooperational arrangements nonetheless develop between enterprises of various sizes (suppliers) as the optimalization of operational size is also taken into consideraton (→ *Operational Size*).

IV. Types

Each and every intercompany cooperation has particular attributes which are determined by its goal orientation. The following discourse distinguishes such characteristic criteria which more or less can be taken into consideration in individual situations. The premise for this undertaking is that such factors can serve as a point of orientation from which to assess whether targeted goals have been achieved.

1. Functions

These are activites which have been integrated into systematic catalogues within the study of business administration. Presenting such a catalogue in the context of this discourse will not be undertaken as practically every industrial management expert has devel-

Table I

Goal	Division	Research and Development	Purchasing	Production	Sales and Marketing	Financing	Administration
Realization of economies of scale	Better utilization of existent means	Single-handed or reciprocal assumption of functions between partners	Collective orders; joint organization/use of transport vehicles; shared warehouse space	Exchange of free capacities	Joint sales agents, service, delivery warehouse bases	Pooling of available short-term, liquid assets for lucrative loans	Uniform, itemized accounting procedures between partners
Realization of economies of scale	Employment of new means	Collective employment of more qualified workers; shared equipment, labs	Shared warehouses with improved facilities; joint fleet; collective import	Joint production of uniform products based on prior agreement	Joint trade exhibitions, customer service organization; shared brands, advertising	Establishment of a joint bank for corporate group or branch	Shared data processing system, common information system
Improvements in proceedings/procedures	Limitation of operational risks (reduction, transferal, avoidance, annulment)	Risk transferal to employees, unions; improved insurance contracts; risk compensation within federation (fire, explosion, etc.)	Risk transferal to suppliers for deadlines, transport, quality; risk compensation for joint transport, warehousing, etc.	Co-operation in control, standardization, better security measures; risk compensation for fire, explosion, etc.	Monopolistic determination of conditions; annulment of risks between partners	Exchange of debtors' credit info.; collective credit guarantees; better conditions for credit collateral	Better insurance policy for legal protection; centralized documentation, information; archive eliminates risk between partners

Source: Hahn, O., Allgemeine Betriebswirtschaftslehre, München–Wien, 1990, p. 587.

Table II

Goal	Division	Research and Development	Purchasing	Production	Sales and Marketing	Financing	Administration
Improvements of capital-basis	Improvements to equity	Co-operation reduces tied capital investment for research and development	Faster transport and inventory turnover reduces each partner's tied-up capital	Better employment of capacities and faster production flow reduce each partners tied-up capital	Collective shared facilities reduce each partner's tied-up capital	Formation of a corporation allows traded stocks to be issued; other legal forms enable federation to accept wealthier investors/members	Efficient management and accounting financial flow and increase return on equity
Improvements of capital-basis	Improvements to borrowed capital	Improve payment terms for contracted work; attainment of special credits form federation	More favorable terms of payment from suppliers; more favorable warehousing for raw materials; bill-jobbing between partners	Better opportunities for off production failities	Archievement of higher down payments from customers; demand better credit conditions based on security of accounts receivable	Affiliation to Volksbanken; issuance of traded bonds	Rationalization of administration in matters to protect creditors (security on accounts receivable; bills of sale)
Realization of economies of scale	Limitation of corporate risks (transferal, reduction, avoidance, annulment)	R & D pool reduces risks between partners; achieve better safeguarding of results with patents	Ensuring quantities and/or prices through collective purchasing efforts; purchasing pool annuls risks between partners	Rationalization, product tests, quality control, reduce risks; production pool annuls risks between partners	Collective delivery; price agreements between partners; set quotas	Improve conditions of insurance for production; stand-stills; collective fund to relieve liquidity short comings	Improve conditions (legal domicile, liability, performance guaranty); standardization of calculation procedures

oped a systematic method of his own. In any case, however, inputs must always be provided (e.g. in purchasing, production, sales) as well as activities which have effects on them (e.g. research and development, accounting procedures, etc.).

2. Geographic Sphere

This is a matter of where the participants and their association have their legal seat (location) and in which areas the cooperation will be active (international or domestic cooperations). → *Joint ventures* are often referred to with regard to international cooperations; these are joint companies and/or partnerships which result through the capital investment of two or more partners. Such cooperations actually do often come into question between domestic and international partners, whereby a shared, collective investment must be at hand.

3. Time Frame

This concerns the extent of time the intercompany cooperation is consenting to. Intercompany cooperations are differentiated into those entered into only for a limited amount of time and those that are open-ended.

4. Procedures (Extent of Ties)

Cooperations can fundamentally function according to two possibilities:
- Exchange of information and experience with regard to the exection of company activities;
- The execution of such company activities;
- A combination of the two.

5. Dimension

This concerns two matters, namely the extent the participating enterprises are tied to the cooperation and the appropriate size of the association, whereby an open or closed number of members should be possible.

6. Direction

Based on the general interrelation of inputs in the economy, ties can be referred to as being either organic or inorganic. Organic ties are those which entail a special connection between inputs (e.g. a yarn factory and a weaving mill). One can further distinguish between horizontal, vertical and diagonal cooperation between companies. Cooperation is deemed horizontal when enterprises co-operate which are on the identical level (e.g. industrial enterprises, wholesale trading companies, etc.). Cooperation is considered vertical when enterprises unite which are on different levels (e.g. industrial enterprises and retail operations, etc.). An intercompany cooperation is characterized as diagonal when enterprises of both identical and different levels are involved in it (e.g. wholesale trading companies and retail operations).

An intercompany cooperation is characterized as inorganic in the sense of the common, ongoing economic process between nature and needs. The general connection between inputs plays a role, thus resulting in a so-called "neutral" cooperation which can accordingly be categorized as horizontal, vertical or diagonal.

7. Complementary Nature

This criterion should determine whether the provided or disengaged inputs are either homogeneous or complentary.

8. External Effects, Legal Scope

The new operational associations naturally have a corresponding effect with regard to third parties. This can be expressed through a particular legal form (e.g. partnership, stock corporation, co-operative, etc. and has corresponding legal consequences, which will not be discussed in particular here due to their variety among individual countries. Each and every legal form can fundamentally come into question. One must however not forget that certain legal forms are particularly appropriate for certain cooperations (→ *Combine, Co-operative*; → *Forms of Cooperation*).

9. Publicity, Visibility

Cooperations can be recognized by non-involved individuals, particularly when a unique legal form is available (see Point 8 above). Even if no written or oral agreements exist, various enterprises can nonetheless act in a uniform manner. In such a situation an tacit or implicit cooperation may be at hand.

Varying types of intercompany cooperations result from the composition of these characteristics in a matrix scheme according to their respective intensity. One can therefore recognize that an abundance of intercompany cooperation type exists (see charts I and II).

V. Realization

Corresponding associations are organized based on the characteristics listed above, whereby the participating enterprises above all are interested in the following considerations:

1) Management of the association;
2) Laws and obligations affecting the individual members of the association;
3) Accounting procedures of the association.

The decision concerning the extent a cooperation should be entered into falls under the management's field of competency, whereby both rational and irrational objectives play a role (as described above).

In this connection it is necessary that the divisions of the enterprise which are predominantly affected by this decision (e.g. production management, etc.) have been appropriately informed and involved in this process.

VI. Assessment of Objectives and Control Mechanisms

The determined objectives must be continually overseen and readjusted as necessary. This assessment includes evaluating the feasibility of certain goals and the actual realization of set objectives. Comparing projected and actual conditions can produce successful results, whereby alterations to certain premises must be taken into consideration in the calculation.

Bibliography

Alsmöller, Horst: Wettbewerbspolitische Ziele und kooperationstheoretische Hypothesen im Wandel der Zeit, Tübingen 1982.
Arbeitskreis für Kooperation und Partizipation e.V. (ed.): Das Zentrum für Kooperation und Partizipation, Baden-Baden 1987.
Bea, Franz Xaver: Diversifikation durch Kooperation, in: Der Betrieb, 1988, pp. 2521 ff.
Bea, Franz Xaver/Dichtl, E./Schweitzer, M.: Allgemeine Betriebswirtschaftslehre, vol. 1, Grundfragen, Stuttgart 1990.
Billig, V./Madauss, B./Schneider, K.: Industrial Cooperation through Project-Management, Köln 1989.
Böhme, Joachim: Innovationsförderung durch Kooperation, Berlin 1986.
Bleicher, Knut: Zum Management zwischenbetrieblicher Kooperation: Vom Joint Venture zur strategischen Allianz, in: Führungsorganisation und Technologiemanagement, Berlin 1989, pp. 86 ff.
Bleicher, Knut: Weltweite Strategien der Unternehmungsakquisition und Kooperation zur Bewältigung des Markt- und Technologiewandels, in: Belz, Ch. (ed.), Realisierung des Marketing, St. Gallen 1986, pp. 211 ff.
Brauer, U.: Die vertikale Kooperation als Absatzwegestrategie für Herstellerunternehmen, München 1989.
BRT-Studie: Zwischenbetriebliche Zusammenarbeit im Schuh-Einzelhandel, in: Die Gewerbliche Genossenschaft, 1989, pp. 8 ff.
Buckley, P.J.: New Forms of international industrial cooperation: A Survey of literature, in: Außenwirtschaft, 1983, pp. 195 ff.
Bundeswirtschaftskammer: Kooperative Forschungsinstitute – Leistungen, Zielsetzungen und Probleme, Studie des Instituts für Gewerbeforschung, series of publications no. 55, Wien 1987.
Clemens, R.: Die Bedeutung des Franchising in der Bundesrepublik Deutschland – Eine empirische Untersuchung von Franchisenehmern und -systemen, Stuttgart 1988.
Clement, W.: Vom Unternehmen zum Netzwerk; einige systematische Anmerkungen zu "alten" und "neuen" Formen der Kooperation (Punktation), in: Konturen – Technologie und Wirtschaft, Wien 1990, pp. 149 ff.
Dülfer, Eberhard: Betriebswirtschaftslehre der Kooperative, Göttingen 1984.
Düttmann, B.: Forschungs- und Entwicklungskooperationen und ihre Auswirkungen auf den Wettbewerb, Bergisch Gladbach 1989.

Eickhof, Norbert: Kooperation, Konzentration und funktionsfähiger Wettbewerb, Tübingen 1975.
Eickhof, Norbert: Wettbewerb, Wettbewerbsfreiheit und Wettbewerbsbeschränkungen, in: Hamburger Jahrbuch für Wirtschaft und Gesellschaftspolitik, Tübingen 1990, pp. 211 ff.
Endress, Ruth: Strategie und Taktik der Kooperation, Berlin 1975.
Eversberg, J.: Aufbau und Nutzung einer Mitgliederdatenbank – am Beispiel Elektronikpartner (EP), in: Der Verbund – Strategie und Praxis der Kooperation, 1990, pp. 9 ff.
Fröhlich, E./Pichler, J.H.: Werte und Typen mittelständischer Unternehmen, Berlin 1988.
Hagemeister, S.: Innovation und innovatorische Kooperation von Unternehmen als Instrumente der regionalen Entwicklung, München 1988.
Hahn, Oswald: Allgemeine Betriebswirtschaftslehre, München – Wien 1990.
Hauri, S.: Laterale Kooperation zwischen Unternehmen: Erfolgskriterien und Klippen, Grüsch 1989.
Heinen, Edmund: Industriebetriebslehre: Entscheidungen im Industriebetrieb, Wiesbaden 1985.
Hinterhuber, Hans H.: Strategische Unternehmensführung, vol. II, Strategisches Handeln, Berlin – New York 1989.
Jenewein, J.-F./Huber, St.: Wettbewerb in der EG, Wien 1989.
Kernforschungs-Zentrum Karlsruhe (ed.): Technologietransfer durch Kooperation, Köln 1989.
König, W.: Zur Förderung der betrieblichen Kooperation mit Unternehmen in Lateinamerika, in: Politische Studien, 1984, pp. 512 ff.
Kück, Marlene: Betriebswirtschaft der Kooperative. Eine einzelwirtschaftliche Analyse kooperativer und selbstverwalteter Betriebe, Stuttgart 1989.
Lechner, Karl/Egger, A./Schauer, R.: Einführung in die Allgemeine Betriebswirtschaftslehre, Wien 1992.
Lengwieler, Ch.: Kooperation als bankbetriebliche Strategie, Bern – Stuttgart 1988.
Lindemann, M.: Co-operative Marktkommunikation, in: Werbeforschung und Praxis, 1990, pp. 155 ff.
Linn, N.: Die Implementierung vertikaler Kooperationen. Theoretische Konzeption und erste empirische Ergebnisse zum Prozeß der Ausgliederung logistischer Teilaufgaben, Frankfurt 1989.
Lipfert, H.: Mitgliederförderndes Kooperations- und Konkurrenzmanjagement in genossenschaftlichen Systemen, Göttingen 1986.
Loitlsberger, E.: Grundriß der Betriebswirtschaftslehre für Juristen, Wien 1990.
Lumbier, L.G./Aranzahl, R.C.: Beispielhafte Kooperation mittelständischer Werkzeugmaschinen-Hersteller; Forschung und Entwicklung und gemeinsam betriebenes Fertigungssystem, in: Werkstatt und Betrieb, 1989, pp. 726 ff.
National Conference on the Advancement of Research (NCAR): Economic Competitiveness through Cooperation in Breakthrough Technologies, Basel 1989.
Österreichischer Genossenschaftsverband (Schulze-Delitzsch): Zusammenarbeit in einer gewerblichen Genossenschaft: Der Leitfaden für eine erfolgreiche Zukunft ihres Unternehmens, Wien 1990.
Olesch, G.: Kooperative Standortpolitik – ein Stufenkonzept, in: Der Verbund – Strategie und Praxis der Kooperation, 1990, pp. 4 ff.
Peters, J.: Unternehmerische Kooperation mit den Entwicklungsländern – Stellenwert und Potential des Mittelstandes, in: Internationales Gewerbearchiv 1989, pp. 261 ff.

Rasche, Hans O.: Kooperation – Chance und Gewinn, Heidelberg 1970.
Rath, Helmut: Neue Formen der internationalen Unternehmenskooperation, Hamburg 1990.
Salje, Peter: Die mittelständige Kooperation zwischen Wettbewerbspolitik und Kartellrecht, Tübingen 1981.
Schrader, St.: Zwischenbetrieblicher Informationstransfer – eine empirische Analyse kooperativen Verhaltens, Berlin 1990.
Schuy, St.: Kooperation ist nicht einfach, aber man kann sie lernen, in: Internationale Wirtschaft, no. 19, 10.05.1984.
Semlinger, K.: Fallstricke und Hemmnisse zwischenbetrieblicher Kooperation, in: JGA 1993, Seite 47 ff.
Staudt, Erich/Bock, J./Tobert, M.: Innovation durch Kooperation, in: Internationales Gewerbearchiv 1989, pp. 141 ff.
Staudt, E. et al: Kooperationshandbuch. Ein Leitfaden für die Unternehmenspraxis, Stuttgart 1992.
Stritzik, P: Unternehmen neu strukturieren. Restrukturierung und internationale Kooperation, Zürich 1989.
Tröndle, D.: Kooperationsmanagement – Steuerung interaktioneller Prozesse bei Unternehmungskooperationen, Bergisch Gladbach – Köln 1987.
Ullrich, W. (ed.): Betriebliche Kooperation mit den Entwicklungsländern, Tübingen 1987.
Wolff, G./Göschel, G.: Führung 2000 – höhere Leistung durch Kooperation, Wiesbaden 1987.
Zeilberger, U.: Kooperation im Export, Wien 1986.

International Co-operative Alliance

BRUCE THORDARSSON

(see also: *Central Institutions*; *International Co-operative Organizations*; *United Nations System*)

I. A Global Movement; II. Main Strategies for Co-operative Development; III. Priorities in the Developed Countries; IV. International Cooperation; V. Co-operatives and Social Needs; VI. Future Challenges.

I. A Global Movement

There are two characteristics of the International Co-operative Alliance which help to describe its nature and structure.
The first is that the ICA is the oldest international non-governmental organization (→ *International Co-operative Organizations*) in the world, with the exception of the International Red Cross. It traces its origins back to 1895, when co-operatives from Western Europe, Eastern Europe, the United States, Argentina, India, and Australia met in London to create an organization that would promote and support their growing movements (→ *History in 19th C.*). The fact that ICA has continued to exist for almost 100 years is a result of the need for a central body to serve as a focal point and representative for the common values and interests of its diverse membership (→ *Corporate Culture*). Of course the actual work of ICA has varied considerably in nature – and quality – during the years.

The second point of note is that, through the size of its membership, ICA is the largest international non-governmental organization in the world, other than religious bodies. Today some 600 million individual members are represented in the co-operative movements from over 100 countries that are affiliated to ICA, either directly or through its regional offices. The small ICA staff – 15 people in Geneva and another 40 in its offices in Asia, Africa, and Latin America – gives a more realistic view of the size and strength of the organization. From the very outset ICA recognized that its role was to concentrate on those common interests of all co-operatives, and that their business interests would be better served through the creation of sectoral committees. During the years Specialized Organizations have been created through ICA to represent the interests of co-operatives in such divers fields as insurance, banking, agriculture, producers, consumers, trade, fisheries, tourism, housing, and training. A separate women's committee exists to promote the role of women in co-operatives (→ *Women and Co-operatives*). Working parties have been established by co-operative professionals in the fields of communications, library-documentation services, and research.
ICA's role, in short, is to promote the growth and strengthening of the co-operative approach in all its forms, and to coordinate and support the common interests of its member organizations.

II. Main Strategies for Co-operative Development

Promoting the growth of co-operatives in developing countries is one of the most important roles of ICA, because co-operatives are one of the best means of overcoming the problems of underdevelopment (→ *Development Policy*).
ICA's role is not to work at the grass roots or local level, however. There are many other development agencies better suited to that task. Our basic function is to help create the most favourable possible environment in which co-operative development can take place. That means, first and foremost, encouraging governments to withdraw from control over their co-operative movements. If there is one fundamental obstacle to successful co-operative growth in the developing countries, it is the fact that governments have regarded co-operatives as such an important development tool that they want to use and control them. But of course this destroys the basic features which make co-operatives so valuable – their ability to respond to members' interests and to give members a feeling of ownership and responsibility.
ICA's regional offices are therefore implementing a variety of programmes for this purpose. In East Africa, for example, ICA brings together on a regular basis all the ministers of co-operatives and gives them an opportunity to establish policies designed to promote co-operative self-reliance.

Another very important strategy is to find ways of strengthening national co-operative organizations – both the apex structures and the national commercial ones in different sectors such as agriculture, insurance, and finance. Without strong national bodies, co-operative movements will never be able to take over from governments responsibility for their own development. ICA helps them with a variety of planning and consultancy services.

A third focus of ICA's development work is to assist and support the efforts of development organizations – especially those which have been established by the co-operative movement itself. ICA members in Europe, North America, Japan, and elsewhere are very committed to supporting co-operative development, and they appreciate the ability of ICA to provide a forum – at both the international and regional level – for them to come together, avoid duplication of effort, and increase their impact by working together in different ways. Similarly, with the big international agencies like the World Bank and the → *United Nations System*, ICA is encouraging them to move in the same direction – more collaboration with co-operative development agencies, and more assistance to co-operatives instead of to government departments (→ *Policies for Promotion*).

III. Priorities in the Developed Countries

ICA's role in promoting co-operatives is by no means confined to the developing countries. However, in the countries of the North it takes a different form, because there co-operatives are facing very different challenges.

One problem is that, in spite of their many successes, co-operatives are still very poorly understood by the public – and maybe even by some of their members. There is a need almost everywhere for more public education about co-operatives. Although this is basically a national responsibility, ICA hopes to assist its members in this effort by having the United Nations declare 1995 as the International Year of co-operatives. Such an international year, which would coincide with the centenary of ICA, could be used by co-operative movements everywhere to generate tremendous amounts of local publicity for their efforts. To convince the UN to make such a proclamation will not be an easy task, but it could be possible if ICA members are able to persuade their governments to offer strong support for this idea.

Another problem common to co-operatives in the North has to do with their continued relevance and competitiveness (→ *Competition*). Conditions have changed dramatically since they were formed 50 or 100 years ago. Today's consumers are well-served by retail outlets, insurance companies, banks, and agricultural marketing firms which are using the same customer-oriented approaches and services that were first introduced by co-operatives. The result is that many co-operative members find themselves wondering what – if anything – is still different about their organization, and why they should continue to support it.

It is in order to answer this question that the ICA has embarked upon a four-year research programme into co-operative basic values (→ *Corporate Culture*) and their implications for economic efficiency. The process began at the 1988 Congress in Stockholm, when the ICA president introduced a discussion paper on basic values. ICA has asked all of its member organizations, including the Specialized Organizations, to think about this topic and its relevance to them. During 1990 and 1991 a variety of meetings will be held – some organized by our members, others by ICA – so that a comprehensive report can be presented to the 1992 Congress in Tokyo. Many of our members have already taken up this task with enthusiasm, for they know that the issue – how co-operatives reflect their distinctive values – is the key to their long-term economic success, and perhaps even their survival.

IV. International Cooperation

It goes without saying that, in order to accomplish these goals, there is a need for all national co-operative movements to collaborate increasingly with each other as well as with the ICA. The key message, I think, is that international collaboration is no longer a luxury for co-operatives, but it is fast becoming a vital necessity. It is rather ironic that our private sector competitors usually practice internatinal co-operation better than we do in the co-operative movement.

This is a natural result of the decentralized nature of our system, but there are signs that our members are aware of the need to work together more and more. There are many examples of how our economic destinies are becoming increasingly affected by events beyond our borders: economic integration in Europe, the U.S.-Canada free trade agreement, the effect on developing countries of trade and investment policies in the North. Co-operatives are very much affected by all these trends.

The European co-operatives are increasingly working together in Brussels to deal with the implications of the European Community (→ *European Community*). The Japanese co-operatives – both agricultural and consumer – are major international importers and exporters. Eastern European co-operatives have been active in establishing a variety of bilateral trading agreements (→ *Development, Eastern Europe*). Co-operative investments are starting to flow across national borders.

The ICA, as a non-commercial organization, has little role to play in direct business transactions between co-operatives. But it has been able to support and facilitate such linkages through its Specialized Organizations which have been created in 11 sectoral fields ranging from banking and insurance to producers and tourism. Several have initiated joint business activities, and others make use of their "informal" contacts to pursue business on a bilateral basis. In the developing world, ICA has been able to stimulate inter-co-operative trade in Asia through a CoopTrade project, which has now been extended to East, Central and Southern Afica.

All of this is very encouraging, but there is little doubt that co-operatives will face increasing pressures as a result of foreign competition. Greater economic collaboration among our members seems to be essential, and the structures provided by ICA – especially the Specialized Organizations – could become increasingly useful in the future.

V. Co-operatives and Social Needs

Most of ICA's members would agree that, although co-operatives are primarily business organizations designed to serve their members' economic needs, they also have a broader social responsibility. How this is defined is very different form country to country. In some countries – Japan and the Soviet Union are two examples – co-operatives area active in supporting peace initiatives. ICA has been able to assist these efforts through presentations to the UN Special Session on Disarmament as a result of its special "category one" status with the United Nations.

Other countries are especially active in promoting movement-to-movement assistance to co-operatives in developing countries. The ICA's development programme is increasingly collaborating with and supporting the efforts of these organizations in such countries as Sweden, Norway, Canada, the Netherlands, and Italy. Other co-operative sectors have special social interests. Many housing and producer co-operatives (→ *Joint-production Co-operatives*) are especially interested in the problems of the disabled, for example. The UN Centre in Vienna is working with ICA to promote this social role of co-operatives. There are many other examples that one could give – co-operative education and the role of women in co-operatives are two especially important issues facing our members in all countries – but in my view one of the most important contributions that co-operatives will make in the years ahead is to provide a true form of economic democracy through which ordinary people can have a voice in the economic and social decisions that effect their lives.

This concept is of course at the heart of all co-operatives. It explains their growth in the developed world during the last one hundred years. But the need is no less today, for increasingly people are questioning whether existing political and economic institutions are serving their best interests. In the socialist countries, too, co-operatives have a unique opportunity today to provide a real alternative to large, unresponsive bureaucracies. China provides a good example of how developing countries can also make good use of co-operatives for agricultural development if the co-operatives are given the freedom to make use of members' initiative creativity (→ *Officialization*). It might well be through going back to their roots – finding out how to meet individuals' needs for a feeling of control over their economic and social destinies – that co-operatives will demonstrate their continued relevance in a rapidly-changing world.

VI. Future Challenges

There is no easy answer to the question of how co-operatives must change in order to respond to current economic, social, and political trends. Much will depend on local circumstances and needs. However, at the risk of grossly oversimplifying a complex subject, if there is one central challenge facing co-operatives everywhere it is the need to become "more co-operative".

In developed countries the fundamental question is how to maintain member loyalty in a highly-competitive market. In socialist countries it is how to respond to greater flexibility in the system (→ *State and Co-operatives, Market Economy*) . In developing countries it is how to move away from governmental control (→ *Officialization*). All of these questions revolve around a common theme – the need to create, or improve, procedures that will enable members to have a feeling of identification with the operation of their organizations.

In the final analysis, this is what co-operative values and principles are all about – service to members. The on-going challenge is to find the most effective ways of translating our abstract concepts into practical action. ICA will certainly not be able to solve this problem for its members, but it will do its best to help them find the right answers.

Bibliography

Böök, Sven Ake: Co-operative Values in a Changing World (Report to the TCA Congress in Tokyo, October 1992), (edited by Margaret Prickett and Mary Treacy), Geneva 1992.

Faucherre, H.: 60 Jahre Internationaler Genossenschaftsverbund (1895–1955), Basel 1960.

ICA (ed.): International Co-operative Alliance – its Aims and Work, London 1963.

ICA (ed.): Annual Report 1989, Geneva.

Krascheninnikov, A. J.: International Co-operative Alliance, Berlin 1984.

Laurinkari, Juhani: Die Zusammenarbeit der Genossenschaftsorganisationen – am Beispiel des Internationalen Genossenschaftsbundes (IGB), in: Laurinkari, Juhani (ed.): Genossenschaftswesen, München 1990, pp. 752–764.

Thodarsson, Bruce: From Stockholm to Stockholm: The Lessons of Three Decades of Cooperative Development, in: Review of International Cooperation (The Official Organ of the International Co-operative Alliance, published quarterly), No. 1, 1988.

International Co-operative Organizations

S.K. SAXENA

(see also: *ICA*; *United Nations System*; *Credit Unions*; *IRU*; *GACOPEA*; *Central Institutions*)

I. Introduction; II. Centre International de recherches et d'Information sur l'economie publique, sociale et co-operative (CIRIEC); III. Committee for the Promotion of Aid to Co-operatives (COPAC); IV. World Council of Credit Unions (WOCCU); V. Regional Organizations; VI. Comite General de la Cooperation Agricole de la CEE (COGECA); VII. European Community of Consumer Co-operative – EUROCOOP; VIII. Association of Co-operative Banks of the EC (ACB); IX. Concluding Remarks.

I. Introduction

The ILO Publication (Int Dir of Coop Orgs, 1988 ed.) lists 32 organizations in this category. Some titles include both the parent organization and the affiliated continental chapters such as the → *WOCCU* and ACOSCA, ACCU etc. For reasons of space, only selected ones are discussed below.

To be included, an organization's membership has to be from more than one country, the geographical spread must be either global or regional and the principal area of interest will be the Co-operative Movement. These criteria will exclude several active national organizations engaged in international work such as the SCC in Sweden, OC/DC in the US, DSE in Germany and the CLEAR Unit in Britain. Moreover, some organizations such as the ICA, UN Agencies and the ILO, FAO, etc., have been excluded as they are treated elsewhere in the handbook. We have included only selected international and regional organizations.

II. Centre International de recherches et d'Information sur l'economie publique, sociale et co-operative (CIRIEC)

Founded in 1947 in Geneva by Professor *Edgard Millhaud*, CIRIEC is a non-governmental international organization devoted to scientific work. Its main areas of investigation are co-operatives and public economy. CIRIEC collects relevant information in its fields of interest, undertakes scientific research, publishes works on economic sectors and activities directed towards serving the general interest, undertakes inquiries in public enterprises at all levels, the social economy, mutual societies and co-operatives self-management and workers participation.

CIRIEC (i) issues a quarterly publication *Annals of Public and Co-operative Economics*, an international scientific journal in the field of Co-operatives; some occasional publications are issued as well (→ *Periodicals, Co-operative*); (ii) organizes an international Congress every two years; and (iii) maintains an International Scientific Commission consisting of academics delegated by the national sections. CIRIEC has both collective and individual members. Its annual budget, derived from member subscriptions, income from publications and government subsidies is about Bfrs. 10,000,000.

The General Assembly is its highest authority. It meets once in two years simultaneously with the congresses. The Assembly appoints the Board (made up of representatives appointed by the national sections), the President, the Vice-Presidents, the Treasurer and the Director. In between the Board Meetings, the Praesidium is responsible for taking and implementing decisions.

CIRIEC's International Secretariat is based in Liege, Belgium.

It has national sections in some 13 countries. Some pursue research and issue their own journals. The collective members, known as national sections and completely autonomous, pay a subscription higher than the individual members.

The International Commission has been concerned lately with the phenomenon of privatization of public enterprises. In 1988–89, three working groups were set up around the themes of: (i) the evolution of the missions and structures of the public enterprises regarding the Single European market of 1993; (ii) the identification and analysis of the social economy sector; and (iii) a comparative international analysis of the economic costs and benefits involved in applying co-operative principles.

CIRIEC maintains contacts with several EEC bodies (the Commission, the European Parliament and the Economic and Social Committee of the Community); it also maintains links with the ICA and the ILO.

III. Committee for the Promotion of Aid to Co-operatives (COPAC)

Established in 1971 and based at FAO premises in Rome, COPAC was created in response to the Second UN Development Decade which emphasized the mobilization of the people, particularly the poor, for their own development through self-help. Its seven International members are: the FAO, ILOM UN, ICA, IFAP, IFFPAW and WOCCU (→ *United Nations System*). ICA and WOCCU work exclusively in the field of Cooperation while the others retain important components of co-operative activity. COPAC promotes aid to co-operatives in the third world. Its initial focus was on coordination of aid but this was found impractical. Members were shy to give advance information on projects they were discussing with aid agencies for implementation in the third world. Its early years were, therefore, marked by territorial jealousies among members. With the passage of time and frequent interaction, the situation has improved. COPAC maintains contacts with non-members as well.

COPAC has succeeded in developing several mechanisms for disseminating information on co-operatives in developing countries. First, its regular member meetings, held twice a year, serve that purpose. The Chairmanship is rotated among members. The meetings are closed events, but lately there is a trend towards inviting more interested outsiders.

Second: COPAC publishes a six-monthly bulletin containing information on co-operative projects that are under consideration or newly approved, details of recent field missions etc (→ *Periodicals, Co-operative*). Such projects are also published annually in the *Current Assistance to Co-operatives in Developing Countries*. To facilitate project preparation, it issued some time ago a document entitled *Guide for the Preparation of Co-operative Projects*.

Since 1979, COPAC has also been publishing a series of country notes. These are factual accounts of national co-operative movements. By the end of 1985, 32 reports had been published. These are good informative documents and are of use to researchers, development agencies etc.

Third: COPAC holds occasional symposia on topical subjects. The discussions in these gatherings are of a high order and the reports are distributed widely. Participants are invited from NGOs, Development Assistance Agencies and others interested in the subject from developing and developed countries.

COPAC has undertaken some work for other agencies as well. For several years running, it has produced drafts for the UN Secretary General's submission on co-operatives to the ECOSOC and the General Assembly, conducted evaluation of UNDP financed co-operative projects, prepared a Technical Advisory Note (TAN) for distribution to the UNDP Resident Representatives to familiarize them with co-operatives and raise their image in developing countries.

COPAC undertakes some field investigations also. However, the output is small. In 1979, it initiated an important investigation and deputed two known experts to design and recommend Proposals for a Co-operative International Interlending Program. Unfortunately, the practical results have not been encouraging.

IV. World Council of Credit Unions (WOCCU)

The WOCCU (→ *Credit Unions*) is the international arm of credit unions, a form of financial co-operative organization which owes its inspiration to *Raiffeisen* and *Schulze-Delitzsch*. The North American pioneers of the credit union movement were → *Desjardins* (Quebec, Canada) and *Filene* (USA). Countries such as India, Sri Lanka and Indonesia have extensive co-operative thrift and credit systems predating the emergence of credit unions; in some countries (e.g. Bangladesh), credit unions are formed around parishes. Historically, thrift and loan societies were confined to rural areas and credit unions, to urban institutions and communities. This distinction, however, is no longer valid.

The structure of WOCCU went through several changes before it assumed its present shape. The Credit Union National Association (CUNA) was formed in the USA in 1935. By the end of 1950s, requests for association from other countries increased and CUNA added a World Extension Department to its structure. Due to the US Credit union movement's funding of programs and the initiation of US assistance programs, considerable development took place in CUNA's international work. As a result, CUNA changed its name in 1964 to CUNA International and in 1970, voted to establish a fourth tier and named it the World Council of Credit Unions. A number of national and regional Confederations emerged and joined the WOCCU.

Article 1 of WOCCU's by-laws describes its objectives as follows: "... the Corporation's mission is to assist members to organize, expand, improve and integrate credit union and related institutions as effective instruments for the economic and social development of people. The Corporation shall serve as a forum for the exchange of ideas and information, provide services for its members, promote membership development and growth, represent members' interests, and extend co-operative financial services to areas where people want and need such services. The Membership Council shall periodically determine the specific activities the Corporation will pursue."

WOCCU has four categories of members: voting, non-voting, associate and observer. Membership Council is WOCCU's Governing Body. Representation on the council is specified in the Constitution and, subject to a ceiling, is based on the number of members in the national organization. Voting members have at least one seat on the Membership Council and the International Credit Union Forum. There are two bodies which may establish policies and directives: the Membership Council and its six elected officers who constitute the Administrative Committee. The Council meets annually and the Committee twice a year. The functions of the Council are to: undertake strategic planning, consider development issues and the concerns of the Forum. These concerns emerge from the debates in national movements or from the deliberations of the Confederations (e.g., Operating Priniciples of Credit Unions, policies and practices to ensure the efficiency of Credit Unions).

WOCCU's sources of funds are (i) membership dues; (ii) charges for services rendered; and (iii) grants, gifts etc. The Membership Council determines the membership dues. The projected budget for 1990 is $7,817,100 of which over 65% is expected to come from the USAID for overseas projects.

The WOCCU Statutes mention the specific activities it should undertake. Among others, these are to: improve the standards of credit unions' operation, promote credit unions and give publicity to their activities (it issues several publications to promote and intensify inter-credit union relationships, ensure the autonomy of credit unions, aid members in developing regional federations and help them achieve technical and financial self-sufficiency.

Financial and technical assistance are the twin elements of WOCCU's international programs. Assistance can be given directly to an organization from funds to which the WOCCU has access; alternatively, it can also try and locate development funds for special programs. Over 40 international Governmental and NGOs provide financial assistance to third world credit unions. The WOCCU provides assistance (i) from its own staff based in its offices in Wisconsin, Washington or Geneva; (ii) through short term consultancies; or (iii) by its staff who may be already in residence in a developing country for an assignment.

The relationship between CUNA, the WOCCU and the US Government provides a basic source of funds for WOCCU's international activities, as it is easy to approach USAID through WOCCU's US member, the CUNA. For this reason, CUNA's Office in Washington liases with USAID for managing development programs and maintains good relations with other US Co-operative organizations involved in overseas work (→ *Development Policy*). CUNA's Global Projects Office and WOCCU were joined together in a restructuring of the organization in 1981.

In 1989, WOCCU concentrated on representation and liason work. This involved visits to Continental confederations for discussion of matters of common interest, assisting projects and programs, advising organizations on their structure, suggesting the creation of regional centres and for intensifying training, studying credit unions (Haiti), inviting national leaders to Wisconsin, helping to strengthen national Federations, (Ecuador and Honduras) by the installation of computerized accounting system in the latter country, advising on the development of micro-enterprise projects (Bolivia) etc. Some multi-regional projects are implemented through continental Confederations. These activities are in addition to the ongoing work of WOCCU such as the provision of information services, production of promotional materials and observance of special events.

Fig. 1 shows the world-wide spread of the credit union movement and gives some basic statistics.

The International Credit Union System

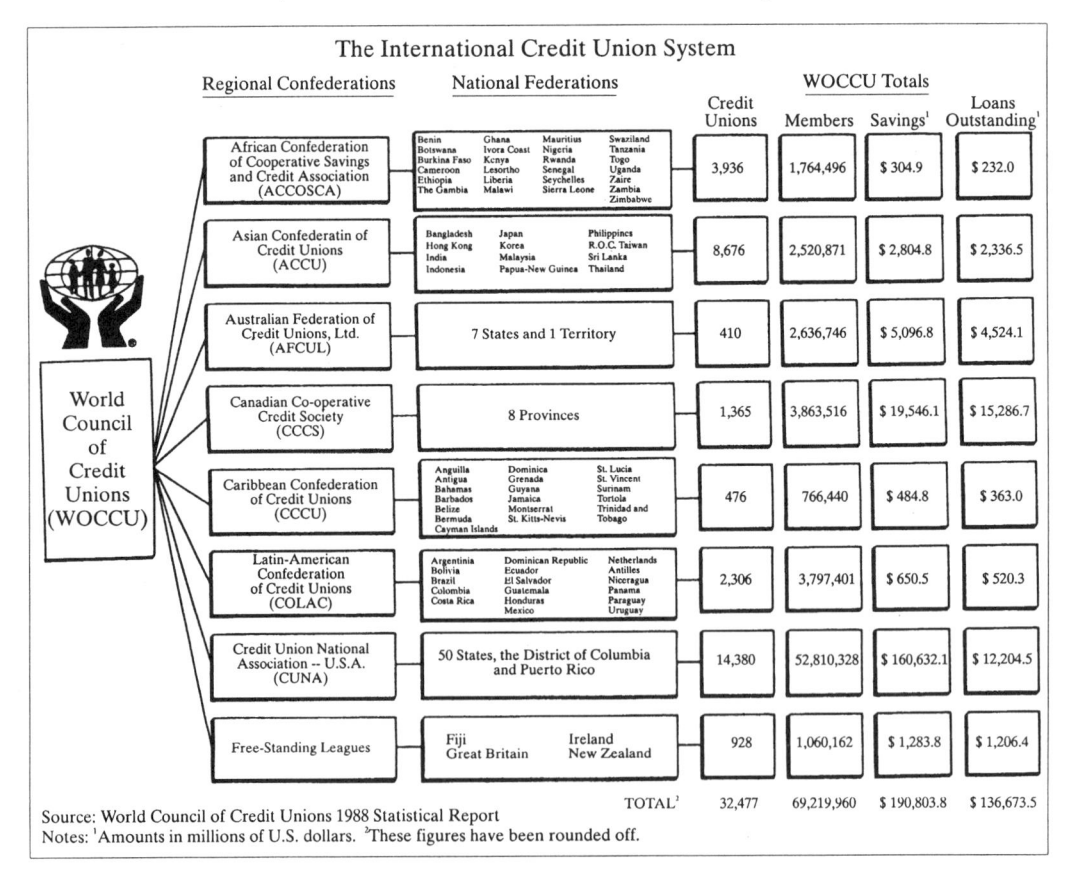

	Regional Confederations	National Federations	Credit Unions	WOCCU Totals Members	Savings[1]	Loans Outstanding[1]
World Council of Credit Unions (WOCCU)	African Confederation of Cooperative Savings and Credit Association (ACCOSCA)	Benin, Botswana, Burkina Faso, Cameroon, Ethiopia, The Gambia, Ghana, Ivora Coast, Kenya, Lesortho, Liberia, Malawi, Mauritius, Nigeria, Rwanda, Senegal, Seychelles, Sierra Leone, Swaziland, Tanzania, Togo, Uganda, Zaire, Zambia, Zimbabwe	3,936	1,764,496	$ 304.9	$ 232.0
	Asian Confederatin of Credit Unions (ACCU)	Bangladesh, Hong Kong, India, Indonesia, Japan, Korea, Malaysia, Papua-New Guinea, Philippines, R.O.C. Taiwan, Sri Lanka, Thailand	8,676	2,520,871	$ 2,804.8	$ 2,336.5
	Australian Federation of Credit Unions, Ltd. (AFCUL)	7 States and 1 Territory	410	2,636,746	$ 5,096.8	$ 4,524.1
	Canadian Co-operative Credit Society (CCCS)	8 Provinces	1,365	3,863,516	$ 19,546.1	$ 15,286.7
	Caribbean Confederation of Credit Unions (CCCU)	Anguilla, Antigua, Bahamas, Barbados, Belize, Bermuda, Cayman Islands, Dominica, Grenada, Guyana, Jamaica, Montserrat, St. Kitts-Nevis, St. Lucia, St. Vincent, Surinam, Tortola, Trinidad and Tobago	476	766,440	$ 484.8	$ 363.0
	Latin-American Confederation of Credit Unions (COLAC)	Argentinia, Bolivia, Brazil, Colombia, Costa Rica, Dominican Republic, Ecuador, El Salvador, Guatemala, Honduras, Mexico, Netherlands Antilles, Nicaragua, Panama, Paraguay, Uruguay	2,306	3,797,401	$ 650.5	$ 520.3
	Credit Union National Association -- U.S.A. (CUNA)	50 States, the District of Columbia and Puerto Rico	14,380	52,810,328	$ 160,632.1	$ 12,204.5
	Free-Standing Leagues	Fiji, Great Britain, Ireland, New Zealand	928	1,060,162	$ 1,283.8	$ 1,206.4
		TOTAL[2]	32,477	69,219,960	$ 190,803.8	$ 136,673.5

Source: World Council of Credit Unions 1988 Statistical Report
Notes: [1]Amounts in millions of U.S. dollars. [2]These figures have been rounded off.

Figure 1

Seven Regional Confederations and four free Standing leagues are affiliated to the WOCCU. Besides Australia, Canada etc., regional Confederations exist in Asia, Africa, Latin America and the Carribeans. The objectives of these confederations are broadly similar. They represent the national members at the Continental and international levels, provide services for the development of credit unions and help arrange exchange of information and experiences among members. This is done mainly through occasional seminars, workshops, visits, provision of technical assistance to members and the distribution of publications. Members' expectations are high and resources, obtained from members' subscriptions, services rendered and overseas assistance, are limited. The policy making body is the General Meeting which meets approx. once a year; the Meeting elects a Board of Directors which is responsible for the implementation of the GM's policies. A CEO is appointed who heads the Secretariat. Member categories are about the same as in the case of WOCCU.

Of the Regional Confederations, we give below some information on WOCCUs Latin American affiliate, the Confederacion Latinoamericana de Cooperativas de Ahorro y Credito.

Founded in Panama in 1970, COLAC has 16 members and its budget fluctuated around US $2 million which it raises mainly from its lending services such as credit and specialized technical assistance. Its objectives are broadly similar to those described earlier. Recent activities have included: drawing up plans for the development of credit unions in Latin America (cf. *Planes de Desarrollo, 1985–1990*), evaluation of its own and members' activities which have provided the basis for the formulation of the "Development Strategy, 1990–92". Priorities identified in the Strategy document are the provision of technical services and technology transfer to credit unions. Self-sufficiency is emphasized and for achieving this, resource mobilization is considered essential. COLAC has contacts with the EEC, IDB, OPIC, USAID and Cuna Mutual.

COLAC's education and training programs are coordinated by FECOLAC, its training foundation based in Pananma. Conferences, congresses, symposia etc. are organized at FECOLAC and short and long-term courses are provided for credit union workers. A broad account of FECOLAC's and COLAC's, activities are described in the publication, *PANORAMA 2 of COLAC*; thumb nail statistical sketches of movement in different countries are included as well.

V. Regional Organizations

Since 1957, EEC wide regional co-operative institutions have grown in number in recognition of the increasing influence of EEC and its authorities in the social and economic affairs of the Common Market countries (→ *European Community*). These groupings are in the sectors of: agriculture, banking, consumer, insurance, savings and thrift and workers' production. The following table gives an overview.

1. Comite General de la Cooperation Agricole de la CEE (COGECA)

COGECA represents the agricultural and fishery co-operatives of EEC countries at the Communty level (→ *European Community*). Its aims are to: represent members' interests in discussion with EEC authorities; undertake, in order to assist the growth of co-operatives, studies of interest to agricultural co-operatives, illustrating, especially, the specificites of co-operatives; promote inter-action between agricultural co-operatives and help to coordinate their activities through appropriate means; and to ensure liasion with the Committee of Professional Agricultural Organizations in the EEC (COPA) and other relevant organizations at different levels (cf. *COGECA: The Agricultural and Fisheries Coops in the EEC*, Brussels, January 1983, 8–9).

COGECA has been active in two main fields: first, from its very inception it has contributed to the development and implementation of EEC market structures policy. It keeps "a critical eye" on new farming policy developments which may affect the market structures and co-operatives. Second: it supports COPA in the preparation and submission of position papers to EEC authorities on subjects affecting agricultural co-operatives' interests. The yearly farm price negotiations are of particular interest to it.

The price policy plays an essential role in the fate of co-operatives and their members (→ *Pricing Policy*). As such, COGECA's input to the EEC's Common Agricultural Policy remains its primary concern. Other subjects which influence the agricultural co-operatives also engage its attention. It lobbies for the improvement of instruments which govern external trade in farm products as rural co-operatives are very active in the processing of agricultural commodities. Agricultural co-operatives' wide experience also provides a good basis for COGECA to make a useful input to the evolution of sound food aid policies to third world countries as well as for assessing the aid possibilities from the Community countries. Information is collected and disseminated on training which is important for the success of agricultural co-operatives. COGECA helps in fostering mutual trade relations across national frontiers in a situation of increasing integration leading to the eventual creation of a Single Market. All this provides a sound basis for international co-operative collaboration. In addition, it has recently set up a Coordination Committee to collaborate with unions at the EEC level. This is rather a loose arrangement meant to lay the foundation for more intensive future collaboration.

Name of Association	Sector	Based	Budget[1]			Staff	Publication
			BFR in Mio	ECU in Mio	Year		
General Committee for Agricultural Cooperation in the European Economic Community (COGECA)	Agriculture	Brussels	75 (*)	1.640	1984	40 (*)	Agricola weekly
Association of Cooperative Banks of the EC (ACB)	Savings & Credit	Brussels	18.2	0.398	1984	11	
Association of Retailer-Owned Wholesalers in Foodstuffs (UGAL)	Independent Retailers	Brussels	4.6	0.100	1983	2	circulaires d'information (ca. 100 p. year)
Association of European Cooperative Insurers (AECI)	Insurance	Brussels	5	0.109	1983	3	Various
European Committee of Workers' Cooperative Productive and Artisanal Societies (CECOP)	Production	Brussels	6[2]	0.131	1983	4	Monthly bulletin
European Community of Consumer Cooperatives (EUROCOOP)	Consumers	Brussels	10.5	0.23	1983	6	Informationsbulletin
The European Union of the Social, Mutual and Cooperative Pharmacies (EUSMCP)	Pharmacies	Brussels	0.2[1]	0.004	1983	1[1]	–
European Committee for Cooperative Tourism (CECOTOS)	Tourism	Brussels	incourse of formation[1]			1[1]	–
European Cooperatives Coordination Committee (ECCC)	Agriculture Credit Retailers Production Consumers Insurance Pharmacies Tourism	Brussel	Not available			1[1]	–
European Cooperatives intersectoral Liaison Committee (CLICE)	Insurance Pharmacies plus 4 national cooperative inter-sectoral organizations (Italy 3 Belgium 1)	Brussels	Not available			1[1]	–

*) Joint secretariat with COPA.
1) Uses the facilities of one or more member organizations.
2) Estimated by the ESC Studies and Research Division.
3) Annual reports are not included.

Source: EEC: The Co-operative, mutual and non-profit sector and its Organizations in the European Community, Luxembourg, 1986)

2. European Community of Consumer Co-operative – EUROCOOP

Euro-coop is the joint body of consumer co-operative organizations → *Consumer Co-operatives*) within the EEC and is based in Brussels. Its objectives are to: represent national organizations as well as associated national organizations of consumer co-operatives outside the EC; defend consumer interests; participate in the implementation of relevant Community decisions; and promote and coordinate joint interests of affiliated consumer co-operative organizations.

I. EURO COOP ORGANISATION CHART

MEMBERS ASSEMBLY

MANAGEMENT COMMITTEE

Secretary-General

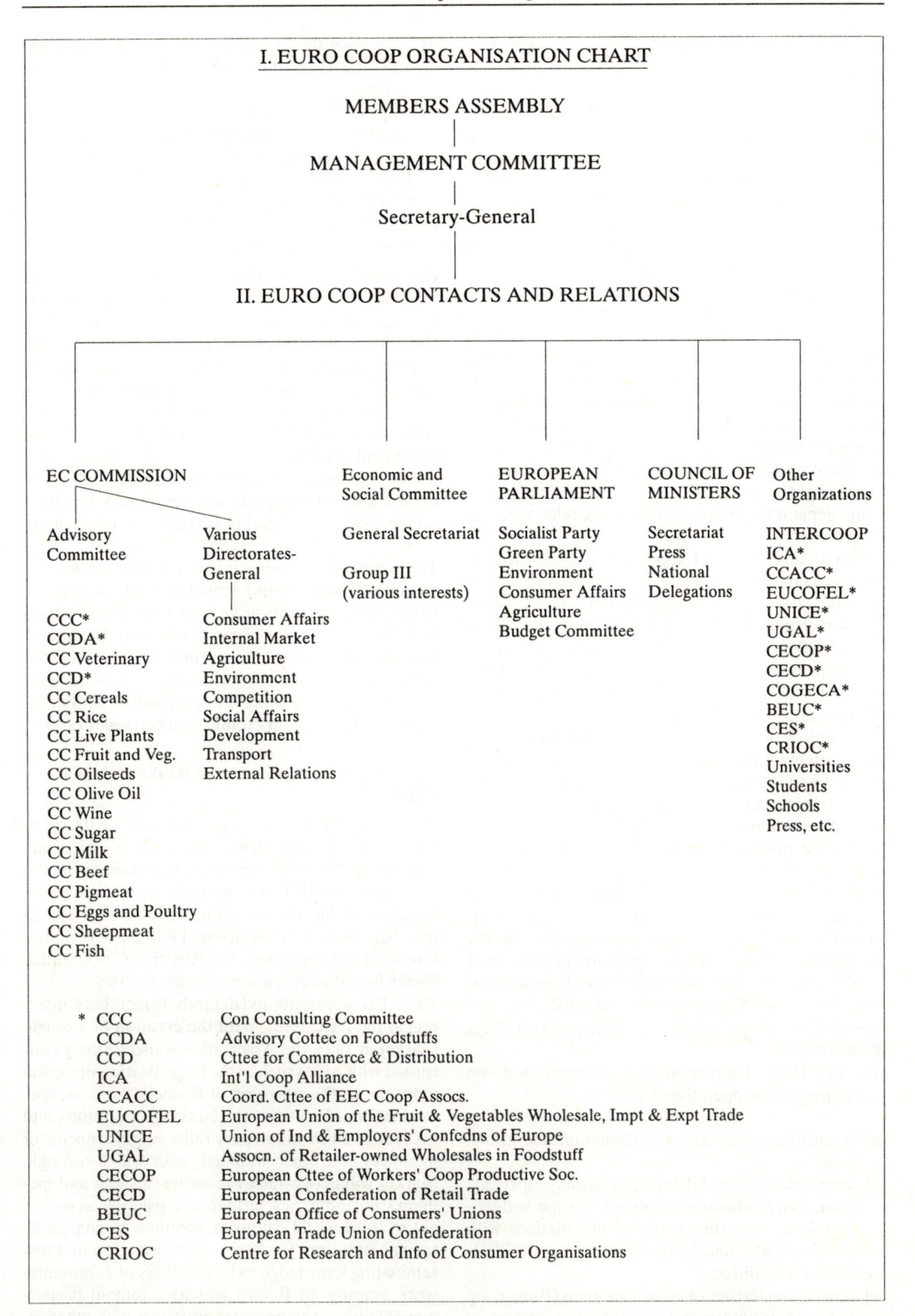

II. EURO COOP CONTACTS AND RELATIONS

EC COMMISSION		Economic and Social Committee	EUROPEAN PARLIAMENT	COUNCIL OF MINISTERS	Other Organizations
Advisory Committee	Various Directorates-General	General Secretariat Group III (various interests)	Socialist Party Green Party Environment Consumer Affairs Agriculture Budget Committee	Secretariat Press National Delegations	INTERCOOP ICA* CCACC* EUCOFEL* UNICE* UGAL*
CCC* CCDA* CC Veterinary CCD* CC Cereals CC Rice CC Live Plants CC Fruit and Veg. CC Oilseeds CC Olive Oil CC Wine CC Sugar CC Milk CC Beef CC Pigmeat CC Eggs and Poultry CC Sheepmeat CC Fish	Consumer Affairs Internal Market Agriculture Environment Competition Social Affairs Development Transport External Relations				CECOP* CECD* COGECA* BEUC* CES* CRIOC* Universities Students Schools Press, etc.

```
*  CCC         Con Consulting Committee
   CCDA        Advisory Cottee on Foodstuffs
   CCD         Cttee for Commerce & Distribution
   ICA         Int'l Coop Alliance
   CCACC       Coord. Cttee of EEC Coop Assocs.
   EUCOFEL     European Union of the Fruit & Vegetables Wholesale, Impt & Expt Trade
   UNICE       Union of Ind & Employers' Confedns of Europe
   UGAL        Assocn. of Retailer-owned Wholesales in Foodstuff
   CECOP       European Cttee of Workers' Coop Productive Soc.
   CECD        European Confederation of Retail Trade
   BEUC        European Office of Consumers' Unions
   CES         European Trade Union Confederation
   CRIOC       Centre for Research and Info of Consumer Organisations
```

Figure 2

Its members are the national consumer co-operative unions, national wholesales and other national consumer co-operative organizations. Its associate members are co-operatives from countries and regions which are "associated" with the EEC and national co-operative or consumer organizations from the EFTA countries and Euro-coop production societies. Euro-coop's organization and contacts are shown in Fig. 2.

The members' Assembly meets once a year, takes decisions on policy matters, considers the Management Committee's report, reviews the Balance Sheet and the proposed budget, determines the fee schedule and elects the Management Committee. The Committee consists of seven members who are distributed widely among Eurocoop's members. Members have a two year term. The Committee oversees the implementation of policy decisions and submits a report to the Assembly as well as a budget for the Assembly's approval. The Secretary-General is the organization's CEO and is responsible to the Management Committee for the work relating to the Secretariat.

Of an annual budget of approx. 15 million Bfrancs, 11 m are raised from member and associate member fees; the latter pay a reduced amount. The EC Commission contributes 4 m Bfrancs for the advice which EUROCOOP proffers to the Commission on consumer protection and consumer policy. Part of the funds are also used for strengthening Eurocoop's Secretariat.

Although in recent years Euro-coop has concentrated on meeting the impending challenge of a Single Market and to prepare its members for that event, its remit to protect consumer rights allows it to undertake a wide range of tasks. Its Management committee has produced an important paper which contains suggestions to members for coping with the forthcoming challenge of 1993. Moreover, it has developed its own program around the five basic consumer rights which have been recognized by the Council of Ministers. These rights are: protection of health; protection of economic interests; compensation for damages; information and education; and consumers' right to be heard on matters which affect their welfare.

During 1989, Euro-coop has concentrated on strengthening co-operatives by:

a) intensifying exchange of information and know-how;
b) emphasizing more bilateral purchasing, especially from own production; creating a Europe-wide assortment; suggesting common negotiations with multinationals and better utilization of INTERCOOP's facilities;
c) advocating the use of a common logo (Euro-coop logo) to facilitate and enhance the impact of advertisement;
d) suggesting the introduction of a European coop VISA card to facilitate payments, encourage tourism etc.
e) emphasizing cooperation across different sectoral activities (with Banks, Agricultural Co-operatives etc.). Euro-coop is also helping to create a European co-operative fund in collaboration with Co-operative Banks; and
f) by creating appropriate mechanisms for the promotion of Cooperation.

On April 17, 1989 on the occasion of the European Day, some other methods for inter-co-operative collaboration were explored and suggestions offered for Community wide activities. These included: control of unfair competition on a Eruopean level, tax harmonization, removal of intra-community barriers on trade by encourging uniformity, (e.g., in health provisions, informative labelling, rules about additives, enactment of a European Co-operative Statute), accordinggreater recognition to co-operative laboratories by taking their work into account. A brochure on the 1993 Single Market was distributed to members.

The Secretariat has made increased efforts to arrange cooperation with the movements in EFTA countries; in fact, in recent years more consumer co-operatives from EFTA have joined the Euro-coop. Euro-coop has also intensified cooperation with specialized committees of the EEC such as the Standardization Committee, the Committee on foodstuffs, Veterinary and Agricultural Product market organizations.

3. Association of Co-operative Banks of the EC (ACB)

Along with the Europe wide structure of the commercial and Savings Banks, the ACB is one of the three representative banking organizations in the EC. Created in 1970 in response to the increasing integration within the Community, ACB now has 23 member organizations from 11 Member States. Greece is not a member; the Austrian Co-operative Banks joined as Associate members in 1988.

The ACB represents and defends its members' interests at the EEC level. With the creation of a Single Market in 1993, the Association is increasingly concerned with issues such as the liberalization of capital movements, the provision of financial services, harmonization of statutes for banking operations and taxation, a uniform solvency ratio, single licencing of members and other widened tasks which a Single Market will necessitate. Financing of small and medium sized industries, farmers and fisheries as well as aid to third world countries continue to engage its special attention. Exchange of information and disseminating knowledge to its members of community work bearing on Banks' activities remain its permanent tasks. It coordinates initiatives with other organizations and maintains contacts, especially, with the European Commission and the European Parliament. ACB's policy making body is its Praesidium. The President is assisted by 2 Vice-Presidents and monitors the implementation of the policies by its General Secretary. A Liasion Office in Strasbourg keeps contacts with the European Parliament. Ten Working Parties investigate special issues and help with drafting statements for submission to community authorities.

ACB's key statistics are as follows

Banking outlets	60,750
Shareholders	35,035,000
Staff	350,000
Deposits	484 bn ECU
Loans	383 bn ECU
Consolidated Balance Sheet	705 bn ECU

4. Concluding Remarks

Three international and three regional organizations have been included in this chapter. WOCCU, however, straddles both categories as it has in its membership Regional Federations as well. While the number of International Organizations has remained steady, those of Regional associations has increased during the past three decades mainly at EEC level where increasing integration is in evidence. Umbrella organizations have been set up in various fields.

The principal objectives of all organizations (with the exception of CIRIEC and COPAC) are to represent their members and promote and defend their rights. This implies monitoring the activities of the organizations at which they represent their members, arranging exchange of experiences, collecting the necessary information for presentation of position papers, doing some lobbying work, holding regular meetings, conferences, symposia and issuing publications.

In all cases, the policy making Body is the Members' Meeting; a smaller body, assisted by a Secretary General, helps in implementing the policies. There are different categories of membership and these are reflected in the differential rates of dues and voting rights exercised.

In additon to member subscriptions and the income derived from services rendered, most organizations receive outside help from Government bodies for work in the third world. Funds are also made available by, for instance, the EEC authorities, for the advisory services rendered by a Co-operative Organization.

There is no formal coordinating arrangement among these organizations. Some loose ties exist among some but mostly they work in isolation with each other. There is no systematic exchange of information.

All international organizations are based in Europe although with the obvious exception of EEC-wide organizations, several have extensions/connections in developing countries.

Two organizations, viz., CIRIEC and COPAC, are somewhat unique. CIRIEC is devoted to research and academic pursuits, fields in which Co-operative Movements are weak. COPAC's members are all international organizations and it is exclusively devoted to the promotion of aid to the co-operatives in the Third World (→ *Development Policy*).

International Raiffeisen Union, The

WILLI CROLL

(see also: *Rural Co-operatives*; *Raiffeisen*; *International Co-operative Organizations*)

I. History of IRU; II. IRU's Tasks at This Time; III. IRU – Internal Matters;

I. History of IRU

1. What Does IRU Mean?

The International Raiffeisen-Union (IRU) is a worldwide, voluntary union of national co-operative organizations, whose work is based on the philosophy of *Raiffeisen's* principles (→ *Principles*). IRU has elected the task to cultivate *Raiffeisen's* ideas, to represent them in public, and to promote their realization worldwide by modern means.

The members of IRU between them consider it their obligation to keep revising their basic economic and social principles, and to exchange experience in doing so. They believe in maintaining the co-operative wealth of ideas in the spirit that "the ideal matter is ineffective without the material matter, but the material matter is aimless without the ideal matter".

IRU is a community of solidarity, i.e. the members who have prospered on *Raiffeisen's* principles of self-aid, self-administration and self-responsibility, make their experience available to member organizations still in the process of developing.

IRU does not enter into competition to existing international institutions (→ *International Co-operative Organizations*). It does not pursue economic activities either, nor is it an institution trying to obtain funds of any kind for financing objects e.g. in developing countries (→ *Development Policy*).

2. What is the Mandate the Founder-Fathers Gave IRU?

IRU was founded on March 30, 1968 in Neuwied/Rhine on the occasion of the 150th anniversary of *Friedrich Wilhelm* → *Raiffeisen* by 20 co-operative organizations from 10 European countries. The foundation had been preceded by the realization that, although *Friedrich Wilhelm Raiffeisen's* ideas had spread all over the world, and that there are institutions of self-aid on all continents based on *Raiffeisen's* ideology, there is little or no contact between these institutions.

This is why IRU is anxious to unite all those believing in *Friedrich Wilhelm Raiffeisen's* ideas throughout the world, and putting his system into effect. The preamble of the statutes is inspired by this spirit: "In reverence and gratitude vis à vis *Friedrich Wilhelm Raiffeisen*, founder and pioneer of a worldwide co-operative movement (→ *History in 19th C.*), anxious to unite all organizations of the world linked by this idea in a community, convinced to be committed to the maintenance and promotion of this idea and to its further development for future generations, *on the day of the 150th anniversary of Friedrich Wilhelm Raiffeisen*, co-operative organizations of his system *have resolved this union on international level* and invite all organizations throughout the world working on the same basis and in the same spirit to join."

Based on this philosophy the statutes identify the purpose of IRU: "... to cultivate the ideas of *Friedrich Wilhelm Raiffeisen*, to represent them in public, and to promote their realization worldwide by modern means, to arrange for a constant exchange of views and experience between its members, and to create, in particular, a documentation centre".

As the founders of IRU see it, the Union should not just be an ideological organization but it should rather seek "practical realizations for the benefit of all, applicable in all countries, also in developing countries. This is why the members should keep in permanent contact by information on ideas put into effect and on experience, which may well inspire other members, by making practical proposals to improve the Raiffeisen system, whose smooth flexibility has stood the test". *Count Christian von Andlau*, Founder-President, points out that, in addition to this rather internal task, IRU is called upon to "defend and spread theory and practice of Raiffeisen co-operatives, i.e. Raiffeisen's doctrine". This doctrine is more topical than ever before because it is in line with the ageless principles of human dignity, the human right to life, happiness and wealth, human rights to freedom, co-determination and co-responsibility.

IRU preamble and statutes underline that IRU is not an organization looking after interests in the field of economic policy. According to the views of its founder-fathers, it should turn to the ideal tasks of co-operative work, detached from the day-to-day problems coming up in the member organizations; it should spread or deepen *Raiffeisen's* ideas in the countries where rural co-operatives do not yet exist, or have only made a moderate start. Preamble and statutes define the road IRU is to take: to support co-operative development aid within its member organizations.

II. IRU's Tasks at This Time

1. General

IRU's statutory tasks include the maintenance of *Friedrich Wilhelm Raiffeisen's* ideas (→ *History of Ideas*), their representation in public, and their worldwide realization by modern means. There is also the steady exchange of views and experience between its members. Both tasks are closely tied to each other.

There is no doubt that it is imperative even today to keep pointing to the Raiffeisen principles of self-aid, self-responsibility and self-administration, as well as to their political and religious neutrality (→ *Principles*). It is of great importance, particularly in the organizations of the industrialized countries, to keep referring to the fact that the co-operative mandate is not fulfilled by economic promotion of the member. There must be the co-operative "More". It is the declared intent, in the spirit of self-determination, self-responsibility, to tie the members into co-operative work.

2. Exchange of Experience

The exchange of experience between members is made possible primarily by members informing the General Secretariat of important developments within their organizations. The General Secretariat functions as a sort of *evidence centre*; it processes these informations within the scope of its possibilities and distributes them to all other member organizations. This is done by circular letters, by inclusion in the annual report and by reference to materials received.

The General Secretariat also carries out *statistical inquiries* with the members (→ *Federation Statistics*), the evaluation of which is made available to all members as a source of information.

Attached to the General Secretariat in Bonn is a documentation centre which is supplied by the members with up-to-date information material. This material is listed. A list of the inventory currently brought up-to-date informs the members on receipt of the latest materials.

In addition to distributing circular letters, important developments within member organizations are included in the annual report or in the *IRU-Courier* published three times a year (cf. II.6) (→ *Periodicals, Co-operative*).

Another channel for the exchange of experience is the Board meeting held once a year, when all Board members report on important developments in their organizations or on the continents from where they come. Basic themes are also discussed in these meetings, with which individual member countries concern themselves.

3. Representation of the Interests of IRU in Public

As a rule, the interests of IRU are represented in public by a brief report on its activities published once a year. This annual report is forwarded to all members with the request to use it for their own publications, e.g. their annual reports. This means that the members refer in their annual reports to their membership with IRU, at the same time reporting, on the strength of the material made available to them, on the work of the Union. In this way, IRU has the chance to point to the Raiffeisen principles and ideas on a large scale.

Moreover, the IRU annual report is forwarded to interested organizations and also to interested journalists. A good chance to point to the work of the Raiffeisen co-operatives is the *cooperation with international organizations* (→ *United Nations System*).

IRU is anxious to entertain friendly contacts with international organizations with a view to make its activities transparent to them. For many years, IRU has been close to WOCCU (→ *World Council of Credit Unions*) through mutual membership. This also results in close friendly relations with ACCOSCA (African Confederation of Co-operative Savings and Credit Associations), with ACCU (Asian Confederation of Credit Unions), and with COLAC (Latin-American Confederation of Credit Unions). IRU also maintains close relation with CLICEC (International Liaison committee of Savings and Credit Co-operatives), ILO (International Labour Office), FAO (Food and Agriculture Organization of the → *United Nations*). There is a loose relation with ICA (→ *International Co-operative Alliance*) via a sort of observer status. As a rule IRU is represented at the functions of these international institutions by its Board members resident in the respective countries or continents.

IRU has stated right from the start that it does not intend to enter into competition with existing international institutions. Such a competitive attitude would make little sense in view of IRU's modest financial means. More important is the fact that many of the member organizations of IRU must be members of these international institutions, be it under economic or competitive aspects. Should IRU therefore enter into competition with international organizations, it would inevitably find itself in a competitive situation vis à vis its own member organizations (cf. also II.5).

Another possibility to make IRU's activities known to third parties, particularly at the General Secretariat, is by looking after *international groups* visiting the Federal Republic of Germany as the country of birth of the co-operative idea Raiffeisen.

4. Documentation Centre

The IRU statutes provide for a documentation centre to be created by the members.

By now such centres exist in Bonn at the General Secretariat, in Bombay/India and in Lévis/Canada. The centre in Bombay was established at the initiative of the Indian member organization "National Co-operative Agricultural and Rural Development Banks Federation". The centre in Canada was established by the "Confédération des Caisses Populaires et d'Economie Desjardins du Québec". Another centre is attached to COLAC in Panama.

In the documentation centres, annual reports and information material made available to the centres by all IRU members, are collected and evaluated as far as possible. This material is primarily available to all members within reach at call. Moreover, these documentation centres are also available to other co-operative institutions of the respective countries and continents, who wish to obtain information on the work of the Raiffeisen co-operatives and their up-to-date experience.

As a sideline, the documentation centres offer the respective service organizations, within the scope of their public relations work, the chance to point to the worldwide relations of the Raiffeisen co-operatives. This is part of IRU's PR work for the purpose of spreading the Raiffeisen idea.

The experience made by IRU so far with the documentation centres is good. It is imperative, though, that the IRU members currently supply the documentation centres with up-to-date information, which are then processed in the field in accordance with the requirements of the respective countries or continents. The ideal state is reached when IRU member organizations and other co-operative institutions have direct access to this information material, possibly with the aid of technical equipment.

5. Cooperation with Third World Countries

Right from the start IRU has been in favour of the co-operatives giving their own development aid (→ *Development Policy*). To that end the European co-operative organizations members of IRU were to make their know-how available.

However, from the beginning it was IRU's declared intent not to engage in technical and financial development aid, because it did not have the funds required. The decisive factor for this attitude was and is that almost all industrialized countries represented in IRU are engaged in co-operative development aid. IRU development projects would inevitably lead to a conflict of interests.

This results in two development-political tasks for IRU: For one, IRU has made it its task to coordinate the various promotional programs of the development organizations engaged in development aid. This means that IRU, the evidence centre, informs its members engaged in development aid about which members are represented in which country in which co-operative development aid projects, with whom they cooperate in that country, and which problems emerge within the scope of these projects. Via these informations, which are exchanged once a year, IRU offers the possibility of cooperation between the individual member organizations, who can take up contact. The funds for co-operative development aid – short everywhere – can be put to appropriate use.

In addition to this function as evidence centre, the IRU members wish most decidedly that IRU should organize, every other year, an International Raiffeisen Co-operative Seminar to promote the advanced training of co-operative executives from Third World countries. The first seminar was held in 1981 in Belgium, followed by Montevideo in 1983, New Delhi in 1985, Rome in 1987, Nairobi in 1989, and Buenos Aires in 1991.

Goal and purpose of these International Raiffeisen Co-operative Seminars are to exchange up-to-date experience made by the co-operative organizations of the industrialized countries with representatives of co-operative institutions from Third World countries (→ *Education, Germany*). In the past, the key themes were saving and credit, co-operative trade, co-operative examinations and training, matters of the conception co-operative institutions have of themselves, the importance of the member as the central target of co-operative work, as well as questions of cooperation between co-operatives and State and international organizations.

These seminars turn to executives of national co-operative institutions involved in everyday co-operative work. The stay of the participants at the venue is financed by IRU for the duration of the seminar.

6. IRU-Courier

IRU publishes the *IRU-Courier* three times a year. The bulletin is published in four languages (German, English, French and Spanish).

The Courier publishes basic articles on topical co-operative matters, as they arise in the IRU member organizations. The authors are both practicians and scientists. Plans are to publish also articles on experience with co-operative development aid in Third World countries, but also briefs on important events in the member organizations.

IRU Courier thus serves as a means of information between the individual member organizations, but also as information organ on IRU activities vis à vis third parties and the interested public.

III. IRU – Internal Matters

1. Membership

Regular members may become IRU members. Regular members are, e.g. national co-operative institutions established on a voluntary basis. Also, legal persons are eligible for supporting membership, who are engaged in co-operative work or who are close to co-operative activities.

At the present time (October 31, 1993), IRU has 91 members from 44 European and non-European countries. Co-operative institutions from the following countries are members of IRU: Egypt, Argentina, Belgium, Bolivia, Brazil, Federal Republic of Germany, Chile, Costa Rica, Denmark, Ecuador, England, Finland, France, Greece, Guatemala, India, Iran, Italy, Japan, Jordan, Canada, Colombia, Korea, Luxemburg, Mexico, Netherlands, Nigeria, Austria, Panama, Paraguay, Peru, Portugal, Zambia, Sri Lanka, Sweden, Switzerland, Spain, Taiwan, Turkey, Hungary, Uruguay, USA, Zaire and Thailand.

The assembly of members, the supreme decision-making organ, meets every three to four years.

2. Board

The Board represents IRU. It performs the tasks assigned him by the assembly of members and carries out the resolutions.

The Board consists of 5–25 persons elected by the Assembly of Members for a period of 6 years, and who work in an honorary capacity. The following countries are represented on the Board: Argentina, Belgium, Federal Republic of Germany, France, India, Italy, Japan, Canada, Luxemburg, Netherlands, Austria, Panama, Sweden, Switzerland and Zambia.

As a rule the Board meets once a year.

3. Presidium

The Board appoints a President and four Vice-Presidents from its midst. These five members form the Presidium. They meet at least twice a year: they confer and resolve on matters related to current IRU work.

At this time (October 31, 1993), the President is *O.W.A. Baron van Verschuer*, Rabobank, Netherlands. Vice-Presidents are: *Dr. Jörg Brixner,* Deutscher Raiffeisenverband, Germany; *Frans Florquin,* Treasurer, CERA, Belgium; *Dr. Herbert Kleiss,* Österreichischer Raiffeisenverband, Austria, *Etienne Pflimlin,* Crédit Mutuel, France.

4. General Secretariat

It is for the General Secretariat to carry out the resolutions of the Presidium and of the Board as well as of the Assembly of the members. The Secretary General works in an honorary capacity. At this time the Secretary General is *Dr. Hans-Detlef Wülker*, Deutscher Genossenschafts- und Raiffeisenverband, Germany.

5. Honorary Presidency

Since taking up its activities IRU has had an Honorary President. The first Honorary President was *Count Christian von Andlau*. The present Honorary President is *Director (Rtd.) Dr. Arnold*

Edelmann, Switzerland. There is also provision for nominating deserving IRU Board members to Honorary Board members. The gentlemen are authorized to attend the Board meetings as well as the Assembly of the Members.

6. Contributions

The financial burden IRU must shoulder is financed by the annual fees of the regular members and by contributions from supporting members. From the outset of IRU there was the declared intent to restrict administrative expenditure as much as possible in order to keep membership fees, i.e. the burden on the members, as low as possible. This is why all functions in IRU are honorary posts, including that of the Secretary General. There is only one full-time employee.

Bibliography

Andlau, Graf Christian von: Feierliche Proklamation der Internationalen Raiffeisen-Union (Solemn proclamation of IRU). Welt-Raiffeisentag 1968, Documentation, published by Deutscher Raiffeisenverband i.V., Neuwied 1968.
Croll, Willi: Die internationale Ausstrahlung der Idee Friedrich Wilhelm Raiffeisens (The international radiation of Friedrich Wilhelm Raiffeisen's idea), Lecture Montevideo, October 1988.
Ditto: Lecture on the occasion of the International Raiffeisen Day, October 1981, Brussels.
Ditto: 10 years IRU, Lecture on the occasion of the World Raiffeisen Day 1978, Wiesbaden.
Edelmann, Arnold: What is the IRU, and what are its intentions?, Lecture on the occasion of the assembly of members if IRU, May 1972, Rome.
Heins, Jürgen: Historical development of the Raiffeisen co-operatives and international radiation of the Raiffeisen idea, in particular promotion of the co-operatives in developing countries. 4th International Raiffeisen Co-operative Seminar 1985, New Delhi.
Sonnemann, Theodor: IRU – a review of 10 years of co-operative activities.
Schiffgen, Werner: IRU, Assembly of the members 1981, Brussels.
Wülker, Hans-Detlef: What is IRU – What are its intentions – What does IRU do?, Lecutre on the occasion of the 5th International Raiffeisen Co-operative Seminar, October 1989, Kenya.
Author not indicated: IRU – Information and coordination platform for co-operatives from all over the world, IRU-Courier 1/1988.

Internationalization of Co-operative Trading Enterprises

ANNEGRET GOBBERS [J]

(see also: *Commercial Co-operatives*; *Marketing*; *Supply Co-operatives*; *Managerial Economics*; *Business Policies*)

I. Introduction; II. The Internationalization of Co-operative Enterprises; III. Empirical Data on Internationalization.

I. Introduction

The rapidly increasing trend towards the opening of international markets (e.g. in the scope of the → *European Community* on the one hand, as well as the turbulent, more frequent sequences of transformations among global economic structures on the other hand constitute the important framework of conditions which corporate management must confront.
This situation is decisive for the fact that international economic activities are no longer relevant only for "large-scale enterprises" but also for trading associations structured as "co-operatives"; such enterprises ascribe to the internationalization of their activities the chance – or even the necessity – to preserve or increase their competitiveness. This can be documented among other things in that several co-operatives in the Federal Republic of Germany were practising cross-frontier management activities at a relatively early point in time, that is as early as the 1930s. A significant expansion of international business in completely varying forms and facets subsequently resulted following the establishment of the European Community in 1950.
From the corporate point of view a plethora of particular management problems accompany the move beyond national borders and activities in unfamiliar environments. One could possibly assume that the international activities of co-operative organizations do not differ in principle from those of other business enterprises. On the contrary, however, it has been proven that "co-operatives" dispose of specific institutional and functional elements compared to other enterprise forms which contradict this assumption (c.f. *Dülfer*, 1982; *Dülfer*, 1981).

1. Co-operative Trading Associations as a Specific Enterprise Form

Enterprises identified as co-operative trading associations (→ *Commercial Co-operatives*), more well-known as "co-operatives", are characterized by the affiliation of multiple independent enterprises in a common business enterprise – the "central co-operative entity" and/or the "co-operative executive entity" (genossenschaftlicher Organbetrieb) (→

Managerial Economics). This occurs with the intended objective of more efficiently meeting the economic goals of the individual members through co-operative means than otherwise possible without the → *combine* of co-operative enterprises. An organizational structure oriented around this premier objective emerges which, when compared to other company conglomerations, includes special elements.

The fundament of these particularities rests in the *specific decision-making behavior* both within the individual member enterprises as well as in the combine relationship between the member enterprises and the "co-operative executive entity". The modification of decision-making behavior assumes concretization in that the executive entity – in its capacity as a business enterprise collectively sustained by autonomous entrepreneurs – does not dispose of instructional authority over these entrepreneurs. The individual member on the other hand is interested in attaining the greatest possible promotion and therefore must be willing to orient his own decision-making behavior in such a manner that the creation of such promotion will be possible within the co-operative combine.

Although the term "co-operative" is widely familiar it can encompass the object of observation only to a limited extent; the legal form of a "registered co-operative" (→ *Legal Form, Co-operative*) is indeed quite frequently chosen for the type of co-operative activity described above (→ *Law, International*), but it is not a compulsory precondition for such activity (c.f. *Dülfer*, 1984; 1983)

A large number of co-operatively structured enterprises have decided to assume a different legal form for various reasons even though they exhibit typical co-operative structural elements – in particular an executively operating entity and independent member enterprises. The more inclusive term "co-operative" and/or "co-operative enterprise" used internationally which is *not* contingent on legal form is therefore to be used in the following discussion.

II. The Internationalization of Co-operative Enterprises

The central question in this matter addresses the particular developments co-operative enterprises witness when they carry on international business, thereby conducting their business activities in a situational context heightened by unfamiliar environmental influences. Internationalization activities undertaken by co-operatives are of interest both under qualitative aspects as well as in their empirically documented quantitative nature.

The *internationalization of co-operatives* in this context should be understood in both a qualitative and quantitative sense as each and every type of international activity undertaken by the executive entity, either as an initial undertaking or as an additional operation. The extensive nature of this definition has the advantage of not limiting the stratified problems of international management from the onset to a mere handful of characteristic categories. Borrowing from the inter-organizational approach and system theory found in business management research, we presume that in principle interdependent relationships of influence exist between organizational structure, the behavior of the participants of the organization and the specific environmental situation of the enterprise. Insomuch it is plausible that the structure of a co-operative enterprise alone does not influence the behavior of the organization participants, but rather also the reverse: regarding the corporate object, certain modes of behavior assumed by the coalition partners can lead to transformations in the formal structure of the organization. This implies that internationalization as a rule is subject to a permanent developmental process, e.g. with respect to the forms of business or country-specific activities; nonetheless, internationalization is not tied to specific, subsequent phases in the sense of an ideal type of evolutionary process (c.f. *Gobbers*).

1. Unfamiliarity with a New Environment: Cause of a Fundamental Change of Situation

As touched on above, organizational structure, the behavior of organizational participants and the environment are locked in an interdependent relationship with each other. The factor "environment" involved in management activities oriented around foreign markets, however, is of particular and exceptionally great importance. Whereas decision-makers in the home country oriented around the domestic market can fall back on a continuously developed cultural potential of experience accumulated from their earliest youth, such a trusted background is to a great extent lacking vis-à-vis the degree of unfamiliarity with the respective environment abroad. On account of this deficit the reactions and modes of behavior employed by the foreign interaction partners can only be assessed with a considerable amount of uncertainty – if at all – by the responsible decision-makers in the home country (c.f. *Dülfer*, 1981).

2. Particularities of the Relevance of Unfamiliar Environments in the Co-operative

Which consequences result for the decision-makers of a co-operative from the fundamental considerations of the environment in the scope of international management? To start with it can be determined irregardless of the particular organizational or decision-making situation, that the variants of unfamiliar conditions confronted by foreign management can represent both a constriction as well as an enlargement of their decision-making lee-way for commercial action compared to the domestic situation. Whether the environmental effects of a business commitment abroad in the end prove to be a special opportunity or a restriction, that is in the sense of a special risk due to increased uncertainty, is on the one hand dependent on the concrete expressions of such effects; on the other hand it is also contingent on the special characteristics and traits of the internationally active enterprise as well as on the strategies it pursues to achieve its defined goals.

The special relevance of foreign environments and/or cultures among enterprises structured in a co-operative manner primarily becomes evident when foreign retailers are drawn into the membership circle in the course of the internationalization (c.f. *Gobbers*).

Whereas such retailers in the case of a non-co-operative wholesale company represent external interaction partners in their capacity as *customers*, they number among the *members* in a co-operative and as such directly belong to the enterprise as "internal partners". The influence of foreign environments assumes a *direct* effect on the enterprise in the face of the special rights allocated to such persons (e.g. all voting rights in the scope of the general assembly, or even controlling and monitoring rights in the case of their election to the supervisory board). This itself is a special situation inasmuch as membership represents long-term affiliation; potential disfunctional economic collaboration with external interaction partners in non-co-operative wholesale enterprises can often be discontinued both more quickly and less problematically.

3. Specific Resources of Co-operative Enterprises: International Competitive Potential

The expectation of successful prospects resulting from different environmental and market conditions in comparison with those at home is surely a crucial factor for the management of a co-operative to decide in the favor of foreign involvement. The assessment of internationalization as "a strategy to seize special chances" presupposes that the combine member enterprise disposes of resources in the form of specific abilities with which it can canvass international markets and which provide particular competitive advantages over competing enterprises in the form of synergy effects. These "specific abilities", also conceived as "skills" in the sense of know-how or information in the literature on the theory of corporate internationalization, can assume a multitude of natures and expressions. Fayerweather for example differentiates between technological, managerial and entrepreneurial skills on the enterprise level and perceives therein essential motives for the realization of international corporate activities (c.f. *Fayerweather*, 1981).

If one draws into relation these theoretical considerations with the category of commodity and service associations under investigation here, special *manage-rial* (and eventually also entrepreneurial) *skills* can primarily be identified as specific, important abilities which differentiate such associations from other corporate forms (→ *Management in Co-operatives*). These assume a concrete form in that management functions originally restricted to the individual enterprise are transferred to the central entity level and realized in an aggregated form, and this *without* members simultaneously dispensing with the dynamic impulses of autonomous entrepreunership in the scope of the combine complex as a whole.

The particular resource transfer potential in the sense of "managerial skills" inherent in the internationalization of co-operative enterprise forms is visible in this combination of the greatest potential, effective centralization occurring on a voluntary basis and beyond national frontiers with the concurrent preservation of decentralized, autonomous economic units. It cannot be answered globally which individual entrepreneurial functions or combinations of the same afford themselves to internationalization. This is contingent in individual cases on the existent tendencies in the respective branches as well as on the given market situations at home and abroad.

III. Empirical Data on Internationalization

The following should illustrate in which form, nature and mode co-operatively structured enterprises pursue international business. This is based on the dimensional traits of internationalization goals and/or motives, alternative target markets, and systems to canvass markets; these dimensions above all serve as indicators to cast light on the particularities of market strategies employed by co-operative enterprises.

1. The Motives behind the Internationalization of Co-operatives

To start with it must be noted that the dimensions listed above are tightly intertwined with each other. The goals and motives of internationalization thus represent important determinants for the selection of foreign markets as well as for the decision favoring certain market canvassing strategies. Close connections exist between the dimensions "target market" and "market canvassing strategies" inasmuch as the regional selection of a specific target market under certain situations avails itself to only quite particular market canvassing strategies due to legal and economic restrictions.

Based on the specific motives for internationalization harbored by co-operative trading enterprises it can be proven empirically that such motives only correspond to those of enterprises structured in a non-co-operative manner in only 37% of all cases. Furthermore, five main motives can be identified which acount for approx. 45% of total, relevant decision-making motives:

Strategy	Rank according to Decision Relevance	Motive
defensive	1 2	Maintaining Market Share Securing the existent German membership body through improved co-operative performance resulting from international activities
offensive	3 4 5	Opening up new markets Creating an additional marketing and/or purchasing opportunity Attaining a competitive edge

When the structure of these five main motives is studied it becomes apparent that it is composed relatively homogeneously from a purely quantitative perspective with each motive having a respective share of approx. 20%. With regard to the qualitative structure a ratio of 2:3 exists between those which entail a defensive market strategy and those which indicate an offensive market behavior (c.f. *Gobbers*).

Seen as a whole, specific ratios and/or relationships cannot be verified under either qualitative or quantitative aspects due to the equivalent share of each motive. The particular specifics in the findings of motive analysis concerning co-operatively structured trading enterprises exist rather much more substantially in the share of relevant decision-making motives which do *not* correspond with those of other enterprise forms.

The following motives are relevant for decision making under this aspect:

1. Creating an international trade brand;
2. Prestige reasons;
3. Attaining economies of scale;
4. A lack of competitiveness in the domestic market;
5. Attaining exclusive purchasing rights;
6. Successfully sharing and exchanging experience with potential foreign business partners;
7. Historic reasons, e.g. territorial changes following World War I;
8. Merging at home with a partner enterprise already involved in international business;
9. Accidental contact between members and foreign colleagues;
10. Political and economic convergence within the European Community.

These additional, relevant internationalization intentions can be subclassified under the categories characterized in the previous analysis as "main motives" in the sense of a concretization of such motives. Nevertheless, it is quite conspicuous that several of these reasons do not represent an intended and conscious planning of foreign commitment as it might have been expected; on the contrary these reasons infer that internationalization processes in co-operative enterprises evolve in part as the result of "accidental environmental constellations".

2. Business Systems

The three classic commercial functions of purchasing, production and marketing represent the potential starting points to open and tap foreign markets. Inasmuch as the relevant category and corporate object for this investigation do not rest in production but rather are concentrated on the trading function, the strategies for foreign business in co-operative enterprises are thus essentially related to the fields of purchasing and marketing (→ *Supply Co-operatives*; → *Marketing*).

Due to systemization reasons the wholesale and retail levels need to be distinguished from each other as well as the business functions of purchasing and marketing. International activities in the field of purchasing solely affect the wholesale level. Although numerous purchasing systems exist for import trade, e.g. those effected through the central warehouse (commodity trading) as well as direct business (as a rule invoiced by the central unit), the executive entity is, nonetheless, also engaged in cases not involving the central store: examples of this include the execution of management functions in the sense of intervening as an organizer between foreign producers and domestic and/or foreign retailers.

a) Direct and indirect import

Fundamental differentiation must be drawn between direct and indirect import.

Internationalization in the form of a direct import strategy takes place in wholesale co-operative enterprises in two manners. One of these options entails the executive entity purchasing goods abroad on its own; the other option is membership in an international purchasing consortium consisting of several national wholesale co-operatives.

The advantage of direct import in comparison with indirect purchasing above all rests in the immediate contact the co-operative enjoys with the relevant foreign markets; such contact involves having direct influence on foreign producers as well as employing marketing instruments oriented around purchasing activities. These measures are of great importance for wholesale co-operatives as the potential accumulation of demand (through the conglomeration of a considerable number of indepedent retailers) represents an outstanding opportunity to exercise influence, for example on policy decisions affecting terms and conditions. This effect is substantially increased when a conglomeration of several co-operatives hailing from various countries develops into an international *purchasing consortium* instead of one lone co-operative entering a foreign market as a buyer. Furthermore, in such a constellation it is possible that the various national federations in turn utilize existing purchasing contacts on their own home market to the benefit of the consortium as a whole.

On the other hand we must proceed from the assumption that tensions between "unification" and "fragmentation" effects arise due to cost considerations (c.f. *Fayerweather*, 1981). This means that not all products collectively purchased on foreign markets (unification) are accepted and can be marketed by every member federation in the consortium in the identical manner regarding quality and quantity (fragmentation).

Furthermore, undertaking direct contact with foreign markets and/or business partners requires extensive, detailed knowledge of the market – in particular of the unfamiliar environmental dimensions; these not only play a role in the relationship with foreign business partners but also encompass other levels of influence. In order to actually take positive advantage of the potential of direct influence in the course of business involvement abroad, or in other words in the sense of member promotion, the employment of special financial and staff resources becomes exceedingly important in comparison with an indirect import strategy – above all as a means to reduce the relatively larger degree of uncertainty (c.f. *Kubcek/Thom*; *Fayerweather*, 1978; *Prahalad*).

It has been proven empirically that *all* surveyed enterprises conduct import business, whereby the largest share of these enterprises are those that import both directly and indirectly, or 58%. Second in line are those enterprises which only conduct direct import, representing a 32% share. The smallest group represents co-operatives which only execute indirect imports, amounting to approx. 10%. These facts clearly indicate that import trade is attributed considerable importance in the process of internationalization.

b) *Direct and indirect export*

International business in the form of export trade is particular for co-operatively organized enterprises in that relationships (of services rendered) can be realized with member enterprises as well as through business with non-members. The qualitative difference between these two variants results from the relevance of the promotion mandate. With regard to transactions conducted with members, such involvement abroad as a rule represents a longterm relationship; the foreign business partners are guaranteed in principle the identical membership rights as fellow partners in the domestic membership body. Business with non-members in contrast is not forced to adhere to the promotion principle: it is typified as a pure market relationship and can therefore occur without any reservations under short-term profitability aspects – either continuous or sporadic – as long as it is advantageous to the combine as a whole, executed by the central entity, and when necessary, terminated accordingly.

This qualitative difference between business conducted with member and non-members, which per se does not represent a specific trait of foreign trade, nevertheless is attributed important significance in the internationalization of co-operative combine organizations.

If one proceeds from the assumption that business with members represents the typical form of co-operative "export activity", it becomes apparent in the face of the extensive opportunities foreign combine partners have to effectuate influence by exercising their membership rights (e.g. holding a seat on the supervisory board, committees or bodies of the combine as well as exercising their voting rights in the general assembly) that the risk aspect of internationalization already touched on a number of times assumes special weight and extensive importance.

Export business conducted with members can occur either on the wholesale or retail level. In the former case, itself rather the exception, the foreign member enterprises function as wholesalers. Some of these are co-operatives in their respective native countries where each maintains a steady membership group of its own, whereas others are organized in varying forms.

The typical form of co-operative export activity – by far the most empirically verifiable form – however, concerns the integration of foreign *retailers* in the German membership body. The average level of foreign members in the respective total membership bodies amounts to a 10% share.

This slight share relativizes quantitatively the problem of risk mentioned above regarding the extensive opportunities foreign members have to exercise influence. That this fact is considered problematic in practical and relevant application is indicated among other things by the fact that a special status is created for the affiliated foreign companies. The so-called "partnership status" represents de facto an intermediate position between membership status and non-membership status. Affiliated foreign companies which have such a status are treated as members by the executive entity with regard to the pure commodity and service relationships. They are likewise entitled to participate in all meetings and organizational bodies with an advisory function but cannot exercise voting rights. This means that they are not entitled to participate in the establishment of corporate policy in the scope of the general assembly or supervisory board.

As in import trade, indirect internationalization strategies are also carried out in the scope of co-operative export trade. Rather than occurring through the active involvement of the co-operative combine itself, indirect strategies take place in the form of marketing relationships which are maintained with another internationally active wholesale combine; relationships oriented around the exchange of information are also frequently maintained.

c) Franchising

In addition to the "indirect" activities for opening up foreign markets discussed above, other strategies exist which are characterized by their intention to establish direct influence on enterprises located abroad. This type of commitment exists both with and without equity participation.

Commitments with direct influence – originally not involving equity participation – are realized among wholesale co-operatives above all in the form of franchise systems (→ *Franchising*). Our quantitative research shows that these represent approx. 16% of the sample and thus rank considerably below import and export trade.

Franchise systems are characterized in that management know-how is transferred from a franchiser to a franchisee located abroad (c.f. *Görge; Tietz/ Mathieu*). As a rule there is no capital tie-in between these enterprises: the advantage of this market tapping strategy is that the franchiser is able to enter a market *without* the risk of investing abroad. A possible explanation must be offered with respect to the relatively marginal empirical importance of franchise arrangements: Differentiation between strategies with direct (e.g. export) and indirect (e.g. franchise systems) influence on the management level of foreign business partners in the co-operative combine cannot be unequivocally drawn. Franchise-like relationships of influence exist between the executive entity (central) and individual traders in the scope of business conducted with members even when international business is restricted to the export function. The importance of such influence for the business partners involved – and thus the potential to construct a systematic analysis of this matter – in the end are contingent on the actual extent of the provided services and the degree of the *voluntary* utilization of them. As a rule it is assumed that voluntary claim to use is more apparent in pure export transactions rather than in the execution of international franchise strategies.

Further particularities in the application of an international franchise strategy in a co-operative combine arise above all in connection with the membership status of the franchisee. The subscription of shares involved in this leads to a capital tie-up between the franchiser and the franchisee. This fact is atypical inasmuch as such a strategy should be avoided in international commitments due to risk reasons, as detailed above. Contracts settled between domestic and foreign partners which are limited in time – and accordingly advantageous in international business because of their capacity to reduce risk – are either nonexistent or else only marginally applicable due to the open-ended nature of membership status.

The lack of a termination date and the de facto, bounded autonomy of the franchisee/member produce tension between co-operative principles, in particular between the principle of autonomy and the advantages of an internationalization process assuming this form. Capital-related risk plays an important role for the franchisee – but also for the franchiser – if one assumes that the transferability of domestic concepts onto foreign markets and into other cultural milieux is only conditionally possible, if at all. The relatively long-term nature of the franchise relationship for the foreign partner in connection with his relinquishment of autonomy as well as the risk of capital investment abroad could represent criteria for a sceptical appraisal of franchise arrangements, at least from the perspective of the individual enterprise level. This problematic situation complicates the application of franchise systems as a strategy for co-operative enterprises to enter or canvass international markets.

d) Participational interests in enterprises

Alongside these methods of opening up and/or tapping international markets which according to their intention do not involve capital involvement abroad, there are other business systems which from their onset presuppose equity participation. With respect to the criterion of direct influence on foreign enterprises this type of commitment can furthermore be differentiated according to the extent of various operational forms. In principle it is possible to realize international objectives through either a 100% foreign branch, or as the case may be by founding a subsidiary company, or else through the establishment of a joint venture (→ *Joint Ventures*).

Approx. 13% of co-operative enterprises undergoing an internationalization process maintain joint ventures abroad. This is therefore a form of foreign commitment which has only been availed of to a minimal degree in the co-operative sector. Based on the desired extent of capital investment and the anticipated degree of influence on corporate policy, parity majority and minority participations exist, whereby the latter clearly predominates. This is surprising inasmuch as minority participations frequently result from pure profit considerations as they do not unconditionally guarantee that business-political measures which are aspired for can in the end be enforced. In contrast, co-operative enterprises primarily attach *entrepreneurial* interest to this form of equity participation abroad. This concerns in individual cases safeguarding export interests and collectively purchasing goods, whereby both cases above all entail taking advantage of the available information channels and contacts to local partners in order to purchase/market goods abroad. Further motives which are closely related to those already mentioned include an intensive exchange of experience with the foreign partner enterprise, the reciprocal transfer of know-how (above all in the field of marketing) as well as jointly taking advantage of the economies of scale which develop.

e) Other methods of opening up foreign markets

Alongside the classic business methods for promoting internationalization the following forms of foreign commitment assume considerable importance for co-operative enterprises:
- *Centralized settlement* in direct business with foreign suppliers provided for either domestic and/or foreign members, or as the case may be, non-members;
- Maintaining *representative offices* and/or agencies abroad to handle the supply relationships between foreign members and the executive entity (central) and/or between the central and foreign suppliers;
- Loose, sporadic, *non-institutionalized forms of cooperation* with foreign enterprises with regard to purchasing and/or marketing;
- Participation in international, branch-specific committees/authoritative bodies which explore new fields of international cooperation;
- *Sharing experience* and maintaining contact with foreign purchasing federations.

These forms of international business are characterized above all in that they avoid risks, e.g. through capital investment abroad or through a fixed institutionalization of international transactions (c.f. *Gobbers*).

3. Target Markets for Co-operatives Underway with Internationalization

The internationalization activities of co-operative enterprises extend over 53 countries and all continents of the earth. Only a few countries, however, can boast of being target markets and of having a high share of business with such enterprises. Italy leads the list with 87%, followed by Austria (approx. 84%), Holland (approx. 84%), Switzerland (approx. 81%), France (approx. 81%), Belgium (approx. 65%) and Hongkong (approx. 55%). Between 30% and 50% of the co-operatives are furthermore involved abroad in Luxembourg, Spain, Denmark, England, Sweden and the former G.D.R. (c.f. *Gobbers*).

The selection of these target markets is closely connected with the marketing or purchasing orientation of the respective business system. It can therefore be concluded that responsible decision makers consider only a handful of countries suitable for the execution of marketing-oriented market canvassing strategies. These countries are Austria, Switzerland, Luxembourg, Holland and Finland. With the exception of the last two, all of these are German-speaking countries. All other target foreign markets are either predominantly or even exclusively chosen based on purchasing-oriented motives of internationalization. Aside from a few exceptions almost all European countries number among this group. The question arises in this context as to the origins of the grave discrepancies involved in the selection of target international markets. One important cause for this is traceable to the varying repercussions of both types of international business on the co-operative's organizational structure and decision-making mechanism.

Domestic and foreign environments are not in direct contact with each other on the membership level of a combine of co-operative enterprises oriented around *purchasing activities* abroad. The executive entity (central) intervenes between these two spheres and assumes a filtering function of sorts. Because of this fact typical problems inherent in international management which emerge from cultural differences among business partners or certain information deficits can be solved directly on the central level. Members are therefore only indirectly affected, if at all. As a result no specific conflicts as a rule develop out of the particular co-operative organizational structure. The choice of target foreign markets thus does not require any special structured criteria focused on cultural selection. The large number and the wide geographic dispersion of target markets abroad is thoroughly plausible in methods of business oriented around purchasing activities.

The situation for *marketing oriented* business systems is completely different, in particular among member enterprises abroad. Since foreign retailers are accepted in the combine, both domestic and foreign environments – and the cultural worlds inexorably tied to them – come into direct contact with each other on the membership level. The membership body can become more heterogeneous an account of the environmental orientation and the varying natures of interests. This situation is in principle surmountable (aside from extreme cases), but adaptational processes are necessary on all communication levels. This in turn results in additional costs which from the economic point of view must be compensated with respective profits (from international business).

In order to facilitate foreign members in their efforts to provide for their domestic market in a competitive manner, for example through the co-operative's palette of services, a diversification of the assortment and/or changes in payment policies might be necessary for the foreign market. A precondition for this in turn is a thorough (as a rule cost-intensive) analysis of the foreign market in question undertaken by the executive entity (central). A systematic structuring and/or modification of international trade relations can only result on the basis of such information.

It is conceivable that such central management activities are not financed by the entire membership body. One reason for this is that domestic members must bear the costs of these specific internationalization measures to the same extent (e.g. in the form of reduced → *reimbursement* dividends, etc.) as their colleagues abroad without, however, attaining a direct advantage from their support.

A comprehensive information policy pursued by the board as well as the involvement of members in the strategic decisions either for or against internationalization are therefore essential factors for the acceptance of consequences which subsequently arise in the form of particular costs and risks.

Bibliography

Doz. Y. Prahalad, C. K: How MNCs cope with host government intervention. In: Harvard Business Review, pp. 149–157, March/April 1980.

Dülfer, Eberhard: Brauchen die Genossenschaften eine eigene Betriebswirtschaftslehre? In: Zeitschrift für das gesamte Genossenschaftswesen, vol.33/1983, p. 252 f..

Dülfer, Eberhard: Betriebswirtschaftslehre der Kooperative, p. 38 ff., p. 54 f., Göttingen 1984.

Dülfer, Eberhard: Internationalisierung der Unternehmung – gradueller oder prinzipieller Wandel?. In: Lück, W./Trommsdorf, V.(ed.): Internationalisierung der Unternehmung als Problem der Betriebswirtschaftslehre, p. 47 ff., Berlin 1982.

Dülfer, Eberhard: Zum Problem der Umweltberücksichtigung im "Internationalen Management". In: Pausenberger, E.(ed.): Internationales Management, Ansätze und Ergebnisse betriebswirtschaftlicher Forschung, p. 1 ff., Stuttgart 1981.

Fayerweather, J.: A Conceptual Framework for the Multinational Corporation. In: Wacker, H./Hausmann, H./Kumar, B.(ed.): Internationale Unternehmensführung, Festschrift für Sieber, p. 19 f., Berlin 1981.

Fayerweather, J.: International Business Strategy and Administration, p. 534 ff., Cambridge/Mass. 1978.

Görge, A.: Die Internationalisierung von Franchise-Systemen, p. 224 ff., Göttingen 1979.

Gobbers, A.: Internationalisierung genossenschaftlicher Handelsvereinigungen, p. 63 ff., Göttingen 1992.

Keller, E. v.: Management in fremden Kulturen, p. 231 ff., Bern/Stuttgart 1982.

Kubcek, H./Thom, N.: Unsystem, betriebliches. In: Grochla, E./Wittmann, W.(ed.): Handwörterbuch der Betriebswirtschaft, 4.ed., cols.4008, Stuttgart 1976.

Marcharzina, K.: Entwicklungsperspektiven einer Theorie internationaler Unternehmenstätigkeit. In: Wacker, W.H./Hausmann, H./Kumar, B.(ed.): Internationale Unternehmensführung, p. 33 ff., Berlin 1981.

Schultz, R./Zerche, J.: Genossenschaftslehre, 2.ed., p. 145 ff., Berlin/New York 1983.

Tietz, B./Mathieu, G.: Das Franchising als Kooperationsmodell für mittelständischen Groß- und Einzelhandel, FIW-Schriftreihe, Forschungsinstitut für Wirtschaftsverfassung und Wettbewerb e. V., Köln, vol.85, p. 351 ff., Köln/Berlin/Bonn/München 1979.

Welge, M.: Management in deutschen multinationalen Unternehmungen, p. 3, Stuttgart 1980.

Joint Stock Company, Co-operative

MARTIN LUTHER [J]

(see also: *Legal Form, Co-operative*; *Law, International*; *By-laws*; *Financing*; *Forms of Cooperation*; *Legal Transformation*; *Organizational Structures, Co-operative*)

I. Background; II. Essential Characteristics of a Co-operative; III. Characteristics of a Co-operative Stock Corporation; IV. Source of Constraints Upon the Transformation Process; V. Formulating the By-laws of a Co-operative Joint Stock Company; VI. Final Comments.

I. Background

In Germany, co-operatives are increasingly adopting the legal structure of a joint stock company (Aktiengesellschaft). This tendency has been particularly promoted by the passage of the "Law amending the Provisions of Commercial Law relating to the Transformation of Company Form", dated August 15, 1969, resulting in the addition of §§ 385 m through 385 q to the German Company Law (Stock Corporation Law) (Aktiengesetz, AktG), and introducing the *possibility of* creating a co-operative joint stock company by *transforming an already incorporated co-operative* created according to the provisions of the Co-Operative Law (Genossenschaftsgesetz, GenG) (→ *Law, National*). Until 1969, a co-operative joint stock company could only be formed by way of establishing a new legal entity.

The members of a traditional co-operative may be induced to opt for the legal form of a joint stock company for a variety of reasons:

- The joint stock company form avoids typical disadvantages associated with the traditional co-operatives, e.g., in the areas of *maintaining and procuring capital.*
- As a co-operative in the form of a joint stock company, the co-operative can *engage in certain types of business* in which traditional co-operatives are not able to engage, such as capital investment and mortgage banking (see § 1, subsection 2, Investment Companies Act (Gesetz über Kapitalanlagegesellschaften, KAGG), § 2, subsection 1, Mortgage Banks Act (Hypothekenbankgesetz, HypBG)).
- Further, by utilising the form of a joint stock company, it is easier to *concentrate the administration and control* of a co-operative.

In most cases, a co-operative opting for the joint stock company legal structure attempts to retain as far as possible the essential features of a co-operative whilst simultaneously reaping the advantages associated with joint stock companies. This hybrid corporate form has become known as the *co-operative joint stock company (Genossenschaftliche Aktiengesellschaft).*

The co-operative joint stock company form is both a feasible and in many cases a recommendable legal structure. Nevertheless, the incorporation of co-operative principles into a joint stock company structure is not without legal difficulties. The purpose of this article is, after discussing briefly the nature of co-operatives (II) and co-operative joint stock companies (III), to highlight some of the ways in which a co-operative may effect this transformation into a co-operative joint stock company and some of the constraints faced by it in the process (IV–V).

II. Essential Characteristics of a Co-operative

A co-operative has three main essential features:

1. Promotion Purpose (Förderungszweck)

Unlike capitalistic corporations, co-operatives are not permitted to have a profit making objective as their main company purpose. Rather, a co-operative must have a *promotion purpose (Förderungszweck)* of seeking to provide its members with direct commercial benefits from its business operations (→ *Promotion Mandate*). The level of commercial benefits obtained by members depends directly on the level of transactions between the co-operative and its individual members. The greater such turnover, the greater the → *Reimbursement (Rückvergütung)* to the members.

2. Principle of Identity (Identitätsprinzip)

Members of a co-operative are also customers of the co-operative – that is, they provide business to the co-operative and, *simultaneously*, their interests are promoted by the business conducted by the co-operative (→ *Theory of co-operative Cooperation*).

3. Personal Structure (Personalistische Struktur)

Co-operatives depend on the *personal participation* of their members, and the rights of the members are tied to that personal participation rather than, as in the case of a traditional stock company, to the level of their respective capital contributions.

Thus a co-operative is a *corporate body structured around individuals* which strives for the economic advancement of its members whilst remaining fundamentally aware of the principle of identity.

III. Characteristics of the Co-operative Stock Corporation

A co-operative joint stock company is a joint stock company characterised by the features of a co-operative:

- promotion purpose,
- the principle of identity and
- the personalistic structure.

Therefore, when transforming a co-operative into a joint stock company, the shareholders of the company must formulate its → *by-laws* in such a manner that the joint stock company retains those co-operative features.

The extent to which it is desired to incorporate → *co-operative principles* and goals into the joint stock company structure will *vary in each particular case*. In all cases, however, provisions have to be made that the co-operative nature of the company is not retained to such an extent that, despite its transformation into the joint stock company form, it remains subject to the limitations associated with the traditional co-operative, the avoidance of which was the motive for the transformation in the first place (see, supra I.).

IV. Sources of Constraints upon the Transformation Process

A co-operative joint stock company is not subject to any special regulations different from a "regular" joint stock company. However, like other joint stock companys, it must respect the *limits imposed* upon its by-laws by § 23, subsection 5, AktG.

According to the first sentence of this provision, the by-laws may only *deviate* from the provisions in the AktG if the AktG expressly allows the articles to do so. Therefore, those provisions of the AktG which apply mandatorily must be observed by a joint stock company irrespective of whether they are consistent with co-operative principles.

According to the second sentence of § 23 subsection 5 AktG, the by-laws may *supplement* provisions of the AktG where those provisions do not purport to exhaustively regulate the particular matter.

Accordingly, § 23 subsection 5 AktG poses a constraint in the creation of co-operative joint stock company since a breach of that provision will result in the *invalidity* of the article concerned in the by-laws. There is, therefore, a limitation as to the extent to which co-operative principles can be applied in a joint stock company.

V. Formulating the By-laws of a Co-Operative Joint Stock Company

The remaining part of this article concentrates on the differences between Co-operative Law and Company Law in relation to these matters. It further suggests, where appropriate, ways in which the by-laws can be formulated so that, to the extent it is desired and legally permissible, the co-operative nature of a company is retained upon its transformation from a co-operative into a joint stock company. In this respect, it shall be distinguished according to the main provisions in the by-laws of a co-operative joint stock company as follows:

- company purpose (1)
- company object (2)
- company name (3)
- membership (4)
- organization (5).

1. Company Purpose

a) The promotion purpose of a Co-operative

§ 1 of the Co-operative Law (GenG) requires that the co-operative has as its *company purpose (Gesellschaftszweck) a promotion purpose*. The description of the promotion purpose in the co-operative's by-laws may elaborate upon the standard formulation in § 1 GenG but may not deviate from it in scope.

Further, § 6 subsection 2 GenG requires that the *company object (Unternehmensgegenstand)* be specified in the by-laws. The company object describes the range of activities in which the company aims to engage in order to fulfill the promotion purpose – that is, it describes the "means" by which the "end", economic advancement of its members, is sought to be achieved.

The definition of the company object complements and gives precision to the very general promotion purpose. As a result, a more concrete purpose emerges, namely the advancement of the co-operative's members through engaging in activities falling within the range specified in the company's object.

The board of directors (Vorstand) and the supervisory board (Aufsichtsrat) are obliged to pursue the promotion purpose in accordance with the company object. If they fail to act accordingly their actions on behalf of the company will be valid, the ultra vires doctrine not being applicable in Germany. They may, however, be liable under §§ 34 and 41 GenG for compensation.

b) The neutrality of the purpose of the joint stock company

The AktG addresses on several occasions the *company object,* being the range of activities in which the joint stock company strives to achieve its corporate purpose, but in contrast to co-operative law, does not contain any requirement of, or indeed any reference to, the *company purpose (Gesellschaftszweck).*

Typically, the purpose of the joint stock company is the *making of profit*. However, in contrast to the co-

operative, it may pursue any legally permissable purpose – that is, it is characterised by neutrality of purpose.
As with co-operatives, the administrative competence of the board of directors and the supervisory board is limited by the object of the company and, where a legally permissible company purpose is set down in the by-laws, also by such purpose. Managing directors and members of the supervisory board can be liable for compensation where they act inconsistently with that object and purpose (§§ 93 and 116 AktG).

c) Anchoring the co-operative promotion purpose in the by-laws

It is possible to anchor the co-operative promotion principle in the by-laws of the co-operative joint stock company because of the neutrality of purpose of the joint stock company. The promotion purpose may be incorporated either as a company purpose or as a business policy (→ *Business Policies*). Such a company purpose or business policy is considered to be a permissible restriction upon the administrative competence of the board of directors under § 76 subsection 1 AktG. However, the power of self-management of the board cannot be taken away completely by determining the corporate purpose or business policy.
There is a limitation to the application of the promotion purpose in the co-operative joint stock company so far as the co-operative institution of reimbursement (Rückvergütung) is concerned (→ *Assessment of Success*). This institution cannot be kept totally intact in a joint stock company because of the *prohibition* under § 57 AktG *against return of capital (Einlagerückgewähr)*. This should more accurately be referred to as the *prohibition against hidden profit distributions*, as "capital" in this sense is to be construed as including the entire company assets and not merely the nominal capital in the technical sense. Further, tax regulations against hidden distributions of profit (verdeckte Gewinnausschüttung) lay boundaries against reimbursements.
This implies the following consequence:
Whilst the joint stock company is characterised by neutrality of purpose, and therefore does not have to strive to make profits, its failure to produce a profit is legally not allowed to be a merely a result of means which constitute a hidden profit distribution under corporate or taxation law (→ *Taxation*).
Therefore, it is only possible within very restricted limits to promote the interests of shareholders by giving them preferential treatment in the price of goods or services purchased or supplied by them (→ *Pricing Policy*). Such preferential treatment of the shareholders must be justified by the advantages which the company actually accrues from reciprocal business relations with its shareholders. For example, a co-operative joint stock company may sell its products to a shareholder at a discount price if the shareholder qualifies just as an independent third party for such a discount in view of large quantities. The total turnover of the transaction justifies the preferential treatment.

2. Company Object

There is *no difference* as to the type of company object required for a co-operative and a joint stock company, except that in relation to the latter, it must be specified more concretely.

3. Company Name

The name of a co-operative joint stock company may retain describing terms, such as "co-operative" (as an *adjective*), which reflects its particular goal orientation, provided the name does not suggest that the company has a legal form which is inconsistent with its nature as a joint stock company. This is why it would not be permitted to use the *noun* co-operative in the name of a co-operative joint stock company.

4. Membership

a) The personalistic structure of membership in the co-operative

The co-operative is, in essence, an association of individuals with a variable number of members. Membership status is attained by personal application for entry into the organization, and terminates through cancellation or death or expulsion of a member.
Numerous *rights* and obligations arise out of membership, such as rights to use the co-operative's facilities and to receive reimbursement from the co-operative. The right to vote is also of a personal nature in that it is based on the principle of "one man – one vote" rather than of the extent of capital contribution. Further, the members are entitled to equal and fair treatment (Grundsatz gleichmäßiger Behandlung) (→ *Group, the Co-operative*).
Obligations of members include those of using the co-operative through purchase and/or supply. The close personal ties in the co-operative produce an increased obligation of loyalty (Treuepflicht) and, as a result, of the majority-based decisions on the legal status of each member, a duty of toleration (Duldungspflicht). As a result, a member is obliged to bear the financial consequences of a majority decision.

b) The capitalitistic structure of membership in the joint stock company

In contrast to the co-operative, the joint stock company is by definition particularly suited to capital intensive operations (→ *Equity Capital*). Its capital requirements are met through the distribution of *shares* which *represent* the *membership rights*. In a joint stock company, the focus is on the extent of the capital investment of the shareholder rather than the shareholder itself. The *right* of the shareholders to equal treatment is incorporated in a modified form in the joint stock company to the effect that shareholders with equal shareholdings are to be treated equally (§ 53a AktG).

The AktG does not impose a special *obligation* of loyalty upon shareholders. The shareholder is, particularly when exercising its shareholder's rights (such as its voting right, right to information and right of avoidance), simply bound to act in good faith and must not misuse its rights.

c) The organization of membership in the co-operative joint stock company

As evident from the above, there are considerable organizational differences between a co-operative and a "normal" joint stock company. However, the AktG allows *some flexibility* as to the organization of membership in a joint stock company and, accordingly, there are numerous ways in which a joint stock company can be made to resemble a co-operative ((aa) to (ff)).

(aa) The issuing of registered shares of restricted transferability (vinkulierte Namensaktie)

Pursuant to the principle of identity, the members of a co-operative are also in a business relationship with it, and accordingly, membership is limited to a discernible, identifiable group of persons.

According to § 68 Subsection 2 AktG, a joint stock company *may issue* registered shares, the effective transfer of which requires the approval of the company. Such shares are called bound name shares (vinkulierte Namensaktien; Latin: vinculatus = fettered, bound), hereinafter, *shares of restricted transferability*.

The by-laws may set out preconditions which have to be satisfied before the company is required to approve the transfer, and circumstances in which approval can be refused. The issue of such shares by the joint stock company can be used to restrict membership, as in a co-operative, to an identifiable group as it enables share transfers to be monitored and for the management to prevent control of the company being vested in individual shareholders, groups of shareholders or undesirable third parties.

(bb) Obligation to tender and right of preemption

The AktG does not contain any further restriction upon the transfer of shares. However, the shareholders may agree in a separate contract on further restrictions. In particular, such a contract can impose on shareholders to first offer the shares to other shareholders *(obligation to tender)*. Further, such a contract may grant the right to the remaining shareholders to enter into a contract of sale of the selling shareholder with a third party *(right of preemption)*.

Whilst preemptive rights only come into consideration in the context of a company with a *few members*, obligations to tender the shares can be utilised in companies with *many members* in order, for example, to remove members who do not continue their business relations with the company. Thus, in the event of a shareholder's failure to remain in a purchaser/supplier relationship with the company the shareholder can be obliged to offer its shares to its fellow shareholders. Such measures can be valuable in enforcing the co-operative nature of a co-operative joint stock company.

(cc) Introduction of shares imposing additional obligations (Nebenleistungsaktie)

Pursuant to § 55 AktG, additional statutory obligations to regularly perform duties other than the payment of money can be imposed on shareholders holding shares of restricted transferability (discussed supra, (aa)).

That provision was introduced as a concession by the legislature to the co-operative sugar factories which amalgamated in the second half of the last century into joint stock companies. The shareholders in each case then imposed upon themselves the obligation to supply their company with sugar beets.

The provision in §§ 55 AktG is generally seen as a foreign element in the joint stock company legislation, because it explicitly enables a personal co-operative element to be introduced into the otherwise capitalistic structure of the joint stock company. In practice, this form of the public limited company with shares entailing additional shareholder obligations has, however, only gained significance in the sugar industry. The reason for the *limited practical* importance of such shares is due to the problem that approval of *all* shareholders is later required to impose further obligations or to increase existing obligations. Therefore, rather than relying on this statutory provision, for practical reasons additional obligations are more likely to be imposed on a contractual basis.

(dd) Non-Voting preferred shares

In order to *improve* its *ability to obtain capital*, the co-operative joint stock company – as all joint stock companies – can issue non-voting preferred shares, i.e., shares conferring no voting rights but increased participation in the profits (§§ 139 et seq. AktG). Thereby, it can take advantage of the capital made available to it by willing third parties without simultaneously being required to grant these new shareholders complete rights of determination as to the future path of the company. Similarly, it is possible to issue non-voting preferred shares to shareholders who want to invest more capital; again, the existing distribution of voting rights will not be affected.

(ee) Limitation of voting rights

The voting right of a shareholder is his most important administrative right.

Conceivably, the voting rights granted to members of a co-operative joint stock company could be made to conform to the *"one man – one vote" principle,* thereby restricting the importance of the number of shares owned. However, it should be recognised that the co-operative "one man – one vote" principle is frequently the very reason why co-operatives opt for the form of a joint stock company in the desire to provide their members with a capital-dependant voting right corresponding with their financial contribution and risk. Where this is the motivation for the transformation of the legal form, adoption of the "one man – one vote" principle is inappropriate.

Rather, the co-operative joint stock company could be concerned to ensure that third parties do not gain *undesired* voting *influence* through the acquisition of shares. This is possible by the company exercising control over share acquisitions. Further, the voting rights and the distribution of votes in a joint stock company can be varied, in order to make the company resemble more closely a co-operative, by introducing voting right restrictions and issuing non-voting preferred shares.

(ff) Facilitating the entry and withdrawal of shareholders

One of the co-operative principles is that *free entry* into, *and exit* from, membership of the company should be possible. How can this be reconciled in the joint stock company, where it is conceivable that a shareholder who wishes to terminate its membership may be unable to find a buyer for its shares?

It would contravene the principle of capital maintenance if a shareholder were able to terminate unilaterally its relationship with the company and, upon such termination, be entitled to demand reimbursement in relation to its surrendered shares. A provision in the by-laws vesting a right of termination for the shareholder, the exercise of which would result in the dissolution of the company, would also contravene the AktG. It would legally only be permissible to provide in the by-laws that a shareholder could demand the company to redeem his shares, but commercially that would leave the company at risk, because it would be obliged to compensate the value of the shares resulting in one of the disadvantages of a co-operative which is often the very reason for transformation into a joint stock company (→ *Financing*).

The co-operative joint stock company can, however, seek to *improve* the limited *fungability* of its shares by concentrating the supply and demand for its shares in the company, engaging as intermediary in the trade of its shares and purchasing its own shares as buying agent.

If then no shareholders have been located ready and willing to sell their shares to interested parties, the company could revert to shares raised at the occasion of capital increases and held by banks upon an agreement with the company. In such an agreement, the company can oblige the bank

- to buy the shares at the price of their emission,
- to hold them until a direction of the company to sell them to a third party,
- and to pay the profit, if any, to the company.

As a result, the company can use such shares (called "Verwertungsaktien", i.e. "utilization shares") to facilitate and increase the trade with its shares.

5. The Organizational Structure

As the joint stock company law served as a model in the formulation of co-operative law, the co-operative and the joint stock company are similar to a large extent in their organisational structure (→ *Organizational Structure of Societies*).

a) The Board of Directors

The *principle of self-administration* laid down in § 9 subsection 2 GenG prescribes that members of the board of directors must also be members of the co-operative. In contrast, there is an implicit principle of third party organization in the AktG, involving the separation of ownership and control. Thus, in the AktG there is no requisite share qualification for appointment to the board.

However, if in an exceptional case it is necessary to incorporate the co-operative principle of self-administration into the organizational structure of the joint stock company, the by-laws can provide for personal qualifications of potential managers for appointment to the board. After considerable debate, it is now accepted that the by-laws can provide that a director's office on the board shall terminate if such qualifications were not satisfied at the time of appointment or if they later cease to be satisfied.

b) The Supervisory Board

The difference in the legal provisions relating to the supervisory board in a co-operative and those relating to a supervisory board in a joint stock company also reflects the application in the co-operative of the principle of selfadministration and in the joint stock company of the principle of third party administration.

Again, if necessary, the *principle of self-administration* can, by virtue of the provisions in the AktG relating to delegation rights (§ 101 subsection 2 AktG) and the power to specify qualifications for appointment in the by-laws (§ 100 subsection 2 AktG), be applied to the composition of the supervisory board in the co-operative joint stock company. Similarly, the articles can provide for the termination of the office of a member of the supervisory board where the statutory prerequisites for appointment have not been satisfied at the time of appointment or if they later cease to be satisfied.

c) The General Meeting

In a general meeting the members of a co-operative theoretically are in a stronger position to exercise *influence over the company* than in the general meeting of shareholders in a joint stock company. In practice, however, primarily because of the lack of activity of the members in a co-operative, through their inadequate exercise of their voting rights, the influence of members in the co-operative has dwindled and the board of directors have assumed more and more power.

As a result of this development, the interests of the members could be protected better in the general meeting of a joint stock company than in the general meeting of a co-operative. The legal position of shareholders of a joint stock company, particularly by virtue of the significant minority rights vested in shareholders under the AktG, is overall stronger than those of the members in a co-operative. Moreover, the *position of the shareholders* in the joint stock company can be improved as follows:

- The position of shareholders of a joint stock company can be even further improved by relaxing, to the extent legally permissible, the preconditions for the exercise of minority rights and by making it more difficult for decisions to be made which disadvantage the shareholders. In particular, the by-laws can provide that a minority of less than 5% as provided for in § 122 AktG – can request that a general meeting be held.
- The position of shareholders can be additionally strengthened by the fact that, pursuant to § 103 subsection 1 sentence 3 AktG, the articles of assocation can provide for the dismissal of persons elected to the supervisory board in a general meeting by a simple majority, instead of a three-quarter majority, of votes casted.
- Alternative majority voting requirements, again increasing the rights of shareholders can also be provided for in the by-laws in relation to resolutions which have serious consequences for shareholders, such as the dissolution of the company or the entry into a control agreement pursuant to which the management of the company would be submitted to another enterprise.
- Where a joint stock company has issued shares of restricted transferability (*see supra* V. 4. c) (aa)) in an effort to preserve characteristics of a co-operative, it would be possible for it to foster its co-operative features by drafting restrictions in its by-laws on the raising of additional capital through the issue of freely transferable shares.
- The by-laws could also require special voting majorities for changes to its provisions, particularly those which would alter the goal orientation of the co-operative joint stock company.

VI. Final Comments

To conclude, it is clearly possible to incorporate essential co-operative principles into the legal structure of the joint stock company. The AktG leaves open numerous possibilities as to how this can be effected. The co-operative joint stock company is, indeed, a noteworthy alternative to the conventional co-operative and is likely to receive even more attention in the future.

As of yet, however, practical experience has not provided a definite prognosis as to the long term effectiveness of transforming a cooperative into a co-operative joint stock company that is, as to whether the company will in the future remain true to its co-operative character or whether it will develop eventually into a typical joint stock company. There are cases in which the co-operative joint stock company has retained substantially the features of the co-operative from which it originated. On the other hand, however, there are also companies which have gone in the other direction and which, today, do not differ in any way from a "normal" joint stock company.

The direction taken by the co-operative joint stock company will depend to a large extent on the will and the degree of interest of those concerned and involved in the company.

Bibliography

Baumbach, Adolf/Hueck, Günther: Aktiengesetz, 13.ed. with additional volume, Mai, 1970, München 1968.

Baur, Jürgen F.: Förderungszweck und Mitgliederselektion im Genossenschaftswesen, BB 71, p.1216.

Birck, Heinrich: Probleme der Eigenkapitalausstattung deutscher Genossenschaften, Festschrift Draheim, p. 109, Göttingen 1968.

Brixner, Jörg: Marktintegration durch bäuerlich-genossenschaftliche Aktiengesellschaften, Karlsruhe 1966

Förschner, Edzard: Zur Problematik der Verwertungsaktien, AG 64, p. 61.

Friedewald, Rolf: Die personalistische Aktiengesellschaft, Köln 1991.

Gadow, W./Heinicken, E.: Aktiengesetz, Großkommentar, Begründet von Gadow, W./Heinicken, E., 3. ed., Berlin 1970–1975, 4. ed., Berlin 1994.

Gail, Winfried: Aktienrechtliche Rückgewähr von Einlagen und steuerliche verdeckte Gewinnausschüttung – Gemeinsamkeiten und Unterschiede, WPg 70, p. 237.

Gessler, Ernst/Hefermehl, Wolfgang/Eckardt, Ulrich/Kropff, Bruno: Kommentar zum Aktienrecht, München 1973–1993.

Gessler, Ernst: Zur zukünftigen Verfassung der Genossenschaft, Festschrift für Reinhardt, p. 237, Köln 1972.
Gessler, Ernst: Bedeutung und Auslegung des § 23 Abs. 5 AktG, Festschrift für Luther, p. 69, München 1976.
Großfeld, Bernhard: Genossenschaft und Eigentum. Zur Problematik des "wirtschaftlichen" Eigentums der Genossen, Tübingen 1975.
Henzler, Reinhold: Investitions- und Finanzierungsprobleme der Genossenschaften in der wachsenden Wirtschaft, Festschrift für Draheim, p. 97, Göttingen 1968.
Hölters, Wolfgang: Stimmrechtsbeschränkungen als Schutz vor Überfremdung, DB 75, p. 917.
Hommelhoff, Peter: Satzungsmäßige Eignungsvoraussetzungen für Vorstandsmitglieder einer Aktiengesellschaft, BB 77, p. 322.
Lang/Weidmüller. Genossenschaftsgesetz, Kommentar, 32. ed., Berlin 1988.
Luther, Martin: § 23 Abs. 5 AktG im Spannungsfeld von Gesetz, Satzung und Einzelentscheidung der Organe der Aktiengesellschaft, Festschrift für Hengeler, p. 167, Heidelberg/New York 1972.
Luther, Martin: Die genossenschaftliche Aktiengesellschaft, Tübingen 1978.
Lutter, Marcus: Verwertungsaktien, AG 70, p. 185.
Meyer/Meulenbergh/Beuthien: Genossenschaftsgesetz, 12. ed., München 1983.
Müller, Klaus: Kommentar zum Gesetz betreffend die Erwerbs- und Wirtschaftsgenossenschaften, 1. ed., Bielefeld 1976–1980, 2. ed., Bielefeld 1991.
Schrötter, Hans Jörg: Vinkulierte Namensaktien als Bremse der Unternehmenskonzentration, DB 77, p. 2265.
Westermann, Harry: Zweck der Gesellschaft und Gegenstand des Unternehmens im Aktien- und Genossenschaftsrecht, Festschrift für Schnorr v. Carolsfeld, p. 517, Köln/Berlin/Bonn/München 1972.
Westermann, Harry: Die unternehmerische Leitungsmacht des Vorstands nach geltendem und zukünftigem Genossenschaftsrecht im Vergleich zur Leitungsmacht des Vorstands der AG, Festschrift für Reinhardt, p. 357, Köln 1972.
Westermann, Harry: Die Umwandlung einer Genossenschaft mit beschränkter Haftung in eine Aktiengesellschaft, Gedächtnisschrift für Rolf Dietz, p. 79, München 1973.
Zöller, Wolfgang (ed.): Kölner Kommentar zum Aktiengesetz, 1. ed., Köln 1970–1985, 2. ed., Köln 1986–1993.

Joint-production Co-operatives

EBERHARD DÜLFER [J]

(see also: *Classification; Conceptions, Co-operative; Classic/Neo-classic Contributions; History in 19th C.; Israel*)

I. Terminology and Manifestations; II. History; III. Legal Provision; IV. Revealed Weaknesses of Joint-production Co-operatives; V. Avoidance Strategies and their Results.

I. Terminology and Manifestations

The joint-production co-operative or producer Co-operative (PC) (workers' co-operative society; Produktivgenossenschaft/Arbeiterproduktivgenossenschaft; société coopérative ouvrière de production) also known in socialistic terminology as "production co-operative", is a co-operative of producers (agricultural, craft trade or small-scale industrial trade) in which the members of the co-operative group not only are the owners (shareholders contributing "paid-up shares" and exercising voting rights based on their person and not on their capital investment) but also at the same time the co-workers of the co-operative enterprise (→ *Classification*). The double characteristic of membership innate in the co-operative (*double qualit*y) – the "identity principle" – thereby rests in the concurrence between co-entrepreneur and co-worker, or between employer and employee on the personnel level. The → *promotion mandate* generally characteristic for the co-operative is addressed according to its original concept through the utilization and marketing of workers' labor input; according to another position it is addressed through the facilitation of attaining joint income.

Specialized literature on the subject casts varying light on the joint-production co-operative with respect to its typological classification. Differentiation can be drawn (Dülfer 1984) between

- the genetic approach and
- the positivistic approach.

The genetic/developmental approach views the joint-production co-operative as the ultimate and most complete integrational form of the entire co-operative complex which consists of member households/enterprises and the co-operative enterprise (→ *Structural Types*). In this case the latter entity has absorbed the member enterprises; the members as individuals are no longer interactive commercial partners of the executively operating co-operative enterprise but rather are a part of the enterprise itself in their capacity as workers. When one views the joint-production co-operative in this light as the final product of the integrational process, one can readily recognize how it is related to the promotional co-operatives, although these in turn qualitatively represent a different phenomenon with respect to their external relationships.

The positivistic approach in contrast trains its view solely on the actual ("positive") phenomenon at hand without taking into consideration its previous genetic/developmental history. This approach, therefore, emphasizes the fundamental and thus qualitative difference in both structure and function to promotional co-operatives oriented around their members' households and/or enterprises.

The fact that joint-production co-operatives could manifest themselves in greatly varied forms under evolutionary aspects was interpreted by *Villegas* (1975) as an important factor for the characterization of this type of organization. He therefore distinguished between the following "development types":

I a,b	Small Groups	PC with united labor or division of labor
II	Large Groups	PC with direct democracy
III	Large Groups	PC with indirect democracy
IV a,b,c	Small or large groups	PC with capitalists and/or wage workers

In the market economy the joint-production co-operative does not enter the market as a combine of enterprises as does the "promotion co-operative" but rather acts as an autonomous individual undertaking. Variational forms range from the "full co-operative" (Infield) encompassing all corners of life, until the quasi-corporation involving non-member employees (e.g. in France), or even borderline forms of (agricultural) multi-purpose co-operatives (group farming) found in developing countries. Delimitations must be drawn on the one hand with regard to compulsory joint-production co-operatives, people's enterprises (Volkseigene Betriebe), people's communes or kolkhozes found in the (former) communist economic systems (→ *State and Co-operatives, Socialism*; → *Rural Peoples Communes*; → *Kolkhozes*) and on the other hand with regard to agricultural production promoting co-operatives (*Schiller-Scheme*) involving private land ownership (in developing countries) (→ *Produktionsförderungsgenossenschaften*), or with regard to forms of worker participation in either capital or management found in market economies (shared property, co-entrepreneurialship) (→ *Partnership Enterprises*). In contrast to these forms the "worker self-management enterprise" assuming varying legal forms and organizational structures (foundation, limited company, the Yugoslavian ASV, the Algerian Entreprise Autogérée) can be classified typologically as joint-production co-operatives.

Specialized literature on the subject characterizes "production co-operatives" as co-operatives whose production facility or enterprise processes their members' products (e.g. dairies, rice mills, oil presses); in such cases the members themselves are not working as employees in their enterprise (→ *Production Co-operatives*). The "work co-operative" (societa cooperativa di lavoro) in Italy represents an intermediate form which does not productively utilize the labor input of its members itself but rather arranges and negotiates the employment of their members (as itinerate laborers) in other companies or projects.

II. History

Borrowing from the previous theoretical conceptions of utopian socialism (→ *Robert Owen*, *Charles Fourier*) and the followers of *Saint Simon*, → *Phillipe J. B. Buchez* (1832) founded the first joint-production co-operative in France. *Louis Blanc* propounded their promotion through state financing in the scope of a national economic system of co-operative socialism; *Ferdinand Lassalle* was a proponent of a related form in Germany. In England *Owen's* concept was embraced by the "Christian socialists". *Karl Marx* in contrast expressed his scepticism but accepted the joint-production co-operative as a potential tool to illustrate the success of socialistic production (→ *Socialist Critics*). The antipodal liberal stance was defended by → *Hermann Schulze-Delitzsch* who conceived the "commercial enterprise on joint account" (Gewerbebetrieb für gemeinsame Rechnung) as a joint production co-operative of industrial workers intended to help them regain in the group their lost independence previously enjoyed as artisan craft workers.

The practical importance of the joint-production co-operative in Germany has remained slight in the meantime; only in the construction sector were the construction joint-production co-operatives successful following the First World War which were established by the trade unions as socialist → "*Bauhütte*" and as Christian-national joint-production co-operatives. The co-operative establishments following 1945, undertaken by refugees and impaired individuals, were likewise short-lived. Only 19 joint-production co-operatives were recorded in the DGRV statistics in 1983. Starting in the late 1980s, new efforts came to light to fuse joint-production co-operatives with ecological goals or to use them as an "alternative" enterprise form to preserve jobs in cases of insolvency. Several thousand small-scale enterprises assuming varying legal forms were founded – in part exhibiting the character of a professional firm, for example in the field of information science.

The development of rural and handicraft joint-production co-operatives in Italy took a different turn. There were more than 11,000 PCs with 428,000 workers in 1981 (*Bonin et al*. 1993). In France, 1,345 PCs existed in 1986, employing 34,276 workers, also joined together in the *Confédération Générale des Sociétées Coopératives Ouvrières de Production* which predominantly encompasses enterprises with non-member workers. The PC has a long tradition in Great Britain, where 3400 PCs existed in 1968, reduced to about half of this figure in 1980 (ibidem).

Following 1945, the joint-production co-operatives witnessed a politically influenced renaissance in the centrally controlled economic systems of Eastern Europe's communist countries. These were primarily forced collectivization efforts which in part transformed themselves back again to self-help organizations after 1989 (e.g. in Poland and Hungary). The attempt to achieve general compulsory collectivization in the agricultural sector via "socialist co-operatives" and "people's communes" even failed in

China, and village co-operatives with partial collectivization have since been reintroduced. The Co-operative Law in the (former) Soviet Union was revised so drastically under *Gorbachev's* presidency in 1987 that three Soviet citizens could found a "co-operative" which also employed wage workers (non-members). This was the first step in the direction of company privatization in the face of the ban on private property with respect to means of production enforceable at that time. This form of production co-operative in the meantime has lost importance on account of the fundamental legal reform which occurred after the dissolution of the Soviet Union.

Up through 1989/90 in Yugoslavia, the "worker's self-management enterprise" formed a basis element of a decentralized national-communist economic system, but in the course of time it has undergone numerous variations and succumbed to state-political intervention. More recent developments are likewise proceeding in the direction of privatization.

A particularly problematic situation arose in the Federal Republic of Germany following reunification with the former German Democratic Republic (GDR). The latter state brought with it 4,000 agricultural production co-operatives ("LPGs") with 900,000 members (1988) and 2,733 (1983) production co-operatives for handicraft industries ("PGHs") (→ *GDR*) which as a whole proved incapable of holding their own in the face of competition in the market economy in their original situation. Furthermore, it was determined in the reunification contract that the LPGs and PGHs were to be transformed into other legal forms by a set date in 1992, or at least into the form of a registered co-operative in accordance with German Co-operative Law in its 1973 version. Considerable difficulties arose concerning the provision stating that all members choosing to withdraw should receive their share of the total value of the co-operative as indemnity in cash.

The forms of workers' co-operatives conceived by immigrants in Israel (after 1909) – the Kibbutz and the Moshav Ovdim (1921) traceable to the Zionist Kwuzah and the Oppenheimer settlement co-operatives – underwent their own development (→ *Israel*; → *Oppenheimer*).

Joint-production co-operatives in developing countries have experienced quite varying developments. In part, these have been borrowed from precolonial forms (Peru: *Ayllu, Minka, Ayni*) or have been established anew (Mexico: *Ejido*, 1910; Algeria: *Entreprises Auto-gérées*, 1953). As a whole, however, results in the agricultural sector with such forms as the "*champs communs*", "group farming" or other special national manifestations such as the "Ujamaa Co-operative" (Tanzania, 1969) have not been inspiring. Joint-production co-operatives in handicraft industries in which members provide their own equipment and tools have only been of temporary developmental-political advantage in connection with the promotion of small-scale industry.

III. Legal Provision

Despite their structural difference with respect to promotion co-operatives, in most countries (as in Germany) joint-production co-operatives are included in the legal provisions for other types of co-operatives; they only are seen as a variant of the legal corporate form of the "registered co-operative". In the German Co-operative Law, which has served as a prototype for numerous other countries – above all in Latin America, the joint-production co-operative is explicitly listed as an exemplary manifestation of the registered co-operative (German Co-operative Law, § 1). In spite of this, suggestions can be found in the literature on the subject proposing that a separate provision be created for the joint-production co-operative.

French law includes a multiple level provision for co-operatives. The basic legal forms are the *Société Anonyme à Capital et Personnel Variable des Code de Commerce* and the Law of 1947 in its 1955 amended version for the *Société Coopérative*. Several special laws grounded on these legal bases exist for individual types of co-operatives, included the form of the joint-production co-operative.

IV. Revealed Weaknesses of Joint-production Co-operatives

Despite the fascination that joint-production co-operatives have instilled for many years in social reformers and social theoreticians of varying schools and persuasions, practical applications of this form have mostly stumbled on certain fundamental problems. In market economic orders joint-production co-operatives have usually exhibited a lack of competitiveness or have transformed themselves after a successful initial phase into corporations (*Oppenheimer*: "The Law of Transformation"). In terms of neoclassic economics it is evident that the *dividend maximizing* PC makes other choices of labour than the *profit maximizing* private firm and – in doing so – does not attain a pareto-efficient allocation of labour (in the short run) because of different institutional conditions. Other results are possible in the long run (*Bonin et al.* 1993). (*For details* → *Labour-Management*).

In centrally controlled market orders, joint-production co-operatives frequently suffer from a lack of motivation among members upon whom membership has been forced, and this to such a degree that they can only maintain their existence on the basis of continual political intervention.

The following reasons document the frequent failure

of practical attempts to establish industrial enterprises with the organizational structure of a joint-production co-operative (*Dülfer* 1984):

a) The contradiction between the egalitarian structure of the membership group and the hierarchical structure of the production enterprise

This conceptional contradiction is apparent in large-scale production enterprises with numerous decision-making levels. Such antagonism can only be ameliorated in part through efforts to introduce a team-oriented organization or a co-operative management style. The theoretical concept of the "democratization" of the enterprise activities runs against social and economic boundaries.

b) The danger of levelling out performance

The egalitarian concept of the membership group, itself contradicting true performance-related participation in the organization's success, encourages the performance level of the weakest member to serve as orientation for work motivation and as a standard for members' willingness to contribute to performance.

c) The disjunction of the membership body

Although the original membership group may be homogeneous the danger can arise that the allocation of management functions and implementation responsibilities can lead to the formation of partial subgroups with varying rights and power positions from which differing group interests can ultimately develop.

d) Conflicts in the distribution of the result

As the membership becomes more heterogeneous, conflicts emerge concerning the distribution of profits and losses. Such conflicts become more heated when bonus systems are in effect for management and professional staff.

e) The lack of a qualified management staff

It is often quite difficult to find the necessary management and professional personnel among the fixed membership body. The employment of qualified management and/or specialized professional staff from beyond the membership body on the other hand is restricted or even prevented through the principle of self-administration.

f) The tendency towards exclusivity

In cases of tight group cohesion a tendency of exclusivity towards outside individuals results based on social-psychological reasons with regard to the turnover and employment goals of the membership group at hand.

g) A lack of adaptability in the face of changes in the business cycle

The fixed nature of the membership body determined by the exclusivity tendency detracts from the organization's ability to adapt to altered market situations and employment outlooks. The assumption of new members is not desired, and members cannot be excluded. The resulting lack of flexibility in the face of the economic cycle leads to competitive disadvantages in comparison to enterprises structured differently.

h) Weak Capital Structure

Because members of joint-production co-operatives normally can only raise relatively small amounts of capital and inasmuch as the principle of "one man – one vote" discourages any incentive for varying levels of capital investment, the capital structure as a rule is chronically weak.

i) A lack of borrowing power

The weak capital structure combined with the lack of opportunities to provide collateral security limits the co-operative's borrowing power.

j) The danger of state intervention

Because the assumption of state financial assistance is often necessary as a result of the weak capital structure, the danger of state intervention arises which can potentially lead to the envelopment of the co-operative in the state's economic administration.

V. Avoidance Strategies and their Results

Recent experience has, nonetheless, shown that the typical structural weaknesses of the joint-production co-operative can be overcome either in part or even in full under certain conditions. This is the case:

a) when the conceptional contradiction between members' equal standing and the organizational structure encompassing all persons is not seen as a disruptive factor. This is the case in small membership groups in which this contradiction does not have an effect, or when hierarchical organizational structures are considered necessary and tolerated in large-scale enterprises;

b) when the performance level is not undermined either because all involved persons strive to contribute according to their abilities or when performance-related participation in the organization's success is accepted;

c) when the allocation of management and implementation functions is voluntarily accepted because varying levels of responsibility with regard to the co-operative group are attached to such tasks.

d) when qualified management staff can be found among the membership body and when specialists from beyond the group can be integrated into the existent organizational culture;
e) when deviating employment levels are compensated by the existent membership group through voluntary overtime in periods of high employment and through voluntary pay cuts in periods of low employment activity.
f) when equity can be accumulated relatively quickly through cutbacks in consumption and/or when borrowing power can be attained either through proven performance potential or the provision of collateral security by a third party.

A particularly grave problem confronts the joint-production co-operative as a rule in that its members are not included in *national social security systems* based on their capacity as members of a corporate-legal body. On the other hand, they are usually not in the position incomewise to cover the corresponding risk through private insurance policies. A bad turn of business therefore not only endangers members' ability to cover a loss and the corresponding liability risks with respect to the creditors of their co-operative; upon the dissolution of the enterprise they also face impoverishment and destitution.

This danger in the meantime has been curbed in numerous countries in that the members of joint-production co-operatives have been granted an employee status in social security law. The handling of this matter is also facilitated in that there is no longer a legal impediment (e.g. in German Co-operative Law) against concluding a completely normal labor contract between the co-operative as a juristic person and the member regardless of his capacity as a shareholder. Although this situation without a doubt does not correspond to the "ideal" co-operative model, it, nonetheless, is possible through the status of the registered co-operative as a legal person. It thus can be utilized by membership bodies true to their co-operative orientation as a useful aid to protect themselves against risk without damaging their co-operative.

The aforesaid opportunities to shape organizational form – at least in central Europe – have been used in the past decades by greatly varied membership groups. They have been utilized in part to implement "alternative" political concepts and ecological efforts as well as in connection with developments in information technology and the expanding commercialization of software production and personal computer service. Typical signs of degeneration appear as long as the structural problems addressed above are unable to be resolved because a solution is made either more difficult – or even prevented – by ideological conceptions, heterogeneity among the membership body, a lack of knowledge in business management matters or the reactional manner of the group; such signs include the disjunction of the membership body, extensive employment of non-members as either workers or as middle-level management staff, the appointment of external management personnel by regulatory authorities, the transformation into a corporation or a state-controlled enterprise, etc.

The majority of the well-known cases of large-scale success in the practical application of joint-production co-operatives were based on special religious (the Hutterite community, the Zionist kwuzah) or on political-ideological fundaments (the Israeli kibbutz, the Basque Spanish project in Mondragon) – cases which cannot be conveyed onto other situations. Mixed forms incorporating either individual or collective structural elements (Israel: Moshav Shitufi) therefore are more steadfast, particularly those in the direction of the integrated co-operative (e.g. taxi co-operatives, co-operative shipping companies, service co-operatives).

Bibliography

Bonin, John P./Jones, Derek C./Putterman, Louis: Theoretical and Empirical Studies of Producer Cooperatives: Will Ever the Twain Meet? In: Journal of Economic Literature Vol.XXXI Sept. 1993), pp. 1290–1320.

Dülfer, Eberhard: Operational Efficiency of Agricultural Cooperatives in Developing Countries, Rome 1974.

Dülfer, Eberhard: Arbeiterproduktivgenossenschaften. In: Gaugler, E. (ed.), Handwörterbuch des Personalwesens, Stuttgart 1975, cols.63–70.

Dülfer, Eberhard: Produktivgenossenschaften. In: Mändle, E., Winter, H.-W. (eds.), Handwörterbuch des Genossenschaftswesens, Wiesbaden 1980, cols.1356–1371.

Dülfer, Eberhard: Betriebswirtschaftslehre der Kooperative: Kommunikation und Entscheidungsbildung in Genossenschaften und vergleichbaren Organisationen, Göttingen 1984.

Dülfer, Eberhard: Gibt es eine Renaissance der Produktivgenossenschaft?. In: Genossenschafts-Forum, Bonn 1985, pp.450–454 und pp.490–493.

Engelhardt, Werner W.: Produktivgenossenschaften In: Handwörterbuch der Sozialwissenschaften, Vol.8, Stuttgart et al 1964, pp.610–612.

Fuchs, H.: Der Begriff der Produktivgenossenschaft und ihre Ideologie, Köln 1927.

Nutzinger, H.G.: Die Überlebensfähigkeit von Produktivgenossenschaften und selbstverwalteten Betrieben. In: Loesch, A. von (ed.), Selbtverwaltete Betriebe. Neue genossenschaftliche und gemeinwirtschaftliche Unternehmen? Überblick und Beurteilung, Beiheft 10 der Zeitschrift für öffentliche und gemeinwirtschaftliche Unternehmen, Baden-Baden 1988, pp.35–58.

Schiller, Otto: Gemeinschaftsformen im landwirtschaftlichen Produktionsbereich. Grundsätzliche Fragen und praktische Handhabung im internationalen Vergleich, Frankfurt am Main 1966.

Seuster, Horst: Genossenschaftsmodelle für die ostdeutsche Landwirtschaft. In: Berliner Schriften zum Genossenschaftswesen, Vol.2, Göttingen 1992.

Villegas, V.R.: Die Funktionsfähigkeit von Produktivgenossenschaften, Tübingen 1975.

Joint Ventures

KLAUS MACHARZINA [J]

(see also: *Intercompany Cooperation*; *Strategic Alliances*; *Management Teams*; *Mergers and Consolidations*; *Managerial Economics*)

I. Theoretical Background; II. Preparation of Formation; III. Joint Venture Contracts; IV. Joint Venture-Stability; V. Problem Areas of the Joint Venture-Management.

I. Theoretical Background

The international joint venture, besides the national joint venture (*jv*), is presently acquiring growing importance because today it is often regarded as the only possibility of presence in a foreign market. This assumption is based on the rapidly progressing internationalization of markets through the intensification of international business relations as well as on the national regulations of many countries which restrict foreign investment possibilities in order to protect domestic markets.

1. Definition of the Concept

A legally and structurally independent company is considered a *jv* (equity joint venture, joint ownership venture or co-operative undertaking) which is established by at least two legally and economically independent partners, whereby their independence remains intact in contrast to group companies (→ *Intercompany Cooperation*). This is based on capital investment shares, the pooling of complementary assets or knowledge as well as the medium- to long-term economic cooperation of the partners set down in contract, which bears the entrepreneurial risk according to the appropriate investment share (*Weder*). The typical *jv* is founded and run by two partners with equal participation ("fifty-fifty" *jv*). Other *jvs* are known in which an equal investment does not exist or where there are more than two companies involved (→ *Producer Associations*).

Cases of purely contractual, temporally restricted cooperation could also be considered a further form of the *jv*. Here no new company is founded with a legal entity, and as a rule it is exclusively limited to the completion of a project. As the so-called "contractual joint ventures" (non-equity joint venture, syndicate business) lack the characteristic of a lasting, long-term cooperation, their association occurs without interlocking capital (*Hellwig*).

The international *jv* is characterized in that at least one of the partner companies has its base in another country, or in that essential activities of the *jv* either predominantly or exclusively take place in a foreign market. In comparison to the purely national *jv*, cooperation above and beyond national borders leads to an increased complexity of problems which is caused by the impact of a heterogeneous environment. The international *jv* presents the dominant form of direct investment for companies pursuing internationalization strategies besides the 100% subsidiary company (legally independent) or the foreign branch office, which is treated as a dependent business establishment for both legal and tax purposes (*Endres*).

2. Joint Venture Typology

Jvs serve the realization of a particular economic goal orientation, the characteristics of which are usually expressed in a *jv* form. Fundamentally, the cooperation could extend to all sectors of the affected company; in such cases the *jv* would be independent and would execute its own purchases, production and sales. In practice, however, the cooperation is usually reduced to a single function or to a few special sectors of the partner companies. In such cases a typology can be undertaken according to the functional differentiation of the sectors of the company to which the cooperation extends.

- In *production joint ventures* only the production, part of the production or final assembly of mass-produced goods are undertaken in order to avoid trade restrictions or to make use of tariff, tax or similar advantages associated with local production. In spite of its legal corporate form, the production *jv* is often structured in a way that a strong technical, economic or financial dependency is related to a partner.
- The *sales joint venture* primarily serves to achieve turnover goals and to obtain direct access to foreign markets through the circumvention of tariff and non-tariff trade barriers such as import duties and bans. Many countries, traditionally above all the countries with state-controlled trade, do not allow the importation of certain foreign products or direct foreign investment, or else only to a limited degree. In such cases the possibility of establishing a *jv* is often the only alternative available for a business operation abroad.
- *Research and development joint ventures* are established with respect to the utilization of synergy effects of know-how transfer by technology intensive companies. These should avoid double investments which are caused by parallel, cost-intensive development projects. Technologically oriented cooperation is increasingly being realized in → "*strategic alliances*", a new form of co-operative competition between two or more companies. The goals of such alliances are the combination of individual strengths in particular business areas, the realization of competitive advantages, and the strengthening or development of success potentials. Strategic alliances are global in magnitude,

concentrating on particular regions and can assume the form of a *jv* (*Contractor/Lorange*).
- If the development of a supply industry of one's own is undertaken at a certain location with favorable wage levels, production costs and resource availability in order to produce for a partner, the transfer prices and conditions of the supply arrangement must guarantee the survival and profitability expectations of the supplier *jv*.
- A further form of application exists in the safeguarding of procurement sources of raw materials through the participation in a *jv* that either undertakes the production or the extraction of raw materials.
- The preferential treatment that local tenderers frequently enjoy when public contracts are awarded makes it attractive to take advantage of this by local *jv* (*Langefeld-Wirth*, 1990b).

A more thorough typological differentiation of *jvs* can be undertaken according to the relation of the partners of the *jv* to each other (*Buckley/Casson*):
- A horizontal *jv* represents the combination of similar types of activities, e.g. a *jv* between companies with competing product lines;
- In a vertical *jv*, complementary activities and resources are pooled;
- In a diagonal *jv*, various technologies are combined in a new product. The partners are active in the same economic sector but do not compete with each other.
- Other combinations are feasible based on these fundamental types.

Formerly, *jvs* predominantly had a complementary function. Today, bringing together the individual strengths of the partners (teaming up) is the primary purpose.

3. Theoretical Explanations

The starting point for the explanation of the motives and driving factors of the potential activity of companies in foreign markets is correspondingly the disadvantage start/up situation of a foreign company compared to the domestic companies there. Reasons for this unfavorable situation include additional preparatory costs to enter the market which themselves are based on various legal, cultural, political and geographic environments. From an economic standpoint, companies which plan on corporate activities abroad must have compensatory advantages at their disposal.
One advantage lies in the possible utilization of property-rights (→ *Institutional Economics*) in the form of know-how in technical, management and organization skills as well as knowledge of the market. These specific business advantages can be evaluated with the help of the internalization theory (Rugman) or the transaction cost approach (*Coase, William-son*). Accordingly, direct investment will be undertaken when the transaction costs of an internal utilization of the competitive advantage are lower than those which arise through a utilization in international markets. The decision favoring the market entry of a *jv* can be explained from the combination of three factors, namely internalization advantages, the indivisibility of resources and barriers to the merging of companies (*Buckley/Casson*). The stronger the influence of the last two factors the higher is the preference for a *jv*. The stronger the latter, the smaller are the internalization effects in comparison to those factors and thus the greater is the probability to opt for the *jv* as the entry strategy.
One internalization advantage of the international equity joint venture in comparison to purely contractual cooperations is the reduction of transaction costs through reciprocal protection by the investment of the partners of the *jv* (*Kogut*, 1988a).
It is possible to empirically ascertain further motives besides these theoretical statements of inherent economic calculation which could play a decisive role in the establishment of a *jv*.

II. Preparation of Formation

1. Joint Venture Motives

There are three essential criteria which lead to the choice of a *jv* as the form of foreign corporate engagement. In the first stage the national regulations of the host country make the participation of domestic capital and labor necessary in the investment plans of a foreign company. The reasons for these investment regulations are based on the fear of foreignization of the national economy as well as in the effort to promote domestic companies and to look after the balance of power structures which guarantee the preservation of national and local interests (*Kumar*, 1975). A second criterion for the decision favoring a *jv* is the endeavor to reduce risks, particularly in host countries with unstable environmental conditions. Business functions dependent on the environment, such as purchasing, sales, personnel and public relations, are intentionally handed over to the partner in the host country as he has special knowledge at his disposal of the market, insider information and experience in dealing with the authorities and other governmental institutions. Finally, companies acquire a domestic character through the presence of the partner from the host country in the international *jv*. Through their proximity to the market they can attain a certain protection from eventual reprisal ranging from dispossession to nationalization by the government of the host country.
The *jv* is regarded as the most intensive and difficult form of international cooperation and thus usually requires an already long and successful business relationship and intensive knowledge of the partner.

2. Partner Selection

An early initiation and establishment of business contacts in the form of cooperation which, in comparison to the *jv*, exhibit a lower degree of cooperational intensity (cooperation agreements, managements contracts, licensing contracts, franchising) help to evaluate and test the business conditions of the future *jv* partner.

Partners in a *jv* can be companies, co-operatives, co-operative organizations and even state institutions. Several country-specific *jv* regulations, like those of the countries with state-controlled trade, prescribe state participation (mixed venture); state enterprises, authorities, ministries or export trade organizations can make use of this.

Western companies, particularly American ones, have been hesitant in the past to start up mixed ventures because of their conviction that private entrepreneurship is not compatible with planned economies. Furthermore, the influence of the state bureaucracy and the possible intervention of the state itself were seen as dangers. A rejection in principle of a mixed venture can, however, mean sacrificing a chance at market entry in an as of yet unopened market which, under the proper conditions, could be very profitable (*Kumar*, 1987). The advantages of a successful business activity through a *jv* in centrally administered economies (above all, the early procurement of market shares or experience) in the recent past may have contributed to the fact that this form of cooperation has found a strong interest in the former Eastern Block against the background of their opening economies.

III. Joint Venture Contracts

1. General Comments

Although the principle of contractual liberty lies behind the joint venture contract (*jvc*), one can notice a certain structural similarity among the most different forms of *jv*. Usually the first step is a rudimentary agreement or a statement of corporate policy with which the necessary permits can be obtained from the authorities. The formation contract contains the constitutive elements and regulates the problems which affect the formation and business operations of the *jv*. It can be amended by additional clauses which may become necessary through specific conditions or situations.

In many countries with state-controlled trade, massive governmental barriers exist in the form of laws, conditions and regulations (controlling the employment of foreign personnel and their pay, the extent of production, difficulties in transferring profit, unclear administrative norms) which inhibit the interest of foreign companies in such forms of cooperation.

2. Content of International Joint Ventures Contracts

a) Domain of Cooperation

The international *jvc* first delineates the tasks and areas of co-operative activities the *jv* will dedicate itself to. Feasability studies or collectively researched business materials help in the decision-making process of such determination of activity.

b) Legal Form

The chosen legal form, the headquarters of the *jv* and its articles of association are defined in the international *jvc*. In principle the participating partners are free in their choice of the legal form of the *jv*. The decision is oriented according to the typical norms for law, taxes, etc. which do not always correspond to the wishes of the partners. Therefore a large amount of willingness to compromise is needed by those involved even in the preparatory phase. *Jvs* are predominantly established in the legal form of a joint stock company (*Endres*) (→ *Law, International*).

Companies within the member states of the → *European Community* have had the opportunity since July 1, 1989, to form a joint venture in the legal form of a European Economic Interest Group. This is the first legal form of European Law for companies and primarily serves the international cooperation between small and mid-sized firms within the Community.

c) Shareholders' Capital

aa) Participation

As long as no legal regulations stand in the way, the allocation of shares in the *jv* can occur as majority, parity or minority participations.

Many countries, above all developing countries and those with state-controlled trade, prescribe a minority participation for the foreign partner in order to control the foreign interests more effectively. It can, however, be mentioned in this connection that the level of influence the *jv* partner exercises on the management can be controlled independently from the formal participation relationship laid down in the *jvc*. In many situations it has been proven that through its particular expert knowledge the domestic partner has more bargaining power than the foreign company; also the legal conditions usually offer more leeway in voting procedures and decision-making rights. Because of this the interest of the domestic partner in an equal participation is frequently not as high as it could be expected.

bb) Opportunities and evaluation of investment

Share capital can be in the form of cash investment, real estate and other tangible property such as plants, equipment and user's rights on them, as well as user's rights on patents and know-how. This means that the partners have leeway in structuring the choice of their investment inputs through reciprocal coordination independent from legal regulations. Those kinds of special legal conditions predominantly in countries with state-controlled trade have recently been relaxed and dramatically improved as a result of massive criticism from companies in the Western industrial countries (e.g. the mandatory recalculation of cash investments into non-convertible currencies). The value of the investment is calculated to the contract prices under consideration of world market prices. If these are not available, a measure of value will be set between the partners through agreement. Furthermore, an agreement must be reached in international *jvcs* concerning the fundamentals of accounting, the calculation of the balance and valuation as no unanimously accepted and enforceable regulations exist on the international level.

d) Authority and management

The authority structures within the *jv* are similarly laid down and the competences, instructional powers and responsibilities are regulated in the *jvc*. Such arrangements concerning the individual responsibilities are left to the partners as no binding norms exist in this regard.

The corporate law of the country in which the headquarter is situated must also be taken into consideration, for example when deciding whether additional control mechanisms such as supervisory or advisory boards should be established besides the business management and general assembly. With respect to the definition of competences, a distribution according to ability and the kind of contribution provided by the partners for the *jv* has proved useful; usually the partner who provides the know-how is granted sufficient influence in the technical areas regardless of his investment share.

The problem of agreeing on the applicable management methods and techniques is particularly difficult in East-West *jvs* because dilemmas of market-oriented business activities must be solved in a centrally organized economy – an environment not familiar with the market system. A solution to the problem cannot occur completely independent from the usual accounting and management practises used by the other company in the respective country (→ *Corporate Culture*).

e) Regulations concerning dissolution

The reasons for dissolution and appropriate regulations are largely dependent on special *jvcs*. The *jv* ceases to exist either upon termination of a time period previously agreed upon or through a bilateral annulment of the contract.

It must be stipulated in the *jvc* if and under what conditions a partner can withdraw and what consequences that will have for the *jv*: whether dissolution, the assumption of corporate shares by another party, the possibility of participation of third parties or alienation, which could be restricted through bans, waiting periods or prior purchase options. In particular it must be set down whether secondary contracts which standardize the relations with suppliers and the like between the partners and the *jv* are to be cancelled or preserved. Before signing a *jvc* with participation from countries with state-controlled trade, one should at first check if a legal convention exists protecting capital which, in the case of the dissolution of the *jv*, provides for the convertibility and transferability of proceeds upon liquidation. If one partner assumes the participatory share of another, the payout of the withdrawing partner must be regulated in the *jvc*; this, in turn, is based on the valuation of contribution and the yardstick to appraise it.

f) Relevant law and the settlement of differences

If the *jv* partners belong to different legal systems it is difficult to formulate the agreement pertaining to relevant law of the *jvc* in the articles of association. This matter is further complicated when the *jv* has its headquarters is a third country. It is therefore expedient in such cases to regulate the arbitration process clearly in the international *jvc*.

IV. Joint Venture-Stability

Seen from the view of competition law, the *jv* is designed to extend over a long-term existence (*Börner*), whereas from the stand-point of business administration it is characterized more as a short- or medium-term phenomenon (*Macharzina*, 1981). Empirical studies of national (*Thompson*) as well as international *jvs* (*Franko*) have confirmed the latter viewpoint and indicate that *jvs* as a whole do not exist for a long duration, but rather present a fairly unstable market entry vehicle. After a certain amount of time and regardless of the satisfaction or general situation of those interested, they are either dissolved or taken over by one of the partners through 100% ownership (*Macharzina*, 1975). A comprehensive empirical study of international *jvs* in the United States (*Kogut*, 1988b) came in particular to the conclusion that around 68% of all *jvs* had a life expectancy of up to six years, whereby the mortality rate varied according to the purpose of the *jv*. Jvs which had sales-related objectives in fields such as marketing show a clearly higher mortality rate than, say, strictly production, research and/or development *jvs*. The way the *jv* ceased to exist, either in dissolution or in a full takeover, seems to depend on the risk potential of the particular spectrum of tasks and activities. *Jvs* which had high risk objects (e.g. development of new products) more frequently liquidated than those with a smaller development risk (e.g. the further development of an existent product), which usually found their end in the form of a total takeover by one of the partners.

Other studies looking at the stability of jvs provide contradictory results. On the one hand, the assumption is supported that the *jv* which is dominated by one of the partners shows a higher level of stability through the reduction of management conflicts (*Killing*'s sample was limited in its survey scope and thus its predictability, and *Beamish*'s was in reference to *jvs* in developing countries). On the other hand, no connection could be found between the share of participation and the stability of the *jv*. (*Janger, Awadzi, et al*).

V. Problem Areas of the Joint Venture-Management

Considerable coordination difficulties arise for the management of an international *jv* because of the presence of two or more parent companies as no clear allocation of competences can be drawn from the degree of ownership for the statement and enforcement of the *jv* behavior as is the case for 100% subsidiary companies. Disregarding the immense coordination requirements in an international *jv* often results in performance levels that do not meet prior expectations, or, in the extreme situation, in failure.

1. Control of Joint Ventures

Let alone the demonstrated problems associated with horizontal coordination and the choice of strategy, a critical variable for the success of a *jv* is the effective control of its activities through the parent companies. The discussion of the control problems of international *jvs* has up to now almost exclusively only touched on individual aspects of control. Three basic dimensions emerge from a synthesis of the various studies and explanations:

- There is an emphasis of research on administrative and control instruments which the parent companies can use (mechanisms of control: *Tomlinson, Friedman/Beguin, Stoppford/Wells*);
- The extent of the control is measured by the relative level of intensity which can be used by the parent companies (extent of control: *Dang, Killing, Beamish*);
- Another focus is on the dimension of the spectrum of selected *jv* activities on which the parent companies can have influence and control (focus of control: *Schaan, Geringer*).

In contrast to the traditional point of view, these three dimensions are not incompatible, but rather complementary and dependent on each other illuminating a different aspect of control. *Geringer* and *Habert* combined all three control dimensions into a complex model of *jv* success incorporating strategy selection and thus developed a collective context for the various approaches.

2. Heterogeneity of Formation Motives and Company Policy

Conflicts of interest between the *jv* partners can be traced back to the differences in motives and intension behind the actual formation. The foreign partner usually pursues a long-term, systematic incorporation of the potential market of the country in question, whereas the domestic partner often wishes to incorporate access to new technologies (*Kumar*, 1975). Similarly, the valuation of previous inputs such as the intangible value of an invention also entails a conflict potential. Differences between *jv* partners in reference to the goal orientation or the appropriate market strategy can frequently only be solved through comprehensive contractual regulations (*Habib/Burnett*).

3. Conflict of Objectives Concerning the Utilization of Profit

The most frequent cause for conflict in international *jvs* concerns the differing views and interests with respect to the calculation, appropriation, distribution and transfer of profit. The foreign partner is predominantly interested in strengthening his strategic position in the country in question during the developmental phase and thus not in the distribution of profit. The domestic partner, on the other hand, is primarily interested in motives of profit orientation. The situation can, however, completely change in the long-term; this is particularly true when the foreign partner does not feel that his expectations in the *jv* have been met and does not intend to develop or invest further. The domestic partner, in contrast, is no longer interested in an increased distribution of profits after the initial consolidation phase in which he must repay loans and credits, but rather in the self-financed expansion of the *jv* made possible through profit accumulation (*Meissner*).

4. Management Conflicts

The partners of an internal *jv* often hail from widely disparate cultural backgrounds and thus differ greatly with respect to their approach and attitude to management and its demands. Expectation discrepancies for planning time frames, quality standards and work motivation considerably complicate the problem-free execution of managerial tasks and thus directly affect the success of the company, as it has been analyzed empirically (*Kumar/Steinmann*, 1987). This is because both (or more) partners are interested in being able to have the largest possible amount of influence on the decisions made by the company's management.

The formation and coordination of a uniform team from personnel with varying ethnic backgrounds, education and language cause further problems in the international *jv* and thus require a high level of sensitivity, adaptability and learning ability from all those involved.

Inspite of careful preliminary considerations, regulations and safeguarding efforts regarding potential problems and conflicts which could arise, all in all risks are still hidden in the international *jv* which are quite difficult to assess. This is essentially a product of the development of the original intentions and interests of the partners over time, which cannot always be forecast, as well as the confrontation of different cultures and political systems with their particular legal orders.

Bibliography

Awadzi, W./Kedia, B./Chinta, R.: Performance implications of locus of control and complementary resources in international joint ventures – An empirical study. Presented at Acadamy of International Business Conference, London 1986.

Beamish, P.M.: The Characteristics of Joint Ventures in Developed and Developing Countries, in: Columbia Journal of World Business, vol. 20/3 (1985), pp. 13–19.

Berg, S.V./Duncan, J./Friedman, P.: Joint Venture Strategies and Corporate Innovation, Cambridge, Massachusetts 1982.

Börner, Bodo: Gemeinschaftsunternehmen im Wettbewerbsrecht von EWGV und EGKSV, in: Huber, U.; Börner, B. (eds): Gemeinschaftsunternehmen im deutschen und europäischen Wettbewerbsrecht, Köln, Berlin, Bonn, München 1978, pp. 189–215.

Buckley, P.J./Casson, M.: The future of multi-national enterprise, London 1976.

Buckley, P.J./Casson, M.: A Theory of Cooperation in International Business, in: management international review, Wiesbaden, special issue 1988, pp. 19–38.

Chowdhury, J.: International Joint Ventures: Some Interfirm-Organization Specific Determinants of Successes and Failures – A Factor Analytic Exploration, Temple University 1989.

Coase, R.H.: The Nature of the Firm, in: Economica, N.S., 4 (1937), pp. 386–405.

Contractor, F.J./Lorange, P.: Competition vs. Cooperation: A Benefit/Cost Framework for Choosing Between Fully-Owned Investments and Co-operative Relationships, in: management international review, Wiesbaden, special issue 1988, pp. 5–18.

Dang, T.: Ownership, control and performance of the multinational corporation: A study of U.S. wholly owned subsidiaries and joint ventures in the Philippines and Taiwan, unpublished doctoral dissertation, University of California, Los Angeles 1977.

Dobkin, J.A. et al.: International Joint Ventures, Washington/D.C. 1986.

Endres, Dieter: Joint Ventures als Instrument internationaler Geschäftstätigkeit, in: Wirtschaftswissenschaftliches Studium, München, vol. 16, no. 8 (1987), pp. 373–378.

Friedman, W.G./Beguin, J.P.: Joint international business ventures in developing countries, New York 1971.

Franko, L.G.: Joint venture survival in multinational corporations, New York 1971, p. 32.

Geringer, J.M.: Criteria for selecting partners for joint ventures in industrialized market economies, Ph.D. dissertation, University of Washington, Seattle 1986.

Geringer, J.M./Herbert, L.: Control and Performance of International Joint Ventures, in: Journal of International Business Studies 1989, vol. 20, no. 2, pp. 235–254.

Geringer, J.M./Frayne, C.A.: Human Resource Management and International Joint Venture Control: A Parent Company Perspective, in: management international review, Wiesbaden, special issue 1990, pp. 103–120.

Gleichmann, K.: Europäische Wirtschaftliche Interessenvereinigung (EWIV), in: Macharzina, K./Welge, M.K. (eds.): Handwörterbuch Export und Internationale Unternehmung, Stuttgart 1989, cols. 488–497.

Habib, G.M./Burnett, J.J.: An Assessment of Channel Behaviour in an Alternative Structural Arrangement: The International Joint Venture, in: International Marketing Review (UK), vol. 6, no. 3 (1989), pp. 7–21.

Hellwig, H.-J.: Joint Venture–Verträge, internationale, in: Macharzina, K./Welge, M.K. (eds): Handwörterbuch Export und Internationale Unternehmung, Stuttgart 1989, cols. 1064–1072.

Janger, A.: Organization of international joint ventures, Conference Board, New York 1980.

Killing, J.P.: Strategies for Joint Venture Success, New York 1983.

Kogut, B.: Joint Ventures: Theoretical and Empirical Perspectives, in: Strategic Management Journal (UK), vol.4 (1988), pp. 319–332.

Kumar, B.: Führungsprobleme internationaler Gemeinschaftsunternehmungen in den Entwicklungsländern (diss.), Meisenheim am Glan 1975.

Kumar, B./Steinmann, H.: Führungskonflikte in internationalen Joint Ventures des Mittelstandes, in: Betriebliche Kooperation mit Entwicklungsländern, Tübingen 1987, pp. 84–97.

Langefeld-Wirth, K.: Joint Ventures im internationalen Wirtschaftsverkehr, Heidelberg 1990a.

Langefeld-Wirth, K.: Rechtsfragen des internationalen Gemeinschaftsunternehmens – Joint Venture, in: Recht der Internationalen Wirtschaft, Heidelberg, vol. 36, no. 1 (1990b), pp. 1–6.

Macharzina, K.: Zum Stabilitätsproblem internationaler Joint Venture-Direktinvestitionen, in: Zeitschrift für betriebswirtschaftliche Forschung, Düsseldorf, vol. 27, special issue no. 4 (1975), pp. 153–164.

Macharzina, K.: Zielkonflikte in internationalen Joint Ventures, in: Pausenberger, E. (ed.): Internationales Management, Stuttgart 1981, p. 139–159.

Meissner, H.-G.: Zielkonflikte in internationalen Joint Ventures, in: Pausenberger, E. (ed.): Internationales Management, Stuttgart 1981, p. 129–138.

Moecke, H.-J.: Gemeinschaftsunternehmen in der Sowjetunion, in: Langefeld-Wirth, K. (ed.): Joint Ventures im internationalen Wirtschaftsverkehr, Heidelberg, 1990.

Rugman, A.M.: Inside the multinationals, London 1981.

Schaan, J.L.: Parent control and joint venture success: The case of Mexico, unpublished doctoral dissertation, University of Western Ontario 1983.

Seibert, Klaus: Joint Ventures als strategisches Instrument im internationalen Marketing, Berlin 1981.

Staudenmeyer, C.: Das Wirtschafts-und Vertragsrecht transnationaler Gemeinschaftsunternehmen in Entwicklungsländern, Berlin 1990.

Stopford, J.M./Wells, L.T.: Managing the multinational enterprise, New York 1972.

Thompson, R.J.: Competitive Effects of Joint Ventures in the Chemical Industry, dissertation outline and supporting documentation, University of Massachusetts, Amherst 1970.

Tomlinson, J.W.C.: The joint venture process in international business: India and Pakistan, Cambridge Mass. 1970.

Weder, R.: Joint Venture, Gruesch 1989.

Kaufmann, Heinrich (1864–1928)

HEINZ STOFFREGEN

(see also: *Consumer Co-operatives*; *History in 19th C.*; *Pfeiffer*; *Schulze-Delitzsch*)

Heinrich Kaufmann (23.11.1864 – 2.7.1928) was the successful organizer of the → *consumer co-operative* movement in Germany. Without knowing much about *Dr. Eduard* → *Pfeiffer*, his ideas and his work, *Kaufmann* brought *Pfeiffer's* efforts to an end, completed his work. *Kaufmann* actually created a genuine consumer movement, unknown until the beginning of this century in Germany.

Kaufmann came from the most northern part of Germany, Schleswig. His father ran a local pub connected with a little shop and operated a small farm. He died when son *Heinrich* was still at school. So *Kaufmann* already very early had to find his own way. His local teacher recognized his talent and promoted him to become a teacher. Thus *Kaufmann* spent six years (1881 – 1887) in teacher training institutes in Apenrade and Hadersleben, towns in the northern part of Schleswig, now belonging to Denmark. After his qualification as a teacher he started work in Kiel, moved to Hamburg in 1891.

As a teacher, he noticed the miserable living conditions of his pupils' families, primarily workers' families. He saw financial problems – but also social problems including educational problems; and when he realized the big thirst for education among uneducated workers he started to spend all his spare time to run evening classes in Barmbek, a typical working class area of Hamburg. He organized and promoted associations for the education of workers until they were banned because of alleged influence of anarchists.

He also assisted in the establishment of the "Freie Volksbühne" (Independent people's theatre) in Hamburg which was a tremendous success, *Kaufmann* being the cashier and book-keeper.

In 1894 he was asked to run the newly established "Volksblatt für Harburg und Wilhelmsburg", a newspaper mainly for social-democratic workers. *Kaufmann* took over this job, moving from a secure employment as a teacher to an insecure position. He lost some income, but he believed that he had to meet the challenge of promoting workers as an underprivileged part of society. This decision became the source for the moving force of all his future life.

Writing and publishing articles on bad living conditions and exploitation practices led to a number of law cases. In one of them *Kaufmann* was convicted to 4 months imprisonment – which did not change his attitude.

Already when teaching workers, *Kaufmann* had learnt about co-operatives. And he had seen that during those years many workers' co-operatives in Hamburg had gone bankrupt and had to be liquidated. Therefore, the climate was not at all favourable for co-operatives (and political workers' organizations were not promoting co-operatives). But *Kaufmann* felt co-operatives to be important instruments to improve the situation of workers. Failures happened mostly due to ignorance! Thus he decided to join a consumer co-operative at Harburg; he started to make this co-operative known, gained many new members, mainly workers, and made it a success within few years.

In 1899, *Kaufmann* was asked to take an active part in the "Großeinkaufsgesellschaft Deutscher Consumvereine" (GEG – Wholesale Society of German Consumer associations), and in 1900 he was put in charge of the "Wochenbericht", a weekly publication issued by the GEG. The bad relations between the workers' party and the consumer co-operatives once more became obvious in the fact that the party officials felt *Kaufmann's* two activities to be imcompatible and asked him to choose! So *Kaufmann* left the social democratic paper and started to work full time for the GEG as from 1.1.1902.

Kaufmann's main task was to develop the GEG publication to become a journal on co-operative affairs (→ *Periodicals, Co-op.*). In his articles he stressed the importance of the Rochdale → *Principles* as the basis for consumer co-operatives and pointed out that consumer co-operatives had an ideology different from that of agricultural, handicraft or urban credit co-operatives. In this respect he followed the line of argument of the consumer co-operatives within the General Federation → *Schulze-Delitzsch*. He wanted to have their special interests also represented but usually they were neglected by the majority of the other co-operatives.

This conflict (which for the first time was expressed by *Eduard Pfeiffer* in 1867) was relevant again in 1894, when the → *consumer co-operatives* within the General Federation decided to create the GEG as a wholesale society. Many members of other co-operatives considered this to be a threat to their existence, especially traders, but also industrial producers and craftsmen.

In 1894, the consumer co-operatives neglected this opposition by the majority of the other co-operatives and by the leadership of the General Federation and went ahead founding the GEG. But this started an argument within the Federation: The majority of member co-operatives and their basic ideology was middle-class oriented – they felt threatened by the consumer co-operatives and the GEG which were consumer-but, at the same time, working class-oriented. Whereas the Schulze-Delitzsch co-operatives wanted to strengthen the middle class entrepreneur against the consequences of industrialization, the Rochdale principles, the consumer co-operatives, and *Heinrich Kaufmann's* ideas very much lead to the concept of a new economic system (for instance without private retail traders) (→ *Conceptions, Co-operative*).

With his ideas, *Kaufmann* gained very strong support from consumer co-operatives but immediately ran into conflict with the leadership of the General Federation. This was part of a more serious conflict within the General Federation, which was solved in 1902 at the congress in Bad Kreuznach (→ *Schulze-Delitzsch*): without prior announcement, a motion was tabled that co-operatives whose activities were directed to destroy middle class economic institutions could not remain members of the Federation. A majority in favour, consequently 98 consumer co-operatives (most of them not even present at the congress) and the GEG were expelled from the Federation on September, 3 in 1902.

The following day, representatives of consumer co-operatives decided to establish their own federation. All other consumer co-operatives were called upon to leave the General Federation – until November 1902 about 400 co-operatives had taken this decision. In May 1903 the "Zentralverband deutscher Konsumvereine" (ZdK – Central Federation of German consumer co-operatives) was established by 585 societies. At the congress in Dresden, *Kaufmann* presented the main policy speech, making the Rochdale Principles (→ *Principles*) the basic philosophy of the new organization.

With the establishment of the ZdK, *Kaufmann's* career as the organizer of the German consumer co-operative movement began: He left the GEG to become the secretary of the ZdK, called Secretary General as from 1907. Until his death in 1928, *Kaufmann* for more than 25 years was the outstanding figure who led the German consumer co-operative movement to become a major economic power in Gemany: In 1928, a total number of 1,024 co-operative societies operated 10,124 shops and had more than 3 million members (→ *Federations*). Quite a number of societies had more than 10,000 members. (To give an example: in 1928, the Stuttgart consumer co-operative society, founded by *Pfeiffer*, had 49,137 members and operated 100 shops.)

A considerable part of German consumer needs were met by consumer co-operative shops with goods produced by GEG production plants. The dream of *Eduard Pfeiffer* had come true – although the economic system had not developed in the way *Pfeiffer* and *Kaufmann* wanted it to.

Kaufmann organized the ZdK on a decentral line –

the primary societies were members of regional unions which also took the responsibility for auditing ('Revisionsverband'). There was a central supply system (GEG in Hamburg) which organized the purchase of goods on wholesale lines. And when there was a boycott of some producers against the GEG, *Kaufmann* led the movement to set up their own production plants.

A widespread information system was introduced: the weekly reports changed to "Konsumgenossenschaftliche Rundschau" (Review of consumer co-operative societies) (→ *Periodicals, Co-operative*) which very soon became a respected (journal/periodical) publication on all co-operative matters. In addition to that there were a special publication for women and a remarkable annual year-book, carefully analyzing the economic situation and development, giving valuable facts and figures. Finally, *Kaufmann* also published books on co-operative principles and practical work: "Wesen und Ziel der Genossenschaftsbewegung" (Nature und objective of the co-operative movement), "Grundsätze der konsumgenossenschaftlichen Praxis" (Guiding principles for the practical work of consumer co-operatives), and "Kurzer Abriß der Geschichte des Zentralverbandes deutscher Konsumvereine" (Short abstract of the history of the Central Federation of German Consumer Co-operatives).

It is impossible to mention all the activities of *Kaufmann* during these decades – but two should not be omitted: Of course, *Kaufmann* remained a teacher – and by exercising the Rochdale principle of education in co-operatives, he became the "teacher" of the German consumer co-operative movement, not only through his articles but also by initiating the "Genossenschafts-Schule" (Co-operative College), where he lectured himself and was a curator all throughout.

Furthermore, there was *Kaufmann's* commitment to international cooperation. Already in 1902, he represented the German consumer co-operatives at the fifth International Co-operative Congress at Manchester and was elected member of the Central Committee of the → International Co-operative Alliance; in 1924, he became member of the Executive Committee.

He contributed to discussions on many occasions, thereby becoming the best known German co-operator. For the German consumer co-operatives, he created structures which remained valid and operational for more than half a century, surviving two world wars.

Bibliography

Faust, Helmut: Geschichte der Genossenschaftsbewegung, Frankfurt 1965.

GEG (Hrsg.): Sechzig Jahre GEG; 60 Jahre Dienst am Verbraucher, Hamburg 1954.

Hasselmann, Erwin: Geschichte der deutschen Konsumgenossenschaften, Hamburg/Frankfurt 1971.

Kolkhozes

Jerzy Kleer

(see also: *State and Co-operatives, Socialism*; *Socialist Co-operative Theory*; *Rural Peoples Communes, China*)

I. Definition and Creation of Kolkhozes; II. The Function of Agriculture and the Collectivization; II. The Financing of Manufacturing Industry; IV. The Development since the 1950s.

I. Definition and Creation of Kolkhozes

The kolkhozes in the Soviet Union are large collective agricultural enterprises possessing co-operative features. They emerged as a result of the process of consolidation (collectivization) of individual peasant holdings. They are based on the principle of group ownership of the means of production and collectively performed work. Production is located on state-owned land which is leased to the kolkhozes for life. The kolkhoz is managed by an elected board and a chairman (→ *State and Co-operatives, Socialism*).

Formation of kolkhozes started shortly after the October Revolution in Russia. Originally, three varieties of Kolkhozes could be differentiated: *communes*, in which all the means of production, residential buildings and the entire livestock were socialized; *artels*, whose degree of socialization of means of production was much lower; and the *Land-Tilling Associations*, which were a rather informal type of a collective organization. Till the 15th Congress of the All-Union communist Party (Bolshevik) in December 1927, the kolkhozes movement had developed slowly and – to a degree – on a voluntary basis. But the need for accelerated industrialization – the decision of the 14th Congress, December 1925, favored the development of heavy industry – caused the 15th Congress to adopt resolutions making changes in the ownership structure faster and subject to control as to their direction.

The causes for collectivizing agriculture can be broken down into two groups. The first has to do with the socialist doctrine, the second with economic practice. The doctrine asserts that the socialist system has to be based on the socialized structure of ownership, which may take a state-owned or co-operative form. In the case of agriculture, it was to be predominantly a co-operative or more accurately, a kolkhoz form. The doctrine precludes the existence of private ownership. In relation to the small and medium-size peasant holdings, it was assumed that the process may be completed through collectivization proceeding, at least formally, on a voluntary basis. It was originally assumed that this process would take a long time. There was also an additional theoretical argument for collectivization, namely a claim that the creation of giant industrial firms should be matched by similar enterprises in agriculture, taking the collective or state-owned form, that is kolkhozes or sovkhozes.

Nevertheless, the causes based on economic practice were more important. They had to do with the idea of subordinating agriculture to the governmental decisions and creating conditions for its inclusion into the structure of the central plan. This was practically infeasible in an environment consisting of many millions of individual peasant farms. Both, the official doctrine of state supremacy over the economy and the role of the central plan, waired some spheres of economic life – and especially agriculture – were left outside the direct central command system.

II. The Function of Agriculture and the Collectivization

One is inclined to think that the conversion of agriculture into one of the leading sources of financing for the industrial and military complex development was even more important. Since the 1930s, that complex has been given an utmost priority in development. The whole system of rechanneling resources from agriculture (described below) and the administrative reallocation of labor to the non-agricultural sector would have been impossible without having collectivized agriculture. The flow of factors of production from agriculture to the industry was based on coercion.

Although it was agreed upon as early as 1927 that the collectivization was to be sped-up, the crucial decision in that respect was made on January 5th, 1930 – Resolution of the Central Committee of the AUCP(B) – (All-Union Communist Party / Bolshevik): "On the speed of collectivization and on the means of helping the kolkhozes construction". This resolution gave the collectivization process a new character: a dramatic acceleration in the process of converting peasants holdings into kolkhozes took place; secondly, coercion was used on a massive scale; finally, richer peasant were subjected to a fast and brutal action of "dekulakization" and deportation. The rate of this process is illustrated in the table below.

Two conclusions can be drawn from this table: first, within only two years (1929–31), over half of all the peasant holdings were collectivized, which must have been achieved through the use of administrative methods and coercion. Second, during the whole period under investigation, 5.7 million peasant holdings vanished, which was the result of deportations and liquidations of the so called "kulak" farms. It is now estimated that some 20 million people lost their lives in connection with the collectivization process, i.e. in the years 1929–1940.

In the process of collectivization, the artel became the basic form of newly created kolkhozes. The com-

Speed of Collectivization, 1928–37 (figures for July 1st of each year)

year	number of collectivized peasant holdings (in millions)	share of farms collectivized (in percent)	number of peasant holdings (in millions)
1929	1.0	3.9	25.6
1930	6.0	23.6	25.4
1931	13.0	52.7	24.7
1932	14.9	61.5	24.2
1933	15.2	65.0	23.2
1934	15.7	71.4	22.0
1935	17.3	83.2	20.8
1936	18.4	90.5	20.3
1937	18.5	93.0	19.9

Source: Kleer, J.: ZSRR – pol wieku przemian gospodarczych, Warszawa 1967 / USSR – Half a Century of Economic Changes, Warsaw 1967/, p.110.

mune was rejected on the grounds that it would socialize the kolkhoz-members' lives too much. The Land-Tilling associations, on the other hand, were abandoned on the grounds that they were not socialized enough and did not change the essence of the peasant ways of farming.

The artel is an organization of collective ownership and collective work. Major means of production are socialized; the brigade, stable in its composition, is the basic unit of work force. The funds at the disposal on the kolkhoz may be classified as non-divisible or divisible. The former are used to expand production undertaken by the collective (investment) and the collective satisfaction of consumption needs (culture, health care, etc.). The latter are used to pay for the labour of the kolkhoz members (individual labour input is measured in standardized work-days calculated according to the quantity and quality of the work done). In the past, the amount of pay corresponding to one standardized work-day was calculated by dividing the income of the kolkhoz minus all of its financial obligations to the state and to the kolkhoz itself (non-divisible funds) by the total number of standardized work-days (credited as) performed in the kolkhoz. It was only after July 1st, 1966, that a new remuneration system was introduced, which stipulated a guaranteed wage to members based on the pay-rates used in the state-owned farms (sovkhozes). The kolkhoz-members were allowed to keep small private plots of land between one fourth to one hectare as a part of their homesteads, which in some periods constituted their major source of income.

The subordination of all agricultural activities to the state, or more precisely, to its specialized agencies (institutions) can be identified as the main goal of collectivization, this ensuring the sources of financing for the development of non-agricultural sectors, mostly that of industry.

In the beginning, the kolkhozes were subordinated both to the MTSs (Machine-Tractor Stations, created in the mid–1930s), which were the owner of agricultural machinery used by kolkhozes, and to the local authorities of the given territory. Both, the MTSs and the local authorities, following the guidelines of the central authorities, designated the economic activities to be undertaken by the kolkhoz, i.e. its crop structure, the scope of livestock-breeding, other agricultural activities, its obligation to the state, etc. In addition, special political departments existed in the structure of MTS contracted to supervise the kolkhozes. The MTSs continued their existence till the end of the 1950s, when kolkhozes were permitted to buy their own machines.

III. The Financing of Manufacturing Industry

Establishing the system of kolkhozes in the 1930s created an important, if not the most important source of financing the industry. This was done through three channels. The first was the transfer of grain to the cities; between 1928 and 1948, total cereal production and land productivity remained roughly the same (yearly crop: 73.6–77.9 million tons; land productivity: 710–750 kg per hectare), while the state purchases of cereals rose dramatically (from 18.2 million tons in 1928–32 to 32.1 million tons in 1938–48). The second was the transfer of labour force to the cities; in the decade between 1929–1939 urban population doubled while that of rural areas according to the official census data decreased by 10 million. The third channel was the introduction of a number of specific devices aimed at taking the resources away from agriculture. The so-called obligatory deliveries of agricultural produce dictated prices more than two times lower than those at the state marketing boards. (In the late 1930s, the average price of cereal grains was 7.50 rouble per hundredweight for obligatory deliveries and 16.40 rouble at the state marketing boards.)

In practice, most of the grain – almost 90% – was appropriated by the state at prices much below production costs. At the end of the 1930s, 37.8% of the state acquired grain was coming from obligatory deliveries, 50.8% from payments in-kind made by kolkhozes to the MTSs (evaluated at reduced prices), and only 11.4% from state marketing boards (at cost-covering prices).

It was only in 1953, that some rather profound changes in the kolkhozes system were initiated. Prices slowly began to increase, and so did the agricultural output which finally reached the pre-collectivization level at the end of the 1950s.

IV. The Development since the 1950s

Since 1950, essential changes in the kolkhozes movement have taken place, the most profound being a fast concentration process. In 1950, there were 123,700 kolkhozes, in 1960 44,600, in 1970 33,500, in 1980 26,300, and in 1988 27,300. This drop in numbers has been caused by two kinds of processes. Firstly, by consolidation of small kolkhozes, the rationale being the necessity for more intensive use of the existing farm machinery and in economies of scale. Secondly, by converting some of the kolkhozes into sovkhozes (state-owned farms), justified by the alleged superiority of state ownership over collective ownership, and by the general tendency of transforming co-operative units into state ones (→ *Socialist Co-operative Theory*).

Since the mid-1950s, there have been several other important phenomena present in the kolkhozes system:

1) the kolkhozes have been given much larger allotments of agricultural means of production (machinery, fertilizers, pesticides, etc.);
2) there has been a systematic increase in the prices paid for the agricultural produce by the state;
3) the gap between incomes of urban and rural population has been closing (nevertheless, the disparity in favor of the former still remains);
4) the output and income generated on the private plots (homesteads) of the kolkhoz-members have been increasing at a pace much faster than those of the kolkhozes themselves;
5) the scope of commands issued by the state authorities to the kolkhozes has been decreasing, although very slowly. Only the recent reforms connected with "perestroika" have laid down certain foundations for larger freedom for kolkhozes, including private (family) tillage of land.

During its entire period of operation, the kolkhozes system as a form of collective economic activity has been a total failure in every respect. It has never provided a sufficient supply of produce, reflected by the fact that the country has been importing grain for almost twenty years. Nor could it offer an acceptable standard of living to the kolkhoz-members. Furthermore, the kolkhozes have never been considered a form of co-operative as documented in the Soviet literature; they have always been subordinated to the state and party organizations and institutions. If the reforms initiated by Gorbachev already some years ago eventually succeed, the existing kolkhozes may possibly be replaced by genuinely co-operative farms – at some future time.

Bibliography

Kleer, J.: ZSSR – pol wieku przemian gospodarczych(USSR – Half a Century of Economic Changes), Warsaw 1967.
Istoria socialisticzeskoj ekonomiki (History of the socialist Economy), Vols. II–VII, Moscow 1967–80.
Statisticzeskij jezegodnik stran-czlenov Sovieta Ekonomiczeskoj Wzaimopomoszczi (Statistical Yearbook of the States-Members of the Comecon), 1989, Moscow 1989.

Labour-Management

ERNST FEHR

(see also: *Joint-production Co-operatives*; *Production Co-operatives*; *Theory of co-operative Cooperation*; *Classic/Neo-classic Contributions*; *Partnership Enterprises*)

I. Definition; II. Labour Management With Tradable Membership Rights; III. Underinvestment and Underemployment Effects in the Absence of a Membership Market; IV. Yugoslavia; V. Market Imperfections.

I. Definition

If the right to control and manage is assigned exclusively to the workers (in their role as workers) of a firm on the basis of the "one worker – one vote" principle we call this firm labour-managed (→ *Joint-production Co-operatives*; → *Production Co-operatives*). According to this definition labour-managed firms (LMFs) are not characterized by the absence of hierarchies or by the prevalence of a particularly egalitarian income distribution or by the existence of collective property rights in the firm's capital stock, although these organizational and distributional arrangements are compatible with the definition of an LMF and may, therefore, be adopted by particular LMFs. Advocates as well as critics of the principle of labour management normally assume that LMFs operate in a market environment. We, too, stick to this assumption. A labour-managed economy (LME) is, therefore, a market economy consisting of LMFs only.

The above definition allows for a wide range of different institutional set ups in a LMF. As we shall show, some of them will be efficient while others will exhibit inefficiency. The definition implies that the transformation of a capitalist firm (CF) into a LMF involves the redistribution of one important right, namely the ultimate right to determine the firm's policy, from the capital owners (with voting rights) to the workers (→ *Workers Co-determination*). This means, for example, that if all capital owners of a firm happen to be also workers (of that firm) and the ultimate decision making power is vested in the workers *in their role as capital owners*, the enterprise is not labour-managed. The reason for this is that the "one worker – one vote" principle is not guaranteed because (i) some workers may own more voting shares than others and (ii) some workers may sell their voting shares to non-workers. If the constitution of this firm rules out the possibility that non-workers hold voting shares and requires each worker to hold the *same* fraction of voting shares it meets the definition of a "pure" LMF because the "one worker – one vote" principle (up to an irrelevant transformation) is fulfilled.

II. Labour Management With Tradable Membership Rights

Tradable membership rights mean that workers who join (leave) a LMF pay (get paid) a certain amount of money to (from) the firm. To the best of our knowledge *Sertel* (1982, chapter 2, 7 and 8; 1987) was the first who examined analytically the consequences of this arrangement for the behavior of LMFs. *Dow* (1986) and *Tütüncü* (1994) extended the idea to an intertemporal framework and showed that workers unanimously choose production plans which maximize the present value of their wealth. In *Fehr* (1993) and *Fehr/Sertel* (1993) the case of unprofitable LMFs and of monopsonistic conditions in the labour market is examined. In addition the equilibrium in a competitive labour market of a LME with tradable membership rights is determined.

Following *Fehr* (1993) and (1994) we assume an economy with perfect information and a large number of LMFs each of which conforms to the following constitutional rules:

(i) the workers and the members of a LMF coincide.
(ii) Each member of the LMF has the right and the duty to supply labour of a prespecified quality.
(iii) Each member has the right to a share of the residual income and the duty to assume a share of the liabilities for the debt of the firm. The share may but need not be proportional to the quantity of labour supplied.
(iv) Each member has the same active and passive (voting) rights regarding the determination of the firms's policy. In particular the "one worker – one vote" rule prevails. The membership size and the investment policy of the LMF are decided by a majority vote.
(v) The membership rights in (ii)–(iv) are acquired through the purchase of the membership deed and expire if the deed is sold to the firm (i.e. the remaining members) or to a new member.

Rule (i) and (v) imply that each worker who joins the LMF has to buy a membership deed and each worker who leaves the firm has to sell his deed. Leaving the firm is, therefore, subject to an agreement. A member cannot be dismissed against his will unless he has violated his duties. Duties are, for example, to supply labour and to refrain from stealing LMF-property.

Vice versa, a member cannot leave the firm by a unilateral decision. He must find somebody who is willing to buy the deed.

It is our aim to show that a (competitive) economy in which each LMF obeys the constitutional rules (i)–(v) will exhibit full employment and an efficient allocation of capital and labour. This proposition holds independently of whether capital goods are rented, individually owned or collectively owned by the members of the LMF. For clarity of exposition we choose a number of simplifying assumptions but our claims have been shown by the above mentioned authors to hold true in a more general framework.

At the beginning of the period the m initial members of the LMF purchase capital goods k on a competitive market at price p_k. The capital stock is owned collectively by all members of the LMF. The LMF (i.e. the majority) requires its initial members to finance this purchase to an equal extent. (In a multiperiod framework this is tantamount to a decision of the majority of members to use retained earnings for the financing of k.)

After the purchase of k the m members choose the employment level n. Each of the n ex-post members supplies one unit of labour. If m>n they offer some of them to buy back their membership deeds. If m<n they sell deeds to new members. After k and n are determined production takes place. q denotes output and q(k,n) represents a twice differentiable concave production function. q and the capital stock k are sold at the end of the period at price p and p_k, respectively. Depreciation is denoted by δ, i.e. (1–δ)k units of capital can be sold at the end of the period. New members of the LMF have to pay a price d for the membership deed. r denotes the competitive interest rate. Under these assumptions the present value of the income of each of the m initial members is given by

$$(1) \quad v = \frac{p\,q(k,n) + p_k(1-\delta)k}{n(1+r)} - \frac{p_k k}{m} + \frac{d(n-m)}{m}$$

$pq + p_k(1-\delta)k$ is the LMF's revenue from selling q and $(1-\delta)k$ at the end of the period. Each of the n ex-post members who contributes one unit of labour to the production of q receives (1/n)th of this revenue which gives a present value of

$$(2) \quad z = \frac{p\,q(k,n) + p_k(1-\delta)k}{n(1+r)}$$

The second term in (1) shows the expenditures for the purchase of k per initial member. Since each of the m initial members bears the same amount of $p_k k$ their income v is reduced by $(p_k k/m)$. The third term in (1) represents the revenue from selling (n–m) new membership deeds at a price d (at the beginning of the period), a revenue which is distributed equally among the m initial members.

Having determined v we must derive the price d that will be charged per deed. To do this let $x \equiv [w/(1+r)]$ denote the present value of the income that a new member could earn elsewhere and assume that m<n. In a competitive economy the alternative income x has to be taken as given by the LMFs. Suppose now that a LMF charges a deed price d^h such that $z-d^h < x$. Then no worker is willing to join the LMF because he can earn more elsewhere. On the other hand demanding only d^l such that $z-d^l > x$, is clearly not in the interests of the initial members because new members are willing to pay $d = z-x > d^l$. Therefore, we conclude that the LMF charges $d = z-x$ for new membership deeds.

What happens if m exceeds n? Then the LMF makes an offer to its initial members to buy back (m-n) deeds at the price $d = z-x$. For suppose that it offers less, i.e. $d^l < z-x$. In this case no initial member is willing to accept this offer because a leaving member earns now (in present values) $\{x + d^l - (p_k k/m) + [d^l(n-m)/m]\}$ whereas those who remain earn $v(d^l) = z - (p_k k/m) + [d^l(n-m)/n]$. Since $x + d^l < z$, the remaining members are better off. If the LMF offers to buy back deeds at d^h such that $x + d^h > z$ the remaining members are worse off than those who leave. It follows that a unanimous reduction of the membership requires a deed price of $d = z - x$. (Our rules preclude non-unanimous reductions.)

The above reasoning shows that the initial members unanimously agree to maximize v subject to $d = z - x$. Inserting $d = z - x$ into (1) and rearranging terms yields

$$(3) \quad v = \frac{1}{m(1+r)} [p\,q(k,n) - (r+\delta)p_k k - w n] + x$$

The term in brackets equals the definition of profits for a CF. Since m, r, p, p_k, w and x are treated parametrically by the LMF maximizing (1) subject to $d = z - x$ leads to the usual marginal productivity conditions of a perfectly competitive CF

(4a) $\quad p\,q_n = w$

(4b) $\quad p\,q_k = (r + \delta)p_k$

We conclude, therefore, that a LME with collective capital ownership and a competitive market for membership rights and the rules set out at the beginning of this section arrives at the same allocation of labour and capital as a perfectly competitive capitalist economy facing the same set of exogenous conditions (technologies, preferences and initial endowments). In particular, full employment prevails in equilibrium. This leads us to conjecture that the set of (Pareto-efficient) allocations that can be implemented as an equilibrium of a perfectly competitive capitalist economy can also be implemented as an equilibrium of a LME with a competitive membership market.

What happens if we allow for unequal residual shares? Suppose for instance that there are two groups of (identically qualified) workers. Members of the first group receive a residual income of z_1 while those of the second group receive $z_2 > z_1$. Assume further that a new member is free to join either group. If he prefers a deed which assigns him an income of z_2 he has to pay a deed price of $d_2 = z_2-x$. If he prefers instead to receive z_1 the deed price is given by $d_1 = z_1-x < d_2$. The membership market will, therefore, price deeds with different residual shares in such a way that the marginal costs of a worker are – independently of his share – given by x (or w if end-of-period values are taken). Or to put it differently: Whatever the distribution of the LMF's revenue from selling q and $(1-\delta)k$ among the ex-post members the LMF will always apply condition (4a) for its employment choice.

Knowing this, it is now easy to extend this argument to the case of differently qualified workers. Suppose for simplicity that there are two groups with $x_1 \equiv w_1(1+r)$ and $x_2 \equiv w_2(1+r)$ as the respective alternative wages and $x_1 > x_2$. Rewrite the production function as $q(k,n_1,n_2)$ where $n_1(n_2)$ denotes the number of workers with type 1 (type 2) qualifications. Furthermore let us demand equality; all workers get paid the same income z. The deeds for type 1 workers are now available at a price of $d_1 = z-x_1$ while those for type 2 workers cost $d_2 = z-x_2$. It follows that the marginal costs of type 1 (type 2) workers are given by $z-d_1 = x_1$ ($z-d_2 = x_2$), i.e. in end-of-period values w_1 (w_2). It is, therefore, in the interest of the incumbents to employ type 1 (type 2) workers until the marginal value product of type 1 (type 2) workers, $p(\delta q/\delta n_1)$ $[p(\delta q/\delta n_2)]$, equals the alternative income w_1 (w_2). Since a competitive CF applies the same rule we can again conclude that the LMF with competitive membership markets allocates labour in the same way as a competitive CF.

III. Underinvestment and Underemployment Effects in the Absence of a Membership Market

In this section we analyse the consequences for efficiency of deviating from the institutional structure set out in section II. First of all – and perhaps most importantly – let us assume that there is no (competitive) market for membership rights, which means that new members don't have to pay for their membership and leaving members don't receive a compensation. Except for d = 0 the other rules of our constitution of section II prevail. Then, as has been argued by *Furubotn* and *Pejovich* (1970), *Pejovich* (1969) and *Vanek* (1975) a so-called underinvestment effect arises. By this these authors mean that the LMF faces a strong disincentive to finance investment projects out of internal funds because the representative member has a finite tenure and has no claim to the LMF's residual income after leaving it. In addition to the *Furubotn-Pejovich-Vanek* effect (FPV effect) another underinvestment effect can arise. As we will show below the FPV effect results from the absence of exit payments while the second underinvestment effect is due to the absence of entry fees. Moreover, while the FPV effect would vanish if the membership tenure were infinitely long or coincided with the duration of the income stream generated by internally financed investment projects the second disincentive to invest is still present under these conditions.

To derive the second effect we assume that desired membership n exceeds initial membership m and that all initial members stay until the end of the period. If d = o the present value of their income is given by

(5) $\quad v' = z - (p_k k/m)$

Maximizing v' w.r.t. k results in

(6b) $\quad pq_k = \{[r(n/m) + \delta] + [(n/m)-1]\} p_k$

It is easy to see that the r.h.s. of (6b) exceeds the r.h.s. of (4b) because n > m. It follows that the LMF faces inefficiently high capital costs which reduces, ceteris paribus, investment. The reason for this is very simple: New members receive the full benefits from past investment but do not bear the burden of financing the investment. The absence of an entry payment is, therefore, tantamount to the expropriation of initial members by new members which gives rise to a disincentive to invest. As one would expect, employment policy is also affected by d = 0. Maximizing v' w.r.t. n yields

(6a) $\quad p\, q_n = \dfrac{p\, q + p_k\, (1-\delta)\, k}{n}$

Notice that the r.h.s. of (6a) exceeds w (weakly) because if w were below $[pq + p_k(1-\delta)k]/n$ the initial members would prefer to close down the LMF and work elsewhere. As a consequence the LMF restricts membership, ceteris paribus, to an inefficiently low level.

In the context of our simple model the FPV effect can be analyzed if we assume that a majority of initial members will leave the LMF after k and n have been chosen but before production starts. Suppose further that the leaving members work elsewhere for the alternative income x. Instead of v the present value of the income of these members is now given as $[-(p_k k/m) + x]$, i.e. they prefer an investment of k = 0. This extreme result is of course due to our simplifying assumptions but qualitatively the conclusion remains unchanged if we allow for a multiperiod framework. As long as there is a majority of workers who know that they will leave the firm after a certain number, say t, of periods the LMF has a strong disincentive to undertake self-financed investments because these incumbents benefit from the investment only during the remaining t periods but have to bear the full financing costs. This limited appropriability of the returns of investment causes the FPV effect.

How does the membership market solve this problem? Each of the leaving members receives now a present value of

$\hat{v} = -(p_k k/m) + [d(n-m)/m] + x + d.)$

Instead of z, the leaving members receive x at the end of the period (in beginning-of-period values). At the beginning of the period they pay $(p_k k/m)$ and receive $[d(n-m)/m]$ *and* d. The last expression denotes the income of a quitting member from selling her membership deed. Substituting the competitive deed price $d = z-x$ into $\hat{v}$ and rearranging terms yields (3). Thus, with a membership market the objective function of leaving members coincides with those of the remaining members and both groups unanimously prefer the efficient choice of n and k.

As an alternative to the implementation of a membership market *Vanek* favoured the financing of investments by bank credit. Both the FPV effect as well as the second underinvestment effect vanishes if investment is financed by credit because the members who receive a share of the per-period revenue z coincide with those who finance the investment. With credit financing the LMF receives $p_k k$ from the bank which is used to buy k; at the end of the period it has to pay back $p_k k(1+r)$. Thus, the present value of the income of ex-ante *and* ex-post members is equal to

$$(7) \quad v'' = z - [p_k k (1+r) / n (1+r)]$$
$$= \frac{p q (k, n) - (\delta + r) p_k k}{n (1+r)}$$

All members will, therefore, unanimously agree to maximize v" w.r.t. k which results in condition (4b). While *Vanek* (1970) argues that LMFs should use credit financing in order to prevent inefficiently low investment levels *Furubotn* (1974) and *Pejovich* (1969) stress that LMFs will exhibit a "natural" tendency towards credit financing because in case of self-financing LMFs will face higher capital costs. Neither *Vanek* nor *Furubotn* and *Pejovich* do, however, consider the efficiency restoring effects of a membership market.

In addition to credit financing and to the absence of a market for membership rights we assume now the following:

(i) Members can be dismissed against their will if a majority agrees on it.
(ii) There are $m_1 > (n/2)$ initial members which form a stable coalition. No member of m_1 is subject to the risk of dismissal, i.e. the desired employment level n is above m_1.
(iii) All (identically qualified) members of the LMF get paid the same income.

We call a LMF which conforms to these assumptions an Illyrian LMF. Under the above conditions the dominant coalition of m_1 members will agree on the maximization of v" w.r.t. n giving rise to the first order condition

$$(8) \quad p q_n = v'' (1+r) = \frac{p q (k, n) - (r + \delta) p_k k}{n}$$

Starting with *Ward* (1958), *Domar* (1966) and *Vanek* (1970) the larger part of the theoretical literature on LMFs deals with maximands like (7) (for a more recent example see *Drèze* (1989), for surveys see Ireland and Law (1982), *Bonin* and *Putterman* (1987), *Fehr* (1988). Keeping, for simplicity, k fixed at some level, say k^0, the maximand (7) or condition (8) has some straightforward (comparative static) implications. If profits $(pq - wn (r+\delta) p_k k)$ of a capitalist twin are positive, $v''(1+r) > w$ holds and the Illyrian LMF employs less labour than the competitive CF or the LMF with competitive membership markets. Secondly, if the output price p rises by $\lambda\%$, pq_n increases by $\lambda\%$ whereas the r.h.s. of (8) increases by more than $\lambda\%$. Thus we have $pq_n > v''(1+r)$ giving rise to the dismissal of some members and the reduction of q. This is the "strange" and famous perverse employment and supply response of the Illyrian LMF. Thirdly, a rise in p_k or r reduces the r.h.s. of (8) while leaving pq_n unaffected. It follows that the LMF increases its membership. Fourthly, LMFs with different production technologies will end up with different levels of income $v''(1+r)$ and, hence, pq_n which indicates an inefficient allocation of labour among LMFs because total output (valued at p) could be increased by reallocating labour from the low- to the high-productivity firm. And finally, for a given number of LMFs an Illyrian LME will in general suffer from involuntary unemployment. This follows simply from the fact that the employment choice of LMFs does not depend on the alternative income w. If all Illyrian LMFs obey condition (8) and aggregate labour demand happens to be below aggregate supply there is (for a given number of firms) no tendency for unemployment to vanish.

IV. Yugoslavia

Yugoslavia is the only country in the world which established the principle of workers control of enterprises on an economy-wide scale. The Yugolsav institution of workers self-management deviates, however, considerably from the institutional set-up of section II. Besides the fact that discretionary state interventions and, hence, interventions by the communist party, at the federal, the republican and the local level seems to have been of considerable scope the market mechanism has been constrained in several ways. First, there is no membership market in Yugoslavia and second, the capital stock is not owned by the LMFs but by the state instead. LMFs only have the right to *use* the capital stock and are required to maintain the book value of their capital assets. In addition there seems to have been a considerable dismissal protection for individual members.

The absence of a membership market leads us to the prediction of underinvestment and underemployment effects and a proclivity for bank financing as discussed in section III. Since without a membership market LMFs do not respond to an excess supply of labour the migration from rural to industrial regions can be expected to create unemployment. In addition the allocation of labour among firms is probably inefficient and Yugoslav LMFs may exhibit a tendency for perverse or at least highly inelastic "Illyrian" responses to changes in prices and fixed costs in the *medium run and the long run*. In the short run dismissal protection will curb these tendencies but in the medium and long run membership reductions can always be achieved by not replacing quitting members. And finally, the capital maintainance requirement and the social ownership of the LMFs' capital tends to strengthen the disincentive of self-financed investments. Within our model it implies that initial members have to buy $(1-\delta)k$ units at the end of the period. The present value of income is then given by

$$(9) \quad v''' = \frac{p\, q\,(k, n) - \delta\, k\, p_k}{n\,(1+r)} - \frac{p_k k}{m}$$

which gives the following first order conditions for k:

$$(10) \quad p\, q_k = [(n/m)\, r + \delta + (n/m)]\, p_k.$$

Capital costs (the r.h.s. of (10)) are now even higher than in condition (6b), i.e. social ownership and the capital maintainance requirement lead to additional underinvestment of internal resources.

V. Market Imperfections

Now we shall be concerned with possible reasons for the non-existence of a smoothly functioning membership market. Our arguments rely on related discussions in *Ben Ner* (1988) and *Dow* (1993a,b). It seems quite likely that workers who are not rich enough to finance the purchase of a membership deed without a credit will face a credit rationing constraint because of the lack of collateral. Since the deed price incorporates implicitly the expected returns to self-financed investments it is higher the larger the (self-financed part of the) capital stock. Credit rationing of potential members of LMFs is, therefore, likely to be a more severe problem the higher the capital intensity of the firm. From section II we know that the deed price varies directly with the share of the residual income a member receives. By reducing the residual share the credit constraint is less likely to be binding. The solution of unequal residual shares for identically qualified workers may, however, have its own costs if notions of fairness and equity play a role. Members with a lower share may consider this as unfair and may e.g. respond by lowering work effort.

Another impediment to the development of a membership market stems from worker risk aversion and the restricted possibilities of members to insure themselves against business risks. "While property owners can spread their risks by putting small bits of their property into a large number of concerns, a worker cannot easily put small bits of effort into a large number of different jobs." (*Meade* (1972), p. 426). By the purchase of a membership deed workers make a risky investment. The returns to their human capital *and* to (parts of) their financial capital is subject to the firm specific risk of "their" LMF. This is the unavoidable consequence of being a residual claimant. Certainly, part of the firm-specific risk may be shared with non-members by issuing non-voting equity shares. But under realistic circumstances (e.g. asymmetric information about LMF returns and worker effort to the disadvantage of investors) workers cannot "sell" the whole risk to outsiders. As a result risk averse workers may prefer to work in a CF where their income is exposed to a lower firm specific risk.

A third difficulty for the establishment of a market for membership deeds arises from its thinness. Unlike in the stock market where exchange of equity holders is easy and not subject to the agreement of the CF membership turnover in LMFs is not likely to function equally smoothly. Since LMFs demand particular qualifications a leaving member is probably not allowed to sell its membership to anybody. But restrictions on sale will curb the volume of sales (and turnover) which in turn may create a thin market. The thinner the market the less likely it is informationally efficient. Potential members may doubt whether the deed price reflects the true expected future returns to membership which makes them reluctant to trade in the deed market.

To summarize, there are reasons which inhibit the spontaneous development of a membership market which in turn (see section III) gives rise to underinvestment and underemployment effects and may thus explain why CFs dominate in western economies. Yet, the fact that CFs are dominant does not imply that they are superior in efficiency terms. A balanced efficiency comparison has to examine both the LMF and the CF in the face of an imperfect market environment. How strong such a comparison is biased against LMFs has recently been demonstrated by *Dow* (1993a,b) who shows that if both the LMF and the CF operate in an imperfect market system the LMF *may* well be superior in efficiency terms. In *Fehr* (1990) it has been shown that if the purchase of jobs is not possible – due to imperfections in the membership and the labour market – a CE *may* exhibit a higher rate of involuntary unemployment than a LME. In addition, *Fehr* and *Sertel* (1993) prove that a LM monopsony employs more workers than a capitalist monopsony. The LM monopsony may even end up at the efficient (competitive) employment level. *Sertel* and *Steinherr* (1984) also show that LMFs may be more efficient than CFs. And finally, the outstanding result in *Dow* (1993a,b) is that a LMF may produce a larger welfare cake than a CF although the latter grows faster and has a higher private value to its members. Or put differently: It is possible that (in the absence of counteracting public interventions) CFs win the evolutionary race against LMFs since they grow faster and since private gains can be made from the transformation of LMFs into CFs although LMFs are more efficient.

Bibliography

Ben-Ner, Avner: The life cycle of worker-owned firms in market economies, Journal of Economic Behavior and Organization, Vol. 10 (1988), pp. 287–313.
Ben-Ner, Avner: Comparative empirical observations on worker-owned and capitalist firms, International Journal of Industrial Organization, Vol. 6 (1988), pp. 7–31.
Bonin, John P. and Putterman, Louis: Economics of cooperation and the labor-managed economy, Chur 1987.
Bowles, Samuel/Gintis, Herbert/Gustafsson, Bo (eds.): Markets and democracy – participation, accountability and efficiency; Cambridge 1993.
Domar, Evsey D.: The Soviet collective farm as a producer cooperative, American Economic Review, Vol. 56 (1966), pp. 734–757.
Dow, Gregory: Control Rights, competitive markets, and the labor management debate, Journal of Comparative Economics, Vol. 10 (1986), pp. 48–61.
Dow, Gregory: Democracy versus appropriability: Can labor-managed firms flourish in a capitalist world? in: Bowles et al., (1993a), pp. 176–196.
Dow, Gregory: Why capital hires labor: a bargaining perspective, American Economic Review, Vol. 83 (1993b), pp. 118–134.
Drèze, Jacques H.: Labour management, contracts and capital markets, Oxford 1989.
Fehr, Ernst: Ökonomische Theorie der Selbstverwaltung und Gewinnbeteiligung, Frankfurt am Main 1988.
Fehr, Ernst: The simple analytics of a membership market in a labour-managed economy, in: Bowles et al. (1993), pp. 260–276.
Fehr, Ernst: Labour-managed and capitalist economics in the absence of entrance fees, Discussion paper, University of Technology, Vienna, Dept. of Economics, 1990.
Fehr, Ernst: The workers' partnership – full employment through changing insider interests, in: Sertel (1994), forthcoming.
Fehr, Ernst/Sertel, Murat: Two forms of workers' enterprises facing imperfect Labor markets, Economic Letters, Vol. 41 (1993), pp. 121–127.
Furubotn, Eirik: Bank credit and the labor-managed firm: The Yugoslav case, Canadian-American Slavic studies, Vol. 8 (1974), pp. 89–106.
Furubotn, Eirik/Pejovich, Svetozar: Property rights and the behavior of the firm in a socialist state: The example of Yugoslavia, Journal of Economics, Vol. 30 (1970), pp. 431–454.
Ireland, Norman J./Law, Peter J.: The Economics of labor-managed enterprises, New York 1982.
Meade, James E.: The theory of labour-managed firms and profit-sharing, Economic Journal, Vol. 82 (1972), pp. 402–428.
Nutzinger, Hans G.: Investment and financing in a labour-managed firm and its social implications, Economic Analysis and Workers' Management, Vol. 9 (1975), pp. 181–199.
Pejovich, Svetozar: The firm, monetary policy and property rights in a planned economy, Western Economic Journal, Vol. 7 (1969), pp. 139–160.
Schlicht, Ekkehard/von Weizäcker Carl C.: Risk financing in labour-managed economies: The commitment problem, Journal of Institutional and Theoretical Economics, Vol. 133 (1977), pp. 53–66.
Sertel, Murat: Workers and Incentives, Amsterdam 1982.
Sertel, Murat: Workers' enterprises are not perverse, European Economics Review, Vol. 31 (1987), pp. 1619–1625.
Sertel, Murat (ed.): Workers' enterprises – alternative in privatization, Amsterdam 1994.
Sertel, Murat/Steinherr Alfred: Information, incentives and the design of efficient institutions, Journal of Institutional and Theoretical Economics, Vol. 140 (1984), pp. 233–248.
Tütüncü, M.M.: An infinite horizon workers' enterprise with finitely-lived members of different ages, in: Sertel (1994), forthcoming.
Vanek, Jaroslav: The general theory of labour-managed market economics, Ithaca 1970.
Vanek, Jaroslav: The basic theory of financing participatory firms. Self-management: Economic liberation of man, Baltimore 1975, pp. 445–455.
Ward, Benjamin: The firm in Illyria: market syndicalism, American Economic Review, Vol. 68 (1958), pp. 566–589.
Wolfsteeter, Elmar/Brown, Murray/Meran, Georg: Optimal employment and risk sharing in Illyria: the labour-managed firm reconsidered, Journal of Institutional and Theoretical Economics, Vol. 140 (1984), pp. 655–668.

Landwirtschaftsanpassungsgesetz – LAG

HORST SEUSTER [J]

(see also: *GDR*; *Rural Co-operatives*; *State and Co-operatives, Market Economy*)

The "Law of Structural Accomodation of Agriculture to the Social and Ecological Market Economy in the German Democratic Republic" (*Landwirtschaftsanpassungsgesetz*, law of structural conformance in the agricultural sector) dated June 29, 1990 as ammended on July 3, 1991 "Amendments to the *Landwirtschaftsanpassungsgesetz* and other Laws" (LAG) forms the legal basis for the future agricultural enterprises on the territory of the former GDR. It can therefore be referred to as "The Basic Law for Reorganization of the East German Agricultural Sector".

Whereas the original version, which was ratified in the former Volkskammer (People's Chamber) of the GDR, only provided for restructuring into the legal form of a registered co-operative, the later amendment passed by the German Bundestag (Federal Parliament) also makes conversions into partnerships or joint-stock companies possible (§ 23, subsec.1) (→ *Law, National*).

The Law at first only prescribes the creation of new legal forms, but this process can in no manner take place without the establishment of new economic structures and institutions (→ *Forms of Cooperation*). Furthermore, the various legal forms in part have certain structural and functional consequences which make alterations necessary with respect to the organization of the former *Landwirtschaftliche Produktionsgenossenschaften* (agricultural production co-operatives, LPGs) (→ *Joint-production Co-operative*). As far as new structures are referred to, the *Landwirtschaftsanpassungsgesetz* takes into consideration:

1. Parcelling and Amalgamating LPGs (§§ 4–22),
2. Converting LPGs through Changes to Legal Form (§§ 23–38),
3. Converting Co-operative Institutions through Changes to Legal Form (§§ 39–40),
4. Dissolving a LPG (§§ 41–42).

The resoluteness of lawmakers with regard to the changes in East German agricultural enterprises is illustrated in § 69, subsec.3: "LPGs and co-operative institutions as defined in § 39, subsec.1 which have not been converted into registered co-operatives, partnerships or joint-stock companies by December 31, 1991 are dissolved by operation of law."

Alongside the possibility of parcelling out a LPG we are interested at this point above all in conversions through an alteration of legal form. According to § 23, subsec.1, the LPG can be converted into:

- a registered co-operative,
- a partnership (non-trading partnership, general partnership [OHG], limited partnership [KG]),
- a company (joint-stock company [GmbH], stock corporation [AG]).

The extent mixed forms (e.g. GmbH and Co.KG) are permissible is not directly stated by the law, but their acceptance in the meantime can be presumed as actual examples illustrate.

When involved in a conversion the board of a LPG must "submit a thorough written report in which the legal conversion and in particular the future membership participation in the company are explained and grounded both legally and economically" (§ 24, subsec.1). All in all one can draw the conclusion from the general tenor of the *Landwirtschaftsanpassungsgesetz* that new organizational forms for the East German agricultural sector are not only allowed but also expressly called for.

Above and beyond this matter, each member of a LPG has the right to terminate his membership through notice. The withdrawing member is entitled to a compensation to the amount of the value of his participatory investment in the LPG. The values taken into consideration aside from land – which always remained the private property of the member – include contributions to inventory, milk datum quantities, and quotas in sugar-beet supply contracts.

The necessary conversion resolution in all cases must regulate the following seven items:

1. The name (company) of the new operation,
2. Members' participational investment,
3. Number, type and extent of shares and/or membership rights which the members should acquire,
4. Rights of the individual members,
5. Legal form,
6. Offered compensation,
7. upon the conversion into a limited partnership: The listing of the limited partners and the amount of their investment.

With respect to the general goal of the LAG, "the restoration of efficient and competitive agricultural enterprises" (§ 3), three critical comments nevertheless appear necessary from the economist's point of view:

1. The substance of the LAG is concerned with providing personal property and corresponding disposing power to the former members – goals which surely should be welcomed. Nevertheless, the question of whether the agricultural enterprise regardless of its legal form is in any position to maintain its existence when all or a vast majority of previous members have their assets payed out – a decision which is solely based on their discretion – is not discussed further on. One can therefore fear that numerous companies will not survive this procedure.
2. The stipulation stating that at most 80% of the original equity capital can be payed out (§ 44, subsec.1, sent.2), or in other words that at least 20% must remain in the company, cannot be considered particularly wise under economic aspects. Namely, when 80% of equity capital from a "normal" functioning company is removed, the company most usually is then on the brink of bankruptcy. The agricultural enterprises in the new German states, presently undergoing a reorganizational progress and suffering from a lack of capital – some of them even having to overcome longstanding debts – can certainly no longer maintain their existence under this stipulation. The lawmaker who permits up to 80% of equity capital to be payed out can also permit the remaining 20% to be payed out, as the company in question is in any case no longer capable of surviving.
3. The provision in the LAG previously mentioned which permits agricultural operations in East Germany to become partnerships and joint-stock companies in addition to co-operatives (§ 23, subsec.1) as a matter of course raises the question of its own expediency. On the one hand, the greater the number of possible legal forms, the greater the number of chances of finding an expedient form for each individual situation; on the other hand, the diversity thereby created by no means makes the correct choice any easier.

The influence the legal form has on the commercial success of a company is well-known to be greatly de-

termined by the extent the management is able to "keep company" with the legal form.
It must therefore be considered doubtfully that the managers of East German agricultural enterprises can handle all the legal forms now at their disposal to an equal extent as they have lacked experience up to now with legal forms found in the market economy – in particular with that of joint-stock companies (→ *Forms of Cooperation*). Such experience cannot be gained overnight, as our experience has taught us. Warnings should therefore be made concerning all too euphoric expectations – particularly in the agricultural sector – that the salvation of the East German agricultural sector is found in the most possible capitalistic legal form (e.g. a stock company). At the moment the new federal states are in a thoroughly experimental stage with respect to the selection of new legal forms, and the results of this are yet to be seen. Before the decision is made for one legal form or another, one should at first orientate oneself to other market economy countries. It is most probably better for the farmers in the new federal states first to consider common legal forms in the agricultural sector of free market economies (co-operative, nontrading partnership) before one opts for a form which has been tried but little in this economic sector. Unfortunately, § 23, subsec.1 of the *Landwirtschaftsanpassungsgesetz* tends to encourage the opposite.

Bibliography

Landwirtschaftsanpassungsgesetz (LAG) vom 3.7.1991 (BGBl. I S. 1418), (Änderungen vom 20.12.1991 gem. BGBl. I S. 2312 und vom 14.7.1992 gem. BGBl. I S. 1257).
Seuster, Horst: Genossenschaftsmodelle für die ostdeutsche Landwirtschaft, Berliner Schriften zum Genossenschaftswesen Vol. 2, Berlin 1992.

Law Concerning Company Groups and Co-operatives

PETER ERLINGHAGEN [S]

(see also: *Legal Form, Co-operative*; *Anti-Trust Laws*; *Combine, Co-operative*; *Financial Accounting Law*)

I. Basic Definitions; II. The Co-operative as Member of a Group of Subordinated Affiliates; III. The Co-operative as Part of a Horizontal Group of Affiliated Companies.

I. Basic Definitions

According to § 18 AktG (German Stock Corporation Law), a company group can be understood as a grouping of several enterprises under a joint management while legal independence of the individual companies is maintained. The differentiation is between a group of subordinated affiliates (§ 18, Sub-sec.1, AktG) and a horizontal group of affiliated companies (§ 18, sub-sec.2, AktG).
A group of subordinated affiliates (1.) is said to exist when there are relations of dependence between the enterprises in the group such that one company as the dominating enterprise exercises the power of direction on the dependent companies. There is a difference between the contract-based group of affiliated companies, which is defined by the conclusion of a control agreement and the de facto group of companies, for which no such contract exists.
In the case of a horizontal group of affiliated companies (2.), the enterprises are grouped under a joint management, but unlike the group of subordinated affiliates, there are no relations of dependence.

II. The Co-operative as Member of a Group of Subordinated Affiliates

1. The Co-operative as a Subordinate Enterprise

A co-operative as part of a group of companies cannot be subordinate to a company with a different legal form, as this would not comply with the co-operative purpose of promotion according to § 1, GenG (Co-operative Law)(→ *Promotion Mandate*) and with the autonomous management of the co-operative by a board of directors (*Metz* in *Lang/ Weidmüller*), because the autonomous board would be replaced by the controlling company's management. This applies not only to a contract-based group of companies, but also to the de facto company group. It is a different question whether a co-operative can be run as a subordinate enterprise in the sense of § 17, AktG, where the companies are not concentrated under a joint management and therefore do not form a group of companies, but where the mere possibility of influence is sufficient (*Merle* in *Emmerich/Sonnenschein*).
In addition to this, should a profit transfer agreement exist, this would be a violation of § 19, GenG (*Schaffland* in *Lang/Weidmüller*). Furthermore, there are reservations in connection with § 105, GenG, as an unlimited obligation to make further contributions during a crisis (→ *Nachschußpflicht*) would mean that the members of the respective co-operative would legally incapacitate themselves, which is inadmissible (*Merle*).

2. The Co-operative as Controlling Enterprise

A co-operative as part of a group of companies may have the function of a controlling enterprise, however, within the limits of § 1, Sub-sec.2, GenG, if this happens to be a measure in support of the running of the co-operative according to the → *by-laws* defining the purpose of promotion (*Müller*).
If a control agreement exists, the subordinate com-

panies are subject to §§ 291 pp, AktG not only if they have the status of an AG (Stock Corporation; → *Joint Stock Company*) or KG (Commercial Partnership Limited by shares – KG a. A.), but also when a GmbH (Limited Liability Company) or partnerships (*Emmerich/Sonnenschein*) are dominated *mutatis mutandis*, the reason being that regulations on the matter are not included in the respective laws. §§ 311 pp AktG can also be applied not only to de facto company groups in respect to the controlling of an AG or KG a. A., but equally of the other types of company.

In what follows, only the regulations for the domination of an AG by a co-operative will be laid out; they are to be applied to enterprises of other forms *mutatis mutandis*.

a) The contract-based group of companies

The nature of the control agreement is laid out in § 291, Sub-sec.1, Sentence 1, AktG. According to this law, it is characterized by the fact that it obliges a company to put its management under the control of another enterprise. Management of a company means the board of management and the company's representation by the board of directors (→ *Management in Co-operatives*). The regular means of subordinating a company to external management is the right of the dominating enterprise to issue instructions to the board of directors of the subordinate company (§ 308, AktG). As a rule, the control agreement runs parallel to a profit transfer agreement, the latter obliging the controlled enterprise to transfer profits to the dominating enterprise. A control agreement without a profit transfer agreement may be sensible in a case where control does not have any economic advantages for the controlling enterprise or where the aim is merely to avoid the applicability of §§ 311 pp, AktG, particularly the necessity of a dependent company report (*Koppensteiner* in *Müller*). As far as the controlling co-operative is concerned, management competence granted by the control agreement is fully subject to the postulation regulating the running of the co-operative in general. In particular, the management of the controlled enterprise has to be run in accordance with the co-operative promotion purpose. The control agreement must subject the dominated enterprise to the co-operative's promotion purpose (*Müller*). Management competence is an integral part of management incumbent on the board of directors in accordance with § 27 GenG. For the co-operative's rendering of accounts, its interconnection with other enterprises must be observed (§ 336 iVm §§ 266, Sub-sec.2 A III No. 1, B III, No. 1, 271, Sub-sec. 2, 275, Sub-sec.2 No. 9, Sub-sec.3 No. 8, 285 No. 11, HGB – German Commercial Code). The regulations concerning group accounts and group management reports (§§ 290–315, HGB are not applicable to co-operatives (§ 336, HGB). Even when a profit transfer agreement is made, the limits of § 1, Sub-sec.2, GenG, must be taken into account.

If a control agreement exists, the following principles from §§ 291pp, AktG apply:

- To become valid, the control agreement requires the consent of the general meeting of shareholders of the controlled enterprise with a majority of at least 3/4 of the share capital present when the resolution is passed, unless the by-laws of the controlled enterprise call for a larger equity majority (§ 293, Sub-sec.1, AktG).
- Furthermore, the general assembly of the co-operative must give their consent to the control agreement, with the respective application of § 293, Sub-sec.2, AktG.
- The agreement requires the written form to be displayed for the attention of shareholders and members (§ 293, Sub-sec.3, AktG) and commented on at the beginning of the general assembly of shareholders and members.
- Apart from that, on request, the shareholders and members must be informed about all the relevant affairs of the company with which the agreement is made that concern the making of a contract (§ 293, Sub-sec.4, AktG).
- The contract must be registered for entry in the register of business names (§ 294, AktG).
- Changes to a control agreement – applying §§ 293, 294 accordingly – also require consent of the general assembly of shareholders and members (§ 295, AktG).
- For important reasons the control agreement may be annulled without observing a period of notice (§ 297, Sub-sec.1, AktG).
- The ending of such a contract must also be registered for entry in the register of business names (§ 298, AktG).
- In order to protect the controlled enterprise and the creditors, special regulations for the statutory reserves to be made have been included in § 300, AktG. Profit transfer by the controlled enterprise is limited to the profit for the year accumulated before the profit transfer, minus a carryover from the previous year and the reserve sum according to § 300, AktG (§ 301, AktG). The controlling co-operative has the obligation for the term of the contract to balance the controlled enterprise's net loss for the year which has not been covered by the profit reserves (§ 302, Sub-sec.1, AktG). If the control or profit transfer agreement ends, the creditors of the controlled enterprise are protected insofar as the controlling enterprise must provide them with security for their claims, if these claims have been announced before the end of the agreement was entered in the register of trade names (§ 303, sub-sec.1, AktG).
- When controlling an AG or a KG a. A., it also has to be taken into account that appropriate compen-

sation for outside shareholders in compliance with § 304, Sub-sec.1, sentence 1, AktG must be provided for in the profit transfer agreement. At the same time, the control agreement must guarantee the outside shareholders a certain yearly share in the profits as appropriate compensation according to the amount set as compensation payment. § 304, Sub-sec.2 lays down the minimal sum to be paid as compensation.
- The control and profit transfer agreement must include the obligation of the controlling co-operative to purchase on request the shares of an outside shareholder for an appropriate compensation sum laid down in the contract.
- The controlling co-operative is entitled to issue instructions to the board of directors of the controlled company concerning the management of the company. This includes instructions to the company's disadvantage, unless stated otherwise in the contract (§ 308, sub-sec.1, AktG). For the conclusion of business deals which require approval by the supervisory board, § 308, Sub-sec.3, AktG must be observed.
- When issuing instructions, the co-operative's board of directors is under an obligation to apply the diligence of a prudent and conscientious business administrator (§ 309, Sub-sec.1, AktG). If they are in breach of this duty, the members of the board of directors are responsible as co-debtors to the controlled enterprise for resulting damage (§ 309, Sub-sec.2, AktG).

b) The de facto group of companies

The existence of a de facto group of companies with a co-operative as the controlling enterprise is also conceivable, as co-operatives may acquire an interest in other enterprises under the prerequisites of § 1, Sub-sec.2, GenG and can therefore have de facto influence on other enterprises through substantial interests within the limits of §§ 311pp, AktG. In this case, too, account has to be taken of the fact that such activities are, according to § 1, Sub-sec.2, GenG, admissible only if the central promotion purpose, which is vital to the nature of the co-operative, is preserved. So if a co-operative exercises the power of direction on another enterprise in the form of relations of control without a control agreement, a de facto group of companies is seen as given (*Müller*).
As far as the co-operative is concerned, the exercising of the power of direction in a de facto group of companies is, as a measure of the board of management, subject to the directing competence of the board of directors. The extension of the co-operative's activities resulting from the forming of the group of companies must be in accordance with the nature of the business laid down in the by-laws. In addition, the forming of the de facto company group must be a measure appropriate to the running of a business on co-operative principles (*Müller*).

Of major importance for the controlled enterprise are §§ 311pp, AktG, whose concept lies in the regulation that from a proprietary point of view, the dependent enterprise must be given a position as if it were independent.
- According to § 311, AktG, the controlling co-operative may not use its influence to instruct the dependent enterprise to do business to its disadvantage, unless the co-operative compensates for resulting disadvantages. If no regulation concerning compensation for disadvantages is agreed upon, the controlled enterprise may claim damages from the co-operative, unless a prudent and conscientious manager from an independent company would have made the same legal transaction. In the case of such a liability for damages, the co-operative's board of directors are liable alongside the co-operative itself as co-debtors.
- If no control agreement exists, the controlled enterprise's board of directors is under an obligation to draw up a report on its relationship to the controlling co-operative, including all its legal transactions with the co-operative (§ 312, AktG), in a so-called dependent company report (→ *Financial Accounting Law*).
- Under the prerequisites of § 313, AktG, the report is to be submitted to the balance sheet auditor, who is to examine it. § 314 regulates the examination of the report by the supervisory board of the controlled enterprise. Furthermore, § 315 grants the shareholders the right to carry out special audits.

III. The Co-operative as Part of a Horizontal Group of Affiliated Companies

A horizontal group of affiliated companies is a group of companies where the enterprises have no relationship of dependence, neither mutually nor towards the company group management. There is no holding company for the group, only a central management supported by mutual agreement (*Schmidt*, 1991).
There are reservations about whether it is admissible to incorporate a co-operative in a horizontal group of companies, as the management of each individual business belonging to the horizontal group is influenced from outside insofar as it is subject to unified overall planning (pro: *Schmidt*; con: *Müller*). The doubts about the admissibility of such are created by the fact that a co-operative's business is directed only by its statutory organs. According to § 27, GenG, a co-operative's management lies in the hands of its board of directors, and in their hands only. Association with a horizontal group of companies whilst at the same time adhering to the co-operative promotion purpose would only be feasible if the board of directors gave its unanimous consent to unified overall planning, the latter thereby receiving full support.

Bibliography

Aschhoff/Henningsen: Das deutsche Genossenschaftswesen, 1985.
Beuthien: Die eingetragene Genossenschaft als verbundenes Unternehmen, in: Mestmäcker/Behrens, Das Gesellschaftsrecht der Konzerne im internationalen Vergleich, 1991.
Emmerich/Sonnenschein: Konzernrecht, 4.ed., Munich 1992.
Ebenroth: Konzernbildungs- und Konzernleitungskontrolle, 1987.
Großfeld/Noelle: Harmonisierung der Rechtsgrundlagen für die Genossenschaften in der Europäischen Gemeinschaft, in: Boettcher, Die Genossenschaft im Wettbewerb der Ideen, 1985, pp. 117ff.
Kölner Kommentar zum Aktiengesetz, 2.ed., May 1987, Köln et al 1987, §§ 291 pp., §§ 304 pp..
Lang/Weidmüller. Kommentar zum Genossenschaftsgesetz, 32.ed., Berlin/New York 1988.
Luther. Die genossenschaftliche Aktiengesellschaft, 1978.
Merle, Werner: Die eingetragene Genossenschaft als abhängiges Unternehmen, Die Aktiengesellschaft, pp.265 ff., 1979.
Meyer/Meulenbergh/Beuthien: Genossenschaftsgesetz, 12th ed., 1983.
Müller, Klaus: Kommentar zum Genossenschaftsgesetz, vol.3, 1.ed., Bielefeld 1980.
Schlarb: Die Verschmelzung eingetragener Genossenschaften, 1978.
Schmidt, Karsten: Gesellschaftsrecht, 2.ed., Munich 1992.
Schmidt, Karsten: Gleichordnung im Konzern: terra incognita?, ZHR 1991, pp.417 ff..
Ulmer (ed.): Probleme des Konzernrechts, 1989.
Welling: Die Beteiligung der eingetragenen Genossenschaft an anderen Gesellschaften nach geltendem und künftigem Recht, 1966.

Law, International Co-operative

HANS-H. MÜNKNER

(see also: *Law, National*; *British-Indian Pattern*; *Principles*; *Anti-Trust Laws*; *Classification*; *Forms of Cooperation*; *Pre-co-operative Forms*)

I. Law for Co-operative Societies; II. Development of Co-operative Legislation; III. Different Models of Co-operative Legislation; IV. Contents of Co-operative Laws; V. Efforts to Standardize Co-operative Legislation.

I. Law for Co-operative Societies

From their origin, co-operative societies are not a legal form of organization, but rather a social and economic phenomenon (→ *History before 1800*; → *History in 19th C.*). Co-operative societies existed before co-operative laws were made. The first "modern" co-operatives in the middle of the 19th century operated without legal recognition or used existing legal patterns for voluntary associations, companies or friendly societies. Only later and only in some countries, special co-operative laws were drafted to suit the needs of co-operative societies (→ *Law, National*). Initially, the co-operative way of working together was a predominantly socio-economic concept (→ *Autochthonous Co-operatives*), a way of living and doing business rather than a legal type of organization.

1. Definition

At an international level, there are two definitions of co-operative societies which are not perceived as being legally binding in the sense that they compel national lawmakers to draft their national laws along the lines of these definitions. However, these international definitions serve as recommendations and have determined to a large extent the profile of the co-operative society as a legal pattern. These definitions at an international level are:

- the list of Co-operative → *Principles* of the International Co-operative Alliance (→ *ICA*) as approved by the ICA congress in 1966 (currently being subject to review), and
- the definition contained in the ILO Recommendation n° 127 of 1966, concerning the role of co-operatives in the economic and social development of the developing countries.

The general ideas expressed in these two documents have served as guidelines for national lawmakers. In the laws of many countries, reference is made indirectly or directly to the Co-operative Principles of the ICA, e.g. in the co-operative laws following the British–Indian pattern of cooperation, where a co-operative society that may be registered is defined as "*a society which has as its object the promotion of the economic interest of its members in accordance with co-operative principles ...*". (Section 4 of the Indian Co-operative Societies Act, 1912; section 4 of the Model Co-operative Societies Ordinance of the British Colonial Office, 1946).

More recent co-operative legislation contains explicit reference to the Co-operative Principles of the ICA, e.g. section 2 of the Zambian Co-operative Societies Act (n° 63 of 1970), where co-operative principles are defined in the interpretation clause as follows:

" 'co-operative principles', except as otherwise provided in this Act, means the following principles and methods used in the operation and administration of a society:

(i) each member or delegate has one vote;
(ii) there is no voting by proxy;
(iii) race, creed or political beliefs are no bar to voluntary membership and, subject to this Act, membership is open to all who can use the services of a society;
(iv) the services of a society are mainly for its members;
(v) the dividend on share capital shall not exceed six per centum per annum;
(vi) the services are available as nearly as possible at cost, allowing for the fact that, except where otherwise provided in this Act, the rules or the

by-laws, the savings arising from yearly operations are paid to members, or members and non-member patrons, in the form of patronage bonus, in proportion to the use made of the services, or to the supply of labour or other contributions made by members and non-member patrons;"

Or in the Co-operative Code of the Philippines of 1990 (R.A. n° 6938 of March 10, 1990), article 4: "Every co-operative shall conduct its affairs in accordance with Filipino culture and experience and the universally accepted principles of cooperation which include the following:

(1) Open and Voluntary Membership – Membership in a co-operative shall be voluntary and available to all individuals regardless of their social, political, racial or religious background or beliefs.
(2) *Democratic Control* – Co-operatives are democratic organizations. Their affairs shall be administered by persons elected or appointed in a manner agreed upon by the members. Members of primary cooperatives shall have equal voting rights on a one-member-one-vote principle, provided, however, in the case of secondary and tertiary co-operatives, the provisions of Article 37 of this Code shall apply.
(3) *Limited Interest on Capital* – Share capital shall receive a strictly limited rate of interest.
(4) *Division of Net Surplus* – Net surplus arising out of the operations of a co-operative belongs to its members and shall be equitably distributed for co-operative development, common services, indivisible reserve fund, and for limited interest on capital and/or patronage refund in the manner provided in this Code and in the articles of cooperation and by-laws.
(5) *Co-operative Education* – All co-operatives shall make provision for the education of their members, officers and employees and of the general public based on the principles of cooperation.
(6) *Cooperation Among Co-operatives* – All co-operatives, in order to best serve the interest of their members and communities, shall actively cooperate with other co-operatives at local, national and international levels."

In other national co-operative laws, the relevant section of the ILO Recommendation n° 127 is used together with reference to co-operative principles in order to define co-operative societies, e.g. section 2 of the Co-operative Societies Act of Tanzania 1991: "'co-operative society' means an association of persons who have voluntarily joined together for the purpose of achieving a common need through the formation of a democratically controlled organization and who make equitable contributions to the capital required for the formation of such an organization, and who accept the risks and the benefits of the undertaking in which they actively participate."

2. Ideological Concept

For many years, two different ideological concepts of co-operative organization (→ *Conceptions, Co-operative*) other than the above-mentioned definitions existed side by side :
On the one hand, the concept of co-operatives as a form of private business organization in a market-economy (→ *State and Co-operatives, Market Economy*) and, on the other hand, co-operatives as instruments for socialist transformation for the implementation of centrally planned programmes under the control of the state and the ruling party (→ *State and Co-operatives, Socialism*).
This co-existence of the two ideological concepts for cooperation under the same general definitions and membership of representatives of socialist countries and countries having a market economy in the ICA and in the ILO was made possible by wide interpretation of key elements determining co-operative organizations, e.g. democratic management and control to include democratic centralism and voluntary membership to include membership made compulsory due to lack of alternatives. Accordingly, co-operative legislation in the socialist countries differed substantially from that of countries having a market-economy. After the political changes that have occurred in the former socialist countries, this dualism of concepts is disappearing.
In the developing countries, state sponsorship and state control over co-operatives constituted an additional element of legislation. Although initially state sponsorship and state control were conceived as temporary measures to help co-operatives to develop on a sound footing (→ *Policies for Promotion*), state involvement in co-operative affairs has continuously increased during colonial times and in the independent states of Asia, Africa, Central America, and the South Pacific. This trend fitted particularly well in developing countries pursuing socialist policies.
The tendency to empower the state under co-operative law to use co-operatives as development tools and to submit them to stringent government control has been a characteristic feature of co-operative legislation in developing countries and seemed to be based on the internationally recognized Co-operative Principles, while containing many provisions contradicting these very principles (→ *Officialization*).
During the last several years, the governments of many developing countries have started to review their ideological concept and perception of co-operative societies under the pressure of structural adjustment programmes as well as their inability to finance overstaffed and costly but largely ineffective government services to control co-operatives. For co-operative legislation this means that the existing laws and regulations have to be revised and excessive government powers to control co-operatives have to be deleted. This trend is in line with a drive already con-

tained in the ILO Recommendation n° 127 on co-operaive legislation, namely,
"to detect and eliminate provisions contained in laws and regulations which may have the effect of unduly restricting the development of co-operatives through discrimination, for instance in regard to taxation or the allocation of licences and quotas, or through failure to take account of the special character of co-operatives or of the particular rules of operation of co-operatives."

3. Organizational Structure of Co-operatives

After the ideological conflicts concerning the objects and role of co-operatives have lost some of their importance, the peculiar structure of co-operatives as voluntary and private business organizations for the promotion of their members' economic and social interests becomes the main common denominator of co-operative societies on the international level, influencing the national lawmakers when drafting new cooperative legislation.

Co-operative societies are organizations characterized by their dual nature as associations of persons (the co-operative group) and a jointly financed, managed, controlled, and patronized business firm (the co-operative enterprise). The typical features of membership in co-operative societies are that members are at the same time capital contributors, goal-setters and decision-makers as well as customers of their joint enterprise. The typical feature of the co-operative enterprise is that its primary objective is to promote the economic interest of its members.

National or regional co-operative laws have to provide a legal framework within which this basic co-operative structure can work effectively. Furthermore, for lawmakers who want to follow internationally recognized co-operative principles, the way in which this basic organizational structure has to be shaped is, to a large extent, predetermined by these principles.

- Goal-setting, decision-making, and control have to be carried out in a democratic manner, giving members as well as their elected representatives the final say in all important matters concerning the co-operative.
- In primary co-operatives, the individual member is the most important denominator. Voting rights and rights of profit sharing are not linked to capital contributions, but to the person and the performance of the individual members (one member – one vote, distribution of surplus in proportion to business done with the co-operative enterprise, patronage refund).
- The role of capital is to serve and not to govern. Transfer of shares is restricted, interest or dividend on capital are deliberately limited, and shares can be withdrawn only at par value. These rules are set to ensure that investment of funds in co-operatives for capital gains or speculative purposes is excluded.

If these general rules are translated into legal norms of national or regional co-operative laws, the co-operative organizations following such laws are likely to succeed in striking the balance between democratic goal-setting and control on the one hand and economic efficiency of the co-operative enterprise as a precondition for effective promotion of the economic and social conditions of their members in competition with commercial business firms on the other.

There are, of course, deviations from these general principles in the national or regional co-operative laws in response to local conditions and circumstances. However, the general principles of co-operative ideology and co-operative structure can be found in a more or less pure form in all co-operative laws, or, where no special co-operative legislation exists, in the by-laws of co-operative societies.

After decades of largely unsuccessful experiments with state-sponsored and state-controlled co-operatives in the developing countries and programmes of socialist transformation by means of state-controlled co-operatives, it is more and more accepted that only such co-operative societies will succeed in the long run as self-reliant and self-controlled → *Self-help Organizations,* which correspond to the above-mentioned definitions and which follow the general principles of co-operative work.

II. Development of Co-operative Legislation

When the first modern co-operative societies were formed in Europe (Association chrétienne des bijoutiers en doré, Paris 1834, the Rochdale Society of Equitable Pioneers, near Manchester in 1844, and the societies formed by → *Raiffeisen* and → *Schulze-Delitzsch* in Germany in 1848) there was no special co-operative legislation for such organizations. In England, the Industrial and Provident Societies Act, under which most of the co-operative societies were registered, was promulgated in 1852. In France, a special chapter on companies having a variable share capital was added to the Companies Code in 1876 to accommodate co-operative societies characterized by variable (open) membership and variable capital. In Prussia, the "Act Governing the Legal Status of Cooperative Societies under Private Law" was promulgated in 1867. This enactment closely followed the recommendations made by *Schulze-Delitzsch.* It was the first law especially drafted for the peculiar organizational pattern of co-operative societies, covering all types of co-operatives. This Co-operative Societies Act was applied to the Northern German Federation of States in 1868, and its application was extended to cover the entire German Reich in 1871.

In Austria, a special law for all types of co-operatives

was promulgated in 1873. In the USA, the first law explicitly recognizing co-operative societies as a specific form of business organization was made in Michigan in 1856. Later, the Sherman Anti-Trust Act of 1890 exempted co-operative societies from provisions of the anti-trust legislation. The first co-operative law of Japan came into force in 1900.

In 1904 the British Colonial Government of India developed a new type of co-operative legislation specially designed for state-sponsored co-operatives, which later became known as the "Classical British Indian Pattern of Co-operation".

Between 1900 and 1926, special Co-operative Societies Acts were promulgated in several countries of Europe, in Canada, the USA, and Australia. The first co-operative laws in Latin America were those of Chile (1925), Argentine (1926), and Mexico (1927). , Before this time, however, a decree dealing with co-operatives already came into force in Guatemala in 1903, and first elements of co-operative legislation were introduced in the commercial codes of Mexico and Argentine in 1899, in Colombia in 1912, and in Panama in 1916.

Among the early co-operative legislation in Africa, the first co-operative law of the former Belgian Congo (today Zaire) can be mentioned, which was made in 1921.

In 1946, the British Colonial Office published a Model Co-operative Societies Ordinance and Model Co-operative Societies Regulations based on experience with the → *"Classical British-Indian Pattern of Cooperation"*. This model was adopted by the colonial governments of most of the former British dependencies in Asia, Africa, the Carribbean, and the South Pacific. With some amendments, this model is still in force today in many of the countries mentioned.

In France, a general Co-operative Societies Act covering all types of co-operatives was promulgated in 1947. It was to supplement special co-operative legislation for the different types of co-operative societies promulgated earlier. The general co-operative law of 1947 was made directly applicable in the French overseas territories of that time; however, this very liberal and incomplete legislation proved inadequate for the use in African countries. In 1955, the French ministry in charge of overseas territories issued a decree governing the legal status of co-operative societies in the territories under its control, to replace a semi-public type of provident society (Société Indigène de Prévoyance et de Secours Mutuel, SIP) and to provide for a governmental development, audit and supervision service for co-operative societies.

After independence, many francophone countries of Africa for some time continued to use this legislation, but also introduced new provisions governing pre-co-operatives and rural groups , e.g. the Associations d'Intérêt Rural (AIR) in Senegal (1960), the Groupements à Vocation Coopérative (GVC) in Ivory Coast (1966), and the Groupements Mutualistes Villageois in Niger (1978).

Some countries in Asia, Africa, and Latin America adopted socialist models of co-operative legislation (e.g. Burma, the Peoples' Republic of China, Cuba, Ethiopia, Guinea/Conakry, Madagascar, Mali, Nicaragua, North Korea, Tanzania and Vietnam).

After the collapse of the socialist systems in Eastern Europe and in the former Soviet Union, the new democratic states in this region have started to develop new co-operative legislation for co-operatives working as private business organizations within an emerging market economy, e.g. in Hungary, the liberation of co-operatives started already in 1968. In 1971, a co-operative law was promulgated which gave co-operatives more power of self-government and reduced the power of the state to control co-operatives. In 1990, a new Liberal co-operative law was drafted which was passed in parliament in 1992.

In Poland, a law was promulgated in 1990 ordering the compulsory liquidation of all regional co-operatives (400 in number) as well as of all national co-operative apex organizations (14), except the Supreme Co-operative Council. However, this law was declared unconstitutional in 1991. Efforts are under way to revise and to update the co-operative law of 1982. To provide a legal framework for the development of private and self-reliant co-operatives, the Czech and Slowakian Federal Republic (CFSR) passed three laws in 1990:

- the Constitutional Law N° 10 amending the constitution of the country to restore private property,
- the Co-operative Farming Act (n° 162/1990), and
- the Housing, Consumer, Producer and Other Co-operatives Act (N° 176/1990) giving co-operatives more autonomy and reducing the influence of the state on co-operatives.

In Bulgaria, a new co-operative law was promulgated in 1991. In Roumania, two new decrees/laws on co-operatives were adopted in 1990, with the aim to decentralize co-operative activities and to reduce state influence.

In the Soviet Union, several decrees of the Supreme Council since 1987 have allowed the formation of new co-operatives in services, catering, and production.

In 1988, a general law on co-operatives accelerated the development of new co-operatives in all spheres of economic activities in rural and urban areas. However, this new law did not create a favourable climate for private and self-reliant co-operatives. In 1990, a new "Law on Changes in and Amendments to the Law of the USSR on Cooperation in the USSR" was made, with the attempt to improve the legal framework for co-operatives, but at the same time, the introduction of high rates of taxation served as a disincentive. After the split of the Soviet Union into the group of independent states, each of these states will promulgate its own co-operative legislation.

III. Different Models of Co-operative Legislation

There are different ways in which the lawmakers provide the legal framework for co-operative activities, ranging from special legislation for all types of co-operative societies as a distinct legal pattern, e.g. in Germany and Austria, in most of the countries of Asia, Africa, the Caribbean, and the South Pacific having experienced the British colonial rule (the Classical British–Indian Pattern of Cooperation), Spain, many countries of Latin America, and some countries of francophone Africa, to the total absence of specific co-operative legislation (e.g. in Denmark) leaving co-operative organizations to choose the legal pattern for their activities from the general law of business organizations with adjustments made in their by-laws.

Between these two extremes there are numerous intermediate forms such as

- special co-operative laws for special types of co-operative societies, like agricultural co-operatives, consumer co-operatives, credit co-operatives, small scale industry co-operatives etc. (This format of legislation is used in France but also, for instance, in Japan and South Korea, in some Eastern European countries, and in Uruguay),
- special chapters or provisions on co-operative societies in general enactments such as the civil code (e.g. Switzerland, Italy), the commercial code (e.g. Belgium, Argentina, Mexico, Nicaragua), the labour code (e.g. France, Nicaragua) or the agricultural or rural code (e.g. Panama, France).

In France, co-operative activities are governed by a very complex system of legal norms. A special chapter for companies having a variable capital was introduced in the General Companies Code in 1876. In the following decades, many special laws for different types of co-operatives were made, specifying conditions to be met in order to qualify for tax privileges, but leaving co-operatives to choose the legal pattern suitable for their activities from the general laws of business organizations. In 1947, a general co-operative law for all types of co-operatives came into force, supplementing the numerous special laws for the different types of co-operatives and the provisions on co-operatives contained in the rural code, the labour code, etc. This general co-operative law was amended in 1992.

In federal states like the USA, Canada, India, and Nigeria, co-operative legislation often is a subject matter of state legislation, while in some states having provinces in which minorities live, such provinces are given autonomy to promulgate their own co-operative legislation (e.g. Italy, Spain).

In many countries, there is a special legislation for co-operative → *credit unions*, e.g. in Canada, the USA, Fidji, Hongkong. Mainly in African countries, special legislation has been developed for pre-co-operatives (→ *Pre-co-operative Forms*) and para-co-operatives, e.g. in Ivory Coast, Burkina Faso, Niger. Similar legislation has also been in force between 1973 and 1990 in the Philippines. Finally, in countries where the government promotes and supervises co-operatives, special laws or decrees or special chapters in co-operative laws contain provisions governing the organization and functions of such government agencies for the promotion and supervision of co-operative societies (British–Indian Pattern of Cooperation) (→ *Officialization*).

IV. Contents of Co-operative Laws

Due to the common ideological base reflected in the co-operative → *principles* of the ICA and the specific co-operative structure referred to earlier in this text, there are similarities and common features which characterize the contents of co-operative laws all over the world.

1. Formation of Co-operative Societies

In most of the industrialized countries, co-operatives like any other business organizations are registered upon application by the founder members in a public register after verification by the registering authority, whether all requirements for registration have been met by the applicants (→ *Register, Co-operative*). Upon registration, the co-operative society is officially recognized and acquires the status of a body corporate (co-operative enterprise). Considering the fact however, that co-operatives are often formed by people of limited means and without easy access to legal advice, special provisions concerning the formation process have been developed, e.g.:

- the requirement to submit an assessment of the development potential of the planned co-operative venture together with the application for registration,
- provisions regarding the steps to be taken by the founder members or a formation committee,
- requirements with regard to pre-membership education offered by co-operative federations or unions, by non-governmental organizations or by government services in charge of promoting co-operative development.

Usually, co-operative societies may be formed with a small share capital in order to make this form of organization accessible to persons with limited means. In developing countries, registration as a co-operative society often is subject to the approval of the registering authority (Registrar of Co-operative Societies or comité d'agrément). In other countries, new co-operatives have to pass through a pre-co-operative stage (→ *Pre-co-operative Forms*) either as registered pre-co-operatives or as provisionally registered co-operatives until they have proved their viability to the registering authority.

The legal norms governing the formation of co-operative societies are often far from the ideal to allow co-operative societies to be formed freely without artificial restrictions and unnecessary formalities. More often than not, co-operatives in developing regions are formed on the initiative of external actors as part of programmes and projects under government plans and/or development aid, i.e. for a target group rather than by a self-help group (→ *Self-help Organizations*).

2. The Legal Status of Members

The legal status of a member in a co-operative society is characterized by his position as the co-owner and customer of the co-operative enterprise.

In co-operative societies as people-oriented organizations, the rights and obligations of the member are linked to the person rather than to the capital contribution. In primary co-operatives, the members usually have equal rights to elect the office bearers and to be elected to serve as an office bearer of the society, (e.g. one member one vote), and personal obligations (e.g. to actively participate in decision making and control, to use the services of the co-operative enterprise, to be loyal to the society, and to comply with majority decisions).

The financial obligations of a member include the duty to contribute to the share capital of the society and to use the facilities of the co-operative enterprise for all or part of his business transactions. In many countries, members have to accept additional personal liability for the debts of the co-operative society in case of bankruptcy. In return, the financial rights of a co-operative member include the right to decide on the appropriation of surplus at the end of a period (→ *Assessment of Success*), the possibility to receive patronage refund on the transactions with the co-operative enterprise and dividend or interest on share capital (→ *Equity Capital*). In some countries, there is the tendency to introduce different categories of members (e.g. members who only contribute capital and full members, associate members in Spain, Italy, and France).

3. Organization and Management of Co-operative Societies

According to their peculiar structure, co-operative societies under the co-operative laws of all countries have at least two organs (→ *Organizational Structure of Societies*): the general meeting of members and a directing body (board of directors or committee of management). For co-operative societies having a large membership or for societies with groups of members belonging to different professions or living in different communities, the general meeting of members may be replaced or supplemented by a meeting of delegates and sectional or area meetings. In most countries, a third organ is also prescribed as a controlling body (supervisory committee). The composition and powers of these organs vary from one country to another and are differently construed under the different legal systems. The co-operative laws usually allow co-operatives to form additional bodies for special tasks such as standing subcommittees or ad hoc committees.

In credit union legislation, provisions are contained for credit committees, education committees, membership committees etc., while for other types of co-operatives like consumers' co-operatives committees for the protection of the environment, social committees and womens' guilds are formed under the societies' by-laws. Japanese consumers' co-operatives are known for their Han-Groups. In general, the persons elected to serve as office bearers in co-operative societies are elected from among the members and are answerable to the members in general meeting. However, in order to allow co-operatives to recruit qualified management, most co-operative laws provide for the appointment of managers either outside or within the board of directors.

In developing countries, where co-operatives are promoted and controlled by government, officials of the government agency in charge of co-operative development are often empowered under the co-operative law or by regulations made under the co-operative law to influence the management of co-operative societies either directly (interventionist powers) or indirectly (decisions of co-operative societies made subject to government approval (→ *Officialization*).

4. Property and Funds of Co-operative Societies

As a form of business organization, co-operative societies need capital to finance their operations (→ *Equity Capital*). Like in any other business organization, the capital consists of members' contributions (shares), non-distributed profits (reserves), and funds obtained from external sources (borrowed capital) (→ *Financing*). The way in which capital is formed in co-operative societies is regulated in different ways, depending on the classification of co-operative societies within the national legal system as

- a special legal pattern of its own,
- a modified company, or
- a way of doing business with free choice of the legal pattern and autonomy to adjust this pattern in the by-laws to meet the requirements of each society.

As a matter of principle, the capital contribution is linked to the person of the member, it is not freely transferable, and it may be combined with a personal liability of the member for the debts of the society in case of liquidation. As a result, in co-operatives with variable membership, the share capital of co-operatives is also variable.

The capital in co-operatives is de-emphasized, which means:
- votes and the right to profit sharing are not linked to the capital contribution but to other criteria (one member one vote, distribution of surplus in proportion to business done with the co-operative enterprise),
- share capital receives only a limited rate of interest or dividend, and
- share capital is paid back to members upon withdrawal at par value or with an adjustment to inflation.

These rules are made to avoid speculative investment in co-operatives.

In co-operative societies, reserves are usually seen and regulated as indivisible social capital, so as to give the co-operative a stable financial base.

With growing size and complexity of co-operative enterprises and increasing demand for investments, the traditional capital structure on which the legal provisions for financing co-operatives are based, has been criticized as a cause of structural weakness of the legal co-operative pattern making it difficult for co-operatives to compete with commercial firms that are not subject to such restrictions.

Accordingly, the following innovations can be found in co-operative laws mainly of industrialized countries (e.g. in France, Italy, and Spain):
- new forms of capital contributions by members (such as non-voting, preferred shares, bonus shares, debentures, qualification loans),
- claims to parts of the reserve fund upon withdrawal (member accounts), and
- non-voting shares offered to the public and sold in the stock exchange.

These new forms of capital formation may help to solve some financial problems of co-operatives. By making co-operatives more and more similar to ordinary companies, however, they also affect the substance of co-operative societies as a special form of organization, having its own distinct identity.

In the developing countries, special problems arise and special provisions are required in co-operative legislation when public funds are made available to co-operatives in terms of shares held by the state (e.g. state-partnership funds in India), and where all decisions concerning the property and funds are subject to government supervision and control (→ *Officialization*).

5. Audit

Co-operative societies are business organizations managed and controlled by their members, who are usually not well versed in matters of bookkeeping and accounting. The need for external audit by professional auditors is universally recognized. Accordingly, most co-operative laws contain provisions on the requirement of annual or bi-annual audit (→ *Auditing*). However, these provisions vary with regard to the scope of this audit, the persons or institutions to whom this audit is entrusted, and the procedures to be followed.

The scope of the co-operative audit reaches from purely financial audit to comprehensive management audit and the assessment of member-oriented efficiency of the co-operative enterprise.

The auditors of co-operatives may be persons appointed by the general meeting of members (commissaires aux comptes), certified public accountants employed by the co-operatives, specially trained co-operative auditors (Verbandsprüfer) of co-operative audit federations or government officials.

6. Secondary and Tertiary Co-operative Organizations

The co-operative laws do not only regulate the legal status, constitution, and working of primary co-operative societies, but usually contain provisions empowering co-operatives to federate and to form or join secondary or tertiary co-operative organizations (→ *Central Institutions*). Such regional and national co-operative organizations can work in the legal form of co-operative society, company or association, depending on their objects, size, and complexity.

Central supply, marketing and banking institutions established among co-operatives are usually exempted from the restrictions of anti-trust legislation. Furthermore, primary co-operative societies are usually affiliated with co-operative federations at regional and/or national levels for representation of their interests, training, audit and consultancy services.

Usually, affiliation of such federate structures is voluntary. In some countries like Germany, however, affiliation to a co-operative audit federation is a legal requirement for registration of primary co-operative societies. Accordingly, membership in an integrated system of co-operatives is compulsory for all organizations established in the legal form of registered co-operative society in Germany.

In some countries (e.g. in the Philippines, Thailand and Singapore), there is a tendency to define the role of secondary and tertiary co-operative organizations and the forms of vertical integration in the co-operative law, while in other countries, the co-operatives are given autonomy to form their central organizations and federations freely according to their needs.

7. The Relationship Between Co-operatives and the State

In the industrialized countries, the relationship between the co-operatives and the state is covered by a co-operative law only to a very limited extent (→ *State and Co-operatives, Market Economy*). The role of the state is reduced to registration, audit or supervision of the proper conduct of audit, normative control (i.e. ensuring that the provisions of the co-operative law are complied with), and dissolution of co-operative societies.

In the developing countries, where co-operatives are promoted and supervised by the state, co-operative laws contain special chapters or provisions regulating the tasks, powers, and duties of the government agencies in charge of co-operative development and supervision. In some countries, these matters are contained in regulations made under the co-operative law for the implementation of the Co-operative Societies Act and the development policy of the state (→ *Policies for Promotion*).

V. Efforts to Standardize Co-operative Legislation

In the developing countries, the introduction of uniform co-operative legislation by colonial governments in the English-speaking countries of Asia, Africa, the Caribbean and the South Pacific Island States (the Classical British–Indian Pattern of Cooperation), and in the French-speaking countries of Africa (the decree n° 55–184 of 1955) has resulted in a standardized co-operative legislation, which continues to be in force in some of these countries even today, while other countries have developed their own national models, implementing their own concepts or following other foreign models.

In 1966, at a conference in Nairobi, the Afro-Asian Rural Reconstruction Organization submitted another model co-operative law. The Recommandation n° 127 of the International Labour Conference in 1966, concerning the role of co-operatives in the social and economic development of the developing countries, also contains a number of guidelines for co-operative legislation in developing countries. In 1973, the Regional Office and Education Centre for South-East Asia of the ICA (New Delhi) also published a model co-operative law for state-sponsored co-operatives (cf. *Weeraman* et al.).

More recent model laws are those of the International Credit Union Organization (1987) and the Organization of American Co-operatives, OCA (1989).

Within the European Community, efforts are undertaken to draft a transnational law for European co-operative societies, i.e. for co-operatives which may be formed by co-operatives having their registered offices in two or more EEC member-states (→ *European Community*). This new European co-operative law will exist parallel to the national co-operative laws of the EEC-member states and, in many instances, will refer to the national co-operative legislation. Although it is not intended to harmonize or standardize the national co-operative legislation within the EEC, in the long run a European co-operative law will inevitably have such effect.

Bibliography

Calvert, H.: The Law and Principles of Cooperation, 5th Edition, Calcutta 1959.

Camboulives, Marguerite: L'organisation coopérative au Sénégal, Paris 1967.

Cracogna, Dante: Estudios de Derecho Cooperativo, Buenos Aires 1986.

Commission of the European Communities: Proposal for a Council Regulation (EEC) on the Statute for a European Co-operative Society, COM (90) 273 final – SYN 388, Brussels, 5 March 1992.

Credit Union National Association, Inc.: Model Credit Union Act and Commentary, Madison 1987.

Ebert, Kurt Hanns: Genossenschaftsrecht auf internationaler Ebene, Bd. I, Marburg 1966.

International Co-operative Alliance (ICA): Report of the ICA Commission on Co-operative Principles, London 1967.

Ministère de la Fonction Publique et du Plan, Délégation à l'Economie Sociale: Recueil de Textes Législatifs et Réglementaires relatifs à la Coopération, La Documentation Française, Paris 1988.

Montolío, José Maria: Legislación Cooperativa en America Latina, Colección Estudios, Serie General n° 6, Ministerio de Tabajo y Seguridad Social, Madrid 1990.

Münkner, Hans-H.: New Trends in Co-operative Law of English-speaking Countries of Africa, Institute for Cooperation in Developing Countries, Papers and Reports n° 4, Marburg 1971.

Münkner, Hans-H.: Ten Lectures on Co-operative Law, Bonn 1982.

Münkner, Hans-H.: The Legal Status of Pre-co-operatives, 2nd Edition, Bonn 1983.

Münkner, Hans-H.: Co-operative Principles and Co-operative Law, Institute for Cooperation in Developing Countries, Papers and Reports n° 5, Marburg 1974.

Münkner, Hans-H. (Ed.): Comparative Study of Co-operative Law in Africa, 6 Country Reports and General Report, Marburg Consult for Self-help Promotion, Theory and Practice of Self-help Promotion, Series B–1, Marburg 1989.

Muralt, Jürgen von: Co-operative Policy and Legislation in Eastern and Central Europe, in Review of International Cooperation, Vol. 84 n° 4, 1991.

Organización de las cooperativas de America, OCA: Proyecto de Ley Marco para las cooperativas de America Latina, America Cooperativa, Documento special n° 3, Bogatá 1988.

Snaith, Ian: The Law of Co-operatives, London 1984.

Torres y Torres Lara, Carlos: La Legislación Cooperativa en el Mundo, Lima 1986.

Weeraman, P. E.: Indian Co-operative Laws vis-à-vis Co-operative Principles.

Sheshadri, P.: International Co-operative Alliance, Delhi 1973.

Law, National Co-operative (Example: Germany)

VOLKER BEUTHIEN [J]

(see also: *History of Ideas*; *History in 19th C.*; *Legal Form, Co-operative*; *Law, International*; *Co-operatives under Public Law*)

I. The Historical Development of the German Co-operative System; II. The Creation of Co-operative Law; III. The Co-operative Law and its Amendments.

I. The Historical Development of the German Co-operative System

The historical development of the German co-operative organizations stretches back to the early Middle Ages; expressions could be found in the guild system as well as in co-operatives for farming land, pastures and dykes (→ *History before 1800*). In contrast to today's co-operatives these early forms were not voluntary associations but rather organizations with compulsory membership (→ *Guilds*). The co-operatives first emerged in their present-day form as voluntary self-help organizations under civil law in the middle of the 19th century (→ *History in 19th C.*). Determining factors for them included the industrial revolution and economic liberalism. Once the guild system was abolished and freedom of trade introduced, broad sectors of the working population – including farmers, artisans, small-scale industrial producers and laborers – were no longer able to stand up on their own against the economic pressure of large companies well provided with capital. Above all, it is thanks to the merit of → *Hermann Schulze-Delitzsch* (1808–83) and → *Friedrich Wilhelm Raiffeisen* (1818–88) that an opportune form of co-operative association was developed in this dire situation. Whereas *Schulze-Delitzsch* is held as the founder of the urban commercial co-operative system, it was *Raiffeisen* who chiefly realized the co-operative idea of collective self-help in rural areas. Each of them likewise organized a banking organization along the lines of a credit co-operative in his respective sphere of influence: the Volksbanken and the Raiffeisenbanken (→ *Co-operative Banks*).

II. The Creation of Co-operative Law

The question inevitably rose whether the extant legal company forms in common law and land law (in particular the Common Prussian Land Law of 1794) took sufficient consideration of the novel organization and method of business inherent in co-operatives, or else whether a special co-operative legal form was necessary. The form of a trading company appeared ill-suited for co-operative associations for one because of its goal of attaining profit. Other company forms likewise did not come under consideration; these either lacked their own legal person for legal interaction, were affected by changes in membership, or were under state regulation. The unique character of co-operative associations needed to be accommodated differently. This occurred through proposed legislation dating 1860, 1862, 1866, and the *Prussian Co-operative Law of 27 March 1867* – each influenced by *Schulze-Delitzsch* in his capacity as a member of the Prussian Chamber of Deputies. The latter law was amended and subsequently promulgated as Northern German Federal Law on 4 July 1868. The so-called 'Declaration Law' of 19 May 1871 stated that business transactions which extended to non-members in principle were permissible. Co-operatives became regulated in a new manner through the *Reichsgesetz concerning Trade and Industrial Co-operatives* dating 1 May 1889, itself a product of year-long preparation. *Schulze-Delitzsch* once again exercised considerable influence through various notice of appeals, this time as a member of the *Reichstag*.

III. The Co-operative Law and its Amendments

1. The fundamentals of the *Genossenschaftsgesetz* (*GenG*, German Co-operative Law), dating from 1 May 1889, are still in effect today. The Law conceives the co-operative as a company of a non-finite number of members which promotes its members' businesses or domestic economies through a common business establishment (*GenG*, § 1, Subsec.1). The registered co-operative is a juristic person under civil law (*GenG*, § 17, Subsec.1) (→ *Legal Form, Co-operative*) and thus of full legal capacity in interactions with third parties through the help of its administrative bodies, above all that of its board of directors (Vorstand) (*GenG*, § 24, Subsec.1). Its guiding concept is natural self-help among all co-operative members for the sake of economic promotion, whereby self-administration and self-responsibility are extended as far as possible (→ *Promotion Mandate*). Self-help transpires in that the members of the co-operative are simultaneously customers of the co-operative undertaking (the so-called identity principle). The fundamental equality of all members corresponds in co-operative law with the objective of self-help, particularly in voting rights (*GenG*, § 43, Subsec.3, Sent.1: one member – one vote).

2. The development of the particular legal form of a registered co-operative is characteristic in that this form has been forced to adjust to changing needs in practical application through the course of the decades, thereby inevitably distancing itself from ideal co-operative conceptions. For example, the direct participation of members in the co-operative administration has diminished considerably. Similarly, members' liability for the co-operative's obligations has decreased decisively. The natural promotion of

members through goods and services is supplemented through manifestations of capitalistic promotion such as interest on paid-up shares in the form of dividends. Trade with non-members exists alongside membership promotion.

3. The GenG has up until today been amended through 29 laws affecting particular issues.

a) With regard to members' liability, the Co-operative Law of 1889 permitted limited liability; the acquisition or loss of membership was contingent on entries in the court-kept list of co-operative members, and the obligation to provide additional contributions (→ *Nachschußpflicht*) as well as the legal audit were introduced. The direct liability of co-operative members with unlimited liability was revoked through the Law of 20 December, 1933. Since then, members can only be called upon by the co-operative for additional contributions in the case of bankruptcy. Following the extensive amendment to the Co-operative Law of 9 October, 1973, the → *by-laws* can exempt members from any obligation to provide additional contributions upon bankruptcy (*GenG*, § 6, Num.3).

b) The Amendment of 1973 also provides incentives for the improved capitalization of co-operatives. The by-laws can prescribe that members' paid-up shares be interest bearing (*GenG*, § 21a) and that the liability level should not be increased upon further investment through additional shares (*GenG*, § 121, Sent.3). Withdrawing members can also have an interest above and beyond the reimbursement of their paid-up share through the so-called internal goodwill; the by-laws can concede them a payment claim to a share of a special reserve formed for this particular reason out of the business result (*GenG*, § 73, Subsec.3, Sent.2). Furthermore, members can recall individual shares in the co-operative (*GenG*, § 67b).

c) In order that they might augment their economic strength, → *consumer co-operatives* were allowed through the Law of 21 July, 1954 to extend their business and encompass non-members as long as the reimbursement of goods does not exceed a limit of maximum 3%. The regulation was rescinded which previously had prevented co-operatives from granting credit to non-members.

d) Reduced member liability necessitated measures to protect creditors. This justified the compulsory membership of all registered co-operatives in an auditing federation and shortened intervals between audits laid down in the Law of 30 October, 1934. The ordinance concerning the audit of credit institutes' financial statements dating 7 July, 1937, prescribes an audit of the annual statement of accounts for all credit institutes which assume the legal form of a registered co-operative. The legal regulations for accounting (*GenG*, § 33) and for mandatory co-operative audits (*GenG*, §§ 53 ff.) (→ *Auditing*) were changed in the wake of the *Bilanzrichtliniengesetz* (Law of Accounting Directives) dating 19 December, 1985 which transformed the 4th EC Directive for the standardization of corporate rules.

e) The influence members exercise on the business management was initially reduced through the Law passed on 1 July, 1992, in which the Assembly of Delegates was introduced into larger co-operatives boasting of more than three thousand members (*GenG*, § 43a, Subsec.1, Sent.1); the assembly of delegates fully acts in the place of the general assembly (→ *Organizational Structure of Societies*). Members in such co-operatives can no longer voice their interests themselves but rather only via their elected representatives in the assembly of delegates. Their right as members to participate in the decision-making procedures of the co-operative is practically limited to their active and passive voting rights in the election for the assembly of delegates; they themselves cannot lay down the particulars of this voting right, but the board of directors and supervisory board rather determine them with the approval of the assembly of delegates (*GenG*, § 43a, Subsec.4, Sent.6).

f) In order to facilitate the mobility of co-operatives in competition the Law dating 3 October, 1973, fortifies the position of the board as a management body. The board must control the co-operative in full responsibility, or in other words free from corporate/political instructions from the general assembly (*GenG*, § 27, Subsec. 1). The co-operative can, furthermore, confer commercial power of attorney and procuration – even to non-members.

g) Altered market relationships effectuate altered membership structures. In earlier times, all or most of the co-operative members were economically weak to a similar degree, but today co-operatives frequently unite members who are both well *and* poorly provided with capital. Because of this the by-laws since 1973 have provided multiple voting rights up to a maximum of three votes for those members which a co-operative especially promotes (*GenG*, § 43, Subsec.3, Sents.2–8). The traditional co-operative principle of "one member-one vote" can thus be restricted in a statutory manner.

4. All amendments to the Co-operative Law have shown that the particular legal form of the registered co-operative is under constant adaptational pressure and has difficulty preserving its unique co-operative identity (→ *Law, International*).

Bibliography

Beuthien, Volker: Genossenschaftsrecht, woher – wohin? Hundert Jahre Genossenschaftsgesetz 1889–1989, Marburger Schriften zum Genossenschaftswesen, vol. 69, pp. 9 ff., 1989.

Faust, Helmut: Geschichte der Genossenschaftsbewegung – Ursprung und Weg der Genossenschaften im deutschen Sprachraum, 1965.

Meyer/Meulenbergh/Beuthien: Genossenschaftsgesetz, Kommentar, introduction, 12. ed., 1983 (with addition 1986).

Paulick, Heinz: Das Recht der eingetragenen Genossenschaft, Ein Lehr- und Handbuch, 1956.
Schachtschabel, Hans Georg: Genossenschaften, Ihre Geschichte und ihr Wesen, 1984.
Seraphim, Hans-Jürgen: Genossenschaftswesen und wirtschaftliche Grundgestalt, Quellen und Studien des Instituts für Genossenschaftswesen an der Universität Münster, vol. 1, pp. 9 ff., 1951.
Westermann, Harry: Das rechtliche Wesen der Erwerbs- und Wirtschaftsgenossenschaft, Quellen und Studien des Instituts für Genossenschaftswesen der Universität Münster, vol. 1, pp. 62–75, 1951.

Legal Form, Co-operative

VOLKER BEUTHIEN [J]

(see also: *Law, National*; *Law, International*; *New Co-operatives*; *Co-operatives under Public Law*)

I. Legal Nature; II. Definitional Characteristics of the Registered Co-operative (eG); III. Types of Registered Co-operatives; IV. Executive Bodies; V. Co-operative Principles; VI. Auditing; VII. The Co-operative Combine.

I. Legal Nature

The registered co-operative (eG, *eingetragene Genossenschaft*) is a *corporate entity* according to its fundamental structure. It is a form of economic association (*wirtschaftlicher Verein*) (BGB, § 22 [Bürgerliches Gesetzbuch, German Civil Code]) regulated through special provisions (the German Co-operative Law [GenG, Genossenschaftsgesetz]) which attains its legal capacity upon entry in the co-operative register (→ *Register, Co-operative*) (GenG, §§ 13; 17, Subsec.1). In contrast to corporations, in particular the AG (joint stock companies) or GmbH (private limited company), the legal form of an eG is not structured in a capitalistic manner but rather in a *personalistic* way inasmuch as this is possible. This is related to the fact that co-operators are both members and customers of the co-operative at the same time. On the basis of the co-operative promotional purpose (GenG, § 1, Subsec.1) the eG is oriented around the personal promotion of its members through goods or services (→ *Promotion Mandate*) and not through the attainment and distribution of a return on equity (dividend). Ideally seen the eG accordingly structures itself around actively pursued membership and not around *co-operators' capital investments* (→ *Equity Capital*), which merely serve members' individual promotion. Because of this reason the eG does not have fixed share capital but rather a capital basis which varies upon members' entry and withdrawal. This in itself exemplifies both a typical and dangerous characteristic of the eG: *equity problems*. Because paid-up co-operative shares as a rule are first raised during the formation of the eG and formed into company shares through payments and profit allocations (GenG, § 7, No.1; § 19, Subsec. 1), they can be reclaimed upon withdrawal (GenG, § 73, Subsec.2, Sent.2, Part 1), which itself can in principle occur at any time (GenG, §§ 65, 67b).

The personalistic structure of the eG is also illustrated in that membership in the co-operative is mandatory for members of the board of directors and supervisory board (GenG, § 9, Subsec.2, Sent.1) (→ *Organizational Structure of Societies*), that all co-operators in principle have only one vote (whereby the bylaws may provide for up to two additional votes [GenG, § 43, Subsec.3, Sents.1–5]), and that a special reciprocal relationship of faithfulness exists between the eG and its members. Summarizing all this, one can classify the eG as a specially regulated, legal *association of persons for economic promotion* that does not strive for profit on its own behalf but which rather endeavors to provide its members with direct and useful promotional outputs and/or services.

II. Definitional Characteristics of the Registered Co-operative (eG)

According to § 1, Subsec.1 of the GenG, the registered co-operative is a company with a non-finite number of members which serves the promotion of its members' commercial enterprises or domestic economies through a joint business establishment; it is likewise entered into the co-operative register (GenG, § 13; § 17, Subsec.1). Companies assuming other legal forms (particularly the AG or GmbH) can, however, also pursue a co-operative promotional purpose (→ *Forms of Cooperation*). In such cases, one refers to co-operatives in an economic sense (cf. *Frotz*, Co-operatives in other Legal Forms of Civil Law).

1. Non-Finite Number of Members

This characteristic of the eG makes its continuance and stability contingent on the entry and withdrawal of co-operative members. This distinguishes it from a partnership which brings together quite particular individuals who are personally bound to one another (non-trading partnership, general partnership; limited partnership). The non-finite number of members also emphasizes the desired contrast to corporations; the AG and GmbH have set share capital broken down into capital shares and therefore a finite number of members. The eG's by-laws cannot completely preclude the admission of new members, but they may prescribe a membership floor or ceiling (→ *By-laws*). Even when the by-laws make membership application contingent on certain personal or material conditions, those people who can meet these conditions in principle have *no title to admittance*. This consideration rests ultimately in the discretion of the responsible co-operative body, usually the board of directors. Title to admittance can only result out of the Law in exceptional situations, in particular when an eG dominates the market in a certain sector through business conducted with its members, and when applicants are seriously dependent on the goods or services of this eG (GWB, § 26, Subsec.2 [Law Against Restraints of Competition).

2. Promotional Purpose

By operation of the Law (GenG, § 1, Subsec.1) the purpose of an eG is necessarily tied to the promotion of the commercial enterprises or domestic economies of its members. This differentiates the eG from general and limited partnerships (OHG or KG) which can have any commercial trade as their purpose and from joint-stock companies (AG or GmbH) which can pursue any object they please. According to its content, fixation to the promotional object mean that the eG must pursue a *non-capitalistic goal which benefits its members*. Its goals must not be capitalistic in nature insofar as the legal forms of the AG and GmbH are already in existence (*case of legal form restriction*). The eG thus is prohibited from distributing corporate profits to co-operative members in the form of a return on equity gained through business transactions with arbitrary third parties (*prohibition of the so-called dividend co-operatives*). The eG can nonetheless attain profits as a means to fulfill its promotion mandate. It may not, however, strive for profits for its own benefit (aside from the accumulation of reasonable reserves), but rather must convert these into promotional outputs and/or service in kind for its members as far as possible. Profit is to be striven for primarily (many people even say exclusively) in business transactions with third parties (so-called counter business transactions), e.g. in a marketing co-operative which purchases goods from its members and sells them to third parties. In its relationship to co-operative members (so-called purpose business transactions) the eG may and even must achieve surpluses which ensure its promotional purpose in order to build reserves out of them (inasmuch as profits from counter business transactions remain insufficient). Furthermore, it is against the promotional purpose to strive for profits at the expense of members as co-operators should be directly supported through the most favorable promotional outputs or services in kind which the eG can provide. Because membership promotion should be pursued along economic lines, the eG *may not pursue exclusively idealistic goals* such as educational or welfare-related objectives. Such objectives can, however, be promoted concurrent to the primary business objective (so-called privilege of secondary purpose).

Members' *commercial operations* are furthered when the promotional output/service of the eG either increases co-operators' income or decreases their expenses in a supplementary manner which cannot be specifically identified in bookkeeping, for example through the creation of employment or marketing opportunities.

The promotion of *domestic economies* is conventionally understood as support for members in their private households. This as a rule occurs by making savings available to members, e.g. through the collective purchase of favorably priced commodities. It is, nonetheless, not particularly appropriate to use the term "members' domestic economies" in a narrow sense to refer exclusively to household economic activities. In the face of the heightened necessaries of life inherent in today's affluent and leisure society, the term should be interpreted more broadly to encompass the entire spectrum of material and ideal necessaries of life found in the private sector both intrinsic and extrinsic to household and home.

3. Joint Business Establishment

The co-operative promotional purpose must be pursued through a joint business establishment. A business establishment is any permanent agglomeration of material or personal means which serves to achieve the object of the undertaking. The eG must accordingly run its own undertaking in the sense of an organized economic unit. The meaning of the term "joint" (*gemeinschaftlich*) is contested. The collective involvement of members is not intended here; to a much greater degree the business establishment should be consigned to the eG in its capacity as a juristic person to manage the business establishment itself with the board of directors serving as its management and representational body. The meaning of the term "joint" insofar is a product of the history surrounding the creation of Article 1 of the GenG. Originally, the term "co-operative business establishment" should have been used; "joint" as defined in GenG, § 1, Subsec.1 thus soley implies "co-operative". The definition of "co-operative" in turn must be determined by the promotional purpose. From this viewpoint only such a business establishment is "joint" which assumes functions originally executed by its members or which are so essentially entwined with its members' economies that they are common needs of all members alike. The eG is not, however, restricted to auxiliary economic functions; it rather can accomplish much more than its members on preceding or subsequent economic levels. Only especially typical forms of co-operative business are listed in GenG, § 1, Subsec.1, No.1–7 (as the word "namely" illustrates). In principle, the eG can therefore include any activity in its by-laws as the object of its undertaking which promotes its membership body (GenG, § 6, No.2).

GenG, § 1, Subsec.1, No.1–7 in part uses obsolete terminology and does not name several types of co-operatives which have acquired importance in today's economy (e.g. transport co-operatives, various service co-operatives as well as liability and guarantee co-operatives for mid-sized crafts industries).

III. Types of Registered Co-operatives

1. Loan and Credit Associations
(GenG, § 1, Subsec.1, No.1)

All types of credit co-operatives are meant under the term "loan and credit associations". Commercial and/or industrial credit co-operatives are usually known as Volksbanken and rural credit institutions as Raiffeisenbanken. As a rule they execute all kinds of typical banking business and thus are universal banks (→ *Co-operative Banks*). In accordance with § 32, Subsec.1 of the KWG (German Banking Code) they need to secure authorization from the Federal Banking Supervisory Office.

2. Associations for Raw Materials
(GenG, § 1, Subsec.1, No.2)

The widely active purchasing co-operatives of today are meant by this outdated term (→ *Commercial Co-operatives*). Their business activity exists in the wholesale purchasing of raw materials and goods as well as other working materials and commodities needed by members for their own commercial enterprises (→ *Supply Co-operatives*). Above all, the purchasing co-operatives for retail traders and craftsmen as well as other commercial undertakings fall under GenG, § 1, Subsec.1, No.2, as well as rural purchasing co-operatives which, as a rule, serve as marketing co-operatives at the same time. The modern, large-scale purchasing co-operatives have developed into sales-oriented, wholesale business undertakings with marketing risks of their own. Their promotion mandate extends beyond the trade of goods to encompass consulting and similar assistance services and even includes the "full-service co-operative" (which supplies goods and services alike).

3. Marketing and Warehouse Co-operatives
(GenG, § 1, Subsec.1, No.3)

→ *Marketing co-operatives* above all are rural merchandise co-operatives (→ *Rural Co-operatives*) which sell their members' agricultural products to third parties and at the same time regularly provide their members with needed agricultural commodities (fertilizer, feed, seed, farm machinery, etc.). They are therefore known as "agricultural supply and marketing co-operatives". GenG, § 1, Subsec.1, No.3 also encompasses rural processing co-operatives such as dairy, fishing and wine-growers' co-operatives. These co-operatives undertake the raw processing of products grown on their members' enterprises or else make new, finished products on joint account. Warehousing co-operatives no longer exist today under this classification. This term originally referred to co-operatives which sold their members' commercial products in public sales and marketing outlets.

4. Joint-production Co-operatives
(GenG, § 1, Subsec.1, No.4)

This term refers to the rather isolated groupings of workers or artisans which collectively produce or process goods or collectively provide services. In contrast to all other co-operative forms the members of a → *joint-production co-operative* (workers' co-operative) place their own labor input at the disposal of the co-operative enterprise. They are the employees of their own co-operative society and simultaneously their own employers. In part the characteristic auxiliary economic trait of the co-operative promotional undertaking is therefore questioned in case of joint-production co-operatives. The promotion mandate of joint-production co-operatives in this connection rests in the best possible utilization of members' labor input from a business point of view. Joint-production co-operatives are understandably often difficult to manage in that all members are equally entitled according to company law but must assume varying tasks (usually subordinate in their importance) according to internal business structure. Nevertheless, an increasing interest in the legal form of the joint-production co-operative can be ascertained today, a phenomenon which is based among other things on high unemployment and widespread social criticism.

5. Consumer Associations
(GenG, § 1, Subsec.1, No.5)

Consumer associations ("Konsumvereine") are known today as → *consumer co-operatives*. They undertake the commercial wholesale purchasing of foodstuffs and other consumer and durable goods for household needs in order to resell them in smaller quantities to their members and, as a rule, third parties (through GenG, § 8, Subsec.1, No.5). Their members are therefore ultimate consumers. The opportunity of granting a co-operative reimbursement is restricted by § 5 of the *Rabattgesetz* (Rebates Law) to 3% in the business year including cash discounts.

6. Works or Use Co-operatives
(GenG, § 1, Subsec.1, No.6)

These serve the purchasing and maintenance of machinery for farming or industrial enterprises to be used by members and borne on joint account, e.g. in the rural sector or craft industries (→ *Machinery Associations/Rings*).

7. Co-operative Housebuilding Societies
(GenG, § 1, Subsec.1, No.7)

A co-operative housebuilding society (→ *Housing Societies*) serves to provide its members with living space. The societies themselves must not build the apartments/homes themselves in contrast to the wording of the law; it is sufficient when they solely obtain living space and make it available. The apartments – either built, purchased or rented – are sold to the members or letted to them. The actual wording of the by-laws determines whether members acquire a general legal title or a general, indefinite claim to the acquisition of an owner-occupied house or the allocation of an apartment in the legal sense of tendering a bid for a house or apartment. The legal title to a certain homestead or particular apartment associated with membership rights is only then actionable when the co-operative member meets the preconditions for promotion laid down in the by-laws; he must submit his application, and the responsible co-operative body (usually the board of directors) must pass the particular allocation resolution prescribed in the by-laws and inform the member accordingly.

The legal nature of the usufructuary relationship which emerges between the co-operative and the member is contested. It is sometimes considered a corporate legal relationship, sometimes a particular co-operative usufructuary relationship, and sometimes a rent relationship. At the root of this matter is the ques-tion whether and/or to what extent the protective provisions embodied in landlord and tenant law are applicable in the co-operative usufructuary relationship. Because it has been unanimously maintained for some time that the protective provisions of the law of tenancy rights found in §§ 556a ff. and § 721 of the ZPO (Code of Civil Procedure) can in any case be applied accordingly in the co-operative usufructuary relationship and can be annulled neither in the by-laws nor in individual contractual situations, the terminological dispute for the most part is superfluous. The *Hausratsverordnung* (decree concerning the household effects) is also applicable. When renting available housing space the co-operative housebuilding societies must respect the co-operative principle of fair and equal treatment of its members.

IV. Executive Bodies

As a juristic person (GenG, § 17, Subsec.1) the eG acts through its executive bodies (cf. Blomeyer, Executive Bodies of Co-operatives). It has three mandatory administrative bodies, namely a board of directors upon which the management and its representatives are incumbent (GenG, §§ 24–35), a supervisory board which watches over the board (GenG, §§ 36–41), and a general meeting as the highest decision-making body (GenG, §§ 43 ff.) (→ *Organizational Structure of Societies*). For co-operatives with more than three thousand members the general meeting must consist of delegates elected by the co-operative members (GenG, § 43a, Subsec.1, Sent.1). Such an assembly of delegates can also be provided for co-operatives boasting more than one thousand five hundred members (GenG, § 43a, Subsec. 1, Sent.2). Aside from these mandatory bodies, further so-called facultative co-operative bodies can be formed, such as advisory boards (GenG, § 27, Subsec.2, Sent.2). These latter bodies, however, cannot be allocated any functions which are to be executed by the mandatory administrative bodies due to the principle of strict adherence to the by-laws (GenG, § 18, Sent.2). In contrast to the board of directors or the supervisory board, the advisory boards can include individuals who are not co-operative members (GenG, § 9, Subsec.2, Sent.1).

V. Co-operative Principles

Whereas legal science primarily trains its view on the *legal form* of the eG, economics conceives the co-operative as an *economic form*. In order to emphasize the functions of this particular economic form, economic science has formulated the so-called → *co-operative principles*. These include, above all, the following:

1) Principle of Self-Help;
2) Principle of Self-Administration;
3) Principle of Self-Responsibility;
4) Principle of Democracy;
5) Principle of Identity between Owner and Customer;
6) Principle of Economic Promotion.

In light of company law these principles are only of note inasmuch as they are entered into the provisions of Co-operative Law. For all that, the following statement is true: The more co-operative "thought" in the sense of the traditional co-operative principles binds the eG to its special legal form in company law, the more "co-operative" the eG is.

The *Principle of Self-Help* states that the co-operative members joined together in the eG are to further and promote themselves through business transactions with the undertaking run by the co-operative. The *Principle of Self-Administration* addresses the situation that the shareholders are to regulate their own matters via organizational-legal rights encompassing control mechanisms and co-administration. Co-operative Law in effect expresses this in that the board of directors and the supervisory board must be composed of co-operative members (GenG, § 9, Subsec.2, Sent.1), that the board in certain management situations can be made subordinate to the approval of the general assembly, and that the general assembly must approve the annual statement (GenG, § 48, Subsec.1, Sent.1) as well as vote to discharge the board of directors and the supervisory board (GenG, § 48, Subsec.1, Sent.2).

The *Principle of Self-Responsibility* means that the co-operative members are personally liable for the obligations of their eG. This is, however, now only partly effective; as of 1974 the by-laws draw limits to the obligation to provide additional contributions in the case that the co-operative goes bankrupt and can even preclude such obligations (GenG, § 6, No.3). The *Principle of Democracy* is expressed in the principle of "one member – one vote" found in GenG, § 43, Subsec.3, Sent.1. This principle of members' equality with respect to voting procedures can, however, be broken by the by-laws, which can prescribe multiple voting rights up to a maximum of three votes to the favor of those members who are especially promoted by the co-operative's business establishment (GenG, § 43, Subsec.3, Sent.2–8).

The *Principle of Identity* states that the co-operators are both members and customers at the same time. The principle of identity thus extends over the principle of self-help promotion in kind for all members via the co-operative business establishment. The most essential and steadfast core of the legal term "eG" thereby is embodied in the *Principle of Promotion* (see II.2).

VI. Auditing

According to GenG, § 63b, Subsec.1 each eG as a registered association must belong to an auditing federation (→ *Federations*) vested by the state with the right to conduct audits (GenG, §§ 54,63) (→ *Auditing*). Affiliation to an auditing federation is not only mandatory for the eG according to company law, but it is an essential precondition for this particular legal form (a). The attestation of an auditing federation that the co-operative has been approved entry is an essential requirement for enrollment in the register (GenG, § 11, Subsec.2, No.4) (b). Furthermore, not belonging to an auditing federation necessarily leads to the legal dissolution of the eG (GenG, § 54a, Subsec.2).

The mandatory audit of the co-operative (GenG, § 53) (→ *Auditing*) serves both the protection of the co-operative members against losses of their investment contributions, additional contributions and setbacks in their own business enterprises as well as the protection of the co-operative's creditors against non-payment of receivables. The audit is indispensible compensation for the fact that co-operative members need not raise a legally set, minimum level of liability capital (see GenG, § 7, No.1), and that the by-laws not only can put a limit to additional obligatory contributions in the face of bankruptcy but can even completely rule out such contributions (GenG, § 6, No.3).

The objective of the audit is to ascertain the economic situation of the eG as well as to confirm that the management has acted in due order and in the sake of membership promotion. As a result of its perennial character the mandatory audit assumes not only controlling functions for past performance but likewise consulting functions oriented around the future (the so-called "attendance audit"). Inasmuch as the auditing federations as a rule are general commercial associations, they also assume other responsibilities (GenG, § 63b, Subsec.4, Sent.1): they look after members' interests as well as the co-operative's entire concerns in the fields of business and legal-political matters, consult members beyond the scope of the audit in management and legal matters, and create collective safeguarding systems (for credit co-operatives) in collaboration with the co-operative apex federation.

VII. The Co-operative Combine

1. Central Co-operatives

As GenG, § 9, Subsec.2, Sent.2 and § 43, Subsec.3, Sent.7 indicate, primary registered co-operatives can join in regional central co-operatives, which in turn join together in national co-operative centers (the so-called three-tiered structure) (→ *Central Institutions*). It is irrelevant which legal form this assumes. Lawmakers permit this multiple-level co-operative economic combine in order that primary co-operatives can avail themselves of market functions in the interest of their members and through the help of the central co-operative(s) – functions which they in their capacity as primary co-operatives either could not fulfill or only to an ineffective degree. It is up to the discretion of the co-operative members with regard to their economic promotion how many tiers they wish to construct. The higher level combine tier in this *vertical economic system* often only directly promotes the level immediately below it, but such promotion in turn serves the indirect promotion of the co-operative basis.

2. Participating Interests in Subsidiary Companies

According to GenG, § 1, Subsec.2 an eG can acquire an interest in any private company regardless of its legal form as well as in public corporations as long as they serve its promotional purpose or its secondary objectives of public benefit. The eG insofar also enjoys *horizontal freedom in forming a combine*.

GenG, § 1 II above all pursues two protective objectives for the eG as a legal form with regard to economic promotion: the protection of promotional capital as well as the protection of the particular legal form of the eG against deterioration into a "non-co-operative" state.

Because participations can also entail losses, the eG first of all should be protected from damages by the imposed prohibition of investment participation which runs counter to the promotional purpose and is possibly speculative in nature; the eG by any means is prone to lack both capital and liability backing because of its structure. In the second place GenG, § 1 II should safeguard the co-operative members from a corporate policy which runs counter to the promotional purpose but which is nonetheless pursued by the board of directors, itself not bound to take any instructions from other co-operative bodies according to GenG, § 27 I, 1. The board of directors could neglect the promotional needs in kind of the co-operative members by undertaking business with non-members (permitted according to GenG, § 8, Subsec.1, No.5) above and beyond pursued company growth levels and even set its eye on an investment policy which was either alien or even counter to the promotional purpose. Participating interests are not immediately beneficial to the promotional purpose when they solely serve the eG's general capital interests; a subsidiary company must rather to a greater degree either pursue promotional economic goals itself with regard to the co-operative members, or else it must serve to strengthen the eG's business establishment in such a manner that it can offer less expensive or more varied promotional outputs/services to its members than previously possible. The eG may not strive for capital yields through investment in subsidiaries in order to pass these returns as such on to their members. Such a *participation co-operative* would be the corresponding counterpart to the inadmissible dividend co-operative.

The eG must certainly be allowed *to invest the reserves of its promotion capital in a profitable manner* like any other business enterprise. Otherwise it would be throwing away potential interest on capital counter to its promotional purpose. The eG must therefore be granted sufficient discretionary lee-way on capital markets. It must also be allowed to invest its reserves of promotional capital in other types of venture capital participation inasmuch as it cannot find a subsidiary which is closely enough related to its statutory promotion mandate as defined in the Law (GenG, § 1, Subsec.1; § 6, No.2). These must, however, ultimately serve the non-capitalistic promotional economy of the eG and therefore must not be out of relationship with business conducted with members to fulfill the promotional purpose or with the need for promotional capital for the execution of such promotional business undertakings. In no way or manner may the investment of the eG predominantly or exclusively serve the interests of the company it is participating in or those of its shareholders. GenG, § 1 II is only applicable to the eG and thus not for co-operatives which assume other legal forms. § 1 II therefore does not extend to shareholdings in central co-operatives run as a joint-stock company. Limits for acquiring an interest in them result only indirectly in that they must promote the primary co-operatives according to their by-laws – in principle through their entire business operation. The central co-operative combine by operation of law is thus less protected from faulty capitalistic developments than its basis.

3. The Co-operative Group of Affiliated Companies

Because GenG § 1 II does not set any ceiling to participation, an eG may also possess a *controlling interest*. Such extensive participation is even expedient inasmuch as it guarantees that the associated company pursues a corporate policy which serves the promotional purpose. On account of its majority of votes in the dependent company's general assembly, the eG is in the position to exercise indirect controlling influence on the other company. This is particularly so for the dependent GmbH because the shareholders' meeting can confer corporate-political directives to the management (Law on Limited Liability Companies, § 37, Subsec.1). The eG can thus be a *dominant enterprise* as defined in the AktG (German Stock Corporation Law), § 17, Subsec.1.

On the other hand, it is questionable whether the eG can be made into a *dependent enterprise* as defined in the law concerning groups of companies through the signing of a *domination contract* according to AktG, § 291, Subsec.1, Sent.1, Case 1. Co-operative literature on the subject has almost unanimously refuted this up to now – nevertheless unjustly. According to Article 9, Section 1 of *German Basic Constitutional Law*, all associations and companies enjoy extensive organizational autonomy. This in principle allows them to formulate their articles of association in a flexible manner with regard to third parties or to enter into business relations of a specific organizational pattern. The eG insofar poses no exception. The principle of strict adherence to the co-operative by-laws (GenG, § 18) only entails the legal relationship between the eG and its members and *not* with the share rights of third parties within or with regard to the eG. The co-operative autonomy remains protected in that the general assembly must ratify a domination contract with at least a three-quarter majority according to AktG, § 293, Subsec.1, Sent.1; the eG must be able to give notice to terminate such a contract at any time according to AktG, § 297, Subsec.1. That the board of directors must independently perform its management responsibilities according to GenG, § 27, Subsec.1, Sent.1 merely means that it does not have to take instructions or directives from other co-operative bodies when executing its management functions. Because it is obligatory for the members of both the board and the supervisory board to be co-operative members (GenG, § 9, Subsec.2, Sent.1) and the dominant company thus can only elect co-operative members to the board of directors or supervisory board, the principle of co-operative self-administration in the executive bodies is not impaired. Members of a controlled eG can counter the danger of being burdened with unforeseeable, personal liability resulting from external instructions via a subordination agreement by limiting the right to give directives in the inter-company agreement; they could likewise reduce or even preclude the obligation to make additional contributions upon bankruptcy fixed in their by-laws (GenG, § 6, Subsec. 3; § 105). Because the controlling company may only give the dependent eG directives which are compatible with the promotional purpose fixed by law (GenG, § 1, Subsec.1) and anchored in its by-laws (GenG, § 6, Subsec.2), no violation of the co-operative principle of promotion occurs.

Within the boundaries of its promotional purpose a dependent eG may obligate itself contractually in accordance with AktG, § 291, Subsec.1, Sent.1, Case 2 to transfer its profit either entirely or partially to a dominant company. The promotional purpose remains guaranteed when the eG secures promotional economic advantages for its members by transferring profits to a third party. This is particularly applicable when the third party has obliged itself to provide the co-operative members with services which serve the promotional purpose. This, furthermore, is the case when the eG secures services for itself from the co-operative combination via a transfer of profits; examples include collective advertising which is advantageous to the eG or security mechanisms for the co-operative combine. A *profit* or *partial profit transfer agreement* can insomuch be useful in the co-operative economic system.

The same holds true for *other types of inter-company agreements* (→ *Intercompany Cooperation*), in particular company lease or surrender agreements. These are fundamentally also permissible for an eG as long as they do not contradict the co-operative promotional purpose as defined in GenG, § 1, Subsec.1. In contrast it would be quite difficult to form a *de facto co-operative corporate group*. The formation of such a group of affiliated companies as a rule flounders in that an eG has no voting right based on capital investment.

Bibliography

Beuthien, Volker: Die eingetragene Genossenschaft als verbundenes Unternehmen. In: Mestbäcker/Behrens (ed.): Das Gesellschaftsrecht der Konzerne im internationalen Vergleich, p. 133 ff., Baden-Baden 1991.
Beuthien, Volker: Genossenschaftsrecht: woher – wohin? Hundert Jahre Genossenschaftsgesetz 1889–1989, Marburger Schriften zum Genossenschaftswesen, vol. 69, 1989.
Lang/Weidmüller: Genossenschaftsgesetz, Kommentar, 32nd edition, Berlin-New York 1988.
Meyer/Meulenbergh/Beuthien: Genossenschaftsgesetz, Kommentar, 12th edition, München 1983 (with addition 1986).
Müller, Claus: Kommentar zum Gesetz betreffend die Erwerbs- und Wirtschaftsgenossenschaften, vol. 1–3, 1st edition, Bielefeld 1976–1980, and vol.1+2, 2nd edition 1992.
Paulick, Heinz: Das Recht der eingetragenen Genossenschaft, ein Lehr- und Handbuch, Karlsruhe 1956.
Schultz/Zerche: Genossenschaftslehre, Berlin-New York 1983.

Legal Transformation of a Co-operative

PETER ERLINGHAGEN [J]

(see also: *Law, National*; *Legal Form, Co-operative*; *Joint Stock Company*; *Co-determination*; *Law, International*)

I. Introduction; II. Preconditions for Transformation; III. Contents of the Resolution; IV. Participation of Co-operative Members; V. Creditor Protection; VI. Advantages of a Legal Transformation; VII. Relevance for Tax Matters.

I. Introduction

The legal transformation of a co-operative society into a stock corporation (AG) (→ *Joint Stock Company*) is the only type of transformation regulated in German corporate law. This transformation option exists on account of *Aktiengesetz*, §§ 385 m ff. (*AktG*, German Stock Corporation Law) which was built into the *AktG* in 1969. This concerns a transformation in legal form in which only the external legal form is altered and not the legal entity as such. A transfer of assets thus does not occur.

The transformation of a co-operative into another legal form as well as the transformation into a commercial entity with a sole stockholder is provided for in German law just as little as companies' option to transform into the co-operative legal form (→ *Legal Form, Co-operative*). In such cases, only singular transformations are possible; in other words, an enterprise must be established in the desired legal form, the enterprise run in the previous legal form must be liquidated, and assets must be transferred – all as individual actions. This is considerably more expensive and troublesome than a transformation. Insofar as a transformation is not directly possible, an additional transformation can by all means be interposed in the process. The transformation of a co-operative into a limited liability company (GmbH), for example, is indirectly feasible in that the co-operative initially is transformed into a stock corporation (AG) which is then transformed into a limited liability company.

II. Preconditions for Transformation

The *preconditions for the transformation* of a co-operative into a stock corporation are established in *AktG*, § 385 m. The transformation resolution of the general meeting is essential for the transformation (*AktG*, § 385 m, Subsec.2, Sent.1). The general meeting is either an assembly of all members of the co-operative or else a delegates' meeting – which is obligatory when membership exceeds 3,000 members. The delegates' meeting is also responsible for the transformation resolution in that it fully assumes the legal position of the general meeting. The general meeting must be called by the board (*GenG*, § 44) with at least a one-week prior notice in the manner prescribed in the by-laws (*GenG*, § 46, Subsec.1). The transformation resolution must be adopted with a three-quarters majority of cast votes, not of total votes (*AktG*, § 385 m, Subsec.2, Sent.4). This corresponds to the necessary majority for amendments to the by-laws in accordance with GenG, § 16, Subsec.2 as well as to the resolution to liquidate in accordance with *GenG*, § 78. It must be taken into account in this matter that voting rights in co-operatives are based on the "one man, one vote" principle (*GenG*, § 43, Subsec.3, Sent.1) in contrast to stock corporations in which they correspond to capital participation.

Protection for co-operative members against unacceptable disadvantages through a transformation which goes against their interests is guaranteed by *AktG*, § 385 m, Subsec.2. in that the agenda and proposal for the transformation resolution must be announced to the co-operative members in written form at the latest when the general meeting is called. Furthermore, this announcement must mention that a three-quarters majority is necessary for the transformation resolution and that it is possible to file an objection (*AktG*, § 385 m, Subsec.5). This communique must likewise be issued to all members when the general meeting assumes the form of a delegates' meeting and the co-operative members are accordingly not entitled to participate. If at least 100 co-operative members file an objection against the transformation resolution up for adoption in a co-operative with over one thousand members or when at least one-tenth of all co-operative members file such an objection in co-operatives with a lower membership level, the transformation can only be passed with a nine-tenths majority of all cast votes (*AktG*, § 385, Subsec.2, Sent.5). The by-laws of a co-operative can prescribe larger majorities, e.g. the unanimous adoption of a resolution, as well as further requirements for the transformation (AktG, § 385 m, Subsec.2, Sent.7). The transformation resolution must furthermore be authenticated by a notary public (*AktG*, § 385 m, Subsec.2, Sent.6).

Furthermore it is necessary that the auditing federation to which the co-operative belongs (in accordance with *GenG*, § 54) submits an expert opinion before the resolution is adopted concerning whether the transformation is compatible with the interest of co-operative members and the creditors of the co-operative alike (*AktG*, § 385 m, Subsec.3). This expert opinion is to be presented in the general meeting in which the transformation resolution is to be adopted before the resolution has been voted on. The auditing federation has a right to participate in the general meeting; it can take up discussion in order to expound on its report, but it does not enjoy voting rights nor the right to file a resolution. The transformation resolution can also be passed against the recommendation of the auditing federation although it is doubtful that the necessary majority for the transformation resolution could be realized in such a situation.

The transformation of a co-operative into a stock corporation does not automatically lead to its withdrawal from the co-operative auditing federation; the stock corporation does not however have any right or claim to maintain its membership. The transformation as a rule represents justification for the auditing federation to exclude the former co-operative (c.f. *Lang/Weidmüller*, § 63 b, margin note 3; § 54, margin note 18).

III. Contents of the Resolution

Necessary *contents for the transformation resolution* include the establishment of the company, its share capital and the nominal value of its shares. Because *AktG*, § 4 is effective, no right exists for the continuance of the enterprise of the co-operative. The minimum level of share capital is DM 100,000. The assets of the co-operative must not be below the nominal value of the share capital after liabilities have been deducted (*AktG*, § 385 m, Subsec.4, Sent.2). The law thus ensures that the share capital is covered by corresponding assets of the stock corporation. If net assets do not amount to the minimum level of share capital a transformation is only possible once the paid-up shares of the co-operative members have been increased. In order to guarantee this precondition the law calls for an audit to take place upon establishment in compliance with *AktG*, §§ 33, 34 (*AktG*, § 385 m, Subsec.5). A balance sheet need not be prepared upon transformation, but an asset and liability statement must be drawn up in order to determine whether the decided level of share capital is covered by the net assets of the company.

The transformation resolution must additionally prescribe necessary changes in the by-laws for the execution of the transformation (*AktG*, § 385 m, Subsec.4, Sent.1). It should thereby be ensured that the by-laws contain the necessary minimum elements in accordance with *AktG*, § 23 and that they do not contradict the preemptory provisions in the *AktG*.

The transformation resolution must also be registered and entered into the co-operative register by the board; the members of the board and the supervisory board must register and enter the stock corporation into the commercial register (*AktG*, § 385 o). The co-operative exists as a stock corporation once the transformation has been entered in the co-operative register (c.f. *Westermann*, p.94). *AktG*, § 385 p, Subsec.2 assumes particular importance: it states that the transformation resolution can no longer be annulled once the stock corporation has been entered into the commercial register.

IV. Participation of Co-operative Members

The *participation of the co-operative members in the stock corporation* is structured in accordance with AktG, § 385 n. Each co-operator takes an equity stake in the share capital of the stock corporation. The decisive factor for the extent of financial participation in the share capital is the relationship of the individual co-operator's paid-up shares to the totality of paid-up shares held by all co-operative members at the end of the completed business year prior to the adoption of the resolution. The paid-up shares of those co-operative members who withdraw from the co-operative prior to the transformation resolution are to be deducted from the sum of the paid-up shares in the calculation of the financial stakes (*Zöllner*, § 385 n, margin note 10).

Because *AktG*, § 8 requires a minimum nominal value of DM 50.00 per share of stock, it is possible for co-operative members merely to acquire a partial right when their paid-up shares are insufficient for the apportionment into stocks with a nominal value of DM 50.00. A precondition for this is that each member must be allotted a partial right amounting to at least DM 5.00 (*AktG*, § 385 m, Subsec.1, Sent.2). These partial rights are salable and inheritable membership rights (*AktG*, § 385 n, Sent.2 with reference to § 385 k), but nevertheless the rights tied to the share can only be made effective and applied when the partial rights are aggregated in one share and represented by a common proxy (*AktG*, § 69).

The automatic transformation of co-operative membership into membership in a stock corporation also occurs for those co-operative members who opposed the transformation in accordance with *AktG*, § 385 m, Subsec.2, Sent.5 but who were outvoted. The law does not provide for the withdrawal of these co-operators before the transformation resolution becomes effective. In other words, the co-operative member becomes a stockholder against his will, but he then naturally has the opportunity to sell his share or partial right. The cooperator who voiced opposition against the transformation resolution can, however, demand that the stock corporation find a ready sale of the shares for him (*AktG*, § 385, Subsec.5 with reference to § 385 i); the cooperator thus has the option of placing his shares at the disposition of the company. The stock corporation thereby does not acquire these shares as property once they are placed at its disposition, but it must rather promptly sell them through a broker in its own name and on the account of the stockholder at the official stockmarket price (*AktG*, § 383, Subsec.2). If there is no listed stockmarket price an official auction must be held. The disadvantage of this option for the stockholder is that he must bear the costs of the auction. Discussion therefore is underway whether a co-operative member who voices opposition to the transformation can be granted the right of an extraordinary cancellation of his membership in the co-operative in accordance with *GenG*, § 67 a. Similar situations which entitle withdrawal of membership in accordance with *GenG*, § 67 a and § 16, Subsec.2 include the alteration of the object of the company and the extension of the period of notice to more than two years. Transformations and substantial alterations to the corporate object are comparable in their nature as particularly incisive measures. A transformation is similar to the preclusion of a right of termination as such a preclusion is unknown in stock corporation law. It could be argued that the co-operative members are protected against termination without notice through AktG, § 385 m, Subsec.5 which refers to *AktG*, § 385 i. The objection could be raised that the right to terminate without notice would exist if this proviso were not necessary. *AktG*, § 385 i, must therefore be interpreted as an additional security for co-operative members which often offers the more economically favorable solution; a right of termination without notice should, however, not be precluded here (c.f. *Zöllner*, § 385 n, margin note 7). Yet another option for withdrawal from the co-operative are contractual agreements made in the course of the transformation. The withdrawal of several co-operative members through contractual agreement can even be necessary in order to achieve the requisite majority for the transformation resolution (c.f. ibid, margin note 8).

An important consequence of the transformation is that the co-operative's board of directors and its supervisory board lose their offices upon transformation (→ *Organizational Structure of Societies*). They must always be elected anew. The newly elected supervisory board must appoint the board of the stock corporation prior to its enrollment of the transformation. Changes in the composition of the supervisory board frequently arise because co-operatives must then provide employee co-determination in their supervisory boards when they employ more than 500 persons (Industrial Constitution Law 1952 [*BetrVG*], § 77, Subsec.3). Stock corporations on the other hand must have co-determination regardless of the number of their employees in accordance with *BetrVG* 1952 , § 76, Subsec.1 (→ *Co-determination*).

V. Creditor Protection

The regulations for a transformation in addition must guarantee *creditor protection*. Because an obligation to make further contributions (→ *Nachschußpflicht*) in accordance with *GenG*, § 105 dissolves upon the transformation, *AktG*, § 385 q maintains this *Nachschußpflicht* for a further two years for those co-operative members who become stockholders in order to protect the co-operative's creditors. Whether or not the co-operator voiced opposition to the transformation resolution is irrelevant. The sale of the share likewise does not discontinue liability during this two-year period; the purchaser of the share does not assume liability. This is also the case when the stockholder places his share rights at the disposition of the company (*AktG*, § 385 i). Because *AktG*, § 385 q endeavors to maintain creditors' chances to be payed off in full, partial rights are also considered shares in the sense of § 385 q.

§ 385 q is disadvantageous for individual co-operators as only those members who withdrew from the co-operative prior to the commencement of bankruptcy proceedings are held liable when the bankruptcy proceedings commence within six months of their withdrawal (*GenG*, §§ 75, 101). If the withdrawal of a co-operative member is effected by the transferral of his paid-up share, his liability is even further limited to the situation in which the purchaser of his share is financially unable to make additional contributions (*GenG*, § 76, Subsec.4). Furthermore it must be emphasized that the *Nachschußpflicht* is not restricted to the satisfaction of those creditors whose outstanding accounts arose before the co-operative was transformed into a stock corporation. *AktG*, § 385 q therefore provides a better position not only for the former creditors of the co-operative but also for the new creditors of the stock corporation (c.f. *Zöllner*, § 385 q, margin note 4).

VI. Advantages of a Legal Transformation

The question is raised at this point as to which *advantages* can arise through the transformation of a co-operative into a stock corporation. The retention of the co-operative legal form first of all does not seem appropriate when the object of the co-operative shifts towards the realization of profits. The most frequently raised argument for a legal transformation however is that a stock corporation enjoys more numerous and simplified options to raise capital. Co-operative membership directed at the person of the members can be dangerous for the co-operative. Because co-operators enjoy the right of termination, the co-operative can be forced at any point in time to reimburse at least partial contributions to the withdrawing members. The equity capital of the co-operative accrued through the paid-up shares is therefore flexible. In contrast to this situation, the capital structure of a stock corporation guarantees the preservation of equity capital in that the share capital is tied to the stock corporation (c.f. *Westermann*, p.84).

The argument must be refuted that the co-operative is a sluggish organization form which cannot quickly make decisions as is required of it. The co-operative board must not acquiesce to individual directives issued by the general meeting or the supervisory board; directives with respect to the intended corporate policy can solely be anchored in the → *by-laws* (c.f. Stehle, p.36 ff.) The co-operative board on the contrary retains control based on its own responsibility (*GenG*, § 27, Subsec.1, Sent.1). The most substantial reason to decide for a transformation can therefore solely be the facilitation of capital acquisition in stock corporations.

VII. Relevance for Tax Matters

The transformation can furthermore result in changes to the liable corporate income tax or the rate of corporate taxation (→ *Taxation*). The transformation to another legal form also affects the calculation of the basis of taxation inasmuch as the co-operative can reduce its profits through → *reimbursements* in contrast to stock corporations (c.f. *KStG*, § 22 [Corporation Income Tax Law], German Civil Code, 1984 I., 217); under certain conditions the co-operative is granted an exemption in accordance with *KStG*, § 25. Tax authorities consider the relevant date to be the day on which the transformation resolution is registered (c.f. *Widmann/Mayer*, Rz.6509, 6512).

The transformation is irrelevant for *tax matters*; it affects neither the scope of income taxes nor transaction taxes. This results from the fact that the transformation of legal form as established in *AktG*, § 385 m ff. solely alters the external legal form and not the body of individuals legally responsible for the enterprise. Assets are therefore not transferred. The Tax Reorganization Law (German Civil Code, 1976 I., p.2641) which exclusively regulates the effects of a transformation undertaken through a transfer is not applicable here.

Shareholders are likewise not taxed as the conversion of co-operative shares into stocks does not bring the shareholders/co-operative members any realized profit. The conversion of co-operative shares into stock on the contrary at best has a neutral effect on profit as a transformation is solely a change in legal form. Shareholders can however be taxed inasmuch as they receive money compensation for ceeding their share to the company in the course of a transformation.

It can therefore be determined that the tax effects are extremely slight in the transformation of a co-operative into a stock corporation in accordance with *AktG*, § 385 m ff.

Bibliography

Beuthien/Becker. Rechtsprobleme bei der Umwandlung der Produktionsgenossenschaften des Handwerks, ZIP 1992, pp. 83ff.

Crisoli/Groschuff/Kaemmel: Umwandlung und Löschung von Kapitalgesellschaften, 1937.
Kothe: Die Genossenschaft – eine Rechtsform der Zukunft? – Neue Impulse aus Brüssel für eine alte Rechtsform, ZIP 1991, pp. 905ff.
Lang/Weidmüller. Genossenschaftsgesetz, 12th ed., 1983.
Luther: Die genossenschaftliche Aktiengesellschaft, 1978.
Meyer/Meulenbergh/Beuthien: Genossenschaftsgesetz, 12th ed., 1983.
Müller, Klaus: Genossenschaftsgesetz, vol. 1–3, 1976–1980.
Ohlmeyer/Philipowski: Die Verschmelzung von Genossenschaften, Deutscher-Genossenschaftsverlag, 3rd ed., 1987.
Turner/Karst: Die Umwandlung Landwirtschaftlicher Produktionsgenossenschaften, DtZ 1992, pp. 33ff.

Liability of Co-operative Boards

PETER ERLINGHAGEN [J]

(see also: *Organizational Structure of Societies*; *Legal Form, Co-operative*; *Law, National*; *Organizational Structures, Co-operative*; *Law, International*)

I. General Introduction; II. Legal Liability of the Board of Directors; III. Liability of the Supervisory Board; IV. Tortious Liability.

I. General Introduction

The legal liability of the members of the board of directors and the supervisory board in a co-operative is anchored in German Co-operative Law (GenG), § 34 and § 41 (→ *Law, National*) as well as in § 93 n and § 93 o in the case of a merger of two co-operatives (→ *Mergers and Consolidations*). The fundamental norm herewith is GenG, § 34, Subsec.2 which states that board members are obligated to provide compensation as joint as several debtors for subsequent damage resulting from their violation and/or neglect of duty.

II. Legal Liability of the Board of Directors

1. Violations of Duty

The board's legal liability always presupposes a violation/dereliction of duty. In connection with GenG, § 27, Subsec.1, Sent.1 the duty of the board is explicitly stated in GenG, § 34, Subsec.1, Sent.1, namely that the self-responsible management must apply "the heedfulness of a prudent and conscientious co-operative top manager".

The term "top management" found in § 27 refers on the one hand to management actions undertaken by the board in internal company matters and on the other hand to the board's representational function beyond the confines of the co-operative in the scope of its power of representation as defined in § 24. The following duties are embraced under careful (and conscientious) co-operative management:

The duty of heedful representation, or in other words, to ensure that the co-operative handles itself correctly to outside parties while adhering to the laws and restrictions in its bylaws with regard to customers (members and non-members) found in GenG, § 27, Subsec.1, Sent.2

The duty of placing co-operative facilities and services at common disposal and the duty of treating members of the co-operative among each other and customers equally (as long as these groups are not identical).

The duty of observing the rules of heedful corporate management with regard to the promotion purpose (productivity and efficiency). This duty encompasses the responsibility of observing norms (law and bylaws); the duty of notifying and orienting members to all relevant legal and corporate-political affairs and developments; the duty to act within the bounds of secure management information, knowledge and experience.

The board should not be liable (very contested!) for executed risky transactions when the transactions seem to have been quite advantageous ex post facto. Other duties worth mentioning include that of optimal co-operation with other co-operative bodies (supervisory board, general assembly, co-operative advisory council), third parties such as the auditing federation and co-operative combine, as well as with other members of the board.

Alongside these general duties for proper management GenG, § 34, Subsec.3 particularly emphasizes a liability for damages in five individual situations, namely: 1) the disbursement of the paid-up shares in an unlawful manner or against by-law provisions; 2) the unlawful distribution of interest or profit shares; 3) the unlawful distribution of co-operative assets; 4) making payments subsequent to the filing of bankruptcy; 5) the impermissible provision of credits. GenG, § 34, Subsec.1, Sent.2 also includes the obligation to preserve secrecy and discretion.

The Law furthermore lists a number of other duties to be upheld by the board, the violation of which can lead to a liability for damage: the obligation to ensure that the necessary books and accounts are kept (GenG, § 3?, Subsec.1); to present the annual statement, profit and loss account and business report (GenG, § 33, Subsec.2); to call for the general assembly (§ 33i, Subsec.1) in the face of an actual or highly probable loss which cannot be covered by half of the total amount available in the paid-up shares and in the reserve fund (with § 44, Subsec.1 as an exception); submitting certification from the auditing → *federation* upon entering the co-operative into the co-operative register, thus confirming the audit and the report of the same to the general assembly (GenG, § 90, Subsec.1, Sent.1); the duty to seek court protection from creditors and/or to file for bankruptcy after determining insolvency as prescribed (GenG, § 99, Subsec.1, Sent.2).

The board likewise acts counter to its duties and can be subject to a claim for damages when it acts contrary to the provisions or binding resolutions passed by the supervisory board or the general assembly.

2. Violation of the Duty of Care

Legal liability in accordance with GenG, § 34 presupposes the fault of the board member in question on whose actions a claim is made. The question of fault cannot be measured solely on the success of a measure prompted by the board. Whether the failure of an action is foreseeable or not therefore is not a basis for determining a fault or offense. Even the situation in which a member of the administration is willing to assume the possibility of damage (dolus eventualis and/or the occurrence of a loss) does not necessarily represent a violation of duty. The circumstances surrounding the individual situation are the determining factors for all business transactions involving risk.

In order to prepare for a decision, the administration must exhaust all sources of information at its disposal (→ *Management in Co-operatives*). Even if it is a matter of immediacy, exaggerated demands should still nonetheless not be made. The decision is to be made "in the interest of the company" and must be defendable from the commercial viewpoint of its success. When the board is not versed in legal matters it must seek advice (like the supervisory board), and if need be, contract for an outside opinion above and beyond the organization's own legal department.

As mentioned above, it is not always a violation of duty to take up business risks. If a measure proves in hindsight to be a failure, the chance still exists that the particular decision also brought along certain advantages; in this matter the outlook at the time of the decision is relevant (ex ante view), and the decision can be considered careful and/or prudent in business terms.

3. Violation of the Duty of Member Promotion

Whereas a violation of the general duty of care as a rule results in the co-operative's monetary claim for damages, particular problems arise in connection with a violation of the specific co-operative obligation of member promotion (→ *Promotion Mandate*). In such cases, it is not the co-operative which incurs an economic loss, but rather the individual member. Due to its lack of a basis for claim, the co-operative is not able to file for damages from the board. Because it is inequitable to release the board from liability in connection with actions contrary to the promotion obligation – a situation which results from the lack of damage incurred by the co-operative and the lack of a claim basis for damages among co-operative members – recent attempts have been under-taken to form a basis for claim based on § 34, Sub-sec.2, Sent.1, in other words, through third party damage liquidation.

For the co-operative, violations of the promotion obligation as a rule represent non-economic losses which must be reversed via natural restitution in accordance with GenG, 34, Subsec.2, Sent.1 and BGB (*Bürgerliches Gesetzbuch*, German Civil Code), § 249, Subsec.1; in other words: the legal act precluding the promotional purpose must be redressed.

Consequences for the individual members of the board who undertake behavior which violates their promotion obligation include the revocation of their appointment and, as the case may be, the immediate termination of their contract of employment.

4. Yardstick for Diligence and Due Care

It is contested whether a uniform, objective yardstick exists for the necessary diligence and due care to be applied by each individual board member, or else whether various subjective criteria should be observed. Such subjective elements of the duty of care primarily include the object and size of the company (→ *Operational Size*), the degree of education of the board mem-bers, an allocation of departmental responsibility, and → *honorary offices*.

a) The object of the company

The by-laws must indicate the object of the company in accordance with § 6, No.2, that is the activity of the company through which the co-operative can promote its form-specific purpose, namely its members' enterprises or households.

According to prevalent opinion in legal decisions and legal studies, this corporate goal of a co-operative represents a criterion for differentiation with respect to the yardstick for due care. The author maintains that this nonetheless is not a suitable criterion for subjectivization as duties arise from the co-operative principles which affect each member of the board equally and which exist irregardless of the corporate object. The best example of this is the → *promotion mandate* found in GenG, § 1, Subsec.1 which must be pursued in an equally intensive manner by all boards. Furthermore, the nature of the corporate object does not play any role at all when this mandate is violated.

a) The size of the company

Another criterion for subjectivization should be the size of the respective company (→ *Operational Size*). In principle, however, the extent of self-responsible management authority which the board assumes in accordance with § 27, Subsec.1, Sent.1 is not contingent on the size of the company as the board of directors is the supreme and fundamentally fully responsible executive entity. Concerning the duties of the board which arise irregard-less of the size of the company, one cannot logically differentiate according to the size of the company as the risk of damages is identical for all co-operatives. A differentiation should only be undertaken for such duties which either arise in smaller co-operatives or which harbor a slighter risk of damage. In such cases, the board members of smaller co-operatives should be subject to less substantial demands and expectations; in the author's opinion a subjectivization seems appropriate for this special situation.

c) The degree of education

Legal studies and pronouncements continually discuss whether the individual board member can plead an inadequate level of education in comparison with the demands placed on him. In order to protect the co-operative and the co-operative members, a uniform and objective degree of average knowledge sufficient for the respective co-operative must be verifiable for each board member. In other words, the board must vouch that it disposes of the necessary level of education and skills and cannot release itself based on lack of knowledge once it has assumed office. In everyday practise and application this has resulted in higher expectations being placed on the abilities of the board members. This is a compulsory step in the face of the high degree of self-responsibility that the board enjoys. This has the indirect positive effect that fewer qualified applicants aspire for such positions and activities (→ *Education, Germany*).

d) Allocation of departmental responsibilities

Fundamentally, each board member bears full personal responsibility not only for his own division or deartment of the business but also for the totality of management decisions made by all members of the board. One school of thought found in literature maintains that if/when specially trained professionals assume individual divisions through an allocation of responsibilities, such members must have higher expectations placed on them as would have been the case for board members without such previous training.

A prerequisite for the allocation of responsibilities is the formal resolution of such passed by the board of directors, the supervisory board and the general assembly. With respect to legal liability in such cases the following distinctions must be drawn:

In the course of management activities some board members could be drawn into an unfamiliar field or division. In some situations a permissible sole representation based on company divisions is at hand in accordance with GenG, § 25, Subsec.2, Sent.1, Case 1 as called for by the internal rules of procedure – one in which the "professional specialist" not vested with representational authority can be charged with a supervisional fault; the other board member in this case is subject to a selectional fault if/when the the "professional specialist" in question is not directly vested with the appropriate departmental authority by the general assembly.

Another manifestation of this situation is when departmental authority is jointly shared by two board members, one of whom does not possess the specific know-how for the particular department and the other of whom does; the board member knowledgeable in this department can be held liable for a violation/dereliction of duty in this situation by the fault of passing responsibility to the non-specialist board member.

In addition, each individual member of the board of directors must exercise a controlling obligation with respect to the other board members in the case of an allocation of departmental responsibilities based on composite board responsibility.

A comprehensive level of basic knowledge and skills encompassing all areas of management therefore results out of necessity for board members undertaking activities in fields other than their specialty. In the simplest of situations, a board member disposing of the necessary professional knowledge for management activities is appointed into his own particular field of specialization; the board member is particularly held legally liable in such a situation as he should be all the more able to recognize and avoid a dereliction of duties as someone less educated and qualified in the field. Nonetheless, the mean objective yardstick for diligence and due care remains intact, thus preventing the allocation of departmental responsibilities from serving as a criterion of subjectivization.

e) Honorary office

One school of thought in literature on the subject maintains that honorary officers should not be subject to a special corporate yardstick for diligence and due care but rather to a more moderate one as they are solely active in a representational manner and do not participate in the management of the co-operative (→ *Honorary Office*). Furthermore, they do not receive monetary compensation. A contractual relationship exists between them and the co-operative in accordance with BGB, § 670 and GenG, § 24, Subsec.3 besides their relationship as board member.

In the author's opinion the particularity of honorary office does not require redress. If and when an honorary member only assumes representational functions no damage "from the co-operative's management" can accordingly arise. On the other hand, if he undertakes damaging activities with corresponding external aftereffects (GenG, § 27, Subsec.2, Sent.1), he is held legally liable for the potential violation of duty based on § 34, Subsec.2, Sent.1; a subjectivization with regard to his honorary involvement cannot be taken into consideration. At most, a slighter level of qualification could be expected solely for representational activities.

f) Joint and several liability

In accordance with GenG, § 93, Subsec.2 board members are jointly and severally liable when they have violated their duty of care. It is contested whether they have observed the heedfulness expected from a diligent and conscientious manager; they are confronted with the burden of proof as established above.

In the case of a violation of legally determined duties by more than one individual it is assumed that each member of the board of directors behaved in a negligent manner until the opposite has been proven. GenG, § 93 therefore heightens the legal liability of the board and at the same time intensifies the protection of the co-operative.

If the co-operative suffers damages through the behavior of its organs – either board of directors or supervisory board – each and every administrative member can be held to compensate such damages. An exception, of course, results when the individual member is able to prove that he had fulfilled his prescribed duty of care and thus did not act culpably.

Concurrent faults undertaken by other administrative members as well as a lack of knowledge and skills thereby cannot lead to their release.

The actual division of management responsibilities among board members does not exempt them from their duties with regard to allround company management. Insofar as the management functions are allocated in a permissible manner (e.g. through the by-laws in large-scale enterprises) and those involved can rely on a reciprocal basis of dutifulness, justification for excuse does exist. However, it must be expected and demanded from each member that he fulfills every controlling function available to him with respect to the other board members and that he bears personal responsibility for the decisions he took part in which were agreed upon in his board. In such cases, the duty of care demanded of a manager is required – that he can orientate himself sufficiently to make independent assessments and decisions.

As joint and several debtors, administrative members among each other are obligated to provide compensation in accordance with BGB, § 426; such compensation is determined according to the degree of their involvement in the arisen fault. A fair compensation among multiple individuals is provided in BGB, § 426 and § 254 based on this notion of involvement.

g) The burden of proof

According to the general principles of providing the burden of proof in the event of court proceedings, the co-operative would have to offer such proof. GenG, § 34, Subsec.2, Sent.2 deviates from this practise and reverses the burden of proof; in other words the individual board member is responsible for providing proof. The provision and presentation of proof in the scope of § 34, Subsec. 2, Sent.1 is structured as follows:

The plaintiff, in this case the co-operative, must present, and if need be, prove

- wrongful action or negligence,
- the calculated extent of the damage (or an estimate according to § 287 of the Procedures for Civil Cases),
- the causal relationship between the behavior of the member in question and the inflicted damage.

The defendant(s) must present, and if need be, prove

- that the heedfulness of a diligent and conscientious co-operative manager was exercised in an objective (an objective violation of duty) and a subjective (fault) manner.

h) Disclaimer of liability upon the pursuance of resolutions passed by the general assembly

The legal liability of the board to the company under its management is not applicable when the damaging action can be traced to a resolution passed by the general assembly (GenG, § 34, Subsec.4).

A legal resolution in accordance with GenG, § 34, Subsec.4 is not however at hand when the resolution of general assembly was contestable. Such is the case when deliberate damage to the co-operative results from the resolution. The board must contest resolutions which damage the interests of the company. A legally permissible resolution in the sense of GenG, § 34, Subsec.4 can however be at hand – and even have been contestable – had resulting damages to the co-operative not been perceiveable at the time the resolution was voted on.

A disclaimer of liability in accordance with GenG, § 34, Subsec.4 likewise is not applicable when a legally permissible resolution was introduced undutifully and when the general assembly was at least negligently misled, similar to the regulation of the intention to deceive.

The board of directors cannot appeal based on a legally permissible resolution passed by the general assembly which was introduced in an undutiful manner, such as through information lying at the heart of the resolution; the board is liable for damages resulting to the co-operative brought about by the resolution. The approval of the measures through the supervisory board also does not preclude liability for damages according to GenG, § 34, Subsec.4, Sent.2.

i) Liability to creditors

The claim for compensation against members of the board in exceptional cases – and only in connection with GenG, § 34, Subsec.3 – can be asserted by creditors of the co-operative when they are not able to procure satisfaction from the co-operative (→ *Financial Accounting Law*). The obligation to pay compensation to creditors cannot be rescinded through a waiver or preventative composition by the co-operative or through the pursuance of a resolution passed by the general assembly.

j) Prescription

Claims for compensation against members of the board of directors are statute-barred for five years.

III. Liability of the Supervisory Board

1. Reference to GenG, § 34

In accordance with GenG § 41, GenG § 34 is effective analogously. Inasmuch as the supervisory board assumes the function "to monitor the board in all fields of administration" (GenG, § 38, Subsec.1, Sent.1), the members of the supervisory board must exercise the heedfulness and diligence that is necessary to monitor the management of the co-operative.

2. Supervisory Board Members' Duty to Participate

Upon assuming office the duty arises for supervisory board members to participate in the orderly execution of the functions of the supervisory board as outlined in both law and company by-laws.

It must be taken into account that supervisory board members as a rule exercise their mandate as an avocational activity, a fact that influences the extent and arrangement of their participational duty.

This participational duty consists of the following functions:

- taking part in supervisory board meetings;
- contributing an individual opinion and decision for resolutions in the scope of the co-operative's interests;
- committing oneself to acquire the most comprehensive information available as a sure basis for competent decisions;
- using special, individual skills while executing tasks assigned by the supervisory board up to a reasonable limit;
- obliging oneself to provide the supervisory board with circumstantial information which could be of importance in the scope of the fulfillment of its function;
- contributing to the proper fulfillment of those tasks subject to the supervisory board;
- obliging oneself to provide the general assembly with information in the face of an impending danger brought upon by a faulty decision of the supervisory board inasmuch as this danger could not have been prevented in another manner (e.g. by contributing to correct the decision);
- above all, in monitoring the activities of the board as a means to delimit its management function.

3. The Object of the Obligation to Monitor

The obligation to monitor and the duty of care held by members of the supervisory board above all always encompass the following responsibilities:

- ensuring that management measures undertaken by the board of directors fulfill and comply with the promotion mandate;
- monitoring the essential corporate-political decisions as well as the general business, personnel and investment policies;
- verifying the year-end financial statement and annual report (GenG, § 38, Subsec.1, Sent.3) as well as making suggestions for the application of the annual surplus.

Further responsibilities for supervisory board members can result from restrictions set to the management function of the board of directors in the essence of GenG, § 27, Subsec.1, Sent.2. Examples of this include the necessary approval from the supervisory board in the face of long-term corporate planning such as the purchase, sale or development of real estate, the establishment of branch offices, or the closure of contracts of considerable importance. Control as a rule assumes the form of sample investigations into the activities of the board, whereby the foci of responsibility and emphasis should be determined which facilitate a fairly effective level of information. Such points of emphasis could, for example, be anchored in the most essential elements of the most important business procedures, in the controlling of systems, in goal-definition and the evaluation of goal-fulfillment.

Furthermore, each member of the supervisory board is obligated to inform the entire supervisory board about the behavior of a member of the board which is damaging to the co-operative.

4. Yardstick of Diligence and Due Care

The identical principles for defining the yardstick of duty to care and fault exist for members of the supervisory board as for members of the board.

IV. Tortious Liability

Direct legal liability to members of the co-operative can result from the statutory definition of the following offenses.

1. BGB, § 823, Subsec.1

Inasmuch as the rights of an individual co-operative member included in BGB, § 823, Subsec.1 are infringed upon by a violation of a supervisory board member's duty to care, the co-operative member is entitled to a claim to damages based on this Civil Code article. Membership rights are thereby treated as other rights in the essence of BGB § 823, Subsec.1, just as the right of receiving promotion.

2. BGB, § 823, Subsec.2

A protectionary clause must be in effect which benefits co-operative members. In the event that such a clause is at hand, a culpable violation against the protectionary clause in question must exist in order to affirm liability.

a) GenG, § 41 in connection with § 34, Subsec.2

Such a protectionary clause could be interpreted as GenG, § 41 in connection with § 34, Subsec.2. The valuation of this article as a protectionary clause must correspond both to the essence and purpose of the law in question. One school of thought found in literature on the subject maintains that § 41 in connection with § 34, Subsec.2 must be considered a protectionary clause in the sense of BGB, § 823; the decisive element in this matter is that the co-operative members are to be protected through the activities of the supervisory board. The author however sees this primarily in connection with the aspect of membership promotion (GenG, § 1); no conclusion can be drawn that § 41 itself represents a protectionary clause.

The prevailing opinion in this matter maintains that § 41 in connection with § 34, Subsec.2 does not represent a protectionary clause in the essence of BGB, § 823, Subsec.2

b) GenG, § 147, subsec.2, nrs. 1, 2

GenG, § 147, Subsec.2, Nrs.1 and 2 (misinformation) are also effective for co-operative members as a protectionary clause in the essence of BGB, § 823.

c) GenG, § 151

GenG, § 151 (obligation to maintain secrecy) likewise is effective as a protectionary clause for the individual co-operative members in the essence of BGB, § 823, Subsec. 2.

d) GenG, § 152

GenG, § 152 (accepting bribes) also serves as a protectionary clause in the sense of BGB, § 823, Subsec. 2 for co-operative members.

3. BGB, § 826

According to prevailing legislation and in accordance with the predominant opinion found in literature on the subject, it is considered sufficient in the statutory definition of BGB, § 826 that the harmful party assumes the possibility of potential damage inflicted on another party and is consciously willing to accept this damage in the event it does occur. The principle of "prima facie" proof is to be applied here inasmuch as the violation of duty is pronounceably large. In such a situation one should proceed from the position that the supervisory board member recognizes the possibility of damages and accepts the situation as such.

In the event the damage is intentional and contra bonus mores in the essence of BGB, § 826, the supervisory board member in question will be held legally liable. Nonetheless, the practical relevance of BGB, § 826 remains remarkably slight as the high demands placed on the statutory definition of BGB, § 826 make it practically impossible to fulfill its preconditions.

Bibliography

Blomeyer/Meyer: Die Verantwortlichkeit des Vorstandes der eingetragenen Genossenschaft aus §34 Genossenschaftsgesetz, ZfG 1985, pp. 250ff.

Frankenberger: Der Aufsichtsrat der Genossenschaft, 2nd ed., 1980.

Golling: Sorgfaltspflicht und Verantwortlichkeit der Vorstandsmitglieder für ihre Geschäftsführung innerhalb der nicht konzerngebundenen Aktiengesellschaft, 1968.

Höhn: Wofür haftet der Vorstand einer Genossenschaft persönlich?, 1979.

Höhn: Wofür haftet der Aufsichtsrat einer Genossenschaft persönlich?, 1981.

Lang/Weidmüller: Genossenschaftsgesetz, 32th ed., 1988.

Metz: Haftung der Mitglieder des Vorstandes und seines Aufsichtsrates, in: Bankpraxis 77. vol.1.

Meyer, Werner F.: Die Verantwortlichkeit des Vorstandes der eingetragenen Genossenschaft aus §34 Genossenschaftsgesetz, 1985.

Meyer/Meulenbergh/Beuthien: Gneossenschaftsgesetz, 12th ed., 1983.

Müller, Klaus: Genossenschaftsgesetz, Vol. 1–3, 1976–1980.

Pottermann, Peter: Die Haftung der Vorstands- und Aufsichtsratsmitglieder einer Kreditgenossenschaft, sowie des genossenschaftlichen Prüfungsverbandes unter besonderer Berücksichtigung des §1 Genossenschaftsgesetz, 1991.

Ringle, G.: Überwachung des genossenschaftlichen Managements durch den Aufsichtsrat, 1984.

Wartenburg, Günther: Stellung und Aufgaben des genossenschaftlichen Aufsichtsrates, 3rd ed., 1983.

Weber: Die organisationsrechtliche Stellung des Vorstandes in der eingetragenen Genossenschaft, 1962.

Weimar: Abschied von der Gesellschafter- und Handelnden-Haftung im GmbH -Recht?, GmbHR 1988, pp. 289ff.

Westermann: Die unternehmerische Leitungsmacht des Vorstandes der Genossenschaft nach geltendem und zukünftigem Genossenschaftsrecht im Vergleich zur Leitungsmacht des Vorstandes der AG, in: Festschrift für Reinhardt, 1972, pp. 359ff.

Linking Banks and Self-Help Groups

HANS DIETER SEIBEL

(see also: *Co-operative Banks*; *Self-help Organizations*; *Policies for Promotion*; *Agricultural Credit*)

I. Background and Origin; II. Guiding Principles; III. Linking Formal and Informal Financial Institutions: a Pilot Project in Indonesia; IV. The Functions of Self-Help Groups and NGOs; V. Performance; VI. Arisan Manjung: an Illustration.

I. Background and Origin

In many developing countries, programmed credit, subsides, and neglect of savings mobilization have undermined rural finance. This has rendered financial institutions unviable and development unsustainable. In recent years, the number of countries has been growing in which banks mobilize savings and practice commercial banking (→ *Agricultural Credit*). But due to excessively transaction costs for both, banks and customers, they rarely reach down to the grassroots level. The rural poor, therefore, have to rely on informal financial institutions which are viable, selfsustained, and adjusted to local conditions. Yet, their resources are insufficient for the local micro-entrepreneurs; they are too weak to reverse the trend of the rural-urban capital flow; and they alone cannot financially support a dynamic development process.

During the early 1980s, a novel approach entered into the debate: linking informal and formal financial institutions (→ *Informal Co-operatives*). In 1986, APRACA took the step from debate to action. Being an association of central banks and major financial institutions in Asia and the Pacific, it took the lead role on the international level, while its members initiated action on the national level.

For more effective financial coverage of the poorer sections of the population, three different approaches were discerned:

- upgrading financial self-help groups of micro-entrepreneurs;
- linking already existing self-help groups and banks;
- adapting banks to their environment ("downgrading").

The linkage approach was selected as a focal approach which may eventually comprise both upgrading and institutional adaption measures. The innovative element of this program is its focus on a financial intermediation system being built around self-help groups (→ *Self-help Organizations*) as grassrootsintermediaries between banks and rural micro-entrepreneurs. The strength of the APRACA initiative lies in the fact that the bottom-up movement of local self-help groups is met by the topdown approach of an association of leading banks.

Subsequently, APRACA member countries carried out surveys in their respective countries. They found that there are many organizational and institutional resources with great potential for micro-enterprise finance and rural development. What stands in the way of the full utilization of these resources is financial market segmentation. There are formal financial markets for the upper 5 to 20 percent of the population. These markets fall under the control of state credit as well as related financial laws and they are supervised by the central bank. They comprise central, commercial, development, savings, and secondary banks as well as non-banking institutions. In addition, there is a small but growing semiformal financial market, which comprises governmental and private voluntary organizations, so-called *Self-Help Promoting Institutions* (NGOs), with their own savings and credit programs. They do not fall under the state's credit law but operate with approval of the state and its organs. Informal financial markets comprise financial self-help groups, other self-help groups with secondary financial functions, and individuals financial agents, such as moneylenders, deposit collectors and trade, crop of land related financial arrangements. From a policy viewpoint, financial self-help groups are of particular importance. They are found in most Asian countries and in most culture areas or ethnic groups within them. Their main financial functions usually are the accumulation and depositing of savings, granting of loans and, to some extent, rendering of insurance services (→ *Insurance, Germany*). They may be found in urban and rural areas, among traders and market-women, farmers and fishermen, craftsmen and small industrialists, wage and salary earners, and among bank employees. Though part of the informal financial sector and lacking legal status, most associations do possess an organizational structure. Typically, they are headed by a staff of elected executives; they have written rules and regulations; they keep membership lists and they practice some form of book-keeping. Local social control mechanisms effectively prevent defaulting or fraud, which plague so many formal credit programs.

II. Guiding Principles

Through a set of interrelated guiding principles, factors of institutional viability and sustainability were systematically built into the design:

- Working through existing institutions
- Respecting the autonomy of participating institutions
- Recognizing SHGs and NGOs as financial intermediaries
- Promoting savings mobilization
- Linking savings and credit

- Using group savings as partial collateral
- Advocating group liability
- Granting financial incentives for timely repayment
- Ensuring fast services through simple procedures
- Achieving financial viability through market rates
- Encouraging banks to assume the credit risk
- Ensuring institutional viability of banks, SHGs, and NGOs through cost coverage from the interest margin.

III. Linking Formal and Informal Financial Institutions: a Pilot Project in Indonesia

1. The Policy Environment

A prerequisite of sound financial market development is an appropriate policy environment. Since 1983, the financial system of Indonesia has been gradually deregulated; inflation was kept under control. The prudential course of deregulation chosen was much in contrast to rapid and wholesale deregulation which had been uncritically applied in Argentina, Brazil, and Chile – with disastrous results.

Depending on costs, risks, and profit expectations, banks in Indonesia are now free to set their own interest rates. Sound banks may engage in foreign exchange at floating rates. It is relatively easy to set up new banks and bank branches. Most subsidized credit programs with their high default rates have been dismantled.

The financial system responded vigorously: banks embarked on innovative approaches to urban and rural finance, they increased in numbers and size, and they embarked on vigorous campaigns of domestic savings mobilization and credit delivery at market rates. The outflow of capital was reversed. Financial savings grew from below 4% in the early 1980s to almost 20% of GDP in 1989, money supply (M_2/GDP) from 15% to 37%: a solid financial basis for economic take-off.

Yet, despite a favorable policy environment and the rapid expansion of the financial system in Indonesia, financial market segmentation continues to underprivilege the poor. The unresolved transaction cost problem effectively keeps the banks from reaching the poorer sections of the population. Only 10% of rural households have access to formal finance, about half of them (1.5 million) to Bank Rakyat Indonesia with its network of about 3,600 branch offices.

2. Institutional Resources

There is a wide network of institutional resources in Indonesia. There are more than 15,000 bank and non-bank institutions offering financial services. There is a great variety of types of *self-help groups* (SHGs). Their number probably surpasses the one-million mark. They have generated their own funds from various sources and, as IFI, have built up their own savings and credit business. There is a small number of non-governmental self-help-promoting institutions (NGOs) which, acting as semiformal financial institutions, have made substantial contributions to the development of a selected number of self-help groups in such fields as group formation, personal development, skill training, income-generating activities, and finance.

Yet, the high transaction costs of formal finance prevent the banks from reaching the poor; self-help groups reach the poor but their funds are insufficient for meeting the growing financial needs of micro-entrepreneurs. A solution is provided by a link between banks and SHGs.

3. History

The linkage approach was initiated in 1986 by APRACA. Together with Bank Rakyat Indonesia and Bina Swadaya, Bank Indonesia (BI) as the central bank started the first pilot project of the region in September 1988, PPHBK. Policy guidance is provided by a national task force comprising banks and NGOs. Technical assistance is rendered by Deutsche Gesellschaft für Technische Zusammenarbeit (GTZ) GmbH.

Training of bank, NGO and SHG staff began in Febr. 1989. The first bank-SHG linkage occurred on May, 31, 1989. In mid–1990, institutionalization became the core strategy of self-sustained linkages: through linkage units in banks and NGOs, financial management training by the bank training institute LPPI and Survey, Training and Consultancy units in major NGOs.

4. Project Design

PPHBK acts as a facilitator between banks, SHGs, and NGOs (Fig. 1). It only provides recommendations, no compulsory scheme. PPHBK aims at im-

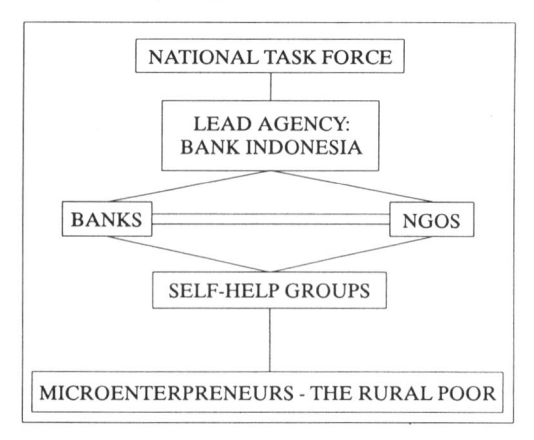

Fig 1: Project Design.

proving access to financial services for the poorer sections of the rural populations by linking SHGs and banks, thus minimizing transactions costs. By bringing the three partners together, business relations ensue in their own self-interest. Since they would prevent viablility and sustainability, no direct subsidies are provided.

The target group comprises self-help groups of rural micro-entrepreneurs in the informal sector, small farmers and tenants, the rural poor, women and men in villages and rural towns.

5. Linkage Models

There are two main linkage models: one of direct linkages between banks and SHGs, which may or may not include NGOs in an advisory function, and another one of indirect linkages through NGOs and additional intermediaries.

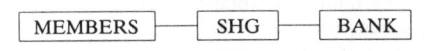

| MEMBERS |—| SHG |—| BANK |

Linkage Model I: Direct Linkages

| MEMBERS |—| SHG |—| NGOS |—| BANK |

Linkage Model II: Indirect Linkages

IV. The Functions of Self-Help Groups and NGOs

Self-Help Groups are local organizations owned by their members (→ *Self-help Organizations*). They may be of indigenous origin, or they may have been initiated by governmental or non-governmental organizations (→ *Autochthonous Co-operatives;* → *Pre-co-operative Forms*). On the local level, the distinctions by origin are frequently only of analytical relevance; in reality, they overlap. An arisan, for instance, may come under the guidance of a government organization, which in turn enlists the training and consultancy services of an NGO.

As a result of proximity, for the group and for the members, i.e., for savers, borrowers, and lenders, the transaction costs in SHGs are very low. Their main functions are:

- providing guidance in all matters
- collecting savings from the members
- building up an internal loan fund
- examining the credit-worthiness of borrowers
- providing financial consultancy services to members
- arranging for informal collateral or guarantees
- granting loans to members
- collecting installments
- applying social control mechnisms to enforce repayment
- acting as a credit guarantee group
- acting as a financial intermediary between members and outside agencies (such as government agencies, donors, NGOs, banks).

NGOs working with financial SHGs may have two basic functions with regard to SHGs:

- guidance, training, and consultancy in financial and non-financial matters
- acting as a financial intermediary between SHGs and donors or banks.

If NGOs act as financial intermediaries, their activities may include any of the following:

- financial extension services
- training in bookkeeping
- training in financial management
- promoting innovative saving schemes, e.g. daily savings collection in the informal sector
- mediating contacts with a bank
- depositing savings of SHGs in a bank
- examining the credit-worthiness of SHGs
- negotiating bank loans for SHGs
- entering into a loan contract with a bank as the legal borrower
- onlending to SHGs
- collecting installments from SHGs
- bearing the credit risk
- repaying the loan.

Apart from entering into a loan contract and bearing the credit risk, NGOs, not acting as financial intermediaries, may still carry out several of these activities. The extent to which financial transactions, such as collecting savings and repayments, are carried out by NGO or bank personnel, depends on the individual case.

Prerequisites are that the NGO possesses

- concerning training and consultancy: the necessary competence in terms of contents and methodology;
- concerning finanical intermediation: financial management skills;
- concerning financial intermediation between SHGs and banks: financial reserves to absorb arrears and bear the credit risk.

V. Performance

During the fourteen months of linkage implementations in the field, i.e. until July, 31, 1990, 19 banks or bank branches, 12 NGOs and 299 SHGs actively participated in the linkages. During that period, the 299 SHGs deposited savings of Rp. 298 million in banks. They obtained 355 bank loans of Rp. 1.48 bn (US-$ 820,000). Outstandings were 1.14 bn. 44% were lent directly to SHGs (model I), 56% through NGOs as intermediaries (model II). Appr. 6,500 members received loans averaging Rp. 220,000: 98,6% of them for income-generating activities. The arrears ratio between banks and SHGs (model I) was 0.8%; between banks and NGOs (model II), all payments were on time.

From the poorer sections of the population, banks have gained new confidence in rural micro-entrepreneurs. They were found to be good savers, prudential investors, and reliable borrowers.

Self-help groups in the informal sector have gained access to bank finance at market rates, Credit supply is no longer limited by scarce subsidies. It is only the capacity of micro-entrepreneurs to save, invest, and repay which may limit their effective demand for credit.

VI. Arisan Manjung: an Illustration

Arisan Manjung in the village of Manjung in Central Java originated in 1971 as a rotating savings association, arisan. In 1975, it came under the guidance of NGO, Bina Swadaya. It then turned into a savings and credit association, retaining the arisan saving practice but in addition building up an internal loan fund from additional savings.

Arisan Manjung now has 52 members, 6 of them women. It is headed by a committee of twelve and employs a book-keeper. There are four major sources of internal funds: initial savings (i.e., equity share), compulsory weekly savings, voluntary savings, and interest income. A major part of the fund is used for loans to members. Another part is deposited as solidarity savings with Bina Swadaya. Excess liquidity is kept on a bank account. Starting in 1975 with Rp. 1,5 million, Bina Swadaya used donor funds to refinance Arisan Manjung at subsidized interest rates, increasing the amount gradually up to RP. 15 million in 1988. Since 1971, there has never been a case of defaulting.

35 out of the 52 members are presently involved in sohun noodle manufacturing as their major microenterprise activity. This has generated employment and income and brought visible wealth to the village. It also spilled over to neighboring villages from which workers are employed, as well as to related sectors such as trade in flour and noodles, transportation, printing of labels, etc. Indirectly, it has influenced farming, animal husbandry, tailoring, and other microenterprises.

Several attempts by Bina Swadaya to promote noodle manufacturing on a group basis have failed. What the members want, is private enterprise. Bina Swadaya contributes to this with group guidance, training, and refinance.

The group has also been innovative in the field of insurance: with life insurance for loan protection and health insurance (→ *Cooperativismo Sanitario*).

On August, 21, 1989, the group deposited savings of Rp. 4 million in the bank and received a bank loan of Rp. 14 million at the market rate of interest through Bina Swadaya in cooperation with the Project Linking Banks and self-Help Groups. The interest rate included a margin for the bank, Bina Swadaya, and the group. In March 1990, the loan had been duly and fully repaid. On April, 21, 1990, the group received another loan, Rp. 30 million, with a maturity of 10 months: Rp. 25 million from the bank through Bina Swadaya and Rp. 5 million from Bina Swadaya's own funds. Outstandings on August, 31, 1990 were Rp. 13 million.

The case study highlights the following points:

- There are self-help groups or pre-co-operatives of local origin which act as informal financial intermediaries.
- They have considerable potential in savings mobilization, capital build-up and credit delivery.
- NGOs may contribute to their development through training and limited refinancing, in the past usually at subsidized rates.
- At market rates, SHGs may gain access to formal finance, only limited by their investment and repayment capacities.
- Repayment performance is excellent.
- Self-help, NGO training, and bank finance may greatly contribute to the advancement of microenterprise activities.

Bibliography

Kropp, E./Marx, M.T./Pramod, B./Quinones, B.R./Seibel, H.D.: Linking Self-help Groups and Banks in Developing Countries, Bangkok/Rossdorf.

Seibel, H.D.: Landwirtschaftliche Entwicklung in Afrika: Durch Einführung moderner oder Modernisierung traditionaler Genossenschaften? Zeitschrift für ausländische Landwirtschaft 3/1968, pp. 219–232.

Seibel, H.D./Massing, A.: Traditional Organizations and Economic Development. Studies of Indigenous Co-operatives in Liberia, New York 1974.

Seibel, H.D./Damachi, U.: Self-Help Organizations. Guidelines and Case Studies for Development Planners and Field Workers: A Participative Approach, Bonn 1982.

Seibel, H.D.: Ansatzmöglichkeiten für die Mobilisierung von Sparkapital zur Entwicklungsfinanzierung: Genossenschaften und autochthone Spar- und Kreditvereine in Nigeria, Forschungsberichte des Bundesministeriums für Wirtschaftliche Zusammenarbeit, vol. 63, München/Köln/London 1984.

Seibel, H.D.: Saving for Development: a Linkage Model for Informal and Formal Financial Markets, Quarterly Journal of International Agriculture 24/4, 1985, pp. 390–398.

Seibel, H.D. et al.: Ländliche Entwicklung als Austauschprozeß/Rural Development as an Exchange Process. Indigenous Social Systems, Governmental Development Organizations and Informal Financial Institutions in Ivory Coast, Saarbrücken/Fort Lauderdale 1987.

Seibel, H.D./Marx, M.T.: Dual Financial Markets in Africa: Case Studies of Linkages between Informal und Formal Financial Institutions, Saarbrücken/Fort Lauderdale 1987.

Seibel, H.D.: Einheimische Selbsthilfeorganisationen im ländlichen Raum in der Volksrepublik Kongo: Ansatzmöglichkeiten für eine Verknüpfung informeller und formeller Finanzinstitutionen, Saarbrücken/Fort Lauderdale 1987.

Seibel, H.D./Shrestha, B.P.: Dhikuti: the Small Businessman's Informal Self-Help Bank in Nepal, Savings and Development 12/2 (1988), pp. 183–200.

Seibel, H.D.: Linking Informal and Formal Financial Institutions in Africa and Asia, J. Levitsky, ed., Microenterprises in Developing Countries, London 1989, pp. 97–118.

Seibel, H.D.: Einheimische Genossenschaften in Entwicklungsländern: Neuere Forschungsergebnisse and entwicklungspolitische Ansätze, J. Zerche, Ph. Herder-Dorneich & W.W. Engelhardt, eds., Genossenschaften und genossenschaftswissenschaftliche Forschung. Regensburg 1989, pp. 193–202.

Seibel, H.D.: Finance with the Poor, by the Poor, for the Poor. Financial Technologies for the Informal Sector, With Case Studies from Indonesia, Social Strategies III/2 (Dec. 1989), Soziologisches Seminar, Universität Basel.

Seibel, H.D./Parhusip, U.: Financial Innovations for Microenterprises – Linking Formal and Informal Financial Institutions, Small Enterprise Development I/2 (1990), pp. 14–26.

Seibel, H.D.: Self-Help Groups as Financial Intermediaries: A Training Manual for Self-Help Groups, Banks and NGOs, Saarbrücken/Fort Lauderdale 1992.

Machinery Associations and Machinery Rings in Agriculture

JOHANNES KUHN [J]

(see also: *Rural Co-operatives*; *Forms of Cooperation*; *Agricultural Trade*; *Producer Associations*)

I. The Mechanization of Agriculture; II. The Main Characteristics of Machinery Associations and Their Dispersion; III. Main Characteristics of Machinery Rings and Their Dispersion; IV. The Effects of Machinery Associations and Machinery Rings from the Members' Perspective.

I. The Mechanization of Agriculture

1. Expansion of Mechanization

The provision of equipment and material resources for those employed in farming is closely connected to the general level of agricultural development in the various regions of the world. At first only man served as a source of energy, and even today in certain areas of Africa and in other regions is farming carried out through the input of human energy and manual tools. In other areas, e.g. in the Near East and in China, animals have been used for tractive force for millenia (*Voss*; *Biswanger*). The tractor entered into farming substantially later. Nevertheless, motor-driven mechanization spread throughout the world at different times. In North America for example, motor-driven mechanization expanded mostly after 1920 and replaced draft animals in approximately 25 to 30 years (*Biswanger*).

Motor-driven mechanization in Japanese and Western European farming took a strong turn in the 1950s. In the meantime, Japan shows the highest level of mechanization, measured by the number of tractors as well as the amount of horse-power. Between 1961 and 1980 the number of four-wheeled tractors there increased 32.5% yearly; the amount of horse-power increased 28% from 1961 to 1983 (*Biswanger* and *Donovan*, p.72). For years other countries, above all those in Asia, have also shown a strong increase in the mechanization of their agriculture. The comparatively lowest rate of increase is in Subsahara Africa (FAO, 1989).

The increased number of tractors and harvester combines in particular is not only variable between countries and groups of countries but also within the countries themselves. In Brazil in 1980 for example, 26% of all tractors were concentrated in the state of Sao Paulo while only 6% of all tractors could be found in the entire north-east of the country (*Biswanger* and *Donovan*, p.17).

2. Multi-farm Application of Machinery

In contrast to divisible means of production such as seed and fertilizer, tractors and other agricultural machines are non-divisible material resources.

Industry has succeeded, however, in constructing individual types of machines with a variety of sizes; machines with smaller sizes and reduced operating capacities are available on the market for a lower price. But even small machines, particularly special machines for field work, have a larger seasonal capacity at their disposal than small and medium sized enterprises require.

In order to reduce the fixed costs per unit of output it is therefore necessary to employ the machines in more than one of such enterprises. These cost considerations as well as other expectations (e.g. in the areas of finance and work efficiency) are essential decision factors favoring a multi-farm application of machinery.

Because of technical and economic reasons one can determine that agricultural machines have a varying rate of suitablity for a multi-enterprise application. By taking into consideration both technical and economic aspects, *Brandes* and *Woermann* conclude that such machines are suitable for multi-farm use which

- require a relatively large amount of field space even for the smallest version because of the large capacity they have;
- have a high purchase price and/or a short period of use, whereby high fixed costs are entailed in their application;
- are available in a variety of sizes, the smallest of which being inferior to the largest when considering its productivity and the utilization costs involved.

The variety of forms and applications of multi-enterprise mechanization is very large as it is dependent on economic-technical development levels, legal relationships and constraints, and the framework of socio-cultural conditions and economic order (*Tschiersch*; *Schmidt*; *Isermeyer*, 1980; FAO, 1985; *Holtkamp*). With the exception of several forms in socialistic countries, multi-enterprise mechanization is concerned with the individual promotion of members rather than some form of collective farming (→ *Joint-production Co-operatives*).

The most widely used forms of multi-enterprise cooperation are listed below, among which definite lines of demarcation do not necessarily exist:

- neighbourhood help, that is informal, periodic or reciprocal help with machinery, with or without manpower assistance, partly involving payment;

- professional contract machine owners who additionally own or run an agricultural enterprise or other business as a secondary source of income;
- contract machine owners working on the side who professionally run their own agricultural enterprise and who earn additional income from other farmers with their machinery;
- professional contract machine owners who practice neither farming nor another occupation on the side;
- machinery associations with the involved farmers using the machines as collective property;
- machinery rings based on individual property of the machines with an organized compensation of supply and demand according to the performance of the machines;
- co-operative machine stations;
- public and partially public machine stations.

Machine stations run or controlled by the government in developing countries have generally not proved reliable (*Biswanger* and *Donovan*; *Bernhard*; *Holtkamp*; *Muckle*). Private contract machine operators can be seen on the other hand as the relatively most successful form of multi-farm mechanization in these countries. → *Rural co-operatives* are only partly involved in this sector. They are showing a downward tendency in many countries after an initial period of expansion.

II. The Main Characteristics of Machinery Associations and Their Dispersion

1. Organizational Characteristics

In the typical form of machinery associations, investment is undertaken by the farmers involved. This mostly follows according to the expected utilization claim on the machine. Through respectively shared financing, an association of machine owners develops hand in hand with an association of machine users. One can note a substantial dispersion of non-co-operative legal forms among machinery associations as well as among machinery rings. (→ *Forms of Cooperation*).

Machines of such associations are generally used in the member enterprises by the respective farmers themselves so that no application of special human labour is needed in the multi-farm machines. There are, of course, machinery associations in which a certain member carries out the employment of the common machine. Through this method, the other members can reduce their own labor application, but they have to pay for it. Furthermore, the maintenance and upkeep of the machines is usually undertaken by one member.

Not only do prospective members join a machinery association who have enterprises with the same production structure, but also those in particular who do not substantially vary from each others with regard to their operational size or their machinery needs; this simplifies the investment financing as well as the organization and administration of the collectively owned machinery (*Brandes/Woermann*; *Tschiersch*). Farmers can concentrate on one or more machinery associations. When a farmer requires a variety of machines which perform different tasks it is also possible that he belongs to more than one machinery association with various machines.

Whereas small machinery associations have between three to five members, the large machinery associations can count fifty or more members (*Schmidt*). They then have various kinds of machines at their disposal and usually also such large models that they can be sufficiently utilized by the larger number of members.

Very large machinery associations (→ *Operational Size*) often have a business manager. With a good management and because of the larger demand for machine tasks they are often in the position to employ their machinery more flexibly and to take better advantage of their capacity than the small associations generally can (*Schinke*).

2. Dispersion of the Machinery Associations

Machinery associations can mostly be found in the industrialized countries (→ *Development, North America*). West Germany experienced a large upswing from the middle of the 1950s through the middle of the 1960s, particularly as they were also promoted by the government (*Isermeyer*). Since then, they have stagnated and their number has even partly decreased; they are being overtaken by the machinery rings.

Likewise, co-operative forms of machinery application developed in other European countries after The Second World War which can be considered machinery associations. These, too, also primarily developed dependent on government support (*Tschiersch*).

Machinery associations furthermore can be found in the developing countries; thorough statistics are, however, not available. There are appropriate references, however, in country and project reports (*May*; *von Erffa*; *Tezer*, *Klingensteiner*). One can assume, though, that they do not have a very extensive dispersion in the developing countries (→ *Development, Africa*; → *Development, Latin America*; → *Development, South Asia*; → *Development, South-East Asia*). Although large differences exist among and between states and regions, the dominant forms of multi-enterprise machine application are the private contract machine operators working either professionally or on the side, and "neighbourhood help involving payment".

3. Two Extra-ordinary Forms of Machinery Associations

Large Machinery Associations in Southern Brazil: This organizational form was started in 1971 as a pilot project and since then has expanded into several machine associations for farmers with a farm size up to 50 hectares. The farmers join such an "association with a co-operative structure" (*Klingensteiner*) by paying a fee upon joining; they have, however, no claim on any type of payment from the assets, reserves, etc. of the organization upon withdrawing. They must additionally pay monthly dues according to the size of their enterprise. The machines, which were purchased through loans and credits, remain solely in the possession of the machine association. The bank credits to purchase the machinery were secured through members' private guarantees. The purchased machines are used in the member farms by salaried personnel against a fixed work payment price. Non-members can also make use of the machines for an additional 10 – 30% fee as long as members are not disadvantaged through this (*Klingensteiner*, p.69). When members have extra capacity on their own machines the business manager can help by using them on a multi-enterprise level in order to achieve a better capacity utilization (→ *Development, Latin America*).

The machinery associations in southern Brazil also support each other reciprocally. In the case that a variety of cultivation areas or climatic conditions are on hand which require a differently timed production and work schedule, an exchange of machinery can take place among the machinery associations (as long as they are not too far apart); furthermore, this can lead to an increase in capacity utilization. The exchange of service personnel between the associations in cases of illness, accident, etc. has also proved its worth.

Large Machinery Associations in Hesse, Germany: In the German state of Hesse, there are public corporations on the level of lower administrative bodies with the task to improve irrigation and drainage and to promote multi-farm application of machinery in agriculture. Members of these so-called "Federations of Water and Land" are owners of agricultural properties. Machinery is purchased through this organization (large machinery association) when demand exists for a particular machine by such a number of members that a sufficiently high level of capacity utilization is guaranteed. A further prerequisite for purchase is the commitment the interested members must make to use the machine annually to a certain extent. The capacity utilization should thus be safely determined from the start. If a member later refuses to use the machine to the agreed upon extent, he must nevertheless pay his share of the fixed costs. Through this method it is made sure that the loans taken out for the investment will be paid back and that the other farmers involved in the employment of the machine are protected against any damages in the form of increased machine operation costs.

The machines themselves remain the property of the organization but are generally used by the farmers themselves. Because some of these machinery associations have several hundred members and thus have a large amount of equipment at their disposal, maintenance and repairs are carried out by personnel of the organization.

The individual water and land federations in Hesse have joined together in a central organization in order to make use of further co-operative advantages such as purchasing machinery together.

III. Main Characteristics of Machinery Rings and their Dispersion

This form of cooperation is a more highly developed organizational form of neighbourhood help. It was first founded in Germany in 1958 by *Geiersberger* in Buchofen, Lower Bavaria. His main desire was to reduce the predominantly high levels of over-capacity the individually owned agricultural machines had by multi-enterprise utilization (*Isermeyer*, 1981). The main characteristics which evolved from the basic form of this organization can be outlined in the following.

1. Offsetting Supply and Demand according to Machine Performance

The co-operative organization among the members is so constructed that a part of the individually owned machines will be employed in their own enterprise, and then used in other member enterprises belonging to the machine pool to utilize the additional machine capacity. The other members, therefore, need not purchase the particular machinery themselves or expand their own machine capacity for their own enterprises. The business management of many machinery rings in West Germany not only distributes and allocates machines but can also supply members with additional manpower help according to demand (see section III, part 3). The prices for using the machinery are periodically reassessed and announced to the members to facilitate billing and payment.

The machines are generally operated by the owners themselves. This produces a direct working income, and the farmer who contracted the work can save the respective labor application for his own enterprise. Offsetting supply and demand according to machine performance in machine pools is thus also connected with offsetting the factor of labor.

2. Membership Structure

In contrast to machinery associations, one can encounter relatively heterogeneous membership structures in machinery rings. Farmers belong who own both small and large agricultural operations. They offer roughly the same amount of machine performance as they require or demand. There are, however, members who require relatively more and those who require relatively less. Moreover, there are members who only offer the machine and manpower capacities not used by themselves. The members of machinery rings are predominantly individual farmers, but also machinery associations and – in many organizations to a great extent – even also contract machine owners. This results from the heterogeneity of suppliers and users.

3. Duties of the Business Management

The chief task of the business manager is offsetting supply and demand based on machine performance. He thus requires dependable information about the business affairs of the members. He must also have a well functioning communication system reaching all members at his disposal (telephone, etc.) as well as business partners, various service sites and extension service.

The organizational goal of "punctual compensation of supply and demand according to machine performance" also implies the effort to maintain an "optimal machine level" of the members of the machinery ring (*Ambros* et al.). Therefore, a very important part of the business manager's duty is advising members about investment matters.

In many machinery rings, an additional area of responsibility has become the so-called farm assistance service. This has developed as a result of the drastically changed labor availability conditions in farming in the industrialized countries. In numerous enterprises, the only labor force is the farmer and his wife – in the household and family. A large risk prevails for the existence of the enterprise when one or both of them are unable to work because of illness, accident, etc. This is similar to the situation when certain work peaks cannot be brought under control. In such situations, farm assistants are placed by the management of the machine pool either in the household or in the operational part of the farm to undertake the necessary functions.

4. Dispersion of Machinery Rings

Various forms of cooperation involving the application of machinery on a multi-enterprise dimension were developed in the industrialized countries especially after the Second World War and were publically promoted to varying degrees. The machinery rings, particularly in Germany, continue to expand, largely involving rings for machinery and farm assistants. One can observe an increase in their number, their membership and the amount of land that they cultivate – above all in machinery rings which have a full-time business manager. Machinery rings which lack a full-time business manager show a stagnating, even lightly decreasing tendency (Bundesministerium für Ernährung, Landwirtschaft und Forsten / Federal Ministry for Food, Agriculture and Forestry).

Machinery rings have also been founded in other European countries, some following the German example and others independent from it. Machinery rings are operated e.g. in Switzerland and Austria (*Grimm*). The Banque de Travail was established in France in 1957 and served as an example for respective foundings in Belgium in 1963. Other European countries also report of machinery rings developed along a variety of lines (*Tschiersch*; *Golter*) and of interest in introducing these organizational forms for the first time into their economies, e.g. in Poland (Janusz GAC) (→ *Development, Eastern Europe*). The first six machine pools have existed in Sweden since 1990 (National report at the convention of machinery rings in Hannover, 1990). A system of machinery rings similar to the German was introduced in Japan in 1972 (*Isoshi Kajii*).

The machinery ring is fairly uncommon in the developing countries. In Kenia, for example, only one machinery ring is spoken about (*von Erffa*). In these countries, there are several main reasons and causes for the rarity of this relatively complicated organizational form: the low development level of general economic-technical affairs including insufficient transportational development, underdeveloped communication networks, pervasive fragmentation of farm holdings, insufficient repair services, and, last but not least, the inherent problems resulting from low sales receipts and income.

IV. The Effects of Machinery Associations and Machinery Rings from the Members' Perspective

The effects of multi-enterpise machine application are determined by members' conditions both internal and external to their individual enterprises as well as by the organizations themselves. The effects of these two types of organizational forms are to a degree very similar, to a degree also very different. They are also rated differently by the members according to their interests and their specific situations. One can assume that the labor alleviation made possible through the employment of machinery has a considerably higher value for farmers suffering from insufficient nutrition and poor health in humid, tropical regions than for farmers in temperate climate zones. Further references are given in the following sections concerning the most important areas of effect that machinery associations and machinery rings have.

1. Reduction in Investment Costs per Hectare

The capital requirements per unit of (farming) area can be reduced through multi-enterprise application of machinery as the machines can be utilized better, thus making fewer machine capacity necessary. Large differences exist according to the organizational form of multi-enterprise cooperation as to the amount of capital the individual members are to contribute for machinery acquisition (*Hanf*). In machinery associations, a proportional reduction of the capital requirements of all involved enterprises can be determined when compared to individual enterprise mechanization. In machinery rings, in contrast, members experience a concentration of their capital requirement who acquire machinery and with it wish to offer output capacity to other members. Those requiring machine output capacities who have partly or completely done without their own machines in their enterprises thus dispense with the necessity of such investments for their own farms. Through this they attain an expanded horizon for other types of capital investment or application (→ *Financing*).

2. Reduction in the Operational Costs of Machinery

Operational costs of machinery can be fundamentally reduced in both organizational forms (in comparison to individual enterprise mechanization) through a higher capacity utilization up to the level of depreciation write-off. Furthermore, a larger and fairly secure demand for machine output capacity can develop into a more efficient – generally a greater – aggregate with the effect of further cost reductions per unit of ouput (procedural degression). A higher capacity utilization through multi-enterprise use reduces the cost per output unit in a decreasing proportion. These diminished savings of expenses could, however, be coupled with mounting organizational problems, resulting from an increasing number of members.

3. Improvement in Liquidity

Members of machinery associations, but moreover those of machinery rings who predominantly require machine output capacities and who have not chosen to invest in the acquisition of such machinery themselves generally have a better liquidity and a better credit rating because of these decreasing expenses for investment. This means that they are in a better position for other financial steps, including an eventual restructuring along more efficient business-organizational lines. This results above all when multi-farm application of machinery lays the groundwork for new methods of labor and work organization.

4. More favorable Conditions for the Application of Technological Advancements

The higher utilization capacity of machinery made possible through multi-enterprise cooperation with respect to individual enterprise mechanization leads to a faster depreciation write-off. Machines can thus be replaced more quickly, providing faster availabilty to mechanical-technical advancements.

Wherever the income and liquidity situation has improved through multi-enterprise mechanization, more favorable conditions for the application of further fields of technological progress also exist – above all in biological-technical progress (fertilizer, seed, pesticides, etc.) Because of the effects on the turnover proceeds eventually resulting from this progress, financing mechanization can also be alleviated.

5. The Effects on Manpower

The availability of machinery application with operating personnel is of particular importance for those who themselves only have a small labor capacity at their disposal. A substantial part of the work they must overcome can be taken care of by contracting through the machinery ring; labor capacity in their own enterprises relieved through such a method can furthermore be put to better use elsewhere. Moreover, those farmers with surplus manpower on their own farms are provided the opportunity to offer other ring members simultaneously their machinery and manpower and thus to earn additional income (*Hanf*). This requires, however, the individual acquisition of one or more machines which is not presently possible for numerous peasant farmers, predominantly in developing countries.

Mechanization – also multi-farm use of machinery as presented in the two organizational forms – must be evaluated differently because of the various conditions in the industrialized and in the developing countries. The most important difference among the group of developing countries is the situation of densely and sparsely populated countries (*Reisch*). Particularly, in densely populated areas, advancing mechanization might run the risk of reaching inappropriate levels with respect to the possible decline (worsening) of employment opportunities.

6. The Contribution to the Social Support and Protection of Members

The possibility that work on an agricultural enterprise can be taken care of by an enterprise-external person with machinery (as is the case in machinery rings and certainly also in some situations in machinery associations) furthermore means a particular economic and existential security for the case that a farmer is periodically unable to work due to illness or the like. The production risk and existential risks of the farmer and his family are considerably reduced through the punctual execution of certain tasks and jobs.

The economic risk in industrialized countries is especially high in the relatively widespread form of one-man enterprises. Numerous machinery rings have therefore included farm assistance services as a special functional area within their organization (see section III, part 3). A further important contribution to the social protection of farmer families is provided through this placement of outside assistants in members' operations.

One can conclude that the effects of machinery rings and machinery associations are quite multifarious and are not simply restricted to savings of costs in machine-executed work. The two organizational forms of multi-enterprise machinery application presented above affect the farm both directly and indirectly in various ways. According to the existent conditions, they provide new opportunities for a more efficient business organization and also for the combination of work and income opportunities both internal and external to the farm.

Bibliography

Ambros, J./Hiemer, J./Weinschenk, G.: Zur Planung des optimalen Maschinenbestandes in einem Maschinenring; Berichte über Landwirtschaft, Hamburg, Berlin 1979, pp. 597– 620.
Binswanger, Hans P.: Agricultural Mechanization, A Comparative Historical Perspective, World Bank Staff Paper No.77673, Washington 1984.
Binswanger, Hans P./Donovan, Graeme: Agricultural Mechanization, Issues and Options, a World Bank Policy Study, Washington 1987.
Brandes, Wilhelm/Woermann, Emil: Landwirtschaftliche Betriebslehre, vol.2, Spezieller Teil, Hamburg, Berlin 1971.
Bundesministerium für Ernährung, Landwirtschaft und Forsten (ed.): Statistisches Jahrbuch über Ernährung, Landwirtschaft und Forsten der Bundesrepublik Deutschland 1989, Münster 1989.
von Erffa, Rüdiger: Financing of Multifarm Used Machinery, Multifarm Use of Agricultural Machinery in Africa, the Middle East and Brazil, Frankfurt 1982, pp. 123–136.
FAO: Multifarm Use of Agricultural Machinery, FAO Agricultural Series No. 17, Rome 1985.
FAO: Production Yearbook 1988, vol.42, Rome 1989.
Gac, Janusz: Der Maschinenring – eine Chance für Bauern in Europa, Kurzfassung eines Vortrages in Hannover zum "Tag der Maschinenringe" 1990 (mimeo).
Golter, Friedrich: Maschinenringe/Maschinengemeinschaften, Handbuch des Genossenschaftswesens, Wiesbaden 1980, cols. 1177–1188.
Grimm, A.: Inter-MR 1990, Länderbericht Deutschland, Österreich, Schweiz, 1990 (mimeo).
Hanf, C.-H.: Auswirkungen der überbetrieblichen Maschinenverwendung, Überbetriebliche Maschinenverwendung in der Landwirtschaft – Ein KTBL-Gespräch, Münster 1980, pp. 8–17.
Holtkamp, Rudolf: Evaluation of Different Systems of Multifarm Use of Agricultural Machinery in Developing Countries, Paper presented at the International Conference on Agricultural Engineering, Paris 1988.
Isermeyer, H.-G.: Auswirkungen überbetrieblicher Maschinenverwendung auf die Betriebsentwicklung, Überbetriebliche Maschinenverwendung in der Landwirtschaft, Münster 1980, pp. 68–83.
Isermeyer, H.-G.: Organisationsformen der überbetrieblichen Maschinenverwendung, Entwicklung und Verbreitung, KTBL-Schrift 244, Münster-Hiltrup 1980, p.18ff.
Isermeyer, Harald: Überbetriebliche Maschinenverwendung und wo sie hinpaßt, KTBL-Schrift 268, Münster-Hiltrup 1981.
Isohsi Kajii: Co-operative Organizations in Agricultural Production in Japan: The New Phase of Activities of Agricultural Cooperatives, Cooperation in World agriculture, Tokyo 1985, pp. 89–95.
Kadner, Klaus: Kosten senken durch überbetrieblichen Maschineneinsatz, Bonn, Bad Godesberg 1979.
Klingensteiner, Peter: Einführung von Maschinengemeinschaften im Süden Brasiliens, Eschborn 1984.
Länderbericht: Schweden – Maschinenringe eine Zukunftschance, Tag der Maschinenringe, Hannover 1990.
Mai, Diethard: Überbetriebliche Mechanisierung der Landwirtschaft in Pakistan, Jordanien und in der Türkei, Multi Farm Use of Agricultural Machinery in Africa, the Middle East and Brazil, Frankfurt 1982, pp. 167–182.
Muckle, T.B.: The Role of the Private Agricultural Contractor in Kenya, Multifarm Use of Agricultural Machinery in Africa, the Middle East and Brazil, Frankfurt 1982, pp. 103–122.
Reisch, Erwin: Probleme der Technisierung in der Landwirtschaft, in: Hohnholz, J.H. (ed.): Die Armut der ländlichen Bevölkerung in der Dritten Welt, Baden-Baden 1980, pp. 121–133.
Schinke, Klaus: Kooperation beim Maschineneinsatz in der Landwirtschaft, in: Zeitschrift für das gesamte Genossenschaftswesen, vol. 29, Göttingen 1979, pp. 119–124.
Schmidt, Karl- Ernst: Landwirtschaftliche Lohnunternehmen, heute und morgen, KTBL-Schrift 286, Münster-Hiltrup 1983.
Tezer, Erkan: Problems of Multifarm Use of Agricultural Machinery in Turkey, Multifarm Use of Agricultural Machinery in Africa, the Middle East and Brazil, Frankfurt 1982, pp. 91–101.
Voss, Charles: Mechanisierung der Landwirtschaft. Handbuch der Landwirtschaft und Ernährung in den Entwicklungsländern, vol. I, Stuttgart 1982, pp. 205–228.

Management in Co-operatives

HELMUT WAGNER

(see also: *Managerial Economics*; *Business Policies*; *Organizational Structure of Societies*; *Strategy Planning*; *Management Teams*)

I. The Term "Management"; II. The Effect of Co-operative Self-image on Management; III. Special Features of the Management of Classical Co-operatives.

I. The Term "Management"

The term "management" refers both to the institution and to the function. Management as a function means the complex of tasks which have to be fulfilled to guarantee the viability of an organisation and the long-term achievement of its aims. Management as an institution describes those persons who fulfill these tasks in an organisation. The managerial employees have to take over certain roles which are connected with the management. This requires special management skills.

1. Managerial Functions

Managerial functions can be classified by several criteria. In accordance with the management process, normative tasks (establishment of the basic values of the organisation, of its objectives and purposes), strategic tasks (creation of potentials and determination of the basic activities to reach the organisational goals), and operative tasks (regulation and controlling of the routine activities of the organisation) have to be distinguished.

In the management process of an enterprise, when its fundamental values are taken as a basis

- the corporate objectives have to be put into operational terms,
- strategies have to be developed which guarantee the supply of necessary material and personnel resources and which permit a long-term achievement of objectives in the chosen fields of business,
- decisions have to be made and plans have to be developed which determine how the resulting tasks can be accomplished,
- the tasks have to be arranged systematically and they have to be allocated to those units responsible for them (organisational structure) and the temporal, functional, local, and personnel sequence of the performance have to be determined and coordinated (process organisation),
- all stages of the process have to be directed and controlled in a way that performances correspond to the goals of the enterprise (directing and controlling).

In addition to these task-oriented duties of management, personnel functions as leading the employees, have to be dealt with. This leadership function is often called the key function of management. It is described by the slogan "management is getting things done with and by other people" and stresses the selection and staffing, the development, the motivation, and the assignment of qualified employees as well as the practice of an effective style of leadership that suits the situation. Moreover, management also includes the representation of the enterprise towards its environment; it thus also includes the responsibility towards the financiers, the clients and the suppliers and towards the public and the society.

In enterprises, usually division of labour is practiced in order to achieve advantages of specialization in both the material and the personnel resources. The subtasks and the complexes of tasks formed within the framework of division of labour, such as marketing management, production management, personnel management, financial management have to be coordinated factually and temporally. The consequent demand for coordination has to be met by the management partly hierarchically by the formation of management and coordination authorities, partly by the formation of coordination committees. The demand for coordination can be reduced by the use of factual instruments of coordination such as plans, programmes, standard routines, budgets, and agreement on objectives the formation of which also represents an essential organisational or managerial task.

In literature, a wealth of catalogues can be found in which the management function is subdivided into subfunctions. As far as the essential basic functions are concerned, however, there is complete agreement on that. The POSDCORB-catalogue (Planning, Organizing, Staffing, Directing, Coordinating, Reporting, Budgeting) by *Gulick* (1937) which takes up *Henry Fayol's* pioneer work and the classical subdivision by *Koontz* and *O'Donnell* (1955) into planning, organizing, staffing, directing, and controlling are the basis of most of the modified catalogues. In practically all of them, however, the relationships between the subfunctions and the demand for permanent feedback in the proceedings are stressed. In management models (manangement by ...), some of these functions are stressed particularly and techniques of fulfilling them are offered.

2. Management Roles

Management as an institution refers to persons who perform management functions. Beside the division into top management, middle management, and lower management which is oriented by the hierarchical levels, classifications by the roles the managers have to take over also exist. Thus, *Mintzberg* (1980) sees in the roles of the superior as figurehead and liaison the realization of interpersonnel relationships, in the roles of the radar screen, the transmitter and the speaker the fulfillment of the information function and in the roles of the innovator, of the problem-solver, of the resources distributor and of the chief negotiator above all the tasks of decision-making. Although all role expectations are valid for practically all managers, the weight of the individual roles differs considerably in accordance with the manager's hierarchical level, the field he is working in, and his personality.

In order to fulfill the management tasks and in order to fulfill the role of the manager successfully, a great number of different abilities are required, which, according to *Katz* (1974), can be reduced to three keyfunctions: technical competence, that is expert knowledge and the ability to use it, social competence, that is the ability to cooperate effectively with other people, and conceptional competence, that is the ability to realize problems and chances in the whole context and to exercise a systematic concept of action.

II. The Effect of Co-operative Self-image on Management

The management functions, roles and abilities presented are valid for all forms of organizations in general regardless of their special orientation, their goals and strategies, their owner, and their legal form. Their special characteristics and importance largely depend on these factors in the particular cases, however. To work out the special features of management in co-operatives, it is necessary to analyze the features of co-operatives which are relevant to management (→ *Managerial Economics*).

1. Features of Classical Co-operatives

In the traditional view, co-operatives are associations formed by their members in order to promote their economic interests (→ *Promotion Mandate*). The members do not only subscribe the capital stock and reserve necessary, but they are also the most important partners in business; they are consequently the suppliers in marketing co-operatives, the buyers in purchasing co-operatives, the investors and borrowers in credit unions. This personal correspondence between the owners and the beneficiaries is called the principle of identity. It has consequences for the functions and the management of a co-operative (*Eschenburg* 1971).

The principle of indentity (→ *Theory of co-operative Cooperation*) is based on the principle of self-help according to which the members, but not other persons, support themselves in their economic affairs. The members carry the responsibility for the co-operative together. All essential decisions have to be made by the members democratically (one man, one vote) (→ *Principles*).

In their macroeconomic function, co-operatives are regarded as a cooperation that primarily aims at the satisfaction of its members' goals (promotion task) which is a necessary and reasonable supplement to gainful corporations which aim at individual self-interest and the public economy which is oriented towards public welfare (*Boettcher* 1980). Unlike public economy, co-operatives are thus oriented towards promotion of the economy of their members only (→ *Promotion Mandate*). Unlike individual enterprises, as promotion companies, they are institutions supporting their members, promoting their members by their services; corporation oriented self-interests have to be of minor importance to the co-operative. The competitiveness and the promotion potential of a co-operative can be increased if several co-operatives cooperate in interconnected operations and associations for the creation and the exploitation of goods and services. It is, however, typical for the classical co-operative association that the co-operatives which work together keep their autonomy and that, in a multistage association, the hierarchy is ordered from the bottom to the top, in other words from the members of the primary associations to the secondary and tertiary co-operatives (*Dülfer* 1984).

The competitiveness and the promotion-potential can often be increased if, with the help of limited business with non-members, a better capacity utilization, a more efficient use of the personnel and factual capacities and thus economies of scale are possible. Apart from this, business with non-members only serves the purpose of enlisting new members and is no end in itself (→ *Business Policies*).

An increase in the efficiency of co-operatives with a complex business might also be possible when the members relinquish parts of the self-administration and management tasks are assigned to professional managers. In these cases, it becomes particularly important to keep the members permanently informed and to control the management especially as far as the interests of the members are concerned.

The way classical co-operative see themselves leads to the fact, in comparison with the management of stock companies, the management of co-operatives show some special features. This does not hold for co-operatives which show a rather institutional self-image.

2. Features of Co-operatives with an Institutional Self-image

The classical principles of self-help, self-responsibility, and self-government lost importance, however, in the course of time because of the growing competition (self-help becomes partly obsolete), the quantitative growth of the co-operatives (necessity of adding professional management or of replacing self-government by it) and because of new financial resources for co-operative (replacement or supplementation of the capital subscribed by the members by earnings retention, capital from certificates of profit sharing and long-term debt capital e.g. from provisions for pension liabilities). This makes the co-operatives see themselves as an institution of their own (*Wagner* 1988).

When the co-operative sees itself as an institution of its own, the long-term preservation and increase of its economic potential and the competitiveness of the co-operative itself, in whatever strategic orientation and organisational structure, are in the center of attention (→ *Strategy Planning*). Ultimately, as institutions, the co-operatives and their associations are ends in themselves which can pursue further autonomously defined within the legal and economic bounds. The management of the co-operatives and of the co-operative associations is thus no longer above all a trustee and lobbyist of the members or of the member co-operatives, it rather has to represent as a stakeholder the interests of all persons and institutions involved. And these are not only the members but also all persons and institutions without membership connected to co-operative as investors, employees and managers, clients and suppliers; and even community, public, state and the society, too.

Above all, managers of big co-operatives which have to face strong → *competition* and whose members have very heterogeneous interests, see their co-operatives as institutions. Direct or individual promotion of the members is practically impossible in these cases; therefore, promotion has to be reduced to profit distribution among the members in accordance with their co-operative share.

This view consequently no longer attributes a dominating role to the interests or the influence of individual members. Management functions are the peak coordinator of the heterogenous interests of all members of the coalition – members or not – and pursue above all the interests of the enterprise respectively its self-interests as far as there is enough scope for it.

As far as the functions and the process of management are concerned, such co-operatives do not have any particularities in comparison with corporations. As equity suppliers the members act as small stockholders. Their demands on the co-operatives are largely reduced to an adequate interest on the capital they have contributed and to their active voting power in the members' general assembly (→ *Assessment of Success*). In connection with marketing activities, one perhaps remembers the fact that they are members of a co-operative. The basic co-operative principles, especially the principle of identity, have become irrelevant, however.

Whatever answer you give to the question whether co-operative with such a self-image can really be called co-operatives, it will probably be easily understandable that in such co-operatives the managerial functions, the management roles and the management process hardly differ from that of a corporation. There might at best be some differences which result from the different legal forms.

III. Special Features of the Management of Classical Co-operatives

The traditional basic co-operative principles influence the whole management process and its stages when they are realized, in fact.

1. Company Philosophy, Corporate Identity, and Corporate Objectives

As mutual benefit organizations, in their company philosophy, co-operatives have to give priority to the needs of their members; the interests of the employees and the other investors, clients, and suppliers have to be treated with lower priority. The long-term economic success the members can achieve by their investments and the exchange of services with the co-operatives is the dominating target figure; success on the market and consequently the achievement, preservation, and growth of market shares are means to an end (→ *Corporate Culture*). This company philosophy has to be reflected inwards by the co-operatives' way of seeing themselves and in its effect on the work of the co-operatives, that is towards the members and the employees, as well as outwards. It has to be accentuated in the management process of the co-operative and it has to be expressed in all decisions and activities.

The translation of this co-operative self-image into operational actions proves to be difficult when the interests of the members are heterogenous. Sufficient operationalization is only possible by means of strategic planning, the ensuing long-term fixation of the business sectors that are to be dealt with and the consequent business policies.

2. Planning in Co-operatives

An essential goal of → *strategic planning* is the identification of the business in which an enterprise can achieve long-term success in order to guarantee its viability and a high achievement of its objectives. Long-term success is to be guaranteed by a focus on markets/market segments with high economic attractiveness and by the achievement of competitive advantages on these markets, not least by the concentration of all economic potentials on business sectors which have an enriching effect on each other (synergy concept). The realization of the strategies than has to take place within the framework of the strategic management which has to guarantee that all medium- and long-term activities correspond to the strategy.

In co-operatives, the attractiveness of business sectors is determined above all by the promotion potential which can be made available to the members by the services offered. The co-operative activities in individual business sectors should make possible a promotion of the members. Owing to the exchange of services with the co-operative, the members must be able to realize bigger successes for themselves than it would be possible if the exchange of services would take place with other market partners.

The identification of long run promotion potentials with high value to the members requires an intensive cooperation between the management of the co-operative and its members (*Wagner* 1984). It also requires a high innovation capability of the co-operative, however, because the competition often absorbs initially existing promotion potentials. The organisation of the strategy in the individual fields and the concrete adaptation of the strategy to the interests of the members within the framework of the strategic management thus presupposes permanent adaptation to the competition especially also a permanent flow of information and lively communication between management and members either personally or through mediating groups such as members' meetings, advisory councils, board of directors, groups of members.

According to the specific situation of the sectors, success of the promotion can be achieved both by the strategy of cost- and quality leadership. As a general rule, the strategy of cost leadership requires big economic unions, however; it is therefore of particular importance for the cooperation in the co-operative association. The strategy of quality leadership aims at a particularly high qualitative benefit for the business partner, the members. It requires a high degree of individual service differentiation. Above all, smaller co-operatives with intensive contact with their members can achieve particular output by means of individual consultation and servicing, a particularly trustful cooperation and a member-oriented service-range. In spite of *Porter's* (1985) warning not to mix the strategy of cost leadership with the differentiation strategy because it might make an enterprise get stuck in the middle with low efficiency, the strategy combination seems to be possible in co-operatives if differentiated service offers by the primary co-operatives are combined with the mass products of the association of co-operatives. If both strategies are possible through the combination of individual services of the individual co-operative with standard performances of the co-operative association, an "outpacing strategy" is also possible if competitors from the non-co-operative sector who adapt themselves with me-too-strategies are excluded with a counterstrategy (*Gilbert, Strebel* 1988).

Since, from the members' point of view, the promotion potential of the individual promotion sectors can subjectively be regarded as being of different importance, if the structure of the members is heterogeneous, broad and differentiated service offers by the co-operative gain significance considerably. It is possible only to arrange a service package that leads to individual promotion with additional benefit in comparison with competitors. Thus, a long-term tie of the members with their co-operative is possible.

3. Organization

There are organizational consequences if the members of a company are regarded as the focus of the company policy (→ *Organizational Structure of Societies*). It is probably evident that without the creation of organizational facilities which establish and keep permanent contact with the members and without activities which show clearly to the members their role as supporting institutions of the co-operative, a consistent orientation towards the members would hardly be possible. Therefore, particular importance has to be attributed to the regular integration of the members into the decision-process of the co-operative by means of honorary cooperation in the management board, the creation of advisory councils and regular discussions with groups of members.

It should, however, be said that such organizational measures do not necessarily facilitate the management of co-operatives by a professional management; the great number of necessary discussions and votes require a lot of time of the co-operative's management and naturally reduces its power.

4. Control of the Management

Whenever the size of the co-operative and the necessary know-how for the business prevent a far-reaching self-administration of the co-operative by its members, the control of the management becomes vital necessity. In order to guarantee reasonable and fair control of the success of the co-operative and its management, operational goals and concrete plans are necessary. Therefore, apart from the supervision of the co-operative performance with the help of the instruments of accountancy, i.e. the annual financial statement and its mandatory audit, establishing promotion plans and accounting for their realization in promotion reports require particular attention. Promotion plans and reports have to show their members the benefits of the co-operative for their members.

5. Leadership

The concentration of the co-operative towards the members' needs has to be taken into consideration in the course of the training of the personnel and its management. Since the promotion of the members by means of anonymous benefits alone is not sufficient it has to find expression especially in personal service, in advisory service and in servicing. These services are not rendered only by the management. Therefore, a member-oriented attitude and a motivation of the entire personnel is necessary because, for most of the members, the employees represent the co-operative in daily life.

If the statement of the leaderhip theory is taken into consideration that styles of leaderhip have to be in accordance with the individual situation, in co-operatives a situation might exist in which a rather co-operative style of leadership seems to be appropriate. Considering the specific interests of the members requires not only know-how and empathy but also flexible reactions and participating. In a participative and member-orientated management, the preconditions for it are far better than with other styles of leadership.

Another argument for a co-operative style of leadership is due to the fact that co-operatives represent the prototype of cooperation, the cooperation between members to promote their economic success. It thus seems to be more than appropriate that the management of a co-operative is actually co-operative and that this has an effect on the personnel management. It is a specific feature of co-operatives, however, that within a participating management system, the specific interests of the members must have priority over that of the employees.

Bibliography

Boettcher, Erik (ed.): Führungsprobleme in Genossenschaften. Beiträge zum genossenschaftswissenschaftlichen Führungsseminar, Tübingen 1977.
Boettcher, Erik (1980): Die Genossenschaft in der Marktwirtschaft. Einzelwirtschaftliche Theorie der Genossenschaften, Tübingen 1980.
Dülfer, Eberhard: Betriebswirtschaftslehre der Kooperative. Kommunikation und Entscheidungsbildung in Genossenschaften und vergleichbaren Organisationen, Göttingen 1984.
Eschenburg, Rolf (1971): Ökonomische Theorie der genossenschaftlichen Zusammenarbeit, Tübingen 1971.
Gilbert, X./Strebel, P. (1988): Strategies to Outspace the Competition, in: Journal of Business Strategies, 1988, pp. 28–36.
Gulick, L. (1937): Notes on the Theory of Organization, in: Gulick, L., Urwick, R. (ed.): Papers on the Science of Administration, New York 1937, pp. 3–45.
Hahn, D. (1975):Führung und Führungsprobleme in genossenschaftlichen Unternehmungen und in Unternehmungen in der Rechtsform der Aktiengesellschaft – ein Vergleich aus betriebswirtschaftlicher Sicht, in: ZfgG, vol. 25, 1975, pp. 79–106.
Hub, H./Metzger, H. (1980): Genossenschaftliches Management, in: Mändle, E./Winter, H.-W. (ed.): Handwörterbuch des Genossenschaftswesens, Wiesbaden 1980, pp. 1095–1129.
Katz, R.L. (1974): Skills of an Effective Administrator, in: Harvard Business Review, vol. 52, no. 5, pp. 90–102.
Koontz, H./O'Donnell, C. (1955): Principles of Management: An Analysis of Managerial Functions, New York 1955.
Mintzberg, H. (1980): The Nature of Managerial Work, 2nd ed., Englewood Cliffs/N.J. 1980.
Nutzinger, H.G.: Führung in Selbstverwaltungsbetrieben und Genossenschaften, in: Kieser, A./Reber, G./Wunderer, R. (ed.): Handwörterbuch der Führung, Stuttgart 1987, pp. 1833–1848.
Porter, M.E. (1985): Competitive Advantage – Creating and Sustaining Superior Performance, New York 1985.
Vierheller, Rainer: Zur Entwicklung genossenschaftstheoretischer Führungsaspekte in der betrieblichen Managementlehre, in: ZfgG, vol. 33, 1983, pp. 31–51.
Wagner, Helmut (1984): Strategische Unternehmensplanung in Genossenschaften. Der Einfluß der Förderprinzips auf Prozeß und Methodik der langfristigen Planung, in: Jäger, W./Pauli, H. (ed.): Genossenschaften und Genossenschaftswissenschaft. Systematische, strukturelle und ordnungspolitische Aspekte des Genossenschaftswesens, Freundesgabe für Prof. Dr. Erik Boettcher, Westfälische Wilhelms-Universität Münster, zum 65. Geburtstag, Wiesbaden 1984, pp. 159–172.
Wagner, Helmut (1988): Organisationstheoretische Überlegungen zur Anzahl der Stufen im genossenschaftlichen Bankensektor, in: Bonus, H./Steiner, J./Wagner, H. (ed.): Dreistufigkeit im genossenschaftlichen Bankenverbund: Luxus oder Notwendigkeit?, Frankfurt/M. 1988, pp. 51–71.

Management Teams

HARTMUT KREIKEBAUM

(see also: *Management in Co-operatives*; *Business Policies*; *Co-determination*; *Industrial Relations*)

I. Introduction: Relevance of Management Teams; II. Structural Elements of Management Teams; III. Objectives of Management Teams; IV. Decision-oriented Aspects.

I. Introduction: Relevance of Management Teams

Managerial decision-making has often been regarded as 'executive' decision-making with emphasis on the individual actions of the entrepreneur on top of the company. It is noteworthy to mention that the co-operative organizations in their long and outstanding history have avoided this pitfall. This is true for almost any type of co-operatives (for a historic and comprehensive overlook cf. *Dülfer* 1980a)(→ *Structural Types*). A common goal-finding process between the members can be regarded as one of the constituents of any co-operative organization. This basic attitude characterizes the specific group-decisions within co-operatives (*Dülfer* 1980b).

Regarding the size of corporations, management teams (MTs) are a prerequisite for big and complex organizations. It seems obvious that not only large companies cannot do without MTs, but that also medium-sized corporations depend upon some form of coordination executed by MTs. This is even true for small companies, if we look upon some basic functions which require a certain form of transfunctional activities (cf. *Kreikebaum* 1989).

Big companies cannot do without an elaborate network of MTs on different hierarchical levels. The complex nature of managerial decision-making requires the integration of staff representatives as well as line managers in MTs. Staff members offer professional business activities in a specific field of knowledge. The professionalization of management has truly invaded almost every area of executive decision-making. Experts exercise a sort of "silent" professional power without which no modern co-operative organization could be guided. This new type of 'knowledge power', however, can only be executed in close cooperation with line managers, i.e., in MTs. In general, MTs lack the bureaucratic controls and information patterns of 'normal' hierarchies and offer a higher degree of organizational effiency (cf. *Rothwell/Zweckfeld* 1982).

II. Structural Elements of Management Teams

It is an open question whether the definition of a team should follow *Marschak's* proposal (1954/55) of a world of group decision-making free of conflict. *Marschak* did not neglect the existence of individual goals, but claimed a team to be an institution where the individual motives of the team members (→ *Motives for Cooperation*) amalgamate into an overall group objective. From research in industrial sociology and organization theory we now know that an organization cannot rely upon everlasting 'given' goals. On the contrary: it is forced to develop a flexible response to changing market conditions (→ *Strategy Planning*). The formulation of the organization's goals has to be regarded as a process rather than a once-and-for-ever stated aim. And this process can reach its fullest efficiency only when different opinions of the various group members are taken into account.

The core element of a MT is 'teamwork'. With this expression we associate a very close form of cooperation and mutual understanding. The individual members share some sort of common belief (→ *Group, the Co-operative*) and concentrate their efforts in this direction. Teamwork means a joint effort towards a common goal, combined with a mutual support in every respect. In this sense, e.g., a soccer team exercises teamwork. The follow-up of the goal ('to win the match') requires an unrestrained input of the members' full potential.

In management, however, there usually are other conditions than those existing in zero-sum games. The goals are not set up once and for ever, but have to be developed and even redefined. The uncertainty of the situation may be great, the degree of intra-team conflict high, and there always exist individual apprehensions.

MTs can develop out of a single governing body or may be formed by members of different institutions. It is, of course, the goal of every board of directors to function like a team, i.e., to regard matters from a basis of mutual understanding and respect.

An interesting example of a team consisting of various governing bodies can be found in Japan's new industrial 'groups', following the old Zaibatsu conglomerates. The biggest one, the FUYO-Group, for instance, is not governed by a single chief executive officer but by a MT of 29 members representing the FUYI-Bank, Hitachi, Nissan, and other core members of the FUYO-Group. This MT is in charge of the most important strategic decisions of the whole group (→ *Group Theory*).

Another structural element concerns the level of hierarchy. MTs may recruit their members from the same level or from different echelons of hierarchy. An example of the first type represents the conference of all personnel managers of a company's operating units or the weekly controllers' meeting. We also find a combination of line and staff people from different levels of hierarchy (e.g., the body responsible for investment decisions, or a planning committee) (→ *Co-determination*).

III. Objectives of Management Teams

1. Corporate Missions

MTs are set up to improve the efficiency and efficacy of managerial decisions. The first element concerns a higher degree of rationality and productivity of the decision process itself. This is not only true for big companies, but also for small and medium-sized forms (cf. *Kreikebaum* 1990, and *Wagner* 1985). MTs have to ensure the purpose and strategic mission of a co-operative. Talking about objectives we may differentiate between top management and middle management levels. Top management is responsible for the basic missions of a company as well as for its philosophy (→ *Corporate Culture*). Goal decisions of this type are embedded in corporate management's responsibility as stated in basic guidelines, the charta of a company, or prescribed by law.

But also in this very specific case of leadership decisions, it is not up to a single person to formulate the long-term policy of a company. A planning committee, an advisory board, or even a joint effort together with the workers' council or the union will be prevalent (→ *Industrial Relations*).

2. Divisional Objectives

Most large co-operatives and a whole number of medium-sized companies are equipped with a divisional type of organization. This kind of structure makes necessary MTs on the branch level as well as a MT which links together overall coporate goals and the divisions' objectives.

According to the basic structure of a divisional organization, the most important functions must be represented within the MT, i.e., production, marketing, R&D, and finance & accounting. It is a prerequisite for this type of organization to react as flexible as possible to customer demands and market changes. Quick decisions have to be carried out, and this requires a free flow of information and open communicaton patters within the leading team.

3. Functional Objectives

Many medium-sized co-operatives are still organized along functional lines. In this case, top management has to fulfill a special task in coordinating the different functional departments. This can become a rather tough job and may require a lot of day-to-day activities on the side of corporate management.

Chester Barnard has already pointed out that the task of coordination can be regarded as the executive's first priority. To secure a well-balanced understanding between, for instance, production and marketing, between finance and advertising, or even between sales and R&D can be a rather time and energy consuming effort which sometimes puts a real burden on the chief executive officer. This burden can be relieved, however, by institutionalizing cross-functional MTs.

Cross-functional MTs, on the other hand, offer a chance for divisionalized co-operatives to establish overall policies within one or more important functions (→ *Management in Co-operatives*). They usually include top management's participation, acting as 'linking pins'.

4. Different Forms of MTs

According to their different tasks and composition, we may differentiate between special assignment teams (task forces, project teams) and permanent institutions working on a team-basis approach. Teams of the first type cooperate during a given time period. They are installed to solve cross-functional problems which are not assigned as regular tasks but arise during the development of a company and its environment. Establishing a computer-based information system within a company, introducing a strategic planning system, or effectuating a major organizational change offer an opportunity for new MTs. The MT members may be recruited only from staff departments. In this case, no formal regulations are required. Such an 'assignment group' (cf. *Kreikebaum* 1972) may be easily formed, it works very informally, and the fulfilling of the assignment also marks the end of this type of MT.

When a MT is organized as a project group or special task force, we usually encounter a much higher degree of formalization. Project groups follow the principles of a project management. A project leader is being assigned, the goals are formally declared, members from staff and line management are chosen to represent their mutual interests and functional aspects, and (sometimes) a budget is set up. The MT members have to fulfill a certain time schedule, and at least the project team leader has to report to upper echelons on a regular basis about results and possible failures. Such a MT may even consist of insiders and outside representatives, e.g., consulting firms. Consultants can be a useful tool in solving an upcoming problem like the strategic response to a decisive legislative change, a new technological invention, unexpected moves of competitors, or preparing solutions for a new environment protection problem.

Every co-operative organization has to solve problems which go beyond a certain department and which require contributions from various functions and hierarchical levels. Investment decisions, for instance, are based upon decisions of an investment committee, installing a new technology has to be discussed in a MT of engineering and production experts, the annual planning cycle relies upon a planning group. All these MTs meet regularly and they even follow an established form of agenda and internal rules. It is in those groupings that we find a rather close cooperation among the team members, no great dissentment from the MT's objectives, and a mutual sense of respect between the individuals participating in the team's decisions.

IV. Decision-oriented Aspects

Regarding the efficiency and efficacy of decision-making, MT have to compete with individual decisions. Managerial decision-making can take up two basic forms: a single person or a group of decision-makers can be responsible for executive actions. Managerial decision-making of the first type enjoys the advantage of avoiding internal quarrels and conflicting ideas. There may be, however, ambiguity of motives within the individual. This problem of intra-conflicting attitudes also exists in group decisions. Individual decisions offer an efficiency advantage compared with the time and energy consuming process of pluralistic decision-making. There exists, on the other side, a definite disadvantage when it comes to efficacy. Regarding this criterion, group decisions have proven to reach a higher degree of goal attainment. A multi-personal approach to solve a problem offers a wider range of options, it does not exclude opponents, it has to take into account different viewpoints and characters, and, after all, it includes the necessity of convergence. Individual choices have to be amalgamated into a single goal of the organization (and of the MT as well). And it should be kept in mind that his can somehow become a demanding process.

Bibliography

Dülfer, Eberhard: Produktionsgenossenschaften. In: Mändle, Eduard/Winter, H.-W. (eds.): Handwörterbuch des Genossenschaftswesens, Stuttgart 1980, pp. 1356–1371.

Kreikebaum, Hartmut: Die Auftragsgruppe als ein Träger der Kooperation von Stabsstellen, Zeitschrift für Organisation, Vol. 41 (1972), pp. 135–140.

Kreikebaum, Hartmut: Strategische Unternehmensplanung, 3. A., Stuttgart, Berlin, Köln 1989.

Kreikebaum. Hartmut: Die Bedeutung von Managementteams in Kleinbetrieben. In: Arbeitskreis für Kooperation und Partizipation e.V. (ed.): Kooperatives Management, Baden-Baden 1990, pp. 55–67.

Marschak, J.: Elements of a theory of teams, Management Science, Vol. 1 (1954/55), pp. 127–137.

Rothwell, R./Zegveld, W.: Innovation in the small and medium sized firms, London 1982.

Wagner, G.R.: Strategische Entscheidungen im Kleinbetrieb – Voraussetzungen und Wirkungen, Bochum 1985.

Managerial Economics of Co-operatives

EBERHARD DÜLFER

(see also: *Theory of Co-operatives*; *Theory of co-operative Cooperation*; *Business Policies*)

I. Concept and Terminology; II. The Co-operative as a Socio-technical Economic System; III. The Business Communication System; IV. The Legal-organizational Communication System; V. The Interpersonal Communication System; VI. The Management Member Information System (MMIS); VII. Further Subjects of Managerial Economics of Co-operatives; VIII. Summary.

I. Concept and Terminology

The co-operative is termed a "co-operative enterprise" in the anglophone scientific literature. This term, however, is not very precise because the total co-operative complex does not only consist of the entrepreneurial operational unit but also includes the member economies. Thus, the so-called co-operative enterprise does not operate autonomously on both market sides, the purchasing side and the marketing side, but is interacting exclusively with the member enterprises on one of these two sides. Supply co-operatives are purchasing on the market and delivering goods and services exclusively to the member enterprises while marketing co-operatives are operating on the sales market by marketing exclusively the products taken over from the member economies. In general, a co-operative enterprise has only *one market relation* while on the other side it is interacting with its member economies. For this reason, the co-operative enterprise is called a "promoting unit" or an "executive operating unit". Its main task is to promote the member enterprises, i.e. to observe their promotion mandate. That constitutes the difference between a private enterprise (operating on both market sides) and the co-operative enterprise.

Inasfar as the co-operative enterprise is operating on the purchase or the sales market, it operates in competition with other private or state enterprises. It is facing the same decision situation, and consequently its decision making observes the same principles and algorithms as any other competitors' enterprise. The co-operative enterprise applies the same principles of general management or managerial economics (micro-economics).

The orientation of this decision making, however, and the fundamental strategies of the co-operative enterprise are influenced by the promotion mandate, i.e. by the fact that the co-operative enterprise has to operate in favour of the member economies. Insofar the whole decision making procedure of the co-operative enterprise is specifically modified. The same is valid for the member enterprises. These modifications of decision making in the co-operative enterprise as well as in the member economies resulting from their inclusion into the overwhelming co-operative organization are not dealt with in the textbooks of micro-economics or general management. It needs special subject matters for these particular aspects; these are formulated in "*managerial economics of co-operatives*" (Betriebswirtschaftslehre der Kooperative).

Managerial economics of co-operatives is based, like any other branch of empirical science (Realwissenschaft), on the following principles:

- take-off aspect of all analytical questions is the scarcity of resources available for goal attainment which requires a decision of choice;
- the processes of decision making in reality are very complex; their analysis requires both empirical approaches as well as theoretical research methods based on the modern logic of science;
- the results of discovery are not the final purpose of the research process but they should produce recommendations for operating towards given goals; normative prescriptions for goal setting, however, are not deducible.

To sum up, managerial economics of co-operatives is dealing with the decision making processes within co-operatives; co-operative seen in the sense of the total co-operative complex. This co-operative complex (co-operative organization) can be defined by four characteristics: there is

- a group of persons who join consciously because of their common interest (→ *Group, the Co-operative*);
- the intention of self-help in the group in order to attain common goals by improving their economic situation through common actions or mutual assistance (→ *Self-help Organizations*);
- the executive operating unit (co-operative enterprise) as the operational means for production or the supply of products or services in favor of the members; and
- the co-operative combine, i.e. the promotion relationship between the co-operative enterprise and the member economies in favour of which the enterprise is performing business functions (→ *Promotion Mandate*).

II. The Co-operative as a Socio-technical Economic System

In the past, the co-operative was mostly dealt with by single scientific disciplines separated from each other, e.g. economics, legal science, sociology etc. The well-known approach of the "double nature" of the co-operative (→ *Dual Nature*) led to the hypothesis that the group of members should be a pure sociological subject while the co-operative enterprise should be a pure subject of economics and general management science. However, such separation makes it impossible to analyse the very complex relationships and dependencies between both phenomena. It takes the application of the general theory of (organizational) systems to attain an interdisciplinary treatment. According to *Hall/Fagen* (1956), "a system is a set of objects together with its relationships". The objects themselves can be analysed as subsystems while the system investigated is itself an element of an overwhelming supra-system.

In the case of the co-operative, the system investigated is the co-operative complex consisting of the co-operative enterprise and the member economies. Thus, the co-operative enterprise and the member economies are (micro-economic) subsystems of the co-operative as a system. The system "co-operative", on the other hand, is a subsystem of the supra-system national economy or national society etc.

It is evident that in this approach, the co-operative enterprise as the executive operating unit of the member economies does not have the same position in the national economy as other private enterprises, because it is an element of the whole co-operative system which also includes the member economies. This phenomenon explains why the decision making in both kinds of entities, in the co-operative enterprise as well as in the member economies (member enterprises), is influenced by the promotion relationship within the co-operative system (the co-operative organization).

The question results from this discovery why these different economic entities are co-operating voluntarily in that way, because we assume that there is not any compulsory relationship between them.

A detailed analysis of the internal cooperation between the different micro-economic sub-systems of the co-operative system shows that three different *communication systems* exist within the complex:

- the business communication system;
- the legal-organizational communication system;
- the interpersonal communication system.

III. The Business Communication System

The business communication system (betriebsfunktionales Kommunikationssystem) comprises the business relationships between the co-operative enterprise and the member economies. The graphic presentation of these business relationships shows for the two fundamental models of the purchasing or supply co-operative on the one hand and the marketing co-operative on the other the well-known "funnel models" of the co-operative complex (→ *Supply Co-operatives*; → *Marketing*).

Well-known forms of the supply co-operative are (→ *Classification*):

- the purchasing co-operative of retailers;
- the supply co-operative of craftsmen, small industrial enterprises or agricultural producers;

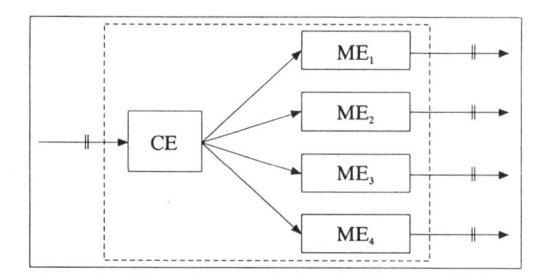

Fig 1: Model of the supply co-operative

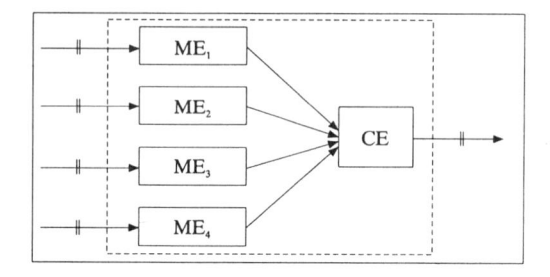

Fig.2: Model of the marketing co-operative

- the supply co-operative of service enterprises (Dienstlcistungsbetriebe);
- the consumer co-operative;
- the housing co-operative society.

The co-operative enterprise in all these cases executes activities of supplying and eventually stocking goods, technical equipment or materials in its capacity as an executively operating unit. In the view of management science, the co-operative enterprise is operating as an merchant wholesaler if the members are retailers, or in the capacity of a retailing enterprise if the members are consumers. As to the details of these activities, please see the keyword articles in this book (→ *Commercial Co-operatives*; → *Marketing* Co-operatives; → *Consumer Co-operatives*; → *Housing Societies*)

The → *housing co-operative societies* are to be classified as supply co-operatives, too because they have the task of suppling the member households with lodging facilities or to assist the members in constructing apartments. Apart from these housing co-operatives, there are house-constructing → *joint-production co-operative*s. They construct apartments or houses for the purpose of giving their members (who are house-building craftsmen) the opportunity to process their manpower potential. Credit co-operatives like peoples' banks, Raiffeisenbanks, credit unions or thrift and loan societies can be classified as supply co-operatives in a wider sense because they execute the financial function in favour of their members, i.e. the supply of borrowed capital. For details of the different business kinds, please see the articles on → *Co-operative Banks* and → *Credit Unions*.

Managerial economics of co-operatives also deals with the activities of the different kinds of co-operatives in their business relationships and with the resulting payment relations.

In this context, it is important in the case of the supply co-operatives that they originally were intended to supply the goods purchased to their members at cost. Insofar, the cost covering principle was relevant for them or – with respect to the time period – the expense covering principle (→ *Assessment of Success*). The preliminary price for the members is indeed always higher ex post than the de facto supply expenses because in the day to day business operations and in view of the time difference between the purchasing operations and supply of the members, eventual risks have to be considered. Thus, a co-operative surplus results. It can be used both to make reserves to cover future risk or to give a → *reimbursement* to the members.

The other case of marketing co-operatives concerns co-operatives of farmers or craftsmen with the purpose of marketing their agricultural or craft products. A special type of marketing co-operative in industrialized countries is the co-operative for crafts services (e.g. for paperhangers, installers, outfit crafts etc.). They work on collective orders. The small industrial crafts marketing co-operative is similar to the industrial marketing syndicate with respect to its structure.

The processing co-operatives which process and market their members' products, e.g. dairy co-operatives, oil mills, rice mills, sugar factories and wineries, also belong to the marketing co-operatives in a wider sense. They are usually named → *"production co-operatives"*, but they are very precisely distinguishable from the joint-production co-operatives as their members do not themselves work in the co-operative enterprise.

The main purpose of marketing co-operatives is to attain as high a price as possible for their members' products. The members receive first a preliminary payment (price) for their products because different risks have to be taken into consideration and reserve stocking is needed in the co-operative enterprise. If a lot of risks have not been realized by the end of the year, a co-operative surplus results. It can be applied to build up reserves in the co-operative enterprise or paid to the members in the form of a → *reimbursement*.

If the co-operative is a multi-purpose co-operative which operates in favour of the members in both the capacity of a supply co-operative as well as a marketing co-operative, more complicated combinations of the above mentioned procedures in both fundamental types are needed. There are hindrances for a precise calculation of reimbursements or further payments with respect to the single business operation. It is also very difficult to calculate the cost of the single operations separately in the case of an integrated business activity. Thus, a precise calculation is not common in practise.

Particular business relations result in the case of the marginal type → *"Produktionsförderungsgenossenschaft"* (production promotion co-operative or Schiller-scheme) which has been introduced by *Otto Schiller* in different countries of the Third World. In this context, the difference in the internal relations of the co-operative complex plays a role, too, which results in the differentiation of structural types.

The joint production co-operative has a completely different structure of market relationships and internal performance relations than the above explained promotional co-operative types. It is also a subject in managerial economics of co-operatives; but for details see the special keyword article (→ *Joint-production Co-operatives*).

IV. The Legal-organizational Communication System

Characteristics of the business communication system are mainly – as explained above – quality and quantity of products and services as well as the structure type of business operations; all this with respect to the exchange of goods and services and to the financial operations. The effectiveness of this system is, however, not only determined by the volume of performance exchanges (turnover, operational size) but also mainly by the continuous running of operations. There is a "flow equilibrium" (Fließgleichgewicht) existing in the sense of the general theory of systems, if there is no blocking through an overboarding input in goods or money and there is no deficit through an excessive outflow. This situation, however, presupposes harmonized behaviour on the part of all participating subsystems and the human decision makers acting within them. This is not always the case in co-operatives, as well as in any other enterprises and societies. Disturbances through conflicts may occur which must be avoided by overwhelming normative regulations the part of the legislator (→ *Legal Form, Co-operative*; → *Law, National* → *Law, International*) and through onlining self-made rules.

It is understandable then, that the co-operative presents a second communication sub-system besides the business communication system. It is the *legal-organizational communication system* which can be understood in part as a component of the national legal order. It comprises all legal norms of behaviour which are attributed to the different microeconomic subsystems of the co-operative society through the legal order in the form of obligations and rights.

These norms indicate how the behaviour of the concerned units and decision makers *should be* in order to avoid interest conflicts and resulting perturbances of the balance within the co-operative. The total of these behavioural norms is an important component of the organizational structure of the co-operative society; they can be called the legal organizational norms. The legal organizational communication system of the co-operative comprises all judical normative bounds resulting from laws, decrees, jurisdiction, societal contracts, articles of associations and bylaws and bilateral contracts within the co-operative society. It is easy to recognize that these norms are important determinants of the factural decision making behaviour within the co-operative. For this reason, their treatment can not only be attributed to a particular consideration by juridical science. It is of course responsible for the development of the legal norms. But the legal-organizational communication system cannot be overlooked in the analytical approach of management science with respect to the co-operative organization.

In the different countries, there are very different expressions of this communication system because it is an element or a part of the respective national legal order. With respect to these details, see the literature on co-operative laws in the different legal areas.

It should be mentioned in this context, however, that the legal regulation of the co-operative society as the basis for the legal organizational communication system in the different countries refers with various intensity to the classical catalogues of co-operative → *principles* of the co-operative pioneers (the *Rochdale* principles, → *Raiffeisen* principles and principles of → *Schulze-Delitzsch*). The structural types, too, have been taken into consideration by the co-operative legislators.

V. The Interpersonal Communication System

There remains a large leeway for actors in co-operative organizations although the legal organizational communication system attributes many obligations and rights to the different units and decision makers when running the business communication system in the co-operative. This leeway must be used in accordance with the system of objectives which itself is a subject of bargaining processes, for instance between the members, the managers and eventually the workers and employees in the co-operative enterprise. The problems resulting have not been dealt with in elder co-operative science. One only referred to the neo-classic model of a profit maximizing enterprise and deduced the logical consequences of action for both the member economies as well as the member-promoting co-operative enterprise. This approach, however, is no longer sufficient in view of the modern theory of organization. In all management science today one refers to the man-models of the theory of motivation when and if the explanation of the motivation of actors and decision makers has to be recognized and the consequences have to be deduced. These motivations and attitudes of the individuals in the interaction process within both the member economies as well as the co-operative enterprise determine the interpersonal relations. These relations are also an important determinant of individual and collective decision-making procedures in the co-operative organization, because there occur manifold effects of the application of social power (*French/ Raven*). The total of these interpersonal relations and the human actors constructing them comprise the *interpersonal communication system* of the co-operative complex.

The interpersonal communication system differs from the business communication system inasfar as the latter comprises the performance and the financial relation between the microeconomic units of the co-operative complex while the former concerns the interaction and influence among the participating natural persons. In the latter point, an overlapping exists between the interpersonal communication system and the legal-organizational communication system because in both systems natural persons are involved. But here the difference is that the legal-organizational communication system indicates how the persons *should behave* while the interpersonal communication system indicates how the persons are in fact operating and acting in accordance to their own motivation. This behaviour may be in contrast to the legal behaviour norms in a marginal case.

The analysis of the interpersonal communication system widened co-operative science with a new aspect which up to now has been considered only by special sociological and psychological investigations (→ *Societal Form, Co-operative*; → *Relationship Patterns*) but which also has great importance for the modern organizational approach to co-operatives. In view of the different effects of interpersonal relations between the different units of the co-operative complex and the addressees within these units, the interpersonal relations can be classified into

- relations between members of the co-operative group;
- relations between the single member and the board members (managers) or staff members in the co-operative enterprise;
- relations between managers and relations between employees or workers, and
- relations between managers and employees or workers within the co-operative enterprise.

These different relations influence each other because the single human actor is involved in not only one but several of these relation networks. Furthermore, we have to take into consideration that the influence on behaviour made by the interpersonal relations is influencing the co-operation of the different units within the co-operative complex and insofar influences the operational communication system, too. To sum up, the interpersonal relations play an important role for the factural coordination of actors within the co-operative organization.

VI. The Management Member Information System (MMIS)

In this study, the three communication subsystems of the co-operative organization which determine and influence cooperation between the member economies and the co-operative enterprise have been explained separately. It is nevertheless evident that they are all linked to each other and influence one another. Structural modifications in the business communication system can be produced by innovative decisions in the strategic management or by technological innovations. In the legal-organizational communication system, modification may result from legal amendments motivated by the legislator's policy or by autonomous agreements of the partners. In the interpersonal communication system, such modifications may occur through a turnover of members or through changes in the attitudes and behaviour of the participants.

An integrated complex of facts, behavioural norms and interaction partners to be dealt with may result for the decision maker from the collaboration of the three subsystems. That creates a permanent informational exchange between the different actors in day to day business and in personal contacts. A net of informational relations is needed which can be constructed technically in very different ways. It must be seen separately from the original communication systems; it is only an institutional consequence of the structure built up by the three other communication systems. Nevertheless, it has its own character and an enormous instrumental importance. The problem of its optimal construction is one of the most important praxeological problems; all forms of informational relations and communication from the traditional oral and telephone communication between two or several persons to the more recent electronic communication systems, must be taken into consideration (→ *Data Processing*).

This information system should be called *management member information system* (MMIS), because it has to fulfill the same function as the well-known management information system (MIS) of enterprises and because it shall facilitate the particular communication relationship between the co-operative enterprise and the member economies. Its most important function will be to diminish the informational difference between the co-operative enterprise and the member economies in day to day business.

It is understandable that the construction of the MMIS will be influenced by the respective structural type (→ *Structural Types*). Very detailed feedback-systems may be graphically presented which describe the situation in the different structural types of the co-operative organization (*Dülfer* 1984).

VII. Further Subjects of Managerial Economics of Co-operatives

1. Structural Dimensions

A further subject of the special approach of managerial economics of co-operatives is the improvement of the typology of structural types. For this purpose, six *structural dimensions* have been formulated which are able in a manifold combination to make a precise typological classification of the single empiric case. (For details see → *Structural Types*).

2. The Success of Co-operation

A further problem concerns content and measurement of the success of co-operation in the co-operative organization (→ *Assessment of Success*). In this respect, a distinction must be made between the success of the co-operative enterprise and the co-operative success of the single member enterprise or member economy. In the case of the co-operative enterprise, a presentation of the commercial success in the sense of the commercial law exists in the balance sheet like in any other enterprise because the co-operative also is submitted to the general principles of accounting and annual financial reporting. But we saw above that the presented co-operative surplus in the balance sheet is not comparable to the usual profit of a private enterprise, instead, the surplus more or less results from the agreement of preliminary pricing between the co-operative enterprise and the member economies and from the agreement of the members with respect to feeding reserves.

Success in any kind of enterprise means the attainment of goals within the respective system of objectives. In the case of the co-operative enterprise, the success of co-operation should be measured by the realistic extent of realized promotion. The promotion of members is the dominant objective of the co-operative. This, however, requires the specification of promotion by concrete single criteria in accordance with the desires of members and the potential of the co-operative enterprise. For these very difficult problems there are until now only some academic recommendations for solutions concerning certain procedures of evaluating co-operative organizations (→ *Evaluation*).

In the same way, the success of co-operation of the single member (respectively, of the single member economy) can only be measured in accordance with the system of objectives of the member economy. In this case, it is equally difficult to find precise criteria of appraisal. For some recommendations in this field see again the evaluation methods.

3. Environment Relations

The interpretation of the co-operative organization as a socio-technical, goal-oriented, open economic system raises questions on its external relations also. In this respect, one originally began with the examination of the market relation. The more recent management science – especially in international management – is however more interested in the subject of environment relations. In this context, the external relationships of the co-operative organization with overwhelming regional and international federation structures have to be taken into consideration. The single co-operative will be confronted, too, with questions of competition structure and competition policy. The co-operation of primary co-operatives on the secondary and tertiary level is limited in some countries by regulations of antitrust laws.

VIII. Summary

The approach of managerial economics of co-operatives shows numerous aspects of internal and external relationships resulting from co-operation. They require consequently a systematization of phenomena and problems in the sense of a particular partial scientific discipline within the economic sciences.

Bibliography

Albert, Hans: Theorie und Realität, 2. ed., Tübingen 1972.
Draheim, Georg: Die Genossenschaft als Unternehmungstyp, 2.ed. Göttingen 1955.
Dülfer, Eberhard: Zielsysteme, Entscheidungsprozeß und Organisationsstruktur im kooperativen Betriebsverbund. – Eine Anwendung kybernetischer Betrachtungsweise –. In: Weißer, G. (ed.): Genossenschaften und Genossenschaftsforschung, Festschrift für *Georg Draheim*, Göttingen 1968, pp.170–195.
Dülfer, Eberhard: Organization and Management of Cooperatives. In: ZfgG, Vol.XX, Sonderheft, Sixth International Conference on Co-operative Science Gießen 1969, Göttingen 1971, pp.74–101.
Dülfer, Eberhard: Guide to Evaluation of Cooperative Organizations in Developing Countries, FAO Rome 1981 (German version, Marburg 1979).
Dülfer, Eberhard: Betriebswirtschaftslehre der Kooperative: Kommunikation und Entscheidungsbildung in Genossenschaften und vergleichbaren Organisationen, Göttingen 1984.
Grochla, Erwin: Einführung in die Organisationstheorie, Stuttgart 1978.
Hall, A.D./Fagen, R.E.: Definition of Systems. In: General Systems, Vol.1, 1956.
Helm, F.C.: The Economics of Co-operative Enterprise, London 1986.
Henzler, Reinhold: Die Genossenschaft – eine fördernde Betriebswirtschaft, Essen 1957.

Marketing Co-operatives

EDUARD MÄNDLE [J]

(see also: *Classification*; *Marketing Strategies; Rural Co-operatives*; *Supply Co-operatives*)

I. Nature and Definition of Marketing Co-operatives; II. The Functions of Marketing Co-operatives; III. The Importance of Marketing Co-operatives.

I. Nature and Definition of Marketing Co-operatives

1. The Term "Marketing Co-operative"

A marketing co-operative is a co-operative enterprise, the fundamental objective of which being the sale of members' products to other enterprises or to consumers. It is predominantly characterized through the following elements:

- It concerns a *promotional co-operative*, as it aims to support its members economically by assuming sales functions through the collective commercial enterprise (→ *Promotion Mandate*).
- The marketing co-operative is in principle a *trading company* which absorbs commodities from its independent member enterprises, if needed warehouses them, and passes them on to the purchaser usually in an unaltered condition – at most with certain typical manipulations common to the trade.
- Furthermore, it is a *consumer co-operative* as its realm of business activity is based on actual objects – grain, cocoa, potatoes, etc. Additional services are to be seen in a supplementary sense to the transfer of commodities, such as information or advice for the buyer of the commoditites.
- The *subjects of the co-operative commercial enterprise* are mostly producers, as a rule farmers and artisans, who are not in the position to carry out their final phase of commercial services because of a lack of organizational and financial preconditions. They thus entrust the co-operative enterprise of which they are both members and suppliers with processing their commercial output, or in other words, the sale of the commodities and all related services (*Identity principle*).
- Marketing co-operatives can be found both in the *primary and secondary levels* of the co-operative organization as not only is a direct promotion of the producers secured but also a promotional service for the → *consumer co-operatives* of the primary level through the co-operative centers.
- Marketing co-operatives are institutions which are specialized in marketing tasks and functions either as a wholesaler or as a retailer. It is important to note that marketing co-operatives are *primarily wholesalers* as they resell the purchased goods mostly to retailers, other wholesale operations or to producers.

In order to define the terms of a marketing co-operative, it is most important that its commercial activity takes place in two phases. The first is the *sales procurement business* by which the supply of raw materials and commodities is carried out from the co-operative members to the collective commercial enterprise. The second is the *sales return business* in which the co-operative enterprise is active in a common sales market. The former exists is such that the farmer sells his self-grown grain to the co-operative company, whereas the latter is represented when the co-operative commercial enterprise resells the purchased grain at attractive prices and conditions to the milling industry or to other wholesale grain traders. The profits attained from the sales return business can then be either directly or indirectly passed on to the members of the co-operative (→ *Assessment of Success*).

2. Types of Marketing Co-operatives

In general practise the following kinds of marketing co-operatives can be distinguished and systematically outlined as follows (→ *Classification*):

a) Marketing co-operatives not involved in processing

Marketing co-operatives which do not have a function in processing are strictly merchandising co-operatives in which only the purchasing, warehousing and marketing of commodities are carried out. Only a collection of the goods produced by the members occurs without any further processing steps. Examples in this category of marketing co-operatives include commercial co-operatives trading grain, cocoa, fruit, eggs, milk and livestock. They are also characterized as the *pure marketing co-operatives*.

b) Marketing co-operatives involved in processing

Those marketing co-operatives which undertake processing functions, which are also known as *production, commercial processing and/or fabrication co-operatives*, carry out comprehensive treatment and processing so that by the end of the process undertaken by the co-operative enterprise a completely new product will be offered in the range of the co-operative sales return business. Co-operatives involved in the processing of dairy, winegrowers', milling, livestock, fruit and vegetable products belong to this kind of specific marketing co-operative. The production activity through which the raw materials attain a higher level of consumption utility is equally important as the merchandising activity of such co-operatives.

c) Service co-operatives with marketing functions

There are quite a few co-operatives both in the developed economies and in the developing countries – primarily service co-operatives and in particular co-operative banks with financial services – which have assumed sales tasks with respect to certain goods. They naturally cannot be primarily considered marketing co-operatives for commodities; from their nature they are co-operative banks.

II. The Functions of Marketing Co-operatives

1. Range of Functions of the Marketing Co-operative

a) Function in the sales procurement business

The main function of the marketing co-operative in the sales procurement business is the promotion of its members (→ *Promotion Mandate*). This is to be seen in the sense of a permanent economic foundation or institution for the utility of each member through the marketing activities of the collective commercial enterprise. One can spot an *immediate and direct promotion* from these marketing activities in the effort to attain the highest possible disbursement for the members of the co-operative. An *intermediate and indirect promotion* in the scope of the sales procurement business results from the counseling and informational services that the co-operative commercial enterprise provides in respect to its members aside the basic sales guarantee it provides for their products (→ *Consulting*).

b) Functions in the sales return business

The business enterprise of the marketing co-operative undertakes the sales return business, which corresponds to typical merchandising and marketing functions (→ *Business Policies*).

- Within the realm of the *contact function* business relations between producers and buyers are established and maintained. This does not only lead to an improvement in market transparency for the purchaser of the product, but also to an increase in the sales possibilities for the members of the co-operative.
- Knowledge of both the market and products are transferred to partners on the market through the *information function* of the business enterprise of the co-operative in a dimension and quality which could not have been carried out by individual co-operative members.
- The *consulting function* avails itself with respect to the buyers of the products from the members' enterprises of the co-operative in that their individual needs in relation to the product application are taken into consideration. When this task is solved it ultimately leads also to a promotion of the marketing of the members' products.
- The business enterprise of the marketing co-operative fulfills the decisive marketing task of making a sensible collection of saleable commodities with

respect to particular groups of buyers through the *assortment function* (→ *Assortment Policies*).
- The *function of bulk arrangement* is seen in that relatively small sales amounts are acquired from the members by the co-operative business enterprise and added together into larger units which correspond to the wishes of the purchasers on the return business side with respect to dimensions and homogenous quality.
- The *function of distance compensation* that the marketing co-operative undertakes exists in that it bridges the geographic distances between the production in members' enterprises and the application in other enterprises or by consumers. To a certain extent the marketing co-operatives assume the transportation function themselves; this is, however, being progressively eliminated from the marketing co-operative and undertaken by forwarding companies specialized in this field. The function of bridging over distance can thus no longer be seen as a typical or exclusive task of the marketing co-operative.
- The *function of temporal compensation* describes the task of reaching a balance between the point in time of production and that of application and/or final consumption. Particularly important here is the concentrated amount of time at harvest for agricultural products as well as the continual consumption of food stuffs by the consumer, whereby warehousing provides a periodic balance. A temporal compensation is also affected by the co-operative business enterprise assuming credit functions between the time of paying the co-operative members for their products and the sale of such products.
- In the scope of the *refining and finishing function* in the sense of typical trade manipulation, certain material and substantial alterations of the merchandise take place through the co-operative business enterprise so that the commodities achieve a higher and qualitatively better consumer grade in the eyes of the purchasers. Examples in the marketing co-operative include drying and grading grain in different quality classes – and not least through initiating producer groups through marketing co-operatives, grading fruit in certain trade classes and packing and presenting the commodities adequately for the consumer.
- The *innovation function* of the business enterprise of the marketing co-operative exists in that numerous productivity and revenue-increasing innovations have been introduced in the sales return business; this is especially true for the agricultural processing co-operatives. Above all, such innovations include: development of new marketing methods, especially in export trade; the creation of new products, particularly of brand products; encouraging the production of new agricultural products, partially of regenerated industrial raw materials, in the product line of the member enterprises. The factual situation that marketing co-operatives have undertaken *service jobs* either directly for their members or non-members to achieve profit for the application of members' promotion can also be considered an innovation.
- The *function of counterbalanced market strength* through the co-operative commercial enterprise (→ *Competition*) means that the relatively small production enterprises of the members can secure an opposing marketing position in the sense of balancing the market strength of those purchasing (→ *Pricing Policy*). This brings about first and foremost a competitiveness and marketability for the products of the member enteprises so that a functional competition can be attained. It naturally becomes problematic when a supply monopoly develops through the marketing co-operatives on a regional or commodity-oriented scale.

3. Changes in the Function of Marketing Co-operatives

a) Emphasis on the retail function

Marketing co-operatives are primarily active in the developing countries as wholesale companies as they mostly sell to other production or trading enterprises. In the developed economies, however, a process in another direction can be observed (→ *Policies for Promotion*); because of the increased inclusion of business with nonmembers – household and garden markets, sales of fuel and building material to an open clientele – a stronger growth has occurred in the function of retail trade. The co-operative aspects of this development can then only be seen as sensible when profits can be attained through these sales activities which benefit the members in the economic promotion of their enterprises.

b) Development of purchasing co-operatives to marketing and full service co-operatives

Originally, the commercial co-operative above all others was structured primarily for the collective purchase of commodities at attractive prices in larger quantities, hence they were called *buying or purchasing co-operatives* (→ *Supply Co-operatives*). In the course of the modern market development these types of co-operatives, above all in the fields of food, toys, shoes, electronics, sporting goods and natural health products, have undergone an alteration in their nature, resulting in an *assumption of marketing functions* in an increased and almost dominating dimension and further service-oriented tasks for the member enterprises. The retail traders organized co-operatively no longer appear isolated on the sales market but rather as a recognized group distinguished through homogenous organizational characteristics. This has substantially strengthened the sales effectivity and is expressed above all through commonly offered assortments (→ *Assortment Policies*), identical advertising and public relations, and local policy. As the co-operative commmercial enterprise has undertaken further tasks with respect to the member retail traders in the form of business consultation, financing, and the education of managers and staff, the designation *full service co-operative* (→ *Structural Types*) is completely justified as it describes purchasing and marketing activities as well as additional services.

III. The Importance of Marketing Co-operatives

1. Marketing Co-operatives in Developed Economies

In the developed economies, the importance of the marketing co-operatives, which almost exclusively appear in the agricultural sector, varies considerably.

- The pure *one purpose marketing co-operative* in which a particular product of the members is sold to a general market has not attained special importance, whereby differences do exist from product to product and region to region. Marketing co-operatives for grain, eggs, fruits and vegetables do not play a dominant role, whereas those involved in marketing live-stock and meat have in part attained considerable market shares.
- The *marketing co-operatives involved in processing* and the *co-operative banks involved in commodities trade* (→ *Multi-Use Credit Co-operatives*) on the one hand, have not attained a leading position in the marketing business of their member's products; they have, on the other hand, shown very large market shares in purchasing capital, investment and consumer goods for both their members and, in ever-growing dimensions, non-members. As the purchasers of these products usually have a possible choice before their decision to buy in respect to the offers of other competitors, the co-operative commercial enterprise should in no way only be seen as a distributor of goods for its members; it must rather also develop marketing activites to a certain extent. In this sense they can also be considered marketing co-operatives, whereby they do not sell the products from their members' enterprises but rather goods that they have purchased from other trade or production companies.

2. Marketing Co-operatives in Developing Countries

As the social, economic and agricultural situations in the developing countries deviate drastically from each other, it is difficult to construe generally valid statements about the nature and importance of the marketing co-operatives (→ *Policies for Promotion*). In spite of this it is possible to recognize several characteristic developments by differentiating strongly by region.

a) Nature of marketing co-operatives in developing countries

Marketing co-operatives in the developing countries are promotional and consumer co-operatives, either specialized or serving multiple purposes, the members of which are principally agricultural producers (→ *Rural Co-operatives*). The general developmental tendency is clearly in the direction of multiple purpose co-operatives in the sense of a combination of marketing and credit functions, marketing and processing functions for members' products, and the purchasing function of semi-durable goods for the members. Above all, the following *instruments for the realization of members' promotion* come into consideration:

- *Price stabilization and the reduction of price variance* for the harvested products and the realization of high sales prices;
- Limitation of the market position of *foreign intermediaries*;
- Establishment of a *network of trustworthy and steady buyers* of the products from members' enterprises;
- Provision of *credits for members*;
- Construction of *warehouse, transport and production facilities and capacities* for processing products produced on the members' enterprises;
- Exertion of influence on the *quality of the agricultural production* on members' enterprises;
- Realization of a *co-operative and commercial way of thinking* among members as well as increasing their professional and general education levels.

It is fairly easy to see that these intentions of the marketing co-operative can only be carried out in reality with great effort. Above all it is very difficult to keep up with the pricing policy of the competition. The company is not large enough to be able to exercise influence on the market, it lacks the capital for investment in such purposes as warehousing, transport and production, and the co-operative management and professional staff suffers from a lack of experience, knowledge and quality.

b) Incidence of marketing co-operatives in the developing countries.

In the regional distribution of marketing co-operatives in the developing countries, a clear concentration can be observed in the *African countries south of the Sahara*, above all in the West African countries which were previously British colonies or belonged to the British Empire. Over half of the co-operatives there are marketing co-operatives which have pre-

dominantly specialized in exporting agricultural products, particularly cocoa, palm seed, coffee, cotton and tobacco. The establishment of such co-operatives structured around agricultural export and many of the marketing co-operatives shouldered by small-scale farmers date back to the 1920s. Because of targeted governmental support, a steady increase in the number of co-operative companies and co-operative members first happened after World War II. Marketing co-operatives hardly play a role in the other remaining regions of Africa.
This is also the case for *Latin America* (→ *Development, Latin America*) where an opportunity for marketing activities could exist in respect to such agricultural products bound for export like bananas, unprocessed sugar, cocoa, coffee, cotton and beef. Although the marketing co-operatives have been very successful in certain regional, internal markets, they have a low overall importance in the Latin American countries for the following reasons:
State trade monopolies exist for the export of agricultural goods so that those co-operatives involved in export trade do not have a chance; large-scale commercial agricultural structures exist in South America which oppose the establishment of co-operatives; there is a strong vertical interdependence between the export companies and the large-scale agricultural operations.
In *Asia* (→ *Development, South Asia*) (→ *Development, South-East Asia*), relatively few marketing co-operatives are present, although in this particular area there are numerous small-scale farming structures already in existence for which the collective marketing of agricultural products would seem sensible. In India and Pakistan, the market share of the agrarian marketing co-operatives is exceptionally low on the total volume of the individual markets. This can be traced back to the traditionally high levels of self-provision in the agricultural sector and the scepticism many farmers harbor to activities from organizations which are supported by the state. Agricultural co-operatives exist in Indonesia for copra, rubber, pepper, coffee and tea. Israel is the only country in the Asiatic region in which marketing co-operatives, particularly for agricultural goods earmarked for export, have attained a strong position.
Marketing co-operatives also exist in *Oceania*; a marketing co-operative for copra was found on the Fiji Islands as early as 1919. Agricultural marketing co-operatives have reached a dominating market position in part on individual island groups in Oceania up to the present; these have been multiple purpose co-operatives which also sell their members' products, as well as consumer co-operatives.
When one realizes the great economic importance of the agricultural sector as a whole in the developing countries, the market share of the marketing co-operatives appears extraordinarily low. This is true for the number of co-operative members, the capital resources of each commercial enterprise and the economic influence. One can only speak of a relative importance of the marketing co-operatives in an entire national economy in states of West Africa, on certain islands in Oceania and in individual Latin American countries (→ *Policies for Promotion*).

Bibliography

Bergmann, Theodor: Die Genossenschaftsbewegung in Indien – Geschichte, Leistungen, Aufgaben. Veröffentlichungen der Deutschen Genossenschaftskasse, vol. 10, Frankfurt/ Main 1971.
Buddeberg, Hans: Betriebslehre des Binnenhandels, Wiesbaden 1959.
Elisseleff, K.: Die Absatzgenossenschaften in Nordamerika. Quellen und Studien des Instituts für Genossenschaftswesen an der Universität Münster, vol. IV, Neuwied 1951.
Endeley, E.M.L.: Die Aufgaben des Genossenschaftswesens in den afrikanischen Ländern, in: ZfgG, vol. 11 (1961), pp. 167 ff.
Ghanie Ghaussy, A.: Das Genossenschaftswesen in den Entwicklungsländern, Freiburg im Breisgau 1964.
Kunze, J.: Bezugs- und Absatzgenossenschaften, in: Handwörterbuch des Genossenschaftswesens, Wiesbaden 1980, cols. 165ff.
Ohm, Hans: Die Genossenschaft und ihre Preispolitik. Quellen und Studien des Instituts für Genossenschaftswesen an der Universität Münster, vol. VIII., Karlsruhe 1955.
Schiedel, E.: Leistungswirtschaftliches Innovationspotential landwirtschaftlicher Absatzgenossenschaften. Veröffentlichungen des Forschungsinstituts für Genossenschaftswesen an der Universität Erlangen-Nürnberg, vol. 28, Nürnberg 1988.
Tietz, Bruno: Absatz und Absatzlehre, in: Handwörterbuch der Betriebswirtschaft, 4th ed., Stuttgart 1974, cols 22 ff.
Weber, Wilhelm: Absatzgenossenschaften in Entwicklungsländern. Marburger Schriften zum Genossenschaftswesen, series B, vol.1, Marburg 1966.

Marketing Strategies of Co-operatives

JERKER NILSSON

(see also: *Marketing*; *Diversification Strategies*; *Pricing Policy*; *Classification*; *Business Policies*; *Managerial Economics*)

I. The Concept of Marketing; II. Classifications of Markets and Co-operatives; III. Consumer and Supply Co-operatives' Marketing to Members; IV. Consumer and Supply Co-operatives' Marketing to Non-Members; V. Other Types of Co-operative Marketing.

I. The Concept of Marketing

The key to the marketing concept is *coordination*. An organization engages in marketing to improve the coordination of activities between itself and its com-

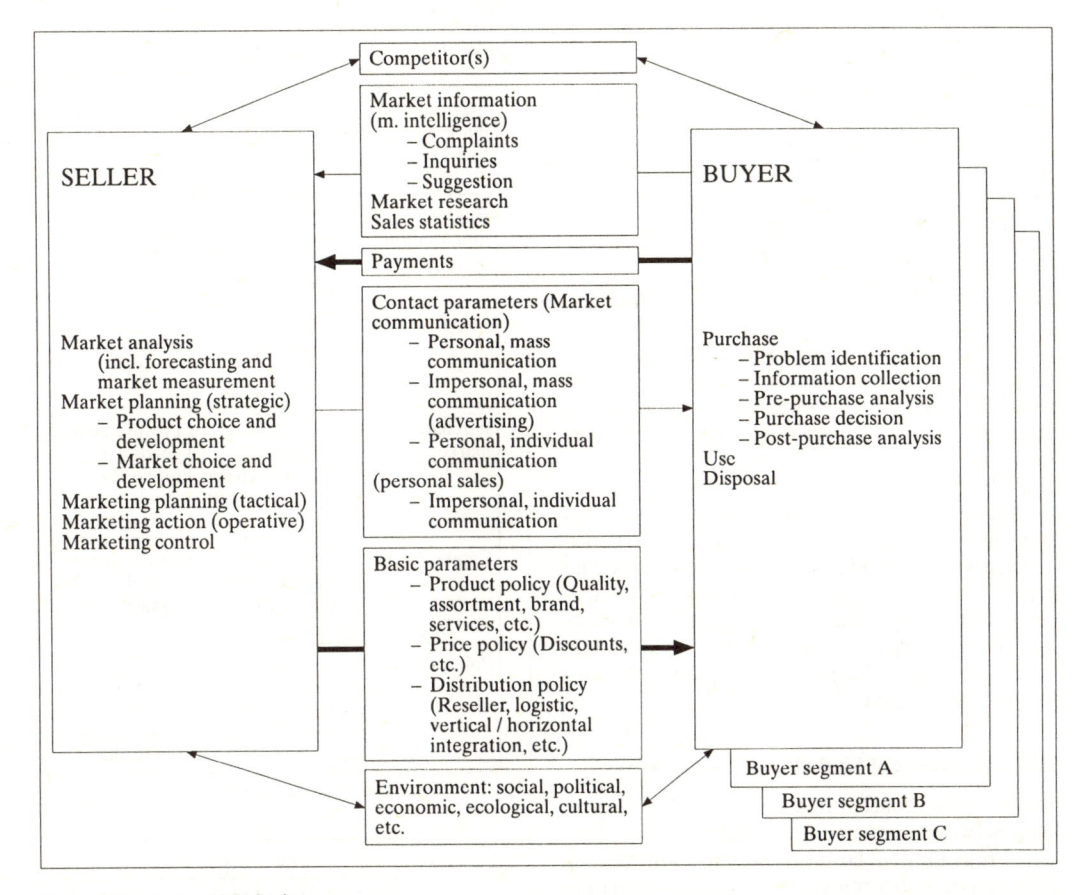

```
┌──────────────────────────────────────────────────────────────────────────────┐
│                         ┌────────────────┐                                   │
│                      ┌─▶│ Competitor(s)  │◀─┐                                │
│                      │  └────────────────┘  │                                │
│                      │  ┌──────────────────┐│                                │
│                      │  │ Market information││                               │
│                      │  │  (m. intelligence)││                               │
│ ┌──────────┐         │  │   – Complaints   ││       ┌──────────┐             │
│ │          │◀────────┼──│   – Inquiries    │◀───────│          │             │
│ │  SELLER  │         │  │   – Suggestion   ││       │  BUYER   │             │
│ │          │         │  │ Market research  ││       │          │             │
│ │          │         │  │ Sales statistics ││       │          │             │
│ │          │         │  └──────────────────┘│       │          │             │
│ │          │◀────────┼──│    Payments      │◀───────│          │             │
│ │          │         │  └──────────────────┘│       │          │             │
```

```
Figure 1: Concepts of Marketing
```

SELLER

Market analysis
  (incl. forecasting and
  market measurement)
Market planning (strategic)
  – Product choice and
    development
  – Market choice and
    development
Marketing planning (tactical)
Marketing action (operative)
Marketing control

Contact parameters (Market communication)
  – Personal, mass communication
  – Impersonal, mass communication (advertising)
  – Personal, individual communication (personal sales)
  – Impersonal, individual communication

Basic parameters
  – Product policy (Quality, assortment, brand, services, etc.)
  – Price policy (Discounts, etc.)
  – Distribution policy (Reseller, logistic, vertical / horizontal integration, etc.)

Environment: social, political, economic, ecological, cultural, etc.

BUYER

Purchase
  – Problem identification
  – Information collection
  – Pre-purchase analysis
  – Purchase decision
  – Post-purchase analysis
Use
Disposal

Buyer segment A
Buyer segment B
Buyer segment C

Figure 1: Concepts of Marketing

mercial environment. Marketing is therefore a concept describing a relationship between two or more actors.

Coordination between an organization and its environment has, however, no meaning. The actors themselves are not being coordinated, but rather their activities. Sellers must see to it that their sales activities are coordinated with the buyers' purchasing activities. Their advertising should be coordinated with buyers' reading habits. Their price policy must be coordinated with the price considerations being taken by the market.

A high *degree of coordination* between activities means that resources (goods, services, information, capital) which constitute outputs from one activity are well suited as inputs for other activities. Coordination is therefore dependent on the characteristics of the resources concerned (outputs/inputs). In an advertising campaign, e.g., it is necessary that its message, design, media and timing (outputs from decision-making processes) match the interests, habits and other preconditions of the recipients, so that they use the advertisements as inputs in their reading activities.

The expression "well-suited" means that the latter activity can be carried out with a high degree of goal achievement. A seller has created good coordination with the consumer when he is experiencing a high degree of need satisfaction while using seller's products. This is positive for the seller in that the consumers can be expected to show a high degree of buying probability, a willingness to pay a higher price, repeat purchases from the same seller again and recommend both the product and the seller to others.

As is the case for all business activity, there are different planning levels, viz., *strategic, tactical and operative marketing* (*Seuster* 1986). Strategic marketing, or *market planning*, refers to changes of the structural characteristics of the firm (→ Strategy Planning). Examples are product development, market choice, capacity changes and competence development. Tactical marketing, or *marketing planning*, refers to actions taken within the existing structure such as product modification, advertising, quality control and market analyses. Operative marketing refers to the current *marketing actions*, i.e., the implementation of the marketing plan.

The two primary components of the coordination

concept are *influence* and *adaptation*. On the one hand, the firm influences the market with the help of market communication – advertising, personal sales, product presentation, sales promotion, etc. – in order to make the market conform to the firm's supply of products. On the other hand, the firm adapts to the market through such mechanisms as → *pricing*, product design, choice of distribution channels, etc.

Adaptation and influence are not mutually exclusive, but, rather, complementary. An actor who wishes to influence another should adapt itself to the other in order to increase his degree of influence. The seller who designs his advertising so that it appeals to the recipients has a greater impact. The reverse is just as true – the seller who has been able to influence his markets well can conduct more effective adaptive measures.

It is obvious from this discussion that the field of marketing is a very wide one, including elements from many other disciplines such as economics, sociology, psychology and political science. There are no generally accepted divisions into sub-fields, especially considering the fact that the subject of marketing finds itself in a period of rapid development. Figure 1 gives a general idea of the contents of the subject. (Cf. *Kotler* 1984).

II. Classifications of Markets and Co-operatives

Marketing is a concept that deals with the relationships between an organization and its environment. Every organization, however, interacts with various segments of its environment – consumers, other organizations, authorities, etc. An organization thus works with a variety of markets, which must be treated with different types of marketing. *Figure 2* shows a classification of markets.

The marketing concept is applicable for all these types of firm/market relations. The literature has, however, a skewed distribution with an emphasis on (1) the consumer market and (2) the buyer organization market, with particular concentration on the former. The other categories are only sporadically covered in literature, with the possible exception of (4) the purchase market. Most often, the marketing concept is associated only with consumer and buyer organization markets. Likewise, this review is also limited to these two categories.

The principles for marketing in co-operative organizations vary also according to the type of co-operative, e.g. a consumer co-operative has a different type of sales to consumers (members) than a producer co-operative. In accordance with Figure 3, four types of co-operatives are suggested, classified on the basis of two criteria – the organization's role for its members and the type of owner-members.

This division into business forms is parallel to the division into market types (Figure 2). Each one of the respective market type actors can function as a

	Market Type	Market Actors	Market's role organization
1	Consumer market	Individuals and household shopping	Sales of outputs from the organization's production
2	Buyer organization market	Firms, purchasing for resale or processing	Sales of outputs from the organization's production
3	Labour market	Individuals, selling their labour	Procurement of labour as an input to the production
4	Purchase market	Goods and service producing firms selling products	Procurement of goods and services as inputs to the production
5	Capital market	Sources of capital (banks, etc.)	Procurement of capital as inputs to the production
6	Political market	Politicians, government authorities, the general public	Acquiring political support for the organization's production

Figure 2: Classification of market types

Organization's role for owner	Type of owner – member		
	Individuals/ households	Private businessmen	Authorities
Procurement of operative goods and services: backward integration	Consumer co-operative	Supply co-operative	Public organization
Disposal of goods and services: forward integration	Labour co-operative	Marketing co-operative	
Capital investment	Capitalistic firm		

Figure 3: Classification of business forms

principal for a firm. If the principals are owners of capital the firm is capitalistic; if the principals are public bodies the firm is a public organization. If individuals and entrepreneurs seek to satisfy their functional needs by becoming principals, the firm is a co-operative in one of its four forms.

As the presentation is limited to four types of co-operatives and two types of markets, eight relationships are analyzed – *see Figure 4*.

Marketing organization		Market Types	
Name	Example	Consumers	Buying org.
Consumer co-op.	Grocery store	A; A*	B
Supply co-op.	Farmer inputs	C	D; D*
Labour co-op.	Workshop	E	F
Marketing co-op.	Slaughterhouse	G	H

Figure 4: Types of marketing relationships in the analysis

Two of these relationships, namely A and D, describe relationships between a co-operative and its members. In these cases, marketing differs considerably from the conventional marketing described in the literature, because the interests of the firm and the members coincide – the task of the firm is to promote member interests. The existing literature more frequently / almost extensively provides examples of firms working for interests in conflict with buyers' interests.

The marketing carried out in relationships A and D purports to create a high degree of coordination for the buyers/members on their own conditions, i.e., coordination must be optimal from the point of view of the member. Marketing in the other relationships is aimed at creating coordination between consumers and purchase organizations while maintaining optimal conditions for the seller.

Hence, the presentation is divided into consumer and supply co-operatives' marketing to members (A and D -Section III) and non-members (A* and D* – Section IV). Analyses of other types of co-operative marketing (B, C, E, F, G, H) follow in Section V.

III. Consumer and Supply Co-operatives' Marketing to Members

Marketing in relation to members in → *consumer* and → *supply co-operatives* differs from standard marketing practices which are based on the assumption that buyer and seller have conflicting interests. Such standard practices explain how the marketing actor can use that conflict in his own best interest.

Such conflicts do not exist in the relationship between the co-operative and its members. The members own the co-operative in order to satisfy certain interests, whereby the goals of the co-operative are identical with member interests. Co-operative marketing is therefore aimed at creating optimal coordination from the point of view of the members.

The view that co-operatives should not have marketing activities in relation to members is sometimes put forward with the argument that marketing is a capitalistic phenomenon (*Cobia & Anderson* 1989, p. 192). When marketing is conceived as coordination, this view is, however, incorrect. Every firm must make decisions about product choice, assortment, quality, service, prices, etc.

The rationale for the existence of co-operatives can explain the relationship between consumer/supply co-operatives and their members. The reason why people join together in co-operative organizations is that the market mechanism under certain conditions does not function satisfactorily for these people.

Co-operative organization represents a partial vertical integration of members' activities (*Ollila* 1989), either forward or backward (Figure 2). This means that co-operative activities act to modify the market mechanism. The coordinations between the co-operative and its members takes place with the help of a combination of the market mechanism and organizational control (coordination by feedback and coordination by plan).

In order for the market mechanism to function perfectly, a number of conditions must be met. Neoclassical economics assumes that the individual has perfect knowledge and maximizes his utility ("Homo Oeconomicus"), that there are a large number of buyers and sellers, and that supply and demand are homogeneous (→ *Competition*). These are the conditions which must prevail for a perfect balance of power between buyer and seller to exist so that both can attain maximum goal achievement (→ *Pricing Policy*).

In situations where reality deviates from these conditions (cf. "Homo Cooperativus"), a disparity in the power balance between buyer and seller arises. In such situations the application of the market mechanism gives rise to *market failures*. The coordination is executed according to the terms of the stronger party, while the weaker party suffers. In such cases, the weak might form a co-operative. They join together to create a countervailing power and to improve their power position. The market mechanism is complemented with internal regulation, contracts, quotas, etc.

There are a large number of potential market failures, e.g.:

a) There is no seller of a product, or the buyer is uncertain if there is any seller, or he is unsure of the seller's conditions.
b) If there is only one seller, he can exploit his monopoly position.
c) Geographical, economic, or other obstacles might prevent the buyer from coming into contact with the sellers.
d) If a seller can restrict the buyer through economic, psychological, or other means, a monopoly situation is created.

e) The buyer might experience high transaction costs.
f) If the buyer is pressed for time, the seller can exploit this.
g) If the buyer has difficulty in assessing the quality and quantity of the products, the seller is able to deceive.
h) If the buyer has limited knowledge, money, abilities and other resources, the seller can exploit this.
i) If the buyer is unable to assess the reliability of the seller, the seller has an incentive to cheat.
j) If the buyer is unclear as to his own needs and choice criteria, the seller can mislead him.
k) The buyer might perceive a need for a public good which, given its nature, cannot be supplied by the market.

These types of market failures (→ *Institutional Economics*) are characterized by a lack of priority given to the buyer in the seller/buyer coordination. Instead, either there is no coordination at all, i.e., the buyer receives no products, or the coordination takes place on the seller's terms, i.e., high prices and poor products.

When buyers establish a co-operative, they can ensure that coordination takes place on their own terms. Hence, co-operative marketing to members eradicates the conditions which led to the market failures. Therefore, the following characteristics can be isolated in co-operative marketing (*Nilsson* 1983).

1) The co-operative eliminates not only the risk that no seller of the product exists (points a and k above), but also the risk that the seller exhibits monopolistic behavior (b, c, d, inter alia).
2) The co-operative works to see to it that members' inputs in their purchases (prices, searching, risk reduction, etc.) should be the lowest possible, given a certain return in the form of product quality, level of service, and other utility values (all points).
3) Likewise, the co-operative ensures that members' benefits (quality, service, etc.) are as great as possible given certain resource inputs (price, transport costs, searching, etc.) (all points).
4) Due to its vertical integrative nature, the co-operative can establish routines that reduce transaction costs (e), e.g., electronic ordering, billing and payment systems, limited assortment, and sales volume contracts. The lower costs are passed on to the members in the form of lower prices.
5) The co-operative can adjust its product assortment according to the limited resources of its members, for example, only sell such products which the buyer needs, irrespective of the buyer's ability to assess that need (f, g, h, i).
6) The co-operative can use advertising and other forms of communication to help its members develop a better overview, analytical capacity, etc. (f, g, h, i), (*Vilstrup & Groves* 1989).

7) The co-operative can adapt its activities to members' diffusely perceived needs and other faults in their goal articulation. This can be done through the choice and design of products which satisfy member needs, even if these are poorly articulated (j).
8) Closely related to this is the ability of the co-operative, through communication with members (advertisement, personal sales, etc.) to influence members to better analyze their needs, be more self-critical, place greater demands, etc. (j).
9) The vertical integrative nature of co-operatives affects the way market information is dealt with. The capitalist firm uses sales statistics and market analyses as the dominant information sources (buyers' actual behavior "exit" according to *Hirschman*). This type of information is also relevant for the co-operative firm, however, in addition, member opinions, wishes, demands and other member-initiated information is of great importance; buyers "voice" their desired behavior (*Hirschman*). This can have consequences for the product policy (→ *Diversification Strategies*), advertising, location, etc. (mostly g, h, i and j). This member information is also necessary for the co-operative to produce public goods (k).
10) The firm can influence the environment of its members so that it is in better harmony with its members' conditions. For example, the co-operative can engage in political lobbying to achieve regulation limiting the capitalistic firms' ability to act exploitatively (k).
11) In terms of inluencing the members' environment, the mere existence of a co-operative has a positive effect on both member and non-member relations to the competing capitalist firms. The fact that a co-operative exists forces the competition to behave less exploitatively. (a, b, c, d inter alia).

It is not possible to determine in which proportions these elements are included in actual co-operative marketing. This varies from case to case, depending on how members perceive their needs. One co-operative can work with a low price profile, with a limited assortment, low service level, etc., while another can have a high quality profile with ensuing high costs and high prices.

IV. Consumer and Supply Co-operatives' Marketing to Non-Members

Consumer and supply co-operatives can use different strategies in relation to consumers and buying organizations which are not members (*Nilsson* 1982; *LeVay* 1983):

1. They refuse to sell to non-members. The consumer or buying organization wanting to buy must first become a member. This is the ideal type of co-operative in its purest form.
2. They sell to non-members but on conditions which are identical to those of the capitalistic forms. The co-operative does not allow non-members any member benefits and transfers the surplus extracted from such exchanges to members. This model is applicable under certain conditions: (a) if the products sold are attractive to non-members so that a surplus can be extracted, (b) if the co-operative has unused capacity, (c) if there are no moral objections among members about making a profit from non-members, (d) if non-member needs are the same as members; otherwise there is the risk that the co-operative will adapt itself to the needs of non-members to the disadvantage of members.
3. They sell to non-members and let them enjoy the same advantages as members to a certain extent. The arguments in favour of this solution are a combination of those in alternatives 2 and 4.
4. They sell to non-members and let them have exactly the same advantages as members. This model is one of degenerated cooperativism, but it is not unusual as an actual type. The following factors support this solution: (a) if the members find it morally objectionable to exploit non-members, (b) if co-operative activities involve significant economies of scale, so that an expansion of activities means a lower cost to members (c) if non-members would not choose to buy at the co-operative if the conditions were worse. The risks are obvious: democracy can hardly function well; membership loses its meaning; the financial solidity of the firm suffers; activities are split up between heterogenous segments.

V. Other Types of Co-operative Marketing

At the tactical and operational level the marketing to consumers and buying organizations carried out by labour and marketing co-operatives differs only slightly from standard marketing practices, that is, those of the capitalistic firm. Both these types of co-operatives attempt to achieve coordination with the market on their own conditions. They try to influence buyers to adjust their behavior in order to receive higher prices and to implement low-cost adjustment behavior on their own part.

There are, however, differences between these types of co-operatives and the capitalistic firm in strategic respects. The co-operatives have limitations in terms of input factors, which means that they have difficulties in undertaking certain adaptive measures. The co-operatives have, at least in the short run, given inputs in the form of raw materials (marketing co-operatives) or labour (labour co-operatives) supplied by members. They cannot change suppliers, location, raw material base, industry or the scope of activities as quickly as the capitalistic firm.

The labour co-operative (→ *Joint-production Co-operatives*) has a staff of members whose competence and other qualifications are the basis of all activity in the firm. In the event that changes in demand occur which require different types of competence, it is not possible to fire staff and hire new. The co-operatives' first option is to train existing staff and recruit new workers with the requisite qualifications. A second option is to collaborate with other firms – purchasing goods and services from others, going into joint ventures, etc.

The marketing co-operative finds itself in a similar situation. It cannot stop acquiring products from its suppliers, just because demand is changing. The farmer-owned dairy cannot go into another industry; it must continue being a dairy. All other types of resources (personnel, know how, machines and plants), however, are variable (*Bateman* 1976, pp. 199 ff.).

The fact that co-operatives are bound to the inputs they receive from their members means that these firms cannot easily undertake structural measures to adapt to demand, which is changeable and heterogeneous. Input dependency means that there are limitations on the development of new products, production techniques, administrative techniques, etc. Depending on the specific circumstances, coordination with markets consequently becomes worse. The firm must compensate for this with lower prices, or by merely intensified influence in the form of advertising, personal sales, etc.

The co-operative's ties to its members can bring with it other handicaps in relation to the capitalistic firm. Besides the input limitation discussed above, there are also geographical, capital and leadership limitations.

The geographical handicap consists of the inability of the firm to be located far away from its members. It cannot locate itself in a country with favorable tax laws, in a region with low wages or an otherwise attractive labour force, or near a market of significant demand concentration. The co-operative thereby incurs the risk of being less able to adapt itself to market conditions. On the other hand, geographical proximity to members means that the degree of coordination with them is high.

A co-operative can not quickly make substantial increases in its risk capital, as the company can. There are also limits on the ability of the co-operative to merge with or have otherwise strong financial ties to capitalistic firms without this leading to negative consequences for members' legitimate influence. This means that the co-operative is limited in its ability to implement structural change to adapt its activities to significant changes in demand.

The board of the co-operative is comprised of people, elected by and from its members – farmers, consumers, fishermen, etc. These people may be very competent in managing their own activities, but these qualifications may not always be the right ones with which to control modern industrial or trading firms (*Cobia & Anderson* 1989).

Bibliography

Bateman, D.I.: Agricultural Marketing: A Review of the Literature of Marketing Theory and of Selected Applications, Journal of Agricultural Economics, Vol. 27, No. 1 (1976), pp. 171–225.
Cobia, David W. & Bruce Anderson: Product and Pricing Strategies, Co-operatives in Agriculture (ed. D. Cobia), Englewood Cliffs, NJ 1989, pp. 174–194.
Hirschman, Albert O.: Exit, voice and loyalty, (Harvard Univ. Press), Cambridge 1970.
Kotler, Philip: Marketing Management. Analysis, Planning and Control, Englewood Cliffs, NJ 1984.
LeVay, Clare: Agricultural Co-operative Theory: A Review, Journal of Agricultural Economics, Vol. 34, No. 1, (1983), pp. 1–44.
Nilsson, Jerker: The Consumer Co-operative's Alternative Strategies Towards Non-Members. Co-operative Systems Development, Stockholm 1982.
Nilsson, Jerker: Det konsumentkooperativa företaget (The Consumer Co-operative Enterprise), Stockholm 1983.
Ollila, Petri: Coordination of Supply and Demand in the Dairy Marketing System – With Special Emphasis on the Potential Role of Farmer Co-operatives as Coordinating Institutions, Journal of Agricultural Science in Finland, Vol. 61, No.3 (1989).
Seuster, Horst: Strategic Planning and Strategic Control of Enterprises as Tasks of Co-operative Management, Co-operatives Today, Geneva 1986.
Vilstrup, Richard H. & Frank W. Groves: Communications, Co-operatives in Agriculture (ed. D. Cobia), Englewood Cliffs, NJ 1989, pp. 339–359.

Marshall, Alfred (1842–1924)

THOMAS BROCKMEIER

(see also: *Classic and Neo-classic Contributions; Mill; Walras and Pareto*)

Alfred Marshall was born in a London suburb on 26 July 1842. Being Professor of Political Economy at the University of Cambridge from 1885 to 1908 (having *Pigou* and *Keynes* among his pupils), he became the founder of the famous Cambridge School of Economics. Some even call him "the great father figure of English economics" (*Hutchinson*, p.62). His major work, "The Principles of Economics" (1890), was the most influential book on economics of its era, serving as *the* textbook for generations of students. ("The Principles" were the first volume of a projected two-volume treatise; the second volume was to cover foreign trade, money, trade fluctuations, taxation, and aims for the future, but it never appeared.)

Marshall's father was a cashier in the Bank of England who intended his son for the ministry. He taught him Hebrew and directed him to the classics at an early age. "(He even) prohibited the mathematics which Alfred loved. Nevertheless, when his father endeavored to send him to Oxford on a scholarship which would have led to the church, the son rebelled. With the aid of a loan from an uncle and another scholarship, he went to Cambridge" (*Lekachman*, p.265), entering St.John's College in 1862.

After being elected to a Fellowship in 1865 (the reason being his brilliant performance in mathematics), *Marshall* began studying the philosophical foundations and moral basis for human behaviour and social organization. He developed an interest in different subjects, such as metaphysics, psychology and, finally, economics. In 1867, he went on a trip to Germany where he met several economists (among them *Wilhelm Roscher*, a leading exponent of the German Historical School of economics).

Upon his return to Cambridge in 1868, *Marshall* became a College Lecturer in Moral Sciences, specializing in Political Economy.

"The reason for his shift (to economics), a little unusual for a man who had expected to make his career in molecular physics, was the not uncommon Victorian wish to do good. *Marshall* wished to end poverty; much more, he hoped to lead the poor to live noble lives. The study of political economy, he hoped, would improve the quality of human existence" (*Lekachman*, p. 265/266).

Marshall stood up for those parts of the population that were less well off and came into contact with the British co-operative movement. In his opening-speech to the Co-operative Congress in Ipswich in 1889 he pointed out his confession to the social ideals of the co-operative movement and explained how he, on the basis of economics, wanted to develop behavioural norms that could be of practical use for the members of the movement in their daily life.

In 1877, the celibacy rules then being in force required *Marshall* to give up his Fellowship because of his marriage to *Mary Paley* who was lecturer in economics in Newham College and had been a student of his. So he left Cambridge to become Principal of the University College at Bristol, holding a chair in Political Economy.

In 1879, his first book, "The Economics of Industry", was published, making him respected as a very promising economist. When *Jevons*, together with →*Walras* and *Menger* one of the three great "fathers of marginalism", died in 1881, *Marshall* became the British leader of the new scientific school of economics.

In 1884, the death of *Henry Fawcett* (a pupil of → *J.St.Mill*), opened up the opportunity for *Marshall* to return to Cambridge, becoming *Fawcett's* successor as Professor of Political Economy. (*Fawcett*, in his "Manual of Political Economy", dedicated one chapter solely to co-operatives, using them as an example to demonstrate "how intimately Political Economy is connected with the practical questions of life", *Hoppe*, page 27, translation by the author.)

Marshall's work in economics was rooted in his stringent mathematical training, but he was also strongly influenced by utilitarianism, evolutionism, and German idealism. Consequently, his economics are a complex combination of the application of theoretical-mathematical tools on the one hand and norms of moral consciousness as well as occupation with the social problems of his time on the other. He tried to make use of the theoretical instruments in economic analysis in a way to most effectively contribute to economic and social progress. Even though to *Marshall* economics meant analyzing aspects of human behaviour open to pecuniary influences, he stressed the human desire for social approbation and the pleasures of skillful activity.

Most likely, he started on economics from *J. St. Mill's* "Principles of Political Economy" (1848). In the 1870s and early 1880s, his readings covered economic development and socialism, much of the literature in German. He was not too interested in the work of *Walras*, and →*Pareto* he almost totally ignored – an interesting and, simultaneously, somewhat surprising fact since *Pareto*, together with *Marshall* (and, among others, *Irving Fisher*, *Eugen von Böhm-Bawerk*) belonged to the "second generation" of marginalists. *Marshall* held his chair in Cambridge until his retirement in 1908. On 13 July 1924, being 81 years of age, he died at Balliol Croft which had been his Cambridge home for a long time.

Bibliography

Blaug, Mark: Economic Theory in Retrospect, Cambridge 1985.
Heilbroner, Robert L.: The Wordly Philosophers, New York 1980.
Hoppe, Michael: Die klassische und die neoklassische Theorie der Genossenschaften, Berlin 1976.
Hutchinson, T.W.: A Review of Economic Doctrines, Oxford 1953.
Starbatty, Joachim: Die englischen Klassiker der Nationalökonomie, Darmstadt 1985.
Stigler, G.J./Coase, Ronald: Alfred Marshall's Lectures on Progress and Poverty, in: Journal of Law and Economics 12 (1), April 1969, pp.181–226.
Whitaker, J.K.: Alfred Marshall, in: The New Palgrave, Vol. 3, London 1987, pp.350–363.

MATCOM

GABRIELE ULLRICH

(see also: *United Nations System*; *Education, Africa*; *Education, Asia*; *Education, Latin America*)

I. MATCOM – an ILO Trade Mark; II. Present Structure and Activities of the ILO MATCOM Project; III. The Project's Development; IV. MATCOM – Training Material; V. MATCOM – Methodology; VI. Review and Outlook.

I. MATCOM – an ILO Trade Mark

MATCOM has become so well-known as a term in quite a number of developing countries that people often do not know anymore that it stands for "Materials and Techniques for Co-operative management Training", a project which the Co-operative Branch of the International Labour Office (ILO) launched in January 1978 with financial support of the Swedish Government. It was meant as a response to the need for practical, job-oriented training in co-operative management.

Already during the 60's, co-operative education and training was one of the crucial issues in the co-operative promotion of ILO. This was endorsed by the ILO Recommendation No. 127 "Concerning the Role of Co-operatives in the Economic and Social Development of Developing Countries". It devoted a special section to education and training under the Chapter "Methods of implementation of policy concerning co-operatives" being equally important as legislation and aid to co-operatives. The lessons learned from ILO's technical cooperation projects and consulations with co-operative policy-makers, lead to the preparation of the ILO/MATCOM Project.

In 1978, the activities were started with a regional focus on Asia and technically on the design and introduction of materials for co-operative management trainers. Since these first beginnings the regional activities were extended to Africa, Latin America, the Pacific and Arab countries. Recently also European countries started using the materials for co-operative management training. Manuals and so-called "learning elements" were developed on over 50 different subjects and in about 35 languages for the use of trainers as well as for self-study of committee members and management.

II. Present Structure and Activities of the ILO MATCOM Project

The ILO inter-regional project MATCOM was first located at the ILO International Centre for Advanced Technical and Vocational Training in Turin. The Centre provided MATCOM with important facilities for the design, illustration, editing and reproduction facilities. Furthermore, the Centre offered the possibility for some training courses using and testing the MATCOM materials. However, due to the rapid expansion of the project and the limited facilities of the Centre, in 1980, MATCOM was transferred to the Vienna International Centre, where office space and various additional facilities needed, were available.

The project operates at present with 4 professionals assisted by administrative personnel who initiate, develop with the help of consultants, coordinate and edit training materials. For the field, ten MATCOM Liaison Officers (MLO) are recruited under the Associate Expert Programme of the ILO financed by various donors additional to those supporting the project itself. The MLOs are a link between the project in Vienna and the training structure of the client country. Their task is to establish contacts with the national training institutions, introduce MATCOM training material to them, assist in training of trainers and of training planners as well as in the adaptation and translation of the MATCOM material.

Counterparts of the MLOs are National MATCOM Liaison Officers (NMLOs). They are selected among national staff experienced in co-operative management and training. They are appointed and paid by their national employer, either Government Departments or Co-operative Organizations. Their tasks are similar to those of the MLOs, however, more inserted into the national structure. In a number of countries with NMLOs they are assisted by sub-regional MLOs. Both are placed or selected in such a way that permits them to collaborate with different co-operative promotion structures. In 1990, the MATCOM project cooperates with about 43 NMLOs in 39 countries. This network is kept informed among others through a MATCOM Bulletin issued twice a year.

The supervisory and technical backstopping of the project lies with the ILO Co-operative Branch. Guidance is given by a Progress Review Committee composed of representatives of the donors, ILO, the project and the ICA. This rather sophisticated structure of the project and its supervision was developed during the course of the different phases. It primarily was needed to ensure the coordination of the extended activities and furthermore, facilitates the links to other project types and promotional instruments. The number of courses and participants increased considerably in course of the last years. The most extended activities took place in India where in 1989 different courses, meetings and programmes were attended by around 57,000 participants. Most of the participants were registered in courses on agricultural co-operatives followed by those on → *consumer co-operatives*. In 1989, the total number of participants in MATCOM programmes world wide amounted to about 64,000. Excluding India, the regions were represented by 1,700 participant in Latin America, 3,500 in Asia and 1,500 in Africa.

III. The Project's Development

The MATCOM Project started operations in January 1978. The first phases until 1983 were financed by the Swedish Government and the following jointly by Denmark, Finland and Norway. The contribution of the European donors were made through the funding of MATCOM – Liaison Officers. The increasing number of National Liaison Officers demonstrated more and more the willingness of national governments and movements to contribute to this network. Moreover, the national training activities themselves are in most cases financed by the national structures, MATCOM makes only relatively small contributions to the training programmes themselves.

The Project was conceived as "service project" which did not anticipate the requests from specific training insitutions governmental and non-governmental co-operative promotion institutions nor was it limited to specific geographical areas. The services were available to any institution and country in developing regions. Criteria for selecting the activities were the objectives of the project and the envisaged target groups.

The ultimate objective to which the Project should contribute was that co-operative enterprises in developing countries provide better services to their members (→ *Development Policy*).

The contribution of the Project to this end should be to achieve that agricultural, consumer and related co-operatives in developing countries apply mamagement techniques taught through MATCOM training programmes. Certainly, the focus of the different phases showed some variations: it started with the preparation, production and dissemination of training materials, development of training techniques and training of trainers. Later on, the aim of the project was for co-operative policy-makers and training planners to become committed to introduce MATCOM and the co-operative training sector to use MATCOM methods and materials. Hence, the activities, although somewhat overlapping, followed generally the sequence:

- production of training material and techniques;
- introduction of these to co-operative policy-makers in developing countries;
- training of training planners and trainers;
- assistance in translation and adaptation of the material to national situations.

The project directs its activities foremost to co-operative trainers but recipients are also other groups who should have a multiplying effect, namely: policy-makers, training planners and co-operative managers. The ultimate beneficiaries should be the co-operative members. The first phases of the Project emphasized more the training of trainers through the production of trainer's manuals and their introduction. Later, the editing of "Learning Elements"

opened the scope of activities to the managers directly and sometimes even to the ultimate beneficiaries.
The geographical extension of the Project was broadened through reinforcement of activities in French-speaking Africa in the early 80's and the take-off of activities in Latin America since 1986.

IV. MATCOM – Training Material

Since 1978, the Project developed training materials for agricultural co-operatives, workers' co-operatives, handicraft co-operatives, consumer co-operatives and credit unions. Under preparation are in 1990 materials on co-operative audit, co-operative banking, training methodology, fishery co-operatives, housing co-operatives and multi-purpose co-operatives.

The training materials exist in form of "trainers's manuals" on various subjects which outline a complete programme for management training. The design is made for courses of a duration from 5 days up to 20 days on one subject.

The manuals are divided into topics and sessions. After a general introduction, the main substance of the manual are "session guides" which indicate to the trainer the objectives of the session, and the process of the session from the trainer's view, however, limiting lecturing to a minimum and giving guidance how to activate the participation of the trainee. Handouts of case studies, exercise, role play-briefs are proposed for each session. The trainer's manual is a loose ringbinder which can easily be supplemented or rearranged.

The trainer' manuals are completed by "learning elements", staff and committee members of co-operative societies. The text and illustrations facilitate self-study and self-testing of a particular subject or the basics for the respective type of co-operative. Learning elements exist in the fields covered by the above mentioned trainer's manuals and for handicraft co-operatives.

V. MATCOM – Methodology

MATCOM claims as its methodological characteristics the following: participation, job-orientation, adaptation to local needs and efficiency. This applies equally to the methods of developing and introducing the training material and to those of training itself.

1. Process of Production and Introduction

The so-called "universal edition of the trainers's manuals" are developed in close collaboration between the MATCOM project staff and an external author. After a first draft has been discussed with other experts on the subject matter, the first version is tested in the field by workshops with potential users. The comments of the workshop participants are incorporated in a final version which thereafter is published.

However, this universal edition may not necessarily respond to the needs in a given situation. Therefore, adaptation to the local context and often translation into local languages is required. The persons and institutions which undertake this adaptation have to analyze carefully the training needs of potential trainees and compose the training materials accordingly. This requires that the trainers have a very good knowledge of practical problems of co-operatives and possess equally good drafting skills. Where these qualifications lack, the persons concerned may be tempted to opt for the easier way of only superficially adapt examples, names etc. or limit themselves to straight foreward translation. Therefore, the adapted version has to be tested again through a similar workshop as described above. However, this is only of help for future use of such material if the comments of participants and the observations of the trainers are carefully noted and integrated into the text.

The fact that all universal editions existed originally in English with reference to examples from Asia and English-speaking Africa made the task of adapation particularly difficult for Latin America and French-speaking Africa. Universal editions were translated from English into Spanish and French but were not drafted according to the prevailing regional context of co-operatives of similar organisations. The task of adaptation to national of local situations was therefore doublefold.

2. Training Methods

The methodological steps to be undertaken in the classroom training are described in the session guides of the trainer's manuals. The overall approach is to mobilize the trainees to participate actively in the sessions. The trainer is supposed to play the role of a facilitator in a "self-learning" process. His main instruments are group work, case method, role plays and planning games. Emphasis is put on the discussion with participants analysis. However, the sequence of the courses is well structured through the session guides, prepared handouts and a rather time schedule. The courses seek to respond to the practical problems of participants through an ex-ante assessment of the training needs and the respective composition of the course's modules. Yet, a complete new composition of modules out of the existing manuals requires long training experience with MATCOM and the concrete target group. MATCOM is at present developing a trainer's manual on methodology. Recently, a first "Trainer's Guide to MATCOM Manuals" was published for India.

3. Methodological Interlinkage of Training Materials, Training and Practical Work

The efficiency and job-orientation of MATCOM is sought to be achieved through the interlinkage of the materials, classroom training and practical work. The materials are elaborated with the support of practitioners and the classroom training ends with a commitment of participants to actions of improvement in their day-to-day work. A good MATCOM trainer would get into contact with his trainees on the job a while after the training course in order to obtain feedback on the application of such commitments. He would then draw conclusions on future class-room training. The training material and its composition should take advantage of the feed-back from participants, the observations of trainers and the assessment of practical work performance. Management training would hence become a continuous process linked with the performance of co-operatives.

It is, however, evident that such methodological approach is subject to a number of factors which figure outside the influence of the MATCOM project: e.g. the availability and continuity of trainers and of co-operative staff, finance for co-operative training, legal and institutional conditions of training. Moreover, the efficiency of training in improving the economic performance of co-operatives is difficult, if at all possible to identify.

VI. Review and Outlook

The MATCOM project was conceived to contribute to economically self-reliant co-operative organizations through training in co-operative management. As a service project, MATCOM was not limited to specific regions. It aimed at producing universally valid training materials and methods in order to ensure an equal quality of managerial standard. The focus on training materials originated from a situation where trainers and training structures exist within a national co-operative setting. Training material was considered to be the foremost needed ingredient to professionalize co-operative management. The universal standard of materials and methods was kept by adapting and translating the materials for the local requirements.

Although the approach was logical and the execution of the activities was performed accordingly, with high quality standards and with an impressive expansion and input, critical views were expressed from outside the MATCOM Project in a number of situations. This criticism was never brought into the open but took rather the form of a certain reluctance in making own inputs into the MATCOM approach and integrating it into existing training and promotion programmes. Attempts to evaluate the Project's activities necessarily showed difficulties as methods to assess the impact of training on the economic performance of co-operatives are hardly existing or too costly to develop. Nevertheless, frequent evaluations and reviews which have to accompany the process of such a service project took into account criticism and positive experiences in integrating MATCOM into regular training, for the necessary adaptations. They will serve also in the development of the future ILO programme of human resources development based on MATCOM:

- The identification of need for job-oriented training materials in co-operative management as described above is still valid in many countries and will require further development and introduction of MATCOM manuals.
- The network of MATCOM liaison persons and institutions offers an excellent basis for disseminating information, materials, training methods and philosophy. The emphasis will be put more on training structures and the integration of MATCOM-based training into regular existing or developing programmes.
- The adaptation process of materials has to be reinforced and innovative mechnanisms be developed which ensure not only in-depth adapted versions of material, but at the same time the process of becoming the local structure's "own material". The interregional standard will continue to be produced through a systematic training methodology applied to local particularities which may differ in the type of organizations and developing structures. Finally, this will lead to local acceptance (not only participation).
- The overall situation of the world economy and hereby for co-operatives in many countries has dramatically changed in the 80's. The deterioration of public finance and services has also affected government services for co-operative promotion. Although the critics of government assistance to co-operatives may see here the only chance for self-reliant organizations and "deofficialization", co-operatives and similar group organizations in developing regions cannot be expected to compensate this decline of outside resources immediately through their own means. As their membership is mostly constituted by the poorer parts of the population, the compensation cannot take place in the short run and not through human resources development only, particularly not when the government contributions to training structures suffer the same decline. External assistance of ILO to co-operatives has to include other elements than promotion of human resources development and its MATCOM activities have to be closely linked to them.
- It became evident that training material and classroom training is only one component of modern co-operative management training. It has to include as well on-the-job training (already started through post classroom contacts of trainer and

trainee), various possibilities of long distance training and particularly a well-adapted mix of these instruments. MATCOM-based promotion of human resources development in co-operatives through ILO will explore these possibilities and take them into account.
- MATCOM-based modular systems and curricula integrated into systematic human resouces development were possible only in some countries. However, the efficiency of MATCOM training has to be backed-up by regular, systematic execution as well as by methodological and political sensitization. Therefore, future activities will have to analyze carefully whether the described conditions are given to develop the efficiency of the co-operative management training or whether the Project or other ILO technical cooperation projects should and could contribute to the development of such conditions. This has to be done in flexible manner and after careful analysis of the concrete needs in the particular case. "Open funds" seem to be the most appropriate instrument for this purpose. Nevertheless, it is equally important to take stock of and then cooperate with existing governmental and non-governmental networks and materials for training in management of co-operative or other grassroot organisations in order to fully develop the synergies of internal and external promotion programmes.

The fourth phase of the interregional MATCOM Project financed jointly by Denmark, Finland and Norway expired end of 1991. Discussions are under way how the interregional activities will be integrated into ILO's Co-operative Branch, the regular work for co-operative human resources development, and how these activities could be strengthened through specialised regional projects which would in turn support the training activities in the field. Based on the passed experiences on an adapted approach, activities development by analysing carefully the gaps of national structures and approaches where MATCOM could give advice and support.

MATCOM will remain ILO's trademark for co-operative management training but it will have to incorporate the feed back from its past experience, the lessons learned in ILO's technical cooperation projects for co-operatives, the changing overall situation and last, but foremost from the ultimate users and beneficiaries.

Bibliography

ILO (ed.): Curriculum Guide for Co-operative Management Training, Geneva 1991.

Mergers and Consolidations in the Co-operative System

ULRICH FEHL/CARSTEN SCHREITER [J]

(see also: *Economic Order; Competition; Operational Size; Business Policies; Anti-Trust Laws; Law Concerning Company Groups*)

I. The Process of Merging and Consolidating: Its Causes; II. Processes and Motives for Mergers and Consolidations in the Co-operative System; III. Effects on Internal Structure, the Co-operative Principles and the Identity of the Co-operative; IV. Consequences on the Position of the Co-operatives Within the Economy as a Whole; V. Outlook and Evaluation.

I. The Process of Merging and Consolidating: Its Causes

1. Process of Consolidation

The phenomenon of consolidation, which continues to emerge in almost all sectors of the industrialized countries, did not initially perturb economists about whether competition was able to function, even under the influence of the works of *Marx* and *Schumpeter*. These concerns from the economist's point of view rather were stirred considerably by *Bain's* hypothesis that a higher degree of concentration in one branch fosters collusion and, because of this, above average rates of profit (*Fehl*). Such profits which accrue in this manner are to be seen as a distortion of allocation. This loss of prosperity results from advantages in company size and aspects of efficiency in certain circumstances; these should be weighed out and could be held responsible for the much lower rate of profitability in smaller companies. Consolidation increasingly enlarges this profit rate discrepancy (*Reekie*).

These correlations become particularly evident in the work of *Nelson* and *Winter* who derive the process of consolidation out of endigenous competitive processes, thus integrating certain dimensions of market development. They elaborate on the reverse neo-*Schumpeter* hypothesis formulated by *Phillips*, according to which technological advancement leads to growth in company size; from this the sphere of management problems arises. The evolutionist perspective emphasizes the connection between present and future levels of success and market share. Based on the consideration that processes of accumulation, themselves dependent on their propensity to attract investment, are determined by profits from the previous business period, it can be demonstrated that the market shares of the relatively successful companies grow more rapidly, and that corresponding profits resulting from their leading position will be reaped. Whether the process of consolidation likewise appears is dependent on:

a) how large the advantages are that companies already on the market have to innovate, or in other words, the opportunities market entry offers;
b) how aggressively the successful companies expand their capacities and, as a result of this, the corresponding price reduction passed on to the final user; this puts relatively strong pressure on conservative suppliers, causes them to withdraw from the market at fairly high rates, and reduces their capacity;
c) how quickly the competition can carry out imitations;
d) whether there are disadvantages to a large company size (for example, organization costs which mount disproportionately) which limit the accumulation tendency of successful companies;
e) the development of demand on the market.

Markets which do not require any specific knowledge and thus do not permit any considerable advantage from know-how in the form of lower production costs or better (sequential) innovation opportunities which affect the other current market participants are thus more greatly endangered by potential competitors. Whether the degree of concentration will actually be lower is, however, not a question of "economies of scale" and "scope" as one might easily think, as these are neither necessary nor sufficient for an explanation of company size (compare with *Teece, Scherer*). Consolidation processes, at least when company growth comes from within, are much more soundly based on superior management efficiency. It thus does not seem implausible that large companies can demonstrate a higher profitability when systematic relationships exist between their former, present and future success. The effectiveness of the "success breeds success" principle is largely based on the so-called "first mover" advantages from learning processes and the transferability of this knowledge to other activities. There is no generally accessible pool of technological knowledge (see *Pavitt*), and thus there are considerable differences in technological opportunities among sectors. External company growth produces an acceleration of the consolidation process as independent market participants disappear. According to the neo-classic stance, this is only problematic for competitive policy when the danger of collusion threatens the adaptive efficiency of the entire economy, such as when a dominating market position is attained or when one already exists. But because the diversity of results and behavior is reduced, the consequence on the dynamic efficiency should be evaluated negatively (*J. Röpke*). The correlation between behavior diversity and an optimally high level of varying activities should not be forgotten (*Willgerodt*). Up to now the successful innovators and early imitators have been observed (*Heuß*). They are able to expand their market shares to the detriment of the conservative entrepreneurs in as far as the latter do not innovate when under pressure to do so (innovation of both process and production), follow suit or achieve lower organizational costs. In this context, it is particularly interesting whether mergers present an opportunity to escape from this pressure.

2. Causes and/or Incentives for Mergers from the Management Viewpoint

In the previous presentation of the consolidation process resulting from a dynamic competitive process, technological change was seen as the catalyst. The explanation of co-operative mergers arises precisely from this point of view emphasizing forced growth (*Fleischmann, Hermann, Hamm*). This compulsory pressure may be caused by a variety of factors:

1) *technological reasons* (on the business level)
   – technological progress and consolidation brought about by an increasing minimum enterprise size needed for optimization (also decentralization effects brought about by innovation)
   – specialization and division of labor
   – savings through increased lot size.

New outputs or services can be provided through competition and the utilization of new technologies. Technical progress is the result of factors incited both from the "demand pull" side and the supply side:

2a) *demand-based reasons*
   – alteration of customer behavior
   – alteration in the demand structure of the customers
2b) *supply side changes*
   – expansion of the assortment of outputs/services
   – changes in product quality and complexity, the necessity for more complementary services, goodwill, serving the flow of information, reputation.

Mergers can also be based on lower average costs on the company level, or in other words, on the organizational structure. This is the case when non-utilized, indivisible production factors exists which cannot be used up by an enterprise whose average costs are rising prematurely (the so-called "multi-unit-economies" by *Blair*). Positive external effects can be integrated which, circumstances permitting, lead to a reduction of costs. Other groups of causes include market strength and counter-market strength, policy factors determining regulation (laws of competition, the regulation of exceptional cases, the definition and enforcement of property rights), fiscal reasons (for example, gross value-added tax on all phases of production), the taxation of conglomerates (interlocking rights and relationships), as well as "managerial economies" (*Blair*) based on the indivisibility of management.

II. Processes and Motives for Mergers and Consolidations in the Co-operative System

1. Consolidation and Merging

The process of consolidation in the co-operative system leaves no level untouched in the structure of co-operative → *federations*:

a) The members' level

The member enterprises themselves can strive for a larger minimum size needed for optimization through merging. An increase in membership level and the growth of the individual member enterprises in affiliation with this can have consequences on higher levels of the association through the changing structures of demand.

b) The primary enterprise level

The merging process of the primary co-operatives is customarily in the limelight of the discussion of consolidation (→ *Operational Size*). Alongside larger minimum enterprise sizes required for optimization, one can also regularly observe causes for mergers among the personnel. Restructuring brought upon by changing membership constellations, or in other words, the active and reactive adaptational processes to the changing demands of the membership, is yet another cause for the observable concentration process. Several exemplary merger motives named by consumer and service co-operatives include the following:

- more favorable purchasing conditions as a result of larger bulk orders
- better capacity
- better starting position for necessary investments
- rationalization.

c) The secondary and tertiary institutional levels

One can in general reiterate everything that was mentioned previously under item 2). The logic behind the emergence of this institutional level indicates a step ahead in development; it is precisely this functional level, extending over and encompassing the primary enterprise level, which then only becomes profitable upon reaching a certain size or capacity. Thus, a certain administrative dominance exists at this level over the member co-operatives. As a result of this, the secondary level becomes a pacemaker for development and thus oftens induces the lower levels to adapt to it. The reversal of the development impulses accompanying this does not leave the relationship between day-to-day co-operative activity and the co-operatives' principles untouched. The motives the credit co-operatives (→ *Co-operative Banks*) have for merging are also exemplary for this level as a whole:

- better clearing
- higher equity and larger credits
- better risk compensation
- division of labor and qualified co-workers
- more extensive palette of services
- rationalization
- more weight on the market.

d) The federation level

The federation level is immediately affected by concentrational processes on the levels previously mentioned (→ *Central Institutions*). A reduction in the number of members hand in hand with an increase in their (enterprise) size, new business fields, and mounting problems in organizational structure directly affect the business structure of the federation and its development of a range of services and outputs. A central motive for merging on the federation level arises from this.

The developmental trend of the German federations could be mentioned here as an example; it points in the direction of the development into a modern service-oriented company (*Lambert*). Traditional services, such as the auditing function, contribute a shrinking share to the business volume. New outputs or services are a reflex reaction to the changing structures of both demand and supply. The adaptational process is accompanied and lead by the services of the federations. Under certain circumstances they also promote mergers, such as when a destitute co-operative must be reorganized. As a rule, they state their opinion and arguments concerning members' plans to undertake a merger.

2. Consolidation and Competition: Compulsory growth?

Consolidation within the co-operative sector would be interpreted as a sign of faltering competitiveness in group competition to other company forms if a) the branch as a whole did not become subject to this tendency, and b) if the market share did not remain constant or even rise somewhat (→ *Competition*). Only first in this context can the consolidation process of the co-operatives be contrasted to a process of competitive displacement. The role of co-operatives in the consolidation process is mostly considered relative. The essence and nature of the co-operative is to promote its member enterprises (→ *Promotion Mandate*) and retain them as members by increasing their competitiveness. With all other things the same, the existence of co-operatives implies a low degree of consolidation compared to a state of affairs without co-operatives at all, under the assumption that the members could not have survived without co-operatives. The thesis reads that co-operatives have the tendency to slow down the concentration process under otherwise identical conditions (*Lambert*). The extent that this function has been able to brake the development of consolidation is contestable in individual situations (for example, *Monopolkommission,* p.114, and *Lambert*, p.61). This statement must in any case be studied closer as cooperation can reduce both variety on the members' level and also their freedom of action. In such a situation, the members would cease being the actual actors on the market (co-operative conglomerate).

A consequence of this "compulsion" theory is that co-operatives must react to the competitive intensity of the branch and, practically as a proxy agent, undertake adaptational processes for their members. Because of this, co-operatives are not particularly enthusiastic about consolidating.

In the strictest sense, this only applies to the members' level. As it is frequently assumed in management theory, the situation becomes apparent on the primary enterprise level that managers pursue growth objectives, and thus that a propensity to consolidate exists at this level (*Boettcher, Eschenburg*) (→ *Theory of co-operative Cooperation*). The extent of the importance of this aspect will not be discussed here; the question concerning the co-operative's inclination and ability to innovate is much more important. As long as co-operatives have a low level of innovational potential at their disposal, they will fall victim to compulsory action in dynamic competition. Consolidation processes would then actually be mostly relative. (*Lenel* criticizes the inevitability of consolidation).

3. The Development of Selected Co-operative Sectors in Germany and Abroad

The following brief overview of several sectors in different countries should illustrate the differences and extent of the consolidation movement.

a) → *Co-operative banks*

Federal Republic of Germany: The strongest process of consolidation has resulted in the credit co-operatives, and within this group particularly among the Raiffeisen banks (rural credit co-operatives) because of the structural changes in agriculture (→ *Rural Co-operatives*). The wave of mergers commenced around 1960 and reached its zenith between 1962 and 1965 with a total of 3,194 mergers. The time period from 1960 to 1967 was the age of technical mechanization in the banking industry (*Hermann*). The mergers between 1967 and 1973 were predominantly caused by an escalation of competition within the banking sector (rescission of the interest and competition agreements). In 1972, the two national associations of → *Schulze-Delitzsch* and → *Raiffeisen* joined together in one union. The mergers which took place between 1977 and 1981 can in part be attributed to legislation increasing the minimum size of a bank's board of directors. 3,241 independent institutes (1989) remained from the original 11,651 credit co-operatives (1969). Within the same time frame, the membership level rose from 3,855,000 to 11,316,000; the business volume increased from DM 22.6 billion to DM 536.6 billion. The eighteen central regional banks of 1960, with transactions amounting to DM 5.4 billion, trimmed down to three institutes as of 1989 with an increase in the amount of their transactions to DM 99.5 billion (1988). The mergers were so conducted that the conveyed banks would be managed as branches. The number of branch offices thus rose from 13,000 in 1950 to 19,500 in 1978 (*Swoboda*). The development of market share, measured as a portion of the balance of all universal banks, indicates an increase from 14.8% to 21.2% in the time frame from 1960 to 1980. Since this point in time the total remained steady at this level until 1989.

Austria: The Austrian Raiffeisen banks show a somewhat slower, but in principle extant process of consolidation which slightly accelerated between 1965 and 1975.

	1950	1955	1960	1965	1970	1975	1977	1983
Credit co-operatives	1760	1754	1754	1732	1596	1353	1312	1045
# of bank offices	2036	2030	1839	2012	1971	1971	2071	1887

(Swoboda, 1980, Column 543 ff., and Pötzelberger)

The total balance of the Raiffeisen banks amounted to 432.4 billion schillings and 119.2 billion schillings for the Volksbanken. This resulted in a total share of 21.3% of all credit institutes (*Pötzelberger*).

Switzerland: The rural mutual loan societies have retained their local-regional character to a great extent. They are still managed by non-paid staff and as a rule do not have full-time tellers. Because of this structure, mergers thus are the exception. In contrast, the Volksbanken in Switzerland merged into one large bank (Schweizer Volksbank).

Great Britain: The first credit co-operatives were established as late as 1964, and of these 78 still exist. There are two national federations. Furthermore there is no differentiation between primary institutes and co-operative central banks. They are not included in the clearing system and do not perform transactions that the universal banks do (see *Poggemann*). Mergers are very unlikely based on the British concept of credit unions, particularly since their membership level is restricted to a maximum of 5,000 members.

Italy: In Italy, small local institutes merged, particularly in the sector of urban credit co-operatives. An expansion in the number of branch offices also occurred here (*Muré*).

b) Agricultural co-operatives

Federal Republic of Germany: The rural consumer, processing and service co-operatives exhibited a numerical decrease from 20,926 to 5,467 enterprises in the time frame from 1960 to 1989. The most pronounced concentration took place among the credit co-operatives active in commodities trade and in the dairy co-operatives. The former were subjected both to the development in the banking sector as well as the structural changes in agriculture, as rationalization and the expansion of agricultural enterprise size produced the demand for larger credits.

The development of the dairy co-operatives was essentially determined by ever-increasing minimum enterprise sizes needed for optimization, improved refrigeration techniques, and an increase in market power for those on the demand side (*Swoboda*). Agricultural restructuring, resulting in a growing demand for working funds, and an increase in supply were responsible for drastically improving the turnover of purchasing and marketing co-operatives up to 1980, even in spite of lower membership levels. The regressive turnover development since then can to a large degree be traced back to farming policy (milk quota regulation in 1984; grain stabilization in 1988; non-cultivation of fields, early retirement legislation).

	1960	1970	1980	1988	1989
Credit co-operatives with commodities business					
# of institutes	8896	4920	2572	1785	1613
turnover mil. DM	1846	3442	7374	6041	5888
# of members	1381	1991	2925	3428	3338
Dairy co-operatives					
# of institutes	5267	3705	1493	925	889
turnover mil. DM	5328	7733	16461	19156	21028
# of members	894	721	452	327	311

(Source: DG-BANK Statistics 1990)

Great Britain: The agricultural co-operatives in Great Britain, first concerning here the purchasing co-operatives, held a market share of 12% in 1945. A process of consolidation resulted, and between 1970 and 1980 the purchasing co-operatives increased their turnover by approx. 225%. By 1986, their market share was able to extend to about 25%. The members developed from co-worker/owners to pure clients to capital investors.

In the sector of → *marketing co-operatives*, a market share of approx. 26% has been maintained since the 1980s. A process of consolidation also took place here which lead to specialization on account of monoculture in the British farming structure. Members are bound to these co-operatives through so-called "member agreements", or in other words, through supplier commitments which include obligatory fee payments (see *Poggemann*, p.51 ff.).

U.S.A.: Three types of farmer co-operatives exist in the United States: the centralized co-operatives (local), the federated (amalgamation of several local co-operatives), and the mixed. The farmer co-operatives reached the apex of their membership level in 1929–30, numbering over 12,000. In 1985, there were still about 5,500, their number reduced by both liquidation and consolidation. 5,109 farmer co-operatives still existed in 1987, of them 3,054 marketing, 1,941 purchasing and 114 service co-operatives. Since the middle of the 1950s and thus around twenty years after the large setback in the number of farmers, the number of co-operative members also started to fall. This is seen as an indicator for the superior market chances of co-operators. 36% of all farmers in 1987 were members. Of these, 66% reported annual production values in excess of $40,000. The structural change among the members can be seen in the structural changes among their capital goods. In spite of a decreasing number of members, the market share of the farmer co-operatives has increased. Almost 39% of all agricultural products sold on the market and more than 25% of all equipment and supplies are purchased through farmer co-operatives. One must, however consider the differentiation of the market structure. The process of consolidation among the farmer co-operatives began between 1915 and 1924; large-scale co-operatives developed. 52 of the largest farmer co-operatives pooled together 51.7% of the total business volume in 1987. The majority of the 5,109 co-operatives (3,417) achieved 8.2% of the total business volume. These figures clearly indicate a high degree of concentration. The smaller local co-operatives only fulfill a few basic functions, for instance purchasing and marketing, but not processing. Merging into a regional co-operative is considered a solution.

A hesitant trend in the direction of processing and thus vertical integration can be observed in the United States, which, because it is so capital intensive, is not as pronounced in the co-operative sector as in the non-co-operative sector. In addition, other companies become incorporated and managed in part like profit-oriented subsidiaries. The result of this development is a resemblance to the structural forms of the large non-co-operative organizations know as "agribusiness conglomerates". Problems arise in these complex co-operatives, managed by professional administrators and integrated both vertically and horizontally, concerning the utilization of capacity. Business conducted with non-members as well as set contracts with members thus gain importance.

III. Effects on Internal Structure, the Co-operative Principles and the Identity of the Co-operative

Ever-growing company size within the co-operative system is reflected both in the development of internal management and control structures as well as in the changing relationship among members and between members and the primary enterprise (→ *Organizational Structure of Societies*). Organizational types like the market-linkage co-operative or the fully integrated co-operative (*Dülfer*) are practically synonymous with these developments.

A separation between management and property results from the increasing complexity of business and the necessary professionalization of the management of the enterprise operation (*Boettcher*). The conflicts which arise between the goals of management and those of the cooperators (*Eschenburg*), hand in hand with the diminishing opportunities individual members have to exercise influence on the business management, altered the co-operative social structure. Ever more complex enterprise operational structures, resulting from the vertical integration of administrational functions, produce ever larger problems for members to see through the activities and contribute to their organization and development. The alienation of members from their co-operative leads to a more poignant emphasis of pure business aspects (→ *Business Policies*).

The opportunities individual members have to exercise influence are quite slight, a result of the asymmetric level of information between the management of large-scale co-operatives and the members/supervisory board. Control and control possibilities are thus strongly undermined to a degree. It is practically impossible for one member to exercise influence in the general assembly in large-scale co-operatives, much less quite costly – not least because the number of members has so drastically risen. Management thus increasingly gains in its importance and ability to pursue its own goals (*Eschenburg*) (→ *Management in Co-operatives*). The control of the enterprise operation through the original basis democracy of the members surrenders to the centralized control of the management. Furthermore, this often leads to a reversal of control and influence. The formation of co-operative conglomerates (EDEKA, REWE) clearly illustrates this (Monopolkommission).

The more pronounced administrative orientation of the managment and its rationalization efforts no longer treats all members fairly. A differentiation among members, a practise never exercised according to the principle of equality, can mean economic advantages for the enterprise operation and its profitability. On the one hand, the capacity of ever-larger enterprise units has lead to a mounting share of business with non-members, a trend resulting from the market-linkage co-operative; on the other hand, the re-integration of members is undertaken (integrated co-operative) on account of mounting reciprocal dependencies (*Dülfer*).

Although this development is only an offshoot of company size, thus occurring without any type of consolidation process, external growth has surely accelerated this change to a great extent.

The amalgamation of members above and beyond the local and regional scope relaxes the social relationships, interests and goals of the members and makes them more heterogeneous. Questions arise concerning the influence of individual members in groups which are becoming more and more differentiated.

This change is characterized by problems concerning group goal orientation, the motivation to work responsibly as a member, changes in the incentive/contribution structure, and the motivation to become a member. The increase in the heterogeneity of the member enterprises complicates both the application of identical standards on all members and the definition of the promotion policy. Such a development has corresponding consequences for the membership structures, the character of the co-operatives, and the quality of the promotion principle.

IV. Consequences on the Position of the Co-operatives Within the Economy as a Whole

Growth within the primary institutes has effects on the distribution of tasks and responsibilities in the co-operative federation, as well as on the demands expected from the associations. Growth on the secondary or tertiary institute level jeopardizes the principle of hierarchical intervention through the consolidation of functions.

Growth itself in the secondary institute level spawns real conglomeration in several fields, something that has nothing to do with the spirit of the co-operative system as it entails a reversal of the direction of influence (see the definition of conglomerates, § 18 of the AktG, Companies Act).

The role and position of co-operatives in the economy as a whole has changed (→ *Economic Order*). Growth processes have created more efficient large-scale units which in some branches have gained additional market shares; in others they have been able to stem decline. Not only where co-operatives have assumed the legal form of a joint-stock company can it be observed that the co-operative is starting to resemble other non-co-operative business forms.

V. Outlook and Evaluation

According to *Swoboda*, consolidation more frequently results in an effort to secure market shares than to reduce costs. One can see from the figures that the market share level has clearly increased. The problematic nature described resulting from consolidation in the co-operatives can be found most extensively in growth of operational size and in the organizational problems which arise. As long as internal growth occurs, management efficiency can be implied. This, however, is not synonymous with success in the co-operative principle of promotion as disparities between members and management can result from growth in operational size. Organizational problems thus can also be expected without a merger; external growth simply exacerbates this tendency. It must not be forgotten that mergers are carried out by the same co-operatives which either in the long term would have no chance of survival or which already find themselves in a grave economic situation. Fundamental existence must thus be weighed against the problems of a merger. In such situations, the merger option will surely be chosen. In as much as the goals strived for through the merger can also be attained through the federation and a redistribution of tasks and responsibilities, it is possibile to preclude member alienation. With respect to the co-operative principles, such a solution should be given priority (*Hamm*), for co-operative decentralization itself is considered a competitive advantage which should be preserved.

Bibliography

Bain, Joe S.: Barriers to New Competition, Cambridge/Mass. 1956.
Becker, Robert: Zur Lage des Farm Credit Systems in den Vereinigten Staaten von Amerika. In: Zeitschrift für das gesamte Genossenschaftswesen, 39 (1989), pp. 45–53.
Blair, John M.: Economic Concentration; Structure Behavior & Public Policy, New York 1972.
Boettcher, Erik: Genossenschaften in der Marktwirtschaft, Tübingen 1980.
Dülfer, Eberhard: Strukturprobleme in der Gegenwart. In: Forschungsinstitut für Genossenschaftswesen an der Universität Wien (ed.): Neuere Tendenzen im Genossenschaftswesen, pp. 5–34, Göttingen 1966.
Dülfer, Eberhard: Betriebswirtschaftslehre der Kooperative, Göttingen 1984.
Eschenburg, Rolf: Ökonomische Theorie der genossenschaftlichen Zusammenarbeit, Tübingen 1971.
Fehl, Ulrich: Wettbewerbliche Dimension des Oligopolmarktes, ORDO, Vol. 37 (1986), pp. 141–153.
Fleischmann, Gerd: Wettbewerbstheorie und Genossenschaften. In: Boettcher, Erik (ed.): Theorie und Praxis der Kooperation, Tübingen 1972, pp. 105–133.
Hamm, Walter: Konzentrations- und Fusionstendenzen. Genossenschaftswesen. In: Laurinkari, Juhani (ed.): Genossenschaftswesen, München/Wien 1990, pp. 350–358.
Herrmann, Albrecht: Genossenschaftliche Identität im Konzentrationsprozeß von Kreditgenossenschaften, Stuttgart-Hohenheim 1988.
Heuß, Ernst: Allgemeine Markttheorie, Tübingen/Zürich 1965.
Klohn, Werner: Die Farmer-Genossenschaft in den U.S.A.. In: Zeitschrift für das gesamte Genossenschaftswesen, vol.41 (1991), 48–61.
Lambert, Klaus: Der Genossenschaftsverband – ein Dienstleistungsunternehmen, Genossenschaftskurier, no.3 (1989), pp. 5–6.
Lampert, Heinz: Genossenschaften und Konzentration. In: Zerche, J./Herder-Dorneich, Ph./Engelhardt, W.W. (eds.): Genossenschaften und genossenschaftliche Forschung, pp. 49–65, Regensburg 1989.
Monopolkommission: Mißbräuche der Nachfragemacht und Möglichkeiten zu ihrer Kontrolle im Rahmen des Gesetzes gegen Wettbewerbsbeschränkungen (Sondergutachten 7), Baden-Baden 1977.
Muré, Guiseppe: Italien. Genossenschaftsbanken in Europa. In: Zeitschrift für das gesamte Kreditwesen, vol.37 (1984), pp. 456–457.
Nelson, Richard R./Winter, Sydney G.: An Evolutionary Theory of Economic Change, Cambridge/Mass. 1982.
W.A.: Die Genossenschaften in der Bundesrepublik Deutschland 1990, Frankfurt a. M. 1991.
Pavitt, Keith: Patterns of technical Change: Towards a Taxonomy and a Theory. Research Policy, vol.13 (1984), pp. 343–373.
Poggemann, Klaus: Genossenschaften in England, Münster 1990.
Pötzelberger: Österreich. Genossenschaftsbanken in Europa, Zeitschrift für das gesamte Kreditwesen, vol.37 (1984). pp. 462–467.
Reekie, W. Duncan: Industry, Prices and Markets, Oxford 1979.
Röpke, Jochen: Externes Unternehmenswachstum im ökonomischen Evolutionsprozeß, ORDO, vol.41 (1990), pp. 151–172.
Scherer, Frederic M.: Industrial market structure and economic performance, Boston/Dallas et al. 2. ed., 1980.
Schumpeter, Josef A.: Kapitalismus, Sozialismus und Demokratie, 2. ed., Bern 1950.
Swoboda, Walter: Fusion/Konzentration im Genossenschaftswesen. In: Mändle Eduard/Winter, Hans-Werner (eds.): Handwörterbuch des Genossenschaftswesens, cols. 532–552, Wiesbaden 1980.
Teece, David: Economies of Scope and Scope of the Economies, Journal of Economic Behavior and Organization, vol.1 (1980), pp. 223–245.
Willgerodt, Hans: Fehlurteile über vielzahligen Wettbewerb. ORDO, vol. 26 (1975), pp. 97–115.

Mill, John Stuart (1806–1873)

THOMAS BROCKMEIER

(see also: *Classic and Neo-classic Contributions; Marshall*)

John Stuart Mill was born on 20 May 1806 as the oldest of six children in Pentonville, London. John Stuart was brought up by his father, *James Mill* (1773–1836), who was one of the leading intellects of the early nineteenth century, "with the advice and assistance of *Francis Place* and *Jeremy Bentham*, to be a repository of advanced thinking on all the great subjects of the day ..." (*Ryan*, p.466). In his works on logic, political economy, liberty, government and utilitarianism, "... (*John Stuart Mill*) constructed an intellectual system which spanned the horizon from syllogism to socialism" (*Ryan*, p.466). His "Principles of Political Economy" (1848) was one of the most influential texts of all time although "the book, as analytical economics, was not original. As late as 1919 it was still being used at Oxford. (Mainly, no doubt, because the superior alternative, → *Marshall's* "Principles", had been written by a Cambridge man)" (*Lekachman*, p.177).

Since *James Mill* largely contributed to his son's later fame, it is worthwhile dedicating a few lines to him. He was born of modest stock in a small village in Scotland in 1773, but "... obtained the patronage of a local leird, *Sir John Stuart*, and by this means was able to attend Montrose Academy and Edinburgh University, where ... he attended *Dugald Stewart's* lectures on moral philosophy and ...(possibly) on political economy" (*Winch*, p.465). In 1817, he published his "History of British India" which gained widespread reception. "In 1819, partly as a result of the reception given to his (book), *James Mill* was appointed to the post of Assistant Examiner with the East India Company (which by this time was important as the government of India, not as a trading company), rising to ...Chief Examiner in 1830, a position which he held until his death in 1836" (*Winch*, pp.465,467). Furthermore, *James Mill*, historian, philosopher and economist, wrote articles for the Encyclopedia Britannica and became a leading figure of the so-called "philosophic radicals" whose movement "...was dedicated to the reform of Parliament and other legal and political institutions according to accepted utilitarian criteria for 'good government'" (*Winch*, p.465). Among his friends was *David Ricardo* who told him about his doubts as to his own capacity to writing down his economic ideas. *James Mill* helped *Ricardo* to overcome these doubts – the result being the publication of *Ricardo's* pathbreaking "Principles of Political Economy and Taxation" in 1817. In 1821, *James Mill* published his *"Elements of Political Economy"* which to some is *"one of the first 'schoolbook' accounts of Ricardo's doctrines"* (*Winch*, p.466).

"*James Mill* had definite ideas about almost everything, and especially about education. His son, *John Stuart Mill*, was the extraordinary result" (*Heilbroner*, p.124). The father decided to treat his son to a Benthamite education and "...took his gifted child's training into his own hands. What hands they were. The tot began Greek at 3, and Latin at 8. When he was 12, his father started him on logic, philosophy, and political economy. During this period, no holiday interrupted the rhythm of his work; no children, except his brothers and sisters...diminished his concentration, and no light reading was permitted" (*Lekachman*, p.181). "(In) his early teens..., he (even) assisted his father in preparing his *Elements of Political Economy*, and finally read *Bentham's* defence of utilitarianism. By his sixteenth year, he was everything his father had hoped – an enlightened young man whose intellect was that of a forty-year-old" (*Ryan*, p.467).

In 1822, *John Stuart Mill* joined his father at the East India Company which he served until 1858, retiring as Chief Examiner – his father's old position. "(But) unlike his father, whose legacy still exists in the Indian legal and educational systems, (John Stuart) *Mill* did not much affect policy" (Ryan, p.467).

In the late 1820s, *Mill* worked for two years as secretary to *Jeremy Bentham*, the man whose writings had so deeply impressed him already when he was a teenager. In his autobiography, *Mill* states that to him, after having read the three volumes of *Bentham's* "Treatise on Legislation", "... the *principle of utility* understood as *Bentham* understood it, and applied in the manner in which he applied it..., fell exactly into its place as the keystone which held together the detached and fragmentary component parts of my knowledge and beliefs. It gave unity to my conceptions of things. I now had opinions; a creed, a doctrine, a philosophy; in one among the best senses of the word, a religion... And I had a great conception laid before me of changes to be effected in the condition of mankind through that doctrine" (*Mill*, p.56).

Between 1825 and 1830, *Mill* and his friends from the Utilitarian Society (founded in 1822/1823) had thorough discussions with adherents of →*Robert Owen*, *Samuel T. Coleridge*, and *William Thompson*. "Thus, he extended his acquaintance to Utopian Socialists, Romantics, and Ricardian Socialists" (*Lekachman*, p.183). (Like the Owenite school of Utopian Socialists, the Ricardian Socialists, *Thompson* being their leading figure, built model communities on co-operative principles. Like the Owenites also, "they exaggerated human goodness and human rationality. However, to this Utopian element they added a faith in scientific psychology which set them apart from the Utopians", *Lekachman*, p.173).

Mill learned that, "if social progress was to be moral and spiritual progress rather than the mere accumulation of wealth, men needed a synthesis of the analytical and the imaginative mind. *Mill* now knew ... (that) politics and economics had to be discussed in a historically sensitive way, utilitarianism had to be enlarged to make sense of the varieties of human happiness, authority and liberty had each to receive their due. This was not mere eclecticism; it was following *Goethe's* motto of 'many-sidedness'" (*Ryan*, p.467).

In his mid-twenties, *Mill* had "... a kind of a nervous breakdown: the delicate dry intellectual world of work and effort on which he had been nourished suddenly became sterile and unsatisfying, and while other youths had to discover that there could be beauty in intellectual activity, poor *Mill* had to find that there could be beauty in beauty. He underwent a siege of melancholy; then he read *Goethe, Saint-Simon* (and other writers...) who spoke of the heart

as seriously as his father had spoken of the brain" (*Heilbroner*, p.124/125). Discovering "that he was a being with genuine feelings restored his happiness" (*Ryan*, p.467).
The greatest happiness, however, was yet to come (and to prove *Mill's* latest 'discovery') – his long friendship and eventual marriage to *Harriet Taylor*. Their relationship was "the great emotional event of his life" (*Lekachman*, p.184). Mrs. *Taylor* was a woman "...full of an intellectual passion quite unlike anything *Mill* knew" (*Ryan*, p.467). He met her in 1830, when she was married and mother of several small children. "Nevertheless, love rapidly ripened and during the next two decades the two occasionally traveled together on the Continent and spent holidays in the English countryside. It was one of the unconventional relationships of which the highly conventional Victorians were capable" (*Lekachman*, p.184). When Harriet's husband died in 1851, they eventually married. "It was a superlative match. *Harriet Taylor* (and later, her daughter, *Helen*) completed for *Mill* the emotional awakening that had begun so late; together, the two women opened his eyes to women's rights and, even more importantly, to mankind's rights" (*Heilbroner*, p.124). "Mill credited *Harriet* with enormous influence upon him. He claimed that the *Essay* on Liberty (1859), his most eloquent piece of writing, was as much hers as his. Her inspiration and persuasion led him to soften his attitude toward socialism in the successive editions of the *Principles*" (*Lekachman*, p.184). Unfortunately, *Harriet* was already ill when they married, and she died in 1858.
In 1843, *Mill* published "A System of Logic", a two-volumed treatise containing an empiricist analysis of logic, mathematics and scientific explanation. In 1848, he published his "Principles of Political Economy", illustrating "an account of the aims and methods of social science which has dominated discussion ever since" (*Ryan*, p.466). As already indicated above, this book "was an enormous success. It went into seven editions in the expensive two-volume edition during his own lifetime, and, characteristic of *Mill*, he had it printed at his own expense in one cheap volume that would be in the reach of the working class" (*Heilbroner*, p.131). In his later works, "On Liberty" (1859), "Considerations on Representative Government" (1861), and "Utilitarianism" (1863), which all became classics in their fields, *Mill* defended "...a secular, utilitarian moral philosophy by showing that it had room for the purest idealism and for the pursuit of individual liberty as a good in itself" (*Ryan*, p.466).
And *Mill's* achievements in the various fields of science aside, "the man himself was so respected; ...more than merely brilliant, he verged on being saintly. When *Herbert Spencer*, his great rival in the area of philosophy, found himself so straitened in circumstances that he was unable to complete his projected series on social evolution, it was *Mill* who offered to finance the project" (*Heilbroner*, p.131).
In the years after *Harriet Taylor's* death, *Mill* led an active public life. During the Civil War, he raised his voice in favour of the North. In 1865, he became Member of Parliament for Westminster and served two terms during which "he...proved to be no mean debater and no gentle critic of his Tory opponents" (*Ryan*, p.467). "He favored extension of male suffrage and the vote for women. He attacked the government's repressive Irish policy. He led the public agitation against Governor Eyre of Jamaica, who repressed disorder in his colony by shooting and flogging..." (*Lekachman*, p.185).
The last few years of his life, *Mill* spent writing about religion, trade unionism, the reform of Irish land tenure and much else. He died in Avignon (where *Harriet* was buried) on 7 May 1873.

Bibliography

Blaug, Mark: Economic Theory in Retrospect, Cambridge 1985.
Hayek, Friedrich August von: John Stuart Mill and Harriet Taylor, London/Chicago 1951.
Heilbroner, Robert L.: The Wordly Philosophers (5th ed.), New York 1980. York
Hollander, Samuel: John Stuart Mill as Economic Theorist, in: The New Palgrave, Vol.3, pp.471–475, London 1987.
Hoppe, Michael: Die klassische und die neoklassische Theorie der Genossenschaften, Berlin 1976.
Lekachman, Robert: A History of Economic Ideas, New York 1959.
Mill, John Stuart: Autobiography, Oxford 1924.
Packe, Michael St. John: Life of John Stuart Mill, 1954.
Ryan, Alan: John Stuart Mill, in: The New Palgrave, Vol.3, pp.466–471, London 1987.
Starbatty, Joachim: Die englischen Klassiker der Nationalökonomie, Darmstadt 1985.
Winch, Donald: James Mill, in: The New Palgrave, Vol.3, pp.465–466, London 1987.

Mondragón

ROBERT HETTLAGE [J]

(see also: *Conceptions, Co-operative*; *History of Ideas*; *Joint-production Co-operatives*; *Production Co-operatives*; *Labour-Management*; *Israel*)

I. General Characteristics; II. The History of its Creation and Other Influential Factors of Genesis; III. The Composition of the Mondragón Co-operative Group; IV. Solving the Traditional Problems of Production Co-operatives.

I. General Characteristics

The Mondragón co-operative group, named after the industrial Basque city of Mondragón in northern Spain, is considered the most successful amalgamation of production co-operatives in the world (*Bradley/Gelb*). For over 35 years it has proven its functional ability in both business and social matters, even in international markets. Mondragón demonstrates that → *joint-production co-operatives* must not inevitably be subject to → *Oppenheimer's* law of transformation.

The Mondragón co-operative group came into existence in 1956, when the co-operative "Ulgor" started producing kitchen appliances. The foundations for its remarkable development into a co-operative complex, currently involving almost 20,000 members, were laid at this time. These members are scattered among 300 enterprises (including branch offices). Of these, 100 are industrial co-operatives (whereby Ulgor only accounts for approx. 15% of total turnover). Among the others are 43 school co-operatives, 14 home-building associations, seven agricultural co-operatives (→ *Rural Co-operatives*), three service co-operatives and one → *consumer co-operative*.

These primary co-operatives are supplemented by four secondary co-operatives which have acquired a particular importance for the development of the entire group: a popular bank (Caja Laboral Popular) with 141 branch offices, a technological research facility (Ikerlan), an insurance co-operative (Lagun-Aro) and an institution for higher technical training (vocational, polytechnic and business schools). The enterprises today are dispersed throughout the Basque region.

II. The History of its Creation and Other Influential Factors of Genesis

The formation of the co-operative complex was closely tied with personal initiative and ideological backgrounds as well as with particular social, political and economic conditions.

1. Promoters and Initiators

The most decisive impulses and the most important encouragement and support emanated from one individual, the Jesuit father *José Maria Arizmendi* who was priest of the Mondragón parish. His engagement began in parish work (in the hospital, home building, and schools) and in mobilizing the population along the lines of self-help in 1941. Out of these efforts an independent technical vocational school was founded in 1943, followed by an educational school co-operative in 1948 (Lega de educación y cultura) and later the polytechnic academy. His objective was to gather young, technically skilled, entrepreneurial, and socially involved individuals with community support together into study groups (e.g. through the Catholic Work Youth) and hence to create initiative groups striving for multi-faceted social development. The initiators of the Mondragón group all hailed from the first graduating class of the local vocational school, who through *Arizmendi* were able to continue their technical studies in Zaragossa. Five of them founded Ulgor in 1956, the heart of the Mondragón experiment. Although *Arizmendi* never assumed an official function within the co-operatives themselves, his manuscripts are still considered today to be the fundamental basis for all subsequent activity. They are based on Catholic social philosophy which supports the interdependence between work and capital instead of class struggle and encourages self-responsibility (solidarity and group liability, limitation of state control, a socially guided market structure, private property, a world view of workers relatively free of class-consciousness). *Ellerman* felt Mondragón to be the best embodiment of such visions of social structure "by associating labor with the ownership of capital, as far as possible, and by producing a wide range of intermediate bodies with economic, social and cultural purposes..." (1984, p.278).

2. The Social and Political Environment

a) Basque Nationalism

The great importance of Basque identity for the success of this co-operative model is constantly emphasized. Euskara, the only pre–Indogermanic language spoken in all of Western Europe, is native to the Basque region; this is an indication of the steadfast existence of the settlements here and the autonomy of the people. A strong cohesiveness between the geographic region, the language and the communities has obviously developed and has in turn affected the co-operatives (*Thomas/Logan*). Expressions of this include the high degree of camaraderie among workers (associations, eating clubs) (*Oakeshott*).

This cohesiveness can be activated against influence from outside. During the years in which *Franco's* unified authoritarian Spanish state attempted to surpress regional particularities, resistance against the central authorities heightened in the Basque region. Even today, the Basque-oriented political parties which promote economic democracy are still elected with an absolute majority of votes (*Bradley/Gelb*).

b) The tradition of self-help

Closely connected to nationalism in this region is the rural tradition of self-help, which has contributed to the thought of interpretating modern co-operatives as living cultural goods ("Hauzo Lan": construction and repair work done within the neighborhood; "Lorra": collective harvesting). Furthermore, local autonomy, decentralization and rural democracy have likewise had great importance. The opportunity to draw from and work within local and rural traditions of thought and social structure proved to be an important factor for modern co-operative self-help, cooperation and self-administration. *Arizmendi* therefore initially focused his efforts on the community, organized social relief organizations and put into force a complex network system of responsibilities and reciprocal trust (*Gutierrez-Johnson*).

c) *The worker's movement oriented along co-operative ideas*

The Basque labor union movement, particularly the Catholic (ELA-STV) but also the socialist (UGT), consistently strove to expand the co-operatives in connection with the nationalist sentiments and the visions of social reform at hand. The union found resonance and support among farmers, workers and small-scale producers. *Bradley/Gelb* (1982), therefore, more strongly emphasize the co-operative spirit than the ethnicity factor. One must, however, also take into consideration that the Spanish central government has supported co-operative business structures since 1960, and that Mondragón has accordingly benefited.

3. The Economic Environment

Alongside the socio-political factors, series of favorable economic factors has also been influential. On the one hand, the tradition of artisan metal working in the Basque region stretches back to the Middle Ages, a factor which facilitated the move to modern metal fabrication. On the other hand, the level of development for the production of household appliances in Spain in the 1950s was low enough to manage with a relatively small amount of initial capital, provided through the traditional self-help network. As the motor of development, "Ulgor" furthermore acquired a firm position for itself on the durable consumer goods market and continued to expand. Not only did market observations prove to be true, but the consciousness and willingness among the initiators to confront problems and adapt organizationally to the market were also quite high. Top priority was therefore placed on capital accumulation and technical innovation, continued training for workers, and the stimulation of their willingness to undertake risks. This also became evident in Mondragón in the typical relationship and interaction between joint-production and credit co-operatives (→ *Co-operative Banks*).

III. The Composition of the Mondragón Co-operative Group

Mondragón did not become known throughout the world only due to its commercial success but also because of its innovative application of the co-operative principles to the exigencies of modern organizational structure.

1. The Industrial Production Co-operative

The Mondragón co-operatives are self-managed enterprises which abide by the principles of identity, solidarity and democracy (→ *Labour-Management*). The principle of identity focuses on the possession of company holdings; it states that (almost) all employees are to be co-operative members so that membership rights cannot be bought but rather can only be acquired through "self-labor". Each member upon entry is obligated to contribute a capital share of approx. DM 7,500, 25% of which must be paid upfront. The remainder can be payed through salary deductions. Annual interest up to 6% is payed on capital.

The → *solidarity* principle refers to the distribution of surplus which is broken down through arrangements about income distribution, dividends and reserves. Compensation for work is payed through monthly "advances" against company revenue according to a "job coefficient" (qualification, experience, responsibility, etc.), whereby the wage span's maximum ratio is 1:3. Profit shares are distributed proportionally to the monthly income (*Thomas/Logan*, 1982, p.154 ff.), but they are only then available upon withdrawal/retirement from the co-operative.

The principle of democracy regulates individual co-determination rights. This is manifested at the annual general assembly (one man – one vote) where the investments and balances are decided upon, where the supervisory board (control authority) and the board of directors (external business management) are elected. The board of directors, as acting executive authority, appoints the president (Gerente) and the department heads; these officers together devise a management plan and present it to the board.

The 'social council' (consejo social) represents members as company employees. This council is elected by the employees; it is a consultational body which is concerned with all aspects of personnel and information.

2. Other Primary Co-operatives

At an early stage of the Mondragón development, the initiators founded a consumer co-operative which was consolidated with eight other rural retail stores into the new co-operative "Eroski" in 1969. Today, this co-operative has around 50 stores throughout the Basque region with over 70,000 consumer-members and 800 worker-members. In accordance with "work primacy", not only do the consumers support and benefit from the co-operative enterprise; employees likewise have the right of co-determination and are included in profit distribution according to their special membership category in the consumer co-operatives. Eroski is thus a hybrid of consumer and production co-operatives (*Ellerman*, 1984, p.14 ff.).

Seven agricultural co-operatives also exist which differ from the usual characteristic type. Not only are farmers members of the co-operative as producers (socios productores), but also the employees in the operational unit (socios transformadores). The agricultural and production types of co-operatives are intermixed in accordance with work primacy.

In the 1970s, co-operative home-building associations (→ *Housing Societies*) were integrated into the co-operative complex to facilitate financing the construction or purchase of housing units (currently over 1200 homes). Furthermore about 50 school co-operatives can be counted with 31,000 school children in pre-school, elementary and secondary levels. In addition to that, there is a schooling program "Lega de educación y cultura" operating separately; parents, teachers and students comprise the membership of this co-operative, which is financed in part through social funds provided by the popular bank and through other co-operatives in the complex at large. The student co-operative Alecoop likewise needs to be mentioned which arranges work for students (mostly jobs in the other co-operatives) as partial financing for their studies. Finally, the service co-operative Auzo-Lagun was organized especially for women who, on account of their situation at home, wish to work part time and/or have flexible work schedules. This co-operative has specialized in kitchen work, company cafeterias, laundries and janitorial work.

3. Secondary Co-operatives

Arizmendi's most important concept was the development of a network of secondary co-operatives which connects the various enterprises. This is of particular importance for financing and education.

a) The Popular Bank "Caja Laboral Popular" (CLP)

"Caja" was founded in 1959, three years after the establishment of Ulgor, in order to solve the predicaments the co-operatives faced concerning capital and credit. This former institution for capital collection is today the normative and controlling center for the Mondragón complex and to a great extent has the identical internal structure as the primary co-operatives (*Saive*, 1980). All co-operatives are in contractual association with CLP, which lays down the legal structure of the individual enterprises (democratic principles, membership rights, tending to accounts, etc.) and determines the co-operatives' relationship to the central banking institution (capital investment share, deposits in CLP, mandatory accounting reports, CLP's right to audit, etc.). Once again, the co-operatives comprise not only the membership of Caja but also the employees of the bank itself. The bank management is thus voted for through a 2:1 ratio from representatives of the co-operatives and bank staff. This results in a combined co-operative form between primary and secondary co-operatives (→ *Central Institutions*).

CLP has had an interventionary role in the individual co-operatives since 1969 beyond the sole fulfillment of banking transactions (division economica). Its management department (division empresarial) undertakes consultational and support work for the affiliated co-operatives and solves financing questions arising from operational restructuring and the formation of new co-operatives. This department works within the fields of business studies, agriculture, industry promotion, consulting (export, personnel, law, administration, marketing), intervention, auditing, urban planning and construction; a management council presides over this department. The divison "industry promotion" analyses new products and future markets, providing individual co-operatives with market studies. In case of founding a new co-operative, advantage can be taken of these various management services by entering into a credit agreement with "Caja".

b) "Ikerlan", the Co-operative Research Insititute

An umbrella organization funded by the co-operatives has been responsible for research since 1979; its internal structure functions similarly to that of CLP. Here, sixty researchers working in the fields of electronics, thermodynamics and computer-aided production develop machine and product prototypes which are then passed on to the affiliated co-operatives.

c) The Insurance Co-operative "Lagun-Aro"

Because co-operative workers in the strict sense of the term are not salaried staff, they are excluded from the Spanish social security system. Social security was thus provided for co-operative members in the scope of CLP's undertakings (Lagun-Aro) (→ *Insurance, Germany*). This field of activity has been operating independently since the beginning of the 1970s. Lagun-Aro ensures retirement for 20,000 members (60% of average income from the last ten years), offers protection against illness, disability and unemployment, and offers retraining and work hygiene programs.

4. Umbrella Organizations for all Branches

The Mondragón co-operatives are not only connected to one another through CLP but also through twelve branch and regional groups. (Ularco is the most well-known and has been in existence since 1964). Returns to scale should be utilized, norms should be made more uniform, social services improved and controls simplified. After deducting its reserve fund from its achieved surplus, each co-operative transfers the remainder to this group; these funds are then accordingly distributed among all enterprises which suffered losses in this business period. New employment opportunities must be provided within the realm of the umbrella organization upon the incursion of job losses as notices of dismissal are not possible (→ *Human Resource Management*).

IV. Solving the Traditional Problems of Production Co-operatives

Joint-production co-operatives frequently suffer from four fundamental weaknesses which make this organizational form seem problematic to many people. Mondragón has proven that these problems can be overcome.

1. Market and Financing Problems

Lack of capital is the basic problem for all joint-production co-operatives as members usually are without means and private lenders are not interested in such an undertaking. Because of this situation the Mondragón group has attained a high rate of self-financing from the beginning through strict regulations. Surpluses are partially accumulated and stored, wages are not raised above the regional average, and dividends are retained in the co-operative until a member withdraws/retires. CLP makes use of the deposits of the general population. Furthermore, 30% of the surplus generated by primary co-operatives must be directed to CLP, and 20% of a co-operative's starting capital is to be raised by members, who furthermore are liable for losses against their equity accounts. On the other hand, CLP offers its specialized know-how in the investigation of markets and market entry preparation.

2. The Problem of Discipline

Co-operatives, like all companies, can only flourish with good management and qualified workers. *Arizmendi* therefore founded numerous training centers which were intended to promote co-operative spirit and technical capability (→ *Education, Europe*). The wage scale also tends to promote solidarity as it allocates varying pay rates to members, but within a limited pay span. Beyond these measures, the performance standards for productivity and discipline are stiff, and the penal sanctions for poor behaviour are severe.

3. The Utilization of Achieved Surpluses

Tension occasionally arises in co-operatives between private and collective needs. The desire to distribute a dividend leads to underinvestment (→ *Financing*). The associational contract with CLP compensates between private and collective interests. One can only join membership ranks with solid financing from the beginning. The co-operatives must reinvest the greater part of their surplus. Strict standards are also enforced among the banks concerning financial and administrative assistance.

4. Open Membership

Older co-operative members frequently tend not to accept new members but rather secure the status of non-members being in salaried employment (non-members) (→ *Selection of Members*). The co-operative slowly transforms itself into a private corporation through this manner. Mondragón, however, regularly endeavors to create new employment opportunities (new co-operatives) and only permits 5% of employees to be non-members. Aside from this, all employees must be willing to switch their particular jobs within the group in emergency situations. Problems concerning co-determination and wages for each job position are looked after by the social works council. Furthermore, newly formed co-operatives are encouraged to keep their operational size relatively small in order that more participational experience can be acquired (*Drimer/Drimer* 1984).

The future problems of the Mondragón complex are threefold in nature:

1) Because of the age structure of their membership, many co-operatives could be facing difficulties when too many equity accounts are liquidated at one time by members entering retirement.
2) Basque nationalism could marginalize the Mondragón group within the Spanish co-operative movement (*Saive*, 1981).
3) Decision-making power frequently does not rest at the basis of the organizations (general assembly) but rather is in the hands of management and/or CLP bank management due to the importance of competitiveness in individual enterprises (*Flecker* et al. 1984).

Up to now, the Mondragón group has, however, proved to be more solid in times of crisis than many private enterprises thanks to its market success and healthy work climate (*Flecker* et al.).

Bibliography

Arismendiarrieta, José Maria: La empresa para el hombre, Bilbao, 1984.
Azurmendi, José: El hombre cooperativo. Pensamiento de Arismendiarrieta, San Sebastian 1984.
Bradley, Keith/Gelb, Alan: The replication and sustainability of the Mondragón experiment. In: British Journal of Industrial Relations 20: pp. 20–33, 1982.
Dolan, Patrick: Mondragón co-operatives. In: Industrial Participation, Spring: pp. 8–12, 1981.
Drimer, Bernardo/Kaplan de Drimer, Alicia: The Mondragón solutions to the traditional problems of work-

ers' co-operatives. In: Review of International Co-operation 77: pp. 29–37, 1984.
Ellerman, David P.: Entrepreneurship in the Mondragón cooperatives. In: Review of Social Economy 42: pp. 272–294, 1984a.
Ellerman, David P.: The Mondragón Cooperative Movement, Harvard Business School (Case No. 1: 384–270), Boston: pp. 1–31, 1984b.
Flecker, Jörg/Gubitzer, Luise/Todtling, Franz: Betriebliche Selbstverwaltung und eigenständige Regionalentwicklung am Beispiel der Genossenschaft von Mondragón. In: Wirtschaft und Gesellschaft 10: pp. 499–526, 1984.
Gutierrez-Johnson, Ana/Whyte, William Foote: The Mondragón system of worker production cooperatives. In: Industrial and Labor Relations Review 31: pp. 18–30, 1977.
Gutierrez-Johnson, Ana: Industrial Democracy in Action: The Cooperative Complex of Mondragón. Cornell University, Ithaca, New York, 1982.
Heisig, Peter: Das Kooperativ-Experiment von Mondragón. Entstehung und Entwicklung des Kooperativ-Komplexes und die Formen der Partizipation in der Leitung. (Diplomarbeit, unveröffentlichtes Manuskript), Göttingen 1987.
Oakeshott, Robert: The Case of Workers' Co-ops., London: pp. 165–214, 1978.
Olabarri, Ignacio: Tradiciones cooperativas vascas. In: Euskal Herria, Historia Y Sociedad, Mondragón: pp. 298–307, 1985.
Saive, Anne-Marie: Mondragón: Ein genossenschaftliches Entwicklungsexperiment im Industriebereich. In: Annalen der Gemeinwirtschaft 49: pp. 223–255, 1980.
Saive, Anne-Marie: Notes sur Mondragón et les aspects doctrinaux du projet coopératif. In: Annalen der Gemeinwirtschaft 50: pp. 369–379, 1981.
Thomas, Henk/Logan, Chris: Mondragón: An Economic Analysis, London 1982.

Motivation for Cooperation

Juhani Laurinkari

(see also: *Incentives*; *Managerial Economics*; *Structural Types*; *Relationship Patterns*; *Group Theory*)

I. Motivation for Participation; II. Fundamental Types of Membership Behavior; III. A Differentiation of Membership based on Motives for Cooperation.

According to all previous empirical studies into the subject, the primary motive for membership in a co-operative is the attainment of economic advantages affiliated with such membership (→ *Incentives*). Participating actively and/or exercising direct influence in the decision-making process are factors of only marginal importance valued by members to varying extents.

I. Motivation for Participation

Members can be classified into the following categories based on their *motivation for participation* irregardless of their formal membership status:

1) *Positive members* are highly motivated and choose to join a co-operative with a clear purpose in mind. Through their membership, say in a consumer co-operative, they hope to keep their expenses for consumer goods as low as possible and thereby maximize their purchasing power.
2) *Negative members* do not have any particular motivation behind their decision to join a co-operative. Tradition and social pressure in part push them into their membership roles, but the lack of alternatives is likewise of importance. Some of them even become members in order to inflict damage on the co-operative; others hope to attain exclusively egoistic advantages.
3) *Neutral members* join upon receiving advice/encouragement from friends and business partners without having personally formulated any clear conceptions of the co-operative or expectations from it.

Empirical studies furthermore indicate that members hailing from lower social classes with lower income levels place higher expectations in their membership – in order to achieve personal advantage – than is the case for better situated members hailing from higher social classes (→ *Group, the Co-operative*). The most important *factors behind motivation* and the willingness to take part in a co-operative are the *level of eduction, income and employment sector*. The lower a member's level of education, the greater his willingness to participate. Members who are employed in manual labor jobs likewise indicate a greater penchant to join.

II. Fundamental Types of Membership Behavior

Stryjan (1987, p.48) differentiates between four fundamental types of membership behavior: resignation, contestation, involvement and loyalty (Figure 1). Unsatisfied members can quit membership on their own accord, raise complaints or quietly hope without offering any contestation that their situation will improve. *Hirschman* added the category of "involved" members to these modes of behavior to describe constructive members who are prepared to take matters in their own hands and solve their problems themselves. Initiative springs from the individual member not in the hope of achieving monetary advantage but rather in order to show personal effort and involvement. *Hirschman* believes there are members who secure themselves certain advantages. Members can value the feeling of "having made a deal" just as much as benefiting from economic or financial profit (*Stryjan*, 1987, p.48).

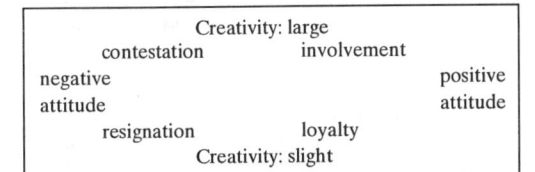

Creativity: large
contestation   involvement
negative   positive
attitude   attitude
resignation   loyalty
Creativity: slight

Figure 1: Member Behavior with regard to the Co-operative Organization (*Stryjan*, 1987, p.48).

Involvement and *contestation* are the most important forms of behavior for participation; they are the most significant factors for motivation and cooperation. The inclination and willingness to cooperate require organizational forms and procedural methods which both promote and co-ordinate engaged behavior; a situation and/or atmosphere must be created in which objections can be converted into constructive criticism. By all means, however, a dissatisfied member should not be forced into behaving "constuctively" at all times; a certain acceptance for criticism is necessary as well as the insight that existant situations might require alteration. Active members quickly distance themselves from co-operatives which brush aside criticism.

There is a close connection between the size of a co-operative (→ *Operational Size*) and the degree of member participation in the general meetings. The greater the number of members and the larger the co-operative, the slighter members' inclination to take part in the general assemblies. The size of the co-operative correlates negatively with member participation, whereas the payment of reimbursements and rebates correlates weakly with the participation level of members (c.f. *Pestoff*, 1988) (→ *Managerial Economics*).

In general, there is a postive correlation between participation in membership meetings and the incentive or inspiration associated with such participation, i.e. the promotion of a living and working democracy and encouraging other members also to contribute actively. The number of elected mandataries correlates negatively with member participation (c.f. *Pestoff*, 1988).

As the co-operative grows in size, it becomes more and more like any other anonymous company found on the market for its members (→ *Structural Types*). Members no longer feel attached or affiliated with their co-operative. A sure indicator of member attachment to their co-operative is loyalty in their purchasing habits (c.f. *Pestoff*, 1988).

As mentioned above, the primary motive for participation according to foregoing empirical investigation can be found in members' efforts to attain economic advantages. Involvement in decision-making processes within the co-operative in contrast to this is of only secondary importance.

In the past, the activization/mobilization of members within co-operatives to encourage membership participation received much too little attention. Such activities will, however, become more important in the future. Above all, the close attachment and affiliation of members to their co-operative will stand in the forefront of such activities. Membership participation paves the way for numerous opportunities to intensify interaction between management and members (c.f. *Ringle*, 1986).

III. A Differentiation of Membership based on Motives for Cooperation

Various efforts have been made to identify and classify members in the co-operative sector. *Suonoja* (1971) developed a model which is based on *Merton's* classification (1957); in part this is linked with the sense of attachment a member shares for the co-operative organization (the motivation to take part in the activities of the co-operative), and in part this takes into consideration the activity of the co-operative. *Attachment* means the extent a member holds the co-operative organization to be important in comparison with other organizations. It is likewise evidence of his motivation and willingness to cooperate within his member organization. *Activity* in turn is determined by the degree of member participation in the decision-making processes within the co-operative undertaking.

The following classification quadrant is the result of this membership breakdown:

		Activity	
		active	passive
Level of	attached	"official"	"morally attached"
attachment	disjoined	"politician"	"total apathy"

Figure 2: Membership Typology in Co-operatives (*Laurinkari*, 1985, p.9).

The "official" type of member can thus be described as being active and attached. In contrast to this typological form, many members are passive even if they are attached to some other commercial undertaking. *Laakkonen* (1981) conceived a comprehensive human typology for co-operatives which was rooted in *Rissmann's* theories (1950). This typology was construed in order to identify the manners and reasons (motivation) behind members' decision to join a co-operative. This typology includes eleven different types of members with varying focal points of orientation; of these, the first three are driven by forces from within, the four middle ones are driven by both internal and external forces, and the final four are driven solely by external forces.

1. homo economicus – thrifty individual
2. homo ludens   – playful individual
3. homo faber   – industrious individual
4. homo socialis   – social individual

5. homo arripens — capricious individual
6. homo ancius — anxious individual
7. homo traditionalis — individual tied to tradition
8. homo institutionalis — individual determined by dynamic/activity in an organization
9. homo adaptans — adapted individual
10. homo ambitius — ambitious individual
11. homo alimentarious — individual clutching his advantages

		Membership Activity	
		instrumental	expressive
Membership	economic-pragmatic	"pragmatist"	"ethicist"
Relationship	ideal-political	"politician"	"passive sympathizer"

Figure 3: Membership Typology in Co-operatives (*Ilmonen*, 1981, p.12; *Laurinkari*, 1985, p.12).

The basic variables in both of these typologies (*Suonoja* and *Laakkonen*) are formulated on the basis of the individual — on his traits and characteristics. In order to provide a more comprehensive answer to the question, however, a classification needs to be presented which is more of a direct extension of membership relationships and/or member activities. One such typology was conceived by *Ilmonen* (1981) which takes into consideration the membership relationship between various organizations such as between the various organizations forms found in the co-operative movement. According to *Ilmonen*, two primary types or forms of expressions of member relationships exist:

The former type is dominated by economic-pragmatic affairs, the latter by ideal-political matters. In this reduced form such a break-down is reflective of the world at large. *Ilmonen* adds that economic and political elements existed side by side in member relationships during the early years of the co-operative movement.

Membership, say in a → *consumer co-operative*, expresses both individual and collective interests. It is defined by the needs and interests of the individual member. Members in turn express their interests in the form of various activities, be they political and/or economic in nature. In everyday practise, members keep in mind both the content and extent of promotional support as well as the co-operative's administration. The second type of member relationship identified by *Ilmonen*, the one with an "ideal-political" character, is shaped by factors which can be of considerable importance as influential controlling factors within the co-operative movement.

The character of the member relationships is also determined by the manner in which the individual functions in the organization in his capacity as a member (→ *Managerial Economics*). Among other things, *Parson's* classification into instrumental and expressive activities (1967) reflects various configurations of member relationships. By cross-tabulating this break-down with the previous classification of membership typology, membership can be subdivided into four parts as follows (see Figure 3).

This quadrant represents a reduction of the ideal model of various types of members in the co-operative movement. The break-downs are always determined by the contractual configuration of the relationship between the member and co-operative.

Ilmonen (1981) described "pragmatists" as members who avail themselves of offered services and act according to accepted principles of reason (e.g. taking advantage of the palette of goods and services at their convenient disposal).

"Ethicists", on the other hand, avail themselves of available promotion out of principle — even when the co-operative enterprise does not offer the most favorably priced goods on the market (→ *Ethics*). Membership in the co-operative represents a question of moral substance for ethicists.

"Politicians", as a rule, are members because they seek to collect votes for their own party and/or use the organization as a "political springboard". The co-operative enterprise represents more of a means to an end than a moral concern for politicians.

"Passive sympathizers" themselves do not take part in the decision-making processes within the enterprise but, nonetheless, generally support the furtherance of the co-operative. The majority of such individuals are "members out of habit" in the organization.

Bibliography

Ilmonen, K.: Elämänolojen Muutos ja E-liikkeen jäsenyys, Helsinki 1981.
Laurinkari, Juhani: Typisierung von Funktionsträgern in Finnland. Veröffentlichungen des Forschungsinstituts für Genossenschaftswesen an der Universität Erlangen-Nürnberg, Publication no.23, Nürnberg 1985.
Laakkonen, Vesa.: Osuustoimintaihmisen muotokuva. E-lehti, n:04, 1981.
Merton, R.: Social Theory and Social Structure, Glencoe 1957.
Pestoff, V.A.: Co-operative Efficiency — A Preliminary Discussion of the Concept in the Swedish Context. Working Party for Research, Planning and Development (ICA), Bologna 1988.
Riessman, D.: The Lonely Crowd, New Haven 1950.
Ringle, G.: Strategien zur Gestaltung intergenossenschaftlicher Gruppenaktivität und Kommunikation. In: Laurinkari, Juhani (ed.): Die Prinzipien des Genossenschaftswesens in der Gegenwart. Festschrift für Prof. Vesa Laakkonen. Veröffentlichungen des Forschungsinstituts für Genossenschaftswesen an der Universität Erlangen-Nürnberg, Publication no. 24, Nürnberg 1986.
Stryjan, Y.: Attäterskapa Medlemskapet. Kooperativ Ärsbok 1987, Stockholm 1987.
Suonoja, K.: E-osuusliikkeen luottamushenkilön muotokuva. E-lehti n:03, 1971.

Multi-Use Credit Co-operatives

EMMERICH BAKONYI [J]

(see also: *Classification; Rural Co-operatives; Co-operative Banks; Linking Banks*)

I. Definition; II. Evolution and Development; III. Development in a Competitive Economy; IV. Outlook.

I. Definition

The term "multi-use credit co-operative" characterizes credit co-operatives (→ *Co-operative Banks*) which carry out non-banking activities, primarily merchandising aimed at clients involved in agriculture, alongside their main business activity of banking transactions. They are also called "*credit co-operatives with supplemental business*", "*all-purpose*" or "*universal co-operatives*". The Raiffeisen banks are typical of this form, which, because of their primary activity, are considered *co-operative banks* or *credit co-operatives*; because of their supplementary merchandising trade, they also belong to the category of "rural consumer and service co-operatives" (→ *Rural Co-operatives*). At least a part of the multi-purpose co-operative societies active in the developing countries likewise belongs to this category of multi-use co-operative (*Ghaussy*, 1964). Their auxiliary business can encompass various undertakings, but it mainly serves to purchase means of production at favorable costs for the agricultural enterprises and household yards of their members, as well as heating material and other consumer goods for rural households. As a rule, economically the most important function is the procurement of fertilizer and feed. This article will attempt to sketch the problematic nature of the multi-use credit co-operatives based on the example of the German Raiffeisenbanken.

II. Evolution and Development

1. Evolution and Organization

Usually, multi-use credit co-operatives are called into being during a transitional phase in which an economy based on self-sufficiency is replaced by the market, or the natural economy by an economy run on a monetary basis. This thus takes place in an age when the traditional agricultural society slowly but surely develops into an industrial society. The lack of a comprehensive network of together with the local or regional monopolistic position of cattle and property traders forces, above all, those farmers with small to medium-sized enterprises into the arms of money and merchandise profiteers (*Faust; Maxeiner*). As an answer to this challenge, sporadic attempts at establishing self-help institutions similar to the multi-use credit co-operatives were undertaken in Germany as early as the 1820s (*Faust*); this form, however, first became wide-spread under the efforts of → *Friedrich Wilhelm Raiffeisen*.

The key to success of the rural credit co-operatives within the financial sector was, above all, the improvement of members' credit solvency through the collective assumption of security and collateral for the individual borrowers (joint warranty). *Raiffeisen* initially counted on the charitable participation of the wealthier classes of rural society for the procurement of credits and credit guarantees, but he was quickly forced to recognize that their willingness to help rapidly disintegrated. After exchanging ideas with *Hermann* → *Schulze-Delitzsch* in 1862, he consequently propagated the principle of self-help: "Concern for one's own interest is the common tenet which must hold organizations of this kind together" (*Faust*, p. 283). By 1862, *Raiffeisen* started participating in the establishment of numerous self-help associations for farmers as chief administrator. In 1866, he published his collected experience in this field in the book *Die Darlehenskassen–Vereine als Mittel zur Abhilfe der Not der ländlichen Bevölkerung* (The Loan Association as a Means to relieve the Need of the Rural Population). This was the impulse for the establishment of numerous multi-use credit co-operatives which, alongside providing credits, also undertook the procurement of production means and, to some degree, the marketing of their production surplus (→ *History in 19th C.*).

2. Innovation for Agriculture and Rural Regions

Raiffeisen's multi-use credit co-operatives, the "loan associations", proved to be an important innovation in two aspects. On the one hand, they *made their members creditworthy through joint warranty* (see above). On the other hand, they, at an early stage, contributed to *involving rural localities in economic development*. Credit institutes with agricultural merchandise trading were founded in locations where turnover levels per community at that time could hardly provide an existence for a company oriented along the lines of the free market.

The association between monetary and commoditiy transactions surely contributed significantly to the rapid development of rural credit co-operatives with merchandise trading. In the early years of the loan associations, the initially low turnover levels in both the financial and merchandising branches called for a close connection between the two; employed resources could thus be utilized better. Above all, those members relying on self-help were financially only burdened with one full-time employee. The connection between financial transactions and merchandise trading also demonstrated *synergy effects*. It is much easier for members to procure both, money and commodities, under the same roof. Those members more interested in purchasing merchandise (→ *Supply Co-operatives*) are thus more strongly integrated in the co-operative. A result of the joint warranty is that all members want each borrower to be able to pay back his loan to the co-operative through successful business transactions. They thus attempt to introduce all technical advances in the enterprises of the borrowers, for example the utilization of mineral fertilizers. They thereby not only strengthen their own self-help organization but likewise the forces of economic progress. The combination of money and merchandise signalizes a welcome risk compensation for the primary co-operative. Conflicts of interest between the financial clients and merchandise clients can, however, arise. This itself is a reason why a competitive model promoted by *Wilhelm Haas* could also gain ground parallel to *Raiffeisen's* model. This second model called for a combination of rural credit co-operatives *without* any supplementary transactions and independent "agricultural consumer societies".

III. Development in a Competitive Economy

1. Cooperation and Consolidation as factors strengthening Competitiveness

Within only a few generations, the market economy in the industrialized Western countries produced almost incredible economic growth with an increased demand for foodstuffs. This also brought new purchasing power to the rural regions and made possible the establishment of progressively more non-farming enterprises. Rural localities also gradually became more attractive locations for savings banks, private banks, and the private rural commodities trade. The credit co-operatives, having initiated the competition against village usurers in the 19th century, slowly began losing their local advantage through the establishment of more and more competitive companies and were constantly challenged in the *competition for the patronage of their members* (*Maxeiner*) (→ *Economic Order*). On the village level, those credit co-operatives engaged in merchandise trading had a difficult position against the regional and supra-regional competitors. Limiting their realm of activity to one village and to a set membership body, generally meant that their turnover was restricted to the needs of this membership and thus remained at a fairly constant level. When purchasing outputs, individuals were not in the position to expect any considerable type of bulk discounts nor were the primary co-operatives able to attain any "size effects" based on their organization. All of this caused no problems for competition; such organizational advantages had already secured the enterprises with larger → *operational size* considerable pricing advantages. Because their own equity level was often too low, the local co-operatives were only able to guarantee loans capped with a low ceiling. In addition, it was quite difficult to remain head on head with the larger companies in the targeted training and specialization of workers (→ *History in 19th C.*).

In order to at least remedy these deficiencies in part, the undertakings of the individual credit co-operatives were gradually integrated into the *co-operative federation*. *Raiffeisen*, already in 1872, had founded an "agricultural co-operative bank" for the transfer of liquid assets in and among the co-operatives. Today, the same function is carried out by the regionally established central co-operative banks. The central banks also serve as a clearing house for transfer business. Rounding out their palette of services, various special co-operative institutes also offer the rural co-operatives assistance in the fields of personal and property insurance, savings for home construction, etc. The agricultural co-operative centers active on a regional level, fulfill particularly important functions for merchandise trading conducted through the multi-use credit co-operatives. By consolidating orders together for their member co-operatives, they are able to negotiate bulk discounts with their suppliers. Their turnover levels also allow them to construct their own production enterprises, for example feed lots, and to offer these products to their members. As early as 1877, *Raiffeisen* had founded a "bar association" which assumed the auditing and consulting work for the loan associations. Today, the services of the regional co-operative federations and the German Raiffeisen Union on the the national level are at the disposal of the rural credit co-operatives. The ever more important tasks of training and continuing education for personnel in the fields of monetary and merchandising transactions is entrusted to the regional co-operative academies and the Academy of German Co-operatives (→ *Education and Training, Germany*). The disadvantages of the rural co-operatives, tailored around the needs of their members, can be alleviated through cooperation in the federation, but cooperation alone cannot check forced economic consolidation.

The stronger the location grows and the economic power increases of the region in which the multi-use co-operatives were founded, the more intense their competition will be. Mounting investment demands by the companies situated at the location, progressive professional employment differentiation and heightened savings practices of (potential) clients necessitate employment specialization as well as adaptation in the economic competitiveness and image of the banks. This requires *consolidation through either growth or mergers*. The easiest method to offset personnel costs is to increase turnover. Aside from these factors of influential size and the ever-present competition, various legislative measures also press for consolidation and the expansion of outputs and services. Among the legal provisions are primarily stipulations in the Moneylender's Act concerning personnel, equity allocation, the extent of credits, etc. Within merchandise trading, the growing average size of the farming enterprises, more fierce competition, and the consolidation among suppliers also require an enlargement of co-operative enterprise and company sizes (see DEUTSCHER RAIFFEISENVERBAND, p.17).

The consolidation process among the multi-use credit co-operatives was particularly accelerated by the rapid upturn of the German economy in the second half of the 20th century. Among other things, this lead to an amalgamation of rural credit co-operatives (Raiffeisenbanken) and industrial/commercial credit unions (Volksbanken) at the beginnning of the 1970s. Whereas the total number of *simple* credit co-operatives in Germany dropped 42.3% between 1960 and 1988 (from 2,755), the number of *multi-use* credit co-operatives fell 80% in the same time period (from 8,896). Membership in the latter increased 147% between 1960 and 1988 (from 1.38 million), but membership in the simple credit co-operatives increased 212% (from 3.85 million, see DG BANK). In a regionally differentiated but altogether dramatic speed, the influence of credit co-operatives with a relatively low level of turnover in merchandising receded. Between 1974 and 1984 alone, the percentile share of credit co-operatives with merchandise trading in the sales category of up to DM 1 million slipped from 60.6% to 24.4%. In the same category, the loss of importance of the agricultural purchasing and marketing co-operatives in comparison fell less dramatically (decrease from 49.2% to 27.0%, see DEUTSCHER RAIFFEISENVERBAND e.V., p.18).

In the larger operating units brought upon by consolidation, the individual member looses his ability to exercise influence personally, this in turn as the highest self-administrational body of the largest co-operatives, in part on account of legal provisions, is no longer the general assembly but rather an assembly of representatives (indirect democracy). This situation, along with other circumstances, causes the member to gradually loose sight of the differences he initially saw between the rural co-operatives and their competitors.

2. The Relationship between the Market Co-operative and its Members

At least the first loan associations counted among the ranks of the "traditional co-operative" (→ *Structural Types*). They stepped into action upon the instigation of their members and were so-called "ancillary undertakings" of and for the members. In the *competitive economy* (→ *Competion*), the multi-use credit co-operatives can only hold their own as "*market co-operatives*", in which the business management pursues a "pricing and output policy independent from the effective orders placed by the membership" (*Dülfer*). This means that the primary co-operative enterprise also offers its services to non-members.

On the other hand, the ties between members and their co-operative noticeably relax in the face of functional competition. Because their credit requirements can now be satisfied on the market, members become less and less willing to participate in a situation of unlimited joint warranty. This is replaced by *limited liability*. As a consumer, the member no longer limits himself to those banking or merchandising transactions offered by his credit co-operative. He much more often explores the offers of the competitors and *selectively chooses his market partner from situation to situation*, when he can expect economic advantages. When the price is the same for the same service, he chooses the nearest supplier, generally the local credit co-operative offering merchandise trading. When he is confronted with differing prices, he orients himself around whether the potential *price savings* surpass the sum of the additional *travel expenses* in addition to an individually defined *mobility threshold*. In the scope of an empirical study concerning the behavior of farmers with respect to their procurement of fertilizer and feed, particularly of those farmers with a low total requirement, only every fourth farmer wanted to unconditionally remain loyal to the nearest supplier. Every fifth farmer, above all the managers of larger farming enterprises, indicated for an additional hour of commuting time a mobility threshold which coresponded to approx. the six-fold hourly wage of a skilled agricultural worker in the year of the study. The mobility threshold for the majority of the mobile farmers in average reached the three-fold hourly wage of a skilled agricultural worker (*Bakonyi*, 1990). No such comparable research studies are known in the financial sector, but one can nevertheless assume that the service recipient would also behave similarly with respect to the supply of services.

The selective utilization of services by the members in the merchandising trade of multi-use credit co-operatives leads to further *adaptational requirements* and problems. In the 1970s and 1980s, an example of this was how the loose transport of fertilizer and feed in the larger agricultural enterprises practically replaced transport of the same in feedbags, as loose transport has a lower price per unit of weight (→ *Pricing Policy*). The rural credit co-operatives which carry out merchandise trading only to a relatively slight extent, were not able to change over to this new technique and retain their interested customers in this field. In their annual statements, this resulted in posted losses within merchandise trading. In many cases, the logical conclusion would be the discontinuation of the entire range of merchandise business. This would, however, mean an alteration of the purpose of the business activity of the co-operative in question, an action which requires the approval of a qualified majority of members. Not only do the smaller (and loyal) warehouse stock purchasers vote against the discontinuation, but also the majority of members no longer loyal with respect to the purchasing of fertilizer and feed. They namely wish to continue to meet their *small requirements* at the *nearest purchase location*. Therefore merchandise trading, inspite of its losses, will continue to be executed for many years to come. Shrinking sales margins and mounting personnel costs, however, rarely provide economic reimbursement of the losses in sales and income (*Glaser*).

IV. Outlook

A superficial comparison of the frequently documented development of credit co-operatives to merchandising trade could cast the impression that the structural change of this kind of co-operative (→ *Structural Changes*) will once again soon decelerate. In relation to the 1970s, the annual rate of decrease in the 1980s was actually lower (6.28% compared to 4.46 based on compound calculation). The numerical weight of the credit co-operatives with merchandising trade alone has, however, also declined as the rate of decrease of *all credit co-operatives* is even lower (4.99% in the 1970s compared to 2,89% in the 1980s). Merchandise trading will most probably continue to succumb to pressure in the 1990s. The geographic mobility of farmers will increase even more through new technological developments, thus further slackening their ties to the local credit co-operatives. The expected continuation of the changes in agricultural structures, above all the increase in farm size, will have a similar effect. This will, for example, increase the share of feed directly purchased by farmers from feed lots. The sporadic direct procurement of fertilizer visible today will most probably also enlarge considerably. The discounts the co-operative centers today still guarantee credit co-operatives involved in the merchandising trade for orders from individual farmers, will sometime also be discontinued. The current tendency already noticeable in agricultural merchandise, purchasing from a two-tiered (farmer ordering/buying from the credit co-operative, which in turn buys from the co-operative central) to a one-tiered system (farmer buying directly from the co-operative central), is expected to continue. This process will surely be accelerated through measures in agricultural policy concerning a further slowdown of surplus production as well as environmental protection measures affecting the ware-housing of chemicals (*Grosskopf*). More and more credit co-operatives will opt to transfer their merchandising business to other corporate entities in the co-operative federations established by them. Only one human generation ahead, multi-use credit co-operatives will presumably be a rarity in Germany.

Bibliography

Bankonyi, Emmerich: Die Strukturanpassung des genossenschaftlichen Landwarenhandels aus der Sicht württembergischer Landwirte. Arbeitspapiere der Forschungsstelle für Genossenschaftswesen an der Universität Hohenheim, vol. 7, Stuttgart 1990.

Deutscher Raiffeisenverband e.V.: Jahrbuch 1985, Bonn.

DG Bank – Deutsche Genossenschaftsbank: Die Genossenschaften in der Bundesrepublik Deutschland 1989. Statistik, Frankfurt am Main 1989.

Dülfer, Eberhard: Integrierte Genossenschaft, in: Handwörterbuch des Genossenschaftswesens, Wiesbaden 1980.

Glaser, Franz Ewald: Kreditgenossenschaften mit Warenverkehr – ihre gegenwärtige und zukünftige Bedeutung im Verbandsgebiet Württemberg, Stuttgart 1985.

Grosskopf, Werner: Neue Wege der Agrarpolitik – Reaktionsnotwendigkeiten für Genossenschaften?, 1987, p. 342 and pp. 392–394.

Faust, Helmut: Geschichte der Genossenschaftsbewegung. Ursprung und Weg der Genossenschaften im Deutschen Sprachraum, Frankfurt am Main 1965.

Ghaussy, A. Ghanie: Das Genossenschaftswesen in den Entwicklungsländern, Freiburg im Breisgau 1964.

Maxeiner, Rudolf: Vertrauen in die eigene Kraft. Wilhelm Haas. Sein Leben und Wirken, Wiesbaden 1976.

Oebser, Arno: Das deutsche Genossenschaftswesen in den Gebieten der ehemaligen Tschecho-Slowakei, in Rumänien, Südslawien und Ungarn, Stuttgart 1940.

Raiffeisen, Friedrich Wilhelm: Die Darlehenskassen–Vereine, 8th ed., Neuwied am Rh. 1966 (1st ed.1866).

Nachschußpflicht (member obligation to make further contributions)

PETER ERLINGHAGEN [J]

(see also: *Legal Form, Co-operative*; *Law, National*; *Law, International*; *Equity Capital*; *Financing*)

I. General Introduction; II. Historical Development; III. Legal Foundations; IV. Amount of Liability; V. Changes in *Nachschußpflicht*; VI. Group of Liable Individuals; VII. Level of Further Contribution; VIII. Expiration of *Nachschußpflicht*; IX. Bankruptcy Proceedings; X. *Nachschußpflicht* upon Membership Withdrawal; XI. Additional Payments upon Liquidation; XII. German Banking Law (Kreditwesengesetz – KWG).

I. General Introduction

Nachschußpflicht (regulated in GenG, § 105 [German Co-operative Law]) is the obligation of the co-operative members in the event of bankruptcy to provide payments to the bankrupt's estate to the extent the bankrupt's creditors cannot be satisfied from the co-operative's assets. It represents additional security for creditors and thereby is a suitable means to supplement share capital and improve the co-operative's creditworthiness.

II. Historical Development

Originally, the concept of co-operatives embraced the policy of unlimited and jointly shared liability of all members. A somewhat more procedural restriction was introduced by the Prussian Law of 1869, which in time was assumed by all German states. This Law limited joint and several liability (which nonetheless remained unlimited and direct) as a secondary liability to the event of bankruptcy.
The Co-operative Law of 1889 entailed two important changes, namely, on the one hand, the opportunity to fix third party liability at a maximum level uniform for all members (§ 2, No.3), and, on the other hand, the opportunity to replace member liability with an unlimited *Nachschußpflicht*.
Direct member liability was completely abandoned in the amendment passed in 1933, and limitations to the *Nachschußpflicht* were approved at a minimum amount corresponding to at least one company share. It ultimately became possible to completely preclude any *Nachschußpflicht* following the amendment passed in 1973 (GenG, § 6, No.3; § 105, Subsec.1).

III. Legal Foundations

The *Nachschußpflicht* is an obligation which results from membership. This obligation does not, however, arise automatically upon the establishment of a co-operative and is not automatically connected to membership. It is based much more substantially on the particulars to be incorporated in the by-laws in accordance with GenG, § 6, No.3; it must be determined in these particulars whether members are obligated to unlimited additional contributions, to a predetermined amount or not to any further contributions.

Even when a *Nachschußpflicht* exists, only the assets of the co-operative are directly liable for the co-operative's obligations to its creditors (GenG, § 2). The *Nachschußpflicht* only exists with respect to the co-operative; it only arises in the event of bankruptcy, and the further contributions are to be payed exclusively to the bankrupt's estate (see IX.).

It is contested whether a member's corresponding obligation is established through the particulars of the by-laws which provide for a *Nachschußpflicht*. The position against this argues that the content of this obligation with regard to the extent of the *Nachschußpflicht* can only first be determined following the commencement of bankruptcy proceedings or in the event a shortfall in the balance sheet is recorded (GenG, § 73, Subsec.2) (*Klaus Müller*, Comments to GenG, § 105, margin no.5). Further proponents argue that it is not even certain whether further contributions actually need to be provided (*Meyer/Meulenbergh/Beuthien*, Comments to GenG, § 105, margin no.3). Both of these arguments do not necessarily oppose the assumption of deferred outstanding claims, the actual extent of which can at least be determined (see *Lang/Weidmüller*, GenG, 31st Edition, § 105, margin no.9). The *Nachschußpflicht* insomuch does not differ from a non-absolute guaranty, bill or check guaranty.

This matter hardly plays a role at all in everday application because even demands for suspensive further contributions only legally become effective upon the incurrence of the condition – the commencement of bankruptcy proceedings – and further contributions are to be exclusively made to the bankrupt's estate. The same holds true accordingly for the liquidation of the co-operative and membership withdrawal. It can in particular be concluded from GenG, §§ 88a and 108, that demands for further payments can in no event be transferable or attachable prior to the commencement of bankruptcy proceedings or the determination of a shortfall in the balance sheet.

IV. Amount of Liability

When the *Nachschußpflicht* is not completely precluded in the → *by-laws* it can be either unlimited or limited to a determined amount (liability amount)

(GenG, § 6, No.3). If it is limited it may, nonetheless, in the by-laws not be fixed lower than the company share (GenG, § 119). It is possible to fix the amount at any arbitrary level, whereby the level of liability as a rule must be uniform for all members.

A varying liability amount can result among members when differing numbers of company shares have been assumed. In such an event liability amount can be increased to the total amount of the acquired shares (GenG, § 121, Sent.1). Upon the subsequent assumption of additional shares the liability amount is not raised provided it was previously higher than the minimum level. It is therefore not necessary to attach the identical liability amount to every company share.

As defined in GenG, § 121, Sent.2 the by-laws can, however, prescribe a higher amount, e.g. the identical liability amount higher than the company share, irrespective of the number acquired, or any arbitrary graduation.

GenG, § 121, Sent.3 even allows a provision according to which the liability amount is not increased at all upon the acquisition of further company shares.

V. Changes in *Nachschußpflicht*

Changes in the extent or dimension of the *Nachschußpflicht* can only be undertaken through amendments to the by-laws; these in turn become effective once the resolutions for such amendments to the by-laws have been entered into the co-operative register (GenG, § 16, Subsec.4).

As defined in GenG, § 16, Subsec.2, No.4, the introduction of a *Nachschußpflicht* or its enlargement requires a three-quarter majority of the votes cast in the general assembly. A larger majority can be fixed in the by-laws or other requirements can be called for (for example the approval of a minimum number of members).

A three-quarter majority is likewise necessary for a reduction of the *Nachschußpflicht*. This is only so in case of doubt; the by-laws can call for larger as well as smaller majorities. Nevertheless, creditors' protection must be heeded through GenG, § 22, Subsecs.1–3, which § 22a refers to in the event a previously unlimited *Nachschußpflicht* is completely revoked or limited; § 120 refers to § 20 when the liability amount is reduced. According to this latter provision, the essential content of the resolution must be stated in the public notification upon its entry into the co-operative register (Subsec.1), and the creditors must be informed that they can demand security (see §§ 232 ff. of the German Civil Code) – or as the case may be – that their (matured) claims be satisfied (Subsec.2). Members may only then be certain about a reduced *Nachschußpflicht* after timely filed claims have been satisfied or guaranteed (Subsec.3).

The introduction or enlargement of the *Nachschußpflicht* according to GenG, § 22a, Subsec.2 does not effect members who had already withdrawn by the time the respective amendments to the by-laws became effective; this also holds true for the situation when further contributions in principle could be requisite at their previous level when the co-operative dissolves within six months following members' withdrawal (GenG, §§ 75; 76, Subsec.4; 155b). If this were not the case, the general assembly would be able to pass resolutions to the detriment of members who are excluded from the decision-making process (also *Lang/Weidmüller*, § 22a, margin nos.6 ff.; *Müller*, § 105, margin no.11).

VI. Group of Liable Individuals

1. General Background

The obligation to provide further contributions in the event of bankruptcy is borne by all co-operative members whose membership is effective at the commencement of bankruptcy proceedings or is simulated according to GenG, § 75, Sent.1. If this is the case, further contributions must be payed based on the number of liable individuals if the by-laws do not state otherwise.

2. Members Once They Have Withdrawn

If a member withdraws from the co-operative he is obliged to provide payments to the co-operative as long as a *Nachschußpflicht* exists and the co-operative's assets including its reserves and paid-up shares do not suffice to cover obligations (GenG, § 73, Subsec.2). His share of the calculated shortfall is thereby of importance, whereby his contribution is limited to the defined liability amount.

This, however, is not the case when the member transfers his co-operative share to another member or third party according to GenG, § 76, Subsec.1; an apportionment thereby does not occur.

The *Nachschußpflicht* is still in effect for a certain duration of time after a member's withdrawal has become effective, that is the end of the year following the death of the share holder or the official entry of withdrawal into the register (GenG, §§ 70, Subsec.2; 77, Subsec.1; 76, Subsec.3). It is particularly important in this connection that withdrawal is not maintained as effectuated when the co-operative is dissolved within six months of the effective withdrawal; this is likewise the case upon the commencement of bankruptcy proceedings (GenG, § 101). Under such circumstances, the former member is obliged to pay further contributions when the assets of the co-operative are insufficient to cover its debts – including the accounts payable accumulated after the member had withdrawn. (Outstanding payments accumulated prior to membership withdrawal are taken into consideration in the apportionment as defined in GenG, § 73.)

If a member withdraws by transferring his company shares, the extended *Nachschußpflicht* only then becomes effective when the purchaser of these shares is not in the position to provide the further contributions he is obliged to. This auxiliary (secondary) *Nachschußpflicht* is likewise temporally restricted to bankruptcy which commences within six months of the official entry of withdrawal into the register (GenG, § 76, Subsec.4).

This six-month time limit is to be extended to a period of 18 months prior to the commencement of bankruptcy proceedings if and when not all creditors can be satisfied through the payment contributions provided by the primarily obligated co-operative members (GenG, § 115b). In other words, former members can be called upon to provide additional contributions up to the determined level of liability as late as a year and a half following their effected withdrawal.

3. A Member's Successors

Upon the death of a co-operative member, membership is transferred to one or all of his successors in accordance to GenG, § 77, Subsec.1; this, however, is limited temporally to the end of the business year in which the death occurred. The *Nachschußpflicht*, numbers among the estate obligations transferred to the successors. It is therefore possible for the successor to limit his *Nachschußpflicht* in the scope of a general reduction of his liability for the estate (see §§ 1975 ff. in the German Civil Code for such regulations).

The by-laws can, however, also provide for membership to be continued through a successor following the death of a co-operative member (GenG, § 77, Subsec.2). In order to avoid the *Nachschußpflicht* the successor only has one opportunity, namely to reject the inheritance in its entirety. Nonetheless, if the successor assumes the inheritance he can terminate membership at the next possible point in time in order to reduce the temporal risk factor of being called upon to provide further contributions.

The provisions detailed above found in GenG, §§ 75 and 115b also are to be applied to the successor(s) in the event bankruptcy proceedings are commenced after a member has withdrawn from the co-operative.

VII. Level of Further Contribution

1. Total Amount

The extent of the further contributions to be provided by co-operative members in the event of bankruptcy is regulated in GenG, § 105. The amount results from the difference between the co-operative's obligations (plus any costs arising in connection with their settlement) and the available assets to cover these obligations. This is not a question of the book value of these assets but, rather, of the amount that is necessary in addition to the available asset value to pay off creditors (*Müller*, § 105, margin no.20). Contribution shortfalls with respect to the book value of these assets following their transformation into cash could arise (particularly for current assets and non-real-estate fixed assets) as well as additional proceeds from the available silent reserves; in particular for real estate property. The final level of the total necessary further contributions as a rule is not set upon the commencement of bankruptcy proceedings but rather is first rendered in the course of such proceedings.

2. Individual Members' Amounts

As defined in GenG, § 105, Subsec.2, members' further contributions are to be provided "per head", that is the total necessary amount of further contributions is to be divided by the number of members obliged to provide such further contributions; a uniform amount thereby must be borne by each co-operative member.

The by-laws can, however, provide for another type of distribution and, for example, make the extent of the individual co-operative member's further contribution contingent on the amount of acquired company shares, or if the level of liability varies (see IV), on the extent of the individual liability amount (→ *Equity Capital*). In the latter situation, the distribution per capita must be modified even without explicit statutory clarification: it is only applicable to co-operative members who have a uniform liability amount. If this were not the case, the member with the lowest liability amount would also necessarily limit the *Nachschußpflicht* of all other members.

3. Redistribution

That a legal *Nachschußpflicht* exists in itself does not state whether the obligated co-operative member is actually in the position to provide his respective contribution to the bankrupt's estate. A particular joint and several liability among the remaining co-operative members comes into action in such a situation; the outstanding amount resulting from a member's inability to perform is equally distributed among the other members according to the general allocation basis.

The inability to perform and fulfill the *Nachschußpflicht* based on individual members' lack of equity can result at the latest point in time from a fruitless execution attempt. It can, however, also result from other circumstances, e.g. a recently pronounced oath of disclosure or the dismissal of bankruptcy proceedings against the assets of a member due to his lack of estate (*Müller*, § 105, margin no.24; *Lang/Weid-*

müller, § 105, margin no.18). According to the purpose of the provision, the inability of the individual member to make addition contributions is to be equated with other situations which de facto prevent the payment of additional contributions. Such situations include the unknown address of a member or procedural difficulties in coming upon assets invested abroad. If necessary the redistribution proceeding is to be repeated.

VIII. Expiration of *Nachschußpflicht*

The *Nachschußpflicht* expires upon its fulfillment, through offsetting (GenG, § 105, Subsec.5) or through company reorganization (GenG, § 112a).

The *Nachschußpflicht* can expire through fulfillment once the claims on the co-operative have initially been raised, that is once the respective amounts have been determined for the appropriate procedure (see IX.). Inasmuch as a member has already met his obligation to provide further contributions by making payments (to a particular account) prior to the commencement of bankruptcy proceedings, such payments are without legal foundation; only a claim on account of unjust enrichment against the co-operative can be grounded. Voluntary contributions following the commencement of bankruptcy proceedings are to be seen as advances which can be calculated together with the determined amount of mandatory further contributions in order to fulfill the *Nachschußpflicht* (see *Müller*, § 105, margin no.26). According to GenG, § 105, Subsec.5, if a member has a claim against the bankrupt co-operative's estate, he can offset it against his mandatory further contribution but not against the demand for advance payments (see IX.). The member must have acquired his claims on the co-operative before bankruptcy proceedings commence (*Müller*, § 105, margin no.30; *Lang/Weidmüller*, § 105, margin no.22; *Meyer/Meulenbergh*, § 105, Note 8). As with the fulfillment of the *Nachschußpflicht*, offsetting becomes effective when the amount level has been fixed, or in other words, upon its calculation; offsetting can, however, be declared at an earlier point in time.

In exceptional situations, the *Nachschußpflicht* can become effected through company reorganization undertaken by the bankruptcy trustee and the co-operative members obliged to make further contributions (GenG, § 112a). According to § 779 of the German Civil Code, company organization is a contract "through which the dispute or uncertainty of parties in a legal relationship" – in this case the existence and/or dimensions of a *Nachschußpflicht* – "can be settled through reciprocal concessions". Uncertainty concerning the *Nachschußpflicht* is equivalent to the insecurity regarding its possible realization. Reciprocal concessions by all means are necessary; in no case can further payments be refused under this provision. Preconditions include approval from the committee of creditors and confirmation of the company reorganization from the bankruptcy court. If the co-operative member falls behind in payments agreed upon in the reorganization – or even with a portion of them –, the company reorganization becomes untenable.

IX. Bankruptcy Proceedings

1. The Commencement of Bankruptcy Proceedings

The *Nachschußpflicht* only arises in the event of bankruptcy. When no unlimited *Nachschußpflicht* exists, bankruptcy proceedings always take place concerning the assets in the event of a co-operative's insolvency as well as in case of debt overload according to GenG, § 98, Subsec.1. If the by-laws provide for a *Nachschußpflicht* limited to a set liability amount, bankruptcy proceedings only take place in the event of debt overload when assets no longer cover debts and when the debt overload exceeds 25% of the total level of liability for all members (GenG, § 98, Subsec.1, No.2; for general bankruptcy proceedings refer to provisions found in GenG, §§ 99 ff and in Bankruptcy Law).

2. Calculation of Advance Payments

Once bankruptcy proceedings have commenced, the bankruptcy trustee must directly draw up a balance and present it to the court. The trustee, using this balance sheet as a basis, must calculate the amount that the members must advance in order to cover the shortfall (GenG, § 106, Subsec.1). In this connection, a list must be drawn up with the names of all co-operative members and their respective payment amounts, whereby it must be noted as thoroughly as possible which individual members are not in the position to fulfill their *Nachschußpflicht* (GenG, § 106, Subsec.2). This tabulation is to be presented to the court in order to have it declared enforceable (GenG, § 106, Subsec.3).

In order for individual members to have the opportunity to raise any objections against the calculations made by the bankruptcy trustee, the court must set a date and invite the co-operative members separately in addition to making public notification. The calculation must be available for inspection at the latest three days prior to this fixed date (GenG, § 107).

Upon the set day of declaration the co-operative board, the committee of creditors and the bankruptcy trustee are to be heard as well as members if they raise objections. The court subsequently decides on the raised objections and declares the calculation (if need be, the corrected calculation) as enforceable. When it can be assumed with all certainty that creditors' claims cannot be satisfied once members have provided their further contributions, the bankruptcy trustee must call upon the members who had withdrawn within the last 18 months to provide contributions and accordingly calculate their mandatory contribution level. The principles listed above are effective respectively (GenG, § 115c).

3. Contestation

Within four weeks, following the declaration of enforceability, each co-operative member can contest the calculation through a court appeal when he had put forward his objection in court on the day of declaration or because of situations beyond his control when he had not been able to put forth his contestation.

4. Collection

The bankruptcy trustee oversees the collection of advances once the calculation has been declared enforceable (GenG, § 109, Subsec.1). The trustee must therewith observe the general co-operative (legal) principles – in particular the principle of equal treatment and promotion mandate – as this concerns claims of the co-operative. This is also the case when installment payments or a respite is granted (*Müller*, § 109, margin no.1; *Lang/Weidmüller*, § 109, margin no.1).

The general provisions of The Code of Civil Procedures are effective for a compulsory execution upon property and the appropriate legal means against such action (GenG, § 109, Subsecs.2,3). Contributions once provided are laid aside (GenG, § 110; Bankruptcy Procedures, §§ 129, Subsec.2; 132) until their final distribution is undertaken (GenG, § 114, Subsec.1); up to this moment, they can only be used for bankruptcy costs and debts.

5. Additional and Closing Calculations for Further Contributions

The calculation for advance payments must state if the tabulated contributions are insufficient to cover the shortfall (GenG, § 113, Subsec.1). This in particular arises when individual members are not in the position to contribute payments themselves or when a raised contention is upheld, such as an incorrect allocation basis. This is likewise the case when it is realized afterwards that the shortfall is larger than originally assumed (see also *Müller*, § 113, margin no.1; *Lang/Weidmüller*, § 113, margin no.1; *Gilbert*, ZBH 1932, p.231).

If necessary, other additional calculations should be drawn up, whereby the regulations for the calculation of advances should be applied respectively (GenG, § 113, Subsec.2).

As soon as the final distribution has commenced, or in other words when the realization of the bankrupt's assets has been concluded, the final calculation of additional contributions is to be undertaken.

X. *Nachschußpflicht* Upon Membership Withdrawal

Nachschußpflicht exists once a member has withdrawn from the co-operative if/when the balance sheet for settlement purposes reveals a shortfall and the withdrawing member is obligated to provide further contributions in the event the co-operative files bankruptcy (GenG, § 73, Subsec.2). The general provisions are effective for determining the extent of the further contributions as well as particulars in the by-laws.

XI. Additional Payments upon Liquidation

The legal provisions for the *Nachschußpflicht* in the event of the liquidation of a co-operative were restated in GenG, § 87 following the amendment passed in 1973. Additional payments to the paid-up shares as well as further contributions upon the determination of a shortfall in the opening liquidation balance sheet can only be adopted to avoid bankruptcy up to the level which corresponds to the total amount of individual members' company shares (→ *Equity Capital*). Certain lee-way must hereby exist in order to avoid as far as possible later resolutions from arising which would otherwise be necessary (*Lang/Weidmüller*, § 87a, margin no.17; also see GenG, § 91, Subsec.1, Sent.2; § 105, Subsec.4, Sent.2).

The general assembly's resolution requires at least a three-quarter majority of all cast votes. Increases of the liability amount in general are barred in the liquidation period.

XII. German Banking Law (Kreditwesengesetz – KWG)

The *Nachschußpflicht* of credit co-operative members acquires particular importance in connection with the calculation of the necessary "appropriate equity" in accordance with KWG, § 19, Subsec.1. As defined in the ordinance passed by the Federal Banking Supervisory Office, co-operatives with unlimited *Nachschußpflicht* must apportion twice the total sum of company shares to equity capital alongside the sum of the paid-up shares and balance sheet reserves; those co-operatives with limited *Nachschußpflicht* must apportion three-fourths of members' total liability amounts. Refer to the article on → *Co-operative Banks* for further details.

Bibliography

Geist, Herbert: Die finanzielle Beteiligung des Genossen an der eingetragenen Genossenschaft, Marburger Schriften zum Genossenschaftswesen, Vol. 56, Göttingen 1981.

Gutherz: Die Verwirklichung der Nachschußpflicht im Konkurs der eingetragenen Genossenschaft mit beschränkter Haftung, 1933.

Hohenleitner: Die Auswirkungen der Reduzierung des Haftsummenzuschlages, 1988.
Lang/Weidmüller: Genossenschaftsgesetz, 32th ed., 1988.
Meyer/Meulenbergh/Beuthien: Genossenschaftsgesetz, 12th ed., 1983.
Müller, Klaus: Genossenschaftsgesetz, vol. 1–3, 1976–1980.
Steding: Mitgliedsorientierte Demokratie – ein tragendes Segment des Genossenschaftsrechts – Eine Betrachtung zur Demokratie als Merkmal der genossenschaftsrechtlichen Rechtsform, BB 1992, pp. 937ff.

New Co-operatives

MARLENE KÜCK [J]

(see also: *Classification*; *Group Theory*; *Group, the Co-operative*; *Theory of co-operative Cooperation*; *Joint-production Co-operative*)

I. New Co-operatives; II. Qualitative and Quantitative Aspects of the New Co-operative Sector; III. Conflicts in Cooperation; IV. Chances of the New Co-operative Sector in the Future.

I. New Co-operatives

New co-operatives were established during the 1970s and '80s in the Federal Republic of Germany and West Berlin. On the one hand, their formation was the result of the current economic development; the increasing imbalance on the job market starting around 1975 induced the creation of new co-operatives, nowadays called *"self-administrated" enterprises*. The problem groups of the job market in particular – women (→ *Women and Co-operatives*), young people and those with an academic background – were the initiators of such companies.

On the other hand, self-administrated companies were and are a result of the changes in the sociopolitical environment. In this context it is important that the "new social movements" obtained lasting influence in Germany by staging numerous political projects starting in 1976/77, such as citizen action programs, neighborhood initiatives and campaigns against restrictions in certain jobs. This development expressed itself in a remarkable way after the "German Autumn of '77", when the first "environment festival" was organized in Berlin (1978) and when the project of a left-wing, alternative daily paper, the *Tageszeitung* (TAZ), succeeded after a very long preparatory phase. As well, the first alternative political party was formed in Germany (the "Alternative Liste für Demokratie und Umweltschutz" AL) in Berlin. All these developments had an influential effect on the new co-operative sector; they promoted the establishment of numerous self-administrated enterprises which settled as a reaction to both the increasing environmental pollution and the expansion of the tertiary sector, predominantly in environmental oriented fields of the market (i.e. the establishment of natural food co-operatives) and in the service branches.

At present, self-administrated companies can be found in all typical small commercial sectors (the trade, handicrafts and service sector). They differ from typical small businesses by their specific company culture (→ *Corporate Culture*), and the "new values" which are expressed in the application of different forms of democratic self-administration, or even fundamental participation.

II. Qualitative and Quantitative Aspects of the New Co-operative Sector

1. Qualitative Aspects

The new co-operative economic sector is restricted and delimitated most differently in the literature. Some authors assign the entire category to "alternative economic forms" (*Kruse*), whereas others identify the co-operative sector as sector of "local employment initiative" (*Bierbaum*). A third position (propounded by *Gessner; Novy; Grottian; Schwendter*) finally subsumes all projects and companies to the co-operative sector, which, by classical delimitation, are included to the self-help, self-administration, co-operative and commonweal sector.

The variety of terminology becomes even more apparent when on the level of isolated economy the various types of co-operative enterprises are named. Among others it is pointed out to the so-called model enterprises (*Flieger*), participational enterprises (*Lezius/Matz*), personnel enterprises, new co-operatives, self-help groups for the unemployed, alternative economic projects (*Bierbaum; Maier; Grottian*) and the already mentioned self-administrated companies. This conglomeration of terms and enterprise forms indicates how difficult it is to formulate a clear definition of the new co-operative economic sector, or the "self-administrated enterprises"(→ *Principles*).

Apart from these rather general remarks, further specific elements concerning isolated economic activity are characteristic for self-administrated companies. First, quite understandably, the *identity principle* (→ *Theory of Co-operative Cooperation*) must be mentioned, i.e. the members of co-operative enterprises have a double function: Each member is employer and employee at the same time.

Fundamental Participation (→ *Principles*), like the identity principle, is also a central component of self-administrated labour. Also known as the principle of democracy, it guarantees the outlined rights of the members to equal and fair participation in formation of opinion and decision-making processes in the enterprise. Fundamental participation establishes the conditions for the provision of non-material benefits and/or advantages as a result of the democratic structure of the enterprise (see above). In this sense, it is the decisive component of the company's system of objectives.

Fundamental participation and the identity principle are usually completed by the demand for *"gradually neutralization of capital"*. Starting point for this demand is the idea, that every self-administrated system requires elimination of private property on productive capital and therefore it is to ensure that the right of disposal of the capital is neutralized by contractual agreements.

Gradual neutralization of capital is understood in a way that the company profits are not distributed to the shareholders (the employees of the enterprise), but remain in the enterprise as "neutralized title" without any collective or individual property right, responsibly administered and held in trust by the employees for production purposes (the first level of neutralization). Gradual neutralization of capital also means, that by accumulation of reserves the initially private held property titles of the employees will be totally restrained by the neutralized titles (accumulated profits) in the course of time (the second level of neutralization).

There are further characteristics for the self-administrated enterprise. The *first* is management according to the → *principle of covering costs*, i.e. the enterprise does not gain profits for the maximization of its employees' individual incomes (which, however, does not imply an exclusion of profits). The *second* characteristic is the attempt *to eliminate sex-specific and role-defined labour distribution*. Women should have the opportunity to break out of the narrow patterns of typical female activity and to participate equally in all functions of the enterprise. It must be noted, however, that this emancipating effort was not always appreciated in the enterprises (*Mohr*, 1985). Women's reaction to this dilemma, among other things, was the establishment of their own enterprises.

The establishment of economic units of their own was also (primarily) a result of the women's movement. One of its articulated needs was for an assortment of feminist products and services which were not produced by the self-managed enterprise (e.g. in the fields of media and health care). The women's enterprises (publishing companies, educational and health projects etc.) thus reacted accordingly with "production efforts" (→ *Women and Co-operatives*). The remaining *third* characteristic of the new co-operative sector refers to *"ecological orientation"* (→ *Environmental Protection*), i.e. the self-managed enterprises avoid the emergence of negative external effects in production or service.

Finally, it is important that self-administrated enterprises in general are small; they are categorized in the sector of *"smallest operating units"*. The characteristic of being "small" has many merits for the operation: On the one hand, it contributes to the preservation of the so-called *"decentralization principle"*, by which the transparancy of processes within the enterprise and the manageability of the company are protected (*Bergmann/Schröter; Schwendter*) On the other hand, it has been observed that the self-administrated enterprise is "only a realistic and viable alternative to the typical companies, if it belongs to the smallest operating units" (*Hahn*, 1987; likewise *Eschenburg*, 1987).

2. Quantitative Aspects

If attention is focused on the size of the self-administration sector or the number of self-administrated enterprises, one realizes that there is no sure data concerning the dimension of co-operative work. First, this is due to the fact that self-managed enterprises are not separately identified in the official statistics. Second, there is no representative study of the size of the co-operative sector in the former entire Federal Republic territory and West Berlin. Available are, however, several regional studies (for Berlin, Bremen, Hamburg, Freiburg, Hanover, Nurnberg, North Rhine-Westphalia). These regional analytic studies partly comprise estimated data for the entire federal territory.

These studies almost concurringly conclude that larger concentration of self-administrated enterprises can be found in cities, above all in large urban areas, than in rural regions. This distribution is not surprising: Large cities obviously seem to have the most favorable background conditions for self-managed enterprises. For one, this is due to the political environment. The "new social movements" (the peace, ecology, women's and "alternative" movements) are concentrated in the cities and thus, as mentioned, to a certain extent, the "germ cells" for experiments in and establishment of participatory enterprises. Likewise, for those partly eccentric production and service ideas of self-administrated companies (partial) markets – and thus positive economical conditions – are easier to find in (large) cities.

Besides the general concentration in heavily populated areas, the two regions of West Berlin (400 enterprises with approx. 3,000 employees) and Hessen (257 enterprises with 1,873 employees according to *Heider*, 1988) have the top positions and show an overproportional enterprise density in relation to the total number of companies. The explanation for this fact is the role of the "new social movements" and their strong presence in both regions. Moreover, West Berlin as well as the Rhine-Main area (sometime later) can be considered the birthplaces of the (new) co-operative economic sector. The first self-managed enterprises started to exist here (during and in the aftermath of the student movement), and business reform concepts were discussed here very early (see *Bartning*, 1980; ASH Frankfurt).

Altogether, the national economic importance of the new co-operative sector in the Federal Republic of Germany is relatively low; the estimated lower level encompasses 4,000 enterprises and 24,000 employees (*Kück*, 1989) while an estimate upper level ranges from between 1,500 and 5,000 enterprises with 15,000 to 30,000 employees (*Beywl*).

III. Conflicts in Cooperation

The democratic economic concept of self-administrated enterprises is linked with several interpersonal problems in decision-making (management), in distribution (organization of decision-making and working processes) as well as in payment (→ *Joint-production Co-operative*). These can lead to strained relations and "conflicts in cooperation".

1. Problems in Decision-making

Decision-making seems to be a fundamental problem of democratic business administrations."Precisely here – ignoring all other adversities for a moment – there is a question mark concerning all the plans for self-management" (*Fischer*). Due to this question mark the special branch of science from a very early point in time was of the opinion that fundamental democratic decision models are only "able to survive" to a limited extent. For *Oppenheimer*, it was the "lack of discipline" in this context (*Oppenheimer*); for *Boettcher*, it was the "lack of specialized knowledge, creativity and flexibility" (*Boettcher*), for *Dülfer*, the problems of the distribution of "management and implementation tasks without the gradual development of sub-groups with divergent authority and interests" which lead to restrictions in decision-making (*Dülfer*).

However, not only co-operative theorists recognize the problem, the practitians of self-administrated economy as well discussed the subject of the management failures of their companies for a long time, which in the essence, are information and coordination problems (see, among others, *Potting; Bartning*, 1980).

a) Information Problems

The everyday work of a self-managed enterprise is often determined by two groups of employees – the *"collective business managers"* and the *"collective employees"*. Both groups essentially differ because of a *different level of information* in relation to the means and methods of pursuing their objectives and because of different interests in cooperation.

The differences caused by limited information between the collective business managers and the collective employees induce conflicts. In decisive situations, both groups come to deviant opinions based on different background information. In such decision situations, however, usually the positions of the collective business managers are carried through (most-

ly after long and quarrelsome negotiations). The result: The collective business managers dominate and outvote all essential decision processes. As such a situation does not comply with the attitude of a democratic enterprise, further conflicts develop in connection with the decision process. The less informed employees rebel and oppose the power position exercised by the informed employees. The conflict, by now often carried out in a latent manner, not only negatively influences the working atmosphere and group cohesion, but also aggravates future decision and agreement-reaching processes.

The causes of the *information difference* between collective business managers and the collective employees can be put down first of all to the fact that there is a differing level of specialized qualification. Well-qualified workers are ahead in terms of information and rather have the opportunity to get and process information than less-qualified fellow workers. This qualitative aspect of the information difference is supplemented by a quantitative difference in the level of information which, above all, is due to the varying informatory activity of the two groups.

The better-informed workers are rather motivated to obtain and process new information concerning business facts. In general, they produce a dynamic conduct concerning information.

The less-informed workers usually behave quite contrarily. They produce informatory activity to a much smaller extent. Furthermore, this behavior is completed by the certainty, that the collective business managers will find and develop information anyway. The insufficient and incomplete level of information is often fed by *"random information"* (*Vierheller*, 1974); the sparse information come from certain sources, linked with the co-worker generally in an emotional approach. Friends (colleagues and acquaintances) are frequently used as informants in order to acquire both information and assessments about a decision-cause in the company. Depending on how this information is come upon, either a qualified or unqualified (random) information level will exist.

Thus, obtained random (or insufficient) information raises a priori the question about equal and fair participation in the decision-making process and objective judgement concerning alternative decisions. It can be assumed in all probability, that selective and incomplete information leads to incorrect decisions, i.e. when the wrong decision alternative is voted for or when the "correct" decision is blocked by unfounded reason.

The information level of the workers decisively influences their *level of demands and/or expectations*. Whereas the better informed workers in general formulate higher demands on the enterprise and its goals, the principle of modesty dominates among the less informed workers. They often consider the ambitious goals and suggestions of the collective business managers as exaggerated and impossible to be realized with the consequence of rejecting them in general.

The fear of lofty goals and projects favours the way for a further phenomenon: the tendency for safety and the efforts to avoid any economic risk. A worker's vote for "security" or for "risk" in the company policy is closely linked with the level of available information; is it a low information level relating to a decision cause, a worker will usually vote for variant without risk because his/her knowledge of the possible economic results, if he/she supports the issue, is insufficient.

If, on the other hand, the level of information (the know-how to evaluate a suggested decision objectively) is given, the person making the decision can "estimate" the possible consequences. The willingness to undertake an economic risk under these conditions is much higher.

To a large degree this is the explanation, why collective business managers rather suggest "ambitious plans" for decision and why collective employees rather tend to understate the case and reject these plans. On the other hand, one must also take into consideration that the individual willingness to take a risk is different. There are simply "pessimistic people thoroughly not prepared to take risks" and, in contrast, "optimistic characters willing to take risks" (*Hahn*, 1983).

Those security – oriented workers with a defensive attitude concerning information, to a large degree, furthermore tend to maintain a position they once took up. These workers are "true to their principles" and present a "calculable" and predictable conduct towards decisions, something which is often seen positively in the enterprises.

This conduct, however, involves considerable risks. Consistent and predictable workers, always true to their position, are often immobile in business-policy matters. They rarely succeed in adequat reactions if general conditions, which affect the enterprise (i.e. fluctuations in the partial market they supply) change. Instead, they behave routine, following the principles they once set.

Routine behavior (in decision situations) is largely an expression of insecurity related to (specific) information: the employees do not have enough knowledge in order to approach the specific decision appropriately.

The (decision) principles (or positions) used as aid are thus frequently reduced to "fundamental-ideological" terms because "debate on general principles" are often instigated by members facing difficult decisions. The result: Decision conflicts evolve between the "ideologists" and the "doers", between the "realists" and "fundamentalists", and thus also between collective employees and collective business managers. Final decisions can, if at all, only be reached in such situations after "multiple attempts".

b) Problems in Voting

Along with these generally described information problems there are predominantly problems related to the applied voting regulations which complicate the decision-making process in an enterprise and contribute to "decision chaos".

The cause of this chaos is the *voting procedure* calculated for consensus, which means, that a decision can be reached only by unanimity. The use of the unanimity criterion usually requires the decision makers to discuss the object of decision throughly in order to convince the other parties. This necessity does not exist to the same extent in other voting procedures. There, members of a group are "simply voted down" without this factor of persuasion (i.e. like the majority principle). The result is that "central elements of the fundamental democracy" get lost.

At any rate, more and more companies are questioning the unanimity criterion. Employees have come to the conclusion that "meanwhile there is almost nobody left who finds the consensus principle as democratic and who is of the opinion, that appropriate decisions are made in the plenum". Aside from this, "many problems are neglected because no one dares to think about it or else is afraid to touch a fragile consensus" (*Fehrle*).

The consensus principle is primarily doomed because of the existing information problems. The illusion that all people can be brought to identical information levels and thus ultimately convinced by thorough discussion, by no means corresponds with reality. In the first place, information problems (i.e. qualification problems) – particularly when the lack of know-how is quite serious – cannot be overcome in plenary meetings. In such a case, a systematic and time-intensive qualification process is necessary. At best, small knowledge gaps can be bridged in collective meetings when the qualification and information levels are about the same. Furthermore, considerable barriers can exist which prevent an adequate reception of information provided in the realm of a meeting. Here, those problems mentioned in connection with the so-called random information are of decisive relevance. Its effect is, that unanimity can only be reached with great difficulty, if at all; the object of decision is reduced considerably.

It is therefore typical, that a "coordinated golden mean", the much criticized compromise, is voted for when differences in information and decision exist. Compromises, however, rarely present an appropriate solution; they "often dilute clear solutions" and lead to a "consensus based on the least common denominator" (*Hoff*).

2. Distribution Problems

Distribution problems in the new co-operative sector arise both through the heterogeneous co-operative fees, which are customarily provided by the members, and through the related problem of distributing the business and/or cooperation result in the form of monetary and non-monetary benefits in a consensus-reaching manner.

In its partial components, the distribution conflict certainly arises most frequently as conflict based on variable collective interests (in co-operative work) and on different qualification levels.

a) Different Collective Interests

As described above, employees in the enterprise either behave as "collective employees" or as "collective business managers". One employee expressed the situation like: "There are people in the enterprises who simply want to work free of repression, at best without a boss. They have had completely negative experiences in normal companies. They know exactly what they don't want. On the other hand, there are people with great involvement, people with political ideas of collective work and initiative". These two types meet each other in the collective and "it can't harmonize right off the bat" (Interview notes).

b) Different Levels of Qualification

The distribution conflict between qualified and less-qualified employees takes place on another level as well. There is tension because "collective work ... means a much higher energy investment from the higher-qualified and thus a general exhaustion. Seen the other way around: the more unqualified someone is, the better position he is in. If something happens they are really priveleged. Those who only provide unskilled work have a regular working day. In contrast, the qualified have 60 to 70 weekly working hours, all under the premise of equality and a uniform wage level" (Interview notes, 1984).

3. Conflicts in Payment

The distribution conflicts based on variable interests in cooperation and variable levels of qualification already discussed lead to heterogeneous activities and input contributions of the employees. If this variability of tasks is rewarded by a uniform wage, distribution conflicts will arise concerning adequate payment.

The uniform wage is moreover the "sacred cow of the collectives". Most self-administered enterprises are oriented according to this principle of payment. The intention is the creation of an "egalitarian income structure" in the enterprises by means of a uniform wage (*Huber*, 1981); all employees receive the identical monthly income regardless of their contribution. This "wage equality" (*Bergmann*) should complete the equality created via the self-administration on the decision-making level. The available budget of material and non-material incentives is thus also subjected to the identical distribution criteria.

The uniform wage is "identical wage for unequal work" (*Bartning*). This method of payment usually does not succeed in distributing the risks and chances of a co-operative enterprise "fairly" (*Eschenburg*, 1971). Imbalances arise which affect the involved, qualified collective business managers negatively and the less-involved and less-qualified collective employees positively. Due to their input contributions, the former group substantially influences the annual figures without having a direct, individual advantage. In other words, the uniform wage remains existent for them as well as for all others. Salary increases are only possible to the extent the wages for the remaining employees are raised, employees who were involved in the business result to a much lesser degree. Independent from the fundamental problem that no exact contribution of each employee concerning success can be calculated as a result of valuation problems, the fact still remains that input incentives get lost by means of the uniform wage principle "because there is no possibility of personal influence on the wages" (TAZ discussion forum). The result of this "absurd wage structure": labour mentality develops with respect to job behavior and indifference to the interests of the enterprise (*Bergmann*). In such a situation, finally there is only one possibility for qualified, motivated employees to get out, "in order not to constantly be at odds with self-exploitation" (*Meding*).

The payment conflict can be reduced decisively when the profit situation of the enterprise allows an appropriate uniform wage level which suits the material expectations of the employees. No wonder that the employees of a successful self-administrated enterprise signalize a relatively high level of contentedness with uniform payment. Distribution conflicts concerning an adequate payment inevitably lose their relevance when people attain a higher level of the needs pyramid (*Maslow*). Vice versa, payment conflict escalates when it concerns "administration of shortage". One worker said: "If we were in the situation to pay us DM 4,000 monthly, we would not have wage disagreements". This, however, is still not possible in many self-administrated enterprises. The uniform monthly wages are often between DM 2,000 and DM 2,800 (gross) per employee. These wages thus provide reason enough for conflict which cannot be alleviated by usual compensational measures, like guarantee of non-material incentives (such as concessions in working hours). Non-material incentive systems fundamentally develop an effect once the material income needs have been substantially covered.

IV. Chances of the New Co-operative Sector in the Future

The decision-making, distribution and payment problems have forced self-administrated enterprises in the past years to a great degree to dissociate themselves from fundamental democracy as their strict management policy. The companies have turned into "co-operative enterprises" to a great extent which practice a levelled-out form of self-administration and which presently are regarded as signs of a (new) co-operative company culture based on the extensive participation of employees. Self-administrated enterprises, on the other hand, which go with the principles of consensus voting and uniform payment as irrevocable principles of commercial and economic activity, are clearly finding themselves in retreat. Such companies are rarely set up nowadays and kept alive respectively. This might also be connected with the fact, that the new social movements, whose dependent partial element the self-administrated companies always were, are now "grown old" and do not emit the political radiance anymore like they undoubtedly did in the '70s and '80s.

Concerning the changes in the present field, only the "transformed collective" has a realistic chance in the future, one which developed from a self-administrated company to a co-operative enterprise, and which still obtains its strength to realize new working principles (co-operative company culture) from the roots of the new social movements.

Bibliography

ASH Frankfurt (ed.): Anders arbeiten – anders leben, Frankfurt/M. 1980.

Berger J. et al.: Alternative zur Lohnarbeit? Selbstverwaltete Betriebe zwischen Anspruch und Realität, Bielefeld 1985.

Bergmann, K.: Ja zur Moral – eine Antwort, in: Schwendter R. (ed.), Die Mühen der Ebenen – Grundlagen zur alternativen Ökonomie, vol. 2, München 1986.

Beywl, Wolfgang: Saure Früchte vom Baum der Erkenntnis, in: Schwendter R. (ed.), Die Mühen der Ebenen – Grundlagen zur alternativen Ökonomie, vol. 2, München 1986, pp. 230–242.

Bierbaum, Heinz: Das Zentrum für Kooperation und Partizipation als zuverlässige Infrastruktur kooperativer Betriebe, in: Arbeitskreis für Kooperation und Partizipation e.V. (ed.), Das Zentrum für Kooperation und Partizipation, Baden-Baden 1987, pp. 13–18.

Boettcher, Erik: Die Genossenschaft in der Marktwirtschaft, Tübingen 1980.

Dülfer, Eberhard: Betriebswirtschaftslehre der Kooperative, Göttingen 1984.

Eschenburg, Rolf: Ökonomische Theorie der genossenschaftlichen Zusammenarbeit, Tübingen 1971.

Eschenburg, Rolf: Das Zentrum für Kooperation und Partizipation: Bedarf, Funktionen, Träger und Organisation, in: Arbeitskreis für Kooperation und Partizipation (ed.), Das Zentrum für Kooperation und Partizipation, Baden-Baden 1987, pp. 96–101.

Fischer, R.: Selbstverwaltung in der Bundesrepublik, in: Fricke, W./ Geissler, A. (eds.), Demokratisierung der Wirtschaft, Hamburg 1973, pp. 139–145.

Flieger, B.: Betroffenenforschung als methodischer Ansatz einer Forschungs- und Bildungseinrichtung für kooperative Betriebe, in: Arbeitskreis für Kooperation und Partizipation (ed.), Das Zentrum für Kooperation und Partizipation, Baden-Baden 1987, pp. 25–34.

Gessner, Volkmar: Zur Organisation des Zentrums, in: Arbeitskreis für Kooperation und Partizipation (ed.), Das Zentrum für Kooperation und Partizipation, Baden-Baden 1987, pp. 119–120.

Goldner, S/Kokigei, M.: Stolpernd unterwegs, Berlin 1982.

Grottian, P.: Hochschulabsolventen im Selbsthilfe- und Alternativsektor oder: über 100,000 innovative Arbeitsplätze im Selbsthilfe- und Alternativsektor durch neue Finanzierungsstrategien realistisch, in: Kaiser, M./ Nuthmann, R/ Stegmann, H. (eds.), Berufliche Verbleibsforschung in der Diskussion, Nürnberg 1985, pp. 645–658.

Hahn, Oswald: Finanzwirtschaft, 2nd edition, München 1983.

Hahn, Oswald: Die Frage nach der Notwendigkeit eines Institus "Selbsthilfe und Selbstverwaltung / Kooperation und Partizipation", in: Arbeitskreis für Kooperation und Partizipation (ed.), Das Zentrum für Kooperation und Partizipation, Baden-Baden 1987, pp. 63–73.

Heider, Frank et al.: Fast wie im wirklichen Leben – Strukturanalyse selbstverwalteter Betriebe in Hessen, Gießen 1988.

Hollstein, W.: Die Gegengesellschaft, Reinbek 1981.

Hollstein, W./Penth, B.: Alternativprojekte, Reinbek 1980.

Hoff, H.: Die Gestaltung von Entscheidungsprozessen in betrieblichen Gremien, Frankfurt/ Bern/ New York 1986.

Horx, M.: Das Ende der Alternativen, München/ Wien 1985.

Huber, J.: Bunt wie ein Regenbogen – selbstorganisierte Projekte und alternative Ökonomie in Deutschland, in: Huber, J (ed.), Anders arbeiten – anders wirtschaften – Dualwirtschaft: Nicht jede Arbeit muß ein Job sein, Frankfurt/M. 1979, pp. 111–121.

Huber, J.: Wer soll das alles ändern – die Alternativen der Alternativbewegung, Berlin 1981.

Kruse, H.: Für ein neues Leitbild kooperativer Wirtschaftsformen, in: Arbeitskreis für Kooperation und Partizipation (ed.), Das Zentrum für Kooperation und Partizipation, Baden-Baden 1987, pp. 102–105.

Kück, Marlene: Neue Finanzierungsstrategien für selbstverwaltete Betriebe, Frankfurt/M. and New York 1985.

Kück, Marlene: Betriebswirtschaft der Kooperative, Stuttgart 1989.

Kück, Marlene/Loesch, Achim von: Finanzierungsmodelle selbstverwalteter Betriebe, Frankfurt/M. and New York 1987.

Laske, Stephan/Schneider, Ursula: "... und es funktioniert doch!" Selbstverwaltung kann man lernen, Wien 1985.

Lezius, M./Matz, C.: Das Zentrum als Brücke zwischen Einzel- und Kooperationsunternehmen, in: Arbeitskreis für Kooperation und Partizipation (ed.), Das Zentrum für Kooperation und Partizipation, Baden-Baden 1987, pp. 102–105.

Maier, H.E.: Selbsthilfe zwischen Markt und Staat, in: Brun, R. (ed.), Erwerb und Eigenarbeit, Frankfurt/M. 1985, pp. 167–179.

Maslow. A.H.: Motivation und Persönlichkeit, Oelten 1977.

Mohr, W.: Emanzipation oder Doppelrolle – Frauen in selbstverwalteten Betrieben, in: Racki, M. (ed.), Frauen(t)raum im Männerraum – Selbstverwaltung aus Frauensicht, München 1988, pp. 21–30.

Novy, Klaus: Renaissance der Genossenschaften – Realismus und Utopie?, in: Berger, J. et al. (eds.), Selbstverwaltete Betriebe in der Marktwirtschaft, Bielefeld 1986, pp. 79–94.

Oppenheimer, Franz: Die Siedlungsgenossenschaft, Leipzig 1922.

Personn, Ch./Thiefenthal, O.: Bedingungen und Strukturen alternativer Ökonomie, Nürnberg 1986.

Potting, C.: Der permanente Zwang zur Identifikation, in: Holenweger, T./ Mäder, W. (eds.), Inseln der Zukunft – Selbstverwaltung in der Schweiz, 2nd edition, Zürich 1979.

Schwendter, R.: Zur Alternativen Ökonomie, vol I and II, Berlin 1978.
Schwendter, R.: Die Mühen der Berge – Grundlagen zur alternativen Ökonomie, vol. 1, München 1986.
Schwendter, R.: Die Mühen der Berge – Grundlagen zur alternativen Ökonomie, vol. 2, München 1986.
Schwendter, R.: Das Zentrum als meta-kooperative Einrichtung, in: Arbeitskreis für Kooperation und Partizipation (ed.), Das Zentrum für Kooperation und Partizipation, Baden-Baden 1987, pp. 88–95.
Vierheller, Rainer: Unternehmensführung und Mitgliederinformation in der Genossenschaft, Göttingen 1974.

Non-Profit Organizations

WOLFGANG PELZL

(see also: *Conceptions, Co-operative; Commonweal Economy; Co-operatives under Public Law; Economie Sociale; Public Benefit Orientation*)

I. Characteristics; II. Assortment of Outputs and/or Services; III. Social Marketing; IV. Financing; V. Measuring the Level of Success.

I. Characteristics

The term "non-profit organization" encompasses a most multifarious spectrum of private and state organizations. Public administration and public enterprises (non-profit organizations for the public economic interest) belong to this category just as do economic organizations (co-operatives, associations), socio-cultural organizations (clubs and groups for culture, sports, and leisure), political organizations (parties), and charitable and religious organizations (welfare organizations and churches).

Non-profit organizations are social systems which primarily differ from profit-oriented enterprises with respect to their goal system and membership structure. The characteristic evident and determined by their name indicates a waiver of profit orientation, or its demand-based economic orientation. Instead of using profit as a formal indicator of systemic efficiency, the fulfillment of various tangible goals is applicable; non-profit organizations provide specific outputs and/or services for their adherents or third parties which in part are not available on the market. The degree of their non-profit economic orientation varies according to their goal system, classification, branch, and output/service assortment. Profit realization is possible as a means of self-financing to attain the tangible goals strived for. The fundamental objectives of non-profit organizations, however, are not to be found in the financial sector.

The members (individuals, enterprises) join together either voluntarily (club, party, association, co-operative, cartel, self-help organization) or on an obligatory basis (state, chamber of commerce) in order to attain common interests within a democratic system collectively formalized through a constitution.

This system consists of three subsystems (in model theory): The membership subsystem undertakes the goal formulation, control functions, and the election of the supervisory body. The supervisory subsystem is responsible for the execution of the members' resolutions, and the realization subsystem attends to their execution. For non-profit organizations in the free economy (→ *State and Co-operatives, Market Economy*), → *solidarity* among members constitutes the central motive of cooperation, supplemented by reciprocity, autonomy, and honorary employment. The duality between avocational and official participation is typical. The decision-making process proceeds either democratically or oligarchically according to the distribution of power. Whereas above all the owners, the management, and the employees determine the commercial goal-orientation in profit-oriented companies, non-profit organizations are considerably under the influence of external institutions (the public, lobby forces, media, and eventually the state). The decision process is thus determined by societal and political influences and conflicts of interest. The formulation of the objective must do justice to the varying member interests, and it is influenced by common fundamental norms or values, through political direction, bureaucratic control or pricing policy. As the membership level increases, the direct democracy is frequently replaced by an indirect democracy. Weaknesses in the system appear when the decision-making process in the membership subsystem proceeds reactively or shows discontinuity, when goal identification between the three subsystems does not exist, when the realization system becomes overly bureaucratic, and when conflicts of interest arise between honorary and full-time functionaries.

II. Assortment of Outputs and/or Services

The assortment of non-profit oriented companies is comprised of marketable/non-marketable, individual/-collective, material/immaterial goods which are offered both, for and without, services in return. Whereas profit-oriented companies primarily offer their goods and services on the market (meeting the demand of others), the recipients of goods and/or services from non-profit organizations in the free market are predominantly members (identity principle, meeting individual demand). Among associations, for example, they receive performance outputs in the form of organization, co-ordination, representation, and economization.

State-managed non-profit organizations frequently fulfill the task of providing certain outputs and/or services which the free economy either cannot make available or only to an insufficient dimension because of a lack of either willingness or capacity to pay for them. In such situations, a direct exchange relationship between the non-profit organization and the customer/comsumer does not exist. The economic principle of cohesion or the common identity of decision makers, financial supporters, and final consumers is not at hand, thus presenting potential inefficiency dangers. Because the assortment of output capacities does not serve as an instrument of profit realization, adaptation to an altered needs structure of the consumers frequently proceeds at a slow pace.

III. Social Marketing

Whereas business marketing (→ *Marketing Strategies*) primarily is an instrument to increase sales, social marketing of the public non-profit organizations should serve to alter value systems or behavior (e.g. health measures, environmental protection, etc.) through information and communication strategies. The goals of marketing and pubic relations are predominantly social or macroeconomic in character; the instruments, however, are drawn from microeconomics (product, service, pricing, distribution and information policies). Planning for a social marketing strategy must evolve from specifically defined tangible goals, as well as from the strengths and weaknesses of the non-profit organization with respect to economic, technical, and social matters, and it must take into consideration the environmental and market situation.

IV. Financing

Non-profit organizations generally finance themselves through membership fees, contributions, grants, subsidies, charges and revenue from assets as well as from the turnover of marketable goods (→ *Financing*). The predominant source of financing is based on the particular kind of the respective non-profit organization as well as on its proximity to the market. Unions and associations, for example, to the most part finance themselves through membership fees, whereby a graduated scale of fees plays an important role in the level of membership satisfaction. Contributions in the form of monetary, material or labor input provide an essential source of financing for charitable organizations, which can be dependent on the general economic cycle. In times of recession, the danger arises that the volume of contributions drops while simultaneously the demand for resources and/or funds increases. Charitable non-profit organizations cannot finance themselves through cost-covering prices as the recipients of their services are usually in need themselves. As they can only compensate subsidy discontinuations with great difficulty, they are severely affected by reductions in public financing.

Whereas the availability of financial resources for profit-oriented companies is either directly (self-financing) or indirectly (outside financing, financing through share investment) dependent on market success, this connection does not exist to such a degree for non-profit organizations. Among public enterprises, for example, budgeted amounts are automatically extrapolated, independent of the efficiency of the output/-capacity made available. Because of their financial dependency on either members or state institutions, many non-profit organization have a much lower equity quota at their disposal in compared to profit-oriented companies.

V. Measuring the Level of Success

In as much as non-profit organizations fulfill a task or mission as a corporate goal which is determined by the members/supporters of the organization, their tangible goals are heterogeneous, without clear prioritization, mostly verbal in character, and defined in terms or categories which cannot be measured. The difficulties involved (→ *Evaluation*) in the operationalization of objectives can likewise only partially be solved through qualitative efficiency criteria or through indicators of social success. In many situations, the actual goals are not outputs or capacities but rather goals of consequence (e.g. influential capacities) which should be attained by the interest group or by the entire general public. Thus, they are external to the non-profit organization and cannot be allocated a specific measure internal to the system or measured in terms of costs and revenue (→ *Principle of Cost Coverage*).

Because the study of business administration (→ *Managerial Economics*), above all, is oriented around profit criteria (either directly or indirectly), its declarative capacity can only with modifications be applied to non-profit organizations. Particular systemic traits induce the development of special managment studies (→ *Management in Co-operatives*) which is structured around a particular type of non-profit organization. Institutional management studies today exist for public administration, public enterprises, co-operatives and associations (→ *Managerial Economics*). Since fundamental differences exist between non-profit organizations in the free economy (associations, parties, churches, welfare organizations) and organizations of the public economy (public administration and state enterprises), general management studies for non-profit organizations can only be extrapolated with a high level of abstraction. The first management research of non-profit organizations was conducted in the late 1960s and early '70s in the USA.

Bibliography

Bea, Franz Xaver/Klötzle Alfred: Planung in nichterwerbswirtschaftlichen Betrieben, in: Handwörterbuch der Planung, 1989.

Bischofsberger, Pius: Plädoyer für Effizienz in gemeinnützigen Institutionen, in: Verbands-Management no. 3 (1989), pp. 11–15.

Blümle, Ernst-Bernd: Führung in Verbänden, in: Handwörterbuch der Führung, Stuttgart 1987.

Blümle, Ernst-Bernd/Kohlas, Jürg: Zur Messung der Leistung von Wirtschaftsverbänden, in: Zeitschrift für betriebswirtschaftliche Forschung, no. 8 (1975), pp. 473–488.

Bruhn, Manfred/Filmes, Jörg: Social Marketing, Stuttgart 1989.

Burla, Stephan: Rationales Management in Nonprofit-Organisationen, Bern 1989.

Byrne, John A.: Profiting from Nonprofits, in: Business Week, 26.3.1990, pp. 46–52.

Cyert, Richard M.: The Management of Nonprofit Organizations, Lexington (Mass.) 1975.

Douglas, James: Political Theories of Nonprofit Organization, in: Powell, Walter (ed.), The Nonprofit Sector: A Research Handbook.

Hasitschka Werner/Hruschka, Harald: Nonprofit Marketing, München 1982.

Hatten, Mary Louise: Strategic Management in NPO, in: Strategic Management Journal, no. 3 (1982).

Herzlinger, Regina E./Krasker, William S.: Who profits from Nonprofits, in: Harvard Business Review, Jan./Feb. (1987), pp. 93–105.

Imboden, Francis: Die Planung im Verband, in: Verbands-Management, no. 1 (1984), pp. 21–30.

Kirsch, Guy: Ziele in verbandlichen Organisationen, in: Zeitschrift für Organisation, no. 5 (1980).

Klötzle, Alfred: Das Planungsverhalten nichterwerbswirtschaftlicher Unternehmen, in: Zeitschrift für öffentliche und gemeinwirtschaftliche Unternehmen, vol. 7, no. 3 (1983), pp. 346–353.

Kotler, Philip: Marketing for Nonprofit Organizations, Englewood Cliffs / New Jersey 1975.

Merkle, Erich: Marketing in öffentlichen Unternehmen und nichtkommerziellen Institutionen, in: Der Markt, Zeitschrift für Absatzwirtschaft und Marketing, vol. 54, no. 2 (1975), pp. 47–56.

Kanter, Rosabeth M./Summers, David V.: Doing Well while Doing Good: Dilemmas of Perfomance Measuring in Nonprofit Organizations and the Need for a Multiple-Consistiuency Approach, in: Powell, Walter W. (ed.), The Nonprofit Sector: A Research Handbook.

Newman, William H./Wallender, Harvey W.: Managing Not-for-Profit Enterprises, in: Academy of Management Review, no. 1 (1978).

Purtschert, Robert: Marketing in Verbänden, in: Die Unternehmung, no. 1 (1979), pp. 61–82.

Raffee, Hans: Perspektiven des nicht-kommerziellen Marketing, in: Zeitschrift für betriebswirtschaftliche Forschung, no. 28 (1976), pp. 61–76.

Reichard, Christoph: Der "Dritte Sektor" – Ansätze zur Strukturierung eines Forschungsbereichs, in: Zeitschrift für öffentliche und gemeinwirtschaftliche Unternehmen, vol. 11, no. 1 (1988).

Schüller, Achim/Strasmann, Jochen: Ansätze zur Erforschung von Nonprofit Organizations, in: Zeitschrift für öffentliche und gemeinwirtschaftliche Unternehmen, vol. 12, no. 2 (1989).

Schwarz, Peter: Erfolgsorientiertes Verbands-Management, Sankt-Augustin 1984.

Schwarz, Peter: Über die Tauglichkeit einer (allgemeinen) Betriebswirtschaftslehre von Nonprofit-Organisationen, in: Verbands-Management, no. 1 (1990), pp. 43–46.

Seibel, Wolfgang: The Nonprofit Sector and the Modern Welfare State – Developing a Research Agenda, in: Zeitschrift für öffentliche und gemeinwirtschaftliche Unternehmen, vol. 11, no. 1 (1988), pp. 82–87.

Shapiro, Benson P.: Marketing for Nonprofit Organizations, in: Harvard Business Review, Sept./Oct. 1973.

Steinberg, Richard: Nonprofit Organizations and the Market, in: Powell, Walter W. (ed.), The Nonprofit Sector: A Research Handbook.

Thiemeyer, Theo: Wirtschaftslehre öffentlicher Betriebe, Hamburg 1975.

Unterman, Israel/Davis, Richard Hart: The Strategy Gap in Not-for-Profits, in: Harvard Business Review, May/June 1982, pp. 30–40.

Wacht, Richard F.: Financial Management in Nonprofit Organizations, Atlanta 1984.

Weisbrod, Burton A.: The Non-Profit Economy, Cambridge (Mass.)/London 1988.

Weisbrod, Burton A.: The Forgotten Economic Sector: Private but Nonprofit, in: Challenge, Sept./Oct. 1978, pp. 32–36.

White, Michelle J. (ed.): Nonprofit Firms in a Three Sector Economy, Washington D.C. 1981.

Zaltman, Gerald: Management Principles for Nonprofit Agencies and Organizations, New York 1979.

Officialization of Co-operatives

ALFRED HANEL

(see also: *Policies for Promotion*; *State and Co-operatives, Market Economy*; *Development Policy*; *Self-help Organizations*)

I. General Characterization; II. Officialization of Co-operatives in Different Economic Systems; III. Officialization of Co-operatives in Developing Countries.

I. General Characterization

The officialization of co-operatives is related to the basic relationships between "the state and co-operatives" (→ *State and Co-operatives, Market Economy*). In co-operative science the term "officialization" is used when the government has charged or commissioned co-operatives to fulfill tasks in which the government is interested (*Draheim* 1955); then, the government or 'the state' directly influences the co-operative activities or controls the co-operative institutions to different extents. Thus, officialization leads to a decrease of the autonomy or independence of the co-operative organizations. The officialization can reduce the external autonomy of co-operatives in their interactions with their environments and in their decisions on the entrepreneurial goals and business policies of the co-operative enterprises, as well as the internal autonomy in self-determining the internal relations and decisions within the co-operative organizations (→ *Managerial Economics*).

II. Officialization of Co-operatives in Different Economic Systems

Different forms of officialization of co-operatives can be found in market economies and in centrally planned economies.

1. Officialization of Co-operatives in Market Economies

Co-operative organizations which are owned by the members and used as instruments of promoting their individual farms, businesses or households, require the existence of sufficient political and economic freedom of action for setting the goals and taking the entrepreneurial decisions of the co-operative enterprise by the organization's participants. Such autonomous co-operatives are compatible with a system (or an "environment") of decentralized planning and coordination of the economic activities in a country – i.e. with a basic type of market-economy. In market-economies governmental policies usually influence indirectly the goals and activities of co-operatives and other "private business institutions" by creating appropriate political and economic framework conditions. However, there also exists direct government control of co-operatives in market economies, which is mostly the result of "voluntary" officialization. This is the case, if and inasmuch co-operatives: (a) decide to integrate themselves (voluntarily) into the implementation of state-financed programmes, which can be channelled through co-operatives for the benefit of their members belonging to specific target groups who are to be supported by these programmes; (b) accept limitations of their autonomy, in order to benefit from governmentally provided privileges (for example: tax reductions and exemptions or subsidies), or (c) undertake activities, (possibly in partnership with state organizations), which in a country are considered to be of particular public or national interest, and, therefore, are directly controlled or supervised by government authorities. Furthermore, the direct governmental sponsorship of the initiation and establishment of co-operatives in market-oriented economies can also lead to a form of officialization which has been observed particularly in developing countries, and will be mentioned in part III (→ *Self-help Organizations*).

2. Officialization of Co-operatives in Centrally Planned Economies

In centrally planned economies, where all economic processes are regulated through a central imperative economic plan, and where the economic enterprises and business institutions are commissioned with the task(s) of fulfilling plan-targets in order to contribute to the achievement of the national economic plan, in principle no autonomous, but only officialized co-operatives are allowed to operate (→ *State and Co-operatives, Socialism*).

Therefore, in countries in which it is intended to establish a system of centrally planned economy, different forms of a "compulsory" officialization of co-operatives can be observed. In centrally planned economies the achievement of the targets as defined by the national economic plan is the primary task of the co-operatives, to which the goal of member-promotion is subordinated and sometimes in extreme cases even impossible. The state-control and integration of the co-operative into the national economic plan is, as a rule, the result of direct administrative or indirect (economic, political and ideological) compulsion, executed by the authoritarian government and also by the political party in power.

An influential model of integrating co-operatives into the comprehensive imperative national economic planning has been developed by the orthodox Soviet concept of constructing a socialistic centrally planned economy (→ *Socialist Co-operative Theory*). In this model state-controlled co-operatives have to perform the following tasks, in particular (cf. *Hartwig* 1985): (a) to transfer the individual private property of small and medium farmers, craftsmen and small businesses into co-operative property which afterwards should be transformed into socialist state property, (b) to function as organs of the central economic administration in order to integrate the individual members' farms and businesses into the central control of the national economy, and, thus, to contribute to the construction of a centrally planned socialist economy, (c) to help to supply the people with consumer goods and housing facilities, (d) to accumulate socialist capital, and (e) to educate the people towards "socialist behaviour", e.g. through executing political functions by the co-operatives which often work as mass organizations of the ruling party. More of less state-controlled co-operatives have been existing in all Eastern European socialist countries (→ *Development, Eastern Europe*). The great difficulties in solving the problems of information, motivation and decision-making in centrally planned economies were the reason for numerous reforms. However, it was not intended to change, but to improve the basic system of central imperative economic planning in the Eastern European countries (with the exception of Hungary and Yugoslavia) until the beginning of the 1980s. Thus, co-operatives were still state-controlled; they were meant to fulfill important so-called "alternative" or "correction functions" in such areas, where, due to their greater internal autonomy and flexibility and their better system of incentives, the co-operatives were able to operate more efficiently than the large, hierarchically organized, bureaucratic state enterprises. The recent reforms, through which it is intended to establish market-economies in Eastern Europe since the (middle of the) 1980s, imply the de-officialization of the state-controlled co-operatives.

III. Officialization of Co-operatives in Developing Countries

In most of the developing countries various governmental promotion policies for the development of co-operatives have been put into practice, and the co-operatives have also been used as instruments for the implementation of different programmes and projects which were planned for the development of the agricultural sector and the rural areas (→ *Policies for Promotion*). As regards the economic system to be established, it was often proclaimed in African and Asian countries to develop a type of a particular "socialist" or "mixed economy" in which, however, either more "market-economy" or "centrally planned economy" oriented development policies dominated. These were frequently not consistently integrated, and, moreover, in many countries often changed through economic reforms. Thus, various forms of direct administrative influences, interventions, and control of the goals, business policies, activities and organizational structures of the co-operatives were undertaken. They were the cause for different forms of officialization.

1. Different Forms of Officialization of Co-operatives

In accordance with the theoretical conceptions of designing promotion policies for co-operatives and of using these co-operative organizations as instruments for the implementation of development programmes in the various countries, three different forms of officialization can be distinguished:

a) Officialization as a consequence of comprehensive state-sponsorship for members' assistance in establishing co-operatives for their (self-)promotion

Since co-operatives were mostly considered as self-help organizations suitable for bringing about socio-economic changes and inducing various development-related effects, comprehensive state-sponsorship in the form of educational, managerial, technical, and financial assistance was often provided in order to initiate and establish co-operatives, which should then efficiently promote their members and develop themselves into relatively autonomous → *self-help organizations* – simultaneously with the creation of secondary/tertiary co-operative institutions.

These co-operatives are often still insofar "state-sponsored", as they depend for their existence on direct governmental assistance given by (para)statal co-operative (self-help) promotion institutions, e.g. co-operative ministries, departments, authorities and others. These often supervise and control the state-sponsored co-operatives' activities and business policies.

In order to assist the self-development of these state-sponsored co-operatives into self-reliance and autonomy, "de-officialization strategies" have been proposed and designed, which imply the "phasing-out" of direct governmental aid and also the correction of (possible) failures made during the implementation of previous supporting policies.

b) Officialization as a result of implementing governmental development programmes through the co-operatives for the benefit of their members

In many developing countries different governmental and para-statal development institutions (such as various ministries, development banks, commercial institutions, extension services and also international development projects) use co-operatives as appropriate organizations in order to channel through them various programmes (for instance in the field of education, training, supply of farm inputs and consumer goods, credits, extension and infrastructural services) for the benefit of the individual members' farms, businesses and households.

The integration of the co-operatives into the planning and implementation of such development-programmes offers the advantages of reaching the "target-groups" more easily and of reducing the transaction costs of the various governmental and para-statal development institutions.

However, when executing these functions, the co-operatives do not operate as self-help organizations, which promote their members through co-operatively undertaken (business) activities. They act more or less as agencies for the distribution of services to their members. These services are provided and financed to a large extent by the government and/or development aid and have to be controlled accordingly.

The members may be satisfied with such forms of state-controlled co-operatives, if (ba) these services are in their interest, (bb) the minimum participation with shares and their own resources in the co-operative is very low (which is frequently found in more market-economy-oriented countries), and (bc) they are not compelled to do their business with the co-operative enterprise. Thus, the members and other participants of the co-operatives may be interested in publicly financed services being available and accept the state-control of their co-operatives as a form of "voluntary officialization". If it is intended to de-officialize such governmentally supported co-operative activities, it is a precondition for designing de-officialization strategies to integrate and harmonize these development programmes with appropriate co-operative self-help promotion policies in order to support the self-development of these state-controlled co-operatives towards self-reliance and autonomy.

c) Officialization of co-operatives as instruments of imperative governmental development planning

In those developing countries which applied a centrally planned development approach, the co-operatives were mostly established and officialized through measures of direct administrative or indirect compulsion and directed and controlled in order to contribute to the achievements of national or sectoral development goals. In these cases the members' individual farms were mostly integrated into the co-operative system. Examples are: the agricultural → *joint-production co-operatives* in countries, in which it was intended to establish a system of a centrally planned socialist economy (like in North Korea, North Vietnam, Cuba, and others); but also the Ujamaa Village Co-operatives in Tanzania; the integrated multi-purpose ("production-promotion") co-operatives established in Egypt under *Nasser* (→ *Produktionsförderungsgenossenschaften*); or → *marketing co-operatives* (in various countries) which had been officially granted the so-called "monopoly right" for the marketing of agricultural products, but which had in fact to execute the business policies as agents of governmental or para-statal trading monopolies (e.g. Marketing Boards).

The introduction of market-economy-oriented reforms, which are proposed and increasingly realized also in developing countries, implies the de-officialization of these co-operatives (for example in Egypt as a consequence of the liberalization policies introduced under *Sadat* and *Mubarak*).

2. Autonomous Co-operatives and Officialized Co-operatives

With due regard to the complex phenomenon of officialization of co-operatives, a general classification distinguishes between autonomous and officialized co-operatives which again may be differentiated into state-sponsored and state-controlled co-operative organizations:

a) "Autonomous co-operatives" or co-operative self-help organizations are characterized as (aa) self-help organizations maintaining member-owned co-operatives enterprises/businesses for the promotion of the members' individual economies, which are (ab) as autonomous in deciding on their organizational goals and business policies as other private enterprises/businesses, and (ac) insofar self-reliant as they do not permanently depend on direct financial and managerial support provided by governmental (or "private") self-help promotion institutions.

b) "State-sponsored co-operatives" are defined as organizations, which are (ba) being supported in their institutional development process in order to become autonomous self-reliant co-operatives, but (bb) are still not able to survive without direct external managerial and/or financial aid provided by the government.

c) "State-controlled co-operatives" can be classified as institutions, which are (ca) legally registered as co-operative societies, but (cb) operate as governmentally controlled organizations and (cc) have developed factual structures which are different in market-economies and in centrally planned economies, but can be clearly distinguished from those of autonomous self-reliant co-operative self-help organizations.

3. Criticism of the Officialization and Arguments for the De-officialization of Co-operatives

Since the criticism of the co-operatives in developing countries in the early 1970s, there have been continuous and sometimes ideological debates on the officialization and de-officialization of co-operatives in the "Third World".

From the point of view of national development policies, the main points of criticism of the officialization and arguments for the de-officialization of co-operatives may be summarized as follows:

a) Effective contributions to national and rural development have been expected from member-efficient, participatory and relatively autonomous co-operative self-help organizations, wherefrom the officialized co-operatives differ considerably. These have largely failed in mobilizing the local resources and the self-help potential of the people.

b) The public resources needed for the direct sponsorship of the co-operatives have been usually planned to be only of a temporary nature. These governmental resources have to be evaluated with high opportunity costs and – due to scarce development budgets – may not be available in the future; and

c) appropriate development policies and projects could also be implemented in cooperation with autonomous co-operatives on a voluntary basis – and even be made more effective – if (ca) these programmes are in the interest of the members, (cb) do not affect negatively the self-help motivation nor the stability of the co-operative organizations, and if (cc) transaction costs involved for the co-operatives are remunerated accordingly.

d) Furthermore, in the context of market-economy oriented reforms in the former socialistic Eastern European and developing countries, autonomous co-operative self-help organizations could contribute to facilitate the transformation processes especially through: (da) supporting the development of small and medium entrepreneurs in agriculture, handicrafts, industry, trade, transport and other sectors; (db) providing consumer goods and housing facilities for the socially weak members, (dc) improving the supply of various local infrastructures and also offering various social services, (dd) contributing to the creation of new markets, the growth of existing markets, the integration of regionaly isolated markets and the intensification of market competition, and (de) helping to improve the framework conditions of the members' individual as well as of the co-operative organizations' activities (cf. *Hanel* 1992).

IV. The De-officialization of Co-operatives in Developing Countries

1. De-officialization and Similar Conceptions

Generally, the term "de-officialization" characterizes the self-development of state-sponsored and -controlled co-operatives into autonomous and self-reliant co-operative self-help organizations. In the scope of co-operative-related development policies, however, this term is often used in order to specify different aspects of de-officialization, such as: the intention or goal; the governmental decision; the strategy to be applied; the process; or also the success of the de-officialization of co-operatives.

Furthermore, it should be mentioned that as a result of the criticism of (officialized rural) co-operatives for having failed to become participatory organizations for the benefit of the "poor" in the 1970s, the terms "officialization" and "de-officialization" are often interpreted either in an ideological or in a negative sense. Therefore, de-officialization is often replaced by "de-bureaucratization", "restructurization", "democratization", "de-regulation" and "decentralization".

However, a systematic analysis and evaluation of the often very hybrid types of co-operatives and even of the different activities within large primary and secondary co-operative organizations may provide the information needed for successful de-officializations; for instance, which co-operatives should be classified either as autonomous, as potentially autonomous or as state-sponsored co-operatives and developed towards self-reliance, and which co-operatives should continue to operate as forms of state-controlled or "public" co-operative institutions (*Hanel* 1992).

2. Principal Conditions for the De-officialization of Co-operatives

If it is intended to develop largely state-sponsored, and state-controlled co-operatives into autonomous co-operative self-help organizations, certain preconditions must be created. A distinction is usually made between "external" conditions providing an adequate framework for the self-development of co-operative organizations and "co-operative movements", and "internal" conditions to be fulfilled within the primary, secondary, and tertiary co-operative organizations:

a) The *basic external conditions* must include the governmental decisions that: (aa) co-operatives self-help organizations are (principally) voluntary and autonomous associations for the promotion of their members; (ab) sufficient political and economic freedom for the self-development of co-operative organizations is (legally) guaranteed; (ac) co-operative self-help organizations are protected from undue interference and control of the various governmental and para-statal institutions as well as from the misuse of market power of large governmental, para-statal and private companies; and the (ad) development related policies, programmes and projects do not discriminate against the (private) co-operative self-help organizations and 'co-operative movements'. Furthermore, self-help supportive global, sectoral, regional, and infrastructural economic policies and co-operative-oriented indirect promotion policies (in particular: adequate co-operative laws, information facilities, and education-, training-, auditing-, and consultation-services) can provide framework conditions which are favourable for the de-officialization of state-sponsored co-operatives towards self-reliance, as well as for their further self-development as autonomous co-operative self-help organizations and "co-operative movements". However, the government must decide the introduction of the "de-officialization" of co-operatives and put this decision into effect, even when this decision is in contrast to the interests and goals of (para-)statal organizations and also when co-operatives should be interested in forms of "voluntary officialization".

b) *The basic internal conditions within the co-operatives* which are relevant for the introduction of successful de-officialization processes are related, in particular, to: (ba) the homogeneity and sizes of the co-operative groups; (bb) the suitable types of the co-operative enterprises and business activities with special attention to the kind and combination of the services to be offered to the members; and the location, size, installations, finance, administration, and a management, which is capable of maintaining and increasing the promotional potential of the co-operatives, and to compete successfully with private and (para-)statal enterprises; (bc) the organizational structures of business relationships between the co-operative enterprise and the individual members' economies; (bd) the active and effective participation of the members in setting the goals, deciding on the activities, as well as on the incentive-contribution-systems and in the internal control and ongoing self-evaluation of their co-operatives.

Furthermore, the establishment of adequately integrated systems consisting of primary, secondary and – if need be – also of tertiary co-operative institutions, is of particular importance for successful de-officialization processes.

3. Some Basic Problems of the De-officialization of Co-operatives

The creation of appropriate framework conditions on the national, the regional and the local level which are favourable for the de-officialization of co-operatives and the design of adequate support for initiating the self-development of state-sponsored and -controlled co-operatives involves the solution of complicated tasks.

Various problems have to be solved, if, for instance, in totalitarian countries with largely centrally planned economies democratic and market-economy-oriented reforms are planned, in the framework of which state-controlled co-operatives shall be successfully de-officialized. Compared with such situations, the de-officialization of potentially or nearly autonomous co-operatives in more democratic ('mixed' or) market economies may be seen as a comparatively simple process. However, if governments intend to develop state-sponsored and state-controlled co-operatives towards self-reliance and autonomy, they may have to deal with various interests and problems which make it difficult to achieve this goal. In governmental and para-statal institutions the fear of reducing the resources, prestige, and direct influence on the co-operatives may develop a strong interest in a sort of compulsory officialization; these institutions may realize the need for financial self-reliance on the part of the co-operatives, but emphasize as well the continuing need for governmental supervision and control.

Co-operative managers and also members may be interested in the continuation or even increase of direct financial government support and accept a kind of "voluntary officialization" or "self-officialization". Thus, the representatives of the co-operative organizations and movements may tend to point out the importance of autonomy and the need for financial sponsorship provided by the state.

A fast withdrawal of the direct managerial and financial sponsorship and supervision may imply the danger that many co-operatives will become dormant or bankrupt, be misused by persons of influence, or, in some cases, develop into economically successful establishments which promote financially well-situated members and neglect the interests and needs of the economically weaker sub-groups of members.

In countries, where strong and self-reliant secondary and apex organizations have been established, these could be assisted in order to support the primary co-operatives.

Yet, the transfer or delegation of external support and supervisory functions to secondary co-operative organizations or apex institutions may turn out to be effective only, where "strong and self-reliant co-operative movements" have already been developed. Often, however, co-operative secondary organizations and apex institutions still do not exist, or they are either rather weak or state-sponsored and state-controlled, so that they have also to be de-officialized and supported in their development towards self-reliance and autonomy.

Consequently, strategies of de-officialization may also provide appropriate support for the (self-)development of central co-operative banks and central co-operative commercial organizations, as well as for secondary co-operative institutions, which are commissioned, for instance, to execute the functions of education, training, and research, of auditing, evaluation, and consultation, as well as the representation of the general interest of the "co-operative movement".

4. The Importance of Appropriate Strategies for the De-officialization

In countries, in which it is intended to initiate and support the self-development of co-operatives towards self-reliance and autonomy, appropriate strategies for the de-officialization have to be developed. The de-officialization strategies must be adapted to the administrative and institutional infrastructures of the country and take into close consideration the internal structures and the level of organizational and economic development, which has been achieved by various officialized primary, secondary and tertiary co-operatives under the prevailing conditions. However, there is sufficient evidence to support the hypothesis that policy-makers do not always have sufficient valid, reliable, and objective information on the factual structures and activities of state-sponsored co-operatives, e.g. on the efficiency of their economy operations, on the extent to which they promote the members, and on their achievements towards self-reliance and autonomy. Policy-makers may have good reasons to assume that feed-back information provided by the governmental agencies – which are commissioned with the sponsorship, audit, and supervision – may sometimes be too optimistic, whereas external observers and critics may often have tended to emphasize the too negative global evaluations of the state-sponsored and controlled co-operatives.

Thus, appropriate detailed evaluations should provide the basic information necessary for starting the design of appropriate de-officialization strategies (→ *Evaluation*).

Considering this and the demands for improving the evaluation (and monitoring) of co-operatives in developing countries, a "tripartite approach of evaluation of co-operative organizations" (*Dülfer* 1981; *Hanel/Müller* 1978) may be mentioned which distinguishes between (a) the evaluation of (co-operative) development projects and (b) the evaluation of co-operatives as institutions. As regards the evaluation of co-operative organizations/institutions it is distinguished between: (ba) the operational efficiency (which is related to the achievement of the co-operative organizations' goals and includes the asssessment of the co-operatives' business policies), (bb) the member-oriented efficiency as the appraisal of the degree to which the members have been promoted according to their interests and aims, and (bc) the development-related efficiency as the evaluation of the co-operatives' contributions to development-processes and, thus, the achievement of governmental development-related goals.

On the basis of such comprehensive evaluations of the officialized co-operatives it could be decided whether a co-operative should be, for example: (a) liquidated or wound up, (b) be transformed into another legal structure, (c) continue to operate as a state-controlled co-operative, (d) be regarded as a "self-reliant, autonomous" co-operative or (e) be classified as a "state-sponsored" co-operative in order to be supported in its self-development towards self-reliance.

Since officialized co-operatives have often been organized to a large extent corresponding to the administrative interests of governmental development institutions, the chances and opportunities of their successful self-development towards self-reliance and autonomy may often be increased considerably, if appropriate institutional reforms can be made. Considering the prevailing structures of largely officialized rural co-operatives some aspects of Indonesian village co-operatives may be mentioned as examples in this regard: (a) The reduction of the size and the degree of heterogeneity of the co-operative groups possibly through forming homogeneous local sub-groups, (b) the concentration of the co-operative enterprises on such activities which (ba) meet the felt needs of the members and which (bb) could be undertaken on a self-reliant basis in due time, (c) improvements of the "incentive-contribution relationships" of the members (→ *Incentives*) and the "rules of distribution" of the jointly produced promotional potential, (d) improvements of the members' participation in goal-setting, decision-making, and control-processes through organizational procedures as well as through the introduction of "promotion reports/promotion plans" and internal participatory self-evaluations, and (e) appropriate consolidations of the high indebtness that has obviously often been caused through governmentally advised investments which then turned out to be rather unprofitable from the point of view of the co-operatives' business policies.

However, effectively operating co-operative-oriented self-help promotion institutions are crucial for providing the assistance which is needed for initiating and supporting the self-development of the state-sponsored co-operatives towards self-reliance and autonomy. Considering the weaknesses of the various governmental and para-statal development organizations in supporting the establishment of autonomous and self-reliant co-operatives, a "de-regulation" of the governmental self-help promotion and the creation of innovative "self-help promotion institutions" seems to be another precondition for the appropriate design and the effective implementation of "strategies of de-officialization".

Bibliography

Baldus, Rolf D./Hanel, Alfred/Münkner, Hans-H. (eds.): Government Promotion of Co-operatives and other Self-Help Organizations for Rural Development, German Foundation for International Development, Food and

Agriculture Development Centre, Berlin (West) 1980 (DOK 1063 A/a S 79-88-80).
Bergmann, Theodor: Social Aspects of De-Officialization of Co-operatives, in: Don, Y. (ed.): Dynamics of Interrelations between the Agricultural Co-operatives and the Government, C.I.R.C.O.M., Tel Aviv 1976, pp. 202-218.
Carroll, T.F.: Deofficializing Co-operatives, Selected Propositions, in: Don Y. (ed.): Dynamics of Interrelations between the Agricultural Co-operatives and the Government, C.I.R.C.O.M., Tel Aviv 1976, pp. 196-201.
Don, Yehuda: De-Officializing Co-operatives. A Model for Policy Optimization, in: Don Y. (ed.): Dynamics of Interrelations between the Agricultural Co-operatives and the Government, C.I.R.C.O.M., Tel Aviv 1976, pp. 221-236.
Draheim, Georg: Die Genossenschaft als Unternehmungstyp, Göttingen 1955.
Dubhashi, P.R.: Principles and Philosophy of Cooperation, Poona 1970.
Dülfer, Eberhard: Evaluation of Co-operative Organization in Developing Countries, FAO, Rome 1981.
Dülfer, Eberhard: The Co-operatives between Member Participation, the Formation of Vertical Organizations and Bureaucratic Tendencies, an Introduction into the Theme, in: Dülfer, Eberhard/Hamm, Walter (eds.): Co-operatives in the Clash between Member-Participation, Organizational Development and Bureaucratic Tendencies, London 1985, pp. 15-39.
Hanel, Alfred/Müller, Julius Otto: Improving the Methodology of Evaluating the Development of Rural Co-operatives in Developing Countries, Case Study Iran, FAO, Rome 1978.
Hanel, Alfred/Müller, Julius Otto: On the Evaluation of Rural Co-operatives with Reference to Governmental Development Policies – Case Study Iran, Göttingen 1976.
Hanel, Alfred: Basic Aspects of Co-operative Organizations and Co-operative Self-Help Promotion in Developing Countries, Marburg 1992.
Hanel, Alfred: Conditions for and Selected Problems of Deofficialization of Rural Co-operatives in Developing Countries – The Lessening of State-Administrative Control, in: Konopnicki, Maurice/Vandevalle, G. (eds.): Cooperation as an Instrument for Rural Development, University of Ghent, ICA, London 1978, pp. 116-123.
Hanel, Alfred: State-Sponsored Co-operatives and Self-Reliance, Marburg 1989.
Hartwig, Karl-Hans: The Conception of Co-operatives in Eastern Europe, in: Boettcher, E. (ed.): The Co-operative in the Competition of Ideas, Tübingen 1985, pp. 237-256.
Institute for Co-operative Research at the University of Vienna: The Co-operatives and the State, Fourth International Conference on Co-operative Science, Vienna 1963, Göttingen 1965.
International Co-operative Alliance (ed.): Report on the Asian Top-Level Co-operative Leaders' Conference, New Delhi 1974.
Koch, Eckard: Officialisation of Co-operatives in Developing Countries, Friedrich-Ebert-Stiftung, Bonn 1986.
Odede, O./Verhagen, K.: The Organization of External Supervision as an Integral Part of Promoting Co-operative Development, in: Konopnicki, Maurice/Vandewalle, G. (eds.): Cooperation as an Instrument for Rural Development, University of Ghent, ICA, London 1978, pp. 98-108.
Soedjono, Ibnoe: Self-help Promotion by Governmental and Semi-Official Bodies (the Indonesian Experiences), in: Dülfer, Eberhard/Hamm, Walter (eds.): Co-operatives in the Clash between Member-Participation, Organizational Development and Bureaucratic Tendencies, London 1985, pp. 275-296.
Wilson, Thomas: The Officialization of the Co-operative System in Developing Countries – Problems and Counter-Strategies, in: Tracy, Mary/Varady, Lajos (eds.): Co-operatives Today, ICA, Geneva 1986, pp. 513-528.

Oligarchy in Co-operatives

RAINER VIERHELLER [F]

(see also: *Business Policies*; *Management in Co-operatives*; *Managerial Economics*; *Organizational Structure of Societies*; *Organizational Structures, Co-operative*; *Labour-Management*)

I. The "Iron Law of Oligarchy" (*Michels*); II. Problems with Oligarchy in Co-operative Democracy; III. Problems with Oligarchy in Co-operatives in Developing Countries.

I. The "Iron Law of Oligarchy" (*Michels*)

The discussion on the problem of oligarchy in democratically structured institutions (i.e., of the dominating role of an elected leadership group) goes back to a classic investigation by *Robert Michels* (1908; 1911/1979). Taking the example of institutions of the socialist workers' movement (political parties, trade unions), *Michels* analyzes the reasons for the discrepancy between the system of values (idealistic expectations) of a democratically organized institution and the reality of the actual situation. *Michels* comes to the following two conclusions, which constitute the "iron law of oligarchy": on the one hand, every democracy requires organization: "Without organization, democracy is inconceivable" (*Michels* 1970). On the other hand, every organization contains within itself an inherent tendency toward the formation of an oligarchy: "Whoever refers to 'organization' also refers to 'tendency to oligarchy'" (*Michels* 1970). *Michels* bases this tendency toward the building up of an oligarchy, brought about by the nature of an organization itself, on two central hypotheses: (1) The increasing size and complexity of a democratic institution lead to the appearance of a bureaucracy and the development of a leadership group. (2) Professional competence is inequally distributed between the leadership and the basis-group; the leadership is able to attain greater influence through its superior expertise ("incompetence of the masses"). The increasing size of the organization leads to a functional division of labour, which in its turn produces elevated positions of leadership: "Technical specialization, which results from every organizational expansion, creates the necessity of a 'professional leadership', which transfers all the decisive qualities of the masses to the leader alone as specific qualities of leadership" (*Michels* 1908). The tendency of leaders to become independent of the basis-group gains momentum, according to *Michels*, through the psychological needs of the basis-group for leadership and through its gratitude to its leaders, as well as through the leaders' charismatic qualities. These postulates by *Michels* on oligarchy stand in contrast to a democratic system of values and have initiated a discussion which is still continuing today. Numerous studies since *Michels'* have succeeded in many cases in confirming at least the tendency within democratic organizations to build up oligarchies; but in other cases these studies have also indicated possible alternatives from which a weakening or an overcoming of the problem of oligarchy can be expected (*Naschold, Röhrich, Ostergaard/Halsey, Hettlage, Witte, Ringle* 1983). In the Yugoslavian workers' self-administration, for example (→ *Joint-production Co-operatives*), it was discovered that in the whole participatory process of decision-making, it was the management who took part in 75% of the discussion, took up 80% of the discussion time, gave 90% of the explanations, and made 75% of the proposals accepted (*Léman*). Whether oligarchy is inevitable, however, in the sense of *Michels'* "iron law", is a highly contested question and is held in doubt, particularly by supporters of the participatory approach.

II. Problems with Oligarchy in Co-operative Demcracy

As an exemplary instance of the tendency toward the formation of oligarchies, one can take the transformation of the structure of the process of decision and policy-making undergone in numerous co-operatives. In particular, the low percentages of participation in this decision-making process, entitled "membership apathy" and referred to as an internationally observable phenomenon (*Draheim* 1952), was early drawn attention to as a problem in co-operative democracy. Not only in other organizations, but also in co-operatives, the development of oligarchies can be traced back mainly to problems of capability, coordination, supervision, and apathy, all of which are closely related to the co-operatives' growing internal and external complexity.

1. Increasing Complexity and Leadership Capability

Traditional co-operatives (*Dülfer*) usually correspond to the type known as "small co-operative", with a relatively simple functional structure (→ *Structural Types*). The resulting low degree of complexity enables the membership to run the co-operative by means of democratic participation in the general meetings, without prohibitive efforts in organizing, in disseminating information, and in learning. A simple functional structure puts the members into a position to provide executives with sufficiently detailed and precise operational instructions that the executives' freedom of action is definitely limited and at the same time can be operationally supervised. But one cannot necessarily deduce from this fact that the members then take advantage of their opportunities to participate or that the general meeting takes advantage of its leadership prerogatives. Studies on the history of co-operatives show that in co-operatives in the 19th century a small and better-educated leadership group (teachers, pastors) possessed a superior position of influence (*Schmid*). According to *Schmid*, it was an exception even in the 19th century for the leadership of a co-operative to be exercised by the general meeting.

In addition to educational advantages, there are other status differences among members (income, size of the member's business, patronage, social background) which contribute to conferring high esteem. When this is the case, the danger arises that persons from a socially superior class among the membership tend to be elected to executive and supervisory positions and that officeholders continue to be recruited from this superior class again and again. The social proximity of executives to members of supervisory bodies creates common interests and can curb the control over the executives from the perspective of the broad interests of the members.

During the course of time, business growth, broadening of functions (full-service cooperation), expansion and diversification of the circle of members, as well as increased intensity of competition (buyers' markets, oligopolistic market forms, and the dynamics of innovation) have, in many co-operatives, led to a growing complexity of enterprise management. Large general meetings are often overburdened by the necessity for dynamic and complex decision-making, because greater demands on expertise, on the individual's capacity for absorbing information, and on the time-allotment in the general meeting often overtax the members (*Hettlage*). Large general meetings tend to be sluggish in reaching decisions and prove themselves too inflexible as leadership bodies (*Klemann*) (→ *Organizational Structure of Societies*). Thus leadership capability and the initiative in decision-making become more and more the domain of executive bodies, which are thereby transformed from administrative into leaderhsip boards. This process is reinforced by the change-over, customary under these circumstances, from an honorary to a professional business management, because professional managers demand independence and can develop their functional abilities only if they are given the necessary freedom of action.

2. Problems of Coordination

In large co-operatives, where direct contacts between the leadership and the membership-base become difficult, a need develops for extending centralized coordinating powers. Problems that arise cannot be solved ad hoc anymore through personal contacts. The general meeting meets too infrequently for current acute problems to be handled adequately. At the same time, the increasing difficulty of face-to-face relationships calls for the use of formalized coordination patterns, in order to guarantee that action be coordinated and unified with the necessary speed. In this way, the co-operative leadership develops into a central coordinating agency which formulates expectations of and rules on coordination and which, on the basis of this, broadens its possibilities for exerting its influence. Its influence grows, the greater the need for coordination becomes and the more important unified action and organizationwide economic synergy potentials become in competition with other organizations.

3. Problems of Supervision

When the general meeting is overburdened, and when the rights of the members become increasingly limited to mere secondary participation, then the professional management of a co-operative tends to be given only general goals to work toward, whose substance is largely undefined. A frequently-mentioned example of this tendency is the unspecified purpose of the co-operative to "serve its members' interests" (→ *Promotion Mandate*). General goals open up wide areas in which the leadership feels free to do as it sees fit; generally-formulated goals render supervision of the actions of the management difficult, particularly because operational instructions are insufficiently precise (as in the above-mentioned purpose of the co-operative to serve its members' interests). Moreover, the withdrawal of the members from the central co-operative leadership causes the professional executives and the membership-base to drift apart, as far as the availability and exchange of information is concerned, whereby the opportunities of the members to supervise the management become further reduced. The members as well as their supervisory bodies become dependent for their information on the management and can therefore no longer call the management fully to account. In addition, those same causes for the transfer of authority from the general meeting to the executive leadership are simultaneously factors which weaken the authority of the members to supervise that leadership. As a result of the status of professional managers as experts, there develops a wide scope in which the co-operative leadership can act at its own discretion (→ *Management in Co-operatives*).

What is more, empirical studies (*Klemann, Glatzner, Ringle* 1984) show that the nomination of candidates for the co-operative supervisory board is not infrequently highly influenced by the management, in other words, that the management co-determines who are to be its supervisors. This nourishes the fear that the selection of people to sit on the supervisory board is not made independently of the interests of the management and that the effectiveness of supervision thereby suffers (*Glatzner, Klemann*). In the economic theory of cooperation (*Eschenburg, Boettcher*), the further deduction is made that the costs and risks involved in voting a manager out of office make the members hesitate to make use of their prerogative to vote a manager out. Discharging a manager requires just as laborious a process of reaching agreement among the members as the choice of a new manager does (→ *Theory of co-operative Cooperation*). Furthermore, the replacement involves productivity risks, because a new manager first has to "learn the ropes"; and his abilities and his behaviour cannot be absolutely reliably predicted in advance. If, besides all this, the members' chances of leaving the co-operative out of dissatisfaction with the manager are limited due to lack of alternative possibilities, then the latent threat of the members to exit the co-operative can lose much of its effect as a mechanism of control. On the other hand, if the members with the greatest business turn-over should threaten to pull out, they can definitely put the management under pressure and cause it to join in with them. In this way, a small but economically important circle of members, together with the management, can come to dominate the co-operative.

4. Problems of Apathy

The limited willingness of the membership-basis to participate actively in the co-operative is generally traced back to the increasingly complex problems of running a co-operative, problems which require of the members a prohibitive investment in time, in learning, and in digesting information of order to reach decisions and determine policy (*Hettlage*). But even the fundamental willingness of members to participate tends to be curbed by the sheer growth of the co-operative. An increase in the size of a group is usually accompanied by a decrease in the cohesiveness of the group, since social and socio-emotional ties are stronger in smaller groups than in larger ones. When cohesiveness dwindles, then the individual's readiness to take an active part in the internal affairs of the co-operative group also dwindles. More than thirty years ago, the "Co-operative Independent Commission Report" drew attention to the fact that the active participation of members drops to the same extent that the organization grows. When the strength of social and socio-emotional ties is reduced, then the members' sense of being the owners of the organization (i.e., awareness of co-operative ownership) becomes weaker and weaker, which is also mentioned as a cause of membership apathy (*Blümle*). Members reduce their relationship with the co-operative to that of clients (*Glatzner*) and tend to remain indifferent toward co-operative self-administration. *Naschold*, on the other hand, points out that possibly the co-operative offers its members too few incentives for active participation, in comparison with interests for active participation, in comparison with interests and burdens which the members have outside the organizations. From the point of view of the economic theory of cooperation (*Eschenburg, Boettcher*), membership apathy is the result of a rational economic calculation. Members decide, on the basis of a logical cost-benefit analysis, that they strike a positive balance in their own favour when they delegate complicated, time-consuming, and information-intensive jobs to a central pool of experts. They recognize the supervisory problems involved in this approach; but these problems are not considered so important as to outweigh the positive balance gained by transferring functions to a professional management.

III. Problems with Oligarchy in Co-operatives in Developing Countries

The factors which have already been mentioned as contributing to the formation of oligarchy in industrialized countries are to a great extent acute in developing countries as well (*Hettlage*). However, additional factors often come into play there which aggravate the problem with oligarchy in Third World countries in comparison to industrialized nations:

1. General education and specialized training are even less equally distributed between management and the membership there than in industrialized countries, particularly when qualified executives are available at all and when they can be induced to assume the management of the co-operative, whereby the scope becomes even wider in which the management can act at its own discretion.
2. The traditional authorities and social structures which still exist or else are still leaving their ex-post-effects in developing countries, especially in rural areas, tend to hinder to a large extent the participation of members in the co-operative process of decision and policy-making. This is true, for example, for social ties in the extended patriarchal family, for traditional feudal structures, for the position of authority of chiefs or elders in tribal societies or for relationships based on religious authority. Often traditional authorities attain a dominating position in the co-operative, or else the co-operative leadership is forced to orient itself to their will, in order not to lose the following of the members (→ *Policies for Promotion*).
3. The static social orders which one finds in developing countries, or the effects of which one still sees, have contributed to a type of socialization among large parts of the population which has produced the attitude that unfavourable external conditions in one's station in life are predestined by fate (*Büscher*). With this mind-set, the people hardly tend to throw given oligarchical co-operative structures into question.
4. In developing countries, co-operatives are often understood to be instruments of state development policy and are therefore founded, developed, and managed by state agencies (→ *officialization* of co-operatives). The founding and promoting of co-operatives from above, as well as the professional and social gap between the membership-base and the management appointed by the state, contribute to the fact that members and potential members fail to view the co-operative as their own concern, that they therefore remain indifferent to internal co-operative affairs, and that they regard the co-operative more as a state service institution (*Büscher, Kuhn*) (→ *Self-help Organizations*). This passivity has to be compensated for by activities on the part of the leadership and thereby favours the formation of oligarchical structures.
5. The alienation between state-dominated co-operatives and the membership-base is worsened when the state co-operative programme is linked with forced membership. No matter how justified forced membership may be in the context of developing countries, it does conflict with the co-operative ideals of self-help and self-responsibility. For this reason, the mechanisms of identification which are connected with these principles cannot be sufficiently activated, which in turn contributes to a passive behaviour on the part of the members and to a corresponding dominance on the part of the leadership.

Bibliography

Bergmann, Herbert: Die genossenschaftliche Demokratie zwischen traditionalen Machthabern und der Entwicklungsverwaltung. Genossenschaften – Demokratie und Wettbewerb, Tübingen 1972, pp. 145–183.

Blümle, Ernst-Bernd: Wachstum und Willensbildung der Primärgenossenschaften, Zeitschrift für das gesamte Genossenschaftswesen, vol. 14, (1964), pp. 453–463.

Boettcher, Erik/Westermann, Harry: Genossenschaften – Demokratie und Wettbewerb, Tübingen 1972.

Boettcher, Erik: Die Genossenschaft in der Marktwirtschaft, Tübingen 1980.

Boettcher, Erik: Kooperation und Demokratie in der Wirtschaft, Tübingen 1974.

Büscher, Horst: Die Rolle der Genossenschaften im Rahmen einer entwicklungspolitischen Konzeption. Genossenschaften und Genossenschaftsforschung, Göttingen 1971, pp. 314–331.

Co-operative Independent Commission Report, Co-operatives Union, Manchester 1958.

Draheim, Georg: Die Genossenschaft als Unternehmungstyp, Göttingen 1952.

Draheim, Georg: Zur Ökonomisierung der Genossenschaften, Göttingen 1967.

Dülfer, Eberhard/Hamm, Walter (eds.): Genossenschaften zwischen Mitgliederpartizipation, Verbundbildung und Bürokratietendenz, Göttingen 1983.

Dülfer, Eberhard: Organisation und Management im kooperativen Betriebsverbund, Zeitschrift für das

gesamte Genossenschaftswesen, special issue 1970: Genossenschaften im Wachstum, pp. 76-103.
Eschenburg, Rolf: Genossenschaft und Demokratie, Zeitschrift für das gesamte Genossenschaftswesen, vol. 22, (1972), pp. 132-157.
Eschenburg, Rolf: Ökonomische Theorie der genossenschaftlichen Zusammenarbeit, Tübingen 1971.
Glatzner, Ludwig: Mitgliederbindung, Arbeitspapiere der Forschungstelle für Genossenschaftswesen an der Universität Hohenheim, no. 5, Stuttgart-Hohenheim 1989.
Grunwald, Wolfgang: Das "Eherne Gesetz der Oligarchie": Ein Grundproblem demokratischer Führung in Organisationen. Partizipative Führung, Bern und Stuttgart 1980, pp. 245-285.
Hasselmann, Erwin: Die Rochdaler Prinzipien im Wandel der Zeit, Frankfurt/M. 1968.
Hettlage, Robert: Genossenschaftstheorie und Partizipationsdiskussion, (Frankfurt/M. 1979), 2nd ed. Göttingen 1987.
Jokisch, Jens: Zur Explikation der Zielbildung in Genossenschaften, Dissertation Hamburg 1974.
Kieser, Alfred: Ehernes Gesetz der Oligarchie, Gresham's Law of Planning, Parkinsons Gesetz, Peter Prinzip. Betriebswirtschaftliche Gesetze, Effekte und Prinzipien, München 1979, pp. 41-47.
Klemann, Peter: Das Management in Genossenschaften des Lebensmitteleinzelhandels, Karlsruhe 1969.
Kranz, Werner: Das Management der Unternehmensgruppe Konsum im Konflikt zwischen Demokratie und Wettbewerbsfähigkeit, Karlsruhe 1968.
Kuhn, Johannes: Aspekte der Mitgliederpartizipation in ländlichen Genossenschaften der Entwicklungsländer, Zeitschrift für das gesamte Genossenschaftswesen, vol.31, (1981), pp. 37-44.
Léman, Gudrun: Das jugoslawische Modell, Frankfurt/M. 1976.
Michels, Robert: Die oligarchischen Tendenzen der Gesellschaft, Archiv für Sozialwissenschaft und Sozialpolitik, vol.27, (1908), pp. 73-135.
Michels, Robert: Political Parties, a sociological study of the Oligarchy Tendencies of Modern Democracy. Zur Soziologie des Parteiwesens, Stuttgart 1970.
Naschold, Frieder: Organisation und Demokratie, 2nd ed., Stuttgart 1971.
Ostergaard, G.N./Halsey, A.H.: Power in Co-operatives, Oxford 1965.
Preuß, Ulrich: Mitgliederinteressen und Wachstum der Genossenschaften, Karlsruhe 1969.
Ringle, Günther: Mitgliederaktivierung und Partizipation in moderne Primärgenossenschaften, Göttingen 1983.
Röhrich, Wilfried (ed.): "Demokratische" Elitenherrschaft, Darmstadt 1975.
Scheiter, Sieghart: Die Mitgliederführung in genossenschaftlichen Handelsgruppen, Göttingen 1982.
Schmid, Günter: Zur Problematik der Leitung von Genossenschaften, Archiv für öffentliche und freigemeinnützige Unternehmen, vol. 14, Göttingen 1985, pp. 231-252.
Vierheller, Rainer: Demokratie und Management. Grundlagen einer Mangementtheorie genossenschaftlichen Managements durch den Aufsichtsrat, Hamburg 1984.
Vierheller, Rainer: Mitgliederpartizipation und professionalle Genossenschaftsführung. Mitgliedschaftsattraktivität als Aufgabe genossenschaftlicher Kooperationspolitik, Göttingen 1991, pp. 214-279.
Weiser, Gerhard: Stilwandlungen der Wohnungsgenossenschaften, Göttingen 1953.
Witte, Erich: Die Genossenschaft als Organisation. Genossenschaften – Demokratie und Wettbewerb, Tübingen 1972, pp. 29-55.

Operational Size of Co-operatives

ERNST-BERND BLÜMLE [J]

(see also: *Theory of Co-operative Cooperation*; *Structural Types*; *Classification*; *Managerial Economics*; *Equity Capital*)

I. Membership as Organizational Size; II. The Community Enterprise as a Standard of Comparison; III. Operational Size and Social Structure of Co-operatives; IV. Organizational Size and Market Influence of the Co-operative; V. Operational Size and Costs.

The term "operational size" describes the scope of total inputs of production factors or their output in the combination process. Operational size can be expressed either through qualitative classifications (small, medium, or large enterprises) or through a quantitative form based on value or volume (turnover, number of employees, final balance). Measurements based on qualitative classifications should also be differentiated spatially (e.g. international, national, regional or local markets) and according to branches (e.g. chemical industry or hatters). Organizational size is always a relative term (large in relation to what?). A small enterprise can play an important role for an isolated valley. Likewise, an enterprise with 20 employees can be the largest in the branch of a certain country (e.g. a hatter).

Because an enterprise is a complex system with multi-dimensional extentions, no uniform terms of size exist which are applicable for all branches and legal forms. In Germany, nevertheless, in the officially required tax audits (i.e. external or company audits) a classification of organizational size is used which, according to the type of business (trading company, finishing plant, free-lance work, credit institutes, insurance company, etc.) and on the basis of business characteristics (such as total turnover, assets and premium revenue) differentiates between large, medium, and small enterprises.

Based on the organizational form of co-operatives and on their membership structures, two points of departure present themselves for measuring the organizational size of co-operatives, namely:

a) the membership, and
b) the community enterprise.

I. Membership as Organizational Size

The members of co-operatives can be private households (users' co-operatives), enterprises (affiliated co-operatives), and people who, as a union of individuals, work together as workers, and enterprise members in co-operatives of production. A precise separation between household and affiliated co-operatives is, however, not necessarily an easy task as co-operatives in the banking and insurance sectors have both, households and enterprises, as members (→ *Group, the co-operative*).

Co-operatives, therefore, can be differentiated according to membership size into large, medium, and small co-operatives. The membership structure of the Raiffeisen banks in Switzerland offers an illustration (see Table 1). In all of Switzerland, the federation has 402,000 members distributed among 1,216 branch offices (1989), whereby the individual Raiffeisen banks show completely different levels of membership. The Raiffeisen bank with the smallest number of co-operators has only 34 members while the largest has 2,502.

The most important characteristics of organizational size in household, enterprise, and production co-operatives will be briefly presented below.

Table I: The Membership Structure of the Raiffeisen Banks

Members per branch	Number of Institutes real	%	Total membership real	%
1,000 +	39	3%	52,182	13%
500 – 1,000	209	17%	140,231	35%
up to 500	968	80%	209,812	52%
TOTAL	1,216	100%	402,225	100

Source: Schweizer Verband der Raiffeisenkassen, St.Gallen (1989).

1. Measuring the Organizational Size of Household Co-operatives

Private households in Switzerland have united through cooperation starting at the middle of the last century (the Zürich Konsumverein was founded in 1851) in order to provide a better economic position for themselves through self-help. The most well-known co-operative associations of private households are the consumer co-operatives, which provide consumer goods and consumer durables, and the building societies, which provide living space. Both of these are so-called supply co-operatives, the goal of which is to offer goods or services to their members under particularly favorable conditions. In a certain sense, the banking, insurance, and health care co-operatives also belong to this group; because of vague classifications, these co-operatives are discussed together with the affiliated co-operatives.

The size of consumer co-operatives (→ *Consumer Co-operatives*) can be measured by the number of households which have joined the particular co-operative. Today, after a wave of mergers and structural changes, 28 independent co-operatives with a total of 1.3 million member households comprise the Coop group of consumer co-operatives. (25 years ago, there were 491 co-operatives with approximately 800,000 members.) In contrast, the building societies in Switzerland are much less diffuse. Today, about 600 co-operatives belong to the Schweizerische Verband für Wohnungswesen (Swiss Housing Federation), which consists of 11 sections with 105,000 associated households or members. The membership levels of the sections differ widely, ranging from 200 to 43,000 households or members.

The importance of the co-operative sector can also be expressed through a relative observation (of the organizational level) – namely, how many households are members of a co-operative in relation to the total number of households. In Switzerland, 50% of all households are members of the consumer co-operative Coop. Only 5% of all Swiss households live in co-operative apartments.

2. Measuring the Operational Size of Affiliated Co-operatives

Above all, small and mid-sized enterprises of the primary, secondary, and tertiary sectors have joined together in cooperation.

Typical forms of this phenomenon are agricultural co-operatives, trade and commercial co-operatives, and credit co-operatives, as well as those for insurance and health care (→ *Classification*). The organizational size in these co-operative forms can also be measured according to the number of members in each co-operative.

As a result of growth, diversification and fusion, such affiliated co-operatives involved in agriculture and trade have undergone a concentration process in the last decade the organizational size, based on membership levels, has therefore risen.

The importance the co-operative sector has for a particular economic branch can be determined by the relationship of the number of enterprises – measured by turnover or some other common characteristic – to the total number of such enterprises in a given branch. Not only can the importance of co-operatives be ascertained through this method, but also which organizational size classes have joined together in co-operatives. One can calculate, for example, that 100% of all small farming enterprises with an area of x hectares are members of a co-operative.

3. Measuring the Operational Size of Production Co-operatives

Because → *Joint-production Co-operatives* are structures free of complicated hierarchies, their membership levels remain fairly low. In Britain, for example, there were just about 900 production co-operatives with 9,000 members in 1984. The problem with an ever-growing number of member-workers is the de facto development of hierarchical structures and the mounting efforts in reaching a consensus and coordination. Consequently, production co-operatives and/or self-administrating enterprises have only attained a modest position in the industrialized countries.

Their relative importance can be determined by comparing the number of employees in production co-operatives to the number of total employees in a particular branch.

II. The Community Enterprise as a Standard of Comparison

The community enterprise is the activity-oriented enterprise which implements decision making and insures co-operative trade. In measuring the organizational size of community enterprises, the same calculation problems and categories apply as is the case with companies with other legal forms. The related economic literature generally lists such characteristics as turnover, market share, and number of employees, whereby branch-specific characteristics provide a variety of different factors. As the general yardstick for measuring the operational size of co-operatives, the sheer number of employees as well as turnover can be chosen. According to individual branches, the following can also be used:

- agricultural co-operatives: output amounts (e.g. kilo, liter) and working material
- production co-operatives: output amounts (kilo, liter) and working material
- retail co-operatives: number of branch shops, amount of sales space
- building societies: number of apartments
- banking and credit co-operatives: final balance
- insurance and health care co-operatives: amount of premiums.

III. Operational Size and Social Structure of Co-operatives

Growth in operational size as a result of expansion and fusion is a general phenomenon in co-operative studies. This growth development into higher size levels has fundamentally changed the structure within co-operatives. If for the Raiffeisen bank of a village or the seed growing co-operative of a region, a small group of members comprises the center of activity, it will become obscure as the co-operative grows in size. The administrator who acted in a state of complete dependency to the will of the members is replaced by a "manager". The most important difference between a manager and an official administrator is the sole responsibility of the manager for the co-operative administration. The context of his contract and orders are not further specified by the members. The manager management acquires near sovereignty with respect to its ever-mounting power and the diminishing possibilities to effectively control it. The ensuing dilemma between management and members expresses itself in deeper member apathy and a lack of identification with the co-operative. Gradually, members lose control over the primary aim of the co-operative: realization of their decisions (→ *Structural Types*) and their own promotion.

IV. Organizational Size and Market Influence of the Co-operative

The concentration process (→ *Structural Changes*) occurring in the co-operative sector results in a growing number of members in each co-operative and, consequently, in a shrinking number of co-operatives.

The concentration process (→ *Mergers and Consolidations*) brings the co-operative into a higher class of organizational size in which it can build up its market position and increase its members' advancement potential. The existing market power of the co-operative – measured by market share – expands fundamentally, not only on the output market but also on the purchasing market. Having joined together, co-operatives can negotiate better supply and delivery conditions on the purchasing market (e.g. securing discounts through larger orders); likewise, each co-operative can reach a better position on the output market than its competitors.

The size of the co-operative's market share, i.e. its economic success, determines its ability to survive, whatever its operational size. This means that success determines the optimal operational size being sought after. Using an example from credit co-operatives, according to *Hahn*, there is "only one yardstick for the optimal operational size: the ability of each institute to satisfy its members; the desires and demands of members in Frankfurt are different from those of members, say, on an island in the North Sea." (*Hahn*, 1986, p.23).

V. Operational Size and Costs

The operational size continually changes because of growth or shrinkage in the co-operative. A change in operational size generally causes a variation in the input factors and brings around new company conditions. When the organizational size grows, one or more sets of similar machines can be added to the current level of input factors (e.g. entire departments or divisions with similar technical equipment, personnel or productions center) which constitute a substantial increase of the former employment level. One refers to this situation of quantitative change in the input factors as a multiple variation in operational size; this causes additional fixed costs in relation to the newly included work units (personnel, equipment). Normally, the amount of output increases through expansion of operational size which, from this point of view, produces a reduction in fixed costs for the co-operative enterprise (→ *Assessment of Success*).

By affecting the quantitative and qualitative capacity of the input factors, a variation in operational size can also bring other changes in its wake. By adding additional input factors, the relation between them can be altered, resulting in the application of new procedures. The more capital-intensive procedures (technical rationalization effect) cause fixed costs to increase and proportional costs to sink. According to various studies, at a certain operational size, capital-intensive procedures will become economical and will bring cost advantages with respect to smaller operational sizes (increasing mass production).

Seen in a nutshell, an increasing size gives a co-operative cost and economic advantages because increasing output levels provide the possibilibty to reduce fixed costs and implement more favorable procedures.

As operational size grows, it is to be feared that a reduction of activities will weaken the co-operative. In this situation, a cost progression occurs, which in turn lowers the flexibility of the entire enterprise.

Bibliography

Andreae, Clemens-August/Niehues, K.: Produktivgenossenschaften als alternative Unternehmensform – dargestellt am Beispiel der Gerätewerke Matrei Gen.mbH, Tirol/Österreich, in: Zeitschrift für das gesamte Genossenschaftswesen, no. 3 (1990), p. 166ff.
Bloech, J.: Betriebs- und Unternehmensgröße, in: Albers, W. et al. (eds.): Handwörterbuch der Wirtschaftswissenschaften, vol. 1, Stuttgart 1988, pp. 556–565.
Blümle, Ernst-Bernd: Genossenschaften: Besinnung tut Not, in: Basler Zeitung – Tribüne der Wissenschaft, no. 59, 10.03.1990. P. 19.
Boettcher, Erik.: Genossenschaften, in: Albers, W. et al. (eds.): Handwörterbuch der Wirtschaftswissenschaften, vol. 3, Stuttgart 1988, pp. 404–556.
Busse von Colbe, Walter: Betriebsgröße und Unternehmensgröße, in: Grochla, Erwin/Wittmann, W. (eds.): Handwörterbuch der Betriebswirtschaft, Stuttgart 1974, col. 566–579.
Dülfer, Eberhard: Produktivgenossenschaften, in: Mändle, E. et al. (eds.): Handwörterbuch des Genossenschaftswesens, Wiesbaden 1980, cols. 1356–1371.
Engelhardt, Werner W.: Die Produktivgenossenschaft, in: Laurinkari, Juhani (ed.): Genossenschaftswesen, München 1990, pp. 664–675.
Hahn, Oswald: Die klassische Raiffeisenbank: Die Dorfbank als Nostalgie oder Notwendigkeit? Veröffentlichungen des Lehrstuhls für Allgemeine, Bank- und Versicherungs-Betriebswirtschaftslehre, Universität Erlangen-Nürnberg, no. 41, Nürnberg 1986.
Hahn, Oswald: Allgemeine Betriebswirtschaftslehre, München 1990, p. 524 ff. and 194 ff.
Jaggi, Ernst: Schweizerisches Genossenschaftswesen, in: Mändle, Eduard. et al. (eds.): Handwörterbuch des Genossenschaftswesens, Wiesbaden 1980, cols. 1697–1718.
Kellerhals, Werner: Coop in der Schweiz. Materialien zur Entwicklung der Coop Schweiz und der Coop-Genossenschaften seit dem Ende des Zweiten Weltkriegs, Basel 1990, p. 136f.
Löwer, Martin: Betriebsgröße, in: Dichtl, Erwin/Issing, Ottmar (eds.): Vahlens Grosses Wirtschaftslexikon, München, vol. 1 (1987), p. 243f.
Patera, Mario: Handwörterbuch des österreichischen Genossenschaftswesens, Wien 1986.
Paulig, Oswald: Konsumgenossenschaften, in: Mändle, Eduard et al. (eds.): Handwörterbuch des Genossenschaftswesens, Wiesbaden 1980, cols. 1036–1041.
Remmer, J.: Genossenschaftliche optimale Betriebsgröße, in: Mändle, Eduard et al. (eds.): Handwörterbuch des Genossenschaftswesens, Wiesbaden 1980, cols. 1326–1334.
Swoboda, Walter: Fusion/Konzentration im Genossenschaftswesen, in: Mändle, Eduard et al. (eds.): Handwörterbuch des Genossenschaftswesens, Wiesbaden 1980, cols. 532–551.
Wöhe, Günter: Einführung in die allgemeine Betriebswirtschaftslehre, 16th ed., München 1986, p. 18f. and 611 ff.

Oppenheimer, Franz (1864–1943)

OSWALD HAHN [J]

(see also: *Conceptions, Co-operative*; *Theory of Co-operatives*; *Theory of co-operative Cooperation*; *Israel*; *Joint-production Co-operatives*)

I. Biographical Sketch; II. The Economist; III. The Co-operative Scientist.

Franz Oppenheimer can be considered one of the great economists and social scientists in the German-speaking regions during the first half of the 20th century who likewise enjoyed extensive international renown. His name at the same time is inexorably tied with the field of co-operative science.

I. Biographical Sketch

Born in Berlin on March 30th, 1864, the son of Rabbi *Julius Oppenheimer* (Hanover) and his wife *Antoine*, née *Davidson* (Pomerania) – a doctor's daughter, *Franz Oppenheimer* took his university preparatory exams in his native city (1881) and subsequently studied medicine in Berlin and in Freiburg/Breisgau (graduation: 1885, full medical accreditation: 1886). During his following ten-year practice as an ear, nose and throat specialist he came into direct contact with the pressing social situation in general and with the land reform movement in particular. *Oppenheimer* was influenced in this context above all by *Theodor Hertzka* (1845–1924), an editor of economics articles who had stirred up a sensation. *Oppenheimer* shut his medical practice, took up work as a free-lance author and studied political economy on the side. His first work (*Freiland in Deutschland*, 1895) was followed the next year by *Die Siedlungsgenossenschaften* (settlement co-operatives) which presented an attempt to overcome communism in a positive manner by solving the co-operative problem and the question of farming. Two years later, the book *Großgrundeigentum und soziale Frage* (large-scale land ownership and the social question) was published. *Oppenheimer* graduated in 1908, following the publication of further works and received non-tenured professor status one year later in Berlin (he studied under *Gustav Schmoller* and *Adolph Wagner*).

For the next ten years, he made his living from well-paid lecture-fees as a non-tenured professor on account of his rhetoric skills, from receipts as an author and from working to provide for the national economy during the War. These activities fundamentally distinguish his career background from that of persons in the present post-war generation. *Oppenheimer* first received a tenured professorship in 1919, in the recently founded Department of Sociology in Frankfurt, a position he filled until his retirement in 1929.

One of his students later became Federal Economics Minister and Federal Chancellor – *Ludwig Erhard* (1924); another of his students – *Erich Preiser* ("students who were critical went to *Oppenheimer*") was only then able to complete his doctoral dissertation by seeking supervision from *Wilhelm Rieger* in Tübingen after *Oppenheimer* had retired due to the aversion directed at his person.

In 1933, *Franz Oppenheimer* was deprived of his retirement pensions; soon afterwards his books fell victim to public book-burnings and he faced ostracism. As a "good German citizen" he refused to emigrate until the Jewish Pogrom instigated by *Josef Goebbels* on November 8, 1938, forced his flight to China and the United States. The 75-year old mustered incredible effort and managed to scrape through as a refugee. Despite poor economic conditions and his own deteriorioating health he founded *The American Journal of Economics and Sociology* in the fall of 1941. Death carried him away two years later shortly after he learned of how fellow Jews were being murdered in the concentration camps by the Waffen-SS or by the combat troops of the German police.

It should seem a disgrace today that the leaders of the German "student revolution" in 1968, and the promoters of a socialist market economy in Eastern Europe were the first ones to bring the name *Franz Oppenheimer* back to the light of day. "The racist extermination policy of the National Socialist regime accomplished its work thoroughly: after 1945, *Oppenheimer* was largely a forgotten person" (*Gerhard Senft*). *Oppenheimer's* memoir from 1931, *Erlebtes-Erstrebtes-Erreichtes*, was republished in an unaltered edition (Düsseldorf, 1964) 21 years after his death.

II. The Economist *Franz Oppenheimer*

The universal scientist *Franz Oppenheimer* is characterized by two essential concepts.

1. The Classification of Economic Science

Oppenheimer considered political economy as well as the entire spectrum of economic sciences to be a sub-discipline of the all-encompassing field of sociology. His fundamental conceptions as well as the entirety of his ideas are embodied in the nine-volume work *System der Soziologie* (Jena, 1922–1935). A general classification of sociology proceeds a *Staatslehre* (tenets of state), a *Theorie der reinen und politischen Ökonomie* (theory of pure and political economics) and finally an abstract of economic and social history spanning from the migration of nations through the 19th century.

2. The Roots of the "Social Market Economy"

Oppenheimer characterized himself as a student of *Karl Marx*. He, nevertheless, did not draw the Marxist conclusion when tracing development from the feudal economy and monopolistic-capitalistic economic degeneration (→ *Socialist Critics*). He was a pronounced opponent of communism from the beginning. As a proponent of a competitive economy he was much more interested in finding an alternative between the two directions – in finding a "third way". This was espoused in the book *Kapitalismus – Kommunismus – wissenschaftlicher Sozialismus* (Berlin-Leipzig, 1919) (capitalism-communism-scientific socialism) which was later entitled *Weder Kapitalismus noch Sozialismus* (Jena, 1932) (neither capitalism nor socialism). His last published book also advocated this position, *Weder so noch so. Der dritte Weg* (Potsdam, 1933) (Neither this nor that. The third way).

Oppenheimer was and remained an advocate of liberal socialism and a proponent of free competition, and it seems thoroughly legitimate to trace *Ludwig Erhard's* concept of the "social market economy" back to the ideas of *Franz Oppenheimer* (→ *History of Ideas*).

III. The Co-operative Scientist *Franz Oppenheimer*

Oppenheimer's ideas refer to co-operative questions only to a slight degree. The equally weighted assessment of *Oppenheimer* as both economist and co-operative scientist is only justified here inasmuch as this volume addresses co-operative science (→ *Theory of Co-operatives*).

1. The "Co-operative State"

The point of departure for co-operative issues is the theory of state. *Franz Oppenheimer* considered the notion of society organized in a co-operative manner to be a counterbalance to the state as an instrument of power (*Der Staat*, Frankfurt a.M., 1900). In formulating his considerations he constructed two state models which the the financial scientist *Antonio Viti de Marco* (1935) and the theoretician for central banks, *Heinrich Ritterhausen* (1962), introduced into currency theory: the state structured along the lines of a co-operative does not produce any inflation which the omnipotent state uses as an instrument.

2. A Call for Agricultural Workers' Co-operatives

The actual precipitant for *Franz Oppenheimer's* socialist ideas was "forcibly controlled ownership of landed property" which drove the former agrarian population into the cities, thereby forming the mass proletariat. *Oppenheimer* saw agricultural workers' co-operatives (→ *Joint-production Co-operatives*) as the alternative to private land ownership and the "land blockade" which subsequently emerged (*Die Siedlungsgenossenschaft*, 3rd Edition; Jena, 1922). His idea formed the scientific basis for the "kibbuz" (6th Zionist Congress in Basel, 1903) (→ *Israel*), which in actual application was structured according to the old Russian "MIR". *Oppenheimer* numbered among the handful of scientists who were not content merely developing models on their desks; in contrast, he tested his notions in a number of practical experiments (fruit farm colony "Eden" near Oranienburg, 1893; settlement colony Eisernach, 1905; settlement co-operative Bärenklau-Brandenburg, 1908; various projects in Palestine, 1910–1913). It is to be noted that the founders of forced collectivization in Eastern Europe painfully avoided any reference to *Oppenheimer* as he conceived the co-operative system to be based on the true voluntary nature of membership both for joining and withdrawing from the membership body.

3. The Renunciation of Commercial Workers' Co-operatives

Oppenheimer was, nonetheless, very skeptical with regard to "commercial workers' co-operatives". He grounded this skepticism on the one hand with a reference to the numerous failures of such establishments (the solitary reason for some modern political economists not disillusioned by reality to be turned off by *Oppenheimer*). On the other hand, he developed the "Law of Transformation" out of this: successful commercial workers' co-operatives become either "parasitic" companies by later engaging individuals who are "only" workers, or else members establish themselves independently and dissolve the workers' co-operative (→ *Conceptions, Co-operative*). This argument, however, elicits criticism: *Oppenheimer* falls victim to the notion that co-operatives as such must live out an "eternal life". As "children of need" co-operatives only maintain their *raison d'etre* until the particular shortcoming has been remedied through the co-operative's activities.

Bibliography

Preiser, Erich: Oppenheimer, Franz, in: Bente, Hermann et. al. (eds.), Handwörterbuch der Sozialwissenschaften, Bd. 8, 1964, pp. 102–104.
Röpke, Wilhelm: Franz Oppenheimer, in: A. Hunold (ed.), Gegen die Brandung, Erlenbach – Zürich 1959.
Schultz, Bruno: Die Grundgedanken des Systems der theoretischen Volkswirtschaftslehre von Franz Oppenheimer, Jena 1948.
Senft, Gerhard: Jenseits der Hegemonie von Staat und Kapital. Franz Oppenheimer und der liberale Sozialismus, in: Zeitschrift für Sozialökonomie, 30. Jg., 96. Folge, März 1993, pp. 3–5.
Wilbrandt, R./Löwe, A./Salomon, G. (eds.): Wirtschaft und Gesellschaft. Festschrift für Franz Oppenheimer, Frankfurt/Main 1924.

Organizational Structure of Co-operative Societies

HANS-H. MÜNKNER

(see also: *Legal Form, Co-operative*; *Law, National*; *Law, International*; *Co-operatives under Public Law*; *Management in Co-operatives*)

I. General Considerations; II. Matters to Be Regulated; III. Different Models of Organizational Structure of Co-operative Societies; IV. Summary.

I. General Considerations

Co-operative societies are organizations characterized by their → *dual nature* as a group of persons linked together by at least one common economic interest (→ *Group, the Co-operative*) and an enterprise established, financed, controlled and used by the group of co-operators as a means to improve the economic situation of their individual enterprises or households (→ *Promotion Mandate*).

The organizational structure of co-operative societies differs from that of other forms of business organizations because in co-operative societies, the members of the group are at the same time the shareholders, the decision-makers and the customers or (in the case of workers' joint-production co-operative societies) employees of the co-operative enterprise (principle of identity).

In this way, the organizational set-up of co-operative societies differs from that of partnerships, where the co-owners provide the capital and are jointly responsible for the management of their joint undertaking but are different from the customers/employees (→ *Legal Form, Co-operative*) and it is also different from that of companies, where the shareholders, the directors and the customers are generally different persons.

The co-operative society as a type of organization has the following characteristics:

- it is a group of persons, usually of a relatively large number, which varies due to admission of new members and withdrawal of members (open door principle);
- it is based on common interests of the members and personal participation, i.e. co-operative societies are organizations centered on personal collaboration rather than on anonymous capital contributions;
- the group of members establishes, finances and uses the services of the jointly managed and controlled enterprise as a means to reach its goals;
- the object of the joint enterprise is to promote the economic and social interests of the members of the group.

These characteristics of the co-operative form of organization require an organizational set-up which enables the co-operative group to take decisions and to act jointly, while the co-operative enterprise has to be organized in such a way that it can be managed efficiently and can compete with commercial firms in the market.

At the same time, measures have to be taken to bind the management of the co-operative enterprise to their principal task of promoting the economic and social interests of the members of the co-operative group.

The appropriate legal framework for this type of organization is to make it a body corporate, which allows perpetual succession of the organization despite changes in membership.

The co-operative law (→ Law, National; → Law, International) has to set out in clear terms in which way decisions binding the organization and/or its members can be made (as decisions of the organization) and how individual persons are empowered to execute such decisions of the organization in dealings with the members and third parties, acting on behalf of the organization.

In most countries, acts of the organs of registered co-operative societies within the scope of their powers as defined in the law or in the society's by-laws, are considered to be acts of the body corporate, i.e. of the co-operative society itself. Hence, the society is directly liable for acts done in its name. In countries following the English legal system, the acts done on behalf of the society by board members are considered to be acts of agents binding the corporate principal within the scope of the authority given to them.

When drawing up the model of co-operative orgnization, the lawmakers are not free to choose the most effective way or the most simple form, but they have to respect the internationally accepted basic ideas and principles characterizing the peculiar structure of co-operative societies, e.g. active participation of members (democratic, control), the specifically co-operative goal system and the general rules governing the national legal system.

II. Matters to Be Regulated

When drawing up models for the organizational pattern of co-operative societies, the following matters are to be regulated:
- setting of common goals,
- decision-making in groups,
- composition, powers and responsibilities of the general body (general meeting of members or meeting of delegates),
- composition, powers and responsibilities of the governing body (board of directors, committee of management, executive committee),
- functions and responsibilities of employed managers,
- composition, powers and responsibilities of the internal control body, if any and
- additional bodies: subcommittees, sectional meetings etc.

1. Setting of Common Goals

In co-operative societies the principal goal is to maximize the long-term benefits of the members. To achieve this objective, the co-operative enterprise has to work efficiently, it has to be able to compete in the market and to earn enough income to cover the operating costs and to render services to members at better conditions than those offered by competitors.

The co-operative way of organizing the setting of common goals is to give members the ultimate authority in determining the policy of the co-operative enterprise either directly in general meeting or through officers elected for this purpose from among the members. It is assumed that where the office-bearers are members, the members' interests will be given due attention in goals set by them.

The employed staff of the co-operative enterprise also influences the goals system directly – if they are represented in the decision-making bodies – or indirectly.

In each co-operative society the goals of promoting the members and of safeguarding the stability and competitiveness of the co-operative enterprise have to be continuously balanced. This can be achieved by distribution of powers between the general meeting of members and the board of directors or by the right mix of elected and employed directors on the board or by the combination of elected members serving as directors and professional management.

2. Decision-making in Groups

Decision-making in groups requires finding ways and means to transform a multitude of individual intentions of the group members into the volition of the group, i.e. the will of the co-operative society as a body corporate.

There are various ways how this can be done:

- by unanimous decision of all members of the group,
- by the majority of all members of the group,
- by unanimous decion of all members present and voting at a meeting or
- by the majority of all members present and voting at a meeting.

For co-operatives as business organizations with a relatively large membership, the requirement of unanimity of all members or even of all members present and voting at a meeting would not allow the co-operative society to function effectively. Accordingly, as a rule, majority vote is accepted as sufficient. This rule is in conformity with the principle of democratic administration and control.

In order to balance the desire to have a maximum of participation of members in the decision-making process even at the risk of having no decision at all and the need to reach valid decisions even without a substantial member participation, the rules of quorum have been developed.

A minimum number of members have to be present in order to constitute a meeting at which decisions binding all members can be taken.

To avoid that the organization is paralyzed by meetings without a quorum, the co-operative laws of some countries do not insist on a quorum, but leave this matter to be decided in the → *by-laws*. In other countries, the laws make provision for further convocations of meetings without a quorum at which all members present form a quorum. In still other countries, there is a split quorum for co-operatives with small or large membership, e.g. 1/4 of all members or 40 whichever is the less (→ *Law, International*).

3. Composition, Powers and Responsibilities of the General Bodies

In co-operatives the general meeting of members is the supreme authority. It represents the democratic basis of the society. Every member has the right to participate in the general meeting, to express his views and to vote. This is usually done according to the principle of one member – one vote or, where a plural voting system is applied, members may have more than one vote given according to objective criteria as laid down in the by-laws, other than share capital contributions, e.g. in proportion to business done with the co-operative enterprise or the use made of the co-operative facilities. Plural voting in co-operatives is subject to an upper limit so as to prevent individual members from having a dominating position in the society, e.g. not more than three votes in the case of the German co-operative law (section 43 (3)) (→ *Law, National*) or not more than 5% of the entire votes in the case of French agricultural co-operative societies.

Where co-operatives have a membership exceeding a certain number (e.g. 3,000 in the case of Germany, 300 in the case of Italy) or where members belong to different professions or live in different areas, the general meeting may either be replaced by a meeting of delegates, representing a certain number of individual members, or it may be split up into sectional meetings, taking over the functions of the general meeting and electing delegates to represent the members of the society at society level.

Another possibility is to have sectional meetings in addition to the general meeting, so as to allow more members to play an active role in the life of the co-operative society (e.g. in the U.K.).

The members in general meeting as the supreme authority of the society have the following key powers, which cannot be delegated to any other body in the society:

- to make and to amend the by-laws,
- to elect and/or revoke the office-bearers,
- to approve the annual returns and decide on the allocation or distribution of the economic results of the co-operative enterprise,
- to decide on amalgamation, affiliation to apex organizations or dissolution of the society.

The members in general meeting are ultimately responsible for the results of the co-operative enterprise. In case of losses, their share contributions may be depreciated or lost, in case of liquidation, they may be personally liable within the limits set by the by-laws for the debts of the society. Accordingly, the members have to exercise democratic control and to do so, they have to be informed on the conditions and financial position of the co-operative enterprise. This is done by reports of the board of directors, the supervisory body and the external auditors in general meeting.

In some countries, decisions of the general meeting are valid only if the audit report has been presented to the members prior to the decision.

4. Composition, Powers and Responsibilities of the Governing body

In co-operative societies the governing body is referred to as the board of directors or committee of management. It usually consists of several persons elected from among the members to direct the affairs of the co-operative society during the time between the general meetings and to represent the society vis-à-vis third parties.

The members of the board of directors or committee of management are usually elected for a term of office of two or three years and may stand for reelection. But there are also co-operative laws according to which board members may be elected for an indefinite period and non-members (professionals) can also be elected to serve on the board.

According to the original concept, service on the

board is not remunerated, except for refund of expenses. However, with the growing size and complexity of co-operative enterprises, full-time board members are considered in many countries as being indispensible and such full-time professional directors have to be paid salaries. In other countries, the original rule of honorary service of office-bearers is upheld and the full-time professional work is carried out by employed managers, rather than by elected board members.

The powers of the board of directors of a co-operative society usually cover all matters except those especially reserved for the general meeting or the control body. They include the power to decide all matters of policy and day-to-day management and to supervise the employed staff. However, the board may delegate some of its executive powers to one or several managers.

In its decisions the board of directors is bound by the law, the by-laws and usually by decisions of the general meeting, however, in some countries like Germany, the autonomy of the board of directors has been strengthened for greater economic efficiency, so that the board can operate without being bound by decisions of the general meeting of members.

The members of the board of directors are jointly and severally liable for damages caused by infringement of the law, the by-laws and, where applicable, contraventions to decisions of the general meeting. They are also liable for negligence in the conduct of the society's business. Many co-operative laws also contain special provisions on criminal liability, e.g. on co-operative breach of trust, which is sanctioned by heavier penalties than ordinary breach of trust.

The board members are subject to control by a special control body and by the members in general meeting, who can revoke any board member any time before the end of his term. In case of emergency, the control body can suspend board members until final decision by the next general meeting of members.

5. Functions and Responsibility of the Manager

The manager is not an elected office-bearer of the society, but rather an employed member of the staff. Co-operatives may operate without having a manager either, because the business of the co-operative enterprise is small and simple and can be conducted by a committee of management or because the governing body has become professionalized and the management functions are carried out by full-time professional board members.

In countries where the service on the board is honorary and the board members are non-professionals elected from among the membership (→ *Honorary Office*), the managers play an important role. This has caused the lawmakers in many countries to include special provisions governing the managers and their liability (→ *Responsibility*) in the co-operative legislation.

In this case, the manager has the powers conferred upon him by the law and delegated to him by the board of directors or under the by-laws of the society. He is responsible for the efficient running of the day-to-day affairs of the co-operative enterprise and is liable for any damage caused by infringement of the provisions of the law or of the by-laws, for acting contrary to decisions of the board of directors or the general meeting of the members and for negligence in carrying out his duties. The liability of the manager does not absolve the board of directors from their overall responsibility for running the affairs of the co-operative society.

6. Supervisory Body

The supervisory body of co-operative societies is referred to as supervisory council or supervisory or audit committee or "commissaires aux comptes" (elected auditors).

There are several models of regulating this matter:

a) The supervisory council is a separate body of three or more persons, elected from among the members at a general meeting to serve for a term of office (between 1 and 3 years) with the possibility to stand for reelection.

The supervisory council does not only scrutinize the accounts and the annual returns, but also supervises the board of directors in performing their duties and especially their task of promoting the interests of the members.

Membership in the supervisory council is incompatible with membership on the board of directors. The supervisory council reports to the general meeting. Service on the supervisory council is honorary except for refund of expenses.

b) The supervisory committee or audit committee may be a subcommittee of the board of directors and may include not more than one board member. In this case, the supervisory committee receives its mandate from the board of directors and reports to the board of directors as well as to the general meeting of members (e.g. in co-operative credit unions).

c) The commissaires aux comptes are persons with knowledge of accounting and auditing, elected by the general meeting of members from within or outside the co-operative group. The elected auditors concentrate on financial audit and are usually not expected to carry out management of performance audit, as in the case of the supervisory council. This form is found in countries following the French legal system.

The control bodies have power to call for information from the board of directors and any employee of the co-operative society, they have access to all books of accounts, documents and other relevant information, as well as the right to call an extraordinary general meeting and to suspend the members of the board of directors.

The liability of the members of the control body is usually the same as that of the board members.

7. Additional Bodies: Subcommittees, Sectional Meetings etc.

Apart from the general meeting, the board of directors and the control body, if any, there are additional bodies that a co-operative society may establish for carrying out its objects. Such bodies may be useful to subdivide tasks and to mobilize members with special skills for active participation in the affairs of the society, e.g.: credit committees, membership committees, education committees, women's guilds, promotion committees (Förderungsbeirat) etc.

Furthermore, a co-operative society may subdivide its membership into subgroups or its area of operation into sections for the purpose of holding sectional meetings and of electing delegates to represent subgroups or sections in the general body (meeting of delegates).

III. Different Models of Organizational Structure of Co-operative Societies

As democratic organizations, all co-operative societies have a general body of members or delegates and office-bearers elected by and answerable to the members. With regard to additional bodies, two different types of organizational structures have been developed, which can be classified as:

- two-tier (or dualistic) systems with two separate bodies in addition to the general meeting of members: the board of directors for management and representation vis-à-vis third parties and a supervisory council as a control body working at the same level but with different functions or
- one-tier (or monistic) systems with only one administrative board in addition to the general meeting of members, within which the functions of management, representation and supervision are carried out: management by an inner board or office-bearers like chairman, secretary, treasurer; representation by the president or chairman and control by a subcommittee of the board or the remaining members of the board.

The co-operative law of a country may prescribe the model to be applied by all co-operative societies (e.g. in Germany and in the model law for co-operatives in Latin America the two-tier model; in the U.K. the one-tier Model) or leave it to the individual society which model to choose (e.g. the draft legislation for co-operative societies of the EEC).

Variations include the possibilities to delegate all management and representative functions to one office-bearer, the president, who may serve at the same time as the general manager for the day-to-day management (PDG, président directeur général, under the French legal system).

With regard to the control body, the co-operative law may contain the provision that small co-operatives, e.g. having less than 25 members, may operate without a supervisory council, while prescribing the two-tier system for larger co-operatives (e.g. in Austria). In the one-tier system additional control may be provided by elected auditors (commissaires aux comptes in countries following the French legal system).

It is furthermore possible to have a supervisory committee or audit committee in addition to the administrative board, which, however, is in practice a subcommittee of the board being appointed by and answerable to the board (e.g. the credit union model).

IV. Summary

Irrespective of the organizational model, the success of a co-opertive society depends on the quality of the persons filling the various posts in the organizational structure and their conviction of the usefulness of the co-operative value system.

Many rules of the original co-operative concept like

- honorary service of office-bearers,
- election of office-beares by the members from among themselves,
- supremacy of the general body in determining the policy,
- exclusion of the professional management from being elected to serve on the board,

were made to safeguard that only co-operatively-minded persons would serve as office-bearers of co-operative societies.

Presently, the development of co-operative enterprises into large-scale and complex business organizations in full competition with commercial firms have brought about changes of these rules:

- full-time, paid office-bearers,
- professional managers appointed by the control body to serve on the board,
- delegation of almost all policy-making powers from the general meeting of members to the board of directors,
- abandoning the idea of separating the service on the board and the management functions and having executive directors on the board.

These changes have brought the co-operative organizational pattern closer to the company structure. Under such circumstances, deliberate and continuous efforts have to be made to maintain the co-operative character of such organizations, even if they are officially registered as co-operative societies.

Bibliography

Camboulives, Marguerite: L'organization coopérative au Sénégal, Paris 1967, pp. 119–139.
Chappenden, W.J.: Handbook to the Industrial and Provident Societies Act, 1965, Manchester 1966, pp. 21–22.
Commission of the European Communities: Proposal for a Council Regulation (EEC) on the Statute for a European Co-operative Society, COM (90) 273 final – SYN 388, Brussels, 5 March 1992, articles 16–48.
Credit Union National Association, Inc.: Model Credit Union Act and Commentary, Madison 1987.
Dülfer, Eberhard: Organization and Management of Co-operatives, in: Co-operatives and Economic Growth, Sonderheft, Zeitschrift für das gesamte Genossenschaftswesen, Göttingen 1971, pp. 74 et seq.
Ebert, Kurt Hanns: Genossenschaftsrecht auf internationaler Ebene, Bd. I, Marburg 1966, pp. 251–352.
International Labour Office: Co-operative Management and Administration, Geneva 1989.
Lemeunier, Francis: Pourquoi et comment constituer une société coopérative? 2e Edition, Paris 1972, pp. C1–18.
Louis, Raymond: Organisation et fonctionnement administratif des coopératives, Bureau International du Travail, Genève 1976.
Münkner, Hans-H.: Co-operative Principles and Co-operative Law, Institute for Co-operation in Developing Countries, Papers and Reports No.5, Marburg 1974.
Münkner, Hans-H.: Ten Lectures on Co-operative Law, Bonn 1982, pp. 65–93.
Organización de las cooperativas de América, OCA: Proyecto de Ley Marco para las cooperativas de América Latina, América Cooperativa, Documento especial No. 3, Bogotá 1988.
Reinhardt, Rudolf: The Legislator and the Co-operatives, in: Fourth International Conference on Co-operative Science, Vienna 1963, Göttingen 1965, pp. 65–80.
Snaith, Ian: The Law of Co-operatives, London 1984, pp. 36–74.
Weeraman, P.E./Dwivedi, R.C./Sheshadri, P.: Indian Co-operative Laws vis-à-vis Co-operative Principles, International Co-operative Alliance, Delhi 1973, pp. 78–110.
Yeo, Peter: Co-operative Law in Practice, A Handbook of Legislation for Co-operative Development, Manchester 1989, pp. 59–102.

Organizational Structures, Co-operative: Mesosociological Aspects of Co-operatives

ROBERT HETTLAGE [J]

(see also: Relationship Patterns; Configuration; Group, the Co-operative; Group Theory; Organizational Structure of Societies; Theory of co-operative Cooperation; Managerial Economics)

I. Base Democracy Versus a Representational Method; II. Management Under the Conditions of Self-Administration.

As the science involved with how all human thought and action is anchored socially, sociology is not merely engrossed with the fundamental conditions and basic forms of social action (microsociology), but rather is also occupied with the goal-oriented, systematically arranged structures and processes ("meso" level) in which membership (entry and exit) is not peremptory but "contingent" (Luhmann). Organizations and their dynamics (enterprises, parties, associations, churches, armies, etc.) thereby become the object of sociological observation, and the functions of individual action are placed in a larger context. This implies that not only people alone and their dispositions are analysed, but structural categories such as ranks/positions, roles, norms and procedural regulations. This is likewise true for the sociology of the organization of co-operatives.

Co-operatives, in compliance with their double character (→ Dual Nature), are not only associations of persons but also *instrumental entities*. The entrusted mission of the organization is the endeavor to achieve performance targets in an efficient manner and to enable utility. Co-operatives must hold their own in markets; their *promotional* character is also rooted in this factor (→ Promotion Mandate). The discrepancies between their internal deportment and external form, between the requirements of structure and the intrinsic meaning of action are apparent and constitute *the* permanent sociological problem of the co-operative as an organizational form.

I. Basic Democracy Versus a Representational Method

As an organization of members empowered with equal rights and responsibilities, the co-operative insists that the instrumental entity established for promotional purposes not only works *for all* those involved (acting as usufructuaries) but also is collectively borne *by all* those involved. Its organizational principle must satisfy the democratic ideal of "one man – one vote" (→ Principles). With regard to the extent and the concrete configuration of the organization, though, two fundamentally differing conceptions of democracy stand in opposition to each other. The "normative" theoreticians of democracy strive after a *lifestyle* based on a collective decision making of will and deed in each and every situation. They therefore emphasize the participational *potentials* of the collective in question and expect democratization in all spheres of life. The advocates of the "elitist" democratic idea, in contrast, concentrate on the *procedure* to elect and depose those in management positions and therefore are more likely to emphasize the participational *barriers* within the base. Among other things, research of both potentials *and* barriers to participation is the task of organizational sociology of co-operation structures. A basic democracy "from below" in all spheres, the identity of those in control and those controlled, and "discourse in absence of hierarchy" (*Habermas*) seems to be unrealistic: a procedure to achieve efficient decisions which is managed "from below" or which in principle can be managed is much more optimal. The (revocable) delegation of power to competences is necessary, that is at least a partial schism between those in control and those under control. This debate is likewise related to the sociology of co-operatives as it refers both in theory and practical application to the conditional requirements of those entities free of hierarchical structures (→ *Oligarchy in Co-operatives*).

1. Co-operative Democracy in Theory and Practice

Co-operative theoreticians allign themselves on the side of the normative democratic ideal insofar as they are also interested in democratization/economic democracy. In practice, however, the situation is fairly grave:

- Markets do not heed time-intensive, democratic decision-making procedures;
- The ability to survive on commodities and service markets and to be successful is only ensured through specialized know-how and competitive performance;
- Know-how, experience, inclination, involvement and performance are rarely distributed equally;
- Members are often quite unable to accomplish the tasks of business management in an appropriate manner;
- Members tend to organize themselves spontaneously but not necessarily efficiently. The functional structure of a division of labor within a business enterprise is necessary.
- Management and execution functions differ for one another.

The conception of basic democracy alters under conditions of pressure and assumes the organizational structures of a representational democracy. It thus is recommendable in practice to differentiate between five distinct *participational levels* within co-operative enterprises with respect to the rights and skills of the members:

1) Sole decision-making rights ("self-management");
2) Shared decision-making rights;
3) Initiative rights (including voting rights);
4) Rights to raise objections (veto);
5) Consultational rights (information, hearings).

Because thorough and consistent self-management is only feasible among largely *homogenous* groups, under surveyable conditions and in non-complex markets, the only remaining alternative in practice is the delegation of responsibilities to differentiated management levels (→ *Labour-Management*).

2. Dangers for the Co-operative

Involved in the inevitable delegation is a fundamental discrepancy – a *strained relationship* – between requirements of structure and the intrinsic meaning of co-operatives: the danger that the group objective will be overlooked in the face of conditions within the organization.

Max Weber, standing at an angle which takes all of society in its perspective, noted that the particular instrumental rationality inherent to modern organizational society can prove to be highly efficient, but that this almost invariably forces a "shell", a matter-of-fact, legally versed, non-personalized domination of bureaucratic officials to be created. The self-responsible personality is threatened with obsolescence under the pressure of impersonal rationalization demands. This "modern cultural problem" is likewise applicable to individual organizations and is particularly true for co-operatives as they originally appeared with opposing action goals and organizational goals. All critics of capitalism (wherever those involved with co-operatives are categorized) felt they must warn about the dehumanizing danger – the unreason – of this rationality. Closely associated with this problem is the tendency of the organization *to grow in size* (→ *Operational Size*). Holding one's own on the market does not only require an efficient organization but also continual, competitive market penetration. Under current (oligopolistic) conditions, efficiency is coupled with concentrational processes involving both capital and decisions (→ *Mergers and Consolidations*). Fragmentation and smallness are "beautiful" in the beginning, but prove to be mostly ineffective over the course of time.

The co-operative, again, cannot escape this trend of growing *self-complexity* (*Luhmann* 1975). The negative effects of size and decision-making efficiency overlap one another, and instead of leading to a gradual expansion of the participational potential of the base they entail a continual limitation of it. From the members' viewpoint, the double nature of the co-operative falls apart, resulting in an identity crisis and *alienation*. The "superstructure" is little aware of this. One party lacks awareness of the problem, the other lacks the necessary lobby to have the problem gain priority status. To date no empirical evaluation of the relationship members have to "their" co-operative, at least in the general sense, has been undertaken. Research along the lines of *Seeman's* five-fold criterion catalogue for the syndrome of alienation, itself more sociological than psychological in nature (powerlessness, normlessness, meaninglessness, isolation, self-estrangement), could be illuminating in this context.

II. Management Under the Conditions of Self-Administration

The problem alluded to above contains a further, more strongly personal facet: not the abstract problem of administration and domination but rather the concrete problem of management, which presents a similar *structural tension*. Co-operatives, like all other enterprises, have a large need for internal and external regulation; in other words, they do not organize and manage themselves on their "own" despite the intention rooted in basic democracy, but rather necessitate the delegation of management tasks to a management personnel. As is the case in other company forms, this is a matter of salaried managers on various levels (insofar as they are not members).

The problem arises in that members must combine and assume the *double role* of responsible supporters and beneficiaries (or workers). On the one hand, they are "entrepreneurs" who, however, seek a de facto business administration for their company which they must up-hold. On the other hand, as members of the base they are subject to the decisions affecting planning, organization, adjustments, supervising, and human resource management made by the manager whom they appointed and who acts independently of them. The reason for this is rooted in the given diffentiation of know-how and the necessary division of labor without which a competitive collective enterprise has no chance of survival, even under the intentions of self-administration. This arrangement vests co-operative participation with particular dynamics of its own.

1. Management-Member Relationships

Management is based to a substantial degree on the ability to execute one's will and realize one's objectives, that is, on the priority of formal power (the authority to give instructions) and informal power, be it based on knowledge and experience ("expert power": *French/Raven* 1959), on a vantage in information, important contact networks, special communicational skills, etc. Such "elite" individuals, set off through their knowledge, necessarily are in conflict with the egalitarian structure of the co-operative (→ *Management in Co-operatives*).

a) Organizational structure and consensus

Theoreticians of harmony do not consider the differentiation of knowledge and power within co-operatives a problem for they see the management-member conflict of interests minimized by:

1) the management bodies as pure executive authorities restricting themselves only to those decisions which are backed by the rulings affecting the company made by the membership body (Basis);
2) administrational bodies and the division of powers successfully counteracting management acting on its own;
3) managers internalizing the fundamental co-operative mission of promoting the membership body ("conviction to duty": *Seraphim* 1936);
4) short- and long-term member interests taking different paths so that managers are confronted with predominantly clear-cut decision-making situations;
5) members either acting in a uniform fashion with a positive approach as a source of know-how, or allowing themselves to be lead in a passive manner.

b) Theoretical adjustments to conflict

As soon as these simplifying assumptions fall to the wayside in favor of more realistic ones, role *conflicts* cannot be precluded (→ *Theory of co-operative Cooperation*). They occur in connection with:

1) siphoning off tasks and the corresponding shift within the structure of tasks and directions (an executively operating, market-linkage and integrated co-operative: *Dülfer* 1984);
2) the localization of different groups and claims to power (bipolarity, multiple polarity) which destroy the assumption of the operating work unit;
3) the influence of various interests, inclinations, rewards, motives for self-esteem, performance and cooperation among managers (manager typologies) as well as among members (member typologies);
4) special consideration of interpersonal communication procedures and negotiation processes which are likewise legitimate for the organization;
5) the only slightly effective opportunities members have with respect to managers to exercise control or influence (*Vierheller*, 1974; *Eschenburg* 1972).

In general, this is all closely related to the assumption that modern co-operatives are developing in the direction of "manager dominance" (*Vierheller*, 1983). However, the varying possible combinations of active and passive behavior, opposition and adherence, distance and proximity, identification and manipulation, as well as the extrinsic and intrinsic motives of the different influential groups make concrete investigation from case to case indispensable.

2. The Risks of an Upset Management-Member Relationship

The designated development perspective cannot, however, conceal the fundamental tension that exists since management and self-management in principle are in opposition with each other.

a) Lack of competence

Self-administration relies on the decision-making competence of all members (→ *Labour-Management*). Success on the market, on the other hand, requires professional management. The source of tension is that members perhaps accept management's vantage as a transitional solution so that they may acquire the necessary qualifications during this time. In reality, however, it quickly becomes evident that management presents a continual demand for policy decisions as well as for their execution. Because management must proceed with a claim on power and control whereas members wish to retain their principle of egalitarian structure, a double-sided, conflict-laden center of power becomes established (*Hettlage*, 1982). Further complications result in that the groups cannot simply be empirically conceived of as a unit; one must reckon with multiple polarity in the settlement of management opportunities and the elements of decision-making. Complications likewise arise when the "desired employees" are not able to be elected but rather for the most part are stipulated as members.

b) Self-management on the job

Experience shows that the most attractive and most sensitive field of economic democracy is the direct arrangement of labor execution due to its closeness to life (*Rothschild-Whitt* 1979). Outside determination or influence finally seems to be done away with; a hierarchy seems superfluous as the group of individuals, vested with equal rights, is in the position to settle its cooperation in a non-bureaucratic and flexible manner, doing justice to its needs. That "utopian" heritage of the co-operative movement which places the social goals of the "association" on equal footing with its economic goals can also be accommodated. In practical application, however, the "community enterprise" frequently cannot be safeguarded against the severity of the market or having to cope with scarcity. Pressure from the competition regarding production efforts and the minimization of risks makes it necessary for managers to enforce a strict work discipline, division of labor, and time management on the members. From the members' perspective of their everyday experiences, management works against them, even when it stems from their own intentions and pursues their well-understood interests. Experience shows that the double role of managing and being managed is latently stressful for all members; in the mid-term it can even provoke a lasting, open conflict, intermittent phases of heated outbursts, or lead to passive frustration (*Paton* 1978).

c) Management exodus (Leadership-drain)

The situation is no less complicated for the managers of a co-operative. On the one hand, they must harmoniously combine economic and social goals which are difficult to bring under one roof. On the other hand, the lack of competencies among members is often too great for them to be in the position to manage themselves; the expectations in the meantime are directed at counteracting the mounting influence from above (the economization of objectives and company structure) and the pressure from below.

Management claiming self-administration falls victim to the *dilemma* of "super-leadership", namely that of simultaneously managing and extinguishing the management position (*Manz/Sims* 1986). The mistrust and misunderstanding inherent in the structure with regard to management's performance as well as incompetent attempts to exercise administrational control produce a high rate of management attrition, demotivate the up-and-coming junior management staff within the co-operative, and have the tendency to make managers "homeless" and ready for migration (*Paton* 1978). This in turn is unjust to the members as they are dependent on management know-how and necessarily must dread the activities of their former, effective managers as future competitors.

Based on these complex experiences a *democratic life cycle* can be reconstructed for co-operatives which proceeds through several phases: the initial conflicts concerning direct democracy, the shift to indirect democratic representation, and the ultimate stage of manager dominance. As *Bastone* already demonstrated, it remains an empirical question whether members slacken in their will to supervise or whether they concentrate their efforts on developing the representational bodies, thereby strengthening management control (which is held to be vital).

Bibliography

Batstone, E.: Organisation and orientation. A life-cycle model of French co-operatives. In: Economic and Industrial Democracy 4: 1983, pp. 139–162.

Dülfer, Eberhard: Betriebswirtschaftslehre der Kooperative, Göttingen 1984.

Eschenburg, R.: Genossenschaftstheorie als Konflikttheorie. In: E. Boettcher (ed.): Theorie und Praxis der Kooperation, Tübingen 1972, pp. 55–71.

French, J./B. Raven: The bases of social power. In: D. Cartwright (ed.): Studies in Social Power. Ann Arbor 1959, pp. 150–167.

Habermas, J.: Theorie des kommunikativen Handelns, Vol. 2: Zur Kritik der funktionalistischen Vernunft, Frankfurt 1981.

Hettlage, R.: Befreite Kompetenz? Wissenssoziologische Einblicke in die neuere Selbstverwaltungsdiskussion. In: Soziale Welt 33: 1982, pp. 5–25.

Hettlage, R.: Solidarität und Kooperationsgeist in genossenschaftlichen Unternehmen. In: M. Kück (ed.): Kooperatives Management, Baden-Baden 1990, pp. 123–152.

Luhmann, N.: Soziologische Aufklärung, Opladen 1975.

Manz, C.C./H.P. Sims: Leading self-managed groups. A conceptual analysis of a paradox. In: Economic and Industrial Demcoracy 7: 1986, pp. 141–165.

Paton. R.: Some Problems of Co-operative Organization. Milton Keynes 1978.

Rothschild-Whitt, J.: The collectivist organization. An alternative to rational-bureaucratic models. In: American Sociological Review 44: 1979. pp. 509–527.

Seeman, M.: On the personal consequences of alienation in work. In: American Sociological Review 32: 1967, pp. 273–285.

Seraphim, H.-J.: Die genossenschaftliche Gesinnung und das moderne Genossenschaftswesen. Karlsruhe 1956.

Vierheller, R.: Informationsgefälle und Entscheidungskoordination in der integrierten Genossenschaft. In: Zeitschrift für das gesamte Genossenschaftswesen 24: 1974, pp. 3–19.
Vierheller, R.: Demokratie und Management, Göttingen 1983.
Weber, M.: Gesammelte Aufsätze zur Religionssoziologie, Vol. 1, 6th ed., Tübingen 1972, (orig. 1920).

Owen, Robert (1771–1858)

SIDNEY POLLARD

(see also: *History in 19th C.*; *Configuration*; *Conceptions, Co-operative*; *Joint-production Co-operatives*)

I. Life and Business Career; II. Social Reforms; III. Owen's Ideas: Socialism and Utopianism.

I. Life and Business Career

Not entirely correctly, Robert *Owen* is often said to have provided one of the few known examples of rags to riches in the British industrial revolution. He was born the son of a village postmaster and saddler in Newton, Montgomeryshire, on 14 May 1771. At the age of twenty, after apprenticeship in the drapery trade and a shortlived attempt as an independent spinning machinery maker and cotton spinner, he became manager of Drinkwater's, one of the largest and most up-to-date Manchester cotton mills. He seemed to have made a success of this demanding job, and came to believe that his experience there provided the basis for his later understanding of industrial psychology and his social theories in the wider sense.

Thwarted in his hopes of a partnership at Drinkwater's, he left to form, with others, the Chorlton Twist Company, another major cotton concern, in 1794 or 1795. In 1799, together with his partners he acquired the New Lanark mills from *David Dale*, a leading Scottish businessman, marrying Anne Caroline Dale, the vendor's daughter, in the same year. He took over the management of the mills in 1800 and, for the next quarter of a century New Lanark became the centre of his business activities as well as of his social experiments.

In contrast to the city location of his earlier mills, the New Lanark establishment was sited in a secluded part of the Clyde valley, the whole village settlement being under the control of the mill owner. Recent research on the archives has confirmed *Owen's* statement in his autobiography that under his management, the mills were highly profitable, but if also has revealed that there was some sharp practice in his financial dealings and that he was not entirely guiltless in the friction which developed with his three consecutive sets of moneyed partners, of which the third set of 1814 was made up of philantropists, in principle favourably inclined towards *Owen's* reforms. However, given how close he was to personal bankruptcy in 1812–14, his engagement in national affairs in those years is all the more remarkable.

It was his undoubted success as manager of one of the country's largest cotton mills that ensured him a respectful hearing among the ruling landed and industrial classes, when he proposed his early schemes of social reform, though in the end none of them was taken up. He left New Lanark in 1824 (resigning formally as manager in 1825) and sank most of his fortune in the unsuccessful communitarian settlement of New Harmony in Indiana. In 1829, he returned to Britain, and after playing briefly a leading part in the co-operative movement and in the trade union acitivity of 1833–4, he devoted much of the rest of his life to propagate and expect rapid millennial changes in society towards a new moral world. He died in Newtown on 17 November 1858.

II. Social Reforms

Before *Owen*, New Lanark had been considered a model factory village, particularly regarding its educational provision for the child apprentices. *Owen* found much to improve. In 1806, when the mills stood idle because of the American embargo on cotton exports, he raised the moral tone of the workforce as well as their motivation to work by continuing to pay their wages for four months. Thereby, he managed to gain the workers' trust and cooperation. His main attention, however, was devoted to the children, for it was his belief that by correct upbringing at an early age, man's character could most effectively be changed for the better. Hours were reduced by stages, and children's work under the age of ten was stopped altogether and a school was provided for them. Older children could continue to attend part-time. By 1812, a new school had been built, to be followed in 1816 by the more famous Institution for the Formation of Character, which did not only house an infant school or Kindergarten as well as a school for children for day and evening classes, but also acted as a centre for adult education and recreation. Many of the numerous visitors who came to view the social experiment at Lanark were impressed above all by its innovative schooling. It was based on the principle that children should be steered by kindness and love rather than punishment, and that they should be taught to cooperate rather than compete. Instead of teaching by rote, as was then the general practice, children were to have their interests roused freely. There were pictures on the walls, and there was much singing and dancing.

In 1815, *Owen* sought to make the limitation of child work more general, first by trying to persuade other Glasgow manufacturers to deal similarly with their factory children and, when his appeal fell on deaf ears, by legislation. Work for children under ten was to be prohibited; to the age of twelve it was to be limited to six hours a day, and to the age of eighteen to twelve hours, including one and a half hours for meals. There were also to be educational tests. A bill to that effect was introduced in 1815, and *Owen* agitated for its implementation and gave evidence before a Select Committee in 1816. However, when after further delay it became law in 1819, it had been so watered down as to become valueless.

Meanwhile, in 1813, *Owen* had come before the public with two essays on *A New View of Society* (1813), to which were added two further essays, written at about the same time but published only in 1816 as a second edition. These gained a widespread response and together probably formed the most influential of his writings. Beside an account of his educational and other reforms in New Lanark, they contained proposals for a system of national education, for Poor Law reform, and for providing work for the unemployed. The widespread unemployment of the post-war years which could not be explained by the then economic theory, was a major issue of public concern and a topic on which *Owen* developed some of his most original ideas. In his second major publication, the *Report to the County of Lanark* (1821), written at the request of the County's magistrates in 1820, he was able to provide a comprehensive plan for social reform. Though extended in some respects in later publications, which also became increasingly millenial, the plans proposed in 1820–21 remained the basis of all his subsequent hopes and ideas.

Among the major evils to be combated were poverty, unemployment, and above all what he termed "immoral" social relations, i.e. a nexus in society based on mutual hostility and competition. The major component in his plan to overcome these failings was the creation of rural settlements (→ *Communal Settlements*) of perhaps 2,000 people, in size similar to New Lanark, whose inhabitants would engage both in agriculture and in some industry, and would live a communitarian life in a huge block built round a court, something like an Oxford or Cambridge college. Since their interests would not diverge, and no one would have cause to envy or take advantage of his neighbour, men's character would be changed towards love and human sympathy – the basis of his New Moral World.

Owen believed that once a model was built, it would be so successful that others would rush to copy it. For the first one, a large sum would be required, and he devised various stratagems to raise funds, especially from the rich and powerful. As noted above, his own funds were spent on the American model at New Harmony.

The rich and powerful remained largely disinterested; however, some of the poor, together with a few philanthropists, were fired with enthusiasm by *Owen's* scheme. Several communitarian settlements were attempted, financed by moneyed sponsors, notably in Orbiston (1825–7), Ralahine (1831–3), and Queen Wood (1839–45). Others without access to ready funds hit upon the idea of opening retail shops (which formed one of the roots of the later co-operative retailing movement pioneered by the *Rochdale Equitable Society* in 1844) (→ *Rochdale Pioneers*). With the surpluses achieved in those shops, members would be employed in co-operative production, realizing yet larger surpluses out of which the founding of true co-operative settlements, the ultimate objective, could be financed. In addition to solving the financial problem, this method would generate a spirit of cooperation and would by-pass capitalist class relations before settlement was entered into. In the following years, the scheme, sometimes attributed to *Dr. King* of Brighton in 1828 (→ *History of Ideas*), was taken up with varying success by several hundred societies.

On his return from the USA in 1829, *Owen* found himself, somewhat to his surprise, the revered prophet of a widespread and growing movement among the working classes, consisting of incipient retailing and producer societies as well as of vigorous propagandist bodies. In 1832, a Labour Exchange or Bazaar was opened in London. This Labour Exchange, where the products of handicraftsmen were exchanged at the "price" provided by the hours of labour put in, was a further extension of the idea of by-passing the capitalist market place. Finally, the trade unions and self-help associations coming together as the Grand National Consolidated Trades Union in 1833–4, were also strongly inspired by *Owen's* ideas.

None had a lasting success, and after their failure *Owen*, with some relief, turned away from these small-scale efforts to devote himself to grander schemes, such as the Society for Promoting National Regeneration (1833) and the Association of All Classes of All Nation (1835) out of which, in 1839, grew the Universal Community Society of Rational Religionists. In such periodicals as *The Crisis* (1832–4) and *New Moral World* (1834–45) as well as the *Book of the New Moral World* (7 parts, 1836–44), he worked tirelessly at what he considered to be his fundamental task – the changing of men's minds. Following the London Institution of 1833, *Owen's* supporters in the 1830's and 1840's, erected "Halls of Science" in provincial cities, in which, beside various cultural activities, Owenist ideas were propagated and non-religious rites of passage performed. The term "science" reflects the Owenists' conviction that theirs was a truly scientific and rational view of society. At this time, rationalism became a growing preoccupation of *Owen*, who by his vigorous denuncation of organized religions in 1817, had alienated much potential support. In his final years, *Owen* also took to spiritualism.

III. Owen's Ideas: Socialism and Utopianism

In his own lifetime, *Owen's* supporters were known as Socialists. Only later did the term came to denote a different body of doctrine as a result of influences from the continent.

Owen's most fundamental belief was that man's character, by which he meant his moral outlook and pattern of behavior to other men, was made by his environment not *by* him but *for* him. In other words, it could be moulded by suitable conditions, at least if the process of education was started early enough in life. Hitherto, he believed, it had been shaped wrongly by a vicious environment and by the errors of organized religion; now that he had discovered the true principle, nothing stood in the way of the regeneration of mankind towards a moral world.

To the problem of action, that is how in a vicious world people could be found who, in contradiction to the principle, had nevertheless become moral (→ *History of Ideas*), *Owen* had two answers: one was his own role as discoverer, which accounts for his dictatorial tendencies wherever he took part in any association; the other was his belief, a relic of the Enlightenment, that men only had to be shown the correct way to adopt it. For *Owen*, character changes were more important than institutional ones and he therefore had little time for politics, which, according to him, attacked the wrong issues. He abhorred violent politics, such as that propagated by some Chartists and trade unionists, and violent revolutions, as they only added to enmity and hostility, the real cause of all social evils. To call him a conservative for that reason, as has been done, seems wholly unjustified: he envisaged nothing less than a complete social revolution, though by precept and persuasion rather than by force. As for economic calculations, he considered the aim to be happiness, not riches.

His communitarian settlements, which apart from the architecture may be likenend to modern Kibbutzim, were clearly socialist in structure. Among their characteristics were common ownership, mainly communal consumption, and no employment or exploitation of one man by another. Capital was to become the servant, not the master. Inter-trading between the settlements was to be done on the basis of the labour value put into commodities. The voluntary decentralized nature of the organization units makes them the forerunners of the co-operative, rather than the state socialist ideal.

To *Marx* and many others (→ *Socialist Critics*), the design of full-blown communities by a single mind instead of their growth in the real world as well as the hope of changing human character were utopian. But *Owen* proceeded from the realities around him, he seemed to have proved in New Lanark that his model was workable, his monetary calculations were sound, his critique of current economic thought was apt, and his understanding of the powers of modern industrialism were second to none. Where he erred most of all, was in his hope of the benign support by the upper classes.

Even *Owen's* enemies recognized his personal human kindness and his philanthropy. Unlike others, he transfered his compassion also to his social and political ideas. He was one of the few who saw even the lowest classes not as hands or potential rioters, but as human beings, deserving full development and recognition of their humanity. That is basically why he was revered and loved, though not always understood, by the great mass of the lowly and the underprivileged of his time.

Bibliography

Butt, John (ed.): Robert Owen, Prince of Cotton Spinners, Newton Abbot 1971.
Cole, G.D.H.: Robert Owen, London 1925.
Cooperative Union: Robert Owen and his Relevance to our Times, Loughborough 1971.
Dolléans, Édouard: Robert Owen, 1771–1857, (Paris 1905), Paris 1907.
Elsässer, Markus: Soziale Intentionen und Reformen des Robert Owen in der Frühzeit der Industrialisierung, Berlin 1984.
Harrison, J.F.C.: Owen, Robert (1771–1857). Dictionary of Labour Biography, London 1982, 6, pp. 205–16.
Harrison, J.F.C.: Robert Owen and the Owenites in Britain and America. The Quest for the New Moral World, London 1969.
Harrison, J.F.C.: Utopianism and Education. Robert Owen and the Owenites, New York 1968.
Hasselmann, Erwin: Robert Owen, Sturm und Drang des sozialen Gewissens in der Frühzeit des Kapitalismus, Hamburg 1958.
Jones, Lloyd: The Life, Times, and Labours of Robert Owen, (London 1889), London 1905.
Miliband, Ralph: The Politics of Robert Owen, Journal of the History of Ideas, Lancaster and New York, 15 (1954), S. 233–45.
Morton, A.L.: The Life and Ideas of Robert Owen, London 1962.
Owen, Robert: Report to the County of Lanark and A New View of Society, (London 1813, 1821), Harmondsworth 1970.
Owen, Robert: The Life of Robert Owen, written by himself, (London 1857), London 1971.
Podmore, Frank: Robert Owen: A Bibliography, 2 vols., London 1906.
Pollard, Sidney and Salt, John (eds.): Robert Owen, Prophet of the Poor, London 1971.
Silver, Harold: Concept of Popular Education, London 1965.

Own Production, Consumer Co-operative

JOHANN BRAZDA / ROBERT SCHEDIWY

(see also: *Consumer Co-operatives*; *Pfeiffer, Conceptions, Co-operative*; *Owen*; *Economie Sociale*)

I. The Early Beginning; II. Own Production on a National Level; III. Own Production on an International Level.

Basically we can distinguish five phases of consumer co-operative own production:
1. The Utopian Phase;
2. The Phase of Small-scale Own Production;
3. The Phase of Large-scale Own Production (initiated around the turn of the century, often under the pressure of boycotts by cartels and oligopolists);
4. The Heyday of Co-operative Own Production from the 1920s to the 1950s;
5. Recent Tendencies to Reduce the Level of Own Production, Mostly for Reasons of Overcapacity and Changes in Market Structure.

I. The Early Beginning

The first ideological commitment to consumer co-operative own production can be found in the long-term ideals of the → *Rochdale Pioneers* (1844) to create a → *"co-operative commonwealth"*. This was an echo of → *Robert Owen's* ideas that co-operatives should basically act as "self-supporting home colonies". In this utopian context the productive character of cooperation was dominant (→ *History in 19th C.*). *The first practical beginnings of co-operatives own production were, however, small scale and took place mostly in the field of bakeries and butchers' shops*. As a matter of fact, many of the earliest → *consumer co-operatives* in the 1860s and 1870s were already incorporating this aspect of small-scale artisan production in the fields of bread and meat production.

II. Own Production on a National Level

The big step forward towards the creation of consumer co-operative industrial production, however, was taking place around the turn of the century when consumer co-operatives were grouping together in most European countries to form *co-operative wholesale societies and unions* (→ *Central Institutions*). Here the British examples of CWS, the English Co-operative Wholesale Society (1863), and of SCSW, the Scottish Co-operative Wholesale Society (1887), led the way and also determined that consumer co-operative own production was preferable to collaboration with producers' co-operatives.
Starting from 1874, the British wholesale societies began to create industrial plants in the fields of textiles, food-production, furniture and printing, that is *basically in the fields of mass consumption articles based on their member societies' needs*. Influenced by the British example European consumer co-operatives founded their own wholesale societies which were to lead the way to consumer co-operative own production: FDB in Denmark was founded in 1884, VSK in Switzerland in 1890, GEG in Germany in 1894, KF in Sweden 1899, SOK in Finland 1904/05, GOEC in Austria 1905. Own production was engaged in by these wholesale societies often in a *defensive way*, because traditional suppliers in oligopolistic markets were not willing to grant wholesale rebates to them. Sometimes suppliers were even pressured by the consumer co-operatives' competitors to boycott them. A typical example was the foundation of the tobacco factory in Esbjerg, Denmark, in 1905 as a result of FDB's fight against the national tobacco trust that had not been willing to give FDB wholesalers' rebates.

In Sweden, the great margarine row between KF and the Swedish maragarine cartel in 1907 to 1911 was provoked by a boycott on KF and later on the whole of the Swedish co-operative movement by the Swedish margarine producers' cartel – a boycott triggered by the pressures of the Swedish retailers' association. In this context KF had no other choice but to buy a margarine production plant of its own, which, however, was inconveniently located and had to be sold off in 1913. Margarine consumption at that time was essential for the Scandinavian lower classes. (Scandinavian countries had the highest per capita consumption of margarine in the whole world.). Thus, it is evident that margarine production plants became an important aspect of Scandinavian consumer co-operative own production during the inter-war years. In this context, a pioneering role was played by the Danish consumer co-operative movement. As KF engaged in building up its own margarine production after World War I, Danish know-how and Danish experts were used.

The Finnish SOK central co-operative was building up its own industrial empire already during the years of World War I. However, it was a little less successful during the inter-war years compared to KF in Sweden, because of the split between the "neutral" and the leftist consumer co-operative movement in 1917, which was aggravated by a civil war in 1918. Other countries engaged in co-operative own production on an industrial scale at that time, too. In 1914, e.g. Switzerland created the world's first "co-op" brand. *The first World War and its concomitant shortage of goods increased the tendency towards vertical integration* and towards the strengthening of consumer co-operative wholesale societies that became privileged importers in the system of "war socialism" – the kind of planned economy that had to be introduced in practically all warfaring states.

On this solid basis the greatly strengthenend co-operative wholesale societies were able to build up large industrial empires during the 1920s and 1930s. The most innovative and daring co-operative entrepreneurs such as KF's *Albin Johansson* in Sweden were then able not only to fight back against cartels that attacked consumer cooperation but to actively break them – thus offering the consumers substantial advantages in fields where oligopolistic market structures had impeded price competition. For example, the Swedish KF, via its own industrial production, not only broke the mill-owners' cartel and the galoshes cartel, it even attacked (via its Luma factory) the gigantic international Phoebus cartel that controlled most of the world's light bulb production (1929–31).

Under the charismatic leadership of *Albin Johansson*, KF even succeeded in making Luma a transnational → *joint venture*, in which the central co-operatives of Denmark, Finland and Norway participated (1931). This was the first international co-operative industrial enterprise (*Kylebäck*) ever. Already at the International Co-operative Alliance's London Congress of 1927, *Albin Johansson* had developed the vision that consumer co-operatives should build up their own *industrial capacity first on a national level, then on an international level*, since international cartels were using their power to dictate prices on an international level, too. At that time, however, it already became evident that international endeavours of this kind needed a dominant partner and that they usually could not follow the federalist model of organisation. Thus, Luma was essentially a KF enterprise and became again so after a number of years.

After 1945, no comparable international industrial undertaking involving consumer co-operatives has been even tried (*Schediwy*, 1990). There have been a number of regional joint ventures, e.g. in the detergent field (1965 with OTK 51%, SOK 45% and KF 4%), or the Nordchoklad venture when the Swedish and Danish co-operative chocolate manufacturing facilities were merged in 1970, with Norway joining in 1975. However, the fact that international co-operative ventures on a federal basis do not seem to work too well is illustrated by the fact that Swedish KF's participation in Nordchoklad had to be raised from 36% to 95% in 1991 during the course of a restructuring program. "Federal" industrial ventures that appear to work rather well during "good times" obviously need a more unified command when difficult decisions have to be taken.

In other countries, where the co-operative wholesale societies did not aquire such a predominant role, there were less important successes in the field of consumer co-operative own production in the 1920s and 1930s. Nevertheless, there were some successes. Even in a country like Austria, where the consumer co-operative movement in the 1930s had serious political difficulties because of a short civil war, the field of own production was a rather successful venture from 1934 to 1938 in the midst of a deep economic depression. Countries with a weak and decentralized consumer co-operative movement such as France and Italy were, however, never able to build up consumer co-operative industrial empires.

It has to be noted, that even during the heyday of centralized co-operative own production *larger regional co-operatives* (→ *Operational Size*) *tended to guard their local production facilities jealously from any tendencies to merge these activities on a national level*. The Helsinki co-operative of Elanto, that was always famous for its good bread, opposed every attempt to have bread production centralized under the wing of the "progressive" wholesale organization OTK (*Schediwy*, 1989). Similarly, the Swedish consumer co-operative of Stockholm always (until the big merger of 1992) guarded its own industrial sector jealously.

The globally positive experiences with centralized and regional co-operative industrial production led to certain over-optimistic visions already at the beginning of the 1930s, such as in the case of German GEG, where the wholesale purchasing society had overestimated the upswing in the German economy and underestimated the efficiency of the co-operatives' competitors (→ *Competition*). This led to surplus capacity in the German co-operative own production plants (*Brambosch*). This aspect then became typical of the post World War II period in many countries. Co-operative products often were high quality products but in many cases had to be sold at rather low prices, because they usually had to be traded at a massive discount compared to well-known branded products. *Attempts to "push" co-operative own products exclusively were also a problematic strategy*, because, if consumers could not find heavily advertised branded products in their "*Konsum*" shops, they might be tempted to go to other shops that held them in stock. For this reason, more than just a few consumer co-operatives in federalized systems tended to buy branded products from other suppliers – even though they were scolded for their "lack of loyalty" to central own production (which thus became a bone of contention between primary co-operative and central institutions). *Often surplus production capacities were the "result of a management ideology which had never questioned the development of consumer co-operative own production. Any rational and business management considerations regarding the wisdom of this constant expansion of co-operative production and of the size of the factories were allowed to be overshadowed by ideological objectives during this period"* (*Brazda*) (→ *Operational Size*).

These problems became more and more evident as during the 1950s and 1960s small individual grocers were being progressively eliminated from retailing markets and consumer co-operatives had to face up to the ever increasing → *competition*. Well integrated chains of retailers and enormous private enterprises started to engage in fierce price → *competition*. Thus, as margins in retailing tended to fall progressively and sellers markets tended to turn into buyers' markets the consumer co-operatives had to face up to the fact that their *central own production was often oversized and saleable only below its true value*. Squabbles about the role of own products in federalist systems of consumer co-operatives became frequent. German GEG and the German consumer co-operative auditing union, for example, were ad odds about the role of own production in the consumer co-operatives' assortment even at the end of the 1950s.

Thus, own production has become a headache for many consumer co-operative movements during recent years, even though this field of activity for a long time tended to retain higher profitability levels than the retailing sphere. As consumer co-operatives were running into increasing economic problems, starting from the end of the 1960s in practically the whole of Europe, there has been a tendency to dispose of productive facilities not only as a ready source of cash but also because excess capacities and a captive market that could not be expanded were increasingly impeding the whole consumer co-operative productive sector.

A country where own production is still very important is Switzerland, not only in the traditional Coop field but also in the field of Migros (a co-operative group that came out of a private enterprise which had to build up its own production also because of boycotts by suppliers). It is, however, significant, that the present merger activities of some of Konsum Austria's and Migros' subsidies have been presented, too, as a method to solve problems of overcapacity in Migros' Swiss plants.

In recent years, the aspect of own brands has played an important role in commerce. However, this low-price alternative to better known international branded products has mostly become important in discount store operations of the Aldi type (→ *Pricing Policy*). Firms of this type do not own their plants, but they are effectively playing off small, medium and even large producers against each other. (Even high quality producers running below full capacity may be tempted to sell some of their produce cheaply to discount stores – and the very anonymity of the discounter's own brand protects their high-class image).

The market structure has changed from suppliers' dominance to buyers' dominance in the whole-saling field as well as in the retailing field: The client has become king and thus it appears to be more profitable for retailers to be able to "squeeze" different suppliers. Equally, it has become more interesting for efficient large scale production plants to opt for the whole retailing market instead of a "captive" but small segment of the market. Thus, traditional own production by co-operatives has lost much of its importance in recent years even in countries where it has played a traditionally strong role such as in Scandinavia. At the same time own brands or even non-branded articles (generic articles just named "toothpaste" or "flour" etc.) are a stable element of retailing in its consumer co-operative as well as in its non co-operative aspect.

III. Own Production on an International Level

The old dream of creating a giant multinational level of consumer cooperation via strong import and production facilities that has been formulated by visionaries like *Albin Johansson*, however, does not seem to be realistic anymore. The "problem of federation" is playing a serious role as an obstacle in this context. *While transnational companies are able to coordinate their international activities rather well, the relatively weak structures of international cooperation between consumer co-operatives were not able to face up to the challenges of the 1970s: Endangered movements had to fight alone*. As the first consumer co-operative movement fell – the Dutch one which had to sell out to private competitors in 1973 – one of the victims of this crisis was the Euro-coop biscuit factory that had been set up by the consumer co-operatives of the common market countries in the Netherlands. It had to be sold because of the collapse of Co-op Netherland (*Schediwy*, 1990). Maybe the proposed Migros-Konsum Austria deal of early 1993, is showing a way for more efficient models of international cooperation between co-operatives, too, which seem to function well only when there is a dominant partner. *In general, however, the future prospects for consumer co-operative own production in its traditional fields have to be regarded as doubtful.*

Bibliography

Brambosch, W.: Coop zwischen Genossenschaft und Gemeinwirtschaft, Münster 1985.

Brazda, Johann/Schediwy, Robert (eds.): Consumer Co-operatives in a Changing World, Geneva 1989.

Brazda, Johann: The Consumer Co-operatives in Germany, in: Brazda, Johann/Schediwy, Robert (eds.), Consumer Co-operatives in a Changing World, Geneva 1989, pp. 173–226.

Kylebäck, Hugo: Konsumentkooperation och Industrikarteller, Stockholm 1974.

Schediwy, Robert: International Cooperation Beetween Consumer Co-operatives – Achievements and Shortcomings, Yearbook of Co-operative Enterprise 1990, pp. 109–121.

Schediwy, Robert: The Consumer Co-operatives in Finland, in: Brazda, Johann/Schediwy, Robert (eds.), Consumer Co-operatives in a Changing World, Geneva 1989, pp. 573–668.

Totomianz, Vahan: Theorie, Geschichte und Praxis der Konsumentenorganisation, Berlin 1914.

Partnership Enterprises

RICHARD WEISKOPF/STEPHAN LASKE [J]

(see also: *Classification; Labour-Management; Joint-production Co-operatives; Organizational Structures, Co-operative; Competition; Economic Order*)

I. Basic Conception; II. The Historic–Ideological Roots of the Partnership Concept in the Economy; III. Preconditions for Acting in Partnership; IV. The Notion of Partnership in the Crossfire of Conflicting Logics; V. Partnership Enterprises in the Capitalistic Market Economy.

I. Basic Conception

1. Social Theory

A critique and classification of "partnership" enterprises can only be undertaken against the backdrop of a thoroughly formulated social theory and theory of economics: It is only possible with the help of a macro-structural approach to critique those specific problems commensurately which arise in the administration and control in each and every type of enterprise organization. An enterprise is by no means an isolated social or technical system but rather is inbedded in a comprehensive system of individual, social and societal relationships (→ *Configuration*). We proceed from the assumption that the existent societal formation – despite partial modifications – can as before be described as capitalistic. The *capitalistic economic system* thereby fulfills three fundamental functions: firstly, the function of utility with regard to invested capital; secondly, the function of co-ordinating actions; and thirdly, the function of reproducing social relationships (c.f. *Türk*, 1987). Even when organizations and the subjects acting in them are not absolutely determined by the societal principle of organization, it, nonetheless, delineates the range for variation within which formative and transformational processes are possible (c.f. *Habermas*, 1973). Differing logics which also collide in enterprise organizations can be derived from a materialistically oriented economic and social theory: the logics of utilization, cooperation and domination (c.f. *Türk*, 1989) form a kind or co-ordinate system which prestructures the political arena. These three logics can also be found in *"partnership enterprises"*.

2. Enterprises

Enterprises can be conceived as social units in which the *transformation of human capital* is organized into usable performance output (c.f. *Seltz/Hildebrandt*). On account of diverging logics and the social interests associated therewith, this transformation is fundamentally viewed as a conflict-ridden process in which actions must be co-ordinated. This primarily constitutes a communicative problem (*Martens*). The organization of work in an enterprise thus serves to expedite actual cooperation between working individuals; it serves the creation of added value and the preservation of social differentiations (*Türk*, 1990, p.177). As such it forms a "political arena" for the conflict revolving around the transformation of human capital into work. Central political realms define the options for varyingly structured (labour) organizations. Enterprise organizations are produced and reproduced through the actions of their members. This reproduction occurs on a *material* as well as on a *symbolic* dimension: "...organizations exist in and through members' communicative and productive interactions" (*Kersten/Deetz*, 1983, p.156). Organizations remain latched to the market with respect to the problem of value realization.

3. Cooperation and Partnership

"Cooperation" constitutes the base definition for this form of work organization; it represents a fundamental anthropological constant. Cooperation is necessary in every society with a division of labor in order to have a social product result from separate partial elements (c.f., for example, *Marx/Engels*). In principle, two forms of cooperation can be differentiated: *antagonistic cooperation* – that is collaboration under conditions of structural conflict – and *"partnership cooperation"*, which in contrast refers to a special quality of cooperation. On the one hand, the social-structural aspect of equality among the interaction participants is addressed, and on the other hand, the socio-cultural aspect of a "trusting, 'prosocial' quality of interaction" is touched upon (*Ulrich*, 1991, p.71). The notion of partnership as a specially distinguished quality of cooperation thus contains a touch of *social utopia* which extends beyond the societal formation at hand. This utopia can be grounded either in communicative-ethical terms (c.f. *Habermas*, 1983; *Ulrich*, 1986) or else from the position of Catholic social doctrine (*Nell-Breuning*, 1973; 1983). The term "partnership" can accordingly be applied either *critically* or in an *affirmative* manner. In a critical sense, it serves to assess existent relationships, using as its yardstick equal participation in the production and consumption of societal wealth. As an affirmative term it serves to shroud de facto interest and power differences. Cooperation occurs under specific social-historic conditions. We do not wish in the scope of this treatise to address the problem of cooperation in general, but rather are concerned with the question of cooperation under the historical conditions of capitalistic production. It is, therefore, necessary to examine this term more closely.

a) Partnership as a process

From an initial view, partnership can be understood as a process of partnership development. From this perspective, it is not a non-recurring matter but rather a social process which must continually prove itself in conflict-ridden decision-making and action situations. The *dynamic* component is herewith emphasized which itself produces contradictions and conflicts. "The most basic, generic contradiction is that between the constructed social world and the ongoing process of social construction. The reification of the organization as a determinate thing standing over against people is contradictory to the ongoing process of production. This contradiction is the essence of social and political alienation" (*Benson*, p.16). We, therefore, conceive the idea of partnership as a *process of community formation* (*Vergemeinschaftung*). In principle, this aims to abolish structural conflicts of interests. With reference to *Max Weber*, *Vergemeinschaftung* is to be understood as the "most radical antithesis" to conflict; it should accordingly always be understood as a *political* process in which truisms are construed socially which become esconced contrary to alternative world views (c.f. *Patzelt*).

b) Partnership as a structure

Partnership can be understood secondly as a structure (→ *Organizational Structures, Co-operative*). On the one hand, structures are a product of human action, but on the other hand, structures also evoke certain actions (c.f. *Giddens*). "Relationships are formed, roles are constructed, institutions are built from the encounters and confrontations of people in their daily round life. Their production of social structure is itself guided and constrained by the context" (*Benson*, p.3). Partnership as a structure suggests an extensive power symmetry, that is in this sense it characterizes a social relationship which is distinguished through an approximate *balance of power* among involved actors. Structural power assymetries are incompatible with the notion of a partnership.

c) Partnership as an instrument

From the instrumental perspective, a partnership can be conceived thirdly and lastly as a medium for the realization of interests. If one fundamentally assumes that interests are diverging and conflicting in an organization, the partnership proves itself as a means of realizing interests based on the *formation of coalitions*. In this connection the potential social-technological character of the partnership can be addressed: the temporally restricted, situation-specific and unilaterally revokable "partnership relationship" serves the "channeled regulation of conflicts" (*Lezius*, p.26) and the reduction of "conflict costs". It represents the attempt to signalize a harmonious community where in actuality contradictory interests are at hand. The addressees of such signals for one are to be found in the environment surrounding the organization, and on the other hand are the organization members themselves who are to be drawn into the "warm embrace of the partnership".

"Partnership enterprises" accordingly can be interpreted as the attempt to emphasize cooperation logic more strongly and to bring to the forefront the "subject character" of those employed. They represent an approach to overcome antagonistic conflicts of interest and to stress "common" or "community" interests ("partnership" vs. "antagonism"): In this regard one can differentiate between superficial models (the ideology of partnerships) and core models (the material safeguarding of the partnership and structural equal opportunity in conflict situations).

II. The Historic–Ideological Roots of the Partnership Concept in the Economy

The idea of structuring enterprise organizations along the lines of → *solidarity* and harmonious collaboration has a variety of historic and ideological origins. The idea of the plant community (*Betriebsgemeinschaft*) for one needs to be addressed. In the face of increasing alienation as a result of the Taylorization of work and in light of the political tumult in the 1920s, the "German Institute for Technical Vocational Training" (*Dinta*) undertook to strengthen workers' emotional ties to their enterprises in order to thwart trade union attempts to exercise influence. This program aimed at counteracting the "destructive effects of Marxism" by means of a harmonistic objective. In the pamphlet "The Battle for the Souls of our Workers" published in 1926, these objectives were delineated as follows: "The liberation of the worker from the loneliness of his isolated, partial function in the production process; to overcome the antagonistic, oppositional stance between the worker and the entrepreneur; the composite improvement of their mental state; the psychological and material satisfaction of workers in the contemporary economic system with the means that the German economy has at its disposal in the present situation" (*Osthold*, p.7). Instead of an organized representation of employee interests, the subordination of partial interests was intended to serve a "communal well-being". In the era of the National Socialists, the plant and work communities were made into the smallest units of the people community (*Volksgemeinschaft*). The de facto disengagement of the unions as an organized counterbalance in the end attained legal legitimacy through the "Law for the Structure of National Labor" issued by the Nazis in 1934. The *Deutsche Arbeitsfront* (German Labor Front, DAF) assumed the position of the unions and in addition to technical rationalization strove in particular to promote the indoctrination of the national socialistic ideology of the *Volksgemeinschaft* (c.f. *Siegel*). The notion of community which so greatly determined fascism – that each individual is bound to unconditional loyalty to the plant and national community – as well as the thoroughly maintained principle of subordination (*"Führer-*Prinzip") formed the two central pillars of the National Socialist "Order of Labor".

The concept of the plant community became discredited on account of its function in National Socialism. Because of this *"partnership enterprises"* emerged in post-war Germany. The majority of these enterprises (currently there are over 500 member companies) are united in the so-called AGP, The Alliance for the Promotion of Partnership in the Economy. The AGP defines a partnership enterprise as a "contractually settled form of cooperation between corporate administration and co-workers intended to provide all parties involved with extensive self-development and to counteract alien determination through various forms of co-participation and co-determination based on the respective assumption of due responsibility" (*Lezius/Beyer*, p.20). It is the stated goal of the AGP to overcome antagonism among structural interests (between labor and capital) and to work towards partnership cooperation. The basis of this concept's legitimation is rooted primarily in the realm of *Catholic social doctrine* (*Kramer, Herr*) and in the recognition in principle of the system of the *"social market economy"*. This involves the fundamental acknowledgement of private property with regard to the means of production and the simultaneous upgrading of the factor of labor. A structural similarity to the plant community can be drawn from the position that "entrepreneurs and employees alike must tolerate disadvantages *for the well-being of the company*" (*Lezius/Beyer*, p.22). The "well-being of the company" is cited as the premier goal factor which is never questioned (c.f. *Laske*, 1979, for a critique on "corporate interests"). This well-being is the scope in which the settlement of conflicts is legimately possible and, at the same time, the point of reference for efforts aiming to regulate conflict.

The idea of a "partnership enterprise" is not isolated to Germany alone. *Fischer* (p.76 ff.) reported of approx. 300 partnership enterprises which existed in Japan in 1970. It is interesting that here, too, the power of the organized representation of interests was weakened and/or was intended to be weakened through a form of labour organization similar to the plant community closely tied to the enterprise.

Whereas in Germany employers had to abandon their efforts to establish "economic associations which organized workers loyal to the enterprise" (*Müller-Jentsch*, p.378 ff.) – the so-called "yellow unions" at a relatively early stage, the Japanese plant communities today appear to complement those initiated by management (c.f. *Bergmann*).

A further root can be distinguished in the *human relations movement*. The fundamental interest in this case existed in the utilization of social relationships as a productivity reserve. Norms and feelings were identified as central determining factors of one's disposition to work and output. Contrary to several abbreviated interpretations, this movement should not be interpreted as a triumph over the Taylor paradigm. It is apparent in numerous cases that the given structural basis conflict also remained unaffected. Instead of conflict regulation using scientific (engineering) methods – as in Taylorism – a technology of cultivating harmonistic relationships emerged which was intended to preserve the appearance of interest homogeneity (c.f. *Perrow*). The idea of interest compensation is carried further in the pragmatic approaches used in organizational and personnel development.

The approach of → *corporate culture* also fits into this context. Above all, the elements intrinsic in the system of organizational symbols are considered media capable of drawing together communities. Management-oriented authors promise a uniform structuring of activities executed by members of a company by means of the formation and influential effect of symbols which promote identity and induce unity, as well as through the influential effect of interpretational methods depicting social reality. By creating a "feeling of 'we'" and through the symbolic demonstration of unity, "harmony and strength" (*Rohlen*) should be realized and conflicts which endanger efficiency and domination should be repressed. Corporate culture as a management approach in harmonistic orientation represents a "renaissance of the plant community" (*Krell*, 1991) (c.f. *Alvesson/Berg; Mark-Ungericht/Weiskopf* for criticism).

These concepts of a "community-making personnel policy" (*Krell*, 1993) share a fundamental harmonistic orientation and likewise attempt to conceive partnership organizations as "intimate associations of people engaged in economic activity but tied together in a variety of bonds" (*Ouchi*, 1981, p.70). They are built on the basis of trusting cooperation between the regular working staff and management (*Bleicher, Fox, Zand*). As *management strategies* (c.f. *Bergmann*) these concepts differ through their fundamental harmonistic orientation to the concepts of → *co-determination* (which aims fabricate and institutionalize countervailing power) and *workers' self-administration* (→ *Labour-Management*) which is usually organized in a co-operative manner (→ *Joint-production Co-operatives*) (itself based essentially on members' property and the democratic principle of "one man one vote") (c.f., for example, *Arbeitskreis für Kooperation und Partizipation*; *Dülfer, Laske/ Schneider* 1985; *Schneider/Laske*). From the position of a materialistically oriented organizational theory, the expressions of a "community-making personnel policy" thus appear as revived and up-dated strategies for employers and management to ensure control over workers and the working process alike (*Littler*). These concepts do not attempt to topple structural contradictions which are inherent in capitalistic production but rather aim to channel and regulate conflicts in the sense of stabilizing the system. The multitude of pragmatically oriented publications among contemporary management literature which propagate consensus formation, harmony, workers' identification, commitment, trust, etc. appear as "euphemisms" uttered by the defenders of the status quo (*Bourdieu*, 1990, p.130) when seen against the backdrop of an essentially conflict-oriented perspective of the capitalistic economic system and its institutions; as such they become suspect to the ideology they expound.

III. Preconditions for Acting in Partnership

1. Personal Preconditions

A fundamental precondition for partnership action is co-operative competence. Alongside linguisitic competence, co-operative competence also encompasses a pragmatic aspect (acting). This term can be extended to include competence in dealing with "things". *Co-operative competence* thus requires competence in interacting with the objective, social and subjective world (c.f. also *Habermas*, 1981). In accordance with our understanding of an enterprise organization as a conflict-ridden arena, we choose to conceive "co-operative competence" as the ability to articulate and realize interests. Co-operative competence necessitates autonomy as detailed by *Giddens* (p.108), or in other words, the "further development of the ability to determine behavior in a reflexive manner". A precondition for the competence of interest articulation is that actors are conscious of their own interests.

2. Institutional and Structural Preconditions

The structural conditions under which economic action occurs in our society can be interpreted as both restrictive and as facilitative general conditions for partnership action. Social structures thus always represent compulsion and restriction but at the same time serve as resources for action (c.f. *Giddens*). Several structural elements are presented in the following according to their importance for partnership enterprises.

a) Ownership structures

To a substantial extent, these determine dispositional rights in organizations. If property is viewed as a social relationship of disposition, the connection between disposition over material goods and disposition over individuals in particular must be analyzed (c.f. *Türk*, 1987). On the one hand, this is a question of material interest: here the appropriation of the return to labor (ouput) is at disposition. "Partnership enterprises", therefore, also strive for employees' material participation in the enterprise capital. (Real) partnership would require an extensively uniform and equal distribution of property shares. Participations usually de facto do not extend so far (c.f. *Köbele/Schütt*, 1992; *Schanz*, 1985; 1987), and one can, therefore, refer to *fictitious partnerships* which primarily fulfill the function of binding people to organizations and securing loyalty. The notion of workers' self-administration, however, is directed at real partnerships (*Laske/Schneider*, 1985). A concept of this nature without a doubt rebuffs the system and is incompatible with the stated intention of the AGP enterprises, namely the "stabilization of the system of the social market economy" (*Lezius/Beyer*, p.21).

On the other hand, this concerns the *non-material* opportunities for participation. In this context, the question of domination in enterprise organizations is at disposition. The following aspects need to be emphasized in this regard:

b) Structural safeguarding of opportunities for the articulation and realization of interests

A real partnership requires a means to safeguard particpational chances structurally. In this sense, those persons affected by decisions must be drawn into the decision-making process as equally entitled partners. This type of co-decision capacity requires appropriate regulation in the by-laws of the organization (c.f. *Gerum*). Power asymmetries and the structural opposition of interests are as incompatible with a partnership as a paternalistic manner of attending to interests: "One may treat a slave humanely, and even ask his opinion regarding matters he is more familiar with than the master. But to transform his basic dependency and this presumption of his incompetence with regard to his own interests, there must be an institutional order or public process whereby the opportunity and capacity for legitimate self-assertion is guaranteed. Such a political process does not mean conflict and struggle as such, but a setting for ordered controversy and accomodation" (*Perrow*, p.133). Cooperation in a partnership is therefore only possible between actors who find themselves in a common situation of interests. "Interests" themselves actually are simply a relationship to an outside entity or force; "partnership" (community) represents the antithesis of interests. Partnership remains an ideology when the material-structural substructure is not at hand. A partnership in a capitalistic organization is therefore only conceivable as a "conflict partnership" (*Müller-Jentsch*, 1991).

c) The question of organizational goal formation (→ Managerial Economics)

If one proceeds from the assumption that differing interests collide with one another in organizations, as a consequence the notion must be cast aside that a uniform or "common" corporate goal could exist. The concrete processes of goal formation are always influenced by the power structures and/or relationships found in organizations. In "partnership enterprises", the participation of employees in goal formation is striven for, but nonetheless the "right to final decision" is in principle retained for the "majority body of capital owners" (*Lezius/Beyer*, 1989). The postulation of (common) corporate goals thereby primarily serves as ideological justification for those individuals who succeed in carrying through their own specific interests, whereby these are shrouded as legitimate corporate goals (*Ortmann*).

d) A further dimension concerns the structuring of labor

In every organization a fundamental conflict emerges which results from the double character of human capital. Labor simultaneously represents an economic resource and is an expression of workers' individual and collective identity (or notions of their identity). Every effort to add structure therefore represents intervention into the autonomy of the actors involved. The structuring of labor is thus also a question of the power actors have, a question addressing disposition over time, claims to identity and the resources of action (*Littek/Heisig*). The extent individuals are able to exercise influence in the structuring of labor by addressing their own expectations and claims is an indicator of how far the real partnership has transcended mere ideological pretentions.

3. Cultural Preconditions

A fundamental precondition on the cultural level appears to be a *system of basic ideas* in which co-operative action appears meaningful to the members of productive organizations. Orientation around this basic ideas in a competitive and competitively oriented society seems to have the tendency to block co-operative action. The capitalistic market economy order is necessarily built on other principles (e.g. individualism regarding ownership, performance ideology, orientation around exchange value). Changes in the assessment of work as well as new, subjectivistic demands placed on work by all means indicate that a transformational process is also underway on the level of "the orientation around the basic ideas" (c.f. "Research into the Transformation of Values"). In part, the tendency can be identified that "co-operative" values (communicative, etc.) are gaining importance (c.f. *Schmittchen*; *Hillman*).

Co-operative action is even increasingly viewed as a "functionable orientation pattern" on the enterprise level (*Schwiering*, 1992). In particular, efforts concerning the formation of corporate culture and its influence can be interpreted as attempts to affect the cultural-ideological preconditions for partnership cooperation. This concerns the attempt to establish a collective orientation of action which can serve as an orientation pattern for overcoming conflict-ridden and contradictory action situations. The notion of "shared meanings" (*Smirchich*) as it is used by proponents of the corporate culture movement in particular illustrate this quite clearly. These findings are, nonetheless, also contradictory.

IV. The Notion of Partnership in the Crossfire of Conflicting Logics

If we proceed from the three fundamental logics identified in the introduction of this treatise, the relationship of cooperation and/or partnership logic to utility logic (1) and to domination logic (2) can be analyzed more closely.

1. Partnership and the Logic of Utilization

The notion of the partnership enterprise can be understood with respect to "utility logic" as an attempt to make the "resources of social solidarity" (*Habermas*, 1981, 1973) useful as a productivity reserve. Proponents of the notion of partnerships hope "to improve motivation and the willingness to perform as well as the opportunities for self-development among workers...through promoting identification with the goals of the company" (*Lezius/Beyer*, p.21).

When one inquires as to the socio-economic context the initiators and the pursued intentions of this notion, it becomes evident that the notion of partnerships and community also has always been an expression of crisis symptoms. This notion is addressed in particular by employers during times of social and economic change (c.f. *Spurk*, 1988). When processes of change and transformation are perceived by those affected as "crises" (c.f. *Habermas*, 1973; *Krell/Ortmann*), a mechanism is needed which cushions them. The notion of community also serves somewhat to "channelize fear" (*Türk*, 1989, p.111). Sociologically, a differentiation is drawn between *Gemeinschaft* (community) and *Gesellschaft* (society): *Gemeinschaft* characterizes proximity where feelings are emphasized, whereas *Gesellschaft* in contrast characterizes anonymous distance. Structuring enterprises according to the principle of *Gemeinschaft* thus entails the attempt of using proximity as a "resource", of channeling emotional energy and ties and making them tenable as a factor of production and productivity.

Alongside the potential economization of the social-integrative dimension, financial considerations are also raised as an argument for the partnership form of an organization: "Equity basis, earning power and efficiency [of the company] should be strengthened in an enduring manner through a combination of material and non-material elements in co-worker participation" (*Lezius/Beyer*, p.21). The notion of the partnership thus does not necessarily contradict the capitalistic principle of utility, but rather it possibly represents a means to tap the last productivity reserves and attain "all-round utility from labor input" (*Deutschmann/Weber*).

2. Partnership and the Logic of Domination

The notion of partnership cooperation tends to stand in conflict with the logic of domination. Enterprise organizations in capitalistic societies are characterized by a fundamental conflict of interests. The given, basic structural conflict between labor and capital is determinant for the capitalistic relationship of production. Partnership enterprises are understood as the attempt to transform antagonistic opposition into collective solidarity. The distinction between *superficial* and *core structures* in organizations is expedient in analyzing the effects of domination structures. Whereas superficial structures encompass that which is directly perceivable, legitimate speech patterns, spoken rules and official declarations of the organization, the core structure concerns the "deeper reality of organizational power relationships" (*Conrad*, p.189); these above all lie in material conditions and set preconditions which are never questioned. If the concept of partnership remains limited to the superficial structure, that is a binding structural securement of participational chances does not ensue (c.f. *Kappler; Laske/Weiskopf*), it foremost serves as pacification and preserves established forms of domination.

Domination is apparent above all in the contradictions which exist between the superficial and core structures. The "partnership" with non-binding organizational principles and policies will become an instrument of ideological justification for the entrenched dominating forces when the symbolic "partnership" is built on given tangible inequalities with regard to power. *Meyer* and *Rowan* (1967) distinguish between two strategies which can be applied in organizations to rip down façades and cast light on real contradictions: the "logic of decoupling" and the "logic of confidence and good faith". When picking up on this theme we can differentiate between two fundamental mechanisms with which the process of community formation (*Vergemeinschaftung*) can contribute to preserve an enterprise's domination structure. The process of community formation in *internal relationships* is helpful in producing acceptance and legitimacy for the existent authority structure: trusted rules and routines are (no longer) questioned. The process of community formation leads to a more intense delimitation of the organization with respect to its *environment*, to individuals propounding different opinions, and to those who "rock the boat". This is apparent in the special procedures used in the selection of personnel; these not only strive to make an objectified investigation of one's professional qualifications but also assume the function of "cooptation based on shared ideologies" (*Kompa*). Loyalty to one's plant community is considered an especially esteemed qualification, especially in times of crisis. The process of community formation is thus frequently a harmonization and defensive strategy which protects "insiders" from the claims of those beyond the confines of the organization.

How can the position of *"personnel"* in partnership enterprises be described against such a background? The role of personnel is composed of social, legal, material and cultural factors and determines the relationship of the working individual to the organization. This relationship is one of distance and alien determination (c.f. *Türk*, 1978). Let us develop this thought consequently a few steps further: partnership must essentially signify the termination of the personnel relationship (as a utopia or a guiding concept). This is the case – at least verbally – when it is postulated that a "partnership" turns employees into "co-entrepreneurs", when the central motive of co-worker participation is said to be the promotion of "entrepreneurial" or "economic thinking", or when motivation and identification or the "abolishment of class antagonism" are named (c.f. *Schanz*, 1987; *Wagner*; for the USA see *Marsh/McAllister*). Furthermore, there are also legal agreements which are intended to ensure the co-partnership of those employed, but these agreements tend only to affect superficial structures on account of the inequalities which continue to exist. Employees as intrapreneurs remain trapped in an "as-if-status" which *Peters* and *Waterman* identify as "simulated entrepreneurship" (p.249). De facto hardly anything changes (materially) in their personnel status. In this sense, the notion of partnership enterprise is understandable as a strategy to collect and bind workers; this strategy latently maintains structural contradictions, thereby supporting the cultural hegemony enjoyed by those in control (*Clegg; Gramsci; Burawoy* 1985). It thus serves to accept the existent social structure as a natural structure, or else to negate this structure in the name of an alleged higher unity in a symbolic manner" (cf. *Bourdieu*, 1990, p.107).

V. Partnership Enterprises in the Capitalistic Market Economy

1. The Problem at Root and Transformational Tendencies

Partnership enterprises are confronted with a myriad of problems in capitalistic market economies – problems both in the enterprise itself as well as beyond its confines which result from the conflux of diverging and, in part, contradicting logics. A number of economic-sociological investigative analyses indicate that the market economy is undergoing a fundamental *structural change* and that new forms of cooperation are emerging along with new requirements (c.f. *Buß*). A "communicative market public" functions as a new control entity on a inter-company level which increasingly forces even traditionally structured enterprises to engage in new forms of cooperation (with suppliers, customers and even with their employees...). Likewise, a new understanding of performance, cooperation and social agreements in many cases seems to develop inside organizations. Social integration in the enterprise also acquires a new, importance to the same extent that productive and creative contributions are needed from employees on account of flexibility demanded by technical production conditions and the market. A slue of labor and personnel-political strategies and instruments therefore aim to promote co-operative forms of work. Developments especially in the field of personnel development indicate this clearly (c.f. *Laske/Gorbach*, 1993).

2. The Future of Co-operative Work and Organization Forms

How can the future of "partnership enterprises" and/or co-operative organizational forms be appraised against such a background?
Our appraisal is quite *ambivalent*. On the one hand, the structural transformations discussed above indicate increasing importance for co-operative forms of economic activity. In this context, it is thoroughly feasible that the notion of partnerships and/or self-administered enterprises will experience a revitalization inasmuch as it can serve as a "teaching model" (*Ulrich*, 1991, p.82). It likewise can be assumed that in times of heightened rationalization pressure efforts will increase for entrepreneurial conflict management. Furthermore, increased efforts are expected to compensate the "lack of legitimacy" (*Meyer/Rowan*, 1977). On the other hand, it cannot be precluded that the macro-economic developments touched upon above (transition to a communicative market public, etc.) will not be interpreted as a replacement for the competition model but rather in the contrary as a model of intensified competition (→ *Competition*). In this sense, the notion of the partnership on the enterprise level would be interpreted as a more potent weapon wielded by employers in the battle to control the work process. It is therefore unforeseeable whether the optimistic perspective or the pessimistic perspective will more closely correspond to reality. The former view assumes that the "practicality of the stronger argument" (*Ulrich*, 1990) will prevail over the newly resulting necessity for cooperation even among commercial organizations. The latter in contrast raises the question whether new lines of fragmentation and segmentation will be drawn between employees which separate those workers willing to cooperate and acquiesce from the remaining staff – and this in the face of increasing, stiffer competition and various selection, promotion and development policies which result from this competition. In such a context, this development would not be considered a stronger appraisal of the cooperation logic but rather as a further continuation and alliance between the logics of domination and utility.

Bibliography

Alvesson, Mats/Berg, Per Olof: Corporate Culture and Organizational Symbolism, Bern/New York 1992.
Arbeitskreis für Kooperation und Partnerschaft (ed.): Kooperatives Management. Bestandsaufnahmen, Konflikte, Modelle, Zukunftsperspektiven, Baden-Baden 1990.
Benson, John Kenneth: Organizations: A dialectical view. In: ASQ, 1977, p.1 ff..
Bergmann, Joachim: Rationalisierungsdynamik und Betriebsgemeinschaft, München/Mering 1990.
Bleicher, Knut: Meilensteine auf dem Weg zur Vertrauensorganisation. In: Thexis, vol.4, 1985, pp. 2–7.
Burawoy, Michael: The Politics of Production. Factory Regimes under Capitalism and Socialism, London 1985.
Burawoy, Michael: Manufactoring Consent. Changes in the Labour Process under Monopoly Capitalism, Chicago/London 1979.
Buß, Eugen: Markt und Gesellschaft. Eine soziologische Untersuchung zum Strukturwandel der Wirtschaft, Berlin 1983.
Conrad, Charles: Organizational Power. Faces and Symbolic Forms. In: Putnam, L.L./Pacanosky, M.E.: Communication and Organizations. An Interpretive Approach, Beverly Hills/London/New Delhi 1983, pp. 173–195.
Clegg, Stuart R.: Frameworks of Power, London 1989.
Deutschmann, Christoph/Weber, Claudia: Das japanische Arbeitsbienensyndrom. Organisationskulturelle und -srukturelle Aspekte der ‚Rundumnutzung der Arbeitskraft'. In: PROKLA, 1987, pp. 31–51.
Dülfer, Eberhard: Betriebswirtschaftslehre der Kooperative. Kommunikation und Entscheidungsbildung in Genossenschaften und vergleichbaren Organisationen, Göttingen 1984.
Fineman, Steven (ed.): Emotion in Organizations, London 1993.
Fischer, G.: Ein Guido-Fischer-Partnerschaftshaus in Japan. In: Personal, vol.3, 1971, pp. 96–97.
Fox, Allan: Beyond Contract: Work, Power and Trust Relations, London 1974.
Giddens, Anthony: Die Konstitution der Gesellschaft:

Grundzüge einer Theorie der Strukturierung, Frankfurt/New York 1988.
Gerum, Elmar: Unternehmensverfassung. In: Frese, Erich (ed.): Handwörterbuch der Organisation, 3.ed., Stuttgart 1992, cols. 2480–2502.
Gramsci, Antonio: The Prison Notebooks, London 1971.
Habermas, Jürgen: Legitimationsprobleme im Spätkapitalismus, Frankfurt am Main 1973.
Habermas, Jürgen: Theorie des kommunikativen Handelns, 2 volumes, Frankfurt am Main 1981.
Habermas, Jürgen: Moralbewußtsein und kommunikatives Handeln, Frankfurt am Main 1983.
Herr, Thomas: Katholische Soziallehre – Eine Einführung, Paderborn 1987.
Hillmann, Karl Heinz: Wertwandel, Darmstadt 1986.
Kappler, Ekkehard: Partizipation und Führung. In: Kieser, A./Reber, G./Wunderer, R. (ed.): Handwörterbuch der Führung, Stuttgart 1987, cols. 1631–1647.
Kompa, Ain: Assessment-Center, Bestandsaufnahme und Kritik, München 1989.
Kramer, Rainer: Arbeit. Theologische, wirtschaftliche und soziale Aspekte, Göttingen 1982.
Krell, Gertraude: Unternehmenskultur: Rennaissance der Betriebsgemeinschaft. In: Dülfer, Eberhard (ed.): Organisationskultur. Phänomen – Philosophie – Technologie, 2.ed., Stuttgart 1991., pp. 147–160.
Krell, Gertraude: Vergemeinschaftende Personalpolitik, München 1993.
Krell, Gertraude/Ortmann, Günther: Personal, Personalwirtschaft und Beschäftigungskrise. In: Staehle, Wolfgang/Stoll, Edgar (ed.): Betriebswirtschaftslehre und ökonomische Krise, Wiesbaden 1984.
Laske, Stephan: Unternehmensinteresse und Mitbestimmung. In: Zeitschrift für Unternehmens- und Gesellschaftsrecht, vol.2, 1979, pp. 173–200.
Laske, Stephan/Gorbach, Stefan (ed.): Spannungsfeld Personalentwicklung. Konzeptionen – Modelle – Analysen, Wien 1993.
Laske, Stephan/Schneider, Ursula: "... und es funktioniert doch!". Selbstverwaltung kann man lernen, Wien 1985.
Laske, Stephan/Weiskopf, Richard: Hierarchie. In: Frese, E. (ed.): Handwörterbuch der Organisation, 3.ed., Stuttgart 1992, cols. 791–807.
Litteck, Wolfgang/Heisig, Ulrich: Rationalisierung von Arbeit als Aushandlungsprozeß. In: Soziale Welt, vol.3, 1986, pp. 236–262.
Lezius, Hans Michael: Das Konzept der betrieblichen Partnerschaft. In: Schneider, Heinz Jürgen (ed.): Handbuch der Mitarbeiterbeteiligung, pp. 24–42, Köln 1977.
Lezius, Hans Michael/Beyer, Heinrich: Menschen machen Wirtschaft. Betriebliche Partnerschaft als Erfolgsfaktor, Wiesbaden 1989.
Littler, Craig: Theorie des Managements und Kontrolle. In: Hildebrandt, Ekkehard/Seltz, Rüdiger (ed.): Managementstrategien und Kontrolle, Eine Einführung in die Labour Process Debate, Berlin 1987, pp. 27–76.
Mark-Ungericht, Bernhard/Weiskopf, Richard: Menschenfertigung und Personalproduktion. Eine ideologiekritische kommunikationstheoretische Betrachtung von Unternehmenskultur und Personalentwicklung, Diss., Innsbruck 1993.
Marsh, Thomas/McAllister, Donald: ESOPs Tables. A Survey of Companies with Employee Stock Ownership Plans. In: Journal of Corporation Law, vol.6, no.3, 1981, pp. 551–623.
Martens, Wil: Kommunikationstheorie der Unternehmung, Frankfurt/New York 1989.
Marx, Karl/Engels, Friedrich: Das Kapital. Kritik der politischen Ökonomie, MEW 23, 16.ed., Berlin 1986.

Müller-Jentsch, Walther: Berufs-, Betriebs- oder Industriegewerkschaften. In: Endruweit, Günther/Gaugler, Eduard/Staehle, Wolfgang (ed.): Handbuch der Arbeitsbeziehungen, Berlin 1985, pp. 369–381.
Müller-Jentsch, Walther: Konfliktpartnerschaft. Akteure und Institutionen der industriellen Beziehungen, München 1991.
Nell-Breuning, Oswald v.: Arbeitnehmer – Mitarbeiter – Mitunternehmer. In: Fricke, Werner/Geissler, Alfred (ed.): Demokratisierung der Wirtschaft, Hamburg 1973, pp. 182–195.
Nell-Breuning, Oswald v.: Worauf es mir ankommt, Freiburg 1983.
Ortmann, Günther: Unternehmensziele als Ideologie, Köln 1976.
Osthold, Paul: Der Kampf um die Seele unseres Arbeiters, Düsseldorf 1926.
Patzelt, Werner: Grundlagen der Ethnomethodologie, Theorie, Empirie und politikwissenschaftlicher Nutzen einer Soziologie des Alltags, München 1987.
Peters, Tom/Waterman, Richard: Auf der Suche nach Spitzenleistungen, München 1990.
Perrow, Charles: Complex Organizations. A Critical Essay, 2.ed., Dallas, Texas 1979.
Rohlen, Thomas: For Harmony and Strength, Berkeley/Los Angeles/London 1974.
Schanz, Günther: Mitarbeiterbeteiligung. Grundlagen – Befunde – Modelle, München 1985.
Schanz, Günther: Mitarbeiterbeteiligungen in den Vereinigten Staaten von Amerika. In: DBW 47, vol.6. 1987. pp. 655–671.
Schmittchen, Günther: Neue Technik – neue Arbeitsmoral. Eine sozialpsychologische Untersuchung über Motivation in der Metallindustrie, Köln 1984.
Schneider, Ursula/Laske, Stephan: Produktivgenossenschaften. Gesellschaften mit beschränkter Hoffnung?, Wien 1985.
Siegel, Tilla: Leistung und Lohn in der nationalsozialistischen "Ordnung der Arbeit", Opladen 1989.
Seltz, Rüdiger/Hildebrandt, Ekkehard: Produktion, Politik und Kontrolle – arbeitspolitische Varianten am Beispiel der Einführung von Produktionsplanungs- und Steuerungssystemen im Maschinenbau. In: Naschold, Frieder (ed.): Arbeit und Politik, Frankfurt/New York 1985, pp. 91–124.
Smirchich, Linda: Concepts of Culture and Organizational Analysis, ASQ, vol.28, 1983, pp. 339.347.
Türk, Klaus : Objektbereich und Problemfeld einer Personalwissenschaft. In: Zeitschrift für Arbeitswissenschaft, vol.4, 1978, pp. 218–221.
Türk, Klaus: Einführung in die Soziologie der Wirtschaft, Stuttgart 1987.
Türk, Klaus: Neuere Entwicklungen in der Organisationsforschung, Stuttgart 1989.
Türk, Klaus: Neuere Organisationssoziologie. Ein Studienskript, Trier 1990.
Ulrich, Peter: Transformation der ökonomischen Vernunft, Bern/Stuttgart 1986.
Ulrich, Peter: Zur Ethik der Kooperation in Organisationen. In: Wunderer, Rolf (ed.): Kooperation. Gestaltungsprinzipien und Steuerung der Zusammenarbeit zwischen Organisationseinheiten, Stuttgart 1991, pp. 69–90.
Wagner, Klaus: Mitarbeiterbeteiligung: Erfolg und Risiko teilen. In: Personalwirtschaft, vol.11, 1990, pp. 13–17.
Weber, Max: Wirtschaft und Gesellschaft (Grundriß der Sozialökonomik, III. Abteilung), Tübingen 1922.
Zand, Dale: Trust and Managerial Problem Solving. In: ASQ 3, 1977, pp. 229–239.

Periodicals, Co-operative

HERBERT WENDT [J]

(see also: *Federations*; *Federation Statistics*; *Marketing Strategies*)

I. Taking Stock and Background Information; II. Structural Changes and Developmental Tendencies.

If one wishes to judge the importance and function of co-operative periodical literature as accurately as possible, one must take into consideration that it itself is an essential component of co-operative public relations. Co-operative enterprises comprise much more than simply fulfilling an economic function: A legitimate and just balance between freedom and order rests at the core and heart of co-operative work, a sensible harmony between the individual and the community. It is the task of co-operative publicity to express this inherent nature.

In our day and age, publicity must not remain restricted solely to what is typically co-operative. It must rather include the entire gamut of effects and consequences! In public opinion today, the activities of a certain co-operative within its own particular branch are much more dominant than the *corporate identity* (→ *Corporate Culture*) of co-operatives as a whole. The objective of modern public relations for the co-operative system can be drawn from this: the visualization and popularization of the total economic output of a modern, affiliated co-operative economy as "productivity oriented collaboration". Co-operative magazines acquire their scope of duties based solely on these considerations.

I. Taking Stock and Background Information

First off, co-operative magazines are a reflection of co-operative activity. The periodical literature is just as multi-faceted as the co-operative system is itself, and ranges from publications for an entire "co-operative union or association" to "customer and company magazines" to "specialized journals". Based on their nature, they are not to be found on the open magazine market, and thus they are relatively unknown to the general public. Their importance, however, is by no means slight as they endeavor to stimulate co-operative trade, promote co-operative thought, document the effects of self-help, and increase the level of awareness – all in correspondence with the characteristic nature of co-operatives. In virtue of their internal structure, co-operatives are in end effect democracies which are experienced and exercised daily. They strive to promote personality development within the community on a wide basis. This requires a permanent dialogue which in turn necessitates above all the written word and its enduring effect.

The main task of all co-operative magazines is thus the permanent activation of a particular "we"-feeling: the acknowledgement of an ideal state of belonging together and the consciousness to participate in solving current questions of the day with a co-operative attitude (→ *Group, the Co-operative*). This is a completely lofty goal, but one hitting at the heart of the matter when one realizes the exigencies of modern corporate culture in the sense of "corporate identity". → *Corporate Culture* is itself the sum total of all value conceptions which have developed within a company as a social organization in the course of its maturity. "If one proceeds from the assumption that the co-operative...is characterized by the identity principle...then it is obvious that the group culture of the co-operative membership circle must be a particularly essential factor in determining the organizational structure of the co-operative. Co-operatives in this point have a long and intensive tradition" (*E. Dülfe*r, "Unternehmenskultur und Corporate Identity bei Genossenschaftsbanken" 1989). Accordingly, a dynamic exchange of thoughts and opinions determined by historical tradition is a criterion typical of co-operative magazines: they strive to give impulses, to achieve a higher level of both intellectual and commercial exchange, and to support the necessary involvement for collective affairs. Their intellectual roots are based on the ideals of "with one another" and "for one another" and guarantee a close affiliation between "member" and "co-operative". Information and identification provide their foundation and backbone.

The pioneers in this field were also aware of this. As early as January 1, 1879, the first journalistic publication for the territory of the German Reich of that time was published, *Das landwirtschaftliche Genossenschaftsblatt* (Agricultural Co-operative Paper), a predecessor to the later *Raiffeisen-Rundschau*. No other than → *F.W. Raiffeisen* was the responsible editor-in-chief of this organ; this task thus must also have seemed necessary and important to him! This likewise was true for → *H. Schulze-Delitzsch*, who, already in 1860, had decided on the publication of the *Innung der Zukunft* (Guild of the Future), a forerunner to the later *Blätter für Genossenschaftswesen*. All of these historic "precursors" later merged into the modern *Genossenschaftsforum* (Co-operative Forum), which is presently continuing this tradition. This is as much a general as a consistent development, and it would certainly be illuminating if one undertook to describe each one individually. In any case, all of these forerunner publications reflect the ups and downs of the co-operative movment in a very revealing manner and are convincing proof that the exchange of thoughts and opinions has always been a vital component of co-operative joint action. Based on the variety mentioned above, this predominantly is applicable for the classical type of "association magazine". Alongside this publication form, there are co-operative "specialized journals" as well as "customer magazines" and "company magazines".

Both the customer and company magazines fulfill different tasks. They are devoted to targeted information for advertising and are exclusively directed at the customers. Co-operatives also find themselves in steep competition on the market and more or less must make use of advertising if they wish to be successful. The situation is similar for company magazines, which endeavor to strengthen the ties between members and their co-operatives. Advertising and information are also priorities for them. Among the group of co-operative "specialized journals", corresponding specialized instruction is clearly given priority, even when from branch to branch this is understandibly treated with varying importance. Typical examples, only to name a few, are the *EDEKA-Handelsrundschau* (published by the EDEKA Union) or *Bankinformation* (published by the BVR, Federal Association of German Co-operative Banks). Because specialized knowledge as a whole has so greatly increased, they have long found their justification and will most likely increase in their importance in view of the evermore pressing tendency of qualified continuing professional education. At the same time, however, they are distancing themselves from their ideological core; "co-operative money" and "co-operative goods" simply do not exist! But because there are so many specialized journals beyond those of the co-operative organization, their boundaries are also set.

Let us now concern ourselves with the periodicals for the co-operative associations and unions. The *regional association magazines* came into being in Germany upon the establishment of the co-operative auditing associations. They were published by the state-level → *federations* and served to maintain the contact to primary co-operatives as informational papers – mostly by reporting about the work of the associations, thus however undertaking numerous subjects concerning co-operative financing and commodity trade as well as discussing special questions relating to the day-to- day business administration, law, and tax structure. Today in Germany, there are ten such informational papers with a total circulation of 40,000 copies per edition. Publication occurs either four, six, or twelve times annually. On an average, they have 340 pages, and most of these publications are for free. What is important is that the annual statement of accounts is published in these periodicals for all local co-operatives.

The prototype of the *modern supra-regional co-operative association magazine* is *Genossenschaftsforum*. This alone is so because it resulted from the amalgamation of the three largest co-operative organizations at the beginning of the 1970s structured along the lines of Raiffeisen and Schulze-Delitzsch and represented the entire co-operative federation on a nation-wide basis to the public. It followed in the tracks of the *Blätter für Genossenschaften* and the *Raiffeisen-Rundschau*. *Genossenschaftsforum* is the organ of those umbrella organizations joined together in the DGRV (German Co-operative and Raiffeisen Federation), which is at the same also its publisher: the DRV (German Raiffeisen Federation), the BVR (Federal Association of German Co-operative Banks), and ZENTGENO (Central Association of the Co-operative Wholesale and Service Agencies). *Genossenschaftsforum* can speak for thousands of co-operatives and millions of members with one voice and, as the only supra-regional magazine, can make the nature and activity of the co-operative as a "productivity-oriented collaboration" known and aware to the vast general public.

The co-operative union organization, which considers itself "unity in the multitude" and which presents itself as "productivity-oriented collaboration", is also reflected in the informational content of the *Genossenschaftsforum*. Thus, its mission in the field of information must be defined very widely. Just because it is a nation-wide publication it cannot restrict itself to merely reporting about work on its own level, but rather it must involve the interested public beyond this: the public must be informed about the undertakings and transactions in the most varied of co-operative branches. Interest for the characteristic co-operative nature must be aroused, and the role of co-operative activity within the context of economic and interactive social-political relationships must be demarcated and uncovered, analyzed and interpreted. Through this, however, the scope of information concerning co-operative internal activity must in no way be neglected. In order to make communication possible between the co-operative management and the economic and social-political surroundings, events, tendencies, and reports of the world around must be explored with co-operative aspects in mind . It is thus self-explanatory that, due to the extent and variety of co-operative activity, an inter-co-operative "glance" into the matters of others must provide information about other branches. It is precisely this dual task of connecting the individual types of co-operatives on the one hand and the general public on the other hand which gives this publication its typical character. Published by the Deutscher Genossenschafts–Verlag E.G. in Wiesbaden (circulation: 8000), this magazine is also highly regarded beyond the organization both, in Germany and abroad, for its treatment of management in co-operative systems. According to its by-laws, it also serves as the organ for publicizing the annual statement; it has a set cover price and can be purchased.

The *Zeitschrift für das gesamte Genossenschaftswesen* (Journal for the Entire Co-operative System), edited by well-known professors since 1950 (→ *AGI*), assumes a particular position in as much as it is exclusively occupied with scientific/academic subjects. It is discussed elsewhere more thoroughly what scientific findings this journal has recently promoted. We find quite noteable what the editors wrote at the time of its initial publication, namely "that this independent scientific publication does not wish to compete with the magazines and other organs of information of the various co-operative associations. The editors are aware how meaningful the work is in the columns of such magazines and how numerous the stimuli are, also for science, which arise from them." (*Zeitschrift für das gesamte Genossenschaftswesen* Vol.1, 1959, p.1). Here, we are primarily interested in publications from the Federal Republic of Germany because Germany was the country of origin for the co-operative movement. Nevertheless, we wish to point out a few corresponding magazines from abroad as far as they are known to us. Without any pretension of entirety, we wish to name:

International: *Review of international cooperation*, Geneva: International Co-operative Alliance (ICA)
France: *Revue des études coopératives mutualistes et associatives*, Nanterre Cedex: Fondation du Crédit Coopératif
Italy: *Rivista della cooperazione*, Rome: IISCLL
Israel: *The journal of rural cooperation*, Rehovat: Centre international de recherche sur les communautés coopératives rurales (CIRCOM)
Poland: *Co-operative scientific quarterly*, Warsaw; *Polish co-operative review; Bi-monthly journal of the supreme co-operative council*, Warsaw
Czechoslovakia: *Czechsolovak cooperator*, Prague: Ustredni Rada Druzstev
Hungary: *Hungarian Cooperation*, Budapest: National Co-operative Council; *Szovetkezeti ipar*: Budapest.

To what extent the development which will be traced in the following pages is also appplicable to these journals can hardly be forecasted here. The developmental trend which can be seen everywhere in the sector of periodical literature, however, also will surely not leave them untouched.

II. Structural Changes and Developmental Tendencies

Developmental tendencies result from structural changes in individual environments. Certain aspects of the future are thus chiefly presented in the type of co-operative magazine in which such changes, as a matter of experience, first become apparent. This is the classic characterization of the association periodical which has grown through time; within German-speaking regions, this is above all *Genossenschaftsforum*. As the solitary supra-regional magazine for the co-operative union, it is not in competition with the regional association magazines. It must, however, be seen in connection with them as they serve to supplement the statements and assertions contained in its contents. If there were not any magazines from regional associations, the task of *Genossenschaftsforum* would necessarily have to be changed. As it is, however, its task remains fairly intense: "This is a high demand. On the one hand, the obligation of a tradition more than 100 years old cannot be overlooked, on the other hand, the location, method of operation, and the goal of the co-operatives must be constantly redefined and adapted to the rapid development of our modern economies." The editors vouched for this lofty goal in the first edition of their new product more than fifteen years ago (*Genossenschaftsforum*, 1/1974, p.3).

This newly created periodical was seen as a great risk through the eyes of that time because it similarly confronted an original and unique situation: it did not have a clearly defined target group. Its readers belonged and still belong to the most varied of co-operative types in a plethora of economic sectors. On the one hand, this variety of sectors revealed a circle of interested readers that was widely divergent, on the other hand, it revealed a corresponding diffentiation in intellectual expectations influenced by the varying problematic situations on the individual levels of the three-tiered organization. One cannot speak of a homogenous group of readers, a necessary prerequisite for any magazine. Far and wide, there is no other such magazine with such a heterogeneous target group! *Genossenschaftsforum* was nevertheless able to develop satisfactorily thanks to the fact that it can base itself on a common denominator valid and true for all, namely that of the co-operative fundament as the common element of unity among the multitude. The building blocks ultimately remain the same, only the houses (the co-operatives) are different! It is precisely this co-operative-specific accent which gives this magazine a status of its own. It is incomparable in its unique ability to encompass co-operatives of every kind. Its subject matter should first and foremost be seen and evaluated under these co-operative aspects. By casting a glance into all types of co-operatives and by surveying the entirety, it likewise speaks for the entirety as "one for all". Through the course of the years it has actually developed an entirely new perspective out of its definition of function and mission, and thus also better prospects.

Genossenschaftsforum, alongside from being a source of information, is simultaneously becoming a component of a modern "corporate identity" policy, even if this is imperceptible. In this function it represents the unity of the entire co-operative sector, something which has also become evident through the constantly growing interest of outsiders to this sector. Business associations and governmental offices, economic institutes and journalists alike have long held this magazine in esteem as an illuminating source of information and use it as a "window" into the development of the modern co-operatives. The co-operative reader, regardless of the position he has as a member in the association, can completely identify himself with it. This modern type of association publication has left clear tracks in its path and has steadily enriched co-operative life in all its years both inside and outside the organization.

In the meantime, the entire landscape has dramatically changed. "The electronic revolution within the media sector awaits us, new communication techniques are gaining importance, and the torrent of information threatens to roll over us... These tendencies, clearly observable, must be taken into consideration in time if we still wish to reach our goal. Thus, the "we" will likewise receive more priority in the future than it has up to now..." (*Genossenschaftsforum*, 12/1983, p.529). From today's point of view, it is quite striking that the magazine questioned its course after ten years of publication, considering that circular letter services, computer technology and many other advancements have guaranteed a substantially speedier transferral of information for many years. In addition, it is well known that the amount of available information doubles every five years. Today's reader is confronted with the difficult task of filtering through a flood of information and finding what is of importance to him alone. This can, however, only be the responsibility of specialized journals, whose future in the co-operative sector also looks secure; as a result of their "advising function", they have the opportunity to go more in-depth into headline news and other short pieces of information. In the case of a periodical for a co-operative association, however, which cannot be a specialized journal, the following results: The original scope of the information transfer dwindles in importance. On the other hand, the "identification function" gains more and more emphasis. Touches of corporate identity and public relations make their way to the fore. The association it serves to both, present and represent, receives more importance in such statements than the individual co-operatives. A magazine serving as a so-called "brand name" for an entire group can hardly exist as a monthly magazine in the traditional sense. The circulation is too small and the mounting purchase price resulting from this would necessarily be too high. Furthermore, the number of advertisements for balance notification will also decrease because, in the future, Brussels rather than Bonn will be deciding who must publicize their annual statements when and where. Income from advertising will inevitably decline, making a monthly edition no longer feasable from the publisher's point of view. In order to guarantee the identification and safeguard the tradition for the future, however, one must be on the look-out for a new sort of magazine which can allow the features of the co-operative soul to be portrayed clearly. In our opinion, that could be a "magazine" which, with a modern layout, should one day assume the role of the *Genossenschaftsforum*. This would be a magazine which could thoroughly treat fundamental co-operative themes under numerous aspects because it would no longer be dependent on monthly publication, a set cover price, a fixed advertising income or on a circulation increase based on profitability. It could surely more or less be financed by all companies in the co-operative union, be printed and presented in a large circulation, better correspond to the communication demands of the future and, at the same time, achieve high levels of synergy. It should be presented in a modern layout and could, above all, provide information about the development of the sector as a type of PR-brochure, but not only for the board level both inside and outside of the organization. Today's economy and society cannot do without the development of this sector: self-responsibility in the co-operative economy!

Whether the development one day will actually take this direction depends on the insight of all those affected, as well as that of the regional association magazines, which are similarly endangered.

Pfeiffer, Eduard (1835–1921)

HEINZ STOFFREGEN

(see also: *Consumer Co-operatives*; *History in 19th C.*; *Kaufmann*; *Own Production*; *Rochdale Pioneers*)

Dr. *Eduard Pfeiffer* (24.11.1835 – 13.05.1921) was the first initiator of a movement of → *consumer co-operative* societies in Germany. Born as a son of a wealthy banker in Stuttgart, he studied economics at the universities of Heidelberg, Berlin, and Leipzig, travelled in France and England and came to notice the social problems in the early period of industrialization. In 1862, he visited the → *Rochdale Society of Equitabel Pioneers* and studied the first successful consumer co-operative society. On one side, he noticed that through the creation of an increasing 'working class', society was falling apart and that there should be institutions to overcome class differences and to integrate workers. On the other side, he realized that co-operative societies could be instruments for reforming society and the economic system (→ *Conceptions, Co-operatives*). The capitalistic system should (in an evolutionary process) be developed into a system of 'co-operatism' in which consumers and workers had a decisive influence on production (→ *"Third Way"*).

After his return from Rochdale, *Pfeiffer* established some organizations in Stuttgart: in 1863, an association for the education of workers, a consumers and savings club in 1865, and a society for the welfare of the working classes in 1866 (the beginning of non-profit housing in the Stuttgart area). Most important was the consumer association which practiced the principle of the open door to unite persons of different classes, pursuing their common interest as consumers. Within 2 years, this co-operative society had 815 members, among them 268 workers, 66 academic professions, 191 other civil servants, 73 traders, 63 craftsmen. The co-operative opened shops and a central store, it operated an active price policy (certain sales below the market price) and, within a few years, it became the biggest food retailer in Stuttgart.

Pfeiffer published his ideas in two important books: "Über Genossenschaftswesen. Was ist der Arbeiterstand in der heutigen Gesellschaft? Und was kann er werden?" (On cooperation. What is the working class in contemporary society? And what could it become? – 1863), and "Die Consumvereine, ihr Wesen und Wirken – nebst einer praktischen Anleitung zu deren Gründung und Einrichtung" (Consumers' associations, their nature and work – with practical instructions for their establishment – 1865). In the beginning, he looked at consumer co-operatives as a preliminary stage for organizing production on co-operative principles – but later found that organizing consumers was an objective in its own importance.

Although the Stuttgart consumer co-operative society under the guidance of Pfeiffer developed rapidly through introducing new business techniques, *Pfeiffer* realized that there was a much bigger potential, if all consumer co-operatives could form one federation and organize bulk-buying or even production according to the needs of their members (→ *Own Production*). This of course, meant the beginning of a conflict with established market structures like retail traders, craftsmen and their organizations.

Pfeiffer saw a consumer movement as a special form of organization which had to fulfill the mission of transforming the whole economic structure (→ *Economic Order*). He, therefore, consequently foresaw conflicting interests with other co-operative organizations of rather middle class membership.

Realizing that a big number of → *consumer co-operatives* had recently been established and hundreds were in the process of foundation, *Pfeiffer* hoped for a strong movement. Therefore, in 1867, he initiated the formation of a 'Verband Deutscher Consum–Vereine' (VDC – Federation of German Consumers' Associations)(→ *Federations*). This first attempt to unite all consumer co-operative societies in Germany was not very successful. Many already existing societies which were affiliated to the General Federation of German Co-operative Societies (→ *Schulze-Delitzsch*) refused to join the new organization. This was especially true for the societies in the northern part of Germany. Thus, the VDC was limited to a smaller number of societies, mainly in the south-west of Germany, with a central office in Stuttgart. Nevertheless, it was taking very specific actions to promote consumer co-operatives.

This proved to be necessary, as some interests of consumer co-operative societies were directly opposed to those of other co-operatives. The General Federation (*Schulze-Delitzsch*) was definitely taking the views of credit and supply societies (especially for craftsmen). If it wasn't for *Pfeiffer* and his federation, the opinion of the consumer co-operatives would have remained unheard.

The most important conflict was the question of liability in the envisaged co-operative law. *Schulze-Delitzsch* expressed that the unlimited personal liability of each member for all debts of a co-operative society was an essential element and should be compulsory for all societies. It would create an attitude of → *solidarity* among the members and increase their credit worthiness – an aspect certainly being true for small societies of entrepreneurs.

But *Pfeiffer* foresaw consumer co-operatives (based on cash sales with little need for outside → *financing*) to develop into big enterprises of tens of thousands of members. He hoped that particularly wealthy people would also join co-operatives together with poorer workers and widows. He argued that consumer co-operatives did not need a liability at all – but if the law should enforce it, it should offer the choice for a limited liability. Consequently, the third annual congress of VDC (in 1869 in Mannheim) voted in this direction – opposing *Schulze*.

But the efforts failed; *Schulze* convinced nearly every legislator in Germany to include his recommended form of liability – thus, throughout Germany (except for Bavaria and Saxonia), the consumer co-operatives after 1871 had no choice of liability – so many of them chose to remain outside the co-operative law, thereby losing the advantages of this particular law (→ *History in 19th C.*).

Only in 1889, when a new co-operative law was introduced, this mistake was corrected. *Pfeiffer's* ideas had been proven right – but it took nearly 20 years, too long a period of time, when consumer co-operatives had to live with the handicap of a less suitable law. This and other arguments showed that *Pfeiffer* also used ideas from abroad, for instance from England. He was well aware of the necessity for an international exchange of experiences. So he studied the French co-operative set-up in Paris in 1866 and participated in the London co-operative congress of 1869. He learnt about the importance of supplies on wholesale terms as the Co-operative Wholesale Society (established by Lancashire co-operative societies in 1863) and the Scottish Co-operative Wholesale Society (esablished in 1868) had started operation. But *Pfeiffer* also understood that he needed as big a number of primary societies as possible. Thus, he still hoped for a successful development of his VDC – and he needed this because *Schulze-Delitzsch* again argued against such a wholesale organization and prevented its establishment within his General Federation. But the VDC never got off the ground. The inaugural meeting in 1867 was attended by delegates of 32 societies, who unanimously agreed to establish this new organization. *Pfeiffer* wrote a detailed letter to 141 consumer co-operatives known to him – but membership in the VDC increased only to 51, some of them with double membership also to the General Federation. Until the end of 1868, there were 63 co-operatives affiliated with the VDC. 35 societies reported, revealing that only two of them (Munich and Stuttgart) had just more than 1,000 members, but 23 societies showed less than 200 members. All 35 reporting societies together had a total of 8,395 members, an average of about 240.

As *Schulze-Delitzsch* mentioned in the very same year, 1868, that he knew about the existence of 555 societies in Germany including Austria (out of which only 75 reported to his federation), that was only a very small part of the German consumer co-operative societies. The vast majority of consumer co-operatives at that stage of development were not prepared to join a federation, to be part of a movement – they rather felt they should develop on their own. This, of course, was disappointing to *Pfeiffer*. He was totally convinced that in the long run only a combined effort could be successful. So he decided to organize a co-operative wholesale organization on his own, even with little support. On June 27, 1869, the 'Einkaufsgenossenschaft Mannheim' (EGM – Co-operative Wholesale Society Mannheim) was established with open membership – but open in a true sense only to consumer co-operatives affiliated with the VDC, a limitation which immediately created big problems.

Although the big co-operatives of Stuttgart and Mannheim were founding members and Munich joined soon, at the end only 19 out of 52 VDC member societies took up business until March 31, 1870, (10 from Württemberg, 5 from Baden, 4 from Bavaria; it was an all-southern German affair). In 1870, the turnover of the EGM was less than 5% of the business of the consumer co-operatives within the VDC – thus, this central wholesale organization proved to be a failure: not even the VDC member co-operatives under *Pfeiffer's* influence recognized the existing potential for development.

Pfeiffer's vision came too early to be acceptable to the young consumer co-operatives and their organizations. The newly created superstructure collapsed soon: At the end of 1871, the VDC member societies joined the General Federation (*Schulze-Delitzsch*), and in 1872, the EGM was transformed into a share holding company – with the majority of shares held by co-operative societies. This majority was lost in 1873 and in 1875, the supply organization was liquidated, shareholders losing 42% of their capital.

After 1871, *Pfeiffer* refused to be involved in co-operative matters other than his Stuttgart co-operative society where he remained chairman of the committee until 1875 (and was elected honorary president in 1905). In 1868, he had been elected Member of Parliament to the Landtag of Württemberg. Until 1876, he held his seat as a respected expert for social welfare affairs. He promoted many social reforms and, in 1917, he donated all his private fortune to an 'Eduard-Pfeiffer-Foundation' to support charitable organizations.

Pfeiffer lived to see that, in 1894, a German Co-operative Wholesale Society (Großeinkaufsgesellschaft deutscher Consumvereine – GEG) was established (→ *Consumer Co-operatives*) in Hamburg, exactly following his ideas of 1869. But he never commented on this in public or on the further fate of consumer co-operatives as members of the General Federation, from which many were excluded in 1902. Now, they had to create a new organization, 30 years after the end of the first federation of consumer co-operatives.

Thus, *Pfeiffer* could realize that his ideas about a consumer movement and its supporting structure proved to be successful after many years – but it was another person to complete the work: → *Heinrich Kaufmann*.

Bibliography

Bittel, Karl: Eduard Pfeiffer und die deutsche Konsumgenossenschaftsbewegung, München 1915.
Faust, Helmut: Geschichte der Genossenschaftsbewegung, Frankfurt, 1965.
Hasselmann, Erwin: ... und trug hundertfältige Frucht; Ein Jahrhundert Konsumgenossenschaftlicher Selbsthilfe in Stuttgart, Stuttgart 1964.
Hasselmann, Erwin: Eduard Pfeiffer und seine Bedeutung für die deutsche Konsumgenossenschaftsbewegung, Hamburg 1954.
Hasselmann, Erwin: Geschichte der deutschen Konsumgenossenschaften, Hamburg, Frankfurt 1971.
Oldewurtel, Günter: Pfeiffer, Eduard. In: Mändle, Eduard/ Winter, Hans-Werner (eds.): Handwörterbuch des Genossenschaftswesens, Wiesbaden 1980, cols. 1336–1339.

Plunkett, Sir Horace (1854–1932)

ELISE BAYLEY

(see also: *Plunkett-Foundation, History of Ideas*)

Horace Curzon Plunkett is justly known in the English-speaking world as the father of cooperation: his influence has extended to Europe, America, Australia, and many other countries (→ *Commonwealth, Co-operative*). Although there was nothing new about co-operative forms of production and distribution, Plunkett was the first to introduce agricultural cooperation into Ireland, and his work there made Irish agricultural cooperation a model for the United Kingdom, as well as for many developing economies in other parts of the world (→ *Development, etc.*).

He believed that cooperation would help the farmer improve his position in at least five different ways: he would produce at less cost, carry his goods at reduced rates and in better condition, he would have greater bargaining power in the market, credit would be more easily available, and his voice would be heard more effectively at legislative level. He believed in self-help through mutual help which, with education and the principles of the Rochdale pioneers, were the way to democratic self-government, political responsibility, and participation in community life. He regarded government action as indispensable – to modernize farming and teach agricultural techniques – but he insisted that local initiative be preserved and that government should work through existent voluntary organizations.

He was born into an aristocratic Anglo–Irish family and educated at Eton and Oxford. But at 25, poor health and a pioneering temperament sent him to America where he bought a cattle ranch in Wyoming and for ten hard years gained the practical experience of farming and farm development he was to use when he went back to Ireland. He frequently returned to the U.S.A. and was one of the most trusted friends of *Theodore Roosevelt*, advising him on his agricultural development campaigns. The work market opening up for agriculture, and the Irish disillusionment with mere politics to better their state gave *Plunkett* the opportunity to start his own long and difficult campaign in a country where political dissension and the apathy of the impoverished and starving peasants hindered the development of new ideas. Although reluctant to enter politics, he realized that his co-operatives would profit from the economic and legislative resources of government and from an influential platform, and in 1892, he sat for south Dublin as a Unionist.

By 1894, some 60 co-operative creameries were in operation and the need for a central organization led to the formation of the Irish Agricultural Organization Society of which Plunkett was president. But for the Society to function effectively, instruction in technical agriculture and legislation were necessary. At Plunkett's suggestion, the Recess Committee of 1896 was set up and its chief recommendation was the establishment (in 1899) of a government department to foster agricultural industries, of which *Plunkett* was vice president. By 1905, there were 718 societies and *Plunkett's* efforts were now universally recognized. In 1903, he was knighted and in 1908, his admirers gave him the fine Georgian house in Dublin which bears his name and is the home of the Irish Co-operative Organization Society today.

The First World War and the Home Rule controversy turned his energies in different directions. From a unique situation as confidential consultant to both British and American governments, he worked untiringly for the promotion of Anglo-American relations and was largely responsible for the American intervention that finally brought peace. In Ireland, he used all his influence to unite the opposing fractions and became chairman of the Irish Convention – a conference of Irishmen of all parties to find a solution to the situation. But despite his efforts the Convention proved abortive: he was converted to the idea of Dominion Home Rule for Ireland and became a member of the Senate of the Free State until 1923.

His beautiful Irish home was destroyed in the ensuing Anglo–Irish war and, in 1923, disillusioned and in constant pain, he made his home in England, to continue nevertheless his work in the cause of cooperation. In 1919, he had established the → *Plunkett Foundation* to work for rural, social, and economic development – a policy summed up in the words "better farming, better business, better living" – and in 1924, he convened the first International Conference on Agricultural Cooperation where, on the recommendation of the delegates from Commonwealth countries, it was decided that the Foundation, with its fine library, should become a clearing house of information for the service of agricultural cooperation throughout the world (→ *International Co-operative Organizations*). Although he gave more time now to England – suggesting ideas of co-operative research to the Agricultural Economics Research Institute at Oxford, setting up rural community councils – he went to South Africa and reviewed the agricultural situation for the Cabinet there and contributed a memorandum on co-operative organization to the Royal Commission on Agriculture in India. In 1929, at the age of 75, he learnt to fly and in 1932, he died at his home in Weybridge. A stoic and an idealist who believed that all human progress is a question of individual moral progress and development of character, he has left the record of a noble and creative mind and a profound and perceptive sensibility in a considerable number of political and co-operative books and pamphlets, and in the correspondence and diaries which he kept daily thoughout his life.

Bibliography

Digby, Margaret: Horace Plunkett: An Anglo American Irishman, Basil Blackwell 1949.

West, Trevor: Horace Plunkett – Co-operation and Politics: An Irish Biography, Colin Smythe 1986.

Plunkett Foundation, The

EDGAR PARNELL

(see also: *Plunkett, Sir Horace; International Co-operative Organanizations; Commonwealth, Co-operative; Development Policy*)

I. Nature and Purpose; II. Objectives and Activities; III. Publications.

I. Nature and Purpose

The Plunkett Foundation is a UK-based independent organization with over 70 years' experience of international activity in assisting people to develop enterprises that improve their economic wellbeing and thus, their quality of life. It is actively involved in the study and development of co-operatives, particularly member-controlled organizations and other types of rural (→ *Rural Co-operatives*) and urban self-managed enterprises in both established and emerging market economies. It is engaged in assisting development and economic restructuring both in the UK and overseas through a "people-centred" and institution-building approach. It works to improve the effectiveness of co-operative enterprises by providing consultancy, information and training services (→ *Consulting*). The purpose of the Foundation is summed up in an adapted form of its Founder's famous slogan: *Better Business – Better Living* (→ *Principles*).

The Foundation was established in 1919 by → *Sir Horace Curzon Plunkett* as an educational trust with charitable status and is registered as a company limited by guarantee. It has established two other bodies: its training arm, the Agricultural Co-operative Training Council (ACTC), and Plunkett Services Ltd., which offers consultancy services to PCBs on a commercial basis. It is supported by patrons of distinguished international standing and a worldwide network of members and associates; and the policies of its Board of Trustees are carried out by its Director and his team of professional support staff, together with external consultants and technical experts. The Foundation also undertakes assignments for, or is in partnership with other organizations. It is financed through the services it provides, with a small income from members' subscriptions, donations and occasional grants.

The Plunkett Foundation provides its services to co-operatives and other people-centred businesses; development agencies and other NGOs; governments and quasi-government bodies; international organizations; and individuals interested in improving their knowledge of "people-centred businesses" (PCBs).

The Foundation is an active member of the → *International Co-operative Alliance* (ICA), and represents the Federation of Agricultural Co-operatives (UK) Ltd. on several Working Groups of the General Committee for Agricultural Cooperation in the EC (COGECA). It is a founder member of ECORD, a consortium of nine leading European agricultural and co-operative organizations formed to provide services to Eastern and Central Europe and the newly independent states of the former USSR. It is also actively involved in the UK Co-operative Council, formed to bring together all the co-operative sectors in the UK.

The Patrons of the Plunkett Foundation are:
- Lord Plumb DL, MEP
- Lord Carter
- Inoke Faletau
- Prof. Dr. Hans-H. Münkner

Chairman: P.M. Bolam
Vice Chairman: J.D. Thirkell
Director: E. Parnell

II. Objectives and Activities

The Plunkett Foundation was established to support the development of enterprises which can bring benefits to people who are seeking to provide themselves with goods, services, and other benefits on a mutual self-help basis. The Foundation is in the business of achieving human development by means of assisting people to develop enterprises which improve their economic well-being, and by this means improve their quality of life, with a particular focus upon those in rural areas.

The prime objectives of the Plunkett Foundation are to:

- *promote* and develop enterprises, particularly co-operatives, farmer-controlled organizations, and other "people-centred businesses", which are driven by the purpose of providing services and other benefits to those involved in them, on a self-help and mutual basis;
- *assist* in improving the viability and effectiveness of such enterprises, in other words: to strengthen their capacity to provide tangible benefits to their members, by means of:
- developing the abilities and performance of the people involved, specifically directors, managers and staff;
- instigating and implementing appropriate systems of organization, governance, and management;
- *initiate* and strengthen organizations and agencies capable of providing support, developmental assistance and training to co-operatives and other people-centred businesses, that is, voluntary and self-sustaining enterprises which encourage people to take responsibility for the process of their own development;
- *formulate* strategies for the implementation of a public policy environment which facilitates the establishment and growth of such enterprises, in particular by ensuring effective equality with other

forms of business, by the provision of a positive framework of legislation and fiscal policies, and by inclusion in the educational system;
- *faciliate* the exchange of experience and information about all aspects of enterprises on an international basis;
- *enable* the provision of training and other means of developing the people involved in the development and operations of people-centred businesses.

The Foundation's activities include:
Consultancy and Advisory Services

- Feasibility and socio-economic studies to examine the possibilities for co-operative growth.
- Advice to governments on co-operative legislation, rural development strategy, and institutional development for the promotion and development of people-centred business.
- Assistance to governments in formulating a public policy to provide the infrastructure for the growth of successful co-operatives.
- Project identification, planning, monitoring, and evaluation.

Project Management
- Major long-term development projects
- Components of short-term national or regional projects in developing countries, Eastern and Central Europe and CIS countries; for UN agencies, European Commission, UK Government, et al.

Research and Policy Development
- Co-operative and institutional development
- Rural development strategy
- Organizational models
- Capital structures
- Farmers' organizations on a national, European and project basis

Information and Communication Services
- Specialized Library and Information Unit containing material on all sectors and aspects of co-operative activity, with full bibliographic service.
- Own annual and occasional publications; mailorder service of books on co-operatives and other people-centred organizations by other publishers.
- Conferences in UK for agricultural co-operative policy-makers to create awareness of matters of current concern and to act as forums for discussion.
- Statistical service and UK agricultural co-operative database.

Study Programmes (→ Education, etc.)
- 3/4 week group planning and familiarization programmes in UK for European and overseas' development policy makers, co-operative managers and members (workshops to identify issues and plan strategies complemented by visits to study UK co-operatives and relevant organizations).

Training
to improve organizational performance and personal skills.
- 2/5 day courses for directors, managers, and staff of UK farmers' associations.
- Short and long courses in Europe and developing countries for planners, trainers, development workers, managers, and members of farmers' and other people-centred businesses.

III. Publications

Publications of the Plunkett Foundation are:

Periodicals:
Yearbook of Co-operative Enterprise
Directory of Agricultural Co-operatives
and Other Farmer-Controlled Businesses in the UK
Facts and Figures about Agricultural Co-operatives

Occasional:
People-Centred Businesses (1991)
Farmer-Controlled Businesses: Bringing Balance to the Market Place (1992)
Farmer-Centred Enterprise for Agricultural Development (1989)
Co-operative Law in Practice (1989)

International Newsletter:
Focus on Plunkett

Bibliography

Digby, Margaret (ed.): Yearbook of Agricultural Co-operation 1969, Basil Blackwell 1969.
Morley, J. A. E.: British Agricultural Co-operatives, Hutchinson Benham 1975.

Policies for the Promotion of Co-operatives in Developing Countries

ALFRED HANEL

(see also: *Development Policy*; *Self-help Organizations*; *British–Indian Pattern*; *Strategies when Establishing Co-operatives*; *Pre-co-operative Forms*; *Autochthonous Co-operatives*; *Informal Co-operatives*, *Officialization*)

I. Introduction; II. Historical Review of Policies for Promoting Co-operatives; III. Analytical Overview of Promotion Policies for Co-operative (Self-Help) Organizations; IV. Selected Aspects and Problems of Direct Support.

I. Introduction

Co-operative organizations have been created in most developing countries as legally registered ("legal" or "modern") co-operative societies or as so-called traditional, indigenous, or informal co-operative organizations. The term "co-operative" is mainly used to characterize the legally registered co-operative societies. The "modern" co-operatives were initiated in some developing countries as early as the end of the last century. Although immigrants from Europe, missionaries, local people and private institutions have worked as co-operative pioneers and initiators, it has been mostly public sponsorship which increased the number of co-operatives, particularly in the rural areas.

II. Historical Review of Policies for Promoting Co-operatives

1. The Early Period

In developing regions attempts have been made at creating favorable conditions for offering prospective members both incentives and the chance to establish co-operative → *self-help organizations* on their own initiative and with the help of private promoters. Thus, co-operative laws were passed in many countries in the first half of this century and – although in varying degrees – indirect support policies (such as assistance in information, education, training, auditing, consultation, tax reduction and financial aid) were implemented. Based on the → *"British–Indian Pattern of Co-operative Development"*, the ("classical") concept of direct governmental initiation of co-operative self-help organizations was developed, which became the model of designing support strategies for co-operatives, especially in the rural areas of many developing countries. According to this concept and in addition to indirect policies, government "promoters" should initiate, motivate and enable (prospective) members to create their own co-operative through self-help activities.

After a comparatively brief learning process, usually in the form of a "pre-co-operative" (→ *Pre-co-operative Forms*), these co-operatives should be able to assert themselves successfully on the markets as relatively autonomous self-help organizations in close cooperation with secondary and tertiary co-operative institutions established simultaneously. Such strategies have been successfully put into effect in various African and Asian countries.

However, in backward, still subsistence-economy-oriented and "poor" regions, the development of viable co-operatives turned out to be a long learning process, and small farmers had often only limited possibilities to contribute to the promotional potential of the co-operatives and to participate effectively in the promotional services. Thus, in the de-colonialization phase and in the First UN-Development-Decade when governments were interested in a rapid spread of co-operatives, particularly agricultural ones, the promotion strategies often deviated from this "classical" concept (→ *Development Policy*).

2. The Period of Political Independence and the First UN-Development Decade (1960–1970)

After the attainment of their political independence many Asian and African countries proclaimed "third ways" of reaching particular social and economic systems, differing both from "Western Capitalism" and "Eastern European Socialism". These "third ways" have been frequently referred to as particular forms of African, Asian (or Islamic) Socialisms and were mostly linked with high expectations of the co-operatives' positive effects on socio-economic and political development and on the establishment of a type of national or agrarian co-operative socialism (→ *"Third Way"*). Therefore, for instance in Africa, frequently "large numbers of co-operatives were created in the spirit of political freedom ... Economic viability of the societies founded was often ignored. (And in the "post-independent period")..." Most newly formed co-operatives reflect government attempts to put into practice their philosophy of "African Socialism". Emphasis is laid on quantitative expansion into as many geographical areas of the country as possible" (*Hyden*, 1973, p.9).

Although the orthodox Soviet model of using co-operatives for the construction of a socialistic centrally planned economy (→ *State and Co-operatives, Socialism*) was followed only by a few developing countries (such as North Korea, North Vietnam and Cuba), some elements of this concept were also attractive in other (socialist) Third World countries. Examples of this include the governmental administrative approach towards co-operatives and the use of direct and indirect coercion in order to enforce co-operative membership and participation; the state-control of the co-operatives and the subordination of individual member promotion to the instrumental use of the co-operatives for the achievement of national development goals; and the integration of co-operative umbrella institutions as mass organizations of the ruling political party. During the first UN-Development Decade (1960–1970), high expectations of manifold positive contributions to national and agricultural development goals (cf. *Dülfer*, 1974) by efficient co-operatives were raised in most developing countries irrespective of their political ideology. Governments often regarded co-operatives as particularly suitable organizations at the village level to efficiently support – with government aid – the small farmers and effect rapid socio-economic change and agricultural modernization.

In many cases, however, no co-operatives existed that were sufficiently viable, and small (poor) farmers could hardly be expected to be capable and willing enough to set up with their own resources (in a short period) co-operative enterprises able to produce the promotional potential necessary for the efficient promotion of the members.

Therefore, another concept (besides the "classical"

one) for establishing co-operatives with more comprehensive government sponsorship was developed. Thus, "co-operative-oriented (self-help) promotion institutions" (SHPs) should provide adequate educative, managerial, technical and financial assistance in order to motivate prospective members and to help them to establish efficiently operating co-operative organizations for their promotion in the short term which in a longer process should develop self-reliance and autonomy.

Although this concept seemed theoretically well designed, the strategies implemented in practice deviated considerably from the principal ideas.

The task of initiating and creating co-operatives was frequently transferred to governmental and quasi-state self-help promotion institutions (SHPs), such as co-operative authorities, ministries, ministerial departments, development banks or other government controlled organizations, and their power over the co-operatives was considerably extended. There was usually a lack of qualified "promoters" who were able to fulfill the functions of "co-operative entrepreneurs" in the villages. Besides, such available persons were absorbed into the rapidly growing bureaucratic organizations and overburdened with administrative tasks. Due to the often unclear responsibilities of several governmental organizations, they were, moreover, often involved in "demarcation conflicts".

Since co-operatives had to be set up as quickly as possible, the members were offered, for instance, undifferentiated financial incentives. Unrealistically high expectations were raised, and measures were also taken to either factually or administratively compel membership – something that was justified as being "educative coercion".

The originally intended participatory approach of promotion, based on information, education, consultation and aid for co-operative self-help was increasingly displaced not only by a paternalistic "top-down approach", but also quite often by adminstrative bureaucratic pragmatism. Co-operatives were often founded according to schemes laid down in directives and decrees which, in principle, provided for member participation but in practice scarcely allowed any adaptation to conditions prevailing in the individual villages. Furthermore, the co-operatives were frequently used as ("multi-purpose") instruments by local agencies for implementing various agricultural policies and projects (e.g. agricultural credits, supply of farm inputs and consumer goods, extension, and marketing of agricultural products in connection with market control and price stabilization). They were also used for carrying through reform programmes, such as land reform and community development. This often lead to considerable officialization of co-operatives, which was criticized in the subsequent Second UN-Development Decade (1970–1980).

3. Criticism and Improvements of Promotion Strategies for Co-operative Self-Help Organizations

In the scope of disappointments from insuffient "Trickle-down-effects" of previous strategies of industrialization and agricultural modernization, the co-operatives were criticized in the early 1970s for having not sufficiently contributed to the development of more egalitarian social structures, to the decrease of economic dualism or to the eradication of the widely spread mass poverty, predominantly in the rural areas of many developing countries.

The subsequent debates concentrated on governmental and international promotion policies and strategies which had been conceptualized to sponsor the development of relatively autonomous and participatory co-operative self-help organizations, but which in practice had often created structures of large officialized co-operatives, i.e. state-sponsored and state-controlled co-operative organizations (→ *Officialization*). Since the late 1970s it has been continuously emphasized that co-operatives and other participatory peoples' organizations could and should play a greater role as instruments of self-help for improving the living conditions of small farmers, craftsmen, traders, self-employed workers and other members belonging to the "poor" part of the rural and urban population. In regard to the promotion of co-operatives, emphasis is placed on the principles of voluntariness, self-help, self-government, member-participation and member-promotion, as well as self-reliance and autonomy. Policy improvements for promoting the "autonomous" co-operatives including the indigenous and informal ones, and the de-officialization of state-sponsored and controlled co-operatives have been proposed, discussed and partly implemented.

III. Analytical Overview of Promotion Policies for Co-operative (Self-Help) Organizations

1. The Relevance of the Economic System and Self-Help Supportive Development Policies

The design and effective implementation of promotion policies must be related to the framework conditions set by the economic system of the country in which the development of the co-operative is to be supported. The initiation and successful development of autonomous co-operatives and other forms of self-help organizations as instruments for promoting the economic interests of their members require the existence of sufficient freedom of action for the establishment of the co-operatives and for deciding on the goals and business policies by the co-operative organizations' participants. It is compatible with a system or an "environment" of decentralized planning and coordination of the individual economic activities in a country, i.e. with a basic form of a market economy – which may be termed as a "capitalistic", a "social" or a "socialistic" market economy. Thus, in compliance with national and sectoral development conceptions based on a market economy and global, sectoral, regional and infrastructural economic policies which provide an adequate basis for self-help activities and individual and group entrepreneurship, different concepts and various policies for promoting the initiation and development of autonomous and participatory co-operatives can be applied (as well as for other self-help organizations).

2. The Creation of Framework Conditions for the Development of Co-operative Self-Help Organizations

A general government concept – through which the "state" is active as an indirect promoter of the self-development of co-operatives – consists of systematic combinations of co-operative-related policies and instruments which create favorable framework conditions for the successful development of co-operative self-help organizations and movements. The main instruments to be integrated in order to create appropriate framework conditions are: (a) adequate co-operative laws and statutory regulations; (b) information, education, and training facilities; (c) auditing and consultation services; (d) equal or preferential treatment when governmental or quasi-state organizations purchase or market goods and services; (e) tax reductions or exemptions; (f) financial assistance in the form of credit as well as subsidies and grants in special cases; (g) antitrust regulations and provisions in order to prevent private and state enterprises from taking unfair advantage of their market power and discriminating, in particular, against the emerging co-operative enterprises. Such governmental policies which are adapted to the socio-economic conditions prevailing in the different countries can provide appropriate framework conditions in order to: (a) improve the opportunities for the continued successful development of the relatively autonomous co-operative societies and co-operative movements; (b) encourage the further self-development of indigenous and informal co-operatives; and (c) to make prospective members favor the creation of co-operatives themselves through the assistance of individual promoters and the support of non-governmental organizations (NGOs) acting as self-help promotion institutions (SHPs).

Such framework conditions can thus also provide an appropriate basis for the implementation of governmental strategies for promoting the initiation and establishment of autonomous co-operative self-help organizations in accordance with either the "classical concept" or the concept "of using more comprehensive support".

3. Direct Support for the Initiation and Establishment of Co-operatives

Direct external aid for supporting the initiation and establishment of autonomous co-operative self-help organizations is provided by public and private resources of the developing countries as well as by funds of multinational and bilateral development assistance organizations. It is implemented by governmental and non-governmental (self-help promotion) institutions (SHPs) and also by individual promoters.

Models for providing direct government support are (a) the already mentioned "classical concept" in which the "state" acts as an initiator of co-operatives, and (b) the "concept of providing (more) comprehensive government support", in which the state is the sponsor of the institutional development of co-operative self-help organizations. Since "state-sponsored co-operatives" have often been created, as a consequence of the latter strategies, this concept has been supplemented by the introduction of a "de-officialization phase" and designed as a three-phased model, like in Iran in the 1970s (cf. *Hanel* 1976; *Hanel/Müller* 1976) and in Indonesia in the 1980s (cf. *Soedjono* 1985).

Thus, the first phase of governmentally supported co-operative initiations and establishments which are state-sponsored to a certain extent is to be followed by a de-officialization phase in which these state-sponsored co-operatives shall be assisted in their self-development towards a third phase of co-operative self-reliance and autonomy.

However, it is widely accepted that further promotional policies should avoid the creation of state-sponsored and state-controlled co-operatives and thus the dependency of supported co-operatives on "donor agencies" right from the beginning.

In order to assist the governments of the developing countries in their endeavors to support the development of co-operatives, new approaches in the multinational and bilateral development cooperation propose the concentration of more aid for the direct promotion of so-called "poor" target groups, thus helping them to organize themselves in co-operatives and other local participatory self-help organizations. Therefore, for example, the "people-centred" approach of the World Bank, the "People's Participation Programme" of the *FAO* (*FAO* 1990, p.4), the combination of food aid with the assistance of co-operatives (COPAC, 1988) and the approach of "fighting poverty through the promotion of self-help" of the bilateral German development assistance may be mentioned. These new approaches include various types of local organizations which are not always clearly defined. With regard to the promotion of co-operative self-help organizations, some principal aspects may be emphasized.

IV. Selected Aspects and Problems of Direct Support

1. Some Basic Preconditions for the Creation of Co-operative Self-Help Organizations

Co-operative self-help organizations can be successfully created under the condition that (at least): (a) prospective members are not satisfied with their economic and social situation and have the aim to actively improve it; (b) they have concrete knowledge of an adequately applicable concept of co-operative organizations as an appropriate instrument of achieving their common interests; (c) potential "advantages of cooperation" exist and can be realized as the best alternative to meet the needs of these persons; (d) they are motivated to join a co-operative group and to make personal and material/financial contributions from a very early stage for the establishment of a jointly owned co-operative enterprise; (e) there are (prospective) members or external promoters who fulfill the entrepreneurial functions of creating and founding the co-operative and (f) neither traditional norms nor legal prescriptions hinder or forbid such innovative activities.

2. The Functions of Co-operative Promoters/ Co-operative Entrepreneurs

Experience from various countries now industrialized and developing shows that agricultural/rural co-operatives of small farmers and other socially weak members have mostly been initiated and created with the help of external promoters, often because such groups of members were not able to satisfy one or more of the above-mentioned preconditions.

In this context, the functions of the co-operative pioneers who acted as primary co-operative promoters should be mentioned – for example the → *Rochdale Co-operative Pioneers*, → *Raiffeisen*, → *Schulze-Delitzsch* and others (cf. Müller, 1976, pp. 110 et seq.). These pioneer co-operative entrepreneurs initiated co-operatives and developed specific concrete organizational concepts which were sufficiently adapted to the needs, interests and concrete situations of the target groups living in different economic and socio-cultural environments. These concepts were simple enough but also adaptable to specific socio-economic environments to such a degree that other persons who acted as secondary co-operative promoters or entrepreneurs and did not have the knowledge and experience of the co-operative pioneers could follow their example and apply these concepts in similar or comparable situations. Thus, the co-operatives created by the co-operative pioneers served as demonstration objects for many other secondary co-operative promoters. In many cases, the co-operative pioneers also established secondary co-operative structures and initiated the development of "co-operative movements".

It is expected that "self-help promotion institutions" (SHPs) fulfill the functions of primary and secondary co-operative promoters or entrepreneurs in the developing countries.

Because of the shortcomings of governmental and parastatal self-help promotion institutions it is often proposed to support the development of co-operatives and other → *self-help organizations* (SHOs) preferably through non-governmental organizations (NGOs) which are considered to be more efficient self-help promotion institutions (SHPs) than governmental organizations (GOs). In his research on NGO activities, *Verhagen* (1987, p.29) has identified the following tasks to be performed or "instruments" to be used for the initiation of self-help organizations and self-help movements: (1.) Identification of target population and target groups; (2.) identification of economic activities through participatory research and planning; (3.) education and mutual training; (4.) resource mobilization and resource provision; (5.) management consulting; (6.) linkage building with third parties; (7.) process extension and movement building; and (8.) ongoing self-evaluation and monitoring. These are general functions related to the creation of SHOs and self-help movements.

In the German bilateral development assistance (The Federal Minister ... 1978, p. 8; *Dülfer* 1981, pp. 57 et seq.), a more specific phased model for supporting the establishment of (primary co-operative) self-help organizations has been developed. In this model, the following seven phases are distinguished in which different combinations of supporting policies have to be adequately designed: (1.) "Initiation of self-help and design of an operational concept"; (2.) "Motivation and training of SHO founding members"; (3.) "Organizational and, if possible, legal foundation of the SHO"; (4.) "Establishment of operational capacity of the subsidiary business unit"; (5.) "Training in continual operations until independence is reached"; (6.) "Independent continuous operation still needing promotion"; and (7.) "Independent continuous operation no longer needing promotion". This phased model may not however be understood as a prescription for an administrative bureaucratic procedure, but rather as a guideline for a concept of strategic planning for the creation of co-operative self-help organizations. Since the initiation of a co-operative is an innovation in its local environment and may be seen as a "voluntary learning process" characterized by the "trial and error" of all its participants, it is impossible to predict and guarantee its success. Furthermore, it is likewise impossible to plan such an evolutionary process in a deterministic sense and regulate it through straightjacket procedures.

The (external) promotion of co-operative self-help requires motivated, capable and experienced (local) promoters who act as innovators in the sense of "co-operative entrepreneurs". It may be remembered that the development of concrete forms of successfully operating co-operative self-help institutions, which are sufficiently adapted to the regional conditions and to the needs of specific target groups and which can serve as "illustrative models" of innovative forms of cooperation, can considerably facilitate the process of their "imitation" and thus the "diffusion" of co-operatives and other self-help organizations.

3. Strategic Aspects of Designing Promotion Policies

It is generally emphasized that the provision of external managerial and financial assistance for establishing co-operative self-help organizations should closely follow the principle of "subordinating giving help to supporting self-help" and be oriented towards (pre-)contributions of members with their own resources. Furthermore, the following aspects of designing promotion policies for the creation of co-operatives (which reflect weaknesses of previous strategies) are usually pointed out: (a) the need to start from the subjectively felt common interests, aims, and risk-perceptions of the members; (b) the importance of an educative, motivating and participatory approach; (c) the promotion of small, homogeneous, and cohesive (local) groups; (d) as far as possible the integration of local co-operative-oriented structures and indigenous forms of self-help and cooperation; (e) the support of local co-operative promoters (local leaders); (f) the development of relatively simple institutional arrangements and adequate management systems which are adapted to the local conditions and oriented towards the principle of "appropriate management technologies"; and (g) assistance in the establishment of an eventual multitiered-system of primary, secondary and tertiary co-operative institutions in a "development process from below". These aspects are relevant for promoting new co-operatives as well as for supporting the state-sponsored co-operatives towards self-reliance and autonomy.

Bibliography

Dean, S./Vilcocq, A. (eds.): Food Aid and Co-operatives for Development, A COPAC-WFP Publication, Rome 1988.
Dülfer, Eberhard: Evaluation of Co-operative Organizations in Developing Countries, FAO, Rome 1981.
Dülfer, Eberhard: Operational Efficiency of Agricultural Co-operatives in Developing Countries, FAO, Rome 1974.
FAO: Participation in Practice, FAO, Rome 1990.
German Foundation for International Development: Government Promotion of Co-operatives and Other Self-Help Organizations for Rural Development (Seminar Report), Vol. 2 (DOK 1063 A/aS 79-99-80) Berlin (West) 1980.
Hanel, Alfred/Müller, Julius Otto: On the Evaluation of Rural Co-operatives with Reference to Governmental Development Policies – Case Study Iran, Göttingen 1976.
Hanel, Alfred: Basic Aspects of Co-operative Organizations and Co-operative Self-Help Promotion in Developing Countries, Marburg 1992.
Hanel, Alfred: Concepts for Establishing Rural Co-operatives through Implementation of Specific Government Policies in Developing Countries with Special Reference to a Three-Phased-Model, FAO, Rome 1976.
Hanel, Alfred: State-Sponsored Co-operatives and Self-Reliance, Marburg/Lahn 1989.
Hedlund, Hans (ED.): Co-operatives Revisited, Uppsala 1988.
Holmen, Hans: State, Co-operatives and Development in Africa, Uppsala 1990.
Hyden, Göran: Efficiency versus Distribution in East African Co-operatives, Nairobi, Kampala, Dar-es-Salaam, 1973.
International Labour Conference: The Role of Co-operatives in the Economic and Social Development of Developing Countries, 1965, 49th Session, Geneva, Report VII (1) 1964, Report VII (2) 1965.
Karva, Dattatreya: Cooperation in a Developing Economy, in: International Problems of Co-operatives, Third International Conference on Co-operative Science, Marburg/Lahn 1960, published by the Institute for Co-operative Research at the Philipps-University Marburg Lahn, Göttingen 1962, pp. 20–35.
Kirsch, Ottfried/Armbruster, Paul G./Kochendoerfer-Lucius, Gudrun: Self Help Institutions in Developing Countries, Saarbrücken, Fort Lauderdale 1984.
Konopnicki, Maurice/Vandewalle, G. (Eds.): Cooperation as an Instrument for Rural Development, Leicester and London 1978.
Kuhn, Johannes/Münkner, Hans-H./Hanel, Alfred (eds.): Promotion of Self-Help Organizations, Konrad-Adenauer-Stiftung, St. Augustin (Bonn) 1985.
Müller, Julius Otto: Voraussetzungen und Verfahrensweisen bei der Errichtung von Genossenschaften in Europa vor 1900, Göttingen 1976.
Münkner, Hans-H. (ed.): Towards Adjusted Patterns of Co-operatives in Developing Countries, Friedrich-Ebert-Stifutng, Bonn 1984.
Münkner, Hans-H.: Co-operative Law as a Tool of Development Policy, in: Tracy, Mary/Varady, Lajos (Eds.): Co-operatives Today, ICA, Geneva 1986, pp. 321–340.
Siegens, Georg St.: The State and the Co-operative in the Developing Countries, in: The Co-operatives and the State, Fourth International Conference on Co-operative Science, Vienna 1963, published by the Institute for Co-operative Reserach at the University of Vienna, Göttingen 1965, pp. 132–146.
Soedjono, Ibnoe: Self-Help Promotion by Governmental and Semi-Governmental Bodies (The Indonesian Experiences), in: Dülfer, Eberhard/Hamm, Walter (eds.): Co-operatives in the Clash between Member Participation, Organizational Development and Bureaucratic Tendencies, London 1985, pp. 275–296.
The Federal Ministry for Economic Cooperation (312–T72410–51/77): Principles of the Promotion of Self-Help Organizations in Developing Countries, Bonn 1978.
Verhagen, Koenraad: Self-Help Promotion, Amsterdam 1987.
Wörz, Johannes (Ed.): Co-operation as an Instrument for Rural Development in the Third World, Witzenhausen (FRG) 1984.

Pre-co-operative Forms of Cooperation

Hans-H. Münkner

(see also: *Classification*; *Autochthonous Co-operatives*; *Development Policy*; *Self-help Organizations*; *different articles on Development of Co-operatives*)

I. Definition of Terms; II. The Pre-registration Stage of Incorporated Organizations; III. The Pre-co-operative Stage in Developing Countries; IV. Conclusion.

I. Definition of Terms

1. Co-operative Society

According to the definition given in Recommendation No. 127 of the International Labour Conference of 1966 concerning the role of co-operatives in the economic and social development of developing countries, a co-operative society is "an association of persons who have voluntarily joined together to achieve a common end through the formation of a democratically controlled organization, making equitable contributions to the capital required and accepting a fair share of the risks and benefits of the undertaking, in which the members actively participate". (para. 12(1)(a)).

In this definition, the importance of members' initiative and of active member participation is emphasized, which characterizes co-operative societies as → *self-help organizations* for the promotion of their members' own economic interests (→ *Promotion Mandate*). It does not preclude that co-operative societies are used as instruments for development (→ *Development Policy*), however, it stresses that even in this case the members' motivation, interest and active participation have to be given priority over other development goals set from outside.

2. Pre-co-operative

The term *pre-co-operative* is used here to cover a co-operative society during all stages of its formative process, starting from the decision of the founder-members to establish the co-operative, to the election of a formation committee, the preparation and conduct of the inaugural meeting, the adoption of the by-laws, the application for registration, up to the registration of the co-operative society (→ *Register, Co-operative*).

A pre-co-operative is not formed as an end in itself but is merely a transitory stage before reaching full registration as a co-operative. However, this transitory stage may last for some time. Pre-co-operatives are characterized by their temporary nature and in this respect they differ from other types of self-help organizations, which are intended as permanent structures pursuing their objectives without the aim of becoming a registered co-operative society.

3. Economic Interest Groups

After the legal pattern of registered co-operative societies has become more and more sophisticated and complex, a new type of simple and flexible organization has developed that has a co-operative structure (i.e. a group of persons joining together to pursue their common economic interests by forming a jointly owned business organization with the object of promoting the economic interests of its members), however, without following co-operative → *principles* (e.g. open membership, democratic management and control, limited return on capital). These economic interest groups (→ *Group, the Co-operative*), which can be registered without share capital but for the debts of which its members have to accept unlimited joint liability, are no pre-co-operatives according to the definition used earlier. However, economic interest groups may transform themselves into co-operative societies, for instance in order to limit the liability of their members. In such case, they may become pre-co-operatives from the decision to undertake the transformation until their registration as a co-operative society.

4. Autochthonous Forms of Self-help Organizations

In developing contries where co-operative societies were introduced during colonial times as "foreign models", it has been widely discussed whether autochthonous forms of self-help organizations (SHO) can be considered as pre-co-operative structures, i.e. as organizations which are a special form of co-operative society or which could gradually develop into co-operative societies.

Autochthonous SHOs (→ *Autochthonous Co-operatives*) are indigenous forms of organization based on local value systems and norms of behavior, without planned influence from outside. The most common forms of such SHOs are rotating savings and credit associations and communal work groups.

II. The Pre-registration Stage of Incorporated Organizations

Incorporated organizations acquire their status as a body corporate by registration in a public register.
Unlike partnerships and similar organizations without incorporation, which can be formed by agreement of their members, incorporated organizations have to apply for registration and do not exist as the intended legal entity before registration is granted by a public authority. The period between the decision of the founder-members to form the organization and its registration is referred to as the pre-registration stage.

1. The Pre-registration Stage under the General Law of Incorporated Business Organizations

Under the general law of incorporated business organizations, the pre-registration stage is usually not covered by special provisions.

There are provisions regarding formation procedures, defining the steps to be undertaken by the founder-members in order to have their new organization registered but, as a rule, the legal status of the organization during the pre-registration stage is left unclear. It is, however, standard practice under general law (and sometimes even prescribed by the respective organization law) that whoever acts in the name or on behalf of the new organization before it is registered, is personally liable for any debts that may be incurred by such acts.

Without entering into discussion of the various theories on the legal nature of organizations seeking incorporation before their registration, it can be stated that the law-makers use the threat of unlimited personal liability of those who act on behalf of such unregistered organizations and the uncertain legal position of the founder-members as a technique to induce founder-members to pass the pre-registration phase without delay and to meet all requirements for registration as quickly as possible.

2. The Pre-registration Stage in Case of Co-operative Societies

In the case of co-operative societies, which are a form of an incorporated business organization, the general rules regarding the pre-registration phase apply. However, there are some special features of co-operative societies that warrant special regulations (→ *Law, International*).

Co-operative societies are characterized by their → *dual nature* being an association of persons and a business enterprise at the same time. Co-operative societies have a special style of organization and operation, they follow specific principles (co-operative principles), they can be formed without rigid requirements as to minimum share capital, and upon registration their members can enjoy the privilege of limited liability. These characteristic features have been taken into account by the law-makers when regulating the pre-registration phase of co-operative societies.

a) Assessment of the co-operative character of the organization before registration

In some countries (e.g. Great Britain) the authority in charge of registration verifies whether the applicants have modelled their organization in line with co-operative principles either defined in the Co-operative Law or in guidelines set by the registering authority.

Conformity with co-operative principles is usually assessed by studying the → *by-laws* of the organization applying for registration as a co-operative society.

b) Assessment of future viability of the organization before registration

As a measure to protect the members of co-operative societies, third parties dealing with co-operative societies and the co-operative movement as a whole against the risks of registering organizations as co-operative societies which have no realistic chance to succeed as business organizations, the co-operative laws of some countries contain provisions which require that the future viabiltiy of a new co-operative society has to be assessed before it can be registered (e.g. §§ 11, 11a Co-operative Societies Act of Germany, 1973) (→ *Law, National*).

III. The Pre-co-operative Stage in Developing Countries

In developing countries where co-operative models of organizations were introduced by colonial government, and where forms of organizations were transferred from the industrialized countries into a different socio-economic and political environment, forming co-operatives was necessarily a different process, because the founder-members of new co-operatives, first of all, had to be made familiar with the new rules and practices they were supposed to apply in their co-operative societies.

The pre-registration phase in developing countries became a learner stage during which the prospective members of the co-operative society were taught the rights and obligations of co-operators. Accordingly, the duration of the pre-co-operative stage was not only determined by the time needed to meet the formal requirements for registration. The registering authority and government staff in charge of co-operative development decided when the members of a new society were considered to be ready for registration. Several models were developed to deal with this pre-co-operative stage:

1. Unregistered Pre-co-operatives

As a rule, unregistered pre-co-operatives are illegal associations, if their membership exceeds a certain number and if they start their business operations before being registered.

Under British law, there are no provisions relating to the pre-registration phase of organizations and, accordingly, none covering pre-co-operatives. However, according to Sec. 434 (1) of the British Companies Act, 1948, associations of twenty or more persons (in the case of banking: 10 or more persons), which are formed with the object of carrying on 'business for gain' either for the association or for its members, are permitted to operate only if they are registered under the Companies Act, the Industrial and Provident Societies Act or similar enactments. Therefore, in developing countries following the British legal system, pre-co-operatives with more than 20 (or in the case of banking: more than 10) members which would start their business transactions before being registered would be considered illegal associations. The provisions of the Co-operative Societies Act would not apply to such organizations and their members, or any persons acting on their behalf, would be jointly and severally liable for any debts incurred in the name of the organization.

Also under French law as a rule the Co-operative Societies Acts do not apply to pre-co-operatives. However, Art. 20 of the Co-operative Societies Act of 1947 (which between 1947 and 1955 was directly applicable in the French overseas territories) provides for uncomplicated formation procedures which enable the founder-members to pass through the unregulated pre-co-operative stage without delay as quickly as they wish. They simply have to deposit copies of the adopted by-laws and a list of all office-bearers of the society (including their names, professions and permanent residences) with the local court not later than one month from the resolution to form the society.

This method of not regulating the pre-co-operative stage may be considered to correspond to the interests of all parties concerned, if it is assumed that it is in the interest of all parties that the group of founder-members passes through the unregulated pre-co-operative stage without delay and that the founder-members themselves can determine when to end this stage by meeting the requirements and by applying for registration.

However, in developing countries, where the co-operative form of organization still is widely regarded as a foreign model, the period between the decision of the founder-members to form a co-operative society and its registration is intended as a learner phase to familiarize the founder-members and prospective members with the principles and rules governing this form of organization. The registering authority has been given power to decide on the date of registration and may insist that members should first gain some practical experience with the co-operative form of organizations and prove their viability before they are registered. In this case, things are different and the European models of dealing with the pre-co-operative stage do not meet the requirements.

a) Unregistered pre-co-operatives under the British Indian Pattern of co-operation

In the former British dependencies in Africa, Asia, the Pacific Island States and the Caribbean, ever since the introduction of the British Indian Pattern of Co-operation with the Indian Co-operative Societies Acts of 1904 and 1912 (→ *British–Indian Pattern*), the pre-co-operative stage has been considered to be a learner phase, during which the officers of the Co-operative Department were supposed to train, guide and advise the prospective members on how to run their co-operative society.

This learner phase often lasted for several months or even for several years, until the officers of the co-operative Department were satisfied that the founder-members had learned enough or the future viability of their co-operative society was established. It was left to the discretion of the Registrar, whether a new society was registered or not ("the Registrar may, if he thinks fit, register the society ...").

The Co-operative Department (→ *Authorities, Co-operative*) tolerated and even encouraged the members of unregistered pre-co-operatives, which had been formed under the guidance of co-operative officers, to take up their business activities as provided in their unregistered by-laws, under the name of 'proposed co-operative society' although, from the strictly legal point of view, these organizations were not governed by the co-operative law, did not have the status of a corporate body, worked with unlimited liability of their members and could be considered to be illegal associations if the number of members exceeded 20. These proposed societies were treated by the Co-operative Departments in a pragmatic manner as if they were already under their supervision and under the Co-operative Societies Act ("proposed societies pending registration").

This way of seeing the pre-co-operative learner stage, which was implied but not expressly laid down in the co-operative laws based on the British–Indian Pattern of co-operation, is clearly expressed in the Zambian Co-operative Law of 1970, according to which the Registrar has the task to see to it,

– that only those new societies are registered which correspond to a real need,
– that the educational standard of members is adequate,
– that the financial means for the commencement of operations are available, and
– that there are some persons capable and willing to take over the duties of direction and management of the affairs of the society.

This way of dealing with the pre-co-operative stage which left new co-operative societies during the most difficult period of its development without the protection of the law and under the complete discretion of the Registrar, was considered to be inadequate and, therefore, models of registered pre-co-operatives were developed.

b) The Credit Union Model

→ *Credit Unions* which are a special type of savings and credit co-operative society based on → *Raiff-*

eisen's ideas and developed initially in the United States of America and Canada among salary earners, were introduced into many developing countries and have established their own worldwide organization, the World Council of Credit Unions.

According to the credit union approach of forming new societies registered either under the Co-operative Societies Act or under special Credit Union legislation, a new credit union starts with a discussion group of founder-members drawn from persons having a common bond (i.e. employment in the same enterprise or administration, residence in the same community or affiliation to the same religious group) under the guidance of promotors or with the help of educational material (guides, manuals etc.) provided by the credit union movement. During several months, these discussion groups make the prospective members familiar with the credit union philosophy. With their practical rules, the members learn how to handle the funds generated by the group. Only after these two preliminary stages, the credit union applies for registration and it starts its lending operations only after registration.

c) Unregistered pre-co-operatives in francophone countries of Africa

After attempts to introduce agricultural and other co-operatives of the European type into the francophone countries of West Africa between 1947 and 1955 (→ *Development, Africa*) failed to bring positive results, efforts were made in Niger and Upper Volta (Burkina Faso) to develop pre-co-operative forms of organizations in dialogue with the local population, without imposing rigid, pre-determined models and without making legal provisions governing the organization and working of these village groups (groupements villageois).

In Niger, the Union Nigérienne de Crédit et de Coopération (UNCC) established in 1962, developed a strategy of encouraging small pre-co-operative mutual assistance groups (groupements mutualistes villageois, GMV) of 30 to 50 farm families of a village to serve as distribution outlets for loans and farm inputs, as savings institutions and collection points for agricultural produce. In 1976, there were 5,300 GMV with approximately 963,000 members in Niger. In 1990, the total of village groups had reached 11.858. The method developed by the Paris-based Institute de Recherche et d'Application de Méthodes de Développement (IRAM) was to create each GMV in close collaboration with the inhabitants of a village as an original form on the basis of existing practical needs of every village, using a special method of adult education corresponding to the mentality of the rural population in Niger. This method of encouraging the people concerned to take an active role in making the (unwritten) rules of their own group, although time-consuming and expensive, proved to be very successful. However, in 1978 the GMV in Niger were given a legal framework and were registered under a new Act governing Rural Organizations of Co-operative and Mutual Character. The following general rules regarding adjusted forms of pre-co-operative organizations can be derived from the experience gained in Niger:

- collective membership of all adult agricultural producers of a village community instead of individual membership,
- no individual share contributions but allocations of part of the annual surplus of the group to a common capital account,
- participation of the individual member essentially in the working of the organizations (attendance of meetings, use of the joint installations) but not necessarily democratic decision-making according to the rule "one member – one vote", no special internal control body.

In Upper Volta (Burkina Faso), unregistered pre-co-operative village groups were introduced in 1966, promoted by regional development organizations (ORD). These village groups existed in a legal vacuum without written by-laws and without registration. The Co-operative Law of 1973 did not provide for such groups. The ORDs recognized them and gave them technical assistance and loans. In 1978, efforts were made to draft model by-laws for the approximately 800 "groupements villageois" with some 20,000 members. (Other sources mention 1,700 to 2,000 village groups with approximately 40,000 members). When a new law on co-operative and pre-co-operative organizations was promulgated in Upper Volta (Burkina Faso) in 1983, based on extensive dialogue with the rural population, it contained special, very flexible provisions for village groups, allowing their members to choose whether to use these village groups as pre-co-operatives or as permanent organizations.

2. Registered Pre-co-operatives

One of the innovations made in co-operative law in developing countries is the development of several forms of registered pre-co-operatives, based on the idea that during the indispensable pre-co-operative learner stage new co-operatives should not be left without protection of the law and without rules governing their operation.

a) Probationary Societies

Dissatisfied with the standard practice in countries following the British–Indian Pattern of Co-operation, namely, to leave a new co-operative before registration in a legal vacuum, but to ask the founder-members at the same time to start operations so as to prove their future viability, the law-makers in the

East African States of Tanzania (in 1963), Kenya (in 1966) and Uganda (in 1970) introduced new legal provisions for probationary societies, granting them provisional registration for a specified period of time. In this way, the difficult task of the Registrar to assess the future viability of a proposed new society and to decide whether it should be registered or not was made easier.

The advantages as compared to the former way of dealing with pre-co-operative societies are the following:

- During its formative stage, the pre-co-operative is given a well defined legal status by registering it as a probationary society, recognizing it officially as a corporate body, limiting the liability of its members in accordance with its by-laws and entitling the probationary society to open a bank account and to participate in programmes for the promotion of co-operative societies.
- Probationary societies have to indicate in their firm name the fact that they are provisionally registered. This reminds the members that they are given a certain time during which they have to meet the requirements for full registration and to learn how to run their society.
- Third parties are informed that they are dealing with beginners.
- The Registrar of Co-operative Societies/Commissioner for Co-operative Development and his staff can concentrate their efforts on preparing the members of probationary societies for their tasks after full registration, but they also have power to cancel the provisional registration at any time.

In the co-operative laws of Tanzania, Kenya and Uganda, provisional registration is an intermediate option between full registration and refusal of registration. It is only applied, if in the opinion of the registering authority the proposed new society does not meet all requirements for full registration, but if the chances are good that these requirements will soon be met. Where the applicants meet all requirements, full registration can be granted immediately.

b) Compulsory two stage formation process

The first legal provisions prescribing a compulsory pre-co-operative stage before full registration as a co-operative society were introduced in Senegal in 1960 (Decree No. 60–177 M.E.R.COOP. of May 20th, 1960).

According to this decree, agricultural co-operatives could only be registered after having gone through a two-year period as an Association d'Intérêt Rurale, A.I.R. (Rural Interest Association).

During this pre-co-operative stage, the members of such A.I.R.s were to be taught co-operative principles and practices (At. 8), local co-operative leaders were to be identified and trained (Art. 10), and the initial capital for the future co-operative society was to be accumulated (Art. 15). During the pre-co-operative stage, the management of the A.I.R. was taken over by the officers of the governmental co-operative development agency (Art. 11, 14). A.I.R.s received financial assistance in the form of short-term loans from the Banque Nationale de Développement du Sénégal (BNDS) but, in return, the members of A.I.R. had to market their cash crops through the government-owned marketing office (OCA/ONCAD). Loan repayments were deducted from the returns for sales of cash crops (Art. 12, 13). If after the lapse of the two-year period the A.I.R. failed to accumulate sufficient capital to finance the operations of the future co-operative, the Regional Governor had the power to dissolve the A.I.R. ex-officio.

This concept failed to work in practice for various reasons:

- The overriding objective was not to promote the creation of self-reliant co-operatives, but rather to reorganize and to control the production and marketing of agricultural produce and to provide an administrative infrastructure for national development programmes (Art. 3, decree 60–177).
- Membership in A.I.R. was supposed to be voluntary, but in practice, farmers could only have access to loans and marketing facilities if they became members of A.I.R.. Therefore, membership became compulsory, due to lack of alternatives.
- The co-operative development service did not have sufficient qualified promoters and trainers for the pre-co-operatives to serve the 12,000 A.I.R. formed between 1960 and 1962.
- There was little motivation for members of A.I.R. to learn how to manage their organization because the management was taken over by officers of the Regional Development Centres (CRAD), and the deductions for share capital and reserve funds from the proceeds of the marketing of produce were not perceived by the members as their capital contributions.
- Finally, it proved to be unrealistic to fix the period for passing the pre-co-operative stage to the maximum of 2 years. Some A.I.R.s continued to exist even 15 to 20 years after their formation.

The new co-operative law of Senegal of 1983 does not contain provisions on A.I.R..

A similar model of a compulsory two stage formation process was introduced in Côte d'Ivoire in 1966 (Act No. 66/251). Under this Act, a pre-co-operative (groupement à vocation coopérative, GVC) was defined as a "group of persons who have declared their intention to establish a co-operative society in conformity with the law, during a period of at least one year and at the most three years, reckoned from the day of such declaration" (Sec.5). Only after lapse of this probationary period, the GVC could apply for official recognition and registration as a co-operative society (Sec.6).

During this pre-co-operative phase, the GVC can commence its business operations. However, the founder-members are personally and jointly liable for the debts incurred by the GVC. Originally, this liability was unlimited.

The GVC model was continuously adapted to the local needs. When the original maximum time limit of three years proved to be too short, a new legal provision made it possible to renew the period if more time was required before a GVC could transform itself into a co-operative society (Act No. 72/253 of December 12th, 1972, Sec.5).

In 1974, the unlimited liability of the members of GVC was reduced to limited liability (Art. 2 of decree No. 74/139), the extent of which had to be determined in the by-laws. GVCs are allowed to establish unions of GVCs, a form of organization that is preferably chosen in Côte d'Ivoire.

After 10 years of experience with the GVC model, the compulsory temporary pre-co-operative learner phase was only retained for agricultural groups (Act. No. 77–332 of June 1st, 1977). In Côte d'Ivoire, more emphasis was placed on encouraging the initiative and active participation of the rural population but, like in Senegal, the GVCs were also supposed to serve as instruments for the implementation of government development policy.

c) *Pre-co-operatives as basic units of a co-operative system*

In 1973, the Government of the Philippines (→ *Development, South Asia*) devised a strategy for rural development based on the idea to combine the organization of farmers in pre-co-operatives (Samahang Nayons – Barrio associations) with the implementation of a land reform.

Only registered members of Samahang Nayons could become beneficiaries of the land reform and could obtain a certificate of land transfer.

Every Samahang Nayon had to build up a village guarantee fund by retaining a percentage of the members' crops in order to guarantee the amortisation payments of the land purchased by the members, and a village savings fund.

The Samahang Nayon was planned as a simple village organization for supply of farm inputs, collection of produce and in general for the improvement of village life. The group size of a Samahang Nayon was fixed to not less than 25 and not more than 200 members (Regulation 3, Letter of Implementation 23). The most important requirement for registration was that all members had to participate in a pre-membership educational course offered by government promoters.

It was not intended to transform the individual Samahang Nayon into a co-operative society, but rather to use the Samahang Nayons as basic units for a co-operative system in which several Samahang Nayons could form a co-operative society (Kilusang Bayan). In 1978, about 18,000 Samahang Nayons with a total membership of 918,000 had been registered with an average membership of 50. In 1990, however, only 1,126, i.e. 6.25% of the Samahang Nayons established in the 70s were still active.

The interesting features of this model are

- the strong emphasis laid on member education before and after admission to membership, even as a legal requirement of registration,
- the use of small and simple pre-co-operatives as grass roots organizations mainly for mobilizing co-operative groups while building co-operative enterprises at a higher level based on several such groups.

However, when analysing the results of this model, several problem areas can be identified, which led to failure:

- The combination of a land reform scheme with a programme of establishing voluntary self-help organizations proved to be difficult to implement.
- A uniform pattern was prescribed for the whole country without regard to large variations in socio-economic conditions prevailing in the different provinces.
- The legal framework was not flexible enough.
- The time tables planned for the learning process were unrealistic (10 weeks for pre-member education to establish a Samahang Nayon, 55 weeks for the education programme to learn how to run a Samahang Nayon).
- It proved to be difficult to plan and coordinate a nationwide education programme, to find a sufficient number of qualified and motivated promotors and to supervise their activities.
- The attempt to use administrative coercion to make the programme successful, failed.

Instead of encouraging the participation in pre-co-operatives, membership in a Samahang Nayon by many members was considered to be a burden rather than an advantage.

A model of pre-co-operatives used as basic units in a co-operative system was also prescribed under the Co-operative Law of Niger in 1978.

3. Neutral Model of Simple Organization

Experience with different models of pre-co-operative organizations leads to two major conclusions:

- What is really needed in the development process are intermediate forms of simple and flexible patterns between informal groups and highly structured and formalized organizations, which allow informal groups to enjoy the advantages of legal protection without forcing them to abandon their

customary values and norms and without submitting them to bureaucratic procedures and heavy supervision.
- Instead of regulating deliberately and exclusively the pre-registration phase of co-operative societies, as originally planned and practiced in most of the known pre-co-operative models, presuming that all persons forming or joining self-help groups do so because their ultimate aim is to form a registered co-operative society, provisions should be made for a simple type of organization, which may develop into a co-operative society or not as the members decide.

Experience and field research have shown that, at the grass roots level, simple and light legal structures which allow the members to choose their own path of development are preferred to pre-determined models leading into one direction (set by external planners).

Such neutral models of simple organization offer their members the following options:

- to develop their organization into a registered co-operative society (e.g. a pre-co-operative in the narrow sense);
- to remain a simple registered group below the level of a registered co-operative society with full autonomy to set their own rules of operation, e.g. to retain autochthonous forms and norms, to combine elements of autochthonous forms with those of "modern" organizations (hybrid structures) or to use the group to introduce new organizational patterns;
- to join a co-operative society as an organized subgroup (pre-co-operative in a broader sense);
- to work together with similar groups by forming a union of groups.

This type of simple and flexible organization, which can be registered easily and which enables the members to determine the direction of their future development, was first introduced in the Ordonnance No. 83-021/CSB/PRES/DR of 13th May 1983 (portant statut des organisations à caractère coopératif et pré-coopératif en Haute Volta, (Law on organizations of co-operative and pre-co-operative character) under the name "groupements villageois" (village Group). This model was later also adopted in Guinea in 1985 (groupement villageois et de quartiers) and is currently (1992) proposed in the new co-operative legislation of Cameroon under the name "*Common Initiative Group*".

These groups have a co-operative structure, e.g. they consist of a group of persons forming a jointly owned and controlled enterprise to promote the interests of their members. However, they do not necessarily follow co-operative principles of operation (open membership, democratic decision-making etc.). They acquire the status of a corporate body and their members enjoy limited liability for the debts of the group, they are exempted from most of the provisions of the Co-operative Societies Act, except those indispensable for protecting the members and creditors against malpractices. They can only be transformed into co-operatives, if their form of organization and operation as well as their by-laws are adjusted to the more stringent requirements prescribed for registered co-operative societies.

These groups can work without equity capital, if their activities do not require a common financial basis. However, if they want to obtain loans, they will have to meet such conditions as a creditor may require regarding collateral security or members' personal liability. Hence, the credit worthiness of these liberal structures will be a limited one, unless the members themselves take measures to increase it.

IV. Conclusion

This survey of the different models of pre-co-operative forms of co-operation is not complete. The selection of models presented was determined by the author's own knowledge and experience.

After decades of testing there are increasing doubts, whether co-operatives can be introduced from outside and from above by government agencies or development programmes to achieve goals set by planners, or whether they can only develop from within, i.e. by persons' own initiatives and needs to work together to solve their own problems.

Accordingly, the manner of assessing pre-co-operative forms of cooperation is changing.

The times of paternalistic governments, making legal provisions for pre-co-operatives in order to use the phase between the decision to form a new co-operative society and its registration to educate and train the members how to run a co-operative society and to assess their future viability at its discretion, are gradually coming to an end. On the one hand, the governments cannot afford to pay for such services of the required quality on a large scale and, on the other hand, the citizens of developing countries resent being guided as if they were incapable of running their own affairs.

Therefore, the *administrative approach*, i.e. prescribing or empowering a government authority in charge of co-operative development to prescribe a pre-co-operative learner phase – as applied for instance in Senegal in case of the A.I.R. model between 1960 and 1983 or in East Africa in the case of probationary societies – appears to be no longer appropriate.

A *technical assistance approach* has proved to be better suited, i.e. to offer the legal pattern of a registered pre-co-operative and to allow those founder-members of new co-operatives who wish to seek protection of the law and access to advice and guidance, to choose this intermediate legal form for a period determined by themselves before applying for registration as a co-operative society.

In times of structural readjustment, liberalization of markets and privatization of economic activities, the *liberal approach* may be most appropriate, i.e. to offer a neutral model of a simple light legal pattern, having a co-operative structure, which the members may use at their choice as a pre-co-operative form of cooperation or as a permanent form of economic grouping if they do not want to apply for registration as a co-operative society, even if they can meet the requirements for registration under a liberal Co-operative Societies Act.

Bibliography

Adeyeye, O.: Co-operative Development through Institutional Adaptation: The Nigerian Experience, ILO Co-operative Information, (1970), pp. 13 et seq.
Agricultural Credit and Co-operative Institute (ACCI), University of the Philippines: The Samahang Nayon Development Program of the Philippines, A Report Prepared for the International Development Research Center (IDRC) of Canada, Executive Summary, Los Baños 1978.
Bavia, Marilen J.: New Approaches to Co-operative in the Philippines, in: Plunkett Foundation, Yearbook of Co-operative Enterprise 1991, pp. 181 et seq.
Bensimon, Josué: Le Groupement Précoopératif, formule plus adaptée à la société rurale sous-développée, Revue des Etudes Coopératives, Vol. XLV, pp. 279 et seq.
Bouman, F.J.A.: The Djanggi, a traditional form of saving and credit in West Cameroon, Sociologia Ruralis, Vol. 16 (1976), pp. 103 et seq.
Bouman, F.J.A.: The ROSCA, Financial Technology of an Informal Savings and Credit Institution, Development Economics, vol. 4 (1979).
Camboulives, Marguerite: L'organisation coopérative au Sénégal, Paris 1967.
de Comarmond, Patrice: Structures sociales traditionelles et coopération moderne, Archives Internationales de Sociologie de la Coopération moderne, Archives Internationales de Sociologie de la Coopération, vol. 23 (1968), pp. 127 et seq.
Department of Local Government and Community Development (DLGCD): Co-operative Development Strategy for Rural Development, Manila 1973.
Dublin, J./Dublin, S.: Credit Unions in a Changing World – The Tanzania – Kenya Experience, Detroit 1983.
Gentil, D.: The Establishment of a New Co-operative System in Niger, Plunkett Foundation: Year Book of Agricultural Co-operation, (1977), pp. 153 et seq.
Institut de Recherches et d'Application de Méthodes de Développement (IRAM): The Role of Grassroot Organizations and the Involvement of the Poor in the Rural Development, Situation in Niger, Paper presented at the COPAC Symposium on Co-operatives against Rural Poverty: Successes and Limitations, Saltsjöbaden, Sweden, 31 July to 4 August 1978, SYM/78/07.
Migot-Adholla, S.E.: Traditional Society and Co-operatives. In: Widstrand, C.G. (ed.): Co-operatives and Rural Development in East Africa, Uppsala, New York 1970, pp. 25 et seq.
Ministère du Développement Rural, Secrétariat Général, Direction des Institutions Rurales et du Crédit: Le mouvement coopératif en Haute–Volta. Sa vie, son développement et sa nouvelle politique, Ouagadougou 1979.
Müller, J.: Basic Conditions and Patterns for a Social Strategy. Leading to Member Participation in Modern Rural Self-help Organizations. In: Baldus, R.D./Hanel, A./ Münkner, H.-H. (eds.): Government Promotion of Co-operatives and Other Self-help Organizations for Rural Development, vol. 2, DSE, Berlin 1980, pp. 47–56.
Münkner, H.-H. (ed.): Credit Union Development in Africa, Institut für internationale Solidarität, Mainz 1978.
Münkner, H.-H.: The Legal Status of Pre-co-operatives, Bonn 1979.
Münkner, H.-H.: Possibilities and Problems of Transformation of Local Village Groups into Pre-co-operatives. In.: INTWORLSA: Third World Legal Studies, 1982, New York 1982, pp. 174–192.
Münkner, H.-H.: Comment créer un cadre juridique approprié pour les organismes d'assistance mutuelle paysanne. Le cas du Burkina, contribution au colloque international du Centre d'Etudes Juridiques Comparatives, Section des Droits Africains, Université de Paris I – Panthéon-Sorbonne, sur le thème: Développement agricole et participation paysanne: L'exemple des politiques de l'eau en Afrique, Paris, 14 et 15 Octobre 1983, Actes du Colloque de la Sorbonne, Paris 1985, pp. 291 et seq.
Nguyen-Manh-Tu: Le droit coopératif en Côte d'Ivoire, l'étape précoopérative, le groupement à vocation coopérative, G.V.C., CENAPEC, Bingerville, sans année (1976).
Ouédrago, L.B.: Associations coopératives traditionelles et développement moderne, Ministère du Développement Rural, République de Haute–Volta, DC/SPCCDR, Quagadougou, sans année (1975).
Sacay, O.J.: Samahang Nayon: A New Concept in Co-operative Development, Manila 1974.
Seibel, H.D./Massing, A.: Traditional Organizations and Economic Development, Studies of Indigenous Co-operative in Liberia, New York, Washington, London 1974.

Pricing Policy Among Co-operatives

ULRICH FEHL / JÜRGEN ZÖRCHER [J]

(see also: *Classic/Neo-classic Contributions*; *Competition*; *Business Policies*; *Managerial Economics*)

I. Introduction; II. The Co-operative in Morphological Classification; III. Co-operative Pricing Policy.

I. Introduction

One of the classic questions of co-operative science is concerning the "correct" price determination of inputs/services involved in transactions with members. The range of propounded solutions encompasses the principle of "current price" in which the co-operative charges the identical price that its competitors do, the "active pricing policy" which allows the co-operative to pursue an independent pricing strategy of its own, and, finally, the "cut-price-principle" which requires the co-operative enterprise to establish prices which simply cover costs and/or expenses (*Henzler*).

For the longest time, the respective procedures involved in pricing policy were legitimized by principles which had been passed down over the years. The chosen procedures varied greatly from branch to branch and from federation to federation. The firm belief in the appropriateness of a strategy frequently superceded the economic analysis of the same. With this in mind, one can clearly recognize the advancement of this debate in the realm of German-speaking countries stirred up by *Hans Ohm's* publication "Die Genossenschaft und ihre Preispolitik" (1955) (The Co-operative and its Pricing Policy). *Ohm's* reception of American literature of the 1940s and '50s (above all, *Emilianoff, Robotka, Phillips*) for the first time informed the German reader about the possibility of approaching the co-operative by using the instruments of "pure" neo-classic theory (→ *Classic/Neo-classic Contributions*). *Ohm's* implicit rejection of thinking in "economic styles" (an analytical tool used by the German Historical School of Economics) likewise marked a turning point in the way German economists addressed co-operative matters and questions (see *Eucken*, for general criticism regarding the Historical School). The discussion resulting therefrom indicated that *Ohm's* conclusions, with regard to co-operative pricing policy, could not be considered the final word, but nonetheless, Ohm's vanguard role justifies renewed deliberation of his work.

II. The Co-operative in Morphological Classification

Ohm based his reflections on price theory on a particular morphological observation which served to differentiate the co-operative as a "new economic entity" from other economic units. The observed self-reliant co-operative character allows the derivation of an ideal type, permitting conclusions with regard to the "optimal" price determination of transactions conducted with members.

1. Objectives of (Co-operative) Cooperation and the Economic Means for their Realization

Ohm assumes members' pure economic motivation to underlie the formation of the co-operative. Members strive to attain the most advantageous individual economic results in the sense of maximizing utility and/or profit. In their endeavors it becomes evident that prohibitively small operational sizes (→ *Operational Size*) make the individual use of specialization advantages impossible (e.g. the formation of departments/divisions). This necessitates resorting to market services provided by specialized suppliers. Interaction on the market however indicates that in the face of market opponents using specialization advantages in order to achieve a dominant market position, the individual member enterprises are inferior trading partners. "Horizontal combination" and "vertical integration" resulting from the formation of a co-operative should provide redress in this situation.

Horizontal combination means the amalgamation of individual enterprises which transfer particular enterprise functions to a commonly managed co-operative enterprise. On the one hand, the participants of this cooperation can make use of cost advantages (decline of marginal unit costs) resulting from their sheer number as well as from the extent of their total demand and/or supply levels now facilitated by possible specialization within the co-operative enterprise. On the other hand, they can collectively improve their trading position on upstream or downstream markets through the execution of *"countervailing (market) power"* (*Galbraith*) made possible through the size of the corporative enterprise.

Vertical integration signifies the unification of controls over consecutive stages of production, which in the course of division of labor "broke apart" and/or were formed completely anew in(to) independent firms, affiliated to each other only through their market relationships. The formation of a co-operative and the achieved supervision of adjacent stages of production (represented through the co-operative enterprises) enable members to reap rents which, as a result of imperfect competition (→ *Economic Order*), previously remained in the sphere of their autonomous market partners.

As the co-operative enterprise should remit surpluses in their entirety to the members, the *principle of cost price* (cost covering price) is a necessary consequence of integration for the co-operative enterprise (→ *Principle of Cost Coverage*).

2. The Co-operative Enterprise as a "New Economic Entity"

Based on the characteristics listed above concerning horizontal combination and vertical integration, *Ohm* concludes that the co-operative enterprise is a "new economic entity" which, on the one hand, does not represent an enterprise and, on the other hand, cannot be treated simply as an (independent) establishment. The lack of two-sided market ties forms the argument against the co-operative exhibiting enterprise characteristics; *Ohm* sees such a two-sided tie as a constitutive trait of a firm alongside the combination of inputs (also see *Henzler*). *Ohm* namely does not see clear-cut market relations emerge between the members as collective owners and the co-operative enterprise, reason enough why the co-operative enterprise is also referred to as an auxilary or supplementary enterprise (see *Draheim* for criticism of this position).

Since it is supported by a number of owner-customers as a result of horizontal combination, the co-operative, on the other hand, is not merely a plant. These owner-customers, through joint action, integrate the "new" stage of production by establishing the co-operative; they collectively bear the risks of the business enterprise and submit the co-operative enterprise to their group decisions, whereby each owner-customer maintains his own economic autonomy. Although *Ohm* does not take position with regard to demarcating "integrated collective companies" with a particular free enterprise character (like a stock corporation), it can be assumed that he interprets the owner-customer identity together with the disassociated status of the individual member enterprises as a sufficiently distinguishing criterion. (From today's viewpoint, the distinction between the German legal form "registered co-operative" and the *economic* characteristics of a co-operative, regardless of the respective *legal* form, tends to raise questions concerning special regulations, e.g. those the by-laws of a corporate entity define, rather than those concerning the legal form; the term "co-operative stock company" should also be understood in this sense.) In the end, the principle of personalism is generally seen to distinguish the co-operative from other corporate commercial companies, and *Ohm* likewise accentuates this distinguishing trait with respect to the cartel.

Aside from the principle of personalism, *Ohm* considers other distinguishing characteristics with regard to cartels and other economic special-purpose associations. He mentions the utilization of productivity advantages and the execution of countervailing power and/or intensification of competition through the installation of an additional competitor. In contrast to this, productivity aspects do not play a decisive role for cartels and non-co-operative administrational business groups (*Ohm* means holding companies, trusts, conglomerates, etc.): here, the goal is rather the creation of (offensive) market power through the elimination of competition on one's own side of the market (*Ohm* does not address the question of classifying cartels for rationalization). According to *Ohm*, both of these reasons are sufficient to clearly draw a line of demarcation.

In closing his morphological observations, *Ohm* deduces that the co-operative is founded to provide its members with productive services, and that the extent of the claim on these services, that is the extent the member enterprises utilize the palette of services provided by the co-operative enterprise, also must serve as the measure of members' participation in the returns as well as in the risks of the co-operative enterprise. Thus, the *principle of turnover (sales) participation* with regard to the distribution of the co-operative enterprise's operating result directly stems from its goal determination, even when exceptions must be allowed for (interest on employed capital in paid-up shares, democratic principle).

III. Co-operative Pricing Policy

The following discourse should serve to reconstruct *Ohm*'s position with respect to co-operative theory – itself inspired by neoclassic thought – using purchasing co-operatives as an example, *Eschenburg's* elaborated version of the standard model serving as a reference.

1. The Components of the Neoclassic Standard Model Describing Co-operative Relationships with Respect to Inputs

The members of a co-operative are rationally behaving economic subjects seeking to maximize profit and/or utility. In order to achieve their individual business goals, they collectively establish a co-operative enterprise. This organization is allowed to provide (promotional) inputs and services exclusively to the co-operative members (owner-customer identity, *Eschenburg*). The members have a free hand in determining the quantity of desired inputs whereas the management of the co-operative enterprise decides on the transfer price at which the inputs/services are to be provided. The members are subject to neither a compulsory purchase clause nor a deviation preclusion with regard to other suppliers and goods. The co-operative enterprise, on the other hand, is obligated to provide services/inputs at appropriate levels as determined by the members.

In the short-term, the co-operative enterprise works with initially decreasing marginal costs (MC), which later rise; the average total cost curve (ATC) thus exhibits the typical U-shaped slope. If, for the sake of simplicity, the co-operative enterprise is assumed to have to bear no fixed costs, the slope of the average total cost curve is identical with that of the average variable costs (AVC).

With regard to the members, it is assumed that the inputs bought from the co-operative enterprise play the role of a limitational input m, the employment of which limits the output of x, the latter being the identical final product produced by all individual enterprises. The remaining inputs can be acquired in appropriate quantities at set prices and, therefore, can be combined optimally, irrespective of the planned output of x and price and quantitiy of m. Ultimately, all members should have the identical net marginal revenue curve (NMR) with regard to m. This curve is declining linearly and in each case independent from the activities of the other member enterprises. With respect to the co-operative enterprise, members behave as "price takers". They base the quantity of their orders on the transfer price and individually are so minute that a variation in their ordered quantities does not have any noticeable effect on the total quantity of M provided by the co-operative enterprise. Furthermore, members do not anticipate any potential reimbursement or subsequent claims from the co-operative enterprise at the end of the period. When all the individual net marginal revenue curves are added together, the aggregate (NMR) represents the average revenue curve (AR) of the co-operative enterprise. This results as the members, in order to maximize their individual profit, extend their input level of m to the point that the aggregate net marginal revenue curve and the individual marginal cost curve correspond. Because the individual marginal cost for factor m, from the viewpoint of the individual member, equals the average revenue (transfer price) of the co-operative enterprise, the net marginal revenue curve and the average revenue curve are the same. This can be illustrated graphically:

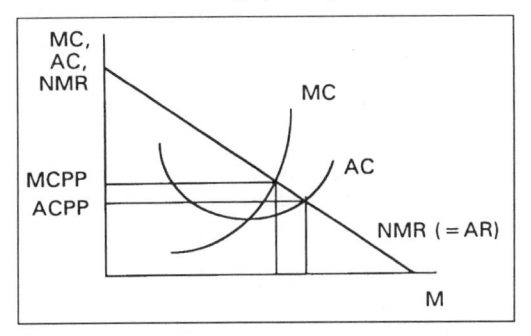

[Cost curve of the co-operative enterprise and the aggregate net marginal revenue curve of the member enterprises]

2. Pricing Principles According to Marginal Cost and Average Cost

The discussion concerning the optimum price determination for membership promotion through the co-operative enterprise, entails two contentious alternatives, namely the pricing principle based on marginal cost (MCPP) and the pricing principle based on average cost (ACPP).

In the former case, the co-operative enterprise charges its members a transfer price which equals its marginal cost at the intersection of the marginal cost curve and its net marginal revenue curve. The ACPP, analogously, requires a transfer price which corresponds with its average cost at the intersection of its average cost curve and the net marginal revenue curve. The alternatives lead to the same results only in the point where the net marginal revenue curve intersects the average cost curve at its minimum. The following discussion assumes that the net marginal revenue curve intersects the average cost curve to the right of the minimum average cost value; thus, the co-operative enterprise produces at a larger output level than at its minimum average cost using either the MCPP or ACPP.

It is uncontested that in this case (for exceptional situations, see *Ohm*, [1960]), the MCPP procedure effects profit maximization for the entire co-operative economic complex (i.e. the co-operative enterprise together with its member enterprises) if members accept the corresponding transfer price as the basis for their individual calculations (absence of anticipation: for evidence, see *Eschenburg*). This results from the fact that an integrated economic unit maximizes its profits if a production level is fixed at which the sum of the marginal costs from the consecutive stages of production within the company equals the marginal revenue the company, for its final product, can achieve on the market (see, for example, *Fehl/Oberender*). The profit of the co-operative economic complex is likewise maximized when the net marginal revenues of the member enterprises with regard to input m correspond with the co-operative enterprise's marginal cost for the production of m. This implies that the profit of each member enterprise will also be maximized given the validity of the principle of turnover participation.

Ohm, nevertheless, recommends the ACPP procedure as the optimal pricing policy. He, first of all, bases this on members' unanticipated reimbursement or subsequent claims which arise at the end of the economic period. This lack of anticipation produces a situation in which members realize ex post facto that their minimum cost combination, involving the utilization of factor m, were astray (for the moment leaving aside the assumption of m representing a limitational factor for the member enterprises): in their calculations, they simply proceeded from an incorrect final transfer price. This problem could only be avoided if the members behaved as "monopsonists" (*Ohm*) with regard to the co-operative enterprise. To achieve influence on the transfer price and/or marginal costs, and to be informed and aware of the resulting reimbursement and/or subsequent claims, they would have to utilize their purchase quantities. In light of the assumptions made concerning the quantity of ordered amounts, each individual member, however, is unable to exercise such behavior. This constitutes *Ohm's* second reason for supporting the ACPP procedure.

The adjustment of the transfer price to the average cost of the co-operative enterprise, in principle not only avoids false expectations from the side of the members, but also, right from the beginning, precludes incorrect combinations of factor inputs in the member enterprises. This preference for the ACPP procedure is justifiably questioned by critics as being theoretically incorrect as the MCPP procedure, without doubt, represents the "optimal" pricing policy for the co-operative enterprise when the objective is to maximize total profit of the co-operative economic complex (*Möller, Timm, Eschenburg*).

3. The Problem of Anticipation

So far, it has been assumed that members, with respect to the co-operative enterprise, act as "quantity adjusters", that is as price takers (based on the transfer price). They do not expect in advance any deviation of the transfer price from the (final) average cost of the co-operative enterprise's output. When this assumption is cast aside, the problem of anticipation arises (e.g. *Beckenstein*).

The members begin to ignore the co-operative enterprise's transfer price as a regulation variable and speculate on the total production quantity M of the co-operative enterprise and the related average costs (final price) at the end of the period. In extreme cases, the transfer prices may no longer play any role (namely, when members' opportunity costs through lost interest revenue (income) are not taken into account). Inasmuch as the members pay tranfer prices in the end surpassing the pure average cost, they, in effect, credit the co-operative enterprise during the period; consequently, they must also take into consideration the additional (opportunity) costs. In this situation, the neoclassic standard model only produces clear results under severely restrictive assumptions (see *Eschenburg*). *Ohm*, therefore, assumes constant reimbursement expectations among members, which in turn leaves way for a clear solution in the form of a parallel shift of the co-operative enterprise's average revenue curve to the right. When this curve is corrected according to reimbursement expectations, the net marginal revenue curve is the result; obviously, the management can then set "correct" transfer prices on the basis of this adjusted average revenue curve.

This makeshift solution appears illfated. The decisive variables for the members' plannings are not the reimbursements (which also depend on the transfer price) but rather the average costs of the co-operative enterprise (which are solely influenced by M). A reasonable basis for expectation can only be rooted in the latter. This results from the fact that each member can improve his individual situation by varying his own demand levels if the net marginal revenue of the member enterprises, based on their utilization of input m, does not correspond with the final transfer price the co-operative enterprise charges (the level of the average cost). Naturally, is this only true when the membership body is very large and inasmuch as each member can assume that the other members will orientate their behavior around the interim prices charged by the co-operative enterprise and/or behave exactly as they did in the previous period. (Seen analytically, group profit maximization and expected individual profit maximization become separate; for evidence, see *Eschenburg*). In the case the member enterprises attain a surplus of their individual net marginal revenue above the final prices of the co-operative enterprise (as the case would be in group profit maximization), it is ceteris paribus possible for each member to ensure noticeable growth of his individual profit by increasing input purchases and his own sales turnover; according to assumptions, this would neither have any noticeable influence on the total purchase amount M nor on the final intercompany price.

When a member expects a certain average cost level differing from that signalized through the transfer price set by the co-operative enterprise, this option becomes effective irrespective of the interim transfer price. The incentive each member has to vary his individual purchase quantity disappears when the expected average cost for the co-operative enterprise's input corresponds with its final average cost. In this case, individual variations of input purchases are no longer worthwhile. Obviously, intercompany prices no longer play any role in these calculations referring to the expected average cost. Therefore, a result similar to the ACPP procedure is realized ex post facto, if the calculations are solely based on the quantity variations of the members acting in their own interests.

In general, each pricing policy which differs from the ACPP procedure instigates the described speculation process in the delineated standard model as long as all surpluses accrued in the co-operative enterprise are reimbursed to the members according to the principle of turnover participation. Thus, the conclusion is drawn that for the management there is no reasonable alternative at hand to the ACPP procedure when the assumptions of the standard model are accurate: Any transfer price which differs from the ACPP cannot exercise a regulation function when the turnover participation principle is in effect and when members develop expectations and behave as to maximize their individual profits. In this case, members' quantity adjustment (price taking) to the *expected average cost* thwarts every effort of the co-operative enterprise to systematically influence member enterprises' purchases of inputs by varying interim transfer prices.

One cannot speak without further ado of the transfer price exercising a control function when anticipation is permissible under the premises of the standard model presented as such. The management would not have any reasonable alternative to the ACPP procedure if the premise was not set that members are "surprised" anew at the end of each period by differences in interim and final transfer prices that the management intentionally charges. This would, however, entail imputing a learning incapacity to the "ideal" members of the co-operative.

The sole unproblematic case appears to be that in which the net marginal revenue curve of the members intersects the average cost curve of the co-operative enterprise at its minimum. In this situation, group profit maximization completely correponds to individual profit maximization just as interim and final transfer prices do; therefore, no contradictory reactions can emerge in the scope of the model between individual and group economic rationality or with regard to members' anticipations.

Bibliography

Beckenstein, A.L.: Theoretical Analysis of Consumer Co-operatives, Journal of Political Economy, vol. 51 (1943), pp. 251–257.
Draheim, Georg: Genossenschaft und Erwerbsunternehmung – Versuch einer Abgrenzung, Zeitschrift für das gesamte Genossenschaftswesen, vol. 4 (1954), pp. 125–148.
Emilianoff, Ivan v.: Economic Theory of Cooperation, Washington D.C. 1948.
Eschenburg, Rolf: Ökonomische Theorie der genossenschaftlichen Zusammenarbeit. Schriften zur Kooperationsforschung, A. Studien No. 1, Tübingen 1971.
Eucken, Walter: Die Grundlagen der Nationalökonomie, (6th edition), Berlin/Göttingen/Heidelberg 1950.
Fehl, Ulrich/Oberender, Peter: Grundlagen der Mikroökonomie, (4th edition), München 1990.
Galbraith, John K.: American Capitalism. The Concept of Countervailing Power, Boston 1952.
Henzler, Reinhold: Die Genossenschaft – eine fördernde Betriebswirtschaft, Essen 1957.
Möller, Hans: Angewandte Preistheorie: Preispolitik der Genossenschaften. Bemerkungen zu Hans Ohm, Die Genossenschaft und ihre Preispolitik, Finanzarchiv NF, vol. 17 (1957), pp. 123–147.
Ohm, Hans: Die Genossenschaft und ihre Preispolitik. Eine theoretische Studie zur volkswirtschaftlichen Problematik der genossenschaftlichen Preispolitik. Quellen und Studien des Institutes für Genossenschaftswesen an der Universität Münster No. 8, Karlsruhe 1955.
Ohm, Hans: Angewandte Preistheorie und Grenzkostenpreisprinzip bei unvollkommener Integration, Weltwirtschaftliches Archiv, vol. 84 (1960), pp. 187–208.
Phillips, Richard: Economic Nature of Cooperative Association, Journal of Farm Economics, vol. 35 (1953), pp. 74–87.
Robotka, Frank: Eine Theorie des Genossenschaftswesens, Zeitschrift für das gesamte Genossenschaftswesen, vol. 5 (1955), pp. 155–175.
Timm, Herbert: Zur Problematik der genossenschaftlichen Preispolitik, Weltwirtschaftliches Archiv, vol.82 (1959 I), pp. 62*–68*.

Principle of Cost Coverage

JENS JOKISCH [J]

(see also: *Business Policies*; *Management in Co-operatives*; *Managerial Economics*; *Pricing Policy*; *Reimbursements*)

I. Description of the Problem; II. The Principle of Cost and Expenditure Coverage from a Theoretical Accounting Standpoint; III. Cost and Expenditure Coverage in Co-operatives from the Standpoint of Corporate Policy.

I. Description of the Problem

In the traditional theoretical literature about co-operatives the specific character of the co-operative as an executively operating economic unit is emphasized; from this it is deduced that the ideal, typical co-operative should orientate itself around the principle of cost coverage in its → *pricing policy* with respect to its members. This position is rooted in the notion that the co-operative operational unit may not strive for profits and that any such profits arising from the co-operative business activity should directly flow to the affiliated member enterprises via more favorable prices. The co-operative thus directly promotes its members in accordance with its fundamental mandate through output/service channels.

Discussion arises in this connection whether the pursued cost coverage applies to the individual transactions or to the co-operative result in a given period. The expenses in a respective period are logically covered by revenue neither through cost coverage based on units and/or job orders nor in cost coverage according to account period. Cost coverage can thus result in losses to be recorded in the co-operative's balance. For this reason, the principle of cost coverage is supplemented and/or made more precise through the principle of expenditure coverage. Refraining from an exhaustive presentation of the similarities and differences between costs and expenditures, we wish to emphasize here that temporal and tangible differences are distinguishable. Inasmuch as the temporal differences in the longer term compensate each other and can furthermore be influenced through the pursued assessment policy, analysis should accordingly concentrate on material differences. It can be determined that the so-called additional costs (costs – never expenditures) can present a more theoretical problem for co-operatives and that the apportionment of calculatory costs can be dispensed with in practical decision-making problems. What remains to be taken into consideration is the share of neutral expenses which will never become costs (additional expenses): so-called non-operating and non-recurrent expenses. These must be covered through revenue in addition to calculated costs. The following discourse addresses the question through a theoretical accounting standpoint and corporate-political point of view whether the principle of cost and expenditure coverage should be taken as a constitutive element of a promotional co-operative's corporate policy.

II. The Principle of Cost and Expenditure Coverage from a Theoretical Accounting Standpoint

When embracing a puristic orientation of pricing policy to the principle of cost and expenditure coverage, a co-operative would have to charge (assign) its members the share of costs for each transaction which arise through the particular transaction itself. This presupposes two conditions, namely that the co-operative can unequivocally determine the individual costs of members' job orders and that the common costs of the co-operative business operation can be allocated to the individual member enterprises and verified by all parties involved. A misinterpretation of accounting and co-operative theory as well as corporate policy rests at the root of this notion of "correct" pricing in transactions with members based on their operational typology.

The attempt to undertake cost allocation true to the origin of costs in individual job orders (allocation objects) is ultimately based on the fundamental thinking behind the concept of cost absorption. Costs accordingly should be allocated to those outputs/services which *incurred* the costs. However, such a cause and effect relationship does not exist between costs and outputs/services similar to causality found in natural science; if this were the case, output as a cause would proceed costs as an effect. Costs (seen as allocated expenditures for the costed operational input of factors), however, come into existence prior to outputs, which represent the outcome of the operational input of factors. Therefore, the relation between costs and output is not *causal* but rather *final*; the relationship is not one of cause and effect but rather of means and ends. Costs are incurred through operational decisions in order to fulfill certain operational objectives. The cost allocation resulting from this according to the principle of finality paves the way for a central pair of terms in accounting theory: direct costs and overhead costs.

The differentiation into direct and overhead costs is based on the allocation of costs to individual and/or allocational objects (here: members' enterprises). The calculated direct costs can be directly assigned to the allocational objects (the cost objective and/or source of revenue); in other words, no allocation formula is necessary because the costs are incurred for one specifiable object and can as such be traced back to a precisely definable operating decision. This is known as allocation according to the identity principle (*Riebel*): Costs and output can be traced back to *one and the same* decision. Overhead costs, in contrast, are incurred for multiple operational objects (here: members' job orders), and each and every apportionment of these overhead costs to the individual cost objectives cannot be logically substantiated. As a result, this cost category cannot be ascribed to individual job orders; it must rather be met through the sum of all contribution margins from transactions with members and non-members alike within a given period.

When basing calculations on absorption costing, overhead costs are divided among the products using allocation bases which are economically implausible. Such calculation results are characterized by their apparent yet faulty accuracy. The intended goal of such calculations (here the calculation of typical co-operative prices in transactions with members) is not achieved. It is a well-known fact that the cost information ascertained using cost absorption (the system being imminent with problems as it is) is not suitable for decisions about pricing policy. The calculation of costs for individual job orders is, however, in the end the accounting goal of traditional absorption costing and traditional co-operative theory. Because of the unsolved allocation problem of overhead costs in the various conceptions of contribution margin calculation, the ascertainment of costs is a task only solved to an unsatisfactory extent. The question about costs in individual job orders between the co-operative and its members is therefore amateurish and cannot be answered unequivocally. As a result of this no pricing policy adequate for co-operatives from a theoretical accounting point of view exists which is based on unit or job order cost information.

The question therefore is posed concerning the extent period-based cost and expenditure coverage can be a goal of co-operative pricing policy. The goal of such an accounting procedure would be the coverage of all overhead costs (with respect to individual job orders) in a given period through the sum of contribution margins achieved in the period (as the difference between price and direct costs). In price calculation, so-called planned contribution margins need to be taken into consideration alongside direct costs. These contribution margins are "arbitrarily" assigned to the direct costs resulting from the job orders according to the extent such margins can be enforced in price policy. The need for coverage (as a sum of the overhead costs and the additional expenses in a given period) is thus divided by the number of job orders expected in the period (similar to a procedure of process costing) in order to ascertain the planned contribution margins of the individual job orders. The assignment of overhead costs does not result from the basic notion of price determination rooted in job order costing. It can be more easily explained pragmatically than proven theoretically and accordingly does not lay claim to any theoretical co-operative or accounting accuracy.

The two elements of price determination, namely on the one hand justifiable, ascertainable (even when not unequivocally determined) direct costs and, on the other hand, planned contribution margins as allocated overhead costs are always indicated separately in internal accounting. The problematic nature of overhead cost allocation is thereby clearly exposed. The distribution of such planned contribution margins can be varied both temporally and in kind. Such tangible criteria include the size of the job order and membership in the co-operative; temporal criteria would involve seasonal deviations (increases or reductions) in the planned contribution margins. Such a pricing policy sets price floors at the level of the direct costs for respective job orders and poses the question of whether the distribution of overhead costs is enforceable in light of sales policy. This naturally does not mean in reality that the management of the co-operative business operation must provide members with all relevant information on price policy.

When the co-operative's planned operating rate proves afterwards to be incorrect, this means that the calculated and budgeted contribution margins were set either too high or too low; a corresponding profit or loss in the co-operative business operation arises due to this which according to the co-operative principles can be distributed (compensated for). Insofar, one cannot state that the co-operative strives for profits on its own by pursuing a profit-oriented policy which takes into consideration the risks of its operating rate.

III. Cost and Expenditure Coverage in Co-operatives from the Standpoint of Corporate Policy

One cannot overlook the fact that a fairly considerable degree of profit orientation exists in everyday co-operative reality. This can be explained in that the management bodies in co-operative business operations on the one hand pursue success-oriented goals and, on the other hand, remain averse to risks. When an all too minimal volume of job orders is realized while pure cost coverage is being pursued or when the risks entered into the cost calculation prove to be too low, the co-operative business operation must record a loss inasmuch as such a loss cannot be prevented in the scope of accounting policy by retransferring silent reserves created the previous year. Because reporting a loss in co-operative business practise likewise cannot be interpreted as successful business activity, the co-operative management – in agreement with its members and federation – attempts to avoid such unfavorable reports which could impair the credit rating of the co-operative on commodity and financial markets. The higher costs in the sectors of service and financing resulting from a degrading of a co-operative's credit rating would have to be taken into consideration when determining prices for transactions with its members; insofar, the competitiveness of the co-operative business operation would be impaired. In the long term, the co-operative can maintain its promotional potential in pricing policy only when it has realized a more favorable cost structure than its competitors.

The risks resulting from the execution of operational functions in the co-operative establishment on the one hand and the necessary interest-bearing nature of co-operative paid-up shares (→ *Equity Capital*) (from the viewpoint of business policy) on the other hand require pricing to overcompensate cost and expenditure coverage. These determinants of co-operative pricing policy are known as *deviation factors* (*Henzler*).

Theoretical accounting problems arise from the "correct" quantitative ascertainment of the deviation factors. Risks rooted in these expenses are incurred discontinuously and cannot be clearly determined as to their extent, the moment of their occurrence, and at times even their cause (the problem of reserves). Because of this the management of the co-operative business operation will be inclined to hold an overly high estimation – measured against past experience – of the positions to calculate *purchasing and marketing risks* in the co-operative enterprise according to the principle of cautious assessment. Such an assessment policy does not inevitably lead to reported profits. From the viewpoint of the co-operative management and its corporate policy it is sensible to make the co-operative less vulnerable to larger discontinuities on purchasing and sales markets by accumulating silent reserves. Nonetheless, one should not fail to recognize that portions of the co-operative profit are de facto no longer subject to the disposition of the general or delegate assembly through such accumulation; insofar a partial departure from the principle of cost and expenditure coverage is undertaken.

This tendency is intensified when *financial risk* as a deviation cause is considered. This is understood as the variability of the paid-up shares as such resulting from open membership and, as the case may be, of the reserves. Upon withdrawal from the co-operative – that is upon the intentional reduction of capital participation in the co-operative – the (former) co-operative members need not sell their shares to other (potential) members; they rather can give notice to membership and individual shares and subsequently receive their paid-up shares (consisting of contributions and retained profit earnings on these shares) and – if specifically provided for in the by-laws – even a portion of the reserves (reserve fund according to GenG, § 73, Subsec.3 [German Co-operative Law]) disbursed following notice and interim waiting periods. In Germany, title to a share of the reserves has been provided for since 1973. In practical application, members have only availed themselves quite guardedly to a share of the reserves and thus of the total value of the co-operative.

Long notice periods provided for in the articles of association (→ *by-laws*) could compensate the co-operative's particular financial risk. Inasmuch as the consequences of mass membership exodus cannot be prevented, many co-operative management bodies attempt to report profits and retain them by deviating from the principle of cost and expenditure coverage when calculating prices for transactions with members. These retained profits are entered into the accounts of statutory and voluntary reserves once the particular financial risks have been indicated rather than being ascribed to the paid-up shares or reserve fund according to GenG, § 73, Subsec.3. Thus, that portion of equity is increased which remains untouched when members choose to withdraw. Such a partial departure from the principle of cost and expenditure coverage may indeed reduce the financing risks of the co-operative but, at the same, time, the management becomes less dependent on members' decisions, and the co-operative's own endeavor to preserve and maintain itself is strengthened.

The third essential cause of deviation from the principle of cost and expenditure coverage is *"interest payment"* on the paid-up shares. Members will expect a dividend on their capital investment as an expression of co-operative promotion upon the fulfillment of three conditions:

1) when members' paid-up and retained shares attain a considerable monetary value;
2) when tangible promotion of the members through pricing advantages does not appear sensible on account of the competition;
3) when profit distribution based on the utilization claims on the co-operative enterprise through → *reimbursements* is not possible on account of the heterogeneity of outputs/services.

According to *accounting conventions,* such interest payments on equity should not be seen as costs or expenditures but rather as profit distributions; it would represent a departure from a puristic interpretation of the principle of cost and expenditure coverage to take such interest payments on capital into consideration in the calculation as budgeted coverage. Nevertheless, from a financial standpoint, the compensation for providing equity is seen as a cost of capital utilization. The payment of dividends on the paid-up shares (which can be discontinued in loss-making years) thus should not be misinterpreted as a grave infraction of the co-operative principle and of the principle of cost and expenditure coverage from a financial point of view in light of the shortcomings of many co-operatives with respect to their equity structure. It is ultimately a question of the extent of such dividends on capital participation. When promotion is the dominant motive for membership application into the co-operative rather than investment potential, interest payments (conforming with market standards) on the paid-up shares must not be seen as an infraction of the principle of cost and expenditure coverage; such interest payment rather is called for from the viewpoint of corporate policy.

Bibliography

Dülfer, Eberhard: Betriebswirtschaftslehre der Kooperative, Göttingen 1984.
Fettel, Johannes: Marktpreis und Kostenpreis, 2.Ed., Meisenheim 1958.
Henzler, Reinhold: Die Genossenschaft – eine fördernde Betriebswirtschaft, Essen 1957.
Kilger, Wolfgang: Flexible Planungskostenrechnung und Deckungsbeitragsrechnung, 8.Ed., Wiesbaden 1988.
Riebel, Paul: Einzelkosten- und Deckungsbeitragsrechnung, 5.Ed., Wiesbaden 1985.
Schweitzer, Marcell/Küpper, Hans-Ulrich: Systeme der Kostenrechnung, 5.Ed., Landsberg 1991.

Principles of the Co-operative System

JUHANI LAURINKARI

(see also: *Conceptions, Co-operative*; *History of Ideas*; *History in 19th C.*; *Rochdale Pioneers*; *Raiffeisen*)

I. The Formation of the Principles; II. Current Principles; III. Criticism of the Principles; IV. The Values and Ideas of the Co-operative System; V. Evaluation of the Principles; VI. The Origin of the Values of the Co-operative System.

The principles of co-operation have been discussed continuously throughout the entire existence of the co-operative movement. They have neither been concretely stated nor amended, and several of them have stopped being pursued over the course of time. The co-operative principles are both temporally and geographically bound. Nevertheless, their main goal has remained the provision of services to their members. The methods of supporting the members' enterprises have varied according to different time periods and different types of co-operatives. The observance of all co-operative principles in the every day business world is by no means simple as no one defining interest identity exists among the members, who, in a sociological manner, are all structured varyingly.

I. The Formation of the Principles

Ideologies always have a recurring theme at their nucleus. Various organizations, which clothe their objectives in the form of different goals, leading ideas, plans of action and principles, must come into being sooner or later in order to realize this central theme or idea. They often construct a hierarchical system in which one certain goal, once reached, becomes an intermediate step from which a subsequent goal will be formulated. This subsequent goal can likewise become an intermediate goal or step on the way to achieving the leading idea.

Co-operatives have been called "the child of want and misery". They are often established under the pressure of material distress – and also frequently of psychic affliction (→ *History in 19th C.*). People, in their efforts to free themselves from their wants and misery, have developed quite diverse methods and means to achieve their ends. Co-operatives have proved themselves to be an expedient solution in this context.

In today's world, the co-operative is no longer the same offspring of want and misery it was at its conception, in any case not in the western countries. It does, however, still strive to increase the living standard of those involved, or at least to prevent a reduction of the same. This cooperation is primarily in economic activity based on the collaboration of those involved to achieve commonly held goals.

In the course of time, co-operatives and their central organizations have created an organized co-operation to carry out their tasks. These tasks are, generally speaking, strictly economic in nature, e.g. the pro-curement of essential commodities, consumer and production goods for members, processing and marketing, granting credits, general use of machines and facilities, etc. But co-operation also involves the participation of the members in determining objectives, resolutions and the revision of the activity. Similarly, voting about the principles of the activity itself is also a part of co-operation. The co-operative organizations have developed a common plan of activity, which is usually called the principle of cooperation. The main principle of the cooperation is serving the customer/members. This main principle was later worked into the so-called co-operative principles, which are most frequently referred to as the seven resolutions formulated in the 1920s and '30s in the scope of the ICA.

Örne, a Swede, and *Thomas*, a Dane, were assigned in 1921 to catalogue the principles of the → *Rochdale Equitable Pioneer's Society* (England) based on statutes and business reports. Thomas was promptly elected the first president of the ILO (International Labor Organization). *Örne* was entrusted with the selection and definition of the principles. He summarized his views of the principles of co-operation in the volume "Kooperativa programmet" (1921), which was also published in Finnish under the title "Osuustoi-minnen ohjelma" in 1923.

The most powerful legal authority of the ICA, the congress, was not willing to recognize and confirm Örne's interpretation of the co-operative principles. A special committee was assigned to address the question, and it surveyed co-operatives and their central organizations in various countries. The responses showed that the organizations were not unanimous about the co-operative principles. In some countries (e.g. Germany, Belgium, USA), certain principles were pursued in the co-operative organizations, but others were not taken into account. The ICA Congress undertook the question again both in London (1934) and in Paris (1937). In the end, the organization confirmed *Örne's* proposal in 1937 – with several alterations, however. The seven principles of the Cooperative System then read as follows:

1) Open membership; voluntary in nature since 1948;
2) Democratic administration;
3) Distribution of the surplus to the members in relation to their utilization of the services the co-operative offers;
4) Limited interest on capital;
5) Political and religious neutrality;
6) Cash sales;
7) Utilization of a determined share of the surplus for educational and campaign goals.

Because only a part of the principles were ratified by all those present, the principles were split into two groups. Principles 1–4 were definitely to be pursued, whereas principles 5–7 were conditional or limited; their observance was not a necessary precondition for membership in the ICA.

If such a compromise had not been made, the ICA as an organization would surely have disintegrated. The delineation of the outline of the principles was not a result of theoretical consideration but was rather dictated by practical experience in order to pursue the goal of creating an organizational unit.

In 1960, the President of the ICA, *Mauritz Bonow* (from Sweden) introduced the idea at the Congress in Lausanne that every organization – regardless of its legal form – could be considered a co-operative as long as it strives to improve the condition of its members and pursues the following principles:

1) Voluntary membership
2) Democratic administration
3) Distribution of the surplus to the members in relation to services utilized.

The question of the co-operative principles was also addressed at subsequent ICA Congresses. At the 1963 Congress, a committee was called which was assigned first off to evaluate the extent the so-called Rochdale Principles were still applicable at that time. Furthermore, the committee was to decide whether the Rochdale Principles corresponded to those of the day and to propose a new form in case that it was decided that a revision of the co-operative principles was necessary (*Laakkonen*, 1965, ICA 22nd Congress Agenda and Reports).

As a result of the committee report, the subject of the co-operative principles was addressed in conclusion at the Congress in Vienna in 1966. The responses of almost 200 co-operative organizations to the question of whether the co-operative principles should be retained form the background of this report. The committee's suggestion for the principles of the co-operative were accepted at this congress so that these principles can furthermore be considered a general opinion of the co-operative organizations about these questions. The committee report found that the co-operative principles, when reduced to a few brief sentences as it was customary in former times, could cause misunderstandings and misinterpretations. Because of this reason they should be so defined as to ensure that no misunderstandings could arise (*Laakkonen*, 1967, pp. 4–5; the original source is the actual committee report).

The committee and the 1966 Vienna Congress defined the co-operative principles as follows:

1) Membership in a co-operative should be voluntary. Each person who can make use of the services provided by the co-operative and who is willing to accept the conditions arising from membership should have the op-portunity to be-

come a member of the co-operative; this should follow without any artificial restrictions and without either social, political or religious discrimination.
2) Co-operatives should be democratic organizations. Responsible functionaries and stewards should be chosen through an election agreed upon by the members and are liable to the members of the co-operative. The members of primary co-operatives should have equal voting rights (member and vote) as well as the opportunity to participate in the decision making of the organization. In other co-operatives (non-primary ones), the administration should be structured along appropriate democratic lines.
3) The interest which is payed on the co-operative capital must be precisely set in the case that it is paid at all.
4) The surplus and/or savings which arise from the business activity of the co-operative are for the good of the members of the co-operative in question and should be distributed in such a manner that no member can derive benefit at another's cost.

Based on the resolution of the members, this can occur in the following methods:

a) The funds are used for the promotion of the co-operative activity;
b) The funds are used for the advancement of the general good;
c) The surplus is distributed among the members according to how they have made use of the services provided by the co-operative.

5) All co-operatives should have means available for campaign projects directed at their members, functionaries, employees and the general public concerning questions about co-operative and economic principles.
6) According to the opinion of the congress, it is important to include the principle of reciprocal co-operation among the co-operatives to the principles already mentioned. In order to work for and serve the good of the members and society as a whole, all co-operative organizations should actively work together and with each other on the local, regional, national and international levels.

The creation and development of co-operatives was outlined above, particularly in the scope of the ICA. The changes which have occurred in society as well as the differentiation of the intrinsic principles and their practical application have found a place in the resulting report. Within the ICA, however, not everyone has completely gotten away from associating the actual principles with suggestions; no consensus was ever reached about the principles of co-operation. Some academics believe that a completely unanimous agreement can never be achieved (*Emelianoff*, 1942). In the course of development, the principles of political and religious neutrality and cash sales have been removed from the so-called Rochdale Principles.

Neither the science of co-operative studies nor the co-operative organizations themselves have always been able to differentiate between the principles and the practical instructions and/or assistance with which the goals and objectives could be achieved.

II. Current Principles

1. Open Membership

Membership in a co-operative should be voluntary, and each person who can make use of the services of the co-operative and who is prepared to accept the demands and requirements set down by the membership should have the opportunity to become a member – without any artificial barriers or social, political or religious discrimination.

This principle originated from the fulfillment of individual desires. When someone needs the services offered by a co-operative and wishes to become a member, he should have the opportunity to do so when he agrees to the rules of the co-operative and when the present membership accepts his application. In this situation, the procedures must follow without any type of discrimination on the grounds of race, religion, or political orientation. The reverse situation must also hold true: Should a member feel that he/she no longer requires the services of a co-operative, he/she should freely be able to withdraw from membership.

One of the more important thoughts from the viewpoint of the fundamental co-operative characteristics is also retained in this principle: The co-operative is an amalgamation of certain consumers of services, not of capital. The co-operative offers services and serves the members. Membership will not be made dependent on whether a certain individual disposes of needed capital or financial means, but rather on whether he immediately requires the services offered by the co-operative. This point manifests the socio-political principle of prosperity inherent to co-operatives. The voluntary nature of membership must also be seen from the standpoint of the other co-operative members. They must have the opportunity freely to accept or reject a membership application and thus safeguard the fundamental tasks of the co-operative – the principle of service.

2. Democratic administration

Co-operatives are democratic organizations. Those invested with the trust of others should be elected or chosen in a manner approved by the members, and these persons are legally liable to the members. Members of primary co-operatives should have an equal voting right (member and vote) regardless of their capital investment, as well as the opportunity to take part in the decision-making process. In non-primary co-operatives, the administration should be structured in an appropriate democratic manner.

This principle is closely related to the previous one. The important ideals of democracy and egalitarianism are brought to light in the character of the co-operative as a group of individuals. Each member has the identical voting right. The employees and administration personnel are responsible for the members. Each member has the same opportunity to evaluate and criticize the activity and to run as a candidate in the election of the management personnel.

Each member can also suggest matters to be discussed by the highest decision-making body of the co-operative, the general assembly or assembly of representatives, which in his opinion are important for the activity and operation of the co-operative. The one precondition is that he does this punctually. Decisions in the administrative bodies are usually made with a simple majority. In certain particularly important questions, the legal protection of minority members is of importance.

The execution of these resolutions presupposes several factors: an everpresent quorum, an increased qualified majority, unanimity, the right to withdraw immediately from membership, or the discussion of important matters at two successive assembly meetings. Through this manner, co-operatives attempt to give their members the opportunity to have an influence on resolutions directly affecting them and to take part in the discussion of more important matters than simply those affecting their own individual enterprises (e.g. Finnish Co-operative Law).

3. Limited Interest payed on Co-operative Equity

Capital also serves as a factor of production in co-operatives and must render an appropriate compensation which has been agreed upon in advance. The interest on co-operative capital must be determined in advance if it is payed out at all.

The investment capital which co-operatives raise from their members is generally rather small – with the exception of numerous production co-operatives in which the investment is closely related to the applied services and utilization opportunites. In this manner, the importance of the investment in relation to the distribution of savings (surplus, reserves) arising during the course of activity is rather slight.

Here it is layed down that a withdrawing member has his investment repaid to him. The investment asset need only be paid once and not annually like membership fees are in various organizations. This is true in the case that the investment is not augmented or that a member does not cause any additional investments as a result of increased turnover through the use of the services of the co-operative. If a member reduces his turnover with the co-operative, he can reduce the number of his shares and forcibly request a part of his investment back from the co-operative. If the investment asset is increased, or when a member is obligated through co-operative regulations to subscribe for additional shares, he must purchase the shares in question.

4. Distribution of the Reserves in relation to the Utilized Services

An amount (surplus or reserves) that resulted from the activity of the co-operative is appropriated to the members and must be distributed in such a manner that no member can derive benefit at the cost of another. Upon the members' decision, the distribution can proceed as follows:

a) The funds will be used for the promotion of the co-operative;
b) The funds will be used to service collective objectives;
c) The reserves are distributed among the members in relation to how they made use of the co-operative services.

This is an extension of the previous fundamental principle. The yield is usually allocated based on the third possibility. A portion of the reserves can be used for so-called non-profit purposes; an effect on the general prosperity of the population as a whole is intended through this action. In as far as the co-operative's palette of services is freely at the disposal of the members, each member can benefit from these services to the extent he/she requires.

5. Continuing Education and Training

All co-operatives should appropriate financial means for campaign projects directed at their members, functionaries, employed staff and the general public concerning questions about the co-operative principles 9as well as the economic and international activities of the co-operative movement.

From the beginning it has been the practise of the co-operative organizations to allocate a certain share of the business return to membership and administration education programs and staff training (→ *Education, Europe* etc.) .

It has namely been determined that co-operative members who do not have a certain degree of knowledge at their disposal are not effectively active in the co-operative, or in other words, that they cannot effectively utilize the services provided by the co-operative. When the present day co-operatives commenced their operation in Europe in the 19th century, they initially had to teach many of their members how to read, write and perfom arithmetic as the state did not provide its citizens with elementary education at this time. Many projects of developmental co-operation thus began with the establishment of a school. From this start one could later delve into instruction concerning the particularities and characteristics of co-operatives. The main question in consideration was what the co-operative system was all about: How can it benefit members, and how can members make use of the services provided by the co-operative?

The informational service work which co-operatives direct at their members is double-natured in the developed countries. Above all, the co-operatives pass on information about co-operative theory to the management personnel. On the other hand, many co-operatives, especially production co-operatives, advise their members in matters concerning work and employment, e.g. in the production of newer and better products and the application of more economical production techniques.

Co-operative organizations have shown many people the way to better job training and thus have given them the chance to assume ever more challenging tasks. This has happened both in the realm of the co-operative movement as well as in society in general. An important and particularly intensive form of training undertaken in recent years has been the delegation of experts to the developing countries and the subsequent training of personnel there.

6. Collaboration in the Various Co-operative Levels

In order to operate in the best possible manner for the wellbeing of members and society, all co-operative organizations should actively work with other co-operatives on the local, national and international levels.

Co-operative undertaking means co-operation on various levels. Co-operation on the primary co-operative level gives members – particularly those in a weak or threatened situation – the chance to maintain or improve their living standard through either their own or collective effort. The primary co-operatives form the co-operative centers for their support, and these in turn are included in organizational structures all the way to the → *ICA*.

The objective and purpose of international co-operation are the collection and exchange of data from co-operative organizations of various countries. In this manner, knowledge about how co-operatives can be run in order to attain their goals can be spread from co-operative to co-operative, from one part of the world to another.

III. Criticism of the Principles

Since the 1960s, a tendency has been making itself noticeable in the co-operative movement of avoiding theory and ideology and concentrating only on economic questions instead. Every organization and institution, however, bases its activity on the ideas which the members believe in and approve of. A co-operative must similarly distinguish its fundamentals, which serve as the springboard of its activities, and continually adapt to them (*Laidlaw*, 1980, p.34). The co-operative principles listed above play an important role in the development of co-operative theory. The principles of co-operation must be particularly observed by every researcher of the co-operative system in his/her undertakings.

The principles have been criticized primarily for two reasons:

– It has been attempted to elevate daily practise to a theoretical level. The principles themselves, however, have never been defined.
– The principles are too heavily structured along the lines of the consumer co-operative sector and cannot be applied to the same extent to different co-operative types (e.g. agricultural, production or home building co-operatives).

The question can be raised of whether the co-operative principles can still claim their validity under the conditions and relations of the 1990s. More precise questions can thus follow:

– Has the practical application of the co-operative principles deviated too drastically from the initial, fundamental ideas?
– Do the principles of co-operation correspond to people's views and expectations (*Ramaekus*, 1983, p.440)?

The training and educational tasks of co-operatives do not significantly deviate from those of other corporate forms in today's society with the exception of matters concerning members and the management staff. Any critical response to this particular task underscores how the level of education and training campaigns has increased in the general population.

It is impossible in practise to describe all the measures that have been developed in co-operatives in the various parts of the earth in order to realize the principles of cooperation. Even when the principles of cooperation are being discussed, the means can be chosen most varingly. It is only important what has been found to be of top priority and desirable and what has proved to be disruptive. One may also not claim that a certain goal can be achieved with only one means. Cooperation is multi-faceted; co-operatives must direct the form of their activity based on their own special tasks as well as on the opportunities defined by their surroundings. As a draft of principles, cooperation is also not an unconditional source of norms which clearly states what is right and wrong.

The fundamental idea in the definition of cooperation is that of collective work, the extent and form of which is determined by the members themselves. If members are able to attain the desired services only with the assistance of the co-operative, from their standpoint the activity is necessary and effective, and the institution is justified. It is also possible that each member on his own can attain the desired service, but that does not mean that it is not more effective collectively.

Cooperation is thus also the result of work distribution. If members have the opportunity to secure services and supplies of needed commodities other than through the help of co-operatives, other criteria concerning effectiveness become more prominent.

The knowledge or recognition of the co-operative principles in a community does not in any way have an influence on the level of cooperation. Nevertheless, one can draw conclusions from certain practical methods of behavior whether a company can be considered co-operative according to the principles of cooperation. The principles of co-operation and the actual activities of the co-operatives are in a constant interaction with each other.

People who live under varying conditions and at different times likewise see and interpret the principles of the co-operative system differently. The definition of the co-operative principles is thus closely tied to social surroundings. This also follows from the observation of the changes of the co-operative principles in the ICA. A close interaction exists between the principles and their realization in practise. The closer one is involved in the practical activities, the greater the inclination to confuse both positions with each other.

Social changes always offer the co-operative organizations new forms of activity and new ways to realize their principles; they even force methods and goals to be checked constantly in order to be able to preserve their applicability and expediency. Experience shows, however, regardless of how well-sounding the principles of the co-operative movement may be, their application in practise is not completely free of problems. The co-operative movement cannot always realize its fundamental task of effectively supporting its members to the extent it wishes.

IV. The Values and Ideas of the Co-operative System

The fundamentals of the co-operative system described above can be summarized in a list of six values: *uniformity, economic efficiency, justice, democracy, freedom* and *enlightenment*. The conception and development of the fundamental principles of the co-operative system within the ICA were examined in the previous pages. One can observe both the influence of societal changes and the distinction between the actual principles and directives for their execution in this development (→ *Corporate Culture*).

Within the international co-operative system, renewed discussion began in the 1980s concerning the values on which the system itself was based. The reason why this discussion commenced was the suspicion that several of the central values of the co-operative system had become outdated over time, and that it was thus necessary to consider completely new values of the system in order to support its work. In the course of development, the ideas of neutrality, cash sales and the goal of creating an ideal society were deleted from the so-called Rochdale Principles.

The ICA World Conference in Stockholm in 1988 was occupied with defining the position to certain questions of the co-operative system concerning principles and values. No decision, however, resulted, and the discussion will be resumed. The Stockholm Congress commissioned the ICA Board to prepare a revision of the principles based on the central values. The ICA central committee called a special committee into life at the conference in Dehli in 1989 to discuss the values of the co-operative system. A fundamental interchange of views and opinions should take place within the ICA concerning principles and values by the time the Tokyo Congress takes place in 1992.

V. Evaluation of the Principles

Hereinbefore it has been attempted to describe how people living under different conditions and at different times have observed the principles of the co-operative system varyingly. The definitions of the co-operative principles are dependent on the environment in which they are drawn. This became particularly obvious in the observation of the changes which have been mentioned within the ICA at various times.

VI. The Origin of the Values of the Co-operative System

Values are normally viewed more generally as goals than attitudes are. The entirety of values (the program) is often called the idea or concept. The analysis of the goals of the co-operative system is therefore in a deeper sense an analysis of the values and ideas of the co-operative system.

Values are related to the goal orientation of human activity. A value, in a more idealistic respect, is a statement of what is good and worthy to be strived after, or in other words, what is ideal. Above it has been demonstrated that the co-operative system has a relatively set content or substance to its principles. Can the same thing be said about its values?

The values of the co-operative system follow from its principles which have been made known (the program). It has been determined above that the principles of the co-operative system have been the object of discussion; they have been checked and revised, and some of them have even been cast aside. The present day ICA principles have been the object of criticism. The central question in this matter might well be whether the principles are only a theorization of practise (idealization), or whether a certain social philosophy lies at their root.

The co-operative system is a social movement; it has a certain social philosophy. The co-operative system must regenerate itself over time by redefining its values and norms in order to keep up with the development of social changes and be in the position to satisfy the needs of both members and those people who wish to become members.

Craig, in his observations of the co-operative system (1980), proposed three central values as the basis of the social philosophy of the co-operative system:

- justice
- equal rights
- reciprocal help (solidarity)

The value of *justice* is reflected in the initial central principles of the co-operative system: in open membership and in democratic management. Justice poses a central philosophical problem in social theory (see, for example, *Rawls*, 1972). Justice, from a philosophical point of view, is valuable. Observing advantages and burdens, as well as the legal standing and relationships of people, is axiological. According to utilitarianism, on the other hand, only that which contributes to utilization is considered valuable.

The equality of rights, as it is mentioned in the principles of the co-operative system, allows people, who are fundamentally equal (with each other), to exert influence on the powers which affect their lives. An individual can become a member of a co-operative without any kind of descriminating restriction, and all members have an equal say in their co-operative. The term "equality of rights" is one of the central values of social philosophy and is closely related to justice. In Aristotelian thought, the two are placed in close relation to each other.

According to Aristotle, *justice* has two characteristic traits. So-called *distributive justice* refers to the fair dispersement of advantages and burdens, or utility and disadvantage, among citizens. *Corrective justice*, on the other hand, refers to the legal position of citizens among each other. According to Aristotle, the former case concerns the principle of *relative equality* and the latter the principle of *absolute equality*.

Corrective justice is particularly expressed in the co-operative principles of democratic management and limited interest payment on co-operative capital, in which case absolute equality is a requisite precondition. Co-operative members fundamentally have an equal say in the management of their co-operative: Each member has one vote, regardless of his/her capital investment. This principle of absolute equality is a unique characteristic of the co-operative system.

The principle of democratic management thus points to a democracy of absolute equality – indicating corrective justice. The actual character of a co-operative as an organization or community of individuals ultimately expresses absolute equality. This fundamental of democracy has been questioned since co-operatives first started operating. It seems possible that the daily operation realized by technocrats creates principles of its own in which the ideals are "forgotten". The principle of absolute equality is also indirectly expressed in the co-operative principle of open membership. The voluntary nature of membership can also be expressed in this manner. The absolute economic equality of the co-operative members also is shown in that one can take part in the economic activity of a co-operative without a large capital investment.

The principle of relative equality, or so-called distributive justice, is expressed in the principles on the one hand by the limited interest on co-operative capital and, on the other hand, in that the distribution of the reserves follows in relation to the utilization of services. These two principles attempt to "adjust advantages according to disadvantages". On an idealistic level, both the interest paid on co-operative capital as well as the distribution of reserves and/or surplus are (visual) expressions of relative equality. The perfunctory principle of relative justice is fundamentally not undertaken in co-operatives, but rather only in connection with solidarity.

The principle of relative justice is more clearly pursued through the distribution of reserves which accumulate through the co-operative operation than through the interest payment on co-operative capital. The business result achieved by and belonging to the co-operative is distributed among the members according to their individual utilization of the co-operative services.

Generally speaking, then, a member who has made good advantage of the services of the co-operative obtains many advantages in the form of reserves or surpluses. In practise, however, this is not particularly visible as a large part of the reserves is often used for the further development of the co-operative, which, in turn, makes the solidarity principle quite evident.

Reciprocal help and responsibility – solidarity – are brought into connection as it is made possible through collective trade and work for people to collectively exercise influence on their future. Reciprocal help plays an important role among the principles of the co-operative system. It emphasizes the importance of co-operative training and education and the collaboration between co-operatives (*Cannon*, 1983, pp. 3–6).

The last two co-operative principles in particular reflect the idea of solidarity, the fourth one also in part. They are: *distribution of reserves in relation to the services used, continuing education and training, and co-operation between the various levels of the co-operative system*. The first principle mentioned here prevents members from deriving benefit at the cost of other members. On the other hand, no one is given preferential treatment as the amount of the reserves depends on each member himself. When the reserves are utilized for the further development of the co-operative operation or for services set aside for collective use, true solidarity is served.

The principle of training and education expresses the conviction to assume responsibility for people both near and distant. Among others, the co-operative system strives to promote the vigor and initiation of the population by increasing knowledge. Instruction and enlightenment campaigns belonged to co-operatives from their inception. This is an expression of practical reciprocal help – → *solidarity*.

The principle of cooperation imbues the entire idea of the co-operative system in the various types of co-operatives. The individual co-operatives as well as the co-operative centers are organized according to the principle of cooperation. The values of the co-operative system and its ideal legacy are discussed in numerous research studies and discussion papers (e.g. *Henzler*, 1960; *Craig*, 1980; *Blümle*, 1981; *Aksnes*, 1982; *Engelhardt*, 1983; *Bager*, 1984; *Dülfer*, 1984; *Rokholt*, 1985; *Laurinkari*, 1986; *Marcus*, 1988; compare with the special committee engaged by the ICA in 1989 which discussed the values of the co-operative system).

Ilmonen (1988, 6) bases his interpretation of the co-operative system on the observation that it should construe its activities based on its central values when striving for a rationality of value in these activities. If the co-operative system does not do this, it should alter its identity and publicize the new values upon which it now intends to structure its activity.

In the discussion of the development of the co-operative system, one can clearly emphasize that the system should not be restricted solely to economic values. One should consider economic solutions at best as a means and not as a value (*Köppä*, 1983, p.55). The explanation of the actual value bases of the co-operative system would then be a particularly pressing task for the movement itself. The co-operative system is certainly a unique combination of economic and social values (and also goals). Changes taking place in society become reflected in the co-operative system.

A clarification of the ideal essence of the co-operative system should greatly be connected with the discussion of the undertakings and value orientations which are strived for in practise. *Tauriainen* (1984, p.34) raises the question of whether the goals of the co-operative system have fallen to the wayside when expansion ideologies and the fight to secure market shares compel work to be structured and oriented around the market in every respect (compare with *Laidlaw*, 1980).

The following must also be discussed: Which value orientation should be the basis of the activity? On which values does a company organization base itself which attempts to have its activity influenced by co-operative behavior (*Tauriainen*, 1984, p. 35)?

If, on the other hand, one wishes to perceive the co-operative system from its conception on entirely as an amalgamation of ideas which exclusively affect economic activity (in other words, the idea of economic cooperation which serves its members), one could be of the opinion that the essence of the co-operative system remained unchanged up to the 1980s (*Tauriainen*, 1981, p.11).

Since the end of the 1970s, alternative movements have been trying to find newly fashioned solutions for the economic activity. There are points of contact in the undertakings of the alternative movements with the traditional ideas of the co-operative system (*Tauriainen*, 1983, pp. 24–25). One can thus also assume that the discussion about the ideal essence of the co-operative system will become more lively considering the rapid changes in social structure happening today. Co-operative thought should be both more flexible and variable. In discussing this matter in the future one must take into consideration the technological development, employment structure in the population and the goods and services required in private households.

A shift in the values of the co-operative system also means a value shift of the principles of the system. The necessity of the co-operative's existence is based on the profitability for the co-operative and not so much on the profitability for the membership. The co-operative must be profitable. This was not the primary goal of the original, ideal co-operative system. Then it was clearly stressed that the co-operative system was to promote the economic interest of its members (see *Henzler*, 1957).

Such changes have taken place in the values of the co-operative system that, all in all, one can realistically speak of a crisis within co-operative thought in the economically developed countries. This crisis can apparently only be overcome through the existence of newer forms and applications of co-operative activity (→ *New Co-operatives*); the existence of so-called ecological banks (in Germany and Finland, among others) and further attempts in the direction of an ecological economy indicated this development.

Ilmonen (1988, p.8) formulated the substance of the identity problem of the co-operative system by stating that the co-operative system in western and northern Europe continues to strive to attach its identity to the old, traditional guiding co-operative values. Cooperation, self-help and democracy, however, no longer guide the co-operative system in practise. According to *Ilmonen*, they predominantly appear in speeches and communiqués. The economy is now the focus of attention for the co-operative system, making other values become secondary.

Bibliography

Bogardus, E. S.: Principles of Co-operation, Wisconsin 1963.
Draheim, Georg: Die Genossenschaft als Unternehmungstyp, 2nd ed., Göttingen 1955.
Engelhardt, Werner Wilhelm: Allgemeine Ideengeschichte des Genossenschaftswesens, Darmstadt 1985.
Lambert: Studies in the Social Philosophy of Cooperation, Bruxelles 1966.
Laurinkari, Juhani: Die genossenschaftlichen Grundwerte, in: Laurinkari, Juhani (ed.): Die Prinzipien des Genossenschaftswesens in der Gegenwart, Festschrift für Prof. Dr. Vesa Laakkonen, Nürberg 1986.
Münkner, Hans H.: Co-operative Principles and Cooperative Law, Papers and Reports, No. 5, Institute for Co-operation in Developing Countries, Marburg 1974.
Hasselmann, E.: Die Rochdaler Grundsätze im Wandel der Zeit, Frankfurt a.M. 1968.

Privatization and Collectivization by Co-operatives

ULRICH FEHL/CARSTEN SCHREITER [J]

(see also: *Economic Order*; *State and Co-operatives, Market Economy*; *State and Co-operatives, Socialism*)

I. Co-operatives in the Organized Market System; II. Co-operatives in Socialism.

I. Co-operatives in the Organized Market System

According to their original characteristic form, co-operatives are self-help institutions (→ *Self-help Organizations*), organizations which strive to maintain individual freedom of action and self-responsibility. The particularly democratic constitution (one man-one vote principle) and the joint-determination of policy reflect this, whereby the changes which have taken place in the meantime (indirect democracy, etc.) should be interpreted as a reflex to the altered size dimensions (*Boettcher*). The strong dependency of the typical auxiliary co-operative on its independent member enterprises represents a further indicator of this organizational form. Even when the so-called "traditional co-operative" (*Dülfer*, 1966) has evolved into a market-linkage or integrated co-operative, its main objective remains the support of its member enterprises (*Dülfer*, 1984). (In the integrated co-operative form, the information and control directions have been reversed, and the member enterprises are closely bound to the co-operative). Alongside the stated goal of promoting the discretionary freedom of the members within the organization, the freedom of action beyond the organization should also be kept in mind. This not least is true for the upholders of the late- and neoclassic who grappled with the phenomenon of "co-operatives" on a theoretical level (→ *Classic/Neo-classic Contributions*). Although their individual reflections differed, their central conviction was the same, namely that co-operatives must hold their own in the field of (imperfect) → *competition* with other company forms (compare to *Hoppe*). The state should only provide for the system of organized competition and not interfere in the competitive development by, say, assuming corporate financing (consider the disagreement between *Lassalle* and → *Schulze-Delitzsch*).

Co-operatives are profit-oriented, capitalistic companies which are spontaneously organized through private initiative in the framework of the market processes and which are initially associated to this organized system (→ *Economic Order*). According to their nature, they are not instrumental, that is they serve neither privatization nor collectivization purposes through political authorities. They rather effect a "correction" of the organized market system through their ancillary character by modifying the distribution of the business result as well as maintaining and promoting the state of the employees/owners. They make state intervention superfluous by the extent they can bring about social and economic improvements and thus influence the level of prosperity. Even when co-operatives fulfill important functions in the scope of the market, they are not in any way a product of state mandate, but rather are the result of private initiative.

II. Co-operatives in Socialism

1. General Remarks

As is well known, the historically dominating form of socialism strives for a centrally administered economy, the functional efficiency of which is dependent on the consistency of planning. In the final stages this means that the economic subjects must be instrumentalized in the sense of being integrated into planning (→ *State and Co-operatives, Socialism*). Seen historically, the co-operatives were not only instrumentalized in this general sense, but rather were also employed as a means of transformation on the path from "capitalism" to "socialism", or in other words, on the path from "market" to "plan". They were meant to practically serve as centers for the collection of information and in this manner play an auxiliary role in fulfilling the execution of the plan. Like all bourgeois institutions, the co-operative should also ultimately perish in the sense of the market economy described above. This development was traced out in Marxist ideology.

2. Ideology and Co-operative Property

According to *Marx* (→ *Socialist Critics*), private property has no place in socialism, the preliminary stage of the classless society called communism. The socialization of the means of production should have taken place during the initial phase of socialism (*Ruwwe*). Co-operatives as an institution of group private property are thus not provided for. Marxist ideology is, however, not completely unequivocal with respect to co-operatives. On the one hand, co-operatives are seen as a model of the Marxist idea of "small scale communism"; co-operatives were rejected, however, because of their tendency to delay the revolution. *Marx* envisioned the revolution as a radical upheaval and not as a peaceful transition into a co-operative society like the "early socialists" did (such as → *Robert Owen*). In Marxist theory, co-operatives are not in the position to transform capitalism into socialistic structures. On the other hand, *Marx* considered co-operatives directly "communist" recognizing their identity principle, or identified "socialized means of production" as "co-operative" (see *Ehm*). Thus, *Marx* himself left room for an interpretation concerning the assessment of co-operatives and their property form, a state of affairs that would play a considerable role in practical economic policy. *Ehm* identifies the ideological stand-points with regard to co-operative group property as the "thesis of inferior standing" and "the thesis of full standing".

3. The Function of Collectivization

a) *Co-operatives as an Instrument of Collectivization*

The nationalization executed by *Lenin* in 1920 clearly illustrates a consistent realization of the thesis of inferiority standing; this action instrumentalized co-operatives in the sense of collectivization. This was facilitated inasmuch as a three-tiered organization structure already existed. Workers were mobilized through obligatory membership and gratuitous admission. Positions of importance were successively filled by party members. The multi-leveled co-operative organization in Poland was even taken advantage of, and the co-operative system thus served as a vehicle of collectivization. Co-operatives in this manner were integrated into the planned economy and so structured as to fulfill tasks based on state purposes. They thus were not only subjected to state control but were also restricted in their activities: "The supreme goal of a socialistic economic system is the material equality of the economic subjects." (*Ehm*, p. 94). Moreover, the purpose of the co-operative was seen in the execution of socialization and educational activities. The promotion mandate, however, was directed in part at the good of the entire socialist society. Because of the particular organizational structure, state influence was quite dominant and extended over various levels, such as in the scope of legal procedures, or special regulations concerning the conditions for formation, operation or organizational structure. The central co-operative federations (→ *Central Institutions*) are thus composed of state representatives as well as representatives from the co-operatives. Upon the formation of a co-operative, the corresponding material obligations of the co-operative with respect to the state budget are determined, and the type and extent of state support are decided on. In order to see in which sectors the co-operatives remain autonomous, it is useful to sketch out in brief the organization and execution procedures of state planning inasmuch as it affects co-operatives (Poland is used here as an example). The planning commission sets its planning coefficients. The parliamentary plan proposal (level 1) forms the basis of the economic plan. The middle planning level (level 2) includes drafting long-term and annual departmental plans as well as fixing the tasks of the plan according to the central plan. The activity of all co-operatives is also determined in this scope. The planning process continues further at the central co-operative federations (level 3). Both co-operative → *federations* and the co-operatives themselves are to be found on the next tier, the state jurisdictional level (the so-called Woiwodschaft); here, the execution of the instruction is completed. The lowest level is the co-operative level, which involves the relationship between the co-operative and its members. The discretionary freedom of the members exists formally on this level.

In history, this idealized process of co-operative instrumentalization for collectivization purposes does not occur as lineally as it is described above. Much more often, counter movements occur which provide more elbow-room for co-operatives; these are conditional to the immanent difficulties inherent in central planning or in the economic and political difficulties which result from it. At the beginning, privatization was carried out following purely pragmatic reasoning in order to establish economic stimuli (initiative, motivation and flexibility functions). This method of action was later bolstered ideologically by the transition and assumption of the thesis of full standing concerning co-operative property. By accepting the thesis of full standing, the groundwork was finally laid which, in the scope of the reform discussion, could ultimately serve to utilize the co-operative as a vehicle of privatization. Group property is fundamentally and ideologically defined as to have a standing equal to state property, which in principle opens the door for the possibilty of effective privatization. This can only be truly effective, however, when co-operative property is combined with commercial rights corresponding to those of an organized market system. Historical development does not directly follow the thesis of full standing either, but is rather characterized by reactionary movements pursuing the thesis of inferior standing, as the following brief historical survey illustrates.

b) Developments in the Former Soviet Union

The system of → *consumer co-operatives* developed in Russia between 1864 and 1914, whereby the development up to 1905 took place only sluggishly. Reasons for this included the drawn-out approval procedure and the arbitrariness of local administrations. This latter feature was based to a considerable degree on a decree issued on July 22, 1866, which granted provincial governors the right to ban assemblies of private companies, thus including co-operatives among others. The first uniform exemplary statute was introduced in 1897 which provided the provincial governors the basis to issue approval. After the so-called "Red Sunday" in 1905, the czarist government was willing to introduce reforms. After this point in time, the consumer co-operatives could develop better. The first worker co-operatives came into being. In 1898, a central union was founded by 18 co-operatives which, in the course of the co-operative integration process, developed into the center of the consumer co-operative movement (→ *History in 19th C.*). Other regional associations joined in increasing numbers up to 1911. The consumer co-operatives were able to continue developing during World War I and received state support. In these years, the consumer co-operatives turned more and more to self-production, and large co-operatives were created. After the dethronement of *the czar* in February 1917, the provisional government passed a co-operative law which was intended to promote the further development of the consumer co-operatives. The Bolsheviks under *Lenin*, who rose to power in October 1917, discontinued this development by commencing the targeted nationalization of "suitable" means of production. Thus, the "Draft Decree for Consumer Communes" was penned in 1918 in order to "nationalize" the consumer co-operatives, which should be restructured into state-managed distribution organizations under strict state control. At this point in time, the rationale was clearly controlled by the thesis of inferior standing. The economic crisis and the strong opposition brought upon a new draft on April 10, 1918, which singularly prescribed the obligation to provide for the population under norms fixed by the state. Moreover, the subordination of consumer co-operatives to state authorities was restructured into a form of voluntary cooperation. The heads of the federations thus should also work and participate in the state provisional authorities. *Lenin* herewith attempted to solve the crisis pragmatically (→ *Socialist Critics*). Nevertheless, the "Decree for Consumer Communes" was issued the following year in an only slightly amended form. The worker's and middle-class consumer co-operatives were fused into one uniform distribution authority. All stores, production enterprises, and warehouses were transferred to this "consumer commune". Membership was mandatory, and a three-tiered organizational structure was called for. From this point forward, all work would only proceed from regulations from the state authorities, which exercised control by appointing personnel to the boards of the consumer communes, the government federations, and the Centrosojuz (highest level co-operative federation). Centralization reached a peak in the decree issued on January 27, 1920, which empowered the Centrosojuz as the top organization for all co-operatives. Credit, rural and artisan co-operatives were fused with the consumer co-operatives, just as their regional associations were with those of the credit communes. The top federations became subdivisions of the Centrosojuz. During the years of "War Communism" (1918–1921), the Soviet Union fell victim to a period of disastrous economic conditions. In 1920, the indications of a total collapse rapidly increased. The most pressing goal was to increase the production level of foodstuffs. *Lenin* thus replaced the model of war communism by the concept of "New Political Economy". The nationalization of land, large and mid-size industries, as well as that of the banks was retained, but the mandatory supply system in agriculture was repealed. In its place a tax in kind was introduced; free surpluses could thus be exchanged for industrial or commercial goods. *Lenin* set his hopes on reprivatized small industry in order to produce the necessary supply level. At the beginning, *Lenin* did not alter his position with regard to co-operatives, but nevertheless, the first draft of a "co-operative plan" dated 1921 signalized practical effects. In July, 1921, co-operatives for artisans, small-scale industries as well as for agricultural purchasing and marketing were allowed with their own enterprises. In the distribution sector, consumer co-operatives were meant to enter into competition with private business and force the latter off the market through superior performance. However, no new ideological basis developed. Rather, this once again was a purely pragmatic manoeuvre. The consumer co-operatives remained chained "on hand and foot", and the free market alone could do nothing. Ultimately, resolutions were passed in March of 1921 concerning the structural and active adaptation of the consumer co-operatives. The decree of April 1922 permitted them to market surplus agricultural products, as well as goods produced by craftsmen and small-scale industries. They were still obligated to continue exchanging agricultural products for goods produced by the state industry. Competition with private enterprises remained a political task which the consumer co-operatives could not fulfill. Reasons for this included the extensive retention of organizational structures, the lack of capital and non-existent means of financing (*Lenin* had abolished money). Compulsory trade in kind put co-operatives in an inferior position with respect to private businesses, and the number of merchants increased. The government finally returned to a monetary economy, allowed credit co-operatives, and repealed stipulations which limited co-operative turnover geographically. A decree dated October 1921 freed the consumer co-operatives from those obligations arising from the plan, and the state-fixed conditions for the exchange of industrial and agricultural products were lifted. At the same time, the state cut off financial help to the co-operatives. The lack of financial equity then lead to a limitation of business to that which could promise a profit with only a minimum of financial investment. Predominant concentration was put on agricultural production at the expense of the state and on the export of agricultural raw material. Private merchants could thus further expand their market share. Caught in this dilemma situation, *Lenin* adopted the thesis of full standing and, in 1923, composed his policy making manuscript "Concerning the Co-operative System". As a result, co-operatives received massive state support in the fight against "capitalistic elements". *Lenin* recognized that co-operatives had an advantage over state enterprises in both their incentive function and their opportunity to comprehend needs more exactly. By 1928, private trade had practically been supplanted.

Industrialization in the Soviet Union became an ever more acute necessity. Investment volume needed to be expanded to a dramatic extent in a situation in which growth potential to the most part was exhausted. Agriculture remained the solitary source of financing, but this could not be accomplished with free market and pricing policies. *Stalin*, therefore, started collectivizing agriculture in 1928/29 (→ *kolkozes*). The first five-year plan was drawn up for the years 1928/29–1932/33. All planning conducted from 1928–1953 was characterized by a sense of strict command. In 1931, private trade was completely done away with, and the consumer co-operatives were instrumentalized as distribution organizations in order to discriminate against the rural population. Consumer co-operatives began being abolished in the urban areas and by 1935 were allowed to provide solely for the rural population. Moreover, the party apparatus undertook an "infiltration of the consumer co-operatives". Although the right of self-management was expressly confirmed in 1935, the candidates for the election of the co-operative administrative body were lined up by the local party organization. The de facto mandatory amalgamation into a federation system which was construed using the tiered legal-administrative framework of the Soviet Union as a model (4–5 levels) had its usual effects. Consumer co-operatives within a rajon (smallest administrative unit) joined together in rajon associations, which in turn were members of the district association. The center of all district associations within a republic of the Union was the republic federation, which itself was subject to the Centrosojuz. The decision making process was centralized and was conducted from the top down: "The system of consumer co-operatives in the *Stalin* years was that of a centralized economic organization with responsibilities in the distribution sector superimposed by the state economic plan." (*Ruwwe*, p.89). In 1956, the last co-operative enterprise in the industrial sector disappeared through administrative channels under *Khrushchev*. Small commercial co-operatives and ones for craftsmen were nationalized, and in 1957, the "Sovkhozation" movement started which converted agricultural collectives (→ *kolkozes*) into state property (sovkhozes). The consumer co-operatives remained spared from direct nationalization, although they could only muster a decreasing share in total retail sales turnover because of administrative limitations and discrimination.

In the following years, co-operative group property ultimately became one of the structural characteristics of the Soviet economic constitution (XXII Party Congress). In the current Soviet reform the ideology has, therefore, yielded once again to a more pragmatic adaptation to economic reality. Not only is the role of the co-operative being discussed but rather also the necessary reforms in the planning and management systems.

4. The Function of Privatization

a) Co-operatives as a Vehicle of Privatization

Following the discussion of the collectivization function of co-operatives, that is their instrumentalization in the sense of the planned economy (→ *Officialization*), at this point the privatization function should be studied which recently has been availed of to a stronger extent. The observed instrumentalization in the direction of the market economy should be illustrated once again using the example of the Soviet Union. This concerns an instrumentalization of the co-operatives inasmuch as the privatization measures up to now have been intended in a gradual or "decelerated" form. The "thesis of equal standing" therefore serves, above all, to replace property seem to have been confiscated by the state as group property; nevertheless, strictly private possession of means of production should remain prohibited or at least discriminated against. The intention behind this is to limit privatization to group property so that the powers in the sense of a "private-law society" (*Böhm*) do not have free reign. In the context of these privatization efforts it should be noted that full success can only be spoken of when corresponding changes in the planning system are simultaneously undertaken, or when the rights of entering into negotiations are altered along the lines of a market economy structure. Therefore, the state monopoly on resources must be abolished in the sense of privatization also. "Pure" enterprising acting, following *Kirzner's* interpretation, does not require resources with respect to "ingenuity" (concerning better opportunity) but, however, the actual ability to take advantage of the "co-ordination gaps" discovered.

b) Reform Developments in the Soviet Union

aa) Objectives of Reform in the Soviet Union

By picking up the threads of *Lenin's* co-operative idea, *Gorbachov* sees a way out of the economic misery whose roots lie in the bureaucracy, the lack of flexibility in the large state enterprises, the lack of competency and motivation, insufficient self-responsibility, and poor methods of rendering accounts (→ *Development, Eastern Europe*). The fundamental tool for this was the ratification of the "Law for Co-operative Systems" passed on May 26, 1988, which established an equal standing between co-operative property and state property. The arbitrariness co-operatives had been previously treated with should thus be called to a stop; competition should be made possible between organizational forms, if only in a limited dimension, in order to remove the causes of the wanting economic situation. The co-operative should "come into being from the ground up"; productivity should increase based on their higher levels of flexibility and adaptability concerning changes in demand, on account of their superior knowledge of local situations, and promotion of the entrepreneurial spirit. Furthermore, the co-operative law should serve to combat the fundamental inhibition to establish companies and produce a framework in which the co-operatives undertake the development and expansion of the service sector which, up to this time, has only existed in a rudimentary state.

bb) Fields of activity

In principle, the extent of the fields of activity remains indeed restricted, whereby the list of prohibitions according to the ministerial instruction "Concerning the regulation of individual types of co-operative activity in concurrence with co-operative law" dated December 29, 1988, is not considered all too restrictive (*Schweisfurth*, 1989). Moreover, certain activites may only be executed by so-called "contract co-operatives". Subject to special regulation, this mandate concerns activity in the fields of industry, construction, transportation, trade, food preparation, and the entire range of services. Among others, the law also is applicable to kolkozes, doctors, lawyers, engineers, etc. It is to be noted that additional special regulations also are effective for kolkozes (*Schweisfurth*, 1988).

cc) General Regulations

The establishment of new companies should be completely free of any obstacles. At least three founders are necessary; citizens over 16 years of age, but also co-operatives and state enterprises can become members. In principle then, pure family co-operatives are possible. In connection with the non-existence of a legal procedure regulating the relationship between members and contractual employers, family enterprises have been created with several hundred employees (*Brazda*, et al.). In spite of the legal co-operative form, a development to a general partnership is visible. The co-operatives can be organized in structural units, and branch offices as well as agencies are permitted. Self-administration and a democracy based on a wide constituency are likewise provided for (→ *Organizational Structure of Societies*): The general assembly is the highest administrative body, and the principle of "one man-one vote" is applicable. Employees may voice their counsel. The chairman is elected by the general assembly; in large co-operatives, the election also encompasses that of the administration as well as of an auditing committee for financial and economic management. In addition, the following regulations are noteworthy, although their realization in individual cases still presents difficulties:

- The capital of the co-operative should be formed by monetary and material investments from members, through co-operative income revenue, by bank credits and investment participation from state enterprises (→ *Equity Capital*).
- The opportunity to issue stock should exist upon approval from the state financial administration.
- The liability obligation for the co-operatives extends beyond its investment reserves; members' liability should only extend so far as it is layed down in the statutes.
- Co-operatives should draw their raw materials from wholesalers and retailers as well as from kolkoz markets.
- The co-operatives should be completely free from the state in matters concerning their financial and production planning.
- Prices can be set either autonomously.(→ *Pricing Policy*) or in the scope of contractual agreements, whereby these must nevertheless reflect "necessary social costs" and demand.
- Co-operatives which have successful products can receive approval to carry out foreign trade directly.
- Production co-operatives are entitled to set up joint ventures both at home and abroad with foreign capital investment participation.
- Co-operatives are free to determine wages and salaries for their members.
- Co-operatives can determine the so-called "fund distribution" as well as profit distribution.

dd) The State and Co-operatives in a new Working Relationship

A strongly debated point prior to the ratification of the Law on Co-operatives was the exemption of co-operatives from mandatory acceptance of state contracts. The state should from now on proceed with a call for tenders. When a co-operative accepts a contract, the state is obligated to supply the raw materials and the co-operative is bound to sell at prices previously set centrally.

The lack of a limit on earnings caused great distribution imbalances under the initial conditions named (see *Peterhoff*) which lead to a rejection of the co-operatives by a great part of the population. A corporation profits tax as well as a a progressive income tax were thus introduced. These were also heavily criticized because a tax ceiling of 90% was established on monthly income exceeding 1500 roubles; tax due on a monthly income of 1500 roubles amounted to 620.20 roubles. The income tax for co-operatives was abolished on July 29, 1988, and a new co-operative tax law became effective as of July 1, 1989.

5. Aspects of Efficiency and Development Opportunities

It is evident that co-operatives have better chances to develop in an economic system that promotes them than in a completely free, organized market system in which competition between company forms is much more stiff. In the socialist countries, competition should primarily develop between state enterprises and co-operatives, whereby this cannot occur in all branches as, for example, the Soviet Law on Co-operatives illustrates. At any rate, competition must surely occur between co-operatives for scarce resources and markets. Compared to a situation in which only state enterprises exist, the liberalization of the co-operative system surely increases prosperity. Compared to a competitive situation involving all possible company and organizational forms, and thus subsequently a better adjustment to transaction costs, an exclusive introduction of co-operatives onto the market appears less than optimal. Although in this case competition between organizational forms occurs, this will be restricted through the mandatory adherence to the co-operative principles. Furthermore, there is much evidence that production co-operatives are at a disadvantage to private companies (*Vélasquez*), and that they are problematic when the entire national economy is viewed (*Wolfstetter*). If the reform measures also allow for private companies, it will not be possible to predict which company form will be able to hold its ground and survive in individual sectors. In the transitional phase, the co-operatives surely have an advantage in that certain restrictions on free entrepreneurial activity exist on both the input and output sides from the planned economy still in force. The unrestricted purchase or sale on markets not yet sufficiently functionable makes the division of labor unsure and, thus, co-ordination through cooperation advantageous. (The "law of large numbers" still cannot reduce the level of risk.) In the long run, this advantage will disappear through the increasing division of labor; free market exchange will then be less expensive.

Bibliography

Boettcher, Erik: Kooperation und Demokratie in der Wirtschaft, Tübingen 1974.

Böhm, Franz: Privatrechtsgesellschaft und Marktwirtschaft, in: ORDO, vol. 17 (1966), pp. 75–151.

Brazda, Johann/Todev, Tode/Laurinkari, Juhani: Ansätze zur Entwicklung einer neuen Genossenschaftsbewegung in den sozialistischen Ländern, in: Juhani Laurinkari (ed.): Genossenschaftslehre, München, Wien 1990, pp. 716–737.

Cholaj, Henryk/Siwek, Tadeusz: Das genossenschaftliche Eigentum im sozialistischen Staat, dargestellt am Beispiel des polnischen Genossenschaftswesens, in: Boettcher, Erik (ed.): Genossenschaften im Systemvergleich, Tübingen 1976, pp. 1–37.

Dülfer, Eberhard: Strukturprobleme der Genossenschaft in der Gegenwart; in: Neuere Tendenzen im Genossenschaftswesen, ed. Forschungsinstitut für Genossenschaftswesen an der Universität Wien, Göttingen 1966, pp. 5–34.

Dülfer, Eberhard: Betriebswirtschaftslehre der Kooperative, Göttingen 1984.

Ehm, Michaela: Die Polnischen Genossenschaften zwischen Privat- und Zentralplanwirtschaft, Münster 1983.

Gorbatschow, Michael: Das Potential der Genossenschaften für die Perestroika. Ansprache des Generalsekretärs des ZK der KPdSU auf dem IV. Unionskongreß der Kolchosen, 23. März 1988, Moskau 1988.

Hoppe, Michael: Die klassische und neoklassische Theorie der Genossenschaften, Berlin 1976.

Kirzner, Israel M.: Entrepreneurship and Competition, Chicago u.a. 1973.

Kleer, Jerzy: Das polnische Genossenschaftswesen, in: Zeitschrift für das gesamte Genossenschaftswesen, vol. 38 (1988), pp. 206–218.

Peterhoff, Reinhard: Kooperative in der Sowjetunion – ein Jahr nach Erlaß des Genossenschaftsgesetzes, in: Genossenschaftsforum, 8/1989, pp. 355–358.

Ruwwe, Hans-Friedrich: Die Stellung der Konsumgenossenschaften im Sozialismus Osteuropas, Tübingen 1972.

Schweisfurth, Theodor: Das neue Genossenschaftsgesetz in der UdSSR, in: Neue Zürcher Zeitung, no. 33, 20.08.1988, p. 33.

Schweisfurth, Theodor: Steiniger Boden für die sowjetischen Genossenschaften, in: Neue Zürcher Zeitung, no. 75, 01.04.1989, p.33.

Vélasquez, Rogelio V.: Die Funktionsfähigkeit von Produktionsgenossenschaften, Tübingen 1975.

Wolfstetter, Elmar: Produktionsgenossenschaften – Mikroökonomische Grundlagen, in: Wirtschaftswissenschaftliches Studium (WiST), (1990), pp. 19–23.

Producer Associations

EGON WÖHLKEN [J]

(see also: *Classification*; *Forms of Cooperation*; *Production Co-operatives*; *Joint-production Co-operatives*; *Federations*)

I. Terminology and Legal Foundation; II. Function and Goal; III. Measures for Goal Attainment; IV. Producer Associations and their Unions as Institutions; V. State Recognition of Producer Associations; VI. Financial Assistance; VII. Legal Competitive Privileges; VIII. The Activity of Producer Associations; IX. Problem Areas for Producer Associations.

I. Terminology and Legal Foundation

Before we begin with closer discussion of the subject at hand, two similar institutions found in the following treatise require differentiation: the producer associations in accordance with the German Market Structure Law (*Marktstrukturgesetz*, *MStrG*) and the producer organizations and/or associations in accordance with European Community Law.

Producer organizations which exist in accordance with European Community Law (Ordinance 1045/72, § 13; Ordinance 3796/81, § 5) are empowered with the function of market intervention for the sake of regulating producer prices in addition to the other tasks which are discussed below (→ *European Community*). Under certain conditions, the expenses accrued in connection with market intervention are reimbursed to an extent from the European Adjustment and Guarantee Fund for Agriculture (*Recke/Sotzeck*).

Producer organizations are primarily found in the vegetable and fruit sector. Producer associations in accordance with the German *MStrG* dominate in sheer number for fishery products (see Table). Producer associations in accordance with European Community Law are planned among other things for hops farmers (Ordinance 1696/71, § 7).

The following discussion is limited to *producer associations* founded in accordance with the German "Law for Adjusting Agricultural Production to Market Requirements" (the *Marktstrukturgesetz*) of 1969. Even in its original formulation, §7 of the *MStrG* drew a clear line between producer associations based on the *MStrG* and producer organizations based on European Community Law: vegetable and fruit producers growing the identical products could belong to either a producer association or a producer organization (*Recke/Sotzeck*). This principle of exclusion was also retained in essence in the recent rewording of *MStrG*, § 7.

II. Function and Goal

Producer associations should fulfill the following functions:

Table: Producer Associations and their Combinations in Germany in accordance with the Marktstrukturgesetz as of December 10, 1992

Product Group	Producer recognized	Association in an initial stage	Combinations of Producer Associations
Quality Grains	477	23	10
Quality Rapeseed	101	12	1
Potatoes	75	15	3
Wine and Grape Must	259	3	2
Flowers and Decorative Plants	22	1	0
Breeding Animals	16	1	0
Milk	121	6	1
Slaughter Animals and Meat	219	24	10
Eggs and Poultry	47	5	2
Fishery Products	1	0	0
Others	29	18	0
TOTAL	1,367	108	29

For Comparison: Producer Organizations or Producer Associations and their Combinations in accordance to European Community Law

Fruit and Vegetables	59	6	5
Fishery Products	25	0	2
Hops	4	1	0

Source: Agrarbericht 1993, Table 133

- The supply of agricultural products is quite fractured due to production in small farm enterprises, but it confronts an increasing concentration of demand on the side of the market occupied by trading and food processing companies. Producer associations are intended to pull together the fractured supply of agricultural products and mold it into a mass capable of more large-scale wholeselling. At the same time, the negotiating position of producers should be strengthened when they sell their goods, thus creating countervailing market power. (→ *Marketing*).
- As consumers become more affluent, demand increases for high quality food products which in turn places higher demands on the agricultural products grown by farmers. The orientation of agricultural production around altered consumer demands for quality should be achieved in producer associations through the implementation of production and quality standards.
- Alongside these main functions, a further objective of producer associations is to agree upon market delivery times; this in turn contributes to the reduction of temporary deviations in market supply.

The goal striven for by producer associations in connection with the functions listed above is "to improve the situation of German agriculture in the Common Market by creating producer associations and unions of producer associations" (*Recke/Sotzeck*, p.105).

III. Measures for Goal Attainment

In order to realize this explicit goal, three interrelated instruments have been provided for by the *MStrG*:
- the creation of the *institution* of the producer association and of the union of producer associations, including their state recognition (*MStrG*, § 1);
- financial *support* of producer associations and their unions subsequent to their recognition from the appropriate (federal) state body (*MStrG*, § 2);
- legal competitive *privileges* for producer associations and their unions (*MStrG*, § 11).

IV. Producer Associations and their Unions as Institutions

Lawmakers define *producer associations* as "consolidated organizations of owners of agricultural enterprises or fisheries who collectively pursue the objective of adjusting production and turnover to market demands" (*MStrG*, § 1, subsec.1). Through a "*List of Products* for which producer associations can be formed and receive recognition" appended to the Law the range of products is defined for which the measures of the Law are applicable. This fundamentally encompasses agricultural products in the state they leave the production enterprise and includes in only a few cases raw food materials and/or food products in an initial processed stage (slaughtered animals, butter, cheese, and curds). The *MStrG* thereby does not extend to finished products in the food and grocery industry.

Unions of producer associations in accordance with the Law are "consolidated organizations of producer associations for a certain product or a group of related products" (*MStrG*, § 1, subsec.3). As an obligatory function they are to further the application of uniform production and quality standards as well as to work towards adjusting production to market demands by providing producer associations with information and consulting services. They furthermore can co-ordinate sales on the various markets for the products of their producer associations as well as assume responsibility for warehousing, market preparatory needs, and packing (optional tasks).

V. State Recognition of Producer Associations

The attainment of state recognition is a precondition for producer associations and/or unions of producer associations to apply for financial support and receive legal competitive privileges. State recognition is tied to several requirements (*MStrG*, § 3):
- the legal form of a producer association (juristic person in private law);
- compulsory payment of membership dues (to ensure personal involvement of members and that business costs are financed);
- the adherence and control of production and quality standards (to structure production around a market-oriented product palette);
- collective tendering for sale (exceptions are possible based on a collective resolution);
- minimum membership duration (at least three years);
- minimum size of the producer association (at least seven members; minimum production levels, minimum cultivated acreage);
- no restraints of competition on the market.

Similar requirements are effective for a union of producer associations to acquire state recognition (*MStrG*, § 4).

VI. Financial Assistance

In accordance with the *MStrG*, producer associations and their unions can receive state support subsequent to their recognition in the form of start-up and investment subsidies.

Start-up subsidies are intended to facilitate the establishment of producer associations and foster their activities during their first five years (*MStrG*, § 5). The ceiling of such subsidies is limited in the first year to 3% of their annual sales receipts, to 2% in the second year, and to 1% in the third, fourth, and fifth years. In the first year, the amount may not exceed 60% of total administration costs including expenses for consulting and quality control; in the second year, it is limited to 40% of the same, and the ceiling the last three years is 20% per year. Furthermore, the total amount of assistance granted to a producer association and/or a union of producer associations may not exceed the sum which results from the following breakdown of their sales receipts from their yearly production: 3% the first year, 2% the second year, and 1% the third year.

Once having attained recognition, producer associations and their unions can receive *investment subsidies* for their initial investments during the first seven years. These are provided for those investments which serve the implementation of production and quality standards as well as processing, packing, and warehousing in line with market conditions (*MStrG*, § 5, subsec.4). The amount of such investment subsidies may not exceed 25% of the investment costs.

Investment assistance can also be afforded to companies which directly purchase products from producer associations (*MStrG*, § 6, subsec.1). Such companies must have signed supply contracts with recognized producer associations, and the investments must serve to improve the quality and marketing of the products covered in the supply contract.

VII. Legal Competitive Privileges

An essential provision of the *MStrG* concerns the partial exemption of producer associations and their unions from cartel stipulations, thus extending beyond the sectoral exemptions for agriculture found in § 100 of the Law Against Restraints of Competition (*GWB, Gesetz gegen Wettbewerbsbeschränkung*en) (*Wendler*) (→ *Anti-Trust Laws*). Producer associations accordingly can pass recommendations on to their members with respect to the maintenance of specific prices for their products or advise them as to which markets should be supplied at which time with which products (*Recke/Sotzeck*).

Unions of producer associations can advise their members on pricing and pass price recommendations on to them (*Hausmann*). The exceptional position with regard to cartel standards is, however, only effective as long as the other remaining provisions of the GWB remain unaffected. Those admissible measures in the *MStrG* which restrain competition are therefore subject to the discretion of the regulatory commission in accordance to *GWB*, § 104 (*Goemann/Gruben/Sotzeck*).

VIII. The Activity of Producer Associations

Since the *MStrG* and the product-specific provisions for its implementation became effective, 1,367 producer associations had been recognized in Germany (including the new federal states) as of December 10, 1992; a further 108 establishments of producer associations are known of, the recognition of which is still pending (*Agrarbericht* [Agriculture Report], 1993, p.162). Most of these producer associations were founded for quality grains (477), wine and grape must (259) as well as for meat animals and piglets (219) (see Table). Seen from their economic importance rather than from their numerical representation, further concentration among producer associations is found in the sectors of poultry animals and early potatoes (*Heim*, 1978). In the majority of cases, the legal form of a registered co-operative (e.G.) or an incorporated society established for non-economic purposes was chosen (*Heim*, 1978; *Weick*), but the incorporated society for economic purposes was also selected (*Elsinger*, 1991).

The number of producer associations and their legal form, however, are not themselves criteria for their effectiveness – aside from the fact that a number of recognized producer associations came into being through the transformation of their existent sales structures. An empirical research study showed that all recognized producer associations involved in wine-growing in the federal states of Rhineland-Palatinate and Hesse developed from previously institutionalized or loosely co-operating producer conglomerations (wine-grower co-operatives, wine-grower combines) (*Weick*). These transformations brought about the proposal to preclude such re-establishments from receiving state funding and support (*Mühlbauer*).

Empirical research analysing producer associations for potatoes (*Heim*, 1982) indicates that enterprises which join together in a producer association

- have an above average amount of potato acreage;
- are not affected by the steady decline in the amount of cultivated acreage in Germany as a whole;
- are found in regions in which large-scale potato growing has been pursued for a great number of years in order to serve a particular processing industry, or where processing enterprises have come into being;
- are concentrated on growing only a handful of potato varieties;
- have achieved a considerable quality advantage by replacing 75% of all seedlings;
- have attained a domestic market share of 15% for potato growing, whereby the individual share for refinement potatoes was 29%, for starch potatoes 78%, and for early potatoes 80%;
- handle their sales on the basis of fixed contractual agreements between the producer associations and direct primary buyers.

Other available studies about market shares held by producer associations, their product-specific and regional distinctions (*Heim*, 1978) as well as their market effectiveness indicate that "producers are more willing to be actively involved the less the prevalent market conditions correspond to the goals of the *MStrG*" (*Hülsemeyer*, p.304). These studies also show that growth in stocks and improvements in the performance level (quality), at least among enterprises producing slaughter pork which are joined together in producer associations, have ensured them a clear advantage over enterprises not organized in this manner; true rationalization effects could be verified in the sector of slaughter cattle based on tangible improvements in the supply structure of meat in the form of smaller commissions for such supply (*Hülsemeyer*). Price stabilization resulting from less variable supply of producer associations could not be determined for the time being (*Heim*, 1978; *Heim*, 1982): the share of production traceable to producer associations is by far too low. Roughly 10% of all pork producers within the former German borders were organized in producer associations in 1977; approx. 16% of all domestic slaughter pork and 10% of all piglets were raised on farms affiliated in producer associations (*Heim*, 1978).

In order to illustrate the extent of production with current figures, the following data for the product groups quality grains, rapeseed, wine, slaughter animals, and meat were collected by the Agricultural Administration in the German state of Hesse for the year 1991:

- Of the 23 recognized producer associations for quality grain in Hesse, 16 of them produced a total of 87,300 tons of quality wheat. In that the total harvested amount of wheat in Hesse was 926,000 tons in 1991 (SBA, 1991, p.17), this represents almost 10%.
- Five producer associations for quality rapeseed with ascertainable production outputs in Hesse produced 5,700 tons in 1991; with the total harvest in Hesse amounting to 186,000 tons (SBA, 1991, p.25), the producer associations thus contributed 3%.
- Three producer associations for wine-growers region with ascertainable production outputs in the Rhinegau produced 29,900 hectoliters of wine. This represented 10% of the 276,000 hectoliters of wine must harvested in the Rhinegau (SBA, 1991, p.130).
- Eleven producer associations for slaughter animals and meat in Hesse which had complete production statistics raised 59,600 tons of beef and 493,000 tons of pork in 1991. With an average weight at slaughter of 310 kilos per cow and 90 kilos per pig and a total production of 84,300 tons of beef and 137,700 tons of pork in Hesse, the producer associations accounted for a 22% share of beef and a 32% share of pork.

The repercussions on company selection in the sector of direct purchasers must also be taken into consideration when evaluating the effects of the *MStrG*. The concentration of supply certainly heightened selectional pressure on small-scale purchasers involved in commercial trade (*Hülsemeyer*).

IX. Problem Areas for Producer Associations

Even though numerous regions and specific product sectors have been successful, the effect of the *MStrG* as a whole has not met the (overly) optimistic expectations of the law's initiators. This indicates that stronger economic impulses (or a change in producers' stance with respect to cooperation) are necessary in order for an extensive institutional and organizational change to occur, thereby resulting in efficiency advantages in the marketing sector.

In this regard, the problem areas of producer associations will be outlined on the basis of empirical research on producer associations in Bavaria, in particular in the sector of slaughter animals; suggestions for the future activities in the producer association sector are accordingly presented (*Elsinger*, 1990; *Elsinger*, 1991).

- Horizontal conglomerations of producers provide an appropriate organizational basis as well as sufficient leeway for the systematic planning of marketing activities. These opportunities up to now have not been exhausted and should be utilized to a better extent.
- Internal enterprise analyses are necessary to detect weak organization points, especially in marketing activities; the extent the producer associations utilize traditional marketing-political instruments was found to be entirely too low, a fact which contributes to their failure to achieve set goals.
- In accordance with the character of producer associations as self-help organizations in the farming sector, decisions concerning the organization and management of these institutions are almost exclusively made by farmers assuming the capacity of honorary officials; only in rare situations are these individuals actually involved in the marketing process. It is therefore necessary to increase the level of potential influence which full- and part-time employees of the producer associations have in decision-making processes. In general, training and continuing education strengthen the qualifications of decision makers. More realistic strategies can be developed in this manner which are co-ordinated around the needs of individual buyers, groups of buyers or market segments.
- A well-known problem of producer associations which in practice has yet to be solved is the irregular behavior of members with respect to their turnover contributions. A satisfactory delivery obligation should be inforced as the fundamental precondition for directed, long-term sales planning. This should be achieved through strengthened membership ties and motivation and, if necessary, through a newly designed form of sanctions.
- The opportunities for cooperation among producer associations in the form of unions of producer associations are frequently not taken advantage of due to the competitive behavior of the producer associations among each other. Such cooperation, however, is necessary in that priority is placed on marketing activities.
- A basic precondition for the development of promising marketing strategies is also the reinforcement of vertical co-ordination with partners on subsequent marketing levels; such co-ordination can only be found in isolated cases.
- Two fundamentally different strategic approaches are recommended. The first strategy is based on producers affiliated in the producer association as initiators of market-oriented activity. In the second strategy, the producer level does not engage itself as the sole initiator of market-oriented sales strategy but rather is integrated in a vertical combine system which has been agreed upon contractually. In the latter model, the involvement of producers in the acquisition of know-how and financial resources from their partners can be appraised in a positive light. Nonetheless, the second variation entails more or less a substantial loss of individual decision-making freedom for each producer association.

The listing of problem areas encountered by producer associations and the related list of suggestions are only an initial step; the implementation of these scientific suggestions in everyday practise by a professional management staff in the producer associations, on the other hand, represents the substantially more difficult endeavor necessary to safeguard the long-term existence of the institution of producer associations.

Bibliography

Elsinger, M.: Erzeugergemeinschaften – Strategie für die Zukunft?. In: Agrarwirtschaft, Jg. 39, H. 9 (September 1990), pp.292–295.
Elsinger, M.: Erzeugergemeinschaften als Organisationsmodell zur Förderung eines marktgerechten Agrarangebots, Diss., Munich 1991.
Gesetz zur Anpassung der landwirtschaftlichen Erzeugung an die Erfordernisse des Marktes (Marktstrukturgesetz), 16 June, 1969 (BGBI.I, No. 39, 20 June, 1969, pp. 423–427) in der Fassung der Bekanntmachung vom 26.9.1990 (BGBI.I, p. 2134 f.) sowie Drittes Gesetz zur Änderung des Marktstrukturgesetzes vom 26.6.1992 (BGBI.I, p. 1159).
Goeman, D./Gruben, H. von/Sotzeck, M.: Marktstrukturgesetz und Absatzfondsgesetz, zwei neue Initiativen zur Ausrichtung der deutschen Agrarpolitik. Berichte über Landwirtschaft, vol. 47 (1969), pp. 283–300.
Hausmann, Friedrich Bernhard: Erzeugergemeinschaften.In: Handwörterbuch des Genossenschaftswesens, pp. 422–439, Wiesbaden 1980.
Heim, Norbert: Erzeugergemeinschaften für Schlachtschweine und Ferkel. Eine Bilanz nach 8 Jahren Marktstrukturgesetz in der Bundesrepublik Deutschland, in: Schweinezucht und Schweinemast, Jg. 26, No.1 (January 1978), pp. 4–9 and Jg.26, No.2 (February 1978), pp. 48–51.
Heim, Norbert: Erzeugergemeinschaften für Kartoffeln in der Bundesrepublik Deutschland. (Ländliches Genossenschaftswesen – Schriften aus dem Institut für ländliches Genossenschaftswesen an der Justus-Liebig-Universität Gießen, H. 22), Gießen 1982.
Hessisches Statistisches Landesamt (HSL): Fleischanfall aus hessischer Erzeugung. (Statistische Berichte CIII 2S – j 91, 3 June 1992).
Hülsemeyer, F.: Kosten und Erträge der Marktstrukturpolitik dargestellt am Beispiel der organisierten Schlachtvieherzeugung Bayerns. In: Schmitt, G./Steinhauer, H.(ed.): Planung, Durchführung und Kontrolle der Finanzierung von Landwirtschaft und Agrarpolitik (Schriften der Gesellschaft für Wirtschafts- und Sozialwissenschaften des Landbaues, vol. 15), pp. 303–312, Munich 1978.
Marktstrukturgesetz (MStrG), see: Gesetz zur...
Mühlbauer, Franz: Die finanzielle Förderung nach dem Marktstrukturgesetz – Ziele, Maßnahmen, Wirkungen sowie einzel- und gesamtwirtschaftliche Effizienz. (Agrarwirtschaft, Sh.87) Hannover 1981.
Recke, H.-J./Sotzeck, M.: Marktstrukturgesetz mit Erläuterungen und Materialien, Hildesheim 1970.
Statistisches Bundesamt (SBA): Landwirtschaftliche Bodennutzung und pflanzliche Erzeugung 1991. (Fachserie 3: Land- und Forstwirtschaft, Fischerei, Reihe 3).
Verordnung (EWG) Nr. 1035/72 des Rates vom 18.5.1972 über eine gemeinsame Marktorganisation für Obst und Gemüse (ABl.EG, L 118 vom 20.5.1972).
Verordnung (EWG) Nr. 1696/71 des Rates vom 26.7.1971 über die gemeinsame Marktorganisation für Hopfen (ABl.EG, L 175 vom 4.8.1971).
Verordnung (EWG) Nr. 3796/81 des Rates vom 29.12.1981 über die gemeinsame Marktorganisation für Fischereierzeugnisse (ABl.EG, L 379 vom 31.12.1981)
Weick, C.: Stand und Entwicklungsaussichten der kooperativen Vermarktung im rheinlandpfälzischen und hessischen Weinbau. Diss. agr. Gießen 1977.
Wendler, D.: Die wirtschaftliche Bedeutung der Bereichsausnahme für die Landwirtschaft im GWB. (Volkswirtschaftliche Schriften, H. 262), Berlin 1977.

Production Co-operatives

THEODOR BERGMANN

(see also: *Classification*; *Joint-production Co-operatives*; *Labour-Management*; *History in 19th C.*; *Produktionsförderungsgenossenschaften*)

I. Basic Principles; II. Stages of Co-operativity; III. From Equality to Economization; IV. Internal Tensions; V. Adaptation of Co-operative Structure; VI. State and Cooperation; VII. Co-operatives and Professional Organizations; VIII. Co-operatives in Developing Countries.

This essay defines as production co-operatives institutions that collect raw materials from agricultural producers, transform them into marketable commodities and commercialize them either directly to the ultimate consumer or indirectly via retail traders. This definition differs from the one hitherto used and usual in countries of planned economies; there the institutions (farms), on which collective farmers jointly produce agricultural commodities, are called production co-operatives.

I. Basic Principles

Co-operatives are defined as institutionalized cooperation with equal rights and binding duties in specific organizational forms (→ *Legal Form, Co-operative*). This implies an organization with regulations, defining the goals. The main economic goal is the economic promotion of the members by joint efforts, mutual and self-aid (→ *Promotion Mandate*). Members have equal rights and offer a contribution that is clearly determined and equal (e.g. land, produce, labour, capital, livestock). The members administer the co-operative from the start or are led to self-administration by government assistance. The social and educational tasks are met by the economic promotion. (*Bergmann* 1967)

Co-operatives are institutions of a dualist character (*Draheim* 1955); they have both economic and social objectives (→ *Dual Nature*), viz to promote the members' economy and to fulfill certain social functions. A specific relationship exists between the two sides of cooperation: they are independent and at the same time contradictory. Only if the members are satisfied with the economic performance of their co-operative, do they identify with it and are they willing to "sacrifice" some part of their "profit" (By definition, co-operatives are non-profit institutions. Thus, the word is put in quotation marks. They only make a surplus, which shall be either distributed to the members according to their contribution, not according to their share in capital (→ *Reimbursements*), or utilized for accepted common aims.) for common and social tasks. A basic principle of cooperation is equality of the members concerning needs, demand for and benefits from cooperation. Equality again contributes to and strengthens identity (→ *Theory of co-operative Cooperation*). Identity implies that all clients are members and that all members are clients. The more services are offered by the co-operative and the more these are vital to and used by the members, the stronger the identity and co-operative nexus. The farmers are producing the raw commodities, which are collected by the co-operative, transformed and processed (to a different degree) and then marketed (→ *Marketing*). The raw materials can be potatoes, sugarbeets, sugarcane, cereals, milk, animals for slaughter, vegetables, grapes, fruits, eggs, coffee, tea, products of home industries etc. Every item has its specific traits regarding processing, perishability, seasonal availability, marketing etc. Production co-operatives are, thus, subsidiary institutions, called to support the more or less independent economy of their members, the individually and differently managed farms or holdings.

II. Stages of Co-operativity

Objective preconditions for the formation of production co-operatives are: Increase of peasant production beyond the need of subsistence and self-consumption, production of commodities and emergence of an urban market of non-agricultural consumers. Subjective prerequisites are: Economic independence of the producers from landlords, moneylenders, middlemen etc., free decision about commercialization of their produce, economic ability to finance a co-operative, socio-cultural ability and political liberty to form and manage a co-operative (→ *State and Co-operatives, Market Economy*).

Thus, there are periods in economic development (history) and countries, in which the ultimate cultivators are in a pre-co-operative stage, be it as serfs, tenants, tenants-at-will, subsistence producers on dwarf-holdings or with low productivity and large families, be it tied to moneylenders or rural middlemen, to whom they are indebted. In fact, formalized and organized peasant co-operation in *Raiffeisen* production co-operatives in Germany started in the middle of the nineteenth century after two important developments: economic and social independence of the peasantry after an agrarian reform (→ *History in 19th C.*); agricultural innovations increased production and productivity beyond subsistence level. Against middlemen, commission agents, merchants, and finally the large market-chains, the producers have to defend themselves, to fight against monopolization of the markets and for their share in the consumers' expenditure for food. The more the market structure changes towards oligopoly or monopoly, the more the individual small producers are compelled to co-operate against the powers in the market. That is the period when small producers need production co-operatives for their very existence.

Logically, there must be a post-co-operative stage, when large-scale producers of agricultural commodities do not need production co-operatives anymore; i.e. when they produce quantities large enough to enable them to make their own direct deal with a processing or marketing enterprise or a retailer.

In countries where smallholdings dominated or dominate the agrarian structure, production co-operatives had and have an important role to play. They are the dominant feature of peasant self-organization. They have educated their members to attain and maintain quality in production, strengthened their ability to form and manage their own organizations and their self-confidence. Such was the case in all scandinavian countries, the Netherlands, France, Germany, Czechoslovakia and Austria. There are regional variations in co-operative coverage, which might be due to historical, cultural and social traditions and to the market position of merchants. (E.g. in the southern regions of viticulture in Germany, production co-operatives are clearly dominant, while in western regions private wine merchants dominate the market.)

III. From Equality to Economization

In the early stages, production co-operatives aimed to organize all producers, small and large, in order to counter market anarchy and producers' competition, favoring the market partner, assure a regular flow of commodities, assure good quality and standards and offer the members a reasonable remuneration for their sales. The market can only be consolidated, when most producers tow the line. Thus, the larger producers must wish to enlist even the small producers. The basic co-operative principle is applied: Equality – all producers receive the same treatment, the same conditions, the same price regardless of the size of the individual delivery. *David* (1922) even asserts, that co-operatives give small holders and small-scale producers the same chance and equal opportunity in the market as offered to the large farmer without co-operatives.

In the later phases of technical innovation and socio-economic development, size and structure of the membership base of production co-operatives change: The number of holdings declines, production increases, socio-economic differentiation grows. Also a changing structure of the market compels the production co-operatives to economize (*Draheim* 1967); they have to apply the "rules of the market". Large-scale producers have a choice between delivery to their production co-operative or to a private firm; small producers on the other hand "lose in weight", i.e. in the market share, while business with them causes higher costs per unit of commodity. Therefore, production co-operatives feel "compelled" to apply unequal treatment: better conditions, higher price for bulk delivery. The co-operative principle of equality becomes uneconomic. Instead of being open and recruiting every producer, even the smaller ones, the co-operative wants to select its members according to their economic capacity. If not, it might lose its large producers.

→ *Oppenheimer* (1896) might have called this development the degeneration of co-operatives; *Draheim* (1967) called it economization. It is in fact the adaptation of co-operatives to the changing structures and forces of their capitalist environment, where profit maximization is the rule and the main yardstick for success. Co-operative principles, formulated about 150 years ago, have to be pushed aside, re-interpreted, in fact deeply changed; they cannot be eternal truth, if the co-operatives want to survive in a new economic world. This also proves that co-operatives do not change the economic system, of which they are part, rather are changed by its developments.

IV. Internal Tensions

The interest of producers in production co-operatives can differ widely, largely according to the type and quantity of their marketed commodity. Small producers (with specialized production and small quantities) might find enough customers in the vicinity, the region, or the next town for direct marketing. Due to adulteration of food and new health consciousness of customers, this direct deal between producer and consumer – without an intermediary – might become important temporarily and on a limited scale. On the other end of the scale, large-scale producers might be or become so strong, offer such large quantities of a standardized commodity, that they can make their own deal, also excluding a mediating co-operative. The stratum in between these two extremes depends on the production co-operatives. The size of this group and thus the share of their co-operative in the total volume of sales depends largely on the size-structure of farm-holdings, their socio-economic differentiation and the structure of the market. This differentiation weakens the co-operative nexus (*Draheim* 1955), since the interests of the members diverge more and more.

Production co-operatives are voluntary organizations. Members' interests are not entirely equal and identical, and their willingness and economic ability to forsake the private economic interest (to contribute to the co-operative interest) differs. Generally, to meet the (urgent) economic and financial needs, the members will demand maximum distribution of the co-operative's revenue; their short-term interest prevails. The responsible leadership, be it honorary or more so paid management, on the other hand, must aim at accumulation of investment funds or for the levelling of seasonal or annual variations in turnover. It must protect the long-term interest of the co-operative.

Production co-operatives have to follow and adapt to modern technical developments, if they shall not fall behind: more processing, grading, classifying, packing of the members' raw material calls for continuous and growing investment in larger processing plants with higher capacity. This has two consequences: a) A clash of interest between short-term "consumption" (distribution) and long-term interest of investment. The balance between the two must be bargained between membership and management (leadership), lest members' trust and delivery discipline be impaired. b) For each processing plant more producers are necessary, whose raw materials are collected, thus less but larger dairies, less slaughterhouses, less wine-caves, more centralization, less local plants, less direct contact between the members and their co-operative and less direct democratic influence and control of leadership and management.

In large, capital-intensive processing plants, large funds cannot be managed by honorary leaders, who are self-employed ultimate producers. These developments rather call for full-time, well-paid, professional managers. Such full-time staff, externally recruited, develops its own views and interests. Direct democratic control by frequent general assemblies of all members becomes more difficult, often unfeasible; the distance between members and management grows, and their interests diverge more and more.

In Sweden, co-operatives have tried to counter the loss of direct democratic contact between the members and their institution by creating a new organizational level of directly elected representatives, whose function is the communication between membership and management. The opportunities for diversion of funds, dishonesty, and embezzlement are given. Indian co-operative statistics report all cases of embezzlement, while in Western Europe newspapers report about criminal cases, i.e. when they have reached a size and a stage, that the courts have to deal with them. (The disclosure and reporting of all cases of bankruptcy, defaulting, and embezzlement in published indian statistics proves the usefulness of publicity and the strength of cooperation that criticizes its own weaknesses. There is definitely as much economic crime in the private economy, but publicity is much less.)

V. Adaptation of Co-operative Structure

The production co-operatives have tried to adapt their structure to the deep changes on both sides (membership and market) by different means (→ *Business Policies*):
1. Formation of secondary firms for processing, marketing etc. by the primary co-operatives, who fund the capital for the new, secondary tier
2. Merger of small primary co-operatives
3. Formation of "peasant shareholding companies" for the processing plants
4. Formation of producer groups (Erzeugergemeinschaften).

In case 1, mostly the secondary tier has acquired the main functions and depleted the primary co-operatives. The centripetal economic and technological forces (concentration, economies of scale) have proved stronger than co-operative self-determination. Mostly for the new types 2–4, the old co-operative principles of openness and equal treatment have been waived. A certain size of production was stipulated by the producer groups (→ *Operational Size*); smallholders were excluded. Members were selected according to economic capacity. In companies of type 3, producers have to put in capital according to their production capacity to pay for the investment in processing capacity. Still, by limiting the number of shares per member, the voting right and the sale of shares by the holder, a certain balance was to be maintained and a brake set against domination by a minority of large shareholders. This new type of firm, originally close to production co-operatives, was quite short-lived. There is a clear interdependence between the development and the changes in co-operatives and the development phases of industrial societies (see also *Engelhardt* 1985).

VI. State and Cooperation

Production co-operatives are economic institutions; the modern state regulates their rules of the game by its legislation, which shapes the conditions of their functioning. The attitude of the state might differ over time and with changing political and economic "ideology". Attitudes can vary from hostility via neutrality to sympathy and promotion and finally to active intervention from control to administrative exploitation. When production co-operatives were founded around 1850 in Western and Central Europe, the state seemed largely disinterested. When their impact on the national economy and their positive effect on their members' economy became tangible, co-operative legislation was initiated. In later critical periods, governments utilized the established network for their own purposes: Compulsory collection of scarce or rationed food commodities in war-time, levies of grain at below-market prices. Government might pay for such administrative assistance. These functions, however, are often contrary to the members' interest and the normal task of co-operatives. Thus, such state-controlled or state-induced activities might alienate the members and induce them to circumvent their "own" organizations, which appear to be the extended arm of public administration, not the advocate and protector of members' interests.

The changing attitude of government and the changing relationship between state and co-operatives can be illustrated by the german case. In imperial Germany – before 1918 – state and legislation were mainly neutral. In republican Germany – 1918–1933 – government was positively interested in such cooperation, since it supported the economy of the millions of smallholders under odd economic conditions (global agrarian crisis). On the other hand, during the period 1918–1933, government also utilized production co-operatives of german-speaking peasants for political purposes in foreign countries. Political subsidies were channelled through such co-operatives to strengthen and expand "germanity" (Deutschtum) beyond the german frontiers (see *Seraphim* 1951). Fascist Germany – 1933–1945 – disliked democratic cooperation, since it was an obstacle to hierarchical uniformity of the almighty state, which aimed at a total control of food production and storage for the preparation of war. Therefore, dairy co-operatives etc. were entirely transformed, integrated in the central organization of all agricultural activities and strata (Reichsnährstand). The democratic structure was abolished; administrative orders prescribed all activities.

After the catastrophy of fascist rule in 1945, the new government took a more distant and neutral stance. Co-operatives could be formed and developed; but no promotion or privilege was offered. Some administrative activities were transferred to them; e.g. co-operative dairies were asked to distribute government subsidies.

VII. Co-operatives and Professional Organizations

Generally, it might be assumed that production co-operatives and professional organizations representing the farmers' demands cooperate without problems or tensions. To a certain extent and in certain periods this is the case. But the changing relations between the members and their co-operative, lack of internal democracy, independence of management etc. might create frictions. A case in point is Sweden. Production co-operatives in Sweden started quite late, in fact only in the 1920's, and reached a high level of organization and efficiency and a high share in the internal market. They are also active in agricultural exports. In the 1970's, a merger of the roof organizations of all production co-operatives (Svenska Lantmännens Riksförbund) with the professional organization (Riksförbundet Landsbygdens Folk) was decided for with the aim of cost-saving and higher efficiency, also in bargaining with government agencies. In the late eighties, however, this merger was questioned by the membership. The critics claimed that both wings have contradictory functions; the professional representation should bargain and fight against the co-operatives for a higher share of the producers in the turnover (distribution of "surplus" against capital formation and investment). This proves a certain alienation of members from their centralized production co-operatives, which are perceived more as employers than as own service institutions.

In the FRG, the heavy decline in the number of farmers has caused several problems for both the commercial co-operatives and the professional farmers union. The latter's traditional advice to their members is questioned; they also look for new tasks and funds to maintain their structure. That leads to competition between the two types of farmers institutions.

Critical and dissatisfied producers feel that co-operatives do not do their best for them and keep a hold on large funds, which, when distributed, could substantially improve their living standard. Finally, they perceive of their production co-operative not anymore as their co-operative property, but rather as a business partner, who tries to minimize their income or as an employer. As a consequence, they expect their professional organization to bargain with the co-operative about the share of revenue to be distributed. That is the case in the FRG in the early nineties. Whatever form and intensity this might take, tension and conflict between basis and management remain as a lasting problem of democratic institutions.

VIII. Co-operatives in Developing Countries

Many issues discussed above are problems of a period of high economic and technical development, of highly industrialized, "mature" capitalist economies. Here, the agrarian sector is on the decline regarding its share both in the numbers of economically active and in GNP, its impact on the national economy. In most developing countries – comprising the majority of mankind – farming is the key sector, though not the leading one. Food production is mainly done in tiny economic units, and most cultivators are in a pre-co-operative stage. Under these conditions, the most urgent issues of production co-operatives are different (→ *Self-help Organizations*). European experts have often and intensively given advice for the formation of production co-operatives. And it could well be that the partial failure of cooperation and the disappointment of the experts is due to their ignorance of the specific problems facing cooperation in a different phase of socio-economic development. Some urgent problems can be seen in Indian production co-operatives (→ *Development, South Asia*).

There was no efficient agrarian reform in most Indian states. Social inequality and inferiority in the village are reflected in the co-operatives. The well-to-do farmers are largely the leaders and officials and they promote their peers, not the poor and needy. Therefore, some Indian cooperators have suggested the "undemocratic" way of excluding big farmers from the management of co-operatives to ensure the emergence and preservation of real co-operative democracy.

The planners of the co-operative movement have tried again and again to link marketing and credit to rid the smallholders from indebtedness and double exploitation by usurious moneylenders amd middlemen. This has largely proved unfeasible hitherto.

Official policy since independence in 1947 has been to promote rural cooperation, particularly in the fields of credit and marketing. Government has given ample support in different ways for the formation of primary societies. At the same time, official tasks were conferred on the production co-operatives, and the official deputies to assist in early organizational steps often outweighed the members and ignored their demands (→ *Officialization*). This has led to a clear call for de-officialization.

Production co-operatives are a substantial element *sui generis* in many national economies. They are vital auxiliary institutions for small-scale producers, particularly in agriculture. Their impact on the economy in general and on the living standard of their members differs from country to country and changes with the development stages of a society. In many developing countries, they have not yet exhausted their capacity in promoting the smallholders (→ *Policies for Promotion*). In highly industrialized countries, they have to adapt to strong external forces. Here, their perspectives are open, but controversial and in the eye of the beholder. Advocates of neo-classical capitalism might assert that co-operatives belong to history. Critics of the drawbacks of capitalism, on the other hand, will see the need to adapt to new challenges, emanating both from economic concentration and technical innovation and from emerging new needs of their members and clients. For the latter group of theoreticians, survival of co-operatives depends upon their ability to self-criticism, reform and meeting new demands.

Bibliography

All–India Rural Credit Survey: General Report, Bombay 1959.
Banerjee, J.: Co-operative movement in India, Calcutta 1961.
Bartölke, Klaus/Bergmann, Theodor/Liegle, Ludwig (eds.): Integrated co-operatives in the industrial society: the example of the kibbutz, Assen, Netherlands 1980.
Benecke, D.W.: Kooperation und Wachstum in Entwicklungsländern, Tübingen 1972.
Bergmann, Theodor/Takekazu B. Ogura: Cooperation in world agriculture – Experiences, problems and perspectives, Tokyo 1985.

Bergmann, Theodor: Die Genossenschaftsbewegung in Indien – Geschichte, Leistungen, Aufgaben, Frankfurt 1971.
Bergmann, Theodor: Funktionen und Wirkungsgrenzen von Produktionsgenossenschaften in Entwicklungsländern, Frankfurt 1967.
Böttcher, Erik (ed.): The co-operative in the competition of ideas, Münster 1986.
Draheim, Georg: Die Genossenschaft als Unternehmungstyp, Göttingen 1955.
Draheim, Georg: Grundfragen des Genossenschaftswesens, Frankfurt 1983.
Draheim, Georg: Zur Ökonomisierung der Genossenschaften, Göttingen 1967.
Engelhardt, Werner Wilhelm: Der Funktionswandel der Genossenschaften in industrialisierten Marktwirtschaften, Berlin 1971.
Engelhardt, Werner Wilhelm: Allgemeine Ideengeschichte des Genossenschaftswesens, Darmstadt 1985.
Guélfat, I.: La coopération devant la science économique, Paris 1966.
Henzler, Reinhold: Der genossenschaftliche Grundauftrag: Förderung der Mitglieder, Frankfurt 1970.
Hough, Eleanor M.: The Co-operative movement in India before partition and in independent India, London 1953.
Infield, Herik F.: Utopia and Experiment – Genossenschaft und Gemeinschaft im Lichte der experimentellen Soziologie, Göttingen 1956.
Kühne, Karl: Marxismus und Gemeinwirtschaft, Frankfurt 1978a.
Kühne, Karl: Neomarxismus und Gemeinwirtschaft, Frankfurt 1978b.
Lopes-Cardoso, A.: Doctrine coopérative et coopération agricole, in: Économie Rurale 62, Paris 1964, pp. 17–24.
Myrdal, Gunnar: Ökonomische Theorie und unterentwickelte Regionen, Stuttgart 1959.
Nell-Breuning, Oswald v.: Produktionsgenossenschaften, in: Staatslexikon Recht-Wirtschaft-Gesellschaft 6, pp. 517–521, Freiburg 1961.
Neubohn, Heinz-Joachim: Entwicklungstendenzen im westdeutschen Genossenschaftswesen, Stuttgart 1972.
Oppenheimer, Franz: Die Siedlungsgenossenschaft – Versuch einer positiven Überwindung des Kommunismus durch Lösung des Genossenschaftsproblems und der Agrarfrage, Leipzig 1896.
Seraphim, Peter-Heinz: Das Genossenschaftswesen in Osteuropa, Neuwied 1951.
Weisser, Gerhard (ed.): Genossenschaften und Genossenschaftsforschung, Göttingen 1968.

Produktionsförderungsgenossenschaften (Co-operatives for the Promotion of Production)

JOHANNES G.F. WÖRZ/OTTFRIED C. KIRSCH

(see also: *Joint-production Co-operatives; Production Co-operatives; Classification; Rural Co-operatives*)

I. Origin of the Term; II. The Concept of Co-operative Promotion of Agricultural Production; III. Practical Examples and Results.

I. Origin of the Term

The term "Landwirtschaftliche Produktionsförderungsgenossenschaft" (co-operative for the promotion of agricultural production) was coined by *Otto Schiller* at the beginning of the 1960s (*Schiller*, 1965, p. 133). Since the mid-twenties, he was involved in professional activities with Soviet agriculture. During the war as a drafted serviceman, he had to "submit recommendations for the abolition of the Kolkhoz system and for the re-introduction of private enterprise" (*Schiller*, 1951, p. 3).
Realizing the necessity of increased mechanization and in view of the shortage of farm equipment and of individual management experience alike, *Schiller* decided to suggest replacement of the collective system by individual family farms of some 4 to 8 hectares each, to be operated under "a new system of farm management", the "farming co-operative" (*Schiller*, 1951, p. 1). To combine the incentives and initiative of private ownership and enterprise with the advantages of large-scale farming, e.g. rational crop rotation and extensive mechanization, the land was not distributed in consolidated units to each family farmer, but in as many parcels as crop rotation fields existed.
Hence, every farmer owned and cultivated one parcel in each of these fields; every field being cultivated uniformly with the crop allotted to it in accordance with the rotation, thus simultaneously ensuring a unified crop rotation for all small holdings. Consequently, the co-operative use of machines was possible even for these small (and individually cultivated) parcels, as those were combined into large units with one and the same crop.
By extending co-operative activities beyond services rendered to the members' farms, right into the agricultural production itself, *Schiller* felt this to be more than a service or auxiliary co-operative. The independence of the member-economies, however, was fully maintained by assuring every member the yield of his individually owned land. In spite of unified crop rotation with the obligation to cultivate the prescribed crops and with partial co-operative work processes, this organization is thus fundamentally different from a producers' (*Schiller*: "production") co-operative, which is characterized by collective land use. Consequently, *Schiller* (1969, p. 8) saw a co-operative sui generis, "an intermediary form between the agricultural production cooperative and the rural service cooperative".
This classification is at variance with that adopted by *Dülfer* (1966), and indeed most other authors, who insist that all co-operatives can be placed under one of two categories: → *service co-operatives*, in which members retain their own individual businesses, and → *producers' co-operatives* (→ *Joint-production Co-operatives*), in which members give up their independent economic status. *Dülfer* then subdivides service co-operatives into traditional, market-linkage

and integrated co-operatives (→ *Structural Types*). In a traditional co-operative, the members control the joint business establishment (Organbetrieb) and regard it as an auxiliary business supplementary to their own individual businesses. In the market-linkage co-operative, the relation between the members' own businesses and the joint business establishment resemble normal market conditions. In an integrated co-operative, the management of the members' own businesses is coordinated by the joint co-operative establishment. According to this system of classification, a co-operative for the promotion of agricultural production is quite clearly an integrated and thus a service co-operative.

Schiller's view, however, is supported by *Digby*, (1957, pp. 8ff.) when she talks of "divided" and "undivided" forms of co-operative farming, and also by *Darling* (1953, pp. 198ff.), when he differentiates between "individualistic" and "collectivistic" forms of co-operative farming. This is in line with *Schiller's* "two ways of cooperative farming" (1962), namely those forms maintaining individual members' businesses (esp. the individual way of harvesting) and those practising collective farming.

After all, *Schiller* (1969, p. 9) admits that "there is no strict dividing line between a service cooperative and a cooperative society for the promotion of agricultural production". Yet, service co-operatives put their emphasis on credit and marketing activities – "concerning the external relations of the agricultural enterprise", whilst co-operative promotion of production is performed by emphasizing "the internal working process of an agricultural enterprise" (*Schiller*, 1969, p. 6).

II. The Concept of Co-operative Promotion of Agricultural Production

One of the most widespread factors impeding agricultural development is submarginal farm sizes, usually combined with a high degree of fragmentation, hampering efforts to increase yields in developing countries as well as attempts to limit production costs. Apart from their weak position on commodity and financial markets (which gave rise to service co-operatives), these prevailing small holdings suffer from:
- hampered production technology transfer due to the traditional attitude of small farmers and their high numbers,
- non-efficient use of machinery due to both small acreage cultivated per farm and large numbers of small parcels,
- inadequate plant protection due to non-synchronized individual actions,
- inappropriate irrigation caused by different crops in any given irrigation unit,
- severe lack of know-how and managerial experience in cases of newly created small holdings, i.e. with agrarian reform or rural settlements.

These hampering factors are particularly grave in developing countries, where fragmentation is still rising due to population pressure. There, additionally liquidity pressure leads to consumption of production credits and lack of know-how to inappropriate use of inputs. On the other hand, co-operative marketing is hampered by large numbers of different crop varieties, being cultivated in small and hence hardly marketable amounts. In the case of commodities meant for industrial processing, the heterogeneity of varieties, fertilization, plant protection, soil cultivation practices and subsequently product quality creates both manufacturing and marketing problems, especially when these products are designated for export markets.

The advantages of inter-farm co-operation to counterbalance these deficiencies have long been recognized. In medieval Germany, a three-field system was in use according to which the arable land in every (historic) reclamation unit was divided into three blocks, with each farmer being allotted strips of land in each block. A compulsory cropping pattern was then followed within each block, thus ensuring a uniform crop rotation and facilitating access to rear parcels without farm road systems, as well as common pasture on both the stubble fields and the fallow land. Modern examples of inter-farm co-operation exist as well in Germany, such as the well-documented experiment carried out in Häusern in the 1930s, when the tractor-drawn reaper-binder was used "on the long line", i.e. ignoring the boundaries of the individual plots (*Münzinger*, 1933).

Schiller's approach, however, is a more comprehensive one. He defines functions within the individual members' agricultural production itself, being coordinated by a service co-operative, as "activities of cooperative promotion of agricultural production". The transformation of such service co-operative into a "cooperative society for the promotion of agricultural production" would only be justified, however, if that co-operative is mainly concerned with such activities, i.e. "if *most* of the operations in farming and animal husbandry are bound by cooperative decisions" (*Schiller*, 1969, pp. 7ff.).

Whereas normally these operations are performed individually, i.e. by each member on his land, they may also be carried out by the co-operative, as for example machinery use or plant protection. However, *Schiller* (1969, p. 7) stresses the necessity that "harvesting is in all cases done individually", to maintain the private incentive through individual rewards for personal initiative.

Schiller also pointed out that his scheme of promotion of agricultural production would facilitate the supervision of → *agricultural credit*, since the uniformity of agricultural production would enable standardized credit packages to be used. In this respect, his approach is very similar to that of *Ruthenberg* (1963), who suggested "production under close supervision", organized by an agricultural extension service within supervised credit schemes. This approach of production promotion is often combined with a special type of vertical integration via contract arrangements (contract farming), especially in connection with capital intensive production and the production of agricultural raw materials requiring immediate processing, thus allowing the processor to act as a quasi-monopolist. In practice, a horizontal integration effect is achieved which replaces the co-operative element of *Schiller's* approach.

III. Practical Examples and Results

Schiller (1960) introduced his system of land distribution in FAO-assisted settlements of the former West-Pakistan, known as the "Schiller-Scheme" (→ *Development, South Asia*). Instead of allocating land in chess-board pattern (i.e. subdivision into holdings in the form of coherent blocks), he suggested subdivision into partitions corresponding to the legs of the crop rotation, allotting every settler one third of his land in each of the three fields in one crop rotation area.

A similar, however more consequent and successful approach was followed in Egypt in the course of the 1952 land reform (*Wörz*, 1967). The expropriated land had been cultivated in large units by the former landlords, partly subdivided for labour input to tenants working under the landlords' upper management. In line with Egyptian cultural traditions, these areas were distributed to the former tenants or labourers, respectively, in small holding units of about one hectare each. "Agrarian reform co-operatives" with obligatory membership for land recipients were introduced in land reform areas, to take over the co-ordinating functions of the former landlords. Agricultural development in Egypt is hampered severely by the pre-dominance of farm sizes of around and below one hectare with subsequent enormous land fragmentation. This results in depressed yields and low product quality, especially in the case of cotton, through:

- an ever increasing percentage of cultivated land being part of the parcels' boundary area, hence harmed by influences from neighbouring parcels' different crops with other requirements towards irrigation water, drainage, fertilization, shade, weeding and plant protection;
- water losses and insufficient irrigation as well as drainage problems due to mixed cropping patterns within irrigation blocks;
- plant protection performed individually and hence inadequate and not within the shortest period of time on all of the village's cotton fields;
- inefficient use of machinery on small parcels causing wasted operation time, e.g. when deep-ploughing by tractor as is required for cotton;
- limited impact of extension service and credit supervision due to excessive fragmentation of crop cultivation.

To minimize these consequences as created by the land reform's subdivision of large units into small farms, an integrated bundle of measures was applied from the reform's very beginning:

- the former crop rotation (and simultaneously irrigation) units with three fields each were maintained, including the uniform cultivation pattern within each field;
- every land recipient was allotted one-third of his land in each of the three fields of one rotation unit, which was to be cultivated individually, however with the very crop assigned to the field in line with the rotation, resulting in large irrigation units of uniform cropping pattern;
- in order to overcome the extension and credit supervision problems resulting from the land recipients' lack of farm management knowledge, all individual cultivation is planned by the agrarian reform co-operative and by the extension officer attached to it, as well as supervised by the latter and the co-operative's board members, as regards to unified crop rotation, quality standards and timing of cultivation work, prescribed application of credited inputs and their recovery by compulsory cotton marketing through the co-operative;
- plant protection measures are performed by the co-operative regardless of individual parcels' boundaries;
- the co-operatively owned and operated machinery is used on individual demand against charge on credit (*Wörz*, 1967).

After successful implementation in the 372 agrarian reform co-operatives, this package of co-operative production promotion measures was introduced from 1955 in Egypt's 4038 "agricultural co-operatives" in the villages with traditional and hence heavily fragmented landownership, however with far less success and – contrary to the land reform areas – not performed as a complete package any more today. Whereas supervised production credit and cotton marketing – both co-operatively channelled – worked by and large as satisfactorily as co-operative plant protection, this was neither the case with unified crop rotation nor with supervising quality standards and timing of cultivation work (*Kirsch/Wörz*, 1985).

In villages with traditional landownership, no homogeneity does exist as regards the size of holdings, number of parcels per holding and the distribution of parcels of anyone holding over the village land area. It is, therefore, impossible to divide the village land into rotation fields in such a way that every co-operative member has anything like one-third of his land in each of three crop rotation fields, allowing him to cultivate cotton, wheat and clover alike.

Hence, those co-operatives had to confine themselves to unify cotton cultivation by preparing a map of the village cultivation area describing the cotton blocks for the coming season. By public notice all farmers were informed of the proposed plan und were given the opportunity to request modifications. In a procedure lasting several weeks, the cotton-growing blocks were adjusted and often had to be subdivided in order to correspond to as many individual wishes as possible (*Wörz*, 1967).

Similar to the Egyptian example, which is outstanding in so far as co-operative promotion of agricultural production was at least partly introduced in all village co-operatives of the country, inter-farm organization of production was introduced in many irrigation schemes, one example being the Gezira Scheme in the Sudan (*Wörz*, 1966). Here, it is not a co-operative but the Gezira Board as settlement authority that centralizes decision-making and implements the planning by "field-inspectors". In addition, the Board delivers irrigation water and drainage facilities as well as credit, inputs and machinery operations (including plant protection) for cotton, ultimately processing and marketing this crop which is harvested individually by the tenants. These, formally being share-croppers, perform all labour operations individually on their holdings under the field-inspectors' strict guidance and supervision. Hence, extension, credit supervision and unified cropping pattern are combined into an informal group approach for the promotion of agricultural production.

In the part of the Gezira Scheme reclaimed prior to 1957, each holding consists of four plots, one of which is devoted to cotton and two half-plots to millet and lubia (a fodder crop). In order to maintain correct crop rotation as well as to restrict each plot to one crop only (for the sake of gravity irrigation), every two neighbouring tenants are obliged to co-operate by growing their millet on the one neighbour's land and their lubia on the other's. Each of the two neighbours cultivates half of the millet-plot and half of the lubia-plot. In the Scheme's Managil Extension, added later, only three (and smaller) plots are available in every holding. Hence, not only millet and lubia, but also cotton has to rotate on two neighbours' holdings. Each tenant cultivates a complete cotton plot, but every second year on the neighbour's land (*Wörz*, 1966).

Other, more recent examples not related to new settlement schemes but to the rehabilitation of old communal irrigation systems can be found in the Philippines (→ *Education, Asia*). There, the National Irrigation Authority encouraged all farmers in villages with old, dilapidated communal irrigation works to organize themselves in irrigation associations, in order to rehabilitate the irrigation systems through joint action and self-administration. In the final stage, the irrigation associations turned into co-operatives which maintained the restructured irrigation systems and organized water distribution, in addition to the usual co-operative services such as marketing (*Kirsch*, 1984).

In many resettlement schemes and land reform programmes, collective farms have originally been organized with a view to overcome difficulties with beneficiaries, who were not professional agriculturalists. After some time, however, many of these collective farms disintegrated. The former producers' co-operatives changed into co-operatives for the promotion of agricultural production or even into service co-operatives.

A typical example of this phenomenon are the semi-collective Ejidos in Mexico (*Schiller*, 1969, pp. 102ff.) (→ *Joint-production Co-operatives*). After disintegration, the farmers are allotted individual plots and cultivate them by applying a combination of collective and individual working procedures. Harvesting is strictly carried out individually and the farmer is remunerated for his work through the yields of his plots and charged with fees for the common services. Thus, the so-called individual Ejidos can be classified as co-operative societies for the promotion of agricultural production, as all Ejidos enjoy access to a supervised production credit programme of the Ejido Bank. These uniform and synchronized credit programmes streamline the production in such a way as to improve marketing by means of attaining a uniform quality of the marketable surplus. The Ejido Bank assists in the co-ordination of marketing, thus playing the role of a vertical integration pole, being strengthened at the same time by horizontal integration at the Ejido level.

In Israel (→ *Development, Israel*), in addition to co-operative settlement and collective farming practised in the kibbuzim and moshav shitufi, a system of co-operative farming with individual land use has long been applied in the moshav ovdim (*Schiller*, 1969, p. 101). There, most of the land was divided into large blocks according to the requirements of the crop rotation and cultivation pattern. Land from each of these blocks is allotted to the families for individual use, thus allowing for a common crop rotation, joint irrigation management and concentration of tree crops in one block. In addition, member families specialize on either cash crop or animal production. On the periphery, farmland is cultivated collectively.

In several sub-Saharan African countries (→ *Development, Africa*) out-growers of sugar-cane plantations and cash crop processing enterprises have been established as co-operative groups for the promotion of agricultural production in order to organize the reclamation of their land. Such co-operative groups can be arranged either as informal sub-groups of one or several out-growers' organizations or as co-operatives, as is the case with the Chemelil Sugar Company in Kenya. This company supports the co-operative groups in reclaiming and jointly preparing their land which subsequently is allotted to the individual members. Land allocation is done in such a way as to allow for unified rotation resulting in larger blocks of cane of the same stage of maturity. Transport of the cane is organized by the co-operative (*Kirsch*, 1976, p. 98).

In Malaysia, rubber settlements have been organized on the basis of group settlements, whereby co-operative promotion of agricultural production is applied. Land reclamation and planting, as well as certain working procedures, are jointly organized at an inter-farm level, whereas the matured plantations are used individually. Such schemes have been promoted by the Federal Land Development Authority (*Kirsch* et al., 1980, pp. 85ff.) (→ *Development, South-East Asia*).

Co-operative promotion of agricultural production has not only been integrated into land reform, land reclamation or resettlement programmes, but has also been adopted as a group approach by many agricultural extension services (→ *Development Policy*) for making beneficiaries familiar with modern farming techniques and hitherto unknown crops. As early as in the 1950s, India's first Five-Year-Plan concentrated on the systematic planning of economic development. From the beginning, the promotion of co-operative farming has been part of the programme for agricultural development. In those days, so-called better farming societies and tenant-farming societies were organized as co-operative farming societies with individual land use (*Schiller*, 1969, p. 112).

Typical cases of co-operative promotion of agricultural production have also been developed in several East-Asian countries under the guidance of the official agricultural extension service. This type was originally established in Taiwan. The farmers were organized in so-called farmers' associations. These can be classified as agricultural co-operative societies, with agricultural extension and production planning integrated as a special service. Registration and supervision of the associations is done by the agricultural extension service (*Schiller*, 1969, pp. 175 ff.).

In rice-growing areas, members of such farmers' associations organize themselves into specialized groups. Guided by agricultural extension workers, these groups are responsible for the production of seedlings, transplanting, plant protection etc. on an inter-farm basis. Weeding and harvesting, however, is strictly done individually. This approach of co-operative promotion of production under the guidance of the official agricultural extension service has spread to other Asian countries such as Thailand and Malaysia, where farmers' associations have been organized in addition to agricultural co-operatives. In Thailand, this new approach resulted in a dual organizational structure. In Malaysia, however, agricultural co-operatives and the new farmers' associations were re-structured into so-called farmers' organizations and subordinated to the new co-operative apex organization, called the Farmers' Organizations Authority (*Kirsch* et al., 1984, pp. 51ff.).

In Turkey, the sugar industry is one example of vertical co-operation between agricultural producers and the processing industry. Here, co-operative societies of the producers are organized for the promotion of agricultural production of the members under the guidance of the sugar factories. In particular, the necessity to organize joint use of machinery led to larger blocks of sugar beets being made up of adjacent individual plots, on the basis of the unified crop rotation (*Kirsch*, 1976, pp. 83ff.).

The basic function of the co-operatives within the agro-industrial combines is that of acting as a mediator between the Turkish Sugar Factory Company and the producers. Each sugar factory issues cultivation quotas in accordance to its capacity. The beet-growing area is determined for each village. The agricultural inspectors of the sugar factories work out a crop rotation plan, with a village plan divided into four sections. Strict attention is paid to ensure that, in any given year, sugar beet is cultivated in one section of the village only. In this way, large blocks of land under sugar beet are achieved, which are suitable for mechanization. These blocks are sown with a seed-drill machine made available by the sugar factory.

In West Germany, co-operative processing societies, such as wine growers' co-operatives, sometimes organize the agricultural production of their members according to the rules of co-operative promotion of agricultural production. In particular, this is the case in such wine-growing areas which have undergone a land consolidation programme (*Schiller*, 1969, p. 153). After land consolidation, replanting of larger blocks (subdivided into individual parcels) was often organized on the basis of inter-farm co-operation under the guidance of the land consolidation association. The different varieties planted in each block of the village area were strictly decided upon by the wine-processing co-operative in close collaboration with the above-mentioned association. In some cases, this inter-farm co-operation practised during replanting continues, e.g. for plant protection. In this way, a wine production of controlled and hence more uniform quality is achieved.

Ultimately, some of the problems of co-operative promotion of agricultural production should be mentioned. Particularly in developing countries, it is difficult to find qualified managers who are able to both farm and organize co-operatives. Furthermore, co-operatives for the promotion of agricultural production based on unified crop rotation are not flexible enough to react to changes in market prices. Often, as in the case of Egypt, the cash crop area was determined by the government, which at the same time was responsible for marketing and export. The government used this instrument for exploiting farmers by imposing extraordinary high export levies. Consequently, the price paid to farmers for their cotton was far below the world market price. The

farmers called it a government crop and therefore did not pay much attention to their cotton fields.
Additionally, promotion of agricultural production by necessity includes a certain element of pressure. Hence, the co-operatives will only be successful if certain pre-requisites exist. These include a number of certain external constraints and restrictions, e.g. in the case of cash crops, which require further capital-intensive processing. Furthermore, the amount of capital invested in settlement and land reclamation projects requires subordination of the settlers to the dominating settlement authority. However, such constraints and restrictions are accepted by the farmers only if the results achieved through inter-farm co-operation are considerably better than those without such co-operation. Finally, there is the danger of co-operatives ending up in bureaucratic structures, if co-operative promotion of production is organized by government support service institutions.

Bibliography

Darling, Malcolm: Co-operative farming in Italy, in: Year Book of Agricultural Co-operation 1953, Oxford 1953, pp. 198–212.
Digby, Margaret: Co-operatives and land use, FAO Agricultural Development Paper No. 61, Rome 1957.
Dülfer, Eberhard: Strukturprobleme der Genossenschaft in der Gegenwart, in: Forschungsinstitut für Genossenschaftswesen an der Universität Wien (Hrsg.), Neuere Tendenzen im Genossenschaftswesen, Wiener Studien, N.F. Bd. 1, Göttingen 1966, S. 5–34.
Kirsch, Ottfried C.: Vertical co-operation among agricultural producers in western Europe and in developing countries, Publications of the Research Centre for International Agrarian Development, Vol. 5, Saarbrücken 1976.
Kirsch, Ottfried C./Benjacov, Albert/Schujmann, Léon: The role of self-help groups in rural development projects, Publications of the Research Centre for International Agrarian Development, Vol. 11, Saarbrücken/Fort Lauderdale 1980.
Kirsch, Ottfried C.: Finanzierungsinstrumente und Selbsthilfeeinrichtungen zur Förderung ärmerer Zielgruppen – Fallbeispiele aus Nepal, Philippinen, Korea und Thailand, FIA-Berichte 84/1, Heidelberg 1984.
Kirsch, Ottfried, C./Armbruster, Paul G./Kochendörfer-Lucius, Gudrun: Self-help institutions in developing countries: Co-operation involving autonomous primary groups, Studies in Applied Economics and Rural Institutions, Vol. 13, Saarbrücken/Fort Lauderdale 1984.
Kirsch, Ottfried C./Wörz, Johannes G.F.: Co-operative promotion of production in Egypt: The failure of unified crop rotation within agrarian reform programmes for old lands, Studies in Applied Economics and Rural Institutions, Vol. 14, Saarbrücken/Fort Lauderdale 1985.
Münzinger, Adolf: Bäuerliche Maschinengenossenschaft Häusern EGmbH, in: Schriftenreihe des RKTL, Heft 54, Berlin 1933.
Ruthenberg, Hans: Produktion unter genauer Aufsicht, Ein Ansatz zur landwirtschaftlichen Entwicklung dargestellt an Beispielen in Ostafrika und in dem Sudan, in: Schmollers Jahrbuch für Wirtschafts- und Sozialwissenschaften, Bd. 83, Nr. 6, Berlin 1963, S. 697–713.
Schiller, Otto: The Farming Co-operative, A New System of Farm Management, in: Land Economics, Vol. XXVII, Number 1, Wisconsin 1951, pp. 1–15.
Schiller, Otto: The field arrangement in new settlements, in: Agriculture Pakistan, The Journal of the Agricultural Research Council, Vol. XI, No. 2, Karachi 1960.
Schiller, Otto: Two ways of co-operative farming, in: Indian Journal of Agricultural Economics, Vol. XVII, No. 2, Bombay 1962.
Schiller, Otto: Die landwirtschaftliche Produktionsförderungsgenossenschaft als neue Genossenschaftsform, in: Zeitschrift für ausländische Landwirtschaft, Jg. 4, Heft 2, Frankfurt (Main) 1965, S. 129–135.
Schiller, Otto: Cooperation and integration of agricultural production, London 1969.
Wörz, Johannes G.F.: Genossenschaftliche und partnerschaftliche Produktionsförderung in der sudanesischen Landwirtschaft, Sonderheft 4 der Zeitschrift für ausländische Landwirtschaft, Frankfurt (Main) 1966.
Wörz, Johannes G.F.: Die genossenschaftliche Produktionsförderung in Ägypten als Folgeerscheinung der Agrarreform und als neues Element der genossenschaftlichen Entwicklung, Wissenschaftliche Schriftenreihe des Bundesministeriums für wirtschaftliche Zusammenarbeit, Bd. 12, Stuttgart 1967.
Wörz, Johannes G.F.: Organizational Forms of Support Service Structures for Small Farms in Egypt and Sudan, in: Quarterly Journal of International Agriculture, Vol. 32, No. 1, Frankfurt (Main) 1993, pp. 106–113.

Promotion Balance Sheet, Promotion Report, Promotion System

WILHELM WEBER / JOHANN BRAZDA [SC]

(see also: *Promotion Mandate*; *Business Policies*; *Law, National*; *Theory of Co-operatives*)

I. Introduction; II. The Historical Purpose of Member Promotion; III. The Theory of Trusteeship; IV. The Balance of Interests Theory; V. The Systemic Theory; VI. The Social Science Concept; VII. The Transaction Costs Concept; VIII. Practical Implementation.

I. Introduction

Today's greatest challenge for modern co-operatives is doubtless the necessity to face up to the realities of the market and yet continue to function as a true co-operative. In Germany and Austria, compared to other countries, the co-operative is characterized by a *legal task based on a legal definition* (→ *Law, National*). Co-operatives serve to promote the income or the economy of their members (→ *Promotion Mandate*). In Latin European countries, co-operatives are regarded as groupings of people with variable membership and variable capital, with capital only playing a subservient role. (These groupings are not necessarily defined by a legal form.) Latin

European law is based on concrete and controllable co-operative criteria which can be adapted to new necessities. For decades, German legal experts, however, have been looking for a *means to concretize the legal duty to promote members' interests*. For the management of co-operative enterprises, this legal obligation for co-operatives to promote their members entails considerable problems. Is a co-operative which is to promote directly the income and economy of its members allowed to be profit oriented? If the economic purpose of the co-operative is situated solely with the members, is the co-operative only an instrument of the economic interests of its members? If member promotion can be based only on the individual member, can it be objectivized for the co-operative as a whole? With regard to co-operatives in changeable economic environments and based on varying theoretical conceptions (→ *Conceptions, Co-operative*) being adapted to co-operative reality in each period of time, the differences between the various conceptions of how to tangibly achieve co-operative promotional activity (situational, social, promotional report, promotional balance, promotional plan) can be based on various historical realities. Thus, for any particular historical perception of co-operatives, a model of co-operative theory (→ *Theory of Co-operatives*) exists.

II. The Historical Purpose of Member Promotion

The formation of co-operatives was one of the numerous new economic strategies developed during the 19th century in a completely new economic situation. The dissolution of the large rural family and the increasing role of the profit motive led to greater disintegration and to a loss of social security. Traditional patterns of social interaction became obsolete. These problems and abuses became the focus of social reform activity. Numerous idealists (mostly of upper and middle class origins) wanted to "rescue" the traditional social orders of artisans and peasants that were threatened by the industrial revolution as well as by the newly emerging working class. To many of them, the co-operative principle appeared as an adequate means. *At that time, there was no question whether at all co-operatives could promote their members and how they should do so*. They arose (often with a little help "from above") as → *self-help organizations* in a situation of want that created → *solidarity*. This was a time of mass poverty during the decline and fall of many branches of traditional artisanry (→ *History in 19th C.*). In the early 19th century, the debt situation of small farmers and the problem of low salaries at the bottom of the bureaucratic and military hierarchies were blatant, and co-operatives were obviously able to alleviate these problems. Even though the self-help principle was an important driving force, the role of well-to-do benefactors as catalyst in this process should not be overlooked. At this moment in time, co-operatives were defined only as a subsidiary organ of their members' economies; they were not to define their own aims and were based on the principle of cost coverage (cost covering price), thus eliminating profit. Among the members according to the Rochdale Principle (→ *Rochdale Pioneers*), excess revenue would be distributed in terms of dividends. Thus the success of a co-operative was directly measurable for its members and no instruments were needed to measure it.

III. The Theory of Trusteeship

After World War, I and even more so after the Second World War, co-operatives became more and more like other enterprises. In order to compete with effective mass distribution enterprises, they heavily invested in machinery, real estate and buildings. They had to face up to the fact that other enterprises were challenging their activities of member promotion by efficient marketing practises centering on customers' needs and desires. Co-operatives had to realize – sometimes after serious crises – that they could only participate in competition by integrating a *qualified management* into their operations. After the turn of the century, elected members' representatives tended to take a less prominent position in day-to-day economic operations and, with regard to internal decision-making in co-operative enterprises, professional managers by the 1920's became dominant. As co-operative enterprises thus became independent and well functioning economic entities, a new theory of member promotion was created in the 1950s: the trusteeship theory. According to this concept, *the managers should act as trustees for their members*. Henzler formulated the "basic task" for a co-operative: "to act under the given circumstances and in adaption to the existing market situations in a way which, in the long run, is favourable to its members' economies". Given the increasing level of competition and the increasing size of co-operatives, the entrepreneurial functions of co-operatives could no longer be realized by the members themselves. These functions were transferred to the co-operative management via a "trusteeship". As members' intentions were not clear anymore, they were superseded by normative rules for co-operative management. The role of the member became reduced to his or her chance to control and challenge management at the annual meetings concerning the co-operative balance, the income statement, and the management report. This chance was rather slim, for the statements and positions of the management were given additional credibility by the supervisory council, by the assent of the co-operative auditing federation as well as by the auditing report itself, the latter being submitted in an abridged form to the co-operative's general assembly.

IV. The Balance of Interests Theory

In the 1960s, the co-operative member structure became more and more heterogeneous and the de-ideologization of co-operative relationships became more and more evident. This opened the way for a *pure economic theory of cooperation* which was exclusively based on the idea of economic members' promotion. Here, the insight that an act of barter between egoistic economic subjects only takes place when both parties are bound to benefit is taken as the main explicative basis of economic cooperation. The idea was to attain an optimal solution for both partners, optimal in the sense that each of them should be convinced that, under the given circumstances, he was unable to attain more so that in fact a balance of interest was established. Thus, based on the *divergency of interests*, a theory was formed which tried to reach conclusions to certain questions, such as whose interests are to be realized to which extent. In this conception, the concrete realization of the co-operative's duty to promote its members was regarded as a decision-making process during which the personal interests of every participant in the organization were transformed into a common goal via certain mechanisms of a balance of interests. *Boettcher* distinguished between the main effects of co-operative collaboration under the headings of productivity effects, power effects and diffusion effects. He also differentiated between the *monetary measurement of market success* and (the less easily measurable) *member benefits* with regard to the extent individual goals are fulfilled. *Blümle* spoke of instrumental and socio-emotional member efficiency. In this context, member benefits are primarily seen as cost and competitiveness benefits under the following aspects:

- rationalization in order to decrease members' costs
- value and quality added to members' products
- information given to members
- sales promotion for members' products
- improvement of members' market situation
- improvement of the structure of the market in which members are competing.

All of these indicators were to be measured quantitatively. In order to more clearly illustrate how co-operative members benefit as a result of dealings with their co-operative, *Boettcher* has proposed to introduce a *promotional plan* at the beginning and a *promotional report* at the end of a given period within the framework of an integrated planning system. According to this concept, the promotional plan should specify the priorities of promotional activity, and, at the end of the period, the proposed plan should be compared to the real outcome via a promotional report. Therefore, management action in terms of its duty to promote co-operative members could be better legitimized than through the purely legal processes of the general assembly which merely accept the co-operative balance sheet.

V. The Systemic Theory

Starting from the 1970s, changes in market structure (high technology, centralization, concentration) and an increasing degree of oligopolization led to the creation of *integrated co-operatives*, especially in retailing. Being small-scale businessmen, the members transferred partial functions of their own enterprises to the co-operatives because of increasing information deficits and market necessities. The co-operative management took over the planning and direction of their members' economies to a considerable extent (This is a process that seems now well on its way in agriculture, too). The co-operatives often created their own enterprises which were primarily to serve the necessities of the co-operative itself. Members were thus integrated "from above" into a co-operative network. Members' economies became dependent on the management of their co-operative. Based on these new conditions, it became unrealistic to assume that members participate in a co-operative only as long as there is a monetarily measurable benefit for them to be expected. *Membership in a co-operative is not only based on one dominant goal but on a complex set of goals rooted in various (monetary and non-monetary) motives interacting between the co-operative and its members in a multipolar goal system.* Thus, the attainment of economic benefits is only one goal among many others. To analyze such an organizational structure, *Dülfer* developed the concept of the "Kooperativ" as a socio-economic system (→ *Managerial Economics*) based on multivariable and multipolar aims which, by using scientific methods of empirical social research, can be measured to determine the degree of their realization. A clear definition of goals and achievements can be given in a *promotional report*. According to *Dülfer*, only the goal system of the "Kooperativ" represents the promotional needs of its membership, and the formulation of this goal system can serve as a guideline for the co-operative management which has to operationalize its promotional duty. Since member promotion falls under short-term strategy and planning, *Dülfer* maintains that it is not necessary to formulate a promotional plan.

VI. The Social Science Concept

The social science concept is even more radical. It postulates the promotional duty of a co-operative in such a way that co-operatives have to serve their members in an *economic as well as in a meta-economic way*. The latter among other things, consists of a certain need for community and democratic participation (*Bänsch, Ringle*). *Blümle*, in order to reduce the increasing distance between co-operative management and members, was vehemently in favour of revitalizing and developing a new element of member participation in co-operatives. This concept has been further developed at the Vienna Institute for Co-operatives where a *promotional balance sheet* has been advocated in both theory and practice. The promotional balance sheet is regarded as an instrument of promotional policy striving to create a balance between economic and community oriented social services in a co-operative (*Patera*). The idea is to provide a flexible framework for a specifically co-operative organizational development process as well as for the development of a co-operative identity adapted to today's world. Based on a broad exchange of opinions, a learning process for all individuals concerned is engaged in, thus improving identification of the co-operative goals. The co-operative management, however, remains in charge of the selection as well as of the balancing and concrete formulation of the goals for the next planning period. At the end of the period, the *promotional plan* is to be compared to the actual data, and a new promotional balance sheet and new bases for the next promotional plan are accordingly determined.

The co-operative promotional balance has, however, not yet been developed into more than an *instrument of legitimizing the actions of the co-operative management*. The problem of how values and norms can be empirically measured and how they should be influenced by co-operative leaders remains as yet unsolved.

VII. The Transaction Costs Concept

In the early 1990s, the *"co-operative consciousness" of members continues to show a downward tendency*. The willingness to participate in the decision-making process of the co-operative, to assume honorary functions, or to engage oneself financially by taking on shares and responsibilities is vanishing. Today, it has to be accepted that it is not too realistic to hope for a clear and early formulation of needs on the part of the members. Therefore, it is said to be the task of the co-operative management to convince members of this specific structure as well as of the reasons for co-operative structural elements (*strategic promotional duty*). The transaction cost principle offers the possibility to operationalize the promotional duty in economic terms (*Bonus*). *The link between the co-operative and its members is defined via the economic cost-and-benefits the co-operative offers* (→ *Institutional Economics*). Of course, there has been an element of this kind in the past, too. However, during the past, not all costs have been reckoned with. In a co-operative, it becomes possible to create relationships of trust and security via the durability of economic links between well defined partners; the single individual, therefore, does not have to pay for the high costs of information and the establishment of contractual relationships in the market. Thus, the co-operative management must make members' transaction cost level as low as possible. *The promotional duty becomes a pure task of the co-operative mangagement* which has to give itself a co-operative identity based on the following main concepts (*Lipfert*): Man has to be the measure of all things, parallel interests have to be realized by grouping together common efforts, and a democratic process of decision-making (→ *Business Policies*).

VIII. Practical Implementation

Practical attempts to formulate promotional reports have been made in several credit co-operatives in Germany, and several co-operative auditing unions, in their standard rules for primary co-operatives, have included that the co-operative management is required to say something about the implementation of its promotional duty in its report. Due to divergent expectations on the part of scientists and co-operative managers, no pragmatic attempts have yet been finalized to create promotional balance sheets as a part of the organizational development of co-operatives. *Thus, realizations have fallen far behind theoretical demands*. Because actors in a co-operative have such complex goal expectations, a consistent goal system can be formulated only with great difficulty, because this entails making a statement about desirable states in the future. Explicit formulations of plans for the future can also be a competitive hazard for an enterprise. Thus, the central problem of developing a multipolar goal attainment control is the tension between necessary and yet risky public utterances based on internal decision-making processes and goal finding processes that correspond to them. The present cost for such organizational development processes also seem too high for many co-operatives.

Translation: R. Schediwy

Bibliography

Bänsch, Axel/Ringle, Günther: Die optimale Größe von Genossenschaften, in: Bänsch, A./Ringle, G.(eds.), Genossenschaftliche Betriebswirtschaften im Ökonomisierungsprozeß, Hamburg 1974.

Blümle, Ernst-Bernd: Probleme der Effizienzmessung bei Genossenschaften, Tübingen 1976.

Boettcher, Erik: Die Problematik der Operationalisierung des Förderungsauftrages in Genossenschaften, in: ZfgG, vol. 29 (1979), pp. 199–215.

Bonus, Holger: Die Genossenschaft als Unternehmungstyp, Münster 1985

Dülfer, Eberhard: Betriebswirtschaftslehre der Kooperative. Kommunikation und Entscheidungsbildung in Genossenschaften und vergleichbaren Organisationen, Göttingen 1984.

Henzler, Reinhold: Betriebswirtschaftliche Probleme des Genossenschaftswesens, Wiesbaden 1962.

Lipfert, Helmut: Mitgliederförderndes Kooperations- und Konkurrenzmanagement in genossenschaftlichen Systemen, Göttingen 1986.

Patera, Mario: Genossenschaftliche Förderbilanz, in Laurinkari, Juhani (ed.), Genossenschaftswesen, München 1991, pp. 285–301.

Promotion Mandate

WERNER GROSSKOPF [J]

(see also: *Principles*; *Legal Form, Co-operative*; *Law, National*; *Law, International*; *Conceptions, Co-operative*; *Assessment of Success*)

I. Introduction; II. The Promotion Mandate as the Specific Principal Goal of the Co-operative Enterprise; III. Economic Success as the Basis of the Promotion Mandate; IV. The Distribution and Control of the Result of Economic Activity as the Content of the Promotion Mandate.

I. Introduction

The majority of co-operative enterprises in all branches within the industrialized countries have faced competition from commercial and/or public competitors for many years on their respective markets. Their business activity on the market as a rule varies only in part from that of their competitors. With respect to their business objectives, commercial co-operatives – like their competitors in other legal and corporate forms – also are forced to attend to the economization of their enterprises in order to maintain their competitiveness (*Engelhardt/Schmid*). They strive to preserve their market share on the various markets and, if possible, to build on it. Profitability, liquidity and security long ago became essential goal factors for co-operative enterprises as well.

Nowadays, expenditure reductions and revenue increases in the scope of the economization measures undertaken by co-operatives, however, by all means must not be goals in themselves. They should solely be a means to achieve subordinate goals of the co-operative enterprise which are pursued through the individual economization measures and derived from the co-operative's ultimate goal (c.f. *Engelhardt/Schmid*). The goal of the registered co-operative according to § 1 of the German Co-operative Law is clearly "to promote their members' enterprises or households through a common business enterprise" (→ *Legal Form, Co-operative*).

The range of action in which co-operative activity is performed today is based on this consideration. On the one hand, co-operatives are exposed to competition in that they are enterprises tied to particular markets. On the other hand, they must unequivocally orientate themselves primarily around the economic interests of their members; as in the past they must continue to fulfill the co-operative promotion mandate. Membership orientation and market requirements – in this order – must thereby influence modern co-operatives' corporate policy structured around future development.

II. The Promotion Mandate as the Specific Principal Goal of the Co-operative Enterprise

1. The Co-operative Identity Principle as the Starting Point

In general, the mandate "to promote members' enterprises or households through a common business enterprise" is held to be the most important co-operative characteristic which differentiates co-operatives from other legal and corporate forms (→ *Principles*); this is likewise its original legal purpose, at least according to German Co-operative Law. The specific principal goal of this enterprise form is indeed therewith delineated, but this statement is nonetheless incapable of fully satisfying the needs at hand. "It is a fact that every economic form of association aims to promote its shareholders" (*Weber*). The co-operative promotion mandate must therefore be understood more specifically if and when it should assist in delimiting non-co-operative legal and corporate forms; in the end, the co-operative strives for the economic promotion of only those persons among its membership who at the same time are its business partners (cf. *Weber*).

One can only then speak of true co-operative collaboration when a group of economic subjects – the members themselves – jointly assumes the legal responsibility for an economic entity (which can be identified as a co-operative enterprise) with the intention of utilizing the economic services/output of "their" enterprise (c.f. *Eschenburg*). The group of members and "their" co-operative enterprise together form the co-operative whose characteristic identification trait, the "identity principle", is described above (→ *Theory of co-operative Cooperation*). "It is first the trait of identity shared by the owner and customer/suppliers of an enterprise which distinguishes co-operatives from other corporate enterprises" (*Eschenburg*). The contextual fulfillment of the promotion mandate is only possible when notice is taken of this principle.

The identity principle allocates the members of a co-operative a two-tiered set of claims from an economic functional point of view (c.f. *Weber*). On the one hand, members in their capacity as clients of "their" co-operative's output rightly expect noticeable economic promotion, or in other words, an economic advantage. If this were not the case, the specific co-operative entity would lack all basis for legitimation. On the other hand, the members are at the same time shareholders of the "co-operative" as an entity of co-operative law through their paid-up share; being the agents of this legal person, they are participants in the decision-making procedures.

The promotion mandate is to be interpreted in economic terms and is derived from the specific co-operative identity principle; it therefore can logically be concluded to be the principal co-operative goal. It is only orientated to members in the scope of their working relationship with the co-operative and is binding to the co-operative for economic and legal legitimation. In this respect, it is truly characteristic for the co-operative method of conducting business affairs.

2. The Promotion Mandate in the Co-operative Goal System

Ever since the science of business management disavowed the classic enterprise model with its univariate objective of profit maximization – *Gutenberg* interpreted this as the "final intensification" of the commercial principle – because such a model was unable to illustrate the potential variety of entrepreneurial decision-making criteria in a sufficiently realistic manner, discussion has been focused around an enterprise goal system (c.f. *Dülfer*, 1980b). This does justice to the fact that a number of different goals can be observed and found in business practise which are pursued simultaneously (c.f. *Wöhe*). Instead of using the univariate approach of setting extremes, one today turns to the multivariate approach of satisfaction, whereby adaptable "claim levels" are formulated in the course of time for individual objectives rather than stipulations for set minimums or maximums (c.f. *Kolbeck*). The goal system can thereby be conceived as a structured whole composed of goal elements between which horizontal and/or vertical relationships either exist or can be established (c.f. *Büschgen*).

This development certainly had effects on co-operative goal formation. The co-operative goal function today can be characterized as multivariate with respect to the numerous individual goals of each member and of the members among themselves, but also in particular with regard to the numerous individual goals of the co-operative enterprise itself or of its management (c.f. *Seuster*, 1978, who furthermore assumes multipolarity or at least bipolarity with respect to the goals of the membership versus those of the co-operative management to be a specific co-operative particularity). Both the legal purpose of registered co-operatives ("to promote members' enterprises or households through a common business enterprise", [§ 1 of German Co-operative Law]) as well as the economic goals of every market-oriented undertaking – regardless of its legal or corporate form – must be taken into consideration for the concretization of the goal system of modern co-operatives. A variety of discussions have been held concerning the relationship between these two goal orientations; in principle these have been superfluous. It can be unequivocally stated that the promotion mandate is understood as a lasting compact placed on the co-operative management by the members which has precedence over all other matters. "This general mandate established by the members is the foundation for every co-operative and for all co-operative activities. This fundamental mandate stretches from the co-operative's formation to its dissolution; it is an element of all co-operatives throughout the world at all times, and as such is the characteristic feature of co-operatives" (*Henzler*, quoting *Seuster*, 1988).

The promotion mandate exclusive to co-operatives and specified through the co-operative identity principle must serve as both a legal and theoretical measure for co-operatives as well as the guiding principle for co-operative action. This observation has clearly found root in the numerous approaches undertaken by co-operative science to operationalize the promotion mandate and to quantify concrete promotion performance. The presumptive openness of the term has thereby resulted in the charge that it is necessary to update its content periodically, for the "forms and options available to realize the co-operative promotion mandate are bound by time, the market and the membership and must therefore be seen dynamically" (*Seuster*, 1988). In order to indicate feasible positionings of the promotion mandate in the goal system of modern co-operatives, the basic arguments in the discussion undertaken in co-operative science literature need to be briefly outlined with respect to this principal goal of co-operative activity. The economic interpretation of the co-operative promotion mandate must hereby be differentiated from the juristic point of view.

It is the task of the economic science disciplines to conceive and understand the self-help entity "co-operative" as an element of social reality, to recognize the specific modes of economic behavior which arise and to describe their correlations (→ *Theory of Co-operatives*). Those characteristics are sought which differentiate the nature of co-operatives and their method of assuming economic functions from other organizations.

In the literature one can find attempted definitions and theses on the subject of the promotion mandate from an economic perspective; these are based on varying premises which can be typified as follows (c.f. *Grosskopf*, 1990 and the annotated literature):

– Commercial/economic interpretations maintain that the promotion mandate is fulfilled when the co-operative organization can produce increases in members' earnings and/or reductions in their costs.
– Interpretations oriented around utility value correlate the fulfillment of members' respective expectations and needs to the substance of the promotion mandate.
– Existential interpretations maintain that the presence of the co-operative alone suffices to fulfill the promotion mandate.

Despite this variety of contents for the promotion goal – which from an economic point of view is evidently sufficiently elastic to encompass concrete economic advantages, the satisfaction of members' needs in the broadest general sense possible, or even alone the existence of co-operatives – there is widespread agreement that the primary purpose of co-operatives and thus their principal goal is the economic promotion of the members in their identity as customers and holders of "their" enterprise.

An extensive variety of interpretations with respect to the co-operative promotion goal can also be determined in the legal literature on co-operatives. From the view of (German) legal science, the promotion mandate is attended to inasmuch as § 1 of the German Co-operative Law is the subject of juristic interpretation. The wording of this provision first of all clearly states that the enrollment into the co-operative register is reserved for those "associations with a non-finite number of members" which strive to promote their members' enterprises or households through a common business enterprise. *Dülfer* (1980a) concludes from this that the statutory promotion mandate is a "conditional declaration" made by lawmakers. Even when intended promotion of the membership group is at hand, the co-operative can be registered. According to this perspective, § 1 of the German Co-operative Law thus does not include any promotion mandate in the sense of a list of directives determined by lawmakers for the co-operative or its management, and thus it likewise does not provide any definition of the same; according to German law, registered co-operatives rather are solely obligated to endeavor to promote their members. *Kirchhof*, for instance, imputes an "action mandate through co-operative law" which obliges membership promotion.

The conclusions and postulates formulated in co-operative science have also found their way into models and explanations of the promotion mandate in everday co-operative practise. It becomes evident in this connection that an obvious concentration of promotion efforts on the membership body is considered a seriously difficult matter to operationalize, particularly for the modern market co-operatives (c.f. *Dülfer*, 1966 on the subject "market-linkage co-operatives").

From this discussion of the promotion mandate as the principal goal of co-operative activity it can be concluded for one that all other components of the co-operative enterprise's goal system – without detracting from their respective individual values – must contribute to the fulfillment of this principal goal. Borrowing from *Dülfer* (as quoted by *Engelhardt/Schmid*), one can speak of a categorical envelopment of the co-operative goal system through the promotion mandate. Secondly, the impression arises that the co-operative promotion mandate cannot experience the effectuation of its actual wording and contents in a competitive economy without pursuing other goals, in particular the most important corporate economic goal – that of attaining profit.

It thus remains established that one can no longer imagine co-operatives in the scope of a market economy without including profit endeavor as a goal dimension. This endeavor represents a dominant economic factor in the goal system of modern co-operatives as a whole with regard to efforts to preserve their security, existence and immediate solvency. The ultimate determination of co-operative enterprises' aspirations to achieve profit is found in the economic effectuation of the identity principle by way of the promotion of members' enterprises or households through a common business enterprise; such promotion represents their principal co-operative goal and is the decisive specific co-operative particularity. Profit attainment is thereby not to be understood exclusively in the sense of the outmoded, one-dimensional maximization thesis but rather as a strong driving force for commercial activity which contributes to fulfill the member-oriented promotion mandate in the scope of utilization claims placed on the services/output of the co-operative enterprise. This in the end can be derived from the specific co-operative identity.

The co-operative goal system must thereby be extended to encompass norms for the distribution of the promotion potential while heeding the co-operative identity principle (c.f. *Lampert*), if and when the promotion mandate is to be actually identifiable and fulfilled in a noticeable economic manner. "In this matter there is a true, potential feature for differentiation from other enterprise forms" (*Blümle*, 1973).

III. Economic Success as the Basis of the Promotion Mandate

19th century co-operatives did not need to pose themselves the questions whether they promoted their members and what exactly their promotion consisted of. Promotion manifested itself in the elimination or alleviation of economic distress into which broad classes of the population had fallen in the course of changes brought about by the industrial revolution and farmers' emancipation (→ *History in 19th C.*). The oppressive plight in which wide circles of self-employed artisans, farmers and the new industrial proletariat found themselves formed the economic-sociological backdrop for the establishment of numerous co-operatives as self-help organizations based on a "solidarity of need". Membership in a co-operative was often the only opportunity to be provided with credit or operating materials at reasonable prices under such market conditions. The scope of co-operative services and outputs was the only channel for members to meet their needs.

Inasmuch as the market structures changed in the course of time – that non-co-operative suppliers offering compatible services and conditions entered the market who were in the position to assume functions previously suitable only to co-operatives – this co-operative "promotion monopoly" disappeared. Co-operatives in part opened themselves to non-member customers, thus expanding the palette of their main (members) business as well as that of their counterdeals on the other market side. The outputs and services which are brought to market by co-operative enterprises today benefit all customers – members and non-members alike – and accordingly are no longer automatically appropriate for the specific promotion of members in the scope of their transactions. The identity principle which once ensured that each cooperation advantage at the same time represented an advantage for the members – and only for them – has lost impact in the economic point of view. The rapidly growing importance of transactions with non-members in numerous co-operatives thereby makes it apparent that these enterprises do not (cannot) behave differently on the market than their competitors with regard to profit attainment in the scope of their business policy.

The nature of the profit distribution (→ *Assessment of Success*) is in this regard the central starting point for the discussion of specific co-operative particularities (c.f. *Henzler*, 1970; *Grosskopf*, 1990). The notion of profit is hereby not interpreted as a feature of bookkeeping but rather conceived in the sense of economic result. The "profit" indicated on the accounts is frequently only a portion of the economic result. It is contingent on the dimension of business conducted with non-members and possibilities to treat market involvement with members and non-members in a differentiated manner.

Membership promotion by means of profit distribution has been a source of passionate discussion time and time again in the (German) co-operative system (c.f. *Volk/Volk; Ehlermann* in particular). The legal adjustments to non-co-operative legal forms which results from the economic conduct of co-operatives in market economy orders, the intensive competition on all markets, the relatively high number of non-member customers, and the apparent far-reaching changes in awareness with respect to the particular nature, reason and object of a method of co-operative economy have, however, led to the situation that this type of promotion today is extensively tied only to the capital participation of the individual member. Tradition and ideology have up to now obstructed obvious new channels for the future. "But quickly changing social and economic factors require an updated approach" (*Volk/Volk*), for the fact is evidently not properly addressed through a traditional manner of "member promotion" via a purely capital-oriented method of profit distribution that such a method by no means is specifically co-operative in nature; it is not in keeping with the co-operative identity principle when enterprises promote their owners as investors through their interest in receiving dividends.

Every enterprise attempts to satisfy its customers – to "promote" them. Every enterprise likewise attempts to fulfill its specific contract as determined by its owners. For commercial companies this means attending to their owners' invested capital in the best possible manner. Such owner promotion purely based on capital as it is currently practised through the distribution of a capital investment dividend in many co-operative branches – above all in the (German) co-operative banking sector – cannot therefore be specific co-operative promotion as long as it is not oriented around additional criteria in the sense of the co-operative identity principle. In any case, it is incompatible with the nature of co-operatives when the dividend rate reaches such a level that the procurement of a capital investment dividend becomes the sole membership purpose, "when a dividend is promised and payed which induces membership out of pure capital investment motives" (*Bänsch*).

A type of profit distribution which conforms to co-operatives fully in the sense of the identity principle – ultimately not a measure of an individual's contribution to the raising of capital but rather a measure of an individual's utilization of offered goods/services, in other words under consideration of the intensity of a member's transactions with "his" co-operative (c.f. *Blümle*, 1980) – can also result when the promotion mandate in (necessarily) profit-oriented co-operatives is still to be fulfilled. The specific co-operative options of such a transaction-oriented distribution of profit enable a dividend based on business participation to be paid to member-customers (c.f. *Münkner*). This is a specific method to promote members particularly when it assumes the form of a co-operative reimbursement (c.f. *Ohlmeyer*) in that the member receives such a business participation dividend according to his turnover with the co-operative from which the profit results (see *Glaser*, 1990). Co-operative → *reimbursements* provided to member-customers which increase in proportion to turnover in principle represent a method that both conforms to co-operatives and which can induce members to either extensively or even exclusively pursue business relationships with "their" co-operative enterprise.

IV. The Distribution and Control of the Result of Economic Activity as the Content of the Promotion Mandate

It has often been discussed whether the promotion result should be equated with the economic result of an enterprise (c.f. *Jäger*). In contrast to this equalization, the position is maintained that membership promotion signifies more than economic promotion (c.f. *Bänsch/Ringle*). This position in part goes as far as to subordinate the pursuance of social and social-political concerns to promotion.

A wider interpretation of "economic promotion" could naturally extend to categories encompassing social and societal life. Through this extension, however, the presentation as well as the control of co-operative promotion become less and less tangible. The co-operative begins to behave in a sovereign manner, which does not correspond to the intention of economic promotion; co-operatives are unequivocally economic institutions.

The fundamental precondition for the effectuation of the promotion mandate is thus the attainment of an economic result. The wording and form of the promotion mandate is therefore provided through the manner the result is distributed among the members. The following approaches must be differentiated while maintaining the identity principle based on the respective structure and orientation of the co-operative:

1. Distribution of Result in the Scope of Current Business Relationships

Here, a direct promotion of members is provided for which takes effect in the short term. This can result from conditions in the scope of price formation, additional services, business hours, etc. Co-operatives choose this method of distributing profit which conduct business exclusively with members and in which only a low level of asset capital is necessary to execute the business activity. Additions to the substance and the maintenance of the co-operative only play a subordinate role in this situation.

2. Distribution of Result through the Development and Extension of the Promotion Potential

The economic result in this situation is "hoarded"; growth in assets and nonmonetary capital for the co-operative enterprise is provided for through this manner. This means for the co-operative that its promotion potential – its "promotion capacity" (*Henzler*) – is increased. Profit attainment is necessary in order to be utilized in securing the existence of the co-operative. In this regard, one can speak of a more indirect, long-term form of promotion of the co-operative members. If the co-operative solely conducts business only with members, the decision between a short-term form of profit distribution and the accumulation of profits to safeguard the success potential in subsequent years is not simple, but it is secured in the sense of member identity when there is no fluctuation in membership.

If a high degree of membership fluctuation is prevalent, those members who withdraw from the co-operative are not included in the profit sharing, whereas the newly joining members can automatically take part in the success of previous years without any involvement of their own. This represents a violation of the identity principle. Attempts should be undertaken to develop solutions to this situation while adhering to the goal of "involvement in the inner value of co-operatives" (c.f. *Henzler* 1969, or more recently, *Blomeyer*).

The identity principle is also violated in the situation in which transactions with non-members are conducted to an extensive degree and when these non-members thus take part in the promotion potential which had been developed in previous years. This method of distributing the result cannot be strictly subordinate to the promotion mandate.

3. Sharing the Result at the End of a Business Period through Profit Distribution

In the case that the result cannot be shared in the course of current business activity due to given market circumstances and/or the fact that a substantial amount of business is conducted with non-members, direct short-term participation in the result – and thus promotion – is only possible through the distribution of the reported profit once the business activity has been concluded. Portions of such profits are a result of the nature and extent of business transactions with non-members. In order to preserve the promotion mandate, it is imperative that the profit distribution is undertaken according to the individual utilization of the co-operative's palette of services/outputs. A distribution of profits through the payment of a capital dividend is only compatible with the guidelines of the promotion mandate, if the co-operative in question is a capital investment co-operative.

In everyday practise, all three forms of distributing the result are combined in application. This poses no problem when business conducted with non-members is insignificant. If, however, transactions with non-members assume a large portion of total business and if membership fluctuation is high, the principles for the distribution of the result elaborated under 1. and 2. above present greater problems for the realization of the promotion mandate with respect to its contents.

The primary problem specific to the clarification of the promotion mandate is that, although there are proven means to characterize market success, no approaches exist to objectivize the promotion output (c.f. *Jäger*). This is surely the case when a high fluctuation of members exists, when the identity principle is violated in the promotion efforts, and when the process of self-management and self-responsibility is stunted.

In all other cases, one can equate market success with member success when the distribution of the result is organized in a co-operative manner.

The numerous approaches to the control of promotion which up to the present have been through the development of promotion plans and reports (c.f. *Boettcher*) do not seem particularly helpful. As a matter of course, a co-operative also proceeds from goal criteria with which it pegs its expected market success through planning channels in order to facilitate control and the determination of factors producing deviation from these criteria. The goals and realities of membership participation, market success and the principles for the distribution of the result should be included in such a promotion plan and/or promotion report. With regard to these three factors, the co-operative's annual report should accordingly include the previously determined goals for the past business year, an explanation of the degree these goals were attained, an analysis of the reasons for eventual deviation as well as a prognostic goal definition for the coming year. The demands placed on the contents of the annual report, combined with the three factors of membership participation, market success and the distribution of the result, are fully sufficient to answer the question of the operationalization of the promotion mandate as well as evidence of its fulfillment.

Bibliography

Bänsch, Axel: Genossenschaften und Kapitalbeteiligungsdividende. In: Genossenschaftliche Betriebswirtschaften im Ökonomisierungsprozeß, Beiträge zu betriebswirtschaftlichen Grundfragen der Genossenschaften, pp. 91–107, Hamburg 1974.
Bänsch, Axel/Ringle, Günther: Die metaökonomische Komponente in der genossenschaftlichen Förderung. In: Genossenschaftliche Betriebswirtschaften im Ökonomisierungsprozeß, Beiträge zu betriebswirtschaftlichen Grundfragen der Genossenschaften, pp. 1–11, Hamburg 1974.
Blomeyer, Wolfgang, with assistance of *Wißmann, Guido*: Die institutionelle Problematik der genossenschaftlichen Kapitalversorgung, Tübingen 1989.
Boettcher, Erik: Die Problematik der Operationalisierung des Förderungsauftrages in Genossenschaften: Förderplan und Förderbericht, (1979), vol. 29, pp. 198–216.
Dülfer, Eberhard: Welche Relevanz hat der "Förderungsauftrag" für die Pflichtprüfung der eingetragenen Genossenschaft? ,vol. 30, pp.47–61, (1980a).
Dülfer, Eberhard: Zielsystem der Genossenschaft, Handwörterbuch des Genossenschaftswesens, col. 1857–1872, Wiesbaden 1980b.
Ehlermann, Rüdiger: Die Kreditgenossenschaften im Spannungsfeld zwischen genossenschaftlichem Förderungsauftrag und universalbankwirtschaftlicher Realität, Diss., Münster 1981.
Engelhardt, Werner Wilhelm/Schmid, Günter: Grundsätzliche Aspekte genossenschaftlicher Ökonomisierung, Das Wirtschaftsstudium (Zeitschrift für Ausbildung, Examen und Weiterbildung), (1987), No.6, pp. 310–316.
Eschenburg, Rolf: Ökonomische Theorie der genossenschaftlichen Zusammenarbeit, Tübingen 1971.
Glaser, Roman: Gewinnerzielung und Gewinnverteilung in Genossenschaftsbanken, Diss., Stuttgart-Hohenheim 1990.
Grosskopf, Werner, with assistance of: *Glaser, Roman/Glatzner, Ludwig*: Strukturfragen der deutschen Genossenschaften, part 1, Der Förderungsauftrag moderner Genossenschaftsbanken und seine Umsetzung in die Praxis, Frankfurt am Main 1990.
Grosskopf, Werner: Mitgliederbindung – Aufgabe und Notwendigkeit, Genossenschaftlich fühlen – genossenschaftlich handeln, Festschrift für Dr. Hermann Hohner, pp. 129–139, Stuttgart 1989.
Grosskopf, Werner/Schüler, Michael: "Sortimentspolitik" in Marktgenossenschaften, neuere Entwicklungen in Betriebswirtschaftslehre und Praxis, Festschrift für Professor Dr. Oswald Hahn zum 60. Geburtstag, pp. 353–366, Frankfurt am Main 1988.
Henzler, Reinhold: Über die Frage einer Beteiligung der Mitglieder am inneren Wert der Genossenschaft. In: Sozialwissenschaftliche Untersuchungen, Gerhard Albrecht zum 80. Geburtstag, pp.81 ff., Berlin 1969.
Henzler, Reinhold: Der genossenschaftliche Gewinn und seine Verteilung unter besonderer Berücksichtigung der Warenrückvergütung. In: Der genossenschaftliche Grundauftrag: Förderung der Mitglieder, Gesammelte Abhandlungen und Beiträge, vol. 8, Veröffentlichungen der deutschen Genossenschaftskasse, pp. 175–189, Frankfurt am Main 1970b.
Jäger, Wilhelm: Der Förderbericht in Genossenschaften als Legitimations- und Motivationsinstrument, vol. 31, (1981), pp.241–247.
Kolbeck, Rosemarie: Bankbetriebliche Planung, Wiesbaden 1971.
Lampert, Heinz: Zur Zielfunktion von Genossenschaften in der wachsenden Wirtschaft (1972), vol.22, pp. 341–355.
Münkner, Hans-H.: Die Genossenschaft – neutraler Organisationstyp oder Abbild gesellschaftlicher Grundauffassungen in Europa?, Tübingen 1989.
Seuster, Horst: Ansätze zur Quantifizierung genossenschaftlicher Förderungsleistungen,neuere Entwicklungen in Betriebswirtschaftslehre und Praxis, Festschrift für Professor Dr. Oswald Hahn zum 60. Geburtstag, Frankfurt am Main 1988.
Seuster, Horst: Zum Zielsystem der Förderungsgenossenschaft (1978), vol. 28, pp. 42–46.
Volk, Karl Otto/Volk, Gerrit: Genossenschaftsbanken zwischen Principal-Agent-Realität und dem Ideal der Wirtschaftsdemokratie, Genossenschaften und genossenschaftswissenschaftliche Forschung, Festschrift des Seminars für Genossenschaftswesen zum 600-jährigen Gründungsjubiläum der Universität zu Köln, pp.139–156, Regensburg 1989.
Weber, Wilhelm: Die Genossenschaft im Wandel der Umsatzsteuersysteme. In: Genossenschaften und Genossenschaftsforschung, Strukturelle und ablaufanalytische, historische und systematische Aspekte der Genossenschaften des 19. und 20. Jahrhunderts, Festschrift zum 65. Geburtstag von Georg Draheim, pp. 290–303, Göttingen 1968.

Public-Benefit Orientation and Co-operatives

HELMUT JENKIS [J]

(see also: *Ethics*; *Commonweal Economy*; *Conceptions, Co-operative*; *Economic Order*)

I. Definition of Terms: Co-operative, Commonweal Economy (Gemeinwirtschaft) and Public-Benefit Orientation (Gemeinnützigkeit); II. The Controversy Between "Co-operative" and "Commonweal economy"; III. The Co-operative Promotion Mandate and Public-Benefit Orientation: A Contradiction?

I. Definition of Terms: Co-operative, Commonweal Economy (Gemeinwirtschaft) and Public-Benefit Orientation (Gemeinnützigkeit)

The terms co-operative, commonweal economy and public-benefit orientation are all used with a great variety of content and meaning.

1. Definition of Co-operative

Aside from the legal definition in § 1 of the German Co-operative Law (GenG, *Genossenschaftsgesetz*), the rights of a registered co-operative are secured by "societies with a non-fixed number of members which strive for the promotion of the employment or the economic situation of their members through a collective commercial enterprise", there are numerous definitions which attempt to capture and explain the character and being of the co-operative. *Engelhardt* (1985) differentiated between the theroretical and the practical, more true to life definition of terms, further distinguishing according to the form of cooperation.

Draheim (1955) provided a concise definition of the co-operative (→ *Dual Nature*) which is still appropriate today:

"Co-operatives are enterprises whose subjects make up a group or body of persons on their own volition in a sociological sense as interpersonally connected individuals; as economic subjects they simultaneously operate a common enterprise whose share capital and administrative bodies solely rest on the members, who have equal voting rights (one member, one vote). Their decisive function is to satisfy those particular needs which arise directly from the members' households in the most advantageous method possible for them... Each co-operative has a *double nature*. It is fundamentally a body of persons, a 'group' in the sense of sociology and social psychology. The members of this group are people who constitute the subjects of the co-operative: a co-operative enterprise of the member households. The subjects of this co-operative enterprise are the same individuals who compose the 'group'".

Dülfer (1966, p.8 ff.) offered a comprehensive definition based on four characteristics. If one sides with *Draheim's* definition and the thesis of the double nature of co-operatives – the social entity and the economic undertaking – then the question obviously arises whether co-operatives do or could both serve the commonweal economy and the public benefit.

2. The Controversial Term "Commonweal Economy"

The term → *Commonweal Economy* (Gemeinwirtschaft) has been and is still used most varyingly. *Thiemeyer* (1975, p.42 ff.) suggests that the commonweal-economic character is used in connection with a great number of considerations: Profitable and non-profitable public-benefit orientation; the social utility function; the maximation of the gross national product and the supply of services; the model of economic welfare; the method of acting "as if" profit was being dispensed with; the idea of commonweal economy in the Law for Non-profit housing; a cost-oriented pricing policy; the application of profit; provisions for existence; the solidarity principle; the obligation of the enterprise in respect to transport, tariffs and rates, timetables, connections, supply and provision. According to *Kloten*, "that all is very unsatisfying and leads to the conclusion that one should completely abandon the term 'commonweal-economic character'" (p.222).

In spite of this criticism, the committee for terminology of the *Gesellschaft für öffentliche Wirtschaft* made the following differentiation of commonweal-economic enterprises:

1) Public enterprises, the agency of which lies in public authority.
2) Independent enterprises involved in the commonweal economy (independent public-benefit-oriented) which are dedicated from their own decision to fulfill public functions, the management of which does not lie in public authority but rather in 'independent' hands of some social groups or forces, respectively.
3) Publically engaged companies which in their being resemble privately operated companies but which are forced to undertake trade and/or business for commonweal-economic purposes because of legislation affecting their operational processes.

If one differentiates between the commonweal economy (or, less precisely: the commonweal-economic character) on the one hand and the public benefit orientation on the other, then one could count the co-operatives among the group of independent enterprises involved in the commonweal economy (need) which do not have to unconditionally dedicate themselves to fulfilling public functions, but which either voluntarily or involuntarily assume public tasks and thus relieve public services or agencies.

3. The Vague Term "Public-Benefit Orientation"

The term "public-benefit orientation" (*Gemeinnützigkeit*) likewise has many meanings; it has become evident that the terms "commonweal economy" (Gemeinwirtschaft) and "public-benefit orientation" (Gemeinnützigkeit) are used synonymously, or at least that they overlap each other. One can come to a variety of conclusions based on the content of the definition that one has chosen. Legislation differentiates between fiscal and non-profit housing enterprises:

In order to carry out §§ 17–19 of the Amended Tax Laws (StAnpG, *Steueranpassungsgesetz* passed on October 16, 1934, Reichsgesetzblatt I., p.925), the so-called Public-benefit Ordinances were issued on December 16, 1941 (GemV, *Gemeinnützigkeitsverordnung*, Reichssteuerblatt I, 1941, p.937) which were replaced by the GemV of Dec. 24, 1953 (Bundessteuerblatt, 1954, I, p.6). This ordinance was worked into §§ 51–68 of the Tax Regulations (AO, *Abgabenordnung*, 1977). According to § 52, subsection 1 of the AO, "a body of persons pursues public-benefit oriented goals when its activity is so structured as to promote the general public selflessly as a whole in material, spiritual or moral matters."

Non-profit housing enterprises were not listed in this catalogue. Although the AO and Law for Non-profit Housing Enterprises (WGG, *Wohnungsgemeinnützigkeitsgesetz* dated February 29, 1940, Reichsgesetzblatt I, p.429) make use of the identical terms, formal and content-related differences exist between these types of public-benefit orientation (*Jenkis*, 1985, p.155 ff.). The WGG similarly does not state any legal definition of public-benefit orientation in the area of housing (non-profit housing) as § 1, subsection 1 of the WGG reads: "Housing enterprises can only then be considered public-benefit oriented when they are recognized in accordance with this law." This is a circular definition; many preconditions are attached to the recognition, and certain practices must be followed upon successfully receiving recognition.

So far, the term public benefit orientation has not been successfully defined in a binding or "final" way; it is much more a matter of an unspecific term or ultimately even an undefinable legal term which can be influenced in content by respective political, economic and/or social norms (*Jenkis*, 1985, p.164 ff.). These norms are intersubjectively non-binding; only conventions can be established.

4. The Difference Between "Real" and "Nominal" Definitions (→ *Classification*)

The three terms co-operative, commonweal economy and public-benefit orientation are vague. This is because no real definitions are possible, but rather only nominal ones (*Essler*, p. 39 ff.).

Real definitions are analysis of nature which can adequately describe the term to be defined; they can either be true or false analytically. On the other hand, a definition is nominal when the term introduced by it has been chosen relatively randomly and can be replaced by another one fairly easily; one encounters a real definition, on the other hand, when such arbitrary substitutions are not permissible. The transition between real and nominal definitions is, however, occasionally indistinct.

Nominal definitions frequently lead to *empty existentialist formulae* (*Topitsch*). This concerns arbitrary moral-political values or with postulates definining the "true" nature of, for example, freedom, democracy, justice or the co-operative, commonweal economy or public benefit orientation. These empty formulae advance the demand for absolute validity, and often a scientific or normative yardstick for decision is taken from such propositions. Ideological supporters use empty existentialist formulae in order to claim in an argument that their definition explains the "true" meaning of a contested term. Such an argument cannot be settled by rational means because the "true nature" or "true meaning" claimed elude any kind of (inter)-subjective verifiability.

The controversy of whether co-operatives are compatible with the commonweal economy and/or the public-benefit orientation can be traced back to the observation that nominal definitions lead to empty existentialist formulae.

II. The Controversy Between "Co-operative" and "Commonweal Economy"

The terms commonweal economy and public benefit orientation are used synonymously in the specialized literature. In this connection, the terms are used and understood with various meanings and contents on account of nominal definitions.

Engelhardt raised the question whether co-operatives are enterprises serving the commonweal economy (1978, p.25 ff.). In agreement with *Weisser*, he held the opinion that the majority of co-operatives are independent enterprises involved in the commonweal economy in the economic sense of the word as self-help organizations or as enterprises servicing self-help which are determined to serve the common good under the supervision of freely formed corporate groups or individuals. *Pfandl* (1983, p.38 ff.) lists the competitive policy, relieving the state and society through promoting economically weaker groups in the population, establishing and preserving self-employment, strengthing demand through price reductions and the educational function as favorable points in the position supporting the co-operative as an enterprise serving the commonweal economy. According to *Weisser* (1954, 1976), other factors permit the co-operative to be seen as an commonweal-economic entity, including the political orientation of such goals as investment, asset accumulation, middle-sized business, consumer, competition, housing development, health, education, research and culture.

In contrast to this comprehensive parallelism between the co-operative and the commonweal economy are, however, the considerations that according to § 1 of the GenG the co-operative is to promote its members and not serve first and foremost the common good. *Pfandl* (p.235 ff.) points out that it is insufficient not to be preoccupied with profit attainment and thus to serve the public at large in an indirect manner; it is much more necessary that the supporters and functions of the enterprise completely and intentionally act to provide advantages for the common good. The promotional purpose is, however, structured around the members and not around the public at large. The argument that co-operatives are to fulfill a market regulatory function and thus serve the public at large is likewise, when at all, indirectly and not immediately at hand.

If one starts out in agreement with the criterion than an enterprise – here, the co-operative – directly or indirectly serves the public at large, then one realizes that a direct service in the interest of the public good would contradict the promotional purpose for the members laid down in § 1, subsection 1 of the GenG. On the other hand, if the indirect effects of the co-operative are referred to, then profit-oriented enterprises could also enlist this service for the public at large (it is referred to in this context as the "invisible hand" described by *Adam Smith*).

III. The Co-operative Promotion Mandate and Public-Benefit Orientation: A Contradiction?

The terminological differentiation between promotion and public benefit orientation has been made because of two reasons:

1) § 1 of the GenG was amended through the Alterations to the GenG dated May 12, 1923, with the inclusion of subsection 2, which currently corresponds in content to Item 2, subsection 2. In other words, co-operatives can have an interest in companies, other associations or public bodies when they "are so determined to serve the public-benefit-oriented endeavors of the co-operative without forming the solitary or predominant goal of the co-operative". The expression "public-benefit-oriented" (*gemeinnützig*) is used here instead of the term "commonweal-economic" (*gemeinwirtschaftlich*).

2) Until the Law for Non-profit Housing Enterprises (WGG) was repealed on Dec. 31, 1989, most of the co-operative housing societies were recognized as non-profit housing enterprises (there has never been a Law for Commonweal Economy). No adjudications of the public-benefit orientation exist according to § 52 of the Tax Regulations (AO).

According to *Pfandl* (p.164), the former statute makes an exception to the promotion of members as it allows for the promotion of public benefit-oriented endeavors. The nature of the co-operative – the promotion of its members (→ *Promotion Mandate*) – is preserved, however, as the participation may not present the predominant or solitary goal.

It was not the amendment to the GenG but rather the circumstance that almost all co-operative housing societies with the exception of 55 at the end of 1982 (most recent statistics available) were recognized as non-profit housing enterprises; these 55 registered co-operatives were so-called artisan-building societies which were not able to attain "public-benefit-orientation-status" on account of the dominating influence of the construction industry. This recognition as a non-profit housing enterprise (gWU, *gemeinnütziges Wohnungsunternehmen*) lead to a lively controversy between the professors *Manfred Neumann* (Erlangen-Nürnberg) and *Erik Boettcher* (Münster). While *Neumann* considered non-profit housing enterprises compatible with the promotional purpose according to § 1 of the GenG, *Boettcher* held there to be a contradiction.

Boettcher differentiates between private industry (promotion of supporters/members, self-help), commonweal economy (promotion of third parties, aid for strangers) and state support (promoting all citizens, state help). Private industry, which strives to make improvements in individual utility, can result from either revenue-oriented enterprises or promotion-oriented enterprises (co-operatives). The advancement of third parties – service for commonweal economy – can result in the form of charitable societies, promotional clubs or public welfare enterprises. Self-help institutions which provide subsidiary service for the state and relieve it from its obligatory duties are public-benefit-oriented. Receiving standing or recognition as a public-benefit-oriented enterprise is an honor or reward from the state for having the identical target group as it has. A conflict can then arise when the state prescribes a particular action, the effect of which causes the affected institution to lose its identity. If the bestowal of the public-benefit orientation for a co-operative housing society is not tied down with conditions, the co-operative autonomy remains preserved, in other words, there is no conflict between the WGG and the co-operative promotional purpose. The WGG, however, contains the so-called 'building obligation' in § 6 WGG. According to *Boettcher*, the heart of the contradiction lies here as the building obligation is easily compatible with servicing the commonweal economy but is only compatible with the co-operative under quite certain conditions. The building obligation is grafted upon the housing co-operative and can, in contradiction to the promotional purpose, go to the wayside, thus benefiting the state's goal orientation. Furthermore, § 5 of the WGG prescribes that housing co-operatives can restrict the transfer of apartments to members, but that they must guarantee admittance to new members. This WGG stipulation poses a breach of the principle of a "non-restricted number of members" because the "open door" principle exists in its place. This stipulation is also in opposition to the GenG as no new members can be accepted, which is against the volition of the members. Co-operatives, including housing co-operatives, are capable of being public-benefit-oriented, but recognition from the state must not level out or eliminate the differences between promoting oneself as self-help and promoting strangers.

Likewise, *Neumann* clearly differentiates between the promotional purpose centered around members of a (housing) co-operative and public-benefit-orientation, which is directed at the public at large. A contradiction between these two goals only exists when the membership promotion and the public-benefit-orientation are simultaneously expressed as goals of the co-operative, and when the administrative management is obligated to both goals. The co-operative housing societies are therefore not public-benefit-oriented because they pursue public-benefit-oriented goals, but rather because they provide services in the interest of their members which lie at the same time in the interest of the common good. *Neumann* also did not see a serious contradiction in respect to the building obligation entailed in the WGG because a demand for housing would also exist in the future. Furthermore, it was remarked that the building obligation in § 6 of the WGG would be fulfilled through a comprehensive modernization of the present housing stock, and the WGG eventually plans a pause in construction.

Irregardless of *Neumann's* position it is necessary to refer to the premises contained in the controversy: They are normative and furthermore avail themselves to nominal definitions (*Jenkis*, 1986). Depending on the selected definition and the unspoken premises included in it, one succeeds in creating an opposition between the co-operative promotional function and the public-benefit-orientation (of housing co-operatives). The majority of the co-operative housing societies have the recognition as non-profit public-benefit-oriented housing enterprises and have not found the restrictions resulting from this to be in contradiction to the co-operative promotional purpose.

This academic dispute of whether public-benefit-oriented and co-operatives are compatible with one another has been mostly overcome through the final appeal of the WGG on December 31, 1989. The differences to the commonweal economy, however, still remain latent.

Bibliography

Aschhoff, Günther: Zur mittelstandsbezogenen Bankpolitik des Verbundes von Genossenschaften – Anmerkungen zu der dreibändigen Veröffentlichung von Dr. Felix Viehoff, in: Zeitschrift für das gesamte Genossenschaftswesen, vol.31 (1981), pp. 13–19.

Boettcher, Erik: Mittelstandspolitik – genossenschaftlich oder gemeinwirtschaftlich? Anmerkungen zu den Anmerkungen Günther Ashhoffs zu der Trilogie Dr. Viehoffs, in: Zeitschrift für das gesamte Genossenschaftswesen, vol.31 (1981), pp. 204–211.

Boettcher, Erik: Genossenschaft oder Gemeinwirtschaft? – Erwiderung auf die Kritiken von Walter Hamm, Ludwig Schnorr von Carolsfeld und Heinz Metzger, in: Zeitschrift für das gesamte Genossenschaftswesen, vol.32 (1982), pp. 253–261.

Brecht, Julius: Die öffentlichen Unternehmen in der Wohnungswirtschaft, Archiv für öffentliche und freigemeinnützige Unternehmen, vol. 3 (1957), pp.13–22.

Brede, Helmut/von Loesch, Achim (eds.): Die Unternehmen der öffentlichen Wirtschaft in der Bundesrepublik Deutschland, Baden-Baden 1986.

Dube, Jürgen: Zur Frage der Ziele bei Genossenschaften, Archiv für öffentliche und freigemeinnützige Unternehmen, vol.9 (o.J.), pp. 97–108.

Engelhardt, Werner W.: Sind Genossenschaften gemeinwirtschaftliche Unternehmen? Schriftenreihe Gemeinwirtschaft, no. 29, Frankfurt 1978.

Engelhardt, Werner W.: Zur Frage der Gemeinwirtschaftlichkeit von Genossenschaften, in: Zeitschrift für das gesamte Genossenschaftswesen, vol.29 (1979), pp. 13–28.

Engelhardt, Werner W.: Das Verhältnis von Genossenschaften und Gemeinwirtschaft, Archiv für öffentliche und freigemeinnützige Unternehmen 1981, pp. 97–122.

Engelhardt, Werner W.: Allgemeine Ideengeschichte des Genossenschaftswesens – Einführung in die Genossenschafts- und Kooperationslehre auf geschichtlicher Basis, Darmstadt 1985.

Finis, Beate: War der Tatchrist Friedrich Wilhelm Raiffeisen ein Gemeinwirtschaftlicher?, Archiv für öffentliche und freigemeinnützige Unternehmen, 1980, pp. 155–170.

Großfeld, Bernhard/Menkhaus, Heinrich: Das Drama 'Gemeinnützigkeit', in: Zeitschrift für das gesamte Genossenschaftswesen, vol.32 (1982), pp. 163–182.

Hahn, Oswald: In eigener Sache: Zum Abschluß der Debatte Aschhoff–Viehoff/Boettcher, in: Zeitschrift für das gesamte Genossenschaftswesen, vol.33 (1983), pp. 9–11.

Hamm, Walter: Mittelstandspolitik und Genossenschaftsbanken, in: Zeitschrift für das gesamte Genossenschaftswesen, vol.32 (1982), pp. 83–90.

Hesselbach, Walter: Die gemeinwirtschaftlichen Unternehmen, Frankfurt 1971.

Jenkis, Helmut W.: Die funktionsgebundene Wohnungsgemeinnützigkeit – Kritische Prüfung eines Vorschlages, Archiv für öffentliche und freigemeinnützige Unternehmen, 1980, pp.187–218.

Jenkis, Helmut W.: Genossenschaftlicher Förderungsauftrag und Wohnungsgemeinnützigkeit – ein Widerspruch? Hamburg 1986, p.146.

Kirchhof, Paul: Die verfassungsrechtlich gesicherte Autonomie von Wohnungsgenossenschaften, Schriften zur Kooperationsforschung, A. Studien, vol.20, Tübingen 1985.

von Loesch, Achim: Die gemeinwirtschaftliche Unternehmung, Köln 1977.

Mändle, Eduard: Zur Frage des genossenschaftlichen Charakters öffentlich- rechtlicher Genossenschaften, Archiv für öffentliche und freigemeinnützige Unternehmen, 1980, pp. 219–232.

Metzger, Heinrich: Anmerkungen zum Beitrag 'Mittelstandspolitik – genossenschaftlich oder gemeinwirtschaftlich' von Prof. Boettcher, in: Zeitschrift für das gesamte Genossenschaftswesen, vol.32 (1982), pp. 213–215.

o.V.: Die Definition des Terminologie-Ausschusses der Gesellschaft zur Förderung der öffentlichen Wirtschaft, Archiv für öffentliche und freigemeinnützige Unternehmen, vol. 1 (1954), pp. 276–279.

Pfandl, Elisabeth: Eingetragene Genossenschaften als gemeinwirtschaftliche Unternehmen – Zulässigkeit gemeinwirtschaftlicher Betätigungen in der Rechtsform der eingetragenen Genossenschaft gemäß § 1 Abs. 1

GenG, Veröffentlichungen des Forschungsinstituts für Genossenschaftswesen an der Universität Erlangen-Nürnberg, vol. 17, Nürnberg 1983 (dissertation).
Richter, Dieter: Möglichkeiten der Operationalisierung des genossenschaftlichen Förderungsauftrages – Zur Frage der Ziele, Maßstäbe und Erfolge genossenschaftlicher Arbeit, Düsseldorf 1981.
Rittig, Gisbert/Ortlieb, Heinz Dietrich: Gemeinwirtschaft im Wandel der Zeit, Festschrift für Hans Ritschl, Berlin 1972.
Rittig, Gisbert: Definitionen des Terminologie-Ausschusses der Gesellschaft zur Förderung der öffentlichen Wirtschaft, Archiv für öffentliche und freigemeinnützige Unternehmen, vol.1 (1954), pp. 214–224.
Röper, Burckhardt: Theorie und Praxis der gemeinwirtschaftlichen Konzeption, Kommission für wirtschaftlichen und sozialen Wandel, vol.128, Göttingen 1976.
Schnorr von Carolsfeld, Ludwig: Zu den Grundfragen der eingetragenen Genossenschaften, in: Zeitschrift für das gesamte Genossenschaftswesen, vol.32 (1982), pp. 1–6.
Schwarz, Peter: Zur Kritik der Bezeichnung 'Freigemeinwirtschaftlicher Unternehmen', Archiv für öffentliche und freigemeinnützige Unternehmen, 1979, pp. 194–224.
Stoll, Gerhard: Die Gemeinnützigkeit von Erwerbs- und Wirtschaftsgenossenschaften im Abgabenrecht – Grundfragen (unter besonderer Berücksichtigung der Gemeinnützigkeit im Wohnungswesen), Vorträge und Aufsätze des Forschungsinstituts für Genossenschaftswesen der Universität Wien, no. 8, Wien 1976.
Stolte, Dieter: Zur Frage der Gemeinnützigkeit von Sparkassen, Schriften der Forschungsstätte für öffentliche Unternehmen, vol.4, Göttingen 1964.
Thiemeyer, Theo: Gemeinwirtschaftlichkeit als Ordnungsprinzip – Grundlegung einer Theorie gemeinnütziger Unternehmen, Volkswirtschaftliche Schriften, vol. 146, Berlin 1970.
Weisser, Gerhard: Die Lehre von gemeinwirtschaftlichen Unternehmen, Archiv für öffentliche und freigemeinnützige Unternehmen, vol.1 (1954), pp. 3–33.
Weisser, Gerhard: Zu den Bemerkungen Gisbert Rittigs über Definitionen des Terminologie-Ausschusses, Archiv für öffentliche und freigemeinnützige Unternehmen, vol.1 (1954), pp. 225–231.
Weisser, Gerhard: Beitrag zur Diskussion über den Begriff 'Gemeinnützigkeit', Archiv für öffentliche und freigemeinnützige Unternehmen, vol.7 (1964/65), pp. 8–13.
Weisser, Gerhard: Die Genossenschaften – freigesellschaftliche Unternehmen im Dienste öffentlicher Aufgaben, vol. 10 (1974), pp.148–166.
Weisser, Gerhard: Einführung in die Lehre von den gemeinwirtschaftlichen Unternehmen, Schriftenreihe Gemeinwirtschaft, vol.24, Frankfurt-Köln 1976.
Weisser, Gerhard: Öffentliche Aufgaben von Genossenschaften, in: Zeitschrift für das gesamte Genossenschaftswesen, vol.27 (1977), pp. 401–413.

Public Services in Latin America, Co-operatives for

HERMANN SCHNEIDER/DANTE CRACOGNA [J]

(see also: *Development, Latin America*; *Co-operatives under Public Law*; *Development Policy*; *Classification*; *Education, Latin America*; *Transport Co-operatives*)

I. Public Services in Latin America; II. Co-operative Solutions; III. Co-operatives for Public Services in Various Countries; IV. Specific Problems; V. Economic and Social Advantages produced by Co-operatives for Public Services; VI. Co-operatives and Privatization; VII. Closing Observation.

I. Public Services in Latin America

In general, the term "public services" is used to characterize the provision of services which aim to satisfy a population's basic needs and which as a rule are regularly required, e.g. the provision of electricity and water or communication and transportation services.

Other services are additionally classified under this term, such as schooling and health care (→ *Health Care System*). These latter services will not be discussed in the course of this treatise even though they are provided in part by co-operatives, such as in Columbia, Brazil and Argentina.

When discussing public services, one generally assumes that the state is bound and obliged to provide for their availability, but that it can meet such obligations in a variety of manners:

– through its own bodies, be they centralized authorities (ministries and subordinate branch offices) or decentralized, autonomous entities, state enterprises, etc.;
– through private organizations authorized by the state.

In the latter case, various legal forms or structures can be assumed, but the state in every case, nonetheless, retains control over pricing and quality considerations for the services in question in order to ensure customer protection (*Cracogna*, 1992).

In this matter, it is important that practically all such service enterprises are de facto monopolies on account of their technical-economic characteristics. Legal considerations also frequently play a role when the state confers respective rights to one supplier, either when it is the state's own enterprise or one run by specially authorized private individuals.

Generally speaking, Latin American countries only provide a low level of public services. These services are often of poor quality, inefficient, produced in an overly expensive manner, and limited in "range" with respect to the geographic area and number of people they are intended to serve. If and when the state directly produces such services itself, an excessive degree of politicization regularly results; a cumbersome and expensive bureaucracy often develops in which the administration suffers from a lack of continuity as well as from a chronic budget deficit. If on the other hand the services in question are furnished by private firms (in the form of concessions or the like), such companies often attempt to generate exaggerated profits – whereby the price of the furnished service does not correspond to its respective quality. This scenario is possible and even facilitated in that the state to a large degree either cannot fulfill or wishes not to fulfill its supervisory obligation and tolerates consumer exploitation (*Cracogna*, 1990).

II. Co-operative Solutions

As a rule, co-operatives can be found in the field of public services in situations in which the required services cannot be provided by the incapable state bureaucracy at hand – or else only to an insufficient extent – or in situations in which private enterprises exercise their market power to the detriment of consumers. Various co-operative solutions have accordingly been established.

1. Consumer Co-operatives

The most widely spread and best developed co-operatives are those in which consumers of one particular service have joined together in order to furnish the respective service and meet their own individual needs (→ *Consumer Co-operatives*). There are usually no specific legal provisions for such co-operatives, and they therefore function as normal consumer co-operatives. Their uniqueness is in the specific service they provide, which in contrast to the other consumer co-operatives is subject to regulations set by the public authorities. The activity of such co-operatives thus results in accordance with terms defined in the concession, license or permit with regard to prices and conditions which are monitored by regulatory authorities (*Cracogna*, 1987).

These types of co-operatives as a rule complement the service palette of the state, which usually provides the co-operatives with the inputs which they in turn distribute among consumers, i.e. electrical energy, drinking water, gas, telephone capacities, etc.

2. Joint-Production Co-operatives

Individuals employed in certain sectors which furnish particular services, especially persons involved in public transport, have joined together in co-operatives (→ *Joint-production Co-operatives*). Only those individuals active in the process of providing this service are members, and the service is provided according to conditions monitored by regulatory authorities. In contrast to the service co-operatives described above, the origin of these co-operatives is rooted in previously existent public service enterprises which were heavily in debt and conveyed to their employees by public authorities as a money-saving maneuver. The means of transport, repair facilities and the like were usually conveyed free of charge or at favorable conditions. In numerous cases, these co-operatives transformed themselves in the course of time so dramatically that they hired employees who were not inducted as members.

3. Co-operatives with State Shareholding

In a few cases, corporate district bodies (communities) joined together in co-operatives in order to attack certain tasks collectively, such as the construction of water purification systems; this is similar to the *régies coopératives* in Belgium (→ *Economie Sociale*). In other cases, services are furnished by mixed co-operatives in which communities and consumers/their organizations collaborate (*Uribe Garzón*).

III. Co-operatives for Public Services in Various Countries

Several countries in Latin America have gathered experience in having their public services provided by co-operative organizations, whereby differences are apparent among countries based on their respective level of development and the particular field of activity.

1. Argentina

In the 1920s, electrification co-operatives began undertaking their activities in the interior of the country. Their goal was to protect the users of electrical energy – their members – from being taken obvious advantage of by the monopoly position of foreign electric companies. The electrification co-operatives at the beginning faced price wars from the former monopolist suppliers in an effort to ruin them; the government even consciously tried to hinder them as it was in league with the interests of the former suppliers. After they consolidated themselves, the electrification co-operatives expanded their services to include the provision of water, the construction of telephone networks both in rural and urban areas, the distribution of gas, etc. They furthermore were involved in the field of so-called "social services", such as funerals, ambulance services, first aid, etc.

At present, over 500 co-operatives of this kind exist which distribute about 10% of the country's electrical energy, thereby reaching about 1.2 million consumers in 900 communities (or about 15% of all consumers in the country). These co-operatives thus assume practically the entire electrical utility provision in the country's rural areas. There are 130 co-operatives which have specialized solely in providing telephone service, and 320 which only provide drinking water (FEDECOBA, 1991). As a whole, numerous small and mid-size communities in the middle of the country are provided with public service through co-operatives.

2. Bolivia

Co-operatives providing public service first undertook their activity in Bolivia in the 1960s and quickly gained considerable importance. This is especially true for Sta. Cruz de la Sierra, the second largest city in the country. Back when the city only counted 80,000 residents, co-operatives began to furnish a variety of public services, starting with the provision of electricity and later expanding to telephone lines and water supply. The co-operative provision of utilities expanded as the city grew, which today has 800,000 residents and in which the most important public services (telephone, water, electricity) are provided by co-operatives.

It is also typical of Bolivia that telephone service in the most important cities – including the capital – is organized by co-operatives. In total, there are 83 co-operatives in the country which provide electricity, 15 for the provision of water and 16 telephone co-operatives (*Antelo Salmón*).

3. Brazil

Co-operatives for public services only recently achieved a degree of importance in Brazil, above all since the 1970s and the beginning of the 1980s. The palette of their services primarily extends to the provision of electricity and telephone service in rural regions, whereby their members have mostly been recruited from local agricultural producers. In numerous cases, these co-operatives can fall back on international loans to construct their utility networks; such monies supplement their local means. At present, there are 202 co-operatives of this kind found primarily in the south and northeast of the country which serve 270,000 consumers. (OCB, p.7).

4. Chile

Co-operatives providing electrical utility service to rural areas came into being in 1945 as the result of a state plan which relied on technical and monetary support from the USA. In the past few years, the number of such co-operatives has not increased, but the number of users drawing their services has: Serving approx. 60,000 consumers they furnish roughly 25% of electrical utility needs in rural areas. Co-operatives have found a further important field of activity in providing small rural communities with drinking water, whereby they were supported by the Interamerican Development Bank in their undertakings. There are 137 co-operatives of this type in the country which serve 30,000 members (Departammento de Co-operativas, p.31 ff.).

5. Columbia

There are practically no consumer co-operatives providing public services in Columbia, but communities have, however, established co-operatives mostly in an effort to organize their water utilities together. Furthermore, there are 294 co-operatives for public transport; in some cases owners of the transport means collaborate, and in other cases it is the employees in the sector. In addition, pre-co-operatives are engaged with recycling garbage and making street improvements (*Uribe Garzón*, p.32 ff.).

6. Costa Rica

Costa Rica likewise has co-operatives which primarily furnish rural areas with electrical service, whereby they too relied on support from the USA during the 1960s. In addition, there are co-operatives providing passenger transportation (60 taxi co-ops and 20 bus co-ops) and merchandise transport (10) (*Vásquez Vargas/Monge Alvarado*, p. 8 ff.).

7. Honduras

→ *Transport co-operatives* have attained some importance in Honduras, both those for the owners of the vehicles as well as those for employees in the sector. This is true not only for passenger transportation but also for merchandise and special transports as well as taxis. As a whole, there are 35 such co-operatives counting 1,172 members dispersed throughout this tiny country which endeavor to organize their cooperation (CHC, p.5).

IV. Specific Problems

Due to the characteristics of the services which co-operatives for public service provide and the specific problems they accordingly face, these co-operatives differ from other co-operatives for the following reasons.

1. Financing

Public services usually require such considerable investments in machinery, distribution networks, repair facilities, depots, motorized vehicles, tools, etc. that they exceed the financing options available to their members/consumers (→ *Financing*). External means are therefore frequently necessary which in the past came in part from public authorities and/or "official" financial institutions and in other cases from international organizations – primarily from the USA – which provided financial and development assistance (→ *United Nations System*). Financing difficulties which result from the high level of such investments and their long-term amortization were thus overcome through the help of third parties.

2. Relationship to Public Authorities

Inasmuch as public authorities determine and control the conditions under which the co-operatives for public service may launch their activities, controversies can arise between the supervisory authority and the co-operatives even when such authorities are composed of the consumers who draw from the services of these co-operatives. Furthermore, politically influenced bodies are responsible for both issuing permits and exercising control; political influence can at times play a role in that officials in the supervisory boards attempt to implement their own criteria to the detriment of those set by the co-operatives (→ *Officialization*).

3. Personnel Qualifications and Management

Many co-operatives require particularly qualified personnel in order to provide their public services (e.g. to construct and run distribution networks for electrical and telephone lines). Because their business partners and in part their competitors to a substantial degree are large-scale public or private companies, high demands are placed on the negotiating and management skills which the co-operative managers must demonstrate. It is therefore quite important for these co-operatives to engage qualified technicians and managers.

4. Enterprise Size and Isolation

Co-operatives for public services in many cases stand out due to their small enterprise size and in that they can be found scattered throughout the country. Small enterprise units providing services for consumers living scattered about do enjoy the advantage of customer proximity, but at the same time they must confront technical and economic disadvantages due to their relatively small enterprise size – disadvantages which are difficult to alleviate or compensate for through cooperation (→ *Operational Size*).

5. Particularities of the Membership

Several consumer co-operatives have in part a considerable number of members, such as those providing urban areas with telephone services. This results in the situation that many members are not aware of the co-operative character of their service enterprises; difficulties accordingly arise in mobilizing members to participate in their co-operatives (→ *Motives for Cooperation*).

V. Economic and Social Advantages produced by Co-operatives for Public Services

The most important economic and social advantages which can be traced back to public services provided by co-operative organizations can be summarized as follows (FEDECOBA).

1. Local Resource Employment

When public services are furnished by local co-operatives, inputs necessary to produce the particular services are employed to a greater extent which are provided locally. Greater local economic impulses accordingly result as would have been the case if the respective service had been produced at a large-scale enterprise located far away to which payments for the utilized service would have been transferred.

2. Impulses for Further Economic Development

If public services are provided by co-operatives due to the lack of other suppliers, not only does the quality of life improve for those receiving the service but the prospects for further economic development likewise increase.

3. Management and Control

→ *Consumer co-operatives* are in a better position to take into consideration the interests of consumers when they furnish public services. This factor is particularly important when the service in question satisfies existential needs which affect the community as a whole. Self-administration and control exercised by consumers themselves have proven more efficient than the bureaucratic control practiced by government officials in a public enterprise.

4. Decentralization

Local control of public service enterprises contributes to the decentralization of decision-making authority and counteracts the concentration of economic and political power. Efficient co-operatives for public services supplement local administrational authorities and are conducive to their consolidation.

5. Infrastructure for Further Fields of Involvement

It has been proven in numerous cases that additional fields of activity have been developed on the basis of a consolidated co-operative infrastructure for the provision of public services. These dynamic effects can be traced back not only to the existent material goods and familiarized organization structure but also to the human capital which has developed in the meantime.

VI. Co-operatives and Privatization

In the course of their efforts to induce structural reforms and a greater market economy, most countries in Latin America are currently involved with executing deregulation and privatization programs (*Crocogna*, 1992). This is especially the case for the sector of public services. In those countries which face high foreign debt and dependency, such privatization moves are frequently undertaken in order to acquire the necessary means to service and repay their debts (in part via debt-for-equity swaps) as well as to reduce their public deficits rather than as a tool to increase efficiency and improve customer service.

It would be desirable if co-operatives – above all consumer co-operatives – were in the position to take part in the privatization processes of public services, particularly since such processes lead to the creation of more enduring structures (→ *State and Co-operatives, Market Economy*). Mixed forms involving state participation are also conceivable when the state does not wish to part from its property but rather entrusts a co-operative with the capacity to provide the particular service.

The difficulties co-operatives confront in their attempts to participate in the privatization process of public services touch on the same factors previously mentioned. The functional processes in question are often technically demanding and require enormous capital expenditures. Potentially interested co-operatives cannot organize themselves efficiently enough in a short amount of time in order to tender a privatization bid due to their geographic dispersion. The problems in raising capital are exacerbated by the time pressure which the state is under to acquire its needed funds. The complexity and magnitude of privatization in many cases exceed the negotiating power and management capacities of interested co-operatives. It is therefore not surprising that co-operatives so far have only had insufficient chances to take part in privatization processes (→ *Development Policy*).

VII. Closing Observation

Public services are furnished to an inadequate extent in numerous Latin American countries, regardless whether they are provided by public authorities or through private suppliers. Co-operatives are successfully involved in this sector in several countries, and in many other cases, such co-operatives could function sensibly and efficiently. In order for this to happen, government authorities must recognize such chances and not preclude co-operative involvement in these fields either purposely or inadvertently.

Bibliography

Carlos, Juan/Salmón: Servicios públicos y cooperativismo, Informe presentado al II Seminario Taller Internacional sobre Prestación de Servicios Públicos a través de Cooperativas, realizado por OCA en Mar del Plata (Argentina) del 27 al 31 de mayo de 1981.

Confederación Hondurena de Cooperativas (CHC): Cifras y estrategias. Movimiento cooperatista hondureno, Tegucigalpa 1991.

Cracogna/Dante: Naturaleza y régimen jurídico de las cooperativas de servicios públicos. In: Cooperativas de servicios públicos, Intercoop, pp. 43–65, Buenos Aires 1987.

Cracogna/Dante: Las cooperativas y los servicios públicos. In: Revista de la Cooperación Internacional, Buenos Aires, No. 1/90, pp. 65–69.

Cracogna/Dante: Problemas actuales del Derecho Cooperativo, Intercoop, Buenos Aires 1992.

Departamento de Cooperativas, Ministerio de Economía, Fomento y Reconstrucción, El sector cooperativo en Chile 1992, Santiago 1992.

Federación de Cooperativas de Electricidad y Servicios Públicos de la Provincia de Buenos Aires (FEDECOBA): Perspectivas de las cooperativas de usuarios en la privatización de los servicios públicos. Informe presentado al II Seminario Taller realizado por OCA en 1991.

Organización de las Cooperativas de América (OCA): Propuesta cooperativa a los gobiernos de América Latina como alternativa en el proceso de privatización de los servicios públicos urbanos y rurales. Documento No. 4, Bogotá 1991.

Organización de las Cooperativas de América (OCA): Derecho Cooperativo. Tendencias Actuales en Latinoamérica y la Comunidad Económica Europea, Antropos (ed.), Bogotá 1991.

Organizacao das Cooperativas Brasileiras (OCP): O sistema cooperativista brasileiro, Brasilia 1991.

Uribe, Garzón/Carlos: Cooperativismo y servicios públicos, Escuela Superior de Administración Pública (ed.), Cuadernos ESAP, No. 25, Bogotá 1991.

Vargas, Vázquez/Angel, José/Alvarado, Monge/Misael: Informe presentado al II Seminario Taller realizado por OCA en 1991.

Raiffeisen, Friedrich Wilhelm (1818–1888)

HORST SEUSTER

(see also: *History of Ideas*; *History in 19th C.*; *Co-operative Banks*; *Rural Co-operatives*; *Credit Unions*)

All over the world, *Friedrich Wilhelm Raiffeisen* today is reputed as the founder of the rural co-operative system. Meanwhile, above the name, the word Raiffeisen has become an institution everywhere. The name Raiffeisen in the whole world stands as a synonym for → *rural co-operatives* in the sense of promoting the enterprise of the members.
Raiffeisen was born on March 30th, 1818, in Hamm/Sieg as son of the mayor there, so he was a contemporary of *Karl Marx*. After visiting primary school and receiving additional lessons by the parson, in 1835, with the intention to go for military career, he entered an artillery regiment at Cologne. Here, he made a relatively fast career until an eye trouble forced him to change place to civil administration.
More important to *Raiffeisen's* development than the imparted school knowledge became the relation to a circle of friends called "Euterpia". Here, he made the aquaintance of literature, music, and of all the friendly intercourse with intelligentsia of his age. Without studying, he became member of a fraternity at Bonn.
In 1843, he took over the position of an urban district secretary in the little "Eifel"-village Mayen. Already at the age of 27, he became Mayor of the rural county borough Weyerbusch/Westerwald including 22 single communities. In 1848, he was transferred to Flammersfeld, the neighboured county borough including 33 communities.
Here, in the "high" Westerwald, he was faced with the difficult social problems of the rural population. At Flammersfeld (1849) and later (1854) at Heddesdorf, he founded his first charitable organization to help the suffering population. Soon he realized that these institutions had no future, since they were born by nothing else but the helpfulness of the wealthy classes.
On his account, in 1864, *Raiffeisen* came to the decision to establish a co-operative based on self-help, namely the Heddesdorfer Darlehnskassenverein, and to continue writing down his idea, finally presenting the first of his epoch-making publications "Die Darlehenskassen–Vereine als Mittel zur Abhilfe der Not der ländlichen Bevölkerung sowie auch der städtischen Handwerker und Arbeiter" (The Remedial Loan Societies as an Instrument to remedy the Misery of the Rural Population as well as the Urban Craftsmen and Workmen, 1866), which under his editorship altogether went through five editions characterized by continious enlargements. This publication of social and reform practice was dedicated to man in his immediate misery and conclusively included, beside the remedial loan societies, consumer, selling, vine grower, dairy, livestock insurance and other co-operatives as well, while on the other side the limitation on rural co-operatives became more precise and finally complete, whereby a difference protruded continually clearer compared with the program of → *Schulze-Delitzsch*.
In 1872, *Raiffeisen* created the first central money equlization board called "Rheinische landwirtschaftliche Genossenschaftsbank e.G.mbH", a central bank for his remedial loan societies. In the same year, the "Arminia, Deutsche Landwirtschaftliche Versicherungsanstalt e.G." (German Agricultural Insurance Company) was formed. Around 1872, all principles were developed, which from this time on determined the essence of local remedial loan societies in the sense of *Raiffeisen*. In 1877, he, by raising the "Anwaltschaftsverband ländlicher Genossenschaften", also carried the for a long time considered project to found a service centre for legal and economic questions for his co-operatives. Finally, in 1879, he founded the "Landwirtschaftliche Genossenschaftsblatt" (Agricultural Co-operative Newspaper).
Still in his lifetime, his co-operatives spread to many European countries. All their → *principles*, which for *Raiffeisen* and many of his former followers were Christian principles, proved to be general ethic axioms of all great religions; generally speaking, of all progressive human societies.
The main task of his co-operatives was and still is the economic promotion of their members, particularly the farmers. Properly speaking, economic promotion logically means support of the members' enterprises, here the rural firms. Concerning the essence and purpose of his co-operatives, *Raiffeisen* stated "...that agriculture as soon as possible will be enhanced, and namely a strong unencumbered peasantry will be brought into being and then also will be conserved".
His significant first-hand performance consisted of the fact that he put in viable forms the things he had seen and known. Surely, he had known of other already existing co-operatives, but the co-operatives as *Raiffeisen* created them did not exist until this time. 'He lived through and invented the co-operative to some extent from the original form once again and in his own way:...the in very present time and in every

not socialistic surroundings efficient and for the future viable, i.e. the at all times suitable "modern" Raiffeisen – co-operative' (*Treue*).
The support of the, as we say today, rural family farms, not their restructing and by no means their dissolution – again expressed in a modern way – implies the philosophy of *Raiffeisen* concerning enterprises. Indeed, it is not a question of the enterprise philosophy or the managerial idea of a single entrepreneur for his enterprise. Moreover, it is by far the corporate image for the many enterprises, particularly the rural agricultural firms in a free enterprise system. In addition, it is characteristic that he in his key co-operative idea and realization had not been influenced by earlier or contemporary developments in co-operative systems. Applicable to him was rather the immediate experience of the rural situation in his surroundings. The ingenuity of his idea was that, in the beginning, it was in accordance with the actual needs of his time. Beyond that, it was flexible enough to also master entirely different situations in other societies, i.e., in all liberal countries, it was also able to develop into the bearing pillar of the rural co-operative system. In doing so, also his orginality and his intellectual independence find expression. Consequently, he clearly created more than simply an economic association for suffering farmers. On the contrary, he accomplished a far-reaching, today more than ever, effective society reform in favor of large parts of the world.

Raiffeisen's further life proceeded plain, but less fortunate. Already in 1864, his chairman of the rural district council was called upon to give a report on the state of health of the nearly blinded. In October 1865, *Raiffeisen* was discharged from civil service, receiving a humble pension. Afterwards, he with less success tried himself as a cigar manufacturer and wine-merchant.

A few days before his 70th birthday, on March 11th 1888, *Raiffeisen* died in his house in Heddesdorf after he had written a detailed comment on the draft of a new co-operative law, which as a result was modified. For more than 100 years, it was tried to solve the social and economic problems of our societies either in the manner of *Friedrich Wilhelm Raiffeisen's* idea or on the basis of *Karl Marx*' (→ *Socialist Critics*). For a long time, it seemed as if in this contest *Marx* would have the upper hand, but in latest time the scale leans to *Raiffeisen* again.

Bibliography

Faust, Helmut: Geschichte der Genossenschaftsbewegung, Frankfurt 1965, pp. 268–307.
Raiffeisen, Friedrich Wilhelm: Die Darlehnskassen–Vereine, unch. repr. of the 5th ed. of 1887, Neuwied 1951.
Treue, Wilhelm: Friedrich Wilhelm Raiffeisen. Große Landwirte, Frankfurt 1972, pp. 177–191.

Ratio-Based Credit Rating Procedures Used by Co-operative Banks

GERT SCHEMMANN

(see also: *Co-operative Banks*; *Discriminatory Analysis*; *Bank Rating*; *Financial Accounting Law*)

I. Credit Risk Appraisals Conducted by Co-operative Banks; II. Ratio Analysis as a Component of Credit Risk Appraisals; III. Ratio-Based Credit Rating: Rule-Based Ratio Assessment; IV. Conclusion.

Introductory Note

The use of ratios and ratio systems to assess companies is a broad field of application within the analysis of annual financial statements (→ *Financial Accounting Law*).
The analysis of solvency risk using ratios is a factor in credit investigations and thus is one of the traditional methods of analysing annual financial statements. The measurement of credit risk using standardized ratio systems can be traced back to research conducted by *Beaver* and *Altman* concerning the extent to which ratios can be used to predict corporate bankruptcy. The combination of certain ratios and certain weightings is considered to be a *standardized ratio system* when the determination of these coefficients and figures is based on statistical procedures rather than on subjective preferences and/or empirical values.

I. Credit Risk Appraisals Conducted by Co-operative Banks

Seen from the theoretical point of view, credit risk appraisals conducted by → *co-operative banks* do not differ from the procedures employed by other banks. Credit analysis encompasses "personal indicators, economic indicators and collateral indicators" (*Schmoll*). Ratio-based credit rating in this connection includes *only* those economic indicators which are reflected in past annual financial statements.
The target customers of co-operative banks, ranging from small through mid-sized to large companies (→ *Operational Size*), are generally heterogeneous in their annual financial statements. For instance, the way in which the various parts of a business are shown on a balance sheet is not particularly revealing. This is a consequence of the frequent splitting of businesses as well as of the common legal forms of partnership and sole proprietorship. As a result, the financial statements reflect only the consequences of splitting operating and holding companies, partners' loans and drawings, real estate preserved as private assets and private taxation above and beyond income tax. Tax optimization in the private sphere, which is

not disclosed, can directly influence the corporate sphere, which is disclosed.

The difficulty in these cases is rooted in the fact that the calculation of aggregate taxable property is the norm although the rendering of accounts is broken down into both private and corporate spheres, where the private sphere is often not disclosed.

A system cannot be expected to predict risks at an early stage if the set of accounting figures provided for the appraisal encompasses only one sphere. On the other hand, a system for measuring financial strength and weakness can be viable when it is able to measure the financial stability and successful economic activity of the sphere which is disclosed.

On this basis, a ratio-based rating system is currently being tested by co-operative banks in the Federal Republic of Germany.

It is important to note that the results of a system limited to *measuring* require further interpretation from the point of view of the company's or proprietor's overall position, as such a system only measures the strengths and weaknesses of those spheres which are disclosed.

II. Ratio Analysis as a Component of Credit Risk Appraisals

Ratio analysis is only one part of a solvency analysis. Within the scope of the analysis of the annual financial statements frequently referred to as balance sheet interpretation, ratio analysis serves to process and present information provided by those figures used in the set of accounting figures. The formulation of ratios therefore accomplishes various informational objectives. The profit situation, the financial position and the structure of assets should be worked out in ratios as components of the company's situation. In this sense, the ratios serve to reflect a company's economic situation. This does not, however, produce a firm result.

1. Ratios and their Measuring Function

Ratios can be used to measure economic facts when a "basis" has been provided. For example, in the case of the equity ratio, balance sheet total is used as a basis on which to measure the equity ratio. An equity ratio of 100% therefore states that equity equals total assets. Grading, however, cannot be accomplished until an appropriate instrument of measurement has been created.

2. Ratios and their Yardstick Function

"The yardstick upon which the extent of a characteristic is rendered is called a scale" (*Schuchard-Ficher*, p.4 et al.). Only when a scale is provided can grading be undertaken. Various scaling is possible in the form of nominal, ordinal, interval or ratio scales. Statements such as "better than", "worse than", "climbing" or "falling" result when ratios are used as a basis of measurement. If the ratios are assessed, qualifications such as "solvent", "insolvent", "sufficient", "acceptable", etc. are attributed to them. For example, when an equity ratio of 10% is said to be unsatisfactory, this is an assessment or evaluation. On the other hand, when it is said that the equity ratio has risen, this is a measurement based on an ordinal scale.

As a rule, such scales are created from empirical values based on experience; the analyst is not in a position to provide an unequivocal point of reference from which his assessment can be derived. This is surely an unsatisfactory situation as the analyst's *background* scale is subjectively determined and thus cannot be reconstructed by others. Furthermore, no guarantee exists that the same scale is used consistently for all assessments.

3. Traditional Ratio Analysis

In order to derive an overall assessment from the ratios utilized, "an individual and subjective weighting system" (*Baetge/Niehaus*, p.159) must be used by analysts employing traditional methods in order to assess balance sheet items and profit and loss positions in the annual financial statements.

The selection of the set of ratios used occurs deductively according to the prescribed objective of the measurement – here, the overall business result and the breakdown into its individual components.

Difficulties arise under traditional ratio analysis when figures of measurement which are not clearly defined are attributed to the target measuring financial strength or weakness. Which criteria of measurement can be allocated to the target of "risk minimization"? How can "financial risk" be defined? Is the debt-equity ratio an adequate device for measuring financial risk? These are the tasks of a theory of balance sheet analysis which has yet to be developed. "The function of a theory of balance sheet interpretation is first and foremost to deduce which financing hypothesis must implicitly be presupposed for each numerical transformation (ratios showing capital lock-up and capital structure, cash flows, etc.) through the creation of models" (*Schneider*, p.642). Predictions that companies are tending towards insolvency are unsubstantiated if they lack justification in the form of financing hypotheses.

4. Statistical Ratio Analysis

Statistical ratio analysis is not a process of defining ratios on the basis of a stated target. Available ratios are taken as a starting point for statistical evaluation without particular ratios having been selected in advance. By applying statistical procedures to available ratios, a ratio or combination of ratios typical of positive or negative trends can be deduced from the underlying values.

a) Discriminatory Functions

The application of discriminatory functions within the scope of the credit investigation process has increasingly gained ground. Discriminatory analysis should not be seen as a procedure for predicting insolvency (→ *Insolvency Prognosis*); however, this was the objective of discriminatory functions during their development. The calculated discriminatory value is useful for making the clearest possible separation between "good" and "bad" companies as early as three years prior to actual insolvency. A random sample of "good" companies – those which proved at a later stage to be without problems – and a group of "bad" companies – those which became bankrupt or in which insolvency led to provisions for doubtful receivables – was drawn up to obtain this discriminatory value. The weightings of the ratio(s) and combinations of ratios were adjusted until the most exact separation of the "good" from the "bad" companies could be attained. This combination provided in turn the formula with which companies not included in the random sample could likewise be classified as "good" or "bad".

As a rule, an alteration in the composition of a random sample results in an alteration in the discriminatory function in this formula deriving procedure. This likewise explains the multitude of discriminatory functions found both in writings on the subject and in practical application.

Nonetheless, justified objections exist to the use of discriminatory analysis in financial statement analysis when the goal is to predict insolvency risk. These objections affect both fundamental preconditions and statistical requirements.

The attraction of this procedure, however, is that its practical application provides an acceptable correlation between those companies rated "critical" and the results of the appropriate classification attained by applying the discriminatory function. This statement must however be qualified. The discriminatory functions presented in the literature on the subject exhibit an unwelcome tendency to err when assessing planned credit commitments. They register bad companies with a good degree of precision but include a considerable number of good companies in the "bad" category. This means that credit applications which are not fundamentally risky are rejected. This is a major shortcoming when the practical use of this method by banks is considered. If one analyses those discriminatory formulas based on the forms classification discussed in German-language writing on the subject, one can determine that "the rate of success within a relevant period of time, that is at least two years prior to insolvency, is under 80%" (*Gemünden*, p.150). The economic consequences of misclassification are of such a dimension that they make the exclusive application of statistical insolvency prognoses obsolete; this can be seen from bankruptcy statistics.

b) Scoring Procedures

Scoring procedures are not tied to numerical evidence, but are nevertheless applied on the basis of numerical evidence. Several trends are evaluated statistically in the development of scoring procedures with respect to their importance in distinguishing "good" from "bad" borrowers. The prediction made on the basis of a scoring system is statistical in nature. It cannot be determined whether the individual credit applicant will or will not repay his loan, but the probability of the individual credit applicant behaving in a satisfactory manner compared with a group of statistically identical credit applicants can be stated. An essential component of the scoring procedure is the allocation of characteristics (attributes) to a numeric value. Grading occurs according to a particular scale for each characteristic. The total score is ascertained by adding together the point values of all characteristics. Whereas scoring procedures are frequently used in retail banking, they are not widely used for analysing annual financial statements.

III. Ratio-Based Credit Rating: Rule-Based Ratio Assessment

1. The Objective

The objective of developing a standard ratio assessment is as follows. The assessment system should be so developed as to provide a machine-calculated ratio assessment of the annual financial statements using selected ratios from those statements.

Ratio assessment should evaluate the structural strengths and weaknesses of a company's financial situation. The assessment is undertaken from the perspective of the creditor. The objective is to ascertain which financial structures result in a situation in which a company is unable to remain solvent without assistance.

It is important to bear in mind that no causal model of a borrower's solvency exists, or in other words, prior knowledge as such does not exist. The lender therefore makes use of empirical values and relies on his own experience of similar credit situations when assessing a credit risk. No model exists in which a future insolvency can be conclusively attributed to specific ratio patterns in the annual financial statements.

2. Presentation

Rule-Based ratio assessment is deduced from the figures in the annual statement which reflect past performance. Assessments of management quality, products, market development and the competitive situation are not taken into account. Viable forecasts can be made only on the basis of figures contained in the planning models of future annual financial statements.

Difficulties arise in obtaining the necessary information from the annual financial statements:
- missing items
- incorrect information
- figures available for only one year
- accounting policy measures.

Furthermore, differences can arise in the structure of the balance sheet because of:
- varying methods of structuring
- a lack of systematic structure
- an incorrect structure.

These impair both the statistical significance of the ratios used as well as the valuation scale applied to them.

The idea of using ratios to determine a credit rating is based on the understanding that ratios, under certain conditions, reflect a company's stability or liability. Ratios are seen as a barometer for gauging a company's resistance under adverse conditions. The method of ratio assessment is therefore formally in accord with that of the discriminatory functions since they also work with ratios based on the annual financial statements. Nevertheless, they vary according to their objective. Discriminatory analysis aims to achieve the most accurate and foreseeable separation of "good" and "bad" companies. Here, the objective is to assess the balance sheet of the borrower using ratio scoring, whereby the results of the risk rating procedure should resemble the results obtained by experts using ratio analysis methods.

a) Components

aa) Ratios

Among the applicable ratios were those which were considered significant for assessing risk. A total of 170 annual financial statements were used as a basis for investigation, and a further 50 annual statements were used as a control.

Statements from both solvent and insolvent companies were used in both groups. In contrast to the discriminatory analysis, however, the number of good and bad companies was not equal; the ratio of good companies to bad companies was approx. 10:1. This ratio is somewhat higher than the expected ratio of repayments to failures in insolvency statistics. It nonetheless avoids the unrealistic assumption that the ratio of good to bad companies is 50:50 in reality and makes the random sample result more applicable to a real-life situation. The investigation was not restricted to certain legal forms or company sizes, nor did it exclude companies with negative equity capital.

These ratios, as well as combinations of them, were studied in iterative procedures to determine the deviation from the results produced by experts in their analyses. The results showed that accuracy could only be achieved by using a combination of ratios and differentiating between four different types of financial statement model. These results would then be accurate enough to guarantee that not one of the companies rated by the experts as "critical" would be considered acceptable and be included.

The following ratios were used in automated calculation procedures:
- equity ratio
- interest coverage
- cash flow to total debt
- rate of return on total capital.

These ratios are used alongside numerous other ratios in traditional ratio analysis and have proved themselves in differentiating accurately between financially stable and unstable companies; this has likewise been verified statistically. "Seen as a whole, in the last 20 years or so of empirical research into insolvency only very few surprising findings have been produced: profitability, liquidity and equity capitalization are the pillars of classic ratio analysis as we know it from many years of credit analysis" (*Gemünden*, p.137).

In order to determine the exact make-up of each financial item used in a ratio, it is necessary to employ uniform procedures in spreading financial statements. For analysis purposes the spread sheet system of German cooperative banks, the so-called "IKBA" format, is used. The composition of the following ratios with reference to the position of the balance sheet items in the IKBA format (in brackets) is as follows:

$$\text{Equity ratio} = \frac{\text{Net worth (2049)} \times 100}{\text{balance sheet total (2129)}} \times 100$$

$$\text{Interest coverage} = \frac{\begin{array}{c}\text{Profit before extraordinary} \\ \text{items and tax (3119)} \\ + \text{interest expense (3111)}\end{array}}{\text{interest expense (3111)}} \times 100$$

$$\text{Cash flow to total debt} = \frac{\begin{array}{c}\text{Profit before extraordinary} \\ \text{items and tax (3119)} \\ - \text{Income tax (3149) [or for} \\ \text{partnerships (3119) } -(5131)] \\ + \text{annual depreciation (3081)}\end{array}}{\begin{array}{c}\text{long-term liabilities (2069) +} \\ \text{current liabilities (2109)}\end{array}} \times 100$$

$$\text{Rate of return on total capital} = \frac{\begin{array}{c}\text{Profit before extraordinary} \\ \text{items and tax (3119)} \\ + \text{interest expenses (3111)}\end{array}}{\text{balance sheet total (2129)}} \times 100$$

bb) Methods of differentiating between different types of financial statement

The above-mentioned ratios have differing values according to the branch or legal form of the company being investigated. For example, the average equity ratio for manufacturing companies is higher than that of trading companies. In the construction industry, this ratio is even lower than that of the trading companies. However, advance payments are a typical feature of construction companies' balance sheets.

Maintaining a uniform scale in scoring the equity ratio for manufacturing, trading and construction companies would necessarily mean that manufacturing companies would always receive a higher score (point value) than trading companies.

The varying equity ratio does not in this case reflect a higher risk for trading companies, but rather indicates that the structural risk of a trading company is lower than that of a manufacturing company; the lower equity ratio of a trading company therefore indicates the same level of risk as the higher equity ratio of the manufacturing company. The ratio values for various branches observed in practice and included in the model are thus taken into consideration in the construction of the point scale. (→ *Equity Capital*).

The structural standards for various types of companies are a means of altering the grading explained above. Structural standards are formulated using structural ratios from the annual financial statements (statement logic). This leads to a general classification of companies similar to a breakdown according to industry. Seen analogously, a separation into manufacturing, trading, construction and service branches can also be made.

One structural standard for trading companies (sales intensive companies) is formulated using capital turnover; all companies which have a capital turnover rate higher than 3 are treated as sales-intensive companies and are assessed using an appropriate rating scale. In the model, further structural standards are used to define sales-intensive companies, but these are not discussed in detail in this paper.

A study of the average capital turnover in selected branches using statistical analysis (using the Bundesbank monthly report for November 1988, Ertragslage und Finanzierungsverhältnisse der Unternehmen in 1986 und 1985) shows that only the wholesale and retail trades have a capital turnover rate higher than 2.2; the majority of firms in manufacturing industry have rates of between 2.1 and 1.2, while the construction industry has a rate of under 1.2.

Such structural peculiarities exist not only with respect to capital turnover but also with respect to interest expenses, depreciation on tangible assets, the share of prepayments on total assets, the operating result as well as the financial result of a company. A further characteristic of ratios which describe the structures of the annual financial statements is that they should not vary significantly on the basis of legal form and company size. Whereas the "capital turnover" ratio, for example, varies comparatively little and thus is suitable as a structural ratio for firms in a certain industry, the equity ratio varies so substantially with joint-stock companies, partnerships and sole proprietors that one cannot draw a correlation between industry and equity share (banks and insurance companies are exceptions).

Four different typical financial statement models using different structural ratios are identified in the system:
- financial statements for "manufacturing" companies
- financial statements for "sales-intensive" companies, e.g. traders
- financial statements for "investment-intensive" companies, e.g. in construction
- financial statements for "usufruct-intensive" companies, e.g. in leasing, rental.

cc) Criteria for Disqualification

Standards registering certain data constellations in the annual statements are considered "disqualifying" if, in the course of the investigation, they are found to be atypical ratios and forestall an assessment based on the experience of the credit analysts. The system indicates "not applicable" and directs the user to the constellation found to be atypical.

This is illustrated by the example of the demarcation results. The system differentiates between the components "operating result" and "financial result" in company earnings before tax and interest. The following definitions are incorporated in the structural system found in the IKBA:

operating result = operating profit (gross) (3099)
financial result = income from investment and participations (3101) + interest income (3102)

If the financial result is larger than investments and participations (1059) plus similar assets (1149), the system will indicate "not applicable". "A particularly high and greatly increased financial result is chiefly observed in parent companies which mobilize the hidden reserves of their subsidiaries." (*Gemünden*, p.137).

Examples of this include strongly increased investment participation values (measured against total assets), strongly increased deductions (measured against total assets), and a financial result which is higher than investments and other interest-bearing assets.

b) How the system works

The calculated ratios are weighted using a point scale so that a total point value can be figured. This in turn is applied to reach an assessment using an appraisal scale. There are four scales for each ratio corresponding to the four types of financial statement models used. In total, sixteen scales are thus used.

Three of the four scales used to measure equity ratio are included as an example. They were calculated using coefficients from the annual statements of German companies in 1986 (Special Issue of the Deutsche Bundesbank 1989, p.52–58). These are average equity ratios for joint-stock companies, partnerships and sole proprietors. The following scales are *not* the same ones as those used in the ratio-based credit rating system.

Score	manufacturing processing	sales-intensive retail trade	investment-intensive construction
6	43.8	34.6	26.4
5	39.1	30.2	22.6
4	34.4	25.8	18.7
3	29.7	21.5	14.9
2	25.0	17.1	11.0
1	20.3	12.7	7.2
0	15.6	8.3	3.4
−1	10.8	4.0	− 0.5
−2	6.1	− 0.4	− 4.3
−3	1.4	− 4.8	− 8.2
−4	− 3.3	− 9.2	−12.0
−5	− 8.0	−13.6	−15.8
−6	−12.7	−17.9	−19.7

Corresponding scales have been created for the ratios "interest coverage", "cash flow to total debt" and "rate of return on total capital".

A complete scale is created for each type of balance, as the following example illustrates (this is only an example and does not correspond to the complete scale used in the system):

Complete Scale for Manufacturing Companies

Equity ratio	41.0	35.9	10.4	−15.1	−20.2
interest coverage		5.3	0.8	− 3.7	
Cash flow to total debt		21.1	3.6	−13.9	
return on total capital		11.3	3.8	− 3.7	
points	6	5	0	− 5	− 6

The points are added up to give the total score, and a solvency range is allocated to that score.

Solvency Range Rating

total score	
18–21	good
10–17	acceptable
8–9	barely acceptable
3–7	unstable
0–2	very unstable
under 0	critical

Ratio-based credit ratings result accordingly from the methods used in scoring procedures. This is evident in the following example. A manufacturing company with an equity ratio of −15.1, interest coverage of 0.8, cash flow to total debt of 21.1 and rate of return on total capital of 11.3 has a total score of 5 and is accordingly rated "unstable".

In the ratio assessment system currently being tested, the scales for the various types of financial statement have been determined by a iterative procedure, whereby a requirement is that the sought-after scale must make possible an assessment whose results correspond with those of the credit analysts in their solvency appraisals.

In contrast to the discriminatory functions formulated in the discriminatory analysis, the scoring procedure adds both positive and negative ratios together; a high negative value in one ratio can be compensated by a correspondingly high positive value in another ratio. Negative equity ratios encountered in business practice, particularly among sole proprietors, are thus taken into account. According to Bundesbank statistics (coefficients, p.58), 40% of the annual financial statements from sole proprietors in Germany have a negative equity ratio, although it can be stated with certainty that a negative equity ratio alone does not lead to insolvency.

There is a wide spectrum of possible applications for ratio-based credit rating:

- balance sheet analysis
- evaluating the actual figures of the balance sheet
- providing consultation in determining planned figures
- appraising credit portfolios
- comparing credit portfolios
- structuring credit portfolios.

IV. Conclusion

Rule-based ratio assessment "uses former values and figures from the annual financial statement alone. Information about markets, management quality, brands, sales channels, and the legal environment are not taken into consideration" (*Schemmann*, p.49). Rule-based ratio assessment does not replace the credit analysts, but as a brief evaluation of the balance sheet and profit and loss account it does make preliminary auditing and sorting of credit inquiries possible. At the same time, it enables analysts to contrast their own results and to review their opinions in the context of a deviation analysis. This procedure is not strictly objective but has been objectified through the experience and knowledge of the experts. It is rooted in risk evaluation in the sense of conventions or norms. As a transparent system with verifiable parameters, the ratio assessment system is a suitable standardized instrument for estimating risk in credit portfolios.

Bibliography

Altmann, Edward I.: Financial Ratios, Discriminatory Analysis and the Prediction of Corporate Bankruptcy, in: The Journal of Finance, #23 (1968), pp.589–609.

Altmann, Edward I.: The Success of Business Failure Prediction Models: An International Survey, in: Journal of Banking and Finance, #8 (1984), pp.171–198.

Baetge, Jörg and Niehaus, Hans-Jürgen: Moderne Verfahren der Jahresabschlußanalyse, in: Bilanzanalyse und Bilanzpolitik: Vorträge und Diskussionen zum neuen Recht, In-

stitut für Revisionswesen der Westfälischen Wilhelm-Universität. Ed. Jörg Baetge, Düsseldorf, 1989.
Beaver, William H.: Financial Ratios as Predictors of Failure. Empirical Research in Accounting: Selected Studies, in: Journal of Accounting Research, #4 (1966), pp.71–111.
Baetge, Jörg: Möglichkeiten der Früherkennung negativer Unternehmensentwicklungen mit Hilfe statistischer Jahresabschlußanalysen, in: ZfbF, #41 (1989), pp.792–811; here p.799.
Douglass, K. Scott and Lucas, Douglas J.: Historical Default Rates of Corporate Bond Issuers, Moody's Special Report 1979–1988, Moody's Investor Service, New York/ 1989) (*interesting study concerning the frequency of insolvencies within a given group of companies under investigation*).
Gemünden, Hans Georg: Defizite der empirischen Insolvenzforschung, in: Krisendiagnose durch Bilanzanalyse, edited by Jürgen Hauschildt, Cologne (1988), pp.135–152; here pp.148–151.
Köllhofer, Dietrich: Moderne Verfahren der Bilanz- und Bonitätsanalyse im Firmenkundengeschäft der Bayerischen Vereinsbank AG, in ZfbF #41 (1989), pp.974–981.
Krehl, Harald: "Zur Verbesserung der Kennzahlenanalyse", in Krisendiagnose durch Bilanzanalyse, ed. Jürgen Hauschildt, Cologne (1988), pp.17–40. Krehl writes on p.40 that "no uniform indication was found in the literature discussing questions. An examination of academic writing on balance sheet analysis on the causes of insolvency and on techniques of credit investigation has yielded no clear indication that any given values used in balance sheet analysis are widely used as insolvency indicators or as crisis warning signals. The instruments of traditional balance sheet analysis are clearly not designed for crisis situations. One should not be surprised when they are inappropriate as an early warning system."
Lampe, Winfried: ibid. Appendix, pp.204–207.
Ohlenroth, Wilfried and Reuter, Arnold: Zensuren für Unternehmen und Bilanzen – Statistische Bilanzanalyse in STS, in: Betriebswirtschaftliche Blätter, #34 (1985), pp.336–342.
Schemmann, Gert: Kennzahlenbasierte Bonitätseinstufung, in: Bankinformation, #7/1989, pp.45–49.
Schneider, Dieter: Eine Warnung vor Frühwarnsystemen – Statistischer Jahresabschluß als Prognose zur finanziellen Gefährdung einer Unternehmung?, in: Der Betrieb, #38 (1985), pp.1489–1494 (*objections to the application of statistical ratio analyses*).
Schneider, Dieter: Erste Schritte..., in: Die Wirtschaftsprüfung, #42 (1989).
Schuchard-Ficher, Christiane/Backhaus, Klaus/Humme, Udo/Lohrberg, Werner/Plinke, Wulff/Schreiner, Wolfgang: Multivariate Analysemethoden, 2nd Edition, Berlin, Heidelberg, New York (1982).
Tamari, Meir: Some International Comparisons of Industrial Financing, A Study of Company Accounts in the U.K., U.S.A., Japan and Israel, Stonehouse, Glos. (1977), pp.124 132. *Weinrich, Günter*: Ein Verfahrensvorschlag zur Erkennung bilanzieller Risiken, in: Die Wirtschaftsprüfung, #40 (1987), pp.341–349; here p.343.
Thomas, Karl: Aussagen quantitativer Kreditnehmeranalysen, in: Innovationen im Kreditmanagement, Entscheidungshilfen, Service aufgaben und Controlling im Firmenkreditgeschäft der Banken, ed. H.-J. Krümmel and B. Rudolph, Frankfurt am Main (1985), pp.196–204.
Thomas, Karl: Erkenntnisse aus dem Jahresabschluß für die Bonität von Wirtschaftsunternehmen, in: Der Jahresabschluß in Widerstreit der Interessen, ed. Baetge, Jörg, Düsseldorf (1983), pp.69–83.

Register, the Co-operative

CHRISTIAN SCHWARZ [J]

(see also: *Law, National*; *Law, International*; *Legal Form, Co-operative*)

I. Terms, Definitions and Legal Bases; II. Register Court; III. Registration Procedures; IV. Entries into the Co-operative Register and into the Membership Lists; V. Effects of Entered Information; VI. Announcements made by the Register Court; VII. Disclosure of the Co-operative Register; VIII. Examination of the Co-operative Register.

I. Terms, Definitions, and Legal Bases

Upon enrollment in the co-operative register, a co-operative attains the status of a "registered co-operative" and thus becomes a juristic person (§§ 10, 13, 17 of the Genossenschaftsgesetz *GenG*, German Co-operative Law). The importance of this registered status is such that the co-operative is considered a merchant by legal structure. The co-operative register is a special form of commercial register for registered co-operatives and, likewise, is an official record of the legal relationships affecting the co-operative and the relevant legal matters involved in legal transactions. By disclosing important legal relationships of the co-operative, it serves both the security and protection of confidentiality. The membership list kept alongside the co-operative register indicates the membership level and the members' participatory interest in the enterprise (→ *Group, the Co-operative*). The co-operative register is kept in accordance with §§ 1–24 of the Verordnung über das Genossenschaftsregister (*GenRegVO*, Regulations for the Co-operative Register) dating from November 22, 1923 (§§ 26–36 regulate the membership list), which was most recently amended through the law passed on November 20, 1986. Further legal foundations for the co-operative register are the *GenG* for industrial and co-operative purchasing associations passed on May 1, 1889, as well as the Gesetz der freiwilligen Gerichtsbarkeit (*FGG*, Law of Voluntary Jurisdiction) dated May 17, 1898. The provisions for the commercial register in the Handelsgesetzbuch (*HGB*) of May 10, 1897 (§§ 8 ff.) are applicable in a supplementary manner (→ *History in 19th C.*). A separate register page (*GenRegVO*, § 12) as well as special records (*GenRegVO*, §§ 13; 27, Subsec.4) are to be kept for each co-operative.

II. Register Court

The co-operative register is kept by the responsible district court which administers the commercial register (*GenG*, § 10, Subsec.2; *FGG*, § 125, Subsec.1). In the jurisdiction of this court, the co-operative has its registered seat (*GenG*, § 10, Subsec.1). In principle, the register judge assumes the responsibilites of a registrar (§ 3, no. 2d of the Rechtspflegergesetz, *RPflG* of November 5, 1969, Law of Judicial Administration); exceptions are outlined in *RPflG*, § 17, No.2 a,b.

III. Registration Procedures

A regular prerequisite for entry into the co-operative register and the membership list is a petition for application, whereby entries must be differentiated between those based on application (*GenRegVO*, § 6) and those based on announcements or declarations (*GenRegVO*, § 7). In principle, entry into the co-operative register requires registration by all members of the board (also deputy members) in an officially notarized form, in other words: the signatures under the typewritten application must be authenticized by a notary public (*GenG*, § 157; *GenRegVO*, § 6). § 6 of the *GenRegVO* likewise lists the applications which this form must satisfy. § 7 of the *GenRegVO* is applicable for other situations of announcements and declarations with respect to the register court. In accordance with *GenG,* § 160, the register court can institute compulsary payment procedures against members of the board who have not fulfilled their registration obligations.

Entries without an official petition are permissible only in exceptional circumstances. Examples include the initiation of bankruptcy procedures concerning the co-operative assets (*GenG*, § 102), dissolvement of the co-operative (*FGG*, §§ 142; 147, Subsec.2; *GenRegVO*, § 22), and deletion of inadmissible entries (*FGG*, §§ 142; 147, Subsec.1; *GenRegVO*, § 9).

IV. Entries into the Co-operative Register and into the Membership List

Only those entries are admissable which are enumerated in §§ 15–23 of the *GenRegVO*. All other entered items are inadmissable.

1. The (initial) registration of a co-operative, aside from the application submitted by the board of directors (Vorstand) and the specification of their power of attorney (*GenG*, § 11, Subsec.3), as well as their official signature samples (*GenG*, § 11, Subsec.4), requires the documents listed in *GenG,* § 11, Subsec.2, or namely the → *by-laws* signed by the founding members, a membership list, a copy of the charter appointing the board of directors and supervisory board, certification from the auditing association regarding the admissability of the co-operative's application, and a report from the auditing association on the establishment of the company.

The register court must check whether the co-operative has been established and registered in accordance with procedures (*GenG*, § 11 a, Subsec.1; *GenRegVO*, § 15, Subsec.1); the by-laws must meet legal prescriptions, and the stated purpose of the co-operative must correspond to the preconditions stated in *GenG*, section 1 (*GenG*, §§ 6–8; 36, Subsec.1, Sent.2; *GenRegVO*, § 15, Subsec.1). The court must only then verify the accuracy of the given information, if and when substantiated doubts arise upon registration or from other circumstances. The expediency of the → *by-laws* is not proved. The register court, however, does have comprehensive verification responsibilities with regard to the content in accordance with *GenG*, § 11 a, Subsec.2. It must check whether the concerns of the co-operators or creditors of the co-operative, in particular with regard to the financial position, are possibly threatened through personal or economic relationships. Herewith, the register court is not restricted to the report submitted by the auditing association upon the formation of the company; if this report is insufficient, it may conduct further investigation (*FGG*, § 12), such as requesting an expert opinion. If the reservations against the proper establishment or registration of the co-operative cannot be dispelled, the register court will deny enrollment, issue a statement listing the reasons for rejection and inform the applicants of the decision (*GenG*, § 11 a, Subsec.1; *GenRegVO*, § 3, Subsec.1). If the registration is permissable, the → *by-laws*, the board members (as well as their proxies), and notification of their power of attorney (*GenG*, §§ 10, Subsec.1; 25,35; *GenRegVO*, § 18) are taken into the co-operative register. Upon being entered into the register, the co-operative acquires the rights of a registered co-operative (*GenG*, § 13). The by-laws are not to be entered into the co-operative register in their totality, but rather only through the enrollment of an excerpt which must contain the necessary information delineated in *GenG,* §§ 10;12, Subsec.2 (*GenRegVO*, § 15, Subsections 2–4). The court will publicist the by-laws excerpt in the Federal Register (*GenG*, §§ 12, Subsec.1; 156; *GenRegVO*, § 5). The original by-laws are placed in the court records (*GenG*, § 11, Subsec.5, Sent.2; *GenRegVO*, § 15, Subsec.5). The signatories of the by-laws are entered into the membership list as members of the co-operative (*GenRegVO*, § 29, subsections 1,2).

2. Amendments to the → *by-laws* must be registered in the co-operative register in accordance with *GenG*, § 157 and *GenRegVO*, § 6 by all members of the board of directors (*GenG*, § 16, Subsec.5, Sent.1). The register court examines whether the registration has followed in due order and whether the wording of the resolution violates either the law or the by-laws, but not whether the legal or statutory stipulations concerning the summoning of the general assembly as well as the voting were adhered to. The registration of amendments to the by-laws follows according to *GenRegVO*, § 16, and the changes must be made public when they affect certain items listed in *GenG*, § 12, Subsec.2, such as the enterprise and location of the co-operative, the object of the company, members of the board or their power of attorney (*GenG*, §§ 16, Subsec.5, Sent.2; 156). Changes in the by-laws first become effective upon their enrollment in the co-operative register (*GenG*, § 16, Subsec.6).

3. The opening of a branch presents a situation which must be entered into the co-operative register. A branch is a geographically business site with its own assets and account books separate from the main headquarters, the manager of which independently conducts business similar to that carried out in the main office; agents or branch offices which merely undertake the execution or settlement of orders are not branches in this sense. The establishment of a branch is to be entered by all members of the board and has to be registered in the co-operative register of the branch at that particular register court where the co-operative headquarter has its registered seat (*GenG*, § 14, Subsec.1, Sent.1; § 157; *GenRegVO*, § 6). The court in which the headquarter has its seat, the registration transfers to the court in whose jurisdiction the branch resides. The establishment of the branch is not announced publically (cf. *GenG*, § 156). A membership list of the co-operators is not kept at the court where the branch is located. Items affecting the branch that are subsequently registered must only be recorded at the court in which the headquarter has its seat; they will be forwarded from there. § 14 of the *GenG* more closely outlines the legal treatment of already existing branches.

4. Every change in the board or in the power of attorney of a board member as well as the appointment of an authorized legal officer must be entered into the co-operative register (*GenG*, § 42, Subsec.1) (→ *Responsibility*). *GenRegVO*, § 18 details the particular content of these changes, and such entries must be made public (*GenG*, § 28, Subsec.1, Sent.3; § 42, Subsec.1, Sent.3; 156). See VII for further information concerning the effects of the disclosure.

5. Any amalgamations occurring to co-operatives (either through incorporation or new formation) must be entered in the co-operative register (*GenG*, § 93, a – s).

a) In a merger process of incorporation (→ *Mergers and Consolidations*), co-operatives are united upon liquidation foreclosure by transferring the assets of the conveyed co-operative as a whole to the co-operative assuming it (*GenG*, § 93 a, Subsec.1). The merger must be registered in the appropriate register courts by all members of the board from both the transferor and transferee co-operatives (*GenG*, § 93 d, Subsec.1; § 157; *GenRegVO*, § 6, Subsec.2, No.7). The merger contract (*GenG*, § 93 c), the report from the auditing association (*GenG,* § 93b, Subsec.2), the merger resolutions from the general assemblies (*GenG*, § 93 b, Subsec.1) as well as the eventual state certification of approval (*GenG*, § 93 d, Subsec.2) are to be included in the registration. Moreover, the co-operative being transferred must submit a final statement of balance upon registration (*GenG*, § 93 d, Subsec.3). The appropriate register court confirms whether the formal preconditions layed down in *GenG*, § 93 a – d, have been fulfilled, the efficacy of the merger contract as well as the legality and compatability of the merger resolutions to the by-laws. The merger is entered into the co-operative registers of the co-operatives involved. The register court to which the transferee co-operative belongs announces the newly entered information and the creditors' summons (*GenG*, §§ 156, 93 f; *GenRegVO*, § 21 a, Subsec.4).

b) In the case of a merger carried out through the formation of a new company upon liquidation foreclosure, the co-operatives are joined in a way that the assets of the (transferor) co-operatives as a whole are transferred to the new co-operative (the transferee co-operative), according to *GenG*, §.93 s, Subsec.1. The formation of the new co-operative follows as dictated in *GenG*, §§ 1–16 inasfar as § 93 s, Subsec.2 of the *GenG* does not designate any deviation. All members of the board of the united co-operatives must be entered into the co-operative register in the court in whose jurisdiction the new co-operative seat is in (*GenG*, § 93 a, Subsec.3, Sent.1; *GenRegVO*, § 21 a). When the new co-operative is entered into the register of the appropriate court, the individual co-operatives involved in the merger are dissolved; their assets and liabilities are transferred to the new co-operative (*GenG*, § 93 s, Subsec.3, Sentences 2,3). After that, the merger is entered into the co-operative registers of the merging co-operatives (*GenRegVO*, § 21a, Subsec.3, Sent.3). No special dissolution of the merging co-operatives is necessary (*GenG*, § 93 s, Subsec.3, Sent.4). The entries are made public along with the creditors' summons through the register court of the newly formed co-operative (*GenG*, § 156; *GenRegVO*, § 21 a, Subsec.4).

6. Dissolutions and subsequent liquidations of co-operatives must also be entered in the register (*GenRegVO*, §§ 20,21). A co-operative can be dissolved through the resolution of the general assembly (*GenG*, § 78), efflux of time (*GenG*, § 79), through judicial decision based on *GenG*, § 80, or upon instruction from government authorities according to *GenG*, § 81. The dissolution must be entered into the co-operative register (*GenG*, § 82). In case of a dissolution following §§ 78 and 79 of the *GenG*, all members of the board must sign into the co-operative register; this can be compelled by imposing enforceable fees (*GenG*, § 160). In the majority of cases, the dissolution is entered without petition. Upon applying for dissolution, the first liquidators as well as the type of power of attorney which they have are to be determined by the board (*GenG*, § 84, Subsec.1, Sent.1; *GenRegVO*, § 20, Subsec.1, Sent.1, Subsec.3; § 18, Subsec.1, Sentences 1,3). The registration of a judicially instigated liquidation proceeds from the authorities (*GenG,* § 84, Subsec.2; *GenRegVO*, § 20,

Subsec.2, Sent.3). The dissolution of a co-operative is made public by the register court in accordance with *GenG*, § 156, Subsec.1, Sent.2, and § 82, Subsec.1.
Following the complete distribution of the co-operative assets (cf. *GenG,* § 90), however, the liquidators at the earliest one year after the creditors' summons (*GenG*, § 82, Subsec.2), must enter into the co-operative register that their right of attorney has expired and that the company is dissolved (*GenRegVO*, § 21).

7. The membership list, above all, is important for the accumulation and loss of membership as well as for the calculation of their liability to contribute upon bankruptcy (→ *Nachschußpflicht*). The growth or loss of membership is dependent on the entries in the list of co-operators upon admission or withdrawal (*GenG*, §§ 15, Subsec.3; 70, Subsec.2). The first members to be enrolled in the membership list are the signatories of the bylaws (*GenRegVO*, § 29, Subsec.2, Sent.1). §§ 26–36 of the *GenRegVO* address other details.

V. Effects of Entered Information

As a rule, entries into the co-operative register are only law-informing (declarative) in their significance. The register, independent from the enrollment of the situation themselves, should only present factual situations which have already taken place. Only the formulation of the by-laws (*GenG*, § 13) and subsequent amendments (*GenG*, § 16, Subsec.6) are law-creating (constitutive) in their effect. "Negative disclosure" of the co-operative register must be differentiated with regard to this (*GenG*, § 29). (see VII following).

Entries into the membership list are mostly constitutive in character. Only the withdrawal due to a member's death or the entry and/or withdrawal of a juristic person upon dissolution or expiration have a declarative effect.

VI. Announcements made by the Register Court

The register court has to make public in only those entries into the co-operative register, public in the Federal Register which correspond to the situations listed in *GenG*, § 156, and in *GenRegVO*, § 5. Entries into the membership list are made known solely to the members affected by the entry and to the board (*GenRegVO*, § 3).

VII. Disclosure of the Co-operative Register

The disclosure of the co-operative register, layed down in *GenG*, § 29, serves to protect confidentiality in business transactions. In contrast to the commercial register, not all entered information must be disclosed, but rather only those changes in the board or in the power of attorney of a board member which must be registered and made public (*GenG*, §§ 28, 156). It can be assured that from the co-operative register, no third party will be able to receive any information concerning changes in the board or in the power of attorney of a board member, when the enrollment of the change has not been undertaken and announced ("negative disclosure", *GenG*, § 29, Subsec.1). A third party must accept changes and effects which have been entered into the register and announced ("positive disclosure", *GenG*, § 29, Subsec.2). Based on his or her trust of the accuracy of the announced information, *GenG*, § 29, Subsec.3 protects a third party from incorrect announcements. Entrusted officials with power of attorney (*GenG*, § 42, Subsec.1, Sent.3) as well as liquidators (*GenG*, § 86) are correspondingly affected by this implementation.

VIII. Examination of the Co-operative Register

Every person, as well as the membership (*GenRegVO*, § 26, Subsec.1), is entitled to look into the co-operative register and the documents submitted to it (*GenG*, § 156, Subsec.1; *HGB*, § 9, Subsec.1). Examination of the remaining documents in the register records and those submitted with the membership list of requires rightful cause (*FGG*, § 34). Every person is entitled to request (notarized) copies of the entries into the co-operative register and into the membership list as well as into the submitted documents to the co-operative register (*GenG*, § 156, Subsec.1; *HGB*, § 9, Subsec.2; *GenRegVo*, § 26, Subsec.2). Likewise, one can request certification concerning a matter of entry when further entries themselves are not available or when a particular entry has not been undertaken ("negative test", *GenG*, § 156, Subsec.1; *HGB*, § 9, Subsec.4).

Bibliography

Bumiller, Ursula/ Winkler, Karl: Freiwillige Gerichtsbarkeit, Gesetz über die Angelegenheiten der freiwilligen Gerichtsbarkeit, 4th Edition, München 1984.
Keidel, Theodor et al.: Handbuch der Rechtspraxis, Vol. 7, Registerrecht, 4th Edition, München 1985.
Kirberger, Petra: Registrar und Genossenschaftsregisterrichter, Rechtsstellung und Aufgabenbereich nach englischem, tansanischem und deutschem Recht, Göttingen 1977.
Lang, Johann/Weidmüller, Ludwig: Genossenschaftsgesetz, 32nd Edition, Berlin and New York 1988.
Meyer, E.H./Meulenbergh, Gottfried/ Beuthien, Volker: Genossenschaftsgesetz, 12th Edition, München 1983 (Supplement 1986).
Paulick, Heinz: Das Recht der eingetragenen Genossenschaft, Ein Lehr- und Handbuch, Karlsruhe 1956.
Werhahn, Jürgen W./Gräser, Bernd B.: Genossenschaft und Registerrecht, Leitfaden für den Schriftverkehr von Genossenschaften mit dem Registergericht, Wiesbaden 1979.

Reimbursements, Co-operative

EBERHARD DÜLFER/CARLOS BIENEFELD [J]

(see also: *Promotion Mandate*; *Legal Form, Co-operative*; *Assessment of Success*; *Taxation*)

I. Reasons for the Co-operative Reimbursement; II. Reasons for the Subsequent Reimbursement in Co-operatives; III. Particular Historical Variations of Reimbursement; IV. Reimbursement in Co-operative Banks?; V. Reimbursement and Taxation.

I. Reasons for the Co-operative Reimbursement

In the headwords of numerous articles found in this book, thorough explanation has been provided concerning how the co-operative enterprise is structured according to the *promotion purpose*: such outputs are produced in the form of goods and services which are congruous to the securement and improvement the eco-nomic and even existential situation of co-operative members and their respective enterprises. The management of the co-operative enterprise must mind and adhere to the → *promotion mandate*.

Correspondingly, this situation has certain consequences on financial management with respect to operational activities. In the case of all types of co-operatives which in the furthest sense of the word can be classified as → *supply co-operatives*, the promotion mandate in its original form meant that acquired goods should be passed on to members at purchase price (→ *Pricing Policy*). The basic notion at the root of this idea is the collective order in which the actual price amount is distributed among all those involved in the collective purchase activity. According to its original concept, the supply co-operative had to pursue the → *principle of cost coverage*.

In the course of later everday practise undertaken`by supply co-operatives, modifications arose with regard to this earlier form. On the one hand, members' purchase orders are not undertaken collectively but rather individually and scattered throughout a given time period. The co-operative management thereby develops the function of consolidating these individual orders into larger purchasing operations as expediently as possible. On the other hand, non-operating and extraordinary expenses start to emerge in the modern co-operative enterprise – just as in any other enterprise form; these expenses likewise must be covered according to the principles of maintaining real-asset values and securing the existence of the enterprise. Such considerations prompted the acceptance of the thesis that the co-operative enterprise needs to follow and adhere to the principle of expense coverage in the account period (business year). Thirdly, deviations occur in simple expense coverage inasmuch as costs and expenses eventually arise which can only be calculated in advance with a considerable degree of uncertainty. Various risks need to be taken into consideration which require members to pay an increased internal price for goods and services based on the commercial principle of "cautious appraisal" (*Schmalenbach*).

Inasmuch as cautiously calculated risks as a rule are not fully realized, a surplus (s) must arise at the end of the year on the basis of this pure policy of expense coverage. The extent of the surplus is an indication that the members of the co-operative who purchased goods at the internal price actually paid too much in the face of expense coverage. The co-operative (c) therefore reimburses (R) this amount to the members in a logical manner based on the turnover (T) achieved by each individual member (m).

The requisite rate of reimbursement results from the following formula:

$$P_R = \frac{S_c \times 100}{T_c}$$

By applying this rate to individual customer's level of turnover, the corresponding reimbursement amount payable to the particular member can be calculated.

$$R_m = \frac{P_R \times T_m}{100}$$

When applying this procedure one must always bear in mind that the co-operative enterprise as a whole confronts risks which company equity must protect against. Insofar as the → *equity capital* in co-operatives remains unstable on account of the opportunity with-drawing members have to receive repayment of their shares, the co-operative company must undertake the accumulation of reserves to which members may only have a claim in the face of company liquidation. The annual contributions to increase these reserves can obviously only be fed out of the surplus described above. The amount of these contributions must be decided upon by the general assembly; this amount is thereupon no longer eligible for use as reimbursement payments (→ *Financing*).

II. Reasons for the Subsequent Reimbursement in Co-operatives

The exact opposite of the situation described above is the case for such co-operative forms which can be classified as → *marketing co-operatives*. According to the promotion mandate of such co-operatives, it is the task of the co-operative to obtain the highest possible market price for the goods and services produced in the member enterprises. The original concept behind this co-operative form is also quite simplistic: the total amount of produced goods are to be sold, and the sales proceeds are to be distributed among the members according to their respective share of the turnover proceeds (T).

This situation becomes rather more complicated in

practical application. Firstly, deliveries made by individual members are scattered throughout the entire year; in contrast, marketing activities are undertaken by the co-operative administration at different points in time and in a much larger dimension based on the current market situation. Secondly, the co-operative enterprise must deduct all expenses which accumulate in the course of the year from the attained sales proceeds. The principle of expense coverage is likewise effective in this calculation. The marketing co-operative must hereby include un-certain risks in its calculation in the identical manner as the supply co-operative. At the end of the year it will become apparent whether all of these risks were realized or not, and whether too much had been retained from the total sales proceeds. A surplus (S) which arises in this manner is to be subsequently distributed to members. The procedure surrounding subsequent reimbursements (SR) accordingly emerged, a measure intended ultimately to correct internal prices which were originally estimated too low.

Nonetheless, the marketing co-operative must likewise put aside funds for its reserves. A respective amount to be deducted from the total amount of the subsequent reimbursement is therefore determined by the assembly of members and transferred to the reserves.

The calculation of the *rate* of subsequent reimbursement occurs using the following formula:

$$P_{SR} = \frac{S_c \times 100}{T_c}$$

The actual *amount* of subsequent reimbursement for the individual member results from his share of total turnover.

$$SR_m = \frac{P_{SR} \times T_m}{100}$$

III. Particular Historical Variations of Reimbursement

In the course of it 150–year history as initiated by the Rochdale Pioneers in 1844, co-operative reimbursement has undergone modifications some several times and has been the object of economic-political discussion for a variety of reasons (*Dülfer* 1984).

1. Reimbursements and Discounts

A well-known example of this situation concerns consumer co-operatives in Germany following the Second World War. In the scope of the reintroduction of the market economy at that time, the permissible customer discount in retail trade was limited to 3% due to considerations of competition policy. Although the co-operative reimbursement according to its nature does not represent a retail discount, it was nonetheless also limited to 3% in order that consumer co-operatives would not develop a competitive advantage over private retailers. Such a limited reimbursement no longer was in keeping with its original essence and intention. The co-operatives therefore chose to pursue an active pricing policy and fully dispensed with reimbursement upon receiving approval from their members.

2. Reimbursements and Price Maintenance

A second and somewhat more recent case which left fundamental affects in its wake likewise arose in Germany in the 1950s. At that time, the Law stated that producers could determine the prices of their goods, and that retailers were obliged to sell these goods at previously prescribed prices. This situation was referred to as "resale price maintenance".

Retailers in this legal situation raised the objection that retail co-operatives (e.g. EDEKA, REWE) could subsequently also provide reimbursements on the turnover of goods falling under the constraint of resale price maintenance. This problem escalated in the case of a quickly selling canned milk (the "Glücksklee" affair). In this instance, no restriction was placed on reimbursement as the regulatory author-ity accepted the following arguments and considera-tions:

The appointed legal experts stated that the purchase price of the canned milk was determined once and for all in the purchase order between the customer and the co-operative based on the practise of resale price maintenance. Although the reimbursement passed on to the customer at a later point in time could very well be calculated on the basis of these purchase prices as a share of turnover, the actual content of this reimbursement does not have anything to do with the purchase price; this situation much rather represents the advantage that members acquire on the basis of their membership in the co-operative. The reimbursement amount, therefore, cannot be considered an ex post facto alteration of the price.

3. Differentiated Reimbursement

Completely different criticism was raised from the view of business management, namely with regard to the method of calculation for simple reimbursement. *R. Henzler* (1962) raised the consideration that a uniform rate of reimbursement is not justified in the face of the varied sizes of orders placed by members. Cost calculation can easily verify that incurred costs as a percentage are slighter in large orders than they are in small orders. *Henzler,* therefore, advocated a "differentiated reimbursement", a notion which has not been taken up in practical application in the meantime.

IV. Reimbursement in Co-operative Banks?

In principle, the credit co-operative (→ *Co-operative Banks*) can be interpreted as a supply co-operative, as in its original form it undertook the function of providing its members with financial means in the form of credits. In this matter, the question arises whether the prices calculated for such credits – or in other words the interest charges – correctly correspond with the principle of cost coverage, or else, whether any attained surplus must be distributed among the members as reimbursements.

1. Counter Arguments

Practical application in the co-operative banking system has yet to realize this consideration. In more cases than not, banks have distributed any acquired surplus in the form of a capital dividend – in other words according to members' paid-up shares. All parties involved in this practise were aware that this is not in keeping with the intrinsic organizational character of the co-operative. Two arguments above all were raised in this case. Bankers, on the one hand, drew attention to the fact that the risks involved in a credit transaction cannot be estimated to a specific point in time as is the case in a purchase transaction: risks exist throughout the lifetime of the loan and can vary in the course of time. On the other hand, modern co-operative banks for a long time have been much more than mere credit banks: Deposit transactions with members and other customers have attained equal importance. Because of this situation the question was raised whether member-depositors should after all be payed a subsequent co-operative reimbursement. This would be possible from the theoretical point of view; in practical application, however, conditions have already been calculated so sharply – especially in the case of large depositors – that a further payment would necessarily produce losses.

Ultimately, the main argument lies in the fact that the introduction of reimbursements in co-operative banks would necessarily result in a considerable reduction of their ability to accumulate reserves. Such a step would have substantial implications in the banking business which is already beset with risks. Furthermore, the calculation and posting of numerous payments (which in part would be quite minuscule) would entail considerable costs. By all means, however, it was recognized that considerable tax savings could be enjoyed by such a distribution – which in turn would increase the potential amount at disposal.

2. The Hessian Initiative: Reimbursement associated with Profit Participation Rights

Irregardless of the presented counter arguments, the attempt was first undertaken in Germany during the 1980s to introduce reimbursements in Raiffeisen banks. In the state of Hesse, approx. 20 Raiffeisen banks active in the rural sector have payed reimbursements since 1986 and accordingly reduced the amounts of reserve contributions and capital dividends. The rate of reimbursement lies between 3% and 4% and is paid on all debit and credit interest.

In all such situations, members have been urged to utilize their attained reimbursements to purchase *profit participation rights*. Such a profit participation right guarantees the owner a share of profits but does not vest him with membership rights. The distributed payments thereby flow back into the co-operative as long-term financing funds for 15 years at 2% interest. Each member must however express his explicity agreement (in writing) to proceed in this manner. An automatic "rebooking" is not permissible as this would raise the suspicion of a "disguised profit distribution" in the view of tax law.

It is apparent that this procedure involving a maximum rate of corporate income tax of 53% is of great advantage for members (→ *Taxation*). The co-operative, on the other hand, can profit so substantially by utilizing these profit participation contributions (according to the leverage effect) that their reserves can maintain a proper level even without reimbursement payments. The repective time needed for making calculations and booking accounts which previously was seen as such a barrier can today be bridged quite easily using special computer programs.

V. Reimbursements and Taxation

As explained above, the executively operating co-operative unit is not structured along the lines of attaining profit but is rather preoccupied with promoting members (and their enterprises). The executive entity cannot, however, dispense with orientation around surplus attainment. Such surpluses can in part be distributed among members but, on the other hand, they are also necessary to ensure the longterm fulfillment of co-operative functions through the accumulation of reserves.

Nonetheless, when a surplus is achieved and a share of it is allocated to the reserves, this still does not represent true market profits; as explained above, these are monetary amounts which members in essence have a rightful claim to. The theoretically plausible question arises in this context whether or not such amounts may be subject to income tax (in this context in the form of corporate income tax). The opinion was held in Germany in the 1950s (among others by *F. Klein*, 1957) that the co-operative does not generate any true "trade profit" in the legal sense and thus must not be taxed according to its profits (→ *Taxation*). This would have led to the financial consequence that the co-operative enterprise would have been taxed based on the priniciple of "encumbrance" via other criteria, for example the promotion it created. This notion seemed too vague for both co-operatives and their federations in that its consequences could not be clearly estimated in advance. This is the reason why the co-operative surplus remains to be taxed as profit reported on the balance sheet, whereas the paid reimbursement and/or subsequent reimbursement can be deducted from taxable income as a business expense. The terminology for profit and co-operative reimbursement is not precisely defined in Co-operative Law, a factor contributing to the long-standing disagreement between theory and praxis concerning the legal nature of reimbursements as well as how they should be treated in tax matters.

Up to the present day, the dominant position in this matter has maintained that co-operative reimbursements and/or subsequent reimbursements represent the characteristic nature of surplus distribution in registered co-operatives when such a surplus is created through the exchange of inputs/outputs between members and the co-operative in the manner described above. Reimbursements are an adjustment or correction of internal prices calculated in the scope of business transactions with members; they are not real profits. As a result, the amount of a member's reimbursement is based on the extent of turnover he has undertaken with the co-operative and not, for example, his capital investment. The German Federal Supreme Court shared this opinion in its ruling of Oct.9th, 1963; the Court refuted an interpretation of co-operative reimbursement as profit allocation or price rebate.

Tax Law also maintains this position. In accordance with § 22 of the Corporation Income Tax Law and Section 66 of the Guidelines to Corporation Income Tax, the co-operative reimbursement does not represent taxable profit but rather a deductible business expense. Nonetheless, various conditions must be fulilled:

- The monies utilized for the reimbursement must have been generated in transactions with members. The distribution of surpluses from other sources to the members is to be treated as a disguised profit distribution.
- It must be noted that surpluses resulting from supplemental business reduce the share of the total surplus that can be reimbursed.
- The extent of the reimbursement is to be calculated based on the level of turnover undertaken between member and co-operative.
- It is impermissible to drawn differentiation between individual members or individual turnover groups. In contrast, differing business branches with varying rates of reimbursement can be calculated. "Branch" in this regard represents in the case of co-operative banks credit transactions, deposit transactions as well as service transactions.
- The co-operative reimbursement must be paid within twelve months following the end of the business year in which it is being provided for. Payment is executed the moment the reimbursment has made it into the domain of the member's control. The member can in turn decide to entrust the co-operative with his reimbursment as a type of loan. In such a situation, a separate loan contract is to be settled for each reimbursement, whereby the decision for such an arrangement must always be on a voluntary basis (ruling of the Federal Financial Court dating Feb.28, 1968; Gazette of the Federal Ministry of Finance II, p.458).
- Subsequent reimbursements from the co-operative for deliveries or services are to be treated as co-operative reimbursements.

§ 22 of the German Corporation Income Tax Law has been applicable in the new German states following reunification on Jan.1, 1991, in an unaltered form. The Corporation Income Tax Law of the former German Democratic Republic did not include any special rules concerning how co-operative reimbursements were to be taxed.

Bibliography

Berge, Helmut: Genossenschaftliche Rückvergütung, in: Mändle, Eduard/Swoboda, Walter (eds.), Genossenschaftslexikon, Wiesbaden 1992, pp.556–557.

Berge, Helmut/Philipowski, Rüdiger: Zinsrückvergütungen in Kreditgenossenschaften, Marburger Beiträge zum Genossenschaftswesen, Nr.11, Marburg 1987.

Dülfer, Eberhard: Betriebswirtschaftslehre der Kooperative – Kommunikation und Entscheidungsbildung in Genossenschaften und vergleichbaren Organisationen, Göttingen 1984.

Dülfer, Eberhard: Pro und Contra zur Rückvergütung bei Genossenschaftsbanken, in: Beyer, Horst-Tilo et al.: Neuere Entwicklungen in Betriebswirtschaftslehre und Praxis, Frnakfurt 1988, pp. 398–420.

Glaser, Roman: Gewinnerzielung und Gewinnverteilung in Genossenschaftsbanken, Veröffentlichungen der Forschungsstelle für Genossenschaftswesen an der Universität Hohenheim, Nr.6, Stuttgart-Hohenheim 1990.

Klein, Friedrich: Aktuelle Fragen zur Besteuerung von Genossenschaften, in: Wiener Studien, Vol.4, Göttingen 1957.

Ohlmeyer, Dietrich: Genossenschaftliche Rückvergütung, in: Mändle, Eduard/Winter, Hans-Werner (eds.): Handwörterbuch des Genossenschaftswesens, Wiesbaden 1980, cols. 1430–1440.

Otto, Reinhard: Rückvergütung bei Genossenschaftsbanken, in: Bankinformation und Genossenschaftsforum, November 1991, pp.45–49.

Relationship Patterns, Co-operative: Microsociological Aspects of Co-operatives

ROBERT HETTLAGE [J]

(see also: *Group, the Co-operative*; ; *Group Theory; Societal Form, Co-operative; Organizational Structures, Co-operative; Self-help Organizations*)

I. Does a Typical Co-operative Relationship Form Exist?;
II. Co-operative Relationships in Practice.

Sociology primarily examines the relatively lasting reciprocal relationships between active individuals ("interactions") insofar as these relationships form a concrete, coherent association (e.g. group, organization) and thereby causing continuous processes of socialization. Every field of interaction can in principle be subjected to sociological research (family, economy, state, etc.). An actual "sociology of co-operations", however, has so far come to a standstill in its initial stages. This has occurred unjustly as co-operatives deserve great note in microsociology (as a pattern of relationships), in mesosociology (as an organizational form) and in macrosociology (as a structural principle for the whole of society). The first topic, that of microsociology, is pointing at the types of social action and nature of social relationships which are both founded in and constructed with the help of the co-operative. The central question of co-operatives is whether a particular "subjectively intended sense" (*Max Weber*) is associated with the collective action.

I. Does a Typical Co-operative Relationship Form Exist?

Many researchers and practicians of co-operative structures have time and time again emphasized the explicit *intention* of the co-operative: to form an action-oriented community whose social character fundamentally differs from that of other economic organizations. *Draheim* (1952) characterized this in the formula of the co-operative "double nature", that of an economic organization and a social group. By that he wanted to express that co-operatives respond to a twofold, reciprocally limiting orientation of their actions, one economic and one social. In this context, recently the concept of "moral economy" has been enforced. Many derive the high regard placed on co-operation among members from the organizational name "co-operative", but that alone is insufficient. In a non-differentiated sense, co-operation as such is inherent to all economic activities which unite a number of people under one goal and certain performance obligations. The private business enterprise can likewise only then function when its employees work together.

The distinguishing feature of cooperation in co-operatives is rather that this collaboration is not only a necessary, purpose-rational means, used to attain a justifiable operating result but also simultaneously a value-rational goal which is esteemed and striven after for its own sake:

1) The central factor of the enterprise no longer is the capital or a prescribed plan but rather the members themselves. The central importance of their individual personal responsibility is expressed in the "joint activity", the voluntary nature of association, and personal connection.

2) Capital as such neither employs labour nor subordinates it to its commercial objectives. Labour and capital as factors of production are brought together through the role of membership and directed to the individual members; the central element of alienation so strongly emphasized by *Marx* should thus be eliminated.

3) Co-operatives are group businesses which were explicitly established to achieve solidarity and reciprocal assistance. The goals usually extend above and beyond pure economic improvement and constitute the co-operatives' orientation around public welfare.

It is not difficult to recognize that co-operatives expect a strong effect on motivation and performance in the organization through the importance placed on collectiveness, attachment and solidarity. They thereby proceed from *fundamental anthropological assumptions* which do not however find unanimous support in specialist circles. Each theory is a "shorthand" version of reality and is necessarily abstract. Social sciences thus attempt to typify human action, dispositions and motives as well as social situations, thereby preparing them for specialized observation of a discipline. Their work also includes certain human stereotypes (models of man). "Homo politicus" is known as the model of man socially bonded; this model can be split up further analytically. Sociology works in part with "homo sociologicus" as the model individual who is mainly seen as the holder of social roles. Organizational theory is familiar with "organizational man", identified through his organization. Further types can be imagined: "homo caritativus", "homo culturalis", "homo traditionalis", etc. The most well-known model is nonetheless "homo oeconomicus", who maximizes utility, calculates and decides selfishly and who is used by economists for the construction of their models. The extraordinary nature of this form is that it is increasingly seen as a *general* representation of human reality and thus is supposed to have a higher value of forecast than the models arising from other social sciences. Whether man loves or hates, steals or gives, sleeps or is awake, eats or fasts; whether man produces goods, buys or sells, whether he does not work at all: the individual always seems to act for his own personal advantage.

Co-operative theory and practise at an early age objected to this ideological form and attempted to set against it another model of man, the *"homo cooperativus"*. They do not rely on the individualist but rather on that type of person inclined to group formation, interested in working together with others on equal footing and prepared to act without a narrowly defined rationality based upon a self-oriented implementation of interests (*"co-operative inclination"*). The elements of co-operative structure reflect this.

This concept has been frequently looked at with scepticism both within and outside co-operatives. The "economic theory of co-operatives" (*Boettcher*) has for some time also applied homo oeconomicus to the co-operative. The preference for solidarity, altruism and reciprocal help are recast in an egoistic light, by saying that co-operation also is conceivable under the assumption of individual utility to widen one's own realm of (possible) actions by working together with others. One must however consider:

1) that "homo cooperativus" is only a model construction, an ideal stereotype which intentionally over-emphasizes certain characteristics of action, a man-made product which does not exist in reality. Reality only offers complex combinations of action motives. This is likewise so for homo oeconomicus;
2) that membership identity and the goodwill of the co-operative enterprises are dependent to a large degree on the will to co-operate, integrate and promote, that is, on the inclination to collective self-help; thereby the actual development and the stability of the enterprises in crisis are influenced by this;
3) that "homo cooperativus" is an action-orientating model which cannot be dispensed with on account of its guiding function and its impulses which change society;
4) that no *a priori* decision can be made whether the inclination to co-operate has a *fundamentum in re*; it is rather much more the task of *empirical* research to discover under which conditions co-operation in its true sense is effective as action or can be successfully trained (*Hettlage*, 1990).

First, it is uncontested that the work- or lifestyle sought after according to the *intention* of the co-operative fundamentally differentiates it from typical human behaviour found in commercial enterprises. This work- or lifestyle namely is based on the "side by side-order" (*Fürstenberg*, 1970) of the members within the promotion organization. This is transformed into certain norms of action and organizational structures. The intention thereby is to break open the core shell of purpose rationality, profit goals and fixation on commercial trade through threefold means:

1. Self-Help

The joint action is based on the norm of *subsidiarization*. The competence of the group has priority over outside influence and decision-making. This in no way precludes complementary outside assistance when it facilitates self-help, since this preserves the intention. In any case, this is based on the fundamental orientation of behaviour directed towards active problem-solving – that is, not a passive resignation in anticipation of provisional measures or assistance from outside sources, but rather a *collective effort* of all involved persons to take fate into their own hands, to seek latitude and to look for opportunities to act. Co-operatives therewith construct action centers which serve to protect the members. On the other hand, it remains an *empirical* question as to how the motives are set, how far it is possible to act upon a problem once it has been recognized, to what degree like-minded people associate together, how far they can rely on their solidarity, and which organizational precautions can guarantee its cohesion.

2. Self-Administration

The co-operative pattern of behaviour becomes clearest in the principle of democratic management. Decision-making authority is not based on majority capital share but rather on the quality of simply being an individual. The internal constitution of the self-help organization must therefore also express an anti-hierarchical tendency. The norm cannot be the elite, top-down order of command (centralized decision-making, the gradual filtering down of information and dependency on "those above"); "collective operation" implies rather the greatest possible participation from members and their personal development. This in practice does not preclude a somewhat top-down structure in *decision-making*, but does nevertheless require high organizational standards in communication, dialogue, collectiveness and a feeling of "togetherness" from all sides.

3. Integrality of Lifestyle

Having the group as "mandate" tends to have effects above and beyond the co-operative enterprise. Members indeed wish to have their economic needs met, but they furthermore seek *social returns* such as participation, emancipation, human closeness and contact, trust, a humane arrangement of work, communal invigoration, etc. This mixed product resulting from co-operation produces a viewpoint *critical of civilization* for many members (at least in the initial phase):

to save the "Lebenswelt", (life-world perceived by the individual) from the assault of a one-dimensional purpose rationality, to work against the dismantling of *interrelations inherent in human life*, and to support "communities" which encourage identity development. This is evidence of how strongly the co-operative as an organization is carried by the far-reaching co-operative *idea (Hettlage,* 1983).

II. Co-operative Relationships in Practice

In everyday practice, one naturally confronts the relationship between ideas and their practical interests as well as intentions and their realization. The danger of idealization in organizations with such high performance expectations, such as in co-operatives, is particularly great. From a sociological point of view, all relationship forms and structures are the result of complicated "negotiation processes" which occur day in and day out. Order is always negotiated and created "negotiated order" both in the horizontal and vertical sense (*Strauss/Schatzman* 1983; *Strauss* 1978). Order pursues certain "micropolitical" lines of communication (pacts, agreements, coalitions, cliques) and is replaced and altered in the course of time. Forces from the external "arena" thereby play an important role, as well as how those people actively involved interpret their organizational structure (*Manning* 1977). This not only throws open a further field of co-operative sociological research, but the risks and transformational dangers are also revealed to which the co-operative goals and structures are continuously exposed. Thereby, the scope of a member-oriented policy is also defined. Three aspects should be emphasized in this regard:

1. Decisions in the Process of Foundation

The motive behind co-operative action is often the desire to prevent shortages, distortions and disturbances (poverty, exploitation, isolation, etc.). Aside from a few exceptional cases, the decision to join together ("solidarity of *action*") is not spontaneous but rather the result of longer term planning, goal determination and clarification of interests. Group formation is not comprehensible without an "intersection of social circles" (*G. Simmel,* 1968, pp. 305 ff). Even the individual's perception of a problem cannot be understood without taking into consideration the individual's previous experiences, dispositions and mooring in tradition, or in other words, without taking into consideration the given social structures of the family, neighborhood, extended family, village, etc. and their supportive or inhibitory effects. Experience furthermore shows that the initiative to establish a co-operative usually does not emanate from "the group" but rather from actively involved individuals (who are also nevertheless anchored in the social context). These can be *promoters*, advisors or assistants who remain outside the group or *initiators* who become group members. Through close association with one another they frequently establish the necessary contacts, provide consultation and encouragement as well as attract future founding members. *The decisive initial "push"* stems from their energy, activity and willingness to assume risks. In the long run, however, their central role (particularly among initiators) is not entirely unproblematic as their position may turn around into explicit and implicit claims with regard to hierarchical and dependency relationships (seniority principle, favoritism, formation of cliques, etc.) (c.f. *Hettlage/Goetze* 1989). The clarification of motives also requires to determine whether the will to co-operate is enduring in nature or whether it is assumed under reservation in the default of others, albeit principally worthy solutions. In particular it is those members, standing out on account of their qualifications from other members, who see the co-operative merely as a stepping stone for a business or political career elsewhere or as preparation for their own enterprise, when their claim to priority status cannot be satisfied in the co-operative

2. Membership Selection

As in all groups, membership selection proves to be crucial for stability. Co-operatives must however confront this particular characteristic: "Solidarity in need" often brings socially weak, disadvantaged or less-qualified individuals together. Each enterprise either stands or falls in the course of time as a result of the readiness for action and specialized competence of its members. Co-operatives must prescribe in part certain requirements from their members which can only evolve through a lengthy learning process. Even this has the tendency to shift the social weights within the co-operative.

An enterprise of individuals on equal footing with each other confronts a further problem: it requires not only specialized competence but also *social competence*. The co-operative is structured according to the principle of dialogue form. A certain readiness must then be present to accept this norm and to provide the necessary time investment for participatory decision-making, to assume responsibilities or at least to execute supervisory competence. Highly developed communication skills also prove to be essential when conflicts need to be worked out, as co-operatives by no means are non-conflictive entities. Many people therefore consider the ideal member profile to be rooted in an extremely large social homogeneity. The tendency of outsider *exclusion* cannot however be overlooked. Entities, once intact with a certain membership level and corresponding performance expectations, shy at the risk of assuming new members – not only on account of the distribution of returns – and thus fall into conflict with the principle of *open membership*.

Social competence and actual readiness to act (performance) are essentially connected with the individual's value system (or lack of socialization) which has become a matter of course. *Michel* 1990, with the help of biographies on co-operative managers from Andulusia, showed the extent previous life experiences ("stock of knowledge") can affect management style. A similar study of member performance remains to be undertaken.

3. Maintenance of Relationships in Co-operatives

(Human Relations)
The egalitarian claim of the co-operative requires to a higher degree than private undertakings that participation lead to relevant organizational experience. This can only become realized through controlled efforts in various "policy fields" within the enterprise:

- through a *communicative style of decision-making* which is not only rhetoric and cosmetic in nature; through individual way of action ("personale Selbstgestaltung"), that is the removal of authoritarian bonds, self-motivation and the mobilization of the individual's willingness to take responsibility for his actions, is the forming principle for all "intentional" joint action communities such as co-operatives (*Fürstenberg*, 1984);
- through intensive, continual training so the necessary general and specialized competences for democratic decision-making procedures can be acquired. For this, as experience shows, an above-average desire for continual organizational and resource development is needed (*Hoppman/Stötzel* 1981);
- through the establishment and practice of conflict-solving procedures. It is frequently underestimated in the initial phase – characterized by idealization – that such procedures are necessary. During conflict conditions it is precisely communication that needs to be exercised;
- through the constant efforts to prevent a *pure* utilitarian interpretation of the co-operative social relationships as the case may be when the co-operative idea becomes lost, when primary groups change into secondary ones, or when membership composition is altered.

It remains to be empirically researched whether co-operatives have become active in these fields and to what extent; whether they have been true to their claims and have been at least as innovative as non-co-operative organizations in the implementation of "workers'", i.e. "members' control". In accordance with the achieved claims of "egalitarianism", participation, communication and solidarity a co-operative relationship *typology* would thus result which could be differentiated into "traditional", "affective", "value-rational" and "goal-rational" versions corresponding to *Weber's* action categories.

Bibliography

Boettcher, Eric: Kooperation und Demokratie in der Wirtschaft, Tübingen 1974.
Draheim, G.: Die Genossenschaft als Unternehmenstyp, Göttingen 1952.
Fürstenberg, F.: Wirtschaftssoziologie, Berlin 1970.
Fürstenberg, F.: Personale Selbstgestaltung in sozialen Systemen, in: Fürstenberg, F./Herder-Dorneich, Ph./Klages, H. (eds.): Selbsthilfe als sozialpolitische Aufgabe, Baden Baden 1984, pp. 201–218.
Hettlage, R.: Genossenschaftsmodelle als Alternative, in: Koslowski, P./Kreutzer, Ph./Löw, R. (eds.): Chancen und Grenzen des Sozialstaats, Tübingen 1983, pp. 192–215.
Hettlage, R.: Die anthropologische Konzeption des Genossenschaftswesens in Theorie und Praxis. – Welche Chancen hat der "homo cooperativus"?, in: Laurinkari, J. (ed.): Genossenschaftswesen, München/Wien 1990, pp. 27–49.
Hettlage, R./Goetze, D. et al.: Selbsthilfe in Andalusien. Kooperativen im Kampf gegen ländliche Arbeitslosigkeit, Berlin 1989.
Hoppmann, K./Stötzel, B.: Demokratie am Arbeitsplatz. Ein Modellversuch zur Mitwirkung von Arbeitnehmern an betrieblichen Entscheidungsprozessen, Frankfurt 1981.
Manning, P.: Police Work, Cambridge/Maas. 1977.
Michel, Th.: Alltagswissen und Macht. Eine empirische Studie zum Management in andalusischen Produktivgenossenschaften, Frankfurt 1990.
Simmel, G.: Soziologie. Untersuchungen über die Formen der Vergesellschaftung, 5th ed., Berlin 1968.
Simmel, G.: Über soziale Differenzierung, in: Gesamtausgabe, vol.2: Aufsätze 1887 bis 1890, Frankfurt, pp. 109–295.
Strauss, A.: Negotiations, San Francisco 1978.
Strauss, A./Schatzman, L. et al.: The hospital and its negotiated order, in: Freidson, E. (ed.): The Hospital in Modern Society, New York 1963, pp. 147–169.
Weber, M.: Wirtschaft und Gesellschaft. Grundriß der verstehenden Soziologie, 5th ed., Tübingen 1964.

Religious Co-operatives, Cloisters

FRIEDRICH FÜRSTENBERG [J]

(see also: *Group, the Co-operative*; *History of Ideas*; *Relationship Patterns*; *History before 1800*; *Group Theory*)

I. Background in the Sociology of Religion; II. Cloister Co-operatives; III. Brotherhood Groups.

The modern concept of the co-operative is applicable to religious confraternities only with reservation. Nevertheless, they display numerous phenomena relevant to co-operatives, in particular from the historical-sociological standpoint, which have contributed to the creation of co-operatives and the discussion surrounding them in other spheres of life.

I. Background in the Sociology of Religion

According to what has been passed down from the great charismatic institutors of religion, circles of disciples gathered around them and communal life was lead together. A high measure of → *solidarity* hereby evolved (*Wach*) which, together with doctrines and rites, formed the fundament for formation of other such communions. Religious brotherhoods functioning as confraternities thus evolved as archetypal church forms in which "the endeavor to revive the oneness of conviction, brotherly equality and communal cultic-organizational life" were manifested (*Wessel*, col. 1427).

Greatly varying local groups initially developed as communal living situations centered around the worship service within the early Christian church. These groups at first only had slight hierarchical features, but personal ties to authority nevertheless existed to a large extent. One can assume that the communal life and experience realized through extensively co-operative forms in this developmental stage acquired a particular immediacy. The reversion to such conditions and/or the emulation of essential characteristics has lead to the formation of religious confraternities up to the present day and age, and this both internal and external to the established popular and state churches, the latter being a form of protest (→ *Informal Co-operatives*). Seen from the perspective of co-operative science, the most important forms should be examined more closely, namely the cloister co-operatives and brotherhood groups.

II. Cloister Co-operatives

The first Christian cloisters, dating from the 4th century, developed out of eremite colonies which laid down an observance for the communal life under one spiritual leader. Their goal was to lead a "completely" Christian life, whereby the monks obliged themselves through vows. Essentially this concerned the pursuance of maxims found in the Gospels: poverty, chastity, and obedience among the co-operative of cloister brothers. In the Catholic church, the monk is accepted into the given order after a probationary period (postulancy, novitiate) by his taking solemn vows. A legally con-doned withdrawal afterwards is only possible in exceptional cases with approval from the Holy See. The fundamental principle of the equality of members reigns within the internal structure of the cloister co-operative; no professional/occupational leadership exists, although in everyday life a hierarchically structured authority in the form of either an abbot constitution or a centralized constitution with a superior general ruling over all cloisters is in effect (→ *Organizational Structures, Co-operative*).

Living expenses are guaranteed by the order, which is not dependent on the performance of the individual. A specific mentality of brotherliness in the scope of a daily life strictly controlled through rules and lead in relative seclusion results out of the shared fundamental orientation. All of these traits characterize cloister co-operatives as "total institutions" as meant by *Erving Goffman*. At the same time, he characterizes them as "social hybrids, on the one hand communal living situations, on the other hand formal organizations" (p.23). A fundamental difference with respect to modern co-operatives is herewith also touched upon: behavior, in principle, is tied to the observance, and membership roles assume a certain universality. The structure of the cloister co-operatives does, however, indeed undergo change under the influence of the varied types of labor often performed beyond the cloister itself. Various degrees of autonomy result from this for the individual member of the order in accordance with his professional position (*Schmelzer*, p.186).

A second type of cloister co-operative exists alongside the cloister in the Catholic church: the congregation, whose members only take a simple vow which, for example, is merely a postponed impediment to marriage. Furthermore, other communities exist as cloister-like co-operatives, the members of which oblige themselves only through a private vow. Protestant efforts to lead communal lives are particularly widespread within Anglican regions. Following World War II, new forms of collective living, known as fraternities or brotherhoods, came into existence, the most reknown of which surely being the brotherhood in Taize-les-Cluny, founded in 1947 (→ *Informal Co-operatives*).

These religious confraternities have several factors in common, namely tight group bonds and the willingness to lead a life solely following the primacy of the worship service, which also can assume the form of service for fellowmen under the most varied of conditions. The history of the cloister co-operatives offers impressive examples of the success as well as the failure of such attempts. Such examples of Christian and, at the same time, communal living practices are manifoldly ascertainable in the history of ideas affiliated with the co-operative system.

III. Brotherhood Groups

This is even more true for the Christian brotherhoods which in part lead communal lives and which in part developed communal activities to heighten their devoutness and promote welfare. Even the existence of funeral co-operatives dating from classical antiquity can be proven. The origin of the brotherhoods in Christianity, as can be observed in other religious communities, lies in prayer fraternities which gradually transformed into influential social groups upon accumulating other functions. The Kalend brotherhoods, emerging in the 13th century, were formed by both priests and laypersons of both sexes. Aside from the communal worship service, they developed numerous social activities, in part religious and in part gregarious in nature. At the time of the Reformation, these brotherhoods were to a great degree wordly in nature. Within the Catholic community, the present-day Marian Congregations or the Brotherhoods for the Adoration of the Sacred Heart of Jesus are examples of the continuation of this form of religious society.

The Brothers for Communal Life were of particular importance in cultural history. These communes gradually came into being as a non-monastic form of living in the late Middle Ages. The members, among whom were important personalities in the Age of Humanism, made a living from their work, e.g. as caligraphers, and later as printers and teachers.

Of particular importance in co-operative history are the Protestant Unities of Brethren on account of their practice of founding parishes (→ *History of Ideas*). The Unity of Bohemian-Moravian Brethren came into being through an altercation with the Hussite movement. Democratically anchored parishes which fully devoted themselves to a life in the Imitation of Christ were founded under the injunction of absolute nonviolence. This free church was forced into exile as a result of the Thirty Years' War. The Bohemian-Moravian brethren, much like other mostly Baptist groups which were able to take hold and expand in the USA, contributed greatly to the development of the principle of self-administration on the parish level, something which also acquired constituent importance for modern co-operatives once rendered to the field of business.

Under pietistic influences, a Revived Unity of Brethren known as the Herrnhuter Brethren Parish resulted in the the 18th century (→ *History of Ideas*). This unity strives for Christian communal living within voluntary association, likewise in the form of community settlements (→ *Communal Settlements*). Korntal, for example, was founded in 1819, both as a religiously independent parish and as a political entity. The settlers joined together to form a purchasing association to collectively acquire the manor Korntal, which is in the vicinity of Stuttgart; this association is considered the oldest savings-bank in Württemberg and the forerunner of *Raiffeisen's* co-operative savings and loan bank. At the same time, it is a type of co-operative for real-estate property and a mutual insurance association. The Brethren parish alone determines its membership circle and strives to emulate the original Christian community as closely as possible. The highest administrative entity is the assembly of parish brethren, that is the entirety of full members, both male and female, which meets quarterly. The business enterprises can be characterized as co-operative in their arrangement and management. This is also true for the "works" (children's homes). The body directly responsible is the Brethren parish which has the individual facilities managed in trust. Parishes of this sort exist in Germany, Denmark, Holland, Sweden, Switzerland, Great Britain as well as in North America.

Communal Christian settlements in the form of brethren farms managed as community property also exist among other religious associations, e.g. among the Hutterite brethren in North and South America. The fundamental organizational characteristics include a democratic parish constitution and voluntary admission which, after a probationary period, extends for life.

These examples indicate that religious communities having more or less co-operative-like traits are closely related to the class of "full co-operatives" (→ *Conceptions, Co-operative*). Individual activities, at least to a certain extent, prove to be similar to partial co-operative organizational forms. The distinguishing trait remains, however, the high degree of member integration and identification brought about by the common fundamental position based on and supported by religion. The realizational chances of each community are accordingly dependent on its continued existence.

In a modern market-oriented society with a division of labor, an at least open if not pluralistic horizon of values and manifold "multicultural" challenges (→ *Corporate Culture*), religious co-operatives are fringe phenomena seen structurally, although their effect as exemplary models must not be disparaged. As social-organizational experiments (→ *Relationship Patterns*) and, in the case of their success, as challenges in that they confront the pure functionality of modern co-operatives with the continued existence of co-operative forms of living, they are of essential importance for the developement of the co-operative system .

Bibliography

Wach, Joachim: Sociology of Religion, Chicago 1944.
Müller-Gangloff, Erich: Bruderschaften III. in der Gegenwart, 2.b), in: Die Religion in Geschichte und Gegenwart I, Tübingen 1957, col. 1430–1432.
Wessel, Klaus: Bruderschaften II. kirchengeschichtlich, in: Die Religion in Geschichte und Gegenwart I, Tübingen 1957, col. 1428–1429.
Goffman, Erwing: Asyle (amer. 1961), Frankfurt 1972.
Grünzweig, Fritz, Die Evangelische Brüdergemeinde Korntal, Metzingen 1958.
Hanstein, Honorius: Ordensrecht, Paderborn 1958.
Dienel, Peter: Die Freiwilligkeitskirche, Dissertation. Münster 1962.
Frank, Karl Suso (ed.), Grundzüge der Geschichte des christlichen Mönchtums, Darmstadt 1975.
Horn, Walter/Born, Ernest: The Plan of St. Gall. A Study of the Architecture and Economy of and Life in a Paradigmatic Carolingian Monastery, Berkeley 1975.
Schmelzer, Günter: Religiöse Gruppen und sozialwissenschaftliche Typologie, Berlin 1979.

Rochdale Equitable Pioneers Society, The

Roy Garratt

(see also: *History of Ideas*; *History in 19th C.*; *Conceptions, Co-operative*; *Consumer Co-operatives*)

The collective of 28 British working men who in 1844 formed the Rochdale Equitable Pioneers Society, a consumer retail co-operative, are rightly regarded as founders of the world-wide Co-operative Movement, particularly in the sphere of consumer Co-operation. However, the → *Principles* of Co-operation which were formulated from the decisions and practices of the Pioneers have had relevance to all forms of Co-operation.

In stating that the Rochdale Pioneers were the founders of the world-wide Co-operative Movement, is not to claim that theirs was the first Co-operative Society in existence or that their little store in Toad Lane, Rochdale, Lancashire, was the very first co-operative shop. This is widely assumed by many people but it is manifestly untrue. There were numerous co-operatives in Britain long before 1844 but most of them faded away through lack of understanding of how best to manage and operate a Co-operative Society and this led to unwise trading practices. The Pioneers were shrewd men – they learned from the mistakes of earlier co-operative societies and from the hard lessons of their own co-operative experience. (There was a Rochdale Co-operative Store in Toad Lane as early as 1833 of which several of the Pioneers had been members. But it collapsed through giving excessive credit to members and it had many bad debtors who never repaid the society). In 1844, the Pioneers decided not to give credit but insist on cash trading and for many years this was regarded as a Rochdale Principle of Co-operation.

What were the Rochdale Principles of Co-operation? They may be summarised as follows (→ *Principles*):

- Open membership;
- Democratic control (one person, one vote);
- Payment of surplus (profit) in proportion to purchases (dividend or patronage refund);
- Limited interest on capital;
- Cash trading;
- Political and religious neutrality;
- Promotion of education for members and workers.

Over the years, these Principles have been subject to expansion and modification in the light of national and international co-operative experience. They were last reformulated by the → *International Co-operative Alliance* in 1966.

Furthermore, it must be remembered that many of the early pre-Rochdale co-operatives made no attempt to promote the idea of Co-operation and establish a Co-operative Movement. They tended to be inward looking and often discouraged the growth of their societies beyond a certain level (for example, closing the membership registers after a certain recruitment number had been achieved). The Pioneers, on the other hand, welcomed all new members over the age of 16 and placed no artificial restriction on the number of members. They welcomed inquiries at their store from neighbouring working people on how to form and run a co-operative society on the Rochdale Pattern. Soon, hundreds of people were visiting the store to obtain this information from the society's directors. Indeed, inquiries became so overwhelming that the Pioneers Society took a leading part in 1869 in the formation of a national federation of co-operative societies – the Co-operative Union – which had the specific task of "establishing and organizing co-operative societies and diffusing a knowledge of the principle of Co-operation", thus relieving the Rochdale Pioneers of the immense burden of inquiries from all over the United Kingdom.

Meanwhile, the Pioneers not only received hundreds of visitors at Toad Lane seeking first hand knowledge of their co-operative system but were also prepared to travel extensively to acquaint working people of the advantages of co-operation and advise them on how to set up their own co-operatives. The Pioneers were truly "missionaries" of Co-operation.

Then again, the Pioneers realised that Co-operation must go beyond the co-operation of individual members in organizing and operating a co-operative society. Co-operative societies must in turn join together for common purposes and for the development of Co-operation as a movement (→ *Federations*).

Consequently, they took a leading part in the formation of the Co-operative Wholesale Society, the national supplier and manufacturer for the consumer Co-operative Movement; the Co-operative Insurance Society, providing insurance protection to societies and eventually to the general public; the Co-operative Press, which publishes the world's oldest national co-operative newspaper (→ *Periodicals, Co-operative*), and the Co-operative Union (→ *Central Institutions*). The Pioneers supported the formation of a CWS Banking Department, now the Co-operative Bank, one of the most innovative banking institutions in Britain.

Not only did the Pioneers seek to establish a fair trading enterprise beneficial to the consumer, but they also sought to enrich the consumer's life by the provision of educational, cultural and social activities (→ *Promotion Mandate*). In 1849, a school for members (many of whom were illiterate) and their children was opened above the Toad Lane co-operative shop. Here they learned reading, writing and arithmetic. As the years passed, teaching these basic skills was augmented with instruction in foreign languages and science subjects.

The Pioneers developed the vision of establishing a

residential Co-operative College (→ *Education, Europe*) in which the philosophy of Co-operation and its practical implementation could be widely and effectively taught. Their dream did not come to fruition until the 20th Century but theirs was the original concept.

These men of vision were, as we said at the outset, 28 working men. Sixteen of them worked in the textile factories. Others held a variety of jobs – woodworkers, a hatter, shoe repairer, and a tailor were among their ranks. Professor *Charles Gide*, the 19th Century French economist and co-operator, perceptively pointed out that the great economists of their day, the learned academics such as *Proudhon* and → *John Stuart Mill* would have been astounded if anyone had told them that a day would come when no more disciples would be found for their learned systems, no more readers for their books, whereas the faithful followers of the Rochdale Pioneers would be numbered by millions.

It is true that the Pioneers held a variety of political and religious doctrines – Chartism, Owenite Socialism (→ *Owen*) and Unitarianism. These beliefs were sincerely held. They included the creation of a co-operative community in which exploitation and economic hardship for working people would be abolished. The vision of a → *Co-operative Commonwealth* in which Co-operation would completely replace the various systems of predatory private enterprise was dear to most of the Pioneers. To create an Owenite co-operative community in Rochdale, the Pioneers launched a corn mill, cotton factory and tobacco factory and built houses for their members and employees. At least they tried but these efforts fell short of creating the self-sustaining co-operative community they had in mind.

It is not the intention of this article to discuss the various nuances of the idealism of the Pioneers and the Utopian and political ideas they held but to emphasize the economic basis on which this ideological superstructure was sustained. The realities of the economic basis proved overriding. The Pioneers abandoned the narrow concept of self-supporting village co-operative communities for the wider, practical view that a Co-operative Movement should be created consisting of national and eventually international co-operative organizations. These organizations should gradually bring about the → *Co-operative Commonwealth*.

The Pioneers were above all realists. It was not the promise of future wellbeing but the here and now of co-operation which was to ensure its success. The fact that co-operatives did not exploit their members, that in co-operatives the goods provided were wholesome and of good quality, that the profits (surplus) were returned to members in the form of dividends which contributed significantly to their economic wellbeing, the fact that they had a democratic right to participate in running co-operative businesses, and that their lives were enriched by co-operatives providing educational, cultural and social activities these were the immediate benefits of Co-operation which ensured its success and not some vague hope and promise of future benefits.

Unfortunately, little is known about the majority of the Pioneers beyond their occupations, area of residence, political or religious persuasions and the place of their burial. However, certain names among them stand out as the natural leaders of the 28.

First place must be given to *Charles Howarth* (1814–1868), textile worker, a man of great courage and vision. Although he lost his savings in the earlier Rochdale Co-operative Store of 1833 to 1835, this did not shake his belief in Co-operation. Despite bitter memories of the failure of the earlier Co-operative society, he assiduously worked for the creation of a new co-operative in Rochdale on a model hitherto unknown. From *Howarth's* fertile brain came the first constitution of the Rochdale Equitable Pioneers Society and he worked out for himself the idea of dividing the profits (surplus) of the Co-operative among members in proportion to their purchases as the most equitable way of enabling the members as shareholders to enjoy the profit made by the society. However, *Howarth* did not invent the dividend principle, as was widely believed. Modern research has revealed that a number of pre-Rochale societies operated various dividend systems but were usually regarded as a peripheral business expedient of no particular significance. On the other hand, the development of the dividend principle in the Co-operative movement, following the establishment of the Rochdale Pioneers Society, made this for many years a cardinal principle of Co-operation in Britain.

But it must be remembered that the 28 Pioneers were a collective – leading men appear in history not only individually but in groups. The force and influence of the perservering *Howarth* were more than trebled by the support of *William Cooper* (1822–1868) handloom weaver, and *James Smithies* (1819–1869) wool worker.

Smithies was probably the best educated of the Pioneers. He had closely studied the works of → *Robert Owen* and *William King*, a Brighton physician, who had earlier advocated the establishment of consumer co-operatives. Like *Howarth, Smithies* was a man of vision as well as of dogged persistence, refusing to succumb to difficulties in organizing the Pioneers' co-operative. He saw beyond the co-operative shop in Toad Lane. He quickly realised that as consumer co-operatives multiplied they would need their own wholesale supplying and manufacturing organization and he took a leading part in forming the Co-operative Wholesale Society. In addition to his brilliant mind, he had a strong sense of humour. During the difficult early days of the society, *Smithies'* merriment kept the Pioneers in good humour and good heart. He encouraged the doubters and made grimfaced members genial. Obviously a born psychologist, he was said to have "laughed the society into existence" and "His happy nature, his wise tolerance... made him exercise the great influence which kept the society together".

William Cooper, the first cashier of the society, was above all a management expert. Self-educated, it was *Cooper* who came to be regarded as the best informed man in Britain regarding co-operative methods of administration. He was responsible for much of the preparatory work in establishing the Co-operative Wholesale Society. He was equally active in forming the Co-operative Insurance Society and was its first secretary. He administered the Pioneers' Society's office, spoke at meetings of many other societies, answered hundreds of letters of inquiry and literally worked night and day according to historian *Percy Redfern*. But he was not as a personality a dry, humourless bureaucrat. On the contrary, he was a boisterous, noisily cheerful man well liked by the members.

The first President of the Society was *Miles Ashworth* (1782–1868) flannel weaver. During the last Napoleonic war, *Ashworth* served in the Royal Marines and, after the defeat of Napoleon by the British at the Battle of Waterloo, *Ashworth* was one of the armed escort which accompanied the ex-Emperor on the warship "Northumberland" to exile in St. Helena.

Five years later, he was back in Rochdale as a flannel weaver and was said to have been at the great working class demonstration in St. Peter's Fields, Manchester, in 1819, which ended in its bloody dispersal by cavalry in what was known as "The Peterloo Massacre". Miles and his son Samuel, who was first manager of the Rochdale Pioneers' shop, took part in operating a "Utopian farm" in Oxfordshire but the experiment failed and they both returned to Rochdale. It is said it was Miles who initially obtained the premises in Toad Lane for the Pioneers.

Although some of the Pioneers were the victims of poverty, most of them were comparatively well paid, skilled artisans, some in business on their own account. They commenced co-operative business with the ultimate aim of pioneering a way to a new and better social order but they kept their feet firmly on the ground and their original Owenite ideals of a self-supporting Utopian community gave way to ameliorating the lot of the worker and consumer within the context of industrial capitalism.

The Pioneers were nothing if not practical men. They were not arm-chair co-operators theorising about common ownership in contrast to private enterprise. Even the most talented of them were not averse to putting up rude shelving prior to the opening of the store, and cleaning the place up and making it ready for its opening.

This combination of men and methods initiated in Rochdale, England, in 1844 was unique. From that combination the modern world-wide Co-operative Movement has arisen.

Bibliography

Bonner, A.: British Co-operation, revised ed., (Cooperative Union), Manchester 1970.
Brown, W. H.: The Rochdale Pioneers: a century of Co-operation in Rochdale, (Co-operative Wholesale Society), Manchester 1944.
Cole, G. D. H.: A Century of Co-operation, London 1944.
Holyoake, G. J.: Self-help by the People: the history of the Rochdale Pioneers 1844–1892, (10th ed.), London 1900.
Robertson, W.: Rochdale: the birthplace of modern co-operation, (Co-operative Printing Society), Manchester 1892.
Watkins, W. P.: Co-operative Principles, Today and Tomorrow, Manchester 1986.

Rural Co-operatives

HANS HEINRICH GESSNER [J]

(see also: *Classification*; *Marketing*; *Supply Co-operatives*; *History in 19th C.*; *IRU*; *Machinery Associations/Rings*)

I. Definition of Terms; II. Historical Development; III. Breakdown of the Rural Co-operatives; IV. Structure of the Rural Co-operative Organization; V. Statistics; VI. Developmental Tendencies.

I. Definition of Terms

Those co-operatives are termed as "rural co-operatives" which were established in the middle of the 19th century (→ *History in 19th C.*) in Germany in rural areas. *Friedrich Wilhelm* → *Raiffeisen*, who is considered their founder, mentioned in the title of his main work on loan associations: "... a means to remedy the needs of the *rural* population."

In addition to these co-operatives, → *Commercial Co-operatives* existed predominantly in urban areas which had been established and organized by *Hermann* → *Schulze-Delitzsch*.

While the Raiffeisen loan associations gradually expanded their activity to the collective purchase of agricultural supplies, the agricultural consumer associations founded by *Wilhelm* → *Haas* after 1872 mainly in the Grand Duchy of Hesse were solely committed to this undertaking at the beginning and later expanded their work to include the marketing of agricultural products. *Haas* later pursued the establishment of → *credit co-operatives*.

II. Historical Development

For over half a century, the Raiffeisen co-operatives, organized in the "General-Anwaltschaftsverband ländlicher Genossenschaften für Deutschland" (General Bar Association of Rural Co-operatives for Germany), and the *Haas* co-operatives, united in the "Reichsverband der deutschen landwirtschaftlichen Genossenschaften" (National Federation of German Agricultural Co-operatives), developed adjacent to and independent of each other. Not until 1930, as a result of inflation and the Great Depression, was a united federation of rural co-operatives founded, "Der Reichsverband der deutschen landwirtschaflichen Genossenschaften – Raiffeisen – e.V.". The separate development of rural and commercial co-operative structures lasted until 1971 in the Federal Republic of Germany. In this year, the Deutscher Raiffeisenverband e.V. and the Deutscher Genossenschaftsverband e.V. joined to make the "Deutscher Genossenschafts- und Raiffeisenverband e.V." (DGRV, German Co-operative and Raiffeisen Union) as the apex organization (→ *Central Institutions*) with three nation-wide associations for the areas of finance, rural commodities and merchandise trading: "Bundesverband der Deutschen Volksbanken und Raiffeisenbanken e.V." (BVR, Federal Federation of German Co-operative Banks), "Deutscher Raiffeisenverbund e.V." (DRV, German Raiffeisen Federation), and "Zentralverband der genossenschaftlichen Grosshandels- und Dienstleistungsunternehmen e.V." (ZENTGENO, Central Federation of the Co-operative Wholesale and Service Agencies), respectively. This development also became generally accepted in most regions of the Federal Republic of Germany in the form of self-contained federations and collective central banks. Only in Oldenburg, a Raiffeisen Federation still exists which is predominately a band of rural co-operatives.

The development of rural co-operatives in Germany in the second half of the 19th century (→ *History in 19th C.*) also served as a model for the remaining German speaking areas. Thus, savings and loan associations were founded in Austria, Switzerland and in Alsace-Lorraine according to the Raiffeisen model around 1880. An agricultural purchasing co-operative had even been founded a few years earlier in Switzerland.

The rural co-operatives, their regional federations and central unions united under the "Österreichischer Raiffeisenverband" (Austrian Raiffeisen Federation) to form a strong organization with considerable market shares in finance and commodities, above all in rural regions. In Switzerland, the regional Raiffeisen federations joined to form the "Schweizer Verband der Raiffeisenkassen" and the co-operative federations for agricultural purchasing and marketing, processing and service amalgamated into the "Vereinigung der landwirtschaflichen Genossenschaftsverbände der Schweiz".

After the end of World War I, the 700 building and loan associations which existed in Alsace-Lorraine and were organized along the lines of the German Raiffeisen co-operatives – although exclusively involved in financial business – united their federation and central reserve with the "Bauern- und Arbeiterkassen" (Farmers' and Workers' Savings Bank), a co-operative organization also in existence. Today, they are a part of the important organization "Credit Agricole Mutuel" which has expanded extensively throughout France.

Prosperous and efficient rural co-operatives also developed in territories belonging to the former Austrian-Hungarian monarchy where the population was predominantly native German speaking. These organizations, however, did not survive long after World War II and were integrated very quickly into the planned economies of the subsequent communist states of the Eastern Block (→ *State and Co-operatives, Socialism*).

In the Soviet occupation zone which later became the German Democratic Republic (→ *GDR*), the rural co-operatives which existed at the end of the War in 1945 were included in the monopolistic state system according to the principles of the socialist planned economy to execute all banking transactions in the scope of fulfilling the plan. The state bank assumed a central role in eliminating substantial leeway in commercial-political decision making by imposing extensive authorization and control mechanisms. The 272 "Bauerliche Handelsgenossenschaften" (BHG, Farmers' Trade Co-operatives), the facility which succeeded the former multi-purpose Raiffeisen and credit co-operatives, were represented in 2,700 towns in the GDR with their main headquarters and branch offices and were solely given the task to process savings and payments of the rural population. Vast departments involved in commodities trade were operated as well, the influence of which outweighed the modest banking transactions in most situations. The BHGs were subordinate to the former "Bank für Landwirtschaft und Nahrungsgüter" (Bank for Agriculture and Foodstuffs) and had to keep their deposits at this bank. They were organized in the "Vereinigung der gegenseitigen Bauernhilfe" (VdgB, Union of Reciprocal Help for Farmers) which was also the holder af all assets on hand.

After the political changes in the fall of 1989 and the introduction of the German mark in the GDR on July 1, 1990, the BHGs have renamed themselves Raiffeisen banks and trading co-operatives and have constructed a modern banking and merchandise trading business with the help of partner co-operatives from the Federal Republic of Germany. The merchandise trading business, in most cases, was not conducted by these Raiffeisen banks and trading co-operatives themselves but, rather, by newly founded merchandise co-operatives. After upon the disolvement of the VdgB, a Raiffeisen federation for the GDR had emerged, and after regional Raiffeisen federations had been built on the territory of the former GDR within the area of the recently revived states, these regional → *federations* were fused with those of the adjacent states of the FRG and Berlin; all this following the unification of the two German states (East and West Germany) in October 1990. An independent co-operative federation only exists in Saxony. All federations and co-operatives have been affiliated to the existing co-operatives apex bodies of the FRG. The DG BANK (German Co-operative Bank) has assumed the central banking functions.

In the over 125 years since the founding of the first loan association which was not a charity association – the Loan Association of Heddelsdorf, 1864 – the rural co-operatives have spread throughout over 100 countries in all parts of the earth and have had great economic importance, particularly in the rural regions of the developing ountries.

III. Breakdown of the Rural Co-operatives

According to their appropriate functions, the groups of rural co-operatives consist of credit co-operatives (→ *Co-operative Banks*), trading and processing co-operatives, and service co-operatives; within the federation, they are seen as either primary co-operatives or secondary co-operatives (co-operative unions).

1. Credit Co-operatives Both Involved and Not Involved in Merchandise Trading

"Volksbanken" (people's banks, i.e. urban/industrial credit co-operatives) are appropriated to the field of commercial co-operatives, whereas the "Raiffeisen Banken" (agricultural credit co-operatives) and building and loan associations to the field of rural co-operatives. Whereas the Volksbanken as a rule only undertake banking transactions, many of the rural credit co-operatives are also operated as multi-purpose commercial and credit co-operatives (in some regions of Germany up to 90% of them). This is because in addition to banking transactions they also perform other tasks involved in the rural commodities trade to a varying degree, including:

- the purchase of requisite agricultural supplies
- marketing agricultural products, above all grain
- trade of necessary foods for house and yard
- trade of solid and liquid fuels
- trade of construction material

The number of multi-purpose commercial and credit co-operatives has been decreasing for many years now, a phenomenon which cannot only be traced to the amalgamation into larger functioning units. If the extent of the rural commodities business reaches a size dimension which cannot economically cover its costs anymore – particularly because of the → *structural changes* in agriculture, this part of the credit enterprise is often removed and transferred to a larger neighboring co-operative or to the regional central co-operative responsible for it.

2. Merchandise and Processing Co-operatives

a) Supply and Marketing Co-operatives

Task/function: The realization of the rural commodities trade (see III.1).
They work predominately in regions in which the rural commodities trade is not carried out by multi-purpose credit co-operatives (separation of finance and trade).

b) Dairy Co-operatives

Task/function: Collection and processing of raw milk produced by their members on the agricultural enterprises and marketing the products made from it. If the activities are limited to the collection of raw milk and the delivery of it to processing enterprises, this organization is called a milk collection co-operative.

c) Livestock Marketing Co-operatives

(The term "processing" as in "livestock processing co-operative" which was commonly used in former times was replaced upon the advent of the modern sales organization by "marketing").
Task/function: Collection, sorting and marketing of the livestock raised by the members on the agricultural enterprises. This can include slaughtering and processing, trade domestick and breeding stock, and the procurement of young animals for fattening (piglets and calves).

d) Fruit and Vegetable Co-operatives

Task/function: Collection, sorting, packing and marketing of fruit and vegetables which were grown on the member enterprises, partly including processing into preserves, juices and deep-frozen foodstuffs and meals and procuring requisite goods for the member enterprises.

e) Winegrowers' Co-operatives

Task/function: Collection and processing of the wine harvests from the member enterprises, developing the must into wine and marketing it or selling the must to a central winecellar (central co-operative of the winegrowers' co-operatives of a wine-growing region), procurement of necessary goods for the member enterprises.

f) Co-operatives for Flowers and Ornamental Plants

Task/function: Collection, sorting, packing and marketing of flowers and ornamental plants grown in the nurseries of the members, centralized purchasing of young plants and other requisite materials for the producing enterprises.

g) Distillery Co-operatives

Task/function: Collection and processing of agricultural products (grain, potatoes, fruit) into alcohol and alcoholic beverages and marketing them.

h) Fishery co-operatives

Task/function: Collection, sorting, packing and marketing – rarely processing – of the catch of the members.

3. Service Co-operatives

a) Grazing Co-operatives

The collective supervision of livestock or the collective use of fields for grazing is one of the oldest forms of the co-operative which stretches back to the Germanic times. The German world for co-operative, "Genossenschaft", stems from the Old High German word "Ginezcaf" – a group who collectively keeps a herd of livestock or shares the use a livestock pasture.
Task/function: Making use of pasture with livestock for agistment.

b) Machinery co-operatives

Task/function: Purchase, maintenance and temporary lending of collectively owned machines to members for payment. The most important example before the advent of the combine harvester: threshing co-operatives (→ *Machinery Associations/Rings*).

c) Livestock Breeding Co-operatives

Task/function: Caring for male breeding animals and temporarily leasing them to members for employment in their agricultural enterprises (stallions, bulls and/or boars). With the advancement of artificial insemination the tasks of the breeding co-operatives have switched over to the insemination co-operatives which keep breeding animals, retrieve their sperm and provide it to the members against payment for artificial insemination. Today, the insemination co-operatives also deal in the trade of sperm and frozen animal embryos which are implanted in the female animals in place of sperm injections (embryo transfers).

d) Utilities Co-operatives (Water, Electricity, Natural Gas and Heating Co-operatives)

Task/function: Retrieval of water or energy, or providing members with utilities through a collectively owned network of mains or lines.

The electricity co-operatives which still exist today almost exclusively tap electricity from the power plants of larger, regional electrical utility companies and distribute it along the co-operatively owned net to their members.

e) Freezer Co-operatives (Coldhouse Co-operatives)

Task/function: The construction and management of collective freezer facilities and leasing freezer space to the members. The number and importance of the freezer co-operatives have been decreasing with the increasing availability of deep freezes and freezers both for households and businesses.

f) Warehouse Co-operatives

Task: Construction and management of warehouse space for the storage of members' agricultural products, e.g. potatoes, grain.

g) Co-operatives for Drying Products

Task: Construction and management of facilities to dry agricultural products (grain, green fodder) against payment.

h) Laundry Co-operatives

Task: Construction and management of a laundry and leasing use of the facility to the members.

IV. Structure of the Rural Co-operative Organization

1. Primary Co-operatives

All of the co-operatives listed as examples in Chapter III are primary co-operatives. Their members are essentially natural persons, and their territory is as a rule restricted to a certain locality or a limited region. The locally founded primary co-operatives are the origin and corner stone of the multi-leveled co-operative organizations which exist today.

2. Central Co-operatives (→ *Central Institutions*)

Even only a few years after founding his first co-operatives, *Friedrich Wilhelm Raiffeisen* recognized the necessity and the advantages of central co-operatives – in the banking sector to serve financial settlements and in the commodities trade to consolidate demand and centralize purchases and sales of goods (unions). Thus, the "Landwirtschaftliche Zentral-Darlehnskasse" was founded in 1876 and the company "Raiffeisen, Fassbender & Cons." was established for the trade sector. Similarly, a few years later a central co-operative for the agricultural consumer association in Hesse emerged within *Haas*' co-operative organization along with a central sales co-operative for the diaries and a central bank.
The members of central co-operatives are either ex-

clusively or predominantly co-operatives. Central co-operatives serve and act for a region or for a specifically limited group of primary co-operatives. They form the second level of the three-tiered co-operative organization structure and are therefore also characterized as secondary co-operatives. They undertake sudsidiary tasks for the member primary co-operatives which either cannot carry them through or else choose to have them taken care of by the central co-operatives because of more practical or economical reasons.

3. Federal Central Organizations

Central national organizations have been formed in many sectors as consolidations of the regional centers which undertake national and international tasks and responsibilities (DG BANK, Deutsche Raiffeisen-Warenzentrale GmbH, Deutsches Milch-Kontor GmbH).

4. Federations

The → *federations* form the organizational structure of the regional and national co-operative organizations. The primary co-operatives of a region and their central organizations belong to the regional federation as their auditing and consulting center, and the regional federations and their co-operatives belong to the approporiate national federation in each branch. The regional and national federations as well as the central national organizations are members and subjects of the head national federation, Deutscher Genossenschafts- und Raiffeisenverband (DGRV, German Co-operative and Raiffeisen Federation).

The regional associations and the DGRV are the legal auditing centers (→ *Auditing*) for their member co-operatives. This means that they have been granted the right by the appropriate governmental advisory authorities to audit the co-operatives which belong to them. This right meets the compulsory examination of the primary co-operative laid down in the "Co-operative Law" (→ *Law, National*). It specifies that each co-operative is obliged to belong to a legal auditing association and allows regular examination. Aside from financial examinations, the federations offer their members consulting and counseling facilities with a comprehensive palette of services including the fields of law, taxation, organization, management, marketing, etc. Furthermore, they provide extensive educational facilities (→ *Education, Germany*) in which the staff of the member co-operatives can continually be educated and trained. Through a shared training conception the regional educational facilities are associated with the Academy of German Co-operatives at Schloß Montabaur as the head of the co-operative education system.

V. Statistics (→ *Federation Statistics*)

5,467 merchandise, processing and service co-operatives belonged to the regional co-operative associations united in the German Raiffeisen Union of the Federal Republic of Germany on December 31, 1989. Among others, they consisted of the following groups:

1,613 Credit co-operatives involved in merchandise trading

697	Purchasing and marketing co-operatives
889	Dairy and milk collection co-operatives
214	Livestock co-operatives
100	Fruit and vegetable co-operatives
311	Winegrowners' co-operatives
1,306	Service co-operatives
54	co-operative centers

Not included in these numbers are the rural credit co-operatives not involved in commodities trade which belong to the BVR (Federal Association of German Co-operative Banks). The BVR no longer differentiates between rural and commercial credit co-operatives in its statistics.

2,161 co-operatives belonged to the Austrian Raiffeisen Federation on January 1, 1990, which were consolidated in the following groups:

851	Credit co-operatives,
165	Purchasing and marketing co-operatives,
542	Dairy and milk collection co-operatives,
42	Livestock processing co-operatives,
43	Wine processing co-operatives,
141	Miscellaneous processing co-operatives (for wood, potatoes, fruit, vegetables, etc.),
5	Electricity transmission co-operatives,
219	Livestock and collective pasturing co-operatives,
14	Machine, mill and sawmill co-operatives,
13	Co-operative electrical power stations,
59	Leasing and promoting co-operatives,
67	Co-operative federations and central co-operatives.

VI. Developmental Tendencies

The functions and type of work of the rural co-operatives have undergone such numerous changes that their number has considerably decreased, particularly after World War II. Whereas 23,735 co-operatives belonged to the regional federations of the German Raiffeisen banks in 1950, only 5,467 did by the end of 1989. This development will continue in the following years and can be traced to the following reasons:

1. Concentration

Co-operatives are economic enterprises which enter into competition. Co-operatives in all branches are

forced to concentrate their work in larger operating units because of increasing competition, mounting technical and human demands and all costs associated with them (→ *Mergers and Consolidations*). As a rule, this is achieved by the merger of two or more co-operatives, but also through co-operative means or the formation of a community enterprise.
The rural merchandise and processing co-operatives have had to adapt to the strong structural changes in their branch within German and European agriculture by adapting to each other as their most important business partners. This adjustment process has run more quickly, been more lasting and has lead to more efficient marketing structures in those countries in the → *European Community* which have traditionally been dependent on the export of agricultural goods (e.g. The Netherlands, Denmark) than in Germany.

2. Separation of Finance and Trade

In spite of exhausting all available rationalization steps, the departments involved in merchandise trading of many multi-purpose credit co-operatives have not been able to cover their costs on account of the decreasing number of clients, shrinking markets and mounting competition. The intensified competition within the banking business no longer permits a long term subsidization of merchandise trading through the financial transactions. The previously existent possibility of transferring the commodites trade to a neighboring co-operative is also more frequently eliminated because the other co-operative often faces the same decision. The commodities trade is therefore increasingly transferred to the appropriate central co-operative (union) as long as it has a network of branch offices which can cover the territory. The co-operative unions, which were formerly only involved as wholesalers for their member co-operatives, are therefore progressively assuming more retail functions as the direct partner to individuals involved in agriculture in rural areas.

3. Fusion of Rural and Commercial Credit Co-operatives

Raiffeisen banks and savings and loan insitutions predominately emerged in villages and small towns in rural areas whereas Volksbanken were almost exclusively situated in the medium-sized and larger cities as urban-commercial institutions.
The competition between these two groups was thus limited to exceptional individual cases. Only after the Second World War and the currency reform of 1948 did the merger of smaller rural co-operatives into larger entities occur which then frequently chose the city situated centrally within its terrritory as the seat of the joint co-operative. On the other hand, the urban Volksbanken established branches in the larger rural localities. The competition between the two increased because the growing Raiffeisen banks could more strongly pursue the business of commercial credits; the Volksbanken likewise discovered and won over a new group of interested customers through their new rural branches. Since the fusion in 1971 of the two former apex federations, the German Raiffeisen Union and the German Co-operative Union, and the formation of joint regional federations and central banks in the majority of regions in Germany, the Volksbanken, Raiffeisenbanken and savings and loan associations, irregardless of their origin or former field of activity, see themselves today as a collective group of credit co-operatives. Together with the → *Building and Loan Society* "Schwäbisch Hall", The R + V Insurance Company (→ *Insurance, Germany*), the Deutsche Genossenschafts-Hypothekenbank AG, the Münchener Hypothekenbank e.G. and other confederated companies they appear in publicity and advertising using the same logos and colors as a united, integrated and self-contained system of financial services. Internal competition within the group at a locality is increasingly resolved through the merger of the Raiffeisen banks and Volksbanken which operate in the same area. By coupling savings from avoidable costs and consolidating personnel and organization, they are thus in a better economic position in the increasingly competitive market with savings banks and large financial institutions (→ *Combine, Co-operative*).
This fusion process of the previously separate rural and commercial credit co-operatives and the formation of larger administrative units will be further accelerated through the opening of the internal European Market in 1993 and the ensuing heightened competition.

4. Development of a Two-tiered Organizational Structure in the Branch of Credit Co-operatives

After the DG BANK assumed the business administration of the Bayerische Raiffeisen-Zentralbank AG at the end of 1985 because of its inability to cover losses in its credit business, the subsequent time was full of intensive discussion concerning the advantages and disadvantages of two- and three-tiered structures within the realm of credit co-operatives. In 1987, the Bayerische Volksbanken AG transferred its administrative activities to the DG BANK as did the Norddeutsche Genossenschaftsbank AG and the Raiffeisen-Zentralbank Kurhessen AG theirs in 1989. Thus, as the new German states of Brandenburg, Mecklenburg–Vorpommern, Saxony, Saxony-Anhalt and Thuringia become integrated into the Federal Republic of Germany, the preponderate part of the co-operative banking system will be two-tiered. It can therefore be expected that the three remaining central co-operative banks, SGZ Bank (Südwestdeutsche Genossenschafts-Zentralbank AG) in Karlsruhe, WGZ Bank (Westdeutsche Genossenschafts-Zentralbank in Düsseldorf), and the Genossenschaftliche Zentralbank AG in Stuttgart, will also have to become incorporated in the DG BANK as a result of the development of the market and competition in the European Common Market after 1993.

Bibliography

Aschhoff, Günther/Henningsen, Eckart: Das deutsche Genossenschaftswesen, Veröffentlichungen der DG BANK Deutsche Genossenschaftsbank, vol. 15, Frankfurt am Main 1985.
Deutscher Raiffeisenverband e.V.: Jahrbuch 1989.
Faust, Helmut: Geschichte der Genossenschaftsbewegung, (3rd edition), Frankfurt am Main 1977.
Mändle, Eduard/Winter, Hans-Werner (eds.): Handwörterbuch des Genossenschaftswesens, Wiesbaden 1980.
Österreichischer Raiffeisenverband: Jahresbericht '89.
Raiffeisen, Friedrich Wilhelm: Die Darlehenskassen–Vereine, Neuwied 1866.

Rural Peoples Communes in China

JERZY KLEER

(see also: *China, Actual Development*; *State and Co-operatives in Socialism*; *Development, South Asia*; *Development, South-East Asia*)

I. Foundation and Characteristics of Rural Communes in China; II. Theoretical Conception and its Implementation; III. Practical Results and Modifications; IV. Rural Communes in China: A Failed Political and Economic Experiment.

I. Foundation and Characteristics of Rural Communes in China

The first *rural communes* were formed in the People's Republic of China in April 1958. The official decision to establish them was made during the meeting of the Chinese Communist Party Political Bureau (Politburo) in Beidahe (August 17–30, 1958).
For the next 25 years or so, they constituted the backbone of the rural organizational structure. A rural commune was a political, economic, social, and cultural organization including 20 to 50 thousand people (members) operating in five areas: industry, agriculture, commerce, education, and national defense. It was an integration of central and territorial authorities with the local (peasant) self-government, to the extent that the latter existed.
Rural communes included members from various professions and walks of life (peasants, industrial workers, wholesale and retail employees, militiamen, etc.) and executed diverse activities (agriculture, animal husbandry, forestry, auxiliary tasks and services). Factories from local industries were also included in the framework of rural communes. They furthermore oversaw the distribution of goods as well as educational and cultural activities. They had their own political organizations and militia.
The rural commune in principle abolished private property and took control of the most important means of production. The work process was structured into a three-tiered organization: a commune management committee, a large production brigade, and a small production brigade (or production team). The state administration and the production organization amalgamated. Each rural commune had its organizational committee and a number of departments responsible for the following fields: water management and irrigation, forestry, animal husbandry, industry, transportation, political affairs, labor, security, financing, procurement, sales, credit, commerce, culture, education, and health. Rural communes also ran their own planning commissions and research institutes.
Rural communes were characterized by: 1) economic self-sufficiency: to a large extent, they became autarkic, at least as far as the traditional rural sector was concerned; 2) extensive decision making authority: they assumed a large part of the prerogatives concerning economic, political, and social decision-making, that had formerly in the hands of the Center. The strong centralization of decision-making power was preserved on the rural commune level.

II. Theoretical Conception and its Implementation

Rural communes were initiated at a time when the Chinese countryside had already been collectivized (in 1956, 96.3% of all peasant farms had been converted into various forms of collective production). The rationale for creating rural communes according to the official version was linked to the thesis that co-operative farms were unable to resolve three existing contradictions. The first was between co-operatives and the private sector (peasants were more inclined to till their own private plots than to work for the co-operative), the second between co-operatives formed by wealthy peasants and those established by poor peasants (the former were more interested in speculating than producing), and the third between the co-operatives and the state (the co-operatives tended to withhold or not disclose a part of their output in order to minimize their supply obligations to the state). The Chinese leadership considered the basis for these contradictions to be found in Chinese traditionalism and attachment to family and private property. In order to overcome this traditional thinking, the existing socio-economic structure needed to be altered, and this was to be achieved through the rural communes (→ *Development Policy*).

In reality, the issue was far more complex. The creation of rural communes was but one element of a larger program which, in policy history, has gone down under the heading of "The Three Red Banners"; the rural communes represented the "General Line" and the "Great Leap Forward".

Under the First Five-Year Plan (1953–1957), industrial output annually rose by 18% and agricultural output by 4.5%, whereas grain production expanded by only 3.7%, a rate being slightly higher than that of the natural population increase. Fertilizers and water were two essential factors of production which were needed to fight the bottleneck of agricultural production. Central authorities were not to relinquish their original priorities; they planned a mass mobilization of the population into units considerably larger than the co-operatives which had previously existed. Between the winter of 1957 and the spring of 1958, at least 100 million peasants were "mobilized" and employed in the realization of irrigation projects (→ *Privatization and Collectivization*). By March 1958, when an additional 60 million peasants were conscripted initially to build and later to operate primative factories and iron furnaces, a labor deficit became apparent. This situation necessitated a reorganization of the rural labor force, above all in order to generate higher work-participation rates for women. The establishment of rural communes facilitated this process through the operation of canteens (messhalls) and kindergartens which enabled women to devote their time to organized "productive" work rather than to "non-productive" household chores.

The strategy of the "Great Leap Forward" was based on two premises. The first concerned the surplus of labor achieved through the "mobilization" of the rural population under the system of rural communes and its ability to be transformed into capital. This surplus was to be utilized not only in irrigation and recultivation projects but also in small-scale industrial production developed in the countryside. The second premise was the possibilty to maximize total output in a situation of technological dualism, or in other words, maximization through the parallel existence of both, traditional and modern, production techniques. The former were to implemented in the traditional sector (subordinated to the rural commune), and the latter in the modern sector (subordinated to the central authorities). Rural communes were to secure the provision of necessary resources from agriculture by drastically reducing consumption among the agricultural population, that is by maximizing aggregate savings (the Marxist equivalent of capital accumulation). The widespread application of labor-intensive small-scale production techniques was to enable the Chinese economy to use in full its existing labor surplus and, thus, to substitute its abundant supply of labor for its insufficient supply of fixed captial and land. In addition, positive externalities also emerged in form of cost reductions in the transport of coal and steel, the opportunity to stimulate development in backward regions, shorter time frames between the initiation of investment projects and their completion, and finally, the possibility to utilize lower quality raw materials productively.

Other long-term goals behind the formation of rural communes included the deliberate deterioration of family ties and the creation of communist man (the opposite of homo oeconomicus), the elimination of the peasantry as a social class, and the transformation of peasants into agricultural workers.

III. Practical Results and Modifications

Regardless of the fact that the concept of rural communes suffered theoretical deficiencies, their actual operation even in the initial period caused a dramatic deterioration of the economic situation in the country. The first symptoms of a coming crisis became visible in 1958, when tens of millions of peasants were forcibly sent to work in the steel smelting factories and in the development of small-scale industries belonging to the rural communes. Because of the insufficient supply of labor left in agriculture, the bounteous crop of 1958 was largely wasted. The decision to save as much as 60–70% of the income of the rural commune severely decreased the level of personal income among the rural population. The urban supplies of agricultural produce dwindled sharply; the Chinese economy began to feel a shortage of raw materials needed for light industry and food preparation. There were riots in many rural regions. These factors combined to produce certain amelioration effects in the "hard" general line adopted by the authorities in 1958. At the same time, rural communes began a process of evolution.

During its almost 25-year existence, the rural commune underwent a quite substantial transformation (for details, see *Cheng, Chu-yuan*: China's Economic Development, 1982). The analysis of the evolution allows to stress certain general characteristics: first, all modifications were not uni-directional; second, politics was an instrumental factor; third, none of the goals laid down were ever achieved, not even for a short time. In general, the modifications in the rural commune model took place in five areas. The first was their number, which varied from 24 to 70 thousand. The obvious result of this is that the number of peasant farms belonging to one rural commune varied (from 1622 to 5000).

The second area concerned ownership structures. Ownership varied greatly from period to period and ranged from full communal ownership of all means of production to, alternatively, the allocation of particular means of production to the large commune (which served as a co-ordinating unit) *and* to the small brigade/production team (which directly controlled land, tractive animals, tools, etc.). In some periods, small private plots (owned by peasants) were allowed, and certain "side" activities were tolerated (the output of which could be retained by the peasants).

The third general area concerned the character of the rural commune. In some periods, it had a joint economic, political, and administrative character, while at other times, it was exclusively a political and administrative unit. This variation of function was based on the particular form of ownership structure prevalent at the time (see above). This further meant that the decision-making process within the rural commune likewise varied in the degree of its centralization over time, along with the extent strictly economic decisions were politicized.

The fourth area of concern was the distribution of produce. Within the consecutive time periods, the state, commune, brigade, and individual peasants contributed varying amounts to the total available supply. In the case of the peasants, the proportion of produce retained in kind changed over time to that retained in cash, as did the proportion of collective consumption to individual consumption.

The final area of concern is usually referred to as the (material) incentive structure and was closely connected to the solutions adopted in the principles of distribution. In certain periods, distribution was effected in an egalitarian manner, in others, it varied according to the labor input. In certain times, it was based on the economic result obtained by the small brigade, family, or even single individual member.

IV. Rural Communes in China: A Failed Political and Economic Experiment

The actual operation and results obtained by the rural communes in the period 1958–1979 prove that the changes in the internal configuration of these organizations were not enough to provide a satisfactory solution to the basic problems faced by the Chinese countryside. They could not ensure adequate supplies of food and raw materials. Furthermore, they could not meet the greatest expectation of the central government, namely that of achieving full territorial self-sufficiency. Rural communes, the great political and economic expirement, turned out to be an utter fiasco.

Since 1979, the Chinese countryside has witnessed the initiation of economic reform which, in essence, rests on a revival of family farming. Two main ideas form the foundation of this reform:

1) The re-establishment of the basic links between economic processes and basic principles of economics. To a large extent, this means abandoning the idea of the primacy of political considerations over economic ones and accepting new rules of the "economic game".

2) The promotion and propagation of the ideas of "grass-roots" entrepreneurship and the self-interest of individuals as motors of their actions.

New solutions have accordingly been tried. For one, the opportunity to lease land has been re-established. Family farms can now be leased (initially for one to three years, with a possible further extension up to 15 years; pastures up to 30 years). In addition, a substantial part (75–90%) of all produce may be retained by the family. Likewise, the regulations governing the structure and operation of the market for agricultural products were transformed, and last but not least, the output composition was adjusted to the needs of specialization and commercialization, i.e. to what the market dictated.

The changes taking place in the lowest tiers of rural structure have had three-fold consequences: 1) the rural commune system has been transformed; 2) towns have been given new controlling functions vis-à-vis the rural regions (For over twenty years, there was no affiliation between towns and rural areas controlled exclusively by rural communes.); 3) co-operatives appeared which were attuned to the requirements of the market economy.

One tangible result of the reforms has been the full dismantlement of the rural communes. This occurred sometime between 1980 and 1983. Rural communes were stripped of their administrative and political powers, but they were allowed to keep certain very limited economic functions. The local xiang (hsiang) governments have assumed the administration of rural regions, while towns have regained their juridical control over rural regions, i.e. counties. A market economy has quickly spread throughout the Chinese countryside. Rural communes no longer play the leading role assigned to them for a period of more than twenty years. The great rural commune experiment, in the end, has proved to be a total failure. The costs of the expirement – human, economic, social, and political costs – have been enormous. Yet another utopia has collapsed.

Bibliography

Cheng, Chu-yuan: China's Economic Development. Growth and Structural Change, Colorado 1982.
Eckstein Elexander: China's Economic Revolution, Cambridge 1977.
Hanxian, Luo: Economic Changes in Rural China, Beijing 1985.
Kleer, Jerzy: Reformy gospodarcze w rolnictwie chinskim, "Wies i Rolnictwo", vol. 1/54, Warzawa 1987.

Schulze-Delitzsch, Hermann (1808–1883)

EBERHARD DÜLFER [J]

(see also: *History of Ideas; History in 19th C.; Law, National; Legal Form, Co-operative; Co-operative Banks; Commercial Co-operatives*)

I. Biographical Dates; II. Political Activities; III. Co-operative Activities.

I. Biographical Dates

Franz Hermann Schulze, called *Schulze-Delitzsch* following German parliamentary custom, was born in Delitzsch on August 29, 1808, the oldest child of *August Wilhelm Schulze*, a Patrimonialrichter (judge appointed by local landowners), and his wife *Wilhelmine, née Schmorl*. This 5,000–soul town in Kurhesse became subject to Prussian rule in 1815. Having completed his secondary exams at the Nicolai-Schule in Leipzig, *Schulze* studied jurisprudence at the University of Leipzig and at the University of Halle-Wittenberg; he passed his first state examination in 1830. Following his clerkship and one-year military conscription, he took his second state examination in 1833, and after passing his third state examination in 1838, he was appointed assistant judge at the higher regional court in Naumburg. Starting in 1839, he worked at the Berlin Court of Appeals but returned to Delitzsch in 1841 and served as Patrimonialrichter in his hometown until 1849.

Since 1847, *Schulze-Delitzsch* had been politically active in favor of the concept of a parliamentary democracy and was therefore elected to the Prussian Parliament as well as to the Frankfurt National Assembly in 1848. Because of this involvement, however, he fell out of favor in his standing as a civil servant in the Prussian monarchy once the position of Patrimonialrichter was abolished in 1849. He had just married *Berta Jakob* when he was transferred to the province of Posen as an assistant judge in 1859, right in the middle of the trial concerning the tax repudiation resolution. On account of his ongoing conflicts with the bureaucratic authorities he filed his resignation from state service in 1851 and returned to Delitzsch as a selfemployed legal consultant. Increasing parliamentary activity, above all following *Wilhelm I.'s* accession to the throne, induced *Schulze* to move to Potsdam in 1862. He received numerous national and international awards following the publication of his treatise "Kapitel zu einem deutschen Arbeiterkatechismus" (Passages in a German Worker's Catechism) in 1863 and accordingly enjoyed extensive renown. In 1873, the University of Heidelberg awarded him the title Doktor jur. honoris causa. *(Franz) Hermann Schulze-Delitzsch* died on April 29, 1883 in Potsdam, where his grave also rests.

II. Political Activities

Schulze-Delitzsch's pioneer contributions to the establishment and development of → *commercial co-operatives* and → *co-operative banks* can only be understood in the context of his political involvement. Schulze was elected to the Prussian National Assembly in Berlin and into the German National Assembly in Frankfurt on May 1, 1848, in light of his capacity as board member in the "Deutscher Volksverein von Demokraten und Liberalen" (Popular German Association of Democrats and Liberals), founded in Delitzsch. In the Berlin Parliament, he distinguished himself above all in connection with the parliament's tax repudiation resolution in opposition to *Brandenburg's* cabinet. The government dissolved the national assembly after this resolution was passed. The subsequent turbulence led to the introduction of the three-tiered system of electoral rights in 1849, a constitutional structure to which *Schulze-Delitzsch* objected due to his democratic beliefs; he, therefore, decided against running for reelection. He was acquitted along with the other defendants in the subsequent trial in connection with the tax repudiation resolution (→ *History in 19th C.*).

At the end of the 1850s, *Schulze* numbered among the promoters of German national unification based on democratic foundations and was therefore once again elected member of the national assembly from a Berlin electoral district. He joined the newly founded "Fortschrittspartei" (Party for Progress) for which he advocated the concept of national unification and liberal economic principles. During the 1860s, he introduced numerous bills in this political direction. He became a representative in the Nord German League in 1867 and a member of the German Reichstag in 1871, a position he maintained until his death.

III. Co-operative Activities

During his term as Patriamonialrichter in Delitzsch (1848) and in the middle of a food crisis haunting the general population, *Schulze* and Rev. *Eduard Baltzer* founded a committee which provided wheat and flour to the needy (→ *History in 19th C.*). After the Prussian National Assembly was established in 1848,

Representative Schulze-Delitzsch was elected to the "Committee for Trade and Industry with Special Consideration given to the Conditions of Artisans and Craftsmen" and appointed its secretary (→ *History of Ideas*).

Schulze assumed chairmanship of the additional special commission addressing artisans' petitions. Here, he experienced first-hand the dispute among artisans and craftsmen concerning the freedom of trade, a matter which *Schulze* strongly supported. In 1849, *Schulze* instigated the founding of the first raw material association for carpenters and cobblers in Delitzsch, and in 1850 of an advance loan society, a kind of credit co-operative open to all people (→ *Conceptions, Co-operative*). During the following years, *Schulze* more fully cultivated this pragmatic concept in the direction of true self-help and self-management. This evolved in part through his contact and exchange of ideas with → *Viktor Aime Huber* and in reference to his 1852 publication "Über die kooperativen Arbeiterassoziationen in England" (About the Co-operative Worker Associations in England). *Schulze* put his ideas to paper in his "Mitteilungen über gewerbliche und Arbeiterassoziationen" (Reports about Commercial and Worker Associations) (1852) and in "Assoziationenbuch für deutsche Handwerker und Arbeiter" (The Association Book for German Craftsmen and Workers) (1853). It is evident here that *Schulze-Delitzsch* identified the "social question" as the largest challenge of his day and age and that he wished to confront this challenge with his co-operative system, which aimed at preserving craftsmen as a class and reestablishing the independent status formerly enjoyed by a portion of factory workers. His system encompassed five types of associations: the savings society (→ *consumer co-operative*), the raw materials and warehousing societies (purchasing co-operatives) (→ *Commercial Co-operatives*), the advance loan societies (credit co-operatives) (→ *Co-operative Banks*), and the cream of the crop – the "Commercial Enterprises on Joint Account" (workers' co-operatives) (→ *Joint-production Co-operative*).

Starting in 1854, *Schulze-Delitzsch* edited the periodic supplement "Innung der Zukunft" (Guild of the Future) in the German Trade Newspaper in order to propagate his ideas; the "Blätter für Genossenschaftswesen" (Leaflet of the Co-operative System) evolved out of this publication (→ *Periodicals, Co-operative*). *Schulze-Delitzsch's* activities as a publicist promoting his co-operative concepts reached a peak in his collaboration in the "Volkswirtschaftlicher Kongress" (National Economy Congress) in 1858. At its second convention (1859), *Schulze* succeeded in replacing the term "Assoziation" with the German word "Genossenschaft" (co-operative). On the one hand, he wanted to draw attention to the older co-operative traditions found in German-speaking regions (→ *History before 1800*); on the other hand, he also wanted to draw a distinction to the socialistic implications of the word *association*.

In the same year, the "First Convention of German Advance Loan and Credit Societies" was held in Weimar. Twenty-nine commercial associations took part, for which *Schulze* was largely responsible. It was decided that a central correspondence office should be opened under *Schulze-Delitzsch's* supervision; the "Anwaltschaft der deutschen Erwerbs- und Wirtschaftsgenossenschaften" emerged from this organization (Legal Representation of German Co-operatives serving Households and Enterprises) (→ *Central Institutions*). The founding of the "Allgemeiner Verband der auf Selbsthilfe beruhenden deutschen Erwerbs- und Wirtschaftsgenossenschaften" subsequently occurred in 1864 (General Federation of German Co-operatives based on Self-help and serving Households and Enterprises).

Schulze was somewhat less successful in his efforts for the workers' movement. One workers' association founded by him in 1862 in Berlin, switched over to *Lassalle's* camp (→ *Socialist Critics*), the initiator of the "Allgemeiner deutscher Arbeiterverein" (Common German Workers' Association). Following an unusually biting literary dispute between *Lasalle* and *Schulze-Delitzsch* the same year, the latter founded the "Vereinstag der deutschen Arbeitervereine" (VDAV, Convention of German Workers' Associations) which, however, soon drifted in a more radical direction. Without a doubt, this development also contributed to the low level of success which *Schulze-Delitzsch's* workers' co-operatives were only able to achieve (→ *Joint-production Co-operative*).

A further scope of *Schulze-Delitzsch's* activity involved contact with the rural co-operative system which had developed following the ground-breaking efforts of → *Friedrich Wilhelm Raiffeisen* (→ *Rural Co-operatives*). Although the *Raiffeisen* co-operatives initially aligned themselves under *Schulze's* legal representation, disputes later arose between these two founding fathers. These disputes were primarily based on the conflict between the concepts of self-help and charitable help for one's neighbours. Differences of opinion concerning the "Landwirtschaftliche Generalbank" (Agricultural General Bank), founded by *Raiffeisen* in 1874, caused a rift to develop, and the independent Raiffeisen Federation was founded in 1874 following the dissolution of the bank.

Perhaps the most important element of *Schulze-Delitzsch's* lifework was the conception and realization of the German Co-operative Law. *Schulze-Delitzsch* had prepared a bill as early as 1860 and made a second draft after the German General Trade Code was ratified in 1862. However, this bill was never discussed as parliament became dissolved. Although the government strove to introduce an obligatory concession for co-operatives, a draft bill was proposed in the lower chamber of the Prussian parliament which strongly borrowed from *Schulze's* ideas. *Schulze* in turn responded with his own draft, a move which ultimately led to the dispensation of a mandatory concession (→ *Legal Form, Co-operative*). The government draft of the bill was accepted on March 27, 1867, assuming all essential points raised by *Schulze-Delitzsch.* The subsequent Prussian Co-operative law became effective on January 1, 1869, for the territory of the North German League and for the entire German Reich on January 1, 1871 (→ *Law, National*).

In 1864, *Schulze-Delitzsch* introduced statutes for statewide and provincial federations at the Federation Convention in Mainz. The following, year he instigated the founding of the "Deutsche Genossenschaftsbank *Parisius, Sörgel* & Co. KGaA" (→ *Central Institutions*), the seminal organization of the Deutsche Genossenschaftskasse (German Co-operative Bank). In the final years of his involvement, *Schulze-Delitzsch* himself recommended mandatory audits for co-operatives as a statutory regulation in their own interest and advocated the idea of limited liability as a means to expand membership circles.

All told, *Hermann Schulze-Delitzsch* assumed a paramount role in the scope of theoretical conceptions concerning co-operatives and cooperation. He designed appropriate organizational forms for numerous commercial sectors and molded them into an entire system which opened up prospects for artisan production to be maintained to an extensive degree in the years of early industrialization; this in turn foresaw small and mid-sized industrial enterprises as societal groups contributing to the solution of the "social question". In the scope of co-operative endeavors as well as their practical realization, *Schulze-Delitzsch* deserves merit for having founded commercial credit co-operatives, which later became the Volksbanken, and commercial commodity co-operatives originally for craft trades and later for the retail sector. These were organizational forms which not only were propagated in Germany but which also quickly spread throughout all of Europe and later to all corners of the world.

Bibliography

Thorwart, F.: Herrmann Schulze-Delitzschs Schriften und Reden, Berlin 1910, 5 Bd..
Dülfer, Eberhard: Das Organisationskonzept "Genossenschaft" – eine Pionierleistung Schulze-Delitzschs, in: Deutscher Genossenschaftsverband (Schulze-Delitzsch) e.V.i.L. (Hrsg.): Schulze-Delitzsch – ein Lebenswerk für Generationen, Bonn 1987, pp. 59–126.

Security Mechanisms Within the Federal Association of German Co-operative Banks (BVR)

WOLFGANG GRÜGER [J]

(see also: *Co-operative Banks*; *Federations*; *Central Institutions*)

I. Historical Overview; II. Essential Characteristics of the Security Mechanisms of the BVR; III. Investigation of the Security Mechanisms; IV. Closing Comments.

The *Volksbanken* (urban credit unions) and the *Raiffeisenbanken* (rural co-operative banks) were the first credit institutions in Germany (→ *Co-operative Banks*) which introduced security mechanisms both in their own interest and in those of their customers. In this way, no depositor or customer of a credit co-operative has had to suffer a deficit or loss since the Great Depression and subsequent banking crisis in the 1930s; for approx. 60 years there has been no occasion in which a Volksbank or a Raiffeisenbank has not been able to fulfill its obligations (→ *Early Warning Systems*).

This 100% functioning ability of the banking security system can conclusively be traced back to the extremely positive development of the Volksbanken and Raiffeisenbanken in the last several decades. This is particularly true for growth in the amount of deposits, the number of members and in market share. At the end of the 1960s, deposits at all credit co-operatives amounted to a mere DM 15.6 billion, which corresponded to a market share of only 15.5%. By the end of 1984, deposits had risen to DM 318.7 billion, whereby the market share of credit co-operatives had climbed up to 27.3%. By 1989, deposits at the credit co-operatives amounted to DM 416 billion, and the market share lay at 26.8%. Development in membership levels likewise occured dramatically. In 1960, membership in the credit co-operatives amounted to 3.8 million members; by the end of 1989, credit co-operatives could count 11.3 million members. These figures provide unequivocal proof for the trust wide sectors of the population have in the soundness and solidarity of the co-operative banks.

I. Historical Overview

The Volksbanken and the Raiffeisenbanken each initially instituted separate security mechanisms on account of their independent historical developments.

1. Security Systems in the Volksbanken

a) In 1937, the Volksbanken decided to create a central security apparatus for the Volksbanken, namely the "Guaranty Fund for Credit Co-operatives". The purpose of this guaranty fund was to alleviate difficulties which occasionally occurred at the Volksbanken through rapid and hushed intervention, to prevent possible distrust from arising among customers, and to increase the security on deposits even further. The guaranty fund was maintained through contributions by the individual Volksbanken; in cases of need, it primarily provided cash grants to a Volksbank requiring assistance.

b) At the end of the 1960s, the discussion concerning deposit security was renewed as a result of certain incidents in the non-co-operative banking sectors; the Volksbanken likewise decided to base their security mechanism on a wider foundation. The "Guaranty Association of the German Volksbanken" thus came into being in 1969 as a complementary institution to the "Guaranty Fund of the Credit Co-operatives", which was endowed with cash means. The "Guaranty Association of the German Volksbanken" assumed the legal form of a registered association and was exclusively defined in its function to provide assistance in balancing the accounts of the banks in emergency situations through granting security or guarantees. Guaranty obligations assumed by the Volksbanken under special declarations to the association constituted the financial basis. According to the articles of association, upon the necessary utilization of such a security or guarantee the cash means provided by the "Guaranty Fund of the Credit Co-operatives" should initially be drawn on and not the liability volume provided by the Guaranty Association.

2. Security Mechanisms of the Raiffeisenbanken

a) In 1941, or four years after the Volksbanken had established the "Guaranty Fund for Credit Co-operatives", the Raiffeisenbanken founded the "Co-operative Assistance Fund". In contrast to the "Guaranty Fund of the Credit Co-operatives" of the Volksbanken, the "Co-operative Assistance Fund" also encompassed all Raiffeisen consumer co-operatives, Raiffeisen agricultural co-operatives and the central business offices in the Raiffeisen sector alongside the Raiffeisenbanken. With regard to the methods of raising cash means and decision making concerning the application of the monies, both funds were quite similar.

b) Under the influence of the discussion previously mentioned concerning deposit security which occured in 1969, the Raiffeisen organization likewise established a second security mechanism, the "Co-operative Guaranty Fund for Deposit Security". This security mechanism was organized similarly to that of the "Co-operative Assistance Fund" of the Raiffeisenbanken but served exclusively to provide security to the Raiffeisenbanken and not to the other Raiffeisen co-operatives.

3. The Joint Security Mechanisms of the BVR for both Volksbanken and Raiffeisenbanken

a) As the Volksbanken and Raiffeisenbanken had in the meantime amalgamated in the (newly formed) Bundesverband der Deutschen Volksbanken und Raiffeisenbanken e.V. (BVR, The Federal Association of German Co-operative Banks), the previous (four) security mechanisms of the Volksbanken and Raiffeisenbanken were brought under one roof in 1977, and the joint "Security Mechanism of the BVR" was created.

b) The security mechanism of the BVR has been newly restructured, a result of the practical experience gained in the subsequent years. The newly formed security mechanism has been in place since January 1, 1986. Its goal is to undertake everything necessary in the endeavor to prevent or reduce as far as possible eventual damages in advance. By determining a common "Code of Behavior", an information system, and an apparatus to undertake effective measures opportunely – even to the extent of excluding a bank from the security mechanism – the organization of credit co-operatives has provided itself with the opportunity to recognize negative developments at an early stage and to confront them in a more effective manner than before.

The Federal Court (among others) decided in its verdict of October 24, 1988 (published in "Wertpapier-Mitteilungen" 1989, 184) that the fundamental elements of the security mechanism of the BVR at hand must be anchored in the articles of association of the BVR. This subsequently occurred. During the extraordinary membership assembly on April 26, 1989, the appropriate resolutions to the articles of association were passed. The entry into the Register of Associations followed on September 12, 1989.

II. The Essential Characteristics of the Security Mechanisms of the BVR

1. Institutional Protection

The security measures of the BVR fundamentally provide comprehensive institutional protection for those co-operative banks which are affiliated in it. These include: Volksbanken, Raiffeisenbanken, savings and loan associations, church-affiliated credit co-operatives, Sparda-Banken, postal savings and loan associations, central co-operative banks, DG BANK, Deutsche Genossenschafts-Hypothekenbank AG, Münchener Hypothekenbank eG, Bausparkasse Schwäbisch Hall AG, etc. (→ *Classification*).

Fundamental, comprehensive banking protection itself can be waived in (extreme) exceptional situations. Therefore, the by-laws of the security measures of the BVR determine those balance sheet items which in any case always require minimum protection. These include in particular the deposits of non-bank customers and the debentures of co-operative banks in the hands of non-bank customers; the most important deposits are savings deposits, savings bonds, time deposits and demand deposits. Furthermore, the corresponding items in the balance are precisely identified in the procedure regulations in the by-laws of the security measures of the BVR. Likewise, those financial means are always protected which credit co-operatives have received external to the co-operative federation for publically supported purposes (such as from the Public Credit Institution for Reconstruction, Bank for the Equalization of Burdens, etc.).

No co-operative bank has legal claim to be assisted in situations of impending or existing economic hardship. Such a legal claim would imply that the corporate risks of a bank would be shifted to the security mechanism. If banks were granted a legal claim to assistance through the security mechanism, the security mechanism itself would be made into an insurance institution. In this case, all statutory conditions for insurance institutions and those subject to legal supervision must be fulfilled and observed; among other things, this would include matters of legal entity, strict equity requirements, high liquidity requirements, an extensive corporate organization, etc. Moreover, such corresponding insurance would be more expensive. Because of these same reasons, and in particular as the self-help structure of the associations can bear the costs of risk considerably more efficiently, all associations of the credit industry (therefore also the security systems of the private banking industry and the organization of savings banks) have precluded a legal claim to assistance. It should, however, be noted in this context that the security mechanisms of the Volksbanken and Raiffeisenbanken in practice are always employed in a manner to cover occurring losses.

2. Guaranty Fund and Guaranty Pool

The security mechanism of the BVR is comprised of a guaranty fund and a guaranty pool.

a) The Guaranty Fund

aa) Contribution System

The guaranty fund is essentially created through the dues raised among the co-operative banks. The amount of compulsory payment is calculated annually using a detailed basis of measurement and a set rate of imposition.

The basis of measurement comprises the risk-bearing assets. These were chosen rather than the deposits as the basis of measurement because the security mechanism of the BVR fundamentally provides extensive institutional protection, and the extent of risk is dependent on the volume of credits.

The base levy for the payment dues to the guaranty fund is $0.5^o/_{oo}$ of the risk-bearing assets. This rate can, however, be quadrupled; the highest annual levy can thus amount to $2^o/_{oo}$ of the risk-bearing assets.

ab) Administration of the Means in the Guaranty Fund

The Volksbanken and Raiffeisenbanken are not only members of the BVR but also of the co-operative auditing associations which are accordingly responsible for them. There are 14 such auditing association within the territory of the Federal Republic of Germany.

The auditing associations administer 90% of the levied dues of the guaranty fund raised from their appropriate member banks in a fiduciary manner for the BVR. The BVR administers 10% of the guaranty fund contributions from all Volksbanken and Raiffeisenbanken as well as those from the central co-operative banks. Furthermore, (the BVR) administers all guaranty fund contributions raised from the interregional institutions (e.g. DG BANK, Deutsche Genossenschafts-Hypothekenbank AG, Bausparkasse Schwäbisch Hall AG, etc.).

ac) Employment of the Means of the Guaranty Fund

In situations in which Volksbanken or Raiffeisenbanken require the assistance of the guaranty fund, the initial financial support would come from the guaranty fund administered by the appropriate co-operative auditing association.

Inasmuch as the means in the guaranty fund managed by the appropriate auditing association and those from a reasonably set special levy imposed on its member banks are not sufficient, the funds centrally administered by the BVR will be utilized. Furthermore, the reserves in the guaranty funds of the other auditing associations can be drawn on proportionally and in accordance with a determined procedure.

ad) Decisions Concerning the Utilization of the Guaranty Fund

The co-operative auditing association to which a needy Volksbank or Raiffeisenbank belongs is entrusted with the discretionary employment of the means in the guaranty fund up to an amount of DM 2 million for stabilization in individual cases.

If the amount of necessary support excedes DM 2 million and the appropriate co-operative auditing association has sufficient means in the fiduciary guaranty fund it administers, the board of the BVR decides based on the recommendation provided by the auditing association.

Inasmuch as the means in the fiduciary guaranty fund managed by the appropriate co-operative auditing association are insufficient, the board of the BVR decides on further security measures following approval from the administrative board of the BVR and two-thirds of the co-operative auditing associations.

ae) The Nature of the Security Measures Imposed on the Guaranty Fund

Means from the guaranty fund of the BVR can be utilized according to the nature and extent of the financial difficulties in the member banks as a tool to balance the accounts of the bank. These means can take the form of guarantees, assistance for liquidity or profitability, as interest bearing and non-interest bearing loans, or as cash grants.

b) Guaranty Pool

ba) Guaranty Obligations of the Co-operative Banks

The guaranty pool does not have cash means at its disposal, but rather a guaranty volume resulting from guaranty obligations each of the co-operative banks have assumed to a determined level with respect to the BVR through corresponding declarations.

bb) Administration of the Guaranty Volume

A (regional) guaranty volume results from the guaranty obligations of the corresponding member banks of a co-operative auditing association. This volume is managed in a fiduciary manner by the appropriate auditing association.
A (central) guaranty volume is formed at the BVR out of the guaranty obligations of the interregional institutions (e.g. DG BANK (→ *Central Institutions*), Deutsche Genossenschafts-Hypothekenbank AG, Bausparkasse Schwäbisch Hall AG (→ *Building and Loan Societies*), etc.).

bc) Utilization of the Guaranty Volume

If Volksbanken or Raiffeisenbanken require assistance from the guaranty pool, the guaranty volume administered by the responsible co-operative auditing association is appropriately engaged.
If interregional institutions require the assistance of the guaranty pool, the guaranty volume administered by the BVR is appropriately engaged.
An auditing association can assume guarantees or provide security (and thus encumbrance the guaranty pool) only to the extent of its (regional) guaranty volume. The BVR can assume guarantees or provide security to the encumbrance of the guaranty pool only to the extent of its (central) guaranty volume. Recourse on an interregional level thus cannot be affected within the guaranty pool in contrast to the guaranty fund.

bd) Decisions Concerning the Application of the Respective Guaranty Volume

The co-operative auditing association to whom a needy Volksbank or Raiffeisenbank belongs is entrusted with the discretionary employment of the respective (regional) guaranty volume up to a limit of DM 2 million for stabilization in individual cases. If the required amount for stabilization exceeds DM 2 million and if the guaranty volume administered by the auditing association is not exhausted, the board of the BVR is responsible for the decision based on the recommendation from the auditing association.
If an interregional institution requires assistance from the guaranty pool, the board of the BVR decides on intervention after receiving approval from the other interregional institutions.

be) The Nature of Involvement of the Guaranty Pool

Banks can be awarded guarantees or provided security (and thus encumbrance the guaranty pool) in order to balance their books. Such assistance is only then possible when it can be anticipated that the guaranty pool will be relieved of the responsibilities of the guaranty or security within five years based on careful analysis of the revenue development of the bank. If this precondition cannot be fulfilled the assistance of the guaranty pool may not be utilized, but rather that of the guaranty fund.

bf) The Utilization of a Guaranty or Security to the Encumbrance of the Guaranty Pool

It is assumed that the actual utilization of a guaranty or security to the encumbrance of the guaranty pool will not occur. Guarantees or the provision of security are ultimately only assumed when an anticipated exemption of the guaranty pool from the guaranty or security within five years can be determined upon careful assessment of the revenue development of the bank. If, however, the utilization of financial means remains necessary contrary to these expectations, the means of the guaranty fund are to be initially employed. The guaranty pool as an instrument in principle should not entail additional cash services. When the involvement of funds becomes necessary beyond the available means of the guaranty fund, the deficit amount must initially be distributed among the underwriting banks according to a previously determined procedure.

3. Banks and Obligatory Diligence

In order to avoid financial encumbrances within the mutual organization as far as possible, the co-operative banks have been entrusted with the responsiblity of acting with diligence. In this regard it must first be clearly stated that all business and related competitive activities which to a foreseeable degree involve normal and/or average credit risks to assets and liabilites should not be submitted to any sort of restriction. These business transactions, in accordance with the organizational structure and the membership ties within the co-operative banks, should predominately be concentrated on regular, local business sectors within the main office and branch locations of the bank, or in other words, on a surveyable territory of business. Alongside this fundamental predominate concentration of business activities, other substantiated, reasonable business relations beyond this sphere are possible. Practically every co-operative bank maintains such business activities to a more or less extensive degree based on the structure and geographic position of its regular business. Thus, meaningful business relations which have been developed over time, such as those with local residents who have moved to other localities or to regions bordering national frontiers, are not affected. Dynamic bank development on sound bases, e.g. business activity in sectors as of yet not sufficiently served by credit co-operatives, as well as normal financial transactions and guaranty provisions should likewise not be negatively influenced.

The following business practices are, however, as a rule incompatible with the objectives of the security mechanism: Not undertaking the prescribed necessary investigation of creditworthiness upon granting a credit, and failing to undertake the prescribed necessary observation throughout the duration of the credit; distributing credits in a poorly balanced manner; assuming guaranty obligations (security, guarantees, etc.) which exceede the limits determined in Art.13, Sec.4 of the Kreditwesengesetz (German Banking Code); raising money to execute transactions which otherwise would not be possible based on the relative size of the bank, etc.

By securing an obligation of the bank with regard to prudence and scrutiny (including intervention and sanctions as well), only those faulty developments among co-operative banks should be prohibited which could lead to the application of the security mechanisms of the BVR (grossly negligent infractions against the diligence obligation assumed by a conscientious co-operative bank manager, e.g. an unrestrained course of expansion, unstable growth, etc.).

4. Information System

In order to recognize damaging developments at a co-operative bank at an early stage and to be able to combat them, a comprehensive information system has been established. Local co-operative banks, DG BANK, the co-operative auditing associations and the BVR are all involved in it. Every time information is discovered or recognized which is or could be of importance to the security mechanism of the BVR, it should be handed over to the responsible post or department. This solely concerns information and instructions concerning the bank itself and not personal information about individual bank customers.

5. Preventative Measures

The BVR is empowered to order an audit at a co-operative bank after meeting with the appropriate auditing association which is responsible for the said bank and gaining approval from the administrative board of the BVR, in which the representatives of the credit co-operative have 50% of total voting authority. This does not, however, mean that the BVR itself can undertake such audits; the BVR cannot, as it has no right to audit. It is solely determined that the BVR is empowered to occasion such audits. The banks and the auditing associations must make audit reports available to the BVR upon its request.

The credit co-operatives are obligated to have their subsidiaries audited by the responsible auditing association or by an auditing office recommended by the auditing association.

Upon attaining agreement from the administrative board of the BVR and from the responsible auditing association, the BVR can investigate claims of a personal and/or material nature in order to avoid a possible utilization of the guaranty fund or the guaranty pool when the business activities of a bank exhibit an unrestrained course of expansion or unstable growth.

6. Demands of a Personal and/or Material Nature

If such business activities of a bank become apparent, the BVR or the responsible auditing association will meet with the board of the bank in order to discuss the entire problematic situation. If this is not sufficient to alter the business policy, the BVR or the responsible auditing association will turn to the supervisory board of the bank in order to energetically affects a change in the business policy of the board. If this likewise does not lead to a change in the course of the business policy, the BVR or the responsible auditing association will ultimately approach the general assembly/assembly of representatives.

Injunctions, either personal or material in nature, are regularly made in connection with concrete security measures to the encumbrance of the guaranty fund or the guaranty pool.

7. Expulsion from the Security Mechanisms of the BVR

A bank can be barred from the security mechanism of the BVR if it severely violates its own obligatory responsibilites to the apparatus.

III. Review of the Security Mechanisms

The administration of the means in the guaranty fund and in the guaranty volume are annually checked by the co-operative auditing associations and the BVR. The board of the BVR informs the administrative board of the BVR, the co-operative auditing associations and the Federal Banking Regulatory Board about the outcome of the investigation; the Federal Reserve Bank is likewise notified about the outcome.

IV. Closing Comments

The organization of co-operative banks has created the means to discover dangerous developments in individual member banks and combat them by defining the principles of behavior for the member banks, through the extensive information system it has developed, through the possibility of intervening in dangerous business activities of a bank, and through the regulation determining expulsion from the security mechanism. The legal and corporate-political autonomy of each co-operative bank – a fundament and typical characteristic of the German co-operative credit institution – thus remain preserved.

Bibliography

Kollbach, Walter: Sicherungseinrichtungen für Kreditgenossenschaften, in: Mändle, Eduard/Swoboda, Walter (eds.): Genossenschaftslexikon, Wiesbaden 1992, pp. 580–581.
Schmid, D.: Einlagensicherung im deutschen Kreditgewerbe, in: Sparkassenheft 60, Stuttgart 1977.
Schultze-Kimmle: Sicherungseinrichtungen gegen Eigenverluste bei deutschen Kreditgenossenschaften, in: Bankwirtschaftliche Studien, 4. Folge, Würzburg 1974.
Statut der Sicherungseinrichtung des Bundesverbandes der deutschen Volksbanken und Raiffeisenbanken e.V.

Selection of Members

JUHANI LAURINKARI

(see also: *Group, the Co-operative; Managerial Economics; Relationship Patterns; Structural Types*)

I. Membership Participation in Organizational Activities;
II. The Selection of Members to the Executive Body.

Co-operative activity according to its fundamental → *principles* must result from voluntary membership in the organization. Rather than representing a constraint or a qualification of this principle, the selection of members refers to the election and/or appointment of existent co-operative members to offices or functions within the co-operative organization which are vested with specific executive authorities.

I. Membership Participation in Organizational Activities

Activity in the executive body of a co-operative represents an integral element of inherent co-operative structure; as such it is a form of social participation and an expression of the exertion of power. A prerequisite for the selection of members, administrators and officials is active participation (→ *Relationship Patterns*). The criteria for selection decisively influence the activities of both members and officials as well as the orientation of the individual co-operative to the co-operative movement as a whole.

The selection process for members to assume executive reponsibilities can be viewed from a variety of angles. In the majority of cases, a descriptive model has been availed of for analysis. *Pestoff* (1979, p.60), for example, devised a model to evaluate membership participation within → *consumer co-operatives* in Sweden. *Pestoff* differentiated between organizational factors (type and structure of the co-operative) and factors on the individual level (socio-economic background and attitude/orientation to co-operative endeavors), both of which sway members to participate. Such factors likewise influence selectivity.

Of the factors stemming from the individual level, social background is certainly of considerable importance for selectivity. More extensive expectations are placed on individuals who enjoy a higher socio-economic standing and who choose to participate than on those persons with a lower socio-economic standing. People from a lower socio-economic background in general have relatively few opportunities to acquire necessary knowledge, much less be in the position to participate.

The term "social participation" is in itself insufficient; only when it is put in connection with human needs, the satisfaction of these needs and particular values does this term acquire fuller content (→ *Group, the Co-operative*). This concerns individual and social reasons behind motivation and subsequent behavior. According to *Maslow's* classification, activity as an inherent co-operative element (in the sense of social participation) is viewed in connection with individual needs, such as for esteem and self-realization (→ *Motives for Cooperation*).

Alderfedler (1969, p.145–147) in turn developed *Maslow's* classification of needs to a further extent. The term coined by him – "relatedness and growth needs" – can be seen in connection with work undertaken by organization officials. The "cycle" of influences and effects is accordingly a means to satisfy attachment needs. The satisfaction of growth needs likewise presupposes the opportunity to exercise decision-making authority. One qualification must, nonetheless, be drawn in this connection. Involvement as an official exemplifies only to a slight degree the opportunities to satisfy personal growth needs. An individual is driven to achieve what he alone desires (e.g. personal advantage), whereas participation in decision and policy-making authority on the other hand is extensively co-operative in nature (→ *Incentives*).

The correlation between social participation and values is quite complicated; the term "value" itself is quite difficult to precisely define and is closely re-

Individual factors:	– demographic factors	Attitude of the co-operative official to the co-operative system
	– socio-economic factors	
	– general level of participational activity	
	– motivation reasons behind co-operative attachment	
	– ties to the co-operative system	
	– co-operative participation	
Situational and Environmental factors:	– background influences (socialization)	
	– ties to neighborhood	
	– regional factors (local norms, etc.)	
Organizational factors:	– position in the organization; extent of trust, responsibility in the organizational body	
	– standing of organization in local eyes	

Figure 1: Factors influencing the attitude and orientation of co-operative officials to the co-operative system and its principles.

lated to the term "needs". Needs can be reflected in values and in that which one maintains to be valuable and desirable. Values (and evaluations) likewise must be seen in light of attitudes and opinions (→ *Ethics*).

In the figure above, the groups of factors in question are presented in a reduced form. Variables assumed as descriptive factors and their respective effects on and among each other are not addressed any closer at this point.

II. The Selection of Members to the Executive Body

The selection of members to serve on the executive body of the co-operative is influenced by various factors. Results from research on the subject indicate that three main influences are dominant in this situation: *individual factors*, *social milieu* and the *organization* itself.

A variety of factors affect the selectional decision for office holders in co-operatives (→ *Organizational Structure of Societies*). Such factors in turn have an

individual factors	situational and environmental factors	organizational factors
	Selection of Office Holders	

Figure 2: Basic Model for the Selection of Members to Executive Bodies.

influence on the actions and behavior of the elected officials themselves. As decision and policy makers for the co-operative, such officials directly determine the structure, development and orientation of the organization. It is therefore necessary to pinpoint how these mandataries view the principles of the co-operative system and how they invision the practical realization of these principles. Furthermore, it is important to analyze how such decision makers behave within the organization.

The components shaping the individual factors encompass social milieu, store of knowledge, attitudes/opinions (values), motives, personal conception and standpoint with regard to cooperation as well as personal self-conception. Social milieu, nonetheless, is the fundamental basis for all other such influencing factors.

Social Milieu
– Age, family standing, home, membership of parents in co-operative organizations, duration of personal membership
– Profession, education/training, income
– Other activities/involvement

Knowledge	Value	Attitude	Self-Conception
– general	system and	towards	
– co-op specific	motivation	cooperation	

Figure 3: Individual Factors.

Situational and environmental factors include mere coincidence, social contact to friends and colleagues at work, the constellation of competition among members as well as the selection process. The socialization process that takes place within the co-operative is not in itself a situational and environmental factor per se as it concerns a previously completed process.

Coincidence	Social Contact among friends and work colleagues	Constellation of competition among members	Selection process

Figure 4: Situational and Environmental Factors.

Furthermore, all-round cultural and social conditions also play a substantial role. The functions and goals pursued by the organization are of importance, but, nonetheless, vary considerably from country to country.

The third factor encompasses the organizational level. Components of this factor include the permanence of the organization and the need/quest for security. An organization which is sure in its ways and has acquired a secured standing within society is recognized in a better manner than one which has yet to define its functions and goals in a clear manner.

| Constellation of competition among various organizations | Importance of the organization seen from cultural perspective | Permanence of the organization | All-round-view of the organization |

Figure 5: Organizational Factors.

The fourth influential factor concerns the entire co-operative system. The greater the movement as a whole has been accepted by society, the greater the need or inclination of the individual to belong to this movement and its respective organizations.

Bibliography

Alderfelder, C.P.: Existence, Relatedness and Growth. Human Needs in Organizational Settings, New York 1972.
Laurinkari, Juhani (ed.): Genossenschaftswesen. Hand- und Lehrbuch, München/Wien 1990.
Milbrath, L.W.: Political Participation, Chicago 1966.
Pestoff, V.A.: Membership Participation in Swedish Consumer Co-operatives, Stockholm 1979.

Self-help Organizations and Third-World-Development

HERBERT KÖTTER

(see *also: Development Policy; Policies for Promotion; Officialization; Pre-co-operative Forms; Autochthonous Co-operatives*)

I. The Activation of Self-help-means and the Objective of Development Processes; II. Basic Characteristics of Self-help Organizations; III. Conditions for the Activation of Self-help Initiatives; IV. People's Organizations as Instruments of Building up Countervailing and Bargaining Power; V. Informal and Formal Self-help Groups; VI. Basic Structural and Functional Problems of Self-help Organizations; VII. Some Characteristics of Self-help Organizations in the Third World; VIII. Transfer of Organizational Models – an Unsettled Question; IX. Promotion of Self-help Inititatives and Corresponding Organizations.

I. The Activation of Self-help-means and the Objective of Development Processes

1. Introductory Remarks

The following analysis concentrates primarily on the role of self-help organizations (SHO's), particularly in the development of the Third World. There, development primarily means the reduction of material and immaterial poverty of broad masses of the population. This poverty is only partly due to the scarcity of natural and human resources. To a considerable extent, these scarcities are "man-made". Political and institutional deficits within developing societies as well as deficits due to relations with other social systems are responsible for a still ongoing process of pauperization and marginalization. Marginalization means that the dominant strata not only exploit the poorer strata but push them more and more to the fringes of the society and economy.

The activation of self-help among the marginal groups seems to be a promising strategy to stop this process of alienations. Such strategy has to take into account the "law of interdependence of orders" (*Küng*, p.60). There do exist close relations between political, socio-cultural, and economic elements within a social system, which must be changed pari passu if substantial development and demarginalization is to take place (→ *Economic Order*).

The socio-economic potential of the marginal groups can be activated by building appropriate people's organizations (→ *Societal Form, Co-operative*). However, this requires considerable institutional changes and a certain redistribution of power and influence. The institutional pattern of socio-political systems in many developing countries still discriminates against the poorer strata. If the poor want to change their situation they have to develop inititatives of self-help and self-reliance, since the ruling "élites" do not offer adequate solutions for the problems of the marginal groups.

2. Some Definitory Observations

In current literature, the term "self-help" in its broadest sense is used for actions taken by individuals and small groups to solve problems by their own efforts, problems which are not taken care of by higher levels of the social system. The endeavour to implement goals for himself by himself or in solidarity with members of primary groups like family or neighborhood seems to be a basic pattern of human behaviour. The aim to change the material situation, sometimes just to survive, certainly plays a primary role. Self-help, however, at the same time by its very nature aims to change socio-political and institutional patterns of a system which discriminates against specific groups (→ *Informal Co-operatives*). The promotion of and the assistance for self-help groups can be looked upon as a strategy of de-marginalization. The development of self-reliance within these groups provokes and strengthens feelings of self-esteem, belongingness, participation, and mutual acknowledgement, as important for socio-economic progress as technical innovations.

In principle, we can distinguish between *indiviual* self-help and self-help approaches in more or less organized *groups*. Individual self-help is oriented towards the improvement of the situation of a person and his closest companions as, f.i., the family. The possibilities of individual self-help are restricted, since the individuals and primary groups usually are not in the position to change the institutional pattern in favour of their own, as f.i. the system of property rights, the access to productive resources, to education and training, political participation and social security. Marginalization is just another expression for the fact that the dominant strata impede the poorer groups to make use of productive resources in their own interest as well as the appropriate usufruct of their own efforts. Only larger self-help organizations have a chance to exert some political influence at different levels, since they, as a rule, can function as a pressure group.

The distinction between self-help organizations with primarily economic aims and others with primarily socio-political ones is somewhat artificial, at least for the real situation in most developing countries. The interdependency of economic and political elements can be characterized by a somewhat simplistic formular. Without a "critical minimum" of socio-political change, self-help organizations are in danger to be "nipped in the bud". Without a minimum of economic efficiency, self-help organizations will hardly be able to articulate and defend their proper interests effectively against the so-called "vested interest" of the dominant strata.

II. Basic Characteristics of Self-help Organizations

SHO's should more or less fulfill the following requirements:

- relatively similar socio-economic positions of the members
  Experience has shown that, at least in the long run, co-operative societies with a socially and economically differentiated membership are not likely to work successfully.
- voluntariness and spontaneity of cooperation
  Establishing SHO's from above or from outside is a contradiction in itself. This, however, does not exclude any promotion from the government or other sponsors.
- co-ordination of individual and group interests and equal rights of cooperation
  The voting system should give every member the opportunity to participate. While members must be able to pursuit their own interest, the principle of cooperation curtails the leeway of individual decision-making. The higher the identity of interests among the members, the more do individual and group interests coincide (*Benecke*, p. 70ff.).
- self-government and participation of members in group decisions and control of management
  Very often, the relations between members and leaders are a crucial problem.
- contribution to group activities and loyalty to the group even in difficult situations
  The "fellow-traveller" (free rider), e.g. the member only looking for advantages without making any own efforts, is not a rare phenomenon.
- appropriate sharing of positive and negative results of group activities

It goes without saying that members must get their proper share. Otherwise, the incentive for cooperation will vanish. The principle of solidarity requires, however, that members are prepared to also carry their fair share of losses and failures.

The importance of effective organizations for the process of "demarginalization" and the formation of a more egalitarian society can hardly be overestimated. A lot of efforts in "institution-building" have been made. The reason that they often failed is that politicians, planners, and other experts did overlook that in the respective societies some of the basic conditions mentioned above were not given. It was not recognized clearly enough that the realization of self-help only partly is a technical and organizational problem. A process of "conscientization" within the different strata of a society is a precondition for institutional change and problem awareness as a basis for self-help activities.

The following quotation from a workshop of the Friedrich-Ebert-Stiftung in 1973 is typical of the situation, which has not changed very much since then. It was recommended "to organize the weak people into groups and institutions through which they could better protect their rights and privileges" (F.E.S., passim). It sounds almost ironical, when at another meeting of the F.E.S., together with FAO and ILO, the following famous vicious circle with regard to peasant organizations was discovered. "The peasants can only be persuaded to join and support an organization, which produces tangible results, but an organization can only produce tangible results if peasants have already joined and supported them" (F.E.S., p.115). To wait for tangible results before joining an organization is absolutely contradictory to the idea of self-help.

III. Conditions for the Activation of Self-help Initiatives

In any case, self-help requires a certain freedom for individuals and groups in decision-making and taking

action. This freedom can be restricted in different ways:
- The social system as a whole and its institutional arrangements may block efforts of self-help, particularly of the lower strata, completely.
- In spite of existing formal regulations, the freedom of action may be curtailed by the existing power structure on the different levels (state down to smaller communities).
- It is also possible that the internalization of traditional patterns by the poor prevents them to make use of an actually existing freedom for self-help initiatives.

This divergency between formally existing and even codified rights and the real distribution of social power is often neglected. That marginal groups are mentally not prepared for self-reliance and self-responsibility, is one to the fact that they often do not seriously put in question the old traditional system of power distribution, the feeling of running a great social risk prevents them to fight effectively for the improvement of their situation. Paternalistic attitudes of members of the establishment vis-à-vis the poor – even with orginally benevolent intentions – are also counterproductive to self-reliance.

The guarantee of freedom of coalition and organization is a conditio sine qua non for the unfolding of proper initiatives (*Wissenschaftlicher Beirat*).

The organization of self-help groups of the marginal population is confronted with internal and external problems. Internal problems are caused by the institutional and organizational pattern of the respective social systems. In this context, the Rural Workers' Organization Convention adopted by the International Labour Conference 1975 should be mentioned. It explicitly states that it "shall be an object of national policy ... to facilitate the establishment and growth, on a voluntary basis, of strong and independent organizations

- continuous in existence;
- democratically controlled;
- reliant on its own resources;
- free from patronage or external influence" (ILO, p.21).

Internal obstacles result from different facts:

- The marginal population is, as already has been indicated above, by no means a homogenous mass. There do exist considerable divergencies of interests and even conflict potentials. Hence, it is difficult to establish the so-called "identity criterion", something absolutely vital for the functioning of an organization of this kind (*Benecke*, p. 71).
- There is a scarcity of autochthonous leaders coming out of the groups themselves. Hence, many organizations rely on leadership and management from outside -a fact at least problematical for the idea of genuine self-help.
- It is extremly difficult to set up self-help groups which are able to extend their influence beyond the local level, so as to fulfill the function of a pressure group.

In this context, the problem of the appropriate size of groups has to be discussed shortly. Under the assumption that self-help groups, as a rule, have a dual function as an economic venture and as a pressure group, the appropriate size depends on the specific aims and the overall socio-political situation. If the group does not exceed a certain size, it can hardly exert any political influence. If it becomes too large, the necessary identity of interests and the personal relations may suffer. Participation and control will become less effective (*Olson*, passim). The way out of this dilemma is to create organizations on the district and even the state level, where the membership consists of locally organized groups.

In many developing countries, however, governements have a tendency to directly or indirectly control organizations which go beyond the village level by appointing the management or influencing election of the leaders in an open or clandestine way. Organizations at the national level very often are "puppets on the string" of the ruling establishment (→ *Officialization*).

IV. People's Organizations as Instruments of Building up Countervailing and Bargaining Power

Any differentiated and pluralistic society produces organizations which try to articulate and defend the interests of specific groups. The state or the government is supposed to act as an "honest broker" between the various interests, without endangering the autonomy of their organizations. However, there exists an inherent tendency with some groupings to wield such an enormous power that they cannot only suppress the interests of conflicting groups but creep into the government structures itself and divert their activities in their own favour (→ *State and Co-operatives, Market Economy*).

Somewhat simplified, one can state that the power of an organization depends on the following elements:
- the extent to which it controls economic resources within the relevant system of property rights;
- its numerical strength, particularly in a parliamentary democracy, where market power to a certain degree can be compensated by organizational power;
- its affiliation with the ruling political powers;
- its specific position and function in economy and society;
- the strength of countervailing power represented by other organizations (*Kötter* 1977).

Measured by this yardstick, the reasons for the weakness of marginal groups organizations become quite evident. They do not have substantial control over economic resources within the prevailing system of property rights. Numerical strength may be high in some cases. But this can provide real political power only under conditions of unmanipulated votings. The identity of interests in larger groups is not only low, but sometimes conflicts will prevail. The marginal groups do not execute a specific function, particularly valued by the societies.

Finally, marginality is just another expression for the fact that there is little or no affinity with the ruling establishment. The social system as a whole and the political climate do not offer the necessary incentives for self-help-acitivities. Moreover, in practice they turn out to be real obstacles for self-reliance. In the long run, self-help strategies will only have lasting success if pari passu institutional change is going to take place. If this is not the case, a considerable revolutionary potential will be built up, especially if the society approaches the two-class-model and the marginal groups are going to form the larger part of it. In view of the extremely high social costs connected with such processes together with the empirical fact that up to now so-called revolutions for the marginalized groups have resulted "in a change of master than in wider economic and political freedom", an evolutionary development seems more appropriate to improve the lot of the poor (*Bavin*, p.186). In some societies, there are possibilities to use already existing formal rights more intensively to foster the development of self-help-organizations (*Wissenschaftlicher Beirat*).

V. Informal and Formal Self-help Groups

Informal groups have a spontaneous and fluctuating character (→ *Informal Co-operatives*). They come into existence very often to tackle with a quite specific problem and may dissolve after some time. Face-to-face relations and a solidarity based on close personal relations as f.i. kinship, neighbourhood, or patron-client-relations play a very important role. In the true sense of the term, these groupings cannot be called organizations because they lack continuity and formal rules.

It is difficult to assess and categorize the manyfold groupings. It would be wrong and even destroy their very essence, if authorities tried to "formalize" them. On the other hand, it is obvious that such groupings will exert only a very restricted influence on institutional change. They often function within the pattern of traditional social structures which may impede a comprehensive development (→ *Autochthonous Co-operatives*).

In the first line, formal organizations can be distinguished from informal ones by the fact that rights and duties of members are fixed in "statutes". As a rule, there must exist a legal basis for their foundation and their field of activities. Insofar they are intermingled with the social system, at the same time making it more difficult and easier to influence the societal frame conditions.

In current literature, the problem of classification and categorization of organizations has been dealt with by quite a number of authors (*Dülfer, Münkner*).

VI. Basic Structural and Functional Problems of Self-help Organizations

Nowadays, lots of studies are available dealing with the "rise and decline" of self-help-organizations in many countries and societies. It has become clear that the one-sided approach to development in the technical and economic sector has not been extremely successful with regard to demarginalization. On the contrary, this approach in a number of cases has widened the gaps between the different sectors of societies. It is at least questionable whether the efforts from many sides to build up organizations have always fostered the idea of self-help. Busy "institution builders" had a tendency to overlook the fact that the philosophy of self-help really has to come from the grassroots. That does not exclude any assistance from outside. But this assistance must be adapted and modified according to the relevant elements of different social systems (→ *Policies for Promotion*).

As a matter of fact, an amazing number of "institutions" and "organizations" has been established all over the Third World. With few exceptions it can be stated that

- these "new institutions" have been mainly superimposed from above without sufficient initiative or even echo from the grassroot level;
- patterns imported from abroad – mainly from developed societies (capitalist or socialist alike) – have been transplanted more or less unrevised;
- even with originally benevolent intentions, these imported patterns have shown a tendency to transpose into instruments of the ruling "elites" and quasi "self-service shops" of the richer part of the populations;
- the euphoria of institution-building has led to the establishment of too many organizations, thereby generating an unnecessary competition and a waste of personnel and funds (*Kötter* 1978).

Many organizations came down to the poor as a kind of gift from above, that is they did not require substantial efforts or sacrifices from the poor themselves. This has led to a considerable erosion of the idea of self-reliance. Institution building from outside, very popular with development experts for some time, is confronted with a basic dilemma. Organizations are built up to act as change agencies. This will work only if the ideology and the structure of such organizations are not to remote from the social reality they try to change. To give an example, it will be very unlikely that a co-operative society based on the "one man-one vote" principle will function properly, if peasants and landlords are grouped together in the same organizations.

The resistance of marginal groups to join such organizations may even be an indicator of their specific rationality. Due to their background, outsiders and bureaucrats have certain difficulties to identify the complicated network of motives, aspirations, and the resulting economic and social behavior of marginalized people. A constant and open dialogue between experts and groups will promote more self-reliance and the feeling of relevance among marginalized people.

How participation, a basic element of self-help, can materialize, depends very much on the character of the social system within which it is supposed to function. Self-help in its broadest sense has a tradition in many societies (→ *Autochthonous Co-operatives*). Such self-help groups were of compulsory character, e.g. he or she became group member with fixed rights and duties (automatically) if, e.g., a person belonged to a family, clan or caste or did reside in a specific location. What distinguishes such traditional institutions from modern ones is this kind of compulsory membership together with a type of leadership and distribution of duties being based on the principle of inequality. These essential differences make it very difficult to use traditional forms as a basis for building up participatory organizations. Participation in the modern sense is an institution, rather alien to hierarchical forms of social organization still prevailing in many developing countries. Participation as the devolution of responsibilities to the most appropriate level may turn traditional social systems upside down. Participation also means to do away with paternalistic concepts of development such as institutional change planned and guided from above (*Blase*). Within the framework of a participatory strategy, even development experts themselves will have to reformulate their own role.

Participation does not mean that everybody can have a say in everything. To contribute to genuine development it must follow the principle of "subsidiarity" (→ *Subsidiarity Principle*) or "devolution". What can be decided at a lower level should be handled there without interference from the higher level. The lower level, however, remains part of the national and sometimes even of the international system. Self-help groups in their function as pressure groups will find themselves in an ambivalent situation. It is their legitimate intention and task to fight for the interests of their group members, their community or village. But, at the same time, the principle of solidarity requires a reconciliation of local initiatives with national strategies. Participation, if interpreted properly, cannot mean simple harmonization. Since interest conflicts will exist always and everywhere, democratic participation in the first line aims at a fair and rational solution of such conflicts. The question to be carefully studied always remains what kind of participation is possible and appropriate in different socio-economic, cultural, and political circumstances. It appears quite promising to distinguish between subject matter related and interest related competencies (*Fürstenberg*).

VII. Some Characteristics of Self-help Organizations in the Third World

It may be useful, however, to describe rather shortly some existing SHO's with regards to their specific problems and goal attainment. We will discuss

- co-operatives,
- people's organizations like small craftsmen and peasant federations,
- trade unions.

Co-operatives are by far the most common organizations to be found in developing countries. Without doubt, they have contributed a lot to economic development. There was a time when governments tried to introduce co-operatives as quickly as possible, while the population was hardly prepared to understand and to deal with co-operative ideas. This has led to an early "officialization" which, to some extent, has eroded the self-help character of co-operatives.

Federations and associations of the poorer strata rather seldom have come to life spontaneously. Very often, socially-minded members of an urban intelligentsia were founders and promoters of such organizations supposed to act primarily as pressure groups. Since these organizations often have difficulties to liberate themselves from paternalism so problematical for self-reliance, authochthonous leadership is rare. Moreover, such associations have often been suspected by governments to be "subversive."

→ *Trade Unions* are typical phenomena of industrial societies, which came into being under conditions hardly present today in developing countries. The organization of trade unions is difficult for a number of reasons, the most important of which are the absence of solidarity among the workers population and the tough competition for jobs. Shortage of labour and the complete lack of a "social net" for the unemployed force the unions to accept more or less any working conditions. Despite the facts given above, trade unions have been very effective in some instances as regards the initiation of a "conscientization process".

VIII. Transfer of Organizational Models – an Unsettled Question

The uncritical transfer of organizational models for SHO's originally elaborated in a completely different socio-cultural and political setting has not seldom proved to be counterproductive in another "ambiente".

Meanwhile, one has become aware that an indifferentiated transfer of production technologies can do a lot of damage. Only recently, one can observe a growing awareness, that the transplantation of organizational patterns from one social system into another requires utter prudence (→ *Development Policy*). The lesson to be learnt is that, if specific development aims are to be attained, the social system, production technologies, and organizational patterns must form a balanced whole.

The foregoing statement does not mean that, in the field of institution building, any help from outside should be stopped. Measures to activate self-help must keep a delicate balance between adaptation to the existing reality as the basis for action and the piece-meal approach to necessary changes.

Failures can discredit the self-help approach. Hence, compromises are necessary to step by step improve the situation in an evolutionary way.

IX. Promotion of Self-help Initiatives and Corresponding Organizations

1. The Role of Government

In theory and practice, the role of government and state in the promotion of self-help is intensively discussed. It has been mentioned above that self-help activities require a better access of the "have nots" to productive chances and services. This normally implies redistribution processes at the expense of the "happy few". From this point of view, one can logically deduct the role of government. Activation of self-help initiatives primarily is a political problem. As already mentioned, the first task of government is to provide conditions without which self-help will not produce lasting results. Under the prevailing circumstances, governments have to defend these changes against "vested interests". Hence, for the starting period, the state has to give assistance and protection to the rather fragile new organizations. For the design of the government strategy two conditions are vital:

- The state should withdraw as soon possible.
- The promotion should be implemented in such a way as not to kill the impetus for own efforts of individuals and groups.

The following phenomena appear to be particularly problematic for the relations of governments and self-help organizations:

- The tendency of bureaucracy not to withdraw after a period of required assistance and to neglect consciously the formation of self-management. This "officialization" easily leads to an erosion of the self-help-idea.
- The not uncommon tendency of politicians to divert SHO's into instruments for political power and to use them for objectives alien to the nature of self-help bodies.
- The fact that opportunities to establish SHO's provided by the government are not or not sufficiently made use of by the marginal groups (see *Baldus et al.*).

2. Self-help Organizations and International Development Cooperation

Self-help initiatives must be born and develop within a social system, that is they cannot be superimposed from outside. Again: without the existence or creation of a favorable political climate, self-help efforts are doomed to fail sooner or later. An essential element of an outside assistance is a "policy-dialogue". Such a dialogue should be oriented not only towards discussion of specific conditions for further technical assistance. Moreover, it should try to convince the ruling strata that in the long run institutional change is in their own interest and the interest of the whole society. The opening and pursuing of such a dialogue on a government level primarily is the task of development bodies of the state. But with their respective counterpart, however, NGO's, too, can play a very important role in this dialogue (→ *United Nations System*).

Bibliography

Baldus, Rolf, Hanel, Alfred, Münkner, Hans-H. eds.: Government Promotion of Cooperatives and Other Self-Help Organizations for Rural Development, Seminar Report, German Foundation for International Development, Berlin 1980.

Baldus, Rolf, Kohlbach, Carl, Ullrich, Gabriele: Selbsthilfe in der ländlichen Entwicklung, Fachseminar DSE–GTZ, Feldafing 1983.

Baldus, Rolf: Zur operationalen Effizienz der Ujama Kooperative Tansanias. Marburger Schriften zum Genossenschaftswesen, Reihe B. Bd. 13, hrsg. von E. Dülfer, Göttingen 1976.

Bavin, T.S.: Trade Union Oriented Type of Organization, in: Friedirch-Ebert-Stiftung op. cit., Bangkok 1974.

Bédard, G. ed.: Saving and credit as instruments of self-reliant development of the poor. International Workshop, German Foundation for International Development, Feldafing 1988.

Benecke, Dieter: Cooperation and Development, Tübingen 1972.

Blase, M.G.: Institution Building, in: A Source book. Agency For International Development AIW, Michigan 1979.

Bundesminister für Wirtschaftliche Zusammenarbeit: Grundsätze für die Förderung von Selbsthilfeorganisationen in Entwicklungsländern, Bonn 1977.

Castillo, Gelia T.: How participatory is participatory development. Some lessons from the Philippine Experiences. Studien zur Integrierten ländlichen Entwicklung, Heft 14, Hamburg 1985.

Dülfer, Eberhard: Guide to evaluation of cooperative organizations in developing countries. FAO, Rome 1982.

FAO: World Conference on Agrarian Reform and Rural

Development. Declaration of Principles and Programme of Action, Rome 1979.
Friedrich-Ebert-Stiftung (F.E.S.): Workshop, Series Report V. Organization of peasants in Asia, Bangkok 1974.
Fürstenberg, Friedrich: Probleme der Mitgliederpartizipation auf verschiedenen Entwicklungsstufen, in: Die Genossenschaften zwischen Mitgliederpartizipation und Bürokratietendenz. Arbeitsergebnisse der X. Internationalen genossenschaftswissenschaftlichen Tagung 1981 in Marburg/Lahn,, hrsg. von Eberhard Dülfer und Walter Hamm, Göttingen 1983, pp. 104–116.
Hoselitz, Bert F.: Sozialer Wandel in unterentwickelten Ländern, Handbuch der empirischen Sozialforschung, hrsg. von R. König, 2. Aufl., Bd. 8, Stuttgart 1977.
International Labour Office (ILO): The challenge of employment, Genèva 1988.
Kirsch, Ottfried: Selbsthilfe und Selbsthilfeorganisationen, in: Gans, O. und Evers, I., (eds.): Handbuch der volkswirtschaftlichen Beratung, Baden-Baden 1988.
Kötter, Herbert: Institutions and Organizations in Rural Development, in: Zeitschrift für Ausländische Landwirtschaft, 1988.
Kötter, Herbert: Involvement of the rural poor – A key factor in development. The present and future role of institutions and organizatons. Rural Aisa-challenge and opportunity. Supplement IV, Asian development bank, Singapore 1977.
Küng, E.: Entwicklungsländer, Entwicklungsprobleme, Entwicklungspolitik. St. Gallen Wirtschaftswissenschaftliche Forschungen, Bd. 34, Tübingen 1983.
Mayntz, Reante und Ziegler, Rolf: Soziologie der Organisation. Handbuch der empirischen Sozialforschung, hrsg. von R. König, Zweiter Band, Stuttgart 1969.
Moore, W.E.: Der soziale Rahmen der ökonomischen Entwicklung. Soziologie der Entwicklungsländer, hrsg. von G. Eisermann, Stuttgart 1968.
Müller, Julius O.: Gesellschaftspolitische Konzeptionen der Förderung von Selbsthilfe durch Fremdhilfe in Afrika, Institut für Kooperation in Entwicklungsländern, Marburg 1981.
Obaidullah Khan, A.Z. and Hexner, Thomas: Poverty oriented rural development and the UN-System: A turning point, Working document for the AAC, UNDP, New York 1976.
Olson jr. Mancur: Die Logik des kollektiven Handelns. Die Einheit der Gesellschaftswissenschaften, hrsg. von E. Boettcher, Band 10, Tübingen 1968.
Rahman, A.: Participatory Organisations of the Rural Poor. – Introduction to an ILO-Programme, Genèva 1984.
Ruttan, V.: Induced Institutional Change, in: Binswanger, H.P., and Ruttan, V. (eds.): Indused Innovation, London 1978.
Schultz, T.W.: Noble Lecture: The Economics of the poor. Journal of Political Economy, Vol. 4, 1980.
Wissenschaftlicher Beirat beim Bundesminister für Internationale Zusammenarbeit: Möglichkeiten und Grenzen der Selbsthilfe im Rahmen einer armutsorientierten Entwicklungspolitik, Bonn 1989.
Wörz, Johannes, (ed.): Kooperation als Instrument der Agrarentwicklung in der Dritten Welt. Vorträge der Witzenhäuser Hochschulwoche 1981. Der Tropenlandwirt. Zeitschrift für Landwirtschaft in den Tropen und Subtropen, Beiheft 14, Witzenhausen 1981.

Social Policy and Co-operative System

VESA LAAKKONEN / JUHANI LAURINKARI

(see also: *Economic Order*; *Economie Sociale*; *State and Co-operatives*, *Market Economy*)

I. The Co-operative System as Social-Economic Activity; II. The Co-operative as a Guarantor of Economic Livelihood and Provider for the Prosperity of its Members; III. The Social-Political Character of the Principles of the Co-operative System; IV. The Co-operative System as a Factor of Social Policy.

I. The Co-operative System as Social-Economic Activity

For those members joined together in a co-operative, co-operative activity is one means of attempting to secure the satisfaction of their own economic needs, be they in production or in consumption. Co-operative activity is economic cooperation; it is a form of social-economic activity, and the co-operative is a company form based on the concept of cooperation. A co-operative is characterized as a community whose level of membership and capital cannot be determined in advance. It is likewise a corporate body which strives to carry out economic activity collectively, that is, according to the principle of member participation. This thus makes the co-operative a "social company", which is characterized by its community-like association of individuals.

In order to understand co-operatives and the co-operative system as a whole as a "social company", one must realize that co-operative activity is often the means used to organize the economy (both in production and consumption) for the middle class spectrum of the population which is less well-off. Its creation and development perfectly fit into to the history of social policy. Many idealists and revisionists have found their place in the history of co-operative science (→ *Theory of Co-operatives*; → *Theory of co-operative Cooperation*) as well as in the history of social policy.

The policy of open membership illustrates the social character of the co-operative system. The business side of the co-operative appropriately shows its economic character. The double character of the co-operative movement is, on the one hand, based on its economic character and, on the other hand, on its social nature (→ *Dual Nature*). In this regard, some people refer to the business (economic) and to the ideal (social) sides of the co-operative.

II. The Co-operative as a Guarantor of Economic Livelihood and Provider for the Prosperity of its Members

The fundamental task of the co-operative is to secure the attainability of necessary → *goods*, services, and commodities as comprehensively and favorably priced as possible. For of this reason, it is difficult for members to realize the importance the co-operative has for them in times of prevailing abundance.

After the supply or attainability of goods has been secured, the co-operative movement is interested in the conditions under which this may happen. In order to provide their members with the greatest possible utility (→ *Promotion Mandate*), the co-operatives have begun to offer their members and customers services, for example the collection of agricultural products, which are produced by such members. The history of the co-operative system (→ *History in 19th C.*) provides many examples of how the establishment of a co-operative decisively improved members' ability to obtain needed goods at favorable prices, and thus how it influenced the prosperity of its membership. This is where its goal orientation overlaps that of social policy.

By improving living conditions and general security – particularly of the less fortunate population groups – social policy, in accordance with egalitarian fundamentals, endeavors to secure an appropriate standard of living for the population. Living standard herewith also includes populations' opportunity to satisfy needs other than only material ones.

This all is in close association with the political character of the co-operative system concerning prosperity. The co-operative system aims at convincing its members to trust their own initiative and strength; added to this is the creation of necessary economic preconditions for improving living conditions. Co-operative activity offers help during the adjustment to changed or changing circumstances. In Finland, one example of this was the support for relocated persons, former soldiers from the front, orphans and widows due to the War. The contribution of the co-operative sector limited itself primarily to the realization of loan allocations for home construction from state revenues; this was primarily lead by the Organization of Co-operative Savings Banks as the other groups of money institutes in the country refused to undertake this task under the same conditions. At any rate, the success of the Organization of Co-operative Savings Banks in Finland in the years after World War II can be traced back to this in part.

Several important researchers of the co-operative movement have also emphasized the partial overlapping of the co-operative system and social policy. At this point, one may mention *Charles Gide* and his work *Les sociétés coopératives de consommation* (1904), *Paul Lambert, La doctrine coopérative* (1959), *Gerhard Albrecht, Die soziale Funktion des Genossenschaftswesens* (1965), and *Georg Davidovic, Towards a Co-operative World: economically, socially and politically* (1967) (→ *Conceptions, Co-operative*).

III. The Social-Political Character of the Principles of the Co-operative System

Along with industrialization in the 19th century, artisans and other small entrepreneurs lost their freedom of self-employment. Company owners or capital investors were able to reap the results of their work. The founders of the co-operatives gathered their money together, generally in small share investments as co-operative capital; with this capital they commenced their business activity. In order to prevent the co-operative from falling into obligation to outside forces and to safeguard its economic independence, they were forced to work with their own money. Since the range of their activity has become much more comprehensive, most of the co-operative organizations have given up this principle today. On the other hand, the co-operatives still maintain the principle of setting non-variable interest rates in advance (→ *Principles*).

In the first years of the co-operative movement, it was not even allowed to sell or transfer one person more than a certain number of shares. It was feared that the solvency of the → *consumer co-operative* could be weakenend when a member who held multiple shares withdrew his membership and received his paid-up shares back. Financially speaking, it was not worth it for anyone to become a member simply because there might be chances to get some shares of the potential revenue resulting from the capital share investment. The priority task of the co-operative is to provide goods and services which the members require to keep their households or to run their enterprises. By providing these goods and services, the co-operative thus satisfies the needs of its members and customers. The more needs the members can have satisfied through the help of their co-operative and the better the method by which this occurs, the higher their living standard.

Today, the co-operative principle that the co-operative may only sell genuine goods and offer customers "the correct amount and weight", might seem completely natural in the so-called developed countries, but that has not always been the case (→ *Principles*). In the formative years of the co-operative movement, the state did not oversee trade sales and did not intervene against the various abuses in this field, exactly as today (in the 1990s) is the case in many developing countries. Co-operatives, particularly consumer co-operatives, put emphasis on the importance of correct and genuine goods. In as much as they closely stuck to the principle of selling non-manipulated goods, the co-operatives practised what in today's language is called "consumer protection". In many developing countries, co-operative organizations must still undertake pioneer work in this respect (→ *Policies for Promotion*). Many experts active in developing countries have determined rampant corruption in the fields of sales and distribution.

It is also possible that in these countries administrative officials could be responsible for such abuse (→ Officialization).

These efforts continue to be pursued in the sense that co-operative organizations demanded and realized the first product analyses, quality control mechanisms, and the introduction of commodity declarations. In the effort to satisfy the needs of their members and customers as best as possible, many co-operative organizations guarantee buyers free exchange or return policies even for goods which, in effect, are not defective.

In the beginning years of the co-operative movement, credit purchases were very common; even though no real credit market existed at that time, necessary production goods were bought on credit as were even consumer goods. The co-operatives, particularly the → consumer co-operatives, attempted to convince their members of the dangers of trade on credit. Many people fell victim to obligations and simultaneously developed a relationship of dependency with regard to their merchants or employers. These debts often were based simply on oral agreements, the conditions were predominantly determined by the lenders, interest payments could be disproportionately high, and the debtors were mostly ignorant of their rights. The result of this scenario was that, when a credit was called in, large amounts of property could be transferred to the creditor on account of minimal debts. Even today, this situation characterizes one of the most crucial problems in developing countries (→ Development Policy).

The requirement to settle accounts with cash sales and the emphasis on the destructiveness of trade on credit were aiming at raising the level of economic autonomy and self-employment among the members and, thus, were aiming at improving their standard of living, particularly when the latter, with regard to the population as a whole, was quite low.

Of the co-operative principles the observation of the "daily market price" is the one most affiliated with the practical operation. Suffering from a shortage of capital, the co-operative often never had the opportunity to enter into price competition, and its employees were not able to avail themselves of the proper preconditions to pursue pricing on their own (→ Competition). When the co-operative offered its members and customers goods at the "daily market price", or at the same price (→ Pricing Policy) other trading companies demanded, either surpluses or savings resulted. Through this conduct, the consumer co-operatives were able to show their members and customers that the "daily market prices" were high. According to how strong they were able to become in one country and which market share they attained with a certain good – at least 15–20% – the co-operative organizations were then able to undertake an active pricing policy. An active → pricing policy means that the co-operative organizations can begin to offer goods and services more favorably than their competitors, initially solely to their members and, later on, also to other customers. This often forces the competitors to follow the example of the co-operative organization, thereby creating a situation advantageous to all consumers of the goods and services in question.

The distribution of the surplus among the members is closely connected with this pricing policy of the co-operative (→ Assessment of Success). Here, the principle is applicable insofar as the surplus (or a part of it) to be allocated to the members of the co-operative must be distributed in the same proportion the members have taken advantage of the services offered by the co-operative. The distribution of the surplus according to the utilization of the co-operative's services is an essential part of the particular form of economic democracy developed by the co-operative system.

In the co-operative system, each member has the same voting right and opportunity to participate in the referendums, regardless of his capital input, assets, age or sex. This economic democracy offers all members of the co-operative the same chance to exercise influence on the interests of the co-operative, for example on the services which the co-operative offers. Thus, members can collectively contribute to the consultation and discussion of questions which affect them personally.

The consistancy of the economic equality is also obvious in that it is possible for the co-operative members to participate in the economic activity without large amounts of capital. Thus, on the ideological level, capital is not essential in the co-operative system. Although the co-operative must award an appropriate compensation on the co-operative capital (→ Financing), its importance in practical application is minimal as, in general, the co-operative capital share (investment) of each member is fairly low. The co-operative, fundamentally, is not a "joint-stock company". Although it concerns economic matters, the principle of absolute equality in the co-operative undertaking holds true on the ideological level; it is in opposition to the motives of common business administration. This principle, above all, should illustrate the social-political character of the co-operative system. The prosperity of the members is, however, also dependent on social motives associated with co-operative participation as well as on knowledge and ability.

The principle of absolute equality in co-operative thought altogether expresses the social-political ideology of the activity. This does not concern a passive reception of advantages but rather the active, collective and social creation of advantages. Co-operative activity can thus be seen as a part of social policy.

Furthermore, the co-operative is the sole company form in which only those people can decide on all matters concerning the activity of the company who take advantage of the services offered by it (→ *Legal Form, Co-operative*). The co-operative can engage its capacities and facilities primarily for the most effective satisfaction of the needs of its members, thereby improving their standard of living. In contrast to a company based on "operational economy", the co-operative must be considered a form based on "requisite economy".

It is because of its "requisite economic" character that the importance of the co-operative and the entire co-operative system as a support mechanism for the economy of its members cannot be measured simply with the help of balances and the closing financial figures in the books of the co-operative; one must, rather, measure the importance based on the extent the co-operative has been able to satisfy the needs of its members (for more on the "Social Balance" see *Weber* and *Brazda*). Such an assessment, however, is a much more difficult task than the determination of the success of the co-operative activity based solely on its balance sheets.

The co-operative movement traditionally has had a visible role in educational policy (→ *Education and Training*). In the formative years of the modern co-operative system, the European governments did not provide general primary schooling. When the first co-operatives layed down in their principles that a portion of savings should be spent on educational purposes, the pedagogical work at the time often meant teaching members how to read and write and how to perform mathematics. At that time, these skills enabled those being taught to solve their problems and comprehend the activity of the co-operative better. In many developing countries, the lack of reading and writing skills among the population is a handicap for the development of the co-operative system. Thus, co-operative organizations made it their responsibilty to provide elementary education for their members. In those developing countries in which the state promotes the co-operative movement as a factor of its social and economic development program, co-operatives can receive financial support from the state. The importance of the co-operatives in such educational campaign work is also exemplified in that they are often the only entities which, in fact, have an organizational network at their disposal, especially in remote areas.

In the developed countries, the character of the educational work carried out by co-operatives has drastically changed compared to the first years of the movement (→ *Education, Asia*; → *Education, Africa*). Now, a central factor is the conveyance of specialized know-how to employees, persons in positions of responsibility and members. The educational work of the co-operative organizations is primarily directed at employees, whereby the propagation and intensification of employees' special skills, understandibly, is an immediate method in the attempt to improve the efficiency of the co-operative. Because of this reason, the central co-operative organizations in particular have founded schools, hosted numerous lectures and courses, and developed training programs. Because these organizations, to a preponderant degree, have assumed workers' training costs, those employees or less well-off but nonetheless energetic and ambitious applicants also have the opportunity to participate in continuing education for their professional work and for promotion to ever more demanding positions.

The educational activity of the co-operative organizations is also aimed at those sitting in positions of responsibility in the organization. Within the administrative ranks of the co-operative organizations, many people have been trained for taking over responsible administrative positions and confidential tasks in state and society.

Even before the term "regional policy" was coined, the co-operative system traditionally had an important regional-political task, and it still has today. Measures to increase the prosperity of the population have often been undertaken in sparsely populated areas quite removed from settled ones. The co-operative banking system, producer co-operatives, and consumer co-operatives bear the responsibilty of the central functions affecting the development of rural areas (→ *Rural Co-operatives*). The co-operative system was and still is a factor of central importance for the further development of prosperity of the rural population in developing countries.

In many countries, co-operative marketing organizations in agriculture and co-operative financial institutions have supported the entire rural population through efforts to further develop their branch of industry and employment. With the help of the co-operative organizations it has been possible for many farmers to be employed on a full-time basis. If this had not been so, many farmers might well have been forced to leave their homes behind to seek other employment opportunities elsewhere. By offering services also to non-members, the co-operative organizations have influenced the living standard of the entire population in a multitude of ways.

IV. The Co-operative System as a Factor of Social Policy

Although the social-political functions of the co-operative system were not always recognized, the co-operative system, as a matter of fact, is related to social policy in many of its expressions, both in practical activity and in its principles (the educational and regional policies were discussed above). To a large degree this is because the co-operative, in general, is only seen from the viewpoint of business administration, or, in other words, only the operational results are taken into consideration. It has been previously mentioned that within the co-operative system it has been almost impossible to determine its social results (may be, the necessary research was not ever desired). Such research would have to focus at least on the following prospects: the extent to which the co-operative, by influencing the economic level of its members through the provision of security, has given its members the opportunity to exercise influence on societal issues and on voting matters; the extent to which the co-operative has raised members' self-awareness, instilling them with the feeling that they are able to master the problems the ever-changing society poses them.

Since its founding in 1920, co-operatives have belonged to the International Labor Organization (ILO) (→ United Nations System). Upon the initiative of *Albert Thomas*, the first president, an auxiliary department named "Co-operative Services" was established in the organizations's office. Since the organization concentrated on improving the living conditions of those population groups living under poor economic and social circumstances, its endeavors after the Second World War were primarily directed at the developing countries (→ *Development Policy*). Grievances and abuses include the poor economic situation of the population, poverty, indebtedness, illiteracy, insufficient vocational education, primitive cultivation and working methods, unfair distribution of land and, above all, the disastrous agency activity – the so-called "middleman system" in which agents often take advantage of the ignorance and the desperate situation of the population.

Committees of the ILO permanently are on the lookout for opportunities to eliminate poverty and other grievances in developing countries. The co-operative system has provided a means to alleviate those impediments to economic growth.

Various co-operatives and other national and international organizations attempt to help the co-operative organizations of developing countries, and the governments of these countries try to establish and strengthen the co-operative system, the ultimate goal being to help the poorest population groups through self-help. Because of the low educational level of the population and the situational urgency, the governments of these countries are much more in a key position than those who actually require the help. In this respect, the beginning of the co-operative movement in developing countries to a certain degree differs from that of the formative years of the co-operative system in the western countries. On the other hand, one must also consider all the help the developed countries gave the developing countries in creating and developing the co-operative system, for example in the form of expert advice, educational help, and campaign work many well-known personalities of the past century contributed to improve societal conditions (→ *Consulting*). By providing the developing countries help and support, the co-operative organizations of the developed countries have contributed to social-political work worldwide.

After the co-operative system in the economically developed countries had grown from a people's movement for satisfying pressing human needs to a company form (among others) being part of the economy as a whole, its social-political essence and content gradually became weaker or even completely disappeared. Its activity no longer primarily consisted of providing services for its members but, as a rule, became rather focussed on attaining a certain economic profitability, regardless of the customers. One exception from this general rule is the emerging interest in new forms of the co-operative system, the "new co-operative movement".

Particularly in the so-called developed countries, many of these "new forms" of the co-operative system have brought back the social-political element to the co-operative system (→ *New Co-operatives*). Examples of these new co-operative forms are neighborhood co-operatives, co-operatives for the care of the elderly, children and the environment, leisure co-operatives, co-operatives for the collective purchase of foodstuffs, and numerous other care and service co-operatives.

Those who live in urban areas do not always have the opportunity to provide themselves on their own with all the services they require. Since taxes seem to be the only way of financing, it would be quite expensive if the state was to offer all of these services. People also would not recognize the supply of goods or services as something of their own as they themselves did not actively participate in the decision-making and realization.

If the so-called "new co-operative system" keeps stressing the satisfaction of personal human needs, the social-political element of the co-operative movement will become stronger again. At the same time, members have the chance to take part in the planning and even in the realization of the activity (compare the Japanese Han Movement as renderer of services for co-operative members).

Bibliography

Engelhardt, Werner Wilhelm: Allgemeine Ideengeschichte des Genossenschaftswesens. Einführung in die Genossenschafts- und Kooperationslehre auf geschichtlicher Basis, Darmstadt 1985.

Lambert: Studies in the Social Philosophy of Cooperation, Bruxelles 1966.

Laurinkari, Juhani: Die genossenschaftlichen Grundwerte, in: Laurinkari, Juhani (ed.): Die Prinzipien des Genossenschaftswesens in der Gegenwart, Festschrift für Prof. Dr. Vesa Laakkonen, Nürnberg 1988.

Socialist Co-operative Theory under Real Socialism

JERZY KLEER

(see also: *History of Ideas*; *Theory of Co-operatives*; *State and Co-operatives, Socialism*; *Economic Order*)

I. Development of the Socialist Co-operative Theory; II. Co-operative Models in the Real Socialism; III. Fundamental Alternations of the Socialist System and its Co-operative Conception; IV. Changes of the Theoretical Concept by O. Lange; V. Consequences of the Political and Economic Reforms since 1980.

I. Development of the Socialist Co-operative Theory

The socialist co-operative theory under real socialism has always been linked to the general co-operative theory (→ *Theory of Co-operatives*) since the basic tenets of the latter have never been rejected. Nevertheless, the changes occuring in real socialism itself were influencing particular elements of that theory. The vision of real socialism has been undergoing rather profound changes in the past seventy-odd years. The theoretical concept of co-operatives under socialism has always been connected with the all-encompassing economic functions of the state (→ *State and Co-operatives in Socialism*). The principle of subordinating economic and social life to the socialist state supremacy (→ *Economic Order*), although in force over the whole life-span of this system, has been subject to evolution. It was reflected in theorectical models of managing the economy, and that in turn influenced co-operative theory.

II. Co-operative Models in the Real Socialism

1. The Basic Hypotheses of Socialism

The theoretical vision of socialism that existed just before the revolution in Russia as well as immediately after its success was not clearly drawn. The new system rather was conceived in opposition to capitalism; there was no clear theoretical concept behind it, especially in the sphere of institutions, mechanisms, and management instruments. The body of concepts which seemed to be so clear and obvious to the first theorists of real socialism may be summarized in the following hypotheses.
A. The dominant and, in future, the omnipresent form of proprietorship will be state ownership of means of production.
B. The economy will be centralized and predominantly characterized by technical rather than economic division of labor.
C. The exchange economy and the market will be replaced by commands and direct barter of goods and services.
D. Income distribution will be relatively flat, although an old principle of "distribution according to the quantity and quality of labor" (credited to *K. Marx*) will continue to be valid to a certain extent (in retrospect, a realization of this principle has never been observed in the economies of real socialism).
Amongst the theoretical concepts of that time there was practically no place for co-operatives. The only publication of that time gaining some importance (*N.L. Mieszczerjakow*, Kooperacija i socialism = Cooperation and Socialism, Moscow 1920) assumed that "Co-operatives will die together with other organizations established with the goal of fighting the capitalist system and its consequences in the area of its supremacy".
In the early stages of the system creation, the above view was frequently presented in the theoretical discussions and had many supporters. As a result, the idea of nationalizing the existing co-operatives was launched *(W. Milutin)*.

2. Three Socialist Co-operative Models

Looking from a theoretical perspective, we may distinguish between three co-operative models in that period (the 1920s) which, to a certain extent, may be considered as being formulated in the works of *W.I. Lenin*. These models exerted a marked influence on theoretical co-operative thought during the later stages of real socialism's development.

1) The first model – in its most general form – has its origins in the concept of the moneyless and non-commodity economy in which centralization of decision making in production and distribution is pushed to its limits. In this model, the co-operatives were to play the role of a "technical apparatus", serving the needs of the economic "Center", and of an apparatus of control over distibution – without the use of money. Co-operatives (of consumers) became the production-cum-consumption communes, whose task it was to integrate the whole population into a network of such communes. In this way, the state gains full control not only over distribution (consumption), but also over the working processes, for distribution is to be closely connected with the process of expending labor. This model may be considered a co-operative one only to the extent it takes over and adapts the existing co-operative structures along with certain external co-operative principles, although generally becoming subordinated to the state. In a later period, the concept of this model played an important role in the field of organizing and running the → *kolkhozes* as well as in the concept of controlling the distribution channels

through which the consumer co-operatives operated in rural areas.

2) The second model is characterized by the fact that the co-operative system is regarded as being one of the forms of state capitalism; this form is to be utilized for the purpose of socialist construction. The essential differences between this and the former model boil down to the following: the co-operatives are independent and operate only under general control of the state; because exchange as well as monetary relations exist, the co-operative, therefore, in fact functions as an enterprise rather than simply performing the functions of a technical apparatus; membership gives the co-operative members certain benefits; finally, the co-operative as a form of state capitalism is limited in its life and, after some (unprecisely defined) time, will become transformed into a purely socialist organization.

In this model, organizing cooperation among small producers (peasants and artisans) is the main task of co-operatives.

3) The third model is characterized by the use of exchange relations and the nation-wide market mechanism. The growth of the co-operative sector and its scope has been regarded here to be synonymous to the advance of socialism. In this model, compared to Model 2 above, the co-operative pains a completely new social characteristic. The co-operatives remain socialist in character because political power (government) is in the hands of the working class, and the essential means of production are under state control. This change in the external environment of the co-operative will influence its character as well as the functions it performs. The co-operative becomes a collective organism which rids itself of the former ties linking it to the private forms of organization. It even fights private forms of business organization (e.g. in commerce) and creates conditions conducive to transforming small-scale undertakings (in agriculture, crafts, and small industry) into collective business organizations. In this latter sense, the co-operative system is a policy instrument used by the government to promote its goals. In this model, one can distinguish between three traits of the co-operative that will continue to be valid, though to various degrees, throughout the entire period of real socialism.

i) The co-operative is a pure collective organism in which the interests of the group dominate that of the individual members.
ii) The co-operatives are subordinated to the state, and they are instrumental in achieving economic and social goals set by the state authorities.
iii) The co-operatives constitute a transitory form of organization that should be used in the process of socializing spheres of production and distribution. They are, however, doomed to be transformed at some point in time into state-owned organizations (all-society property).

III. Fundamental Alternations of the Socialist System and its Co-operative Conception

Changes taking place in the Soviet economy in the 1930s and 1940s led to fundamental alternations in the blueprint (as well as in the realization) of the economic system of real socialism. They greatly influenced the shape of the theoretical concept of the co-operative system. A fully centralized model entering the scene at that time is characterized by: full socialization of the means of production, i.e. by the elimination of private ownerhsip of those means; introduction of an all-encompassing central plan having a command (binding) character expressed in non-monetary terms (quantities); shifting the economic calculation (cost-benefit analysis) from the micro to the macro level. The enterprise becomes a purely "technological unit"; actual cost-benefit analysis is not carried out at this level. The only criterion in evaluating economic performance is the fulfillment of the central plan's goals. All the market relationships that are left in existence (prices and wages) are defined by the plan according to the preferences of the state authorities (the Center).

The concept of real socialism, construed along the lines discribed above, was the basis for a new approach to the co-operative system. Although the co-operative is still recognized as a legitimate element of the socialist economy, the views on its role have been radically modified in comparison to the so-called "Third Lenin-Model". Only rural regions are considered to be the primary area of co-operative activity. As a result of massive collectivization projects (→ *Kolkhozes*), the → *consumer co-operatives* have been virtually "deported" to rural areas. The grounding rationale for this move was found in the theorem stating that coexistence of the state-owned enterprises (higher level of socialization) with the co-operatives (lower level of socialization) may hamper the development of a truly socialist economy. This was the basis for advancing the concepts of minimizing the co-operative forms of business organization and, later on, terminating the co-operative activity in towns. The theoretical finishing touch to the actual process of minimizing the co-operatives presence until the point of disappearance was added by *J. Stalin*. His work "Economic Problems of Socialism in the USSR" (1952) contains three lines of thought which are important in the context of co-operative theory under real socialism. The first is connected with the issue of commodity production, the presence of which, according to *Stalin*, being a consequence of the existence of two forms of property, and mainly a result of the co-operative form. Since *Stalin* regarded commodity production as an "element foreign to socialism", its liquidation, therefore, should be considered a prerequisite for attaining a higher stage of system development. The state sector may develop without commodity relations, while the very existence of the co-operatives strengthens such relations. A second line of thought follows similar lines. It is pointed out that the contradictions between the town and the countryside are related to the existence of two different forms of property. Only by liquidating that duality, one can create conditions conducive to solving those contradictions. Therefore, certain ways of minimizing the scope of commodity exchange (through the use of barter) are sketched; transformation of the co-operative property (→ *Kolkhozes*) into state property should be the result. One can see, therefore, that the Stalinist model assumed liquidation of the co-operative sector and realization of a socialist society unified in terms of ownership structure. As such, the model agreed with *Lenin's* theoretical concept, the only difference being that *Stalin's* model made use of coercion to a much larger extent and, in addition, was to be implemented quickly.

IV. Changes of the Theoretical Concept by O. Lange

In the late 1950s, negative consequences resulting from the fully centralized Stalinist model prompted the introduction of some corrections. In the Soviet Union, as well as in Middle and Southeastern Europe, some timid attempts at economic reforms were made, which had some effect on changing the theoretical attitude toward the co-operative system. An important role in the formation of a new theoretical concept of the co-operative system was played by *Oskar Lange* (Rola Spódzielczosci w Budowie Socjalizmu, = The Role for the Co-operative Movement in the Construction of Socialism, 1958). He put forward several new theses which differed from the Stalinist model. His theses are not only important but also highly representative for the co-operative theory. Later on, they became the centerpiece of several theoretical debates on co-operatives – not only in Poland, but in the majority of countries under real socialism.

Lange lists two features which differentiate between co-operatives and state enterprises. Although both stem from the group character of ownership, co-operatives make use of specific economic incentives which motivate the economic agents in ways somewhat similar to those present in private enterprises and which are much stronger than those found in state enterprises. Moreover, co-operatives create a tradition of democratic management under the form of self-government. Both of these long-lasting, traditional co-operative features which had been eliminated in the Stalinist model should be used in the socialist construction. *Lange*, however, goes on and introduces two further theoretical propositions. The first states that the co-operative has responsibilities not only for its members, but also for society as a whole. The other says that transformation of the co-operative into a fully socialist unit requires making it subject to the planning mechanisms and structures. The whole theoretical discussion that followed was focused on the following issue: what should have priority in the co-operative – its constitutional features (i.e. voluntary membership, self-government, and benefits to the members) or the functions it fulfills for the whole society and the economy, as prescribed by the central plan? As far as theory is concerned, the controversy has never been fully and finally settled, mainly because two different underlying theoretical concepts existed. The first won official government recogniztion and was institutionalized as such; the second was parallel to the official theory and had many elements contradictory to those officially accepted. The officially accepted theory may be summarized by the following theses.

1) The co-operative is based on certain general co-operative priniciples that are valid under any political system. The extent to which those principles (independence, members' benefits, election of the board, freedom of decision making) were in fact respected, depended upon two considerations: the general model of the economy and the type of the particular co-operative.

2) It has been acknowledged that the co-operative system constitutes a continuing element of the socialist eocnomic structure. The Stalinist idea of accelerated transformation of co-operative ownerhsip into state property was – at least in theory – abandoned, although in practice the very concept of carrying out that transformation was not given up until the early 1980s. It was only agreed that it would be an issue for the future, the process of which may be carried out step by step.

3) The proposition that co-operative ownership represents a lower degree of socialization than state ownership was still accorded official recognition. Nevertheless, at least in some countries (Hungary, Poland), the officially accepted theory would more and more frequently contain a postulate granting equality to the two kinds of ownership in many respects.

4) Despite the recognition of the co-operative as a separate and independent economic unit, a general provision existed that subordinated all the the economic units (including co-operatives) to the requirements of the central plan. The organization of structural links between the co-operatives was serving the needs of that provision. The structure was hierarchical (multi-tiered) and branch-oriented (the scope of permitted activities was clearly delineated) – a fact making it similar to the organization of the state sector.

Beside this officially accepted theory of co-operatives under real socialism, another -unofficial- theory existed, the influence of which varied from country to country depending on the scope of tolerated open dissent. The major propositions differentiating it from the official theory can be summed up as follows:

i) co-operatives are based on voluntary membership and independence;
ii) their goal is to maximize the benefits of the members;
iii) in the first place, co-operatives are market-oriented; any links with the central plan, if at all necessary, should be as flexible as possible;
iv) co-operatives are primarily local organizations;
v) state authorities must not compel a co-operative to fulfill certain goals if, firstly, the fulfillment of those goals falls outside the range of its standard activities and, secondly, if they conflict with the interests of its members.

V. Consequences of the Political and Economic Reforms since 1980

In numerous countries under real socialism, the economic reforms beginning in 1980 changed the relationship between the state and the co-operatives. Those reforms provide conditions for the development of genuine co-operatives which are formed as a result of a grass-roots movement, rejecting the strongest forms of subordination to the political and administrative authorities. Frequently, for the first time ever, the legislators in some countries have passed laws regulating the legal status and operational rules for co-operatives.

These new conditions, however, have not created any new theoretical concepts of the co-operative system operating under real socialism. They only meant that the former unofficial current of thought which used to exist at the periphery of institutionalized science, has gained more recognition and more influence on practical matters. This new current runs parallel to the old officially accepted theory, which has not been fully abandoned.

It is hard to predict what will be left of the co-operative theory of real socialism in the future, mainly because many countries of that system are now changing their political, social, and economic order. At the same time, it is not at all clear what the new socio-economic institutions taking shape in Eastern and South-Eastern Europe will look like and, as consequence, what changes will take place in the co-operative sector of those countries. To what extent will the co-operatives become private in character, and to what extent will they continue to rely on collective operation? Finally, it is not clear whether and where some mutants of real socialism will survive (the former Soviet Union, China).

Bibliography

Kleer, Jerzy: Zarys ekonomicznej teorii spóldzielczosci (An Outline of the Economic Theory of Co-operatives under socialism), Warsaw 1979.
Lange, Oskar: Rola Spóldzielczosci w budwie socjalizmu (The Role of the Co-operative Movement in the Construction of Socialism), 1958. In: Oskar Lange, Dziela Works, Vol. II, Warsaw 1973, p.213.
Stalin Josef: Ekonomiczne problemy socjalizmu w ZSRR (Economic Problems of Socialism in the USSR), Warsaw 1952.

Socialist Critics of Co-operatives

KARL-HANS HARTWIG [J]

(see also: *History in 19th C.*; *History of Ideas*; *Conceptions, Co-operative*; *Co-operative Socialism*; *Buchez*; *Schulze-Delitzsch*)

I. Ferdinand Lassalle; II. Karl Marx; III. Vladimir Iljitsch Lenin.

The *socialist critics* did not fundamentally reject the co-operative. What they fought against was primarily its orientation as a self-help organization along the lines of private enterprise as it was promoted by *Schulze-Delitzsch*. They rather had in mind associations above all in collective production – production co-operatives – though with state support or even under state control. The individual views and opinions of the socialist critics diverged considerably; their positions were ambivalent and unclear in individual points. The most eminent figures among this group include *Ferdinand Lassalle* (1825–1864), *Karl Marx* (1818–1883), and *Vladimir Iljitsch Lenin* (1870–1924).

I. Ferdinand Lassalle

Above all, *Ferdinand Lassalle* acquired his historical importance as the founder and leader of the German workers' movement. The co-operative ideas he introduced while pursuing his political and social goals as well as the intellectual arguments he had with the co-operative leaders of his era, in particular → *Schulze-Delitzsch* and → *Huber*, make him , however, also interesting for the co-operative movement. *Lassalle* was born on April 11, 1825, in Wroclaw (Breslau), the son of a well-off merchant family. He was considered highly talented, almost obsessed in his personal ambition and gifted with incredible rabble-rousing abilities. After secondary school, he attended trade school in Leipzig in order to fulfill the wishes of his parents of following a merchant's career path. However, he realized very quickly that this profession did not meet his own expectations and preferences and rather felt himself drawn to be a political author and politician.

Afterwards, *Lassalle* went to Berlin and studied philosophy, history, and classical languages. In 1845, he spent time in Paris in order to study source material of the philosopher *Heraclitus*. This not only brought him together with the German emigrants living there, including *Heinrich Heine*; he also became acquainted with the writings of the French co-operative socialists. Under the influence of the socialist thought of *Saint Simon, Fouriers*, and *Blancs* (→ *Co-operative Socialism*) which was concentrated in Paris, *Lassalle* relatively early developed into a supporter of the socialist movement which was just showing its first life-signs in Germany at this time. Because of this support, his participation in the Revolution of 1848, and a number of trials and prison sentences for high treason he also met *Karl Marx* and *Friedrich Engels*, who sat on the editorial board of the "Neue Rheinische Zeitung" in Cologne, a paper with a leftist orientation *Lassalle* also worked for.

At this time, *Lassalle* lived in Düsseldorf as a political writer and legal counsel for the *Countess Sophie von Hatzfeld*. She was involved in a legal dispute with her husband which appeared completely hopeless when *Lassalle* undertook the case and, after 36 trials which had been becoming increasingly political in nature, successfully won it for her. While *Lassalle* was heavily involved in the Hatzfeld trial, he wrote an exhaustive treatise on *Heraclitus*. After moving to Berlin, his treatise was published in 1858 and received great recognition within the field. The wish for an academic career, however, never came true even after the publication of another great philosophical work on law in 1861. He kept himself occupied with various publications handling political problems of the time and with numerous lectures concerning the question of the workers' situation. In this connection, the Central Committee for the Establishment of a General German Workers' Congress in Leipzig 1863 requested that he put together a social-political program for the workers. In particular, he therewith was to give his opinion on the value of the co-operatives founded by and operated according to the principles of *Schulze-Delitzsch*. In little more than two weeks, *Lassalle* published his "Open Response", the core of which included the principles for the General German Workers' Association which was founded in May, 1863. *Lassalle* assumed the presidency of this organization from which the German Social Democratic Party later developed.

The "Open Response", above all, was an appeal to workers to found a political party and to strive for a general and direct voting right. This process should be economically promoted by production co-operatives – initially by industrial workers and followed by laborers – to which the state should provide the necessary means of credit and whose members are guaranteed individual freedom and compensation for their work. The co-operatives founded by → *Schulze-Delitzsch* as self-help organizations were rejected by *Lassalle*. In the commentary to his response and in his controversial treatise "Herr Bastiat-Schulze von Delitzsch, der ökonomische Julian, oder Kapital und Arbeit" (1864), he argued that the co-operatives for craftsmen and for credit lending established by *Schulze-Delitzsch* were completely worthless for the ever-mounting number of destitute industrial workers and as a solution as such for the social dilemma. They would only be able to help small groups of craftsmen and industrial workers. In as much as their replacement represents a necessary process in the face of industrialization, the co-operatives for raw materials and credit would only slow down the social revolutionary development.

Lassalle also considered the → *consumer co-operatives* inappropriate. On the one hand, they could protect the workers in the short term from profiteering in the trade and provide them with inexpensive goods. On the other hand, though, everything that the workers could win as consumers they would lose again as producers. This is because the work market is ruled by an "iron law of wages" the population is accustomed to; this always limits the average working wage to a necessary minimum needed to eke out an existence and reproduce . This "law" of economics, which had already been formulated by *Ricardo, Malthus*, and *Turgot*, would bring about a reduction in the working wage; this occurs to the same extent as the consumer co-operatives make foodstuffs less expensive for the workers and as the workers join such co-operatives.

Because *Lassalle* nevertheless considered free and individual co-operatives as a driving force of social development, only production co-operatives involving factory-like mass production were of importance to him. The destitute worker, however, did not have the means at hand to raise the financial resources for such large enterprises. *Lassalle*, therefore, demanded help from the state in the form of credits and interest guarantees. His liberal critics feared governmental intervention and patronage as well as a demotivating effect on the readiness to contribute to the economic output. In rebuttal, *Lassalle* pointed out that the most holy duty of any state is to promote workers' associations; ultimately, the state itself is nothing more than a large association of the working class (*Lassalle*, 1893).

After being elected the first president of the General German Workers' Association, *Lassalle* plunged into his new office with zeal and fervent optimism. He was not only able to familiarize *Bismarck* with the idea of universal suffrage and to convince him of the necessity for production co-operatives; at the same time, he managed to win over the king through *Bismarck's* intercession, having him finance the establishment of a production co-operative out of his own privy purse. Nonetheless, this co-operative ended up in a financial fiasco. Likewise, extreme differences in opinion brought *Bismarck* and *Lassalle* further and further apart. *Lassalle* also lacked success in his activities in the workers' association. When he professed a people's monarchy, the workers withdrew. He thus began his agitations among the workers anew and attended countless assemblies in order to win over followers. In the end, a woman became his fate. Out of love, he provoked a duel for her and, as a consequence, he died on August 31, 1864, at the age of 39.

II. Karl Marx

Lassalle never developed a close relationship to *Marx* and *Engels* although he was in close intellectual and spiritual contact to them. They considered his analytical abilities to be shortcoming. *Marx* explicitly explained the necessity of a preface in the first volume of his *Capital* by the fact that *Lassalle*, in his treatise against *Schulze-Delitzsch*, not only used *Marx's* ideas and terms without providing information about the source, but he also used them in incorrect and misleading ways (*Marx*, 1867).

Marx certainly had characterized the co-operative namely as "useful in principle" in his early writings. But he considered it fully inappropriate to free the masses from their misery and society from capitalism. He even went so far as to suspect co-operatives of contributing to the delay in the necessary revolutionary transformations in society as well as to the unnecessary prolongation of capitalism's survival. The increasing propagation of co-operative thoughts and ideas was a very clear sign for him:. "...those very same people from the ruling classes who are well enough aware to admit that the present system cannot possibly continue – and there are many of them – have posed as impertinate and loudmouthed apostles of co-operative production" (*Marx*, 1871). Since the social revolution would necessarily come to be, it was therefore completely useless, even "ridiculous", to want to prevent the unavoidable through social improvements in the form of co-operatives. He deemed *Lassalle's* suggestion to establish co-operatives with support from the bourgeois-capitalistic state as downright "confusion".

One cannot find a rejection of co-operatives throughout *Marx's* work. In particular, the co-operative factories interested him very much; they could prove that it is possible to remove the social contradiction between capital and labor and to eliminate alienation. Nevertheless, *Marx* considered them as he always had – as capitalist in their impact. At the same time, however, he saw in them a demonstrative model for communism in the future which would then be achieved when the entire society became co-operatively organized on the basis of collective property and steered according to a common plan (*Marx*, 1871).

This vision of communism was the result of a deep conviction and decade-long study, the foundation of which was laid between 1836 and 1841 in Berlin, where *Marx*, who was born on November 5, 1818 in Treves, studied law, philosophy, and history. He came into contact with the group of Young Hegelians who derived aesthetic and revolutionary ideas from *Hegel's* philosophy. After being awarded his Doctorate in Philosophy in Jena, *Marx* first worked on the staff and, later, as a managing editor of the "Rheinische Zeitung", a newspaper which under his influence increasingly acquired revolutionary characteristics. When the Prussian government banned this paper, *Marx* went to Paris with his wife, *Jenny*. In Paris, under the influence of the German and French workers' movements and after meeting with *Friedrich Engels* in 1844, *Marx's* final commitment to communism took place. This can also be seen in the large number of fundamental texts which, among others, include: *Economic and Political Manuscripts* (1844);
A Critique of Hegelian Legal Philosphy (1844); *Foundations of a Critique of the National Economy* (1844); *The Misery of Philosophy* (1846–47). Together with *Engels*, *Marx* also joined the "Group of the Just" which steadily developed into a revolutionary communist party. This organization commissioned them to write *The Communist Manifesto*, which was published in London in 1848 and was to have an enormous influence on the workers' movement.

In 1848, *Marx* was called back to Germany by the revolution. Under his supervision, the "Neue Rheinische Zeitung", for which *Engels* also worked, was printed starting in July. This publication was solely dedicated to the revolution and to subversion of the constitution in power. The end of the revolution also signalized the end of the "Neue Rheinische Zeitung", which had to cease publication on May 19, 1849. *Marx* was expelled from Cologne as a "dangerous person". He went to London with his family via Paris where he likewise was not welcome. He lived in London until his death. Along with the more than 300 articles he penned for the "New York Daily Tribune" and numerous other smaller publications, he wrote his most important works on economics, *Capital* and *Theories of Surplus Value*. Marx himself only experienced the publication of the first volume in 1867. After long and arduant work on *Marx's* outline, the second and third volumes of *Capital* were published by *Engels* from left-behind material in 1885 and 1894. The series *Theories of Surplus Value* first followed between 1905 and 1910 through the work of *Karl Kautsky*.

The misery that *Marx* was fighting followed him and his family for decades. "I do not believe that anyone has ever written about money while experiencing such a lack of it," he wrote in London. The family had modest resources at its disposal, though. *Marx* inherited a fairly large sum from *Wilhelm Wolff*, to whom he dedicated the first volume of *Capital*. He also received fees for his newspaper articles that he wrote between 1851 and 1862. But he never managed to find himself with money. Furthermore, *Marx* did not want to assume any steady employment in order not to change into a "bourgeois money machine". He received financial support from his friend and comrade-in-arms, *Friedrich Engels*, who came from a well-off family of manufacturers in Barmen (Wuppertal). In contrast to *Marx*, who had so good as no personal relation to wage earners, *Engels* was well acquainted with the world of factory workers. In 1859, he joined his family's enterprise in Manchester. In 1869, he had his shares bought out and laid aside a retirement pension for *Marx* which made it possible for him to lead a bearable life.

In London, *Marx* worked at the library of the British Museum, which at that time had around 150,000 volumes. Throughout many years, he not only meticulously studied economic texts but his unquenchable thirst for knowledge also attracted his attention to the fields of history, natural science, and languages. At the same time, he became active in the International Workers' Association which was founded in London in 1864. Its goal was to unite the individual national proletarian movements. *Marx* composed the inaugural address, the founding charter, and the provisional statutes of the workers' association and, as its intellectual and spiritual leader, maintained steady contact with *August Bebel* and *Karl Liebknecht*. With solidarity campaigns and advice from London, he supported the revolution which broke out in Paris on March 18, 1871.

Marx committed the results of his extensive studies to paper in notebooks of excerpts and extracts which then served as the basis for his later economic texts. The rough outline of *Capital* was worked out in 1857 and 1858; the three volumes that resulted were actually suppossed to be the first of six planned parts. The rough outline itself was first published between 1939 and 1941 by the Foreign Languages Publishing House in Moscow under the title *Foundations in the Criticism of Political Economy*. The second outline was written between August, 1861, and July, 1863, from which the first volume finally appeared on September 14, 1867. Only very few newspapers published reviews; even the French version which Marx himself edited and the Russian version (St.Petersburg, 1872) did not initially have their anticipated effect. This was first to be reserved for the future when *Capital* would become one of the spiritual platforms of international socialism. But *Marx* experienced that just as little as the reaction to the English version of his work (1887). He lead the withdrawn existence of a private scholar and increasingly became ill. He could not recuperate from the deaths of his wife (1881) and his favorite daughter, *Jenny* (1883). He died on March 14, 1883, and was buried in London.

III. Vladimir Iljitsch Lenin

Lenin's opinion and position on the co-operative movement, like *Marx's*, was ambivilant. He initially decried it as "a completely ordinary form of petit-bourgeois reform" (*Lenin*, 1902) because he did not expect any substantial political changes to result from it. He did, however, see a preliminary organizational form of the workers' struggle in the co-operative if it could be molded into a center for revolutionary propaganda, agitation, and organization. In contrast to *Marx*, *Lenin* leaned towards the consumer co-operatives because in his opinion the production co-operatives simply consisted of small entrepreneurs and large-tract farmers who obviously had no interest in revolutionary changes. In spite of this all, Lenin conceded the consumer co-operative's function in the organized prolitarian struggle only in the temporary revolutionary phase. For him, the group collective property of the co-operative was compatible with neither communism nor its preliminary societal stage, socialism.

This appraisal of Lenin became poignantly expressed in the resolution sketch which he worked out for the Soviet Social Democrats at the Socialist Congress in Copenhagen in 1910. He maintained his position up to the beginning of the 1920s when, under the impression of the rapid economic decline in Russia, he advocated strengthening the co-operatives in his famous article "About Co-operatives" (1923). Even though he considered them relics of capitalism as he had before, he now also saw them as "schools of socialism" in which the members could develop a socialistic consciousness. Additionally, the co-operative property had automatically assumed a new, socialist quality on account of the socialization of the means of production. *Lenin* counted co-operative property among the components of societal-social property; rather than state property it was a preliminary stage.

When *Lenin* changed his position on co-operatives, he already was beyond the peak of his political power. He was standing before the end of a strenuous but successful career as a scholar, career revolutionary, and politician, which had lead to the radical upheaval of one of the largest empires of its time. *Lenin* was born on April 18, 1870 as *Vladimir Ilyich Ulyanov* in Simbirsk; he came from a lower-aristocratic / bourgeois family. The most important experience of his youth was the fate of his older brother, *Alexander*, who was incarcerated during the preparation of an assasination attempt on *Czar Alexander* and executed on May 28, 1887. In the same year, *Ulyanov* began studying law and political science at the University of Kasan where he quickly came into contact with the revolutionary movement. Because of his participation in student disturbances, he was expelled and banned from the university. Although he was not allowed to study any more, he was granted permission to take the state law exams in St.Petersburg, in 1891.

After *Ulyanov* had established his legal practise in St.Petersburg he joined an outlawed circle of social democrats and founded the "League of Struggle for the Emancipation of the Working Class" in St.Petersburg. An illness forced him to leave the country in 1895; abroad he met the founders of Russian Marxism, *Plechanov* and *Axelrod*, as well as *Marx's* son-in-law, *Paul Lafarge*. Upon his return to Russia, he gained the leadership of the Marxists in St.Petersburg. At year's end, 1895, *Lenin* was imprisoned and banished to East Siberia for three years. There he married *Nadeshada Krupskaya*, who was also banned and who helped him to complete his first work on economics, *The Development of Capitalism in Russia*. This book was published under a pseudonym as was his second book, *The Goals of the Russian Social Democracry*, which followed shortly after and for which he used the name *Lenin* for the first time.

After his banishment, *Lenin* emigrated and worked in London, Munich, and Geneva constructing a strictly organized Russian social democratic party. The newspaper "Iskra" – the spark – served as the official organ. It was initially printed in Leipzig and later in London and was distributed in Russia by agents. By the end of 1902, all the Social Democratic Party Committees in Russia belonged to the "Iskra" network. Nonetheless, at the Second Party Congress of the Russian Social Democratic Workers' Party in London and Brussels in 1903, a split in the party resulted from the centralized status which *Lenin* had prepared. The majority of the members (the Bolshevists) backed *Lenin* whereas the minority group (the Menshevists) stood behind *Martov*.

In 1905, *Lenin* returned to Russia where he witnessed the collapse of the revolution lead by *Trotsky*. He emigrated to Switzerland via Finland and Sweden and moved to Paris in 1909. He wrote his comprehensive philosphical paper *Materialism and Emperical Criticism* (1909) and completed his main work on economics, *Imperialism as the Highest Level of Capitalism* (1916), while living in exile. In Prague in 1912, he split the Russian Social Democratic Workers' Party for good and founded a Bolshevik Central Committee. Starting in May of that year, the official organ, "Pravda", commenced publication. In order to edit "Pravda" better and to organize the Bolshevist activities in Russia better, *Lenin* moved to Krakow in July, 1912, where he was put in prison for espionage in 1914.

Lenin returned to Switzerland where he stayed throughout the duration of the First World War. Because he was fairly isolated from the Bolshevik movement in Russia, he only had a few followers there. His name was hardly known there at the outbreak of the February Revolution in 1917. He was seen as a coffeehouse conspirator by the Social Democrats of Western Europe, as the Russian with the big theories and the small group of followers (*Shub*). That all was to change quickly. After *Lenin*, via Sweden and Finland, had returned to Russia through the help of the German military command in April, 1917, he gained great popularity immediately. He ran into opposition from close party comrades, though, with his "April Theses" in which he openly called for a revolution. Nevertheless, he was able to assume complete leadership of the All Russian Bolshevik Party in May.

In July, *Lenin* was forced to flee after an insurrection against the provisional government. He went to Finland and returned illegally on October 20th in order to prepare for the armed coup d'état. On November 7th and 8th, in St.Petersburg, *Lenin's* plans were executed under Trotsky's supervision , and power was seized. The revolution then spread throughout the entire country.

In the first new government *Lenin* became the chairman of the Supreme Soviet of the People's Commissar. The following year was filled with the conclusion of the peace treaty at Brest-Litovsk and the ruthless consolidation of power in the civil war. An assisination attempt on *Lenin* served as an excuse to go against the competing social democratic movement with full force. *Lenin* also succeeded in centralizing power within the party by establishing the Secretary and the Politburo. At the same time, he tried to realize a world-wide prolitarian revolution by founding a Communist International. His political success became clouded, however, by the rapid economic decline. As a result of the communist struggle and its centralist methods, Russia found itself on the verge of an economic collapse in March, 1921, facing a new revolution. The sailors from Kronstadt who had helped *Lenin* to power in 1917 rebelled against him. *Trotsky* ruthlessly crushed the rebellion and *Lenin* tried to stabilize the economy with his "New Economic Policy".

The new course in policy seemed to be more hopeful, but *Lenin's* health seriously started deteriorating around the end of 1921. The 11th People's Congress was the last one he attended; *Stalin* was appointed General Secretary. A series of strokes followed which increasingly impaired *Lenin's* capacity to act, even when he was periodically able to fight against his illness. In the meantime, a power struggle developed in the party which *Lenin*, in expectation of his death, continued to try to influence until the end with his "Political Testament". His demand for the immediate recall of *Stalin* was without effect. *Lenin* died on January 21, 1924, after a further stroke.

Bibliography

Faust, Helmut: Ursprung und Aufbruch der Genossenschaftsbewegung, Neuwied am Rhein 1958.
Friedhelm, Richard: Karl Marx – Sein Leben und seine Zeit, München 1981.

Lassalle, Ferdinand: Herr Bastiat-Schulze von Delitzsch, der ökonomische Julian, oder Kapital und Arbeit, Berlin 1864.
Lassalle, Ferdinand: Reden und Schriften, ed. by Eduard Bernstein, Berlin 1893.
Lenin, Wladimir–Iljitsch: Revolutionäres Abenteuertum (1st ed. London 1902), Lenin-Werke, Berlin vol. 6 (1959).
Marx, Karl: Der Bürgerkrieg in Frankreich (1st ed. Leipzig 1871), Marx-Engels-Werke, Berlin vol. 17 (1962).
Marx, Karl: Das Kapital (1st ed. Hamburg 1867), Marx-Engels-Werke, 4th ed., Berlin vol.23 (1969).
Shub, David: Lenin, Wiesbaden 1957.

Societal Form, Co-operative as a

ROBERT HETTLAGE [S]

(see also: *Relationship Patterns*; *Organizational Structures, Co-operative*; *Configuration*; *Group, the Co-operative*; *Group Theory*; *Autochthonous Co-operatives*; *Informal Co-operatives*)

I. Dualism of Social Constitutions; II. Historical Lines of Development of the Co-operative Societal Form; III. Modern Life and the Co-operative Societal Form.

For a long time, research on co-operatives was limited to the co-operative as a form of economic organization competing with other types of business; this distorted the view of the further-reaching, macrosociological aspects of the co-operative system (→ *Configuration*). Not always, though, for there was and still exists a tradition in research concentrating on policies with respect to economic orders, which is relevant to co-operatives, one that asks about the principles which form a certain type of society, about the system of social relations emerging from the historical conditions of life and the urge for creation, including the distribution of duties, rights, claims in state and society. Diametrically opposed solutions are conceivable in this context.

I. Dualism of Social Constitutions

1. Rule and Co-operative

Even in the last century, → *Gierke* pointed out in connection with German Law that constitutional reality was marked by the opposing principles of the rule and co-operation.
Rule applies, when a group or a protagonist is in a position to monopolize "integral" power even in a case of conflict (*Geiger*, p. 344). Social formations follow the principle of cooperation, when nobody possesses this integral power, because it is "executed by everyone on everybody in the form of circle " (ibid).
Rule-defined and co-operative forms of relations thus differ insofar as for the former, power is divided unequally (vertically), whereas the latter divides it equally (horizontally). Rule aims at subordination of subjects, co-operation at equality of people who hold power. Consequently, co-operation is in no way devoid of conflict and power, although sociologically speaking it is rule-less, as no decision-leader has a monopoly on exercising integral power. Ideally, power is everybody's, yet nobody's. So the chances of life and influence are balanced differently from those in rule-oriented social formations.

Following on from that, important areas of social structuring adopt a different shape. Typically, a ruler will, for example, attempt to secure his monopoly on power and to establish obedience. Any imaginable division of power, therefore, merely serves the purpose of increasing the chance of "obtaining obedience in answer to an order" (*Weber*) (divide et impera). The co-operative principle of division of power (*Montesquieu*), on the other hand, seeks to avoid any concentration of power by primarily transferring sovereignty to the level of citizens, members of an organization, participants, etc. This does not exclude a partial transferral of power to intermediate levels (and the state apparatus) (*Coleman*). Co-operation aims at a balance of power in social relations, creates scope for action through different potentials of influence and helps solve conflicts of interest in a form of self-enforcing contracts. (*Williamson, Weipert*, 1963).

In consequence, the co-operative societal system is not limited to segmented societies (consisting of homogenous parts unconnected with one another and not differentiated in terms of division of labour), but can just as well be transferred to functionally integrated formations operating on a complexity of interests and division of labour.

2. The Combination Theory of Rule and Co-operation

So far, only an ideal image of two basic social conditions not tied to a specific time or space has been given. Rule and co-operation are "terms of direction" (*Tönnies*), typical form of human togetherness and the communal making of decisions. In "pure" form, they do not exist, they combine in the course of concrete, social chances and necessities for creation.

- Thus, cross-connecting social circles can each be constituted differently: e.g., there can be rule-based structures of families and co-operatively structured forms of village communities.
- Apart from that, different sensitivities and structural prerequisites that have developed historically favor one or the other form of society.
- Finally, one structure may transform into the other. "In a co-operative system, a ruler may come to the top, in a rule-based system, there may devel-

op a co-operation of servants, but there will be no inner reconciliation of the two principles. One or the other will alternately be dominating in the forefront" (*Gierke*, 1897, p. 13).

Gablentz interprets this up and down movement as a constant state of tension between the two elements, which permanently endangers the unity of the system of relations and absolutely necessitates a balance (between the people and the state, freedom and order, individual and common interests, law and power). For order has to be arranged on the principle of freedom; freedom has to be integrated responsibly. Power has to be legitimized legally, law has to be secured by authority. "Law has to be accepted, cooperation needs to have an order." (ibid, p. 55 f.). Emerging from this complementary condition of principles, the interaction of bases of legitimation historically leads to a "swing of the pendulum" from predominantly co-operative to predominantly rule-oriented social structures (on a macro-, meso-, and micro-sociological basis) and vice versa. Important historical manifestations can only be interpreted as a combination of these two types, just as occidental history is dominated by events that run a course between polis and empire, a system of estates and absolutism, pluralism and totalitarianism (*Gablentz*).

II. Historical Lines of Development of the Co-operative Societal Form

1. Archaic and Tribal Societies

Vierkandt is of the opinion that kinship groups and tribal peoples do not have any pronounced social stratification because of their limited spatial interaction and are unfamiliar with rule-based positional power, knowing only the power of a leader's reputation (primus inter pares). The (full) members are not superior or inferior to one another, but equal on a co-operative basis. The same applies to archaic peasant farmers and peasant societies. Corporative and class-based differentiations of power are comparatively late phenomena.

Systems of rule are often formed as a consequence of being infiltrated by tribes of nomadic horsemen ("Equestrian herdsmen" – *Rüstow,* p. 74). Even so, quite often a co-operative structural principle spreads as a counterbalance. Already the first theocracies in the Mediterranean knew about the *Fraternity of Worship* or the Divine Community of the Faithful (e.g. the Israelites). The later Christian Church state at some stage also counted on co-operatively organized religious orders (e.g. the Dominicans).

The Germanic peasantry, with its thinking centered on the farm, is an example of the significance of the co-operative form of society. It revolves around the kinship group as a community of blood ties, defense, worship and economic ties. The borderland community has its origins in the tribes settling there. Administration of "the march" as a living area is organized in such a way that it grants all full members equal status in their rights and duties; at least in the beginning, before nobility was clearly defined. The idea of differentiating between the members as a whole and as individuals has not yet emerged: therefore, common property and common usufruct dominate, whereas demand-oriented privileges have only limited validity *(Gierke,* 1895).

2. The Autonomy of Communities and "Free People's States"

Gasser (1977) indicates that these principles have been preserved up to the present day in the nation-state type of administratively decentralized, authority-resisting "people's state" (of the Anglo-Saxons, Scandinavians, Dutch and Swiss). Local self-administration strengthened law-abidingness and the feeling of citizenship and made the local authorities take responsibility for themselves. For such reasons, these peoples remained relatively untainted by excesses of state authoritarianism and totalitarian temptations. "States formed from the bottom upwards on a basis of local federacy have an overwhelming tendency of forever remaining worlds of local and regional self-administration – just as much as the rule-defined states, the worlds of administration based on a hierarchic command system show overwhelming inertia" *(Gasser,* 1947). Principles of order defined by local structuring and people's rights, respectively by the rights of authoritarian rule for him even form the constants of social history.

3. Corporate Society and Its Eclipse by Overlordship

Under the military regimes of the Romans and the Franks, the free communities of the ancient times in Greece, Italy, Spain, France, and Germany had perished. Since then, the co-operative societal form could only and temporarily re-form in medieval towns. The influence of the rule-defined administrative system kept large parts of the population used to a "Master's Law" *(Gasser,* 1945). After the period of migration of the peoples, the peasants were forced back into a state of dependence by the military and religious ruling classes. The upper ranks, following the Roman provincial conditions, took over the now hereditary right of disposal of the farms and the land ("manorial system", 7th to 13th centuries), but made the peasants do the agricultural production work in exchange for goods in kind, money or work. Thus, a corporate ruling class spread its roots *(Kötter),* and took over the economic, political and often legal power (feudal system). Social acceptability was now dependent on the belonging to the nobility, which in turn was differentiated into a class system of ranks – dating from Byzantine late antiquity – whereas the peasants materially became serfs, tied to the soil and held in bondage. Nevertheless, co-operative principles were not lost completely. They remained a custom mainly in the areas where properties were large (socage farms as court authority for farm members). Also, neighborhood communities possessing common land had compulsory schemes for the co-ordinated cultivation of all the fields, while the common land (woodland, poor ground) could be utilized by everybody. The community of village companions formed the supreme authority ("Märkerding"). Sometimes, these communities and regions developed niches where corporate rulers could not reach (Swiss cantonal communities with their "council democracy").

A further characteristic of Medieval society is the merchants' guild democracy (→ *Guilds*). Their guilds took over public functions (jurisdiction) and were able to extend their political positions of strength. At the same time, the patricians were challenged by the craftsmen. Where guilds prevailed, forms of democratic self-administration developed (craftsmen's guilds), which in the beginning concentrated on their own business, but later often extended to local governments (merchants' Hanseatic towns, Italian and Dutch guild towns of the 13th/14th centuries). The resulting factionalism between guilds (arti maggiori – arti minori) and between masters and journeymen was one of the reasons for the cities to open to the rulers again. In the 15th century, they began to form modern administrative states without intermediary authorities (estates, vassals) – founded on direct rule over the citizens.

4. Bourgeois Society and Economic Co-operatives

With the population's increasing interdependence and growing need for culture, regional and national trade replaced the former economy limited to the individual cities. It brought the transition from customer-oriented to anonymous market production. High capital investments and risks encouraged the appearance of the self-dependent entrepreneur and large capital assets. This development combined with modern individualism, which favored the autonomous subject, its individual nature and its civil rights (freedom of trade, of contract). Everybody was supposed to be responsible for himself, nobody was to be submitted to anyone's rule. So, citizens' self-determination and their freely defined purpose of welfare were declared principles of society. Thus, the state could only be the sum of individual wills and could only become active after majority decisions. The economy had to be organized similarly, through profit-oriented motivations for action of the participants in the market and competition. The market was now a guarantee for everyone that they could determine their chances for themselves. Laissez-faire had become an end in itself.

This prompted a "great transformation", which shook the existing cultural foundations of the societies. This ideally constructed atomistic juxtaposition of market participants could not become real, as the different distribution of capital and success on the market created extreme opportunities for domination. "The working people hardly had a part in this great movement, the consequence of which, figuratively speaking, was that it enabled them to survive the journey between the decks. They had about as much say in the determination of their own destiny as the " black freight" aboard Hawkins' ships. However, especially the fact that the ... working class did not actively take part in deciding about its own destiny determined the course of ... social history..." (*Polanyi*, p. 213). The massive pauperization of large portions of the population in particular made a co-operative correction imperative. The Workers' Movement partly counted on class solidarity and nationalization, but also on co-operative enterprises, economic democracy, and self-administration. Both directions, under different premises, aim for the distribution of profits gained from the cooperation of capital and labour. Ownership rule is to be forced back and to be replaced by co-operative heteronomous or autonomous labour. On the one hand, the workers resorted to self-help by uniting in *trade unions (labour market price cartels)* and parties, on the other hand they tried to disarm capitalism on the goods market (through consumer associations, purchase and sales co-operatives). The latter were also utilized by parts of trade and the middle classes.

Co-operative theorists and practitioners with different far-reaching proposals joined this debate about the "social question" (→ *Conceptions, Co-operative*). The "monists" saw *co-operatives* as a chance to form an economic organization that would be able to uproot the capitalist economic order completely. Thus, the early Socialists experimented with settlement co-operatives (*Fourier*, → *Owen*) and → *joint-production co-operatives* (*Proudhon, Buchez, Blanc*). Others saw the approach to a rule-less social system in the consumer co-operative (*Owen, later Bourgeois, Poisson, Gide*). Others again – such as the anarchists (*Kropotkin, Landauer*) – viewed co-operatives as a possibility of doing away with the state or at least of controlling it democratically. (*Lavergne*) (→ *History of Ideas*).

But in general, the "pluralists" with their re-dimensioned claims to social reform have prevailed. For them, the co-operative executively operating enterprise is merely an addition to the market system, whose competition system they do not wish to be touched. Economic co-operatives are supposed to gain power "within the system" in order to influence all participants in the economy in such a way that the system will be improved, as a type of opponent whose actions are socially motivated. Or in order to initiate a transformation from inside the system towards a co-operative social system on a long-term basis. In the debate on developing countries of the 1960s to 90s, co-operative transformation models also played a not inconsiderable part (kibbutzim in Israel, the Ujamaa movement in Tanzania, the idea of a Co-operative Commonwealth in India) (→ *Autochthonous Co-operatives*). Nevertheless, it has to be emphasized that even by members of co-operatives, the question of the co-operative societal form was in most part changed into a debate about the creation of a specific type of enterprise – although a type which could never completely deny its socio-political expectations.

III. Modern Life and the Co-operative Societal Form

1. The Victory of Industrialism

The social and cultural changes brought about by the "great transformation" are deeper and more global than any earlier change. They include the forms of organization, industrial relations, habits of thinking, and all facts of social behavior. Huge economic and urban agglomerations are developing, where rule is concentrated. The urban middle class and its style of living dominates and is gaining control of the industrialization process. Mass media and mass consumption are setting new standards for work and leisure. The industrial form of civilization is the most aggressive one mankind has ever known. Although it has been developing for only 200 years, it will have replaced most pre-industrial societies by the middle of the 21st century. Everywhere there is

– a division between ownership and management,
– an organizing of the workers,
– an increase in state activity (security, competition policy, settling of conflicts, sharing of income, employment, etc.).

Market, state regulations and group negotiations merge. As a consequence of growing interdependence, calculability, efficiency of administration, continuity, balance of interest, and pragmatism are what counts. "In essence, the new realism is conservative. The status quo is only changed gradually, the 'balance' has to be maintained ... One may have the impression, that parliamentary life is more and more falling into decline and that political parties are merely additional bureaucratic machines. The great political disputes of the past are possibly reduced almost completely to an analyzing of technical problems, the verbal duels are giving way to committee ... The century of 'great debate' is replaced by the period of major and minor compromises" (*Kerr/Dunlop* et al., p. 335).

2. A Renaissance of Co-operative Thinking

An unintentional consequence of the actions of bureaucratic and legal organization and rule is that the efforts to achieve "fundamental democratization" typical of co-operatives are strengthened at the same time. On the one hand, the official machinery seems to concentrate on the level of the means of production and the political and military instruments of power, thereby furthering the rule status of small minorities, which results in a "feudalizing of political, economic and cultural life" with new elitist knowledge and administration (*Mannheim*, p. 54). On the other hand, one of the features of the structure of our modern industrial society is that it becomes increasingly sophisticated in political and regional respects (federalism), in the individualization of lifestyles and the organizational apparatus of self-help, "so that the individual cells cannot be monitored by the centre any more" (*Mannheim*, p. 56).

The complicated machinery of rule of a large social system by itself produces the reserve tendency of only being able to function if it is sure of the small units' support (individual companies, associations, local administration). So the constitution of rule at the same time serves as a "social elevator" for the development of co-operative social structures. The main reason for this lies in the dynamics of technology and society itself. The industrial society needs to constantly improve the training of its population in the use of complicated plant and machinery in order to keep the system of production going at all. *Education* becomes the decisive productive force, but has the tendency of diffusing influence, responsibility and power ("new systems of production", workers' aristocracy, the winners of the rationalization process, stripping away of hierarchic structures). At the same time, a rising standard of living, consumers' opportunities, mobility and spare time make people more independent and demanding. Education and emancipation merge. All this must lead to a situation where the managers' formerly unchallenged position of power is limited by a system of checks and balances (co-determination). The sharing of power becomes significant to the population in a way similar to the sharing of income (cf. *Kerr/Dunlop* et al.). In a pluralistic society, the idea of progress is linked with claims to participation. They relate to control of the place of work and the opportunity of co-determining the social system of norms – a tendency which is to some extent being internationalized with global interaction and possibilities of comparing and pressurizing. Concentration of power, uniformity, and discipline are no longer sufficient. Higher qualifications necessitate consent; they make counteraction, differentiation, and the pluralistic forming of centres possible, as well as co-operative social levelling. "The fully developed industrial society is centralized and decentralized *at the same time*; it takes for granted a set of norms, but also sets free the individual. In contrast to many visions of the future, none of these contradictory tendencies will prevail alone, but there will develop a fluctuating balance between them ..." (*Kerr/Dunlop* et al., p. 342f.).

3. The Crisis of Modernity and the Search for Alternatives

Apart from that, the search for co-operative forms of life receives greater significance through the crisis of modernity. It seems as if the dominance of rationalization and the increase in efficiency are perceived as an unhealthy "colonization of the 'Lebenswelt' (individual living conditions)" (*Habermas*) and that they come up against their own limitations through the destruction of the environment. At the same time, over-complexity, pluralism, and de-institutionalization place the people in a situation of "having no answers". Market capacity and the capacity of the state of solving problems, the whole ruling "shell" of one-dimensional purposeful rationality of organization can hardly find an answer to the "feeling of discontent in modernity" (*Berger/Berger/Kellner*).

This gap may be filled by the efforts to find alternative forms of living and resistance, (guild-type) social networks, "intentional communities", which are all directed against exaggerated planning, centralization, hierarchy and bureaucracy. Instead, they stress the unity of work and living, self-help, group solidarity, communal work, contact, communication, mutual harmony, and variety. These strategies of escape and search give the co-operative social system new relevance – at least on a limited scale. They are all based on self-determination, self-responsibility and self-administration in mutual association. The members are mainly looking for a form of life which, apart from economic advantages, can also integrate social ones (basic participation, human organization of work, inspiration of local communities) into the concept of rationality and efficiency. This may be typical of the co-operative commitment to the promotion mandate, but nowadays it extends more and more to the structuring of income-oriented "business communities". A similar shift from patriarchal and conflict-oriented confrontation to negotiation dominated by comprise and co-ordination can be observed in the mutual relations between parties to an agreement.

The spheres at the core of modern society are therefore defined such that (at least as a postulate) "hierarchic structures are replaced by the heterarchic principle: no commands from the top down, but rotation of responsibilities; not the élitist, but the co-operative model of decision-making; no dependence on the upper ranks, but interdependence; not structured and filtered information, but the free distribution of knowledge in all directions; not central, but decentralized co-ordination" (*Gretschmann*, p.50).

A further global variety of the model of a community constituted on principles of egalitarianism and discourse can be found in the women's emancipation movement and to some extent in the changing style of upbringing (specific to the middle classes). While in a corporate society the relation between the sexes and generations had a strongly rule-oriented character, in this field, too, tendencies towards a co-operative arrangement of relations are beginning to show. The fact that because matters of education are changing, women no longer accept a subordinate social status, but can depend on equal rights, equal strength and equal experience, may be the greatest revolution as the 20th century draws to a close. This similarity applies to the modern youth movement, which claims self-responsibility and its own style of living (→ *Informal Co-operatives*). The changes in education and the style of upbringing meet these criteria. Parents' and educators' superiority shows a tendency to make way to comradely advice. "In the 'century of the child', educators have more of a co-operative than a rule-defined relation to their charges" (*Eisermann*, p. 123). And: "It is a well-known fact that women had to fight for such a status. In the case of children one, of course, cannot speak of fighting. So it is all the more significant that the same change has taken place: adults voluntarily gave up a great part of their former power and took a completely different approach in their behavior towards youth, bordering on equality. This is clearly a result of the fact that the tendency towards a shift of power is deeply rooted in modern society and its direction of development" (ibid).

So the co-operative societal form as a cultural ideal plays a dominant part in the present dynamics of development. It also assumes the role of "midwife" for a practical introduction to a new style of thinking and behavior. This tendency towards "co-operativization", though, is often misjudged, because it seeks to form a synthesis of values and organization with industrial constructs and constraints, and therefore rarely occurs in a pure form. Their chance lies in the fact that they both practice the autocentric principle without turning against the basics of human existence in a self-destructive manner (*Klages*).

Bibliography

Berger, Peter L./Berger, Brigitte/Kellner, Hansfried: Das Unbehagen in der Modernität, Frankfurt/New York 1975.
Coleman, James S.: The Asymmetric Society, Syracuse, New York 1982.
Eisermann, Gottfried: Wandlungstendenzen der modernen Gesellschaft. In: op. cit. (ed.): Wirtschaft und Kultursystem, Zürich/Stuttgart 1955,
Gablentz, Otto von der: Einführung in die politische Wissenschaft, Cologne/Opladen 1965.
Gasser, Adolf: Gemeindefreiheit als Rettung Europas, 2nd edition, Aarau 1947.
Gasser, Adolf: Herrschaft und Genossenschaft. In: Verband

schweizerischer Konsumvereine (ed.): Einführung in die Genossenschaft, Basel 1945, pp. 18–38.

Gasser, Adolf: Zum Problem der autonomen Kleinräume. Zweierlei Staatsstrukturen in der freien Welt. In: Aus Politik und Zeitgeschichte, vol. 1/1977, pp. 3–15.

Gehlen, Adolf: Die Sozialstruktur primitiver Gesellschaften. In: Gehlen, A./Schelsky, H. (ed.):Soziologie. 2nd edition, Düsseldorf/Cologne 1966.

Geiger, Theodor: Vorstudien zu einer Soziologie des Rechts, Neuwied/Berlin 1964.

Gierke, Otto von: Deutsches Privatrecht. Vol. 1: Allgemeiner Teil und Personenrecht, and vol. 2: Sachenrecht, Leipzig 1895/1905.

Gierke, Otto von: Die Genossenschaftstheorie und die deutsche Rechtssprechung, Berlin 1897.

Gierke, Otto von: Das deutsche Genossenschaftsrecht, Vol. 1: Rechtsgeschichte der deutschen Genossenschaft, Graz 1954.

Gretschmann, Karl: Wirtschaft im Schatten von Markt und Staat. Grenzen und Möglichkeiten einer Alternativökonomie, Frankfurt 1983.

Hettlage, Robert: Vergenossenschaftlichung in kultur-soziologischer Sichtweise. Eine Studie zum Wiederaufleben abgesunkener Sinngehalte. In: Schweizerische Zeitschrift für Soziologie. Vol. 7/1981, pp. 85–111.

Hettlage, Robert: Genossenschaftsmodelle als Alternative. In: Koslowski, P./Kreuzer, P./Löw, R. (ed.): Chancen und Grenzen des Sozialstaates. Staatstheorie – Politische Ökonomie – Politik (Civitas-Resultate, vol. 4). Tübingen 1983, pp. 192–215.

Hettlage, Robert: Genossenschaftstheorie und Partizipationsdiskussion, 2nd edition, Göttingen 1987.

Kerr, Clark/Dunlop, John T./Harbison, Frederick H./Myers, Charles A.: Der Mensch in der industriellen Gesellschaft, Frankfurt 1966.

Klages, Helmut: Wertedynamik. Über die Wandelbarkeit des Selbstverständlichen, Zürich/Osnabrück 1988.

Kötter, Herbert: Agrarsoziologie. In: Gehlen, A./Schelsky, H (ed.): Soziologie, Düsseldorf/Cologne 1955, pp. 198–227.

Mannheim, Karl: Mensch und Gesellschaft im Zeitalter des Umbaus, Darmstadt 1958.

Oppenheimer, Franz: Wege zur Gemeinschaft. Gesammelte Reden und Aufsätze, vol. 1, Munich 1924.

Oppenheimer, Franz: Machtverhältnis. In: Vierkandt, A. (ed.): Handwörterbuch der Soziologie, pp. 338–348. 2nd edition, Stuttgart 1959.

Pfeffer, Karl-Heinz: Die sozialen Systeme der Welt. In: Gehlen, A./Schelsky, H. (ed.): Soziologie, pp. 313–343, Düsseldorf/Cologne 1955.

Polanyi, Karl: The Great Transformation. Politische und ökonomische Ursprünge von Gesellschaften und Wirtschaftssystemen, Vienna 1977.

Rüstow, A.: Ortsbestimmung der Gegenwart, vol. 1, Zürich 1950.

Vierkandt, Alfred: Die genossenschaftliche Gesellschaftsform der Naturvölker. In: op. cit. (ed.): Handwörterbuch der Soziologie, 2nd edition, Stuttgart 1959, pp. 191–201.

Weber, Max: Wirtschaft und Gesellschaft, Tübingen 1964.

Weippert, Georg: Zur Soziologie des Genossenschaftswesens, In: Zeitschrift für das gesamte Genossenschaftswesen, vol. 7 (1957), pp. 112–144.

Weippert, Georg: Vereinbarung als drittes Ordnungsprinzip. In: Jahrbuch für Sozialwissenschaft, vol. 14 (1963), pp. 169–178.

Williamsom, O. E.: The economics of organization. The transaction cost approach. In: American Journal of Sociology, vol. 86 (1981), pp. 548–577.

Solidarity

MARIO PATERA [J]

(see also: *History of Ideas*; *Conceptions, Co-operative*; *Relationship Patterns*; *Group, the Co-operative*; *Principles*)

I. Terminological Definition of Solidarity; II. Contrasting Perspectives; III. The Concept of Solidarity in Co-operatives; IV. Future Perspectives for Co-operative Solidarity.

I. Terminological Definition of Solidarity

The western tradition of thought has been occupied with questions concerning solidarity for the past 2,500 years, if one begins tracing this occupation back to the notion of man as *"zoon politikon"*. The conceptions of solidarity, in part greatly disparate, can only be sensibly understood in the context of the greatly differing political-economic circumstances in which they were developed – a context which is also of significant importance for the term solidarity in co-operative organizations. Emerging from the "mother of all sciences", philosophy, a number of disciplines in the humanities and social sciences have proposed explanations and interpretations of the various forms of solidarity; thorough presentation of these would substantially overstep the bounds of this brief abstract (→ *History of Ideas*). The following models, which have also clearly influenced discussion about co-operative solidarity, can be differentiated in rough terms from each other (*Amann*, 1986):

– *anthropological "a priori" assumptions*:
Solidarity is an innate, inherent human characteristic, traceable to the inclination to form communities (c.f. for example Montesquieu's "innate propensity for community").

– *purely biological frames of thinking*:
Expression of reciprocal dependency in an organism model.

– *social-interactive paradigms*:
Solidarity first arises when individuals commence social action.

Regardless of these schematic criteria, forms of "deviant solidarity" (*Prisching*, 1992) must be referred to for the sake of entirety even if they are not addressed any closer. "Deviant solidarity" can be found in criminal or terrorist associations – consider the dubious infamy associated with the mafia or how it can be affixed to political protection and corruption.

One is confronted with a confusing variety of terms which frequently lack more precise definitions as well as with more or less timeworn, banal formulations of position vis-à-vis the abundance of literature on the subject of solidarity – or perhaps precisely because of it (*Hettlage*, 1990A) (→ *Relationship Patterns*). Treatises discussing co-operative solidarity in particular offer many authors a welcome opportunity to establish moralizing norms. In those situations in which argumentation lacks conviction, reference is drawn to an existent moral which can be clearly traced to upbringing. Many of these treatises, thus, succumb to the methodological error of simply presupposing the particular phenomenon (i.e. solidarity) rather than actually explaining it in empirical-theoretical terms (e.g. *Weber*, 1980). Solidarity formulas, themselves abundantly available, can only obscure their extant empirical-theoretical inadequacies with considerable difficulty; apodictic statements like "only solidarity which emphasizes individual utility can release vitality" (*Jäger*,1992) do nothing to change the situation.

Co-operative solidarity's "need for affirmation" can perhaps be explained in that prevailing opinion (occasionally also referred to as "Zeitgeist") which considers solidarity in co-operatives merely an antiquated relic from an earlier age of need (→ *Conceptions, Co-operative*). Solidarity is seen to have degenerated to an anachronism in a society determined by economic contrivance, venality, materialism, personal isolation, and selfishness (at least in western industrial countries whose interests primarily occupy western science); solidarity so seen is accordingly replaced by the market and the state. This relation between politics, economics, and co-operatives as well as its consequences on co-operative solidarity will be addressed in detail below.

Returning to the problem of a uniform terminological definition for such disparate phenomena as class solidarity in the workers' movement, world-wide women's solidarity, solidarity with the poor in one's own country or with those people facing starvation and other such calamities in the Third World – ultimately also addressing solidarity in the co-operative context – it becomes evident how impossible it is to make an all-encompassing, collective definition. One fails in the attempt to capture the entire range of application associated with the term solidarity in one definition, such as what solidarity can express in a small group or in a global perspective. "We are involved with numerous solidarities – types or expressions of behavior showing elements of solidarity – which can be brought together under a single, unifying social science definition." (*Prisching*, 1992).

We choose to proceed from the following definition to indicate the connection to co-operative solidarity – to be more precise, one must refer to *self-help based on solidarity* on an egalitarian, democratic basis according to the interdependence of co-operative characteristics (*Patera*, 1986): "Solidarity is a principle of orientation and action which attains a different sense according to concrete historical situations; this sense changes in the course of time, involves expediency, emotionality and orientation with regard to non-rational (economic) goals, and is likewise affected by external conditions which induce people to find a way to free themselves of their dependencies in a co-operative manner" (*Amann*, 1986) (→ *Principles*). Behavior along the lines of solidarity should be understood as a *process to be acquired through learning* whose motives can be quite multifarious in character, and which among other things is dependent on the size of the group (ibid.).

Such a concept perceives solidarity to be "a general form of behavior organization which follows particular requirements but which experiences only one specific form or expression in co-operatives" (ibid.). The following will clearly indicate that this specific form or expression stands in contrast to the position maintained by numerous authors. Because the problem of solidarity in co-operative literature has been perpetually controversial (→ *Theory of co-operative Cooperation*), the most important positions of this debate will be presented before the author proceeds to reveal his own position.

II. Contrasting Perspectives

It is an uncontested fact that the original co-operative idea had been quite strongly connected with the notions and principles of solidarity following its modern genesis in the previous century. The dispute has crystalized around the question whether co-operative solidarity should be seen as a precondition or as a result of cooperation in co-operatives. One can roughly outline both poles of interpretation found in the relevant literature (→ *Conceptions, Co-operative*):

- *Solidarity as an inherent characteristic of the co-operative*: Behavior along the lines of solidarity is seen as "a priori", individual action (compare with the "a priori assumption" above) and/or as an existential reason of joint co-operative collaboration (*v.Bretano*, 1980).
- *Solidarity as individualistic-utilitarian behavior*: that is, a rational, expedient behavior which primarily serves direct interests. According to this point of view, co-operatives owe their establishment to their members' rational, self-serving behavior.

A superficial classification of these two perspectives into the positions of altruistic versus egoistic behavior provides further confusion. It would be advantageous to clearly differentiate the levels of argumentation: it can easily be shown that solidarity and/or individualism is a question of the number of actors, whereas altruism or egoism, on the other hand, is a question of the chosen direction of action (*Hettlage*, 1990B).

Furthermore, co-operative solidarity has also been referred to as the result of specific structural characteristics – "*structural solidarity*". This perception of solidarity is born in the joint organization or on the business enterprise level. The morphological peculi-

Inclination to Solidarity	Condition of Solidarity (corporate structure)	Behavior of Solidarity
Life Experience ("Need") – Biography – Social Situation – Social Mileu (Reference Groups) Collective Consciousness (Common Fixation) – Morals, Traditions – Values, Norms – Ideology, *Weltanschauung*	Self-Help Integration Participation Promotion	Possibilities for Performance – Personality – Knowledge, Competency Decisions for Performance – Intensity – Duration

Figure I: Connections between Solidarity and Co-operative Undertakings

from: *Hettlage, Robert,* (1990A), "‚Solidarität' und ‚Kooperationsgeist' in genossenschaftlichen Unternehmungen", in: *Kück, Marlene* (ed.): Kooperatives Management, Baden Baden 1990.

arities of this association of individuals (self-help, the integrational character of the co-operative, egalitarian participation and the promotion purpose) are expressions of the solidarity principle: "It serves as the grounds for a certain corporate concept whose structure of relationships and influences in turn induces solidarity; a process of circular causation is thus put into motion." (*Hettlage*, 1990A). This structure of solidarity and the concrete behavior along such lines, nonetheless, are subject to a typical life cycle which leads to an extensive degeneration of the initial solidarity in the course of economization undergone by the co-operative (ibid.).

Figure I provides an overview of the important connections between solidarity and the co-operative undertaking.

III. The Concept of Solidarity in Co-operatives

In order to develop more fully the understanding of solidarity-based behavior in co-operatives as a learning process which can assume a great variety of forms according to given concrete situations, the constitutive characteristic of co-operatives' double nature (*Draheim*, 1952) must be addressed (→ *Dual Nature*). Co-operatives accordingly represent social systems which have a dichotomized complex of functions:

- market-oriented, economic functions of a business undertaking;
- group-oriented, social functions of an association of individuals.

Co-operatives fall under two paradigms, one goal-rational and economic, the other socio-cultural and psychical (*Pater*, 1990). Solidarity can thus be conceived as that systemic, constitutive process which represents the intercessional connection between sociological and social-psychological elements of the self-managed organization on the one hand, and market-specific, economic action on the other (*Amann*, 1986). "A network is necessary in which a plethora of individual conditions must be firmly anchored; solidarity should develop out of their reciprocal interrelations." (ibid). If cooperation in co-operatives is understood as a compromise solution between market coordination or coordination through a bureaucratically organized hierarchical unit, it requires solidarity as a fundamental basis.

Solidarity, at least in its initial phase, has both market-oriented and social-interactive aspects (ibid.). Members' motivation for approving solidarity is thereby unseparably tied to both intrinsic motives (internal dispositions) and extrinsic motives (external incentives). A purely economic explanation is just as unsuitable to capture the reality of co-operative solidarity as is a purely non-economic explanation.

IV. Future Perspectives for Co-operative Solidarity

As is the case in the scope of society as a whole, co-operatives confront the problem of defining their specific tasks under perpetually changing conditions in order to guarantee their continued existence in the future (*Patera*, 1989). A number of constitutive, basic contradictions can be diagnosed for co-operatives found today in industrialized countries (*Patera*, 1992). Among other things, co-operatives pursued an emancipational program which can be characterized by two opposing logics (*Amann*, 1993):

- *"Vergemeinschaftung"* directed at integration, a common living situation, an identity of interests and solidarity for collective action goals, and
- *"Vergesellschaftung"* which aims at fragmentation, isolation and competition, pitting everyone against each other.

If the most important fields of involvement for co-operatives and the corresponding media for their control are examined in a systemic, theoretical manner:

a) Market/Money
b) Politics/Power
c) Community/Solidarity

unequivocal findings can be established (*Prisching*, 1992): Numerous social theoreticians are in agreement that the "community orientation" of former societal formations could no longer be maintained. Such orientation was eroded by state intervention and administrative programs and was equally annihilated through the installation of market-like procedures in all sectors of life. Just as solidarity has been replaced by the market and the state on the level of society as a whole, the alliance between the market and politics has caused co-operatives to lose influential weight in the community sector. Is there a further sense in being occupied with the medium "solidarity" against such a background aside from making mere entreaties? Solidarity cannot be implemented in its intended manner in a historic process in which the controlling media of power and money increasingly supplant it. Solidarity can, however, be forced, learned and practiced in the course of creative reorganization (*Amann*, 1986) in those situations where gaps in the supply of goods and/or services become poignantly obvious due to market failure and where the alliance politics/power (more clearly formulated: political abuse of power) prevents important goals from being attained and/or occasions of contradictions between alternatives or a general lack of alternatives to arise.

Nevertheless, solidarity's operationalization will become a central question everywhere in order to open the door to new engagement opportunities and to enable new relationships between members to develop. Each operationalization, however, requires precise knowledge of members' needs and wishes, the likes of which can only be gained through membership surveys (*Patera*, 1986).

Despite the diagnosis of the degeneration of solidarity in wealthy societies, one central theoretical learning/socialization fact must be alluded to in the scope of today's co-operatives: the ability to act along the lines of solidarity is contingent on actual "practice". Only solidarity which is exercised in practical application induces further solidarities to follow in its wake. (*Prisching*, 1992).

Bibliography

Amman, A.: Soziologischer Abschnitt. In: Patera (ed.): Möglichkeiten und Grenzen demokratischer Mitbestimmung in Genossenschaften, pp. 33–38, Vienna, 1984.

Amman, A.: Soziologie und Genossenschaft. In: Patera, Mario (ed.): Handbuch des österreichischen Genossenschaftswesen, pp. 441–511, Vienna 1986.

Amman, A.: Sozialwissenschaftlicher Teil. In: Patera, Mario (ed.): Bestandssicherung und Zukunft von Wohnbaugenossenschaften, Frankfurt 1993.

Brentano, Dorothee von: Die Bedeutung der Solidarität in Genossenschaften und bei genossenschaftlichen Gründungsvorgängen. In: Archiv für öffentliche und freigemeinnützige Unternehmen, pp. 11–31, Göttingen 1980.

Draheim, Georg: Die Genossenschaft als Unternehmungstyp, Göttingen 1952.

Hettlage, Robert: "Solidarität" und "Kooperationsgeist" in genossenschaftlichen Unternehmungen, 1990A. In: Kück, Marlene (ed.): Kooperatives Management, pp. 123–152, Baden Baden 1990.

Hettlage, Robert: Die antrophologische Konzeption des Genossenschaftswesen in Theorie und Praxis – welche Chancen hat der ‚homo cooperativus'?, 1990B. In: Laurinkari, Juhani (ed.): Genossenschaftswesen, pp. 27–49, Munich 1990.

Jäger, Wilhelm: Solidarität. In: Mändle, Eduard/Swoboda, Walter (ed.): Genossenschaftslexikon, pp. 585–586, Wiesbaden 1992.

Neumann, Manfred: Konflikt- oder Harmonietheorie der Genossenschaften. In: Zeitschrift für das gesamte Genossenschaftswesen, vol. 23, pp. 46–62, 1973.

Patera, Mario: Genossenschaftliche Förderbilanz, Theoretische Grundlagen – praktische Durchführung. In: Zeitschrift für das gesamte Genossenschaftswesen, vol. 31, pp. 212–225, 1981.

Patera, Mario: Genossenschaftliche Förderbilanz. In: Patera, Mario (ed.): Handbuch des österreichischen Genossenschaftswesen, pp. 515–556, Vienna 1986.

Patera, Mario: Zukunftswerkstatt Genossenschaft. In: Gemeinwirtschaft 2–3/1989, pp. 7–26.

Patera, Mario: Genossenschaftliche Förderbilanz. In: Laurinkari, Juhani (ed.): Genossenschaftswesen, pp. 285–301, Munich 1990.

Patera, Mario: Doppelnatur der Genossenschaft. In: Mändle, Eduard/Swoboda, Walter (ed.): Genossenschaftslexikon, pp. 140–141, Wiesbaden 1992.

Prisching, M.: Solidarität in der Moderne – zu den Varianten eines gesellschaftlichen Koordinationsmechanismus. In.: Journal für Sozialforschung, 32nd Jg. (1992), pp. 267–281, vol.3/4.

Schachtschabel, Hans Georg: Artikel Genossenschaften (III), Soziologisch-volkswirtschaftliche Problematik. In: HdSW vol. 4, pp. 379–392, 1965.

Seraphim, Hans-Juergen: Die genossenschaftliche Gesinnung und das moderne Genossenschaftswesen, Karlsruhe 1956.

Weber, Wilhelm: Genossenschaftliche Solidarität. In: Mändle, Eduard/Winter, Hans-Werner (ed.): Handwörterbuch des Genossenschaftswesens, col. 1468–1476, Wiesbaden 1980.

Weippert, Georg: Zur Soziologie des Genossenschaftswesens. In: Zeitschrift für das gesamte Genossenschaftswesen, vol. 7, pp. 112–144, 1957.

Weisser, Gerhard: Genossenschaften, Hannover 1968.

State and Co-operatives in a Market Economy

WALTER HAMM [J]

(see also: *Classic/Neo-classic Contributions*; *State and Co-operatives, Socialism*; *Officialization*)

I. Fundamental Elements of a Market Economy; II. Directions of Co-operative Development in the Free Market; III. Co-operatives: An Instrument of State Policy? IV. The Importance of Co-operatives for a Free Market System.

I. Fundamental Elements of a Market Economy

A liberal political structure, the likes of which is normally realized in parliamentary democratic countries, must ensure that the extent of state domination remains limited in all sectors of human interaction, and thus also in the economy; it must furthermore provide the citizens of the state extensive rights of self-discretion. Those economically active in the market economy are guaranteed extensive liberties within state-determined limits (see Sec. II.3). In contrast to consumers in a centrally planned and controlled economy, those in a market economy are not allotted anything by the state; they decide about their consumption independently. Producers must align themselves along the desires of their customers if they wish to be economically successful. They are, however, free to choose which markets they wish to supply and which production methods and marketing devices they wish to employ.

Companies remain unimpeded with respect to their initiative and innovation. Because many different companies find themselves in competition with each other for customer patronage, only those producers prevail who provide their buyers advantageous offers. The market economy is oriented around consumers' interests, ensures frugal utilization of factors of production (increasing productivity, decreasing unit price), constantly shaves off entrepreneurial profit in pricing competition, and thus serves to benefit consumers as a result of successful corporate endeavors.

In order that a free market structure can emerge, the following provisions are essential: The preconditions for private entrepreneurial activity in potentially lucrative fields of engagement include the right of private property regarding means of production, and freedom of trade, business location and professional undertaking. Markets must be made accessible; no state-imposed restrictions to market accessibility should exist as far as non-essential professional qualifications are concerned (e.g. medical requirements for doctors). Each individual must be able to decide freely which partners he wishes to engage and to which conditions the output-obligation relationship is determined. No one may be forced to sign, accept, and fulfill contracts against his/her will.

A further important characteristic of the market economy structure is the market's free determination of pricing (→ *Pricing Policy*). State intervention into price determination, particularly in the form of binding state pricing regulations, regularly causes either production deficiencies or surpluses and results in a misappropriation of the forces of production. Moreover, monetary stability must be guaranteed in order for the pricing system to function satisfactorily. Experience shows that high rates of inflation greatly increase the risks of entrepreneurial activity, thus greatly inhibiting investment and advances in competition. Ensuring monetary stability is one of the responsibilities of the state (normally under the control of the central bank or finance ministry).

The protection of all trading participants from the abuse of economic strength is of primal importance for the functioning of a free economic structure (→ *Competition*). Competition is normally the most effective instrument to prevent the maleficent use of power. In any case, however, the state must ensure that contractual freedom is not used to restrict competition. The behavior of market participants must be subjected to state supervision on markets in which competition is not sufficiently effective despite open accessiblity to the markets. Permissive international economic relationships are particularly suited to intensify competition on domestic markets. The relaxation of administrative trade restrictions and tariffs as well as the assurance of unhindered capital movements across national frontiers thus gains considerable importance. State authorities also bear the responsibility for such measures.

Corporate dispositions, often long-term in nature, can be ruined by state policy when unforeseen interventions alter the bases of administrational planning. The continuity, dependability and predictability of state policy are thus essential. Otherwise the typical momentum of free market development can be decelerated or even completely stopped. A comprehensive system of social security and compensation, moreover, is a factor of the political stability of a free economic system. Those in need must be cared for in an appropriate manner; weaker participants must be guaranteed sufficient protection against the exploitative undertakings of stronger market participants (e.g. employment contracts). Nonetheless, these measures must be so structured in a free economic system as not to paralyze performance incentives and the forces shaping general prosperity.

II. Directions of Co-operative Development in the Free Market

1. Freedom of Business Activity

The fundamental freedoms of trade, professional activity, and contractual agreement remain likewise unrestricted for those who wish to join together in a co-operative or who have chosen a co-operative as a business partner. Hindrances from the side of the state with regard to the formation and business operation of co-operatives would contradict the basic principles of a liberal market system. Inasmuch as weaker members of a society frequently join together in a co-operative in order to consolidate their inputs and achieve the necessary strength to hold their ground on a competitive market, co-operative activites are often promoted from the state, or support subsidies upon formation are provided in exceptional

cases (e.g. for amalgamations of alternative commercial companies or for production co-operatives).
Freedom of business activity, moreover, means that state bodies should attempt to refrain from any type of intervention in the co-operative business policy. This freedom is only enfringed upon when state support collaborates with co-operative self-help; state authorities usually determine how the public resources can be attained and how they should be utilized. The price for state support is compensated for in the form of losses in personal autonomy and discretionary freedom.
Co-operatives can also suffer losses in their independent status and economic self-reliance when they become attached to an ideology or party policy (such as in Belgium and Italy). Such developments in this direction in Germany (such as among the consumer co-operatives) have failed; the German co-operatives emphasize and practice political autonomy.

2. Free Choice of Legal Form

In economies structured by a market system, each individual is free to select the most expedient legal company form to pursue certain economic goals. Law-makers normally take particular care as not to benefit or disadvantage one legal form with regard to another and thus influence the choice of the legal form itself.
On account of varying company organization among enterprises with differing legal forms (prescribed by law-makers), it is particularly expedient to select the co-operative legal form when economic subjects (private households, small and mid-size companies) strive to promote their own interests in a collective business enterprise (→ *Law, National*). The dual identity of shareholders and business partners (→ *Dual Nature*), the participation of the shareholders in the administrative bodies of the company, the particular (democratic) method of policy making, and the financial participation of shareholders in both revenue making and risk taking contribute to make the co-operative a particulary well suited legal form in numerous cases.
The free choice of legal form certainly also means that existing co-operatives can reform themselves and select another legal form (→ *Joint Stock Company*; *Forms of Cooperation*). Very large co-operatives, above all, have taken advantage of this opportunity; as a rule this has not meant that the company objectives (particularly the promotion of the membership) have been changed. The reasons for this alteration of legal form will not be discussed here.

3. General Limitations Set by the State

Freedom of action irrespective of any bond or commitment would be a contradiction of a free market structure. One central provision must guarantee that the interests of an individual do not result an encumbrance of the general good. It is the responsibility of the state to set regulations for private economic activity which prevent the extensive discretionary leeway of the individual from being used to the detriment of third parties. Income discrepancies and capital advantages may only result from economic performance. State policy delimitations are intended to ensure a strict relationship between financial advantages and individual output.
The first important precondition for this is a well functioning system of competition. Damages to contractual partners and competitors brought upon by the abuse of economic strength must be prevented (→ *Competition and co-operatives*). Competition which functions successfully provides the opportunity for market partners to defend themselves against those with exploitative means or market encroachment practices. State supervision of market competition becomes involved inasfar as competition itself is not sufficiently effective. Competitive regulations which prevent the encroachment of competition and the abuse of power are essential for a free market system (→ *Anti-Trust Laws*).
Secondly, legal regulations must ensure that the freedoms of economic discretion and action remain inseparable from their resulting consequences. The aftermath of poor or faulty performance must not be transferred to third parties. Self-responsibility does not solely include the right to reap the fruits of commercial undertakings but also the responsibility for the occurrance of losses. Otherwise the door would be left open for an irresponsible disposal of scarce resources.
In the third place, labor laws and social legislation must ensure that wages and labor conditions are not set unilaterally to the detriment of workers. Comprehensive legal regulations concerning rights of co-determination and availability of information ensure that workers councils and unions participate in the formation of company policy affecting all social matters. This is applicable for job security as well as for physical and psychological stress brought upon by work. Regulations for labor disputes determine how to proceed in cases of non-conciliation with regard to wage increases and reductions of working hours (strike laws). The state, keeping the whole of the economy in mind, must safeguard that neither of the negotiating partners attains an overly dominant position and thus is in the position to dictate conditions to the other side.
In the fourth place, a portion of the total related production costs must not be transferred to the general public in the form of environmental polution. Laws of environmental protection (→ *Environmental Protection*) should ensure that the general public should not be disturbed or inconvenienced any more than it is absolutely necessary through the withholding of

permits, the imposition of taxes, and control measures.

These conditions as well as others in the scope of the law are valid for companies of any and every legal form to the same extent, including co-operatives. State influence on business planning should solely serve to ensure a free market structure and peaceful cohabitation between all people, if when necessary, through the prompt redress of conflicts. The goal of conditions set by the state in the scope of the law is not to impose stipulations controlling individual behavior, but rather solely to forbid behavior which is detrimental to the public as a whole. The freedom of discretion with regard to the numerous possible actions which remain open to the individual remains intact.

4. Special Regulations for Co-operatives

Alongside the general conditions in the scope of the law which are applicable for all company forms, special stipulations exist which are exclusively applicable to co-operatives. These above all are corporate-legal regulations which concern the particular nature of the co-operative form (→ *Legal Form, Co-operative*). The obligatory examination of the books (→ *Auditing*) by an auditing association serves the protection of confidentiality of co-operative members who often are not very experienced in business matters. Other co-operative specific stipulations are related to the fact that state authorities occasionally use co-operatives as an instrument to pursue political objectives (see following section).

III. Co-operatives: An Instrument of State Policy?

1. The State and the Principle of Non-intervention

Co-operatives were created in Europe as self-help organizations. The co-operative founders in Germany, above all → *Schulze-Delitzsch* and → *Raiffeisen*, put particular emphasis on the fact that the self-help character should not be undermined through outside assistance (charitable support from wealthy fellow citizens) or through help from the state. Practical experience shows that help from third parties or from the state weakens (or even completely does away with) the willingness to mobilize the power from within and overcome hardships through collective action. Waiting for outside assistance is much easier than exerting one's own strengths. The recognition of this, as well as the experience from the formative years of the first modern co-operatives, has been confirmed a thousand times over. The self-help character of the co-operatives in numerous countries has thus more or less been strictly maintained.

It always happens that, when the state takes action through assistance, state controls as well as restrictions in self-determination and self-administration inevitably are involved. There are numerous cases in which co-operatives (in individual developing countries) have completely lost their autonomy and have become an extended arm of state administration (→ *Officialization*). It therefore is understandable that many co-operatives energetically emphasize their self-help character and simultaneously call for the principle of state non-intervention (→ *Policies for Promotion*). In many industrial countries with free market structures, the co-operatives' assertion of autonomy is respected.

2. Co-operatives as an Instrument of Small Business Policy

In the discussion of policy affecting mid-sized companies, one hears time and time again the argument that small and mid-sized companies cannot hold their ground on their own in competition with large companies, that they require state assistance and receive tax benefits, and must be protected from the competition from large companies which outmatch them. Inasmuch as many small and mid-sized companies (→ *Operational Size*) are amalgamated in co-operatives, these demands are also extended to co-operatives (→ *Structural Changes*).

These considerations are, however, refuted by facts. Many small and mid-sized companies hold their own, and often with great success, because they have specialized in supplying goods and services which can be produced both better and less expensively in mid-sized companies than in large companies. Small and mid-sized companies in particular frequently attain superior results in stiff competition. One cannot speak of a general indigence among mid-sized companies. Focusing production and marketing to the particular abilities and talents of one's own company is an integral corporate task. State policy regarding mid-sized companies, in the interest of the general good of the public, must not consist of constructing protectionary barriers around mid-sized company structures. In the course of increasing competition it must be decided which companies prevail on which markets.

Subsidizing co-operatives consisting of mid-sized companies is likewise as unjustifiable as mid-sized companies requiring general state assistance. Co-operatives (e.g. for artisans and retailers) are a successful means to aid the improvement of output production and cost reduction for small and mid-sized companies. The experience of several decades with regard to protectionist duties and subsidies indicates that state assistance, nevertheless, leads to complacency and to the expectation (usually fulfilled) that the state will increase its assistance when the hitherto subsidy level can no longer ensure the survival of the enterprise.

The resulting conclusion should be adhered to: A successful policy for small businesses consists of methods to increase the performance ability of small and mid-sized companies. Fair competition and protection from the abuse of economic power by large companies are the most effective methods to ensure this. Co-operatives are by nature suited to compensate for disadvantages resulting from company size (such as in purchasing). State assistance for co-operatives of mid-sized companies is, however, not necessary.

3. Co-operatives and Their Social-political Functions

There are certain sectors of activity in which co-operatives can be seen only to a limited extent as self-help organizations for their members and in which the assumption of state influence on business policy has increasingly undermined the self-help character. These tendencies among certain (not all) co-operative home-building associations are the most extreme. When tenants for available apartments are assigned by the municipal administration because subsidies for the construction of social housing have lead to occupancy regulations on the local level, the self-help character becomes undermined (→ *Commonweal Economy*). In such a situation, one must question to what degree the co-operative can still be considered an appropriate legal form and whether state or municipal authorities could not be served more expediently by companies with other legal forms to pursue housing policy goals.

→ *Consumer co-operatives* have likewise distanced themselves in part from their membership mandate. By expanding their business to encompass non-members they have developed into companies which are barely differentiable from joint-stock companies. The relationship to their members has been essential reduced to customer contact. Along with higher unemployment and an increasing share of the population becoming dependent on social assistance, political interest likewise increases to provide the poorer levels of the population above all with foodstuffs. State promotion of consumer co-operatives is, nevertheless, not an expedient policy procedure. The intensification of competition within retailing (as well as permitting various forms of sales and marketing) can quite effectively reduce the costs of providing for the population without the instigation of state aid for individual commercial enterprises, as the case in Germany proves. German consumer co-operatives are having a more difficult time holding their ground in competition. There are likewise no convincing arguments to subsidize co-operatives based on social-political reasons.

4. State Assistance: A Risk for Co-operatives

Inasmuch as co-operative self-help and self-responsibility at the same time unintentionally serve to benefit the outcome of state policy (e.g. reinforcing the active competitive elements of mid-sized companies in a free market system), state intervention is superfluous. Co-operatives thus do not run the risk of degenerating as a result of state assistance and losing their driving internal forces (→ *Officialization*).

On the other hand, there are, nevertheless, political objectives that can only be achieved through state influence on the business management of co-operatives, or in other words, through restrictions in self-administration and self-responsibility. Social-political goals should be mentioned in this context as well as immediate assistance for otherwise nonviable enterprises which politically are seen as worthy of promotion. The perennial subsidies for production co-operatives in the → *European Community (Union)* should also be alluded to.

The uncommon success and the most remarkable development of co-operatives in the last 150 years have, however, not been based on state help and promotion, but rather on the mobilization of the strengths of the co-operative members and their active participation to do their utmost for their common goals. It has been proved that active cooperation, willingness to be responsible for one another (→ *Solidarity*), as well as the utilization of professional knowledge, ideas and willing input from members have been decisive in bringing co-operatives forward. These forces would be lacking if outside help were permanently expected; they have ensured the dynamic development of independent co-operatives and the prosperity of members. Just as → *Schulze-Delitzsch* ruminated, only those people can completely develop their capabilities and powers who are not dependent on outside assistance. Subsidies either reduce or destroy the willingness of companies to adapt agilely to changing market relationships and to increase efficiency by mobilizing their own energy. Perpetual dependence on state aid and state intervention would thus result.

The conclusion drawn from experience is that state assistance for co-operatives should be mistrusted; in its place one must rather opt to engage collective co-operation as decisively as possible. The key to success: Confirmation and reinforcement of the notion of self-help.

IV. The Importance of Co-operatives for a Free Market System

A free market system is only then stable when the strength and security of its fundaments are consciously worked on and maintained. This includes:

- limiting state influence;
- determining ethical and economic rights and obligations for the individual with respect to the common good;
- upholding the freedom to choose one's professional activity independently, including that of self-employment;

– preventing the abuse of private power;
– strengthening competitive controls by establishing numerous decision-making centers;
– preparing for and securing against the plight of individuals or entire population groups; only then can a wide-based identification with the free market system be expected.

The experience of the past confirms up to this day that co-operatives have contributed and continue to contribute decisively to safeguarding the free market system. By emphasizing self-help and refusing state aid as strongly as they do, co-operatives serve as a model of the limitation of state power. The inner co-operative democracy is based on ethical and economic regulation of benevolent behavior within the community, the effects of which radiate beyond the actual co-operative sectors (→ *Corporate Culture*).

The activities around the initial establishment of co-operatives as well as the preservation of mid-sized companies through co-operative action clearly indicate several achievements and sectors of co-operative work:

– strengthening the independent middle class;
– increasing the number of independent business decision-making centers;
– encouraging economic dynamism;
– contributing to effective control of private power;
– improving the competitive control functions.

Co-operatives, which originally came into being as "children of want and need" in today's industrialized countries, continue to prove themselves a successful instrument for self-help and offer the developing and second-world countries a chance (as of yet unused) to overcome plight through consequential self-help. In other words, one can establish close reciprocal influences between a free market system and co-operatives as self-help organizations. The market economy offers the freedom and space for co-operatives to develop as they may. Likewise, energy is generated from co-operative activities which contribute to safeguard and reinforce the fundaments of the free market system.

Bibliography

Boettcher, Erik: Die Idee des Genossenschaftswesens und dessen ordnungs- und gesellschaftspolitischer Standort, in: Boettcher, Erik (ed.): Die Genossenschaften im Wettbewerb der Ideen, Tübingen 1985, pp. 27–48.
DeutscherGenossenschaftsverband (Schulze-Delitzsch) e.V. i.L. (ed.): Schulze-Delitzsch – ein Lebenswerk für Generationen, Wiesbaden 1987 (with articles by R. Aldenhoff, E. Dülfer, V. Beuthien and W. Hamm).
Dülfer, Eberhard: Betriebswirtschaftslehre der Kooperative, Göttingen 1984.
Eucken, Walter: Grundsätze der Wirtschaftspolitik (Bern, Tübingen 1952), 5th edition, Bern, Tübingen 1975.
Genossenschaften und Staat. Bericht über die IV. Internationale genossenwissenschaftliche Tagung in Wien 1963, in: Zeitschrift für das gesamte Genossenschaftswesen, Göttingen, vol. 14 (1964), pp. 125ff.
Gutmann, Gernot: Volkswirtschaftslehre. Eine ordnungstheoretische Einführung, Stuttgart 1981.
Kluthe, Klaus: Genossenschaften und Staat in Deutschland, Berlin 1985.
Münkner, Hans-H.: Selbstverständnis und Rechtsverfassung von Genossenschaftsorganisationen in EG-Partnerstaaten, in: Boettcher, Erik (ed.): Die Genossenschaften im Wettbewerb der Ideen, Tübingen 1985, pp. 87–116.
Schultz, Reinhard/Zerche, Jürgen: Genossenschaftslehre, Berlin 1983.
Willgerodt, Hans: Wertvorstellungen und theoretische Grundlagen des Konzepts der Sozialen Marktwirtschaft, in: Schriften des Vereins für Sozialpolitik, N.F., vol. 190, Berlin 1990, pp.31–60.
Woll, Artur: Wirtschaftspolitik, München 1984.

State and Co-operatives in Socialism

TADEUSZ KOWALAK

(see also: *Socialist Co-operative Theory*; *Socialist Critics*; *Economic Order*; *State and Co-operatives, Market Economy*; *Development, Eastern Europe*)

I. Preliminary Remarks; II. Types of Relations between Co-operatives and the State; III. Trends of Further Development.

I. Preliminary Remarks

Co-operatives, first introduced after the Russian October Revolution of 1917, were the only form of economic activity taken over from capitalism and implemented into the new socialist system. The first theoretical justification for the existence of co-operatives in socialist Russia was found in the writings of *Karl Marx*, the discussions of which, although dispersed throughout his works, were never developed into a systematical concept. The theory of co-operatives in socialism was developed by *V.I.Lenin* in several articles, the most important of which being entitled "On Cooperation", written in 1923. Although interpreted differently by theorists and practitioners, *Lenin's* co-operative theory was considered permanently true and as such was implemented in all countries of middle and eastern Europe after the Second World War (→ *Socialist Critics*).

According to *Lenin's* theory, co-operatives were the simplest way to implement the socialist concept of society in Russia after the revolution was accomplished; hence, in March 1919, obligatory affiliation of all Russian citizens to consumer co-operatives was imposed in order to introduce the principle of equality into the sphere of consumption. Equality in the sphere of production was to be introduced by socializing all means of production. Lenin considered the co-operative form the most suitable method to change private ownership into collective ownership, particularly in agriculture and handicraft trade. Thus, co-operatives became instruments in the process of constructing a new socialist economic and political system. Their main purpose and, at the same time, the justification of their existence, was to build up Socialism, i.e. to primarily serve the interests of society as a whole. The most important instrument of the socialist economic system was a centrally conceived and implemented plan of economic and social development. Therefore, co-operatives, as tools in the process of building socialism, were subordinated to the state, which was simultaneously the supreme political organization of the society, the supreme manager of the national economy, and the owner of most (if not all) means of production. Consequently, co-operative ownership as group ownership was considered a lower form of socialist ownership. This justified its subordination to state political and economic authorities.

Through coefficients provided by plans of economic and social development, the state regulated almost everything concerning co-operatives: the fields of co-operative economic activity, the changes in co-operative functions, the organization of co-operatives and their unions, the supply of the means of production as well as capital, investments, the prices of the most important goods, the channels of distribution, the number of persons employed, and their wages. Only decisions of minor significance were left to the co-operative management. The subordination of co-operative property to the state authorities resulted in the occasional transfer of co-operative enterprises to economic sectors belonging to the state. Also known were transfers in the opposite direction, that is from the state to the co-operative sector. In the Soviet Union, for instance, the number of kolkhoses between 1950 and 1975 fell from over 100,000 to about 30,000, mainly because of the take-over of kolkohoses by state farms. In Poland in 1975, all small scale state industrial enterprises were transferred to the Central Union of Work Co-operatives and integrated with existing work co-operatives. In both cases, neither co-operative members nor their organizations were consulted. Between 1956 and 1960, the Soviet workers' productive (or work) co-operatives were transferred to the state industrial enterprises. In Czechoslovakia, → *consumer co-operatives* were eliminated from urban areas and assigned only to rural regions in the early 1950s. Their town property was assumed by state wholesale and retail trade enterprises.

The monopolistic systems of state banks and state sup-ply and marketing wholesale enterprises insured that the economic plan would be fulfilled. On the other hand, the rigid control by the state bureaucratic structures played a role which cannot be overestimated. The system of "*nomenklatura*", i.e. the designation of top functionaries in co-operatives and their unions by the Communist Party, facilitated the functioning of the totalitarian machinery in the co-operative sector of the economy.

Of course, this description gives a simplified picture of the relation between the state and co-operatives. There are significant differences between the various socialist countries as far as their economic and social conditions are concerned. These differences, as well as the process of relaxing the rigidity of the socialist system in particular countries, generated differences in the mutual relations between the state and co-operative movements.

II. Types of Relations between Co-operatives and the State

At the end of the 1980s, three types of relations between the state and co-operatives could be identified.

1. State-controlled Co-operatives

As a result of the rigid implementation of the rules characteristic for the doctrine of Leninist-Stalinist Communism described above, this type of relation functioned during the Stalinist period in all Eastern European countries under Soviet domination. Since 1956 in Poland and 1968 in Hungary, changes in the rigid relations between the state and co-operatives have gradually been introduced, stemming from the process of relaxing the general socialist system. As in the end of 1989, only the former Bulgarian, Czechoslovakian, Romanian, and former East German co-operatives could be defined as state-controlled co-operatives, openly manifested in the regulations of each respective country's co-operative law.

The East German Act on Agricultural Co-operatives of 1982 stated that agricultural production co-operatives (LPG) (→ *Joint-production Co-operative*s) fulfilled their tasks according to the decision of the Socialist United Party of Germany (Sozialistische Einheitspartei Deutschlands, SED), that they were a part of the integrated socialist national economy, and that they organized their economic activity according to plans approved by the state. Only → *consumer co-operatives* were affiliated to the co-operative unions on regional and state levels. Their central federation, the Verband der deutschen Konsumgenossenschaften (Federation of German Consumer Co-operatives), was responsible for consumer co-operatives to realize the economic policy of the former GDR and to coordinate their development. In the statutes, it is explicitly stated that the principle of democratic centralism is obligatory within the organization. What has been decided on a higher level must be followed by lower level organizations. → *Co-operative banks* in the GDR had their Central Federation, the

Verband der Genossenschaftskassen (Federation of Co-operative Saving Banks), which was subordinated to the East German State Bank. → *Supply and marketing co-operatives* of handicraft industries were directly subordinated to the District Chamber of Handicraft, a state authority; housing co-operatives were subordinated to the District Councils; agricultural production co-operatives, horticultural co-operatives, and co-operatives of the working fishermen (→ *Rural Co-operatives*) were subordinated to the Department of Agriculture and Food in the respective District Councils; artisans' productive co-operatives were subordinated to the Department of Local Supply Economy of the District Councils, and fishing productive co-operatives to the Union of State Sea Fishery Enterprises. All the authorities and/or enterprises mentioned were subordinated to the proper ministries, either directly or indirectly.

Bulgarian co-operatives were in a very similar, if perhaps less drastic, situation. State authorities could assign their central and district co-operative unions to allocate the tasks of the state plan among the respective co-operative organizations and enterprises. The Union itself was to play an active role in the construction of both, the material and technical, bases of socialism and in building the developed socialist society in Bulgaria. The power and authority of the Central Co-operative Federation were very much like those of a state ministry, making it the central management system for national economic decisions in all fields concerning the activities of affiliated co-operatives. According to the Bulgarian Law on Co-operative Organizations (1983), Bulgarian co-operatives were an inseparable part of the national economic organization. By law, they were defined as "socialist public economic organizations". The state was to assist, encourage, and co-ordinate their economic activities.

In Czechoslovakia, the economic activity plans of the co-operatives were also based on targets and directives laid down in the socio-economic development plans of the state. The stress, however, was put on the state's function and the obligation to create conditions for the realization of the economic and social development of co-operatives, mainly through a system of generally binding legal regulations. Nevertheless, co-operatives were to follow the decisions of the People's Councils, which were state organizations. In Czechoslovakia, the relationship between co-operatives and the state differed from those in the GDR and in Bulgaria in that the state was obliged by legal regulations to fully reimburse material losses resulting from state interference. Although being controlled by the state, co-operatives in these countries used to be defined "voluntary" organizations, respecting the principles of equality among members and democratic management.

There were some differences between particular countries as far as the organizational set-up of the position and role of co-operatives in the respective national economies is concerned. A high level of state interference resulted in a loss of voluntary involvement, the equality of rights, and democracy.

2. State-sponsored Co-operatives

After 1968, the process of change in the relations between the state and co-operatives in Hungary developed so far that their status could almost be defined as that of state-sponsored co-operatives. According to Hungarian Co-operative Law (1971) (→ *Law, International*), the purpose of the state's activity concerning co-operatives was to bring about harmony between social, group and individual interests. To achieve this goal, the state acted through legal regulations, economic directions, and the involvement of public authorities. State authorities were restricted in exerting influence on co-operative activities, being authorized to do so only so far as being provided for by Acts of Parliament, legal and governmental decrees and resolutions. Ministers could issue regulations influencing the economic activites of co-operatives if the proper co-operative federation expressed its consent. The opinions of national co-operative federations had to be solicited as far as outlines of legal regulations from higher levels were concerned. Proper ministries were obliged by law to help the development of co-operatives. They were, however, to exercise professional supervision in order to assure that co-operative activities remained in accordance with the interests of society.

Co-operatives were supervised by Executive Committees of People's Councils and by co-operative federations. The National Council of Co-operatives, the highest co-operative institution in Hungary, was supervised by the Council of Ministers. If statutes or → *by-laws* were infringed upon, appropriate state authorities were empowered to abolish resolutions made by the co-operative's corporate management, to suspend presidents of co-operatives in their terms of office, and even to dissolve a co-operative or federation. The road for further emancipation of Hungarian co-operatives have however been opened. The definition of the co-operative gave the promotion of members' material welfare priority over its "planned and profitable participation in satisfying manifold requirements of the society."

According to the comprehensive Co-operative Law passed by the Soviet Parliament (Act on Co-operative Movement of 26th May, 1988), Soviet co-operatives have been made much more independent from state interference than Hungarian ones, and they may therefore be viewed as being in a partnership relation with the state. Because "of the great importance of the co-operative movement to the economic and social development of the society, to the rational use of material and human resources, and to the process of democratization, the State promotes with all its might the co-operative movement, contributes to its popularization, safeguards the rights and just interests of co-operatives and their members ... State guidance of co-operatives is realized by the Soviet of People's Delegates and by the State organs in full accordance with the Act". State authorities conclude agreements with co-operatives which contribute to the co-operative's participation in accomplishing the tasks of the economy as a whole; they provide necessary raw materials and grant investment credits for this purpose; they assign land and premises to co-operatives for production purposes; they promote the introduction of new technologies; they help in developing social activities and training personnel. The control over co-operatives (→ *Authorities, Co-operative*) exercised by state authorites is limited to the latter's compliance with regulations concerning conditions of work, fire prevention, fighting animal and plant diseases, and fulfilling commitments to the state budget and statistics. Co-operatives may be suspended for misusing natural resources by the proper state authority, or even liquidated in case of "brutal and permanent violation of law." The interference of the state authorities and/or co-operative federations with the economic activities or similar undertakings a co-operative, however, is not permitted.

If a state authority or a superior co-operative union transgresses its field of competences or offends against the law, the co-operative involved may take it to court or to a state arbitration committee in order to legitimize the incompatability of such acts with the law. Losses caused by such actions shall be compensated. All relations between co-operatives and state authorities, enterprises and institutions, between co-operatives and their unions, as well as relations between individual co-operatives themselves were to be based on agreements rather than orders.

3. Autonomous Co-operatives

The first breach in the rigid system of state control over co-operatives, that existed and functioned in the Eastern European countries since the end of the 1940s, was to be noted in Poland. There, after the famous Polish October of 1956, dairy, horticultural and credit co-operatives originally liquidated in the era of Stalinism, were re-established (1957) and plants and facilities were repossessed from state enterprises. The Law on Co-operatives and their Unions of 1963 included the principle of democratic self-government in the co-operative definition (→ *Development, Eastern Europe*). In Poland, the position of the co-operatives with respect to the state could be considered autonomous at the end of the 1980s. The new Co-operative Law of 1982 contained a remnant of the old concept of "co-operatives conducting their economic activities being guided by assumptions laid down in central and territorial socio-economic plans", but in this respect there was no mechanism for state interference provided by the Law. The economic reform of 1981/82 revoked the obligatory economic indices imposed on co-operatives by state planning authorities up to that time through co-operative federations as intermediary agencies. Co-operatives regained their freedom of economic decision-making and started to take advantage of it as far as their economic resources allowed them to.

By this Law, all levels of state administration were obliged to collaborate with co-operatives in the execution of their socio-economic tasks and to extend appropriate assistance to them. This regulation is to be interpreted as a declaration of intentions rather than a source of actual state activity. Proper organs of state administration, according to the Law of 1982, have the right to impose new tasks on the co-operatives' plans or to assign to them tasks which were not originally included in their plans. But this is only the case if there are indispensable national demands such as help for defence or relief in case of natural disaster. In such situations, the proper ministry in the state administration should provide co-operatives with all means necessary to carry out the imposed tasks. The execution of such tasks should be based on appropriate agreements. If losses result, the co-operative can claim damages from the department which imposed the task.

In Poland, the old controversy about the nature of co-operative ownership has been solved by the new Law on Economic Activity (January 1, 1990), which provides full equality of the rights of state, co-operative and private enterprises (→ *Legal Form, Co-operative*). This provision was fundamental for maintaining the autonomous position of co-operatives in their relations to the state.

In order to guarantee this position, the Co-operative Law provides that co-operatives, in cases their right's have been infringed upon, may sue state authorities, enterprises and institutions, as well as co-operative federations. Thus, the courts function as independent institutions, enforcing respect for legal regulations on all levels of state authority and co-operative organizations.

III. Trends of Further Development

During the decade of the 1980s, even in the most orthodox conservative Marxist Countries like the GDR (until 1990) or Bulgaria, a general trend towards the limitation of governmental influence on co-operatives was to be noticed. In Poland and Hungary, economic reforms resulted in reducing the influence of state authorities on the formulation of the business activity plans for the co-operative sector. Obligatory economic indices were either cancelled or reduced in number. As far as the influence of the state on organizational and decision-making processes was concerned, remarkable changes were taking place. The East German Act on Agricultural Productive Co-operatives (1982) introduced co-operative bodies into the decision-making process in all forms of inter-co-operative collaboration, as well as in cooperation between co-operatives and state farms. In Bulgaria, where, according to the Law on Co-operatives of 1948, the → by-laws of all new co-operatives were subject to approval by the Council of Ministers before their official registration, the Co-operative Law of 1983 no longer required any approval or opinion prior to the registration of a co-operative. At the end of 1989, model by-laws, which were obligatory in all countries of Eastern Europe during the three decades between 1950 and 1980, were binding only in the former GDR.

In Poland, neither statements of intention from the central co-operative union nor opinions from the proper local state authority have been needed for a new co-operative's registration application since 1983. In 1987, the association of Polish co-operatives in central co-operative unions was no longer obligatory. Changes of the Hungarian Law on Co-operatives of 1971, introduced in the 1980s, secured co-operatives more independence in their planning processes and in the establishment of their internal organizations. The tendency to grant co-operatives more independence from governmental and lower level state authorities also materialized in the introduction of the co-operative's right to appeal in court in cases of illegal interference into co-operative activities by the state or co-operative federations (Poland, Hungary, the Soviet Union).

The critical political changes which took place in the end of 1989 brought about new co-operative laws or amendments to co-operative laws in all post communist countries of Eastern Europe between 1990 and 1993. The unification of Germany granted the co-operatives operating on the former territory of the GDR important support from West German co-operative organizations and brought that region under the rule of the German Co-operative Law of 1889 with its later amendments (→ *Law, National*). This resulted in a relatively rapid restructualization of the co-operatives according to the requirements of a democractic political structure and market economy system (→ *LAG, Germany*). For the rest of post-Communist Eastern European countries, this process will require much more time.

An example for severe state interference into co-operative structures is the Law on Changes in the Organization and Functioning of Co-operatives adopted by the Polish Parliament in January, 1990. This law was aimed at destroying the monopolistic and bureaucratic upper level co-operative structures formerly serving as agents of the centrally planned economy, as well as eliminating top and middle-level co-operative personnel, which, in the past, was designated to their posts by the Communist Party. This incidental law, characteristic of the transition period from a socialist to a capitalistic system, was to promote the further introduction of the market economy.

The present wave of criticism of the concept of state-controlled co-operatives, together with the changes presently taking place in the political and economic systems of the Eastern European countries, do indicate the most probable development of mutual relations between the state and co-operatives. In the minds of the population, the centrally planned economic system created a generally disapproving image of co-operatives – as organizations ruled by the state. The reintroduction of genuine co-operatives is now being demanded. In many respects, they are to be different from what they became in the system of "real socialism". It seems to be generally accepted that, in order to create genuine co-operatives and co-operative structures at the regional and national level, they must meet certain requirements and must have certain characteristics, respectively: they have to be independent from any state interference into their structures and activites; they have to be democratically managed, i.e. free in choosing their administration, as well as in planning and controlling their activities through a democratic system of decision-making; they must be free to affiliate with co-operative unions; and self-financing. Their primary and predominant purpose should be to support and promote the enterprises and households of their members. Co-operatives should be based on the principles of self-help and solidarity (→ *Principles*). The material and non-material links between members and their co-operatives should be strengthened to create an organization really owned and controlled by their members (→ *Managerial Economics*). Such co-operatives would have the potential to play an adequate economic and social role in the market economy system developed within a democratic political environment.

The Co-operative Law passed by the Polish Parliament on 16th of May, 1993, responds to the ideas presented above. Co-operatives became organizations independent from the interference by state authorities at all levels. In some other countries of Eastern Europe like Hungary (1992) and Czechoslovac Republic (1990), co-operative laws certainly created the same conditions of independence from the state as well as equal rights with respect to other forms of enterprises; this will secure the development of genuine co-operative structures.

In the Eastern European countries, co-operatives have never been the decisive economic force. Their future situation depends on new legal regulations as well as on the market. The new legal regulations are based on principles of equality for all forms of enterprises (private, co-operative, and state) and on independence and democracy. Co-operatives have lost their former privileges. It is therefore most probable that, under the pressure from the rules of a free market economy, they will be of minor importance for economies of the Eastern European countries.

Bibliography

Lenin, Wladimir I.: On Co-operatives (1923). Polish edition in: Lenin o spóldzielczosci, Warszawa 1974, pp. 673–684.
Kleer, Jerzy: Panstwo i spóldzielczosc w socjalizmie (State and Co-operatives in Socialism), Warszawa 1973.
Janic, J.: Udzial spoldzielczosci w gospodarce narodowej krajów RWPG (The Share of Co-operative Movement in National Economies of CMED Countries), Spóldzielczy Kwartalnik Naukowy (Co-operative Scientific Quarterly), Warszawa, No. 4, 1981, pp. 133–155.
Texts of Laws on Co-operatives from Bulgaria, Czechoslovakia, German Democratic Republic, Hungary, Poland, Rumania and the Soviet Union.

Strategic Alliances

DIETGER HAHN/LUTZ KAUFMANN

(see also: *Intercompany Cooperation*; *Joint Ventures*; *Strategy Planning*; *Institutional Economics*)

I. Context; II. Definition of Strategic Alliances; III. Forms of Strategic Alliances; IV. Objectives of Strategic Alliances; V. Forming Strategic Alliances; VI. Potential Pitfalls of Strategic Alliances; VII. Re-forming Strategic Alliances.

I. Context

Alliances represent one of the buzzwords from the field of *strategic management*. Literally, strategic management has to invent the future of a company, a task that requires management of change (→ *Strategy Planning*). Conceptually, strategic management has

- to determine the *corporate philosophy*; and
- to design the desired *corporate culture*;
- to shape the *vision of the corporation*, and to define the *mission of the business*, both are an outflow of the system of *general objectives* of the company;
- to formulate *strategies on the corporate, business, and functional level as well as regional strategies for all of these levels*;
- to plan the *organizational structure*, the *legal form(s)*, and the *managerial infrastructure* (including management development systems, incentive systems and information systems) of the company;
- to *implement* the respective programs; and
- to *control* the appropriateness and execution of the strategies (*Hahn* 1991; *Hahn* 1994, *Hax/Majluf* 1991).

The central task is the formulation and implementation of sound corporate, business, functional, and regional strategies. A company has two *generic alternatives to pursue its strategies*. One is to go-it-alone and the other is to cooperate. Strategic alliances belong to the second group: They are a way of pursuing the strategies of a company through cooperating with one or more other companies in order to achieve competitive advantages (→ *Intercompany Cooperation*).

Due to increasing challenges imposed by an ever changing environment the difficult question whether to *build, buy or cooperate* in order to grow recently attracted significant attention in theory and practice alike (*Harrigan* 1987; *Porter/Fuller* 1986, *Contractor/Lorange* 1988).

For an indepth understanding of the theoretical context and the nature of strategic alliances we have to start with our basic understanding of the *nature of the firm*. The firm can be seen

- as a *nexus of interests and activities*; and
- as a *nexus of contracts*.

As contracts are the "glue" between interests and activities, both perspectives are fully compatible: The stakeholders of a firm (e.g. shareholders, creditors, employees, customers and suppliers) have certain *interests* in the firm which they want to be satisfied. These interests can be satisfied if the stakeholders themselves supply the firm with certain *skills or competencies* (resources), that is if the stakeholders make contributions. Management therefore offers specific *incentives* to specific groups of stakeholders in exchange for specific *contributions* (stakeholder inputs). If stakeholders take this offer, a *contract* comes to life. This contract must not necessarily be a contract in the legal sense, it can be an informal "treaty" or a mental bond only. At this point, *Torger Reve* differentiates internal and external contracts, and he interprets the firm as a function

a) of organizational incentives and core as well as special skills (internally), and
b) of interorganizational incentives and complementary skills (externally) (*Reve* 1990).

Following this notion, we may view the *firm* as consisting of a *strategic core and special skills* and of *strategic relationships* or alliances with external parties. Traditional management literature focuses on managing the strategic core, not on managing strategic relationships. This focus shifts as firms increasingly utilize the flexibility of being a temporary partner in different alliance-networks. While still concentrating on their core activities (the vital parts of its business), firms can move relatively freely within alliance-networks as they anticipate and respond to changes in the environment.

II. Definition of Strategic Alliances

An alliance is a *specific kind of cooperation* and thus can be located as a hybrid governance mechanism *between hierarchies and markets* (*Williamson* 1990). Figuratively "the image is perhaps neither that of the "visible hand" nor the "invisible hand" but of the continuous handshake" (*Teece* 1989). Following the

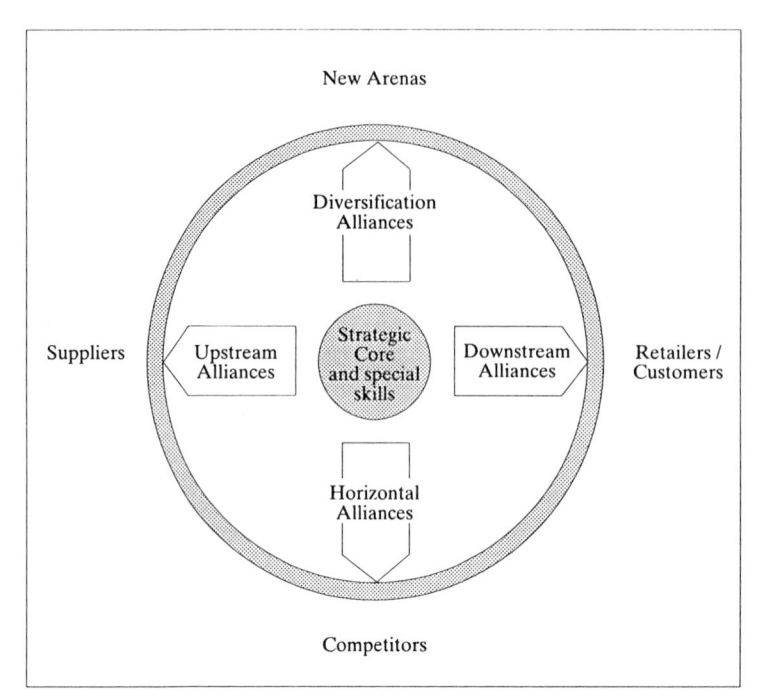

Figure 1: Strategic core and special skills and alternative strategic relationships of a firm (see *Reve* 1990)

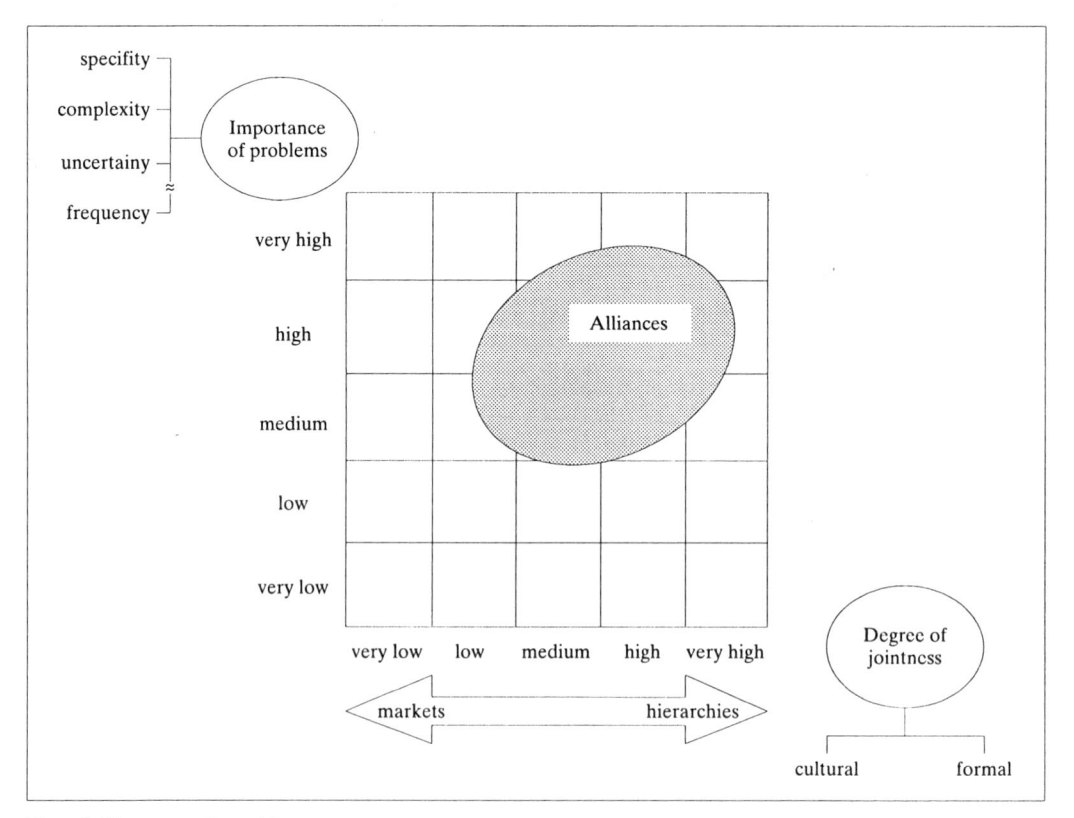

Figure 2: The cooperation grid

so-called Decision Theory of Management (*Heinen* 1971) and focusing on the process of cooperating, *cooperation* in short is *joint problem solving between independent firms*. It is characterized by a *pooling of interests* and a *pooling of activities* spelled out in *formal contracts*.

We can analyze cooperations in a two-dimensional way, in what we term the *cooperation grid*. The y-axis of our grid shows the importance of the problems that have to be solved (in a cooperative mode). The x-axis shows the *degree of "jointness"* with the extremes market and hierarchy. *Alliances* serve for solving problems of strategic importance and they are characterized by the fact that the *degree of jointness* is usually, but not necessarily *high* (but lower than in the case of a merger, which is not a form of alliance) (*Kaufmann* 1993).

Alliances are a specific *form of cooperation*. Here, the partners come together to achieve strategic objectives (*Harrigan* 1988) resp. *competitive advantages* vis-à-vis non-partners. For this end, they combine certain activities along their value chains. The overall objective, therefore, is to achieve competitive advantages through cooperative advantages.

While this categorization of alliances as a kind of strategic cooperation is commonly accepted in theory and practice alike, there has not emerged a commonly accepted complete definition of alliances so far. Sometimes the term alliance is used relatively restricted: In its most narrow approach, German management literature and German antitrust authorities define only horizontal strategic cooperations as alliances. This definition includes only "strategic cooperations between firms from the same industry or with related technologies" as (strategic) alliances (*Backhaus/Piltz* 1990; *Kartte* 1992; *Macharzina* 1993). In international management literature, we do find the term alliances applied in a less narrow fashion: Here, not only horizontal and conglomeral strategic cooperations (coalitions), but also strong relationships between buyers and their suppliers are called (forward or backward) alliances (*Heide/John* 1990; *Burgers, W.P./Hill, C.W.L./Kim, W.C.* 1993).

Sometimes nearly every form of cooperation is called an alliance: In some instances, the term alliance is also applied to intense cooperations between firms and not-for-profit organizations. This is frequently the case when university-industry collaboration is discussed (*Teece* 1989).

As they always serve as means to obtain competitive advantages, *alliances are per se strategic in nature*. We may therefore drop the term "strategic" as we leave it aside when talking about acquisitions and not about "strategic" acquisitions.

With reference to the Japanese *Keiretsus*, Horst Albach recently introduced the *concept of the strategic family* which goes beyond that of alliances: He describes a group of institutions whose successes are interdependent and whose strategies are complementary to each other as members of a strategic family. He sees e.g. the suppliers as well as the house-bank of a firm – in short, the *company-external key-stakeholders* of a firm – as part of the strategic family of this firm (*Albach* 1992). This new approach opens up a real *network-perspective* for further research in the field of alliances.

III. Forms of Strategic Alliances

Alliances can take different forms. From a *legal standpoint*, we can differentiate alliances where a *separate legal entity* exists (→ joint ventures, sometimes called equity joint ventures) and alliances where the partners do *not* hold equity in a *separate legal entity* as is the case with licensing agreements or supply agreements (sometimes called contractual joint ventures) (*Macharzina* 1993; *Weder* 1989). The definitions of alliances given above include equity joint ventures, but are not limited to this kind of venture (*Burgers, W.P./Hill, C.W.L./Kim, W.C.* 1993).

Depending on the *kind of activities on the value chains* of the partners which are *included* in the alliance we can differentiate alliances in *one functional area* (like pure R&D-alliances, e.g. research consortia) and alliances including *different functional areas* (like cross-licensing- and cross-marketing-agreements between two firms or joint ventures that include joint product development, joint manufacturing and marketing).

Depending on the position of the alliance-partners vis-à-vis each other, a third categorization can be used that distinguishes horizontal, vertical and conglomeral alliances: *Horizontal alliances* are agreements between actual or potential competitors from the same industry. *Vertical alliances* are strategic backward (between buyers and suppliers) or forward cooperations (e.g. between manufacturers and retailers). Here the partners operate in adjacent stages of the value chain. In *conglomeral alliances*, the partners come from different industries, e.g. a fiberoptics manufacturer and a computer company.

Alliances can also be categorized according to the *primary objective* of the alliance (*Backhaus/Plinke* 1990; *Pausenberger* 1993).

IV. Objectives of Strategic Alliances

Generalizing statements about objectives for alliances cannot be easily made. As alliances always serve as *means to better achieve the overall objectives* of companies, *objectives for an alliance always depend on the specific context of a company* and must be formulated on a case by case basis. Alliances are a way of pursuing corporate, business and/or functional objectives and strategies (*Abravanel/Ernst* 1992).

The success of a company depends on gaining competitive advantages. For the firms considering an alliance the alliance therefore is *instrumental in gaining competitive advantages* – at least vis-à-vis non-partners. Consequently, future success of an alliance depends on gaining "joint competitive advantages".

Depending on whether targeted customers attribute more value to the financial aspects (price) or the non-financial aspects (like quality) of a product or service, *cost leadership* or *differentiation* is the appropriate overall strategy to achieve competitive advantages (*Porter* 1985). Consequently, general objectives for allying, such as increasing market share, sales volume and productivity must be complemented by other operational *cost-, quality- and time-related performance-measures* (*Bleeke/Ernst* 1991). These central criteria can be influenced by the company in it's interplay with alliance partners and they allow for judging the success of an alliance. Because competitive advantage is itself a moving target, the priorities within the set of operational performance-measures will evolve over time and the appropriate configuration of alliances will, too.

Though a clearcut distinction is not possible, we can state that the *most common alliance motives* in practice fall into the following categories:

a) To establish *global* operations.
    Alliance partners often use an alliance as a vehicle to global scale production and to a local presence close to customers from around the world. The ultimate objective is to realize *economies* of scale and/or of scope.
b) To be able to generate a constant flow of *innovations*.
    In this case, the partners usually bring together complementary competencies. The objective is to *create new markets* and to secure an *advantageous position in traditional markets* without taking the full risk of failing (burden sharing).
c) To *outpace* non-partners.
    This is done mainly by shortening R&D-times through R&D-alliances, and by quickly penetrating markets through production and distribution alliances. The ultimate goal is to achieve a *quick and broad commercialization* of new products and services.

Alliances are prevalent in industries where high competitive interdependence and quickly changing demand conditions exist. Competitive uncertainty and demand uncertainty therefore seem to be the driving forces behind most alliances: The more *global* an industry, the larger the *product/service variety* in that industry, and the more *volatile* the environment of a business, the more likely is it that a company lacks the financial and know-how-resources to maintain a go-it-alone strategy. Examples are the automotive industry and the electronics industry. The global electronics industry e.g. is characterized by a convergence of telecommunications, computers and consumer electronics at an unprecedented pace (*Burgers, W.P./Hill, C.W.L./Kim, W.C.* 1993). Here we find all kinds of alliances: horizontal, conglomeral and vertical.

V. Forming Strategic Alliances

Forming an alliance requires gathering large volumes of data which must be analyzed thoroughly. This makes the process a demanding and time-consuming effort. Broken down into a few single *steps, the formation process includes* (see figure 3) (*Bleicher* 1992; *Bronder/Pritzl* 1992, *Lorange/Roos/Bronn* 1992):

- Stating the *objectives* for an alliance;
- Assessing and achieving *strategic fit* with potential alliance partners;
- Assessing and achieving *cultural fit* with potential alliance partners;
- Designing the *organizational, legal and managerial infrastructure* of the alliance.

1. Objectives for an Alliance

For stating the *objectives* a firm wants to achieve through an alliance, several informational prerequisites must be fulfilled. The alliance formation starts with a company-internal analysis: First and foremost, a thorough analysis of the own strengths and weaknesses of this firm must be conducted. Simultaneously, an analysis of the opportunities and threats evolving from the environment of the firm is necessary in order to obtain a *clear picture of the overall situation of the firm*.

Next, the own *corporate vision* as well as the *general objectives of the firm* must be taken into account. Among the strategies that are feasible to achieve *targeted competitive advantages*, a rough segmentation should be made. The set of alternative strategies must be roughly divided into two groups: one group of strategies that should be executed autonomously (e.g. through internal growth or through acquisitions), and the other group of strategies where cooperations resp. alliances should be analyzed more thoroughly. Empirical studies suggest that acquisitions are more promising for expanding core businesses and for expanding into existing geographic regions while *alliances* are more effective for entering or expanding *non core businesses* and/or for expanding into *new geographic areas* (*Bleeke/Ernst* 1991).

For the group of strategic problems which might be solved through an alliance, it can be decided company-internally what degree of jointness will be necessary to accomplish this task. The desired position of the co-operative venture in the cooperation grid should be depicted at this point in time. Management should now decide upon the *desired type of alliance* by answering the following questions (*Lorange/Roos/Bronn* 1992):

Figure 3

Objectives for an alliance	Strategic fit	Cultural fit	Alliance infrastructure	Ongoing management of the alliance
Strengths/ Weaknesses, Oppertunities/ Threats-analysis	compatible visions	culture profiles	organizational interfaces	
corporate vision, general objectives, targeted competitive advantages	win-win-possibilities	cultural misfits	legal contracts	
	complementary strengths	impacts of misfits on the alliance	equity links	
potential areas for an alliance: produkts, markets, regions, functions → search profile	letter of intent	management of acculturation	planning system	
	business, functional, and regional strategies		MIS and EDI	
			key personell	

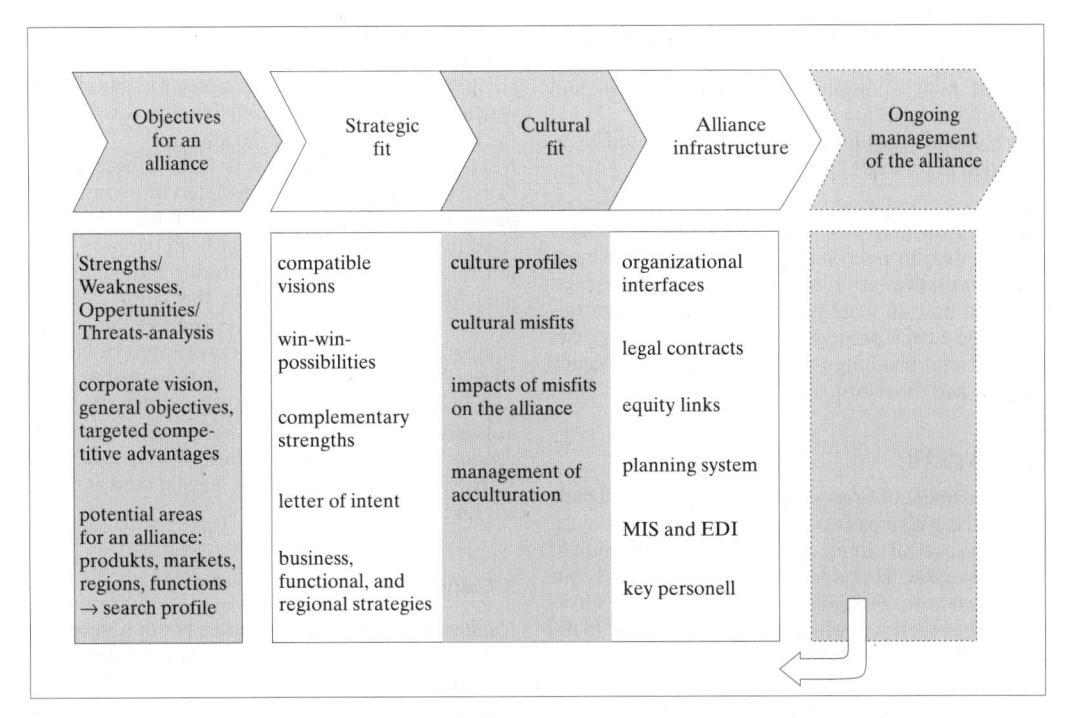

Figure 3: Key aspects in the formation process of an alliance

Figure 4

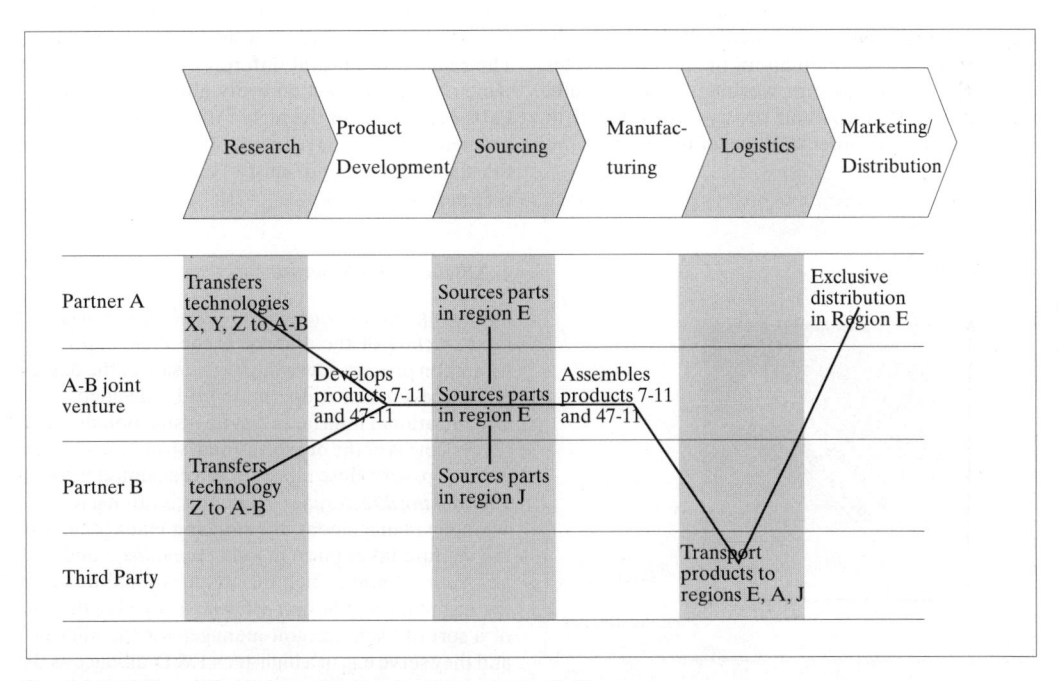

	Research	Product Development	Sourcing	Manufacturing	Logistics	Marketing/ Distribution
Partner A		Transfers technologies X, Y, Z to A-B	Sources parts in region E			Exclusive distribution in Region E
A-B joint venture		Develops products 7-11 and 47-11	Sources parts in region E	Assembles products 7-11 and 47-11		
Partner B		Transfers technology Z to A-B	Sources parts in region J			
Third Party					Transport products to regions E, A, J	

Figure 4: Activity profile of a cross-functional and cross-regional alliance

- Should the alliance be horizontal, vertical or conglomeral?
- What kind of businesses (which products and which markets) are considered?
- Which activities along the value chain should be included in principle?

Having specified what *kind of products, markets, regions and functions* should be covered by the alliance, it is possible to point out which of the above mentioned *objectives* are *specific to the alliance* in question and how an ideal partner would look. On this basis, the search process for an alliance partner can start. Useful planning tools at this stage are *search profiles and checklists*.

2. Strategic Fit

An assessment of *strategic fit* between potential partners starts with a basic check of the following points: First, the overall *visions* of the two companies should be compatible. That does not mean that the visions must lead both companies in exactly the same direction. Nevertheless, it will not make much sense in the long run to cooperate with a company that has declared that it's strategic intent is to drive the potential partner out of major markets. Second, both partners must clearly see broad *benefits for both* of them (winwin situation) through allying. Third, the two parties must see areas where they can *complement each other* such that they *create common strengths* that yield advantages in the market place and the financial benefits desired (*Bronder/Pritzl* 1992).

Now the partners can develop a *"letter of intent"* which should not be legally binding. It should simply demonstrate the commitment of the senior management of both sides to start working together, while still keeping the formation process open-ended in this initial phase in order to allow for flexibility in the latter phases of the process (*Bery/Bowers* 1991). The letter of intent can be interpreted as a *statement of common objectives*: The objectives *for* the alliance which both partners have individually, now become the common objectives *of* the alliance.

Next, the mutual willingness to form a successful alliance has primarily to be translated into sound *business plans* by a joint working team. It has to be translated into the business plans of both partners and – in case of a (equity) joint venture – into a business plan for the joint venture. In the latter case, the market potential has to be assessed and the general competitive approach of the venture must be laid out (*Bery/Bowers* 1991). The formation process then proceeds by an in-depth analysis of the combined *business, functional and regional implications of the venture*. A helpful planning tool for this task is the activity profile diagram which may be used at different levels of precision.

3. Cultural Fit

Cultural fit between the partners is not a necessary condition for successful alliances; nevertheless, it is a desirable situation (*Pohle* 1990). As the → *corporate culture* can be a source for competitive advantages, compatible cultures may be sources of co-operative advantages. What is necessary for alliance-success is in any case a certain degree of tolerance or openness toward the culture of the partner: the partners must develop an *informed respect for their cultural differences* (*Lewis* 1990). In the course of an alliance there may well emerge an alliance culture as the partners interact over time and as acculturation takes place. The remaining cultural differences do not have the same negative impact on every alliance. The potential for conflict rises the higher the importance of the problems is which have to be solved collectively, and the higher the cultural "misfit" between the partners is (*Kaufmann* 1993).

4. Alliance Infrastructure

Designing the *organizational, legal and managerial infrastructure* of the alliance is the final step in the formation process. Here the formal side of the degree of jointness in our cooperation grid is decided.

Organizational interfaces can be institutionalized on several levels of the organizational structure. Starting at the top, very close alliances are cemented through *interlocking directorates*. While this is often a form of symbolic management, the ongoing management of the venture takes place in *joint committees*, and *project-teams*. Another helpful organizational device is the installation of *liaison officers:* They play the role of a sort of "key account manager for the alliance" and they serve e.g. in a high-tech R&D-alliance as the gatekeepers who make sure that the alliance does not

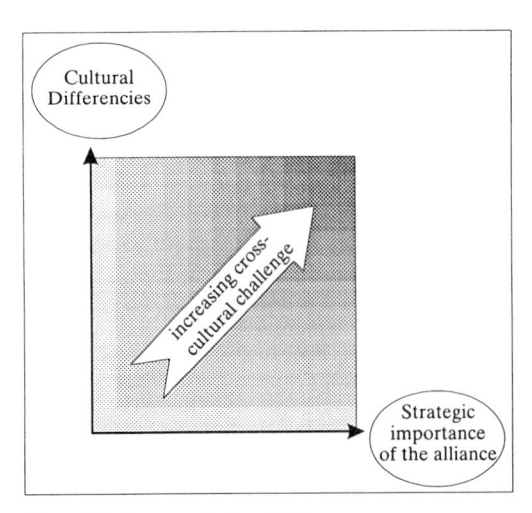

Figure 5: Relevance of cultural differences

become a know-how drain for their respective companies. In case of a full-blown → *joint venture*, a whole new *organizational structure* must be developed in addition to the creation of organizational interfaces between the partners (*Hahn* 1992).

The *contract* between the alliance partners is a legally recognized mutual plan for the co-operative venture. Changes to contracts must be mutually accepted. Therefore, highly structured contracts usually don't leave sufficient room for adjustments to changing conditions. In order to allow for flexibility, certain risks have to be left open in contracts. However, in every contract the termination clauses should be included to prevent serious problems at the time the alliance is dissolved (note that dissolving an alliance may well be a sign of it's success!).

The time horizon of the alliance and the contract duration should be the same, such that investment decisions have a safe ground to be based on. There are some *contract types* that support longer term alliances (*Lewis* 1990). One is the so-called "evergreen" or "rolling" contract. This is a multiyear agreement (e.g. over ten years) that is renewed periodically (e.g. every year). Another type is the contingency agreement, which implies that certain rights and obligations come into effect provided that certain events occur. An example is that one partner grants options for licenses if certain technical results are achieved during a R&D-agreement. The problem associated with contracts in which the partners agree to discuss a new agreement after certain milestones are completed is that the uncertainty resulting from renegotiations after each stage discourage substantial long-term risktaking. The focus then is on negotiating every single foreseeable aspect ("the fine letters of the contract") rather than on forming a flexible cooperation under an umbrella of shared objectives.

Other tools for binding alliance partners are direct and indirect *equity links* (*Teece* 1989). In joint ventures, the partners create indirect links between each other by holding equity in the joint venture. Direct equity links are when the partners hold stock of each other. This is more common in horizontal and conglomeral alliances, and relatively uncommon in backward alliances between buyers and their suppliers – at least in Western economies (*Kaufmann* 1993).

The important points about the managerial infrastructure which might have to be adapted to the alliance strategy are the *managerial and the technological aspects of the management information system*. The managerial part is to shape the *planning and reporting systems* according to the objectives, the strategies, and the organization of the alliance (*Lorange/ Roos/Bronn* 1992). It has to be made clear who decides what and when and what the critical performance measures are. The (information-)technological part is to make sure that the *MIS* (Management Information Systems) of the partners (and possibly the joint venture) are compatible and have smooth interfaces such that no major bottlenecks for efficient *EDI* (Electronic Data Interchange) exist.

A very important task for securing the success of an alliance is the *human resources management* of key personnel. Special attention should be given to the staffing policies, management development, and the incentive system. The most critical success factor is to develop managers who are willing and able to manage both people and business at the interface of two companies. *Knut Bleicher* has pointed out several practices that also contribute to the goal of achieving cultural fit with alliance partners (*Bleicher* 1989):

- appoint managers to the alliance on a full-time basis;
- transfer managers to the alliance partner;
- develop "alliance managers", that is managers with strong pragmatic and conceptual skills for the alliance setting and with open-mindedness towards their counterparts;
- make the alliance success a basis for the promotion and the rewards of individual managers.

VI. Potential Pitfalls of Strategic Alliances

1. Insufficient Stakeholder Blessing

If stakeholders do not agree with the alliance idea, the formation process might be politicized – and delayed – in latter phases. The major stakeholders internal and external to the company must accept and promote the idea of forming an alliance in general and with a specific partner. As pointed out earlier, the stakeholders have certain interests which they want to have satisfied by the company. The same applies to an alliance. Therefore, it is necessary to assess in advance what *effects* potential alliances may have on different groups or subgroups of stakeholders (e.g. a potential loss of jobs for some employees) and what their *reactions* will be. Depending on the effects and the reactions, the relevant groups must be informed and possibly convinced in an *open dialogue* which is one of the most important tasks of top management in the early stages of an alliance formation. The top management should try to gain and to foster understanding and support for the alliance idea through explaining the alliance idea with all its consequences – especially to the managers and functional specialists (e.g. decreasing autonomy for certain researchers) – in a way that lets them see the opportunities of allying without neglecting the risks (*Lorange/Roos/Bronn* 1992).

2. Poorly Designed Reward Systems

While information is important, it is only one of the tools that should be applied. As information and reward systems *both* play a critical role in order to overcome the mental walls within people's minds that hinder successful alliance management, the *rewards* must be made dependent on the *achievement of milestones* in the alliance process. Especially if the rewards and the appraisal of full-time managers depend on properly structuring the alliance, they should be more motivated to ensure alliance success (*Bery/Bowers* 1991).

3. Bad Planning and a Lack of Adaptability

Another potential pitfall is the *expectation of stability* as an assumption in the planning process. Alliances almost always include a "give-something-to-get-something"-situation. Depending on who gives and gets what and especially at what point in time, the *bargaining position* of the firm *will change* over time. Another source of problems lies in the challenges imposed by *changing competitive environments.* Therefore, the focus in setting up an alliance should always be on designing *flexible plans. Contingency planning* (e.g. for what to do if a joint R&D-project fails or is delayed) can prevent the partners to some degree from becoming inflexible. But despite having contingency plans, there must be an *openness to change* – or put differently a willingness to continuous learning and improvement – while the alliance grows and evolves over time.

4. Decreasing management attention

Over time another pitfall may appear: *decreasing management attention* to the alliance (*Bleicher* 1989). Here it is advisable to schedule regular informal meetings between the top management of the partners and to install a steering committee that supervises the alliance continuously. Making a high-level executive as a 'mentor' responsible for the development of the alliance may prevent diminishing top-management attention.

VII. Re-forming Strategic Alliances

The performance of an alliance should be evaluated continuously against it's initial objectives. Nevertheless, there may come a point for one or both partners where the alliance does not yield results that can be seen as satisfactory. At this point, it has to be decided whether the cooperative effort should be continued or whether it should be terminated.

The process of rebuilding an alliance starts with a thorough *analysis of the reasons that made the current alliance ineffective.* The causes of the problem have to be discovered. Did the objectives change? Did the partner not contribute its share to the venture and why did it not do so? Did the competitive environment change and in what respect? Answers to questions like these can e.g. be obtained from interviewing key personnel, industry experts and customers. Such a review is basically the starting point for a *new formation process* as discribed above: The partners must update the objectives for and of the alliance, reassess strategic as well as cultural fit, and they must analyze whether the organizational, legal and managerial infrastructure of the cooperative venture is appropriate.

It seems psychologically important not to start the reformation process by criticizing the partner's past actions and to focus on negotiating a new legal contract: After an unsuccessful performance of the venture often mistrust has come up, and the partners have in most cases to redevelop their cooperative spirit first, in order to *focus on formulating new joint objectives and strategies* afterwards. Legal aspects should play a minor role at the beginning of rebuilding an alliance. Also the parties should not try to achieve quick fixes. The restructuring of an alliance may well take the same amount of time as did the initial formation process (*Bery/Bowers* 1991).

It may speed up the rebuilding process to *use a neutral third party, like a consulting firm.* This third party can act as a catalyst in the communication processes between the partners. If problems have mounted up extremely, partners may at first want to discuss problems indirectly through the consultant. The consultants may also play the role of a vertical communication link between the senior management of both sides and the joint working-team(s).

Bibliography

Abravanel, R./Ernst, D.: Alliance and acquisition strategies for European national champions. In: The McKinsey Quarterley, 1992, No. 2, pp. 44–62.

Albach, H.: Strategische Allianzen, strategische Gruppen und strategische Familien. In: Zeitschrift für Betriebswirtschaft, Vol. 62, 1992, pp. 663–667.

Backhaus, K./Piltz, K.: Strategische Allianzen. In: Backhaus, K./Piltz, K. (eds.): Strategische Allianzen, ZfbF-Sonderheft 27/1990, pp. 1–10.

Backhaus, K./Plinke, W.: Strategische Allianzen als Antwort auf veränderte Wettbewerbsstrukturen. In: Backhaus, K./Piltz, K. (eds.): Strategische Allianzen, ZfbF-Sonderheft 27/1990, pp. 21–33.

Bery, V./Bowers, T.: Rebuilding an alliance. In: The McKinsey Quarterley, 1991, No. 4, pp. 94–105.

Bleeke, J., Ernst, D.: The way to win in cross-border alliances. In: Harvard Business Review, Vol. 69, 1991, No. 6, pp. 127–135.

Bleicher, K.: Der Strategie-, Struktur- und Kulturfit Strategischer Allianzen als Erfolgsfaktor. In: Bronder, C./Pritzl, R. (eds.): Wegweiser für Strategische Allianzen, Frankfurt/Wiesbaden 1992, pp. 267–293.

Bleicher, K.: Kritische Aspekte des Managements zwischenbetrieblicher Kooperation. In: Thexis, 1989, No. 3, pp. 4–8.

Bronder, C./Pritzl, R.: Ein konzeptioneller Ansatz zur Gestaltung und Entwicklung Strategischer Allianzen. In: Bronder, C./Pritzl, R. (eds.): Wegweiser für Strategische Allianzen, Frankfurt/Wiesbaden 1992, pp. 17–44.

Burgers, W.P./Hill, C.W.L./Kim, W.C.: A Theory of Global Strategic Alliances. In: Strategic Management Journal, Vol. 14, 1993, pp. 419–432.

Contractor, F./Lorange, P.: Why Should Firms Cooperate? In: Contractor, F./Lorange, P. (eds.): Cooperative Strategies in International Business, Lexington 1988, pp. 3–30.
Hahn, D.: Entwicklungstendenzen der strategischen Führung. In: technologie & management, Vol. 41, 1992, No. 2, pp. 10–21.
Hahn, D.: PuK – Controllingkonzepte, 4. A., Wiesbaden 1994.
Hahn, D.: Strategic Management – Tasks and Challenges in the 1990s. In: Long Range Planning, Vol. 24, 1991, No. 1, pp. 26–39.
Harrigan, K.R.: Strategic Alliances and Partner Asymmetries. In: Contractor, F./Lorange, P. (eds.): Cooperative Strategies in International Business, Lexington 1988, pp. 205–226.
Harrigan, K.R.: Strategic Alliances – Their new role in global competition. In: The Columbia Journal of World Business, Vol. 22, 1987, pp. 67–69.
Hax, A.C./Majluf, N. S.: The Strategy Concept and Process, Englewood Cliffs 1991.
Heide, J.B./John, G.: Alliances in Purchasing. In: Journal of Marketing Research, Vol. 27, 1990, pp. 24–36.
Heinen, E.: Der entscheidungsorientierte Ansatz der Betriebswirtschaftslehre. In: Zeitschrift für Betriebswirtschaft, Vol 41, 1971, pp. 429–444.
Kartte, W.: Wettbewerbspolitische und wettbewerbsrechtliche Probleme Strategischer Allianzen. In: Bronder, C./Pritzl, R. (eds.): Wegweiser für Strategische Allianzen, Frankfurt/Wiesbaden 1992, pp. 401–424.
Kaufmann, L.: Planung von Abnehmer-Zulieferer-Kooperationen, Gießen 1993.
Lewis, J.D.: Partnerships for Profit, New York 1990.
Lorange, P./Roos, J./Bronnn, P.S.: Building Successful Strategic Alliances. In: Long Range Planning, Vol. 25, 1992, No. 6, pp. 10–17.
Macharzina, K.: Unternehmensführung: Das internationale Managementwissen, Wiesbaden 1993.
Pausenberger, E.: Unternehmenszusammenschlüsse. In: W. Wittmann et al. (eds.): Handwörterbuch der Betriebswirtschaft, 5. A., pp. 4436–4448.
Pohle, K.: Strategische Allianzen in der chemisch-pharmazeutischen Industrie. In: Backhaus, K./Piltz, K. (eds.): Strategische Allianzen, ZfbF-Sonderheft 27/1990, pp. 67–76.
Porter, M.E./Fuller, M.B.: Coalitions and Global Strategy. In: Porter, M.E. (ed.), Competition in Global Industries, Boston 1989, pp. 315–342.
Porter, M. E.: Competitive Advantage, New York 1985.
Reve, T.: The Firm as a Nexus of Internal and External Contracts. In: Aoki, M./Gustafsson, B./Williamson, O.E. (eds.): The Firm as a Nexus of Treaties, London et al. 1990, pp. 133–161.
Teece, D.J.: Competition and Cooperation in Technology Strategy, Working Paper, University of California at Berkeley, Berkeley 1990.
Weder, R.: Joint Venture, Grüsch 1989.
Williamson, O.E.: The Firm as a Nexus of Treaties. In: Aoki, M./Gustafsson, B./Williamson, O.E. (eds.): The Firm as a Nexus of Treaties, London et al. 1990, pp. 1–25.

Strategies Employed When Establishing Co-operatives

JULIUS OTTO MÜLLER

(see also: *History in 19th C.*; *Conceptions, Co-operative*; *History of Ideas*; *Relationship Patterns*; *Organizational Structures, Co-operative*; *different articles concerning Co-operative Pioneers*)

I. Term; II. Objectives, Function, Types; III. Historical Approaches; IV. Modern Approaches.

I. Term

Used originally to designate the art of warfare and the organization of political and economic processes of decision (→ *Strategy Planning*), strategy in cooperation means the art of combining all the operations which, in consideration of the contemporary cultural situation, especially of political, economic and socio-cultural data, influence positively the foundation, stabilization and maintenance of co-operative groups. Thus, cooperation strategies include the totality of the instrumental operations which, as the ideal type, is oriented towards achieving the main group of objectives when promoting the members' economic activities (households, family smallholdings, businesses) in co-operative groups.

II. Objectives, Function, Types

The objectives are, thereby, to motivate, educate, guide and sponsor the individual members or cooperative groups (→ *Group, the Co-operative*) for active participation in all co-operative tasks of self-help, self-responsibility and self-administration (→ *Principles*). Co-operative strategies were originally put forward by the promoters of the co-operative concept and its pragmatic transposition into the social reality: the early philosophers of co-operative development concepts, charismatic leaders, pedagogues and other secondary promoters and mandatories of the foundation, stabilization and maintenance of co-operative groups until the subsequent organization and guidance of associations for promoting co-operatives.

Public and private, national and international, political, religious and neutral supporting organizations joined them at a later stage. Today, when development strategies are applied to organize co-operatives in developing countries, they play a considerable role in → *development policy*.

In view of the possibility to approach the individual and his integration into a co-operative community of persons and economy, two strategical types of development must be differentiated in practice; they have different intentions and methods when cooperation is being motivated:

(a) The objective is the fast economic independence

of cooperation by means of self-help and self-responsibility ('from within'), either
(aa) usually with the help of selfless promoters not belonging to the group ('from outside') or,
(ab) more rarely, with the help of leaders of the groups promoting a certain amount of self-help oriented towards satisfying the needs expressed autonomously ('from within').
(b) The objective is the political and economic guidance and control of cooperation by an interested, powerful promoter out of political interests which are not those of the group ('from above and from outside').

As far as the first type is concerned, the autonomously expressed needs to be satisfied by self-help and the early or immediate self-determination (self-reliance regarding the objectives, methods, decisions and distribution of profits) are characteristic. Regarding the second type, it is the patronal regimentation in all spiritual and physical cooperation views and activities by a politically and socially superior authority, in most cases with the purpose of enforcing its political and economic interests. Within the context of such a strategy of making cooperation official, there is generally no incitement to self-help even if it is announced that it will cease to be official at an unspecified date. Eventual self-help plans are hindered or even suppressed in the case of both types when thoughtlessly planned external financial aid is granted as a component of the strategical procedure (→ *Officialization*). Cooperation usually fails when such external aid is stopped.

III. Historical Approaches

Individual, operational procedures which have been combined to form a coherent co-operative strategy and which have stood the test of time, result from a long-lasting historical process of a systematic conversion of positive and negative experiences and knowledge gained from previous co-operative organizations, especially from the failure of earlier efforts in the 19th century (→ *History in 19th C.*). These historical experiences gained from individual cooperation strategies as well as from the combination of individual procedural approaches into a strategical overall concept are, independent of time, of great informative value as long as they can be transposed from one culture to another – because they are based on human experiences that are universally valid. The implementation of the co-operative concept in the overall cultural historical situation in the 19th century called for specific strategical measures to resist three phenomena antagonistic to co-operative activities:

1. the power of capital,
2. the political influence of the upper strata in society and government power, and
3. human weaknesses, namely, selfishness, indifference and lack of discipline.

This task was most often fulfilled by outside-promoters ('fathers', 'pioneers') of the development of viable co-operatives. The comparative analysis of historical documents dating from the origin and consolidation of co-operatives, which have been able to achieve great economic and social success, gives evidence of the following basic modalities of the strategical procedure adopted by their primary and secondary promoters:

1. Maintenance of the individual's personal values.
2. Microsociological access to individuals in a group.
3. Activation of self-help 'from above and outside' but, at the same time, 'from below and from within'.
4. Selection of the members and formation of an elite among them.
5. Production of own capital.
6. Co-operative education.
7. Primary and secondary organization.

For the individual member, the maintenance of personal values means one's own experience of the voluntary decision as to join and quit, enjoyment of justly distributed individual advantages, democratic formation of intent and decision ('one man, one vote'), and autonomy of individual business. The maintenance of individuality proved to be a basic condition for the spiritual and physical involvement in cooperation. It was expressed in the assumption of co-operative roles in view of responsible collaboration.

The microsociological access as a partial strategy aims, in the first place, at selecting economically and morally particularly capable individuals who are, at the same time, disciplined and have organizational talent and who then guarantee the organization of a major economic and social cooperation group in view of forming a nucleus group through its dynamic development. (*King* in Brighton, *Cooper* and *Howarth* in Rochdale (→ *Rochdale Pioneers*), Ludlow, *Maurice* and *Vansittart Neale* in London, → *Schulze* in Delitzsch and → *Raiffeisen* in the Neuwied area). The application of macrosociological concepts by → *Owen*, *Fourier* and *Blanc* in large groups or masses under a paternalistic-authoritarian access from 'above and outside' led to failure either because the co-operative concept and the organization's forms did not reach the individual so as to initiate self-help activities or because the individual's existential basic needs did not agree for long with the political-ideological objectives imposed from above.

In the partial stratgy of the activation of self-help 'from above and ouside' but, at the same time, 'from below and within', 'from above and outside' meant the intellectual and organizational initiative of the exogenous promoters who had an economic, social and political overview and moral authority. 'From below and within' meant, in the economic sector, the rational orientation of the material objectives of cooperation towards the requirements of the people concerned, the gradual formation of own capital due to saving measures and the rapid assumption of the tasks of self-responsibility and self-administration by those concerned. In the social sector, 'from below and within' meant the intensive co-operative pedagogical work with didactic methods adjusted to the local conditions. 'From below and within' referred finally to the formation of social → *solidarity* as a consequence of economic solidarity and loyalty to the co-operative. The latter had been achieved through the enjoyment of permanent individual advantages as a result of strict discipline in the application of the 'golden rules' of cooperation (Rochdale). Solidarity and loyalty were encouraged by the individual promoters who founded reading and discussion circles and included women and women's interests in the co-operative activities.

As far as *Bellers* and *King* are concerned, the → *selection of members* is the salient strategical nucleus in the historical institution of co-operatives. It aimed at forming a reliable co-operative group animated by the co-operative spirit of a friendly community sharing the same opinions which, simultaneously, was to contribute to the decent organization of work and life for the lower social strata. *King* submitted a catalogue of qualification criteria which go far beyond the average capacities to be expected and strive toward a spiritual and moral elite. The selection criteria for the individual candidates are as follows:
– 'good and skillful workmen, able to earn a certain sum per week' – 'industrious, sober, steady and quiet' – 'not ignorant and prejudiced' – 'desirous of adding to their knowledge and improving their minds as far as their circumstances and opportunities allow' – 'of good general health, not liable to constitutional disorders' – 'if they are too old they may become superannuated before the Society can receive the fruits of their labour' – 'in the infancy of the Society, too many unproductive members might become a serious evil' – 'it is necessary that the wife of a proposed member should approve the Society and understand something of its principles, otherwise the husband cannot be hearty in the cause, and he will be liable to interrupt the harmony of the Society' – 'labour will be directed by knowledge and therefore the cooperators will acquire all the useful knowledge they possibly can.'

However, the concept of an ideal type was not up to reality since it was precisely the weaknesses of character of the 'elite' which caused, in practice, the failure of the institutions created according to *King*. In the meantime, in 1844, the Rochdale Pioneers succeeded, as *King's* followers, in constituting an economically capable, resolute and steadfast nucleus of members with the provable moral support their wives provided. They had deliberately derived their name of 'pioneers' from that of the "able-bodied, valiant forerunners who had settled in the virgin forests in the west of North America" (*Huber*). The self-responsible individual economy according to Rochdale's rules demanded, in the first years, strategical perception for waiving the claims to individual benefits, for strict discipline and patience according to the motto: 'work and wait.'

In the case of the Rochdale Pioneers and of *Schulze* in Delitzsch (as already claimed by *King*), the other nucleus of the strategy was the formation of own capital by contributing the smallest amounts and waiving the individual claims to benefits, interests and dividends until the payment of a specific number of shares (or more) had been effected.

In 1853, *Schulze-Delitzsch* demanded of an applicant for selection "that he should have contributed as an ordinary member over a period of at least three months; that no dishonourable offence or business be imputed to him; that he does not owe to the bank any arrears on earlier loans, nor that he had caused any damages to any guarantors; that his circumstances offer the necessary security for the refund of the loan."

Moreover, the beneficiary was also to be carefully screened as cooperator. *Schulze-Delitzsch* imposed upon the candidates for the craftsmen's co-operative a probationary period whose objectives was to "to show that one was credit-worthy so as to become creditable." Thereby, he proceeded liberally when admitting candidates in order to give them an opportunity but was again consequent in taking it back in the case of failure to cooperate. Those were strategical measures which guaranteed the economic success. Similarly, *Raiffeisen* effected selection according to moral and economic criteria, but he entrusted the leadership over a long period to an elite that was not personally concerned and which consisted of spiritual leaders belonging to the upper strata in order not to leave cooperation to chance. However, this paternalistic gesture could also be antagonistic to the formation of self-help. In the case of *Raiffeisen*, the ideal method – since it was secure – during the foundation phase was to limit the activities, because they could be submitted to a better economic and social supervision, to the controllable area of a parish, the 'civil community' (a maximum of three villages).

Co-operative education and formation, connected with the selection of members adequate for cooperation, is the third nucleus of the historical co-operative strategy. The concept of the co-operative as an 'educational school' has an historical tradition: *Bellers* (1696) already refers to the strategy of merging economic, social and pedagogical tasks into an integral unit when forming a co-operative community independent of external economic and political influences. *Pestalozzi's* and *Goethe's* ideals of education (not only) for the lower social strata are based on co-operative school institutions. The first co-operative school for public education established in view of arousing subjective 'autonomous power' in a community goes back to *Fellenberg's* Pedagogical Institution in Hofwyl near Bern. Practical work, technical-economic general education and character training under the aspect of guidance towards autonomy and responsibility to oneself and to others (curbing selfish interests) make up the integral concept. The similarity with *Goethe's* 'Pädagogische Provinz' in 'Wilhelm Meister' (1821) is undeniable. *King* was the first to abandon the paternalistic access to individuals that is practised there. For *King*, 'from below' meant mutual instruction and discussion, social influence by example and precedent, democratic determination: equal votes, promotion possibilities in all offices of the co-operative according to competence and confidence.

The Equitable Pioneers of Rochdale put *King's* educational theory from 'The Co-operator' in practice (1828–1830) in the specific co-operative and general education and achieved great effects on the education of autonomous members in the co-operative and in society. Thereby, itinerant teachers of cooperation played an important strategical role. Special reference must be made to the propagation of documents of the foundation of co-operatives and socio-pedagogical formation as a further spiritual component of co-operative strategies in all the movements in the main European countries. The Christian Socialists (*Ludlow* et al.) achieved a considerable educational and journalistic task (working men's colleges). *Schulze-Delitzsch's* educational concept based on economy (business management and book-keeping) focussed on the transmission of real economic advantages, as far as possible within the framework of the basic needs and of the few co-operative functions which were appropriate for an early takeover. *Raiffeisen* combined deliberate pedagogical plans with the duty of attending the regular meetings, general assemblies and associations' afternoons on Sundays. Feelings of joint responsibility for the rational utilizations of the capital formed by personal financial contributions under personal privations, consolidated cooperation. Thus, strategical effects result that bind society and stabilize cooperation; that is, social solidarity is based on economic solidarity (*Schulze-Delitzsch*). The economic organization of the operational dimension and the internal structure of co-operatives, their combination into associations whose tasks are to advise, supervise, audit the balance of capital and the relations to private banks, in particular establishing the legislative conformity of statutes in view of protecting the co-operative institutions was the crowning work of the primary promoters' strategical procedure (the Christian Socialists in England, *Schulze-Delitzsch* in Germany). The decentralization of the organization soon proved to be more favourable under the strategical aspect than the initial centralization.

IV. Modern Approaches

In the wake of the growing development in the overall economy and the co-operatives' increasing competition with non-co-operative enterprises in the industrial societies of the 20th century, the strategical measures were then concentrated on increasing the economic efficiency and maintaining the co-operative undertakings. Democratic training of will-power and economic member decisions are transformed into professional management decisions which, adjusted to the specialization and concentration processes of the overall economy assumed more and more the sole economic responsibility (forfeiture of democracy and recession of social goals). As a result of the propagation of material welfare, the initial self-help co-operative for preventing economic and social misery gradually became a productive and competitive co-operative – often not to be differentiated from non-co-operative enterprises.

During the economic and social crises since the last third of the century, the co-operative concepts had found new possibilities of being applied in alternative movements, concepts of dual economy and citizens' initiatives, often, however, without the power of the co-operative spirit that motivates joint partnership and economic stability. Discipline and competence, experienced, altruistic leadership and proved strategical modes of procedure are lacking in the materially and egocentric affluent society.

On the other hand, new strategical approaches for promoting co-operative activities are applied by governmental and non-governmental organizations in the so-called developing countries in view of motivating self-help and participation among economically and socially destitute craftsmen, farmers and households (→ *Policies for Promotion*). There is a lack of unselfish independent promoters from the middle and upper strata. It is necessary to develop strategies adjusted to the specific socio-cultural situation and to the local requirements, with the help of which it would be possible to eliminate ignorance and illiteracy as well as fill the gap between the poor and the rich. Concepts and attitudes that do justice to cooperation and commercial and administrative abilities should be transmitted, the formation of own capital encouraged and the access to credit organized. In particular, the forms of cooperation should be guarded from misuse because of the external political and economic interests of third parties – local and national pressure groups, including the government and its administration. This is why, in every case, an attempt should be made to combine locally adjusted partial strategies which dispel the dangers of growth before the application of paternalistic and bureaucratic strategical approaches based on requirements. If external interests, authoritarian access and working methods are eliminated, the strategies of an immediate partnership, pedagogical leadership and guidance by non-governmental organizations generally have better chances of promoting self-help and self-responsibility in groups at the basis than government institutions. The access to easily controllable, socio-economically homogeneous groups having their own – not external – goal concepts allows the initiation of leaders belonging to the group and followers to have mutual confidence while utilizing the local cultural identity. This strategical procedure has better prospects regarding participation and the autonomous assumption of self-help activities than the access from above through a mass organization that remains anonymous for the individuals at the base while identity with the interests is insufficient or lacking, or when the goal structures are regimented. Under the strategical aspect, the promoting organization should proceed in such a way that the groups's self-help potential is mobilized. Thereby, the promoter should retain the character of a catalyst. The potential agents of development of self-help cooperation (Self-help Development Organizations) are on the side of donors and beneficiaries: parties and political associations, paragovernmental institutions (e.g., development authorities, marketing boards), religious institutions, unions, ministerial, regional and communal agencies, non-profit associations and, finally, existing → *self-help organizations* as well.

The strategical efforts of such agents of development should be orientated principally towards the main objectives of a policy based on peace and human rights, the motivation, protection and organization of self-help and thereby, namely, the development of participatory organization forms. The overriding strategical measures to be applied successively are grouped according to a canon of seven indispensable tasks to be performed carefully:

- indentification of the target group, of the socio-cultural potential, of the problems and structures concerning socio-economy and power policy, of the structures of needs and self-efficiency, of the motivating powers and formation of will-power on the one hand, and the factors preventing self-help, on the other hand;
- experience of the possibilities and abilities to participate in view of an immediate motivation to participate in real tasks;
- training in all the specific functions of cooperation (group organization, situation analysis, decision-making, operation plans in production, processing, marketing, management training, administration, etc.) in a mutual dialogue and permanent communication between partners;
- planning resources in terms of the mobilization of own and external funds, planning credit and forms of credit liability;
- management counselling and establishment of vertical and horizontal organizational structures.

- Creation of a network for the further exchange of experience and of other forms of contact with other similar groups;
- monitoring and evaluation, learning self-evaluation and feedbacking the evaluation results to the own or other groups.

The people to be promoted belong to complex sociocultural systems whose social institutions are alive and, internally, still closely related and strive after other cultural objectives in addition to the realization of economic goals (→ *Relationship Patterns*). Thus, one-sided economic concepts would lead to a proportionately limited, less efficient combination of strategical instruments and endanger the durability of self-help. The creation of official, legal framework conditions for cooperation, which leave a sufficient margin to the groups concerned, allowing them to include proved, i.e., familiar local-cultural requirements for regulations, has, in practice, often stood the test of time as a strategical measure of legal protection within and outside the groups.

The promotion of autochthonous self-help organizations on foreign initiative with a view to strengthening the self-help capacity was also to take into consideration the following measures (selection):

- the rehabilitation (so far as rational) of useful, precious (people's) knowledge;
- the defence of primary self-help and of the felt needs against external interests;
- the transformation of problems into objectives of the activities and discussion of the relation between goals and means in the course of time;
- help to establish socio-economic contacts with (eventually official) external institutions regarding, for example, supply and marketing functions, extension techniques, financing, technical aid, etc.;
- the supply and joint testing of simple techniques;
- the provision of modest financial means that complement the existing own means and that must be repaid within realistic terms, i.e., no gifts;
- the distribution of tasks and roles as well as the eventual exchange of roles within the course of time;
- the creation of conditions leading to a threefold participation: in decisions, in practical work and in the benefits of the self-help activities.

In all these strategical measures, the specific role played by women and women's groups, their objectives, and their approaches towards solutions within the context of the local self-help must be taken into consideration. To that end, it is, of course, necessary

- to designate appropriate and capable leaders from within the own ranks;
- to define the internal regulation of self-help organizations, of meetings and of the chronology of spiritual and physical activities;
- to establish, right at the beginning of the activities,

a minimum amount of rules for the informal cooperation, internal agreements or temporary statutes which must be developed (definition of simple rights and duties).

The greatest strategical consideration should permanently be given to the self-determination of objectives and to the conditions for creating self-responsibility and self-administration independent of government and of the world market as well as of the obligations of an extended family. Under government régie, co-operative activities run the risk of preventing a priori the free genesis of self-help, self-help objectives, self-responsibility and self-administration.

Contacts and the exchange of experience between government and non-governmental agents are desirable in view of a future, more flexible organization of development policy and political procedure. With regard to practice, in comparison with the historical approaches of strategical influence exercised on the formation and furtherance of co-operatives, it is evident that modern development strategies tend to concentrate on the partial sectors of training and administration and that the above-described canon of an ideal type in the modern strategical overall concept of co-operative development is applied, if at all, by non-governmental organizations. The historical strategical modes of procedure, the selection of people, their education and training, discipline in and loyalty to cooperation but especially concerning the personal contribution to cooperation dependent upon self-help have not lost their importance even when modern strategical methods are worked out flexibly. If the great economic success of European co-operatives in the 19th century caused these pioneer co-operative groups to be taken as models for developing societies, the strategical conditions and modes of procedure that were indispensable for the rise from misery and loneliness at the time have, very often, been forgotten.

Bibliography

Bardeleben, Manfred: Grundsätze für die Förderung von Selbsthilfeorganisationen. Friedrich-Ebert-Stiftung, Bonn 1979.
Bellers, John: Proposals for Raising a College of Industry, London 1696.
Cheikh Dieng, M./Beloglavec, M./Münkner, H.-H./ Ullrich, G.: Guide pour la gestion appropriée des coopératives de petits explotants agricoles (GACOPEA) en Afrique francophone, 2e ed., DSE/FAO, Feldafing 1985.
Crüger, Hans: Anleitung zur Gründung von Handwerkergenossenschaften, Berlin 1900.
Environnement et Développement Africain (ENDA): Intiatives paysannes au Sahel. Sér. Etudes et Recherches No.97–98, Dakar 1985.
Fassbender, Martin: Ländliche Spar- und Darlehenskassenvereine. Vollständige Anleitung zur Gründung und Geschäftsleitung, Münster 1883.
Holyoake, George Jacob: The History of Cooperation in England: its literature and its advocates. Vol. I–II (London 1875, 1879), New York 1906.
Huber, Victor Aimé: Ausgewählte Schriften über Sozialreform und Genossenschaftswesen, Berlin 1894.
Hughes, Thomas/Vansittart Neale, Edward: A Manual for Co-operators, London 1881.
Imfeld, Al/Meyns, Peter et al.: Mit Bauerngruppen arbeiten. Burkina Faso: Einsichten in ein Ausbildungsprojekt (Weltfriedensdienst), Berlin 1985.
Janssen, Volker/Schwedersky, Thomas (eds.): Promouvoir l'Autopromotion Paysanne. Fondation Allemande pur le Développement International (DSE), Feldafing 1985.
King, William: The Co-operator (Brighton 1828–1830), Manchester 1922.
Kuhn, Johannes/Münkner Hans-H./Hanel, Alfred (eds.): The Role of Non-Governmental Organizations in Promoting Self-Help Organizations, A Follow-up Seminar, Internat. Inst. of the Konrad-Adenauer-Stiftung e.V., Sankt Augustin,1985.
Lanzendörfer, Matthias (ed.): Organisation et gestion de coopératives et d'autres organisations d'autopromotion (cours international de formation), Fondation Allemande pour le Développement International (DSE), Feldafing 1987.
Müller, Julius Otto: Kritische Anmerkungen zu Selbsthilfe, Fremdhilfe und Partizipation in fremdbestimmten ‚Selbsthilfe'-Organisationen der Entwicklungspolitik, Verfassung und Recht in Übersee, 13, (1980), pp.213–226.
Müller, Julius Otto: Autopromotion – Problèmes et conditions d'un instrument de développement. Bliss, R./Hemann, H. (eds.): Communication et développement rural. Séminaires spécialisés destinés aux journalistes de la Radio Rurale de l'Afrique Francophone. (GHK, Onde Allemande), Der Tropenlandwirt, Beih. 42, 1989, pp. 67–94.
Münkner, Hans-H. (ed.): Instrumente der Selbsthilfeförderung – Bestandsaufnahme – Weiterentwicklung, Marburg/L. 1990.
Raiffeisen, Friedrich Wilhelm: Die Darlehnskassen–Vereine ... als Mittel zur Abhilfe der Not der ländlichen Bevölkerung, 3rd ed., Neuwied 1881.
Schulze-Delitzsch, Hermann: Associationsbuch für Deutsche Handwerker und Arbeiter, Leipzig 1853.
Seibel, Hans Dieter/Damachi, Ukandi G.: Self-Help Organizations. Guidelines and Case Studies for Development Planners and Fieldworkers (FES), Bonn 1982.
Verhagen, Konraad: Self-help Promotion, a challenge to the NGO-community, Amsterdam 1987.

Strategic Planning in Co-operatives

HARTMUT KREIKEBAUM

(see also: *Business Policies*; *Managerial Economics*; *Management in Co-operatives*; *Policies for Promotion*)

I. Introduction: The Need for Strategic Planning in Co-operative Organizations; II. Specific Influences of Objectives on the Planning Structure of Co-operative Organizations; III. Competitive Determinants of the Planning Process in Co-operative Organizations; IV. Basic Instruments of Strategic Planning; V. Introducing and Implementing Strategic Planning in Co-operative Organizations; VI. Future Planning Problems to be faced in Co-operative Organizations.

I. Introduction: The Need for Strategic Planning in Co-operative Organizations

Strategic planning has been established in a variety of companies as a valuable tool for corporate management since many years. It has proven its existence by its basic features. In controversy to non-planning or improvisation, every planning process consists of three main elements:
- it takes into account future risks and developments,
- alternative actions are considered to cope with uncertainty,
- the planning process includes a decision to be executed.

The core element of strategic planning is the formulation and implementation of strategies. Strategies express how corporations use their present and potential strengths to put into action the long-term objectives and policies. They are influenced by the prevalent attitudes and philosophy of corporate management as well as the set of circumstances and conditions the company is facing in its environment (cf. *Kreikebaum* 1989; for the specific conditions of small companies see *Kreikebaum* 1984).

Environmental conditions of co-operates differ according to the specific type of organization. It is, therefore, necessary to treat first of all the main objectives of different types of co-operative agencies and describe their influences on strategic planning. We also have to analyze the elements of the planning process, since every co-operative organization acts within the specific realm of a given industry. Furthermore, basic instruments of strategic planning will be presented as they pertain to co-operatives. We will also describe the process of introducing and implementing a strategic planning system within a co-operative organization, its hardships and prerequisites. In this respect, we can rely on some results of an empiricial study in this special field of organizational development. Finally, some actual problems of strategic planning in co-operates will be tackled.

II. Specific Influences of Objectives on the Planning Structure of Co-operative Organizations

Co-operative organizations differ widely in size (→ *Operational Size*), scope, membership, and objectives. Since long-term objectives form an integer part of strategic planning, we will concentrate on this core element.

We may distinguish three types of co-operatives (cf. *Boettcher* 1981, pp. 542):

1) Purchase or procurement co-operatives (of farmers, consumers, retail sellers, craftsmen) which concentrate on buying goods or services at a low price and good conditions (→ *Supply Co-operatives*). Strategic objectives of these companies are clearly focussed on excellent sources of procurement, good deliveries, troublefree logistics, and low prices. Basic strategies include searching for competent delivery firms, balancing procurement risks by a policy of diversity and stability, and securing long-term delivery contracts. Necessary actions to execute these strategies include, among others, excellent working relations with the delivering companies, an internal control system to supervise the quality of purchased goods and services, and forecasts of the various purchase markets.

2) Sales co-operatives (→ *Marketing*), on the other hand, serve the consumer. They concentrate on selling, e.g. dairy products, wine, or horticultural and agricultural equipement on the market. These co-operatives compete with other suppliers. Their main objective, therefore, consists of maintaining or developing a certain market share and establishing satisfying consumer relations. Marketing facilities of these companies cover the whole range of product-/market activities. This is also true for co-operative organizations which combine sales and production activities (like wineries or dairy-famers' associations) (→ *Classification*).

3) Co-operative credit institutions (like loan banks) compete with all other banking institutions (→*Co-operative Banks*). In the whole field of business banking, co-operatives have gained a substantial influence over the years. In the Federal Republic of Germany, about 3,223 co-operatives ('Volksbanken', 'Raiffeisenbanken') with a consolidated balance sheet of 515 billion DM hold an important market share in this sector. They follow the same objectives as their main competitors (the big banking institutions like Deutsche Bank AG as well as the decentralized saving banks). Besides these business goals, co-operative organizations follow a second pattern of aims: the wellbeing and personal development of their members (cf. *Dülfer* 1980, pp. 1857–1863). This represents another important mission which results in consequent strategies. Co-operatives seriously follow the purpose of solidarity, sustaining the individual members of the association. They are committed to personal development of their membership like training and career building strategies (→ *Education, Germany*).

III. Competitive Determinants of the Planning Process in Co-operative Organizations

As all other companies within a market-oriented structure, co-operatives face the up-coming of new entrants, they rely upon the bargaining power of customers and suppliers, they are dependent on movements and developments among their contestants (→ *Competition*). Those are the external forces co-operative organizations have to cope with in their different industry positions (cf. *Porter* 1979, and *Porter* 1980).

Evaluating the strengths and weaknesses of the most important competitors is a prerequiste for successful companies operating within a market-oriented economy. There exists, however, a definite lack between this theoretical insight and the actual behavior and decision pattern of many firms.

Since co-operative organizations compete with non-co-operative ones, they have to analyze the different sales markets and their conditions as well as the potential threats caused by substitute products. They also have to review the potential strength of competitors and the existing rivalry among them. This rivalry is enlarged by many strong competitors, high sunk costs, saturated markets, homogenous products, heterogenity of competitition, and high exit barriers.

IV. Basic Instruments of Strategic Planning

Strategy formulation requires a certain set of instruments. The strategic planner needs a variety of tools to cope with uncertainity, starting with the generation of scenarios. A newer tool of strategic analysis is called 'strategic issue analysis' (cf. *Ansoff* 1980). Also widely used are analyses of the company's potential, indicated by its strengthes and weaknesses. These instruments describe the external and internal environment of any co-operative organization. For co-operatives which sell their products to different customers, an analysis of the different markets as well as the competitive forces are a prerequisite for defining product-/market strategies (→ *Assortment Policies*). Finally, portfolio analyses are also common tools of strategic planning.

In co-operative organizations operating under market conditions (→ *Economic Order*), the strategic options center on a product-market strategy. According to *Ansoff*, there are four different types of product-market strategy (cf. *Ansoff* 1957, p. 114):

1) *Market penetration* by improving business performance without departing from the original product-market strategy (e.g., through advertising or price policy).
2) *Market development* by adapting the present product line to new missions and customers.
3) A *product development* strategy aims at developing products with new and different characteristics, to improve the performance of the existing mission.
4) Finally, a *diversification* strategy (→ *Diversification Strategies*) calls for new markets (missions) as well as for new products. Virtually every co-operative organization operating under market conditions is forced to investigate its procurement and its sales markets.

Analysing the procurement markets becomes a prerequisite for co-operatives that concentrate on a co-ordinated bying effort for their members. In this respect, companies have to review the risks linked to the supply of important goods and services used in production and/or for sale. Furthermore, the strategic analysis has to look out for possible substitutes, the suppliers structure, strategic reactions of the supplying firms, and tendencies of concentration among the suppliers.

Analysis of the procurement markets also includes a permanent appraisal of the personnel market. Securing line executives and staff people of a wanted high calibre requires a careful analysis of the different labor markets.

The most obvious field of market analysis is the sales market. For co-operatives offering their goods and services on different markets, a thorough study of customer problems becomes a necessity. These customer-centered companies have to perform a careful and lasting appraisal of their products' functions, including the product life cycle, the experience curve, the competitors' analysis, and the portfolio analysis. The portfolio matrix serves as a basis for defining strategic alternatives. It first of all opens the planner's eye for the present status of the company's product-/market positions in different segments. Furthermore, it underlines the high correlation between a big market share and the exploitation of a firm's long-term levels of potential success. On the other hand, one should not overemphasize portfolio analysis as a means of developing so-called 'norm strategies' of strategic norms. A certain business area does not represent a homogenous cluster but is influenced by a host of strategically relevant factors in the future.

V. Introducing and Implementing Strategic Planning in Co-operative Organizations

Strategic planning starts with strategy formulation, continues with strategy implementation, and ends up with strategy control. The most important first step to strategy formulations is an analysis of the internal capabilities and the external environment of the company. This strategic analysis is required in order to efficiently and effectively direct the firm's resources. It also offers valuable information for the first phase of strategy formulation: goal-setting by defining the company's mission and purpose (→ *Corporate Culture*).

We may define this process as the necessary step towards a conceptual scheme of strategic planning. In this first stage of the planning process, competitive strategic alternatives have to be developed in order to reach a sustainable competitive advantage and a long run profitability. Decisions regarding the following operational programmes are included in this phase of the planning process.

In a second step, the concept of strategic planning has to be implemented within the total planning structure of a company. Organizing for strategic planning includes the set-up of a new strategic planning system as well as the development of an already existing planning structure. During this phase, existing planning barriers have to be overcome. In many cases, pressing for change on the side of decision-makers may arise suspicion on the part of the employees. Resistance to change is due to many reasons. It is not easy to develop an overall policy for overcoming resistance to change on the different levels of hierarchy. There is no simple answer to this particular problem. A basic attempt, however, should be made for winning employee commitment (→ *Human Resource Management*).

Resistance to change may be matched by involving management on all levels in the process of implementing the planning system. Empirical evidence underlines a positive correlation between a broad degree of participation in the process of formulating company goals and the efficiency of implementing subsequent company policies (cf. *Kreikebaum/Suffel* 1981).

Based on a questionnaire study of 460 firms in six industrialized countries (U.S.A., Japan, Canada, England, Italy, and Australia), *Schöllhammer* investigated the most important pitfalls of long-range planning (*Steiner* and *Schöllhammer* 1975, pp. 2–12). 'Top management assumptions that it can delegate the planning function to a planner' was ranked by respondents to the questionnaire as the most important pitfall to be avoided. These results particularly show the need for top management's commitment to planning (cf. *Kreikebaum* 1986, pp. 198–199).

VI. Future Planning Problems to be faced in Co-operative Organizations

In general, co-operative organizations share the actual planning problems of their various competitors, some of them even in the realm of multinational corporations (→ *Internationalization*). There exist, however, two distinctive features. Relating to the original purpose and organizational set-up, co-operatives offer a unique opportunity for a favorable 'planning climate' for introducing and smoothly implementing a strategic planning system within an organization. This assumption follows from the basic self-understanding of co-operative decisions as a conflict-solving activity (cf. *Dülfer* 1984, pp. 186–193). It is also due to the basic mission of a co-operative that ecological issues are embedded in strategic thinking. If not already at present, both factors may be regarded as a future challenge to top management.

Incorporating ecological issues in the strategic planning function becomes a must for future strategic planning (→ *Environment Protection*). During the past two decades, the ecological limits to growth have become well known. East and West are aware of the imminent dangers and future threats of the present ecological situation. It took, however, quite some time for the majority of companies to react to the ecological crisis. Still today there are many companies that neglect their responsibility for better environmental protection. In spite of the many writings and public declarations on the issue, ecological goals today still play a minor role in product development strategies (cf. *Töpfer* 1985). The environmental problems of the least developed countries are augmenting from month to month. They range from energy, water, and food shortages in the rural areas over lacking refuse and faeces disposal in urban (congested) areas to water and air pollution and soil destruction through industrial development.

It is particularly in the developing countries that co-operative organizations form an integrating factor within society (→ *Development Policy*). This could enable them to counteract the ecological crisis especially in those countries. Many examples indicate that co-operatives have redefined their missions in order to reach out for a policy of sustainable development and qualitative growth (cf. *Kreikebaum* 1990).

Integrating environmental considerations in strategic planning requires the restructuring of 'normal' economic decision-making. For instance, it shifts the attention to preventive environmental protection. Integrated technologies replace end-of-pipe technologies, the principle of responsibility or liability will help to foster ecological self-regulation of business activities, and a 'low waste economy' substitutes a 'through-put-economy'.

Integrating the natural environment into business activities will become one of the central future problems of co-operative organizations. It will be of decisive importance to form an environmentally concerned, innovative organizational structure to implement strategies having a long-term perspective.

Bibliography

Ansoff, Igor: Strategic Issue Management, Strategic Management Journal, Vol.1 (1980), pp. 131–148.

Ansoff, Igor: Strategies for Diversification, in: Harvard Business Review, Vol. 35 (1957), No.5, pp. 113–124.

Boettcher, Erik: Genossenschaft I: Begriff und Aufgabe. Handwörterbuch der Wirtschaftswissenschaft, Vol. 3, Stuttgart et al. 1981, pp. 540–556.

Dülfer, Eberhard: Betriebswirtschaftslehre der Kooperative, Göttingen 1984.

Dülfer, Eberhard: Zielsystem der Genossenschaft. Handwörterbuch des Genossenschaftswesens, Stuttgart 1980, cols. 1857–1872.

Gälweiler, Aloys: Portfolio-Management. Handbook of German Management, Stuttgart et al 1990, pp. 1878–1799.

Kreikebaum, Hartmut: Der Einsatz "sanfter" Technologien in den Entwicklungsländern, Unpublished Manuscript, Frankfurt 1990.

Kreikebaum, Hartmut: Introducing and Implementing a Strategic Planning System. Research on Organizational Decision-Making, Amsterdam et al. 1986, pp. 189–202.

Kreikebaum, Hartmut: Small Business Management in den USA. Mögliche Konsequenzen für die Theorie und Praxis

der Unternehmensführung mittelständischer Unternehmen. In: Betriebswirtschaftslehre mittelständischer Unternehmen, Wissenschaftliche Tagung des Verbands der Hochschullehrer für Betriebswirtschaft e.V., Stuttgart 1984, pp. 645–659.
Kreikebaum, Hartmut: Strategische Unternehmensplanung, Stuttgart, Berlin, Köln 1989.
Kreikebaum, Hartmut/Suffel, Winfried: Der Entwicklungsprozeß der strategischen Planung, Thun/Frankfurt 1981.
Porter, Michael E.: How competitive forces shape strategy, Harvard Business Review, Vol.57, March-April (1979), pp. 137–145.
Porter, Michael: Competitive Strategy. Techniques for analyzing Industries and Competitors, New York/London 1980.
Steiner, George A./Schöllhammer, Hans: Pitfalls in Multinational Long Range Planning, Long Range Planning, Vol. 8 (1975), pp. 2–12.
Töpfer, Armin: Umwelt- und Benutzerfreundlichkeit von Produkten als strategische Untenehmensziele, in: Marketing-ZFP, Vol. 7 (1985), pp. 241–251.

Structural Changes Among German Co-operative Banks

BERND KUBISTA [J]

(see also: Co-operative Banks; Multi-Use Credit Co-operatives; Mergers and Consolidations)

I. Merger Policies; II. Growth; III. Deposit Structure; IV. Market Shares; V. Changes on the Secondary Level.

In no other branch of the German credit business were the structural changes following World War II as enduring as in the co-operative banking group. "Raiffeisenbanken" (rural co-operative banks) and "Volksbanken" (urban peoples' banks) at the same time comprised the most successful group within the entire Federal Republic of Germany, measured according to the development of market shares. The decisive factor for this development was that Volksbanken and Raiffeisenbanken at a very early stage established a comprehensive and functioning all-round finance federation.

I. Merger Policies

A clearly evident process of concentration (→ Mergers and Consolidations) is characteristic for the structural development of the co-operative banking group within the last 30 years. Whereas there were 11,795 independent co-operative banks in 1957 (the first year statistics were collected being comparable to those of today), their number dropped to 2,855 in 1990 and (including East Germany) to 2,909 by the end of 1992 (see Table 1). A systematic merger policy, above all since the middle of the 1960s, has cleary reduced the number of independent Volksbanken and Raiffeisenbanken. This process has been facilitated since the beginning of 1972 inasfar as reorganization of the federation structure eliminated certain barriers preventing mergers between Volksbanken and Raiffeisenbanken which had existed up to then. Until the end of 1971, mergers as a rule only occurred within the individual Raiffeisenbank or Volksbank sectors.

The prevailing criterion of this merger policy was always to create larger operational units (→ Operational Size) which, in the interests of customers and members, could operate more economically and, therefore, were more efficient. At the same time, a dynamic policy concerning branch offices ensured that customer proximity was maintained and even improved. The number of Volks- and Raiffeisenbank branch offices increased from 2,305 in 1957 to 17,700 in 1992. Within this identical time frame, the number of bank locations increased from 14,100 to 20,609. Thus, the Volksbanken and Raiffeisenbanken thus had approx. 45% of all domestic bank locations at their disposal, controlling the tightest network of bank location in the FRG.

Table 1: Number of Volksbanken and Raiffeisenbanken

Year	Main Offices	Branch Offices	Total
1957	11,795	2,305	14,100
1965	10,266	6,603	16,869
1970	7,059	11,280	18,339
1975	5,196	14,004	19,200
1980	4,226	15,474	19,700
1985	3,660	16,029	19,689
1990	2,855	15,977	18,832
1992*	2,909	17,700	20,609

* including East-Germany

II. Growth

The concentration process in the co-operative banking group was accompanied by dynamic growth. Total assets of Volksbanken and Raiffeisenbanken climbed from DM 22.1 billion in 1960 to DM 685.2 billion in 1992. Accounts receivable in this identical time frame grew from DM 10 billion to DM 404.4 billion; accounts payable likewise increased from DM 15.4 billion to DM 551.2 billion (see Table 2).

The causes of this positive development were rooted both within the group itself as well as in the economic and social framework conditions. Work and performance morale of the local, fully self-responsible management staff guaranteed a high degree of flexibility in the entire, dynamically expanding market. The ambitious development of credit co-operatives into true all-round banks (→ Co-operative Banks) enabled the Volksbanken and Raiffeisenbanken to profit overproportionally from the increases in both income and affluence enjoyed by wide sections of the population.

In the first third of this observed time frame, large populational groups became familiar with banks and integrated into them; today, these groups comprise the traditional retail banking clientele among Volksbanken and Raiffeisenbanken. In addition, today small and mid-sized companies in particular profited from the economic growth and expansion of the 1960s and '70s, companies which number among the regular customers of co-operative banks.

Table 2: Development of Volksbanken and Raiffeisenbanken in DM billion

Year	Total Assets	Accounts Receivable	Accounts Payable
1960	22.1	10.0	15.4
1970	78.7	46.1	66.2
1980	284.7	180.9	333.6
1985	411.9	259.9	333.6
1990	555.7	325.7	447.9
1992*	685.2	404.4	551.2

* including East-Germany

Membership in Volks- and Raiffeissenbanken tripled during the past three decades. At the end of the 1960s, Volksbanken and Raiffeisenbanken together had 3.8 million members; by the end of 1992, they could count 12.1 million members. In the course of time, growth associated with membership gains has clearly altered the structure of these banks. Membership share including white- and blue-collar workers and civil servants has more than doubled in the past 30 years, whereas the share of mid-sized commercial customers/entrepreneurs has steadily decreased. The loss of membership share from the sector of mid-sized companies in part reflects the decrease in the number of self-employed persons in the Federal Republic of Germany. Between 1960 and 1989 the number of self-employed persons fell by 62%. This development can likewise be traced back to the fact that the weights resulting from the strongly increasing absolute number of members hailing from non-self-employed branches have naturally been shifted to their advantage (see Table 3).

Analogeously to the development within the membership structure, the customer structure has changed. Whereas more than 80% of all credits were granted to corporate clients in 1960, this rate had decreased to just over 50% in 1992 (see Table 4). In the sectors of agriculture, lumber and trade, the relative decrease in the importance of commercial clients is particularly evident. The share these customer groups have in the total allotment of credits from Volksbanken and Raiffeisenbanken has drastically diminished over the past decades. The steady structural changes including the enormous reduction in the number of self-employed persons/sole proprietors is reflected in these economic sectors. Although credits to agricultural and timber operations only amounted to 5.9% of total credit commitments from co-operative banks, this by no means implies that Volksbanken and Raiffeisenbanken, have have relinquished their position as the most important financier for the agricultural sector (→ *Early Warning Systems*). Volksbanken and Raiffeisenbanken continue to maintain a 50% market share for all credits that the agricultural sector raises. In the meantime, the largest portion of total credits granted by Volksbanken and Raiffeisenbanken are raised by wage and salary workers. This share increased from 10.6% in 1960 to 39.3% in 1992. Loans to companies in the service industry have likewise increased, as have those to public budgets, although this has remained at a low level.

III. Deposit Structure

When the development of savings deposits is analysed according to the classification of depositors, one can likewise see that private individuals constitute the most important group of depositors. Their share of total deposits, amounting to over 50% in 1960, has increased in the course of the past decades to over 80% (see Table 5). The shift itself among the groups of depositors initially occurred in the 1960; since then, the structures have remained relatively constant. Wide sections of the population, then for the first time, found themselves in the position to

Table 3: Development of Membership Structure (Share of Total Membership in Per Cent)

	1960	1970	1980	1990	1992**
Craftsmen	13.9	7.4	3.2	1.9	1.9
Trade, Industry	17.0	11.8	4.4	5.5	5.6
Agriculture	27.9	14.9	4.8	4.3	4.8
White- and blue-collar; Civil Servants	28.7	47.8	60.2	58.1	57.6
Free-lance workers	2.9	2.9	2.6	3.3	3.4
Others*	9.6	15.2	24.8	26.9	26.7

* Housewives, Retired Persons, Students, Public Budgets
** including East-Germany

Table 4: Accounts Receivable (Credits) According to Occupational Group in Per Cent

	1960	1970	1980	1990	1992
White- and blue-collar workers; Civil Servants	10.6	21.8	33.8	39.8	39.3
Retired Persons	1.4	1.5	1.6	1.9	1.9
Other Private Persons	3.8	3.9	4.0	5.4	5.6
Agriculture & Timber	22.7	16.0	7.8	6.1	5.9
Industry, Manufacturing, Construction	17.8	16.5	19.6	18.0	18.1
Service Branch Companies	10.1	12.8	14.4	14.8	15.3
Trade	26.3	21.6	11.9	9.2	9.3
Other Businesses	5.8	3.9	2.7	1.8	1.6
Public Budgets	1.6	1.9	4.2	3.0	3.0

(Craftsmen 14.8 11.3 7.56 15.6)

Table 5: Savings According to Depositor Classification in Per Cent

	1960	1970	1980	1990	1992*
White- and blue-collar workers; Civil Servants	30.1	39.8	41.7	42.2	42.2
Retired Persons	10.3	12.2	16.5	22.1	22.5
Other Private Persons	12.2	13.9	21.8	22.9	23.2
Agriculture & Timber	19.1	12.6	6.8	3.7	3.9
Industry, Manufacturing, Construction	7.2	4.7	2.9	1.8	1.8
Service Branch Companies	9.7	8.7	4.2	1.8	1.9
Trade	8.3	5.9	2.2	1.0	1.0
Other Businesses	2.3	0.9	1.3	0.5	0.5
Public Budgets	0.8	1.3	2.6	3.0	3.0
(Craftsmen	10.7	6.3	1.9	0.9	0.9)

* including East-Germany

build savings in the 1960s as a result of the economic boom and the positive income developments resulting therefrom.

The importance of deposits for the total liabilities of Volksbanken and Raiffeisenbanken has nonetheless clearly fallen over the course of time. If one studies the development of the various types of deposits (see Table 6), one can see that the share of savings with respect to total customer deposits has dropped from 76% to 36% in the past twenty-five years. The share of time deposits (including certificates of deposit [CDs]), on the other hand, has dramatically risen, recently amounting to 40%. Among demand deposits, no such drastic change has resulted in the course of time: their share has altered merely 2 percentage points in the past 25 years, including intermittent fluctuations.

IV. Market Shares

The overall positive development of Volksbanken and Raiffeisenbanken in the past thirty years is clearly visible in the growth of their market shares (see Table 7). Between 1960 and 1990, Volksbanken and Raiffeisenbanken increased their share of total business volume among all banks in Germany from 5.9% to 11.3%; their share of total credits granted to non-bank customers increased from 5.9% to 12.5%. Over the past 30 years, Volksbanken and Raiffeisenbanken can also boast of considerable gains in market share with respect to deposits from domestic non-bank customers. Their share of demand deposits increased by a good 75% between 1960 and 1990, whereas their share of savings deposits/certificates of deposits even increased by 93%. Their market share of time deposits climbed to 13.5% in 1992.

This dynamic business development, together with the process of concentration discussed above (→ *Mergers and Consolidations*), has resulted in substantially increased (→ *operational size*) among Volksbanken and Raiffeisenbanken. Whereas the average business volume of the credit co-operatives amounted to a mere DM 1.5 million in 1957, business volume had increased to DM 235 million by 1992. As the average operational size has grown, the demands the local banks have on services, inputs, and general

Table 6: Deposit Structure among Volksbanken and Raiffeisenbanken in Per Cent

Year	Demand Deposits	Time Deposits [CDs]	Savings Deposits
1968	20.1	4.2	75.7
1970	18.4	6.9	74.7
1975	17.6	8.0	74.4
1980	15.8	22.3	61.9
1985	13.9	32.6	53.5
1990	16.0	41.0	43.0
1992*	18.0	46.0	36.0

* including East-Germany

performance from the federation and, in particular, from the regional central bank level, have likewise changed. For example, the regional central banks' function of offsetting liquidity has been reduced – at least to a relative degree – as the number of local banks decreased while their operational size increased. At the same time, the demand local banks have for quality, high-value financial services has also increased. Individual Volksbanken and Raiffeisenbanken either cannot offer such services themselves, not offer them at the necessary quality level, or not provide them at a justifiable price.

V. Changes on the Secondary Level

Larger operational sizes, altered market requirements resulting from this, as well as changing domestic and international markets have all lead to a concentration on the level of the regional central banks. There were 18 regional central banks (→ *Central Institutions*) in 1957 – without counting DG BANK; this number had been reduced to three by the end of 1989. This development has entailed considerable alterations of the functions and tasks of DG BANK. On the one hand, the demands the remaining regional central banks place on DG BANK have changed; on the other hand, DG BANK now exercises the direct function of a central bank for wide sections of the co-operative banking group.

Bibliography

BVR (ed.): Bericht – Zahlen (annual report), Bonn (several volumes/years).

BVR (ed.): Bankinformation und Genossenschaftsforum, Bonn/Wiesbaden (published monthly).

Structural Types of the Co-operative

EBERHARD DÜLFER [J]

(see also: *Managerial Economics*; *Classification*; *Theory of Co-operatives*; *Theory of co-operative Cooperation*; *Relationship Patterns*)

I. Introduction and Point of Departure; II. The Structural Types of the Promotion Co-operatives; III. Typological Distinctions; IV. Structural Types in a Generalized Form; V. Further Developments of the Concept of the Integrated Co-operative; VI. The Co-operative's Structural Dimensions.

I. Introduction and Point of Departure

The tenets of co-operative "structural typology" published by *Dülfer* (1966) arose in the scope of discussion pursued during the 1950s and '60s in German-speaking regions concerning symptoms of degeneration afflicting co-operatives (→ *Conceptions, Co-operative*). At that time, empirical studies indicated that among the "promotion co-operatives" important factors of the organizational and management relationships between the member enterprises and the jointly borne business unit (co-operative enterprise) deviated from the *ideal theoretical model* of the co-operative. This model describes that particular structure for the co-operative complex as a whole which was formulated by such pioneers as the *Rochdale Weavers* (→ *Rochdale Pioneers*), → *Friedrich Wilhelm Raiffeisen* or → *Hermann Schulze-Delitzsch* in the 19th century, and which at least served as the basis for the legal corporate form of a registered co-

Table 7: Market Share of Volksbanken and Raiffeisenbanken expressed as Percentage of Total Bank Activity (of all Banks)

Year	Business Volume	Credits to Non-banks	Deposits from Domestic Non-Bank Customers		
			demand	time	savings/CD
1960	5.9	5.9	11.1	–	14.2
1970	7.7	7.9	14.5	6.8	17.8
1980	10.9	11.5	19.2	10.4	22.4
1985*	12.6	12.9	20.4	11.8	26.9
1990	11.3	12.5	19.4	13.5	27.4

*Bistapflicht for all Stock Companies

operative found in German Co-operative Law (until 1973) (→ *Law, National*). *Dülfer* first propounded his observations in 1956, namely that the circumstances around such symptoms of "degeneration" (as they were more or less classified) were an expression of certain "typical" interaction relationships between the member enterprises on the one hand and the co-operative business unit on the other; inasmuch as these typical configurations represented the result of certain developmental processes (→ *Managerial Economics*), Dülfer differentiated three "developmental models of co-operatives". In 1966, he restated these more precisely, refining them according to organizational theory, as three *"structural models" of promotion co-operatives*. Workers' co-operatives must be treated separately as a fourth model. These structural types were previously formulated as follows.

II. Structural Types of the Promotion Co-operative

According to the 19th century conception held by the founding co-operative pioneers who oriented their endeavors around social reform (→ *History in 19th C.*), the characteristic nature of the co-operative organization was to enable small-scale, market oriented companies or households to join together in co-operative groups (→ *Group, the Co-operative*) in order to collectively establish a business unit which in turn could promote them through purchasing and marketing services. The double nature of membership (*double qualité*) which accordingly results from this was emphasized in French co-operative science from the beginning; in German language studies, this was named "*Identitätsprinzip*" (*Eschenburg*, 1972) and maintained to be the most important co-operative characteristic (→ *Theory of co-operative Cooperation*). The original concept also called for members to jointly manage the co-operative business affairs on the basis of equal voting rights. Surpluses attained as a result of risk policy are to be distributed among the members in the form of → *reimbursements*. This serves to explain why the co-operative enterprise itself does not make any profit although it promotes its member enterprises through encouraging their profit (or utility) maximization. Because academic tenets (→ *Theory of Co-operatives*) and practical corporate policy alike originally oriented themselves around this concept, the author identifies this formative model as the *"traditional co-operative"*. This model is by no means solely a historical phenomenon but rather remains a contemporary type in the varied co-operative sectors, above all in developing countries (→ *Development Policy*).

Following the revitalization of co-operatives in Germany after World War II, it quickly became apparent in the scope of the market economy's rapid growth that the relationships between co-operative business units and their member enterprises relaxed in many co-operatives. The business management in the co-operative enterprises saw themselves forced through heightened competition to standardize promotional services for their members to a greater extent due to cost considerations (→ *Principle of Cost Coverage*). Furthermore, numerous co-operatives decided to offer non-members purchasing and marketing services originally intended solely for members in order to gain economies of scale (→ *Operational Size*). This automatically resulted in greater independence for the co-operative management with respect to members' wishes and, therefore, lead to a relaxation of the ties in the co-operative combine. The co-operative business unit acquired the character of a quasi-autonomous enterprise (Unternehmung) (*Draheim*, 1952: "Die Genossenschaft als Unternehmungstyp").

Members likewise sensed their relations loosened; as a result, they felt less obligated to their own co-operative enterprise and obtained services/outputs in part from competitors (→ *Competition*). The original, closely-wedded service/output and settlement relationship between the co-operative enterprise and its members thereby increasingly changed and headed in the general direction of a quasi-market relationship. This model was therefore quickly identified as the *"market co-operative"* and its expression can be found above all in → *consumer, credit* (→ *Co-operative Banks*), → *supply* and → *marketing co-operatives*. In → *co-operative science*, there was hesitation for some time to recognize this manifestation as a type of its own; G. *Draheim* (1952) characterized this development merely as the "economization of the co-operative", whereas *R. Henzler* (1956) spoke of a "marginal co-operative form" ("Grenztyp der Genossenschaft").

It became apparent at an early stage, however, that strong interests existed among the member enterprises in certain classes of co-operatives (in particular, co-operatives of retailers (→ *Commercial Co-operatives*), small transport enterprises (→ *Transport Co-operatives*) and farmers (→ *Rural Co-operatives*)) to preserve or reinstitute exclusivity in member relationships as they had previously functioned. These members were prepared to entrust the co-operative enterprise with certain independent decision-making competencies in order to resolve the management's policy dilemma which accordingly arose. The co-operative management acquired the new role of "group management", or in other words, it also started making decisions with regard to and/or for the member enterprises. Thus, whereas the member enterprises had originally controlled how the co-operative business operation provided services/outputs, the general direction of control to a large extent was reversed. As a result, the co-operative enterprise (on the wholesale level) as well as the member enterprises (on the retail level) became more competitive. In this regard, however, the voluntary nature of the member enterprises' affiliation had to be preserved so that the particular form of cooperation would not violate § 1 GWB (Law Against Restraints of Competition) because Germany has witnessed intensified legal cartel control and surveillance. *Dülfer* characterized this new structure within the entire co-operative combine as the *"Integrated Co-operative"*, thereby taking into consideration the fundamental re-integration in the complex as a whole.

III. Typological Distinctions

In daily co-operative practice – above all among purchasing co-operatives active in retail trade – the latter structural model is often referred to as a *"fullservice co-operative"* (→ *Commercial Co-operatives*). In this connection it is important that the integrated co-operative is not simply identified with the *multi-purpose co-operative* (→ *Classification*) which, according to its corporate policy, can restrict itself to providing supply and marketing services solely based on decisions made by the member enterprises. It can therefore assume activity according to the structure of the traditional co-operative as well as that of the market-linkage co-operative. In contrast, the true purchasing co-operative (→ *Supply Co-operatives*) bears the structure of an integrated co-operative as it recommends marketing activities to its members. The difference between the integrated co-operative and the *workers' co-operative* (→ *Joint-production Co-operative*) ultimately rests in that the members in the latter no longer dispose of their own operating units (enterprises). The members work as employees in the co-operative enterprise. The borderline between these two structural types is most evident in the case of → *Produktionsförderungsgenossenschaften*. In this type of agricultural promotion co-operative (introduced by *Otto Schiller* in Third World countries), land (and, as the case may be, equipment) remains the personal property of the member-farmers, although cultivation up through the harvest is planned and undertaken collectively. If need be this occurs through the (informal) consolidation of private fields.

IV. Structural Types in a Generalized Form

In the face of the world-wide tendency affecting the transformation of co-operatives into other and variously named legal forms, the author undertook the following generalization of these three structural types in the scope of his 1984 publication "Betriebswirtschaftslehre der Kooperative" (→ *Managerial Economics*): the traditional co-operative as an "*organwirtschaftliches Kooperativ*" (executively operating co-operative); the market co-operative (in order to differentiate it from the marketing co-operative) as a "*Marktbeziehungs-Kooperativ*" (market-linkage co-operative); and the integrated co-operative as the "*integriertes Kooperativ*". These three generalized structural types are to be understood as modifications to the co-operative which presently is interpreted from the viewpoint of general systems theory as a socio-technical, open, goal-oriented and economic "system".

V. Further Developments of the Concept of the Integrated Co-operative

The conflict potential and resolution options among market-linkage co-operatives and integrated co-operatives were addressed by *Eschenburg* (1971). Among other things, he pointed to the danger of a "control deficit" rooted in member dependency on management for information; on the other hand, this deficit can be alleviated through goal congruency as long as the heterogeneity existing in the membership body is not thereby reduced.

Vierheller (1974) chooses to commence his detailed discussions with the situation of members' low information level representing a source of danger. He assumes that the high degree of integration in this structural model causes a mounting decision-making interdependency between members' enterprises and the co-operative enterprise. He, therefore, isolates the main problem in the decision-making co-ordination between "anticipated management decisions and subsequent decisions made by the members based on the former". This co-ordination can however be endangered in that differing opinions could exist between the members and the co-operative management concerning the nature of goal pursuance; "realization conflicts" arise as a result of this. In contrast to a group of companies, the group management does not dispose of any possible sanctions, and a regulation of the conflict is thus only possible through a strategy of persuasion. The necessary decision-making co-ordination must therefore be striven for primarily through improvements to the level of membership information. With regard to this structural type, it is therefore imperative that the typical management information system is developed into a *management-member information system* (→ *Managerial Economics*).

Continuing with this idea, *Zimmermann* (1978) discusses the co-ordination problems in integrated co-operatives found in the retail food industry, particularly with regard to the typical heterogeneity of enterprise forms common in this sector. The conflicts and friction resulting from this, logically cannot be redressed through a standard program; in this case, rather, it is more imperative to have a differentiated information policy. The degree of differentiation of such a policy is determined not least by cost aspects. In this connection, the strategy of market segmentation is applicable analogously by developing a strategy of "member segmentation", applying known techniques to isolate the respective characteristics of the member enterprises and personalities.

There are numerous references in the literature concerning the application of co-operatives in Third World development policy programs (e.g. *Böttcher*, 1972; *Dülfer*, 1979) (→ *Development Policy*) that the integrated co-operative can be advantageous for the diffusion of technological progress (→ *Policies for Promotion*). One must, however, mind the danger of → *"officialization"* becoming too pronounced (*Hanel*, 1974).

Seuster (1975) provides a continuation of structural typology for the sector of agricultural co-operatives (→ *Rural Co-operatives*). He also proceeds from the notion of a "traditional co-operative" which corresponds with that type mentioned at the beginning of this treatise. *Seuster* distinguishes three subcategories which are analogous to the market co-operative: the "*centralized co-operative*", the "*concentrated co-operative*" (a market co-operative which is simultaneously a multi-purpose co-operative), and the "*decentralized co-operative*" (which represents the latter type with decentralized control over operation divisions). *Seuster* then also formulated the *integrated co-operative* as a fifth type which has "only gradual differences to the type proposed by *Dülfer*". These differences primarily rest in the emphasis placed on the integration of the individual primary co-operatives into the secondary organizational combine, which itself can be born by various institutions. *Seuster*, in this particular manner, considers it expedient to differentiate the term "integration" for the sector of rural commodity co-operatives.

VI. The Co-operative's Structural Dimensions

The more recent development of co-operatives and similar organizations, both in industrial countries and in the Third World, indicates that the diversity of co-operative organizational forms aiming at "self-help" continues to expand (→ *Self-help Organizations*). The respective structures are clearly determined by internal and external factors in the respective *situation*. This realization was formulated for organizational theory in general and not only for co-operative organizations. The term "*situational approach*" ("situativer Ansatz") is referred to in this context. On the basis of this approach, considerations can be made following the concept of structual types mentioned above. The objective is to ascertain which criteria can set the groundwork for a sensible differentiation. Such an analytical instrument should be able to make a more precise and praxiological structural recommendation in individual situations. By borrowing terminology from general organizational theory, we can identify these factors as *structural dimensions of the co-operative*. Following the interpretation of the co-operative given by general systems theory, suggestions for such structural dimensions can include the following (*Dülfer*, 1984):

- Dimension I: Configuration of the participating individual enterprises
- Dimension II: Member characteristics
- Dimension III: Intensity of cooperation
- Dimension IV: Allocation of competencies for goal definition and decision making
- Dimension V: Formalization of cooperation
- Dimension VI: Stability of cooperation

1. Dimension I: "The Configuration of the Participating Individual Enterprises"

The base characteristic is the "*systemic fundamental structure*" referring to the classification of the individual subsystems "member enterprises" and "co-operative operational unit" (→ *Managerial Economics*). In most cases, this classification or "configuration" is expressed in the name of the co-operative form (e.g. purchasing association, marketing co-operative, loan bank). The designation addresses the question whether the operational unit is to be found on the purchasing or on the marketing side of its member enterprises, or whether it only maintains internal relationships with its members as a workers' co-operative (→ *Joint-production Co-operative*). The basis for further characteristics are laid in part by this configuration. The *extent and nature of the delegation of functions* (single or multi-purpose co-operative) play a role in this context.

2. Dimension II: "Member Characteristics"

Although the configuration of the individual economic units in individual cases is clearly determined by the *nature of the members* (e.g. in consumer co-operatives), this is not true in general application. Farmers, for example, can be members of supply, marketing or multi-purpose co-operatives. On the other hand, the quality of the output/service relationship cannot be judged from the configuration of the individual economic units if and when further characteristics of the members or member enterprises are not provided.

These characteristics predominantly are associated with the *macro-economic functions* of the member enterprises. In connection with other structural dimensions, it is important whether the member enterprises avail themselves of production, distribution or credit functions, or combinations of such functions. The member's *profession* also plays an important role, for example, whether he is a retailer in the foodstuffs industry or a farmer. This is particularly the case in those co-operatives which boast of a heterogeneous membership group, such a credit co-operatives and consumer co-operatives.

As a rule, the *nature of the member's enterprise* is closely related to his practiced profession. Such enterprises could include those in farming, crafts, retailing, transportation, navigation, etc. The extent of legal and/or *economic independence* is likewise relevant for various types of promotion or workers' co-operatives. The *size of the member's enterprise* (→ *Operational Size*) and the nature of its *resources*, i.e. both staff and equipment, is ultimately also of interest.

3. Dimension III: "Intensity of Cooperation"

The *degree of intensity* in the co-operative relationship between members and/or the member enterprises is important for several aspects. The *degree of specialization* of the operational cooperation in turn plays a role for the intensity of co-operative ties between the various individual economic units. This intensity obviously increases with the *number* of operational functions of the member enterprises involved and included in the cooperation. Intensity, as a rule, is thereby higher in a multi-purpose co-operative than in a single purpose co-operative. The degree inevitably increases when consultational and/or management functions are provided above and beyond the processual operating functions (i.e. purchasing, marketing, etc.), as is the case with integrated co-operatives.

Furthermore, it has been proved empirically that the intensity of cooperation is contingent on the *value* the member enterprises place on such operational functions or services (the latter being the object of cooperation) in the scope of their allround activity. A co-operative dairy, for example, has a different significance for a specialized milk producer than for a grain farmer who keeps a few dairy cows on the side. The value placed on the operational functions promoted by the co-operative is thus relevant to ascertain the degree the overall situation of member enterprises is contingent on the success of the cooperation.

Yet another yardstick for measuring the intensity of cooperation is the extent the member enterprises avail themselves of the operational unit; this is referred to as the *"frequency of cooperation"*. The *proportion of total business volume* undertaken with member enterprises compared to the share carried out with non-members provides an interesting ratio in this connection.

4. Dimension IV: "Allocation of Competencies for Goal Definition and Decision Making"

This structural dimension is quite complex. In order to attain a characterizing statement, the relevant "goal subjects" (e.g. members, managers, employees) must first be taken into consideration within the observed co-operative, according to their nature, number, and constellation. In this connection, the processual particulars for constructing an "operational goal-defining system" for the operational unit as a whole are of considerable importance. In this regard, the following aspects should be taken into consideration (*Dülfer*, 1984):

"– the degree the goal system of the co-operative group has been concretized; seen the other way around, this degree in turn determines the extent the manager of the operational unit must make an interpretation of this goal system himself;
– the nature of the communication process through which the goal system of the co-operative group is realized;
– the amount of lee-way the management of the operational unit has for decision making;
– the nature and extent of the influence exercised by the manager's personal individual goals;
– the expression and extent of "co-determination" exercised by the employees of the operational unit and/or their delegates (→ *Workers Co-determination*);
– the nature of the management style used in the co-operative operational unit and the corresponding management concept;
– the number of decision-making levels in the operational unit responsible for member communication;
– the nature and influence of business interaction and informational communication with companies involved in the co-operative combine on the interregional level (→ *Combine, Co-operative*);
– the nature and extent of legal supervision and/or specialized intervention from state authorities (e.g. state development agencies)."

In addition, the nature and influence of *"external centers"* such as social groups, business federations, political parties, trade unions, etc. are of interest when analyzing how the process of goal formation is conceived.

The extent of member enterprises' *commitment to decision recommendations* made by the operational unit is of particular importance; this is not only influenced by formal organizational regulations but also through informal interpersonal relationships. This is a question of the degree of *acceptance* members have for such recommendations. Various gradations between the "typical" structures of the market likage co-operative and the integrated co-operative can fall under consideration. In this regard, the composition and voting mechanisms of the relevant *decision-making bodies* are important.

5. Dimension V: "Formalization of Cooperation"

On the one hand, long-term continuity is striven for in cooperation, whereas a certain extent of flexibility and adaptability is necessary on the other hand. The *degree of detail in the behavioral rules* affecting the members of the co-operative group is thus quite important. This *"behaviour codex"* itself is multifarious: it is grounded in various legal norms (laws, regulations, by-laws), but professional and social behaviour norms (role expectations) are, nonethe-

less, also taken into consideration (→ *Corporate Culture*).
Interaction within the co-operative must be formalized through contracts and internal organizational regulations to the extent *the processes of task fulfillment become programmed* (*Grochla*), such as franchising agreements. The nature of documentation used in internal co-operative communication processes (bookkeeping, standardized forms, data processing, etc.) plays an important role for the co-operative's control systems.

6. Dimension VI: "Stability of Cooperation"

It is obvious that the co-operative is, in principle, less "stable" than individual companies due to the fact that it is composed of relatively autonomous individual economic units (subsystems). In the majority of cases, these participating individual economic units are not unconditionally dependent on cooperation; in fact, they can even act against the interests of the group as a whole. On the other hand, they frequently cannot be replaced by other economic units without further ado if they choose to withdraw from the co-operative. A further complication for the *"stability of cooperation"* in several countries is a competition policy which assumes a critical stance to intensive cooperation patterns (in Germany, for example, the prohibition provisions in the Law Against Restrictions of Competition, GWB (→ *Anti-Trust Laws*). With regard to classic co-operative principles, civil law does permit voluntary membership withdrawal without entailing the dissolution of the co-operative, but the withdrawing member has the right to receive his paid-up share reimbursed upon withdrawal (→ *Equity Capital*). This circumstance means that the operational unit must confront the disadvantage of "fluctuating" share capital which can only partly be alleviated through the accumulation of nonpayable reserves.

It thereby is apparent that the *co-operative's degree of stability* is a particulary important structural characteristic and that it is primarily contingent on members' *"inclination to cooperate"* (*Draheim*: Kooperationsneigung) and on the *necessity for cooperation* felt by the member enterprises. Included among these classic *indicators of stability* are the following considerations:

- members' willingness to adapt to the internal co-operative structures;
- the willingness to accept decisions and/or recommendations made by the co-operative operational unit;
- management's willingness in the operational unit to orient activity around group goals.

As a basis for internal co-operative stability, sufficient *adaptability to environmental changes* must, furthermore, be at hand.

Bibliography

Draheim, Georg: Die Genossenschaft als Unternehmungstyp, 2nd ed., Göttingen 1955.
Dülfer, Eberhard: Strukturprobleme der Genossenschaft in der Gegenwart, in: Forschungsinstitut für Genossenschaftswesen an der Universität Wien (eds.), Neuere Tendenzen im Genossenschaftswesen, Wiener Studien N.F. vol. 1, Göttingen 1966, pp. 5–34 (passim).
Dülfer, Eberhard: Organisation und Management im kooperativen Betriebsverbund, in: ZfgG Sonderband 1970 (IV. Internationale Genossenschaftswissenschaftliche Tagung Gießen 1969), pp. 76–103.
Dülfer, Eberhard: Betriebswirtschaftslehre der Kooperative, Göttingen 1984.
Dülfer, Eberhard: Operational Efficiency of Agricultural Co-operatives in Developing Countries, Rom 1974/77 (frz. und span. A. 1975, arabische A. 1976)
Eschenburg, Rolf: Genossenschaftstheorie als Konflikttheorie, Tübingen 1972.
Seuster, Horst: Die strukturelle Entwicklung der ländlichen Warengenossenschaften, in: ZfgG 1975, pp. 104–122.
Vierheller, Rainer: Unternehmensführung und Mitgliederinformation in der Genossenschaft, Göttingen 1974.
Zimmermann, Peter: Konsequenzen der Betriebstypenheterogenität für das genossenschaftliche Gruppenmarketing, Göttingen 1978.

Subsidiarity Among Co-operatives

RAINER VIERHELLER [J]

(see: *Principles*; *Economic Order*; *State and Co-operatives, Market Economy*; *Managerial Economics*)

I. General Fundamentals; II. Subsidiarity in the Co-operative Scope of Reference; III. The Subsidiarity Principle in Application.

I. General Fundamentals

The principle of subsidiarity is closely tied to Catholic social doctrine and has become a commonly discussed socio-philosophical principle. The focus of the subsidiarity principle (→ *Principles*) is directed at the distribution of functions between individuals and social entities or between social entities of varying hierarchical importance (lower and higher standing). The subsidiary distribution of functions in its essence is oriented around the following principles (*Schneider*):

1. The collective body may not divest the individual of what he is capable of accomplishing on his own (*divestiture injunction*).
2. The divestiture injunction includes an obligation of the collective body to provide "auxiliary assistance" (*Nell-Breuning*) inasmuch as the individual's capacity to accomplish tasks or functions necessitates compensation (*assistance-precept*).

3. The collective body should undertake what the individual cannot accomplish himself (*help-precept*), whereby the principle of "help for self-help" should remain in effect.
4. What the individual can accomplish on his own at a later time, resulting from either altered conditions or improvements in individual performance ability, should be retransferred from the collective body to the individual (*subsidiary-reduction*).

These principles are applicable analogously for the distribution of functions between social entities with higher and lower hierarchical standing (in the co-operative scope of reference: competency regulation between individual and central co-operatives). Consequently, subsidiarity is a principle of competence which regulates the relationship between decentralized and centralized units: the centralized function position is conceived as *supplemental* help for the decentralized limbs of the organization and/or members, whose decentralized autonomy should remain as untouched as possible (→ *Principles*). Concerning the distribution of functions, decentralized units enjoy precedence over centralized ones – over the "subsidiary assistance" (*Schneider*) of the center. In the end, the concept of the entitled self-responsible individual based on primordial natural rights lies at the root of this fundamental socio-ethical stance. Despite his social ties and involvements, the individual should not be treated by the collective body as a dependent and non-personal component: "That which an individual is capable of doing on his own should not be taken away from him through social activity, as this represents neither aid nor enrichment but contrarily an infringement, an impairment and a curtailment of personality development which is for ever tied to the incitement of one's own strength" (*Nell-Breuning*). The principle of subsidiarity consequently assumes a position between the two fundamental socio-philosophical stances of individualism and collectivism. Collectivism absolutizes the social conditionality (sociality) of the individual, whereas individualism neglects this altogether. The principle of subsidiarity involves the social attachment of the individual through the subsidiary function and importance of the collective body; at the same time, however, it emphasizes the relatedness of the community to the individual through the subsidiarity of community functions.

II. Subsidiarity in the Co-operative Scope of Reference

Co-operatives as self-help communities (→ *Self-help Organizations*) are closely tied to the principle of subsidiarity in a threefold manner:

1) Cooperation in co-operatives fundamentally concerns the question of deciding between private self-help and outside assistance from the state (→ *State and Co-operatives, Market Economy*).
2) The question is raised in the context of co-operative self-help concerning the distribution of functions between individual members and the co-operative as well as the distribution of competencies between the general assembly of members and the management bodies (→ *Organizational Structure of Societies*).
3) The question is also finally raised concerning the distribution of functions between lower and higher level co-operatives when individual co-operatives choose to amalgamate into central co-operatives (→ *Central Institutions*) in order to overcome limits imposed by → *operational size*.

Subsidiarity as such fundamentally embraces the opinion that public assistance need not to be drawn on or accepted as long as co-operatives are able to improve the living conditions of economically weaker population groups. This standpoint is maintained by most co-operatives in the industrial age. In particular, the German co-operative pioneers → *Schulze-Delitzsch* and *F.W.* → *Raiffeisen* were critical opponents of outside public assistance. They held the position that state assistance is not possible without state influence and say into matters (loss of decentral autonomy); furthermore, outside assistance would threaten to lame individual efforts (damage to self-help). The experience of the housing co-operatives clearly indicates the loss of co-operative autonomy caused by state assistance (*Brecht*).

Co-operatives of the industrial age traditionally emphasize their character as an association of persons. This emphasis should express that individual human values have precedence over economic-material values. Seen from this angle, the economic functions of co-operatives are structured to safeguard the economic preconditions of value goals, themselves personal in nature. Co-operatives in the age of industrialization have been closely entwined with the principle of subsidiarity since their beginning because of their position with regard to personal values: "The value assumptions which develop their expression in the principles of solidarity and subsidiarity are to the most part identical with those in the general philosophical direction of personalism, which, seen as a doctrine of values, postulates that all values emanate from the individual (and not from the subject) and that the individual is not only the source of values but also the measure and goal of them" (*Staehle*). The principles of self-help, self-management and, self-responsibility stressed by *Schulze-Delitzsch* (as well as co-operative federalism which results from these) stem from the fundaments of personalism and simultaneously form the basis of the values expressed in the subsidiarity principle. This close connection between personalism and subsidiarity was clearly expressed by *Schulze-Delitzsch*: "Only where the strengths of the individual are insufficient in the face of a disfavorable *external* situation does the *free co-operative* become involved in a supplementary manner in order through the unification of strengths to achieve those matters at which the individual failed. The personality of the co-operator should not be touched...but rather the goal [of the co-operative] is to aid him in attaining full worth in life" (*Schulze-Delitzs*ch).

The guiding co-operative maxims of voluntariness and participational democracy (→ *Principles*) are likewise addressed through claims to subsidiary function distribution. Members of co-operatives for economic assistance not only are free in their decision to enter or withdraw from the co-operative, but in the essence of the principle of voluntariness they are also are not subject to to any utilization mandates with respect to the palette of co-operative services. Members can decide on their own which decentralized tasks are to be transferred to the co-operative on the basis of participational democracy, just as the general assembly of members – in the scope of legal provisions – can consider and determine the distribution of competencies between the general assembly and the management bodies.

The characterization of the co-operative as a "partial collectivization" aimed at the promotion of the *individual* is also cleary related to the principle of subsidiarity: "The goal of this partial collectivization is the promotion and support of the co-operators' individual business enterprises. On the one hand, the economic character of this organizational form is shown, on the other hand, the functions of the co-operative with regard to personalism and economic independence are clearly expressed" (*Seraphim*). *Back*, therefore, sees modern co-operative organizations – in contrast to pre-industrial, historical co-operatives – as "the development and extension of collective organizations and facilities [serving] as the superstructure encompassing the realm of autonomous individual economy according to the principle of subsidiarity."

III. The Subsidiarity Principle in Application

Within the co-operative scope of reference, the subsidiarity principle is part of an ethical-normative economic doctrine. Forecasted ethical-normative statements are, however, only then immediately effective in application when definite situational directives for their application can be derived from them. The application of the subsidiarity principle is, however, bound to certain preconditions which themselves are difficult to determine: a centralization of functions in the sense of the subsidiarity principle is only then justified when it has been sufficiently proved in the interrelated chain of actions that a decentralized task can be accomplished better on the central co-operative level and that this improvement is of great importance for the decentralized members. In other words: The application of the subsidiarity principle presupposes that the choice between a decentralized or centralized execution of certain functions can be unequivically determined with regard to consequences on quality and the importance of these functions to the decentralized members. Nonetheless, the subsidiarity principle does not provide any uniform indications as a prescriptive-normative statement. The burden of proof alone is settled through the subsidiarity principle: If the central level wishes to divest the decentralized units of their functions, it must be able to sufficiently justify the necessity of centralization. It cannot be discerned from the subsidiary value system, whether or not the centralization arguments provided correspond to objective circumstances. As long as the importance and quality of both a centralized and decentralized execution of functions cannot be unequivocally determined, the subsidiariry principle does not provide any guarantee against overcentralization within co-operatives. The consequences of the distribution of functions between centralized and decentralized levels are particularly difficult to determine when the goal of "membership promotion" remains too vague in its definition, when argumentation involves synergy effects which are difficult both to predict and measure, or when uncertainties exist concerning future market demands and co-ordinational requirements. Therefore, an investigation of the body and content of centralization arguments usually becomes quite difficult. Such conditions facilitate the arguments of a superior professional central management for excessive centralization.

A decentralized independent execution of functions entails a multi-polar decision-making system which facilitates the implementation of partial interests and necessitates a higher degree of co-ordination. Such effects are likewise difficult to quantify and weight, thus explaining the uncertainty associated with the determination of an appropriate subsidiary distribution of functions. The decision concerning a subsidiary distribution of functions then becomes complicated when such functions and inputs are closely interlocked with each other. By no means, however, does each transfer of decentralized functions to the collective co-operative enterprise result in a corresponding loss to decentralized functions. Collective advertising campaigns can, for example, on the one hand be tied to a partial divestiture of decentralized publicity activities. On the other hand, new publicity activities can be launched by the central organization which the individual members themselves are not in the position to execute. When the decentralized members are involved in part in the scope of these new activities (e.g. in advertising committees or through supportive decentralized sales promotion campaigns), centralized advertising undertaken by the collective body thus represents not only a partial functional loss but also a partial functional gain for the decentralized spheres. The larger the role such interlocking inputs play, the more difficult it becomes to decide on a subsidiary distribution of functions. The questions raised above concerning the distribution of co-operative functions must be settled to a sufficient degree in order for subsidiarity to function properly. Nevertheless, ambiguity and uncertainty arise in connection with the explanation of these questions which consequently cause the subsidiarity principle to exhibit a minimum of instructional capacity for individual situations.

Bibliograpy

Back, Josef M.: Genossenschaftsgeschichte, in: Handwörterbuch der Betriebswirtschaftslehre, vol. II., Stuttgart 1958, cols. 2191–2210.
Brecht, Julius: Selbsthilfe und Staatshilfe am Beispiel der Wohnungsbaugenossenschaften, in: Zeitschrift für das gesamte Genossenschaftswesen, vol. 2 (1952), pp. 81–100.
Nell-Breuning, Oswald v.: Solidarität und Subsidiarität im Raume von Sozialpolitik und Sozialreform. Sozialpolitik und Sozialreform, Tübingen 1957, pp.213–226.
Pfüller, Reiner: Der Genossenschaftsverbund, Göttingen 1964.
Schulze-Delitzsch, Hermann: Die praktischen Mittel und Wege zur Hebung der arbeitenden Klassen. Anthologie des Genossenschaftswesens, Berlin 1922, pp. 63–67.
Seraphim, Hans-Jürgen: Die genossenschaftliche Gesinnung und das moderne Genossenschaftswesen, Karlsruhe 1956.
Totomianz, Vahan: Anthologie des Genossenschaftswesens, Berlin 1922.
Utz, Arthur F. (ed.): Formen und Grenzen des Subsidiaritätsprinzips, Heidelberg 1956.

Supply Co-operatives

WERNER GROSSKOPF [J]

(see also: *Classification*; *Commercial Co-operatives*; *Rural Co-operatives*; *Consumer Co-operatives*)

I. Definition of Terms; II. The Promotional Expectations of the Members; III. Initial Establishment and Historical Development in the 19th Century; IV. Development of Supply Co-operatives in the 20th Century; V. Outlook for the Future.

I. Definition of Terms

All co-operative self-help organizations (→ *Self-help Organizations*) can be considered supply co-operatives which strive to promote their members through *favorable procurement of inputs* for the enterprises or households of their members. Their common characteristic which distinguishes them from all other co-operatives is that they wish to promote their members primarily through the purchasing activity of their organization (→ *Promotion Mandate*). Thus, the supply co-operatives can either acquire the necessary economic inputs for their members from the market or they can provide them through their own management organization, e.g. in a special enterprise of their own. In this latter case, along with the "processing co-operatives" for farmers and craftsmen as well as the → *"joint-production co-operatives"*, a common characteristic comes to light, namely that of a co-operatively owned production enterprise. The supply co-operatives vary from the two organizations last mentioned in as much as the self-produced services of the supply co-operatives generally serve to *improve the situation* of their members *in their purchase* of sought after inputs. The provision of services in the common enterprise of the processing co-operatives, on the other hand, serves to improve the situation of the members in the marketing of the goods produced in the members' enterprises. The collective production enterprise of the members of a production co-operative should ultimately secure a better utilization of the working force comprised of members.

Aside from the consumer, building, and credit co-operatives (→ *Classification*), the supply co-operatives for farmers and/or craftsmen and the purchase co-operatives for independent merchants also belong to these co-operatives. The youngest member of the family of this type of co-operatives is the service co-operative, which primarily strives to meet the information and data processing needs of its members as economically as possible. Among others, this group includes co-operatives of self-employed persons which attend to the accounting or invoicing tasks for the members' enterprises.

II. The Promotional Expectations of the Members

The members of co-operatives expect their self-help organizations to improve in the economic activity of their enterprises or households from. In as far as supply co-operatives are concerned, this improvement as a rule means a *reduction in price or time expenditure* for the member in the provision of inputs (→ *Pricing Policy*). In situations where a standardized input cannot be offered and where the *quality of the input* plays a very large economic role for the member, e.g. the quality of purchased fodder in agriculture, a high quality level of the inputs also numbers among the particularly valued expectations of the members.

As one can see from empirical research analyses, the members of supply co-operatives generally expect a reduction in their own *information costs* (Sager-Röhm and Bakonyi). They lay particular value in the banking sector (→ *Co-operative Banks*) on member-oriented consulting and personal attention. In general, the time aspect (e.g. transport time) also has a high priority among the customers. The pricing conditions (→ *Pricing Policy*) and considerations first play an important role in business transactions with a larger economic importance. The stronger the *unit costs per purchase unit* can be reduced (→ *Principle of Cost*

Coverage) through the collective provision of inputs important for a member, the more the member is dependent on his supply co-operative. When member enterprises increase their purchase of inputs, the fixed costs associated with information procurement, transport, etc. will be spread out among relatively many input units without straining the supply co-operative. As a result of a *mounting scope of business activity*, members become geographically more mobile and more *critical* of their supply co-operative. Particularly the younger members view the offered products and services of the co-operatives critically. Self-employed merchants likewise react with respect to their provision co-operatives when they are up against stiff competition (→ *Competition*), as, for example, in larger urban areas.

Those critical members do not simply count on their co-operative without undertaking anything further, but rather frequently acquire additional information from the market. The readiness of the members increases with a growing scope of business activity to overcome the greater distance between their own enterprise (household) and the location of a *more favorable supplier* on grounds of a more advantageous price offer (→ *Operational Size*). The "co-operative loyalty" of the members negatively correlates to the range of the total input requirements of the member enterprises.

III. Initial Establishment and Historical Development in the 19th Century

Present-day supply co-operatives are predominantly a result of industrialized societies. On the other hand, they are particularly promoted by the state in various developing countries as democratic organizations (→*Policies for Promotion*). Their initial formation took place in the industrial European countries in the *early years of capitalism*. This replaced feudalism, unwillingly assumed its strains and burdens, and initially exacerbated social problems, unemployment, and malnutrition. At this time, workers, small and midscale farmers and craftsmen hardly had any type of liquidity reserves and only rarely sufficient creditworthiness. In emergency situations, they had to make use of *commodity credits or monetary credits* from usurers. They thus easily fell into an economic dependency they could rarely escape from. Furthermore, *with respect to the far stronger suppliers*, these social groups, in many ways, were in a very weak economic bartering position. Upon the introduction of capitalistic economic methods, no efficient *transportation system* was in existence. Because harnessed animals were the only non-human energy source, the transport of both people and goods was expensive. Every very strong storm restricted the transportation possibilities between localities on the unsurfaced roads and repeatedly *isolated communities* from each other for weeks on end. As a result, almost insurmountable hurdles stood in the way of the exchange of goods and services between different towns and regions as well as of the physical mobility of both labor and capital. Altogether, this strongly *reduced competition* between the various suppliers and offerers of inputs and jobs, and benefitted the creation and preservation of a "sellers' market" to an extreme degree. In this market, the sole supplier, who was frequently the only one accessible, dictated his conditions. In such situations, those negatively affected often resorted to self-help and founded supply co-operatives.

Over time, though, most of those spontaneously founded co-operatives have been forgotten. Those organizations called into being by the "fathers" of the various co-operative movements are the ones which have gone down in history. One of the few examples of a spontaneously founded establishment which has become well-known is the co-operative store founded in 1764 in the Scottish town of Fenwick, which was a forerunner of the present day consumer co-operative (→ *History before 1800*). In 1821, the establishment of an agricultural loan society was reported in Southern Germany (→ *History in 19th C.*). This society had an organization similar to the contemporary credit co-operatives. These self-help institutions could only then become part of the "movement" when they fulfilled two *conditions*. Those addressed did open themselves up to co-operative thought only when it could be made clear and sensible to the potential members through convincing arguments that *the incentives* (→ *Incentives*) *exceeded the expected contributions* of each cooperation (see *Eschenburg* for more on the Incentive-Contribution Relationship). A successful emulation of such a "model" also assumed that a very convincing and willing person availed himself *to the dissemination of co-operative ideas* (compare *Faust* and *Preuss*).

IV. Development of the Supply Co-operative in the 20th Century

At least in their "developmental years", the supply co-operatives were mostly called into being as "*traditional co-operatives*" (see *Dülfer*). The needs of their members or the rising competition in their fields of activity then led them to the developmental path in the direction of "market co-operatives" or to "integrated co-operatives" (→ *Structural Types*). The "traditional supply co-operative" was also known as a "relief organization" to its members. In this early time period, the → *consumer co-operatives* or the supply co-operatives for farmers or craftsmen generally did not keep stock of wares but rather executed the procurement of goods in individual cases. Non-members were generally not served; the subjects (members) and the input recipients (customers) of the co-operative were identical (Identity Principle). In this developmental stage, the collective purchasing activity limited itself to the only slightly differentiated "basic needs" of the members. As it did not need any working business enterprise, this traditional organizational form had no capacity problems. The disadvantages of this "ordering co-operative", though, quickly became apparent. This method of function assumes that the individual members have a long-term stock of goods in their households and/or family enterprises. The advantages of bulk orders could also not always be seized. The more diffuse the needs of the members are and the more mounting competition rules out a "market failure" in the course of economic development, the more forcefully the co-operatives will be obliged to adapt themselves to what is offered by their competitors. They will be prevailed upon to maintain stock, establish a working enterprise and pursue further measures for the business administration.

Having a *working enterprise of its own*, the co-operative has more administrative opportunities but, at the same time, limits its freedom of disposition and activity in other areas. By opening its own working enterprise, a supply co-operative at first has the opportunity *to permanently offer goods* to its members, something up to then being possible only periodically. It is possible that with warehousing the co-operative can purchase considerably larger amounts at one time than it could without warehouse facilities. The *price reductions* attained through this then contribute to a reduction in the purchase costs. When the co-operative can always offer its members expected inputs and when its condition continues to appear lucrative, it can *promote its members better* than through periodic orders. The members, as recipients of inputs, remain loyal to their co-operative. By establishing a working enterprise, the supply co-operative more readily prepares itself for the *pressures and constraints of the market forces* (→ *Competition*).

By retaining the identity principle (→ *Theory of Co-operatives*), *it is disadvantaged in competition*. As long as it only satisfies the needs of its members it, is limiting its volume of turnover to the demands of its members. Then, the co-operative can only make use of its size and reduce its unit price at a certain minimum turnover level. If, as a result of its limited growth potential, the co-operative no longer is able to offer its members improvements in their situations in respect to the market, the relationship between the incentives for membership and the members' own contributions to the co-operative deteriorates. This can lead to a breach in loyalty within the co-operative. In such a situation, various possibilities become available for each individual co-operative to improve its performance. The easiest is to increase the turnover between the working enterprise and the members through an *intensification of the business relations*, in which the co-operative expands its realm of activity into new fields of business. The purchasing power of the members of → *consumer co-operatives* as well as the turnover in the enterprises of those self-employed members grow with mounting levels of real income. This causes a differentiation of the members' structure of needs and permits an expansion of the assortment in the working enterprise. Alongside the requisite capital investments, which in many ways presupposes a differentiation of the business activities, other "costs" must also be reckoned with. When there is *no homogeneous expectation structure* from the members in respect to the differentiated offer from the working enterprise, the promotion of at least a part of the membership will suffer.

The growth constraints on the individual supply co-operatives can be reduced if more and more primary co-operatives establish *secondary co-operatives* (→ *Central Institutions*). The secondary co-operatives then assume those functions from their members, the primary co-operatives, through which they can attain price advantages because of collective trade. The lower the yield a primary co-operative turns over, the more it can profit per input unit from the *efficiency* and the *"countervailing-market power"* of its secondary co-operative. Based on this reason, the agricultural supply co-operatives, which are involved in numerous community levels (and very frequently run as a side enterprises of credit co-operatives), as well as the consumer co-operatives, established regional co-operative centers at a relatively early point in time (see *Preuss*). Despite the concentration of demand in co-operative centers, the supply co-operatives do not dispose of sufficient market power to eliminate excessive profits from their suppliers. If this is the case and if *cost advantages are guaranteed by producing on their own*, various supply co-operatives will engage in the production of products for their members. Thus, both construction planning and supervision are among the standard functions of a co-operative building society. The consumer co-operatives, above all in the Scandanavian countries, are equipped with their own production enterprises. Various agricultural co-operative centers, for example in Germany, run their own factories to produce concentrated feed primarily to create a more favorable arrangement of the purchasing trade in agriculture. Many supply co-operatives of retail grocers also deliver their members self-produced goods (*Preuss*). With the help of their own production enterprise, supply co-operatives can have rationalization profits passed on to their members. An important precondition must, however, be fulfilled: A high utilization of the output capacity of the co-operative itself. The two organizational forms "market co-operative" and "integrated co-operative" offer such capacity utilization (→ *Structural Types*).

The *market co-operative* no longer exclusively offers its outputs and services to its members but rather also to other input recipients. It widely *abandons* the important principle (→ *Principles*) of co-operative theory, namely the *identity of agents (members) and input recipients (users) of the co-operative*. The more mobile its members are in the selection of their market partner, the better the offers the competitors of the co-operative working enterprise can make the members, and the fewer the number of members dependent on the working enterprise, the earlier will the co-operative take this step. These conditions occur most frequently in the consumer and banking branches in the developed industrial societies. Upon expanding the working enterprise for non-members, *a differentiation of the input expectations* can be forecasted *through the heterogeneity of the input recipients* as well as a loss of influence of the promotional expectations of the members (*Preuss*). In the relinquishment of the identity principle, the *self-help* character of the supply co-operative *becomes partially lost*. Eventually, the co-operatives' competitors are successful in *slowly reducing or even abolishing the privileges the co-operatives were granted by state policy makers*. For example, the opportunities to promote the membership can be dramatically deteriorated through taxing the transfer of inputs and/or services, through legally restricting the methods of reimbursement or by imposing special disadvantages on the members. Slowly but surely the co-operative becomes a procurement source like any and all others for its own members.

Retail merchants often find themselves confronted with oligopolistic markets from which they must purchase their goods (→ *Economic Order*). The fewer the chances they reckon with in the "free market" for determining trade conditions with their suppliers in a market with ever-mounting competition, the earlier they will state their willingness to transform their traditional co-operative into an *"integrated co-operative"*. They thus *entrust their co-operative with relatively many decision competences*, strongly binding and committing themselves to them in respect to planning and consulting beyond the mere purchase of goods. This strong integration enhances the competitiveness of each member but also considerably reduces his mobility in the selection of his suppliers. In the second half of this century, the grocery retailers in various industrialized countries have fallen into such a situation.

Concentration through fusion or *individual enterprise growth* (→ *Mergers and Consolidations*) has been a frequently useful means to increase the efficiency of the co-operative itself. The concentrational undertakings have lead to a filialization of the individual co-operatives, predominantly in the consumer co-operatives in numerous industrialized countries. Many considerable cost degressions were achieved as well as a reduction in the marketing mechanism from the production enterprise to the final consumer. Through this, however, an essential co-operative characteristic lost extensive influence – *the self-administration characteristic*. The members could barely survey the activities of the large-scale co-operative, much less control them.

V. Outlook for the Future

The co-operatives are *in competition* with other organizations *for the utilization of capacities from both agent/members and input recipients*. The better they fulfill the promotional expectations of their (potential) members, the larger the run they can expect to draw. The supply co-operatives are especially capable of promoting their members when and where the preconditions for pure competition do not exist on the local or regional market level. Their promotional performance is most apparent when they can *prevent monopolists or oligopolists from prevailing with inflated prices*. In new markets, generally in developing countries, their performance record can be seen relatively easily. The *proximity* of a supply co-operative in the sparsely populated regions of industrialized countries continues to pay off for the expansion or preservation of membership. In the future, the factor cannot be left out of consideration that in numerous branches of the economy the *continued concentration of supply* could again play the function of revitalizing competition into the hands of the co-operatives and result in strengthening membership ties. In general, the co-operatives can only maintain their competitive position or build on it through particularly good outputs and services; this assumes a *constant readiness for innovation and timely structural adaptation* when necessary. In one respect the co-operatives could be a step ahead of the competitors because of their organizational form – *in the field of information procurement and consulting*. Based on the identity of both agents and input recipients, members can rightfully expect the most thorough information and consultation from their co-operatives. When the co-operatives are thereby able to acquire and maintain a justifiable improvement in their membership loyalty, they are in a better position than their competitors to contribute to a reduction in their members' transaction costs (*Schuler*).

Bibliography

Bakonyi, Emmerich: Mitgliedererwartungen in Bankgenossenschaften, Stuttgart 1983.

Boettcher, Erik: Die Genossenschaften in der Marktwirtschaft, Tübingen 1980.

Dülfer, Eberhard: Integrierte Genossenschaft, in: Mändle, Eduard/ Winter, Hans-Werner (eds.): Handwörterbuch des Genossenschaftswesens, Wiesbaden 1980, cols. 995–1005.

Eschenburg, Rolf: Anwendung der Anreiz-Beitrags-Theorie, in: Zeitschrift für das gesamte Genossenschaftswesen, vol.38 (1988), pp. 250–262.

Faust, Helmut: Geschichte der Genossenschaftsbewegung. Ursprung und Weg der Genossenschaften im deutschen Sprachraum, Frankfurt am Main 1965.

Preuss, Walther: Das Genossenschaftswesen in der Welt und in Israel, Berlin 1958.

Sager, Hans-Peter/Röhm, Helmut: Kooperationsbereitschaft und Kooperationsverhalten mittelständischer Unternehmer des Textil-Einzelhandels, Stuttgart 1977.

Schuler, Michael: Sortimentspolitik und Förderungsauftrag in Bankgenossenschaften, Stuttgart 1989.

Taxation of Co-operatives

RÜDIGER PHILIPOWSKI [J]

(see also: *Managerial Economics*; *Financing*; *Assessment of Success*; *Reimbursements*)

I. Taxable Income; II. Tax Rates; III. Co-operative Reimbursement; IV. Tax Exemption for Rural Co-operatives.

When a co-operative supplies goods or provides services it must pay turnover tax; when it purchases real estate property it must pay property acquisition tax, etc. In such situations, the co-operative itself is not being taxed but rather the economic transaction in which the co-operative is participating. In the context of this treatise, only those types of taxes are of interest which (intend to) encumber the co-operative as such. This primarily involves corporate income tax (Körperschaftssteuer).

Discussion has been underway for years in Germany, whether the taxation of co-operatives is fair at all in the scope of the tax system (→ *Managerial Economics*). One school of experts responds negatively to this question, basing its stance on the following argument: Corporate income tax is intended to encumber the *income* of a corporate body. The object of a co-operative is, however, not the attainment of (the highest possible) income but rather the promotion of its members' enterprises. To achieve this objective, the co-operative maintains a common business enterprise comprised of its members. Inasmuch as a surplus is realized through transactions with members, this surplus does not belong to the co-operative, but rather to its members. It consequently should not also be taxed at the co-operative (→ *Reimbursements*). At best, it is permissible to calculate the distribution of the surplus to the individual members and to tax the partial amounts then and there. If this is too cumbersome for the tax authority, taxation should not be undertaken.

Despite this argument, German legislators decided in favor of taxing co-operatives. The following considerations played a critical role in this decision: If and when a surplus is achieved through transactions with members and distributed in the form of reimbursements, it in fact must not be taxed at the co-operative; each member must rather be taxed in relation to the partial amount he is due (see below under III.1). If, however, the co-operative does not distribute the surplus – or else distributes a part of it as reimbursements – but rather retains it (or a part of it), the co-operative intends to use the surplus for its own purposes, e.g. to increase its reserves or to pay a dividend on accepted paid-up shares. The co-operative's decision to retain a surplus for its own purposes is justification to tax this amount as a part of its income.

The extent of the corporate income tax is determined from the base of assessment (taxable income) and the rate of taxation. In some international discussions, emphasis is solely placed on the tax rate level, which is understandable in that percentage rates can be easily compared with each other. The specialized expert, on the other hand, knows that much greater attention should be paid to the respective provisions which determine the taxable assessment base. Such provisions vary from country to country.

The following article will discuss the legal situation in Germany and is intended to incite the reader to make appropriate comparisons with the tax code of his/her own country.

I. Taxable Income

1. Calculation of Income

The amount of taxable income is ascertained using the following calculation:

Business capital at the conclusion of the business year	......
Minus business capital at the end of the previous business year	– ......
Plus non-tax-deductible company expenses	+ ......
Plus disguised profit distributions	+ ......
Plus 50% of the supervisory board's pay	+ ......

The level of business capital results from the tax balance sheet. The first question to be posed and decided is: which items must be included in the tax balance sheet and which may be excluded?

2. Obligations, Prohibitions, and Options to Include Certain Items in the Balance Sheet

The co-operative must include all assets and all liabilities in its tax balance sheet (Law of Complete Reporting; Principle of Balance Sheet Integrity). This principle also holds true for the commercial balance sheet (which is published and serves to inform both members and business partners).

It may occur in everday practise that a co-operative either accidentally or intentionally omits an asset in its commercial balance sheet (thereby showing lower company assets), or that it omits a liability (thereby indicating higher business capital). It is furthermore imaginable that this balance sheet mistake is discovered sometime afterwards, but that the commercial balance sheet is not accordingly revised. Nevertheless, the state's claim to tax monies must not be contingent on whether the co-operative corrects the faulty commercial balance sheet or not. As a consequence, the tax balance sheet must always indicate those items under legal obligation to be either capitalized or carried as liabilities, even when they were not actually included in the commercial balance sheet (because the amount of liable taxes is calculated from the tax balance sheet) (→ *Financial Accounting Law*). The tax authority makes sure that this principle is maintained when it audits the co-operative. Large co-operatives undergo such audits regularly, whereas smaller co-operatives are only occasionally audited (→ *Auditing*).

Prohibitions against the inclusion of certain items in the balance sheet are a measure of creditor protection. Expenses incurred in founding the co-operative and raising equity, for example, may not be capitalized. Asset items may also not be reported for self-generated goodwill nor for the establishment of a regular clientele which results from the co-operative's own efforts. These prohibitions against inclusion in the balance sheet are in effect for both the commercial and tax balance sheets.

It is imaginable that asset items of this nature are accidentally included in the commercial balance sheet and that this mistake is not rectified due to one of numerous reasons. The respective items must accordingly be omitted when the tax balance sheet is drawn up.

In certain situations, an option to include items in the balance sheet exists, as the following example illustrates: A co-operative borrows a credit for 1 million marks. It is agreed that the lender will retain a disagio of 6% upon disbursing the loan proceeds and that the credit will be payed back after five years. In this situation, the co-operative must carry the loan as a liability on the balance sheet and capitalize the payed out amount of DM 940,000. With respect to the disagio, however, the co-operative has an option in the commercial balance sheet. It may capitalize the DM 60,000 (and write off the amount within five years according to plan), or it can dispense with capitalizing the DM 60,000; in the latter case, it will indicate DM 60,000 less in business capital and profit to its members and business partners. The co-operative must nonetheless indicate the amount of DM 60,000 in the tax balance sheet as a prepaid item. It thus cannot reduce its taxable income in the year it borrows the credit by negotiating a disagio. The following rule is generally applicable: An item which *may* be capitalized in the commercial balance sheet *must* be capitalized in the tax balance sheet even when it was not actually included in the commercial balance sheet.

Working in the other direction, however, an item which may be carried as a liability (but does not have to be) in the commercial balance sheet must not be carried as a liability in the tax balance sheet – even when the item was allocated for in the commercial balance sheet. The following serves as an example of this situation: Repairs should have been executed in the business year which just expired, but they were never undertaken. These repairs are undertaken in the following business year some several months subsequent to the balance sheet date. In such a situation, the co-operative may set aside reserves in the previous year's commercial balance sheet for such maintenance expenses yet to be undertaken; it can, however, choose not to create such reserves. Regardless of the option it chooses, no reserves for postponed maintenance expenses may be allocated for in the tax balance sheet.

3. Capitalizing Assets at Purchase or Production Cost

Assets purchased by the co-operative are to be reported at their purchase cost. This includes all expenses necessary in order to purchase the individual asset and to transform it into an employable state. The purchase price must be capitalized (minus deductible prior turnover tax) as well as all incidental costs which can be allocated to the purchased object. Those assets produced in and by the co-operative itself (above all buildings and commercial goods) must be reported at their cost of production. Such costs include all expenses which arise when other goods are used or worn out or when services are availed of in connection with the production of the asset.

4. Appreciation

In the course of time, many assets appreciate in value. This is above all the case for real estate property and occasionally for participatory investments. Despite their increased value, such assets are to be reported in the tax balance sheet in the subsequent years at their historical purchase or production cost. The increase in value thus does not result in an increase in the reported value in the balance sheet and does not raise taxable income. A tax obligation first arises in this situation when the increase in value is actually realized once the asset is sold.

5. The Principle of Nominal Value

In inflationary periods, the principle of nominal value taxes fictitious profit. The following example should clearly illustrate this phenomenon:

(historical) purchase or production cost of a good	100
(present day) replacement cost of this good	120
turnover attained upon sale of this good	130

When the co-operative sells the good and replaces it with an identical good with the turnover proceeds, its real profit is (130–120 =) 10. German tax code, however, does not take into consideration the increases in the sales and replacement prices which arise due to inflation. The nominal profit of (130–100 =) 30 is taxed instead. At a tax rate of 50%, the co-operative must pay 15 in taxes. Because it in actuality had only earned 10, the tax liability can substantially undermine the foundation of the co-operative enterprise. The dimension of this risk is contingent on the annual inflation rate. When inflation remains low it is admissible to keep to the principle of nominal value. This is in particular the case when special provisions exist which reduce taxes on fictitious profit. Such provisions existed and/or still exist in Germany, but only in narrowly defined situations, namely

- when certain capital goods are sold: taxable profits can be avoided by shifting revealed quiet reserves to other capital goods;
- when the market price of goods increases by more than 10% annually: reserves which reduce profit can be accrued for inflation;
- when certain imported raw materials are subject to volatile price swings on the world market: a downward valuation adjustment of up to 20% can be undertaken which reduces profit;
- when purchasing and selling merchandise: the valuation method of "last in, first out" is used.

All of these provisions do not ultimately prevent fictitious profits from being taxed but postpone such taxation to a future point in time.

6. Depreciation of Commercial Buildings

In Germany, it was originally assumed that the majority of buildings could remain standing and be used for 100 years. As a result of this, the write off for depreciation (DWO) was so calculated that the building would be completely written off within a period of 100 years; the DWO rate accordingly was set at 1%.

Lawmakers decided in the mid 1960s to reduce the duration of utilization to only 50 years when calculating the DWO rate, which was accordingly raised to 2%. The DWO rate was once again increased in 1985, this time to 4%. This corresponds with a typical utilization duration of only 25 years. Every co-operative manager knows, however, that a solidly constructed building can remain standing for at least 25 years (and sometimes for substantially longer). The utilization duration set by tax code legislators does not correspond with reality: The 4% DWO rate is much higher than the actual extent of wear and tear and corresponding value depreciation.

The high DWO is intended to provide a tax incentive to undertake construction investment. The law is, however, formulated in such a manner that the co-operative *must* use the 4% rate (not a lower rate). This situation has consequences for co-operatives which invest very large amounts of money into buildings but which subsequently do not achieve the gross profits they had expected through their undertaken business involvement with goods or services. It can even happen in such a case that a taxable loss arises solely due to the 4% DWO rate, a situation which is sometimes not desired. Such a loss can, nonetheless, be either retroactively transferred to the past or carried forward to the future (see under I.12.) The important issue here is that the co-operative has an option with regard to its commercial balance sheet: It can either write off the building at a 4% annual depreciation rate or it can use a lower DWO rate which represents the actual extent of wear and tear and value depreciation. The co-operative thus does not need to indicate a loss in the commercial tax balance.

Instead of choosing the linear DWO method outlined above, the co-operative can use a degressive DWO method. For commercial buildings, the rate is calculated as follows:

$$\begin{array}{rl} 4 \text{ years at } 10\% & = 40\% \\ 3 \text{ years at } 5\% & = 15\% \\ \underline{18 \text{ years at } 2.5\%} & = \underline{45\%} \\ 25 \text{ years} & = 100\% \end{array}$$

If the co-operative chooses the degressive DWO method, it must use it uniformly in both the commercial and tax balance sheets.

The percentages in the degressive DWO method certainly do not represent the actual extent of wear and tear on a building. The rates are set as high as they are primarily due to economic considerations and reasons based on business cycle policy. In the course of the years and decades to come, these reasons could lose their importance and have less value placed on them. This is likewise the situation in Germany. Commercial buildings which are constructed and finished by 1994 should be subject to new degressive DWO rates presently under debate in Parliament which only correspond to

$$\begin{array}{rl} 5 \text{ years at } 7\% & = 35\% \\ 6 \text{ years at } 5\% & = 30\% \\ \underline{14 \text{ years at } 2.5\%} & = \underline{35\%} \\ 25 \text{ years} & = 100\% \end{array}$$

7. Depreciation on Machines and Motor Vehicles

The co-operative can choose between the linear and the degressive DWO method. If it chooses the linear method, the purchase or production costs are equally distributed over the years of its useful life expectancy. If, for example, the purchase cost amounts to 100,000 and the useful life expectancy is 8 years, the co-operative can write off 12,500 annually, or 12.5% of the 100,000.

The degressive DWO rate amounts to a maximum of three times the linear DWO rate; the highest rate is, however, 30%. This percentage remains constant throughout the entire write off period. Starting in the second year, the rate is applied to the residual value, and so on. Using the numerical example illustrated above, the degressive DWO method proceeds as follows:

Purchase cost	100,000
DWO of Year 1: 30% of 100,000	−30,000
Residual value after Year 1	70,000
DWO of Year 2: 30% of 70,000	−21,000
Residual value after Year 2	49,000
DWO of Year 3: 30% of 49,000	−14,700
Residual value after Year 3	34,300

... and so on.

By the end of the eighth year, the total remaining book value has been deducted.

8. Retirement Reserves

Many co-operatives are obligated to pay retirement pensions to their (board of) directors and, occasionally, to their higher level staff upon their retirement. A profit minimizing reserve can be accumulated for these future retirement liabilities under certain preconditions. When the insured event occurs, the amount of reserves equals the cash value of the sum of probable future retirement contributions to be disbursed (using the discounting process). A 6% discount rate should thereby be used, and the recognized rules of actuarial theory must be taken into consideration.

A reserve should be formed in the balance sheet prior to the occurrence of the insured event; it should start to accrue in the year in which the retirement commitment has been promised. The reserve contribution mentioned above is to be accrued through uniform, annual partial contributions, and a discount rate of 6% must likewise be taken into consideration. The allocated contributions to these reserves in theory should be distributed through the time frame spanning from the beginning of the employed status (for salaried staff at the earliest upon reaching age 30) up to the previously determined moment when the pension payments are to be disbursed.

Retirement reserves play a fairly substantial role in the balance sheets of German co-operatives.

9. Non-deductible Company Expenditures

Expenditures which (objectively) are related to the co-operative enterprise and (subjectively) serve the co-operative enterprise are, in principle, tax deductible. Many of these expenses cannot, however, be deducted because they affect other people's private lifestyles. Examples of such non-deductible expenses include: gift expenses for business partners amounting annually to more than DM 75 per person; 20% of restaurant expenses for business partners (regardless of whether the meal was held in an expensive restaurant or in the company cafeteria); fines for offenses against antitrust regulations or other commercial laws.

Such non-deductible company expenses should be included in the profit calculated according to the tax balance sheet. This likewise is the case for contributions payed for corporate income tax and net worth tax. To a certain extent, expenses which promote charitable, religious, church-related, scientific, cultural and public benefit purposes are tax deductible. Contributions to political parties are also tax deductible to a certain degree.

10. Disguised Profit Distribution

Contributions distributed among members in a disguised manner (either alongside or in place of an open distribution) are to be included in taxable income. Such disguised distribution arises when the co-operative conducts business with members and non-members alike but offers the former more favorable conditions (special advantages) due to their affiliation to the co-operative.

Contributions which in the course of the business year are payed to members and, as a result, no longer are found in the company assets of the co-operative at the end of the business year are to be included in the profit calculated according to the tax balance sheet.

When a co-operative hosts its general assembly it is customary that it invites its members to a meal. By providing food and drink the co-operative creates a pleasant atmosphere which serves to fulfill a two-sided purpose. On the one hand, members' willingness to conduct all possible business with the co-operative (and not with competing companies) should be furthered; in order to encourage such willingness, the board attempts in an appropriate manner to direct attention to the efficiency of the co-operative during the general assembly. On the other hand, an incentive is given to the members to participate in the general assembly the following year so that the necessary resolutions can be passed.

The German tax administration decided to treat this situation as follows: food and drink up to DM 25 per participant is occasioned through the customer relationship (80% of these eating expenses are tax deductible; 20% are non-deductible business expenses). Food and drink exceeding 25 DM per participant is occasioned through the membership relationship; this portion of expenses is allocated to the disguised profit distribution and is not fully deductible.

11. Remuneration for the Supervisory Board

The salaries which a co-operative pays the members of its board of directors can always be deducted from taxes even when these salaries are quite high. Remuneration the co-operative pays to the members of its supervisory board, on the other hand, can only be deducted up to half of their total amount, even when such compensation is quite modest (→ *Organizational Structure of Societies*).

This law can only be explained historically. In the preceding century, many corporations namely began to pay the members of their supervisory boards (who were simultaneously the principle shareholders) disproportionately high compensation for serving on the supervisory board. This abusive situation was offset by tax laws. Today, the restrictions placed on the deductability of supervisory board members' remuneration are not longer justified, above all by the compensation payed by co-operatives.

Nevertheless, the tax code provision continues to be in effect, and 50% of the pay given to supervisory board members must be included in the profit calculated according to the tax balance sheet.

12. Tax Loss Carrybacks and Carryovers

If a loss occurs on the tax balance sheet due to the consideration of the points explained in parts I.9–11 above, it can be carried back up to an amount of DM 10 million and deducted from the positive income of the two previous years. The tax authorities will reimburse the co-operative the corporate income tax it had collected for these two years. A portion of the remaining loss can be carried forward and deducted from the positive income in the succeeding years. The law previously restricted carryovers to only five years, but this temporal restriction was lifted in 1990.

II. Tax Rates

1. Historical Development

For decades, the co-operatives in Germany were treated differently than stock corporations, but since 1981 both corporate forms have been subject to the identical tax rates.

Through the end of World War I (1918), co-operatives were never accounted for at all with regard to taxes. In the 1920s, they were accounted for but remained extensively exempted from taxes related to their member-oriented businesses. Their tax obligation first materialized in the 1930s, but the tax rates were reasonable for that time. Furthermore, completely varying provisions were in effect for the different types of co-operatives (credit co-operatives, trading co-operatives, farming co-operatives) (→ *Classification*).

The development of the credit co-operatives (→ *Co-operative Banks*) is particularly interesting. Lawmakers involved with the tax code became convinced that these co-operatives had become larger and more competitive over the course of the years, and therefore it could be expected of them to contribute more to the financing of public expenditures. Following the turbulence of World War II and the post-war years, the tax rate initially was at 15% (1955); it was then raised to 19% (1958), later to 32% (1968), 41% (1976), 46% (1977), and finally to the full 56% (from 1981 through 1989).

A critical examination of this development must take into consideration the fact that the entirety of co-operative income has no longer been subject to the listed tax rates since 1977. Special regulations (see under the following, **II.2**) have been effective since 1977 for that portion of income which is set aside for profit distributions.

The tax rate for co-operatives as well as for stock corporations was reduced from 56% to 50% in 1990. According to a bill presently under debate in parliament, this rate should be lowered to 44% by 1994. The current 50% rate is applicable to all portions of income which should be allocated to reserves or to the financing of non-deductible expenses (e.g. in order to pay net worth tax). This is likewise applicable for the future 44% rate.

2. Taxing Profit Distribution (Imputation System)

The legal situation can be presented and explained most clearly using a numerical example:

(1) A co-operative sets aside for profit distribution   1,000,000

(2) Of this sum, it pays 36% corporate income tax   *–360,000*

(3) Dividend sum agreed to and passed by the general assembly   640,000

(4) Of this, the co-operative pays 25% capital gains tax   *–160,000*

(5) Remaining distribution amount   480,000

If one chooses to start with the dividend sum (3), the corporate income tax to be paid (2) with regard to this always amounts to 56.25%. The following procedure is contingent on member affiliation to a particular group.

a) The first group includes all members who receive a dividend (3) valued at a maximum of DM 100. If a member has a right to a dividend valued at DM 80, for example, initially he is only entitled to a pay out amount of DM 60 (DM 80 minus 25% capital gains tax). The co-operative is in the position, however, to request a reimbursement from the tax authorities for the corporate income tax (56.25% of DM 80 = DM 45) and the capital gains tax (25% of DM 80 = DM 20), to be payed in one lump amount. It hereby does not need to provide the name of the member in question. In the course of preliminary financing, it pays the member the DM 60 as well as DM 45 and DM 20, or, in other words, DM 125 in total. This payment is executed in one single sum.

b) The second group includes all members who are entitled to a dividend (3) valued above DM 100 and who have informed the co-operative that they wish to utilize their legal tax exemption for interest and dividends for their co-operative dividend. (This exemption amounts to DM 6,100 for singles and DM 12,200 for married couples). If such a member has a right to a DM 400 dividend, he initially only has disposition over a payment amounting to DM 300 (DM 400 minus 25% capital gains tax). The co-operative can, however, request from the tax authorities to receive in one lump sum the corporate income tax (56.25% of DM 400 = DM 225) and the capital gains tax (25% of DM 400 = DM 100) which arise in connection with the dividend. In this case, the co-operative must provide the name and address of the member in question in order that the tax authorities may still exercise an optional control function. In the course of preliminary financing, the co-operative simultaneously pays out both the DM 225 and the DM 100 on top of the DM 300 to the member, or DM 625 in total.

c) The third group includes all those members who are entitled to a dividend (3) exceeding DM 100 but who either cannot or do not wish to take advantage of the exemption described above under b. When such a member has a claim to a DM 400 dividend, the co-operative will pay him DM 300 and at the same time issue an attestation for DM 225 in payable corporate income tax and DM 100 in payable capital gains tax. The member must subsequently declare the entire DM 625 as gross income when he files his income tax. The DM 225 and the DM 100 will be included in his income tax liability (just like an income tax prepayment).

Seen formally, the corporate income tax on profit distributions represents a tax liability and a tax expenditure for the co-operative. As a result, the tax amount is to be indicated in the profit and loss account. Seen from the economic point of view, this does not represent an encumbrance on the co-operative but rather a prepayment of members' eventual income tax liability. The corporate income tax on dividends, therefore, has a similar function as the capital gains tax withheld by the co-operative for its members' accounts.

The described procedure pursues several purposes. On the one hand, all dividends should be accounted for with regard to taxes. In the case of members in group c, the tax authorities even receive the payable taxes when a member "forgets" to include his dividend income when filing his income tax statement. On the other hand, the co-operative dividend should not be encumbered with the tax rate (presently amounting to 50%) which is normally in effect for co-operatives. The dividends should rather be encumbered with the marginal tax rates the individual members must bear, which fluctuate between 25% and 40%. If a member has not exhausted his tax exemption elsewhere, he should receive his co-operative dividend without any type of encumbrance. Ultimately, the situation should be avoided in which one and the same dividend is first taxed at the co-operative and subsequently again when the member files his taxes (avoidance of a double taxation burden). This procedure may seem technically complicated, but with the help of electronic data processing it can be resolved without any large problems.

The decisive advantages of the imputation system can be summarized as follows: the dividends are burdened with fewer taxes than before; the "after-tax profit" therefore increases for members (although the co-operative's costs for the dividend remain the same); on account of the higher return, members are more willing than before to subscribe to additional shares; the co-operative accordingly can improve its equity basis and fulfill its promotion mandate better than before.

III. Co-operative Reimbursement

1. Calculating Tax-Deductible Contributions

When a co-operative determines at the end of the business year that it has generated a surplus which it does not need in its entirety to strengthen its equity level, it can make a distribution among its members which reduces it tax obligation when:

- it supplies goods or provides services, thereby collecting remuneration from its members; this takes the form of a → *reimbursement*;
- it purchases goods or services and pays remuneration to its members (above all in marketing and production co-operatives); this takes the form of a subsequent reimbursement (Nachvergütung).

The first step in this procedure is to ascertain which partial amount of the total surplus comes into question for a reimbursement, which in turn reduces taxes. To achieve this purpose, taxable income is to be reduced by the profit arising from non-member business. The balance which results from this is to be allocated in proportion

- from the remuneration the co-operative collected from its members to the total amount of collected payments, or
- from the remuneration the co-operative payed to its members to the total amount of payed out remuneration.

The resulting partial amount is considered profit from the business conducted with members and as such defines the upper limit for the tax-reducing re-

imbursement. Nonetheless, the following preconditions still play a role for tax deductibility:
- that it is measured according to the level of turnover between the co-operative and the individual members;
- that it is actually payed out (that is, deducted from the co-operative's assets);
- that the member has a legal right to the reimbursement; it is irrelevant whether this legal right results from the co-operative's by-laws, from a resolution passed by the general assembly or from a resolution passed by the board and announced to the members.

2. Economic Importance

Co-operative reimbursement held an enormous importance up through 1976, above all for those co-operatives fully liable in taxes. If a co-operative at that time had applied a portion of its income for dividend payments, the following taxes would have been payable: 49% corporate income tax (for the co-operative) and on top of that a maximum of 53% income tax (for the member) on the remaining amount. As a result, less than 25% of the original amount would "make it" to the member (double encumbrance of the dividend with an asset-eroding effect). In order to avoid this overtaxation, those co-operatives subject to a full tax liability dispensed with dividend payments. In their place they distributed reimbursements.

Although this dividend policy was quite intelligent from the vantage point of tax policy, it proved to have quite disadvantageous effects on the capacity of many co-operatives to accumulate equity. Numerous members namely referred to the fact that the co-operative reimbursement was fully tax deductible and demanded the highest possible distribution. This precipitated a situation in which reserves could not be sufficiently accumulated. Nevertheless, there were no voluntary payments on paid-up shares as they were not endowed with dividends. The consequence: the equity which needed to increase with the growing dimension of the business activity remained below the necessary requirements. In order to attain equity despite this situation, many co-operatives saw themselves forced to introduce mandatory participation graduated according to the level of members' turnover. At first, this participation form appeared the ideal solution; it became problematic, however, as soon as individual members' turnover level with the co-operative continued to slack off.

These problems have been extensively resolved since 1977 when the imputation method was introduced (see above under II.2.). The question of whether distribution payments assume the form of reimbursements or dividends now only influences the level of trade tax, which is a local tax in Germany levied in addition to corporate sales tax.

Certain particularities exist for credit co-operatives. Since 1981, when they became fully liable for corporate income tax, they can also deduct reimbursements (e.g. interest reimbursements) as company expenses. Less than 20 of the 3,000 odd credit co-operatives in Germany presently distribute an interest reimbursement.

IV. Tax Exemption for Rural Co-operatives

→ *Rural co-operatives* are tax exempt as long as they limit their business enterprise to the following activities:
- the joint utilization of facilities, tools, and equipment;
- services or work orders for the production executed in members' enterprises;
- working with or processing products grown by members as long as such processing still can be categorized under farming.

The tax-exempt status is not effected when ancillary, non-favoured activities are executed which do not exceed a maximum level of 10% of total income. This means that if the 10% income margin is respected, the co-operative remains tax exempt for the profits resulting from its favoured activities; only the profits from other activities are taxable (partial tax liability). If, however, the 10% income margin is not adhered to, the co-operative and its entire income will be taxable.

The 10% limit allows rural co-operatives a certain amount of lee-way in determining their corporate policies.

Bibliography

Philipowski, Rüdiger/Hofkens: Besteuerung von Genossenschaften im internationalen Vergleich, vol.14, Vorträge und Aufsätze des Forschungsinstituts für Genossenschaftswesen der Universität Wien, Wien 1990.
Zülow/Schubert/Rosiny: Die Besteuerung der Genossenschaften, 7.Ed., München 1985.

Theory and Science of Cooperation

WERNER WILHELM ENGELHARDT [F]

(see also: *Theory of co-operative Cooperation*; *Conceptions, Co-operative*; *History of Ideas*; *Managerial Economics*; *Classic/Neo-classic Contributions*; *Promotion Mandate*; *Dual Nature*)

I. Distinctions from the Viewpoint of Science Theory; II. On the individual Nature of Co-operative Science; III. The Position of Co-operative Research in the System of the Sciences; IV. The Place of Co-operative Theory in the History of Ideas in the Science of Economics; V. A Concept of Co-operative Theory.

I. Distinctions for the Viewpoint of Science Theory

In principle there must be a distinction made between statements "by" co-operatives (co-operatives in a legal sense, co-operatives in an economic sense, and various other forms of cooperation) and statements "on" co-operatives. The latter – just like statements on other organizations as well – can be arrived at not only by scientists in various disciplines, and they serve not just scientific purposes. But insofar as these statements do originate with scientists and the purpose of research and teaching are being pursued, then varying points of view play a role in arriving at and applying these statements (such as an emphasis on different aspects or the development of scientists' utopias) (→ *Conceptions, Co-operative*). These varying points of view result in widely differing formulations of questions and answers to questions. The co-operative as an "object of experience" is thus turned into divers objects of analysis and of study by numerous branches of science. There is today, however – at least in its approach, also a specific discipline known as "co-operatives science", which manifests itself in Germany, among other ways, in scientific journals (→ *Periodicals, Co-operative*), book publication series, and co-operative institutes of universities. The resulting statements are of a descriptive, typological, or theoretical kind directed at either theories of basic laws or at applied theories; in the latter case they have an explanatory, prognosticating, or technological character. In addition to the empirical type of theory, which is a prerequisite for and includes typological laws, a distinction is also made between a type of theory based on the logic of decision-making and a normative type of theory which is more controversial. (cf. *Albert, Engelhardt, Haller, Popper* et al.)

II. On the Individual Nature of Co-operative Science

Draheim has raised the question as to which points of view are fundamentally possible when scientific statements on co-operatives are concerned. The author was thinking primarily not of distinctions according to criteria such as normative validity. Logical correctness, or empirical truth, but of distinctions involving closeness to reality, systematics. and applicability in everyday practice. He rejected the "merely empirical" point of view, that is, the merely descriptive approach, which – often mixed with normative aspects – has the longest tradition in the practical literature of co-operatives and in scientific treatises on co-operative organizations. But he also rejected the "purely economic" theory, which jumps overhurriedly to generalized assumptions and wins the logical correctness of its statements at the price of estrangement form reality (e.g. *Emelianoff, Ohm, Robotka*). The only point of view to win *Draheim's* acceptance was the "morphological" one, which supposedly as a science of co-operatives as entireties enables one to understand their organized dual nature as groups and as business enterprises and to study them typoligically (e.g. *Sombart, Weippert, Weisser; Henzler* is somewhat similar). But this point of view, which works with specific terms such as "tendency to cooperate" and "homo co-operativus" (*Henzler*, e.g.: "basic objective to promote members' interests") (→ *Promotion Mandate*), presupposes careful study of co-operatives as objects of experience as well as sytematic comparisons.

Later *Draheim* modified this position. While the present author has kept the basic position – nontheless with important corrections, usually in the direction of methodological individualism – *Draheim* ultimately stated that adaptations of the morphological theory of co-operatives to other theories would take place. Since competition as the main driving force in social change plays an ever greater role, it must also be taken into account theoretically. *Draheim* said that he could envisage that co-operative theory will be grouped into two parts: into a general part on a very high level of abstraction, which could be derived form a theory of cooperation of organization, and into special applied theories, for example of credit and housing co-operaitves (*Grünfeld* has already written similarly).

In sociology, on the other hand, *Fürstenberg* and *Hettlage*, picking up the ideas of *Trappe, Weippert*, and others, have expressed regret that the classic approaches of co-operative theory (cf. *von Gierke* and *Tönnies*) have been somewhat pushed aside by a sociology of the predominance of an individual or group in society which has largely taken over ever since the work of *Max Weber* (→ *Societal Form, Co-operative;*→ *Organizational Structures, Co-operative* → *Configuration*). In the eyes of *Fürstenberg* and *Hettlage*, the co-operative's task of promoting the concerns of its members (*Henzler: Förderungsauftrag*) should be carried out in a quite specific way, that is to say, under the condition that there be a consensus arrived a through membership participation. This comprehensive participatory character, relatively free of the influence of a predominating individual or group, constitutes for them the specific feature of co-operatives. The significance of this feature as a topic for scientific research in the course of the century and also as a topic for practical implementation has, in their view, by no means been fully dealt with.

In the more recent system-oriented theory of business administration, the Swiss economists *Blümle* and *Schwarz* are probably the strongest proponents of this emphasis; in Germany, they are *Kück, Ringle*, and *Vierheller*, for example; in Austria, an example is *Patera*, who also takes into consideration the developement of organizations and research on action. They consider particularly those co-operatives which promote members' interests as a special type of productive social system or as a special need-oriented type of organization within non-profit organizations. They maintain that this type of organization has the privilege of having long been a subject of an institutionally separate and distinct science, althrough its fund of knowledge is of course heterogenous in a double respect: on the one had, because it has to do with an interdisciplinary conglomeration; on the other hand, because with respect to business administration it breaks up into different schools of though and explanatory approaches, which are based upon diverging concepts.

A decidedly theoretical analysis of the co-operative as a system has been submitted by *E. Dülfer*, who pays less attention to these heterogeneous tendencies, and who answers the question as to what constitutes a special science of cooperation primarily in favour of a business amdinistration solution (→ *Managerial Economics*). Whereas *Henzler* and, more recently, *Wagner* have clearly rejected special business adminstration theories for co-operatives, *Dülfer*, just like *Hahn*, approves of them fully for scientific as well as for didactic reasons. *Dülfer* sees the theory of business administration for co-operatives, in consideration of institutional organizational aspects and of the special relevance of the interdependence of structure and function in co-operatives in their initial approach, as a supplementation to the general theory of business administration. However, it does extend into the realm of problems faced by specialized theories of business administration which are oriented to types of enterprises. According to *Hahn*, the typoligical approach is above all suited to those special fields of business administration "in which homogeneity within the industry is missing." This is largely the case today with respect to the placement of co-operatives within the economy. According to *Zerche*, the co-operative as an "object of experience" can be the subject of several scientific disciplines, as a special field of research. The respective "object of cognition", on the other hand, is "the subject of only one discipline," presumalby "because of the specific type of questions to be posed" (*Schultz/Zerche* 1983, p. 19). Problems which economics and business administration have in common belong to a "general economic theory of action." For the clarification of special co-operative problems, the author attributes great significance to this "praxeology", which is strictly system-oriented and strongly application-related. To be mentioned in this connection are the ladership functions of co-operative management and the regulations for co-determination, which at the same time are also of interest to the scientist in social policy (→ *Social Policy*).

In recent decades, economists belonging to various schools of thought, but particularly "new political economists" and "new institutional economics", have tried to pull away from the purely eocnomic view of co-operatives criticized by *Draheim* (for example, *Boettcher, Bonus, Eschenburg*) (→ *Institutional Economics*). In Germany today, it is generally observed that co-operative pioneers have striven for specific achievements – which of course can be last again – that even in the process of competition remarkable effects of cooperation can be noted (cf. for example *Fleischmann, Hamm, Neumann*) (→ *Competition*) and that the hybrid form of organization which has emerged nonetheless contains within it an unmistakeable, modern concept of enterpise, one which is and will be of great significance (*Bonus*). Of course, co-operative theory represents in the last analysis only a theory of enterprise, a theory of organization – naturally one which devotes itself to special features and relationships of its object of investigation (*Eschenburg*) (→ *Theory of co-operative Cooperation*).

Outside Germany (cf. *Treacy/Varady* ed. 1986), the Swede *Nilsson* has recently expressed the opinion that to identify the special character of co-operatives and of co-operative research, it would be necessary to have a macrotheory of co-operative enterprises (→ *Assortment Policies*). The goal would be to reach a better understanding of the prerequisites for such individual enterprises in a "society of mixed economy of a western type." To reach this goal it would be necessary to identify characteristics a) of all forms of enterprise, as well as b) of societies as a whole, and finally c) of forms of research and, to be precise, by means of using ideal types. In the enterprises as well as in the societies involved, *Nilsson* differentiates among three types: co-operative, capital-controlled, and state-controlled enterpises. These are to be analyzed through ideal-type research using the categories of "society", "individuality", and "collectivity". What matters today in the long run is to prevail upon the capital-controlled as well as the state-controlled societies as a whole, and on the corresponding enterprises within these socieites, too, to adapt themselves more than heretofore to the co-operative form of enterprise, but at least to slow down the movement in the direction of state-controlled or capital-controlled forms of enterprise (with reference to *Boulding, Cujes, Polanyi, Sorokin* et al.).

What the author of the present text has taken up again in his work are primarily historical questions in co-operative research. However, what is important to him are not purely historical representations of a narrative kind (as, for example, is the case with *Faust* and *Hasselmann*), but rahter the clarification and explanation of events from a theoretical stand-point (as with *Pollard* and *Novy*, among others). In combination with morphological-typological research aims, which are current in economics and business administration, an argument is made here on behalf of co-operative science on a historical basis (→ *History of Ideas*), which is conceived of as a supplement to and also as a corrective for primarily system-related research (*W.J. Mommsen*, 1972). It incorporates the fact that, in addition to individual and class concepts,

concepts in typoligical relations also play a role in this research, among which concepts in systems of effectiity are of course also included. (cf. the article on "Classification and Typology of Co-operatives")

III. The Position of Co-operative Research in the System of the Sciences

Thus far, it has been assumed that an independent science of co-operatives exists, at least rudimentarily, and that at the present time efforts are being made to develop it further. But quite apart from this assumption, it remains to be said that questions with regard to co-operatives can be dealt with in widely differing sciences and actually are dealt with by them. These disciplines include the following sciences or groups of sciences: basic sciences, legal sciences, historical sciences, social sciences., economic sciences, and agricultural sciences.

1. Basic Sciences

In these disciplines, it is primarily social philosophers, but also antrhopologists, who have dealt with co-operative phenomena, for example in connection with the interpretation of instinct and utopias (*Buber*, *Plessner*, and *Watkins*, among others). Even ethnologists and ethologists, who have studied the behaviour of the most highly developed animals, have de facto gone into questions for co-operative science (ever since *Kropotkin*, *Mead*, and *Totomianz*). The same is true for theologians and ontologists, metaphysicists, ethical writers and moral philosophers, who have furthered co-operative research through discussion, for example, of the basic value of community and solidarity or of rational value-oriented or purpose oriented behaviour. Even scientific theoreticians, ligicans and methodologists have often enriched this branch of science in a similar way, for example by analyzing the process of trial and error which bears specifically co-operative characteristics or could be early detected in co-operatives (*Warbasse*).

2. Legal Science

In this group of sciences, it is constitutional history, in particular, which has long shown an interest, since the priod of historicism, in co-operatives in the legal sense (*Gasser*, *von Gierke* and *von Maurer*, among others). With maternal law as the starting-point for research, the medieval German (Germanic) sytem of law has been especially closely studied, which as "social law" bore specific co-operative traits. These characteristics had their effects not only on households and communities, but even on cities and urban federations (for example, the Hanseatic League), on → guilds, monasteries (→ *Religious Co-operatives*) and universities (cf. *Planitz*, among others). In addition to constitutional and legal history and the development of Natural Law, one must not forget the systematically laid down areas of enacted law in the group of disciplines, as well as the more of less participation-oriented legislation policy (jus de lege ferenda).

3. Historical Sciences

In historically-oriented co-operative research, the emphasis can be placed on the Middle Ages, which should receive recognition, by the way, for other socio-economic and cultural achievements besides just legal ones (cf. for example, *Bader*, *Kuczynski*, or *Juske*). Or one can place emphasis on other historical periods: prehistorical times, ancient periods, or the modern or industrial age, right up to current history (→ *History before 1800*; → *History in 19th C.*). If one adopts the point of view of universal history (like → *von Gierke, E.R. Huber*, and the present author), and does not accept the absolute separation – result of the influence of historicism – of "historic" and "modern" co-operatives (as *Back* and *Grünfeld*, among others, have done) – for example, because early forms of co-operatives oriented to the public benefit (contrary to the opinion of *North* and *Schnabel*, among others) also appear in the industrial age, although mostly under different conditions of development and with decreasing frequency – then it will be impossible for scientific research not to pay more attention to historical forms of association with a co-operative character. This is true even for the previous century, which has reveiced a comparatively large amount of attention, and for current times, for example as far as the connection of co-operative with social movements and the triggers for transformations are concerned (cf., for example, *Eisenberg, Jenkis* and *Novy*).

4. Social Sciences

In addition to ethnology, which has already been mentioned, sociology, socio-psychology, political science, the science of social policy, and social education are all important for co-operative research (→ *Group Theory*). Although co-operatives and similar organizations were early on analyzed under the apects of utopias and spontaneity, the more exact study of their structures under social-scientific aspects began relatively late (→ *Group, the Co-operative*). However, in many places in Euorpe and North America, this occurred before the "fateful decision" (*Hettlage*) in favour of a paradigm reflecting patterns of social domination. Usually, a choice of aspects was made in favour of the co-operative principle of identity (for example, *von Durkheim, von der Gablentz,* and *Vierkandt*), less often one critical of co-operatives from the outset and of tendencies to create a co-operative economy of too "officialized" co-operatives (for example, *M. Weber* and *Th. Geiger*) (→ *Officialization*). In the recent past, there has been a revival of social-scientific co-operative research, under the influence of grass roots. Alternative, participatory political and reform movements (for example, *Amann, Behrendt, Eisermann, Kück, Lezius, Nutzinger, Schwendter,* and *Patera*, in addition to authors mentioned earlier).

5. Economic Sciences

Coming into consideration in this group of disciplines are primarily the sciences of economics, business administration and public finance, in each case with theoretical and applied sub-disciplines. In the science of economics, earlier known as "political economics", co-operatives have never been predominant. However, in connection with questions on cartels, concentration of business, and price policies, as well as of welfare economics, their role has not been just a more one either (cf. → *Marshall*, → *J.St. Mill*, → *Walras* and *Pareto*, among others). Co-operatives have also been dealt with by the science of public fincance, at first in connection with questions on enterprises for public benefit (cf. *Thiemeyer*, 1970) (→ *Public Benefit Orientation*), and later within the theory of public, collective, and written → *goods* (*Boettcher, Gretschmann, Grossekettler, Ritschl, Schäffle,* and *A. Wagner*, among others). The emphasis in economic scientific research in the field of cooperation shifted, of course, toward the science of business administration. This took place at the time and after when, on the one hand, co-operatives in a legal or economic sense, under increasing emphasis upon "economization" (*Draheim*), presented themselves less as groups and mainly as business undertakings, and when, on the other hand, the science of business administration was developing into a fully-established discipline. Togehter with business programmes for public enterprises, for enterprises of public benefit, and for business associations and other organizations, the science of business administration has developed individual explanatory and guiding programmes which are oriented more or less along lines of morphology and structure, including "organization development" and "action research", and also more commonly to functions and processes (in addition to previously mentioned authors, especially on co-operatives and public enterprises, cf. for example *Bänsch, Eichhorn, Hildebrandt, Jenkis, Oettle, Ringle, Thiemyer,* and *Vierheller*).

6. Agricultural Sciences

In this group of disciplines, there have been intellectual approaches to cooperation ever since the first teaching programmes on agriculture at the beginning of the previous century (*von Thünen*). These approaches were later continued and have been carried on up to the present time by other teachers of business administration and agricultural policies (for example, *Aereboe, Großkopf, Jäger, Seuster,* and *Röhm*). However, not until recent times have well-founded empirical studies comparing systems been carried out (or are soon to be made with international participation). One of the emphases here has been the co-operative-like agricultural system in communist countries (cf. *Bakonyi, Th. Bergmann, Boettcher, Cholaj, Kleer, Kowalak, Laakkonen, Laurinkari* and others). Yet another emphasis in research has been on self-run organizations of a more or less co-operative sort on the part of agricultural population groups in Africa, Asia, and South America. In addition, both private and government aid to support these tpyes of reform measures have been intensively investigated (by *Dülfer, Hanel, Kuhn, J.O. Müller, Münkner, O. Schiller,* and *E.G. Schumacher* among others) (→ *Policies for Promotion*).

IV. The Place of Co-operative Theory in the History of Ideas in the Science of Economics

If within theoretical co-operative research one makes distinctions between an "approach stressing concepts of utopia", and "approach from the life-situations of members", and "approach dealing with the creation and development of co-operatives", and an "approach emphasizing aspects and tenets" (*Engelhardt*, 1985), then, particularly in connection with the approach emphasizing aspects and tenets, one can further subdivide economic research as follows:

1. Early Socialists

In the thought and action, often called "utopian", of the early socialists – "utopian" action in so far as precursors or pioneers of actual co-operatives were involved (cf. article on the → *History of Co-operative Ideas*) – cooperation in general, and the → *joint-production (settlement) co-operative* in particular, played an outstanding role. This is the reason why some of the authors, who were professed Christians or atheists or agnostics, were also called "co-operative socialists" (for example, *Gide* and *Rist*). The change-over from them to later anarchists, syndicalists, guild socialists, and fabians was gradual, with overlappings.

2. Late Classical Economists

In contrast to the physiocrats and early classical economists, and due to the influence of the early socialists, the late classical political economists in Great Britain and Germany were receptive to co-operatives (→ *Classic/Neo-classic Contributions*). Their ideas came partly from individualistic, utilitarian axioms and partly from more problematical assumptions on laws of evolution and development (*J.St. Mill* among others). In Germany, the influence of *Kant's* criticism is unmistakable in the works of several authors (particularly in *von Thünen's*). There is already talk here of a competition among types of enterprises.

3. Marxists

The Marxist school of thought, which considered itself to be scientific socialism, and to which the Leninists later belonged, took for granted various possibilities for co-operatives and other forms of conscious or unconscious cooperation to take action and achieve results. However, in contrast to the early socialists, this school of though warned against an over-estimation of co-operatives and especially of → *consumer co-operatives*, because of the validity of the "iron wage law", which supposedly prevents co-operatives form achieving an increase in real income for its members. However, for later periods of developed socialism and communism, *Engels* prophesied great opportunities for agriculture in production co-operatives (→ *Socialist Critics*).

4. Fabians

This specifically English form of socialism (*Heer*), which succeeded Owenism, the Chartists, and Christan social reformers, and which also helped to bring reformism into being in German social democracy (*Bernstein* and *Lindemann*), put its hopes not only in public ownership but also in decentralized forms of business of a co-operative type. Public property, according to the Fabians, does not need to be administered by the state. Therefore, in addition to the developemt of production co-operatives, forms of "municipal socialism" were given priority (*Potter-Webb*, among others). The Fabian school of thought had considerable influence on later guild socialism (*Cole*, among others) as well as on German religious socialists (for example, *Heimann*).

5. Co-operativists

This movement, which was especially significant in France ("École de Nîmes"), but which was also important in Germany for a time, and which overlapped, among others, with "solidarism", which was in turn influences by the Cristian religion (*Pesch*, among others), placed its hopes, in contrast to Marxists and Leninists, particularly – and at times exclusively – in the development of consumer co-operatives and other co-operatives for households. The conviction of the co-operativists was that household co-operatives might make progress only in slow stages but that, according to developmental laws,

they were definitely predistined to succeed in achieving a complete change in the existing market economy system, in the direction of an economy determined by *homo cooperativus* and oriented to the fulfillment of needs (later *Lambert*, *Lassere*, and *Lavergne*, among others).

6. Historical Schools of Thought

Representatives of both the German Historical Schools of economics (ever since *Roscher*), as well as the Anglo-American institutionalist, were open to doing research on co-operatives. Moreover, they took an active interest in self-help solutions in the sense of a "principle of social reform" (*Gehrig*), without over-estimating measures of that type or falling victim to a dogmatization of co-operative structures according to developmental laws. *Von Schmoller*, however, considered it not unthinkable that ever since the previous century, thanks to co-operatives, a new structuring of economic and civic life was finally managing to set itself up.

7. Classical Theory of an Economy for Public Benefit

The first systematic teachings on the co-operative "free economy for public benefit" (*A. Wagner* and *A. Schäffle*) can be traced back to the classical theory of an economy for public benefit (so called by *Thiemeyer*), whose adherants were active in Germany at the same time as the historical schools. These social-conservative or social-liberal authors were influenced by philosophers of the "criticism" school in their analysis of voluntary co-operative associations, which did not include forms of association for charitable purposes. Later on, both religious socialists (for example, *Heimann*) and more liberal socialists (for example, *Weisser*) picked up the ideas of the literature of the classical theory on an economy for public benefit and developed them further.

8. Neo-Classics

The predominant opinion of thinkers in this group found expression in purely economic statements, also called decision-logical statements today. According to these statements, co-operatives belong entirely to the sphere of individual economic activity. For this reason, they have nothing or only indirectly something ("rationalistic concept for the common weal") to do with an economy for public benefit. However, the authors, who are mostly Brititsh and American, admit that in contrast to other enterprises in the private sector of the economy (above all, joint-stock companies) and to mergers of enterprises (for example, cartels), co-operatives disply special characteristics. With respect to economic policies, they can prove themselves useful in the process of welfare maximization → *Marshall, Pareto, Pigou,* and → *Walras*; in German-speaking countries von *Wieser* and *R. Liefmann*, for example).

9. Neo-Liberals and Ordo-Liberals

At first, the opinion was widespread among these authors (for example, *Eucken*) that co-operatives were hardly distinguishable from "collective monopolies" (opinion corrected by *Hamm, Lampert,* and *M. Neumann*, among others). At the same time, however, ordo-liberals and neo-liberals often belonged to those who, in contrast to the neo-classics, have tried and are still trying, through observing "market morphology" and thinking according to economic systems, to overcome the purely economic aspect and the merely decision-logical character of earlier statements on co-operatives and on a "third independent sector" between government and profit-oriented sectors (cf. *von Hayek*). They consider co-operatives just as well suited to a social market economy as other private initiatives (*F. Böhm, Reinhardt, Seraphim, and Weippert*, among others).

10. New Political Economists

As has already been mentioned, some political economists of this school of thought have begun to disengage themselves from a purely economic view of the kind criticized by *Draheim*. Although they continue to draw on the neo-classic rationalistic axiom and, in practicing theoretical "imperialism" (*Boulder*), to apply economic thinking even to an analysis of politics (following the example set by *Downs* and *Olson Jr.*, among others), they are nonetheless endeavouring at the same time to base their knowledge on more empirical studies. Taking up modern concepts involving theories of organization and conflict (by *Barnard, Dahrendorf, Leibenstein, March,* and *Marris*, among others), they are trying to replace mere decision logic with empirically-based theory (*Boettcher, Eickhof,* and *Eschenburg*, among others).

11. New Institutional Economists

This new Anglo-American institutionalism, which is related to the "economic theory of politics" just dealt with above, the one flowing into the other, is now beginning to influence German research on co-operatives (→ *Institutional Economics*). This "New Institutional Approach" unites theories on rights of use, on the economics of transaction costs, on the principle-agent approach and on the control approach. They all go back to the neo-classics (beginning with *Coase*), but also to theories on limited rationality (*Simon*, among others). In comparison to New Political Economists, the New Institutional Economists devote more attention in their methodolgoy to a re-

gained awareness fo the importance of empirically-based theory. According to this, co-operatives are indeed considered as a hybrid form of organizations; but on the other hand, this form is seen to have considerable chances for development in the present as well as in the future. The hybrid form makes it possible to supplement mere market relationships with new kinds of organizational relationships and competition among types of enterprise (*Bonus, Eschenburg,* and *Williamson*; *North* is more empirical).

V. A Concept of Co-operative Theory

1. The Aim is Empirically-based Theory

In reference to the different types of theory which were distinguished from each other at the beginning of this article, what is important here is "empirical theory" (*Albert* and *Popper*; earlier *von Schmoller* and *Whewell*). This theory, however, does not always follow the concept of "methodoligical individualism" (in the sense of *Popper* and *Down,* among others), for example, when non-individualistic oddurrences in the area of co-operatives are incorporated into the theory with a certain sympathetic understanding. What is meant by empirical theory is neither purely economic decison theory, nor an all-encompassing doctrine in the sense of a normative "theory of society" (*R. König*), but rather "social theory". The main thing is to arrive at and to substantitate falsifiable hypotheses on laws and clarified conditions of growth and development of co-operatives – including their transformation – as individual enterprise organizations (institutions) in their respective fields (growth and development approach).

2. The Frame of Reference is, as a rule, the Market Economy.

Thus, in addition to advance decisions on the perspective and the theory pattern, a selection of the frame of reference for the investigation is also made. Aside from planned economies (centrally administered economies), which today are of less and less importance, one can as a rule promise a frame of reference which holds co-operatives and organizations related to them to be relatively constant structures and functional processes of mutual solidarity and self-help, which may possibly be supplemented by external sources of private and governmental aid, but which in principle function in a market economy. Through co-operatives and other co-operative-type organizations, it is possible to shape this economic environment and even alter it step by step, without basically putting the market economy into question. Whoever supports or does research on co-operatives turns his back at least hypothetically on the view that the problems of a society solve themselves "automatically", or that they can be overcome by the government alone (a third, logically independent principle of co-ordination, according to *Weippert*).

3. Fundamental Questions

Empirical co-operative theory of the type represented here is at one and the same time research on purposes and on effects. With regard to effects, one can ask, for example, how a co-operative deals with its members and what consequences this has for competitors, business partners in the market, and the whole competitive process (*Fleischmann* in *Boettcher*, ed., 1972). These problematic questions lead to hypotheses such as this: one can never carry out reforms without strengthening the forces pulling in the opposite direction (*Mändle*). But this theory also involves questions like the following: how do co-operatives arise, and what subjective or objective factors produce, apart from their "self-organization", change or even digression from their original purpose? Problematic questions of this type lead to the following generally formulated suppostions. One can never initiate and implement reforms, until individual persons have developed selective utopias and applied their beliefs to groups and thereby made them take effect.

4. Noteworthy Groups of Characteristic Features

In particular, co-operative theory should bring various features with regard to purpose and levels of individual goals and means into relationship with features of action and the resulting effects of action of the respective owners, directors, and the persons participating in co-operatives and co-operative-type organizations, whereby in the area of the latter groups of features, one should also take note of unintended side-effects and delayed reactions (for example, of a cultural nature; cf. *Dülfer*, ed., 1988). However, no matter how important effects are of the most varied sort (effects of achievement and style), attention should be given first and foremost to the subjective characteristics of models and the utopias of the pathfinders, pioneers, and persons currently active in co-oeperatives which lend a sense of purpose and stimulate action. Via the clarification of differing legal, social, and business concepts – e.g. via the structure of co-operative law, the fostering of a co-operative spirit ("co-operate identity", according to *Lipfert*), or the formulation of the requirement to promote the interests of members – these subjective features lending meaning and purpose lead to the "instituional purpose" inherent in individual enterprises or in an economy, which purpose is then given the character of an often objective, binding value (*Thiemeyer* and *Weisser*). (For the approach according to concepts of utopia, cf. the article on Concepts of Cooperation)

Subjective purpose derived from models and other utopias, and the institutional purpose in legal norms and other arrangements which stem from subjective purpose, is usually only effective, of course, in a situation of widely existing great need which a whole group of persons or a social class of society must have come to experience. The well-known saying that co-operatives are the "children of need" is an expression of this fact. It would be important to make analyses of the life situations of potential or actual co-operative members and to ascertain their specific outward or inward needs, similar to the analyses of life situations which social-policy researchers have developed (among others, *Weisser* and *Amann*). According to the opinion advocated in this treatise, and approach analysing members' life situations would be very important as a basis of the actually experienced history of co-operatives and even of analyses related to the present time, especially for developing countries.

Bibliography

Arbeitskreis für Kooperation und Partizipation e.V. (ed.): Das Zentrum für Kooperation und Partizipation, Baden-Baden 1987.
Arbeitskreis für Kooperation und Partizipation e.V. (ed.): Kooperatives Management, Baden-Baden 1990.
Attems, Rudolf: Organisationsentwicklung und Genossenschaften, Wien 1982.
Backhaus, Jürgen: Ökonomik der partizipativen Unternehmung, vol. I. Tübingen 1979.
Back, Joseph M.: Die kulturelle, soziale und ökonomische Lage der Genossenschaften in der Gegenwart, in: Zeitschrift für das gesamte Genossenschaftswesen, special volume, Göttingen 1959.
Blümle, Ernst-Bernd/Schwarz, Peter: Die Genossenschaft als Kooperativ-bedarfswirtschaftlicher Organisationstyp, in: Zeitschrift für das gesamte Genossenschaftswesen, Göttingen, vol. 27 (1977), pp. 306–315.
Boettcher, Erik (ed.): Theorie und Praxis der Kooperation, Tübingen 1972.
Bonus, Holger: The Co-operative Associaton as a Business Enterprise: A Study in the Economics of Transactions, JITE, Tübingen, 142 (1986), pp. 316–339.
Draheim, Georg: Zur Ökonomisierung der Genossenschaften, Göttingen 1967.
Draheim, Georg: Aktuelle Grundsatzprobleme des Genossenschaftswesens, Marburg 1972.
Dülfer, Eberhard: Systemcharakter und Strukturdimensionen des Kooperativs, in: Zeitschrift für das gesamte Genossenschaftswesen, Göttingen, vol. 31 (1981), pp. 93–107.
Dülfer, Eberhard/Hamm, Walter (eds.): Die Genossenschaften zwischen Mitgliederpartizipation, Verbundbildung und Bürokratietendenz, in: Zeitschrift für das gesamte Genossenschaftswesen, special volume, Göttingen 1983.
Dülfer, Eberhard: Betriebswirtschaftslehre der Kooperative, Göttingen 1984.
Dülfer, Eberhard (ed.): Organisationskultur, Stuttgart 1988.
Engelhardt, Werner Wilhelm: Allgemeine Ideengeschichte des Genossenschaftswesens, Darmstadt 1985.
Engelhardt, Werner Wilhelm: Zu theoretischen Analysen genossenschaftsspezifischer Vorteile und positiver Effekte, in: Finanz-, Bank- und Kooperationsmanagement, Frankfurt am Main, 1989, pp. 139–155.

Emilianoff, Ivan V.: Economic Theory of Cooperation, Washington, D.C. 1948.
Eschenburg, Rolf: Ökonomische Theorie der genossenschaftlichen Zusammenarbeit, Tübingen 1971.
Hettlage, Robert: Genossenschaftstheorie und Partizipationsdiskussion, 2nd ed., Göttingen 1987.
Hofmann, Werner: Ideengeschichte der sozialen Bewegung des 19. und 20. Jahrhunderts, 6th ed., Berlin 1979.
Hoppe, Michael: Die klassische und neoklassische Theorie der Genossenschaften, Berlin 1976.
Lasserre, Georges: Coopèratives contre Cartels et Trusts (Paris 1938), 2nd ed., Paris/Basel/Brüssel 1956.
Laurinkari, Juhani (ed.): Genossenschaftswesen, München/Wien 1990.
Ohm, Hans: Die Genossenschaft und ihre Preispolitik, Karlsruhe 1955.
Popper, Karl R.: Logik der Forschung (Wien 1935), 9th ed., Tübingen 1989.
Schultz, Reinhard/Zerche, Jürgen: Genossenschaftslehre, 2nd ed., Berlin/New York 1983.
Seuster, Horst: Von der Genossenschaftswissenschaft zur Kooperationswissenschaft, in: Zeitschrift für das gesamte Genossenschaftswesen, Göttingen vol. 27 (1977), pp. 392–400.
Thiemeyer, Theo: Gemeinwirtschaftlichkeit als Ordnungsprinzip, Berlin 1970.
Tracy, Mary/Varady, Lajos (eds.): Co-operatives Today, Geneva 1986.
Weippert, Georg: Vereinbarung als drittes Ordnungsprinzip, Jahrbuch für Sozialwissenschaft, Göttingen 14(1963), pp. 169–178.
Weisser, Gerhard (ed.): Genossenschaft und Genossenschaftsforschung, Göttingen 1986, 2nd ed. Göttingen 1971.
Williamson, Oliver E.: The Economic Institutions of Capitalism, New York/London 1987.
Zerche, Jürgen/Herder-Dornreich, Philipp/Engelhardt, Werner-Wilhelm (eds.): Genossenschaften und genossenschaftswissenschaftliche Forschung, Regensburg 1989.

Theory of Co-operative Cooperation

ROLF ESCHENBURG

(see also: *Theory of Co-operatives*; *Managerial Economics*; *Institutional Economics*; *Classic/Neoclassic Contributions*; *Business Policies*)

I. Theory of Co-operative Cooperation; II. Cooperation and Individual Welfare; III. Cooperation and Social Welfare; IV. The Emergence of a Co-operative Association; V. The Co-operative Democratic Structure; VI. Agency Problems in a Co-operative Association.

I. Theory of Co-operative Cooperation

On the one hand, cooperation means the process of collective action of two or more economic subjects deliberately restricted to a common goal. On the other hand, cooperation means an organization within which co-operation in the former sense takes place. In the latter sense, a cooperation may be a club, a trade union, a professional association, a cartel, or a co-operative association like a farmer's co-operative (→ *Rural Co-operatives*), a housing co-operative (→ *Housing Societies*), a → *consumer co-operative*, and so on. In other words, the institutional concept of cooperation restricts the set of all types and forms of organizations to a subset of organizations with – in a wide sense – a democratic structure (→ *Organizational Structures, Co-operative*).

Within the area of economics, cooperation thus means collective self help action on the one hand and self help organization on the other (→ *Self-help Organizations*). A theory of cooperation has to deal with both concepts. Some of the main questions of a cooperation theory are: Why do economic subjects cooperate at all? Why do economic subjects cooperate only sometimes? What are the gains from cooperation? Why do economic subjects cooperate in different types and forms of organizations? What are the specific advantages and disadvantages of the different types and forms of cooperation? (→ *Institutional Economics*). We will deal with all this and some more questions in an indirect manner. A theory of co-operative cooperation is – in a narrow sense – restricted to cooperation as collective action in the form of a co-operative association. Nevertheless, as a specific theory it should refer to the general theory of cooperation where the latter holds true for the specific case of co-operative associations and the cooperation within them (→ *Theory of Co-operatives*).

II. Cooperation and Individual Welfare

By the efficient use of his resources (capital, labour force, time, knowledge and so on), the individual economic subject is maximizing his individual welfare. An economic subject always intends to realize that situation or outcome of his activity which is to his knowledge and in his mind the most favourable for him. If collective action promises a more favourable outcome than individual action he will choose it if it is possible. To be chosen, collective action has to offer a net gain from cooperation to every participant.

In the area of individual action, each subject decides independently about the autonomous use of his resources. In the area of collective action, the individual sacrifices a part of his freedom of choice or souvereignty by pooling a part of his resources in order to decide collectively how to use them.

Switching from individual to collective action does not increase the total amount of resources which all the cooperating subjects in total have at their disposal. Hence, pooling of resources can increase total benefit only insofar as "effects of synergy" (or in other words: economies of large scale) exist, can be utilized, and result in a common surplus. There are three different types of "effects" which serve as sources of the common surplus of collective action and thus allow a mutually advantageous cooperation: the effect of productivity, the effect of power, and the effect of diffusion.

1. The Effect of Productivity

One has to distinguish between the different cases of the effect of productivity. The *first* case is the combination of labour (or other resources) in order to overcome indivisibilities. Serving as an example is the very simple case of a large stone in the road, which is too heavy for a single man, but can be removed by the cooperation of two or more men.

The *second* case is the division of labour, which is highly important. Cooperation allows the individual participant to specialize in certain activities. This has several positive results. By reducing the quantity of changes between activities, division of labour allows the reduction of the corresponding costs. A man who has to fulfill several activities, inevitably incurrs costs of changing between them. A very simple example is provided by every small firm such as that of a coal merchant, who has to fulfill certain black-collar activities like storing, weighing, packing, and loading coal, besides the white-collar activities of buying, advertising, selling, and book-keeping. Changes between black- and white-collar activities obviously require handwashing and thus need time.

Furthermore, division of labour allows the emergence and utilization of more specific and far-reaching experience in one's domain of specialization. The longer the time working in a specialized manner the greater the experience and the greater the productivity in that specialized activity. Finally, division of labour allows the utilization of the personal comparative advantages of some or all of the participants. Human beings have different knowledge, experiences, capabilities, and attitudes. Division of labour allows putting the right man on the right job.

The *third* case is avoiding double activities. This can be seen as a special case of division of labour. Buying and processing information collectively gives us an important and illustrative example. Without collective action, many economic subjects have to buy and process identical or very similar information in order to become sufficiently informed. Cooperation allows one member (probably with comparative advantages) to search out a certain type of information, process it, and provide the whole group with processed information at lower costs.

The *fourth* case is the internalization of external effects. This means the production of a public good. Individual action causes damage to a common resource by overusing it, because private costs are lower than social costs. Protection of a common natural resource like a fish population in a sea or a big lake is only possible by collectively imposing certain restrictions on individual action and installing corresponding checks to assure compliance. Very often, this can successfully be done by a cooperative organization.

2. The Effect of Power

The outcome of individual action depends on the relative ability and strength of the economic subject in all the negotiations about the exchange conditions in the market. Collective action allows improvement in the relative strength of the participants in two different ways. The first way is to create and/or increase the marketpower of the cooperating group. The second way is to reduce the marketpower of the opposite side in the market. Pooling resources and founding a cooperative association changes the structure of the market by the entrance of an additional firm on the opposite side of the market. This weakens the power of the already existing firm(s).

3. The Effect of Diffusion

The outcome of individual action depends on the amount and quality of information and knowledge utilized in the corresponding decisions. Collective action facilitates diffusion of information within the groups from the better informed persons to the worse informed ones. This means in the short run, diffusion of information about facts and, in the long run, about techniques of production, administration, organization, and so on. Long run diffusion of information can also be an additional vocational training and thus mean an additional investment in human capital. A co-operative organization as a firm which is owned by its clients or employed persons facilitates the diffusion of all types of information including that about innovations.

III. Cooperation and Social Welfare

That all participants gain from cooperation is necessary but not sufficient for an increase in social welfare. Clearly a cooperation may cause welfare-losses to outside persons. Hence, there is no possibility for a doubtless a priori judgement of the welfare-effects of cooperation. This holds true for all types of cooperation and thus for cooperative associations as well. And it also holds true for developing countries (→ *Development Policy*).

Individual gains from cooperation which result exclusively from productivity effects of cooperation probably increase social welfare. But to be certain of this, one has to prove it by a more detailed evaluation which also analyzes the effects of the cooperation on its environment. Cooperation always requires pooling of resources and thus always causes effects of power which may cause welfare losses to outside persons. Despite the impossibility of a certain a priori judge-

Figure 1

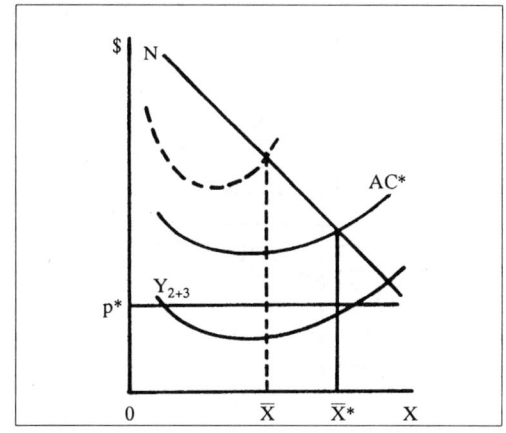

Figure 2

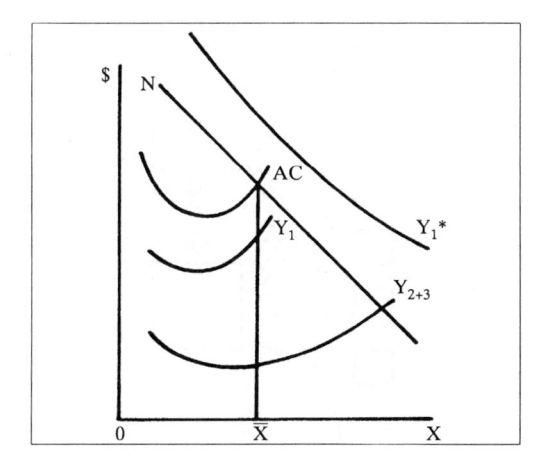

ment of – also co-operative – cooperation, there are sufficient reasons to expect a positive impact on development and thus an increase in social welfare by founding and running a cooperative association in certain situations, especially in developing countries. A dualistic structure because of low and insufficient economic integration is a very big problem in most developing countries. The economy of a developing country consists normally of two sectors, the advanced sector and the underdeveloped sector which includes subsistent economies, too. The advanced sector is highly integrated into the world market with fully developed trade relations and transfer of technologies. In contrast, we find low integration between advanced and underdeveloped sectors, with incomplete trade relations and a poor transfer of technologies. Within this economic environment, founding and running cooperative associations may have positive effects (→ *Policies for Promotion*).

1. The Creation of a Market

At least since *Adam Smith*, we know that missing trade may follow from a too small market. This means that the expected volume of trade is too small in relation to the minimum possible firm size. Missing trade forces a firm to "make" instead of "buy", thus resulting in a high degree of vertical integration within the firm. Without expecting a sufficient volume of trade, nobody would invest in a specialized firm despite the availability of a corresponding technology. Sometimes, many small economic subjects in a very similar situation are producing with a highly integrated production technology very similar goods, as in the case of small farmers who all produce bread by grinding wheat, preparing the dough, and baking it. It might be that in a situation like this, co-operative cooperation would allow the creation of a market by specializing in one of the integrated activities. *Figure 1* serves as an illustration.

Figure 1 shows the situation of the individual economic subject who produces bread. AC is his total average cost curve of bread production, which is the sum of the average cost curves Y_{2+3} (preparing dough and baking it) and Y_1 (grinding wheat). N is his own demand for bread. X limits the range within which bread baking is worthwhile with his small scale technology. The optimal amount of bread would be a quantity between O and X. The curve Y_1^* represents a large scale technology of wheat grinding. This situation contains the possibility of mutual advantageous co-operative cooperation. When all entities would stop, at the same time, small scale wheat grinding and would instead start to buy flour, their aggregate demand could be high enough to make specialization in the large scale technology worthwhile.

Figure 2 shows the situation of the individual economic subject after the creation of the flour market. This entity now is buying flour at the price P^* which corresponds to the average cost of grinding a great quantity of wheat. The total average costs of his bread production is AC^* and equals now the sum out of Y_{2+3} and P^*. The quantity limiting the range within which bread production is worthwhile increased from X to X^*. He is better off now, because the cost of flour decreased. This result does not depend on the type of firm which is selling flour at price P^*. If flour is sold at P^*, the outcome is the same whether the specialized firm is a co-operative or a non-co-operative firm. This presents the question whether the co-operative solution is more advantageous or not. Three arguments can be stressed in favour of the co-operative solution. Firstly, the co-operative way seems to offer an easier solution to the problem of necessary coordination. With a cooperative association, it seems more probable to guarantee the simultaneous termination of individual wheat

Figure 3

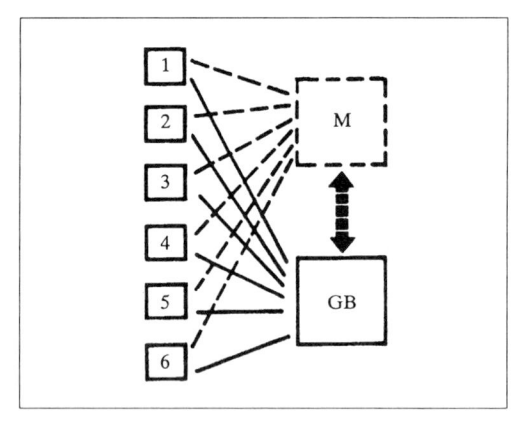

Figure 4

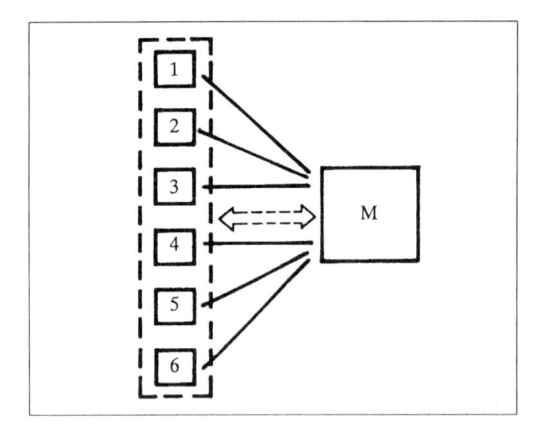

grinding and actualization of flour demand within a certain group of economic subjects. Secondly, the co-operative solution guarantees flour delivery to the members, i.e. stopping individual grinding does not result in high uncertainty of provision with flour. Thirdly, a co-operative firm is obliged to sell to members at cost determined prices. Hence, a well functioning co-operative association allows avoidance of overcharging.

2. The Widening of a Market

Especially in underdeveloped regions, markets sometimes are so small that only one firm can survive in the situation of a natural monopoly. But most monopolistic firms are artificial monopolies, which make use of certain barriers to entry. But in both cases, monopoly power results in exploitation. *Figure 3* serves as an illustration. The small firms 1 to 6 have to bear the risk of being exploited by the monopolistic firm M. There are two different strategies of cooperation to defend the group of small firms against monopolistic exploitation. The first strategy consists on the formation of countervailing power. The 6 small firms can form a cartel in order to increase their own power substantially by changing the situation into that of a bilateral monopoly. However, a cartel solution always suffers from the problem of free riding. The greater the group, the greater the probability of a break down of cartel discipline. From time to time, even small groups face the problem of loss of cartel discipline by free riding.
Figure 4 illustrates the second strategy. Instead of forming a cartel, the group of the 6 small firms can found a co-operative association and install the co-operative firm GB besides the up to now monopolistic firm. In both cases, existing besides the up to now monopolistic firm or replacing it, the co-operative solution would offer certain advantages in comparison to the cartel solution. A well functioning co-operative association offers cost determined prices and allows hence the optimal trade volume, which normally means a widening of the market. A co-operative association is designed to include great groups of members without increasing problems of free riding. A co-operative association provides a solution by diminishing power instead of increasing it. Summing up shows that, within underdeveloped regions and markets, co-operative associations can contribute substantially to the development of markets and thus economic integration. The obvious comparative advantages of a co-operative firm in comparison to a non-co-operative firm result from the fact that, within a less developed economic environment, a co-operative association provides a lower risk of a given high asset specifity of the specialized technology or of a given high site specifity.

IV. The Emergence of a Co-operative Association

Net gains from cooperation for each participant are necessary but not sufficient for the emergence of a cooperation. Creating a cooperation means the production of a public good. This holds especially true in the case of a co-operative association which is designed to include large groups of members. The emergence of a cooperation requires the combination of organizational knowledge and experience with political entrepreneurship.
If an intended cooperation promises net gains from cooperation to every prospective participant, he will in principle be prepared to contribute to cover the costs of founding that cooperation. Hence, a person with the corresponding situation-specific knowledge, the necessary organizational experience and in addition an attitude to political entrepreneurship may find it worthwhile to engage in founding it. For this reason, the emergence of a co-operative association depends on whether such a person starts founding activity and finishes it successfully. Governmental pro-

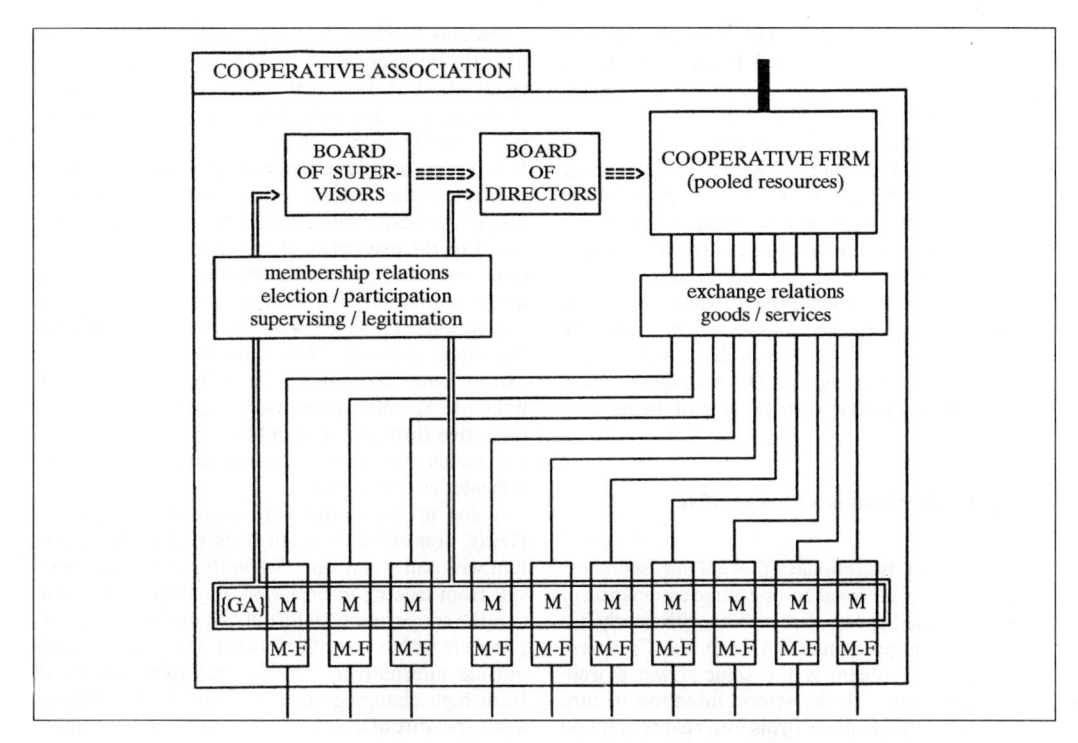

Figure 5

motion programs may help but also can fail (→ *Officialization*).

Clearly, the more people tend to follow a co-operative ideology, the more they are prepared to contribute in an active and direct manner to found a co-operative association. But co-operative ideology, enthusiasm or even fanaticism does not serve as a proper substitute for organizational knowledge. And despite all the belief and confidence in the usefulness of co-operative associations, only a detailed well-done analysis can identify the probable gains from cooperation and thus help to justify the necessary long run investment in cooperation.

V. The Co-operative Democratic Structure

In a co-operative association, the pooled resources are invested in the co-operative firm which in principle functions as a special sort of common resource. This is because the co-operative firm produces goods and/or services in favor of the member firms which are its exclusive or at least main clients. There are twofold relations between the members of the co-operative association and the co-operative firm: the exchange relations on the one hand and the membership relations on the other. This is depicted in *Figure 5*.

Besides the exchange relations between the co-operative firm and the member-firms *(M-F)*, *Fig. 5* shows the membership relations which are organizational relations. The members, which are individually running their *M-F*, form as a group the general assembly *GA* which is one of several decision-making bodies. From the idea of cooperation and democracy, it follows that the *GA* has ultimate decision-making power. At least such important issues like changes of by-laws, entry to liquidation, and merger require legitimating decisions made by the *GA*. It follows, too, that the members of the co-operative association participate as members of the *GA* in nominating and/or electing the members of the board of directors and the board of supervisors or at least in legitimating their nomination and/or appointment by a corresponding decision.

One finds that division of labour takes place in the process of decision making within a co-operative association. *Fig. 5* allows to identify the different decision-making entities: GA, Board of supervisors, Board of Directors, The Co-operative Firm, and all M-F. *Fig. 5* corresponds to the legal situation in Germany (→ *Legal Form, Co-operative*). Legal situations in other countries (→ *Law, International*) may result in less or even more decision-making bodies of the co-operative association. Clearly, each member firm will always be a separated decision-making entity. But despite that a co-operative association always has at least two different decision-making bodies: the general assembly on the one hand and the co-operative firm run by a manager on the other.

In a democratic structure, the GA always has to have ultimate decision making power. From this it follows that the manager be in charge of promoting the associated member firms. For a long time it was thought that this charge could serve as a clear-cut guideline for managing the co-operative firm in favor of the member firms. But *J.K. Arrow's* proof of the impossibility of an individualistic-founded social welfare function holds for a co-operative association, too. Hence, the manager has the freedom or duty to follow his own imagination of what might be a proper policy to promote member firms. And the members have – individually as well as collectively – the problem of ensuring that the manager's policy corresponds with their own feeling of being promoted.

VI. Agency Problems in a Co-operative Association

The problem of discretionary powers may seem less important in a traditional co-operative association of a relatively small group of members with nearly homogenous member firms (→ *Group, the Co-operative*). But the problem is the same. Even a well-minded manager with the strong intention to turn promotion of the member firms into reality can't be certain to avoid a policy which causes discontent of some, a majority, or even nearly all of the members. A well-minded manager would be very much interested in receiving as soon as possible an indication of content or discontent of the members in order to adjust his policy (→ *Managerial Economics*). Having in mind the possibility of even a bad minded manager, the members would be very much interested in being able to give as soon as possible a clear signal of discontent to the manager in order to govern him to follow a more corresponding policy. The members can give a signal of their discontent by using the "exit"-option. The fact that a member left the co-operative association shows undoubtedly that the former member prefers to be outside. Once realized, the exit option reveals an obvious preference for the outside situation in comparison to the inside situation. This gives a clear indication of discontent.

The exit option has a threefold effect. Firstly, exit informs the manager, the other members, and outside persons about discontent of a member by revealing the corresponding preferences. Secondly, exit works as a negative sanction to the manager by reducing the co-operative firm's total volume of exchange with member firms and reducing the number of members of "his" co-operative association. Thirdly, exit works as a challenge to the manager by provoking him to react, in order to prevent more loss of economic power and personal image and to offset the loss already incurred. Furthermore, the exit option within a co-operative association is a two-step exit option. The first step means that a member – partly or totally – abstains from exchanging goods and/or services with the co-operative firm. The second step means termination of the membership in the co-operative association. In principle, both steps have the above mentioned threefold effect.

But if a co-operative association serves at least in principle as the preferable organizational solution of division of labour with considerable site- and/or asset specifity, the exit option does not seem to be the optimal means to govern the manager. This rises the question whether instead of the exit option the non-exit option could serve as well. Because exit indicates discontent, it should be possible to expect that non-exit indicates content. Unfortunately, this does not hold true. Keeping up exchange relations with the co-operative firm and/or membership in the co-operative association cannot indicate clear content like exit indicates clear discontent.

Keeping up behaviour may have several reasons. *Firstly*, non-exit may result from well-founded content with the status quo. *Secondly*, non-exit may result from lacking information about the world outside the cooperation; before choosing the exit option, one at least has to get informed about the possible outside alternatives. *Thirdly*, non-exit may result from high changing costs; the greater the site- or asset-specifity of the co-operative and/or the member firm, the greater the cost of exit. *Fourthly*, non-exit may result from loyalty; despite actual discontent, the member may chose non-exit in order to support the co-operative association during a period of adjusting policy. *Fifthly*, non-exit may result from fear of repressive activities, which would be a special type of cost of exit. *Sixthly*, non-exit may result from resignation.

Instead of the exit option members may express their discontent also by the "voice" option. Voice means criticizing in a direct or indirect manner and with more or less intensity. Voice may consist of critical remarks, heavier verbal attacks, apostasy, rebellion, or voting out. The voice option, at least in principle, serves – like the exit option to govern the manager – to follow a policy which prevents members from giving signals of discontent. But like the non-exit option, the non-voice option does not serve well as an indicator of content because there are several reasons to do without the voice option. Whether a member in a certain situation feels content or not depends heavily on corresponding information about choosable alternatives. In order to prevent members from bad decisions, they should be provided with sufficient and objective information. What members need, too, is information about problems and solutions within other, more or less comparable, co-operative associations. Information of this type – in principle – is available from an auditing union. Hence, an auditing union may be another important entity within the division of labour in co-operative decision making.

Bibliography

Boettcher, Erik: Kooperation und Demokratie in der Wirtschaft, Tübingen 1974.
Eschenburg, Rolf: Ökonomische Theorie der genossenschaftlichen Zusammenarbeit, Tübingen 1971.
Eschenburg, Rolf: Konflikt- oder Harmonietheorie der Genossenschaften, Bemerkungen zur gleichnamigen Kritik Manfred Neumanns, in: Zeitschrift für das gesamte Genossenschaftswesen, Vol. 23, 1973, pp. 101–114.
Eschenburg, Rolf: Der ökonomische Ansatz zu einer Theorie der Verfassung: die liberale Verfassung im Spannungsverhältnis zwischen Produktivität und Effektivität der Kooperation, Tübingen 1977.
Neumann, Manfred: Konflikt- oder Harmonietheorie der Genossenschaften, in: Zeitschrift für das gesamte Genossenschaftswesen, Vol. 23, 1973, pp. 46–62.
Olson, Mancur: Die Logik des kollektiven Handelns (Kollektivgüter und die Theorie der Gruppen), Tübingen 1968.

"Third Way", Co-operatives as a

PAUL TRAPPE

(see also: *Economic Order; State and Co-operatives in Market Economy; State and Co-operatives in Socialism; History of Ideas; Socialist Co-operative Theory; Informal Co-operatives*)

I. Introduction; II. Functional Levels; III. Complex Societies.

I. Introduction

Of those concepts advocated in social and economic policies, the course of time evidences that the "third way" is usually an empty formula, since it seems possible to resolve or defuse virtually any contending extremes with a "tertium gaudens", i.e. an uncommitted compromise. With regard to co-operatives, however, it is legitimate to bring coherent contents to bear on this concept in order to offer a viable alternative to common conceptions of social and → *economic order*. Following common usage, the term "third way" refers to an intermediary force negotiating fixed opposites, such as rich and poor, free and constrained. In more general terms, it is an intermediary force between socialism and capitalism; "labour and capital"; private ownership and a state economy system; marketing opportunities for individuals and corporate organizations (self-employers and stock corporation); individualism and collectivism; weak population and weak state, or between weak population and a powerful state. In most general terms, the "third way" is a possibility to overcome and adjust deeply fixed contending extremes. With respect to co-operatives, the third way usually concerns the improvement of the marketing opportunites of specific products, or raising their market potential (→ *Marketing Strategies*).

Obviously, associations of those sharing common interests can improve such opportunities considerably. Furthermore, the foundation of co-operatives need not occur immediately; often, as for example in "groupements paysans", or in so-called "associations" (machinery associations), simple forms of co-operation may lead to improvements.

Various other approaches to the "third way" generally appear to suggest that the foundation of a 'more human' ('emancipated'), 'solidarity-based' and 'free' society is possible on an "intermediary level", i.e. between contending extremes that cannot be implemented (→ *Informal Co-operatives*). Often, conceptions of this kind are utopian (→ *Conceptions, co-operative*), such as those of pioneering and "utopian socialists" (→ *History of Ideas*) like Robert → *Owen* ("New Harmony") and *Jean Cabet* ("Journey to Ikaria"). In such utopianism, it is not unusual for "right" and "left-wing" conceptions of the world to converge, as for example in the contending extremes of a free market economy (cf. *Gilbreth*) and of a society based upon "voluntary associations" (cf. *Marx*). In *Friedrich Pollock's* description of the extreme position of a centralized authority or a form of state capitalism, corporatism is advocated as a mandatory third way to enforce strict social hierarchy at the expense of liberal democracy. Thus, corporatism officially stifles an independently operating "third way".

II. Functional Levels

On the macro-level, the comparative analysis of social structures in sociological theory distinguishes between ruling and co-operative forms of society (cf. *Oppenheimer, Rüstow*) (→ *Communal Settlements*), while a society based on private autonomy, reported by liberalist thinkers, is marginalized and termed irrelevant. In theory and practice, the macro-level indicates various transitions to socio-political reality, including Catholic social teaching, within which Neo-Thomism, which follows traditional Thomistic social principles, occupies the space between Neo-Liberalism and Neo-Marxism (cf. *Utz*). Thomist principles provided the basis both for the foundation of co-operatives in the Renaissance (e.g. *di Terni*) as well as the nineteenth-century formations of groups on the intermediary level (e.g. journeymen's associations, cf. *Kolping*). However, consideration of the "third way" in the aligned Rerum Novarum (1891), Quadragesimo Anno (1931), Centesimus Annus (1991), and in other aligned so-called "development encyclopaedias", such as Mater et Magista (1961) and Pacem in Terris (1963), is crucial. As *A.F. Utz* puts it in his commentary on Pacem in Terris: "Intermediary level associations, that is those positioned between the individual and the state, comprise the entire socialization of the economic and social orders. In particular, diversified intermediary socialization is all-important in a democracy ..." (→ *Group Theory*). In 1910, referring to the extant intermediary levels in the social structure, *Max Weber* had already demanded that more attention should be paid to "the intermediary level between the politically organized and institutionalized powers – state, municipality and state church – and the organic development of the family community ...". In theory and practice, the "free (social) market economy" is related to this intermediary level as well as the interplay of "mixed economy" enterprises.

On the micro-level, the "*third* way" has been assigned special functions in particular in development aid projects involving costly economic infrastructural measures (irrigation, dissolution of latifundia of minifundia by fusions) by the admission of support groups (including co-operative groups); this has even involved the authorized (temporary) enforcement of co-operative organization in favour of the beneficiaries. Some examples may serve as an illustration: the agrarian reform regions in Spain, the "ejidos" in Mexico, and irrigation projects in Mediterranean countries, Maghreb and in the Sudan (Ghezira) (→ *Autochthonous Co-operatives*). Incentives for a "third way" were often harnessed to the co-operative marketing of cash crops, the introduction of new products, together with the foundation of co-operative (or co-operative-like) associations, given that they made explicit sense and were profitable to members, for the purposes of marketing, transportation, refinement and so forth. According to British colonial administration and a large amount of relevant documentation, this often involved tough competition with established tradesmen, agents with economic power, money-lenders, and other agents dominating the market.

III. Complex Societies

In complex societies, a "third way" has taken shape long ago with reference to *intermediary* political and social powers, including the co-operative. Since the co-operative is one of the most wide-spread forms of oganization, it is hoped that the co-operative spirit of self-help, self-management, and self-responsibility will contribute to overcoming economic and social grievances. All co-operative movements have been founded on this legitimately voluntary and belligerent spirit; all traceable co-operatives have attempted to surmount or temper a deplorable state of (economic) affairs by co-operative associations. Their legitimacy and attraction was founded on their mediating, intermediary and promotive role, which individual members were incapable of implementing without the co-operative structure. Orientation of the co-operatives was both economic as well as social. Regarding the former, there is unanimous agreement in the relevant research that economic goals can be realized better by associations of individuals with common interests. As to their social orientation, this secondary goal can be pursued by co-operatives, such as in large-scale European and → *consumer co-operatives*. However, socio-political goals can also manifest primary co-operative intentions. Social goals can be promoted by flanking "ideal groups" or similar subgroups of the co-operative membership. *Richard F. Behrendt*, considering the social goals of co-operatives, has referred to "the human need to share being" as a means to fight "isolation in a complex society". Among similar forms of organization, *Behrendt* regards the co-operative "undoubtedly as the most liberal and simultaneously most constructive form". In psychology, psychiatry, and medicine, the numerous self-help groups are factual co-operatives in the broadest sense, attempting to provide likeminded or mutually affected individuals with a means of surmounting the alleged signs of the modern, complex world, i.e. disintegration, isolation, dependence. In education, the work of *Johann Heinrich Pestalozzi* and *Philipp Emanuel von Fellenberg* attests that social goals have a certain tradition, even if they were poverty-stricken in practice. Today, parents' associations, in particular in developing countries, have similar objectives by initiating and establishing primary schooling where state institutions are defunct (e.g. African "bush-schools").

By integrating the allegedly isolated individual into a group of like-minded individuals, the western-European co-operative opens up a "third way" without giving rise to a collectivist unit or the group being subjugated to a centralized authority, which eliminates or forces the co-operative spirit into conformity. Thus, the co-operative is a viable intermediary solution between the contending extremes of individualism and collectivism (→ *Informal Co-operatives*).

In developing countries, co-operatives have been used recurrently, and with some success, to promote the policy of a "third way" (→ *Policies for Promotion*). In his outline of Tanzania's social policy concept, *Julius K. Nyerere* made the explicit demand that it be developed in accordance with the existing agrarian social structure rather than in terms of abstract, "academic" socialist or capitialist conceptions. In the absence of a class struggle, the task was to modernize the traditional co-operative structure to enhance a specifically African process of development. "Third ways" are wide-spread in Africa (→ *Development, Africa*). In an independent "African socialism", there is outspoken support for community development and co-operative societies among its major representatives (*L.S. Senghor, Anta Diop, S. Touré, T. Mboya, M. Obote, K.Kaunda*, and others). This concept goes back to *Karl Marx* and other pioneers. Following a resolution of the 20th Communist Party congress, Soviet development policy tried to put this concept into practice. At a later stage, however, Ujamaa-socialism lost its specifically African sense to apply the notion of the collectivism of the large collectives of the People's Republic of China (these were soon faced with internal and external demands for liberalization).

For many years, theories of mobilization in developing countries have been demanding the implementation of a "third way" with explicit reference to establish mobilization through co-operatives (cf. *Lenin, Mao Tse-tung*, and others (→ *Socialist Co-operative Theory*). In recent theories, attempts are made to define a compromise between "unusable capitalist means of production" and the "questionable usability of Soviet and Cuban methods" (cf. *Mansilla*). In practice, however, the insufficient implementation of the "third way" is striking.

The tendency towards community-development, villagization, and co-operative association was strongly promoted under British colonial administration. In India, *S.K. Dey's* work has highlighted the co-operative form of organization in the agrarian environment. Several years ago, the UN commissioned Geneva-based UNRISD to do research on "rural institutions" world-wide. Uncountable examples of the promotion of existing and the implementation of new agrarian institutions with relevant (and corresponding) forms of institutional organizational forms are furnished by Christian missionaries and non-government organizations. Co-operatives can only prosper and pave the way for a "third way" under favourable conditions. Again and again, however, co-operatives have failed, which has fuelled recent development policies and aid with not entirely warranted scepticism.

In critical debate, it is often not ascertained whether the institutional framework (including the already existing power relations) or the organizational form of the co-operative is responsible for the failure. Equally, there is the problematic tendency of foreign relief workers to couch ideologically different social conceptions in characteristic jargon, e.g. collapsing all forms of the co-operative association of the underprivileged into notions of "co-operative" and "root community" and mystifying the promise they hold. According to much recent research, the development policy for co-operative organization has failed. However, such undifferentiated judgement should not be accepted.

Translation: Mark Kyburz

Bibliography

Adler, Max: Die solidarische Gesellschaft (Soziologie des Marxismus, Bd. 3), Wien 1964.
Behrendt, Richard Fritz: Eine freiheitliche Entwicklungspolitik für materiell zurückgebliebene Länder, Ordo, Jahrbuch für die Ordnung in Wirtschaft und Gesellschaft, vol. 8, Düsseldorf-München 1956, pp. 67–122.
Dessauer, Friedrich: Kooperative Wirtschaft, part I: Das co-operative System, Bonn 1929.
Dey, S.K./Sahakari Samaj: The Cooperative Commonwealth, London 1967.
Dia, Mamadou: Contribution à l'étude du mouvement coopératif en Afrique noire, 3e éd., Paris 1952.
Infield, Henrik F.: Utopia and Experiment, Essays in the Sociology of Cooperation, New York 1955.
Kantowsky, Detlef/Sarvodaya: The Other Development, Konstanz o.J.
Lerner, Daniel: The Passing of Traditional Society, New York 1958.
Mansilla, H.C.F. (ed.): Probleme des Dritten Weges, Mexico, Argentinien, Bolivien, Tansania, Peru (Sammlung Luchterhand), Darmstadt, Neuwied 1974.
Nyerere, Julius Kambarage: Ujamaa, The Basis of African Socialism, Dar es Salaam 1962.
Oppenheimer, Franz: System der Soziologie, 4 Bde., Jena 1922–1934.
Pollock, Friedrich: Stadien des Kapitalismus, München 1975.
Rüstow, Alexander: Ortsbestimmung der Gegenwart, 3 Bde., Zürich 1950–1957.
Schasching, Johannes: Der Gesellschaftliche Ordnungsgedanke in Rerum Novarum und Quadragesimo Anno. In: Utz; Arthur F. (ed.): Die katholische Soziallehre und die Wirtschaftsordnung, Trier 1991, pp. 67–84.
Schachtschabel, Hans G.: Genossenschaften III, soziologische-volkswirtschaftliche Problematik. In: Handwörterbuch der Sozialwissenschaften, 4. Bd., Göttingen 1965, pp. 379–392.
Schumacher, Ernst Günter: Grundprobleme der Entstehung von Selbsthilfeorganisationen in Entwicklungsländern, Berlin 1985.
Sik, Ota: Humane Wirtschaftsdemokratie, Ein Dritter Weg, Hamburg 1979.
Trappe, Paul: Die Entwicklungsfunktion des Genossenschaftswesens am Beispiel ostafrikanischer Stämme, Neuwied u. Berlin 1966.
Utz, Arthur F. (ed.): Die Friedensenzyklika Papst Johannes' XXIII., Pacem in Terris, Freiburg-Basel-Wien 1963.
Utz, A.F.: Zwischen Neoliberalismus und Neomarxismus, Die Philosophie des Dritten Weges, Köln 1975.
Utz, A.F.: Arbeitskampf und Wirtschaftsethik, Basel 1989.

Trade Unions and the Co-operative System

ACHIM VON LOESCH [J]

(see also: *Conceptions, Co-operative*; *History in 19th C.*; *History of Ideas*; *Socialist Critics*; *Schulze-Delitzsch*)

I. The Emergence of Co-operatives and Unions; II. The Relationship between the Housing and Joint-production Co-operatives and the Trade Unions; III. The Ideological Disputes with the Socialists; IV. The "Marriage" of the Consumer Co-operatives and the Unions; V. The Disadvantages of Undertakings Imbued with Ideology; VI. Consumer Co-operatives as Employers and the Unions; VII. The End of the Cooperation between the Consumer Co-operatives and the Trade Unions in Germany.

When discussing the relationship between co-operatives and trade unions, it is important that both came into being around the same time for similar reasons. They likewise experienced parallel developments during the following 150 years. A branch of the co-operatives, the → *consumer co-operatives*, entered into a "marriage" with the trade unions in the first half of this century, an occurrence international in character. This affiliation produced advantages for the consumer co-operatives but also brought along disadvantages which certainly contributed to their decline in Germany during the 1980s. The trade unions, however, remained essentially unaffected from this temporary cooperation.

I. The Emergence of Co-operatives and Unions

Both co-operatives and unions came into being in the previous century as "children of need". They strove to alleviate situations of need through the means of → *solidarity*. Both were self-help measures stemming from the economically weaker populational groups caught in pre-industrial circumstances: farmers, artisans, traders and workers. The rapid increase in population since the 18th century, the revocation of farmers' bondage and the introduction of unrestricted commercial and labor freedom brought upon the end of guilds for artisans, the end of "corporations" for traders, and the annulment of labor regulations for workers (→ *History before 1800*).

Initially, however, only a few individuals could take advantage of the new legal opportunities to engage in entrepreneurial activity and enter into new work relationships. The new living situations exposed many people principally to new perils. A multitude of farmers, artisans, traders and workers fell victim to enormous difficulties. "The battle for profits between producers and for wages between workers which immediately ensued when the barriers of the former guilds fell appeared to be the greatest social danger." This indicated in advance "that competition would lead to the monopoly position of the largest capitalist" (*Gide, Rist*).

Co-operatives and trade unions arose around the middle of the 19th century in Germany on account of this need, albeit initially in rudimentary forms (→ *History in 19th C.*). "Their founders wanted neither competition nor monopoly situations; the co-operative seemed to them the sole means to surpress competition without either inhibiting freedom or the necessary conditions of production" (*Gide, Rist*). They also enjoyed a prosperous success. By the end of the 19th century, they had developed into extensive → *federations* encompassing the entire territory of the German Reich; they likewise had united with corresponding organizations abroad into worldwide, international alliances (→ *ICA*).

Both union and co-operative associations were initially hindered by coalition prohibitions. Artisans and laborers had been forbidden to join together since the onset of the Middle Ages. Artisans in the late Middle Ages namely saw fewer and fewer chances to become masters themselves, and journeymen had begun to unite in order to have influence on working conditions and on the training of apprentices. Reaction to this took the form of coalition prohibitions imposed by civic authorities and later enforced on the national level.

Even the forces of the great French Revolution fought against co-operatives, which were seen as remnants of the *ancien regime* (→ *Socialist Critics*). It was maintained that all associations interrupt the free flow of forces. Co-operatives and unions were therefore not included in the list of human rights; in contrast, they were universally prohibited. The *Loi Chapelier* ratified in 1791, for example, declared violations of the ban on professional organizations to be an attempt against freedom and human rights and accordingly prosecuted co-operatives.

Only once awareness of the liberal stance started fading in the course of time with regard to the polarity between "individual" and "community" did a change occur. Freedom of association eventually became seen by the general public as an expression of individual freedom, and the ban on associations was lifted. With regard to the coalition prohibition, the "Nationalökonomie" (economics) declared that the freedom of coalition was not detrimental to the natural wage. It often became recognized that the ban was practically aimed against workers in that it was not possible to lay hold of agreements made among employers. The coalition prohibition therefore was gradually lifted during the second half of the century. Since then, co-operatives and trade unions have more and more often appeared where failed or insufficient state institutions and/or civil regulations once were present which had previously regulated the markets of these population groups and provided numerous social services.

The co-operatives and unions were also similar to the former state institutions in several important points. They likewise had two sides: outwards an economic face, and inwards a social substance. With regard to the outside world, they arranged purchasing or sales cartels of products and/or workers for the "producers" of these products; in their internal relationship they served as an association offering → *solidarity*, not infrequently also maintaining social facilities for their members.

More and more motives thereby fused co-operatives and unions together: idealistic movements, radical indignation about existent inequalities, a new class consciousness – but at the same time prospects for profits and wages, better and cheaper products, better sales turnover, and an easier means of earning income. They simply needed to find the correct mixture of → *motives* which would further those affected economically, morally, and socially and to take measures suitable to these motives which would bring about the actual relief hoped for (*Gustav Schmoller*).

II. The Relationship between the Housing and Joint-production Co-operatives and the Trade Unions

In order to address in detail the relationship between the co-operative system and the unions we must first differentiate co-operatives according to whether they are involved with unions, and if so, to the extent of this involvement.

On the one hand, there are those co-operatives which the unions encounter simply as employers, such as those found in agriculture and industry, including the credit co-operatives (→ *Co-operative Banks*). These promote primarily middle class population groups who themselves are not typical wage-earners and who ideologically have very little in common with unions. We, therefore, will not be concerned to any further degree with these types of "middle-class" co-operatives in this treatise.

On the other hand, there are those groups of co-operatives which exhibit common similarities with the unions based on sociological and ideological reasons but which, however, do not have a "relationship" with the unions in the usual context of union activity – the employer/employee relationship – because such co-operative groups do not employ wage-earners. The housing (→ *Housing Societies*) and → *joint-production co-operatives* will be discussed in brief at this point as an example.

Housing co-operatives are alluded to here principally because they are almost inevitably treated as housing societies. This is, however, incorrect. The housing system for lower income groups in Germany namely is regulated mostly by the housing societies, which neither are co-operatives nor represent a form of self-help; these rather are either state undertakings exhibiting a commonweal economic character which are entrusted with social-political tasks, or else social institutions established by large public or private companies which above all serve their employed staff. The housing societies practically represent public property in the form of a foundation of sorts provided from housing subsidies. There is no opportunity in this case to exercise self-help through solidarity.

Because they, nonetheless, are of great importance for wage-earners, German unions have operated the largest housing company for more than 30 years as their own undertaking, amassing a housing stock that counts almost 500,000 apartments. The relations this company carries on with its workers resembles those of the consumer co-operatives which will be discussed below. That this undertaking was on the brink of bankruptcy in the 1980s, accordingly divided and to the most part distributed among the German states can be traced back to neither the unions nor to the state of the undertaking but rather primarily to management errors which from time to time are encountered in all enterprises.

The housing co-operatives on the other hand, which exist alongside the housing societies, do not boast of any special union "relationship" as they do not employ wage-earners, or else only very few. The situation rarely arises for typical union members – industrial workers – to become participants in a housing co-operative; a mandate for the union to provide consultation, therefore, is not present here which would be similar to that of the housing societies. Wage-earners are namely also not in the position today to raise the necessary capital, something that is only possible for better paid civil servants and salaried personnel who typically are not organized in unions. Housing co-operatives for wage-earners have mostly been formed where particular circumstances enhance such development. In this case, they rapidly assume a vocational character which frequently contradicts the solidarity notion propagated by the unions.

The majority of unions likewise do not have any special relationship with the → *joint-production co-operatives* (our second example) as true joint-production co-operatives also do not employ wage-earners. Nonetheless, the joint-production co-operatives embrace an ideology many union members find engaging, and for a while they were in the center of the reform discussion. Experiments were continually made with them in the socialist camp, but this notion was not taken up by either the unions or the SPD (Sozial-demokratische Partei Deutschlands).

Joint-Production co-operatives were not particulary attractive to the unions for a very simple reason: they all rapidly came to an end. All true joint-production co-operatives either consistantly failed or "degenerated" into companies.

Joint-production co-operatives namely attempt to "harmonize" the contradictions inherent in companies and enterprises by incorporating the functions of equity owner, entrepreneur/industrialist, employer and employee in the person of the co-operator – a feat that rarely succeeds. If, on the other hand, certain functions were made distinct, say for example that of the equity owner from that of the employer, the character of the joint-production co-operative would change; seen from the morphology of the undertaking, the co-operative would transform itself into a company, and the co-operative members would become corporate share holders.

Furthermore, the joint-production co-operative maintains implicitly that all of its workers are equal. As a result, all of them receive the identical voting right and the identical wage. This, however, contradicts the operational need of basing remuneration on performance; jobs are strongly differentiated according to their degree of difficulty, and members' performance levels in a productive co-operative – as is the case for all people in all situations – vary greatly. Added to this is the rapid formation of management positions in productive co-operatives which contradicts the articles of association and → *by-laws* as they are oriented around the ideal of equality. This in turn weakens management functions (which, nevertheless, remain necessary) and paves the way again and again for disputes.

The fact arises – itself hardly motivating – from the experience gained from joint production co-operatives that, if they want to hold their own in competition with private companies, they must adapt their organization and salary structures to such private companies which strive for the highest possible level of productivity. This means that the various identities mentioned above, the equality postulate and the call for democracy must all be abandoned.

III. The Ideological Disputes with the Socialists

The → *consumer co-operatives* and unions forged a special relationship with each other only for a short period of time, and this only after reconciling differences. Of these, the most important for a long time was that the decisive socialist current embraced by many union members did not have a positive opinion of the co-operatives. First of all *Ferdinand Lassalle*, the founder of the SPD, raised general objections against the co-operatives (→ *socialist critics*). In his "Open Reply", which is considered the founding proclamation of this party, *Lassalle* voiced his opinion about co-operatives. He solely propagated joint-production co-operatives; only with their help could the working classes become their own employers, for only alone "could that iron and terrible law be overcome which determines the working wage." If the working classes organized themselves using joint-production co-operatives to become their own employers, the distinction between profit and working wage would disappear. In its place, output would serve as compensation for labor, and the working wage would simply, peacefully and legally disappear. For *Lassalle* this was the sole non-illusionary improvement of workers' conditions (→ *Schulze-Delitzsch*).

Lassalle did not think much of the consumer co-operatives. Price reductions brought about by the consumer co-operatives would only lead to wage decreases as a result of the iron law of wages, thus not leading to any improvement of workers' situation. For him, the consumer co-operatives were even "completely incapable of effecting improvements to the situation of the working classes."

The consumer co-operatives were also criticized by the Marxists. *Karl Marx* (→ *socialist critics*) and *Friedrich Engels* saw co-operatives as a great social experiment which indicated that exploitation could be replaced through a republican system of free and equal producers. The capitalistic system could, however, only be shaken to its foundations by joint-production co-operatives; consumer co-operatives could not achieve this as they merely touch the surface. Seen from the revolutionary point of view, all co-operatives are irrelevant for workers: as single enterprises they could not mold the revolutionary forces capable of reshaping society.

This revisionist change was supported and furthered by a new variable of consumer co-operative ideology advocated by *Heinrich Kaufmann*, at that time the most important personality involved in consumer co-operatives. This "new" consumer co-operative ideology extended considerably further than the existing liberal notions of consumer co-operatives. The consumer co-operatives had previously seen themselves politically as the medium through which democracy would be introduced into the economy. Since the times of → *Heinrich Kaufmann*, the consumer co-operatives also embraced a new interpretation – an anticapitalistic goal: instead of a capitalistic "profit economy" a co-operative "economy of need satisfaction" should emerge.

This became magnified and strengthened in the subsequent decades under the influence of the English socialists, in particular the *"Fabians"* Sidney and *Beatrice Webb* (→ *Rochdale Pioneers*). Concepts of a "consumer co-operative socialism" – a commonweal economy along consumer co-operative lines – were also being developed in Germany according to which the consumer co-operatives would serve as the premier enterprises in a more just economic system. This co-operative concept was in turn embraced by *Fritz Naphtali*, the economic expert of the free unions following the First World War, who utilized it in his "economic democracy", the much discussed economic concept of the free unions at the end of the 1920s. This concept also played a role after the Second World War in the scope of the discussions about co-determination and the undertakings of the German unions serving the commonweal.

IV. The "Marriage" of the Consumer Co-operatives and the Unions

Parallel to the revisionists gaining acceptance among important segments of the working classes, the consumer co-operatives additionally removed their organization from the other remaining co-operatives – a move that is frequently traced back to the rapprochement between consumer co-operatives and both the SPD and trade unions; it was, however, primarily based on economic reasons. The consumer co-operatives had namely founded a common purchasing center, the GEG, in 1894 as well as a number of factories from which they supplied local consumer co-operatives. In addition, they also accepted deposits from their members. This "modern" dimension of organization strengthened them and made them dangerous for private retailers, wholesalers and producers. A new economic contradiction became added to the political-ideological contradiction be-

tween the mostly liberal co-operatives serving midsized businesses and the social-democratic consumer co-operatives: the consumer co-operatives themselves became producers and money institutions.
This contradiction led in 1902 to the exclusion of the consumer co-operatives from the Allgemeiner Genossenschaftsverband (General Co-operative Federation) at the federation's co-operative convention in Kreuznach (which is why it is referred to as the "Kreuznach Inquisition") (→ *Schulze-Delitzsch*). "The liberal middle class opposed those socialistically inclined; those in small business wanted a divorce from workers" (*Helmut Faust*). Organized small and mid-sized producers and loan associations separated themselves from the large complex of self-support enterprises. This development led to the establishment of a consumer co-operative federation of its own in 1903, the Zentralverband Deutscher Konsumvereine (Central Federation of German Consumer Associations). With this move the consumer co-operatives established themselves as an independent social movement with its own goal orientation and central organization.
It should not be overlooked when discussing the transition to revisionism and the separation of the consumer co-operatives from the other co-operative organizations that the actual reason for the alliance between consumer co-operatives and the unions was economic in nature, namely the hope of improving workers' situation as a whole and not just that of the members of the consumer co-operatives. This itself was rooted in an interpretation which *Karl Marx* and *Friedrich Engels* had already put to paper in 1848 in the *Communist Manifesto*. In this work, they had propounded that workers were "exploited" not only by employers in their role as producers but likewise in their function as consumers by retailers, property owners and money lenders. The *Communist Manifesto* states: "if the exploitation of the worker through the factory owner concludes by the former receiving his working wage payed out in cash, the other segments of the bourgeoisie then pounce on him – the property owner, the merchant, the pawn broker, etc." (→ *Socialist Critics*).
The interest of workers not to be exploited by shopkeepers directed them to consumer co-operatives; their will not to fall into the hands of pawn brokers encouraged them to found their own insurance companies; to improve their position as renters they opposed property owners with the assistance of housing co-operatives.
Summarizing, the experience proved true that nominal wage increases effected by the unions alone were insufficient. The price and quality of the most important consumer goods for workers needed to be adapted to the needs of these segments of the population through the assistance of co-operatives and undertakings with a commonweal economic character. In other words, the fixing of real wages through the co-operatives must take place alongside the nominal wage increases effected by the unions. A quasi "natural" collaboration and sense of shared identity therefore developed between consumer co-operatives and unions.
This collaboration between the free consumer co-operatives and free unions also continued until 1933 among the Christian consumer co-operatives and Christian unions and was likewise based on the same reasons. Alongside the organization of labor in the unions it was intended for purchasing power to be organized in the consumer co-operatives and savings to be collected in worker banks (*Adam Stegerwald*). The identical alliance between consumer co-operatives and unions can also be found in the other German speaking countries as well as in Scandinavia and Great Britain. It is particularly well developed between unions and co-operatives in England.
This led to the "marriage" mentioned above between consumer co-operatives and the unions at the turn of the century. Since then, whoever was a member of the union was also in most cases a member of the appropriate consumer co-operative, and vice versa. Consumer co-operatives formed the third "pillar" of the worker movement (*Erwin Hasselmann*). Alongside the large political organization of the Social Democratic Party (SPD) and the large trade union organization of free unions, the consumer co-operatives entered the stage as the large organizer of consumers; all three were set in the framework of numerous culture and sport organizations for workers within the "worker's movement" as this grouping has generally been referred to.
The collaboration between the SPD, the free unions and the consumer co-operatives in the Central Federation greatly increased membership in the consumer co-operatives in Germany at that time. The number of members in the free consumer co-operatives surged from 500,000 in 1900 to 2 million in 1913; this means 2 million families, which represented between 9 and 10 million consumers. The consumer co-operatives grew through this manner to become one of the largest organizations in Germany and remained so through the 1960s despite two world wars and national-socialist persecution. It should, however, not be forgotten that this collaboration also brought the consumer co-operatives certain disadvantages. "The consumer co-operatives for many people became the 'red consumer associations'; the co-operative store became stigmatized as the 'poor people's shop'" (*Erwin Hasselmann*) – an image that became dangerous considering the dismantlement of political ideology, a decrease in the number of workers, and an increase in the number of salaried employees with a differing mentality in the population as a whole. The Christian consumer co-operatives which were united with the Christian unions and the Zentrum-party underwent a similar experience, albeit to a lesser extent.

V. The Disadvantages of Undertakings Imbued with Ideology

This collaboration between the SPD and the unions, as well as between the "Zentrum" and the Christian unions, presented German consumer co-operatives of both persuasions with disadvantages, above all on account of associated ideological orientation. The consumer co-operatives were fundamentally neutral with regard to party politics both in their official statements and in their practical business policy. Both rejected class struggle and were open to all consumers. As a rule, they only became politically active when general consumer interests were concerned. As an offshoot of the political movements, the worker movement and political Catholicism, the consumer co-operatives of both persuasions did, however, fall victim to ideological turbulence.

It should be noted here that ideological orientation among business undertakings itself is a general problem. Both advantages and disadvantages always arise for the enterprise in question when economic activity becomes subject to ideology, as was the case with the consumer co-operatives. Initially, the advantages are predominant as workers become motivated by the ideology and are more strongly inclined to join together in a community of solidarity than those workers in other enterprises. Ideological orientation also creates sympathizers. During the further course of affairs, however, non-economic goals mostly prove disadvantageous for companies which are in competition with enterprises lacking this element of ideological orientation. The opponents of the ideology then also become opponents of the business undertaking in question. The competitors of the particular undertaking imbued with ideology will also seek to portray the ideological ties in a bad light to the less motivated segments of the population; the front rejecting such ideology thereby grows in strength.

This situation is particularly applicable for emancipation ideology which endeavors to create new political or social conditions; those groups and companies in question are presented as the germinating seeds of a new social order as was the case with business undertakings during the workers' movement. They boast of their superiority and wish to completely convert their opponents and/or prevail over them. This above all activates their opponents, whereby the opponents of the social and reform movement in turn become opponents of the companies ascribing to this movement. Antagonism among business undertakings considerably exceeds amiability in quantity, intensity and duration.

Internal company problems also frequently arise. Ideological goals often entangle those companies embracing ideologies in the type of disputes that regularly befall every movement, above all disputes between reformers and revolutionaries, confrontations which absorb great amounts of energy and time.

Ideological orientation is above all detrimental when demands are drawn from it to promote or discriminate (i.e. boycott) certain companies or states based on political or moral reasons; furthermore, detriment occurs in this connection when business relations and revenue are forsworn but not accordingly rewarded by a certain, equally political behavior among like-minded compatriots.

Ideological or even active political action or abstention usually results in non-operating expenses that the non-politicized competitors do not have to bear. Ideological orientation accordingly deteriorates the competitive situation of the company in question in more than one aspect. In the first place, boycotters direct additional business to the non-politicized competitors; common experience has shown that the goods and services of the ideologically oriented company remain in demand despite the boycott measures. Secondly, their role as a competitor disappears; the non-politicized companies can sell their goods and services at correspondingly higher prices and at a higher rate of turnover, thus achieving additional profits.

VI. Consumer Co-operatives as Employers and the Unions

In addition to the difficulties that ideologically charged companies have in general, co-operatives also had to confront the situation of the free trade unions striving for union success within the consumer co-operative organizations. Alone, it proved insufficient merely to strengthen employees in their role as consumers. Both organizations were divided for a long time about work relations in the consumer co-operatives – above all in their production plants. Only after the consumer co-operatives in the Central Federation conceded in this matter and signed a collective wage agreement with the unions (the first of its kind in Germany) could a long-lasting agreement be made. In the subsequent years, those employed at the consumer co-operatives could demand and receive higher wages, better working hours, improved working conditions and more social benefits than those employed in competing private retail companies and their suppliers. The consumer co-operatives amassed considerably higher personnel costs than their competitors in private industry. Inasmuch as retail trade is a quite wage-intensive sector, these higher wages added greatly to operational costs.

This would have been tolerable had the employees in the co-operatives worked better than those in the competing private companies. In contrast to the hopes of numerous socialists, workers in the consumer co-operatives did not behave substantially different as would have been the case if they had worked for private companies. Some malicious individuals even maintained that work in consumer co-operatives was cushier than in private retail and production enterprises.

A cause for further disadvantages in comparison to private competitors was the prevailing union tendency of more strongly addressing lower wage and salary groups than higher ones. This also posed many difficulties for the co-operatives because the new wage relations drove qualified co-workers to their private competitors. Further differences resulted in that workers in the co-operatives were granted more co-determination rights than employees in private companies after the unions had demanded more control over production.

Through these activities, the unions often pursued the goal of setting precedents in the consumer co-operatives with regard to wage and work relations which they then could argumentatively apply in the wage settlements with private companies. Because these efforts as a rule did not have an effect on the competition – as wage relations illustrated – the unions in reality only created privileges for the workers in the consumer co-operatives compared to their colleagues working in private enterprises, thus at the same time creating competitive disadvantages for consumer co-operatives.

In effect, the boards of the consumer co-operatives owed it to the members of their consumer co-operatives to react like private employers with regard to the employees of the consumer co-operatives and refuse their further demands. They were, however, unsuccessful in many cases as a result of the numerous cases in which the same persons held leader's positions in both organizations simultaneously. The unions enjoyed such strong influence in the delegates' assembly in the consumer co-operatives that the boards which remained firm in this issue never remained in office for an extended amount of time. This fact was known by all, and everyone acted accordingly.

This one-sided involvement to the benefit of the workers and unions was to the detriment of the consumer co-operatives' promotion mandate and thus to the detriment of their members and the reimbursement entitled to them. Those co-operatives with lower union representation and accordingly less ideologically bound to the unions requested from their workers and their unions that they should not demand more from them than they would from their private competitors.

The unions, on the other hand, were often able to push through their demands with the German consumer co-operatives belonging to the Central Federation. The consumer co-operatives signed the first collective wage agreement in the Reich with the General Commission of the Free Trade Unions in 1904 – an era in which the notion of collective agreements was not yet propagated in the economy. Through this agreement, the workers and salaried employees of the consumer co-operatives received the highest wages in all of Germany prior to World War I. In 1911, the Central Federation also introduced the eight-hour working day to the consumer co-operatives when throughout the country the twelve-hour working day was the norm. The Federation thereupon granted a paid, two-week annual vacation – one of the first employers in Germany to do so. A retirement plan was even established in the consumer co-operatives in 1906, which was maintained up through the 1980s (with intermittent interruptions).

VII. The End of the Cooperation between Consumer Co-operatives and Trade Unions in Germany

Cooperation between the consumer co-operatives and trade unions in Germany was revived once again for almost three decades after World War II, but it never attained its former intensity. Categorical two-class thinking, differentiating between "bourgeoisie" and "proletariat", which forms the basis of the "worker movement subculture" faded in importance. The uniting ideological bond which the term "workers' movement" had signalized also became less and less prevalent.

Actual historic reasons for one were responsible in Germany for this. Political practices in the Soviet-occupied zone, later to become the GDR, were shocking. There, during the 1950s, the "capitalists" were disposessed – namely industrialists, independent farmers, small commercial operators, numerous artisans and home owners. This often occurred under inhumane circumstances, and many people were even coerced to leave the country. Other consequences of the War made two-class thinking a thing of the past. The War and its aftermath, such as the expulsion of 9 million Germans out of the territories east of the Oder-Neisse frontier, contributed to the equalization of property distinctions in that they affected rich and poor alike. Those in the possession of monetary or nominal capital assets were practically dispossessed through currency reform. Reconstruction on the other hand, the so-called "economic miracle", offered enterprising individuals with incredible prospects which were hardly present in normal times.

Thinking in two-class categories, therefore, lost ground for reasons inherent in industrial development itself and applicable to all industrial countries, including such factors as the decline of poverty and the increase of living standards for all people to their present-day level. The visible, superficial differences between the classes became blurred in connection with the drop in the number of children per family and increased employment among women. The progressing rationalization ultimately reduced the proportion of workers – the main proponents of two-class thinking – in the total number of employed individuals and increased the proportion of salaried employees who often fostered a completely different ideological approach. These two groups of employed persons in part also varied substantially with regard to qualification and income. The development of the education system, coupled with the increase in the number of academics from 3% to almost 20% of the population born in a given year and including more and more women, in the end overcame the "class barriers" in this sector.

Compared with the years prior to World War I and those between the Wars, the social conditions after World War II in general became emancipated from ideology. The "Cultural Revolution" in 1968, however, itself did bring about a Marxist renaissance and revitalize the long-forgotten word "workers' movement", but it primarily remained limited to cultural problems and restricted to the universities. The ideologies found in the scope of the ecological and peace movements addressed questions affecting humanity as a whole and not social conditions.

The loss of ideological orientation following the Second World War was influenced by the fact that it corresponded with important, concrete needs of the three organizations primarily addressed in this treatise. In the first postwar years, the consumer co-operatives and unions overcame their long-time differences between the consumer co-operatives affiliated with the free unions and those affiliated with the Christian unions. The consumer co-operatives as well as the unions each evolved into one unified organization.

On the other hand, the SPD, which likewise played an important role in this development, freed itself from its Marxist foundations and oriented itself around the goals of a people's party, as embodied in the *Godesberger Programm* (1957), after losing several federal parliament elections. This, likewise, produced a trend away from ideological orientation.

A decisive factor for the removal of ideological orientation in the consumer co-operatives was that the market situation in the sector of foodstuffs retailing fundamentally changed after World War II. An immense concentrational process also occurred. Today, only a handful of large retail conglomerates dominates the markets for foodstuffs and semiluxury goods, each of which employs several thousand workers. At the same time, they enlarge their product assortment with more extensive groups of goods.

The transition from small shops providing customer assistance to large self-serve supermarkets, furthermore, eradicated ideology inasmuch as trade itself became anonymous. Political and personal contacts to individual co-operative members could no longer be maintained in the large supermarkets, which likewise were forced to extend their business beyond their politically like-minded clientele on account of increasing pressure from fixed costs. Both of these factors contributed to making co-operative democracy as irrelevant and/or abstract as in the large, publicly owned companies.

The primary reason why the consumer co-operatives and the unions each went their own way and terminated their "marriage" was, however, grounded in the fact that neither organization needed the other no longer in a reciprocal manner. On the one hand, the unions no longer needed the consumer co-operatives. The consumer co-operatives had more or less made themselves superfluous through their consumer-friendly competition policy. Competition had escalated so dramatically in the 1960s, that one could no longer speak of consumer "exploitation". The correctional function of the consumer co-operatives with regard to both price and quality was no longer a pressing matter; the same was true for the social dependency on retailers which many workers previously had to cope with. In the meantime, lawmakers also occasionally addressed grievances which continued to arise, themselves pushed to action by consumer organizations and the press and supported by consumer-friendly legislation. They usually outperformed the consumer co-operatives in this matter which, when under union influence, were often forced to take consideration of jobs in the production sectors in question.

At the same time, however, the co-operatives also no longer needed the unions; the contrary was rather true. In the beginning, the unions often brought the consumer co-operative new members and maintained their contacts to them. As described above, this often vested the co-operatives with the reputation of "proletarian shops" – of "red" consumption – which impeded their access to more "middle-class" salaried employees, civil servants, self-employed individuals, and workers who associated themselves with such groups. It is precisely the more well-off individuals which make the better customers from a businessman's perspective.

During this restructuring process, close cooperation between the consumer co-operatives and the unions was temporarily reestablished in the 1970s. At this time, a great number of consumer co-operatives namely fell victim to considerable economic difficulty, and the unions jumped in to help them. They created a holding company in 1974, the co op Zentrale AG, which in the course of the following years took over a large number of economically weak consumer co-operatives, among which included in part several quite large consumer co-operatives as well as important central facilities such as the GEG and its production operations. The co op Zentrale AG ultimately consolidated in its organization almost half of the total turnover of German consumer co-operatives. Without its assistance, i.e. support from the unions, the consumer co-operatives incorporated in it would have faced bankruptcy.

The transformation of a number of consumer co-operatives into the legal form of a joint-stock company occurred in more than one case. A large group of consumer co-operatives split off and assumed the legal form of a joint-stock company, led by the consumer co-operatives in the Saar. Alongside this development, a third "remnant" of the former consumer co-operative movement exists, the consumer co-operative Coop Dortmund-Kassel eG. It functions according to the older form, thereby serving to contradict the claim of the two joint-stock companies that modern grocery retailing no longer can be pursued in this manner.

In the 1980s, the unions once again called an end to their involvement benefiting consumer co-operatives which themselves fell victim to difficulties and in the course of time had to be sold off. The first to be sold was the co op AG, the name the former co op Zentrale AG had meanwhile assumed. Since 1986, it has been a large foodstuffs company. It is no longer associated with the unions; it also no longer propounds any consumer-political goals.

The sale of co op AG is indeed a very sad incident from the point of view of the unions and the commonweal economy as much as one can empathize with this development while keeping the disaster of the unions and their huge housing society "Neue Heimat" in mind. Granted, it resulted in the face of the facts – presented above – that the correctional function was hardly necessary anymore. It took place, however, at the same time that the concentration of retail trade in the sectors of foodstuffs and semiluxury goods reached a dimension never before seen. It would naturally be of great interest to the unions to have "a foot in the door" with one of the large retail trade companies dealing with foodstuffs and semiluxury goods. In the end, between a fourth and a third of workers' wages lands in the registers of the grocery retailers – wages from groups of workers who are especially strongly organized in the unions. One gathers the impression that the unions divested themselves of a corrective precisely in the moment that it once again began to get interesting.

Bibliography

Engelhardt, Werner Wilhelm: Allgemeine Ideengeschichte des Genossenschaftswesens, Darmstadt 1985.
Faust, Helmut: Geschichte der deutschen Genossenschaftsbewegung, Frankfurt 1965.
Hasselmann, Erwin: Geschichte der deutschen Konsumgenossenschaften, Hamburg 1971.
Hesselbach, Walter: Die gemeinwirtschaftlichen Unternehmen, Frankfurt 1971.
Loesch, Achim von: Die gemeinwirtschaftliche Unternehmung, Köln 1977.
Loesch, Achim von: Die gemeinwirtschaftlichen Unternehmen der deutschen Gewerkschaften, Köln 1979.

Transport Co-operatives

ULRICH SCHUMACHER [J]

(see also: *Classification*; *Federations*; *Structural Types*)

I. Types and Characteristics; II. Inland Navigation; III. Roadway Transport.

I. Types and Characteristics

Owner-entrepreneurs of mid-sized companies in the transport industry joined together before the turn of the century (→ *History in 19th C.*) in order to promote the goals of their individual enterprises through co-operative organizational forms in the following sectors:

Inland Navigation
– Freight Navigation
– Passenger Navigation

Roadway Transport
– Road Haulage
– Freight Forwarding
– Passenger Transport

As a rule, the objective and substance of co-operative activity is membership promotion oriented around marketing practises. In particular situations, the co-operative confines its involvement to the fulfillment of secondary goals expressed by individual entrepreneurs.

Individual owner-entrepreneurs are more or less strongly or even completely dependent on the various co-operative forms according to their varying degree of integration in the co-operatives.

II. Inland Navigation

Shipping co-operatives have existed in part since 1898. They undertake the promotion of their members through a joint business operation which is completely oriented around the goals of the individual members. The promotional expectations placed on freight and passenger navigation have lead to different co-operative structures; this itself is contingent on the different conceptions and practises inherent in the shipping industry.

1. Freight Navigation

The establishment of co-operatives of inland navigators (co-operatives of independent barge-owners) addressed the exigencies of freight navigation at an early day and age. Co-operatives traditionally also boast of the most extensive organizational structure. The inland navigator who runs his ship himself must decide from the beginning whether to join a shipping company and/or a forwarder ("Hauspartikulier") or seek integration in a co-operative. This pressure becomes all the stronger the more differentiated the demands are which the forwarder places on the size, fittings, and operative capacity of the ship's hold.

On the other hand, the association of individual inland navigators with various types freight ships in a co-operative results in an efficient and flexible transportation option for the forwarding trade. It can be compared to other large-scale company forms and even in part outperforms their fleets.

Extensive attachment of the individual members to the organization is a result of the pooled economic resources in the group. The individual owners in part relinquish disposition over their own ships and subject themselves to the contracting directives of the registered co-operative.

This attachment is compensated in that the co-operative's goal system corresponds extensively with the composite goal systems of the individual members. The members have conveyed essential functions of their individual enterprises to the co-operative, namely acquisition, conclusion of contracts, disposition of cargo capacity, collection of freight, regulation of transport costs, customs charges, fees, etc. Only the less important functions remain to be executed – such as to hire the crew and maintenance, as well as fundamental decisions (assumption of trade, investment decisions, financing).

The barge-owners joined together in the co-operative come upon their freight loads exclusively through the co-operative. The co-operatives in turn exclusively assign and employ the freight capacity of their members. The co-operatives do not dispose of freight tonnage themselves in order to prevent goal conflicts between the co-operatives and the members from arising.

Inasmuch as the paid co-operative management completely addresses and covers interests, it is out of question that they would pursue their own interests to the detriment of the individual members. The members, on the other hand, can assess the planning goals of the co-operative business operation and their realization against the operational figures of their individual enterprises.

A strong level of member participation in co-operative affairs – in particular in the general assembly – results from the exclusive economic motivation inherent in the relationship between members and their co-operative, from the interdependency between the business goals of the individual members on the one hand and the goal system of the co-operative group on the other hand, and ultimately from the insight the individual members have concerning the importance of integrated promotion through the co-operative group.

Around 700 members are joined together in the 12 inland navigation co-operatives, a level which represents approx. one-half of all independent inland navigators in Germany. In relation to cargo capacity, the co-operative organization comprises one-third of the fleet of German barge-owners, a figure which in turn represents approx. one-sixth of total German cargo tonnage (excluding tankers).

2. Passenger Navigation

In contrast to freight navigation, co-operatives involved in passenger navigation are without exception associations utilizing means of production. Members regularly place one or more ships at the disposal of the co-operative, and the number of members therefore remains fairly low.

The employment of the ships (individually owned by the members) is regulated solely by the co-operative, which likewise must bear all costs associated with the operation of these ships. Members are obligated to collect transport proceeds for the co-operative's account; in turn, the co-operative uses them to cover operating and administrative expenses and to distribute cost reimbursement and, as the case my be, as a surplus among the members as compensation.

III. Roadway Transport

The history of roadway transport co-operatives is relatively young as they were first initiated in the 1930s. A differentiation must be drawn in this connection on the one hand between associations of road haulage and freight forwarders and, on the other hand, associations of operators who undertake passenger transport (taxi business, bus companies).

1. Road Haulage

In a narrower sense, roadway transport co-operatives are associations of owner-operators involved in road haulage who, in the scope of their allotted licenses, independently undertake freight transport or short-haul traffic. The roadway haulage co-operatives (SVGs) as well as the registered co-operative of truckers in the German railway system (GdB) thereby limit their activity to the realization of secondary goals of the individual truckers incorporated as members. The co-operatives themselves do not provide or arrange any services for the transport sector, neither as haulage contractors nor as freight forwarders.

The SVGs endeavor to oversee compliance with the general legal obligation to abide with transport rates regulated in the Law on Road Haulage (GüKG) and, if the occasion should arise, instigate recalculations and subsequently collect freight discounts.

This freight check capacity was conveyed to the SVGs as licensed freight check sites after 1945. The SVGs check over 80% of all freight accounted for in long-haul trucking and are themselves shouldered by their members, that is companies involved in road haulage. Therefore, the SVGs are in competition

with licensed, non-co-operative freight check sites which offer their services to all truckers, regardless of whether they are co-operative members or not.
In competition with third parties, the SVGs and the GVB also provide their members with merchandise such as fuel, spare vehicle parts and accessoires, services (insurance brokerage, personnel training, information services) or motor-courts. Business with nonmembers is permissible in all cases, but as a rule has not been intensely cultivated.
On account of limitations to market accessiblity because of concession licensing as well as the application of regulated transport rates (RKT), competition – in particular price competition – has become so extensively restricted that the individual operators no longer have any direct incentive or pressure to shift further operational functions to a co-operative establishment.
On the other hand, isolated large-scale enterprises have sprung up in the meantime through the concentration process in the trucking business which in turn exhibit interest for a co-operative organization; usually, they would be competitors.
Around 6,900 freight transporters are joined together as members in a total of 17 SVGs. The SVGs insofar do not assume any marketing functions for them.
Co-operative marketing services for the members of the GdB are likewise unnecessary. The members of this co-operative are bound to the Deutsche Bundesbahn (DB, German Railway Co.) through individual employment contracts and provide the Bundesbahn with transport services. The registered co-operative, therefore, need not fulfill any acquisition functions. The co-operative primarily limits its activity to the invoicing of its members' transport services with the DB, the collection of freight and paying its members.

2. Freight Forwarding

The small number of freight forwarding co-operatives essentially are associations of freight forwarders striving for promotion of their member enterprises through a federated structure. As such, they are not marketing-oriented group organizations. In only one case does a loading association of freight forwarders pursue the forwarding interests of its members.

3. Passenger Transport

Despite concession licensing and rate levels in passenger transport, the pressure for optimal intensification of economic efficiency has effected a more extensive convergence of individual operators' goals. The introduction of radio communication itself exercises continual pressure to more strongly economize the performance process; such economization is only possible through the merger of individual taxi companies.
Aside from maintaining radio communication to arrange the provision of services, a taxi co-operative (with radio transmission) also assumes marketing functions for its members inasmuch as admissible transport contracts are concluded above and beyond the fixed tariff rates for passenger transport, for example with large corporations, health insurance companies, etc. regardless of the general passenger rates. Although the co-operative is forced to have its individual members furnish these transport services because it does not dispose of vehicles itself, individual taxi owners could not realize such extra services themselves on account of their insufficient transport capacities. In this connection, the co-operative not only executes the contracting side of such rides but also collects payments resulting from such transport services.
Because the co-operative itself does not undertake any transport services, the goals of the individual members extensively correspond with the goal system of the co-operative. Consequently, the co-operative members to a great degree have entrusted the co-operative with the advertising functions for their transport services. The co-operative represents the interests of its members when transportation rates are refixed.
Owner-operator associations in the sector of bus transportation are practically insignificant when compared to the 30 existing taxi co-operatives.

Bibliography

Aschoff, Gunther/Henningsen, Erkart: Das deutsche Genossenschaftswesen, Frankfurt 1985.
Draheim, Georg: Zur Ökonomisierung der Genossenschaft, Göttingen 1967.
Draheim, Georg: Grundlagen des Genossenschaftswesens, Frankfurt 1983.
Dülfer, Eberhard: Strukturprobleme der Genossenschaften in der Gegenwart, in: Forschungsinstitut für Genossenschaftswesen an der Universität Wien (ed.), Neuere Tendenzen im Genossenschaftswesen, Göttingen 1966.
Dülfer, Eberhard: Die Effizienz der Genossenschaft, in: ZfG (1972), pp. 324 ff.
Hamm, Walter: Straßenverkehrsgenossenschaften vor neuen Aufgaben, in: Genossenschaften und Genossenschaftsforschung, Festschrift für Georg Draheim, Göttingen 1971.
Hettlage, Robert: Genossenschaftstheorie und Partizipationsdiskussion, Frankfurt/New York 1971.
Kress, Herbert: Entwicklung, Arbeitsweise und Struktur der Schiffahrtsgenossenschaften, Marburg 1963.
Kress, Herbert/Kessler, Hans-Joachim: Entwicklung, Arbeitsweise und Struktur der Straßengütergenossenschaften, Marburg 1967.
Lipfert, Helmut: Mitgliederförderndes Kooperations- und Konkurrenzmanagement, Göttingen 1986.
Münkner, Hans-H.: Genossenschaftliche Identität und Identifikation mit ihrer Genossenschaft, Frankfurt 1990.
Nehammmer, Dieter: Ansatzpunkte für eine Erfolgsfeststellung bei Genossenschaften, Nürnberg 1977.
Schultz, Reinhard/Zerche, Jürgen: Genossenschaftslehre, Berlin 1983.
Varnholt, N.T.: Förderleistungsoptimierung in Handelsgenossenschaften, Köln 1989.

United Nations System and Co-operatives

JÜRGEN VON MURALT

(see also: *ICA*; *International Co-operative Organization*; *MATCOM*; *GACOPEA*; *Development Policy*; *different articles on Co-operative Development and Education and Training in the Third World*)

I. Introduction; II. The United Nations Organizations and the Specialized Agencies and their Particular Interest in Co-operative Development; III. Selected Activities of UN Organizations in Favour of Co-operative Development.

I. Introduction

The United Nations Organization as the political world body has taken an early active interest in co-operatives and has established relations with the world-wide co-operative movement. Its General Assembly and the Economic and Social Council have endorsed recommendations from member states urging the UN and the world community to assist countries in the development of co-operatives as a means to organise popular participation and self-help in the development process and to promote a more equal distribution of income.

The United Nations family is made up of a large number of specialized agencies which are organised according to sectoral interests or other thematic concerns such as agriculture, industry, education, labour, trade and environment. Whilst many of these organizations will have had, from time to time, contacts with co-operatives in their field of specialisation there are only four which have regular and close working relations with co-operatives: The Food and Agriculture Organization, the International Labour Organization, the United Nations Industrial Development Organization and the United Nations Educational, Scientific and Cultural Organization. The following description will focus on the activities of these four specialized agencies. There are also two UN organizations which provide resources in support of co-operative self-help as part of their anti-poverty oriented development activities, namely the World Food Programme (WFP) and the International Fund for Agricultural Development (IFAD). There are furthermore several other inter-governmental organizations which will be mentioned although they are not formally part of the United Nations. These are the Bretton Woods institutions, particularly the World Bank but also the regional development banks in Africa, Asia and the Americas, and in fact, they often provide the funds for investment which is so badly needed to put the co-operatives in developing countries on their own feet.

The world co-operative movement, represented by the International Co-operative Alliance, welcomed the assistance provided by UN organizations in the ICA Declaration on the occasion of the 47th International Co-operative Day in the following terms: "Acclaims its full agreement with the aims of the United Nations and its Agencies and welcomes a Resolution now adopted by the General Assembly of the UN at its 23rd Session, in which, recognizing the important role of the co-operative movement in the development of various fields of production and distribution, the General Assembly invites member States to provide increasing help to developing countries and request the UN Specialized Agencies together with the International Co-operative Alliance to render increased assistance within the possibilities in the realisation of the objectives of the Resolution".

II. The United Nations Organizations and the Specialized Agencies and their Particular Interest in Co-operative Development

1. The United Nations Organizations

Over the years, the General Assembly of the United Nations and the Economic and Social Council (ECOSOC) have adopted a series of resolutions concerning co-operatives and their role in national development (→ *Development Policy*). As far back as 1951, ECOSOC recommended inter alia in its Resolution 370 on land reform, that governments take appropriate measures to promote co-operative organizations for servicing agriculture. A certain landmark came in 1968 with General Assembly Resolution 2459 on the role of the co-operative movement in economic and social development. In this resolution, the International Labour Organization and other specialized agencies were requested, in cooperation with the → *International Co-operative Alliance*, to render increased assistance to co-operatives in developing countries. It also recognized the contribution co-operatives could make in the implementation of the goals of the second United Nations Development Decade. Similar resolutions have been adopted subsequently by the UN, the latest being a resolution on national experience in promoting the co-operative movement in December 1989.

In order to be able to monitor the effect given to these resolutions and review the progress of co-operatives in development, the Secretary-General has been requested to submit every second year a report to the General Assembly.

Taking into account the profound social and economic changes which resulted from structural adjustments and the transition to a market economy in many former socialist countries, the report which was submitted to the General Assembly in 1992 dealt with the "Status and Role of Co-operatives in the Light of the New Economic and Social Rends". The report was based, amongst others, on a major study prepared by COPAC, the Committee for Promotion and Advancement of Co-operatives. Following the discussion of the report by both the Economic and Social Council and the General Assembly, the latter adopted in December 1992 a resolution with the same title, which inter alia welcomes the recommendation in the Secretary-General's report and invites governments and international organizations to maintain and increase their programmes of support to the international co-operative movement.

These reports, which are prepared in collaboration with all UN organizations concerned, document the involvement of the UN system in co-operative development and the progress made at national levels. In addition to this policy-oriented action of the UN, there are a variety of operational activities undertaken by the Secretariat itself, particularly through the UN Centre for Social and Humanitarian Affairs which carried out studies and activities in the field of co-operatives and their involvement with the ageing, youth and disabled, the Regional Economic Commissions and various UN bodies such as the Centre for Human Settlements (HABITAT), the Population Fund (UNFPA), the Office of the United Nations High Commissioner for Refugees (UNHCR), the Research Institute for Social Development (UNRISD), the United Nations Development Programme (UNDP) and the World Food Programme (WFP). The UNDP has become the central funding institution which finances a major part of the UN system's technical cooperation activities in favour of co-operatives. There is also the International Fund for Agricultural Development (IFAD) which provides financial resources in support of co-operative self-help activities of the rural poor (→ *Self-help Organizations*).

While the UN Secretariat and the Regional Social and Economic Commissions mainly organize meetings and seminars on specific aspects of co-operative development, the other institutions directly support co-operatives through advisory services or technical cooperation projects. The UNFPA, for example, funds population education programmes which are implemented with the help of co-operatives and HABITAT has a sizeable programme to support low-cost and self-help settlement and housing schemes including housing co-operatives. Within the UN, these activities date back to 1954 when the then UN Housing and Town and Country Planning Section organized a seminar on housing co-operatives in Latin America. In the late 1960s, the United Nations Research Institute for Social Development reviewed the status of co-operatives in the different developing regions of the world. A major research project was launched under the title "Rural institutions as agents of planned change" which resulted in several volumes of regional papers and national case studies which served as a basis of a synthesis report. This report was rather critical of the role of co-operatives as genuine autonomous self-help institutions and advocated major policy reforms which would enable co-operatives to play a positive role as agents of change in economic and social development.

While there is no permanent structure for the promotion of co-operatives in the UN itself, there is a continuous commitment for assisting in their advancement and a recognition of their contribution to economic and social progress. This commitment was reconfirmed by the Secretary-General himself when he addressed the XXIXth Congress of the International Co-operative Alliance (Stockholm, July 1988).

2. The International Labour Organization (ILO)

Among the specialized agencies of the UN system the International Labour Organization assumes a particular role as regards co-operatives. Only a year after its establishment in 1919, this organization, under the leadership of its first Director-General, *Albert Thomas*, created a co-operative service which has continued to operate to this day. The common roots and the similarity of objectives of the co-operative movement and the ILO characterize the special relationship which exists between the two and which is even recognized in Article 12 of the ILO Constitution. The concept of labour and social questions of *Albert Thomas*, a man who had many personal links with the co-operative movement, was closely related to the co-operative idea and, therefore, became an element of the ILO's policy. As early as 1921, the Third International Labour Conference decided that "the ILO should pay special attention to the study of certain aspects of cooperation which are connected with the improvement of the economic and social conditions of workers".

Between the two World Wars, research and the collection and dissemination of information were the ILO's main activities in the field of co-operatives. One of the regular outputs of this work was the publication of an international directory of co-operative organizations of which the thirteenth edition appeared in 1988. Over the years, the ILO organized a large number of expert meetings and conferences, often on a regional basis, which offered delegates from member States i.e. government representatives, employers' and worker delegates an opportunity to discuss and exchange experiences on co-operative matters. Of special importance was an expert meeting in Geneva in 1962 which examined the rends and developments of the co-operative movement throughout the world. The conclusions reached at that meeting comprised practical suggestions and proposals regarding the major aspects of co-operative development, for instance the role of the State in the growth of co-operatives. The work carried out at these meetings and conferences culminated in the adoption by the International Labour Conference, in 1966, of Recommendation No. 127 concerning the "Role of Co-operatives in the Economic and Social Development of the Developing Countries". This Recommendation is designed to provide governments of developing countries with guidelines for effective co-operative development. Its scope extends to all types of co-operatives. It calls on governments of developing countries to formulate and carry out a policy under which co-operatives receive economic, financial and administrative aid and encouragement without affecting their independence. As regards the methods of implementing such a policy it defines the role of governments in respect to legislation, education and training, and their financial, administrative and supervisory responsibilities. The Recommendation emphasises especially the requirements of members, elected office bearers and managerial staff to receive education and training in co-operative principles, methods and techniques. It further calls on member States to collaborate in providing aid and encouragement to co-operatives in developing countries, through increased provision of technical assistance, exchange of information and qualified personnel, the grant of fellowships, the organization of international seminars, inter-co-operative exchange of goods and services, and the initiation of systematic research into the structure and problems of the co-operative movements in developing countries. Although mainly meant for action at the national level, the Recommendation also greatly inspired the further work of the ILO in this field, as will be explained below when the various instruments for the promotion of co-operatives are examined.

3. The Food and Agriculture Organization (FAO)

As the leading international body for food and agriculture, the FAO, founded in 1945, concentrates on finding ways to eliminate the hunger and poverty affecting millions of people in developing countries. In accordance with the Preamble of its Constitution, a principal objective of the FAO is to improve the conditions of rural people and raise their levels of nutrition and standards of living. The organization aims at improving the production and distribution of all food and agricultural products. In pursuing these goals, the FAO carries out a major programme of technical advice and assistance for the agricultural community on behalf of governments and development funding agencies; it advises governments on policy and planning; it collects, analyses and disseminates information and it provides opportunities for governments to meet and discuss food and agricultural problems. Within this broad mandate, millions of farmers, fishermen and forestry workers and their families are being assisted by or are involved in activities, projects and programmes supported worldwide by FAO (→ *Rural Co-operatives*). The focus on people and their participation through their own organizations in the development process was considerably strengthened by the World Conference on Agrarian Reform and Rural Development in 1979 which gave rise to the FAO's People's Participation Programme. But already long before this World Conference, the FAO had developed active programmes for support to co-operatives through research and technical assistance to which reference will be made below. It held many regional technical meetings on co-operatives in the 1950s and 1960s several of which were jointly organized by the FAO and the ILO, as for example the Technical Meeting on Cooperation in Asia and the Far East (Kandy, 1954) the Technical Meeting on Fishing Co-operatives (Naples, 1959), the Technical Meeting on Cooperation in the Near and Middle East (Cairo, 1959) and the Expert Meeting on Rural Cooperation (Mexico, 1967).

Between 1953 and the end of 1968, the UN, the ILO, the FAO and various donor countries – Denmark, in particular – organized 35 regional or inter-regional seminars for many hundreds of co-operative leaders from over fifty countries. In addition, the FAO and the ILO jointly sponsored in Cyprus in 1952 a training course for co-operative leaders and operated together in 1959, in Nairobi, a temporary training centre for co-operative staff from 16 African countries. The collaboration between the FAO and the ILO in the co-operative field was very much facilitated by the existence of a Memorandum of Understanding, supplementing the general agreement between these two organizations, which spells out in some detail the respective responsibilities of the two bodies in the co-operative field and describes the modalities of collaboration.

4. Other Specialized Agencies – UNIDO and UNESCO

Among the other specialized agencies of the UN there are several which include activities relating to co-operatives in their work programmes. Foremost among these is the United Nations Industrial Development Organization (UNIDO) which actively promotes industrial co-operatives as part of its endeavours to develop small-scale industries in developing countries. This is done either through direct assistance at the country level in the framework of UNIDO's technical cooperation programme or through the organization of meetings, seminars and workshops dealing with co-operative matters and providing a forum for the exchange of experience and the discussion of problems. The working agreement between UNIDO and the ILO includes a section of co-operatives which notes their mutual recognition of the need for a comprehensive and coherent approach to the development of industrial co-operatives in developing countries. It also provides for the exchange of information on their respective on-going and projected activities especially in connection with country programming exercises, and the promotion of joint or co-ordinated programmes of action.

The United Nations Educational, Scientific and Cultural Organization (Unesco), although not primarily concerned with co-operatives, undertakes from time to time activities which involve them. For example, in 1970 UNESCO collaborated with the International Co-operative Alliance in organising the International Conference of Co-operative Education Leaders in Switzerland which was directly supported by co-operative organizations from Austria and Switzerland. UNESCO has long recognized the importance of the role of co-operatives in the development of human resources. In fact, in the same year, the UNESCO General Conference approved at its 16th Session Resolution 9.15 on the importance of co-operative education for the achievement of the goals of the Second UN Development Decade. The educational aspects of co-operatives are clearly a major concern of UNESCO, particularly in view of its policies and programmes to promote adult education and functional literacy. Good use is being made by co-operative leaders and educators of UNESCO's travel grant programme. In addition to the field of education, the participation aspects of co-operatives are of interest to UNESCO and in this connection it organises seminars to discuss the institutionalization of people's participation in social and economic development and publishes reports and studies on the subject.

5. Development Banks and Funding Institutions

In addition to the specialised agencies, there is a group of institutions related to the UN system which has an important role in supporting co-operative development. These are the financial agencies such as the World Bank, and the regional development banks. None of these institutions has yet developed a coherent policy vis-à-vis co-operatives as part of their lending policies. However, there are indications that their interest is growing to work with grass-root level institutions such as co-operatives. A 1986 study showed that about half of the World Bank's agricultural operations had involved co-operatives and co-operative-type associations. The study concluded that the performance of Bank financed co-operative components has been mixed. One of the reasons for the limited impact on co-operatives was the fact that loans were mostly channelled through government agencies, thus increasing the dependency of co-operatives on state institutions. A significant step towards reviewing its position concerning co-operatives was the convening, in early 1990, of a Seminar on Donor Support for the Promotion of Rural Co-operatives in Developing Countries. Also it appears that increased recognition is being given in operational activities to the potential role of co-operatives and funds are being set aside to strengthen the operation of co-operatives, often in close collaboration with technical agencies such as the FAO and the ILO. These programmes, particularly in Africa, have assumed growing significance in connection with structural adjustment measures.

Regional development banks seem to place even less emphasis on a systematic involvement of co-operatives. However, the Inter-American Development Bank has developed a facility, namely the Small Projects Fund which allows the IDB to deal directly with co-operatives and other non-governmental organizations and many co-operatives have benefited from this possibility. Moreover, it finances urban development projects which may involve housing co-operatives. Likewise, the projects of the African and the Asian Development Banks sometimes include elements which involve different types of co-operatives, although there is no systematic approach toward co-operatives. In the context of providing financial resources for co-operative development, IFAD must be mentioned. This specialised development bank has been established with the clear mandate to support agricultural development with a definite anti-poverty focus. Much of its lending is on concessional terms and many loans are supplemented by grants for technical assistance. The conscious support of co-operatives as a self-help institution can be seen as part of its development policy and there are many examples where funds are channelled through co-operatives or where they are used to establish structures for credit, supplies of inputs and marketing of products.

Among the funding organizations, the United Nations Development Programme (UNDP) plays a key role in financing technical cooperation within the UN system; in fact, many activities undertaken by the specialised agencies in support of co-operative development are to a significant extent programmed together with, and funded by, UNDP. Particularly relevant in the investment context is the United Nations Capital Development Fund (UNCDF) which forms part of UNDP and funds small capital investments in least developed countries (LDCs) which are often linked to technical assistance projects. Since raising capital is a major obstacle in establishing co-operative enterprises, UNCDF's assistance can be particularly useful. UNIFEM, the Development Fund for Women of UNDP, also provides financial and technical support to co-operative activities of women.

6. Coordination of Activities

As the interest of UN organizations in co-operatives developed and direct assistance expanded, the question of coordination arose and the need for establishing regular relations with representative organizations of co-operatives was recognised. Thus, in the late 1960s discussions started among interested organizations which led, in January 1971, to the establishment of COPAC, the Committee for the Promotion of Aid to Co-operatives (in 1989 renamed Committee for the Promotion and Advancement of Co-operatives). Originally, the membership consisted of the International Co-operative Alliance, the International Federation of Agricultural Producers, the International Federation of Plantation, Agricultural and Allied Workers, the FAO and the ILO. In its resolution 1668 of June 1972, ECOSOC included a recommendation that the membership of COPAC should be broadened. In response to this, the UN joined in 1972 and the World Council of Credit Unions in 1973. Thus, COPAC is currently made up of seven intergovernmental and non-governmental organizations which jointly finance and support the COPAC secretariat which is located with the FAO headquarters in Rome. COPAC was established to provide a forum for action-oriented consultation between its members and for the exchange of information about programmes and plans for co-operative development, thus avoiding duplication of efforts. In addition to its activities related to the needs of members, it maintains relations with a great number of other international and national organizations and agencies concerned with co-operatives. The COPAC secretariat also publishes an information bulletin, carries out research and studies on specific co-operative issues, organizes occasional symposia and seminars and provides initial assistance in formulating co-operative projects. It has, for example, assisted UNDP in an evaluation of co-operative development programmes and issued a Directory of Agencies Assisting Co-operatives in Developing Countries. COPAC's country information notes, over 30 of which have been published so far describe the current status of co-operatives in individual countries.

III. Selected Activities of UN Organizations in Favour of Co-operative Development

1. Collection and Dissemination of Information

Between the years 1929 and the end of the Second World War, the ILO's co-operative service laid the foundations for what the former ICA Director, *P.W. Watkins* described as follows: "For over half a century the Co-operative Service of the ILO known under various titles at different periods, has been one of the greatest – and is now probably the world's greatest – repository of knowledge about cooperation. The ILO's relations with its Member governments and, along with them, employers' and workers' organizations, have afforded opportunities and facilities for gathering information which no other institution can match." (*Watkins*, 1970). In fact, during these years most efforts of the ILO co-operative service were concentrated on collecting information on co-operatives, analysing trends, maintaining relations with co-operative organizations and publishing the results of this work. The Directory of Co-operative Organizations is one of the outputs of this research, as is the periodical Co-operative Information, which was first issued in 1924 and which published between 1932 and 1955 a complete list of all co-operative laws and regulations enacted in the world. This information is regularly updated and stored in a data bank.

After the Second World War, a Co-operative Advisory Committee was set up by the ILO following a proposal by the International Labour Conference in 1945 and the Co-operative Service "had prepared and published two important volumes which were of immense value in drawing the attention of all agencies concerned with rehabilitation and reconstruction to the achievements of cooperation in its various forms and its unique advantages, as a means of restoring health to economic life, and repairing the wastage caused by the war" (*Watkins*). These volumes were respectively entitled "Co-operative Organization and Post-war Relief" and "The Co-operative Movement and Present-day Problems".

To a varying degree, research relating to cooperation matters continues to be undertaken by most organizations concerned and the results are published regularly. Since the establishment of COPAC, a certain part of the studies are carried out by this jointly supported body.

2. The Role of UN Agencies in Providing International Fora for the Debate of Problems Relating to Co-operatives

In this context, it is not possible to give an exhaustive list of all the international conferences and meetings relating to co-operatives which have been held in the different regions of the world, nor of the reports and studies which were presented to them. It is, however, worth mentioning that many of these meetings are jointly organized by several UN agencies or in close collaboration between them. As early as 1949, the FAO and the ILO held a joint meeting in Lucknow, India, on agricultural co-operatives and joint farming co-operatives. In 1989, UNIDO had its first consultation on Small and Medium-Scale Enterprises including Co-operatives in which the ILO participated. The UN organized in Moscow, in May 1987, a seminar on the role of government in promoting the co-operative movement in developing countries. A truly co-operative effort was the organization of an International Symposium on Food Aid and Co-operatives in September 1988 in Vienna, jointly by COPAC and the World Food Programme with the financial assistance of the Government of Norway. As mentioned above, ILO Recommendation No. 127 was the outcome of discussions at the ILO General Conferences in 1965 and 1966. An ILO meeting of experts held in 1969 undertook a first review of the impact of the Recommendation. A further examination took place at another co-operative expert meeting in April 1993 which recommended a revision of this recommendation with a view to make it applicable at a global level and not only to developing countries, and to strengthen the division of responsibilities between the state and co-operatives. Other important issues discussed at that expert meeting included the role of co-operatives in the promotion of employment and income in the rural and informal sectors and the role of human resources development in the economic viability, efficient management and democratic control of co-operatives. The situation of co-operatives on a whole continent was reviewed by the ILO's Seventh African Regional Conference which met in Harare in late 1988. The basis of the discussion was a report on the status of co-operatives in Africa (→ *Development, Africa*; → *Development, Northern Africa*). The Conference adopted a set of conclusions for the attention of African member States of the ILO and a resolution which, amongst other things, called on the ILO to reinforce its technical cooperation activities for the promotion of co-operatives in Africa.

3. Technical Cooperation for Co-operative Development

As the co-operative idea and practice began spreading in the developing countries of Africa, Asia and Latin America (→ *Development, South Asia*; → *Development, South-East Asia*; → *Development, Latin America*), the specialized agencies of the United Nations were increasingly called upon to advise and assist in the establishment and management of co-operative associations. Technical assistance became, in fact, the principal instrument of the UN family for co-operative promotion. In the case of the ILO, the first advisory mission was undertaken in Morocco in 1937 to assist the Government in preparing a co-operative law. Such advisory missions of ILO and FAO specialists and the assignment of resident experts became a regular feature from the early 1950s, financed mostly by UNDP and its predecessor institutions (EPTA and the Special Fund).

The assistance rendered by ILO experts to governments and the co-operative movements related mainly to the following:

- the preparation or revision of co-operative laws and regulations;
- the organization and operation of administrative services responsible for the promotion and supervision of co-operatives;
- the organization and structure of co-operative movements (establishment of co-operatives, their unions, federations or specialised apex organizations);
- strengthening the management capacity of co-operatives and their secondary organizations (including consultancy services to help solve particular problems);
- co-operative education and training and the establishment of specialized institutions for these purposes.

Several thousand expert missions or assignments have concerned one or the other of these fields. In the case of FAO, there would clearly be a strong bias towards agricultural, fishing and forestry co-operatives and their specific technical problems. In larger technical assistance projects of that agency, there is often a combination of expertise, i.e. agronomic and economic functions supplemented by assistance in setting up farmers' associations such as co-operatives.

Agricultural credit, co-operative supply of inputs and marketing or produce, co-operative farming and livestock raising etc., have received the particular attention of FAO. This assistance is usually directed at specific problems and can lead to large-scale capital investment in agriculture. Finding answers to the problems of the smallest and poorest farmers is stressed through policies and programmes that promote integrated rural development – through the cultivation of food and fodder crops, animal husbandry, small-scale fisheries and forest industries, either individually or jointly – for greater food production and economic self-reliance.

The World Conference on Agrarian Reform and Rural Development (1979) and its Programme of Action strengthened the focus of FAO's work on people and their participation through their organizations in the development process and led to the establishment of the People's Participation Programme. PPP's main emphasis is on the formation of small, informal, self-reliant groups of the rural poor as part of a longer-term strategy to build institutions serving their interests. These groups allow members to engage in new income-generating activities, serve as receiving mechanisms for development services and provide a voice for members in dealing with local authorities. Other UN agencies similarly promote co-operatives in the sectors falling within their particular mandate. This applies particularly to industrial co-operatives (→ *Joint-production Co-operatives*; → *Production Co-operatives*) in the case of UNIDO and low-cost housing co-operatives which are supported by UNCHS (→ *Housing Societies*).

As an organization concerned with the social advancement of working people, the ILO has a clear mandate to promote co-operative self-help enterprises. ILO's activities, therefore, embrace all areas which are of interest to all types of co-operatives, such as co-operative legislation, organizational structure, management development, education and training. All possible variations can be found in the form of assistance given. Sometimes requests can be satisfied by sending a staff member to provide ad hoc advice, in other cases small teams of specialists are fielded on longer assignments. But there are also cases where projects are sustained for several years to assist and advise in a number of technical fields. In most projects, the human resources development element is dominant, with many activities oriented towards the education of members and the training of officers and managerial personnel (→ *Education and Training*). Often the international experts assist in the establishment and operation of specialized co-operative colleges or training institutions. In support of their overall co-operative training programmes, both the FAO and the ILO have developed global or regional approaches and structures for improved methodologies and training materials. The FAO created, in collaboration with other institutions, a programme for the development of Appropriate Management Systems for Small Farmers' Agricultural Co-operatives (AMSAC) whose principal objective is the mobilisation of unused resources for increased production of food crops, increase of productivity and improvement of the living conditions of small agricultural producers (→ *GACOPEA*). This objective is to be reached through the formation and establishment of an integrated co-operative management system with vertical and horizontal linkages. The training of co-operative managers who can perform as development entrepreneurs and the development of the capacity to diversify economic activities on the basis of the opportunities available in rural areas. Through its projects and advisory functions, FAO provides assistance to governments in policy and programme formulation and in the implementation of activities included in national co-operative development policies.

As its major instrument for co-operative training, the ILO has developed → *MATCOM* (Materials and Techniques for Co-operative Managerial Training). It came into existence in 1978 and at present operates in about 60 countries. It is based at the UN Centre in Vienna. It has developed training material for almost every economic activity of co-operatives, translated partially into 38 different local languages. Some countries have based their co-operative training activities largely on MATCOM materials and methods. Countries are assisted by specially trained junior experts and national liaison officers who work in close cooperation with MATCOM headquarters. In order to help countries in South and South East Asia to achieve a professionalisation of co-operative management, the ILO operated with financial support of the government of Norway a regional project entitled: Setting Effective Co-operative Training Policies and Standards. This project has greatly contributed to the creation of awareness for the need of manpower planning for the co-operative sector and the transfer of training functions from government institutions to the co-operative movement.

These few examples show that the types of technical cooperation projects in the co-operative field, undertaken by the UN agencies, seek to respond to the changing needs and the challenges faced by co-operatives. A dynamic concept and innovative approaches are particularly important in dealing with the problems resulting from effects of structural adjustment policies which many developing countries are compelled to implement. The breakdown of certain services formerly provided by governments or parastatal organizations and the need to protect the weaker strata of the population from the impact of austerity measures put great demands on economic self-help institutions such as co-operatives.

An example of a project designed to respond to such challenges is ILO's ACOPAM project (Appui Coopératif aux Activités de Développement assistées par le Programme Alimentaire Mondial en zone soudano-sahélienne). This large-scale multi-country project operates in six countries of West Africa and consists of 15 sub-projects. It started its activities in 1978 and is now preparing for its fourth phase. Its approach is characterised by the fact that it gives priority to activities which can satisfy the basic needs of the most vulnerable populations but is at the same time looking for longer-term solutions which are compatible with the macro-economic and environmental conditions and constraints. An important aspect of its work is the promotion of such activities which the beneficiaries will be able to manage themselves. It, therefore, puts special emphasis on education, training and organization of the beneficiaries in order to contribute to the social dynamics of self-reliance. In its work it adopts a methodological approach to learning from experimenting at the local level while adopting the know-how for replication under similar conditions. Within this overall approach, activities for sub-projects are identified and developed in close cooperation with the target groups and national authorities. While the tasks vary from country to country, they can be viewed within the context of the economic and social conditions prevailing in this sub-region. In general terms, they strive to attain self-sufficiency in food by increasing and diversifying agricultural production and achieving food security by irrigation management, improvement of storage and markets. Thus, the principal aim is the better utilization of existing infrastructures and the development of local human, natural and financial resources. The ACOPAM sub-projects seek to contribute to these objectives by strengthening participation and the productive capacity of the poor. Up to now, ACOPAM promoted the self-management of groups for cereal banks, seed stores, village consumers' shops, village dispensaries, irrigation schemes and drilling of wells, cotton markets and cereal mills. The individual sub-projects are developed with the active participation of the population in the identification of target groups who also decide about activities on the basis of their priority needs. At the beginning stands a process of self-organization of the beneficiaries in order to manage the new economic activities. This process is supported through education, literacy campaigns and training programmes. Only when the management of an economic activity is ensured are diversifications planned.

ACOPAM as a whole tries to link as much as possible with other agencies and organizations in order to share the experiences gained and eventually cooperate in the execution of activities. Close collaboration with the World Food Programme (WFP) has made it possible to use food aid for pump-priming a self-reliant process for increasing production, incomes and food security of the target group. Other partners of this project, which is financed by Norway, range from multi-lateral institutions such as UNDP, UNCDF, World Bank to bilateral agencies, other ILO-projects and non-governmental organizations. The dialogue and cooperation with international and sub-regional bodies and national policy-makers constitute an essential dimension of the project. The two-pronged approach, which establishes linkages and feed-backs between experience at the grass-roots level and policies at macro-level, characterizes a new concept in development assistance which takes into account past experiences from project work and the evaluation of such activities.

The → *evaluation* of the impact of international assistance to co-operative development is obviously an important aspect of technical cooperation itself. The FAO has played a certain pioneering role developing methodologies for the evaluation of agricultural co-operatives (*Dülfer* 1974, 1981; *Hanel* 1977). The ILO has established a system of project design which facilitates an on-going monitoring and expert evaluation of technical assistance projects. The ILO's Governing Body in turn has monitored the progress of operational activities in the field of co-operatives by carrying out a major review of the programme implemented between 1969 and 1983. More recently, COPAC has undertaken to carry out work on evaluation of co-operative projects.

Most of the technical assistance projects executed by UN agencies in the co-operative field are based on requests received through government channels. An important role in the preparation and the implementation of such projects is played by UNDP, which coordinates and often finances the interventions of UN organizations. Sometimes, project proposals originate also from sectoral review missions undertaken by the different agencies. The ILO, FAO and the International Co-operative Alliance have in recent years jointly undertaken such diagnostic missions in some African countries and the ILO has carried out co-operative country surveys for the World Bank. For such missions, use is made of the specialized outposted regional co-operative advisers who are also available on request to provide advice and direct assistance to individual government agencies or co-operative organizations. While UNDP remains the main funding source for technical cooperation carried out by UN organizations, a substantial number of co-operative projects executed by the ILO are funded through arrangements with individual donor countries.

In conclusion it can be considered that programmes for the promotion of co-operatives and technical assistance projects for their support fit very well into the anti-poverty and basic needs oriented development strategies which are pursued by several UN agencies. Under the influence of structural adjustment policies with the accompanying liberalization and privatization of trade and services, co-operatives are assuming an increasingly important role. This trend is confirmed by the increasing number of requests for assistance in training, operational counsultancies, and legislation. Many developing countries are currently revising their co-operative legislation in order to adapt it to changed conditions. The ILO is not only actively involved in such exercises there but it also assists countries in Central and Eastern Europe to adjust co-operative laws and regulations to the requirements of a market economy.

Bibliography

Colombain, Maurice: Cooperation: A Workers' Education Manual, ILO Geneva 1956.
COPAC/WFP: Food Aid and Co-operatives for Development, Report of the International Symposium on Food Aid and Co-operatives, Rome 1988.
COPAC: Consolidated Report: COPAC member activities in support of co-operatives in developing countries, Rome 1987 (and previous reports).
COPAC: Rural Co-operatives in World Bank assisted projects and some relevant development issues, Rome 1986.
Dülfer, Eberhard: Operational Efficiency of Agricultural Co-operatives in Developing Countries, FAO, Rome 1974.
Dülfer, Eberhard: Guide to Evaluation of Co-operative Organizations in Developing Countries, FAO Rome 1981.
Economic Commission for Africa: Report of the Expert Consultation on the Role of Rural co-operatives in the productive Sectors in Africa, Addis Ababa 1985.
FAO: Agricultural Credit through Co-operatives and other institutions, Rome 1965.
FAO: Co-operatives and Land Use, Agricultural Development Paper No. 61, Rome 1957.
FAO: Training and Extension in the Co-operative Movement, Paper No. 74, Rome 1962.
ICA: Review of International Cooperation, ICA/UN Historical Collaboration, vol. 83, No. 1, Geneva 1990.

IFAD: The Role of Rural Credit Projects in Reaching the Poor, Oxford 1985.

ILO: Co-operative Management and Administration, 1960, Second (revised) edition, Geneva 1988.

ILO: Co-operatives. A Review of co-operative development in the African region: Scope, impact and prospects. Seventh African Regional Conference, Harare, November-December 1988, Report III, Geneva 1988.

ILO: Conclusions concerning Co-operatives and Resolution on the Promotion of the Co-operative Movement in Africa, Official Bulletin, Vol. LXXII, Series A, No. 3, Geneva 1989.

ILO: International Directory of Co-operative Organizations, 13th Edition, Geneva 1988.

ILO: Recommendation No. 127 Concerning the Role of Co-operatives in the Economic and Social Developing Countries, Geneva 1966.

ILO: Review of ILO Operational Activities in the Field of Co-operatives, Governing Body, Committee on Operational Programmes, Geneva 1985.

ILO: Setting Effective Co-operative Training Policies in South and South-East Asia, Report on a Regional Symposium, Chiang Mai, Thailand, 17–21 November 1986, Bangkok 1987.

ILO: The Co-operative Movement and the ILO in: Co-operative Information, Geneva 1969.

ILO: The Role of Co-operatives in the Economic and Social Development of Developing Countries, International Labour Conference 1965 and 1966, Reports VII (1), VII (2), IV (1) and IV (2).

Oakley, Peter: The Monitoring and Evaluation of Participation in Rural Development, FAO, Rome 1988.

Sabry, Omar: Agricultural and Rural Co-operatives in Africa, FAO's Experience and Outlook, Seminar on Donor Support for the Promotion of Rural Co-operatives in Developing Countries, World Bank, Washington 1990.

Silberman, Murray: The Role of Co-operatives in the Production, Marketing and Consumption of Food, UN Center for Social Development and Humanitarian Affairs, Vienna 1986.

UN: Activities within the United Nations System dealing with Co-operatives, Social Development Newsletter, No. 22, January-June 1985.

UNRISD: A Review of Rural Cooperation in Developing Areas, Geneva 1969.

UNRISD: Rural Co-operatives as Agents of Change – a research report and a debate, Geneva 1975.

von Muralt, Jürgen: Co-operative Issues and Policies: Legislation, Entrepreneurship, Training, Co-operative Perspective, Vol. 24, No. 2, July-September 1989.

von Muralt, Jürgen: The ILO's Approach to Co-operative Promotion and Development, Seminar on Donor Support for the Promotion of Rural Co-operatives in Developing Countries, World Bank, Washington 1990.

Von Muralt, Jürgen: Self-help Organization, Rural Infrastructure and Food Security, in: H.U. Thimm/H. Hahn (eds.): Regional Food Security and Rural Infrastructure, Vol. 50 and 51, Schriften des Zentrums für regionale Entwicklungsforschung der Justus-Liebig-Universität Gießen, Münster-Hamburg 1993.

Watkins, W.P.: The International Co-operative Alliance 1895–1970, London 1970.

Walras, Léon (1834–1919) and Pareto, Vilfredo (1848–1923)

THOMAS BROCKMEIER

(see also: *Classic and Neo-classic Contributions; Marshall; Mill*)

I. Léon Walras; II. Vilfredo Pareto.

I. Léon Walras

As were → *John Stuart Mill* and *John Maynard Keynes*, *Léon Walras* was the son of an economist. In all three cases, the fame of the son exceeded that of the fathers. To some, his "Eléments d'Économie Politique Pure" is the towering achievement of all economics. Today, *Walras* (as one of the three "Great Marginalists" – *W.Stanley Jevons* and *Carl Menger* being the other two) is regarded the founder of the modern theory of general economic equilibrium.

Walras was born on 16 December 1834 in Evreux, France, and christened Marie Esprit Léon. His father, *Antoine Auguste Walras*, had been a secondary school teacher before becoming professor of philosophy at the Royal Colleges in Lille and in Caen. The economic writings of *Antoine A. Walras* "...received some limited attention, chiefly because some of his views and economic concepts influenced his son, Léon" (*Walker* 1987, pp. 851/852).

In 1854, after having received the bachelier-ès-lettres (1851) and the bachelier-ès-sciences (1853) from the Lycée of Douai, *Léon Walras* entered the School of Mines of Paris. "(But) finding the course of preparation of an engineer not to his liking, he gradually abandoned his academic studies in order to cultivate literature, philosophy and social science. Although those efforts resulted in a short story and a novel ("*Francis Sauveur*" 1858)..., it rapidly became apparent to him that his true interests lay with social science" (*Walker* 1987, p.852). So, in the late 1850s, *Walras* decided to follow his father's request to devote himself to economics.

From 1859 to 1862, he worked as a journalist for the Journal des Economistes in Paris, and in 1860 he published "L'Economie politique et la justice", confuting the normative economic doctrines of *Proudhon*. In 1865, he became managing director of a co-operative association bank and gave lectures on co-operative associations. From 1866 to 1868, he (together with *Jean Baptiste Say*) co-edited and published the journal Le Travail, a review largely devoted to the co-operative movement (*Walker* 1987).

During the 1860s, *Walras* unsuccessfully tried to obtain an academic appointment in France. In 1870, however, his appointment to an untenured professorship of economics at the Academy (later University) of Lausanne was secured by *Louis Ruchonnet*, a Swiss politician whom he had met during a congress on taxation in Lausanne ten years before. In 1871, he was made a tenured professor of economics in Lausanne, a position he held until his retirement in 1892.

Walras' professional life can be divided into the study on pure theory, economic policies, and normative goals. Among his most important writings are "Théorie mathématique de la richesse sociale: quatre mémoires" (1877), "Eléments d'économie politique pure; ou théorie de la richesse sociale" (two parts: 1874 and 1877), "Etudes d'économie sociale" (1896), "Etudes d'économie appliquée" (1898), and "Equations de la circulation" (1899).

More than a mathematician, *Walras* was a land reformer, even something of a socialist (but he rejected, on theoretical grounds, the *Marxist* theory of value). As a practical reformer, he contemplated a good deal of state intervention in order to improve the effectiveness of resource allocation in cases when the market mechanism did not work well. (Among his wishes or requests, respectively, were the restriction of working hours, compulsory education, and curbs upon monopoly.)

Walras' contribution to economics can hardly be overestimated. In the late 1860s, when he seriously began his research, economics in continental Europe were hardly more than a mixture of normative prescriptions. In England, through the works of →*John Stuart Mill*, matters had gone further, but were also lacking a clear view of the relationships of distribution and production as well as a theory of supply and demand in multiple markets. *Walras* constructed or refined many of the fundamental building blocks of modern economic theory. Furthermore, he developed the idea of the general equilibrium of the economic system (his conception being the economy as a whole) and implemented it through devising a system of equations, thereby providing the substantial beginning for the mathematical analysis of the interrelations of all parts of the economy.

As to his influence, *Walras* felt neglected by several economists – → *Alfred Marshall* being a case in point. But others, such as *Vilfredo Pareto*, borrowed many ideas from him and, through their own publications, worked on their widespread dissemination. *Walras* was given recognition even in the USA, where he was made a honorary member of the American Economics Association in 1892.

Walras's personal life was somewhat unconventional: In the late 1850s, he formed a common law union with *Célestine Aline Ferbach*, who had a son by a previous marriage. "(She) and *Walras* had twin daughters in 1863, one of whom died in infancy. In 1869 he married Célestine, thereby legitimizing their daughter...and adopted Célestine's son" (*Walker* 1987, pp.852/853). In 1879, being 45 years of age, Célestine died. Five years later, *Walras* married *Léonide D. Mailly*. But this marriage also did not last too long: Léonie died in 1900. This further loss left *Walras* disconsolate, spending the last years of his life almost in isolation at his home in Clarens, close to Lausanne, where he died on 5 January 1910.

II. Vilfredo Pareto

1. General Remarks

Pareto was *Walras'* successor in the chair of Political Economy in Lausanne. He extended the general economics of his predecessor, but he avoided everything to continue *Walras'* reformist politics. Being an aristocrat and a pessimist, *Pareto* found no unilateral progress in history and, in contrast to →*Marshall*, he stressed the conflict and hostility in social affairs. These misantropic observations became systematisized by his massive sociological investigations.

2. Education and Early Professional Life

Pareto was born in Paris on 15 July 1848. His father was a civil engineer, who after 1852, when the family had moved to Italy, tought accounting and agricultural economics at the Leardi Technical School in Genoa. Vilfredo was a gifted child who studied Greek and Latin and attented classes in mathematical physics at an early age. In November 1864, *Pareto* entered the University of Turin, enrolling in mathematical sciences. Three years later, after having received his degree in mathematical and physical sciences, he enrolled at the engineering school, receiving his doctorate in 1870.

In the early seventies of the nineteenth century, *Pareto* worked as an engineer for several companies and published articles in support of free trade, fighting against protectionism, custom duties, and subsidies in industry. (He became one of the founders of the *Adam Smith Society*, an institution aiming at spreading and preserving the doctrine of economic liberalism.) He wanted to prevent any form of state intervention in economic activity since he believed social legislation to be a sure way to waste money and wealth, slowing down the accumulation of capital.

In the late seventies and early eighties of the nineteenth century, *Pareto* traveled to several European countries (Belgium, France, Germany, and Switzerland), searching for capital and technical assistance to improve the competitiveness of the industrial plant he, as the technical director, was responsible for since 1875.

3. Academic Career as an Economist

Despite all his efforts *Pareto* could not modernize the plant and so, in July 1890, he left the company to spent all his time studying, becoming interested in the application of mathematics to political economy.

Shortly after, he met *Maffeo Pantaleoni* who advised him to read the works of his teacher *Walras* whom *Pareto* then met himself in September 1890. In the meantime, *Pareto* continuously published articles harshly criticizing the Italian government for its economic policy. Because most of these articles – particularly "L'Italie économique" (Oct. 1891) – were so fiercely liberalist, a storm of protest was unleashed and a sharp controversy arose (without changing *Pareto's* mind, of course...).

In 1891, several of *Pareto's* theoretical articles on pure economics were published, establishing his reputation as one of the leading Italian figures in economics. In this situation, *Pareto* then being at the forefront of the field of the new economic theories, *Pantaleoni* heard of *Walras'* plans to give up his chair in Lausanne and recommended *Pareto* as his successor. So, in April 1893, *Pareto* was appointed associate professor of Political Economy at the University of Lausanne, becoming a full professor in April 1894.

His first book, the "Cours d'économie politique" (1896/1897), "...contains an exposition of economic theory illustrated with numerous empirical facts. The theory is presented in a more precise and refined way than that of his intellectual predecessor *Walras* and the emphasis is consistently and unequivocally on the interdependence of economic phenomena and the idea of general equilibrium." (*Kirman*, p.804)

"One of *Pareto's* major contributions has long been considered as that, even though utility may not be measureable, an ordinal notion is sufficient for the construction of equilibrium theory" (*Kirman*, p.805). Another important contribution was the famous analysis of 'indifference curves' *Pareto* developed in his "Manuel d'économie politique" (1909) – in contrast to the approach of *Egdeworth*. It was also in this "Manuel", that he established the so-called 'first theorem of welfare economics'. But of "...all *Pareto's* contributions to economics, it is (the) notion of ...efficieny or ('Pareto-)optimality' that has made the greatest impact. The real insight that *Pareto* had was that his notion of efficiency or optimality was independent of all institutional arrangements and of all distributional considerations" (*Kirman*, p.806)

4. Pareto and Socialism

In 1893, *Pareto* published his refutation of *Marx's* theory of value, starting widespread debates and criticism in socialist magazines. Interestingly, despite these controversies, *Pareto* believed the socialists to

be more honest than others, particularly the conservatives and those in government.
In one important chapter of his "Cours d'économie politique", he analyzed the distribution of income, concluding "that the stratification imposed by the distribution of wealth in a society has in fact changed very little over time. A different distribution of wealth would not solve the overall problem of actual social divisions, neither would it improve the conditions of mobility between classes and social levels. This phenomenon ... is known as *Pareto's Law*" (*Busino*, p.801). *Pareto* did not have faith in progress and believed history to be "a mechanical sequence of events...because man remains the same. Repetitions and cyclical recurrences are therefore inevitable. He even broke with liberalism in believing that most individuals in a civilized society are the opposite of the theoretical rational homo oeconomicus." (*Busino*, p.801)
Pareto continued studying socialist doctrines and, in 1902 and 1903, he published "Les systèmes socialistes" in which he critized any doctrine solely based on reason, liberalism being a case in point. "*Pareto* maintained that socialism took advantage of the desire which every man has of transcending his own state,..., of living in a better world. In brief, socialism mobilized new energies. Liberalism calls on reason; socialism plays on feelings. And since feeling is at the root of all human action, socialism is politically more effective than liberalism." (*Busino*, p.802)

5. Pareto as a Sociologist

In 1905, *Pareto* published his "Manuale d'économica politica". Although homo oeconomicus was still the focal point of this book it ended as follows (*Busino*, p.802): "Whoever wants to make a scientific study of the social facts has to take account of reality and not of abstract principles and the like.... In principle, men act in an nonlogical way, but they make believe that they are acting logically."
As a result, *Pareto* gave up economics, exclusively concentrating on sociology, since he believed it to be of major importance for understanding (the two-sided) human behaviour -logical and nonlogical action- and for providing a sound basis to economics (*Busino*).
In 1916, five years after his retirement, he published his famous "Trattato di sociologia generale", according to which "there is no scientific solution to the problem of human behaviour, to the problem of social order or to the problem of socio-political organization. Democracy, socialism, liberalism, human rights, justice and liberty are all abstract notions, ... just like all revolutionary beliefs. Revolutionaries promise to change everything... . No sooner have they gained power than they create a society which does not have anything to do with what they promised before the revolution. ...social heterogeneity does not exist...(except for the) one fundamental barrier, that which exists between the masses and the elite. The elite... is always deprived of power by another elite, who may speak on behalf of the ...exploited. History is therefore the history of elites who alternate in the position of command." (*Busino*, p.803) To *Pareto*, this "circulation of elites" was the main characteristic of any society.
"Even after having resigned from his chair (in 1911), he remained on very good terms with the University, which in 1917 organized formal celebrations in his honour. In 1922 he became a citizen of the free state of Fiume thus enabling him to divorce his first wife" (*Busino*, p. 803). *Pareto* died on 19 August 1923, just two months after he had married *Jeanne Regis*, the woman he had been living together for more than twenty years, in Celigny in the Swiss canton Geneva.

Bibliography

Busino, G.: Pareto, Vilfredo, in: The New Palgrave, Vol.3, London 1987, pp.799–803.
Eisermann, Gottfried: Vilfredo Pareto als Nationalökonom und Soziologe, Tübingen 1961.
Hamann, Rudolf: Paretos Elitentheorie und ihre Stellung in der neueren Soziologie, Stuttgart 1964.
Hoppe, Michael: Die klassische und die neoklassische Theorie des Genossenschaftswesens, Berlin 1976.
Kirman, A.P.: Pareto as an economist, in: The New Palgrave, Vol.3, London 1987, pp.804–808.
Schlieper, Ulrich: Pareto-Optima – Externe Effekte und die Theorie des Zweitbesten, Köln, Berlin, Bonn, München 1969.
Stavenhagen, Gerhard: Geschichte der Wirtschaftstheorie, Göttingen 1969.
Walker, Donald A.: Léon Walras in the light of his correspondence and related papers, in: Journal of Political Economy 78 (4), July-August 1970, pp. 685–701.
Walker, Donald A.: Walras, Léon in: The New Palgrave, Vol.4, London 1987, pp. 852–862.
Zauels, Günter: Paretos Theorie der sozialen Heterogenität und Zirkulation der Eliten, Stuttgart 1968.

Women and Co-operatives in Developing Countries

SABINE BECKER

(see also: *Development Policy; Self-help Organizations; Relationship Patterns; Group, the Co-operative*)

I. Introduction; II. Gender and Co-operatives; III. Women's Participation in Mixed Co-operatives; IV. Women's Co-operatives; V. Conclusions.

I. Introduction

Women's participation in co-operatives is surprisingly low, even though it differs with regard to various countries, types of co-operative, the co-operatives' degree of formality etc. Only few women are members and even less, often none, take part in the co-operatives' management and decision-making. The case of the Gambian Co-operative Produce Marketing Societies is typical where only 10% of the members are women (*Jallow*; p. 11) just as in agricultural co-operatives in Indonesia (Centre for Women Resources Development; p. 1). This is not a phenomenon specific to co-operatives but it reflects the subordinate position of women in our societies. However, in the case of co-operatives, women's low participation questions the co-operative principle of free membership and/or the appropriateness of this organizational form for women.

Lately, the women's role in mixed co-operatives has been increasingly a subject of discussion; in conferences, annual meetings, workshops of co-operative movements, and development agencies. Yet, in terms of research and practical action little has been done so far.

Still excluded from the mainstream access to resources, women in developing countries organize themselves more and more in co-operatives, formal and informal, to meet the increasing responsibility they have for their households' survival. Collectively, they provide credit and transport, undertake income-earning activities, and organize the marketing of their products- with more or less success.

The first part of this article gives a brief overview of the development of gender roles with reference to co-operatives. The second part evokes some co-operative inherent constraints to women's equal participation and asks whether co-operatives would profit from a higher participation of women and whether women would really benefit from participation in mixed co-operatives. The third part gives examples of women's co-operatives; their potential and their specific problems are highlighted.

II. Gender and Co-operatives

1. Modernization, Co-operatives, and Gender

In many developing countries, co-operatives based on the European model were imposed either by the colonial powers or later by the national governments as instruments to implement agricultural policy (→ *Development Policy*), to bring forward the modernization of agriculturual production, and to introduce and improve cash crop production (*Mayoux*) (→ *British–Indian Pattern*). This modernization of agricultural production has led to a decline in women's property rights and to a marginalization of farming women worldwide and co-operatives contributed to this process. Generally speaking, agricultural labour became divided in a way that men were increasingly involved in market production and therefore integrated in the cash economy while women's role in producing food for their families' subsistence was strengthened.

Furthermore, land reforms, settlement programmes, and changes through outside development assistance which aimed at a more egalitarian distribution of resources, have often reinforced the gender division of labour. Development projects meant to create new opportunities for access to land, to credit, to new agricultural technology, and extension services were oriented towards the male "breadwinner" and women were left out or expected to profit through a male parent (*Lamming*). Where land reforms took place, e.g. in Costa Rica, land titles were given almost exclusively to men even though both men and women had been involved in the previous political fight. Many of those new landowners formed co-operatives (*ICA, 1991*). Also the registration of land which recently started in some countries' agricultural adjustment and privatization process is to a large extent done in the name of the male head of household.

Yet, with regard to labour force utilization, co-operatives usually involve the whole family of their members (*Primera Conferencia Nacional, Peru*). Women contribute directly to co-operatives as unpaid family labour on co-operative land or in cash crop production but they often do not benefit directly from their work. In fact, women might even be adversely affected through the withdrawal of their time from other activities such as food production. While the mechanization of agricultural production lightens the labour burden of "men's tasks", women's work load even increases as increased hectarages have to be manually weeded and harvested (*Lwenje, Sala*).

The co-operative movements in developing countries have not been able to respond to the growing number of landless and of migrants entering the urban labour market. These masses and among them an extremely high percentage of women are forced to create their own employment and income in the informal sector while co-operatives exist so far mainly in the formal economy of urban areas.

2. Gender Roles

When discussing women's and men's socio-economic and political roles, the concept of "gender" is a useful tool. As compared to "sex" which refers to the biological difference of women and men, "gender" implies the differences between men and women which are determined by social, cultural, historical, and psychological conditions. By gender roles we mean learned behaviours in a given society, conditioning which activities, tasks, and responsibilities are considered male and female. In the following, some characteristics of women's gender role are highlighted which affect directly their opportunity to join mixed co-operatives.

Women's work consists on the one hand of unpaid, unregistered and, therefore, "invisible" housework, food preparation and child rearing aiming at the reproduction of the families' work force. On the other hand, women work in the "productive" sphere: in urban areas, they are engaged mostly in informal commerce, services, and small-scale manufacturing (e.g. textile); in rural areas, they are involved in cash crop production and they are often the main producers of food-crops. According to UN-estimates, women's contribution to the agricultural labour force represents to the production of stapelfood, 70% in Africa (*Holt, Ribe*).

Men are rather involved in productive market-oriented labour and they rarely contribute to the reproductive work of their household. This division of labour between men and women is not rigid, it changes over time and at different places. But while women are more flexible and step in for "men's duties" when needed, either by doing additional work or financially, men do not step in for "women's duties.". The gender division of labour leads to limited opportunities for women to join mixed co-operatives. First, given the co-operative orientation towards male-dominated activities, women and their respective productive and reproductive activities are to a large extent excluded from co-operative membership and action. Secondly, women's triple role as worker/farmer, mother, and home-carer leaves them less spare time than men and thereby limits their opportunities to participate in mixed co-operatives' activities which are not immediatiely remunerative (*Mayoux*).

Another crucial factor of restriction is women's lack of access to essential resources. In spite of the important role women play in the economy, they lack access to fertile land and water, to inputs like credit and tools, to institutional support, to know-how and to storage and marketing facilities much more than men. Women's work is still considered to be supplementary to men's and, therefore, they are expected to benefit through their husbands' or fathers' access to resources and income. This is especially difficult for female heads of households whose number is growing worldwide due to male landlessness, migration, unemployment, and social change (e.g. divorce). The percentage of men who are able to economically maintain their families is decreasing. Therefore, more and more women are left to be the main food provider for their families without having the necessary inputs.

In many countries, women's lack of access to means of production is cemented by national legislation which descriminates against them regarding wages, personal and property rights. Access to land for instance is a crucial problem for women in most developing countries.

The above mentioned characteristics of women's gender role (the division of labour, the lack of access to resources including land legal discrimination) result from the most fundamental reason for women's subordinate position in society and economy: their limited political power as compared to men's (*Staudt*). In society, in co-operatives and in the single household, women's power does not correspond at all to their economic and social responsibilities. This lack of power also leads to national development plans, agricultural policies, and legal provisions such as co-operative laws which do not reflect the needs of women.

Increasing women's power and influence in decision making is however closely linked to gaining access to education and training opportunities – education and training which is so far rather oriented to boys and men than to girls and women. Training for women if it exists is often limited to subjects reinforcing women's domestic role such as health and child care or to "traditional" female handicraft skills (knitting, sewing) for which there is no market (*Staudt*). What women need as well is training in management, in new skills to take up remunerative activities and in book-keeping.

III. Women's Participation in Mixed Co-operatives

1. Co-operative-Specific Constraints

Most co-operative laws do not discriminate against women directly; it is rather the conditions for membership as interpreted by men which exclude women (*Swedish Co-operative Centre*). In practice, most co-operatives accept only one person per family as a member to avoid that a family has more than one vote. This means also that co-operative services such as credit and training are oriented towards this one person. Most of the time it is the male "head of household" who becomes a member of a co-operative.

This rule is based on the idea of the Western family as a production unit with a common interest represented in public by the husband. In countries where the production unit is the household including various families, where men and women of the same family have separate productive activities and work on separate accounts and where men migrate while women are the de facto heads of household, family members might have diverging interests. An example of the Gambian Co-operative Production and Marketing Society shows that male members take loans from the co-operative to lend it on with additional interest to their wives. Loans and trade among couples are quite common in the Sahel (*Champagne*).

The exclusion of women in this regard could be avoided by extending co-operative membership to all those persons engaged in a certain economic activitiy or by creating the status of co-membership.

In the case of most agricultural co-operatives, membership depends on the property of land or usufructuary rights. Thereby, women, young men, and the growing number of landless farmers are excluded from the co-operatives to a large extent. In some countries, women are still not allowed by law to possess land (*Holt*; *Ribe*). The percentage of female members in agricultural co-operatives is lowest as compared to other types of co-operatives (such as consumer and financial co-operatives) even though their share in agricultural labour is high and in some regions even higher than that of men. To remove this restriction, the de facto usage of land or the work contribution could be used as a requirement for becoming a member instead of ownership of land.

Evidence from Côte d'Ivoire shows that female members in mixed co-operatives tend to let men make decisions whereas men are reluctant to share responsibility with women (*Cissoko*). Mixed co-operatives rarely permit women to develop leadership and management skills. In some districts of India, 20% of the existing dairy co-operatives are even managed by women. However, at the district level, women leaders are not respresented (*Kumari*). Legal structures need to be created to allow for women's representation at all levels, including decision-making. Provisions for quota-systems can be included in co-operative laws and by-laws which reserve a minimum number of seats for female members in the co-operatives' management committees like it is foreseen for the first Namibian co-operative law in 1992.

Furthermore, where the requirements to enter a co-operative are membership subscription or initial savings, poor women's opportunities of becoming full members in a mixed co-operative are restricted. Women dispose of less cash income than men to save money and the fact that women's responsibility for family needs even increase in situations of economic crisis hinders them to build up savings. Additionally, institutions in some countries, including credit unions and co-operative banks require a signature of a male or a "No Dues Certificate" in the husbands' name to enter into an agreement with a woman (*Kumari*).

Another constraining factor for women's membership in co-operatives is the orientation and planning of co-operative activities. Co-operatives' schedules for training, meetings, and work on co-operative land tend to ignore women's labour burden and, therefore, do not allow for their participation.

On the other hand, women might not wish to join a mixed co-operative for several reasons. In cases where co-operatives and their male members are very much controlled by the government, women might prefer to stay out or create their own more independent structures. Moreover, many agricultural co-operatives continue to be single purpose and oriented towards assistance to the production of cash crops and offer their services accordingly. For farming women who are involved in all kinds of productive activities in addition to their reproductive work, there might be no economic incentives to join the co-operative as it does not respond neither to their producer nor to their reproducer needs.

2. Co-operatives' Benefits from Women's Participation

Women's participation in co-operatives became a subject of discussion at a time when the sustainability of development assistance as a whole was questioned. With respect to co-operatives, assisted or not by development projects, many of them have not been able to significantly improve the economic and living situation of members and their families. Agricultural co-operatives still concentrate on the production of "traditional" export goods, while other needs of the members' households such as food production, processing, and marketing of other products than cash crops are not responded to by co-operative services. So far, government policies and structural adjustment programmes enhance this lack of flexibility by emphasizing export production. Presently, however, food security is increasingly difficult to obtain in many regions while incomes from cash crops export become more and more fragile. Including food production, to a large extent done by women, and other economic activitites such as craft production in the co-operatives' activities would help to improve the living standard of the members' households and stabilize the income of the co-operative. Only then would women have a real interest in joining mixed co-operatives.

The economic rationale for co-operative enterprises to open up for women is the fact that, due to market liberalizations, they have to be increasingly competitive. The economic performance of co-operatives depend, among other factors, on the full utilization of human resources and the productive potential of all persons involved. If women had access to co-operative services including training, credit, and infrastructure, they would be able to improve their productivity and as a consequence they would maximize the co-operatives' economic results.

Furthermore, in the field of financial services, women have proved to be interesting clients. In the "Union des Caisses d'Epargne et de Credit du Burkina Faso" only 25% of the members are female but 40% of the total savings in 1991/92 belong to them (Solagral Courrier de la Planete). Credit unions and co-operative banks have an economic interest in members/clients who are reliable and whose repayment rates are above average. Empirical evidence in many countries shows that these qualities are very much found in women.

In the process of structural adjustment, co-operatives in many countries emphasize democratic member participation and management instead of obligatory membership and State control. Free membership and democracy in co-operatives, however, is not serious without the participation of half of the working population, as members and in decision making.

3. Women's Benefits from Membership in Mixed Co-operatives

Participation in mixed co-operatives can improve women's economic position as well as their political influence. According to *Moser's* distinction of practical and strategic gender needs, co-operatives can respond to both, women's practical needs, i.e. what they need to earn a livelihood (e.g. access to inputs) and their strategical needs which is reducing inequalities (*Moser*). Also, the Nairobi Forward Looking Strategy elaborated at the end of the UN women's decennium (1975–85) recommends the participation in co-operative organization, mixed or women only as means towards women's empowerment.

Membership in a mixed co-operative can respond to one of the most urgent economic (practical) needs women have, which is access to resources such as credit, land, water, tools, technology. Moreover, opportunities for marketing of products would significantly improve through organization. Women, by becoming members, would be able to make use of the already existing infrastructure of a co-operative. This is especially essential in those countries where co-operatives are the main channels for input distribution. In urban areas, participation in a mixed co-operative especially can improve women's access to the labour market, their job-security, and their working conditions. In countries where co-operatives are the only structures at village level offering education and training, membership is especially for women the only way to enjoy some formal → *education and training* .

The above mentioned advantages of joining a mixed co-operative such as access to and control over resouces, improved working conditions and training opportunities will help women to gain economic independence and self-esteem. Thereby their influence in the household's and in the community's decision making will increase. In addition to empowerment through economic advancement, co-operatives can be a direct tool and serve female members as a platform to express their economic and political problems and needs. Condition is however that the respective co-operative functions according to democratic principles. In fact, the application of participatory methods in mixed co-operatives should lead to internal democratization and emancipation of members, men and women.

IV. Women's Co-operatives

Many women groups and co-operatives emerged to respond to the situation of economic crisis prevailing in most developing countries; co-operative organization is especially for poor women the only way to obtain production inputs and make an income. Activities which are frequently taken up collectively are food processing, animal husbandry, vegetable gardening, and handicraft production. Other women co-operatives organized in times of structural adjustment programmes in order to substitute for former State services, e.g. in health or day care. And again other such as most women groups in rural West-Africa have been initiated by governments and development agencies to take up income earning activities and/or to reduce women's labour burden (cereal mills) (*Champagne*).

Women in many countries (Côte d'Ivoire, Nepal, Indonesia etc.) are rather organized in informal groups than in officially registered co-operatives. Often they are based on a long tradition of mutual aid such as the rotating savings assoiations ("tontine" in West-Africa, "dikuti" in Nepal) and rotating labor associations ("harambee" in Kenya) (*March, Taqqu*). One of the reasons women seem to prefer informal structures is that the transformation of an informal self-help group to a formal level tends to provoke a shift from female dominated to male dominated structures (Centre for Women Resources Development). Another explanation might be that administrative barriers to establish a co-operative are too high (Primera Conferencia Nacional Peru). From Côte d'Ivoire, it is reported that women are not aware of possible advantages of formal co-operatives (*Cissoco*).

The most famous examples of successful formal women's co-operatives derive from India. The Self Employed Women's Association, SEWA and the Working Women's Forum, WWF are best documented among them. In Nepal, where women are rare among the members of the formal agricultural co-operatives (*Sajhas*), recently more and more women groups and co-operatives emerged. Most of them start by saving collectively small amounts of money; when savings are high enough they give loans to each other permitting members to invest in productive activities. In the Andean region, Peru and Bolivia, women get organized in "Clubes de Madres" in order to improve their income situation. In Peru, the clubs' economic activities have been quite successful and even the husbands joined in to do work on the mother clubs' land. In Bolivia, organization is quite high and the clubs have formed a confederation. Unfortunately, the confederation seems to have moved away from its basis which is partly due to too much outside assistance by development agencies.

In principle, women co-operatives have to fulfill the same requirements as mixed co-operatives in order to survive in a competitive market. However, in addition to those general requirements, women co-operatives have some special attributes: they face specific problems but, at the same time, they seem to dispose of a strong potential.

1. Potential

Women groups are engaged in a large variety of activities. Some organize collectively certain areas of reproductive work such as child care or food preparation which has a time-saving effect for the members. Others, the majority, are involved in the productive sphere of women's work. Through co-operative organizations women and especially poor women largely improve their chances to obtain access to the production inputs as they need them. In the field of credit, most poor women cannot provide sufficient collateral towards banks to take up loans. With the group collateral, the women become more credible to the banks.

Participation in women groups not only increases women's ability to raise their proper income but it also helps to control and manage this income themselves. This usually has a positive impact on the living situation of the whole family as women tend to use their income according to their responsibilities mainly for their families' subsistence or for reinvestment and only to a lesser extent than men for social events. In several countries, e.g. Bangladesh, women co-operatives are reported to be economically more efficient than the male dominated mixed co-operatives (*ICA* 1992). Evidence from Côte d'Ivoire shows that women co-operatives are often more dynamic and that member participation tends to be higher as compared to mixed co-operatives (*Cissoko*).

Women co-operatives motivate women to solve their own problems regarding their work and help to break the social isolation some women might be in. As compared to mixed co-operatives, women in their own organization have more opportunities to gain experiences in leadership and management. They attain an improved self-perception and raise consciousness about their own rights, both of which women necessarily need before integrating into mixed co-operatives. Women increase their bargaining power in economic as well as in political terms. The Working Women's Forum (WWF) in India and other women's organizations from developing countries consider "empowerment" of women and awareness-building to be their priorities.

2. Problems

Women co-operatives in most countries are not strong enough to influence development policies and efforts, especially since separate apex-organizations at a national level do rarely exist. Therefore, women even when they are organized in groups run the risk of being marginalized by institutions and development organizations.

Beyond the general political pressure in some countries against popular movements, women who want to organize themselves often meet additional political hindrance by male political leaders or reluctance from male family members to varying degrees. In several countries, e.g. in Egypt, in Mali, and in Indonesia, governments attempt to integrate women groups into the national co-operative structure without giving them the right to develop their own legal entity.

A serious problem for women co-operatives is the phenomenon that as soon as economic activities undertaken by women become economically interesting and marketable, men tend to enter the respective sector and might even be able to take over with improved tools (*Lamming*). Examples from Nepal and West Africa illustrate this. In a Nepalese village (Sunkhani, Dolkha-District), a women group had applied for economic usage of a forest close to the village when village men became aware of the economic benefits, put pressure and obtained it instead. In West-Africa, vegetable gardening is predominantly done by women as long as it is for subsistence and local markets. As soon as production reaches the export level, men take over.

Depending on the social differentiation of the society and the degree of homogenity within a women's co-operative, class differences create conflicts like in any mixed co-operative. Women from the poorer strata of the population might be dominated by middle or higher class women, e.g. wives of partly leaders and women from higher casts or "noble" families who are likely to take over the leading roles in a women group. This is especially true for groups and co-operatives which have been organized from outside. In Nepal, women are obliged to respect the cast system and join groups and co-operatives with women of their own cast.

Many co-operatives, whether mixed or women, only suffer from management problems. However, due to lack of education, of appropriate training opportunities, little spare time and less experience with management than men, women co-operatives and groups are often especially affected. The high illiteracy-rate, mainly of rural women, forces women co-operatives to rely on outsiders for the administrative work (*Kumari*). Especially smaller and more informal women groups run the risk of not being able to really improve women's income situation or to provide regular employment. It has been reported also from some women co-operatives that participation mainly lead to additional working hours, to increased labour burden and, therefore, to self-exploitation (ICA Bangladesh 1992). The low level of formalization of most women's groups contributes to a lack of credibility in the eyes of male dominated formal bureaucracies.

V. Conclusions

The question whether it is more appropriate for women to integrate into mixed co-operatives or to form separate women groups and co-operatives, formal or informal, can only be answered by taking into account each particular situation, women's needs and interests, the economic activities of women and men, and the division of labour between them. In practice, women often opt for separate women co-operatives as those might permit them to build up organizational and management capacity first and to increase their bargaining power before joining a mixed co-operative.

Mixed co-operatives, however, ought to have a strong economic and political interest in attracting more women as members since this would enhance their performance with regard to democratic member participation, diversification of productive activities and the full use of resources, all of which are closely linked to women's participation in co-operatives.

To increase the membership of women in mixed co-operatives, changes need to take place in several fields:

a) Legislation

Legal arrangements have to be made to ensure that women participate as members, in management, and in decision making according to their numerical strength. Membership in co-operatives needs to be redefined:

- to enable and encourage more than one household member to join a co-operative and
- to allow for membership without having to own private property.

b) Human Resources Development

In co-operative training courses (including management, accountancy, technical skills etc.), quota-systems should be used which provide for a minimum of female participants per course: this would accelerate the slow process of increasing women's participation, enable women to better influence decision-making and attract women for membership.

Gender Awareness Training should become part of co-operatives' member education programmes in order to raise men's and also women's consciousness about gender roles and their consequences in society and economy. Co-operative training centers in the cities might not at all be accessible to rural women; instead, mobile training teams should go to the rural areas and provide training there.

Gender-sensitive training material has to be developed; so far, most training materials used in co-operatives are oriented towards male members. Adequately qualified personnel and more female co-operative extension officers need to be promoted as a pre-condition for improvement of women's participation in co-operatives.

c) Economic Activities

Co-operatives need to be more flexible in responding to the changing needs of current and potential members by diversifying their services and promoting the production of "non-traditional" products. Thus, co-operatives would improve their economic performance and women, who are involved in a large variety of reproductive and income-earning activities would have an interest in becoming members.

Co-operatives should become active with regard to households' reproductive tasks, which are so far mainly executed by women. Infrastructures could be established, e.g. day care services and improved water supply systems, and labour saving technologies could be introduced.

d) Research

Co-operatives and their apex-organizations should reorient their research activities in a way that women and their respective activities and needs are covered as well.

Bibliography

Archives de Sciences Sociales de la Cooperation et du Developpement: Economies Sociales ... au feminin, Jan.-March 1987, Paris, Bureau d'Etudes Cooperatives et Communautaires.

Centre for Women Resources Development: Study on Potential Partners for the Women's Component of the ILO Co-operative Project, Jakarta 1991.

Champagne, Suzanne: Cooperation Feministe et Pouvoir des Femmes au Sahel, Quebec 1991.

Cissoko, Alain: Integration de la Femme dans le Mouvement Cooperatif en Côte d'Ivoire, Abidjan 1990, ILO Project Report "Appui à la Consolidation et la Restructuration des Cooperatives de Commercialisation".

Dean, Susan: Women in Cooperatives, COPAC 1985.

Department Social R.I.: Study on Women Groups/Women Cooperative Activities, Report for ILO Co-operative Project, Jakarta 1991.

Desroche, Henri (ed.): Femmes, Entreprises et developpements, Oulessebougou (Mali), 21–27 January 1988, International Cooperative University.

Holt, Sharon/Ribe, Helena: Developing Financial Institutions for the Poor: A Focus on Gender Issues, Washington 1990 (draft for the World Development Report on Poverty).

International Co-operative Alliance: Bases para una Strategia de Integracion, Santiago 1991.

Jallow, Jufe Manneh: Role of Women in Development of Horticultural Cooperative Activities in The Gambia, July 1992, ILO and UNDP.

Lacher, Christine: Das Selbsthilfepotential von indonesischen Frauengenossenschaften, Marburg 1990, Marburg Consult.

Lamming, G.N.: Women in Agricultural Cooperatives; Constraints and Limitations to Full Participation, Rome, 1983, FAO.

Lwenje, Ndimanye/Sala, Maija: Women Participation in Co-operative Development in the International Cooperative Alliance, Regional Office for East, Central and Southern Africa: An Analysis and Practical Proposal, Finland 1991, Oy Kosana LTD Consulting.

March, Kathryn S./Taqqu, Rachelle L.: Women's Informal Associations in Developing Countries: Catalysts for Change? London 1986, Westview Press/Boulder.

Mayoux; Linda (ed.): All Are Not Equal – African Women in Cooperatives, London 1988, Conference Report, Institute for African Alternatives (10.–11– Sept.).

Meghji, Zakia: Women Involvement in Economic Develop-

ment in Developing Countries; The Case for Co-operatives in East, Central and Southern Africa, Moshi-Tanzania 1980, ICA-Regional Office for East and Central Africa.
Moser, Caroline: Gender Planning in the Third World: Meeting Practical and Strategic Gender Needs; in: World Development 1989, 17,II.
NN.: Regional Consultation on Gender Integration and Women in Co-operative Development, Sri Lanka, 27 April–2 May 1992, Different National Reports.
Primera Conferencia Nacional: La Mujer y el Movimiento Cooperativo, Lima, Peru, 20.–22.04.1990.
Sala, Maija: Women's Involvement in Cooperatives in Africa. Rationale and problems, in: Seminar Report on Rural Development and the Challenges to Cooperative Movements in Developing Countries, Helsinki, Finland, 5.–8. May 1992.
Schujman, Lon: La Participacion de la Mujer en el Movimiento Cooperativo International; Experiencias Regionales en el Sur de la America Latina, 1988, draft for the Interregional Consultant Meeting on Women in Co-operatives, Plovdiv, Bulgaria, 20–24 June 1988.
Instraw (United Nations International Research and Training Institute for the Advancement of Women): Implications for Development, Santo Domingo 1988, Report on International Consultative Meeting on Women in Co-operatives: Plovdiv, Bulgaria, 20–24 June 1988.
Swedish Cooperative Centre (SCC): Bring Women Into Co-operative Development, Stockholm 1989, Guidelines.
Staudt, Kathleen A.: Women's Organizations in Rural Development, Washington 1980, USAID, Office for Women in Development.

Worker Co-determination in Co-operatives

KLAUS BARTÖLKE

(see also: *Co-determination*; *Labour-Management*; *Legal Form, Co-operative*; *Promotion Mandate*; *Organizational Structure of Societies*)

I. Co-determination: A comparatively neglected Field in the Discussion on Co-operatives; II. Co-operative Associations and Worker Co-determination – Concepts and Intentions; III. Development of Co-operatives and the Relevance of Worker Co-determination; IV. Reflections on the Effects of Worker-co-determination and Participative Management in General.

I. Co-determination: A comparatively neglected Field in the Discussion on Co-operatives

Many co-operative associations have undergone a change that makes them similar to regular economic organizations (*Duhm; Springenberg/Jander*). Performance in economic terms for many becomes the main objective (*Purtschert*). This is associated with growth as regards sales and number of employees (*Hamm* 1990). Also, concentration, → *joint ventures*, and merging (→ *Mergers and Consolidations*) have not left the co-operative sector, untouched of the necessity to cope with the requirements of competing in a market economy (*Grosskopf*).

In a large number of co-operatives, therefore, employees have become a major element of organizational activities. Nevertheless, including employees into the framework for analyzing the reality of co-operatives remains the exception (*Männicke*) or even meets resistance if decision-making processes are concerned (see the arguments in *Beuthien* 1976, *Blomeyer/Painz* and *Stuchlik*). This phenomenon applies to most of the literature. Therefore, the following considerations are mainly conceptual, do not have a strong empirical basis, and rely on plausibility. They might apply as general theoretical guidelines across different societal conditions, although it cannot be denied that they are probably biased by the German legal situation where co-determination laws (→ *Co-determination*) do apply to co-operatives and therefore have initiated some discourses.

II. Co-operative Associations and Worker Co-determination – Concepts and Intentions

In order to understand the relationships, it appears to be appropriate to delineate basic properties of co-operatives and co-determination.
Considering co-operatives first, there is a vast variety of organizational forms coming under the heading of co-operatives (→ *Forms of Cooperation*). Here, the term co-operative refers to organizations (associations of members) that define their purpose as promotion and support of their members on a personal (one person – one vote) basis which might – although this is not a necessary condition – foster societal reforms in general and economic reforms in particular, for example the movement in the direction of a → *third way* between capitalism and communism.
The normative principles under which governance of co-operatives should be pursued, comprise self-help, → *solidarity* among members, democratic procedures for decision-making, freedom and equality among members and altruism (*Dülfer* 1984, *Engelhardt, Hettlage, Laurinkari/Brazda*). More specifically, for the legal construction of co-operative economic activities three principles have been formulated, namely voluntariness of membership, openness of the group, and equality among members (*Dülfer* 1984). The concrete form of institutional transformation of these → *principles* will depend on the regulations of company law in different countries (→ *Law, International*) (for the German case, see *Beuthien* 1990 → *Legal Form, Co-operative*).
Worker co-determination refers to any concept of governance of organizations which includes institutionalized opportunities for employees – workers without ownership rights as regards the organization on the basis of labor contracts which include regulations about expected contributions and offered in-

ducements, specifically about job duties and renumeration – to become involved in decision making. The form that → *co-determination* takes might vary. For example, there might be work councils and worker representatives in supervisory boards based on laws (the German case). There might be shop stewards acting in the context of collective bargaining. There might be direct negotiations of unions with corporate management on behalf of the employees of one organization (a summary of forms is provided by *Hettlage*). In any case, the term co-determination does not indicate, that existing governance institutions – like the executive board or a managerial board combined with a supervisory board or the management of an individual plant – are replaced. It rather indicates that they are supplemented by additional non-managerial, non-owner representatives and/or that organizational decision-making procedures are modified by the involvement of actors from the group of dependent salaried workers.

The reasons for such institutionalized inclusions of employees are manifold. They depend on legal, socio-cultural and economic factors (see *Dülfer* 1984, for a discussion of different legal systems) but will generally include the importance of human dignity and self-determination, the claim for equality between capital (property rights) and labour, the promotion of the democratic idea by transferring it into the economic sphere, and the control of economic power (→ *Organizational Structures, Co-operative*). Co-determination, thus, has a political connotation as it presumes the possibilty of differences in interests based on the existence or non-existence of ownership rights. It is political participation of employees as distinct from motivational participation that – via co-operative, participative leadership behavior or management concepts – tries to take into consideration the needs and expectations of individual employees and groups of employees with the aim of improving organizational performance. As such, the introduction of motivational participation, is in principle, voluntary, the institutionalization of political participation (co-determination), again in principle, obligatory (*Bartölke/Eschweiler/Flechsenberger/Palgi/Rosner*).

III. Development of Co-operatives and the Relevance of Worker Co-determination

Considering the kind of task and the immediacy of member-co-operative relationship, one can differentiate between primary co-operatives – e.g. rural producer, consumer trading, finance, housing, worker co-operatives – as well as secondary and tertiary co-operatives. In principle, members of secondary are primary and members of tertiary are secondary co-operatives. Secondary serve for the primary and tertiary for the secondary as support or superstructures. Whereas in primary co-operatives, the personal element prevails – for example in joint production co-operatives, ideally, all workers are members and all members are workers – in secondary and tertiary co-operatives, relationships become more abstract, more determined by immediate economic considerations. Combined with this phenomenon and the growing size of the organizations, including primary co-operatives, there are a growing number of employees as well as a professionalization of management. Managers might even no longer be members or, if they are, their membership only has a formal basis and is not connected with any consumption or production activity for which regular members search institutionalized support.

From a somewhat different perspective, this development can be described as a change from traditional co-operatives to market-linkage and integrated co-operatives (*Dülfer* 1976, 1984, *Blümle, Niessler*) (→ *Structural Types*). In traditional co-operatives, there is a very close link between members and the co-operative. Members determine the activities of the co-operative which only acts in support of its members ("executively operating co-operative", *Dülfer* 1984, S. 91). Such restrictions do not hold for market-linkage co-operatives. In market-linkage co-operatives, one often finds that business activities directed at non-members by far dominate the amount of business done with members. In such "market-linkage co-operatives" (*Dülfer* 1984, S. 94), the co-operative and its members to a large extent become independent of each other and their relationships are similar to regular market connections. This does not hold true for the third type, the integrated co-operative, where there is a network of often rather intense relationships between members and the co-operative. But here, compared to the traditional idea, the direction of control has been reversed. The co-operative provides support to members, but at the same time, also directs their activities. Again, in combination with size, the development away from traditional forms or the addition of new forms means the appearance of an institutionalized management and of employees (who might formally become members but would nevertheless have interest differing from those of the founding members).

For many co-operatives today, a situation therefore exists where at least three stakeholders can be identified. Stakeholders are defined as individuals, groups or institutions that through their interactions co-produce the results of the co-operative while pursuing at least partly differing interests (e.g. *Quarter/Wilkinson*).

In such an understanding, stakeholders obviously are the members (as individuals or organizations), the management of the co-operative enterprise, and the employees (*Männicke, Niessler*). The concrete objectives of members in connection with activities of the co-operative will vary with the reason of being of the co-operatives. In abstract terms, they are the support and promotion of their interests. The employees interests will vary, too, but in general they will be related to the job, to the working conditions, safety, remuneration, career opportunities, and security of employment. The interests of the management will show some variance, too, depending on whether they are genuine members or employed professionals and on their individual aspirations.

The character of the relationships between these sets of interests differs. The connection between members and management has to be understood in terms of a principal-agent perspective which is not of systematic concern for co-determination as long as opportunism of managers is not in specific ways typical of co-operatives. The relationship of members to employees is an indirect one, mediated via management decisions. The relationship of the management as the representative of the members to the employees is a hierarchical one, based on asymmetric work contracts in which the employee's role is defined as the duty to follow orders, a duty that is not basically changed by co-determination.

On the level of such an abstract analysis, conflicts of interests between stakeholders are likely, but ambiguous. The way members interests will be affected, will, first, depend on the precision with which objectives of the co-operatives are linked with members' objectives. This link will be close in traditional co-operatives and rather loose in market-linkage co-operatives. The situation appears less obvious in integrated co-operatives (for a more detailed discussion see *Dülfer* 1976). It will, secondly, vary with the way the management performs its role, that is whether it is more inclined to consider workers' or members' interests. In any empirical case, the effects of worker co-determination on the objectives of members will therefore depend on structural conditions in combination with orientations of actors and the factual power differentials (*Niessler*).

IV. Reflections on the Effects of Worker Co-determination and Participative Management in General

If an → *evaluation* is attempted about the effects of worker co-determination on the co-operative and its mission of supporting and promoting its members, a first impression provided by the literature – as mentioned – is the suspicion that co-determination, at least in its strongest version of "parity" representation in supervisory boards (see Co-determination in Germany), is detrimental to the idea of a co-operative on the assumption that co-operatives are different from capitalist companies (*Beuthien* 1976). This includes in the German case the complaint that co-determination in co-operatives limits the amount of support for members (*Hamm* 1976, *Metz*). Apart from the zero-sum nature of such claims and the ambivalence and perspective dependency of evaluations (*Stern*), doubts about such assumptions have to be raised.

The doubts to be raised suffer somewhat from a lack of empirical studies about co-determination in the co-operative sphere. In one German study, though, it has been found that, with respect to the influence of the works council, there does not appear to be much of a difference between co-operatives and regular firms (*Kliemt*). Assuming that this finding can be generalized, the results of research about co-determination in private and public organizations become applicable to co-operatives as well.

Interpreting the results of this research, which mainly concerns the influence or power of works councils (*Bartölke/Henning/Jorzik/Ridder*), with respect to the question whether company objectives are restricted or modified, the answer in general is negative. Co-determination occurs in a reactive mode, protection rather than design is the orientation. Often there is a missing interest of and support by workers for the activities of their representatives. Representatives have interests of their own that might be at odds with the interests of the workers in general (another principal-agent problem which the management might use to pursue the objectives of the organization). There are differences in interests between groups and layers of employees that weaken representatives' activities. Management's interests and objectives remain dominant.

The effects of co-determination on the operation of the co-operative nevertheless remain ambiguous. Employees and how they are involved are a main determinant of the performance of the co-operative and therefore of the support and promotion members receive. And on the one hand, co-determination might – because of the explicit inclusion of the expert knowledge of worker representatives – improve the quality of decisions, enlarge creativity, lead to the acceptance of decisions, diminish absenteism and resignations, heighten motivation, integrate employees, and make employees sensitive to the specific properties of a co-operative. On the other hand, one might claim that among others co-determination slows down the process of decision-making, reduces flexibility, produces undue financial burden, is disadvantageous because of qualification deficits of worker representatives, shuts off the members of the co-operative, is ineffective because of diminished motivation in the constituency of the worker representatives (*Männicke*).

Although some arguments about potential negative effects of worker co-determination appear to be based on the bias that the management could handle the mentioned problems if co-determination would not interfere, they hint at potential deficits of representative, indirect, political participation. Co-determination has a collective orientation based on structurally founded interests of dependent workers that might not cover their specific individual needs and aspirations. For these, direct participation opportunities might be of greater importance. Such opportunities, in general, will be provided by participative management concepts like semi-autonomous work groups or quality circles and participative leadership behaviour. These concepts of motivational participation are not systematically linked with political participation – e.g. in the German law, participative management is of no concern (*Bartölke/Jorzik*). These and similar concepts are nevertheless adequate for a co-operative context (e.g. *Hettlage*), specifically if in practice they are integrated into co-determination activities as well as the management process.

Such an evaluation is normative in the sense that, considering the democratic intentions of both co-operative and worker co-determination on the one hand and the performance orientation defined by the managerial role on the other, it provides a prescription that makes worker co-determination a desirable, justifiable and legitimate element of co-operative associations.

Bibliography

Bartölke, Klaus/Eschweiler, Walter/Flechsenberger, Dieter/Palgi, Michal/Rosner, Menachem: Participation and Control, Spardorf 1985.

Bartölke, Klaus/Henning, Heiner/Jorzik, Herbert/Ridder, Hans-Gerd: Neue Technologien und betriebliche Mitbestimmung, Opladen 1991.

Bartölke, Klaus/Jorzik, Herbert: Mitbestimmung, Führung bei, in: Alfred Kieser/Gerhard Reber/Rolf Wunderer (eds.), Handwörterbuch der Führung, Stuttgart, 1987 col. 1461–1472 (new edition in print).

Beuthien, Volker: Die Arbeitnehmermitbestimmung in Genossenschaften, Zeitschrift für das gesamte Genossenschaftswesen, 26(1976), S. 320–336.

Beuthien, Volker: Die Organstruktur der Genossenschaft. In: Juhani Laurinkari (ed.), Genossenschaftswesen, München-Wien 1990, S. 413–421.

Blomeyer, Wolfgang/Painz, Elfriede: Die eingetragene Genossenschaft im Mitbestimmungsurteil des Bundesverfassungsgerichts vom 1. 3. 1979, Zeitschrift für das gesamte Genossenschaftswesen, 29 (1979), S. 240–249.

Blümle, Ernst-Bernd: Die Genossenschaft als Zusammenschluß von Wirtschaftssubjekten und als Gemeinschaftsbetrieb. In: Juhani Laurinkari (ed.), Genossenschaftswesen, München-Wien 1990, S. 78–85.

Duhm, Rainer: Wenn Belegschaften ihre Betriebe übernehmen, Frankfurt/New York 1990.

Dülfer, Eberhard: Arbeitnehmer-Mitbestimmung in Genossenschaften aus betriebswirtschaftlicher Sicht, Zeitschrift für das gesamte Genossenschaftswesen, 26(1976), S. 302–319.

Dülfer, Eberhard: Betriebswirtschaftslehre der Kooperative, Göttingen 1984.

Engelhardt, Wilhelm Werner: Die Genossenschaftsidee als Gestaltungsprinzip. In: Juhani Laurinkari (ed.), Genossenschaftswesen, München-Wien 1990, S. 10–26.

Grosskopf, Werner: Grundlagen genossenschaftlicher Strukturen und deren Wandlungen als Folge von Marktzwängen. In: Juhani Laurinkari (ed.), Genossenschaftswesen, München-Wien 1990, S. 363–378.

Hamm, Walter: Gesamtwirtschaftliche Aspekte der Paritätischen Mitbestimmung in Genossenschaften, Zeitschrift für das gesamte Genossenschaftswesen, 26(1976), S. 337–344.

Hamm, Walter: Konzentrations- und Fusionstendenzen. in: Juhani Laurinari/Johann Brazda (eds.), Genossenschaftswesen, München-Wien 1990, S. 350–358.

Hettlage, Robert: Genossenschaftstheorie und Partizipationsdiskussion, Göttingen 1987.

Kliemt, Rudolf: Die Praxis des Betriebsverfassungsgesetzes in genossenschaftlichen Unternehmen – Aus der Sicht des Betriebsratsvorsitzenden, Archiv für öffentliche und freigemeinnützige Unternehmen, 10 (1978), S. 227–266.

Laurinkari, Juhani/Brazda, Johann: Genossenschaftliche Grundwerte. In: Juhani Laurinkari (ed.), Genossenschaftswesen, München-Wien 1990, S. 70–77.

Männicke, Andreas: Mitarbeiter-Mitbestimmung in Genossenschaften aus betriebswirtschaftlicher Sicht. In: Juhani Laurinkari (ed.), Genossenschaftswesen, München-Wien 1990, S. 176–187.

Metz, Egon: Die Mitbestimmung aus der Sicht der genossenschaftlichen Praxis, Zeitschrift für das gesamte Genossenschaftswesen, 26(1976), S. 345–350.

Niessler, Eva: Arbeitnehmer-Mitbestimmung und Mitglieder-Förderung in Genossenschaften, Göttingen 1978.

Purtschert, Robert: Zur Ökonomisierung der genossenschaftlich organisierten Wirtschaft. In: Juhani Laurinkari (ed.), Genossenschaftswesen, München-Wien 1990, S. 264–275.

Quarter, Jack/Wilkinson, Paul: Recent Trends in the Worker-Ownership Movement in Canada: Four Alternative Models, Economic and Industrial Democracy 11 (1990), S. 529–552.

Springenberg, Maria/Jander, Martin: Gewerkschaften, Genossenschaften, Demokratisierung. In: Werner Fiedler, Reiner Hoffmann, Klaus Kost (eds.), Gewerkschaften auf neuen Wegen, Marburg 1987, S. 60–84.

Stern, Robert N.: Participation by Representation, Work and Occupation, 15(1988), S. 396–422.

Stuchlik, Karl-Heinz: Die deutschen Konsumgenossenschaften als Schrittmacher unternehmensverfassungsrechtlicher und sozialpolitischer Reformen, Archiv für öffentliche und freigemeinwirtschaftliche Unternehmen, 14(1982), S. 275–292.

List of Contributors

Akpoghor, P.S.
Lagos (Nigeria)
Ali Khan, Mahmood Prof. Dr.
Lahore (Pakistan)
Aschhoff, Gunther Dr.
Deutsche Genossenschaftsbank
Frankfurt/M. (Germany)

Bänsch, Axel Prof. Dr.
Universität Hamburg
Aumühle (Germany)
Baetge, Jörg Prof. Dr.
Universität Münster
Münster (Germany)
Baker, Christopher
World Council of Credit Unions Inc.
Madison, Wisconsin (USA)
Bakonyi, Emmerich Dr.
Universität Hohenheim
Metzingen (Germany)
Bartölke, Klaus Prof. Dr.
Universität/Gesamthochschule Wuppertal
Wuppertal (Germany)
Bausch, Walter Direktor i.R.
FIDUCIA-Informationszentrale AG
Karlsruhe (Germany)
Bayley, Elise
Plunkett Foundation
Oxford (United Kingdom)
Becker, Hartmut
Universität Marburg
Marburg (Germany)
Becker, Sabine Dipl.Vw.
International Labour Office
Neuenrade (Germany)
Benecke, Dieter W. Prof. Dr.
Inter Nationes
Bonn (Germany)
Bergmann, Theodor Prof. Dr.
Universität Stuttgart
Stuttgart (Germany)
Beuthien, Volker Prof. Dr.
Universität Marburg
Marburg (Germany)
Bhatti, Mohammed H. Dr.
Lahore (Pakistan)
Bienefeld, Carlos Dipl.Kfm.
Universität Marburg
Marburg (Germany)

Blomeyer, Wolfgang Prof. Dr.
Universität Erlangen-Nürnberg
Erlangen (Germany)
Blümle, Ernst-Bernd Prof. Dr.
Universität Fribourg
Fribourg (Switzerland)
Böök, Sven Ake
Kooperativa Förbundet
Stockholm (Sweden)
Bonus, Holger Prof. Dr.
Universität Münster
Münster (Germany)
Boos, Werner Dr.
Schöneich (Germany)
Bratschitsch, Rudolf Prof. Dr.
Universität Innsbruck
Innsbruck (Austria)
Brazda, Johann Ass.Prof. Dr.
Universität Wien
Wien (Austria)
Brockmeier, Thomas Dipl.Vw.
Universität Marburg
Marburg (Germany)

Chaabouni, J. Dr.
Universite de Sfax
Sfax (Tunisia)
Chukwu, S.C. Prof. Dr.
Institute of Management & Technology
Enugu (Nigeria)
Cracogna, Dante Dr.
CIEDLA
Buenos Aires (Argentinia)
Craig, J.G. Prof. Dr.
York University
King City/Ontario (Canada)
Croll, Willi Präsident i.R.
Deutscher Raiffeisenverband e.V.
Bonn (Germany)

Don, Yehuda Prof. Dr.
Bar-Ilan University
Ramat-Gan (Israel)
Dülfer, Eberhard Prof.em. Dr.
Universität Marburg
Marburg (Germany)
Duymaz, Ismail Dr.
Istanbul (Turkey)

Eckardstein, Dudo von Prof. Dr.
Universität Wien
Wien (Austria)
Engelhardt, Werner Wilhelm Prof. Dr.
Universität Köln
Köln (Germany)
Erlinghagen, Peter Prof. Dr. Dr.h.c.
Universität Hamburg
Hamburg (Germany)
Eschenburg, Rolf Prof. Dr.
Universidad Austral de Chile
Valdivia (Chile)

Fairbairn, Brett
University of Saskatchewan
Saskatoon/Saskatchewan (Canada)
Fehl, Ulrich Prof. Dr.
Universität Marburg
Marburg (Germany)
Fehr, Ernst Prof. Dr.
Universität Wien
Wien (Austria)
Feidicker, Markus Dr.
Universität Münster
Münster (Germany)
Fürstenberg, F. Prof. Dr. Dr.h.c.
Universität Bonn
Bonn (Germany)

Garratt, Roy
Rochdale Pioneers Museum
Manchester (United Kingdom)
Gessner, Hans Heinrich
Genossenschaftsverband
Hessen/Rheinland-Pfalz/Thüringen e.V.
Kassel (Germany)
Gobbers, Anette Dr.
Tutzing (Germany)
Großfeld, Bernhard Prof. Dr.
Universität Münster
Münster (Germany)
Grosskopf, Werner Prof. Dr.
Universität Hohenheim
Stuttgart (Germany)
Grüger, Wolfgang Präsident
Bundesverband der Deutschen Volksbanken und Raiffeisenbanken (BVR)
Bonn (Germany)

Gupta, Ganesh P. Dr.
Maharshi Vedvyas Foundation
for Studies in Co-operation
Varanasi (India)

Hana, Korinna Dr.
Universität Marburg
VW-Forschungsprojekt, Peking
(China)
Marburg (Germany)
Hahn, Oswald Prof. Dr.
Universität Erlangen-Nürnberg
Rückersdorf (Germany)
Hahn, Dietger Prof. Dr. Dr.h.c.
Universität Gießen
Gießen (Germany)
Hamm, Walter Prof.em. Dr.
Universität Marburg
Marburg (Germany)
Hanel, Alfred Prof. Dr.
Universität Marburg
Marburg (Germany)
Hartwig, Karl-Hans Prof. Dr.
Universität Bochum
Bochum (Germany)
Henningsen, Eckhart
Deutsche Genossenschaftsbank
Frankfurt/M. (Germany)
Hettlage, Robert Prof. Dr. Dr.
Universität Regensburg
Regensburg (Germany)
Hetzler, H.W. Prof. Dr.
Universität Hamburg
Hamburg (Germany)
van Hulle, André Dr. †
Leuven (Belgium)

Jenkis, Helmut W. Prof. Dr.
Verbandsdirektor i.R.
Hannover (Germany)
Jokisch, Jens Prof. Dr.
Universität Stuttgart
Stuttgart (Germany)

Kamdem, Emmanuel Dr.
International Labour Office
Genève (Switzerland)
Ketilson, Lou Hammond Prof. Dr.
University of Saskatchewan
Saskatoon/Saskatchewan
(Canada)
Kaufmann, Lutz Dr.
Universität Gießen
Gießen (Germany)
Kieser, Alfred Prof. Dr.
Universität Mannheim
Mannheim (Germany)
Kirsch, Ottfried Dr.
Universität Heidelberg
Heidelberg (Germany)

Kleer, Jerzy Prof. Dr.
Universität Warschau
Warszawa (Poland)
Kleiner, Horst
Bausparkasse Schwäbisch Hall AG
Schwäbisch Hall (Germany)
Kötter, Herbert Prof.em. Dr.
Universität Bonn
Lollar (Germany)
Kowalak, Tadeusz Prof. Dr.
Universität Warschau
Warszawa (Poland)
Kramer, Jost W. Dipl.Vw.
Humboldt-Universität Berlin
Berlin (Germany)
Kreikebaum, Hartmut Prof. Dr.
European Business School, Koblenz
Schlangenbad (Germany)
Krug, Carl E. Dipl.-Volkswirt
Marburg Consult
Marburg (Germany)
Kubista, Bernd Dr.
Bundesverband der Volksbanken und Raiffeisenbanken
Bonn (Germany)
Kück, Marlene Prof. Dr.
Freie Universität Berlin
Berlin (Germany)
Kuhn, Johannes Prof. Dr.
Universität Marburg
Marburg (Germany)

Laakkonen, Vesa Prof. Dr.
Universität Helsinki
Helsinki (Finland)
Laske, Stephan Prof. Dr.
Universität Innsbruck
Innsbruck (Austria)
Laurinkari, Juhani Prof. Dr.Dr.
Universität Kuopio
Kuopio (Finnland)
Nürnberg (Germany)
Lenfers, Guido
Universität Münster
Münster (Germany)
Linneborn, Friedel
Stuttgart (Germany)
Lipfert, Helmut Prof.em. Dr.
Universität Hamburg
Hamburg (Germany)
von der Lippe, Peter Prof. Dr.
Universität/Gesamthochschule
Essen
Essen (Germany)
von Loesch, Achim Dr.
Frankfurt (Germany)
Luther, Martin RA Dr.
Hamburg (Germany)

Macharzina, Klaus Prof. Dr.
Universität Hohenheim
Stuttgart (Germany)
Mändle, Eduard Prof. Dr.
Fachhochschule Nürtingen
Geislingen (Germany)
Malt, Friedbert
Deutsche Genossenschaftsbank
Frankfurt/M. (Germany)
Mariadis, Stavros Dr.
Thessaloniki (Greece)
Mose, Konrad WP Dipl.-Kfm.
Wabern (Germany)
Müller, Julius Otto Prof. Dr.
Universität Göttingen
Bovenden (Germany)
Münkner, Hans-H. Prof. Dr.
Universität Marburg
Marburg (Germany)
von Muralt, Jürgen Dr.
International Labour Office
Genève (Switzerland)
Mussons, Salvador Dr.
Barcelona (Spain)

Nchari, A.N. Dipl.Kooperations-Ökon.
Pan African Institute for Development - IPD
Buea, South West Province
(Cameroon)
Neumann, George C. Dr.
Frankfurt (Germany)
Nilsson, Jerzy Prof. Dr.
The Swedish University
of Agricultural Sciences
Uppsala (Sweden)
Novy, Klaus Prof. Dr. †
Berlin (Germany)

Oved, Yaacov Prof. Dr.
International Communal Studies Association
Ramat Efal (Israel)

Parnell, Edgar
Plunkett Foundation
Oxford (United Kingdom)
Patera, Mario Dr.
Universität Wien
Wien (Austria)
Pelzl, Wolfgang Prof. Dr.
Universität Leipzig
Nürnberg (Germany)
Pfeiffer, Thomas Dipl.Vw.
Universität Marburg
Marburg (Germany)
Philipowski, Rüdiger Prof. Dr.
Deutscher Genossenschafts-

und Raiffeisenverband
Alfter-Oedekoven (Germany)
Pohling, Roland Dr.
Universität Marburg
Marburg (Germany)
Pollard, Sydney Prof. Dr.
Universität Bielefeld
Bielfeld (Germany)

Ramirez, Benjamin Prof. Dr.
Universidad Santo Tomás
Bogotá D.E. (Columbia)
Renken, Cornelius
Universität Münster
Münster (Germany)
Ringle, Günther Prof. Dr.
Universität Hamburg
Hamburg (Germany)
Rinn, Hermann Siegfried
WP/StB
Westfälischer Genossen-
schaftsverband
Münster (Germany)
Röpke, Jochen Prof. Dr.
Universität Marburg
Marburg (Germany)
Rönnebeck, Gerhard Dr.
Humboldt-Universität Berlin
Berlin (Germany)

Saxena, S.K. Dr.
Markham/Onatario (Canada)
Schmale, Ingrid Dr.
Universität zu Köln
Köln (Germany)
Schreiter, Carsten Dr.
Universität Marburg
Marburg (Germany)
Seibel, Hans Dieter Prof. Dr.
Universität zu Köln
Köln (Germany)
Seidel, Eberhard Prof. Dr.
Universität Siegen GHS
Siegen (Germany)
Seuster, Horst Prof. Dr.
Universität Gießen
Gießen (Germany)
Swoboda, Walter Dipl.-Kfm.
Akademie Deutscher Genos-
senschaften e.V.
Montabaur (Germany)

Schediwy, Robert Dr.
Wien (Austria)
Schemmann, Gert Dr.
Deutsche Genossenschaftsbank
Berlin (Germany)
Schiemenz, Bernd Prof. Dr.
Universität Marburg
Marburg (Germany)
Schinke, Eberhard Prof. Dr.
Universität Gießen
Gießen (Germany)
Schneider, Herrmann Dr.
Fundacion Konrad Adenauer
Buenos Aires (Argentina)
Schumacher, Ulrich WP/StB RA
Hamburg (Germany)
Schwarz, Günther Christian Dr.
Universität Marburg
Marburg (Germany)
Schwarz, Peter PD Dr.
Universität Luzern
Eggersriet (Switzerland)
Staehle, Wolfgang Prof. Dr. †
Freie Universität Berlin
Stoffregen, Heinz Prof. Dr.
Universität Marburg
Marburg (Germany)

Thiemeyer, Theo Prof. Dr. †
Universität Dortmund
Thordarsson, Bruce
International Co-operative Alliance
Genève (Switzerland)
Trappe, Paul Prof. Dr.
Universität Basel
Mühleturnen (Switzerland)
Todev, Tode Dr.
Universität Wien
Wien (Austria)

Ullrich, Gabriele Dr.
International Labour Office
Genève (Switzerland)

Varadi, Layos
International Co-operative Alli-
ance
Grand-Saconnex/Geneva (Switz-
erland)
Vienney, Claude
Savieny Sarge (France)

Vierheller, Rainer Prof. Dr. †
Hochschule für Wirtschaft und
Politik
Hamburg (Germany)
Vir, Dharm Dr.
Maharshi Vedvyas Foundation
for Studies in Co-operation
Varanasi (India)
Vyas, Arvind Prof. Dr.
J. Nehru University
New Delhi (India)

Wagner, Helmut Prof. Dr.
Universität Münster
Münster (Germany)
Weber, Wilhelm Prof. Dr.
Dr.h.c.mult.
Universität Wien
Wien (Austria)
Wehlmann, Hans-Dieter RA
R+V Versicherungen
Wiesbaden (Germany)
Weinerth, Erich WP Dipl.-Kfm.
Verbandsdirektor i.R.
Rhodt unter Riedburg (Ger-
many)
Weiskopf, Richard Prof. Dr.
Universität Innsbruck
Innsbruck (Austria)
Wendt, Herbert Dr.
Bonn (Germany)
Wöhlken, Egon Prof. Dr.
Universität Gießen
Gießen (Germany)
Wörz, Johannes Prof. Dr.
Universität/Gesamthochschule
Kassel
Witzenhausen (Germany)
Wurl, Hans-Jürgen Prof. Dr.
Technische Hochschule Darmstadt
Darmstadt (Germany)

Zerche, Jürgen Prof. Dr. Dr.h.c.
Universität Köln
Köln (Germany)
Zörcher, Jürgen Dr.
Universität Jena
Jena (Germany)

Index of Persons

Aaker, D.A. 271
Abdallah, C. 234
Abel, W. 435
Abele, P. 194; 197/198
Abelidis, P. 16
Aberle, G. 135
Abrahamson, M.A. 224; 226
Abravanel, R. 835; 840
Ackermann, K.-F. 36; 462; 464
Ackoff, R.L. 162
Adair, P. 234
Adams, D.W. 10
Addes 292
Adelhelm, R. 385
Adewunmi, W. 205
Adeyeye, O. 700
Adickes, F. 446
Adler, M. 887
Aereboe 875
Ahrends, K. 396
Ait-Amara, H. 234
Akpoghor, P.S. 42; 45/46
Aksnes 715
Albach, H. 162; 277/278; 280/281; 835; 840
Albert, H. 101; 105; 135ff.; 592; 872; 877
Albrecht, G. 104; 406; 448; 803
Alchian, A.A. 472; 475ff.
Aldenhoff, R. 828
Alderfelder, C.P. 794; 796
Alderson, W. 31f.; 35
Alexander, P. 178
Ali Khan, M. 242
Ali, M. 227; 229
Alix 292
Alley, R. 91
Alonso Soto, F. 178
Alsmöller, H. 488
Altman, E.I. 262; 264; 761
Alvarado, M. 752; 754
Alvesson, M. 673; 677
Alwabil, E.A. 262; 264
Aly, I.M.M. 262; 264
Amann, A. 820; 822/823; 875
Ambros, J. 577; 579
Anagnostiadis, Ch. 16
Andel, N. 403
Anderson, B. 35/36; 599; 602
Andlau, Ch. Conte de 500; 502/503
Andreae, C.-A. 654

Angel, J. 754
Ansoff, H.I. 70; 74; 150; 157; 162; 277ff.; 280; 848/849
Aoki, M. 841
Apthorpe, R. 205
Aristotle (Aristoteles) 714
Arizmendi, J.M. 616; 618/619
Armbruster, P.G. 10; 692; 736
Armin, B.v. 343
Arnazahl, R.C. 488
Arnod, E. 128
Aschermann, R. 41
Aschhoff, G. 80; 85; 321; 484; 543; 749; 784; 897
Ashby, W.R. 190; 193
Ashworth, M. 778
Astor 451
Athos, A.G. 180; 186
Attems, R. 150; 878
Attwood, D.W. 258/259
Awadzi, W. 526/527
Axelrod, R. 136; 141; 814
Azurmendi, J. 178; 619

Bachof 170ff.
Back, J. 103; 137; 860/861; 874; 878
Backhaus, J. 403; 878
Backhaus, K. 762; 835; 840
Bader, K.S. 435; 874
Badura, B. 422
Baetge, J. 3; 7; 192/193; 255; 259ff.; 264; 274; 280f.; 757; 761/762
Bager 715
Bahve, V. 50
Bain, J.S. 607; 613
Baker, Ch. 186
Bakonyi, E. 141; 396; 623f.; 626; 861; 864; 875
Balandier, G. 405/406
Baldus, R.D. 44; 62; 203ff.; 256; 259; 361; 646; 700; 801
Baldwin, J.M. 262; 264
Balla, B. 142; 145
Ballachey, E.L. 362
Ballesteros, E. 178
Baltzer, E. 787
Banerjee, J. 730
Bänsch, A. 28; 46; 69; 72; 74; 136; 265; 271; 738/739; 743; 745; 875

Bar-Niv, R. 262; 264
Bardeleben, M. 47; 51; 846
Barnard, Ch.I. 73/74; 461; 464; 585; 877
Bartning 633/634; 636
Bartölke, K. 730; 916ff.
Bartu, F. 51
Bascom, W.R. 47; 51
Bastone, E. 664
Bateman, D.I. 600; 602
Baudin, L. 222
Bauer, E. 53
Bauer, P.T. 361
Baum, H.-G. 162
Baumann, H. 20/21; 23; 484
Baumbach, A. 76; 78; 516
Baumgarten 449; 453
Baur, J.F. 516
Bausch, W. 194; 197/198
Bavia, M.J. 700
Bavin, T.S. 799; 801
Baviskar, R.S. 258/259
Bayley, E. 684
Bea, F.X. 488; 639
Beamish, P.M. 526/527
Beaujour 16
Beaver, W.H. 262; 264; 280; 762
Bebel, A. 813
Beckenstein, A.L. 704/705
Becker, H. 74; 562
Becker, R. 613
Becker, S. 909
Beckmann, L. 381
Bédard, G. 801
Bedrani, S. 232; 234
Beer, M. 458; 460
Beer, St. 192/193
Beguin, J.P. 526/527
Behrendt, J.-U. 422
Behrendt, R.F. 142; 143; 886/887; 875
Behrens 543
Belenes Juarez, R. 178
Bellers, J. 423/424; 437; 843; 846
Beloglavec, M. 846
Below, G.v. 417; 435
Ben Lalah, A. 234
Ben Ner, A. 537/538
Benecke, D.W. 169; 216ff.; 222; 329; 730; 797/798; 801
Bengelsdorf, R. 396
Benjacov, A. 736

Benseler, H. 195; 197/198
Bensimon, J. 700
Benson, J.K. 672; 677
Bente, H. 656
Bentham, J. 613/614
Benya 153
Berg, P.O. 673; 677
Berg, S.V. 527
Berge, H. 5; 7; 141; 343; 769
Bergengren, R.F. 188; 198/199
Berger, B. 819
Berger, J. 637
Berger, P.L. 819
Bergmann, H. 650
Bergmann, J. 673; 677
Bergmann, K. 633; 636/637
Bergmann, T. 4; 7; 145
Bergmann, Th. 498; 596; 647; 726; 730/731; 875
Bermann 376
Bernhard 575
Bernsdorf, W. 143; 145
Bernstein 424; 876
Bertalanffy, L.v. 193; 466; 468
Bertrand, L. 64
Bery, V. 838:840
Beseler, G. 397
Bessaoud, O. 233/234
Bestor, A. 131
Betsch 141
Beuthien, V. 20; 23; 36; 38/39; 40/41; 41; 77/78; 102/103; 112; 114; 140; 376; 441; 444/445; 517; 543; 552/553; 559; 562/563; 568; 627; 630; 632; 765; 828; 916; 918/919
Beyer, H. 410; 412; 673ff.; 678
Beywl, W. 634; 637
Bhaduri, A. 242
Bhatti, Y. 242
Bhinta, R. 527
Bienefeld, C. 766
Bierbaum, H. 632; 637
Bilderbeeck, J. 262; 264
Billerbeck, K. 361
Billig, V. 488
Binswanger, H.P. 574/575; 579; 802
Birck, H. 516
Birr, J. 456
Bischofsberger, P. 640
Bismarck, O. Fürst v. 419; 439; 811/812
Bittel, K. 684
Blair, J.M. 608; 613
Blanc, L. 63/64; 93; 144; 424; 437/438; 518; 811; 817; 842
Blase, M.G. 800/801
Blau. P.M. 105

Blaug, M. 603; 615
Bleeke, J. 836; 840
Blei, R. 280
Bleicher, K. 193; 275; 488; 673; 677; 836; 839/840
Bleier, E. 262; 265
Bloech, J. 654
Blomeyer, W. 103; 140; 568; 744/745; 916
Blümel, W. 402/403
Blumenroth, U. 448
Blümle, E.B. 28; 30; 42; 71; 74; 105; 141; 371; 422; 640; 649ff.; 654; 715; 738/739; 742/743; 872; 878; 917
Bock 428
Boettcher, E. 28; 30ff.; 74; 100; 102/103; 113/114; 120; 135; 139; 141; 162; 346; 399; 403; 429; 543; 581; 584; 610; 613; 634; 637; 650; 654; 664; 716; 721; 731; 738/739; 744/745; 748/749; 771; 773; 828; 847; 849; 856; 864; 875; 873; 877/878; 885
Bogardus, E.S. 716
Böhm, F. 719; 721; 877
Böhme, J. 488
Böhret 136
Bolam, P.M. 686
Bonin, J.P. 518/519; 536/537
Bonnemère, J-E. 435
Bonner, A. 778
Bonus, H. 2ff; 7; 135; 256/257; 259; 273; 371; 472; 473ff.; 584; 739; 873; 877/878
Böök, S.A. 491
Bookchin, M. 470
Boos, K-J. 343
Boos, W. 52
Borana, G. 472
Bordeaux Szekely, E. 435
Born, E. 775
Börner, B. 525; 527
Borries, R.v. 385
Bouami, A. 234
Boulanger, F. 16
Boulder 877
Boulding 873
Boulet, D. 234
Bouman, F.J.A. 700
Bourdieu 674; 676
Bourgeois 136
Bowers, T. 838; 840
Bowles, S. 528
Bradley, K. 616/617; 619
Brambosch, W. 669/670
Brandes, W. 574/575; 579
Bratschisch, R. 484

Brauer, U. 488
Braun, R. 414; 417
Brazda, J. 123; 127; 150; 157; 309; 345/346; 422; 668ff.; 720/721; 736; 805; 916; 919
Brecht, J. 749; 859; 861
Brede, H. 749
Bredendiek, W. 456
Brelay, E. 440
Brentano, D.v. 144/145; 410ff.; 424; 429; 821; 823
Brentano, L. 440
Brisbane, A. 128
Brixner, J. 502; 516
Brockmeier, T. 602; 613; 907
Bronder, C. 836; 838; 840
Bronn, P.S. 836; 839; 841
Brown, M. 538
Brown, R.K. 464; 469
Brown, W.H. 778
Bruhn, M. 640
Brümmerhoff, D. 403
Brycesson, D. 205
Buber, M. 135; 424; 429; 472; 874
Buchanan, J. 402
Buchez, Ph.J.B. 63/64; 93; 115; 121; 144; 424; 437/438; 518; 817
Buckley, P.J. 488; 523; 527
Buddeberg, H. 596
Bühner, R. 271
Bumiller, U. 765
Bungenstock, W. 111/112; 114; 368; 371
Burawoy, M. 676/677
Burgers, W.P. 835/836; 840
Burla, St. 640
Burnett, J.J. 526/527
Busch, E. 13; 15
Busche, M. 396
Büscher, H. 141; 650
Büschgen, H. 343; 381; 741
Busino, G. 909
Busse v. Colbe, W. 654
Bussel, J. 212
Buß, E. 677
Butt, J. 667
Byrne, J.A. 640
Byzycki, H.v. 472

Cabet, J. 128; 439; 456; 469; 885
Calvert, H. 58; 62; 550
Camboulives, M. 550; 661
Campanella 469
Cannon 714
Carlos, J. 754
Carroll, T.F. 647
Carter, Lord 686
Cartwright, D. 664

Casson, M. 523
Castan, E. 101; 105
Castano Colomer, J. 179
Castillo, A. 329
Castillo, G.T. 801
Castro 289; 292
Cathari 431
Chaabouni, J. 226
Chakravorty, B. 308
Champagne, S. 911; 913; 915
Chappenden, W.J. 661
Chattopadhyay, P. 242
Chaulet, C. 234
Cheikh Dieng, M. 846
Chekir, H. 234
Chen Han-Seng 91
Chen Jiyuan 91
Chen Wei 92
Chen Yan 92
Chen, K.H. 262; 265
Cheng, Ch. 785/786
Child, J. 465; 469
Chmielewicz, K. 107; 110; 381
Cholaj, H. 721; 875
Chowdhury, J. 527
Chukwu, S.C. 199
Cicero 431
Cirpka, E. 68
Cissoko, A. 912ff.
Claessens, D. 135; 411/412
Clapham, J J. 435
Clark, M.M. 131
Clausen, L. 145
Clegg, St.R. 676/677
Clemens, R. 488
Clement, W. 488
Coase, R. 256; 523; 527; 603; 877
Cobia, D.W. 35/36; 226; 599; 602
Cock, P. 131
Coenenberg, A.G. 162; 381
Cole, G.D.H. 53; 96; 425; 446; 666; 778; 876
Coleman, J.S. 815; 819
Coleridge, S.T. 614
Colombain, M. 905,
Comboulives, M. 700
Conrad, Ch. 676/677
Contractor, F.J. 523; 527; 833; 841
Cooley, G.H. 404; 406
Cooper, W. 437; 777/778; 842
Cory 47
Cotterill, R. 225/226
Cracogna, D. 550; 750/751; 754
Craig, J.G. 157; 219; 222; 225/226; 258/259; 715
Crawford, R. 475; 477
Crisoli 563
Croll, W. 499; 503

Croteau, J.T. 169
Crüger, H. 440; 846
Crutchfield, R.S. 362
Cujes 873
Cuvillier, A. 64
Cyert, R. 181; 461; 464; 640
Czar Alexander 813

Dahrendorf, R. 466; 468; 877
Dale, D. 665
Dalinas Ramos 178
Damachi, U.G. 572; 846
Damaschke, A. 448
Danforth, A. 226
Dang, T. 526/527
Darling, M. 736
Dassan, M. 527
David 727
Davidovic, G. 803
Davidson, A. 654
Davidson, G. 131
Davis, R.H. 640
Deal, T.E. 180; 186
Dean, S. 692; 915
Deetz 671
Delors, J. 178
Derfuß, J. 141
Deschamps, J. 294; 299
Desjardins, A. 163; 188; 198/199; 223/224
Desroche, H. 289; 292; 915
Dessauer, F. 887
Deter, W. 120
Deutsch, M. 70; 74
Deutschmann, Ch. 676/677
Dewey 137
Dey, S.K. 50/51; 887
Dhanani, K.A. 262; 265
Dia, M. 887
Diallo, F. 294; 299
Dichtl, E. 361; 381; 488
Diehl, K. 447
Dienel, P. 775
Dietz, R. 517
Digby, M. 685; 687; 732; 736
Dinata 672
Diop, A. 886
Disraeli, B. 309
Dobkin, J.A. 527
Dobkowski, M. 146
Dolan, P. 619
Dolléans, É 667
Domar, E. 536; 538
Domarmond, P. de 700
Don, Y. 211
Donavan, G. 574/575; 579
Dopsch, A. 435
Douglas, J. 640
Douglass, K.S. 762

Dow, G. 533; 537/538
Downs 877
Doz, Y. 510
Draheim, G. 29; 42; 46; 65; 68; 70; 74; 101; 104/105; 114; 120; 126; 136; 141; 169; 186; 216; 222; 272ff; 338; 344; 346; 404; 406; 409ff.; 412; 423; 516/517; 592; 642; 647/648; 650; 705; 716; 726; 728; 731; 745/746; 770; 773; 822/823; 854; 858; 872; 875; 877/878; 897
Drèze, J.H. 536; 538
Drimer, B. 619
Du Ying 92
Dube, J. 749
Dubhashi, P.R. 647
Dublin, J. 700
Dublin, S. 700
Duby, G. 435
Duhm, R. 916; 919
Dülfer, E. 3; 4; 5; 7; 9; 10; 12; 15; 28; 29; 30/31; 39; 41; 43; 101/102; 104/105; 110; 114; 117; 136; 139ff.; 150; 159/160; 162; 166; 169; 179; 183; 186; 192/193; 203ff.; 223; 234; 268ff.; 272ff.; 276/277; 280; 294/295; 299; 355/356; 358; 361; 367; 370; 406; 462; 464; 488; 503/504; 510; 517; 519; 581; 584; 586/587; 591/592; 610; 613; 624; 626; 634; 637; 646f.; 648; 650; 654; 661; 663/664; 674; 677; 679; 688; 691/692; 708; 715/716; 721; 731; 736; 738/739; 741/742; 745/746; 766/767; 769; 787; 789; 799; 801; 828; 847; 849; 853/854; 856/857; 862; 864; 873; 875; 878; 897; 905; 916ff.
Duncan, J. 527:
Dunlop, J.T. 466ff.; 818ff.; 820
Durau 92
Durkheim, E. 47; 404/405; 406; 465; 468; 874
Düttmann, B. 488
Duttweiler, G.v. 151; 153; 155; 428
Duymaz, I. 248

Ebenroth 543
Eberhard, W. 50
Ebers, M. 186
Ebert, K.H. 5; 7; 41; 77ff.; 103; 136; 140; 550; 661
Eckardstein, D.v. 457
Eckardt, U. 516
Eckhardt, J. 53
Eckstein, E. 786
Edelmann, A. 503

Edminster, R. 262; 265
Egdeworth, F.Y. 908
Egger, A. 488
Ehlermann, R.9 743; 745
Ehm, M. 211; 717; 721
Ehrlich, S. 406
Eichhorn 875
Eickhof, N. 488; 877
Eisenberg 874
Eisermann, G. 143; 145; 819; 875; 909
El Ghazouani, A. 234
Elam, R. 262; 265
Elias, N. 406
Elisseieff, K. 596
Ellerman, D.P. 616f.; 620
Elleuch, T. 234
Ellinger, A. 54ff.
Elm, v. 427
Elsässer, M. 424/425; 429; 667
Elser, F. 279; 281
Elsinger, M. 725/726
Elvers, R. 456
Emilianoff, I.v. 701; 705; 873; 879
Emmerich 540/541; 543
Emory, C.W. 362
Endeley, E.M.L. 596
Endres, D. 527
Endress, R. 488
Endruweit, G. 110; 468; 678
Engelhardt, W.W. 85; 100/101; 104/105; 120; 125ff.; 135ff.; 141/142; 145; 182; 273; 370; 372; 410; 423; 429; 440; 450; 453; 519; 573; 613; 654; 715/716; 729; 731; 740; 742; 745ff.; 749; 806; 871/872; 875; 891; 916; 919
Engels, W. 343; 428
Engels, F. 121; 671; 678; 811ff.; 890/891
Ephrata 127
Erdland, A. 277; 280
Erffa, R.v. 575; 577; 579
Erhard, L. 655
Erlinghagen, P. 540; 559; 563; 627
Ernst, D. 835/836; 840
Eschenburg, R. 70; 74; 92; 100; 103; 110; 114; 169; 218; 222; 280; 329; 345/346; 402/403; 461; 464; 581; 584; 610; 613; 633; 636/637; 649/650; 663/664; 702ff.; 705; 740; 745; 854/855; 858; 864; 877; 885; 873; 879
Eschweiler, W. 917; 919
Espriu, J. 174ff.; 179
Essler 747

Etzione, A. 28; 362; 462; 464
Eucken, W. 135ff.; 287; 705; 828; 877
Everling 151
Eversberg, J. 488
Eze, E.A.E. 295/296; 299

Fagen, R.E. 588; 592
Fahrion, R. 192/193
Fairbairn, B. 329
Falkenstein, L. 484
Farmer, R.N. 179/180; 186
Fassbender, M. 846
Faucherre, H. 423/424; 429; 440; 491
Fauquet 137
Faust, H. 51; 120; 139; 182; 321; 418; 422; 423ff.; 428/429; 440; 456; 474; 477; 529; 552; 623; 626; 684; 756; 784; 814; 864; 891; 895
Fawcett, H. 602
Fayerweather, J. 505/506; 510
Fayol, H. 580
Feder 295
Fehl, U. 398; 607; 613; 700; 703; 705; 716
Fehr, E. 533; 537/538
Fehrle 635
Feidicker, M. 259
Feineisen, A. 418
Fellenberg, P.E.v. 423; 437; 454; 844; 886
Ferbach, C.A. 908
Fettel, J. 343; 381; 708
Feuerborn, S. 77/78
Fiedler, W. 919
Filaretos, G. 16
File, R.G. 85; 262; 265
Filene, E.A. 163; 188; 198/199
Filmes, J. 640
Findikoglu, Z.F. 254
Finemann, St. 677
Finis, B. 139; 144/145; 427; 749
Fink, U. 422
Finnel, E.V. 162
Fischer, G. 673; 677
Fischer, P.H. 205
Fischer, R. 634; 637
Fischer, Th. 192/193
Fishbein, M. 362
Fite, G.C. 224; 226
Flanders, A. 468
Flechsenberger Dieter 917; 919
Flecker, J. 619/620
Fleischmann, G. 608; 613; 873
Flieger, B. 632; 637
Florquin, F. 502
Flume, W. 170; 172

Flürschheim, M 448
Fogarty, R.R.S. 131
Förschner, E. 516
Forster, G. 454
Forster, Th. 454
Förster, W. 53; 57
Forsthoff, E. 170/171
Fourier, Ch. 16; 63; 93; 121; 424; 437; 456; 469; 518; 811; 817; 842
Fox, A. 673; 677
Franco 616
Frank, K.S. 775
Frankenberg 568
Frankenberger, W. 7
Franko, L.G. 525; 527
Franz, G. 436
Frauendorfer, S.v. 436
Frayne, C.A. 527
Freidson, E. 773
French, jr. J.R.P. 226; 362; 590; 663/664
Frese, E. 678
Fricke, W. 637; 678
Friederich II. (d.Gr.) 164
Friedewald, R. 516
Friedhelm, R.K. 814
Friedman, P. 526/527
Friedman, Y. 345; 472
Frieteema, H.J. 272/273
Fröhlich, E. 488
Fuchs, C.J. 448; 450; 453; 461
Fuchs, H. 519
Fuiller, M.B. 833; 841
Fürstenberg, F. 136; 138/139; 141; 406; 409; 411ff.; 771; 773; 800/801; 872
Furubotn, E. 535/536; 538

Gabelmann, E. 44; 46
Gablentz, O.v.d. 103; 816; 819; 874
Gac, J. 579
Gadow, W. 516
Gail, W. 516
Galbraith, J.K. 701; 705
Gälweiler, A. 849
Gandhi, M. 50
Garbei, A. 57
Garratt, R. 776
Gaskin, St. 129
Gasser, A. 143; 145; 816; 819f.; 874
Gaudin, J. 291/292
Gaugler, E. 468; 678
Gayer 100
Gbenebichie, S.A. 292; 299
Gebhardt, G. 29; 262; 265
Gehlen, A. 820

Gehrig 137; 876
Geiersberger 576
Geiger, T. 143; 145; 404; 815; 820; 875
Geilen, B. 112; 114
Geissler, A. 637; 678
Geist, H. 631
Gelb, A. 616/617; 619
Gemünden, H.G. 758; 760; 762
Gentil, D. 700
Gentry, J.A. 262; 265
Georg, H. 448
Georgiou, I. 16
Gerhard, S. 341; 343; 382
Geringer, J.M. 526/527
Gerlen, B. 371/372
Gerum, E. 674; 678
Gessler, W. 516/517
Gessner, H.H. 778
Gessner, W. 632; 637
Ghai, Y. 63
Gharajedaghi, J. 162
Ghaussy, A.G. 596; 623; 626
Ghazali, A. 233; 234
Gheroune, N. 234
Giddens, A. 672; 674; 677
Gide, Ch. 29; 93; 96; 122; 126; 137; 141; 144; 216; 289ff.; 292; 425; 440; 777; 803; 875; 888
Gierke, O.v. 101ff.; 106; 136; 143; 145; 170; 172; 397ff.; 406; 414; 436; 440; 772; 815/816; 820; 874
Gilbert 631
Gilbert, X. 584
Gilbreth 885
Gintis, H. 538
Giordano, Ch. 145/146
Gitzinger, S. 194; 197/198
Gladstone, A. 110
Glandorf, K.-H. 67/68
Glaser, F.E. 626
Glaser, R. 743; 745; 769
Glatzner, L. 649; 651; 745
Gleichmann, K. 527
Glueck, W.F. 278; 280
Gobbers, A. 503/504; 506; 509/510
Goebbels, J. 655
Goemann, D. 724; 726
Goethe, J.W.v. 437; 614; 843/844
Goetze, D. 772/773
Goffman, E. 774/775
Goldner, S. 637
Golling 568
Golter, F. 577; 579
Goodman, P. 470
Gorbach, St. 677/678

Gorbachev (Gorbatschow), M. 519; 720; 721
Görge, A. 508; 510
Göricke, F.N. 10; 205
Göschel, G. 489
Gossen, H.H. 448
Graft-Johnson, J.C.de
Gramsci, A. 676; 678
Granges, C. 234
Granovskii, A. 239; 242
Gräser, B.B. 765
Gretschmann, K. 125/126; 139; 141; 819/820; 875
Grießinger, A. 413/414; 417
Grimm, A. 577; 579
Grochla, E. 110; 114; 372; 381; 510; 592; 654; 858
Groschuff 563
Gross, H. 387
Grossekettler, H. 875
Grosskopf, W. 31; 135; 140ff.; 475; 477; 626; 740/741; 743; 745; 861; 875; 916; 919
Großfeld, B. 3; 7/8; 17; 20; 23; 111; 114; 120; 140; 142; 170; 441; 444/445; 517,543; 749
Grottian, P. 632; 637
Groves, F. 600; 602
Gruben, H.v. 724; 726
Grüger, W. 789
Grünfeld, E. 136; 138/139; 426; 429; 440; 872; 874
Grunwald, W. 651
Grünzweig, F. 775
Gu Cunwei 92
Gu Yikang 92
Gubitzer, L. 620
Guélfat, I. 731
Guen, M. 234
Gueslin, A. 288; 292
Gulick, L. 580; 584
Gümberl, R. 31; 35
Gupta, G.P. 299ff.; 308
Gurjewitsch, A. 415; 417
Gustafsson, B. 538; 841
Gutenberg, E. 343; 741
Guthardt, H. 85; 113f.
Gutherz 631
Gutierrez del Alamo, J. 179
Gutierrez-Johnson, A. 617; 620
Gutmann, G. 287; 828
Guttman, L. 362

Haas, W. 36ff.; 80; 139; 216; 314ff.; 418ff.; 427; 439; 624; 626; 778/779
Habermas, J. 661; 664; 671; 674/675; 678; 819
Habib, G.M 526/527

Habicht, H. 472
Häcker, A. 142
Haederic, L.J. 308
Haffner, F. 396
Hagedorn, E. 194; 197/198
Hagemeister, S. 488
Hagen, O.v.d. 403,
Hahn, D. 162; 274; 280; 584; 833; 839; 841; 873
Hahn, O. 101; 106; 135; 142; 163; 169; 275; 343; 381; 486; 488; 633; 635; 637; 653/654; 745; 749
Halbach, A.J. 362
Hall, A.D. 588; 592
Hall, F. 429
Haller 873
Halsey, A.H. 648; 651
Hamann, R. 909
Hamel, W. 458; 460
Hämke, K. 164; 169
Hamm, W. 12; 15; 30; 103; 106; 131; 135; 205; 281; 608; 613; 647; 692; 749; 823; 828; 873; 877/878; 897; 916; 918/919
Hammel, W. 362
Hammer, R. 163
Hana, K. 85
Hanel, A. 62; 136; 141; 204/205; 272; 362; 641; 644; 646/647; 687; 690; 692; 700; 801; 846; 856; 875; 905
Hanf, C.-H. 12; 15; 578/579
Hanstein, H. 775
Hanxian, L. 786
Harbison, F. 468; 820
Hardenberg 435
Harder, P.C.v. 112; 115; 484
Hardin, G. 338
Harding, K.F. 226
Hardy, D. 131
Häring, D. 449
Harrigan, K.R. 833; 835; 841
Harrison, J.F.C. 667
Hartwig, K.-H. 396; 642; 647; 810
Hasitschka, W. 640
Hasselmann, E. 135; 140; 425; 428; 429; 529; 651; 667; 684; 716; 891; 895
Hatten, M.L. 640
Hatzfeld, Gräfin S.v. 811
Hauri, S. 488
Hausmann, F.B. 724; 726
Hausmann, H. 510
Havermann, H. 7
Hax, A.C. 841
Hayek, F.v. 132; 287; 446/447; 449; 615; 877

Hazar, N. 254
Heckmann, J.H. 43; 46
Hedlund, H. 692
Heer, F. 876
Hefermehl, W. 516
Hegel, G.W.F. 273; 812
Heide, J.B. 835; 841
Heider, F. 633; 637
Heidrich, R. 15
Heigl, A. 159; 163
Heilbroner, R.L. 603; 614/615
Heim, N. 724; 726
Heimann 876
Heine, H. 811
Heinen, E. 186; 381; 488; 841
Heinicken, E. 516
Heins, J. 503
Heisig, P. 620
Heisig, U. 675; 678
Heister, M. 429
Hellwig, H.-J. 522; 527
Helm, F.C. 592
Hemmer, H.R. 362
Hempel 101
Hendcke-Hoppe, M. 396
Henning, H. 422; 918; 919
Henningsen, E. 80; 85; 484; 543; 784; 897
Heno, R. 260; 265
Hensel, K.P. 287
Henzler, R. 2/3; 7; 26; 28; 30; 70/71; 74; 104; 106; 111; 114; 136; 139ff.; 216; 272; 273; 406; 517; 592; 701; 705; 707/708; 715; 731; 737; 739; 741; 743ff.; 745; 767; 854; 872/873
Heraclitus 811
Herbert, L. 526/527
Herder, Dorneich, Ph. 573; 613; 773; 879
Herdzina, K. 135
Herlinger, R. 640
Hernandez, S. 179
Herod 431
Herr, Th. 673; 678
Herrmann, A. 139; 426; 608; 610; 613
Hertzka, Th. 448; 654
Herzog, H.-J. 211; 397
Hess, K. 472
Hesseler, H.L. 280
Hettlage, R. 136ff.; 141ff.; 145/146; 411/412; 429; 615; 648ff.; 661; 664; 770ff.; 815; 820/821; 823; 872; 874; 879; 897; 916
Hetzler, H.W. 464; 469
Heuß, E. 217; 222; 608; 613
Hexner, Th. 802

Hiemer, J. 579
Hiertsiefer, H. 449
Hildebrand, K. 36; 39; 41; 42
Hildebrandt, E. 671; 678; 875
Hilferding 53
Hill, C.W.L. 835/836; 840
Hill, D. 371/372
Hill, G.W. 71; 280
Hillman, K.H. 675; 678
Hinds, W. 131
Hinterhuber, H.H. 163; 280; 488
Hirschfeld, A.O. 217; 222; 228; 234; 592; 600
Hitler, A. 128
Hobbes, Th. 465; 468
Hoff, H. 635; 637
Hoffmann, R. 919
Hofmann, M. 150
Hofmann, W. 879
Hofstätter, K. 280
Hohenleitner 631
Höhn, R. 568
Hohner, H. 745
Holenweger, T. 637
Hollander, S. 615
Holloway, M. 131
Hollstein, W. 472; 637
Holmberg, A.R. 51
Holmen, H. 692
Hölscher, R. 277; 280
Holt, S. 911/912; 915
Holterhus, G. 280
Hölters, W. 517
Holtkamp, R. 574/575; 579
Holyoake, G.J. 151; 425; 440; 778; 846
Homann, W. 397
Homeyer, K.G. 397
Hommelhoff, P. 517
Homrighausen, F.H. 135
Hoppe, M. 100; 603; 615; 716; 721; 879; 909
Hoppman, K. 773
Horlacher, H. 111; 114
Horn, W. 775
Horne, J.C.van 73/74
Horváth, P. 163
Horx, M. 472; 637
Hoselitz, B.F. 802
Hostetler, J. 131
Hough, E.M. 731
Howard 437
Howarth, Ch. 425; 777; 842
Hruschka, H. 640
Hu Bin 91
Hub, H. 584
Huber, E.R. 874
Huber, F.L. 454
Huber, J. 472; 636/637

Huber, M. 454
Huber, St. 488
Huber, U. 527
Huber, V.A. 29; 101; 136; 182; 425/426; 438; 440; 446; 450; 453ff.; 788; 810; 843; 846
Hubert-Valleroux, O. 440
Hueck, A. 76; 78
Hueck, G. 516
Hughes, Th. 437; 846
Hulle, A.v. 346
Hülsemeyer, F. 724ff.
Humme, U. 762
Hunsel, L. 422
Hüsken 36; 41
Husserl 273
Huß, M. 262; 264
Hutchinson, T.W. 602/603
Huter, J. 128
Hyden, G. 204/205; 293ff.; 299; 688; 692
Hyman, R. 465; 468

Ibbetson, Sir D. 58; 60; 63
Ilmonen, K. 157; 622; 715
Im Hof, U. 51
Imagawa, N. 309
Imboden, F. 640
Imfeld, A. 846
Infield, H.F. 472; 731; 887
Inoke Faletau 686
Ireland, N. 528
Irriger, U. 172
Irsigler, F. 412; 417
Isermeyer, H.-G. 574ff.; 579
Isohsi, K. 577; 579
Issing, O. 381
Iwu, E. 51

Jackson, J.H. 163
Jacob, H. 1; 5; 7/8
Jäger, W. 112; 114; 427; 442; 444/445; 456; 584; 743ff.; 823; 875
Jaggi, E. 654
Jakob, B. 787
Jallow, J.M 910; 915
Janberg, H. 343; 381
Jander, M 916; 919
Janger, A. 526/527
Janic, J. 210/211; 833
Janssen, A. 398
Janssen, V. 846
Jantsch, E. 338
Janzen, H. 163
Jaques 181
Jarchow, K. 472
Jaures 289
Jaurs, J. 122

Jay, P. 198
Jeetun, B. 202; 204; 392:
Jenewein, J.-F. 488
Jenkis, H.W. 101; 425; 429; 445; 449; 453; 456; 745; 747; 749; 874/875
Jeserich, W. 281
Jessen, L. 12; 15
Jevons, W.S. 602; 907
Johansson, A. 151; 310; 428; 669/670
John, G. 835; 841
Jokisch, J. 23; 28; 651; 705
Jones, G.N. 150
Jones, L. 667
Jorzik, H. 918/919
Jünger, E. 174; 179

Kadner, K. 579
Kaemmel 563
Kaiser, M. 637
Kalefeld, K.-H. 13; 15
Kalveram, W. 381
Kamdem, E. 407
Kaminski, P. 292
Kant, I. 138; 192
Kanter, R. 640
Kantor, R. 131
Kantowsky, D. 50; 362; 887
Kaplan de Drimer, A. 619
Kappler, E. 676; 678
Karst 563
Kartte, W. 841
Karva, D. 692
Katterle 137
Katz 179; 580; 584
Kaufmann, H. 80; 150; 427; 528/529; 684; 890
Kaufmann, L. 833; 835; 838/839; 841
Kaunda, K. 886
Kautsky, K. 53; 812
Kedia, B. 527
Keidel, Th. 765;
Kellerhals, W. 654
Kellner, H. 819
Kelter, E. 414; 417
Kempski, v. 101
Kengerter, G. 195; 197/198
Kennedy, A.A. 180; 186
Kerr, C. 468; 818ff.; 820
Kersten 671
Kessler, H.J. 897
Ketilson, L.H. 329
Ketteler, W.E.v. 424; 439
Keutgen, F. 412; 417
Keynes, J.M. 602
Keysberg, G. 265
Khan, M.A. 247

Khrushchev (Chrutschow), N. 719
Kieser, A. 412; 584; 651; 919
Kievelitz, U. 164; 169
Kikuchi, K. 92
Kilger, W. 708
Killing, J.P. 526/527
Kim, W.C. 835f.; 840
King 666
King F. Wilhelm IV 454
King, W. 424/425; 437; 440; 777; 842ff.; 846
Kingsley 437
Kirberger, P. 765
Kirchgeorg, M. 338
Kirchhof, P. 742; 749
Kirman, A.P. 908/909
Kirsch, G. 640; 692; 731; 733ff.; 736
Kirsch, O.C. 8/9; 10; 30; 202; 205; 802
Kirsch, W. 275; 281
Kirzner, I.M. 719; 721
Kißling, R. 441; 445
Klages, H. 773; 819f/820
Klausmann, W. 280
Kleer, J. 530; 532; 721; 784; 786; 807; 810; 833; 875
Klein, B. 475; 477
Klein, F. 171/172; 768/769
Kleiner, H. 64; 68
Kleinheyer, G. 397/398
Kleiss, H. 462; 464; 502
Klemann, P. 648/649; 651
Klepper, O 428
Klient, R. 918
Klingensteiner, P. 575/576; 579
Klohn, W. 613
Kloten, N. 746
Klötzle, A. 639/640
Klugkist, A. 454
Klugmann, N. 472
Kluthe, K. 428/429; 828
Knapp, J.G. 224; 226
Köbele 674
Koch, H. 382
Koch, P. 484
Koch,E. 647;
Kochendoerfer-Lucius, G. 10; 692; 736
Kogut, B. 523; 525; 527
Kohbach, W. 794; 801
Kohlas, J. 640
Köhler, H. 112; 114
Koinecke 7
Kokigie, M. 637
Kolb, Ch. 460
Kolbeck, R. 382; 741; 745
Koll, M. 47; 51; 205

Köllhofer, D. 762
Kolping 885
Kompa, A. 676; 678
König, U.-K. 281
König, W. 488
König, R. 802; 877
Konopnicki, M. 63; 647; 692
Konrad 5; 7
Koontz, H. 158; 163; 580; 584
Köppä 715
Koppensteiner 541
Kopplin, D. 14; 15
Kordatos, G. 16
Korp 151
Korten, D.C. 257; 259
Korthaus, K. 139; 314/315; 428
Koschka, H. 343; 382
Kosiol, E. 343; 382
Koslowski, P. 773; 820
Kosmanos, D. 16
Kost, K. 919
Kothe 563
Kotler, P. 598; 602; 640
Kötter, H. 796/797; 799; 802; 816; 820
Köttgen, A. 172; 170
Kowalak, T. 205; 828; 875
Kraenzle, C.A. 226
Kraft, V. 135
Kramer, J.W. 4; 7; 271; 274ff.; 280
Kramer, R. 673; 678
Kranz, W. 651
Krascheninnikow, A. 313; 491
Krasker, W.S. 640
Krebs, C. 397
Krech, D. 362
Krehl, H. 762
Kreikebaum, H. 163; 584ff.; 846/847; 849
Krell, G. 673; 675; 678
Krelle, W. 12; 15
Kress, H. 897
Kreutzer, P.H. 773
Kreuzer, P. 820
Krischausky, D. 450; 453
Krockov, v. 137
Kropff, B. 516
Kropotkin, P. 131; 137; 144; 817
Kropp, E. 10; 11; 572
Krug, C.E. 146; 150
Krümmel, H.-J. 762
Kruse, H. 632; 637
Kubcek, H. 507; 510
Kubista, B. 850
Kück, M. 103; 106; 488; 632; 637; 664; 822; 872; 875
Kuczynski 874
Kühl, R. 12; 15

Kuhn, J. 136; 141; 205; 277; 362; 383; 574; 651; 692; 846; 875
Kuhn, W. 142
Kühne, K. 731
Kulischer, J. 436
Kullmer, L. 403
Kumar, B. 510; 524; 526/527
Kumari 912; 914
Kunczik, M. 145
Küng, E.; 802
Kunze, J. 596
Küpper, H.-U. 159; 163; 708
Kuske, B. 436
Kylebäck, H. 157; 669/670

Laakkonen, V. 344; 346; 621/622; 709; 716; 802; 806; 875
Lacher, Ch. 915
Lafarge, P. 814
Laidlaw, A. 225/226; 715
Lambert, K. 609/610; 613
Lambert, P. 64; 106; 136; 716; 803; 806; 876
Lamming, G.N. 910; 914/915
Lampe, W. 762
Lampert, H. 136; 371/372; 424; 742; 745; 877; 144; 817
Landauer, G. 144; 472; 817
Landrat Brandt 447
Lang, J. 7; 40; 42; 74; 78; 376; 517; 540; 543; 559/560; 563; 568; 628; 630ff.; 765
Lange, O. 808; 810
Langefeld-Wirth 523; 527
Lansbury, R. 110
Lanza del Vasto 130
Lanzendörfer, M. 392; 846
Larenz, K. 75; 78
Laske, St. 637; 671; 673f.; 676; 678
Lassalle, F. 104; 183; 424; 439; 518; 716; 810ff.; 890
Lasserre, G. 136; 429; 876; 879
Latapi, P. 329
Laurinkari, J. 120; 123; 127; 142; 163; 344ff.; 422; 429; 491; 613; 620ff.; 654; 708; 715/716; 721; 739; 794; 796; 802; 806; 875; 879; 916; 919
Laux, H.8 68
Lavergne, B. 136; 144; 146; 817; 876
Law, P. 538
Le Coutre, W. 382
Le Coz, J. 234
Leary, T. 470
Leber, G. 56
Lechner, K. 488
Leffson, U. 1; 2; 5; 14; 114

Lehmann, W. 64; 68
Lehnhoff, J. 343
Leibenstein, H. 877
Leidel, H. 172
Leipold, H. 287
Lekachman, R. 602; 614/615
Léman, G. 648; 651
Lemeunier, F. 661
Lenel, H.O. 610
Lenfers, G. 33; 112; 114
Lengwieler, Ch. 488
Lenin, W.I. 207; 392; 428; 718ff.; 807/808; 828; 833; 810ff.; 815
Leo XIII, Pope 424; 428
Lerner, D. 887
LeVay, C. 600; 602
Levitsky, J. 573
Lewis, J.D. 838/839; 841
Lezius, H.M. 632; 637; 672/673; 674ff.; 678; 875
Licht, W. 339; 343
Liebknecht, K. 813
Liefmann, W. 139; 877
Liegle, L. 730
Lincoln, A. 198
Lindemann 876
Linn, N. 488
Linneborn, F. 397
Linneke, R. 55
Linse, U. 472
Lipfert, H. 56; 69ff.; 74; 115; 184; 186; 341; 343; 382; 464; 488; 739; 878; 897
Lippe, P.v.d. 363; 367
Lippert 457
Lipset, S.M. 406
Littek, W. 675; 678
Little, I.M.D. 362
Littler, C. 678
Lockhart, J. 351
Loesch, A.v. 57; 120; 137/138; 142; 519; 637; 749; 887; 895
Logan, Ch. 616/617; 620
Löhr, A. 344; 346
Lohrberg, W. 762
Loitlsberger, E. 488
Lopes-Cardoso, A. 731
Lorange, P. 523; 527; 833; 836; 839; 841
Loris, B. 262; 264
Louis, D. 464
Louis, R. 661
Love 387
Löw, R. 773; 820
Löwe, A. 656
Löwer, M. 654
Lucas, D.J. 762
Lück, W. 510
Ludlow 424; 437; 842; 844

Luft, H. 396
Luhmann, N. 661/662; 664
Lührig, K. 343
Lumbier, L.G. 488
Lüneborg, K. 262; 265
Lürig, R. 371/372
Lütge, F. 414; 417; 436; 449
Luther, M. 511; 517; 543; 563
Luzzatti, L. 198; 221; 254
Lwenje, N 910; 915

Maaß, H.-C. 397
Mac Pherson, I. 222; 226
Machancoses, F. 179
Macharzina, K. 835; 841
Mackscheidt, K. 450; 453
Madauss, B. 488
Mäder, W. 637
Mai, D. 579
Maier, H.E. 632; 637
Mailly, L.D. 908
Maini, K.M. 63
Majluf, N.S. 833; 841
Malon, B. 289
Malt, F. 352
Malthus 811
Mändle, E. 24; 28; 29; 120; 127; 150; 171; 273; 343; 382; 445; 584; 592; 613; 654; 684; 749; 769; 784; 864
Manewald, P. 5; 12; 14; 142
Mangoldt, K.v. 447
Mangoldt, R.v. 447; 449
Mann, R. 278; 281
Mannheim, K. 143; 146; 818; 820
Männicke, A. 916; 918/919
Manning, P. 772/773
Mansilla, H.C.F. 887
Manuel, F. 429
Manz, C.C. 664
Mao Tse-tung 887
March, J.G. 461; 464; 181; 877
March, K.S. 913; 915
Marcharzina, K. 510; 522; 525; 527
Marcus 715
Marcuse, H. 470
Mariadis, St. 15; 29; 32
Mariátegui, J.C. 49ff.
Mark-Ungericht, B. 673; 678
Markowitz, H.M. 71; 74
Marris 877
Marschak, J. 584; 586
Marsh, Th. 676; 678
Marshall, A. 92/93; 97ff.; 100; 614; 875; 877; 907
Martens, W. 671; 678
Marthelot, P. 234
Martin, D. 262; 265

Martov 814
Marx, J. 812
Marx, K. 50; 121; 144; 146; 273; 392; 439; 518; 607; 655; 667; 671; 678; 716/717; 755/756; 770; 807; 810ff.; 815; 828; 886; 890/891
Marx, M.T. 572
Marzouki, I. 234
Maslow, A. 100; 184; 636/637; 794
Massing, A. 51; 572; 700
Matenaar, D. 186
Mathieu, E. 386/387
Mathieu, G. 508; 510
Matz, C. 632; 637
Mauniel. F. 429
Maurer, v. 874
Maurice 424; 437; 842
Maxeiner, R. 418; 624; 623; 626
Mayer 562
Mayer, E. 100; 162/163
Mayntz, R. 56; 802
Mayoux, L. 910/911; 915
Mc Allister, D. 676; 678
Mc Auslan, J.P.W.B. 45/46; 63
Mc Bride, G. 226
Mc Lanahan, J.& C. 226; 330
Mc Laughlin, C. 131
Mead, M. 51; 874
Meade, J.E. 537/538
Meding 636
Meffert, H. 338
Meghji, Z. 915
Meier-Dallach, H.-P. 405/406
Meissner, H.-G. 526/527
Meitzel,C. 457
Menger, C. 602; 907
Menkhaus, H. 749
Menn, H. 339
Mentrup, H. 343
Meran,G. 538
Merkle, E. 640
Merle, W. 540; 543,
Mersmann, A. 57
Merton, R. 621/622
Mesarovic, M.D. 191; 193
Mestmäcker, E.J. 543
Metersky, M.L. 362
Metz, E. 5; 7; 111; 114; 540; 568; 918/919
Metzger, H. 584; 749
Meulenbergh, G. 38ff.; 77f.; 444f.; 517:543; 552; 559; 563; 568; 627; 630; 632; 765
Meyer 676/677
Meyer, A. 14/15
Meyer, B. 51; 77f.; 142

Meyer, E.H. 38ff.,42; 376; 444/445; 517; 543; 552; 559; 563; 568; 627; 630; 632; 765
Meyer, O. 164
Meyer, P.A. 277; 281
Meyer, W.E. 568
Meyns, P. 846
Michailidis, I. 15; 16
Michels, R. 405; 647/648; 651
Middleton, J. 47; 51; 406
Mieszczerjakow, N.L. 807
Migot-Adholla, S.E. 293; 299; 700
Milbrath, L.W. 796
Milhaud, E. 136; 492
Miliband, R. 667
Mill, J.St. 63; 92ff.; 100; 602; 613ff.; 615; 777; 875f.; 907
Mill, James 614
Miller, J.G. 192/193
Milutin, W. 807
Minc, A. 179
Mingo, K.A. 262; 265
Mintzberg, H. 580; 584
Miquel, v. 428
Mirrlees, J.A. 362
Misael 754
Mithat Pascha 250
Mladenatz, G. 64
Moecke, H.-J. 527
Mohamed Ali 224; 226
Mohr, W. 633; 637
Molitor, B. 344; 346
Möller, H. 703; 705
Mommsen,W.J. 873
Moncef, D. 234
Montesquieu 815
Montolfo, J.M. 550
Moody, J.C. 53; 85; 224; 226
Moore, W.E. 464; 469; 802
Moragas, R. 172; 179
Moreau, J. 285; 292
Morley, J.A.E. 687
Morris, D. 131; 472
Morton,A.L. 667
Morus 423; 469
Mose, K. 36/37; 39; 42
Moser, C. 913; 916
Moutsopoulos, N. 16
Moxter, A. 3; 7
Mubarak 643
Muckle, T.B. 424; 575; 579
Mühlbauer, F. 724; 726
Müko-Reuter 76
Mülayim, Z.G. 254
Mulford, Ch.L. 362
Müller, A. 74/75; 234
Müller, C. 559
Müller, H. 423; 429; 436

Müller, J.O. 64; 70; ; 78; 181; 186; 362; 423; 425/426; 429; 436; 440; 469; 472; 647; 690ff.; 700; 802; 841; 846; 875
Müller, K. 517; 627; 628ff.; 632; 540ff.; 543; 646; 563; 568
Müller, W. 412; 417
Müller-Gangloff, E. 775
Müller-Jentsch, W. 673; 675; 678
Munding, K. 457
Münkner, H.-H. 42/43; 46; 51; 57; 62/63; 79; 101ff.; 106; 124/125; 127; 136; 140ff.; 182; 186; 203ff.; 254/255; 259; 292; 295/296; 299; 392; 397; 409; 453; 543; 550; 646; 656; 661; 686; 692/693; 700; 716; 743; 745; 799; 801; 828; 846; 875; 897
Münstermann 424
Münzel, F. 92
Münzinger, A. 732; 736
Muralt, J.v. 550; 898; 906
Murdock, G.P. 47; 51
Muré, G. 610; 613
Musgrave, P.B. 403
Musgreave, R.A. 403
Mussons, S. 173; 179
Musto, S.A. 254; 362
Muzik, J. 313
Myers, Ch.A. 468; 820
Myrdal, G. 217; 222; 731

Na Aman 424
Naphtali, F. 890
Napoléon Bonaparte, L. 63; 778
Napoleon III. 439
Naschold, F. 648/649; 651; 678
Nathan, A.S. 92
Naucke,W. 406
Nauyen-Manh-Tu 700
Nchari, A.N. 292ff.; 299
Nehammer, D. 897
Nehru, P. 245
Neide, K.v.d. 397
Nell-Breuning, O.v. 136; 404; 671; 678; 731; 858ff.
Nelson, R. 607:613
Neubohn, H.-J. 731
Neumann, G.C. 385
Neumann, M. 70; 74; 115; 748/749; 823; 873; 877; 885
Neumann, R. 442; 444/445
Neurath, O. 53
Newbold, P. 262; 265
Newman, W. 100; 640
Nicholson, F.A. 57; 63
Niehaus, G. 277; 278

Niehaus, H.J. 262ff.; 265; 281; 575; 761
Niehues, K. 654
Niessler, E. 917; 919
Nilsson; J. 31; 34; 35; 157; 596; 600; 602; 873
Nishida, Takeshi 130
Nishida, Tenko 130
Noelle, Th. 110; 114; 444/445; 543
Nonow, M. 709
Nordhoff, Ch. 131
North 874; 877
Novy, K. 53; 57; 101; 103; 139; 142; 453; 632; 637; 874
Nowak, G. 385
Noyes, J.H. 127; 131
Nuthmann, R. 637
Nutzinger, H.G. 103; 410; 412; 875; 519; 538; 584
Nyerere, J.K. 48; 51; 144; 202; 294; 299; 886/887

O'Connor, F. 131
O'Donnell, C. 158; 163; 580; 584
Oakeshott, R. 616; 620
Oakley, P. 906
Obaidullah Khan, A.Z. 802
Oberender, P. 703; 705
Obote, M. 886
Odede, O. 63; 647
Oebser, A. 626
Oelsch, G. 120
Oertzen, v. 51,
Oettle 875
Oexle, O.G. 413; 417
Ohlenroth, W. 762
Ohlmeyer, D. 4; 7; 120; 376; 563; 743; 769
Ohlson, J.A. 262; 265
Ohm, H. 596; 701ff.; 705; 873; 879
Ojo, A.T. 205
Okereke, O. 294; 299
Olabarri, I. 620
Oldewurtel, G. 684
Olesch, G. 488
Ollila, P. 599; 602
Olson, M. jr. 9; 221/222; 798; 802; 877
Olson, J.A. 265
Olson, M. 401; 403; 462; 464; 885
Oncken, H. 423
Oppen, v. 426
Oppenheimer, F. 54; 101; 143/144; 146; 212; 410; 448; 519; 616; 634; 637; 654ff.; 728; 731; 820; 885; 887
Oram, B. 92
Örne, 709

Ortlieb, H.D. 750
Ortmann, G. 675; 678
Osgood, C.E. 362
Ostergaard, G.N. 648; 651
Osthold, P. 672; 678
Otto, R. 769
Ouchi, W.G. 180; 186; 673
Ouma, S.Y. 294; 299
Oußedrago, L.B. 700
Oved, Y. 127; 131
Owen, R. 16; 121/122; 128; 131; 144; 309; 405; 410; 424; 437; 454; 456; 469; 518; 614; 665ff.; 668; 717; 817; 842; 885

Pacanosky, M.E. 677
Packe, M.S.J. 615
Paeplow, F. 53
Painz, E. 916
Palandt, O. 79
Paley, M. 602
Palgi, M. 917
Pandit Nehru 241
Pantaleoni, M. 908
Pareto, V. 92/93; 96/97; 100; 603; 877; 907ff.
Parhusip, U. 573
Parker, S.R. 464; 469
Parkinson 651
Parnell, E. 686
Parsons, T. 466ff.; 469
Parvinen, J. 345; 346
Pascale, R.T. 180; 186
Patera, M. 141; 273; 654; 739; 820ff.; 872; 875
Paton, R. 664
Pattnaik, U. 242
Patzelt, W. 678
Pauli, H. 584
Paulick, H. 77; 79; 102/103; 106; 120; 140; 553; 559; 765
Paulig, O. 654
Paulsen, I. 457
Pausenberger, E. 835; 841
Pavitt, K. 608; 613
Payot, A. 234
Peacock, A. 287
Pecqueur, C. 289
Peemöller 7
Pejovich, S. 535/536; 538
Pelzl, W. 194; 197/198; 452; 638
Penth, B. 472
Penty, A.J. 53
Pepelasis, A. 16
Pergande, H.-G. 449
Pergande, J. 449
Perrow, Ch. 673/674; 678
Persé, H.-J. 164
Personn, Ch. 637

Pesch 136; 876
Pestalozzi, J.H. 423/424; 437; 843; 886
Pestoff, V.A. 621/622; 794; 796
Peterhoff, R. 720/721
Peters, H. 171ff.
Peters, J. 472; 488
Peters, K.-H. 449
Peters, T. 676; 678
Peters, T.J. 180; 186
Petersen, H.-G. 403
Pethig, R. 403
Pfandl, E. 747ff.
Pfeffer, K.-H. 820
Pfeiffer, E. 80; 137/138; 142; 150; 425; 438; 440; 528f.; 682ff.
Pfeiffer, T. 392
Pfimlin, E. 502
Pfrunder 51
Pfüller, R. 110; 114; 860
Philipowski, R. 7; 563; 769; 865; 871
Philipps, R. 268; 272/273; 607; 701; 705
Piasny, J. 453
Pichler, J.H. 488
Pifer, H.W. 277; 281
Pigou, A.C. 92/93; 99/100; 602; 877
Piltz, K. 835; 840
Pinches, G.E. 262; 265
Pirenne, H. 436
Pius XI, Pope 198; 424
Place, F. 613
Plandt-Heinrichs 75
Planitz 874
Plato 423
Plechanow, 814
Plessner 874
Plinke, W. 762; 835; 840
Plockhey, P.C. 423; 437
Plum, W. 228; 234
Plumb, Lord 686
Plunkett, Sir H. 182; 439; 684ff.; 686
Podmore, F. 667
Poggemann 610/611
Poggemann, K. 78/79; 613
Pohle 31
Pohle, K. 838; 841
Poisson, E. 122; 144; 151
Polanyi, K. 820; 873
Pollard, S. 424; 429; 665; 667
Pollock, F. 885; 887
Pommerehne, W.W. 403
Popenoe, C. & O. 131
Popper, Sir K. 137; 273/274; 872; 877; 879

Porter, M.E. 69; 74; 583ff.; 833; 836; 841; 848; 850
Pössinger. H. 205
Potter-Webb, B. 102; 106; 876
Pottermann, P. 568
Potting, C. 634; 637
Pötzelberger 610; 613
Powell, W. 640
Power, E. 435
Pozo, C. 49
Prahalad, C.K. 507; 510
Pramod, B. 572
Preiser, E. 655/656
Preuss, W. 429; 440; 863/864
Preuß, U. 651
Prickett, M. 491
Priewasser, E. 197/198
Prinz, M. 57
Prisching, M. 820ff.
Pritzl, R. 836; 838; 840
Probst, G.J. 163; 192/193; 338
Proudhon, P.J. 144; 777; 817; 907
Prüße 12; 13; 14
Purtschert, R. 71; 74; 370ff.; 640; 919
Putman, L.L. 677
Puttermann, L. 536/537

Quadflieg, F. 170ff.
Quarter, J. 917; 919
Quinones, B.R. 572

Raab, G. 277; 281
Rabindra Nath Tagore, L. 308
Racki, M. 637
Raffee, H. 640
Rahman, A. 802
Raiffeisen, F.W. 9; 16; 28; 29; 36ff.; 42; 64/65; 80; 102; 110; 121; 139; 163; 165/166; 182ff.; 188; 198ff.; 205; 216; 224; 254; 275; 309; 313ff.; 321; 345; 386; 396; 418; 426; 438/439; 445; 453; 456; 474; 479; 499f.; 503; 543; 551ff.; 590; 610; 623/624; 626; 679/680; 691; 749; **755ff.**; 774; 778; 784; 788; 826; 842ff.846; 853; 859
Raki, M. 234
Ramirez, B. 321; 329
Rana, J.M. 309
Rasche, H.O. 489
Rath, H. 489
Rathenau, W. 136; 141
Rauter, A.E. 372
Raven, B. 362; 590; 663/664
Rawls, J. 714
Reber, G. 462; 464; 584; 678; 919

Reboul, C. 234
Rechaud, A. 397
Recke, H. 722ff.; 726
Redfern, P. 778
Reekie, W. 607; 613
Reemann 3; 7
Regis, J. 909
Reich, Ch. 470
Reichard, Ch. 640
Reiners, J. 110; 114
Reinhardt, R. 139; 517; 568; 661; 877
Reisch, E. 385; 578/579
Remmer, J. 654
Renken, C. 170
Reuter, A. 762
Reve, R. 841
Reve, T. 833/834
Rheinberg, W. 142
Ribe, H. 911/912; 915
Ricardo, D. 435/436; 614; 811
Rich 136
Richman, B.M. 179/180; 186
Richter, D. 141/142; 750
Richter, O. 5; 7
Ridder, H.-G. 918/919
Riebandt-Korfmacher, A. 449; 453
Riebel, P. 708
Rieger, W. 655
Riessman, D. 621/622
Ringle, G. 71; 74; 185/186; 371/372; 440; 442/443; 445; 461; 568; 622; 648/649; 651; 738/739; 743; 745; 872; 875
Rinn, H.S. 1; 7
Rist 875; 888
Ritschl 102; 875
Ritter 222
Ritterhausen, H. 656
Rittig, G. 750
Rius Mosoll, R. 179
Rius, R. 179
Roberts, B.C. 467; 469
Robertson, W. 778
Robotka, F. 272/273; 701; 705; 872
Rohlen, Th. 673; 678
Röhm, H. 141; 861; 864
Röhrich, W. 648; 651
Roider, W. 205
Rojas, A. 329
Rokholt 715
Römer, A.U. 403
Rondinelli, D.A. 259
Rong Lin 92
Rönnebeck, G. 392
Roos, J. 836; 839; 841
Roosevelt, Th. 685
Röper, B. 750

Röpke, J. 150; 254/255; 259; 284; 608; 613
Röpke, W. 287; 656
Roscher, W. 602; 876
Rosembuj, T. 179
Rosicrucians 431
Rosiny 871
Rösler, J. 262; 265
Rosner 917
Rossei, G. 472
Roszak, Th. 472
Rothschild, E. 211
Rothschild-Whitt, J. 664
Rothwell, R. 584; 586
Rousseau 423
Rovira, J. 179
Rowan 676/677
Roy, A. 226
Roy, E.P. 43; 46; 226
Rubin, P.H. 472; 477
Ruchonnet, L. 907
Rudolph, B. 343; 762
Rugman, A.M. 523; 527
Rundra, A. 238; 242
Runge, B. 422
Rüstow, A. 816; 820; 887
Ruthenberg, H; 9; 11; 732; 736
Ruttan, A. 802
Ruwwe, H.F. 716; 719; 721
Ryan, A. 613/614; 615

Sablonier 51
Sabry, O. 906
Sacay, O.J. 700
Säcker, F.J. 110
Sadat 643
Sager, H.P 861; 864
Sagmeister 151
Sahakari Samaj 887
Saint-Simon, C.H. Conte de 63; 121; 424; 437; 518; 614; 811
Saive, A.-M. 620
Sajhas 913
Sala, M 910; 915/916
Salinas Ramos, F. 179
Salje, P. 489
Salmón, A. 752; 754
Salomon, G. 656
Salt, J. 667
Salter, M. 271
Samaj, S. 51
Samiuddin 309
Samuelson, P.A. 402/403
San, Tenko 130
Sarvodaya 887
Sauer, K. 34; 35
Saxena, S.K. 157; 492
Say, J.B. 907
Schaan, J.L. 526/527

Schachtschabel, H. G. 103; 553; 823; 887
Schäfer, O. 68
Schäfer-Kehnert 10; 11
Schäfers, B. 406
Schaffland, H.-J. 4; 7; 540
Schäffle, A. 125; 875/876
Schanz, G. 676; 678
Schasching, J. 887
Schatzman, L. 772/773
Schauer, R. 488
Scheder, T. 172
Schediwy, R. 150; 157; 668ff.
Scheer, A.-W. 163
Schein, E.H. 180/181; 184; 186
Scheiter, S. 651
Schelsky, H. 820
Schemann, G. 277; 281; 756; 762
Scherer, F.M 608; 613
Schiedel, E. 596
Schiemenz, B. 189; 191/192
Schierenbeck, H. 1/2; 7; 140; 281
Schiller, O. 409; 519; 589; 731ff.; 736; 855; 875
Schimmelmann, W. v. 197/198
Schinke, E. 382
Schinke, K. 575; 579
Schlack, P. 428
Schlarb 543
Schlicht, E. 538
Schlieper, U. 909
Schlüter, C. 145
Schlüter, M. 4; 7,
Schmale, I. 123
Schmalenbach, E. 382; 766
Schmelzer, G. 774/775
Schmid, D. 740; 742; 794
Schmid, G. 141/142; 648; 651; 745
Schmidt, F. 42; 47; 140
Schmidt, G. 476/477
Schmidt, K. 543; 574; 579
Schmitt, G. 406; 726
Schmittchen, G. 675; 678
Schmitz-Dräger, R. 163
Schmoll 756
Schmoller, G.v. 427; 655; 876/877; 888
Schmorl, W. 787
Schnabel, H.X. 464; 874
Schneider 674; 858/859
Schneider, B. 406
Schneider, D. 7; 197/198; 343; 382; 757; 762
Schneider, H. 750
Schneider, H.J. 678
Schneider, K. 488
Schneider, U. 637; 678

Schnorr v. Carolsfeld, L. 102/103; 517; 749/750
Schobert, R. 361
Schöllhammer, H. 849/850
Scholz, Ch. 192/193
Schotenroehr, H. 7
Schrader, St. 489
Schramm, B. 371/372
Schreiner, W. 762
Schreiter, C. 607; 716
Schröder, J. 397/398
Schröter 633
Schrötter, H.J. 517
Schubert, R. 75; 79; 871
Schuchard-Ficher, Ch. 757; 762
Schudt, H. 343
Schuhmann, L. 736
Schujman, L. 916
Schuler, H. 279; 281
Schüler, M. 745; 864
Schulin, B. 172
Schüller, A. 287; 640
Schulte, B. 179
Schulte, H.-W. 5; 8; 142; 278; 281
Schultz, B. 656
Schultz, D. 404; 406
Schultz, R. 8; 11; 30; 110; 113/114; 135; 422; 450; 453; 510; 559; 828; 873; 879; 897
Schultz, T.W. 802
Schultze Kimmle 794
Schulz, U. 367; 415
Schulze, A.W. 787
Schulze, F.H. 787
Schulze-Delitzsch 16; 28; 36ff.; 42; 77; 80; 95; 101/102; 104; 110; 115/116; 119; 121; 138/139; 165/166; 182ff.; 188; 198ff.; 205; 216; 224; 254; 275; 309; 313ff.; 321; 386; 396; 406; 418/419; 422; 424; 426; 438f.; 453ff.; 493; 518; 528; 543; 551ff.; 590; 610; 623; 679/680; 683; 691; 716; 755; 778; **787ff.**; 810/811; 826f.; 842ff.; 846; 853; 859/860; 890
Schumacher, E.G. 875; 887
Schumacher, U. 891
Schumpeter, J. 56; 217; 222; 607; 613
Schürmann, K. 13; 15
Schütt 674
Schuy, St. 489
Schwan, B. 449
Schwarz, Ch. 762
Schwarz, P. 101; 105/106; 367; 369; 372; 462/463; 464; 640; 750; 872; 878

Schwedersky, T. 846
Schweisfurth, Th. 720/721
Schweitzer, M. 488; 708
Schwendter, R. 632/633; 637/638; 875
Schwier, D. 14; 15
Schwiering 675
Scott, R. 105
Seeman, M. 662; 664
Seibel, D. 47; 50; 51; 199; 205
Seibel, H.D. 569; 572; 700; 846
Seibel, W. 640
Seibert, K. 527
Seidel, E. 334; 339
Seiwert, L.J. 279; 281
Sekerak, E. 226
Seki, H. 444/445
Selchert, F.-W. 42
Selden, M. 92
Seltz, R. 671; 678
Semlinger, K. 489
Semmelroth, D. 259
Senft, G. 655/656
Senghor, L.S. 294; 886
Seraphim, H.J. 29; 30; 103; 114; 120; 138; 427; 429; 553; 663/664; 729; 731; 823; 860/861; 877
Serfling, K. 163
Sertel, M. 533; 537/538
Seuster, H. 141; 341ff.; 376; 382; 418; 519; 538; 540; 602; 741; 745; 755; 856; 858; 875; 879
Shaker 127
Shapiro, B.P. 640
Sheshadri, P. 550; 661
Shils, E.A. 466; 469
Shimerda, T.A. 262; 265
Shrestha, B.P. 573
Shub, D. 815
Siegel, T. 673; 678
Siegens, G.St. 692
Siepmann 426
Sik, O. 887
Silberman, M. 906
Silver, H. 667
Simmel, G. 465; 469; 772/773
Simon, H.A. 181; 192/193; 461; 473; 477; 877
Sims, H.P. 664
Sinkey, J.F. jr. 262; 265; 277; 281
Sira, F.N. 258/259
Siwek, T. 721
Skaupy 387
Skinner, B.F. 129; 471
Smirchich, L. 675; 678
Smith, A. 289; 338; 435; 436; 748; 881
Smithies, J. 777

Snaith, I 550; 661
Soedjono, I. 647; 690; 692
Sombart, W. 138; 872
Sonnemann, Th. 503
Sonnenschein 540/541; 543
Sorokin 873
Sotzeck, M. 722ff.; 724; 726
Southern, R. 79
Spector, B. 458; 460
Spencer, H. 100; 615
Spiethoff, A. 449
Spremann, K. 162
Springenberg, M. 916; 919
Spurk 675
Staatz, J.M. 33; 36
Staehle, W. 106; 110; 468; 678; 859
Stalin, J. 719; 808ff.; 814
Stamm, Th. 448
Starbatty, J. 603; 615
Staudenmeyer, C. 527
Staudinger 427
Staudt, E. 489
Staudt, K.A. 911; 916
Staufer, W. 77; 79
Stavenhagen, G. 909
Steder, K.H. 75; 79
Steding 632
Steger, U. 339
Stegerwald, A. 891
Stegmann, H. 637
Stehle, W. 279; 281; 562
Stein , J.H. v. 262; 265; 278/279; 435
Steinberg, R. 640
Steinbuch, K. 192/193
Steindorff, E. 23
Steiner, G. 849/850
Steiner, J. 584
Steiner, R. 470
Steinhauer, H. 726
Steinherr, A. 537/538
Steinmann, H. 344; 346; 526/527
Stern, R.N. 919
Stettena, P.L. 309
Stettner, N. 92
Stewart, D. 614
Steyrer, J. 150
Sticher, J. 110
Stigler, G.J. 603
Stober 170ff.
Stockhausen, J.v. 11
Stoffregen, H. 362; 528; 682
Stoll, G. 750
Stolte, D. 750
Stopford, J.M 526/527
Stötzel, B. 773
Straaten 141
Strasmann, J. 640
Strauss, A. 772/773

Strebel, P. 584
Streim, H. 343
Strickland, C.F. 42; 46; 60; 63
Stritzik, P. 489
Strümpell, H. 20; 23
Stryan, Y. 620
Stuchlik, K-H. 916; 919
Stürmer, M. 415ff.
Stutz, H.-R. 146; 150
Stützel, W. 382
Suci, G.J. 362
Suffel, W. 849/850
Sugakawa, K. 309
Summers, D.V. 640
Sumner W.G. 465; 469
Sun Yixian 86
Suonoja, K. 621/622
Surridge, B.J. 63
Süssmuth, R.v. 470
Svensson, C. 157
Svensson, R. 154
Swoboda, W. 120; 126; 150; 273; 313; 321; 382; 610/611; 613; 654; 769

Tacitus 431
Taffler, R.I. 262; 265
Tait, D. 47; 51; 406
Takekazu B.O. 730
Tamari, M. 762
Tannenbaum, P.H. 362
Tanner 151
Taqqu, R.L. 913; 915
Tauriainen 715
Taylor, B. 53; 162; 274; 280
Taylor, G. 615
Taylor, H. 615
Teece, D. 608; 613; 833; 835; 839; 841
Teichmann, A. 77; 79
Ter Woorst, G.J. 268; 270; 273
Terni, di 885
Terry, B. 49
Tezer, E. 575; 579
Thiefenthal, O. 637
Thieme 103; 136
Thiemeyer, T. 101; 105f.; 120; 124ff.; 136; 138/139; 142; 422; 640; 746; 750; 875; 879
Thier, E. 457
Thirkell, J.D. 686
Thom, H. 507; 510
Thomas 709
Thomas, A. 806; 899
Thomas, H. 616/617; 620
Thomas, K. 263ff.; 762
Thompson, R.J. 527
Thompson, W. 525; 614
Thordarsson, B. 489; 491

Thorwart, F. 789
Thünen, J.H.v. 875/876
Tiedtke, H. 120
Tietz, B. 101; 106; 386/387; 508; 510; 596
Tillman, N.H. 429
Timm, H. 703; 705
Tobert, M. 489
Todev, T. 309; 721
Todtling, G. 620
Tolstoy, L. 131
Tomlinson, J.W.C. 526/527
Tönnies, F. 103; 126; 143; 145; 404; 429; 815; 872
Töpfer, A. 850
Torres, L.C. 550
Totomianz, V. 51; 429; 440; 670; 860; 874
Touré, T.M. 886
Tracy, M. 647; 692; 879
Trappe, P. 46; 51; 136; 140; 144/145; 192/193; 403; 406; 872; 885
Trautmann, W. 234
Treacy, M. 142; 273; 491; 873
Treu, T. 110
Treue, W. 756
Trommsdorf 510
Tröndle, D. 489
Trotzsky 814
Trux, W. 275; 281
Tsambasis, P. 16
Tschiersch 574/575; 577
Tullock, G. 110; 114
Turban, E. 362
Turgot 811
Türk, K. 671; 674ff.; 678
Turner 563
Tütüncü, M.M. 533; 538

Ulitin, A. 51
Ullrich, G. 388; 392; 603; 801; 846
Ullrich, W. 489
Ulmer 543
Ulrich, H. 192/193
Ulrich, P. 339; 671; 677/678
Ulyanow, V.I. (Lenin) 813/814
Unterman, I. 640
Uphoff, N. 259
Uribe, G.. 751/752; 754
Uribe, G.C. 329
Urwick, R. 584
Usui 85
Utz, A.F. 861; 885; 887

Válcarcel, L. 48; 51
Vallender, H.W. 640
Vandevalle, G. 63; 647; 692

Vanek, J. 535/536; 538
Vansittart Neale, E.A. 437; 842; 846
Váradi, L. 120; 142; 273
Varady, L. 692; 647; 873; 879
Vargas, V. 752; 754
Varnholt, N.T. 897
Velarde Fuertes, J. 179
Vélasquez, R.V. 721
Velaverde Fuertes 178
Verhagen, K. 647; 691/692; 846
Vernikow, A.V. 242
Verschuer, O.W.A. Baron van 502
Vidal, I. 179
Viehoff, F. 749
Vienney, C. 291ff.
Vierheller, R. 142; 159; 163; 584; 638; 647; 651; 663/664; 855; 858; 872; 875
Vierkandt, A. 46; 51; 103; 143; 146; 404ff.; 410; 412; 816; 820
Viggo, H. 35
Vikas 5
Vilcocq, A. 692
Villegas, V.R. 517; 519
Villiers, G. de 234
Vilmar, F. 422
Vilstrup, R. 600; 602
Vincent, F. 299
Vir, D. 299ff.; 309
Viteles, H. 211
Viti de Marco, A. 655
Volk, G. 743; 745
Volk, K.O. 743; 745
Vollmar, K.-B. 472
Vormbaum, H. 343; 376; 382
Voss, Ch. 574; 579
Voßkamp, W. 429
Vyas, A. 234; 242

Wach, J. 774/775
Wacht, R.F. 640
Wachtel, F. 443ff.
Wächter, H. 110
Wacker, H. 510
Wagner, A. 192/193; 655; 875/876
Wagner, G.R. 163; 586
Wagner, H. 579; 581/582; 584/585
Wagner, H.-J. 53ff.; 120; 125; 145
Wagner, K. 676; 678
Wales 435
Walker, d.A. 907; 909
Wallerstein, I. 405; 407
Wallimann, I. 146

Walras, L. 92/93; 95; 100; 139; 292; 602/603; 877; 907ff.
Walther, U. 341; 343
Wang Shiying 92
Wapenhans, W. 397
Warbasse, J.P. 137; 142ff.; 146; 874
Ward, B. 536; 538
Warren, R.D. 362
Wartenburg, G. 464; 568
Waterman, R. 180/181; 186; 676; 678
Watkins, W.P. 101; 135; 137; 140; 142; 211; 425; 429; 778; 874; 802; 906
Webb, B. 440; 464; 469; 890
Webb, S. 440; 464; 469; 890
Weber 568
Weber, C. 677
Weber, H.-O. 7
Weber, J.L. 162/163; 292
Weber, M. 7; 8; 30; 101; 143; 146; 151; 181; 407; 414; 417; 662; 664; 676; 678; 770; 773; 805; 815; 820; 872; 875; 886
Weber, W. 596; 736; 740; 745; 823
Weder, R. 522; 527; 835; 841
Weeraman, P.E. 247; 550; 661
Wehlmann, H.-D. 477
Weibel, P.F. 261; 265
Weick, C. 725/726
Weidmüller, L. 7; 40; 42; 74; 78; 517; 540; 543; 559/560; 563; 568; 628; 630ff.; 765
Weimar 568
Weinerth, E. 372; 442; 445
Weinhold, W.A. 267
Weinkauf, W. 149/150
Weinrich, G. 262; 265; 762
Weinschenk, G. 579
Weippert, G. 30/31; 103; 135ff.; 142; 144ff.; 407; 409; 412; 815; 820; 823; 872; 877; 879,
Weisbrod, B.A. 640
Weiskopf, R. 671; 673; 676; 678;
Weiss, M. 110; 469
Weisser, G. 101; 102; 104; 106; 120; 124; 136; 138/139; 273; 420; 422ff.; 651; 731; 747; 750; 823; 872; 876/877; 879
Weiß, C. 362
Weitling, W. 121
Weizäcker, C.C.v. 538
Welge, M.K. 163; 510; 527
Welling 543
Wells, L.T. 526/527
Wendler, D. 726
Wendt, H. 679
Werbik, G. 57

Werhahn, J.W. 765
Wernli, F. 436
Wesche, R. 385
Wessel, K. 774/775
West, T. 685
Westergaard, P.W. 294; 299
Westermann, H. 103; 110/111; 115; 120; 140; 407; 517; 553; 562; 568; 650
Wettschurek, G. 362
Weuster, A. 345/346; 423ff.; 428
Whewell 877
Whitaker, J.K. 603
White, M.J. 640
Whitford, D.T. 262; 265
Whyte, W.F. 620
Widmann 562
Widstrand, C.G. 63; 204
Wiener, N. 187; 192/193
Wiesenthal 136
Wilbrandt, R. 656
Wilhelm I 439
Wilhelm I. 787
Wilkinson, P. 917; 919
Willeitner, S. 464
Willgerodt, H. 287; 608; 613; 828
Williamson, O.E. 256; 259; 472ff.; 477; 523; 815; 820; 833; 841; 877; 879
Willke, H. 465; 469
Wilpert, B. 110; 468
Wilson, Th. 647
Winch, D. 614; 615
Wind, J. 31; 36
Winkler, K. 765
Winter, G. 339
Winter, H.-W. 343; 382; 584; 613; 684; 784; 864
Winter, S.G. 607; 613
Wissell, R. 412ff.; 417
Wißmann, G. 745
Witte, E. 102; 136; 141; 648; 651
Wittmann, W. 126; 343; 510; 654
Wittvogel 50; 51
Woermann, E. 574/575; 579
Wöhe, G. 382; 654; 741
Wöhlken, E. 11; 722
Wolf, E. 398
Wolff, G. 489
Wolff, H.W. 170ff.; 198; 812
Wolfsteeter, E. 538; 721
Woll, A. 135; 287; 828
Wondung, S. 245
Woodward, S. 472:477
Wörz, J.G.F. 692; 731; 733/734; 736; 802
Wright, D. 129
Wu Yihuan 92
Wu Yuzhang 92

Wülker, H.-D. 502/503
Wunderer, R. 584; 678; 919
Wurl, H.-J. 157
Wurm, Sh. 472

Xiahzou, X. 85
Xyts, V. 16

Yamagishi, Miyoso 130
Yamey, B.S. 361
Yang Jianbai 92
Yang Peilun 92
Yeo, P. 661
Yetley, M.J. 362

Zablocki, B. 131
Zaltman, G. 640
Zand, D. 673; 678
Zander, E. 110
Zangemeister, Ch. 362
Zauels, G. 909
Zavgren, C.V. 262; 265
Zeidler, H. 440
Zerche, J. 110; 113; 115; 123; 126/127; 135; 141/142; 419; 422; 449/450; 453; 510; 559; 573; 613; 828; 873; 879; 897
Zheng Gang 92

Zhou Jinting 92
Zhou Wanjun 92
Ziegler, R. 802
Zimmermann, P. 855; 858
Zipp, W. 150/151
Zöller, W. 517
Zöllner 561/562
Zörcher, J. 700
Zorn, W. 412/413; 417
Zülow, 871
Zünd, A. 163
Zur, E. 163
Zweckfeld, W. 584; 586

Subject Index

20-point-programme, 1986 239; 311/312
AACE 348
Abgabenordnung 4; 747
absence of hierarchy 145
abuse of market power 133
Academy of German Co-operatives 317ff.
accounting 1; 2; 4; 5; 7
Accounting in Co-operatives 1
accounting system 7
ACCU 301
ACFSMCs 305
achieving efficiency 257
ACOPAM 904/905
ACOSCA 202; 296
activity profile 837
acts of the Apostles 431
additional bodies 660
additional payments 28
addressees of evaluation results 357
administrative bodies 276
administrative model 9
advisory committees 71
Afghanistan 300
Africa Cooperative Saving and Credit Association (ACOSCA) 202; 296
african socialism 48,203; 886
african way of life 294
aftermath of the audit 39
agency problems 884
ager compascuus 431
AGI 29
AGR 195
Agrarhandelsunion der Vereinigten Landwarenkaufleute GmbH 12
agrarian communism 49
agrarian reform in 1972 231
agrarian revolution 233
agricultural circle 383
agricultural co-operatives 222ff.; 229; 239; 249
agricultural commodities trade 11; 13; 14
agricultural consumer associations 427
Agricultural Credit and Co-operatives 8

agricultural credit co-operatives (ACCs) 250
agricultural extension services 9; 733
agricultural production co-operatives 207; 830
agricultural service co-operatives for French farmers 227
Agricultural Trade 11; 12; 13
AHVA 1915 211
AIFCOSPIN 235
Akademie Deutscher Genossenschaften 318ff.
Aktiengesetz 559
ALCECOOP 221; 323
alcoholics anonymous 422
algerian entreprise autogérée 518
algerian experience 232/233
all-credit co-operatives 626
all-finance package 112
all-purpose co-operative Banks 165; 168
all-russian Bolshevik Party 814
all-society property 808
Allgemeine Geschäftsbedingungen 75
Allgemeiner deutscher Arbeiterverein 788
Allgemeiner Genossenschaftsverband 891
Allgemeiner Verband der auf Selbsthilfe beruhenden deutschen Erwerbs- und Wirtschaftsgenossenschaften 37; 314; 788
alliance infrastructure 838
alliances 835
Allmende 432
allocation of competencies for goal definition 857
alternative co-operative 144
alternative economy 143
Alternative Liste für Demokratie und Umweltschutz 632
alternative political concepts 521
Amana (1842) 127
Ambelakia Syntrofia 15
American Constitution 435

American Economics Association 907
American Insitute of Cooperation (A.I.C.) 331
Amish 410
AMSAC 388ff.; 904
ANCD 120
ancien régime 888
ANGKASA 304
Anglo-Irish War 685
Angola 201
annual business report 376
annual financial report 2; 7
annual financial statement 1/2; 38; 373
ANP 231
anthroposophy 470
anti-trust authority 17
Anti-Trust Laws 17
anti-trust laws of the European Community (European Union) 387
Anwaltschaft der deutschen Erwerbs- und Wirtschaftsgenossenschaften 788
Anwaltschaftverband 37
apostles 127
application of multivariate disciminatory analysis procedures 262
appreciation 866
Arbeiter-Lesebuch 424
Arbeiterfrage 424
Arbeiterselbsthilfe Frankfurt 470
Arbeiterwohnungsbaugenossenschaften 394,
Arche (France) 471
Argentina 751
Arisan Manjung 572
aristotelian logic 101
article 85 of the EC (EU) Treaty 387
artifacts and creations 180
artisans' settlement co-operatives 251
Arusha Declaration 203
Asian and Pacific Regions 299
asiatic despotism 406
ASKO 153
assembly of delegates 443

assessment center methodology 279
Assessment of Success 23ff.
associate members of the World Council 187
association 16
association d'intérêt rural (AIR) 408
Association for the Consolidation of Landholders 172
Association of Co-operative Banks of the EC (ACB) 347; 498
Association of Co-operative Science Institutes (AGI) 29ff.
Association of Cooperative Educators (A.C.E.) 332
association of production enterprises 23
Association of social building Enterprises 55
Association ouvrière de Production 63
Associations for Raw Materials 555
associations of agricultural producers 347
assortment 31
Assortment Policies 32
Assoziation 788
Assoziationsbuch für deutsche Handwerker und Arbeiter 426; 788
AUCP(B) (All-Union Communist Party/Bolshevik) 530
audit 549
audit compensation 41
audit of a merger 41
audit of a resumption 41
audit of conveyance 41
audit of custodianship accounts 41
audit of enforced settlement 41
audit of the financial position 39
audit report 39
audit upon formation 40
audit upon restructuring 41
auditing 80; 84; 148; 222; 235; 557
auditing federation (Prüfungsverband) 36
Auditing, Co-operative 36
Auroville (India) 471
Australia 300; 307
Austrian Co-operative Law of 1873 205
Authorities, Co-operative 42ff.
Autochthonous Co-operatives 46ff.; 886

autochthonous forms of self-help organizations 693
autochthonous self-help organizations 844
Autogestio Sanitaria 175
autonomous co-operatives 643; 831
autonomous self-help organizations 10
average variable costs 702
AWG 394,
ayllu 49; 217; 519
Ayni 519

B.E.G.Bank 353
backward diversification 268
balance sheet 1; 2; 26/27
balance-sheet law 7
Banco Cooperative Espanol 83/84
Bangladesh 300/301
Bangladesh Co-operative College (BCC) 301
Bank Europäischer Genossenschaftsbanken 353
Bank für Gemeinwirtschaft 57
Bank für Landwirtschaft und Nahrungsgüterwirtschaft 393
Bank of Israel 216
Bank Rating 52
Bankinformation 680
Banking Management Seminar 316
bankruptcy proceedings 630
basic assumptions 180
basic co-operative Gestalt 103
basic democracy versus a representational method 661
basic modalities of the strategical procedure 842
basic model for the selection of members 795
basque nationalism 616
Bäuerliche Handelsgenossenschaften 392; 779
Bauhaus 56
Bauhütte 518
Bauhütte Movement 53ff.; 450
Bausparkasse der Deutschen Volksbanken AG 66
Bausparkasse Schwäbisch Hall 790
beginnings of co-operative education 314
Behavioural Options with Regard to Environmental Protection 335
Benin 295

Berliner gemeinnützige Baugesellschaft 425; 446
Berliner Kammergericht 18
Betriebsfunktionales Kommunikationssystem 588
Betriebsordnung 108
Betriebsverfassungsgesetz 106
Betriebswirtschaftslehre der Kooperative 855
Betriebszweig-Gemeinschaft 383
BHG 392; 379
Bhutan 300/301
BIK 194
Bilanzrichtliniengesetz 4; 37; 552
Bina Swadaya 572
biographical questionnaire 279
bisectoral world-view 139
bivariate discriminatory analysis 261
BJSU 301
BKS 105
black box analysis 264
black market 9
Blätter für Genossenschaftswesen 314; 679; 788
Blessed Sacrament 414
bloodbrothers 412
BNDS 697
board of directors 71; 91; 279
Bohemian Brothers 435; 469
Bolivia 752
bookkeeping 36
Botswana 295
bottom-up 250
Bourgeois Society 817
brands 34
Brazil 752
British-Indian Pattern of Cooperation 42; 57ff.; 200; 546
brotherhood 15
brotherhood groups 774
brothers for communal life 775
Bruderhof movement 128
Brunei 300
Building and Loan Associations, Co-operative 64
building and loan societies 164
Building and Loan Society „Schwäbisch Hall" 783
Building Societies 64
building-saving contract 66
Bulgaria 311/312; 830/831
bulletin Cooppresse 333
Bürgerliches Gesetzbuch (BGB) 398
Bürgschaftsgenossenschaft 164
Burkina Faso 296

business communication system 588
business features 104
Business Policies, Co-operative 69
business policy 25; 26; 69
BUUD 246
BVR 5; 317; 680; 779
by-laws 1; 3; 19; 28; 36; 75ff.; 95; 103; 118; 139; 170; 182; 209; 229/230; 342; 367; 443; 540
by-laws of a co-operative joint stock company 512
By-laws of the Co-operative Society 74ff.
Byzantine late antiquity 817

C.C.A. 333
C.C.C. 333
CAB 302
cabinet 787
Caisse Centrale des Banques Populaires (CCBP) 82; 84; 166
Caisse Centrale Desjardins, Quebec, 84
Caisse Centrale du Crédit Mutuel (CCCM) 81/82
Caisse Centrale Raiffeisen, Luxembourg 80
Caisse Nationale de Crédit Agricole (CNCA) 81; 84; 165
Caixa Cental de Crédito Agricola Mutuo 84
Caja Laboral Popular 616
Cajas Rurales 83/84
Calgary Consumers Co-operative 225
Cameroon 295ff.
Cameroon Co-operative law (1992) 298
Cameroonian law No. 92/006 of August 14,1992 407
Canada 332
Canadian Co-operative Association (C.C.A.) 333
Canadian Co-operative Credit Society, Toronto 84; 224
Canadian Co-operatives Association 223
canon for the formation of informal co-operatives 472
CAPAM 231
CAPCS 232
capital 812/813
capital costs 26
capital life span 378
capitalist firm (CF) 533ff.
capitalizing assets 866

capitulare de villis 431
CAPRA 232
CAPS (Coopérative Agricole Polyvalente communale de Services 231
CARMEL winegrowers co-operative 211
Carolingian villicationes progresses 431
cartel agreement 17
cartel authority 22
cartel decision 17
cartel office 21/22
cartels 17; 20; 71; 103; 105; 112; 119; 133; 151; 284
CASE (computer aided software engineering) 197
cash/export crops 202
categories of equity capital 340
catholic church 774
catholic social doctrine 673
CATIC 90
Caudillo principle 217
causal structure of co-operative policy 255
CCA 232
CCAM (Caisse Centrale de Crédit Artisanal et Maritime 229
CCC 223
CECODHA 348
CECOP 348
CECOTOS 348
CEFDEC 44
Celts 430
Centesimus Annus (1991) 885
central co-operative banks 111
Central Co-operative Institutions 80
central co-operatives 80/81; 112; 781
Central Committee of the Communist Party 209
Central Council of Supply and Marketing Co-operatives of Vietnam 304
Central Federation of German Industrial Co-operatives 139
central institutions 194
central institutions in selected countries 80
central issuing and/or underwriting authorities 164
central organization of rural co-operatives, Teheran 302
central plan 809
Central Union of Consumers' Co-operatives 306

centrally planned economic system 206
centrally planned economies 641/642; 281/282
Centrosojuz 206; 313
Centurai settlements 430
CEPAL 326
CEPRA (Cooperative d'Elevage Pastorale de la Révolution Agraire) 232
CERA Centrale Raiffeisenkas, Louvain 80; 84
certified public accountant (Wirtschaftsprüfer) 37; 38
CET Programmes in Australia and the Pacific 307
CET Programmes in Central Asia 306
CET Programmes in Northern-Eastern Asia 305
CET Programmes in South-East Asia 303
CET Programmes in Southern Asia 300
CET Programmes in Western Asia 307
chamber of certified accountants 38
chambers of commerce 170
Chambers of Handicrafts and Craftsguilds 172
Chambers of Industry and Commerce 172
champs communs 519
Changes on the Secondary Level 953
Characteristics of the International Co-operative Alliance (ICA) 419
charismatic management 181
charitable or philanthropical associations 291
Charte Coopérative 233
Charter of social economy in 1982 288
Chemelil Sugar Company 734
chengbao system 86
chest 414
Chile 49; 752
China 49; 300; 305
China International Famine Relief Comission 86
China, Actual Co-operative Development in 85ff.
Chinese Constituion of Dec. 1982 86
Chinese economy 785
choice of legal Form 825

christian and socialis social reforms 437
christian building productive societies 55
christian socialists 63; 121; 182; 424; 844
christian trade union 54
christian unions 892
CICA 85
CICP 354
CICTAB 301/302
CIRCOM 681
CIRDAP 301
CIRIEC 492
CIUDEC 221; 323
class-struggle 151
Classical and Neoclassical Contributions to Co-operative Theory 92
Classical British Indian Pattern 42; 57ff.; 200; 546
classical literature 437
Classification and Typologies of Co-operatives 100
classification of economic science 655
classification results from parent population data 262
classifications of markets 598
cloister co-opertives 774
CLT 304
club goods 403
Clubes des Madres 913
CMSC 303
CNLAMCA 288
co op Zentrale AG 894
co-determination 143; 182; 673; 916
Co-determination Act of 1976 106ff.
Co-determination in Germany 106
co-operate identity 70/71; 878
co-operation 815ff.
co-operatism 86; 96; 88
co-operative as a socio-technical economic system 587
co-operative as a system 873
co-operative as controlling enterprise 540
co-operative assistance fund 790
co-operative autonomiy 111
Co-operative Banks 163ff.; 185; 194; 207; 275; 278/279; 789ff.; 829; 850
co-operative bodies 229
Co-operative Code of the Philippines 544
Co-operative College 305; 777

Co-operative College of Malysia 304
Co-operative College Stanford Hall 29
Co-operative Colony Merhavia 212
co-operative combine 110ff.; 185; 557
co-operative commonwealth 128; 137; 144; 425; 668; 777
co-operative community 309
Co-operative Community of New Harmony 121
Co-operative Congress in Ipswich 1889 602
co-operative consciousness 739
co-operative corporate philosophy 159
co-operative credit institutions 847
Co-operative Credit Societies Act 235
Co-operative Credit Societies Bill 58
co-operative culture 135
co-operative democracy 662
co-operative democratic structure 883
co-operative departments 43/44; 60ff.
co-operative development in the Post Mao Era 86
co-operative education 225; 300
co-operative education in Latin-America 323/324
co-operative entrepreneurship 256/256
co-operative equity 375
co-operative evolution 123/124
co-operative executive entity 503
co-operative factories 812
co-operative failure 254
co-operative federation 148/149; 252
Co-operative Guaranty Fund for Deposit Security 790
co-operative hospital 176
co-operative housebuilding societies 556
Co-operative Housing Foundation of Canada 333
co-operative idea 423
co-operative identity 184; 370
co-operative ideology 25; 136
co-operative law 12; 20; 43; 45; 74; 111; 139; 276; 279; 450
co-operative law for Guangdong province 86

Co-operative Law in the (former) Soviet Union 519
co-operative law no. 1163 passed in 1963 250
co-operative league 199
Co-operative League of Thailand 304
co-operative models 116
co-operative movement 42/43; 137/138; 207
Co-operative Network 196
co-operative organization 75
co-operative organizational structures 142
co-operative ownership 285
co-operative philosophy 135
co-operative plan 207
Co-operative Policies in Primary Co-operatives 70
co-operative principles 39; 78; 89; 136; 138; 142; 234; 356; 543; 556
co-operative principles and the identity 612
co-operative register 75
co-operative republic 122
co-operative rules 431
co-operative rural bank 241
co-operative savings banks in Finland 803
Co-operative Scientific Quarterly 681
co-operative self-image 581
co-operative services 806
co-operative settlements 201; 410
co-operative social structure 142
Co-operative Societies Act of 1925 235
Co-operative Societies Act of 1947 695
co-operative society 143
co-operative society law 48
co-operative strategies 135
co-operative success 376
co-operative surplus 122
co-operative system 411
co-operative theory 24
co-operative theory in the history of ideas 875
Co-operative Training College at Lyalpur 303
co-operative training opportunities in Africa 295
co-operative union 208
Co-operative Union of Philippines 304
co-operative universities 312

Co-operative University of Paris 295
Co-operative Wholesale Society 683; 777
Co-operative/Credit Union Dictionary and Reference 330
co-operatives as public bodies 420
co-operative combines in Western Europe 113
co-operatives during the colonial era 227
co-operatives for commonweal 101
Co-operatives for drying products 781
Co-operatives for flowers 781
Co-operatives for public services 751
co-operatives for the promotion of agricultural production 9
co-operatives for vocational trades 115
Co-operatives in socialism 716
Co-operatives in South Asia 238
co-operatives in the Arctic amongst the Inuit 223
co-operatives in the economic sense 103
co-operatives in the legal sense 103
co-operatives of agricultural circles 207
Co-operatives under Public Law 170ff.
co-operativistic pluralistic ideologies 137
co-operativists 876
co-operativization 144; 819
co-ordination of activities 282
co-ordination of the combine 370
Coady International Institute 333
code of behavior 790
COGECA (General Committee of Agricultural Cooperation in the EEC 347; 311
COLAC 323
COLACOT 222; 323
collective business managers 634
collective goods 399
collective interests 636
collective property 87
collectivism 138
collectivization of agriculture 207
collectivization process 207
College Cooperatif 29

College of Agricultural Banking 302
collegia 469
colonial times 405
Columbia 752
combine systems 7
Combine, Co-operative 110
Comite General de la Cooperaiton Agricole de la CEE (COGECA) 495
commercial co-operatives 182
Commercial Purchasing and Service Co-operatives 115ff.
Commission Centrale de Surveillance des Societé Indigène de Prévoyance 44
Committee for Trade and Inndustry 788
common alliance motives 836
common companionship 15; 16
common initiative groups 298; 407; 699
Common Man's Charta 49
common market 468
common purpose 17
commonweal economic enterprises 285
commonweal economy (Gemeinwirtschaft) 123ff.; 125; 138; 746
commonweal Sector 124
commonweal undertakings 123
Commonwealth, Co-operative 120ff.
communal settlements 127ff.
Communaucratie 49
communautés 435
communidades 49
Communist Manifesto 121; 812; 891
Community of the Ark 130
Community of Independent States (CIS) 313
company group 111ff.
company philosophy 582
competition 12; 14; 27; 93ff.; 112; 119; 131; 159; 195; 258; 282ff.; 285; 291; 356; 457; 862/863
Competition and Co-operatives 131ff.
competition as a process of discovery 132
competition policy 21; 69; 132
competitive advantages 835
competitive economy 256
competitive-evolutionary process 259
comptroller of the currency 280
comptrollership (Revision) 36

compulsory co-operative 144
compulsory economic system 102
compulsory measures 170
compulsory membership 201
COMSEC 293
Concentration 371
Concept of Marketing 596/597
concept of plight 182
concept of synergism 70
concept of the strategic family 835
conceptions of the 19th century 182
Conceptions, Co-operative 135
concepts of equity capital 339
conciliation commitee (Einigungsstelle) 109
Concordia 454/455
concurrent evaluation 358; 360
Confederation des Caisses Populaires d'economie Desjardins du Quebec 224
Conféderation Générale des Sociétées Coopératives Ouvrières de Production 518
confederations 187
Configuration of Co-operative Society 142
conflict and cooperation 465
conflict and harmony theory 345
conflict theory 70
conflicts in Cooperation 634
conflicts in payment 636
Conseil canadien de la coopération (C.C.C.) 333
Consolidation and Competition 609
Constituent National Assembly 1848 106
constitution of 1945 245
constitution of the economy 281
constitutive elements 433
construction guild movements 53
consulting 11
consulting concept of organization development 150
Consulting for Co-operatives 146ff.
consumer and supply co-operatives 599
Consumer Associations 555
consumer co-operative chain UNI-COOP 218
Consumer Co-operatives 28; 32ff.; 94/95; 97; 113; 121; **150ff.**; 163; 182/183; 185; 204; 207; 222; 225; 243; 251; 405;

552; 827; 718; 753; 794; 803; 811; 829; 862/863; 886; 890ff.
consumer co-operatives as employers 892
consumer protection 803
consumers cooperation 212
consumption credit 8
Consumvereine 683
contents of co-operative laws 547
continuing education 711
continuous handshake 833
contract between the alliance partners 839
contract co-operatives 720
contract portfolio 67
contract-based group of companies 541
contracts and resolutions 23
contractual joint ventures 522
control 190/191
control and/or surveillance system 276
control of joint ventures 526
controlling 5
controlling economic power 132
Controlling in Co-operatives 157ff.
controlling instruments 160f.
convergence theory 144
Coop Dortmund 153
Coop Dortmung Kassel eG 895
coop-AG 153
cooperation and individual welfare 879
cooperation and social welfare 880
cooperation grid 834/835
cooperation in ownership 103
cooperativas 216
Cooperativas en America Latina 221
Cooperative Alumni Association 330
Cooperative Business Journal 331
Coöperative Centrale Raiffeisen Bank 165
Cooperativismo Sanitario (Health care co-operativism) 173
COPAC 492; 690; 899; 902/903
CORC 302
corporate crises 259/260
corporate culture 4; 7; 180; 673; 679
Corporate Culture of Co-operatives 179
corporate ethics 344

corporate identity 582
corporate mergers 134
corporation 170
Corpus Christi procession 413
corruption 284
cost curve of the co-operative enterprise 703
cost-covering contribution margins 26
Costa Rica 752
Council of Ministers 349
Council of the National Salvation of Romania 210
countervailing (market) power 701; 863
countervailing-power-effect 402
countries of Spanish and of Portuguese language 321
country banks 250
Country survey 152
coup d'état in 1965 232
CPA (certified public accountant) 37/38
CPD 304
craftsguilds 170
craftsman's honourableness 413
creation of co-operative law 551
Crédit Agricole Mutuel 165; 779
credit and savings co-operatives 8
credit co-operative 5; 28; 88; 104; 112; 135; 140/141; 215/216; 235; 242; 250
credit co-operatives involved in commodities trade 12
credit in kind 9
credit programmes 10
credit risk appraisals 756
Credit Schemes and Types of Co-operatives 9
credit system law 22
Credit Union Act of Massachusetts 199
credit union model 695
Credit Union National Association (CUNA) 199; 223ff.; 331
Credit Union National Extension Bureau (CUNEB) 199
credit unions 9; 163/164; 203/204; 222/223
Credit Unions Operating Principles 187
Credit Unions, World Council of 186ff.
creditor protection 561
criteria for disqualification 760
critical issues facing co-operatives 225
critical judgement 5

critical minimum of socio-political change 797
criticism of political economy 813
criticism of the principles 712
CTI 300
CUAC 305/306
cultural environment 145
cultural fit 838
Cultural Revolution in 1968 894
cultural system 145
CUM 304
CUNA 188
current principles 710
CWS (Co-operative Wholesale Society) 668
Cybernetics and Cooperation 189ff.
Czechia 313
Czechoslovac Republic 832
Czechoslovak cooperator 681
Czechoslovakia 206/207; 830

dairy co-operatives 207; 780
danish production communes 130
Darlehnskassen-Vereine 755
data from government statistics 365
Data Processing in Co-operative Organizations 194ff.
DATEV 321
de facto group of companies 542
de facto purchasing concentrations 19
de-bureaucratization 644
de-centralization 644
de-officialization of co-operatives 205; 643; 644
de-regulation 644
decision-making in groups 657
decline of the guild 415
definition of Kolkhozes 530
definitional characteristics of the registered co-operative 553
Degania 1909; 212
degree of urgency 463
DEKOPIN 303
delcredere 118
délégation à l'économie sociale (DES) 288
delphi method 278
democratic administration 710
Democratic Peoples' Republic of Korea 306
democratic principles 436
demonstrative model for communism 812

denationalization of land 209
deposit structure 851
depreciation of commercial buildings 867
depreciation of machines 867
DESEC in Cochabamba (Bolivia) 217
destructive cooperation 98
detribalization policies 49
Deutsche Akademie für Wohnungswesen 447
Deutsche Arbeitsfront 673
Deutsche Bau-AG 56
Deutsche Bausparer AG 65
Deutsche Bundesbank 760
Deutsche Entwicklungshilfe für soziales Wohnungs- und Siedlungswesen e.V. (DESWOS) 452
Deutsche Genossenschafts-Hypothekenbank 783; 790
Deutsche Genossenschaftskasse von Soergel, Parrisius & Co. 110
Deutsche Landliga 448
Deutsche landwirtschaftliche Genossenschaftspresse 316
Deutsche Raiffeisen Warenzentrale 12
Deutscher Bund für Bodenbesitzreform 448
Deutscher Genossenschafts- und Raiffeisenverband e.V. (DGRV) 317
Deutscher Genossenschafts-Verlag 680
Deutscher Genossenschaftsverband (Schulze-Delitzsch) e.V. 315; 317
Deutscher Raiffeisenverband 316
Deutscher Verein für Wohnungsreform 447
Deutscher Volksverein von Demokraten und Liberalen 787
developed countries 256
developing countries 42/43; 45; 136; 145; 254; 295; 803; **909**
development efficiency 359
development fund 122; 22
development in the 19th century 862
development of co-operative legislation 545
Development of Co-operatives in Africa, South of Sahara 199
Development of Co-operatives in Eastern Europe 205
Development of Co-operatives in Israel 211
Development of Co-operatives in Latin America 216
Development of Co-operatives in North America 222
Development of Co-operatives in Northern-Africa 226
Development of Co-operatives in South Asia 234
Development of Co-operatives in South-East Asia 242
Development of Co-operatives in Turkey 248
development policy 841
Development Policy, Co-operatives in 254
development tendencies 370
development types 517
deviant solidarity 820
deviation analyses 72
deviation factors 707
DEWOG 55
DG Bank (Deutsche Genossenschaftsbank) 80/81; 84; 112; 166; 197; 780; 783/784; 789ff.
DGRV 4; 5; 37; 317; 680; 779
different forms of officialization 642
different models of organizational structure 660
different organizational patterns 357
differentiation of membership 621
dikkuti 913
dimensions of ecology-oriented business management 336
direct and indirect export 507
direct and overhead costs 706
director of Co-operatives 42/43
discrete versus cumulative incentives 473
Discriminatory Analysis Procedures for Corporate Assessment 259
discriminatory function 264; 758
disguised profit distribution 868
distillery co-operatives 781
Distribution of Benefits and Surplus 23ff.
distribution of earnings 7
distribution of functions 369
distribution of surplus 141
distribution of the reserves 711
diversification 370/371
diversification activity of marketing and purchasing co-operatives 265/266; 268

Diversification Strategies of Co-operatives 265
diversification strategy 848
diversification through business with non-members 267
diversification through taking up processing 266
dividend on the basis of purchases 28
dividends 89
division of labour among the sexes 47
division of power 815
dominant market position 285
double nature 126
DPRK 300
Drittorganschaft 441
DRV 317; 779
dual nature 147; 404
Dual or Double Nature of Co-operatives 271ff.
dual system 109
dualistic development 217
Duff & Phelps 52

early identification system 275
early socialists 875
early warning for federation auditors 280
Early Warning Systems for (Credit) Co-operatives 274ff.
early warning systems for bank management 276
Eastern Europe 311; 355
EC Commission 349
EC Directive, 4th 552
EC standards 109
ECA 293
ecological orientation 633
ecology-oriented framework of regulations 337
Economic and Social Committee (ESC) 347
Economic Order and Co-operatives 281ff.
economic philosophy of the guild 414
economic priniple 357
economic promotion 743
economic service chains 69
economic theory 96
economic theory of co-operatives 771
economics of industry 602
Economie Sociale 136; 287
economies of scale 98; 194
economization of co-operatives 272
Economy for Public Benefit 876

ECOSOC 898; 902
EDEKA 321
EDEKA-Handelsrundschau 680
Eden (Germany) 471
education 200; 818
education agencies in the United States 330
education and training 43; 62
Education and Training in Africa, Co-operative 292ff.
Education and Training in Asia, Co-operative 299ff.
Education and Training in Canada 332ff.
Education and Training in Europe, Co-operative 309ff.
Education and Training in Germany, Co-operative 313ff.
Education and Training in Latin America, Co-operatives 321ff.
Education and Training in North America, Co-operative 329ff.
education and training system 93
educational concepts for credit co-operatives 319
educational concepts for merchandise and service co-operatives 320/321
educational concepts of the commercial co-operatives 321
educational model 9
EEC 293
effect of diffusion 880
Effect of Government Intervention 8
effect of power 880
effect of productivity 880
efficiency 93; 863
Eidgenossenschaft 50/51
ejido 50; 519
Ejido Bank 734
ejidos 217; 734; 886
EKA 154
ELANTO 154
electronic data processing 194ff.
elementary law of social relationships 70
elements of price determination 706
ELG 393
elite 843
élites 796
emancipation 818
empirically-based theory 877
employment of human labor 384
ENC (Ecole Nationale de Coopération) 230
english legal system 78

English Quakers 469
enterprise as such 141
enterprise autogérée 231
Entreprises Auto-gérées 519
environment relations 591
environmental balance sheet 337
environmental context 467
environmental factors 795
environmental influences 182
environmental protection 287
Environmental Protection and Co-operatives 334
épargne-logement 64
Ephrata 127
EPTA 903
equilibrium size of an economic organization 256
Equitable Pioneers Society 120
equity capital 111; 377; 766
equity joint venture 522
equity problems 553
Erfolgswertvermögen 280
Erster Vereinstag deutscher Vorschuß- und Kreditvereine 314
Erwerbsgenossenschaften 104
Erwitte 470
Essay on Liberty (1859) 615
Essenes 120; 127; 431
essential elements of economic orders 282
essentialisms 136
esteem by others 184
esusu 47
Ethics and Co-operatives 344ff.
Etiopia 203
EUROCOOP 496
Europe's Development Regions 50
European Community (Union) 346
European Community of Consumer Co-operatives (EUROCOOP) 347
European Cooperation of Co-operative Central Banks 352ff.
European Economic Interest Groupings 350
European Limited Company 350
European national constitutions 143
European Statute of a Co-operative Society 351
European Union 346
Euterpia 755
evaluation 1; 5; 27; 918

Evaluation of Co-operative Organizations 355
evaluation of the principles 713
evolution 132; 143
evolutionary dynamics 258
evolutionary policy regime 255
evolutionary process 94
ex-ante evaluation 358; 360
ex-post evaluation 358; 360
examples for cooperation agreements 354
executive Bodies 556
executive council (Sprecherausschuß) 107
executively operating co-operative 272; 855
exemptions 22/23
exosystem 144
experience obtained from an investigation 262
external effects 99/100; 487
external funds 10
Extra-ordinary forms of machinery associations 576
extraordinary audits 40

fabians (Fabier) 182; 876
FACMOA 246
factoring bank 119
factors influencing attitude of co-operative officials 795
familia militaris 432
FAO (see: Food and Agriculture Organization)
Farm Bill, 1990 330
farm credit system 165; 224
Farmers Organization (Idara-i-Kisan-IK) 246
farmers-groups 407
farming on co-operative lines 203
farmstead co-operative 143
faza 47
FDB 154; 668
February Revolution in 1917 814
FEDECOBA 753
FEDECOCAGUA 217
Federal Association of German Co-operative Banks 790ff.
Federal Bank of Co-operatives 238; 241
Federal Benefit Fund 420
Federal Cartel Office 40ff.
Federal Intermediate Credit System 165
Federal Reserve Bank of New York 280

Federal Supervisory Office for the Banking (BAK) 22
Federation of Egalitarian Communities 129
Federation Statistics 363ff.
federations 80/81; 140; 163; 222; 310; 782
Federations of Commercial Co-operatives 119
federations service programme 368
Federations, Co-operative 367
feed-forward 191
feedback control 190
FELCRA 304
FELGA 304
Fellachen 230
feudal manor theory 412
FIDUCIA 195/196; 281
Fifth Directive 350
fifty-fifty jv. 522
Fiji Co-operative Union Ltd. 307
final auditing meeting 39
finance controlling program 278
Financial Accounting Law 372ff.
financial audit 40
financial risk 707
Financing 5; 11; 26; 376ff.
Findhorn (England) 131; 471
Finkhof (Germany) 47/48
first co-operative wholesale company 115
First Directive on the structure of public limited companies 109
First Five-Year Plan (1953-157) 719; 785
first franchise system 386
first oil crisis (1973) 274
first theorem of welfare economics 908
First UN-Development-Decade 688
First World War 518; 668; 685; 814
fishermen's associations 47
fishery co-operatives 172; 781
Fitch Investors Service 52
FLN (Front de Libération Nationale) 231
flow equilibrium (Fließgleichgewicht) 589
Fluchtliniengestz 446
Flurzwang 431
FNCC 154
Fokonolona 48
Fondation Desjardins 333

Food and Agriculture Organization (FAO) 293; 302/303; 690; 792; 900f.; 902/903
Förderungsauftrag (see: Promotion Mandate)
foreign trade policy 286
forestry co-operative 172
formalization of cooperation 857
formation of goals 24
formation process of an alliance 837
Forms of Cooperation 382ff.
forms of franchising 386
forms of MTs 586
Fortschrittspartei (Party for Progress) 787
forward diversification 268
foundation „St. Theobaldi" 455
foundation-type co-operatives 102
founding fathers 137
Fourierism 128
Fourth EC Directive 341
Franchising 385/386; 472; 508
franchising in co-operatives 387
Franksh Era 431
fraternities 50
Fraternity of Worship 816
fratres coniurati 413
free co-operatives for public benefit (freigemeinwirtschaftliche Genossenschaften) 101
free genesis of self-help 846
free market system 827
free religious „communautés" 469
free self-help co-operatives 437
free-rider 400/401
free-rider-mentality 443
Free-Standing Leagues 187
freedom of trade (Gewerbefreiheit) 17
freezer co-operatives 781
Freie Volksbühne 528
freight forwarding 897
freight navigation 895
freiwillige Gerichtsbarkeit 76
French Revolution 63; 120; 344; 435; 446; 888
french socialists 93
Friedrich-Ebert-Stiftung 797
friendly societies 43
Frühe Bauernbefreiung 432
Fruit and Vegetable Co-opertives 780
Fruitères 432
Führer-Prinzip 673

full co-operatives 104; 775
full-service functions 118
function of collectivization 717
functional groups 105
functions and responsiblities of the manager 659
functions for controlling 158
functions of an Honorary Office 442
functions of marketing co-operatives 593
Fundación Espriu 177
fundamental democratization 143
fundamental participation 632
further diversification strategy 267
Furubotn-Pejovich-Vanek effect (FPV effect) 535

Gaborone Declaration for a Regional Development Decade 294
GACOPEA (Concept; Materials; Methodology; Network) 388ff.; 904
GAD 195
GAEC 383
Gambia 47
gandu 47
gaya 47
GDR 208; 519; 538ff.; 829; 831/832; 893
GDR, Co-operatives in the Former 392
GDUD HAAVODA (Labour Battalion) 213
GEG 668; 890; 894
Gehöferschaften 434; 438
Geitskell-report 152
Gemeinschaft 103; 143; 404
Gemengelage 431
gender roles 910
General Co-operative Law No. 1163 251
general co-operative law of 1947 546
general economic theory of action 873
General German Workers' Association 811
general meeting 91
General Systems Theory 466
General-Anwaltschaftsverband ländlicher Genossenschaften 779
generation problem 184
genossenschaftliche Gesellschaftsform 405

Genossenschaftsforum (Co-operative Forum) 679
Genossenschaftsgesetz (German Co-operative Law) 551
Genossenschaftsgesetz, 1 420
Genoz 430
German Agricultural Co-operative School 418
German Aid to Developing Countries for Social Housing and Settlements 452
German Banking Law (Kreditwesengesetz - KWG) 631
German Co-operative Law (Genossenschaftsgesetz) 742; 788
German Democratic Republic 197; 205; 779
German Fiscal Code (AO) 125
German General Trade Code 788
German Health Insurance System 420
German Institute for Technical Vocational Training 672
German Law against Restraints of Competition 17; 21ff.
German Millenarian Sects 127
German National Assembly in Frankfurt 787
German Reich 789
German Reichstag 787
German Social Democratic Party (SPD) 811
German Union of Construction Workers 54
German universities 311
German Work Front (DAF) 56
German youth movement 471
Gesamtverband Gemeinnütziger Wohnungsunternehmen e.V. 37; 452
Gesellschaft 103; 143; 404
Gesellschaft des Bürgerlichen Rechts 383
Gesellschaft für Wirtschafts- und Sozialkybernetik (GWS) 192
Gesellschaft für zweitstelligen Grundkredit 66
Gesetz gegen Wettbewerbsbeschränkungen, GWB 17; 21ff.
Gesetz über Bausparkassen 65
gesetzliche Krankenversicherung 419
Gewinnverfassung 432
Gezira Scheme 734
Ghana 47; 201ff.; 295
GHG 393,395
GIS 194

GmbH 103
GmbH & Co KG 103; 539
goal formulation process 24
goal system 24
GoB 4
Godesberger Programm (1957) 894
GOEC 668
government departments 205
Government Involvement 45
governments' intervention 244
governments' technical assistance 243
gradual neutralization of capital 633
grazing co-operatives 781
great depression 151
great leap forward 86; 785
great pioneers 425
greatest happiness of the greatest number 93
green movements 470
Großeinkaufsgesellschaft 427
Großeinkaufsgesellschaft Deutscher Consumvereine (GEG) 528; 684
group enterprise 383
group farming 202
group management 357
Group of Affiliated Companies 558
Group of Liable Individuals 628
group of subordinated affiliates 540
Group of the Just 812
group solidarity 71; 404
group stability 402,
Group, Common Initiative (groupe d'initative commune) 407ff.
Group, The Co-operative 409
groupement à vocation coopérative (GVC) 201; 408
groupement agricoles 385
groupement d'intérêt économique 408
groupement villageois (GV) 408
Groupements à Vocation Coopérative (GVC) 546
Groupements Mutualistes Villageois in Niger 546
groupements mutualistes villageois, (GMV) 408; 696
groupements regionaux de la cooperation (GRC) 288
grouping of companies 371
groups of producer associations 23
growing self-complexity 662

GRZ 195
Guaranty Fund for Credit Co-operatives 790
Guaranty Pool 791/792
Guide to Evaluation 356
guiding moral principles 346
guiding principles 569
guild festivities 414
guild mentality 386
Guild socialism 53
guild's jurisdictional functions 413
Guilds 47; **412;** 434
Guinea 49
Gung Ho 91
Guomindang 86
GVC model 697
GWB, (Gesetz gegen Wettbewerbsbeschränkungen) 724
GWGs 394,
gWU (gemeinnütziges Wohnungsunternehmen) 748

HABITAT 899
HAKIBBUTZ HAARTZI 213
HAMASHBIR 212
HAMERKAZI 212
Hammurabi Codex 430
Han 155
Han Movement 806
Handwörterbuch des Wohnungswesens 448
Hanse 433/434
harambe 913
harmonization of company law 349
Harmony 127
HASHOMER HATZAIR 213
Hatzfeld trial 811
Hauberggenossenschaften 434
Hauptverband deutscher gewerblicher Genossenschaften 315
Hauptverband deutscher Wohnungsunternehmen 37
Health Care System 419
Hebrew Essenes 469
heretic sects 127
Herr Bastiat-Schulze von Delitzsch 811
Herrnhuter Brethren Parish 775
HEVER HAKVUTZOT 214
hexagonal boundaries 291
HGB (Handelsgesetzbuch) 373/374
hidden reserves 341
hierarchical coordination 38
Hierarchy 191
High Middle Ages 432

Hilfsgenossenschaften 100
hippy 471
Histadrut 212/213
historical approaches 842
historical schools of thought 876
History of Co-operative Ideas 423
History of Co-operatives before 1800 429ff.
History of Co-operatives in the 19th Century 436
history of industrial relations 466
homo caritativus 770
homo co-operativus 345; 409; 771
homo culturalis 770
homo economicus (oeconomicus) 33; 179; 345; 770
homo politicus 770
homo sociologicus 770
homo traditionalis 770
Honduras 752
Hong Kong 300; 305
honorary board 369
honorary leadership 367
Honorary Office 440ff.; 565
horizontal diversification 265
horizontal group of affiliated companies 542
horizontal structure of financing 376
horticultural co-operatives 207
hostility toward innovations 414
housing /joint-production co-operatives and Trade Unions 889
Housing co-operatives 113; 207; 215; 222ff.; **449;** 452; 830
housing co-operatives in Pakistan and Malysia 244
Housing Reform Movement 445ff.
housing societies 182
housing society „Neue Heimat" 895
HR-strategies 457; 460
human capital 95
human relations movement 673
Human Resource Management 457; 839
human ressource development 299ff.
human rights 436
human suffering 95/96
humbe 47
Hungarian Trade Act of 1875 206
Hungary 312; 829; 831/832

hunting co-operative 172
Hussite movement 775
Hutterite community 521
Hutterites 128; 410,435

I.E. – NO-Hikari 306
ICA 85; 154; 223; 302; 681; 686; 709/710
ICA Regional conference 388
Icaria movement 128
IDB 901
ideal types 101; 410
Idealtyp 101; 410
Identitätsprinzip 854
identity consciousness 184
identity principle 124; 740; 743; 862/863
ideological concept 544
ideological desputes 890
ideological differences 310
IFAD 899; 901; 905
IHUD HAKIBBUTZIM VE-HAKVUTZOT 215
IKBA format 759
Ikerlan 618
IKOPIN 303
IKS 105
ILDEC 307
illiteracy 309
Illyrian responses 37
ILO 293; 302; 806; 900
ILO African Regional conference 388
ILO inter-regional project MAT-COM 603
ILO Recommendation no 127 of 1968 243; 543ff.
important framework conditions 285/286
inborn limitations 73
Inca 49
Inca Empire 217
incentive compatability 402
incentives 26; 94; 132
incentives for mergers 608
Incentives of Co-operatives 461ff.
independence 61
India 50; 235; 245; 300/301
Indian Co-operative Societies Acts of 1904 and 1912 59
Indian Farmers' Fertilizer Co-operative Limited (IFFCO) 299
indicator systems 274
indigenismo movement 49
indigenous forms of cooperation 199

indigenous rotating savings and credit associations 202
individual factors 795
individual goods 398
individual needs 794
individual self-help 797
individual value of incentives 463
individualism 138
indogenous co-operatives 226
Indonesia 243; 245; 300; 303
Indonesian Institute of Co-operative Management 303
inducement/contribution theory 461
Industrial Age 423
Industrial and Provident Societies Act 58; 78; 424
industrial co-operative school 305
industrial co-operatives 88; 243
industrial commodity and service co-operatives 113
industrial conflict 466
industrial purchasing and marketing co-operatives 28
Industrial Relation Systems 466
Industrial Relations 464ff.
industrial revolution 42; 309
Informal Co-operatives 469
informal sector 46
information system 276
information system of a centrally planned economy 284
informational infrastructure 364
INICEF 293
INIFEM 901
initiation rituals 414
Inland Navigation 895
inner colonization 425
innovation 370/371
Innung der Zukunft 438; 679; 788
Institut de recherche et dénseignement pour les co-oératives de l'Université de Sherbrooke (I.R.E.C.U.S.) 334
Institute for Development of Agricultural Co-operative in Asia (IDACA) 306
institutes for co-operative studies at universities 29/30
institution building 406; 799
institutional characteristics of the guild 416
Institutional Economics 472

institutional organizations in South and South-East Asia 242
institutionalism 137
institutionalization of industrial conflict 466
institutionalized training facilities 311
Institutions 11
instruments of small business policy 826
instruments of strategic planning 848
insurance co-operative „Lagung-Aro" 618
Insurance, Co-operative 477
integrated approach 356
integrated co-operatives 101; 105; 117; 167; 183; 738; 855; 862ff.
integrated world market 310
Integrierte Gemeinde 131
Integriertes Kooperativ 855
intensity of competition 13
intensity of cooperation 857
Inter-African Credit Union Training Workshop 296
intercompany comparison 365/366; **484ff.**
intercompany cooperation 99
intermediary culture 470
internal auditing 159
Internal Co-operative Alliance 489ff.
internal federation statistics 366
internal statistics 363
internalization theory 523
International Co-operative Alliance (ICA) 28; 119; 124; 140; 184; 235; 425; 439; 452; 543; 776; 898
international co-operative law 40
International Co-operative Organizations 492ff.
International Co-operative Science Conferences 30
international comparison of co-operative auditing 41
International Construction Guild Association 53
international development organization 300
International Industrial Relations Association 468
International Labour Office (ILO) 468

International Labour Organization (ILO) 899f.; 902ff.
International Workers' Association 813
International(e) Raiffeisen Union 499
internationalization 310
Internationalization of Co-operative Trading Enterprises 503
internationalization process 157
Interpersonal Communication System 590
Interpersonales Kommunikationssystem 590
Interpretation of GWB, 1 17
interpretative paradigm 181
Invalidity of Clauses 75/76
investments 2
invisible hand 833
IRAM 696
Iran 300; 302
Iraq 300; 307
Iron Law of Oligarchy 647
Iron Law of Wages 424; 811
IRU 85
IRU-Courier 502
Iskra 814
Islamic Revolution in Iran 274
Israel 300; 307
Istituto Centrale delle Banche Populari Italiane 82
Istituto di Credito delle Casse Rurali ed Artigiane (IC-CREA) 82; 166
Itoen 130
Ivory Coast 47; 201ff.; 296

Jans 454
Japan 300; 305
Java 50
Jewish Palestine 211
JICA 306
joint business establishment 554
joint guarantee funds 10
joint ownership venture 522
joint production co-operatives 55; 93ff.; 113; 158; 182
joint stock companies 373
Joint Stock Company 511
joint venture contracts 524
joint venture motives 523
joint venture typology 522
joint venture-management 526
joint venture-stability 525
Joint Ventures 522ff.
joint-production co-operatives 450; **517;** 555; 643; 861

joint-stock company (AG) 103; 279
Jordan 300
Journal for Comprehensive Co-operative Studies 31
journal Wohnungswirtschaft 55
Jugendbewegung 469
juntas de vigilancia 217

Kaira District Co-operative Milk Producers Union Ltd. 245
Kampuchia 300
Kazakhstan 300
Kensan 130;
Kenya (Kenia) 48; 201ff.; 295
KF in Sweden 151ff.
KIBBUTH MEHUHAD 214/215
Kibbutz 212ff.; 519; 405
kinship-based group 406
KKKUD 303
Kolka Rolnicze 383
Kolkhozes 405; 530ff.
Kollegien der Rechtsanwälte 394
Kombinate 281; 284; 394,
Kommunistisches Manifest 121; 812; 891
Konsumgenossenschaftliche Rundschau 529
Kontrollratsgesetz 106
Kooperationsfibel 20
Kooperativ 101; 738
Kooperativa programmet (1921) 709
Korea 300
Körperschaftssteuer 865
Kreditwesengesetz 320
Kreuznach Inquisition 891
kulak farms 530
KWG (Kreditwesengesetz) 1; 38; 277/278
Kwuzah 519; 521

L'atelier 63
L'Ouiza 227
labor contract 521
labor law 286/287
Labour and Marketing Co-operatives 35
labour co-operatives 32; 104
labour-managed economy (LME) 533ff.
labour-managed firms (LMFs) 533ff
Labour-Management 533ff.
Lake Chad 47
Land Bank system 165
Land Reform Movement 447

land settlement programmes in Thailand 244
Landschaft 164
Landschafts-Zünfte 434
Landwirtschafltiche Generalbank 788
Landwirtschaftsanpassungsgesetz – LAG 538ff.
Laos 300
large group 410
late classical economists 875
Late Middle Ages 433
lateral diversification 265
Latin America 49
Latin American countries 750
Laundry Co-operatives 781
Law Concerning Company Groups 540
Law for Co-operative Systems 1988 720
Law of 1967 (general status of co-operatives) 229
Law of 1982 831
Law of Accounting Directives 552
law of increasing costs 96
law of interdependence of orders 796
law of public benefit 183
law of requisite variety 190
law of structural conformance in the agricultural sector 538
Law on Housing for Public Benefit 451
Law, National Co-operative 551
laws in Thailand, Philippines, Indonesia and Singapore 242
LCB 353
Le Conseil Canadien de la Cooperation 223
Le mouvement des caisses populaires Desjardins 198
leadership 583
leadership style 460
leadership-drain 664
League of Struggle for the Emancipation of the Working Class 814
Lebenswelt 819
legal competitive privilieges 724
legal forms 384/385
legal fundaments 119
legal person 170
legal spheres in co-operative law 140
Legal Status and Responsibilities of Auditing Federations 37
legal status of members 548

Legal Statute in the EEC 349
legal transformation of a co-operative 559
Legal-organizational Communication System 140; 589
legal-organizational framework 1
legislation 86/87
Lennoxtown Victualling Society 425
Lesotho 203/204
levels of interaction 467
levels of qualification 636
levels of the co-operative education 324/325
Lex Adickes 446
Leyes de Indias 49
liability capital 339
Liability of Co-operative Boards 563
liability of the board (of directors) 373
liability of the supervisory board 567
liberal societal structure 344
liberalism 446
limitations set by the state 825
limited company (KG) 193
limited interest 711
line of products 11
linear discriminatory function 257
linear multivariate discriminatory analysis 260
link-up system 9
linkage models 571
linking formal and informal financial institutions 570
LIP 470
liquidation of the enterprise 342
liquidation report 360
liquidity 378
Livestock Breeding Co-operatives 781
Livestock Marketing Co-operatives 780
Llano del Rio (1914-1938) 128
loan and credit associations 555
local area network (LAN) 197
local community networks 470
logic of domination 676
logic of utilization 675
logical-deductive ration system 276
Loi Chapelier 1791 888
London & Continental Bankers Ltd. 353
long-term loans 9
Longo Mai (France) 130; 471
lord of the manor 430

Loughborough Co-operative College 295
LPG (Landwirtschaftliche Produktionsgenossenschaft) 394; 519; 539

Maàouna 226
Maastricht, Treaty of 1992 355
machine stations 575
Machinery Associations 282; 574
machinery co-operatives 781
machinery rings 382/383; **574;** 576
Macrosociological Aspects of Co-operatives 142
Maghreb 226ff.
maintaining stock 11
Malawi 202
Malaysia 300; 303
Maldives 300; 302
Mali 49; 201
management 579
management assessment 39
management functions 5; 39
Management in Co-operatives 579ff.
management roles 580
Management Teams 584
management-member information system (MMIS) 105; 462; 591; 855
management-member relationships 663
Managerial Economics of Co-operatives 587
managerial functions 580
managing directors 91
mandatory audit 36
Mandatory Co-operative Audit 38
mandatory duties 38
manor Korntal 775
manuel d'économie politique 908
Mapuche 49
MARA 233
marginal co-operative form (Grenztyp der Genossenschaft) 854
marginal groups 796/797; 800
marginal revenue curve 703
märkerding 817
market co-operatives 105; 862
market coordination 38
market development 848
market economies 641/642
market economy 2; 281; 283; 824
market failures 38; 400
market for agricultural goods 11

market imperfections 537
market penetration 848
market shares 14
Market Structure Law (Marktstrukturgesetz, MStrG) 722
market-linkage co-operative 4; 105; 117; 166; 183; 272/273; 357; 742
marketing 5; 33
marketing and warehouse co-operatives 555
marketing board system 202
Marketing Co-operatives 9; 32/33; 202; 224; 266; **592;** 766
marketing policy 462
marketing societies 202
marketing strategies 32
Marketing Strategies of Co-operatives 596
Markgenossenschaft 432
Marktbeziehungs-Kooperativ (market linkage co-operative) 855
marxism 121; 309
marxist criticism 289
marxist-leninist ideology 392
marxists 876
MAS 395
MASHBIR 212
mass media 818
mass organization in the GDR 394
MATCOM 603; 904
MATCOM-Methodology 605
Mater et Magista (1961) 885
materialism and emperical chriticism 814
Mauritius 202
measuring the level of success 639
mechanization of agriculture 574
medieval corporations 433
medieval craft guilds 53
medium-term loans 9
Mehringhof 470
member characteristics 856
member education 244; 300
member information system 159
member participation 71
member segmentation 855
member's successors 629
member-oriented efficiecy 359
members' consulting 147
membership as organizational size 651
membership group 182
membership list 763
membership participation 794

membership typology 622
Mennonites in Paraguay 217
Mercantilism 446
merchandising co-operatives 104
merchant guilds 412
merger policies 850
mergers 284
Mergers and Consolidations 607
Mesican Revolution 217
Mesosociological Aspects 661
method called „verstehen" 181
methodology interlinkage 606
Mexican revolution 50
Mexico 321
Microsociological Aspects of Cooperatives 770
Middle Ages 100/101; 103; 136; 182; 430/431; 446; 419
migros 151; 153; 428
Ministry of Agriculture MARA 231
Minka 519
Mir 405
misery of philosophy 812
mixed forms 281
mobility threshold 625
model by-laws 140
models of co-operative legislation 547
models of man 770
modes of assumption of responsibility 290
modification of the by-laws 76/77
Mondragón 521
Mondragón Co-operative Group 617
monetary and currency policy 286
money-lenders 8; 234
Mongolia 300; 306
monists 817
Montan-Mitbestimmungsgesetz of 1951 106ff.
Monté Vérita 469
Montepio de Prevision Social 177
Moody's Investors Service 52
Moroccan Experience 233
Morocco 233
Moshav 213
MOSHAV OVDIM 214; 519
MOSHAV SHITUFI 214; 521
Motivation for Cooperation 620
motivation for participation 620
motivation of the individual economic entities 283
motives 462

motives behind the internationalization 505
motor-driven mechanization 574
mouvement coopératif Algérien 231
Mouzarat 227
Mt. Kilimanjaro 47
MTSs (machine-tractor stations) 531
multi-enterprise machine employment 283
multi-farm application of machinery 574
multi-national agencies 293
multi-purpose 104
multi-purpose co-operative societies (MCPS) 236
multi-purpose co-operatives 10
multi-state co-operative Societies Act 245
multi-use credit co-operatives 623
multicultural challenges 775
multivariate discriminatory analysis 260
Münchner Hypothekenbank 783; 790
Mussakat 227
mutual societies of insurance and credit 290
Mynamar (Burma) 300

NACF 306
Nachschußpflicht 342; **627ff.**
Nachtwächterstaat 446
nafir 47
nanjing era 86
narrative interview 181
Nation Council of Farmer Co-operatives 223
national advisory council 44
National Agricultural Co-operative Federation (NACF) 306
National Agricultural Co-operative Marketing Federation of India (NAFED) 235
National Association of Co-operative Training Centres Inc. (NATCCO) 303
National Bank for Agriculture and Rural Development (NABARD) 235
National Board for Co-operative and Dev. Aid - ONCAD 201
National Centre for Co-operative Education 301
National Co-operative Businees Association 223

National Co-operative Council of Sri Lanka 303
National Co-operative Development Corporation (NCDC)/India 245
National Co-operative Organization of Turkey (TMKB) 252
National Co-operative Union 241
National Co-operative Union of India (NCUI) 235
National Connection Committee of the Co-operative, Mutual and Associative Activities 288
National Cooperative Business Associaton (N.C.B.A.) 331
National Council for Co-operative Training 301
National Dairy Development Board (NDDB) 299
National Development Council (NDC) 235
national development plan 239
national equitable labour exchange 121
National Federation of Credit Associations 82
National Federation of Credit Co-operatives 82
national federations 235
National Finance Corporation for Co-operative Development 244
national plans of socialist countries 243
national social security systems 521
national workshops 438
nature of co-operative science 872
NCBA 223
NCCE 301
NCCT 301
NCDFI 235
NCFC 223
NCHF 235
NCSLDBF 235
NCUI 301
need for strategic planning 847
neighbourhood help 574
neo-classics 876
Néo-Destour Party 228
neo-liberals 877
neolithic revolution 405
Nepal 50; 300; 302
Neue Heimat 56
neutral model of simple organization 698

new Co-operative law 207
new Co-operative law in 1990 210
new co-operative law of 1988 210
new co-operative movement 806
new co-operative order 309
new co-operative sector 636
new co-operative system 806
New Co-operatives 632
new consumer co-operatives 156
new cooperation 177
New Economic Policy (NEP) 814
new forms of training and education 312
New harmony 128; 405; 424
new institutional economics 273; 472; 873
new institutional economists 877
New Lanark model 121; 665ff.
new political economists 873; 877
new view of society 424
New Zealand 307
newspaper, co-operative 470
NFCSF 235
NFCUB 235
NFIC 235
NFLC 235
NGOs (non-governmental organizations) 243; 247; 293; 298; 571/572; 690/691
Niger 201
Nigeria 43; 45; 47; 49; 201ff.; 295
nomenklatura 829
Non-Co-operative Legal Forms 382ff.
non-co-operative types of cooperation 103
non-economic goals 96
non-finite number of members 553
non-institutional credit 241
non-profit character 369
non-profit housing enterpises 747/748
non-profit organization 123; 289; 638
non-registered co-operative 75
non-statutory functions 59
Nordisk Andelsförbund 151
Norinchukin Bank 82
normative dimension of co-operative management 337
North American Students of Cooperation (N.A.S.C.O.) 332
North German League 787ff.

object of cognition 873
objective of analysis 259
objectives for an alliance 836
objectives of management teams 585
objectives, interests and expectations 1
objects and method of the audit 38
obligatory membership 206
obligatory reserve 373
OCA/ONCAD 697
occupational risk, co-operative 171
ODCO 233
Office Chérifien Interprofessionel du Blé (CIB) 227
Office Interprofessionel du Blé (ONIB) 227
Office National de Promotion Rurale (ONPR) 297
office theory 412
officialization of co-operatives 145; 253; 257; 388; 641ff.; 800
Okobank, Helsinki 81; 166
OKS 105
Oligarchy in Co-operatives 647ff.
oligopolistic competition 310
OMRVA 233
OMVA 233
One for all, and all for one 345
Oneida 127,
ONI (Office National de la Modernisation Rurale) 233,
ONMR (Office National de la Modernisation Rurale) 233
open door principle 748
Open Land 471
opentrading company (OHG) 103
operational efficiency 358
operational size 169; 859
operational size and costs 653
operational size and social structure 653
operational size of affiliated co-operatives 652
Operational Size of Co-operatives 651ff.
operational size of production co-operatives 652
operative empirical-inductive ration systems 277
Oppenheimerian colonizatory blueprint 212
opportunism 476
options for ecology-oriented business management 335

orderly book-keeping 1
Ordo-liberals 877
Organbetrieb 105
organisation du travail 424
Organisationsrechtliches Kommunikationssystem (legal-organizational communication system) 140; 589
Organization 583
Organization of Co-operatives of America (OCA) 221; 323
organization of official national statistics 364
organization of seminars and symposiums 297
organizational culture 180
organizational factors 796
Organizational Integration of Controlling 160/161
organizational participants 181
organizational principles 427
organizational size and market influence 653
organizational size of household co-operatives 652
organizational structure 96; 515
Organizational Structure of Co-operative Societies 656
organizational structure of co-operatives 545
Organizational Structures, Co-operative 661
Organwirtschaftliches Kooperativ 855
orta 51
ortak 51
Österreichische Volksbanken AG (ÖVAG) 83/84; 166
Österreichischer Raiffeisenverband 779
Ottoman Empire 250
outside financing 379
outside-promoters 842
Owen's ideas: socialism and utopianism 667
Owenite ideals 778
Owenite school of Utopian Socialists 614
own production 151,
Own Production 668
Oxford approach 468

PACCA 300
Pacem in terris (1963) 885
Pädagogische Provinz 844
Padanaram (God's Valley) 129
PAID's Educational and Training Programmes 294
PAID's guiding principles 294

Pakistan 241; 246; 300; 303
palette of insurance services 480
Pan African Institute for Development 292
Pardes 211
Pareto and socialism 908
Pareto's Law 909
Parsonian model 466
partial collectivization 860
partial integration 33
participation 143; 462; 800
participation of co-operative members 561
participational interests 508
participatory financing 377
partner selection 524
partnership 383; 671
Partnership Enterprises 671
passenger navigation 896
passenger transport 897
Pathfinders 423
Patrimonialrichter (judge appointed by local landowners) 787
patrons of the Plunkett Foundation 686
payment conditions 31
pension payments 373
people of the early Middle Ages 412ff.
people's banks 241
people's communes 86; 88; 518
people's participation 244
People's Participation Programme 903
People's Republic of China 784
people's state 816
people-centred businesses 686
perestroika 532
perfect society 120
period of political independence 688
Periodic Auditing Report 360/361
periodicals 87
peripheral vs. central positioning 473
personal characteristics 289
personal structure (Personalistische Struktur) 511
personality assessments 279
personnel assessment 40
Peru 49
Peterloo Massacre 778
PGH 393; 519
Phalanstéres 16
phased model for the establishment of self-help organizations 691

phenomena antagonistic to co-operative activities 842
Philippines 246; 300; 304
Philipps-Universität Marburg (Germany) 295
philosophy of enlightenment 437
Pingmin Study Society 85
Plan Nacional de Desarrollo Popular 49
plastic production factor 472
Plunkett Foundation 685/686
pluralists 817
Poland 207/208; 829; 831/832
Policies for the Promotion of Co-operatives in Developing Countries 687
political environment 145
political structures 47
Politische Offensive Verkaufsorganisation (POVO) 470
pollution of the natural environment 337
portfolio concept 278
position of co-operative research 874
post office savings system 202
post-degree formation programmes 328
post-independence governments 255
post-independent period 688
power controls 284
Pravda 814
pre-co-operative forms 226
Pre-co-operative Forms of Cooperation 693
pre-co-operative stage in developing countries 694
pre-co-operatives 46; 75; 408; 693
pre-Columbian civilizations 217
pre-independence racial oppression 201
precarious relations 473
preconditions 149
precursors of the co-operative movement 423
present crisis of consumer co-operatives 155
Preußische Central-Genossenschaftskasse 84
Preußische Genossenschaftskasse 428
price policy of co-operatives 25/26
pricing policies 97; 705; 804
Pricing Policy Among Co-operatives 700
principle catalogues 184

principle of a self-operation executive unit 441
Principle of Cost Coverage 705ff.; 766
principle of covering costs 633
principle of democracy 419
principle of identity (Identitätsprinzip) 141; 419; 511
principle of imparity 341
principle of localization 410
principle of nominal value 866
principle of non-intervention 826
principle of open membership 772
principle of regionalism 337
principle of securing just nourishment 414
principle of self-administration 441
principle of subsidiarity 800
principles 3; 96; 116; 121/122; 124/125; 135f.; 140ff.; 151; 205; 216; 251; 275; 344; 425ff.; 590; 709; 776; 794; 803; 843; 916
principles of financing 377
principles of health care co-operativism 174
principles of housing 426
principles of political economy 615
Principles of the Co-operative System 708
Prinzip der vertrauensvollen Zusammenarbeit 109
prisoners dilemma 110; 400
Private Goods 399
privatization 754
Privatization and Collectivization 716
privatization of co-operatives 210
probationary societies 201; 408; 696
problems of apathy 649
procedure of discriminant analysis 277
procedure of evaluation 356
processing chain 35
processing co-operatives 780
procurement co-operatives 847
Producer Associations 722ff.
production campaigns 8
Production Co-operatives 163; 190; 518; 726ff.
production credit associations 165
production enterprises 23

production under close supervision 9; 733
production units 229f.
Productivity advantages 117
Productivity and Cost Advantages in Co-operative Organizations 116/117
Produktionsförderungsgenossenschaften 731ff.
professional associations 421
professional organizations 729
Profi-Märkte 387
profit and loss account 1; 374
profit distribution 3; 89
profit from balance/loss from balance 374
profit participation rights 343
Profitability 377
programme Seneca 311
project accounting 5
Project Completion Report 360
project evaluation 357/358
Project Feasibility Study 360
Project interim Checking Report 360
promotion balance sheet 1; 2; **736; 739**
promotion mandate 20; 111; 136; 141/142; 158; 182; 337; 356; 367; 475/476; **740ff.; 766**
promotion of member's interests 72
promotion purpose 766
promotion report 736
promotion system 736
promotional plan 739
promotional plus 141
promotional purpose 554
promotional report 738
proper bookkeeping 4
property and funds of co-operative societies 548
proto-democratic 47
Prussian Central Co-operative Bank 139
Prussian Co-operative Law (1867) 426; 789
Prussian Law of 1869 627
Prussian National Assembly 787
public benefit housing companies 125
public goods 258; 398
Public Limited Company Act 108
public ownership of the means of production 285
public services (in Latin America) 750

Public-Benefit Orientation (Gemeinnützigkeit) 125; 745/746
Publications 189
publications of the Plunkett Foundation 687
publicity 487
Puget Sound 128
purchasing and marketing associations 384
purchasing and marketing risks 707
purchasing co-operatives 20
pure economic theory of cooperation 738
purely savings co-operatives 202
purpose of promotion 19
PUSKOPKARS 246

Quadragesimo Anno (1931) 885
Quadrogesimo 424
Quakers 127
quasi-feudal rural structures 250
Quebec Co-operative Syndicates Act 198
Quick Schuh 387

R + V Insurance Company 783
R + V Versicherungsgruppe 478
Rabobank, Nederland, Utrecht 83/84; 165/166
racially segregated co-operatives 201
Raiffeisen Federation 788
Raiffeisen libraries 315
Raiffeisen organization 112
Raiffeisen Zentralbank Österreich (RZB) 83/84; 166
Raiffeisenbanken (agricultural credit co-operatives) 80/81; 780; 789; 850
rates of inflation 286
ratio analysis 757
ratio based credit rating (1989) 277
rationalization pressure 14
RBG 195
RBI 302
re-distribution of benefits 74
REA 224
real socialism 311; 807ff.; 832
real-time processing 196
reality of co-determination 109
recommendation no.127 900
reform in 1989/1990 395
regalia 430
régies coopératives Belgium 751
Regional Centres for Development Aid-CRAD 201

regional data processing centers 194
regional development organizations (ORD) 696
Regional Economic Commissions 899
Regional Education Facilities 318
regional policy 804
Register Court 762
Register, Co-operative 762
registered association (e.V./ eingetragener Verein) 103
registered co-operative (e.G./ eingetragene Genossenschaft) 103; 553; 702
registrar 42; 58ff.; 200; 235; 242
registration 22
registration procedures 763
regulated transport rates (RKT) 897
regulation CEE Nr 26/62 346
Regulations for Co-operatives 826
Reichs-Heimstättengesetz 448
Reichsnährstand 316
Reichsverband der deutschen landwirtschaftlichen Genossenschaften-Raiffeisen-e.V. Berlin 37
Reichsverband der deutschen landwirtschaftlichen Genossenschaften 315; 779
Reimbursement 3; 6; 28; 341; 375; 766ff.; 870
Reimbursement associated with Profit Participation Rights 768
Reimbursement in Co-operative Banks 768
Reimbursements and Taxation 768
Relationship Patterns 770
Religious Co-operatives, Cloisters 773
Religious communes 127
religious fraternities 469
remedial loan societies 755
renaissance of ethics 345
Rentenbank-Kreditanstalt 316
report of Gide 290
representatives'assemblies 3
Republic of (South) Korea 44
Republic of Cameroon 44
Republic of Indonesia 44
reputation 476
Rerum Novarum (1891) 424; 885
Reserve Bank of India (RBI) 235

reserve capital 26
reserve fund 372
reserves 7
restraints of competition 17; 18
restructuring in the combine 371
retail co-operatives 117
Review of consumer co-operative societies 529
Review of International Cooperation 681
Revisionsverband deutscher Konsumgenossenschaften e.V. 37
revival of solidarity groups 9
Revue des études coopératives mutualistes et associatives 681
REWE 321; :
Rheinische Landwirtschaftliche Genossenschaftsbank 755
Rheinische Zeitung 812
Ricardian Socialists 614
RISDA 304
Riverside 1941 130
Road Haulage 895/896
roadway transport 896
Rochdale 15
Rochdale Co-operative Store 1833 777
Rochdale consumer co-operative 92
Rochdale Equitable Pioneers Society 682; 776ff.
Rochdale model 201
Rochdale Pioneers 28; 58; 120ff.; 135; 138; 151; 182; 216; 344; 425; 668; 776; 843
Rochdale principles 425:776
ROK 300
role-defined labour distribution 633
Rolls of Qumran 431
Roman Centuria Settlements 431
Romans 430
roots of the „Social Market Economy" 655
Rouiza 226
rule 815ff.
rule-based ratio assessment 758
rules of financing 378
rural co-operatives 251; **778**
rural commodities co-operatives 12
rural commune 471
rural electric associations 224
Rural Peoples Communes in China 784
rural reform experimental zones 87

rural share-holding co-operative enterprises (SCEs) 87
Russian social democratic party 814
Rwanda 298

SAARC 302
Saemaul Undong 44
Sahel 48/49
sailors form Kronstadt 814
sales channels 481
sales co-operatives 847
Salik 470
Samahaang Nayon 246; 408
Saporog cossack samp 51
saving and loan associations 64
Saving Funds 10
savings and credit co-operatives 198
savings and credit unions 203
savings and loan co-operatives 28
savings banks 164; 278
scale 98/99
Scandinavian Luma-project 151
SCEs 89/90
Schiller-Scheme 733
school co-operatives 207
Schulze-Delitzsch Institut 317
Schwäbisch Hall Building Society 65
SCIAS-Barcelona 175
science theory 872
scientific socialism 183
Scoring procedures 758
Second World War 806
Secondary Co-operative Institutions 204
secondary co-operatives 863
secondary group 410
secteur associatif 126
secteur d'économie sociale 125
secteur mutualiste 126
Security Mechanisms 789/790
security systems 789
SED (Sozialistische Einheitspartei Deutschlands) 395
Selbstorganschaft 124; 441
selected innovative experiences 245
Selection of Members 794ff.; 843
Selex+Tania-Gruppe 18
self-employed Women's Association (SEWA) 913
self-administrated enterprises 632
self-administration 4; 771
self-financing 341; 377
self-fulfilling prophecy 145

self-help 47; 139; 254; 420; 771; 796/797; 818; 821
self-help from above and outside 842
self-help groups 103; 571/572
self-help organizations 97; 217; 250; 355/356; 407; 689ff.; **796ff.**; 844
self-help promotion institutions (SHPs) 689
self-management on the job 664
self-organisation of small farmers 389
self-reliance 798
self-responsibility 5
sellers-market 310; 862
Senegal 47; 49; 201
service co-operatives 222; 781
Service d'Etudien, d'Assistance et de Developpement 44
Service de contrôle 44
Service de l'information et de la propaganda 44
services of Credit Unions 188
Services Provided by Commercial Co-operatives 118
settlement co-operatives 9; 519
settlement schemes 203
settlement societies 202
seven elements 440
seven principles of the Co-operative System 709
Seventh African Regional Conference 903
SGCC 154
SGZ Bank 783
Shaker settlement 127
share-holding co-operative organization 87; 89
shareholding form 166
SHGs 571
shirka 47
shop stewards (Vertrauenstelle) 109
short-term crop advances 9
short-term production loans 9
short-term solvency for a company 260
SHOs 797ff.
side-effects 92
SIDEFCOOP 221; 323
Siedlungsgenossenschaften 654
SINAMOS farming advisors in Peru 221
SINERA 176
Singapore 300; 304
Singapore Co-operative Union 304

Singapore National Co-operative Federation 304
single-purpose 104
situational approach 356; 856
Slowakia 313
small group 410
small service co-operatives 225
small workers co-operatives 208
Small-scale Farmers in Traditional Agricultural Societies 8
SMCs 305
SOCAP in Morocco (Societés de Crédit Agricole et de Prévoyance) 228
social balance sheet 2
social construction enterprises 450
Social Democratic Party 451
social economy 289
social elevator 818
social environment 144
social law 103
social marketing 639
social participation 794
Social Policy 104; 286/287; **802ff.**
social question 151; 788; 817
social reforms 436
social science concept 738
social sciences 289
social security 173
social security crisis 173/174
socialism destourien 229
socialist co-operative doctrine 207
socialist co-operative models 807/808
Socialist Co-operative Theory 807
socialist co-operatives 518
socialist co-operatives models 116
Socialist Congress in Copenhagen 1910 813
socialist countries 116; 242
Socialist Critics of Co-operatives 810ff.
socialist trade unions 54
socialization of privately owned handicraft 207
Societal Form 815
Société Anonyme à Capital et Personnel Variable 519
Société Mutelle de Developpement Rurale (SMDR) 200
Société Mutuelle de Production Rurale (SMPR) 200

Sociétés Agricoles de Prévoyance, SAP 228
Sociétés de Crédit et de Secours Mutels, SCSM 227
Sociétés de Prévoyance et de crédit Agricole, SPCA 227
Sociétés Indigenes de Prevoyance (SIP) 200
Sociétés Indigenes de Prevoyance, Secours et Préts Mutuels 227
socio-economic change 25
sociological analysis 410
sociology of co-operations 770
sociology of religion 774
SODIMAC 218
SOK 152ff.; 668
solidarité paysanne 432
Solidarity 111; 123; 192; 249/250; 291; 344; 638; 715; **820ff.**; 822; 843; 888
solidarity of need 742
SONADER model 203
sorting process 32
sources of equity capital 340
Soviet Union 312
soziale Baubetriebe 450
Soziale Bauwirtschaft 55
Sparkassen-Haftungsgesellschaft 278
SPD (Sozialdemokratische Partei Deutschlands) 889ff.; 894
special characteristics of co-operative equity capital 342
spontaneous co-ordination 132
spreading of the British-Indian Pattern 60
Sri Lanka 50; 236; 240; 243; 300; 303
St. Francis Xavier University in Antigonish Nova Scotia 223
Stability 378
stability of Cooperation 858
Staff Representation Act (Personalvertretungsgesetz) 107
Stalinist model 809
Standard & Poors Corporation 52
start-up subsidies 723
statal institutions 312
STATBIL balance interpretation system 278
State and Co-operatives in a Market Economy 823ff.
State and Co-operatives in Socialism 828ff.
State Bank of Pakistan 238
state bureaucracy 284
state failure 402

State Federation of Co-operatives in Western Australia 307
state property 809
state-controlled co-operatives 643
state-sponsored co-operatives 643; 830
statistical documentation of co-operative development in Latin America 218/219
statistical financial statement analysis 260
statistical ratio analysis 757
statutes 15
Sternverträge 19
Steueranpassungsgesetz 747
Strategic Alliances 157; **833ff.**
strategic controlling 275
strategic cor and special skills 834
strategic fit 838
strategic management 833
Strategic Planning 274/275; **846**
strategic shift in co-operative policy 259
strategical measures 844
Strategies Employed When Establishing co-operatives 841
strategies for co-operative development 489
strategies for de-officialization 646
Structural Changes 780; **850**
structural dimensions of the co-operative 856
structural elements of management teams 584
structural features of consulting 146
structural models and legal forms 117
structural models of promotion 854
structural solidarity 821
Structural Types 165; **192; 853ff.**
structural typology 159; 853
structural-functional approach 466
structure of the co-operative system 232
Strukturtypen der Genossenschaften 192
Sub-Saharan Africa 47
subsidiarity 111; 192
Subsidiarity Among Co-operatives 858
subsidiary-reduction 859
subsitute ways of financing 381
substantive audit 36

success in member promotion 24
success in the market 24/25
success in the promotion of members' interests 24
success of co-operation 591
Success Orientation 4
Sudan 295
suitabilitiy of available incentives 463
supervisory board 5; 7; 91; 108; 171; 276; 279; 443/444; 868
supervisory body 659
supplemental help 859
supply and marketing co-operatives 88; 207; 780; 830
supply co-operatives 32ff.; 224; 275; **861**
support and consultancy 297
Supreme Soviet 814
surplus distribution 28
Svanholm Collective 130
Swedish Building Co-operative Association 55
sworn brothers 413
symbolic value of honour 413
symbols 52
syndicates 103
synergy effects 623
system of logic 615
systemic fundamental structure 856
systems „without rulers" 47
Systemstreit 110

tafar 47
Taiwan 300; 306
Taize-les-Cluny 1947 774
Tanzania 48; 201ff.; 295;
tax balance sheet 2
tax exemption 871
tax loss carrybacks and carryovers 869
tax matters 251
tax obligations 119
tax rates 869
tax regulations 25
tax repudiation resolution 787
taxable income 865
Taxation of Co-operatives 1; **865**
taxes 26
TCZB 251
Tendenzbetrieb 126
terminological catalogue 385
terms characterising the group 403,
terra familia 431
tertiary co-operatives 104

texts of laws on co-operatives 833
Thailand 246; 300; 304
The „Co-operative State" 655
The Co-operator 424
The Farm (USA) 129; 471
The jounal of rural cooperation 681
Théorie de l'Association Ouvrière 63
Théorie de l'Unité Universelle 424
theories of surplus value 812
Theory and Science of Cooperation 871
Theory of Co-operative Cooperation 879/880
theory of eventual consequence 18; 19
theory of purpose 18; 19
theory of subject matter of contract 14; 17
theory of trusteeship 737
thiasis 431
third - progressive - way 255
third principle of economic order 137
third sector 125
Third Way, Co-operatives as a 885
Third World 796ff.; 799/800
third-party transactions 118
Third-World-Development 796
Thirty Years War 128; 446; 775
three types of co-operative banks 163
three-tiered co-operative organization 117
time of maturity 378
TNUVA 213
TOBACCf 235
Togo 203/204
TOKP 251
Tönniesian ideal type 137
tontines 47; 913
top-down method 250
top-down intervention 143
Toyasato 130
trade 11
trade co-operatives 230
trade union movements 121
trade unions 106; 109; 152; 817; **887**
traditional co-operative theory 20
traditional co-operatives 104; 117; 166; 183; 272; 856; 862
traditional financial statement analysis 260

traditional ratio analysis 757
traditional self-help groups 408
training centre at Var Gard 311
training institutes 310
training programs 311; 328
transaction cost approach 523
transaction costs 273
transaction-specific quasi-rents 475
transparence of the market 11
Transport Co-operatives 113; **895**
Treaty of Rome 346
Trends of Change 209
trickle down effects 217
trickle down hypothesis 242
Tripartite Approach of Evaluation 356; 358.
tripartite-sytem 466
trust form 166
Tunisian Experience 228
Turkey 300; 307
Turkish Agricultural Bank, TCZB 250
Turkish Republic in 1923 250
Turkish Sugar Factory Company 735
Turkish system of co-operatives 250
tutelage and autonomy 251
TVEs 88/89
TVEs development 87
Twin Oaks 129; 471
two definitions of co-operative societies 543
two stage formation process 697
two-land-system 88
two-sided stream of information 35
types of basic objectives 101
types of co-operative organizations 367
types of co-operative structure 117
types of co-operatives 323; 847
types of consulting 146
types of economic orders 281
types of marketing co-operatives 593
types of membership behavior 620
types of registered co-operatives 555
types of structures 368
typical distinctions 855

U.S. Central Credit Union. Overlan Park, Kansas 84

UCCC (Union centrale des Coopératives de Consommation) 230
UCPA, Unité Co-opérative de Production Agricole 229
UEPSMC 347
UFCC 119
UGAL 347
Uganda 201ff.; 295
UGTA 231
UGTT (Union Générale des Travailleurs Tunisiens) 229
ujamaa 48:61; 144
Ujamaa Co-operative 519
Ujamaa of Tanzania 203
Ujamaa policy 48
Ujamaa villages 294
Ujamaa-villagization-schemes 405
ultra vires doctrine 171
UN agencies 300
UNCC 696
UNCDF 901
UNCHS 903
UNDP 293
UNDP 899; 901ff.; 905
UNESCO 293; 900/901
unfair competition 133
Unfallversicherung 419
unfamiliar environments 504
UNFPA 899
UNHCR 899
Unico Banking Group 353/354
UNIDO 900ff.
unification theory 412
Union des Groupements d'Achat Cooperatifs de Detaillants de L'Europe 119
Union of Productive Co-operatives 210
unions 892
United Kibbutz Movement (TAKAM) 215
United Kingdom communitarianism 131
United Nations Organizations and the Specialized Agenices 898
United Nations System 898
Unity of Bohemian-Moravian Brethren 775
universitas 103
University of Wisconsin 331
unregistered pre-co-operatives 694
UNRISD 887; 899; 906
Unternehmenskultur 180
Urban Development 432; 434/435

USA 52
USDA 225
Use of Collective Land 226
USSR 236
utilitarian principle 345
utilitarianism 93; 615
utilities co-operatives 781
Utopia (1516) 423
utopias 101; 137

value of income 534
values 180
variations of reimbursement 767
various plan documents 239
VDC 683
VdgB 395
Veräußerungswertbilanz 280
Verband der Baugenossenschaften 37
Verband der deutschen Konsumgenossenschaften 829
Verband der hessischen landwirtschaftlichen Konsumvereine 315
Verbund 110ff.
Verein für Socialpolitik 449
Verein Reichswohnungsgesetz 447
Vereinstag der deutschen Arbeitervereine 788
Vergemeinschaftung 404; 822
Vergesellschaftung 822
Vermögensbildungsgesetz 68
vertical co-operative combine 167
vertical cooperation 105
vertical diversification 265
vertical flow of financing 376
vertical integration 33
Vienna Congress, 1966 709
Vietnam 300; 304
village and township enterprises 86
village development co-operatives 251
Villages of Cooperation 16
villagization 49; 203
Violation of the Duty of Care 564
Violation of the Duty of Member Promotion 564
Violations of Duty 563
Visibility 487
VMCC 246
VMNICOM 302
Volksbanken (people's banks) 80/81; 780; 789; 850
Volksblatt für Harburg und Wilhelmsburg 528
Volkseigene Betriebe 392

Volksgemeinschaften 404; 673
Volkskammer 538
Volkswirtschaftlicher Kongress 1858 788
Vollgenossenschaften 410
voluntary functions 38
voluntary officialization 643
voluntary unpaid management 203
Vorschußvereine 426
vote for women 615
VSK 668

wage theories 94
warehouse co-operatives 781
warning signals 260
water and land associations 170/717
weak signals 274/275
weaknesses of joint-production co-operatives 519/520
welfare associations 102
WFP 899; 905
WGG (Wohnungsgemeinnützigkeitsgesetz) 747/748
WGZ Bank 784
WHO (World Health Organization) 293
wholesale trading functions 115
Wilaya 231
Winegrowers' Co-operatives 780
Wirtschaftsgenossenschaften 104
Wissenschaftlicher Beirat 798/799
WOCCU 85; 302
Women and Co-operatives 909
women's co-operatives 235; 913
women's groups in Nigeria 298

women's participation 911
women's programmes 293
work co-operative (societa cooperative di lavoro) 518
work design 460
Worker Ownership Development Foundation 333
worker production and artisan co-operatives 230
worker's self-management enterprise 519
Workers Co-operative Alliance (INKOPAR) 246
workers' co-operatives 63
workers' productive co-operatives 207
Working Women'Forum (WWF) 913
workmanship 11
Works Constitution Act 107ff.
works council 107/108
Works Council Act of 1920 (Betriebsratgesetz) 106
works or use co-operatives 555
World Bank 293; 901; 905
World Conference on Agrarian Reform and Rural Development (1979) 903
World Council of Credit Unions (WOCCU) 224; 493
World Food Programme 903
World War I 446ff.; 737; 894
World War II 448; 774; 779; 894
Württembergische Genossenschafts-Akademie Hohenheim 316
WWF 913

X-efficiency 93

Yardstick for Diligence and Due Care 564
yardstick function 757
Young Hegelians 812
Yugoslav institution of workers self-management 536
Yugoslavian ASV (Arbeiterselbstverwaltung) 518

Zaire 203f.
Zambia 201/202; 295
Zambian Humanism 49
Zeitgeist 821
Zeitschrift für das gesamte Genossenschaftswesen (Journal for the Entire Co-operative System) 29; 31; 680,
ZENKYOREN (National Mutual Insurance Federation of Agricultural Co-operative Association) 305
ZENTGENO 120; 317; 321; 680; 709
Zentralverband deutscher Konsumgenossenschaften 37
Zentralverband deutscher Konsumvereine 427; 529; 891
Zentrum 892
Zimbave 201
Zionist 519
Zionist immigrants in Palestine 211
zoon politikon 820
Zünfte 433
ZVN Decision 18

Journal for the study of cooperatives

Zeitschrift für das gesamte Genossenschaftswesen (ZfgG)

Organ für Kooperationsforschung und -praxis

Herausgegeben von Wolfgang Blomeyer, Ernst-Bernd Blümle, Eberhard Dülfer, Ulrich Fehl, Bernhard Großfeld, Oswald Hahn, Wilhelm Weber. Im Auftrag der Genossenschaftsinstitute an den Universitäten Berlin, Erlangen-Nürnberg, Fribourg/Schweiz, Gießen, Hamburg, Hohenheim, Köln, Marburg, Münster, Wien/U, Wien/WU.

An interdisciplinary quarterly for the study of cooperatives. Editorial board and authors represent various academic disciplines and approaches: economy, business, law, and sociology. At the same time, close contact with actual cooperative practice is of fundamental significance.

Inhalt
(konstante Rubriken in den Heften):
In wenigen Sätzen *(über den Heft-Inhalt)*
Was wir meinen *(zu aktuellen Themen)*
Sektorenanalyse
Abhandlungen
Länderbericht
Personalia
Forschungsergebnisse
Rechtssprechung
Buchbesprechungen und Anzeigen

4 monograph series for the study of cooperatives

Berliner Schriften zum Genossenschaftswesen

Herausgegeben vom Institut für Genossenschaftswesen an der Humboldt-Universität zu Berlin: Volker Beuthien, Eberhard Dülfer, Werner Großkopf, Gerhard Rönnebeck, Rolf Steding, George Turner.
5 titles published 1983 – 1994

Hamburger Schriften zum Genossenschaftswesen

Herausgegeben von Axel Bänsch, Peter Erlinghagen, Dietrich Hill, Helmut Lipfert, Rolf Lürig, Günther Ringle.
9 titles published 1983 – 1994

Marburger Schriften zum Genossenschaftswesen

Herausgeber im Namen des Vorstandes des Instituts für Genossenschaftswesen an der Philipps-Universität Marburg: Volker Beuthien.
77 titles published until 1994

Organisation und Kooperation in Entwicklungsländern

Veröffentlichungen des Instituts für Kooperation in Entwicklungsländern der Philipps-Universität Marburg, herausgegeben von Eberhard Dülfer.
24 titles published until 1994

For detailed information ask:
Vandenhoeck & Ruprecht,
D – 37070 Göttingen

V&R
Vandenhoeck & Ruprecht